The Sky Their Battlefield

Air Fighting and the Complete List of Allied Air
Casualties from Enemy Action in the First War

British, Commonwealth, and United States
Air Services 1914 to 1918

Trevor Henshaw

GRUB STREET · LONDON

Published by
Grub Street
The Basement
10 Chivalry Road
London SW11 1HT

Typeset by Pearl Graphics, Hemel Hempstead
Printed and bound by Biddles Ltd, Guildford and King's Lynn

This book is dedicated to Patrice Leavold and to John Henshaw, my father

Contents

ACKNOWLEDGEMENTS 6

INTRODUCTION 7

Using this book 10

Glossary of terms and abbreviations 15

Part I THE WESTERN FRONT 1914–1918 18

Part II AMERICANS IN THE GREAT WAR 1916–1918 456

Section A: L'ESCADRILLE LAFAYETTE 1916 — 1917 456
Section B: UNITED STATES AIR SERVICE AERO SQUADRONS 1918 459
Section C: AMERICANS KNOWN TO HAVE BEEN CASUALTIES 472
WHILST SERVING WITH THE FRENCH AIR FORCE IN
1918 — ENTRY VIA THE LAFAYETTE FLYING CORPS
Section D: AMERICANS KNOWN TO HAVE BEEN CASUALTIES 473
WHILST SERVING WITH THE FRENCH AIR FORCE IN
1917–1918 — DIRECT ENTRY

Part III UNITED KINGDOM and HOME WATERS 1914–1918 475

Part IV ITALY and THE ADRIATIC 1917–1918 481

Part V THE DARDANELLES and THE TURKISH
COAST 1915–1918 493

Part VI MACEDONIA and THE AEGEAN 1916–1918 499

Part VII EGYPT and PALESTINE 1914–1918 508

Part VIII MESOPOTAMIA 1915–1918 526

Part IX EAST AFRICA 1914–1917 536

Part X THE NAME INDEX 537

Statistical Appendices 572

Appendix I: Losses on the Western Front 1914–1918 by Category, 575
Cause, and Nature of Operation

Appendix II: Losses on the Western Front 1914–1918 by Machine Type 576

Appendix III: Important AIR1 Files in the Public Record Office, Kew, 577
relating to Air Casualties in the Great War

Acknowledgements and Author's Note

Four people who must be singled out for their help and support in the writing of this book are Russell Guest, Peter Andersson, Brad King, and Martin Gladman. Each in their different way has helped me beyond measure to realise this work and I am deeply grateful to them. It would also not have been possible without the help of the staffs at the Public Record Office at Kew, the Imperial War Museum, the Royal Air Force Museum, and the National Archives of the United States in Washington. The primary sources in their care are the bedrock of the information presented here. I am also indebted to the work which has been done by several individuals in the field of First World War aviation. Besides affording me their great insights and hard-won understanding, their work has given me stimulation and pleasure over many years. Those whose writings have been of particular value include Jack Bruce, Ray Sturtivant, Gordon Page, Norman Franks, Christopher Shores, Frank Bailey, Christopher Cole, EF Cheesman, SF Wise, James Sloan, Chaz Bowyer and Alex Imrie. In the preparation of the accompanying text, reference has been widely made to the the six volumes of the official history, *The War In The Air* by Sir Walter Raleigh and HA Jones. Gorrell's *History of the American Expeditionary Forces Air Service 1917–1919* has been the key reference for the section on the involvement of the United States. I owe a special debt of thanks to Russell Guest and others for the sharing of their work on RFC, RNAS, and RAF squadron combat victories, particularly in the period after 1916, as well as to the authors of *Above The Lines* for access to Jagdstaffel records which they hold. Thanks must also go to Stuart Leslie and Jack Bruce for access to, and use of images from, their photograph collection. Unless otherwise noted, all photographs are from either the Bruce-Leslie collection or that of the author. I thank the others who have supported and aided me in my efforts but who I have been unable to mention here. My final thanks go to Patrice Leavold, who shares the dedication of this work with my father. Without her there would be no book.

Introduction

This book is about the young airmen of the First World War who made the sky their battlefield — the first to meet this great and difficult challenge. Some were destined to excel in what was a completely new form of warfare, whilst for the vast majority of these earliest fighting airmen it was achievement enough simply to fight and survive. It was the fate of so many, however, to suffer and die high above the earth in an unforgiving sky. In four years of war, almost eight thousand airmen from Britain, Australia, Canada, and the United States were shot down and killed, taken prisoner, or wounded in action. Although other aspects of the air war are explored in this book, its central purpose is to record the bravery and contribution of these men.

Air operations were a constant companion to the ground fighting from the earliest days of the war. Both sides showed a steadily growing commitment to the air war, so that airmen were not only quickly drawn into the action, but also into the ethos of the fighting. Even from the first months, however, the airman's lot was identified as being different, and this is particularly reflected in the air casualties. From the perspective of the losses on the ground, which cast a shadow over an entire generation of the world's youth, those few thousand in the air seem so minor. What must be remembered, though, is that the air services, for all their profound influence, were always small and concentrated, full of highly trained and motivated individuals, for whom even the relatively low levels of losses were often devastating.

Flyers also fought a very different war from those on the ground. They usually saw their opponents, and survived or fell in combat with them through the most demanding blend of skill and bravery. Unlike the infantry, this stark challenge of war confronted the airman nearly every day of his active service. His was an unremittingly watchful existence, and if it was concentrated into a few hours a day over the battle, it was no easier for that. Life was risked constantly, and life was lost virtually every day, but so crucial were airmen to the fighting that those remaining simply had to press on. The sense of personal loss which could have pervaded so many squadron messes was instead directed into a force for greater effort, purpose, and comradeship. Amongst all the qualities displayed by airmen on both sides of the conflict this was one of their very greatest achievements — to rise above the fear of sudden and painful death and focus upon the job in hand. This devotion to duty matches any in war.

The enormous changes in air warfare, which both they and burgeoning technology were responsible for, had been scarcely credible at the outset of fighting. What began as a somewhat suspect instrument of reconnaissance gathering had become, by the end of the war, a weapon which could win battles. The usefulness of the aeroplane to armies soon became a revelation. At first it fed commanders with a new understanding of the forces opposing them, as well as providing detailed information about the positions of their own troops. Not long afterwards it was directing artillery fire and dropping the first bombs on the enemy.

As the usefulness of the air arms to both sides grew, so did the price of their work, and it became necessary to fight for the sky above the battlefield. Air fighting was slow to start; casualties remained light whilst there were no purpose-built fighters with appropriate armament. The main enemies until late 1915 were primitive anti-aircraft fire, a stray bullet from the ground, and mechanical failure. The need for control of the air nevertheless began to unleash the airman's fighting temperament. The revolution which brought about a real awakening of air fighting, however, was the appearance of the Fokker E-type monoplane fighter in the autumn of 1915. From this time onwards the sky could become a battleground at any time.

The continuous development of fighter aircraft thereafter was a natural response to this escalation, as each side sought to out-perform and destroy the enemy. Fighter tactics were enunciated and perfected, so that survival became ever more demanding and control of the air ever more important. All air fighting took place, however, to protect and facilitate the more mundane work which was happening over the battlefield. The organisational capabilities of the air arms were expanding very rapidly, enabling increasing diversification of roles for aircraft. Photographic reconnaissance, bombing, artillery co-operation, and close contact work with advancing armies were all essential services provided by the Royal Flying Corps by the time of the battle of the Somme in July 1916.

From this time the numbers of aircraft involved in the fighting greatly increased — the RFC grew enormously, whilst the German Air Force began to concentrate its best aircraft and pilots against it. Air

combat became widespread and took on a new ferocity through the spring of 1917, as the British sought to survive "Bloody April" and its aftermath, and by early summer dogfights of forty or more fighters were not uncommon. These saw some desperate confrontations, in which losses were high. Initially, fighting took place between formations of German single-seaters of the highest quality pitted against greater numbers of markedly inferior British aircraft. In time, however, a distinct transformation took place as a new generation of Allied fighters and two-seaters became available. Not only were these as good or better than their German counterparts, but they were soon to be considerably more numerous. Increasing production began to deliver aircraft such as the Sopwith Camel, the SE5, the DH4, and the Bristol Fighter to British front line units in great numbers.

The Royal Flying Corps had suffered terribly in March and April, however, and lack of proper training had played quite as big a part as had poor equipment in the events which had just passed. Therefore, as part of the upheavals in the RFC at this time, training was completely overhauled. Developments in operational organisation had already begun to make the force a more formidable weapon, and by the middle of 1917 these factors — improved organisation, better production, quality new equipment, and proper training — ensured the RFC would survive and eventually prosper.

The RFC rebuilt itself through late 1917, only to be thrown into the appalling fighting in Flanders. It was during these battles, however, that the aircraft emerged as a battlefield weapon. Just as the tank promised a revolution in ground warfare, it is fair to say the aeroplane, used as a low attacking weapon against the enemy, made a similarly profound impact. From the first reconnaissance flights of 1914 the aeroplane had removed the element of secrecy from an opposing army, or at least made it much more difficult to operate without its own defensive shield in the air. When aircraft began strafing and bombing the enemy as part of a co-ordinated assault, they unleashed untold disruption and chaos. This role was to be developed until it became an essential element of any ground offensive. It was particularly well used in theatres other than the Western Front in 1918 when on several occasions low bombing and shooting up of retreating armies was almost catastrophically effective. In France, where ground defences were more organised, it was a very costly operation in terms of air crew.

In the upper air, the British policy of an unflinching offensive launched deep into German territory also led to hundreds, maybe thousands, of casualties in the air. It became a daily ritual for so many fighter squadrons to operate in sweeps east of the lines, searching out and attacking enemy formations and confounding their plans. As well as the fighters, however, the bombers also roamed far from home, attacking distant enemy lines of communications, ammunition dumps, aerodromes and troop concentrations. The bombing offensive grew dramatically in 1918, and it will be seen that the crews involved sustained some of the highest casualties of all groups in that year. During their raids, often made in inadequate aircraft to targets at the very limits of their range, many formations suffered violent and sustained attacks by enemy fighters, whose aerodromes were often close at hand, and who found them easy prey.

A vital point to remember when considering Allied air casualties is that most of the air fighting took place to the east, over German-held territory. Although this owed something to the prevailing westerly wind, the air policies of the two protagonists were the chief reasons. The British strategy of an air offensive meant that its units went in continuous search of the enemy. On the other hand, the numerically smaller German Air Force needed to marshal its strengths and launch carefully structured attacks when the situation was most favourable. The most advantageous environment in which to fight was naturally over their own territory, where they could mass quickly and meet the Allied airmen on their own terms, and they also worked in close co-operation with their anti-aircraft batteries. There was an odd synchronicity between the two opposing air forces: offensive patrolling over enemy territory meant the Allies could restrict their opponents' access to the lines, whilst fighting here also suited the tactics of the German Air Force. Its policy of selective aggression meant that when German fighter aircraft chose to approach the front lines they usually did so purposefully and in large formations, looking to impose themselves and cause maximum trouble. Having achieved this they were content to retire again in order to fight another day. Allied air intelligence was such, however, that its fighter units were usually alert to enemy activity and would go east to confront these formations before they reached the lines. All these aspects of the air war are explored in the text, but as regards an overview of casualties, these circumstances meant that Allied losses were very high east of the lines, explaining why so many air crew were posted missing in action.

If Allied airmen managed to escape from attack whilst on offensive patrol or bombing, they still faced a very substantial trip home. They needed to work west again, against the prevailing wind, eventually passing over the front lines where they could expect further attention from ground fire. If they made the

safety of their own lines but then needed to land because of a shortage of fuel or the condition of their aircraft, their forced landing was made in the ruined and desolate landscape of the Western Front, which in places stretched twenty miles deep. A crash often resulted, increasing the likelihood of injury or death.

Crews flying corps machines are also encountered repeatedly in this book, usually operating very locally with their army groups near the battlefield, providing reconnaissance or supporting the artillery. They have been touched on before, and it was noted that it was in order to give them protection that the air war first intensified. One measure of the effectiveness of the Allied air arm, therefore, is to see how these machines were faring at particular times as they carried out their crucial duties. With few exceptions, it is fairly clear that during the biggest battles they decidedly maintained their viability, their losses being light when compared to fighter and bomber casualties in the same periods. Statistical appendices of losses have been provided to assist the reader in making sense of these trends.

If the first two years of the development of the air weapon could be seen as a period in which its roles were discovered and refined, then the last two years saw ever increasing complexity and weight of effort as air activity vastly multiplied. By the time the Royal Flying Corps had become the Royal Air Force in April 1918, it had become a vital part of a huge war effort, simultaneously capable of intricate deployment as well as being used to deliver killer-blows upon the enemy. How these changes came about can be traced in this book, whilst the men who fought and died in this process, as well as many who survived to celebrate a great victory, are listed in its pages.

Using this Book

The contents

The Sky Their Battlefield is a chronological listing of the air activity on all fronts on every day of the First World War. It records the details of every casualty sustained by British, Commonwealth, and American airmen due to enemy action during the fighting. By reference to German material it proposes links for over two thousand of these with German Flak and Jagdstaffel claims. Whilst air crew losses are the central study of this work, it also incorporates several other groups of entries and accompanying text to form a comprehensive record of all fighting in the first air war, including a detailed exploration of how these forces interacted with the armies fighting on the ground.

The entries

All activities of the Royal Flying Corps, the Royal Naval Air Service, the Royal Air Force, the Independent Force, and the Australian Flying Corps are given in detail. All British aircraft and crews who were shot up or suffered attack by the enemy on any day are listed, even if the crew escaped uninjured. Details of virtually every engagement with the enemy by the Royal Flying Corps on the Western Front, from August 1914 until late spring 1916, are also given. This is to enable a close study of the development of the air war from the earliest reconnaissances made for the British Expeditionary Force in the first days of the war, through the growth of air fighting and the era of the Fokker Eindekkers, to within a few months of the Somme when air activity suddenly rose to much greater levels. From this time onwards comprehensive listing becomes impractical, although extensive coverage of air combats is continued, albeit selectively. Those included after this time typically describe air fighting involving every British and Commonwealth ace, as well as action which can throw further light on particularly important events in the air war. The roles in battle of every squadron, all types of operation, as well as changing equipment and technology are covered, including every British aircraft type which flew in action. There are roughly eight thousand casualties, and well over nine thousand entries. Many airmen appear several times, and all names of personnel mentioned in the book are indexed in Part X: The Name Index (see below).

The text

To draw all this information together a comprehensive history of the air war accompanies the data. Its main purpose is to contextualise the entries so that the reader can move from the specific to the general and have a greater understanding of the currents running through the air activity. The text describes the following:

- the development of the organisational structures of the RFC, RNAS, RAF, as well as the German Air Force, both at command and operational level

- all British air concentrations assembled for every major battle, which are given in detail, usually with each squadron's roles described

- the course of every ground battle, in so far as it can illustrate the tasks of the air arm and, by implication, the growing involvement and importance of aircraft in battle plans

- the arrival and departure of all British air units in all theatres

- overviews covering tactical and technological developments affecting the air war, including the war service of virtually every Allied aircraft type

- any additional information which expands on a particular entry or group of entries.

The structure

The book is divided into ten parts. Parts I and II cover the Western Front; the first examines the RFC, RNAS, and RAF operations in France from 1914 to 1918, whilst the second records the activities of the Lafayette Escadrille in 1916 and 1917 and then the United States Aero Service in 1918. Parts III to IX cover British operations in all other theatres from 1914 to 1918. Within each part the entries are set out in date order, and then within each day, in squadron order, and within each squadron, by serial number.

RFC and RAF units come first, with RNAS, US Aero, and Australian units following. At the end of each month the occasional untraced airman is noted.

The Name Index

Part X is an expanded index of all the names of personnel mentioned in the first nine parts. It comprises over 10,800 separate names which are indexed by the dates of the relevant entries. The Name Index is envisaged as a research tool in its own right. As well as being the means of accessing the chronological listings by giving relevant dates for each and every airman it also notes further key information if he was a casualty, for instance if he was killed in action, was made a prisoner of war, etc. The index is described in more detail in Part X.

Appendices

Two of the three appendices towards the rear of the book are statistical examinations of flying personnel losses on the Western Front. Appendix I considers losses by category, cause, and nature of operation. Appendix II looks at losses by machine type. These have been done in unprecedented detail and it is hoped they will particularly illuminate the several evolutionary steps the air war took in four years of fighting. Appendix III lists AIR 1 files in the Public Record Office relating to air casualties which may be useful for further study.

What is a casualty?

All casualties noted, with only a few exceptions, occurred as a result of enemy action. This means that the airman either went missing, was killed, was taken prisoner, was wounded, or died of wounds sustained from enemy fire. Enemy fire might variously mean machine-gun exchanges during aerial combat, anti-aircraft fire and other ground fire, shells and shrapnel, bombing of aerodromes, and so on. The list also includes all airmen who were driven down for whatever purpose over the lines — through, for instance, engine failure or disorientation. For the purposes of completeness, casualties are expanded to include death or injury incurred subsequently in crashes after combats to which the latter might have contributed by the damage inflicted on the aircraft.

As a rule, it does not include reference to airmen killed or injured in flying accidents in which the opposing forces had no part. The exceptions are occasional entries covering the service of particular, usually famous, individuals, for instance the death of the British ace James McCudden in a flying accident in 1918. All casualties of a purely accidental nature will be included in a subsequent book by the author which will look at all British aircraft and the units and personnel associated with them.

As has been noted, there are thousands of other entries which deal with air combats and illustrate the general course of the air war.

Interpreting the entries

There is a huge amount of information contained in this book so it has been written as consistently as possible. Consequently, there are some basic structural rules governing the layout of all entries.

On any particular day, entries in squadron order are set out as follows. The first line in **bold** gives the aircraft serial number if known, the aircraft type, and the relevant squadron or unit. If a serial number has a suffix following a dot then this is a known Flight aircraft marking. Squadron numbers of units of the Independent Force are given an "(I.F.)" suffix to distinguish them. Names given to an aircraft by its crew are also noted on occasions. The details are then given in this order:

Mission Type comes first.
eg. P: Patrol; AOb: Artillery Observation; EscRec: Escorting Reconnaissance (see glossary below). Preceding this are either two stars: "**" or a cross and a star: "+*". Both refer to involvement in enemy action and point to the key source of the information; in this case, respectively a casualty or combat report. Sources are discussed in more detail below. Following the mission type the destination of that operation is usually given.

A *description* of events as they unfolded *for that particular air crew* is then noted in strict order: the nature of enemy fire or the number and type of enemy machines if known; then any information relating to victory claims is given in square brackets (see below); then *where* the engagement or enemy fire was met; *the altitude*; *the time*; and then what happened afterwards to the Allied crew, for example a crash at X or

return to aerodrome Y, with further times, map references, or place names which may be relevant. An example might be:

**B VALENCIENNES combat with Fokker DVIIs~16000'
2pm AA shot up seen ldg in control EoL 2-30pm

This can be read as a bombing operation to Valenciennes during which the patrol met a formation of Fokker DVIIs and fighting took place at around sixteen thousand feet at 2pm. Following this, the crew was hit by anti-aircraft fire and eventually forced to land in control in enemy territory at 2-30pm.

As noted above, if a **combat victory** was claimed by the Allied crew, a brief note of the key data is always given in square brackets with a "+" denoting a victory. All information within these square brackets describes what befell the German victim of a claim. It is important to realise that everything which is noted outside of these square brackets is happening to, or relates to, the Allied crew. Taking a fictitious example:

combat with 5 AlbatrosDVs[+ooc+flames,des] wCAMBRAI 12000'
6am controls shot up dam ftl cr wr 6-25am OK(Capt P McDonough)

This means that five German Albatros DV fighters were engaged by a patrol west of Cambrai at twelve thousand feet at 6am and that this pilot claimed two of them shot down: one seen going down out of control and the other destroyed in flames. Additionally, this example describes how during the fight the Allied machine's flying controls were damaged and the pilot was forced to land but crashed and wrecked his aircraft, coming down at 6-25am. The pilot was uninjured.

Otherwise, if a combat is simply generally mentioned as in the first example, then it can be considered inconclusive in terms of Allied claims. Alternatively, in cases where there is some residual doubt, a question mark is used to show this: [+?driven down].

The Allied **crew** is then given in round brackets, the pilot always named first and separated from the observer, where relevant, by a slash. If they escaped unhurt then a general upper case "OK" is given ahead of the brackets. If they were reported missing in action then "**MIA**" is given here. If the action resulted in injury, wounding, death, or being taken prisoner this is then given after the names of each crew member. If an airman died of wounds subsequently then that date is given next. Finding out the fate of air crew from "other ranks" is often very difficult, but every effort has been made to settle these details.

On occasions only one member of a two-man crew has been able to be identified from the sources. In this case, if he was known to be the pilot then his name is given followed by a slash. If he was known to be an observer then his name is given after a slash.

If the **nationality** of the airman is known to be different from British this is noted, although this aspect of the book is not exhaustive. The exceptions to this rule, for obvious reasons, are entries for American or Australian squadrons; however, the nationalities of these air crew are specified in the Name Index. If there is any British air crew flying with either of these air services then this is noted.

Ancillary information then follows, usually consisting of a departure time; other details about the destination; more details about an injury or whether the airman went to hospital; if the aircraft was captured or if the airman was interned; extra notes about any name or initials or date queries; dates of repatriation or escape; possible Jasta claims from secondary sources; background information about aces' victory scores, etc. Most of this is necessarily abbreviated.

Finally, if there is a **German Air Force** combat or Flak claim or other official record which is thought to match these events then this is given in square brackets. In fact, it is worth stressing again that anything inside square brackets is happening to the enemy or is from a German source (see notes about sources below). This information is also set out in a particular format. The British machine type is quoted verbatim and in inverted commas from the Abschusse lists or other sources consulted: hence "Vikkers" (sic) and "Sopwith" claims typically abound. Then comes any place name noted in German records, then the time (always British time: see below), and finally the German pilot and his unit number.

Time

German time was usually one hour ahead of Allied time for most of the war. Forms of daylight saving were used by both sides however, and from early 1917 there were a few weeks in both spring and autumn when the systems used by the opposing sides were out of phase. This meant that there were periods when German and Allied time matched. Until now, the author suspects this has not been fully resolved, and the dates involved are given below. There have been some disparities in references in the past owing to

confusion about time, so this book began with a clean slate and built up the picture on both sides from primary sources, or transcriptions of primary sources, making the choice, however, to give all times throughout the entire book always as *Allied time*. This is the case even when referring to German-sourced material where times have been converted. In this way, comparisons can be reliably made. AM/PM time is always used.

Variations between British and German time
1917
Until 24.3.1917 German time was one hour ahead of British time.
From 25.3.1917 until 15.4.1917 German and British times matched.
From 16.4.1917 until 17.9.1917 German time was one hour ahead of British time.
From 18.9.1917 until 5.10.1917 German and British times matched.
From 6.10.1917 until 9.3.1918 German time was one hour ahead of British time.

1918
From 10.3.1918 until 15.4.1918 German and British times matched.
From 16.4.1918 until 15.9.1918 German time was one hour ahead of British time.
From 16.9.1918 until 5.10.1918 German and British times matched.
From 6.10.1918 until 11.11.1918 German time was one hour ahead of British time.

Dates, terminology, queries
One strength of these listings should be the considerable number of primary and official sources which have been consulted. As much care as possible has been taken to assemble what could be called the viable truth of the events. Looking so widely has not only built up a much more detailed picture, but has also meant that sheer weight of evidence has ironed out many anomalies. There are still unknown areas, and doubtless there are faults. It is by no means the final word, but as many details as possible have been included to lead the reader as close as the author can take him to the facts.

If there is any query in the information provided then this has been assiduously pointed out; nor has anything been added other than from a reliable source. If there are few queries it is only because the author has returned to the primary sources so many times for yet another look. Dates are one area where this book may propose an occasional new one. A good many casualty reports were written and filed the day *after* the event, and only by careful reading of the entries are many dates properly revealed. Dates supplied in casualty reports have been checked at least twice for this record.

The linking of German records to Allied casualties is one area where an attempt has been made to bring together material from what are essentially two parallel universes. The making of these connections is emphatically not the central purpose of this book — they are very often put forward as suggestions which will hopefully open up further research, and it will be seen that many are queried. German claims should not be read in isolation with the entries to which they are appended, although extensive effort has been made to reach the most viable connections. German material should be seen in the wider context by looking at all entries for a given day, as others may prove more appropriate as work is done. In making the connections, aircraft types, times, and place names have been the means of filtering out extraneous material. Research into times has been discussed, but place names have been given equal scrutiny. Over twelve hundred towns, villages and hamlets have been tracked down and used to locate the events described.

The general terminology used in the entries follows the original wording of the primary sources as closely as possible. This is in order to preserve the mood and atmosphere as much as the veracity of the information. German aircraft types mentioned in combat and casualty reports are often difficult to be certain about. Where types are noted they have naturally been given, but this area remains somewhat vague.

All map references are given exactly as they appear in reports save that nearly all place names have been sorted out and their spellings resolved, and all names of air crew checked for correctness. All place names are given in upper case.

The sources
The main primary sources for this work are the combat and casualty reports held in AIR1 files at the Public Record Office at Kew in England. Where information has come from a RFC, RNAS, or RAF

Casualty Report it is preceded by two stars: "**". Every casualty report at Kew has been recorded in research for this book. There are two additional AIR1 sources which have this reference. This book begins its examination with the very first casualties in the air war. At this time there was no formal method for reporting these events — the earliest casualty reports began to be collected around May 1915, and even these had little system to them. In order to assemble events up until this time the only option open to the researcher is to minutely examine individual squadron and wing records, aircraft returns, reconnaissance reports, and so on, until a picture begins to form. The entries built up in this manner, until the summer of 1915, have also been given the source reference ** as a catch-all.

The other records which have been given a ** reference are those which have no corresponding casualty report but appear in the files AIR1/967/204/5/1097 to AIR1/969/204/5/1102. These list RFC and RAF pilot and observer casualties from June 1915 until April 1919. The names in these files are indexed and list most, but not all, casualties caused by enemy fire as well as by accidents. As it was assembled retro-spectively it often gives extra information such as a map reference for a crash or the fate of a missing airman. Although it gives a few hundred additional names of airmen who were casualties in action but who are not found in any casualty report, it is not always accurate as details were being transferred once removed from the event. A classic example of this is 2Lt J Gay and Lt G Leeson of 16 Squadron who were Max Immelmann's fourth victims on the 10th of October 1915. AIR1/967/204/5/1097 gives their aircraft as BE2c 2003, and so it has remained for all researchers for seventy years, until now, when it can be assuredly proven to be BE2c 2033. The 16 Squadron record book makes this perfectly clear. The names obtained from these files are also prefixed with ** but they can be usually identified by the fact that they do not include a mission type, and are rather brief. Records commenced with +* mean they have been derived from squadron combat reports.

Other sources of primary or official information for British and Commonwealth air crew include:

– Hundreds of AIR1 files at Kew dealing with personnel and aircraft at Wing and Squadron levels throughout the war. Over three hundred of these relating specifically to casualties are given in the bibliography.

– The 70,000 RFC and RAF Casualty Cards held at the RAF Museum, Hendon, all of which have been examined and recorded on computer by the author. The balance of this material will appear in subsequent publications.

– The Roll of Honour, Royal Flying Corps and Royal Air Force for the Great War 1914-18 and The St Catherine's Register, dealing with other ranks.

– The List of Officers Taken Prisoner in the Various Theatres of War Between August 1914 and November 1918.

– Regimental Rolls of Officers who Died in the War.

– Logbooks held at the RAF Museum Hendon and in the Imperial War Museum.

German source material regarding combat and Flak claims has mostly come from the lists contained in *Abschusse Feindlicher Flugzeuge*, the copy consulted being in the library of the Imperial War Museum, as well as the transcriptions of Jasta claims lists in the possession of the authors of *Above the Lines*.

United States Air Service source material has come mostly from the Gorrell Reports, especially Series M: Miscellaneous, Volume No. 38, "Compilation of confirmed victories and losses of the AEF Air Service as of May 26, 1919".

In the research which involved working through all the above, secondary cross-reference was made to countless articles contained in Cross and Cockade Journals of both American and British origin, as well as to numbers of *Over the Front* magazine. Many hundreds of books were consulted as well, but several deserve special mention. They are:

– The six volumes of the official history, *The War in the Air* and its appendices, by HA Jones and Sir W Raleigh

– *Royal Navy Aircraft Serials and Units 1911–1919* and *The Camel File* by R Sturtivant and G Page

- *Above the Trenches* by C Shores, NLR Franks, and R Guest

- *Above the Lines* by NLR Franks, FW Bailey, and R Guest

- *The Aeroplanes of the Royal Flying Corps (Military Wing)*, by JM Bruce

- *The Air Defence of Britain 1914–1918*, by C Cole and EF Cheesman

- *The Australian Flying Corps*, vol. 8 of *The Official History of Australia in the War of 1914–1918*, by FM Cutlack

- *Canadian Airmen in the First World War*, by SF Wise

- *Wings of Honor*, by JJ Sloan Jr

- *The Roll of Honour, Royal Flying Corps and Royal Air Force for the Great War 1914–1918*, by HJ Williamson.

Glossary of terms and abbreviations

*AmmDrp	Ammunition Dropping	*LP	Line Patrol
*AOb	Artillery Observation Patrol	*LRec	Line Reconnaissance Patrol
*AP	Artillery Patrol	*LowB	Low Bombing Patrol
*ARec	Artillery Reconnaissance Patrol	*LowP	Low Patrol
*AReg	Artillery Registration	*LowRec	Low Reconnaissance Patrol
*AS	Aerial Sentry Patrol	*NB	Night Bombing Operation
*AShoot	Artillery Shoot	*NFP	Night Flying Patrol
*AStr	Artillery Strafe	*NOP	Northern Offensive Patrol
*AmmDrop	Ammunition Drop	*NRec	Night Reconnaissance Patrol
*B	Bombing Operation	*OP	Offensive Patrol
*BOP	Low Bombing and Offensive Patrol	*ObP	Observation Patrol
*CAP	Counter-Attack Patrol	*Phot	Photographic Patrol
*CentP	Central Zone Patrol	*PhotB	Bombing Photography
*COP	Central Offensive Patrol	*prac	Practice Flight
*COP	Close Offensive Patrol	*RFL	Returning from forced landing
*CP	Contact Patrol	*Rec	Reconnaissance Patrol
*Comm	Communications Flight	*RecB	Bombing Reconnaissance Patrol
*Counter	Counter-Attack Patrol	*Sent	Aerial Sentry Patrol
*DBP	Detached Balloon Patrol	*Shoot	Artillery Shoot
*Deliv	Delivery Flight	*SitP	Situation Patrol
*DKBP	Defensive Kite Balloon Patrol	*SOP	Southern Offensive Patrol
*DOP	Deep Offensive Patrol	*SpM	Special Mission
*DOP	Distant Offensive Patrol	*SpP	Special Patrol
*DnRec	Dawn Reconnaissance Patrol	*Str	Strafing Patrol
*EscPhot	Escorting Photographic Patrol	*SubP	Anti-Submarine Patrol
*EscRec	Escorting Reconnaissance Patrol	*targprac	Target Practice
*EvRec	Evening Reconnaissance Patrol	*Test	Testing Flight
*Famil	Familiarisation with Lines	*travel	Travelling Flight
*FleetP	Fleet Patrol	*TrB	Trench Bombing
*FoodDrp	Food Drop	*Trg	Training Flight
*GroundP	Ground Patrol	*TrRec	Trench Reconnaissance Patrol
*gunprac	Gunnery Practice	*TrpSht	Troop Shoot-up
*HAP	Hostile Aircraft Patrol	*Visit	Visiting the lines
*HD	Home Defence Patrol	*WTInt	Wireless Interruption Patrol
*HOP	High Offensive Patrol	*ZepP	Anti-Zeppelin Patrol
*InfProt	Infantry Protection Patrol	1Lt	First Lieutenant (US Aero Service)
*InnP	Inner Patrol		
*IOP	Inner Offensive Patrol	2Lt	2nd Lieutenant
*Insp	Inspection Patrol	2Str	Two-seater
*KBP	Kite Balloon Patrol	A	Acting
		AA	Anti-aircraft fire

a'c	aircraft
AD	Aeroplane Depot
Adj	Adjutant
AFC	Australian Flying Corps
AKN	Abwehr Kommando Nord (German defence command)
A.L.G.	Advanced Landing Ground
AM	Air Mechanic
AP	Aeroplane Park
ARD	Aeroplane Repair Depot
ARS	Aeroplane Repair Section
A-type	German two-seater monoplane (1914–1915)
Aust.	Australian national
B-type	German two-seater biplanes (1914–1915)
Bgde	Brigade
Bogohl	Bombengeschwader (German bombing unit)
btwn	between
Can.	Canadian national
Capt	Captain
capt	captured
Cdt	Cadet
conv	converted
Cpl	Corporal
cr	crashed
cr ldg	crashed landing
C-type	improved German two-seater biplane (1915–1918)
c'wind	crosswind
dd	driven down
des	destroyed
Det.Flt.	Detached Flight
DFC	Distinguished Flying Cross
DFM	Distinguished Flying Medal
DFW	Deutsche Flugzeug-Werke (two-seater)
DoI	Died of Injuries
DoW	Died of Wounds
DRO	Daily Routine Orders
DSC	Distinguished Service Cross
DSM	Distinguished Service Medal
D-type	German single-seater fighter
d'wind	downwind
EA	Enemy Aircraft
eAMIENS	east of Amiens (typically)
Ens	Ensign (US Navy)
EoL	east of lines
Esc	Escadrille (French flying unit)
E-type	German single-seater monoplane fighter
FAb	Flieger-Abteilung (German aviation unit)

FAb.A	Artillerieflieger-Abteilung (German artillery spotter aircraft unit)
FCdr	Flight Commander
FFAb	Feldflieger-Abteilung (German field aviation unit)
Flak	German anti-aircraft fire
FlgM	Flugmeister (German Naval airman)
Flgr	Flieger (German Private)
Flt	Flight
FLt	Flight Lieutenant (RNAS)
FMAS	First Marine Air Service (US)
Fr.	Freiherr (German Baron)
French.	French national
FSgt	Flight Sergeant
FSLt	Flight Sub-Lieutenant (RNAS)
ftg	fighting
ftl	forced to land
GAF	German Air Force (Luftstreitkrafte)
GHQ	General Headquarters
GL	Gun-layer
Gfr	Gefreiter (German Private)
Gnr	Gunner
Grk.	Greek national
HA	Hostile Aircraft
HF	Henri Farman
HMS	His Majesty's Ship
HMT	His Majesty's Trawler
hosp	to hospital
HP	Handley Page
hp	horsepower
Hpt	Hauptmann (German Captain)
HQ	Headquarters
hrs	hours
I.F.	Independent Force
Ind.	Indian national
Irl.	Irish national
inj	injured
INT	Interned
IWM	Imperial War Museum
Ja,Jasta	Jagdstaffel (German single-seater fighter unit)
JG	Jagdgeschwader (Permanent German fighter wing)
JGr	Jagdgruppe (Temporary German fighter wing)
Kagohl	Kampfgeschwader der Obsten Heeresleitung (German combat squadron)
KASTA	Kampfstaffel (German fighter section)
KB	Kite balloon
KBS	Kite Balloon Section

KEK	Kampfeinsitzer-Kommando (German single-seater fighter command)		prop	propeller
			proto	prototype
			Pte	Private
KEST	Kampfeinsitzer-Staffel (German single-seater fighter unit)		rep	repairable
			repat	repatriated
KG	Kampfgeschwader (German fighter-bomber unit)		resc	rescued
			RFC	Royal Flying Corps
KIA	Killed in Action		Ritt	Rittmeister (German Cavalry Captain)
KIFA	Killed in Flying Accident			
Kld	Killed		Rlwy	Railway
lb	pound weight		RNAS	Royal Naval Air Service
LM	Leading Midshipman		RoH	Roll of Honour
Lt	Lieutenant		R-type	Riesenflugzeug (German Giant aeroplane)
Ltn	Leutnant (German 2nd Lieutenant)			
			SA.	South African national
LtnzS	Leutnant zur See (German Naval Lieutenant)		sAMIENS	south of Amiens
			SchSt	Schlachtstaffel (German ground support unit)
LVG	Luft-Verkehrs Gesellschaft (German two-seater)			
			s-e, se	south-east
Maj	Major		sev	severely (wounded)
MC	Military Cross		SFS	Seefrontstaffel (German marine unit)
M.E.	Middle East			
MF	Maurice Farman		Sgt	Sergeant
MFJa	Marine-Feldjagdstaffel (German marine fighter unit)		Sig	Signalman
			SLt.	Sub-Lieutenant
mg	machine-gun fire		snd	spinning nose dive
MIA	Missing in Action		Sqn	Squadron
Mid,Md	Midshipman		ss	side-slipped
mins	minutes		SS	Seaplane Station (German)
MM	Military Medal		Stn	Station
M.S.	French Morane Saulnier Escadrille		s-w, sw	south-west
			tk off	take off
nAMIENS	north of Amiens		TLt	Temporary Lieutenant
nd	nose dive		U-boat	Unterseeboot (German submarine)
n-e, ne	north-east			
n.m.l.	no man's land		u'c	undercarriage
nrAMIENS	near Amiens		UK.	United Kingdom national
NZ.	New Zealand national		Untoff	Unteroffizier (German Corporal)
ObFlgM	Oberflugmeister (German Naval Senior NCO)		US.	United States national
			USAS	United States Air Service
Oblt	Oberleutnant (German 1st Lieutenant)		USMC	United States Military Corps
			USNR	United States Naval Reserve
OffSt	OffizierStellvertreter (German Warrant Officer)		VC	Victoria Cross
			Vzfw	Vizefeldwebel (German Sergeant)
OK	refers to personnel: okay, uninjured		wAMIENS	west of Amiens
			WCdr	Wing Commander
ok	refers to aircraft: okay, undamaged		WIA	Wounded in Action
			WO, w'o	write off
ooc	out of control		WoL	west of lines
o't	overturned		wr	wrecked
ovAMIENS	over AMIENS		WT	Wireless Telegraphy
PO	Petty Officer		~	approximate (time)
PObs,Prob	Probationary Observer		+	Allied victory claim (when used within square brackets)
POW	Prisoner of War			
PRO	Public Record Office			

Part I

THE WESTERN FRONT 1914–1918

1914 THE OUTBREAK OF WAR

The Great War changed the world in ways undreamt of in 1914. The conflict was to immerse entire nations for many years, and the forces which would drive it extended well beyond the lives of those many millions involved. National character and resilience, and certainly native skill and inventiveness, would all play a part and all be relentlessly tested. It was clear in August 1914 that there was no simple solution to the crisis because the forces which had brought about the war ran so deep. The aspirations of nations now conflicted so openly that it was inevitable that it should be left to two great armies to resolve matters.

The war set in motion a sweeping tide of events, driven by battle plans which at the outset were appropriately vast. That which Germany pursued, almost to victory, had been nurtured for a generation. Its architect was Graf Alfred von Schlieffen, and it was devastating in its simplicity. Rather than frontally attack France's well defended eastern borders, Germany would launch a great flanking movement through Belgium. This would then pivot down through eastern France, behind her armies, isolating them from Paris and cutting their supply networks and lines of retreat. The additional hook, which would assure France's destruction, would be a deliberate fall back of German forces in the Alsace and the Lorraine. This would lure the French eastwards, pulling them into the feint, to find themselves enveloped and defeated. With some telling modifications, this plan duly unfolded in the days following the 4th of August, as Germany finally made its decisive gesture and began its surge into Belgium.

THE AIR SERVICES MOBILISED

As hostilities commenced, both the Allied Powers and Germany possessed a varied collection of aircraft. Some military leaders hoped they could be found useful to their armies. A small number of machines had been built up through the years of slow discovery and development of the new air weapon, and within the opposing military structures were gathered into units. At the outbreak of war, most other civilian machines were quickly commandeered as well.

Annual military manoeuvres had been conducted as usual in 1913 in Britain, France, and Germany. The use of aeroplanes had been incorporated into these, but exactly what use they could be to commanders in war was far from clear. Germany and France were both more resolved than Britain on finding a role for aircraft. This was best demonstrated on the Continent by the relatively generous support offered to designers and builders of aircraft by the military authorities. In Britain, many in influence felt they were, and would remain, a novelty. In spite of the developments made up until August 1914, what all countries possessed by then was little more than an ad hoc collection of types, with no single machine convincingly designed or suited for war.

The air arms of the protagonists shared one central characteristic, which was that all their efforts were subordinated to the armies on the ground. This relationship would survive until the end of the war, preserved and fostered through an ever growing, unbreakable interdependence with the army staffs. It was known that aircraft and balloons could gather reconnaissance, but in 1914 so could horse and foot patrols. Many felt that airmen flying two thousand feet above the ground could not grasp the essentials of what

was being played out on the ground and that they would make errors. But perhaps their reports could add to the picture, so long as those reading them felt they could be trusted. In other words, the new arms would need to prove their effectiveness.

There was not a single armed aircraft in the air at this time. German flyers were required to wear their sabres when aloft, and British pilots were made to carry tools, a stove, soup-making equipment and spare goggles. Air crew were expected to carry service revolvers in the event of needing to land in hostile territory. The machines they flew were slow and their engines unreliable. Forced landings were a way of life, and repairs were usually carried out on the spot by whichever member of the crew showed the most aptitude for the problem. Flying in general was hugely dependent on the weather to be effective and safe. Britain also had to get its aircraft across the Channel, which even in normal times would have given any flyer in 1914 a long pause for thought.

At this time the British Royal Flying Corps (RFC) had one hundred and seventy-nine aircraft, a mere forty of which were finally deemed capable of making the crossing. Another twenty-four were packed up ready to be shipped. On the 8th of August this force began to find its way to Dover from its various locations for mobilisation. Nos. 2, 3, 4, and 5 Squadrons, Headquarters and the Aircraft Park made up the strength.

On the 13th of August machines began to set out for Amiens in France. Nos. 2 and 4 Squadrons had BE2s, No.3 Squadron had a mixture of Blériots and Henri Farmans and No.5 Squadron had Henri Farmans, Avros and BE8s. One flight of No.4 Squadron remained behind to continue coastal patrols, and was replaced in that unit by a small wireless flight. The RFC comprised sixty-three aircraft when it crossed to France, one having been lost in the final stages of mobilisation. On the 16th, most of the British force flew on to Maubeuge, where the British Expeditionary Force's (BEF) General Headquarters were situated. The BEF at this time was a tiny force in the overall picture, consisting of two corps and a cavalry division. It was to position itself on the French left. Its air arm, the RFC, carried out the first aerial reconnaissances of the war within three days of its arrival.

The first war duties of the Royal Naval Air Service (RNAS) were patrols of England's eastern coast, ordered within days of the declaration of war. In combination with these it watched over the passage of the British Expeditionary Force to France. It claimed to have ninety-three aircraft, and the first unit to cross to the Continent would be the transfer of Commander CR Samson's Eastchurch Squadron to Ostende on the 27th of August. A typical assemblage of types would make up this group: BE and Sopwith biplanes, Blériots, a Henri Farman, a Bristol biplane and a converted Short seaplane.

The German Air Service consisted of forty-nine sections of aircraft, including twenty-nine Feldflieger Abteilungen (field aviation sections) and four Festungflieger Abteilungen (fortress flights) positioned on the borders. The remainder were home training sections. Each had a theoretical strength of six machines, or four in the case of the fortress flights, but in August 1914 the total number of flyable aircraft was two hundred and eighteen. The German units were composed of the lovely Taube monoplane and several types of two-seater tractor aircraft (so called for having the propeller at the front, pulling the aircraft through the air) built by the manufacturers LVG, DFW, Albatros and Aviatik. The German airmen were still, at this stage, a branch of the Signal Corps. Finally, the French had twenty-three escadrilles at mobilisation, two of which were cavalry escadrilles. Each had a maximum of six machines and in all the French aircraft numbered one hundred and thirty-eight. Another four escadrilles were formed shortly after hostilities began.

August 1914

16th August

625   **BE8**   **3Sqn**
* stall at 150′ on take off cr AMIENS fire wr(2Lt EWC
Perry **KIFA**/2AM HE Parfitt **KIFA**)

These were the first RFC casualties on active service in France. The first casualty of the air war had been a French observer wounded by fire from the ground on the 8th, whilst Oblt R Jahnow was reported as the first German air casualty of the war on the 12th. He was shot down and killed, also by ground fire, crashing near Malmedy.

19th August

Blériot XI-2   **3Sqn**
*Rec left 9-30am NIVELLES-GENAPPE cloudy lost ftl
TOURNAI OK(Capt PB Joubert de la Ferte) no
observer

242?   BE2   4Sqn
this a'c? *Rec left 9-30am NIVELLES-GEMBLOUX
cloudy OK(Lt GW Mapplebeck)

These were the first two reconnaissances carried
out across the lines in France by the RFC. They
were begun together but each pilot subsequently
took his own route.

22nd August

The RFC carried out twelve reconnaissances on the
22nd, one of them offering vital confirmation to
headquarters that the German Army was commencing an enveloping movement. This flight had
seen a significant force moving westward on the
Brussels-Ninove road, turning south-west at
Ninove, and in consequence moving into a position
to outflank the British Army. This ominous news
galvanised headquarters to commence a general
retreat from Mons, begun almost immediately and
just in time to save the BEF. It took the form of a
retreating arc, pivoting southwards around the
fortress of Verdun.

BE2?   2Sqn
**Rec seLESSINES rifle fire OLLIGNIES then ground
fire from Cavalry Regiment swGHISLENGHIEN &
finally shot up ovMAFFLE seATH(2Lt MW Noel OK/
SgtMaj DS Jillings **WIA**)leg

SgtMaj Jillings was the first RFC air crew to be
wounded in action. He was back on strength of
2 Squadron by October 1914.

390   Avro 504   5Sqn
**Rec BELGIUM probably shot down by German
ground fire cr **MIA**(2Lt VE Waterfall **KIA**/Lt CGG
Bayly **KIA**) left 10-16am

This was the first British crew to be missing in
action and likely to have been brought down by
enemy fire. For the German High Command it
imparted the first real proof that the British
Expeditionary Force was in the field before them.

One other thing of note which occurred this day
was the appearance of the first German aeroplane
seen in the air by the RFC. It was a two-seater
Albatros. It came over Maubeuge aerodrome about
2-25pm and three aircraft duly took off to chase it.
In two BE2s from No.2 Squadron were Maj
Longcroft and Capt Dawes, and Lt L Dawes and
Maj CJ Burke (probably in BE2a 372), whilst Lt
LA Strange with Lt Penn-Gaskell of No.5
Squadron ascended in Farman 341. In Strange's
typically indefatigable way, he had unofficially
mounted a Lewis gun to his aircraft and his
observer managed to fire it off at the fast escaping
enemy machine. The gun also painfully diminished

the aircraft's performance and it was ordered to be
removed, so that next time they took a rifle. Flyers
were already experimenting with taking such
weapons aloft. Before the Albatros had come over
they had already seen enemy aircraft on the
ground, and attempts had even been made to drop
the occasional bomb on these, without success.
Pilots were already thinking about warfare in the
air, but it all lay in the future to be discovered. The
current thinking was that bombs or even hand
grenades might be dropped onto passing enemy
machines. One suggestion being considered was to
dangle a grappling hook and snare the opponent!

23rd August

THE BATTLE OF MONS

The battle of Mons commenced on the 23rd. What
had at first been planned as a British offensive
became the general retreat. The RFC began its own
retirement on the same day, moving its headquarters from Maubeuge to Le Cateau. It was the
first of several moves as the RFC was forced back
before the army, its headquarters occupying ten
towns between the 23rd of August and the 4th
September. Many aircraft had to be abandoned or
burnt in this retreat and these have been mentioned
where possible. The strains imposed on headquarters and squadrons alike were enormous in
these days. It was essential for crews to maintain a
steady flow of intelligence, and to ensure that this
was possible the ground crews worked around the
clock to keep machines operational.

The preservation of the Allied cause rested
entirely on the orderly withdrawal of its troops.
The German Army strove desperately therefore to
edge around the western flank of the retiring army,
or to find a dislocation in the line, either of which
would have almost certainly led to disaster. Their
command was also being informed by the efforts of
its aviators so that relentless pressure could be
maintained. German airmen searched constantly
for thin sections of the British line or points where
a lack of resources was evident.

24th August

The RFC worked just as tirelessly to interpret the
unfolding events, particularly at the edge of line
where circumstances were most critical. One of the
most important reconnaissances was that made by
Capt GS Shephard and Lt IM Bonham-Carter of
No.4 Squadron on the 24th which brought
conclusive evidence that von Kluck's right wing
was likely to outflank the British Army unless the

retreat was maintained. Not only could airmen alert the retreating army to impending danger of this kind, but also began to provide information about other matters, such as the enemy's guns. Naturally the usefulness of this flow of information was dependent on being properly assessed at head-quarters and the organisational structure for this process was in many ways still in its infancy. Without doubt, however, the British retreat would have been severely compromised without the new element of air reconnaissance. In a time of certain crisis the RFC was finding its feet.

355	MFLH	5Sqn

** engine trouble, a'c abandoned MAUBEUGE in move to LE CATEAU engine salvaged

25th August

The RFC brought down the first enemy aircraft this day. Three 2 Squadron machines so alarmed the pilot of a German Taube with feinted attacks that he was forced to land. Lt HD Harvey-Kelly and Lt WHC Mansfield landed nearby and chased the pilot off into a wood. Later in the same day, another enemy aircraft was forced down near Le Quesnoy by a 4 Squadron crew.

608?	RE1?	Aircraft Park (for 2Sqn)

this a'c? ** hit by bullet, ftl cr nrMONS(2Lt C Gordon-Bell **inj**)shaken, possibly on the 23rd? (see below)

This casualty is listed in AIR1/871/204/5/550 with the date 25.8.14. 2Lt C Gordon-Bell, the noted pioneer test pilot, was listed as being in the original Expeditionary Force, at the Aircraft Park. It is known that a hurried request was sent back to England on the 22nd of August for any spare machines to be flown to France. Five were found, including RE1 608, which Gordon-Bell flew over on the 23rd. He may have been shot up on the journey, or on subsequent testing of the aircraft. The RE1 was off strength by the end of the month.

299	BE2a	4Sqn

**Rec shot up by French: 6 shots dam OK(Maj GH Raleigh/Capt Small)

Crews on both sides at this time ran the gauntlet of ground fire from foe and friend alike. National markings were as yet barely considered, and the presence of any aircraft above a fighting army was still not only utterly novel but also undoubtedly disconcerting. Already, the troops on the ground had learnt how difficult it was to hide from the view of aircraft above them, and if in any doubt they naturally took steps to protect themselves. Enemy airmen were the only combatants not shooting at one another.

26th August

220	BE2a	4Sqn

* burnt at LE CATEAU

389	Blériot XI-2	3Sqn

**Armed Rec LE CATEAU-VALENCIENNES-CAMBRAI dropped single bomb on transport BLAUGIES then engine hit by ground fire wCAMBRAI ftl burnt a'c returned to WoL OK(Lt GF Pretyman/Maj LB Boyd-Moss) joined French cavalry to ARRAS, and eventually back to squadron.

The full reconnaissance report of these events also appears in vol. I of *The War in the Air*, but the serial of the Blériot given there is 387, which is incorrect.

27th August

THE ROYAL NAVAL AIR SERVICE IN FRANCE

The RNAS Eastchurch Squadron arrived in Ostende on the 27th in an attempt to set up a coastal unit for attacks on German bases. Three days later it was decided that Ostende could not be defended and the RNAS was ordered back to England. It first travelled to Dunkirk, where it was delayed by a serious crash of one of its Blériots. Several days of bargaining between Britain and France then followed, with the result that the unit was permitted to remain in Dunkirk and operate with the French. Samson was ordered to "operate against Zeppelins and enemy aeroplanes and to carry out reconnaissances as required by the French general". As it happened, most of their first operations were made using armoured cars, operating in tandem with aircraft. The Eastchurch Squadron was renamed No.3 Squadron RNAS on the 1st of September 1914.

NOTE: An effort will be made throughout this book to keep track of the multitudinous name changes which the RNAS went through in the first two and a half years of fighting in order that there be some basis for understanding the unit names when they arise. For detailed analysis of this subject, and much else besides, the best reference is Sturtivant and Page's book *Royal Naval Aircraft Serials and Units* (see bibliography).

September 1914

1st September

239	BE2a	2Sqn

* engine failed ftl, a'c abandoned in retreat burnt (Lt Lawrence)

608   RE1   2Sqn
* damaged while landing to warn troops of enemy advance,
then burnt in retreat(Maj Longcroft/Lt Holbrow)

2nd September

356   MFLH   5Sqn
* a'c burnt & abandoned JUILLY: needed repair so was to
be evacuated late, but damaged on take off, engine
salvaged, NB not No. 456 as some sources

6th September

THE FRENCH COUNTER-ATTACK

The French Commander in Chief, Joffre, ordered a
major counter-attack against the Germans on the
6th. The German Supreme Command had interpreted the substantial retreats it had imposed on the
British and the French as a rout, and decided to
hasten the encirclement by ordering its armies still
east of Paris, to wheel south-east and eastwards. In
this action, the von Schlieffen plan was effectively
abandoned, and Germany found itself committed to
bearing down on an army which was in fact far from
defeated. The concentration of troops into this drive
suddenly created a vulnerable flank, open to attack
from the French Army in front of Paris, and they
took their chance and drove in on Kluck's forces to
the north-east of the capital.

It was because the relatively small force of the
Royal Flying Corps had offered such a high quality
of intelligence about the German movements that
the French command felt able to take this momentous gamble of a counter-attack. Joffre's staff would
pay great tribute to their work in these critical days,
saying "The British Flying Corps had played a
prominent, in fact vital part, in watching and following this all-important movement on which so much
depended. Thanks to the [British] aviators he had
been kept accurately and constantly informed of
Kluck's movements. To them he owed the certainty
which had enabled him to make his plans in good
time."

7th September

479   BE8   3Sqn
** burnt nrSIGNY by enemy? **MIA**(Lt VSE Lindop
POW) to Holland 6.2.18

Lt Lindop was the first Royal Flying Corps prisoner
of war as well as being 3 Squadron's first casualty.

318   BE2a   4Sqn
**Rec MELUN bullet through main spar OK(Lt HJA
Roche/Lt KP Atkinson)

8th September

HF 806   Henri Farman   5Sqn
**Rec bullet hit spar OK(2Lt DC Ware/Capt RA Boger)

9th September

The Allied counter-attack from the west finally
stopped the German advance. Kluck had crossed
the Marne unprepared for the attack which came
on his right flank and he had no option but to
reorganise and face it. Furthermore, German air
reconnaissance now reported that British troops in
their turn were about to cross the Marne. The
British had moved forward with tremendous accuracy, crucially aided by the detailed intelligence
provided by the RFC. Faced with these compound-
ing events the German High Command made the
momentous decision to retire its troops northwards.

471   BE2a   2Sqn
* engine failed ftl NANTEUIL burnt to stop
capture(Capt FF Waldron/Lt HD Harvey-Kelly)

372   BE2a   2Sqn
* thought MIA but OK(Lt L Dawes/Lt DSK Crosbie)

Bl 809   Blériot XI   3Sqn
* wr & burnt DOUEX(Lt GF Pretyman)

On the 9th of September the remaining C Flight of
4 Squadron arrived in France. It had remained
behind at Dover to carry out coastal patrols, but
now its Maurice Farman Shorthorns were brought
across. Notably these were fitted with machine-
guns and were the first armed machines to arrive
in France.

Until the 9th the weather had been remarkable
for flying, and this had contributed considerably to
the effectiveness of the RFC. It now deteriorated
dramatically and flying was impossible for a few
days. Terrible gales struck the RFC machines at
Fère en Tardenois on the night of 12th/13th of
September and several were wrecked.

12th September

384   BE2   2Sqn
**Rec ground mg engine hit ftl LAON-SOISSONS EoL
cr woods to wreck a'c OK(Lt L Dawes/Lt WR Freeman)

This crew spent the night escaping westwards,
finally swimming the Aisne and reaching the
British guns.

** **MIA**(F.Sgt D Goodchild **POW**/A.M. Chilton? or
1A.M. Foley? **POW**)

13th September

THE BATTLE OF THE AISNE

The battle of the Aisne commenced on the 13th of September. This saw the British forces advancing along the river until impasse was reached around the 20th.

On the Aisne, the fledgling Wireless Flight of 4 Squadron was used effectively for the first time, gaining great notoriety for their work above the battle. Lts DS Lewis and BT James in their BE2as were the first airmen to observe for the artillery, a completely novel aspect of army co-operation work. In time this task would assume major proportions.

15th September

| | | 3Sqn |
*PhotRec ovBELGIUM OK(Lt GF Pretyman), 5 plates exposed

This was the first ever photo-reconnaissance.

16th September

No.2 Squadron RNAS arrived at Dunkirk on the 16th of September but stayed only briefly. It was based at Antwerp and Ostende before returning to England to be disbanded on the 10th of October.

20th September

| 242 | BE2a | 4Sqn |
**B: Kite Balloon, prop shot up returned to a'dr, but re-started only to be shot up again OK(Lt GW Mapplebeck)

22nd September

| 242 | BE2a | 4Sqn |
**Bombing Kite Balloon exchanged shots with Albatros 2Str shot up ftl 2Sq DHUIZEL(Lt GW Mapplebeck WIA)leg

Mapplebeck was the first RFC pilot to be wounded by fire from an enemy aircraft.

| 906 | Sopwith 3 Seater | 1Sqn RNAS |
**B raid to DUSSELDORF Airship Sheds OK(Lt CH Collet)

This was the first British raid on Germany itself. Only Collet reached the target, and a single bomb of the four he dropped exploded. All the aircraft involved in the attack returned safely.

27th September

| 917 | Bristol TB8 | 3Sqn RNAS |
**B shot up ftl sea 10m off CALAIS salved OK(FLt CF Beevor)

28th September

| 372 | BE2a | 2Sqn |

** dam in retreat & burnt LA FÈRE OK(Lt L Dawes/ Lt DSK Crosbie)

THE FIRST RFC SCOUTS IN FRANCE

This day saw two Bristol Scout single-seaters join active RFC Squadrons in France. It was the first allocation in the field of a type of aircraft which would be used primarily for air fighting — the fast single-seater scout — and as such it demonstrated a crucial new awareness, that of opposing combatants in the sky. No. 644 went to 5 Squadron and No. 648 to 3 Squadron. The new offensive mood was evident in the elaborate armament these machines received. 5 Squadron hastily fixed a Lee-Enfield rifle angled off from the propeller arc, provided a Mauser pistol and fixed an external rack with five grenades. 3 Squadron also fitted a rifle on each side of the Scout's fuselage, angled out at 45 degrees.

30th September

| 314 | BE2a | 4Sqn |
** fuselage shot up by French mg & by French a'c dam(Lt WGS Mitchell/Capt DLeG Pitcher)

| 26 | RE5 | Dunkirk |
**B CAMBRAI Railway Station OK(SCdr. AM Longmore/FLt E Osmond)

October 1914

THE RACE TO THE SEA

Throughout September the Allied counter-offensive had pressed hard at the German retirement, but eventually it halted in entrenched deadlock on the Aisne. What then took place is known as "The Race to the Sea", in which the two armies drove north-westwards pressed together in a battle for advantage. The first efforts centred on attempts to outflank one another but a raging, deadly battle soon evolved as both sides strove for position all the way to the Channel coast. Generally deteriorating weather and the expansive extent of the fighting meant that air support could only take a reduced role in these events. The value of air reconnaissance was no longer in any doubt, however, and the presence of aircraft was now demanded wherever possible by the ground forces. On the other hand, the ever increasing scale and intensity of the fighting taxed the meagre resources and experience of the flying corps. It was now essential to reorganise and nurture its activities, and this would characterise the growth and diversification of the RFC in the coming months.

A battle line began to settle itself onto north-eastern France, and by mid-October it would extend from

northern Flanders, at Nieuport on the coast, all the way to the Swiss border. The war of movement would be ended, and operations imposed by this deadlock would come to dominate the four long years of fighting which remained. It would become a static war of vast opposing defensive fortifications from which attritional, unforgiving and deadly fighting would be conducted. The air forces which presently flew over the deepening entrenchments had already proved of inestimable value to the participants during the war of movement, but now they too would have to adapt to the new circumstances.

1st October

916	Bristol TB8	3Sqn RNAS

** fuel tank shot up ftl field unsalvable OK (Lt TA Rainey)

4th October

465	BE2a	4Sqn

+* shots exchanged with DFW ovCRAONNE 4000' ~8-20am OK (Capt EF Chinnery/Cpl Piper)

5th October

638	Avro 504	5Sqn

**Rec left 2pm BAPAUME MIA (Capt R Grey POW/ Capt RA Boger POW) both to Holland 6.2.18

	Voisin III	Esc. VB24 (French)

** 47 rounds fired at Aviatik [+destroyed] ovJONCHERY-SUR-VESLE OK (Sgt Frantz/Cpl Quenault) German crew killed were Schlienting and Zangen

This was probably the first aircraft brought down by fire from another machine.

7th October

6 Squadron RFC proceeded to Ostende on the 7th of October. At the outbreak of war it had been little more than a nucleus, and its personnel and equipment had been mostly transferred to 2 Squadron. It was reassembled and dispatched in great haste to help relieve Antwerp, bringing types including the BE8, BE2a, BE2b, and the Henri Farman. Immediately on arrival it began reconnaissances but within a week it had retired to Dunkirk and then Poperinghe. It would continue in a strategic reconnaissance role until the end of the year, but at the same time would be developing what would later be its specialist fields — co-operation with the artillery and tactical reconnaissance.

8th October

167	Sopwith Tabloid	2Sqn RNAS

1Sqn RNAS? **B to KÖLN Airship Sheds but met poor weather, lost, so bombed KÖLN Railway Station OK (SCdr. Spencer DA Grey)

168	Sopwith Tabloid	2Sqn RNAS

1(N)? **B to DUSSELDORF Airship sheds, dh on sheds with 4 x 20lb bombs from 600' [+destroyed Zeppelin Z.IX] AA?, low fuel ftl 20m from ANTWERP on return OK (FLt RL Marrix) a'c abandoned in retreat

9th October

167	Sopwith Tabloid	2Sqn RNAS

** hit by ground fire ANTWERP dam then a'c abandoned in retreat

10th October

No.2 Squadron RNAS returned to England on the 10th of October. It was reformed at Eastchurch where it undertook the training of air personnel. It was renamed No.2 Wing RNAS on the 21st of June 1915 and would return to France briefly in August before being sent to the Dardanelles.

15th October

633	MFSH	4Sqn

** shots exchanged with Albatros 2 Str ovFLEURBAIX 5500' [+? nose-dive, then into clouds] ~3-30pm OK (Lt Barton/Capt T Crean)

19th October

THE FIRST BATTLE OF YPRES

Very poor weather in the second half of October made observation work almost impossible. Nevertheless, enough was carried out to alert the British to an impending German offensive of great magnitude. Fighting in the first battle of Ypres broke out on the 19th of October and would last for a month, conducted by both sides at times with a terrible desperation. Their air arms were now carrying out reconnaissances whenever it was possible to get machines into the air, increasingly targeted for effect.

26th October

317	BE2a	4Sqn

this a'c? **Rec shot down by Allied rifle fire ovPOPERINGHE 1000' cr fire (Lt CG Hosking KIA/ Capt T Crean KIA)

BE2a 317 had an ensign painted on both wings, but this had not saved the crew from being fatally shot down. As the numbers of aircraft over the battlefield multiplied so did the ground fire directed at them. The red cross at the centre of the ensign dominated its pattern from a distance and it is likely they had been mistaken for German crosses. This fatality hastened the adoption of a form of the French cockade for the British in which the colours were swapped.

27th October

469   BE2a   6Sqn
Rec LILLE strong westerly gale **MIA(Lt K Rawson-Shaw **POW**/Lt HGL Mayne **POW**) left 8-30am, both to Holland 24.2.18

This crew was the first lost in action by 6 Squadron RFC.

30th October

5Sqn
Rec HOLLEBEKE-HOUTHEM rifle fire shot up(Maj JFA Higgins **WIA/Lt RM Vaughan OK)

371?   MFSH   4Sqn
**B attacked ground targets: shot up enemy convoy, firing 250 rounds w Lewis gun OK(Lt GN Humphreys) probably MFSH 371

This was most likely the first ever ground attack by an aircraft.

November 1914

THE FIRST RFC WINGS AND AN EXPANDING ROLE

In November the RFC took the first formal steps towards decentralising into workable units appropriate for the widening war. The squadrons were divided into two Wings, one allocated to each of the two new armies about to be formed. 2 and 3 Squadrons became 1 Wing at St Omer on the 19th, and 5 and 6 Squadrons formed 2 Wing on the 29th. 4 Squadron, the Communications Wing, and the Aircraft Park remained with RFC Headquarters at St Omer. The concept of attaching a wing to an army would be fully adopted by the beginning of 1915.

At the same time, the technology which could enable the air arms to contribute more effectively to the changed nature of the war took a sudden leap. With the battle lines now static there was a desperate need to understand the dispositions in depth of the enemy before them. Dumps, camps, lines of communication and defences would all have to be mapped and then continually observed in minute detail in order to reveal where some sudden breakout might occur. Tactical understanding was especially vital for the Allies, because in terms of terrain and communications the Germans had retired to highly advantageous positions. The Allies had been left facing them on often difficult and inferior ground, none of which could be lightly relinquished however. It was therefore essential that air reconnaissance provide an edge where it could.

Two types of work arose from this situation which would remain central to the air war from this time onwards. Ultimately their protection would be the reason why air fighting developed. One was aerial photography, which was to prove the prime method for reconnaissance. But first, experiments in ranging guns for the artillery began to gather pace, and it would soon become obvious that using aircraft for this was without comparison. German positions were often set well down into the landscape, invisible from the British batteries, and it was only aircraft which could hope to expose them. In order to communicate what they could see on these operations more aircraft were carrying wireless transmitters, 4 Squadron continuing to be pre-eminent in pioneering this work.

1st November

633   MFSH   4Sqn
+* combat with EA ovCHEVREUX 6500′ ~8-30am(Lt Barton/Lt Smith)

5Sqn
Rec OOSTLAVERNE-HOLLEBEKE shot up ftl YPRES(Lt RM Vaughan **WIA/Lt CEC Rabagliati OK) Observer flew home

3rd November

Bl807   Blériot XI   2Sqn
** dam shell fire, taken to ST OMER(Lt WR Freeman)

3Sqn
*? (Lt WR Read **WIA**?) inj?

4th November

487   BE2b   4Sqn
** longeron shot through OK(Capt GS Shephard)

5th November

1220   Bristol TB8   Dunkirk
travelling to Dunkirk shot down in sea(FLt CF Beevor **KIA/SLt Earl of Annesley **KIA**)

6th November

BE2a?   4Sqn
AReg then attacked snipers: shot up(Lt IM Bonham-Carter **WIA)

8th November

314   BE2a   4Sqn
**P fuel tank shot up & shrapnel ftl cr OK(Lt WGS Mitchell/Capt HH Hughes-Hallett)

465   BE2a   4Sqn
+*AOb saw DFW below ovYPRES 5500′ but could not get shot off OK(Lt PHL Playfair)

18th November

371   MFSH   4Sqn
**HAP AA shot up: 50 holes but repairable(Lt GN
Humphreys **WIA**/AM Barter **WIA**) name JN
Humphries?

19th November

314   BE2a   4Sqn
**Rec shelled at 2800′ dam but repairable(Lt WGS
Mitchell OK/Capt HH Hughes-Hallett **WIA**)

21st November

873   Avro 504A   RNAS
**B FRIEDRICHSHAFEN Zeppelin Sheds ground mg
fuel tank hit ftl(SCdr. E Featherstone-Briggs DSO **POW**)
a'c captured, pilot allegedly attacked and injured after
landing, but some doubt this

874   Avro 504A   RNAS
**B FRIEDRICHSHAFEN Zeppelin Sheds released
bombs and returned OK(FLt SV Sippe)

875   Avro 504A   RNAS
**B FRIEDRICHSHAFEN Zeppelin Sheds OK(FCdr.
JT Babington)

These three machines set off from Belfort and
attacked the Friedrichshafen Zeppelin sheds across
Lake Constance. A fourth pilot, FSLt RP Canon in
Avro 179, failed to take off. To reach the target a
difficult and circuitous route of one hundred and
twenty-five miles had to be negotiated. Over the
sheds bombs were dropped which damaged the
airship and destroyed the gas works. This attack on
such a distant target led to a significant strengthening of its garrison and defences. In a real sense it
drew off enemy resources that might have been put
to better use for it was never bombed again.

In Flanders the first battle of Ypres came to a
halt with terrible losses having been suffered for
very little territorial gain by either side. It brought
to a close the main campaign in the west for 1914.

22nd November

683?   Avro 504   5Sqn
outside chance this is 683? **Rec dived on EA 2 Str[+
shot up ftl WoL nrNEUVE EGLISE] shot up dam(Lt
LA Strange OK/Lt FG Small **WIA**)finger, left 7-30am,
EA was met on return, first seen going East towards
BAILLEUL 7000′, EA fired back with pistol

This machine carried a Lewis gun (still against
squadron orders) mounted for use by the observer
and was used to bring the enemy aircraft down on
this occasion.

27th November

1823   Henri Farman   5Sqn
*Rec shrapnel: 28 hits, ldg ok BAILLEUL(Lt HF
Glanville? OK/Lt Arkwright **WIA**)foot, a'c unserviceable
so dismantled.

December 1914

6th December

635   BE2a   4Sqn
** shell fragment in rudder

8th December

The RFC Headquarters Wireless Unit was
redesignated 9 (Wireless) Squadron RFC on the
8th of December. It continued to supply wireless
machines to the other squadrons from St Omer
until the following March.

17th December

829   Short 830   RNAS Grain
** engine failed ftl sea HOOK OF HOLLAND
MIA(SCdr JW Seddon **INT**/LM RL Hartley **INT**) a'c
salvaged & crew saved by Norwegian ship SS *Orn* &
interned until repatriated 20.12.14.

1240   MFSH   Dunkirk
**B to BRUGES Submarine sheds, a'c shelled cr
BRESKENS(FLt TA Rainey **INT**) interned Holland

21st December

1241   MF F27   3Sqn RNAS
*NB OSTENDE OK(Cdr CR Samson/FLt WH Wilson)

This was the first ever night bombing raid.

25th December

120   Short Folder   HMS *Engadine*
**CUXHAVEN Zeppelin Sheds bombed, low fuel ftl sea
nNORDENEY GAT Light House, taken in tow but
eventually abandoned(FLt AJ Miley) bombed by
Schutte-Lanz Airship, sunk by gunfire

136   Short 135   HMS *Riviera*
**B CUXHAVEN Zeppelin Sheds, chased Airship, AA
heavily shot up engine ftl OK(FCdr. CF Kilner/Lt R
Erskine-Childers) left 7am, carried out comprehensive
survey of shipping

814   Short S74   HMS *Empress*
**B CUXHAVEN Zeppelin Sheds, a/c abandoned
nrNORDERNEY GAT(FSLt V Gaskell-Blackburn/CPO
Bell) left 7am, bombed by Airship, crew saved by
Submarine

815   Short S74   HMS *Empress*
**B CUXHAVEN Zeppelin Sheds, a/c abandoned
nrNORDERNEY GAT(FCdr DA Oliver/CPO Budds)
left 7am, crew saved by submarine

This raid was made by seven seaplanes, operating from three seaplane carriers. Its purpose was not only to attack the Zeppelin sheds but also to gain intelligence about German shipping.

28th/29th December

A violent storm overnight wrecked or damaged thirty RFC aircraft. Sixteen were completely written off, a sizeable proportion of a still small force.

31st December

By the end of the year the RFC had received eighty-four additional machines to complement or replace the original sixty-three with which it had arrived in France.

1915 THE AIR WAR AWAKENS

The deadlock of trench warfare had now imposed itself comprehensively on the combatants. The air arms were in increasing demand to supply intelligence about the opposing forces and, as the armies grew and a picture began to emerge, so the air services were widened and fostered. Through 1915, virtually all the main activities to be undertaken for the rest of the war would emerge and take concrete form. The continual need for reconnaissance would occupy the vast majority of their energies, bringing forward not only photographic reconnaissance, but the wider introduction of fast single-seater scouts, which would soon all be armed, to carry out deeper sweeps. In the hands of often spirited and aggressive pilots the capabilities and potential of these aircraft would soon become apparent. From this would evolve "patrolling", and with it the first steps toward combat flying. Artillery co-operation would also become a paramount activity, contact patrolling would be experimented with, a programme for aerial bombing would be established, and even the first night operations would be attempted. In 1915 a small number of pilots would begin to claim several victories in combat, to become the first aces of the air.

All of these developments relied on new technologies and equipment to advance, and in turn gave tremendous impetus for solutions to be found. The greatest step forward in the coming months would be the wedding of armament to aircraft by Anthony Fokker to make the first true fighter, the Fokker Eindekker EI. In general, however, both sides on the Western Front in 1915 would strive to find an increasingly specialised group of aircraft, rather than all-purpose types, to achieve their air aims. Just as the value of air reconnaissance and artillery patrolling was now established, there was a corresponding demand for ways to be found to prevent the enemy from carrying out these same activities. Air services were soon charged with intercepting and shooting down aircraft, and at the same time with protecting their own machines by providing armed escorts. The side with the most technologically advanced aircraft, flown with the greatest tactical sophistication, would prevail in these circumstances, so the drive for supremacy was on. Many of the crucial advances would be slow at first. For instance, intensification in air fighting was only likely to happen when specialised, more highly powered aircraft with better armament found their way into wider operational use. Air fighting might be increasingly engaged, but until the technology was available to really drive home an attack it would remain mostly inconclusive. The casualty statistics in the appendices of this work clearly demonstrate this: it took the appearance of proper air fighters in the early summer of 1915 to begin the escalation of casualties, but this also took time, as the new combat techniques were gradually worked out. All of these developments were ultimately dependent on increasing production in the home countries, and 1915 saw the first real reorganisations to co-ordinate and raise provision of what was needed at the front.

A summary of developments in 1915 must include mention of the appointment on the 19th of August of Col HM Trenchard as General Officer commanding the RFC in the field. His appointment was part of a general reorganisation of leadership commensurate with the rapid expansion of the air war. It goes without saying that his influence was to be enormous, for he undoubtedly came to the position with a clear vision of how the RFC would have to fight in order to be supreme in the skies, and this set the character of its operations for the rest of the war. Trenchard believed that the air services must act to support the armies on the ground, and that this could only be possible through a comprehensive control of the skies above. His method of achieving this was to be unflinchingly aggressive. This policy will be met many times in this book, as it quite simply drove the efforts of the RFC.

January 1915

10th January

1241	MF F27	3Sqn RNAS

**B OSTENDE dam OK(Lt CH Collet DSO/FLT WH Wilson)

	Morane Parasol	Esc MS (French)

** exchanged fire with EA biplane[+shot down cr] nrAMIENS OK(Sgt Gilbert/Lt dePuechredon)

18th January

	BE2?	4Sqn

? (/Capt EF Chinnery **KIA)

19th January

	BE2?	4Sqn

P to attack troops GHISTELLES bombs exploded cr sea en-route nrST MALO 6-40am(Capt HJA Roche **KIA) left from OSTENDE, possibly hit by French mg?

Four machines made this raid, the others, piloted by Maj GH Raleigh, Capt RP Wills, and Lt TW Mulcahy-Morgan, all returning safely.

22nd January

1845	Morane L	3Sqn

Deliv lost ftl(Lt AJ Evans **INT) interned Holland

Twelve German aircraft in loose formation flew in from the sea and bombed Dunkirk on the 22nd. It was an almost unique attack for the time, flying in such numbers together, and was a portent for the future. British, French and Belgian machines all took off to challenge the Germans and succeeded in bringing one down with rifle fire. The RFC pilot responsible was either Capt FV Holt or Lt RP Mills, both of 4 Squadron and both flying BE2cs.

23rd January

1241	MF F27	3Sqn RNAS

B submarines at ZEEBRUGGE AA fire shot up dam(SCdr R Bell-Davies DSO **WIA) hit prior to bombing, but carried on

February 1915

5th February

1848?	Morane L	3Sqn

this a'c? ** exchanged fire with Aviatik[+forced down ftl 2m from its a'dr at LILLE] nrMERVILLE OK(2Lt VHN Wadham/Lt AE Borton) saw rifle fire from as close as 50' hit EA

Possibly in this aircraft as this crew crashed in Morane L 1848 on 27.2.15.

10th February

16 Squadron RFC was formed at St Omer on the 10th of February. It comprised elements from Nos. 2, 5, and 6 Squadrons and made its first reconnaissance flight on the 26th of February. It took on a typical mixture of roles for a unit of the time: tactical reconnaissance, photography, artillery co-operation, and bombing. It also carried out offensive patrols.

16th February

875	Avro 504	Dover

ZEEBRUGGE Raid forced return lost at sea **MIA(FLt EG Riggall **KIA**)

813	Short S74	Felixstowe

ZEEBRUGGE Raid lost at sea **MIA(FLt Hon D O'Brien? **KIA**) but could be FSLt T Spencer, see 817

817	Short S74	Felixstowe

ZEEBRUGGE Raid lost at sea **MIA(FSLt T Spencer? **KIA**) but could be FLt Hon D O'Brien, see 813

17th February

1199	W&T No3 Flying Boat	Dover

** AA ftl sea WESTER SCHELDE **MIA**(FLt DG Murray **INT**) interned Holland

22nd February

No.1 Squadron RNAS moved to Dunkirk on the 22nd of February (see also the 21st of June) to relieve No.3 Squadron RNAS which was being withdrawn for service to the Dardanelles. No.3 Squadron returned to England on the 26th and sailed for the Mediterranean on the 11th of March.

27th February

1852	MFSH	9Sqn

** hit by shell fire OFF 27.2.15

28th February

621	Vickers FB5	16Sqn

Rec left 9-30am **MIA(2Lt MR Chidson **POW**/2Lt DCW Sanders **POW**) a'c captured, pilot to Holland 1.3.15, observer to Switzerland 30.5.16

The loss of this Vickers was a blow to the RFC as well as to the two men who found themselves prisoners. It delivered a barely used example of Britain's first ever purpose-designed fighter to the enemy. It was, in fact, the first FB5 to reach France, having been briefly with 2 Squadron before coming on to 16 Squadron. The Vickers was a development of that company's pre-war efforts to design a gun-carrying aircraft. It had a pusher configuration, with the propeller placed behind the nacelle, in which the crew sat. The observer

manned a Vickers machine-gun in the nose, from where he had an unobstructed field of vision, and could rotate the gun to some degree as well. The type held much promise at the time of its arrival in France, and indeed it would see much action for over a year. By that time it would be totally outclassed, and have become a liability to all associated with it. For the first several months of its operational use, when it could have had substantial effect, the slowness with which it appeared lost it the initiative. It took until the 25th of July for a unit fully equipped with the type, 11 Squadron, to arrive in France. Allocations before this had been sporadic, only 5 Squadron having them in any numbers. Its poor rate of climb and general performance was soon evident, and engine troubles beset its operational use. In May, an RFC memorandum about the type noted that one Vickers pilot had suffered twenty-two forced landings in thirty flights because of engine problems.

March 1915

7th March

1 Squadron RFC arrived in France at St Omer on the 7th of March and carried out its first operations on the 10th. Its early flying would involve reconnaissance, photography, and bombing.

8th March

1864   Voisin LA   4Sqn
**Rec prop shot up ftl OK (2Lt AL Russell/Lt H Lygon) no dam to a'c

1754   BE2c   16Sqn
** mist lost low fuel ftl PAULINAPOLDER **MIA**(Capt FE Fryer **INT**/2Lt GH? Eastwood **INT**) initials EH?, interned Holland, observer escaped 2.8.15, date 10.3?: 8.3 via AIR1/826,204/5/123

9th March

1858   Voisin LA   4Sqn
**Rec radiator shot up ftl dam OK (Lt GN Humphreys/ 2Lt TEH Davies) II Corps Det, 7-10am until 8-50am, 43 holes in a'c

10th March

THE BATTLE OF
NEUVE CHAPELLE

The battle of Neuve Chapelle began on the 10th of March. Great efforts in Britain had resulted in considerable numbers of troops now arriving in France. This had enabled a gradual relief of the French in Flanders, so that by March a continuous British line stretched from Langemarck in the Ypres Salient to Givenchy on the La Bassée Canal. The British efforts would centre mostly at the southern end of this front, north of the La Bassée Canal. It was decided that a preliminary assault by the First Army should attack the enemy adjacent to Neuve Chapelle. At one point it had been hoped it would form part of a combined operation with the French. The deeper British objective was to take the Aubers Ridge and threaten Lille, whilst to the south Foch would secure the heights of the Vimy Ridge. The major French effort planned in Champagne soon began to dominate their minds and resources and it was clear that Vimy would have to wait. Sir John French never the less decided to proceed independently. Given the shortage of ammunition, guns, and other war making potential it was undeniably a gamble to seek a rupture of the line so close to Lille — one of the enemy's major communications centres. Few reserves were in place when the battle started, amounting to little more than the cavalry who, should a breach develop, were expected to rush on the city.

It was the first of three successive attempts by French to break the impasse of the trenches, and it was hoped that valuable fighting experience could be gained in this battle before more major operations took place. Indeed, those involved were to discover in one short battle nearly all of the gruesome elements of a trench war offensive — a pattern of bombardment, attack, and then stalemate and costly sacrifice as those involved were unable to exploit early promise. It was a pattern which would become all to familiar in the coming years.

The techniques and strategies with which this war would be fought were being explored not only on the ground but in the air as well. It was during the preparations for this battle that aerial photography came of age as an essential tool for artillery cooperation. Both the British and French had experimented with trench mapping using this technique before the end of 1914, and it was decided that an attempt would be made to map the entire German lines at Neuve Chapelle to a depth of as great as 1500 yards. Vertical rather than oblique shots would be made, and then assembled into a mosaic from which a map could be drawn. The work was undertaken by 2 and 3 Squadrons, who had overcome tremendous difficulties to complete the work by the end of February. When one remembers that at this time the aerial camera was a crude and difficult apparatus requiring a minimum of ten separate operations to expose a single plate, and that each required leaning over the side into the slipstream of the aircraft, the magnitude of their achievement becomes clearer. When the advancing troops left their trenches at

7-30am on the 10th, thousands of them carried maps of the terrain they were advancing over, giving a new-found understanding of their objectives.

In preparation for the battle the Royal Flying Corps had also carried out a widespread programme of registering the opposing guns of the enemy. As soon as fighting had begun and the initial bombardment subsided, one of the main tasks of the airmen became counter-battery work. This was carried out by wireless machines which every squadron now possessed.

The British Army was only too aware that the Germans would rush troops to the area. In consequence, the RFC was also ordered to bomb transport and towns where these reserves were massing. They carried this out, however, with only the most primitive of bomb racks and other equipment. Of note was the fact that specific targets were allocated for their attention. 3rd Wing was assigned Lille, Douai, and Don stations, whilst 2nd Wing machines attacked Courtrai Station and Menin junction. Some of the airmen involved in these attacks are noted below. Finally, the RFC flew reconnaissances and generally saw to it that they held a presence in the air over the battle.

The weather was poor as the battle opened, but early progress was extremely good. By noon Neuve Chapelle had been entered and was mostly secured. The advance then slowed as the troops met a number of German strong points which could not be overcome. This problem became the crux of the battle and three days of fighting would see virtually no deeper penetration, and that only achieved with greatly increasing casualties. Aerial photography and reconnaissance had been unable to gauge the strong points accurately, but of course in time such insight would be possible when these new techniques came of age. What had also been apparent was that the British commanders had been unable to understand how the fighting was unfolding. This was one reason why there had been a near total failure to exploit the gains which had been made. Communications were extremely primitive, and contact patrolling of troops from the air lay well into the future. This vital aerial role was however presaged when Capt GF Pretyman of 3 Squadron attempted to follow events at the face of battle by making two low reconnaissances on the 12th.

It is interesting to note that the RFC Order of Battle for Neuve Chapelle listed eleven types of aircraft, but that amongst these only two were rather rudimentary scouts (Martinsyde Scouts and SE2s), and there was a solitary Vickers FB5 fighter. The British air units which had been assembled

were as follows: Nos. 2, 3, and 16 Squadrons of 1st Wing; Nos. 5 and 6 Squadrons of 2nd Wing; and Nos. 1 and 4 Squadrons of 3rd Wing.

BE2c?	3Sqn

**B Divisional HQ FOURNES ~6am OK(Capt EL Conran/Maj JM Salmond) came down to 100′ to drop bombs

BE2c?	3Sqn

**B Divisional HQ FOURNES ~6am OK(Lt WCK Birch)

BE2c?	3Sqn

**B Divisional HQ FOURNES ~6am OK(Lt DR Hanlon)

BE2c?	5Sqn

**B railway nMENIN hit by blast and rifle fire, returned at 200′ OK(Capt GI Carmichael) left 3-30pm

1748?	BE2c	6Sqn

possibly this a'c? **B troop train COURTRAI Rlwy Stn OK(Capt LA Strange) AA en-route, silenced sentry at station with hand grenade, 75 dead & wounded troops in bombed train

11th March

487	BE2b	4Sqn

**NB rail junction seLILLE MIA(Capt GW Mapplebeck POW) left ~4-45am, a'c captured, escaped to UK 4.15

703	BE2b	4Sqn

**NB rail junction seLILLE cr MIA(Lt AStJM Warrand POW DoW 19.3.15) left ~4-45am

These two pilots undertook the first night bombing operation by the RFC. A third machine was involved, piloted by Capt Barton, but crashed soon after take-off. Each aircraft carried two 100-lb bombs on carriers designed and built by the squadron. Preparations included fitting the cockpits with electric light and, to direct the crews, two signalling lamps were placed on the ground five miles apart.

12th March

The third day of the battle was stormy and very difficult for flying. It was marked by a series of intense enemy counter-attacks before the fighting eventually subsided.

2132	BE8	1Sqn

**B rail bridge neDOUAI-DON MIA(2Lt O Mansell-Moullin POW)

This pilot was lost on a bombing operation undertaken by four pilots of 1 Squadron. The others involved were Capt ER Ludlow-Hewitt, Lt EO Grenfell, and Lt VA Barrington-Kennett. Only Ludlow-Hewitt's bombs, which he dropped

mistakenly on Wavrin instead of Don, were in any way effective. Mansell-Moullin was the first loss for the Squadron.

16th March

1832	Blériot XI	3Sqn
616	Blériot Parasol	3Sqn
715	Avro 504	3Sqn

** a'c shot up damaged, all reported sent to AP 16.3.15

20th March

1855	Morane L	3Sqn

** longeron shot through, no further details yet known

1876	Voisin L	4Sqn

Vs.533 **Rec left 8-15am **MIA**(Lt GN Humphreys **POW**/2Lt TEH Davies **POW**) pilot to Holland 1.3.18, observer to Holland 23.8.18

21st March

753	Avro 504A	1Sqn

** AA engine hit ftl **MIA**(2Lt JC Joubert de la Ferte **INT**/Lt DMV Veitch **INT**) interned Holland, pilot repat 2.18, observer escaped 12.10.15

24th March

1001	504B	1Sqn RNAS

B HOBOKEN Submarine Depot clouds, lost, engine trouble ftl KRUININGEN 9am **MIA(FLt B Crossley-Meates **INT**) interned Holland

22nd March

9 Squadron RAF temporarily ceased to exist in France on the 22nd of March. For four months it had been providing wireless machines to various units, but in early 1915 it had been decided that each squadron should have its own Wireless Flight and this led to its dispersal. It reformed at Brooklands in England on the 1st of April and would return to France in December.

26th March

1872	Morane L	3Sqn

this a'c? ** damaged by shrapnel(Capt EL Conran **WIA**)arm, 27.3?

28th March

	BE2c	16Sqn

** shot up(Lt CH Stringer **WIA**)back

This was the first casualty for 16 Squadron.

Untraced casualty in France in March 1915

? (2AM AC Hawkins **KIA)

NEW MACHINES FOR THE GERMAN AIR SERVICE

In March, Germany began a programme to improve the efficiency of its air service. The number of Feldflieger Abteilungen had increased to seventy-one by this time, and it was decided that a new office, that of Feldflugchef, would be created to take on responsibility for equipment and armament. This would leave the units still operationally responsible to the army units they served. A new two-seater reconnaissance machine, the C-type, was also developed to replace the old B-types. This incorporated a more powerful engine giving greater speed and climb. It also reversed the previous positions of the pilot and observer, so that the latter sat in the rear, in a better position to defend against attack. Many of the new C-types were armed with machine-guns from an early stage. It is interesting to note that none of these plans yet included the development of a fighter-type, for it was felt that superior performance was defence in itself.

April 1915

THE FIRST COMBAT REPORTS AND THE FIRST AIR FIGHTERS

RFC Wing headquarters only ordered the forwarding of combat reports from squadrons from the 20th of April 1915. It is evident from the entries that combat reports exist from shortly before this date, but in general it is only from this month that a comprehensive picture of air fighting can be assembled. The sudden growth in entries should therefore not be interpreted as evidence of a raising of tempo in the air war, although this was in fact gradually occurring. Orders directly requiring the attacking of enemy aircraft during patrols were now appearing. In the first few months of 1915 significantly more aircraft were also in the sky, carrying out a greater range of activities, so that an increasing number of engagements and casualties were to be expected. However, April was indeed to be a momentous month in the history of air warfare. Before it ended, the first true air fighter would be a reality.

The French air service stood out in the first year or two of the war for its often far-sighted organisation. It was the first air power to recognise the advantages of specialised groupings of aircraft and pilots, and by March 1915 had already reorganised its entire fighting force into four groups:

Reconnaissance, Infantry and Artillery Co-operation, Bombing, and Fighting. For each of these groups it then allocated a particular aircraft, respectively a new Maurice Farman pusher, the Caudron, a new Voisin model, and the Morane Saulnier monoplane. All other types were retired from the front.

The Morane was quite agile and fast for its time, but it was no "fighter". It could only be armed as had been the Bristol Scout, with a rifle or machine-gun set obliquely to fire well away from the propeller. One of the French Escadrilles to fly as fighters in the reorganisation was M.S.23 (M.S. for Morane Saulnier), and it gathered together a number of distinguished pre-war French pilots. One of these was Roland Garros.

For a true fighter aircraft to evolve, a way had to be found to make the machine-gun an effective weapon in the air, for it was now apparent that it was the only way that sufficient fire could be delivered at the enemy. It also made sense to mount it firing forwards, because this was the way a pilot flew his machine, and in combat he could therefore use his flying skills not only to manoeuvre but to aim his gun at the same time. Most fast scouts had the tractor configuration, so that there was the immediate obstacle of the propeller. The British side-stepped the problem for the time being by developing aircraft with the pusher configuration.

Garros' Morane was a tractor, and he was determined that if he was to be a fighter pilot he would find a way of firing at the enemy through the propeller arc. Working with his mechanic, Hue, he mounted a single 8mm Hotchkiss machine-gun onto his Morane and then fitted steel deflector plates onto each blade of his propeller. With this device the first true fighter was created. At last a pilot could direct an attack at an enemy by aiming his aircraft and opening fire. Garros shot down his first victory on the 1st of April, and by the 18th had caused consternation in the German air service by accounting for a number of other machines.

1st April

Morane L   M.S.23 (French)
** combat with EA 2 Str[+shot down] just sDIXMUDE?
OK(Lt R Garros) left from DUNKIRK, German crew
brought down were Gfr A Spacholz & Ltn W Grosskopf

This French Morane was fitted with a machine-gun firing through the propeller which in turn was protected by deflector blades. With it, Garros claimed his first famous victory.

8th April

368   BE2a   6Sqn
** shrapnel damage, a'c to 1AP 8.4.15

7 Squadron RFC arrived in France on the 8th of April, with RE5s and Vickers FB5s. Within days the Vickers Fighters had been transferred to 5 Squadron, and replaced by a flight of Voisins. Its primary duty was reconnaissance, but by July it had become an independent unit working with Headquarters RFC. After this time it would carry out more strategic patrols and bombing.

15th April

8 Squadron RFC arrived in France with BE2cs. It was the first unit fully equipped with this type to be posted overseas. This unit would come to specialise in long reconnaissance and day bombing.

16th April

2822   Martinsyde S1   6Sqn
+*P YPRES combat with EA ovPOPERINGHE 6500'
6-10am OK(Capt LA Strange) inconclusive

17th April

1669   BE2c   4Sqn
+*Rec BRUGES combat with Albatros
nrZUYDSCHOOTE [+shot up ftl cr] 6000' 6-30am
OK(Capt RM Vaughan/2Lt JF Lascelles) met EA on
way to BRUGES, 24 rifle shots fired from ~80yds range,
EA pilot hit in head? & killed, then ldg by EA observer
nrBOESINGHE-French lines, who was captured. RFC
crew watched crash then went on to BRUGES

The observer used a cut down service rifle to force the enemy down. This combat is described in Volume 2 of *The War in the Air*, which ascribes a date of the 15th of April. This is probably an error. The original combat report exists in a 1st Wing RFC AIR1 file, dated the 17th of April.

18th April

1894   Morane L   1Sqn
+*P drove off 2 Aviatiks then combat with Fokker[+?
steep dive, wobbled considerably] YPRES-COMINES
9000' 6-30am OK(Capt ER Ludlow-Hewitt/Cpl
Fitzgerald) Aviatiks down nrMENIN?

This was the first claim made in air fighting by 1 Squadron RFC. This crew, and others from the unit, were intently involved in the struggle for Hill 60 — an eminence to the south-east of Ypres which afforded the Germans a good view of the city. The attack had commenced the previous evening and 1 Squadron had spent that day patrolling the sky so as to prevent any enemy aircraft from detecting

preparations for the assault. The unit was subsequently involved in all counter-battery work as British troops strove to hold the hill under an onslaught of repeated shelling. German troops eventually re-took the hill on the 5th of May and all subsequent efforts failed to dislodge them. Long before this, however, attention had sharply switched northwards with news that a new German offensive was about to be launched on Ypres.

1668 BE2c 4Sqn
+*Rec RUMBEKE-ROULERS 25min combat with Otto Pusher 6-45am OK (Capt T? Carthew/Lt HM? Hankin)

1780 BE2c 6Sqn
**B GONTRODE Airship Sheds shot up dam OK (Lt LG Hawker)

Hawker hoped to destroy LZ35 which he believed was housed at Gontrode, and obtained two hits on the shed. Unfortunately it was no longer there, having crashed five days earlier. Hawker had come to France with 6 Squadron in October 1914 and within weeks had begun to stand out for his daring and bravery. He was one of the very first pilots on either side to engage the enemy in the air. Until late spring virtually all his flying was done in BE2cs, much of it in this machine, carrying out typical reconnaissance and artillery spotting duties. For consistent bravery, culminating in this lone operation, he was awarded the DSO and was subsequently promoted to Captain.

Morane L M.S.23 (French)
EscB ground fire nrCOURTRAI shot down ftl EoL nrINGELMUNSTER **MIA (Lt R Garros **POW**)

THE FOKKER EINDEKKER

Lt Garros had shot down his third enemy aircraft earlier in the day. He was patrolling near Courtrai when he was hit by ground fire and forced to land east of the lines near Ingelmunster. His attempts to burn his Morane failed and the aircraft, along with its armament system, was captured. Within a week, the authorities had asked Anthony Fokker, the Dutch aircraft designer, to replicate the device. One reason that Fokker became involved was because his own new single-seater monoplane was similar to the Morane.

In only a few days, so the story goes, Fokker's staff at his Schwerin factory had improved on the deflector plate system and produced a workable interrupter gear. This was a mechanical linkage which allowed bullets to be fired through the propeller arc by interrupting their flow whenever a blade passed through the line of fire. The device was tested out using a Parabellum machine-gun fitted to his monoplane, and was clearly effective. An imme-

diate production of this armament and aircraft was ordered — this potent combination going into service as the Fokker Eindekker EI and evolving into the first ever purpose-designed single-seat fighter type. With it, a new aerial weapon was born. Its introduction would be gradual: following a demonstration tour of operational units in May there would be eleven Fokkers with interrupter gear in service by mid-July. Initially there was to be one attached to each Flieger Abteilung in sectors where the Allies held control of the air. Its introduction would soon loosen their grip.

20th April

368 BE2a 6Sqn
+*AReg nrYPRES combat with Albatros 2 Str 5500' OK (Lt WC? Adamson/Capt Bovill) pilot's initials?

22nd April

THE SECOND BATTLE OF YPRES

The German offensive which began the second battle of Ypres commenced on the 22nd of April. This grim event saw the first use of poisonous gas, blown onto French positions from the German trenches on the first evening of fighting. Intelligence of the imminent use of this terrible weapon had reached the Allies on the 15th, but a special patrol from 6 Squadron, sent to search for information the next day, had been unable to see anything of note. The Germans had been waiting for the wind to change, and when it came the gas caused chaos, decimating the defenders in their trenches at a stroke.

Within 48 hours of the battle opening, the Germans had exploited their advantage and broken through the salient at St Julien. The situation could have been far more critical had the Germans not underestimated the effectiveness of the gas attack and committed more reserves. The first contact patrols were to be used over this battlefield, commencing on the 25th of April. This saw aircraft shadowing the advance of troops in order to keep commanders advised of their progress. It was another natural use for aircraft in war, but in these first attempts, many mistakes were made because of difficulties in identifying friendly troops. Proper methods of recognition and signalling had yet to be worked out.

23rd April

1894 Morane L 1Sqn
**P combat with "big pusher" ovZONNEBEKE-MOORSLEDE 8000' 7am then AA dam OK (Capt ER Ludlow-Hewitt/Lt L Playfair) chased EA down to 4500', inconclusive

2859   Avro 504   1Sqn
+*TacRec combat with Aviatik or Albatros[+?seen dive
steeply & land in field 1m ePASSCHENDAELE] 7500'
8-30am OK (Capt JDG? Sanders/Lt C Court-Freath) EA
possibly not damaged

238   BE2a   6Sqn
+*AReg YPRES combat with Aviatik 6000' 6am OK (Lt
Hargrave/Lt Morton)

1675   BE2c   6Sqn
+* combat with EA BOESINGHE-HOUTHULST 7000'
5-30am OK (Capt LA Strange/Lt Hawkins)

24th April

6 Squadron's aerodrome at Poperinghe was shelled
in consequence of the German advance and the unit
was compelled to move back to Abeele. The
squadron was operating in desperate circumstances
with V Corps, adjacent to the French Corps so
recently struck down by gas. It was this unit's
airmen who reported the enemy pressing in on St
Julien on this day, as well as bringing the grim news
that German troops were flooding south from Poelcappelle and Langemarck. The German Army was
bent on exploiting its breakthrough if it could.

25th April

1780   BE2c   6Sqn
P shot up LANGEMARCK (Lt LG Hawker **WIA)slight

26th April

687   BE2b   2Sqn
**LowB troops shot up nrCOURTRAI returned a'dr
~4-15pm (2Lt WB Rhodes Moorhouse **DoW** 27.4.15) left
3-05pm WIA in thigh & abdomen: to hospital
MERVILLE

Rhodes Moorhouse was awarded the first Victoria
Cross for an airman in this incident. The battle in
the Ypres Salient had developed to a critical phase,
and it was known that German reinforcements were
gathering in the Ghent area. Air operations were
mounted against adjacent centres of rail communications in an effort to disrupt their deployment. 7
and 8 Squadrons were mainly involved in these
bombing attacks, but they were helped by four
additional machines from 2 Squadron. These were
allotted the stations at Roubaix, Tourcoing, and
Courtrai. Rhodes Moorhouse flew alone on this
bombing mission, carrying a single 100-lb. bomb.
Coming down to three hundred feet he released his
bomb onto track near Courtrai station, but as he did
so he was met with a barrage of fire from the
assembled troops below, as well as from a machine-
gun in the belfry of Courtrai church. He was also
caught by the shrapnel blast of his bomb. By the

time he had made his escape he had been wounded
seriously in his thigh and abdomen, but fighting
back unconsciousness from loss of blood, he
managed to return to his aerodrome and land his
machine. He then insisted on giving his report of the
operation to his Squadron before allowing himself to
be removed to hospital at Merville, where he died on
the 27th. His aircraft had ninety-five holes from
bullets and shrapnel.

1626   Vickers FB5   5Sqn
+*Rec YPRES VLAMERTINGHE combat with Aviatik
wYPRES 6000' 3-15pm OK (Lt S Graham-Gilmour/2Lt
Andrews) gun jam, 2nd inconclusive combat shot up
3-45pm

1780   BE2c   6Sqn
**Rec combat with Aviatik ZONNEBEKE[?+driven
down by his rifle fire] 4500' 4pm OK (Lt LG Hawker/Capt
Wyllie)

Despite being wounded on the previous day,
Hawker insisted on carrying out another sortie, so
desperate was the ground battle. He had to be lifted
into the cockpit. Some days later he received a
period of sick leave.

27th April

Following a few critical days' fighting, the command
of the British Army in front of Ypres was hastily
reorganised on the 27th. As a temporary measure,
all troops in the neighbourhood of that city came
under the command of Gen Sir HCO Plumer and
this body was given the name "Plumer's Force".
Within days this Force was preparing to fall back to
a new line nearer Ypres which was accomplished
roughly a week later. In tandem with this, the RFC
in the area was also regrouped. 2nd Wing would
consist of Nos. 5, 6, and 8 Squadrons and was to
operate entirely with this new Force. 3rd Wing now
contained Nos. 1, 4, and 7 Squadrons. The two
groups divided their activities in the salient north
and south of the Ypres-Roulers railway line.

28th April

748?   Martinsyde S1   1 Sqn
this a'c ** combats: attacked 2 LVGs & 3rd EA
nrHANDZAEME 5500' ~4-30pm armed only with 2
revolvers, drove off OK (2Lt MMcB Bell-Irving) several
other attempted engagements followed

Bell-Irving was convinced that if he had been
armed with a machine-gun he could have accounted for at least one EA in this fight. However he
added that "at 5500 ft the Martinsyde without
machine-gun has to be flown at 65mph in order to
fly level, and with a machine-gun its speed would

be reduced to below this". His responsibilities that day were to protect the 2nd Corps batteries, and his tactic had been to dive on a selected enemy aircraft of a group as they appeared. This usually resulted in its departure, but then each attack had to be followed by a laborious climb back to altitude to mount a further attack. In the time it took to achieve this, the enemy reconnaissance could be continued quite unmolested. This report shows a number of the limitations widespread in air fighting at the time.

1Sqn
** AA(2Lt L Parker **WIA**)head slight, but see 29.4.15?

206   BE2a   6Sqn
+* combat with 2 Albatros YPRES-LANGEMARCK 4-30am OK(Lt Kinnear/Capt Wyllie)

1675   BE2c   6Sqn
+*P YPRES combat with EA ovBOESINGHE 6000' 5am OK(Capt LA Strange/Lt Hawkins) seen going down steeply but ok?

737   RE5   7Sqn
+*Rec combat with LVG 6500'-6000' 7-05am OK(Capt GD Mills/Lt Murray)

This was the first recorded combat for 7 Squadron.

29th April

4Sqn
*? (2Lt L Parker **WIA**)

30th April

715   Avro 504   5Sqn
Rec mg shot down YPRES EoL **MIA(2Lt CA Gladstone **POW**/Capt DSK Crosbie **WIA POW**) left 11-30am, pilot to Holland 23.3.18

2449   Martinsyde S1 6Sqn
+* combat with Albatros YPRES-HOUTHULST 6000' 7pm OK(Capt LA Strange) "EA tried to break prop by ball at end of copper cable"

RE5   7Sqn
** (Lt NC Spratt **WIA**/Lt CW Anstey **WIA**)

These were the first casualties in action for 7 Squadron RFC.

May 1915

Important Note:

INCLUSION OF
AIR COMBAT DATA

Although this record of airmen is primarily concerned with British air casualties in action, the list has also set out to record nearly all early air combats — for the purposes of this book this means until the early summer of 1916. This has been attempted in order to provide the fullest picture possible of the development of air fighting on the Western Front, from the first exchanges of rifle fire until the beginning of dogfights between fighters. It is hoped that this additional area of record will be found of interest. After that time, records of many combats will continue to be given, but it is important to understand that these then become selective. Why certain combats are chosen for inclusion is explained more fully in a note at the end of the entries for March 1916. Air combat rose to such intensity from this time that to follow all events would have been simply impossible. Nevertheless, there are several hundred additional combats described through the last years of the war to help illustrate various developments and events in the fighting.

2nd May

468   BE2a   6Sqn
+*AReg combat with Aviatik POPERINGHE 6000' 8am OK(Lt Hargrave/Capt Bovill)

3rd May

2130   BE8   1Sqn
+*P BOESINGHE combat with Aviatik ovHOUTHULST WOOD 6000' 7pm shot up so had pull out OK(Lt VA Barrington-Kennett/Lt Richard) chased EA off twice, but then wireless drift wire hit so had to return

242   BE2a   6Sqn
+*AReg drove off EA preventing firing nYPRES 6000' 8-10am OK(Lt Adamson/Capt Bovill)

1748   BE2c   6Sqn
+*AOb combat with Aviatik ovYPRES 6000' OK(Capt LA Strange/Lt CH Awcock) EA was going towards COMINES

1656   BE2c   16Sqn
+*Rec combat with Albatros nORCHIES[+seen ftl field d'wind 5m eORCHIES] 7500' 7-12am to 7-30am then 2nd combat with decoy Albatros 8-22am, which lured them down onto ground fire ovSECLIN(Lt EGS Walker OK/Lt CFO Master **WIA**)leg, to hospital AIRE

4th May

2130   BE8   1Sqn
+*P combat with Aviatik neYPRES 8000' 6am OK(Lt Barrington-Kennett/2Lt Wells-Bladen) EA seen ldg nr sheds ePOELCAPPELLE

5th May

1849   Morane L   3Sqn
+* combat with EA nrDON[+?driven down ftl] ~6pm OK(Capt GF Pretyman/Capt JHS Tyssen) [this "Morane" type or "Fokker Parasol" was seen ldg in

ploughed field nrLILLE, before another "Morane" drove them off]

This "Fokker Parasol" was of course the older two-seater AIII. Tyssen later served with 22 Sqn before commanding 58 Squadron RFC in 1918, which was a night reconnaissance and bombing unit.

1637   Vickers FB5   5Sqn
+* combat with EA ovYPRES 5500′ 10-15am shot up OK(2Lt R Maxwell-Pike/2Lt Andrews) gun jam, inconclusive, had earlier combat 10am

206   BE2a   6Sqn
+*AOb combat with EA YPRES-HOUTHULST WOOD 7000 OK(Lt Cunningham/Lt Wenden)

7th May

748   Martinsyde S1   1Sqn
+*P combat with "big EA pusher" nrGHELUVELT 6000′ 4-30am chased & caught it nrZANDVOORDE[+ ?looked ooc but seen glide down engine off towards MENIN 4000′] OK(2Lt MMcB Bell-Irving) first mistook EA for Voisin & got shot up

8th May

An extremely heavy German attack was launched on sections of the V Corps front on the 8th, sections of which were broken through. There were further heavy attacks for another two weeks but none took any significant amount of ground.

**   Voisin LA   4Sqn**
Rec shrapnel hit ~6am(Capt EF Unwin/2Lt WL Robinson **WIA)arm

1616   Vickers FB5   5Sqn
+* sYPRES combat with Ago nrDICKEBUSCH 6000′ 7-25pm then ground fire OK(Lt S Graham-Gilmour/ 1AM Rogers) inconclusive

1748   BE2c   6Sqn
+*AOb ZONNEBEKE combat with Otto ovHOUTHULST WOOD 7000′ 8-10am OK(Capt LA Strange/Lt CH Awcock)

9th May

THE BATTLE OF AUBERS RIDGE

On this day the battle of Aubers Ridge commenced — an attempt by the Allies to advance onto what had been an earlier objective of the battle of Neuve Chapelle. The British First Army would make the attack. Air fighting continued to escalate through the week and the 9th was easily the busiest day yet of the air war. Especially notable was the plan to use aerial bombing prior to the general bombardment. Its intent was to disrupt communications in the back areas but crude bomb aiming techniques comprehensively reduced its effectiveness. All the early attempts to use tactical bombing in battle were handicapped by this.

Contact patrolling was tried again, with 16 Squadron ordered to carry out an associated reconnaissance for army headquarters whilst 2 and 3 Squadrons operated directly with the corps. All these units belonged to 1st Wing. 16 Squadron's work attempted to advance the methods of tactical contact patrolling significantly, for instance reporting the arrival of troops at various key positions who were to deploy white signalling sheets. Special wireless receiving facilities were provided on the ground, and machines managed to send some forty-two messages. These, it has to be said, were of little actual use, as objectives were never reached. More effective contact patrolling would have to wait for the specialised training of the future involving much greater use of low flying. Of all the air services provided for the Allies in this battle, that of artillery co-operation was the most successful.

1860   Voisin LA   4Sqn
**SpM shot up hit through boot OK(Capt EF Unwin)

1623   Vickers FB5   5Sqn
+*Rec combat with EA ZONNEBEKE 8000′ 7am OK(Lt WHD Ackland/Lt Andrews) inconclusive

1626   Vickers FB5   5Sqn
+*Rec sYPRES Salient combat with Albatros? nrZILLEBEKE 7000′[+? shot down cr ground eWYTSCHAETE] 5-30pm OK(Lt S Graham-Gilmour/ 1AM Sutcliffe) EA seen on nose on ground fr 3500′

238   BE2a   6Sqn
+*AReg combat with Aviatik eYPRES 8000′ shot up? OK(Lt Hargrave/Capt Bovill)

484   BE2b   6Sqn
+*AReg combat with EA eYPRES 6500 OK(Capt Macdonnell/Capt BT? James)

**   Voisin   16Sqn**
B DON AA hit(Lt HF Glanville **WIA)leg, to hospital

**   Voisin   16Sqn**
LRec left 3-50am shot down EoL **MIA(Lt FH Eberli **POW**/Lt SA Sanford **POW**) both to Holland 10.4.18

1854   Maurice Farman   16Sqn
AP dhAA steep glide down then nd folded 2000′ 7-30am (Lt CB Spence **KIA/2Lt Hon FW Rodney **KIA**) left 4-35am, killed at the end of a long, continuous ranging of guns which had vitally silenced several German batteries.

1877   Voisin LA   16Sqn
B DON BRIDGE AA ovCAMBRAI 4am fell nrLines **MIA(Capt AG Fox **KIA**) left 3am

10th May

**   2Sqn**
? (Lt JL Jackson **WIA)face

1872   Morane L   3Sqn
** AA shot down ovFOURNES 1-30pm? **MIA**(Lt D

Corbett-Wilson **KIA**/2Lt IN Woodiwiss **KIA**) ovRADINGHEM ~12-45pm?

1860   Voisin LA   4Sqn
**Rec dam by shrapnel OK(Capt EF Unwin/Lt H Lygon)

1616   Vickers FB5   5Sqn
+*Rec YPRES-LILLE 10000'-2000' combat with Albatros ovLILLE[+? saw bits fly off then nose-dive 1500' wr] 10-45am OK(Lt WHW Acland/1AM Rogers)

1637   Vickers FB5   5Sqn
+* YPRES heavy AA then combat with 2 Albatros & other ovSTADEN 5am shot up then down for 2nd combat shot up ftl POPERINGHE OK(2Lt R Maxwell-Pike/2Lt Andrews)

2449   Martinsyde S1   6Sqn
+*AOb BOESCLARE-MENIN combat with Otto ovPOLYGON WOOD 8000' 8-30am (Capt LA Strange) pilot was thrown out after combat but managed to crawl back in: see 'Recollections of an Airman'

11th May

234   BE2a   4Sqn
**Rec spar shot up dam OK(Capt RM Vaughan/Lt Hankin)

12th May

1655   BE2c   4Sqn
**AP left 3-50am shell shot up, fuel leak ftl OK(Lt GWG Lywood/2Lt Benett)

1856   Voisin LA   4Sqn
+*P COURTRAI combat with EA ovWARNETON 5700' 7-03am on return OK(Capt Murphy/Lt H Lygon)

3823   Voisin   1Sqn RNAS
this a'c? St Pol **ZepP ftl DIXMUDE EoL **MIA**(FLt JO Groves **POW**/LCdr H Dobell **POW**) left to attack Zeppelin returning from UK, to Switzerland 22.5.18

14th May

The first FE2b pushers, Nos. 4227 and 4228, arrived in France and went to 6 Squadron at Abeele.

15th May

1864   Voisin LA   4Sqn
Rec shot up engine ftl cr tree 100yd short of a'dr 6-45am wr(Capt EF Unwin **inj/Lt.Hon H Lygon OK) Lygon shaken & to hospital

**   BE2c?   8Sqn**
** shrapnel(Capt AD Gaye **WIA**/Lt G Graham **WIA**)

These air crew were the first casualties in action for 8 Squadron RFC.

17th May

The Allied advance on the Aubers Ridge crucially

hesitated at this time. This was partly brought about by a lack of clarity about their true position. A persistent mist also fell over the battlefield from the 17th.

20th May

**   4Sqn?**
? (2Lt JA Johnstone **KIA)

**   5Sqn**
** shot up(Capt HC MacDonnell **DoW** 23.5.15)

23rd May

**   1Sqn**
Rec (2Lt HF Boles **DoW 24.5.15) operation on 24.5?, attached 1Sqn

**   1Sqn**
Rec (Lt C Court-Freath **WIA)

299   BE2a   4Sqn
**Rec left 6-15am hit by shell case ftl returned a'dr 7am dam OK(Capt Burdett/2Lt Capel)

314   BE2a   4Sqn
**Rec left 5am main spar shot through dam returned a'dr 6-50am OK(2Lt Mitchell/Lt JR? Parker)

737   RE5   7Sqn
** shrapnel broke up 300' nrVIEUX BERQUIN cr(Lt RCH Bewes **DoW**/2Lt FH Hyland **DoW**) own grenade exploded?

24th May

1748   BE2c   6Sqn
+*Rec ZONNEBEKE combat with Aviatik 6500' 4-30am OK(Capt LA Strange/2Lt GA Parker) EA dived until very low, typical role of "driving off" EA

1756   BE2c   8Sqn
8Sqn? **P shell hit? dam OK(2Lt HR Nicholl/Lt Greenslade)

The battle for Ypres had continued for a month now, with virtually no respite for the opposing forces. German attempts to create a decisive break-through had become increasingly desperate, and included another gas attack this day to the east of Ypres. For a while this caused the situation to became highly critical as the Allies fought for cohesion, but eventually the German attack faltered. By the end of the month their efforts had been generally halted and, at tremendous cost, their counter-offensive had been thwarted. The size of the Allied salient around Ypres had been reduced and the German gains had left British positions much more difficult to defend, surroun-ded as they were now by German guns on important stretches of high ground. At the same time Allied fighting about Aubers Ridge had also

died away, with minimal results to show for it.

The RFC had taken an increasing part in both these areas of fighting. Not only had they directed the fire of many hundreds of guns over the previous month, they had followed the progress of their own troops and reconnoitred and bombed the enemy forces. They had also begun to fight for the sky — limiting the scope of German airmen to support their own armies.

26th May

1637   Vickers FB5   5Sqn
+* ZONNEBEKE-PASSCHENDAELE combat with Aviatik[+? shot down? nose-dive then ss to ground ooc? nrKEERSELAARHOEK] 7300'-5000' 5-30am OK(2Lt R Maxwell-Pike/2Lt RV deHalpert)

1676   BE2c   16Sqn
+* combat with EA HENIN LIETARD 6000' 5-55pm then engine failed ftl OK(Lt Nicholson/Capt Cairnes)

Some authorities believe the first successful aerial combat by a German aircraft took place on this day. A C-type machine in transit between FAb.12 and FAb.20 claimed to have shot down an Allied aircraft.

29th May

5002?   Morane L   3Sqn
this a'c **Rec shrapnel ovILLIES ldg ok(Capt JHS Tyssen **WIA**)leg

1616   Vickers FB5   5Sqn
+* MOORSLEDE combat with 2 Aviatiks nrPOLYGON WOOD[+shot up ss cr woods E.5.c.] 5-35pm shot up shelled on return dam OK(Lt WHW Acland/1AM Sutcliffe)

5008   MFSH   16Sqn
+*Rec combat with Albatros going west from DOUAI 7000' 5-45pm shot up OK(Capt Porter/Capt Bradley) inconclusive

31st May

1668   BE2c   4Sqn
**AP left 10-05am dam shell fire returned a'dr 11-55am OK(Capt Kennedy)

114   Henri Farman Seaplane RNAS
** AA hit off OSTENDE 3000' bad damage dived into sea wr OK(Lt HG Wanklyn)saved, towed in by French

Untraced casualty in France in May 1915
? (1AM Hanley **KIA)

June 1915

1st June

1623   Vickers FB5   5Sqn
+*ZepP BECELAERE combat with 2Str

nrLANGEMARCK 7500'-5100' 5am then attacked KB on ground & heavily shot up dam OK(Lt WHD Ackland/Lt Sampson) combat inconclusive

BE2c?   8Sqn
? shell exploded(/Capt JNS Stott **WIA)

2nd June

1623   Vickers FB5   5Sqn
+* ZONNEBEKE-MOORSLEDE combat with Aviatik 5500'-3000'[+ftl but not hit? nrPASSCHENDAELE] then 2 more combats heavily shot up dam OK(Lt WHD Ackland/Lt Sampson) combat inconclusive

1637   Vickers FB5   5Sqn
+* had 3 combats POLYGON WOOD-ZONNEBEKE 6000'-4500' 5-45am to 7-20am OK(Capt Rees/Lt RV deHalpert)

1675   BE2c   8Sqn
DuskRec shot up ftl KADZEND **MIA(Capt AD Gaye **INT**/Capt FH Pritchard **INT**) one injured in cr ldg, interned Holland

3rd June

4228   FE2a   6Sqn
+*P combat with EA ovHOUTHULST WOOD 7000' OK(Capt LA Strange/Lt GA Parker) EA last seen very low

This was the first recorded combat for the FE2a two-seater. 6 Squadron were now relinquishing their BE2cs in exchange for FEs and Bristol Scouts, to become what was in effect the first homogeneous fighter unit in the RFC.

4th June

1666   BE2c   8Sqn
+*Rec combat with Aviatik ovLEDEGHEM? 7500' 6-10pm OK(2Lt Monkton/Capt Arkwright)

5th June

1677   BE2c   8Sqn
Rec engine ftl cr **MIA(Lt EE Hodgson **INT**/2Lt CM Morrell **INT**) interned Holland, pilot escaped

6th June

1616   Vickers FB5   5Sqn
+*P nrYPRES 5000' combat with EA POLYGON WOOD[+sh up then down ooc cr wood J.5-J.6] 3000' 5-15pm shot up dam OK(2Lt CH Barfield/Cpl Fineran) so close could see pilot's helmet ribbons

4228   FE2a   6Sqn
+*Rec combat with EA POLYGON WOOD 8000' EA driven off OK(Capt LA Strange/Lt GA Parker) EA last seen very low

631   RE5   7Sqn
+*Rec DOUAI-VALENCIENNES combat with

Albatros then pusher 7000′ 5pm to 5-30pm shot up dam OK(Lt FM Adams/2Lt GER Meakin)

7th June

1609 Bristol Scout C 6Sqn
+*P combat with EA neYPRES 4000′ 7-30pm OK(Capt LG Hawker) inconclusive

Not long after Hawker's return to the front he was given Bristol Scout C 1609, the first of two scouts he used to achieve some notable victories. He was to be awarded the Victoria Cross for an action in the other, serial no. 1611, on the 25th of July. On both machines he fitted a Lewis machine-gun to the side of the fuselage pointing forwards and outwards, and with this armament he began to challenge an increasing number of enemy machines.

1783 BE2c 8Sqn
+*Rec combat with EA ovSTADEN 6700′ 12pm shot up by EA rifle fire & shelled(Capt AE Borton **WIA**/Capt Marshall OK) WIA severe

3253 Morane Parasol L 1Sqn RNAS
**HD left 1am attacked airship LZ37[+shot down] ovBRUGES OK(FSLt RAJ Warneford) left from FURNES

FLT SUB-LIEUTENANT WARNEFORD

FSLt Warneford received the Victoria Cross for shooting down LZ37. It was the first time an airship had been shot down by an aircraft. He had spotted the airship over Ostende, and spent 45 minutes gradually overhauling it, so that near Bruges he began to attract its fire. Warneford only carried bombs, and so set about climbing above it. At 11,000 feet he dived from directly behind, and coming down to within 150 feet flew along the airship's length, dropping his six bombs. After some seconds an explosion commenced which soon developed into an enormous disintegration of the craft, throwing the Morane out of control in its blast. The airship crashed to the ground in seconds. Warneford's engine had stopped and so he was forced to land in enemy territory. He found that a separated fuel line was the cause. He managed to take off again, and flying in thick mist he eventually reached safety on the sands at Gris Nez. By 10-30am he was back at Furnes.

The sad epitaph to this story is that Warneford died of injuries received in an aeroplane accident ten days later, on the 17th of June. On the afternoon following his investiture with the Legion d'Honneur he crashed in a Henri Farman he was due to ferry back to his squadron.

8th June

1626 Vickers FB5 5Sqn
**P AA dam ftl wr OK(Lt S Graham-Gilmour/AM Sutcliffe)

9th June

1626 Vickers FB5 5Sqn
+*P combat with EA[+cr] eWYTSCHAETE OK(Lt S Graham-Gilmour/AM Sutcliffe)

12th June

234 BE2a 4Sqn
**AP shell hit prop ftl on return dam OK(Lt Vaughan/Lt Kennedy) fragment fell in observer's lap, pilot Capt RM Vaughan?

1609 Bristol Scout C 6Sqn
+*P combat with EA POELCAPPELLE 8000′ OK(Capt LG Hawker) inconclusive

15th June

746 BE2b 4Sqn
**Rec shell passed through planes shrapnel dam OK(Lt WGS Mitchell/Lt JF Lascelles) exploded above a'c

16th June

1849 Morane L 3Sqn
+* combat with LVG BOIS DE BIEZ-FOURNES 6-5000′ 10-15am OK(Capt GF Pretyman)

398 Avro 504 5Sqn
+*Rec combat with EA 6500′ 5pm shot up dam OK(Lt Swart/Lt Andrews)

4228 FE2a 6Sqn
+*Rec combat with LVG POLYGON WOOD 3000′ 6-30am[+? EA seen ldg in field 2m neMOORSLEDE] OK(Capt LA Strange/Lt GA Parker)

1694 BE2c 16Sqn
+*Rec combat with Aviatik 4-55pm? OK(Lt EGS Walker/Cpl T? Bennett) EA in nose-dive but recovered

This may be the first British crew to become casualties through fire from an enemy aircraft during combat. It should be noted that Lt CFO Master of 16 Squadron was wounded in the leg in BE2c 1656 after combats on the 3rd of May, and that Capt AE Borton was also wounded in BE2c 1783 on the 7th of June. Although enemy aircraft were fought on both these patrols, the two casualties were almost certainly due to ground fire afterwards.

5019 MFSH 16Sqn
+* RICHEBOURG ST VAAST-ESTAIRES combat with EA 7-20am? OK(2Lt HS Shield/Capt FWK Davies)

17th June

1609 Bristol Scout C 6Sqn?

+*BECELAERE combat with Aviatik 11000' 9am —10-15am OK(Lt MMcB Bell-Irving) inconclusive, details as per Combat Report but Bell Irving with 1Sqn?

368   BE2a   16Sqn
+*Rec combat with Aviatik SECLIN 8000' OK(2Lt HM Goode/2Lt McL Holme)

19th June

1694   BE2c   16Sqn
+*Rec combat with EA nrCAMBRAI 8500' 6-15pm OK(Lt EGS Walker/Lt Ackroyd)

20th June

5028   Voisin LAS   4Sqn
**Rec left 3-15pm AA hit engine returned 5pm OK(Capt Macdonell/2Lt JF Lascelles)

1642   Vickers FB5   5Sqn
Rec combat with AgoC ovPOELCAPPELLE[+one engine hit ftl] 4000' 6am then AA on return, fuel tank hit set on fire ftl Sh28NW C27.c.5.8. burnt wr OK(2Lt WHD Ackland **WIA?/2Lt RV deHalpert **inj**)

1609   Bristol Scout C   6Sqn
+* combat with DFW or LVG 2Str[+shot down trailing smoke then nose-dive, unconfirmed] sePOELCAPPELLE 8000'-5000' 7-45pm OK(Capt LG Hawker)

4227   FE2a   6Sqn
+* combat with EA ROULERS 7000' 7-15am OK(Lt Kinnear/Lt GA Parker)

21st June

No.1 Squadron RNAS was renamed No.1 Wing RNAS on the 21st of June.

BE2c?   8Sqn
** shrapnel(/Capt JNS Stott **WIA**)

22nd June

5029   Morane L   3Sqn
+*Rec combat with EA ovLENS 12-9000' shot up ftl? wr OK(2Lt A Payze/2Lt JK Summers) broke off at LE BAS

1609   Bristol Scout C   6Sqn
** 3 combats then low fuel ftl cr o't OK(Capt LG Hawker)

24th June

4Sqn
? (Capt EF Unwin **WIA)

THE GROWTH OF AIR FIGHTING

Many RFC operations at this time began to adopt important distinctions in the way they were carried out. Whilst crews performing work directly for adjacent army groups in or around the lines continued to be armed mostly with rifles and revolvers, those needing to go further afield, for longer reconnaissances, patrols and bombing, were now regularly armed with machine-guns and were adopting an increasingly offensive approach. The reasons for this were simple, for the axis of air control, around which the fight for supremacy would be waged, was almost as established now as were the trench networks on the ground. Air fighting was making its appearance, the clearest proof of this being the first Allied losses due to air combat earlier in the month. These losses, and the many other aerial skirmishes that were taking place almost daily, as yet only involved exchanges between two-seaters, with the occasional intervention of a fast armed scout. For want of effective offensive armament most engagements were inconclusive. In the coming weeks, however, the first purpose-designed single-seater fighters would make their appearance, changing the face of air war for ever. They would extend the battlefield into the skies.

The character of this new battlefield was very distinctive. Many factors were involved, but it came to be that the centre of activity would be tilted generally eastwards. The aggressive policies of the Allies, being experimented with in these months, saw the RFC holding the air space above the lines by pressing increasingly beyond them. It was not only the prevailing westerly wind which pushed patrols forever eastwards, but also Germany's preference for engaging above its own territory which ensured that virtually all crucial air fighting for the rest of the war would take place east of the lines. Therefore, so long as air supremacy was maintained by the Allies, those involved in artillery co-operation and contact operations close to the line could concentrate on their job without needing an offensive capability. This divergence of roles would be formalised in early 1916 into the distinct corps and army squadrons of the RFC.

For the Germans, on the other hand, it brought into focus what they would have to do if they were to survive. They would have to develop fast, well armed two-seaters for reconnaissance, escorted by fighters, together capable of selectively penetrating the offensive curtain. As importantly, they needed to be capable of fleeing eastwards again. Finally, below the air battles, the Germans began to assemble a substantial anti-aircraft network on the ground, which would eventually co-ordinate extremely well with these tactics of the airmen. The German strategy would not always be so defensive, because such a stance could never utilise an air service to its full potential. Nor would the Allies always be in the ascendant, as German technology, inventiveness, and the skill of its fighter pilots was about to ensure. On the 1st of July Ltn Kurt Wintgens would claim a

French Morane Parasol, shot down while flying the new Fokker Eindekker fighter.

July 1915

1st July

Morane Parasol   M.S.48 (French)
this a'c & unit? ** combat: dived on Fokker then shot down, but ldg ok(Capt du Peuty **WIA**/Lt de Boutiny **WIA**), [unconfirmed "Morane" claim combat eLUNEVILLE 2000m-2500m 5pm Ltn K Wintgens FAb6]

There is some doubt whether this Morane was the actual two-seater Wintgens believed he had shot down for the very first Fokker Eindekker claim. Some facts match, but others show disparities. The French casualty report mentioned meeting a Fokker monoplane over the Forêt de Parroy and fighting it for several minutes until the observer had exhausted his ammunition. The pilot was also wounded by this time, and they also thought they had hit the German. They broke off the combat and eventually landed. On the other side, Wintgens wrote home about the combat he had experienced. He noted how the Frenchmen had first dived on him firing, but were wide of the mark. Wintgens reached the same level as the Morane, and each machine put in a number of attacks. He then described how it suddenly fled, at which time he rapidly turned to chase down behind and bring it into his sights. He wrote that in four seconds he had shot it down. Only the Fokker, with its forward firing gun, could have taken full advantage of this most natural chasing manoeuvre, the dispatch of fire perfectly in harmony with the flight. The first Allied machine had made the mistake of fleeing before a Fokker.

3rd July

1875   Morane L   3Sqn
+* combat with Aviatik ovDON 8-9000' 10-30am but gun jam AA?(2Lt A Payze **WIA**/2Lt JK Summers OK) **WIA** slight (NB: **WIA** record gives 4.7.15?)

674   RE5   7Sqn
Rec shot up GHENT 12-30pm ftl SAS-VAN-GAND **MIA(2Lt GER Meakin **INT**/Lt FP Adams **INT**) burnt a'c, interned Holland, repat 2.7.18 [a'c had logged 103'40 hrs when lost]

4th July

1694   BE2c   16Sqn
Rec engine failed ovDOUAI **MIA(Lt EGS Walker **POW**/Capt JC Leech **POW**) left 3-35am, on the run for 4 days before capture, to Holland 23.1.18, pilot repat 7.12.18

OSWALD BOELCKE'S FIRST VICTORY

Oswald Boelcke gained his first victory this day, shooting down a French Morane in a twenty-five-minute combat while flying an LVG two-seater (serial 162/15) of FAb.62. His observer was Lt Heinz. In this aircraft, Boelcke had been one of the first German pilots to show an offensive spirit, having already chosen to attack the enemy on several earlier occasions. However, his aggression was also combined with tremendous skill and insight. His early talents led to his selection to fly one of the first Fokker EI monoplanes, in fact one of the machines Fokker had used on his demonstration tour (serial E3/15). His great abilities would soon bear richly, not only through his air fighting, but also through his skills as an instructor and an organiser, in which context his legacy would be profound.

5th July

4223   Avro 504   1Sqn
+*Rec MENIN-TOURCOING-MOUSCRON combat with AviatikC?[+shot down dest] for 25 mins ovMENIN 7000' 4-33am till gun jam OK(Capt DE Stoddart/2Lt MS Stewart) Report that EA was brought down BELLEGHEM-ROLLEGHEM & crew KIA 4-30am

6th July

4223   Avro 504   1Sqn
+*AOb combat with 2 Aviatiks met earlier ovST JULIEN 5000' 11-40am shot up engine hit ftl OK(2Lt OD Filley/Lt L Playfair **KIA**) earlier chased 2 Aviatiks ~10-15am & other ~11-10am going towards PASSCHENDAELE

1890   Voisin LA   4Sqn
**Phot shot up radiator ftl ERQUINGHEM OK(Cpl V Judge/2Lt JF Lascelles)

1680   BE2c   6Sqn
+*AOb combat with EA pusher BOESINGHE 7600'-7800' 6am OK(Capt BT James/2Lt CH Awcock) EA like FE, EA almost hit by Allied AA

1883   Voisin LA   7Sqn
+*Rec ARMENTIÈRES-QUESNOY combat with EA 7000' 5-25am to 5-45am shotup(2Lt LW Yule **WIA**/2Lt RH Peck **WIA**) hit by exploding cartridges

1702   BE2c   8Sqn
+*Rec combat with double nacelle EA sTHOUROUT 8000' 3-49pm OK(2Lt HR Nicholl/Lt Greenslade)

9th July

1613   Bristol Scout C   8Sqn
P shell hit 700' nose-dive ooc cr eDICKEBUSCH(Lt MH Monckton **KIA) attached from 2Sqn? (a'c was at

1AP in wrecked condition 10.7.15, with 1hr 45m on a'c log)

10th July

1602   Bristol Scout C   1Sqn
+* climbed to attack Taube HOUTHEM-PLOEGSTEERT 10700' 5-40pm OK(Capt EO Grenfell) EA had not seen him, actually got too close to bring fixed Lewis to bear

BE2?   6Sqn
** (Capt RH Austin-Sparks **WIA**)

13th July

1898   Voisin LA   4Sqn
+*Rec sCOMINES combat with big pusher from behind shot up 2-50pm OK(Capt REB Hunt)

241   BE2a   6Sqn
AReg AA fire nose-dive 6000' cr nrVERLORENHOOK **MIA(Capt BT James **KIA**)

179   Avro 504   Dunkirk
** ground fire CANVEY Island shot up ftl dam OK(FSLt JC Croft)

14th July

2003   BE2c   16Sqn
Rec **MIA(Lt HM Goode **WIA POW**/2Lt WM Crabbie **WIA POW**) WIA: pilot in neck, observer in head, to Holland 10.4.18

This aircraft serial is often given as that which Immelmann shot down for his fourth victory. This is incorrect, see BE2c 2033 (See AIR1/2148/209/3/195, amongst others).

19th July

1602   Bristol Scout C   1Sqn
+*HAP POLYGON WOOD combat with fast LVG? ovHOUTHULST WOOD 7500' 4-41pm OK(Lt MMcB Bell-Irving) called up by WT, EA dived away

1870   Morane L   3Sqn
+* combat with EA VILLE CHAPELLE-BOIS DE BIEZ 8000' 8am OK(Lt Saunders/Sgt JTB McCudden) inconclusive

21st July

1659   BE2c   2Sqn
+*Phot combat with Aviatik ovSECLIN 9600' 6-10pm OK(Capt JG Hearson)

1710   BE2c   2Sqn
+*Rec I Army area combat with EA neDOUAI 11000' 6-15pm shot up dam OK(Capt J Collins/Lt R Marshall)

1800   BE2c   4Sqn
**Rec CAMBRAI-PERONNE combat with Albatros ovDRIENCOURT 4-20am shot up ailerion controls dam ooc but recovered ftl hit wires cr OK(Lt GWG Lywood/

Lt EL Foot) EA came from behind (Combat Report filed with those of 3 Sqn)

1858   Voisin LA   4Sqn
Rec combat with EA ftl **MIA(Cpl V Judge **DoW**/2Lt JR Parker **POW DoW**) left 4-20am, observer hit in brain & shoulder, German message dropped later, saying they "died in an honourable fight"

678   RE5   7Sqn
Rec shot up engine ftl WUIJCKHUYSEPOLDER 6-10am burnt a'c **MIA(Capt REB Hunt **INT**/Lt FH Jackson **WIA INT**) interned Holland

2458   RE5   7Sqn
+*Rec CAMBRAI combat with EA 7000' OK(Capt GD Mills/2Lt RC Macpherson)

24th July

1678   BE2c   4Sqn
+*LRec combat with EA BILMCOURT-BUS 5800' 5-50am shot up OK(Capt.Hon LJE Fiennes/Lt EL Foot) inconclusive, later shot up again

25th July

A new German weapon, the flame-thrower, appeared for the first time in fighting on the 25th. It was used to deadly effect, and a serious breach was forced in the line north of the Menin Road, at Hooge. This brought about intensified fighting in the air as well as on the ground for several days, culminating in an Allied counter-attack in early August. 5 and 6 Squadrons were involved in most of the fighting.

1611   Bristol Scout C   6Sqn
Lewis Gun obliquely mounted **OP combat with EA[?+ driven down] nrPASSCHENDAELE, then AlbC[+of FAb3, driven down ftl] ovHOUTHULST, then combat with AlbC[+in flames] ovHOOGE 10000' 7pm OK(Capt LG Hawker)

Capt Hawker was awarded the Victoria Cross for this action, the first given for combat between aircraft. It was the most successful fight the air war had seen — Hawker accounting for perhaps three of the enemy. It firmly presaged the era of combats between single-seaters.

2864   FE2a   6Sqn
+*Rec combat with EA LINSELLES 9500' 4-50pm OK(2Lt MK Cooper-King/2Lt EW Leggatt)

Nos. 10 and 11 Squadrons RFC arrived in France on the 25th of July. 10 Squadron was equipped with BE2cs and would be attached to the First Army for reconnaissance purposes. Later in the year, in the battle of the Loos, it would carry out strategic reconnaissance and artillery co-operation.

No.11 Squadron's complete compliment of Vickers FB5s made it the first two-seater fighter

unit to serve with the Expeditionary Force. The FB5 had so far contributed effectively to the Allies' control of the air. Despite its reasonably poor turn of speed, its armament had ensured it was treated with respect by its adversaries. Unfortunately for 11 Squadron it was about to be comprehensively outclassed by the Fokker. Until 18 Squadron arrived in November, also with the Vickers Fighter, 11 Squadron remained the only RFC unit operating as a concentrated fighter outfit. There had been suggestions that the French system of grouping fighters be taken up, but this was over-ruled, and existing squadrons continued to have the use of at least one or two scouts within their ranks. The Bristol Scout remained the most common type.

The first of the RFC Communiqués was issued. These were intended to summarise battle related events occurring in the air war.

26th July

1602	Bristol Scout C	1Sqn

+*Rec combat with small LVG? ovROULERS 7500' 6-30pm poor engine OK(Lt MMcB Bell-Irving)

1669	BE2c	2Sqn

+*Rec I Army area combat with Fokker TOURNAI 8000' 4-30pm OK(Capt T Carthew DSO/Capt Milne)

The combat report of this engagement included the first definite reference to the engaged aircraft as a "Fokker", meaning a Fokker E-type. The end of July is known to be when British crews began to meet the new monoplane.

1678	BE2c	4Sqn

+*Rec eALBERT-CAMBRAI combat with EA shot up then 2nd combat with pusher[+ftl?] 7-8500' 5-40am OK(Lt FE Hellyer/2Lt Capel) "Lt AG Weir & Lt HM? Hankin caused EA to descend" (in BE2c 1698)

1698	BE2c	4Sqn

**Rec combat with EA MIA(Lt AG Weir POW/Lt HM? Hankin POW) initials HF?, both to Holland 10.4.18

5028	Voisin LAS	7Sqn

+*RecP forced EA to dive fast 5m seYPRES 7000' 6-45pm OK(2Lt LW Yule/2Lt BG James)

27th July

783	Avro 504	5Sqn

+*Rec nrLILLE combat with "Morane" LILLE-ZONNEBEKE 5-10am OK(Capt Abercromby/2Lt CSL Whidborne WIA?) some records give WIA 24.7.15

1898	Voisin LA	7Sqn

+*Rec MENIN combat with EA 7000' OK(Lt DL Allen/2Lt RH Peck)

28th July

2864	FE2a	6Sqn

+*Rec combat with Aviatik YPRES-PASSCHENDAELE 8000' 6-45pm engine failed (shot up?) ftl OK(Capt LA Strange/Lt EC Braddyll)

1649	Vickers FB5	11Sqn

+* combat with Fokker[+dd] OK(Capt LWB Rees/FSgt JM Hargreaves)

This was the first combat for 11 Squadron, within only days of arrival at the front.

29th July

1687	BE2c	2Sqn

+*Phot combat with 3 Fokkers ovSECLIN 10000'-7300' 8-15am OK(Capt TW Smith/Lt AW Davies) see BE2c 1703

1703	BE2c	2Sqn

+*Phot combat with 1 Fokker then 2 Fokkers[+?these driven down] SECLIN 10000'-7300' OK(Capt JG Hearson/Lt R Marshall) 1st Fokker seen off with help of BE2c 1687

1649	Vickers FB5	4Sqn

+* combat with Fokker ovBUCQUOY 6am shot up dam OK(Capt Reese/Capt Kennedy) EA driven off

1656	BE2c	4Sqn

+*Rec CAMBRAI-PERONNE combat ovEPEHY 7000' 6-20am OK(Capt RM Vaughan/2Lt Lawes)

4732	DH2	5Sqn

prototype **P BOESINGHE combat with large Aviatik 7-40am shot up OK(Capt R Maxwell-Pike)

Maxwell-Pike had been chosen to carry out the service evaluation of the new DH2 single-seat pusher fighter, having first flown it at Hendon on the 22nd of June. It had come to France on the 26th of July, and this was its first recorded combat.

631	RE5	7Sqn

**Rec dhAA tail & engine hit ftl MIA(Lt PA Broder POW/2Lt RC Macpherson POW) both to Holland 10.4.18

2458	RE5	7Sqn

+*Rec OSTENDE-BRUGES-GHENT combat with EA 8400' but gun jam OK(Capt JA Liddell/2Lt HH Watkins)

31st July

4223	Avro 504	1Sqn

+*AOb CORTEMARCK-HOUTHULST WOOD combat with Aviatik 7500' OK(2Lt OD Filley/2Lt M Jacks) inconclusive

1611	Bristol Scout C	6Sqn

+* combat with large Albatros ovYPRES 11000' 10-15am but gun jam OK(Capt LG Hawker)

4253	FE2a	6Sqn

+*Rec combat with Albatros ovTOURNAI 8400'
7-15am OK(Lt Mansfield/Lt EC Braddyll)

2457   RE5   7Sqn
**Rec BRUGES-GHENT combat with 2Str shot up
AA(Lt JA Liddell **DoW** 31.8.15/2Lt RH Peck OK) WIA
leg: taken to FURNES hospital

Lt Liddell received the Victoria Cross for this
action. He and Peck were heading away from
Ostend, at about 5000 feet, when they were
attacked by an enemy two-seater. Fire was
exchanged, but whilst Peck was changing drums a
very accurate burst hit the RE5 and severely
wounded Liddell in his right thigh. He lost consciousness and the machine dropped some 3000
feet, during which time Peck could only hold on
grimly to his gun. Liddell partially regained
consciousness and managed to right the RE5. It
was very substantially shot up and difficult to
control, but he chose to attempt to fly it back to
Allied lines rather than for he and Peck to be taken
prisoner. In intense pain he flew for some thirty
minutes before making an almost perfect landing at
La Panne, a Belgian airfield. He was rushed to
hospital but died of his wounds a month later.

5028   Voisin LAS   7Sqn
+*Rec combat with EA wGHISTELLES-OSTENDE
7000' 5-15pm OK(2Lt LW Learmount/2Lt HH Watkins)
had also encountered EA nZARREN-DIXMUDE 6000'

August 1915

THE "FOKKER SCOURGE"
BEGINS

By the beginning of August, numbers of Fokker
fighters had grown to a point where they could
begin to be effective. The combats of the final days
of July are evidence of their growing menace. The
aeroplanes which were fighting this week were an
interesting group for the range of types involved.
The entries record several machines involved in
daily action which had already seen front line
service for nearly a year. These included the
Voisins, the Avro 504, and the BE2c. In contrast,
one or two of the others were destined to make an
emphatic new impact on the air war, albeit still
several months hence. The DH2 prototype is an
obvious example, and the FE2a was to be
developed into a highly successful two-seater
reconnaissance fighter. Both showed the Allied
commitment to the pusher configuration, and were
destined to become the fighter mainstay of the RFC
for much of 1916. Bristol Scouts continued to
provide a fighting capability for many squadrons,

patrolling and protecting reconnaissance operations, and were flown by many of the pilots who
were now instigating a new era of air fighting. Most
now had some arrangement of machine-gun, fitted
to fire obliquely beyond the propeller arc, but this
in turn demanded double deflection shooting,
allowing not only for your opponent's movement,
but your own as well, and was rarely effective
beyond very close range. But the Bristol Scout, like
the Vickers FB5, had a very unreliable engine,
ensuring it would never make a full contribution.

The RFC Command was beginning to recognise
the importance of having numerical superiority in
the air, and this was to become a vital prerequisite
of achieving their policy. Now, with the growing
presence of the Fokker as well, a few uneasy months
of sparring began, when the old and the new
survived together. The outcome was never in
doubt, however, for the new order would soon
impose itself. It was a true turning point in the air
war.

Until this time, the RFC had felt able to operate
over the battle with relative security and impunity.
Its airmen had little more to contend with than
anti-aircraft fire and the reliability of their own
machines. The BE2c remained the staple reconnaissance aircraft of the RFC — some two thirds
of its squadrons being equipped with it in 1915 —
and indeed it would still be in widespread use well
into the following year. However it was already
known to be very inadequate as a fighting machine.
Unlike the relatively new German C-types, whose
capabilities had benefited so much from a thorough
redesign, the BE2cs had some insuperable dis-
advantages. The observer sat in front of the pilot
and thus had a dreadful field of fire. Various
machine-gun mountings had been experimented
with, but to little effect.

Until this time, however, if an RFC pilot saw an
enemy machine he nearly always attacked it as a
matter of course, most times seeing it off, even if
flying a BE2c. On some occasions the enemy would
even be shot down. The Fokkers totally changed
this balance of engagement, removing the initiative
from the British. The Fokker first appeared as an
escort machine protecting those on reconnaissance
work. The aircraft did not turn German pilots into
aggressive fighters overnight. This was most
unlikely to occur, because from the outset the
fighter pilots' role was primarily one of protection.
Orders forbidding flying beyond their own lines, as
part of the general defensive ethos of the German
air service, saw to this. However, the Eindekker
was a new and potent weapon, and it cried out to
be experimented with tactically. It was the ability

of a few early exponents of the Fokker to evolve the essentials of air fighting with such skill which made it the great weapon it became. These included aspects of manoeuvrability and superior positioning, which will be looked at later. The Fokker was to have its problems, but at its peak it was an extremely dangerous weapon because it combined several telling attributes which made it superior in combat to anything else in the sky. The "Fokker Scourge" was beginning.

1st August

1897   Morane L   1Sqn
+*P WARNETON-LILLE combat with fast LVG ovYPRES 8000' 9-15am OK(2Lt MMcB Bell-Irving) could not get close

1662   BE2c   2Sqn
B VITRY combat with EA shot up ftl DOUAI ldg ok **MIA(2Lt W Reid WIA **POW**)arm, operating with no observer, to Switzerland 30.5.16 Imm1 [combat nrDOUAI 5-15am Ltn M Immelmann FAb62]

MAX IMMELMANN'S FIRST VICTORY

This was the first official victory for Max Immelmann, one of the greatest of the early German aces. He was flying an armed Fokker EI for the first time in battle. There were still very few Fokkers in service, but FAb.62 was one unit which now had its initial allocation of two machines. One likely reason for this was that since the spring this unit had been gaining a reputation for war flying, inspired by the leadership of Hptm Kastner and made possible by the presence of not only Immelmann, but also Boelcke, amongst its flyers. Both these great pilots were now beginning their flying with the type. Immelmann had been itching to fly the new fighter in combat, and his chance came when he took off to attack enemy machines which were bombing his aerodrome. Boelcke was already aloft in his Eindekker but had to return with a gun stoppage. The few RFC aircraft which he and Boelcke had sought to attack then headed towards Arras, and catching sight of a lone BE2c he headed for it while it was bombing Vitry. He climbed above the enemy and then dived, expending some 450 to 500 bullets during the ten-minute combat which followed. His manoeuvring finally forced the BE2c down, and landing beside it he was able to meet his wounded opponent and offer him assistance.

1874   Morane L   3Sqn
+* combat with Fokker ovVIMY 8000' 6-15am

OK(Capt M Barratt/Lt CT Cleaver) previous combat with Aviatik 6am ovANNEQUIN

2864   FE2a   6Sqn
+*Rec LILLE combat with EA POLYGON WOOD 8000' 9-20am to 9-30am OK(2Lt MK Cooper-King/2Lt EW Leggatt)

1649   Vickers FB5   11Sqn
+*Esc 5am to 7-30am combat sBAPAUME 7200'-5500' OK(Capt LWB Rees/Lt CW Lane)

2nd August

1713   BE2c   6Sqn
+*Phot HOOGE combat with EA 6000'-7000' 8-10am to 8-20am OK(2Lt MK Cooper-King/2Lt EW Leggatt)

2864   FE2a   6Sqn
+*Rec combat: dived on 2 2-seaters[+1st left in nose-dive nrHOUTHEM ftl EoL] WYTSCHAETE 7500' 8am OK(Capt LG Hawker/Lt HJ Payn) chased other down to 5000', later attacked 3rd EA (PS not in FE2a 4227 as some sources give)

Hawker described this combat in a letter home written four days later: "Last Monday in an FE on our way home we came up behind a couple ranging. Left No1 diving steeply after 140 rounds, attacked and chased No2 well home until we got too low over their lines — 5000' — and later attacked a third, who made off into the clouds. We since heard No1 landed just behind their trenches . . . so evidently we at least did in his engine — unluckily there was a strong wind in his favour. They are all armed with machine-guns now, of course, and don't hesitate to use them. Further south I believe they are giving the French an awful lot of trouble."

3rd August

11Sqn
? (2Lt GM Allen **WIA) inj?

6th August

RFC
** (2Lt C Dollingsworth **POW**) to Holland 10.4.18

RFC
** (Lt W Dalzell **POW**) to Holland 10.4.18, to UK 23.10.18

8th August

2875   Vickers FB5   11Sqn
+*P GRANDECOURT-BAPAUME combat with EA 8500' 7-15pm OK(2Lt LA Tilney/2Lt C Jones)

9th August

4732   DH2   5Sqn
**P HOOGE AA combat with Albatros 2Str, hit by

single shot ftl cr o't WESTHOEK 2.5m eYPRES
MIA(Capt R Maxwell-Pike **DoW**)head, a'c captured
[shot down by ObltzS Ritscher/Ltn S Maass MFAbII]

The terrible loss of Maxwell-Pike, flying the DH2
prototype, delivered an example of the new fighter
type into German hands. There is a German record
of these events, which describes how Maxwell-Pike
was most likely seeing off the enemy reconnaissance
machine when a lucky shot from the observer's gun
hit him in the head. He brought the machine down
well enough, but overturned on rough ground. He
died soon afterwards. The DH2 was taken off for
lengthy evaluation.

1611   Bristol Scout C   6Sqn
+*P POLYGON WOOD combat with Halberstadt?
ovHOOGE 9000' but gun jam OK(Capt LG Hawker)
(not 2.8 as per RFC Communiqué No.4)

The successful counter-attack by the 6th Division
at Hooge came this day. Nos. 1, 5, and 6 Squadrons
carried out important counter-battery work. The
first effective shelling occurred as early as 4am and
most of the enemy positions were soon silenced.

11th August

1687   BE2c   2Sqn
+*Phot combat with Fokker ARMENTIÈRES-
VIOLAINES 5pm OK(Capt TW Smith/Lt AW Davies)
with BE2c 1703

1703   BE2c   2Sqn
+*PhotRec ARMENTIÈRES-VIOLAINES combat
with Fokker 5pm shot up dam OK(Capt JG Hearson/
Capt Milne) with BE2c 1687

4227   FE2a   6Sqn
**Rec HOUTHEM-ZILLEBEKE combat with Albatros
then 2Halbs then combat with Aviatik 8000'-7000' 6am
to 6-45am[+down in nose-dive nrHOUTHEM, landed?]
then combat with Fokker ovLILLE-ROUBAIX 9000'
7-15am[+vertical nose-dive cr] OK(Capt LG Hawker
VC/Lt N Clifton)

2875   Vickers FB5   11Sqn
+*P BUCQUOY combat with EA 8500' 6-45pm?
OK(2Lt LA Tilney/2Lt C Jones) time am?

12th August

3717   Sopwith Schneider   Felixstowe
this a'c? **B ZEEBRUGGE MOLE then AA shot down
sank **MIA**(FSLt JM D'Arcy-Levy **POW**) to Holland
9.4.18, a'c salvaged & displayed by Germans

15th August

No.2 Wing RNAS had been formed at Eastchurch
on the 21st of June from elements of 2 Squadron
RNAS which had been disbanded after early
service in the war in 1914. In turn, No.2 Wing

began to arrive in St Pol in order to relieve No.1
Wing RNAS on the 2nd of August. Almost
immediately however the decision was taken to
send it to reinforce the RNAS in the Dardanelles
and embarkation took place on the 15th of that
month. It operated in the East for the rest of the
year and through the evacuation of the Peninsula
in December, after which time it remained serving
in the region.

16th August

2006   BE2c   8Sqn
RecP dhAA ftl **MIA(2Lt DD Drury **POW**/2Lt WA
Maclean **WIA POW**) left 4pm, slight WIA, Drury to
Switzerland 27.12.17

18th August

1637   Vickers FB5   5Sqn
+* combat with EA 9200' Sh28.D. 5-30pm shot up dam
OK(Lt Greig/1AM Nicholls) EA first seen going south
ovHOUTHULST WOOD, inconclusive

19th August

**   BE2c?   2Sqn**
** combat with EA fuel pipe shot up ftl nARRAS
OK(Capt JG Hearson/Capt Barker)

21st August

2866   Vickers FB5   11Sqn
** combat with LVG shot up dam OK(Capt PHL
Playfair/Lt JS Cemlyn-Jones)

22nd August

1687   BE2c   2Sqn
+*Phot combat with Fokker ovSECLIN 8800' 6pm badly
shot up OK(Lt RT Heather?/Lt AW Davies) EA used
steel core bullets

2034   BE2c   2Sqn
Phot dhAA EoL **MIA(2Lt GC? Gallie **KIA**/2Lt WM
Wallace **KIA**) initials JC?, "fell like a stone"
ovSAINGHEM

1603   Bristol Scout C   5Sqn
+* combat with "Aviatik" ovBOESINGHE shot up
10800' 3-15pm to 3-45pm OK(Capt Read) had red white
& blue rudder so did not know it was HA until fired on,
then "escorted it back to Houthulst"

2874   Vickers FB5   5Sqn
+* combat with Fokker going east ovYPRES 6000'
7-45am OK(Lt S Graham-Gilmour/1AM Buckerfield)
inconclusive

1648   Vickers FB5   11Sqn
+*P COLINCAMPS combat with LVG 8500' 5-45pm to
6-15pm OK(Lt LA Pattinson/Lt JS Cemlyn-Jones)

23rd August

4666   Bristol Scout C   8Sqn
+*HAP 7-25am to 8-15am combat with 2Str nrALBERT
6000' shot up? dam repairable OK(2Lt ERC Scholefield)

5454   Vickers FB5   11Sqn
+*P HAMEL-SERRE combat with LVG 9000' 8am
OK(2Lt HA Cooper/2Lt AJ Insall)

25th August

2866   Vickers FB5   11Sqn
+*P BERTRANCOURT combat with LVG SAILLY-
AU-BOIS 7600' 6-10pm shot up engine dam OK(Capt
PHL Playfair/Lt JS Cemlyn-Jones)

26th August

1897   Morane L   1Sqn
1894?: probably not +*ACoop WYTSCHAETE combat
with new 2Str ovHOUTHEM 8000' 12-30pm OK(Capt
MMcB Bell-Irving)

1870   Morane L   3Sqn
+*Rec LA BASSIE combat with Aviatik nDON 1-30pm
with 5147 OK(Lt Saunders/Cpl Roberts) gun jam,
inconclusive

1712   BE2c   16Sqn
+*Phot combat with EA ovHAUBOURDIN 7000'
OK(Lt PB Greenwood/Capt TE Lombridge)

3623   Henri Farman   1 Wing RNAS
St Pol **Bombed U-boat[+destroyed, seen sink] 4m
nnwNIEUPORT OK(SCdr AW Bigsworth)

27th August

1863   Morane L   3Sqn
+* combat with EA LILLE 9-50am OK(2Lt CA Ridley/
Cpl Roberts)

1601   Martinsyde S1   6Sqn
+* combat with Aviatik HOOGE-POLYGON WOOD
12-30pm OK(2Lt MK Cooper-King)

2031   BE2c   6Sqn
+*AOb 10-10am to 11-20am combat with EA
HOLLEBEKE-HOOGE 6500'-8000' wireless shot up
but returned to a'dr OK(Lt Collis/2Lt GA Parker)

2037   BE2c   16Sqn
+* drove off EA ovLILLE OK(2Lt HS Shield/Lt D
Leeson Can.)

28th August

1863   Morane L   3Sqn
+* combat with 2Aviatiks ovLILLE 5-30pm OK(2Lt CA
Ridley/2Lt CT Cleaver), A Flt

5055   Morane L   3Sqn
+*Phot LA BASSIE-DON combat with Aviatik
ovGIVENCHY 11-30am OK(2Lt AC Collier/2Lt JK
Summers)

1678   BE2c   4Sqn
+*Rec combat with large Aviatik ePERONNE 9am
OK(2Lt E Harrison-Mitchell/Lt W Collon-Minchin) EA
probably hit

1706   BE2c   6Sqn
+*AOb combat with EA from ROULERS 7000' 10am
OK(Lt Collis/2Lt GA Parker)

1632   Vickers FB5   11Sqn
+*P nrHEBUTERNE chased Fokker 7700' 4-45pm: led
over AA then bad storm OK(2Lt AL? Neale/Lt CW
Lane)

30th August

1704   BE2c   8Sqn
+*Rec HAMELINCOURT combat with EA 9000'
9-45am OK(2Lt ERC Scholefield/Capt FJC Wilson)

31st August

BE2c   7Sqn
**Rec DOUAI combat with EA[+chased down, gunner
hit?] shot up, engine poor at 5000' so pulled out(2Lt
Fairburn OK/2Lt BG James **WIA**)

2032   BE2c   10Sqn
+*LRec combat with LVG?[+?EA observer probably
hit] swDOUAI 7000' 7-45am OK(2Lt CO Fairbairn/2Lt
HH James) bad engine so gave up chase at 5500'

1649   Vickers FB5   11Sqn
+*P BUCQUOY-BAPAUME combat with LVG[+?saw
dive into clouds, seen badly hit] ACHIET LE PETIT
7000'-8000' then engine problems OK(Capt LWB Rees/
FSgt JM Hargreaves) had returned for fuel and then
re-found EA, 2Lt Cooper/2Lt Insall saw EA going down
in odd spirals

5454   Vickers FB5   11Sqn
+*P SERRE-ACHIET LE PETIT saw combat of FB5
1649 7000' 9-30am? OK(2Lt HA Cooper/2Lt AJ Insall)

Untraced Casualty in France in August 1915

? (Sgt BF Barnard **KIA)

September 1915

For a few short weeks in September the Fokker E-
types were actually grounded as service aircraft.
This was due to three fatal crashes occurring in the
Fokker training unit at Doberitz. These happened
on the 27th and 31st of July, and 29th August, and
led to the remaining aircraft there being sent back
to Schwerin and the unit being disbanded. The
Fokker was then generally grounded. The pressure
was so great for its use, however, that in a few
weeks the order had been rescinded and training
reorganised.

1st September

1704   BE2c   8Sqn
**Rec combat with Albatros nrBAPAUME shot down
7-45am **MIA**(2Lt ERC Scholefield **POW**/Capt FJC
Wilson **POW**) both a'c seen nose-dive but thought OK?,
observer to Switzerland 12.8.16, pilot to Holland 10.4.18

2866   Vickers FB5   11Sqn
+*P BUCQUOY-BOYELLES 7-30am to 8-15am
combat with LVG 7000' then Rumpler OK(Capt PHL
Playfair/2Lt A Murray)

4th September

2875   Vickers FB5   11Sqn
+*Phot DOUCHY-AYETTE combat with LVG[+
driven down EoL, landed ok] 9000' 8-45pm? OK(2Lt HA
Cooper/2Lt AJ Insall) time am?

5th September

1863   Morane L   3Sqn
**P combat with 2 Aviatiks ovLILLE 7000' 5-30am, gun
jammed & engine shot up: chased by EA to 1km WoL(Lt
CA Ridley **WIA**/2Lt CT Cleaver OK)foot, a'c suffered
40-50 hits

4227   FE2a   6Sqn
AP AA shot down **MIA(Capt WC Adamson **KIA**/Lt
EC Braddyll **POW DoW**) earlier drove off 3HA in
combat Sh28 1.30.d.8.

5454   Vickers FB5   11Sqn
+*P GOMMECOURT combat with LVG[+smoke & in
flames nose-dive towards SARS, seen cr destroyed]
COURCELETTE neALBERT 7500' 5-45pm to 6-15pm
engine failed as hit twice so forced to return OK(2Lt HA
Cooper/2Lt AJ Insall)

6th September

12 Squadron RFC arrived at St Omer from
England on the 6th of September. It was attached
to Headquarters RFC and began carrying out
reconnaissance work.

5455   Vickers FB5   11Sqn
+*PhotP ALBERT-SOMME RIVER combat with 2
LVGs[+?1st nose-dived to within few feet of ground]
ovBOYELLES 9000'-5000' ~9-45am OK(2Lt GSM
Insall/2Lt G Manley)

3177   Nieuport 10   RNAS
**Bombed U-boat[+claimed probably sunk] 20 miles off
NIEUPORT OK(FSLt RH Mulock)

This is the first record of a Nieuport Scout in action
for the British in France. The RNAS were flying
Nieuports some months before the RFC. A few
Nieuport 16 Scouts would join Nos. 1 and 11
Squadrons RFC in March 1916.

7th September

1894   Morane L   1Sqn
**P YPRES-COURTRAI combat with 2 Albatros "firing
seriously at us" over X-roads Sh28 J.29 but driven off by
pointing telescope! 6500-7000' 9-45am to 10-05am
OK(2Lt R Balcombe-Brown/Lt TMcK Hughes)
Albatros' attacked from behind (Morane had forward
firing gun), also earlier combat with Albatros

1611   Bristol Scout C 6Sqn
+*P combat with EA ovBIXSCHOOTE 9000'[+shot
down ooc] OK(Capt LG Hawker) Lt Baldwin of 5Sqn
saw EA down ooc nose-dive

This was Hawker's last victory before being posted
back to England to form 24 Squadron, the RFC's
first single-seater fighter squadron. It was probably
his seventh victory, and he returned to England as
the first British ace of the war.

1647   Vickers FB5   11Sqn
+*Phot BAPAUME combat with Aviatik 9000' 10am
gun jam OK(Capt CC Darley/Lt E Robinson)

2866   Vickers FB5   11Sqn
+*Phot combat with LVG ALBERT-BOIS D'AVELUY
8500' 7-40am OK(Capt PHL Playfair/2Lt A Murray)

2033   BE2c   16Sqn
+*Rec combat with Aviatik ovBOIS DE BIEZ 9-15am
OK(2Lt J Gay/Lt D Leeson Can.) EA seen to nose-dive
after being hit?, not seen again

8th September

1632   Vickers FB5   11Sqn
+*SpP RAMNEVILLE combat with Aviatik ovHAMEL
4pm OK(2Lt AL? Neale/Capt CW Lane)

5454   Vickers FB5   11Sqn
+*P HEBUTERNE LVG tried to lure onto AA 9800'
10-05am OK(2Lt HA Cooper/2Lt AJ Insall)

9th September

2866   Vickers FB5   11Sqn
+*Phot combat with Aviatik nrBOYELLES swARRAS
8500' OK(Capt PHL Playfair/2Lt AJ Insall)

10th September

1601   Martinsyde S1   6Sqn
a'c to UK 28.8.15, but?: +* combat with EA YPRES
7500'-8000'10am OK(Capt TW Mulcahy-Morgan)

2031   BE2c   6Sqn
+*AOb YPRES combat with EA 8500' shot up dam
OK(Lt RA Archer/2Lt GA Parker)

2039   BE2c   8Sqn
+*Rec combat with EA nrGOMMECOURT 10000'
8-05am OK(2Lt AV Hobbs/2Lt AH Goldie) 2nd combat
nwST QUENTIN 12000' 9-50am: being drawn onto AA

1648   Vickers FB5   11Sqn

+*P DOUCHY combat with LVG nrGOMMECOURT 8000'-4500' 9-10am shot up dam & close AA OK(2Lt LA Pattinson/2Lt AL Findlay) there was 2nd LVG higher up

| 2235 | RE7 | 12Sqn |
+*Rec combat with EA Scout ARMENTIÈRES 8500' 5-05pm OK(Capt GAK Lawrence/Lt Birch)

11th September

| 2033 | BE2c | 16Sqn |
+*P YPRES combat with two-engined EA 9am then AA OK(2Lt J Gay/Lt D Leeson Can.) EA was possible lure for AA, went off towards MENIN

12th September

| 2864 | FE2a | 6Sqn |
+*P combat with Aviatik ovWESTROOSEBEKE Sh28 D.27.d.0.8. 9000' 3pm OK(2Lt MK Cooper-King/Lt MW? Thomas)

| 1647 | Vickers FB5 | 11Sqn |
+*Phot ALBERT-PERONNE combat with Aviatik[+ engine hit?, nose-dived ftl field, EA observer WIA?] 6500' 8am OK(Capt CC Darley/Lt E Robinson)

13th September

| 5056 | Morane L | 1Sqn |
+*HAP GAAPORD combat with Albatros[+?chased & fired from 150', dived straight down, still diving at 5000'] WYTSCHAETE-MENIN 14000'-9500' 7-40am OK(Lt EO Grenfell) only EA pilot on board, later drove off Albatros eCOMINES 10200' 7-55am

| 1680 | BE2c | 6Sqn |
**SpM:spy drop ftl nrOYGEM cr tree ldg 5-15am MIA(Capt TW Mulcahy-Morgan WIA POW/spy) left 4-20am, to hospital in COURTRAI, pilot escaped to UK 9.4.17

This was the first attempt to drop a spy behind the lines. After the machine crashed, friendly civilians were able to remove incriminating papers from the scene.

| 2671 | BE2c | 10Sqn |
+*Rec seTOURNAI combat with Fokker 9000' 1pm badly shot up difficult trip home OK(2Lt JC Quinnell/ Lt WH Sugden-Wilson)

| 2037 | BE2c | 16Sqn |
+*P BOIS DE BIEZ combat with Albatros 2Str[+EA engine hit brought down] ovARMENTIÈRES 10000' 7-15am to 7-30am OK(2Lt HS Shield/Cpl T? Bennett) [EA crew from FAb24 both killed]

14th September

| 2039 | BE2c | 8Sqn |
+*Rec combat with Fokker ovDOUAI 8000' 5-35pm OK(2Lt HR Nicholl/Capt Stolt)

15th September

| 5006 | Morane L | 1Sqn |
+*Rec LILLE-ROUBAIX combat with Aviatik ovLILLE 8000' 5-46pm to 6-15pm OK(2Lt VS Strugnell/2Lt KA Creery) inconclusive

18th September

| 2457 | RE5 | 7Sqn |
+*Rec combat with Fokker out of sun 8000' 5-30pm OK(Capt GD Mills/2Lt Layton)

| 4670 | Bristol Scout C | 16Sqn |
+*combat with Aviatik nrGHELUVELT 7-55am then Albatros nrSOUCHEZ ~9-30am OK(Capt AAB Thompson)

19th September

| 1734 | BE2c | 2Sqn |
+*AOb HENIN LIETARD-DOUAI combat with Albatros[+steep nose-dive on fire 4m nVITRY] nrLENS 9500'-5000' 9-10am then 2nd Albatros[+ftl] OK(2Lt HW Medlicott/2Lt EM Gilbert)

| 1651 | Vickers FB5 | 5Sqn |
+*P ePOLYGON WOOD 5-25am to 7-20am combat with large 3Str 2eng EA 6000' nrHOUTHULST[+EA engine hit seen diving over tail with one smoking engine] then 3rd combat with Albatros OK(Lt FJ Powell/1AM J Shaw) had earlier combat with LVG 6000' chased EA down towards MENIN, gun jam problems

| 1740 | BE2c | 6Sqn |
+*AReg combat with two-engined EA ZILLEBEKE-TENBRIELEN 8000' 10-50am[+? brought down BISSIGHEM] shot up dam OK(Lt A Sommervail/Lt CE? Ryan) EA was "two-engined tractor with nacelle"

| 1782 | BE2c | 7Sqn |
**Rec LEDEGHEM combat with Ago ovROULERS A'dr 8300' 7-05pm shot up sump dam ftl OK(Capt Mansfield/Capt Holt)

| 2008 | BE2c | 8Sqn |
**Rec combat with EA shot down nrST QUENTIN(2Lt WH Nixon KIA/Capt JNS Stott WIA POW) observer to Holland 10.4.18 [combat nrST QUENTIN Hpt H-J Buddecke FAb23]

| 4668 | Bristol Scout C | 10Sqn |
+*P combat with LVG? 2m sDON 8000' 7-05am[+?EA engine hit: dived down to field from 2000'] OK(Capt C Gordon-Bell)

| 1647 | Vickers FB5 | 11Sqn |
+*AReg combat with EA 10m sARRAS 8500' 3pm OK(Capt CC Darley/Lt E Robinson)

| 1649 | Vickers FB5 | 11Sqn |
+*P ALBERT combat with Albatros 2Str 8500' 10am OK(Capt LWB Rees/FSgt JM Hargreaves)

20th September

| 1735 | BE2c | 7Sqn |
+*Rec seROULERS combat with Albatros 8000' 7am OK(2Lt NJ Bengough/2Lt AD Bell-Irving)

21st September

PREPARATIONS FOR THE BATTLE OF LOOS

The preliminary bombardment for the battle of Loos began on the 21st of September, four days ahead of the infantry advance. The attack was to be undertaken by the British First Army under Sir Douglas Haig, coupled with the French Tenth Army to its right. The First Army would launch its attack between Lens and La Bassée, with the objective of the ground around Henin-Liètard and Carvin.

The RFC were to play an increasingly complex part in this battle, which was a subsidiary attack to much larger French efforts further south. The French felt their resources had grown sufficiently to attempt another great breakthrough, this time to the south of Rheims. Whilst the size of the Expeditionary Force had also grown continually through the summer, there were fears about its own means to launch a battle, a particular concern being the shortage of shells. It therefore fell to the RFC to comprehensively reconnoitre the enemy positions before the battle, so that best use could be made of the resources. Once the fighting began, the RFC was then to provide unprecedented support for both the continuing bombardment and counter-battery work. Crews were expected to be constantly in the air directing fire, whilst photography would provide a comprehensive picture of the effectiveness of the shelling as well as alerting commanders to the changing circumstances before them.

In the weeks preceding the battle the weather was superb for information gathering. Squadrons were put into place and began their allotted operations some time before the fighting, so that the transition into battle duties was a relatively smooth one. Most of the operations directly in support of the First Army were undertaken by units of 1st Wing, namely Nos. 2, 3, 10, and 16 Squadrons. The First Army front was divided into four zones each roughly between three and six miles in length. These corresponded to the four corps moving into position north to south, namely III Corps, the Indian Corps, and I and IV Corps. Each of the squadrons of 1st Wing was then allotted to one of these zones, carrying out work with the relevant divisional artillery, so that Nos. 16, 10, 3 and 2 Squadrons corresponded to the above. The heaviest fighting was to occur in the two southern zones and so once the advance commenced this would enable one Flight from 16

Squadron to be reserved for tactical reconnaissances over the battlefield and one from 10 Squadron to fly strategic reconnaissances. The latter would press as deeply as Valenciennes.

The battle plan also involved the use of units from 2nd and 3rd Wings to provide bombing capability and protective patrols for 1st Wing's artillery work. Machines from Nos. 1, 5, 6, and 7 Squadrons of 2nd Wing, as well as four Vickers FB5s from 11 Squadron of 3rd Wing, were to patrol and guard the skies over the battlefield. Bombing of various enemy targets would be carried out by other machines provided by 2nd and 3rd Wings, as well as by 12 Squadron who operated with Headquarters. The two remaining units not mentioned as yet, Nos. 4 and 8 Squadrons of 3rd Wing, were involved in this work. The bombing programme began on the 23rd of September and is described in more detail below.

1784   BE2c   5Sqn
+* combat with Aviatik 8000' 5-15pm OK(Lt Williams/ Cpl Harrison) inconclusive

1718   BE2c   6Sqn
+*Phot POLYGON WOOD combat with EA 7500' OK(2Lt HBR Grey-Edwards/2Lt TD O'Brien)

2864   FE2a   6Sqn
+*AOb HOOGE combat with twin-engined EA 9000'-7000' OK(Lt Kinnear/Lt RC? Morgan)

2864   FE2a   6Sqn
+*Rec HOOGE combat with EA ovPOLYGON WOOD[+? EA diving smoking towards MENIN] 7200' 11-40am to 11-50am OK(Lt Kinnear/Lt RC? Morgan)

2004   BE2c   10Sqn
Rec shot down eNEUVILLE cr **MIA(2Lt SW Caws **KIA**/Lt WH Sugden-Wilson **WIA POW**) message: a'c & crew burnt, observer WIA spine, to Holland 10.4.18, Imm3 [combat nrWILLERVAL, eNEUVILLE ~9am Ltn M Immelmann FAb62]

This crew were the first casualties in action for 10 Squadron RFC.

1649   Vickers FB5   11Sqn
+*Phot DOMPIERRE-FLAUCOURT combat with twin nacelled Ago?[+engine hit seen glide down towards PERONNE smoking] 8000'-4000' 11am OK(Capt LWB Rees/FSgt JM Hargreaves)

5030   MFSH   16Sqn
+*AOb shot up Albatros nrARMENTIÈRES with rifle 10-15am then shot up dam OK(Capt AAB Thompson) pursued EA as far as WYTSCHAETE

22nd September

1729   BE2c   2Sqn
+*AP LENS-VIMY combat with EA 9500' 11am OK(2Lt KDP Murray/Lt HB Russell)

2673   **BE2c**   2Sqn
+*AP combat with twin nacelled Albatros? nrLENS
5-40am OK(2Lt HW Medlicott/Lt AW Brown), later
met Fokker 6pm

2673   **BE2c**   2Sqn
+*AP LENS-ARRAS combat with EA 11000'-5500'
7-40am OK(2Lt HW Medlicott/Lt AW Brown)

617   **RE5**   7Sqn
+*Rec THOUROUT-LICHTERVELDE-ISEGHEM
combat with EA 8000' 8am OK(Capt NC Spratt/2Lt AD
Bell-Irving) 5 other EA about

1711   **BE2c**   8Sqn
+*Rec combat with EA HEBUTERNE-RANSART
7-15am[+?EA seen down at LASIGNY FARM 7-30am]
OK(2Lt DA Glen/2Lt LC Drenon?) earlier combat with
Aviatik sARRAS 6-30am

1648   **Vickers FB5**   11Sqn
+* combat with LVG ovLA BASSÉE 7000' 5pm OK(2Lt
LA Pattinson/Lt WA Skeate) filed with 3Sqn Combat
Reports

1649   **Vickers FB5**   11Sqn
+*PhotRec combat with Albatros C-type[+driven down
ovLE SARS] seALBERT 7000'-3500' 5-50pm OK(Capt
LWB Rees/FSgt JM Hargreaves)

23rd September

Aerial bombing was another relatively new service
of the RFC which was now in increasing demand.
An effort had been made to co-ordinate raids with
the French, but all bombing operations were still
being impeded by unreliable sights. An official
report in the summer had found that of the one
hundred and forty-one attempts to bomb enemy
troops and communication lines up until that time,
only three were known to have succeeded.
Improved sights were now slowly making an
appearance, and the potential for aerial bombing
was most certainly recognised — some five-and-a-
half tons of bombs would be dropped at Loos. The
special bombing programme developed for the
battle commenced on the 23rd, the British effort
concentrating on the important railway triangle of
Lille-Douai-Valenciennes. It aimed to strike at
various junctions, engine sheds, and the trains
themselves, thus disrupting troop and supply
movements. Its effectiveness would become one of
the prime victims of the weather, however, which
was about to worsen. The ultimate impact of the
bombing programme on this battle was not easy to
judge, although in truth it was probably rather
minor. Strikes were made on targets as deep as
thirty-six miles behind the lines and trains and
other targets were known to have been hit. Reports
showed that the disruption had soon been made

good, however. The RFC would persist with aerial
bombing, but in 1915 it was still developing its
basic techniques and strategies.

1658   **BE2c**   4Sqn
+* combat with DFW swARRAS 8-30am OK(2Lt JW
Woodhouse/Lt EL Foot)

2035   **BE2c**   4Sqn
+* combat with "Fokker 2Str" 4m seDOUAI-4m
sARRAS shot up OK(2Lt AT Whitelock/2Lt WF
Balmain) "Fokker shot through prop"

2030   **BE2c**   8Sqn
+*ARec swBAPAUME combat with 2EA 8000' 8-30am
shot up dam OK(2Lt AV Hobbs/2Lt LAJ Orde)

5455   **Vickers FB5**   11Sqn
+*Rec FOUCAUCOURT combat with Aviatik 5800'
10-25am OK(2Lt Small/2Lt AL Findlay)

5456   **Vickers FB5**   11Sqn
+*Rec nrHAM combat with Fokker[+?probably hit:
nose-dive & ss to earth] ovROUPY 5000' 2pm then
ovPERONNE 7500' 3-10pm OK(2Lt R Hughes-
Chamberlain/Capt CW Lane) main combat at
1-25pm?(via Communiques), pilot's initials REAW?

5030   **MFSH**   16Sqn
+* combat with EA nrARMENTIÈRES 11-15am
OK(Capt AAB Thompson/2Lt LAK Butt)

24th September

The weather began to deteriorate in the final few
days preceding the attack. Rain set in on the 24th
and bombing was halted, although reconnaissance
and artillery work was continued with difficulty.
Rain was still falling when the battle commenced
the next morning and a mist hung in the air.

25th September

THE BATTLE OF LOOS

The infantry advance for the battle was set in
motion around dawn on the 25th. Early progress
was very good, the first British troops reaching
Loos by 8am. Artillery support had been maintained with widespread effectiveness, although not
all the information provided by the airmen was
acted upon by those on the ground. General air
reconnaissance was more flawed, the conditions
causing some important matters about enemy
strength and dispositions to remain obscure
throughout the day.

Contact patrols were tried again as their potentially great benefits were now acknowledged. There
were attempts to incorporate increasingly sophis-

ticated liaison between the ground and aircraft, and all four squadrons of 1st Wing devoted a few aircraft to this task. In the case of 3 Squadron, two men were despatched directly into the front line to organise signalling. Regretably, both were subsequently wounded and one died of his wounds (see entries on the 28th and the 30th). Continuing rain and poor visibility over the battlefield meant the contact patrols faltered once again, however, and generally failed. The first British use of gas also contributed to the general confusion.

? (Capt AM Read **KIA)

1723   BE2c   8Sqn
+*B combat with EA 1500' 6-15am? shot up dam OK(2Lt DA Glen/2Lt DC Rutter)

4301   BE2c   8Sqn
Rec shot down sMETZ-EN-COUTURE, wCAMBRAI(2Lt JN Washington **POW DoW 2.10.15/ 2Lt MW Greenhow **POW**) left 7-11am, observer to Holland 10.4.18

Despite the poor conditions, bombing was resumed on the day of the advance and saw attacks by fourteen aircraft of 2nd and 3rd Wings on the Douai-Valenciennes railway line. The two 8 Squadron machines mentioned above were involved in these raids.

5054   MFSH   16Sqn
+* combat with EA ovBOIS DE BIEZ 6500' shot up dam?(2Lt HR Deighton-Simpson OK/2Lt EL Hyde **WIA**)slight, pilot's initials HD?

26th September

On the 26th the weather worsened further, with thick fog hanging over the battlefield until late morning. Once it cleared operations continued. 7 Squadron and others were heavily involved in both bombing and reconnaissance of rail networks around Valenciennes.

1726   BE2c   4Sqn
** shot through by 3 shells ftl dam(2Lt EH Mitchell **WIA**/Lt FE Hellyer **WIA**) to hospital, AA hit pilot?, rifle fire hit observer

617   RE5   7Sqn
+*Rec nrROULERS combat with Fokker 7000' 1-35pm OK(Capt NC Spratt/2Lt AD Bell-Irving) EA vol-planed steeply

1719   BE2c   7Sqn
ArmyRec engine problems ftl HEVELE EoL(2Lt LW Yule **KIA/2Lt BG James **KIA**) via later message

2010   BE2c   7Sqn
+*B SECLIN combat with LVG?[+? "probably brought down nrHAUBOURDIN"] 8000' 1pm OK(2Lt LW Learmount)

2457   RE5   7Sqn
+*Rec combat with Albatros 2m sLILLE 9000' 3-15pm OK(Capt GD Mills/2Lt Layton)

1743   BE2c   12Sqn
+*EscB combat with Albatros 7-8m swLILLE 9500' 4-15pm OK(Capt GAK Lawrence/2Lt McArthur) "guard machine to two bombing a'c"

1744   BE2c   12Sqn
B AA shot down 4-30pm sPHALEMPIN ftl(Capt FB Binney **WIA POW) seen bombing train from 500' then ldg on nose, repat 14.6.18

Capt Binney was the first loss in action for 12 Squadron RFC.

27th September

Fighting on the ground had slackened after the initial advances, the British having resolved to dig in and secure their positions. General Headquarters was not at all clear about the strength of the enemy opposed to them, and with conditions as they were the RFC could be of little use. Fog and rain continued to make most flying impossible.

2033   BE2c   16Sqn
+*Rec combat with Albatros ovCOURRIÈRES 6-30am chased EA down to 1800' then ground fire OK(2Lt J Gay/Lt D Leeson Can.) then attacked KB which was hauled down

28th September

**   3Sqn**
** hit by shrapnel in forward position on the ground whilst signalling with lamps to Contact Patrols(FSgt W Burns **DoW**) head

617   RE5   7Sqn
DistRec CHARLEROI low fuel ftl(Capt NC Spratt **WIA POW/2Lt HB Stubbs **POW**) both to Holland 4.18

**   Vickers FB5   11Sqn**
Rec shrapnel(/2Lt JS Cemlyn-Jones **WIA) to hospital

This was most likely the first casualty in action for 11 Squadron, surprising given it had engaged in so much action with the enemy over the previous two months.

2037   BE2c   16Sqn
+*Rec neWAVRIN combat with Albatros[+EA hit and dived but recovered, though smoking] 7-05am OK(2Lt HS Shield/Cpl Bennett) passed so close EA crew's faces could be seen

30th September

From this time onwards the battle of Loos fell into a series of defences against German counterattacks. Whenever the weather permitted, Allied bombing of the enemy rail network continued, as

did co-operation with artillery, reconnaissance, and contact patrolling. The German attacks took place over two weeks but were withstood, so that the fighting eventually died down. The French offensive in Champagne was to be a failure, and the wider objectives at Loos had also been denied to the British. The weather no doubt played a part in this and the High Command drew a few small crumbs of comfort from what had taken place. The persistence and breadth of effort made by the RFC had been encouraging and duly received much praise. On the other hand, as a fighting force, the air arm was beginning to suffer increasing casualties.

3Sqn
** hit by shrapnel in forward position on the ground whilst organising signals for Contact Patrols(Maj EW Furse **WIA**) skull, severe

6Sqn
? (Lt A Sommervail **WIA/) to hospital

1735   BE2c   7Sqn
+*B ROULERS-HOUTHULST WOOD combat with Fokker 8000' 3-45pm OK(2Lt NJ Bengough)

1649   Vickers FB5   11Sqn
+* combat with Albatros C-type[+lost wing nose-dived from 5000', a'c captured] nrGOMMECOURT 8000' 8-15am OK(Capt LWB Rees/FSgt JM Hargreaves) (Filed in 2Sqn Combat Reports)

Untraced date in France in late September 1915

1678?   BE2c   4Sqn
this a'c? **B left 8-30am MIA but OK(Capt.Hon LJE Fiennes) ps: no observer

October 1915

THE FOKKER SUPREMACY

The Allies were in deepening trouble in the air by October. The number of RFC squadrons in France had grown to twenty-five, and in six months the number of machines at the front almost doubled. However, it was only by virtue of this rapid expansion that the Allies preserved some ability to contest the air. The Fokker E-Type was still not plentiful, and although developments in the forms of Types EII and EIII were appearing, poor engine reliability combined with its scarcity to rob it of its full impact. Even with these shortcomings, however, it was already dismantling the Allies' air supremacy. The "flying gun", as it was pithily known, was easily the match for any Allied machine in general use. Its manoeuvrability and

fire power made it a most effective weapon, and its perceived supremacy provided a great psychological threat.

In particular, Immelmann and Boelcke were able to extract the greatest potential from the Eindekkers, and between them they established new tactical standards for air fighting. The Fokker could be flown into positions of great advantage in combat, stalking the enemy and then diving onto its prey. Superior height and speed gave the attacker the advantage, and coming from concealed positions such as from clouds or out of the sun, the attack was deadly. Where possible this concealment would be used to approach the enemy from a blind spot, to come as close as possible unseen before steadying the machine and then firing short, accurate bursts. Often the sound of machine-gun fire was the first sign of being attacked by a Fokker. Its machine-gun being belt fed from within the fuselage meant its fire power far exceeded the drum fed machine-guns of the Allies.

Where concealment was not an option, or once combat was engaged, the Fokker could also be flown with great agility, so that to manoeuvre in a combat into a position of apparent superiority with an Eindekker was no assurance of safety. A flying repertoire was being developed by the German pilots which challenged accepted tactics. The greatest manoeuvre to come from 1915 was one perfected by Max Immelmann: the "Immelmann Turn". This involved a half roll at the top of a half loop, and had many advantages and many opportunities for use in combat. It enabled a pilot when pursued to pull into a loop, and then when inverted to roll out again so that guns pointed once more at the attacker, and usually from a superior height. It could also be used to reassert height and position after an initial dive of engagement, or to gain relative height repeatedly through a fight.

Finally, Boelcke's way of deploying Fokkers increasingly gathered into self-protecting teams heralded the start of group tactics. Whilst one Fokker searched and led, it was protected from attack by two others. As the leader engaged the enemy, the others would remain standing off, warily on guard, until summoned if required. These tactics, and others like them for the protection of two-seaters, will be increasingly encountered in the entries drawn from RFC combat reports.

The machine and the new tactics were so shockingly effective that for a while the Allied pilots appeared almost mesmerised. This led to concern at RFC Headquarters that pilots were choosing to break off combat, doubtless something to which

Headquarters would be sensitive. Looking at hundreds of combat reports from the time, however, there seems to be little breaking off because the pilots were hesitating in any way. On the contrary, it was more often because of a failing engine or jammed gun, neither of which left much option but to retreat. The factor which was changing was the intensity of the fighting: increasingly, it left one in a precarious position if something went wrong. The Allied pilots soon knew they would also have to learn the new skills if they were to have a chance of survival. The only thing that would then be lacking was an effective British fighter.

2nd October

773   Avro 504A   1Sqn
+*Rec attacked by 2 Albatros & LVG wLILLE 7500′ 7-30am OK(Capt CC Miles/Capt L Prickett) all 3 attacked from behind & above

2673   BE2c   2Sqn
+*AP ARRAS-HENIN LIETARD combat with Albatros going towards DOUAI 8am OK(2Lt HW Medlicott/2Lt EM Gilbert)

5455   Vickers FB5   11Sqn
+*Rec HAM combat with LVG 7500′ 9-13am to 9-21am OK(2Lt GSM Insall/2Lt E Robinson)

5460   Vickers FB5   11Sqn
+*P nARRAS combat with Albatros 10000′ 9-45am OK(2Lt HT Kemp/Capt CW Lane)

3rd October

2677   BE2c   2Sqn
+*AP VERMELLES combat with 1 Fokker & 3 Aviatiks WINGLES 9000′ 5-15pm OK(Lt GH Turton/Lt HV Stammers) went off towards DOUAI

1658?   BE2c   4Sqn
this a'c? **SpyDrop to swSERAIN, 10m seCAMBRAI shot up so dropped at BANTOUZELLE ~5-30pm engine problems but returned dam ldg OK(2Lt JW Woodhouse/agent) left 4-30pm

This was another very early attempt at a spy drop. The agent, dressed in French uniform with civilian clothes underneath, took two baskets of pigeons, one on his knees and another tied onto the lower plane beside the fuselage. After having dropped the agent, Woodhouse encountered problems with his engine on take-off but, insisting the agent be on his way, started the engine himself and climbed back on board as the machine began to move. Engine failure caused him to land almost immediately again, but eventually he managed to take off and recover the lines, landing in the dark sixteen miles east of Amiens around 6-40pm.

1651   Vickers FB5   5Sqn
+*P sePASSCHENDAELE-BECELAERE 10-50am to 11-25am combat with LVG 4800′ OK(Lt FJ Powell/1AM J Shaw), then attacked by Albatros

8460   REP Parasol   1 Wing RNAS
**ZEEBRUGGE SHEDS British shells ftl ZUIDZANDE MIA(FSLt JED Errol Boyd INT) British ships fired on a'c, interned Holland

7th October

5052   Morane L   1Sqn
+*LRec COURTRAI-TOURNAI combat with Halberstadt? Scout 11000′ 10-30am OK(2Lt JG McEwan/Lt M Jacks)

1669   BE2c   2Sqn
+*AP combat with large 2 nacelled Albatros ovPONT À VENDIN 9500′ 11-30am headed for CARVIN then gun jam OK(Capt T Carthew DSO/Lt EM Gilbert) EA was trying to draw BE2c over AA

8th October

168   Sopwith Tabloid   1 Wing RNAS?
**DUSSELDORF Zeppelin Sheds ftl on return nrANTWERP OK(FLt RLG Marix) Zeppelin Z.IX destroyed in raid

10th October

1703   BE2c   2Sqn
+*AOb combat with Fokker 8000′ 3-15pm OK(Capt Babington/Lt Chadwick)

2673   BE2c   2Sqn
+*Rec combat with AlbC nrCARVIN 11000′ 2-50pm OK(Lt HW Medlicott/2Lt BC Rice) earlier met Fokker nrLA BASSÉE 2pm, driven off towards LILLE

1874   Morane L   3Sqn
+*Phot combat with EA ovHULLUCH 2-15pm shot up but returned a'dr ok OK(2Lt HR? Johnson/Cpl Roberts WIA)

1706   BE2c   5Sqn
+*Rec combat with Albatros ovHOUTHULST WOOD 9000′ 3-30pm OK(Capt Parker/Lt H French) combat lasted 20mins, EA left for MENINOFF

1728   BE2c   5Sqn
+* combat with Aviatik ovHOUTHULST 9000′ 4-45pm OK(Capt Read/Capt Freeman) also Albatros ovPOELCAPPELLE

1720   BE2c   10Sqn
+*Phot combat with Albatros 3m seLILLE 8000′ 4-30pm fuel tank & prop hit ftl dam OK(2Lt Lloyd-Williams/2Lt T Henderson)

1717   BE2c   16Sqn
+*Phot combat with Albatros nrLILLE 2-45pm OK(2Lt HS Ward/1AM BC Digby) later met 2Albatros

2033   BE2c   16Sqn
**Phot AA combat with 2EA shot down ovLILLE Sh36

1.6.a. at 2-25pm **MIA**(2Lt J Gay **DoW**/Lt D Leeson Can.
WIA POW) Imm4 [combat 4k nwLILLE 2pm Ltn M
Immelmann FAb62] PS: Immelmann's 4th victory was
this aircraft, 2033, not BE2c 2003 as some sources give

5030	MFSH	16Sqn

+*AOb combat with LVG ovLAVENTIE 6500' 4-45pm
OK(Lt GH Eastwood/2Lt Hardie) EA was attacking RE

RFC

** (Lt R Potter **POW**) to Holland 10.4.18

11th October

	BE2c	2Sqn

+*AOb ovCITE ST ELOI combat with Albatros
C-type[+ftl a'c captured, EA of FAb202] 7500'-8000'
8-40am OK(Lt WDS Sanday/2Lt Ellison) shared with
BE2c 1716 & 3Sqn Morane crew

1716	BE2c	2Sqn

+*AP combat with Albatros[+ftl a'c captured, EA of
FAb202] NOYELLES-LES-VERMELLES 7800'
8-40pm OK(Lt CE Clarke/Lt HV Stammers) shared

2019	BE2c	2Sqn

+*test combat with Albatros LA BASSÉE 10am OK(2Lt
HW Medlicott/Sgt Craven)

2019?	BE2c	2Sqn

+*AReg combat with Albatros C[+EA engine hit: smoke
ftl o't SAILLY SUR LYS] ovHAUBOURDIN ~3pm
OK(Lt HW Medlicott/Lt HB Russell) EA earlier
softened up by Capt Mitchell/Lt Shepherd 10Sqn, earlier
met 2 nacelled Albatros

4667	Bristol Scout C	2Sqn

+*P LENS-ARRAS combat with 4 Albatros[++?one
seen ldg at a'dr VIMY, other in field nrROUVROY,
FAb62?] 10500' OK(2Lt HM Medlicott) EA reported
down nrSAILLY

4667	Bristol Scout C	2Sqn

probably later?: +*P nrLENS combat with LVG HENIN
LIETARD-DOUAI[+shot down ooc into mist] 12000'
between 3pm & 4-15pm OK(2Lt HM Medlicott) took
45mins to get above EA

	Morane	3Sqn

+*AOb ovCUINCHY combat with Albatros[+ftl a'c
captured, EA of FAb202] NOYELLES-LES-
VERMELLES 7800' 8-40pm OK(Capt M Barratt/Lt CT
Cleaver) landed beside EA, shared victory with two 2Sqn
crews, including that of BE2c 1716

1651	Vickers FB5	5Sqn

+*P HOOGE combat with Biplane 5000' 10-01am then
AA hit, nacelle shot up ftl(Lt FJ Powell OK/1AM J Shaw
WIA)leg

5459	Vickers FB5	5Sqn

2 Lewis +*P combat with Fokker neVOORMEZELE
8500' 10-30am OK(Capt R Loraine/Cpl Fineran)

4071	BE2c	7Sqn

+*Rec wROULERS combat with 3 Albatros then Fokker
8500' 9-30am then AA OK(Capt Mansfield/Capt Holt)

2047	BE2c	8Sqn

ArmyRec MIA(2Lt AJ Burnie **POW**/2Lt BO Wilkin
POW) both to Holland 19.4.18 [?combat VILLERET
Ltn M Zander KEK.*Nord*]

1737	BE2c	10Sqn

+*AReg LA BASSÉE combat with Albatros 8000'
4-15pm shot up dam OK(Capt Mitchell/Lt Shepherd)

12th October

2235	RE7	12Sqn

+*EscSpM combat with Albatros & LVG 3m sLILLE
8500'-7500' 4pm OK(Capt GAK Lawrence/Lt C
Gordon-Burge) to protect Capt Christie to TOURNAI-
MOUSCRON-MENIN-GHELUVELT

13th October

1733	BE2c	10Sqn

+*Rec combat with Albatros DOUAI 4pm OK(Capt RG
Gould/Lt Vaucour)

4675	Bristol Scout C	10Sqn

+*P combat with Albatros C[+? seen ss & turn over into
clouds] eLENS 9000' 3pm then attacked by large LVG
~3000' OK(Capt C Gordon-Bell) 2nd combat indecisive,
EA was seen ldg eLILLE

14th October

2036	BE2c	10Sqn

+*LRec combat with Aviatik ovVALENCIENNES
8000' 4pm but gun jam OK(Capt Mitchell/Capt Bruce)

18th October

1714	BE2c	6Sqn

+*Phot combat with EA VERLORENHOEK 7000' 3pm
shot up in mist OK(2Lt HBR Grey-Edwards)

3177	Nieuport 10	RNAS

**B airship sheds BERCHEM STE AGATHE engine
failed on return ftl nrBRAY DUNES cr(FSLt JT Bone
Killed)

19th October

13 Squadron RFC arrived in France on the 19th of
October equipped with the BE2c. Initially its work
consisted of artillery co-operation, reconnaissance,
and photography. It would come to greater promi-
ence the following summer when it pioneered
formation bombing in the Somme campaign.

4672	Bristol Scout C	1Sqn

+*HAP HOLLEBEKE CHATEAU-WERVICQ
combat with Aviatik[+?seen going down ooc?:"heavy"]
10200' 11-43am OK(Capt EO Grenfell) EA was
watching Morane when Grenfell attacked, left EA at
3000' ovWERVICQ-MENIN because he felt wire snap
and dare not chase on down

1611	Bristol Scout C	6Sqn

+*P combat with EA ovMERKEM 10800' 11am OK(Lt
Kinnear)

5642   FE2a   6Sqn
+*PhotRec combat with Albatros LANGEMARCK
10500' 12pm then later EA & AA dam OK(2Lt Impey/
2Lt MAJ? Orde)

4072   BE2c   7Sqn
+*Rec combat with two-engined EA nrZARREN 9000'
11-15am OK(2Lt DAC Symington/2Lt ST Welch)

4450   BE2c   7Sqn
+*Rec combat with Albatros? ovLILLE 9000' 1-45pm
OK(2Lt HH Kitchener/Lt CC Haynes)

20th October

The first FE2b arrived in France for service
appraisal on the 20th of October. This was 5201,
and by the 30th of that month it was allotted to 16
Squadron.

21st October

5034   Morane L   3Sqn
**Grenade Drop to LA BASSÉE, combat with Fokker,
shot up but escaped when another BE2 came up (Sgt F
Courtney DoW/Sgt G Thornton DoW) to hospital,
"Fokker with deflector blades", Courtney WIA leg,
Thornton WIA hand

2866   Vickers FB5   11Sqn
+*Rec combat with Fokker & LVG ST QUENTIN-
PERONNE 7000' 3-30pm to 4-15pm OK(Capt PHL
Playfair/2Lt AL Findlay)

1705   BE2c   16Sqn
** AA fuel tank shot up ftl CROIX DU BAC dam(Lt JP
Greenwood? OK/Cpl T Bennett? WIA?) this crew?, after
combat with Albatros nrDOUAI

22nd October

5095   Morane N   3Sqn
**travel from Paris to HQ, met clouds ftl ESEMAEL
nrTIRLEMONT(2Lt AC Collier POW) had set out
16.10.15, with Lt Henderson, to Holland 19.4.18

4075   BE2c   8Sqn
+*EscLRec LE CATEAU combat with 2 Fokkers[+shot
down in vertical nose-dive towards CAMBRAI, cr trees
in "cloud of dust"] 1-30pm OK(2Lt DA Glen/Cpl E
Jones) other Fokker made off

1649   Vickers FB5   11Sqn
+*P NURLU combat with Albatros[+?saw bullets enter
EA nacelle & piece fly off or fall out] 7000'-2700' 11-30am
OK(Capt LWB Rees/Lt WA Skeate)

23rd October

1669   BE2c   2Sqn
+*AReg combat with Albatros ovLA BASSÉE 8500'
2-30pm OK(Capt T Carthew DSO/2Lt LC? Chapman)

1649   Vickers FB5   11Sqn
+*P left 10am combat with Ago PERONNE 7500'
10-30am OK(Capt LWB Rees/2Lt RJ Slade)

5457   Vickers FB5   11Sqn
+*P combat with drove off Aviatik? 8000'-10000'
12-40pm OK(2Lt AL? Neale/Lt WA Skeate)

2017   BE2c   13Sqn
**EscRec combat with EA sST QUENTIN MIA(Capt
CH Marks KIA/2Lt WG Lawrence KIA) left 1-32pm
[combat ST QUENTIN Hpt H-J Buddecke FAb23]

These airmen were the first losses in combat for 13
Squadron RFC. Lawrence was the brother of TE
Lawrence.

26th October

1729   BE2c   2Sqn
+*AReg VERMELLES-LOOS combat with Albatros
9000' 11am OK(Lt AL Russell/2Lt AW Brown) EA
wavered but recovered

1732   BE2c   2Sqn
+*AOb combat with Albatros ovVERMELLES 9500'-
10000' 9-45am to 10-10am low fuel OK(Capt GT Porter/
Cpl Welch)

5077   Morane N   3Sqn
+*EscPhot combat with Aviatik ovLILLE 10-15 to
10-35am OK(2Lt RJ Lillywhite OK/Lt WS Fielding-
Johnston)

1736   BE2c   5Sqn
+*RecCB ZONNEBEKE-LANGEMARCK combat
with Fokker 9000'-5000' 10-16am OK(Lt Swart/Capt
Simpson) then attacked by Aviatik and Albatros

5459   Vickers FB5   5Sqn
+*P combat with 2 Albatros[+first was hit by AA then
chased down cr WoL Sh28 U.13.a.5.6., captured crew
were from FAb33] ovHOUTHEM 9000' 9-30am chased
EA down to 700' then engine failed ftl OK(Capt R
Loraine/Lt EFP Lubbock) see RFC Communiqué No17
for POW report

5643   FE2a   6Sqn
+*Rec BOESINGHE combat with EA 8000' 11-25am
OK(Lt Kinnear/2Lt JEP Howey)

          BE2c   10Sqn
**Phot nrLILLE combat with Fokker shot down, then
ldg by observer(2Lt Lloyd-Williams WIA/2Lt W Hallam
WIA) to hospital, ldg WoL French Sector Sh36 M.25,
pilot hit in arm & shoulder then lost consciousness and
fell into spinning nose-dive, pilot thrown out as a'c o't

5075   Vickers FB5   11Sqn
+*P LE SARS-NURLU combat with EA OK(Lt LA
Pattinson/2Lt AL Findlay)

5462   Vickers FB5   11Sqn
**P combat with EA CAMBRAI ftl(Capt CC Darley
WIA POW/2Lt RJ Slade POW) pilot to Holland 19.4.18,
Darley to Switzerland 30.5.16 & to UK 14.6.17 Imm5
[combat ECOUST ST MIEN 9-05am Ltn M
Immelmann FAb62]

1760   BE2c   16Sqn

+*Phot sLILLE combat with 3EA between 10-15am & 11am OK(2Lt G Merton/2AM Milne)

2056   BE2c   16Sqn
+*P combat with LVG ovESTAIRES on return 10000'
10-40am OK(2Lt BC McEwen/2Lt Catherall) chased EA
EoL

27th October

2019   BE2c   2Sqn
+*AP combat with Albatros LA BASSÉE-
VERMELLES 4-55pm shot up dam OK(Lt AL Russell/
2Lt AW Brown)

31st October

1649   Vickers FB5   11Sqn
+*P left 10am combat with LVG?[+?] BAPAUME
7000'-800' 9am then found themselves over AA & rifle
fire, shot up dam OK(Capt LWB Rees/FSgt Raymond)
EA chased down very low and seen with maps falling out
or fabric coming off nrPYS-IRNES

Untraced casualty in France in October 1915

? (2AM HG Shields **KIA) is this 2Lt HS Shield of
16Sqn?

November 1915

2nd November

1857   MFSH   12Sqn
travel to 3AP GHQ, left LE CROTOY **MIA(2Lt JB
Robinson **POW**)

4th November

1651   Vickers FB5   5Sqn
+*Phot combat with 3 successive EAs 1m seYPRES
7000' 12-40pm OK(Lt FJ Powell/Lt EFP Lubbock)

2043   BE2c   5Sqn
+*Rec combat with Aviatik then Fokker ovSh20 ~U.18.
down to 7000' 12-05pm, then AA shot up dam OK(Lt
McConnochie/Lt C Porri)

1714   BE2c   6Sqn
+*Rec II Army front combat with 2 Albatros
WESTROOSEBEKE 9000'-8000' 12-30pm to 12-50pm
OK(Lt Danby/2Lt JEP Howey)

2031   BE2c   6Sqn
+*AOb combat with large pusher EA & others 9500'
12-30pm to 12-45pm shot up badly, fuel tank hit rudder
jammed(2Lt H Bright OK/Capt CE Ryan **WIA**) saved
by crew of 5644

5644   FE2a   6Sqn
+*Phot combat with Fokker over 'HILL 60' 9500'
12-45pm[+saw flip and then down ooc sZILLEBEKE]
OK(2Lt CH Kelway-Bamber/Lt HJ Payn) saved crew of
BE2c 2031 who were being attacked

5460   Vickers FB5   11Sqn
**P combat with Albatros 2m nNESTLE 10000'-7000'
4-15pm gun jam OK(2Lt HT Kemp/Cpl H Monks) EA
landed 5m nNESTLE

5th November

5644   FE2a   6Sqn
**Rec MERKEM-YPRES combat with Aviatik 10800'
4-30pm OK(Capt Kinnear/2Lt JEP Howey)

7th November

1715   BE2c   10Sqn
**Rec combat with EA nrARRAS chased down in spiral
cr nrQUIERY ~2-45pm(Lt OV Le Bas **KIA**/Capt TD
Adams **KIA**) See report of Capt C Gordon-Bell in Bristol
Scout 4675 in RFC Communiqué No.19, Imm6 [combat
wLILLE 2-45pm Ltn M Immelmann FAb62]

4675   Bristol Scout C 10Sqn
+*EscLRec DOUAI combat with Fokker & Aviatik[+
?Fokker dived as if hit] 9000'-4000' 2-45pm then engine
problems ftl o't field nrVERQUIGNY? OK(Capt C
Gordon-Bell) escorting BE2c 1715, which he saw hit &
then circled by Fokker until it crashed nrQUIERY, could
do nothing

By this time, German aggressiveness had risen to
such a degree that the escorting of RFC patrols had
become all but essential. These lists show the
degree to which air fighting was increasingly widespread and intense. Escorting of reconnaissance
machines would be formalised by the Allies early
in the new year as the Fokker menace caused ever
greater problems for them.

5074   Vickers FB5   11Sqn
**OP combat with AviatikC[+driven down] 4m
seARRAS then ground mg shot up ftl OK(Lt GSM Insall
VC/AM TH Donald DCM) combat in pm, Aviatik had
attempted to draw Vickers onto "rocket battery"

Lt Insall was awarded the Victoria Cross for this
action. He and his observer had forced an Aviatik
to land after hitting its engine with machine-gun
fire. Once on the ground, the German crew was
forced to abandon it after more fire from Donald's
gun and attempts by Insall to destroy it with an
incendiary bomb. Continuing westwards they
found enemy trenches to shoot up but were in turn
subjected to intense rifle and machine-gun fire.
Their own machine was so badly shot up that they
made a forced landing near a wood only five
hundred yards from the front line. German artillery
soon located it and began shelling in an attempt to
destroy it. This failed, however, and the crew
remained on hand, repairing their Vickers throughout the night and successfully flying it back to their
airfield at Bertangles in the morning.

10th November

1Sqn
? (2Lt CC Miles **WIA/2Lt LJ Baily **WIA**) inj?

2673   BE2c   2Sqn
Rec shot down nwBAPAUME **MIA(2Lt HW Medlicott **POW**/Lt AW Brown **WIA POW**) pilot shot in escaping 6.18, Brown to Switzerland 19.1.17

5077   Morane N   3Sqn
+*Rec combat with EA ov LILLE 8000' 9-20am OK(2Lt AV Hobbs/2Lt CEG Tudor-Jones)

4072   BE2c   7Sqn
+*B GITS A'dr combat with Albatros 8000' 9-35am OK(2Lt DAC Symington)

11th November

5056   Morane L   1Sqn
+*Phot ARMENTIÈRES 3 combats 7500'-11200' 9-20am to 10-10am OK(Lt EO Grenfell) Alb, then large EA, then Albatros or Aviatik

1669   BE2c   2Sqn
+*EscRec combat with Fokker & 2 Albatros eDOUAI 9000' 11-30am OK(2Lt W Allcock/1AM Bowes)

1703   BE2c   2Sqn
+*Phot VENDIN LE VIEIL fired at 3 Albatros 7000' 9-30am OK(Capt Babington/Lt Chadwick)

1729   BE2c   2Sqn
+*EscRec VALENCIENNES combat with LVG nrLOOS-VERMELLES 6000' 9-30am OK(2Lt KDP Murray/2Lt EM Gilbert)

1730   BE2c   2Sqn
+*AReg combat with LVG MAZINGARBE ~9-30am OK(2Lt WDS Sanday/Sgt Hodgson) a'c was not armed with a machine-gun as "all in use".

2019   BE2c   2Sqn
+*Rec combat with EA VALENCIENNES 8500' 9-30am OK(Lt AL Russell/2Lt BC Rice)

5644   FE2a   6Sqn
Rec combat with 2HA ROLLEGHEMCAPELLE shot down(2Lt CH Kelway-Bamber **KIA/2Lt JEP Howey **WIA POW**) to Switzerland 13.2.17

1711   BE2c   8Sqn
B combat with EA, shot down EoL **MIA(2Lt VM Grantham **POW**) to Holland 19.4.18

1725   BE2c   8Sqn
B shot down EoL **MIA(Lt WA Harvey **WIA POW**) interned Switzerland, died Switzerland 7.11.18 [combat Hpt H-J Buddecke FAb23]

These two 8 Squadron machines were lost during a bombing raid on the German aerodrome at Bellenglise. A combined attack was planned with bombing aircraft from Nos. 4, 8, and 13 Squadrons and with other units providing protection. The bombers were to rendezvous over the target and bomb simultaneously. Very adverse weather, including high winds and cloud, led to several of the BE2cs and their escorts becoming lost, and inevitably some fell prey to attack in the confusion.

4670   Bristol Scout C   16Sqn
** left 9-45am to attack LVG, engaged ovBOIS DE BIEZ but engine failed ftl OK(2Lt G Merton)

14th November

2680   BE2c   7Sqn
LRec combat with AgoC[+prop stopped & glided down] ovROULERS 9200' 1-45pm shot up ftl ABEELE ok(Lt GSM Ashby **WIA/Lt RA Preston OK)

4080   BE2c   13Sqn
+*Rec combat with Fokker HERBECOURT(sic) 7000' 3-40pm but gun jam shot up dam ftl nrALBERT OK(Lt AH Morrison/2Lt EH Grant) excess oil caused jam

1760   BE2c   16Sqn
+*Phot shot at Albatros ovLE MAISNIL 11am OK(2Lt G Merton/2AM Milne)
? (2Lt R Corbett **WIA) inj?

15th November

Dull and foggy weather significantly restricted flying for the remainder of November.

4071   BE2c   7Sqn
+*Rec ZARREN-ROULERS combat with EA 9000' 3-20pm OK(Capt Mansfield/Lt Moffatt) EA down in steep, spiral but ok?

4675   Bristol Scout C   10Sqn
+*EscPhot LILLE combat with large Albatros[+? diving steeply] 2-30pm then AA began OK(Capt C Gordon-Bell) also earlier combat with EA nrLENS 13000' 10-30am NB Cas Report dated 15.11, given wrongly as 16.11 in Communiqui No. 20?

4086   BE2c   16Sqn
+*P LA BASSÉE-LILLE combat with Ago 6000'-4500' 12-30pm then AA OK(Lt DW Grinnell-Milne/Lt SE Buckley)
? (Lt OD Filley **WIA) inj?

17th November

6Sqn
? (Capt MK Cooper-King **WIA) inj?

18th November

RFC?
? (Lt JP Inglefield **WIA) inj?

1732   BE2c   2Sqn
+*EscLRec combat with Fokker 8500' 8am shot up dam OK(Capt GT Porter/Lt Davey)

19th November

18 Squadron arrived in France on the 19th of

November armed primarily with the Vickers FB5 Fighter, although it also had a few Bristol Scouts on strength. It carried out fighter-reconnaissance work with these obsolete FB5s until February, long after it should have been replaced with something less dangerous. 11 Squadron was to be saddled with the type until July, such equipment showing how few options were available to the RFC at this time.

RFC

** (Lt TC Shillington **POW**) to Switzerland 12.8.16, to UK 11.9.17

20th November

1713   BE2c   6Sqn
+*AOb combat with EA POLYGON WOOD 700' 12-45pm OK(2Lt EHP Cave/2Lt MW Thomas) then 2nd combat with Albatros ovZANDVOORDE, both inconclusive, had seen off earlier Aviatik ovBIXSCHOOTE 10am (see BE2c 2674)

2674   BE2c   6Sqn
+*Phot HOOGE shared combat with the second EA mentioned above under BE2c 1713, 6000' 12-45pm OK(2Lt NA Bolton/2Lt G Price) Combat Report gives BE2c 2764, but error?

4072   BE2c   7Sqn
+*Rec ZARREN combat with Fokker 9000' 10-25am OK(2Lt DAC Symington/Lt Boyton)

4086   BE2c   16Sqn
**EscLRec combat with EA OK(Lt DW Grinnell-Milne/ Capt CC Strong) pilot involved in several other combats in November

4670   Bristol Scout C   16Sqn
** combat with Albatros seARMENTIÈRES 11-20am OK(2Lt G Merton)

5071   MFSH   16Sqn
** dam by AA: salved for spares

25th November

2001   BE2c   4Sqn
+*ACoop ALBERT-BRAY combat with 3EAs between 2-45pm & 3-30pm OK(2Lt AT White/2Lt WF Balmain)

4100   BE2c   7Sqn
+*B GITS A'dr combat with Fokkers & Ago on return 9000'-10000' 2-30pm OK(Sgt GJ Lusted)

4086   BE2c   16Sqn
**EscLRec combat with Albatros 11am(Lt DW Grinnell-Milne/Capt CC Strong)

26th November

2061   BE2c   4Sqn
+*AOb combat with EA sFRICOURT 10-45am OK(2Lt Robinson/2Lt Bottrell)

2875   Vickers FB5   11Sqn
+*Phot BRAY SUR SOMME-MORLANCOURT combat with Albatros 7500' 11am engine failed OK(2Lt HA Cooper/2Lt AJ Insall) EA appeared to shoot through trap in floor

4070   BE2c   13Sqn
+*EscRec combat with Aviatik[+?steep dive into cloud at 2000' EoL ovFRICOURT, steam from engine] on return 11000'-4000' ~12pm OK(2Lt HMD O'Malley/ FSgt WH Harrison) pilot opened fire from 25yds

27th November

5051   Morane L   1Sqn
**AP WARNETON combats with EAs: driven off OK(Capt JD Saunders)

5060   Morane L   1Sqn
**LRec LILLE combat with 2 Albatros HAUBOURDIN 9000' 3-20pm OK(2Lt CC Godwin/Lt M Jacks)

1717   BE2c   16Sqn
+*Esc combat with Albatros ovLA BASSÉE 12-30pm OK(2Lt HS Ward/Lt Veitch)

28th November

5067   Morane N   3Sqn
**HAP left 9-30am NOEUX-LES-MINES combat with Albatros 8000'[+?driven down to 1500' ovVENDIN-LE-VIEIL] then other combats OK(Lt GLP Henderson)

1701   BE2c   4Sqn
+*Phot CLERY combat with Fokker CLERY-CURBE 12-30pm OK(Capt JC Halahan/Capt McLeod)

5459   Vickers FB5   5Sqn
+*P nYPRES combat with Aviatik ovHONDSCHOOTE 10000' after stalking to eHOUTHULST WOOD 8-15am to 8-50am OK(Lt FJ Powell/Lt EFP Lubbock) waited to cut off EA, but then gun jam

4103   BE2c   8Sqn
+*B combat with Fokker sPERONNE 9-15am OK(Lt WS Douglas)

1733   BE2c   10Sqn
+*AReg combat with Albatros from LA BASSÉE to AIRE 1-55pm to 2-10pm OK(Capt RG Gould/Lt Vaucour)

2036   BE2c   10Sqn
+*Rec combat with Aviatik DON-LILLE on return 7000' 12-30pm OK(Capt Mitchell/Capt Bruce)

4675   Bristol Scout C   10Sqn
+*SpP combat with two-engined EA ovBOIS DE BIEZ 12000' 10-15am but gun jam OK(Capt C Gordon-Bell)

4070   BE2c   13Sqn
+*EscRec combat with Fokker ovBAPAUME 8000' 12-30pm to 1pm engine failed, required return then badly shot up OK(2Lt HMD O'Malley/FSgt WH Harrison) escorting Lt Richarson & Lt Kyffin, continual gun jams

4086   BE2c   16Sqn
+*P combat with Albatros C-type[+destroyed, seen o't nrSEQUEDIN] NEUVE CHAPELLE-LILLE 9000′ 10-15am then combat with 4EA then AA OK(Lt DW Grinnell-Milne/Capt C Strong) Albatros joined by 2 Fokkers, but managed close range hit, then Fokkers joined by Aviatik & Albatros: 15min combat: found it hard to change gun from left to right side of cockpit

5201   FE2b   16Sqn
+* drove off Aviatik ovARMENTIÈRES 8000′ 11-30am OK(2Lt AR Tillie/2Lt FR Hardioe)

5201   FE2b   16Sqn
+* drove off Albatros ovBETHUNE 7500′ 3pm OK(Lt GH Eastwood/Lt LN Gould)

2343   Vickers FB5   18Sqn
+*P combat with LVG[+?driven down]4m eLA BASSÉE 8000′-4000′ 9-50am OK(Capt JA Cunningham/1AM Smith) "EA never saw me" but Smith was on his first trip so made inexperienced firing

5621   Vickers FB5   18Sqn
2 Lewis guns +*P chased away DFW then LVG ovLA BASSÉE prop shot up by DFW 8000′ 9-30am dam OK(Lt G Strover?/Lt T McKenna)

These were the first combat victory claims for 18 Squadron.

3620   Henri Farman   1 Wing RNAS
St Pol **Bombed U-boat[+broke apart, sunk?] 6m wMIDDELKERKE OK(FSLt TE Viney/Lt Comte de Sincay)

30th November

5072   Morane LA   3Sqn
**AReg LA BASSÉE-BOIS DE BIEZ combat with Albatros C-type 8000′ 11-45am OK(Capt WCK Birch/ Lt HO Long)

5642   FE2a   6Sqn
+*Rec VI Corps front combat with Aviatik then Fokker ovZONNEBEKE-MOORSLEDE 9000′ ~12-30pm shot up ftl POPERINGHE OK(Lt EHP Cave/Lt EW Stubbs) Fokker "fired apparently through prop" then headed towards ROULERS

1733   BE2c   10Sqn
+*AReg combat with large EA BOIS DE BIEZ 8000′ 11-30am OK(Capt RG Gould/Lt Vaucour)

4675   Bristol Scout C   10Sqn
+*P combat with large 2Str LVG[+suddenly turned tail towards DOUAI & fell from 4000′ & ss into field HENIN LIETARD-BEAUMONT] nrLENS 11500′ 10-55am OK(Capt C Gordon-Bell)

1717   BE2c   16Sqn
Phot combat with EA shot down **MIA(2Lt HS Ward **WIA POW**/Lt SE Buckley **POW**) combat nr German front line trenches, Ward escaped 4.16, Buckley escaped to UK 16.6.17

Flying was also affected as poor weather closed in from November.

THE ESCALATION OF AIR CASUALTIES

Looking at the statistics of casualties in Appendix I for the last six months of 1915 — namely since the "Fokker Scourge" had commenced — one can see that RFC losses certainly rose to a new level in this period. However, whilst the numbers were higher, it was hardly an escalating crisis. Operations came to be increasingly restricted by the Fokker, but until the early months of 1916 the actual losses remained relatively light. This once again bears out how psychological the impact of the machine-gun armed Eindekker was. The numbers of Allied machines in France increased greatly in these months, so that hours of war flying were almost doubled through the autumn (to around 4700 hours in September). In contrast, the number of Fokker E-Types in France, which were causing these problems, climbed to barely forty by the end of the year. 45% of the British aircraft involved in losses in these six months had sustained their casualties in air combat, compared with 7% in the first half of the year. What is noteworthy is that German AA also accounted for 20% of the total in the same period. The damage from the Fokker, ably assisted by AA, was to continue into 1916, peaking in January and February.

The way in which the various developments of the Fokker reached the fighting are also worth noting. The first Eindekkers, the EIs, were essentially makeshift aircraft, based on a test-bed for a new combination of scout and armament system. When they proved successful, further versions of this relatively crude machine were rushed to the front. Its reliability was very poor, even dangerous, and the compromises which had been made in order to produce it meant that a proper purpose-designed fighter version had to come forward. This was the EII, the first true fighter aircraft. Not only the flight characteristics were refined, but the armament as well. Around sixty-five EIs and EIIs were eventually built, the first EIIs arriving in France in July. However, by October there were still only eight operational; problems continued to plague the early Eindekkers' use, but this is not to say its impact was anything less than immense. Much of this was due to the next version, the Fokker EIII, which appeared in August and became the preferred machine for all the great Fokker pilots. Most of these still had single gun armament. Around two hundred and fifty were to

be produced. It probably had the best blend of engine and armament, resulting in the best fighting performance, for whilst the EIV which followed had the bigger Oberursel 160hp engine, which enabled multiple machine-gun armament, the manoeuvrability and performance of this latter type were to be somewhat handicapped by the extra weight involved. Only a few EIVs seem to have appeared due to shortages of engines, and they were restricted to the best pilots, Boelcke receiving his in mid-December, for example. These then were the Fokkers causing such problems to the RFC.

December 1915

1st December

4086   BE2c   16Sqn
LRec engine ftl nST QUENTIN EoL burnt a'c **MIA(Lt DW Grinnell-Milne **POW**/Capt CC Strong **POW**) pilot escaped to UK 4.18, observer to Holland 19.4.18

A very strong westerly wind contributed to the loss of this crew. Engine trouble developed over Valenciennes and they could only press to within eight miles of the lines before being forced to land in enemy territory.

2nd December

1669   BE2c   2Sqn
+*AReg combat with fast Albatros ovLA BASSÉE 7000' 12-30pm OK(Capt T Carthew DSO/Lt Milne) also later combat with Albatros neDON 3pm which was being attacked by Morane

2081   BE2c   2Sqn
+*B combat with Albatros 2Str eDON 6000' 3pm OK(2Lt W Allcock)

4673   Bristol Scout C   2Sqn
+*EscB DON combat with LVG? 3pm OK(Capt GT Porter) believed EA hit, but inconclusive

5067   Morane N   3Sqn
EscB DON combat with "Morane" type 8500' shot up(Lt GLP Henderson **WIA)above eye, had to withdraw as temporarily blinded by blood, Fokker?

1733   BE2c   10Sqn
+* combat with Albatros LA BASSÉE 8000' 1pm OK(Capt RG Gould/Lt Vaucour)

2683   BE2d   10Sqn
+*EscB DON combat with Albatros 8000' 2-45pm OK(2Lt PEL Gethin/Lt Shepherd)

5th December

5643   FE2a   6Sqn
+*P POLYGON WOOD combat with EA 8500' 11-45am then it made off toward GITS OK(Lt EHP Cave/Lt O Nixon)

2049   BE2c   13Sqn
EscPhot BELLENGLISE combat with EA nrBAPAUME **MIA(2Lt ARH Browne Aust. **DoW**/1AM WH Cox **POW**) shot from behind?, fell with 4092 [BE claim combat ACHIET LE GRAND 2pm Ltn G Leffers KEK.*Bertincourt*]

4092   BE2c   13Sqn
EscPhot BELLENGLISE combat with EA **MIA(Lt GA Porter **KIA**/1AM H Kirkbride **KIA**) shot from behind?, fell with BE2c 2049, Porter Died 6.12.16 [?combat wROYE Oblt E Althaus KEK.*Vaux*]

7th December

5101   Morane LA   1Sqn
**Rec combat with Albatros, Aviatik, Albatros 5m wTOURNAI 9-50am OK(Capt EO Grenfell)

                            3Sqn
? (Lt CG Heaston **WIA?)shock, non combat?

                            3Sqn
? (Lt Marburg **WIA?)head, inj

                            6Sqn
? (Lt EG Bowen **WIA?)nose, inj?

2683   BE2d   10Sqn
+*Rec nrPONT À VENDIN-LILLE combat with EA 8500' 10-45am to 11am OK(2Lt PEL Gethin/Lt Shepherd) later met Fokker

8th December

2682   BE2c   10Sqn
P AA dam(2Lt L Moss **WIA/2Lt T Henderson OK)

4079   BE2c   13Sqn
**SpM shot up PERONNE ftl trenches SUZANNE cr dam OK(2Lt CEH Medhurst) left 8am HERVILLY

10th December

? (Cpl O'Giollagain **WIA) to hospital, ~10.12.15 inj?

13th December

1733   BE2c   10Sqn
+* combat with Albatros LA BASSÉE 8000' 11-30am OK(Capt RG Gould/Lt Vaucour)

4675   Bristol Scout C   10Sqn
+*P combat with Albatros 11000' 11-40am gun jam OK(Capt Mitchell)

2876   Vickers FB5   11Sqn
**P BIENVILLERS chased off LVG 7500' 9-20am OK(2Lt HVC deCrespigny/2Lt AJ Insall)

5471   Vickers FB5   11Sqn

+* CUGNY-FRIÈRES combat with Ago[+?down erratically ooc until more level at ~2000'] seHAM 9-40am OK(Lt GH Norman/Cpl TH Donald) Fokker came up so fate of combat was unseen

14th December

2035   BE2c   4Sqn
**SpM chased by Fokker shot up but returned ldg a'dr ok OK(2Lt AT Whitelock) left 11-30am

4671   Bristol Scout C   5Sqn
+*P HOUTHULST-ROULERS-YPRES combat with Aviatik attacking FB5 5466 ~11am fuel tank shot up dam OK(Capt Read) chased it down ovWESTROOSEBEKE, but suffered gun jam, saw off 2nd Aviatik on escape

4671   Bristol Scout C   5Sqn
and later: +*P combat with 2EA WESTROOSEBEKE-STADEN 10,500' ~3-30pm fuel tank shot up OK(Capt Read), pilot noted that ". . . the [enemies'] bullets' greatly assisted one's aim . . ."

5466   Vickers FB5   5Sqn
+*Phot VI Corps front combat with Fokker ovST JULIEN [+?saw bullets hit, EA dived] 8000' 1-15pm OK(Lt AWH James/Lt C Porri) earlier combats: Aviatik 6500' 10-35am eYSER Canal(Capt Read in 4671 saw EA off) & Fokker ovLANGEMARCK 5000' 10-45am

4680   Bristol Scout C   6Sqn
+*P POELCAPPELLE combat with Fokker 5000' then Aviatik 4000' 10am to 10-30am shot up: bullet through seat back dam OK(Capt Kinnear)

2060   BE2c   7Sqn
Rec combat with Fokker shot up & AA ftl cr ldg YPRES wr(Capt OM Guest **WIA/Lt AD Bell-Irving **WIA**) to hospital, Irving also injured in cr ldg

It was a relatively rare event to be attacked and shot down by a Fokker west of the lines.

4100   BE2c   7Sqn
+*Rec LICHTERVELDE combat with 2 Fokkers[+? one did bump in air when hit then shaky turn and dive] 9500' 9am OK(2Lt Fernihough/Lt Moffatt)

4075   BE2c   8Sqn
+*B HERVILLY combat with EA shot up prop hit dam 12-45pm OK(Lt WT? Douglas)

2671   BE2c   10Sqn
+*Rec combat with Albatros ovDON ~12pm[+?EA seen fly into bullet trail & nose-dive over tail: last seen diving steeply ovPONT À VENDIN] OK(Lt HM Sison/ 2Lt AR Goodson) then attacked by two-engined EA ovLILLE

5074   Vickers FB5   11Sqn
ArmyP combat with Fokker, AA? engine dam? seen going down **MIA(2Lt GSM Insall VC **WIA POW**/Cpl TH Donald DCM **WIA POW**) Insall escaped to UK 9.17

5457   Vickers FB5   11Sqn
+*Esc nPERONNE combat with Albatros 8000' 12-55pm OK(2Lt AL? Neale/2Lt JB Quested)

1707   BE2c   16Sqn
+*EscLRec combat with 3 Albatros & 4 Fokkers nrDOUAI 10am OK(Capt Boddam-Whitham/2Lt Catherall) escorting FE2b 5202, one Fokker appeared hit but recovered

5202   FE2b   16Sqn
+*LRec combat with 3 Albatros & 4 Fokkers nrDOUAI OK(Capt GH Eastwood/Lt Veitch) helped by crew of BE2c 1707

3971   Nieuport 10   1 Wing RNAS
+* combat with enemy seaplane[+shot down in flames neLA PANNE] but engine problems ftl sea sank OK(FSLt CW Graham/FSLt AS Ince) crew rescued

15th December

5087   Morane LA   3Sqn
Rec combat with EA ovVALENCIENNES shot down cr nrRAISMES **MIA(2Lt AV Hobbs **KIA**/2Lt CEG Tudor-Jones **KIA**) newspaper report: one crew fell from the a'c, Imm7 [combat RAISMES Ltn M Immelmann FAb62]

4091   BE2c   13Sqn
+*AOb combat with EA[+?glided down with no engine, met AA] ovMAILLY 6000' 10-15am OK(Lt Morrison/ 2Lt Johnson) fired from 80 yards, saw EA crossing lines low 10-30am

19th December

Very heavy air fighting took place on this day, coinciding with a German gas attack on a part of the Second Army front. Fairly relentless enemy attacks were made, especially on RFC reconnaissance machines north of the River Lys. Official records showed forty-six fights taking place. As the year drew to a close, there had been no let up for either side in the air war. Fighting was in many ways the most intense it had ever been, simply because the numbers of aircraft had grown to such an extent on one side, matched by technological superiority on the other. There could be no winners, only an increasing amount of fighting.

The year had begun with opposing aircraft offering very little harm to one another. The air arms of both sides had been able to go about their constantly evolving work, developing their roles and their reputations so that their contribution to the war had reached completely new levels. Operations in the air had begun to revolutionise many aspects of warfare on the ground. But to sustain this revolution, another one had occurred above the fighting — the sky was now a battlefield, and an increasingly dangerous one.

5069?   Morane L   1Sqn
this a'c? **HAP left 9-15am combat with EA ovQUESNOY 11000'[+driven down, smoking] (Capt MMcB Bell-Irving **WIA**) a'c still diving but recovering?

7000′, pilot hit by British AA fragment after later combats

4673 Bristol Scout C 2Sqn
+*EscRec DON-WINGLES-LENS combat with Fokker 9000′ 8-45am OK(Capt GT Porter)

5077 Morane N 3Sqn
+*AOb HAINES-LA BASSÉE combat with Aviatik[+ dived steeply ftl cr o't field eSALOME]ovBOIS DE BIEZ 10-35am to 11-10am OK(2Lt RJ Lillywhite/Lt HO Long) Aviatik previously chased by Bristol Scout, other combats w Albatros & Aviatik, then 1Aviatik

5088 Morane LA 3Sqn
+*Esc DOUAI-VALENCIENNES combat with Fokker 8000′ shot up OK(Lt Saunders/Sgt JTB McCudden)

5099 Morane LA 3Sqn
+*LRec LILLE-DOUAI combat with Fokker ovWATTIGNIES 10000′ OK(Capt Steinbach-Mealing/ Lt CT Cleaver) Fokker "from behind"

4501 BE2c 5Sqn
+*CB combat with Fokker & others ovELVERDINGHE 8000′ ~10-15am fuel tank shot up dam ftl OK(2Lt Cooper/2Lt Glenny)

5459 Vickers FB5 5Sqn
+*Phot VI Corps front combat with Aviatik HOUTHULST WOOD[+? piece seen leave EA, chased down to 1000′, smoking] 8000′ 10-30am then bad AA shot up ftl OK(Lt FJ Powell/Lt EFP Lubbock) shot up 2nd Aviatik & LVG on return, also earlier Fokker

5465 Vickers FB5 5Sqn
+*Rec combat with EA ovPOELCAPPELLE 8-50am OK(2Lt Pemberton/2Lt Murlis Green) also 2nd combat with Aviatik

5466 Vickers FB5 5Sqn
+*P combat with large Aviatik[+? EA smoking] 8200′- 10500′ 10-20am OK(Lt AWH James/Lt C Porri) went to help Powell & Lubbock in 5459

2082 BE2c 6Sqn
+*CB ST JULIEN combat with Fokker[+? appeared hit seen diving at 1500′ ovLANGEMARCK] 10000′ then shot at by Aviatik OK(2Lt EHP Cave/2Lt A Duguid)

2679 BE2c 6Sqn
+*AOb BOESINGHE-YPRES combat with EA[+ bullets seen hit EA, an EA pusher seen on ground 12-15pm by Lt EHP Cave] 9-40am OK(Capt Moore/Lt Moncrieff) name Moor?

5645 FE2a 6Sqn
+*Rec BIXSCHOOTE-YPRES combat with 3EA heavily shot up OK(2Lt GEH Fincham/2Lt G Price) tracer bullets caused jams, brave attempt by French Maurice Farman to assist

2680 BE2c 7Sqn
+*Rec DIXMUDE-CORTEMARCK combat with 2 Albatros & Fokker 8500′ between 8-50am & 9-30am OK(2Lt Horn/Lt Moffatt) lost escorting a'c at start of combat

4109 BE2c 7Sqn
**Rec combat with 3 Fokkers & 1 EA pusher nrZARREN 9000′ 9-30am fuel tank shot up returned a'dr OK(2Lt Horsbrough?/Lt Haynes)

4672 Bristol Scout C 7Sqn
+*P YPRES combat with EA 1200′ 11am OK(2Lt DAC Symington) head to head firing

4675 Bristol Scout C 10Sqn
+*P BETHUNE-ARRAS drove off Albatros & LVG 12000′ between 10-15am & 11am engine hit dam OK(Capt Mitchell)

5471 Vickers FB5 11Sqn
**Phot nrBUCQUOY combat with Ago 6500′ 10-30am OK(Capt LA Pattinson/2Lt E Robinson) others in area

1741 BE2c 12Sqn
Rec BRUGES combat with Albatros [+?EA observer appeared hit after 10 mins] YPRES-POPERINGHE shot up dam ftl nrCASSELL (Lt CO Fairbairn Aust. **WIA/ Capt EC Perrin OK)arm, got back WoL

2074 BE2c 12Sqn
EscRec combat ovBRUGES shot down OOSTCAMP **MIA(Lt N Gordon-Smith **KIA**/Lt DF Cunningham-Reid **KIA**) headstone made of a'c tail [combat OOSTKAMPE-BRUGES Ltn O Parschau KG1]

5202 FE2b 16Sqn
+*AReg combat with Albatros ovERQUINGHEM OK(Capt GH Eastwood/2Lt LAK Butt)

5476 Vickers FB5 18Sqn
2 Lewis guns+*P saw off DFW ovLAVENTIE 9500′ 11-15am OK(Lt H Henderson/2Lt OJF Scholte)

5618 Vickers FB5 18Sqn
+*P saw off LVG ovCUINCHY 10000′ 9-55am OK(2Lt M LeBlanc-Smith/2Lt DS Hall) no fight?

20th December

Increasingly bad winter weather reduced flying until the last days of the month.

9 Squadron RFC had been reformed in England and returned to France as of the 20th of December equipped with BE2cs. It was to be mostly concerned with artillery co-operation, having specialised in experimental wireless work when building up at Brooklands in Kent.

23rd December

15 Squadron RFC arrived in France on the 23rd of December equipped with BE2cs. It was initially an army squadron but became a corps unit the following spring.

27th December

4673 Bristol Scout C 2Sqn
Rec left 9-25am I Army area ftl wLILLE burnt a'c **MIA(Capt GT Porter **POW**) to Holland 19.4.18

28th December

5093   Morane LA   3Sqn
+*P HANTAY combat with 2Aviatik, Albatros & larger
a'c dam OK(Lt Gould/2Lt SE Pither)

4678   Bristol Scout C   4Sqn
+* ALBERT-ARRAS combat with EA ovHEBUTERNE
1-45pm OK(2Lt JW Woodhouse) later saw EA ldg?

5465   Vickers FB5   5Sqn
+*P combat with Aviatik ovPASSCHENDAELE 8800'
10-55am OK(2Lt Pemberton/1AM Nicholls) bullets seen
enter EA

4680   Bristol Scout C   6Sqn
+*P LANGEMARCK-PASSCHENDAELE-ST
JULIEN combat with EA 10000'-6000' OK(2Lt EHP
Cave)

2670   BE2c   8Sqn
**ArmyRec combat with Aviatik ovSANCOURT,nHAM
MIA(2Lt GL Pitt **KIA**/2Lt M Head **KIA**) [combat Oblt
E Althaus? KEK.*Vaux*]

4075   BE2c   8Sqn
+* combat with Albatros nrADINFER WOOD 12-40pm
OK(Capt CM Crowe/Lt LC Drenon)

4675   Bristol Scout C   10Sqn
+*P ARMENTIÈRES-LILLE combat with large
Albatros 11000' 12-30pm then engine failed ftl SAILLY
OK(Capt C Gordon-Bell) EA dived toward LILLE

Gordon-Bell was almost certainly the RFC's
second ace. He later commanded 41 Squadron in
England.

1606   Bristol Scout C   18Sqn
+*P ENNETIÈRES? combat with Aviatik
ovFLEURBAIX 8200' 2-35pm chased EA into clouds
4000' then ground rifle fire OK(Capt JA Cunningham)

2343   Vickers FB5   18Sqn
**P AA shot down nLENS ftl but recovered dive 300'?
MIA(Lt EJ Strover **POW**/1AM W Holden **POW**) left
8-45am, pilot to Holland 19.4.18

This was the first crew lost by 18 Squadron in
action.

3113   FBA Flying Boat   1 Wing RNAS
Dunkirk ** combat with 4 enemy seaplanes[+1 EA nose-
dived cr sea & sank] 3m nWESTENDE OK(FSLt JBP
Ferrand/AM1 Oldfield)

29th December

1729   BE2c   2Sqn
+*AP HULLUCH combat with 2 Albatros 7500' 12pm
OK(2Lt KDP Murray/2Lt BC Rice) tracers seen hit EA
fuselage

2061   BE2c   4Sqn
+*EscB combat with Albatros HERVILLY OK(Capt
ED Horsfall/2Lt Bottrell) assisted by arrival of FB5

2039   BE2c   8Sqn
**EscLRec combat with 2 Fokkers, forced to spiral down
to 2000' then flattened out but cr swARRAS to prevent
capture? **MIA**(2Lt DA Glen **KIA**/Sgt E Jones **POW**) left
9-25am, see Combat Report of BE2c 4087: 2Lt Glen seen
WIA [?possible BE claim combat MARQUION 11am
Ltn G Leffers KEK.*Bertincourt*]

4087   BE2c   8Sqn
+*EscRec CAMBRAI 15-20min combat with 6 Fokkers
spread over a period[+?hit then nose-dived] 6500' 11am
then chased down to 20' by 3 Fokkers and managed to
return very low OK(Lt WS Sholto-Douglas/Lt Child)
escorting Lt DA Glen & Sgt E Jones who were attacked
and spiralled down hit? & cr nrARRAS

5468   Vickers FB5   11Sqn
+* combat with LVG & Fokker nrHERVILLY 8500'
11am OK(Capt LA Pattinson/2Lt JF Morris)

5483   Vickers FB5   11Sqn
+*EscB HERVILLY combat with EA nrNURLU 8000'
OK(Lt GH Norman/Cpl GJ Morton)

**   Bristol Scout C   18Sqn**
+*P combat with Aviatik 2Str[+?driven down]
ovPROVIN 9500' then other combats OK(Capt JA
Cunningham)

1606   Bristol Scout C   18Sqn
+*P combat with Albatros then Aviatik PONT À
VENDIN 11500' 12-30pm OK(Capt JA Cunningham)
had met one of these EA ovPROVIN 9500' 11-55am,
inconclusive

1606   Bristol Scout C   18Sqn
+*P LAVENTIE-HAUBOURDIN combat with small
EA 11000' 1-10pm OK(Capt JA Cunningham)
inconclusive

30th December

4134   BE2c   7Sqn
+*Rec COURTRAI-INGELMUNSTER-
LICHTERVELDE combats with 5EA 11000' between
9-30am & 10am eg Albatros ovCOURTEMARCK[+?
steep bank & "went down"] OK(2Lt LW Learmount/Lt
Moffatt)

2882   Vickers FB5   18Sqn
2 Lewis +*P combat with 2Aviatiks eLOOS 9200' 10am
then AA ovLOOS shot up dam OK(Lt GH Hall/2Lt H
Welch)

5619   Vickers FB5   18Sqn
+*P chased off Aviatik ovWINGLES 7000' 9-45am
OK(2Lt G Teale/1AM G Mackie)

**   Nieuport   1 Wing RNAS**
+* combat with EA[+ooc] DIXMUDE OK(FSLt RH
Mulock)

At the end of 1915 there were eighty-six Fokker E-
types on the Western Front.

Untraced casualty in France possibly in 1915

(Lt E Lister **KIA?)

1916 PREPARATIONS FOR A WAR OF ATTRITION

With the exception of the first few weeks of fighting on the Western Front, all attempts to defeat the German army had relied on battles which hoped to break through their defences by a bombardment, followed by an infantry assault. These had also been reasonably localised affairs, with the hope that once the breach had been made the damage would ripple and reverberate along the front. When prospects for Allied victory in 1916 had been reviewed the previous December it was concluded that this strategy, if continued, had little chance of success because experience showed that German reserves could always be brought up effectively to oppose it.

In 1916, therefore, scale of effort became all important, for the Allied command resolved to launch a great battle of attrition on the Somme in the coming summer. The whole year's war for the British in the west was to revolve around this offensive. With this strategy, one side simply sought to exhaust and outstay its opponent, so that in a final assault he would be too weak to resist. The original planning had been to commence with a series of subsidiary battles so as to impose immediate pressure on Germany's reserves. Meanwhile, Britain and France would attempt to build up their strength. This was completely mollified, however, by Germany's own attack on Verdun in February which, it will be seen, swept all initiative away.

By the time preparations for the Allies' own campaign needed to gain real momentum, France could only contribute what could be spared from Verdun. The offensive would have to become a largely British affair, whilst one of its primary goals had now become the removal of the German Army from around the French fortress. Only once this was achieved could the principal British objectives be tackled. The build-up on the Somme would nevertheless be unparalleled, and it was hoped that this tremendous weight of arms could drive through the enemy's front and capture the German positions around Bapaume.

An integral part of the new British Army would be a greatly enlarged Royal Flying Corps. Trenchard strove to create a force which could meet the challenges of the coming offensive — one he knew would be conducted between vast armies on a huge scale. Between the battles of Loos and the Somme, fifteen new squadrons appeared in France, hugely increasing its capability. The Allies would also learn a great deal from the defence of Verdun which would bear on the fighting in the summer. The air forces, in particular, would have taken several major steps forward in tactics and strategic approach by the end of the spring. Finally, the RFC would at last have the aircraft capable of delivering air supremacy back to the Allies so that as the battle opened in July they would have control of the skies.

The new year began with a long period of strong gales and rain. Apart from some activity on the 5th, virtually all flying was restricted until the 10th.

January 1916

5th January

1734   BE2c   2Sqn
**EscRec combat with 3 Fokkers 8-15am shot down ooc cr
MIA (2Lt WE Somervell **WIA POW**/Lt GC Formilli **WIA POW**) to hospital, to Holland 19/18.4.18 [combat HARNES, nHENIN LIETARD Ltn O Boelcke FAb62]

2019   BE2c   2Sqn
**SpB DOUAI combat with Fokker engine dam ooc cr
MIA (2Lt AL Russell **POW**) left 11-20am, to Holland 19.4.18 [BE claim combat VITRY 12-30pm Ltn E Hess KEK.*Douai*]

2766   BE2d   2Sqn
+*TacRec combat with 3 Fokkers LILLE 6000' 8-15am OK (Lt Wynne-Eyton/Lt Davey) 2 Fokkers remained after combat, escorting 2Lt WE Somervell/Lt GC Formilli, who were lost after combat & did not return

5081   Morane BB   3Sqn

+*Esc combat with 2 Fokkers ovDOUAI 9000' 12-45pm shot up OK (Sgt TH Bayetto/Sgt JTB McCudden) second Fokker attacked nearby BE2c, first spiralled down but ok?

2014   BE2c   7Sqn
+*TacRec sLILLE-RONCHIN combat with large 2-engined EA & Fokker unseen in sun 9200' 9-05am to 9-20am OK (2Lt Hagon/2Lt Boyton) large EA went down steeply

4682   Bristol Scout C   8Sqn
**HAP left 10am combat with 2Aviatiks ovBOIS D'ADINFER 7000' 10-15am engine ftl bad ground dam OK (Capt CM Crowe)

2688   BE2c   16Sqn
+*B DOUAI combat with Fokker then another[++both shot down vert snd ooc] 7500' 12-30pm shot up dam ftl BRUAY OK (Lt RH deBrasseur) first Fokker just after bombing, many tracers seen hit home

5201   FE2b   16Sqn
+*AReg combat with LVG? ovBOIS GRENIER 6000' 10am OK (Capt AAB Thompson/2Lt Caton)

5469   Vickers FB5   18Sqn
+*P combat with LVG CAMBRAI-sSALOME 6200'
10-05am OK(2Lt G Teale/2Lt HS Paynter) a'c fitted
with 2 Lewis guns.

10th January

5091   Morane LA   1Sqn
**LRec shot down ovTOURNAI 7000' MIA(2Lt JG
McEwan WIA POW/2Lt F Adams POW) left 1-40pm
Second Army front, both to Holland 19.4.18 [combat
LILLE Ltn A Dossenbach/Ltn Schilling FAb22 (FAb5?)]

12th January

The 12th was sunny and clear, so air activity
increased.

5100   Morane LA   1Sqn
**LRec combat with EA ROUBAIX MIA(2Lt R Barton
KIA/Lt ES Wilkinson KIA) left 7-08am Second Army
front

This was the second unsuccessful attempt in three
days to carry out this reconnaissance.

1732   BE2c   2Sqn
+*AOb combat with Albatros ovLENS 7500' 11am
OK(Lt Wynne-Eyton/Lt Davey)

2685   BE2c   2Sqn
+*AReg combat with Albatros PONT À VENDIN 9500'
OK(2Lt W Allcock/2Lt BC Rice) returned WoL as 3
Fokkers seen

4114   BE2c   5Sqn
+*EscRec combat with Albatros & Aviatik nROULERS
9800' 8-45am to 9-15am OK(2Lt Nethersole/2Lt
Hemming) escorting BE2c 2684

5481   Vickers FB5   5Sqn
+*P combat with 4EA BOESINGHE-WYTSCHAETE
6000' 10am then AA OK(Capt FJ Powell/Lt GW Murlis
Green) combat over Sh28 E.8.

5460   Vickers FB5   11Sqn
**Esc combat with EA 8000' engine hit ftl BAPAUME
MIA(2Lt HT Kemp WIA POW/2Lt S Hathaway KIA)
left 7-23am, to Holland 19.4.18 Imm8 [combat
TOURCOING ~8am Oblt M Immelmann FAb62]

2287   RE7   12Sqn
**RecEsc clouds lost a'c ovLILLE MIA(2Lt Kingdon
KIA/Lt KW Gray WIA POW) left 7-55am, to Holland
19.4.18 [?combat MOUSCRON, neTOURCOING am
Ltn O Boelcke FAb62]

12 Squadron were due to carry out a long reconnaissance for Headquarters on this day, but the
machines were turned back by the conditions. This
escort machine failed to make the early rendezvous
with the patrol, and carried on thinking they would
meet up over the lines. Pressing on eastwards
alone, they were probably shot down by Boelcke,
for whom they would have been an easy target.

1712   BE2c   16Sqn
**AReg AA ovLIGNY 4000' 10-15am then dive in
flames(Lt EFW Cobbold KIA/Lt CVG Field KIA) men
fell out

5469   Vickers FB5   18Sqn
+*P combat with Aviatik 5000' 10-45am then engine
failed ftl OK(2Lt G Teale/2Lt RGH Adams) earlier
combat with LVG ovGIVENCHY 8000' 10-10am

14th January

4087   BE2c   8Sqn
**Rec eACHIET LE GRAND combat with EA dials shot
up engine failed ftl trenches nrBECOURT CHÂTEAU
WoL wr(2Lt JH Herring WIA/Capt R Erskine WIA) left
8-07am, a'c shelled [combat BECOURT CHÂTEAU
nrFLERS ~9-15am Ltn O Boelcke FAb62]

4117   BE2c   8Sqn
**AOb a'c shelled(/2Lt RA Denne WIA)

5479   Vickers FB5   11Sqn
+*P combat with Fokker[+des:last seen wr in field]
nrBERTINCOURT 8300'-3500' 10am then engine
problems OK(Capt HVC deCrespigny/Lt JLMdeC
Hughes-Chamberlain)

**   Vickers FB5   11Sqn**
** combat shot up(/2Lt HB Milling WIA)

THE RISE OF
FORMATION FLYING

A great majority of the British squadrons would
still be flying the BE2c as their basic equipment for
many months to come, but already its crews and
headquarters alike knew that it was woefully
inadequate as a fighting machine. Its stable flying
qualities and sedate ways might make it a
dependable and useful machine for observation of
the battle below, but if attacked it rarely escaped
some mauling. The observer was seated in the front
cockpit in the BE2c, and hence was in the worst
position for bringing fire to bear on an attacker. He
was surrounded with bracing wires and faced the
arc of the propeller. Even though he could move
the Lewis gun onto other mounts during combat,
his freedom to do so was also very restricted. The
layout of this seating was probably a greater factor
than its performance in understanding why the
BE2c suffered so much at the hands of the Fokker.
The Eindekker was now reaching the Western
Front in greater numbers but, just as incisively,
was now being grouped more tactically. This had
begun at the close of 1915 with a more careful
allocation of the type, and coupled with an
increasing proficiency of its pilots, had meant that
Allied reconnaissance flights were now being
critically restricted.

Rapid and important changes effecting the whole nature of air fighting were about to occur. The result was to be a considerable increase in the numbers of aircraft operating together on both sides, with a commensurate intensifying of air combat. On the 14th of January RFC Headquarters issued an unusually candid order in response to the damage that was being inflicted by the Fokker. Until Allied units with aircraft capable of countering it could be assembled in France, all reconnaissance and photographic machines would be accompanied by at least three escorts — in practice, considerably more than this number would often be deployed. The Fokker menace had spawned the concept of formation flying, ever afterwards a key element of air warfare. The immediate effect of this was, of course, to reduce the practical amount of work a squadron could carry out. The German airmen might now find it harder to disrupt the work of the BE2cs, but they had also forced the Allies to spread their available machines more thinly. Not only the squadron's scouts, but also its other BE2s usually made up the escorts.

15th January

5077   Morane N   3Sqn
AP ftl GIVENCHY(2Lt RJ Lillywhite OK/2Lt CE Sherwin **WIA) pilot probably Lillywhite

16th January

Immelmann was known to have taken delivery on the 16th of a Fokker EIV armed with three synchronised machine-guns. Allegedly, he used it to bring down a few of his victims, but the weight of guns and ammunition must have seriously handicapped its performance.

17th January

5068   Morane N   1Sqn
+*EscRec MENIN-HOUTHULST combat with 3-4EAs ovHOUTHULST WOOD[+?2 Fokkers driven off, one ftl, then Albatros shot up, then Fokker driven down] btwn 8am & 8-40am OK(Capt EO Grenfell)

Two slightly varying Combat Reports exist for Capt Grenfell's engagement. They demonstrate the growing intensity of combats. From this time Allied reports begin to reflect a shift in intent, with the attack now being increasingly taken to the enemy. Notwithstanding the limitations of formation flying, it also imparted a timely impetus to the British. There had been a growing resolve in the actions of a certain number of pilots, evident also in the language they had begun to use in their reports, that "seeing off" an enemy was not enough — he needed to be shot down. Operating until now on lone patrols or in pairs had meant, despite the intention, that the odds were still against success. However, in only a few weeks the new patrol structure brought the future of air warfare into focus. The details of Capt Grenfell's combat seem to be that he was dived on by two fast Fokkers, the first of which he sent into a dive, and the second which he shot up sufficiently to force it to land in a field south of Moorslede. He then attacked an Albatros C-type, which he shot up inconclusively. Finally, seeing a third Fokker below him, in the midst of some BE2cs, he dived and attacked it. He watched his tracers enter its cowling and fuselage, and saw it go down.

5076   Morane N   1Sqn
**Phot HOLLEBEKE combat with Scout 5000' 9-40am shot up OK(2Lt CC Godwin) EA like Morane

5113   Morane LA   1Sqn
SpRec AA shot down WYTSCHAETE nrDADIZEELE **MIA(2Lt W Watts **KIA**/2Lt CC Hayward **KIA**) left 7-06am

5466   Vickers FB5   5Sqn
+*Phot combat with EA POLYGON WOOD 6000' 10-50am many hits OK(Lt AWH James/Lt GW Murlis Green)

7457   FE8   5Sqn
+*P combat with Aviatik[+?possibly shot down?] ovBECELAERE 8000' 11-10am OK(Capt FJ Powell)

This was the second prototype of the FE8 single-seater pusher. It had joined 5 Squadron from 1AD on Boxing Day 1915 for evaluation. In the next few months it was to take part in several fights, particularly in the hands of Capt Powell.

4309   BE2c   6Sqn
+*AReg combat with 3Aviatiks incl first 10am[+?30 shots then dropped suddenly & rapidly ovPOLYGON WOOD] 5000' then combat with Fokker on return 11am OK(Lt Danby/Lt G Price) many other combats for 6Sqn btwn 10am & 11am YPRES-POPERINGHE

4680   Bristol Scout C   6Sqn
P YPRES SALIENT combat with Aviatik 8000' 9-20am shot up ftl nrZILLEBEKE LAKE dam(2Lt EHP Cave **WIA)thigh, unconscious but recovered at 4000'

4735   Martinsyde G100   6Sqn
+*P combat with Fokker[+?second burst of fire caused spurt of flame from EA & then dived]ovGHELUVELT 10000' 8-45am then engine poor & AA ftl OK(2Lt NA Bolton) first seen ovPOLYGON WOOD 2000' below, flames were possibly tracers

5643   FE2a   6Sqn
+*P YPRES SALIENT combat with LVG nYPRES but gun jam OK(2Lt Raymond-Barker/2Lt Young)

FE2   6Sqn
+*AOb combat with Aviatik YPRES-POPERINGHE
6000' 9-50am OK(Capt Moore/2Lt G Price) cut off EA
& possibly hit it

4119   BE2c   9Sqn
+*EscB combat with Fokker[+pilot hit? driven
down?]sIRLES 8000' 10-40am OK(2Lt VD Bell/Lt L
Eardley-Wilmot) EA pilot's gun seen to swing out

BE2c   9Sqn
B shot up(2Lt RB Jenkins **DoW 18.1.16)

This was the first casualty for 9 Squadron RFC
after returning to France.

4667   Bristol Scout C   10Sqn
+* combat with Fokker seLA BASSÉE but gun jam 9am
OK(Capt C Gordon-Bell) suspected EA had two guns
due to noise, saw bullets hit a'c but inconclusive, second
combat with large Albatros 11am

5472   Vickers FB5   11Sqn
+*Esc combat with 2LVGs ovPERONNE 8000' 11am
OK(2Lt HA Cooper/Cpl H? Monks)

4662   Bristol Scout C   12Sqn
2 Lewis +*HAP combat with EA ovBAILLEUL 10000'
11-05am dam OK(Capt GAK Lawrence)

2105   BE2c   15Sqn
EscRec left 7-35am cr **MIA(Capt VHN Wadham **KIA**/
Sgt Piper **KIA**) [?unconfirmed BE claim BAPAUME Ltn
G Leffers FAb32 KEK.*Bertincourt*]

This was the first crew lost by 15 Squadron in
action.

4107   BE2c   15Sqn
**EscRec FAUST-HOUTHULST combat with
Fokker[+chased down, last seen spiralling down] 9000'
8-30am then shot up OK(Lt CB Wilson/2AM Lathean)

BE2c   15Sqn
+*Esc saw off Aviatik ovCORTEMARCK 8500' 8-30am
OK(2Lt ED? Tempest/2Lt O Nixon) initials ER?

BE2c   15Sqn
later: +*Esc MOUSCRON combat with 2Aviatiks[+
?EA badly shot up then ss steep dive ooc almost
ovCOURTRAI] 11000' 10am OK(2Lt ED? Tempest/2Lt
O Nixon) initials ER?, EA was lost to sight as Fokker
attacked

5470   Vickers FB5   18Sqn
2 Lewis guns +*P combat with Aviatik ovBOIS
GRENIER 8000' 11-05am OK(2Lt CH Johnston/2Lt JA
Slater)

19th January

1732   BE2c   2Sqn
+*AReg combat with Albatroses ovLENS & ovLOISON
10000' 11am OK(Lt Wynne-Eyton/Lt Davey)

5110   Morane LA   3Sqn
+*EscRec combat with Albatros ovLILLE 7000'

11-20am OK(2Lt FE Goodrich/Cpl James) saw EA ldg
nrLILLE

5465   Vickers FB5   5Sqn
**Phot combat with 3EA BECELAERE-
PASSCHENDAELE ovSh28 J.11. 6000' 12-05pm drew
EA on & fired from 40yds [+?tracers seen hit: last seen
in steep nd over ePOLYGON WOOD 3000'] OK(Lt
AWH James/Lt GW Murlis Green)

2683   BE2d   10Sqn
+*AReg combat with LVG wBOIS DE BIEZ 9000'
11am OK(2Lt L Feltum?/2Lt Bush)

4667   Bristol Scout C   10Sqn
+* 10min combat with large Albatros BOIS DE BIEZ
12000' 10-25am OK(Capt C Gordon-Bell)

2694   BE2c   15Sqn
+*Rec LINSELLES-COURTRAI combat with Fokker,
2 Aviatiks, 2 Albatros 8500' 10am OK(Capt PC Maltby/
2Lt CR Robbins)

4107   BE2c   15Sqn
EscRec shot down TOURCOING 8-40am **MIA(Lt
CW Wilson **WIA POW**/2Lt WA Brooking **KIA**) to
Holland 19.4.18

4123   BE2c   15sqn
**EscRec LINSELLES-COMINES combat with Fokker
& Aviatiks COURTRAI-MOUSCRON 8500' 9-55am
but AA hit observer & had to exit, but then attacked by
Aviatik which Nott, who had revived, drove off(Capt G
Henderson OK/Cpl CN Nott DCM **WIA**)eye

Cpl Nott was awarded the DCM for this action; it
was the first gallantry medal for 15 Squadron.

BE2c   15Sqn
+*P combat with Aviatik ovBOESINGHE 9000' 2-30pm
to 3pm: cartridge case had jammed aileron but saved by
"the arrival of an FE8" OK(2Lt FN Hudson/Cpl
Edwards)

5084   Vickers FB5   18Sqn
2 Lewis guns +* combat with Aviatik RICHEBOURG-
NOEUX LES MINES 7-8000' 10-45am to 11-15am
OK(Capt Hutcheson/2Lt RGH Adams)

5919   DH2   18Sqn
+*P combat with Albatros ovSOUCHEZ 12500'
10-15am OK(Capt H deHavilland) later combat with
Aviatik BOIS GRENIER 11000' 10-40am, problem that
tracers could not be seen over sight

20th January

7457   FE8   5Sqn
+*P combat with Aviatik ovHOUTHULST 7500' 11am
shot up dam engine failed ftl Sh28 B.19.d. OK(Capt FJ
Powell)

4309   BE2c   6Sqn
+*AReg YPRES combat with Aviatik 6000'[+? steep
dive ovPOLYGON WOOD] OK(Lt Danby/Lt G Price)
had 3 combats btwn 10am and 10-25am, then met Fokker

on way home at 11am, after this: "noticing several other hostile machines cruising about we thought it advisable to give up any endeavour to continue registration and proceed to carry out a policy of aggression", but despite looking failed to find another

2876   Vickers FB5   11Sqn
**P AA nrALBERT nacelle damaged OK(2Lt HVC deCrespigny/2Lt JLMdeC Hughes-Chamberlain) ALBERT-BAPAUME-BIENVILLIERS

23rd January

Both Nos. 20 and 21 Squadron RFC arrived in France on the 23rd. The latter brought RE7 two-seaters whilst 20 Squadron was the first unit to be fully equipped with the promising FE2b. This was a development of the FE2a, retaining the two-seater pusher configuration, and possessed an increasingly useful performance. FE2as, followed by a few FE2bs, had already reached France in late 1915, and had shown themselves to be the match of any German aircraft over the previous four or five months. Only two FE2as had been lost in 1915, and only one of these in air combat (on the 11th November). However, until the arrival of 20 Squadron, the improved FE2b had been in only token use in France, for extended evaluation purposes. The defensive as well as aggressive intent of RFC Squadrons was still resting with the crews of Vickers FB5s, Moranes, and single-seater scouts such as the Bristol Scout. All these aircraft were now usually outclassed in combat. The Fokker remained in the ascendant, increasingly so as its numbers multiplied, and as will be seen, continued to take a mounting toll of Allied two-seaters and scouts alike. The arrival of a squadron of FE2bs was therefore most welcome. It was intended to use it for reconnaissance as well as a fighter. Increasingly desperate for a counter to the Fokker, it was only with the wider operational appearance of machines like this, as well as the Nieuport Scouts and the new single-seat pusher fighter, the DH2, that the balance began to be hauled back.

2685   BE2c   2Sqn
+*CB combat with Albatros eLA BASSÉE[+engine stopped then planed down nrHULLUCH] 9500′ 10am shot up OK(2Lt W Alcock/2Lt BC Rice) fuel short so had to retire, NB: not 25.1.16

2882   Vickers FB5   18Sqn
+*P combat with DFW BETHUNE 7000′ 3-05pm OK(Lt GH Hall/1AM G Mackie)

5916   DH2   18Sqn
** AA ftl 10Sq a'dr CHOCQUES OK(Capt JA Cunningham)

3182   Nieuport 10   1 Wing RNAS

St Pol +*Bombed U-boat 10m wOSTENDE OK(FSLt EW Norton)

3963   Nieuport 10   RNAS
+*Bombed U-boat 10m wOSTENDE OK(FSLt HR Simms)

24th January

3977   Nieuport 11   RNAS
St Pol +* combat with 2Str[+?ftl nrWESTENDE] OK(FSLt RH Mulock)

25th January

5296   Bristol Scout C   2Sqn
+*HAP combat: drove off Albatros ovLA BASSÉE 9-10000′ 10-25am OK(Lt Wynne-Eyton) hit EA engine & fuselage, earlier combat with Albatros ovBETHUNE 9-45am

2672   BE2c   4Sqn
+*Phot combat with Fokker & Aviatik ovBOUCHAVESNES 7000′ 2pm OK(Lt GA Burney/2Lt JS Quinlan) no escort about, fired at continually by Fokker for 7mins

2679   BE2c   6Sqn
+*AReg combat with Aviatik YPRES-POPERINGHE 7500′ 10-55am OK(Lt ER Tempest/Lt G Price)

5295   Bristol Scout C   10Sqn
+*P combat with 2 Albatros ovANNEQUIN 12000′ 1-10pm but engine stopped, had to pull out OK(Capt C Gordon-Bell)

5483   Vickers FB5   11Sqn
+*SpP attacked KB ovLE BARQUE swBAPAUME 4500′-2000′ 12-45pm OK(Capt LA Pattinson/2Lt JE Morris) shot up once

4105   BE2c   13Sqn
+*AOb combat with A-type ROCLINCOURT 8500′ 1-30pm OK(2Lt FCA Wright/Maj ASW Dore)

2694   BE2c   15Sqn
+*Rec GHELUWE combat with 3 Fokkers attacking formation 8000′ 8-20am OK(Capt PC Maltby/Sgt HJ Gardowner)

4126   BE2c   15Sqn
+*Esc combat with Fokker[+?engine hit?: dived steeply & landed in control] neTOURCOING 8000′ 11-30am OK(2Lt FN Hudson/2AM Lathean)

4127   BE2c   15Sqn
+*Esc combat with 3 Fokkers GHELUWE attacking formation 7800′ 8-20am OK(2Lt J Stuart/Sgt FH Middis)

4129   BE2c   15Sqn
+*Esc TOURCOING combat with Albatros then Aviatik[+?ooc: saw hit EA then down steep spiral]nrCOURTRAI 8000′ btwn 11am & 12pm OK(Lt B Adams/2Lt HAD Mackay)

4670   Bristol Scout C   16Sqn

+*P combat with 2 Albatros neARMENTIÈRES 9500'
11-45am OK(2Lt G Merton) possibly hit EA observer as
he could not fire second drum

2882   Vickers FB5   18Sqn
+* combat with Aviatik GIVENCHY 7000' 9-30am
OK(2Lt G Teale/1AM G Mackie)

5621   Vickers FB5   18Sqn
+* combat with Aviatik 9000' 9-30am to 9-45am OK(2Lt
E Millar/2Lt HS Paynton)

5916   DH2   18Sqn
+*P combat with Albatros LA BASSÉE[+engine hit,
smoke driven down] OK(Capt JA Cunningham)

5919   DH2   18Sqn
+*P combat with Albatros ovFESTUBERT 9500'
10-10am but gun jam OK(Capt H deHavilland) had got
behind & below. Later combat (in this a'c?): +* combat
with 2 Albatros ovLA BASSÉE 12500' 1-15pm but gun
jam

The first skirmishes involving production versions
of the DH2 on the Western Front are those above,
recording combats by 18 Squadron pilots. It would
not be until the arrival of 24 Squadron on the 7th
of February, that a unit fully equipped with the
DH2 would appear.

26th January

3977   Nieuport 11   RNAS
St Pol +* combat with 2Str[+des] NIEUPORT 3pm
OK(FSLt RH Mulock)

THE FIRST RFC
BRIGADES FORMED

January saw the reorganising of pairs of wings into
brigades, one allocated to each army. Within each
brigade, there was now a corps wing and an army
wing. The corps wing carried out artillery observation, photography, reconnaissance, and reasonably
localised bombing, and was responsible to the
corps headquarters. The army wing was responsible to an individual army headquarters, and had
an air fighting role whether through mounting
offensive patrols or later in protection of the corps
machines. Its aircraft also carried out long reconnaissances and deep bombing raids. Each brigade
also had a headquarters, an aircraft park and a
balloon wing. It soon became apparent that the
work of the squadrons of the army wings required
aircraft with more fighting capability, and this set
in motion, in embryo form, the natural specialisation of types into units which would be the way
of the future. In the coming months fighters would
be gradually extracted from corps squadrons and
concentrated into the army wings. By the time of

the Somme Battle in July, only a few somewhat
obsolete fighting types would still be on strength
with corps squadrons, and by August there would
be none. In this way the principle was established
whereby the job of air fighting in order to maintain
an offensive policy was kept separate from the day
to day corps operations over the battlefield.

The first two RFC brigades were formed on the
30th of January. I Brigade with the First Army
comprised the 1st(Corps) Wing and 10th(Army)
Wing; whilst III Brigade with the Third Army
comprised the 3rd(Corps) Wing and the 12th
(Army) Wing (but see also the 29th of February).
On the 10th of February II Brigade was formed for
the Second Army, and this included the 2nd
(Corps) Wing and the 11th(Army) Wing. How
these brigades had evolved by the time of the battle
of the Somme is given in more detail in text
associated with the July 1916 entries. Finally, on
the 16th of February, those units retained by RFC
Headquarters for special strategical and patrol
work were formed into 9th (Headquarters) Wing.
At this time it comprised Nos. 12 and 21
Squadrons.

February 1916

1st February

5296   Bristol Scout C   2Sqn
+* combat with Albatros? LENS-MAZINGARBE 9000'
1-30pm to 2pm OK(Lt Wynne-Eyton) EA "made off"

2nd February

1730   BE2c   2Sqn
+*P combat with A-type nrLA BASSÉE 920am OK(2Lt
Ward/2Lt GR Moser) EA had 2 guns

5th February

5069   Morane N   1Sqn
+*P combat with LVG?[+hit wing & fuselage, front man
slumped & nd into clouds]seARMENTIÈRES 9000'-
5800' 11-10am to 11-32am OK(2Lt VS Strugnell)
observer crouched, also had combat with LVG 10500'
10-09am to 10-50am: several hits, EA dived into cloud

7457   FE8   5Sqn
+*HAP combat with large Aviatik wYSER CANAL[?+
EA probably hit from below: going down in control
towards ROULERS A'dr] 7000' 10-40am OK(Capt FJ
Powell) went up twice more to see off EA: first was sent
diving steeply ovPLOEGSTEERT WOOD 7000'
11-25am, second seen off 2-35pm

1716   BE2c   2Sqn
+*AReg combat with Albatros ovPONT À VENDIN

8000' 11am then AA hit wires & forced to return a'dr OK(2Lt Henderson/Lt Faure)

2082   BE2c   6Sqn
+*P BRIELEN combat with Aviatik 8000' 10-25am: 4 sessions of circling & combat then gun jam OK(2Lt H Bright/2Lt A Duguid)

2096   BE2c   9Sqn
+*Esc INCHY-BAPAUME combat with 2 Fokkers & 3Albatros[+tracers entered second Albatros then stall ss cr in flames] 6500' 8-45am to 9-15am OK(Lt R Egerton/ 2Lt TE Gordon-Scaife) other EAs afterwards did not approach, BE2cs 2102 and 4132 also submitted combat reports

2102   BE2c   9Sqn
+*EscRec HAVRINCOURT WOOD combat with 3Albatros[+tracer seen hit & down ooc smoke] 6500' ~9am OK(2Lt HR Deighton-Simpson/2Lt CWP Selby) matching claim from BE2cs 2096 & 4132

4132   BE2c   9Sqn
+*EscRec combat with Fokkers[+shot down smoking] 4m eBAPAUME 8000' ~9-10am OK(2Lt C Faber/2Lt AE Wynn) shared claim with BE2cs 2096 & 2102

4091   BE2c   13Sqn
**EscRec combat with EA ftl EoL MIA(2Lt LJ Pearson POW/2Lt EHEJ Alexander WIA POW) left 7-45am, a'c captured, to Holland 17.10/19.4.18 [?BE claim combat GREVILLERS-IRLES Ltn R Berthold KEK.*Vaux*]

5916   DH2   18Sqn
** combat with "new Albatros"[+?tracers hit nose then black smoke & nd, ldg eCARVIN, but ok?] ovSALOME nrLA BASSÉE 11000' 10-35am OK(Capt JA Cunningham)

5916   DH2   18Sqn
** second combat with Aviatik ovLOOS 10000' 10-45am OK(Capt JA Cunningham) "flying downhill and moving very fast", inconclusive, third combat with Aviatik ovPONT À VENDIN 11am

4735   Martinsyde G100   20Sqn
prototype +*InterceptP ST OMER-CASSEL-STEENVOORDE combat with LVG? ovFORÊT DE CLAIRMARAIS 9500' 11-45am to 12-30pm OK(Capt JR Howett) sent up to intercept Fokker ovCASSEL

7th February

The DH2-equipped 24 Squadron arrived in France. It was the first RFC unit to be composed purely of single-seat fighters.

1784   BE2c   5Sqn
+*P drove off EA POPERINGHE-YPRES 5-7000' 9-30am OK(Sgt Noakes/AM Crossley)

7457   FE8   5Sqn
+*HAP drove off large Aviatik[+?possibly EA observer hit or had gun jam, last seen diving ok] POPERINGHE 10000' 9-45am OK(Capt FJ Powell)

2127   BE2c   6Sqn
+*AReg YPRES combat with Albatros & Aviatik 6-7000' 9-20am to 9-50am then dived ovPOPERINGHE to avoid EA fire OK(2Lt N Howarth/2Lt G Price) also saw BE2c on ground eVLAMERTINGHE

2077   BE2c   15Sqn
**EscRec combat with EAs shot up VLAMERTINGHE(Lt J Prestwich DoW/Cpl Alton OK) left 7-20am, also exchanged fire with 2 EA bombers after main combat once lines had been reached, WIA leg

2578   BE2c   15Sqn
+*Esc 14EA seen to rear & 1 attacked & driven off 8000' 8-45am OK(2Lt FN Hudson/2Lt EA Parke)

4116   BE2c   15Sqn
+*LRec POPERINGHE-VLAMERTINGHE combat with Aviatik 7000'-4000' 9-25am OK(Capt L Jenkins/2Lt HAD Mackay) Second Army Rec

**   FE2b   20Sqn**
+*EscRec combat with Fokker[+ss then fell rapidly with smoking engine] ROULERS 8200' 9am OK(2Lt GPS Reid/Lt HF Billinge)

This was the first combat claim for 20 Squadron. During a long reconnaissance for the Second Army, in which BE2cs of 15 Squadron were escorted by FE2bs, a formidable series of enemy patrols was met. Only by retaining tight formation did they manage to survive a harrowing morning's work. The first Fokker appeared over Roulers, to be joined soon afterwards by another seven. A further two Fokkers then mounted a direct attack but were driven off. Over Cortemarck another six Fokkers arrived, so that on the return journey, the formation was pursued by an enemy force which had grown to fourteen aircraft. Notably, none of these made any further attacks, and the RFC machines successfully regained the lines. Unfortunately, the pilot of an escorting BE2c was wounded in further fighting once the formation had recrossed the lines, and he later died.

8th February

5917   DH2   5Sqn
+*P HOOGE combat with Aviatik ovPOLYGON WOOD 9000' 10-30am OK(Capt R Loraine) EA fuselage hit?

2127   BE2c   6Sqn
+*AReg YPRES saw off Aviatik 9-10000' 10-30am OK(2Lt N Howarth/2Lt G Price)

2104   BE2c   15Sqn
+*NorthRec combat with 2 Fokkers & 3Aviatiks HOUTHULST WOOD-ROULERS 7000' 9-25am OK(2Lt C Danby/Cpl Kennedy)

4127   BE2c   15Sqn
+*Esc combat with 2 Fokkers & 3 Aviatiks

HOUTHULST WOOD-ROULERS 8000' 9-25am
OK(2Lt J Stuart/Cpl Cormack)

9th February

5299   Bristol Scout C   6Sqn
+*P ZONNEBEKE combat with Fokker & 2 larger EAs
9000' 10am heavily shot up dam finally gun jam and then
engine failed over VLAMERTINGHE ftl OK(2Lt NA
Bolton) petrol leak had caused difficulty breathing but
returned to continue combat

10th February

2018   BE2c   9Sqn
+*Rec dived on Fokker 7000' 11am OK(2Lt VAH
Robeson/2Lt TE Gordon-Scaife)

4132   BE2c   9Sqn
**EscRec combat with 2Fokker[+?tracers seen hit first
Fokker but then attacked by second Fokker] ovROISEL
7000' 11am then shot up lost control until 2000' ftl 12pm
(2Lt C Faber **WIA**/2Lt RA Way **WIA**) also rifle fire?,
crossed Lines low, no dam to a'c

BE2c   9Sqn
+*EscRec combat with Fokker nROISEL[+?saw tracers
hit cowl then dived & landed steeply in field wROISEL]
11am OK(Lt R Egerton/2Lt BH Cox)

13th February

2801   BE2c   2Sqn
+*AReg combat with double-fuselaged EA with Albatros
ovARRAS 9000' 5pm OK(Capt Babington/Lt
MacClintock)

6331   FE2b   20Sqn
+*P combat with RumplerC[+ooc?] wMOUSCRON
3-40pm OK(2Lt PG Scott/2Lt FS Moller) name Miller?

6336   FE2b   20Sqn
+*EscRec combat with two-engined EA[+appeared hit:
another observer saw EA fall to ground & cr
wMOUSCRON] 7400' btwn 4am & 4-30am OK(2Lt JT
Kirton/Lt HF Billinge) also met Albatros ovMENIN &
Rumpler ovHALLUIN

This was the first certain combat victory for 20
Squadron. The Combat Report was only dated
"Feb", but an appended note refers to the 13th of
February, as does RFC Communiqué No. 30.

14th February

From the 8th of February the Germans launched a
number of minor attacks in the Ypres Salient to
divert attention from their impending assault on
Verdun. The fiercest of these occurred on the 14th,
when a small hill was taken on the north side of the
Ypres-Comines Canal. It was retaken on the 2nd of
March. During this fighting, the artillery work and
most of the air interception was done by 6

Squadron who carried out their registering of
enemy positions with a new system of co-ordinated
patrolling. Mist and high winds prevailed throughout these days.

15 February

Lt Albert Ball arrived in France and came on
strength of 13 Squadron RFC.

19 February

BE2c   4Sqn
**NB CAMBRAI A'dr bombed shed from 30' & shards
dam a'c OK(Capt JE Tennant)

BE2c   4Sqn
**NB CAMBRAI A'dr OK(Capt ED Horsfall) bombs
failed to release over a'dr, dropped later

These two machines carried out one of the earliest
night bombing raids. It was reasonably successful
and influenced headquarters to call for further such
attacks. The lack of resources resigned this duty to
a very minor position, however, and it was almost
three months before another was attempted. Night
flying practice was nevertheless increased.

5621   Vickers FB5   18Sqn
P gun fire shot down wr(Lt C Hart Collins **WIA/1AM
H Briggs **WIA**) left 8-35am, a'c shelled on ldg [Flak
claim: down nrCUINCHY]

20th February

25 Squadron arrived in Flanders on the 20th of
February. They were the second squadron to be
completely equipped with the FE2b pusher, which
was proving itself a sturdy and reliable aircraft. Its
excellent field of view from the nacelle, its speed
and strength and its ease of flying all lent
themselves to the air fighting of the period. Indeed,
it is often forgotten that the FE2b was a key front
line combat machine for more than a year and was
involved in a great deal of action (see Appendix II:
Losses on the Western Front 1914-1918 by
Machine Type). These same characteristics of
strength and straightforward flying qualities, in
particular when landing, were two valuable assets
much later in its operational life when it became a
night bombing and night reconnaissance machine.

Morane   1Sqn
+* saw Albatros & Aviatik? ovPOLYGON WOOD shot
up Albatros fr 100yd then chased Aviatik down 10-50am
OK(Capt RA Saunders), Albatros disappeared into
clouds

5069   Morane N   1Sqn
**P YPRES-COMINES combat with Aviatik 12000'-
7000' 2-40pm to 3-30pm OK(2Lt VS Strugnell) EA dived

fr 12000', seen low ovCOMINES, EA likely to be from FAb102b?

2054   BE2c   13Sqn
Esc combat with Fokker but seen diving smoking 4m sFINS **MIA(2Lt FAA Garlick **KIA**/Capt W Knox **KIA**) left 7-45am, a'c captured? [BE claim combat AIZECOURT-LE-BUS 8-45am Ltn G Leffers KEK.*Bertincourt*]

5476   Vickers FB5   18Sqn
P combat with EA, then AA ftl BULLY GRENAY wr **MIA(Lt M Henderson **WIA POW**/2Lt OJF Scholte **POW**)

3981   Nieuport   11 RNAS
+* combat with EA[+?des] NIEUPORT OK(FSLt RS Dallas)

21st February

THE BATTLE OF VERDUN: THE LESSONS FOR AIR STRATEGY

The battle of Verdun commenced on the 21st of February 1916. The German concentrations of its air weapon around that fortress gave a welcome respite to the Allied squadrons in the north. Although the accompanying chapter of the air war is outside the scope of this work its ramifications were profound and should be described.

The German Army Air Service planned a very substantial use of their air weapon to disrupt and eliminate French reconnaissance gathering. They had assembled one hundred and sixty-eight aircraft — twenty-one of these were Eindekkers and were expected to play an important part.

Over the winter, several new Kagohls (combat squadrons or battle groups) had been gradually assembled to bring together the best two-seater pilots and their machines. Five would be operational by March and each included six Kampfstaffeln (KASTAS: fighting sections). These stood ready to be moved to a required section of virtually any front in order to carry out bombing or indeed engage the enemy in the air if necessary.

At Verdun, Kagohls I and II were brought up and further strengthened. They were to bomb railway junctions and French airfields as well as forming an aggressive presence in the air. Ten Feldflieger Abteilungen were to turn their attention from photography to protection flights to exclude French aircraft from the battle area, whilst six Artillerieflieger Abteilungen were to co-operate with the guns. Finally, the twenty-one single-seat fighters, mostly Fokker and Pfalz E-types, were grouped into three Kampfeinsitzer Kommandos (KEKs) to carry out intensive fighter patrols in

support of the two-seaters. Until this time, these fighter commands had been integrated into Flieger Abteilungen, albeit that some of these, such as Nos. 32 and 62, were already specialising in the use of fighters. At Verdun the KEKs now became semi-permanent groups. They were named after their airfields and were initially at Avillers, Jametz, and Cunel.

The French began their defence of Verdun very under-prepared, and in the face of mounting losses an order was made on the 29th that brought in aircraft from elsewhere along the front. This concentrated six French fighter squadrons, mostly comprising Nieuports, and eight reconnaissance squadrons for the battle. It was decided that these would be operated in formations, the fighters undertaking offensive patrols of three or four aircraft actively seeking out enemy machines in order to destroy them. This aggressive policy immediately brought results, but at a cost, in that the French infantry at the face of battle was often left with virtually no tactical air cover.

The Fokkers in the area of the German Vth Army were themselves constituted into groups of as many as a dozen aircraft, but even in such numbers they were unable to suppress French intelligence gathering and artillery patrols in the way they had hoped. Many units were positioned far from the front, and operations were not always effective once ordered up because of a lack of intelligence about the enemy's movements. The next German response was to begin virtually continual "barrage" patrolling in an attempt to comprehensively deny the French access to the skies, but the effort simply dissipated the effectiveness of the Fokker. German armed two-seaters were gradually forced to assume the role, foregoing their bombing duties in order to carry out more patrolling and air fighting. Their work therefore supplemented that of the single-seaters, but to use the latter for more or less continuous patrol work over the battle field was found to have been misguided. The relatively poor performance of the Fokker as an aircraft was stretched to the limit in these conditions and its value was lost. The increased patrolling duties laid upon the two-seater machines also drew them off from more valuable work, notably losing their bombing capacity — by April the Kagohls were almost exclusively involved in the protection of the troops on the ground.

The lessons both sides learnt from these events led to another major step forward in air war planning and tactics.

Oswald Boelcke was amongst the pre-eminent German movers for change. He had requested that

his unit be moved closer to the battle and it was relocated from Jametz to Sivry, only seven miles from the front. He then had a system of forward observation and intelligence gathering instituted. With such developments the KEKs were able to conserve some of their strength and marshal their efforts where they were most effective: directly into combat. These improvements were adopted up and down the line with the formation of other KEKs, and had a further important consequence in that it brought about an ever stronger and more permanent concentration of fighter aircraft into their own discrete units. This would coalesce into the system of Jagdstaffeln in the autumn.

At the same time there had been close liaison between the Allies during the battle. The effectiveness of the French tactics of taking the fight to the enemy had not gone unnoticed by the British, whose generally offensive policy it reinforced. It would continue to take a heavy toll of casualties, but Trenchard was more convinced than ever that well directed aggressive patrols of fighters penetrating far over the lines would be the best means to strike at the enemy and free the skies for reconnaissance. By the time of the Somme Offensive the control of the air would have been regained and aircraft capable of carrying out these patrols would be in place.

5120	Morane LA	3Sqn

**AP AA ovLA BASSÉE rudder shot away ftl OK(2Lt FE Goodrich/2Lt CW Short)

5468	Vickers FB5	11Sqn

+*P combat with two-engined EA ovHANSART 9500' 11am OK(Capt LA Pattinson/Lt WB Moorhead)

	BE2c	15Sqn

Rec AA(2Lt FN Hudson **WIA/)head

2120	BE2c	15Sqn

+* combat with AlbatrosC[+dd,ooc] nMENIN 5pm OK(2Lt DK Johnstone/Cpl Cormack)

24th February

5142	Morane BB	1Sqn

**HAP DICKEBUSCH combat with Albatros eHOLLEBEKE 11000' ~11-55am OK(Maj GF Pretyman/Cpl R Mumford)

2801	BE2c	2Sqn

+*AP LOOS-BETHUNE-HULLUCH combat with Albatros 7000' 3pm OK(Capt Babington/Lt MacClintock) had dropped tinsel or paper just eBETHUNE, several hits seen

25th February

1737	BE2c	10Sqn

+*Phot BOIS DE BIEZ combat with LVG 9000'

12-50pm OK(2Lt HE vanGoethem/1AM Hooker)

26th February

5069	Morane N	1Sqn

**P combat with Aviatik BAILLEUL 9000' 2-15pm OK(Capt RA Saunders)

21 RFC aircraft also bombed Don Railway station.

29th February

5068	Morane N	1Sqn

+*P combat with Albatros MESSINES 10500' 10-45am OK(2Lt EP Plenty) EA lost to view

5119	Morane LA	1Sqn

+*ACoop YPRES-WESTROOSEBEKE combat with 4Aviatiks[+chased one, but then two more:tracers hit EA observer followed by smoke & flames fr engine & dive towards woods beyond PASSCHENDAELE] 12000'-5000' 10am to 10-35am OK(Capt RA Saunders/2Lt CB Joske) then 4th, EA"softened up" initially by Capt Powell 5Sqn FE8

1710	BE2c	2Sqn

AP AA ftl ldg ok(2Lt WSR Bloomfield NZ. **WIA/Capt SR Stammers OK) left 10-40am

2801	BE2c	2Sqn

+*Phot/AP combat with 2 Type-A's 8000' 10-30am OK(Capt Babington/Lt MacClintock) first hit & went down steeply, then chased other

5296	Bristol Scout C	2Sqn

+*P combat with Albatroses LENS-LA BASSÉE-BETHUNE 10000' 10-15am & 10-45am OK(Lt Wynne-Eyton)

7457	FE8	5Sqn

+*HAP combat with Aviatik & DFW 7-10000' 10-10am OK(Capt FJ Powell) (see Morane 5119 above)

1737	BE2c	10Sqn

+*HighP nBETHUNE-LA BASSÉE CANAL combat with Albatros MERVILLE[+EA prop seen to slow then chased down in dive towards BOIS DE BIEZ & cr o't 2m sMERVILLE: EA pilot wounded in leg, captured, **POW**] 8000' 10-50am to 11-10am OK(2Lt EW Leggatt/2Lt TS Howe) earlier combat with Albatros 6500'

4195	BE2c	16Sqn

+*HAP combat with Albatros ovYPRES 7500' 11-50am then AA OK(2Lt AR Tillie/2Lt HDW Wilson)

6338	FE2b	20Sqn

Rec combat with EA 7700' ftl ok nrMENIN **MIA(2Lt LA Newbold **POW**/2Lt HF Champion **POW**) a'c captured, to Holland 30.4.18 for duty, observer to UK 3.16? [? claim combat MENIN Vzfw Wass]

This crew was the first lost in action for 20 Squadron.

3981	Nieuport 11	RNAS

+* combat with LVG[+shot down] flooded area nrDIXMUDE 10-30am OK(FSLt HR Simms)

III Brigade of the Royal Flying Corps had been formed at the end of January in support of the Third Army in the area north of the Somme river. The army had been in this sector since the previous July, with 3rd Wing (Nos. 4, 8, and 11 Squadrons) attached to it. With the formation of the new brigade, 3rd Wing became its corps wing, and 12th Wing its army wing. When the Third Army was moved to the Arras sector at the end of February, to relieve the French Tenth Army, the III Brigade went with it. The newly created Fourth Army, under Sir Henry Rawlinson, thus took up the Somme front from Gommecourt to Curlu. III Brigade left behind the 3rd(Corps) Wing as a nucleus for the new IV Brigade to be formed for the Fourth Army and this brigade came into being on the 1st of April (see below). III Brigade was subsequently reconstituted so that by the summer fighting it comprised 12th Wing, now a corps unit, with Nos. 8, 12, and 13 Squadrons, and a new army wing, the 13th, with Nos. 11 and 23 Squadrons.

March 1916

1st March

March 1916 could be considered the beginning of the end of the Fokker's supremacy on the Western Front. It would see British concern extending even to its Parliament, where Noel Pemberton Billing MP would articulate many people's fears by describing the BE2s and other products of the Royal Aircraft Factory as "Fokker Fodder". On the other hand, it would also witness the widening active use of British machines capable of defeating it.

On the 1st of March the three Flights of No.1 Wing RNAS were formed into "A" and "B" Squadrons at St Pol when Dunkirk Headquarters was set up on the same day. "A" Squadron 1 Wing concentrated on reconnaissance, coastal patrols, and air fighting, and it would reform as No.1 Squadron RNAS once more on the 1st of December 1916, based at Furnes. "B" Squadron 1 Wing carried out spotting and reconnaissance work and became No.2 Squadron RNAS on the 5th of November 1916. The original No.2 Squadron RNAS, which has been encountered in 1915, had become No.2 Wing RNAS in June of that year and been transferred to the Dardanelles in August.

27 Squadron RFC arrived in France on this day equipped with the new Martinsyde G100 Scout. It soon began operational patrolling but the Martinsyde very quickly proved a poor fighter and

the unit took up more reconnaissance and photographic work. It eventually proved to be most suited to bombing and it was primarily used in this role. The type is discussed in later commentary.

2nd March

5142	Morane BB	1Sqn

**ACoop drove off 2 Aviatiks YPRES 3500-4000' 12-01pm OK(Capt RA Saunders/2Lt AF Organ)

5067	Morane N	3Sqn

+*EscRec ovDOUAI 1 Fokker came up then 4 more, dived on Fokker[+shot down in woods nrVALENCIENNES on fire] 12500' OK(Sgt TH Bayetto) Fokker chased down hit?, then escorted 2Str Morane & met two more groups Fokkers, total: nine Fokkers between 7-45am & 9-45am

5137	Morane BB	3Sqn

Rec combat with 5EA shot down VALENCIENNES EoL **MIA(Lt CW Palmer **POW DoW** ~29.3.16/Lt HF **Birdwood KIA**) left 7-40am, Imm9 [combat SOMAIN am Oblt M Immelmann FAb62]

2127	BE2c	6Sqn

*CB YPRES combat with Fokker in & out of clouds 3500' 12-20pm OK(2Lt GEH Fincham/2Lt G Price) Morane answered signal & saw off EA

5916	DH2	18Sqn

** combat with EA shot up dam OK(Capt JA Cunningham) left 9-30am NOEUX LES MINES-FIEFS-BETHUNE

3rd March

No.5 Wing RNAS was installed at Coudekerque by the 3rd of March. This had formed at Dover on the 31st of July 1915 taking over the Westgate Defence Flight.

5th March

2099	BE2c	9Sqn

EscRec combat with Fokker ftl dam(2Lt CW Seedhouse **WIA/)

6th March

Thirty-one RFC aircraft bombed railheads and billets at Carvin, without casualty.

8th March

5069	Morane N	1Sqn

+*P YPRES combat with 2 large EA chased EA towards COMINES 12000' 11-15am but engine failing OK(2Lt RP Turner)

4077	BE2c	16Sqn

+*Phot KEMMEL combat with Aviatik? 9400' 10-30am shot up prop hit dam OK(Lt LN Gould) hit but continued photography

9th March

5069   Morane N   1Sqn
**HAP combat with 10-37am shot down
seHOLLEBEKE **MIA**(2Lt RP Turner **KIA**) a'c
captured [?Morane claim nWYTSCHAETE, sYPRES
Ltn Patheiger/UntOff Groescher FAb 213]

4181   BE2c   6Sqn
**AReg combat with Fokker nrKRUISSTAAT-YPRES
ftl cr(Lt GEH Fincham **WIA KIA**/2Lt G Price **WIA**)
pilot killed in cr

6339   FE2b   20Sqn
**EscRec combat with EA wTOURNAI 8000' (Capt JR
Howett inj/Sgt T May **WIA**) left 9-45am [?claim: shot
down by Rumpler crew]

6356   FE2b   20Sqn
**EscRec combat with Fokker nrANNAPES 9-45am
steam seen coming from FE2b ftl nrLIGNY **MIA**(Lt LR
Heywood **POW**/2Lt DB Gayford **POW**) pilot to Holland
7.10.18, observer to Switzerland 24.4.18

12th March

Morane   1Sqn
** (Lt OM Moult **POW**?)

5089   Morane LA   1Sqn
+*P combat with Albatros eYPRES 7000' 8-30am
OK(Lt Saunders/FSgt TFB Carlisle)

5142   Morane BB   1Sqn
+*P combat with Aviatik & Albatros eYPRES 1-30pm
then again nrWESTROOSEBEKE 1-50pm OK(Capt
RA Saunders/2Lt CB Joske)

7457   FE8   5Sqn
+*P combat with Fokker[+EA diving until dense smoke
seen at 2000'] 3m nMOORSLEDE 7000' 12-20pm, then
attacked by Aviatik so unconfirmed final fate of EA
OK(Capt FJ Powell) EA first seen in se corner
HOUTHULST WOOD

5302   Bristol Scout C   16Sqn
**HAP combat with A-type then Fokker[+engine hit
then seen in vertical dive until glide & ldg ENGLOS
FORT-LILLE] 10000' 2pm OK(Capt WT Allcock) AA
firing all the way down

13th March

4678   Bristol Scout C   4Sqn
**HAP mg rifle fire ovLIGA combat? 11-45am cr
nrSERRE **MIA**(Maj VA Barrington-Kennett **KIA**)
Imm10 [EA claim combat SERRE ~11-30am Oblt M
Immelmann FAb62]

4151   BE2c   8Sqn
**EscRec combat with Fokker shot up 2-53pm spiralled
down ftl wINCHY Sh57.C.d.5. **MIA**(2Lt MAJ Orde
WIA POW/1AM P Shaw **POW**) Fokker also landed, all
seen by BE2c 4180: see entry below, pilot to Switzerland
27.12.17 ["BE" claim combat nCAMBRAI &
BOURLON Ltn R Berthold KEK.*Vaux*]

4180   BE2c   8Sqn
+*Rec MOEUVRES-FONTAINE combat with 3
Fokkers 7000' 2-55pm OK(Capt Morton/Lt Robinson)
saw BE2c 4151 spiral down chased by two Fokkers, one
of whom followed, and both landed in field together

4197   BE2c   8Sqn
**EscRec AA spin cr VIS-EN-ARTOIS Sh51B.o.21.(Lt
GDJ Grune **KIA**/2Lt BE Glover **KIA**) AIR1/967/204/5/
1097 gives AA hit RH wing [EA claim combat PELVES
wBEAUMONT 5-40pm Oblt M Immelmann FAb62]

2575   BE2c   16Sqn
**Phot combat with C-type near Sh36NW N.12. 7500'
1pm to 1-20pm OK(2Lt RA Logan/Lt A Nesbitt)

14th March

5107   Morane LA   1Sqn
**Phot combat with 3 Fokkers mg LA CLYTTE 9-55am?
wr Sh28 N.1.c.4.5(Capt RA Saunders **WIA DoW**)
stomach, 11-15am?, 2Lt Strugnell was witness: saw Capt
Saunders hit EA: smoke was seen but it didn't dive. At
same time Saunders' Morane dived steeply but in control,
finally ldg on left wing

5128   Morane LA   3Sqn
AP dhAA VIMY spin broke up **MIA(Lt DPB Taylor
KIA) left 12-20pm

4404   BE2c   13Sqn
**EscRec AA below: heavy dam then followed by combat
with Fokker ftl cr nrLE TOURET wr(Lt CJ? van
Nostrand OK/1AM T Parkes **KIA**) left 10am, Parkes was
hit after his mg had been hit & put out of action

4153   BE2c   15Sqn
**EscRec combat with Fokker ovACHIET LE GRAND
10-40am **MIA**(2Lt JC Cunningham **KIA**/1AM JW
Newton **KIA**) FAb32 [combat sBAPAUME 11-15am Ltn
G Leffers FAb32 KEK.*Bertincourt*]

4162   BE2c   16Sqn
+*AReg combat with B-type ovSh36 I.29.c.8.8. 8000'
11-20am OK(2Lt Petit/2Lt King)

6332   FE2b   20Sqn
+*Rec combats with 2 Fokkers & another EA
ovROULERS 7000' 8am OK(2Lt NG McNaughton/2Lt
G Chancellor)

6339   FE2b   20Sqn
**EscRec THOUROUT-ROULERS combat with 3
Fokkers 8300' 8am, then observer was hit by shrapnel but
shot up Fokker well (Capt JR Howett OK/Lt HF Billinge
WIA)eye, Fokker ascended from GITS A'dr, then
observer was hit, long skirmish, shot up including a head
on clash: "we missed colliding by not more than 5-10'"

6359   FE2b   20Sqn
+*EscRec combats with 2 Fokkers & other EA
ovROULERS 7000' 8am OK(2Lt RJ Morton/Cpl May)

16th March

23 Squadron RFC arrived in France on the 16th of

March. It would become fully equipped with FE2bs but at first it also flew a few Martinsydes. It would carry out fighter-reconnaissance work and was to become heavily involved in offensive patrolling through the autumn.

5309   Bristol Scout C   7Sqn
+*HAP combat with LVG ARMENTIÈRES 9000′ 10-05am but tracers jammed gun OK(Capt JC Quinnell)

6353   FE2b   23Sqn
**Travel from UK, mg ovBLAGNY fuel tank hit ftl ARRAS Race Course OK(Lt SHB Hanis/2Lt EB Harvey) had met clouds ovFRUGES, dh from shell when on ground 4-10pm, a'c destroyed

18th March

4077   BE2c   16Sqn
+*RecP combat with 3Aviatiks[+last EA dived: HA reported brought down by mg after diving steeply to 200′ cr] ovRADIGHEM 6000′ 4-45pm, then AA on return OK(Lt FH Thayre/Lt CR Davidson Can.?)

6328   FE2b   20Sqn
**Rec combat with Fokker fuel tank shot up nrYPRES ftl Sh28 I.26.c.38. OK(Lt RH Anderson/Capt EW Forbes) left 9-30am

6332   FE2b   20Sqn
+*Central Rec combats with 3EA ovMENIN 9000′ 11-10am OK(2Lt NG McNaughton/1AM Talbot) saw 1FE forced down (6328)

19th March

5089   Morane LA   1Sqn
+*EscAOb OOSTAVERNE combat with Albatros [+ ?EA badly hit as it turned & then did heavy ss & dive ooc towards 28.P.8] 6500′ 10-53am OK(FSgt TFB Carlisle/Lt JA McKelvie)

20th March

A large bombing raid was carried out against the German floatplane base at Zeebrugge, involving nineteen British, nineteen French, and sixteen Belgian aircraft.

3621   Henri Farman   5 Wing RNAS
Coudekerque **B HOUTTAVE A'dr ZEEBRUGGE OK(FSLt SJ Woolley)

3632   Henri Farman   5 Wing RNAS
Coudekerque **B HOUTTAVE A'dr ZEEBRUGGE then chased by EA but flew out to sea & returned ok OK(FSLt AM Hughes)

8346   Short 184   HMS Vindex
**B ZEEBRUGGE Raid OK(FLt HF Towler/SLt EG Hopcroft)

5119   Morane LA   1Sqn
+*P CASSEL-POPERINGHE combat with Aviatik 9500′-4500′ 6-50am to 7-05am OK(2Lt TA Oliver/2Lt DA Carruthers)

5917   DH2   5Sqn
+*P saw off 2 EAs ovYPRES 11000′ 5pm OK(2Lt J Latta) inconclusive

2612   BE2c   16Sqn
+*P combat with Scout? ovFORÊT DE NIEPPE 8500′ 7-30am OK(2Lt PGA Harvey/1AM Milne)

23rd March

8346   Short 184   HMS Vindex
**B HOYER Airship Raid shot up dam OK(FLt HF Towler/SLt EG Hopcroft)

25th March

A Bristol Scout fitted with interrupter gear and a machine-gun capable of firing through the propeller arc arrived in France for assessment on the 25th. It was No. 5313 and after being used by 12 Squadron it subsequently went to 11 Squadron. It was the first machine so adapted to fly in active service with the RFC.

29 Squadron arrived in France on this day equipped with DH2 single-seat fighters.

5930   DH2   24Sqn
**ArmyP left 7-30am met very strong westerly wind ftl EoL MIA(2Lt O Lerwill POW) pilot to Holland 30.4.18

Lt Lerwill's capture was 24 Squadron's first casualty, and the first loss of a production DH2 on active duty. The aircraft was captured undamaged in enemy lines.

8153   Sopwith Baby   HMS Vindex
**B HOYER Airship Base ftl MIA(FSLt JF Hay POW) to Holland 19.4.18

8040   Short 184   RNAS
**B HOYER Airship Sheds shot down off BELGIUM(FLt GH Reid POW/CPO Mullins POW) a'c captured, pilot to Holland 27.6.18 [?possible "English 3Str" claim Ltn Schurer/Ltn Ratazzi]

8383   Short 184   RNAS
**B HOYER Airship Raid ftl MIA(FSLt CG Knight POW/Md SE Hoblyn POW) Hoblyn to Holland 30.4.18 [?possible claim Ltn Rogge/Ltn Lowe]

29th March

4105   BE2c   13Sqn
+*AOb combat with 2 Albatros ovVIMY 5000′ 10am shot up dam OK(2Lt GA Parker/2Lt SA Villiers) dived on first then shot up by second during drum change: behind seat was hit, etc

5215   FE2b   23Sqn
** known to have been shot up in combat, crew not yet known

6352   FE2b   23Sqn
**EscRec combat with EA, shot down in controlled spiral ovQUEANT MIA(2Lt FG Pinder WIA POW/2Lt EA Halford POW) a'c captured, pilot to Switzerland 9.12.17,

observer to Holland 7.10.18, Imm12 [combat
eBAPAUME-BETHINCOURT(Bertincourt?) 10am
Oblt M Immelmann FAb62]

This crew was the first lost in action by 23
Squadron.

6364   FE2b   23Sqn
+*Esc shot up Fokker from below ovQUEANT 8200'
10-15am then shot up dam OK(Lt SHB Harris/2Lt LC
Powell) saw FE2b previously attacked by Fokker
spiralling down in control?

30th March

5157   Morane BB   1Sqn
+*Esc to Sh28 Sq. O & U, combat with 3 Albatros [+
?first EA went home, second badly hit, third shot up]
10000' ~10-30am OK(FSgt TFB Carlisle/Lt JA
McKelvie)

1778   BE2c   8Sqn
+*Rec combat with Fokker VILLIERS 7600' 11-30am
OK(Lt A Stanley-Clarke/1AM Evans) inconclusive

2605   BE2c   8Sqn
**EscRec combat with Fokker shot down nrMONCHY-
AU-BOIS 11-15am MIA(Lt TC Wilson WIA POW/
1AM A Walker KIA) [?"BE" claim combat
BANCOURT- BAPAUME Ltn Schmedes/Ltn Lehman
FAb32]

4136   BE2c   8Sqn
+*Esc combat with Fokker VILLIERS 7500' 11-30am
OK(2Lt A Goodfellow/Lt Stevens) inconclusive

5471   Vickers FB5   11Sqn
**Phot AA in flames? down FAMPOUX-MONCHY LE
PREUX MIA(2Lt JS Castle WIA POW/2AM ERA
Coleman POW) left 8-45am, pilot to Holland 30.4.18
["Vickers" claims all with combats nWANCOURT: Ltn
M Müzer Fab5b (FAb62?); Oblt Wimmer FAb5; Oblt
Kraft FAb5b]

4116   BE2c   15Sqn
**Phot combat with EA nrQUESNOY FARM 11am? cr
MIA(2Lt GJL Welsford KIA/Lt WJ Joyce WIA POW)
left 9-30am, observer to Holland 30.4.18 Imm13 [combat
ABLAINZEVELLE 10-15am driven down wSERRE?
Oblt M Immelmann FAb62]

31st March

5492   FB5   11Sqn
+*P combat with Aviatik ovSOUCHEZ 9500' 9-45am
OK(2Lt JW Toone/Lt HB Milling) EA had rings on side,
simulating cockade

7665   FB9   11Sqn
**P combat with Aviatik[+?appeared hit as did not fire
back: dived & was chased down to 2500', lost sight of
almost on ground] ovVILLERS AU BOIS 10500'
9-45am OK(Capt HVC deCrespigny/2Lt JLMdeC
Hughes-Chamberlain)

2290   RE7   21Sqn

**Rec AA EoL on fire ftl cr ldg burnt(Capt DC Ware
WIA)

This was the first casualty for 21 Squadron.

6342   FE2b   25Sqn
**EscRec combat with Fokker ovGHELUWE shot up(Lt
Norris OK/Capt H Seagrave **WIA**)leg

This was the first casualty for 25 Squadron.

Important Note:

INCLUSION OF
AIR COMBAT DATA

*This book is first and foremost about air casualties.
Through the first eighteen months of the war, which have
now been covered, the scale of air fighting was such that a
very complete record of those involved has been possible. For
instance, virtually every recorded air combat has been
described up until now, in addition to all the casualties in
action. This structure consciously changes at this point,
however, for practical reasons.*

*As the ground war escalated into the summer battle of
the Somme, the amount of air fighting also became vastly
greater. To keep recording these events comprehensively is
beyond the scope of this work and so, from this point
onwards, it will concentrate on its central purpose of
recording those British airmen and machines shot down in
fighting. The wider picture of air fighting will not be
ignored, however — important combats and achievements
of hundreds of other airmen will be recorded where they
throw light and interest on the developing air war. Whilst
these are selective, they will amount to several hundred
additional entries. They will cover air fighting of virtually
all Commonwealth aces; combat which saw a squadron or
individual achieving early victories, or perhaps saw an
aircraft type finding its mettle or beginning to lose its edge.
The structure of the book is discussed in more detail in the
introduction.*

April 1916

THE EXPANSION OF
THE ROYAL FLYING CORPS

The three or four months preceding the Somme
Offensive saw the operational introduction of
Allied aircraft types which would regain a clear air
superiority for their armies. The arrival of new
fighter units armed specifically with the new pusher
fighters are noted throughout as they occurred.
Long before Verdun had run its full course, preparations for the growth of the RFC had begun in
earnest, and the scope of the expansion undertaken

was remarkable. Between the battles of Loos and the Somme the following squadrons arrived in France: No.13 (BE2cs) 19th October 1915; No.18 (Vickers Fighters) 19th November; No.9 (BE2cs) 20th December; No.15 (BE2cs) 23rd December; No.20 (FE2bs) and No.21 (RE7s) both on 23rd January 1916; No.24 (DH2s) 7th February; No.25 (FE2bs) 20th February; No.27 (Martinsyde G100s) 1st March; No.23 (FE2bs) 16th March; No.29 (DH2s) 25th March; No.22 (FE2bs) 1st April; No.70 (Sopwith Strutters) had Flights appearing on the 24th May, 29th June, and 30th July; No.32 (DH2s) and No.60 (Moranes) May 28th. By the end of June, in total, the RFC had twenty-seven squadrons in France, seven of them equipped with new DH2 and FE2b fighter pushers. It was the operational appearance of these machines in particular which made possible the change in approach that Verdun had signalled.

From early April onwards these aircraft could operate with increasing freedom and effect, and were clearly the match and more for the Fokker. The aggressive patrols now being flown would typically fly deep behind the enemy lines so as to have the sun behind them in the morning, and to cut off retreat to the east. There they would search for and attack any German aircraft which appeared, and so great was the concentration of fighters destined for this front that the effectiveness of these tactics would be considerable. The BE2cs were able to redouble their vital intelligence gathering in increasingly secure skies. One can see the losses of these aircraft falling in the casualty listings. Since the Fokker fighter had reached the Western Front the BE2c had been the main target of their attentions. Combats between fighters had still been relatively rare. This situation now began to change as the German fighters were consciously hunted down. In March the RFC had also begun to receive the first examples of the French Nieuport Scout, passed on to them by the RNAS, no doubt at some sacrifice. These were Nieuport 16s, and in the coming weeks the type was to become fully active with 1 and 11 Squadrons. They were to prove among the best Allied aircraft of the period. It was powered with the larger 110hp Le Rhône engine and had a forward firing Lewis gun fixed on the top plane above the cockpit, which could be fired by the means of a Bowden cable.

April also saw the appearance in France of a new two-seater tractor biplane called the Sopwith One and a Half Strutter. It came on strength of No.5 Wing RNAS at Coudekerque. The performance of this aircraft was a revelation, and it was chosen to be the first production type to be fitted with inter-rupter gear so that it could fire through the arc of its propeller. Its impact was so great, in fact, that the new RFC Squadron, No.70, was formed in England to train up on the new type using machines directly transferred from the RNAS for the purpose.

By this time, the removal of the single-seater fighters of the corps wings for amalgamation into army wing squadrons was also well under way. The single-seater pilots naturally went with them, and inevitably this concentration of talent threw up some personalities of note. The first British pilots that we now consider great aces began to emerge at this time. Albert Ball was one such flyer, and his early progress is followed in the lists. In May and June he would be flying his Nieuport with 11 Squadron, developing the techniques and tactics with which he would soon begin to shoot down many of the enemy.

1st April

Very bad weather continued in the Ypres sector as April opened. Small, relatively surgical skirmishes were still occurring as both sides attempted to straighten out the line in places. 5 and 6 Squadrons continued their work there.

22 Squadron RFC arrived in France with FE2bs on the 1st. It would fly this type, or its more powerful variant, the FE2d, until July 1917. In spite of the growing limitations this equipment would impose on the unit it was to acquire a great reputation for its fighting qualities. It would re-equip at that time with Bristol Fighters.

IV Brigade Royal Flying Corps was formed on the 1st of April to support the Fourth Army in the Somme sector. It comprised 3rd(Corps) Wing (now Nos. 3, 4, 9, and 15 Squadrons) and 14th (Army) Wing (Nos. 22 and 24 Squadrons). The units of 3rd Wing would therefore be given most of the responsibility for the corps work leading up to and during the battle of the Somme.

2129   BE2c   5Sqn
P shot down HOLLEBEKE MIA(Lt FN Grimwade **WIA POW/Lt HA Frost **WIA POW**) left 2-34pm, pilot to Switzerland 6.6.17, observer to UK 11/13.9.17

**   BE2c?   7Sqn**
**Phot (/2Lt Bramwell WIA)slight

4138   BE2c   8Sqn
** AA neADINFER WOOD shot up but repairable OK(Lt RS Lucy/AM Clark)

2683   BE2d   10Sqn
+*HighP combat with Albatros[+?driven down in nose-dive nLA BASSÉE Canal, disappeared into clouds 4000"] LA BASSÉE-DON 10000' 8-15am OK(Capt PEL

Gethin/Capt Scott) later combat with Albatros wLENS 9am

5079   Vickers FB5   11Sqn
+*P attacked KB then combat with LVG[+?driven down: suddenly dived, chased down & lost sight of] ovBOYELLES 6000′ 8-15am OK(2Lt WC Mortimer-Phelan/Cpl GJ Morton)

5316   Bristol Scout C   13Sqn
+*P dived on and saw off 2 LVG wLENS 9000′ 10am OK(Capt Cooper)

2nd April

7665   Vickers FB9   11Sqn
**P combat with 5HA controls shot up ooc 1000′ ftl LE HAMEAU wr OK(Capt HVC deCrespigny/2Lt JLMdeC Hughes-Chamberlain) "saved by perfect rigging"

5924   DH2   24Sqn
+*OP combat with 2Str Albatros[+dived & chased down, ftl] nALBERT 9000′ 6-50am shot up OK(2Lt DM Tidmarsh) single Lewis, dived to assist Sibley, shared with 5948

5948   DH2   24Sqn
+*OP combat with 2Str Albatros[+dived & chased down, ftl] nALBERT 9000′ 6-50am shot up OK(2Lt SJ Sibley) two fixed Lewis guns, first spotted half mile sBAIZIEUX and was first to attack, AA report that EA came down between GRANDCOURT-RIVER ANCRE, shared with 5924

These two pilots shared the first DH2 victory in air combat, probably over a crew from FAb263.

5079   Vickers FB5   11Sqn
+*P combat with Albatros MONCHY AU BOIS 5000′ 11-20am OK(Maj TO'B Hubbard/2Lt AJ Insall) EA had gun jam & last seen diving

8th April

The first Fokker Eindekker forced to land in Allied territory came down this day. It was an EIII, E210/15, and was salvaged intact and taken for assessment.

9th April

5132   Morane LA   1Sqn
ARec dh AA eWYTSCHAETE 7000′ tail off 4000′ 11-30am(LtCol DS Lewis DSO **KIA/Capt AWG Gale DSO **KIA**) 10.4?, unsalvable

BE2c?   5Sqn
** AA shell(/Capt IAJ Duff **WIA**)

1737   BE2c   10Sqn
+*Phot LA BASSÉE-DOUAI combat with Albatros 8000′ 10-45am to 11-10am OK(2Lt EW Leggatt/1AM Hooker) inconclusive?

10th April

5472   Vickers FB5   11Sqn
+*Phot combat with LVG[+EA observer hit: started steep dive, driven down] ovBAILLEUL 6000′ 4-30pm OK(Capt HA Cooper/2Lt HC Vickery)

11th April

The first aircraft of No. 4 Wing RNAS arrived at Petite Synthe on the 11th of April. These were to be mustered into two squadrons, "A" and "B", and their equipment included two-seater Nieuports, Caudron GIVs, and an Avro 504C.

13th April

Poor weather from the 13th until the 16th of April.

16th April

2097   BE2c   9Sqn
AOb combat with EA shot down in flames eMARICOURT EoL A.18.d at 10-15am **MIA(2Lt WS Earle **KIA**/2Lt CWP Selby **WIA POW**) to Switzerland 24.12.16, to UK 11.9.17 [combat sMAUREPAS Ltn R Berthold KEK.*Vaux*]

Vickers FB5?   11Sqn
** AA(/2Lt HC Vickery **WIA**)slight

BE2c   15Sqn
*AOb shrapnel(Lt EGE Donaldson **WIA**/)

6344   FE2b   25Sqn
**P LA BASSÉE AA shot up dam, returned 1-05pm OK(Lt CJ Hart/Cpl JH Waller) left 5-01am

9117   Caudron GIV   Coudekerque
**delivery, AA hit WESTENDE then combat with Fokker ftl OOST DUNKIRK OK(FSLt R Souray)

17th April

Poor weather from the 17th until the 19th of April.

21st April

2625   BE2c   13Sqn
+*AP combat with 2 A-types & 1 B-type ARRAS-LENS 9500′-10000′ 7am to 8am OK(2Lt GA Parker/2Lt Joel)

2625   BE2c   13Sqn
+*AOb headed off A-type ovARRAS 12000′ 10am OK(2Lt GA Parker/2Lt SA Villiers)

6332   FE2b   20Sqn
EscRec combat with 2HA ovZONNEBEKE(2Lt NG McNaughton **WIA/1AM S Catton OK)

6361   FE2b   20Sqn
**EscRec combat with 2HAs, engine failing? ftl YPRES RACE COURSE Sh28 I.20.c.2.5. OK(Capt CEH James/ 2Lt GA Exley)

5929   DH2   24Sqn
**? shell through nacelle OK(2Lt DM Tidmarsh)

22nd April

Flying mostly rained off.

8382	Short 184	Dunkirk Seaplane Stn

** shot up wings dam

23rd April

5079	Vickers FB5	11Sqn

**Phot combat with EA ovARRAS, FAMPOUX?
MIA(2Lt WC Mortimer-Phelan POW/2Lt NAG? Scott-
Brown POW) initials W?, left 8-45am and then failed to
rendezvous, pilot to Holland 30.4.18 Imm14 [combat
MONCHY-LE-PREUX am Oblt M Immelmann
FAb62]

5210	FE2b	25Sqn

**P combat with EA 11-30am ESTAIRES AA 6000'(Lt
WE Collison OK/2AM GF Atwell KIA) [combat
nrESTAIRES Ltn M Mülzer FAb62]

3981	Nieuport 11	RNAS

+* combat with EA 2Str[+?des] WESTENDE-
MIDDELKERKE 4-35am shot up dam OK(FSLt RS
Dallas)

3213	Breguet de Chase	5 Wing RNAS

**B OSTENDE A'dr shot up dam OK(FSLt CR
Blagrove)

Eight RNAS machines bombed Mariakerke Aerodrome, west of Ostende.

24th April

2683	BE2d	10Sqn

+*AReg DOUVRIN-MARQUILLIES-FOURNES
drove off 6EA[+?possibly 1 driven down] 7-30am to
9-30am OK(Capt PEL Gethin/2Lt HM Parsons)

This was only one of very many of combats this
day.

25th April

8140	Sopwith Baby	HMS *Cantatrice*

**AZep ftl sea 40m off ditched saved(FSLt SG Beare
INT) interned Holland

	BE2c	15Sqn

**Rec discovered Third Line trench system from
ABLAINZEVELLE-IRLES-LE SARS-FLERS OK(Lt
AB Adams/2Lt CR Robbins) escorting BE2cs and 24Sqn
DH2s saw off attacking Fokkers

It was this reconnaissance which brought the
earliest news of the formidable defences Germany
was constructing behind the Somme front.

26th April

2119	BE2c	10Sqn

**AReg AA ovFROMELLES shot down 1-55pm dam
but repairable (Capt? RG Gould OK/2Lt J Milner KIA)
rank Lt? Gould

4200	BE2c	13Sqn

+*AOb LENS-MERICOURT-FRESNOY-OPPY met
EA five times 11am to 12pm OK(2Lt GA Parker/2Lt SA
Villiers)

4105	BE2c	13Sqn

+*Rec combat with 2 Fokkers CAMBRAI-
MASNIÈRES-ARRAS 9000' 12-30pm OK(2Lt FCA
Wright/2AM Edwards)

4173	BE2c	13Sqn

+*Rec combat with Fokker[+?appeared hit: went down
steeply but other EA about] 10m eARRAS 9000' 12-50pm
OK(2Lt Hodgson/1AM N Casty) EA dived from above

5232	FE2b	18Sqn

**PhotAP combat with Fokker Sh36b.w.11. mg ftl(2Lt JC
Callaghan OK/2Lt J Mitchell WIA)

27th April

A116	Nieuport 16	1Sqn

+*HAP combat with Albatros ovMESSINES 13000'
9-30am OK(Lt EP Plenty) EA first seen ovNEUVE
EGLISE

A118	Nieuport 16	1Sqn

**HAP combat with Albatros[+?fuselage seen
hit:probably driven down] BAILLEUL-Lines 6000'
4pm? shot up dam blinded by splinters but ldg ok(2Lt CE
Foggin WIA) time am?

These were the first combats reported by RFC
Nieuport pilots, and Foggin's wounding was
therefore the first casualty in the type.

29th April

6332	FE2b	20Sqn

**EscPhot combat with Fokker ftl nrPOPERINGHE cr
fire destroyed (2Lt RD Sampson WIA/1AM S Catton
KIA)

5209	FE2b	25Sqn

+* combat with Fokker[+des] HULLUCH-LA BASSÉE
11-105am OK(2Lt.Lord Doune/2Lt RU Walker)

30th April

A116	Nieuport 16	1Sqn

+*P combats with 2 Aviatiks HOUTHEM 12000' 5am
to 5-40am OK(FSgt TFB Carlisle) separate combats,
tracers seen hit fuselage & dive. Carlisle complained that
with more than the maximum 47 bullet burst available
that both would have been shot down: the EA seemed to
know drum was finished so opened fire.

7457	FE8	5Sqn

**P shot up dam(2Lt RK Shives WIA)

This was the first casualty involving the FE8
pusher in action.

A117	Nieuport 16	11Sqn

+*P ARRAS combat with Albatros[+shot down]
ECURIE-DOUAI 9000' 6-40am OK(Capt LA

Pattinson) EA was chasing BE2c, III Bgde AA report: EA seen ldg ooc 6-30am Sh51B B.6. after attack by British Nieuport

This was the first confirmed RFC Nieuport Scout victory.

6345   FE2b   23Sqn
Phot AA AYETTE dam(Lt SHB Harris **WIA/Lt AN Solly OK)

5965   DH2   24Sqn
+*EscFE's combat with Fokker[+des] ovBAPAUME OK(2Lt DM Tidmarsh) described as "F-type" on Combat Report. Fokker apparently dived so steeply in attack that it crashed ooc onto roof of building, without Tidmarsh firing a shot

May 1916

3rd May

1729   BE2c   2Sqn
**AReg AIX NOULETTE engine on fire 3500', from mg?, ftl and made cool safe ldg OK(2Lt RJ Mounsey/Lt GR Moser) a'c shelled on ground

4th May

4109   BE2c   7Sqn
AReg combat with Fokker shot down in flames ePLOEGSTEERT WOOD(2Lt EG Ryckman **KIA/2Lt JR Dennistoun **KIA**) left 2-10pm, crew jumped [combat sWARNETON Vzfw W Frankl KEK.*Vaux*]

5966   DH2   24Sqn
+*OP attacked 2Str[+ftl but cr o't] low down nrCLERY 9am then gun problems ftl but took off again & made WoL OK(2Lt SE Cowan) fired on EA from 50yds

5212   FE2b   25Sqn
**P FROMELLES rad shot up ftl dam OK(2Lt H Dixon/Lt ER Davis)

8412   BE2c   4 Wing RNAS
B MARIAKERKE A'dr engine failed ftl(FSLt RE Greensmith **INT) interned Holland

9118   Caudron GIV   5 Wing RNAS
B MARIAKERKE A'dr forced to return ftl **MIA(FSlt KM van Allen **POW DoW** 11.5.16)

5th May

A126   Nieuport 16   11Sqn
+* combat with Fokker ovSOUCHEZ 10000' 11-10am but going too fast OK(Capt HVC deCrespigny)

8904   Nieuport 12   1 Wing RNAS
** combat with EA shot down cr sea(FSLt HR Simms **KIA**/SLt CJA Mullens **KIA**) [combat Ltn E Bönisch 1SS]

6th May

Poor weather set in from the 6th to the 10th of May.

11th May

2748   BE2c   16Sqn
AReg AA sARMENTIÈRES 4000' ftl by observer 300yards WoL(Capt AR Tillie **KIA/2Lt JG Howell OK) a'c shelled

16th May

5312   Bristol Scout C 11Sqn
+*P combat with Albatros A-type[+?dived on EA from 12000' & chased EA down: EA turned upside down at 2000' but engine was missing so pulled off] ovGIVENCHY 5000' 8-45am OK(2Lt A Ball)

This unconfirmed but likely combat victory was Albert Ball's first action since arriving with 11 Squadron, although it is likely that this machine was fitted with interrupter gear to enable fire through the propeller arc. According to the Combat Report it was not made in Bristol Scout C No. 5313 as some sources give.

5301   Bristol Scout C 11Sqn
P seen going south 5-30pm nrBERLES? shot down **MIA(2Lt MM Mowatt **POW DoW**) Imm15 [combat IZEL ~5pm Oblt M Immelmann FAb62]

2026   BE2c   12Sqn
+*P combat with Fokker 2m nARRAS 7000' 6-45pm to 7pm shot up? cr ldg OK(Capt Rowell/Lt Turner) Fokker attacking BEs: see BE2c 4105

4105   BE2c   13Sqn
** AA combat with Fokker shot up ftl ok 700yd nANZIN ST AUBIN(2Lt FCA Wright **WIA**/Capt GB Lucas **DoW**) AA battery reported BE2c ldg L.6.b.

6359   FE2b   20Sqn
EscRec combat with EA YPRES ldg by observer, cr wr (Lt E Trafford-Jones **KIA/Capt EW Forbes **WIA**)

6341   FE2b   25Sqn
EscRec AA then combat with 4EA shot down FOURNES **MIA(Capt D Grinell-Milne **POW**/Cpl D McMaster **POW**) left 7-55am, a'c captured, pilot to Holland 30.4.18

17th May

5238   FE2b   25Sqn
P 6-30am LA BASSÉE CANAL combat with EA (Capt W Milne **WIA/2Lt ER Davis OK)

18th May

5163   Morane BB   1Sqn
**P AA engine dam(2Lt TMB Newton/Lt DA Carruthers)

A116   Nieuport 16   1Sqn
+*P combats with 2 Aviatiks[+3rd drum at 50yds hit EA: fell in vertical dive Sh20 V.20.2, destroyed] sHOUTHULST WOOD 10000' 10-40am to 10-50am shot up dam OK(FSgt TFB Carlisle)

4160   BE2c   5Sqn
+*P combat with Fokker[+got very close: believed to be shot down ooc] YPRES SALIENT 11500' 3-50pm shot up dam OK(2Lt FGS Williams/Cpl Harvey)

19th May

5173   Nieuport 16   11Sqn
+*ArmyP shot up Scout ovVIMY 12000' 12pm OK(Capt HA Cooper) closest range was 300yd

A117   Nieuport 16   11Sqn
+*P ARRAS combat with 3 type-As SOUASTRE-ARMENTIÈRES 13-9000' 4-30am to 5am OK(Capt LA Pattinson) "showed a wonderful turn of speed and climb, the Nieuport having little advantage in this respect.They also appeared to be able to fire nearly all around . . ."

7280   Mart G100   23Sqn
+*P combat with 3 Type-Bs wARRAS 9000' 5am OK(2Lt AK Tylee) EA hit nrSOUCHEZ but carried on ok

20th May

2731   BE2c   12Sqn
+*P combat with Fokker[+fell to ground & cr upside down 5m s-seBEAUMETZ, crew had fallen out] 9200' 9-30am OK(Lt Farrow/2Lt Carden) nearby FE dived on EA, then attacked it when it reached their level, Casualty Report note: "also Adam's claim?" refers to 23Sqn FE2b 6354

6351   FE2b   23Sqn
+*P combat with Aviatik[+?des: cr trees 3m eneADINFER WOOD] 9-5000' 9-30am OK(2Lt DC Cloete/Cpl P Havens) saw Adams get within 20yds, & also saw 12Sqn BE2c 2731

6354   FE2b   23Sqn
+*P combat with Aviatik[+?des: after second drum EA nose-dived then cr trees 3m eneADINFER WOOD] 9-5000' 9-30am shot up: almost had fuel tank hit OK(Capt RN Adams/1AM DAR Chapman) & see 12Sqn BE2c 2731 [German crew from FAb4]

This combat saw 23 Squadron achieve its first certain victory.

7278   Martinsyde G100   27Sqn
**P combat with Roland Sh36 s.16.C.D., ftl ooc LORGIES EoL MIA(2Lt MD Basden KIA)a'c shelled, killed by shells?

Basden was the first combat casualty for 27 Squadron on Martinsyde single-seaters. Other squadrons had the type in small numbers, but only this unit was fully equipped with them. It was designed as a fighter reconnaissance aircraft, but although it achieved some early successes in combat, they were not sustained. Its rather poor manoeuvrability and performance saw it resigned to bombing duties by the time of the Somme offensive. Even in these circumstances, a heavy toll of its pilots continued.

3993   Nieuport 11   1 Wing RNAS
+* combat with EA Seaplane[+shot down sunk] 4m off BLANKENBERGHE 7am OK(FSLt RS Dallas)

21st May

The German attack on the Vimy Ridge opened this day, the brunt being taken by IV Corps. 18 Squadron artillery machines were mostly involved in the air work.

           FE2b   20Sqn
** combat with 2EA shot up(Lt AH Francis WIA/)

5206   FE2b   20Sqn
**EscRec combat with 2EA? seen ldg ZANDVOORDE EoL MIA(Capt CEH James POW/Lt HLC Aked POW) observer to Holland 30.4.18 [combat HOUTHEM Ltn W Frankl KEK.Vaux]

3992   Nieuport 11   1 Wing RNAS
St Pol +* combat with two 2Strs[+?ooc] off NIEUPORT 2pm OK(FSLt RH Mulock) had another victory earlier in the day.

22nd May

Hazy weather conditions around Vimy in the next few days limited air operations on both sides.

5173   Nieuport 16   11Sqn
+*P combat with Albatros A-type ovACHEVILLE 10000' 8-40am OK(2Lt A Ball) inconclusive

23rd May

A letter written at this time by Gen Sir Henry Rawlinson outlined the conviction that the Fokker was finally being matched by the DH2s accompanying reconnaissance operations. Although they had been met by several aggressive Fokkers early in the month, three of these had been successfully driven down. He continued, "The fact remains that since this occurrence we have successfully photographed the whole of the enemy's trenches in front of the Fourth Army . . . without once being attacked by the Fokkers. This was done on the 15th, 16th, 17th, and 18th of May and clearly shews that for the moment at any rate we have command of the air by day on the Fourth Army front. . . . the de Havilland machine has unquestionably proved itself superior to the Fokker in speed, manoeuvre, climbing, and general fighting efficiency."

24th May

The first Flight of 70 Squadron Sopwith Strutters arrived in France on the 24th. These, and the Strutters of the second flight which came out a month later, were fitted with the Vickers gun, with that company's own interrupter system. The third

and last flight, which had been transferred directly from the RNAS, used the Scarff-Dibovsky system. The latter soon showed its superiority and became standard on the Strutters.

FE2b   **18Sqn**
**NightRec LENS AA 3-30am shot up tail dam so returned 4-40am, crew OK, left 2-40am, second recon of night to monitor unusual rail movement nr LENS associated with fighting on VIMY RIDGE (crew not yet established).

26th May

6932   **FE2b**   **25Sqn**
**P AA shot up nARRAS cooling system dam OK(Capt BM Hay/2Lt JCM Stewart)

27th May

6232   **BE2c**   **2Sqn**
this a'c? **Rec shot up(Capt CJ MacKay **WIA**/) name Mackay?

28th May

32 and 60 Squadrons RFC arrived in France on the 28th. No.32 was equipped with DH2 single-seat fighters. 60 Squadron RFC, in contrast to other British units, arrived without aircraft and was brought to strength with French Morane types. Initially it received a flight each of nine Type N Bullet monoplanes, four Type BB biplanes, and three Type L and LA Parasols, but the latter were replaced almost immediately by more Type N machines. Over the winter the Morane Bullet had proved to be the match of the Fokkers as the offensive mainstay of 1 and 3 Squadrons RFC, but in no way could its qualities be compared with those of the new Allied pushers and the Nieuports. The Morane monoplanes were also notoriously difficult to fly at operating level, owing to their high wing loading and the use of balanced elevators in place of tail planes. The vicious flying characteristics of the Morane Parasol are described at some length in Cecil Lewis' superb book *Sagittarius Rising*. 60 Squadron were to fly the Morane Bullets throughout the early months of the Somme battle, but were fated to suffer significant losses.

29th May

5311   **Bristol Scout C**   **6Sqn**
+*P combat with Aviatik ovYPRES SALIENT[+ ?seemed ooc ovABEELE-POPERINGHE & possibly hit again ovMENIN] 10000' 3-50am OK(Capt NA Bolton)

5173   **Nieuport 16**   **11Sqn**
+*P combat with Albatros A-type ovBOIRY 7000' 7-45am ended combat at 3000' when unable to change drums OK(2Lt A Ball) dived from 10000'

5173   **Nieuport 16**   **11Sqn**
+*P combat with Albatros A-type[+?ooc] ovMOYENNEVILLE 6000' 8am OK(2Lt A Ball) EA seen dive vertically

5173   **Nieuport 16**   **11Sqn**
+*P combat with Albatros A-type[+?ftl] ovDOUAI 1000' 8-30am OK(2Lt A Ball) waited for 2 Fokker escort to leave Albatros & turn towards OPPY, then engaged EA & forced it to land

These were Albert Ball's first confirmed claims for victories.

5946   **DH2**   **29Sqn**
P combat with 2EA nose-dived cr nrVOORMEZEELE **MIA(Capt EW Barrett **KIA**) left 7-45am, down nrROULERS, a'c shelled

30th May

Rain prevented most flying.

31st May

5215   **FE2b**   **23Sqn**
+*EscRec CAMBRAI-ARRAS RD-MARQUION-ADINFER WOOD combat with 3 Fokkers nrMARQUION 6-7000' 9-15am OK(Capt H Wyllie/Lt AN Solly) helped by keeping tight formation, one Fokker disappeared

5235   **FE2b**   **23Sqn**
EscRec combat with Fokker on return from CAMBRAI 8000' 9-30am returned a'dr(2Lt EF Allen OK/Lt LC Powell **KIA) Fokker dived down from 2000' above "raining lead into the engine". Observer suggested a stall to get shot over top plane, but then was hit in head, EA drew off

5249   **FE2b**   **23Sqn**
+*EscRec CAMBRAI-ADINFER WOOD combat with 3 Fokkers 6-7000' 9-15am, shot up once by EA OK(2Lt AT Watson/2Lt CL Blake)

6345   **FE2b**   **23Sqn**
EscRec combat with EA wCAMBRAI down ooc? in dive 7-05am **MIA(2Lt A Cairne-Duff **WIA POW**/Cpl G Maxwell **WIA POW**) both to Holland 30.4.18 [combat INCHY Ltn M Mülzer FAb62]

6354   **FE2b**   **23Sqn**
+*Esc combat with 3 Fokers out of the sun nrADINFER WOOD 9-7000' 9-30am OK(2Lt DC Cloete/2Lt CE Pither)

7280   **Mart G100**   **23Sqn**
+*Rec combat with 3 Fokkers[+?saw EA which was attacking Capt Wyllie hit then ss & nose-dive] nrCAMBRAI 11000' 10am engine poor: had to pump all the way home OK(1AM DAR Chapman)

7287   **Mart G100**   **23Sqn**
+*EscRec combat with 3 Fokkers CAMBRAI-ADINFER WOOD 11500'? 9-18am OK(2Lt JC Griffiths)

This combat amply demonstrated that on some fronts the German Fokker formations were still very game for a fight. On this reconnaissance for the Third Army, three Fokkers took on seven machines.

June 1916

1st June

A130   Nieuport 16   1Sqn
**HAP combat with LVG? ovMÉRVILLE 13000'-8000' 2pm OK(2Lt JD Latta)

4172   BE2c   10Sqn
+*AReg combat with Albatros then Fokker [+?seen hit from point blank: banked over, box? fell out, nose-dived & then last seen spiral down]ovMARQUILLIES 11800' 4-45pm OK(Capt? RG Gould/Lt FG Pearson) Fokker reported in nose-dive in ne corner BOIS DE BIEZ, rank Lt? Gould

5173   Nieuport 16   11Sqn
+*P combat with Albatros A-type & 1 Fokker ovDOUAI 10000' 10-10am OK(2Lt A Ball) prevented a'c from leaving vicinity of DOUAI A'dr by forcing back down

2612   BE2c   16Sqn
**EscRec shot up dam OK(2Lt R Buck/2Lt GF Westcott)

3176   Nieuport 10   4 Wing RNAS
St Pol +* combat with EA shot up ftl ABEELE(FSLt IdeB Daly **inj**)

A5   FE2d   1AD
delivery from UK, ldg HAUBOURDIN swLILLE undamaged **MIA(Lt SCT Littlewood **POW**/Capt DL Grant **POW**) a'c captured, pilot to Holland 30.4.18, passenger to Holland 30.4.18 [Abschusse lists "2Lt CT Middlewood/Cpl DL Grant down in Vickers B5136]

This mishap delivered a completely new type directly into the hands of the Germans. The FE2d differed from the FE2b in that it had a larger 250hp engine which gave it a higher ceiling and slightly increased speed. Possibly of more importance, it enabled a second Lewis gun to be carried aloft for the pilot's use without compromising performance. It was not to prove the significant variant that was hoped for, however, as the bigger engine was less reliable and, more crucially, it was no match for the German machines soon to make their appearance.

2nd June

Following their small gains at Vimy, the Germans began a more substantial and serious attack at Hooge. They quickly captured over a mile and a half of trenches and advanced up to seven hundred yards. This battle lasted until the 13th, when a Canadian force made a successful counter-attack. 6 Squadron was once again notable in artillery co-operation work. The 7 Squadron casualty below occurred during this fighting.

3rd June

2750   BE2c   7Sqn
** brought down in control eWYTSCHAETE **MIA**(2Lt C Goodson **POW**) to Holland 30.4.18 [AA fire claim]

2732   BE2c   10Sqn
+*B combat with 2 Fokkers & 4 Albatros' [+?Fokker seen fall ooc but recovered 3000'] BAPAUME 6-7000' 6-45am to 7am then running fight with Albatros OK(2Lt O'Hara-Wood) with BE2c 1737 in combat

1737   BE2c   10Sqn
+*B combat with 2 Fokkers & 4 Albatros' [+?Fokker seen fall ooc but recovered 3000'] BAPAUME 6-7000' 6-45am to 7am then running fight with Albatros: strut shot up so re-crossed lines OK(2Lt HC Marnham) with BE2c 2732 in combat

4th June

6938   FE2b   25Sqn
P AA BETHUNE dam(Lord Lt Doune OK/2Lt RU Walker **WIA)

8th June

A130   Nieuport 16   1Sqn
**KBP ALBERT-BAPAUME attacked KB[+shot down] 1m nLE SARS 2500' 4pm shot up dam OK(2Lt JD Latta)

5173   Nieuport 16   11Sqn
+*SpP combat with Albatros ovMÉRICOURT 7000' 6-15am OK(2Lt A Ball) gun jam

5173   Nieuport 16   11Sqn
+*SpP combat with Albatros ACHEVILLE-ROUVROY 6-7000' 6-30am OK(2Lt A Ball) EA dived

5173   Nieuport 16   11Sqn
+*SpP combat with EA[+?driven down] DOURGES 7000' 6-40am OK(2Lt A Ball)

5173   Nieuport 16   11Sqn
+*SpP combat with Albatros[+driven down ftl nFLERS] ovFLERS nDOUAI 10000' 7am OK(2Lt A Ball)

5173   Nieuport 16   11Sqn
+*SpP combat with LVG ovROUVROY 3-2000' 7-10am OK(2Lt A Ball) had no ammunition but came up very close behind and it went down very low

All the combats for Ball's morning patrol have been given because they so clearly illustrate his cunning, tenacity, and fighting spirit.

2375　　RE7　　　　21Sqn
+*EscRec engine failed so returned ~7am then combat with EA shot up, observer hit & engine stopped so glided down ftl 3m WoL(2Lt EA Rice OK/Lt W Russell **WIA**) also AA?, crossed Lines at 2000′

5976　　DH2　　　　29Sqn
P combat with EA ovYPRES hit by mg of another DH2 ftl a'dr(Capt AC Clarke **WIA) left 6-40am

6005　　DH2　　　　32Sqn
P combat? shell? ftl fainted on ldg FREVIN CAPELLE cr wr(2Lt RA Stubbs **DoW) WIA in combat & injured in cr

2Lt Stubbs was the first airman lost to 32 Squadron in action.

10th June

4077　　BE2c　　　16Sqn
+*AP combat with Fokker[+hit EA on turn then fast dive: pilot saw EA cr nrHARBOURDIN ~o.23. or o.24.] EoL 6500′ 5-50pm OK(2Lt AAND Pentland/Capt WH Walker)

13th June

During the Canadian counter-attack on the 13th, which recovered the ground at Hooge, poor weather prevented any artillery co-operation. The guns relied instead on the registrations mapped over the previous weeks. These had been done so well that most of the fire was effective.

17th June

5164　　Morane BB　　1Sqn
Phot AA ovHOUTHULST WOOD cr ldg S27.L.22.d.(Capt MMcB Bell Irving **WIA/2Lt AW Smith **WIA**)

18th June

6940　　FE2b　　　25Sqn
P combat with EA 3000′ ftl neARRAS **MIA(Lt CE Rogers **KIA**/Sgt H Taylor **WIA POW**) left 2-35pm, Imm16 [?unconfirmed "Vickers" claim combat BUCQUOY 4pm Oblt M Immelmann FAb62]

4909　　FE2b　　　25Sqn
P combat with 2 Fokkers engine hit? shot down ovWINGLES 7-45pm **MIA(2Lt JRB Savage **DoW**/2AM N? Robinson **WIA POW**) initial N?, Imm17 [combat nrLENS 8-45pm Ltn M Mülzer KEK.*Nord*, after ?combat nrLENS]

THE DEATH OF MAX IMMELMANN

It was in this combat that the first great German ace, Oblt Max Immelmann, was killed. It is possible that Immelmann may have done the damage to FE2b 4909 which was then capitalised on by Mülzer. Immelmann was claimed by another 25 Squadron crew, 2Lt GR McCubbin and Cpl JH Waller, but his machine was seen to disintegrate and it is likely he was the victim of one of the greatest technical shortcomings of the Fokker. The official German report on his death concluded that he had shot off his own propeller, and that the Fokker had collapsed under the strain of the self-destructing engine and his attempts to save himself. This was a terrible blow for the German Air Service, who were hit by this loss just as they were commencing a comprehensive restructuring of their air service. One outcome was that Boelcke received an Imperial Decree forbidding him from active flying until further notice, and he used the time to tour the South Eastern front to gather intelligence.

5983　　DH2　　　　32Sqn
P opposite LENS gunshots: engine shot up ftl dam(2Lt WE Nixon **WIA)

8357　　Short 184　　RNAS
** engine fire ftl German mine field nOSTENDE then 3 enemy seaplanes attacked but were driven off by mg fire OK(FLt GW Price/CPO Ellen) towed home

20th June

2488　　BE2c　　　8Sqn
AOb AA 9-55am ldg EoL nrPUISSEUX? **MIA(2Lt DWS Paterson **KIA**/2Lt J Cooke **DoW**)

22nd June
AIR CONCENTRATIONS FOR THE BATTLE OF THE SOMME

Final preparations for the Somme Offensive were well underway. The 1st of July had been chosen as the date for the launching of the infantry offensive, and as the armies continued to train and build, the air offensive began to intensify. The newly formed Fourth Army was to spearhead the attack with the assistance of the XIII Corps from the Third Army. The Corps assembled, running north to south, were Nos. VIII, X, III, XV, and XIII. These forces had been allotted the principal sector north of the river, with the French attacking to the south.

The Fourth Army's air support was provided by the squadrons of IV Brigade. To re-state its constituents, these were the units of the 3rd (Corps) Wing, namely Nos. 3, 4, 9, and 15 Squadrons, who would typically carry out the artillery and contact work, and the 14th (Army) Wing, consisting of 22 and 24 Squadrons. The Brigade also included No.1 Balloon Squadron. These IV Brigade squadrons would be the first to benefit from the decision to increase unit strengths from twelve to eighteen

aircraft. In addition, the squadrons of the 9th (Headquarters) Wing were available, namely Nos. 21, 27, and 60. Finally, two flights of 70 Squadron Sopwith Strutters would also be on the Somme soon after fighting began. This unit would join 9th Wing. Its four squadrons would be respectively responsible for strategic reconnaissance (No. 70), distant bombing of communications (No. 21), and offensive patrolling to restrict German activity in the air and to protect RFC bombing machines on their raids (Nos. 27 and 60).

The bombing offensive was aimed at disrupting the enemy's lines of communications — principally to isolate the rail network behind the battle area by tactical bombing of trains, bridges, junctions, and other railway targets. The part of the network which would receive the heaviest attention was Cambrai-Busigny-St Quentin-Tergnier. Ammunition dumps at Namur and Mons would also be hit. BE2cs of units from other brigades were drawn in to do this work, namely from Nos. 2 and 10 Squadrons of I Brigade, Nos. 7 and 16 from II Brigade, and Nos. 12 and 13 from III Brigade. The extent of the air forces which were being assembled for this battle indicates how substantial the expansion of the RFC had been.

Intensive strategic reconnaissances for RFC Headquarters had begun well in advance of the fighting and were usually escorted. Enemy lines of communications and supply were also being steadily bombed by this time, protected by co-ordinated offensive patrolling. Escorting of these raids was given a relatively low priority, however — the control of the skies was to be used primarily in support of the army in the forward areas. The weather would not be as favourable for their plans as it might have been, but the programme of air activity was to be far in excess of anything attempted before.

The Allies' numerical air superiority would be the essential factor in maintaining control of the air. The strengths of the British units supporting the Fourth Army amounted to one hundred and nine aircraft of IV Brigade and fifty-eight of 9th (Headquarters) Wing, a total of one hundred and sixty-seven machines. Importantly, seventy-six of these were new fighter types. Eighteen additional BE2cs of 8 (Corps) Squadron of III Brigade would assist in a subsidiary attack. The French had massed slightly more than this number.

In contrast, the German Army Air Service had only one hundred and twenty-nine aeroplanes in the sector, many of their machines still being held back for Verdun. Within weeks this number would be substantially swelled, but for the present it

would leave them unable to counter the intentions of the RFC. Of still greater relevance, however, was that only nineteen of these were actually fighters — those belonging to Kampfeinsitzer Kommandos attached to the Second Army. Furthermore, most were still Fokkers and clearly technically inferior to those of the British. The legend that had built up around the Fokker Eindekkers had been a result of very successful use by only relatively few pilots. For most of their operational life they had suffered continual problems. Stoppages which were very difficult to clear and synchronisation errors were two failings of its armament which seriously handicapped its effectiveness. Between June 1915 and April 1916, some one hundred and eighty German single-seaters found their way to the front, but only a relatively small number at a time could be deployed because of these doubts.

The units with the German Second Army consisted of six reconnaissance flights (Feldflieger Abteilungen), four artillery flights (Artillerieflieger Abteilungen), a bomber-fighter squadron (Kampfgeschwader), and KEK.*Nord* at Bertincourt and KEK.*Süd* at Château Vaux. The fact that so many German machines remained in place around Verdun, and would do so for several weeks, contributed markedly to Allied air superiority in the opening stages of the offensive. The final obstacle for the German Air Service as the battle neared was its very low morale. For the present, therefore, the balance of air superiority was clearly with the RFC.

A131   Nieuport 16   1Sqn
+*HAP MESSINES-HOLLEBEKE saw off 2 Albatros ovHOUTHEM between 9am to 11am OK(2Lt BJ Moore) also combat with Albatros ovST ELOI

7335   BE2c   6Sqn
+*AReg combat with 6EA ovHOOGE-HOLLEBEKE-DICKEBUSCH 9-30am to 10-30am but only hit once by EA fire OK(Capt NA Bolton/Lt Brymer)

5573   Bristol Scout D   11Sqn
+*SpP chased down B-type ovBOISLEUX ST MARE 4000′ 6-55am OK(Lt CM Gibson)

5209   FE2b   25Sqn
**P combat with Fokker EoL ldg nHULLUCH 7-30am MIA(2Lt JLP Armstrong POW DoW/Sgt G Topliffe POW) ["Vickers" claim combat LOOS Ltn M Mülzer KEK.*Nord*]

6334   FE2b   25Sqn
**P SOUCHEZ AA dam(2Lt LC Angstrom WIA/2Lt HC Hadwick OK)

6378   FE8   29Sqn
**P combat with EA WOESTEN Rd nwYPRES shot down cr wr(Capt LH Sweet KIA) left 11-10am

6003   DH2   32Sqn
**P LENS engine problems ftl: glided then AA 7-15am
cr ldg dam OK(2Lt OV Thomas) engine was vibrating:
due to earlier AA hit?

3963   Nieuport 10   1 Wing RNAS
St Pol +* combat with LVG?[+shot down cr sea]
WENDUYNE-BLANKENBERGHE 12500' 10-30am
OK(FLt T Hinshelwood)

23rd June
2609   BE2c   8Sqn
**AOb AA dam ftl OK(2Lt WO Phillips/2Lt V Bayley)
left 7-18am VII Corps front

4907   FE2b   25Sqn
**AReg BOIS DE BIEZ shot up dam ftl 2Sqn 8-20am(Lt
HB Davey OK/Lt SRP Walter WIA) left 7-15am, the
crew of this machine is as per RFC Casualty Report. That
entered in AIR1/967/204/5/1097 has crew of 2Lt JJ
Lynch OK/2Lt Rickards WIA, but error.

24th June
The Allied bombing offensive was due to intensify
on the 24th. There had been a very heavy storm in
the Somme area on the previous afternoon, and
rain and low cloud lingered on from this through
the day. Most efforts to commence the programme
were therefore thwarted and flying was all but
eliminated.

25th June
The bombardment gained momentum on the
second day and brought the first retaliation from
the German guns. Recording of these positions by
counter-battery crews therefore began in earnest.

A116   Nieuport 16   1Sqn
+*KBP ALBERT-BAPAUME dived on KB[+smoke &
in flames after 10 seconds & then fell to earth] ovFLERS
at 4000' 3-45pm OK(2Lt BJ Moore) left 3-45pm with 2
BE2cs, dived from 6000', used Le Prieur rockets in attack,
just missed collision

This was one of the Nieuports involved in
concerted attacks on the German balloon line on
the Somme. Of the twenty-three balloons known to
be up, fifteen were attacked, and there were others
brought down besides the one mentioned here. The
attacks were repeated the following day.

6350   FE2b   23Sqn
*P left 2-20pm BOIRY ST RICTRIDE combat with EA,
rudder controls shot away so cr ldg cross-wind
WAGNONLIEU dam(2Lt KL Gopsill **inj**/Sgt HN
Johnson **WIA**)severe

26th June
2759   BE2c   9Sqn

**AOb left 7-50am AA ovBERNAFAY WOOD dam(2Lt
JA Coates WIA/2Lt GC Stapylton OK)

6348   FE2b   23Sqn
**B combat with EA eARRAS shot down MIA(Lt HB
Russell WIA POW/Lt JR Dennistoun POW DoW
9.8.16) left 8-50am, pilot to Switzerland 9.12.17, to UK
24.3.18

5212   FE2b   25Sqn
**B combat with EA MAZINGARBE 6-55am wr(Lt
RCB Riley WIA/Lt EH Bird DoW 27.6.16) [?claim Ltn
M Mülzer KEK.*Nord*]

6334   FE2b   25Sqn
**B combat with EA shot down CAMBRAI(2Lt R
Sherwell OK/2AM H Chadwick KIA) left 6-55am

6346   FE2b   25Sqn
**B combat with EA shot up nrBEUVRAY(2Lt GR
McCubbin WIA/Cpl JH Waller OK) left 7-15am

The losses on bombing operations had been
notably heavy in the preceding days.

27th June
As the bombardment gained momentum the RFC
had carried out very extensive co-operation with
the artillery for as long as the conditions permitted.
Finally, however, the weather closed in and for the
last few days before the assault nearly all flying was
impossible. This would have major repercussions
on the accuracy and effectiveness of the closing
British barrage.

2496   BE2c   2Sqn
**B/AP AA hit ovPONT À VENDIN 6000' 9-30am(2Lt
AES Story OK/Lt R Hilton WIA) left 8-30am

7303   Martinsyde G100   27Sqn
** hit by AA engine dam ftl BEAUQUESNE OK(Sgt
DAR Chapman)

29th June
5763   BE2d   8Sqn
**AP left 10-20am combat with HA(2Lt AH Vaisey
WIA/2Lt GM Pickthorn OK) returned a'dr 11-15am

5963   DH2   24Sqn
**OP combat with HA shot down in spiral ovCLERY,
chased down MIA(2Lt KP McNamara KIA) HA seen
come from behind ["1Str" claim:"Lt SKP Mekamare"]

June had seen the pace of the war generally
increasing in preparation for the Somme Offensive.
It had seen the death of the first great innovator
and ace of the war, Max Immelmann, but already
the air fighting he had pioneered was being
adapted and changed by new tactics. Whenever the
weather permitted both sides flew constantly,
resulting in increasingly heavy combat. The
numbers of aircraft at the front had been steadily

climbing: records showed that in the previous year the RFC had taken on 2,568 aircraft, and struck off 1,427. A further 8,403 were now on the order list. The month had been brought to a close by four days of poor weather, so the last week before the Somme battle had been relatively quiet for both the RFC and the German Army Air Service. A brilliant sunny day dawned for the start of the offensive, so the entire weight of air power was now expected to make its presence felt in the tremendous battle about to begin. For all involved, deafened by the guns for miles behind the lines, nothing would ever be the same again.

July 1916

1st July
THE BATTLE OF THE SOMME AND THE ROLE OF THE RFC

The British offensive of the first battle of the Somme opened on the 1st of July 1916. One asset the great army clearly had was control of the skies and they would retain this throughout all the early fighting. The role of the fighter squadrons of 14th (Army) Wing was to give immediate protection to the corps machines as they worked with the advancing ground forces. They did this by flying continuous line patrols and mounting offensive sweeps throughout the sector. Of all the work carried out by the RFC it was, of course, the corps squadrons' operations which were the most vital. Co-operation with the artillery was assuming ever more importance, and on the Somme new gun ranging techniques were being used extensively for the first time. These were based on "Zoning", whereby targets could be identified by simple combinations of letters. Wireless technology, to facilitate these developments, was advancing keenly as well. The burgeoning scope of artillery work also meant much greater demands on those carrying out reconnaissance and photography work, a great deal of which had been done in preparation for this battle. The systematic photographing of enemy positions was proving so useful that by the spring every corps and army reconnaissance squadron had been allotted a small photographic section.

Besides artillery co-operation, close bombing, and reconnaissance, the corps squadrons would undertake increasingly involved contact patrolling to keep headquarters in touch with the advance.

Techniques of signalling and co-ordination were improving and, for the first time, these patrols were to be made lower down. The success of these operations would still be heavily dependent on the weather and prevailing conditions over the battle.

The role laid out for the RFC was an ambitious one, and it has to be said that the air crews who were to carry it out were not so highly trained as they might have been. This was a key factor in the first few days' work, which in truth took some time to gain momentum. The huge scale of the operations was another clear reason for this.

The British knew they faced German defences of exceptional strength and scale, the defenders having been in possession of this territory for most of the war. It was hoped that this could be mitigated by a truly vast bombardment preceding the assault. Eight days of continual and intense shelling had been carried out to this end. The tragedy was that this key operation was to fail in its intention, the machine-gun defences, in particular, being spared. The huge and hopeful army which had been assembled for this great battle commenced the fighting unaware of the true hell that still faced it. This was to be such a battle as the world had never seen. By the evening of the 1st, the British would have 60,000 dead and wounded.

7338	BE2c	6Sqn

B seen 12-30pm ovCAMBRAI **MIA(2Lt CH Coxe **DoW**) left 11-15am

2689	BE2c	9Sqn

**CP AA shot up dam OK(Capt JTP Whittaker/2Lt TE Gordon-Scaife) arrived over Lines 10am

These two airmen took part in a notable contact patrol. 9 Squadron machines were operating over the XIII Corps, on the British right. They were watching the advance of men of the 30th Division, informed of their progress by mirrors some of them were carrying on their back. They then attacked and shot up a machine-gun position in Bernafay Wood from 700', as well as German troops nearby. Returning to the line they spotted the 18th Division moving up the ridge west of Montauban, and in a moment of mutual exhilaration flew up along the lines of men exchanging waves and cheers of delight.

2640	BE2c	12Sqn

B left 12-42pm ST QUENTIN **MIA(Lt CJ vanNostrand Can. **POW**) to Holland 16.5.18

4196	BE2c	12Sqn

B ST QUENTIN **MIA(Lt LA Wingfield **POW**) left 12-31pm, escaped to UK 21.10.17 [?"BE 4146" claim, possibly shot down by Ltn W Frankl KEK.*Vaux*]

2648.3   **BE2c**   **13Sqn**
****B ST QUENTIN combat with EA MIA(2Lt C
Monckton KIA) left 4-40pm**

2763   **BE2c**   **13Sqn**
****B ST QUENTIN left 4-31pm MIA(Capt TWPL
Chaloner POW) to Holland 16.5.18**

2578   **BE2c**   **15Sqn**
****CP shot up(2Lt KS Henderson Aust. OK/2Lt NP
Tucker WIA)**

15 Squadron was supporting the left flank of the
Fourth Army, in the Serre-Thiepval area.

6365   **FE2b**   **22Sqn**
****P shot down high over CLERY-LONGUEVAL EoL
MIA(Lt JH Firstbrook Can. WIA POW/Lt R Burgess
DoW) left 6-38am, to Switzerland 13.12.16, to UK
11.9.17**

6928   **FE2b**   **22Sqn**
****P AA ftl DOUCHY MIA(Capt GW Webb KIA/Lt
WO Tudor-Hart WIA POW) left 10-02am**

22 Squadron were carrying out the offensive patrols
protecting the corps machines in the northern area
of the front between Douchy and Miraumont. They
were maintained by pairs of aircraft throughout the
entire day, their job being to fly high and engage
any enemy machines coming over to attack the
corps aircraft below. The two crews noted above
were the first losses for 22 Squadron in action.

5213   **FE2b**   **23Sqn**
****Rec combat with 5 B-types ovVAULX 7000' 5-10pm
shot up & hit once by AA(Capt H Wyllie OK/Lt AN
Solly WIA) two bullets in observer's thigh**

5235   **FE2b**   **23Sqn**
****RecP left 3-20pm BAPAUME-CAMBRAI RD combat
with 5 B-types[+?1EA down in steep spiral] ovVAULX
7000' 5-10pm then later combat radiator shot up
ovFAMPOUX engine blew ftl OK(2Lt KL Gopsill/Cpl
AJ Cathie)**

6369   **FE2b**   **23Sqn**
**+*RecP combat with 5 B-types ovVAULX 7000' 5-10pm
OK(2Lt GJ Firbank/FSgt Adams)**

6969   **FE2b**   **23Sqn**
**+*RecP combat with 5 B-types ovVAULX 7000' 5-10pm
OK(2Lt AT Watson/2Lt CL Blake) EA went down in
controlled nose-dive but was unobserved**

6002   **DH2**   **32Sqn**
****Esc left 6-53pm shot up dam(Capt SG Gilmour
WIA)ear**

6015   **DH2**   **32Sqn**
**** combat with 4EAs[+driven down] shot up but ldg
ok(Maj LWB Rees WIA)leg, to hospital, first seen
approaching FESTUBERT**

Maj Rees, Commanding Officer of 32 Squadron,
was awarded the Victoria Cross for this action. A

large formation of enemy aircraft was spotted
approaching Festubert, and Rees took on four of
them when his group of DH2s engaged them. He
forced the second machine he attacked to descend
and land, but the third managed to get a burst into
his own aircraft and he was wounded in the leg.
Continuing the fight, however, he shot up and
wounded the observer of the third machine and
then turned his attentions to the fourth aircraft he
was fighting, firing at it until he had expended all
his ammunition.

THE RESULTS OF
THE FIRST DAY'S FIGHTING

The first day on the Somme had yielded mixed
results for the RFC in that whilst German interference in the air had soon melted away, the
effectiveness of the artillery calling and contact
patrolling had been variable; events on the ground
had also not gone as planned, most of the fighting
having unfolded in continuing chaos and misfortune. Thick early morning mist had prevented
effective observation at the initial attack, and many
of the RFC reports that came in that day were to
be over-optimistic or mistaken. Other crucial
intelligence they provided was not acted upon.
Accurate shelling was laid onto many artillery
positions but the German machine-guns could not
be eliminated and it was these which caused the
carnage. Against terrible odds several deep penetrations were made into enemy territory, but in
many places even these could not be held after
nightfall, and withdrawals were carried out.
However, the scale of these tragic events can in no
way be laid at the feet of the RFC, who had an
onerously difficult and largely untried role to play,
and who were required to operate within an
abiding battle plan which was found to be
essentially flawed from the outset.

Most progress had been made on the British
right and by the French forces south of the river.
Haig decided that the British effort should be
concentrated into the area where these gains had
pressed deepest; namely south of La Boisselle.
From this time Rawlinson became solely responsible for this section of the front; the two most
northerly corps of the Fourth Army, the VIIIth
and the Xth, were placed under General Sir
Hubert Gough and his command was designated
the Reserve Army. Their front stretched from La
Boisselle to Serre, and whilst maintaining pressure
on the enemy, they were to provide the pivot for
the main attack. The Reserve Army was to become
the British Fifth Army at the end of October.

In order to provide the new Army with air support, V Brigade would be formed. With VIII and X Corps had come Nos. 4 and 15 (Corps) Squadrons and these were removed from 3rd Wing and formed into 15th (Corps) Wing. The 14th (Army) Wing continued to provide fighter protection along the whole front for the present.

To the left of the Reserve Army was the British Third Army. III Brigade RFC served this force and, being adjacent to the battle area, its squadrons were to become increasingly involved in the Somme offensive. A few of its Corps units have already been noted as being amongst those used in the bombing offensive. At this time its strength was as follows: the 13th (Army) Wing (Nos. 11 and 23 Squadrons); and the 12th (Corps) Wing (Nos. 8, 12, and 13 Squadrons).

N500	Sopwith Triplane	1Wing RNAS

+* attacked 2 EAs 6m nLA PANNE gun jam forced to break off OK(FSLt RS Dallas) saw hits on one

This was the prototype Sopwith Triplane, in action for the first time, fighting off the Flemish coast. Dallas, who was to become one of the greatest Australian aces of the war, had initially flown the machine on an offensive patrol to Ypres a week before. Regrettably, it was to be months before production types of this startling aircraft reached France.

2nd July

5195	Morane N	3Sqn

**OP AA lost cowl ftl wBRAY OK(2Lt TH Bayetto) (attached 24Sqn)

2654	BE2c	9Sqn

AOb AA combat with 2 Fokkers eBAPAUME fire **MIA(Lt IC MacDonnell **KIA**/2Lt HA Williamson **KIA**) left 6-30pm, hit by rocket? [claim combat sBAPAUME Ltn S Kirmaier KEK.*Jametz*][combat MIRAUMONT 1pm Ltn M Mülzer KEK.*Bertincourt*]

2598	BE2c	10Sqn

EscRec AA hit 7-20am LILLE dam(2Lt JE Evans OK/ Lt GW Panter **WIA) LENS-SECLIN-LILLE

6357	FE2b	11Sqn

Phot combat with EA BAPAUME seen chased down in dive by EA 2-30pm **MIA(2Lt JW Toone **POW**/2Lt EB Harvey **POW**) left 12-50pm, pilot to Holland 16.5.18

A134	Nieuport 16	11Sqn

+*P combat with 6Rolands[+shot up then dived crMERCATEL-ARRAS RD] ovMERCATEL 10000' 5-30pm OK(2Lt A Ball) Ball's victory was witnessed by FB5 7820, also another Roland seen cr after attack by FE2b

A134	Nieuport 16	11Sqn

+*P combat with Aviatik[+direct hit into EA: ss to earth cr ~Sh36 v.11] nrLENS 11000' 6pm OK(2Lt A Ball) suffered gun jam at first

2382	RE7	21Sqn

**B shot up BAPAUME dam OK(2Lt TR Irons) in pm

Six RE7s attacked Bapaume in the afternoon, each aircraft carrying a 336-lb bomb. Their targets were an infantry headquarters and an ammunition dump, in which they caused a huge fire. They were escorted by 27 Squadron, with 60 Squadron flying offensive patrols in the proximity, but no enemy attacks were encountered.

7462	Martinsyde G100	27Sqn

**EscRec radiator & engine shot up ftl dam OK(Capt OT Boyd)

3rd July

Reconnaissance patrols reported heavy German reinforcements pouring into Cambrai by rail. From there they were being sent on to Bapaume and Peronne. It was imperative therefore to step up the bombing of trains. From 5-30 am, crews began going out in pairs to do this work, once again protected by 27 and 60 Squadrons. Several casualties to both the bombers and their escorts occurred on this work.

5170	Morane BB	1Sqn

+*HAP combat with 2 Albatros[+?1 in vertical dive, destroyed?] ovHOUTHULST WOOD 10000'-6000' OK(Lt TA Oliver/Sgt R Mumford) the 2 Albatros had WT aerials, which on the one shot down streamed out behind, crew adamant of victory, several other combats between 6-50am & 7-50am

A116	Nieuport 16	1Sqn

+*KBP ALBERT-BAPAUME dived on KB ovLE SARS 1000' 10-30am "green onions" & much AA OK(2Lt BJ Moore) KB not hit

2607	BE2c	4Sqn

**CP THIEPVAL shot up dam OK(Capt CAA Hiatt/Lt GEF Sutton)

2645	BE2c	4Sqn

AP combat with 2HAs, dive cr **MIA(2Lt RC Stoddard **KIA**/2Lt JF Quinlan **KIA**) left 4-05pm for MIRAUMONT-GRANDCOURT

2752	BE2c	5Sqn

**B DOUAI-CAMBRAI mg shot up dam OK(Lt JS Scott Can.) was bombing train nrCAMBRAI

5780	BE2d	5Sqn

B **MIA(Lt WB Ellis **POW**) to Holland 16.5.18

II Brigade machines from 5 and 16 Squadrons (see 16 Sqn entry below) were also bombing trains, and suffered two crews missing in action.

6945   FE2b   11Sqn
****ArmyP combat with EAs shot up ftl 4Sqn 10-30am
dam(Capt Rough/Capt ACW Field) left 7-25am

A134   Nieuport 16   11Sqn
+*SpP attacked KB ovPELVES with darts &
Buckingham bullets 5-3000' 2-15pm OK(2Lt A Ball)

2644   BE2c   13Sqn
**B ST QUENTIN AA hit nrBRIE on Somme River ftl
3Sqn(Lt PR Meredith **WIA**) head

4173   BE2c   13Sqn
B left 5-45am ST QUENTIN **MIA(2Lt WFL Castle
POW) to Holland 16.5.18

Following the losses on these BE2cs of 13
Squadron, its Commanding Officer wrote that
"Experience has shown that hostile machines avoid
Allied machines flying in formation and attack
isolated machines. This increases the likelihood of
being attacked when the patrol is not at hand."
These, and the other losses suffered this day by 5
and 16 Squadrons, were on unescorted operations
to bomb designated rail targets behind the lines.
Their protection was notionally provided by
offensive patrols in the locality, but this co-
operation was not working. Further, it has to be
remembered that the pilots were flying alone,
owing to the weight of their bombs, and they were
more or less in no position to defend themselves
from attack. Given that the value of their bombing
was highly questionable, units like these from II
and III Brigade were taking unacceptable losses.
Trenchard subsequently removed the BE2s from
these raids.

5746   BE2d   16Sqn
B AA fire **MIA(2Lt SH Ellis NZ. **WIA POW**) a'c
captured, to UK 7.1.18 [?"Bristol 5746: but name is 2Lt
Howard" claim combat sPERONNE Oblt F Walz
KASTA2]

6339   FE2b   23Sqn
**B LA BASSÉE shot down AA FESTUBERT dam(2Lt
R Sherwell **KIA**/2Lt JCM Stewart **KIA**)

7850   DH2   24Sqn
ArmyP dhAA spin cr nPUISIEUX **MIA(Lt DH Gray
Aust. **KIA**)

A175   Morane N   60Sqn
**OP combat with EA ovCAMBRAI, shot down
EPINOY 8-24am **MIA**(Maj FF Waldron **POW DoW**)
[A175 Morane claim]

The loss of Maj Waldron, 60 Squadron's Commanding Officer, was their first casualty in France,
and a bitter blow.

4th July

Low cloud restricted flying from the 4th until the

6th. Those continuing with artillery work in this
quiet period saw very few German machines. The
conditions, as well as the absence of the enemy in
the air, suited the Allies in the sense that Haig was
already organising reinforcements of squadrons
from quieter fronts. Improved weather was
essential to the RFC's chances of maintaining air
superiority and the next main attacks would benefit
immeasurably from increased Allied air presence.

6th July

Progress on the ground had been made despite the
odds, and by the 5th the first defence system, from
the Brickfields to La Boisselle, had been taken. The
advance then turned its attention to the fortifications in Mametz Wood. 3 Squadron was ordered
to reconnoitre these positions in the afternoon, as
well as continuing their reconnaissances of the rail
movements.

5098   Morane LA   3Sqn
**Phot combat with 5 LVGs 9-55am ftl a'dr(2Lt TA
Tillard **WIA**/FSgt Hall **WIA**)

5308   Bristol Scout C   4Sqn
**OP shell wPOZIÈRES 5000' ftl ALBERT "broke in
half" on ldg cr wr OK(Lt PB Prothero) left 9-05am
AUCHELLES

7th July

2638   BE2c   4Sqn
**CP shot up ftl FORCEVILLE cr wr(2Lt JH Ross
WIA/Lt GEF Sutton OK) left 7-30am

7336   BE2c   4Sqn
AP AUTHVILLE WOOD(Capt GA Burney **KIA/Lt
JW Halcrow **KIA**) left 7-40am

6236   BE2d   9Sqn
**CP AA ovMONTAUBAN dam OK(Capt JTP
Whittaker/2Lt TE Gordon-Scaife) left 8-20am

8th July

Fighting began to rise in intensity again, the area
around Mametz Wood becoming the focus for some
terrible exchanges of artillery fire. Airmen were
flying in behind the barrages to register fire in the
most dangerous circumstances. German resistance
would prove very stubborn, all ground attacks
failing until the 10th and 11th of July, when the
enemy positions were finally relinquished.

6231   BE2d   2Sqn
**AReg LIEVIN combat with A-type but returned
a'dr(Lt RG Gould **WIA**/2Lt LC Chapman OK)

2634   BE2c   4Sqn
+*AP combat with 2Str ovGRANDECOURT 3500'
12-30pm OK(Lt MW Thomas/2Lt EH Stevens)

5765   BE2d   4Sqn
Phot snd cr MIRAUMONT **MIA(Lt EC Jowett **KIA**/ Cpl R Johnstone **KIA**) HA came out of clouds? [?combat MIRAUMONT Ltn M Mülzer KEK.*Bertincourt* FAb32]

4 Squadron was involved in an extensive programme of photography which was being carried out in advance of the next main phase of the battle. This was the attack on the second line, on the ridge from Longueval to Bazentin-le-Petit, and was due to be launched in the middle of the month. This crew was lost on these duties.

5794   BE2d   9Sqn
**AP AA seats shot up dam OK(Lt BT Coller/2Lt VA Strauss)

6375   FE2b   22Sqn
**P combat with 3HA ftl FREMENT OK(Capt WA Summers/2Lt RM Chaworth-Musters) a'c shelled

5719   Sopwith Strutter   70Sqn
Rec CAMBRAI shot up ftl ST OMER 5-45am(Capt GL Cruikshank OK/2Lt AJT Cruickshank **WIA DoW)

A384   Sopwith Strutter   70Sqn
Rec dhAA down in flames ooc eARRAS **MIA(Capt DMV Veitch **KIA**/Lt JL Whitty **DoW**) a'c captured

The two casualties above were the first suffered by 70 Squadron in action. Much of their work on the Somme involved escort work with 27 Squadron Martinsydes. They, and the other headquarters units, flew beyond the areas covered by the army squadrons. Their patrols commonly went as far as Marcoing, Epehy, Cambrai, and Le Catelet. 27 and 70 Squadrons went further, as far as Valenciennes, Solesmes, Le Cateau, and Bohain. It was on these lengthy and exposed operations that many of their casualties occurred and where their heaviest fighting took place.

9th July

With the weather improving, this was the most intense day yet of air fighting, and the entire front saw many combats and many casualties. In the previous few days the rail networks had been very closely watched for signs of reinforcements. What had become apparent was that substantial numbers of troops were being removed from around Lens and Thelus in order to reinforce the German Army south of the Somme. In turn, large numbers of troops were being brought down from Lille in the north to take their place. The great upsurge in German air activity was no doubt to facilitate and cover these redeployments. It was also to hinder the Allied bombing programme on these rail centres, which was now in full swing. 21 and 27 Squadrons were involved in this.

6949   FE2b   11Sqn
OP burnt EoL **MIA(Lt HTL Speer **KIA**/2Lt WA Wedgwood **KIA**) left 4-29am, crew burnt

6952   FE2b   11Sqn
OP left 6-05 **MIA(2Lt DH Macintyre **WIA POW**/2Lt J Floyd **DoW** 11.7.16) FAb32?, DoW at FABREUIL, to Holland 16.5.18 for duty [?combat MIRAUMONT Ltn G Leffers AKN]

2192   RE7   21Sqn
B left 4-30pm seen ovMARCOING Stn in combat with 7HA shot down nrMASNIÈRES **MIA(2Lt CV Hewson **KIA**)

7301   Martinsyde G100   27Sqn
B seen 5-45am going toward MARCOING **MIA(2Lt RW Nichol **POW**) to Holland 16.5.18

3043   Bristol Scout C   Dunkirk
+* engaged EA 5m wYPRES OK(FSLt RA Little) EA was ftl EoL

3994   Nieuport 11   1 Wing RNAS
+* combat with Fokker[+shot down] MARIAKERKE A'dr 3-10pm K(FSLt RS Dallas)

8749   Nieuport Scout   1 Wing RNAS
**combat with Fokker[+] off MIDDELKERKE 10000' 3pm then shot down by EA, engine hit ftl NIEUPORT BAINS OK(FSLt LH Irving) a'c shelled, destroyed

10th July

34 (Corps) Squadron arrived in France on the 10th of July equipped with BE2es. It joined the 3rd (Corps) Wing of IV Brigade and fought in the battle of the Somme, being particularly involved in artillery co-operation and contact patrolling. It would re-equip with RE8s at the end of January 1917.

5824   BE2d   5Sqn
NB MOORSLEDE shot up mg dam(2Lt WG Pender **WIA)

5754   BE2d   7Sqn
B Billets left 11-50am ftl 5Sqn bomb exploded ldg wr(Capt JC Quinnell **WIA)leg, injured in explosion?

6230   BE2d   9Sqn
AP AA hit controls dam down spin **MIA(Lt WJM Tomson **inj POW**/Capt WW Jefferd **POW**) left 1-05pm, both to Holland 16.5.18

11th July

6011   DH2   24Sqn
ArmyP **MIA(2Lt C Kerr **POW**) a'c captured, to Holland 16.5.18

A878   Sopwith Strutter   70Sqn
**Rec CAMBRAI combat with 3EA shot up dam OK(2Lt Selby/2Lt Ocling)

12th July

Showers limited most flying.

14th July

The next big attack of the Somme Offensive began on the 14th of July. This was on the second trench system and was launched at 3-25am, taking the enemy by surprise. The ground had been well reconnoitred and contact patrolling was generally effective, so that the successful advance was able to drive on towards Delville Wood.

A120   Morane LA   3Sqn
Rec left 6-50pm LIGNY-TILLOY combat with EA [+?] shot up ftl cr(Capt AJ Evans OK/Lt HO Long **WIA)face, EA used explosive bullets

2500   BE2c   9Sqn
CP shell burst hit 500' ovLONGUEVAL shot down ftl neMARICOURT dam(Capt JU Kelly **WIA/2Lt HAV Hill **WIA**) left 3-50am, hit whilst following progress of attack, pilot temporarily blinded so helped to land by observer.

The advances on the first morning had been very substantial, despite low cloud which brought the contact patrols well down. To exploit the situation GHQ ordered that a completely erroneous wireless message be sent from an aircraft that was assured of being picked up by the enemy. It was to report a comprehensive rout of the enemy. This is likely to have been the first ever use of such a ruse. By the late afternoon, part of Longueval had been captured and the decision was made to advance on High Wood. An act of some bravery ensued when the 3 Squadron Morane crew of Capt AM Miller and 2Lt CW Short spotted German infantry concealed in long corn and ready for the assault. They took their machine low down over the enemy to draw their fire and thus make them reveal themselves. They continued to shoot up the troops and disrupt them, despite heavy fire, until the danger had lessened. They also brought a very effective sketch of the enemy positions back with them.

15th July

6980   FE2b   22Sqn
P rifle fire HEBUTERNE engine hit ftl a'c shelled(2Lt RH Sievwright OK/2Lt JL Reid **DoW) left 5-15pm on strafe

On earlier 22 Squadron patrols that day, at least two other crews had engaged in effective ground strafing of enemy troops. These were some of the earliest such attacks, made to help infantry fighting around High Wood, near Bazentin-le-Petit. It was also one of the first uses of Buckingham incendiary

tracer ammunition. It proved too difficult to hold on to gains in High Wood, and a withdrawal was made that night.

3963   Nieuport 10   1 Wing RNAS
St Pol +* combat with seaplane[+shot down in flames] 10m off OSTENDE ~4pm OK(FSLt DHMB Galbraith)

16th July

The bombing offensive north of the Ancre river was carried out by the squadrons of III Brigade and their work succeeded in drawing off quantities of German air activity from the immediate battle area. The squadrons involved were Nos. 8, 12, and 13, all with BE2cs, and these were escorted by the FE2bs of 11 and 23 Squadrons (60 Squadron took over from 23 Squadron from September). The escorting aircraft usually carried smaller bombs to drop as well.

A197   Morane LA   3Sqn
Rec LIGNY-THILLOY **MIA(Capt AJ Evans **POW**/Lt HO Long **POW**) left 5-10am, Long to Holland 15.6.17, Evans escaped to UK 16.6.17

4189   BE2c   9Sqn
**CP shot up dam OK(Lt BT Coller/2Lt TE Gordon-Scaife)

5233   FE2b   18Sqn
NB ftl no man's land 1am **MIA(2Lt HW Butterworth **KIA**/Capt JHF McEwan **POW**) left 12-30am, ftl Sh36c.H.2.s., observer to Holland 15.6.18

6374   FE2b   25Sqn
P AA hit 8-45am(Lt Chadwick OK/Pte WH Truesdale **WIA) to hospital

17th July

THE END OF
THE FIRST PHASE OF
THE BATTLE OF THE SOMME

There was mist and rain as the 17th dawned. The remorseless pressure to move the advance onwards saw Pozières as the target for the next day. In preparation, its fortifications were heavily bombarded, but conditions had made it impossible to assess the real damage. An evening air reconnaissance in a clear spell revealed little damage had been done and, if anything, the German positions had been strengthened. With this intelligence, the next day's assault was cancelled, and so the first phase of the Somme Offensive was effectively brought to a close. Yet, as the weather continued to deteriorate, there would be little pause in the terrible and bitter fighting.

The British had fought their way up the slopes

to the rim of the plateau and established themselves on a crest at Delville Wood. In the process they had broken through both primary and secondary defensive systems. But to achieve this foothold, along the valley of the Somme hundreds of thousands of British, French and German soldiers now lay dead and wounded; a staggering human disaster was unfolding. By mid-November the British Army alone would have suffered nearly half a million casualties, and some German estimates of their own dead and wounded were also to match this figure.

The Allies had already managed to achieve one of their aims, which was that the German Army had halted its offensive at Verdun. Fortunately for the British, it would be several weeks before German aircraft were re-deployed in numbers from that front. The RFC still held air superiority, and felt that in its own right it had performed extremely creditably in the face of the appalling events on the ground. The doctrine of offensive flying, which would dominate British operations in France for the rest of the war, was remaining effective through its most severe test to date, and the work of the corps squadrons had been permitted to flourish, and was showing ever increasing competence.

With the end of this first phase it is worth looking at the casualties suffered by the RFC and to consider what they reveal about the effectiveness of its policies and tactics to this time. The most striking fact is that in the first phase of the Somme, only three corps machines were lost due to air fighting whilst carrying out co-operation duties. These were BE2cs 2654 on the 2nd, 2645 on the 3rd, both on artillery patrols, and 5765 on the 8th, doing photography. The protection of corps aircraft by offensive patrolling was almost complete. This handed a tremendous advantage to the British, whilst no doubt perplexing the German air forces who were denied access to the battlefield. Only bad weather prevented an even more comprehensive use of the dominance of the skies. The British contact patrols could also operate widely and, remarkably, not a single one was lost to enemy fire. This fact revealed that low flying aircraft over a battle were surprisingly free from attack, so absorbed were the ground troops in the actual fight for survival around them. This is not to say that those being attacked on occasions were not highly demoralised by the RFC operating so freely just above them.

The balance of air superiority was about to be challenged, however, for the Germans themselves were galvanising their forces on the Somme and steadily reinforcing their existing units. As the German First Army was reconstituted and came into the battle on the right of the Second Army, it brought with it the following new air units: three Feldflieger-Abteilungen, one Artillerieflieger-Abteilung, one Kampfgeschwader, and one Kampfstaffel. Complementing these were two new Kampfeinsitzer-Staffeln, composed of single-seater fighters, so that by the third week of July Germany would have almost one hundred and seventy aircraft in the sector.

18th July

On the 18th the Germans launched the first of their counter-attacks. It was these which would characterise the second phase of the battle, as each army struggled for possession of the main ridge. The fiercest fighting was to be on the British right. The British were anxious to take high ground which overlooked their new positions at Longueval and Delville Wood. This stretched from Guillemont around to High Wood. Plans for this arduous undertaking had been ready for at least four days, but had been delayed by the weather. In the breathing space this gave to the enemy, he prepared and launched a counter-stroke so that by evening of the following day it was Longueval which had been largely lost. Fighting to wrestle back the village was understandably intense, but only moderately successful.

2655	BE2c	9Sqn

** left 7-55am AA dam OK(2Lt AL Macdonald)

19th July

5190	Morane LA	3Sqn

**AP combat with EA fuel tank shot up ftl seFRICOURT o't OK(2Lt WB? Young/2Lt Rickards)

7333	BE2c/d	13Sqn

**SpM:NB engine problems ftl EoL MIA(Lt H Clements-Finnerty POW) left 2-25am BIACHE ST VAAST, to Holland 15.6.18

5235	FE2b	23Sqn

**EscB combat with HA shot up dam(Lt ER Manning WIA/2Lt CVJ Borton WIA) left 6-02am

7288	Martinsyde G100	27Sqn

**Esc seen BAPAUME ~9am MIA(2Lt AHW Tollemache KIA)

7874	DH2	32Sqn

**EscOP combat with FokkerEIII[+ooc] ovPROVIN EoL 5am shot up forced to return cr WoL nrNOEUX LES MINES, sBETHUNE(2Lt J Godlee Aust. DoW)

32 Squadron was an army unit operating in the 10th(Army) Wing of I Brigade. This Brigade provided air support to the First Army who were responsible for the front running from opposite

Lille down to Vimy. Its other units were as follows: 25 Squadron in 10th Wing, and Nos. 2, 10, and 18 Squadrons in the 1st (Corps) Wing. To the north of this again was the British Second Army, on the front stretching up into Flanders. Its air support was offered by II Brigade, comprising the 11th (Army) Wing (Nos. 20 and 29 Squadrons), and 2nd (Corps) Wing (Nos. 1, 5, 6, 7, and 16 Squadrons). As noted previously, a number of these units were providing tactical bombing capability for the main battle, but in general the northern fronts remained relatively quiet whilst the main battle raged to the south. On the 19th of July, however, there was a significant British attack launched near Armentières which utilised units from both brigades. 25 and 32 Squadron carried out offensive patrols, comprehensively denying the enemy the sky, whilst air co-operation for the attack was provided by Nos. 2, 10, and 16 (Corps) Squadrons.

A386   Sopwith Strutter 70Sqn
**OP combat with EA nrCAMBRAI shot down?
MIA(Lt HR Hele-Shaw **KIA**/2Lt RC Oakes **KIA**)
["Sopwith 9653" claim combat ARRAS Ltn K Wintgens KEK.*Vaux*] ps: 9653 was the old RNAS serial of the machine before transfer to the RFC.

20th July

5172   Nieuport 16   1Sqn
+*HAP combat with Roland[+EA observer seen collapse & a'c glide down with no engine] ovYPRES 10000'-7000' 1-45pm combat finished far to East then met heavy AA on return OK(2Lt AM Walters)

2481   BE2c   4Sqn
AOb combat with 8HA nrCONTALMAISON shot up ftl cr(2Lt GV Randall **KIA/2Lt GM Angier **inj**) left 5pm, observer injured in crash

2507   BE2c   9Sqn
+*AOb COMBLES-FLERS-MARTINPUICH combat with Fokker[+tracers hit then smoke seen, ss & down in flames cr nrBAZENTIN-LE-PETIT Railway S.7.a.]7000' 8-30pm OK(Lt BT Coller/2Lt TE Gordon-Scaife) Fokker was chasing DH2 so followed down & fired, later met two other Fokkers

6351   FE2b   23Sqn
Rec seen low swPERONNE **MIA(2Lt DSC Macaskie **WIA POW**/2Lt CI Sandys-Thomas **WIA POW**) left 6.15pm, pilot to Switzerland 24.12.16 to UK 14.9.17, observer to Holland 15.6.18

6932   FE2b   25Sqn
BOP combat with HA[++] shot up(2Lt LL Richardson **WIA/1AM LS Court OK) left 4-50pm

5721   Sopwith Strutter 70Sqn
OP shot up CAMBRAI dam(2Lt J Manley **WIA/2Lt WB Saint OK)

21st July

There was heavy fighting at times through the 21st. The weather was fine and many of the new German machines in the sector came out to fight for the first time. 24 Squadron DH2s were especially active in patrols with 22 Squadron, meeting large enemy formations of Fokkers and Rolands at dawn over Roisel, and again in the evening the two squadrons had a thirty-minute fight with fifteen German scouts over Bapaume. These were notable fights, for perhaps as many as six of the enemy were shot down and more were driven off. Although both RFC units had machines shot up and damaged, neither suffered a casualty.

On the 21st of July 32 Squadron was transferred from the First Army front to the Somme. In August it would be attached to the 15th (Army) Wing and later combined with this to form the new V Brigade.

2754   BE2c   4Sqn
+*AOb combat with 2 Albatros ovPOZIÈRES 7000' 11-35am OK(Capt CJ MacKay/2Lt A Hughes)

2100   BE2c   12Sqn
**B combat with 2 Fokkers AUBIGNY-AU-BAC
MIA(2Lt RM Wilson-Browne **POW DoW** 21.7.16)
["Bristol 2100" claim combat sDOUAI pm Ltn K Wintgens KEK.*Vaux*]

5795   BE2d   12Sqn
**B rifle fire AUBIGNY-AU-BAC dam(Lt Philpott)

12 Squadron was bombing the junction and rail bridge at Aubigny-au-Bac, escorted by 23 Squadron. These escorts shot down two enemy machines.

2388   RE7   21Sqn
B AA shot down BEAULENCOURT **MIA(Capt JO Cooper **KIA**/Lt AV Oliver-Jones **KIA**) left 2-50pm

The last RE7 loss to 21 Squadron before re-equipping with the BE12 single-seat fighter.

6966   FE2b   22Sqn
OP left 6-03am combat with EA badly shot up dam but returned a'dr 8-06am(Lt RD Walker **inj/Cpl Capper **inj**)

A128   Morane N   60Sqn
OP left 5-30pm combat with Fokker shot down in flames **MIA(Capt NA Browning-Paterson **KIA**) ACHIE-LE-PETIT [combat COMBLES pm Ltn K Wintgens KEK.*Vaux*]

22nd July

BE2e   34Sqn
*Rec BAZENTIN-LE-PETIT — HIGH WOOD OK(Capt CHB Blount/2Lt TS Pearson)

The weather was poor for flying from the 22nd until

the 28th. It was essential that air reconnaissance still be carried out with the next phase of the advance onto the ridge about to begin. One of these, made by the recently arrived 34 Squadron, proved very important. A number of flights were returning with reports of extensive strengthening of enemy positions, but few of these were certain because of fog. This crew now spotted a completely new and elaborate trench system immediately opposing the proposed advance. Once this was known, attempts were made to revise the battle plan.

A881   Sopwith Strutter   70Sqn
**Rec CAMBRAI shot up ftl ALBERT OK(2Lt RMS Shepherd/2Lt JW Gunton)

23rd July
THE SECOND PHASE BEGINS

The first general British attack of the second phase took place early on the 23rd after a night of bombardment on the entire front from Trones Wood to Pozières. The enemy was found in great strength, however, and it failed. Subsequent attacks in the following days were also very stiffly met. The weather meant that most efforts to obtain photography or to co-operate with artillery were severely limited. Progress was to be made, however, in every area except on the right flank, which continued to be the greatest and most dangerous obstacle. Fighting to gain Guillemont continued into the next month.

5807   BE2d   9Sqn
**CP shot up dam OK(Lt BT Coller/2Lt TE Gordon-Scaife)

BE2c?   15Sqn
** shell fire(/2Lt RW Settle **KIA**)

7296   Martinsyde G100   27Sqn
EscRE7s gunfire sALBERT(2Lt FG Hogarth **WIA) to hospital

24th July

819   Short 830   Dunkirk
** shot down by U-boat ZEEBRUGGE **MIA**(FLt JF Bailey **POW**/FLt FW Mardock **POW**) later picked up

25th July

2744   BE2c   7Sqn
CP left 4-55am THIEPVAL-POZIÈRES **MIA(2Lt ED Steytler **KIA**/2Lt JG Robertson **WIA POW**) attached 4Sqn, to Holland 15.6.18

7 (Corps) Squadron had been operating in the Ypres salient as part of II Brigade and working with 1 Anzac Corps. When this corps was brought down to the Somme at the end of July, 7 Squadron came down with it, a Flight at a time. These were initially attached to 4 Squadron but all had arrived by the 30th and 7 Squadron became part of the 15th (Corps) Wing serving the Reserve Army (later the Fifth Army).

2615   BE2c   9Sqn
**AP shot up dam OK(2Lt ERH Pollack/2Lt CP Creighton) name Pollak?

2653   BE2c   9Sqn
AP combat with EA ovDELVILLE WOOD shot down in mist, in flames? **MIA(2Lt JA Brown **KIA**/2Lt F Bowyer **KIA**) left 3pm

26th July

A149   Morane BB   60Sqn
Rec combat with LVGs nrBETHUNE shot up VERQUIN ftl(Lt LE Whitehead OK/2AM ER Deal **WIA) left 7-30pm

28th July

5752   BE2d   8Sqn
B AA ROCLINCOURT on return ftl in flames **MIA but OK(Lt HH Watkins **WIA**)burnt, left 6-05pm railway at AUBIGNY-AU-BAC, escorted by 23 Squadron, a'c shelled by Germans after landing (see below)

6972   FE2b   22Sqn
**P combat with EA dam OK(Capt WA Summers/2Lt RM Chaworth-Musters)

FE2b   23Sqn
** shrapnel(Lt LTN Gould **WIA**/) pilot of FE2b 6974 with Collinson?

6974   FE2b   23Sqn
EscB AUBIGNY-AU-BAC combat with EA(/2AM F Collinson **WIA)

23 Squadron were again escorting 8 and 12 Squadrons on an evening raid to bomb the rail junction and bridge at Aubigny-au-Bac. Fighting was continuous during the raid, a formation of Fokkers being fought off.

29th July

2491   BE2c   4Sqn
+*Phot combat with 2 LVGs[+?first seen go down ftl BAPAUME RD, nrLIGNY] ovCOURCELETTE 6500' 7-30pm OK(Capt CJ MacKay/2Lt AP Kelly)

5767   BE2d   6Sqn
B shot up ARMENTIÈRES ftl 6Sq(2Lt RJ Bennett Aust.? **WIA)

7261   Martinsyde G100   27Sqn
*B combat with EAs shot up cr ldg?(2Lt HJW Collins **WIA**?)

7307   Martinsyde G100   27Sqn
**B gunfire shot up ROISEL dam OK(Lt JC Turner)

7465   Martinsyde G100   27Sqn
**B ROISEL combat with EAs shot up dam OK(Capt
OT Boyd)

27 Squadron were bombing enemy aerodromes
between Bertincourt and Velu. The unit provided
its own escorts and was attacked by fighters during
the operation. It sent down one of the enemy.
Notably, relatively few casualties were sustained
whilst bombing these aerodromes, indicating that
this direct offensive on the German air force was
one very effective way of striking at the enemy. A
sizeable tonnage of bombs was dropped in these
weeks, but to meet enemy aircraft, as 27 Squadron
had done on this day, had been unusual until now.
This situation would soon change, however.

6002   DH2   32Sqn
**OP left 6pm shot up BAPAUME returned 7-30pm(2Lt
E Lewis **WIA**)foot, to hospital

30th July

19 Squadron joined the RFC in France on the 30th
of July, flying BE12s. Their arrival coincided with
the widening of the bombing offensive, in which the
unit was to play an important part. The squadrons
mainly responsible for the attacks south of the
Ancre, besides No. 19, were Nos. 21 and 27. Their
most common targets were the railway networks in
the triangle formed by the junctions at Marcoing,
Epehy, and Velu, and the stations at Bapaume and
Cambrai. These operations not only materially
hindered the German disposition of troops and
equipment, but also drew off valuable resources
from the front line which were soon deployed to
counter them, in the same way as the raids on
aerodromes were doing. These, of course, included
aircraft, and the degree to which the RFC bombers
came to be attacked was an indication of the
problem they posed.

The weather was slightly clearer on the 30th, and
the German fighters came out in force. Some
twenty-five managed to cross the lines of the Fourth
Army, which was more than had ever been met
before. From midday the fighting was ceaseless for
some hours as attempts were made to drive them
off. RFC fighter squadrons again came through
these combats without loss, and with perhaps two
enemy destroyed. After this day's fighting, activity
dropped again.

2491   BE2c   4Sqn
+*Phot combat with 2 Fokkers & 3LVGs[+?sudden dive
after 20 rounds & down ooc?] COURCELETTE-
MARTINPUICH 6000' 12-10pm OK(Capt CJ

MacKay/2Lt GR Bolitho)

BE2c?   4Sqn
** AA(/2Lt A Hughes **WIA**)

5795   BE2d   12Sqn
**B ST LEGER AA 12-22pm ftl dam OK(Lt Philpott)

7304   Martinsyde G100   27Sqn
B EPEHY combat with EA? **MIA(Lt ER Farmer
POW) combat in afternoon, to Holland 15.6.18 ["Mart
4704" claim] Formation of 8 Martinsydes were attacked
both going an returning form target.

7471   Martinsyde G100   27Sqn
B EPEHY shot down **MIA(2Lt LN Graham **WIA**
POW) combat in afternoon, to Holland 15.6.18 ["Mart
7471" claim combat ePERONNE Ltn K Wintgens
KEK.*Vaux*]

5162   Morane BB   60Sqn
**Rec combat with 5HA ovESTRÉES ftl BAIZIEUX(Lt
LE Whitehead **WIA**/2Lt WEG Bryant **WIA**) to hospital,
left 4-10pm

5193   Morane BB   60Sqn
Rec seen going down smoking ovESTRÉES **MIA(Capt
LS Charles **POW DoW**/Lt C Williams **KIA**) left 4-10pm

31st July

2491   BE2c   4Sqn
+*AOb combat with EA COURCELETTE 9000'
1-45pm OK(Capt CJ MacKay/2Lt WH Buckeridge)
then EA engaged by DH2s

2686   BE2c   10Sqn
**AP shot up by shrapnel 7pm(2Lt EJ Garland OK/2Lt
JH Bickerton **WIA**)

5242   FE2b   22Sqn
**P combat with EA BRAY ftl cr burnt(2Lt FD Holder
OK/Pte Welford **inj**) left 8-45am, observer injured in ldg

6963   FE2b   22Sqn
**P shot up AA BASIEUX dam ftl 4Sqn a'dr(2Lt WRC
DaCosta OK/2Lt CG Riley **WIA**) left 8-36am

5967.4   **DH2   24Sqn**
**OP Fourth Army area combat with EA dam(Lt RHMS
Saunby **WIA**)

5998   DH2   24Sqn
**OP combat with 8EA BAPAUME 10000'-15800' btwn
6pm & 7-30pm OK(Capt JO Andrews) fast HAs & Fokkers

7282   Martinsyde G100   27Sqn
**B MARCOING attacked by LVG & 3 or 4 Rolands on
return fuel tank shot up dam(Lt RHC Usher **WIA**)leg,
left in afternoon, limped back WoL at 50'

After its losses of the previous day 27 Squadron was
escorted on this raid by 70 Squadron. Soon after
crossing the lines, mist rolled in and machines
became separated. Only two Martinsydes reached
Marcoing, including the one above, although they
still had some escorts.

August 1916

The second phase of the Battle of the Somme was now well into its deadly way and would last another six weeks or so whilst the German Army made repeated and desperate attempts to dislodge the British.

Major changes in the organisation of the German air weapon were about to be instigated at this time, their need all the more pressing because of the continued failure to wrestle back a degree of air control. For the Germans, the first month of the Somme had seen a return to the tactic already found wanting at Verdun — of blanket patrolling. This situation had been forced upon the units as much by failing, over-rigid organisation as by the inferiority of their aircraft or the difficulty in dealing effectively with the aggressive tactics of the RFC. German Army Headquarters had direct control of the Kampfeinsitzer-Kommandos and the Kampfeinsitzerstaffeln (KESTs), and this was now a real obstacle as the requirement for single- and two-seater units on the Somme burgeoned.

The existing command chain had been increasingly unable to cope, and so an intermediary control to manage the fighter units was introduced. This culminated in the order for the formation of the first German Jagdstaffel on the 10th August, formalising the concentration of what were already semi-permanent groups of fighter aircraft in the German Air Service. These "Jastas", as they were abbreviated, had a planned establishment of fourteen D-type single-seater fighters, and seven such units would be in place by early October to serve the I,II, and V Armies, the first two by the end of the month. They brought together experienced single-seater pilots from the Feldflieger Abteilungen as well as from the KEKs and KESTs, and their role was to be purely offensive. German fighter pilots had been at an increasing disadvantage with their aircraft, but the new types about to be supplied to the Jastas were to change the situation profoundly. As the numbers of German machines mounted in the sector, so the volume of combats rose.

However, as with the Allies, the German fighter units were there as a means to an end, to maximise the work of reconnaissance and artillery machines, which in turn was to facilitate the work of the ground forces. In practical terms, the work of these less glamorous units was the most important of all the duties of the German Army Air Service. The fighters, however, were also increasingly essential to their effectiveness. The aircraft performing this reconnaissance, photography and co-operation were grouped into Fliegerabteilungen (FAb), and those with artillery co-operation duties into Fliegerabteilungen-A (FAb(A)).

1st August

4278   FE2b   22Sqn
**P AA hit swBAPAUME down in flames destroyed nrALBERT 2-10pm MIA(Capt WA Summers MC KIA/ FSgt LC Clarkson KIA) left 11-43am ["Vickers" found completely burned 2-14pm swBAPAUME]

6990   FE2b   25Sqn
**B LA BASSÉE-FROMELLES AA hit dam(Capt CH Dixon OK/2Lt JB Hinchcliff WIA)

2nd August

There were some notable bombing operations on the 2nd, the first being a long range attack on Zeppelin sheds at Brussels involving six BE2cs with three Moranes as escort. The mission took five hours. The RFC also bombed Courtrai and Bapaume stations, whilst sixteen RNAS machines hit St Denis Westrem airfield, south-west of Ghent. One purpose of these raids was to attack enemy locations weakened by the transfers of units required for fighting on the Somme.

The first flight of 40 Squadron FE8s arrived in France at Treizennes on the 2nd August (the remaining two flights arrived on the 25th of the month). Its duties were to include bomber escort, offensive patrolling, and balloon attack work, all activities which were made more difficult by their already obsolete machines. With a clear similarity to the other single-seat pusher fighter, the de Havilland DH2, the FE8 was also meant to be an Allied counter to the Fokker, but by the time it appeared in France the problem of the Eindekkers had long passed. A few prototypes had been flying in combat for several months, making a reasonable impression whilst they were still competitive, but the type suffered much delay from red tape, and by the time 40 Squadron arrived in France to be fully operational with them, they met a German air force about to re-emerge with far superior machines. Some early versions of the FE8 were handicapped by an awkward gun mounting, and pilots found its acrobatics unreliable after the pleasures of the DH2, for it had a reputation for locking into a spin. 40 Squadron would begin to receive Nieuport Scout replacements in March 1917.

2616   BE2c   5Sqn
**B left 10-50am AA ovLEDEGHEM ftl MIA(Capt CW Snook POW) to Holland 15.4.18 ["BE & Capt CW Snook" down by AA]

2753   BE2c   7Sqn
**P AA 5-55pm dam ftl OK(2Lt HW? Tagent/Capt MacCallum)

In order to sustain pressure on the German air service and to remind it again of the penalties of drawing off reserves for the Somme, Trenchard ordered four more big bombing raids on distant targets on the 2nd. These were carried out by II Brigade machines (from Squadron Nos. 5, 6, 7, and 16), as well as escorted RNAS aircraft from Dunkirk. Five RFC BE2cs and three Moranes bombed airship sheds at Brussels. The 5 Squadron machine lost above was hit on the way out, but it was the only one to go down on the raid. RNAS Caudrons and a Henri Farman attacked the big aerodrome at St Denis Westrem and the ammunition dump at Merelbeke. There was also a diversionary bombing raid to Courtrai railway station by thirteen BE2cs.

2688   BE2c   16Sqn
**SpRec to P.31.d.8.6., AA dam repairable OK(2Lt Massey/2Lt G Westcott) probably bombing raid to Brussels airship sheds, as above

            FE2d   20Sqn
P AA (/2Lt EH Lascelles **WIA)

The first FE2d casualty due to enemy action.

3990   Nieuport Scout   4 Wing RNAS
Dunkirk ** AA hit nYPRES shot up ftl cr(FLt RGA Baudry **KIA**)

5177   Morane BB   60Sqn
P AA 11000' POUILLY shot down ooc(Lt JAN Ormsby Can. **POW DoW 5.8.16/2Lt HJ Newton **KIA**) left 4pm [combat sPERONNE pm Ltn K Wintgens KEK.*Vaux*] [?combat BEAUMETZ pm Ltn W Frankl KEK.*Vaux*, or Morane below?]

5181   Morane BB   60Sqn
P dhAA POUILLY 11000' down in spin wnwST QUENTIN (Sgt A Walker **KIA/2Lt LL Clark **KIA**) observer fell, left 4pm

3rd August

A5594   FE2b   11Sqn
**AP combat with EA shot up ftl BERLES-AU-BOIS Sh51c W.22 dam OK(2Lt JM Drysdale/) salvaged

4272   FE2b   25Sqn
P combat with Fokker LENS 4-35pm seen in flames(2Lt K Matthewson **KIA/Sap EM desBrisay **KIA**) ["Vickers 384" claim combat LENS 4pm Ltn M Mülzer FAb32]

7307   Martinsyde G100   27Sqn
B NAMUR Sidings AA shrapnel shot down CHAMPION **MIA(Lt JC Turner **POW DoW**) DoW NAMUR

This distant raid was typical of some of the ambitious attacks that were being attempted at this time. Two machines went on to bomb the airship sheds at Cognelée.

A143   Morane LA   60Sqn
SpM:spy drop seen DOUAI engine failed ftl nrCAMBRAI **MIA(2Lt CA Ridley **POW**/French agent) left 7-10pm, a'c captured, escaped to UK

The pair involved in this spy drop had many adventures after they had been forced to land through engine trouble. Ridley and the agent escaped from the scene of the landing and proceeded to carry out covert surveillance of the rear areas for two weeks before crossing into Belgium. Ridley then travelled westwards, disguised as a deaf mute, one time being arrested in Mons but then escaping. He finally crossed the Dutch frontier on the 8th of October. A week later he was back on the Somme, revealing a mine of information about enemy positions behind the lines.

This happened to be the last loss to 60 Squadron before it was pulled out from the Line. So heavy had been its losses on the Moranes that it was withdrawn for a time to be rebuilt and rested. In seven separate engagements it had lost its Squadron Commander, two Flight Commanders, and incurred losses of eight dead and three wounded airmen in a month.

The new structure of 60 Squadron was based around the two new flights of Nieuport Scouts, one of which had been transferred directly from 11 Squadron (this unit then became fully equipped with the FE2b two-seater). The third flight retained its Morane Bullets. By the 23rd of August 60 Squadron was back in position, this time at Izel Le Hameau, and its pilots now included Albert Ball.

5th August

2649   BE2d   4Sqn
B left 5pm combat with HAs shot down GREVILLERS burnt **MIA(Lt MN Thomas **KIA**) ["BE" found completely burned 6-15pm nwBAPAUME]

4917   FE2b   18Sqn
EscPhot LENS AA engine cut then combat with Fokker shot up nrMONT ST ELOI(Capt FC Baker OK/2Lt EV Maclean **WIA)

4922   FE2b   25Sqn
**Esc AA swHAUBOURDIN brought down Sh36 N.2. OK(2Lt WH Rilett/1AM LS Court)a'c shelled

6th August

5250   FE2b   22Sqn
**P left 2pm combat with EA shot up(Capt JG Swart

OK/2Lt WS Mansell **WIA**)

7268   Martinsyde G100   27Sqn
**OP shot up nePERONNE dam OK(Lt H Spanner)

7th August

A380   Sopwith Strutter   70Sqn
**Rec shot down in control cr WALINCOURT
MIA(2Lt CW Blain **POW**/2Lt CD Griffiths **POW**)
deliberate crash, pilot escaped 8.18, observer to Holland
12.10.18

8th August

4286   FE2b   22Sqn
**P left 4-32pm combat with EA ftl 4Sq(Lt GHA
Hawkins **WIA**/2Lt CM Clement OK)

4288   FE2b   22Sqn
**P combat with EA propeller dam ftl 4Sq(2Lt CPF
Lowson OK/2Lt LWB Parsons **WIA**)

7878   DH2   24Sqn
**DP nrBAPAUME shot up dam ftl repairable OK(2Lt
HC Evans)

9th August

5741   BE2d   2Sqn
test/HighP left 2-40pm **MIA(Capt EW Leggatt **POW**)
escaped to UK 8.18

5792   BE2d   7Sqn
**CP POZIÈRES shot up mg ldg a'dr ok OK(2Lt L
Minot/2Lt GH Wood)

5964?   DH2   24Sqn
this a'c? **OP stalked LVG then combat wFLERS[+?]
~7am 11000'-5000', shot up: suffered hits from cockpit
splinters in forehead & blinded so ftl(2Lt SE Cowan
WIA)slight, patrol from 5-30am to 7-30am, EA was going
sw from BAPAUME

6996   FE2b   25Sqn
**P left 3-05pm shot down 7pm? burnt(Lt CJ Hart
KIA/Lt IA Mann **KIA**) ["Vickers" found completely
burnt]

A881   Sopwith Strutter   70Sqn
OP AA then EA swBAPAUME broke up **MIA(2Lt
RMS Shepherd **KIA**/2Lt JW Gunton **KIA**) chased down
by EA: air collision with EA?

10th August

Poor weather from the 10th until the 19th of August
restricted flying.

12th August

6540   BE12   19Sqn
**OP BAPAUME combat with HA 6-45am dam but
repairable OK(Capt CR Tidswell)

This was the first combat involving the BE12

fighter, an ill-fated attempt to develop a single-
seater from the BE2c. There was an ever increasing
demand for fighter units on the Western Front, and
19 Squadron had now arrived in France with the
new type. 21 Squadron had also begun operating
with it. Its main armament was a single forward-
firing Vickers gun, with Vickers interrupter gear.
It was mounted on the port side of the fuselage
because of the large engine air scoop immediately
in front of the cockpit and, equally awkwardly, the
gun aiming rings were placed here too. With
ominous foresight, some were given an additional
rear-pointing Lewis gun, also on the port side, in
an attempt to protect against attack from behind.
Retaining the inherent stability of the BE2c it could
never achieve any success as a fighter for single-
seaters relied on their manoeuvrability and fire
power to survive.

6015   DH2   32Sqn
**OP shot down COURCELETTE spun down ooc
3-50pm **MIA**(Sgt EH Dobson **KIA**) left 2-30pm LE
SARS ["Vickers" found completely burnt 4pm
nrCOURCELETTE]

7894   DH2   32Sqn
**OP AA ovOXFORD COPSE damaged prop ftl cr shell
hole wr(Capt SG Gilmour **WIA**)

13th August

                BE2c   10Sqn
** AA(/2Lt IM Harris **WIA**)neck

6542   BE12   19Sqn
**OP BAPAUME combat with HA & shells shot up
6-45pm returned a'dr ok repairable OK(Lt GGB
Downing)

6549   BE12   19Sqn
**OP left 5-48pm seen before combat with HA
BAPAUME 6-45pm **MIA**(2Lt C Geen **POW**) to Holland
12.10.18 [combat nrBAPAUME 6-45pm Ltn A
Dossenbach/Oblt H Schilling FAb22]

This was the first BE12 lost in action. The RFC
Casualty Report is dated 14.8, but 13.8 is more
likely: an error of one day late owing to the aircraft
having been missing in action?

15th August

42 (Corps) Squadron arrived at Bailleul to become
the second new unit in France equipped with BE2d
and BE2e corps machines. These types were
developments of the BE2c, having much improved
performance and control in the air. It was also
fitted with dual controls and had been initially
projected as a long range aircraft but, like a
number of RFC machines coming into operation at
this time, it would suffer heavy casualties at the

hands of the new German fighters. In the absence of proper replacements it would need to battle on until the summer of 1917. "Bloody April" would see its worst moments, however, with a quarter of the machines shot down in that month being one of these variants (see Appendix II).

16th August

A201   Nieuport 17   11Sqn
+*Esc combat with 4 A-types & Roland[+?dived on Roland & forced it to land seST LEGER] 8000′ 9-10am OK(Lt A Ball) after Roland, returned to A-types & forced two down

5929   DH2   24Sqn
OP combat with many HAs ftl ldg ok BAISIEUX OK(Capt REAW Hughes-Chamberlain **WIA) Fourth Army front

17th August

A187   Nieuport 16   11Sqn
+*SpP combat with Albatros ovBAPAUME 5000′ 7-30am OK(Lt A Ball) EA dived into clouds

19th August

7464   Martinsyde G100   27Sqn
**B BAPAUME combat with HA shot up engine problems ftl OK(Lt PC Sherren)

20th August

2613   BE2c   2Sqn
EscB ftl HARNES? EoL **MIA(2Lt RT Griffin Can. **WIA POW**/Lt HH Whitehead Can. **POW DoW** 21.8.16) left 8-35am, DoW REMY, pilot to Holland 12.10.18

5120   Morane LA   3Sqn
**AP left 9-40am AA dam on return 10-40am OK(Capt CC Miles/Lt CT Cleaver)

9067   Short 184   Dunkirk
** shot down off Belgian coast **MIA**(FLt BC Tooke **POW**/TFLt OH Crowther **KIA**) spotting for HMS *General Craufurd* off coast [?"Seaplane" claim Ltn zS Boenisch]

21st August

2647   BE2c   4Sqn
+*AP several combats with EAs[+second Fokker 6-30pm went down into clouds apparently ooc ovLE SARS-PYS 4500′] CORCELETTE-PYS ~6000′ 4-40pm to 7-15pm OK(Capt JTP Whittaker/2Lt EH Stevens)

A201   Nieuport 17   11Sqn
+*SpP saw off A-type ovGIVENCHY 10000′ 9-30am to 9-50am OK(Lt A Ball) later again ovSOUCHEZ 9-55am to 10-47am

22nd August

**   BE2d?   7Sqn**
** AA (2Lt WRE Harrison **WIA**/)

6552   BE12   19Sqn
+*OP shot up EA from 400yd range swBAPAUME 9000′ 6-10pm then engine failed ftl OK(Lt RF Talbot) HQ commented on 400yd range on Combat Report

A201   Nieuport   11Sqn
+*EscB WARLENCOURT VALLEY combat with 20EAs in 3 groups[+++first was rear of 7 Rolands, shot down cr, second down in flames, third shot down cr house] shot up ftl SENLIS OK(Lt A Ball)

On his last day of operations with 11 Squadron, Ball was escorting bombing aircraft of III Brigade with FE2bs from the unit. After these combats he was forced to return to the lines very low, being shot up on the way. He re-armed at 8 Squadron's aerodrome and then headed east again to fight. After further fighting he was finally forced to land and spent the night by his machine before flying on to his new posting with 60 Squadron.

23rd August

The first German Jagdstaffel, Jasta 1, was formed on the 23rd under the command of Hpt M Zander. Jasta 2, under Boelcke, was officially formed a week later.

1737   BE2c   10Sqn
AReg dhAA cr fire, both fell out over S.27.d. (2Lt HC Marnham **KIA/Lt CL Tetlow **KIA**) left 5-37pm

2629   BE2c   15Sqn
AOb AA ldg ok(2Lt RJ Hudson OK/2Lt GSW Wood **WIA)

**   BE2e   34Sqn**
P combat with EA(2Lt HM Probyn **WIA/2Lt LTS Smith **WIA**)

These were the first casualties in action for 34 Squadron and, incidentally, the first on the BE2e.

24th August

4129   BE2c   15Sqn
Phot shot up ftl a'dr dam(2Lt CD Kershaw **WIA/2Lt EVD Mathews **WIA**)

6532   BE12   19Sqn
+*OP combat with LVG BAPAUME 11000′ 5-30pm to 6-45pm OK(Capt GGA Williams)

6545   BE12   19Sqn
**OP BAPAUME-CAMBRAI combat with 4 Rolands & 3 Fokkers[+?1Fokker seen shot up then down in vertical nose-dive] 11000′ 5-30pm to 6-45pm OK(2Lt EC Callaghan) shared "possible" with BE12 6548

6548   BE12   19Sqn
+*OP several combats including 3 Fokkers & 4 Rolands[+?1 Roland nose-dived ovEQUANCOURT but

unable to follow] 11000′ 5-30pm OK(Capt IHD
Henderson) see BE12 6545, had met 2 Fokkers
ovFLESQUIÈRES, then later: LVG ovACHIET LE
GRAND, Fokker & LVG ovVAUX

6557   BE12   19Sqn
+*OP combat with 4 Rolands & 3 Fokkers 6m
eCAMBRAI 11000′ 5-30pm? to 6-45pm OK(Capt GWD
Allen)

7002   FE2b   25Sqn
B dhAA ftl trenches(Lt MT Baines **WIA/Lt WE
Harper **WIA**) left 5-30pm sARMENTIÈRES, a'c shelled

A879   Sopwith Strutter 70Sqn
**OP shell hit MARCOING spin but recovered?
MIA(Capt RG Hopwood **KIA**/Gnr CR Pearce Can.
KIA) got left behind

A890   Sopwith Strutter 70Sqn
** AA swCAMBRAI then combat with 2EA shot up
engine hit & failed ftl 1m sCARNOY OK(2Lt AM
Vaucour/Lt AJ Bott) [?Sopwith claim combat eMETZ-
EN-COUTURE? 5-30pm OffSt L Reimann Ja1]

When A890 was hit by AA it ignited a section of
the fuselage which Bott was forced to tear away
with his hands. They were then attacked on their
way home, but limped back west of the lines after
a fight (see entry below for incident whilst the
aircraft was being salvaged).

25th August

Delville Wood was finally cleared of the enemy.

                 Morane   3Sqn
TrenchRec rifle fire(Capt CC Miles **WIA)

                 BE2d?   4Sqn
** mg fire(/2Lt GR Bolitho **WIA**) but see Capt JTP
Whittaker

                 BE2d?   4Sqn
P combat(Capt JTP Whittaker **WIA/) but see 2Lt GR
Bolitho

6554   BE12   19Sqn
+*B combat with EA BAPAUME 9500′ 10-30am
OK(2Lt RH Johnson) biplane EA

                 FE2b   22Sqn
** (/Sgt BF Murray **DoW**)

4285   FE2b   22Sqn
Rec engine problems ftl EoL safe ldg **MIA(Lt RD
Walker **POW**/2Lt C Smith **POW**) left 6-49am, a'c
captured [?"Vickers" claim combat GUEDECOURT
Hpt M Zander Ja1]

4289   FE2b   22Sqn
+*P GUEDECOURT combat with 2 Fokkers
ovCOMBLES fuel tank hit, engine failed ftl s.26.b.9.6.
OK(Capt JHS Tyssen/Lt SH Clarke) saw tracers hit EA

5994   DH2   29Sqn
P left 9-35am shot down eYPRES? control? cr **MIA

(Lt KK Turner **POW**) a'c captured

9396.A4   Sopwith Strutter 5 Wing RNAS
Dunkirk **B COGNELÉE Airship Shed low fuel ftl
SCHOONDIJKE **MIA**(FSL CW Jamieson **INT**)

A187   Nieuport 16   60Sqn
**OP AA BOISEUX-AU-MONT dam(Lt Drysdale
WIA) to hospital

A201   Nieuport 17   60Sqn
+* combat with RolandCII[+ooc] sARRAS 11am
OK(Lt A Ball) first victory for Ball in 60Sqn, achieved
ten in this a'c with Nos.11 and 60 Sqns

A890   Sopwith Strutter 70Sqn
**RFL combat with 3EA swALBERT then AA fuel tank
& observer hit ftl nwBOUZINCOURT cr(2Lt AM
Vaucour OK/1AM HP Warminger **DoW**)

As noted above, this machine had force-landed the
previous day. On the 25th, Vaucour returned to the
machine with Warminger to carry out repairs and
bring the machine back. On their way back they
were attacked, but it was a fragment from an AA
shell which damaged the machine and wounded
the passenger. Vaucour managed to reach his
aerodrome but Warminger died of his wounds.

26th August

6743   BE2d   7Sqn
*AReg AA nd crSh57d x.11.a.(2Lt LD Russell NZ.? **DoW**
2.9.16/2Lt D? Clarke **KIA**) observer's initials JW Clarke?

6513   BE12a   19Sqn
B ldg EoL: mistook a'dr? **MIA(2Lt RF Talbot **KIA**)
grave found?, patrol met storm? after bombing

6532   BE12   19Sqn
B ldg EoL: mistook a'dr? **MIA(2Lt AW Reynell **POW**)

6545   BE12   19Sqn
EscB ldg EoL: mistook a'dr? **MIA(2Lt EC Callaghan
KIA)

6548   BE12   19Sqn
+*EscB combat with 6 LVGs on return
ovBOUVINCOURT 11000′ 6-30pm, then another LVG
OK(Capt IHD Henderson) earlier combat LVG
ovHOLNON WOOD

6551   BE12   19Sqn
B left 5-20pm ldg EoL: mistook a'dr? **MIA(2Lt HM
Corbold Can. **POW DoW**) DoW ROISEL

6562   BE12   19Sqn
**B left 5-20pm HAVRINCOURT WOOD ldg EoL:
mistook a'dr? **MIA**(2Lt SP Briggs **POW**)

This black day for 19 Squadron occurred on a raid
to the railway triangle, to bomb troops suspected
of de-training in Havrincourt Wood. After bombing, the patrol met a heavy storm and most likely
became disoriented. All five aircraft were lost.

Sopwith Strutter   70Sqn
** AA(/2Lt JC Taylor **WIA**)neck

27th August

V Brigade RFC was formed on the 27th to serve
the Reserve Army. It grouped 32 Squadron with
15th (Corps) Wing (Nos. 4, 7, and 15 Squadrons).
23 Squadron joined them from III Brigade on the
5th of September and, with No.32, made up the
new 22nd (Army) Wing.

2629   BE2c   15Sqn
**AOb engine shot up dam ftl ldg a'dr OK(2Lt RJ
Hudson/Cpl Whitehead)

28th August

4926   FE2b   11Sqn
**EscB MONTAUBAN combat with EA: rudders dam
ftl cr wr OK(2Lt HH Turk/Lt DH Scott)

4187   BE2c   15Sqn
**AOb shot down sAUCHONVILLERS WoL(Lt R
Burleigh **KIA**/2Lt RC Harry **KIA**) a'c shelled ["BE"
claim combat sAUCHONVILLERS 11-05am Oblt H
Bethge Ja1]

A173   Morane N   60Sqn
**OP combat? BAPAUME-PERONNE seen going east
6-30pm **MIA**(2Lt BM Wainwright **POW**) a'c captured

9892   Sopwith Strutter   70Sqn
OP seen dive on EA nBAPAUME 6pm **MIA(Lt HF
Mase **POW**/Lt VG Odling **POW**) observer to Holland
12.10.18

A888   Sopwith Strutter   70Sqn
+*OP combat with several EAs incl LVGs &
AlbatrosDII[+ooc] BAPAUME 11000'-7500' btwn
5-45pm & 6pm OK(Capt HA Salmond/Lt DA Stewart)
1EA came out of the sun was sent down ooc from point
blank, first victories for 70Sqn

A3432   Sopwith Strutter   70Sqn
+* combat with several EAs incl Albatros DII[+snd,
completely ooc] BAPAUME 6pm OK(Lt AW Keen/
Capt FG Glenday) last of five combats, first victories for
70Sqn

29th August

This was an important day in the general progress
of the war for the Chief of the German General
Staff, General von Falkenhayn, was replaced by
Field-Marshal von Hindenburg. Under the new
leadership a reorganisation and reappraisal of their
war position was made, the greatest consequence
of which was that their offensive at Verdun was
finally suspended. The battles in the north had
been gaining increasing attention throughout
August, but the formal decision to concentrate on

the defence of the Somme was now made. The
ramifications for the air service were as great as
those for the ground forces, and the transfer of
resources soon began.

A big storm occurred on the 29th which
destroyed a hangar containing BE12s of 21
Squadron. Five were totally wrecked, whilst
another seven were damaged.

5836   BE2e   34Sqn
AOb storm ftl EoL **MIA(2Lt DS Cairns **POW**/2Lt KE
Tulloch **POW**) a'c captured, left 3-45pm ST QUENTIN,
last wireless message was at 4-37pm, observer to
Switzerland 10.7.18

31st August

The first fine day after a week of wet weather on
the Somme saw an upturn in fighting. The
Germans were immediately more active, and it was
found that several new aerodromes had also been
completed around Douai. Air fighting took place as
deep as thirty miles east of the line. Ball was active
in his Nieuport, breaking up a formation of twelve
Rolands over their aerodrome near Cambrai. DH2
squadrons were also busy, meeting a new German
fighter type for the first time (see below).

6542   BE12   19Sqn
**EscB(27Sqn) shot up HAVRINCOURT WOOD(2Lt
RS Carline **WIA**)

6579   BE12   19Sqn
**EscB(27Sqn) HAVRINCOURT WOOD engine shot
up dam OK(Lt AT Williams)

5235   FE2b   23Sqn
EscB seen eBAPAUME **MIA(2Lt FG McIntosh **WIA**
POW/2Lt JDA Macfie **WIA POW**) left 9-10am, pilot to
Switzerland 9.12.17, to UK 24.3.18, observer to
Switzerland 13.12.16, to UK 14.9.17

5998   DH2   24Sqn
**DP combat with 3 EA nrGINCHY OK(Capt JO
Andrews)

This combat was the first sight of the new German
fighter, the Albatros DI, these three being from
Jagdstaffel 1.

7873   DH2   24Sqn
**DP combat: dived on HA shot up ftl 9Sq dam(2Lt RS
Capon **WIA**)

7287   Martinsyde G100   27Sqn
EscB left 6-20am HAVRINCOURT WOOD **MIA(2Lt
HM Strange **POW**) ["Mart" claim combat
BEAUMETZ, nrCAMBRAI 7am Ltn H vKeudell
Ja1][?claim Ltn W Fahlbusch/Ltn H Rosencrantz KG1]

7299   Martinsyde G100   27Sqn
**B ldg in control? HAVRINCOURT WOOD a'c burnt
MIA(Capt OL Whittle **POW**) left 6-20am, one

subsequent enemy report said pilot was "unrecognisable"?, but incorrect. pilot repat to UK 18.12.18?

7479   Martinsyde G100   27Sqn
EscB HAVRINCOURT WOOD shot down **MIA(2Lt AJ O'Byrne **WIA POW**) left 6-20am, to Switzerland 27.12.17 & to UK 24.3.18 ["Mart" claim combat FINS 7-15am Oblt H Bethge Ja1]

7482   Martinsyde G100   27Sqn
EscB combat: seen dive with HA shot down in flames **MIA(Capt A Skinner **KIA**) left 6-20am HAVRINCOURT WOOD [?Mart claim Ltn W Fahlbusch KG1] ["Mart" claim combat MOISLAINS 7-40am Ltn G Leffers Ja1]

These four machines were amongst several lost this week whilst bombing billets in the heavily defended Havrincourt Wood. They were attacked after releasing their bombs.

September 1916

AIR FIGHTING ON THE SOMME INTENSIFIES

In the early days of September the Allies still maintained an almost complete aerial superiority, but this circumstance was about to be challenged. Fighting for control of the air had become an ever present and increasingly intense aspect of the war. For the Allies it meant the sky remained relatively free for reconnaissance and in turn was denied to the enemy. German air power had been kept in control by a mixture of offensive patrolling which kept them from the corps machines, and a programme of widespread bombing which drew off resources needed to deal with it. To achieve this, the British bombing squadrons had absorbed some punishment in the previous two months.

However, the Germans were about to display their resilience in the closing months of the year with the gradual introduction of several new fighters, and in time these would swing the odds away from the British. 24 Squadron had already met them in action, in their ominous encounter with the first to reach the Western Front. The combat had lasted half an hour, and although the RFC pilots all managed to return, they knew that they had been outclassed. The combat also highlighted another changing aspect of the air war, which was that individual combats were becoming less common, and instead were taking place between larger formations of opposing aircraft.

The relatively poor manoeuvrability of the Fokker monoplane, coupled with a failure to greatly develop its performance or solve the problems of its armament, meant that its days were almost over. The German fighter pilots had known, however, what they wanted in order to regain the initiative. In essence this was a tractor biplane with light wing loading which could be reliably thrown about to its limits in the tight confines needed for combat, with an engine powerful enough to give a higher rate of climb and ceiling, and the ability to carry increased armament. Three or four such scouts now appeared on the Western Front: the Fokker DII, the Halberstadt DII and the Roland DI, and finally the Albatros DI. All but the Fokker were powered by water-cooled units, the Fokker being powered by a rotary. This machine lacked performance, but the Halberstadts and Rolands were decidedly fast and manoeuvrable. The Roland also managed to carry an armament of twin Spandau machine-guns. However it was the Albatros fighter which soon showed itself to be the most formidable of the new types. Its streamlined shape and very powerful engine made it a significant step forward in fighter design and was the first of a number of superb fighters from that factory. It was still not quite as agile as the Allied pushers, but superior in every other respect. This could be said, in fact, about all four of the new German machines. Not the least important characteristic of the new Albatros was that it also carried two machine-guns, a factor which, combined with its great speed, was going to tell dearly in the next six months.

At first, the new types mostly fled eastwards when confronted, but as their numbers increased through the autumn, and combats became more frequent, their superiority was obvious. Their advantage was two-fold, for the German machine could not only deliver deadly fire, usually from a superior position, but it could also flee from danger with ease. In this respect it was an aircraft perfectly suited to the German air fighting tactics — selective aggression from within a generally defensive method of approach.

1st September

6373   FE2b   18Sqn
HAP LA BASSÉE-LILLE combat with Fokker shot up then spiralled down to safety dam(2Lt GK Macdonald **WIA/Lt FS Rankin OK)

    BE2e   34Sqn
** AA(/2Lt SA Gibbons **WIA**)

2nd September

4290   FE2b   11Sqn

OP left 6-15pm **MIA(2Lt E Burton **POW**/2Lt FW
Griffiths **POW**) observer escaped in 1918

7008	FE2b	11Sqn

**OP combat with Roland shot down wr(2Lt GN
Anderson **WIA**/2Lt GM Allen **KIA**) left 6-15pm, a'c
salvaged

6542	BE12	19Sqn

** combat? shot up(Lt GGB Downing **WIA**)toe

6547	BE12	19Sqn

**B combat with EA HAVRINCOURT 10000' 7pm then
bad ldg dam OK(Lt FS Schell) biplane EA

6554	BE12	19Sqn

B combat? shot up(2Lt RH Johnson **WIA)eye

6561	BE12	19Sqn

**B HAVRINCOURT WOOD shot up dam ldg ok
OK(Lt AT Williams)

A week after losing an entire patrol in a raid, 19
Squadron had another difficult journey to
Havrincourt Wood. After bombing billets once
more they were attacked and were lucky to make
their escape with no losses.

7895	DH2	32Sqn

**OP combat with 4HA BAPAUME Sh62 M.3.B.5.5.
engine hit ldg ok? EoL **MIA**(Capt RE Wilson **POW**) left
4pm, burnt a'c ["BE" claim combat THIEPVAL 6-15pm
Ltn O Boelcke Ja2]

This was Boelcke's twentieth victory and the first
for his new Jagdstaffeln 2. He was flying one of the
new Fokker DIII fighters.

A888	Sopwith Strutter	70Sqn

**OP low combat with HAs nrBOURLON WOOD
down in control? **MIA**(Capt HG Salmond **WIA POW**/
Lt D Stewart **POW**) left 7pm, observer escaped 4.17
["Sopwith" down nrBOURLON 7-20pm]

A892	Sopwith Strutter	70Sqn

+*OP combat with 6EAs nrCAMBRAI incl FokkerEIII
[+smoking,des] BOURLON WOOD 7-05pm then
another FokkerEIII [+absolute vertical dive ooc]
SAILLY 7-25am OK(2Lt AM Vaucour/Lt AJ Bott Can.)
met other EAs later

3rd September

Allied progress was substantial over the next four
days. After a considerable amount of photography,
reconnaissance, and counter-battery work had
prepared the way, another assault was launched on
a wide front as far as Beaumont Hamel. Troops
were finally able to move on Guillemont, and other
successes occurred towards Ginchy.

5766	BE2d	4Sqn

** AA controls shot up ftl ss nose-dived ldg a'dr
12-25pm(2Lt HE McCutcheon **KIFA**/2Lt Rennie **inj**)

	BE2c	8Sqn

** **MIA**(2Lt APV Daly **POW**) ?

5817	BE2e	9Sqn

**CP longeron shot through ftl OK(2Lt SW Mann/Lt
MG Begg)

2732	BE2c	10Sqn

**EscB combat with EAs shot up(2Lt JA Simpson OK/
Pte JVW Phillips **WIA**) to hospital, left 7-30am, Phillips:
leg amputated

6548	BE12	19Sqn

+*OP combat with 5 LVGs ovLE SARS 10000' 1-20pm
OK(Capt IHD Henderson)

6596	BE12	19Sqn

+*OP combat with 2 EAs wCAMBRAI 3000' 9-30am
OK(2Lt HGH Stewart) biplane EAs

6591	BE12	19Sqn

**OP combat with Fokker nrBAPAUME 10000' 8am
OK(2Lt RH Edwards)

4918	FE2b	23Sqn

+*PhotOP combat with 6 Rolands RUYAULCOURT?
seBAPAUME 7000' 8am OK(Lt CJW Crichton/2AM H
Brothers) EAs dived away but ok

6976	FE2b	23Sqn

+*Phot/OP combat with 6 Rolands RUYAULCOURT?
seBAPAUME 7000' 8am OK(2Lt EG Wheldon/1AM
Bayes)

4288	FE2b	22Sqn

**OP left 8-07am combat with EA prop hit ftl
BAIZIEUX dam repairable OK(2Lt CM Clement/Cpl
JK Campbell)

6930	FE2b	22Sqn

**Phot LE SARS engine shot up fuel pipe hit ftl Sh57C
s.15.c.31 dam OK(Capt GR Howard/2Lt JH Chester-
Walsh)

6934.6	FE2b	23Sqn

**OP combat with 5EAs shot down nBAPAUME
MIA(2Lt FDH Sams **POW**/Cpl W Summers **WIA
POW**) left 6-16am, shot down by captured Nieuport
Scout!, a'c captured ["FE 6934" claim combat MORY
8am Ltn G Leffers Ja1, who was possibly killed in this
Nieuport on 27.12.16]

7887	DH2	24Sqn

**OP combat with 3HA shot down FLERS safe ldg?
N.20.a. at 11-05am **MIA**(2Lt HC Evans DSO Can. **KIA**)
killed ldg?, a'c shelled

A1563	Martinsyde G102	27Sqn

**B left 1-25pm AA nrALBERT ftl dam(Lt PA Wright
WIA)

9123	Caudron GIV	4 Wing RNAS

**B GHISTELLES A'dr shot up dam OK(FSLt AL
Thorne)

5th September

7916 DH2 32Sqn
**OP left 6-50am DELVILLE WOOD MIA(2Lt EF Bainbridge KIA)

6th September

2637 BE2c 15Sqn
**B shot up wr ldg nrFRICOURT(2Lt FH Hodgson WIA) attacking aerodromes between BERTINCOURT and VELU

6538 BE12 19Sqn
** combat(Capt GGA Williams WIA)leg

6540 BE12 19Sqn
+*EscB combat with fast LVG ovLE TRANSLOY 12000' 3-30pm OK(Capt CR Tidswell)

6546 BE12 19Sqn
+*B combat with fast LVG ovLE TRANSLOY 12000' 3-30pm OK(2Lt RD Herman)

6580 BE12 19Sqn
+*B combat with fast LVG ovLE TRANSLOY 12000' 3-30pm OK(Lt GBA Baker)

5238 FE2b 25Sqn
**P LOOS combat with Fokker shot down in flames cr 1000yd WoL(2Lt JL Roberton KIA/2Lt EC Kemp KIA) left 3-30pm, pilot jumped

5985 DH2 29Sqn
+*OP HOUTHEM-MENIN combat with Aviatik 2Str[+] nrYPRES 14000' ~12pm shot up dam OK(Sgt JTB McCudden)

This was the first air combat victory for McCudden, whose tally was eventually to reach fifty-seven.

7070 BE2e 42Sqn
**B left 5-30pm combat with HA? QUESNOY shot down MIA(2Lt CLS Thomas KIA)

2Lt Thomas was the first loss in action for 42 Squadron.

A886 Sopwith Strutter 70Sqn
**Rec high combat with EA sCAMBRAI 3-30pm seen going north MIA(2Lt JK Tullis POW/2Lt JC Taylor WIA POW) pilot escaped 8.18, observer to Switzerland 27.12.17

A3431 Sopwith Strutter 70Sqn
+* combat with Roland CII[+flames] ELINCOURT 6-45pm OK(Capt WJS Sanday/Lt Busk) Sanday commanded 19Sqn in 1917

7th September

In an act of further intimidation, Trenchard ordered a second series of bombing raids to distant targets, in which the RNAS was again involved. II Brigade aircraft mostly bombed airfields in front of the Second Army.

2634 BE2c 4Sqn
**AP LE SARS shot up fuel pipe ftl dam(Lt RH Jarvis/ 2Lt EH Stevens)

BE2c? 15Sqn
** mg(/2Lt CR Cook WIA)

4267 FE2b 22Sqn
**Phot left 8-10am combat with EA engine problems ftl nrGROVETOWN Railhead o't on bad ground dam OK(2Lt FD Holder/Lt E Ambler)

6010 DH2 24Sqn
**OP pipes shot through ftl ALBERT W.27.c. dam OK(2Lt LC Burcher)

9127 Caudron GIV 4 Wing RNAS
**B ST DENIS WESTREM A'dr shelled then met enemy seaplane dam OK(FSLt HG Brackley)

8th September

A8 FE2d 20Sqn
**P AA ovLILLE dam ftl 1m sFLEURBAIX a'c shelled(2Lt DH Dabbs WIA/1AM F Dearing OK) left 1-30pm, injured by shell, after ldg?

4921 FE2b 22Sqn
**Phot combat with EA 5-29pm fell in flames nLE SARS MIA(Lt EGA Bowen KIA/Lt RM Stalker KIA) left 4-15pm ["Vickers" claim combat FLERS 5-25pm Hpt O Boelcke Ja2]

A1567 Martinsyde G102 27Sqn
**B mg hit fuel tank ftl 4Sq dam(Lt ED Hicks WIA)burns

9th September

The capture of Ginchy and part of High Wood on September the 9th marked the end of the second phase of the Somme. The British forces had now overrun the last main obstacles on the upper part of the ridge. Air fighting was typically heavy that day, some RFC patrols meeting as many as twenty-five enemy at a time.

The final phase of the battle would last until mid November, as the British extended their gains down the forward slopes of the plateau, capturing Morval, Thiepval, and the Thiepval Ridge.

2742 BE2c 5Sqn
+*Phot ST JULIEN combat with Fokker[+seen nose-dive cr ground LANGEMARCK-POELCAPPELLE] 7000' 2-10pm OK(Lt WH Hubbard/Lt HB Rickards)

2507 BE2c 9Sqn
**CP shot up OK(Lt BT Coller/2Lt TE Gordon-Scaife) pilot's seat shot up from behind

6988 FE2b 11Sqn
**EscB combat with 20 Rolands ftl POMMIER dam ldg(2Lt WHC Buntine WIA/Sgt GJ Morton OK) escorting III Brigade machines on a big raid to dump nr railway at IRLES

6593   BE12   19Sqn
**OP shot up ldg a'dr dam OK(2Lt Smyth)

6596   BE12   19Sqn
+*OP combat with EA BOURLON WOOD 11000'
6-30pm OK(2Lt HGH Stewart) biplane EA

6366   FE2b   22Sqn
**EscPhot seen going West ovMARTINPUICH
nrCONTALMAISON, but down in flames **MIA**(Lt H
Strathy Mackay **KIA**/Lt AJ Bowerman **KIA**) left 3-53pm

7842   DH2   24Sqn
Esc22Sqn combat with EA 5-15pm **MIA(Lt NP
Manfield **KIA**) 4-15pm? [?"Vickers" claim combat
swBAPAUME 5-40pm Hpt O Boelcke Ja2]

7613   FE8   40Sqn
**P left 1-45pm LA BASSÉE-VIMY combat with EA,
drum through prop ftl nrARRAS wr OK(2Lt KS
Henderson)

              Sopwith Strutter   70Sqn
** mg shot up(2Lt HA Howell **WIA**/)

A1911   Sopwith Strutter   70Sqn
**OP BAPAUME-FINS shot up ftl French Lines(2Lt EJ
Henderson OK/2Lt GN Cousans **KIA**)

10th September

Poor weather from the 10th until the 13th of
September restricted most flying.

5861   BE2e   34Sqn
**Shoot combat with HA shot up ovMARTINPUICH ftl
18Sqn dam(2Lt EJ Campbell **WIA**/2Lt EJH Douch OK)

11th September

              BE2c?   9Sqn
CP(/2Lt DL Reed **WIA)back

6546   BE12   19Sqn
**OP shot up ftl French a'dr dam repairable OK(2Lt T
West)

4851   FE2b   23Sqn
OP in format then dived on EA **MIA(2Lt GJ Firbank
KIA/2Lt LGH Vernon **KIA**) left 6-21am

7901   DH2   24Sqn
OP Fourth Army front seen EoL **MIA(Lt LR Briggs
WIA POW) to Switzerland 9.12.17

13th September

              BE2c?   9Sqn
** rifle fire(2Lt CS Hollinghurst **WIA**/)shoulder

A1914   Sopwith Strutter   RFC
*ferrying a'c to France ftl EoL **MIA**(2Lt AF Organ
POW) repat 18.12.18 [note: Abschusse Lists give "2Lt
Organ" down in Clerget Sopwith]

14th September

2652   BE2c   4Sqn
**AP AA hit dam ftl OK(Lt RH Jarvis/Lt CB Bird)

6594   E12   19Sqn
+*P combat with 2 Albatros & 5 Rolands 11000' 8-30am
drifted towards LE CATELET during combat then WIA
by shrapnel and left unconscious for seconds, but
managed return(Lt V Brown **WIA**)head, left 7-15am,
had earlier combat 2 Fokkers & French Nieuport with
crosses

6546   BE12   19Sqn
+*P attacked by small fast rotary EA[+? down ooc
sideways] nrHAVRINCOURT OK(2Lt T West) see
BE12 6561

6561   BE12   19Sqn
+*P attacked by small fast rotary EA[+? saw tracers hit
& dive with black smoke] nrHAVRINCOURT OK(2Lt
RD Herman) see BE12 6546

6579   BE12   19Sqn
+*P combat with 2 Albatros & 5 Rolands 11000' 8-30am
OK(2Lt GC Baker)

The 19 Squadron combats for the last month have
been comprehensively listed because they show the
singular ineffectiveness of the BE12 in combat.
Again and again there was no result: either they
were bested by an opposing aircraft or else the
enemy made an easy escape.

7873   DH2   24Sqn
OP left 7-55am shot down **MIA(2Lt JV Bowring **WIA
POW**) a'c captured, ["Vickers" claim combat
DRIENCOURT 9-10am Hpt O Boelcke Ja2]

7284   Martinsyde G100   27Sqn
+*combat with EA[+ftl] (Lt WHS Chance)

5821   BE2e   34Sqn
**Phot AA shot up ovMARTINPUICH OK(Lt JS
Barnes/Lt H Simons)

A897   Sopwith Strutter   70Sqn
**Rec combat with HA sBAPAUME nose-dived broke
up(2Lt JH Gale **KIA**/Spr JM Strathy **KIA**) [?"Sopwith"
claim combat MORVAL,sBAPAUME 8-15am Hpt O
Boelcke Ja2]

A1908   Sopwith Strutter   70Sqn
**Rec combat with EA dam(Capt WJCKC Patrick OK/
2Lt EW Burke **KIA**)

15th September
THE BATTLE OF
FLERS-COURCELETTE

The third phase of the Somme Offensive began at
dawn on the 15th of September. This was the battle
of Flers-Courcelette. Its ambitious plan required
the Fourth Army to overwhelm the enemy's third

line system between Morval and Le Sars, and then to mount a cavalry charge through the gap onto high ground. The attack was to use air support to its fullest, and by the end of the day the RFC had fought its heaviest battle of the war. The assault would also see the first exploratory use of tanks in battle, including direct aerial co-operation with them. An interesting aside to this was that aircraft were set patrolling ceaselessly over the battlefield the night before attack to drown the sound of their deployment.

The artillery barrage had begun three days in advance of the fighting, and was being directed by a more sophisticated "zone-calling" system. It was increased in intensity through the last hours before dawn, until at 6-20am the infantry moved forward in thin mist. Their progress was watched by corps squadrons, and these provided valuable intelligence about the advance. At one point in the fighting, as it approached High Wood, 34 Squadron's contact patrolling certainly saved a sizeable British force. All three tanks assigned to this attack had failed, and the troops found themselves opposing an enemy of uncertain strength. Repeated patrols by Capt CHB Blount and Lt TS Pearson established that it was in fact about to encounter a formidable force, and to attack it would be a grave error. As a result, the orders for the assault were cancelled.

Much of the work the RFC carried out proved invaluable in directing the battle and enabling enemy batteries to be engaged effectively. Genuine progress was made through the day, although it in no way matched the earlier aspirations. On a six-mile front, two main enemy defensive lines had been broken, and Courcelette, Martinpuich, and Flers had been taken, with only relatively light losses. There was extremely heavy air fighting, as is evident from the casualties, for the air war had taken a decisive step in intensity. This only strengthened the resolve of the RFC to maintain its highly offensive tactics. It was an obvious thing to do for the side possessing numerical superiority, but by this time they were also long committed to it philosophically. Unfortunately, it was a policy meeting diminishing success as the availability of quality German machines rose.

A293?   Morane Parasol   3Sqn
this a'c? **AP left 9-55am dhAA LES BOEFFS(Capt AM? Miller **WIA**/Lt H Tatton? **WIA**) names Millar?,Taylor?

6947   FE2b   11Sqn
OP ldg neFRISE 6pm? **MIA(2Lt FE Hollingsworth **KIA**/2Lt HMW Wells **KIA**) left 4-06pm

FE2b   11Sqn
EscB to railway targets at BAPAUME combat shot up (/Sgt DB Walker **DoW)

BE2c   12Sqn
B railway targets at BAPAUME (Capt EG Tyson **WIA)slight, escorted by 11 Sqn

5220   FE2b   18Sqn
*CP mg fire FLERS 1200′ 10-50am shot up dam ftl OK(2Lt FC Biette/2Lt PJ Smyth)

18 Squadron had been brought onto the Somme to co-operate with the anticipated cavalry charge.

6580   BE12   19Sqn
**CP rifle fire EoL shot up dam but returned a'dr ok OK(Lt GBA Barker)

6164   BE12   21Sqn
BP left 4-30pm **MIA(Lt G Klingenstein **WIA POW**) repat to UK 7.1.17

6583   BE12   21Sqn
BP left 9-30am **MIA(2Lt C Elphinston **WIA POW**) [?"BE 6583" claim combat MANANCOURT 11-30am Ltn K Wintgens Ja1]

7484   Martinsyde G100   27Sqn
EscB for BOURLON WOOD shot down emitting smoke **MIA(2Lt CJ Kennedy **POW**) left 7-45am, attacking General von Below's headquarters, were attacked over château

A136   Nieuport 16   60Sqn
KBP left 8-30am AA? sBAPAUME in flames **MIA(Capt ASM Summers **KIA**) [?poss Nieu claim combat PERONNE Ltn W Frankl Ja4]

A200.A6   Nieuport 17   60Sqn
**KBP BAPAUME shot up ftl ldg 60Sq repairable OK(Lt A Ball)

A895   Sopwith Strutter   70Sqn
OP combat with HA nrYTRES shot down(Capt GL Cruikshank DSO MC **KIA/Lt RA Preston **KIA**) left 6-40pm

A1903   Sopwith Strutter   70Sqn
OP BAPAUME-CAMBRAI shot up ftl cr(2Lt N Kemsley OK/2Lt CJ Beatty **KIA) killed in crash

A1910   Sopwith Strutter   70Sqn
OP BAPAUME-CAMBRAI **MIA(2Lt FH Bowyer **WIA POW**/2Lt WB Saint **DoW**) pilot repat 7.1.18 [2 "Sopwith" claims combats HESBECOURT 7am, ETERPIGNY 7-15pm Hpt O Boelcke Ja2]

A1913   Sopwith Strutter   70Sqn
OP BAPAUME combat with HA shot up dam ftl 15Sqn(Capt WJCKC Patrick OK/Capt FG Glenday **KIA)

This was a grim day for 70 Squadron, meeting Boelcke over Havrincourt Wood at the height of his confidence and skill. The Strutter formation was split up in early fighting, and suffered as a result.

Despite occurrences such as this, the Strutter was undoubtedly one of the best British machines in France. In these same combats, 70 Squadron still managed to drive down three enemy, and another two of the enemy collided in heated fighting on the way home. The stakes for both sides were increasing dramatically. The Strutters they flew had both synchronised forward fire through the propeller and a machine-gun behind for the observer, which meant the machine combined protection with attacking qualities. It was a genuine two-seater fighter scout, and the techniques of formation flying which were employed added to its usefulness. The observer's gun was now fitted to a Scarff ring-mount, which gave great scope for fire. It was the model for nearly all mountings for years to come. There was a single-seater bombing variation as well, which only the RNAS used. The drawbacks of the Strutter centred on the reliability of its synchronised firing mechanism. A separate trigger for the gun was provided in case it failed, which betrayed the basic lack of confidence in it. In this instance, the pilot chanced firing direct through the propeller with no interrupter system. In the face of increasingly powerful armament being fitted to the new German types, a single forward gun also looked a little under-armed. One bonus the Strutter was to enjoy was that it successfully adapted to a larger, more powerful engine in 1917, extending its useful life.

16th September

4495   BE2c   2Sqn
B left 5-20am DOUAI Stn combat with Fokker shot down **MIA(2Lt D Cushing Can. **POW**)

2 and 25 Squadrons carried out several important bombing raids to the rail system around Douai, Valenciennes, and Somain in the coming days. These were a part of a general bombing intensification on the Somme, intended to hinder German efforts to reinforce its armies.

A180   Morane LA   3Sqn
**AP left 1pm shot up dam returned a'dr ok 2-20pm OK(Lt JK? Summers/Lt CT? Cleaver)

6999   FE2b   11Sqn
Rec shot down smoking but in control wMARCOING **MIA(2Lt AL Pinkerton **POW**/Lt JW Sanders **POW**) left 5-40pm ["FE" claim combat MANANCOURT but 5pm? Ltn O Höhne Ja2]

2617   BE2c   15Sqn
AOb combat with 3EA ovMIRAUMONT STATION out of clouds 4000' 3-30pm gun jam shot up ftl Albert(2Lt Vinson OK/Capt A Brooke-Murray **DoW 23.9.16) observer hit in leg after gun jam

4842   FE2b   18Sqn
**EscPhot combat with 3Rolands nrFLERS shot up dam OK(Capt FC Baker/2Lt AV Shewell)

4854   FE2b   18Sqn
**EscPhot FLERS fuel tank shot up nrTALIS BOISE ftl Sh57C A.9.c. OK(2Lt F Hall/2Lt HS Royffe)

4863   FE2b   18Sqn
**Esc combat with 2 of 4HA shot up dam but returned a'dr ok OK(Sgt T Jones/Lt A Nesbitt) left 4-15pm Fourth Army front

6971   FE2b   18Sqn
*TacP fouled KB cable cr wr(2Lt CC Hayward Aust. **DoI**/2Lt PJ Smith **DoI**) left 10-20am

17th September

2624   BE2c   8Sqn
**Phot VII Corps shot up OK(2Lt C Holland/2Lt JB Pirie)

4844   FE2b   11Sqn
EscB combat with HAs MARCOING ftl **MIA(2Lt TPL Molloy **POW**/Sgt GJ Morton **WIA POW**) left 9-05am, ldg ok?: burnt a'c [claim combat EQUANCOURT? am Ltn W Frankl Ja4]

6994   FE2b   11Sqn
EscB wMARCOING seen in control? **MIA(2Lt H Thompson Can. **POW DoW** 18.9.16/Sgt JE Glover **KIA**) left 9-12am [?"FE" claim combat sTRESCAULT 10-35am? possibly 11-35am? Ltn L Reimann Ja2]

7018   FE2b   11Sqn
Esc wMARCOING down control? EoL **MIA(2Lt LBF Morris **POW DoW**/Lt T Rees **KIA**) left 9-10am, DoW CAMBRAI, "Lt Turk saw all" ["Vickers" claim combat VILLERS PLOUICH 10-40am Ltn M Fr vRichthofen Ja2]

MANFRED VON RICHTHOFEN'S FIRST VICTORY

This victory was the first for Manfred von Richthofen, the most famous fighter ace of the First World War. He would come to be known as the "Red Baron", and in the next twenty months would claim eighty victories. In this, his first, he was flying an Albatros DII, part of a group of Jagdstaffel 2 pilots led into battle by Boelcke, for the first time in formation. They met and fought eight BE2cs from 12 Squadron which were being escorted by FE2bs of 11 Squadron. The results of this one combat were four FEs shot down along with two 12 Squadron aircraft. An offensive patrol from 60 Squadron helped extricate and rescue the survivors. It was a devastating introduction for the new German fighter types, which the Jasta had received only the day before.

In fact, in the last three days' air fighting there

had been a total of eighteen RFC air crew killed and fifteen more taken prisoner. The aerial superiority which the RFC had enjoyed through the spring and summer of 1916 was in the process of being ended. A report by Trenchard to Headquarters at this time reminds one of the scale of commitment of the RFC's offensive policy. The purpose of the report was to register his dismay over the increasing presence of the enemy over Allied lines. He went on: ". . . the Germans have brought another squadron . . . of fighting machines to this neighbourhood and also more artillery machines. One or two German aeroplanes have crossed the line during the last few days . . . With all this, however, the anti-aircraft guns have only reported 14 hostile machines as having crossed the line in the Fourth Army area in the last week... whereas something like 2,000 to 3,000 of our machines crossed the lines during the week."

7019   FE2b   11Sqn
EscB combat with EA wMARCOING ftl down in control? **MIA(Capt DB Gray **POW**/Lt LB Helder **POW**) left 9-05am, Gray escaped 8.18 [?"FE" claim combat EQUANCOURT? 10-35am Hpt O Boelcke Ja2]

2741   BE2c   12Sqn
B MARCOING **MIA(Lt RRN Money **POW**) [Ja2?]

5873   BE2d   12Sqn
B MARCOING combat with EA shot down **MIA(2Lt AFA Patterson **POW DoW** 25.9.16) DoW at CAMBRAI

6169   BE12   21Sqn
**OP BAPAUME mg dam ftl FLAUCOURT-BARLEUX OK(Capt E Digby-Johnson)

4852   FE2b   23Sqn
Rec combat with EA then down control? **MIA(Sgt B Irwin **KIA**?/2Lt FG Thiery **KIA**) left 6-07pm for VELU-EPEHY-MARCOING triangle [?"Vickers" claim combat HEUDICOURT 8am Hpt M Zander Ja1]

**   FE2b   25Sqn**
B DOUAI combat with 2 Fokkers(/Lt R Spiers **WIA)

7286   Martinsyde G100   27Sqn
B VALENCIENNES engine failed 50 miles EoL ftl **MIA(Lt WHS Chance **POW**) left 7-10am for rail targets [?"Avro" claim CAMBRAI Ltn R Berthold Ja4]

The listings show a high number of casualties to bombing operations at this time. Bombing continued to be carried out both to damage particular targets and to cause redeployment of valuable aircraft from the front. Increasing numbers of these raids were being directed at enemy aerodromes. This was one more response to the growing threat of German air power. As a reflection of these changes the proportional rise of casualties through air combat as opposed to other

causes was particularly marked in September 1916 (see Appendix I).

9420.A3   Sopwith Strutter   5 Wing RNAS
B ST DENIS WESTREM AA ground fire ftl WESTCAPELLE 3-30pm **MIA(FLt DE Harkness NZ. **WIA** INT) interned Holland

A1913   Sopwith Strutter   70Sqn
Rec mg HA seen ovCAMBRAI **MIA(2Lt O Nixon **KIA**/2Lt R Wood **WIA POW**) observer to Holland 9.4.18, to UK 2.7.18 ["Sopwith 2Str" claim combat nwHERVILLY 6-45am Ltn E Böhme Ja2]

18th September

Poor weather prevented most flying.

19th September

6951   FE2b   11Sqn
**Rec shot up dam ok ldg a'dr OK(Sgt Coupal/Sgt Parke) left 5-05pm

6985   FE2b   11Sqn
Rec combat with EA ftl DELVILLE WOOD wr(Lt WP Bowman OK/Cpl G Munk **WIA) left 5-10pm, a'c shelled on ldg

6992   FE2b   11Sqn
** combat(/2Lt AJ Cathie **WIA**)arm

11 Squadron were on a reconnaissance escorted by 60 Squadron when they were attacked by Boelcke's unit near Queant. This assault was so effective that the operation was abandoned.

6330   FE2b   18Sqn
**Phot mg shot up ftl nrSUZANNE 6-15pm dam OK(2Lt SF Heard/2Lt GT Richardson)

6595   BE12   21Sqn
BP shot up nrBAPAUME ftl 18Sq(2Lt ES Duggan **WIA)

A204   Morane V   60Sqn
Esc seen with HA on tail ovACHIET LE GRAND snd with wing off **MIA(Capt HC Tower **KIA**) left 5-30pm ["Morane" claim combat ovGREVILLERS WOOD 6-30pm Hpt O Boelcke Ja2: found completely burned]

See entries for 11 Squadron above.

20th September

4934   FE2b   22Sqn
P seen WoL going north, met clouds lost PUISIEUX **MIA(2Lt RN Carter **POW**/2Lt WJ Gray Can. **POW**) left 12-27pm

21st September

**   Morane   3Sqn**
** combat(/2Lt C Baines **WIA**)arm

22nd September

4937　　　FE2b　　　　18Sqn
**Phot combat with EA 8-55am down nrGINCHY(2Lt
F Hall **DoW**/Lt BF Randall OK) landed by observer,
a'c shelled, EA possibly a Roland, & possibly first hit by
a shell [? combat COMBLES Hpt H-J Buddecke Ja4]

The weather had been dull for a week, but the next
general Allied attack was planned for the 25th, and
work could not stop. Machines of IV Brigade spent
these days comprehensively photographing the
enemy positions, generally reconnoitring, and
registering guns. On the 22nd its corps machines
spent three hundred and three hours in the air on
these duties. It was much clearer on this day, and
this brought out aircraft on both sides in force. The
Germans were becoming ever more active and
dangerous, with many more aircraft crossing the
line. The crew above fell victim to one of these
enemy fighters. The observer, Randall, landed the
machine after his pilot had been hit and fallen
unconscious. There were very few other attacks on
the vital photographic machines, however, as they
were strongly protected by single-seaters.

6937　　　FE2b　　　　18Sqn
Esc combat with 2HA ERVILLERS AA? **MIA(Sgt T
Jones **inj DoW** 29.9.16/2Lt FAA Hewson **WIA POW**)
left 9am nBAPAUME

6544　　　BE12　　　　19Sqn
**OP combat with HA br down nrLE TRANSLOY?
MIA(2Lt G Hedderwick **KIA**) ["BE" claim combat
sSAILLY-SAILLISEL OffSt L Reimann Ja2]

6561　　　BE12　　　　19Sqn
OP brought down nrBAPAUME? **MIA(2Lt RD
Herman **DoW** as **POW**) DoW at EPHEY [?"BE" claim
combat BERTINCOURT Ltn R Berthold Ja4]

6591　　　BE12　　　　19Sqn
OP brought down BAPAUME? **MIA(2Lt RH
Edwards **KIA**) ["BE" claim combat COMBLES Ltn O
Höhne Ja2]

19 Squadron flew offensive patrols to bomb Velu
aerodrome, east of Bapaume, on this day. Two
patrols were made and both met fierce opposition.

6578　　　BE12　　　　21Sqn
**B VELU A'dr shot down in flames BOIS
D'OUVRAGE(2Lt CD Higgins **KIA**) left 7-55am [?poss
"Sopwith" found completely burnt in ST PIERRE
FOREST 9-15am on 22.9]

4938　　　FE2b　　　　22Sqn
**P combat with HA shot down sHARDECOURT cr o't
dam(2Lt HJ Finer **inj**/Cpl A Winterbottom **KIA**) left 7-
25am, observer hit & killed whilst moving mg position,
which then fell on pilot's head. Pilot was effectively
unconscious when he landed

6993　　　FE2b　　　　25Sqn
B AA shot down low eDOUAI **MIA(2Lt KF Hunt
POW/Cpl LO Law **POW**) left 6-40am

This was another loss inflicted during the bombing
programme to the enemy rail networks behind the
Somme front.

7263　　　Martinsyde G100　　　27Sqn
**B HAVRINCOURT WOOD shot up dam OK(Sgt H
Bellerby)

6384　　　FE8　　　　40Sqn
+* combat with Fokker[+shot down] OK(Capt DO
Mulholland)

This was the first combat victory for 40 Squadron.

23rd September

Air activity was high again on another bright day.

2533　　　BE2c　　　　5Sqn
+*AOb combat with 2 Rolands over V.28. 7500' 1-15pm
OK(Lt Skeate/Lt HB Rickards) hit EA from 60 yards
before gun jam, then seen bank

4853　　　FE2b　　　　18Sqn
**P combat with EA LE TRANSLOY chased down ftl
T.5.c.5.5. **MIA**(2Lt JL Tibbetts **WIA POW**/Lt WG
Warn **KIA**) left 3-15pm Fourth Army front

6167　　　BE12　　　　21Sqn
OP BAPAUME left 8am **MIA(Lt JMJ Kenny **POW**
DoW) [combat SAILLY 8-55am Hpt H-J Buddecke Ja4]

7910　　　DH2　　　　24Sqn
**EscOP combat with Fokker dam ftl nGINCHY-
DELVILLE WOOD OK(2Lt WE Nixon)

7911　　　DH2　　　　24Sqn
**EscOP combat with Fokker dam OK(Lt PAL Byrne)

7475　　　Martinsyde G100　　　27Sqn
**OP combat? MARCOING? collided with HA? smoke
MIA(2Lt EJ Roberts **KIA**) left 8-40am [?"Mart" claim
combat HERVILLY 8-55am Ltn E Bvhme Ja2]

7480　　　Martinsyde G100　　　27Sqn
**OP smoke? air collision with HA? LE TRANSLOY?
MIA(2Lt OC Godfrey **KIA**) [Vzfw L Reimann Ja2 in air
collision with EA ovBUS 8-50am but both survived?]

7481　　　Martinsyde G100　　　27Sqn
OP collision with HA? combat? **MIA(Sgt H Bellerby
KIA) MvR2 ["Mart" claim combat sBEUGNY 8-50am?
Ltn M Fr vRichthofen Ja2]

Six 27 Squadron Martinsydes left for a morning
patrol to distant Cambrai, but met a formation of
new German fighters. Besides the three losses
above, 2Lt LF Forbes had an air collision with an
enemy, which plummeted to earth. Forbes' wing
was damaged but he managed to nurse his machine
back to the lines. As he attempted to land at 24
Squadron's aerodrome he crashed his aeroplane.

5814   **BE2e**   **34Sqn**
AP combat with Roland shot up cr sMAMETZ(2Lt PR Pinsent **DoW/Lt JAR Buller **WIA**)

24th September

The day began with dense mist which lasted until late morning. Photographic work was therefore hindered for most of the day, but a large offensive sweep, planned for the afternoon, still took place. This involved sixty RFC machines, and targeted the enemy aerodromes around Cambrai from which many of the new German fighters were operating. It was moderately successful, but the BE12s of 19 Squadron suffered heavily. What is more, they suffered at the hands of enemy two-seaters as well as fighters, being completely out-manoeuvred by them in the battle which took place over Havrincourt Wood. The losses to Nos. 23 and 27 Squadron below also happened on this raid.

6546   **BE12**   **19Sqn**
** combat with HA HAVRINCOURT in flames broke up **MIA**(2Lt T West **KIA**) a'c captured [?"Mart" claim combat FLESQUIÈRES Ltn K Wintgens Ja1] [?claim combat MORCHIES 5-10pm Ltn A Dossenbach/Oblt H Schilling FAb22]

6579   **BE12**   **19Sqn**
** HAVRINCOURT combat with HA in flames broke up **MIA**(2Lt G Edwards **KIA**) a'c captured [?"Mart" claim combat FLESQUIÈRES Ltn K Wintgens Ja1]

So unsuccessful had the BE12 been as a fighter in its brief few weeks at the front, that on the 24th Trenchard finally attempted to abandon it. He wrote: "I have lost a very large number of them, and I am afraid that we are losing more of these machines than we can afford in pilots, and certainly more, I am afraid, than they bring down . . . Although I am short of machines to do the work that is now necessary with the large number of Germans against us, I cannot do anything else but to request that no more be sent out to this country." Any replacement aircraft were far from ready, however, and a switch to a bombing role was the solution devised.

4857   **FE2b**   **23Sqn**
SpP engine shot up ftl MILLENCOURT(2Lt JC Griffiths OK/2Lt RS Osmaston **KIA) attacked by a Roland? over BERTINCOURT, which was then shot down by 6964 (see below)

6964   **FE2b**   **23Sqn**
+* combat with 1Str[+ooc] ovBERTINCOURT 5-05pm OK(2Lt KL Gopsill/2Lt FWA Vickery)

7498   **Martinsyde G100**   **27Sqn**
OP left 3-40pm shot down **MIA(2Lt EN Wingfield **POW**) to Holland 12.10.18, a'c captured and later shown in Delka display

In this period of increasingly heavy fighting the Martinsydes and BE12s between them had their heaviest week of losses so far in the war. In three days seven BE12 pilots were killed whilst four Martinsydes were shot down, a single pilot surviving to become a prisoner.

25th September

This was a bright, fine day for the commencement of the next stage of the British advance. The main objectives for the infantry were from between Guedecourt down to Morval, and their progress was closely watched by contact patrols. By the afternoon most of the objectives were close to capture. The air fighting accompanying the battle was a little unusual, for the German machines, which were very active and numerous, remained high up where they could not be reached. Occasionally some dropped down to attack corps machines, or cross the lines, but there was generally little interference.

A140   **Morane LA**   **3Sqn**
**AP LE TRANSLOY explosion ftl dam OK(Lt JK Summers/2Lt L Reynolds) bullet hit grenade?

    BE2c?   **4Sqn**
LowRec THIEPVAL AA(2Lt NES Simon **WIA)slight

    FE2b   **11Sqn**
** shrapnel(/Capt ACW Field **WIA**)chest

2669   **BE2c**   **16Sqn**
CB LIBERCOURT Stn AA ovVIMY 5000' ooc ftl cr Sh36.C.s.26. a'c shelled wr(2Lt RS Haward? OK/2AM HHR Rolfe **DoI) left 1-30pm?, name Howard?

6553   **BE12**   **19Sqn**
**CP shot up dam ldg ok at a'dr, repairable OK(2Lt FHB Selous) involved in fighting around THIEPVAL

6383   **FE8**   **40Sqn**
**EscB AA prop shot off ftl Sh36C c.13.d wr OK(2Lt R? Gregory)

40 Squadron were involved in some elaborate escort duties on the 25th, all of which were associated with the bombing programme. The main target for the day was the station at Libercourt, which was bombed by BE2cs of 16 and 25 Squadron, with 40 Squadron in attendance. In order to prepare for this attack, however, three nearby enemy aerodromes were attacked in advance. FE2bs of 25 Squadron also did this work, again escorted by 40 Squadron, and their loads included smoke bombs to further hinder the Germans on their air strips. It was reported that only one German fighter managed to get into the air, and could offer little resistance to the attackers.

A382   Sopwith Strutter   70Sqn
**OP shrapnel hit ftl cr OK(Lt JB Lawton/Pte Jones)

26th September

Guedecourt still remained in enemy hands on the
26th, and the day's fighting concentrated on this
village. Between the British and their objective was
an important enemy trench, and a 3 Squadron crew
assisted greatly in its taking. They were Lt LG
Wood and Lt HJL Cappel on contact patrol. In
effect, their final strafing and bombing of the
occupants led to their surrender. The increasing
harassment meted out to German troops by the
RFC at this time, of which this was a prime
example, was to be well documented by the enemy
infantry.

A192   Morane LA   3Sqn
**AP shell hit ftl MARICOURT A.9.D. at 9-30am cr
OK(Lt Williamson/Lt MMA? Lillis) left 8am

6254   BE2d   5Sqn
+*Phot combat with Roland nPOLYGON WOOD 7000'
12pm to 12-15pm OK(2Lt GW Pender/Lt HJ Duncan)

BE2c?   8Sqn
** AA(/Capt PE Welshman WIA)ankle

7079   BE2e   9Sqn
**CP dhAA ovLESBOEFFS 3pm MIA(Lt BT Coller
KIA/2Lt TE Gordon-Scaife KIA) left 2-20pm

7020   FE2b   11Sqn
**OP combat with EA shot up but ldg ok dam OK(2Lt
LR Wren/LCpl Young) left 4-15pm

A8   FE2d   20Sqn
**P combat with EA[+] ovYPRES ftl
VLAMERTINGHE dam(2Lt AF Livingstone WIA/
1AM F Dearing WIA) left 6-25am

7478   Martinsyde G100   27Sqn
**OP combat with EA shot up dam OK(Lt JM McAlery)

A201.A2 Nieuport 17   60Sqn
** AA shrapnel BAPAUME 11-30am(2Lt G Phillipi
WIA)

A1916   Sopwith Strutter   70Sqn
**OP combat with 6EAs swBAPAUME 10-20am
MIA(2Lt FStJFN Echlin KIA/1AM A Grundy KIA)
[?possible EA claim combat ERVILLERS 11-25am Ltn
A Dossenbach/Oblt H Schilling FAb22]

27th September

Before heavy rain set in later in the day there was
another period of heavy fighting. An attack on the
Martinsydes of 27 Squadron by five of Boelcke's
unit was one of the most destructive.

4839   FE2b   25Sqn
** combat with EA[+] TOURMIGNIES shot down
OK(2Lt VW Harrison/Sgt LS Court) [?FE2b claim

combat TOURMIGNIES Ltn A Dossenbach/Oblt H
Schilling FAb22, who was shot down but OK]

7491   Martinsyde G100   27Sqn
**OP BAPAUME combat with EA shot up dam OK(2Lt
RW Chappell)

7495   Martinsyde G100   27Sqn
**OP left 9-20am MIA(2Lt S Dendrino POW DoW)
[?poss "Avro 7495" unconfirmed claim Vzfw L Reimann
Ja2, however Boelcke describes shooting this machine up
and then grimly becoming aware that it was flying around
in circles with the pilot mortally wounded at the controls
(see War in the Air, vol. II)]

A1562   Martinsyde G102   27Sqn
**OP combat with EA ftl MAROEUIL dam(2Lt BUS
Smith WIA)

A1568   Martinsyde G102   27Sqn
**OP left 9-20am combat with EA MIA(2Lt HA Taylor
KIA) [?claim combat neERVILLERS Hpt O Boelcke
Ja2]

A1569   Martinsyde G102   27Sqn
+*OP combat with 7EAs[+?down in vertical nd]
BAPAUME-CAMBRAI 13000'-9000' 11am OK(Lt H
Spanner) EA was very fast Nieuport type, after 4 drums
EA eventually went down, but in control?

A1909   Sopwith Strutter   70Sqn
**Rec combat with EA Scout & AA shot down
MARQUION in control? MIA(2Lt MS Faraday WIA
POW/2Lt JH Lowson WIA POW)

28th September

2742   BE2c   5Sqn
**B seen on ground nrGHELUVELT ~3pm hazy
MIA(Lt AT Eason? POW) joined Sqn 16.9.16, name
Easom?

3992   Nieuport 11   1 Wing RNAS
+* combat with enemy seaplane[+?ooc] off CALAIS
~11am dam OK(FSLt DHMB Galbraith)

A253   SPAD 7   60Sqn
+*P combat with 4Albatros[+] AVESNES-LES-
BAPAUME ~6-10pm OK(Capt EL Foot)

This was the first victory achieved on the new
SPAD 7 French fighter by the RFC. SPAD fighters
were to be amongst the best of the war, and were
already proving themselves in battle with the
French.

29th September

No real war flying because of conditions.

30th September

The last day of the month was fine and warm, and
a great deal of air work was carried out. This was
mainly to assess the next area for advance — for

example, over five hundred aerial photographs were taken of the battle area. The Pozières ridge and the ground generally overlooking the Ancre valley had finally been taken. This denied a substantial amount of high ground for observation to the enemy, so efforts to restrict their air reconnaissances became even more important. Much of this offensive patrolling was done by RFC Nieuports. 12 and 13 Squadrons also carried out bombing of Lagnicourt, escorted by Moranes and Nieuports of 60 Squadron and FE2bs of 11 Squadron.

6973   FE2b   11Sqn
EscB combat with seBAPAUME? 10-45am shot down in flames **MIA(Lt EC Lansdale **POW DoW** 1.12.16/Sgt A Clarkson **KIA**) left 9-10am, MvR3 ["Vickers" claim combat FREMICOURT 10-50am Ltn M Fr vRichthofen Ja2]

6968   FE2b   18Sqn
**HAP combat with 9HA nrBAPAUME shot up ftl Sh62d L.11. dam OK(2Lt C Parkinson/Lt FS Rankin) left 4-40pm Fourth Army front

6931   FE2b   22Sqn
**DP left 4-37pm LIGNY Lewis drum into prop during combat ftl BRAY OK(2Lt CS Duffus/Cpl F Johnson)

6000   DH2   24Sqn
OP left 10-55am combat with EA BAPAUME ftl wr(2Lt CPV Roche **WIA)

A206   Morane I   60Sqn
**EscB LAGNICOURT combat with EA shot up dam OK(Capt EO Grenfell)

N500   Sopwith Triplane   1 Wing RNAS
+* combat with 2Str[+?shot down] swST PIERRE CAPPELLE then drove off EA attacking Belgian Farman OK(FSLt RS Dallas)

THE LOSS OF ALLIED AIR SUPERIORITY

It is clear from the entries for these last weeks of September that the aerial superiority of the Allies had been dealt a critical blow. The Germans had revived their fighting spirit and vigour. RFC squadrons had flown a record 22,500 hours in September in an effort to contain their opponents, but the casualties suffered by fighter units had dramatically climbed. Trenchard wrote a letter to Haig full of concern and foreboding on the last day of the month. In it he noted: "Throughout the last three months the Royal Flying Corps in France has maintained such a measure of superiority over the enemy in the air that it has been enabled to render services of incalculable value. The result is that the enemy has made extraordinary efforts to increase the number, and develop the speed and power of

his fighting machines. He has unfortunately succeeded in doing so and it is necessary to realise clearly, and at once, that we shall undoubtedly lose our superiority in the air if I am not provided at an early date with improved means of retaining it. Within the last few days the enemy has brought into action on the Somme front a considerable number of fighting aeroplanes which are faster, handier, and capable of attaining a greater height than any at my disposal with the exception of one squadron of single-seater 'Nieuports', one of 'FE Rolls Royce', and one of 'Sopwiths'. . . All other fighting machines at my disposal are decidedly inferior. The result of the advent of the enemy's improved machines has been a marked increase in the casualties suffered by the Royal Flying Corps, and though I do not anticipate losing our present dominance in the air for the next three or four months, the situation after that threatens to be very serious unless adequate steps to deal with it are taken at once."

Haig himself was reflecting deeply on the worsening situation, and wrote the telling observation that as a result of the increasing losses, the British were now doing less distant fighting, "with the result that an increasing number of German machines now come up to the lines . . . It is the fighting far behind the enemy's lines that tells the most."

Facing these men as they wrote these words were the British air personnel losses for this terrible month. The listings above show that over France the RFC had lost sixty-two airmen dead, another thirty-six taken prisoner, and thirty-six wounded. Over half of the losses had occurred in only nine days, between the 15th and the 23rd. These figures also excluded another forty or so occasions during September when Allied aircraft were forced down through enemy action but with no casualty to the crew. At this time of growing concern the RFC took welcome encouragement from the fact that Albert Ball had accounted for ten enemy machines between the 15th and the 28th.

Since the 12th of June the RFC as a whole had consumed 1,195 aircraft whilst taking on 1,725.

October 1916

1st October

Two significant British pushes began on October 1st. The first was a drive against Eaucourt l'Abbaye, for which 3 and 34 Squadrons supplied contact patrols. One of the 3 Squadron machines

had a shell pass right through a wing and was
forced to return. Such was the precision and force
of the advancing barrage that all objectives were
reached in under one hour, including the entering
of Le Sars. The other operation involved Canadian
troops in fierce and desperate fighting north and
west of Courcelette.

4863	FE2b	18Sqn

**HAP combat with 5HA 11am ldg a'dr ok(2Lt FC Biette
WIA/2Lt WA Mackay OK) left 9-05am Fourth Army
front

7892	DH2	32Sqn

**LP left 8-15am PUISIEUX combat with EA shot down
HEDAUVILLE dam OK(2Lt G King)

A2533	DH2	32Sqn

**LP POZIÈRES-COURCELETTE combat with EA
shot down cr shell hole a'c abandoned OK(Capt HWG
Jones) [?Scout claim combat nwFLERS Hpt O Boelcke
Ja2]

2nd October

4190	BE2c	15Sqn

AOb left 8-15am MIA(Lt WD Miller **KIA/2Lt WRC
Carmichael **WIA POW**) last wireless message 8-15am,
observer to Switzerland 17.12.17, to UK 24.3.18

9658	Sopwith Strutter	5 Wing RNAS

**B EVHRE Airship sheds, BELGIUM MIA but
OK(FSLt AJ Chadwick) escaped back WoL

The 2nd was the first of several days of often
continuous rain, producing very little fighting over
the battlefields. If anything, German aircraft were
most in evidence in this week, carrying out photography and occasional attacks on troops on the
ground. The records show that in contrast, the
RFC machines remained mostly in their hangars,
and the ensuing lack of reconnaissance prior to the
next phase of the attack on the 7th had ramifications on its effectiveness. It was, in fact, the start
of a period of appalling weather, stretching well
into November, and which undoubtedly hindered
and frustrated Allied plans in the later stages of the
Somme Offensive. The British High Command felt
it had achieved a number of successes ripe for
exploitation in the last months of 1916. The
German Army had suffered a series of significant
defeats and was now perceived as vulnerable. So
long as it could be denied time to regroup it would
remain so, and this circumstance drove the Allied
war plan. The RFC was still far from beaten and
would at least be in a fighting position to help drive
home any further progress. It was therefore
extemely regrettable that the weather closed in, for
it gave the German Army exactly what it needed
most: time. On the other hand, it has to be said

that in some respects the terrible weather should
have been anticipated for the season. The closing
months of the year in northern Europe were no
time or place for all-out war, but the lesson was not
learnt in 1916. It would take the calamities of the
early winter campaign in Flanders a year later to
demonstrate this truly.

7th October

The weather was still extremely poor when the
British infantry moved forward on the 7th, this
time to help the French Army against Sailly-
Saillisel. The machines on contact patrol met a
very strong westerly wind, reducing their progress
on their homeward flights to almost a standstill.
Many machines were heavily shot up and crew
were wounded.

	BE2c?	15Sqn

CP? bullet from trenches(2Lt A Rice Oxley **WIA)

6564	BE12	21Sqn

**OP left 7-30am nrYTRES shot up then dam ldg
18Sq(Lt JA Stewart **WIA**)back [?poss "BE" claim
combat COMBLES ~9am? Oblt H Berr Ja5]

6618	BE12	21Sqn

OP left 7-30am shot down YTRES cr **MIA(2Lt WC
Fenwick **KIA**) MvR4 [combat EQUANCOURT 9-10am
Ltn M Fr vRichthofen Ja2]

	BE2e	34Sqn

CP? AA (/2Lt SA Gibbons **WIA)slight

	BE2e	34Sqn

CP? rifle ground fire(/2Lt RStJ Hartley **WIA)bad

8th October
THE FORMATION OF
THE GERMAN AIR FORCE

The ongoing reorganisation of the German air
weapon now saw the formal establishment of the
Luftstreitkrafte (The German Air Force) on the 8th
October. Its remit was the "amalgamation of all
means of air combat and air defence in the army,
in the field and in the home areas, into one unit".
Its formation took place in a week or so which was
a watershed for the German air arm. Not only was
the morale of the service being recovered, through
the widespread introduction of the new types
coupled with more effective organisation, but the
middle of October also saw the German Air Force
reach its greatest concentration on the Somme.
Production at home, as well as the re-dispositions
from Verdun and elsewhere, were enabling a
steady and highly effective build-up. By the 15th of
October there were thirty-eight units on the

German First Army front between Hannescamps and Peronne. These were made up of seventeen Feldflieger-Abteilungen, thirteen Artillerieflieger-Abteilungen, three Jagdstaffeln, three Kampf-geschwader (bombing units), and two other fighter-bomber units. Their combined strength numbered three hundred and thirty-three aircraft.

9th October

Morane?   **3Sqn**
** rifle bullet(/2Lt CT Cleaver **WIA**)foot

4494   **BE2c**   **16Sqn**
P BRUAY-BETHUNE-HOUDAIN-BRUAY **MIA(2Lt C Kennard **WIA POW**/1AM BC Digby **POW**) left 4-15pm, pilot escaped 8.18

10th October

A brief period of fine weather saw much more flying again. Offensive patrols were sent out in strength, and all met German formations and engaged them. Sopwith Strutters of 70 Squadron had a big engagement over Velu aerodrome with Jagdstaffel 2, and although assisted by some DH2s and FE2bs, the RFC machines found the new German scouts extremely difficult opponents.

6992   **FE2b**   **11Sqn**
OP combat with HA neBAPAUME down in flames **MIA(Sgt E Haxton **KIA**/Cpl BGF Jeffs **KIA**) left 2-40pm, observer jumped [?FE claim combat MORVAL, nePOZIÈRES pm, but see 4918 Hpt O Boelcke Ja2]

4162   **BE2c**   **16Sqn**
CB mg from trenches(2Lt RV Franklin **WIA/)

4856   **FE2b**   **18Sqn**
**HAP MORVAL combat with 4 HAs ftl shell hole Sh57d x.21.a.9.10. wr OK(2Lt CG Shaumer/1AM L Hardinge) left 7-15am

4918   **FE2b**   **23Sqn**
OP combat with HA ovACHIET LE GRAND cr shell hole MEAULTE(Capt RN Adams **KIA/2Lt GJ Ogg OK) left 7-10am, wounded pilot fell onto control stick so observer was forced to land a'c

A2540   **DH2**   **24Sqn**
OP combat with EA ovTRANSLOYseen diving in control going west 10-10am **MIA(2Lt N Middlebrook **POW**) left 8am, ok but then met 5-6 more fast EA [combat MORY-VRAUCOURT 10am Ltn M Müller Ja2]

A2556   **DH2**   **24Sqn**
OP left 3-15pm combat with EA fuel tank shot up ftl MEALTE(Sgt S Cockerell **WIA) to Fourth Army front [?combat BEUGNY 4-30pm Hpt M Zander Ja1]

4292   **FE2b**   **25Sqn**
B combat with HA shot down ldg EoL? OPPY? **MIA(2Lt M Hayne **KIA**/Lt AHM Copeland Can. **WIA**

POW) left 3-30pm [claim combat ROEUX Vzfw F Kosmahl/Oblt Neuburger FAb22, one source nortes that they who finished it off after MvR?]

A2539   **DH2**   **32Sqn**
**OP combat with EA controls shot away, shot down MOUQUET FARM cr a'c abandoned OK(2Lt MJJG Mare-Montembault) left 6am POZIÈRES, a'c shelled [?combat eLONGUEVAL 8-50am Ltn E Bvhme Ja2]

A382   **Sopwith Strutter**   **70Sqn**
OP combat with EA ovBAPAUME 4pm **MIA(Lt JB Lawton **POW**/2Lt FM Lawledge **DoW**) ["Sopwith 2Str" claim combat LAGNICOURT Ltn H Imelmann Ja2]

A1921   **Sopwith Strutter**   **70Sqn**
OP combat with HA AA dam(2Lt CE Ward OK/2Lt FC Corry **WIA)

11th October

Low cloud again restricted flying.

2513   **BE2c**   **13Sqn**
SpM(B) left 11-05pm DOUAI A'dr **MIA(Lt G Wadden **POW**)

Night bombing of Douai aerodrome and Vitry railway station was carried out by 13 Squadron and this loss occurred on this raid. 18 Squadron also bombed Cambrai, whilst 19 Squadron attacked Marcoing.

12th October

An attack was made along the whole Fourth Army front on the 12th, and the casualties below were all received in work associated with this. The advance was only minimal, the poor weather having severely limited artillery preparation.

5178   **Morane BB**   **3Sqn**
CP left 1-50pm AA dam ftl wr(Lt LC Kidd **KIA/Lt FES Phillips **KIA**)

2512   **BE2c**   **4Sqn**
*AOb British shells ovM.9.d. at 900' but recovered ftl M.26.d.8.8. OK(Capt TM Scott/2Lt JR Hopkins) II Corps front

    BE2c?   **9Sqn**
** rifle fire(/2Lt SM Smith **WIA**)

    BE2c?   **15Sqn**
** trench mg(/LCpl G Pilkington **WIA**)

9176   **Breguet Concorde**   **3 Wing RNAS**
B OBERNDORF Raid AA shot down **MIA(FLt CD Newman **POW**/GL Vitty **POW**?)

9181   **Breguet Concorde**   **3 Wing RNAS**
B OBERNDORF Raid AA shot down **MIA(FSLt J Rockey **POW**/GL Sturdee) [?claim OBERENZEN 3-59pm Ltn O Kissenberth KEK.E]

9660.1   **Sopwith Strutter   3 Wing RNAS**
**B OBERNDORF Raid combat with EA shot down ftl
FREIBURG A'dr(FSLt CH Butterworth **WIA POW**) a'c
captured [combat FREIBURG-IM-BREISGAU
~2-15pm Ltn L Hanstein FAb9] [?also Sopwith claim
combat OFFENBURG Ltn K Haber Ja15]

This raid to the Mauser small arms factory at
Oberndorf was the first major operation for 3 Wing
RNAS, which in turn was the first British unit set
up for purposes of strategic bombing. The French
also took part in the bombing and sustained losses.

14th October

              BE2d?   **6Sqn**
** AA(/Capt TR Duff **WIA**)

A882   Sopwith Strutter   70Sqn
**prac shot up mg dam ftl SAULTY OK(2Lt EB Mason/
2Lt LF Struben) clouds: strayed EoL

15th October

Two new RAF squadrons arrived in France on the
15th. The first was 41 Squadron, equipped with
FE8 single-seat pusher fighters; the second was 45
Squadron with Sopwith Strutters. The latter
machines had the Scarff-Dibovsky interrupter gear
for forward fire through the propeller, and Scarff
ring-mountings for the rear machine-gun.

6346   FE2b   18Sqn
**NB left 11-15pm moon ldg HAVRINCOURT WOOD
MIA(2Lt AR Crisp **POW**/1AM L Hardinge **POW**)

5965   DH2   24Sqn
DP AA(Lt WE Nixon **WIA)slight, to hospital

16th October

Fine weather brought aircraft out from before dawn
until the early evening.

No.3 Wing RNAS came up to full strength at
Luxeuil-les-Bains on the 16th of October. The wing
had been reformed again in England on the 28th
of April and had come to France to carry out
strategic bombing. Its equipment at this time
included Short Bombers and Breguet Type Vs. For
reasons which will be discussed later, this squadron
only operated until the end of June 1917.

A137   Morane BB   1Sqn
**EscRec engine failure? seen going down
neCOURTRAI nrHARLEBEKE **MIA**(2Lt C Moore-
Kelly **WIA POW**/2Lt TGG Sturrock **KIA**) left 1-37pm,
a'c captured [?combat ENNETIÈRES? 4-45pm Vzfw A
Ulmer Ja8]

              BE2c?   **4Sqn**
** AA(Lt CR Clapperton **WIA**/)arm

7085   BE2e   9Sqn
** bombed on a'dr in dark, damaged

6745   BE2d   15Sqn
**AOb combat with 5EA HEBUTERNE ftl cr trenches
a'c shelled & destroyed(Sgt F Barton **KIA**/Lt EM Carre
KIA) left 12-15pm, last wireless message 1-29pm ["BE"
claim combat eHEBUTERNE 1-20pm Hpt O Boelcke
Ja2][?"BE" claim combat swTHIEPVAL 1-05pm OffSt
L Reimann Ja2]

6580   BE12   19Sqn
B shot down **MIA(2Lt J Thompson **KIA**) MvR5
["BE" claim combat YTRES 4pm Ltn M Fr vRichthofen
Ja2]

6620   BE12   19Sqn
B combat with EA shot down **MIA(Capt CR Tidswell
KIA)

Seven BE12s from 19 Squadron bombed Hermies
station and aerodrome, as well as Ruyaulcourt in
the afternoon.

A2542   DH2   24Sqn
**OP combat with 12 fast EA Scouts nLE TRANSLOY
6000' ooc but recovered? **MIA**(Lt PAL Byrne **KIA**) left
3-15pm Fourth Army front [combat
neBEAULENCOURT 4-45pm Hpt O Boelcke Ja2]

5818   BE2e   34Sqn
**AOb combat with EA shot up ovWARLENCOURT
dam(Lt HT Horsfield OK/Lt CKM Douglas **WIA**) left
12.30pm

7107   BE2e   42Sqn
FlP dhAA cr 1000yd EoL(2Lt V Hugill **KIA/2Lt A
Douglas **KIA**) left 4-10pm

17th October

A new naval air unit, soon to be known as 8
Squadron RNAS, was ordered to make ready for
dispatch to the RFC on the Somme this day. It
would arrive at Vert Galand on the 26th.

The 17th was a second fine day, and the high
level of air activity continued.

A259   Nieuport 20   1Sqn
EscB in clouds dhAA? down Sh28.0.36.b. **MIA(2Lt CC
Godwin **KIA**/Lt PC Ellis **KIA**)

6965   FE2b   11Sqn
**Phot combat with ~20EAs, chased down by EA
ovQUEANT? **MIA**(2Lt CL Roberts **POW**/2Lt JL
Pulleyn **KIA**) left 10-10am [?claim combat
wBULLECOURT 11-10am Hpt O Boelcke Ja2 but see
7670] [?also possible "FE" claim combat swBAPAUME
11am Ltn G Leffers Ja1]

7670   FE2b   11Sqn
**Phot combat with ~20EAs MORY-QUEANT
MIA(Lt WP Bowman **KIA**/2Lt G Clayton **KIA**) left
10-11am ["Vickers" claim combat nMAUREPAS Ltn R
Theiller Ja5] [claim combat neBAPAUME 11-10am
Oblt S Kirmaier Ja2]

4866   FE2b   23Sqn
Rec combat with HA seen ooc ovVELU **MIA(2Lt JK
Parker **WIA POW**/2Lt J Cooper-Wilson **KIA**) left
8-57am

18th October

Poor weather the 18th and 19th brought a pause in
air fighting.

19th October

5239   FE2b   18Sqn
HAP seen ovALBERT **MIA(2Lt RL Dingley **POW**/Lt
WHN Whitehead Can. **POW**) left 4-40pm

20th October

From the 20th until the 22nd of October some of
the heaviest combats of 1916 took place. The two
opposing air forces, now at their greatest strengths,
were lured out by a few days of good weather. Most
of the air fighting occurred over the immediate
battle area where the German fighters were concentrating their attacks on corps machines.

      Morane?   3Sqn
** combat with EA ftl French Lines ldg ok(2Lt WB
Young **WIA**/2Lt R Davis **KIA**)

4867   FE2b   11Sqn
Phot down in control ovDOUAI **MIA(2Lt NR
dePomeroy **KIA**/2Lt W Black **WIA POW**) left 8-15am
for Third Army front, a'c shelled, observer to Switzerland
27.12.17 [?FE claim combat nwMONCHY 9-30am Ltn
E Böhme Ja2]

7674   FE2b   11Sqn
**Phot combat with HA ovACHICOURT shot down cr
WoL sARRAS wr(Lt RP Harvey **WIA**/2Lt GK Welsford
KIA) left 7-51am for Third Army front, observer fell out
[?combat wAGNY? 9-30am Hpt O Boelcke Ja2]

A6   FE2d   20Sqn
**Rec ground fire? combat BAC ST MAUR sLILLE
dam(2Lt GG Callender NZ. **WIA**/2Lt HW Soulby OK)

A9   FE2d   20Sqn
**Phot trench mg ftl LA CLYTE dam OK(Lt HE
Hartney/2Lt WT Jordan) left 11-30am ST ELOI-
MESSINES, name Jourdan?

6608   BE12   21Sqn
**P left 11-30am seen dive ovBAPAUME in combat
MIA(2Lt CJ Creery Can. **KIA**) ["BE" claim combat
swGREVILLERS WOOD 4-50pm OffSt M Müller Ja2]

7782   Sopwith Strutter   45Sqn
**DP combat with HA shot up dam ldg OK(Capt Hon
EFP Lubbock/2Lt GB Samuels) Fourth Army front

3956   Nieuport Scout   1 Wing RNAS
Furnes +* combat with two-engine seaplane[+shot
down] off OSTENDE OK(FLt GV Leather)

3994   Nieuport 11   1 Wing RNAS
+*KBP shot down KB[+des] nrOSTENDE 800'
11-35am OK(FLt EW Norton) Le Prieur rockets used

21st October

Fighting on the ground flared up around the
Schwaben Redoubt on the 21st, with both sides
using the better weather to seek advantage. The
Allies had the better of the fighting and made most
of their objectives. 4 and 7 Squadrons were
involved in contact patrolling and the artillery co-
operation.

5857   BE2d   10Sqn
AReg AA LA BASSÉE(2Lt JA Simpson **DoW
22.10.16/2Lt AJ Gregor OK) left 3-50pm

      FE2b   11Sqn
OP AA(/FSgt J Helingoe **WIA)

2546   BE2c   12Sqn
**B combat with HA down ooc cr nBULLECOURT
MIA(2Lt AB Raymond-Barker **WIA POW**) left 9-05am
[?BE claim combat COURCELETTE OffSt L Reimann
Ja2] ["BE" claim combat ECOUST ST MIEN am Ltn
S Kirmaier Ja2]

12 and 13 Squadron carried out big bombing raids
to Queant, escorted by 11 and 60 Squadron. A total
of thirty aircraft were involved and bombs were
dropped from as low as three hundred feet.

A892   Sopwith Strutter   70Sqn
Rec seen nrCAMBRAI **MIA but OK(2Lt EJ
Henderson/2Lt RD Elliot), Henderson later KIA 25.3.17

N500   Sopwith Triplane   1 Wing RNAS
+* combat with LVG[+destr] DIXMUDE OK(FSLt
RS Dallas)

22nd October

The 22nd was the last fine day of the month and
there was deadly and determined air fighting.

3986   Nieuport 11   1 Wing RNAS
St Pol +* combat with EA Seaplane[++dived into sea]
2.5m off BLANKENBERGHE 3-30pm OK(FSLt
DHMB Galbraith Can.)

A247   Morane LA   3Sqn
this a'c? ** shot up **MIA**(2Lt FWG Marchant **DoW**
25.10.16/2Lt CC Hann **DoW**) [?"Morane" claim combat
nwSAILLY-SAILLISEL 10am Oblt H Berr Ja5]

      BE2d?   6Sqn
** shot up bullet(/2Lt A Koch **WIA**)back

7027   FE2b   11Sqn
**OP eGOMMECOURT AA dam OK(Capt CN Lowe/
2AM RE Tollerfield) left 2-20pm, returned 4-10pm

7669   FE2b   11Sqn
**OP combat with EA[+] TILLOY 4-20pm dam ftl
Sh51b A.26.B. OK(2Lt JB Graham/Lt FD Lutyens) [?FE

claim combat BAILLEUL 4-40pm Ltn H Imelmann Ja2]

7684   FE2b   11Sqn
**OP very low combat with HA eGOMMECOURT
MIA(2Lt ALM Shepherd **POW DoW** 3.11.16/1AM NL
Brain **DoW**) left 2-10pm

5797   BE2d   16Sqn
*AOb combat with Monoplane ovAVION 7500'
10-50am(2Lt H Martin-Massey **inj**/Capt Waller OK)
EA last seen with FE on tail

4929   FE2b   18Sqn
**EscPhot combat with 6HAs[+] shot up nrBAPAUME
on return, ftl WoL M.23.b.9.9.(2Lt FL Barnard **inj**/Lt FS
Rankin **KIA**) to Fourth Army front, observer hit in head

Rankin was hit attempting to drive off continued
attacks from enemy scouts. The front observer's
position in the FE2b was very exposed at the best
of times, the nacelle being little more than a low
aerodynamic skirt. In combat, the gunner often
stood up and fired back over the top plane as his
pilot tilted the aircraft up into a stall, and it was in
these circumstances that Rankin was hit. He was
only just prevented from falling out of the cockpit
by Barnard who grabbed him from behind.
Barnard then climbed over into the front position
to haul Rankin back on board and then made an
emergency landing. The machine had been under
continual attack and, despite having lost most of
his controls, a landing was made. Regrettably,
Rankin was found to be dead.

6180.4   **BE12   19Sqn**
B left 12-00pm LOUVERAL **MIA(2Lt R Watts **POW**)
a'c captured

A263   SPAD 7   19Sqn
**Esc combat with EA[+ooc] seLAUNERAL shot up
dam but returned a'dr ok OK(2Lt EW Capper)

6654   BE12   21Sqn
**OP attacked by many HA, seen down wr
nrWARLENCOURT a'c shelled **MIA**(2Lt WT Willcox
POW) left 12-45pm [?"BE" claim combat
seLAGNICOURT 1pm OffSt L Reimann Ja2][?"BE"
claim combat swGREVILLERS 2-40pm Hpt O Boelcke
Ja2]

6963   FE2b   22Sqn
**P combat with 3EAs ovLE TRANSLOY(2Lt A
Cropper **DoW**/Capt RH Rushby OK) left 8-15am, pilot
died soon after landing

5952   DH2   29Sqn
**P left 10am snd EoL 1m ePOLYGON WOOD
MIA(2Lt JN Holthom **KIA**) [claim combat BAPAUME
11am Vzfw H-K Müller Ja5]

5855   BE2e   34Sqn
**AP combat with HA then spin down to avoid HA, cr
shell hole OK?(Lt JHC Minchin/2Lt HA Pearson)

7777   Sopwith Strutter   45Sqn
OP BAPAUME-PERONNE **MIA(Capt L Porter
POW DoW 24.10.16/2Lt GB Samuels **KIA**) left 10-15am
["Sopwith 2Str" claim combat DRIENCOURT 10-45am
Ltn W Frankl Ja4][?"Sopwith 2Str" claim combat
swGREVILLERS WOOD 10-50am Hpt O Boelcke Ja2]

7786   Sopwith Strutter   45Sqn
OP BAPAUME-PERONNE **MIA(2Lt OJ Wade **KIA**/
2Lt WJ Thuell **KIA**) left 10-15am, German message of
deaths [?"Sopwith 2Str" claim combat LES BOEUFS
10-50am Ltn E Böhme Ja2]

A1061   Sopwith Strutter   45Sqn
OP BAPAUME-PERONNE **MIA(Sgt P Snowdon
KIA/2Lt WFH Fullerton Can. **KIA**) left 10-15am
[?possible Sopwith claim combat OffSt L Reimann Ja2]

A1066   Sopwith Strutter   45Sqn
**OP combat with 5AlbatrosDII[+ooc] ovBAPAUME
8-40am? shot up dam(2Lt HH Griffith OK/Lt F Surgey
WIA) 10-45pm?

BRITISH AIR REINFORCEMENTS
ON THE SOMME

These four aircraft involved in casualties for 45
Squadron were their first, and came at a time of
very heavy fighting. This unit would eventually
become the highest scoring Sopwith Strutter
squadron, but in these early days its crews were
paying the price for being rushed into battle so
quickly. On this day they had the misfortune to
meet the finest fighter squadron on the Western
Front.

45 Squadron was part of Trenchard's attempts
to reinforce the beleaguered RFC over the Somme.
In recent months, Nos.19, 34, 41, and 42
Squadrons had also come out from England. In the
fast evolving air war, 41 Squadron's FE8 pusher
fighters were already effectively obsolete, and it was
lamentable that pilots would still be fighting in this
type nine months later: the last airman shot down
in combat on the FE8 was lost on the 14th of July
1917. 46 Squadron, with Nieuport two-seaters,
were also about to arrive on the 26th of October.

Trenchard brought another five units onto the
Somme from elsewhere in France, two of which
were DH2 fighter units. The first was 29 Squadron,
relocated from the Ypres front. This sector had
seen nothing approaching the same activity as the
Somme and had provided its pilots with some
invaluable experience. The other, 32 Squadron,
was moved down to Lealvillers to be closer to the
action. Three corps units, Nos. 5, 7, and 18, also
joined the RFC in the south.

Set against this expansion, however, was the fact
that most of the existing squadrons on the Somme
had been engaged in four months of generally

continuous and bitter fighting, and many were in a state of exhaustion. Furthermore, the RFC had been forced to re-deploy some units because of the ineffectiveness of their equipment; those flying the BE12 single-seater were the prime example. As the month continued, the enemy air concentrations remained at their height, so that opposing the British and French airmen on the Somme was more than a third of the whole German Air Force.

Indicative of the worsening situation was the unprecedented RFC request to the Royal Naval Air Service for help. As noted above, one of the newly forming units, soon to be known as 8 Squadron RNAS, was offered. It comprised Flights from Nos. 1, 4, and 5 Wings RNAS at Dunkirk. On the 26th of October it somewhat reluctantly left St Pol and arrived at Vert Galand to begin operations on the Somme and flew its first patrols on November the 3rd. It was the first complete RNAS unit to work with the Army on the Western Front. At this time its equipment consisted of a flight each of Nieuport Scouts, Sopwith Strutter two-seaters, and a very recently introduced type, the Sopwith Scout, which was to become known as the Sopwith "Pup". At this time the Pup was solely on strength of the RNAS, and had almost immediately shown itself to be not only a delight to fly but also one of the best fighting aircraft available. 1 Wing RNAS at Dunkirk had operated a flight of Pups since September, and in two months they had convincingly shot down several enemy aircraft without loss. Through November and December, more Pups were to become available to 8 Squadron RNAS. Its performance and high manoeuvrability made it just about a match in combat for the existing German scouts, and victories continued to mount. Only its armament of a single Vickers machine-gun left it at a disadvantage.

Whilst this hurried programme of reinforcements provided some welcome new resources for the RFC, the essential technological inferiority of their machines was becoming a desperate problem for them. The numbers and types of opposing aircraft are set out below, but the slight numerical superiority of RFC machines over the Germans in October 1916 is misleading. The actual ratio of fighters was in favour of the German Air Force, and they were flying undoubtedly superior types. In the Pup the British had glimpsed the future, but fighter units would endure a long and costly wait for production to deliver this and the other emerging new types.

The RFC also looked with some envy at the SPAD VII fighters which were now operating effectively with the French. As noted, the British had one or two early examples, but were to receive only a relatively small number, and then only after several months. It was the intention of the RFC to re-equip their Nieuport Scout squadrons with British manufactured machines (such as the de Havilland DH5), but this took longer than planned. The early Nieuports remained in RFC use until casualties on the types began to mount in the following spring, and the SPADs and later versions of Nieuports became an option the British could not ignore.

The numerical advantage of the RFC, which had counted for so much through the autumn battles, was now at an end. On the 15th of October, machines of IV and V Brigade and of the Ninth (Headquarters) Wing numbered two hundred and ninety-three (consisting of one hundred and twenty-five corps reconnaissance two-seaters; fifty-two FE2bs; thirty-six DH2s; eighteen Martinsyde G100s; thirty-five BE12s; twenty-six Sopwith Strutters; and one SPAD 7). Added to this the five squadrons of III Brigade, who operated not only against the German First Army but the Sixth Army in front of Douai as well, had ninety aeroplanes (eighteen FE2bs; fifteen Nieuport Scouts; two Moranes; one SPAD 7; the remainder being two-seater corps machines). This gave the RFC three hundred and twenty-eight serviceable aeroplanes on the Somme, if one included the fighting machines of III Brigade. The forces were therefore numerically similar (see 8th October). Telling as these statistics are, the fact that the German Air Force had begun to reorganise itself from top to bottom was just as vital to its growing strength.

25th October

No.8 Squadron RNAS was officially formed at St Pol, Dunkirk, on the 25th of October. It joined the V Brigade Royal Flying Corps on the Somme on the following day (see above).

2524	BE2c	4Sqn

AOb left 8-45am **MIA(2Lt SN Williams **KIA**/2Lt GR Bolitho **KIA**) II Corps front [?"BE" claim combat GOMMECOURT 10-50am Ltn O Höhne Ja2]

5831	BE2d	7Sqn

CB combat with EA ovPUISIEUX shot down in flames **MIA(2Lt W Fraser **KIA**/2Lt J Collen **KIA**) left 10-10am MIRAUMONT ["BE" claim combat PUISIEUX 11-10am Hpt O Boelcke Ja2]

6629	BE12	21Sqn

P combat with EA neMARICOURT dive 1500' chased down by EA **MIA(2Lt AJ Fisher **KIA**) left 7-45am [BE claim combat swBAPAUME 8-50am Ltn M Fr vRichthofen Ja2, ps: *NOT* 6654]

26th October

Virtually none of the reinforcements described above were in place at this time, and the burdens of this heavy week of fighting lay with the existing units. Around eighty combats had been recorded on the 20th, and on the 26th, the morning and the afternoon were consumed by two typically intense battles. Around 7-15am five DH2s of 24 Squadron confronted nearly twenty enemy aircraft near Bapaume. The fight continued evenly for some time until the DH2s finally withdrew and struggled slowly back to the lines against a strong head wind. The differing attributes of the two opposing aircraft had left honours even: the Halberstadts had been faster and could outclimb the DH2s, but the British aircraft kept their height well in turns — the manoeuvre that made up so much of air fighting — and this enabled them to hold their own.

In the afternoon, Boelcke led Jagdstaffel 2 in an attack on 5 and 15 Squadron BE2cs engaged in artillery work near Ancre. DH2s of 32 Squadron and a Nieuport Scout from 60 Squadron (see Nieuport 16 serial A165 below) subsequently joined the fighting, with mixed results. 32 Squadron shot down one enemy fighter, whilst the Nieuport was driven down and crashed.

46 (Corps) Squadron arrived at Droglandt, flying Nieuport two-seaters. Until the spring of 1917 it would be occupied in reconnaissance, photography, and artillery co-operation. At that time it would convert to a fighter squadron flying Sopwith Pups.

5781   BE2d   5Sqn
AOb combat with 2EAs PUISIEUX cr K.34.b.9.5. a'c shelled(2Lt Smith **WIA/Lt JC Jervis **KIA**) left 2pm ["BE" claim combat swSERRE 3-45pm Hpt O Boelcke Ja2]

6235   BE2d   7Sqn
CB nCOURCELETTE **MIA(2Lt FG Parsons **KIA**/2Lt GA Palfreyman **KIA**) left 3-10pm [?combat GRANDCOURT-LE TRANSLOY 3-50pm Oblt S Kirmaier Ja2, but see 4205]

4205   BE2c   15Sqn
armoured a'c **AOb last WT 3-25pm wr **MIA**(2Lt LC Fawkner **KIA**) left 2-50pm

4933   FE2b   18Sqn
HAP ldg nrLE TRANSLOY? 4-20pm **MIA(2Lt PF Heppel **WIA POW**/2Lt HBO Mitchell **WIA POW**) to hospital, left 2-35pm, both to Holland 9.4.18, to UK 18/16.8.18 ["FE" claim combat LE TRANSLOY 5pm Oblt Berr Ja5]

A2549   DH2   24Sqn
**OP Fourth Army front left 6-20am combat with 20 Halberstadts[+ooc] nrBAPAUME shot up dam(2Lt K

Crawford **WIA**) Crawford eventually claimed 5EAs, this being the first (see above)

A133   Nieuport 16   60Sqn
OP GREVILLERS-SERRE combat with EA 2-40pm **MIA(2Lt WM Carlyle Can. **KIA**) left 2-05pm ["Nieu" claim combat GREVILLERS 2-40pm Ltn H vKeudell Ja1]

A165   Nieuport 16   60Sqn
**OP combat WoL 1500' shot down ftl sHEBUTERNE fire a'c burnt OK(Capt EL Foot MC) left 2-05pm, joined fight in support of Artillery BE2c's being attacked by Jasta 2 ["Nieu" claim combat SERRE 3-30pm Ltn H Imelmann Ja2]

28th October

4543   BE2c   7Sqn
**Phot PYS shot up dam OK(Capt L Minot/Lt P Cawdwell)

6483   BE12   21Sqn
P combat with HAs ovCOURCELETTE steep dive **MIA(2Lt M Sharpe **KIA**) left 7-45am [?"BE" claim combat COURCELETTE 8-30am Ltn H vKeudell Ja1, but some sources date 29.10?]

THE DEATH OF OSWALD BOELCKE

The great German air fighter and unit leader Oswald Boelcke was lost during air fighting on this day. In the context of the developments which were occurring his death had an enormous impact. The Allies could take some small crumb of comfort from the fact that they were surviving, but the operational use of aircraft that would enable the British actually to regain the ascendant again was still a very long way off. It was the German Air Force which was carving out a substantial superiority of the skies, a superiority which the RFC was only able to counter with very great losses. Allied reconnoitring and patrolling was being comprehensively hindered, and furthermore, the Allies could only see this situation worsening.

It was therefore a terrible blow for the Germans to lose Boelcke, at a time when his influence on events had led the Germans to a real ascendancy, and when without doubt his future impact would have been profound. He was the consummate tactician of air combat and a formation leader with few equals. In a wider sense he had contributed deeply to the development of fighter unit organisation as well as in the evaluation and development of new types. At the moment of his death he was engaged in a dogfight with DH2s of 24 Squadron when he collided in mid-air over Pozières with one of his own men, Ltn Erwin Böhme. Boelcke's

Albatros fell to earth and he was killed in the crash. Böhme survived but was naturally inconsolable at these events. Following this disaster, however, he went on to become a high scoring ace in his own right.

30th October

The British Reserve Army was renamed the Fifth Army on the 30th of October.

31st October

A887   Sopwith Strutter   70Sqn
**LP shell fire dam OK(2Lt JS Cooper/Sgt R Dunn) planes needed replacement

A1919   Sopwith Strutter   70Sqn
**LP dam shell fire ftl wMAROEUIL(2Lt CE Ward WIA/2Lt HA Chuter OK)

A1923   Sopwith Strutter   70Sqn
**LP left 3-15pm MIA(Lt GH Nicholson POW/Lt TM Johns POW)

October 1916 ended with a grim pattern of loss emerging for the RFC. On the four days mostly available for war flying in the week between the 22nd and the 28th, they had lost sixteen aircraft in action. Twenty-four airmen were dead, four taken prisoner, and another five wounded. Not only were the casualties being sustained by aircraft on offensive patrols, but giving great concern was the fact that around forty per cent were occurring to the machines of corps squadrons. Most revealingly, eighty-six per cent of casualties in this period were caused by enemy fighters, whose time had truly come.

November 1916

1st November

5874   BE2d   7Sqn
**AOb combat with Roland LE SARS 1-35pm ftl WoL M.20.(2Lt Percival OK/2AM P Brindle WIA)a'c shelled

6265   BE2e   9Sqn
**Phot combat with EA nrROCQUIGNY at o.13., shot down in spin 2-30pm MIA(2Lt SW Mann KIA/2Lt EA Wynn KIA) left 1-15pm [?"BE" claim combat LE SARS 2-40pm Oblt S Kirmaier Ja2, but poss 5874]

4162   BE2c   16Sqn
**CBt shot up ldg BRUAY dam(2Lt RV Franklin WIA/ Lt CN Jones WIA) left 2-15pm

2nd November

5760   BE2e   7Sqn
**AReg shot down 4-45pm cr LE SARS? MIA(Sgt Bromley DoW/2Lt GH Wood DoW)

A2546   DH2   32Sqn
**OP left 2-45pm AA MARTINSAART WOOD ooc wr(2Lt RH Wallace WIA)

A224.C3   Nieuport 16   60Sqn
**OP left 3-45pm eARRAS combat with EA shot up dam ldg SAVY OK(2Lt PS Joyce)

3rd November

Fine weather saw significant levels of air fighting.

5806   BE2d   16Sqn
+*Phot combat with 2LVGs? sLENS 6-6500' 3pm shot up OK(Sgt J Drew/2AM Russell)

7010   FE2b   18Sqn
**HAP combat? with 2HA AA ooc cr eENGLEBELMER a'c shelled MIA(Sgt CG Baldwin KIA/2Lt GA Bentham KIA) left 11-35am [FE claim combat neGREVILLERS 1-10pm Ltn M Fr vRichthofen Ja2]

5250   FE2b   22Sqn
**Esc BANCOURT MIA(Capt AJM Pemberton Can. KIA/2Lt LCL Cook WIA POW) left 1pm, observer to Holland 9.4.18 [?"FE" claim combat wLE MESNIL 1-45pm Ltn R Theiller Ja5][?FE claim combat MORY Ltn A Dossenbach/Oblt H Schilling FAb22]

6374   FE2b   22Sqn
**Esc combat with EA engine hit ftl by wind MIA(2Lt WE Knowlden WIA POW/2Lt BWA Ordish POW) left 1pm BANCOURT, observer to Holland 9.4.18, to UK 7.9.18

7026   FE2b   22Sqn
**Rec combat with 3HA shot up seen ss cr MIA(Capt Lord AT Lucas KIA/Lt A Anderson inj POW) left 1-37pm BANCOURT, Lucas hit in head & leg, a'c landed by observer [FE claim combat BARASTRE 2-25pm Ltn E König Ja2][FE claim combat HAPLINCOURT 2-40pm Ltn M Müller Ja2]

A125.B4   Nieuport 16   60Sqn
**OP combat with 4EA[+ooc] ovADINFER WOOD shot down F.4. at 4pm MIA(Lt JMJ Spencer KIA) DoW as POW? ["Nieu" claim combat DOUCHY 3-45pm Ltn H Imelmann Ja2]

1459   Handley Page 0/100   3 Wing RNAS
*ferry to France OK(SCdr JT Babington/Lt JF Jones/Lt P Bewsher)

This Handley Page 0/100 was the first of the new twin-engined heavy bombers to reach France. For its time it was a big machine, and was rightly marvelled at by those who saw it come into operation. Handley Page had acquired a reputation for designing and building large aircraft, and was a natural choice for the Air Department of the Admiralty when it sought a new heavy bombing and coastal reconnaissance type for the RNAS. From their classic phrase to describe what they

wanted — "a bloody paralyser of an aeroplane" — came the line of huge twin-engined bombers which were to serve the RNAS and, much later, the RAF so well. By the spring of 1917 they were carrying out deep night bombing raids for the Naval arm. These were often attacks on strategic targets hitting the enemy's means of production. Some day operations were also tried but were abandoned when a machine was lost (see the 25th of April 1917).

5th November

No.2 Squadron RNAS was formed from "B" Squadron 1 Wing RNAS on the 5th of November (refer 1st March of 1916). At this time it flew wireless-equipped Farman F56s and Sopwith Strutters, and its duties were mainly gun-spotting, reconnaissance, and photography. No. 3 Squadron RNAS was also reformed at St Pol on this day from "C" Squadron 1 Wing RNAS (the latter had been formed at St Pol the previous June). Its equipment included Nieuport 11s, Sopwith Pups, and Sopwith Strutters. It was destined to go to the RFC in February to help in the Somme area, in fact, relieving 8 Squadron RNAS. By that time it would be fully equipped with Sopwith Pups as a single-seat fighter squadron.

6270	BE2e	9Sqn

*AOb AA ovGINCHY-LESBOEFFS ftl OK(2Lt A Gray/2Lt CP Creighton) a'c shelled

9th November

November had begun with a period of wet and windy weather, presaging one of the worst European winters for decades. Relatively little aerial activity was possible for a few days, until conditions improved on the 9th. There were several sizeable battles that day, including the biggest the war had yet seen. This occurred during a large bombing raid on a German ammunition dump at Vraucourt. 12 and 13 Squadron BE2cs, escorted by fighters from Nos. 11, 29, and 60 Squadrons, made the attack. German machines had been increasingly prevalent over the battlefields, in particular carrying out some very effective low strafing of troops and defensive positions. The purpose of the raid therefore was to draw off enemy resources from the immediate battle areas, and the operation certainly attracted a response. A large body of German fighters met the formation when it had barely crossed the lines, soon after 9am, and as the target was neared the attacks were intensified until around thirty enemy machines began to cause mayhem. Effective fighting tactics enabled

the Germans to divide the bombing formation into several smaller groups, and Allied casualties climbed alarmingly. The results of this ill-conceived operation are clear from the entries below, three bombing machines and four escorts being lost or their crews wounded.

7023	FE2b	11Sqn

OP combat with HA ftl 8Sq wr(Lt W Baillie OK/Lt GE Goolden **WIA) left 2-13pm

7701	FE2b	11Sqn

EscB combat with HA ovBAPAUME seen going s-w ftl nrSOMME WoL **MIA(2Lt JD Cowie **WIA**/Cpl CGS Ward **KIA**) left 8-15am

2502	BE2c	12Sqn

B left 8-15am engine hit ftl nr MORY? **MIA(Lt GF Knight **POW**) see 2506, escaped to UK 13.9.17 [claim combat HAPLINCOURT Ltn H Imelmann Ja2]["BE" claim combat MORY 9-30am? Oblt S Kirmaier Ja2]

2506	BE2c	12Sqn

B left 8-05am ooc SAPIGNIES? **MIA(2Lt IG Cameron **POW DoI**) see 2502, MvR8 ["BE" claim combat BEUGNY 9-30am Ltn M Fr vRichthofen Ja2]

4589	BE2c	12Sqn

B combat with HA shot up eADINFER dam(2Lt T Haynes **WIA) left 9-10am

4258	FE2b	18Sqn

HAP combat with 7HAs shot down ovGOMMECOURT 4pm ldg CONTALMAISON(Capt GH Norman **WIA/2Lt CP Murchie OK) left 2-40pm

7915	DH2	29Sqn

EscB left 8-30am **MIA(Capt AC Bolton **WIA POW**) [?possible combat LE SARS 9-30am Oblt FO Bernert Ja4]

7925	DH2	29Sqn

P left 11-30am combat with EAs shot up **MIA(2Lt HA Hallam **POW**) met the new Albatros DII [?combat swWANCOURT 12-40pm Ltn G Leffers Ja1]

7928	DH2	29Sqn

P combat with EAs ftl lines eARRAS & escaped back WoL over-night **MIA(2Lt N Brearley **WIA**) left 11-30am, met the new Albatros DII, a'c shelled & burnt [?claim combat WANCOURT-TILLOY 1pm Ltn H vKeudell Ja1]

A2543.5	DH2	29Sqn

EscB **MIA(2Lt I Curlewis **WIA POW**) repat to UK 7.1.18 [?claim combat seGREVILLERS-BAPAUME 9-30am Ltn H vKeudell Ja1]

A later 29 Squadron patrol on the 9th also met and fought a formation of the new German Albatros DII fighter, encountered for the first time (see DH2s 7925 & 7928 above). Those who survived did so by holding tight formation during their fighting retreat to the lines.

5865 BE2e 34Sqn
**AOb LE SARS combat with EA shot up ftl 9Sq
dam(2Lt AA Patterson **DoW**/)

6409 FE8 40Sqn
OP combat with HA shot down nwCAMBAI **MIA(2Lt
HF Evans **POW**) left 1pm, repat to UK 2.6.18 [?combat
Oblt FO Bernert Ja4][?claim combat ARLEUX 2-10pm
Ltn E Böhme Ja2]

7624.6 **FE8 40Sqn**
OP LA BASSÉE dhAA cr **MIA(Capt T Mapplebeck
WIA POW) a'c captured

These were 40 Squadron's first combat losses.

A272.B1 **Nieuport 17 60Sqn**
**OP combat with EA dam ldg a'dr OK(Capt JD Latta
MC) [possible "Nieu" claim combat swLE TRANSLOY
9-55am Ltn Wortmann Ja2]

A pilot of another 60 Squadron patrol brought back
the first evidence of extensive new enemy digging
occurring around Queant. These positions were
well behind the present front, in a region into which
the enemy airmen had fiercely prevented intrusion.
In fact the reconnaissance had stumbled on the
early workings of the famous Hindenburg Line.
The trenches at this time ran from west of Bourlon
Wood, around Bullecourt, across the Sensee river
and continued southwards to meet the present
German line south-east of Arras. In the coming
months these works would be developed into a
truly formidable chain of fortifications, to which the
Germans would make a brilliant tactical retreat in
the spring. It was little wonder that the German
Air Force offered such stiff resistance in front of
these hidden and secret locations.

10th November

4179 BE2c 16Sqn
+*P combat with LVG? wVIMY 5500' 10-15am OK(Lt
AV Burlton/2Lt AH Steele)

FE2d 20Sqn
** (/1AM H Alexander **WIA**)

6174 BE12 21Sqn
**P combat with 2HA shot up nCOMBLES dam
OK(2Lt FS Wilkins) left 12-30pm

6648 BE12 21Sqn
**DP left 9-30am LE TRANSLOY-ROCQUIGNY
combat with 3HA nrROCQUIGNY fuel tanks shot up ftl
swGUILLEMONT o't dam OK(2Lt J Duncan) left
9-30am

4841 FE2b 25Sqn
OP prop burst broke up(2Lt ESP Hynes **KIA/2Lt CH
Bidmead **KIA**) left 12-50pm, tail broke

A385 Sopwith Strutter 70Sqn
**OP combat with HA shot up ftl 9Sq

MORLANCOURT dam(Capt AG Saxby OK/2Lt CE
Macrae **KIA**) *name* Saxty?

A885 Sopwith Strutter 70Sqn
**OP combat with HA shot down HAVRINCOURT
WOOD broke up cr K.14(2Lt M Allport **KIA**/Lt TM
Bennet **KIA**) ["Sopwith 2Str" claim combat
HAVRINCOURT WOOD 11-30am Ltn H vKeudell
Ja1]

8016 Short 184 Dunkirk
B OSTENDE **MIA(FLt GGG Hodge **POW**) a'c
captured

13th November
THE BATTLE OF THE ANCRE

The last significant fighting of the Somme
Offensive, the battle of the Ancre, started on the
13th of November. The preparatory bombardment
had commenced on the 11th as the Fifth Army was
moving into its final positions. The commanders
were encouraged by the weather conditions which
were cold and misty but dry. At dawn the continuous, heavy bombardment of the enemy
trenches shifted into a creeping barrage and the
infantry began their advance. The fog prevented
nearly all contact work, but was of net benefit to
the attackers on the ground who pressed right into
Beaumont Hamel and beyond. The following day
the mist cleared and the air co-operation was more
effective.

15th November

FE2d 20Sqn
**combat with EA[+ooc] 2-15pm YPRES(2Lt RBW
Wainwright OK/Sgt S Birch **WIA**)

9321 Short Bomber 4 Wing RNAS
**B OSTENDE DOCKS AA ftl OOST DUNKIRK
beach OK(FSLt R Darley/AM Kirby)

This week had seen several operations by the
RNAS to bomb the docks at Ostende and
Zeebrugge, as well as strategic strikes to Volklingen
Steel Works.

16th November

BE2c? 5Sqn
AP bullets from trenches(/2Lt HB Rickards **WIA)
initials HG?

2518 BE2c 7Sqn
CB cr eBEAUMONT HAMEL **MIA(2Lt DA
Macniell **KIA**/2Lt RGR Allen **KIA**) left 9-05am, last
wireless message 10-32am, seen on ground

BE2d 8Sqn
**AP attacked by Albatros DII[+driven down ftl]
OK(Capt GA Parker/2Lt HE Hervey) 16Nov.18

This was the first Albatros DII fighter captured intact, forced down after a sustained duel over the lines. It is likely that the engine of the fighter had been hit.

7080   BE2e   9Sqn
AOb LE TRANSLOY combat with EA shot up dam(Lt CW Hyde OK/Lt JV Barry **WIA) [?"BE" claim combat neFLERS 9-45am OffSt M Müller Ja2, but see 2518?]

A37   FE2d   20Sqn
**P combat with 3HA shot up ftl nrABEELE wr OK(2Lt JW Francis/Lt FRC Cobbold) left 12-15pm [?"FE" claim combat swYPRES UntOff WA Seitz Ja8][?"FE" claim combat wYPRES Vzfw Glasmacher Ja8]

7003   FE2b   25Sqn
B SOMAIN JUNCTION hit on return(2Lt H Sellers OK/2Lt WW Fitzgerald **WIA)

A225   Nieuport 16   60Sqn
OP left 7am combat with Roland GOMMECOURT 10-30am **MIA(Lt DH Bacon **KIA**) ["Nieu" claim combat seSERRE-BEAUCOURT 8am Ltn H vKeudell Ja1]

A1907   Sopwith Strutter   70Sqn
**OP shrapnel fire dam ftl CROIX-CONTES OK(Capt WJCKC Patrick/2Lt HI Newton)

A3432   Sopwith Strutter   70Sqn
OP ok at 2-30pm **MIA(Sgt RS Evans **KIA**/2Lt LF Struben **KIA**) to BAPAUME-FINS-HERMIES, Evan's grave found. Serial here is as per Casualty Report:A3432 (note serial mis-numbering), not Strutter 9677 ["Sopwith 2Str" claim combat sBANCOURT 2-45pm Ltn S Kirmaier Ja2]

17th November

                Morane   3Sqn
** combat(/2Lt RV Tivy **WIA**)

4952   FE2b   18Sqn
HAP combat with EA BOUZINCOURT 8am shot up(Lt CH Windrum OK/Lt AV Shewell **WIA)

6950   FE2b   22Sqn
EscPhot combat with EA controls dam ftl nrPOZIÈRES cr(2Lt MR Helliwell **WIA/Pte FD Cox **WIA**) injured in cr [claim combat GUEDECOURT 11am Ltn H vKeudell Ja1]

A2577   DH2   24Sqn
Esc22Sq left 9-20am combat with EA shot down cr nrLIGNY(2Lt WC Crawford **KIA) [?claim combat seBAPAUME-WARLENCOURT 10-30am Ltn O Höhne Ja2, but see 6950]

A2555   DH2   29Sqn
OP broke up **MIA(Capt SE Cowan **KIA**)

A2565   DH2   29Sqn
OP left 9-30am **MIA(2Lt WSF Saundby **KIA**) [?claim combat swYPRES Ltn W Göttsch Ja8]

These two machines probably collided whilst diving to attack an enemy formation.

9324   Short Bomber   4 Wing RNAS
**B OSTENDE DOCKS AA engine hit ftl nrNIEUPORT PIER OK(FSLt GP Powles/GL Young)

18th November
FIGHTING ON THE SOMME DRAWS TO A CLOSE

The last ground attacks of the Somme battle took place on the 18th. A thaw had turned the earth to a sea of mud, whilst snow and blizzard conditions made the circumstances appalling and the fighting short-lived. The RFC could therefore take little part in operations, but in truth, the whole offensive was grinding to a halt for the winter.

The battle of the Somme ended with the enemy pushed into a highly exposed salient between the Ancre and the Scarpe. The four and a half months of mostly continuous fighting had been a dogged and attritional affair; at terrible cost the British had regained the initiative but won back territory only to a depth of some seven miles. In doing this some profound blows had been inflicted on the German Army, but in turn, a great part of the new British Army had been cruelly depleted. For both sides the sacrifices made on the Somme would resound until the end of the war. As for the air services, the British defence of the skies had been so notable and determined that, even as their control was in decline, Germany would devote the coming winter to completing the reorganisation of its air force so that it could concentrate the greater part of its strength against the RFC.

Between now and the end of the year, the status quo of impending German ascendancy, held off only at terrible cost to the Allies, would continue. It had become the norm for both sides to carry out operations whenever conditions permitted, and no quarter was given. The volume of work which the RFC maintained in these months is well illustrated by noting that between the 23rd June and the 20th October 1916 it observed for just over two thousand separate artillery shoots and bombardments.

Both sides had no doubt now that control of the skies above the battlefield was essential to success. Any superiority would need to be held with unflinching determination along a number of fiercely contested fronts. The RFC continued to take the war aggressively to the enemy, often far over his Lines, and it is a tremendous tribute to its crews that they kept the skies open with significantly inferior machines for as long as they did.

52 (Corps) Squadron arrived in France on the 18th of November equipped with the new RE8 corps machine.

20th November

2767   BE2c   15Sqn
AP combat with HA shot down brought down ovMIRAUMONT o't 8-45am **MIA(2Lt JC Lees **WIA POW**/Lt TH Clarke **POW**) [?"BE" claim nMIRAUMONT 8am Oblt S Kirmaier Ja2]

4848   FE2b   18Sqn
HAP WARLENCOURT shot down **MIA(2Lt GS Hall **POW DoW** 30.11.16/2Lt G Doughty **KIA**) left 1-15pm, MvR10 ["FE" claim combat seGUEDECOURT 3-15pm Ltn M Fr vRichthofen Ja2]

22nd November

A248   Morane LA   3Sqn
Phot combat with EA wFLERS(Lt EP Roberts **WIA/ Capt GL Watson **WIA**) left 12-45pm [combat LONGUEVAL 1-10pm Ltn E Böhme Ja2]

7677   FE2b   11Sqn
**OP combat with EA shot down nrHEBUTERNE dam OK(2Lt F Crisp/2Lt JAV Boddy) [?"Vickers" claim combat HEBUTERNE 3-50pm Ltn E König Ja2]

A2607   DH2   32Sqn
OP BEUGNATRE combat with EA neBAPAUME shot up 1-30pm chased by EA ftl **MIA(Lt R Corbett **WIA POW**) seen in combat by Lt FH Coleman of 32Sqn, to Switzerland 27.12.17 [combat BIEFVILLERS 1-15pm Ltn H vKeudell Ja1]

23rd November

A146   Morane LA   3Sqn
AP combat with 5HA nrHIGH WOOD shot up ftl BAZENTIN-LE-PETIT(Lt Forshaw OK/Lt Dormor **WIA) left 7-40am

          FE2b   11Sqn
Phot AA (/Lt AL Harrow-Bunn **WIA)

6976   FE2b   23Sqn
Rec combat with neACHIET-LE-GRAND 9-45am dam(2Lt EG Wheldon **WIA/2Lt AW Phillips OK)

5964   DH2   24Sqn
DP combat with 8HAs ovACHIET shot down cr **MIA(Maj LG Hawker VC **KIA**) left 1pm [combat sLIGNY 2pm Ltn M Fr vRichthofen Ja2]

THE DEATH OF MAJOR HAWKER

Major Hawker's death was a bitter blow for the RFC and came, like Boelcke's shortly before him, at a critical time for his air service. He had set a superb example of leadership and bravery, and his alert mind had been a real asset to the RFC as it moved towards its operational maturity on the Western Front. He had extracted the very best from the men under his command and as the balance had swung away from the RFC his contribution had been one of those which ensured it still survived to fight.

He was the eleventh victim of Manfred von Richthofen who was flying an Albatros fighter. In a fight which lasted over half an hour its superior fire power was matched against the agility of the DH2. There had been little gain by either pilot until Hawker's engine began to fail and he dived for the British lines. Richthofen followed him down and it was then that Hawker was hit in the head and killed instantly, virtually at ground level and seconds from safety.

A2554   DH2   24Sqn
Esc22Sq Fourth Army front left 9-15am **MIA(2Lt HB Begg **KIA**) [?possible "Vickers" claim nLE SARS 10am Ltn Collin Ja2]

7683   FE2b   25Sqn
OP(2Lt FS Moller **WIA/Sgt C Butler OK)

N5182   Sopwith Pup   8Sqn RNAS
+* combat with Aviatik C-type[+shot down cr woods nrCOURCELETTE? destroyed] 9-50am OK(FSLt RA Little Aust.)

This was Little's first confirmed victory of an eventual total of forty-seven enemy aircraft. He would become the most successful Australian pilot of the war. The loss of FLt Hope noted below was the first loss in combat for 8 Squadron RNAS since it had joined the RFC in operations on the Somme.

N5190   Sopwith Pup   8Sqn RNAS
** combat with EA shot down nrMOEUVRES **MIA**(FLt WH Hope **POW DoW**)

24th November

A4019   BE12a   21Sqn
OP left 7-20am THIEPVAL-COMBLES **MIA(2Lt BW Blayney **POW**)

          BE2e   34Sqn
** ground mg(2Lt BHM Jones **WIA**/)

26th November

5947   DH2   29Sqn
left 10an to travel back from 41Sqn, ldg nrLILLE? **MIA(2Lt WB Clark **POW**)

6454.6   FE8   41Sqn
P PICANTIN low fuel ftl ROULERS **MIA(2Lt GS Deane **POW**) tried to burn a'c, but captured

Deane was the first 41 Squadron pilot to be lost in action.

27th November

7084   BE2e   9Sqn
**AReg in flames cr 1m nGUEDECOURT EoL 2-40pm
MIA(2Lt JT Hanning Can. **KIA**/Lt VA Strauss **KIA**)
left 2-15pm

4915   FE2b   18Sqn
**P combat with HA nrGINCHY in flames(Lt FA
George **WIA**/1AM O Watts **KIA**) left 11am [?poss
"Vickers/BE" claim combat sBAPAUME 1-15pm Ltn W
Voss Ja2, but 9Sqn BE 7084 poss apart from time]

A281.A1 **Nieuport 17   60Sqn**
OP seen 9-40am BAPAUME shot down **MIA(Capt
GA Parker **KIA**) Voss1 ["Nieu" claim combat
MIRAUMONT 8-40am Ltn W Voss Ja2][?"Nieu" claim
combat HEBUTERNE 8-45am Ltn M Müller Ja2]

28th November

Fog made flying almost impossible from the 28th
until the 3rd of December but some bombing raids
to rail centres were still carried out.

December 1916

On the 12th of December 1916 the Army Council
approved expansion of Royal Flying Corps to one
hundred and six active Squadrons and ninety-five
reserve squadrons. Subsequently, two night-flying
squadrons were also added. At present, the RFC
had only eight single-seater fighter squadrons on
the Western Front, in a total of some thirty-eight
in active service. Only two of these, 60 Squadron
with its Nieuport Scouts, and 8 Squadron RNAS
with its Pups, were not operating obsolete aircraft.
The opposing German Jagdstaffeln numbered
twenty-five. Their machines included growing
numbers of Albatros DIs and DIIs. RFC reconnaissance squadrons still laboured on with their
BE2cs, now critically overdue for replacement; the
RE8 two-seater, still some months away from its
troubled introduction, would provide this. The
year in France would end with the arrival of the
first RFC Squadron equipped with the Sopwith
Pup — No. 54 Squadron. The Pup was the first
new machine for many months, and heralded a new
generation of RFC aircraft capable of taking the
fight back to the enemy. For now though, the two
sides were forced to reduce their operations due to
steadily worsening weather. For the RFC crews it
was a mercy. Both sides set about preparing for
another year of war they knew would be ever more
bloody and protracted.

1st December

No.1 Squadron RNAS was formed from "A"

Squadron 1 Wing RNAS on the 1st of December
(refer the 1st of March 1916). During February
1917 it became known as 1(Naval) Squadron to
avoid confusion with 1 Squadron RFC.

4th December

Over the following week there were heavy losses to
crews on photographic reconnaissance operations.

BE2d?   4Sqn
Phot combat with 2HA shot up(2Lt PJ Long **WIA/)

6732   BE2d   4Sqn
**AOb combat with 2HA ovMIRAUMONT shot up ftl
by observer wCOURCELETTE cr wr(2Lt HD
Crompton **KIA**/FSgt GW Halstead **WIA**)

4592   BE2c   16Sqn
+*AOb combat with Roland ovBAILLEUL 5000' 1pm
OK(2Lt RV Franklin/2Lt WJ Lindsey) also saw FE8
shoot down EA: a 40Sq claim: probably that of Capt DO
Mulholland in FE8 6384, but possibly Lt EL Benbow's
in FE8 7627

2633   BE2c   16Sqn
+*AOb combat with Roland ovSOUCHEZ 3000'
11-25am OK(2Lt FH Gay/Lt JP Greenwood)

FE2b   25Sqn
Phot AA shell(/Cpl AO Bower **WIA)

7022   FE2b   25Sqn
**P combat with HA shot down cr EoL nrTHELUS
Sh51.B.B.7.c **MIA**(2Lt DS Johnson **KIA**/Lt I Heald
KIA) left 9-05am [combat FARBUS Ltn O Splitgerber
Ja12]

3956   Nieuport Scout   1 Wing RNAS
Furnes +* combat with Albatros DI[+shot down]
neBAPAUME OK(FSLt GG Simpson) shared with
Nieuport Scout 8750

8750   Nieuport Scout   RNAS
+* combat with Albatros DI[+shot down]
neBAPAUME 11am OK(FLt CR Mackenzie) see
Nieuport 3956

3957   Nieuport Scout   8Sqn RNAS
** combat with EA WoL shot down nrFLERS
MIA(FLt.Hon AC Corbett **KIA**)

5th December

After only a single fine day the weather turned poor
again until the 9th, permitting only limited air
activity.

7th December

A5447   FE2b   23Sqn
**Phot BEAUMONT HAMEL AA ftl 200yd WoL(2Lt
JC Griffiths **WIA**/Lt R Affleck OK) left 1-40pm,
unsalvable

11th December

BE2c?   **2Sqn**
Esc AA(/2Lt RB Davies **WIA)

7153   **BE2g**   **10Sqn**
EscPhot combat with HA 2000yd nANNEQUIN shot down in flames cr 11am(2Lt GW Dampier **KIA/2Lt HC Barr **KIA**)

5986   **DH2**   **32Sqn**
Esc left 9-20am MORCHIES **MIA(Lt BPG Hunt **WIA POW**) to Holland 9.4.18, MvR12 [combat MERCATEL 10-55am Ltn M Fr vRichthofen Ja2]

A278   **Nieuport 17**   **60Sqn**
.C1? **OP left 10am combat with AlbCII[+capt] DAINVILLE 10-30am shot up ftl cr nrARRAS L.16.b.(Capt EO Grenfell MC **WIA**) last of several victories

12th December

Flying was curtailed by poor weather from the 12th until the 15th of December.

16th December

57 Squadron arrived in France equipped with FE2d pushers.

A270   **Morane LA**   **3Sqn**
**AP GUEDECOURT-BEAULENCOURT combat with EA dam ldg cr OK(Lt HA Whistler/Lt AD deRoss)

4204   **BE2c**   **12Sqn**
Phot combat with HAs 10-30am shot down NEUVILLE VITASSE nrAGNY(2Lt T Thomson **inj/Lt HG Murray **KIA**)

BE2d?   **16Sqn**
Rec trench mg(/Lt JP Greenwood **WIA)

17th December

Weather yet again poor from the 17th until the 19th December.

19th December

A2614   **DH2**   **29Sqn**
OP combat with HA shot up ldg a'dr ok(2Lt WKM Britton **WIA)

20th December

Jasta 2 took a heavy toll of aircraft on the 20th, including two claims by von Richthofen.

FE2b   **11Sqn**
Rec AA(/Lt WO Boger **WIA)

4884   **FE2b**   **18Sqn**
OP combat with 2HAs seen in flames Sh57C.1.8. 12-55pm **MIA(2Lt R Smith **KIA**/2Lt H Fiske **KIA**) left 11-25am [?"FE" claim combat neBEUGNY 12-45pm Ltn H Imelmann Ja2]

A5446   **FE2b**   **18Sqn**
OP seen ok ovLines at LE TRANSLOY 1-15pm but **MIA(2Lt LG D'Arcy **KIA**/2Lt RC Whiteside **KIA**) left 11-15am, MvR14 [combat NOREUIL 12-45pm Ltn M Fr vRichthofen Ja2]

A5452   **FE2b**   **18Sqn**
OP left 11-25am GOMMECOURT shot down seen gliding SAPIGNIES **MIA(Lt CH Windrum **POW**/Lt JA Hollis **POW**) [?"FE" claim combat SAPIGNIES 1-05pm Ltn Wortmann Ja2]

5956   **DH2**   **29Sqn**
*P combat with HA shot up ldg a'dr ok OK(2Lt AN Benge)

7927   **DH2**   **29Sqn**
OP AA snd eADINFER WOOD **MIA(Capt AG Knight **KIA**) left 9-45am, down x.28. [claim combat MONCHY-AU-BOIS 10-30am Ltn M Fr vRichthofen Ja2]

A2552   **DH2**   **29Sqn**
**OP fuel tank shot up ftl sBEAUMETZ cr OK(2Lt HB Hurst)

21st December

5782   **BE2d**   **7Sqn**
CB combat with EA eBEAUCOURT EoL **MIA(Lt DW Davis Can. **WIA POW**/2Lt WMV Cotton Can. **KIA**) last WT message 9-45am, to Holland 7.5.18, Voss3 [?BE claim combat MIRAUMONT 10am Ltn W Voss Ja2]

24th December

54 Squadron arrived in France on the 24th of December. It was the first RFC squadron to be equipped with the Sopwith Pup single-seat fighter.

26th December

53 (Corps) Squadron arrived in France on the 26th of December flying the BE2e. In the following spring it would be re-equipped with the RE8.

6228   **BE2d**   **2Sqn**
Phot AA shot down LOOS(Capt JR Gould **WIA/Lt CAW Thompson **inj**) left 9-40am, shot down Sh57d X.4.d.

BE2d?   **5Sqn**
B shot up?(2Lt WH Hubbard **WIA) [?BE claim combat COURCELETTE 2-15pm Ltn E Böhme Ja2]

4498   **BE2c**   **5Sqn**
B left 9-15am VAULX VRAUCOURT **MIA(2Lt HE Arnold **Kld**) [?"BE" claim combat BEUGNY 11-10am Oblt H Bethge Ja1]

6254   **BE2d**   **5Sqn**
B left 9-15am VAULX VRAUCOURT **MIA(Lt FN Insoll **POW**) [?"BE" claim combat SAPIGNIES 11-10am Vzfw Bona Ja1]

A5450   FE2b   18Sqn
****OP shell exploded nr a'c ftl cr shell hole o't wr(2Lt GA
Masters **WIA**/2Lt PS Taylor **inj**) Fifth Army front

A5453   FE2b   18Sqn
**OP combat with HA nrVELU? ftl cr shell hole Sh57T
18.a.4.7.(Capt HLH Owen OK/Lt R Mayberry **inj**)
[?"Vickers" claim combat 1km wSAILLY 9-55am Ltn R
Theiller Ja5]

7712   FE2b   23Sqn
**LP combat with 5 Halberstadts ftl(2Lt WB Kellog?
WIA/2Lt TB Jones **WIA**) left 9-40am, pilot's name
Kellogg?

7885   DH2   24Sqn
**OP left 9-35am combat with EA 10-15am cr
REINCOURT wr **MIA**(2Lt EL Lewis **KIA**) [combat
eMORVAL 10-20am Ltn D Collin Ja2] [NB:
vonTutschek claimed his FAb6b observer Ltn Fr vStein
shot down a "pusher" in a big fight this day, but the claim
went to Jasta instead]

A3294   Nieuport 12   46Sqn
was Nieuport 9332 **Phot combat with Roland
ovRAILWAY WOOD Sh28 I.11. nd(Capt JWN Nason
KIA/Lt CAF Brown **KIA**) [?"Nieu 2Str" claim combat
Vzfw A Ulmer Ja8]

This crew was the first lost by 46 Squadron.

27th December

A119   Morane LA   3Sqn
**AOb GUEDECOURT combat with 4HA shot up dam
ftl M.28.b.5.0. OK(Lt KA Creery/Lt J Claudet) left
11-40am

7666   FE2b   11Sqn
**Rec combat with EA[+] WANCOURT 11-15am then
ftl(Capt JB Quested OK?/2Lt HJH Dicksee **WIA**)
combat victory was probably over Ltn G Leffers of Jasta
1 in Nieuport? [?FE claim nrCHERISY 11-20am OffSt
W Cymera Ja1][NB: MvR's FE2b claim this day is at
3-25pm]

A36   FE2d   20Sqn
**OP POELCAPPELLE mg 100' ftl BERTHEN
burnt(2Lt DC Cunnell OK/Capt CM Carbert **inj**)

28th December

A1569   Martinsyde G102   27Sqn
DP dhAA BEAUMONT HAMEL **MIA(Capt H
Spanner Can. **KIA**)

29th December

Bad weather affected all flying from the 29th until
the 31st of December.

31st December

Four new RNAS units were formed on the 31st of
December. The first two were from existing
Squadrons of No.5 Wing RNAS (refer 3rd of
March 1916) at Coudekerque. No.5 Wing was
disbanded at this time but would be back as an
entity in France by March 1917. The first unit was
No.4 Squadron RNAS, which was reformed from
"A" Squadron 5 Wing. No.4 Squadron had
originally come into existence on the 25 of March
1915 from the Defence Flight Dover but this unit
had been renamed No.4 Wing RNAS when it
moved to Eastchurch on the 3rd of August of that
year. At first No.4 Squadron was a bombing unit
with Sopwith Strutters and two-seater Nieuports.
It began to re-equip with Sopwith Pups in March
1917 and would be transferred to 4 Wing RNAS at
Bray Dunes as a fighter squadron. The second unit
was 5 Squadron RNAS, formed from "B"
Squadron of No.5 Wing RNAS. "B" Squadron 5
Wing had been at Coudekerque as a bombing unit
for several weeks and it was in this role that No.5
Squadron RNAS continued for the rest of the war.
Its equipment at this time was Caudron GIVs and
Sopwith Strutters.

The other two new squadrons were formed at
Petite Synthe, from units of No. 4 Wing RNAS
(refer 11th of April 1916), which was also disbanded on this day. The first of these was No.6
Squadron RNAS, formed from "A" Squadron 4
Wing. In this present incarnation it was to survive
only until August 1917 when its personnel and
aircraft went to 9 and 10 (Naval) Squadrons. In all
this time it remained near the coast, and whilst it
originally flew mostly Nieuport two-seaters, it soon
acquired Nieuport single-seater scouts and by June
it was equipped with Sopwith Camels. The final
new unit was No.7 Squadron RNAS formed from
"B" Squadron 4 Wing RNAS. Its equipment was
a mixture of Caudron GIVs and Short Bombers
but it later received Sopwith Strutter bomber types,
and ultimately, it was flying exclusively Handley
Page heavy bombers by the summer of 1917.

Untraced Casualty in France in 1916?

** (FSLt HM Burton **POW**)

1917 SURVIVAL, EXPANSION, DIVERSITY

The ground war saw a considerable lessening of activity through the winter of 1916/17, which meant a commensurate reduction in war flying. The weather continued to be generally poor for many weeks, which was a major contributory factor. In any event, a pause of sorts was timely for both sides, for it gave the opportunity to develop and strengthen positions significantly, both on the ground and in the air, in preparation for the spring battles which would surely follow. In terms of survival, this hiatus was probably more of a godsend for the Allied air forces who had begun to bend under relentless German pressure. Only a numerical superiority and considerable endeavour on the part of the Allied air crews held an increasingly sophisticated and well organised enemy at bay.

Neither weight of numbers nor sacrifice could be more than temporary solutions without innovative new machines to take the evolving air war to the German pilots, but for months that is what the Allied response amounted to, as new units and old machines flooded into France. There were already aircraft in the hands of the Allies which once into full production could recover the initiative in the air, but regrettably they would not be seen in any quantity for months. In the meantime, the Royal Flying Corps would have to do both its fighting and its day to day war work with inferior aeroplanes.

It was certain that if it could survive this period, then the effort invested in its considerable expansion programme would begin to bear fruit. The numbers of aircraft that could be deployed above the fighting were but the tip of an iceberg for the expansion that the RFC had embarked upon was comprehensive. After the shock of the Somme battles had alerted the High Command to the imperative value of air power, a demand for fifty-six squadrons for the following year's campaigns had been made. By November 1916 another twenty more were requested, only to be increased to a plan for one hundred and six active and ninety-five reserve squadrons by mid-December. For each new fighting machine in every one of these new squadrons, there had to be trained aircrew, skilled personnel to build, service, and maintain the aircraft, and effective means of supply to the front line in the form of new air parks and ferrying schemes. These manpower demands for the air services occurred at exactly the time when every other branch of the war machine was desperate for the same commodity. There is little doubt that the near disaster that the RFC suffered in April 1917, "Bloody April", was due not only to a critical short-fall in the quality of its machines, which nevertheless were deployed in an unflinchingly offensive manner, but also to the arrival of hundreds of under-trained air crew who had not been able to benefit from the new organisation in the way those who followed would.

On the other hand, the Germans continued to introduce machines of proven quality into their front line units, and to consolidate the methods whereby they hoped to destroy the Allied air forces. This they nearly succeeded in doing in the spring. Only the lack of experience of many of the German pilots, unable to exploit the full potential of their aircraft in many cases, prevented a greater calamity.

Certainly, all the initiative was to be Germany's in the first months of 1917, as it presented the Allies with one of the most striking gambits of the entire war: the withdrawal of its armies back to the Hindenburg Line. Most of the events which occurred on the Western Front in the first half of 1917 were to be coloured by this.

Learning from the previous summer on the Somme, the German High Command sought to avoid a further devastating year of attritional fighting. Certainly, they wished to delay any potentially decisive battles until events had been settled in Russia. The key to survival was a secure defensive position, and so a colossal system of defences was devised linking Douai, Cambrai and St Quentin, all important railway centres. This, the Hindenburg Line, was not only designed to be very strong, but also shortened the German front very significantly, so that troops could be more effectively deployed. It also meant Germany completely dictated the field of battle, and in the weeks preceding the German withdrawal in March, virtually the entire region in front of the new line was laid waste to ensure maximum effect. The scope of this strategy was vast, for the Hindenburg Line stretched from the Oise almost to the Scarpe, and thus covered a great deal of the French line as well as all that occupied by the British. The extent of the withdrawal, some thirty miles at its deepest point, was not fully understood until the middle of March, by which time the destruction of the countryside was nearly complete. The advance across this wasteland, against the remaining rearguard forces, was therefore extremely difficult, absorbing weeks of difficult

fighting. By the time the Allies finally came to face the Hindenburg defences in early April, they were already breathing hard.

During the winter Joffre was also replaced as Supreme Commander of the French forces by General Nivelle, whose intention it was to launch another great assault on the German Lines. The difference from those of the past was that Nivelle planned this to be the great decisive and overwhelming one, which would see an end to the conflict. Whilst his plans were in preparation, however, the great withdrawal to the Hindenburg Line occurred, and although this effected a large section of the front he proposed to attack, he felt unmoved to modify much of his intentions. In this way battles were planned, and their fate decided even before they had begun. This, then, is the background to the first months of 1917.

January 1917

1st January

1463   HP 0/100   RNAS
travelling to France, lost then ftl CHALANDRY, nrLAON EoL **MIA(FLt HC Vereker **POW**/Lt SR Hibbard **POW**/AM D Kennedy **POW**/AM Wright **POW**/AM Higby **POW**) a'c captured [German record of HP lost and ftl nLAON]

This well documented disaster delivered a new twin-engined British heavy bomber directly into the hands of the enemy. Two attempts had been made to fly the Handley Page to France in December, but each had been turned back by engine problems. The 1st of January was a foggy, wintery day, but another attempt was made, only this time the machine lost its way and was forced to land in enemy territory. It landed at the aerodrome of Flieger Abteilung (A) 208 at Chalandry. The amazed members of this unit found themselves in possession of not only a new bomber type but also comprehensive performance documentation. This 0/100 was subsequently flown and tested by the Germans until it was crashed at Johannisthal aerodrome on the 22nd of August 1917.

4th January

A626   Sopwith Pup   8Sqn RNAS
OP combat with 7EAs nrBAPAUME ~3-15pm shot down nRHEIMS **MIA(FSLt JC Croft **POW**) left 2-30pm, a'c captured, Ja10? [?"Sopwith" claim combat NEUCHATEL, nRHEIMS Ltn Mallinckrodt Ja10]

N5193   Sopwith Pup   8 Sqn RNAS
OP ACHIET LE GRAND combat with 7EAs shot down nrBAPAUME **MIA(FLt AS Todd **KIA**) left 2-30pm, last seen attacking EAs 3-15pm, MvR16 ["Sopwith" claim combat METZ-EN-COUTURE 3-15pm Ltn M Fr vRichthofen Ja2]

The pilots of Sopwith Pups were amongst the very few British pilots who could fight the German Jagdstaffeln on something approaching equal terms. It was a much loved aeroplane to fly, being beautifully responsive and manoeuvrable, if somewhat under-powered, and certainly under-armed with its single Lewis machine-gun. Nevertheless, it was highly respected by the best German pilots, a point demonstrated by von Richthofen's report of the above combat: "One of the English planes attacked us and we saw immediately that the enemy plane was superior to ours. Only because we were three against one, we detected the enemy's weak points. I managed to get behind him and shoot him down."

5th January

7190   BE2g   6Sqn
AOb combat shot down fire a'c destroyed(2Lt H Jameson MC **KIA/Lt WD Thomson **KIA**) left 8-35am YPRES SALIENT ["EA" claim VOORMEZEELE seYPRES 10am Vzfw W Göttsch Ja8]

A2581   DH2   24Sqn
OP left 10-15am shot up(Lt WFT James **WIA)thigh, to hospital

7th January

6238   BE2g   6Sqn
AOb YPRES SALIENT combat with Halberstadt Scout 4000' 12pm rear fuel tank hit shot up(Lt AJCE Phillippo OK/2Lt EGW Bisset **DoW)head

A39   FE2d   20Sqn
OP combat with 2 Albatros[+spun down ooc?] shot up 9000' fuel tank hit ftl in flames cr o't 3m nBAPAUME(Sgt TT Mottershead VC **DoI 12.1.17/Lt WE Gower MC **inj**) Ja8 ["Vickers" claim combat YPRES-KEMMEL 12pm Ltn W Göttsch Ja8]

Sgt Mottershead was awarded the Victoria Cross for his actions on the 7th. This and another crew were carrying out an offensive patrol over Ploegsteert Wood. Almost immediately after commencing they were attacked by two Albatros Scouts, and the FEs became separated. Gower sent one of the enemy machines down, but bullets from the other hit their petrol tank and a fire began. Mottershead, in the pilot's position immediately in front of the engine, was soon suffering burns but

dived away and pressed westwards to safety. The fire was enveloping most of the machine as it eventually touched down. It overturned and, as so often occurred in a pusher crash, the observer was thrown clear whilst the terribly burnt Mottershead was pinned beneath the engine. He was extricated and rushed to hospital, where four days later he succumbed to his injuries. Gower was awarded an MC for his efforts to save his pilot.

7851   DH2   32Sqn
OP left 11am MIA(2Lt EGS Wagner **KIA)
[?"Vickers" claim combat BEUGNY 11-30am Ltn E Böhme Ja2]

A74   RE8   52Sqn
Phot combat cr nrALLAINES 1pm **MIA(Maj L Parker **KIA**/2Lt FA Mann **POW**) left 11-40am ALBERT ["EA A74" claim combat nwPERONNE 12-40pm Ltn G Schlenker Ja3]

This was the first casualty in action for 52 Squadron in France and the first involving an RE8. The unit had arrived the previous November equipped with this new corps reconnaissance machine. It then suffered a series of miserable and morale-sapping accidents with the type — eleven in fact — which left its air crews convinced that it was a death trap. Most of these accidents involved spinning in on landing, usually made all the more deadly by the engine being rammed back into the fuel tanks. So mortified was the Squadron that the very unusual step was taken to exchange No.52's RE8s for 34 Squadron's BE2es, and this began soon after the loss of A74. The whole design of the RE8 was reappraised and modifications made which substantially improved its safety. It has to be said, though, that many of the accidents which 52 Squadron suffered in these months owed as much to inadequate flying training as anything else.

N5198   Sopwith Pup   8Sqn RNAS
** combat with EA shot up(FSLt AHS Lawson **WIA**)

11th January

BE2cs 2529, 2580, 4446, 4587, & BE2d 5771   16Sqn

All these aircraft were damaged in their hangar at Bruay by enemy bombing in the early hours of the 11th of January. By this time there were regular night bombing raids of Allied aerodromes and dumps being carried out by Germany.

13th January

5755   BE2d   5Sqn
pracAP left 2-30pm **MIA(2Lt GW Bentley **KIFA**/2Lt DR Hinkley **KIFA**) possibly KIA?

17th January

43 Squadron RFC arrived in France on the 17th of January. It was equipped with Sopwith Strutter two-seaters and its work began with reconnaissance, photography, and line patrols. By the beginning of 1917 the Strutter was becoming increasingly obsolete, but the unit persevered with the type until September, suffering high losses at times.

23rd January

5868   BE2g   6Sqn
Phot combat with Roland Scout? ovSh28 J.20 6000' 12-30pm shot up dived towards POPERINGHE(Capt EA Beaulah **WIA/FSgt F Slingsby OK)

6388.4   FE8   40Sqn
EscLP combat with 5EAs shot down in flames nrLENS 3-05pm(2Lt J Hay Aust. **KIA) left 1-12pm, cr R.30.A.9.2. seAIX-NOULETTE, MvR17 ["Vickers" claim combat swLENS 3-10pm Ltn M Fr vRichthofen Ja11]

7613   FE8   41Sqn
P combat with 4EAs spiral down nose dive 600' eBOESINGHE MIA(2Lt SF Cody **KIA) left 2-24pm, combat nrPASSCHENDAELE Albatros & Roland ["Vickers 7613" claim combat BIXSCHOOTE Ltn W vBülow Ja18]

Sopwith Strutter   45Sqn
** combat? shot up(/2Lt TF Northcote **WIA**)leg

A1078   Sopwith Strutter   45Sqn
EscPhot YPRES seen ovDADIZEELE 12-30pm MIA(2Lt JN Lyle **KIA/Bdr A Harrison **KIA**) ["Sopwith" claim combat GHELUVELT Ltn W vBülow Ja18]

A1083   Sopwith Strutter   45Sqn
+* combat with AlbatrosDII[+ooc] MENIN 12-30pm OK(Capt WGB Williams/2Lt J Senior)

24th January

7175   BE2g   6Sqn
EscPhot shot up(2Lt EG Waters **KIA/Sgt F Slingsby OK) ldg by observer at Sh28 H.17.c.

FE2b   22Sqn
** combat? shot up(/Capt RH Rusby **WIA**)

FE2b   23Sqn
LP combat?(/Sgt L Booth **KIA)

6997   FE2b   25Sqn
Phot combat with Albatros ovROUVROY shot down, ldg ok nrVIMY MIA(Capt O Greig **POW/Lt JE MacLennan **POW**) left 9-50am ["FE 6937" claim(but 6997 correct) combat VITRY nrARRAS 11-15am Ltn M Fr vRichthofen Ja11]

6417   FE8   41Sqn
**OP YPRES combat with EA nose dive 6000' cr wr

~3-50pm WoL(Sgt CS Tooms **KIA**) left 2-35pm [?"FE" claim combat wWYTSCHAETE 3-50pm Vzfw A Ulmer Ja8]

6453   FE8   41Sqn
P combat shot up ftl 28.B.25.c.1.9. dam(2Lt A Denison **WIA)arm, left 12-50pm

6308   BE2e   53Sqn
Phot WARNETON seen going down **MIA(Lt TF Preston **KIA**/Lt CM Buck **KIA**) ["Bristol" claim nWARNETON: between HOUTHEM-WYTSCHAETE Vzfw Ulmer Ja8]

These airmen were the first casualties in action for 53 (Corps) Squadron.

N5198   Sopwith Pup   8 Sqn RNAS
OP BAPAUME combat with EA shot down nrFAVREUIL **MIA(FCdr CR Mackenzie **KIA**) left 11-25am, seen 12pm ovBAPAUME going east after EA ["Sopwith 5198" claim combat BIHUCOURT 12-10pm Ltn H vKeudell Ja1]

25th January

A34   FE2d   20Sqn
Rec met EA ovMENIN, down ooc but seen regain control, ftl RONCQ **MIA(2Lt S Alder **WIA POW**/Lt RW White **WIA POW**) ["Vickers A34" claim combat BOUSBECQUE Oblt Grieffenhagen Ja18][also "A34" flak claim swMENIN FkB336]

A81   RE8   52Sqn
+*Phot combat with 2Str[+dive ooc] MARICOURT 7000′ 12-45pm OK(2Lt DHM Carbery/2Lt HAD Mackay) EA seen ldg MORLANCOURT-BOUCHAVESNES c.25.

This was the first victory claim for 52 Squadron.

6311   BE2e   53Sqn
this a'c? **Phot shot up(Capt FWH Simpson OK/2Lt J Houghton **WIA**) [?possible "Sopwith" claim combat WARNETON-MESSINES Vzfw W Seitz Ja8]

A635   Sopwith Pup   54Sqn
+* combat with AlbatrosDII[+des] nPERONNE 10-30am then 2Str[+capt] MARICOURT 10-50am OK(Capt A Lees)

This was the first combat victory for 54 Squadron.

26th January

6278   BE2g   6Sqn
AOb combat with Albatros seYPRES 6000′ ~2-45pm shot up(Capt SP? Smith/2Lt PC Hollingsworth **WIA) EA in sun from behind, observer wounded early [?possible "BE" claim combat nrWYTSCHAETEBOGEN Ltn Brenninger/Ltn Ompteda FAb.3]

A35   FE2d   20Sqn
Rec combat with EA ovWESTROOSEBEKE ftl cr ST MARIE CAPELLE wr(Sgt CJ Cox **inj/2Lt LG Fauvel **inj**)

A1074   Sopwith Strutter 45Sqn
EscPhot combat with EA, down in flames Sh28 R.21.c **MIA(FSgt WG Webb **KIA**/Cpl RD Fleming **KIA**) to HALLUIN [?"Sopwith 4072" claim combat RECKEM Ltn W vBülow Ja18]

N5181.T   Sopwith Pup   8 Sqn RNAS
**EscPhot(15Sq) left 2pm GRANDCOURT combat with EA ftl wr PICQUIGNY MIA but OK(FSLt RR Soar)

27th January

A305   Nieuport 17   24Sqn
+* combat with 2Str[+des] nrBAPAUME 10-05am OK(Capt SH Long)

A81   RE8   52Sqn
+*AReg combat with EA & seen off ovMOISLAINS WOOD 3500′ 11-15am OK(Lt Woodhouse/Lt HQ Nickalls) EA reported down MAUREPAS

A307.B1   Nieuport 17   60Sqn
** combat with AlbatrosC HANNESCAMPS engine problems ftl 8Sqn OK(2Lt KL Caldwell NZ.) a'c shelled but salvaged (see below) ["Nieuport" claim dn nrHANNESCAMPS by Flakzug58]

28th January

2514   BE2c   4Sqn
AOb AA spiral sPUISIEUX(2Lt PCE Johnson **KIA/Lt CB Bird MC **POW DoW**) left 1-30pm, last WT 3-40pm ["Bristol 2514" Flak claim eSERRE]

6646   BE12   21Sqn
DP AA crGUEDECOURT-LE TRANSLOY(2Lt FG Russell **KIA) left 1-10pm

             FE8   41Sqn
** combat? shot up(2Lt AF Barker **WIA**)

                            60Sqn
** hit while salvaging A307 nr trenches which had come down on the previous day(Lt EG Herbert **WIA**)

29th January

A239   Morane P   3Sqn
Phot shot up ftl nrMAMETZ WOOD(Lt AH Whistler **WIA/Cpl EJ Hare **inj**) observer injured in ldg

             BE2e   9Sqn
AOb shell fire(/2Lt A Matthews **WIA)

6981   FE2b   11Sqn
**OP left 1-25pm ARRAS AA 3-10pm ftl WoL R.5.D. cr wr OK(Capt BL Dowling/Lt CF Lodge)

             FE2d   20Sqn
** shot up(/Lt HM Golding **WIA**)

A782   FE2b   25Sqn
Phot HENIN LIETARD combat with 12 Halberstadts[+hit point blank, down ooc] ovHARNES 10000′ 10-50am engine shot up dam(2Lt AW Shirtcliffe OK/2Lt AV Blenkiron **WIA)thigh, escort was provided by three 40Sqn FE8s

A87   **RE8**   **52Sqn**
+*Phot combat with EA[+driven down ooc in flat spin]
BOUCHAVESNES-MARRIERS WOOD 7500'
12-30pm OK(Lt HC Mulock/Cpl Boult)

February 1917

In January, thirty-five aircraft had been involved in casualties, twenty-nine of which were caused by air combat. Air fighting continued to dominate the way casualties were now caused. December's worrying trend of increasing numbers of Allied corps machines being attacked also continued, but much greater problems surfaced in February. In this month, thirty-three of the sixty-five casualties were aircraft involved in artillery or photographic work — duties offensive patrolling was designed to protect.

1st February

No.9 Squadron RNAS was formed at St Pol, Dunkirk on the 1st of February from a nucleus supplied by 8 Squadron RNAS. It was equipped with Sopwith Pups and Nieuport Scouts but would soon replace the latter with Pups and then Sopwith Triplanes in the summer. On the 15th of June it was made available to the RFC, relieving 3 (Naval) which returned to Dunkirk.

    BE2e   **2Sqn**
AOb AA (/Lt KB Brigham **WIA)leg

2643   **BE2c**   **8Sqn**
**AP combat with EA dam ftl nrBEAUMETZ OK(2Lt DH Robertson/AM EM? Harwood)

    BE2e   **15Sqn**
** ground fire fr trenches(Capt GM Moore **WIA**)

6742   **BE2d**   **16Sqn**
Phot THELUS combat with 4EAs ftl ldg ok EoL Sh51B A.10.d. 3-10pm **MIA(Lt PW Murray **POW DoW**/Lt DJ McRae Can. **DoW**), a'c shelled & destroyed, both DoW 2.2.17 ["BE 6742" claim combat nrVIMY swTHELUS 3-10pm Ltn M Fr vRichthofen Ja11]

    FE2d   **20Sqn**
** shot up(Lt JK Stead **KIA**/)

A28   **FE2d**   **20Sqn**
PhotRec combat with EA shot down 1km eMOORSLEDE **MIA(2Lt ED Spicer **KIA**/Capt CM Carbert MC **KIA**) seen ok going towards ROULERS 4-05pm, Ja8 ["Vickers A28" claim combat 1km eMOORSLEDE pm OffSt W Göttsch Ja8]

A1951   **FE2d**   **20Sqn**
Rec combat shot down BONDUES nLILLE **MIA(2Lt WA Reeves **WIA POW**/2Lt FH Bronskill **POW**) seen ok 4-05pm going towards ROULERS, Ja8 ["Vickers A1951" claim combat BONDUES nLILLE pm Ltn W Göttsch Ja8]

A2614   **DH2**   **29Sqn**
OP combat BEAUMONT HAMEL shot down(Capt APV Daly **WIA POW) left 3-30pm ESSARTS-ACHIET LE PETIT, seen ok 3000'?, pilot to Holland 7.5.18, Voss4 ["Vickers 1Str A2614" claim combat ESSARTS-ACHIET LE PETIT 4-30pm Ltn W Voss Ja2]

N6161   **Sopwith Pup**   **1 Wing RNAS**
3(Naval)? ** shot down nrBLANKENBERGHE **MIA**(FSLt GL Elliot **POW**) a'c captured [?combat nrBLANKENBERGHE Obfm K Meyer SFS1]

2nd February

7711   **FE2b**   **22Sqn**
EscPhot hit sBAPAUME ftl cr wr(/2Lt JMR Miller **WIA) cr shell hole ROZIÈRES

7705   **FE2b**   **23Sqn**
EscRec combat with EA chased down diving in mist neBAPAUME 1-15pm **MIA(2Lt RT Whitney **POW**/Lt TG Holley **WIA POW**) left 11-40am ["Vickers 7705" claim combat swHENDECOURT 1-25pm Vzfw P Bona Ja1]

A2570   **DH2**   **32Sqn**
OP combat ftl? ePUISIEUX in control? 2-45pm **MIA(2Lt H Blythe **POW DoW** 10.2.17) left 2pm [?"Vickers" claim combat nrGOMMECOURT 2-30pm Ltn Gutermuth Ja5]

N5191   **Sopwith Pup**   **8Sqn RNAS**
EscPhot BAPAUME-CAMBRAI shot down nrHERMIES **MIA(FSLt WE Traynor **KIA**) left 12pm, attached from 3(N) ["Sopwith 5191" claim combat nrHERMIES OffSt F Kosmahl/Ltn R Schulz FAb261]

3rd February

No.8 Squadron RNAS returned to Dunkirk for six weeks' rest on the 3rd of February. By the end of this period it would have exchanged its Pups for Sopwith Triplanes. No.3 Squadron RNAS replaced it shortly afterwards, arriving for duty with the RFC fully equipped with Pups. They would fly these until the summer when the Sopwith Camel fighter became available. By the end of February, No.3 Squadron would be known as 3(Naval) Squadron, in common with virtually all other naval units so renamed, in order to avoid confusion with RFC squadrons. One exception to this change appears to have been No.2 Squadron RNAS.

    BE2e   **4Sqn**
AOb AA (Capt JC McMillan **DoW 6.2.17/)

4th February

    FE2b   **11Sqn**
OP ftl n.m.l. nrHEBUTERNE cr(2Lt AB Coupal **inj/

2Lt HL Villiers **KIA**) left 11-03am, shot down?, Coupal:
shock ["Sitter EA" claim combat GOMMECOURT-
COURCELETTES 11-55am Vzfw P Bona Ja1]

7105   BE2e   15Sqn
AOb last WT 2-05pm **MIA(Sgt JF Shaw **KIA**/2Lt
GWB Bradford **KIA**) left 1-50pm, ldg ok Sh57D L.25.c.,
KIFA? [?"BE" claim combat HEBUTERNE-
PUISIEUX 2-30pm Ltn E Böhme Ja2]

2768   BE2c   16Sqn
**AOb combat with EA shot up ftl cr WoL 50yd
nBERTHONVAL FARM(Lt JW Boyd **DoW**/2Lt AH
Steele **DoW**) both DoW 5.2.17 [?"BE" claim combat
sGIVENCHY nrNEUVILLE 2-30pm Ltn E König Ja2]

5797   BE2d   16Sqn
**AOb combat with 2EAs shot down in flames WoL
Sh36C X.30(2Lt H Martin-Massey **inj**/2Lt NMH
Vernham **KIA**) pilot burnt [BE claim combat
nrGIVENCHY 2-40pm Ltn W Voss Ja2]

A2536   DH2   32Sqn
** combat with AlbatrosDII[+ooc] ACHIET 3-35pm &
AlbatrosDIII[+des] ABLAINVILLE 4pm but shot up
dam(Capt WGS Curphey MC **WIA**)head [?"Sopwith
1Str" claim combat SAILLY-LE TRANSLOY 2-05pm
Ltn E Böhme Ja2]

5th February

A3274   Nieuport 12   46Sqn
+* combat with AlbatrosDII[+des] eYPRES 2-20pm
OK(Capt GM Boumphrey/Capt F Findlay)

This was the first 46 Squadron victory in France.

6th February

7144   BE2e   15Sqn
**AOb combat with EA shot down in flames
sPENDANT COPSE WoL cr K.34.d.2.4.(2Lt HL
Pateman **KIA**/2Lt HJ Davis **KIA**) left 10-20am last WT
10-30am

A31   FE2d   20Sqn
Phot combat with 6EAs MOORSLEDE **MIA(Lt TCH
Lucas **KIA**/2Lt JT Gibbon **KIA**) left 3-11pm, seen low
down in control after combat, Ja8 ["Vickers A3 . . ."
claim combat eMOORSLEDE Ltn Traeger Ja8]

A38   FE2d   20Sqn
Phot combat with 6EAs MOORSLEDE **MIA(2Lt ME
Woods **inj POW**/Lt EB Maule **KIA**) left 3-05pm, down
in control: seen low, Ja8 ["Vickers 38" claim combat
seGHELUVELT Oblt Fr vEsebeck Ja8]

4971   FE2b   22Sqn
**Esc combat ftl cr EAUCOURT L'ABBAYE wr(Lt WN
McDonald **WIA**/2Lt E Galley OK) [?"Vickers" claim
combat neFLERS, HAPLINCOURT 12-10pm Vzfw P
Bona Ja1]

**   FE2b   23Sqn**
** shot up(/2Lt FWA Vickery **WIA**)

7th February

7789   Sopwith Strutter   45Sqn
**Phot MENIN combat with 4EAs, wings folded
5000'(2Lt EE Erlebach **KIA**/Gnr F Ridgeway **KIA**) a'c
fell for 2 minutes ["Sopwith 7789" claim nrLINSELLES
12-25pm Ltn W vBülow Ja18]

N5102.1   **Sopwith Strutter 5 Wing RNAS**
** BRUGES shot down ROXEM **MIA**(FLt CR Blagrove
KIA/2AM J Milne **KIA**) a'c captured ["Sopwith 2Str"
claim combat ROXEM Vzfw J Wirtz MFJa1]

This machine may have been lost on RNAS
bombing raids to German shipping in Bruges
harbour. Air reconnaissance had shown that the
severe winter conditions had frozen over the canals
and locks leading to the harbour, effectively
trapping the ships at their moorings. This gave an
excellent opportunity for attack, and raids were
carried out over the next few days by 4 and 5 Wing
based at Dunkirk.

These units were by now performing valuable
work in the coastal region. Virtually all of their
bombing efforts were directed at German U-boat
and destroyer bases on the Belgium coast. The
above casualty was on one of these raids. They also
attacked hostile aerodromes in the north from
which bombing operations on England were being
made. Machines at Dunkirk in February were
Sopwith Strutters, twin-engined Caudrons for
night bombing, and Short seaplanes. Their work
would expand as the year progressed and better
and more potent aircraft were put at their disposal.

8th February

**   BE2e   4Sqn**
** combat? shot up(Lt WHK Copeland **WIA**/)arm

Retaliation for the bombing of Bruges harbour
came on the 8th and the 14th of February. Enemy
bombers attacked Dunkirk and killed sixteen
people.

9th February

**   BE2e   5Sqn**
** combat with EA shot up(2Lt HV Puckridge **WIA**/Lt
AN Nesbitt **WIA**)

6936   FE2b   25Sqn
* shot down AA: crew not yet known but OK?

A1084   Sopwith Strutter   45Sqn
**LP HOUTHULST combat with EA shot up edge of
tail folded but managed ldg nrCHÂTEAU LOUVIE
OK(Capt EFP Lubbock/2Lt FM Austin) this crew had
claimed an AlbatrosDII nrMENIN on 7.2.17

10th February

No.10 Squadron RNAS was to be formed at St Pol on the 12th of February. It was a fighter unit equipped with Sopwith Triplanes, but it also had Nieuport two-seaters on strength for some months. In May it was withdrawn from Dunkirk for attachment to the RFC.

A2741   **BE2g**   **10Sqn**
AOb AA in flames WoL 3-45pm(Lt WA Porkess **KIA/2Lt E Roberts **KIA**) left 2-12pm, burnt

A2548   **DH2**   **32Sqn**
LP (Capt LP Aizlewood **WIA) ["Vickers 1Str" claim combat nrPUISIEUX, wSERRE 11-25am Ltn W Voss Ja2][?is this "Vickers 2Str" claim combat GOMMECOURT 11-20am Ltn E Böhme Ja2]

A1107   **Sopwith Strutter**   **43Sqn**
DP AA ovNEUVE CHAPELLE cr(Lt TS Edelston **WIA)wrist & injured in crash

A2386   **Sopwith Strutter**   **43Sqn**
P combat with 7EAs ovCAMBIN(Lt JMJCJI Rock **WIA/2Lt AEP Smith **WIA**)badly

     Sopwith Strutter   **43Sqn**
P combat with 5EAs shot up(/Lt RJ Docking **DoW)

These were the first combat casualties for 43 Squadron.

11th February

2498   **BE2c**   **13Sqn**
AOb ROCLINCOURT combat driven down EoL cr fire ~G.12.b.9.5. **MIA(Capt J Thorburn **KIA**/2Lt JK Howard **KIA**) a'c burnt ["BE" claim combat ST LAURENT-ROCLINCOURT, nrARRAS 2-20pm Ltn E König Ja2]

2520   **BE2c**   **13Sqn**
EscPhot AA(/Cpl GO Cottingham **WIA)leg

     BE2c   **15Sqn**
AOb combat with 6EAs shot up(/2Lt LL Brown **WIA)

13th February

59 Squadron arrived in France on this day equipped with RE8 corps machines. It was to become known throughout the RFC for its photographic work.

A266   **Morane P**   **3Sqn**
Phot combat with EA 3-30pm, broke up in dive, cr WoL M.29.d.5.5.(Lt T Seeman-Green **KIA/2Lt WK Carse **KIA**) left 3-10pm, Ja1? ["Morane" claim combat nrLE TRANSLOY 3-35pm OffSt Behling Ja1]

14th February

2543   **BE2c**   **2Sqn**
AReg combat? shot up(Capt GC Bailey **WIA/2Lt GWB Hampton OK) [?"BE" claim combat swMAZINGARBE nrLENS 3-45pm Ltn M Fr vRichthofen Ja11]

6231   **BE2d**   **2Sqn**
AOb combat ovCITÉ ST AUGUSTE seen spiral down **MIA(2Lt CD Bennett **WIA POW**/2Lt HA Croft **KIA**) left 9-45am LENS, MvR20 ["BE 6231" claim combat LENS-HULLUCH ROAD 11am Ltn M Fr vRichthofen Ja11]

A6652   **Morane P**   **3Sqn**
AOb combat with 8EAs shot down in flames broke up cr WoL 9-25am(Lt FC Young **KIA/Lt AGS de Ross **KIA**) left 9-10am, cr N.27.d.33 [?"Morane" claim nrGUEDECOURT Ltn Gutermuth Ja5]

     BE2e   **8Sqn**
** shot up(/2Lt WJ Pearson **WIA**) [?possible "BE" claim combat ETERY nwPERONNE Vzfw Eck Ja3]

A15   **FE2d**   **20Sqn**
P combat with EA ftl hit wires cr(2Lt FJ Taylor **inj/2Lt FM Myers **KIA**) left 2-48pm [?"FE" claim combat ZUIDSCHOOTE 4pm Ltn P Strähle Ja18]

A1960   **FE2d**   **20Sqn**
** combat with AlbatrosDII[+?des+?ooc] PASSCHENDAELE 5pm prop shot up, control wires gone ftl cr wr(Capt HE Hartney Can. **inj**/2Lt WT Jordan **inj**) WIA?, both in hospital [?poss "FE" claim combat HOUTHULST WOOD" Untoff Flemmig Ja18]

A642   **Sopwith Pup**   **54Sqn**
Esc seen ovCAMBRAI shot up ftl **MIA(2Lt JV Fairbairn **WIA POW**) left 11-15am, to hospital, to Holland 15.4.18 ["Sopwith A642" claim combat ETERPIGNY, sPERONNE 11-45am Ltn G Schlenker Ja3]

Fairburn was the first Sopwith Pup pilot lost in action by the RFC.

15th February

No.1 Squadron RNAS moved to the Somme to operate with the RFC on the 15th of February.

A6610   **Nieuport 16**   **1Sqn**
+*combat with Albatros DIII [+flames] VLAMERTINGHE 5pm OK (2Lt VH Collins) see 46 Sqn below

A6622   **Nieuport 17**   **1Sqn**
P combat with 3EAs seen nose dive ovGHELUVELT WOOD 12-26pm **MIA(Capt JME Shepherd **KIA**) left 11-52am BOESINGHE-WYTSCHAETE ["Nieu 1Str 6622" claim combat sBIXSCHOOTE 12-30pm Vzfw Glasmacher Ja8]

1 Squadron RFC was converted to a single-seat fighter unit in 1917 and this was its first loss in action on Nieuport Scouts.

     FE2d   **20Sqn**
** shot up(Lt RBW Wainwright **WIA**/)

7932   **DH2**   **32Sqn**
**LP heavy combat with EA low ovBOIS DE

LOUPART **MIA**(2Lt CH March **WIA POW**) to
GREVILLERS, seen in control after combat ["Vickers
7932" claim combat nrMIRAUMONT 9-45am Vzfw
Bassing Ja5] ["Vickers claim combat nrMIRAUMONT
9-45am Ltn R Theiller Ja5]

A2535   DH2   32Sqn
LP combat with EA shot up(Capt HWG Jones **WIA)

7635   FE8   40Sqn
**LP LA BASSÉE CANAL AA hit cr WoL 2-55pm
OK(2Lt LB Blaxland) [some give this as the "FE 2Str"
claim on 16.2? combat LIEVIN-GRENAY 2-55pm Vzfw
S Festner Ja11, but relevant RFC Casualty Report dated
16th refers to action on 15th]

A229   Nieuport 20   46Sqn
+* combat with AlbatrosDIII[+flames] HOSPITAL
FARM-VLAMERTINGHE 4-30pm OK(2Lt SH Pratt/
2Lt G Bryers) victim was German ace Ltn H von Keudell
Ja27, shared with 1 Sqn

A87   RE8   52Sqn
**Phot left 11-50am combat with EA, shot down
C.7.c.3.9. **MIA**(Lt HC Mulock **KIA**/Pte TA Booth **KIA**)
[?"BE" claim combat RANCOURT-COMBLES Ltn G
Schlenker Ja3]

There were only two RE8s actually lost in combat
by 52 Squadron before it completed its exchange to
BE2es, this being the last (see the 7th of January).

A645   Sopwith Pup   54Sqn
**EscFEs GREVILLERS-ROCQUIGNY combat with
EA **MIA**(2Lt EH Hamilton **KIA**) left 11-40am
[?"Sopwith 1Str" claim combat nrSAPIGNIES-
DOUCHY Ltn Fr vStenglin Ja1, but see other 54 Sq a'c]

A647   Sopwith Pup   54Sqn
**EscFEs BAPAUME shot up dam ftl 3Sq OK(2Lt NA
Phillips)

A654   Sopwith Pup   54Sqn
**EscFEs left 11-40am left formation in combat
MIA(Capt CLM Scott **KIA**) ["Sopwith A654" Flak
claim LIGNY-TILLOY, BAPAUME 1Army Flak]

16th February

BE2e   5Sqn
** combat? shot up(Sgt HG Smith **WIA**/Lt JA Aldred
OK)slight

4179   BE2c   16Sqn
familiarisation with Lines **MIA(2Lt EW Lindley **POW
DoW** 18.2.17/2Lt LV Munn **KIA**) left 11-50am [?"BE
4179" claim combat eARRAS 12pm? Ltn K Allmenröder
Ja11]

25th February

A2557   DH2   29Sqn
**OP combat with EA shot down ooc nrARRAS cr wr(Lt
RJS Lund **WIA**) Voss7, left 12-35pm ["Vickers" claim
combat nrARRAS-LE SAUVEUR 1-55pm Ltn W Voss
Ja2] ["Vickers 1Str" claim combat nrARRAS 1-45pm
Ltn E König Ja2]

9735   Sopwith Strutter 3 Wing RNAS
**B BREBACH combat with 4EAs[+?] CHÂTEAU
SALIRES shot up ftl SIECHAMPS OK(FLt E Potter/
AM LA Dell) started late

9739   Sopwith Strutter 3 Wing RNAS
**B BREBACH RAID combat with EA shot down
SAARGEMUND **MIA**(FSLt LE Smith **POW DoI**/AM1
RS Portsmouth **KIA**) Ja24 ["Sopwith 9739" claim
combat SAARGEMUND Offst Vohlnecht Ja24]

As far back as November 1916 it had been known
that Germany was constructing formidable new
defences well back behind the Somme area.
However, it was only during a patrol by 54
Squadron Pups on the 25th, which had managed
to penetrate to the Hindenburg Line, that the first
definite proof was gathered when great fires were
seen burning in nearly every village.

26th February

BE2e   5Sqn
** combat? shot up(Capt E Fletcher **WIA**/2Lt AM
Morgan **WIA**)

2535   BE2c   16Sqn
**AOb combat with Halberstadt ECURIE shot down,
chased to ground by EA(Lt HE Bagot **WIA**/2Lt RLM
Jack **DoW** 27.2.17) left 2-15pm, Voss9 [BE claim combat
nrECURIE 3-50pm Ltn W Voss Ja2]

A5460   FE2b   18Sqn
**LP combat with EA shot down cr
nrGUILLEMONT(2Lt G Vaughan-Jones **KIA**/Lt JF
Ferguson **WIA DoW**?) left 1pm

18 Squadron carried out a follow-up reconnaissance of the Hindenburg Line after the
discoveries of 54 Squadron the previous day. They
brought back details of the elaborate defences now
in place, as well as signs in the intervening territory
of substantial fortifications and strong points. The
crew above was lost during this operation.

DH2   29Sqn
** combat? shot up(2Lt LL Carter **WIA**)leg

BE2e?   52Sqn
** AA(/Lt HQ Nickalls **WIA**)hand

3981   Nieuport 11   1 Wing RNAS
**B ZEEBRUGGE ground fire fuel tank hit ftl
CADZAND(FSLt GP Powles **INT**)

27th February

2530   BE2c   8Sqn
**AOb combat with EA 9-45am cr wr R26a.51c.SE
MIA(2Lt EA Pope **KIA**/2Lt HA Johnson **KIA**) Ja2 Voss
["BE" claim combat BLAIREVILLE 9-45am Ltn W
Voss Ja2]

7197 BE2e 12Sqn
**AOb combat with 5EAs, fell in flames ovARRAS(Capt
JH McArthur **KIA**/Pte J Whiteford **KIA**) left 2-55pm,
Ja2 Voss11 ["BE" claim combat ST CATHERINE,
wARRAS 3-48pm Ltn W Voss Ja2]

BE2e 13Sqn
** combat? shot up(2Lt HF Mackain **KIA**)

28th February

3 (Naval) Squadron arrived at Bertangles on the
Somme for operations with the RFC on the 28th of
February.

Untraced Casualty in France in February 1917?

RNAS
** (FSLt G Bowles **INT**) interned Holland

March 1917

THE GERMAN WITHDRAWAL
TO THE HINDENBURG LINE

All air intelligence now being brought in by the
RFC was pointing to the fact that a staged German
withdrawal to the Hindenburg Line was being
made. On the 14th of March detailed plans for this
were discovered in a captured dug-out, and three
days later a general British advance was ordered.

It was not around the Somme, however, but
further north where I Brigade RFC was operating
with the First Army, that the air war intensified in
the coming weeks. The corps units there were Nos.
2, 5, 10, and 16 Squadrons and the Army units
were Nos. 25, 40, and 43. These, and the other
British units being assembled for what would
become the battle of Arras, are given in detail on
the 4th of April. Reconnaissance and photographic
units in particular were stretched to the limit as
they strove to understand what the enemy was
doing, and through March their losses rose
accordingly. The statistics show that their escorts
were also being hit heavily.

The Germans were about to deliver an onslaught
— the British losses in the air in March 1917 were
to equal all those lost in the whole of 1915, and
eighty-eight per cent were to be brought about by
air fighting. German single-seat fighters, which had
dominated the air war since the previous autumn,
were now being joined by new and more powerful
types. The prime example of this was the Albatros
DIII, which arrived on the Western Front in late
January 1917. It was a notable machine in many
ways, not least of all for the fact that the aircraft it
replaced, the Albatros DII, was even then the best

fighter in the war. By the beginning of March there
were also fifty-eight of the highly regarded
Halberstadt DVs in France. Not only these, but
new two-seaters also appeared, some of which had
operational ceilings substantially higher than the
machines which were supposed to be intercepting
them. An example was the Rumpler CIV which
went about photographing the front lines from its
ceiling of 21,000 feet. It was beautifully designed
for its purpose: its pilot and observer were
positioned close together to maximise co-operation
on patrol and it was very well armed, the observer
having the luxury of a pair of Parabellum machine-
guns if required, as well as a front firing Spandau.
It was the first aircraft to carry oxygen equipment.

1st March

4 (Naval) Squadron transferred to No.4 Wing
RNAS at Bray Dunes as a fighter squadron on the
1st of March. It was equipped with the Sopwith
Pup and became responsible for offensive patrolling, escorting, and protection of naval units from
air attack.

5821 BE2e 4Sqn
**AP combat with 6EAs ovACHIET LE PETIT, engine
problems ftl bad ground cr Sh57D x.13.c. dam(2Lt DRC
Gabell **inj**/Lt GE Craig OK)

Kite Balloon 14Bal Co
** balloon brought down by EA burnt(Lt GK Simpson
DoW 7.3.17)

FE2b 25Sqn
EscPhot shot up(/2Lt GRF Waner **DoW
2.3.17) stomach

A782 FE2b 25Sqn
+* combat with AlbatrosDIII[+ooc] MERICOURT
3pm OK(2Lt JL Leith/Lt GMA Hobart-Hampden)

N6164 Sopwith Pup 9 (Naval) Sqn
**combat with EA[+] dam ftl sea nrCADZAND
MIA(FSLt FV Branford **INT**) interned Holland

3rd March

A2571 DH2 29Sqn
** combat with AlbatrosDIII[+capt] TILLOY 3-50pm
OK(2Lt AJ Pearson) shared in last? DH2 victory for
29Sqn

6419 FE8 40Sqn
**EscP combat with HA ftl 4pm dam OK(2Lt KS
Henderson) left 1-42pm ANNOEULLIN-OPPY

4th March

5785 BE2e 2Sqn
** combat? shot up(Lt JB Crosbee OK/Sgt JE Prance
WIA)leg [?"BE" claim combat neLOOS 11-45am Ltn M
Fr vRichthofen Ja11]

6252   BE2e   8Sqn
**AOb combat with EA BERNEVILLE WoL, shot down
in flames(Sgt RJ Moody **KIA**/2Lt EE Horn **KIA**) left
9-25am, Voss12 (not MvR) ["BE" claim combat
BERNEVILLE, swARRAS 10-30am Ltn W Voss Ja2]

BE2c   15Sqn
** AA(2Lt FHE Reeve **WIA**/)slight

4895   FE2b   18Sqn
**Phot AA shot up dam ftl ldg a'dr OK(Lt CG Shaumer/
2Lt RC Doughty) to Fifth Army front

A789   FE2b   18Sqn
**EscPhot combat shot up ftl cr 3Sqn a'dr(Lt H
Lambourne **WIA**/Pte J Collison **WIA**) left 9-25am Fifth
Army front

7707   FE2b   22Sqn
**LP combat fuel tank shot up ftl glide cr
nrMONTAUBAN OK(2Lt EA Mearns/Lt H Loveland)
Fourth Army front

A5441   FE2b   22Sqn
**LP combat with EA fire began but put out ftl WoL ok
but a'c destroyed Sh57c S.30.a. OK(2Lt LW Beal/2AM
AG? Davin) to Fourth Army front, initials FG? ["FE"
claim combat BOUCHAVESNES 4-15pm Ltn R Theiller
Ja5]

4965   FE2b   23Sqn
**EscPhot combat with HA M.32.c.8.2. dam ftl WoL(2Lt
WE Jones OK/2Lt WA Golding **WIA**)knee, left 9-26am,
severely wounded

A4872   FE8   40Sqn
**EscP combat with HA shot down ftl Sh36A x.2.5.
3-45pm dam OK(Lt CO Usborne) left 1-42pm
ANNOEULLIN-OPPY

A961   Sopwith Strutter   43Sqn
+* combat with 2Str[+ooc] neVIMY 9-35am OK(2Lt
CP Thornton/Sgt R Dunn)

This was the first air combat victory for 43
Squadron.

A1108   Sopwith Strutter   43Sqn
P combat with 3EAs shot down sVIMY **MIA(2Lt HJ
Green **KIA**/2Lt AW Reid **KIA**) left 1-40pm, left format
then combat 3-45pm, MvR23 ["Sopwith A1108" claim
combat ACHEVILLE 3-20pm Ltn M Fr vRichthofen
Ja11]

A1109   Sopwith Strutter   43Sqn
P ovLENS 10-55am then EA **MIA(2Lt PL Wood **KIA**/
2Lt AH Fenton **KIA**) left 8-40am ["Sopwith 4594?" claim
combat swHAISNES 10-50am Ltn K Schaefer Ja11]

A285   Nieuport 20   46Sqn
+* combat with AlbatrosDIII[+ooc] BIXSCHOOTE
5pm shot up OK(2Lt GP Kay OK/2Lt WW Steuart
DoW 5.3.17)

This was the last Nieuport two-seater victory for 46
Squadron.

A633   Sopwith Pup   54Sqn
**EscRec combat with 2EAs engine hit, in spin down
ovST QUENTIN but recovered? **MIA**(Capt A Lees **WIA**
POW) left 10-33am ["Sopwith A633" claim combat nrST
QUENTIN Ltn G Schlenker Ja3]

At this time 54 Squadron Pups were escorting 22
Squadron FEs on deep reconnaissances systematically photographing the Hindenburg Line.

A4163   RE8   59Sqn
**Phot EA shot down nwMONCHY cr WoL W.28.
wr(Lt BW Hill **KIA**/2Lt W Harms **KIA**) left 2-44pm
["BE" claim combat nMONCHY 3-30pm Ltn R Theiller
Ja5]

These were the first combat casualties for 59
Squadron.

N5188   Sopwith Pup   3 (Naval) Sqn
*Esc shot up dam cr ldg a'dr dam OK(FSLt HF
Beamish)

N6165   Sopwith Pup   3 (Naval) Sqn
**LP combat with EA shot down nrVIS-EN-ARTOIS
EoL **MIA**(FSLt JP White **KIA**) left 11-15am
GOMMECOURT-LE TRANSLOY, Ja1 ["Sopwith
6165" claim combat VIS-EN-ARTOIS 1-05pm Oblt H
Kummetz Ja1]

N6166   Sopwith Pup   3 (Naval) Sqn
LP combat with EA shot up(FSLt LA Powell **DoW
7.3.17)stomach, this a'c?

N6170   Sopwith Pup   3 (Naval) Sqn
**LP combat with EA shot down nrVIS-EN-ARTOIS
EoL **MIA**(FLt HR Wambolt **KIA**) left 11-15am
GOMMECOURT-LE TRANSLOY, Ja1 ["Sopwith
6170" claim INCHY-SAINS LES MARQUION
12-50pm Ltn H Schröder Ja1]

These were the first casualties for 3 (Naval)
Squadron.

6th March

55 Squadron RFC arrived in France on the 6th
March equipped with one of the great aircraft of
the war, the new two-seater Airco DH4. It was
destined to be used as both a bombing machine and
a fighter reconnaissance type, and would still be
operating in the last days of the war. It was a
tractor biplane utilising several engines, depending
on its intended role, a factor which complicated its
production, and which must have perplexed more
than one equipment officer. Those which 55
Squadron flew out had 250hp Rolls-Royce engines
and were fitted with Constantinesco interrupter
gear for the forward machine-gun. For a large
machine it was extremely handy. Its ability to
account for itself and to absorb damage were
valuable assets in war flying, and it soon proved its

superiority. For a time it even flew without fighter escort. The type would arrive in numbers in late spring, flying with 25 and 57 Squadrons RFC and 2 (Naval), and taking over a substantial amount of the photo-reconnaissance and day bombing duties of the RFC for a year or more. Like any really good machine, however, it was used remorselessly, and hundreds of casualties on the DH4 found in these pages are testimony to this.

A268   Morane P   3Sqn
AOb shot down nrLIGNY N.19. WoL 12-30pm(Lt CW Short MC **DoW/Lt SMcK Fraser **WIA**) left 10-50am, a'c shelled [?"Parasol Monoplane" claim combat nrGUEDECOURT 12-45pm OffSt E Nathanael Ja5]

6273   BE2e   7Sqn
+*ARec combat with 2Str ovCHAULNES 8-43am OK(2Lt PB Pattisson/2Lt FA Prescott) EA appeared to fire through bottom of fuselage

5856   BE2d   16Sqn
Phot combat shot down ooc nrGIVENCHY 11-35am into glide nr ground cr Sh36C s.18. **MIA(2Lt GM Underwood **KIA**/2Lt AE Watts **KIA**) left 10-15am FARBUS, Wolffl ["BE 5856" claim combat nrGIVENCHY 11-30am Ltn K Wolff Ja11]

6823   BE2e   16Sqn
+*AOb combat with "Fokker" NEUVILLE ST VAAST 3500' 3-40pm shot up(Lt OR Knight **WIA**/2AM ED Harvey OK)slight, earlier combat with Halberstadt 3-10pm

A2785   BE2e   16Sqn
AOb VIMY combat WoL shot up cr wr(2Lt GMG Bibby **KIA/Lt GJO Brichta Can. **KIA**) left 1-50pm ["BE" claim combat nrSOUCHEZ 4pm Ltn M Fr vRichthofen Ja11]

4957   FE2b   23Sqn
EscPhot combat ftl nrBELLEVUE(Sgt EP Critchley OK/2AM G Brown **WIA) left 1-31pm

7699   FE2b   23Sqn
**Phot combat radiator shot up ftl nrST LEGER dam cr OK(Capt CE Bryant DSO/2Lt HS Elliot)

A5471   FE2b   23Sqn
EscRec combat shot up cr nrBAVINCOURT WoL(2Lt GH Harrison **WIA/2Lt OGS Crawford **WIA**) left 1-50pm

7503   Martinsyde G100   27Sqn
**B HEBUTERNE-SAILLISEL shot up dam OK(Lt J Gilmour)

7882   DH2   32Sqn
EscRec **MIA(2Lt MJJG Mare-Montembault **POW**) ["Vickers 7882" claim combat BEUGNY-BEUGNATRE 3-30pm Oblt A Rt vTutschek Ja2]

7938   DH2   32Sqn
LP shot up(Lt CEM Pickthorn **WIA)slight

7941   DH2   32Sqn
EscRec **MIA(Capt HG Southon **WIA POW**) ["Vickers 1Str 7941" claim combat nrVILLERS AU FLOS 3-35pm Ltn W Voss Ja2]

A978   Sopwith Strutter   43Sqn
OP shot down in flames ovLENS ~11am **MIA(Lt SJ Pepler **KIA**/Capt JD Stuart **KIA**) left 9am ["Sopwith" claim combat ovLENS 11-45am Ltn K Schaefer Ja11, also second Strutter claim 11-55am]

A1072   Sopwith Strutter   45Sqn
P combat with 5EAs shot up dam ftl(Capt JE MacKay OK/2Lt DE Greenhow **DoW) combat HOUTHULST FOREST-Lines ftl 41Sq ABEELE

A1082   Sopwith Strutter   45Sqn
**P LANGEMARCK shot up engine dam OK(Capt EFP Lubbock MC/Lt J Thompson)

5823   BE2e   52Sqn
Phot combat with EA shot up brought down cr WoL Sh62C A.12.c.6.5.(Lt JW Lockhart **WIA/2Lt GK Walker OK) left 10-55am [?possible "BE" claim Gefr Ophaus SS11]

A1948   FE2d   57Sqn
DOP SAILLY combat eBAPAUME down in control ADINFER WOOD? **MIA(2Lt FE Hills **POW**/2Lt AG Ryall **POW**) left 11am ["Vickers 1948" claim combat MORY 12-15pm Ltn H Gontermann Ja5]

A1953   FE2d   57Sqn
DOP met EA eBAPAUME, down ADINFER WOOD? **MIA(Capt WSR Bloomfield **POW**/2Lt VO Lonsdale **POW**) left 11am GOMMECOURT-SAILLY ["Vickers A1953" claim combat nrERVILLERS-BOIRY 12-20pm Ltn A Schulte Ja12]

A1963   FE2d   57Sqn
DP combat swARRAS down BERNEVILLE cr wr **MIA(Lt WFW Hills **KIA**/2Lt W Sutton-Gardner **KIA**) left 11am GOMMECOURT-SAILLY ["Vickers" claim combat with EAUCOURT L'ABBAYE 12-35pm Oblt H Kummetz Ja1]

These were the first combat losses for 57 Squadron.

A208   Nieuport 16   60Sqn
Phot ACHIET LE GRAND seen going west attacking EA ovBAPAUME 8000' 11am **MIA(Lt PS Joyce **KIA**) left 9-15am, presumed killed ["Sopwith 1Str" claim combat ACHIET LE GRAND 10-30am Oblt H Kummetz Ja1]

The BE2e, FE2b & d, and RE8 units who usually carried out all photographic reconnaissance were finding this work so difficult that single-seat fighters were conscripted. Joyce was lost after one of these operations, but mystery surrounds his death for although he was escorted back to within close range of his aerodrome he never landed. Neither he nor his aircraft were ever found.

A213.A1   **Nieuport 17**   **60Sqn**
**OP combat with EA nrRIVIÈRE down in flames cr
WoL nrRIVIÈRE Sh51C.R.21.1.4. 12-30pm(Maj EP
Graves **KIA**) left 12-10pm [?"Sopwith 1Str" claim
SAILLY-AGNY 12-50pm OffSt W Cymera Ja1]

8th March

48 Squadron RFC, equipped with the new Bristol
F2a two-seater, arrived in France on the 8th
March. The air crews had been given a little over
two months to work up on the machines before
being hastened into battle. The Squadron already
harboured a certain lack of confidence in their new
aircraft due to a series of mishaps and crashes in
England. These seemed to result from some
fundamental structural weaknesses. Two months,
however, had been too short a time to learn the true
capabilities of the Bristol Fighter; unfortunately
they would need to be discovered in battle.

11 (Naval) Squadron was formed on the 8th of
March at Petite Synthe. It was part of No. 4 Wing
RNAS at Dunkirk but would be disbanded in
August owing to a shortage of pilots.

9th March

A2571   **DH2**   **29Sqn**
**Esc left 9-20am dive in flames(2Lt AJ Pearson MC
KIA) MvR25 ["Vickers 1Str" claim combat
swBAILLEUL 10-55am Ltn M Fr vRichthofen Ja11]

6397.4   **FE8**   **40Sqn**
OP combat with EAs shot down **MIA(2Lt WB Hills
POW) to LA BASSÉE CANAL-BAILLEUL ["Vickers
6397" claim combat FASCHODA, PONT-À-VENDIN
10-20am Ltn K Schaefer Ja11]

6399   **FE8**   **40Sqn**
**OP combat with EAs shot up in flames ftl cr WoL
Sh36c G.21. 9-30am(2Lt RE Neve **WIA**) jumped from
burning a'c ["FE 1Str" claim combat wHULLUCH
9-30am Ltn K Allmenröder Ja11]

6425   **FE8**   **40Sqn**
** combat with EAs[+ooc] eLENS shot up 9-25am ftl
2Sq dam OK(2Lt HC Todd)

6456.4   **FE8**   **40Sqn**
OP shot down nrANNAY cr ldg o't **MIA(2Lt T
Shepard **POW**) left 8-45am LA BASSÉE CANAL-
BAILLEUL, a'c captured, Ja11 Wolff2 ["FE 1Str 6456"
claim combat ANNAY 9-20am Ltn K Wolff Ja11]

7636   **FE8**   **40Sqn**
**OP left 8-45am combat with EAs engine shot up ftl wr
OK(Lt W Morrice) to LA BASSÉE CANAL-
BAILLEUL

A4874.4   **FE8**   **40Sqn**
OP shot down o't **MIA(2Lt GF Haseler **POW**) left
8-45am LA BASSÉE CANAL-BAILLEUL, Ja11, a'c

captured ["Vickers 4874" claim combat PONT À
VENDIN 10-20am Ltn K Schaefer Ja11]

The sudden escalation of air fighting and the
suffering being meted out to the Royal Flying
Corps is all too apparent on these pages. The
terrible price demanded of the service to keep
reconnaissance and photographic machines in
operation was now becoming apparent. And it
would all become much worse. The 40 Squadron
FE8s noted above were on offensive patrol when
they were attacked. These operations were a lynch
pin of Allied air policy still determined that the
fight should be taken unflinchingly to the enemy.
Nine FE8s were dived on by an enemy formation
led by von Richthofen and the ensuing fight lasted
for thirty minutes. Four FE8s were shot down
whilst another four were driven down hopelessly
shot up. Two German machines were hit and
forced to land.

11th March

4541   **BE2c**   **2Sqn**
**AOb combat with EA, fell in flames in snd WoL
10-30am WoL(2Lt GC Hoskins **KIA**/2Lt GWB
Hampton **KIA**) left 9-15am LOOS ["BE" claim combat
ovLOOSBOGEN 10-20am Ltn K Schaefer Ja11]

6232   **BE2d**   **2Sqn**
**Phot combat ovGIVENCHY 10-45am shot down EoL
MIA(2Lt J Smyth **KIA**/2Lt E Byrne **KIA**) left 10-30am
["BE 6232" claim combat sLA FOLIE WOOD 10-50am
Ltn M Fr vRichthofen Ja11]

2545   **BE2c**   **4Sqn**
**PhotAOb left 10-45am COURCELETTE u'c shot off
ovCOURCELETTE ftl wr ldg OK(2Lt JD Hewett/2Lt
FG Taylor)

7155   **BE2e**   **7Sqn**
**AOb combat with 3EAs shot up dam(Capt FR Hardie
DSO **WIA**/2Lt AE Turner **WIA**?) left 9-40am
CHAULNES, ldg a'dr

A785   **FE2b**   **18Sqn**
**EscPhot Fifth Army front combat with HA shot down
WoL(2Lt JE Lewis **inj**/Lt R Mayberry **WIA**) shelled a'c
destroyed [?"FE" claim combat VIMY-GIVENCHY
10-45am Ltn Krefft Ja11][?possible "FE" claim combat
nrGUEDECOURT-LIGNY Ltn Schulte Ja12]

A5475   **FE2b**   **18Sqn**
EscPhot combat shot down **MIA(Sgt HP Burgess
KIA/2Lt HM Headley **KIA**) left 9-45am Fifth Army
area, down in flames? ovBAPAUME?

7685   **FE2b**   **22Sqn**
**LP combat with EA shot up ftl nrCOMBLES(2Lt LW
Beal OK/2AM AG Davin **WIA**) controls shot away
[?"FE" claim combat RANCOURT 9am Ltn W Voss
Ja2]

A5454   FE2b   22Sqn
EscRec combat with EA shot up(2Lt JFA Day **WIA/
2Lt LC Davies MC **WIA**) to hospital, Fourth Army front,
Day: slight WIA [possible "FE 464" claim combat
sBEUGNY Vzfw F Kosmahl/Oblt Neuburger FAb261]

7713   FE2b   23Sqn
EscPhot driven down neBAPAUME **MIA(2Lt CAR
Shum **POW**/2Lt FC Coops **POW**) left 9-08am
["Vickers" claim combat sBAPAUME 11-45am Ltn H
Gontermann Ja5]

A5443   FE2b   23Sqn
EscPhot combat with EA ftl cr **MIA(2Lt A Holden
POW/2AM AG Walker **POW**) left 9-08am eBAPAUME
["Vickers A5443" claim combat nrBEUGNY 10-40am
Ltn F Hengst/Ltn Criege SS3]

7898   DH2   32Sqn
**LP combat shot up ftl nrBAPAUME o't bad ground
wr OK(Lt CEM Pickthorn)

7903   DH2   32Sqn
**LP IRLES combat with EA engine shot up ftl
n.m.l.(2Lt WAG Young **WIA inj**)unsalvable, a'c riddled

**   DH2   32Sqn**
LP shot up(2Lt G Howe **WIA)head:slight

A2535   DH2   32Sqn
**LP nrWARLENCOURT shot up cr
nrBAPAUME(Capt JM Robb **WIA**)legs

A2548   DH2   32Sqn
**LP ovSCOTLAND TRENCH combat with D-type[+
ooc] BAPAUME 10-10am engine shot up ftl
nrBAPAUME dam (2Lt AC Randall **WIA**)slight

A5025   DH2   32Sqn
**LP combat with EA shot up ftl cr nrBAPAUME (2Lt
JH Cross **inj**) [?possible "Vickers" claim combat LE
SARS Ltn Fr vStenglin Ja1]

There are a number of possible "Vickers" claims
which could be considered regarding these heavy
losses to 32 Squadron. They include the following:

[?"Vickers" claim combat nrNOREUIL Offst W Cymera
Ja1] [? "Vickers 1Str" claim GIVENCHY-VIMY
10-10am Ltn Kresst Ja11] ["Vickers 1Str"
nrGREVILLERS WOOD Vzfw Grigo Ja12]

A78   RE8   34Sqn
**AOb combat with HalberstadtD BARLEUX 5000′
9-50am OK(Lt HR Davies/StfSgt Dennis)

A972   Sopwith Strutter 43Sqn
**OP left 9-10am sLENS AA ftl field HERSIN cr wr
10-45am OK(Lt J Potter/2Lt CJ Poole)

A1071   Sopwith Strutter 45Sqn
P fell YPRES MOAT wr(2Lt HGG? Bowden **KIA/2Lt
DB Stevenson **KIA**) Bowden's initials HGC?

A1082   Sopwith Strutter 45Sqn
**P shot down RAILWAY WOOD nrYPRES wr(Capt
EFP Lubbock MC **KIA**/Lt J Thompson **KIA**) [?"Nieu"
claim combat ZILLEBEKE 11-15am Ltn P Strähle Ja18]

**   BE2e   52Sqn**
** rifle fire(/2Lt NJ Bredner **WIA**)

A279.C3   Nieuport 17   60Sqn
**Esc combat with EA shot down in flames
nrBAILLEUL 1-40pm, cr Sh51B B.14 **MIA**(Lt AD
Whitehead **WIA POW**) Casualty Report gives AA?,
Voss15 ["Nieu" claim combat BAILLEUL 1-30pm Ltn
W Voss Ja2]

13th March

A6604   Nieuport 17   1Sqn
**Rec WYTSCHAETE-MESSINES dhAA cr wr
OK(2Lt VWB Castle)

15th March

A250   Morane LA   3Sqn
**AOb FREMICOURT AA shot down ftl WoL wr
OK(Lt EP? Wilmot/Lt Morris)

**   BE2   12Sqn**
** combat? shot up(/2Lt ASH O'Brien **WIA**)slight

A5459   FE2b   22Sqn
**P combat with HA shot up ovST QUENTIN(2Lt EA
Mearns OK/2AM CS Belton **WIA**) [?possible "Vickers"
claim combat PERONNE-BOUCHAVESNES 4-30pm
Ltn K Küppers Ja6]

16th March

**   FE2b   25Sqn**
** combat? shot up(/Sgt C Buchannan **WIA**)

7693   FE2b   25Sqn
**OP combat ftl CAMBRAI L'ABBÉ cr(2Lt RNL
Munro **WIA**/Sgt CH Nunn OK) left 1-55pm LA
BASSÉE-ARRAS, down 3-30pm

A780   FE2b   25Sqn
**OP combat shot up ftl BRAY wr(2Lt WD Matheson
WIA/Sgt G Goodman **WIA**) left 1-55pm LA BASSÉE-
ARRAS, AIR1/968/204/5/1099 gives 15.3?

A5484   FE2b   25Sqn
**OP patrol of 6 FE2bs met ~16 enemy Scouts[+ooc]
ovNEUVIREUIL 10000′ 3-15pm OK(Lt J Whittaker/
2AM F King)

1460   HP 0/100   3 Wing RNAS
*NB railway junction nrMETZ(SCdr JT Babington/)

This was the first night raid carried out by Handley
Page 0/100s. They dropped their bombs with only
a little trouble and returned confident in the new
type. Their report noted: "It is considered the
machine as a 'night bomber' will prove entirely
satisfactory and reliable. No difficulty has been
experienced in easily lifting the 12 bombs carried
and five and a half hours fuel, although the state of
the aerodrome was not very favourable owing to
the heavy rainfall."

N5134   Sopwith Strutter French
on loan ? ** combat with EA shot down(Serg L Pivette)
a'c captured ["French Sopwith 5143(sic)?" claim combat
Ltn Kaemmel Ja23]

17th March

The general British advance into the area now
being abandoned by the German Army was commenced on the 17th, including the occupation of
Bapaume. Of critical importance for the British
was to maintain effective lines of communications,
for every mile took them further from prepared
positions they had used for years. The job of the
RFC was therefore to keep in touch with the most
forward of the troops, essentially acting as
messengers. In the area of the advance the RFC
met little air opposition and in this the Germans
knew exactly what they were doing. They were
conserving their forces for when the real fighting
would occur — in this lay another reason for the
control the German Air Force exerted in the
coming month. By their ruthless wasting of the
countryside the German High Command had
ensured that the area in front of the Hindenburg
Line would be no place from which the Allies could
launch an offensive. They knew instead that the
attack would come from around Arras and in the
Champagne, as their airmen had seen British and
French preparations in these sectors. Of more
importance, they had also managed to capture full
details of Nivelle's plans. They knew, therefore,
exactly where to concentrate their air power and to
prepare for the coming battles, which they did with
vigour.

A6617   Nieuport 17   1Sqn
**EscFEs combat 8EA seen in spin nrLILLE 10-05am cr
MIA(2Lt AJ Gilson **KIA**) left 9-31am LILLE-MENIN-
COURTRAI ["Nieu 1Str" claim combat WERVICQ,
nwLINSELLES 10-20am Ltn P Strähle Ja18]

6740   BE2d   4Sqn
**AOb combat with 6EAs shot up ftl WoL R.11.b.1.5.
wr(2Lt NH Colson **WIA**/2Lt HB Mann OK) left 1-20pm
II Corps front

6241   BE2e   6Sqn
**Esc combat with 5EAs 12-05pm shot down in
flames(2Lt A Appleton **KIA**/Cpl A Cooper **KIA**) left
11-05am POLYGON WOOD [?possible "BE 5179?"
claim combat nrGHELUVELT Oblt Griessenhagen
Ja18]

4979   FE2b   11Sqn
**Rec combat shot up ftl GREVILLERS WoL(Lt AC
Woodman OK/2Lt RC Cox **WIA**) left 9am

7694   FE2b   11Sqn
**Rec combat with HA brought down nrFRICOURT
dam OK(Lt NH Read/2Lt L Nevile-Smith) left 9-30am

7695   FE2b   11Sqn
Rec combat WARLENCOURT shot down **MIA(2Lt
RW Cross **POW**/Lt CF Lodge **POW**) left 8-55am,
Voss16 [?"FE" claim combat neWARLENCOURT
11-15am Ltn W Voss Ja2]

6275   BE2e   12Sqn
**AReg left 6-40am combat with HA ovARRAS shot up
dam OK(Lt Thomson/Lt OD Norwood)

A2814   BE2e   16Sqn
**AOb combat broke up 1000' cr WoL S.27.a.5.9.(2Lt
CM? Watt **KIA**/Sgt FA Howlett) initials GM?, left
3-25pm FARBUS, NB: serial in Casualty Report without
prefix is very likely an error ["BE" claim combat
wVIMY, sGIVENCHY 4pm Ltn M Fr vRichthofen
Ja11]

4896   FE2b   18Sqn
**EscPhot Fifth Army area shot up cr ldg a'dr dam(Lt C
Parkinson OK/2Lt PS Taylor **inj**)

4990   FE2b   18Sqn
**EscPhot Fifth Army area combat with HA engine &
radiator shot up ftl trenches THIEPVAL dam OK(Lt
VH Huston/Lt EA Foord)

A6634   SPAD 7   19Sqn
+* combat with EAs HAVRINCOURT-BAPAUME
15000'-10000' btwn 10-30am to 12pm OK(Capt GWD
Allen) all 4 SPADS entering combat reports from this
operation were plagued with gun jams

A27   FE2d   20Sqn
Phot LILLE-MESSINES AA hit seen ok **MIA(Lt W
Anderson MC **POW**/Lt DB Woolley **POW**) a'c captured,
left 8-50am, FAb.(A)227 [?claim combat LOMME 10am
Untoff W Hippert FAb.(A)227]["BE A27" claim
nrLOMME, LILLE FlkB Lille]

4900   FE2b   22Sqn
**LP combat controls shot up ftl WoL wr Sh62C C.2.c
Central(2Lt FR Hudson **WIA**/2AM W Richman **WIA**)
[?possible claim combat ST PIERRE 1-30pm Ltn H
Gontermann Ja5]

FE2b   25Sqn
**Phot combat with EA shot up(2Lt IW Parnell
WIA)ribs

A5439   FE2b   25Sqn
**EscPhot ANNOEULLIN-VITRY shot down EoL
MIA(Lt AE Boultbee **KIA**/2AM F King **KIA**?) left 9am,
MvR27 ["Vickers A5439" claim combat seOPPY
10-40am Ltn M Fr vRichthofen Ja11]

A2583   DH2   32Sqn
**LP wTHILLOYS combat with HA shot down
nrBAPAUME wr(Lt TA Cooch **WIA**) Voss17 ["Vickers
1Str" claim combat neWARLENCOURT 11-25am Ltn
W Voss Ja2]

Sopwith Strutter 43Sqn
** combat?(/2Lt HE Ward **WIA**)foot

A1097   Sopwith Strutter 43Sqn
OP BEAUMONT **MIA(2Lt RA Constable **KIA**/2Lt

CD Knox **KIA**) left 9-10am, Wolff3 [?"Sopwith" claim combat PONT DU JOUR, ATHIES 10-45am Ltn K Wolff Ja11]

A1111   Sopwith Strutter   43Sqn
OP left 9-10am BEAUMONT **MIA(2Lt JC Rimer **KIA**/2Lt RH Lownds **KIA**) ["Sopwith A1111" claim combat nrATHIES-OPPY 10-45am Ltn K Allmenröder Ja11]

A2779   BE2e   53Sqn
EscPhot shot up damaged, into spin on landing due to wind, hit pole wr(2Lt A Pascoe OK/Cpl TW Willis **inj)

N6163   Sopwith Pup   3 (Naval) Sqn
**OP left 9-45am neBAPAUME combat ftl nrCONTALMAISON CHÂTEAU cr ldg wr OK(FSLt FD Casey)

18th March

Peronne was occupied. 66 Squadron arrived at Vert Galand on the 18th of March equipped with Sopwith Pup fighters.

2755   BE2c   4Sqn
AOb combat shot down B.24.D.3.a at 1-45pm **MIA(2Lt J Thwaytes **KIA**/2Lt GHT Bourne **KIA**) left 12-35pm XI Corps front

5748   BE2e   8Sqn
P shot down ground fire cr(Capt C Holland **WIA/2Lt AC Heaven OK) left 9-55am to M.4.c.9.5., combat with Voss18?, name Heavan? [?"Sopwith 5784" claim combat nrNEUVILLE 5-40pm Ltn W Voss Ja2, but see BE2c 5784 lost "next day"?]

5770   BE2d   13Sqn
Rec combat BOYELLES ftl ok? **MIA(Capt GS Thorne **DoW**/2Lt PEH van Baerle **POW**) left 5-25pm FAMPOUX [?"BE 5770" claim combat nrBOYELLES 5-50pm Ltn W Voss Ja2]

**   RE8   59Sqn**
** combat? shot up(/2Lt J Muirhead **KIA**)?

19th March

5784   BE2e   8Sqn
AOb combat with EA ftl EoL N.25. **MIA(2Lt CR Dougall **POW**/2Lt S Harryman **POW DoW** 24.3.17) left 5-10pm, Casualty Report dated 19.3 but POW listings give 18.3 [?"Sopwith 5784" claim combat nrNEUVILLE 5-40pm Ltn W Voss Ja2 on 18.3?]

A312   SPAD 7   19Sqn
**OP CAMBRAI combat with 2EAs BOURLON WOOD-MARQUION 8-40am engine hit? ftl GINCHY OK(Capt WJ Cairnes)

A6633   SPAD 7   19Sqn
OP seen combat with EA nrLE CATELET 9am **MIA(2Lt SSB Purves **POW**) left 8-10am CAMBRAI-MARQUION-LE CATELET, later escaped ["Sopwith" claim combat ROISEL-TEMPLEUX 8-40am Hpt P vOsterroht Ja12] ["Sopwith 6633" claim HOMBLIÈRES

9-10am Ltn K Schneider Ja5] ["A6633" ftl with no petrol HOMBLIÈRES eST QUENTIN]

This was the first casualty in a SPAD 7 fighter suffered by the RFC. The British had decided as early as May 1916 to order this most promising French single-seater, and the first one, A253, had briefly gone to 60 Squadron in September. 19 Squadron was the first RFC unit to be fully equipped with the SPAD, but despite pleadings from the very highest levels, deliveries were very slow, and it was not until the 12th of February that it came up to full strength. By this time, the French had been using it widely for many months. It was built on different principles from the Nieuport Scouts, the other famous contemporary French machines. Whilst the Nieuports were designed with a rotary engine and small, compact wing area to out-manoeuvre an opponent, the SPAD was a heavier, sturdier machine, very fast and devastating in a diving attack, which was how its greatest exponents used it. There were drawbacks: the machine-gun was built into the engine and was thus unable to be cleared in combat, leaving one at a distinct disadvantage if it failed, and it was also known to be capable of simply dropping out of the sky if its engine failed in a dive. The RNAS also ordered SPADs but, as will be discussed later, a deal was struck releasing all of these SPADs to the RFC in return for access to all Triplanes.

A6662.C SPAD 7   19Sqn
**Rec ST QUENTIN-GUISE-RIBEMONT-LA FÈRE shot up engine dam ftl MELICOCQ dam OK(Lt AT Hope)

7499   Martinsyde G100   27Sqn
**B combat with EA engine dam fuel tank shot through ftl BRIE dam OK(Lt WS Caster)

7503   Martinsyde G100   27Sqn
B AULNOYE shot down EoL **MIA(2Lt JG Fair **KIA**) [?"Mart" claim combat nrBRIE, sPERONNE 9-19am Ltn A Mohr Ja3]

7508   Martinsyde G100   27Sqn
B AULNOYE shot down **MIA(2Lt TW Jay **WIA POW**) Ja3 ["Mart 7508" claim combat nrROISEL ePERONNE 8-45am Ltn G Schlenker Ja3]

A79   RE8   34Sqn
Rec combat with Scout nMONS EN CHAUSSÉE 1200' 10-50am shot up(2Lt MacGeorge OK/Lt AA Murray **DoW) WIA?, Combat Report gives KIA from ricochet to back of head?

A88   RE8   34Sqn
CP combat with AlbatrosD ~o.33. 10-50am shot up dam ftl(Lt HR Davies OK/2Lt B Farmer **WIA)slight

**   BE2e   52Sqn**
** rifle fire(Lt S Guillon **WIA**/)

A4165   RE8   59Sqn
P ST LEGER AA(Capt EW Bowyer-Bowyer **KIA/Lt
E Elgey **KIA**) Voss20 ["Sopwith" claim combat ST
LEGER 8-30am Ltn W Voss Ja2]

A4168   RE8   59Sqn
**EscP AA ftl ST LEGER cr 600yd swECOUST-ST-
MIEN C.7.a. **MIA**(Capt CP Bertie **KIA**/Lt FH Wilson
POW) ["Sopwith A4168" claim seARRAS 9-25am Ltn F
Bernert Ja2]

From the 19th of March the casualties to units of I
Brigade were becoming so calamitous that
machines of III and IV Brigades were ordered to
commence offensive patrols around Douai.

21st March

100 Squadron RFC arrived in France on the 21st
of March. This was the first ever specialist night
bombing unit, equipped with FE2bs specially
adapted for night operations. By the 1st of April it
was at its base at Izel Le Hameau where it temporarily acquired some additional BE2es.

A3154   BE2f   16Sqn
**AOb combat with EA ooc cr WoL Sh51b A.15.d at
4-30pm(Sgt SH Quicke **KIA**/2Lt WJ Lidsey **DoW**
22.3.17) left 3pm, MvR29 ["BE" claim combat
NEUVILLE ST VAAST 4-40pm Ltn M Fr vRichthofen
Ja11]

A305   Nieuport 17   24Sqn
**OP seen in spin ooc ovROUPY ldg 500m AUBIGNY
MIA(Capt HWG Jones MC **WIA**) left 3-15pm Fourth
Army front

**   FE8   40Sqn**
**LP AA nrABLAIN STRAZAINE(Lt EL Benbow MC
WIA)

A2390   Sopwith Strutter 43Sqn
**LP combat ftl MAZINGARBE 2-45pm fire(Lt HWL
Poole **inj**/2AM AJ Ball **DoI**) ["BE" claim combat
sVERMELLES, nrLOOSBOGEN 2-30pm Ltn K
Allmenröder Ja11]

22nd March

**   Morane   3Sqn**
** (Maj M Elphinstone **Kld**) KIA?

6750   BE2e   9Sqn
**CP shot up dam OK(Lt RWP Hall/2Lt WB Cramb)

**   FE8   40Sqn**
** mg fire(2Lt SJ Stocks **WIA**)stomach [?slight
possibility of "Vickers?(sic)" claim combat nrDOUCHY
Ltn Hilf/Ltn Olsen FAb 23]

9708   Sopwith Strutter 3 Wing RNAS
**B BURBACH combat engine shot up ftl WoL(FSLt
NM MacGregor/1AM Allen) ldg MALZEVILLE

23rd March

**   BE2c   4Sqn**
** rifle fire(/2Lt FG Taylor **WIA**)thigh

A3149   BE2g   52Sqn
Rec shot up ftl wr(2Lt CM White **WIA/2Lt DM
McLeay **KIA**) to NURLU-TINCOURT, combat ftl
nrNURLU

24th March

5769   BE2d   8Sqn
**Phot combat with EA shot down BOYELLES WoL(Lt
H Norton **KIA**/2Lt RAW Tillet **KIA**) left 2-15pm,
Voss21? ["BE" claim combat BOIRY-BOISLEUX
3-45pm Ltn W Voss Ja2][?"EA" claim combat
nrPRONVILLE Ltn FO Bernert Ja2]

7248   BE2e   8Sqn
**Phot combat, in flames nrACHICOURT 10am cr
WoL(2Lt HW Tagent **KIA**/2Lt GT Gray **KIA**) left 9am,
a'c burnt

4949   FE2b   11Sqn
**Phot shot up mg ftl a'dr dam OK

A803   FE2b   11Sqn
Rec left 7-45am **MIA(Lt JR Middleton **POW DoW**
21.6.17/2AM HV Gosney **KIA**) VAULX-MORCHIES?,
Voss?

A5442   FE2b   11Sqn
**Rec combat brought down nrCROISILLES wr
ldg(Capt CN Lowe **inj**/2Lt G Masters OK) left 7-58am,
Voss? ["FE" claim combat nrCROISILLES 10-30am
Untoff R Jorke Ja12][?claim combat swHENDECOURT
10-30am Ltn A Schulte Ja12]

2515   BE2c   13Sqn
**AOb AA lost tail ooc nose dive 6000' cr WoL wr(Capt
GO Brunwin-Hales **KIA**/Lt AR Legge **KIA**) left 1-29pm
ST CATHERINE

7254   BE2e   15Sqn
**Phot AA combat 3-15pm shot down WoL Sh57C 1.16.a
wr(Sgt JF Ridgway **WIA**/2Lt EF? Hare **KIA**) initials
EJ?, left 2-15pm

5777   BE2d   16Sqn
Phot shot down WoL 2-40pm(2Lt FH Gay **DoW/2Lt
AA Baerlein **WIA**) left 1-15pm to Sh36C SqS

A263   Spad 7   19Sqn
+* combat with EAs seLENS 10000'-11000' 10-50am
gun stoppage OK(2Lt FL Harding) gun stoppages nearly
every flight

A6663   SPAD 7   19Sqn
+* combat with HalbD[+?ooc] DOUAI 11am OK(Lt
AH Orlebar) not confirmed but possible first SPAD
victory once fully equipped with the type

A6706   SPAD 7   19Sqn
OP seen 5m seLENS engine ftl EoL **MIA(Lt RP Baker
WIA POW) MvR30, to LENS-HERMES-BAILLEUL,
a'c still on strength 5.17?, but there is a photo of it in

shreds ["SPAD 6607" claim combat GIVENCHY
10-55am Oblt M Fr vRichthofen Ja11]

FE2d   20Sqn
** shot up(/2AM CC Riach **WIA**)hand

4986   FE2b   22Sqn
**Phot combat with EA shot up ftl ESTRÉES(Capt WE
Salter OK/2Lt EDG Galley **WIA**) left 6-30am, combat
ovHESBECOURT(Hendecourt?) [?"FE" claim combat
nrHENDECOURT" Vzfw Patermann]

4960   FE2b   23Sqn
**PhotEsc left 1-20pm combat with EA shot up ftl
MARTINSART cr wr OK(Lt WF Fletcher/2Lt HS
Elliott)

A5485   FE2b   23Sqn
**EscPhot combat shot up ftl ACHIET LE GRAND
wr(Sgt EP Critchley **WIA**/1AM F Russell **KIA**) left
1-13pm [?"FE" claim combat VAULX-MORCHIES
3-10pm? Ltn W Voss Ja2 but 11Sq a'c possible]

A1954   FE2d   57Sqn
+* combat with AlbatrosDII[+ooc] eLENS OK(2Lt HR
Harker/2Lt VD Fernauld) [Ja5?]

This was the first of a few FE2d victories for 57
Squadron.

A956   Sopwith Strutter   70Sqn
**Rec combat with 12EA shot up dam(Capt AG Saxby
OK/Lt HF Duncan **DoW** 29.3.17) to hospital, left
6-30am CAMBRAI-DOUAI

A957   Sopwith Strutter   70Sqn
**Rec combat 12HAs DOUAI-CAMBRAI, seen going
west then cr **MIA**(Capt AM Lowery **DoW**/Lt GWW
Swann **DoW**) left 6-35am [?"1Str" claim combat
ECOUST ST MEIN 8am OffSt E Nathanael Ja5]

A1907   Sopwith Strutter   70Sqn
**Rec combat 12HAs DOUAI-CAMBRAI, seen going
west after **MIA**(Capt WH Costello **POW**/Lt HS
Whiteside **POW**) left 6-35am, Gont4 ["Sopwith A1907"
claim combat OISY-LE VERGER 7-55am Ltn H
Gontermann Ja5] ["Sopwith" claim combat ANZIN
8am Ltn K Schaefer Ja11]

A1925   Sopwith Strutter   70Sqn
**Rec CAMBRAI combat 12EA shot up dam(Lt H
Butler OK/2AM AG McMillan **inj**) left 6-35am,
repairable

A2983   Sopwith Strutter   70Sqn
**Rec combat 12HA CAMBRAI shot up dam(Lt Peter
inj/Lt B Balfour OK) left 6-35am

25th March

Until now, German time had been one hour ahead
of British time. From the 25th of March until the
15th of April German and British times matched
(all times given are British time).

A799   FE2b   11Sqn
**Rec DOUAI combat with EA mg shot up dam OK(2Lt
Morrison/AM Tooley) left 6-20am

A5469   FE2b   11Sqn
**Rec left 6-27am combat with EA[+?ooc] shot up dam
OK(2Lt H Calvey/2AM F Hadlow)

A6689   Nieuport 17   29Sqn
Esc left 7-05am shot down **MIA(2Lt CG Gilbert **POW**)
MvR31 ["Nieu" claim combat TILLOY 8-20am Oblt M
Fr vRichthofen Ja11]

BE2e   52Sqn
** combat? shot up(2Lt R Littlejohn **WIA**/2Lt AD
Collins **WIA**)

A630   Sopwith Pup   54Sqn
**EscFEs seen going down on back after combat 3-4 m
swST QUENTIN **MIA**(2Lt NA Phillips **KIA**) left
8-40am [?"EA" claim combat nrGISSECOURT? Ltn F
Mallinckrodt Ja20]

A306.C4 **Nieuport 17   60Sqn**
**DP combat with AlbatrosDII[+destr] nST LEGER
5pm shot through ftl dam OK(Lt WA Bishop) Bishop's
first of 72 victories

7763   Sopwith Strutter   70Sqn
Rec combat 9EA ovCAMBRAI **MIA(Lt CS Vane-
Tempest **DoW**/2Lt F Allinson **POW DoW**) left 7-10am,
both DoW 27.3.17 ["Sopwith 7763" claim combat
nrPOUCHAUX Ltn K Deilmann Ja6][also some say
"Sopwith" claim combat SABLONNIÈRES Vzfw
Hausler Ja6, but this is sCHÂTEAU THIERRY?]

A884   Sopwith Strutter   70Sqn
Rec combat 9EA ovCAMBRAI **MIA(Lt H Butler
KIA/2Lt LA Norris **KIA**) left 7-25am ["Sopwith"
nrVELU & "Sop 1Str" nrBEUGNY 9-20am OffSt E
Nathanael Ja5]["Sopwith" nrHAPLINCOURT 9-25am
Ltn H Gontermann Ja5]["Sopwith" nrBEUGNY Vzfw
Hoppe Ja5]

A954   Sopwith Strutter   70Sqn
**Rec seen start combat with 9EA ovCAMBRAI cr WoL
wr(Lt JS Cooper **KIA**/Lt NA MacQueen **KIA**) left
7-10am [met Ja5?, see entry for A884]

A958   Sopwith Strutter   70Sqn
**Rec seen start combat with 9EA ovCAMBRAI
MIA(Lt LS Ward-Price **KIA**/Lt HA Chuter **KIA**) left
7-10am [met Ja5?, see entry for A884]

A2986   Sopwith Strutter   70Sqn
**Rec seen start combat with 9EA ovCAMBRAI
MIA(Capt EJ Henderson **KIA**/2Lt JM Sim **KIA**) left
7-10am [met Ja5?, see entry for A884]

These many onerous losses for 70 Squadron,
sustained over two consecutive days, occurred on
deep reconnaissances to the Hindenburg Line. This
work was seen as being absolutely essential to the
understanding of the enemy withdrawal and was

undertaken fully in the expectation of meeting intense attacks. The Strutter was no longer capable of fighting in this new air war, however, and its crews would suffer high casualties for several months.

27th March

8 (Naval) Squadron was once again attached to the RFC, now equipped with the Sopwith Triplane. It mostly carried out offensive patrols but also did specialist Wireless Interruption work (see below).

28th March

A6615   Nieuport 17   1Sqn
OP combat with 5EAs seLILLE 10-45am lost in mist ftl field cr **MIA(2Lt H Welch **KIA**) left 9-30am ["Nieu A6615" claim combat nrROUBAIX 10-24am Oblt H Bethge Ja30]

BE2c   16Sqn
** AA(2Lt WDB Taylor **WIA**/)arm

BE2c   16Sqn
** combat? shot up(2Lt OR Knight MC **WIA**/)hand

BE2c   16Sqn
AOb AA(/2Lt RH Lloyd **WIA)thigh

7715   FE2b   25Sqn
P combat driven down EoL 5-15pm **MIA(2Lt NL Knight **WIA POW**/2Lt AG Severs **KIA**) left 2-30pm LA BASSÉE-ARRAS ["Vickers" claim combat eVIMY 5-20pm Ltn L Fr vRichthofen Ja11]

7862   DH2   32Sqn
**Phot MORCHIES combat with EA shot up dam OK(2Lt AVH Gompertz)

2560   BE2e   52Sqn
prac combat then brought down EoL(SLt HW Owen **POW) had earlier been forced to land at 59Sqn, a'c captured ["BE 2560" lost so ftl nrRIENCOURT]

30th March

A2857   BE2e   13Sqn
** to XIII Corps front, French dhAA tail hit ftl dam OK(2Lt JHO Jones/Lt GJ Farmer)

A6680   Nieuport 17   40Sqn
+*LP combat with 2Halberstadts[+?ooc into clouds towards BAILLEUL] sVIMY 2-15pm OK(Capt R Gregory) Ltn Lubbert KIA Ja11

This was the first 40 Squadron claim on Nieuport scouts.

A6780   Nieuport 23   40Sqn
LP LA BASSÉE-RIVER SCARPE **MIA(Lt DMF Sinclair **KIA**) [?"Nieu" claim combat nrBAILLEUL, nrARRAS 2-15pm Ltn K Allmenröder Ja11]

A273   Nieuport 17   60Sqn
OP left 10-55am seen ovFAMPOUX cr **MIA(Lt WP

Garnett **KIA**) Wolff4, to ARRAS-VITRY-DOUAI ["Nieu" claim combat FRESNOY, nwARRAS 11-45am Ltn K Wolff Ja11]

A6774   Nieuport 23   60Sqn
** combat shot up FOUQUIÈRES 11-45am ftl nrALBERT(2Lt F Bower **DoW** 31.3.17)

31st March

7691   FE2b   11Sqn
Rec combat ftl nrVITRY-EN-ARTOIS cr **MIA(Lt LAT Strange **POW**/2Lt WGT Clifton **DoW**) left 6-02am seen BOIRY, a'c captured, Wolff5 ["FE" claim combat nrGAVRELLE 7-50am Ltn K Wolff Ja11]

A6769   Nieuport 23   60Sqn
+* combat with AlbatrosDII[+destr] sGAVRELLE 7-30am OK(Lt WA Bishop Can.) Bishop obtained 6 victories in this Nieuport

When No.5 Wing RNAS was disbanded in France at the end of 1916 it re-emerged at Dover from elements of 4 Squadron RNAS which had been left there. It returned to Coudekerque at the end of March, probably to replace No.4 Wing RNAS.

April 1917

BLOODY APRIL

So began "Bloody April", as the RFC would come to know it. Preparations for Nivelle's great offensive were entering their final stages, yet there was little for which the German forces felt unprepared. The plan General Nivelle had devised required the British forces to fight a subordinate role, effectively creating a diversion on the Arras front to draw the enemy's efforts into a defence of Cambrai. Once this was achieved the French would then launch the major offensive aimed at breaking through between the Oise and Reims. If the French attack failed for any reason, the British would be left to fight a protracted and probably costly battle. The Germans, on the other hand, were highly informed and in the ascendant, and would no doubt dispose their forces, on the ground and in the air, well.

In contrast, RFC Headquarters was already distinctly anxious. Trenchard and his staff were battling with preparations for the Arras offensive in the certain knowledge that it would be an air war of unprecedented ferocity. As many reserves as possible were to be held back, including the use of the new machines such as the Bristol Fighter, the DH4, and the SE5 fighter, all of which would be unleashed as the battle began. They were being counted on to have a significant impact, but very many of the machines available for operations, for

instance the BE2 types and FE2bs and ds, were in dire need of replacement and losses were expected to be high. Some cheer could be drawn from the new generation of machines reaching France, but those fighter squadrons already in place, equipped with only Nieuports, SPADs, and Pups, would be kept intensely busy.

1st April

4954   FE2b   11Sqn
DP seen wBOYELLES lost in storm **MIA(Cpl A Wilson **POW**/2AM F Hadlow **POW**) left 2-20pm

2561   BE2c   15Sqn
AOb combat with EA ovST LEGER brought down WoL Sh57 B.18.c. at 11-45am(Capt AM Wynne **WIA/Lt AS Mackenzie **KIA**) left 9-25am, Voss23 ["BE" claim combat eST LEGER 11-45am Ltn W Voss Ja2]

2nd April

6746   BE2d   2Sqn
**ASReg combat with EA shot up dam OK(2Lt WJ Stonier/2Lt HCW Strickland)

2521   BE2c   12Sqn
+*AOb combat with Albatros ovCITÉ CALONNE 3000' 10-50am OK(Capt H Fowler/Lt FE Brown)

2510   BE2c   13Sqn
**Phot left 9-50am combat with 4EAs cr 2Sqn a'dr wr OK(2Lt CF Fox/2AM JH Bolton) ["BE 7061" claim combat ANGRES, swLENS 10-35am Ltn K Allmenröder Ja11]

5841   BE2d   13Sqn
Phot left 7-47am **MIA(Lt PJG Powell **KIA**/1AM P Bonner **KIA**) ["BE 5841" claim combat FARBUS, neARRAS 8-35am Oblt M Fr vRichthofen Ja11]

A3161   BE2e   15Sqn
**AP AA ovCROISILLES ftl S.30.d dam ftl o't wind dam OK(2Lt JH de Conway/2Lt ME Mealing) left 6-30am, a'c left 48hrs before salvage

6953   FE2b   22Sqn
Phot combat with 18EAs ovGOUZEAUCOURT, seen ooc in flames cr **MIA(2Lt PA Russell **KIA**/Lt H Loveland **KIA**) left 6-35am ["EA" claim combat neGOUZEAUCOURT WOOD am Offst E Nathanael Ja5]

A2401   Sopwith Strutter   43Sqn
Phot eVIMY combat 11-10am then shot down into clouds eVIMY **MIA(2Lt AP Warren **POW**/Sgt R Dunn **KIA**) left 10-30am MvR33 ["Sopwith A2401" claim combat nrGIVENCHY 11-15am Oblt M Fr vRichthofen Ja11]

A1944   FE2d   57Sqn
LP combat with 6EAs LENS **MIA(Lt HP Sworder **KIA**/2Lt AH Margolouth **KIA**) left 8am LENS-ARRAS-BAPAUME [?"Vickers" claim combat AUBY, nDOUAI 10-50am Vzfw S Festner Ja11]

A1959   FE2d   57Sqn
+* combat with AlbatrosDIIIs[+flames+ooc] seARRAS 9-45am OK(2Lt EEE Pope/Lt AW Nasmyth) British AA reported 2EAs shot down in engagement

A5151   FE2d   57Sqn
LP combat with 6EAs[++] LENS 9-45am **MIA(Capt H Tomlinson MC **POW DoW**/Lt NC Denison **WIA POW**) left 8am LENS-BAPAUME ["FE A5151" claim combat nDOUAI 9-50am Ltn Krefft Ja11]

A6763   Nieuport 23   60Sqn
OP left 7-15am combat shot down in flames FONTAINE-LES-CROISILLES 7-45am(2Lt VF Williams **KIA) to ARRAS-GOMMECOURT [possible ?"Nieu" claim combat nrQUEANT 8-30am Ltn F Bernert Ja2]

3rd April

2532   BE2c   4Sqn
**AOb ANZAC Corps front AA hit dam OK(2Lt RMH Young/2Lt W Wallace) left 3-15pm

A808   FE2b   11Sqn
Rec dhAA seen cr Sh51B H.27.D. **MIA(Lt ETC Brandon SA. **KIA**/2Lt G Masters NZ. **KIA**) left 1pm

7236   BE2g   15Sqn
Phot combat with Ja12 then hit by AA ~5-30pm & shot down nrCROISILLES **MIA(2Lt JH Sayer **KIA**/2Lt VC Morris **POW**) left 4-25pm ["Bristol 7236" claim combat nrBULLECOURT 4-20pm Hpt P vOsterroht Ja12]

A5486   FE2b   22Sqn
** combat shot down ftl nrMOISLAINS OK(2Lt GM Hopkins/1AM H Friend) left 4-20pm, a'c shelled on ground

4897   FE2b   23Sqn
EscPhot PRONVILLE combat shot up(Sgt JA Cunniffe? OK/2AM J Mackie **WIA) name Cunliffe? [?"FE" claim nrST LEGER Ltn Schulte Ja12]

A6371   FE2d   25Sqn
Phot combat driven down EoL nrLENS 4-30pm **MIA(Lt L Dodson **WIA POW**/2Lt HS Richards **DoW**) left 3-30pm ["FE A6371" claim combat nrAVION, sLENS 4-20pm Ltn K Schaefer Ja11]

A6382   FE2d   25Sqn
Phot combat driven down EoL nrLENS 4-30pm **MIA(2Lt DP MacDonald **POW**/2Lt JIM O'Beirne **KIA**) left 3-30pm ["FE A6382" claim combat LENS-LIEVIN 4-15pm Oblt M Fr vRichthofen Ja11]

A2536   DH2   32Sqn
LP combat with EA eLAGNICOURT shot down cr EoL **MIA(Lt EL Heyworth **WIA POW**) [?possible "English Sitterrumpf" claim combat nBOURSIES OffSt E Nathanael Ja5, but see 4897?]

A5012   DH2   32Sqn
**LP nrVAULX VRAUCOURT badly shot up dam repairable OK(2Lt LW Barney)

A6674   Nieuport 17   40Sqn
Esc left 1-55pm **MIA(2Lt SA Sharpe **POW**) ["Nieu 6674" claim combat with eARRAS 1-55pm Ltn Nernst Ja30]

4th April
THE BATTLE OF ARRAS

The air offensive for the battle of Arras began on the 4th of April. The British front line ran from Givenchy-en-Gohelle south to Croisilles. The key to the fighting was the capture of Vimy Ridge, the task being allocated to the First Army which was significantly composed of Canadians. Elsewhere, the attack was to be launched by corps of the Third Army.

The air units in support of these groups were as follows: I Brigade with the First Army comprised the 1st (Corps) Wing, made up of Nos. 2, 5, 10, and 16 Squadrons, the latter attached to the Canadian Corps. All these units operated BE2 types. The 10th (Army) Wing also worked with the First Army and comprised the following fighter squadrons: Nos. 25 (FE2bs and FE2ds), 40 (Nieuport Scouts), 43 (Sopwith Strutters), and 8 (Naval) Squadrons (Sopwith Triplanes). 40 and 8 (Naval) Squadrons were to attack kite balloons and fly offensive patrols, whilst Nos. 25 and 43 were to provide line and offensive patrols in protection of the corps machines and carry out reconnaissance.

Air support for the Third Army came from III Brigade RFC, made up of the 12th (Corps) Wing, comprising Nos. 8, 12, 13 (all BE2 types), 35 Squadron attached to the Cavalry Corps (with the new Armstrong Whitworth FK8), and 59 Squadron (RE8s). It also included the 13th (Army) Wing, comprising Nos. 29, 60, and 6 (Naval) Squadrons (all Nieuport Scouts), and Nos. 11 (FE2bs) and 48 Squadrons (Bristol Fighters). The Nieuports were to be used on offensive patrols and attacks on kite balloons, 11 Squadron FE2bs were variously allocated reconnaissance, photography, and night bombing, whilst 48 Squadron was to be used as a fighter-reconnaissance unit.

The final British air support for the battle of Arras came from the seven squadrons of the 9th (Headquarters) Wing. These were Nos. 19 (SPAD 7s), 27 (Martinsyde Scouts), 55 (DH4s), 56 (SE5s), 57 (FE2ds), 66 (Sopwith Pups), and 70 (Sopwith Strutters), and finally, there were the night bombers of 100 Squadron (FE2bs). At the start of the air offensive the British machines concentrated for the battle therefore numbered three hundred and sixty-five, comprising twenty-five squadrons, although the SE5s of 56 Squadron would be with-

held from use until later in the month. Opposing the British on this front was the German Sixth Army with an air strength of one-hundred and ninety-five aircraft. This was made up of eighteen reconnaissance and artillery flights, seven protection flights, and five fighter flights. At this time the majority of the German Air Service on the Western Front was on the Aisne ready to oppose the French armies.

At the commencement of air operations the RFC was therefore numerically superior to the German Air Force, but still markedly inferior in terms of equipment, although some of the units equipped with new types which had been kept back so as to have the greatest impact were now to be deployed. It was expected that German air reinforcements would flood the region as required and, vitally, the morale of their pilots was known to be very high.

The British, for their part, had only one approach to the air war — an implacable offensive so as to control the skies over the battlefield. The ground offensive was one week away and, in order that it be given the greatest chance of success, air fighting immediately rose to intense levels. Much of this early skirmishing was done through periods of low clouds and rain. Constant reconnaissances systematically registering and photographing the effect of bombardment on enemy positions were also carried out. In the first four days of April sixty per cent of RFC casualties were suffered on photographic missions, including the loss of eleven aircraft.

2563   BE2f   12Sqn
AReg ARRAS combat shot down wr(2Lt KC Horner **DoW/Lt AE Emmerson **DoW**) left 8-10am, died in hospital ["BE" claim combat ARRAS 8-10am Ltn H Klein Ja4]

5th April

A2855   BE2e   12Sqn
**AP combat from behind dam ftl H.28 OK(Lt Lascelles/Lt Rycroft)

2520   BE2c   13Sqn
Phot hit by British shells ovST CATHERINE(2Lt OFG Ball **KIA/Lt H Howell-Evans **KIA**)

5787   BE2d   13Sqn
Phot trench mg shot down DUISSANS WoL(2Lt GE Brookes **WIA/2AM JH Bolton **KIA**)

4967   FE2b   18Sqn
Phot combat with EA shot down nr BAPAUME WoL(Lt HAR Boustead **DoW 5.4.17/2Lt C Mackintosh **KIA**) left 11-05am Fifth Army front

A805   FE2b   23Sqn
EscPhot combat shot down **MIA(Lt L Elsley **KIA**/2Lt

F Higginbottom **DoW**) left 10-45am, chased down ovPRONVILLE, DoW 6.4.17 ["FE A805" claim combat MOEUVRES-BOURSIES 12pm Ltn G Schlenker Ja3]

A2592　　DH2　　　　　24Sqn
OP combat with 4EAs, seen in spin ooc eHONNECOURT **MIA(2Lt JK Ross **DoW** 9.4.17) left 10-05am Fourth Army front, 5 DH2s in patrol ["EA A2592" claim combat nrRIBECOURT Untoff Mackeprang?/Ltn Wolluhn FAb210]

7485　　Martinsyde G100　　27Sqn
B left 11am HIRSON ftl ORIGNY EoL burnt a'c(2Lt WTB Tasker **POW)

A1578　　Martinsyde G102　　27Sqn
B HIRSON down nrCHÂTEAU D'OSSEMONT burnt(2Lt M Johnstone **KIA) down 12k eCOMPIÈGNE ["Martinsyde G100" ftl due to engine failure nrLA BOUTEILLE]

A6684　　Nieuport 17　　　29Sqn
+* combat with AlbatrosDIII[+ooc] VITRY EN ARTOIS 6-35pm OK(2Lt CVdeB Rogers) first Nieuport claims for 29Sqn

A6752　　Nieuport 17　　　29Sqn
+* combat with AlbatrosDIII[+ooc] VITRY EN ARTOIS 6-35pm OK(2Lt EJ Pascoe) shared first 29Sqn Nieuport victory

A6791　　Nieuport 23　　　29Sqn
OP left 6-10pm VITRY EN ARTOIS found G.24.d.7.8. **MIA(Lt NA Birks **WIA POW**) [?"BE 1Str" claim combat ATHIES 7-15pm Vzfw C Menckhoff Ja3]

A1073　　Sopwith Strutter　　43Sqn
SpM seen combat with EA **MIA(2Lt CP Thornton **POW**/2Lt HD Blackburn **KIA**) left 10-15am to Sh36C D,J,P ["Sopwith A1073" claim combat nrBOUVROY Ltn Nernst Ja30]

**　　　Bristol F2a　　　48Sqn**
+* combat with AlbatrosDIIIs[+ooc] DOUAI ~10-15am OK(Capt A Wilkinson/Lt LG Allen)

A3320　　Bristol F2a　　　48Sqn
OP combat with AlbatrosDIIIs ovDOUAI shot down **MIA(Lt HA Cooper **WIA POW**/2Lt A Boldison **WIA POW**) ["Bristol A3320" claim combat nrMONCHECOURT 10am Ltn Simon Ja11]

A3337　　Bristol F2a　　　48Sqn
OP combat with AlbatrosDIIIs[+ooc] MERICOURT-DOUAI 10-15am shot down ~11am nrDOUAI **MIA(Capt W Leefe-Robinson VC **POW**/2Lt ED Warburton **POW**) ["Bristol" claim combat MERICOURT 11am Vzfw S Festner Ja11] first Sqn victories

A3340　　Bristol F2a　　　48Sqn
OP combat with Albatros DIIIs ovDOUAI shot down **MIA(2Lt AN Leckler **WIA POW**/Lt HDK George **POW DoW** 6.4.17) pilot to Holland 9.4.18, MvR35 ["Bristol A3340" claim combat LEWARDE, seDOUAI 11-08am Oblt M Fr vRichthofen Ja11]

A3343　　Bristol F2a　　　48Sqn
OP combat DOUAI shot down **MIA(Lt HT Adams **POW**/Lt DJ Stewart **WIA POW**) MvR36 ["Bristol" claim combat QUINCY 11-28am Oblt M Fr vRichthofen Ja11]

The new Bristol Fighter, of which so much was expected, finally came into action on the 5th. For 48 Squadron's first ever operation, six Bristols made an offensive patrol over Douai. Leading them was Capt Leefe-Robinson VC, famous by this time for having shot down the SL11 airship. They had the great misfortune to meet Manfred von Richthofen and the Albatros DIIIs of Jasta 11 and in the disastrous air battle which followed the patrol was virtually destroyed.

These events caused great anxiety for the RFC whilst a surge of confidence passed through Germany's fighting units. Richthofen, who had accounted for two of the victims, declared that the Albatros was unquestionably superior to the Bristol both in speed and climbing power, and this led to a general consensus amongst the German pilots that it offered little to be feared. Fortunately for the Allies, this was a judgement they would subsequently need to revise, but throughout April they would be heavily mauled. The loss of Leefe-Robinson was also a great blow to the Squadron and the RFC. He was to spend a miserable time in captivity, singled out for his fame, and fated to return to England in December 1918 a broken man, succumbing almost immediately to the influenza epidemic and dying soon afterwards.

A6693.C4　Nieuport 17　　　60Sqn
KBP nrCAMBRAI combat with EA shot down BAILLEUL-SUR-BERTHOULT 1pm **MIA(Lt EJD Townesend **WIA POW**)severe, left 12-15pm ["Nieu" claim combat swBAILLEUL 1pm Vzfw S Festner Ja11]

N3202　　Nieuport 17　　　6 (Naval) Sqn
OP combat shot down, circled then in snd nrARRAS 6-45pm **MIA(FSLt RK Slater **WIA POW**) left 4-50pm ARRAS-CAMBRAI

Slater was the first casualty in action for 6 (Naval) Squadron.

6th April

5834　　BE2d　　　　　2Sqn
Phot combat with HA in flames **MIA(Capt VJ Whitaker **KIA**/2Lt AR Brown **KIA**) left 9-15am combat 10-15am LIEVIN, Frankl?(his claim to south) [?"BE" claim combat GIVENCHY 10-20am Ltn K Schaefer Ja11]

A2879　　BE2e　　　　　8Sqn
Phot left 8-35am **MIA(Lt GJ Hatch **KIA**/Cpl E Langridge **KIA**)

A811   FE2b   11Sqn
Rec seen ldg eARRAS? H.33 **MIA(Sgt FH Evans
POW/2AM E Wood **KIA**) left 7-35am ["FE" claim
FEUCHY 8-50am combat Ltn W Frankl Ja4]

A5500   FE2b   11Sqn
**Rec ARRAS combat with EA ovARRAS-ST POL Rd
shot down ftl Sh51C L.16 at 9am wr OK(2Lt DS
Kennedy/2AM JF Carr) left 7-35am ["FE" claim combat
ARRAS 8-55am Ltn W Frankl Ja4]

A3157   BE2e   15Sqn
**Phot combat with EA 9-30am driven down WoL
Sh57C C.29.d. OK(2Lt AH Vinson/2Lt ELC Gwilt) left
8-50am, a'c shelled & destroyed

6823   BE2e   16Sqn
AOb combat in flames nrTHELUS 10-30am **MIA(Lt
OR Knight **KIA**/2Lt UH Seguin **KIA**) left 9-20am
eNEUVILLE ST VAAST

A6358   FE2d   20Sqn
**B LEDEGHEM shot down BELLEWAARDE
MIA(2Lt R Smith **KIA**/Lt R Hume **KIA**) Ja8 [combat
nePOLYGON WOOD 10-30am OffSt W Göttsch Ja8]

A6709   SPAD 7   23Sqn
+* combat with AlbatrosC[+des] Sh57c R.9.a. 7-30am
OK(Capt KC McCallum) first SPAD victory for 23Sqn

7025   FE2b   25Sqn
**EscBEs combat GROSVILLE cr ~9am wr(2Lt DP
Walter **WIA**/2Lt C Brown OK) left 7-43am LENS-
BAILLEUL

7465   Martinsyde G100   27Sqn
**B ATH combat with Halberstadts shot down nrATH
MIA(2Lt JRS Proud **DoW** as **POW**) ["Sopwith 7665"
claim combat ATH 8-15am Ltn J vBertrab Ja30]

7478   Martinsyde G100   27Sqn
**B ATH combat with Halberstadts shot down nrATH
MIA(Lt JHB Wedderspoon **KIA**) ["Sopwith" claim
combat seLEUZE 8-30am Ltn J vBertrab Ja30]

A6667   Nieuport 17   40Sqn
**SpM(KB) left 9-15am SALLAUMINES shot down
EoL wr **MIA**(2Lt HS Pell **KIA**) [MFlak60]

A6677   Nieuport 17   40Sqn
+*SpM(KB) dived on KB from 8000' to 500' fired 3
rockets at 10 yards' range[+flames] nrNEUVIREUIL
~10am AA, flaming onions, rifle fire OK(2Lt HC Todd)
recrossed lines ARRAS 2000', saw 2EA in flames E
beyond ARRAS

7806   Sopwith Strutter   45Sqn
Rec left 9-10am LILLE **MIA(2Lt JE Blake **KIA**/Capt
WS Brayshay **KIA**) ["Sopwith 7806" claim combat
nrTOURNAI 10-48am Oblt H Bethge Ja30]

A1093   Sopwith Strutter   45Sqn
Rec left 9-10am **MIA(2Lt JA Marshall **KIA**/2Lt FG
Truscott MC **DoW**) LILLE ["Sopwith" claim combat
BECQ 10-48am Ltn J vBertrab Ja30]

A2381   Sopwith Strutter   45Sqn

Rec LILLE **MIA(2Lt CStG Campbell **KIA**/Capt DW
Edwards MC **KIA**) left 9-10am ["Sopwith" claim combat
BECQ 10-50am Ltn J vBertrab Ja30]

A6165   Sopwith Pup   54Sqn
** combat with EA sLAGNICOURT(2Lt RM Foster)
["Sopwith" claim combat nrLAGNICOURT,
neBAPAUME 9-45am Ltn W Voss Ja2]

A21   FE2d   57Sqn
**OP combat with 6EAs nrMARQUION? 9-30am
MIA(2Lt DC Birch **POW**/Lt JK Bousfield MC **POW**)
left 7am SOMAIN-BEAUVAIS ["FE A21" claim
combat THIAUT 8-25am Ltn O Splitgerber
Ja12][?"FE" claim combat nrLAGNICOURT 7-30am?
Hpt P vOsterroht Ja12]

A22   FE2d   57Sqn
OP combat with 6EAs CAMBRAI **MIA(Lt RTB
Schreiber **POW**/2Lt M Lewis **POW**) left 7am SOMAIN-
BEAVAIS, Pte Sibley saw 3 a'c in combat
nrMARQUION 9-30am, one in steep dive, one of two
pushers seen ldg by AA at Sh57C H.16.c [?claim combat
sANNEUX but 8-30am? Oblt A Rt vTutschek
Ja2]["Sopwith 22" ftl nrANIS(sic) SUR SERRE,
nLAON]

A1952   FE2d   57Sqn
**OP combat with 6EAs CAMBRAI 9-30am cr Sh57C
NW.C.16.(Capt AC Wright **WIA**/Pte R Sibley OK) left
7am SOMAIN-BEAUVAIS? [?possible unconfirmed
"FE A652?" claim nrANNEUX?]

A1959   FE2d   57Sqn
OP combat with 6HA CAMBRAI **MIA(Lt TF Burrill
POW/Pte F Smith **WIA POW**) SOMAIN-BEAUVAIS?
(BEAUVOIR?), combat MARQUION 9-20am
["Vickers 1959" claim combat NEUVILLE
swVALENCIENNES 8-15am Ltn H Gontermann Ja5]

A6388   FE2d   57Sqn
**OP combat with 6EAs MARQUION 9-20am
MIA(2Lt HD Hamilton **WIA POW**/Pte E Snelling
POW) SOMAIN-BEAUVAIS, five FEs lost [?"FE A6
..." claim DOUCHY swVALENCIENNES 8-20am?
OffSt E Nathanael Ja5]

The lack of experience in war flying which had
limited the potential of the new German types now
melted away, and several great pilots began to
emerge amongst the Jastas. The more measured
use of its smaller air force meant that Germany's
pilots survived longer, and so had the potential for
learning and imparting their skills. Scouting
patrols on either side did not have to search long
for opponents as each sought the other out. On this
day it was the turn of 57 Squadron, in their now
obsolete pusher two-seaters, to meet and be
destroyed by the enemy. A few days previously, IV
Brigade RFC had ordered that FE2bs were to be
no longer used on their own for offensive patrols.
    The impact of the superior German machines

derived not simply from their ability to destroy the enemy comprehensively in this way; they imparted a great tactical initiative because they could engage or break off to best advantage, whilst the British crews were expected to stand and fight. The German edge also crucially constrained British operations. In the same way as the Fokker threat had led to the adoption of protective formation flying, diminishing the Allies' effective forces, so now the demand for high numbers of escorting aircraft had the same effect. As many as fifteen fighters escorted three photographic machines. The desperate need for air crew for these operations also meant that many of the subsidiary activities which the RFC had undertaken during the Somme battles, such as bombing, were now much reduced — even marginalised — in comparison.

A112 RE8 59Sqn
EscRec VITRY-ARRAS **MIA(2Lt RWM Davies **KIA**/2Lt JCD Wordsworth **KIA**) left 9-35am [?"EA" claim combat ROEUX 10-15am Ltn FO Bernert Ja2]

A3206 RE8 59Sqn
EscRec VITRY-ARRAS **MIA(Lt CF Bailey **KIA**/2AM VN Barrie **KIA**) left 9-35am, Bailey's real name was Alban ["BE" claim combat THELUS-ROUVROY 10-30am Vzfw C Menckhoff Ja3]

A3421 RE8 59Sqn
EscRec VITRY-ARRAS combat ftl cr wr EoL **MIA(2Lt AC Pepper **POW**/Lt WL Day **DoW**) left 9-35am, Wolff6 ["Sopwith A3421" claim combat nrBOIS BERNARD 10-15am Ltn K Wolff Ja11]

7714 FE2b 100Sqn
NB left 2am DOUAI A'dr **MIA(2Lt ARM Richards **WIA POW**/2AM EW Barnes **POW**) casualty occurred on the night of 5th/6th, Frankl ["FE 7714" claim combat LA MOTTE-DOUAI A'dr 2-30am Ltn W Frankl Ja4]

Whilst there were insufficient resources to expand bombing in the same way as other RFC operations, a bombing scheme related to the offensive was nevertheless carried out. The intention was to force the enemy to withdraw anti-aircraft batteries and aircraft from the front lines in order to deal with this bombing. As well as some long distance raids carried out by Nos. 27 and 55 Squadrons of 9th (Headquarters) Wing, plans for the first time also included night bombing. The casualties noted above were the first for 100 Squadron who were pioneering this work, and occurred on their first night of operations. They bombed Douai aerodrome, the home of Richthofen, where they left four sheds burning. This crew was lost on the second show of the night and was to be a rare instance of an FE2b night bomber being brought down by an enemy fighter.

N5448 Sopwith Triplane 1 (Naval) Sqn
OP seen climb EoL combat shot down nrMARQUION **MIA(FSLt LMB Weil **KIA**) earlier combat with 2 Halberstadts saved by Triplane N5444, Ja12 ["Tripe N5448" combat MALAKOW? Stn 11-15am Hpt P vOsterroht Ja12]

N5457 Sopwith Triplane 1 (Naval) Sqn
OP combat ovDOIGNIES EoL 12000' 8am ftl nrMONS **MIA(FSLt NDM Hewitt **POW**) combat Ja11? or Voss24?, a'c shelled ["Sopwith" claim combat wVIMY 10-37am Ltn K Schaefer Ja11]["Dreidecker" 5457 ftl nrMONS]

Although the Triplane had seen limited action for the RNAS for several months now, these losses for 1 (Naval) Squadron appear to be the first casualties arising from enemy action. The aeroplane would have a relatively brief period of glory in this summer's intense fighting, but its contribution would be great.

The Sopwith Triplane was a revolutionary machine. As a single-seater it derived many of its details from the Pup, but was designed trully to excel in the new demands of combat. First tested in the summer of 1916, the authorities were to remain too indifferent to the Triplane for too long. Whilst two prototypes were operating in France by the end of the year, and were soon joined by a trickle of production aircraft, the machine was destined never to reach the front in great numbers. For some reason the agreement which gave all available SPADs to the RFC and all Triplanes to the RNAS resulted in a significant reduction in orders for the type.

The Triplane sought to maximise a blend of nimble handling, speed, as well as a high rate of climb and a wide field of view in a single radical design. Its bank of short span wings gave tremendous lift with great manoeuvrability and the short chord of the wings meant it remained a compact aircraft and obstructed little of the cockpit view — all characteristics essential to a fighting machine. And a fighting machine it certainly was; the Triplane would be at its height in the coming months, as half a dozen RNAS squadrons were equipped with the type. It first proved itself the match of the best enemy machines in the battle of Arras when it began to shoot many of them down.

Four Naval squadrons, Nos. 1, 3, 9, and 10, were in the process of moving south to reinforce the RFC at this time, so that the remaining RNAS units at Dunkirk were reorganised. This grouped squadrons with like roles into their own wings. No. 1 Wing at St Pol took over the administration of seaplanes at Dover and Dunkirk. Its duties were co-operation with the naval forces off the Belgian

coast, including spotting, reconnaissance, and photography. No. 4 Wing contained the fighter element of the Dunkirk Command and by the end of April its headquarters had moved to La Panne. No. 5 Wing comprised units carrying out day and night bombing. These were Nos. 5 and 7 (Naval) Squadrons, of which the latter amalgamated with the squadron of Handley Page heavy bombers at Coudekerque. 2 (Naval) Squadron, re-equipped with the new DH4, subsequently joined No.5 Wing RNAS as well.

7th April

A6605   Nieuport 17   1Sqn
KB:at 22.9.8 left 8-42am met & shot down by 3 Albatros guarding KB **MIA(Lt RJ Bevington **POW**) ["Nieu A6605" claim combat BECELAERE, eYPRES Hpt vHunerbein Ja8]

A1961   FE2d   20Sqn
B combat with EA in flames WoL(Capt GJ Mahony-Jones **KIA/2Lt WB Moyes **KIA**) left 5-13pm sPLOEGSTEERT WOOD, a'c burnt ["FE" claim combat sPLOEGSTEERT 6-15pm Ltn W vBülow Ja18]["FE" claim combat nrROUBAIX 6-20pm OffSt M Müller Ja28]

A6400   FE2d   20Sqn
B combat shot up ftl sPLOEGSTEERT WOOD cr ditch(2Lt J Lawson OK/2Lt HN Hampson **DoW)

A6692   Nieuport 17   29Sqn
SpM left 4-40pm combat shot down cr wr(Capt A Jennings **KIA) Ja4 ["Nieu A6692" claim combat FRESNES-BIACHES Vzfw Paterman Ja4]

A6775   Nieuport 23   29Sqn
SpM left 4-40pm **MIA(2Lt JH Muir **KIA**) ["Nieu 6775" claim combat ROEUX, eARRAS 5-15pm Ltn FO Bernert Ja2]

A6745   Nieuport 17   40Sqn
+*EscSpM(KB) SALLAUMINES-NOYELLES 8000' 4pm attacked from 3500' but suffered heavy AA OK(2Lt HC Todd)

A3317   Bristol F2a   48Sqn
** combat with EA neARRAS 6-30pm engine ftl SAULTY(Lt JW Warren OK/2Lt GC Burnand **KIA**) [?possible "Sopwith" claim combat MONT ST ELOI-MAROEUIL 5-50pm Vzfw S Festner Ja11, but also possibly Nieu A6645?]

A6645   Nieuport 17a   60Sqn
OP combat nwWANCOURT 5-45pm **MIA(2Lt GO Smart **KIA**) left 4-40pm, found burnt at N.7.d.5.3., MvR37 ["Nieu" claim combat neMERCATEL Rittm M Fr vRichthofen Ja11]

A6766   Nieuport 23   60Sqn
OP left 4-40pm shot down in flames **MIA(2Lt CS Hall **KIA**) Wolff7 ["Nieu" claim combat ovMERCATEL

5-45pm Ltn K Wolff Ja11] [?"Nieu" claim combat MERCATEL 5-45pm Ltn K Schaefer Ja11]

A6773   Nieuport 17   60Sqn
OP left 6-05pm combat with EA FAMPOUX? ftl **MIA(Capt MB Knowles **POW**) Frankl [?"Nieu 4635?" claim combat seFAMPOUX 7-25pm Ltn W Frankl Ja4]

B1517   Nieuport 17   60Sqn
** combat with EA GUEMAPPE shot up dam OK(2Lt HE Hervey)

8th April

56 Squadron arrived in France on the 8th of April fully equipped with the new SE5 fighter. It was withheld from action until the 23rd.

A2815   BE2g   16Sqn
Phot FARBUS combat EA, down 4-40pm 1000yd wVIMY B' DE BONVAL **MIA(2Lt KI MacKenzie **KIA**/2Lt G Everingham **KIA**) left 3pm ["BE2 A2895" claim combat nrVIMY 4-40pm Rittm M Fr vRichthofen Ja11]

A813   FE2b   25Sqn
B seen on return MONT ST ELOI 7pm shot down **MIA(2Lt EAV Bell **POW**/2Lt AHK McCallum **POW**) left 5-25pm

A6765   Nieuport 23   29Sqn
OP left 6-35pm **MIA(2Lt TJ Owen **KIA**)buried HENIN ["Sopwith" claim combat CROISILLES 7-10pm Ltn G Schlenker Ja3]

A2406   Sopwith Strutter   43Sqn
LP combat glided down through clouds 11-30am **MIA(2Lt JS Heagerty **POW**/Lt LH Cantle **KIA**)MvR38, left 10-30am, south of First Army ["Sopwith" claim combat FARBUS 11-40am Rittm M Fr vRichthofen Ja11]

A156   Nieuport 20   46Sqn
Phot combat with 3EAs shot down wr(2Lt JE deWatteville **WIA/Lt RA Manby **WIA**) left 3-45pm, a'c shelled burnt [?"EA" claim combat eYPRES Ltn W vBülow Ja18]

A3330   Bristol F2a   48Sqn
OP met EA eARRAS, seen glide down nrREMY **MIA(2Lt OW Berry **KIA**/2Lt FB Goodison **POW DoW**) left 2pm, DoW 26.5.17 ["BE A3330" claim combat REMY-ETERPIGNY-BAILLEUL 3-10pm Ltn FO Bernert Ja2]

A2140.2   DH4   55Sqn
B CHÂTEAU HARDENPOINT combat with EA then dive **MIA(Lt RA Logan **POW**/Lt FR Henry **WIA POW**) a'c captured, left 1-07pm ["BE A2140" claim combat EPINOY 2-40pm Ltn K Schaefer Ja11]

A2141   DH4   55Sqn
B CHÂTEAU HARDENPONT combat seen ftg several EAs **MIA(Lt B Evans **KIA**/2Lt BW White **KIA**) left 1-07pm, Wolff8 ["BE A2141" claim combat BLECOURT 2-30pm Ltn K Wolff Ja11]

A2160   DH4   55Sqn
B AA shot up 2m wAMIENS(Lt AJ Hamar **DoW/2Lt
JA Myburgh **DoW** 10.4.17) to CHÂTEAU
HARDENPONT nrMONS

These three losses to 55 Squadron were the first for
the unit as well as the first suffered in combat by
the DH4. The unusual target for four DH4s had
been the headquarters of Crown Prince Rupprecht,
near distant Mons. Two machines were shot down
returning from the raid, and the third was hit by
AA. The squadron had commenced operations on
the 6th, bombing Valenciennes, and although these
three disastrous losses occurred on the 8th, there
were already signs that the DH4s could generally
out-manoeuvre and out-distance the enemy.

**   FE2d   57Sqn**
** shot up(/2Lt WW Glenn **WIA**)

A1955   FE2d   57Sqn
**OP shot up nrARRAS Sh51C L.16A.56(Lt AD Pryor
WIA/2AM C Goffe **WIA**) left 12pm ARRAS-
CAMBRAI, a'c riddled with bullets

A3418   RE8   59Sqn
**EscPhot combat with EA shot up ETAING dam(Lt
EG Leake OK/Lt PL Hogan **WIA**)

A4178   RE8   59Sqn
EscPhot ETAING **MIA(Lt KB Cooksey **KIA**/2AM
AH? Jones **KIA**?) Jones' initials RH? [victim of Frankl?]

A4185   RE8   59Sqn
**EscPhot ETAING combat with EA shot up dam
OK(Lt EL Hyde **WIA**/Lt RM Grant **WIA**)

A311.C1 Nieuport 17   60Sqn
OP AA ovARRAS engine ftl 2m EoL **MIA(2Lt HE
Hervey **POW**) left 8-35am

A6764.C6 Nieuport 23   60Sqn
OP left 8-35am combat with EA VIMY **MIA(Maj JAA
Milot **KIA**) ["Nieu23 2865.C6" combat eVIMY 9-30am
Vzfw S Festner Ja11]

7669   FE2b   100Sqn
NB left 3am **MIA(Lt L Butler **POW**/2AM R Robb
POW) 7/8th ["FE" claim combat seDOUAI 4-20am Ltn
H Klein Ja4]

Fine weather through the day turned to snow
squalls in the evening. By the following morning,
the time for the general attack, there was a drizzle
of thin snow and visibility was very poor.

9th April

The infantry attack of the battle of Arras commenced on the 9th of April after some three weeks
of preparatory bombardment. Relatively large
numbers of tanks were accompanying the troops for
the first time. Flare systems had been designed to

further assist contact patrolling, but in the
conditions Klaxon horns and Very lights fired from
the aircraft had to be resorted to. In these very
trying conditions the advance was generally
followed from the air, this work being carried out
by aeroplanes of Nos. 12, 13, and 16 Squadrons.
Artillery spotting was also maintained as a high
priority, but a south-westerly gale at high altitudes
led to the abandonment of the bombing progamme
for the assault and many of the offensive patrols
were also curtailed.

As the first phase of the battle developed through
the day, British and Commonwealth forces
achieved their objectives with great success and
valour. The Canadian Corps stormed and took the
formidable Vimy Ridge, almost reaching Lens.
Elsewhere, General Allenby's Third Army attacked
and broke through the enemy lines either side of
the Cambrai-Arras Road.

5742   BE2d   4Sqn
**Rec ANZAC front combat with 5EAs Sh57c NW
C.24.d. at 6-55pm shot down wr(Lt JHE Brink **DoW**
11.4.17/Lt RC Heath **WIA**) [?"BE" claim combat AIX-
NOULETTE 7-10pm Ltn K Schaefer Ja11]

**   BE2e   12Sqn**
CP? combat? shot up(/2Lt OD Norwood **WIA)back

A3159   BE2e   12Sqn
**CP mg longeron shot up ftl dam OK(Lt Croft/Lt JM
Musson)

4493   BE2c   13Sqn
**CP MAQNONLIEU shot up engine ftl dam OK(Lt K
Capel/Lt J Brooker)

5437   BE2c   13Sqn
**AP to H.7.b. mg fire brought down in n.m.l. dam
OK(Lt FAV Cook/Lt JAER Daly)

A2878   BE2e   13Sqn
**CP left 6am shellfire cr n.m.l. Sh51B NW G.11.B.9.9.
wr OK(Lt JH Norton/Capt TL Tibbs) a'c shelled

6818   BE2g   16Sqn
CP mg shot down 6-30am **MIA but OK(2Lt EB
Smythe **WIA**/2Lt S Cooper **WIA**) left 5-47am, British
mg?, message: ok in dugout GIVENCHY

A3315   Bristol F2a   48Sqn
**OP left 6pm eARRAS combat shot up(Lt JHT Letts/
Lt HG Collins **KIA**)

N3190?   Nieuport 17   6 (Naval) Sqn
this a'c? **DistP CAMBRAI combat(FSLt JdeC Paynter
WIA) combat?

N3205?   Nieuport 17   6 (Naval) Sqn
this a'c? **DistP CAMBRAI combat with EA[+ooc]
then storm cr ldg(FSLt AL Thorne **KIFA**)

6 (Naval) Squadron carried out the only distant
patrols possible on the opening day of fighting.

10th April

The weather on the 10th still worsened. Nieuports of 60 Squadron were forced to carry out tactical reconnaissances, needing to fly as low as two hundred feet.

A2839   BE2e   8Sqn
AOb ftl BULLECOURT shelled(2Lt PB Pattisson **WIA/2Lt EM Harwood OK) left 7-15am

A2829   BE2e   12Sqn
CP gun fire ftl made safe ldg ~H-27d. but blown over(2Lt JH Cooper **WIA/2Lt WA Winter OK) left 11-55am, a'c unsalvable

During these contact patrols, crews repeatedly shot up the troops on the ground.

          DH4   55Sqn
** (2Lt A Lindley **WIA**/)

11th April

The weather improved on the 11th, and with it came the return of the German fighter units. Fighting broke out all over the sector in one of the heaviest days of air fighting of the war.

A6722   Morane P   3Sqn
AOb combat with HA shot down WoL nrLAGNICOURT C.24.c.7.5. at 12-30pm(Lt MMA Lillis **KIA/AM A Fyffe **KIA**) left 10-45am [?"Parasol Morane" claim combat NOREUIL-LAGNICOURT 12-40am Ltn FO Bernert Ja2]

          BE2e   4Sqn
** combat? shot up(2Lt AFT Ord **WIA**/)slight

2769   BE2c   4Sqn
B left 7-08am CAMBRAI combat with HA shot down **MIA(2Lt F Matthews **WIA POW**) ["BE 2769" claim combat nrHEM LENGLET Ltn Roth Ja12] [?"Sopwith" claim combat nrNEUVIREUIL 9-05am Ltn A Schulte Ja12]

5849   BE2d   4Sqn
B left 7-08am CAMBRAI combat with HA shot down **MIA(Lt FL Kitchin **KIA**) ["BE 5849" claim combat nrTILLOY 8-55am Ltn A Schulte Ja12]

5811   BE2e   8Sqn
AOb seARRAS combat with 4EAs shot down wr(Sgt JV? Bell **WIA/Lt HJQ Campbell **WIA**) initials VJ? ["Sopwith" claim combat eFRIEDHOF nr ARRAS 9-50am Ltn K Schaefer or "BE" claim FAMPOUX Vzfw S Festner Ja11]

A2813   BE2e   8Sqn
AP left 12-20pm NEUVILLE VITASSE ftl cr wr N.19.a (2Lt EJE Stafford **WIA/Lt GE Gibbons OK) ["Sopwith" claim combat neFAMPOUX 12-35pm Ltn L Fr vRichthofen Ja11]

7242   BE2e   12Sqn
CP left 10-55am combat ftl wr(2Lt GH Jacob **WIA/

2Lt PL Goudie **WIA**) to H.22.c.

2501   BE2c   13Sqn
AOb combat with EA cr French Lines wr(Lt ECE Derwin **WIA/Gnr H Pierson **WIA**) left 8-05am XVII Corps front, cr trenches and escaped to WoL, MvR40? [?"BE" claim combat WILLERVAL 9-25am Ritt M Fr vRichthofen Ja11]

5848   BE2d   13Sqn
AOb XVII Corps front combat with EA ftl wr(Lt ER Gunner **WIA/Lt C Curtis **WIA**) left 8-25am [?"BE" claim combat nFAMPOUX 9-05am Vzfw S Festner or "Sopwith" claim Ltn K Schaefer Ja11]

5851   BE2d   13Sqn
AOb **MIA(2Lt ET Dunford **POW DoW** 23.4.17/Capt G Stewart **KIA**) left 8-45am XVII Corps front, DoW DOUAI [?2 "BE" claims combat BIACHES 10-20am & Fluchy 10-50am Ltn H Klein Ja4]

          FE2b   18Sqn
** shot up(/2Lt JR Smith **WIA**)stomach

A6690   SPAD 7   23Sqn
Esc left 7-55am seen by 3(Naval) nrCAMBRAI ftl **MIA(2Lt S Roche **POW**) a'c captured ["Sopwith A6690" claim combat CUVILLERS, neCAMBRAI 9am Ltn H Frommherz Ja2]

A6696   SPAD 7   23Sqn
**SpM BULLECOURT combat wires shot away dam ftl ECOUST ST MIEN OK(Lt FC Troup) left 11-40am

A3318   Bristol F2a   48Sqn
OP combat with EAs[++] shot down FAMPOUX Sh51B at 9-05am **MIA(2Lt RE Adeney **DoW**/2Lt LG Lovell **KIA**)Ja11, DoW as POW, Schaefer ["BE" claim combat FAMPOUX 9-10am Ltn K Schaefer Ja11]

A3323   Bristol F2a   48Sqn
OP combat with EA[+] shot down GAVRELLE 9-05am **MIA(2Lt GN Brockhurst **WIA POW**/2Lt CB Broughton **WIA POW**) left 7-35am, Ja11 ["BE A3323" claim combat MOUVILLE FERME, sARRAS 9-15am Ltn L Fr vRichthofen Ja11]

A3338   Bristol F2a   48Sqn
OP combat with AlbatrosDIII[++des] FAMPOUX shot down nFRESNES Sh51C 9-10am **MIA(Capt DM Tidmarsh MC **POW**/2Lt CB Holland **WIA POW**) left 7-35am, shared, Wolff["BE A3338" claim combat MOUVILLE FERME? 9-10am Ltn K Wolff Ja11]

The 11th was a dark day for many British units, but for 48 Squadron it was the end of a truly ghastly week in which they had lost crew from ten aircraft. At the same time, however, they were beginning to understand what was happening to their machines in battle. The air crews had been taught to use their Bristols in an orthodox two-seater fashion in which the pilot actively manoeuvred to give his gunner firing positions on the enemy, but the intensity of the German attacks

was making a disaster of these methods. Slowly the realisation came that the wonderful performance of the Bristol F2b meant that it could be flown like a fighter, the pilot concentrating on the use of the front gun, whilst the observer used his own gun to protect the rear. A few 48 Squadron pilots began to fly the machine in this way, and slowly but surely one of the greatest fighting aircraft of the entire war began to account for itself.

A2838   BE2e   52Sqn
P left 1-25pm French Lines **MIA(Capt AF Baker **KIA**/ 2Lt AJE Etches **KIA**)

A4190   RE8   59Sqn
LP found Sh51B B.28.a.8.5. **MIA(Lt GT Morris **KIA**/ Lt JM Souter **KIA**)

A6158   Sopwith Pup   3 (Naval) Sqn
** combat with Albatros[+ooc] then another[+cr] then Halberstadt[+crCAMBRAI] shot up ftl SAVY OK(FSLt JST Fall)

N5199   Sopwith Pup   3 (Naval) Sqn
** shot up dam(FSLt S Bennett)

12th April

Snow blizzards blew all day, retarding nearly all air work. Those reconnaissances which were possible showed the enemy destroying his positions and about to retreat.

4984   FE2b   18Sqn
EscPhot **MIA(Lt OD Maxted **POW**/Lt A Todd MC **POW DoW** 16.4.17) left 8-50am Fifth Army area ["FE 4984" claim combat DURY-ETERPIGNY Vzfw Schorisch Ja12]

4995   FE2b   18Sqn
EscPhot left 9-10am Fifth Army area **MIA(Lt OT Walton **KIA**/2AM JC Walker **KIA**) air collision?, buried EPINOY ["FE" claim combat RUMAUCOURT-BARALLE 10-40am Ltn A Schulte Ja12]

A104   RE8   34Sqn
Phot ASCENSION FARM Sh62c 30.c. combat with black AlbatrosDV 5000' ~11am shot up chased down ftl at L.15.c.6.2. wr(Capt FLJ Shirley **WIA/Lt LT Smith OK) dh by shell on a'c, destroyed, serious stomach wounds, Albatros had streamers

N6172.M **Sopwith Pup   3 (Naval) Sqn**
EscPhot combat with EA[+] then shot down ftl EoL QUEANT-PRONVILLE (AFCdr RG Mack **inj POW) left 9-45am, escorting 25Sqn, a'c captured, Ja12 ["Sopwith" claim combat MARQUION-BOURLON 9-30am Hpt P vOsterroht Ja12]

13th April

This was the first day since the offensive began when the weather was good enough to permit a full day's work in the air. The German airmen were now concentrating on protecting the withdrawal of their own forces, mostly flying low over the battle. 11 and 29 Squadrons, flying line patrols, met most of the action. The finer weather enabled a big resumption of bombing. A total of thirty-eight machines, gathered from 25, 27, 19, 40, and 66 Squadrons, bombed the German de-training centre of Henin-Lietard.

A6760   Morane P   3Sqn
Phot combat with 3EAs shot down WoL cr Lines Sh51B N.4.Central wr(Lt LF Beynon **WIA/2Lt AC Lutyens MC **WIA**) left 5-25pm

7156   BE2g   5Sqn
**LRec OPPY combat shot up ftl WoL cr wr(2Lt NC Buckton/2Lt GL Barritt) left 5-20pm, 29 hits

A819   FE2b   11Sqn
OP combat shot up cr nrLines wr(Lt ET Curling **WIA/ 2Lt J Rothwell OK) left 5-35pm [?"FE" claim combat PONT DU JOUR, LIEVIN, nrARRAS 6-30pm Ltn K Schaefer Ja11, but see FE2b 4877?]

A831   FE2b   11Sqn
OP left 11-25am shot down WoL wr(Sgt JA Cuniffe **WIA/2AM WJ Batten **WIA**) ["Vickers" claim combat MONCHY-FEUCHY 12-45am Rittm M Fr vRichthofen Ja11][?"FE" claim combat sBAILLEUL 12-35pm Ltn K Wolff Ja11]

A6649   SPAD 7   19Sqn
+* combat with AlbatrosD[+ooc] BREBIÈRES 8-40am OK(Lt GS Buck)

**   FE2b   22Sqn**
** shot up(Lt EA Thomas **WIA**/)

4997   FE2b   25Sqn
B shot down on return EoL 7-30pm **MIA(2Lt AH Bates **KIA**/Sgt WA Barnes **KIA**) left 6-40pm HENIN LIETARD ["Vickers 4997" claim combat NOYELLE-GODAULT, nrHENIN LIETARD 7-35pm Rittm M Fr vRichthofen Ja11]

A784   FE2b   25Sqn
B shot down EoL on return 7-30pm **MIA(Sgt J Dempsey **POW**/2Lt WH Green **WIA POW**) left 6-40pm HENIN LIETARD ["FE A784" claim combat with HARNES-ANNAY 7-30pm Vzfw S Festner Ja11][?"FE" claim combat nrHARNES, sLA BASSÉE Ltn E Bauer Ja3]

A6372   FE2b   25Sqn
B combat with shot down EoL on return 7-30pm **MIA(Capt LL Richardson Aust. **KIA**/2Lt DC Wollen **KIA**) left 6-40pm HENIN LIETARD [?"FE" claim combat nrVIMY 7-10pm Ltn H Klein Ja4]

FE2bs from 25 Squadron had set out for Henin-Lietard escorted by Nieuports of 40 Squadron, but were attacked after the raid by a formation led by Richthofen. The Nieuports had left immediately after the bombs had been dropped, and when the

German fighters approached they were apparently mistaken for the escort until it was too late.

A1564   Martinsyde G102   27Sqn
B HENIN LIETARD left 6-05pm shot down **MIA(2Lt M Topham **KIA**) Wolff13 ["FE A1564" claim combat nrROUVROY 6-52pm Ltn K Wolff Ja11]

A6768   Nieuport 23   29Sqn
DP combat with HA MONCHY shot down wr(2Lt B Scott-Foxwell **WIA) left 3-55pm, Wolff 12 ["Nieu" claim combat sMONCHY-LE-PREUX 4-30pm Ltn K Wolff Ja11]

B1519   Nieuport 17   40Sqn
+*OP combat with AlbatrosC[+ooc,cr] COURRIÈRES 11-30am OK(Lt HEO Ellis)

Nieuport 12   46Sqn
** (/2Lt CP Long **KIA**)

This was the last casualty for 46 Squadron before re-equipping with Sopwith Pups as a single-seat fighter unit.

A3322.5   **Bristol F2a   48Sqn**
LP shot down 4pm seen low neARRAS **MIA(2Lt HD Davies **POW**/2Lt RSL Worsley **POW**) left 2-50pm eARRAS, a'c captured [?"Sopwith A3322" claim combat nrDOUAI but 16.4? Untoff Stendel/Ltn Figulla SS4][?some list combat neARRAS 4pm Ltn L Fr vRichthofen Ja11]

A1950   FE2d   57Sqn
OP left 7am **MIA(2Lt GW Gillespie **KIA**/Pte RE Sibley **KIA**) [2"EA" claims combat GAVRELLE-OPPY 9am Ltn K Schneider Ja5]["FE" claim combat BIACHE-HAMBLAIN 8-56am Ltn H Klein Ja4]

A5150   FE2d   57Sqn
OP left 7am **MIA(Capt LS Platt **KIA**/2Lt T Margerison **KIA**) ["Vickers A5150" claim combat VITRY-EN-ARTOIS 9-05am Ltn H Gontermann Ja5]

A3190   RE8   59Sqn
PhotEsc ETAING **MIA(Capt JM Stuart **KIA**/Capt MH Wood **KIA**)burnt ["FE" claim combat VITRY-BREBIÈRES 8-56am Rittm M Fr vRichthofen Ja11]

A3199   RE8   59Sqn
Phot ETAING **MIA(Lt A Watson **WIA POW**/Lt ER Law **WIA POW**) ["BE A3199" claim combat ETAING-DURY 8-51am Vzfw S Festner Ja11]

A3203   RE8   59Sqn
Phot ETAING **MIA(Lt PB Boyd **KIA**/Lt PO Ray **KIA**) ["new EA" claim combat VITRY 8-55am & "BE" claim eROEUX-PELVES 8-56am Ltn L Fr vRichthofen Ja11]

A3216   RE8   59Sqn
Phot ETAING **MIA(Capt GB Hodgson **KIA**/Lt CH Morris **KIA**)

A3225   RE8   59Sqn
Phot ETAING in flames **MIA(Lt AH Tanfield **KIA**/

Lt A Ormerod **KIA**) Wolff10 ["BE 9625" claim combat nVITRY-EN-ARTOIS 8-56am Ltn K Wolff Ja11]

A4191   RE8   59Sqn
Phot ETAING **MIA(Lt HGH Horne **KIA**/Lt WJ Chalk **KIA**)

This disaster for 59 Squadron occurred in the morning. A patrol of RE8s had left at 8-15am to carry out a photographic reconnaissance of the line from Quiery-la-Motte to Etaing. This sector was dangerously close to Douai, an important base for Richthofen's operations. There had been escorts arranged for this work but all were dependent on the unfolding of other events — some of the escorts left late for the operation and the others never arrived, so that 59 Squadron was left at the mercy of the German fighters. All six RE8s were shot down in a few minutes.

14th April

Another attempt was made to photograph the same section of the line on the 14th, this time with proper escort and timed to coincide with nearby offensive patrols. 11 Squadron FE2bs were used, escorted by 29 Squadron Nieuports. Again they were fiercely attacked by Albatros and Halberstadt Scouts, this time over Vitry, and although the Nieuports prevented a repeat of the previous day, the photography was still not accomplished.

2527   BE2d   2Sqn
AP to BOIS DE L'HIRONDELLE combat shot down **MIA(Capt GB Lockhart **KIA**/Lt AP Wilson **KIA**) [?"RE" claim LA COULOTTE wAVION 4-20pm Ltn K Schaefer Ja11, but also consider 5Sqn a'c 6184?]

6814   BE2g   5Sqn
RecP WILLERVAL-BAILLEUL cr wr(Capt LC Coates **WIA/Lt JC Cotton **WIA**)

2567   BE2f   10Sqn
SpM:NB left 4-20am HENIN LIETARD **MIA(2Lt CWD Holmes **POW**) a'c captured ["BE 2562" claim combat nrRIBECOURT 8-30am Ltn H Frommherz Ja2]

7702   FE2b   11Sqn
PhotRec left 8-10am combat with EA shot up dam(/ Cpl W Hodgson **KIA)

A6746   SPAD 7   19Sqn
OP BAILLEUL-VITRY-SAINS in flames **MIA(Lt EW Capper **KIA**) Wolff15 ["SPAD" claim combat nrBAILLEUL 6-30pm Ltn K Wolff Ja11][?"Sopwith" claim combat VIMY-FARBUS 6-23pm Ltn L Fr vRichthofen Ja11]

4877   FE2b   25Sqn
P combat, down in flames nrLIEVIN 4-44pm wr(2Lt WE Davies **KIA/Lt NW Morrison **KIA**) left 4pm LENS-ARRAS ["FE" claim combat LIEVIN-ELEU 5-05pm Ltn K Schaefer Ja11]

A6794   Nieuport 23   29Sqn
Esc left 8-40am down EoL **MIA(2Lt EJ Pascoe **KIA**)

A78   RE8   34Sqn
EscPhot left 9-20am **MIA(Lt HR Davies **POW**/Lt JR Samuel **POW**) [?"RE" claim combat LA COULOTTE, wAVION Ltn K Schaeffer Ja11]

7241   BE2g   52Sqn
Phot left nrMETZ burnt(2Lt CTL Donaldson **KIA/SR Carter **KIA**) to Front Lines ["BE" claim combat METZ-EN-COUTURE Ltn H Gontermann Ja5]

Sopwith Pup   54Sqn
OP left 6-30am XV Corps combat shot up(Lt RNS Smith **WIA)

A6772   Nieuport 23   60Sqn
OP eDOUAI shot up ftl **MIA(Capt A Binnie **WIA POW**) left 8-30am, shot down eFOUQUIÈRES, lost arm ["Nieu 6792/2976" claim combat eFOUQUIÈRES 9-20am Ltn L Fr vRichthofen Ja11]

A6796   Nieuport 17   60Sqn
OP eDOUAI combat with EAs BOIS BERNARD shot down **MIA(Lt WO Russell **POW**)MvR, left 8-30am ["Nieu A6796" claim combat sBOIS BERNARD 9-15am Rittm M Fr vRichthofen Ja11]

B1511   Nieuport 17   60Sqn
OP left 6-30am eDOUAI combat with EAs DROCOURT **MIA(2Lt JH Cock NZ. **KIA**) Wolff14 ["Nieu B1511" claim combat seDROCOURT 9-20am Ltn K Wolff Ja11]

B1523   Nieuport 17   60Sqn
OP left 8-30am eDOUAI combat with EA 9-15am shot up ftl **MIA(2Lt LC Chapman **POW DoW** 16.4.17) ["Nieu" claim combat GAVRELLE 9-15am Vzfw S Festner Ja11]

60 Squadron were patrolling in the general area of the attempted photo-reconnaissance by 11 Squadron, and became involved in a related fight with Jasta 11.

9667   Sopwith Strutter 3 Wing RNAS
B FREIBURG AA shot down **MIA(Capt GRS Fleming **POW DoW** 17.4.17/AM AG Lockyer **POW**)

N5117   Sopwith Strutter 3 Wing RNAS
B shot down neCOLMAR **MIA(FSLt H Edwards **POW**/GL JL Coghlan **POW KIA**?) ["Sopwith 5117" claim combat nrSCHLETTSTADT Vzfw R Rath Ja35]

N5171   Sopwith Strutter 3 Wing RNAS
B combat shot down nwCOLMAR **MIA(FLt C Rathborne **POW**/GL V Turner **KIA**) pilot escaped ["Sopwith 5171" claim combat nrSCHLETTSTADT Vzfw G Schindler Ja35]

This was a reprisal raid to Freiburg and was the last raid carried out by this specialist strategic bombing unit before it was disbanded. So much assistance had been offered to the RFC by the Admiralty in the previous weeks that 3 Wing RNAS could no longer be maintained, and its resources were re-allocated to 10 (Naval) Squadron so that it too could be available to the RFC if required. It officially ceased to exist on the 30th of June long after it had been broken up.

German reinforcements had been pouring onto the Arras front, and by now almost double the number of troops compared with the opening day of the battle were engaged. In the air, too, the Germans had heavily reinforced. Four new reconnaissance and artillery units, one close escort unit, and two new Jagdstaffeln had come into the sector. The RFC continued its attempts to understand how the German air forces were operating, so that counters might be developed. The latest thinking was set out in a memorandum, which is worth describing. Enemy aircraft were known to be no longer patrolling at height, but were commonly slipping below Allied patrols and coming up through low cloud to launch surprise attacks on photographic and artillery machines from below. Whilst this meant that the Allied high patrols must be having some effect, it also led the RFC to conclude it should incorporate similar tactics for some of its own fighting. In this way it would also have an increased number of fighting machines at the levels at which the corps machines operated to offer a degree of protection. What the RFC failed to fully recognise was the meticulous care with which the German Supreme Command was disposing its available aircraft. It took great care to follow what the British were doing in the air through a highly organised network of information gathering. German machines were usually sent up only when the RFC was most active, thereby ensuring that their fighters were brought into action when the circumstances were most telling.

15th April

2525   BE2c   2Sqn
** shot up(2Lt W Brettell **WIA**/Lt E Leggett **OK**)

16th April
NIVELLE'S OFFENSIVE

The first phase of the British offensive came to an end at this time. The breach in the enemy's lines had been successfully achieved, and the German command had also been forced to focus its attention on Arras. On the 16th of April General Nivelle launched the great French attack in the south, but after a promising start it soon collapsed. Well prepared German reinforcements flooded into the battle area and soon checked any possibility of

success. Whilst this took a few days to become apparent, it was of course grievously disappointing. Not only did it lead France into despair but also committed the British forces to weeks more of almost pointless fighting. Haig was driven to apply ceaseless pressure upon the enemy at Arras in order to distract him. For three long weeks his armies could not afford to slacken, by which time the battle had sunk into one of pure attrition. British plans to mount its own major offensive, intended to take place in Flanders, would also be threatened as Arras drew off precious resources.

From the 16th of April German time reverted to being one hour ahead of British time (all times given are British time).

5869   BE2d   7Sqn
AOb AA shot down SAVY wr(2Lt W Green **WIA/2Lt CE Wilson **KIA**) left 1-05pm

7163   BE2e   9Sqn
P shot up dam(2Lt WR Balden **WIA/2Lt HH Riekie OK)

A3156   BE2e   13Sqn
AOb combat with HA ftl o't(2Lt A Pascoe **WIA/Lt FS Andrews **DoW** 29.4.17) left 2-50pm XVII Corps front, a'c unsalvable ["BE" claim combat BAILLEUL-GAVRELLE 4-30pm Rittm M Fr vRichthofen Ja11]

7804   Sopwith Strutter 43Sqn
RecLP LA BASSÉE **MIA(2Lt JGE? Frew **WIA POW**/1AM F Russell **KIA**) initials JGH?, left 6-30am LA BASSÉE-BAILLEUL

A6769   Nieuport 23   60Sqn
OP VITRY combat with EA shot down ROEUX **MIA(2Lt RE Kimbell **KIA**) left 8-05am [?"Nieu" claim combat neROEUX 9-30am Ltn K Wolff Ja11][?"Nieu C . . . IV" claim combat neBIACHE 9-30am Vzfw S Festner Ja11: "IV" could be squadron marking]

B1501   Nieuport 17   60Sqn
OP left 8-05am VITRY combat with EA PLOUVAIN-ROEUX 9-15am **MIA(2Lt DN Robertson **POW DoW**) ["Nieu" claim combat ROEUX-PELVES 9-30am Ltn L Fr vRichthofen Ja11]

B1507   Nieuport 17   60Sqn
OP VITRY combat with EAs shot down **MIA(Lt T Langwill **POW DoW** 17.4.17) left 8-05am, combat BIACHE ST VAAST

B1509   Nieuport 17   60Sqn
OP left 8-05am VITRY combat with EAs shot down VITRY-MONCHY 9-15am **MIA(Lt JMcC Elliot **KIA**)

On the Arras front the weather suited flying on the 16th, and yet another attempt was made to photograph the line between Drocourt and Queant. This time, a very heavy escort was provided and the reconnaissance was a success. The only component to meet trouble was 60 Squadron. They were due

to make offensive patrols in the vicinity but as the formation crossed the lines they saw a BE2c being attacked and diverted to assist. The enemy was Richthofen's Jasta, and four Nieuports were shot down.

17th April

The resumption of the offensive was delayed by very bad weather for the next four days. Virtually all flying was halted.

20th April

A2868   BE2e   15Sqn
AOb combat with EA ftl C.17a.7.9. shelled(Lt FF Wessell **WIA/2Lt SE Tomer OK) left 7-35am V Corps area

2553   BE2c   16Sqn
P(Phot?) AVION-WILLERVAL **MIA(Sgt J Dangerfield **POW**/2AM ED Harvey **POW**) left 4-10pm

A1098   Sopwith Strutter 43Sqn
LP LOOS Salient **MIA(2Lt AE Crisp **WIA POW**/2Lt GA Newenham **WIA POW**) left 1-05pm ["Sopwith" claim neBEAUCAMP Flakzug46]

B1566.C5 Nieuport 17   60Sqn
+* combat with 2Str[+shot down flames] BIACHE ST VAAST 2-58pm OK(Capt WA Bishop) Bishop claimed 29 victories in this machine

21st April

Air activity resumed again on the 21st. German kite balloons were attacked all along the Arras front, three being brought down. Patrolling formations were sent out in force, at one time an estimated fifty British machines were active, but the air fighting was comparatively light.

A2766   BE2e   16Sqn
Phot VIMY combat with EA 4-20pm ftl seVIMY(Capt EJD Routh **WIA/2Lt MacKenzie OK) left 3-10pm, a'c unsalvable, Wolff17 [?"BE?" claim combat nwARLEUX 4-30pm Ltn K Wolff Ja11]

A2888   BE2g   16Sqn
AOb VIMY dhAA hit cr wr(2Lt Bishop OK/2Lt CN Milligan **WIA) left 1-45pm

A2915   BE2g   16Sqn
Phot combat with 2HA? shot down in flames VIMY-MARICOURT **MIA(2Lt JPC Mitchell **KIA**/Capt GC Rogers **KIA**) left 3-10pm [?"BE?" claim combat nwARLEUX Ltn L Fr vRichthofen Ja11, but possible 29Sq Nieu?]

A6755   Nieuport 17   29Sqn
OP left 4-30pm **MIA(2Lt CVdeB Rogers **KIA**) [?"Nieu" claim combat eFRESNES 4-45pm Ltn K Wolff Ja11]

A6797   Nieuport 23   29Sqn
OP left 4-30pm **MIA(2Lt F Sadler **KIA**) [?"Nieu"
claim combat eFRESNES 4-45pm Ltn K Schaefer Ja11]

B1568   Nieuport 17   29Sqn
OP left 4-30pm down EoL **MIA(2Lt AB Morgan **KIA**)
found dead 22.4.17

22nd April

A313   Nieuport 17   1Sqn
**OP left 5-44am combat 8Albatros ovLILLE seen shot
down cr on nose **MIA**(Lt AW Wood **WIA POW**) to
LILLE-SECLIN-CARVIN, a'c captured ["Nieu" claim
combat COULIN?, eWAVRIN 7-10am Ltn A Hanko
Ja28]

A6727   Morane P   3Sqn
**trav combat shot down broke up nrBAPAUME
~7-30am **MIA**(2Lt FL Carter **KIA**/Cpl A Morgan **KIA**)
had left 11-30am for A.L.G., 3(N) saw a'c shot down by
EA: crew was taking photos (originally thought to be due
to weather) [?"Morane" claim combat with
HAVRINCOURT 7-05pm Ltn K Wolff Ja11]

FE2b   11Sqn
** shot up(/2AM JF Carr **WIA**)slight, probably morning
patrol, met by 2 Albatros D-types

FE2b   11Sqn
** shot up(/2Lt PA deEscofet **WIA**)leg, probably
morning patrol

7020   FE2b   11Sqn
**PhotRec shot down ftl cr o't 3 times Sh57c.03c(Lt WF
Fletcher **WIA**/Lt W Franklin **WIA**) badly wounded,
MvR46? ["Vickers" claim combat LAGNICOURT
4-10pm Rittm M Fr vRichthofen Ja11, other 11Sq a'c
possible]

A810   FE2b   11Sqn
*Phot left 2-50pm combat shot up cr ldg 4pm dam(Capt
ER Manning Aust. OK/Cpl R Tollerfield **WIA**)

A820   FE2b   11Sqn
**Phot combat with EAs fell & burst into flames ldg cr
wr(Lt CA Parker OK/2Lt JEB Hesketh **DoW**) left
2-30pm, observer shot soon after start of combat, then
held in by pilot who attempted to land with most controls
shot away, a'c had dh by shell on ground as Parker
carried observer away [?"FE?" claim combat
nwMONCHY-TILLOY, but 7-20pm? Ltn K Schaefer
Ja11]

A5500   FE2b   11Sqn
Phot combat with EA shot up cr wr (2Lt JJ Paine **inj/
2Lt J Rothwell **inj**) left 2-45pm, injured in ldg

A5501   FE2b   11Sqn
Phot left 2-40pm **MIA(Sgt JK Hollis **WIA POW**/Lt
BJ Tolhurst **KIA**) Wolff19 [?"FE" claim combat
HENDECOURT 4-10pm Ltn K Wolff Ja11]

There were two further attempts by 11 Squadron
to reconnoitre the Drocourt-Queant line, both of

which failed as a result of fierce attacks. The worst
casualties occurred in the afternoon when Jasta 11
met them. Of those that limped home with dead
and wounded aboard, four subsequently crash-
landed.

FE2b   18Sqn
**B CAMBRAI A'dr AA splinter(Capt HLH Owen
WIA)knee

SPAD 7   23Sqn
**EscB(18Sqn) combat with EA shot up(Capt KC
McCallum **WIA**)foot

A6682.4   SPAD 7   23Sqn
**EscB(18Sqn) left 5-27pm CAMBRAI combat with EA
eCAMBRAI **MIA**(2Lt FC Craig **POW**) SPADs joined
EA patrol in error, a'c captured ["SPAD" claims combat
sMARCOING 7-05pm Hpt P vOsterroht Ja12 &
?unconfirmed claim combat wHAVRINCOURT 7-10pm
Untoff R Jorke Ja12]

A6695   SPAD 7   23Sqn
EscB combat eCAMBRAI **MIA(2Lt KR Furniss **POW**
DoW) left 5-27pm CAMBRAI ["SPAD" claim combat
wCAMBRAI 7-05pm OffSt E Nathanael Ja5]

23 Squadron was escorting six FE2bs on an evening
bombing raid when this fighting took place. Six
Pups of 3 (Naval) Squadron were also involved.
The SPADS lost the main formation and met a
patrol of Albatros fighters which the flight leader
apparently mistook for British aircraft and climbed
to joined them. They were then attacked and lost
two machines.

9376.A5   Sopwith Strutter   5 Wing RNAS
B engine failed ftl OOSTBURG **MIA(FSLt DAH
Nelles DSC **INT**) interned Holland

23rd April

British infantry attacks recommenced in earnest on
the 23rd. There were many enemy machines
operating over the battlefield which no doubt
inhibited the forward troops from revealing much
of their position to contact patrols. Artillery and
reconnaissance machines were attacked and, in
general, the corps machines were constantly harassed in their vital work throughout the day, despite
the presence of as many as fifty Allied single-seaters
in the air. This can be seen from the casualties
below — a relatively unusual list, even in these
dark days. Despite the appalling casualties of April
1917 the RFC was managing to keep the corps
machines operating, a goal often achieved at great
cost to the men protecting them.

A final element of the day's fighting which
deserves mention was the development of several
skirmishes into general dogfighting, never seen to
such intensity. Certainly, there were a great many

machines in the air on both sides, and only a perceived mood of caution by the Germans prevented greater numbers of decisive engagements. One of the biggest was in the evening, after FE2bs of 18 Squadron and their Pup escort from 3 (Naval) Squadron had been attacked by two formations of Albatros and Halberstadt scouts. It subsequently swept up into a fight variously involving Triplanes of 1 (Naval) Squadron, Nieuports of 60 Squadron, Pups of 66 Squadron, and Bristol Fighters of 48 Squadron.

A2843   BE2g   10Sqn
**SpM:B ST POL AA ftl nrST POL dam OK(2Lt AW Watson)

7099   BE2e   12Sqn
P main spar shot up cr a'dr dam(Lt Lavarack OK/Lt Budgett **inj) spar broke ldg, repairable

7182   BE2e   12Sqn
AOb left 3-15pm fell in flames burnt(Lt A Ralphs **KIA/Lt LW Mott **KIA**)

7089   BE2e   13Sqn
**CP XVII Corps front ground mg shot down nFAMPOUX OK(2Lt HS Robertson/Lt GJ Farmer) left 6-44am, a'c shelled

**   BE2e   15Sqn**
** AA(/2AM FA Blunden **WIA**)face

A2876   BE2g   16Sqn
Phot eVIMY combat with 5Halberstadts shot down Sh51b A.6.b wr(2Lt CM Crow **KIA/2Lt ET Turner **WIA**) left 9-45am ["BE" claim combat nVIMY 11-10am Ltn L Fr vRichthofen Ja11][?possible "Sopwith" claim combat NEUVILLE Vzfw Grigo Ja12]

A3168   BE2f   16Sqn
Phot shot down in flames Sh36C T.16.a. **MIA(2Lt EA Welch **KIA**/Sgt AG Tollerbey **KIA**) left 9-25am eVIMY, MvR47 ["BE" claim combat MERICOURT 11-05am Rittm M Fr vRichthofen Ja11]

A823   FE2b   18Sqn
B 4EA closed in[+several hits: "EA went ooc" snd, last seen 2000'] ovBARELLE 10000' 5-30pm then EA above which shot up radiator & hit pilot(2Lt EL Zink **WIA/2Lt GB Bate OK)shoulder

Of passing interest is that casualty and combat reports were now being phrased in a much more consistent language, such as in this case simply summarising the victory as the "EA went ooc".

SPAD 7   19Sqn
OP combat?(Lt WE Reed **WIA)

6929   FE2b   22Sqn
OP combat EA, air collision with DH2 7909, broke up cr nrLE VERGUIER (Lt EA Barltrop **KIFA/2Lt FO Sullivan **KIFA**) ["EA" claim combat BELLENGLISE (with 7909) 6pm Ltn K Schneider Ja5]

7681   FE2b   22Sqn
Phot HA fire shot down in spiral in flames o't(2Lt JA Rossi **WIA/2Lt PH West **WIA**) to Fourth Army front, crew burnt [?earlier "FE" claim for day: combat BELLENGLISE 7-15am Ltn K Schneider Ja5]

7909   DH2   24Sqn
*P left 6-30pm air collision with FE2b 6929 nrLE VERGUIER(2Lt MA White **KIFA**) ["EA" claim combat BELLENGLISE (with 6929) 6pm Ltn K Schneider Ja5]

7501   Martinsyde G100   27Sqn
B combat with EA shot up(Lt MH Coote **WIA) [?"Mart" claim combat ITANCOURT OffSt Weckbrodt Ja26]

A6752   Nieuport 17   29Sqn
OP left 5-45pm combat shot up dam(Capt EF Elderton **WIA)leg

B1516   Nieuport 17   29Sqn
**Esc left 3-15pm combat with EA shot down OK(2Lt JD Atkinson) a'c unsalvable

B1520   Nieuport 17   29Sqn
Esc left 3-15pm combat with EA shot down(Lt WPT Watts **WIA) a'c unsalvable

A88   RE8   34Sqn
NFP combat with 4HA cr 6-35pm burnt(2Lt HO Hill **KIA/Lt HP Illsley **KIA**) left 5-45pm, Hill hit in head ["BE" claim combat seARRAS 6-25pm Ltn H Gontermann Ja5]

A2694   A.W.FK8   35Sqn
LP heavy mg shot up eARRAS on return dam(2Lt MW Wilson OK/2Lt NC Yonge **WIA) to hospital, left 9am

This was the first combat casualty for 35 Squadron and the first in the Armstrong Whitworth FK8 corps machine. The type was to become a well liked and respected machine for its qualities of sturdiness and reliability, but was to be oddly under-used, being finally allocated to only five operational squadrons in France. Early problems with its weak undercarriage, unable to cope with the rough usage typical of the Western Front, were soon overcome and its crews fought some notable battles during its long period of service in France and in the Middle East.

Bristol F2b   48Sqn
** AA shot up(/Lt LE Porter **WIA**)

DH4   55Sqn
B BOUE (/2Lt FL Oliver **WIA)

A2147   DH4   55Sqn
B BOUE Ammunition dump neETREUX mg ftl ldg a'dr ok(Lt IV Pyott DSO OK/2Lt AD Taylor **WIA)arm, left 3-30pm

A7408   DH4   55Sqn
B BOUE combat shot down URVILLERS(Capt AT Greg **KIA/1AM RW Robson **WIA**) left 3-50pm

A7410   DH4   55Sqn
**B BOUE combat engine shot up ovEDGEHILL dam
cr nrBUIRE OK(Lt T Webb/1AM W Bond) left 3-30pm

These losses occurred after eight DH4s from 55 Squadron had set off to bomb an ammunition dump at Boue, north-east of Etreux. Two crashed before reaching the lines, and then on the return journey seven enemy fighters attacked the formation.

A4850   SE5   56Sqn
+* combat with AlbatrosDIII[+destr] CAMBRAI
11-45am OK(Capt A Ball) followed morning victory on
Nieuport (see below)

B1522   Nieuport 17   56Sqn
+* combat with AlbatrosC[+destr] ABANCOURT-
TILLOY Road 6-45am OK(Capt A Ball)

Albert Ball's dawn victory in Nieuport B1522 above was his first with 56 Squadron, and in fact was the first achieved by that unit. Later in the morning he scored a second, this time in SE5 A4850, which was his first in this type. He shot down another two enemy machines in this SE5 three days later.

24th April

A6738   Nieuport 17   1Sqn
+* combat with AlbatrosC[+flames] BOIS GRENIER
12pm OK(2Lt TF Hazell) early victory for this ace whose
score was over 40

A2769   BE2e   8Sqn
**AOb combat with 4HA ovVIS-EN-ARTOIS shot up
dam OK(Capt BC Rice/2Lt AC Heaven)

7195   BE2e   9Sqn
**B left 5-40am AA hit? MIA(Lt GE Hicks POW)
[?"BE" claim combat nrLE CATELET 8-40am Oblt FO
Bernert Ja2]

A2937   BE2e   9Sqn
**B left 5-40am AA hit MIA(2Lt FA Matthews KIA)
[?possible 5 claims, including 4"BEs" combat nrLE
CATELET ~7-40am Ltn FO Bernert Ja2]

A2941   BE2e   9Sqn
**B left 5-40am AA hit cr burnt MIA(Lt CL Graves
KIA) burnt to death [?"BE" claim combat nrLE
CATELET ~7-45am Ltn FO Bernert Ja2]

A5144   FE2d   20Sqn
**Esc combat with EAs, in flames ftl YPRES a'c burnt(Lt
NL Robertson WIA/Capt RM Knowles MC WIA) left
6-14am ["FE" claim nrYPRES 8-40am Ltn W vBülow
Ja18]

A6385   FE2d   20Sqn
**EscRec YPRES MIA(2Lt AR Johnston KIA/Lt HR
Nicholson KIA) ["FE" claims combat eYPRES 8-10am
OffSt W Göttsch & Lt W Junck Ja8][see A6403 re Vzfw
J Wirtz]

A6403   FE2d   20Sqn
**EscRec YPRES combat with 5HAs[+] shot up ftl dam
OK(2Lt EO Perry/2AM EH Sayers) [shot down by Vzfw
J Wirtz MFJaI who claimed 2 FEs in combat
ovPOLYGON WOOD & BECELAERE]

A4858   SE5   56Sqn
+* combat with AlbatrosC[+ooc] BELLONE 11-10am
OK(2Lt LM Barlow) first victory of 20 for Barlow

A2149   DH4   55Sqn
**B LA BRIQUETTE combat then ftl wr
nrDOULLENS(Lt AMN deLavison WIA/2AM K
Oliver KIA) left 5-55am [?combat 7-50am Ltn FO
Bernert Ja2]

**   RE8   59Sqn**
** mg fire shot up(/Lt RS Stone WIA)

A6777   Nieuport 23   60Sqn
**KBP combat with 3EAs eARRAS ftl in flames cr
1-15pm(2Lt RB Clark DoW 1.5.17) left 12-35pm

A6152   Sopwith Pup   66Sqn
**Esc LENS-BREBIÈRES-LECLUSE combat shot up
dam OK(2Lt Morley)

A6175.5   Sopwith Pup   66Sqn
**Esc SOLESMES seen nrCAMBRAI brought down
MIA(2Lt RS Capon WIA POW) slight WIA, Ja33
["Sopwith" claim combat BOURLON? 7-05am Oblt H
Lorenz Ja33]

2Lt Capon was the first combat loss for 66 Squadron in France.

A7305   Sopwith Pup   66Sqn
**Esc LENS-BREBIÈRES-LECLUSE combat with EA
shot up dam OK(Capt R Oxspring)

A1002   Sopwith Strutter 70Sqn
**Rec sCAMBRAI fell in flames MIA(2Lt CH Halse
KIA/2AM WJ Bond KIA) left 5-35am [?"BE" claim
combat VAUCELLES 7-30am Ltn FO Bernert Ja2]

Many of the above machines were involved in a combined reconnaissance and bombing operation. This type of raid was finding increasing favour with the British because of the clear advantages of co-ordinating air activity. By blending the roles of several different squadrons, it was not only more economical on resources, but also proving more effective. As one party left an area, another's arrival coincided with it, so that help could be given if necessary, or the burden of protection shared. Such were the benefits beginning to flow from the organisational expansion of the RFC. On this day, six Pups from 66 Squadron escorted nine Strutters from 70 Squadron. The long reconnaissance they were embarked on could not be completed because of low cloud, and they were attacked over Solesmes. Martinsyde bombers from 27 Squadron, with 19 Squadron SPAD escorts, had already followed into

the area, and then six DH4s of 55 Squadron finally arrived to drop their bombs, all units returning to their aerodromes by mid-morning.

N5467   Sopwith Triplane   8 (Naval) Sqn
OP combat with 3Albatros shot down BAILLEUL 8-05am(FSLt EBJ Walter **KIA) ["Tripe" claim combat BAILLEUL 8am Ltn H Gontermann Ja5]

25th April

Around this time the decision was taken to abandon immediate plans for a British offensive in Flanders. Continued support for the French cause was far more critical politically, for in the space of barely two weeks the heart had been all but torn out of the French Army, leaving it close to open revolt. In these circumstances, the British effort at Arras redoubled, whilst France sought to reorganise its High Command. The infantry advance paused for a few days and most of the air activity, conducted under low cloud, concentrated on the protection of corps squadrons.

A2899   BE2g   10Sqn
AOb combat with Albatros shot down 7-45pm(Lt RV Kann **WIA/2Lt C Bousfield OK) left 5-25pm CITÉ ST PIERRE, WIA back, a'c unsalvable

7191   BE2e   12Sqn
AOb **MIA(Lt T Thomson **KIA**/2Lt AM Turnbull **KIA**)

A837   FE2b   25Sqn
EscLP combat with EA shot down in flames WILLERVAL-BAILLEUL 9-35am(2Lt CV Darnell **KIA/2AM G Pawley **KIA**) left 8-50pm LENS-ARRAS ["FE" claim combat BAILLEUL 9-40am Ltn K Schaefer Ja11]

Sopwith Strutter   43Sqn
LP combat?(/2Lt ESW Langton **WIA)foot

A3352   Bristol F2a   48Sqn
COP eARRAS combat with EA then seen going down **MIA(2Lt WJ Clifford **KIA**/2Lt HL Tomkies **KIA**) left 6-20pm ["Bristol" claim combat ROEUX Stn 7-30pm Ltn K Schaefer Ja11]

A3213   RE8   59Sqn
** left 5-15am **MIA**(Sgt FC Smith **POW**/Lt EJ Dillnutt **POW**) [?possible "Austin 2Str" claim combat GUEMAPPE but 9-30am? Ltn K Allmenröder Ja11]

3115   HP 0/100   7Sqn RNAS
Day Bombing German destroyers off OSTENDE combat with enemy seaplane, seen 3m nNIEUPORT fuel tank hit ftl in sea **MIA(FSLt TSS Hood **KIA**/GL RH Watson **POW DoW**/AM FC Kirby **WIA**/AC2 WC Danzey **POW DoW** 6.12.17) Kirby saved by French flying boat

This was the first Handley Page bomber involved in a casualty due to enemy action. Two days

previously, on the 23rd, Handley Pages had been used to carry out their first daylight bombing operations, attacking five German destroyers off Ostende. This had been reasonably successful, but on the 25th 3115 strayed from its fighter escort and was attacked. Two French flying boats attempted to rescue what crew they could, but only one of these managed to take off again before German motor boats from Ostende apprehended all those left on the water. After the failure of this operation it was decided to restrict Handley Pages to night bombing.

26th April

A6671   Nieuport 17   1Sqn
KBP left 12pm attacked KB[+] seen attkg second KB cr wr **MIA(Lt AV Burbury MC **POW**) a'c captured

A2806   BE2g   5Sqn
AOb shot down in flames nrGAVRELLE? 3-30pm **MIA(Lt HBT Hope **KIA**/2Lt LE Allan **KIA**) left 3pm, NB: not 2808 as some sources, and has prefix "A": see A2814, Wolff21 ["BE2" claim combat eGAVRELLE 3-35pm Ltn K Wolff Ja11]

BE2e   9Sqn
** shot up(Capt RJ Lowcock **WIA**)shoulder

5870   BE2e   10Sqn
Phot seen going down spirals HULLUCH-WINGLES 5-25pm **MIA(Lt F Roux **DoW** as **POW**?/2Lt HJ Price **POW**) ["BE" claim combat with HAISNES Ltn Erbguth Ja30]

A2826   BE2e   16Sqn
AOb eVIMY shot down in flames Sh36sw T.26. ~6-30pm **MIA(2Lt WS Spence **KIA**/2Lt WA Campbell **KIA**) left 4-35pm ["BE" claim combat seVIMY RIDGE 5-40pm Ltn L Fr vRichthofen Ja11]

A2859   BE2g   16Sqn
AOb VIMY combat 6-30pm shot down hit tree wr(2Lt LWK Mercer **WIA/Pte Pea OK) left 3-05pm ["BE2" claim combat VIMY-HOHE(Ridge?) 6-30pm Ltn K Allmenröder Ja11]

FE2d   20Sqn
** combat?(/Sgt A Clayton **KIA**)

FE2b   22Sqn
Phot shot up(Lt LW Beal **WIA/)

4883.B1   FE2b   22Sqn
B shot down ovBRANCOURT? **MIA(Capt HR Hawkins **POW**/2Lt GO McEntee **POW**) left 5-45pm BOHAIN, lost in mist ovESSIGNY-LE-PETIT [?"FE" claim combat BRANCOURT 7pm Offst Sturm Ja5]

A825   FE2b   22Sqn
B shot down BRANCOURT? **MIA(2Lt GM Hopkins **POW**/2Lt JDM Stewart **POW**) left 5-45pm BOHAIN STN, see FE2b 4883 [?possible "FE" claim combat nST QUENTIN 7-05pm Ltn Nebel Ja5]

B1549   Nieuport 17   60Sqn
*OP left 8-45am AA hit ftl lake cr(2Lt NP Henderson **inj**)

8171   Sopwith Baby   Dunkirk Seaplane Stn
** shot down 7m neDUNKIRK wr MIA but OK(FCdr WL Welsh)

27th April

10 (Naval) Squadron came south from Dunkirk to operate with the RFC on the 27th of April. It was flying Sopwith Triplanes and would first join the 11th (Army) Wing in support of the Second Army. Later it would move north to work with the Fifth Army in the battle of Ypres.

2713   BE2c   2Sqn
AReg LENS ground fire cr wr ST PIERRE **MIA(2Lt WJ Stonier **KIA**/2Lt FR Croker **KIA**) seen low 11-15am, man fell out

4850   FE2b   11Sqn
LP left 5-20pm **MIA(2Lt JA Cairns **POW**/1AM EG Perry **POW**) [?possible "Vickers" claim combat FRESNES 7-15pm Ltn Fr L vRichthofen Ja11, but others?]

7698   FE2b   11Sqn
LowP shot up? ftl cr trench o't 8pm(2Lt P Robinson **WIA?/2AM H Tilley **inj**) Robinson inj? [?"FE" claim combat sGAVRELLE 7-20pm Ltn K Wolff Ja11]

B1570   Nieuport 17   60Sqn
delivery from 2AD left 8am lost ftl DOUAI **MIA(2Lt F Stedman Aust.? **POW**)

28th April

The British infantry advance was renewed on the 28th and with it came a return to contact patrolling and other tactical work. The units involved were heavily mauled by the German fighters, who concentrated their efforts on the BE2es. Low clouds assisted their attacks.

2551   BE2f   5Sqn
AP shot up dam(Lt AE Clark **WIA/2AM A Morley OK)leg

2557   BE2f   5Sqn
**Phot GAVRELLE combat with EA shot down wr OK(2Lt NC Buckton/2Lt O'Sullivan) left 4-25pm, Wolff23 ["BE" claim combat wGAVRELLE 10-20am Ltn K Wolff Ja11]

BE2e   9Sqn
** shot up(2Lt HJ Gogarty **WIA**/)

7221   BE2e   13Sqn
AOb XVII Corps front **MIA(Lt RW Follit **DoW**/Lt FJ Kirkham **WIA POW**) left 7-20am ["BE" claim combat ePELVES 8-30am Rittm M Fr vRichthofen Ja11]

A1843   BE2e   13Sqn
**CP XVII Corps front trench mg shot down OK(2Lt

JH Jones/2Lt G Hall) a'c unsalvable, left 5-42am

A2745   BE2e   16Sqn
AReg left 9-40am combat with EA **MIA(2Lt JV Wischer Aust. **WIA POW**/2Lt AA Baerlein **POW**) Wolff23 [?"BE" claim combat OPPY-GAVRELLE 10-20am Ltn K Wolff Ja11]

A2896   BE2e   16Sqn
AOb left 5-05am mg hit fuel tank 6am ftl cr wr(/2Lt AC Perryman **inj)

A2944   BE2e   16Sqn
AP? THELUS shot down by British shells(Maj McMurty **KIA/Lt Mason **KIA**) left 10-05am

A993.A6   Sopwith Strutter 43Sqn
LP LENS-NEUVIREUIL ftl RONCY **MIA(2Lt CM Reece **POW**/2AM A Moult **WIA**? **POW**) a'c captured

7165   BE2e   52Sqn
+*P combat with HA chased down R.19.c.5.5. dam OK(2Lt WD Thom/2Lt MH Armstrong)a'c shelled

29th April

The weather improved, and the fighting became intense.

BE2d   7Sqn
** shot up(2Lt JH Hayward **WIA**/)

6768   BE2e   12Sqn
CP left 6-10am mg ftl cr wr(Lt NH Mackrow **WIA/Lt JM Musson **WIA**) Third Army front ["BE" claim combat LE PAVE 6-45am Ltn F Kempf Ja2]

7092   BE2e   12Sqn
AOb combat shot down **MIA(Lt CJ? Pile **DoW** 1.5.17/ Lt JH Westlake **DoW**:7.5.17) initials EJ?, left 4-58pm

A2738   BE2e   12Sqn
AOb left 4-45pm shot up(2Lt DE Davies **KIA/Lt GH Rathbone **KIA**) ["BE"combat sROEUX 6-25pm Rittm M Fr vRichthofen Ja11] ["BE" claim combat neMONCHY 6-25pm Ltn L Fr vRichthofen Ja11:Lothar shared with Manfred, as the "other" 12Sqn BE2 lost that day, 7092, came down WoL?]

A technical point: the serial of this machine is given on the original RFC Casualty Report as 2738, and has been given as this in subsequent research. It is, however, in a range of serials where there is some likelihood it should have an "A" prefix. It is the author's opinion that this entry, as well a later one (A2814), should be prefixed by "A". 2738 was not a BE2e but a BE2c, and was known to be with 36HD Squadron at Seaton Carew in November 1916.

Jasta 11 attacked these 12 Squadron BE2es in the evening after they had already successfully fought and shot down the FE2bs of 18 Squadron noted below. Some Triplanes of 8 (Naval) Squadron tried to intervene in the evening fight,

and although there is some uncertainty about the exact identity of the claim, Richthofen probably shot down one of these, N5463, for his fourth individual victory of the day (see below).

4898   FE2b   18Sqn
Esc combat shot down over front Line cr **MIA(Sgt G Stead **KIA**/Cpl A Beebee **KIA**) left 2-20pm Fifth Army area, MvR50 ["Vickers" claim combat swINCHY 3-55pm Oblt M Fr vRichthofen Ja11]

A5466   FE2b   18Sqn
+*Phot combat with 4 red EAs ovMARQUION-BARELLE 10000' ~4pm shot up snd into cloud 3000' ftl FREMICOURT (2Lt RW Reid OK/2Lt RC Doughty **WIA**)observer got off only 1 shot before being wounded, chased down by EA but seen off

A5483   FE2b   18Sqn
Esc combat with EA over front line shot down(2Lt GH Dinsmore OK/2Lt GB Bate **KIA) left 2-20pm Fifth Army area, Wolff26 ["Vickers" claim combat sPRONVILLE 4pm Ltn K Wolff Ja11]

A6681   SPAD 7   19Sqn
OP LENS **MIA(Maj HD Harvey-Kelly DSO **DoW**) to LENS-FONTAINE-NOREUIL Wolff25 ["SPAD" claim combat SAILLY 11-10am Ltn K Wolff Ja11]

A6753   SPAD 7   19Sqn
OP LENS-FONTAINE-NOREUIL **MIA(Lt WN Hamilton **POW**)LvR Ja11 ["SPAD" claim combat IZEL 11-15am Ltn L Fr vRichthofen Ja11]

B1573   SPAD 7   19Sqn
OP LENS-FONTAINE-NOREUIL down EoL **MIA(2Lt R Applin **KIA**) ["SPAD" claim combat eLECLUSE 11-05am Rittm M Fr vRichthofen Ja11]

A19   FE2d   20Sqn
B combat with 20HAs after crossing Lines ftl EoL **MIA(Sgt S Attwater **POW**/2Lt JE Davies **POW**) left 4pm, Ja18 ["Vickers" claim combat nCOURTRAI 5-50pm Ltn E Wiessner Ja18]

A29   FE2d   20Sqn
B combat 7HA 6pm but ground fire ftl nwSANITARY WOOD(2Lt EO Perry **WIA/2AM TE Allum **WIA**) left 4pm, combat 6pm, burnt [?possible "FE" claim eZILLEBEKE Ltn Nolte Ja18]

A1956   FE2d   20Sqn
**B left 4pm AA hit dam OK(2Lt GC Heseltine/2Lt FJ Kydd)

A6391   FE2d   20Sqn
B combat with 20HAs 6pm ftl EoL(2Lt VLA Burns **POW/2Lt DL Houghton **POW**) left 4pm, Ja18 ["Vickers" claim combat nCOURTRAI pm Ltn P Strähle Ja18]["Vickers 6391" ftl with engine problems nCOURTRAI]

A6684   Nieuport 17   29Sqn
OP left 11-50am seen ldg EoL **MIA(Sgt G Humble **POW**) a'c captured

B1579   Nieuport 23   29Sqn
OP left 11-50am seen ldg EoL **MIA(Lt HB Milling **POW**)

A6739   Nieuport 17   40Sqn
OP left 6-45am down EoL **MIA(Lt JAG Brewis **KIA**)

A6745   Nieuport 17   40Sqn
OP left 6-20pm message:down EoL(Capt FL Barwell **KIA) ["EA" claim combat nwDOUAI 8pm OffSt E Nathanael Ja5]

             DH4   55Sqn
** (Lt CG Sturt **WIA**)

A6355   FE2d   57Sqn
LP combat with EA nrNOYELLES **MIA(2Lt FAW Handley **POW**/2Lt E Percival **POW**) left 9-10am LIEVIN-NOREUIL, seen on EA's tail 1000' ["FE" claim combat BARALLE 9-55am Untoff F Gille Ja12]

As the larger dogfight came into the ascendant, combats and casualties of the various squadrons became increasingly inter-linked; the events of the 29th were prime examples of this. Three SE5s on offensive patrol from 56 Squadron had been attacked by six Albatros fighters and, although the SE5s were surviving the engagement, the dogfight was spotted by a formation of five 57 Squadron FE2ds who came down to assist. It was at this time that the FE2d noted above was shot down. None of the SE5s were lost. It is understood that this German patrol then joined Jasta 11 in an attack on SPADs of 19 Squadron, some of which are also noted above. Finally, the 1 (Naval) Sopwith Triplanes noted below joined this fight.

N5425.16 **Sopwith Triplane   1 (Naval) Sqn**
**OP combat with EA[+ooc] 11-50am then engine ftl nrBETHUNE bad ground o't dam OK(FSLt HV Rowley) shared

N5437   Sopwith Triplane   1 (Naval) Sqn
**OP combat with EA[+ooc] CAGNICOURT 11-50am OK(FLt CB Ridley) shared

N5441   Sopwith Triplane   1 (Naval) Sqn
OP shot up engine ftl sBETHUNE 6-30pm(FSLt AP Heywood **WIA) left 5pm, thought landing had been made EoL so burnt a'c [Ja11?]

A6160   Sopwith Pup   3 (Naval) Sqn
** combat shot down nrELINCOURT **MIA**(FSLt SL Bennett **KIA**) ["Sopwith" claim combat ELINCOURT 10-30am Ltn K Schneider Ja5]

N3192.15 **Nieuport 17   6 (Naval) Sqn**
OP combat with EA[+]then shot down eHARCOURT **MIA(FSLt AHV Fletcher **WIA POW**) dived on by 12EA combat 1-15pm

N5463   Sopwith Triplane   8 (Naval) Sqn
"DORIS" ** combat with EA shot down nrCOURRIÈRES **MIA**(FSLt AE Cuzner **KIA**) MvR52

[?MvR gave "Nieuport" in combat report, but possible "Tripe" claim in Abschusse: combat BILLY-MONTIGNY, sHENIN-LIETARD 6-40pm Rittm M Fr vRichthofen Ja11]

Triplanes of 8 (Naval) Squadron attempted to come to the assisitance of the 12 Squadron BEs being attacked by Jasta 11 (see above).

30th April

The 30th of April witnessed a major development in German fighter tactics for it saw the combining of several units into one group, the predecessor of the so called "Richthofen Circus". It was intended that this group act as a massed fighter formation, moving bodily to different parts of the line in order to operate when and wherever it could be most effective. It made its first sweep from Douai in the morning and consisted of twenty fighters. The Allied parties they variously met included 57 Squadron FE2ds, escorted by 8 (Naval) Squadron Triplanes, some Bristol Fighters on reconnaissance, 56 Squadron SE5s, in which fighting the first SE5 was lost (see below), and then a patrol of eight 18 Squadron FE2bs, who also suffered casualties.

A2916   BE2e   9Sqn
**Phot MIA(2Lt RPC Freemantle KIA/2Lt P Sherman KIA) left 10am

A2949   BE2e   9Sqn
**Phot? MIA(2Lt D McTavish WIA POW/Capt AS Allen MC Can. KIA) left 5-40am

A2910   BE2e   13Sqn
**Phot combat shot down wr(2Lt WK Trollope DoW 3.5.17/2Lt A Bonner KIA) left 3-08pm XVII Corps front, Wolff29 [?possible combat wFRESNES 4-35pm Ltn K Wolff Ja11]

7060   BE2e   15Sqn
**AOb last WT 3-30pm MIA(Lt DJ Paris MC POW/2Lt AE Fereman POW) left 1-30pm Corps area

A2768   BE2e   16Sqn
**Phot FRESNES mg shot up dam OK(2Lt Bishop/2Lt Lytton)

A2851   BE2g   16Sqn
**Phot eVIMY combat with HA 8-30am brought down nARRAS wr OK(2Lt VF? Stewart/2Lt Boyle)

A2942   BE2g   16Sqn
**CP shot down in flames 300yd eVIMY 6-10am MIA(2Lt NA Lawrence KIA/2Lt GRY Stout KIA) left 5-40am ["BE" claim combat VIMY-WILLERVAL 6-15am Ltn L Fr vRichthofen Ja11]

6998   FE2b   18Sqn
**EscPhot combat ftl 22Wing A.L.G. cr dam(Sgt T Whiteman WIA/2AM JH Wynn DoW) very shot up, u'c collapsed on ldg cr (18Sq in combat BARALLE-

MARQUION area ~9-30am) [?possible "FE A" claim combat RIBECOURT 11am Ltn H Klein Ja4]

A5481   FE2b   18Sqn
**EscPhot combat with EA shot up fuel tank hit ftl nrMONCHY-AU-BOIS cr ldg wr OK(2Lt SH Bell/Lt DW McLeod)

B1562   SPAD 7   19Sqn
**OP LENS-FONTAINE blown up in air MIA(Capt DAL Davidson MC KIA)

           FE2d   20Sqn
** (2Lt HM Coombs WIA/)

A5143   FE2d   20Sqn
**B AA on return controls shot up ooc ftl EYKHOEK, nPOPERINGHE o't fire(Lt DY Hay inj/2AM EH Sayers inj)

B1601   Nieuport 17   29Sqn
**Esc left 4-50pm MIA(2Lt RH Upson POW) ["BE" claim combat CANTIN 5-50pm Vzfw C Menckhoff Ja3]

German two-seater aircraft were becoming increasingly active in battle, and one way this manifested itself was a surge in low flying machine-gun attacks on British front line trenches. They also used these close attacks to shoot up corps machines, several of which, it can be seen, were shot down. To counter this, fighters from 19, 29, and 60 Squadrons began carrying out low flying line patrols of their own. This brought them into constant contact with the enemy, and much fighting ensued.

A1080   Sopwith Strutter 45Sqn
**EscPhot shot up nrLILLIERS dam(2Lt WA Wright OK/2AM BG Perrott KIA) [?"EA" claim combat ARMENTIÈRES 9-05am OffSt M Müller Ja28]

A4866   SE5   56Sqn
**OP VITRY-VILLERS combat with EA seen shot down in flames cr nrVILLERS burnt MIA(Lt MA Kay KIA) [?combat eFRESNOY 9-05am OffSt E Nathanael Ja5]

NEMESIS SURVIVED

This was the first SE5 fighter casualty lost, as has been mentioned, in an encounter involving the first efforts of the Flying Circus. In a month which had been a true watershed in the course of the air war, the fighting on the morning of the 30th was an apotheosis. Here were the new tactics of increasingly massed flying, pursued by both sides in their own ways, now evolving almost daily. The appearance of yet another new and famous Allied aircraft in battle was also indicative of the direction matters were taking. The SE5 took its place alongside the other new British machines which had appeared this month — the Bristol Fighter and the DH4. The

operational use of the very effective Sopwith Triplane had also increased, and the Pup was flown into battle with utmost confidence. These would soon be joined by the most famous World War One fighter of all, the Sopwith Camel.

Callous as it may sound, the Allied losses of the last week of April were casualties with a purpose when contrasted with those at the start of the Arras campaign. At that time the RFC was being comprehensively outclassed, in fact they were close to being overwhelmed, so that casualties had been imposed on them by an almost rampant enemy air service. The high RFC losses nevertheless had a grim purpose — at all costs to sustain a fighting presence over the battlefield. By comparison, by the end of the month the technology was in place, and the organisational framework built, with which the initiative could be regained. Only the barest signs of these changes were in evidence in the present fighting, but in terms of the casualties the losses were the result of the fact that the fight was once more being taken to the enemy: the RFC and the RNAS had survived, and from these small beginnings they would re-emerge to wrestle back control. Through their worst month of the war they had maintained their offensive policy despite terrible odds: of the three hundred and nineteen air crew lost in April, two hundred and fifty-two had been taken prisoner or killed east of the lines.

A1966   FE2d   57Sqn
**LP seen combat with HAs nrDOUAI shot down wr OK(Lt CS Morice/Lt F Leathey) left 6am LIEVIN-NOREUIL, heavy combat but ok

A6352   FE2d   57Sqn
LP combat with many HAs DOUAI MIA(2Lt ED Jennings **POW/2Lt JR Lingard **POW**) left 6am LIEVIN-NOREUIL ["Vickers" claim combat IZEL 6-55am Ltn L Fr vRichthofen Ja11]

A6380   FE2d   57Sqn
LP combat shot up cr wr(Lt JH Ryan **DoW 2.5.17/2Lt B Soutten **WIA**) left 9am LIEVIN-NOREUIL

A6402   FE2d   57Sqn
LP seen in combat with many HAs nrDOUAI MIA(Lt PT Bowers **POW/2Lt ST Wills **POW**) left 6am LIEVIN-NOREUIL ["FE" claim combat IZEL 6-55am Oblt A Rt vTutschek Ja12]

These three FE2ds were the first early morning victims of the "Flying Circus", carrying out its first group operation.

N6175   Sopwith Pup   3 (Naval) Sqn
** shot down ROUMAUCOURT wCAMBRAI ~5-30pm **MIA**(FSLt JJ Malone DSO **KIA**) left 4-15pm ["Sopwith" claim combat ROUMAUCOURT 5-10pm Ltn P Billik Ja12]

Untraced casualty in France in April 1917

** (LtCol CEH Rathbone **POW**) escaped 10.17

May 1917

Early in May, the character of the air war changed as the tremendous exertions of the previous month's fighting began to take their toll. Richthofen himself took leave back to Germany on the 1st of May, and seemed to take some of the momentum of the German effort with him. Their tactics of attack with grouped Jastas continued however — the Germans after all still flew superb machines — and these larger fighting formations now contained many battle hardened and brilliant pilots. In Richthofen's absence, for instance, Jasta 11 could be lead into combat by his brother Lothar, as well as by Kurt Wolff, who already had between them nearly fifty victories.

In a wider perspective, the grouping of Jastas into fighting formations did have a contrary effect, for it concentrated fighting effort into a smaller area, so that whilst some British pilots found themselves facing a very formidable foe, the wider operations of the RFC once more found the skies opened up. This played into their hands, for it was irretrievably committed to expansive, offensive action, their very aim to secure possession of as much sky as possible. Finally, the effect of increased operational co-ordination within the RFC at this time can not be underestimated. From it would flow a measure of strength and security for those carrying out reconnaissance, bombing, and artillery work. By targeting when and where the enemy was likely to be most active, his impact was bound to be diminished.

1st May

A6668   Nieuport 17   1Sqn
** combat with 2Strs[+des] WARNETON 9-15am then combat with 2Str[+des] PLOEGSTEERT 10am shot up dam(Capt CJQ Brand **WIA**)hand, last of 7 victories with 1Sqn, achieved another 5 on home defence night fighter Camels

A6678   Nieuport 17   1Sqn
combat with EA shot up ftl ELVERDINGHE 12pm(Capt ED Atkinson **WIA) ["Nieu" claim combat ePOPERINGHE-WOESTEN 12pm Ltn K Schaefer Ja28] Atkinson was 10 victory ace, mostly on SE5as

A9997   A.W.FK8   2Sqn
AReg combat fuel tank hit shot down in flames & exploded wr(Lt WP Eastwood OK/2Lt RB Davies **KIA) left 5-30am nARRAS, a'c burnt out

RE8   6Sqn
** shot up(Capt SP Smith **WIA**/)

A2850   BE2e   8Sqn
AOb shell hit 7-15pm cr wr(2Lt EP Morris **KIA/Lt VR
Pfrimmer **KIA**) left 5-25pm WANCOURT

4968   FE2b   18Sqn
NB Fourth Army **MIA(2Lt EWA Hunt **KIA**/2Lt GB
Miller **KIA**) left 9-30pm

    FE2b   25Sqn
** combat?(/Sgt L Emsden **WIA**)hand

A782   FE2b   25Sqn
**LPB combat with 4HA ftl cr ARRAS Racecourse
6-15pm(2Lt B King OK/Sgt HG Taylor **WIA**) left
4-50pm

A815   FE2c   25Sqn
**B EPUERCHIN 9EA shot down in flames on return
ovROUVROY 6pm **MIA**(Lt GS French **WIA POW**/Lt
GP Harding MC **POW**) later escaped, Wolff28 ["FE"
claim combat sBOIS BERNARD 6pm Ltn K Wolff Ja11]
["Vickers" claim combat wACHEVILLE? 6pm Ltn L Fr
vRichthofen Ja11]

    Martinsyde G100   27Sqn
B EPINOY A'dr? (2Lt SJ Stewart **WIA)

6471   FE8   41Sqn
**OP left 3-02pm combat with 4EAs shot down
ABEELE(2Lt ECHR Nicholls **WIA**)

A8252   Sopwith Strutter   43Sqn
Phot DOUAI ftl **MIA(Lt CR O'Brien **POW**/2Lt EL
Edwards **POW**) left 10-55am, a'c captured ["Sopwith"
claim combat HENIN LIETARD Ltn Riegel/Vzfw
Totsch FAbA211]

N6186   Sopwith Pup   3 (Naval) Sqn
*EscRec(FEs) CAUDRY shot down ftl cr ECOURT-ST-
QUENTIN **MIA**(FSLt AS Mather **POW**) a'c captured,
left 9-20am (11-30am?) ["Sopwith" claim combat
nrCANTAING 10-40am Oblt A Rt vTutschek Ja12]

N5434   Sopwith Triplane   8 (Naval) Sqn
**P combat with 7Albatros shot down ooc n.m.l. VIMY
RIDGE wr(FSLt DM Shields **WIA**) hid in shell hole, a'c
unsalvable [?"Tripe" claim combat ROUVROY 9-20am
Ltn K vDöring Ja4]

N5474   Sopwith Triplane   8 (Naval) Sqn
"GWEN" **OP left 8-40am shot down sSECLIN EoL
MIA(FSLt ED Roach **KIA**) left 8-40am, Wolff28
["Tripe" claim combat sSECLIN 9-50am Ltn K Wolff
Ja11]

2nd May

6281   BE2e   12Sqn
**AOb shot up ftl WoL cr wr shaken(Lt JE Turner/Lt
PS Laughton) left 10-30am [?"BE" claim combat
nrPLOEGSTEERT WOOD but 3-15pm? OffSt M
Müller Ja28]

6429   FE8   41Sqn
**P combat engine vibrat ftl Sh36.N.7.a. dam OK(2Lt
AF Barker) left 7-55am ARMENTIÈRES

A3345   Bristol F2a   48Sqn
**OP combat with AlbatrosDIIIs[+] shot up(2Lt LG
Harrison **WIA**/2Lt HLE Richards **WIA**)

A3347   Bristol F2a   48Sqn
+* combat with AlbatrosDIIIs[+flames+ooc]
BIACHE-VITRY 7-45pm OK(Lt OFJ Scholte/2AM FW
Dame)

A3348   Bristol F2a   48Sqn
+* combat with AlbatrosDIIIs[++ooc+des]
BREBIÈRES-BIACHE btwn 7-30pm & 7-40pm OK(2Lt
WOB Winkler/2Lt ES Moore)

B1539   Nieuport 17   60Sqn
+* combat with AlbatrosDIII[+des] VITRY-
BELONNE 4-30pm OK(Lt SB Horn)

In the evening there was a big air fight east of
Arras, involving some forty aircraft, but there were
no British casualties.

3rd May

The British infantry attack recommenced at 3-45
am on the 3rd, and extended for 16 miles along the
fronts of the First, Third, and Fifth Armies. V
Brigade RFC was in support of the Fifth Army. It
comprised the 15th (Army) Wing (Nos. 3, 4, and
15 Squadrons) and the 22nd (Army) Wing (Nos.
18, 23, 32, and 3 (Naval) Squadrons). Objectives
were typically optimistic and demanding, and little
real advance was achieved. The German Army was
operating a new counter-attack system known as
"elastic defence", whereby a relatively light front
line could be quickly reinforced at critical places by
troops specifically held back for the purpose. In this
way any real advances being made by the attacking
British were quickly stifled. The British were aware
of these tactics, and one of the new roles of the air
arm in this fighting was to fly low patrols watching
for these counter-attacks, reporting any developments to the artillery. In the endemic fog of such
warfare, with its constant readjustment of
positions, this task was extremely difficult.

    Morane P   3Sqn
CP rifle fire(/Lt CT Cleaver MC **WIA)

A6698   Morane P   3Sqn
**CP rifle & shell dam ftl A.L.G. wr ldg(Lt Barrington/
Lt Jones) left 7-45am, fuselage broke in two on ldg

    BE2e   15Sqn
AP rifle fire(/Lt FE Elliot **WIA)

A6390   FE2d   20Sqn
**B combat after bombing ftl VLAMERTINGHE
wr(2Lt RG Dalziel **WIA**/Lt LG Fauvel **WIA**) left 4-06pm

7622   FE8   41Sqn
**OP seen start combat with EA nrHOUTHULST
engine fail ftl EoL **MIA**(2Lt A Fraser **WIA POW**) left

4-07pm LICHTERVELDE [?"Vickers" claim combat ovHOUTHULST WOOD pm Ltn E Wiessner Ja18]

A4873   FE8   41Sqn
OP combat with EA seen going down in spin e HOUTHULST WOOD **MIA(Capt SF Browning **KIA**) left 4-03pm LICHTERVELDE [?"Vickers" claim combat DREIBANK, nLILLE pm OffSt W Göttsch Ja8]

          Sopwith Pup   66Sqn
** (2Lt AJ Lucas **WIA**)leg

4th May

The weather continued to improve, and with it came an increased presence of German fighters.

          BE2e   15Sqn
CP ground mg fire(Sgt WG Bennett **WIA/)leg

          RE8   53Sqn
** AA(/Lt JR Geddes **WIA**)head

A2157   DH4   55Sqn
PhotRec VALENCIENNES shot up ftl dam(Lt BJ Silly MC DFC OK/Lt RK Abram **WIA)leg, attacked by a single EA?, NB: Silly's DFC awarded later

          RE8   59Sqn
** AA(Lt EG Leake **WIA**/)slight

          Sopwith Pup   66Sqn
OP (Lt JT Collier **WIA)burn

A1001   Sopwith Strutter 70Sqn
Rec combat with EA engine ftl ok EoL nwTOURNAI **MIA(2Lt VH Adams **POW DoW** 5.5.17/2Lt IL Pinson **DoW**)burnt a'c, left 10-25am, crew murdered ["Sopwith" claim combat nLILLE 12-17pm Vzfw W Göttsch Ja8]

A3431   Sopwith Strutter 70Sqn
Rec TOURNAI combat with HA AA ftl BAILLEUL WoL(Lt DG Allen OK/Lt BL Franklin **KIA) left 10-25am

Nine Strutters of 70 Squadron were conducting an unescorted reconnaissance to photograph new aerodromes around Tournai. Some of their work was accomplished, but before long they were forced to withdraw, and were required to fight all the way back to the lines.

N6207   Sopwith Pup   3 (Naval) Sqn
"BLACK BESS" **OP seen ECOURT-ST-QUENTIN 7-40pm shot down FRESNES-VITRY **MIA**(FSLt HS Murton **POW**) left 6pm, Ja12 ["Sopwith" claim combat FRESNES-VITRY 7-30pm Oblt A Rt vTutschek Ja12]

5th May

Many RFC units in the Arras sector were given a nominal rest on the 5th. No bombing or recon-naissance was ordered. In effect, the battle of Arras was ending, although over the next two weeks significant fighting was still to break out on

occasions. General air fighting continued to accompany this, and to be evident elsewhere, notably in Flanders where activity was increasing. Attention was shifting to the south, for the way was now clearing for the British to mount their intended offensive.

7228   BE2g   10Sqn
AOb dhAA 7-15am 7000' cr(Capt HC Lomer **KIA/Lt CT Bruce **DoW**) left 5am

               BE2e   15Sqn
CP ground mg fire(Lt TG Poland **WIA/)leg

A1942   FE2d   20Sqn
B **MIA(2Lt LG Bacon **WIA POW**/2AM G Worthing **KIA**) ["Vickers" claim combat SCHAAP-BAILIE OffSt W Göttsch Ja8]

A5147   FE2d   20Sqn
**OP combat with EA on return ftl nrBAILLEUL OK(2Lt GC Heseltine/2Lt FJ Kydd) left 4-35pm [?"FE" claim combat nrST ELOI Ltn E Wiessner Ja18] [?"FE" claim combat ZILLEBEKE SEE Vzfw Flemmig Ja18]

B1525   SPAD 7   23Sqn
KBP BOURLON WOOD, seen by escort crossing Lines ok nBAPAUME-CAMBRAI Rd going east **MIA(2Lt CC Cheatle **KIA**) left 11-16am

A4853   SE5   56Sqn
+* combat with AlbatrosD[+ooc] MONTIGNY btwn 6-45pm & 7-45pm OK(Lt CA Lewis) Lewis' first of 8 victories in this a'c

6th May

A9999   A.W.FK8   2Sqn
AOb GIVENCHY combat with 5HAs 3-15pm, in flames crew fell out **MIA(2Lt G Wood **KIA**/2Lt JCG Coupland **KIA**) left 12-15pm ["Bristol" claim combat seGIVENCHY 9-50am Ltn L Fr vRichthofen Ja11]

A3469   RE8   16Sqn
**EscPhot left 8-50am AVION combat with HA ~9-55am dam OK(2Lt Carter/2Lt Alder) repairable

A4596   RE8   16Sqn
Phot combat with EA 10am ftl FARBUS(2Lt AC Sanderson **WIA/Lt Lytton OK) left 8-45am, a'c shelled

A2627   DH2   32Sqn
**LP shell hit low ftl o't ldg A.L.G. dam OK(Lt TA Cooch)

B1522   Nieuport 17   56Sqn
+* combat with AlbatrosDIII[+cr,destr] SANCOURT 7-30pm OK(Capt A Ball)

This was Albert Ball's forty-fourth and last victory. He shot down Vzfw Jager of Jagdstaffel 20.

B1514.A4 Nieuport 23   60Sqn
EscPhot combat with EA ftl BOURLON WOOD **MIA(2Lt CW McKissock **POW**) a'c captured, left

4-50pm, Ja5 ["Nieu" claim combat nBOURLON 5-40pm OffSt E Nathanael Ja5]

B1597   Nieuport 17   60Sqn
EscPhot combat ECOURT ST QUENTIN shot up ftl **MIA(2Lt GD Hunter **WIA POW**) left 4-50pm ["Sopwith" claim combat nECOURT ST QUENTIN 5-45pm Ltn K Schneider Ja5]

A5480   FE2b   100Sqn
SpNB left 10-10pm **MIA(Lt TG Holmes **KIA**/2AM AW Ekins **KIA**)

7th May

A6738   Nieuport 17   1Sqn
**OP left 10-32am COURTRAI engine shot up ftl VOORMEZELE OK(Lt L Drummond)a'c shelled ["Nieu" claim combat eYPRES 11am Ltn A Hanko Ja28]

A2801   BE2e   7Sqn
Phot AA nST QUENTIN shot down 2-15pm **MIA(2Lt GW Jackson **KIA**/Lt CV Gaulter **KIA**) left 1-10pm [?possible "BE" claim combat 2-40pm nST QUENTIN Ltn FO Bernert Ja6]

7215   BE2g   12Sqn
**Phot combat ovHAMBLAIN-LES-PRES shot up dam OK(Lt Mann/Lt Webster) left 2-10pm, a'c repaired

4595   BE2c   13Sqn
Phot combat with HA shot down wr(2Lt IR Owen **DoW/2AM R Hickling **DoW**) left 10-40am XVII Corps front [?"BE" claim combat FRESNOY 11-45am Ltn K Allmenröder Ja11]

A5487   FE2b   18Sqn
EscPhot left 9am Fifth Army area **MIA(2Lt MM Kaizer **POW**/Sgt F Russell **POW**) [?possible "FE" claim combat wCAMBRAI 10-40am Ltn Reisen Ja5]

A5149   FE2d   20Sqn
B shot down EoL ftl Ja18 a'dr(Lt AW Martin **POW/ Pte WC Blake **POW**) a'c captured ["FE" claim combat Ja18 a'dr MENIN 11am Ltn W vBülow Ja18][?"FE" claim combat BOESINGHE 11-15am OffSt M Müller Ja28]

A6609   Nieuport 17   29Sqn
P? left 3-45pm combat with EA brought down ooc nrFRESNES **MIA(2Lt CS Gaskain **KIA**) [?"Nieu" claim combat GAVRELLE, wBIACHES 5-30pm Ltn L Fr vRichthofen Ja11]

A6733   Nieuport 17   40Sqn
+*SpM attacked KB[+destr] QUIERRY LA MOTTE 9-35am OK(Lt EC Mannock)

This was the first of sixty-one confirmed victories by the great British ace "Mick" Mannock.

B1541   Nieuport 17   40Sqn
**SpM(KB) left 8-58am fuel tank shot up ftl cr CAMBLAIN L'ABBÉ 9-30am OK(2Lt HR Parry)

B1631   Nieuport 17   40Sqn
SpM(KB) left 8-58am combat FRESNES **MIA(Capt

WE Nixon **KIA**)

A patrol of 40 Squadron attacked kite balloons for a second time in a week, using a very low, ground-hugging approach to come upon their targets unobserved. A formation of Triplanes also flew high up to distract attention. Seven balloons were claimed destroyed, but Nixon was lost, and many of the others were shot up.

A1075   Sopwith Strutter 45Sqn
**P YPRES AA hit tail fell ooc cr nrOUDERDOM wr OK(Lt H Forrest/Gnr.1AM FARC Lambert) left 9-05am

A4850   SE5   56Sqn
P left 5-30pm combat with EA **MIA(Capt A Ball VC DSO MC **KIA**) [?"Tripe" claim combat ANNOUEULLIN 7-30pm Ltn L Fr vRichthofen Ja11]

A4856   SE5   56Sqn
P left 5-30pm ARRAS-CAMBRAI-DOUAI shot up nrGOUZ(Lt JO Leach MC **WIA)leg hospital

A4867   SE5   56Sqn
P left 5-30pm shot down **MIA(Lt RM Chaworth-Musters **KIA**) [?possible "Sopwith" claim combat nrLECLUSE 6-25pm Ltn W Voss Ja2] [?possible "English EA" claim combat nrDOUAI Untoff Orth SchSt4]

A8900   SE5   56Sqn
P combat with AlbatrosDIIIs[+ooc] nCAMBRAI btwn 6-30pm & 7-45pm shot up(Capt H Meintjes **WIA)

THE DEATH OF ALBERT BALL

In this combat, in the evening of the 7th of May, Albert Ball was killed. The success of the men of Jasta 11 at Douai had drawn such attention upon the unit that the Allies had determined to treat its operations as a special case. To this end in early May the RFC established regular morning and evening offensive patrols into the area in order to attempt to stifle its activities. It was on one of these patrols that eleven SE5s from 56 Squadron, including Ball in A4850, set off to find and engage the Germans. There was mist and cloud, and the SE5s lost formation on the outward journey. As expected, they were met by Albatros fighters of Jasta 11, and furious fighting broke out, passing in and out of the cloud cover. Ball was last seen chasing a red Albatros into a cloud, and whilst most believe this was Lothar von Richthofen, there is less certainty about Lothar's claim that he subsequently shot Ball down. In the first place, his claim was for a Triplane. The final fate of Albert Ball is uncertain: he might have been the victim of ground fire. What is certain is that the air war lost one of its greatest fighter pilots, for he blended exceptional flying skill with unstinting bravery and determination. At his best, an enemy had no counter for him.

A3426   RE8   59Sqn
LP nrFICHEUX combat ftl(Capt WW Leete **WIA/Lt
BA Wilson **WIA**) crew in hospital ["Sopwith" claim
combat nrTILLOY 2pm Vzfw C Menckhoff Ja3]

4989   FE2b   100Sqn
**SpB left 12-50am shelled on return 2-40am dam(2Lt
HEK Eccles **WIA**/)

9th May

A2746   BE2e   8Sqn
**AOb left 4pm combat with EA VIS EN ARTOIS-
GUEMAPPE ~5pm dam OK(2Lt JW Brown/Lt A
Hollingworth)

A4195   RE8   16Sqn
**AOb GIVENCHY combat, engine hit ftl cr(Sgt PWE
Millington **inj**/Lt WC Rowe **inj**) left 4pm

         FE2d   20Sqn
Phot (/2Lt HR Wilkinson **WIA)head

A6429   FE2d   20Sqn
**B AA shot down VLAMERTINGHE ftl(2Lt EJ Smart
OK/2Lt HG Neville **DoW** 10.5.17) left 11-53am YPRES

4991   FE2b   22Sqn
Phot combat with 3EAs ftl EoL swLESDAIN **MIA(2Lt
CAM Furlonger **POW**/2Lt CW Lane **POW**) left 2pm,
earlier combat with 7EAs, Voss27 ["FE" claim combat
LE BOSQUET 3-50pm Ltn W Voss Ja2]

A887   Sopwith Strutter   43Sqn
Phot seen WINGLES 2-15pm **MIA(2Lt FD Woolliams
POW/Lt JBBdeM Harvey **POW**) left 1pm BOIS-
HUGO-GAVRELLE

         Sopwith Strutter   45Sqn
P (/Lt J Senior **DoW)

7803   Sopwith Strutter   45Sqn
OP ARMENT-LA BASSÉE **MIA(Lt WL Mills **KIA**/
2AM JW Loughlin **WIA POW**) left 3-20pm [?Sopwith"
claim combat ovWARNETON but 6pm Ltn K Schaefer
Ja28]

A8269   Sopwith Strutter   45Sqn
+* combat with AlbatrosDIII[+des] FOURNES
OK(2Lt WA Wright/2Lt ET Caulfield-Kelly)

A7108   Bristol F2b   48Sqn
+* combat with AlbatrosDIII[+++ooc] eVITRY btwn
5-25pm & 5-30pm OK(Lt FP Holliday/Capt AHW Wall)
had also shared in LVGC in morning; other victories for
this crew in A7108

A7110   Bristol F2b   48Sqn
**OP combat with AlbatrosDIII[+des] neFAMPOUX
5-25pm shot down(2Lt WT Price **WIA**/Lt CG Claye
WIA) left 4-25pm for eARRAS, LvR["F2b" claim
combat ROEUX-GAVRELLE Road 5-30pm Ltn L Fr
vRichthofen Ja11]

This fighting involved the first losses in combat to
air crew of a Bristol Fighter F2b, the improved
version of the relatively short lived F2a.

7209   BE2e   52Sqn
**AOb combat with EA HAVRINCOURT shot down
WoL wr(Lt RH Coles **KIA**/2Lt JC Day **KIA**) left
10-55am for Lines, Voss26 ["BE" claim combat
nrHAVRINCOURT 1pm Ltn W Voss Ja2]

A6174.I   Sopwith Pup   54Sqn
**Esc combat chased down in flat spin ftl LESDAIN but
ldg ok **MIA**(2Lt GCT Hadrill **POW**) left 2-23pm, a'c
captured, Voss28 ["Sopwith" claim combat LESDAIN
3-45pm Ltn W Voss Ja2]

A7420   DH4   55Sqn
Rec shot up ftl ~2-15pm(2Lt F McQuistan **WIA/AM
FG Ellis OK)slight

A994.B4   Sopwith Strutter   70Sqn
Rec **MIA(2Lt WJ Gayner **KIA**/2AM GD Breakfield
KIA) left 12-50pm CAUDRY-NEUVILLY [?possible
"Sopwith" claim combat ST HILAIRE LES CAMBRAI
Vzfw Dilcher Ja5]

N5458   Sopwith Triplane   8 (Naval) Sqn
OP combat shot up(FSLt LEB Wimbush **WIA)leg
["Tripe" claim combat nrFARBUS 7-50am Vzf C
Menckhoff Ja3]

10th May

7703   FE2b   22Sqn
(Maj LW Learmount **WIA/)

A800   FE2b   22Sqn
PhotRec (/2AM AG Whitehouse MM **WIA)slight

A2581   DH2   24Sqn
**Esc combat VILLERS-GUISLAIN shot down 4000yd
eEPEHY(Lt HC Cutler **KIA**) left 1-30pm [unconfirmed
"Sitterrumpf" claim ftl after combat VILLERS
GUISLAIN 2-45pm Ltn K Schneider Ja5]

A3349   Bristol F2b   48Sqn
**OP left 4-05pm eARRAS radiator shot up ftl(2Lt GE
Hawksley **WIA**/2Lt L Speller **WIA**)

A668   Sopwith Pup   54Sqn
**OP shot up ftl wing buckled 50' cr o't shell hole Sh57C
w.30 (Capt RGH Pixley **inj**)

A2150   DH4   55Sqn
**PhotRec NEUVILLY shot up dam ldg a'dr ok OK(Lt
CA? Stevens/Lt FL Oliver)

A7413   DH4   55Sqn
**Phot shelled GOUZEAUCOURT(Capt N Senior
WIA/Cpl PH Holland **KIA**) shell fire [?"EA" claim
neGOUZEAUCOURT 2-10pm Ltn W Blume Ja26]

A7416   DH4   55Sqn
**Phot AA shot down in flames ovLE CATEAU cr
MIA(2Lt BW Pitt **KIA**/2Lt JS Holroyde **KIA**) left
12-55pm CAUDRY-NEUVILLY [?"EA" claim combat
nLE CATEAU, sSOLESMES 2pm Vzfw F Krebs Ja6]

A7419   DH4   55Sqn
Phot dhAA broke up ovLE CATEAU **MIA(2Lt T

Webb **KIA**/1AM W Bond **KIA**) left 12-55pm CAUDRY-NEUVILLY

A6178   Sopwith Pup   66Sqn
OP DOUAI-BREBIÈRES **MIA(Lt TH Wickett **WIA** POW**) [?possible "Sopwith" claim combat VITRY 6-40am Ltn K Allmenröder Ja11][?possible unconfirmed "Sopwith" claim combat MONCHY 12-20pm Oblt A Rt vTutschek Ja12]

A7303   Sopwith Pup   66Sqn
OP DOUAI-BREBIÈRES down EoL **MIA(2Lt DJ Sheehan **KIA**) ["Sopwith" claim combat SAILLY-VITRY 6-50am Ltn L Fr vRichthofen Ja11]

A8174   Sopwith Strutter 70Sqn
Rec combat ftl MORLANCOURT(Capt RS Lucy OK/2Lt N Butterworth **KIA) left 12-50pm CAUDRY-NEUVILLY

N6185.A Sopwith Pup   4 (Naval) Sqn
"*ANZAC*" **EscB left pm shot down nrZEEBRUGGE **MIA**(FLt CJ Moir **KIA**)

11th May

For the first time, British aircraft were used to directly assist attacking troops by carrying out low machine-gun strafing of the enemy. FE2bs of 11 Squadron, and the Nieuports of 60 Squadron did this work, in support of the Third Army in their attack on positions on the Scarpe River. The aircraft preceded the infantry attack and then operated beyond the creeping barrage in order to disrupt defensive preparations. The flyers followed up with subsequent strafing during the battle, all of which contributed to the success of the attack.

6276   BE2e   7Sqn
AP AA ovPONTRU ooc fire at 1000' burnt(2Lt AW Mason **KIA/Lt WE Davies **KIA**) left 6-25am VERMAND, observer jumped from 600'

B1533   SPAD 7   23Sqn
**OP left 5-14pm combat with HA dam returned a'dr ok OK(Sgt CE Evans)

A6787   Nieuport 23   29Sqn
+* combat with AlbatrosDIII[+destr] SAILLY 10-15am OK(Lt AS Shepherd DSO Aust.) first of 10 victories, also see B1504 on 20.7.17

A3347   Bristol F2b   48Sqn
OP left 3-05pm eARRAS(/2Lt FM Magenais **WIA)

A7101   Bristol F2b   48Sqn
OP eARRAS shot down in flames nrFRESNES **MIA(Capt AT Cull **KIA**/1AM A Trusson **KIA**) left 3pm [?"Bristol" claim combat nOPPY 4-15pm Ltn K Allmenröder Ja11]

A7104   Bristol F2b   48Sqn
+* combat with AlbatrosDIII[+ooc] BIACHE-DURY 12-45pm(Capt JHT Letts **WIA**?/2Lt J Jameson OK)slight?, shared

A7111   Bristol F2b   48Sqn
OP shot down GAVRELLE **MIA(2Lt WOB Winkler POW **KIA**/2Lt ES Moore **POW**) left 3pm eARRAS, Winkler given as KIA in Roll of Honour, but repat? ["Bristol" claim IZEL 4-10pm combat Ltn L Fr vRichthofen Ja11]

A6168   Sopwith Pup   54Sqn
+* combat with 2Str[+des] WALINCOURT 6-40pm then AlbatrosDIII[+des] BEAUREVOIR OK(Capt WV Strugnell)

A7307   Sopwith Pup   54Sqn
**P ST QUENTIN AA shot up dam, repairable OK(Lt FJ Morse)

A7308   Sopwith Pup   54Sqn
OP combat with 3HA spun down in flames cr **MIA(2Lt HC Duxbury **KIA**) left 7am Fourth Army front ["Sopwith" claim combat sLESDAIN 8-35am Vzfw F Krebs Ja6][?poss"Sopwith" claim combat nrHAGNECOURT? Vzfw Reissinger Ja12]

A3472   RE8   59Sqn
Phot combat with EA shot up dam returned a'dr ok(Capt FD Pemberton **WIA/Lt TW McConkey **WIA**)hospital

N6162?   Sopwith Pup   3 (Naval) Sqn
this a'c? ** combat(FSLt HS Broad **WIA**)face

N6464.D Sopwith Pup   3 (Naval) Sqn
Esc seen BOURLON shot down ftl **MIA(FSLt J Bampfylde-Daniel **WIA POW**) a'c captured Ja12 left 3-15pm [?possible "Sopwith" combat CROISILLES 2-40pm? Oblt A Rt vTutschek Ja12]

N3189   Nieuport 17   6 (Naval) Sqn
OP combat with 4HA shot down forced to dive into n.m.l. VILLERS OUTREAUX WoL o't wr(FSLt OJ Gagnier **inj) injured in crash ["Nieuport" claim combat neHARGICOURT 7-45pm Ltn K Küppers Ja6]

12th May

RE8   16Sqn
AOb (/Lt E Adler **WIA)

B1560   SPAD 7   19Sqn
OP CROISILLES-BAILLEUL **MIA(Capt WD Bransby-Williams MC **KIA**) left 6-23am [?possible "SPAD" claim combat nrIZEL but time? Ltn P Billik Ja12]

A23   FE2d   20Sqn
B left 6-34am shot down ftl **MIA(2Lt H Kirby **POW**/Sgt TE Wait **POW**) a'c captured

A1935   FE2d   20Sqn
**B combat with HA shot up dam returned a'dr(2Lt FF Babbage/Sgt B Aldred)

B1544   Nieuport 17   29Sqn
OP left 6am **MIA(2Lt CR Sloan **KIA**) [?"Nieuport" claim combat INCHY 7am Untoff F Gille Ja12]

A3243   **RE8**   **53Sqn**
Phot AA? shot down nrMESSINES **MIA(2Lt F Adams
KIA/2Lt OR Kelly **KIA**) left 1-45pm, AA say down by
AA, Müller10 ["EA" claim combat HOLLEBEKE,
sYPRES 2-25pm Ltn M Müller Ja28]

A4860   **SE5**   **56Sqn**
**OP eLA BASSÉE-VIMY AA hit seen in spin & break
up down ovLENS **MIA**(Lt AJ Jessop **KIA**) left 6-30pm

A664   **Sopwith Pup**   **66Sqn**
OP BOIRY-LENS down EoL shot down? **MIA(Lt JR
Robertson **KIA**) ["Sopwith" claim combat BARALLE-
MARQUION 9-50am Oblt A Rt vTutschek Ja12]

N5154   **Sopwith Strutter**   **2 (Naval) Sqn**
"FIREFLY" ** engine failed ftl CADZAND but ldg ok?
MIA(FSLt HV Tapscott **INT**/GL GA Richardson **INT**)
on standby Wireless Duty, interned Holland

This machine had been on standby wireless duty
for ranging the attack on the lock gates at
Zeebrugge. This operation hoped to seal the
important German shipping harbour by shelling
the entrance, but to do this required extremely
accurate firing from a great distance. It was
calculated that firing would need to be sustained
for almost 90 minutes. There was a delay in
bringing up one of the ships, and this was probably
fatal for both the operation as well as the crew
above. They waited too long before turning for
home and were forced to come down. Other
Sopwiths involved were delayed, so that despite
many shells being aimed at the target none actually
hit it, or else they failed to explode.

N5456   **Sopwith Triplane**   **10 (Naval) Sqn**
**FleetP AA hit ovZEEBRUGGE, cr sea
BLANKENBERGHE **MIA**(FSLt MWW Eppstein **KIA**)
seen 8m off shore [?"Sopwith" claim sea off OSTENDE
Oblt T Osterkamp MFJaI][other MFJaI pilots claim
similar: Ltn Saschenberg & Ltn Heinrich]

13th May

7130   **BE2e**   **13Sqn**
**AOb combat with HA brought down B.16.D. OK(2Lt
F Thompson/Lt ACC Rawlins) left 9am XVII Corps
front, a'c shelled & unsalvable ["BE" claim combat
ARLEUX Wood, wFRESNOY 10-35am Ltn L Fr
vRichthofen Ja11]

A4245   **RE8**   **16Sqn**
**AOb ARLEUX combat with EA shot down ooc
10-40am wr(2Lt VF Stewart **KIA**/2Lt JG Troup **KIA**)
left 10am ["BE" claim nrrARLEUX 10-45am Ltn K
Allmenröder Ja11]

A6354   **FE2d**   **20Sqn**
+* combat with 2Str[+des] MENIN 11am OK(Lt AN
Solly/2AM C Beminster)

A6443   **FE2d**   **20Sqn**
**B combat with several HAs ftl EVERDINGHE cr dam
OK(Lt AC Lee/Pte C Lloyd) left 9-34am

A6445   **FE2d**   **20Sqn**
**B combat with several EAs ftl BRANDHOEK cr(2Lt
GC Heseltine **WIA**/2Lt LG Fauvel OK)Ja18, left 9-34am
["FE" claim combat POLYGON WOOD Ltn P Strähle
Ja18]

A6665   **Nieuport 17**   **29Sqn**
OP left 7-05pm combat with EA engine hit ftl **MIA(Sgt
WH Dunn **POW**) ["Nieuport" claim combat FRESNES
8-20pm Ltn Hintsch Ja11]

B1567   **Nieuport 23**   **29Sqn**
OP left 7-05pm combat with 3EAs ftl **MIA(2Lt AM
Sutherland **POW**) [?"Sopwith" claim combat
OSTRICOURT 8-25pm Ltn K Allmenröder Ja11]

B1640   **Nieuport 17**   **40Sqn**
OP left 6-28am **MIA(Lt AB Raymond **POW**)

14th May

2555   **BE2e**   **8Sqn**
AOb combat with HA shot down 0.25.c.5.7. **MIA(Lt
JW Brown **KIA**/Lt EJ McCormick **KIA**) left 8-40am
[?"BE" claim combat GUEMAPPE 10-30am Ltn K
Allmenröder Ja11]

A2622   **DH2**   **32Sqn**
**LP:KBP combat with EA, in flames 20' cr
eLAGNICOURT **MIA**(Capt WGS Curphey MC **POW**
DoW 15.5.17) ["FE 1Str" claim combat VIS EN
ARTOIS, nSEVERIN FERME 10-15am Hpt F Walz
Ja2] Curphey had claimed 6 victories

A4800   **DH2**   **32Sqn**
**LP PRONVILLE-MARQUION combat with
AlbatrosC[+des] seBARALLE 10-30am badly shot up
dam OK(2Lt CC Tayler) Tayler's 2nd claim of an
eventual 10

A6158.WB   **Sopwith Pup**   **3 (Naval) Sqn**
**OP seen ECOURT ST QUENTIN 11-30am, prop
destroyed, shot down **MIA**(FSLt WR Walker **POW**) left
10-20am, left 1pm?, Ja33, a'c captured ["Sopwith" claim
combats ESTRÉES 12-25pm Oblt H Lorenz Ja33]

15th May

               BE2e   **15Sqn**
CP ground mg fire(2Lt JH deConway **WIA/)

A6446   **FE2d**   **20Sqn**
P shot down nLILLE **MIA(SLt EJ Grout **POW**/2AM
A Tyrrell **POW**) left 5-34am QUESNOY, a'c captured
["FE" claim combat nLILLE 7-20am Ltn J vBertrab
Ja30]

17th May

Bullecourt village was captured in heavy fighting.

7687   **FE2b**   **11Sqn**
CP EA? cr Sh51B H.24.B seen o't(2Lt LA Fuller **KIA/

Cpl C Beauchamp **WIA**) left 5-45pm, a'c unsalvable, not known why a'c lost

18th May

A6619   Nieuport 17   1Sqn
** combat with EA[+] shot up(Lt HJ? Duncan MC **WIA**)thigh

A6644.6 **Nieuport 17   1Sqn**
KBP left 8-10pm shot down KB[+] then shot down **MIA(2Lt TH Lines **POW**) a'c captured

B1555   Nieuport 17   1Sqn
KBP left 8-10pm **MIA(2Lt MG Cole **KIA**)

B1636   Nieuport 17   1Sqn
KBP left 8-10pm **MIA(Lt L Drummond **KIA**)

These heavy losses for 1 Squadron were suffered in further raids on the enemy balloon line. Observation balloons were nearly always protected by substantial anti-aircraft defences and were therefore very dangerous targets. They needed to be shot up from close range, and were quickly hauled down when attacking aircraft appeared, so that the machines involved needed to come down very low. Some units, for example 84 Squadron, were to specialise in this work in 1918.

                    BE2d?   2Sqn
** AA(2Lt WO Hatcher **WIA**/)

7074   BE2e   12Sqn
NFP combat with 6HA broke up cr WoL(Lt B Strachan **KIA/Lt AG Mackay **KIA**) left 6-30pm to nrFOSSÉE FARM [?"BE" claim combat wMONCHY 7-05pm Ltn K Allmenröder Ja11]

B1588   SPAD 7   19Sqn
OP eCROISILLES-BAILLEUL engine ftl **MIA(2Lt JDV Holmes **POW**) a'c captured, left 5-58am, seen 7am seARRAS

                    Sopwith Strutter 45Sqn
** AA(/2Lt W Wallace **WIA**)

A6770.A1 **Nieuport 17   60Sqn**
OP broke up in dive on EA(2Lt RJ Grandin **KIA) left 8am OPPY-GUEMAPPE, hit by EA observer's fire?

19th May

B1627   SPAD 7   19Sqn
OP eCROISILLES-BAILLEUL AA ftl **MIA(2Lt SF Allabarton **POW**) a'c captured, left 6am, seen seARRAS

A5457   FE2b   22Sqn
LP combat with 5HA shot down in flames nrGOUZEAUCOURT cr burnt(2Lt MS Goodban **KIA/2Lt PHB Ward **KIA**) left 4-15pm Fourth Army front [?unconfirmed "Vickers" claim combat VILLERS GUISLAIN 4-20pm? Ltn FO Bernert Ja6] ["Vickers" claim ditto Vzfw Holler Ja6]

A5510   FE2b   22Sqn

**LP combat with 4EAs shot up ftl 9Sq dam OK(2Lt GW Foreman/2Lt ND Robison) to Fourth Army front

A6711   SPAD 7   23Sqn
HAP left A.L.G. 9-55am **MIA(Sgt CJ Abrahams **KIA**) [?"Sopwith" claim combat nSAILLY 10-10am Ltn J Schmidt Ja3] SAILLY nrCAMBRAI?

                    Sopwith Strutter   43Sqn
LP combat? shot up(/Pte J Johnston **KIA)

N5461   Sopwith Triplane   1 (Naval) Sqn
OP combat 3EAs shot down in flames nrETERPIGNY EoL 8-10am **MIA(FSLt GG Bowman **KIA**) left 7am, shot down at p.16. ["Tripe" claim combat nrDURY 8-05am Oblt A Rt vTutschek Ja12]

N5488   Sopwith Triplane   1 (Naval) Sqn
** combat with EA shot down in flames eARLEUX 12000' **MIA**(FSLt OB Ellis **KIA**) seen enter clouds ovHENIN LIETARD, pilot fell out, Ja4 ["Tripe" claim combat DROUCOURT 7-55pm Ltn G-W Groos Ja4]

20th May

A4240   RE8   5Sqn
AOb combat with 5 Albatros OPPY-BAILLEUL 4500' 11-35am shot up(2Lt APM Sanders **WIA/Lt HC Stephens OK)arm, EA bright red & silver, copper covered steel core bullet found in observer's seat

A2908   BE2e   8Sqn
P rifle fire ftl C9.a.4.5. dam ldg(2Lt J Mundie **WIA/ Sgt BC Budd **WIA**) to hospital, left 6-40pm

                    FE2b   11Sqn
CP (2Lt RWG West **WIA/2Lt JT Johnson **WIA**) hit shoulder/thigh

A5507   FE2b   11Sqn
+* combat with AlbatrosDIII[+ooc] SENSÉE CANAL 12-15pm OK(2Lt AW Gardner/Lt DD McIntosh)

On the 20th, the British began their assault on the section of the Hindenburg Line between Bullecourt and the British front line west of Fontaine-les-Croisilles. In this action 11 and 60 Squadrons repeated their co-operation with the infantry, low strafing the enemy positions in advance of the attack. The above casualties were probably caused at this time.

A5511   FE2b   11Sqn
PhotRec AA ooc **MIA(2Lt TJ Hudson **KIA**/2Lt LH Horncastle MC **KIA**) left 10-20am, in spin cr Sh51B 2.5.a.

A5517   FE2b   11Sqn
+* combat with AlbatrosDIII[+ooc] SENSÉE CANAL 12-15pm OK(Capt ER Manning/2Lt AM West)

These were the last FE2b victory claims for 11 Squadron before re-equipping with Bristol Fighters.

FE2b   **18Sqn**
KBP AA shot up(/2Lt TP Johnston **KIA)

A6444   **FE2d**   **20Sqn**
OP combat radiator shot up ftl cr(2Lt HB Howe **inj/
LCpl R Bradley **KIA**) left 8-15am, cr ST SYLVESTRE
CAPELLE, observer crushed by a'c o't ldg

A6457   **FE2d**   **20Sqn**
OP MENIN shot down **MIA(Lt AC Lee **POW**/
2AM C Beminster **POW**) left 8-20am Ja28 [?is this "FE"
claim dated 18.5 in Abschusse: combat HOLLEBEKE
10-10pm Ltn K Schaefer Ja28]

B1587   **SPAD 7**   **23Sqn**
HAP left A.L.G. 9-50am **MIA(2Lt HT Garrett **KIA**)
["SPAD" claim combat nrRIENCOURT 10-10am Oblt
A Rt vTutschek Ja12]

6448   **FE8**   **41Sqn**
**OP NOORDHOEK 2 AA shells ftl Sh28 T.7.d.8.8.
OK(2Lt T Perkins) left 9-45am, turned-turtle in air, mg
smashed so thrown out

             FE8   **41Sqn**
P AA shot up(2Lt EBW Bartlett **WIA)arm

A8246   **Sopwith Strutter**   **45Sqn**
**OP LILLE cr wr Sh28s 17b.8.1.(Capt CH Jenkins
DoW/Lt DC Eglington OK) DoW 23.5.17

A3341   **Bristol F2a**   **48Sqn**
**OP eARRAS combat with EA shot down wr OK(2Lt
JA Armstrong/2Lt G Baines) left 11-05am

A7112   **Bristol F2b**   **48Sqn**
+* combat with AlbatrosDIII[+ooc] BREBIÈRES
12-30pm OK(Capt R Raymond-Barker/2Lt RNW Jeff)

A8912   **SE5**   **56Sqn**
**OP eCROISILLES-HERMIES AA brought down
EoL **MIA**(Lt CE French **POW**)

N5366   **Sopwith Triplane**   **10 (Naval) Sqn**
**LP combat with EA[+] shot up ftl(FSLt CE Pattison
WIA)shoulder

21st May

The first bombardments preceding the battle of
Messines (see the 1st of June) commenced on the
21st of May, mostly directed from the air.

A6447   **FE2d**   **25Sqn**
LP combat with 4EAs **MIA(2Lt JH Blackall **WIA**
POW/2Lt BC Moody **WIA POW**) left 2-35pm
HULLUCH-GAVRELLE, driven down eVERMELLES
["FE" claim combat HULLUCH 4-10pm Ltn E
Mohnicke Ja11]

23rd May

B1554   **Nieuport 17**   **1Sqn**
*OP combat with AlbatrosDIII[+ooc] sBECELAERE
6pm cr ldg dam OK(Lt LF Jenkin) his first of 22 victories
with 1Sqn

FE2b   **18Sqn**
Phot shot up(2Lt W Birch **WIA/)neck

FE2b   **18Sqn**
Rec AA(/Lt DW McLeod **WIA)foot

A5502   **FE2b**   **18Sqn**
Phot combat shot down wr(2Lt WF Macdonald **KIA/
Lt FC Shackill **KIA**)Ja5, left 11-45am combat
CAMBRAI-BAPAUME Voss29 ["FE" claim combat
CAMBRAI-BAPAUME ROAD 1-25pm Ltn W Voss
Ja5]

A6466   **FE2d**   **20Sqn**
**OP combat with EAs ftl nrVLAMERTINGHE(2Lt W
Howarth **WIA**/Sgt F Bird **KIA**) left 9-46am, Ja28?

A6467   **FE2d**   **20Sqn**
OP combat with EAs EoL **MIA(2Lt RG Masson **KIA**/
2Lt FW Evans **DoW**) Ja28 ["FE" claim combat
WARNETON Ltn K Schaefer Ja28]

A6468   **FE2d**   **20Sqn**
OP combat with EAs **MIA(Lt RAP Johns **WIA POW**/
Sgt B Aldred **KIA**) ["FE" claim combat HOUTHEM-
WARNETON 3-15pm OffSt M Müller Ja28]

A665   **Sopwith Pup**   **46Sqn**
**P combat with EA nrKEMMEL brought down cr
wr(2Lt JP Stephen **KIA**) Casualty Report dated 24.5, but
error? ["Sopwith 1Str" claim combat WYTSCHAETE-
BOGEN 5-45pm, on 23.5 Ltn K Schaefer Ja28]

This was the first combat casualty on Sopwith Pups
for 46 Squadron.

A8909   **SE5**   **56Sqn**
+* combat with D-type[+ooc] AUBIGNY btwn 7pm &
7-15pm OK(Capt PB Prothero) shared, first of 6 with
56Sqn

             Sopwith Triplane   **8 (Naval) Sqn**
** combat shot down(FSLt FV Hall **WIA**)slight

N5481   **Sopwith Triplane**   **8 (Naval) Sqn**
OP shot down nrLENS-DOUAI EoL **MIA(FSLt HA
Pailthorpe **KIA**) left 7-15am Ja11["Tripe" claim combat
swFASCHODA 8-15pm Ltn H Hinsch Ja11]

24th May

7672   **FE2b**   **11Sqn**
**Rec AA ftl cr Sh36B Q.22.c. dam(Lt SNS Kennedy
WIA/Cpl C Beauchamp **WIA**) left 6-15pm, injured in
crash?

A5517   **FE2b**   **11Sqn**
**Rec shot down flames nrCHERISY(2Lt WGD Turner
KIA/2Lt L Holman **WIA POW**) left 6-55am [?"FE"
claim combat BOIRY-NOTRE DAME 7-50am Ltn K
Allmenröder Ja11]

A6374   **FE2d**   **20Sqn**
**OP combat with HAs mg shot up ftl hit wires ldg
nrBRANDHOEK cr(2Lt WP Scott **inj**/2Lt ES Cogswell
inj) pilot shaken, observer severely injured

B343   DH5   24Sqn
prac left 7-55am **MIA(Lt JHH Goodall **POW**)

This was the first de Havilland DH5 loss, and in common with a number of other aircraft in their early days at the front, a new fighter type was delivered almost intact to the enemy. 24 Squadron was the first unit to receive the DH5, initially coming on strength from the 1st of May.

The DH5 was yet another new Allied single-seater, welcomed into service at the time of its arrival because its design provided a number of features important to a fighter. One recognised essential for air fighting was a good view from the cockpit, and the DH5 sought to achieve this by its back-staggered wings. In this way, the view forward which had been such an asset in the earlier de Havilland DH2 pusher, could be emulated for a tractor aircraft, which in turn could give a much superior performance. It did indeed give a marvellous view forwards and upwards, which was no doubt why it became the first aircraft type to specialise in the precarious role of ground strafing, but views rearwards or above were non-existent. This was a recipe for disaster in air fighting. It was provided with a single machine-gun and Constantinesco interrupter gear, which was to become another source of intense concern for its pilots. Within weeks of arrival in France, every DH5 of 24 Squadron, as well as those of 32 Squadron who were next to receive them, was grounded with armament problems. Repeated forced landings due to engine failure linked to the failure of bearing plates were also to plague its use. High expectations were set on the DH5 by RFC Headquarters, indicated by the relatively high numbers ordered. That the DH5 proved deficient in several ways meant that an inferior machine was kept in fairly widespread use long after a replacement should have been found. It survived until the end of the year.

A3474.18 **RE8   34Sqn**
Det Flt **AOb left 7am ldg nrLAON **MIA**(2Lt CCF Osborn **POW**/Sgt J Lewis **POW**) left 7am ST QUENTIN-BELLENGLISE, a'c captured

B1642.2 **Nieuport 17   40Sqn**
OP left 6-05pm shell hit shot down cr nATHIES 7-35pm(2Lt LL Morgan **WIA) WIA by shell splinter hit [?"Nieu 1Str" claim ST ELOI, WYTSCHAETE-BOGEN 7-50pm OffSt M Müller Ja28]

Sopwith Strutter   43Sqn
LP combat 9 Albatros shot up(2Lt EH Jones **WIA/)leg

A973   Sopwith Strutter   43Sqn
PhotLP going down in flames 8-10am **MIA(Lt GM Goode **KIA**/2Lt J Gagne **KIA**) left 7-20am

NEUVIREUIL [?"Tripe" claim combat IZEL-FERME 8-02am Ltn K Allmenröder Ja11]

Sopwith Strutter   45Sqn
OP combat? shot up(/2Lt CG Stewart **WIA)leg

Sopwith Strutter   45Sqn
OP AA(/2Lt FH Austin **WIA)thigh

A3350   Bristol F2a   48Sqn
HAP combat with EA[+] shot up(Capt JHT Letts OK/Lt LW Allen **WIA)

A6183   Sopwith Pup   54Sqn
+* combat with AlbatrosDIII[+des] PREMONT 8-10am OK(Lt OM Sutton) collided with EA, managed to return to a'dr with damaged wing, claimed 5 of his 7 EAs in this a'c

A8910   SE5   56Sqn
+* combat with AlbatrosDIII[+ooc] sDOUAI btwn 7pm & 8pm OK(Capt CM Crowe) shared, Crowe claimed 15 victories

A6194.4 **Sopwith Pup   66Sqn**
OP eCROISILLES-HERMIES ftl **MIA(Capt LA Smith **POW**) a'c captured, escaped to Switzerland 27.12.17 [?possible "Sopwith 1Str" claim combat NOYELLES, nrLENS Ltn Kellein/Ltn Haugg FAb48][?possible "Sopwith" claim combat MONCHY. 8-40am Ltn J Schmidt Ja3]

N5450   Sopwith Triplane   8 (Naval) Sqn
"TIKI" **OP DOUAI combat with EA shot down FLERS **MIA**(FSLt HL Smith **KIA**) Ja11 ["Tripe" claim combat ovFLERS 8-02am Ltn Maashoff Ja11]

25th May

A6678   Nieuport 17   1Sqn
OP combat: dive by 4EAs ovHOUTHEM 12000' **MIA(Lt JR Anthony **POW DoW**) left 6-57am TENBRIELEN-PERENCHIES ["Nieuport" claim combat nWERVICQ 7-45am Ltn P Strähle Ja18]

A1841   BE2e   13Sqn
**AP left 7pm XVII Corps front combat with 7 EA ftl dam OK(2Lt WJ Wyatt/2Lt WW Boyd)

RE8   16Sqn
AOb combat? shot up(/Capt JF Davidson **WIA)shoulder

SPAD 7   19Sqn
OP (Lt HGP Okenden Aust. **WIA)

A3   FE2d   20Sqn
OP left 6-58am combat with EA ftl(2Lt RG Dalziel **WIA/Lt WH Chester OK)

A6366   FE2d   20Sqn
OP combat with EA ftl IRISH FARM(2Lt JH Baring-Gould **WIA/Lt CA Hoy **inj**) left 6-58am, a'c shelled, Gould: gunshot in back ["FE" claim combat wWYTSCHAETE 8-07am Ltn A Hanko Ja28]

A6471   FE2d   20Sqn
**OP combat with EA ftl PLOEGSTEERT(Lt RE

Johnston **inj**/2Lt LG Fauvel **inj**) left 6-58am, injured in crash?, initials LF?

SPAD 7   23Sqn
** (2Lt EW Hallam **WIA**) [possible ?SPAD claim combat neMONCHY Untoff F Gille Ja12]

A9363   DH5   24Sqn
+*Esc/OP LESDAIN-LIGNY combat with 9AlbatrosDIII[+steep dive, cr nrLIGNY Sh57b O.2.&.3] 11-45am OK(Lt S Cockerell) engaged EA on Lt HW Woollett's tail (DH5 A9166) then 10 min combat, 5 DH5s in patrol, first DH5 claim for 24Sqn

This was the first air combat victory for the DH5. Cockerell scored seven victories, this being his only one on the DH5.

A4881   FE8   41Sqn
OP left 4-54am AA shot down in flames **MIA(Lt CG Eccles **KIA**)

Sopwith Strutter 43Sqn
LP AA hit(2Lt NH England **WIA/)foot

A963   Sopwith Strutter 45Sqn
OP left 9-10am **MIA(2Lt J Johnstone **WIA POW**/2Lt TS Millar **POW**) [?possible "Sopwith" claim combat LANGEMARCK Vzfw Bärenfänger Ja28]

A7409   DH4   55Sqn
B CANTIN A'dr combat with EA lost tail in dive nrNOYELLES ooc **MIA(Lt RE Jeffery **KIA**/Lt PR Palmer **KIA**) left 11-55am

A6776   Nieuport 23   60Sqn
P combat with Albatros C shot down in spin EoL **MIA(2Lt W Gilchrist **WIA POW**) left 9-15am ROEUX-SAILLY, combat Sh51B 0.16.["Sopwith" claim BOIS DU VERT 9-45am Ltn K Allmenröder Ja11]

N3209   Nieuport 17   6 (Naval) Sqn
P combat with EA[+] nwBOHAIN 11-40am(FSlt BPH deRoeper **WIA)

26th May

Nieuport 17   1Sqn
OP (Lt JCC Piggott **WIA)

B1559   Nieuport 23   1Sqn
+* combat with AlbatrosDIII[+ooc] LOMPRET 10-40am OK(Lt PF Fullard) first victory of 40 for Fullard

B1685   Nieuport 17   1Sqn
OP left 5am ftl but destroyed a'c **MIA(2Lt RR MacIntosh **POW**) to TENBRIELEN-PERENCHIES [?"Nieuport" claim combat wROUBAIX 6am Ltn P Strähle Ja18]

A.W.FK8   2Sqn
AReg ground mg fire shot up(/Lt RC Rogers MC **WIA)leg

B1626   Nieuport 23   29Sqn
OP left 7-15pm **MIA(2Lt GM Robertson **WIA POW**) [?"Nieuport" claim combat nrDOUAI 7-55pm Oblt H Bethge Ja30]

A6188   Sopwith Pup   46Sqn
P left 6-40pm combat shot up ftl nrDICKEBUSH wr(2Lt AS Lee **WIA)

A6168   Sopwith Pup   54Sqn
EscFE combat with 6EAs shot down wGONNELIEU wr(2Lt MB Cole **WIA) to hospital, left 1-30pm, Voss30 ["Sopwith" claim combat swGOUZEAUCOURT 2-45pm Ltn W Voss Ja5]

A8902   SE5   56Sqn
OP eBAILLEUL-CROISILLES combat with 2Str **MIA(2Lt Y? Toogood **WIA POW**) initial J? left 6-30pm, seen start combat ovGOUY-SOUS-BELLONE

A6186   Sopwith Pup   66Sqn
OP CAMBRAI **MIA(2Lt CF Smith **POW**) FAb32 [?"Sopwith" claim combat nrETAING 7-50pm? Untoff O Rosenfeld Ja12] ["Sopwith" claim combat ETAING 7-15pm Untoff R Jorke Ja12] [?"Sopwith" claim combat nrCAGNICOURT Ltn Hochstaetter Ja12]

N5963   DH4   2 (Naval) Sqn
EscRec OSTENDE **MIA(FSLt W Houston-Stewart **KIA**/Lt CL Haines **KIA**) seen ovOOST DUNKIRK BAINS 1m off shore, lost?

27th May

BE2g   10Sqn
PhotRec (2Lt B Ord **WIA/)

A5474   FE2b   18Sqn
**Rec combat with AlbatrosDV[+ooc] shot up flames ftl OK(2Lt E West-White/Sgt JR Cumberland) left 5-35am Fifth Army area ["FE" claim combat QUEANT 7-30am Ltn K Schneider Ja5] last FE claim for 18Sqn?

A3200   RE8   42Sqn
AOb combat with HA nrCOMINES shot up dam(2Lt H Blofeld **WIA/2Lt WA Hunter **WIA**) to hospital, left 3-52pm

These were the first casualties in action for 42 Squadron in France.

A8226   Sopwith Strutter 45Sqn
OP down EoL **MIA(Capt LW McArthur MC **KIA**/2Lt AS Carey **KIA**) ["Sopwith" claim combat neYPRES 11-15am OffSt M Müller Ja28]

B1704   Sopwith Pup   46Sqn
P left 10-30am mg shot up dam ldg ok a'dr(Capt NG? Caudwell **WIA)

Bristol F2b   48Sqn
OP shot up(/2Lt G Baines **DoW 3.6.17)

A4868   SE5   56Sqn
**OP combat with HA fuel tank shot up ftl DULEY GRENAY wr OK(2Lt APF Rhys Davids) left 5-30am to 10m eBAILLEUL-CROISILLES [?poss"SE" claim combat nrHAMBLAIN Ltn Hesselink Ja33], Rhys Davids claimed first 6 victories in 4 days in this a'c, from 23.5.17

A8905   **SE5**   **56Sqn**
**OP eBAILLEUL-CROISSILLES seen in combat with
Scout sCORBEHEM shot down **MIA**(2Lt EAL Lloyd
WIA POW) ["SE" claim combat nrCORBEHEM OffSt
Altmeier Ja33][also ?possible "English 1Str" combat
nrCORBEHEM MG-Sch Hegger/Vzfw Rebbe SS11]

A7340   **Sopwith Pup**   **66Sqn**
OP eCROISILLES-HERMIES **MIA(Lt SS Hume
POW)

28th May

         BE2e   **15Sqn**
** (Sgt HA Milnes **WIA**/)

         FE2b   **18Sqn**
Rec AA hit(/Lt J Tanglin **WIA)arm

A32   **FE2d**   **25Sqn**
Rec **MIA(2Lt EH Stevens **POW DoW** 16.6.17/LCpl C
Sturruck **WIA POW**) left 11-15am DOUAI-ST
AMAND-ORCHIES ["FE" claim from 25Sq combat
DOUAI 1pm Ltn W Voss Ja5]

A6378   **FE2d**   **25Sqn**
Rec **MIA(Capt A deSelincourt **WIA POW**/Lt H
Cotton **WIA POW**) left 11-15am DOUAI-ST AMAND-
ORCHIES, possible not WIA ["FE" claim from 25Sq
combat nrMONTIGNY-EN-OSTREVENT 12-50pm
Ltn K Schneider Ja5]

A6410   **FE2d**   **25Sqn**
Rec DOUAI-ST AMAND **MIA(Lt TN Southorn
POW/Lt V Smith **WIA POW**) left 11-15am ["FE" claim
from 25Sq combat BEAUMONT 12-50pm Vzfw O
Koennecke Ja5]

         Nieuport   **29Sqn**
OP left 8am shot up(2Lt AM Wray **WIA)knee

B1684   **Nieuport 17**   **40Sqn**
+* combat with AlbatrosDIII[+ooc] neDOUAI 7-50pm
OK(Lt AE Godfrey Can.) shared

         Sopwith Strutter 45Sqn
OP shot up(/Lt EC Kelly **WIA)thigh

         SE5a   **56Sqn**
OP (2Lt GM Wilkinson **WIA)

B1575.B1 **Nieuport 23**   **60Sqn**
+* combat with AlbatrosD[+?dr dn] MONCHY LE
PREUX 7am shot up ftl OK(Maj AJL Scott MC)

B1624   **Nieuport 23**   **60Sqn**
**P left 11am combat with EA eLENS EoL 12pm
MIA(2Lt RU Phalen **KIA**) ["Nieuport" claim combat
nLENS 12-10pm Ltn Schuhmann Ja5]

B1715   **Sopwith Pup**   **66Sqn**
OP BUSIGNY **MIA(Lt RM Roberts **POW**)
["Sopwith" claim combat nrMALINCOURT 12-30pm
Ltn W Blume Ja26]

         FE2b   **100Sqn**
NB AA ovLILLE(2Lt GL Castle **WIA/)

29th May

A4221   **RE8**   **5Sqn**
**AOb GAVRELLE combat 1EA flames(2Lt JL Murray
KIA/Lt GM Dick **KIA**) left 3pm, fell eBAILLEUL
burnt, pilot fell out [?"BE" claim nGAVRELLE 4-50pm
Ltn K Allmenröder Ja11]

A841   **FE2b**   **100Sqn**
**NB LILLE ground fire ftl in flames a'c burnt(Lt EA
Worrall **WIA**)arm, left 10-45pm, ftl nrSTEENWERCK

30th May

B1721.3 **Sopwith Pup**   **54Sqn**
**EscFEs combat with 8HA 14000' chased down by EA
MIA(Lt FW Kantel **POW**) a'c captured, left 5-45am,
chased down eHESBECOURT, Ja6 Vzfw Holler
["Sopwith 1Str" claim nrPONCHAUSE?
eBEAUREVOIR Vzfw Holler Ja6]

31st May

The main bombardment for the battle of Messines
opened on the 31st May.

         FE2b   **18Sqn**
OP AA splinter(Sgt C Evans **WIA/)

A3191   **RE8**   **21Sqn**
**AOb left 4-15pm YPRES AA hit dam OK(Lt G
Leckie/2Lt V Hughes)

A4239   **RE8**   **53Sqn**
**ACoop to 0.8.a 8002 AA dam ftl OK(Sgt GL Haydon/
Lt HM Jackson)

Untraced casualty in France in May 1917?

         RNAS
** (FSLt WR Wing **POW**)

June 1917

THE FLANDERS FRONT

With the failure of the Nivelle offensive on the
Aisne, the Allied emphasis eventually switched to
the British front in Flanders. The broad intention
was to remove the enemy from the Belgian coast,
so that pressure could be imposed on the northern
flank of his vast defensive system. As well as this
the Royal Navy was anxious to remove the threat
posed by the German U-boat bases in this region.
Some felt that without this problem being
eliminated the Channel would be impossible to
hold. All efforts in Flanders would have to remain
mindful of France's precarious position in the war,
ensuring that the new offensive could not be interpreted as an abandonment of Britain's troubled
ally.

The first prerequisite for the offensive was the

capture of the Messines-Wytschaete Ridge in order to deny the enemy a position from which the preparations for fighting could be observed. From Messines, the important Lys Valley could be watched, whilst the Ypres battlefields spread out to the north. The British Second Army were allocated the task of taking the ridge, and the battle would start on the 7th of June. To assist them, in excess of three hundred British aircraft were made available in the Messines battle area, over a third of them fighters, whilst along the whole front to the sea there was something like five hundred British machines. In the immediate battle area there were eighteen squadrons. Some RFC units operating on the edges of the sector facing the ridge also extended their operations to include it, whilst others were kept in the Arras sector until late into May to give the impression that this remained the main area of fighting.

The full elements of the British air concentration at the time of the battle of Messines were as follows:

I Brigade RFC in support of the First Army consisted of the 1st (Corps) Wing: Nos. 2 (FK8s), 10 (BE2e/f/g), and 5 and 16 Squadrons (both RE8s), as well as the 10th (Army) Wing: Nos 23 (SPADs), 25 (FE2ds), 40 (Nieuport Scouts), 43 (Sopwith Strutters), 8 Naval (Sopwith Triplanes), and 100 Squadron (FE2bs and BE2es).

II Brigade RFC in support of the Second Army consisted of the 2nd (Corps) Wing, Nos. 4, 6, 21, 42 and 53 Squadrons (RE8s) as well as 7 Squadron which had temporarily had its machines redistributed to Nos. 6, 21, and 42 Squadrons. It also included the 11th (Army) Wing comprising Nos.1 (Nieuport Scouts), 20 (FE2ds), 41 (FE8), 45 (Sopwith Strutters), 46 (Sopwith Pups), and Nos.1 and 10 Naval Squadrons (Sopwith Triplanes).

III Brigade RFC in support of the Third Army consisted of the 12th (Corps) Wing, Nos. 3 (Morane Parasols), 8, 12, 13 (BE2es), and 15 and 59 Squadrons (RE8s). It also had the 13th (Army) Wing consisting of Nos.11 and 18 (FE2bs), 29 and 60 (Nieuport Scouts), 32 (DH5s, but still a few DH2s on strength), 48 (Bristol Fighters), and 3 Naval (Sopwith Pups).

IV Brigade in support of the Fourth Army consisted of the 3rd (Corps) Wing, Nos. 9, 34, and 52 (RE8s) and 35 Squadron (FK8s), and the 14th (Army) Wing, Nos. 22 (FE2bs), 24 (DH5s), 54 (Sopwith Pups), and 6 Naval (Nieuport Scouts)

Finally, the squadrons of the 9th(Headquarters) Wing consisted of Nos.19 (SPADs), 27 (Martinsydes), 55 (DH4s), 56 (SE5s), 57 (re-equipping with DH4s), 66 (Sopwith Pups), 70 (Sopwith Strutters), and a Special Duty Flight (BE12s and BE2es).

The German forces were only too aware, however, that the pivotal fighting was moving to Flanders. As soon as the Arras offensive had slackened in early May, substantial numbers of both troops and air units had begun moving north. Between the 4th of May and the 7th of June, the German Fourth Army, which held the line through Flanders to the sea, had its air support increased from ten to nineteen artillery and reconnaissance flights, the Jagdstaffeln increased from five to eleven, with six additional fighter-bomber groups, and eight protection flights. In the area of the Messines Ridge the numbers of aircraft opposing one another were about equal — around three hundred — but the Germans had more fighters. Elsewhere in the north, the British had a marked numerical superiority. The German commanders knew that their greatest obstacle in the air war was the British, and they continued to concentrate their best efforts against them.

In the battle of Messines it was essential that the British guns gained supremacy. The German positions completely overlooked those of the British, and this advantage had to be nullified. The artillery brought up for the fighting overshadowed anything previously seen and the RFC was crucial to its successful use. It was not only responsible for laying its fire and reconnoitring its effect, it also had to prevent knowledge of preparations from reaching the enemy.

1st June

A3162   BE2e   2Sqn
Phot mg shot down ePUITS **MIA(2Lt BF Rowe **KIA**/2Lt BS Lister **WIA POW**) left 9am BOIS HUGO

A3265   RE8   16Sqn
AOb combat shot down 11am WoL(Lt WE McKissock **KIA/2Lt AWL Nixon **KIA**) left 9-25am, ground fire? [?"RE" claim combat MERICOURT 11am Ltn O Brauneck Ja11]

        FE2b   18Sqn
** combat? shot up(/Lt MT Trotter **WIA**)foot

B1561   SPAD 7   23Sqn
+* combat with AlbatrosDIII[+ooc] nLENS 11am OK(2Lt FJ Gibbs)

B1583   Nieuport 23   29Sqn
LP left 4-30am **MIA(Lt EA Stewardson **POW**) ["Sopwith" claim combat nrBOIRY 5-20am Oblt H Lorenz Ja33]

        Nieuport   40Sqn
OP combat eLENS(Lt WE Bassett Aust. **WIA)

A4887   FE8   41Sqn
OP combat with HA shot down wHOUTHEM **MIA(2Lt PCS O'Longan **KIA**) left 6-56pm ["FE" claim

combat wHOUTHEM, neWARNETON 8-30pm Oblt H
Bethge Ja30]

A2393   Sopwith Strutter 43Sqn
**Phot AA dam ftl 1500yd eROCLINCOURT 10-45am
OK(Lt J Potter/2Lt WB Giles) to DOUAI, down Sh51B
H.8.a.9.4.

A3690   RE8   53Sqn
**AOb AA controls shot up cr WoL(Lt JS Harvey OK/
2Lt MDR Paton **DoW** 12.6.17) left 5am

N3209   Nieuport 17   6 (Naval) Sqn
OP shot up(SqCdr CD Breese **WIA)slight

2nd June

Fine weather prevailed for virtually all the first
week of June, so that the full RFC flying programme in advance of the assault could be carried
out. The corps machines suffered very few casualties during these preparations in comparison with
those from the army squadrons. Air fighting at this
time, however, was only sporadic, several
casualties being caused by anti-aircraft fire. The
heaviest combats occurred behind Messines, in the
Ypres-Roulers-Menin triangle.

In the usual way, the RFC sought to achieve
freedom over the battlefield through offensive
patrolling, but Messines differed from previous
large engagements in that this time there was to be
more concentration of effort over the immediate
battle zone. In practical terms this meant the area
stretching from the fighting back some 10,000 yards
to the enemy balloon line. There would also be a
reduced number of distant patrols into the area
beyond, but no enemy aircraft were to be allowed
westwards of the balloon line for the full seventeen
miles between Perenchies and Langemarck. This
would keep the German observers at an ineffectual
distance whilst enabling the British corps machines
to do their work. This beat was divided up into
Northern and Southern Sector Offensive Patrols,
and references to these are found in the listings as
**NOP and **SOP respectively. The two sectors
met roughly over the centre of the battle, and there
were also separate barrage patrols of this area to
ensure a greater presence here. Should enemy
aircraft break through, as they inevitably would,
then the burgeoning technology of wireless interception would locate the machines involved.

Wireless interception was being increasingly
used to direct air attacks onto the enemy. It was
being adapted into a highly useful system of intelligence gathering. Ground stations to pick up and
locate the signals of German spotting machines had
been used since October 1916, but by now, each
army had its own pair of Aeroplane Compass

Stations as well as an Aeroplane Intercepting
Station. It was their sole function to track and
interpret enemy aircraft activity continuously.
They might be in direct contact with a Wing headquarters, an Anti-Aircraft command, Corps
Artillery headquarters, or even a specific squadron.
This flow of information was of immense value, as
it not only enabled more effective engagements
with enemy machines, but also elucidated what
were often quite major trends occurring in air
tactics, enabling a more effective and focused
response to be made. Both sides were availing
themselves of this new technology in their own way,
and it was during the battle of Messines, where the
artillery war was bound to prove decisive, that it
came into general use.

B1691   Nieuport 17   1Sqn
**OP left 7-50am WERVICQ etc with 11 others
MIA(2Lt HE Waters **POW**)

A3241   RE8   4Sqn
Phot dhAA in flames **MIA(2Lt JC McNamara **KIA**/
2Lt GH Fletcher **KIA**?) left 9-25am, fell J.13.a.9.5.o.5.

               RE8   6Sqn
AOb combat? shot up(/Lt CN Bennett **WIA)shoulder

A6675.3 **Nieuport 17   19Sqn**
OP left 11am AA ftl eCOURRIÈRES **MIA(2Lt F
Barrie **POW**) a'c captured

A2716   A.W.FK8   35Sqn
**AOb VERMAND AA hit shot down 12-45pm wr(2Lt
ER Bottomley **KIA**/2Lt GA Griffiths **KIA**) left 12-15pm

B1709   Sopwith Pup   46Sqn
+* combat with AlbatrosDIII[+ooc] HOUTHULST
6pm OK(Lt CA Brewster-Joske)

B1760   Sopwith Pup   46Sqn
+* combat with AlbatrosDIII[+ooc] MENIN 8-55am
OK(2Lt F Barrager)

This was the first 46 Squadron Sopwith Pup victory

               Bristol F2b   48Sqn
OP shot up(/2Lt G Rogers **WIA)arm

               RE8   53Sqn
AOb combat? shot up(/Lt RR Gyles **WIA)leg

B1566.C5 **Nieuport 17   60Sqn**
+*HAP(solo patrol for EAs) to enemy a'drs in
ESTOURMEL area, attacked 7Albatros on ground at
either ESNES or AWOINGT a'dr[+++2 shot up &
destroyed attempting to take off, then shot down third at
1000'] 4-23am to 5am, heavily shot up by ground fire but
returned a'dr ok 5-30am OK(Capt WA Bishop Can. VC
DSO MC) Bishop awarded Victoria Cross for this lone
raid

The Canadian ace Billy Bishop was awarded the
Victoria Cross for these engagements. He had left

before dawn, with the intention of attacking Neuville aerodrome. Mist and rain hung over the entire area and, apparently finding no sign of life at Neuville, he pressed on until he found an aerodrome showing some activity. Two machines that were being run up attempted to take off but were attacked and shot down. Of another two which then took off he shot down one about three hundred yards from the aerodrome. He then drove off other attackers and made for the lines. The full story of this lone raid has never been totally consistent in its details, and will be a point of discussion for many years to come. The above description follows the original RFC Combat Report, and a letter which his Commanding Officer wrote subsequently.

N6194   Sopwith Pup   3 (Naval) Sqn
*travel, shot up wounded then lost control o'shot ldg A.L.G. cr(FSLt WE Orchard **DoW**) left 8-25am, WIA head, & inj in ldg

N6294   Sopwith Triplane   10 (Naval) Sqn
*EscPhot combat broke up nrPROVEN cr Sh27.F.7.(FSLt IS Dissette **KIA**) fell woods [?"Tripe" claim combat ovCOXYDE Ltn G Nolte Ja18]

3rd June

It had been learnt that the Germans intended to defend their positions by a prearranged scheme of artillery fire, which made it especially important to locate and disrupt this plan by extensive counter-battery work. To force the Germans to reveal their positions at large, it was decided to feign a full-scale artillery barrage and smoke demonstration, exactly as had been planned for the main assault. It was hoped the Germans would believe they were being attacked and begin to fire their guns whilst British aircraft would be aloft to record their positions. Thirty-one corps machines observed the result, but the German guns were probably aware of what was being attempted and their fire was minimal. The ruse was repeated on the 5th with slightly more success. Armed with this information the counter-battery work intensified.

B1639   Nieuport 17   1Sqn
OP left 8-44am combat with 5HA ovGHELUWE shot down(2Lt LM Mansbridge **WIA) to LANGEMARCK-TENBRIELEN [?"Nieuport" claim combat nYPRES FlMt B Heinrich MFJaI]

B1690   Nieuport 17   1Sqn
**OP left 8-44am combat with 5HA ovGHELUWE fuel tank hit ftl cr ldg OK(Lt LF Jenkins) to LANGEMARCK-TENBRIELEN

A6413   FE2d   20Sqn
OP left 7-15am LOCRE mg fire ftl LOCRE(2Lt EK? Robins **WIA/Pte C Lloyd OK) initials ER?

7926   DH2   32Sqn
LowP combat? shot up (Lt FJ Martin **WIA) shoulder

This was the last casualty in action on the DH2 on the Western Front.

DH5   32Sqn
LowP shot up(2Lt CFH Ley **WIA)

A8272   Sopwith Strutter   45Sqn
OP seen break up cr EoL **MIA(2Lt ED Haller **KIA**/2Lt FH Foster **KIA**) left 4pm, Müller14 ["Sopwith" claim combat QUESNOY 6-10pm OffSt M Müller Ja28]

A6204   Sopwith Pup   46Sqn
OP HOULTHULST seen 10min after combat **MIA(Lt DR Cameron **POW**) left 4-25pm [?"Sopwith 1Str" claim nYPRES FlMt Kunstler MFJaI]

B1618.B3 Nieuport 17   60Sqn
HAP shot up VITRY 6-30am(2Lt WH Gunner **WIA)head [?"Avro" claim nrMONCHY 6-30am Ltn K Allmenröder Ja11]

A981   Sopwith Strutter   70Sqn
PhotRec seen going down ROLLEGHEM 4pm **MIA(Lt AS Bourinot Can. **POW**/Cpl A Giles Can. **KIA**) left 2-30pm, ok nrMENIN, observer fell, Ja8 ["Sopwith" claim combat nrPOMBROUCK? 3-35pm Vzfw R Francke Ja8]

A1012   Sopwith Strutter   70Sqn
PhotRec seen nr MENIN **MIA(2Lt RM Neill **KIA**/Lt FW Harley **KIA**) left 2-30pm ROULERS-COURTRAI-MENIN-TOURCOING [?possible "Sopwith" claim combat MENIN 3-45pm Untoff Meinberg Ja8]

N6297   Sopwith Triplane   10 (Naval) Sqn
OP seen MOORSLEDE-BEYTHEM 6pm shot down **MIA(FSLt PG McNeil **KIA**) seen approach 12 Albatros engine failed? ftl? down EoL, Ja27 ["Sopwith" claim combat nrWERVICQ OffSt Klein Ja27]

4th June

A6687   SPAD 7   19Sqn
OP combat with HA shot up ftl DICKEBUSCH wr(Capt G Chadwick **WIA)knee, to ROULERS-MENIN-YPRES

A115   RE8   21Sqn
Phot YPRES SALIENT **MIA(2Lt HF Paton **KIA**/2Lt GRD Gee **KIA**) left 8-20am

A1566   Martinsyde G102   27Sqn
B ST DENIS WESTREM combat 9 Albatros on return shot down **MIA(2Lt DT Steeves **POW**) left 12-15pm [?"Mart" claim combat AELTRE nrGHENT Ltn Kruger MFJaI]

St Denis Westrem was occupied by two German bombing units currently carrying out daylight attacks on England. The nine Martinsydes which bombed the aerodrome were escorted by Pups.

A8223   Sopwith Strutter   45Sqn
**OP AA ftl cr wr nrBAILLEUL OK(2Lt AEJ Dobson/
Lt CT Ward)

B2151   Sopwith Pup   54Sqn
**Esc combat with EA LE CATELET shot down
MIA(Capt RGH Pixley MC **KIA**) left 5am Fourth Army
area, seen ftl Sh57B.s.28, Voss32 ["Sopwith" claim
combat AUBENCHEUL-LE CATELET 6-10am Ltn W
Voss Ja5]

A7420   DH4   55Sqn
**B left 12-10pm combat seen in spin down
swINGELMUNSTER **MIA**(2Lt DJ Honer **KIA**/Pte G
Cluncy **KIA**) ["EA" claim combat MOORSLEDE
1-10pm Ltn K Schaefer Ja28]

Soon after crossing the lines on the way to bomb
the rail network near Ingelmunster, a formation of
DH4s from 55 Squadron were attacked by ten
enemy scouts and the fight developed into a running battle all the way to the target and then back
again. 55 Squadron claimed one enemy shot down.

A8920.B4 SE5a   56Sqn
**OP combat with EAs spiral wMOORSLEDE cr
MIA(Lt TM Dickinson **WIA POW**) a'c captured, left
6-30am HOUPLINS-YPRES, spiral down from 15,000'
to 9,000' (see below)

5228   FE2b   100Sqn
*NB CAMBRAI pom-pom blew up ftl cr 12-15am
OK(2Lt Chaplin) left 11pm 3.6.17, a'c shelled

The night bombers of 100 Squadron were busy in
these days making use of the full moon to attack
rail networks and trains behind the front. The
incident described above must have been an
unpleasant one, for the Vickers "pom-pom" was a
quick-action gun firing one pound shells from a
forty round belt. It was mounted in an FE2b
specially modified as a single-seater and to have
blown up must have caused some consternation for
2Lt Chaplin. Two of these went to France on the
7th of April and joined 100 Squadron. At least one
attack using the gun was carried out on a train on
the night of the 17th of April.

N5480?   Sopwith Triplane   1 (Naval) Sqn
this a'c? ** shot up bullet(FSLt LH Cockey **WIA**)leg

N5440   Sopwith Triplane   1 (Naval) Sqn
** combat 15-20Albatros[++ shot down] 7-50am to 8am,
shot up ftl MOORSLEDE dam OK(FCdr TFN Gerrard)
second victory shared with 1Sqn Nieuport

The Triplanes of 1 (Naval) Squadron were
involved in one of the few dogfights in these days
before Messines. 1 Squadron Nieuports, SE5as of
56 Squadron, one of which was lost (SE5a A8920
above), and SPADs were also involved. They may
have been fighting Marinefeld Jasta I.

N6347   Sopwith Camel   4 (Naval) Sqn
+*P attacked enemy Scout[+?dived away into sea haze
eMIDDELKERKE] 15m off NIEUPORT 3pm
OK(FCdr AM Shook)

This was the first recorded combat of what was
arguably the most famous aircraft of the Great
War. 4 (Naval) Squadron had received this Camel
on the 26th of May, and others were coming on
strength with that unit at the time this combat took
place. This uncertain engagement was followed the
next day by two definite victories (see below)

5th June

FE2b   11Sqn
Rec AA hit(/Lt GE Leishman **WIA)skull

A6747   SPAD 7   19Sqn
**OP left 10-01am ROULERS-MENIN-YPRES
MIA(2Lt CD Grierson **POW**) [?combat
eFRELINGHIEN 11-45am Oblt H Bethge Ja30] (see 45
Squadron comments below)

A6384   FE2d   20Sqn
**OP combat 15EAs ovYPRES-MENIN Road shot up ftl
YPRES SALIENT(Lt WW Sawden **DoW**/Lt RMcK
Madill OK) left 1-48pm, a'c unsalvable [via *War In The
Air. Vol. IV*: shot up by red Albatros which was itself
subsequently shot down (see A6469 below) and found to
be piloted by the German ace Ltn KE Schaefer Ja28]

A6392   FE2d   20Sqn
**OP combat with HAs mg shot up dam OK(Lt HGET
Luchford/Pte C Lloyd) left 6-53am, ldg a'dr ok

A6469   FE2d   20Sqn
+*OP combat 15EAs[+shot down destr] BECELAERE-
ZANDVOORDE shot up OK(Lt HL Satchell/2Lt
TAMS Lewis) 15 min combat, Ltn KE Schaefer Ja28 shot
down

20 Squadron had already been fighting in the
morning, only to meet about fifteen Albatros scouts
over the Ypres-Menin road in the afternoon. An
extended combat developed, lasting in all over
twenty minutes, in which Sawden was shot down
and died of his wounds, and the German ace
Schaefer was killed.

RE8   21Sqn
PhotRec AA hit(/Lt HB Hammond MC **WIA)

A857.B1 FE2b   22Sqn
Rec combat with 6EAs **MIA(Capt FP Don **WIA
POW**/2Lt H Harris **WIA POW**) a'c captured, to Fourth
Army front, combat 8-30am controls hit, seen spiral down
ftl 2000yd swLESDAIN ["FE" claim combat
MASNIÈRES-VAUCELLES 8-30am Ltn W Voss Ja5]

A5461   FE2b   22Sqn
+* combat with AlbatrosDIIIs[+des+ooc]
nwVAUCELLES-LESDAIN btwn 7-15am & 7-30am
OK(Capt CM Clement Can./2Lt LG Davies)

This was the last FE2b victory for 22 Squadron before they re-equipped with Bristol Fighters.

B1655   Nieuport 23   29Sqn
OP left 7-45pm combat 9~9-30pm shot down wr(2Lt WH Stevenson **KIA)

B1548   Nieuport 17   40Sqn
OP left 7-22pm **MIA(Capt WTL Allcock **KIA**)

A1925   Sopwith Strutter   45Sqn
OP left 9am shot down **MIA(Lt RS Bennie **KIA**/Lt TA Metheral **KIA**) [?combat Sopwith claimed 10-20am Ltn O Brauneck Ja11][ditto sYPRES 10-30am Ltn A Niederhoff Ja11, but also see A8268?]

A8268   Sopwith Strutter   45Sqn
OP left 9am shot down **MIA(Sgt EA Cook **KIA**/2AM HV Shaw **KIA**) ["Sopwith" claim combat nrDADIZEELE 10-30am Ltn R Runge Ja18]

A8280   Sopwith Strutter   45Sqn
OP left 9am shot down EoL **MIA(Lt B Smith **WIA POW**/2AM S Thompson **WIA POW**) German message came that the crew were "Dead", but they were later found to be alive and prisoners.

A8291   Sopwith Strutter   45Sqn
**OP fuel tanks shot up ftl ST SYLVESTRE CAPPELLE OK(Lt JCB Firth/2Lt J Hartley) left 9am

A8293   Sopwith Strutter   45Sqn
OP shot up ftl WESTANTRE(Lt PT Newling **WIA/2Lt WG Corner **WIA**) left 9am, gunshots, both WIA legs

Sopwith Strutter   45Sqn
+* combat with AlbatrosDVs[+ooc] ovMENIN ~10-15am OK(2Lt MB Frew/2Lt MJ Dalton)

Sopwith Strutter   45Sqn
+* combat with AlbatrosDVs[+ooc] ovMENIN ~10-15am OK(2Lt N Macmillan/2Lt PFH Webb)

These disastrous losses for 45 Squadron occurred while they were carrying out a photographic reconnaissance to the Menin area. They were initially attacked by five Albatros, and others later joined in the fighting. The Sopwith Strutter was now markedly outclassed, and although two Albatros fighters were destroyed and another sent down out of control, the patrol barely limped back to the lines. It is believed that the German formation then found a formation of Pups from 46 Squadron near Polygon Wood and attacked them, as well as fighting with 19 Squadron SPADs which had appeared. One of the latter was also lost in the fighting (see A6747 above), and a further Albatros was shot down.

A6216   Sopwith Pup   46Sqn
**SOP combat shot up cr a'dr on return dam OK(2Lt PW Willcox)

B1729   Sopwith Pup   54Sqn
**EscFEs low combat with 3HAs engine hit ftl seen ldg

& burn a'c **MIA**(2Lt BG Chalmers **POW**) [?"Sopwith 1Str" claim combat nrMASNIÈRES 7-40am Ltn F Kempf Ja2]

A995.B5   Sopwith Strutter   70Sqn
**Rec combat with EA shot up dam OK(2Lt JH Gotch/Lt LA Kiburz) to ROULERS-COURTRAI-MENIN-TOURCOING, repairable

N6347   Sopwith Camel   4 (Naval) Sqn
+*P attacked 15EA[++first shot down cr beach, second 2Str shot down ooc] between NIEUPORT-OSTENDE 7pm to 7-30pm OK(FCdr AM Shook)

These were the first firm Sopwith Camel victories.

6th June

BE2e   13Sqn
PhotRec combat with 7EAs ovFAMPOUX(2Lt LR Neville **WIA/Cpl L Tucker **WIA**) shot up but ldg a'dr ok

A6480   FE2d   20Sqn
P shot down by British AA ftl nrABEELE cr wr(2Lt RE Conder **WIA/Sgt JJ Cowell OK)shaken, Conder claimed 6EAs

A2693   A.W.FK8   35Sqn
AOb shot down in flames nrPREMONT **MIA(Lt GW Devenish **KIA**/Lt HGK Cotterill **KIA DoW**?) left 10-30am ["EA" claim combat seLE CATELET 11am Vzfw F Krebs Ja6]

A3235   RE8   42Sqn
Phot trench mg fire shot down dived 3-55pm B.6.D.8.5.9.6. **MIA(2Lt E Jacot **KIA**/2Lt CJ Baylis **KIA**) left 3-10pm

A7306   Sopwith Pup   54Sqn
EscFEs combat swCAMBRAI seen going down ooc on back **MIA(Lt EJY Grevelink **KIA**) left 10-45am to ANNEUX [?"Sopwith 1Str" claim combat btwn MOEUVRES-INCHY Vzfw Reisinger Ja12] [?"EA" claim combat MOEUVRES 12-10pm Untoff O Rosenfeld Ja12]

B1730   Sopwith Pup   54Sqn
EscFEs ANNEUX combat swCAMBRAI ooc **MIA(Maj CE Sutcliffe **KIA**) left 10-45am, seen going down on back [? unconfirmed claim combat swSAINT-LES-MARQUION 12-20pm Ltn H Becker Ja12]

DH4   55Sqn
B RECKEM A'dr(/2Lt WH Bolam **WIA)

The last of the three raids on the aerodrome at Reckem met and attacked three two-seaters on the return journey, shooting one down. 2Lt Bolam may have been wounded in this fighting. The day bombing carried out at this time by 27 and 55 Squadron had limited effect as the targets were small, and the attacks were made from high altitude. As usual, however, their purpose was not only disruption, but also the drawing off of resources from the battle area.

A8899   SE5   56Sqn
OP nROULERS combat shot up **MIA(Lt H Harmer
KIA) ["Sopwith" claim combat GITS, neHOOGLEDE
9-30am Ltn R Francke Ja8]

N3204   Nieuport 17   6 (Naval) Sqn
**OP going down after EA then into spin & broke
up:engine failure?(FLt FP Reeves **KIA**) to BOIS DE
BOURLON ["Nieuport" claim combat wCAMBRAI
12-10pm Ltn W Voss Ja5]

N6193   Sopwith Pup   9 (Naval) Sqn
** badly shot up dam OK(FSLt HF Stackard)

N5490   Sopwith Triplane   10 (Naval) Sqn
+*OP combat with 15EA[+++ shot down, first 2 in
flames, third ooc] ovPOLYGON WOOD btwn 10-50am
& 11-10am OK(SLt R Collishaw) EA formation was
escorting 2Strs

To counter the attacks on their artillery machines,
the Germans were now regularly providing them
with fighter escort. Such was the group met by the
Triplanes of 10 (Naval) Squadron. They achieved
several victories over the Albatros fighters, with no
losses to any of their own machines. The Canadian
ace FSLt R Collishaw was prominent in the
engagement, scoring three victories. In the first
week of June he would achieve ten victories in
N5490. The Triplanes of 1 (Naval) Squadron were
also active that morning, shooting down at least
two Albatros fighters also without loss. The
Triplane was proving itself deadly effective in
combat.

7th June

THE BATTLE OF MESSINES

The battle of Messines opened on the 7th of June.
It was preceded by an enormous mine explosion of
four hundred tons of ammonal at 3-10am laid
under German positions on the ridge. This feat had
taken five months of tunnelling. A vast artillery
barrage immediately followed, beneath which the
infantry began its advance.

The work of contact patrolling was now a well
developed component of the battle, and a presence
was constantly maintained over the fighting. Flares
were lit at regular prearranged times to show the
position of the advance, guaranteeing a more
accurate picture of events. The success of these
operations was ultimately dependent on the
willingness and experience of the ground troops to
send their signals, and the operation was handicapped by the use of green flares, which were hard
to see in the morning light. The situation was,
however, reasonably assessed and understood.

Counter-battery work proved highly successful,
and British guns remained in the ascendant. The
RE8s of 21 Squadron were particularly prominent
in these operations, sending down ninety-six
separate zone-calls through the day. This
supremacy not only enabled successful movement
up onto the ridge, but kept open lines of communication. As a consequence, the advance was well co-
ordinated and enemy counter-attacks quickly
covered.

A6676   Nieuport 17   1Sqn
KBP QUESNOY-WERVICQ seen in clouds **MIA(2Lt
WG Milliship **KIA**) left 1-17pm [?"Nieuport" claim
combat wGHELUVELT 1-45pm Hptm Stenzel Ja8] [?
also "Nieuport" claim GHELUVELT Ltn Kunstler
MJaI]

Morane P   3Sqn
AOb AA(2Lt RA Powell **WIA/)arm

RE8   6Sqn
CP (Capt LP Prior **DoW)

RE8   6Sqn
CP shot up(/Lt CE Williamson-Jones **WIA)leg

RE8   6Sqn
CP gunshot(2Lt JR Wilson **WIA)leg

RE8   6Sqn
CP bullet(/2Lt CCG Girvan **WIA)thigh

A3214   RE8   6Sqn
CP left 5-50am shot up cr EoL **MIA(Sgt L Gray **KIA**/
Lt MFJ Halliday **KIA**)

A4210   RE8   6Sqn
Phot seen cr eHOLLEBEKE **MIA(Lt AJCE Phillippo
KIA/Lt FV Durkin **POW**) left 3-50pm [?"RE" claim
combat HOLLEBEKE Ltn Weissner Ja18]

Barrage patrolling by fighters held off most
German attempts to break through to the corps
machines in the battle area. One formation which
managed to penetrate the defences in the afternoon
consisted of four Albatros fighters, and they
attacked and shot down this crew from 6 Squadron.

A6403   FE2d   20Sqn
OP left 3-17pm flak? **MIA(2Lt BS Marshall MC **KIA**/
Pte C Lloyd **POW**) ["FE" Flak claim nrWARNETON
Oblt vWolfskeel K.Flak60]

B1524.1   SPAD 7   23Sqn
OP combat with EA nrBONJOUS **MIA(2Lt FW
Illingworth **WIA POW**) a'c captured, left 6-35am, seen
in combat with JG1 ["SPAD" claim combat COUCOU?
nrMENIN 7-15am OffSt P Aue Ja10]

B1527   SPAD 7   23Sqn
**OP BONJOUS seen low after combat down in control?
MIA(2Lt GC Stead **POW**) left 6-30am, Müller15
["SPAD" claim combat COMINES-WARNETON
8-15am OffSt M Müller Ja28]

B3460   SPAD 7   23Sqn
**OP ROULERS combat with EA then seen after
MIA(2Lt Count LTB diBalme **POW**) a'c captured, left
4-22am [?"SPAD" claim combat sRUMBEKE 6-20am
Untoff Brettel Ja10]

B1552.4 Nieuport 17   40Sqn
+*OP combat with AlbatrosDIII[+ooc] nLILLE
7-15am OK(Lt EC Mannock) left 5-58am

This was Mannock's first victory over an enemy
aircraft.

B1674   Nieuport 17   40Sqn
OP left 9-50am LILLE-YPRES area? **MIA(Lt JW
Shaw **POW**)

6437   FE8   41Sqn
**OP YPRES shelled low down cr WoL wr(Capt H
Jackson **DoW**) left 6-18am

6465   FE8   41Sqn
**LowP left 11-10am COMINES seen ldg ok EoL
MIA(2Lt NB Hair **POW**) [?possible "FE" claim combat
nrKOELBERG(Koelenberg?) Untoff Heiligers Ja30]

              RE8   42Sqn
CP shell fire(/2Lt JJ Gaynor **WIA)

A3487   RE8   42Sqn
**Phot combat with 3 Albatros shot up dam ftl a'dr ok
OK(Lt WF Anderson/AG.2AM Kirwan)

Another of the few corps machines to be attacked
was this RE8. It met a small patrol of three
Albatros fighters in the morning and was forced
down. One German aircraft was shot down in the
fighting. That so few corps machines were lost on
the 7th was a great achievement, as it was their
work which really gave form to the advance. It was
in the deeper areas that the heaviest air fighting
took place, involving RNAS Triplanes.

A4213   RE8   42Sqn
**CP tail shot off ftl shell hole OK(2Lt WG Breen-
Turner/Lt RS Hudd) left 4-05am, cr shelled area, a'c
unsalvable

A8221   Sopwith Strutter 43Sqn
GroundAttk seYPRES **MIA(Capt DC Rutter MC
KIA/2Lt JB Jackson **KIA**) left 4-10am

A8248   Sopwith Strutter 43Sqn
**GroundAttk shot up cr 5-30am(2Lt Hon SH D'Arcy
WIA/Lt AE Pickering OK) left 4-30am to
WARNETON, cr PLOEGSTEERT WOOD

Ground attacks on troops and other appropriate
targets were repeated at Messines following their
successful use in the last days of Arras. The
relatively rigid structure of the first efforts was
considerably loosened, so that many of the pilots
were now ordered to roam freely about as soon as
the battle had begun. They were to cause as much
mayhem as they could: columns of troops, guns,

trains and transport were all attacked. Aerodromes
also came in for special attention, and were
bombed and shot up throughout the day. Crews
were also expected to absorb what they were seeing
on their raids and to report enemy movements and
strengths immediately on their return. In the
opening days at Messines, the units and machines
which carried out this work were 43 Squadron
Strutters, 66 Squadron Pups, Nieuports from 1
Squadron, FE8s from 41 Squadron, SPADs of 19
Squadron, and 56 Squadron SE5as.

It was, of course, very dangerous work. Looking
among the day's entries for both 41 and 43
Squadron, a number of casualties were suffered on
low patrols. Some pilots undoubtedly took to its
free-ranging and demanding nature. There is a 19
Squadron combat report from October 1917 which
gives a brief insight into the challenge of ground-
strafing. 2Lt JD dePencier described shooting up
troops in Moorslede, in company with 2Lt RA
Hewat. He noted that he was attacking from below
the level of the church spire . . . and that Hewat
was flying beneath him (see 26th October 1917).

A8296   Sopwith Strutter 45Sqn
** seen on road wDEULEMONT **MIA**(Lt AEJ Dobson
KIA/2Lt GAH Davies **KIA**)

A6157   Sopwith Pup   46Sqn
SOP POLYGON WOOD seen combat 10HA **MIA(Lt
AP Mitchell **WIA POW**) left 9-10am, Müller16 ["SPAD"
claim combat seROULERS 10-45am OffSt M Müller
Ja28]

A3240   RE8   53Sqn
*FlRec combat with HA shot down WoL 6-05pm cr shell
hole(2Lt FP Brown **WIA**/2Lt HE Wells **WIA**) to
OOSTTAVERNE LINE

A4308   RE8   53Sqn
CP British shell hit wing snd cr(Lt NJ Wenger **inj/2Lt
EB Hamel **inj**) left 7-15am WYTCHAETE

A2159   DH4   55Sqn
**B RAMEGNIES CHIN shot up dam ftl dam OK(Lt
CC Knight/2Lt JC Trulock) repairable

A8903   SE5a   56Sqn
**OP combat with EA engine failed ftl cr wires dam(2Lt
JS Turnbull **inj**) left 4-30am HOUTHULST-
ROULERS-MENIN-QUESNOY

A1957   FE2d   57Sqn
B CHÂTEAU DU SART **MIA(2Lt GH Pollard **POW**
DoW/2Lt FS Ferriman **KIA**) left 6-10am

This was the last crew to be lost by 57 Squadron
before it re-equipped with DH4 reconnaissance
bombers.

              RE8   59Sqn
AOb (Lt EG Leake **WIA/)shoulder

A7314   Sopwith Pup   66Sqn
OP HOUTHULST-ROULERS-QUESNOY **MIA(Lt
RM Marsh **POW**) ["Sopwith" claim combat ROULERS
10-45am Vzfw H Oberländer Ja30]

B1719   Sopwith Pup   66Sqn
**OP HOUTHULST WOOD-ROULERS-QUESNOY
shot up dam OK(2Lt AV Shirley)

N5484   Sopwith Triplane   1 (Naval) Sqn
** combat with 2EAs[+] eYPRES 6-15am then ftl
TENBRIELEN **MIA**(FSLt JF Nalder **WIA**)severe
[?possible "unconfirmed Sopwith" claim combat
GHELUVELT]

N5361   Sopwith Triplane   10 (Naval) Sqn
this a'c? **OP gunshot(FSLt JH Keens **WIA**)chest
[?Tripe claim combat BOUSBECQUE? 10-10am Ltn A
Niederhoff Ja11]

8th June

By the previous evening, progress onto the ridge
had been made with almost overwhelming success.
Only the situation to the east of Messines was still
uncertain, where II Anzac Corps were still battling
hard in confused fighting. Early on the 8th two 42
Squadron machines reconnoitred their positions
and matters became clearer. In general, the day
was spent consolidating gains until the German
counter-attack came in the evening. This was
quickly neutralised by artillery, and the main phase
of this short, intense battle came to a close. The
taking of the Messines-Wytschaete Ridge was one
of the most notable successes of the entire war for
the British, not least because this important victory
against defences which the Germans had considered all but impregnable had been achieved with
relatively low losses.

B1641   Nieuport 17   1Sqn
**NOP combat with EA engine shot up ovBECELAERE
ftl cr wr OK(2Lt EG Nuding) left 5-25am
POELCAPPELLE-PASSCHENDAELE-WERVICQ

B1644   Nieuport 23   1Sqn
**NOP combat with 7EAs ovBECELAERE engine going
down EoL **MIA**(2Lt RSL Boote **POW**) left 5-25am
POELCAPPELLE-PASSCHENDAELE-WERVICQ
[?"Nieuport" claim combat wDADIZEELE Oblt vVoigt
Ja8]

B1656   Nieuport 17   1Sqn
**NOP left 5-25am combat with 6EAs BECELAERE
going down with EA on tail **MIA**(2Lt FD Slee **POW**)
POELCAPPELLE-PASSCHENDAELE-WERVICQ
["Nieuport" claim combat nrMOORSLEDE 6-30am Ltn
H Göring Ja27]

A4687   RE8   6Sqn
**CounterCP left 3-15pm shot up dam OK(FSgt
Halstead/Lt Lees)

A1965   FE2d   20Sqn
**OP AA controls shot up ldg a'dr ok OK(2Lt W
Durrand/Sgt EH Sayers) left 7-21am

A6393   FE2d   20Sqn
**OP AA hit ftl dam shelled OK(Lt HL Satchell/Lt AN
Jenks) left 1-03pm COMINES, ldg nrLE BISET Sh36C
8.D.2.4.

A6360   FE2d   25Sqn
**B combat with 4 AlbatrosDIII[+ooc]
wHAUBOURDIN 10-12000' 7-35am shot up(Sgt R
Mann **WIA**/2AM J Harris OK) attacked after drop,
Mann WIA early in thigh, EA hit by fire back over top
plane & down in flat spin

6445   FE8   41Sqn
**OP ftl YPRES SALIENT shelled a'c destroyed (Capt
WI Bailey **WIA**) left 3-05am YPRES

A3684   RE8   53Sqn
CP dhAA 5-45am cr wr(2Lt TCS MacGregor **KIA/2Lt
RW Spooner **KIA**) to OOSTTAVERNE LINE

A6181   Sopwith Pup   66Sqn
**OP shot up bad dam OK(Lt AB Thorne)repairable

A6207   Sopwith Pup   66Sqn
**OP ROULERS air collision with Pup B1745(2Lt AG
Robertson **KIA**) [2 "Sopwith" claims combat
MOORSLEDE 1-20pm Oblt K Mettlich Ja8]

B1726   Sopwith Pup   66Sqn
**OP ROULERS cr VOORMEZELLE(Capt JD Latta
WIA) [?possible "Nieuport" claim combat
wDADIZEELE 1-15pm Oblt vVoigt Ja8]

B1745   Sopwith Pup   66Sqn
**OP ROULERS air collision with Pup A6207(2Lt AV
Shirley **KIA**)

N5491   Sopwith Triplane   1 (Naval) Sqn
SpM left 9-40am shot down MOORSLEDE **MIA(FLt
TG Culling DSC **KIA**) [?possible one of 2 "Sopwith"
claims combat MOORSLEDE Ltn Mettlich Ja8]

N6293   Sopwith Triplane   1 (Naval) Sqn
**HAP shot down nrQUESNOY EoL flames(FSLt TR
Swinburne **KIA**) Müller17, Ja28 ["Tripe" claim combat
QUESNOY 6-10pm Offst M Müller Ja28]

N5451   Sopwith Triplane   9 (Naval) Sqn
** combat with Albatros[+] shot up controls ftl cr
FURNES-COXYDE RD(FSLt HF Stackard **WIA**)
[?possible "Tripe" claim combat nWARNEFORD? Ltn
Bossler MFJaI]

9th June

From the 9th until the 17th the air war generally
quietened, low clouds and poor weather also
contributing to this. Corps aircraft remained the
prime target for German machines but were mostly
protected. Richthofen returned from leave on the
14th, and much of the fighting that arose derived
from his reappearance.

There were no further bombing attacks on the front, and as the RFC offensive lessened, so did the German efforts to meet it. As always, the air weapon was there on both sides to serve the masters on the ground. The new technologies such as wireless interruption, coupled with a new culture of information gathering which was being almost feverishly promoted, meant that each side had much more understanding of the others' activities. In this climate, air power was being used with increasing precision. War flying surged or declined in unison on both sides, as resources were saved for when they could be most effective. The British, who now increasingly held the initiative, were conserving their aircraft for the main Flanders offensive. Heavy fighting in the air throughout the spring had eaten deeply into the reserves of men and machines, and a plea went out from Trenchard to the squadrons on the 10th of June to do everything possible to preserve and look after what remained. He knew the very success of the offensive policy would rest on this.

B1550   Nieuport 17   1Sqn
OP combat with 6 Albatros ovOOSTHOOK seen eGHELUWE **MIA(2Lt WJ Mussared **POW**) left 7-35am, last seen with 3EAs on tail 2000' ["Nieuport" claim combat wMENIN 8-40am Ltn R Francke Ja8]

B3481   Nieuport 17   1Sqn
NOP combat with spun down wGHELUWE with 3EA behind **MIA(Lt F Sharpe **WIA POW**) left 1-27pm POELCAPPELLE-PASSCHENDAELE-WERVICQ [?"Nieu" claim combat ZANDVOORDE, nrHOLLEBEKE 2-15pm Oblt K vDöring Ja4]

A6430   FE2d   20Sqn
B combat with EA **MIA(Capt FJH Thayre MC **KIA**/ Capt FR Cubbon MC **KIA**) left 5-30am COMINES, Thayre had claimed 20 victories, 19 in this a'c & most with Cubbon

FE2d   20Sqn
OP AA(2Lt ER Robins **WIA)head, initials EK?, see 3.6.17?

A6789   Nieuport 23   40Sqn
**LP combat with 12EA including AlbatrosDIII[+des] & AviatikC[+ooc] ovDON 7-20am shot up dam ftl OK(Lt JL Barlow) left 5-45am DON-WINGLES

B1545   Nieuport 17   40Sqn
+* combat with AlbatrosDIII[+ooc] nDOUAI 8-20pm OK(Lt WA Bond)

FE8   41Sqn
OP AA(Lt AW Hogg **WIA)leg

A3463   RE8   53Sqn
ACoop combat with 1 2Str & 5Albatros[+ooc] eHOUTHEM ovSh28.o.24. 6000' 2-10pm shot up dam(2Lt JA Loutit **WIA/2Lt VJ Holland MC **WIA**) first

burst from EA hit pilot in leg then observer hit after EA had been sent down, EA was hit from 100yds did half loop then ooc

10th June

A7469   DH4   55Sqn
PhotRec combat mg ftl cr ALVERINGHEM wr(Lt PJ Barnett OK/2Lt RM Dixon **WIA) left 2-30pm NIEUPORT-MIDDELKERKE

11th June

B1689   Nieuport 17   1Sqn
HighOP AA ovPILCKEM wings fell off EoL **MIA(2Lt RWL Anderson **KIA**) left 5-27pm POELCAPPELLE-PASSCHENDAELE-WERVICQ

A8284   Sopwith Strutter   70Sqn
**PhotRec AA hit dam on return 2-15pm OK(Lt G Budden/SLt K Wallace) left 11-55am WERVICQ-MENIN-MOORSLEDE

12th June

A.W.FK8   2Sqn
AP AA(2Lt G Allsop **WIA/)arm

A2823   BE2e   8Sqn
AOb shell ovHENIN cr wr(2Lt A Curruthers **inj/Capt KG MacDonald **inj KIA**?) left 8-05pm HENIN-SUR-COJEUL

Sopwith Strutter   43Sqn
LP shrapnel hit(/Cpl JW Collins **WIA)arm

Bristol F2b   48Sqn
OP (/Pte AM Dolan **WIA)face

A4207   RE8   53Sqn
Phot combat with EA OOSTTAVERNE 8-20am, fell in flames(2Lt W Turnbull **KIA/Lt WB Protheroe **KIA**) to WARNETON [?"RE" claim combat WYTSCHAETEBOGEN Vzfw Wittekind Ja28]

A8283   Sopwith Strutter   70Sqn
**PhotRec AA ftl POPERINGHE dam OK(Lt WE Gossett/Lt JA Sully)

13th June

B1522   Nieuport 17   1Sqn
OP combat with 2EAs ovGHELUVELT dam ftl 28.N.5.d. cr(2Lt RS Davies **inj) left 9-28am, a'c had come from 56Sqn but wrecked in one week

N6362   Sopwith Camel   4 (Naval) Sqn
** Interception of 16 Gothas 12pm, broke up: wing lost, fell 5m nwBRUGES-GHENT **MIA**(FSLt LFW Smith DSC **KIA**)

This was the first Sopwith Camel casualty to occur on active service.

14th June

A8919   SE5   56Sqn

**OP left 6pm HOUTHULST-ROULERS-QUESNOY
MIA(Lt H Rogerson **POW**) [?"Sopwith" claim combat
neDADIZEELE 7-30pm Ltn K Küppers Ja6]

N5470   Sopwith Triplane   10 (Naval) Sqn
**OP combat with 7EAs nrZONNEBEKE 7-20pm shot
down **MIA**(FSLt LH Parker **KIA**) Ja6 ["Tripe" claim
combat SCHLOSS POEZELHOEK 7-30pm Vzfw F
Krebs Ja6]

B1654.B6 Nieuport 23   60Sqn
+* combat with AlbatrosDIII[+ooc] DROCOURT
9-55am OK(Lt KL Caldwell NZ.)

15th June

9 (Naval) Squadron was made available to the
RFC on the 15th of June so that 3 (Naval) could
be relieved. 9 (Naval) flew Sopwith Triplanes and
Pups. In July, as it began to be equipped with
Sopwith Camels, it was moved north to the coastal
area to operate with I Brigade RFC in support of
the First Army.

**   Morane P   3Sqn**
Phot shot up(2Lt AMcN Denavon **WIA)hand
[?unconfirmed "English monoplane" claim combat
nrBULLECOURT Ltn Billik Ja12]

A4310   RE8   15Sqn
AOb Corps area **MIA(2Lt JH de Conway **KIA**/2Lt
CH? Powell **KIA**) initials AH?, left 12-55pm

B1589   SPAD 7   19Sqn
**P ROULERS fuel tank shot up ftl THERONANNE
dam OK(Lt CRJ Thompson Aust.) Thompson claimed
6EAs

**   SPAD 7   23Sqn**
** shot up bullet(2Lt CL Adamson **WIA**)chest

A1019   Sopwith Strutter   45Sqn
**COP combat shot up cr eYPRES(Capt IG Elias
shaken/Rfn P Hammond **DoW**) DoW gunshot in side &
leg [?"Sopwith" claim combat nrVORMEZEELE
8-30pm Vzfw K Wüsthoff Ja4]

A8230   Sopwith Strutter   70Sqn
**Phot AA shot up ldg a'dr ok 2-15pm(Lt CS Workman/
2AM SA Groves) left 11-55am ROULERS-WERVICQ-
LINSELLES

16th June

B1700   Nieuport 17   1Sqn
+* combat with AlbatrosC[++des] HOUTHEM btwn
9am & 9-10am then 2Str[+des] QUESTNOY 9-40am
OK(2Lt WC Campbell) Campbell claimed 11 of 23
victories in this a'c

**   A.W.FK8   2Sqn**
PhotRec shot up(/ 2AM WH Poole **WIA)

**   RE8   4Sqn**
Rec combat? shot up(2Lt WFEdeB Maclaren **WIA/)
foot

A6572   FE2d   20Sqn
**OP combat with Albatros[+des] neYPRES 12-30pm
shot up(2Lt PJ Gardiner **WIA**/Pte J MacLeod
OK)throat

**   RE8   21Sqn**
** PhotRec combat mg(/2Lt JR Currington **WIA**)

A381   Sopwith Strutter   45Sqn
P left 5pm **MIA(2Lt TSC Caulfield **KIA**/Rfn G
Edwards **KIA**?) [?"Sopwith" claim combat HOUTHEM
6-05pm Oblt E vDostler Ja6]

A1021   Sopwith Strutter   45Sqn
**OP combat shot up ftl BAILLEUL bad dam OK(2Lt
WA Wright/2Lt DC Eglington MC) [?unconfirmed
"Sopwith" claim nrWARNETON seMESSINES 6-06pm
Feld Ltn Schubert Ja6]

A8911   SE5a   56Sqn
** (2Lt KJ Knaggs **WIA**)

B1610   Nieuport 23   60Sqn
**OP MARQUION seen follow EA down: air collision
2000' **MIA**(Lt DRC Lloyd **KIA**) left 7-35pm

17th June

**   RE8   4Sqn**
Phot mg fire(2Lt WE Davies **WIA/Sgt W Studholme
WIA)

A4705   RE8   4Sqn
**Phot combat with 9EA shot down H.16.d. 10am wr(2Lt
H Stroud **WIA**/Lt L Ansell **WIA**) left 9-25am

A7141   Bristol F2b   11Sqn
+* combat with AlbatrosC[+ooc] SAILLY EN
OSTREVERT 6-35am OK(2Lt FJ Foster/Lt DG
Davidson)

This was the first Bristol Fighter victory for 11
Squadron.

A6368   FE2d   20Sqn
**COP AA hit ftl WEEGSCHEEDE dam OK(Lt HW
Joslyn/Lt SF Trotter)

A6469   FE2d   20Sqn
**OP combat with EA ST ELOI 9-20pm, shot down
flames(Lt N Boucher **WIA**/Lt W Birkett **inj**) left 7-10pm,
bruised & burnt ["FE" claim combat ST ELOI 8-20pm?
Oblt E vDostler Ja6]

**   SPAD 7   23Sqn**
HAP EA shot up(Capt AB Wright **WIA)foot [?un-
confirmed SPAD claim combat LIEVEN 7-40pm Ltn J
Schmidt Ja3]

A4862.C3 SE5   56Sqn
**OP combat ovHAUBOURDIN shot down cr o't
MIA(Lt HD Spearpoint **POW**) left 8am HOUTHULST-
ROULERS-MENIN ["SE5" claim combat
BEAUCAMPS wLILLE 9-02am Vzfw F Krebs Ja6]

A8922.C3 SE5   56Sqn
**OP left 8am combat ovHAUBOURDIN shot down

MIA(Lt W Turner-Coles POW) to HOUTHULST-
QUESNOY [?unconfirmed "SE" claim combat
BEAUCAMPS 8-55am Ltn Pollandt Ja6]

A2173   DH4   57Sqn
+* combat with AlbatrosDV[+ooc] sLANGEMARCK
12-40pm OK(Lt WB Hutcheson/Sgt AT Rose)

This was the first DH4 victory for 57 Squadron.

18th June

B1638   Nieuport 17   1Sqn
**HAP combat with 4EAs seen cr Sh28 J.7. EoL
MIA(2Lt RS Lloyd KIA) left 8-05am BECELAERE-
YPRES, seen cr by Fullard [?"SE" claim combat
VALORENHOEK 8-50am Ltn K Allmenröder Ja11]

RE8   6Sqn
**EscPhot combat? shot up(Lt GC Body WIA/)leg
[?possible "RE" claim combat nrMESSINES Ltn Klein
Ja4]

A3255   RE8   9Sqn
**PhotRec dhAA shot down MIA(2Lt BH Bean KIA/
2Lt ET Philip KIA) left 11-25am to Sh28.C.1, message:
dead, "AA"?

A4290   RE8   9Sqn
**Phot dhAA MIA(Lt RW Ellis KIA/Lt HC Barlow
KIA) left 11am, MvR?: but see A4617?

A4617   RE8   53Sqn
**AOb combat with EA brought down cr wr 12pm(Lt
ME Newton KIA/2Lt HM Jackson KIA) shot down
U.4.B.20.25. [?"RE" claim combat neYPRES 12-15pm
Rittm M Fr vRichthofen JG1, "some say this victory was
over A4290 of 9Sqn, but Casualty Report notes AA for
this loss]

19th June

B1680   Nieuport 17   1Sqn
**OP ZONNEBEKE-PERENCHIES separated in cloud
MIA(2Lt GC Atkins POW)

B3504   SPAD 7   23Sqn
**OP seen going west in heavy AA seYPRES at 2000′
MIA(Capt T Davidson POW) a'c captured FAb33, left
5-36am

6420   FE8   41Sqn
**IP to 20.U.20. combat with 3HA ftl cr ldg ABEELE
OK(Lt LJ MacLean)

6468   FE8   41Sqn
**IP left 5-36am shot down Sh28C 26.a.4.3. a'c shelled
(Lt Hartridge inj)hospital

9057   Short 184   Dunkirk Seaplane Stn
** combat with enemy seaplanes 8m nneNIEUPORT
5-30am shot down MIA(FSLt LP Paine DSC POW/Lt T
Rogers KIA) combat

N1015   Sopwith Baby   Dunkirk Seaplane Stn
** combat with enemy seaplanes 5-30am shot down 12m
neNIEUPORT MIA(FSLt JE Potvin KIA)

20th June

A7125   Bristol F2b   11Sqn
**PhotCP sROEUX AA dam returned a'dr OK(Lt AE
McKeever Can./2Lt HD Duncan) left 8-05am

SPAD 7   23Sqn
**HAP AA hit(2Lt A Hurley WIA)head

21st June

On the 21st, 56 Squadron returned to England and
66 Squadron went to Calais in order to counter the
German bombing raids on London. Fourteen
Gothas had attacked the City and the East End of
London on the 13th, causing heavy casualties, and
the public had let out a cry to their leaders for
protection. In only a week, two of the best units on
the Western Front found themselves withdrawn to
perform a home defence role. They were removed
from 9th (Headquarters) Wing, leaving 19
Squadron SPADs as its only fighter unit — such
was the power of political necessity. In France, the
German fighter units took advantage of this
weakening, and in particular attacked British
observation balloons for most of the next week.

B3495   Nieuport 17   1Sqn
**OP seen in combat with 4EAs ovPOLYGON WOOD
driven down by 1EA MIA(2Lt TM McFerran KIA) left
9-23am ZONNEBEKE-PERENCHIES [?"Nieuport"
claim combat neBECELAERE Ltn Wewer Ja26]

A7139   Bristol F2b   11Sqn
**COP left 5am OPPY seen going east ~BAILLEUL-
OPPY 6-45am MIA(2Lt DCH MacBrayne KIA/Sgt W
Mollison POW) [?"Bristol" claim combat wPETIT
VITRY Ltn Fuchs Ja30]

This was the first loss on Bristol Fighters for 11
Squadron.

B1709   Sopwith Pup   46Sqn
**HAP left 9-10am seen ov Lines ~10-30am MIA but
OK?(2Lt HAC Tonks Aust.) seen later with no EAs,
Tonks not listed dead or POW ["Sopwith" claim combat
ROLLENBERG? 9-55am? Hpt O Hartmann Ja28]

A2171   DH4   57Sqn
**Phot AA hit cr wr ldg AIRE dam OK(2Lt JF Hillier/
2Lt DRC Drury-Lowe) left 7-25am STEENBECK
FARM

A7443   DH4   57Sqn
**OP combat shot up ftl cr wr nrPOPERINGHE(2Lt R
Trattles inj/Lt PH Bigwood KIA) left 10-05am
BIXCHOOTE-HOUTHEM

These were the first combat casualties for 57
Squadron on DH4s.

N5376   Sopwith Triplane 10 (Naval) Sqn
"BLACK SHEEP" ** flak ftl dam OK(FSLt HW Taylor)

23rd June

FE2b	20Sqn

** AA (/Pte J Macloud **KIA**)

RE8	21Sqn

AOb trench rifle fire(Capt NA Bolton **WIA/)

B1603   Nieuport 23   29Sqn
OP left 3-20pm seen ldg EoL **MIA(2Lt GT Harker **POW**)

24th June

RE8	9Sqn

AOb AA hit(2Lt WG Nicholls **WIA)head

A4625   RE8   9Sqn
**AOb AA hit shot down wr OK(Lt WA Smith/2Lt AS Goodwin) to VLAMERTINGHE

B1531   SPAD 7   23Sqn
OP nwST JULIEN combat shot up ftl DICKEBUSCH 10am(2Lt DP Collis **inj) left 9am

B1607   Nieuport 23   29Sqn
OP left 5-55pm **MIA(Capt WP Holt **KIA**) [?"Nieuport" claim combat nrBEAUMONT Untoff Heiligers Ja30]

A4925   FE8   41Sqn
P left 2-35pm ftl EoL **MIA(2Lt TM Sturgess **POW**) seen fire green Very light and land Sh28.J.34.

A7473   DH4   57Sqn
Phot combat with EA, in spin down ovBECELAERE 9000' 8-30am **MIA(Capt NG McNaughton MC **KIA**/Lt AH Mearns **KIA**) left 7-40am, MvR55 ["DH" claim combat BECELAERE 8-30am Rittm M Fr vRichthofen JG1]

N5358.Q   Sopwith Triplane   10 (Naval) Sqn
OP combat shot down ZONNEBEKE-MOORSLEDE ~8am **MIA(FSLt RG Saunders **KIA**) left 7-30am, Ja11 [?"Tripe" claim combat POLYGON WOOD 8-05am Ltn K Allmenröder Ja11, but see N6306]

N6306   Sopwith Triplane   10 (Naval) Sqn
OP shot down ovZONNEBEKE in control Sh28.J.34 ~8am **MIA(FSLt AB Holcroft **WIA POW**) Ja11, lef 7-30am ["Tripe" claim combat nrZONNEBEKE: btwn KEIBERGMOLEN-LICHTENSTEINLAGER 8-20am Ltn G-W Gross Ja11, but see N5358]

25th June

A6511   FE2d   20Sqn
OP AA ftl 28.N.27.d. cr wr(2Lt M McCall **inj/Rfn WJ Benger **inj**) left 5-20am

B1552.4   Nieuport 17   40Sqn
+* combat with AlbatrosDV[+ooc] neDOUAI 8pm then second[+des] 5m eLA BASSÉE 8-40pm OK(Lt GB Crole)

A3847   RE8   53Sqn
**AOb combat shot down nd trenches 4-35pm cr Sh28

U.16.A. wr(Lt LS Bowman **KIA**/2Lt JE Power-Clutterbuck **KIA**) ["RE" claim combat GRABEN, nrLE BIZET 4-20pm Rittm M Fr vRichthofen JG1]

N5376   Sopwith Triplane   10 (Naval) Sqn
"BLACK SHEEP" **LP combat shot down eMESSINES **MIA**(FSLt GE Nash **WIA POW**) seen going down after combat EoL in control 6-10pm ["Tripe" claim combat wQUESNOY 5-46pm Ltn K Allmenröder Ja11]

26th June

B1649   Nieuport 17   1Sqn
OP combat with 6EAs shot down snd 2nd line trenches wr(Lt CC Street **KIA) left 7-56pm ZONNEBEKE-PERENCHIES [?"Nieuport" claim combat nrYPRES 9pm Ltn K Allmenröder Ja11]

B1681   Nieuport 17   1Sqn
+* combat with AlbatrosDV[+ooc] BECELAERE 9pm OK(Sgt GP Olley)

A7144   Bristol F2b   11Sqn
+* combat with AlbatrosDIII[+ooc] ETAING-DURY 6-45pm OK(Lt AE McKeever Can./2Lt E Oake)

This was the first victory for this top scoring Bristol Fighter ace who finally achieved thirty-one victories, five in this particular aircraft.

A7154   Bristol F2b   11Sqn
+* combat with AlbatrosDIII[+ooc]eCAMBRAI 6-50pm ftl but returned a'dr? (2Lt PC Ross **DoW**/2AM W Woodward OK) pilot hit below heart

27th June

A2800   BE2e   7Sqn
Phot ovST JULIEN AA EoL cr 6-35pm **MIA(2Lt FE Vipond **POW**/2Lt GP Simon **POW**) left 5-15pm

Bristol F2b	11Sqn

OP AA(Lt TE Wylde **DoW/)chest

B1663   SPAD 7   19Sqn
OP seen low eHOULTHULST WOOD 6-45pm **MIA(Lt M Lowe **KIA**) left 5-56pm MERCKEM-YPRES ["SPAD" claim combat HOEKSKE, nBIXSCHOOTE 7pm Oblt vVoigt Ja8]

B1572   Nieuport 23   29Sqn
OP left 6pm down EoL **MIA(Lt JDJ Bird **KIA**) [?"Nieuport" claims CROISILLES-VIS EN ARTOIS Ltn vRostitz & Ltn Knake Ja12]

Sopwith Strutter	45Sqn

OP ground mg fire(/AG.Rfn E Sharp **DoW)

A6718.A3   Nieuport 17   60Sqn
OP seen ovBEAUMONT, combat 7-45pm? **MIA(Lt DCG Murray **WIA POW**) left 7pm BEAUMONT-AVION, Ja29 Wolff31[?"Nieuport" claim combat AVION, SALLAUMINES 7-30pm Ltn K Wolff Ja29]

A1872   BE2e   100Sqn
Rec AA FRELINGHEN nrARMENTIÈRES cr 11pm wr(Capt WTF Holland **WIA) to hospital, left 10-20pm to locate enemy a'dr

28th June

N5471   Sopwith Triplane   8 (Naval) Sqn
** mg fire eVERMELLES shot up ftl trenches dam OK(FSLt WL Jordan)

29th June

B1677   Nieuport 17   29Sqn
OP left 6-50am **MIA(Lt VA Norvill Aust. **WIA POW**) Ja29?[?"Nieu 1Str" claim combat nrFRESNOY-OPPY 6-08pm OffSt Gregor Ja29][?"Nieuport" claim combat nrPLOUVAIN 8-10am Ltn P Billik Ja12]

A7488   DH4   57Sqn
Phot AA shot down wr 1000yd from front lines(Lt DM Goodyear **KIA/2Lt FR Martin **KIA**) left 12pm

B1652   Nieuport 23   60Sqn
.A1? +* combat with AlbatrosDIII[+cr,des] DOUAI-ESTRÉES 6pm shot up ftl GAVRELLE 6-15pm OK(Capt WE Molesworth Irl.)

30th June

The Seaplane Defence Flight was formed at St Pol on the 30th of June. It became the Seaplane Defence Squadron on the 23rd of September and would be redesignated 13 (Naval) Squadron on the 15th of January 1918. The unit came about as a result of continued attacks by German fighters on the seaplanes at Dunkirk. It was decided in June that seaplanes should be phased out of this base and concentrated at Dover. They had been unable to counter the enemy and so the new Defence Flight was equipped with land aircraft fitted with flotation gear. The first machines used were Sopwith Pups but the Camel was the predominant type by autumn. Seaplanes were still operating from Dunkirk in late September.

July 1917

ALLIED INTENTIONS FOR THE FLANDERS OFFENSIVE IN 1917

The battle for the Messines Ridge had been an essential but subsidiary action to the main preparations for the offensive in Flanders. These had been continuing on a vast scale through the summer, although a note of caution was unmistakable, as Haig's entire battle plan was still not formally approved by his political masters. That would eventually come later this month, opening the way for another huge battle on the Western Front. This, the third battle of Ypres, was crucially fated never to break out beyond a relatively minute sector of the line, however, and it was conducted with appalling concentration and intensity in terms of both effort and sacrifice.

In contrast, the original plan set the Allies a major and sweeping objective: the Belgian coast. To confront the German Army north of Ypres was potentially very advantageous, for it was the one part of the entire line where it could not simply withdraw to a new prepared position, as it had done so effectively in the spring. To do this would mean the incalculable loss of its submarine and air bases adjacent to England. Germany would be forced to fight, perhaps risking too much. The coast was to be reached in three stages. The first was an advance on a seven- to eight-mile front between Hooge and Steenstraate, with the object of capturing the Passchendaele-Staden Ridge some eight miles eastwards. From there, crucial supply lines to the north, including sections of the rail network, would be taken and cut. Finally, seaborne landings near Ostende would combine with an attack inland from Nieuport to roll back the German-held territory. The Fifth Army was given the task of achieving Passchendaele, whilst the Fourth Army, combining with divisions from both Belgium and France, would fight operations on the coast. The British Second Army, south of the Fifth, would form a defensive flank. The date for the opening attack was still to be settled, but it was hoped to be before the end of July. Air concentrations being assembled for the battle are given in the entry for the 8th of July.

2nd July

Crews engaged on photographic reconnaissance suffered many casualties in the next few days.

RE8   4Sqn
Phot AA(2Lt FT Wakeman **WIA/)slight

RE8   16Sqn
AOb (Lt FL Barker **WIA/)leg

A1575   Martinsyde G102   27Sqn
B seen break up nrVILLERS swCAMBRAI EoL **MIA(Capt F Wyatt **KIA**) left 10-35am PRONVILLE A'dr

Sopwith Strutter   43Sqn
Phot (/Lt W Gaunt **WIA)arm

Sopwith Strutter   45Sqn
Phot combat shot up(/AG LCpl F Russell **DoW)back [?possible "Sopwith" claim POPERINGHE Vzfw Zehe/ Ltn Druckhammer FAb40]

A3249   RE8   53Sqn
EscPhot combat with EA shot down ftl snd wr(Capt WP Horsley MC **KIA/2Lt AG Knight **WIA**) to TENBRIELEN, badly wounded ["RE8" claim combat nrMESSINES 9-25am Ltn G-W Gross Ja11]

A3538   RE8   53Sqn
EscPhot shot down flames nrCOMINES 8-40am(Sgt HA Whatley **KIA/2Lt FGB Pascoe **KIA**)MvR57, to TENBRIELEN ["RE" claim combat DEULEMONT 9-20am? Rittm M Fr vRichthofen JG1]

3rd July

B3486   Nieuport 23   1Sqn
*OP chased & shot down in spin over 42Sqn a'dr by 46Sqn Pup(2Lt T Littler **KIFA**) Pup had streamer, headed south afterwards

         Sopwith Strutter 43Sqn
Phot AA(Capt TS Wynn MC **WIA/)head [?possible "Sopwith" claim combat nrVAULX 9-30am Oblt A Rt vTutschek Ja12]

A7153   Bristol F2b   48Sqn
+* combat with AlbatrosDV[+ooc] QUEANT 9-30am OK(2Lt A Riley/2Lt W O'Toole)

B1585   Nieuport 17   60Sqn
OP left 5pm DOUAI combat LAGNICOURT 6pm **MIA(Lt AR Adam **POW DoW**) a'c captured ["Nieuport" claim combat CAGNICOURT 6-20pm Ltn P Billik Ja12] Cagnicourt 2m nLagnicourt

4th July

         FE2d   20Sqn
OP AA(/2Lt M Lingard **WIA)

4857   FE2b   100Sqn
**NB AA hit 12-55am cr nrRICHEBOURG wr OK(Capt VE Schweitzer/Lt JS Godard) left 12-05am RAMEGNIES-CHIN A'dr

5th July

56 Squadron returned to France from its brief home defence duties, whilst on the next day, 66 Squadron was also withdrawn from Calais. 46 Squadron then returned to England for this work and their Sopwith Pups were at Sutton's Farm by the 10th. They would be back in France at St Marie Cappel by the 31st of August.

6th July

A2726   A.W.FK8   2Sqn
AOb LIEVIN combat with 6EAs shot down on return nrCITÉ CALONNE(2Lt LW Brookes **KIA/Lt W Campbell **KIA**) left 11-30am [?possible "BE" claim nrLENS 2-45pm Ltn Pastor Ja29]

                          4Sqn
PhotRec AA(2Lt DG Money **WIA/)slight

A3581   RE8   4Sqn
**AOb combat with 5EAs controls shot away OK(Lt AJ Longton/Sgt W Studholme) left 5-10pm? XI Corps front

A4313   RE8   4Sqn
**AOb combat with 5EAs shot down in flames 1.28.b.

MIA(2Lt JY Taylor **KIA**/Lt G Mutch DSO **KIA**) left 5-10pm? XI Corps front, Wolff32 ["RE" claim combat ZILLEBEKE 8-20pm Ltn K Wolff Ja11]

A6419   FE2d   20Sqn
OPCent combat with EA shot up ftl cr(2Lt W Durand OK/Lt SF Trotter **DoW) left 9-53am

A6448   FE2d   20Sqn
**OP combat formation of up to 40 EA including red Albatros's[+ooc] ovWERVICQ 10-30am OK(Lt CR Richards/2Lt AE Wear)

A6512   FE2d   20Sqn
**OP combat formation of up to 40 EA including red Albatros's[++++(+?) 4 claimed ooc & another not claimed but seen hit & spin away] ovWERVICQ 10-30am OK(Capt DC Cunnell/2Lt AE Woodbridge)

The fifth enemy aircraft noted above, which was seen hit and then to spin away, was almost certainly piloted by Manfred von Richthofen, who was shot down and wounded this day in his Albatros DV. A formation of six FE2ds had met and been attacked by Jasta 11, and forming a defensive circle, had begun fighting their way back towards the lines. Numerous other German aircraft soon joined the attack, until about forty were opposing the FEs. Four Triplanes from 10 (Naval) Squadron came to their assistance and managed to shoot down four of the enemy. Cunnell and Wood-bridge described the fifth aircraft they had hit as a red Albatros, but did not enter a claim as they did not see it crash. Richthofen had actually been hit in the head and lost consciousness. He spun down but came too at around five hundred feet and managed to make a landing near Wervicq. He was rushed to hospital at Courtrai, where he was nursed mostly back to health. He would not return to the front before the first days of August.

B3475   SPAD 7   23Sqn
OP seen combat seHOUTHULST FOREST 11-40am **MIA(2Lt WH Clark **KIA**) left 10-46am ["SPAD" claim combat ST JULIEN 11-45am Ltn W vBülow Ja36]

B3519   SPAD 7   23Sqn
+* combat with AlbatrosDVs[+des+ooc] TOURCOING 12-35pm OK(Capt RG Neville) Neville claimed 5 victories

A7109   Bristol F2b   48Sqn
DOP combat with EA shot down in flames **MIA(Lt HC Farnes **KIA**/Cpl JT Park **KIA**) left 7-50am eCAMBRAI ["BB" claim(sic) combat nrSAILLY 9-50am Lt F Jacobsen Ja31]

A7137   Bristol F2b   48Sqn
DOP combat shot down in flames **MIA(2Lt H Smither **KIA**/2Lt HC Clarke **KIA**) left 7-50am eCAMBRAI ["Bristol" claim combat nrTILLOY 9-20am Ltn K Wissemann Ja3]

B714   Sopwith Strutter   70Sqn
Phot seen going down ovLANGEMARCK **MIA(2Lt HJ Watlington **KIA**/2AM E Gilchrist **KIA**) left 12-55pm [?"Sopwith" claim combat nYPRES-ZONNEBEKE 2-25pm Ltn H Klein Ja4]

N5435   Sopwith Triplane   1 (Naval) Sqn
Phot shot down RECKEM EoL **MIA(FSLt EC Hillaby **KIA**) ["Tripe" claim combat RECKEM FlM B Heinrich MFJaI]

7th July

Nieuport   1Sqn
OP gunshot(2Lt JMSG Stevens **DoW 14.7.17)leg

A6498   FE2d   20Sqn
OPCentral left 5-21pm **MIA(Lt J Crafter MC **POW DoW**/Sgt WDA Backhouse **KIA**) ["FE" claim combat ovHOOGE 6-40pm Ltn W vBülow Ja36][?"FE" claim combat seYPRES 7-45pm Ltn H Bongartz Ja36]

A4606   RE8   21Sqn
AOb YPRES SALIENT combat shot down ooc wr **MIA(Lt G Leckie **KIA**/Capt HP Osbourne **KIA**) left 7-30am ["RE" claim combat nWARNETON 10-35am Vzfw F Krebs Ja6]

A7505   DH4   25Sqn
+* combat with AlbatrosDV[+ooc] DORIGNIES 1pm OK(Capt J Fitz-Morris/Lt DL Burgess)

This was the first DH4 claim for 25 Squadron.

A4937   FE8   41Sqn
LP ARRAS-ST QUENTIN mg fr hostile KB 11-15am **MIA(Lt JC MacGown **inj POW**) left 10am

A1029.A3 Sopwith Strutter   45Sqn
OP combat with EA cr o't EoL **MIA(Lt T Hewson Aust. **KIA**/Lt FCH Snyder **KIA**) a'c captured, left 3-30pm [?possible "Sopwith" claims HOUTHEM-WYTSCHAETE-HOLLEBEKE Ltn Anders Ja4 & Vzfw Lautenschlager Ja11: several claims by 45Sq in area]

A8281   Sopwith Strutter 45Sqn
OP left 3-30pm **MIA(Lt JVA Gleed **KIA**/Lt JB Fotheringham **KIA**) [?"Sopwith" claim nrCOMINES 5-07pm Ltn H Klein Ja4][?possible "Sopwith" claim combat QUESNOY Vzfw Block/Vzfw Haasler SS21]

A6172, A6183, A6210, A7330, and A7344

These Sopwith Pups of 54 Squadron were damaged on Bray Dunes aerodrome by an enemy bombing attack. Its purpose was to deplete the Allied resources in the coastal sector in preparation for the German surprise attack at Lombartzyde (see July 10th). Most were repairable, but had to be taken off strength.

A7493   DH4   55Sqn
B down in control ovLILLE **MIA(Lt PW Battersby **KIA**/Capt WW Fitzherbert **KIA**) left 8-50am RAMEGNIES-CHIN A'dr ["Sopwith" claim combat swWARNETON 11am Oblt E vDostler Ja6]

SE5   56Sqn
** got separated, attacked by EA out of the sun shot up but returned a'dr(Lt CA Lewis **WIA**)back, slight

A8934   SE5   56Sqn
+* combat with AlbatrosDV[+ooc] HENIN-LIETARD btwn 8-30am & 9-15am OK(Lt RA Maybery) first of 21 claims with 56Sqn, first 6 in this a'c

DH4   57Sqn
B combat(/2Lt LA Rushbrooke **WIA)leg

B1747   Sopwith Pup   66Sqn
OP ARRAS ftl 2AD(2Lt EL Ardley **WIA) to hospital, inj?

A1026   Sopwith Strutter   70Sqn
**PhotRec AA hit 11-50am dam OK(Lt CS Workman/ 2AM SA Groves)

N5480   Sopwith Triplane   1 (Naval) Sqn
EscPhot shot down ovDADIZEELE EoL **MIA(FSLt DW Ramsay **KIA**) Ja24 ["Tripe" claim combat BOUSBECQUE 10-05am Vzfw F Altemeier Ja24][?possible "Tripe" claim combat BOUSBECQUE Ltn A Niederhoff Ja11, but see N6291]

N6291   Sopwith Triplane   1 (Naval) Sqn
EscPhot shot down ovDADIZEELE EoL **MIA(FCdr CA Eyre **KIA**) Ja4? ["Tripe" claim combat wWERVICQ Ltn R Kruger Ja4]

N6309   Sopwith Triplane   1 (Naval) Sqn
EscPhot shot down ovDADIZEELE EoL **MIA(FSLt KH Millward **KIA**) Ja11 Wolff33["Tripe" claim combat COMINES 10am Ltn K Wolff Ja11]

N6460   Sopwith Pup   3 (Naval) Sqn
**Intercepting 22 Gotha bombers, engine failed ftl sank sea 1m swNIEUPORT OK(FSLt LL Lindsay) saved [?possible Sopwith claim combat MANNEKENSVEERE-NIEUPORT 6-05pm Sergt Haefer/Vzfw O Tranker SS16]

N5974   DH4   5 (Naval) Sqn
B GHISTELLES A'dr shot up by Albatros on return dam(/LM WJ Edwards **WIA)

N6462   Sopwith Pup   9 (Naval) Sqn
P BULLECOURT combat with EA[+] ~5-30pm then snd 2000' (FSLt JC Tanner **DoI) [Ja4]

8th July

PREPARATIONS FOR
THE BATTLE OF YPRES
AND JAGDGESCHWADER 1

Throughout July the final preparations for the Flanders Campaign continued, although the high level of air fighting and casualties occurring in the sector already presaged the ferocity of this battle. Offensive patrols were taking the strain of fighting in the air — on the 7th, for example, fifteen British

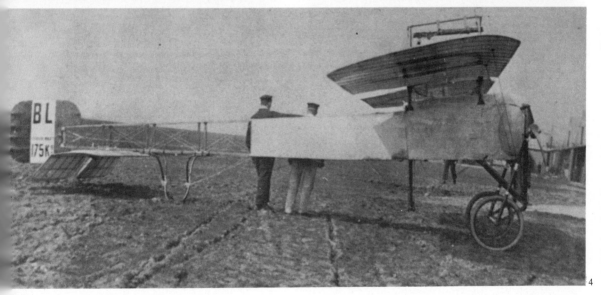

A group of pre-war aviators at Eastchurch in 1912.
k row left to right: Capt GWP Dawes, Lt VHN
dham, Lt PHL Playfair, Lt Charteris, Lt AEB Ashton,
L'Estrange Maloney, Lt Spencer DA Gray,
AG Fox (KIA in 16 Sqn Voisin 1877, 9 May 1915); front
: Lt G deHavilland, Capt R Gordon, Major HRM
oke-Popham, Major FH Sykes, Cdr CR Samson,
A Barrington-Kennett (KIA in 4 Sqn Bristol Scout
578 on 13 March 1916).

2 & 3. The three RNAS Avro 504As which took part in
the raid on the Zeppelin sheds at Friedrichshafen on 21
November 1914. They are 873, 875, and 874. SCdr E
Featherstone-Briggs' machine, No. 873 on the left, was hit
and captured.

4. An early Blériot Parasol notable for the machine-gun
mounted above the propeller arc.

1. A Morane Saulnier in service with the RNAS in early 1915, possibly 941. This crash probably occurred on 26 February 1915 but neither of the crew was hurt. The photograph is notable for the markings on the underside of the wings - both an ensign and early RNAS red ring around a white centre being visible.

2. Early members of 4 Squadron in France beside BE2a 234. They are Lt RM Vaughan, Lt Kennedy, and Lt Clarke. The first two named were shelled and forced to land in this BE2a on 12 June 1915. Vaughan had been wounded on 1 November 1914 whilst with 5 Sqn.

3. Capt GW Mapplebeck of 4 Squadron went missing and was captured whilst flying this BE2b, No. 487, on 11 March 1915. He subsequently escaped and was back in England within a few weeks.

4. This, the prototype DH2 pusher fighter 4732, came down in enemy lines near Ypres on 9 August 1915. Its pilot, Capt R Maxwell-Pike, had been hit in the head by shrapnel and later died, although he managed to land the machine. *(T Foreman, via JMB/GSL)*

The BE2c 1744 of Capt FB Binney of 12 Sqn is seen
on after having been shot down whilst he was bombing a
in near Phalempin on 26 September 1915. He was
unded and taken prisoner. *(K Kelly, via JMB/GSL)*

One of the greatest airmen of the war, the German
wald Boelcke, sits in the cockpit of his FAb 62 Fokker
ndekker at Douai in the autumn of 1915. He was killed
action a year later on 28 October 1916.

3. A German Albatros BII takes off from its snowy
airfield in late 1915, probably on a test.

4. Members of the German unit FAb 23 celebrating
Christmas in 1915. As numbered: Ltn Köchel, Ltn Kraft,
Ltn Euringer, Ltn Ungewitter, Oblt Rudolf Berthold,
Ltn Rieger, Oblt Fillisch, Ltn Riezler, Hpt Christenn,
Oblt Schröder.

1. Fokker Eindekker EIII 410/15, possibly with FAb 23, in late 1915. It was delivered to the front on 16 December 1915 and was known to be in repair at Schwerin in March 1916.

2. Capt AJ Evans of 3 Sqn in the cockpit of his Morane N in late 1915. He was forced down east of the lines on 16 July 1916 in Morane LA A197 and taken prisoner along with his observer Lt HO Long. Evans escaped to England the following summer. Note the machine-gun and deflector blades on the propeller.

3. This crashed Vickers FB5 is 2343 of 18 Sqn, having come down in enemy territory after being hit by AA on December 1915. The crew of Lt EJ Stover and 1AM W Holden were taken prisoner.

4. Morane BB 5137 of 3 Sqn was brought down and claimed by Max Immelmann on 2 March 1916. The observer Lt HF Birdwood was killed in the combat while the pilot, Lt CW Palmer, died of wounds at the end of March.

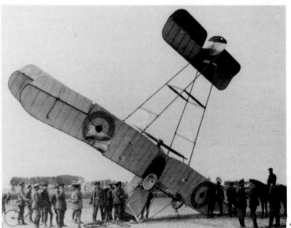

This British crew coming to terms with their captivity
e Lt LR Heywood and 2Lt DB Gayford, of 20 Sqn.
ey had been forced down after combat whilst flying
E2b 6356 on 9 March 1916.

2Lt GJL Welsford and Lt WJ Joyce of 15 Sqn were the
ctims of Immelmann's guns on 30 March 1916 when he
ot down their BE2c 4116. The pilot was killed and the
ounded observer taken prisoner.

3. FE2b 6341 of 25 Sqn, Zanzibar No.1, was forced down
and captured on 16 May 1916 . The crew was Capt D
Grinell-Milne and Cpl D McMaster.

4. A pristine FE2d, serial A5, is seen here having landed
east of the lines, near Lille, during a delivery flight on
1 June 1916. The crew was Lt SCT Littlewood and Capt
DL Grant who were taken prisoner.

1. Albert Ball whilst with 11 Sqn at Savy in the summer of 1916.

2. A portrait of Oblt Max Immelmann. He was killed after engaging in combat with 25 Sqn FE2bs on 18 June 1916.

3. FE2b 4909 of 25 Sqn was shot down in combat on 18 June 1916. The pilot, 2Lt JRB Savage, was killed and th wounded observer, 2AM Robinson, taken prisoner.

4. The wreckage of Max Immelmann's Fokker Eindekke in which he crashed to his death on 18 June 1916. The terrible force of impact on the nose is very evident.

The great early German ace Kurt Wintgens, in the [cen]tre marked by a cross, surveys the result of his latest air [co]mbat: the destruction of 60 Sqn Morane BB 5177 on 2 [Au]gust 1916. The pilot, Lt JAN Ormsby, died of wounds [thr]ee days later whilst the observer, 2Lt HJ Newton, lies [dea]d in the foreground.

[B]E2d 5780 of 5 Sqn sits on a German airfield shortly [aft]er capture in the early days of the Somme Battle, on [Ju]ly 1916. The pilot, Lt WB Ellis, was carrying out [bo]mbing operations, probably near Cambrai.

3. This Sopwith Strutter A1914 was lost whilst being ferried to France by 2Lt AF Organ. It was off strength by 13 September 1916 and was very likely lost on that day.

4. A group of 32 Sqn officers in 1916. From left to right: Capt WGS Curphey (shot down 15.5.17 in DH2 A2622 and died the next day), 2Lt E Henty, Lt FH Coleman, 2Lt MJJG Mare-Montembault (POW in DH2 7882 on 6.3.17), and Capt RE Wilson (POW 2.9.16 in DH2 7895: by Boelcke - the first victory for Jasta 2).

1. Martinsyde G100 7498 is seen here with German markings after having been shot down on 24 September 1916 - a day after its arrival at the squadron. The captured pilot was 2Lt EN Wingfield of 27 Sqn.

2. BE2c 2546 of 12 Sqn having been brought down in combat on 21 October 1916 whilst on bombing duties. The pilot, 2Lt AB Raymond-Barker, was taken prisoner.

3. The Australian ace FLt Rodney Dallas stands in front of

a Nieuport 11 of 1 Wing RNAS. He was to be killed in combat on 1 June 1918 in SE5a D3530 of 40 Sqn when h tally was in excess of thirty.

4. Nieuport 17 A201 of 60 Squadron at Filescamp Farm in January 1917 – a notable machine in which Albert Ba scored ten of his victories with 11 and 60 Sqns. 2 Lt G Phillipi was also wounded by shrapnel in it on 26 September 1916.

ix pilots of 60 Squadron photographed in the spring of
7. The first three from the left are probably 2Lt JL
d, Lt HH Balfour, Lt H Meintjies (WIA in SE5 A8900
6 Sqn on 7.5.17), whilst the fourth is the New Zealander
ot KL Caldwell.

he German ace Oswald Boelcke, killed in action
October 1916.

Canadian FSLt AJ Chadwick of 5 Wing RNAS was
ted missing on a bombing raid in this machine, Sopwith

Strutter 9658, on 2 October 1916 but escaped back to his
lines. The words 'Buster Brown' are painted on the
fuselage side. Chadwick drowned on patrol 10 months
later.

4. "A" Flight 41 Sqn in front of two FE8 pushers on 10
October 1916. The machine on the right is 6438. Seated
on the left is Sgt SF Cody (KIA in FE8 7613 on 23.1.17);
fourth from left is 2Lt SF Browning (KIA in FE8 A4873
on 3.5.17).

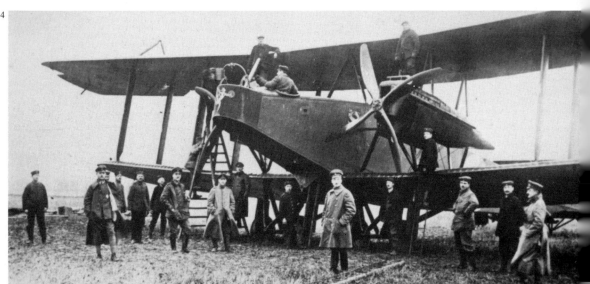

1. Four RNAS inmates of Clausthal Camp, all from Dunkirk. Left to right, with dates on which they were lost in brackets: FLt GGG Hodge (10.11.1916); FLt BC Tooke (20.8.1916); FLt JF Bailey and FLt FW Mardock (both 24.7.1916).

2. Adolph von Tutschek in the forward cockpit of an Albatros CVII of FAb 6a, with his observer Ltn Ferdinand Fr von Stein. The two were involved in combat on 26 December 1916. Von Tutschek would progress onto fighters and become a great ace as well as the first leader of JGII, a position held until he was killed in combat on 15 March 1918.

3. Three Nieuport 17s of A Flight 60 Sqn in early 1917. Lt DCG Murray was wounded and taken prisoner in A6718 on 27 June 1917. The three pilots are 2Lt CS Ha[...] killed in action in A6766 on 7 April 1917; Lt H Kirton; 2Lt GO Smart who was killed in A6645 on 7 April 191[...] Manfred von Richthofen.

4. Handley Page 0/100 1463, seen here at Laon, was for[...] to land in enemy territory on 1 January 1917. The five crew were all taken prisoner and a pristine example of [...] new bomber delivered to the enemy (see text).

WE Molesworth, an Irishman, claimed 18 victories
60 and 29 Sqn. Here he is with 60 Sqn in early 1917.

e very high scoring Canadian ace William Bishop in
perations room of 60 Sqn in February 1917. With him
t WE Molesworth and Lt HW Guy, the unit's
rding Officer.

is pile of wreckage is probably all that remained of
ith Strutter A1078 after being shot down on 23

January 1917 by Ltn W von Bülow of Jasta 18. The 45
Squadron crew of 2Lt JN Lyle and Bbr A Harrison were
killed.

4. Two notable pilots, Lt HH Balfour and 2Lt d'UV
Armstrong of 60 Sqn in early 1917. Armstrong came to be
considered by many as the finest acrobatic pilot in the
British air services. He survived the war, however, only to
be killed stunting.

1. This wreckage of a FE2d in enemy hands, with Flight marking 6 on its nacelle nose, may be A28 or A31 of 20 Sqn. Both were specifically claimed shot down over the lines in the first week of February 1917 and both crews killed. Note the snow on the ground.

2. Sopwith Pup N6165 at Dover in February 1917. FSLt JP White of 3 (Naval) Sqn was killed in combat in this machine on 4 March 1917 by Oblt H Kummetz of Jasta 1.

3. FE8 6397 of 40 Sqn was brought down by Ltn K Scha on 9 March 1917. Its pilot, 2Lt WB Hills, was taken priso

4. A group of 1 Sqn pilots in full flying kit at Bailleul i March 1917. Front row left to right: 2Lt EM Wright, 2Lt MG Cole (KIA 18.5.17 in Nieuport 17 B1555), Lt McKercher, 2Lt EST Cole MC, Lt JR Anthony (POW DoW 25.5.17 in Nieuport 17 A6678), Lt DJ Macdonal 2Lt LM Mansbridge (WIA 3.6.17 in Nieuport 17 B163

pt James McCudden VC DSO and Bar, MC and Bar,
of Britain's greatest aces with an eventual tally of 57
ries, is photographed here possibly whilst on a visit to
qn in early 1917. He was killed in a flying accident in
ce on 9 July 1918 on his way to command that squadron.

n O Seitz and observer in a Roland CII Walfisch of

FAb(A) 292 in early 1917.

3. A type AE German kite balloon.

4. The German crew of a Rumpler CIV of FAb(A) 292
with a most interesting twin-gun armament: a
combination of British Lewis and German Parabellum
machine-guns. The pilot is Ltn O Seitz.

1. This wreckage in enemy territory may be 48 Sqn's Bristol F2a A3330 lost on 8 April 1917 near Eterpigny and claimed by Ltn Bernert of Jasta 2. The pilot 2Lt OW Berry was killed and the observer 2Lt FW Goodison died of his wounds six weeks later.

2. Lt A V Burbury was shot down and taken prisoner whilst attacking kite balloons in this aircraft, Nieuport 17 A6671 of 1 Sqn, on 26 April 1917.

3. FSLt WR Walker of 3 (Naval) Sqn was shot down and captured in Sopwith Pup A6158 on 14 May 1917.

4. Manfred Fr von Richthofen, the Red Baron, sits in the cockpit of his Albatros DIII flanked by other members of Jasta 11 on their airfield near Douai. The date is 23 April 1917 and the unit is celebrating its hundredth victory. Standing from left to right are Ltn K Allmenröder, Ltn Hintsch, Vzfw S Festner, Ltn K-E Schaefer, Ltn K Wolff, Ltn G Simon, Ltn O Brauneck. Seated: Ltn Esser, Ltn Krefft, and Ltn Lothar Fr von Richthofen in front.

1

2

3

4

elieved to be Sopwith Triplane N5357 of 10 (Naval) shot down and captured on 11 July 1917. The pilot of machine was FSLt RL Kent.

FW Winterbotham of 29 Sqn was taken prisoner on uly 1917 in Nieuport B1577 having been forced down

after combat. In WW2 he was the leading principal in the Ultra Secret Organisation.

3. Line up of Albatros DIIIs of Jasta 30, spring 1917.

4. An Albatros DIII D767/17 of Jasta 30, spring 1917.

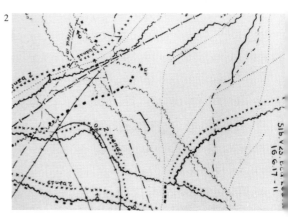

1 & 2. An aerial photograph with its corresponding annotated tracing - the first detailed step in the vital task of interpreting images.

3. The Photographic Section of 35 Sqn RAF in November 1918.

4. The wreckage of a British machine being assembled Westende beach may be the remains of Sopwith Came B3806 of 4 (Naval) Sqn which was seen diving steeply combat over Westende on 20 July 1917. The pilot, FS W Akers, was killed.

airmen had been killed in action. The 25th had now been chosen for the opening infantry assault, but weather and other factors would delay it until the 31st. The air offensive, on the other hand, was begun on the 8th. This would enable time for the organisational network to settle into a rhythm, as well as permitting preliminary operations to be undertaken. Already there was concern, however, at the amount of air and artillery co-operation being carried out by the enemy.

The RFC air concentrations being assembled in support of the British armies were considerable. At this time there was still much to do, but as most of the units involved in the main battle were fighting in Flanders in the preceding weeks, it is useful to summarise them here. By the 31st the Fifth Army would have the use of V Brigade RFC, consisting of the squadrons of the 22nd (Army) Wing, Nos. 23 (SPADs), 29 (Nieuport Scouts), 32 (DH5s), 10 Naval (Sopwith Triplanes), and the bombing unit, 57 Squadron (DH4s). The corps units of 15th (Corps) Wing were Nos. 4, 7,9, and 21 Squadrons (all RE8s).

The IV Brigade RFC, supporting the Fourth Army, comprised the units of the 14th (Army) Wing, Nos. 48 (F2bs), 54 (Sopwith Pups), 6 Naval, now with the new and formidable Sopwith Camel, already blooded in combat, and 9 Naval (Sopwith Triplanes and Pups). The latter would also have Camels by the 4th of August. With these was the 3rd (Corps) Wing, Nos. 34 and 52 Squadrons (both RE8s). II Brigade RFC to the south contained the 11th (Army) Wing, consisting of Nos.1 (Nieuport Scouts), No.1 Naval (Sopwith Triplanes), No.20 (FE2d), and No.45 Squadrons (Sopwith Strutters and Camels). It also included the 2nd (Corps) Wing, with Nos. 6, 42, and 53 Squadrons (all RE8s).

The French First Army and the Belgian forces had around two hundred and forty aircraft, so that in total the Allied air concentration from the Lys Valley to the Channel amounted to approximately seven hundred and fifty machines. Three hundred and thirty of these were fighters. Most of these were now a match for the German fighters pitted against them, but were typically a mixture of both older and more advanced types. The battle proven machines, such as Pups and SPAD VIIs, were nevertheless fighting at an increasing disadvantage, whilst others, notably the Camels and the F2bs, were poised to fulfil their tremendous promise.

With the centre of the fighting moving northwards to Flanders the units of the Dunkirk Command also found themselves much busier. Many important enemy targets were brought within range of its bombing squadrons, and fighter units increasingly met enemy formations using sea approaches for their reconnaissance work. As a result, units of 4 Wing RNAS began a programme of offensive patrols off the coast to counter this activity, which they continued until the offensive began. After this time, circumstances forced them to return primarily to co-operation work with the fleet as the naval mine barrage off Belgium took shape (see below). The units involved were Naval Squadrons 3, 4, and 11, but it should be remembered that five other naval fighter units were already in service with the RFC. Day and night bombing units from Dunkirk were still able to operate widely in support of the land battle, however, and flew repeatedly until the year's fighting ended. The bombing units of 5 Wing RNAS were Naval Squadron Nos.5 (DH4s) and 7 (Handley Pages). The latter was subsequently divided to form 7A (Naval) Squadron before the end of the month and in December this unit was the nucleus of 14 (Naval) Squadron.

The German Air Force had also made itself as ready as it possibly could be for the battle, the numbers of aircraft available to the German Fourth Army being roughly doubled throughout June and July, until they had amassed around two hundred fighters and four hundred other types. Neither of the totals given in this summary includes opposing strengths of aircraft operating on the coast. Here again, the Allies enjoyed a numerical superiority.

Of special importance was the presence of the new German fighter wing, Jagdgeschwader 1 (JG1), commanded by Manfred von Richthofen. Although at present out of action and in hospital, he would return to the unit in early August, and be fighting again by the 16th. JG1 grouped Jagdstaffeln Nos 4, 6, 10, and 11, bringing together much of the cream of German fighter pilots and aircraft. Exactly how formidable it was is well illustrated by its achievements the day following Richthofen's wounding, when it was led into battle in his absence by Oblt von Doering: it claimed nine victories, without loss to itself. It was to be used tactically, as a concentrated force which could be moved wherever necessary to counter the numerical superiority of the Allies. This role was clearly spelled out in orders authorising its formation: "The Wing is a closed unit. Its task is the achievement of air superiority in important operational areas." It was a development of the German experiments towards the end of the battle of Arras, where tactical grouping had been tried with reasonable success. Immediately prior to its formation there had been attempts to use German Jastas

assembling in Flanders in groups in order to cope with the larger British formations being encountered. These efforts had been sporadic and lacked organisation and cohesion, and it was clear that more permanent groups under steady and experienced leadership would be more effective. This is how the new Jagdgeschwader came about, and during the battle of Ypres JG1 would be effectively under the control of von Richthofen.

There was, however, a price to pay for the Jagdgeschwader and the other German concentrations on this front, for they had been made possible only by a ruthless transfer of Jagdstaffeln from other areas. It also meant that experienced and more expert pilots no longer permeated units in other sectors as they had done, so that skills were not passed on so freely. Even along the Flanders front itself the best equipment and men had been drawn off for the Jagdgeschwader.

The appearance of JG1 also coincided with the eclipsing of the main German fighter type, the Albatros DIII, by the wider operational use of several superior Allied types. The seeds of recovery for the RFC, first evident in fighting at the very end of April, had now matured. Its organisation, machines, and tactics had all imposed themselves in two or three short months, and the German Air Force found itself on the defensive.

Oddly, the tactics which the German High Command were laying down for the Jagdstaffeln this summer were a throwback to previous, failed methods. The fighters effectively occupied sections of the sky in standing patrols, resembling the barrage patrols of the Verdun battle which had already proved to be an ineffective use of fighters. Only Jagdstaffel 11 escaped this dictum and subsequently, of course, Jagdgeschwader 1. This unit would be capable of taking aerial superiority in most sections of the line, especially at higher altitudes. The problem for the German Air Force was how to hold on to this by its normal operations. The ordinary Jastas suffered high casualties through the summer because the superiority of the British units was bound to tell on their German equivalents, depleted of talent and experience.

The final point to mention, in the middle of July 1917, is that these records show that the Royal Flying Corps was still sustaining significant casualties on what were becoming the "quiet" fronts to the south. These background notes necessarily trace the events of the major battles. It has to be remembered that whilst the predominantly active front varied with time, the British presence was now so extensive that its armies stretched along a front seventy-five miles long. For most of this the RFC provided the only operational air presence. Fighting was apt to flare up virtually anywhere, and even during the long periods of calm that many sectors knew, it was essential to maintain general reconnaissance and air protection. For this reason, with its resources stretched to the very limit prior to a major battle, very few squadrons would escape casualties.

B1725   Sopwith Pup   66Sqn
OP LANGEMARCK-BIXSCHOOTE shot up ftl 2m nDICKEBUSCH(2Lt WR Keast **WIA) date as per Casualty Report, but AIR1/968/204/5/1100 gives 7.7?

B1758   Sopwith Pup   66Sqn
OP LANGEMARCK-BIXSCHOOTE shot up dam cr ldg? BAILLEUL No1 a'dr(Capt GW Robarts MC **WIA) date as per Casualty Report, but AIR1/968/204/5/1100 gives 7.7?

10th July

In the midst of the Allied preparations, the Germans launched a surprise attack in the coastal area. As has been described, an important element of the Allies' own plans in Flanders was for an eventual landing of troops on the coast, designed to take place between the Yser and Ostende. Elaborate efforts had been made to keep the preparations for this secret, but the German Command was well aware of it. They had watched the handing of the Nieuport sector from the French to the British, and strengthened their army there accordingly. The central part of this sector offered little scope for defence to the new occupants, and so an attack was launched at Lombartzyde on the 10th. Through the preceding few days, preparations for this had gone virtually unseen by air patrols because of low clouds and mist. The Germans had also bombed 66 Squadron practically out of action on its own aerodrome.

The fury with which the bombardment opened at dawn totally shocked the defenders, and when the attack came at 7pm the British forces quickly found themselves pinned back against the Yser and taking heavy losses. It took two days of fighting to bring German victory. 52 (Corps) Squadron was hurriedly reinforced so that counter-battery work could be stepped up, but German smoke screening made this almost impossible. The potential long term consequences of this short battle were never to be fully realised because the coastal operations planned as part of the Flanders offensive were dependent on the Fifth Army reaching Roulers. This never happened, so fighting in the far north and on the coast never took place. Had the Flanders offensive been fully played out, this small German victory which denied the Allies a foothold

east of the Yser might have proved very important.

A7141   Bristol F2b   11Sqn
COP controls shot up ftl 41Sq dam(2Lt FJ Foster **inj/
2Lt HJ Day **inj**) left 6-50pm

B1575.B1 Nieuport 23   60Sqn
**OP combat with AlbatrosDIII[+flames] QUIERY-
LA-MOTTE 8-10pm shot up(Maj AJL Scott MC
WIA)arm

N6361   Sopwith Camel   4 (Naval) Sqn
**P combat with 4EAs ovPERVYSE shot down cr
nrRAMSCAPELLE ~7-50pm(FSLt EW Busby **KIA**)
[unconfirmed German claim COXYDE-FURNES]

This was the first Sopwith Camel casualty due to
combat.

11th July

The same few days of bad weather that had prevented effective air reconnaissance at Lombartzyde,
also delayed the start of the air offensive for the
battle of Ypres until the 11th.

A4240   RE8   5Sqn
**EscPhot IZEL combat with EA shot up dam returned
a'dr 11-15am OK(Lt WG Pender?/Lt Down) left 9-35am,
Pember?

A1963   FE2d   20Sqn
**LP ZANDVOORDE combat with EA prop shot up ftl
cr shell hole o't nrST ELOI OK(2Lt RM Makepeace/2Lt
WD Kennard)

A6370   FE2d   25Sqn
**LP left 4-30pm LA BASSÉE-SCARPE River combat
with 3AlbatrosDV[+des] OPPY WOOD 5-30pm shot up
ftl cr MONCHY FOSSE FARM 6pm(2Lt FHStC
Sargant **WIA**/Lt JH Kirk OK) ["FE" claim combat
nrMONCHY 5-45pm Oblt A Rt vTutschek Ja12]

This was the last FE2d victory for 25 Squadron.

A9385   DH5   32Sqn
+*OP combat with AlbatrosDV[+ooc] HOOGE 9-15am
ftl dam OK(Lt StCC Tayler)

This was the first DH5 victory for 32 Squadron.

B344   DH5   32Sqn
**OP combat shot down in flames wGHELUVELT
MIA(2Lt KG Cruickshank **POW DoW** 12.7.17) joined
EA patrol in error ~8-35am ["Nieuport" claim
nrBECELAERE 8-40am Ltn R Runge Ja18]

A7484   DH4   57Sqn
B seen spiral down ovROULERS 10000' **MIA(2Lt A
Trattles **POW**/2Lt AJ Savory **POW**) left 5pm
INGELMUNSTER ["Sopwith" claim combat
nrLEDEGHEM 6-45pm Ltn O Creutzmann Ja20]

N5357.K Sopwith Triplane   10 (Naval) Sqn
**OP combat with Albatros ovPOLYGON WOOD, seen
dive WERVICQ with EA on tail, shot down 8-45pm

MIA(FSLt RL Kent **POW**) "Tripe" claims: [combat
COMINES 8pm Ltn W Blume Ja26][?"Sopwith" combat
TENBRIELEN 8am Ltn H Bongartz Ja36][?combat
COMINES 8-15pm Ltn E Mohinicke Ja11]

12th July

The 12th of July saw the heaviest air fighting yet
of the entire war. It lasted all day and occupied
every part of the line, being particularly heavy
opposite the Fifth Army, where some major dogfights developed. It was the start of a period of
more or less continuous and intense fighting until
the start of the main offensive.

B3463   Nieuport 23   1Sqn
+* combat with AlbatrosDV[+ooc] MENIN 8-55pm
OK(2Lt WW Rogers Can.) shared

B3484   Nieuport 17   1Sqn
**OP left 7-25am combat with EA shot up ftl cr(2Lt RE
Money-Kyrle **WIA**)leg

B3496   Nieuport 17   1Sqn
**HAP BAILLEUL combat with EA shot up cr a'dr dam
OK(2Lt JB Maudsley) name Mawdsley?

A7154   Bristol F2b   11Sqn
DOP dhAA snd cr in flames BUISSY **MIA(Capt CE
Robertson **KIA**/Sgt JF Carr **KIA**) left 6-35pm

A6663   SPAD 7   19Sqn
**OP RONCQ-MENIN-COURTRAI-ROULERS
combat nLILLE **MIA**(Lt DS Weld **POW**) left 1-20pm
[?possible "SPAD" claim combat QUESNOY Oblt Jahns
Ja18]

B1863   FE2d   20Sqn
LP MENIN AA ftl wr(Capt DC Cunnell **KIA/Lt AG
Bill **inj**)ldg by observer, left 3-35pm, observer badly
shaken in ldg

A3195   RE8   21Sqn
AOb YPRES Salient **MIA(2Lt JC Griffith **POW**/2Lt
WA Strickland **WIA POW**) left 8-30am, last WT
8-40am, slight WIA

A6782   Nieuport 23   29Sqn
OP left 9-55am **MIA(2Lt HH Whytehead **KIA**)
[?"Sopwith 1Str" claim combat btwn HOUTHEM-
HOLLEBEKE 10-50am Oblt E vDostler Ja6]

B1625   Nieuport 23   29Sqn
OP left 7-15pm **MIA(2Lt HM Lewis **POW**) Squadron
was fighting in ZONNEBEKE-ROULERS area
[?"Sopwith" claim combat ZILLEBEKE 8-45pm Oblt
Dostler Ja6]

B1658   Nieuport 17   29Sqn
OP left 9-55am down EoL **MIA(2Lt JW Fleming **KIA**)
[?"Nieuport" claim combat HOLLEBEKE 10-50am Ltn
K Deilmann Ja6]

B1682   Nieuport 17   40Sqn
+*OP combat with DFWCV[+shot down ftl] AVION
10-10am OK(Lt EC Mannock) left 9-50am, EA from

Sch12 captured, another victory in this a'c on 13.7.17

B1693   Nieuport 17   40Sqn
+* combat with 2Str[+ooc] BREBIÈRES 12-15pm
OK(2Lt W MacLanachan)

MacLanachan was the noted World War One
aviation writer "McScotch" and a close friend of
Mannock.

A1025   Sopwith Strutter   43Sqn
**LP combat with EA controls shot away ftl cr
VERQUINEL 7-10pm(2Lt S Thompson OK/2Lt
AKAM Buschmann **WIA**) left 6-40pm [?"Sopwith"
claim combat eDICKEBUSCH 5-35pm Ltn H Adam
Ja6]

A7112   Bristol F2b   48Sqn
**OP OSTENDE shot up dam returned a'dr 7-15pm
OK(2Lt G Colledge/Sgt ASC Lindfield) left 4-45pm

A4621   RE8   53Sqn
**AOb combat with EA shot down 9-10am(Sgt R Kay
WIA/Lt BW Binkley **KIA**)

A4563.B6   SE5   56Sqn
+* combat with DFWC[+capt] nARMENTIÈRES then
combat with AlbatrosD[+ooc] eRONCQ btwn 2pm &
3pm OK(2Lt APF Rhys Davids) first of 8 victories in this
a'c

A4861.L   SE5   56Sqn
.L? **OP MENIN combat shot up ftl LE BESQUE(2Lt
JS Turnbull **WIA**)legs, left 6pm [combat
ZANDVOORDE 8pm Oblt T Osterkamp MFJaI]

A8918   SE5a   56Sqn
**OP left 6pm MENIN combat with EA shot up ftl(Capt
EW Broadberry **WIA**)leg [?"Sopwith" claim combat
WYTSCHAETE 6-40pm Ltn K Küppers Ja6, but see
Nieuport B3496?] Broadberry had claimed his 8th victory
in this a'c the day previously

A8929   SE5   56Sqn
**OP left 6pm MENIN-ROULERS combat forced low
engine failed ftl POPERINGHE OK(Capt ED Messervy)

A7449   DH4   57Sqn
B engine cut then left format seen wYPRES **MIA(Sgt
T Walker **POW**/2AM W Harris **POW**) left 6-05am
INGELMUNSTER

B1566.C5   Nieuport 17   60Sqn
+* combat with AlbatrosDIII[+destr] VITRY-DOUAI
1-40pm OK(Capt WA Bishop)

Combat reports show that two great Allied aces,
Little and Bishop, were hunting together for a
while on this day.

B1760   Sopwith Pup   66Sqn
+* combat with AlbatrosDIII[+ooc] neYPRES ~8pm
OK(Lt TV Hunter)

B3756   Sopwith Camel   70Sqn
** combat with AlbatrosCX[+capt] BELLEVUE
12-15pm OK(Capt NW Webb)

This was the first Sopwith Camel victory for 70
Squadron.

N6350   Sopwith Camel   6 (Naval) Sqn
**P combat with Albatros shot down in flames SLYPE
10-45am **MIA**(FSLt EK Kendall **KIA**) [?"Sopwith 1Str"
claim nrSLYPE Ltn Götte Ja20]

B3759   Sopwith Camel   8 (Naval) Sqn
+*OP combat with EA ECOURT ST QUENTIN-
VITRY 16000'-3000' btwn 10am & 11am OK(FLt PA
Johnston) inconclusive fight, but this was the first Camel
Combat Report by 8(N)

N5364?   Sopwith Triplane   10 (Naval) Sqn
this a'c? **OP AA splinter ftl(FSLt JAM Allan **WIA**)leg

N5368   Sopwith Triplane   10 (Naval) Sqn
**OP combat with 3EAs shot down ZILLEBEKE
8-50am **MIA**(FSLt CR Pelger **KIA**) left 7-45am, down in
spin ovPOLYGON WOOD, but then in control?
[?"Tripe" claim combat nrZILLEBEKE 7-50am? Ltn W
Güttler Ja24]

13th July

B1666   Nieuport 17   1Sqn
**OP combat with AlbatrosDV[+ooc]
ZANDVOORDE-WERVICQ 8-15pm then engine failed
ftl cr o't shell hole cr Sh28.H.11.d.1.1. dam OK(Lt PF
Fullard) to ZANDVOORDE-MENIN-LILLE, last of 4
victories in this a'c

B3483   Nieuport 17   1Sqn
**OP chased down by 3EAs ovGHELUVELT 7-30pm
MIA(2Lt WC Smith **WIA POW**) left 5-55pm
ZANDVOORDE-MENIN-LILLE-ARMENTIÈRES

            Bristol F2b   11Sqn
OP combat shot up(/AG Cpl S Brett **KIA)heart

B1580   SPAD 7   23Sqn
**OP left 8-16am lost canvas on plane diving on EA
"after loud retort" ftl nrYPRES 9-15am dam OK(Capt
WJC Kennedy-Cochran-Patrick MC)shaken, Cochran-
Patrick had claimed at least 9 of his 21 victories in this a'c

A1579   Martinsyde G102   27Sqn
**B ATH AA hit ftl NOEUX LES MINES cr wr
OK(Capt HOD Wilkins)

A6260   Martinsyde G102   27Sqn
**B left 4-40am ATH shot up dam returned to a'dr(2Lt
BC Jones **WIA**)slight

B1506   Nieuport 17   29Sqn
**Esc left 9-50am seen in combat ovGHELUVELT
MIA(Lt AWB Miller **KIA**) [?"Nieu" claim combat
eYPRES 10-30am Ltn H Adam Ja6][?"Nieu" claim
combat ZANDVOORDE 10-20am Lt K Deilmann Ja6]
Miller made two claims the previous evening
nrZONNEBEKE

B1577   Nieuport 17   29Sqn
Esc seen combat ovGHELUVELT **MIA(Lt FW
Winterbotham **POW**) seen 9-50am ["Nieuport" claim
combat nZONNEBEKE 10-40am Oblt E vDostler Ja6]

A9193   DH5   32Sqn
**OP eYPRES AA hit ftl dam OK(2Lt HJ Edwards)

A6240   Sopwith Pup   54Sqn
**SpRec left 6-30pm seen BRUGES-OSTENDE
MIA(Capt FN Hudson MC **POW**)

A7421   DH4   55Sqn
**B combat with 6EAs wAUDENARDE seen going
down in steep spiral **MIA**(Lt AP Matheson **KIA**/2Lt FL
Oliver **KIA**) left 1-30pm ["DH" claim combat btwn
AUDENARDE-DYCKE 3-30pm Ltn E Hess Ja28]

**   DH4   57Sqn**
Rec shot up by Belgian Nieu(/Lt ACM Pym **WIA)

A1028   Sopwith Strutter   70Sqn
**PhotRec combat with EA then AA dam ftl 45Sq a'dr
OK(2Lt CNL Lomax/SLt K Wallace)

A8335   Sopwith Strutter   70Sqn
Phot combat fell in flames nrBECELAERE **MIA(2Lt
MO Baumann **KIA**/Bdr E Fletcher **KIA**) left 9am
GHELUWE-ZONNEBEKE [?"Sopwith" claim combat
sBECELAERE 10-35am Oblt E vDostler
Ja6][?"Sopwith" claim combat ST JULIEN-
ZONNEBEKE 10-30am Vzfw F Krebs Ja6]

A8786   Sopwith Strutter   70Sqn
**Phot combat with EA fell in flames BECELAERE
MIA(Lt CG Mathew **POW**/Lt ED Sliter **WIA POW**)
left 9am GHELUWE-ZONNEBEKE [?possible
"Sopwith" claim combat btwn ZONNEBEKE-
MOORSLEDE 10-30am Vzfw F Krebs Ja6]

These were the last losses on Sopwith Strutters for
70 Squadron.

14th July

B3466   Nieuport 17   1Sqn
** combat with 4HA shot up ftl OK(Lt CSI Lavers)

2562   BE2f   9Sqn
**CP heavy AA ovST QUENTIN shot down 11am(2Lt
WB Cramb **KIA**/Lt W Harle **WIA POW**) left 9-15am

A863   FE2b   18Sqn
**LP combat controls shot up ftl shelled area nrAGNY
7-55am dam OK(2Lt W Birch **WIA**/2Lt D Logan **WIA**)
left 5-45am, inj in ldg [?"RF" claim(sic) combat HENIN-
LIETARD 6-50am Ltn J Schmidt Ja3]

7500   Martinsyde G100   27Sqn
B left 5-20am LA BRAYELLE EoL **MIA(2Lt TE
Smith **KIA**) ["Sopwith 1Str" claim combat ovLENS
6-45am Ltn J Schmidt Ja3]

A1572   Martinsyde G102   27Sqn
B left 5-20am LA BRAYELLE shot down **MIA(2Lt
DH? Palmer **POW**) initials GH?, Ja30? [?possible "Avro
1Str" claim nrLEFOREST? Untoff Heiligers Ja30]

A6266   Martinsyde G102   27Sqn
B left 3pm ZARREN **MIA(Lt CM De Rochie **KIA**)

B349   DH5   32Sqn
**OP combat with EA fuel tanks shot up dam ftl o't shell

hole nwBREILEN OK(Lt SRP Walter) Walter claimed
6EAs, the first 2 in this a'c

A3489   RE8   34Sqn
**CP ground mg ovNOSE TRENCH shot up 8-20pm
dam OK(Lt TC Thomson/2Lt HV Jones) left 7-35pm

A6783   Nieuport 23   40Sqn
OP left 5-25am DOUAI ftl cr **MIA(Lt G Davis **POW**)
Ja31? [?"Nieuport" claim combat BERSÉE,
nrCAPELLE 6-20am Ltn E Böhme Ja29]

A4885   FE8   41Sqn
LP seen eBAPAUME 3-35pm **MIA(Lt WG Thompson
KIA) left 2-57pm [?possible "FE" claim combat
BOURSIES Vzfw Oefele Ja12]

This was the last casualty suffered on the FE8.

**   Bristol F2b   48Sqn**
** (/Lt VWG Nutkins **WIA**)slight

A3254   RE8   52Sqn
**AOb combat shot up dam ldg ok a'dr OK(2Lt AGB
Davidson/2Lt B Farmer) to "WEST END BAINS"

**   Sopwith Pup   54Sqn**
OP (2Lt LW Osman **WIA)

15th July

B3485   Nieuport 23   1Sqn
**OP fuel tank shot through ovMENIN 8-10pm ftl cr wr
OK(Lt CSI Lavers) left 7-20pm POLYGON WOOD-
MENIN-LILLE-PERENCHIES

**   A.W.FK8   10Sqn**
** AA(/AG 2AM H Watson **WIA**)hand

A7490   DH4   18Sqn
ViewLines **MIA(Lt VC Coombs **WIA POW**/Lt HM
Tayler **WIA POW**) left 4-05pm [?"Sopwith" claim
combat FRESSAIN 5-20pm Lt K Jacob Ja31]

These were the first losses on DH4s for 18
Squadron.

A4225   RE8   52Sqn
**AOb AA DUNKIRK-NIEUPORT cr OK(Capt
RWP Hall **WIA**/Capt G Davies OK)

B1575.B1 Nieuport 23   60Sqn
**OP combat 1m wDOUAI 7-30pm fuel tank shot up ftl
in control **MIA**(Lt GAH Parkes **WIA POW**) left 7pm
["Nieuport" claim combat sDOUAI 7-25pm Oblt A Rt
vTutschek Ja12]

B3758   Sopwith Camel   8 (Naval) Sqn
** left 7pm combat with EA shot down in flames VIMY
MIA(FSLt F Bray **KIA**) [?"Mart" claim combat
LOISON-HARNES? 8-10pm Oblt H Bethge Ja30]

16th July

B3478   Nieuport 17   29Sqn
**KBP left 4pm AA hit cr ELVERDINGHE ~5-15pm
dam OK(2Lt PE Palmer)

B1780   Sopwith Pup   54Sqn
**OP eNIEUPORT AA ftl o't sand BRAY DUNES
OK(Capt SH Starey) left 4-20am

A8931   SE5   56Sqn
**OP combat with EA engine shot up ftl DRANOUTRE
dam ldg OK(2Lt RG Jardine) left 5-45pm
MOORSLEDE-POLYGON WOOD ["Sopwith" claims
combats neYPRES 7-05pm Ltn H Göring & Vzfw Krauss
Ja27][?"Sopwith" claim combat neYPRES 7-05pm Ltn H
vAdam Ja6]

17th July

Bristol F2b   11Sqn
OP bullet(/Lt PD Macintosh **WIA)thigh

A6468   FE2d   20Sqn
+* combat with AlbatrosDVs[+ooc+des] MENIN btwn
10-30am & 10-40am OK(Lt CR Richards Aust./2Lt AE
Wear) this crew made a further 3 claims in the evening:
AlbatrosDVs [+des+flames+ooc] POLYGON WOOD
Sh28.Q.28. btwn 9-45pm & 9-55pm

B3453   Nieuport 23   29Sqn
**IP left 10-50am combat shot down cr 12-15pm(Lt PE
Palmer **KIA**) a'c unsalvable["Nieuport" claim combat
NORDSCHOOTE 12-15pm Ltn A Niederhoff
Ja11]["Nieuport" claim combat swST JEAN, nrYPRES
11-50am Ltn W Göttsch Ja8]

B3462   Nieuport 17   29Sqn
**IP left 7-25pm combat with EA oil tank shot up dam
ftl a'dr ok OK(2Lt AB Hill)

A7166   Bristol F2b   48Sqn
Phot seen ldg neNIEUPORT BEACH **MIA(Lt RB
Hay MC **DoW**/Lt OJ Partington **WIA POW**) left
7-05am OSTENDE

B1713   Sopwith Pup   54Sqn
**OP combat shot down in steep glide cr water
SUYVEKEUSKERKE EoL 6-30am **MIA**(2Lt CT
Felton **WIA POW**) to MIDDELKERKE LAKE
[?"Sopwith 1Str" claim combat 6-30am Vzfw J Buckler
Ja17]

B3779   Sopwith Camel   70Sqn
**OP ROULERS-ISEGHEM-MENIN seen in combat
MIA(Lt CS Workman MC **DoW**) to hospital, left 7-30pm
["Sopwith 1Str" combat eCOMINES 8-05pm Ltn Tuxen
Ja6]

N6332   Sopwith Camel   70Sqn
**OP ROULERS-ISEGHEM-MENIN seen in combat
with EA **MIA**(Lt WE Grossett **POW**) left 7-30pm
["Sopwith" claim combat WATERDAMHOEK 8-20pm
Vzfw R Francke Ja8]

18th July

13Sqn
CentP combat(/Lt HS Porter **KIA)

19th July

RE8   52Sqn

AOb AA(2Lt AGB Davidson **WIA/)shoulder

20th July

Bristol F2b   11Sqn
LP bullet(/AG Cpl S Mee **WIA)calf

B1504   Nieuport 23   29Sqn
IP left 7-30pm **MIA(2Lt AS Shepherd DSO MC **POW
DoW**) ["Sopwith" claim combat ZONNEBEKE 8-10pm
Ltn A Niederhoff Ja11]

RE8   52Sqn
**AOb combat with 5AlbatrosDs[+ss,nd] WESTENDE
7000' 3-30pm shot up oil tank hit ftl 3(Naval) a'dr
dam(Capt RJ Lowcock MC **WIA**/Lt Manley OK)leg

DH4   55Sqn
B (/AG 2AM A Tibbles **WIA)

A8921   SE5   56Sqn
**OP left 6-50pm ROULERS-MENIN seen eYPRES
climbing to attack EA **MIA**(Lt RG Jardine **KIA**) ["SE5"
claim combat PASSCHENDAELE 7-25pm ObFlM K
Schoenfelder Ja7]

A8945   SE5   56Sqn
**OP ROULERS-MENIN seen eYPRES climbing to
attack EA **MIA**(Capt ED Messervy **KIA**) left 6-50pm
[?"Sopwith" claim combat ZANDVOORDE-
HOLLEBEKE 8pm Ltn H Kroll Ja24]

B3806   Sopwith Camel   4 (Naval) Sqn
**P steep dive with 2EAs on tail ovWESTENDE
nrOSTENDE **MIA**(FSLt FW Akers **KIA**) ["Sopwith
1Str" combat btwn MIDDELKERKE-WILSKERKE
Ltn Jons Ja20]

N5974   DH4   5 (Naval) Sqn
**B AERTRYCKE A'dr combat shot up on return
dam(FSLt WF Cleghorn OK/1AM WR Burdett **WIA**)

N6360   Sopwith Camel   6 (Naval) Sqn
**OP combat Avtk[+ooc] then shot down 2-35pm
MIA(AFCdr GC Maclennan **KIA**) MIDDELKERKE,
down EoL [?"Sopwith" claim combat btwn
MIDDELKERKE-WILSKERKE Ltn H Jons Ja20]

N5429   Sopwith Triplane   10 (Naval) Sqn
this a'c? **OP combat shot up(FSLt HW Taylor
WIA)arm

21st July

B3479   SPAD 13   19Sqn
First RFC SPAD13 +* combat with AlbatrosDIII[+ooc]
neYPRES 7-30pm OK(Capt F Sowrey) possibly a second
EA ooc

B3538   SPAD 7   19Sqn
**OP DOUAI shot up ftl 18Sq OK(2Lt JGS Candy)

A3436   RE8   21Sqn
**Phot YPRES AA shot down cr in flames D.19.c.
MIA(2Lt SF Brown **KIA**/Rfn H Davis **KIA**) left 2-30pm

B1694   Nieuport 27   40Sqn
OP shot down BOURSIES(2Lt FW Rook **KIA) left

6-50pm ["Nieuport" claim combat CAMBRAI-
BAPAUME ROAD 8-30am Oblt A Rt vTutschek Ja12]

A7164   Bristol F2b   48Sqn
+* combat with AlbatrosDIII[+ooc] SLYPE 6pm
OK(Lt RD Coath/2Lt KE Tanner)

A7451   DH4   57Sqn
**B combat elevator shot away ftl dam OK(Sgt EV
Bousher/Sgt AG Broad) left 4-47pm

B1569.A1 Nieuport 23   60Sqn
**OP DOIGNIES combat with EA engine shot up ftl
a'dr OK(2Lt GC Young)

22nd July

A6610   Nieuport 17   1Sqn
**DOP combat shot up ftl trenches nrWYTSCHAETE
wr(2Lt JB Maudsley **WIA**) left 6-30pm POLYGON
WOOD-LEDGEHEM-MENIN-LILLE ["Nieuport"
claim combat OOSTTAVERNE 7-50pm Oblt K vDöring
Ja4]

**   A.W.FK8   10Sqn**
** AA(Capt WR Snow MC **WIA**/)leg

**   RE8?   13Sqn**
AP shot up(Capt AA Greenslade **WIA/)arm

B1628   SPAD 7   19Sqn
**OP combat with AlbatrosDIII[+ooc] eBOESINGHE
8-05pm shot up ftl ABEELE dam(Capt WE Young **WIA**)
to ROULERS-MENIN

A6709   SPAD 7   23Sqn
**OP left 5-05pm combat with EA radiator & fuel tank
shot up ftl OK(2Lt D Langlands)

A9209   DH5   32Sqn
**OP shot up swVLAMERTINGHE engine dam ftl cr
OK(2Lt TE Salt)

A9412   DH5   32Sqn
OP AA shot down EoL cr eHOOGE 5000′ **MIA(Lt
WH Coates NZ. **KIA**)

B1688   Nieuport 17   40Sqn
OP AA fell ovSALLAUMINES ooc broke up **MIA(Lt
WA Bond MC **KIA**) left 6-05am, wing blown off

**   RE8   42Sqn**
Esc Phot combat bullet(/2Lt EG Humphrey **WIA)arm

A3446   RE8   42Sqn
**Phot combat with EA shot down? nrFRELINGIEN
MIA(Lt BH Smith **KIA**/Pte A McLaughlin **KIA**?) left
8-20am [?"EA" claim combat nrDEULEMONT 9-20am
Vzfw A Heldman Ja10]

A1032   Sopwith Strutter   45Sqn
EscPhot left 8-35am shot down EoL **MIA(Lt RH
Deakin **KIA**/Lt R Hayes **KIA**) [?"Sopwith" claim
combat swYPRES 9-45am Hpt O Hartmann Ja28]

A1036   Sopwith Strutter   45Sqn
**PhotRec combat with EA[+] MENIN 10-30am shot
up ftl(Lt JCB Firth OK/2Lt JH Hartley **KIA**) Ja11?

A5245   Sopwith Strutter   45Sqn
**EscPhot shot up dam OK(Lt OL McMaking/Sgt WS
Wickham)

B2576   Sopwith Strutter   45Sqn
**PhotRec combat with AlbatrosDIIIs[+flames]
WARNETON 10-35am but shot down **MIA**(Capt GH
Cock MC **WIA? POW**/Lt M Moore **POW**) left 8-30am,
last of 13 victories ["Sopwith" claim combat
seZONNEBEKE 10-30am Ltn A Niederhoff
Ja11][combat WARNETON 10-30am Oblt W Reinhard
Ja11]

A7508   DH4   55Sqn
**B fired Very light seGHENT ftl TERNEUZEN
MIA(2Lt CC Knight **POW**/2Lt JC Trulock **POW**) left
4-58am, burnt a'c

B1629.B4 Nieuport 23   60Sqn
**OP shot up engine ss 100′ ldg cr 11-15am(Lt AWM
Mowle **WIA**)leg, left 9-40am, bullet in leg

BE2e's A2849 & A2883, and FE2b A5503 100Sqn

These three machines were destroyed when 100
Squadron's aerodrome was shelled in the early
morning. Treizennes was close to a steel works
which was often bombed at night, and the Germans
were well aware of the location of 100 Squadron
nearby. This unit was now regularly bombing
enemy aerodromes around Courtrai in the
evenings. These housed sections of the new
Richthofen Circus, and this raid was no doubtless
a retaliatory strike for the trouble they were
causing. Air Mechanics AM Evans and J Sowerby
were killed in one of the hangars.

N5478   Sopwith Triplane   10 (Naval) Sqn
**combat with EA[++?] ovYPRES-MESSINES
~8-15am then shot down BECELAERE **MIA**(FSLt JA
Page **KIA**) Ja11["Sopwith" claim combat
eKORTEWILDE, BECELAERE 10-25am Ltn O
Brauneck Ja11]

N6307   Sopwith Triplane   10 (Naval) Sqn
"BLACK DEATH" **OP combat with EA ovYPRES-
MESSINES dhAA ~8am broke up cr wCOMINES
MIA(FCdr JE Sharman DSO **KIA**) [possible "Sopwith"
claim wCOMINES 10-30am Oblt W Reinhard Ja11]

23rd July

A4197   RE8   6Sqn
**AP combat shot down cr in flames WoL(Lt OL Burt
KIA/Lt MW Briscoe **KIA**) left 5-05pm

B1865   FE2d   20Sqn
**OP combat with EA engine hit shot down WoL ftl Sh28
N.15.D.6.6. dam(2Lt M McCall **WIA**/Lt RMcK Madill
KIA) left 5-33pm MENIN, pilot WIA in face

B1606   Nieuport 17   60Sqn
+* attacked KB[+?driven down] RECOURT 12-30pm
OK(Lt F Parkes) unconfirmed, shared

B1608   Nieuport 23   60Sqn
+* attacked KB[+driven down] RECOURT 12-30pm
OK(2Lt AR Penny) unconfirmed, shared

B1652   Nieuport 23   60Sqn
+* attacked KB[+driven down] RECOURT 12-30pm
OK(Capt WE Molesworth Irl.) unconfirmed, shared

This was the last Nieuport claim for 60 Squadron.

24th July

B1546   Nieuport 17   29Sqn
IP left 5-40am shot down ftl **MIA(2Lt AB Hill **POW**)
a'c captured ["Nieuport" claim combat eYPRES 6-10am
Untoff F Classen/Ltn Wolter FAb221]

          Bristol F2b   48Sqn
DP AA(/Lt GR Spencer **WIA)slight

A7176   Bristol F2b   48Sqn
+* combat with AlbatrosDIII[+ooc] offRAVENSYDE
5-40pm OK(Lt KR Park NZ./2Lt AW Merchant) first of
20 victories for Park, all with 48Sqn, also with 2Lt AR
Noss

B3825   Sopwith Camel   70Sqn
**OP combat with 4EAs spiral down ok? EoL 7-30pm
MIA(Lt HD Tapp **KIA**) left 6-40pm DADIZEELE-
GHELUVELT-POLYGON WOOD ["Sopwith 1Str"
claim combat seMOORSLEDE Oblt E Fr vAlthaus Ja10]

N5364   Sopwith Triplane   10 (Naval) Sqn
**OP dive on EA folded up nrMOORSLEDE 7-15pm
AA? **MIA**(FSLt TC May **KIA**) ["Tripe" claim
sePASSCHENDAELE 7-15pm Ltn H Dilthey Ja27]

25th July

          SPAD 7   23Sqn
HAP ground fire(2Lt D Langlands **WIA)foot

A1020   Sopwith Strutter   45Sqn
LP left 5-15am **MIA(2Lt HN Curtis **KIA**/Sgt WS
Wickham **KIA**) [?possible "Sopwith 1Str" claim combat
eYPRES 7pm Vzfw Oehler Ja24]

26th July

An enormous and lengthy dogfight took place in
the evening near Polygon Wood. It is estimated
that on roughly four levels, stretching from 5000 up
to 17000 feet, there were almost one hundred
aircraft engaged in combat. According to the
Official History, seven Triplanes at the top fought
ten Albatros scouts; below them, around thirty
assorted RFC single-seaters were fighting another
ten Albatros; then up to about 8000 feet there was
a dogfight between seven DH5s and maybe thirty
enemy fighters. Below all of these some two-seaters
were firing at one another. In the confused circumstances, most of the fighting was inconclusive.

The second night bombing unit, 101 Squadron
RFC, arrived in France on the 26th of July.

B3562   SPAD 7   19Sqn
**OP seen combat MENIN-Front Lines 7-45pm
MIA(2Lt A Wearne Aust. **POW**) left 5-56pm
ROULERS-ISEGHEM-COURTRAI-MENIN

A8925   SE5   56Sqn
**OP combat 7-45pm ooc broke up neHOUTHEM
14000' **MIA**(Capt PB Prothero **KIA**) left 7pm
ROULERS-ISEGHEM-COURTRAI-MENIN

B507   SE5a   56Sqn
+* combat with AlbatrosDV[+ooc] ROULERS-
MENIN Road btwn 7-30pm & 8-30pm OK(2Lt LM
Barlow)

B1756   Sopwith Pup   66Sqn
+* combat with AlbatrosDV[+?ooc] GHELUWE
8-15pm OK(Capt JTB McCudden) possible victory
during his brief stay as Flight Commander

B3756   Sopwith Camel   70Sqn
**OP MENIN-ROULERS combat with EA shot down
ftl dam OK(Capt NW Webb) left 7-05pm, returned
8-55pm [?possible "Sopwith" claim combat
sBECELAERE Vzfw Muth Ja27]

B3814   Sopwith Camel   70Sqn
**OP left 6-15pm DIXMUDE-YPRES combat with EA
shot up dam OK(2Lt JC Smith) [?unconfirmed
"Sopwith" claim combat nrDIXMUDE Ltn Götte Ja20]

N6356   Sopwith Camel   6 (Naval) Sqn
this a'c? **OuterP shot up(FSLt AC Campbell-Orde
WIA)

27th July

A reconnaissance by 9 Squadron on the 27th found
that the enemy seemed to have made a significant
withdrawal. The offensive had already been postponed once so that the British guns could be
brought up closer. Ceaseless counter-battery work
had forced the Germans to withdraw many of their
batteries. They now appeared to have abandoned
a large section of their trench system, so an advance
was ordered and the new positions consolidated by
the following day. Guns needed to be re-registered
onto their targets and the army settled, so that it
was not until the morning of the 31st that the Allies
felt ready to begin the battle.

          RE8   7Sqn
Low Rec ground fire(2Lt CC Marsden **WIA/)back

          RE8   7Sqn
Phot(Lt JLMdeC Hughes-Chamberlain **WIA/2AM
HV Bennetto **WIA**)slight

A3615   RE8   7Sqn
**AOb combat with EA shot up ftl LA LOVIE(2Lt JC
Foden Aust. **WIA**/2Lt AE Turner MC **WIA**) left 5-15pm

A7134   Bristol F2b   11Sqn
**COP seen ok going north-east ovVIS-EN-ARTOIS
7-50pm but then going down with smoke trail **MIA**(2Lt

J Chapman **POW**/Lt WB Mackay **POW**) left 6-30pm

A8794   SPAD 7   19Sqn
**OP ROULERS-ISEGHEM shot up dam returned a'dr
OK(2Lt FE Barker)

A1956   FE2d   20Sqn
+*OP MENIN lured EAs to dogfight rendezvous,
combats with Albatros DVs[+shot down in flames,+ooc]
nMENIN OK(Lt HGET Luchford/Lt MW
Waddington)

A6415   FE2d   20Sqn
**OP MENIN lured EAs to dogfight rendezvous,
combats with Albatros DVs[+ooc] MENIN-
MOORSLEDE then AA dam, u'c fail ldg a'dr cr OK(Lt
HW Joslyn/2AM FA Potter)

A6512   FE2d   20Sqn
+*OP MENIN lured EAs to dogfight rendezvous,
combats with Albatros DVs[++first broke up, other
destroyed] eMENIN OK(2Lt GTW Burkett/2Lt TAMS
Lewis)

A6528   FE2d   20Sqn
+*OP MENIN lured EAs to dogfight rendezvous,
combats with Albatros DVs[+ooc LILLE-MENIN]
MENIN-POLYGON WOOD OK(2Lt RM Trevethan/
Lt CA Hoy)

A6548   FE2d   20Sqn
+*OP MENIN lured EAs to dogfight rendezvous,
combats with Albatros DVs[+++destroyed, another
shot down in flames, third destroyed swPOLYGON
WOOD] MENIN-POLYGON WOOD OK(2Lt RM
Makepeace/Pte SE Pilbrow)

See entries for 56 Squadron below, regarding these
20 Squadron victories.

A7479   DH4   25Sqn
**Phot combat shot down crFOUFFLEN 4-15pm(2Lt
WL Lovell **KIA**/2Lt WW Fitzgerald **KIA**) left 2-15pm
DOUAI

A9399   DH5   32Sqn
*OP combat with 2Str[+des] GHELUVELT 2-45pm
shot up then hit hangar ldg cr dam OK(Lt WRG
Pearson) shared

A7170   Bristol F2b   48Sqn
+* combat with AlbatrosDV[+flames]neNIEUPORT
5-10pm OK(Capt BE Baker/Lt GR Spencer) shot down
Vzfw Brandt of MFJa1

A4303   RE8   53Sqn
**ACoop combat shot down 3pm wr o.28.c. (2Lt PJ
Rodocanachi **KIA**/2Lt NL Watt **DoW**) ldg by severely
wounded observer ["RE" claim combat btwn
MESSINES-WYTSCHAETE 3-35pm Ltn E Hess Ja28]

A7509   DH4   55Sqn
**B GONTRODE shot down cr HOOGSTADE(2Lt
RWC Morgan **DoW**/Lt WR Cooke OK) shot down?,
Morgan WIA stomach

A8900   SE5   56Sqn

+*OP combat with AlbatrosDVs[++des] wROULERS
then HOUTHULST WOOD btwn 7-30pm & 8-45pm
OK(Capt GH Bowman) to ROULERS-MENIN-
COURTRAI

A8911   SE5   56Sqn
+*OP combat then ooc neROULERS **MIA**(2Lt TW
White **POW**) to ROULERS-MENIN-COURTRAI
[?possible "SE5" claim combat wMOORSLEDE Ltn
Ziegler Ja26]

A8914   SE5   56Sqn
+*OP combat with AlbatrosDVs[+ooc] neROULERS
btwn 7-30pm & 8-45pm OK(Lt RTC Hoidge) to
ROULERS-MENIN-COURTRAI

A8934   SE5   56Sqn
**OP left 6-45pm combat with AlbatrosDVs[+ooc]
neROULERS btwn 7-30pm & 8-45pm OK(Lt RA
Maybery) to ROULERS-MENIN-COURTRAI, EA
from Ja33?

Remarkably, SE5 A8911 was one of only two
British machines lost in a huge fight over Polygon
Wood (the other being Triplane N5492 of 10
(Naval) Squadron). A decoy formation of eight 20
Squadron FE2ds was used to lure the enemy
machines to a prearranged trap where fifty-nine
RFC and RNAS aircraft were waiting in layers for
them. This ensnarement was planned to deal a
body blow to the enemy fighter formations
operating with such effect in the sector. The FEs
had set out towards Menin with the aim of attract-
ing the attentions of a fighter group. Some twenty
Albatros Scouts gathered, and during a fighting
retreat 20 Squadron led them towards Polygon
Wood. A tremendous fight then broke out as the
full body of aircraft met, drawing in every other
English, French, and German machine in the area.
The fighting lasted from about 7-45pm until
8-40pm, when the last German aircraft retired. The
FE2ds had fought very successfully, five crews
claiming victories, with possibly six enemy shot
down. The Triplane pilots made six claims, and
those on SE5s made four.

A7467   DH4   57Sqn
**B HEULE A'dr shot down DE COENINCK
FARM(Lt AJL O'Beirne **DoW** 28.7.17/2Lt NR Rayner
KIA) left 3-20pm

B3963   DH4   57Sqn
+* combat with AlbatrosDVs[+++ooc]
HOUTHULST 5-30pm (Capt L Minot/Lt AF Britton
WIA)calf

**   DH4   57Sqn**
B combat(2Lt ACS Irwin **WIA/)foot

**   DH4   57Sqn**
B combat shot up(/2Lt NM Pizey **KIA)heart

B1703   Sopwith Pup   66Sqn
**OP shot up dam OK(2Lt RA Stedman) [?possible
"Sopwith" claim ROESELAERE, OSTRAND?-YPRES
6-40pm Ltn A Thurm Ja24]

B3864   Sopwith Camel   70Sqn
**prac LANGEMARCK combat shot up returned 8-
30pm dam OK(Capt CF Collett) left 7-15pm

B3877   Sopwith Camel   8(Naval)Sqn
+* combat with 2Str[+cr destr] ovLOOS 4pm OK(FCdr
RA Little) EA shelled by Allied guns, crew killed

This was Robert Little's last victory with 8 (Naval)
before being rested.

N533   Sopwith Triplane   10 (Naval) Sqn
"BLACK MARIA", twin Vickers +*OP combat with
Albatros DVs[++first broke up nMENIN, second ooc
POLYGON WOOD] 7-45pm to 7-50pm OK(FCdr R
Collishaw Can. DSC DSO) These were probably
Collishaw's 37th and 38th victories

N5483   Sopwith Triplane   10 (Naval) Sqn
"BLACK ROGER" +*OP combat with Albatros DVs[+
++first shot down MENIN, second ooc COURTRAI-
MENIN, third broke-up destroyed] 7-50pm to 8-05pm
OK(FSLt EV Reid Can. DSC] killed by Flak the next day

N5492   Sopwith Triplane   10 (Naval) Sqn
**OP combat brought down ooc nrMOORSLEDE
7-45pm **MIA**(FSLt G Roach **KIA**) Ja11 ["Tripe" claim
combat BEYTHEM 7-40pm Ltn K vSchönebeck
Ja11][also unconfirmed "Tripe" claim combat nMENIN
7-40pm Ltn Thurm Ja24]

The Triplanes of 10 (Naval) were involved in the
huge fight over Polygon Wood (see text above
relating to SE5 A8911 of 56 Squadron).

N6302   Sopwith Triplane   10 (Naval) Sqn
+*OP combat with Albatros DVs[+ooc]
wTOURCOING 7-30pm OK(FCdr AW Carter)

N6174   Sopwith Pup   11 (Naval) Sqn
** engine failed in dive on EA ftl sea nOSTENDE(FSLt
EJK Buckley OK)salvaged [?"Nieuport" claim combat
OSTDUNKIRK FlM B Heinrich MFJaI]

This casualty may have occurred during operations
to lay net mine barrages off the Belgian coast.
Between the 25th and 27th this work was undertaken by the Royal Navy to isolate Zeebrugge and
Ostende, and Sopwith Camels and Pups offered
protection to the ships. German air attacks were
attempted but mostly neutralised. On the 27th,
German seaplanes attempted to drop torpedoes
near Ostende but these were also driven off. From
the following day, once the barrage had been laid,
fighting formations patrolled the area. This work
was dangerous because pilots ran the risk of
needing to ditch if they suffered engine trouble.
Indeed, on the 29th FCdr. AJ Chadwick was forced

to alight on the sea off La Panne in Sopwith Camel
N6369 and subsequently drowned.

28th July

7A (Naval) Squadron was formed from 7 (Naval)
Squadron on the 28th of July.

A6680   Nieuport 17   1Sqn
**DOP combat ovHOOGE dive chased down by 4EAs
9-25am **MIA**(2Lt GB Buxton **KIA**) left 8-55am
POLYGON WOOD-LILLE-MENIN-LEDEGHEM
[?"Nieuport" claim combat nwPOLYGON WOOD Gefr
Scheerer/Untoff Sandner SS30][? unconfirmed
"Nieuport" claim YPRES]

B1547   Nieuport 17   1Sqn
+* combat with AlbatrosDVs & 2Str[++des]
ZANDVOORDE btwn 10am & 10-10am OK(Lt LF
Jenkin) most of Jenkin's 22 victories achieved in this a'c,
of which these were the last

A4691   RE8   4Sqn
**Phot combat with 5EAs, pilot hit and fainted, ftl by
observer cr GODEWAERSVELDE(Sgt WR Clarke
WIA/2Lt FP Blencowe **inj**) left 11-25am

              RE8   5Sqn
AP AA(/2Lt CJL Harrison **WIA)

              DH4   18Sqn
** trench mg(/2Lt GR Willis **WIA**)

B3565   SPAD 7   19Sqn
**P ROULERS-ISEGHEM-MENIN shot up ftl
BAILLEUL dam OK(Lt FB Best) [?possible
unconfirmed "SPAD" claim combat nrBIXSCHOOTE
Vzfw R Franke Ja8]

A3986   Martinsyde G102   27Sqn
**B LICHTERVELDE left 5-10pm seen 1m neHOOGE
going west 7pm?, shot down **MIA**(Capt HOD Wilkins
POW) [?"Mart 1Str" claim combat sLINDEKEN,
nrSTADEN OffSt Sattler/Ltn Horauf FAb45]

A9421   DH5   32Sqn
**OP AA engine hit ftl cr nrBRIELEN o't dam OK(2Lt
TE Salt)

B1678   Nieuport 17   29Sqn
Esc left 10-30am **MIA(2Lt JK Campbell **KIA**) JG1
["Nieuport" claim combat eBECELAERE 11-10am Ltn
H Adam Ja6] [?"Nieuport" claim combat sDADIZEELE
10-50am Vzfw Küllmer Ja6] [?"Nieuport" claim combat
BECELAERE 11-10am Ltn J Schmidt Ja3]

B353   DH5   32Sqn
**OP combat with 2EAs 4000' seen in vertical dive down
nrZANDVOORDE **MIA**(2Lt RG Ottey **KIA**)
POLYGON WOOD [?possible "DH" claim combat
nrKRUIS Station 6pm Ltn Stock Ja6]

A4566   RE8   42Sqn
**AOb FRELINGHIEM AA cr WoL(2Lt GN Goldie
WIA/Lt GF Dracup **DoW**) left 8-45am

A8787   Sopwith Strutter   43Sqn
**LP shot down ground mg HULLUCH 7-40pm?
MIA(2Lt LA McPherson **KIA**/2AM F Webb **KIA**) left
5-35pm HULLUCH-RIVER SCARPE

Sopwith Strutter   45Sqn
OP gunshot(/Dvr WA Fellows MC **DoW
29.7.17)buttocks

A1031   Sopwith Strutter   45Sqn
** combat ovPOLYGON WOOD MIA(Lt GH Walker
KIA/2Lt BG Beatty **KIA**) left 7-45am ["Sopwith" claim
combat WESTHOEK, wYPRES 10-10am Ltn E Hess
Ja28]

A8228   Sopwith Strutter   45Sqn
**OP shot up u'c dam ftl cr a'dr dam OK(2Lt MB Frew/
Lt GA Brooke) left 4-30pm, Frew claimed 5EAs on
Strutters [?"Sopwith" claim combat nePLOEGSTEERT
5-10pm OffSt M Müller Ja28]

A4274   RE8   52Sqn
**AOb British AA hit WoL cr WULPEN DAM(2Lt CG
Winter **inj**/Lt EG Richardson **inj**) to Front Lines

A8914   SE5   56Sqn
+* combat with AlbatrosDVs[+des+ooc] wROULERS
& DADIZEELE btwn 7-30pm & 8-30pm OK(Capt RTC
Hoidge) last of at least 9 victories in this a'c, had a total
of almost 30

A7537   DH4   57Sqn
+*B combat with AlbatrosDVs[+ooc+des]
INGELMUNSTER 6-30pm OK(Maj EG Joy/Lt F
Leathley)

A8936   SE5   60Sqn
+* combat with AlbatrosDIII[+flames] ovPALEMPIN
6-10pm OK(Capt WA Bishop Can.)

This was William Bishop's first SE5 victory with
60 Squadron and the first for unit on the type.

A7448   DH4   57Sqn
B INGELMUNSTER MIA(Lt HNS Skeffington **KIA/
Lt AC Malloch **WIA POW**) left 4-15pm [2 DH4 claims
combat neCOURTRAI 5-50pm, OOSTROOSEBEKE
6pm Oblt E vDostler Ja6]

A7538   DH4   57Sqn
B INGELMUNSTER MIA(2Lt HWB Rickards **KIA/
2Lt RH Corbishley **KIA**) left 4-15pm [?"DH" claim
combat eINGELMUNSTER Ltn Tuexen Ja6][?"DH"
claim combat swTHIELT 5-50pm Ltn Czermak Ja6]

A7540   DH4   57Sqn
**B left 4-15pm INGELMUNSTER MIA(Capt L Minot
KIA/2Lt SJ Leete **KIA**) [?possible "English EA" combat
OOSTROOSEBEKE 5-55pm Ltn H Adam Ja6]

Sopwith Pup   66Sqn
** shot up(2Lt T Luke MC **WIA**)

A6216   Sopwith Pup   66Sqn
**OP nrTHIELT seen nDIXMUDE going west 5000'
8-30am MIA(2Lt JB Hine **POW**)

B3823.C5 Sopwith Camel   70Sqn
**OP left 7pm seen combat ovROULERS shot down
MIA(2Lt RC Hume **POW**) a'c captured, ROULERS-
MENIN ["Sopwith 1Str" claim combat MOORSLEDE
8-05pm Oblt O vBoenigk Ja4, or B3874?][?"Sopwith
1Str" claim combat btwn GULEGHEM?-
MOORSLEDE 8-20pm Lt H Auer Ja28]

B3874   Sopwith Camel   70Sqn
**OP ROULERS-MENIN seen combat ovROULERS
MIA(2Lt JC Smith **KIA**) left 7pm [?"Sopwith 1Str"
claim combat ROULERS 8pm Oblt Weigand
Ja10][?"BE" claim combat BECELAERE-
MOORSLEDE 8pm Ltn E Mohnicke Ja11]

N6358   Sopwith Camel   6 (Naval) Sqn
** combat with Albatros[+?] over sea 5-10pm shot up
ftl(FSLt JH Forman **WIA**)

N5493   Sopwith Triplane   8 (Naval) Sqn
** combat AA? badly shot up dam OK(FSLt ED
Crundall)

N5483 Sopwith Triplane 10 (Naval) Sqn
**OP combat with Albatros DV[+destroyed]
DADIZEELE-BECELAERE 8am, later shot down
nrARMENTIÈRES MIA(FSLt EV Reid DSC **KIA**) seen
~8am DADIZEELE-ROULERS, AA? or combat? seen
going down ovROULERS ok? [K.Flak 21 claim
nrARMENTIÈRES] [possible "Sopwith" claim
nrMOORSLEDE 8-05pm Ltn O Fr vBoenigk Ja5]

29th July

Large numbers of British troops were now concentrating in the forward areas in preparation for the
assault, and it was ordered that for the next two
days offensive patrols were to be drawn in closer
and were to prevent any enemy knowledge of this.
The weather was poor on the 29th so few German
aeroplanes were met. On the 30th it was even
worse, and there were no combats. On the eve of
the Ypres battle a summary of air activity would
note: "The enemy has shown less individual
activity and does not cross our line as often as he
used to do. He works now in large formations
which we have successfully encountered on many
occasions, and nearly all encounters have taken
place on the enemy side of the lines".

A3683   RE8   5Sqn
**AOb AA nrVIMY T.5. dam(Lt JP Colin OK/Pte W
Milton **WIA**) left 5-10pm, returned 5-45pm

RE8   7Sqn
AOb AA(/Lt RA Airth **DoW)back

B3531   SPAD 7   19Sqn
**OP left 8am ROULERS-MENIN seen eYPRES
9-30am MIA(Lt FB Best **KIA**) Ja29 ["SPAD" claim
combat POELCAPPELLE Vzfw Misch Ja29]

Bristol F2b   22Sqn
+* combat with 2Strs[+ooc] TORTEQUESNE 6-50am

OK(2Lt EAH Ward/Lt GG Bell)

A7174   Bristol F2b   22Sqn
+* combat with 2Strs[+flames] TORTEQUESNE
6-50am OK(Capt CM Clement/2Lt LG Davies)

These were the first Bristol Fighter claims for 22
Squadron.

B1696   SPAD 7   23Sqn
HAP left 6am seen 4m eYPRES 7-05am **MIA(Sgt AE
Parry **POW DoW**) ZONNEBEKE-GHELUVELT
[?"EA" claim combat HOOGE-WESTHOEK 6-55am
Ltn A Heldman Ja10]

A4607   RE8   52Sqn
**AOb combat shot down in flames eNIEUPORT ~6am
MIA(Lt WM Roskelly **KIA**/Lt HQ Nickalls **KIA**) left
5-25am ["RE" claim combat eNIEUPORT MOLE Ltn
Mattheus MFJaI]

A8937   SE5   60Sqn
**OP seen above EA ovDOUAI then engine failed
combat with EA shot down **MIA**(2Lt WH Gunner MC
KIA) left 6-15am ["SE5" claim combat nrHENIN-
LIETARD 7-05am Oblt A Rt vTutschek Ja12]

B1629.B4 Nieuport 23   60Sqn
+* combat with AlbatrosDIII[+shot down ooc ftl]
eLENS 6-30pm OK(Lt WE Jenkins)

The victim of this combat was believed to have
been Oblt A vonTutschek of Jasta 12, forced to
land but uninjured. Jenkins scored ten victories
before being killed in an air collision on 23.11.17.

B3780   Sopwith Camel   70Sqn
**OPcombat with EA 5m EoL on return shot down
nrWASSENMOLEN **MIA**(Lt HO McDonald **POW**) left
8-15am to ROULERS-COURTRAI-MENIN
["Sopwith" claim combat HOUTHULST-
LANGEMARCK 9-25am Ltn R Wendelmuth Ja8]

N5452   Sopwith Triplane   1 (Naval) Sqn
OP seen WoL flak shot down eMESSINES **MIA(FSLt
VG Austen **WIA POW**)

30th July

Very poor weather.

A9179   DH5   32Sqn
**OP combat with AlbatrosDVs[++ooc]
LANGEMARCK btwn 7pm & 7-05pm shot up(Capt A
Coningham **WIA**)slight head, last of 9 claims in this a'c,
returned with 92Sqn in 1918

B336   DH5   32Sqn
**OP shot up ftl cr shell hole nVLAMERTINGHE(2Lt
AW Gordon **inj DoW** 12.8.17) injured in crash

31st July

THE THIRD BATTLE OF YPRES

The general offensive for the third battle of Ypres

began on the 31st of July. The attack was made on
a front stretching from the Lys Valley in the south
to the flooded area at Jansboek in the north. The
infantry moved forward at 5-30am, and dull, lowering clouds made air work difficult. The day's
objectives, of taking three German trench systems,
were at first successfully achieved, so that by 10am
the first and second of these were in Allied hands.
Stiffer resistance was met in fighting for the third
line, including low flying attacks which accompanied German counter-actions. It was now also
raining, so that the extensive plans for air co-
operation which had been planned for the assault
were seriously reduced. Those on contact patrols
were forced very low to obtain their information,
whilst offensive patrolling suffered the most. These
operations became largely a series of low ground
attacks and strafes on enemy positions near the
line, rather than attempts to confront the enemy in
the air. Though lacking co-ordination, they had
some morale-boosting effect. One new form of
attack not unrelated to this work was also tried —
bombing and strafing attacks by single-seaters on
enemy aerodromes to disrupt the use of German
fighters early in the battle. 56 Squadron did this
work, each SE5 carrying four 25-lb Cooper bombs.
19 Squadron SPADs were also planned to be used,
but bomb racks could not be successfully fitted.
Normal bombing of these aerodromes was also
done by 27 Squadron.

B3474?   Nieuport Scout   1Sqn
this a'c? **SpM attacking KB? combat with EA shot
up(Capt WC Campbell DSO MC **WIA**)thigh [?"Nieu"
claim combat wBELLEWARDE 1-05pm Oblt E vDostler
Ja6]

Campbell had shot down two kite balloons in this
aircraft on the 28th, making him the first RFC
balloon ace.

A4724   RE8   4Sqn
InfantryProtection, left 11-45am **MIA(Lt AJ Longton
KIA/2Lt TL Carson **KIA**) to XI Corps front [?"RE"
claim combat DEIMLINGECK 12pm Ltn Meyer Ja11]

            RE8   5Sqn
AOb AA(/2Lt HK Budgen **WIA)forearm

            RE8   6Sqn
** mg fire(/Lt GC Smith MC **DoW**)

A111   RE8   6Sqn
**FlRec mg shot up dam(Lt Barraclough OK/Lt HJ
Snowden **WIA**) left 4-45am

            RE8   7Sqn
CP ground fire(Lt HH James **WIA/)knee

A4636   RE8   7Sqn
AP mg shot up dam(Capt GA Lascelles **WIA/2Lt MA
O'Callaghan OK) left 4-40am

RE8   **9Sqn**
CP ground fire(/Lt VC Roberts **WIA)leg

A3233   RE8   9Sqn
**InfProt shot up dam ldg ftl Sh28 I.6.b.(Capt EH
Bedson/2Lt AT Miller) [?possible "RE" claim combat
12-10pm FREZENBERG Ltn Schoenebeck Ja11]

A3644   RE8   9Sqn
**InfantryProtection, shot up dam OK(Capt EH
Bedson/2Lt G Leal)

A3860   RE8   9Sqn
**CP engine oil pipe shot up ftl OK(Lt P Warberton/2Lt
TN Robinson)

B3568   SPAD 7   19Sqn
SpM left 11-55am eSTADEN-DADIZEELE **MIA(2Lt
WB Kellog **WIA POW**)

FE2d   20Sqn
OP combat gunshot(/2Lt AE Woodbridge **WIA)chin
["FE" claim combat MOORSLEDE 12-40pm Ltn W
Göttsch Ja8]

A1956   FE2d   20Sqn
** to VERBRANDENMOLEN combat with EA 2-45pm
shot down **MIA**(Lt CH Beldam **POW**/2Lt WH Watt
WIA POW)Ja4, left 2-32pm, Wüsthoff6 ["FE" claim
combat VERBRANDENMOLEN 2-45pm? Vzfw K
Wüsthoff Ja4]

A3229   RE8   21Sqn
**CP YPRES shot up Verys exploded ftl dam OK(Lt
RH? Williamson/Capt SleG Cutler) left 5am

A9213?   DH5   32Sqn
this a'c? **OP gnd fire(2Lt CC Tayler **WIA**)side & arm,
Tayler had claimed 3 victories in this a'c in the previous
5 days

RE8   53Sqn
CP bullet(/2Lt L Collier **WIA)arm

August 1917

1st August

The 1st of August should have seen the advance
being pressed with increasing momentum, but the
weather turned from bad to worse, and the armies
were literally stopped in their tracks. It poured for
the next five days, and flying was all but grounded.
This had a profound effect on the ground fighting,
as General Sir Hugh Gough wrote: ". . . all our
counter-battery work was also made most difficult,
if not impracticable, by our being largely deprived
of the use of our eyes owing to the bad weather
interfering with flying and the capacity of the Air
Service for observation". The appalling conditions
in which the infantry found itself fighting can be
barely imagined. The Allies had chosen a battlefield of clay, which under the intense levels of

shelling that were now part and parcel of this war,
was pulverised into a deadly and impassable sea of
mud. The delay of the offensive, which it was now
recognised would have to wait for better weather
and a recovery of the ground, was a disaster for the
Allies. It alerted the enemy, or rather confirmed to
them, most of the intentions of the attack, whilst
also giving them plentiful time to recover and
assemble reinforcements.

4th August

A9404   DH5   32Sqn
**OP nrKEMMEL AA hit brought down cr ldg dam(2Lt
LCF St Clair **DoW**)

RE8   52Sqn
AP (/2Lt TFP Dennett **DoW 5.8.17)stomach

5th August

The rain ceased on the 5th, permitting more
activity, but the damage to the offensive had been
done.

A4369   RE8   9Sqn
**Phot fuel tank shot up dam ftl OK(Lt AG Peace/Lt GD
Gillie)

A6264   Martinsyde G102   27Sqn
**B CORTEMARCK Station AA controls shot away ftl
WoL OK(2Lt AE McVittie) left 12-50pm

B1609   Nieuport 23   29Sqn
**IP left 12-40pm combat with EA shot up dam ftl(2Lt
AR Penny **WIA**) [?possible "Nieuport" claim combat
wYPRES 2pm Vzfw K Wüsthoff Ja4]

B3454   Nieuport 23   29Sqn
**IP combat with EA shot up dam ftl cr(2Lt WP
Hawgood **WIA**)arm

A4709   RE8   34Sqn
**NFP AA shot down cr sea 3-40pm swam in to
Lines(2Lt AW Little **WIA**/2Lt JG Sharpe OK) left
2-50pm, a'c sank ~M14.b.45.

A975   Sopwith Strutter   43Sqn
**Phot HULLOCH-RIV SCARPE AA dam OK(2Lt RP
Hood/Lt HGS deCarteret) left 4-50pm, returned 7-15pm

A4852   SE5   56Sqn
**OP ROULERS-MENIN-COURTRAI brought down
nrBORRE cr wr OK(Lt DA Page) left 6-40pm

B2304   Sopwith Camel   70Sqn
**OP DIXMUDE-WERCKEN combat seen dive
smoking ovWERCKEN then no smoke **MIA**(2Lt HJ
Ellam **WIA POW**) left 12-50pm [?Sopwith claim combat
wSTADEN 2-15pm Ltn O Fr vBoenigk Ja4]

B3792   Sopwith Camel   70Sqn
**OP left 6-35pm combat with EA shot up dam ftl
nrBAILLEUL(Lt G Budden **WIA**) to BIXSCHOOTE-
ROULERS-MENIN ["Sopwith" claim 7-15pm combat
Ltn H Göring Ja27]

6th August

A99   **RE8**   **34Sqn**
**Shoot AA engine hit ftl sea 100yd off LA PANNE 3pm OK(2Lt RT Barlow/LtJR Orrel) left 2-02pm, a'c salvaged

7th August

A4255   **RE8**   **4Sqn**
AOb combat with EA shot down WoL wr(2Lt A Walsh **DoW 8.8.17/2Lt DJ Fendall **DoW**) left 5-30pm II Corps front

A4375   **RE8**   **9Sqn**
InfProt dhAA **MIA(Capt EH Bedson **KIA**/2Lt G Leal **KIA**) left 4-30pm

             Bristol F2b   **11Sqn**
OP shot up (/2Lt HJ Day **DoW 8.8.17)thigh

A9372   **DH5**   **32Sqn**
**GroundP nrELVERDINGHE AA dam ftl cr OK(Capt RC Phillips)

8th August

It has been noted that although the fighter squadrons from 4 (Naval) Wing at Dunkirk had co-operated with the army in the days before the offensive, they were mostly returned to work with the navy in August. One exception was their involvement in specialist operations known as wireless-interception which were begun on the 8th. In this, enemy artillery machines were located by the signals they were sending down and patrols were then sent up to attack them. 3 (Naval) Squadron Camels from Dunkirk were also allocated low bombing and strafing duties during the fighting.

A3623   **RE8**   **4Sqn**
**AOb combat with 4EAs controls shot away, ftl nrPYPEGAATE OK(Capt WH Gilroy/Lt HK Thompson) left 2-40pm II Corps front

A6528   **FE2d**   **20Sqn**
+* combat with AlbatrosDV[+ooc+des] eMESSINES btwn 10-30am & 10-40am OK(Lt RM Trevethan/Lt CA Hoy) Trevethan claimed 12EAs, Hoy claimed 10

9th August

A6700   **Morane P**   **3Sqn**
** combat (Lt D King **WIA**/Lt W Pierce **WIA**) thigh(8.8?)

             RE8   **7Sqn**
AP combat (2Lt EV Gibson **WIA/2Lt OG Lewis **WIA**) crew? arm/foot, but see 14.8.17?

             Bristol F2b   **11Sqn**
COP (/Capt JA Revill **WIA)foot

A7114   **Bristol F2b**   **11Sqn**

COP shot up ftl nrZOCCS dam(2Lt MS West OK/2Lt F Adams **WIA)spine, left 6-55pm ARRAS-BUCQUOY Rd [?"SE5" claim combat FEUCHY 8pm Ltn V Schobinger Ja12] West claimed 5 enemy by September

B3519   **SPAD 7**   **23Sqn**
OP left 8-14am seen eYPRES after combat **MIA(Lt WH Howes **POW**) ["SPAD" claim combat nrYPRES 9-35am Ltn E Hess Ja28]

A3978.B4 Martinsyde G102   **27Sqn**
B seen nMOUVAUX 6000' going west AA? shot down o't(2Lt WRK Skinner **POW) Ja28 [?unconfirmed "EA" claim combat NEUVE EGLISE 6-50am Ltn E Hess Ja28]

             Nieuport   **29Sqn**
OP combat(Sgt AR Harvey-Bathurst **WIA)leg

B1553   **Nieuport 17**   **29Sqn**
+* combat with 2Str[+ooc] MENIN 6-30pm OK(Lt WB Wood)

B3456   **Nieuport 23**   **29Sqn**
OP seen in combat shot down? nrWESTROOSEBEKE **MIA(2Lt HB Billings **POW DoW**) left 5pm [?"Nieuport" claim combat POELCAPPELLE 5-55pm Oblt E vDostler Ja6]

B512   **SE5a**   **56Sqn**
OP shot up nrROULERS? ftl o't dam(2Lt I Carmichael-MacGregor **inj)

A8928   **SE5**   **60Sqn**
**COP CAGNICOURT AA aileron control shot away ftl 7-25am ooc o't dam OK(2Lt A Beck)

6547   **BE12**   **9thWing Special Duty Flt**
NB left 1-55am **MIA(Lt CAS Bean **POW**) a'c captured

N6290   **Sopwith Triplane**   **8 (Naval) Sqn**
"DIXIE" **OP combat ovPOLYGON WOOD 12-10pm shot down, seen spin from 11000' into cloud **MIA**(FSLt KR Munro **KIA**) Ja24 ["Sopwith" claim combat nrEESEN, eDIXMUDE 12-10pm Ltn W Güttler Ja24]

B3870   **Sopwith Camel**   **9 (Naval) Sqn**
OP combat with EA seNIEUPORT shot down in flames **MIA(FSLt MG Woodhouse **KIA**) ["Sopwith 1Str" claim combat seNIEUPORT 6-45am Vzfw J Buckler Ja17]

10th August

A6618   **Nieuport 23**   **1Sqn**
OP POLYGON WOOD-LILLE-LEDEGHEM-MENIN combat with EA **MIA(2Lt LJF Henderson **POW**) left 1-27pm [?"Nieuport" claim combat with HAASY GUT, nrST MARGUERITE 2-40pm Ltn K Wissemann Ja3, could be either 1Sqn Nieuport lost?]

B1559   **Nieuport 23**   **1Sqn**
DOP combat with EA seen spin down ovBOUSBECQUE then flattened out at clouds? **MIA(Capt AB Jarvis **KIA**) left 1-27pm POLYGON WOOD-LILLE-LEDEGHEM-MENIN

A.W.FK8   **2Sqn**
Attached 5 Sqn **AOb combat with EA(2Lt ETL Jones **WIA**/)neck

A4293   **RE8**   **6Sqn**
AP combat shot up dam ldg a'dr ok(Lt AC Pickett OK/ Lt JG Gibson **DoW 11.8.17) left 6-15pm [?"RE" claim combat MESSINES 8-20am Ltn E Hess Ja28]

A3593   **RE8**   **9Sqn**
Phot **MIA(2Lt CG Mallous **POW**/2AM T Hughes **WIA POW**) left 12-50pm [?"RE" claim combat VERLORENHOEK 1-25pm Ltn J vBUSSE Ja3]

B3523   **SPAD 7**   **23Sqn**
** seen ovZILLEBEKE 9000′ 9-30am ftl **MIA**(2Lt DP Collis **POW**) a'c captured, left 8-14am, Müller20 ["SPAD" claim combat GODSHUIS, nrWERVICQ 9-10am? Ltn M Müller Ja28]

B357   **DH5**   **24Sqn**
COP dive on EA ovNIERGNES 6-20am engine failed seen at 5000′ gliding west ovCAMBRAI **MIA(Capt HE Read **KIA**) left 5am Third Army front [?"Sopwith" claim combat MALINCOURT 6-40am Vzfw O Könnecke Ja5]

B1687   **Nieuport 17**   **29Sqn**
OP lost prop in combat ftl cr wr Sh20 T.14 dam 7am(2Lt JD Payne **inj) instruments stolen while unconscious

A9213   **DH5**   **32Sqn**
SpP seen ovPOLYGON WOOD 1000′ 5-15am **MIA(2Lt E Seth-Ward **KIA**)

A9396   **DH5**   **32Sqn**
**SpP neKEMMEL shell hit cr ldg dam OK(2Lt WR Fish)

         Sopwith Strutter   **45Sqn**
OOP gunshot(/2Lt JW Mullen **WIA)legs

A1004   **Sopwith Strutter**   **45Sqn**
OP combat fuel tank shot up ftl KEMMEL 6-15am dam(2Lt A Campbell OK/2Lt AE Peel **WIA) left 4-55am [?unconfirmed "Sopwith" claim combat nYPRES Ltn M Muller Ja28]

B2579   **Sopwith Strutter**   **45Sqn**
**OP AA nrSTEENWERCK engine hit dam ftl RABOT OK(2Lt EJ Brown/Pte Tappin)

A4666   **RE8**   **52Sqn**
AOb combat with EA shot up Lines dam(Lt HOW Hill OK/2Lt CE Wharram **WIA)slight

         RE8   **53Sqn**
ACoop combat(Lt A Binnie **WIA/2Lt JT Long **WIA**)

A3260   **RE8**   **53Sqn**
AOb combat shot down 3-30pm wr(Lt GIL Murray Aust. **WIA/2Lt SH Short Can. **WIA**)

B1761   **Sopwith Pup**   **54Sqn**
**OP left 5-55am MIDDELKERKE AA hit fuel tank dam OK(2Lt AL MacFarlane)

A8923   **SE5**   **56Sqn**
OP combat then seen eMENIN-ROULERS ROAD down EoL **MIA(Capt WA Fleming MC **KIA**) left 12-50pm ROULERS-COURTRAI-ISEGHEM [?possible "Sopwith" claim combat nDADIZEELE Ltn Stock Ja6]

B504   **SE5a**   **56Sqn**
*OP combat with EA shot up dam ldg a'dr ok OK(Lt VP Cronyn)

A7513   **DH4**   **57Sqn**
Phot left 5-30pm **MIA(2Lt HE Biedermann **KIA**/Lt A Calder **KIA**)

A7529   **DH4**   **57Sqn**
Phot seen going west 14000′ 7-30pm **MIA(2Lt AN Barlow **POW**/Lt CD Hutchinson **POW DoW** 12.8.17) left 6-05pm wHOUTHULST WOOD, Müller21 ["DH4" claim combat INGELMUNSTER 7-30pm Ltn M Müller Ja28]

A6201   **Sopwith Pup**   **66Sqn**
OP **MIA(2Lt SJ Oliver **KIA**) [?"Sopwith 1Str" claim combat SLYPSHOEK, nrMOORSLEDE 3-30pm Vzfw Weber Ja8][?"Sopwith" claim combat ePASSCHENDAELE 7-45pm Ltn H Auer Ja26]

A5652   **FE2b**   **100Sqn**
NB left 2-05am bad weather lost ftl nrCOURTRAI **MIA(2Lt EP Fulton Aust. **POW**/2AM AW Hawkins **POW**)

N5449   **Sopwith Triplane**   **8 (Naval) Sqn**
"JOAN" **SpM BAILLEUL shot up ground fire ftl dam(FSLt ED Crundall **WIA**) shrapnel in back

11th August

A3863   **RE8**   **21Sqn**
Phot YPRES combat shot down **MIA(2Lt CE Holoway **KIA**/2Lt PG Harris **KIA**) left 6-25pm, Ja36 ["RE" claim combat wZONNEBEKE 7-10pm Ltn T Quandt Ja36]

         Bristol F2b   **22Sqn**
** shot up (Lt RN Treadwell **DoW** 9.9.17/)back

A7169   **Bristol F2b**   **22Sqn**
COP combat with 5EAs **MIA(Capt PW Chambers **POW DoW**/2AM W Richman **WIA POW**) left 6-55am III, dive on EAs ovARLEUX 7-45am ["BF" claim combat BIACHE 8-10am Oblt A Rt vTutschek Ja12]

A7179   **Bristol F2b**   **22Sqn**
DOP combat with 6EAs seen 6000′ neDOUAI after combat **MIA(Lt EAH Ward **KIA**/Lt KW Holmes Aust. **KIA**) left 5-15pm [?"Bristol" claim combat nrHENIN LIETARD 5-30pm Oblt A Rt vTutschek Ja12]

A6784   **Nieuport 23**   **29Sqn**
+* combat with AlbatrosDV[+ooc] & 2Str[+des] 5m nROULERS OK(Capt TA Oliver)

B1518   **Nieuport 23**   **29Sqn**
OP combat ovHOUTHULST WOOD seen in spin 6-40pm ch down by 3EAs **MIA(Lt CG Guy **POW DoW**

12.8.17) left 5-50pm ["Nieuport" claim combat
KOELKERKE, nrCORTEMARCK 6-30pm Ltn F
Wendland Ja35]

DH5   **32Sqn**
Ground Targets, ground fire(2Lt GA Wells **WIA)arm

A3482   RE8   34Sqn
**TrenchReg AA hit dam ftl 4pm OK(Lt WD Thom/
1AM Chegwidden) left 12-30pm

A5244   Sopwith Strutter   45Sqn
**OP combat with EA ftl POPERINGHE wr(Capt
JMcAM Pender **WIA**/Pbr WT Smith OK)

A7177   Bristol F2b   48Sqn
**Phot OSTENDE ftl EoL Sh12 M.28.B. in control?
MIA(2Lt G Colledge **POW**/2Lt RNW Jeff **POW**) left
11-15am

A4645   RE8   52Sqn
AOb combat with EA shot down EoL **MIA(Lt DB
Davies **KIA**/Lt RH Sawlor? **KIA**?) left 12-40pm, name
Sawler? [?"RE" claim combat wSPERMALIE 1-15pm
Ltn J Buckler Ja17]

N5482   Sopwith Triplane   8 (Naval) Sqn
"MAUD" **OP combat with Albatros ovACHEVILLE
shot up ftl FARBUS wr OK(FCdr CD Booker) left
6-15pm ["Tripe" claim combat FARBUS 7-40pm Ltn V
Schobinger Ja12]

12th August

B1648   Nieuport 17   1Sqn
**DOP left 11-20am seen in combat with 7EAs
ovMENIN **MIA**(2Lt FM McLaren **KIA**) POLYGON
WOOD-MENIN-LILLE-PERONNE [?"Nieuport"
claim combat VIERKAVENHOEK, BROONSEINDE
12-52pm Ltn H Dilthey Ja27]

B3482   Nieuport 17   1Sqn
**DOP left 11-20am seen in combat with 7EAs
ovMENIN **MIA**(2Lt L Read **POW**) POLYGON
WOOD-MENIN-LILLE-PERONNE [?"Nieuport"
combat swMOORSLEDE 12-45pm Vzfw W Kampe
Ja27]

RE8   4Sqn
AP combat(/2Lt HW Hamer **WIA)arm

A4282   RE8   5Sqn
Det Flt **EscPhot DIXMUDE AA shot up ldg a'dr ok
dam OK(2Lt AD Martin/2AM S Hookway)

A3475   RE8   9Sqn
**Phot mg driven down nrBOESINGHE WoL(2Lt HA
Churchward OK/Lt W Nuttall **WIA**) to
eZONNEBEKE? [?possible "English EA" claim combat
BOESINGHE 7-50am Vzfw Hoffman Ja36]

B1660   SPAD 7   19Sqn
**P ROULERS-MENIN-ISEGHEM shot up returned
a'dr ok OK(2Lt AAND Pentland)

B3507   SPAD 7   19Sqn
**OP ROULERS-MENIN-ISEGHEM-COURTRAI

seen ok EoL **MIA**(2Lt SL Nichols **KIA**) left 1-17pm
["SPAD" claim combat wGHELUWE 2-55pm Oblt E
vDostler Ja6]

B3491   SPAD 7   23Sqn
**EscPhot left 2-56pm seen combat several EAs
eLANGEMARCK 4-10pm **MIA**(2Lt CW Elliot **KIA**)
[?"SPAD" claim combat Vzfw Fritzsche Ja29]

A1573   Martinsyde G102   27Sqn
**B MOUVAUX A'dr combat with EA shot down in
flames nLILLE **MIA**(2Lt SC Sillem **KIA**) ["Mart" claim
combat WERVICQ-COMINES 1-10pm Hpt O
Hartmann Ja28]

A9398   DH5   32Sqn
**GroundP seen wHOUTHULST 5000' 5-20pm
MIA(Capt RM Williams **KIA**) left 4pm, due back 5-
30pm [?"Sopwith" claim combat nPOELCAPPELLE
4-10pm? Ltn J Schmidt Ja3]

A6771.I   Nieuport 23   40Sqn
P left 7-10pm **MIA(2Lt WD Cullen **POW**)

RE8   52Sqn
AOb combat(/AG.2AM R Bestford **KIA)

DH4   55Sqn
** (/2Lt HKR Bent **WIA**)severe

B3966   DH4   55Sqn
**B combat 12EA ovISEGHEM on return ftl wr(Capt
GW Frost **inj**/2Lt H Dunstan **WIA**) left 3-07pm
INGELMUNSTER

13th August

FE2d?   20Sqn
DOP combat shot up(/2Lt J Cawley **WIA)arm

B1698   SPAD 7   23Sqn
**P left 9am seen going down in spin nrLANGEMARCK
but flatten out & go south **MIA**(2Lt HG Tinney **POW**)
[?"SPAD" claim combat FREZENBERG 10-04am? Ltn
F Loerzer Ja26]

A4268   RE8   34Sqn
**NFP AA shot up dam OK(Capt GC Pirie/2Lt WC
Thompson)

A8276   Sopwith Strutter   43Sqn
**LP AA prop hit ftl dam MAZINGARBE 6-45am(Lt
CL Veitch **inj**/2Lt F Marshall-Lewis **inj**) left 5-45am
HULLOCH-SCARPE

A1044   Sopwith Strutter   45Sqn
**P left 4-55pm shot up ftl 1Sq(Capt AT Harris OK/2Lt
PFH Webb **WIA**)

A2157   DH4   55Sqn
**B GHENT combat with EAs on return fell ooc
nrMELLE **MIA**(Lt PB McNally **KIA**/2AM C Kelly
KIA) left 6-33am [?"EA" claim combat SCHELLEBEKE,
eGHENT 8-20am Ltn Bockelmann Ja11]

A7429.3   DH4   55Sqn
**B DEYNZE combat with EA after bombing ftl WoL
wr(Lt CW Davyes OK/Lt WR Cooke **inj**)

A7475 DH4 55Sqn
**B DEYNZE Rail Jctn combat with EA on return
ovROULERS nd fire **MIA**(Capt PG Kirk **KIA**/Lt GT
Young-Fullalove **KIA**) left 6-42am, observer jumped

B4852 SE5a 56Sqn
*EscBOP shot down ftl nrBORRE eHAZEBROUCK cr
OK(2Lt LW Ramage) left 7-50am MELLE-DEYNZE

14th August

A4370 RE8 7Sqn
**CP combat shot up dam ldg ok(Capt CH Gardner
WIA/Lt WH Davies **WIA**) left 6-05am, returned to a'dr

A4734 RE8 7Sqn
**AOb combat shot up dam returned a'dr ok(Lt N
Sharples OK/2Lt OG Lewis Aust. **WIA**) left 7-55am,
severely wounded in lung & arm

A3699 RE8 9Sqn
**AOb LANGEMARCK shot up dam OK(Lt H Turner/
Sgt AL Corson)

B3406 RE8 9Sqn
AOb left 9am combat with 3EAs **MIA(2Lt FW Curtis
KIA/Lt FB Doran **KIA**) [?"RE" claim combat
BOESINGHE 9-40am Oblt Reinhard Ja11][possible
?"RE" claim combat ZILLEBEKE 9-15am Ltn E
Loewenhardt Ja10]

B228 A.W.FK8 10Sqn
**AOb AA down in ss but slight control? 5-10pm
MIA(Lt D Gordon **KIA**/Lt PG Cameron **KIA**) left
3-30pm

SPAD 7 23Sqn
OP combat(2Lt CK Smith **WIA)foot [?possible
"SPAD" claim combat BOESINGHE Oblt W Reinhard
Ja11]

A2159 DH4 25Sqn
**B left 6-05pm combat with 20EAs broke up, seen in
pieces nrWINGLES 7-35pm **MIA**(2Lt PL McGavin
KIA/2Lt N Field **KIA**) to DOIGNIES A'dr ["Mart"
claim combat PONT À VENDIN 7-30pm Ltn E Udet
Ja37]

B1557 Nieuport 17 29Sqn
** left 8-30am down EoL **MIA**(Capt TA Oliver **KIA**)

A3828 RE8 53Sqn
FlRec left 2-15pm **MIA(2Lt JE Goodman **KIA**/2Lt FE
Kebblewhite **KIA**) [?possible "RE" claim combat
sKEMMEL 3pm Untoff Reinhold Ja24] [?possible "RE"
claim combat BIXSCHOOTE 5-50pm Vzfw W Seitz
Ja8]

A7410 DH4 55Sqn
**B ABEELHOEK A'dr combat with EA ftl WoL cr
wr(Lt Whitehead/2Lt HB Macdonald) left 4-05pm
["English EA" claim combat HOLLEBEKE 4-40pm Ltn
W Blume Ja26]

A7470 DH4 55Sqn
**B ABEELHOEK combat with EA shot up dam

returned a'dr ok(2Lt CA? Stevens OK/2Lt BF Sandy
WIA)slight

A4868 SE5 56Sqn
+* combat with 2Str eWESTROOSEBEKE btwn
5-30pm & 6-30pm OK(2Lt RH Sloley)

A8943 SE5 56Sqn
**OP spiral down after combat ovHOUTHULST ok
low?: flattened out **MIA**(Lt JG Young **POW**) left 5pm
ROULERS-MENIN-COURTRAI-ISEGHEM
["Sopwith" claim combat HOUTHULST 6-35pm Ltn H
Adam Ja6]

B509 SE5a 56Sqn
**OP combat ovHOUTHULST shot down then not seen
MIA(2Lt DA Page **POW DoW**) left 5pm ROULERS-
MENIN-COURTRAI-ISEGHEM [?"Sopwith" claim
combat neST JULIEN-POELCAPPELLE 6-30pm Oblt
E vDostler Ja6]

B3820 Sopwith Camel 9 (Naval) Sqn
**OP combat with AlbatrosD nrNIEUPORT shot down
in spin **MIA**(FSLt MN Baron **KIA**) seen EoL alone
["Sopwith 1Str" claim combat wSLYPE 5-40pm Ltn O
Fitzner Ja17]

N536 Sopwith Triplane 10 (Naval) Sqn
2-gun Triplane **OP AA hit nrZILLEBEKE LAKE
4pm shot down, seen going west under heavy fire
MIA(FSLt SH Lloyd **KIA**)

15th August

FIGHTING FOR HILL 70

A day before fighting at Ypres re-intensified, a
subsidiary action was fought opposite Lens, in the
First Army area to the south. This was organised
to draw German resources from Flanders, and
centred around a successful Canadian attack on
Hill 70 at Loos. Some of the RFC squadrons which
were involved in this fighting were No 16 (RE8s),
who were attached to the Canadian Corps and did
the essential corps work of artillery co-operation,
photography and contact patrolling; Nos.10 (FK8),
25 (DH4), and 27 (Martinsydes), who carried out
important bombing of railway junctions, billets and
aerodromes prior to the attack; and Nos. 40
(Nieuport Scouts) and 8 Naval (Triplanes), who
managed highly effective offensive patrolling and
protection of the corps machines. Strutters from 43
Squadron also spent all day in a variety of demanding roles that not only included challenging any
enemy aeroplanes, but also general observation,
attacking of artillery positions, and low strafing of
counter-attacking troops. As can be seen from the
entries below, the Strutter crews paid heavily for
this work.

A4630   RE8   6Sqn
**AP combat with HA fuel tank shot up ftl cr OK(Lt
GAS Nicholson/Lt FL McCreary) left 7-35am

RE8   16Sqn
AP AA shell(/2Lt J Douglas **WIA)slight, shoulder

A3648   RE8   16Sqn
**AOb LENS ground mg dam returned a'dr ok OK(2Lt
Burnand/2Lt Harle) left 4-40am

A5152   FE2d   20Sqn
**P AA engine hit ftl DICKEBUSCH wr(2Lt CH
Cameron OK/Pte SE Pilbrow **KIA**), Voss36? [?probable
"FE" claim combat ZILLEBEKE LAKE 6-10pm Ltn W
Voss Ja10, but see A6500?]

A6500   FE2d   20Sqn
**OP combat with EA nYPRES shot up ftl Sh28NW
H.6.a.5.5.(2Lt JM McLean **WIA**/Gnr A Owen **DoW**)
gunner hit in head, Ja24, Kroll (or Voss?) ["FE" claim
nYPRES 5-55pm combat Ltn H Kroll Ja24, but see
A5152?]

B1682   Nieuport 17   40Sqn
OP left 6-50pm seen ok eLA BASSÉE **MIA(Capt WG
Pender MC **KIA**) ["Nieuport" claim combat wANNAY
7-45pm Oblt H Bethge Ja30]

Sopwith Strutter 43Sqn
SpM ground mg fire(2Lt CA Hargreaves **DoW/)
stomach

Sopwith Strutter 43Sqn
SpM ground mg fire(/2Lt EW Pritchard **WIA)foot

Sopwith Strutter 43Sqn
SpM ground fire(2Lt AN Maplestowe **WIA/)leg

A1079.B6 **Sopwith Strutter 43Sqn**
SpM neLENS **MIA(2Lt HDB Snelgrove **KIA**/2AM W
Addison **KIA**) left A.L.G. 8-10am ["Sopwith" claim
combat with HARNES 9-25am Ltn E Udet Ja37]

A8294   Sopwith Strutter 43Sqn
SpM left A.L.G. 9am neLENS **MIA(2Lt CG Moore
KIA/2Lt JB Smith **KIA**)

A8906   SE5   56Sqn
**OP radiator shot up engine seized ftl LENS dam
OK(Capt GH Bowman) left 6-15pm

A6212   Sopwith Pup   66Sqn
**OP shot up ftl 11Sqn a'dr dam(Lt OD Hay
WIA)hospital

16th August

THE DEVELOPMENT OF LOW
FLYING IN THE BATTLE OF YPRES

The Ypres operations recommenced on the 16th.
These were concentrated in the northern part of the
sector, in front of Langemarck, and fighting lasted
for three days. The weather was again disadvan-

tageous, being cloudy. On the left, progress was
made to Langemarck and beyond, but in the
centre, especially north of St Julien, new German
"pill-box" strongpoints caused huge problems.
These were heavily constructed machine-gun
points, numerous and well defended. Ludendorff's
"elastic defence" was also in full flow, whereby
guns and most of the infantry were withdrawn from
areas suffering bombardment and turned to make
fierce counter-attacks elsewhere on the line. Low
cloud and drifting smoke made it very difficult for
air observers to make sense of these. The British
were unsure of how to proceed against either of the
new tactics. The new weapon of the tank might
have helped, but the mud made it almost
impossible to use.

The plans for air support were ambitiously conceived and were most notable for the increasing
emphasis being placed on low-flying infantry
protection and ground attack. Some of its effectiveness was robbed by the weather and the confused
fighting, but it was clear from this battle onwards
that ground attack was to be a regular activity for
the RFC. It was planned to be used in a number
of ways. For instance, two DH5s were allotted to
each divisional front with orders to strafe and
attack any enemy strong points as the final
objectives were being reached. Some 32 Squadron
DH5s managed to do this. Other low flying fighter
patrols went behind the Fifth Army front to
machine-gun enemy counter-attacking build-ups.
Operating over the German forward positions they
were also expected to disrupt the opponent's
contact patrolling. 29 Squadron Nieuports and 19
Squadron SPADs spent most of the day doing this
work. These activities were deriving the benefits of
greater co-ordination. For example, these last
mentioned fighter patrols extended their remit
deeper into enemy territory later in the day, in
order to attack reinforcements which would be
coming into the area. Ground attacks were also
widely made on targets beyond the immediate
battle zone. In the back area west of Staden and
Dadizeele, machines from both corps and army
squadrons were encouraged to go down low and
attack ground targets, whilst further east, fighters
from 9th (Headquarters) Wing would strafe and
bomb airfields once again. These same squadrons,
namely Nos. 56, 66, and 70, the latter now equipped with Sopwith Camels, would provide
continuous offensive patrols through the day,
although the weather meant that not much air
fighting was decisive. 27 and 55 Squadrons would
bomb airfields and rail targets on several missions,
both units losing crews on this work.

Nieuport 1Sqn
DOP gunshot(2Lt JHC Nixon **WIA)head

B3455 Nieuport 17 1Sqn
+* combat with AlbatrosDV[+ooc] HOUTHULST
7-45pm OK(Capt TF Hazell Irl.) 20th & last victory for
Hazell with 1Sqn

A3848 RE8 4Sqn
**CP shell hit ftl 4Sq ok(2Lt DR Starley OK/Lt BCR
Grimwood **WIA**) to hospital, left 1-10pm

This crew is probably the one described in the
Official History, who were about to transmit news
of a counter-attack forming when their machine
was hit by a shell. Their wireless was wrecked and
so a message bag was dropped at divisional headquarters. Another 4 Squadron machine on contact
patrol attacked troops on the ground with machine-
gun fire.

A3856 RE8 7Sqn
CP broke up cr **MIA(2Lt D Townsend **KIA**/Lt LV
Gray **KIA**) left 7-25am LANGEMARCK-"WINNIPEG
RD"

A3875 RE8 7Sqn
**CP shelled ovPILCKEM ftl cr fire on ldg wr(Lt WH
Luxton **inj**/Lt B Mason **inj**) left 8-15am
LANGEMARCK-"WINNEPEG RD"

RE8s of 7 Squadron also shot down two Albatros
Scouts on their contact patrols through the day.

RE8 9Sqn
CP ground fire(/2Lt TN Robinson **WIA)arm

A3208 RE8 9Sqn
PhotRec **MIA(2Lt HA Churchward **KIA**/Lt EH Ward
KIA) left 12-15pm

A3591 RE8 9Sqn
**AOb combat with EA? shot up dam returned 21Sqn
a'dr OK(Capt B Weil/2Lt GJ Fogarty)

A3626 RE8 9Sqn
**CP combat with 3EAs 2000' but gun jam, then down
to attack EA ovBROENBEEK 400' 3-45pm but heavy
ground mg & observer **WIA**(Capt SJ? Sutton OK/2Lt
WF Leech **DoW** 18.8.17)thigh, had been 30 minutes early
for flare call, so attacked EAs

A4364 RE8 9Sqn
CAP **MIA(2Lt MT Wright **POW**/Lt AES Barton
POW) left 9-20am

B3426 RE8 9Sqn
**CAP shot up OK(2Lt VW Burgess/Lt CH Dixon)
repairable

A3676 RE8 12Sqn
+*AOb combat with AviatikC[+?des] ovFONTAINE
5600' 5-45pm OK(Lt Marm/AM Cartwright) EA stalled
& possibly dived to ground

A6634 SPAD 7 19Sqn
P combat ~12-10pm eYPRES shot down **MIA(Lt AT

Shipwright **POW**) left 11-56am [? possible "SPAD" claim
combat nrPASSCHENDAELE OffSt Klein Ja18]

B1622 SPAD 7 19Sqn
**OP left 7-25am shot up dam returned a'dr 8-45am
OK(Lt OC Bryson) eventually claimed 12 victories with
19Sqn

B1653 SPAD 7 19Sqn
**P combat with EA shot up ftl ldg ok H18.a-96(Lt HL
Waite **WIA**)leg hospital [?"SPAD" claim combat
nrLANGEMARCK 8-35am? Oblt B Loerzer Ja26]

B3471 SPAD 7 19Sqn
OP left 12-02pm seen combat eYPRES **MIA(Lt CD
Thompson **POW**) a'c captured [?possible "SPAD" claim
eBELLEWARDE Untoff Brandl/Untoff Emmerich SS24,
but other SPAD claims in area?]

B3615 SPAD 7 19Sqn
**OP left 7-56am shot up dam returned a'dr 9-46am
OK(2Lt AAND Pentland) a'c repairable [+?possible
"SPAD" claim neYPRES 9-45am ObFlm Schönfelder
Ja7]

A6448 FE2d 20Sqn
**OP left 10-40am AA hit dam ftl Sh28H 15.b.1.8.
OK(Lt HGET Luchford/2Lt J Tennant)

A3599 RE8 21Sqn
**FlRec left 7-42am YPRES combat with 9AlbatrosDs
[+ooc+BritAA] BELLEWARDE LAKE 7000' 10-20am
AA fuel tank & engine shot up ftl Sh28H 10.D.2.8.
OK(Sgt AAL Moir/2Lt ML Hatch) [?poss "RE" claims
ST JULIEN 6-25am Ltn Trager & Ltn Wendelmuth
both Ja8]

This was the first of a few victories for 21 Squadron
in RE8s.

A4638 RE8 21Sqn
**InfProt shell hit 9-15am engine dam ftl cr shell hole wr
nrYPRES(2Lt CJG Etheridge OK/2Lt HD? Scudamore
inj) *initials* HG?, left 7-10am, observer shaken

B3414 RE8 21Sqn
CP ground fire dam ftl 7-40am(Capt JS Barnes **WIA/
Lt VH Hughes OK) left 6-40am

SPAD 7 23Sqn
SpM combat(2Lt WR Brookes **WIA)leg

A6261 Martinsyde G102 27Sqn
**B seen MENIN-COURTRAI going south-east 5000'
MIA(2Lt AR Baker **KIA**) left 10-40am COURTRAI
["Mart" claim combat nLINSELLES 11-20am Ltn E
Mohnicke Ja11]

A6611 Nieuport 17 29Sqn
** combat with 2EAs sHOUTHULST WOOD 6-50am
MIA(2Lt WHT Williams **POW DoW** 22.8.17) left
6-25am ["Nieuport" claim combat swHOUTHULST
6-55am Rittm M Fr vRichthofen JG1]

A108 RE8 34Sqn
TrReg shot up ftl 3-10pm(2Lt ET Molyneux **WIA/2Lt
A Robertson **DoW** 17.8.17) to hospital, left 2pm

B2560   Sopwith Strutter   45Sqn
**OP gunshot shot up dam cr nrESTAIRES(Lt AJ
Heywood OK/AG.Pte W Whittington **WIA**)leg

A7495   DH4   55Sqn
BPhot LYS VALLEY A'dr **MIA(Lt CB Waters **POW**/
2Lt GM Smith **POW**) left 10-40am

DH4   57Sqn
B hit by explosive bullet(/AG.Cpl CR Goffe **WIA)arm

57 Squadron was attacking railway targets at
Ingelmunster and Courtrai, as well as aerodromes
at Heule and Reckem.

B3756   Sopwith Camel   70Sqn
**OP seen dive on 2EAs ovPOLYGON WOOD combat
4000′ 7-45am **MIA**(Capt NW Webb MC **KIA**)Voss, left
6-05pm ["Sopwith 1Str" claim combat nrST JULIEN
8pm Ltn W Voss Ja10]

B3873   Sopwith Camel   70Sqn
**B left 4-55am ARMENTIÈRES-COURTRAI A'dr,
seen nrBISSEGHEM **MIA**(Capt AR Hudson **POW**)

B3890   Sopwith Camel   70Sqn
**B left 4-45am ARMENTIÈRES-BISSEGHEM A'dr
mg fire shot up after attacking train at RUMBEKE ftl
dam in ldg 6am OK(2Lt JG Crang) also destroyed a'c in
hangar at a'dr?

N6304.K Sopwith Triplane   1 (Naval) Sqn
**OP left 9-50am seen ovYPRES 11am, shot down
ZILLEBEKE LAKE **MIA**(FSLt AT Gray **POW DoW**)
["Tripe" claim combat HOLLEBEKE-ZILLEBEKE
LAKE 10-20am? Ltn G-W Gross Ja11]

Sopwith Triplane   10 (Naval) Sqn
OP combat(FLt HJT Saint **WIA)side

17th August

RE8   4Sqn
CP (/2Lt CA Barlow **DoW)side

A4363   RE8   7Sqn
**AOb combat with EA shot down dived into cloud &
out, cr wr(2Lt HL Sayer **KIA**/2Lt JG Tobin-Willis
DoW) left 4-35pm [?"English EA" claim combat
nZILLEBEKE LAKE 7-10pm Vzfw F Altemeier Ja24]

A6376   FE2d   20Sqn
**OP combat with AlbatrosDVs[++++ooc]
HALLUIN ~10-10am shot up engine controls hit ftl
nrDICKEBUSCH dam OK(2Lt OHD Vickers/Lt JA
Hone) [combat ST JULIEN 10-10am Ltn K Deilmann
Ja6] Vickers claimed 13EAs

B1891   FE2d   20Sqn
OP **MIA(Lt HW Joslyn Can. **KIA**/2Lt A Urquhart
Aust. **KIA**) Ja26, left 8-12am ["FE" claim combat
nrZONNEBEKE 10-10am Vzfw F Kosmahl
Ja26][unconfirmed "FE" claim combat ST JULIEN
Ja26]

Bristol F2b   22Sqn
OP (Lt MW Turner **WIA/2Lt CR Edson Aust. **DoW**)

A7162   Bristol F2b   22Sqn
**EscB/OP CORTEMARCK seen shot down in flames
nrHANDZAEME 9-10am after combat(Lt R Cornford
KIA/2Lt SE Raper **KIA**) left 7-40am

A7201   Bristol F2b   22Sqn
OP shot down ftl(2Lt RS Phelan **WIA POW/Lt JL
Macfarlane **POW DoW** 26.9.17) left 6pm ["Bristol"
claim combat nrSTADEN 7-15pm Ltn H-G vOsten Ja11]

B368   DH5   32Sqn
**GroundP seen ovBELLEWARDE LAKE 6-10am
MIA(2Lt W Chivers **KIA**)

A2413   Sopwith Strutter   43Sqn
+* combat with AlbatrosDIII[+flames] HENIN
LIETARD 9-45am OK(2Lt LSV Gedge/Pte C
Blatherwick)

A8224   Sopwith Strutter   43Sqn
+* combat with AlbatrosDV[+ooc] LA BASSÉE-LENS
7-40am OK(Lt FM Kitto/1AM AW Cant)

These were the last claims on Sopwith Strutters
made by 43 Squadron before the unit re-equipped
with Sopwith Camels.

A7210   Bristol F2b   48Sqn
**OP combat with EA[+] engine shot up but ldg ok
7-30am (2Lt HS Gough **WIA**/Capt LF Reincke **KIA**) left
6-10am

A8903   SE5   56Sqn
** combat ovPOLYGON WOOD shot down seen low
after combat going west **MIA**(Lt DS Wilkinson **POW
DoW** 26.8.17) left 5-40am, Müller22 ["BE" claim combat
neQUESNOY 6-05am Ltn M Müller Ja28]

B2.M   SE5a   56Sqn
+* combat with AlbatrosDV[+des] sMOORSLEDE
btwn 6-15am & 7-15am OK(Capt GH Bowman)
Bowman made 8 of his 32 claims in this a'c

B514   SE5a   56Sqn
OP left 5-40am combat ePOLYGON WOOD **MIA(Lt
RT Leighton **WIA POW**) ["SE" claim combat
wPASSCHENDAELE 6-25am Ltn G-W Gross Ja11]

A7461   DH4   57Sqn
B COURTRAI **MIA(Lt TS Roadley **KIA**/2Lt CR
Thomas **POW DoW**)

A7563   DH4   57Sqn
**B COURTRAI-MENIN combat with EA[++]
7-30am shot up engine ftl VLAMERTINGHE dam
OK(Maj EG Joy/Lt F Leathley) [?"Mart" claim combat
nMENIN 7-10am Oblt E vDostler Ja6]

B1732   Sopwith Pup   66Sqn
**OP seen HOULTHULST WOOD-SLADEN(sic)
12000′ **MIA**(2Lt PA O'Brien **POW**) STADEN?, escaped
11.17

B2319   Sopwith Camel   70Sqn
**OP left 7-30am seen dive on EA eYPRES nrLines
MIA(Lt AMT Glover **KIA**) [?possible "Sopwith" claim
combat nrBECELAERE 9-15am Ltn Ohlrau Ja10]

B3783   Sopwith Camel   3 (Naval) Sqn
** combat with EA NIEUPORT shot up(FSLt RFP
Abbot **WIA**) [?"Sopwith" claim combat NIEUPORT
Ltn G Meyer Ja7]

N6334   Sopwith Camel   6 (Naval) Sqn
** combat seen shot down ovZEVECOTE **MIA**(FSLt FS
Strathy **KIA**)

B3757   Sopwith Camel   8 (Naval) Sqn
**OP combat air collision with B3877 ovWINGLES EoL
MIA(FCdr PA Johnston **KIA**) left 6pm ["Sopwith" claim
combat sWINGLES 6-05pm Oblt H Bethge Ja30]

B3877   Sopwith Camel   8 (Naval) Sqn
** combat air collision with B3757 ovWINGLES EoL
MIA(FSLt EA Bennetts **KIA**) left 6pm ["Sopwith" claim
ovWINGLES 6-05pm Oblt H Bethge Ja30]

18th August

After the battles around Langemarck had died
down, fighting in the sector became more localised.
The weather in Flanders until the end of the month
continued wet and generally poor for flying; on the
ground the conditions could also not be much
worse.

                    RE8   4Sqn
PhotRec (/AG.2AM E Perrott **WIA)leg

A7126   Bristol F2b   11Sqn
DOP seen 6-15am ovDOUAI **MIA(2Lt TW Abbott
KIA/2Lt M Nicholson **KIA**) left 5-15am

A7147   Bristol F2b   11Sqn
DOP left 5-25am DOUAI **MIA(2Lt GA Rose **POW**/
Cpl HG Bassinger **POW**) seen 6-15am ovDOUAI ["BF"
claim combat LALAING Ltn V Schobinger Ja12]

A7191   Bristol F2b   11Sqn
**DOP left 5-25am DOUAI seen ~6-15am ovDOUAI
MIA(2Lt LO Harel **KIA**/Capt WH Walker Can. **POW**?)
Walker not in Roll of Honour

A4177   RE8   16Sqn
**Shoot LENS left 7-45am AA hit shot off u'c cr ldg a'dr
9-30am dam OK(Lt Douglas/Lt Williams)

A4367   RE8   21Sqn
+*Phot combat with EA(2Lt J Whitworth-Jones OK/2Lt
EE Wallace **WIA**)

A6701   Nieuport 17   29Sqn
OP left 6-15am seen sYPRES WoL 7am **MIA(2Lt WB
Styles **WIA POW**) ["Nieuport" claim combat
PASSCHENDAELE 7-40am Untoff R Besel/Ltn Zichaus
SS30]

A9438   DH5   32Sqn
**GroundP seen in spin wST JULIEN 4000' 11-20am
MIA(2Lt TR Kirkness **KIA**) no EA seen

B3871   Sopwith Camel   45Sqn
**HAP attacked 2Str shot up(Maj HA vanRyneveld
WIA)head

This was the first casualty on Sopwith Camels for
45 Squadron.

A4295   RE8   53Sqn
** damaged in hangar by enemy bombs

                    Sopwith Pup   54Sqn
OP AA(Capt AL MacFarlane **WIA)

                    DH4   55Sqn
**pracCP lost went EoL AA shot up(2Lt GF Mackay
WIA)

A7471   DH4   55Sqn
**B LA BRIQUETTE A'dr AA hit nrOCRE re-crossing
lines broke up **MIA**(Lt HJ Forsaith **KIA**/2Lt H Dunstan
KIA)

B517   SE5a   56Sqn
OP seen chase EA eROULERS going west **MIA(Capt
HN Rushworth **WIA POW**) left 6am COURTRAI-
MENIN

B519   SE5a   56Sqn
+* combat with AlbatrosDV[+ooc] eHOUTHEM btwn
6-30am & 7-30am OK(Capt JTB McCudden)

This was McCudden's first victory with 56
Squadron.

A7454   DH4   57Sqn
**B COURTRAI last seen diving with 3EAs on tail
nwROULERS **MIA**(Sgt CJ Comerford **KIA**/2Lt N Bell
KIA) left 5-45am

A7510   DH4   57Sqn
**B combat with 3EAs 14000' 7-15am, nd swROULERS
MIA(Lt J Hood **KIA**/2Lt JR MacDaniel **KIA**) left
5-50am [?"DH4" claim combat eROULERS, but time?
Oblt E vDostler Ja6]

A7535   DH4   57Sqn
**B left 5-45am COURTRAI AA dam wr ldg
nrDROGLANDT OK(Lt DS Hall/Lt AF Britton)

B3938   Sopwith Camel   4 (Naval) Sqn
** combat with EA shot down smoke ooc eDIXMUDE
MIA(FSLt CRW Hodges **KIA**) ["Sopwith 1Str" claim
combat VLADSLO, eDIXMUDE 8-10am Ltn P Billik
Ja7]

19th August

B1683   Nieuport 17   1Sqn
**DOP left 4-07pm combat with 5EAs ovMENIN
MIA(2Lt HEA Waring **WIA? POW**) but Waring not
seen involved in fighting, a'c captured ["Nieuport" claim
combat nrMENIN 5-10pm Ltn M Müller Ja28]

A779   FE2b   18Sqn
**SpM(low patrol/straffe) trench mg shot up dam ftl a'dr
ok 7-55am OK(Lt JF Bryom/Lt EA Foord) left 4-45am
Third Army area

Low strafing and ground attacks were not only
being used in Flanders, but in virtually all the other
minor actions now being fought. Such direct co-

operation with the infantry had been used on the 9th of August in fighting around Boiry Notre Dame on the Third Army front. 41 Squadron DH5s were in action then, as well as FE2bs from 18 Squadron. When other such attacks were launched in the sector, such as that south of Vendhuille on the 19th, a quite extensive programme of low air strafing and ground attacks was incorporated. On this occasion, 18 and 41 Squadrons were joined by Nos. 24 and 60, and between them they attacked troops in their billets behind the battle area as well as targets around the German headquarters town of Bohain. Some 9000 rounds of ammunition were fired into troops and various enemy strong points.

B1890   FE2d   20Sqn
Phot shot down ldg ok eWERVICQ **MIA(2Lt CR Richards Aust. MC **WIA POW**/2Lt SF Thompson **WIA POW**) left 3-51pm ["FE" claim combat LE QUESNOY 5pm Ltn E Hess Ja28] Richards had claimed 12 victories, the last 4 in this a'c

A7160   Bristol F2b   22Sqn
**DP AA shot up ftl 5Sq a'dr 7-25am dam OK(Capt H Patch/2Lt LM Quelch) left 6-15am Fifth Army area

A7172   Bristol F2b   22Sqn
OP combat with ovLANGEMARCK 7-35pm **MIA(Capt CM Clement Can. **KIA**/Lt RB Carter Can. **KIA**) left 5-50pm, Clement made 14 victory claims, 4 on the 12th of August with Carter

A9168   DH5   41Sqn
+*SpM attacked gnd positions VENDHUILLE 1200'-500' btwn 5-40am & 6-15am OK(Lt M Thomas)

A8298   Sopwith Strutter   45Sqn
COP broke up nrZANDVOORDE **MIA(Lt CM Ross **KIA**/2Lt JO Fowler **KIA**) seen by 53Sq

A7171   Bristol F2b   48Sqn
OP combat with 2 EAs ovOSTENDE driven down **MIA(2Lt R Dutton **KIA**/2Lt HR Hart-Davies **WIA POW**) left 5-45pm [?"Bristol" claim combat OUDENBERG Ltn Brachwitz Ja17]

A649   Sopwith Pup   54Sqn
**OP left 5am combat with 3EAs shot up dam OK(2Lt FW Gibbes)

A4266   RE8   59Sqn
LP ground mg fire shot up **MIA(Lt FB Tipping **KIA**/2Lt GS Gordon **KIA**) left 6-15am GILLEMONT FARM ["RE" claim combat nrEPEHY 7-20am Vzfw F Rumey Ja5]

**   Sopwith Camel   70Sqn**
** (2Lt AM Epps Aust. **WIA**)arm

B2307   Sopwith Camel   70Sqn
OP left 6am seen EoL nrPOLYGON WOOD **MIA(2Lt JW Gillespie **POW**) to STADEN-INGELMUNSTER-COURTRAI-MENIN [?possible "Sopwith 1Str" claim combat LINSELLES 6-52am Vzfw

F Jacobsen Ja31 but some sources give 18.8]

20th August

A3603   RE8   21Sqn
PhotAOb combat shot down H.9.B.Sh28 (2Lt AN Donnet **WIA/2Lt CB Payne **KIA**)severe WIA, left 8-40am YPRES

**   SPAD 7   23Sqn**
OP combat(2Lt CW Warman US. **WIA)shoulder, Warman had made 12 claims, his last in SPAD B1581 on 18.8.17

A8336   Sopwith Strutter   43Sqn
LP engaged 4EAs ovVITRY **MIA(2Lt FE Winser **KIA**/2Lt HF Young **KIA**) left 6-45am VITRY ["Sopwith" claim combat VITRY 8-20am Vfzw R Jorke Ja12]

A7216   Bristol F2b   48Sqn
+* combat with AlbatrosDVs[+des+ooc] GHISTELLES 7-15pm OK(Capt JT Milne/2Lt W O'Toole) EAs from MFJa1, Milne claimed 9 EAs, O'Toole claimed 8

A7522   DH4   55Sqn
B FARMARS A'dr engine glide down EoL towards BREBIÈRES A'dr **MIA(2Lt CP Adamson **WIA POW**/2AM FJ Smith **DoW**)

A7567   DH4   55Sqn
B LEDEGHEM DUMP controls shot away ftl cr wr(2Lt AB Cook OK/2Lt RN Bullock **WIA) ["English EA" combat wBECELAERE 11-20am Vzfw W Kampe Ja27]

**   DH4   57Sqn**
Phot combat PILCKEM-YPRES(/Lt AF Britton **WIA)

B3876   Sopwith Camel   70Sqn
OP left 6-50am format dive on EA ovDOUAI **MIA(2Lt HD Turner **KIA**) ["Sopwith" combat RUMAUCOURT 8-05am OffSt J Mai Ja5]

N5355   Sopwith Triplane   10 (Naval) Sqn
** combat with 5AlbatrosDs nrLANGEMARCK 10000' 3-20pm shot down forced to dive into clouds **MIA**(FSLt CH Weir **POW DoI** 21.8.17)

21st August

B1613   Nieuport 23   1Sqn
DOP last seen combat 12EA ovHOULTHULST 7-10pm shot down **MIA(2Lt CA Moody **KIA**) left 6-20pm POLYGON WOOD-MENIN-LILLE-PERENCHIES ["Nieuport" claim WESTROOSEBEKE 7-15pm Ltn F Loerzer Ja26]

B3558   Nieuport 17   1Sqn
** combat with EA[+] HOULTHULST 7-10pm OK(2Lt WS Mansell) [?"Nieuport" claim combat nrWESTROOSEBEKE 7-15pm Ltn F Loerzer Ja26, but see B1613?]

**   RE8   6Sqn**
EscPhot combat(2Lt GAS Nicholson **DoW 22.8.17/

AG.Pte F Lankshear **DoW**) crew? [?"RE" claim nrYPRES 6-30pm Untoff R Besel SS30]

FE2d? **20Sqn**
COP combat shot up(/AG.Pte H Greenner **WIA)leg

A3622 RE8 21Sqn
AOb shot down in flames nrFREZENBERG **MIA(Capt AH Smith MC **KIA**/2AM C Hallam **KIA**) left 9-05am YPRES ["RE" claim combat VERLORENHOEK 9-25am Ltn E Hess Ja28]

Bristol F2b 22Sqn
** shot up(/AG.1AM G Brown **WIA**)head

7276.A6 **Martinsyde G100 27Sqn**
B to LEZENNES A'dr combat with EA eSECLIN shot down seen chased down by EA ovLILLE ftl **MIA(2Lt S Thompson **POW**) a'c captured ["Mart" claim combat DOUVRIN?-BOUILLY 7-20am Ltn M Müller Ja28]

A3992.C3 **Martinsyde G102 27Sqn**
B combat eSECLIN air collision with A6259 on return nrLILLE then driven down by EA **MIA(2Lt DP Cox **KIA**) [?"Mart" claimed ENNOVELIN, eSECLIN 7-05am Oblt H Bethge Ja30]

A6259 Martinsyde G102 27Sqn
B combat with EA eSECLIN air collision with A3992 **MIA(Capt GK Smith MC **KIA**) to LEZENNES A'dr, seen going east in control [?"Mart" claim combat nSECLIN 7-10am Ltn K Bolle Ja28]

Sopwith Strutter 43Sqn
LP AA(/2Lt HHG Lamb **WIA)thigh

B2583 Sopwith Strutter 45Sqn
+* combat with DFWC[+flames] ePLOEGSTEERT WOOD 10-25am OK(2Lt N Macmillan/2Lt RSV Morris) MacMillan author of *Into the Blue, Offensive Patrol*, and others, claimed 9 EA in France with 45Sqn, mostly on Camels, but also flew on the Italian front.

B1759 Sopwith Pup 54Sqn
**OP shot up dam OK(Lt FJ Morse) repairable

B2156 Sopwith Pup 54Sqn
**OP AA shot up 2 large bits hit u'c dam cr ldg FURNES A'dr OK(2Lt TL Tebbit) left 9-15am, repairable

A7566 DH4 55Sqn
B RAISMES Ammunition Factory engine ftl in control? EoL nrVALENCIENNES **MIA(2Lt CW Davyes Aust. **WIA POW**/2Lt JL Richardson **KIA**) left 5-48am, seen fire green light

A2132 DH4 57Sqn
B left 5pm LEDEGHEM DUMP fuel tank shot up engine ftl cr wr(Sgt EV Bousher **WIA/1AM W Hamilton? **WIA**) name Harmston?, both hit in legs ["DH4" claim combat LEDEGHEM 6-25pm Ltn M Müller Ja28]

A7555 DH4 57Sqn
B seen ok nrMENIN 3000' **MIA(Lt WB Hutcheson **POW**/Lt TE Godwin **KIA**?) left 5pm LEDEGHEM DUMP, Godwin noted KIA only in AIR1/968/204/5/

1100 ["DH" claim combat HOOGE 6-30pm Ltn A Hanko Ja28]

A7577 DH4 57Sqn
Rec left 5-30am **MIA(Lt C Barry **KIA**/2Lt FB Falkiner MC **KIA**) to ROULERS-MENIN [?possible "DH" claim combat ASCQ, seLILLE 7-45am Ltn E Udet Ja37]

A3535 RE8 59Sqn
PhotRec shot down ooc Sh57b M.33. **MIA(Capt FD Pemberton **KIA**/Lt JA Manners-Smith **WIA POW**) left 12-15pm ["RE" claim combat nrLE PAVE? 3-05pm Vzfw O Könnecke Ja5]

B1762 Sopwith Pup 66Sqn
+* combat with AviatikC[+ooc] swROULERS 11-45am OK(2Lt WA Pritt)

B1775 Sopwith Pup 66Sqn
OP seen dive on EA nwROULERS **MIA(2Lt WR Keast **DoW**) [?"Sopwith" claim btwn YPRES-FRESENBERG 8-50am combat Ltn E Hess Ja28]

B2177.3 **Sopwith Pup 66Sqn**
OP seen dive on EA nwROULERS **MIA(Lt PH Raney **KIA**) [?"Sopwith 1Str" claim eYPRES Ltn Weiss Ja28]

N6308 Sopwith Triplane 1 (Naval) Sqn
COP combat shot down ePLOEGSTEERT WOOD wr **MIA(FSLt FC Lewis **KIA**) Ja28 ["Tripe" claim combat TERHAND? 6-35pm Hpt O Hartmann Ja28]

N5425 Sopwith Triplane 10 (Naval) Sqn
** combat with EA ~14000' seen go down ooc MENIN 6-40pm **MIA**(FSLt C Lowther **KIA**) [?"Sopwith" claim combat btwn YPRES-FREZENBERG Ltn Hess Ja28]

22nd August

B3459.2 **Nieuport 17 1Sqn**
+* combat with DFWC[+des] POELCAPPELLE 6-35pm OK(Capt PF Fullard) left 5-17pm, last of 16 victories in this a'c

RE8 21Sqn
AOb AA(/AG.Dvr FJ Moore **WIA)shoulder

Bristol F2b 22Sqn
OP (/AG.2AM SC Boxall **WIA)foot

SPAD 7 23Sqn
OP combat(2Lt HO Brown **WIA)leg

B3473 Nieuport 17 40Sqn
OP seen dive low on EA DOUAI **MIA(Lt HA Kennedy **KIA**) left 5-40pm DOURGES-DOUAI, combat ~6-45pm?

A7219 Bristol F2b 48Sqn
HAP chasing Gotha to sea shot up(Capt JHT Letts **inj/2Lt HR Power **KIA**) Letts hit by Lewis Gun as Powers slumped

B7125 Bristol F2b 48Sqn
OP combat shot up(/2Lt JHR Price **WIA)

B1767 Sopwith Pup 66Sqn
SpM engine failed seen ftl EoL eOSTENDE(2Lt EH Garland **POW)

B2317   Sopwith Camel   70Sqn
**OP ROULERS-MENIN shot up? cr ldg Sh28
H.20.c.6.4. wr(Lt EM Letts **WIA**)hospital ["English EA"
claim combat YPRES 7-35pm Ltn J Schmidt Ja3]

B2318   Sopwith Camel   70Sqn
**OP ROULERS-MENIN combat with EA shot up
dam(2Lt BCL Barton **WIA**)leg, to hospital, left 5-35pm
[?"Sopwith" claim combat HOUTHULST WOOD
6-45pm Untoff Horst Ja7]

B3895   Sopwith Camel   3 (Naval) Sqn
+* combat with AlbatrosDV[+ooc] sMIDDELKERKE
3-50pm OK(FSLt ET Hayne SA.)

23rd August

SPAD 7   19Sqn
OP combat shot up(Capt AL Gordon-Kidd DSO **DoW
27.8.17)thigh

A7204   Bristol F2b   22Sqn
OP combat with 5EAs 7-30am **MIA(2Lt HG Tambling
POW/FSgt W Organ **POW**) Fifth Army front [F2b claim
combat ISEGHEM 7-40am Ltn H Böhning Ja36]

B1101   Bristol F2b   22Sqn
**OP combat with 5EAs 7-30am shot down in flames
MIA(Sgt CL Randell **KIA**/1AM JV Hurley **KIA**) Fifth
Army front [F2b claim combat neZILLEBEKE LAKE
7-30am Ltn H Hoyer Ja36]

A1048   Sopwith Strutter   45Sqn
+* combat with AlbatrosDV[+ooc] BELLEWARDE
LAKE 9-15am OK(2Lt ED Clarke/Lt GA Brooke)

A1053   Sopwith Strutter   45Sqn
St Marie Capelle +* combat with AlbatrosDVs[+ooc]
BELLEWARDE LAKE 9-15am OK(2Lt KB
Montgomery/2Lt RC Purvis)

These were the last Sopwith Strutter victory claims
made by 45 Squadron before they re-equipped with
Sopwith Camel fighters.

B3768   Sopwith Camel   70Sqn
**OP left 6pm POELCAPPELLE-HOUTHEM AA then
combat cr Lines **MIA**(2Lt L Wigley **POW**)

25th August

RE8   5Sqn
AP mg trenches(2Lt CW Adkin **WIA/2Lt AW Mackay
WIA)

A3758   RE8   9Sqn
AOb BOESINGHE shell hit(2Lt EB Greenheus **KIA/
2Lt GJ Fogarty **KIA**) blown to bits

B758   RE8   9Sqn
**AOb BOESINGHE combat shot down wr(2Lt JB
Finch **WIA**/Capt JM Beaufort **inj**)

B3524   SPAD 7   23Sqn
**OP left 7-32am fuel tank shot through ftl Lines
eLANGEMARCK o't dam OK(2Lt EGC Quilter) *initials*
EDC?

A9207   DH5   32Sqn
**GroundP shot through engine failed ftl cr shell holes wr
OK(2Lt C Turner)

A9212   DH5   41Sqn
**COP seen ovSOREL-LE-GRAND going s-east
MIA(Capt JSdeL Bush **POW DoW** 25.8.17) left 5-26am

B3917   Sopwith Camel   45Sqn
+* combat with AlbatrosDV[+ooc] ePOLYGON
WOOD 7-30pm OK(2Lt N Macmillan)

This was the first Sopwith Camel victory for 45
Squadron.

B3918   Sopwith Camel   70Sqn
**OP GHELUWE-HOUTHULST combat shot up
returned 7-30pm(2Lt OC Bridgeman **WIA**) to hospital,
left 5-50pm [?"Sopwith" claim combat swYPRES 7-45am
Oblt H Göring Ja27]

3137   HP 0/100   7A Sqn RNAS
**B attkg ST DENIS WESTREM A'dr, flak shot down
nrGHENT **MIA**(FSLt HH Booth **POW**/AM SA
Canning **KIA**/AM PM Yeatman **KIA**) ["HP" Flak
claims nrURSEL Flkz51,FlkB537,27]

N5367   Sopwith Triplane   10 (Naval) Sqn
** seen ok ovROULERS 7-30am: very strong west wind
MIA(FSLt ADM Lewis **POW**) Ja11 ["Tripe" claim
LANGEMARCK-PASSCHENDAELE 6-30am Ltn H-G
vOsten Ja11]

26th August

A3770   RE8   9Sqn
**AOb combat Scouts ovBOESINGHE 5000' 11-30am
tracers seen hit(Lt F Maden OK/2Lt HC Dumbell
WIA)leg broken, observer hit in first few rounds

A4390   RE8   9Sqn
AOb combat with 7EAs shot down **MIA(Capt AL
Macdonald MC **KIA**/2Lt FJA Wodehouse **KIA**) to
BIXSCHOOTE area ["RE" claim combat
LANGEMARCK 9-05am Vzfw C Menckhoff Ja3]["RE"
claim combat BIXSCHOOTE 9-05am Oblt W Reinhard
Ja11]

B3492   SPAD 7   19Sqn
**Esc left 5-18am seen combat COURTRAI 6am
MIA(2Lt CP Williams **KIA**) ["SPAD" claim combat
POELCAPPELLE-LANGEMARCK 6-30am Rittm M
Fr vRichthofen JG1]["SPAD" claim combat
ZONNEBEKE 5-45am Vzfw C Menckhoff Ja3]

B3570   SPAD 7   19Sqn
**P shot down after combat with EA WoL wr(Lt FE
Barker **WIA**)thigh [?unconfirmed "SPAD" claim combat
swBECELAERE 5-55am Ltn K Wissemann Ja3]

B3556   SPAD 7   23Sqn
+* combat with AlbatrosDV[++ooc]
nPASSCHENDAELE 6-50am then combat with
AlbatrosDV[+ooc] nCOMINES 7am OK(2Lt SC
O'Grady Irl.)

B3572   SPAD 7   23Sqn
+* combat with AlbatrosDIIIs[+des+ooc] COMINES-
POLYGON WOOD btwn 7am & 7-15am OK(Capt DU
McGregor Can.)

A9178   DH5   24Sqn
**LowP left 5-15am trench ground fire ooc nd 200' cr
MIA(2Lt JG White **KIA**)

24 Squadron was trench strafing again with 41
Squadron in the Third Army area.

RE8   34Sqn
Rec mg bullet(Lt HWW Bean **WIA/)thigh

A.W.FK8   35Sqn
**EscPhot combat with EA(2Lt RSG MacLean US?
WIA/)arm

A6184   Sopwith Pup   54Sqn
**OP left 9-15am AA longerons dam ftl OK(2Lt SJ
Schooley)

27th August

6 (Naval) Squadron was disbanded on the 27th of
August, its Sopwith Camels and air crew going to
9 and 10 (Naval) Squadrons. It would be re-formed
on the 1st of January 1918 at Dover as a day-
bomber squadron.

A4760   RE8   21Sqn
**CP AA hit cr WoL OK(Lt GFW Zimmer/2Lt BR
Worthington)

31st August

46 Squadron returned to France from home defence
duties.

A4422   RE8   9Sqn
**AOb combat with EA fuel tank hit shot down
flames(2Lt VW Burgess **inj**/2Lt F Foster OK) hand
burnt

A7217   Bristol F2b   48Sqn
+* combat with AlbatrosDV[+ooc] ZARREN 9-05pm
OK(2Lt HJ Pratt/2Lt H Owen) shared

B521   SE5a   56Sqn
**OP left 6pm shot up dam OK(2Lt GN Wilkinson) to
HOUTHULST WOOD-POELCAPPELLE-
MOORSLEDE-GHELUVELT [?combat
ovZONNEBEKE 6-50pm Ltn H Adam Ja6]

B1794   Sopwith Pup   66Sqn
OP seen ovHOUTHULST WOOD **MIA(2Lt ES
Bacon **KIA**)

B3889   Sopwith Camel   70Sqn
**prac left 6-25pm combat with EA shot up dam
OK(Capt CF Collett)

September 1917

August in Flanders had been one of the wettest in
living memory, and although the worst of it had

passed, conditions remained terrible. It was
considered that at least another three weeks would
be needed to recover from the rains and to complete
preparations for another main offensive. Troops on
both sides had been exhausted by the slow and
desperate struggle demanded of them, so the pause
was used to relieve some sectors and to reorganise
the fighting groups. Part of the Second Army would
now fight directly with the Fifth, along a proposed
front of some eight miles, and the air support for
the battle would be the most complex of the whole
offensive. Details of the RFC air concentration
concerned are given in the notes on the 19th of
September.

1st September

B782   RE8   6Sqn
**AOb combat ovPOLYGON WOOD seen go down in
spin **MIA**(Lt JBC Madge **WIA POW**/Lt W Kember
KIA) left 5-50am last WT 6-40am, MvR60 ["RE" claim
combat nrZONNEBEKE 6-50am Rittm M Fr
vRichthofen JG1]

B3569   SPAD 7   19Sqn
**P combat shot down in spin nrHOUTHULST WOOD
MIA(2Lt EM Sant **KIA**) left 6-33am [?possible "SPAD"
claim combat WERVICQ Ltn Hammes Ja35]

2nd September

A4624   RE8   7Sqn
**AOb combat shot up ldg a'dr ok 7-50am(2Lt LG
Brazier OK/Lt S Wilmott **WIA**) left 6-50am, thigh

A312   SPAD 7   19Sqn
P left 7am seen combat nrMENIN 7-40am **MIA(2Lt
WAL Spencer **WIA POW**) ["SPAD" claim combat
wROUBAIX 7-50am Ltn H Dilthey Ja27]

B3921   Sopwith Camel   8(Naval)Sqn
+* attacked KB[+des] QUIERY LA MOTTE-
BREBIÈRES 8pm OK(FLt RB Munday Aust.) Munday
shot down 2 other KBs in this a'c

3rd September

B1582   Nieuport 17   1Sqn
**P going down steep with 2EAs on tail neGHELUWE
MIA(2Lt C Pickstone **KIA**) left 6-10pm ROULERS-
MENIN ["Nieuport" claim combat KOELENBERG
6-50pm Ltn H Adam Ja6]

A4651   RE8   4Sqn
**Phot combat with 3EAs shot down spin nr
"STIRLING CASTLE" 3pm(Lt GF Ward shaken/Sgt W
Studholme **DoW** 5.9.17) ["RE" claim combat
wTENBRIELEN 9-40am Ltn H Hoyer Ja36]["RE"
claim combat eZILLEBEKE 4pm Vzfw K Wüsthoff Ja4]

RE8   6Sqn
AOb shot up combat(/Lt RFL Bush **WIA)leg

A4309   RE8   6Sqn
**Phot low combat with EA, seen low ovHOUTHEM in
control with 1EA on tail **MIA**(Lt AC Pickett **POW**/Sgt
HS Foulsham **WIA? POW**) left 8-50am Sh28.P [?"RE"
claim combat nwHOUTHEM 11-10am Ltn K vDöring
Ja4]

B3559   SPAD 7   19Sqn
+* combat with AlbatrosDV[+des] seCOMINES
8-30am OK(Capt J Leacroft)

A7214   Bristol F2b   20Sqn
+* combat with AlbatrosDV[+flames] MENIN-
WERVICQ 10-10am OK(2Lt RM Makepeace/Lt MW
Waddington)

This was the first Bristol Fighter victory for 20
Squadron.

A7120   Bristol F2b   22Sqn
**OP shot up ftl nrYPRES due to wounding(Lt GR
Carmichael OK/2Lt S Cleobury **WIA**) left 8-20am, a'c
damaged in salvage

B3917   Sopwith Camel   45Sqn
**NOP combat with EA nHOUTHEM 9-25am made to
cr **MIA**(Lt AT Heywood **KIA**) left 8-15am, last seen
going west ovCOMINES 4000' ~11am, German
message: Dead [?"Sopwith" claim combat
ZANDVOORDE-HOUTHEM Ltn W Voss Ja10 is too
late at 8-25am]

A7333   Sopwith Pup   46Sqn
OP left 9-30am seen ovLINSELLES 10-30am **MIA(Lt
SW Williams **POW**) [?"Sopwith" claim combat
eWERVICQ 10-30am Ltn O Fruhner Ja26]

B1716   Sopwith Pup   46Sqn
**SOP left 9-30am combat shot up ftl 23Sq dam(Lt FB
Baragar **WIA**)leg

B1754   Sopwith Pup   46Sqn
OP left 5-48am combat ovMENIN 6-45am **MIA(Lt
KW MacDonald **POW DoW**) DoW at MENIN
["Sopwith" claim combat btwn WERVICQ-
TENBRIELEN 6-30am Ltn E Mohnicke Ja11]

B1795.Z Sopwith Pup   46Sqn
OP left 5-45am **MIA(Lt AF Bird **POW**) MvR61
["Sopwith" claim combat sBOUSBECQUE 6-35am
Rittm M Fr vRichthofen JG1]

A7222   Bristol F2b   48Sqn
+* combat with AlbatrosDVs[+flames+ooc]
nDIXMUDE 8-15am OK(Lt R Dodds Can./Lt TCS
Tuffield)

**   DH4   57Sqn**
Phot Rec combat(/Lt GM Guillon **WIA)foot [?"DH"
claim combat nLAMPERNISSE 6-55pm Ltn H Göring
Ja27]

B3872   Sopwith Camel   70Sqn
**OP left 6am combat with EA fuel tank shot up ftl dam
OK(Capt FH Laurence) to LICHTERVELDE-
LEDEGHEM-INGELMUNSTER

Other "Sopwith" claims for the morning include:

> [combat TENBRIELEN 7-30am Ltn W vBülow
> Ja36][combat TENBRIELEN 7-30am Ltn K Wüsthoff
> Ja4][?combats nrDIXMUDE ~7-25am Ltn C Degelow,
> Ltn P Billik & Ltn G Meyer Ja7]

A5547   FE2b   101Sqn
NB left 9-10pm **MIA(2Lt F Scarborough **POW**/2AM
TH Taylor **POW**)

This crew was the first lost in action for 101
Squadron.

N5381   Sopwith Triplane1 (Naval) Sqn
**OP seen dive on EA chased by 6EAs WYTSCHAETE
MIA(FSLt GBG Scott **KIA**) [?"Tripe" claims combat
eHOLLEBEKE 9-05am Ltn K vSchönebeck &
ovWYTSCHAETE 9-30am Ltn Stapenhorst Ja11]

B3796   Sopwith Camel   3 (Naval) Sqn
*P ftl EoL 5-45am **MIA**(FSLt ND Hall **POW**)

B3879   Sopwith Camel   4(Naval)Sqn
+* combat with AlbatrosC[+ooc] 1m sGHISTELLES
4-50pm OK(FLt JEL Hunter) first of 12 claims

B3898   Sopwith Camel   9(Naval)Sqn
+* combat with AlbatrosDV[+des] sePERVYSE
6-30pm OK(FCdr JST Fall) Fall's first victory with
9(Naval)

4th September

B3411   RE8   7Sqn
**AReg combat with EA WoL AA? shot down(Lt TE
Wray **KIA**/2Lt WSL Payne MC **KIA**) left 6-20am
[?"RE" claim combat nYPRES 7-25am Oblt R Berthold
Ja18]

A3778   RE8   9Sqn
AReg down EoL **MIA(Lt BKB Barber **KIA**/Pte AW
Brimmell **KIA**) left 1-30pm, Brimmell is name given in
AIR1/968/204/5/1100, Pte AM Brunell? ["RE" claim
combat POELCAPPELLE 3-30pm Ltn J Schmidt Ja3]

A4372   RE8   9Sqn
**AOb combat with 3EAs VLAMERTINGHE shot
down dam(2Lt GN Moore **WIA**/Lt FF Munroe OK)
initials GM Moore? [?"RE" claim combat ST JEAN,
nYPRES 4pm Oblt R Berthold Ja18]

A7156   Bristol F2b   11Sqn
**COP shot down in flames seHAVRINCOURT 8-30am
MIA(2Lt JF Wightman **KIA**/2AM J Heedy **KIA**) left
7-40am Third Army front ["Mart" claim combat ovLE
CATELET 8-15am Ltn R Matthaei Ja5]

A7405   DH4   25Sqn
+*B combat with 12AlbatrosDIIIs[+flames] sLA
BASSÉE 6-50pm OK(Lt DGE Jardine/2Lt G Bliss)
shared

A7487   DH4   25Sqn
**B combat with 12AlbatrosDIIIs[+flames] ovLA
BASSÉE 6-50pm shot up(Lt CA Pike OK/2Lt AT
Williams **DoW**) shared, EA hit on banking [?2 "Bristol"

claims combat LA BASSÉE btwn 6-45pm & 6-50pm Oblt
H Bethge Ja30]

A7480   DH4   25Sqn
P combat with 10EA fell ooc nrLA BASSÉE **MIA(2Lt
CJ Pullen **KIA**/2Lt EDS Robinson **KIA**) left 5-35pm
PONT À VENDIN-DOUAI [?2 "Bristol" claims LA
BASSÉE 6-45/6-50pm Oblt H Bethge Ja30]

A6679   Nieuport 17   29Sqn
**OP seen combat ovZONNEBEKE 3000′ ~6-50am
MIA(2Lt JH Binns **KIA**) left 5-40am ["Nieuport" claim
combat nwPOLYGON WOOD 7-05am Vzfw K
Wüsthoff Ja4]

B1777.4 **Sopwith Pup   46Sqn**
Izeau le Hameau +* combat with AlbatrosDV[+ooc]
nePOLYGON WOOD 5pm OK(Lt AG Lee) possibly
shared in earlier victory at 4-30pm

A6172   Sopwith Pup   54Sqn
**OP pipe hit shot down behind Belgian Front Line
nrBOITSHOUCKE cr wr OK(Lt K Shelton) left 6-15am

B1838   Sopwith Pup   66Sqn
**OP combat ovROULERS-MENIN RD shot down
MIA(Lt SA Harper MC **WIA POW**) [?"Sopwith" claim
combat BECELAERE 7-40am Ltn E Mohnicke
Ja11][?"Sopwith" claim combat sBECELAERE 7-40am
Ltn Stapenhorst Ja11]

B2197   Sopwith Pup   66Sqn
**OP seen combat ovROULERS-MENIN RD
MIA(Capt CC Sharp **WIA POW**) [?"Sopwith" claim
combat sYPRES 9-45am Vzfw K Wüsthoff Ja4]

5th September

A4280   RE8   6Sqn
**AOb shot up ftl cr a'c on a'dr 5-55am dam OK(Lt
Wright/Lt Haley) left 5-55am to J.2.39.

            RE8   9Sqn
AReg combat(Capt BE Sutton DSO MC **WIA/2Lt F
Forster **WIA**)

            FE2d   20Sqn
PhotRec combat(/AG.2AM W Harrop **WIA)

A3776   RE8   21Sqn
**AOb dh shell 5000′ cr C.19.6.Sh28(Sgt AAL Moir
WIA/2Lt ADK Craig **inj**) to hospital, left 11-05am, Moir
severely WIA

A9374   DH5   32Sqn
**OP combat with EA shot down cr in YPRES
CANAL(Lt WE Sandys **KIA**)

B3838   Sopwith Camel   45Sqn
**NOP left 7-10am nrCOMINES? shot down n.m.l.
wr(Lt W Shields **KIA**)

B3863   Sopwith Camel   45Sqn
**NOP left 7-10am seen combat COMINES-WERVICQ
MIA(2Lt AO MacNiven **KIA**) [?"Sopwith" claim
combat seZILLEBEKE 9am Vzfw K Wüsthoff Ja4]

B1842   Sopwith Pup   46Sqn
**SOP shot up eYPRES dam OK(2Lt CW Odell)
[?"Sopwith" claim combat nrST JULIEN 2-50pm Ltn W
Voss Ja10]

A7331   Sopwith Pup   54Sqn
**OP left 9-10am AA hit shot up dam OK(2Lt PC
Norton)

A2170   DH4   55Sqn
**B MELLE several EAs shot up dam ldg ok OK(Lt
Whitehead/2Lt HB Macdonald) [?combat with Ja18]

A7530   DH4   55Sqn
**B MELLE combat with EA nrGITSBERG down
smoke **MIA**(Lt JWF Neill **WIA POW**/2Lt TM Webster
WIA POW) left 12-04pm [?"BE" claim combat
nrTHIELT 2-28pm Oblt R Berthold Ja18]

B519   SE5a   56Sqn
**OP shot up dam ldg a'dr ok OK(Capt JTB
McCudden) to LICHTERVELDE-LEDGEHEM-
INGELMUNSTER

B3777   Sopwith Camel   70Sqn
**EscB chased down by 2EAs ROULERS-
WESTROOSEBEKE spiralled from 4000′ then flattened
MIA(2Lt JC Huggard **POW**) left 1pm
ARMENTIÈRES, "Sopwith" claims:[?combat ST
JULIEN 2-15pm Ltn E Loewenhardt Ja10, but see 46Sq
Pup?][combat HOUTHULST WOOD 2-30pm Ltn J
vBusse Ja3]

B3807   Sopwith Camel   3 (Naval) Sqn
+* combat with AlbatrosDIII[+ooc] nrLEKE 6-20pm
OK(FLt LH Rochford) first Camel claim by this 29
victory ace

6th September

B1895   FE2d   20Sqn
**OP combat ovBOESINGHE Sh28.C7, shot down in
flames(Lt JO Pilkington **KIA**/2AM HF Matthews **KIA**)
left 2-35pm, Voss42, Ja10 ["FE" claim combat
nrBOESINGHE 3-35pm Ltn W Voss Ja10]

            RE8   21Sqn
CAP AA(Capt JW Thomson-Glover **WIA/)slight

            Bristol F2b   22Sqn
(/AG.2AM F Scott **WIA)knee

B3488   SPAD 7   23Sqn
**WTIntP left 7-25am shot down, seen WoL 8am 5000′
going down to land in thick mist **MIA**(2Lt EGC Quilter
WIA POW) [?"SPAD" claim combat nrSCHAAP-
BALIE Ltn P Billik Ja7][?is this also "Sopwith" claim
combat ELVERDINGHE 8-10am Ltn W Göttsch Ja8]

A9218   DH5   41Sqn
+* combat with AlbatrosC[+ooc] MASNIÈRES-
LESDAIN 1-35pm OK(Lt R Winnicott) indecisive: EA
apparently ooc in nd 5000′, Winnicott made 7 of the 15
DH5 claims for this unit, all in this a'c

This was the first DH5 victory claim for 41
Squadron.

B6226   Sopwith Camel   10 (Naval) Sqn
+* combat with AlbatrosDV[+ooc] seDIXMUDE 8am
OK(FSLt HS Broughall)

This was the first Camel victory for 10 (Naval)
Squadron.

9th September

69 (Australian) Squadron arrived in France on the
9th of September. It was a corps unit flying RE8s,
and was the first Australian squadron to serve on
the Western Front, although No.1 Squadron
Australian Flying Corps (by now named 67
(Australian) Squadron) had been operating in the
Middle East since 1916. In January 1918 it would
be renamed No.3 Squadron, Australian Flying
Corps.

B3558   Nieuport 17   1Sqn
**SP combat with 3EAs chased down in dive by 2EAs
into clouds ftl nTENBRIELEN 2-24pm MIA(2Lt
WEdeB Diamond WIA POW) left 1-10pm ["Nieuport"
claim combat COMINES 2-20pm Ltn J Schmidt Ja3]

A3710   RE8   21Sqn
**PhotAP combat shot up(2Lt LN Waddell WIA/)

A7189   Bristol F2b   22Sqn
**EscP combat shot up ftl cr o't ldg X.28.d.2.3.Sh27 at
4-25pm dam(2Lt EO Peel shock/1AM SWT Ottey WIA)
to hospital, left 2-25pm

A7207   Bristol F2b   22Sqn
**Esc shot down in flames ovWAMBRECHIES
MIA(Sgt JH Hamer KIA/Sgt GE Lambeth KIA) left
2-25pm ["Mart" claim combat seFRELINGHIEN
3-30pm Ltn E Hess Ja28]

A6713   SPAD 7   23Sqn
**OP seen combat with 3m ePOELCAPPELLE 6000'
11-45am MIA(2Lt KR Sayers KIA) left 10-55am
[?"SPAD" claim combat btwn ZONNEBEKE-
FREZENBERG 11-50am Ltn Stapenhorst Ja11]

A3597   RE8   52Sqn
**AOb combat shot down in flames wr(Lt AGB
Davidson KIA/2Lt BB Bishop KIA) left 1-40pm [?"RE"
claim combat MANNEKENSVEERE 2-25pm Untoff P
Bäumer Ja2]

B2341   Sopwith Camel   70Sqn
**OP combat with 2Str[+ooc] GHELUVELT 5-05pm
then another[+des] 5-25pm & an AlbatrosDV[+des]
5-50pm both GHELUVELT-HOUTHULST WOOD
from 13000' down to 40' shot up dam(Capt CF Collett
NZ. MC WIA)finger, last of 11 victories

B3916   Sopwith Camel   70Sqn
**OP GHELUVELDT-HOUTHULST fuel tank shot
up cr trenches 4-45pm(2Lt H Weightman WIA)abdomen
[?"Sopwith" claim combat neYPRES Ltn L Luer Ja27]

B3928   Sopwith Camel   70Sqn
**OP combat ovHOUTHULST ~6pm shot down

MERCKEN? cr o't MIA(Lt NC Saward WIA? POW)
left 4-45pm GHELUVELDT, Sopwith claims:[combat
WESTROOSEBEKE 6pm Vzfw F Kosmahl
Ja26][combat POELCAPPELLE 6-05pm Ltn O Fr
vBoenigk Ja4][combat HOUTHULST 6-10pm Ltn
Hammes Ja35]

N5477   Sopwith Triplane   1 (Naval) Sqn
**OP combat shot down YPRES seen dive past Pat
MIA(FSLt LE Adlam KIA) Ja4 [?"Tripe" claim combat
BELLEWARDE Ltn H Kroll Ja24][?possible "Sopwith"
claim combat LANGEMARCK-POELCAPPELLE
6-05pm Oblt O Fr vBoenigk Ja4, but see Camel B3928?]

10th September

A9435.E **DH5 24Sqn**
**COP left 4-10pm fell ooc sCAMBRAI MIA(2Lt GP
Robertson POW) Third Army front, a'c captured

B3787   Sopwith Camel   70Sqn
**OP HOULTHULST WOOD combat with EA
LANGEMARCK 4-55pm MIA(2Lt OC Pearson KIA)
left 4-45pm, seen ROULERS-STADEN ~5-20pm?(via
AIR1/968/204/5/1100), Voss44 ["SE" claim combat
nrLANGEMARCK 4-55pm Ltn W Voss Ja10] [NB? also
"Sopwith" claim combat nwHOUTHULST WOOD
6-30pm Ltn F Ray Ja28]

B3927   Sopwith Camel   70Sqn
**OP HOULTHULST WOOD combat LANGEMARK
4-50pm MIA(2Lt AJS Sisley KIA) left 4-45pm, seen
ROULERS-STADEN 5-20pm? (via AIR1/968/204/5/
1100), Voss43 ["1Str" claim combat LANGEMARCK
4-50pm Ltn W Voss Ja10] [?Sopwith claim combat
BLANKARTSEE 6pm? Ltn E Hess Ja28]

11th September

B3635   Nieuport 27   1Sqn
**NP low after combat 9EA ovWESTROOSEBEKE
chased down in control MIA(Capt LF Jenkin MC KIA)
left 3-45pm ROULERS-MENIN [?unconfirmed
"Nieuport" claim combat neBIXSCHOOTE 6-30pm
Oblt O Schmidt Ja29]

B3648   Nieuport 27   1Sqn
**SpP MENIN-QUESNOY dhAA sHOUTHEM down
ooc broke up MIA(2Lt WS Mansell KIA) left 10-43am

A.W.FK8   2Sqn
**PhotRec combat with EA(/Lt F Yorke WIA)foot

A3701   RE8   21Sqn
**AOb YPRES combat with EA shot up dam OK(2Lt
LN Waddell/Sgt A Frazer) left 4-45pm

B1105   Bristol F2b   22Sqn
**OP left 8am combat EA shot up ovSCHAPP BAILLIE
2000'(2Lt RdeL Stedman WIA/2Lt HE Jones DOW?)
DoW 12.10.17?

B3775   Sopwith Camel   45Sqn
**P left 7-40am MIA(2Lt EB Denison POW) [?Sopwith
1Str" claim combat ROULERS-YPRES 9-05am Vzfw
Wackwitz Ja24][?unconfirmed "Sopwith 1Str" claim

combat PASSCHENDAELE 8-55am Vzfw Heller
Ja24][?combat MOORSEELE 8-50am Vzfw C
Menckhoff Ja3]

B6236   Sopwith Camel   45Sqn
**P left 1-50pm combat with DrI ST JULIEN 3-25pm
shot down in flames ovLANGEMARCK, chased down by
DrI **MIA**(Lt OL McMaking **KIA**) Voss47 [?"EA" claim
combat eST JULIEN 3-25pm Ltn W Voss Ja10]

B2191   Sopwith Pup   46Sqn
+* combat with LVGC[+ooc] sSCARPE River 10-55am
OK(Capt MDG Scott) shared

A7187   Bristol F2b   48Sqn
EscDH4s seen ok sNIEUPORT 16000' **MIA(Sgt WH
Roebuck **KIA**/2Lt HT Batson **KIA**) left 9-35am
BRUGGES [?possible "Bristol" claim combat
WYNENDACHE Ltn vGotz MFJaI]

A7220   Bristol F2b   48Sqn
+* combat with DFWC[+ooc] DIXMUDE 10-15am
OK(Lt J Binnie/2Lt TCS Tuffield) FAb(A)224?

RE8   52Sqn
AP combat shot up(Lt WGB McKechnie **WIA/)thigh

A3477   RE8   52Sqn
**AOb combat shot down COST DUNKERQUE(2Lt
HC Smith **KIA**/2Lt EFC Budd **DoW**) left 11-40am

B1799   Sopwith Pup   54Sqn
**OP left 11-30am combat with EA shot up dam OK(2Lt
G Clapham)

DH4   57Sqn
B combat shot up(2Lt CRB Halley **WIA/)foot

A7439   DH4   57Sqn
**B COURTRAI SIDINGS seen wCOURTRAI 17000'
12-40pm **MIA**(Sgt SF Edgington **KIA**/2Lt ETH Hearn
KIA) left 10-45am

A7582   DH4   57Sqn
**B seen wCOURTRAI SIDINGS 12-40pm, combat
with EA shot down 12-50pm **MIA**(2Lt JA Mackay **KIA**/
2Lt EJ Halliwell **KIA**) left 10-45am

B3932   Sopwith Camel   70Sqn
OP left 9-05am HOUTHULST shot down **MIA(2Lt
EHP Streather **KIA**) to COURTRAI-LEDEGHEM-
ROULERS-HOUTHULST WOOD ["Sopwith" claim
combat HOUTHULST WOOD 10-01am Ltn H
Böhning Ja36]

B3845   Sopwith Camel   8 (Naval) Sqn
+* combat with 2Str[+ooc fire?] PONT À VENDIN-
COURRIÈRES 11-50am OK(FLt RR Thornely)

B3884   Sopwith Camel   9(Naval)Sqn
+* combat with AlbatrosDVs[+des] LEKE 5-30pm
OK(FSLt AR Wood) shared, probably Ltn ZS Gotz
MFJaI shot down

12th September

B3425   RE8   6Sqn
**AOb dh shell VERBRANDENMOLEN cr

Sh28.I.28.D.4.3.(Lt GH Miles **KIA**/2Lt NC Whittall
KIA) left 5-10pm, a'c salvaged

B3506   SPAD 7   23Sqn
**OP neMENIN seen combat ovMENIN 12-15pm shot
down **MIA**(2Lt SW Dronsfield **POW**) left 10-35am
["SPAD" claim combat swLINSELLES 12-15pm Ltn H
Kroll Ja24]

13th September

A8325   Sopwith Strutter   43Sqn
**Phot dhAA eOPPY 11-40am broke up cr WoL wr(Capt
AT Rickards **KIA**/2Lt F Marshall-Lewis **KIA**) left
10-45am OPPY

N5429.11 Sopwith Triplane   1 (Naval) Sqn
** combat shot down ovMENIN **MIA**(FSLt JR Wilford
WIA POW) Ja4 ["Sopwith" claim combat sWERVICQ
7-30pm Vzfw K Wüsthoff Ja4]

B3933   Sopwith Camel   10 (Naval) Sqn
**OP combat with EAs wROULERS 3000' 7-10am
MIA(FSLt ED Abbott **WIA POW**) seen at rear of
formation about to be attacked, in control after?
["Sopwith 1Str" claim combat TERHAND,
nrBECELAERE 7-10am Ltn W vBülow Ja36]

14th September

A7203   Bristol F2b   20Sqn
**P shot up dam returned a'dr ok OK(2Lt HF Tomlin/
2Lt RSV Morris) left 3-07pm

A6292   Martinsyde G102   27Sqn
**B COURCELLES petrol pipe broke in air ldg 20m
EoL sCOURTRAI **MIA**(2Lt SH Taylor **POW**) left
3-15pm

A8234   Sopwith Strutter   43Sqn
**LP AA ftl cr shell hole 7-55am dam(2Lt S Thompson
WIA inj/1AM EP Croll OK?) left 6-15am WINGLES-
DROCOURT, WIA leg

A3238   RE8   53Sqn
**AOb AA hit 6-25am cr Sh28 o.27.a wr(2Lt HW
Westaway **WIA**/2Lt L Hodkinson **KIA**) to P.27.b.25.25.,
slight WIA

Sopwith Pup   54Sqn
OP (Lt JW Sheridan **WIA)

B516   SE5a   56Sqn
**OP left 5pm seen combat nrMENIN shot down
MIA(2Lt NH Crow **KIA**) LICHTERVELDE-
LEDEGHEM-INGELMUNSTER ["SE" claim combat
DE RUYTER, VIERKAVENHOEK 6-05pm Vzfw C
Menckhoff Ja3][?unconfirmed SE5 claim combat DE
RUYTER 6pm Ltn J Schmidt Ja3]

A8918.W SE5   60Sqn
**OP combat ovMENIN 4-40pm shot down mg fire ftl
MIA(Lt HT Hammond **POW**) left 3-10pm, AA as well?

B2333   Sopwith Camel   70Sqn
**OP fuel tank hit chased down by 2EAs wROULERS

7-50am seen losing fuel **MIA**(2Lt ESC Sen Ind. **POW**)
left 7am HOUTHULST-ROULERS-GHELUWE
["Sopwith 1Str" claim combat MENIN 7-50am Vzfw G
Schneidewind Ja17]

B3829   **Sopwith Camel**   **9 (Naval) Sqn**
** combat controls shot up ftl n.m.l. nrPERVYSE
OK(FSLt AC Campbell-Orde) pilot saved, a'c
abandoned

15th September

B1672   **Nieuport 17**   **1Sqn**
NP seen low neYPRES 3-30pm EoL **MIA(2Lt ED
Tyzack **KIA**) left 1-40pm ROULERS-MENIN
["Nieuport" claim combat WESTROOSEBEKE?
(Rousbecque?) 3-25pm Oblt B Loerzer Ja26]

B765   **RE8**   **9Sqn**
**AOb IRISH FARM combat shot down WoL
nYPRES(2Lt WGC Hackman OK/2Lt AJ Powney
DoW) observer WIA abdomen

A3773   **RE8**   **12Sqn**
**LP mg fuel tank shot up ftl eWANCOURT dam
OK(Capt Stevenson/Lt Webster) left 4-45pm CHERISY
["RE" claim combat WANCOURT 5-10pm Untoff F
Gille Ja12]

Bristol F2b?   **20Sqn**
OP combat shot up(/2Lt JEL Skelton **WIA)lung

A9251   **DH5**   **32Sqn**
**OP combat with EA shot down ftl nrGHELUVELT
a'c abandoned(Lt JRM Simpson **WIA**) to
SANCTUARY WOOD, gunshot **WIA** ftl eZILLEBEKE
[?possible "Sopwith 1Str" claim combat WERVICQ Ltn
Berkemeyer Ja27]

A2130   **DH4**   **55Sqn**
B seen going down ok LILLE **MIA(Lt EEF Loyd
POW/Lt TG Deason **POW**) left 12pm WORTEGHEM
[?"Sopwith" claim combat ZILLEBEKE LAKE
1-10pm(2-10pm?) Oblt R Berthold Ja18][?"Sopwith
2Str" claim combat FREZENBERG? 11-45am Ltn H-G
vOsten Ja11]

B2341   **Sopwith Camel**   **70Sqn**
**OP left 5pm MENIN-ROULERS combat with EA ftl
cr Sh28.G.25(2Lt RSCD Ashby **WIA inj**) injured in
crash

B2343   **Sopwith Camel**   **70Sqn**
OP left 5pm MENIN-ROULERS **MIA(2Lt H
Ibbotson **POW**) [?"Sopwith 1Str" claim combat
nYPRES 6pm Ltn H Adam Ja6]

B3753   **Sopwith Camel**   **70Sqn**
**OP seen glide down ok nrHOUTHULST FOREST
11-30am **MIA**(Lt GB McMichael **POW**) left 11am

B6250   **Sopwith Camel**   **70Sqn**
**OP left 11am HOUTHULST WOOD-MENIN
MIA(2Lt JBH Wyman **WIA POW**) escaped?: interned
Holland 7.5.18

B3833   **Sopwith Camel**   **6(Naval)Sqn**

+* combat with DrI[+flames] ovWERVICQ 4-50pm
OK(FSLt NM MacGregor) death of 33 victory ace Oblt
Kurt Wolff Ja11

This was the first Fokker DrI Triplane lost by the
German Air Force.

16th September

B3621   **Nieuport 17**   **1Sqn**
**SP combat with EA lost format ftl 7Sq a'dr o't ldg dam
OK(2Lt FG Chown) left 5-40pm LEDEGHEM-
MENIN-QUESNOY

RE8   **4Sqn**
Phot combat(2Lt WH Weller **WIA/2AM F Farmer
DoW 17.9.17)

B9435   **DH4**   **18Sqn**
+* combat with AlbatrosC[+ooc] BOURLON 2-20pm
OK(2Lt JF Byron/2Lt EJ Detmold)

This was the first DH4 victory for 18 Squadron.

A4728   **RE8**   **4Sqn**
**Phot combat shot down "GLENGORSE WOOD"
5-30pm(2Lt LG Humphries **KIA**/2Lt FL Steben **WIA**)
left 5pm ANZAC CORP FRONT [?"RE" claim combat
nwBOESINGHE 5-30pm Ltn J Veltjens Ja18]["RE"
claim combat ZONNEBEKE 5-25pm Oblt R Berthold
Ja18]

A4693   **RE8**   **6Sqn**
**Phot combat with 2EAs ovSWANNHOEK shot down
in controlled spin 4-50pm **MIA**(Lt H Haslam **KIA**/Cpl
AJ Linlay **KIA**) left 3-55pm ["RE" claim combat
wBECELAERE 5pm Oblt R Berthold Ja18]

B3618   **SPAD 7**   **19Sqn**
**SpM seen low 2m swPASSCHENDAELE 10-30am
MIA(Lt RL Graham **KIA**) left 9-52am

A6251   **Martinsyde G102**   **27Sqn**
**B HOOGLEDE left 2-55pm flak shot down seen going
west 1m EoL, south of flooded area 3000' 5-05pm
MIA(2Lt AH Skinner **WIA POW**)

A6287   **Martinsyde G102**   **27Sqn**
**B HOOGLEDE combat with 2EAs in spin nrSTADEN
MIA(Lt NW Goodwin **KIA**) left 2-55pm ["Mart" claim
SLEIJHAGE 5pm Ltn A Hanko Ja28]["1Str" claim
combat PASSCHENDAELE-POELCAPPELLE 5pm
Ltn E Hess Ja28]

A673   **Sopwith Pup**   **46Sqn**
**COP left 12-15pm seen before combat with 7EAs
ovECOURT ST QUENTIN **MIA**(2Lt LM Shadwell
POW) ["Sopwith 1Str" claim combat MONCHY Vzfw
R Jorke Ja12]["Sopwith 1Str" claim combat
nrLECLUSE 1-20pm? Ltn V Schobinger Ja12]

A8909   **SE5**   **60Sqn**
**OP left 6-10pm combat TENBRIELEN 6-30pm shot
up ftl **MIA**(2Lt JJA Hawtrey **POW DoW** 17.9.17)
[?"Sopwith 1Str" claim combat GHELUWE 6-45pm?
Ltn O Fitzner Ja17]

B3836   Sopwith Camel   70Sqn
OP left 11am HOUTHULST FOREST shot down seen glide down in control nrHOUTHULST ~11-30am **MIA(2Lt LF Wheeler **WIA POW**) Sopwith claims:[STADEN-HOUTHULST ROAD 11-45am Oblt K vDöring Ja4][?combat neDIXMUDE 12pm Ltn F Ray Ja28][?combat HOUTHULST WOOD Vzfw R Francke &Lt W Göttsch Ja8]

17th September

A7185   Bristol F2b   22Sqn
**OP shot up mist ftl COYECQUE cr dam OK(Lt WM Yool/Pte DW Clement) to Fifth Army area

A9409   DH5   41Sqn
OP combat ovPELVES btwn 7-30am & 7-45am ooc or broke up ~7-45am **MIA(2Lt RE Taylor **KIA**) left 6-35am SCARPE VALLEY [?"DH5" claim combat IZEL Untoff Liebert Ja30]

A9410   DH5   41Sqn
OP combat with EA ovPELVES btwn 7-30am & 7-45am shot down broke up **MIA(Lt GC Holman **KIA**) left 6-35am SCARPE VALLEY ["DH5" claim combat IZEL 7-30am? Ltn E Udet Ja37]

A7222   Bristol F2b   48Sqn
OP combat with EA ftl FERME LE MOULIN(Sgt J Oldham OK/AG.2AM W Walker **inj) WIA?

A7492   DH4   57Sqn
Rec left 6-20am **MIA(2Lt CF Pritchard **KIA**/2Lt T Grosvenor **KIA**)

18th September

From the 18th of September until the 5th of October German and British times matched (all times given are British time).

A9208   DH5   41Sqn
COP seen in combat wCAMBRAI 11-20am going west shot down **MIA(2Lt AJ Chapman **KIA**) left 10-25am CAMBRAI [?"Sopwith 1Str" claim combat nWAMBAIX? 11-20am Ltn W Ewers Ja12][?"Sopwith 1Str" claim combat wMOEUVRES 11-05am Vzfw R Jorke Ja12]

A9426   DH5   41Sqn
COP seen combat ovSCARPE VALLEY 10-50am shot down **MIA(Lt HF McArdle **KIA**) left 9-50am ["Sopwith 1Str" claim combat VIS-EN-ARTOIS 10-35am Oblt H Bethge Ja30]

A4319   RE8   52Sqn
**AOb combat mg fire shot down dam ftl A.L.G. OK(2Lt S Canning/2AM TH Lea) ["RE" claim combat MORY 8-40am Ltn V Schobinger Ja12]

19th September
FIGHTING FOR THE MENIN ROAD RIDGE

The third main battle of the offensive at Ypres was planned to begin the following day, on the 20th of September. Fighting had never really ceased, however, and an unrelenting period of terrible weather had turned the conflict into a form of nightmare for the troops. In a landscape devastated by war and flooded by rains and by rivers burst apart by shelling, the conditions were truly horrific. For seven weeks of effort and sacrifice the advance had been less than two miles. There was increasing consternation as to how a way could be found across a battlefield which was little more than a series of lakes, bogs and endless shell holes filled with deadly mud. The battle, when it flared, was a series of numbing attacks and counter-attacks that brought almost no movement. Already the objectives of the offensive looked increasingly unachievable, and were fast contracting. However, even if by tremendous endeavour the ridges and high ground immediately to the east could be taken, what additional hell would be met on the flat, bleak Belgian plain beyond? Those unlucky enough to be fighting this ghastly battle were probably approaching the limit of what it was possible to withstand.

The Allies were desperate for the progress which they felt the weather had denied them. But it was not simply progress, but the whole reason for the offensive which they had lost. For a highly complex set of reasons, however, these terrible circumstances did not cause a cessation or re-evaluation of fighting, but an intensification. With the year fast closing, this new attack was to be a very considerable effort. Its objective was the Menin Road Ridge, and air services were to play an integral part.

Once again there was to be a big emphasis on disruption of the enemy forces by low patrolling. As before, this would fall into several categories. There would be the usual co-operation with the advancing infantry, strafing defended positions and opposing troops; billets behind the immediate battle area and the rail networks serving these would be bombed; enemy aerodromes would be attacked throughout the day; and every effort would be made to break up German counter-attacks as they formed. Raids by both day and night bombing units were to concentrate on the enemy aerodromes and complement the attacks by fighters. Ground attacks by fighters would be restricted to those of II Brigade, who were to keep a constant presence east of the barrage line throughout the day. Operating at no higher than 500 feet they were to reconnoitre and attack any troop build-ups. The fighters of V Brigade had a slightly more traditional role, involving sweeps of

offensive patrols, but they too were to come down lower on their return and attack any reinforcements that could be found. They would also operate low offensive patrols specifically to protect corps machines and attack enemy two-seaters.

There were twenty RFC squadrons directly concerned. These were the seven corps squadrons Nos. 4, 6, 7, 9, 21, 42, and 53, all flying the RE8; two fighter-reconnaissance squadrons, Nos. 20 and 22, with Bristol Fighters; twelve fighter squadrons, namely Nos.1 (Nieuports), 19 (SPADs), 45 (Sopwith Camels), 60 (SE5s), and 1 Naval (Sopwith Triplanes) of II Brigade; and Nos. 23 (SPADs), 29 (Nieuports), 32 (DH5s), 70 (Sopwith Camels), and 10 Naval (Sopwith Camels) of V Brigade; and Nos. 56 (SE5s) and 66 (Sopwith Pups) of 9th (Headquarters) Wing. Day bombing would be carried out by Nos. 27 (Martinsydes), and 55 and 57 Squadrons (DH4s), and night bombing by 100 and 101 Squadrons with their FE2bs. RNAS Handley Page heavy bombers from Coudekerque were also allotted rail junction targets on the night before the attack, but the weather made this impossible. Regrettably, on the eve of the battle, it rained again all night.

A234   Morane BB   3Sqn
prac seen eESTOURMEL shot down **MIA(Lt E Golding **KIA**/Cpl LS Goss **POW DoW**) left 10-45am on training flight, see A6655 [?"Morane" claim seCAMBRAI 12-03pm Oblt Flashar Ja5]

A6655   Morane P   3Sqn
prac combat shot down EoL **MIA(2Lt CA Sutcliffe **POW**/2Lt T Humble **POW**) left 10-45am on training flight: led formation nCAMRAI-ESTOURMEL then attacked by EA ["Morane" claim MARETZ 12-17pm Ltn R Matthaei Ja5]

B3427   RE8   4Sqn
Phot ANZAC CORP FRONT cr Sh28.J.10.D. **MIA(2Lt JS Walthew **KIA**/Lt MC Hartnett **KIA**) left 9-45am [?"RE" claim combat wYPRES 10am Ltn H Adam Ja6]

B5012   RE8   9Sqn
AOb combat shot down WoL(Lt HL Devlin **KIA/2Lt FA Wright **KIA**) left 9-45am nrLANGEMARCK [?"RE" claim combat BOESINGHE 10-47am Ltn E Böhme Ja2]

A7130   Bristol F2b   11Sqn
DOP seen 8-45am wBULLECOURT **MIA(2Lt NJ Taylor **WIA POW**/Lt GW Mumford **WIA POW**) left 7-45am BULLECOURT [F2b claim combat swSAILLY 8-50am Untoff F Gille Ja12]

A3264   RE8   13Sqn
AOb combat controls shot up driven down(Lt ELP Evans OK/Lt BC Gay **WIA)leg, left 2-35pm ST ELOI

A7528   DH4   18Sqn
**View engine failed then AA on glide back, dam cr wr

OK(2Lt AC Atkey/1AM T McGrath)

A8864   SPAD 7   19Sqn
WTInt left 2-54pm badly shot up ftl(Lt RJ Patterson **WIA)shoulder [?"SPAD" claim combat VERBRANDENMOLEN 3-20pm Oblt H Auffahrt Ja18]

B3528   SPAD 7   19Sqn
**WTInt left 2-53pm shot up ftl ldg ok dam rep OK(Lt W Jones) [?Ja18]

A7246   Bristol F2b   20Sqn
Phot combat with AlbatrosDVs[+flames++ooc] BECELAERE-POLYGON WOOD 10am shot up ftl 4Sqn a'dr ~10-30am(2Lt AVG Taylor OK/2Lt H Dandy **WIA)

These were the first definite victories for 20 Squadron after having re-equipped with Bristol Fighters.

**   Sopwith Strutter 43Sqn**
** AA(/2Lt SMacG Peterkin **WIA**)buttocks

B2571   Sopwith Strutter 43Sqn
LP dhAA eGAVRELLE 7-25am broke up **MIA(2Lt MGM Oxley **KIA**/2AM CA Blatherwick **KIA**) left 6-40am WINGLES-DROCOURT [?possible "Sopwith 1Str" claim combat FRESNES 7-30am Oblt H Waldhausen Ja37]

These were the last casualties for 43 Squadron in Strutters before the unit re-equipped with Sopwith Camel fighters.

B3871   Sopwith Camel   45Sqn
+* combat with AlbatrosDV[+ooc] WESTROOSEBEKE 11-05am OK(2Lt KB Montgomery) made 10 claims in France, 2 in Italy

N5446.16 Sopwith Triplane   1 (Naval) Sqn
P gunshot(FSLt CFD Ash **WIA)back

N5490   Sopwith Triplane 1 (Naval) Sqn
** combat with EA[+] swDOUAI 6pm then seen glide down ok? ftl EoL neST JULIEN **MIA**(FSLt RE MacMillan **POW**) Ja26 ["Tripe" claim combat PASSCHENDAELE 5-55pm Vzfw F Kosmahl Ja26]

N6292   Sopwith Triplane 1 (Naval) Sqn
** combat with 2Albatros[+ooc] BECELAERE 10-10am but seen chased down EoL nrKRUISHER **MIA**(FSLt JH Winn **KIA**) shared, [Ja10?] some sources give 20.9 for date of death but Casualty Report dated 19.9?

N6374   Sopwith Camel   10 (Naval) Sqn
combat with EA eYPRES fell in flames seHOUTHULST WOOD 10am **MIA(FSLt EJV Grace **KIA**?) a combat seen occurring btwn 10am & 10-15am but possibly not involved in this: fell ~10am? [?"Sopwith" claim combat HOUTHULST WOOD 10-05am Ltn H Adam Ja6]

20th September

The assault began at 5-40am. The rain had stopped at dawn but a wet mist hung over the battlefield.

The Menin Road Ridge was an invaluable piece of high ground in the context of future operations, and so was fought for without restraint. By nightfall virtually all the objectives had been won, but in recognition of the importance of the victory, the enemy had launched eleven separate counter-attacks through the afternoon and evening. These, and the many others which followed in the coming few days, were all effectively repulsed, but only by virtue of the most intense and bitter fighting.

The air co-operation provided by the RFC was of the highest order in this battle. The corps machines were forced low by the clouds on their contact patrols and artillery spotting, but the fullest picture possible was relayed back. For example, three hundred and ninety-four separate zone calls were laid onto German batteries and other targets. Their work was little troubled by attacks from enemy fighters, as can be seen from the entries below. Virtually all the hundred or so combats recorded through the day were between single-seaters away from the main battle zone, from which enemy fighters were largely denied access; most of the casualties occurred behind the fighting. Low flying attacks by fighters on enemy aerodromes were not undertaken because of the mist, but they were still bombed the previous night and then again through the day. 27 Squadron attacked all four "Circus" airfields simultaneously. Rail stations were also bombed.

The most important work of the day however, was the warning those in the air were able to give of approaching German counter-attacks. Virtually every airman in one way or another was on the lookout for these, and for once the clearing conditions enabled the situation to be understood. It meant that artillery fire could be directed onto enemy concentrations as they gathered, and counter-attacks were often broken up before they began.

A6721   Nieuport 23   1Sqn
**SpM North area left 8-25am MIA(2Lt CGD Gray WIA POW) had landed at 40Sqn at 10-40am for fuel, then left and not seen again

B3632   Nieuport 27   1Sqn
**SpMCent seen after combat ovGHELUVELT MIA(2Lt RH Garratt KIA) left 11-55am ["Nieuport" claim combat ZILLEBEKE LAKE 1-20pm Ltn R Runge Ja18]

B6755   Nieuport 27   1Sqn
**SpM:North area, shot down WoL MIA(2Lt FJ Chown KIA) left 12-55pm

RE8   7Sqn
**CP (Capt CH Gardner WIA/)slight

A3650   RE8   7Sqn
**AOb AA or British guns? down nrLANGEMARCK o't shell hole filled with water WoL(2Lt GW McKenzie KIA/2Lt JB Bailey KIA) left 9-25am

B5019   RE8   7Sqn
**CP LANGEMARCK mg & shell fire shot down WoL dam(Lt N Sharples KIA/Lt BW Ryan KIA) left 7-35am

A3637   RE8   9Sqn
**CAP mg shot down behind EAGLE TRENCH(2Lt FP Watts WIA/2Lt AN Burrow WIA) name Burrows?

A3770   RE8   9Sqn
**AP LANGEMARCK combat shot up dam(2Lt F Maden OK/2Lt GD Turner WIA)leg [?possible unconfirmed "English 2Str" claim combat wHOOGE Ltn J Veltjens Ja18][?claim combat ZILLEBEKE LAKE Ltn F Ray Ja28]

RE8   16Sqn
**AP trench mg fire(/Lt A Willans WIA)hand

A6516   FE2d   20Sqn
**P combat with EA shot up dam returned a'dr ok, repairable OK(Capt FD Stevens/2Lt WC Cambray) left 5-40pm

A4745   RE8   21Sqn
**CP ground mg shot up dam returned a'dr 8-20am(Lt GFW Zimmer WIA/2Lt E Wilson inj) left 7-45am YPRES, WIA finger

B3493   SPAD 7   23Sqn
**OP left 12-45pm shot up ftl(Lt F Bullock-Webster? DoW) name Webster-Bullock? [?"SPAD" claim combat wLANGEMARCK 2-30pm Vzfw K Wüsthoff Ja4]

B6756   Nieuport 27   29Sqn
**GroundP seen over trenches eYPRES going east 11am MIA(2Lt SL Crowther KIA) left 10-45am

A9179   DH5   32Sqn
**OP seen shell hit seST JULIEN 9am MIA(2Lt WO Cornish DoW) [?"Sopwith" claim combat nrBECELAERE 9-40am Ltn H Adam Ja6]

A9434   DH5   32Sqn
**OP ZILLEBEKE combat with EA fuel tanks shot up ftl cr(2Lt RGR Townsend inj) ftl nrHOOGE [Ja6?]

B345   DH5   32Sqn
**OP neYPRES engine shot up ftl shell holes wr OK(Lt A Claydon)

B6205   Sopwith Camel   45Sqn
**NOP left 11-50am MIA(Lt BR Davis KIA)

A4859   SE5   56Sqn
**OPleft 1-15pm CORTEMARCK-MENIN shot up? cr eAIRE OK(2Lt ER Taylor)

A8931   SE5a   60Sqn
**B ftl eZONNEBEKE MIA(Sgt JW Bancroft POW) left 8-55am [?"Sopwith 1Str" claim combat wBELLEWARDE 9-50am Ltn H Adam Ja6]

B522   SE5a   60Sqn
** combat with EA shot up dam OK(Capt JK Law)

B535   SE5a   60Sqn
** combat with AlbatrosD ZONNEBEKE shot up
4-55pm? ftl nrST MARIE CAPPEL dam OK(Capt JK
Law)

A6183   Sopwith Pup   66Sqn
SpP:B enemy a'dr YPRES FRONT **MIA(2Lt CHF
Nobbs **POW**)

B2342   Sopwith Camel   70Sqn
**GroundP AA shot up ftl 11-10am(2Lt FH Bickerton
WIA)thigh, to hospital, left 10-45am

B2359   Sopwith Camel   70Sqn
**GroundP left 11-15am AA gunfire dam returned
11-45am OK(Lt NO Vinter)

N5459   Sopwith Triplane   1 (Naval) Sqn
**GroundP unseen EoL shot down
nrPASSCHENDAELE **MIA**(FSLt EW Desbarats **POW**)
["Tripe" claim combat nrPASSCHENDAELE 11-50am
Vzfw F Kosmahl Ja26]

**   Sopwith Triplane   1 (Naval) Sqn**
GroundP gunshot(FSLt E Anthony **WIA)foot

B3906   Sopwith Camel   9 (Naval) Sqn
**OP combat with 4AlbatrosDV[+ooc] 3-10pm shot
down n.m.l. ST PIERRE CAPELLE(FSLt R Sykes
WIA) returned WoL, a'c abandoned ["Mart" claim
combat RAMSKAPELLE 3-10pm Untoff P Bäumer Ja2]

B6226   Sopwith Camel   10 (Naval) Sqn
**LowP seen clouds neYPRES 11-35am shot down
MIA(FSLt HS Broughall **POW**) [?"Sopwith" claim
combat swSTADEN 12-10pm? Ltn Lange Ja2][?possible
"Sopwith" claim combat GRAVENSTAFEL 11-30am
Oblt B Loerzer Ja26, but see Nieu B6756 or 60Sq SE5]

21st September

68 (Australian) Squadron arrived in France on the
21st of September equipped with DH5 fighters. It
was to be re-named No.2 Squadron, Australian
Flying Corps in January 1918.

A4298   RE8   4Sqn
**AOb combat with 5EAs POLYGON WOOD dam
OK(Lt T Owen/2Lt LVW Clark) left 9-55am, returned
a'dr ok

**   RE8   9Sqn**
** combat(/AG.Sgt SD Pearce **WIA**)

B270   A.W.FK8   10Sqn
**Phot combat with 4EAs cr WoL 1pm(Maj GB Ward
MC **KIA**/2Lt WA Campbell **DoW**) left 10-45am

B3533   SPAD 7   19Sqn
**NOP seen start combat ovDADIZEELE shot down
MIA(2Lt FW Kirby **KIA**) left 9-22am [?"SPAD" claim
combat wMENIN 9-50am Oblt R Berthold
Ja18]["SPAD" claim combat AMERIKA 9-50am Ltn R
Runge Ja18]

B3557   SPAD 7   19Sqn
NOP seen start combat ovDADIZEELE **MIA(2Lt RA

Inglis **KIA**) left 9-16am [Ja18?]

B3642   SPAD 7   19Sqn
**NOP left 9-16am seen start combat nDADIZEELE
MIA(2Lt WG McRae) **KIA** 26.10.17?: **DoW** as **POW**?
[?unconfirmed "SPAD" claim combat nwMENIN
9-40am Ltn H Auffahrt Ja18]

A7234   Bristol F2b   20Sqn
**OP combat shot down in control WERVICQ-MENIN
MIA(Lt CHC Woods **KIA**?/2Lt TW McLean **KIA**) left
4-36pm, Ja27, Göring ["F2b" claim combat
SLEYHAGE, wROULERS Ltn H Göring Ja27, but see
A7224]

B1110   Bristol F2b   20Sqn
**OP combat with EA fuel tanks shot up ftl dam OK(Sgt
F Hopper/2Lt RS Morris) left 6-35am

B1892   FE2d   20Sqn
+* combat with AlbatrosDV[+ooc] BECELAERE 11am
OK(2Lt W Durrand/Lt AN Jenks)

This was the last FE2d claim for 20 Squadron
before completely re-equipping with Bristol
Fighters. It is also the last record in these lists of
the FE appearing in a daytime fighter-reconnaissance role. FE types would be involved in active
service for longer than virtually any other type,
however. The first FE2as had come to France in
late 1915 and the FE2b would be night bombing
on the last evening of the war.

A7149   Bristol F2b   22Sqn
**OP air collision with A7233 eYPRES broke up 10000'
8-15am (2Lt SM Spurway **KIA**/1AM H Friend **KIA**) left
6-15am Fifth Army front

A7233   Bristol F2b   22Sqn
**OP air collision with A7149 eYPRES broke up 10000'
8-15am (2Lt AH Gilbert **KIA**/2AM C Loveland **KIA**)
left 6-15am Fifth Army front

**   DH5   24Sqn**
OP (2Lt LV Thorowgood **WIA)slight

B3914   Sopwith Camel   45Sqn
NOP left 10-35am **MIA(2Lt EA Cooke **POW**)

A7321   Sopwith Pup   46Sqn
**COP combat with 6EAs then down in control BOIRY
NOTRE DAME Sh51B I.35. **MIA**(2Lt RS Asher **KIA**)
left 8-55am, combat 10-35am? ["Sopwith" claim combat
eMONCHY LE PREUX 9-15am Untoff U Neckel Ja12]

A7224   Bristol F2b   48Sqn
**COP combat with many EAs: seen spin down 10m
eROULERS **MIA**(2Lt RL Curtis **POW DoW**/2Lt DP
Fitzgerald-Uniacke **WIA POW**) left 8pm OSTENDE
[possible F2b claim HOOGLEDE Ltn F Kieckhafer
Ja29, but Göring a possibility], Curtis had claimed 15
EA, including 6 in this a'c

A3617   RE8   53Sqn
**AOb combat seen brought down in control

nrWARNETON 6-55am **MIA**(Capt RNF Mills **KIA**/Lt WA Browne **KIA**) left 6-35am [?"RE" claim combat KEMMEL? 8-52am Ltn E Böhme Ja2]

A4857   SE5   56Sqn
OP left 8am combat ovVERLINGHEM WOOD shot down **MIA(Lt WJ Potts **KIA**) to LICHTERVELDE-LEDEGHEM-INGELMUNSTER ["Sopwith" claim combat eYPRES 8-21am Vzfw G Schneidewind Ja17]

A7581   DH4   57Sqn
+* combat with AlbatrosDVs[++des] DADIZEELE 10-50am OK(Lt AT Drinkwater Aust./Lt FTS Menendez) this crew claimed 6 victories in DH4s

A8914   SE5   60Sqn
OP left 8-55am combat with AlbatrosD eYPRES shot down **MIA(Capt JK Law **KIA**) [?possible "English EA" combat WERVICQ OffSt Weckbrodt Ja26]

A8932   SE5a   60Sqn
+* combat with AlbatrosDV[+des] & 2Str[+des] LANGEMARCK 6-15pm OK(Lt RL Chidlaw-Roberts) claimed 9 victories with 60Sqn & a KB with 40Sq

Sopwith Camel   70Sqn
** combat with EA(2Lt HD Layfield **WIA**) [?"Sopwith" claim combat BOESINGHE 5-50pm Untoff P Bäumer]

A856   FE2b   101Sqn
NB left 3-32am LEDEGHEM **MIA(2Lt AI Orr-Ewing **POW**/Capt E Marshall **POW**)

A5672   FE2b   101Sqn
NB left 3-32am ROULERS **MIA(Capt AC Hatfield **POW**/2Lt RR Macgregor **POW**) both WIA?, left 3-32am, ie early hours of 21.9

These were the first losses for 101 Squadron, sustained in attacks on Menin and other de-training centres. Considerable reinforcements were pouring into these locations and 55 Squadron continued the attacks throught the day. Then 101 Squadron was back again the following evening (see below). 100 Squadron also took part in these bombings.

B3818   Sopwith Camel   9 (Naval) Sqn
+* combat with DFWC[+ooc] ZARREN 5pm OK(FSLt OW Redgate) shared, early victory of probably 16, 8 in this a'c

B6217   Sopwith Camel   9 (Naval) Sqn
+* combat with DFWC[+ooc] ZARREN 5pm OK(FCdr ST Edwards Can.) shared, eventually claimed 16 victories

22nd September

A3448   RE8   4Sqn
**AOb shell hit rear fuselage ftl cr H.15 c.5.8. dam OK(2Lt NF Northam/2Lt S Chadwick) left 2-25pm

A7205   Bristol F2b   22Sqn
OP down in flames nrHOLLEBEKE EoL **MIA(2Lt EA Bell **KIA**/2Lt RE Nowell **KIA**) left 8am Fifth Army

front ["Sopwith" claim combat ZILLEBEKE LAKE 9am Oblt R Berthold Ja18]

B3617   Nieuport 24   40Sqn
+* combat with AlbatrosDV[+des] ePONT À VENDIN 8-30am OK(Lt JH Tudhope SA.) first of 10 claims

B2376.E Sopwith Camel   45Sqn
**NOP left 8am combat with EA bad shot up dam OK(2Lt KB Montgomery)

A7335   Sopwith Pup   46Sqn
+* combat with AlbatrosDIII[+des] nBREBIÈRES 10-15am OK(Capt CA Brewster-Joske Aust.) shared

B6   SE5a   60Sqn
+* combat with 2Str[+des] YPRES-ROULERS 6-45pm OK(Lt WJ Rutherford Can.)

B4860   SE5a   60Sqn
OP combat with Albatros D ZONNEBEKE 10-35am shot up cr WoL(Lt IC MacGregor **WIA) left 9-25am, gunshot to leg [?possible "Sopwith" claim combat WESTROOSEBEKE 10-30am Oblt B Loerzer Ja26, but see 45Sq Camel]

B4864   SE5a   60Sqn
OP combat with Albatros seZONNEBEKE 10-30am **MIA(Lt JO Whiting **KIA**) left 9-25am

B402   FE2b   101Sqn
**NB ROULERS gunfire shot up dam returned a'dr OK(2Lt WH Jones/2AM Muff)

B6213   Sopwith Camel   4 (Naval) Sqn
** combat with enemy seaplane[+dd] then ftl sea off OSTENDE sank OK(FSLt AC Burt)rescued

This combat occurred during protection duty for monitors bombing Ostende. Enemy fire was returned by virtue of an enemy seaplane operating in low cloud. It was this machine the Camel came upon and attacked. It was driven down onto the water and salvaged by the British destroyer Nugent. Sopwiths B3867 (FSLt KV Turney) and B3879 (FLt JEL Hunter) were also involved in this action, in which at least one other enemy seaplane was forced down and crashed.

23rd September

B3485   Nieuport 23   29Sqn
OP left 12pm combat shot down WoL 1-30pm wr(2Lt E Holdsworth **KIA) [?"Nieuport" claim combat WARNETON Ltn W vBülow Ja36]

B3624   Nieuport 27   29Sqn
OP diving on 4EAs ovLANGEMARCK 1-10pm **MIA(2Lt H Rothery **POW DoW**?) left 12pm, probably ok as POW, Ja8, "Sopwith" claims:[?combat sKRUISTRAAT 12-30pm Oblt K Mettlich & nYPRES 12-30pm Ltn R Wendelmuth Ja8][?"Nieuport" claim combat ST JEAN 12-30pm Vzfw W Seitz Ja8]

A9258.B2 DH5   32Sqn
OP last seen 1m wST JULIEN shot down **MIA(2Lt

GR Baynton **POW**) a'c captured [?possible "Sopwith"
claim combat wFREZENBERG 6-30pm Ltn R
Wendelmuth Ja8]

B1670   Nieuport 17   40Sqn
**OP dive on EA cr nrARLEUX Sh51b.B.11.d.8.2. wr
5-30pm(2Lt JL Barlow **KIA**) left 3-50pm ["Nieuport"
claim combat OPPY-WILLERVAL 4-55pm Ltn H
Becker Ja12]

B3541   Nieuport 23   40Sqn
+* combat with 2Str[+flames] ovOPPY 4-45pm OK(Lt
EC Mannock) left 3-50pm, EA broke up

A4563.L SE5   56Sqn
**OP LICHTERVELDE-LEDGHEHEM combat with
EA shot through dam OK(Lt VP Cronyn)

B1.K   SE5a   56Sqn
**OP LICHTERVELDE-LEDGEHEM combat shot
through badly dam OK(Lt RA Maybery)

B525   SE5a   56Sqn
**OP combat with Fokker DrI & later Albatros DV
which came to assist[+Albatros shot down ooc but
landed, +DrI shot down spiral down ooc] neYPRES
SALIENT ~6pm shot up OK(Lt APF Rhys Davids MC
DSO) [Ltn W Voss Ja10 shot down and killed after long,
lone combat against tremendous odds]

B4863   SE5a   56Sqn
**OP combat with EA 2str[+destr] then joined in main
fight with DrI(see SE5a B525 above) shot up OK(Capt
JTB McCudden)

The above encounter between a patrol of 56
Squadron SE5s and the German ace Werner Voss
was a famous fight. Voss was commander of Jasta
10, and at the time the second highest scoring ace
of the German Air Force with forty-eight victories.
He fought a tremendously brave and long fight
with seven of the best RFC pilots, including the
three mentioned above, finally succumbing to fire
from Rhys Davids. Ltn Karl Menckhoff of Jasta 3
who had come to his aid in a red nosed Albatros
was also shot down and credited to this pilot,
although the German managed to crash-land his
machine and survived. McCudden paid his tribute
to Voss with these words from *Five Years in the Royal
Flying Corps*: ". . . as long as I live I shall never
forget my admiration for that German pilot, who,
single-handed, fought seven of us for ten minutes,
and also put some bullets through all of our
machines. His flying was wonderful, his courage
magnificent, and, in my opinion, he is the bravest
German airman whom it has been my privilege to
see fight."

A7643   DH4   57Sqn
**B combat with EA 8-30am shot down ROULERS
MIA(2Lt SLJ Bramley **KIA**/2Lt JM deLacey **KIA**) left
7-50am HOOGLEDE, seen WoL nrHETSAS?, Voss48

["DH" claim combat ROULERS-LEDEGHEM 8-30am
Ltn W Voss Ja10]

B539   SE5a   60Sqn
**OP combat with EA shot up bad driven down ftl 29Sq
6-55pm OK(Capt HA Hammersley)

B557   SE5a   60Sqn
OP left 9-20am combat with EA EoL **MIA(2AM HH
Bright **KIA**) fell in Lines

B3894   Sopwith Camel   3 (Naval) Sqn
** combat with Albatros DV[+ooc] MIDDELKERKE
~11am(FSLt GS Harrover **WIA**) [?"Sopwith" claim
combat nNIEUPORT 10-55am Ltn F Ray Ja28]

24th September

The third RFC night bombing unit, 102 Squadron,
arrived in France. They flew FE2bs until the end
of the war.

A3862   RE8   15Sqn
Phot AA tail shot off cr nrINCHY(2Lt WE Hall **POW/
2Lt PJ Casey **POW**) initials ME? left 2-15pm to
E.1.C.4-4., last WT 2-26pm

B3619   SPAD 7   19Sqn
**NOP shot up dam ftl LA LOVIE a'dr OK(2Lt AAND
Pentland)

A3976   Martinsyde G102   27Sqn
**B combat nrSAUCHY LESTRÉE 2-50pm shot down
seen dive steeply in control **MIA**(2Lt W English **WIA
POW**) left 11-50am ATH STATION ["1Str" claim
combat CAGNICOURT 2-45pm Oblt H Waldhausen
Ja37]

B1826   Sopwith Pup   66Sqn
OP ROULERS area? **MIA(Lt D Moir-Paton **KIA**)
[?"Sopwith" claim combat nwDIXMUDE 1pm Oblt B
Loerzer Ja26]

B2361.C Sopwith Camel   70Sqn
**OP combat ftl cr ldg HONDSCHOOTE dam OK(2Lt
CW Primeau) [?possible "Camel" claim combat
MOORSLEDE 4-50pm Ltn K Wüsthoff Ja4]

N6343   Sopwith Camel   8 (Naval) Sqn
OP combat with EA(FSLt WL Jordan **WIA)thigh
[?"Sopwith" claim combat RAMSCAPELLE 3-30pm Ltn
F Ray Ja28]

B3883   Sopwith Camel   9 (Naval) Sqn
+* combat with AlbatrosDIII[+ooc] LEKE 3-45pm
OK(FSLt HF Stackard) shared, possibly later combat:
with AlbatrosDV[+ooc] MIDDELKERKE 4-30pm,
Stackard claimed 15EAs

B6279   Sopwith Camel   10 (Naval) Sqn
**OP seen nHOUTHULST WOOD 9-40am shot down
MIA(FSLt B Foster **POW**) seen before he crossed Lines,
Ja4? [?"Sopwith" claim combat MOORSLEDE, but
time? Vzfw K Wüsthoff Ja4]

9042   Short 184   Dunkirk
this a'c? **B destroyer snd sea **MIA**(FSLt AW Phillips

POW/CPO EA Boyd **POW**) picked up by ship

25th September

The Official History notes that the German airmen were very active on this day, but as can be seen the RFC suffered very few casualties. On the other hand, as a result of the many combats, thirty-two enemy aeroplanes were claimed driven down, of which nineteen were seen to crash.

A4216   RE8   6Sqn
CP combat shot up cr ldg wr(Lt J Wolstenholm **KIA/Lt FL McCreary **WIA**) left 8-45am, pilot was killed in combat and observer made landing but spun in from 200'

A7124   Bristol F2b   11Sqn
DOP combat broke up 1000' ooc ovLE CATELET 11-10am (Lt GE Miall-Smith **KIA/2Lt CC Dennis **KIA**) left 9-30am

**   DH4   18Sqn**
PhotRec combat(/Lt GC Langford **WIA)

B3520.A   SPAD 7   19Sqn
SpM left 4-08pm **MIA(Lt BA Powers **KIA**) [?"SPAD" claim combat GHELUVELT 4-30pm Oblt R Berthold Ja18]

B1116   Bristol F2b   20Sqn
OP combat with EA shot up ftl(Lt JC Kirkpatrick OK/Capt AA English **WIA) left 9-30am

B3607.L   Nieuport 24   40Sqn
+* combat with RumplerC[+ooc] SALLAUMINES 3-10pm OK(Lt EC Mannock) left 2-55pm, 5th of 8 patrols for the day, Mannock's last Nieuport victory with 40Sqn

A6211   Sopwith Pup   54Sqn
+* combat with AlbatrosDIII[+des] nMIDDELKERKE 11-30am OK(Capt O Stewart)

B1776   Sopwith Pup   54Sqn
**OP left 10-40am combat with EA shot up dam cr wr OK(Lt N Clark Aust.?) [?Sopwith claim combat sLANGEMARCK Ltn H Kroll Ja24]

A796   FE2b   100Sqn
**NB left 10-47pm shot up dam returned 11-58pm OK(Lt FW Wells/Lt RC Pitman)

B3920   Sopwith Camel   10 (Naval) Sqn
OP cr eYPRES(FSLt AF MacDonald **WIA) inj?

B6240   Sopwith Camel   Seaplane Defence Flt
Dunkirk **P attacked Fried'hafen seaplane[+shot down in sea] oil tank hit then engine failed ftl sea 10m nMALMO-LES-BAINS OK(FCdr R Graham) pilot rescued by destroyer, a'c salvaged, EA crew was Vzfwgm Plattenburg WIA/Ltn Brettman

26th September

Although heavy fighting had continued around the Menin Road Ridge, a further main assault was undertaken on this day into the area of Polygon Wood. The front for the advance was more concentrated than before, stretching northwards from just south of the ridge to a little beyond St Julien. The purpose of this fighting was to gain a good position for the intended attack on Passchendaele. Most of Polygon Wood was taken in fierce and costly fighting through the day, and by the evening of the 27th was completely in Allied hands. The Germans flew more low ground attack patrols than usual in this fighting, but lost six of their fighters to machine-gun fire from the ground. Pilots of 70 Squadron Camels, for their own part, suffered onerously from the same work. One of the RFC's greatest contributions through the day was giving warnings of impending counter-attacks, many of which were dealt with by artillery.

A8863   SPAD 7   19Sqn
SpM left 7-02am **MIA(2Lt GB Roberts **KIA**) Sqn operating COMINES area [?"SPAD" claim nwDADIZEELE BECELAERE 7-20am Ltn K Stock Ja6]

B3620   SPAD 7   19Sqn
** left 7-04am shell hit cr wr(2Lt AAND Pentland Aust. **WIA**)face, gunshot?, Pentland achieved at least 7 of perhaps 23 victories in this a'c

B3640   SPAD 7   19Sqn
SpM left 9-35am shot up dam on return 10-11am(Lt W Jones **WIA)foot

A4615   RE8   21Sqn
CAP shot down nrZONNEBEKE **MIA(2Lt DG Rouquette **KIA**/2Lt AL Sutcliffe **WIA POW**) left 7-30am ["English EA" claim combat POLYGON WOOD Ltn W vBülow Ja36]

B3490   SPAD 7   23Sqn
OP left 10am combat shot up cr Lines wr(2Lt E Taylor **DoW 26.9.17) [?"SPAD" claim combat BECELAERE 10-40am Vzfw K Wüsthoff Ja4]

A9175   DH5   24Sqn
OP seen ok BELGIUM Sh12 T.18 going ene at 2000' 2-45pm **MIA(2Lt A Taylor **POW**) left 2-15pm to nr T.18

B3649   Nieuport 27   29Sqn
IP seen 7-30am nrHOUTHULST shot down EoL **MIA(2Lt HV Thompson **KIA**) left 7-15am ["Nieuport" claim combat nrGHELUVELT Ltn H Böhning Ja36]

A9194   DH5   32Sqn
OP British shell seen o't in air MENIN RD-POLYGON WOOD 1-45pm **MIA(2Lt FC Andrews **POW**) report: fell out?

B2363   Sopwith Camel   45Sqn
**OP AA shot up dam OK(2Lt KB Montgomery)

B2374   Sopwith Camel   45Sqn
** combat with 5Albatros ovPASSCHENDAELE shot down EoL **MIA**(2Lt CF Risteen **KIA**) left 10-45am

[?"Sopwith" claim combat GREFENSTAFEL 11am Oblt
B Loerzer Ja26 (or 70Sqn casualties?)][?"Sopwith" claim
combat eBECELAERE 11-15am Ltn R Runge Ja18]

B2358   Sopwith Camel   70Sqn
**OP seen low swPASSCHENDAELE going sw to Lines
12-15pm MIA(Lt WHR Gould **KIA**) left 11-05am
[?"Sopwith" claim combat BECELAERE 12pm Oblt R
Berthold Ja18]

B3915   Sopwith Camel   70Sqn
**OP seen low nrPASSCHENDAELE going se to Lines
12-15pm MIA(2Lt TB Fenwick **POW**) left 11-05am

B5151   Sopwith Camel   70Sqn
**OP seen low nrPASSCHENDAELE going se to Lines
12-15pm MIA(2Lt CE Stuart **POW**) left 11-05am
["Sopwith 1Str" claim combat sHOUTHULST WOOD
Ltn R Klimke Ja27, also second Sopwith claim
sSCHLOSSES VIERCKENHOCK(Verlorenhoek?)]

B6237   Sopwith Camel   70Sqn
**OP left 10-05am combat with EA shot up dam returned
10-55am OK(Lt GR Wilson)

B6275   Sopwith Camel   70Sqn
**OP seen low nrPASSCHENDAELE going se to Lines
MIA(2Lt CNL Lomax **POW**) left 11-05am, seen
12-15pm [?"Sopwith 1Str" claim combat
BLANKAARTSEE 12-15pm? Ltn W Rosenstein Ja27]

N1232   Short 184   HMS *Vindex*
** low fuel ftl sea OK(FLt EG Hopcraft/PO EJ Garner)
crew released, a'c interned

         Sopwith Triplane   1 (Naval) Sqn
GroundP shot up(FSLt CWL Calvert **WIA)foot

N5388   Sopwith Triplane   1 (Naval) Sqn
** French pilot **KIA** [?"Tripe" combat "PLANQU.46",
COMINES? Vzfw F Altemeier Ja24][also "Tripe claim
COMINES Vzfw Wackwitz Ja24]

This Triplane had been loaned to the French Air
Force.

N5421   Sopwith Triplane   1 (Naval) Sqn
** combat with EA shot down HOUTHULST WOOD
MIA(FSLt JC Akester **WIA POW**) [?"Sopwith" claim
combat HOUTHULST WOOD Ltn H Bongartz Ja36]
name Akeston?

N5440   Sopwith Triplane   1 (Naval) Sqn
** combat with EA shot down EoL MIA(FSLt WG?
Burnett **KIA**) initials WJ?, Ja36 ["Tripe" claim combat
PASSCHENDAELE 12-10pm Ltn T Quandt Ja36]

B6258   Sopwith Camel   9 (Naval) Sqn
SpM left 5-33am MIA(FSLt W Ingleson **POW)

N6359   Sopwith Camel   10 (Naval) Sqn
this a'c? **OP AA hit(FSLt RH Daly DSC **WIA**)

27th September

B3441   RE8   9Sqn
**Phot combat with EA shot down WoL(2Lt CB

Andrews **WIA**/Spr AG White **KIA**) [?"RE" claim
combat FARBUS WOOD 5-10pm Oblt H Waldhausen
Ja37]

A7248   Bristol F2b   20Sqn
**PhotRec combat with EA shot up dam returned a'dr
OK(Lt JP Dalley/Lt OA Rowan) left 12-33pm

B331   DH5   24Sqn
**OP Fourth Army front shot up dam OK(2Lt AK
Cowper)

A7150   Bristol F2b   48Sqn
**OP OSTENDE combat shot down in flames cr
6-55pm(Sgt H Clarke **KIA**/Bdr EA Nash **DoW**) left
4-45pm OSTENDE-DIXMUDE [?possible "Sopwith"
claim combat PERVYSE 6-40pm Ltn X Dannhuber
Ja26, but see N6355]

A7452   DH4   55Sqn
**B HESDIN L'ABBÉE lagging behind on return
combat 11EA shot up(Capt Owen OK/2AM WA Fraser
WIA) left 1-38pm

A5526   FE2b   101Sqn
**NB RUMBEKE fuel tank shot through ftl dam
OK(2Lt TJC Martyn/2Lt HW Steele)

B6227   Sopwith Camel   8 (Naval) Sqn
+* combat with AlbatrosDV[+ftl] SOUCHEZ 6-45pm
OK(FCdr CD Booker) EA of Ja7 captured, last victory
with 8(Naval) for this ace

N6355   Sopwith Camel   10 (Naval) Sqn
**OuterOP seen sHOUTHULST WOOD shot down
MIA(FSLt JS de Wilde **KIA**) seen lagging behind
3-10pm [?possible "Sopwith" claim combat PERVYSE
Ltn X Dannhuber Ja26]

28th September

The lack of effectiveness of the German "elastic
defence" in fighting around Polygon Wood
materially disrupted their organisation in the
following days, and German activity in the air
dropped noticeably. The RFC used this opportunity to concentrate heavy bombing onto enemy
road and rail networks. Several corps units also
carried out this work, so that on the 28th, for
instance, twenty separate bombing attacks were
made.

9 (Naval) Squadron was withdrawn from attachment to the RFC and returned to Dunkirk for some
months. It came under the command of No.4 Wing
RNAS and before the end of the year would re-
equip with Bentley-powered Sopwith Camels.

A7210   Bristol F2b   20Sqn
**PhotRec combat with EA down WERVICQ-MENIN
12-30pm MIA(Capt JS Campbell **KIA**/Dvr G Tester
KIA) left 11-40am ["English 2Str" claim combat
sWERVICQ 12-30pm Oblt H Auffahrt Ja18]

A7241   Bristol F2b   20Sqn
**PhotRec combat in flames cr wr(2Lt HF Tomlin KIA/
2Lt HT Noble KIA) left 11-40am WERVICQ-
HOLLEBEKE 12-30pm [?"English 2Str" claim combat
eHOLLEBEKE 12-30am Ltn J Veltjens Ja18]

A9211   DH5   32Sqn
**OP AA shell hit 1pm broke up(Capt AT Lloyd KIA)

A9276   DH5   41Sqn
**DOP driven down by 3EAs ovPELVES down in
control 6-17pm Sh51B C.22 MIA(2Lt JL Haight WIA
POW) left 4-50pm CAMBRAI ["DH5" claim combat
BIACHE Stn 6-15pm Ltn U Neckel Ja12]

B2366   Sopwith Camel   43Sqn
+* combat with AlbatrosDIII[+ooc] PONT À
VENDIN 6-15pm engine shot up dam ftl WINGLES
OK(Capt TS Wynn)

This was the first Sopwith Camel victory for 43
Squadron.

B6209   Sopwith Camel   43Sqn
**OP SECLIN-DOUAI shot down in flames ovPONT À
VENDIN 6-20pm MIA(2Lt RP Hood KIA) left 5-40pm
[?one of 2 "SE" claims combat wWINGLES 6pm Ltn E
Udet Ja37]

This was 43 Squadron's first Camel casualty. At
this time they were operating in the First Army
area to the south.

A5686   FE2b   101Sqn
**NB shot up dam OK(Capt LGS Payne/Lt FP
Worthington)

29th September

B277   A.W.FK8   10Sqn
**AOb RICHEBOURG combat with 5EAs ftl WoL
6pm(Lt EL Burrell WIA/2Lt EA Barnard KIA)
[?possible "Sopwith" claim combat FLEURBAIX Vzfw
Buckler Ja17]

B1124   Bristol F2b   48Sqn
**B combat AA engine left formation, seen glide towards
Holland ftl SLUIS 3pm MIA(2Lt FL Smith INT/2Lt JW
Frost INT) left 2-20pm ZEEBRUGGE

A5599   FE2b   101Sqn
**NB GONTRODE shot down MIA(Lt GF Westcott
POW/2Lt EAV Ellerbeck POW) left 8-15pm

30th September

The temporary hiatus in the fighting ended with
German counter-attacks being launched north of
the Menin Road, followed by another six over the
next three days. These attacks were fiercely made,
but none caused serious reversals and were generally repulsed. Fine weather prevailed through
much of this time, and some of the most useful work
the RFC did was to photograph the enemy lines
thoroughly.

A3736   RE8   5Sqn
**Phot combat with EA 12-05pm shot down
ovGAVRELLE wr(Lt EH Pember KIA/2AM A Morley
KIA) left 11-10am ["RE" claim combat eTILLOY Vzfw
Hamster Ja37]

Bristol F2b   11Sqn
**OP shot up(2Lt AR Browne WIA/)calf

A3731   RE8   13Sqn
**Phot combat shot down in flames MIA(Sgt AO Stanley
KIA/1AM AH Wardlaw KIA) left 10-50am XVII Corps
front

A9440   DH5   41Sqn
**DOP combat fuel tank shot up ftl CANDAS A'dr
4-30pm dam(2Lt GA Gillings WIA) left 2-45pm

Sopwith Pup   46Sqn
**OP shot up(2Lt E Armitage DoW 4.10.17)calf

B1768   Sopwith Pup   66Sqn
**OP seen in slow spin ovGHELUWE MIA(Lt JW
Boumphrey POW) [?"Sopwith 1Str" claim combat
WAMBEKE 11-55am Ltn H Auffahrt Ja18][Sopwith
claim combat ST MARGUERITE 11-50am Ltn R Runge
Ja18]

B2185   Sopwith Pup   66Sqn
**OP seen going down in spin sGHELUWE MIA(2Lt
JG Warter KIA) [?"Sopwith" claim combat
PLOEGSTEERT WOOD 11-55am Ltn J Veltjens
Ja18][?"Sopwith" claim combat DEULEMONT
11-50am Oblt R Berthold Ja18]

B2377   Sopwith Camel   70Sqn
*OP hit Camel B6283 ldg dam: later damaged in evening
enemy bombing raid

B2398   Sopwith Camel   70Sqn
**OP left 11am combat many Albatroses
seHOUTHULST FOREST ~11-20am MIA(Lt C
Dalkeith-Scott KIA)

FE2b   100Sqn
** shot up(2Lt CO Bean WIA/)leg

A822   FE2b   100Sqn
**SpNB left 8pm GONTRODE Zeppelin Sheds, engine
hit by AA nrTHIELT on return ftl nrMEULBEKE
MIA(2Lt JF Bushe POW/2Lt LA Colbert POW)

**Untraced casualty in France in September
1917?**

RNAS
** (Lt DF Lewis? POW) Sep.17?

October 1917

1st October

B6753   Nieuport 27   1Sqn
+* combat with DFWC[+ooc] HOUTHULST 11-10am
OK(Capt RA Birkbeck) shared, Birkbeck claimed 10 EA

on Nieuports, most in this a'c

RE8   **7Sqn**
AOb combat(2Lt BH Caswell **WIA/)

RE8   **7Sqn**
AOb (/SLt DB Laughton **DoW)

A7231?   **Bristol F2b**   **11Sqn**
this a'c? **OP combat with EA shot up(2Lt H Scandrett **WIA**/Lt C Watson MC **WIA**) this crew had scored 2 victories in A7231 on 30.9.17

B5014   **RE8**   **21Sqn**
**CP YPRES shot up by EA on return 11-30am AA? OK(Lt GFW Zimmer/2Lt JE Mott)

A7405   **DH4**   **25Sqn**
B CARVIN combat shot down 2pm cr nrBURBURE on return wr(2Lt CO Rayner **KIA/2Lt JL Hughes **KIA**) left 12-35pm

A8928   **SE5a**   **56Sqn**
OP combat with EA broke up ovOOSTNIEUKERKE seen going down(2Lt RH Sloley **KIA) left 4-30pm ["Sopwith 1Str" claim combat WESTROOSEBEKE 5-50pm Ltn X Dannhuber Ja26]

2nd October

B1508   **Nieuport 17**   **1Sqn**
+* combat with DFWC[+ooc] COMINES 11-05am OK(2Lt GB Moore Can.)

A7138   **Bristol F2b**   **11Sqn**
DOP combat WASNES-AU-BAC **MIA(2Lt JM McKenna **KIA**/2Lt S Sutcliffe **KIA**) left 4-45pm, seen combat DOUAI-CAMBRAI ~6pm ["Bristol" claim combat swMARQUETTE Vzfw H Oberländer 6-10pm Ja30]

           DH5   **24Sqn**
OP AA(2Lt RC Davies **WIA)

A4376   **RE8**   **53Sqn**
FlRec combat with AlbatrosD[+flames] YPRES 9000' in dark 6-30pm, fired close burst, then lost ftl DROGLANDT cr(T2Lt SA Gilray OK/Lt HW Smith **WIA)ankle, pilot's first service flight EoL, became lost because observer was "out of it" & ftl

A7642   **DH4**   **55Sqn**
B MARKE seen nrYPRES re-crossing lines **MIA(2Lt WR Bishop **KIA**/2Lt G Mathews **KIA**) left 8-59am ["DH4" claim combat MEULEBEKE 10-40am Ltn H Klein Ja10]

           DH4   **57Sqn**
B combat(2Lt FA Martin **WIA/)foot

A7451   **DH4**   **57Sqn**
B seen combat ovROULERS **MIA(2Lt CRB Halley **KIA**/1AM T Barlow **KIA**) left 11-45am ABEELE, seen at rear of patrol ["DH4" claim combat ROULERS 1-30pm Ltn R Runge Ja18]

A7581   **DH4**   **57Sqn**
B combat ovROULERS **MIA(2Lt CGO MacAndrew

KIA/2Lt LP Sidney **KIA**) left 11-45am ABEELE [?"DH4" claim combat nrROULERS 1-30pm? Oblt R Berthold Ja18]

A7583   **DH4**   **57Sqn**
B seen combat ovROULERS **MIA(2Lt CG Crane **POW**/2Lt WL Inglis **KIA**) left 11-45am [?"DH4" claim combat nrROULERS Ltn Kleffel Ja18]

A9271   **DH5**   **68 (Australian) Sqn**
COP seen after combat ovVILLERS OUTREAUX engine failure **MIA(2Lt ICF Agnew **POW**) left 4-45pm (10-10am?)

This was the first loss in action for 68 (Australian) Squadron.

3rd October

           RE8   **9Sqn**
Phot combat(Lt WF Findlay **WIA/)

B1641   **Nieuport 17**   **29Sqn**
OP left 10-15am seen ovYPRES 10-50am going east, lost ftl ST AMAND EoL 11-40am **MIA(2Lt FM Nash **POW**)

           Bristol F2b   **48Sqn**
OP (/2Lt GR Horsfall **WIA)slight

4th October

Although the period of relatively good weather ended on the 3rd, the next main assault, planned for the 4th, still took place. This saw an attack along a seven-mile front between the Menin Road and the Ypres-Staden railway. Its aim was to press on to Poelcappelle and Broodseinde, on the Passchendaele Ridge — a significant advance in the context of the Ypres campaign. Despite the return of rain, and with high winds and clouds down to as low as four hundred feet, a significant amount of the air co-operation immediately associated with the assault was somehow carried out, although deeper work was impossible. Beneath them, the infantry fought with tremendous fortitude and sacrifice, and the objectives were reached by the afternoon. What actions followed were mainly to fight off the inevitable counter-attacks, which was done successfully. The Germans suffered severe casualties in this fighting.

B6794   **SPAD 7**   **19Sqn**
GP left 8-55am **MIA(Lt HC Ainger **KIA**)

A4763   **RE8**   **21Sqn**
**CP combat? then strong winds ftl SALVATION CORNER OK(Lt AC Youdale/2Lt JE Mott) left 9am

5th October

The weather remained terrible all through this week. Whatever expectations the British High

Command had as regards the weather — and that subject must have been constantly before them in this campaign — it is hard to understand how at this time the decision could be made to press on with the offensive. This they did, however, on the basis that the capture of the Passchendaele ridge would be the only acceptable position in which to halt for the winter. No doubt it was also advantageous for the Allies to keep drawing the enemy into Flanders, as the next French offensive was planned for later this month on the Aisne. There was absolutely no sign, however, that the weather was improving, nor would it until the spring.

B1536   SPAD 7   19Sqn
Wireless Interruption, seen going east EoL **MIA(2Lt JG Stevenson **POW**) left 9-51am

B1133   Bristol F2b   20Sqn
OP combat with EA nDADIZEELE **MIA(Capt DD Walrond-Skinner **POW**/Pte FJ Johns **POW**) left 7-39am, seen going north ovROULERS ["Bristol" claim combat DADIZEELE 8-15am Ltn E Böhme Ja2]

A9312   DH5   32Sqn
OP shot up nZILLEBEKE ftl wr ldg(2Lt JE Johnston **WIA)slight [?possible "DH" claim nrWESTROOSEBEKE 3-25pm Vzfw Patzer Ja36]

B524   SE5a   56Sqn
OP left 7am seen combat with ovROULERS-MENIN ROAD **MIA(2Lt CH Jeffs **POW**) ["Sopwith" claim combat MENIN 8-20am Oblt B Loerzer Ja26]

B527   SE5a   56Sqn
**OP combat with EA shot up ftl dam OK(2Lt RJ Preston-Cobb)

B507.A   SE5a   60Sqn
OP engine failed ftl BAVICHOVE(2Lt JJ Fitzgerald **POW) left 10-15am, a'c captured

N5377.4   **Sopwith Triplane   1 (Naval) Sqn**
** shot down DADIZEELE EoL 6-50am seen dive ne ovZONNEBEKE **MIA**(FSLt MJ Watson **POW**) Ja4? ["Sopwith" claim combat DADIZEELE Ltn Wilde Ja4]

6th October

From the 6th of October German time reverted to being one hour ahead of British time (all times given are British time).

B5039   RE8   9Sqn
AOb dh from British shell cr Sh28.C.14(2Lt EP Lewis **KIA/Lt HG Holt MC **KIA**)salvaged?

B3508.C   **SPAD 7   19Sqn**
WTInt seen ovLILLE prior hail storm **MIA(2Lt GR Long **WIA POW**) left 9-26am

A5680   FE2b   102Sqn
NB **MIA(2Lt RH Richardson **POW**/2Lt CE Carroll **POW**) 5/6Oct.17

This was the first loss for 102 Squadron RFC in action.

7th October

A7280   Bristol F2b   22Sqn
EscP seen ovKRUISEIKE 7-30am **MIA(2Lt JC Bush MC **KIA**/Lt WW Chapman **KIA**) left 6-28am ["Bristol" claim combat MENIN 7-40am Ltn H vHaebler Ja36]

B3612   Nieuport 24   40Sqn
+* combat with AlbatrosDV[+des] LA BASSÉE 7-45am OK(Capt GL Lloyd)

This was the last Nieuport victory for 40 Squadron.

A7401   DH4   55Sqn
B combat several EAs ftl DICKEBUSCH(Sgt M Coomer-Weare **WIA/Gnr WG Osborne **WIA**) observer 2AM S Moreman? [?possible "English EA" combat wGHELUVELT Untoff Duschner/Untoff Besel SS30]

8th October

Rain fell all through the 7th and 8th as preparations continued for the next attack, which had now been ordered for the 9th.

28 Squadron arrived in France with Sopwith Camels on the 8th of October. It was only briefly on the Western Front before being transferred to Italy within a month.

A4315   RE8   7Sqn
AOb left 8-30am **MIA(2Lt CB Wattson **KIA**/Lt J Diamond MC **KIA**) last WT 8-50am [?unconfirmed "RE" claim swTERHAND: Vzfw Reichenbach?]

9th October

The attack on the 9th, designed to broaden the salient to the north between Yser and Houthulst Wood, began at 5-20am. Again it was raining. The troops involved should have been used to it by now, except that it was too deadly an enemy. It restricted flying once again to the immediate battlefield, where contact patrols managed to keep a detailed track of developments, and those on artillery co-operation work managed to break up several German counter-attacks. 9 Squadron's efforts were particularly notable in this regard, flying in and about the barrage. Their endeavours also made them targets, as can be seen from the casualties noted below.

B3577   Nieuport 17   1Sqn
HighOP seen low ovMENIN 1-35pm combat with 3EAs **MIA(2Lt MA Peacock **POW**) left 12-42pm ["Nieuport" claim combat GHELUWE 1-30pm Ltn Müller Ja11]

B6767   Nieuport 27   1Sqn
**LowOP combat with 5EA ftl nrPOLYGON

WOOD(Capt WVT Rooper **DoW** 25.10.17) left 2-50pm, fractured thigh [?Ja11], Rooper had claimed 8 EAs, the last 4 in this a'c

1 Squadron were one of the very few units to carry out offensive patrolling on the 9th. One patrol met nine enemy fighters and another met five later in the day.

A3675   RE8   6Sqn
FlRec hit by British shell ftl HOOGE cr(Lt NW Wadham **WIA/Lt Tyler OK) hit 9-45am

**   RE8   9Sqn**
AOb (2Lt AJD Torry MC **KIA/)

A3663   RE8   9Sqn
CAP left 7-40am **MIA(2Lt IU MacMurchy **KIA**/2Lt FT Brasington **KIA**) buried Sh20 U.12.c.60.10. ["RE" claim combat LANGEMARCK-BIXSCHOOTE 9-10am Oblt B Loerzer Ja26]

A4387   RE8   9Sqn
CAP combat shot down ftl 23Sqn a'dr(2Lt WGC Hackman **WIA/2Lt GF Sogno **DoW**)

B3638   SPAD 7   19Sqn
LowNP AA? shot through ftl(Lt RI Van-Der-Byl **WIA)knee[?"Sopwith" claim POELCAPPELLE 10-15am Ltn H Dilthey Ja27]

B1125   Bristol F2b   20Sqn
SpRec ROULERS-MENIN engine failed ftl EoL on a'dr of FlAbt(A)217 **MIA(Lt WD Chambers **POW**/2Lt FH Berry **POW**) left 3-19pm, a'c captured

B1135   Bristol F2b   20Sqn
**P AA hit shot up ftl OK(Lt JC Kirkpatrick/AM J McMechan)

A4729   RE8   21Sqn
AP:Zone Calls to YPRES AA ftl cr dam(Lt CW MacAloney **WIA/Lt D Alexander **WIA**) left 2pm

4969   FE2b   102Sqn
NB **MIA(Lt DG Powell **POW**/Lt RF Hill **POW**)

10th October

B3637   Nieuport 27   29Sqn
OP left 5-35am combat shot up dam ldg ok a'dr(2Lt CW Hamilton **WIA)

B6791   Nieuport 27   29Sqn
OP left 5-35am GLOUCESTER HOUSE ftl by EA? wr(2Lt GB Wigle **WIA)face

B360   DH5   41Sqn
Esc ECOURT ST QUENTIN AA 4-15pm but seen going down in control ovHENDECOURT & ldg ok **MIA(2Lt AW Edwards **KIA**) ["DH5" claim combat HENDECOURT 4-05pm Ltn W Ewers Ja12]

B23   SE5a   56Sqn
OP left 3-40pm combat with EA eYPRES **MIA(Lt GM Wilkinson **KIA**) ["Sopwith" claim combat sBECELAERE 5pm Ltn X Dannhuber Ja26]

A2138   DH4   57Sqn
B OOSTNIEUKERKE seen WoL on return **MIA(Sgt FV Legge OK?/1AM JS Clarke **KIA**) left 3pm ["DH" claim combat WESTROOSEBEKE 4pm Ltn H Bongartz Ja36]

B2356   Sopwith Camel   70Sqn
+* combat with AlbatrosDV[+flames] WESTROOSEBEKE 8-05am then AlbatrosDV[+ooc] sHOUTHULST WOOD 8-25am OK(2Lt FG Quigley Can.) first of 33 victories

11th October

A4330   RE8   5Sqn
AP combat with 3EAs shot up sFARBUS ftl(Lt FCE Clarke **DoW 11.10.17/Lt P Mighell **DoW** 12.10.17) combat 8-40am ["RE" claim combat ROCLINCOURT 8-45am Ltn J Buckler Ja17]

A7127.U   Bristol F2b   11Sqn
Post combat shot down nrHAM 51B.I.18 at 3-50pm wr **MIA(2Lt AE Turvey **POW**/2AM W Hewitt **WIA POW**) left 2-40pm

A7181   Bristol F2b   22Sqn
OP left 8-25am **MIA(Lt RIV Hill **POW**/2Lt RS Gilbert **POW**) [?"Bristol" claim combat BOVEKERKE 10-15am Ltn H Viebig Ja57]

A7223   Bristol F2b   22Sqn
**OP combat with EA shot up dam ftl ok OK(Lt WG Meggitt MC/Capt FA Durrad), left 8-50am

B6314   Sopwith Camel   28Sqn
*pracform seen going west POPERINGHE-YPRES strayed EoL **MIA**(2Lt WH Winter **POW**) left 3-05pm, a'c captured ["Sopwith" claim combat ARMENTIÈRES 4-20pm Ltn J Buckler Ja17]

This was the first loss in action for 28 Squadron.

B2180   Sopwith Pup   46Sqn
DOP BOURLON WOOD seen combat ovMARQUION **MIA(2Lt AA Allen **KIA**) left 3-25pm ["DH5" claim combat SAINS-LES-MARQUION 4-45pm Ltn W Ewers Ja12]

This was the last Sopwith Pup casualty for 46 Squadron before it became a Sopwith Camel unit.

A4861.L   SE5   56Sqn
OP PONT À NIEPPE combat? ftl(2Lt JN Cunningham **DoW 19.10.17) left 6-15am, gunshot in back

B525.I   SE5a   56Sqn
+* combat with AlbatrosDV[+ooc] neYPRES-BECELAERE btwn 7-30am & 8-15am OK(Lt APF Rhys Davids) his last of 25 victories, including his last 8 claims in this a'c

B542   SE5a   56Sqn
OP left 6-15am combat with EA eYPRES **MIA(Lt RJ Preston-Cobb **KIA**) to CORTEMARCK-COURTRAI-MENIN, Ja36 ["SE5" claim combat KOELENBERG 7-30am Ltn H Hoyer Ja36]

B577   SE5a   56Sqn
*OP left 3-40pm shot up? ftl ZILLEBEKE dam OK (Lt GB Shone)

N6358   Sopwith Camel   9 (Naval) Sqn
OP left 2pm combat with 3EAs ZARREN seen diving on trenches **MIA (FSLt N Black **DoW** 12.10.17) [?"Sopwith" claim combat EESEN, eDIXMUDE 3-05pm Ltn X Dannhuber Ja26]

12th October

The Official History, normally sanguine of events, could only say of the plans still in place for a continuance of the offensive that "they were not yet impossible". This is another way of saying that to carry on with them for much longer would be utterly foolhardy. The next attack, planned for the 12th of October, was countermanded, again because of rain, but only after it had already begun and become totally bogged down in the flooded valleys west of the main ridge. The halt did not come until the early afternoon, but mercifully it was before any major German counter-attacks had begun. Low patrolling carried out by no less than ten squadrons had made life a complete misery for the German infantry, and they were constantly and heavily shelled in their positions as well. Had the advance continued, no doubt there would have been bloody fighting in the counter actions

The appalling conditions took a high toll on the squadrons co-operating with the fighting, as can be seen in the listings below. German fighters were also out in numbers and caused casualties to offensive patrols in the back areas. Once again, very little ground had been gained at so much cost. Even now, however, when the British High Command knew that the ridge could not be gained before winter, the fighting ground onwards. Daily skirmishes and attacks continued, and it can be seen from the casualty lists that the next main move would not occur until a break in the weather permitted it, around the 22nd. Yet on nearly every day of this gruelling and painful progress on the ground there were also losses to the air services. The fighting in Flanders would press on to conceal intentions for a new battle, this time further south, in the sector opposite Cambrai.

B5040   RE8   4Sqn
Phot **MIA (2Lt WG Morgan **POW DoW** 23.10.17/Lt JM Atkinson **POW**) left 2-20pm I ANZAC CORPS, observer interned Holland 30.4.18

B6458   RE8   7Sqn
**CP mg fuel tank shot up ftl OK (Lt WMB Skinner/Lt CE Prescott) left 11-40am POELCAPPELLE-ST JULIEN RD

B3574   SPAD 7   19Sqn
GroundP left 12-50pm down EoL **MIA (2Lt HR Hicks **KIA**)

A3768   RE8   21Sqn
AOb AA ftl cr Sh28D.20.H.93. (Capt JHC Minchin **WIA/Lt CS Vandyke **WIA**) to hospital, left 9-45am YPRES, injured in crash?

B5072   RE8   21Sqn
**CP left 12-05pm AA shot up ftl made ldg ok OK (Capt AC Youdale/Lt JE Mott)

**   SPAD 7   23Sqn**
OP (Lt FH Hiscock **WIA)

A7426   DH4   25Sqn
B BEYTHEM **MIA (Sgt AL Clear **POW**/2Lt FW Talbot **POW**) left 10-35am, Talbot interned Holland 9.4.18

B1635   Nieuport 17   29Sqn
**IP AA ftl a'dr 10-25am dam OK (2Lt ES Meek Can.)

B2375   Sopwith Camel   45Sqn
NOP left 10-45am seen combat eHOUTHULST **MIA (Capt HB Coomber **KIA**) [?unconfirmed "Sopwith 1Str" claim combat swCOURTRAI 11-20am Untoff J Kaiser Ja35]

B2386   Sopwith Camel   45Sqn
NOP left 10-45am seen combat eHOUTHULST **MIA (2Lt KH Willard **KIA**) [?possible "Sopwith 1Str" claim combat nwMOORSLEDE 11-15am Ltn H vHaebler Ja36, but see 66Sqn Pups?][?possible unconfirmed "Sopwith 1Str" claim combat nwCOURTRAI 11-15am Untoff Stumpert Ja35]

A2135   DH4   57Sqn
BRec eROULERS **MIA (2Lt GW Armstrong **POW**/2Lt H Pughe-Evans **POW**) left 11-45am ["DH" claim wRUMBEKE 12-40pm Ltn F Kieckhafer Ja29]

A7515   DH4   57Sqn
B seen sSTADEN 10000′ **MIA (Lt SH Allen **KIA**/2Lt GCE Smithett **KIA**) left 10-07am ["DH4" claim combat ROULERS 10-55am Ltn H vBülow Ja36 but see A7426]

**   Sopwith Pup?   66Sqn**
OP shot up (2Lt GL Dore **WIA) leg

A635.D   Sopwith Pup   66Sqn
OP seen with format ovYPRES 12000′ **MIA (2Lt M Newcomb **POW**) a'c captured, Ja36 ["Sopwith 1Str" claim combat ROLLIEMOLENHOEK? 11-15am Ltn T Quandt Ja36][?"Sopwith 1Str" claim combat LAUWE 11-20am Ltn H Klein Ja10]

B1798   Sopwith Pup   66Sqn
**SpP shot up ldg ok OK (2Lt FDC Gove) repairable

B1830   Sopwith Pup   66Sqn
OP seen with formation ovYPRES 12000′ **MIA (2Lt RWB Matthewson **POW**) [?possible "Sopwith 1Str" claim combat nwMOORSLEDE 11-15am Ltn H vHaebler Ja36, but see 45Sqn Camel?]

B1836   Sopwith Pup   66Sqn
OP seen with formation ovYPRES 12000' **MIA(Lt AW
Nasmyth **KIA**) Ja36 ["Sopwith 1Str" claim combat
WESTROOSEBEKE 11-15am Ltn H Hoyer Ja36]

B6206   Sopwith Camel   70Sqn
**OP combat with AlbatrosDV[+ooc] seHOUTHULST
WOOD 5-30pm then ftl AVIATIK CHÂTEAU 11-45am
OK(2Lt EB Booth Can.)

13th October

The weather continued unsettled and poor for a
week or more.

B5038   RE8   6Sqn
**AOb combat with EA engine shot up forced down by
EA ftl Sh28.I.5.B.Cent(FSgt Halstead OK/Lt TP Heald
KIA) left 6-20am [?"Mart" claim combat sWIELTJE
6-42am, but 14.10 date? Ltn K Gallwitz Ja2]

A3752   RE8   21Sqn
**AOb ZONNEBEKE AA ftl cr wr OK(2Lt SE
Dreschfield/Lt Moore) left 9-05am

B5026   RE8   21Sqn
**CP AA hit 7-25am returned a'dr ok OK(Capt AC
Youdale/Lt JE Mott)repairable

B5065   RE8   21Sqn
**CP ZONNEBEKE AA ftl cr wr OK(Lt GFW Zimmer/
2Lt BR Worthington) left 9-45am

A7344   Sopwith Pup   54Sqn
**OP ST PIERRE CAPPELLE-ZARREN combat EoL
shot down **MIA**(2Lt PC Norton **POW**) left 6-45am,
French saw "several fall" [Ja2?][?Pup claim combat
KAYEM-BEERST 8-05am Ltn R Francke Ja8]

B1800   Sopwith Pup   54Sqn
**OP left 6-45am combat EoL down ovZARREN
MIA(2Lt FW Gibbes **KIA**) to ST CAPELLE-ZARREN
[?"Pup" claim combat swKOKELAERE 7-50am Ltn E
Böhme Ja2]

B2161   Sopwith Pup   54Sqn
**OP left 6-45am combat EoL down ovZARREN
MIA(2Lt JHR Salter **KIA**) to ST PIERRE CAPELLE-
ZARREN ["Sopwith 1Str" claim combat PRAAT
BOSCH 7-55am Ltn H Klein Ja10]

B5918   Sopwith Pup   54Sqn
OP combat EoL fell ooc nrZARREN **MIA(2Lt WW
Vick **POW**) left 6-45am ST PIERRE CAPELLE-
ZARREN ["Sopwith 1Str" claim combat
BOUVEKERKE 8am Vzfw Körner Ja8][?unconfirmed
"Pup" claim eDIXMUDE 8am Ltn A Heldmann? Ja10]

A9277   DH5   68 (Australian) Sqn
COP shot down cr(Lt DG Morrison **WIA)arm, shelled
a'c destroyed [?possible "DH5" claim combat QUEANT
Ltn Staats Ja12]

14th October

64 Squadron arrived in France on the 14th of

October bringing DH5s with which it would carry
out mostly low patrolling and ground work. In
1918 it would re-equip with the SE5a.

A3652   RE8   6Sqn
AOb 6Sq saw 3-50pm WoL? **MIA(Lt C Smythe MC
POW/Lt AA Ward **POW**) left 2-35pm, last WT 3-05pm

B1137   Bristol F2b   20Sqn
**Phot combat with EA shot up ftl 6Sq a'dr(Lt NV
Harrison OK/2Lt JPF Adams **KIA**) left 10-15am

A4444   RE8   21Sqn
**Phot combat with EAs shot down EoL Sh28D.18.A
MIA(2Lt BF Braithwaite **WIA POW**/2Lt JC Garrett
WIA POW) left 2-55pm, Infantry Report: WIA POW
[?"RE" claim combat ZONNEBEKE Ltn H Bongartz
Ja36]

B6778   Nieuport 27   29Sqn
**OP combat with EA shot down cr Sh28 D.7(2Lt HD
MacPherson **KIA**) left 5-45am, a'c unsalvable
["Sopwith" claim combat WIELTJE 6-42am Ltn E
Böhme Ja2]

RE8   34Sqn
**Phot combat with EA shot up mg(/Lt J Duncan
WIA)neck

This was the last casualty suffered by 34 Squadron
before it was transferred to the Italian Front at the
end of the month.

15th October

A4460   RE8   9Sqn
**Phot combat with 3Albatros?[+?EA on tail brought
down?] sHOUTHULST WOOD 4000' 12-30pm 2EAs
on right opened up & hit observer(2Lt WJH Courtis OK/
Lt PW Malthouse **WIA**)slight

B3616   SPAD 7   19Sqn
**SP combat with EA shot up on return OK(Lt MRM
Jenning)repairable

A7269   Bristol F2b   20Sqn
OP combat with EA BECELAERE 3-10pm? **MIA(2Lt
JP Dalley **KIA**/Lt LH Gould **KIA**) left 1-12pm, seen
ovWERVICQ, observer POW:DoW? [?"DH4" claim
combat BECELAERE 2-10pm? Ltn H Hoyer Ja36]

A7244   Bristol F2b   22Sqn
**OP chased by several EAs smoking but seen in control
MALDEGHEM(Maaneghem?) 7000' 1-15pm **MIA**(Lt
HS Wellby **POW**/2AM W Nicol **POW**) [?"Bristol" claim
combat AERSEELE eTHIELT 1pm Oblt B Loerzer
Ja26]

B558   SE5a   84Sqn
+* combat with AlbatrosDV[+destr] MENIN-
COURTRAI 1pm OK(2Lt EO Krohn)

This was the first combat victory for 84 Squadron,
whilst below, Vernon-Lord was their first loss in
battle.

B574.F   SE5a   84Sqn
**OP COURTRAI seen going south ovCOURTRAI
1-15pm MIA(2Lt T Vernon-Lord POW) a'c captured

B3880   Sopwith Camel   9 (Naval) Sqn
**OP dive on 2EAs sOSTENDE 12-30pm combat with
4EAs shot down MIA(FSLt WEB Oakley POW) left
11-30am [unconfirmed "Sopwith 1Str" claim
eNIEUPORT]

B6202   Sopwith Camel   10 (Naval)Sqn
+* combat with 2Str[+ooc] seZARREN 1-45pm
OK(FSLt WA Curtis Can.) Curtis made 13 claims, 7 in
this a'c

B6297?   Sopwith Camel   10 (Naval) Sqn
**OP (FSLt IF Sutherland WIA)

16th October

A7159   Bristol F2b   11Sqn
+* combat with AlbatrosDVs[++des] BREBIÈRES-
DOUAI btwn 10-20am & 10-25am OK(Lt AE
McKeever Can./2Lt LA Powell) probably the last of
perhaps 10 victories by McKeever in this a'c

B3639   SPAD 7   23Sqn
**OP left 5-55am combat fuel tank shot through ftl
28.C.19.b OK(2Lt CJ Fowler)

B3598   Nieuport 17   29Sqn
**WEA seen ST JULIEN 5000' 8-25am shot down & a'c
captured in tact MIA(Lt FJ Ortweiler POW) left 7-58am,
pilot later escaped ["Nieuport" claim combat
MAGERMEIRIE? 8-25am Ltn E Böhme Ja2]

A9209   DH5   32Sqn
**OP combat with EA ftl cr shell holes 28.c.20.G wr
OK(Capt WR Fish)

A9284   DH5   68 (Australian) Sqn
**COP left 10-35am GOUY combat with EA on return
to a'dr shot up dam but ok 12-35pm OK(Lt RW Howard
MC)

17th October

B3432   RE8   6Sqn
**Phot mg shot up ftl a'dr 10-25am dam OK(Lt FStK
Anderson/Pte Docker)

A7209   Bristol F2b   11Sqn
**Phot combat vert dive ovSENSÉE CANAL ~10am
MIA(2Lt SE Stanley POW DoW 19.10.17/2Lt EL Fosse
POW) [?"Bristol" claim combat RECOURT 10-20am
Vzfw J Buckler Ja17]

A7231   Bristol F2b   11Sqn
**PhotRec combat with EA seen shot down in controlled
glide ovCAMBRAI 10-45am MIA(2Lt E Scholtz POW/
2Lt HC Wookey POW) left 8-50am DOUAI-DENAIN-
CAUDRY, a'c captured [?"Bristol" claim combat
swCAMBRAI Vzfw Bey Ja5]

A postscript to this loss of a Bristol Fighter crew
was that upon capture they received a sentence of

"10 years' penal servitude for dropping enemy
proclamations". This aircraft was probably the
captured Bristol which subsequently had "Nicht
Schiessen . . . Gute Leute" painted on the upper
surfaces of its planes.

Bristol F2b   20Sqn
** (/Lt S Veacock DoW)abdomen

A7271   Bristol F2b   20Sqn
**P combat with EA seen nrZONNEBEKE MIA(2Lt
AGV Taylor POW DoW/Sgt WJ Benger POW DoW)
left 7-40am, Ja36 ["English EA" claim combat
POELCAPPELLE 8-30am Ltn T Quandt Ja36]

B1793   Sopwith Pup   54Sqn
**OP combat shot up ftl NIEUPORT OK(Lt K Shelton)
left 1-45pm ["Sopwith" claim combat sNIEUPORT
3-20pm Oblt B Loerzer Ja26]

DH4   57Sqn
**Phot combat(2Lt FD Grant WIA/) [?"DH4" claim
combat wHOUTHULST WOOD 6-30pm Ltn H
Bongartz Ja36]

18th October

A.W.FK8   2Sqn
** combat(/AG.ACpl H Burrell KIA)

A7125   Bristol F2b   22Sqn
**OP seen combat ovARDOYE 8-45am MIA(2Lt BB
Perry POW/2Lt CH Bartlett POW) left 7-30am, a'c
captured? ["Bristol" claim combat nrINGELMUNSTER
STN 8-45am Obflm K Schoenfelder Ja7]

A7247   Bristol F2b   22Sqn
**OP combat ovARDOYE 8-45am MIA(2Lt CE
Ferguson KIA/2Lt AD Lennox KIA) left 7-30am
["Bristol" claim combat ARDOYE 8-50am Ltn E
Loewenhardt Ja10]

A7264   Bristol F2b   22Sqn
**OP combat ovARDOYE 8-45am MIA(Capt H Patch
POW DoW 19.10.17/Pte R Spensley POW?) ["Bristol"
claim combat nrROULERS 8-55am Ltn H Klein
Ja10][?possible "Bristol" claim combat
WILDERMANN? Vzfw Eck Ja3]

A9494   DH5   24Sqn
**OP NIEUPORT seen on patrol 8000' 8-30am
MIA(2Lt GW Forbes POW) left 7-45am

B6814   Nieuport 27   29Sqn
+* combat with AlbatrosC[+ooc] 2m nwMENIN
11-05am OK(2Lt JD Payne) first of 5 claims in this a'c, in
total of 14

A9218   DH5   41Sqn
+* combat with AlbatrosDV[+ooc] ARLEUX 3-30pm
OK(Lt R Winnicott)

The victories on the 18th were the last in DH5s for
41 Squadron.

A9406   DH5   41Sqn
**DOP combat nwHAVRINCOURT WOOD 4pm

cr(2Lt GH Swann **KIA**) down control, wr 1000yd
eLINES nwBOURLON WOOD ["DH5" claim combat
neBOURSIES 3-40pm Ltn U Neckel Ja12]

A9408   DH5   41Sqn
+* combat with AlbatrosDV[+ooc] ARLEUX 3-30pm
OK(2Lt RM Whitehead)

A9465   DH5   41Sqn
**DOP combat with EA shot up 4-05pm ftl a'dr,
repairable OK(2Lt J Cushny)

B528   SE5a   56Sqn
**OP left 8-10am combat with EA nBAS WARNETON
then entered clouds **MIA**(Lt JD Gilbert **KIA**) to
ROULERS-COURTRAI

B588   SE5a   56Sqn
**OP left 8-10am combat cr nrST JULIEN flames Sh28
6.c.6.(Lt GB Shone **DoW** 19.10.17) died in Ambulance
Train No27 [?"Sopwith 1Str" claim combat eCLERKEN
8-40am Ltn H Dilthey Ja27]["Sopwith" claim combat
wPASSCHENDAELE 8-50am Vzfw W Kampe Ja27]

B2429   Sopwith Camel   70Sqn
**OutOP combat with EA ftl Sh28B.30.c.9.8.
12-45pm(2Lt AH Hepworth **WIA**) left 11-45am

B546   SE5a   84Sqn
**EscB THIELT combat 1EA ovPOELCAPPELLE
9-20am **MIA**(2Lt SM Park **POW**)

20th October

                    RE8   9Sqn
AOb combat(/2Lt H Hirst **WIA) [?"RE" claim
combat HOUTHULST WOOD 1-15pm Ltn J vBusse
Ja3]

A7245   Bristol F2b   20Sqn
**OP combat engine & controls shot up ftl 6Sqn a'dr
cr(2Lt RB Slade **WIA inj**/Lt GB Booth **inj**) left 7-27am

B3887   Sopwith Camel   28Sqn
**OP combat with EA controls shot up ftl cr o't OK(Lt
HE Singh-Malik) [?possible "Sopwith 1Str" claim
combat swMOORSLEDE 11-30am Ltn L Hanstein
Ja35]

B6313.1C   Sopwith Camel   28Sqn
+* combat with AlbatrosDIII[+destr] ROULERS
12-15pm OK(Capt WG Barker)

This was the first victory for both Barker and 28
Squadron, made in one of the most famous aircraft
of World War One. William Barker claimed forty-
six victories at its controls — some in France, but
mostly on the Italian front in 1918.

B6344   Sopwith Camel   28Sqn
+* combat with Albatros DIII[+des] ROULERS
12-15pm OK(Lt J Mitchell)

B2370   Sopwith Camel   70Sqn
OP combat MENIN-COMINES RD mist **MIA(2Lt
FB Farquharson **POW**) left 10-30am MENIN-
ROULERS ROAD ["Camel" claim combat

ePASSCHENDAELE 11-20am Ltn G Bassenge Ja2]

B6352   Sopwith Camel   70Sqn
**OP combat ovMENIN-COMINES RD mist
MIA(Capt JR Wilson **KIA**) left 10-30am MENIN-
ROULERS ROAD ["Sopwith 1Str" claim combat
GRAFENSTAFEL 11-20am Ltn F Kempf Ja2]

The two 70 Squadron Camels noted above were
lost on a relatively unusual and ambitious
operation. This was a massed fighter attack on
Rumbeke aerodrome, which involved forty-five
single-seaters from three squadrons. The idea of
grouping fighters together in this manner, forming
a huge tactical attacking force, had been proposed
earlier in the year. It was felt this might be one way
of dealing with similar but smaller German formations when they were particularly active. This was
not done in 1917, but the force which attacked
Rumbeke was intended to be similarly uncontain-
able and overwhelming. Eleven Sopwith Camels
with bombs from 70 Squadron, escorted by another
eight, were to attack and strafe the aerodrome,
whilst another eighteen Camels from 28 Squadron
were to destroy any machines attempting to take
off. High above, seven SPADs of 23 Squadron
covered the Camels with an offensive patrol. The
operation was a notable success, much damage
being inflicted on the enemy machines and
buildings. Additionally, seven single-seaters were
shot down in air fighting. The two 70 Squadron
pilots were the only RFC losses.

B4876.H   SE5a   84Sqn
EscB left 10-55am seen ok EoL nwYPRES **MIA(2Lt
WE Watts **POW**) a'c captured, escorting DH4s from
THIELT

B3919   Sopwith Camel   10 (Naval) Sqn
this a'c? **OP combat(FSLt WN Fox **WIA**)

21st October

                    Bristol F2b   11Sqn
COP (/2Lt JT Johnson **WIA)nose

                    Bristol F2b   11Sqn
OP combat(/2Lt HL Walter **WIA)

A7157   Bristol F2b   11Sqn
COP seen WoL but engine failed **MIA(Sgt CJ Butler
POW/1AM WT Long **POW**) left 9-30am, seen firing
lights

A7503   DH4   25Sqn
**Phot left 11-30am LOPHEM-COOLKERKE A'drs
MIA(2Lt D McLaurin **POW**/2Lt OM Hills MC **POW**)

Continuing the preparation for the next assault, a
huge amount of last minute air photography was
done. 1304 exposures were made. DH4 A7503 was
lost on these duties.

B6335   Sopwith Camel   28Sqn
OutOP combat with EA fuel tank shot up ftl cr water dam(2Lt D Shanks **inj) to hospital, left 7-45am KRUSE-ABEELE

A9450   DH5   32Sqn
**OP combat with EA shot up ldg ok OK(2Lt B Monkhouse)

A3540   RE8   52Sqn
test, but seen PUNCH TRENCH brought down EoL **MIA(Capt HOW Hill MC **KIA**/2AM TC Robertson **KIA**?) left 2-30pm NIEUPORT

B3961   DH4   55Sqn
B BOUS seen ok 7m EoL **MIA(Capt D Owen **POW**/Lt B Harker **POW**) Owen interned Holland 30.4.18

B521   SE5a   56Sqn
**OP left 7-15am combat with EA shot through nrYPRES ftl OK(2Lt SJ Gardiner)

B4863.G **SE5a   56Sqn**
+* combat with RumplerC[+ftl] eMAZINGARBE btwn 12-10pm & 2-10pm OK(Capt JTB McCudden) EA from FAb5 captured, last of 9 victories in this a'c

A3859.C1 **RE8   59Sqn**
B nrVITRY seen down in control nrETERPIGNY **MIA(2Lt GR Edwards **WIA POW**/1AM F Pollitt **WIA POW**) a'c captured, left 1-30pm, Ja12 ["RE" claim combat LECLUSE 2-40pm Ltn V Schobinger Ja12]

B547   SE5a   84Sqn
OP RUDDERVOORDE combat with 15EA nrROULERS **MIA(2Lt AE Hempel **POW**) seen ovROULERS 3-15pm [?"SE5a" claim combat VIERKAVENHOEK 3-10pm Ltn K vDöring Ja4]

B551   SE5a   84Sqn
OP RUDDERVOORDE combat with 15EA nrROULERS seen ovROULERS 3-15pm **MIA(2Lt RB Steele **POW DoW** 22.10.17) a'c later at 1ARD

B560   SE5a   84Sqn
OP RUDDERVOORDE combat with 15EA nr ROULERS **MIA(2Lt FL Yeomans **POW**) seen ovROULERS 3-15pm ["SE5a" claim combat LINSELLES 2-45pm Ltn H Göring Ja27]

A5678   FE2b   102Sqn
NB left 5-05pm down EoL **MIA(Lt EH Kann **KIA**/2Lt HD Barbour **KIA**) probably to BISSEGHEM A'dr

All three night bombing squadrons were operating on the final evenings before the battle, typically bombing aerodromes, rail stations and transport.

           DH5   68 (Australian) Sqn
Esc (2Lt CL Johnson **WIA)face

B3937   Sopwith Camel   4 (Naval) Sqn
** combat with EA ICHTEGHEM[+AlbD flames] shot down **MIA**(FSLt EG Eyre **KIA**) ["Sopwith 1Str" claim combat WYNENDAALE 10-30am Oblt B Loerzer Ja26]

N6363   Sopwith Camel   4 (Naval) Sqn

+* combat with AlbatrosDIII[+ooc] sGHISTELLES 10-25am shot up ftl(FCdr AM Shook **WIA**)

22nd October

The ground advance was recommenced on the 22nd, but once again it was forced to be made in heavy rain. This cleared in the afternoon, when most air activity took place. Contact patrols followed the battle effectively, whilst single-seaters carried out ground strafing and low flying attacks. Losses were few. The advances of the first day gave the impetus to push further, and progress was made towards Houthulst Forest and into territory beyond Poelcappelle.

B5064   RE8   7Sqn
**Phot AA engine hit ftl dam OK(Lt IA Johnson-Gilbert/2Lt JO Durham) hit 3-50pm OOSTVLETEREN

B3443   RE8   9Sqn
**CAP HOUTHULST mg shot through dam OK(Lt FR Walker/Lt ERB Playford)

B2422   Sopwith Camel   28Sqn
OP left 3-05pm dhAA seen ooc ROULERS 4pm **MIA(2Lt WRS Smith **KIA**)

B1782   Sopwith Pup   54Sqn
OP combat EoL air collision with Pup B1834 broke up **MIA(2Lt G Cowie **KIA**) left 1-45pm ST PIERRE CAPELLE-HOUTHULST [2 "Camel" claims wBEERST 3-25pm Ltn M Müller Ja28]

B1834   Sopwith Pup   54Sqn
OP combat EoL air collision with Pup B1782, in spin slight cr **MIA(2Lt P Goodbehere **POW**) left 1-45pm KEYEM, Müller28 [2 "Camel" claims wBEERST 3-25pm Ltn M Müller Ja28]

           FE2b   101Sqn
** shot up(/2Lt Dd'H Humphreys **WIA**)arm

24th October

B5896   RE8   16Sqn
AOb combat with EA MERICOURT 3-27pm spun down ooc to 600′ then nd in flames Sh36C T.22.c.7.3.(Lt AO Balaam **KIA/Lt DSP Prince-Smith **KIA**) [combat MERICOURT 3-20pm Ltn J Buckler Ja17]

A6627   SPAD 7   19Sqn
NOP separated in combat **MIA(2Lt JD Laing **POW DoW** 28.1.18) left 8-11am [?2 "SPAD" claims nrARRAS ~10am Ltn W vBülow Ja36]

A6709   SPAD 7   19Sqn
NOP left 8-30am separated in combat **MIA(2Lt KL Golding **POW**) ["SPAD" claim combat LINSELLES 9-05am Ltn W vBülow Ja36]

B3489   SPAD 7   19Sqn
**NOP shot up dam ftl Sh28J 19.D.7.3. OK(2Lt WP Delamere) a'c unsalvable as too near Lines [?"SPAD" claim combat sWESTROOSEBEKE 1-27pm Ltn H

Hoyer Ja36, but see 23Sqn SPAD? time?]

B3615   SPAD 7   19Sqn
**NOP shot up dam but returned a'dr OK(2Lt JGS
Candy)

B3571   SPAD 7   23Sqn
**OP seen with patrol ZILLEBEKE-YPRES 2-15pm
going east **MIA**(2Lt WFG March **POW DoW**) left
1-05pm [?possible "SPAD" claim combat
sWESTROOSEBEKE 1-27pm Ltn H Hoyer Ja36, but
time?]

B6762   SPAD 7   23Sqn
**OP EA? ftl cr KOREK FARM 28D.9.c.1.7.(2Lt FJ
Sharland **KIA**)a'c abandoned, left 1AD at 8-01am
[?possible "Sopwith" claim combat swBECELAERE
8-50am Ltn R Klimke Ja27]

**   DH5   24Sqn**
** AA(2Lt PA MacDougall **WIA**)slight

A7155   Bristol F2b   48Sqn
** combat with EA[+] gunshot(2Lt HF Jenkins **WIA**/
1AM EJ Dunford OK)arm

B1117   Bristol F2b   48Sqn
OP shot down MERCKEM **MIA(Capt JT Milne MC
KIA/Lt S Wright MC **KIA**) French saw F2b shot down
4-25pm ["Bristol" claim combat nrHOUTHULST
4-20pm Ltn F Kieckhafer Ja29]

A6182   Sopwith Pup   54Sqn
**OP DIXMUDE AA combat? shot up dam on return
ok(2Lt CG Wood **WIA**)arm

A5702   FE2b   100Sqn
NB left 6-30pm **MIA(2Lt LM Archibald **POW**/Lt RS
Greenslade **POW**) FALKENBERG-SAARBRÜCKEN
Rlwy

A5706   FE2b   100Sqn
NB left 6-45pm **MIA(2Lt WH Jones **POW**/Lt JS
Godard **POW**) [14'08] FALKENBERG-
SAARBRÜCKEN Rlwy

N5476   Sopwith Triplane   1 (Naval) Sqn
**P HOUTHULST seen wGHELUVELT shot down
EoL **MIA**(FSLt JEC Hough **KIA**) to HOUTHULST
FOREST Ja29? [?"Tripe" claim combat TENBRIELEN
11-50am Ltn Blume Ja26]

3120   HP 0/100   A Sqn RNAS
NB flak shot down nrHANDZAEME **MIA(FSLt A
McDonald **POW**/FSLt JM Smith **POW**/GL EE Smith
POW) to SAARBRÜCKEN

3141.A   HP 0/100   A Sqn RNAS
**NB SAARBRÜCKEN shot down ftl nrPIRMASENS
MIA(FSLt HGB Linnell **POW**/FSLt GS Smith **KIA**)

These losses occurred on the first night bombing
raid made by nine machines of "A" Squadron
RNAS. This was a Handley Page heavy bomber
unit which had been formed at Manston on the 5th
of October. It had come into being in response to
the demands being made for a British long distance

strategic bombing capability. A year or more of
raids on the English mainland had convinced the
politicians of the need for some retaliatory action,
which would additionally strike at Germany's war-
making potential. Some bombing of this nature had
been undertaken by 3 Wing RNAS at Luxeuil
before it had been disbanded earlier in the year,
but in early October, Trenchard was instructed to
begin attacks in the Nancy area where there were
several strategically important German targets. In
order to carry out these raids 41st Wing was
created comprising 55 Squadron (DH4s) for day
bombing, and 100 Squadron (FE2bs) and the
newly formed "A" Squadron RNAS (Handley
Pages) for night bombing. "A" Squadron was to be
redesignated 16 (Naval) Squadron on the 8th of
January 1918. The Wing was the forerunner of the
Independent Force and would typically raid
factories and power stations in towns such as
Mannheim, Trèves, and Thionville. The easterly
limit of these operations was the region including
Cologne, Frankfurt, and Stuttgart, in which lay
coal and iron fields, and industrial and production
centres contributing directly to Germany's war
effort. From the very start of its operations, 41st
Wing's bombing potential was restricted to these
strategic raids; neither it, nor the Independent
Force it was to become, was allowed to be used in
a tactical role except in the most exceptional
circumstances. 55 Squadron made the Wing's first
day bombing raid to the Burbach works at Saarbrücken on the 17th. The raids on the 24th were
its first night attack, made on the same target, and
sixteen FE2bs from 100 Squadron accompanied
"A" Squadron. These light bombers also suffered
two casualties. Bad weather contributed to the
misfortunes.

25th October

A801   FE2b   101Sqn
NB left 11-20pm **MIA(2Lt JAM Fleming **POW**/2Lt
ECS Ringer **POW**) attacking RUMBEKE and ABEELE
A'dromes, Fleming escaped

26th October

Another infantry surge was made around Poelcappelle on the 26th. Hopes that the weather was
improving for the assault were dashed by heavy
rain through the night which continued into the
day. Rain was now no reason for corps machines
to remain on the ground — it was almost expected
on the day of an assault — and their crews
laboured gamely. Ground attacking aircraft of the
fighter squadrons were also very busy, and several

casualties were sustained from ground fire whilst shooting up enemy troops. The day's advances along the whole line would have been a total success except that a withdrawal was required around Gheluvelt because mud-choked rifles became useless. The fighting continued on into the 27th.

A3850   RE8   6Sqn
FlRec shell hit nrYPRES down nrDUMBARTON LAKES cr a'c shelled **MIA(Lt HL Marvin **KIA**/Lt CH Barton **KIA**) left 10-50am

A6662   SPAD 7   19Sqn
LowP GHELUWE combat with 2Str[+completely ooc at 200'] nGHELUWE 800' 10-20am despite heavy ground fire then shot up while fixing stoppage, dam but returned a'dr(2Lt RA Hewat Can. **WIA)head

B6776   SPAD 7   19Sqn
+* combat with 2Str[+ooc] swGHELUWE 10-20am OK(2Lt E Oliver)

Sopwith Camel   28Sqn
LowRec (Lt JB Fenton **WIA)

B5406.5C **Sopwith Camel   28Sqn**
GroundP combat with EA[+] 450 hits returned a'dr ok(2Lt HE Singh-Malik **WIA) to hospital, left 10-45am VLAMERTINGHE

B2327   Sopwith Camel   45Sqn
LowP left 8-15am mg br down cr 20SE.3.20.D.7.3.(Lt ED Clarke **WIA)arm

B5152.M **Sopwith Camel   45Sqn**
GndP left 8-15am **MIA(2Lt EALF Smith Can. **POW**) [?"Camel" claim KRUISTRAAT 8-50am Ltn J vBusse Ja3]

3122   HP 0/100   7ASqn RNAS
NB shot down **MIA(FSLt G Andrews **POW**/2Lt WW Kent **KIA**/GL GA Kent **POW**) to ST DENIS-WESTREM a'dr, nrGHENT

27th October

65 Squadron arrived in France with Sopwith Camels.

RE8   6Sqn
Phot AA(/AG.2AM G Kirton **WIA)leg

B6776   SPAD 7   19Sqn
pracP(solo) seen ovZILLEBEKE going west **MIA(2Lt SL Whitehouse **WIA POW**) left 6-25am ["SPAD" claim combat nWERVICQ 7-30am Ltn Seifert Ja24]

B5178   Sopwith Camel   28Sqn
OutOP left 3pm seen wDIXMUDE going west **MIA(Lt RA Cartledge **POW**)

B6364   Sopwith Camel   28Sqn
+* combat with AlbatrosDV[+?ooc] ROULERS 1-43pm OK(2Lt AG Cooper)

28 Squadron was involved in its last intense air fighting in France on the 27th before being withdrawn for service on the Italian front.

Sopwith Camel   43Sqn
** combat (2Lt OC George **WIA**)

B6249   Sopwith Camel   43Sqn
**OP PLOUVAIN-SALOME combat ftl n.m.l. cr 11-35am OK(2Lt CRF Wickenden) [?"Sopwith 1Str" claim combat sMERICOURT Ltn Brachwitz Ja17, but see B6374?]

B6374   Sopwith Camel   43Sqn
OP combat with 5EAs in spin ooc in flames ovSALLAUMINES 9-45am **MIA(2Lt GP Bradley **KIA**) to PLOUVAIN-PERENCHIES [?"Sopwith 1Str" claim combat with HARNES, sLA BASSÉE Ltn Fuchs Ja30, but see B6249?]

B2382   Sopwith Camel   45Sqn
NOP seen driven down by 4EAs EoL MOORSLEDE **MIA(2Lt CI Phillips **KIA**) left 9-45am [?"Sopwith 1Str" claim combat DADIZEELE Ltn Kuke Ja33]

RE8   52Sqn
AOb combat with 3-4AlbatrosDVs ovNIEUPORT 5000' 4-15pm shot up ftl(Capt GC Rogers **WIA/2Lt EG Henderson OK)hip? [?"RE" claim combat nGHELUVELT 1-20pm Vzfw F Hemer Ja6]

B5916   Sopwith Pup   54Sqn
**OP AA shot up ftl cr LAMPERNISSE OK(2Lt A Thompson) left 1-45pm ST PIERRE CAPPELLE-ZARREN-HOUTHULST WOOD [?"Sopwith" claim combat wDIXMUDE Oblt B Loerzer Ja26, but possible 70Sq Camel?]

B31   SE5a   56Sqn
OP seen after combat with swROULERS **MIA(Lt APF Rhys Davids DSO MC **KIA**) left 10-35am CORTEMARCK-COURTRAI-MENIN [combat POLTERRJEBRUG 11-10am Ltn K Gallwitz Ja2]

Arthur Rhys Davids was killed whilst leading a patrol which met an enemy formation and he was last seen in heavy fighting. He had probably twenty-five victories to his credit.

DH4   57Sqn
Phot (Capt AB Cook **WIA/)

B534   SE5a   60Sqn
OP left 12-40pm combat with EA? shot down in flames EoL **MIA(Lt WB Sherwood **KIA**) to MOORSLEDE-DADIZEELE [?"SE" claim combat BELLEWARDE 2-50pm Vzfw C Menckhoff Ja3]

B2349   Sopwith Camel   70Sqn
OP combat with EA eROULERS seen going east **MIA(2Lt CW Primeau **KIA**) left 1-15pm HOUTHULST FOREST, Ja36 [?"Camel" claim combat ST ELOI 3-45pm Ltn H Böhning Ja36]

B2361.C **Sopwith Camel   70Sqn**
**OP combat with EA eROULERS seen going east

MIA(Lt RJEP Goode **POW**) left 1-15pm HOUTHULST FOREST, Ja36 [?"Camel" claim combat ROULERS 2pm Ltn H Bongartz Ja36]

B2463   Sopwith Camel   70Sqn
OP combat shot up 2-15pm dam returned to a'dr rep(Capt CN Jones **WIA) to HOUTHULST WOOD, Ja36 ["Camel" claim combat HOUTHULST WOOD 2-10pm Ltn H vHaebler Ja36]

A5662   FE2b   102Sqn
NB radiator shot up engine o'heat ftl cr dam(Capt IAJ Duff **WIA/Lt Davis) left 7-50pm, bearings ran, a'c sent to 1AD

On this night 101 and 102 Squadron bombed German aerodromes and rail junctions.

N5455   Sopwith Triplane   1 (Naval) Sqn
this a'c **OP (FSLt WM Clapperton **WIA**)arm ["Tripe" claim combat nrHOOGE 1-45pm Vzfw K Wüsthoff Ja4]

N6371   Sopwith Camel   10 (Naval) Sqn
** combat with 6 Albatros Ds shot down in flames seen in vertical dive neDIXMUDE 1-20pm **MIA**(FSLt GH Morang **KIA**)

28th October

Fog over the battlefield restricted flying.

A4426   RE8   16Sqn
AOb combat shot down cr CARENCY? 4pm burnt wr(Lt EH Keir **KIA/Capt CWC Wasey **KIA**) left 3-10pm LENS [unconfirmed "RE" claim combat MONT ST ELOI 4-05pm Ltn J Buckler Ja17]

B5885   RE8   21Sqn
**CP left 9-30am AA hit dam OK(Capt AC Youdale/Lt JE Mott)

B565   SE5a   60Sqn
NOP combat with Albatros shot through ftl swVLAMERTINGHE 9-55am cr Sh28b G.11.a.4.5.(Capt CJ Temperley **WIA) left 9-05am

B4873   SE5a   60Sqn
OP AA WESTROOSBEKE-POELCAPPELLE 9-40am **MIA(Capt JCA Caunter **KIA**) left 9-05am, gunfire?

B566   SE5a   84Sqn
EscOP HARLEBEKE A'dr seen 2m eYPRES **MIA(2Lt AW Rush **POW**) left 6-45am

29th October

B3630   Nieuport 27   1Sqn
NOP combat dive with 7EAs on tail HOUTHEM 11-35am **MIA(2Lt AW MacLaughlin **KIA**) to DADIZEELE-GHELUWE [? combat eHOUTHEM 11-10am Ltn J Buckler Ja17]

A9474.F   DH5   41Sqn
COP seen BULLECOURT going west then lost in clouds 7-45am **MIA(2Lt FS Clark **WIA POW**) a'c captured

This was the last DH5 casualty for 41 Squadron.

B2357   Sopwith Camel   43Sqn
OP combat with EA shot down swOPPY WOOD 10-10pm(2Lt CH Harriman **KIA) left 9-20am PLOUVAIN-SALOME, a'c unsalvable

FE2b   102Sqn
NB (/2Lt CL Shaw **WIA)ankle

30th October
PASSCHENDAELE

The final infantry assault of the Flanders campaign of 1917 began on the 30th, with Passchendaele itself as the target. The gruelling and terrible months of fighting were now drawing to a close, but another week or ten days' agony remained to be endured as its final limits were drawn. On this day, the Canadians forced an entry to the outskirts of Passchendaele. Rain poured down on their efforts from late morning. In the air, the RFC met little action and got on with its work while it could.

B3627   Nieuport 27   1Sqn
NOP EA on tail 8-50am cr WESTROOSEBEKE **MIA(2Lt ED Scott **KIA**) ["Nieuport" claim combat WESTROOSEBEKE 8-45am Oblt B Loerzer Ja26]

B5070   RE8   4Sqn
AOb shell down in spin ooc cr D22.a.8.5. **MIA?(Lt FT Wakeman **KIA**/Lt GDA Heys **WIA**) left 6-25am 1st ANZAC CORPS

Bristol F2b   20Sqn
OP combat(/AG.Pte CM Snoulton **WIA)

SPAD 7   23Sqn
SpRec (Capt JM M'Alery **WIA)

3123.D3   HP 0/100   A Sqn RNAS
** MANNHEIM shot down **MIA**(FLt LG Sieveking **POW**/AM H Brooks **POW**/GL HL Dodd **POW**)

31st October

The following days were drier, but mist affected flying.

B2425   Sopwith Camel   3Sqn
COP left 9-30am seen nrWANCOURT **MIA(Lt HB New **KIA**) [?"Sopwith 1Str" claim combat BOIRY-NOTRE DAME 10-15am Ltn H Becker Ja12]

This was the first casualty for 3 Squadron on Sopwith Camels.

B6484   RE8   6Sqn
Phot combat with 5EAs shot up returned a'dr ok dam OK(Lt FStK Anderson **WIA/Pte HG Dockree **WIA**) left 10-10am

B319   A.W.FK8   10Sqn
Phot combat shot down in flames nLA BASSÉE 10-40am but extinguished at 1500' (Lt W Davidson **KIA/

Lt W Crowther Can. **KIA**) left 9-30am ["RE" claim
combat nLA BASSÉE 10-30am Ltn J Buckler Ja17]

A7235   Bristol F2b   11Sqn
**DOP Third Army area shot up ftl Lines Sh51B.U.29.4.
4-15pm(Sgt TF Stephenson OK/1AM SH Platel **WIA**)
toe shot off, a'c unsalvable

B1109   Bristol F2b   11Sqn
DOP seen FRESSIE **MIA(2Lt SW Randall **KIA**/2Lt
WdeC Dodd **POW DoW**) left 2-34pm, FRESSAIN?, EA?
[?"BF" claim combat sMARQUION 4-10pm Ltn V
Schobinger Ja12]

A3827   RE8   13Sqn
Phot down ooc BIACHE STV **MIA(Lt WLO Parker
KIA/1AM HL Postons **KIA**) left 11-25am XVII Corps
front, BIACHE ST VAAST [?"RE" claim PLOUVAIN
12-10pm Oblt H Bethge Ja30]

B1565.M SPAD 7   23Sqn
**OP seen YPRES after combat nrROULERS 8am
MIA(2Lt NH Kemp **POW**) to ROULERS-MENIN
[?"SPAD" claim combat NEUVILLE 7-40am Ltn H
Bongartz Ja36]

B3551   SPAD 7   23Sqn
**OP combat then seen 7-45am ovROULERS behind
and above formation **MIA**(2Lt RM Smith **POW**)
[?"SPAD" claim combat WERVICQ-BECELAERE
Road 7-45am Ltn H vBülow Ja36]

A3865   RE8   53Sqn
**ACoop combat with EA shot up dam returned ok(Lt J
Barker **WIA**/2AM Kitsun **WIA**?) to J.36.a.40.60. [?"RE"
claim combat sPOELCAPPELLE 7-20am Ltn H
Bongartz Ja36]

A4214   RE8   53Sqn
AP down in control seGHELUVELT **MIA(Capt WAL
Poundall MC **KIA**/2Lt ER Ripley **KIA**) left 11-25am to
P.11.a.99.00.

A8944.H SE5   56Sqn
.H? +* combat with 2Str[+des] STADENBERG btwn
9-05am & 11-15am OK(Lt KK Muspratt) last of 8
victories with 56Sqn

B544   SE5a   84Sqn
OP left 2pm seen engage EA MENIN **MIA(2Lt GR
Gray **POW DoW**) to ROULERS-MENIN-COURTRAI
[?"SE5" claim combat seZILLEBEKE LAKE 4-15pm
Ltn E Böhme Ja2]

B4874   SE5a   84Sqn
OP left 2pm seen engage EA MENIN **MIA(2Lt EW
Powell **KIA**) to ROULERS-MENIN-COURTRAI
[?unconfirmed "Sopwith" claim combat ROULERS-
MENIN Road 3-10pm Ltn H Bongartz Ja36]

**   FE2b   102Sqn**
NB (/Lt AR Robertson **WIA)slight

Untraced Casualty in France in October 1917?

** (FSLt JS Sercombe-Smith **POW**) Oct.17? see Handley
Page 3120 on 24.10?

November 1917

The weather was very poor for flying through much
of November — especially at night. For instance,
41 Wing's long distance strategic work, which was
naturally very sensitive to cancellation through bad
weather, was virtually eliminated for the month.

2nd November

A5579   FE2b   101Sqn
**B shot through dam ftl ldg a'dr ok OK(2Lt RS Larkin/
2Lt S Ellis) hit on way out

3rd November

**   Nieuport   1Sqn**
SpM trench gunfire(Capt EL Bath **WIA)foot

4th November

A3823   RE8   5Sqn
Detached Flt **Phot combat with 6Albatros[+? drove
one off in nd] ovT.30 8000' shot up dam(Capt BC
Douglas OK/2Lt F Whitehead **WIA**)foot

B1796   Sopwith Pup   54Sqn
+* combat with AlbatrosDIII[+des] nDIXMUDE
1-50pm OK(2Lt SJ Schooley) shared with 2Lt HH
Maddocks

This was the last combat victory for 54 Squadron
on Sopwith Pups before re-equipping with Sopwith
Camel fighters.

5th November

C5028   RE8   6Sqn
**AOb combat with 4EAs shot down ftl cr 28.I.24.B.(Sgt
Eddington **WIA**?/2Lt FA Dormer **WIA**) left 11-45am
[?"RE" claim nZILLEBEKE LAKE 1-37pm Ltn W
Blume Ja26]

B5175   Sopwith Camel   45Sqn
OP seen ooc ovMOORSLEDE EoL 11-40am **MIA(2Lt
RG Frith **WIA POW**) left 10-55am [?"Sopwith" combat
sST JULIEN 11-50am Vzfw P Bäumer Ja2][?"Camel"
claim combat POELCAPPELLE 11-45am Vzfw K
Wüsthoff Ja4]

N6341   Sopwith Camel   10 (Naval) Sqn
** combat[+] nwDIXMUDE shot up ftl OK(FSLt AA
Cameron) ["Sopwith" claim combat
nwBLANKAARTSEE Ltn L Luer Ja27]

6th November

This day saw the final push by the Canadians into
Passchendaele, which they took after bitter

fighting. The most the RFC could do to assist them was to shoot up the defenders on the ground. 11,000 rounds were fired on this day from the air at German troops and guns. Rain, low mist, wind and cold all made the airman's efforts difficult. The fighting was not over with the taking of the village, however, and the last desperate actions unfolded a few days later, on the 10th.

B6827   Nieuport 27   1Sqn
LowP left 8-08am to POELCAPPELLE-ROULERS Rd seen going towards Lines wPASSCHENDAELE **MIA(2Lt FG Baker **POW**)

B5160   Sopwith Camel   3Sqn
COP seen btwn BAPAUME & BULLECOURT: lost, low fuel ftl **MIA(2Lt RC Taylor **POW**) left 7-35am, driven east by wind, came down to land nrNAMUR, then re-took off to fly west, but travelled south — finally driven down by weather and no fuel, to be captured at Rheims.

B6355   Sopwith Camel   3Sqn
COP seen btwn BAPAUME & BULLECOURT: lost, low fuel ftl **MIA(2Lt AG Cribb **POW**) left 7-35am, see Camel B5160 above

B6382   Sopwith Camel   3Sqn
COP seen btwn BAPAUME & BULLECOURT: lost, low fuel ftl **MIA(2Lt EP Wilmot MC **POW**) left 7-35am, see Camel B5160 above

B6392   Sopwith Camel   3Sqn
COP seen btwn BAPAUME & BULLECOURT: lost, low fuel ftl engine fail, unable to re-take off with others so burnt a'c **MIA(2Lt TB Bruce **POW**) left 7-35am, see Camel B5160 above, pilot went on run and eventually escaped to Holland

All the above 3 Squadron Camels were victims of the atrocious conditions of the battlefield. The patrol of four machines was caught by the strong westerly wind and poor visibility, and found itself having strayed far into enemy territory. Not having a clue where they were, the leader eventually brought the patrol down where he could. Enquiries revealed that they were near Namur. Bruce could not take off with the others because of engine problems, so burnt his machine and went on the run (see above). The other three attempted to fly back to the lines but were eventually driven down a hundred miles later by failing fuel and the terrible conditions. The irony was that they were captured at Rheims: they had flown south, not west, in their efforts to escape.

A3643   RE8   6Sqn
CP broke up in dive cr in mud in DICKEBUSCH POND nr a'dr, (Lt GMWG Cato **KIA/Lt RH Richardson **KIA**) crew drowned

**   RE8   15Sqn**
OP bullet(/2Lt NA Arthur **WIA)

B3641   SPAD 7   19Sqn
LowNOP cr PASSCHENDAELE? 7-40am **MIA(2Lt F Gartside-Tippinge **KIA**) left 6-20am

**   Bristol F2b   20Sqn**
OP combat shot up(Lt ES Brander **WIA/2AM A Townsend **WIA**)

B1139   Bristol F2b   20Sqn
NOP left 7-22am flak? **MIA(2Lt CB Simpson **KIA**/2Lt JHW Duggan **KIA**)

B6779   Nieuport 27   29Sqn
*GndP left 7-15am **MIA**(2Lt HG Downing MC **KIA**) ["Sopwith 1Str" claim combat wPASSCHENDAELE 7-50am Ltn H Ritt vAdam Ja6]["Nieu" claim combat ZONNEBEKE 7-50am Vzfw Stumpf Ja6]

**   RE8   42Sqn**
OP (/2Lt AV Farrier **WIA)back

B512   SE5a   60Sqn
** combat POLYGON WOOD shot up 8-45am ftl dam OK(Lt W Duncan)?

B2408   Sopwith Camel   65Sqn
LowP YPRES clouds mist Patrol lost? **MIA(Lt WL Harrison **POW**) strong sw wind ["Sopwith" claim claim combat SCHERMINKELMOLEN 10-50am Ltn E Böhme Ja2]

B2414   Sopwith Camel   65Sqn
LowP YPRES clouds mist Patrol lost? **MIA(2Lt EH Cutbill **POW**) strong sw wind, Casualty Report gives B2414, sortie time? [?"Sopwith 1Str" claim combat VIERLAVENHOEK 7-25am Vzfw P Bäumer Ja2] [?"SE" claim combat swPASSCHENDAELE 7-45am Ltn R Plange Ja2]

B2441   Sopwith Camel   65Sqn
LowP YPRES clouds mist Patrol lost? **MIA(Lt EGS Gordon **POW**) strong sw wind [?combat STADEN 10-50pm Ltn G Bassenge Ja2]

These were the first combat losses for 65 Squadron.

N5081   Sopwith Strutter   2 (Naval) Sqn
** AA hit EoL LOMBARTZYDE ftl(FSLt HP Salter **POW**/GL HW White **POW**) [claim LOMBARTZYDE Flak 514]

This was the last Sopwith Strutter lost on the Western Front.

7th November

A3746   RE8   4Sqn
CAP **MIA(2Lt AG Grose **POW DoW** 9.11.17/2Lt BCR Grimwood MC **KIA**) left 6-25am 1 ANZAC Corps ["RE" claim combat swMORSLEDE 7-10am Vzfw P Bäumer Ja2]

A3696   RE8   5Sqn
Det Flt **AOb AA ftl bad ground cr wr A.28.A.40. OK(2Lt JA Higham/AM JM Dixon) to Sh20NW B.11

A7633   DH4   27Sqn
**HeightTest strayed: lost, mg shot up ftl BAILLEUL
dam OK(2Lt WJ Henney/2Lt PS Driver)

A5577   FE2b   102Sqn
**NB left 9-35pm MIA(Capt EE Barnes KIA/Lt EDS
Casswell KIA)

8th November

B5032   RE8   7Sqn
**AOb hit by British shell?(Lt ES Livock KIA/Lt HR
Morgan KIA) left 1-10pm

A7283   Bristol F2b   22Sqn
*OP combat with EA in spin down ooc 2m
nMOORSLEDE MIA(2Lt HG Robinson POW/Lt FJB
Hammersley WIA POW) left 12-50pm Fifth Army front
[?"Bristol" claim combat wMOORSLEDE Ltn Dahm
Ja26]

A7517   DH4   18Sqn
**B seen ok VITRY-HENIN LIETARD 12pm MIA(2Lt
WC Pruden POW/2AM J Conlin WIA POW) left
10-05am First Army area [?"DH" claim combat
MONCHECOURT 12pm Vzfw H Oberländer Ja30]

B6777   SPAD 7   19Sqn
**NOP left 8-07am combat? MIA(Lt GA Cockburn
KIA) ["SPAD" claim combat HOUTHEM 8-50am Ltn
W vBülow Ja36]

B5071   RE8   21Sqn
**Phot ground fire shot up YPRES ftl LA LOVIE
A'dr(Lt GFW Zimmer OK/2Lt CE Stewart WIA)

B1120   Bristol F2b   22Sqn
**OP combat with EA shot up ftl dam rep OK(2Lt EC
Bromley/2Lt AH Middleton) left 12-53pm

B1123   Bristol F2b   22Sqn
**OP combat then two separated: ooc in spin 2m
nMOORSLEDE MIA(Lt WG Meggitt MC WIA POW/
Capt FA Durrad KIA) pilot repat 2.6.18, Ja36 ["Bristol"
claim combat LEDEGHEM 2-05pm Ltn H Bongartz
Ja36]

B6812   Nieuport 27   29Sqn
2 mgs +* combat with AlbatrosDV[+flames]
eWESTROOSEBEKE then combat with 2Str[+flames]
HOUTHULST WOOD 4pmOK(Capt WE Molesworth)
Molesworth's first with 29Sqn, final total 18 victories

         Sopwith Camel   46Sqn
+* combat with AlbatrosDV[+ooc] CAMBRAI OK(2Lt
EG MacLeod)

This was the first Sopwith Camel combat claim for
46 Squadron.

A4664   RE8   53Sqn
**ACoop dh by shell down in flames n.m.l. 8-55am
MIA(2Lt LW Middleton KIA/2Lt FJ McCullough KIA)
pilot's grave Sh28 O.11.D.95.70.

B1.K   SE5a   56Sqn
**OP NEUVE EGLISE engine shot through ftl dam
OK(Lt MH Coote)

B630   SE5a   56Sqn
**OP combat patrol split ooc MOORSLEDE MIA(Lt
FRC Cobbold WIA POW) left 8-25am
CORTEMARCK-MENIN-COURTRAI [?"Sopwith"
claim combat nOOSTNIEUWKERKE 9-10am Ltn F
Loerzer Ja26]

B4883   SE5a   56Sqn
**OP left 8-30am combat with EA 9-20am in spin ooc
ovCOMINES MIA(Capt PC Cowan KIA) ["SE" claim
combat TENBRIELEN 9-10am Ltn H vHaebler Ja36]

A4619   RE8   59Sqn
**Phot combat with EA shot up dam but ldg ok(2Lt
Dagleish OK/2Lt A Pickford WIA)

B622   SE5a   60Sqn
**OP combat shot up ftl cr 500yd wPOELCAPPELLE
4-15pm OK(Lt JD McCall)a'c shelled [?"Sopwith 1Str"
claim combat nZILLEBEKE 3-45pm Vzfw P Bäumer
Ja2]

B4869   SE5a   84Sqn
**OP chasing EA ovWESTROOSEBEKE 2-15pm
MIA(Lt JH Deans Can. KIA) left 1-05pm ["SE5" claim
combat PASSCHENDAELE, ROULERS 2-10pm Ltn T
Quandt Ja36]

B4877   SE5a   84Sqn
**OP chasing EA 2-15pm WESTROOSEBEKE
MIA(2Lt WR Kingsland WIA POW) left 1-05pm
ROULERS-MENIN-COURTRAI ["SE" claim combat
wROULERS-MOORSLEDE 2-10pm Ltn H Hoyer
Ja36]

9th November

A3761   RE8   5Sqn
Det Flt **AOb combat with 6EAs DIXMUDE 10-50am,
wing off broke up cr(2Lt EW Morris KIA/2Lt NE
Williams KIA) [?"RE" claims combs OOSTKERKE-
PERVYSE 11am Ltn W Schwartz & Ltn R Wendelmuth
Ja20]

         RE8   7Sqn
**Phot combat(/AG.1AM H Franks WIA)

B6454   RE8   21Sqn
**Phot EA fire shot up ftl 28H.11.A dam OK(Lt CE
Abell/Lt Chard) [?possible claim combat
nBELLEWARDSEE 9-30am Vzfw K Wüsthoff Ja4]

B6821   Nieuport 27   29Sqn
**OP combat tank shot up lost all fuel ftl field nr a'dr
9-45am dam OK(2Lt LC Tims) left 8am ["Sopwith 1Str"
claim combat seDIXMUDE-EESEN 9-40am Ltn R
Francke Ja8]

B6822   Nieuport 27   29Sqn
**OP engine shot up ftl 28 D.5.d.8.8. 9-40am wr OK(Lt
FWW Wilson)a'c unsalvable, abandoned

B1757   Sopwith Pup   54Sqn
**OP 2EAs on tail into clouds in control eDIXMUDE
MIA(2Lt A Thompson POW) left 8-30am [?possible
"Sopwith" claim combat sST JULIEN 9-40am Ltn F
Loerzer Ja26]

Thompson was the last Sopwith Pup pilot lost with 54 Squadron.

B6290   Sopwith Camel   8 (Naval) Sqn
**OP lost clouds nrLENS last seen going north 6000′
10-30am ftl by EA **MIA**(FSLt WS Magrath **POW**) a'c captured and used as German evaluation machine

10th November
THE LESSONS OF AIR FIGHTING IN THE YPRES BATTLE

In the hours between dawn and the late afternoon, the last fighting of the third battle of Ypres took place in what had once been fields north of Passchendaele. This took a few more yards along the road towards Staden, and at this point, the end was signalled.

The advance of the last three months was the most costly enterprise endured in the whole history of the war. What was spent in human life and killed in the spirit of those who survived its terrible progress, was all the more pitiful for the meagre advances it had made in territory. If the four or five miles of actual ground taken seem slight, the strategic gains were still more negligible.

Reflecting on the role of the Royal Flying Corps in the third battle of Ypres, it is clear that a rapid evolution of their work occurred. The greatest innovation to take root was structured ground work in direct co-operation with infantry attacks. Responding to the close, chaotic nature of Ypres sector fighting, air power was made into an additional battlefield weapon. It no longer simply followed the ground fighting, or helped direct it, it now took part in it. Air fighting itself was more likely to take place as the armies prepared for battles, offensive patrolling holding back the attempts of the enemy to make sense of what was happening. Fighting between larger formations, almost as set pieces to establish priority and dominance in the air, were more common. The character of the ground fighting at Ypres was heavily affected by the conditions, and so too were the tactics of the air arms. The weather was so relentlessly bad that in many ways low patrolling was not only the most effective work that could be done but was on many days the only kind possible. In fact, many of the traditional activities of the air arms that had been established since the Somme fighting were compromised by the weather.

The artillery could not play its proper part in this battle either. In fact, it failed the British armies because of the havoc it wrought on the terrain, and once this was realised it was used more carefully. This put more pressure on the artillery co-operation and low reconnaissance machines, whose crucial duty it became to find and direct fire onto German counter-attacks. Even more responsibility was laid on these crews at Ypres as the ground conditions often made traditional communications impossible.

Another shift in tactics saw enemy machines attacked almost as much on the ground as in the air. Direct attacks on the German Air Force by bombing and strafing its aerodromes not only destroyed aircraft, as did air fighting, but also disrupted options for their deployment at source. Aircraft were highly vulnerable on their airfields, and there is no doubt that at this time it was carried out with fewer casualties than air fighting inflicted. Additionally, whilst fighters were very suitable for this work, it could also be effectively sustained over the longer term by a programme of bombing. This was another area of expansion during the battle of Ypres, for by the end of the fighting in November all manner of day bombing was being undertaken, whilst night bombing had also become common place.

In these notes, at the beginning of 1917, it was mentioned that the German High Command sought a way to limit their losses and conserve their strength in the west whilst matters in Russia were resolved. The withdrawal to the Hindenburg Line gave them the perfect secure defensive position on which to build just such a war strategy. In fact, it gave them more than this — it gave them the initiative. Until mid-summer, most activity on the Western Front was played out in the shadow of this great strategem: anything of significance Britain and France had achieved in these months was in reaction to the new balance of tensions it imposed. When they tried to ignore it, such as during Nivelle's French offensive, their efforts became futile and irrelevant.

For the bloody and disastrous campaign in Flanders to follow this, which saw wanton wastage of thousands of first class British and Commonwealth troops and resources, played into the hands of the German commanders. Aided to a high degree by the weather, the enemy had succeeded in his design of yielding the minimum of ground whilst imposing the heaviest possible losses on the Allies. A German offensive was surely coming in 1918 in the west. The United States of America was entering the war, and Germany now had its eastern armies to deploy in France. Opposing them now would be a British Army which had effectively lost the greatest battle of attrition of the war and was depleted and exhausted, with only the endurance and bravery of its troops to admire. The fighting

for 1917 was still not over, however — the battle of Cambrai was only ten days away.

A9512   DH5   24Sqn
OP mg dam fuel tanks? ftl cr Sh17.M.33 wr 4-20pm(2Lt WH Statham **inj)

11th November

A9439   DH5   32Sqn
**OP combat with EA fuel tanks shot through neYPRES ftl o't dam OK(Lt A Claydon) [?"SE5" claim combat WIELTJE 11-20am Ltn M Müller Ja2]

RE8   52Sqn
Phot (/Lt B Head **WIA)face

12th November

Two DH4 flights of 49 Squadron RFC arrived in France on the 12th of November. This squadron was to engage in fighting in a very short space of time, taking part in the battle of Cambrai.

B5086   RE8   5Sqn
Det Flt **AOb combat very fast Scout wDIXMUDE 2000' driven down to 20' by EA when it retired & able to return a'dr(2Lt JA Higham **WIA**/1AM S Hookway **WIA**) pilot hit foot, observer in chest & arm [?"RE" claim combat eMERKEM 10-35am Ltn H Bongartz Ja36]

RE8   6Sqn
Phot combat with EA(/AG.2AM G Wyatt **WIA) [?"RE" claim combat nrOOSTKERKE 2-45pm Ltn J Buckler Ja17]

RE8   6Sqn
Phot combat(/Cpl WA Elliot **WIA) [?possible "RE" claim combat nYPRES 9-35am Ltn F Hemer Ja6]

B2255   RE8   7Sqn
ViewLines AA cr n.m.l.(Lt WA Sewell **KIA/2Lt SLH Symonds **KIA**) to French front

A6748   SPAD 7   23Sqn
**NOP left 9-43am DADIZEELE combat with EA radiator shot up ftl OK(Lt JI Bundy)

A8913   SE5a   40Sqn
+* combat with AlbatrosDIII[+ooc] ANNAY 12-20pm OK(Lt W MacLanachan)

This was the first SE5a victory for 40 Squadron.

B2413   Sopwith Camel   65Sqn
OP shot up(Lt GH Pitt **WIA)

B2405   Sopwith Camel   65Sqn
OP dive on LVG QUESNOY-LILLE 4000' 11-50am **MIA(Lt KS Morrison **WIA POW**) no EA seen above, interned Holland 14.4.18

B2417   Sopwith Camel   65Sqn
OP DADIZEELE-QUESNOY shell hit cr EoL wr(Lt DH Scott MC **KIA)

B2420   Sopwith Camel   65Sqn
**OP QUESNOY-LILLE combat with EA shot up fuel tank dam OK(Lt B Balfour) [?"Sopwith 1Str" claim combat sARMENTIÈRES 12-05pm Ltn H Kroll Ja24]

B5651   Sopwith Camel   1(Naval)Sqn
+* combat with PfalzDIII[+flames] DIXMUDE 3-45pm OK(FSLt JH Forman Can.) shared

This was the first Sopwith Camel claim for 1(Naval) Squadron.

B6341   Sopwith Camel   10 (Naval) Sqn
OP dive on EA 2Str broke up nrFORTHEM-DIXMUDE **MIA(FSLt GL Trapp **KIA**)

13th November

A.W.FK8   35Sqn
** (/2Lt WJ Matthews **WIA**)

15th November

B6789   Nieuport 27   1Sqn
+* combat with DVs[++des] ZANDVOORDE 11-55am, OK(Capt PF Fullard) left 10-33am, Fullard's last victories (broke leg playing football 2 days later)

B6819   Nieuport 27   1Sqn
**NOP left 10-36am shot up ftl dam OK(2Lt CE Ogden) [?claim combat neZILLEBEKE LAKE 10-35am? Ltn H Bongartz Ja36]

A6687   SPAD 7   19Sqn
*LowLP cr wr(2Lt HJ Stone **DoI**) to hospital, DoW?

B3646   SPAD 7   19Sqn
WTInt combat with EA shot up ftl Sh28J.15.B.3.4.(2Lt T Elder-Hearn **WIA) left 10-20am, combat?

B6773   SPAD 7   19Sqn
** combat with EA shot up ftl cr 28.J.c.11.C.8.5. wr OK(Capt P Huskinson)

A4652   RE8   21Sqn
AOb YPRES combat with EA ftl cr Sh28.C.8.D. (2Lt WA Barnett **DoW/Lt GJ Bakewell **DoI** 16.11.17) left 6-50am, observer injured in crash ["RE" claim combat neYPRES 7-45am Ltn J Buckler Ja17]

B6792   Nieuport 27   29Sqn
NP left 1-45pm seen eZONNEBEKE EoL 2-50pm **MIA(2Lt SS Henry **POW**)

B6800   Nieuport 27   29Sqn
HAP seen sZANDVOORDE shot down **MIA(Lt JM Leach **WIA POW**) left 10-35am

B2430.B **Sopwith Camel   45Sqn**
+* combat with AlbatrosDV[+ooc] POELCAPPELLE 9-40am OK(Lt EMcN Hand Can.) Hand claimed at least 5 EAs

B3929.L **Sopwith Camel   45Sqn**
+* combat with AlbatrosDV[+flames] LANGEMARCK 9-35am OK(Lt KB Montgomery) [Ltn H Adam **KIA** Ja6], EA also claimed by 29Sqn

B5182.G **Sopwith Camel   45Sqn**
+* combat with 2Str[+des,cr] neHOUTHULST
WOOD 9-10am OK(Lt P Carpenter)

B6423.T **Sopwith Camel   45Sqn**
+* combat with AlbatrosDV[+ooc] eCOMINES 9-45am
OK(Lt JCB Firth)

This was the last of Firth's nine victories in France
and the last for 45 Squadron in France before they
were sent to the Italian front. Firth scored another
two victories in this aircraft in Italy.

B2411   Sopwith Camel   65Sqn
+* combat with AlbatrosDV[+ooc] DADIZEELE
7-40am OK(Lt GM Cox)

B2418   Sopwith Camel   65Sqn
+* combat with AlbatrosDV[+ooc] DADIZEELE
7-40am OK(Lt HL Symons)

These were the first combat victories for 65
Squadron.

B2458.R **Sopwith Camel   65Sqn**
**OP DADIZEELE-QUESNOY combat ovCOMINES
10am **MIA**(2Lt TP Morgan **POW**) a'c captured
["Sopwith 1Str" claim combat ST
MARGUERITE, sCOMINES 9-55am Vzfw O Esswein
Ja26]

B2444   Sopwith Camel   70Sqn
**SOP seen combat with EA TENBRIELEN 11-50am
MIA(Lt R Mayberry **KIA**) [?possible "Sopwith 1Str"
claim combat eZILLEBEKE LAKE 12-25pm Untoff
Reinhold Ja24]

B5409   Sopwith Camel   70Sqn
**WEA left 7-50am combat shot up dam OK(2Lt FC
Gorringe)

B6398   Sopwith Camel   1 (Naval) Sqn
+* combat with AlbatrosDVs[+ooc+des] BEERST-
nDIXMUDE btwn 1pm & 1-15pm OK(FSLt SM
Kinkead DSC)

B6427   Sopwith Camel   1 (Naval) Sqn
+* combat with DFWC[+des] RUGGEVELDE 9-15am
OK(SCdr RS Dallas Aust.)

B6430   Sopwith Camel   1 (Naval) Sqn
** badly shot up dam OK, pilot not yet established

16th November

A9269   DH5   32Sqn
**OP shell passed through fuselage dam return a'dr
OK(2Lt WR Jones) to Second Army area

18th November

A3669   RE8   9Sqn
**AOb shot down LANGEMARCK Sh28U.11.C.8.3.,
a'c shelled OK(2Lt WJH Courtis/2Lt ET Taylor)a'c
shelled, left 10-20am ["RE" claim combat
BIXSCHOOTE 1-15pm Ltn J Buckler Ja17]

B6817   SPAD 7   19Sqn
**NOP shot down ftl nr Lines Sh28D.13.B.3.1. OK(2Lt
A Reid-Walker) [?"SPAD" claim combat nYPRES
8-25am Vzfw Wawzin Ja10]

           Bristol F2b   20Sqn
** (/2Lt FB Wallis **WIA**)

           Bristol F2b   20Sqn
** (/Lt LH Phelps **WIA**)

B3575   SPAD 7   23Sqn
**WTInt seen ok nwPASSCHENDAELE 10-20am
MIA(2Lt GA Cranswick **KIA**) left 9-28am

A7282   Bristol F2b   48Sqn
**OP DIXMUDE combat 12-40pm shot down in flames
Sh20NW A.29.D. (2Lt WS McLaren **DoW** 19.11.17/2Lt
DW Hardie **KIA**) ["F2b" claim combat
LAMPERNISSE 12-10pm Ltn R Wendelmuth Ja20]

B35.5   **SE5a   56Sqn**
+* combat with RumplerC[+des] eRONNSOY 9-40am
OK(Capt JTB McCudden) first of 7 victories in this a'c

B519   SE5a   60Sqn
**NOP combat with DFW shot up dam ftl in water crater
nrST JULIEN Sh27.C.17.d.5.2. at 11-50am(2Lt SLG
Pope Irl. **WIA**) Pope claimed 6EA, 1 in this a'c

19th November

B3560   SPAD 7   19Sqn
+* combat with 2Str[+des] neOOSTNIEUWKERKE
12-10pm then combat with JunkersC[+des]
PASSCHENDAELE 12-30pm OK(Capt AE McKay)
first of his 6 victories with 23Sqn

           DH5   32Sqn
** (Capt WR Fish **WIA**)

AIRCRAFT AND TANKS AS BATTLEFIELD WEAPONS — FIGHTING AT CAMBRAI

The casualties for the previous ten days were very
slight, virtually all occurring as the battles in
Flanders subsided, allowing the opposing positions
to settle down into their winter defences. The calm,
however, was all of the Allies' making, because
unknown to the German High Command, the
British had one more intense and lightning assault
to make, opposite Cambrai. Its very secrecy,
enabled by the comprehensive use of a tank assault
as a substitute for an opening artillery barrage, was
the key to its success.

The art of surprise had been lost on the Western
Front. Whilst an enormous preliminary bombardment might offer initial success in an offensive, it
also telegraphed exact intentions to the enemy, and
then so devastated and confused the objectives that
in the end it was a hindrance to the advance. Both

sides were seeking a solution to the impasse of trench warfare. Ludendorff was developing schemes for fast disposition of troops to where they were most effective for the fighting. The Allies looked to the battlefield weapon of the tank. In this regard, it is interesting to see that at this time the use of the aeroplane was fast developing in the same direction. Indeed, operations involving aircraft in low attacking patrols were now called "Battle Flights". Tanks had been tried at Ypres, but the mud and rain had defeated them. On higher ground they promised much more. The problem for the British was that the battle was coming at the end of a terrible, weary year, and their resources were now heavily depleted. For this reason their efforts were bound to remain fairly exploratory, so that in one of the typical ironies of the Great War, if the battle plan to unlock the fighting proved a success, it could not then be pressed. There were genuine inconsistencies in the thinking of the Allied command, whose conflicts of purpose were never resolved and could have proved fatal.

The battle was to take place on a narrow front, but its objective was very ambitious. It was aimed at the heart of the Hindenburg Line, opposite Cambrai. The terrain here was excellent for the tank, being hard, rolling downland, and since the withdrawal to the Hindenburg Line, the area had been mostly inactive and had suffered little. If a breach could be made here it had the potential to disorganise the German defence system throughout the whole of the Western Front. It was calculated that the element of complete surprise might give the British commanders as much as two days' advantage before reinforcements would reach the German defences. Cambrai itself was not the objective, rather the attackers would push through to Bourlon and then spread the assault northwards into the rear of the defences. Perhaps if these tactics were successful they might force the Germans to make a strategic withdrawal on a very large scale: this was the hope.

The task was entrusted to the Third Army, largely rested since Arras. Preparations were made with the utmost secrecy, with remarkable results for the time. The troops involved did not know until forty-eight hours before the assault what was intended of them. The moving up of tanks was again masked by low flying aircraft over enemy positions, but this work was on a much larger scale. Six hundred additional guns were secreted into the sector, and even these were denied any form of pre-registering shots at their targets. This put significantly more responsibility on to at least two groups

of airmen involved in the battle. The corps artillery machines had now to locate the enemy positions as quickly and as accurately as possible from the moment fighting began. Additionally, the gunners were heavily dependent on the battle flights, who were now not only to carry out their low attacks but were to be mainly responsible for searching out and elucidating the enemy's gun positions and troop movements.

The air co-operation for the battle utilised a reinforced III Brigade RFC with additional fighting and bombing elements brought in from I Brigade and 9th (Headquarters) Wing. III Brigade had six corps squadrons of 12th (Corps) Wing: Nos. 8 (AW FK8s) and 12, 13, 15, 35, and 59 (all with RE8s), and seven fighter squadrons of 13th Army Wing: Nos. 3 (Sopwith Camels), 41 (SE5as), 46 (Sopwith Pups and Camels), 56 (SE5as), 64 (DH5s), 68 Australian (DH5s), and 84 (SE5s) ; 11 Squadron's Bristol Fighters for fighter reconnaissance work; and those parts of 49 Squadron recently arrived from England to carry out day-bombing with DH4s. Brigade strength numbered two hundred and eighty-nine aircraft.

I Brigade operated mostly in the northern part of the sector. Its bombers were to target Somain and Dechy railway stations, whilst its fighters were to carry out offensive patrols between Douai and the Sensée river and to ground attack troops and other targets as far east as Denain. The units involved formed the 10th (Army) Wing, and were Nos. 8 Naval (Sopwith Camels), 40 (SE5as), and 43 Squadrons (Sopwith Camels). All reconnaissance in this northern area was also the responsibility of this wing, carried out by the DH4s of 18 Squadron. Their corps machines made up the 1st (Corps) Wing, and were AW FK8s from 2 Squadron and RE8s from 4, 5, and 16 Squadrons. These units were to be held in reserve to co-operate against any significant counter-attacks.

The 9th (Headquarters) Wing units were to bomb major railway targets further eastwards, including Valenciennes, Busigny, Denain and Douai, and to reconnoitre the deeper locations behind the lines where build-ups might first be noticed. Its squadrons were Nos. 25 (DH4s) and 27 (Martinsydes and DH4s) day bombing; Nos. 101 and 102 (FE2bs) night bombing; and 22 Squadron (Bristol Fighters) fighter reconnaissance.

What is very apparent in this line up of RFC machines on the eve of Cambrai is how the revolution of providing new and formidable types into front line service had now been achieved. It was not simply the appearance of such a comprehensive array of improved aircraft which was so

impressive. The generations of machines which would finally win the war were already being trialled in Britain. These would be characterised by ever more specialisation for their purpose, whether this meant performance, manoeuvrability, bomb carrying capacity, or armament. In many ways the aircraft being built up in numbers at this time on the Western Front were the first of these, for they reaped the rewards of technological excellence and production. Operationally, they grew enormously in potential by virtue of much improved training and battlefield organisation. There were now virtually no second rate or obsolescent types, and crews knew to a high technical degree what was expected of them. At Cambrai, the Allied air forces assembled gave the Third Army enormous air superiority, for opposing the total of one hundred and thirty-four RFC fighters at the outset were twenty Albatros DVs of Jasta 5.

20th November
THE BATTLE OF CAMBRAI

The infantry advance of the battle of Cambrai began at 6-20am. Troops went over the top alerted not by the deafening roar of a huge barrage, but by a shell fired from a single gun. They moved off in the shelter of their three hundred and eighty-one tanks in fog, which favoured the surprise. The tanks easily broke through the wire entanglements and barriers, destroying machine-gun nests as they went, so that an almost hectic pace of advance was made, unlike anything the war had seen. By night-fall in some places the teams of tanks and men had moved four and a half miles into enemy territory, so that Graincourt and Anneux in the north, down to Masnières and Lateau Wood in the south were all captured. Some niggling salients persisted, however, such as the hill at Flesquières, and the delay this caused was to prove crucial in the course of the battle. Notably, the losses to the infantry were extremely light for the extent of front line overrun.

The corps machines and battle flights all had a busy day's fighting, made very difficult by low clouds and mist. Whilst these units struggled to do their work, that allocated to the bombing units of the 9th Wing was all but abandoned. Distant reconnaissances also suffered, and night bombing could not take place.

10 (Naval) Wing was withdrawn from service with the RFC on the 20th of November and returned to 4 Wing RNAS in the north.

B2421   Sopwith Camel   3Sqn
B left 6-55am VAUCHELLES WOOD **MIA(2Lt

WCV Higginson **KIA**) to Battery M.28 in Wood

B3824   Sopwith Camel   3Sqn
B left 6-45am ESTOURMEL A'dr **MIA(2Lt MWB Stead **POW**)

B3875   Sopwith Camel   3Sqn
**deliv shot up ftl AIZECOURT OK(2Lt FH Stephens) (crashed on re-take off on 26.11.17)

B5159   Sopwith Camel   3Sqn
B left 6-55am CARNIÈRES A'dr shot down **MIA(2Lt GW Hall **KIA**) Ja5 ["Sopwith 1Str" claim combat 1km eESTOURMEL A'dr 7-40am OffSt J Mai Ja5]

B5181   Sopwith Camel   3Sqn
**B shot up dam ftl A.L.G. OK(Capt DB King)

B5207   Sopwith Camel   3Sqn
**B left 6-45am ESTOURMEL A'dr mg fire shot up dam returned a'dr 8-15am OK(2Lt R Coop)

B6373   Sopwith Camel   3Sqn
B left 6-50am ESTOURMEL A'dr **MIA(2Lt HP Ledger **KIA**) forced to return

B6385   Sopwith Camel   3Sqn
B left 6-45am ESTOURMEL A'dr AA ftl **MIA(2Lt TJ Kent **POW**) a'c captured

This terrible day for 3 Squadron began in a series of dawn raids to bomb and shoot up enemy aero-dromes. There were nine Camels detailed to attack Estourmel, Carnières, and Caudry. When three of these arrived in mist over Estourmel at around 7-30am they found twelve fighters of Jasta 5 with pilots ready in their cockpits. Two of these managed to get off whilst the attack was driven home, and they managed to shoot down 2Lt GW Hall in B5159. Two more machines apparently crashed into trees in the mist on their return, whilst a fourth, attacking the other nearby aerodromes, was also lost. This was probably B6385. Exactly what machines were lost where on this operation is still uncertain, because the raid was generically noted as being to "Estourmel" on most of the Casualty Reports. 2Lt WVC Higginson was lost in other duties whilst attacking batteries around Lateau and Vaucelles Woods with 46 Squadron.

B279   A.W.FK8   8Sqn
CP mg shot up 7am dam ftl(Capt GEW Hitchcock **WIA/Lt AA Browne NZ. OK) to A.12.c.9.5.

B312   A.W.FK8   8Sqn
** fuel tank shot through ftl nrAUBIGNY(crew not known) crashed on re-take off in soft ground from this forced landing on 22.11.17 (Lt D Maclean)

Bristol F2b   11Sqn
CP (/2Lt PJ Cayley **WIA)

A7153   Bristol F2b   11Sqn
**Rec shot up dam return a'dr 11-15am OK(Capt JCL Barnett/Cpl J Mason) left 9-15am Third Army area

A7292   Bristol F2b   11Sqn
Rec left 7am **MIA(Sgt TF Stephenson **KIA**/Lt TW
Morse **WIA POW**)

A3640   RE8   13Sqn
AP left 10am XIII Corps front **MIA(Sgt RW Taylor
KIA/2AM WH Swift **KIA**)

      RE8   15Sqn
CP (Lt TC Creaghan **WIA/)

      RE8   15Sqn
CP (2Lt WF Mayoss **WIA/)

A4398   RE8   15Sqn
CP mg shot down in flames **MIA(2Lt GJT Young
KIA/2Lt AL Wylie MC **KIA**) left 10-15am

B5031   RE8   15Sqn
**CP 15lb shell hit 7-15am ftl ok(Capt HS Robertson
WIA/2Lt WC Davey **DoW** 21.11.17) to 57 Q.16.d.

B5894   RE8   15Sqn
**AP AA dam shot up return a'dr OK(2Lt GW
Armstrong/2Lt R Kearton) left 12-30pm

A4383   RE8   21Sqn
AOb YPRES shell hit cr(Lt ACNMP deLisle **KIA/Lt
SM Goodeve Can. **KIA**) left 9-10am, a'c unsalvable

      DH5   32Sqn
** (2Lt DW Lane **WIA**)

      Sopwith Camel   46Sqn
SpM (2Lt JK Smith **WIA)

A6188   Sopwith Pup   46Sqn
**B left 6-40am CAMBRAI mg fire? ftl ERVILLERS
cr(Sgt J Leigh **WIA**) inj? in cr

This raid was most likely to other aerodromes
around Cambrai. Because of mist, only that at
Awoingt was found and attacked and 46 Squadron
suffered their first casualties on Camels in the
fighting.

B2186   Sopwith Pup   46Sqn
**B HAVRINCOURT shot up dam return a'dr 8-40am
OK(2Lt EG Thomson) left 6-40am

B2466   Sopwith Camel   46Sqn
**B mg fire shot up return a'dr ok OK(Capt C
Courtneidge)

B2491   Sopwith Camel   46Sqn
**B mg fire shot up ftl AUBIGNY 10-50am OK(2Lt SR
Hanafy)

      Bristol F2b   48Sqn
** combat(/2Lt GR Horsfall **KIA**)

B548   SE5a   56Sqn
**P engine shot up ftl EQUANCOURT OK(Capt RTR
Townsend)

A7568   DH4   57Sqn
*Met found wrLES ALLEUX **MIA**(Capt DS Hall
KIFA/Lt EP Hartigan **KIFA**) left 9-45am

A3417   RE8   59Sqn
**P AA shot down GOUZEAUCOURT cr wr(Capt C
Eales OK/2Lt CE Kennedy **WIA**) left 6-40am

A9201   DH5   64Sqn
GndP left 7am shot down? BULLECOURT? **MIA(2Lt
OW Meredith **KIA**)

A9235   DH5   64Sqn
**GndP mg fire shot down cr n.m.l. BULLECOURT
7-50am OK(Lt RG Hardie)

A9298   DH5   64Sqn
GndP left 7am shot down? BULLECOURT? **MIA(Lt
JP McRae **WIA POW**)

A9335   DH5   64Sqn
GndP left 7am shot down? BULLECOURT? **MIA(Lt
RE Angus **KIA**)

A9486   DH5   64Sqn
**GndP ground fire shot up plane blown off in air nd cr
n.m.l. BULLECOURT 7-45am(2Lt LB Williams
WIA)hospital

A9492   DH5   64Sqn
**P shot up dam ftl A.L.G. OK(Lt EE Ashton)

The low clouds and mist which were such an asset
for the tank assault proved problematic for the low
flying aircraft throughout all of the first day. Some
machines were certainly lost because of these
conditions. One unit engaged heavily in this work
was 64 Squadron, with their DH5s. On the first day
of the advance they bombed gun-pits and other
ground targets around Flesquières. They had come
to France as specialists in low-patrolling, and these
heavy losses were the first of many for the
Squadron in this dangerous work. The other units
principally involved in this were 46 Squadron and
68 (Australian) Squadron. During this fighting
these units suffered casualties approaching thirty
per cent.

A9278   DH5   68 (Australian) Sqn
**P fuel tank shot up dam MIA but OK(Lt LH Holden
MC)

A9378   DH5   68 (Australian) Sqn
**GP shot down n.m.l. cr wr joined advanced infantry &
fought OK(Lt H Taylor) left 8-20am, found DH5 A9473
& tried to fly out

A9399   DH5   68 (Australian) Sqn
LowB left 8-20am seen low ovMARCOING **MIA(2Lt
LN Ward **inj POW**) injured in crash ldg

A9457   DH5   68 (Australian) Sqn
SpM shot up? cr wr(2Lt FH Shepherd **WIA) a'c
unsalvable

A9473   DH5   68 (Australian) Sqn
**TroopB forced low by fog rifle fire shot down
X.3.D.57.C dam(Capt J Bell **DoW** 27.12.17) left ~dawn
to Sh57C X.3.D.

A9483   DH5   68 (Australian) Sqn
**P shot up dam ftl A.L.G. dam OK(Lt WA Robertson)

21st November

Poor conditions restricted most of the Allied flying.

A2718   A.W.FK8   35Sqn
CP ground fire shot down MARCOING(Capt RN Walton **WIA/Capt GW Surne? OK) WIA cheek

22nd November

The resistence at Flesquières on the 20th had caused a crucial delay, despite the fact that the Germans abandoned it that night. That the advance had been heavily dependent on the reconnoitring of low patrolling aircraft and fighters for its structure might be seen as a flaw. The conditions of mist, and the general confusion of the action made their task doubly difficult, because they were there first to attack, and only then to reconnoitre. If the problems at Flesquières had been detected earlier, perhaps the battle might have developed differently.

The flaws of the Cambrai offensive were not this simple, however. The advance on the second day had been tangible but slower, and the inconsistencies deep within the battle plan had begun to emerge. The high point of Bourlon Wood was the next objective, but there was no general reserve to bring forward, and the High Command was nervous, as usual, of using the cavalry. It had staked all on success in the first forty-eight hours of fighting, and although it appeared to have won this gamble, the opportunity presented was simply handed away in the following days. A stiffer kind of opposition was met around the critical strong point of Bourlon, and developed into a grim and costly struggle for the next five days. It was bristling with machine-guns, and troops were attacked remorselessly by low-flying German aircraft. It was clear that the enemy air services had been reinforced, for increasing numbers of fighters were in action over the fighting. Four SE5as of Nos. 41 and 84 Squadron begun offensive patrols on the 22nd to counter these, and suffered only one casualty, 2Lt PJ Moloney of 84 Squadron who was wounded (see below). In the delay caused by these events, however, German troop reinforcements also flooded into the area.

B5180   Sopwith Camel   3Sqn
**Rec mg fire shot up 8-25am ftl ok OK(Lt RSS Brown)

A3730   RE8   15Sqn
**CP combat fuel tank shot up FLESQUIÈRES 12-30pm ftl OK(Lt CKM Douglas/2Lt WH Steele)

A2703   A.W.FK8   35Sqn
**Rec combat shot up MARCOING ftl 12pm OK(Lt R Buchanan/Lt D Taylor)

B581   SE5a   41Sqn
+*COP combat with AlbatrosDV[+capt] swCAMBRAI 11am engine ftl n.m.l. NIERGARES OK(Lt R Winnicott) a'c abandoned

This was the first SE5a victory for 41 Squadron, although it is not certain that the combat and abandonment were sequential. The casualty below was also the first for the Squadron on SE5as.

B629   SE5a   41Sqn
P shot up ftl cr ldg A.L.G. dam(Lt J Cushny **WIA)hospital

B2366   Sopwith Camel   43Sqn
SpLowRec left 10-35am DOUAI **MIA(2Lt EF Marchand **POW**)

B6267   Sopwith Camel   43Sqn
SpLowRec left 7-55am DOUAI **MIA(Capt GB Crole MC **WIA POW**) ["Sopwith 1Str" claim combat ovMARCOING 8-10am Ltn F Rumey Ja5]

B1747   Sopwith Pup   46Sqn
B left 8-40am BOURLON WOOD **MIA(Lt TL Atkinson **POW**)

B2457   Sopwith Camel   46Sqn
**B left 11-05am CAMBRAI ftl EoL but escaped to safety MIA but OK(Capt ASG Lee) a'c captured

Captain Lee's reminiscences of low flying at Cambrai are quoted in *The War in the Air*, vol. IV, pp. 236-237. They are an evocative witness to the demands of low patrolling. He noted how essential it was first to hunt down objectives by virtually skimming to them a few feet above the ground. In this way, one was past the enemy before they knew of one's approach. The battle area would be marked by a hazy cloud of smoke and exploding shells, and one would fly straight into this, still virtually at ground level. He found that moment very unpleasant, and indeed many low patrolling machines were lost during the war by flying into the ground at these times. He would then rise up through the smoke, mist, and ground fire over the fighting and make his attacks. The strafing and bombing was carried out in a general atmosphere of chaos and confusion, one's aim being to deliver bombs and fire effectively whilst avoiding that fatal burst of AA or colliding with other machines.

B597   SE5a   84Sqn
*DOP ftl field BELLE EGLISE 9-45am o't dam OK(2Lt AFW Beauchamp-Proctor)

B4866   SE5a   84Sqn
DOP CAMBRAI gunfire dam ftl nrBUS(2Lt PJ Moloney **WIA)

B4886   SE5a   84Sqn
+* attacked KB[+des] nRAILLENCOURT-
BOURLON WOOD 8-50am OK(Capt ER Pennell)

A5593   FE2b   100Sqn
** dam by EA while in hangar

A9265   DH5   68 (Australian) Sqn
**SpM:57.C.J.6.d. left 10am AA ftl cr Lines dam(Lt AJ
Pratt **inj**)

A9294   DH5   68 (Australian) Sqn
*P combat EoL shot up dam fog ftl 56Sq OK(Lt RW
Howard) left 10am

A9461   DH5   68(Australian) Sqn
+*LowP shooting up troops swRAILLENCOURT then
attacked AlbatrosDV[+des] OK(Lt FG Huxley) "It was
a gift"

This was the first combat victory for 68 (Australian) Squadron.

A9477   DH5   68 (Australian) Sqn
**SpM going east ovBOURLON WOOD 10-30am? shot
down by ground fire EoL **MIA**(2Lt DG Clark **KIA**) left
10-30am BAPAUME

23rd November

The British attempted two big infantry attacks on
Bourlon Wood and Fontaine-Notre Dame on the
23rd, but ultimately these were mostly repulsed.
Notably in this fighting, the Germans used mobile
anti-aircraft guns against tanks, with some effect.

Very high casualties continued to be suffered by
the low-patrolling pilots of Nos. 3, 46, and 64
Squadrons. These units flew fifty machines over the
fighting throughout the day. The weather for flying
had improved, and from dawn onwards relays of
between four and fifteen machines kept a constant
presence over troops and gun emplacements in
Bourlon Wood. German air reinforcements into the
area now included Jagdgeschwader I, led by
Manfred von Richthofen. This group was composed of Jagdstaffeln 4, 6, 10, and 11. Richthofen's
presence was of vital assistance to the German
effort, and he took general command of the air
operations. Jagdstaffel 5 had been also joined by
Jagdstaffel 15 on the 22nd. The ground co-
operation work rose to a crescendo of activity
around 1pm, when fifteen machines were fighting
over Bourlon and Fontaine. This happened to
coincide with the first patrol of the Richthofen
Circus, who mounted a fierce attack on them.
DH5s of 64 Squadron were particularly singled out.

B2369   Sopwith Camel   3Sqn
**LP left 11am BOURLON WOOD forced to return
MIA(Lt JW McCash **KIA**)

B5153   Sopwith Camel   3Sqn
**LP left 11am BOURLON WOOD forced to return

MIA(Lt FH Stephens Can. **KIA**)

B316   A.W.FK8   8Sqn
B seen ovCAMBRAI combat with 7EAs **MIA(2Lt WA
Booth **KIA**/2Lt GJ Howells **KIA**) left 1-15pm [?"F2b"
claim combat swMARCOING 12pm? Vzfw F Rumey
Ja5]

              Bristol F2b   11Sqn
Rec (Lt RD Coath **WIA/)

B1116   Bristol F2b   11Sqn
Rec seen ovCAMBRAI **MIA(2Lt ED Perney **KIA**/2Lt
EJ Blackledge **KIA**) left 12-35pm [?"F2b" claim combat
wSERANVILLERS? 1pm Ltn L Fr vRichthofen Ja11]

              DH4   18Sqn
** AA(Capt ER Cottier **WIA**/Capt JA Mansfield **WIA**)

A7501   DH4   18Sqn
**B AA clouds ftl A.L.G. 8-50am BAPAUME dam
OK(2Lt DA Stewart/Lt HW Macleay)

              SPAD 7   19Sqn
OP (2Lt JD dePencier **WIA)

A2170   DH4   25Sqn
B SOMAIN seen ovARRAS **MIA(2Lt R Main **POW**/
1AM GP Leach **POW**?) left 10-15am

Day bombing of distant objectives was finally
possible on a broad scale on the 23rd, and 25
Squadron went to Douai, Denain, Dechy, and
Somain stations in company with Nos. 18 and 27
Squadrons. This loss of a 25 Squadron crew, and
the 18 Squadron casualties noted above, occurred
on these operations. Night bombing of Dechy and
Douai by 102 Squadron was also carried out and
was moderately successful.

              A.W.FK8   35Sqn
CP (/2Lt ACT Perkins MC **WIA)

B5767   A.W.FK8   35Sqn
**Rec mg shot up ftl LONGAVESNES A'dr(Lt LG
Paling OK/2Lt DO Duthie **WIA**) to hospital, left 3-45pm

B2316   Sopwith Camel   46Sqn
**B/OP left 9-58am FONTAINE mg shot up ftl OK(2Lt
HNC Robinson)

B2326   Sopwith Camel   46Sqn
B/OP left 11-30am BOURLON WOOD **MIA(Lt SR
Hanafy **DoW**) ["Sopwith" claim combat FONTAINE
12-20pm Vzfw O Könnecke Ja5]

B2497   Sopwith Camel   46Sqn
**P mg shot up ftl A.L.G. dam rep OK(Lt RLM Ferrie)

B2513   Sopwith Camel   46Sqn
**B/OP left 10-30am BOURLON WOOD mg shot up ftl
OK(2Lt CW Odell) [?"Camel" claim combat
ovBOURLON WOOD 11am Vzfw F Rumey Ja5]

B5208   Sopwith Camel   46Sqn
P shot up ftl A.L.G.(Capt C Courtneidge **WIA)

B5410   Sopwith Camel   46Sqn
**B/OP mg shot up ftl cr nrCAMBRAI 11-58am wr
OK(Lt RE Dusgate)

B511   SE5a   56Sqn
**P left 11-30am shot up ftl ldg ok dam OK(Maj R
Balcombe-Brown)

A9237   DH5   64Sqn
**GndP mg shot up ftl BOURLON WOOD cr wr
trenches 12-10pm (Capt AC StClair-Morford **WIA**)
attacking troops, a'c unsalvable

A9295   DH5   64Sqn
**TroopShoot, mg shot up ftl seen cr BOURLON
WOOD OK(Lt AA Duffus) left 12-40pm, a'c unsalvable

A9299   DH5   64Sqn
**TroopShoot, mg shot up ftl cr BOURLON WOOD(Lt
JAV Boddy **WIA**) to hospital, left 12-40pm BOURLON
WOOD, severely WIA in head, a'c unsalvable ["DH5"
claim combat seBOURLON WOOD 1pm Rittm M Fr
vRichthofen JG1]

A9313   DH5   64Sqn
**TroopShoot mg shot up ftl seen cr BOURLON
WOOD OK(Lt RC Hardie) left 2-55pm, a'c unsalvable

A9490   DH5   64Sqn
**TroopShoot, mg shot up ftl seen cr BOURLON
WOOD OK(Capt HT Fox Russell) left 12-40pm, a'c
unsalvable

A9508   DH5   64Sqn
**TroopShoot, mg shot up ftl seen cr BOURLON
WOOD OK(2Lt VW Thompson) left 2-55pm, a'c
unsalvable

B2409   Sopwith Camel   65Sqn
**NOP combate BECELAERE 11-05am air collision
with B5222 ooc **MIA**(2Lt A Rosenthal **KIA**) left 10-45am
DADIZEELE-STADEN [2 "Camel" claims(including
1 unconfirmed) combat BECELAERE 10-50am Ltn H
Bongartz Ja36]

B2415   Sopwith Camel   65Sqn
**NOP combat with AlbatrosDV 11-25am seen
eBECELAERE-DADIZEELE **MIA**(2Lt L Marshall
KIA) Ja36 [?possible "Camel" claim combat
BECELAERE 10-50am Ltn H Bongartz Ja36, but his 2
claims(1 unconfirmed) were probably a collided pair of
Camels]

B2493   Sopwith Camel   65Sqn
**NOP combat BECELAERE shot down ftl cr shell hole
Sh28 D.26.C.75. a'c shelled(2Lt CP Tiptaft MC **WIA**)
left 2-45pm STADEN-DADIZEELE ["Sopwith 1Str"
claim combat wMOORSLEDE 3-30pm Ltn W vBülow
Ja36]

B5222   Sopwith Camel   65Sqn
**NOP combat eBECELAERE 11-05am air collision
with Camel B2409 ooc **MIA**(Lt CF Keller **POW**) left
10-45am DADIZEELE-STADEN [?"Camel" claim
combat BECELAERE 10-50am? Ltn H Bongartz Ja36]

SE5a   84Sqn
DOP (2Lt DJ Rollo **WIA)

A9263   DH5   68 (Australian) Sqn
**SpM shot up ground fire ftl nr Lines but cr(Lt SW
Ayres **DoW** 24.11.17) taxied into road, a'c unsalvable

A9326   DH5   68 (Australian) Sqn
**LowB combat with EA heavily shot up dam ldg ok
12-25pm OK(Lt LH Holden)

A9428   DH5   68 (Australian) Sqn
**SpM seen ok? ovBOURLON WOOD 3-45pm shot
down by ground fire **MIA**(Lt A Griggs US. **DoW**
23.11.17) low patrolling over BOURLON WOOD. Died
trying to save a Company of the Royal Irish rifles

B6230   Sopwith Camel   9 (Naval) Sqn
+* combat with AlbatrosDV[+ooc] sDIXMUDE
12-20pm OK(FCdr FE Banbury Can.)

24th November

B263   A.W.FK8   10Sqn
FlRec left 8-50am shot down **MIA(2Lt A Muir **POW**/
Gnr J Dunsmuir **POW**)

            Sopwith Camel   65Sqn
** (2Lt TF Pilcher **WIA**)

            RE8   69 (Australian) Sqn
** (/AG.Sgt TH Barrell **WIA**)

This was the first combat casualty suffered by the
corps unit 69 (Australian) Squadron.

26th November

The fighting at Bourlon was a grizzly affair, with
the village desperately fought for and taken, only
to be lost again. The air support in the final days
of this fighting could only be patchy because of the
conditions. Deeper bombing was also restricted by
the low clouds, and with Richthofen marking his
presence, these called for ever more escort. An
example of this was when 49 Squadron attempted
their first active bombing raid on the 26th it took
fourteen SE5 escorts with it. The delays caused by
this resistance imposed an increasingly limited
battle on the attackers, who were more than ever
concerned about the safety of their own protruding
salient. By the last days of the month, Haig's
superiority had crumbled, and once more, tired
and exhausted men faced the prospect of a deadly
counter-attack. The salient was extremely vulnerable being poorly connected to the original front as
well as being under supplied. The majority of the
tanks had been used in the opening offensive, and
were also now in a sorry state, and air reconnaissances told an uneasy story of a formidable enemy
build-up.

Nieuport   **29Sqn**
NOP (2Lt CA Mulligan **WIA)

B6405   Sopwith Camel   46Sqn
** mg fire fuel tanks shot through ftl FLESQUIÈRES
dam OK(Capt AS Lee)

A5676   FE2b   102Sqn
**NB left 7pm shot up engine hit ftl cr wr OK(Lt PH
Cummings/Lt HA Parry)

27th November

Most of the air casualties until the end of
November were occurring in Flanders. Opposite
Cambrai, troops were being rested and, in places,
relieved, but most ominously a German counter-
attack seemed imminent.

A3826   RE8   21Sqn
**TrenchB combat with EA shot up 3-45pm returned to
a'dr(Lt WW Fielding **WIA**/2Lt CW Dunsford **WIA**) to
hospital

B3578   Nieuport 17   29Sqn
NP left 11-30am **MIA(Lt L Kert **POW**)

28th November

A4458   RE8   7Sqn
Phot left 11-45am **MIA(2Lt WG Mann **KIA**/2Lt RA
Forsyth **KIA**) [?"RE" claim possible combat
GHELUVELT Vzfw P Bäumer Ja2, but see B6492]

B6492   RE8   9Sqn
**Phot AA? ftl YPRES cr Sh28 L.11.B.3.8.(Lt JA Pullan
KIA/Lt CH Dixon **KIA**) [?"RE" claim combat
nGHELUVELT 1pm Vzfw P Bäumer Ja2]

B227   A.W.FK8   10Sqn
**OP ground mg fire shot up dam OK(2Lt JA Pattern/
2Lt PW Leycester) to POLDERHOEK CHÂTEAU

DH5   32Sqn
OP (2Lt D Francis **WIA) [?possible "DH5" claim
combat PASSCHENDAELE-POELCAPPELLE
12-40pm Ltn E Udet Ja37]

B2427   Sopwith Camel   65Sqn
**DawnP seen in clouds ZONNEBEKE-
PASSCHENDAELE 7-40am **MIA**(2Lt JF Mackinnon
KIA) left 7am

B2452   Sopwith Camel   70Sqn
LP mg fire shot up ftl seBECELAERE EoL **MIA(2Lt
CH Brown **WIA INT**) left 8am, seen get out & walk to
farm, interned Holland

29th November

B6758   SPAD 7   19Sqn
OP YPRES left 2-30pm **MIA(2Lt AH Rice **KIA**)
["SPAD" claim combat PASSCHENDAELE 3-35pm Ltn
W vBülow Ja36]

A7253   Bristol F2b   20Sqn
**NOP combat with EA MOORSLEDE 1pm seen

nrWESTROOSEBEKE **MIA**(2Lt EV Clark **KIA**/2Lt G
Noon **KIA**) left 10-54am [?"Bristol" claim combat
nMOORSLEDE Ltn H vBülow Ja36]

C4817   Bristol F2b   20Sqn
**NOP combat with EA engine shot up ftl
STEENWORDE OK(2Lt W Beaver/1AM JM? Thomas)
left 9-32am

A7704   DH4   49Sqn
**B combat with AlbatrosD & AA, down in flames
nrTHUN ST MARTIN 10-10am **MIA**(2Lt CB Campbell
Aust. **KIA**/AM WAE Samways **KIA**) left 9am
eCAMBRAI

This was the first casualty in action for 49
Squadron RFC.

A7740   DH4   49Sqn
**B eCAMBRAI mg shot up AA dam OK(2Lt GS
Stewart/Lt DD Richardson) left 9am, returned a'dr
10-40am

B4890.C SE5a   56Sqn
**DOP III seen attk many EA ovAWOIGNT 8-45am
MIA(Lt A Dodds **POW**) left 10am, a'c captured, Ja5?
["SE" claim combat WAMBAIX 8-45am FwLtn
Schubert Ja6, but see Ja10 claims of DH5 A9517?]

A9517   DH5   68 (Australian) Sqn
**P BOURLON combat with EA[+ftl] shot up dam
OK(Lt RW Howard) left 7-40am, returned a'dr 9-25am
[+?possible "Sopwith 1Str claims sCAMBRAI 9am Ltn
H Klein & Ltn A Heldmann Ja10, but outside alternative
is SE5 B4890]

30th November
THE GERMAN
COUNTER-ATTACKS

The British High Command was now convinced
that a counter-attack was massing. Wireless interruption was showing that German artillery aircraft
were increasingly registering opposing guns.
However, the generals clung to the belief that the
attack would come through Bourlon in the north,
despite mounting conflicting evidence. Troops were
seen spreading to either side of the salient, and
Richthofen's red machines were plainly in place in
the south on the British right. The German Command wanted the attention kept on Bourlon, for
indeed it had other plans. It had hastily assembled
sixteen fresh divisions, and whilst it would strike
from Bourlon, the heaviest attack would come from
the south, around Gonnelieu, wrapping up the
exhausted defenders in a pincer. They had also
quickly relearned the value of surprise, for they too
embarked on their counter-attack with virtually no
preliminary barrage. Instead, the German assault
came at Gonnelieu at 7-30am, after only a short,
albeit intense bombardment, and this time was

driven home with low flying aircraft strafing and bombing troops. Most of this work was done by the specialised two-seaters of Schutzstaffeln, or "Protection Flights". Their work was highly co-ordinated with the ground advance. In ninety minutes the Germans had pushed right through the bewildered British line and on into Gouzeaucourt, which they held for a day. The defending troops managed counter-attacks of their own once the initial thrust had been halted, 3 Squadron fighting the German low-patrols and 68 (Australian) Squadron being very active in the ground work.

In the north, around Bourlon Wood, these new surprise tactics were not so much used, although co-operating ground strafing was also done here by the German Air Force. The British line which was attacked at Bourlon had been prepared in strength and the troops held out through five successive counter-attacks on the opening day. Offensive patrols higher up were also sent out in the early hours of fighting in the north, SE5as of 41 Squadron being typically involved. However, when they found nothing to attack they came down lower to the more immediate battle area. Then followed an absolute scrap for the rest of the day, with one pilot's report quoted in the Official History recording that "the air was thick with DH5s, some SE5s, RE8s, and Bristol Fighters". The work of the co-operating machines on either side suffered the most in this fighting, being repeatedly denied a clear sky. In contrast, the ground patrols caused most damage and mayhem to the infantry.

When a British Court of Inquiry came to examine the German counter-attack some months later, it focused on the effectiveness of the German low-flying patrols with the following words: "These aeroplanes came over in considerable numbers at the time of the assault and flew . . . lower than 100 feet, firing their machine-guns into our infantry both in the front-line trenches and in rearward positions. The moral effect of this was very great and no doubt tended to facilitate the enemy's successes. Our men did not seem to know what to do to minimise the moral effect of these low-flying machines . . . fire on them produced no result." The Germans had been scrupulously careful in the disposition of their aircraft, ensuring that maximum strength was applied to the most decisive points of the battle. And their High Command was impressed with the results. The above was effectively a description of the new air war, fore-shadowing so many future battles. In five months, the fighting arena had descended from ten thousand to just one hundred feet.

B2496   Sopwith Camel   3Sqn
LowB left 12-25pm INCHY-BOURLON **MIA(2Lt LW Timmis **POW**)

B5220   Sopwith Camel   3Sqn
LowB AA shot up ftl cr bad ground 1-30pm o't Sh57c.D.27. (2Lt R Coop **WIA)

B6336   Sopwith Camel   3Sqn
LowB left 12-25pm INCHY-BOURLON **MIA(Capt DB King **POW**) ["Sopwith 1Str" claim combat MOEUVRES-BOURLON WOOD 2-45pm Ltn E Loewenhardt Ja10]

B308   A.W.FK8   8Sqn
CP combat ovMASNIÈRES shot up dam(2Lt AM Kinnear OK/Lt AA Browne? **WIA)finger, left 11-30am, returned 12-40pm, Brown?

B5780   A.W.FK8   8Sqn
CP ground mg shot up ftl cr LONGAVESNES dam(Lt CL Philcox OK/Lt RCG Rowden **KIA)heart, to eGOUZEAUCOURT

A7288.7   Bristol F2b   11Sqn
+* combat with AlbatrosDVs[++++des] sCAMBRAI btwn 11-50am & 11-55am OK(Capt AE McKeever Can./ 2Lt LA Powell) last victories of this crew, McKeever with 31, Powell with 19

RE8   12Sqn
P (/Lt LB Nicholls **WIA)

A4453   RE8   15Sqn
**P combat engine shot up ftl cr FLESQUIÈRES o't mud 8-05am OK(Lt CKN? Douglas/2Lt WK Whittle) initials CKM?

B6504   RE8   15Sqn
AP combat fuel tank shot up ftl Sh57C K.14.c.3.9. 1-45pm(Capt TS Malcomson OK/Lt LV Desborough **KIA) left 12-30pm

A9304   DH5   24Sqn
+* combat with AlbatrosDV[+ooc] eBOURLON WOOD 12-55pm OK(Capt BPG Beanlands)

A9509   DH5   24Sqn
COP seen combat with EA BOURLON WOOD shot down 1pm **MIA(2Lt ID Campbell **KIA**) left 12-15pm ["DH5" claim combat sBOURLON WOOD 12-45pm Ltn H-G vOsten Ja11]["DH5" claim combat MOEUVRES 1-25pm? Ltn S Gussmann Ja11]

B644   SE5a   41Sqn
COP combat with EA MOEUVRES nrCAMBRAI 1-30pm shot down in flames **MIA(Lt DADI Macgregor **KIA**) MvR63 ["SE5" claim combat MOEUVRES 1-30pm Rittm M Fr vRichthofen JG1]

B2512   Sopwith Camel   46Sqn
COP seen ovCAMBRAI **MIA(Lt RE Dusgate **POW DoW** 19.12.17) left 2-15pm [?"Sopwith 1Str" claim combat swMARCOING 2-45pm Ltn J Janzen Ja6, but possibly 3Sqn a'c]

B40   SE5a   56Sqn
**OP combat with EA shot down in flames nrCAMBRAI

MIA(Capt RTR Townsend **KIA**) left 2-15pm ["SE5" claim combat LE PAVE 2-48pm Vzfw J Mai Ja5]

B4871 SE5a 56Sqn
OP seen dive on EA CAMBRAI combat with EA MASNIÈRES 11-15am broke up **MIA(2Lt GA Cawson **KIA**) [?possible unconfirmed "SE5" claim combat LE PAVE]

RE8 59Sqn
** **MIA**(/Sgt? Bastick **POW**)

RE8 59Sqn
Rec mg fire(/2Lt AER Aldridge **WIA)

A9458.U DH5 64Sqn
+* combat with DFWC[+ooc] BOURLON WOOD 10-45am OK(Capt JA Slater) Slater's final score was 24 claims, mostly on SE5as

This was the first combat victory for 64 Squadron.

A9507.E DH5 64Sqn
+*combat with AlbatrosDV[+ooc] nwBOURLON WOOD 3-20pm OK(Capt ER Tempest) first of 17 victories

B562 SE5a 84Sqn
+* combat with AlbatrosDV[+des] MALINCOURT 12-30pm OK(Capt J Child) last of 7 claims

A5586 FE2b 101Sqn
NB left 11-40pm DOUAI AA? shot up cr ldg(Capt T? Grant **WIA/2Lt Shand OK)leg, Grant's initial J?

A9532 DH5 68 (Australian) Sqn
**SpM left 8-40am BOURLON combat shot down CANTAIN Sh57C F.27.d.6.8. cr OK(2Lt HC Cornell), left 8-40am, spent 24hr in shell hole after coming down before re-making lines, a'c unsalvable

Untraced casualty in France in November 1917?

RNAS
** (Lt AAD Grey **POW**) Nov.17?

December 1917

ALLIED FAILURES AT CAMBRAI

The remarkable gains of the tank offensive at Cambrai had been lost, and these actions had been followed by an almost as bold and effective counter-attack in the south by the Germans. By the early days of December, however, the fighting was again subsiding. In the air, mist and low clouds restricted action as well. Some old ground had been won back around Gouzeaucourt and the German efforts were exhausted, whilst heroic fighting at Bourlon ensured there would be no disaster for the British Army.

The Cambrai offensive left the British with an untenable front, however, from which a withdrawal was inevitable. Between the 4th and the 7th, the army pulled back from Bourlon and Marcoing onto the Flesquières ridge. What had begun for the British as a most hopeful enterprise for the future became exactly that for the Germans. The tank had been proven in battle, and the enemy were never to find an answer to it. But although each side lost about the same quantity of prisoners and guns, it was the Germans who had successfully carried out their first important offensive since Verdun. It came as a great boost to their morale, especially so at this time when the initiative was passing into their hands, as they eagerly awaited the spring and their decisive offensive in the West.

1st December

B314 A.W.F.K.8 8Sqn
CP mg MERICOURT fuel pipe shot through dam ftl(2Lt AM Kinnear **WIA/Lt MA O'Callaghan OK) left 2-30pm

A.W.FK8 35Sqn
CP mg fire(/2Lt EL Shaw **WIA)

B5778 A.W.FK8 35Sqn
*CP to nrVILLERS GUISLAN **MIA**(Lt J MacKenzie **KIA**/2Lt C Hyde **KIA**) left 12-30pm ["RE" claim combat NOBLE VILLE 12-50pm Vzfw G Schneidewind Ja17]

B2191 Sopwith Pup 46Sqn
+* combat with AlbatrosDIII[+des] CAMBRAI 9-10am OK(Lt EY Hughes) Ja17?

This was the last Sopwith Pup claim for 46 Squadron.

A9341 DH5 68 (Australian) Sqn
**SpM shot up GOUZEAUCOURT 12-05pm dam OK(Lt L Benjamin)

A9451 DH5 68 (Australian) Sqn
+* combat with AlbatrosDV[+des] nwVILLERS-GUISLAIN 12-15pm OK(Lt RW MacKenzie)

A9466 DH5 68 (Australian) Sqn
**SpM ground fire GOUZEAUCOURT shot down 12pm dam OK(Lt WA Robertson)

2nd December

B3303 A.W.FK8 8Sqn
AP combat with 5-6EA shot down in flames VILLERET a'c destroyed(Lt TR Hepple **inj/1AM F Rothwell **KIA**) left 10-30am, pilot burnt, hospital

A7167 Bristol F2b 11Sqn
**Rec AA hit sump ftl dam OK(2Lt LA Rivers/Pte JW Scott)

A6662 SPAD 7 19Sqn
NOP left 10-48am seen ovYPRES 12pm **MIA(2Lt SG Spiro **POW**)

A7270   Bristol F2b   20Sqn
**OP combat with EA seen ok sePASSCHENDAELE
10-30am **MIA**(Capt HGET Luchford MC **KIA**/Capt JE
Johnston **inj POW**) left 9-45am ["Bristol" claim combat
BECELAERE 10-35am Ltn W vBülow Ja36], Luchford
had 24 claims

B3583   Nieuport 17   29Sqn
Ni23? **NOP seen ovPASSCHENDAELE going south
9-45am **MIA**(2Lt GGW Petersen **POW**) left 8-45am

A7422   DH4   57Sqn
B left 8am **MIA(2Lt D Miller **WIA POW**/2Lt AHC
Hoyles **KIA**) Müller33 ["DH4" claim combat
nwMENIN 8-45am Ltn M Müller Ja2]

A7679   DH4   57Sqn
BPhot **MIA(2Lt JT Orrell **KIA**/2Lt JG Glendinning
POW DoW 16.12.17) left 10-10am [?"English 2Str"
claim combat neMOORSLEDE 11-05am Ltn H
Bongartz Ja36]

A.W.FK8   10Sqn
CAP mg fire(/Lt WE Dexter **WIA)

A.W.FK8   10Sqn
CAP (/Lt SW Rowles **DoW 13.12.17)side

3rd December

A7141   Bristol F2b   20Sqn
NOP combat seen nHOLLEBEKE 12-10pm **MIA(2Lt
W Bevan **KIA**/2Lt FB Gloster **KIA**) left 11-25am

B1153   Bristol F2b   22Sqn
**OP engine failed seen going down nrYPRES 5000′
MIA(2Lt AF Goodchap **POW**/2Lt AH Middleton
POW) left 10-10am [combat BELLEWALDE LAKE?
12-20pm Untoff R Besel SS30]

4th December

The British began their withdrawal back to the
Flesquières ridge and it was completed by the 7th.

A5651   FE2b   100Sqn
** damaged by enemy bombing of OCHEY A'dr

Machines of the 41st Wing were bombed at Ochey
on the 4th and the 5th of December. There was
considerable damage, but mostly to the French
units sharing the aerodrome. Ochey had been
attacked twice in November as well, and it was
feared that an enemy campaign to halt the strategic
work was commencing. However, there were no
more attacks after these.

**B6358   Sopwith Camel   Special Defence
Sqn(RNAS)**
** attacked KB[+des] then fog lost fuel ftl crPITGAM
dam OK(FSLt JE Greene)

5th December

B6753   Nieuport 27   1Sqn
**left 8-50am seen low eMOORSLEDE 1000yd EoL

MIA(2Lt CE Ogden **POW**) ["Nieu" claim combat
sHOUTHULST WOOD 9-30am Ltn O Löffler Ja2]

Sopwith Camel   3Sqn
OP mg(Capt H Brokensha **WIA)thigh

B6234.A **Sopwith Camel   3Sqn**
COP left 10-45am **MIA(2Lt LG Nixon **POW**) a'c
captured, Ja6 [?"Sopwith" claim combat
SERANVILLERS 9-30am? Vzfw O Könnecke Ja5]

A7143   Bristol F2b   11Sqn
PhotRec left 8-50am **MIA(Sgt MH Everix **POW**/Lt H
Whitworth **POW**) [?"BF" claim combat nCAMBRAI
10-20am Vzfw Barth Ja10]

A7266   Bristol F2b   11Sqn
**PhotRec CAMBRAI combat with EA shot up dam
OK(2Lt HR Child/Lt A Reeve) left 8-45am, return a'dr
10-50am

A4317   RE8   13Sqn
**AOb combat HA shot down in flames 7000′(2Lt WK
Nunnerley **KIA**/2Lt GA Carter **DoW**) left 9-08am, pilot
jumped, observer burnt [?"RE" claim combat ATHIES
11am Vzfw Wackwitz Ja21]

A6642   SPAD 7   23Sqn
NOP seen ovYPRES 10-40am **MIA(2Lt S Kendall
WIA POW) ["SPAD" claim combat btwn COMINES-
WARNETON 10-50am Vzfw W Kampe Ja27]

A9300   DH5   32Sqn
+* combat with 2Str[+ooc] BECELAERE 8-55am
OK(Capt WRG Pearson) shared

B4916   DH5   32Sqn
+* combat with 2Str[+ooc] BECELAERE 8-55am
OK(Lt WA Tyrell) shared

Sopwith Camel   54Sqn
OP combat(2Lt HV Young **DoW 8.12.17)

The first casualty on Sopwith Camels for 54
Squadron.

DH4   55Sqn
B AA(/Lt A Sattin **WIA)

B4891.6 **SE5a   56Sqn**
+* combat with RumplerC[+des] HERMIES 12-40pm
OK(Capt JTB McCudden) first of over 30 victories in
this a'c, including 13 in December 1917

B2470   Sopwith Camel   70Sqn
**NOP AA EA? shot down in flames
seWESTROOSEBEKE(2Lt CVG Runnels-Moss **KIA**)
left 12-50pm [?"Sopwith 1Str" claim combat
MERCKEM Untoff M Schumm/Untoff Scheuchl SS26]
[?possible "SE5" claim combat WESTROOSEBEKE-
POELCAPPELLE 1-30pm Ltn E Udet Ja37]

B6428   Sopwith Camel   1 (Naval) Sqn
+* combat with AlbatrosDV[+des] VLADSLOO
eDIXMUDE 2-10pm OK(FSLt SW Rosevear Can.) first
of his 14 claims in this a'c, final total was 25

6th December

B5774   A.W.FK8   10Sqn
****AOb combat with EA shot down cr(2Lt AC Ross
DoW/Lt CWM Nosworthy DoW) both DoW 6.12.17, a'c
unsalvable**

A7250   Bristol F2b   20Sqn
****Phot combat mg shot up ftl in shelled ground cr(Sgt F
Hopper WIA/Capt RH Warden inj) observer shaken**

B1623   SPAD 7   23Sqn
****ResP left 8-42am seen neYPRES 9-25am(2Lt W
Whitaker KIA) ["SPAD" claim combat
PASSCHENDAELE 9-35am Ltn J Jacobs Ja7]**

A3642   RE8   52Sqn
****trav left 9-45am MIA(2Lt CS Read KIA/2Lt LGH
Brown KIA) from BRAY DUNES**

B6535   RE8   59Sqn
****P shot down neHAVRINCOURT WOOD(2Lt D
Parker inj/2Lt OI Norton inj) left 11-15am, broken legs:
to hospital**

B2464   Sopwith Camel   65Sqn
****SpM left 2-15pm COMINES seen going towards
HOLLEBEKE MIA(2Lt HA Dyer KIA) seen
nrBAILLEUL going towards ARMENTIÈRES 2-30pm
[?SPAD claim combat nBECELAERE 3-35pm Vzfw W
Kampe Ja27]**

4980   FE2b   100Sqn
** a'c damaged by enemy bombs on a'dr

A9279   DH5   68 (Australian) Sqn
****SpM combat with EA shot up dam OK(Lt Johnson
Aust.)**

A9544   DH5   68 (Australian) Sqn
****SpM combat shot up aileron controls shot away ftl
OK(Lt RW McKenzie)**

This was the last report of a DH5 being shot up in
France, occurring just as 68 (Australian) Squadron
were exchanging the type for SE5as. Ground patrol
work was difficult and dangerous enough without
having to carry it out in poor and unreliable
machines. The greatest change which had occurred
in the air war since the summer battles had been
the rise of low-flying attacks on infantry, as has
been described before as the making of the aeroplane into a battlefield weapon. What the RFC
needed to face, however, was that this work was
terribly wasteful of men. The many airmen lost in
this way were all highly trained, courageous, and
precious commodities. If the RFC was to maintain
its offensive policy it would have to reserve this new
strike force for use when it really mattered: during
major operations or in dire emergency.

7th December

The battle of Cambrai ended on the 7th of

December. The remaining records for 1917 show
fighting continuing in Flanders, a sector unlikely to
really quieten for the rest of the war.

RE8   12Sqn
** AA(2Lt J Sturrock WIA/)slight

B5020   RE8   13Sqn
****AP left 9-40am MIA(2Lt TW Calvert WIA POW/2Lt
AW Palmer POW) [?possible "Mart" claim combat
MERCATEL, sARRAS 10-30am Untoff Reinhold Ja24]**

RE8   15Sqn
**AP (/Lt JR Hodgkinson WIA)leg

RE8   16Sqn
** combat(/AG.2AM G Lawrence WIA)

B3559   SPAD 7   19Sqn
****NOP seen eMOORSLEDE ~10-30am combat? shot
up ftl MIA(Lt HA Yeo POW) left 9-47am [?"SPAD"
claim combat MOORSLEDE 10-55am Ltn M Müller
Ja2][?"SPAD" claim combat ZONNEBEKE 10-55am
Vzfw P Bäumer Ja2]**

B3552   SPAD 7   23Sqn
***NOP AA? going down in spin sPASSCHENDAELE
11-10am MIA(2Lt MG Gunn KIA) left 10-43am,
elevators hit?**

8th December

B5784   A.W.FK8   10Sqn
****FlRec combat with EA shot up ftl dam OK(Lt FW
Burdick/2Lt LM Fenelon)**

A7605   DH4   25Sqn
****Phot combat shot through ftl hit wires ldg cr(Capt CT
Lally MC WIA/Lt JE Cole WIA) left 11-40am**

B6365   Sopwith Camel   43Sqn
****OP left 12-10pm ldg nrARMENTIÈRES MIA but
OK(2Lt VS Parker)**

9th December

7A (Naval) Squadron became 14 (Naval)
Squadron on the 9th of December. It remained a
heavy bombing unit flying Handley Pages.

10th December

C5030   RE8   15Sqn
****Phot left 10-50am hit by Flak? MIA but OK?(Capt TS
Malcomson OK?/2Lt HTA Honeyman KIA) [? claim
INCHY 11-45am Flakzug505]**

C5032   RE8   15Sqn
****Phot left 11am MIA(Lt LH Thierry KIA/2AM RT Lee
KIA?)**

A7299   Bristol F2b   20Sqn
****NOP AA high nd cr wr(Lt JC Kirkpatrick KIA/2Lt
WTV Harmer inj) left 8-26am**

A9257   DH5   24Sqn
+* combat with AlbatrosDV[+des] sHONNECOURT

12pm OK(Lt IDR MacDonald)

This was the last DH5 claim for 24 Squadron.

12th December

N6330   Sopwith Camel   10 (Naval) Sqn
** combat with AlbatrosDs 14000' shot down ooc
nDIXMUDE 3-45pm MIA(FSLt JG Clark POW) Ja7
["Sopwith" claim combat KAYEM, DIXMUDE 3-30pm
Ltn P Billik Ja7]

13th December

         RE8   12Sqn
**AP AA(/2Lt TR Scott WIA)

B5209   Sopwith Camel   46Sqn
**COP pressure pump failed ftl nrMERVILLE 102Sq
then left MIA(Lt AL Clark POW) left 9-20am & again
4-15pm

15th December

B1651   Nieuport 23   29Sqn
**ResP left 8-45am seen gliding west nrYPRES but lost
to sight MIA(2Lt HV Caunt POW)

16th December

         RE8   9Sqn
**AOb combat(/2Lt H Keeton WIA) [?possible "RE"
claim combat nBOESINGHE 1-10pm Vzfw P Bäumer
Ja2]

17th December

A3816   RE8   69 (Australian) Sqn
**AOb combat with 6Albatros DVa[+ftl]
ovARMENTIÈRES(Lt JLM Sandy KIA/Sgt HF
Hughes KIA) to DEULEMONT-ARMENTIÈRES

Although the crew of this RE8 were killed in
combat the aircraft circled for two hours and
landed fifty miles away on the Bruay–St Pol Road
around 3pm.

18th December

The first Sopwith Camels of 71 (Australian)
Squadron reached St Omer on the 18th of
December. It was soon up to strength and moved
to its airfield at Bruay. This unit would be redesignated No.4 Squadron Australian Flying Corps on
the 19th of January.

B6824.R Nieuport 27   1Sqn
**OP left 10-45am cr ABEELE(2Lt RO Phillips WIA)

B5899   RE8   21Sqn
**AOb shot down in flames MIA(2Lt FG Flower KIA/
2Lt CW Cameron KIA) left 9-10am, a'c burnt, Ja36
["RE" claim combat nrZONNEBEKE 10-40am Ltn H
vHaebler Ja36]

B2388   Sopwith Camel   65Sqn
**OP combat with HAs CLERCKEN-QUESNOY
2-10pm MIA(2Lt RH Cowan POW) left 1-30pm, seen in
combat ovROULERS ["Camel" claim combat
KAPHOEK? (Kappelhoek?) 2-25pm Ltn H Bongartz
& Ltn H vHaebler Ja36] [?one of these 65Sq combat
wBECELAERE Vzfw P Bäumer Ja2]

B2419   Sopwith Camel   65Sqn
**OP combat with HAs CLERCKEN-QUESNOY
2-10pm MIA(2Lt DM Sage KIA) a'c salvaged, Ja26?
[?Camel claim combat nwSTADEN 2-30pm Ltn K Bolle
Ja28]["Sopwith" claim combat HOUTHULST WOOD-
DIXMUDE 2-45pm Ltn J Jacobs Ja7]

B6271   Sopwith Camel   65Sqn
**OP combat with HAs CLERCKEN-QUESNOY
2-10pm MIA(2Lt ID Cameron POW) left 1-30pm, seen
in combat ovROULERS, Ja36? [?possible "Sopwith"
claim combat nZILLEBEKE LAKE Untoff Werner
Ja26]

B9166   Sopwith Camel   65Sqn
+* combat with AlbatrosDV[+flames] & 2Str[+ooc]
ROULERS btwn 2-25pm & 2-35pm OK(2Lt JI
Gilmour) first of almost 40 Camel victories with 65Sqn
for Gilmour

B6426   Sopwith Camel   70Sqn
+* combat with 2Str[+cr] nCOMINES 12-45pm
OK(2Lt FC Gorringe) early victory of around 14 scored
with 70Sqn, several in this a'c

19th December

B3585   Nieuport 23   29Sqn
**ResP AA?(Flak108) engine failed ftl 1-45pm OK(2Lt
HR Gates) a'c abandoned

B506   SE5a   56Sqn
**DOP combat with EA[+flames] 1pm but then ooc
BOURLON WOOD MIA(Capt RA Maybery MC KIA)
left 12-20pm

N6008   DH4   5 (Naval) Sqn
**B BLANKENBERGHE cr sea MIA(FSLt SS
Richardson KIA/GL RA Furby KIA) [?combat off
BLANKENBERGHE ObFlM A Buhl 12-47pm SFS]

22nd December

B3321   A.W.FK8   8Sqn
**Phot combat with EA GOUZEAUCOURT-
HAVRINCOURT WOOD shot up ftl bad ground dam
ldg OK(Lt AM Kinnear/Lt MR Picot) left 10-20am

B3403   RE8   16Sqn
**AOb combat with 2Str shot down cr 12-05pm wr(2Lt
FE Neily KIA/2Lt LL Medlen KIA) [?possible "RE"
claim combat nrLIEVIN Untoff Marczinke/Ltn Hertel
FAb235]

         Bristol F2b   20Sqn
**OP combat(/Lt NM Sanders WIA)eye

23rd December

B5088 RE8 21Sqn
Rec flak hit, down in flames **MIA(Capt AC Youdale
MC **KIA**/2Lt JE Mott **KIA**) left 2-25pm, burnt

24th December

A7465 DH4 55Sqn
**B MANNHEIM combat engine hit shot down
SPEYER **MIA**(2Lt GF Turner **POW**/2Lt AF Castle
POW)

This was the first raid undertaken on the factories
and railways at Mannheim, made by ten DH4s.
Two machines needed to turn back.

26th December

B5898 RE8 16Sqn
**Phot combat AA 3-20pm in spin fr 6000' cr fire on
gnd(Lt EH Read **KIA**/2Lt HR Donovan **inj**)

28th December

B3555 Nieuport 17 1Sqn
OP seen ovMOORSLEDE 12-10pm flak hit? **MIA(2Lt
J Brydone **POW**)

C4801 Bristol F2b 22Sqn
**EscB seen going down ovNIEPPE FOREST 11am
MIA(Lt DG Barnet **DoW**?/2AM GL Sims) a'c found LE
HAVRE

B6734 SPAD 7 23Sqn
**OP combat with 2Str GHELUVELT-DADIZEELE
12-15pm **MIA**(Capt AE McKay **KIA**)

DH4 25Sqn
** (/AG.2AM R Ireland **WIA**)

B598 SE5a 40Sqn
+*combat with 2Str[+destr]DROCOURT-VITRY
11-20am OK(2Lt GEH McElroy Irl.) EA from
FAb(A)224, first of possibly 47 victories, at least 7 in this
a'c in the next 7 weeks

B2311 Sopwith Camel 70Sqn
+* combat with AlbatrosC[+des] ZARREN 11am
OK(2Lt GR Howsam Can.) first of 13 victories

B6447 Sopwith Camel 8 (Naval) Sqn
+* combat with AlbatrosDV[+ooc] MERICOURT
11-25am OK(FSLt WL Jordan) first victory of perhaps 4
in a week in this a'c

29th December

Sopwith Camel 3Sqn
B (2Lt DM Christie **WIA)

A8834 SPAD 7 19Sqn
+* combat with AlbatrosDV[+ooc] neHOUTHULST
WOOD 10-15am OK(Capt AD Carter Can.) Carter's
15th and last victory on a SPAD

B6780 SPAD 7 19Sqn
OP left 9-30am seen with 2EAs on tail **MIA(2Lt HE
Galer **POW**) ["SPAD" claim combat DRAAIBANK
10-20am Vzfw C Menckhoff Ja3]

Untraced Casualty in France in December 1917?

(Lt J Brent **INT) interned Holland Dec.17?

1918 THE BALANCE OF POWER ON THE GROUND AND IN THE AIR ON THE WESTERN FRONT

The year 1917 had closed gloomily for the Allies. Very significant and costly attempts to force a breakthrough on the Western Front had all failed. So many strategies had been found so ill-advised and wasteful of effort that in six months the whole character of warfare had undergone a sea change in a search for a different, less attritional approach. One prime example of this evolution was the abandonment of colossal bombardments, which had once been mandatory before an assault. The guns did their work to some extent, but they also gave full warning of an attack and so comprehensively destroyed the ground that sustained progress across it was extremely difficult. The Allied experience at Cambrai showed that the tank could be a more than adequate substitute for artillery in prising open enemy defences. Indeed the tank and that other new battlefield weapon, the ground-strafing aeroplane, were capable of changing the whole complexion of the fighting. Now however, only weeks after Cambrai, it was not the potential value of these great weapons which stood out in the minds of the battle planners. Rather, it was the ultimate and almost disastrous failure of that campaign which haunted their memories for the present. Time would be needed to learn the lessons of Cambrai.

Time, however, was a problem for the Allies. There had been such loss of life and general exhaustion of the resources of the British and French armies that their war-making capability was now in serious

difficulty. For instance, the inability to make good the losses of 1917 meant that the establishment of the British infantry was reduced by twenty-five per cent in February, namely from twelve to nine battalions in each division. At the same time, dwindling French forces meant that the British front line needed now to be extended south of the Somme, as far as the river Oise.

Through the winter of 1917-1918 the Allied Command had become ever more certain that there would be a very major German offensive in the spring. Germany was regrouping and massing its fighting strength, bolstered by men, guns, and aircraft from the concluded Russian campaign, and to some extent benefiting from an eased situation in Italy as well. Between October 1917 and March 1918 over a million troops were transported back from the Eastern Front.

The German Air Force had also been greatly fostered and expanded, so that as the year turned it was fully on course for doubling the size of its fighter strength in eight months. Favoured status for the allocation of raw materials had enabled the aircraft manufacturers to reach a pitch of production, whilst training had also kept pace with developments. Although for the present the Allies held the balance of air supremacy, a great amount was expected of the German Air Force in the coming months, for it had never been stronger. The final great incentive for a decisive German offensive early in the year, in fact hugely important to the plans of both sides, was the imminent arrival of many thousands of American troops into the fighting. Germany would have an infinitely greater chance of victory before America became a full participant.

Faced with these factors, all centred on the strong expectation of a huge attack on their depleted forces, the Allies knew the only viable policy for the early months of 1918 would be a defensive one. Haig began his pleadings to London for the troops he believed he needed, but the politicians were extremely wary after the waste of 1917 and promised only moderate reinforcements. The immediate objectives would have to be the building up and training of what armies could be assembled, and most importantly, to ascertain when and where the attack would come. The contribution of the RFC and RNAS was therefore considerable, for it was their intelligence gathering which would provide the first evidence of German intentions. As the offensive approached they would then have the vital task of attacking and bombing the distribution network behind the lines, the disruption of which would be essential. The final task for the RFC before the offensive began would be to maintain its offensive challenge to the German Air Force for possession of the skies.

For the British armies, one great asset they assuredly posessed was the Royal Flying Corps, growing to a new maturity in terms of both its size and the scope of its operations. Re-emerging from the desperate days of "Bloody April", in fighters such as the Sopwith Camel and the SE5a, and two-seaters like the Bristol Fighter and the DH4, its squadrons had slowly reasserted Allied air dominance. Their fighter opponents were now mostly flying the elegant and agile Pfalz DIII or the latest variant of the Albatros, the DV. The latter was a development of the very successful DIII, with a bigger engine and other changes, but its extra weight somewhat offset these improvements. Some very notable German pilots were also flying the Fokker DrI triplane. Its inspiration, no doubt, was the Sopwith Triplane but its design incorporated some highly sophisticated concepts. Its wing area and compactness gave it a remarkable rate of climb and outstanding manoeuvrability so that it was extremely useful in dogfighting. For all its fame, however, its operational use was to be quite limited.

The opposing air arms were both on a course of rapid development, but the RFC was able to maintain its air superiority because in several ways its machines were given the edge. A reorganised and more well-informed operational structure certainly contributed to its effectiveness. At a time when the RFC had needed to develop quite radical changes in its tactics in 1917, such as the growth of massed dogfights and low-flying attacks in support of the ground forces, it had been essential to have the organisation in place to co-ordinate it. Increased emphasis on careful and thorough training, which stressed standardisation of technical matters as much as the development of flying and fighting skills, was also helping the RFC develop its mettle.

The British had also been able to call on increasing numbers of air crew and aircraft as training and production at home continually expanded. This, coupled with great aircraft, would finally decide the air war as Germany was numerically and tactically overwhelmed in the autumn. The proven fighters and two-seaters were, in effect, in mass production, whilst development programmes for new types were beginning to deliver the next generation of specialist machines to units on the front line. One notable example was the Sopwith Dolphin.

The RFC would now have to meet new challenges, however, for just as it had mastered the skills and tactics associated with attack in 1917, it would have to adapt once again. It was destined, as always, to

maintain its air offensive, but it would also have to develop ways of supporting an army which was, for the present, completely committed to defence.

Virtually all discussion related to ground offensives had died down to a whisper after Cambrai. Instead, attention turned to understanding and perfecting methods of defence. The first lesson to come from the soul searching about Cambrai was that the British tactics of elastic defence, copied from the Germans, would need to be better learnt and executed. Elastic defence relied on the presence of very strong points along an otherwise thinly held line which could support one another and provide the basis of quick and significant reinforcements to points of attack as needed. At Cambrai the conditions had permitted the Germans to make surprise attacks which could not be repulsed before the gaps formed became critical. Training would therefore concentrate on minimising surprise, and aircraft would naturally play a very important part in this.

The "Memorandum on Defensive Measures", issued on the 14th of December 1917 by General Head-quarters, set out the principles by which the enemy must be held when the attack came. As the terms it used will be met with again they are summarised here. There were to be three zones of defence in depth, each with its system of trenches, strong-points and emplacements. The "Forward Zone" was effectively the front line which would take the initial assault. Behind this was the "Battle Zone" which was a well prepared and, it was hoped, advantageous area for fighting, up to two miles deep, and then behind this, was the "Rear Zone", between four and eight miles further back, defining the ultimate fall-back position.

January 1918

1st January

	RE8	7Sqn

AOb (2Lt GA Williamson **DoW)

C5332	SE5a	60Sqn

+* combat with 2Str[+ooc] wROULERS 10-50am OK(Lt FO Soden Can.) made 17 victory claims with 60Sqn in total of 27

B665	SE5a	40Sqn

+* combat DFWC[+shot down captured] ovFAMPOUX 11-35am OK(Capt EC Mannock) EA from FAb(A)288

This was Mannock's last victory with 40 Squadron and his first in a SE5a. It was shared with the two 8 (Naval) pilots noted below.

B2513	Sopwith Camel	46Sqn

COP left 2-20pm seen eHAVRINCOURT going north **MIA(2Lt AL Kidd **POW**)

B6321	Sopwith Camel	8 (Naval) Sqn

+* combat with HannoverC[+des] ovFAMPOUX 11-38am OK(FSLt GK Cooper) shared

B6340	Sopwith Camel	8 (Naval) Sqn

+* combat with HannoverC[+des] ovFAMPOUX 11-38am OK(FCdr RJO Compston) shared

3rd January

B9131	Sopwith Camel	3Sqn

LowB seen nwMARCOING 1000' EoL **MIA(2Lt ES Davenport **KIA**) left 7-10am, Ja30?

	Sopwith Camel	3Sqn

B (Lt RSS Brown **WIA)

C3521	A.W.FK8	10Sqn

**AOb BECELAERE combat with 5EA shot up 3-15pm

ldg ok(2Lt AB Cochrane OK/2Lt VC Baker **WIA**)

B2087	DH4	27Sqn

**B MARIA AELTRE combat with EA shot up dam returned a'dr OK(2Lt WJ Henney/Lt PS Driver)

	SE5a	29Sqn

OP combat(2Lt CD Skinner **WIA)

B2516	Sopwith Camel	46Sqn

COP dive on EA combat then spin ovMETZ-EN-COUTURE 11-30am(2Lt RLM Ferrie MC **KIA)

	Bristol F2b	48Sqn

** combat(/2Lt L Lambe **WIA**)

B9143	Sopwith Camel	54Sqn

+* combat with DFWC[+flames] eST QUENTIN 8-25am OK(Capt HH Maddocks) claimed several other victories

This was the first Sopwith Camel victory for 54 Squadron.

C1753	SE5a	56Sqn

DOP left 10am seen ftl near enemy EoL(2Lt RJG Stewart **WIA POW) Ja35 ["Camel" claim combat wLE CATELET 11-10am Lt L Hanstein Ja35]

A7687	DH4	57Sqn

Phot left 10-50am down EoL **MIA(Capt AFE Pitman **KIA**/Lt CW Pearson **KIA**) Ja26 [?"Bristol" claim combat swGHELUVELT 12-30pm Oblt B Loerzer Ja26]

B539	SE5a	84Sqn

+* combat with 2Str[+ooc] neST QUENTIN OK(2Lt AW Beauchamp-Proctor SA.)

This was the first of fifty-four victories for this most notable British ace. His first five were made in this aircraft through January and February.

B6447	Sopwith Camel	8 (Naval) Sqn

+* combat with HannoverC[+cr destr] ovARRAS 10-05am OK(FSLt PM Dennett) EA cr wARRAS, shared

B5658   Sopwith Camel   10 (Naval) Sqn
**HOP combat with EA wLILLE seen 1-50pm
MIA(FSLt F Booth **KIA**) [?"Camel" claim combat
sARMENTIÈRES but 11-35am? Vzfw O Fruhner
Ja26][?"Camel" claim combat MEURCHIN Untoff
Liebert Ja30]

N6351   Sopwith Camel   10 (Naval) Sqn
**HOP combat with AlbatrosDs wLILLE seen shot down
1-50pm **MIA**(FSLt AG Beattie **POW**) in pm, Ja30
["Sopwith" claim combat PROVIN, BILLY-BERCLAU
1-50pm Vzfw H Oberländer Ja30]

4th January

B2074   DH4   27Sqn
**B combat with EA 13000' AA engine ftl EoL possibly
gliding down? swDENAIN **MIA**(2Lt KP Ewart **KIA**/Lt
AN Westlake MC **KIA**) left 9-50am

A7424   DH4   57Sqn
Phot left 11-45am **MIA(Capt EEE Pope **POW**/Lt AF
Wynne **POW**) [?possible unconfirmed "DH" claim
combat NEUVILLE 12-50pm Ltn O Fruhner Ja26]

C5334   SE5a   60Sqn
**OP dive on EA then air collision ovMENIN EoL cr
MIA(Capt FHB Selous MC **KIA**) 11-45am, other source
gives: broke up in dive on EA 1.5m eMENIN [?"SE" claim
combat GHELUVELT 11-45am Ltn Papenmeyer Ja2]

B2413   Sopwith Camel   65Sqn
**ResP left 9-45am combat with HA 10-45am
DADIZEELE **MIA**(2Lt RE Robb **KIA**) [?possible claim
combat ROLLEGHEM 10-45am Vzfw W Kampe Ja27]

B5612   Sopwith Camel   65Sqn
+* combat with large 2Str[flames] sROULERS 10-40am
then AlbatrosDVs[+ooc+des] sROULERS-
sGHELUVELT btwn 11am & 11-10am OK(Capt JI
Gilmour)

A2971   BE2e   100Sqn
**NB MEZIÈRES low fuel saw EA ftl in snow cr
nrCOLOMBEY 10-45pm OK(Capt HTO Windsor) left
7-30pm

B6278   Sopwith Camel   8 (Naval) Sqn
**SpM combat with DFWC[+cr] NEUVIREUIL-OPPY
but shot down EoL ooc 10-30am **MIA**(FSLt AJ Dixon
KIA) shared victory, Ja30?

5th January

               RE8   13Sqn
AP mg fire(2Lt S Grossberg **WIA)

6th January

               Bristol F2b   11Sqn
DOP combat(2Lt NE Gwyer **WIA/2Lt EH Church
WIA) crew? both WIA?

A4300   RE8   16Sqn
**AP mg fire 8am then combat ovMERICOURT engine
cut ftl cr wr(2Lt GW Ferguson **WIA**/Lt FW Howitt OK)
left 7-40am

A7706   DH4   27Sqn
**B CAMBRAI ftl nrAMES bombs exploded on ldg
flames wr(2Lt GR Vickers **KIA**/Lt GE Rodmell **inj**)

               SE5a   29Sqn
ResP combat(Capt RH Rusby **WIA) made 10 claims
with 29Sqn

B633   SE5a   41Sqn
**DOP DOUAI shrapnel hit engine failed ftl cr
nrLAVENTIE OK(2Lt AS Hemming)

B4885   SE5a   60Sqn
OP left 12-10pm for YPRES ftl BRIELLE **MIA(2Lt O
Thamer **INT**) interned Holland

8th January

The RNAS Handley Page bomber unit "A"
Squadron was redesignated 16 (Naval) Squadron
on the 8th of January. It continued to carry out deep
strategic bombing with 41st Wing.

9th January

The Sopwith Camel fighter unit 73 Squadron
arrived in France on the 9th of January.

B3607   Nieuport 24   1Sqn
ResP left 9-58am seen in formation 10-25am **MIA(Lt
EK Skelton **KIA**)

B6768   Nieuport 27   1Sqn
ResP last seen in formation 10-25am **MIA(Lt RC
Southam **KIA**)

B6830   Nieuport 27   1Sqn
+*ResP combat with 2DFWC[+ooc] GAPAARD-
COMINES 9000' 10-25am then gun stoppage OK(Capt
WD Patrick) made 4 of his 7 claims on this type

This was the last Nieuport Scout victory for 1
Squadron.

C4816   Bristol F2b   48Sqn
**Phot combat with EA 11-45am wings shot away, fell ooc
eESTRÉES(Capt AW Field **KIA**/2Lt WS Smith **KIA**) left
10-45am CAMBRAI-ST QUENTIN ["Bristol" claim
combat NAUROY Vzfw Meinke/Untoff K Ungewitter
SS5]

10th January

The FE2b night bombing unit 58 Squadron arrived
in France on the 10th of January.

B9163   Sopwith Camel   3Sqn
**LowP last seen 2500' 1m wMARCOING going east
MIA(2Lt CW Leggatt **POW**) left 7-30am

A3655   RE8   5Sqn
**AReg British AA hit 12-15pm ftl cr(2Lt HPJG Hamel
KIA/2Lt LCS Tatham **KIA**)

12th January

B5023   RE8   12Sqn
**Rec mg engine hit 800' ftl cr OK(Lt Harman/Lt

Steele)shelled

B283   A.W.FK8   35Sqn
AP shot down ftl in control? Sh62B G.28b.1.7. **MIA(2Lt
TA Urwin **POW DoW** 15.1.18/2Lt JH Young **POW
DoW**) Ja35 ["AW" claim combat sNAUROY 11-50am
Ltn L Hanstein Ja35]

B2354   Sopwith Camel   43Sqn
OP left 3pm **MIA(Lt J Boyd **POW**) [?possible
unconfirmed "Camel" claim combat BEAUMONT
3-30pm Ltn H Stutz Ja20]

3140   H.P. 0/100   16 (Naval) Sqn
"BLUE BIRD"? * noted shot down by French nrNANCY
OK, but error?: a'c cr wr 17.2.18

13th January

B5602   Sopwith Camel   71 (Australian) Sqn
**OP combat with 2 AlbatrosDVs 5m eLA BASSÉE
11-40am shot down in dive spin **MIA**(2Lt FB Willmott
POW) lagging behind, cut off by 3 EA Scouts, Ja29
["Camel" claim combat LIBERCOURT 11-50am Ltn G
Schuster Ja29]

Willmott was 71 (Australian) Squadron's first
combat casualty, and was incidentally shot down
during the unit's first air fight.

B5826   A.W.FK8   8Sqn
**Phot combat with EA shot down ovBANTOUZELLE
WoL 11am(Lt FH Hall **WIA**/Lt AS Balfour **KIA**)to
hospital [?"Bristol" claim combat GONNELIEU-
HONNECOURT 12-28pm Ltn Schlömer Ja5]

A7174.F Bristol F2b   11Sqn
DOP DOUAI seen going east smoking **MIA(2Lt HV
Biddington **POW**/2Lt JH Corbet **KIA**) left 9-50am ["BF"
claim combat sBEAUMONT 11-30am Ltn F Rumey Ja5]

DH4   25Sqn
** (/2Lt JH Haughan **WIA**) also frostbite

SE5a   41Sqn
COP (Capt RW Chappell SA. **WIA)face

C5329.G SE5a   84Sqn
**OP seen with patrol neST QUENTIN 11-30am shot
down AA cr wr **MIA**(2Lt HE Davies **POW**) left 10-35am,
a'c captured

14th January

6 (Naval) Squadron arrived at Petite Synthe
Dunkirk as a day-bomber unit on the 14th of
January. It had been reformed at Dover at the end of
1917 from personnel of the Walmer Defence Flight
and No.11 Squadron RNAS. It would fly DH9s but
its first raid did not take place until the 9th of March,
when training had been completed. On this day 17
(Naval) Squadron was also formed to replace the
Seaplane Base at Dunkirk. This was part of the
ongoing process to replace the seaplanes

here with land-based machines. Its work became
mostly anti-submarine patrolling and bombing.

15th January

The Seaplane Defence Squadron based at St Pol
became 13 (Naval) Squadron on the 15th of
January.

18th January

B273   A.W.FK8   2Sqn
**AReg combat with EA wHULLUCH shot down G.23
10-25am cr fire(2Lt WK Fenn-Smith **KIA**/2Lt NL
Cornforth **KIA**) ["AW" claim combat LOOS 10-45am
Vzfw U Neckel Ja12]

Sopwith Camel   54Sqn
** (2Lt WG Ivamy **WIA**)

B4629   Sopwith Camel   65Sqn
**OP combat with 5HA 10-30am WESTROOSEBEKE
down ooc cr **MIA**(2Lt AE Wylie **KIA**) [?"Sopwith" claim
combat nPASSCHENDAELE 10-20am Ltn K Gallwitz
Ja2]

19th January

68, 69, and 71 (Australian) Squadrons were
redesignated Nos. 2, 3, and 4 Squadrons, Australian
Flying Corps on the 19th of January.

RE8   16Sqn
** mg(/Lt FD Howitt **WIA**)

A7193   Bristol F2b   20Sqn
**P left 10-16am ROULERS seen nrWYTSCHAETE
MIA(2Lt B Starfield **KIA**/Lt A Hutchinson **KIA**)

B6208   Sopwith Camel   43Sqn
**OP combat with EA 10-55am shot down VITRY snd
ooc **MIA**(2Lt CN Madeley **KIA**) [?possible "Camel"
claim combat BIACHE Ltn Koch Ja12]

B5423.6 Sopwith Camel   54Sqn
OP seen 6000' RAMICOURT 9-15/9-30am **MIA(2Lt
FM? Ohrt **POW**) initials AM?

SE5a   56Sqn
DOP (2Lt EHM Fetch **WIA)

DH4   57Sqn
Phot (Capt FD Grant **WIA)

B2468   Sopwith Camel   65Sqn
**P combat with EAs WESTROOSEBEKE-STADEN
chased down by 2 Albatros, seen spin but flatten out? mist
MIA(2Lt ET Baker **KIA**) 5 Camels vs 17EA [?"English
EA" claim combat sHOUTHULST WOOD 1-45pm Ltn
K Gallwitz Ja2]

B6369   Sopwith Camel   8 (Naval) Sqn
+* combat with AlbatrosDV[+ooc] WINGLES 11-25am
OK(FSLt WL Jordan) shared

** (Capt Biheller? **POW**)

20th January

B3313   A.W.FK8   35Sqn
Phot combat with EA ftl 12pm(2Lt R Buchanan **WIA/
Lt TG Mather **OK**)WIA arm, to hospital [?possible
"RE" claim combat sDRAAIBANK 12-05pm Vzfw C
Menckhoff Ja72, but this claim on 22.1.18?]

21st January

A5695   FE2b   100Sqn
NB left 8-40pm **MIA(2Lt AH Peile **POW**/Lt CW Reid
POW)

22nd January

80 Squadron arrived in France on the 22nd of
January. It was equipped with Sopwith Camels
and was destined to spend much of its operational
life carrying out the dangerous tasks of strafing and
low bombing. As a headquarters unit it was constantly moved about the front, taking part in nearly
every great battle of 1918. For this it paid dearly
in casualties.

C4825   Bristol F2b   20Sqn
OP ST JULIEN seen 11-10am **MIA(2Lt AR Paul
POW DoW/2AM A Mann **POW DoW**?) left 10-30am,
pilot DoW in transit ["Bristol" claim combat
OOSTNIEUKERKE 11-05am Ltn K Gallwitz
Ja2]["Bristol" claim combat ST JULIEN 11-05am Oblt
T Cammann Ja2]

B6426   Sopwith Camel   70Sqn
BOP left 12-20pm last seen MENIN **MIA(2Lt FW
Dogherty **POW**) ["Sopwith" claim combat COUCOU,
WERVICQ 12-55pm Ltn O Fruhner Ja26]

N6370   Sopwith Camel   9 (Naval) Sqn
** AA hit? ftl cr nrHOUTHULST WOOD(FSLt JE
Beveridge **WIA**)

23rd January

B2463   Sopwith Camel   43Sqn
**OP controls shot away 2-05pm LAVENTIE ftl cr
OK(Capt JN Metcalf)

B7184   Sopwith Camel   3 (Naval) Sqn
** seen going west ovZARREN 2pm then combat with
EAs shot down **MIA**(FSLt HStJE Youens **POW**) combat
with 4 DFWs then 3 other EA [possible combat
nrSTADEN Ja36?]

B5663   Sopwith Camel   10 (Naval) Sqn
** combat with 9EA ~2-50pm then air collision with
Albatros fell ooc locked together cr nrSTADEN
MIA(FSLt RA Blyth **KIA**) Ja36? [2"Camel" claims
nrSTADEN Ltn Wandelt Ja36]

24th January

B6774   Nieuport 27   1Sqn
*engine test broke up north of a'dr 12-25pm wr(Capt HG
Reeves **KIFA**) Reeves had claimed 4 of his 13 victories
in this a'c in 1917

B2527   Sopwith Camel   4Sqn AFC
+* combat with DFWC[+des] nLA BASSÉE 12-27pm
OK(Capt AH O'Hara-Wood)

This was the first combat victory for No.4
Squadron AFC.

A7912   DH4   57Sqn
B HARLEBEKE down EoL **MIA(Lt JO Beattie **KIA**/
1AM WJ Belchamber **POW**?) left 11-50am, St Catherine's
Register gives Pte WJ Belchamber died 1919 [?"DH"
claim combat nCOURTRAI 1-20pm Ltn Lotz Ja7]

B4897   SE5a   60Sqn
**OP air collision with EA 12-10pm swBECELAERE
EoL 12000' cr **MIA**(Lt AW Morey **KIA**) [SE? claim
combat BECELAERE 12-50pm Ltn Moebius Ja7]

A852   FE2b   100Sqn
**NB left 5-30pm TREVES AA hit rudder controls then
fouled by balloon barrage ESCHE, LUXEMBURG ftl
EoL **MIA**(Lt LG Taylor **POW**/Lt FE LeFevre MC
POW) AA hit near Central Station

N5985   DH4   2 (Naval) Sqn
** shrapnel hit fuel tank ftl LA PANNE OK

B6321   Sopwith Camel   8 (Naval) Sqn
+* combat with AlbatrosDV[+des] FRESNES-VITRY
11-40am OK(FSlt JB White Can.) first of 12 claims

25th January

B883   Bristol F2b   20Sqn
OP combat AA? ftl **MIA(Sgt HO Smith **WIA POW**/
2Lt HS Clemons **WIA POW**) left 11-40am [?claim combat
COURTEMARCK 12-15pm Ltn C Degelow Ja7]

B2085   DH4   27Sqn
**B ROULERS AA combat with 9EA ftl HOUPLINES
2000yd WoL dam OK(2Lt DTC Rundle-Woolcock/2Lt
JH Holland)

B6348   Sopwith Camel   12 (Naval) Sqn
** shot down EoL seDIXMUDE ~2.15pm flames
MIA(FSLt JHT Carr **POW**)

N6363   Sopwith Camel   13 (Naval) Sqn
+* combat with Fokker DrI[+ooc] STADEN 3-25pm
OK(FCdr MJG Day)

This was the first combat victory for 13 (Naval)
Squadron.

28th January

B5089   RE8   5Sqn
**Phot combat with 2EA ftl 11-30am(Lt JPB Harold
WIA/2Lt FM Woolner **WIA**)

A7288.7   Bristol F2b   11Sqn
COP shot down EoL **MIA(2Lt S Reay **KIA**/2AM A
Paterson **KIA**) left 10-05am CAMBRAI, pilot jumped,
Ja5 [2 "Bristol" claims combat GRAINCOURT &
BOURLON WOOD 11-15am Vzfw F Rumey & OffSt J
Mai Ja5]

B1189   Bristol F2b   11Sqn
COP CAMBRAI **MIA(2Lt JM Milne-Henderson **KIA**/

2Lt EA Cunningham **KIA**) left 10-05am, Ja5 [?"Bristol" claim combat GRAINCOURT 11-15am Vzfw F Rumey Ja5]

B2066   DH4   18Sqn
**Phot AA combat with 2str ovCARVIN engine ftl 4Sqn 12-30pm OK(Lt Ritch/Capt Roberts) left 10-20am First Army front

B6836   Nieuport 27   29Sqn
+* combat with AlbatrosDV[+ooc] sROULERS 12-20pm OK(Lt JG Coombe) made 8 claims

          Sopwith Camel   54Sqn
** (2Lt DF Lawson **WIA**)

B610   SE5a   56Sqn
DOP dive on EA ovBOURLON WOOD 2pm wr **MIA(Lt LJ Williams **POW**) [?unconfirmed "SE5" claim nCAMBRAI]

29th January

62 Squadron flew to France on the 29th of January. They were equipped with Bristol Fighters and made their first patrol, against kite balloons, on the 17th of February.

B5427   Sopwith Camel   3Sqn
COP dive on 2Str seen break up ovBOURLON WOOD cr Sh57C E.11.D. **MIA(2Lt CL Van-der-Hoff **KIA**) left 11am

B1593   SPAD 7   19Sqn
this a'c?: +* combat with AlbatrosDVs[++ooc] HOUTHULST WOOD 7am OK(Capt P Huskinson MC) made several claims on SPADs and Dolphins

This was the last combat victory in a SPAD 7 for 19 Squadron before the unit re-equipped with the Sopwith Dolphin fighter.

A7600   DH4   25Sqn
Phot **MIA(Capt AG Whitehead **KIA**/Lt WJ Borthistle **KIA**) left 9-05am ["Bristol" claim combat ST QUENTIN 11-10am Vzfw F Rumey Ja5]

A9233   DH5   32Sqn
+* combat with AlbatrosDV[+des] STADEN 3-25pm OK(2Lt CJ Howson)

This was the last DH5 victory for 32 Squadron, the last likely claim having been on 5.12.17

          Sopwith Camel   46Sqn
** (2Lt PWS Bulman **WIA**)

B3890   Sopwith Camel   70Sqn
ResP combat with 10EA MOORSLEDE-ROULERS 3-30pm in dive 1500' chased down by EA **MIA(Lt KM Rodger **WIA POW**) left 2-10pm [?claim combat ePOELCAPPELLE 3-10pm Ltn K Bolle Ja28]

B3909   Sopwith Camel   13 (Naval) Sqn
+* combat with enemy seaplane[+des] off BLANKENBERGHE PIER 2pm OK(FSLt JE Greene Can.)

30th January

C4832   Bristol F2b   22Sqn
OP combat shot down in flames Sh36 M.6.d wr(2Lt GG Johnstone **KIA/Dvr RA Duff **DoI**) [?possible "Camel" claim combat NEUVE CHAPELLE 11-45am Oblt H Auffahrt Ja29]

          DH4   25Sqn
** (/AG.2AM CN Harvey **KIA**) KIA?

B6401   Sopwith Camel   3 (Naval) Sqn
fan pattern on tail +* combat with AlbatrosDV[++ooc] GHELUVELT 10-45am OK(FCdr LH Rochford) shared

N5982   DH4   5 (Naval) Sqn
** OOSTCAMP shot down EoL **MIA**(FSLt FTP Williams **KIA**/GL CA Leitch **KIA**) [? claim combat eWILSKERKE 1-20pm Ltn K Bolle Ja2]

31st January

          Sopwith Camel   65Sqn
** (Lt D Shanks **WIA**)

February 1918

The approaching crisis for the Allies quickened through February and March. Poor weather in January had hindered air reconnaissance, but as February opened, the huge extent of the German build-up was becoming clear. At first there was uncertainty about where the attack would be concentrated, but in time, reports confirmed that it would be focused on the British Third and Fifth Armies to the south, opposite the Cambrai salient, with Amiens as their objective. Local German activity had become quite intense, with the construction of new aerodromes, dumps, sidings and encampments. Amiens was a vital railway junction, upon which an enormous amount of supply to the entire British line depended, and to force a breach here would also divide the British and French forces.

The British High Command formed the view that upon such a massed attack, so long as major losses could be contained within that area, their armies could afford to give ground in front of Amiens. There was room to manoeuvre, and the German Army would need to press deep before reaching valuable objectives. It was also hoped that by the tactical surrender of some ground, the advance might be held, even if by the slimmest of margins, without the need for large reinforcements from the north. There lay the enemy's greatest goals — the Channel ports. Haig knew that he must leave his main strength and reserves in front of these. The forces before Amiens would have to fight more or less as they stood, and as the Official

History states, "only by the thinnest of margins was disaster averted".

2nd February

The grouping of the German Jagdstaffeln into the larger operational unit of Jagdgeschwader I had proved a success, and on the 2nd of February, two more were created. These were JG2 (Jastas 12, 13, 15, and 19) under the command of Hptm Adolf Ritt. von Tutschek, and JG3 (Jastas 26, 27, 36, and Jagdstaffel Boelcke) under Hptm Bruno Loerzer.

B8273   SE5a   41Sqn
DOP combat with 3HA 6000′ AUBERCHICOURT 2-45pm shot down **MIA(Maj FJ? Powell MC **WIA POW**) initials JF?, left 1-30pm ["SE5" claim combat BOUCHAIN 2-30pm Lt Kühn Ja10]

B5436   Sopwith Camel   54Sqn
WTInt combat with EA engine ftl VERMAND dam(2Lt G Russell **inj)to hospital, left 9-48am

3rd February

**   RE8   12Sqn**
** (/2Lt JOM Turnbull **WIA**)

A7873   DH4   25Sqn
B MELLE Rlwy Sdgs **MIA(Lt EG Green MC **POW**/ Lt PC Campbell-Martin **POW**) left 7-40am ["DH" claim combat MARIAKERKE, GHENT 9-40am Ltn O Löffler Ja2]

B38   SE5a   41Sqn
** combat with AlbatrosC[+ooc] nwDOUAI 10-10am OK(Capt LJ MacLean) shared

B60   SE5a   41Sqn
** combat with AlbatrosC[+ooc] nwDOUAI 10-10am(2Lt GA Lipsett **WIA**) shared

B471   FE2b   58Sqn
NB fog ftl DROGLANDT cr ldg(2Lt RK Fletcher OK/ 2Lt H Kearley **KIA) left 3-40am, misjudged flare height as flares were on poles so overshot ldg

This was the first death on active duty for 58 Squadron.

B2419   Sopwith Camel   65Sqn
**OP combat with Albatros[+ooc]swROULERS shot up dam OK(2Lt GM Knocker)

B6377   Sopwith Camel   8 (Naval) Sqn
+* combat with DFWC[+des] SALLAUMINES 12-25pm OK(FSLt EG Johnstone) shared, pilot made several victories in this a'c

B6430   Sopwith Camel   9 (Naval) Sqn
** combat with Fokker DrI[+des] 2m seROULERS 2pm then shot down EoL folded? **MIA**(AFCdr RR Winter **KIA**) shared [?"Sopwith" claim combat SLEYHAGE 3-15pm Vzfw O Fruhner Ja26] Winter claimed 5EAs

B6204   Sopwith Camel   10(Naval)Sqn
"ALLO! LIL BIRD" +* combat with AlbatrosDV[+seen

cr] swRUMBEKE A'dr 3-15pm OK(FLt WGR Hinchliffe)

B6370   Sopwith Camel   10(Naval)Sqn
** combat ovRUMBEKE a'dr 12000′ shot down swRUMBEKE 3-15pm **MIA**(FSLt WH Wilmot **KIA**) [?3 "Camel" claims combat eLANGEMARCK 3pm-WESTROOSEBEKE 3-15pm OffSt O Esswein Ja26]["Camel" claim combat SLEIGHEN? (SLEIJHAGE?) 3-15pm Vzfw O Fruhner Ja26]

4th February

A7798   DH4   18Sqn
**B combat SSDIIIs[++ooc] ovMESSINES 11-15am OK(2Lt AC Atkey Can./Lt CRH Ffolliott)

These two Siemen Schuckert fighters were the first of thirty-eight victory claims on two-seaters by this high scoring pilot — most were to be achieved on Bristol Fighters with 22 Squadron.

**   Bristol F2b   20Sqn**
** (2Lt FD Miller **KIA**)

**   Sopwith Camel   54Sqn**
** (2Lt P Barker **WIA**)

B474   FE2b   58Sqn
NB left 5-25pm **MIA(2Lt A Holmes **KIA**/2Lt PAB Lytton **KIA**)

5th February

A7255   Bristol F2b   20Sqn
**OP mg shot up engine COMBEKE ftl cr wr OK(Lt DG Campbell/2Lt WH Nash)

A7680   DH4   25Sqn
B combat with 15EA DEYNZE gliding down but lost in clouds **MIA(2Lt EO Cudmore **POW**/1AM LJW Bain **POW**?) left 1pm, Ja36 [2 "DH4" claims combat THIELT 2-40pm Ltn H Bongartz Ja36]

A7865   DH4   25Sqn
B combat with 15EA DEYNZE in flames **MIA(2Lt RP Pohlmann **KIA**/2AM R Ireland **KIA**?) left 1pm, Ja36 [2 "DH4" claims combat OUDENBURG 2-43pm Ltn H Bongartz Ja36]

**   DH4   25Sqn**
** (/AG.Sgt Hupper **WIA**)

B6466   RE8   53Sqn
Phot shot up ground mg fire 11-10am at Sh28J.15.c. cr(2Lt FA Lewis US. **KIA/Lt TMcK Hughes **KIA**) unsalvable

B533   SE5a   60Sqn
OP left 10-40am AA HOUTHULST 11-30am ftl **MIA(2Lt AC Ball **POW**) [?"Sopwith" claim combat eSTADEN 11-25am OffSt O Esswein Ja26]

B2394   Sopwith Camel   65Sqn
OP shot up ROULERS 1-30pm ftl cr shell hole(2Lt HVC Luyt **WIA)head [?"Sopwith 1Str" claim combat 1-35pm Ltn H Dilthey Ja27]

B3832   Sopwith Camel   8(Naval)Sqn
+* combat with AlbatrosDV[+des] sPONT À VENDIN
12-45pm OK(FSLt HHS Fowler Can.) first of 6 claims

N6379   Sopwith Camel   8(Naval)Sqn
OP dive on EA broke up Sh36c.O.2 12-45pm **MIA
(FSLt H Day DSC **KIA**) left 11-45am, Ja29 ["Sopwith"
claim combat nwANNAY 12-45pm Ltn G Schuster Ja29]

6th February

C1552   Sopwith Camel   3Sqn
**COP left 3-05pm seen REMY then shot down in flames
MIA(2Lt PF Kent **KIA**)

C6706   Sopwith Camel   3Sqn
COP left 3-05pm seen in combat ovREMY **MIA(2Lt
AGD Alderson **POW**) ["Camel" claim combat REMY
4pm? Ltn H Becker Ja12]

8th February

9 (Naval) Squadron returned to England on the 8th
of February to be rested. It would return to
Dunkirk on the 20th of March but then hurried
onto the Western Front to work with the RFC.

9th February

A3766   RE8   12Sqn
**LRec combat with 6EA 6200' ovSh51B. shot up on
return OK(2Lt Harman/Lt Wood)

B5417.11 Sopwith Camel   54Sqn
WTInt left 9-35am seen EoL SISSY 800' **MIA(2Lt
GAC Manley **POW**) a'c captured

B439   FE2b   100Sqn
NB COURCELLES engine failed ftl EoL **MIA(2Lt OB
Swart **POW**/2Lt A Fielding-Clarke **POW**) left 5-51pm

12th February

DH4   55Sqn
B (Lt WB Andrew **KIA/2Lt FG Todd **KIA**) both KIA?

13th February

RE8   52Sqn
DawnRec (Capt HHW Bean **WIA)knee

14th February

B1254   Bristol F2b   48Sqn
*SpRec flak seen low going eST QUENTIN **MIA**(Capt
SJ Sibley **POW**/Lt OGS Crawford **POW**) left 10-05am

16th February
THE ALLIED BOMBING
OFFENSIVE

Through late February and early March Germany
continued to restrict its air activity so as to conceal
everything possible about its concentrations.
Bombing of their aerodromes therefore became one
of the main offensives which could be carried out

against the enemy air force before the battle opened,
and this programme began in earnest in early
March. The railway network and other centres
where troops and equipment were massing were also
targets. All of these destinations were very well
defended by anti-aircraft batteries, and the bombing, which took place around the clock if possible,
attracted many casualties. In order to gain the
greatest benefit from these operations, squadrons
were advised to concentrate their attacks, and quite
often would be ordered to return day after day to the
same location, as long as the weather permitted.
Squadrons were also given alternative targets to
ensure some flexibility. The problem they faced,
however, was that there were so many targets available, spread over a very large area, which was bound
to lead to some lessening of its impact.

The same bombing crews added reconnaissance
to their tasks, and for the first time this also
included a programme of night reconnaissance,
particularly of the rail system. The usefulness of
this work is obvious when one remembers that the
great majority of troop movements prior to the
offensive were done under cover of darkness. The
huge German army assembled for the Ludendorff
Offensive was, nevertheless, moved up largely
covertly and its size and strength were barely
anticipated. Germany was also operating a bombing programme at this time to hinder Allied reconnaissance making. This was most intense on the
Croisilles-Havrincourt front where they were determined their preparations should not be seen.

B4881   SE5a   1Sqn
+*HAP BAILLEUL combat with AlbatrosDV[+driven
down,ftl] ovMONT ROUGE 4000'-2000' 11-30am
OK(2Lt PJ Clayson) Ja30 EA ftl 27x22Cent & then
captured: pilot seen walking, Clayson's first of 29 victories
with 1Sqn
  This was the first SE5a victory for 1 Squadron.

B2252   RE8   4Sqn
B left 10-05am **MIA(2Lt DG Money **KIA**)

A4423   RE8   5Sqn
B left 10am COURRIÈRES **MIA(2Lt FC Gilbert
POW) [?2 "RE8" claims combat MEURCHIN-
CARVIN 11-15~11-20am Vzfw R Heibert Ja46, but
consider A4756]

A4455.4 RE8   5Sqn
B left 10am COURRIÈRES ftl **MIA(2Lt R
MacDonald **POW**) a'c captured, Ja46 [?"RE" claim
Vzfw P Heibert Ja46]

A4756.1 RE8   16Sqn
**B driven down in control by EA ovPONT À VENDIN
MIA(Capt FS Thomas **KIA**)

A7724   DH4   18Sqn
**B combat with 10EA ovCOURRIÈRES shot down ftl

16Sqn 11-05am(Lt Hudson OK/Lt T Nicholson **WIA**)

B120   SE5a   24Sqn
** combat with AlbatrosDV[+ooc] MONT D'ORIGNY
A'dr ~12-30pm shot up(Capt JS Ralston **WIA**) in B891?

This was the first SE5a victory for 24 Squadron.

A2688   A.W.FK8   35Sqn
**Phot BELLICOURT AA dam OK(Lt HH Wilson/
Capt JS Gregory) left 10-20am, returned 12-05pm

B5620   Sopwith Camel   43Sqn
+* combat with AlbatrosDVs[+ooc+des]
COURRIÈRES 11-15am OK(Capt HH Balfour) first of
several claims in this a'c

A7229   Bristol F2b   48Sqn
P shot down in flames 12pm(Sgt ET Hardeman **KIA/
2Lt GW Croft **KIA**) left 11am, Ja6 ["Bristol" claim
combat wST QUENTIN 12-45pm Oblt W Reinhard Ja6]

B6379   Sopwith Camel   8(Naval)Sqn
+* combat with AlbatrosDV[+flames] PRONVILLE
11-15am OK(FCdr GW Price) shared, last of 12 claims

17th February

C5043   RE8   3Sqn AFC
**AOb hit by British shell? broke up ovOOSTAVERNE
12-35pm(Lt H Streeter **KIA**/Lt FJ Tarrant **KIA**)

B5207   Sopwith Camel   4Sqn AFC
**OP on tail of EA 2-15pm ovLILLE then broke up(2Lt
CH Martin **KIA**) hit by shell?

DH4   18Sqn
B (/Lt AC Morris **KIA)shot through head

B1177   Bristol F2b   20Sqn
+* combat with PfalzDIIIs[+ooc+des]
nrMOORSLEDE btwn 11-20am & 11-30am OK(Sgt F
Johnson/Capt JH Hedley) both crew were high scoring
two-seater aces

B1209   Bristol F2b   20Sqn
**OP combat with EA dam ftl cr WOESTEN OK(2Lt P
Roberts/2Lt W Noble)

B8231   SE5a   24Sqn
**OP dive on EA broke up folded ovLEVERGUES 8000'
MIA(2Lt DN Ross DCM MM **KIA**) ["SE" claim combat
12-40pm nBEAUMETZ Untoff Schweppe Ja35]

B2077   DH4   27Sqn
**B combat with Pfalz DIII ovMARQUAIN ~12-30pm?
shot down in flames(2Lt AW Greene **KIA**/Sgt A
Hughesden **KIA**) MARCOING?, Ja29 [?"DH4" claim
combat HAM 12-30pm Oblt H Auffahrt Ja29]

A.W.FK8   35Sqn
AP AA(2Lt WH Martin **WIA)ankle

A.W.FK8   35Sqn
SpRec mg ground fire(/2Lt DF Hurr **WIA)leg

B37.U   SE5a   56Sqn
+* combat with AlbatrosDV[+ooc] FRESNOY 2-45pm
OK(Capt WS Fielding-Johnson) claimed several victories
in this a'c

B6549   RE8   59Sqn
**Phot combat with EA shot through ftl ALG
10-30am(2Lt RH Williams **WIA**/1AM SW Egan **WIA**)

18th February

79 Squadron came to France on the 18th of
February. It was the first unit to arrive equipped
with Sopwith Dolphin fighters, although 19
Squadron already had a few and 23 Squadron
would receive them in April. From the earliest
prototypes this machine had impressed both the
authorities and pilots alike. It was very fast and
responsive at virtually all levels, and had a very
good ceiling. It was easy to fly and sturdy, but one
of its greatest assets as a fighter was the field of view
from the cockpit. The mainplanes were negatively
staggered and there was an open centre section of
the top plane, making the pilot position very
favourable, if a little exposed. This same asset
became a liability in a crash, however, and various
ideas were tried to protect the pilot in a turnover
on landing, and also to give him a means of escape
from the cockpit. Its Hispano-Suiza engine also
made for some misgivings. On balance, however, it
was one of the best fighters of the period.

B211   A.W.FK8   2Sqn
*Phot broke up diving to help FK8 fighting 6 Pfalz wLA
BASSÉE 12-25pm(Lt AJ Homersham **KIA**/Capt S
Broadbent **KIA**) ["BF" claim wLA BASSÉE 12-15pm
Ltn M Gossner Ja23]

Sopwith Camel   3Sqn
** (2Lt DS Judson **WIA**)

SE5a   29Sqn
** (2Lt FW Chambers **WIA**)leg

B8260   SE5a   40Sqn
**Esc combat with Albatros shot up MAZINGARBE ftl
12-10pm(2Lt LA Herbert)

B2499   Sopwith Camel   70Sqn
**OP combat with 18 AlbatrosDs HOUTHOULST
FOREST & seen after combat **MIA**(2Lt CJW McKeown
POW) left 11am ["Camel" claim combat HOUTHULST
WOOD 11-50am Oblt B Loerzer Ja26, but see N6347]

A5601   FE2b   100Sqn
NB left 6pm **MIA(Lt GG Jackson **POW**/2AM JC
Guyat **POW**)

B7188?   Sopwith Camel   8(Naval)Sqn
**OP combat with EA shot down nrARLEUX(FSLt CR
Walworth **KIA**)

B7198   Sopwith Camel   8(Naval)Sqn
+* combat with AlbatrosDV[+ooc] 2m neVITRY
11-15am OK(FSLt WL Jordan) his last victory with 8(N)

B7204   Sopwith Camel   8(Naval)Sqn
** VITRY-DOUAI area combat with EA shot up
MIA(FCdr GW Price DSC **KIA**) [?"Sopwith 1Str" claim

combat GIVENCHY-LEZ-LA-BASSÉE 12-20pm Ltn T
Rumpel Ja23]

N6347   Sopwith Camel   10(Naval)Sqn
** combat? cr wr WoL(FSLt RE Burr **DoW** 20.2.18)
[?possible "Camel" claim combat Oblt B Loerzer Ja26]

19th February

C4837   Bristol F2b   20Sqn
**OP combat 1pm Sh28.c.22 in flames(Lt DG Campbell
KIA/Lt JH Stream **KIA**) [?"2Str" claim combat
POTYZE 2-50pm OffSt O Esswein Ja26]

B3305   A.W.FK8   35Sqn
**AOb combat with HA shot down in flames at F.9.c.29
(2Lt HH Wilson **KIA**/Capt JS Gregory **KIA**) [?"AW"
claim combat seEPEHY 7-10am Ltn F Schleiff Ja56]

A7468   DH4   55Sqn
**B seen 15m from TREVES turning back but in control
MIA(Lt W Ross **POW**/2Lt HA Hewitt **POW**)

DH4   55Sqn
** AA(/Lt JM Carroll **WIA**)

Sopwith Camel   80Sqn
** gunshot(Lt SLH Potter **WIA**)

B9171   Sopwith Camel   80Sqn
**LP left 11-55am combat with HA eLA BASSÉE
MIA(2Lt E Westmoreland **KIA**) this or Camel B9185
went down ooc in flames [?"Sopwith 1Str" claim combat
MARQUILLIES 1-05pm Ltn H-G Marwitz
Ja30][?"Sopwith 1Str" claim combat nLORGIES
1-05pm Oblt H Bethge Ja30 but see B9185]

B9185   Sopwith Camel   80Sqn
LP left 11-55am combat neLA BASSÉE **MIA(2Lt SR
Pinder **KIA**) this or Camel B9171 went down ooc in
flames [?"Camel" claim NEUVE CHAPELLE 1pm Oblt
H-J Buddecke Ja30, but see B9171]

These were the first combat casualties suffered by
80 Squadron.

C5310   SE5a   84Sqn
+* combat with AlbatrosDVs[+des] nLA FÈRE then
AlbatrosDV[+ooc] ST GOBAIN WOOD btwn 10-15am
& 10-20am OK(2Lt JA McCudden) brother of James
McCudden: several victories claimed in this a'c

A5744   FE2b   100Sqn
FE2c? **NB caught during enemy bombing raid of
OCHEY A'dr ftl hit wires cr dam OK(2Lt HJ Crofts/2Lt
JCE Price) crew shaken

B485   FE2b   100Sqn
**NB HA shot up over own a'dr ftl wr OK(Lt HL Miles/
Lt HA Sampson)

B434, B445, B447   all FE2c   100Sqn
**All shot up and damaged by enemy boming raid on
OCHEY A'dr while preparing for raid

The FE2c was a variant of the FE2b in which the
pilot and observer positions were reversed, namely,

with the pilot in the front of the nacelle. There were
very few of these types built and still fewer used as
night-bombers. There is also little evidence to show
there were any pure FE2ds used in night
operations.

1455, 3130   H.P. 0/100s   16(Naval)Sqn
** damaged on OCHEY a'dr in enemy bombing raid

These last seven machines noted were caught in an
enemy raid on Ochey aerodrome, which housed
two of the three strategic bombing units of 41st
Wing. Two of the 100 Squadron FEs damaged in
this attack were over the aerodrome as it was
launched. They may have been followed back after
their own operations and were probably shot up as
they approached to land — a time when an aircraft
was particularly vulnerable. Ochey aerodrome was
to be bombed again a few nights later.

20th February

B5815   A.W.FK8   82Sqn
**Phot combat with Fokker DrI shot up ftl hit mole hill
dam u'c OK(2Lt WG MacKenzie/2Lt EHS Morris)

21st February

SE5a   2Sqn AFC
** combat with 10 Albatros shot up(2Lt R Lang MM
UK. **WIA**) Lang attached from RFC

B619.E   SE5a   2Sqn AFC
NOP left 11-35am seen making for Lines **MIA(2Lt GC
Logan Can. **POW**)

RE8   3Sqn AFC
AOb AA fire(/2Lt AO'C Brook **WIA)

RE8   4Sqn
** mg ground(/2Lt DS Gordon **KIA**)

B5552   Sopwith Camel   4Sqn AFC
**OP combat with 5 Albatros shot down 10-50am
nrHAUBOURDIN **MIA**(2Lt A Couston **POW**) left
10am ["Camel" claim combat WAVRIN 11am Ltn R
Matthaei Ja46]

RE8   16Sqn
** (/Lt WJ Blitch **WIA**)

A7524   DH4   18Sqn
** shot up dam, crew not yet known

B664   SE5a   24Sqn
+* combat with AlbatrosDV[+ooc] sHONNECOURT
10am OK(Capt GEH McElroy Irl.) McElroy's first
victory with 24Sqn

A7220   Bristol F2b   48Sqn
**OP combat with EA shot up ftl eSAVY 10-45am(2Lt
CDB Stiles OK/Lt WCS Gregson **WIA**)

B4860   SE5a   60Sqn
**ResP seen nrHOUTHULST WOOD 9-15am down

EoL **MIA**(2Lt WM Kent **KIA**) left 7-40am ["SE5" claim
combat HOUTHULST WOOD 9am Ltn R Klimke
Ja27]

C5325   SE5a   60Sqn
**OP combat with EA HOUTHULST shot up ftl
MIA(2Lt GB Craig US. **POW DoW** 22.2.18) left 7-40am
["SE5" claim combat LEDEGHEM 9am Oblt H Göring
Ja27]

C4630   Bristol F2b   62Sqn
+*P PLOEGSTEERT WOOD combat large 2Str[+
smoke cr] ovARMENTIÈRES 7000' OK(Capt GF
Hughes Aust./Capt H Claye) EA in vertical dive & cr
200yd EoL

This was the first combat victory for 62 Squadron.

B5600   Sopwith Camel 65Sqn
+* combat with AlbatrosDV[+flames] 3m eDIXMUDE
2-50pm OK(Capt HL Symons Can.) made 6 claims

**   Sopwith Camel   70Sqn**
LP AA(2Lt R Longman **WIA)

**   FE2b   101Sqn**
** severe gunshot wounds(/Lt A Fudge **DoW** 22.2.18)

As part of the bombing programme 101 Squadron,
in the Fifth Army area, had been ordered to bomb
Etreux aerodrome, from which German night-
bombers left to attack Paris and Allied communications. Raids were ordered to take place from the
20th until the 4th of March but the sole night it was
possible to make them was the 21st — the weather
at night being continually unfavourable. Night
flying was constrained by a completely different set
of factors from day operations and was much more
susceptible to cancellation due to bad weather.
Whereas day flying might still be viable in some
conditions of rain and mist, at night it was impossible. The main obstacle was navigation, which
relied on the highly trained observation of ground
features as well as the use of a network of signalling
beacons. One often finds night operations "washed
out" following a day which might have been quite
brilliant for flying because fog and mist or rain had
rolled in.

B451   FE2b   102Sqn
NB **MIA(2Lt BCW Windle **POW**/2Lt SG Williams
MC **POW**) left 6-45pm, observer escaped, returned UK?
1.5.18

A793   FE2b   16(Naval)Sqn
** bombed and wrecked on OCHEY A'dr by EA

24th February

As certainty grew about where the German attack
would be made, so attention switched to resolving
when it would come. The German forces ensured
there was as little evidence as possible to help

determine this, but one tell-tale sign would be the
appearance of greater numbers of aircraft. It was
known that many were being held back in reserve,
awaiting the final phase of the preparations to be
brought up and then to be used directly in the
fighting. Little could be told in this regard from the
reconnoitring of enemy aerodromes, for the
Germans used the clever expedient of erecting
similar numbers of temporary hangars on all new
airfields along the entire length of the line, only
some of which were actually housing machines.
What was all too apparent from air reports and
photography was the enormous build-up of enemy
forces.

**   Sopwith Camel   3Sqn**
LowP (Capt C Sutton **WIA?)

B7317   Sopwith Camel   4Sqn AFC
**OP seen btwn Lines-LA BASSÉE 2pm shot down
MIA(2Lt WB Randell **POW**) left 1-45pm

**   SE5a   40Sqn**
** combat shot up(2Lt LA Herbert **WIA**)

B2293.17 RE8   52Sqn
AP left 12-40pm **MIA(2Lt GRT Marsh **POW**/2Lt IM
Dempster **KIA**) [?"RE8" claim combat MARCY? OffSt
F Altemeier Ja24]

B7320.P   Sopwith Camel   70Sqn
** AA dam OK(2Lt J Todd?)

26th February

A3531   RE8   16Sqn
**Phot combat with 5EA shot down sLENS 11-55am wr
ldg(2Lt WG Duthie **WIA**/2Lt RWStG Cartwright **KIA**)
["RE" claim combat MERICOURT 11-50am Ltn F Ritt
vRöth Ja23]

B6871   SPAD 7   19Sqn
**ResP combat with Fokker DrI then glide s-w from
COMINES **MIA**(2Lt JL McLintock **KIA**) left 9am
[?combat WARNETON 10-10am Ltn R Plange Ja2]

C3841   Sopwith Dolphin 19Sqn
+* combat with Fokker DrI[+ooc] COMINES 10-05am
OK(Lt JD dePencier)

This was the first Sopwith Dolphin victory for 19
Squadron. The unit was still coming up to full
strength on the type.

**   Bristol F2b   22Sqn**
** combat(/Sgt C Hagan **WIA**)

B6732.A   SPAD 7   23Sqn
**OP seen starting combat with HAs 14000' 10-15am
LAON ldg in control? **MIA**(2Lt DC Doyle **POW**) a'c
captured, Tut24 ["Spad" claim combat neLAON
10-20am Hpt A Rt vTutschek JGII]

B548.Z   SE5a   24Sqn
**OP left 3pm last seen in combat nLAON 4-10pm

MIA(2Lt CH Crossbee? **POW**) name Crosbie? [?"SE5" claim combat eVAUXAILLON? Vzfw U Neckel Ja12]

C9542   SE5a   24Sqn
**OP left 9am combat with HA shot up returned a'dr 9-30am OK(Lt HVL Tubbs)

A7697   DH4   25Sqn
PhotRec LAON **MIA(Lt GM Shaw **WIA POW**/Lt CHS Ackers **WIA**? **POW**) left 11-40am

25 Squadron had been commonly involved in photo-reconnaissance work, as well as bombing, since the beginning of the year. As a unit operating with headquarters it had a typically wide remit, with objectives as far apart as Roulers and Cambrai. When it was moved to the Fifth Army area on the 6th of March it concentrated on bombing rail targets in the south, but it also continued its photographic role.

C5336   SE5a   40Sqn
OP AA nrPLOUVAIN ov Sq 1.9. ldg? ok 200yd EoL eFAMPOUX 9-15am **MIA(2Lt RC Wade **KIA**) left 8-05am

B3434   RE8   52Sqn
**AOb AA dam ftl cr wr OK(Capt W Deane/2Lt TAW Foy)

B5249   Sopwith Camel   54Sqn
OP left 11-05am combat last seen LAON-LA FÈRE **MIA(Lt JR Law **POW**)

B9193   Sopwith Camel   54Sqn
OP left 11am combat with EA LAON-LA FÈRE spiralled down **MIA(2Lt HF Dougall **POW**)

B4891.6 **SE5a   56Sqn**
+* combat C-types[++des] OPPY then CHERISY btwn 11-20am & 11-30am OK(Capt JTB McCudden)

These were James McCudden's last victories, leaving him with a probable total of fifty-seven.

A7804   DH4   57Sqn
B going down wCOURTRAI **MIA(2Lt JM Allen **POW**/Capt FR Sutcliffe **POW**) left 9-10am ["DH4" claim combat COURTRAI 10-25am ObFlM K Schoenfelder Ja7]

27th February

B8900   RE8   5Sqn
AReg AA hit BAILLEUL cr then fire on ldg destroyed(2Lt LN Gaskell **DoW 1.3.18/Lt LMcC Ritchie **WIA**)

A7733   DH4   25Sqn
test but shot down? into sea **MIA(Lt MW Dickens **KIA**/Sgt FJ Swain **KIA**) (salvaged from sea 23.6.18)

N6363   Sopwith Camel   13(Naval)Sqn
** seen attacking 6 enemy seaplanes but shot down in flames into sea 25m nDUNKIRK **MIA**(FCdr MJG Day DSC **KIA**) clung on but drowned [?combat FlM Dreyer/Ltn Frantz SFlgII], Day made a few claims in this a'c

28th February

C5379   SE5a   84Sqn
OP combat with 3EA 4-35pm ovST GOBAIN WOODS, seLATERE **MIA(2Lt EO Krohn **KIA**) left 3-25pm ST QUENTIN ["SE5" claim combat ST GOBAIN WOODS Vzfw U Neckel Ja12]

March 1918

1st March

B6293   Sopwith Camel   54Sqn
**SpRec combat with EA shot up ftl OK(Lt GC Cuthbertson) Ja11

B9259   Sopwith Camel   54Sqn
**DKBP combat 11-30am seen well WoL 15000', later crashed MIA but OK(2Lt JL Horne) left 10-40am

B5837   A.W.FK8   82Sqn
AOb combat with 2 Fokker DrIs FLAVY gun jam ftl spiral down cr ldg fire(Capt ERH Pollack OK/2Lt JA Moir **WIA)

2nd March
ROYAL FLYING CORPS CONCENTRATIONS FOR THE DEFENCE OF AMIENS

Depending on where the attack was expected to fall, RFC Headquarters had issued various options for air concentrations for the battle on the 19th of February. After a meeting on the 2nd of March, the scheme relating to an expected attack in the south on the Third and Fifth Armies was adopted and put into operation. The aircraft assembled were as follows. In support of the Third Army was III Brigade, consisting of 12th (Corps) Wing with Nos. 12, 13, 15, and 59 Squadrons, all with RE8s; and 13th (Army) Wing with Nos. 3, 46, and 70 Squadrons with Sopwith Camels, Nos. 41, 56, and 64 Squadrons with SE5as, as well as 11 Squadron with Bristol Fighters and 49 Squadron with DH4s. V Brigade consisted of 15th (Corps) Wing, comprising Nos. 8, 35, and 82 Squadrons with Armstrong Whitworth FK8s, and 52 and 53 Squadrons with RE8s. It also included the 22nd (Army) Wing, being 54 Squadron with Sopwith Camels, Nos. 24 and 84 Squadron with SE5as, 23 Squadron with SPADs, 48 Squadron with Bristol Fighters, and 5 (Naval) Squadron with DH4s.

Additionally, 9th (Headquarters) Wing also sent a substantial number of its squadrons south. Many of these were new units which had arrived in France since Christmas. Three fighter squadrons, Nos. 73 and 80 (Sopwith Camels), and 79 (Sopwith Dolphins) went to the Fifth Army area with two

DH4 day-bomber squadrons, Nos. 25 and 27, as well as 62 Squadron, a fighter-reconnaissance unit with Bristol Fighters. The night-bombers of 101 Squadron was already flying with V Brigade, and another 9th Wing night bombing unit, No. 102, went to the Third Army area.

The total concentration in support of the Third and Fifth Armies therefore amounted to thirty-one squadrons with a total of five hundred and seventy-nine serviceable aircraft. Two hundred and sixty-one of these were single-seat fighters. The German forces facing these armies would consist of their Seventeenth, Second, and Eighteenth Armies, with air support amounting to seven hundred and thirty aircraft, of which three hundred and twenty-six were single-seater fighters. For the first and only time, the German air concentration assembled for a battle on the Western Front would exceed that of the Royal Flying Corps.

Long before all the British units mentioned above had completed their move to the battle zone, those already in the area were busy disrupting and harassing the enemy. The substantial bombing operations have already been mentioned, but there were other important components. Virtually all the work of the corps squadrons before the offensive was with the artillery, particularly in counter-battery ranging and directing fire onto enemy ammunition and supply railheads. To enable this programme of interference with the enemy's preparations required control of the skies, and this was achieved by widespread and intense offensive patrolling. These were either "Close" or "Distant" Patrols. "Close" meant from between the lines back to about five miles into enemy territory, whilst "Distant" meant the zone five miles further distant behind this. Large engagements with enemy formations were not common — the German Air Force had reason to conserve and conceal its strength, but on occasion these patrols did draw them out.

The Dover-Dunkirk Command was one RNAS body reorganised as part of the impending formation of the Royal Air Force. It too, however, would be swept up into the fighting in March. The intention had been to create three new RAF wings from the forces around Dunkirk. One wing, the 61st, was to be kept for direct naval operations, but the other two, Nos. 64th and 65th, were to be made available to General Headquarters. After the formation of the RAF, the 61st Wing was to consist of Squadrons 201, 210, and 213 (Sopwith Camels), 202 (DH4s and DH9s), and 217 (DH4s). The other two were to be grouped into the new VII Brigade, consisting of 64th Wing: Squadrons 203, 204, 208, and 209 (all Sopwith Camels), and 65th Wing:

Squadrons 206 and 211 (DH9s) and 207, 214, and 215 (Handley Pages). The latter was initially envisaged as a northern strategic bombing force which would complement the operations of the Independent Force in the south. Its targets would be German naval targets on or around the Belgian coast, in particular the submarine bases at Zeebrugge and Bruges. The huge demands of the German spring offensive were to ensure this never eventuated. In fact, as the fighting became increasingly desperate, every fighter and every unit which could be spared was to be redeployed southwards. By the end of the month, Nos. 201, 203, 208, 209, and 210 had all been dispatched, along with the DH9s of 206 Squadron.

5th March

A4748   RE8   4Sqn
PhotRec combat with 4EA over Sh36a G.14.b.7.8. ftl o't 3-05pm(2Lt WH Boston **WIA/Lt JEG Mosby OK)

                RE8   15Sqn
** (/2Lt RS Fear **DoW**)

B1168   Bristol F2b   22Sqn
HAP combat with HA[+des+ooc] LENS 3-35pm shot up prop shot off ftl(2Lt SA Oades **WIA/2Lt SW Bunting **WIA**) last of 11 claims by Oades, 7 with Bunting

B145   SE5a   24Sqn
OP shot up VILLERS OUTREAUX **MIA(2Lt WF Poulter **POW DoW** 6.3.18) left 12-55pm

                A.W.FK8   35Sqn
Phot (/2Lt TW Cave **WIA)

6th March

83 Squadron arrived in France on the 6th of March. It was an FE2b night bombing unit operating in the north with 9th (Headquarters) Wing.

B9283   Sopwith Camel   3Sqn
**LowB left 6-10am shot up dam returned a'dr OK(2Lt AP Freer)

B2296   RE8   5Sqn
Phot EA shot up 11-10am on return wr(2Lt CP Virgo **WIA/Lt NG Morris **WIA**)

A4460   RE8   9Sqn
Phot AA shot down ftl dam(2Lt S Jones **WIA/2Lt FT Taylor OK)

A7658   DH4   18Sqn
**B shot up by many HA 11am ftl wr OK(2Lt J Balderstone/2Lt J Baird)

A7797   DH4   18Sqn
B combat many HAs combat with PfalzDIIIs[++ooc] & AlbatrosDVs[++ooc] LENS-PONT À VENDIN ~11-15am shot up controls dam cr wr ldg(2Lt DA Stewart OK/Lt HWM Mackay **DoW) 11am?, Stewart

was high scoring two-seater ace

B9436   DH4   18Sqn
**B combat engine shot up ftl 2Sq a'dr hit ditch ldg cr
11-40am OK(2Lt W Rochelle/LtJ Brisbane) left 9-40am
First Army area

C4810.N   **Bristol F2b**   **22Sqn**
+* combat with PfalzDIII[+ooc] eLA BASSÉE 11-15am
OK(2Lt GW Bulmer US./2Lt SJ Hunter) first of several
victories for Bulmer

C1057.C   **SE5a**   **24Sqn**
**OP left 1-20pm seen in combat with HA nLA FÈRE
MIA(2Lt APC Wigan **POW**) a'c captured, Tut26
["SE5" claim combat 1-45pm Hpt A Rt vTutschek
JGII]

C9494   SE5a   24Sqn
+* combat with AlbatrosDV[+ooc] ST QUENTIN
10-15am OK(Capt AJ Brown) shared, first of 5 claims in
a week in this a'c

C9535   SE5a   24Sqn
**OP left 1-20pm air collision with EA cr wr(2Lt DM
Clementz **KIA**)

A7713   DH4 25Sqn
**PhotRec combat with 6EA ovLE CATEAU shot up on
return 11-15am OK(2Lt C Ross/Lt HE Pohlmann) left
8-30am ANOR-HIRSON

B201   A.W.FK8   35Sqn
**AOb left 9-45am BELLICOURT combat with EA shot
up dam returned 1-45pm OK(Lt Fry/Lt Knivecon)

C1068   SE5a   40Sqn
+* combat with AlbatrosDV[+des]nwLENS 4-20pm
OK(2Lt JW Wallwork) most of his 5 claims were in this
a'c

Sopwith Camel   43Sqn
OP (2Lt AJS Doble **WIA)

B9153   Sopwith Camel   46Sqn
+* combat with HannoverC[+ooc] eDOUAI 1-45pm
OK(2Lt DR MacLaren) MacLaren's first of possibly 54
victories, all in Camels with 46Sqn (almost half in this
a'c)

B1265   Bristol F2b   48Sqn
** combat with PfalzDIII[+des] LA FÈRE 9-50am shot
up(Lt RH Little OK/Lt LN Jones **WIA**)

C1569   Sopwith Camel   54Sqn
**OP AA engine shot up ftl 10-20am BOUCLY OK(2Lt
EA Richardson)

DH4   57Sqn
B (/Sgt J Lowe **WIA)

B5838   A.W.FK8   82Sqn
**Phot combat with 5EA eSERY 1-10pm shot down in
flames ovMEZIÈRES I.8.6.(2Lt DL Sisley **KIA**/Lt AC
Gilmour **KIA**) left 10-55am [?possible claim combat
1-10pm Ltn K Küppers Ja48]

A8946   SE5a   84Sqn
**OP left 8am seen going west 9-40am wRENANSART

12000' **MIA**(Lt RE Duke **POW**) [?"Sopwith" claim ST
QUENTIN Lt R Rienau Ja19]

B7215   Sopwith Camel   10(Naval)Sqn
+* combat with AlbatrosDV[+ooc] seDIXMUDE
8-30am OK(FCdr WM Alexander Can.) first of several
victories in this a'c

7th March

B2266   RE8   12Sqn
C2266? **LP left 4-40pm mg fuel tank shot up 3000' dam
OK(2Lt Worsley/2Lt Harman)

8th March

RE8   4Sqn
Phot (/Lt CR Pilcher **WIA)

A7835   DH4   25Sqn
**PhotRec shot up LE CATEAU ftl 10-30am(2Lt RM
Tate **WIA**/Sgt AH Muff OK)

B2094   DH4   27Sqn
B combat with HA shot down BUSIGNY **MIA(2Lt
JFRI Perkins **KIA**/Lt RG Foley MC **KIA**) ["Bristol"
claim combat nwFRESNOY LE GRAND 10-10am
OffSt J Mai Ja5] a'c possibly captured?: there exists
a photo of a DH4, serial B209- visible, with German
cross painted on the tail

A7298   Bristol F2b   48Sqn
+* combat with AlbatrosDVs[++ooc] MONT
D'ORIGNY 8am OK(2Lt LA Payne/Lt GHH Scutt)
Payne claimed 11EAs

B1190   Bristol F2b   48Sqn
+* combat with AlbatrosDVs[+ooc] BOHAIN 10-40am
OK(Capt NC Millman Can./2Lt HA Cooper) made
another claim that day: AlbatrosDV[+ooc] BOHAIN
3-55pm, pilot's last of 6 claims

C5057   RE8   52Sqn
**Phot shot up returned a'dr 11-45am OK(2Lt AFW
Gregory/Lt WAB Savile) left 10-30am

B8264.C   **SE5a**   **64Sqn**
**COP combat seen chased down by EA ov Sh51B.x.28c
10-40am but pulled out at 9000' & seen going west
MIA(2Lt RH Topliss **WIA POW**) left 10am [?"SE5"
claim combat BOURLON WOOD 10-40am Ltn W
vManteuffel-Szoge Ja35]

C8241   Sopwith Camel   70Sqn
**OP seen dive into combat with HA ROULERS 1-15pm
seen later? **MIA**(2Lt FG McNeil **KIA**) left 12-55pm

B3905   Sopwith Camel   12(Naval)Sqn
**prac seen ovGRAVELINES combat with EA shot
down nrMENIN SLEYHAGE **MIA**(FSLt HR Casgrain
POW) left 1-45pm, Ja36 ["Sopwith" claim combat
ROULERS-MENIN 1-30pm Ltn H vHaebler Ja36]

9th March

There was a large-scale combined bombing raid on
enemy aerodromes on the 9th, involving fifty-three

fighters. The operation had been planned well in advance, and the pilots involved had practised techniques of low bomb dropping and generally prepared for the attack. The raids were timed to find the enemy on their aerodromes making ready for their afternoon patrols, so that maximum damage could be inflicted. 23 Squadron SPADs attacked Bertry aerodrome, supported by 24 Squadron, whilst 48 and 54 Squadrons, protected by 84 Squadron SE5as, bombed Busigny and Escaufort. All fifty-three machines returned safely.

RE8	9Sqn

AOb (/2Lt EF Taylor **WIA)

A.W.FK8	10Sqn

AOb mg fire(/2Lt T McGovern **WIA)

B6518	RE8	15Sqn

Phot combat with 15EA shot up 11-30am(2Lt WF Mayoss **WIA/2Lt W Haddow OK) left 10-05am

C3822	Sopwith Dolphin	19Sqn

**OP shot up ftl HAZEBROUCK wr OK(2Lt GG Irving)

Bristol F2b	22Sqn

HAP:attacked spotter EA shot up ftl(Maj LW Learmount DSO MC **WIA/) loss of blood but ldg ok, 22 Sqn C.O., sent home

B664	SE5a	24Sqn

**OP combat with HA u'c shot up dam ftl 9-15am cr ldg dam OK(2Lt AK Cooper)

SE5a	40Sqn

OP (Capt RJ Tipton **WIA)

C5348	SE5a	40Sqn

OP new pilot: lost? seen going towards AUCHEL? 5pm **MIA(Lt PLaT Foster **POW**) left 3-05pm

C9538	SE5a	40Sqn

OP combat 4-15pm broke up? diving on HA ovCOURCELLES **MIA(Maj LA Tilney **KIA**) [?"SE5" claim combat NOYELLE-VION 4-10pm Ltn P Billik Ja52]

B5597	Sopwith Camel	65Sqn

+* combat with Fokker DrI[+flames] WESTROOSEBEKE 4-40pm OK(Lt G Bemridge) last of 5 claims

B7475	Sopwith Camel	70Sqn

+* combat with AlbatrosDV[+flames] 9-30am then AlbatrosDV[+des] MENIN 9-45am OK(Capt FG Quigley Can.) in afternoon shot down 2 more AlbatrosDV[++ooc] QUESNOY 1-10pm, Quigley made almost half of his 33 claims whilst flying this a'c

10th March

From the 10th of March until the 15th of April German and British times matched (all times given are British times).

B9147	Sopwith Camel	3Sqn

LowP seen diving on transport neMARQUION **MIA(2Lt EPP Edmonds **WIA POW**)10Mar.18 left 7-20am, interned Holland

Sopwith Camel	3Sqn

** (Lt BA Cooke **WIA**)

A7719	DH4	18Sqn

B combat with HA OIGNES 12pm seen going down in control **MIA(2Lt JNB McKim **KIA**/Lt CRH Ffolliott **KIA**) left 10-55am ["DH4" claim combat ALLENNES 12-10pm Oblt H Bethge Ja30]

RE8	52Sqn

** (/2Lt G Gilham **WIA**)

A7556	DH4	55Sqn

B STUTTGART combat with HA fuel tank shot up ftl BURNVILLE-AUX-MIRROIS wr(2Lt C Cavaghan OK/Lt JM Carroll **WIA)arm

A7569	DH4	55Sqn

B STUTTGART combat with HA gave Green light then down control seOBERKIRCH **MIA(2Lt R Caldecott **POW**/2Lt GPF Thomas **POW**)

The strategic bombing target of Stuttgart lay one hundred and four miles east of the lines. 55 Squadron had been restricted from making its deep strategic bombing raids by rain and snow through the early days of March, but then had a busy week in which it mounted operations on most days. On this occasion it was striking the Daimler motor works near the town, but was met by enemy machines as the target was reached. All crews pressed on to deliver their bombs, but some casualties were sustained.

B484	FE2b	58Sqn

NRec shot down ftl ROEUX cr wr(Capt CH Brewer MC **inj WIA/2Lt DS Broadhurst **WIA**) left 10-30pm, pilot wounded saving observer

These casualties were caused during the relatively new work of night reconnaissance. Their objective had been to assess the activity on the Lille-Valenciennes railway. The conditions would normally have ruled out all flying but the work was seen as essential. Brewer was driven down to below 300' by fog in order to carry out the reconnaissance and this exposed them to considerable ground fire. The radiator was hit and they were forced to land in no man's land. They crashed and overturned in the darkness and Brewer's jaw was broken whilst Broadhurst was pinned unconscious beneath the machine. Under heavy fire, Brewer managed to lift the aircraft and rescue his observer whom he carried to a shell hole. In performing the rescue he was shot in the thigh.

After two hours Broadhurst regained consciousness and they crawled to the safety of some trenches.

C9603.3 **SE5a** **64Sqn**
+* combat with LVGC[+ooc] MARQUION 1-50pm OK(Capt RStC McClintock)

B5572 **Sopwith Camel** **73Sqn**
+* combat with Fokker DrI[+des] wBOHAIN 2-15pm OK(Capt M LeBlanc-Smith)

B7291 **Sopwith Camel** **73Sqn**
+* combat with Fokker DrI[+des] wBOHAIN 2-25pm OK(Lt GS Hodson)

B9209? **Sopwith Camel** **80Sqn**
this a'c? +* combat with AlbatrosDVs[+ooc] BOHAIN-RIBEMONT OK(Capt StCC Taylor)

B9325 **Sopwith Camel** **80Sqn**
this a'c? +* combat with AlbatrosDV[+ooc] BOHAIN-RIBEMONT OK(2Lt D Gardiner)

The four combat victories noted above were the first for the two respective squadrons.

C6719 **Sopwith Camel** **80Sqn**
**OP BOHAIN-RIBEMONT seen in combat with Fokker DrI 5m neST QUENTIN 14000' MIA(2Lt CH Flere POW) ["Camel" claim combat MONTBREHAIN, LE CATELET 2-30pm Vzfw F Hemer Ja6]

C5384 **SE5a** **84Sqn**
+* combat with 2Str[+ooc] BELLICOURT 2-20pm OK(2Lt WH Brown Can.) Brown made 9 claims

B7230.T **Sopwith Camel** **3(Naval)Sqn**
**P combat shot down nrLENS in spin from 11000' but seen going east & ldg ok 9-50am MIA(FSLt KD Campbell POW) a'c captured (later used by Otto Kissenberth of Jasta 23?)

11th March

B835 **RE8** **5Sqn**
**AReg combat with HAs ovOPPY 4pm ftl brought down FRESNOY PARK MIA(Lt JA Convery KIA/Lt JLP Haynes KIA) left 2pm ["RE" claim combat ARLEUX-EN-GOHELLE 4-15pm Ltn H Viebig Ja57]

C5096 **RE8** **5Sqn**
**AOb combat with 9EA shot up ovARRAS-SOUCHEZ ftl cr 4pm(Maj EJ Tyson DSO MC DoW 11.3.18/2Lt B Bidmead WIA) [?"RE" claim combat Gfr Sielemann Ja57]

       Bristol F2b **48Sqn**
**P (/2Lt JH Robertson DoW)

A7227 **Bristol F2b** **48Sqn**
**OP combat with EA shot up ST QUENTIN ~12pm OK(2Lt WL Thomas/Cpl J Bowles) ["Bristol" claim combat nFRESNOY-LE-PETIT 1-10pm Ltn L Fr vRichthofen Ja11]

RE8 **13Sqn**
** (/2Lt EMcL Cleland WIA)

B54 **SE5a** **56Sqn**
**COP left 12-10pm combat with 5EA shot down WoL(2Lt D Woodman KIA) ["SE5" claim combat HOLNON WOOD 1-10pm Vzfw E Scholtz Ja11]

B8296 **SE5a** **64Sqn**
**DOP combat with HA shot up dam ftl 59Sq(2Lt JW Bell WIA) to hospital

N5965 **DH4** **2(Naval) Sqn**
**Esc combat? lost ftl sea LA PANNE(FSLt CG MacDonald Kld/1AM PJ Capp Kld) [?claim LA PANNE MFl B Heinrich MFJaI]

12th March

B4889 **SE5a** **1Sqn**
**ResP combat with 4EA 10-30am nSTADEN MIA(Lt AH Fitzmaurice KIA) Ja20?, left 9-45am ["SE5" claim combat DIXMUDE 9-45am Vzfw R Heibert Ja46][? combat HOUTHULST 10-50am Ltn H Steinbrecher Ja46]

C4847 **Bristol F2b** **11Sqn**
+* combat with 2Str[+ooc] 11-15am then combat with Fokker DrIs[++++ooc] CAUDRY btwn 11-45am & 11-55am OK(2Lt JS Chick/2Lt P Douglas) Chick eventually claimed 16 victories

B891.T **SE5a** **24Sqn**
**OP combat prop shot off ftl 9-30am, broke in half ldg OK(2Lt PA MacDougall)

C6400 **SE5a** **24Sqn**
**OP shot up OK(2Lt PJ Nolan) [?"Camel" claim combat VILLEVECQUE Oblt K Mettlich Ja8]

B9157 **Sopwith Camel** **46Sqn**
**B seen in formation 7am MOEUVRES MIA(2Lt JW Muir KIA)

B9317 **Sopwith Camel** **46Sqn**
**B left 6-30am in formation 7am MOEUVRES MIA(2Lt GD Falkenberg POW)

A7290 **Bristol F2b** **48Sqn**
**OP combat with Fokker DrIs[++shot down ooc]LE CATELET 12pm ftl 12-30pm cr ldg soft ground(2Lt CH Hore OK/Cpl J Cruickshank KIA)

B1247 **Bristol F2b** **62Sqn**
**OP shot down ooc eCAMBRAI 11-10am MIA(Capt DS Kennedy KIA/Lt HG Gill KIA) left 9-30am, LvR28 ["Bristol" claim combat MARETZ 11am Ltn L Fr vRichthofen Ja11]

B1250 **Bristol F2b** **62Sqn**
**OP combat with EA 11-10am seen going down eCAMBRAI MIA(2Lt CB Fenton POW/Lt HBP Boyce POW) left 9-30am, LvR29 ["Bristol" claim combat CLARY 11-10am Ltn L Fr vRichthofen Ja11]

B1251 **Bristol F2b** **62Sqn**
**OP combat with EA eCAMBRAI shot down in flames

11-10am **MIA**(2Lt LCF Clutterbuck **WIA POW**/2Lt
HJ Sparks MC **POW**) left 9-30am, MvR64 ["Bristol"
claim combat neNAUROY 11-15am Rittm M Fr
vRichthofen JG1]

C4824   Bristol F2b   62Sqn
**OP combat with EA going down eCAMBRAI 11-10am
MIA(Lt JAA Ferguson **WIA POW**/Sgt LSD Long
WIA POW) left 9-30am ["Bristol" claim combat
BEAUVOIS 11am Ltn W Steinhauser Ja11]

These were the first losses in combat for 62
Squadron, one of the 9th (Headquarters) Wing
units which had been moved down to the Fifth
Army area on the 7th of March. All of these
units found themselves operating on the
boundary between the two armies, namely
where the coming offensive was expected to to
be delivered and where it was likely there
would be the hottest action. 62 Squadron were
on offensive patrol when they met large formations led by Richthofen on this and the following day, and in all suffered six losses. On both
occasions they were co-operating with DH4
bombers from 25 and 27 Squadrons.

B6429   Sopwith Camel   1(Naval)Sqn
+* attacked KB[+des] nrKEMMEL 1-15pm OK(FLt
HV Rowley) shared, Rowley claimed 9EAs, last 4 in this
a'c

13th March

C6705   Sopwith Camel   3Sqn
**LowP left 6-35am Third Army area ground targets, mg
dam returned 7-10am OK(Lt JKvonI Peden)

            Bristol F2b   20Sqn
** (/2Lt DE Stevens **KIA**)

C1070   SE5a   24Sqn
**OP combat with EA wing shot off ovLA FÈRE
MIA(2Lt EA Whitehead **KIA**) left 9-35am [?possible
"SE5" claim combat HONNELIEU 10-30am Vzfw
Piechulek Ja56]

B5429   Sopwith Camel   46Sqn
**LowP left 6-30am shot up dam returned 7-50am
OK(2Lt MM Freehill) to Third Army area

            Bristol F2b   48Sqn
** (/2Lt EG Humphrey **WIA**)

B9279   Sopwith Camel   54Sqn
**WTInt combat with EA controls shot away ftl cr
ldg(2Lt JR Moore **inj** hosp) left 11-30am

A7489   DH4   55Sqn
B FREIBURG **MIA(2Lt RB Brookes **KIA**/Sgt H
Gostling **KIA**) [?"DH" claim combat
RUSTENHORT? 4-50pm Ltn G Schlenker Ja41]

A7579   DH4   55Sqn
B FREIBURG **MIA(2Lt TS Wilson **WIA POW**/2Lt
L Cann **KIA**) [?"DH4" claim Ltn Schulz Ja41]

B3966   DH4   55Sqn
B FREIBURG **MIA(2Lt A Gavaghan **KIA**/Sgt A
Brockbank? **KIA**) name Brocklebank?

Munition factories at Freiburg were the target
of this raid but the formation was attacked by
fifteen fighters over the town and suffered
heavy casualties.

B1207   Bristol F2b   62Sqn
**OP combat with EA going down eCAMBRAI
MIA(2Lt C Allen **KIA**/Lt NT Watson **WIA POW**) left
9am, ten F2bs vs several EAs ["BF" claim combat
MARCOING 10-16am Ltn Heins Ja56]

B1268   Bristol F2b   62Sqn
OP combat with HAs eCAMBRAI **MIA(2Lt NB
Wells **POW**/Lt GR Crammond **POW**) left 9am, 10
F2bs vs several EAs ["Bristol" claim combat sLA
TERRIÈRE 10-20am Ltn F Schleiff Ja56]

The attack on the 62 Squadron formation
followed one on the 73 Squadron Camels noted
below.

B2523   Sopwith Camel   73Sqn
**OP left 9-35am combat with EAs seCAMBRAI then
not seen after **MIA**(Lt EE Heath **WIA POW**) [M vR
65?]

B5590   Sopwith Camel   73Sqn
**OP combat with EAs seCAMBRAI in flames by
Fokker DrI **MIA**(2Lt JNL Millett **KIA**) left 9-35am,
MvR? ["Camel" claim combat BANTEUX 10-35am
Ritt M Fr vRichthofen JG1, but see B2523?: MvR
reported EA airman **WIA** only][?this "Camel" claim
VAUCELLES in flames 10-40am Vzfw E Scholtz
Ja11]

B7282   Sopwith Camel   73Sqn
+* combat with AlbatrosDV[+ooc] then combat with
Fokker DrI[+des] seCAMBRAI 10-15am OK(Capt
AH Orlebar) DrI broke up

These were the first losses in combat for 73
Squadron.

            Sopwith Camel   80Sqn
** (2Lt FJ Milligan **DoW**)

14th March

A2732   A.W.FK8   8Sqn
*SpRec controls shot away ftl nrBUS 4pm dam OK(2Lt
AM Kinnear/2Lt EI Wells)

B85   SE5a   24Sqn
SpM shot up(2Lt PJ Nolan **WIA)neck slight

C4640   Bristol F2b   48Sqn
**Low Shoot ESTRÈES mg 100' cr trenches(2Lt HH
Hartley **KIA**/2Lt G Dixon **inj**) pilot hit in heart

            Bristol F2b   62Sqn
** (/Sgt J Lake **WIA**)

15th March

A.W.FK8   8Sqn
** (Lt SH Kerr **WIA**/)

B79.Y   SE5a   24Sqn
+* combat with Fokker DrI[+ooc] nrPREMONTE
~10-30am OK(2Lt HB Redler SA.) shot down Hpt A
von Tutschek, commander of JG2, 27 victory ace, Redler
finally claimed 10 victories

C1075   SE5a   84Sqn
+* combat with AlbatrosDV[+des] MESNIL ST
LAURENT 9-45am OK(Lt EA Clear) Clear claimed
several of his 12 victories in this a'c

16th March

B9139   Sopwith Camel   3Sqn
*LowGndP mg shot up dam OK(Lt FL Hird)

B5208   Sopwith Camel   4Sqn AFC
**OP combat with HAs ANNOEULLIN shot down
MIA(2Lt WH Nicholls **POW**) Ja36?, left 9-10am, seen
about to attk HAs 10-05am [?"Camel" claim Vzfw
Wagner Ja29]

RE8   5Sqn
** (2Lt AW Fraser **WIA**/)

A8043   DH4   18Sqn
B shot down in control ovFROMELLES? **MIA(2Lt
RA Mayne **WIA POW**/Lt VW Scott MC **KIA**) place?
left 2-10pm [?"DH4" claim combat nrAMIENS
3-55pm Oblt H Auffahrt Ja29]

A7161   Bristol F2b   22Sqn
+* combat with PfalzDIII[+ooc] BEAUMONT 11am
OK(2Lt WFJ Harvey/Sgt A Burton) first of over 20
victories for Harvey

C5398   SE5a   24Sqn
**OP shot up ESSIGNY LE GRAND ftl 10-50am cr
OK(2Lt W Selwyn)

B5442   Sopwith Camel   46Sqn
LowP AA? seen ovLAGNICOURT 6-45am **MIA(2Lt
ALT Taylor **POW**) left 6-30am

B121.2   SE5a   56Sqn
**DOP seen attacking 2Str nBOURLON WOOD
12-30pm shot up then broke up cr nrHAMEL **MIA**(2Lt
KJ Knaggs **KIA**) left 10-45am

B595   SE5a   56Sqn
*DOP left 10-45am damaged in dive on EA ftl ALG
12-45pm OK(Lt ME Mealing) Mealing scored most of
his 14 victories in this a'c, including his first

A5710   FE2b   83Sqn
**Rec left 3pm! AA shot down eMERICOURT in control
MIA(2Lt WH Taylor **POW**/2Lt CV Shakesby **POW**)
"behind balloon line"

A5791   FE2b   83Sqn
**DayRec! AA mg shot down cr ldg AVION(Capt OE
Ridewood **WIA**/Lt FF Hutchison OK) Rec "behind
balloon line"

These were the first losses in action for the
night-bombers of 83 Squadron. The fact that
FE2bs had been sent out on active duties in
daylight caused some consternation amongst
other night flying units for it was not a
machine in which to be caught aloft by the
enemy without cover of darkness. It was of
course common for night bombing squadrons
to test and fly their aircraft well back from the
battle zone during the day — a tribute, incidentally, to the effectiveness of Allied offensive
patrolling, for they were usually unarmed
whilst testing — but in daylight they were
normally never allowed near the lines.

C9500   SE5a   84Sqn
**OP flak shot off prop ST QUENTIN cr ldg OK(2Lt
HO MacDonald)

A7908   DH4   5(Naval)Sqn
B BUSIGNY DUMP combat with EAs **MIA(FCdr
LW Ormerod DSC **KIA**/FSLt WLH Pattisson DFC
KIA) left 9-46am [?"Bristol" claim combat ST
BENIN EoL 11-10am Vzfw J Mai Ja5][possible
"DH4" claim combat VILLERET 11-30am Ltn Heins
Ja56]

N6001   DH4   5(Naval)Sqn
+*B combat with several AlbatrosDVs[+des+ooc]
BOHAIN-LE CATELET OK(FLt SR Watkins/SCdr SJ
Goble Aust. DSO DSC)

N6005   DH4   5(Naval)Sqn
**B BUSIGNY DUMP combat with HA on return ftl
DOULLENS(FSLt GM Cartmell **WIA**/AGL RB
Wilcox **WIA**) left 9-46am

The Fifth Army had no day-bombing squadron
until the arrival of 5 (Naval) on the 6th of
March. In anticipation of the imminent amalgamation of the RFC and RNAS into the Royal
Air Force, virtually all Naval squadrons were
put under the command of Haig in the last
weeks leading up to the offensive. 5 (Naval)
was the only one to leave Dunkirk at this time,
however, and had been brought down to bomb
enemy aerodromes and dumps.

17th March

From the 17th until the 20th of March thick clouds
and rain set in, so that reconnaissance making was
limited. There was still no certainty as to the day
planned for the opening of the offensive and the
restrictions of the weather were therefore all in
Germany's favour. Just at this time, however, the
first definite dates were extracted from a captured
pilot who revealed the attack was planned for the
20th or the 21st. This was subsequently confirmed
by other prisoners and by the latest reports of RFC

crews who now knew better what to look for. Below them, the German front lines bristled with guns, weaponry, and the undeniable signs of a huge army in the last stages of preparation.

B6738 SPAD 7 23Sqn
**OP AA shot prop off ftl OK(Capt HFS Drewitt NZ.)

B6843 SPAD 13 23Sqn
OP combat with HA seen shot down in flames cr nwBELLICOURT A.20.b.6.7.6. **MIA(2Lt TG Shaw **KIA**) left 3-27pm

B6860 SPAD 13 23Sqn
**OP combat? 10-25am neLA FÈRE 10000′ going n-e MIA but OK(2Lt RJ Smith) turned up later

B8407 SE5a 24Sqn
+* combat with PfalzDIII[+des] sRAMICOURT 6-20pm OK(2Lt AK Cowper Aust.) Cowper made 11 claims in March 1918, including 6 in this a'c

DH4 27Sqn
** (/Sgt AJ Perkins **WIA**)

B1231 Bristol F2b 48Sqn
**OP AA shot up ST QUENTIN ftl OK(2Lt N Roberts/ Cpl T Ramsden) [?"Bristol" claim combat LE CATELET 4-20pm Vzfw F Piechulek Ja56]["Bristol" claim combat BONY 4-25pm Oblt F Schleiff Ja56]

DH4 57Sqn
** (Capt A Roulstone MC **WIA**/2Lt WC Venmore **WIA**)

C4632 Bristol F2b 62Sqn
**OP AA ftl cr o't shell hole OK(2Lt JW Symons/Sgt WN Holmes)

B673.A SE5a 64Sqn
**COP shot up ftl ldg a'dr 11-45am dam OK(2Lt JFT Barrett) [?"SE5" claim combat MARCOING 10-25am Ltn F Rumey Ja5]

B684.Y SE5a 64Sqn
**COP shot up ldg a'dr ok OK(2Lt PS Burge) [?possible "SE5" claim combat HOLNON WOOD 10-30am Vzfw Weimar Ja56]

B5632 Sopwith Camel 65Sqn
+* combat with AlbatrosDV[+des] ZUIDHOEK 11-25am OK(Maj JA Cunningham) made 10 claims

B9209 Sopwith Camel 80Sqn
OP left 9-30am combat sCAMBRAI 10-20am **MIA(Capt StCC Tayler **KIA**)

B9229 Sopwith Camel 80Sqn
OP combat with HAs sCAMBRAI 10-20am shot down nrLESDAIN **MIA(2Lt JL Holt **KIA**) left 9-30am

B6420 Sopwith Camel 1(Naval)Sqn
HighOP combat with Pfalz ovROULERS shot down ovHOUTHULST FOREST **MIA(AFCdr RP Minifie DSC **POW**) ?combat MOORSLEDE 12-15pm Vzfw F Ehmann Ja47]

18th March

C4844 Bristol F2b 11Sqn
DOP shot down FRESNOY LE GRAND-BOHAIN **MIA(Capt AP Maclean **POW DoW**/Lt FH Cantlon MC Can. **KIA**) left 9-30am ["Bristol" claim combat JONCOURT 11-15am Ltn G Geigl Ja16][F2b claim combat sLONCOURT 11am Ltn S Gussmann Ja11]

B1152.C Bristol F2b 22Sqn
+* combat with AlbatrosDV[+des] CARVIN 10-15am OK(Capt FGC Weare/Lt GS Hayward) Weare claimed 11 victories in 5 weeks, Hayward eventually 25

A2171 DH4 25Sqn
PhotRec MAUBEUGE **MIA(Lt JH Wensley **POW**/ 2Lt AW Matson **POW**) left 9-10am

B3605 Nieuport 24bis 29Sqn
+* combat with PfalzDIII[+des] seRUMBEKE 11-45am OK(Lt FJ Williams)

B6823 Nieuport 27 29Sqn
OP left 10-45pm combat with HA seROULERS 11-45am **MIA(2Lt RE Neale **KIA**) ["Nieu" claim combat HOOGLEDE 12-05pm Vzfw F Ehmann Ja47]

B6836 Nieuport 27 29Sqn
OP left 10-45am combat 11-45am seROULERS **MIA(Lt LA Edens **KIA**) Ja28?

B5243 Sopwith Camel 54Sqn
OP left 10-10am large EA formation 2m eBUSIGNY **MIA(2Lt WG Ivamy **POW**) MvR66 ["Camel" claim combat AUBIGNY 11-15am Rittm M Fr vRichthofen JG1]

B5421 Sopwith Camel 54Sqn
OP left 10-10am combat with large EA formation 2m eBUSIGNY **MIA(Lt N Clark **KIA**)

C1566 Sopwith Camel 54Sqn
OP left 10-10am combat large EA formation 2m eBUSIGNY **MIA(2Lt G Russell **KIA**) possibly **DoW** as **POW** ["Camel" claim combat ST MARTIN 11-10am Vzfw K Bohnenkamp Ja22]

C1576 Sopwith Camel 54Sqn
OP left 10am combat large EA form 2m eBUSIGNY **MIA(2Lt EB Lee **POW**) [?"Sopwith" claim combat eBOHAIN 11-15am Vzfw E Scholtz Ja11]

C6720 Sopwith Camel 54Sqn
OP left 10-10am combat large EA formation 2m eBUSIGNY **MIA(Capt FL Luxmoore **POW**) ["Camel" claim combat swVAUX-AUBIGNY 11-10am Ltn H Kirschstein Ja6, but possibly dam in combat and ftl]

These five Camel casualties for 54 Squadron made up only a part of the heavy losses suffered on a big raid to Busigny aerodrome. On the previous day there had been a completely successful raid to the same area, which involved not only bombing but an attempt to lure the defenders up so that a surprise attack

could be launched on them up-sun from the east. The units involved were 5 (Naval) and 84 Squadron. When the ruse was attempted again on the 18th, two Flights of 54 Squadron Camels were added to the fighter component so that a total of twenty-four fighters were available for the surprise attack. When the German formations came up to confront 5 (Naval)'s DH4s it is likely they were ready to fight this time for they numbered perhaps fifty aircraft, and a huge dogfight was soon raging. The action drifted eastwards towards Le Cateau and was very intense, Richthofen's Circus being involved. All Allied units lost machines and suffered other casualties.

A7548   DH4   55Sqn
**B MANNHEIM shot up engine dam ftl nr a'dr OK(2Lt RC Sansom/Sgt J Ryan)

C5385   SE5a   60Sqn
+* combat with AlbatrosDV[+des] RUMBEKE 12-50pm OK(Capt HA Hamersley Aust.) Hamersley claimed 13 EAs with 60Sqn

B169   SE5a   84Sqn
OP left 10am combat 15000' BUSIGNY **MIA(2Lt HA Payne **KIA**)

B172   SE5a   84Sqn
OP left 10am combat with EAs 15000' ovBUSIGNY **MIA(2Lt JA McCudden MC **KIA**) brother of James McCudden [?"SE5" claim combat ESCAUCOURT 10-15am Ltn HJ Wolff Ja11]

B7217   Sopwith Camel   3(Naval)Sqn
** seen in dive with EA on tail nrHAUBOURDIN 11-05am after combat **MIA**(FSLt JL Allison **KIA**) left 10am [?"Sopwith" claim combat GONDECOURT 11-20am? Ltn H vHaebler Ja36]

A7587   DH4   5(Naval)Sqn
B combat with 3 Fokker DrIs engine hit ftl ESTRÈES cr(FSLt CE Wodehouse **WIA/AGL L James OK) left 9-44am BUSIGNY a'dr

A7663   DH4   5(Naval)Sqn
B seen in dive nrPREMONT **MIA(FSLt RB Ransford **KIA**/AGL G Smith **KIA**) [?"DH4" claim combat ST SOUPLET 11-05am Hpt W Reinhard Ja6]["English EA" claim combat BEAUREVOIR Ltn F Pütter Ja68]

B3781   Sopwith Camel   10(Naval)Sqn
** combat with EA seCOURTRAI 12-30pm then seen going east sROULERS 12-45pm **MIA**(FSLt GT Steeves **POW**) combat ovHOUTHULST WOOD? [?"Sopwith" claim combat wSWEVEZEELE 12-50am Ltn E Thuy Ja28]

19th March

RE8   5Sqn
AA fire (/Lt CKS Metford **WIA)

20th March
THE ROLE OF THE RFC IN THE GERMAN SOMME OFFENSIVE

There was rain and low cloud on the 19th which worsened on the 20th, to the extent that nearly all air activity was impossible. In addition, a mist hung over the battlefield. The British armies and the Royal Flying Corps were as ready as they could be as they waited for the inevitable, but the poor conditions limited last minute reconnaissance and heightened the uncertainty.

In this battle the support of the RFC would have to be reactive and flexible as never before in order to adapt to the unfolding crisis. Priorities and duties for the air arm to be followed once the offensive began had been laid down since January and varied only slightly between the two armies. Events were to overwhelm this orderly framework of tasks, however — in particular that of the corps squadrons — but to appreciate the scope of the air work it is worth summarising these schemes. All corps machines were to remain focused on counter-battery work, artillery patrols, counter-attack patrols, counter-battery photography, harassment of enemy troops and transport, and night bombing if resources permitted. The Army squadrons, in order of importance, were to protect the corps machines; to attack battery positions, de-training points, enemy troop concentrations and transport in order to disrupt the attack; to carry out low bombing of front line troops; and to provide high offensive patrols to protect the work down below.

In general, Camel squadrons were to concentrate on the protection of the corps machines, but for the Third Army they would also carry out low attacking patrols; Bristol Fighter squadrons were also to make disruptive attacks and low bombing, but would also do some offensive patrolling for the Third Army; and the SE5a squadrons were to make the offensive patrols over the whole battle area, where it was expected the enemy would be found operating in support of their own armies, mostly below 2000 feet. Some 48 Squadron machines were kept back to continue long reconnaissance work. It is clear from the above that there was an appreciation of how important low patrolling and ground work might be. It would soon dominate the entire programme of operations and would be the key to survival.

9 (Naval) Squadron returned to Dunkirk from its period of rest in England on the 20th of March. A few days later it was called onto the Western Front.

21st March

THE GERMAN OFFENSIVE
IN PICARDY

The German Offensive finally burst on the Western Front on the 21st of March. There was no warning it had finally arrived until a huge and continuous deluge of shelling began at 4-45am, pouring onto the British and French positions to a depth of twenty miles. The scope of the bombardment was enormous, pounding battle zones, defences, lines of communications and headquarters along a fifty-four mile front. Mixed with the explosives were gas shells which rained down on the waiting defenders neutralising their gunners and creating chaos and disruption. The five hours of shelling which followed was so intense in places that some recalled later how they found the hands of their watches stopped at the time when the barrage opened. The bombardment was selectively delivered onto key points so that when the attack came important sections of terrain remained relatively unscathed. Sixty-two German divisions were launched against the British Third and Fifth Armies between the Oise and Scarpe, with reserves standing ready. The defenders amounted to barely thirty weakened British divisions.

The Germans moved forward in the persistent fog which had thickened from the previous day. It was perfect for the initial stages of attack for it blinded the defenders and left them unable to co-operate with one another. RFC pilots generally went out despite the fog but could see little until the weather improved in the afternoon. These same conditions somewhat handicapped the plans of the German Air Force. It had been their intention to launch an intense attack on the British fighters so as to permit their army co-operation machines as much access to the battle as possible. There were also plans to comprehensively disrupt the RFC reconnaissance work and to attack balloons. The element of surprise secured the Germans early control of the air over the fighting and the co-operation machines were mostly protected. The air fighting, which developed particularly later in the day, is noted in more detail below.

Byng's Third Army was able to mount some resistance opposite Cambrai but the damage was worst in the south, where elements of the Fifth Army had been stretched and weakened in order to take over the line from the French. Contact patrolling by 15th (Corps) Wing crews was limited by fog, but their reports formed an alarming picture of enemy advance south of St Quentin.

Air fighting was intense in the afternoon and evening as German aircraft crowded the skies over their armies and the first major British efforts to meet them began to be organised. Hundreds of enemy machines were involved in contact patrol work and artillery co-operation, whilst German fighters attempted to shoot down the British corps machines on similar operations. One can see they were reasonably successful in this endeavour as all but two British corps units suffered casualties. The biggest air fights took place on the Third Army front where conditions were clearer. The most decisive was between formations from 56 and 64 Squadrons and about twenty-six enemy fighters over Bourlon Wood. Four of the enemy were claimed shot down in this dogfight. Finally, bombing of rail junctions and bridges by DH4s continued through this most critical of days but with, it has to be said, little effect.

> **Sopwith Camel   3Sqn**
> ** (2Lt J K von I Peden **WIA**)

> **B5245   Sopwith Camel   3Sqn**
> **SpRec shot up mg then dam bad ldg OK(2Lt HTW Mainwaring)

> **B5450   Sopwith Camel   3Sqn**
> **Rec shot up mg dam OK(2Lt HE Stewart) [?possible combat with Ja35]

> **B9155   Sopwith Camel   3Sqn**
> **SpRec shot down VAULX VRAUCOURT 4pm OK(Capt CM Leman) [?"Sopwith" claim combat nrBERTINCOURT 4-20pm Ltn W vManteuffel-Szoge Ja35]["Sopwith" claim combat BAPAUME, but 5-45pm? Ltn L Hanstein Ja35]

> **B2535   Sopwith Camel   4Sqn AFC**
> +*OP combat with AlbatrosDVs[+ooc+?des] sBREBIÈRES 9-05am OK(Lt AH Cobby) Cobby's first of 29 victories

The fighter squadrons attached to the First Army in the north, of which 4 Squadron AFC was one, were diverted to fight on the adjacent Third Army front during the battle. The other units involved were 2 Squadron AFC and 40 Squadron (SE5as), 43 Squadron and 3(Naval) Sqn (Sopwith Camels), 22 Squadron (Bristol Fighters), and 18 Squadron (DH4s), all of the 10th (Army) Wing.

> **B5830   A.W.FK8   8Sqn**
> **AP controls shot up ftl cr wr ldg OK(Lt JT Quick/2Lt AJ Ord)

> **C3562   A.W.FK8   8Sqn**
> **AP **MIA**(2Lt CB Banfield **POWDoW**/2Lt FK Kneller **POWDoW**) left 3-25pm, both severely injured

> **B833   RE8   12Sqn**
> **CP CROISILLES shot up ground mg dam OK(2Lt

JLS Hanman/Lt CR Cuthbert) left 10-20am, returned
12-05pm

B2273   RE8   12Sqn
**P shot up EA(2Lt HC Adams OK/Lt HC? Batchelor
WIA) initials EC?

B2292   RE8   12Sqn
**Phot mg shot down SAPIGNIES cr nrLines 1-15pm
OK(2Lt CJS Dearlove/2Lt WM Irvine) burnt a'c,
destroyed

B2297   RE8   12Sqn
**CP shot up ground mg dam OK(2Lt EC Hucklebridge/
2Lt LG Warren) left 1-10pm CROISILLES, returned
2-25pm

B5119   RE8   12Sqn
**P ECOUST shot up ground mg dam OK(2Lt JA
Scrivener/2Lt F Catterall) left 12-20pm?(sic), returned
12-25pm

RE8   12Sqn
** (Capt ET Owles MC **WIA**/)

12 Squadron operations were in the northern sector
of the Third Army front.

B8895   RE8   13Sqn
**P left 3-55pm shot through mg OK(Lt FRG McCall
MC/Lt G Dario)

A4393   RE8   15Sqn
**P shot up ground mg fire dam OK(2Lt VJ Reading/
2Lt M Leggat)

B8388   SE5a   24Sqn
**GndP left 2-35pm shot up ftl 7Cps HQ cr
abandoned(Lt HVL Tubbs **WIA**)

C1798   SE5a   24Sqn
**OP shot up ftl 1-20pm OK(Capt BPG Beanlands)

D279.A   SE5a   24Sqn
+* combat with PfalzDIII[+ooc++des]
BELLICOURT ~2-15pm OK(Lt HB Richardson) made
15 victory claims, many in this a'c

SE5a   29Sqn
** mg fire (2Lt RBE Turnbull **WIA**)

B3311   A.W.FK8   35Sqn
**P left 1-30pm ROISEL shot up dam OK(2Lt BL
Norton/2Lt RW Briggs) returned a'dr 2-50pm

B698   SE5a   41Sqn
**COP QUEANT shot down seen going down eastwards
ovQUEANT in control **MIA**(Lt AT Isbell **WIA POW**)
left 1-20pm

B6405   Sopwith Camel   46Sqn
**LowP left 11-05 shot up dam returned 1-05pm OK(Lt
JH Smith) Smith claimed several victories on Camels

C1558   Sopwith Camel   46Sqn
**LowP mg fire shot up MORY ftl 2-50pm dam OK(2Lt
RK McConnell)

C1613   Sopwith Camel   46Sqn
**LowP mg fire ftl 2-40pm OK(Lt WJ Shorter)

C1627   Sopwith Camel   46Sqn
**LowP left 1-20pm shot up dam returned 3-10pm
OK(Capt GE Thompson MC) made almost half of his 21
claims in this a'c: mostly EA reconnaissance 2Strs in the
weeks leading up to the Offensive

46 Squadron made its first low patrols, strafing
troops and batteries, as early as 6am, and continued them through the day.

C1641   Sopwith Camel   46Sqn
**travelling from 59Sq, left 6pm ldg ok WoL MIA but
OK(2Lt EEF? Elliott **WIA**) initials GEF?

B1187   Bristol F2b   48Sqn
**RecOP mg ST QUENTIN ftl WoL wr OK(2Lt CGD
Napier/2Lt JMJ Moore)

B1269   Bristol F2b   48Sqn
** combat with LVGC[+ooc] eEPHEY 2-45pm shot up
ftl(Lt E Stock OK/Cpl JH Bowler **WIA**)

A4259   RE8   52Sqn
**CP mg fire ftl ROUPY burnt a'c(Capt RE Bryson
WIA/Lt BT Head OK)

B6519   RE8   52Sqn
this a'c? **AP mg fire HAM engine ftl cr 5-35pm(2Lt JH
Reeves **WIA**/2Lt LF Goodwin OK) but see 22.3.18 ref
pilot?

B6517   RE8   59Sqn
CP ground fire shot through dam(Lt AP Kelly **WIA/
2Lt R Hegan OK)

B6547   RE8   59Sqn
**P/Rec shell hit LAGNICOURT shell passed through
fuselage at 1000' ftl OK(Capt DH Oliver/2Lt WH
Leighton)

59 Squadron carried out some very important
reconnaissances in the afternoon, including this one
by Oliver and Leighton which first revealed the
scale of the German incursions into the Third
Army front. Before they were hit they established
that the enemy was within reach of Vaulx-
Vraucourt, on a wide advance between Bullecourt
and Doignies.

B147.U   SE5a   64Sqn
+* combat with AlbatrosDV[+des] INCHY EN
ARTOIS 12-05pm then Fokker DrI[+ooc] &
AlbatrosDV[+ooc] BOURLON WOOD 1-35pm
OK(Capt JA Slater) Slater scored 24 victories

B9321   Sopwith Camel   73Sqn
*OP left 4-15pm ground fire shot up bad cr nrHAM bad
dam OK(Lt GL Graham)

B2456   Sopwith Camel   80Sqn
**P combat with HA ST QUENTIN-ROUPY shot down
ftl abandoned OK(2Lt CSL Coulson) a'c burnt
[?"Sopwith 1Str" claim combat swVERMAND 2-25pm
Oblt Ritt R vGreim Ja34 JG10]

B5839   A.W.FK8   82Sqn
**CP mg shot up dam OK(Capt GI Paterson/Lt TI Findley)

C3640   A.W.FK8   82Sqn
Rec ground mg fire dam(2Lt LS Kiggell OK/2Lt AO Matt **inj)

22nd March

In desperate fighting in the coming days, the defenders were swept from their positions in the battle zone and driven back across the Somme by the tremendous onslaught. The most critical losses of territory continued to occur here in the south, where the defenders found themselves pressed back into their most rearward positions, with orders to hold the line at all costs. It appeared for a while that the objective of Amiens might be there for the taking. The RFC units attached to the Fifth Army were already in withdrawal, with one, 5 (Naval), having been bombed out of its aerodrome.

Air fighting increased steadily all along the front on the 22nd as the RFC strengthened its presence in the air and began to focus its energies more effectively into the defence of key areas. This was particularly noticeable on the Third Army front before Arras and Bapaume, where a strong resistance to the advance was about to develop. Most fighting further south occurred in the afternoon again, as a result of the indifferent weather. The control of the air here was still generally with the German Air Force, but it was hoped that the increasing size and scope of Allied patrolling would slowly begin to assert itself. All corps machines were now carrying bombs on their co-operation flights, which they mostly dropped from very low heights. German activity on the ground behind the lines was intense and drew all the efforts of the day and night bombing squadrons.

** (Lt RW Coutts **POW**)

C9539.V   SE5a   2Sqn AFC
+* combat with 2Str[+ooc] neST QUENTIN 3-10pm OK(Lt HG Forrest) Forrest's first of 11 victories in this a'c

D212   SE5a   2Sqn AFC
P seen eEPEHY at 5000' going west combat with EAs shot down **MIA(Capt RW Howard **DoW**) left 5pm, Howard had scored several victories in this a'c in the previous three weeks

B3376   A.W.FK8   8Sqn
**CP shell fire nrPERONNE dam OK(2Lt R Grice/2Lt MR Picot) left 12-40pm, returned to MOISLAINS 1-15pm but a'c abandoned

A3626   RE8   12Sqn
**P ground mg shot down ovST LEGER nrLines 5-30pm

OK(2Lt Achton/Lt DM Cassidy MC) burnt a'c destroyed

B4040   RE8   12Sqn
P left 4-20pm IV Corps front **MIA(Capt JM MacIlwaine **KIA**/2Lt WM Irvine **KIA**)

             RE8   15Sqn
** (/2Lt LJ Bayley **WIA**)

C1797   SE5a   24Sqn
**OP engine shot up ftl 5pm abandoned burnt a'c OK(2Lt PJ Nolan)

D272   SE5a   24Sqn
OP left 3-15pm(Capt BPG Beanlands **WIA) was MIA, 24.3?

B327   A.W.FK8   35Sqn
**P combat with EA shot down POEUILLY destr a'c OK(2Lt MGW Stewart/Lt LC Keen)

C8201   Sopwith Camel   43Sqn
*OP AIZECOURT engine ftl 8Sqn abandoned burnt a'c 12-30pm OK(2Lt GA Lingham) left 11-25am

C8243   Sopwith Camel   43Sqn
*OP left 11-55am engine ftl 8Sqn abandoned burnt a'c OK(2Lt AK Lomax)

B1255   Bristol F2b   48Sqn
OP shot up ST QUENTIN(2Lt NH Muirden OK/2Lt ES Herring **WIA) destroyed on a'dr prior to evacuation

B1301   Bristol F2b   48Sqn
OP shot up seFLEZ(2Lt CA Hore MC **WIA/Lt SR Parker **WIA**) unsalvable

C4606   Bristol F2b   48Sqn
** combat with EAs[+capt+ooc] seFLEZ shot up(2Lt ACG Brown **WIA**/2Lt GC Bartlett OK)

B6565   RE8   52Sqn
B mg fire ftl burnt a'c(Lt TE Logan **WIA/2Lt SW Swaine OK) left 4-40pm

B7803   RE8   52Sqn
Rec mg fire ftl burnt a'c(2Lt JH Reeves **WIA/Lt AW Foy OK) left 1-30pm, but see 21.3.18 ref pilot **WIA**?

             RE8   52Sqn
** (/2Lt FL Heigham-Plumptre **WIA**)

A4400   RE8   53Sqn
** **MIA**(2Lt TEH Birley **POW**/2Lt E Dennis **KIA**) [?"RE8" claim combat ESSIGNY LE GRAND-LIEZ 2-40pm OffSt F Altemeier Ja24, but see RE8 A4438?]

A4438   RE8   53Sqn
** (2Lt BG Poole **KIA**/2Lt GF Moseley **WIA**) was MIA [?"RE8" claim GENLIS WOOD 3pm Ltn H Kroll Ja24, but see RE8 A4400]

C1657   Sopwith Camel   54Sqn
OP left 2-50pm combat with EA shot up ftl cr wr(2Lt EA Richardson **WIA)

            Sopwith Camel   54Sqn
** (2Lt NM Drysdale **WIA**)

B536   SE5a   56Sqn
**OP combat with EA shot up ftl dam OK(Lt KW
Junor) [?"SE" claim combat VERMAND Ltn H Böhning
Ja79]

Sopwith Camel   65Sqn
** (Lt CB Matthews **WIA**)

C8214   Sopwith Camel   70Sqn
**OP combat with HA nwCAMBRAI dived & glided
west but ftl Lines (2Lt JRW Thompson **DoW**)to
hospital, left 2-30pm, a'c abandoned[?"Sopwith"
claim combat HAVRINCOURT 3-55pm OffSt O
Esswein Ja26][?Sopwith claim combat
GRAINCOURT-FLESQUIÈRES 3-55pm Ltn F
Loerzer Ja26]but these swCAMBRAI?

C8235   Sopwith Camel   70Sqn
**OP left 2-25pm combat with HA nwCAMBRAI
MIA(2Lt HK Cassels **POW**)

C1619   Sopwith Camel   73Sqn
+* combat with AlbatrosDV[+destr] DOUCHY 2-30pm
then attacked LVGs[++destr] nrROISEL 3-10pm
OK(Capt TS Sharpe)

B7282   Sopwith Camel   73Sqn
**OP combat with AlbatrosDV[+flames] HAM 2-30pm
shot up(Capt AH Orlebar **WIA**)leg

Typical of the continuous offensive patrols
carried out on the 22nd was the one by 73
Squadron in the afternoon. The eleven Camels
met a large enemy formation near Ham on
their way out on patrol, where Sharpe and
Orlebar each shot down an Albatros. Half an
hour later they met and fought another eight
Albatroses north-west of St Quentin.

A.W.FK8   82Sqn
** (2Lt JEA Kernahan **WIA**/)

B5823   A.W.FK8   82Sqn
**CP combat with 2 Fokker DrIs ovLA NEUVILLE ftl
destr a'c(2Lt D Adams **WIA**/2Lt EW Keep **WIA**?)

B8337   SE5a   84Sqn
+* combat with PfalzDIII[+des] FOYET 2-45pm?
OK(Capt FE Brown MC Can.) pilot had a total of 10
victories

A7665   DH4   2(Naval)Sqn
** AA cr PERVYSE 4pm(FSLt FEA Bembridge **inj**/
AM1 HG Lovelock **KIA**) left 2-15pm

B7216   Sopwith Camel   3(Naval)Sqn
**OP air collision with B7219 in dive on EA folded cr
nrST QUENTIN **MIA**(FSLt LA Sands **KIA**) left 1pm

B7219   Sopwith Camel   3(Naval)Sqn
**OP air collision with B7216 in dive on EA folded up cr
nrST QUENTIN **MIA**(FSLt WA Moyle **KIA**) left 1pm

B7229   Sopwith Camel   3(Naval)Sqn
+* combat with AlbatrosDV[+ooc] MARQUION
12-30pm OK(FSLt AB Ellwood) made several claims in
this a'c

23rd March

101 and 102 Squadrons had bombed enemy troop
billets behind the Fifth Army overnight and
brought back news of huge movements westwards
along the Mont d'Origny — St Quentin Road. This
convinced the commander of the Fifth Army that a
withdrawal west of the Somme was now essential.
At least by these actions his army might be saved
from defeat and the decisive battle for Amiens
delayed. In consequence, the right of the Third
Army was forced to retire from the Flesquières
salient as well, but they suffered a fatal delay and
for a time the two armies lost touch. A crucial
weakness at the junction of the two armies
developed and through the day the British forces
were pushed back past Peronne. The developing
crisis was watched and reported on by contact
patrols, and although artillery co-operation was
maintained throughout the day much information
was wasted because the British batteries were
themselves on the move and in retreat.

Ludendorff read these events as the beginning of
the end for the two British armies. As a consequence, he issued new orders so as to build on the
successes made on the Somme, making the capture
of Amiens the immediate goal. The effect of this,
however, was to divide the efforts of his own
armies, and in consequence deflect some pressure
away from the weak junction of the British armies
in front of Albert. It took him two days to realise
he had missed his chance of a killer blow to the
centre, and by the time he reversed these orders the
Allied armies had linked again. By then Gough
was standing firm around Arras and the Fifth
Army was beginning to receive the support it
needed to defend Amiens.

B9167?   Sopwith Camel   3Sqn
** (2Lt WC Dennett **WIA**) see 27.3

C4574   RE8   5Sqn
**Phot combat shot up BOIS VILAIN dam OK(2Lt PW
Woodhouse/Lt CH Brown) [?2 "RE8" claims nTILLOY
3-45pm & sDOUAI nBEUGNATRE 4-15pm Vzfw P
Bäumer Ja2]

C8429   A.W.FK8   8Sqn
**AP combat with EA shot up TEMPLEUX(2Lt LA
Buddwin OK/2Lt V Beeton **WIA**)

C8430   A.W.FK8   8Sqn
**CP shot up ground mg CHIPILLY 10am dam OK(2Lt
Hooten/2Lt H Wisnekowitz)

C3940   Sopwith Dolphin 19Sqn
+* combat with 2Str[+flames] eLILLE 3-40pm OK(Lt
AB Fairclough Can.) Fairclough eventually claimed
19EAs, incl 5 with 23Sqn

B1171   Bristol F2b   22Sqn
OP seen CAMBRAI EoL **MIA(Capt P Thompson
KIA/2Lt DW Kent-Jones **POW**) left 9-05am

C4827   Bristol F2b   22Sqn
**OP combat with HA ftl HOM 11-30am OK(2Lt HL
Christie/Lt NT Berrington) a'c shelled destroyed

B167   SE5a   24Sqn
**OP mg dam ESMERY MALLON a'c abandoned
OK(2Lt WF Warner) left 3-40pm

C9627   SE5a   24Sqn
**OP left 3-40pm mg dam CHAMPIEN wr OK(Lt RG
Hammersley)

B3622   Nieuport 27   29Sqn
+* combat with 2Str[+des] ePASSCHENDAELE
10-50am OK(Capt RH Rusby) made 10 claims with
29Sqn, including several on SE5as

This was the last victory claim in Nieuport scouts
for 29 Squadron before fully re-equipping with
SE5a fighters.

A.W.FK8   35Sqn
** (/2Lt BJ Bevan **WIA**)

B3369   A.W.FK8   35Sqn
*P engine shot up ftl 3-40pm dam burnt a'c OK(2Lt GN
Hardwick/2Lt H Hanson) left 3-10pm

C3631   A.W.FK8   35Sqn
**OP combat with HA shot down MONS 11-30am burnt
a'c OK(Capt LG? Paling/Capt Fasson)

C1752   SE5a   41Sqn
+* combat with AlbatrosDV[+des+ooc]BOURLON
WOOD 11-30am OK(Lt FH Taylor)

41 Squadron claimed five combat victories in the
day's fighting.

B5247   Sopwith Camel   46Sqn
**LowP shot up dam OK(2Lt MM Freehill)

C1564   Sopwith Camel   46Sqn
**LowP seen in combat ovMORCHIES snd? 2pm
MIA(2Lt ERH Edelston **POW**) left 12-20pm
[?"Sopwith" claim combat LAGNICOURT Ltn H
Bongartz Ja36]["Sopwith 1Str" claim combat sST
LEGER 1-30pm Vzfw P Bäumer Ja2]

The situation for the Third Army was not as severe
as that for the Fifth Army, but a breakthrough in
front of Bapaume clearly threatened and several
squadrons were called on to supplement low
strafing and bombing attacks, particularly around
Beugny and Vaulx Vraucourt. Amongst those
involved on the 23rd were 46 Squadron, which
suffered the above casualty, Nos.3, 3 (Naval), and
4AFC all in Sopwith Camels, 41 Squadron in
SE5as, and 59 Squadron in RE8s. German
Jagdstaffeln were also attempting to carry out this

work in the same area, and some of the fighter units
mentioned above met and fought them in the
heaviest air fighting of the day. In general, the RFC
units had the better of these battles — 46 Squadron
for example claimed the staggering figure of nineteen fighters and two-seaters in the day's combats.

C4707   Bristol F2b   48Sqn
+* combat with LVGC[+des] & PfalzDIII[+des]
MATIGNY 4-25pm OK(Capt WL Wells/Cpl W Beales)
also shot down LVG nwHAM 11-24am that day, this air
crew scored several victories

DH4   49Sqn
B (2Lt RA Curry **WIA/)

RE8   52Sqn
** (Capt W Deane **WIA**/)

B59.3   SE5a   56Sqn
**OP left 6-20am shot up dam ftl 8-15am OK(Lt EDG
Galley)

A3600   RE8   59Sqn
P left 6-30am **MIA(2Lt F Naylor **KIA**/2Lt HJC
Reynish **KIA**)

RE8   59Sqn
** (Lt LS Gray **WIA**/)

B7478   Sopwith Camel   70Sqn
**OP shot up CAMBRAI ftl nrBAPAUME abandoned
burnt a'c(2Lt G Richardson **WIA**) [?possible "Sopwith
1Str" claim combat sCHERISY Ltn F Loerzer Ja26,
but see 46Sq a'c?]

C1672   Sopwith Camel   70Sqn
+* combat with AlbatrosDV[+ooc] nwCAMBRAI
8-35am OK(Lt A Koch Can.) last of 10 victory claims

C8205   Sopwith Camel   70Sqn
+* combat with 2Str[+des] VITRY 5pm OK(Lt EH
Peverell) claimed 5 victories

C8238   Sopwith Camel   70Sqn
**LowP left 4-15pm shot up BIHUCOURT ftl(Lt KA
Seth-Smith **WIA**) claimed several victories

C8244   Sopwith Camel   70Sqn
**OP left 7-55am CAMBRAI seen neBAPAUME
MIA(2Lt CH Clarke **POW**) seen by Lt HW Ransom
& Lt KA Seth-Smith ["Camel" claim combat HAM
am Vzfw U Neckel Ja12]

C3905   Sopwith Dolphin 79Sqn
**OP ROISEL-SERANCOURT seen 1m ePERONNE
MIA(2Lt AFG Clarke **POW**) left 10-30am
[?"Dolphin" claim combat CARTIGNY 1-20pm? Ltn
F Rumey Ja5]

This was the first Sopwith Dolphin shot down in
action.

B637   SE5a   84Sqn
+* combat with AlbatrosDV[+des] neHAM 4-55pm
OK(Capt KMGStCG Leask) last of 8 victories

Squadrons in support of the Fifth Army were also thrown into operations involving low-flying strafing attacks on the enemy. They were seen as a key means of hindering their advance. 84 Squadron typically added them to their offensive patrolling, bombing and shooting up troops as they moved about the battlefield.

B7185   Sopwith Camel   3 (Naval) Sqn
+* combat with PfalzDIII[+ooc] VAULX-BEUGNATRE 5pm OK(FCdr FC Armstrong)

3 (Naval) made four claims in low fighting on the 23rd.

24th March

Notwithstanding the change of emphasis in Ludendorff's plans, the fighting around the junction of the two British armies reached its most critical phase on the 24th. The German forces seemed about to burst through between them as Combles and Lesboeffs fell in the afternoon, taking the front line some fifteen miles west of the position of three days previously. In desperation, troops were mustered, handed machine-guns, and told to delay the German advance for as long as they could whilst new defences were feverishly erected. Low flying patrols and bombings were ordered from every available machine that could be spared. Their effectiveness is evident in a German regimental history which recorded that "During the hot hours of the afternoon there was a pause, especially as the very active fighting and bombing squadrons of the enemy in the clear air imposed a very cautious advance on us".

B5433   Sopwith Camel   3Sqn
**LowB mg fire ftl 10-50am burnt a'c OK(2Lt AP Freer)

B5437   Sopwith Camel   3Sqn
LowP left 1-35pm **MIA(Lt JO Butler **POW DoW** 11.4.18)

C1615   Sopwith Camel   3Sqn
**LowP shot down mg fire 10-15am cr OK(Capt DJ Bell SA.) high scoring Camel ace, many in this a'c

B5016   RE8   16Sqn
**AOb LENS combat nwLENS 5-15pm shot up ftl BRUAY 5-35pm dam OK(2Lt HL Whittome/2Lt R Wallace) left 3-10pm

B1122   Bristol F2b   20Sqn
**OP mg fire dam ftl nwYPRES OK(2Lt L Campbell/Lt A Mills)

B6856   SPAD 13   23Sqn
**OP combat with 2Str[+flames] & PfalzDIII[+ftl] VIEFVILLE btwn 2pm & 2-15pm shot up CHAMPIEN engine dam returned a'dr OK(Capt J Fitz-Morris MC) left 1-28pm, last of over a dozen victories

B6859   SPAD 13   23Sqn
**OP left 8-07am shot up engine wROYE ftl OK(Lt JB Allen)

B6862   SPAD 13   23Sqn
**OP left 8-06am shot up I.17.d. ftl burnt a'c OK(Capt HFS Drewitt NZ.)

**   SPAD 13   23Sqn**
** (2Lt ER Varley **WIA**)

C1795   SE5a   24Sqn
**GndP shot up VILLERS BRETONNEAUX ftl 6pm abandoned OK(Capt AK Cowper MC)

B2079   DH4   27Sqn
**B combat LANDRECIES ftl cr a'dr OK(2Lt GR Norman/2Lt BCD Oliver)

B2108   DH4   27Sqn
**B LANDRECIES combat WoL seen with EA on tail MIA but OK?(2Lt BI Johnstone/2Lt Lord CC Douglas)

The RFC Headquarters bombing squadrons, Nos. 25 and 27, continued to attack rail centres. They had suffered relatively little interference in their work since the offensive had begun but on the 24th, as they returned home, 27 Squadron was attacked by eleven enemy fighters and heavily shot up. 49 Squadron in the Third Army area, and 5 (Naval) on the Somme were also regularly bombing rail targets and bridges.

**   A.W.FK8   35Sqn**
** (2Lt LE Jones **WIA**/2Lt H Hanson **WIA**) crew?

Hanson may be the 35 Squadron observer mentioned in the Official History who called up vital fire onto the Bethancourt Bridge, until he was wounded by ground fire. This delayed the advance appreciably.

A7221   Bristol F2b   35Sqn
**travelling(to Sqn?) shelled whilst taxying, a'c burnt and abandoned

C3532   A.W.FK8   35Sqn
**B CHIPILLY A'dr shot up gunfire dam returned a'dr 4-45pm OK(2Lt AG Hanna/2Lt RA Burnard) left 2-45pm

C3534   A.W.FK8   35Sqn
**P combat with HA shot down CARBONNEL ftl 2pm OK(Lt RMC MacFarlane/2Lt AE Lancashire)

C3549   A.W.FK8   35Sqn
**Phot combat BETHANCOURT ftl 12-20pm burnt a'c OK(2Lt E Pybus/2Lt WW Jones)

C8433   A.W.FK8   35Sqn
**B left 11am shot up gunfire returned a'dr OK(2Lt AG Hanna/2Lt RA Burnard)

C1054   SE5a   41Sqn
OP left 2-10pm HAVRINCOURT **MIA(2Lt JP McCone US. **KIA**)

C6399   SE5a   41Sqn
OP left 2-05pm HAVRINCOURT **MIA(2Lt DC Tucker **KIA**) ["SE5" claim combat COMBLES 2-45pm Rittm M Fr vRichthofen JG1, but see C1054]

C8240   Sopwith Camel   43Sqn
+* combat with AlbatrosDV[+des] BULLECOURT 11-30am OK(2Lt HC Daniel SA.) most of his 9 claims were made in this a'c

C8270   Sopwith Camel   43Sqn
**OP combat with DFWCs[+des+flames] then AlbatrosDV[+des] eMERCATEL, then in afternoon, combat with 2 AlbatrosCs[++des] & 2Str[+des] SAILLY SAILLISEL 3-20pm OK(Capt JL Trollope), first DFW shared, 6 EA shot down in 1 day

On a day of heavy fighting Trollope excelled all others by being the first man to shoot down six enemy aircraft in two engagements in the same day. The total air fighting claims were twenty-four shot down on the Third Army front, where Trollope was operating, and seventeen on the Fifth Army front.

C1554   Sopwith Camel   46Sqn
LowP left 3pm with formation SAILLY SAILLISEL **MIA(Lt JD Currie **POW**) [?"Sopwith 1Str" claim combat neCHAUNY 3-45pm OffSt F Altemeier Ja24, but CHAUNY nrST QUENTIN?]

C1559   Sopwith Camel   46Sqn
**LowP left 12-45pm MARQUISE shot up ftl OK(Lt EE Lindsay)

C4710   Bristol F2b   48Sqn
**LowP ground mg engine shot up ftl wFOUCAUCOURT Sh62c M.26.c. at 6-15pm OK(Capt CR Steele/2Lt EH Stanes) left 5-05pm VOYENNES, unsalvable as traffic was too heavy & the enemy too near

B5061   RE8   53Sqn
** **MIA**(Capt RH Martin **KIA**/2Lt GH Parker **KIA**) [?"RE" claim Ltn F Rumey Ja5]

RE8   53Sqn
** (/Lt FJ Pullen **WIA**)

RE8   53Sqn
** **MIA**(2Lt AA Miles **POW**/2Lt CW Cook **POW**)

C1553   Sopwith Camel   54Sqn
OP left 5pm seen 2m swPERONNE 1500' **MIA(2Lt W Knox **KIA**)

A7562   DH4   55Sqn
B MANNHEIM Chemical works seen in combat with large enemy formation of EAs over target **MIA(2Lt CF Westing **POW**/Sgt H Hodge **POW**) [?DH4 claim Ltn O Creutzmann KEST4b]

A7661   DH4   55Sqn
B MANNHEIM down in control ovPIRMASENS **MIA(2Lt NH Thackrah **POW**/Lt WG Fluke DSO **POW**)

DH4   55Sqn
B MANNHEIM (/Sgt J? Ryan **KIA)

B182   SE5a   56Sqn
OP left 4-55pm combat C-type ovLE TRANSLOY but then ground fire? **MIA(Lt ME Mealing **KIA**) was chasing UntOff Zetter/Ltn Tegeder of FAb245, Mealing had scored his 14th and last victory in this a'c at 1-15pm wTINCOURT

B666   SE5a   56Sqn
**OP combat with EA shot up ftl a'dr 7-10pm OK(Lt EDG Galley)

C1076   SE5a   56Sqn
**OP combat with EA shot up ftl a'dr 1-40pm OK(Lt KW Junor)

C5389   SE5a   56Sqn
OP left 12-35pm combat with HA wPERONNE **MIA(2Lt W Porter **KIA**) Ja34b? ["SE5" claim ETERPIGNY 1-14pm combat Oblt Ritt vGreim Ja34]

B1267   Bristol F2b   62Sqn
TrStr PERONNE-HAM **MIA(Lt AR James **POW**?/Lt JM Hay **KIA**) left 4-20pm

Bristol F2b   62Sqn
** (/2Lt F Keith **WIA**)

Sopwith Camel   70Sqn
** (2Lt GR Howsam **WIA**)

B9261   Sopwith Camel   73Sqn
GndStr left 4-30pm not seen but ftl EoL **MIA(2Lt HP Blake **POW**) [?"English EA" claim combat ASSEVILLERS? 5pm Ltn F Pütter Ja68]

C1639   Sopwith Camel   73Sqn
GndStr left 4-30pm shot down cr nrPARGNY nNESLE **MIA(2Lt V Hyatt **KIA**) nrBEAUVOIS?

D6421.D   Sopwith Camel   73Sqn
**GndStr combat with LVGC[+flames] POEUILLY-VERMAND 10-40am mg shot up dam ftl CACHY abandoned OK(2Lt WS Stephenson) left 9-05am

C3802   Sopwith Dolphin   79Sqn
** dam in hangar by EA bombs

B9239   Sopwith Camel   80Sqn
**P left 4-45pm PERONNE shot up ftl dam OK(2Lt WA Pell)

B7220   Sopwith Camel   3(Naval)Sqn
+* combat with AlbatrosDV[+ooc] VAULX 3-30pm OK(FLt AT Whealy Can.) shared, Whealy claimed many of his 27 victories in this a'c

B3774   Sopwith Camel   13(Naval)Sqn
** combat with PfalzDIII, shot down ooc cr sea & sank DEEP off NIEUPORT 11am(FSLt LC Messiter **Resc**) was MIA [?claim combat NIEUPORT 11-30am FlM C Kairies SFS]

25th March

Enemy advances by the morning of the 25th made a very grave picture. On the Third Army front the

German Army had reached the Ancre and was preparing to take Albert. A desperate order went out from Major-General JM Salmond to the 9th Wing to "send out your scout squadrons and those of No. 27, No.25, and No. 62 Squadrons that are available onto the line Grevillers-Martinpuich-Maricourt. These squadrons will bomb and shoot up everything they can see on the enemy side of this line. Very low flying is essential. All risks to be taken. Urgent." Ten more squadrons from I Brigade, normally operating up around Lille, were swept into the area to carry out low attacks, including five corps units: Nos. 2, 4, 5, 16, and 42. All but one of these squadrons were to suffer casualties in this dangerous and desperate work. Until this time most of the air attacks on ground targets had been directed at German infantry reserves, but now the enemy advance needed reinforcements of ammunition, guns and food and it was these, clogging the roads in enormous convoys behind the battle, which the ground patrols now sought to disrupt.

In the air in general, the German Air Force was being increasingly held by the weight of Allied reinforcements now entering the battle zone. Whereas in the first two days of fighting they had been able to restrict and control the many efforts of the RFC to reach the battle, the latter were now commonly penetrating the defensive screen and doing their work effectively. The RFC was, however, presiding over the gravest of situations on the ground. The increasing air support was one of the few bright features the Allies could look to at this time.

C3518   **A.W.FK8**   **2Sqn**
**LowB AA MAILLY MAILLER ftl wr OK(Lt GA Barry/Lt LR Rice)

         A.W.FK8   **2Sqn**
** (Lt CA Chisnall **WIA**/)

C1562   **Sopwith Camel**   **3Sqn**
LowB seen ovBEAULINCOURT **MIA(2Lt D Cameron **KIA**) MvR68, left 3-30pm ["SE" claim combat BAPAUME-ALBERT Rd 3-55pm Rittm M Fr vRichthofen JG1]

B7303   **Sopwith Camel**   **4Sqn AFC**
*LowB shot up BASSEUX ftl just WoL shelled OK(2Lt HG Watson)

         RE8   **4Sqn**
** (2Lt FT Jackson **WIA**/)

         RE8   **5Sqn**
** (2Lt N Bury **WIA**/)

B6572   **RE8**   **5Sqn**
**B mg shot up GOMMECOURT ftl 5-05pm burnt a'c OK(2Lt HC Cooke/2Lt R Key)

C4552   **RE8**   **5Sqn**
**B mg shot up AYETTE ftl 7-15pm burnt a'c OK(2Lt RS Durno/Lt RD Stewart)

B3378   **A.W.FK8**   **8Sqn**
**AP left 1pm shot up ftl bad ground dam OK(Lt JT Quick/2Lt WJT Shirlaw) returned 2-25pm

C8438   **A.W.FK8**   **8Sqn**
** shot up: not flyable so burnt & destroyed in advance

B6578   **RE8**   **12Sqn**
**CP shell hit ERVILLERS ftl OK(2Lt FS Clark/2Lt CCR Millington) burnt a'c

B5860   **RE8**   **16Sqn**
*SpM BAPAUME seen going south with others **MIA**(2Lt GG Newbury **POW**/Lt EM Chant **POW**) left 5pm

         RE8   **16Sqn**
** (/2Lt CCF Ekins **WIA**)

         RE8   **16Sqn**
** (/Capt MM Pakenham **WIA**)

B9434   **DH4**   **18Sqn**
B left 12-25pm **MIA(Capt RP Fenn **KIA**/Capt HWE Barwell MC **KIA**)

B171   **SE5a**   **24Sqn**
B left 12-30pm **MIA(2Lt RH Kirkaldy **KIA**)

C8440   **A.W.FK8**   **35Sqn**
**P engine shot up ftl nrALBERT dam OK(2Lt MGW Stewart/Lt LC Keen) left 6-30am, burnt a'c

         A.W.FK8   **35Sqn**
** (2Lt J Edelsten **WIA**/)

         A.W.FK8   **35Sqn**
** (/2Lt GJ Mortimer **WIA**)

B624   **SE5a**   **41Sqn**
+* combat with AlbatrosDV[+des] SAILLY 10-40am OK(Capt RW Chappell SA.) scored several of his 11 victories in this a'c

C8216   **Sopwith Camel**   **43Sqn**
OP air collision with DH4 12-50pm PUISIEUX-AU-MONT **MIA(2Lt HV Highton **KIA**) collided with DH9? [?"Camel" claim combat Ltn H Becker Ja12]

C1572   **Sopwith Camel**   **46Sqn**
**LowP left 1-55pm shot down sBAPAUME bad dam abandoned OK(2Lt VM Yates)

         Bristol F2b   **48Sqn**
** (/Lt DW Orr **WIA**)

C4520   **DH4**   **49Sqn**
**B combat with EA shot up VILLERS BRETONNEAUX ftl 10am cr dam OK(2Lt C Bowman/Sgt Kelsall)

Owing to the diversion of most bombing units into low ground work, 49 Squadron remained the only unit carrying out distant bombing through the daytime. FE2b night-bombers of 101 and 102

Squadrons also made raids on troops and dumps although the conditions were extremely adverse — storms, hail, and snow persisted through the night.

C4573   RE8   52Sqn
**B left 11-20am mg ftl burnt a'c OK(2Lt AD Pope/Lt HS Redpath)

B9265   Sopwith Camel   54Sqn
OP left 10am seen control eBETTONCOURT **MIA but OK?(2Lt HC Deeks)

          Sopwith Camel   54Sqn
** (2Lt AEI Clifford **WIA**)

          Sopwith Camel   54Sqn
** (2Lt HJ Richardson US. **WIA**) inj?

B6656   RE8   59Sqn
**P left 11am LOUPART WOOD shot up dam OK(Lt EG Leake/2Lt TH Upfill)

A7248   Bristol F2b   62Sqn
*deliv mg? engine cut ftl ALBERT OK(2Lt VK Hilton/Cpl J Borwein) burnt & abandoned a'c

C8217   Sopwith Camel   70Sqn
+* combat with AlbatrosDV[+des] nBAPAUME-CAMBRAI Rd 4-45pm OK(Capt FH Hobson) made 15 victory claims

B9223   Sopwith Camel   80Sqn
P left 7-20am sBAPAUME **MIA(2Lt RSFD Radcliff **KIA**)

C6724   Sopwith Camel   80Sqn
P left 7-20am sBAPAUME **MIA(2Lt G Miller **POW DoW** 31.3.18) ["Sopwith 1Str" claim combat BAPAUME am OffSt W Kühne Ja18]

          A.W.FK8   82Sqn
** (2Lt JGW March **WIA**/)

B7218   Sopwith Camel   3(Naval)Sqn
TrenchStrafe then seen fall in flames sERVILLERS re-crossing Lines **MIA(FCdr FC Armstrong **KIA**)

26th March
A CRUCIAL DAY OF AIR OPERATIONS

The wholesale redeployment of machines into low ground-attack work continued. The Third Army area north of the junction between the armies remained the critical part of the battlefield and consumed most of this effort. The Somme river itself had become the boundary between the two and the front stretching up to Albert, which would fall that day, saw the heaviest fighting.

The 9th (Headquarters) Wing again sent out every one of its machines to break up concentrations of enemy troops and transport, this time west of Bapaume, whilst V Brigade was ordered to send as many as possible in support; three of its units

sent aircraft: Nos. 5 (Naval), 54, and 84. All the fighter squadrons of I Brigade continued to come south to operate in the Third Army area and even these were joined on the 26th by four army squadrons of II Brigade, who had fought until now in Flanders. These were Nos.1 (SE5as), 19 (Sopwith Dolphins), 20 (Bristol Fighters), and 57 (DH4s). All of the units new to the sector went quickly into action and some perhaps suffered for their inexperience: No.1 Squadron, for example, lost three pilots on the first day. Including the III Brigade machines already operating there, on the 26th the RFC had concentrated twenty-seven squadrons into the offensive against ground targets on the Third Army front. In addition, Nos. 22, 41, 43, 56, 60, and 64 were carrying out offensive patrolling above the fighting.

On paper, it was by far the greatest British air concentration of the war, scraping bare significant sections elsewhere along the Western Front. It has to be remembered, however, that some of these squadrons were carrying out what was in effect relief work. So many units attached to the Third and Fifth Armies had themselves been driven back in the chaos of retreat and, in consequence, many were now seriously dislocated or operating with greatly reduced means. Aircraft were abandoned and destroyed in great numbers in these weeks of fighting. In the circumstances, the only way of making up this shortfall was to draw units in from other sectors. Nevertheless, the fighting on the ground north of the Somme had reached its decisive hour, and hundreds of airmen would play an essential role in the outcome. One can see from the casualties below that an awesome, and perhaps vital, effort was made. Crews returned repeatedly to the face of battle to make attacks and to attempt to make sense of the fighting for headquarters.

The most crucial operations for aircraft in the Fifth Army area were in defence of Roye, south of Peronne. The enemy had commenced an advance on the town that morning, clearly with the intention of dividing the British and French armies. All squadrons were drawn south of the Somme in the afternoon to strafe and bomb troops.

German AA was reasonably quiet as field guns had been given preference on the crowded roads, and this enabled the RFC to work very effectively. In general, there was also very little air fighting on the 26th. Allied pilots found the German pilots' reticence to engage a curious thing on such an important day of battle. The regimental histories of the German infantry, which bore the low attacks, showed they too could not understand it and felt betrayed. For instance, on the Fifth Army front

only 24 Squadron recorded any decisive combats. Offensive patrols in the Third Army area were made by Nos. 22, 41, 43, 56, 60, and 64 Squadrons who all reported only moderate activity. The occasional enemy fighter made an appearance, but only briefly. Pilots felt that between the numerous offensive patrols up above and the swarming aircraft on ground work below, the enemy had made little impression on the British presence in the air that day.

There were more deep-seated reasons for the absence of German fighters, however. In the first days of fighting the units had suffered heavy casualties. It will be recalled that air fighting was a major preoccupation of both sides through the first four days of the offensive. On the 25th, when the RFC made a conscious strategic decision to channel the majority of its effort into low attacks, they had already seriously depleted the German stock of machines. This was just as well as, had the RFC continued to be attacked and been forced to recommence high patrolling, their plans might have failed.

Supply difficulties were not the only enemy of the German Air Force. The success of the advance imposed its own difficulties, for in a very short time the airmen found themselves a further ten or twenty miles behind the fighting, and the pace of battle was such that liaison between the ground and air forces had begun to break down. Only when some advanced landing grounds were established in the ravaged countryside behind the fighting, and some replacements arrived, did Germany return to the air in numbers. Much of this happened too late to deflect Allied strategy.

The RFC also struggled to overcome what were almost overwhelming supply and logistical problems, but were in a slightly better position to adapt. For instance, whilst virtually all units were at some time forced back as their aerodromes were overrun by the advance, a mixture of excellent organisation and the removal of the usual formalities ensured that locations for new landing grounds were found and swiftly made ready. Between the 21st and the 5th of April, feverish activity built forty-five new aerodromes. Having a network of aerodromes to work with made the problems of supply infinitely easier — as soon as a new aerodrome was completed it was stocked in advance. This was a factor crucially lacking for the German Air Force.

B32   SE5a   1Sqn
**B combat with EA shot up AMIENS ROAD ftl 1-30pm OK(Capt HJ Hamilton)Ja26, left 12-55pm

B511   SE5a   1Sqn
SpM mg fire BAPAUME **MIA(2Lt AMcN Denovan Can. **KIA**) Ja26 [?"SE5" claim combat BIHUCOURT 5pm Ltn C Riemer Ja26]

B641   SE5a   1Sqn
SpM mg fire seen ftl o't nrBAPAUME EoL **MIA(2Lt WMR Gray SA. **POW**)

B643   SE5a   1Sqn
SpM BAPAUME seen in combat with EA **MIA(2Lt A Hollis **POW**) Ja26 [?"SE5" claim combat FAMECHON WOOD 5-20pm Ltn O Fruhner Ja26]

B8265   SE5a   1Sqn
**B mg fire? ftl LEALVILLERS 8-30am abandoned a'dr OK(Lt DM Bissett)

B2478?   Sopwith Camel   4Sqn AFC
this a'c? ** combat with EA shot up(Lt JW Wright DFC **WIA**)to hospital, ground fire?

B742   RE8   15Sqn
BP left 4-10am shot down ovALBERT **MIA(2Lt VJ Reading **KIA**/2Lt M Leggatt **KIA**) MvR70 ["RE" claim combat neALBERT 5pm Rittm M Fr vRichthofen JG1]

C3790   Sopwith Dolphin 19Sqn
LowP **MIA(2Lt FW Hainsby Can. **KIA**) [?"Mart" claim combat 5-45pm OffSt O Esswein Ja26][?"Mart" claim combat ST PIERRE 5-30pm Ltn H Lange Ja26]

C3793   Sopwith Dolphin 19Sqn
LowP strafing then going down in flames **MIA(2Lt EJ Blyth **KIA**) [?"Mart" claim combat GREVILLERSWALD 5-15pm Ltn R Plange Ja2]

B1196   Bristol F2b   20Sqn
OP ftl ALBERT 3-15pm(Lt RD Leigh-Pemberton **WIA/Capt NW Taylor OK)unsalvable

B79   SE5a   24Sqn
+*LowP combat with D-type[+flames] CROIX 2-15pm OK(Lt JEAR Daley)

B8411   SE5a   24Sqn
+*LowP combat with 2Str[+des]FRESNOY LES ROGER-GUYENCOURT 5pm OK(Lt RT Mark)

C1081   SE5a   24Sqn
+*LowP combat with 2Str[+flames] ESTRÉES-BARLEUX 9-30am OK(2Lt HB Redler)

D279   SE5a   24Sqn
+*LowP combat with 2Str[+des] DRESLINCOURT 2-30pm OK(2Lt HB Richardson)

A7526   DH4   25Sqn
B shot up mg BAPAUME ftl(2Lt CJ Fitzgibbon **WIA/2Lt RW Hobbs MC OK) left 6-40am, burnt a'c

B2076   DH4   27Sqn
B combat with 5EA controls shot up BAPAUME cr(Capt MH Turner **WIA/Lt PS Driver **KIA**) left 10-30am, abandoned & burnt a'c

B2101   DH4   27Sqn
**B combat with 3EA shot up nrFRICOURT-

CAMBRAI ftl dam OK(Lt GE Wait/2Lt WG Hurrell)
left 10-20am

B2111   DH4   27Sqn
B BAPAUME shot down **MIA(2Lt GR Norman
POW/2Lt RCD Oliver **POW**) left 7-45am

DH4   27Sqn
** (/2Lt J Mitchell **WIA**) 27Sq?

Of the five day bombing squadrons assembled for
attacks on troops around Bapaume, 27 Squadron
suffered the heaviest casualties.

A.W.FK8   35Sqn
B AMIENS(2Lt JB Coward **KIA/2Lt CG Pugsley
DoW 26.3.18)

C9540   SE5a   40Sqn
**OP left 2-50pm mg shot up SONCAMPS engine hit ftl
OK(Lt CO Rusden)

C9579   SE5a   40Sqn
**OP mg fire ftl 3(Naval)Sqn a'dr OK(Capt I Napier)

C9561   SE5a   41Sqn
OP left 12-10pm BAPAUME(2Lt GD Robin **WIA)
was MIA

Bristol F2b   48Sqn
** (/2Lt RS Herring **WIA**)

RE8   52Sqn
** (2Lt HCE Daggett **WIA**/Lt WAB Savile **WIA**) crew?

B822   RE8   52Sqn
**trav shot up dam OK(2Lt ED Jones)

B6464   RE8   52Sqn
 **B fuel tank shot up ftl burnt a'c OK(2Lt G Carter/2Lt
L Fenlow) left 2-30pm

C5052   RE8   52Sqn
B left 1-50pm **MIA(2Lt TH Buswell **KIA**/Lt CE
Wharram **KIA**)

C1568   Sopwith Camel   54Sqn
OP left 12-45pm seen ovROYE in control **MIA(2Lt
ATW Lindsay **POW**)

B6533   RE8   59Sqn
 B left 6-30am **MIA(2Lt JR Aikins? **KIA**/Lt WT
Saidler **KIA**) name Aikens?

B7689   RE8   59Sqn
B shot up ftl LEALVILLERS(2Lt RC Richards **WIA/
2Lt TW Barlow **WIA**) burnt a'c

C8255   Sopwith Camel   70Sqn
LowP shot up mg ftl 8-15am(2Lt RG Mitchell **WIA)

C1619   Sopwith Camel   73Sqn
**GndStr mg fire ftl ALBERT a'c abandoned OK(2Lt G
Pilditch)

C3859   Sopwith Dolphin 79Sqn
**OP HAM-NESLE seen going west PERONNE-
AMIENS RD **MIA**(Capt JGJ Kilkelly **KIA**) left 11-45am

B9179   Sopwith Camel   80Sqn
*P mg fire ftl nrALBERT?(Capt DDG Hall MC **DoW**
27.3.18)

C8448   A.W.FK8   82Sqn
**LP mg shot down ftl cr ldg looking for ambulance
11-15am(Lt RCStJ Dix OK/Lt RM Montgomery **WIA**)
burnt a'c, 25.3.18

B7223   Sopwith Camel   3(Naval)Sqn
** combat shot up(FLt WH Chisam **WIA**)hand, claimed
several victories in March

In the evening, the night bombing undertaken was
the heaviest the war had seen. FE2bs of Nos. 58,
83, 101 and 102 Squadrons dropped tons of bombs
on troops and transport around Bapaume in
repeated raids which continued until dawn.

27th March

The direst circumstance faced the Fifth Army on
the 27th. The right corps of the Third Army had
mistakenly withdrawn along the north bank of the
Somme the previous afternoon, leaving the Fifth
Army left flank completely exposed. This was hotly
exploited by the enemy, who needed only to cross
the river in order to launch an attack on the rear
of the army. The British had no option but to
abandon their positions and withdraw. Proyart
soon fell and it seemed as though the remnants of
the fighting force which now made up the Fifth
Army front line might be driven southwards from
the Somme and pushed into defeat. In what was a
truly great feat of endurance and bravery, the
exhausted army managed to halt the German
advance just after the abandonment of Framerville.

The skies above this fighting were thick with air
assistance, the RFC shifting its attention from
Albert down to the Somme in the first hours that
it was known the enemy had found an open flank
and were crossing the river. Ground attacks were
made by machines of corps and army units from I,
II and III Brigades. Enemy fighters had also
appeared again, mostly in similar low attack work
for their army. As a consequence, the majority of
combats occurred well down.

North of the Somme the situation had stabilised
somewhat. This was just as well as the the Third
Army was now pushed hard up against its most
rearward positions. Albert had fallen overnight but
the enemy had finally been held there. The day
bombing squadrons and ground-attack machines
worked tirelessly all day to stall the advance. In the
fighting, one of the crews of a 2 Squadron FK8 took
part in an action for which the pilot was awarded
the Victoria Cross. The crew was McLeod and
Hammond, noted below.

They had set out to bomb and strafe troops east of Albert but en route attacked and shot down a Fokker Triplane. They were then set upon by another eight Triplanes and through a long and intense fight Hammond's rear gun accounted for another two. By this time, however, McLeod had received five wounds and his gunner six, so that when an enemy bullet hit their petrol tank and it burst into flames the situation became desperate. McLeod nevertheless climbed out onto a wing and by steep side-slipping of the aircraft, kept the flames from engulfing them whilst enabling Hammond to keep up some defence with his gun. They eventually crashed in no man's land and, despite appalling wounds, McLeod pulled his gunner from the burning aircraft and dragged him to safety. This was done under heavy enemy machine-gun fire and shelling, and the pilot was wounded once more by shrapnel whilst he was saving his comrade. McLeod was able to be returned to his native Canada but succumbed to his wounds in November. Hammond required the amputation of his leg, but survived.

B288   A.W.FK8   2Sqn
**LowB left 3-20pm ALBERT MIA(2Lt ET Smart KIA/ 2Lt KP Barford KIA)

B5773   A.W.FK8   2Sqn
**SpLowB ALBERT attacked Fokker DrI[+ooc] then combat with 8 Fokker DrIs[++flames] shot up engine caught fire ftl cr n.m.l. MIA(2Lt AA McLeod Can. DoW 6.11.18/Lt AW Hammond MC WIA) left 2-50pm, VC Action ["2Str" claim combat swALBERT 3-20pm Ltn H Kirschstein Ja6]

**   A.W.FK8   2Sqn**
** (Lt JS Dunkerley WIA/)

**   A.W.FK8   2Sqn**
** (/Lt WHM Wardrope WIA)

D3502   SE5a   2Sqn AFC
**P EA gunfire EoL BOUZINCOURT ftl 9-30am cr OK(Lt G Brettingham-Moore) [?"SE5a" claim combat nPOZIÈRES 10-30am Ltn F Friedrichs Ja10]

B9167   Sopwith Camel   3Sqn
**Low B left 6-40am seen ovFRICOURT MIA(2Lt WC Dennett KIA) [?"SE5" claim combat BRAY-SUR-SOMME 7-15am Oblt H Auffahrt Ja29] [?"1Str" claim combat swALBERT 8am Ltn H Bongartz Ja36]["Camel" claim combat ALBERT 7-15am Vzfw K Pech Ja29]

B9319   Sopwith Camel   3Sqn
**LowB left 9-05am Third Army front ground mg shot up(2Lt HE Stewart WIA)arm, returned 10am

C1570   Sopwith Camel   3Sqn
**LowP left 2-50pm seen nrFRICOURT MIA(2Lt TF Rigby KIA) ["Camel" claim combat neALBERT 3-25pm Ltn H Kirschstein Ja6]

B7347   Sopwith Camel   4Sqn AFC
*LowB mg fire? LAMOTTE cr o't shell hole(2Lt AW Adams WIA)to hospital, combat?, a'c captured?

B2272   RE8   5Sqn
**B mg controls shot up PROVILLE ftl dam OK(2Lt AE Burton/Lt WA Milton) left 10-15am

C3611   A.W.FK8   8Sqn
**CP mg shot up dam returned 3-15pm OK(2Lt LC Hooton/2Lt H Wisnekowitz) left 1-15pm
MORLANCOURT

C3662   A.W.FK8   8Sqn
**AP mg rifle shot up dam OK(Capt AV Milton/Lt JW Campbell-Dick) left 12-05pm, returned 2-25pm

C8435   A.W.FK8   8Sqn
**CP radiator shot up ftl cr ldg 4-45pm OK(2Lt AM Kinnear/Lt H Fenton) left 11-30am

B5840   A.W.FK8   10Sqn
*NB left 10-20pm MIA(Lt FJ Westfield WIA POW)

B1332   Bristol F2b   11Sqn
**Rec left 11-15am ALBERT-SOMME MIA(Capt HR Child KIA/Lt A Reeve KIA) see Bristol Fighter B1156 of 20 Squadron below

B3418   RE8   16Sqn
**SpM left 3-05pm ALBERT MIA(2Lt G Gornall KIA/ 2Lt RA Steel KIA) [?"RE8" claim combat swALBERT Ltn R Plange Ja2][?"RE8" claim combat ALBERT but 9-55am? Ltn F Ray Ja49]

B5028.15   RE8   16Sqn
**SpM shot up ftl then MIA(2Lt L Playne KIA/2Lt H Carbines KIA) landed at 84Sqn a'dr, left 3pm for home but disappeared

A7767   18Sqn   DH4
**B left 9-25am MIA(2Lt RB Smith US? POW/1AM H Sinclair POW?) ["DH4" claim combat BAPAUME 11am Ltn H Habich Ja49]

B1156   Bristol F2b   20Sqn
**LowB ALBERT MIA(Capt RK Kirkman POW/Capt JH Hedley POW) [?"BF" claim combat FOUCAUCOURT 4-30pm Rittm M Fr vRichthofen JG1, but some time doubt: did they leave in morning?] [F2b claim combat sALBERT 11am Ltn K Gallwitz & Vzfw E Scholtz Ja2]

Regarding von Richthofen's victories on the 27th of March there have been assorted Dolphins, DH4s, etc put forward as alternatives to the two Bristol Fighters which were once believed to be his victims that day. Without attempting to solve this problem, if von Richthofen's claim times were wrong in some way but still seen as a pair, then claims for F2bs B1156 and B1332 are still possible in the light of other factors. However, the "Dolphin" theory has strong claims — see C4016 of 79 Squadron below which, being still a relatively new type, he may have mistaken for a Bristol Fighter (also refer 11 Squadron entries above).

B6848.C   SPAD 13   23Sqn
RecB mg fire? seARVILLERS ftl cr EoL **MIA(2Lt RD Kennedy **KIA**) left 10-38am

A7535   DH4   25Sqn
**B shell hit u'c axle cr ldg 1-15pm dam OK(2Lt BL Lindley/Sgt A Remington) left 11-25am sBRAY

A7664   DH4   25Sqn
B left 7am eALBERT **MIA(2Lt CG Pentecost **KIA**/Lt A Rentoul **KIA**) [?"DH4" claim combat wMIRAUMONT 7-50am Ltn E Loewenhardt Ja10][?"Bristol" claims combat ALBERT 7-55am Ltn H Bongartz Ja36][?"Bristol" claim combat AVELUY WOOD 8am Serg A Hübner Ja36]

D8372   DH4   25Sqn
**B AA combat with EA shot up ftl seAEQ 7-50am dam OK(2Lt FF Keen/Cpl T Ramsden)

B5828   A.W.FK8   35Sqn
**B shot up dam returned 12-15pm OK(2Lt JLS Fry/2Lt G Hall) left 11-15am [?possible "RE8" claim combat ALBERT 11-50am Ltn E Udet Ja11]

C8490   A.W.FK8   35Sqn
**P mg shot up VILLERS BRETONNEAUX ftl dam OK(2Lt AG Hanna/2Lt RA Burnard) left 12-25pm

D3507   SE5a   40Sqn
EscOP left 9-05am **MIA(2Lt FCB Wedgwood **WIA POW**)slight

**   RE8   42Sqn**
** (/Capt MF Bridge **WIA**)

B6528   RE8   42Sqn
RecB left 10-50am(Lt JVR Brown **WIA/2Lt CF Warren **WIA**) was MIA [?"RE" claim combat sMORCOURT 11-40am Hpt W Reinhard Ja6]

B7311   Sopwith Camel   46Sqn
LowP combat with HA ALBERT 6-15pm ftl(Lt GD Jenkins **WIA) was MIA, a'c found but unsalvable

**   Sopwith Camel   46Sqn**
** (2Lt RE Lindsay **WIA**)

**   Bristol F2b   48Sqn**
** (/2Lt HJ Finnemore **DoW**)

B3409   RE8   52Sqn
**B mg? shot up engine seized ftl LA HOUSSOYE dam OK(2Lt AD Pope/Lt HS Redpath) left 11-40am

C1574   Sopwith Camel   54Sqn
OP left 10am mg fire ALBERT **MIA(Capt WR Fish **KIA**)

C1633   Sopwith Camel   54Sqn
**OP mg ftl cr nrMORLANCOURT ~8-30am wr OK(2Lt ACR Hawley) unsalvable, MORCOURT?

**   Sopwith Camel   54Sqn**
** (2Lt MS Pettitt **WIA**)

B119.1   SE5a   56Sqn
**P left 5-40pm seen in combat with HA

BERNANCOURT? **MIA**(2Lt WS Maxwell **KIA**) BERTRANCOURT? [?"SE5" claim combat nwALBERT Ltn H Vallendor Ja2][?"SE5" claim combat swALBERT Ltn R Plange Ja2]

B8266   SE5a   56Sqn
+* combat with AlbatrosDV[+des] seBRAY 1-15pm OK(Lt HJ Walkerdine) shared

A2155   DH4   57Sqn
**BPhot BAPAUME AA shot up ftl dam OK(Lt Powell/2Lt A Leach)

A5762   FE2b   58Sqn
NB nrBRAY engine ftl **MIA(2Lt JD Vaughan **POW**/Lt JC Thompson **WIA POW**) left 8-30pm, whilst attached to 102Sq

B465   FE2b   58Sqn
*NB engine cut ftl cr nrSAVY hit tree(2Lt TE Carley **inj**/Lt FC Dixon OK) to hospital

**   FE2b   58Sqn**
**NB bombed several ammunition dumps CROISILLES-ST LEGER: enormous explosion, 5 dumps destroyed OK(Lt GN McBlain/Lt JF White) very stormy night

B7722   RE8   59Sqn
*P mg? controls shot up ftl cr wr OK(2Lt WL Christian/Lt JE Hanning) left 6-15am [?possible "RE8" claim combat sBOIS D'AVELUY 9-20am Ltn Janzen Ja6]

C5094   RE8   59Sqn
**CP GOMMECOURT mg shot down cr wr OK(2Lt CL Hilborn/2Lt WL Kingwell MC) left 2-30pm [?"RE8" claim combat MIRAUMONT Ltn H Müller Ja18, but see B3418]

B1305   Bristol F2b   62Sqn
**LowP AA nrMAILLY MAILLET ftl cr abandoned OK(2Lt HN Arthur/2Lt J Bruce-Norton) left 12pm

**   Bristol F2b   62Sqn**
** (2Lt VK Hilton **WIA**/)

**   Sopwith Camel   70Sqn**
** (Capt FG Quigley **WIA**)

C8219   Sopwith Camel   70Sqn
LowP left 8-55am shot down ALBERT a'c abandoned(2Lt CJ Wilsdon **WIA)to hospital

C8234   Sopwith Camel   70Sqn
LowP left 9am ALBERT **MIA(2Lt HW Ransom **KIA**) Ja36?

C8297   Sopwith Camel   70Sqn
LowP mg shot up POZIÈRES 9-45am(2Lt A Koch **WIA)to hospital

C6733   Sopwith Camel   73Sqn
GndStr left 7am combat with 3EA eALBERT **MIA(Capt TS Sharpe DFC **WIA POW**) ["SE" claim combat neAVELUY 9am Rittm M Fr vRichthofen JG1, some say C8234 of 70Sq but it left 9am?]

Sopwith Dolphin   79Sqn
** (Lt BS Cole **WIA**)

C3798   Sopwith Dolphin   79Sqn
**P ground mg EA shot up ftl LAVENTIE-ALBERT
7-45am cr OK(2Lt DW Lees) left 7am to shoot up
trenches from 500', unsalvable, burnt a'c ["BF" claim
combat seALBERT 7-50am Vzfw F Hemer Ja6]

C3967   Sopwith Dolphin   79Sqn
P left 7am **MIA(Capt EB Cahusac **POW**)

C4016   Sopwith Dolphin   79Sqn
P left 3-30pm **MIA(2Lt GH Harding US. **KIA**)
MvR73? [?"BF" claim, but described as "covered over":
combat with Dolphin?(a relatively new type)
neCHUIGNOLLES 4-35pm Rittm M Fr vRichthofen
JG1] see entries above for Nos. 11 and 20 Squadrons

C4050   Sopwith Dolphin   79Sqn
P left 7am **MIA(Capt PV Tanner **KIA**)

C3630   A.W.FK8   82Sqn
**B mg fuel tank & engine hit CHIPILLY glide then ftl
cr destroyed a'c burnt OK(2Lt FB Wilson/2Lt Potter)

D8379   DH4   5(Naval)Sqn
B left 3-29pm FOUCAUCOURT **MIA(FSLt EC
Stocker **KIA**/AGL AM Rendle **KIA**)

Although Albert had fallen, and the Fifth Army in
the area south of the Somme barely clung to life, it
was on this day that the German advance showed
the first small signs of faltering. The situation was
still highly critical, but a number of factors had also
suddenly coalesced to allow the Allied situation to
ease slightly. The first had been the timely arrival
of Australian and New Zealand divisions into the
heart of the fighting on the previous day. It is
recognised that their actions in stalling the German
advance around Beaumont Hamel were to be
instrumental in stabilising the situation north of
Albert. The remnants of the British Fifth Army had
fought valiantly through another day, and although
its reserves were down to barely two thousand men
it remained attached across the Somme and still
held the approaches to Amiens. On the 26th,
General Foch had also been appointed to co-
ordinate the efforts of the Allies on the entire front
and he immediately breathed life into the French
Army and Air Force in front of Amiens and at last
promised fresh reserves for its defence.

28th March

The Germans launched a new series of assaults at
Arras on the 28th, roughly on the boundary
between the First and Third Armies. It would
transpire that these were preparatory incursions
connected with the next great German offensive,
planned for a month's time in the Lys. The British
line in front of Arras had given little since the first

day of the main offensive and it held firm again,
the initial German advance failing to penetrate the
battle zone. In the attack on the 28th there was no
fog to aid the attackers, the British systems of
elastic defence operated well and very heavy
German losses were inflicted. Another attack north
of the river Scarpe in the afternoon failed
completely.

In this fighting the RFC not only carried out
ground attacks but also directed British fire on to
massing enemy troops, causing great chaos. In this
defensive battle on the 28th some of the long-
forgotten schemes which had formed part of the
original defensive plan could be put into action.
The all-abiding emphasis on ground attack formed
the central role for the Royal Flying Corps however. It had proven to be of inestimable value, and
the fighter squadrons of II Brigade, for instance,
who had been flying tirelessly down in the Third
Army area, swung their operations and their battle
experience northwards. These units comprised 2
and 4 Australian Flying Corps, 3 (Naval)
Squadron, and Nos. 1 and 40 Squadrons. 18
Squadron from this Brigade also carried out
bombing. II Brigade was reinforced on the 28th by
9 (Naval) Squadron (Sopwith Camels) and three
days later by 6 (Naval) Squadron (DH4s), both of
which had come down from Dunkirk.

The fighting for Amiens in the south remained
as intense as before, but the crisis was passing and
the next steps for the Allies had some inkling of
order to them. The Germans launched a general
assault on the Fifth Army and the French forces at
dawn, leaving the Allies no option but to make a
structured withdrawal along the whole front.
Whilst this was happening, 9th (Headquarters)
Wing squadrons were prominent in attacks on
towns all the way back along the Somme valley,
which were still teeming with enemy troops and
supplies. Typically, Fifth Army corps squadrons
(Nos. 35, 52, and 82) bombed and carried out
contact patrols further south, towards Montdidier
and to the edge of the French front, whilst its army
squadrons made low-flying attacks. In general, the
losses for the RFC were high on the 28th, but most
were caused by ground fire rather than during
attacks on enemy aircraft. These were seen but only
rarely came down to engage.

A8913   SE5a   2Sqn AFC
P left 9-40am seen ovOPPY **MIA(2Lt T Hosking **KIA**)
["Sopwith" claim combat MERCATEL 10-10am Ltn E
Koch Ja32]

B102   SE5a   2Sqn AFC
**P left 11-15am seen ovOPPY-LENS shot down
MIA(2Lt OT Flight **POW**)

B181   SE5a   2Sqn AFC
**P left 9-45am PROYART-ALBERT mg fire shot up
dam OK(Lt LH Holden MC) returned a'dr 10-20am

B9277   Sopwith Camel   3Sqn
**LowB left 11-20am MIA(Lt JKvonI Peden KIA)

B2395   Sopwith Camel   4Sqn AFC
*LowB left 9-30am seen ovOPPY engine ftl seARRAS
MIA(Lt CM Feez POW) [?possible "Spad" claim
combat FAMPOUX 9-50am Ltn P Billik Ja52]

B6574   RE8   5Sqn
**AP combat with EA shot up dam returned a'dr
OK(2Lt R Parkhouse/2Lt R Key) left 8-55am

C5027   RE8   5Sqn
**AP left 9-40am MIA(2Lt PW Woodhouse KIA/Lt S
Collier MC KIA)

C3636   A.W.FK8   8Sqn
**CP left 8-25am MIA but OK(2Lt WT Chard WIA/Lt
JB Martin WIA)

C3679   A.W.FK8   8Sqn
**AP AA rifle mg radiator dam ftl CORBIE OK(Lt JT
Quick/2Lt Brabrook) left 6-45am, took off again &
returned a'dr 11-40am

C8454   A.W.FK8   8Sqn
**AP mg rifle fire ftl dam returned a'dr 10-40am OK(2Lt
WM Butler/Lt CHL Cox) left 8-20am

RE8   9Sqn
** (/Lt J Wedgwood WIA)

RE8   13Sqn
** (/2Lt H Pickles WIA)

DH4   18Sqn
** (2Lt DO Robinson WIA/)

B8884   RE8   21Sqn
**NB MENIN left 10-10pm MIA(2Lt EW Pickford
POW/ballast)

SE5a   24Sqn
** (Lt FV Heakes WIA)

DH4   25Sqn
** (/Sgt AM Muff WIA)

B175   SE5a   32Sqn
**OP AA seARRAS ss for 2000' cr wr abandoned(2Lt
CF Palmer inj)to hospital, WIA?

B3221   A.W.FK8   35Sqn
**P combat with EA nrVILLERS BRETONNEAUX
radiator hit ftl OK(2Lt BL Norton/Lt RW Briggs)burnt
a'c, left 4-30pm

C8224   Sopwith Camel   43Sqn
**OP left 8-10am seen EoL MIA(2Lt CR Maasdorp
POW DoW) Ja11 [?"SE" claim combat ALBERT-
BAPAUME 9-10am Ltn E Udet Ja11]

C8259   Sopwith Camel   43Sqn
**OP left 8-10am combat with AlbatrosDV[+des]
eALBERT 9-30am MIA(2Lt RJ Owen POW) Ja4, also

Owen's last claim of 7 with 43Sqn, incl 3 in this a'c on
24.3.18 ["Camel" claim combat neSUZANNE 9-30am
Ltn V vPressentin Ja4]

C8267   Sopwith Camel   43Sqn
**OP left 8-10am MIA(2Lt HT Adams KIA)
[?"Sopwith" claim combat BRAY-SUR-SOMME
9-10am Ltn F Rumey Ja5]

C8270   Sopwith Camel   43Sqn
**OP left 8-10am attacked KB[+des] then combat with
AlbatrosDVs[++des] eALBERT ~9-30am shot up
MIA(Capt JL Trollope WIA POW) Ja52 ["Camel"
claim combat SAILLY 10am Ltn P Billik Ja52] Trollope
had claimed 17 victories, many in this a'c

D1777   Sopwith Camel   43Sqn
+* combat with AlbatrosDV[+des]4m eALBERT-
BRAY Rd 9-35am(2Lt CF King WIA)

D6404   Sopwith Camel   43Sqn
**OP left 8-10am MIA(2Lt WJ Prier POW) Ja56?
[?"Sopwith" claim Ltn Heins Ja56]

C1649   Sopwith Camel   46Sqn
**LowP combat with EA shot down cr nrLines burnt
a'c(2Lt C Marsden inj)WIA?, left 9-25am BOIRY
NOTRE DAME, came to after crash [?possible
"Sopwith" claim combat BAILLEUL 9-55am Ltn J
Werner Ja14, but possible 43Sq Camel]

Bristol F2b   48Sqn
** (2Lt EG Humphrey WIA/)

B1273   Bristol F2b   48Sqn
**OP mg shot up ftl ALLONVILLE dam OK(2Lt ER
Stock/2Lt WD Davidson) left 9-55am, radiator hit & ftl
11-30am [?"Bristol" claim combat SAILLY 11-15am Ltn
H Weiss Ja11]

C4701   Bristol F2b   48Sqn
** (Capt WL Wells WIA/Cpl W Beales WIA)

C4501   DH4   49Sqn
**B BRAY left 10-30am MIA(2Lt GS Stewart KIA/Lt
DD Richardson POW)

B6571   RE8   52Sqn
**B left 11-40am MIA(2Lt AD Pope POW/Lt HS
Redpath POW) [?"RE" claim combat
FOUCAUCOURT 12-35pm Ltn H Schaefer Ja15]

D4686   RE8   59Sqn
**P left 6am mg shot down COLLINCAMP cr wr destr
OK(Lt EG Leake/2Lt TH Upfill)

Bristol F2b   62Sqn
** (2Lt SW Symons WIA/)

Bristol F2b   62Sqn
** (/1AM A Boxall WIA)

B1211   Bristol F2b   62Sqn
**TrenchStrafe, left 12pm MIA(2Lt MH Cleary KIA/
2Lt VG Stanton POW DoW 29.3.18) to eVILLERS
BRETONNEAUX

B1281   Bristol F2b   62Sqn
Rec controls shot away ftl cr(2Lt HN Arthur **WIA/Cpl
J Borwein OK)

C4613   Bristol F2b   62Sqn
**TrenchStrafe, bad mg hit eVILLERS
BRETONNEAUX ftl cr nrLines abandoned OK(2Lt ET
Morrow Can./Lt HE Merritt) left 12pm

D1798   Sopwith Camel   70Sqn
trav DOULLENS left 3-45pm **MIA(2Lt FD Shreeve
POW)

C1673   Sopwith Camel   80Sqn
**SpP shot up engine dam ftl REMAISNIL A'dr
OK(2Lt AL Code) left 10-15am ALBERT

C8444   A.W.FK8   82Sqn
Rec seen EoL but shot down? **MIA(2Lt JB Taylor
KIA/2Lt E Betley **KIA**) lost EoL? ["AW" claim combat
eMERICOURT? 12-30pm Rittm M Fr vRichthofen JG1]

C8456   A.W.FK8   82Sqn
BRec seen EoL **MIA(2Lt T Watson **KIA**/2Lt T Taylor
KIA) [?"2Str" claim combat MARQUEVILLERS?
2-25pm Ltn K Bohny Ja17]

A7976   DH4   5(Naval)Sqn
B FOUCAUCOURT **MIA(FSLt JG Carroll **KIA**/Gnr
GE Daffey **KIA**) left 9-35am ["DH4" claim combat
VILLERS BRETONNEAUX Oblt Ritt vGreim JG10]

N6001   DH4   5(Naval)Sqn
+* combat with Fokker DrIs[++des:collided]
RAINECOURT ~10am OK(FCdr CPO Bartlett/AGL
W Naylor) last of 8 claims by Bartlett, Naylor had 14 by
this time

THE DEFENCE OF
THE WEST ACHIEVED

The line to which the Allies withdrew was designated the Amiens Defence Line, running from
Mezières to Ignaucourt and Hamel. The front thus
straightened and reduced offered the first chance of
denser, more co-ordinated defence, behind which
the exhausted infantry could be relieved at last in
relative safety and reserves and reinforcements
slowly drawn in. Reasonable stability of British
positions stretched further north to Albert,
Beaumont Hamel and on up to the First Army area
north of Arras, so that it appeared the first great
attack of the German spring offensive had been
finally halted. The German Army was as exhausted
as some sections of their British and French
counterparts and nothing more of a decisive nature
could be asked of them. Their progress had been
startling and awesome, advancing in eight days to
within ten miles of their objective, three-quarters of
the forty-odd miles which lay between the old front
line in front of St Quentin and the objective of
Amiens. In a little more than a week they had

regained most of the territory for which the British
had needed six months of terrible fighting to win
in 1916. Time would show all this was not enough,
however, to earn them victory in the west. In the
coming weeks and months there would be other
attempts to press what seemed like those last few
miles to victory, but the opportunities they created
for themselves in March 1918 would never come
again.

The Allies achieved their great defence of the
west through a magnificent feat of arms by the
infantry, who refused to yield and somehow found
the strength and means to abide. This would have
been impossible without the endeavours of the
Royal Flying Corps and the other Allied air units.
The planning and organisation which enabled the
British air effort to be so highly co-ordinated
showed a new level of sophistication, but tactically,
there was nothing of great subtlety about it. At
every hour of the offensive Allied aircraft were in
numbers over the battlefield, carrying out the most
dangerous operations with no other thought than
to crush the life out of it. In the absence of extensive
British artillery, which was often dislocated
because of the scale of the retreat, and with the
great weapon of the tank inappropriate in this
battle, it was left to the aeroplane to be the decisive
Allied weapon. In Volume 8 of the *Official History
of Australia in the War of 1914-1918*, Cutlack describes
the contribution of the airmen in this great defensive battle thus: ". . . while it was the heroic
infantry of outnumbered British and French
divisions which held up the enemy advance . . . it
was principally the untiring exertions of the airmen
in delaying the enemy's reserves, and throwing his
whole transport system out of gear, which enabled
the Allied infantry to succeed." The pilots, their
gunners and observers, their bomb layers and
armaments officers, their air mechanics and operations staff had together saved the British Army. In
a matter of days the Royal Flying Corps and the
Royal Naval Air Service would pass out of existence as the Royal Air Force was formed. They left
the new body a staggering legacy of achievement.

29th March

Air casualties were the lightest since the start of the
offensive, although part of the reason for this was
worsening periods of weather. Losses were spread
between fighting in front of Arras and south of the
Somme. Most of the line in the latter sector was
held through the day by what remained of the Fifth
Army and its reserves. This force had now been
renamed the British Fourth Army. The heaviest

German attacks during this and the following day were made on the borders of the French line north of the Luce and there was some reappearance of German fighters.

C3661   A.W.FK8   8Sqn
AP combat with EA shot down J.21.d. 2pm(Capt EW Monk **KIA/Lt CB Wilkinson **KIA**) as per Casualty Report: some sources give Wilkinson KIA on 28.3.18?

B1162   Bristol F2b   22Sqn
+* combat with 2Strs[+++des] LIHONS-VAUVILLERS btwn 3-30pm to 3-40pm OK(Sgt EJ Elton/2Lt R Critchley) Elton & his crews had claimed 14 EA in March 1918

B6731   SPAD 7   23Sqn
**RecB shot up ~3pm WARFUSÉE-ABANCOURT engine dam ftl OK(2Lt ER Varley) a'c burnt after ldg

      SPAD 13   23Sqn
** (Lt MS Maclean **WIA**)

      SPAD 13   23Sqn
** (2Lt HV Lewis **WIA**)

B593   SE5a   32Sqn
+* combat with AlbatrosDV[+des] sPROYART 4-15pm OK(2Lt HF Proctor)

This was the first SE5a victory for 32 Squadron.

C9625   SE5a   32Sqn
**OP left 1-50pm combat with EA fuel tank shot up ftl nAMIENS OK(2Lt WA Tyrell)

D282   SE5a   32Sqn
**OP AA controls shot up ftl dam OK(2Lt KGP Hendrie)

B5015   RE8   52Sqn
 **B shot through dam returned a'dr 4-05pm OK(2Lt JK Watson/2Lt JW Benton) left 2pm

B9267   Sopwith Camel   54Sqn
OP left 8am mg fire WARFUSÉE(2Lt ACR Hawley **WIA)to hospital, unsalvable ["Sopwith 1Str" claim combat nwABANCOURT Ltn K Schattauer Ja16]

D1780   Sopwith Camel   65Sqn
prac left 2-55pm Flak? seen trying to land on German a'dr at VILLERS BRETONNEAUX-LAMOTTE-WARFUSÉE then o't(Lt FAW Nunn **Kld) seen walk away, DoW 2.4.18?

      A.W.FK8   82Sqn
** (/2Lt P Hardy **WIA**)

30th March

The British strategy now rested on stifling the enemy advance against the southern extremities of their line a day or two longer. To this end they concentrated many attacks around the junction with the French Army, for instance along the Amiens to Roye Road. V Brigade corps squadrons

(Nos. 35, 52, and 82) dropped one hundred and nine 25-lb bombs and fired 17,000 rounds of ammunition into German troops whilst on their reconnaissances and contact patrols. 2 Squadron AFC (SE5as) and 65 Squadron (Sopwith Camels) had been recently transferred to this brigade and together with its other fighter units, Nos 23, 24, 48, 54, and 84 Squadrons, concentrated on ground attacks through the day. Headquarters fighter and bombing squadrons were also operating in this area.

74 Squadron, equipped with SE5a fighters, arrived at St Omer from England on the 31st.

B72   SE5a   1Sqn
** mg fire shot up(2Lt AE Sweeting **WIA**) [?"SE5" claim combat ARRAS 7-20am Ltn C Reimer Ja26]

C3650   A.W.FK8   8Sqn
**AP rifle fire mg shot up dam returned 9-50pm OK(Lt JT Quick/2Lt AJ Ord) left 6-30pm

      RE8   13Sqn
** (/2Lt FH Thorp **DoW** 31.3.18)

      RE8   16Sqn
P(Capt GHB Streatfield **WIA/Lt BW Sims **WIA**)

B6835   SPAD 13   23Sqn
**RecB left 6-28am AA shot up dam forced to return OK(2Lt HAF Goodison)

B6879   SPAD 13   23Sqn
**Rec VILLERS BRETONNEAUX AA shot up prop dam ftl OK(Capt JF Morris) left 1-13pm, burnt a'c

      RE8   59Sqn
** (/2Lt AR Harrison **WIA**)

D6454   Sopwith Camel   65Sqn
OP ESSENBANK ftl cr ldg o't(2Lt DG Brown **WIA)

C3791.R   Sopwith Dolphin 79Sqn
P left 9-15am combat shot down **MIA(2Lt HW Browne **POW**) ["Sopwith" claim combat eVAIRE 12-30pm Ltn R Stark Ja34]

C3893   Sopwith Dolphin 79Sqn
P left 9-15am combat with EA shot up(2Lt DW Lees **WIA) was MIA

C3647   A.W.FK8   82Sqn
CP mg shot up ovASSEVILLERS ftl burnt a'c(2Lt AM McTavish OK/2Lt HA Somerville MC **KIA) left 7-15am

C8460   A.W.FK8   82Sqn
**CP left 5-25pm mg dam cr OK(2Lt WG MacKenzie/2Lt EHS Morris)

C6382   SE5a   84Sqn
OP combat with 5HA VILLERS BRETONNEAUX contoured away but hit wires cr(2Lt CT Travers **inj) left 8-55am

N5992   DH4   5(Naval)Sqn
** shot up dam(FSLt CJ Heyward OK/AGL TW Jones

WIA) unit bombed troops & transport eVILLERS BRETONNEAUX

31st March

C8451 A.W.FK8 8Sqn
**AP shot up radiator ftl D.15.d. dam OK(Lt D Maclean/Lt EJ Brabrook) left 2pm, a'c shelled destroyed

C8482 A.W.FK8 35Sqn
*OP left 4-40pm **MIA**(2Lt AS Hanna **POW**/2Lt RA Burnard **WIA POW**)

RE8 52Sqn
** (2Lt W Dancy **WIA**/Capt JE Greenall **WIA**?) crew?

A2161 DH4 57Sqn
B BAPAUME **MIA(2Lt ESC Pearce **KIA**/2Lt CB Coleman **WIA POW**) left 2-20pm [?"BF" claim combat BEUGNATRE Ltn G Geigl Ja16]

A7674 DH4 57Sqn
Phot left 12-50pm **MIA(Capt PD Robinson MC **KIA**/2Lt JQF Walker **KIA**)

With the passing of the most critical period of fighting some of the DH4 units returned to high bombing operations.

April 1918

1st April
THE ROYAL AIR FORCE

The Royal Air Force came in to being on the 1st of April, amalgamating the Royal Flying Corps and the Royal Naval Air Service. For the vast majority of British and Commonwealth airmen serving in France its birth was hardly noticed — they were too busy fighting. There would be time enough to reflect on the new Third Service, to which they all now belonged. A more noticeable change was the renumbering of the old RNAS units which now had 200 added to their number. For example, 3 (Naval) Squadron became 203 Squadron RAF. In the Dunkirk area, only the following eight units were left: 202 reconnaissance Squadron, 204 and 213 fighter Squadrons, 211 day-bomber Squadron, 217 anti-submarine Squadron, and Nos. 207, 214, and 215 heavy night-bomber Squadrons. At this time these were formed into 5 Group, and not long after, VII Brigade was disbanded. Many of these units were striking military, as opposed to naval, targets at this time. Whenever possible, however, they co-operated with naval operations directed at Zeebrugge and Ostende throughout April and May, the primary purpose of which was to block the entrances to harbours and canals. Work related to this is noted below where relevant.

On the 1st of April, whilst there was not much activity on the ground, there was heavy air fighting. Virtually all of this was low down, where German fighters were again busy. Some of the orders for the day showed a shifting of emphasis; for instance, Ninth Wing fighter squadrons were to ". . . work at low altitude, their first objective being hostile machines, and their second, ground targets". Air casualties were some of the heaviest for the offensive, a high number of these being on offensive patrols. There were also many accidents across the whole spectrum of the RAF. For instance, 58 Squadron had suffered virtually no casualties through ten nights of hard, intensive night bombing, but on the 1st it accumulated five wrecked machines. These were caused by a mixture of enemy action, engine failure, and landing on poor ground — no doubt exhaustion played its part as well. Having averted defeat so narrowly, the effort involved was telling on both men and aircraft.

98 Squadron arrived in France equipped with DH9 bombers.

B2253 RE8 3Sqn AFC
**AOb COMINES-WARNETON AA? engine cut EoL ftl cr 10-25am(Lt JL Smith/Lt JL Withers)

RE8 5Sqn
** (/Lt CH Brown **WIA**)

C3684 A.W.FK8 8Sqn
AP ftl wHERNICOURT dam(Lt D Maclean **WIA/Lt EJ Braebrook **WIA**) left 6-20am, name MacLean?

A7240 Bristol F2b 20Sqn
** AA shot down cr nrWULVERGHEM OK(Maj JA Dennistoun/2Lt HG Crowe) left 5-25pm

C4615 Bristol F2b 20Sqn
** AA shot down ftl PYPEGALE 9-58am(2Lt RBT Hedges **WIA**/Lt AG Horlock **WIA**) name Harlock?

B6858 SPAD 13 23Sqn
Rec left 12-50pm combat with EA? **MIA(2Lt NR Joyce **KIA**)

B2102 DH4 27Sqn
**B PERONNE AA cr 11-10am dam OK(2Lt F Carr/2Lt JH Holland) left 8-50am

C6413 SE5a 32Sqn
**Esc ground fire HA? engine shot up ESCLAINVILLE ftl OK(Capt DM Faure) left 9am, burnt?

D265 SE5a 32Sqn
OP left 9-10am combat with AlbatrosDV[+ooc]MEZIÈRES 10-30am shot up(2Lt HF Proctor **WIA) was **MIA** [?"SE5" claim combat wMOREUIL 10-45am Ltn H Schaefer Ja15]

B3380 A.W.FK8 35Sqn
**P rifle fire radiator hit ftl wood burnt a'c OK(2Lt BL Norton/Lt RW Briggs) left 7-30am VILLERS BRETONNEAUX

C3642   A.W.FK8   35Sqn
**OP VILLERS BRETONNEAUX combat with EA
shot through dam OK(2Lt A McGregor/2Lt M Balston)
[?2 "BF" claims combat wswAUBERCOURT Ltn G
Geigl Ja16]

D3526   SE5a   40Sqn
+* combat with 2Str[+des] wIZEL LES EQUERCHIN
12-20pm OK(2Lt WL Harrison Can.) made 12 claims

          Bristol F2b   48Sqn
** (2Lt CDB Stiles **WIA**/)

          Sopwith Camel   54Sqn
** (2Lt EE Stock **WIA**)

B9281   Sopwith Camel   54Sqn
**OP left 3pm AA ground fire ftl dam(2Lt NF Spurr
WIA?)

D6529   Sopwith Camel   54Sqn
*OP combat? mg fire? ftl field o't(Capt GC Cuthbertson
MC **WIA**) left 3pm, a'c unsalvable

C5433   SE5a   56Sqn
**OP combat with Fokker DrI ovFRICOURT 12-45pm
ftl **MIA**(Lt F Beaumont **POW**) fired green Verys light
4000' below patrol ["SE5a" claim combat ALBERT
12-45pm Vzfw O Könnecke Ja5]

C6351   SE5a   56Sqn
**OP combat with Fokker DrIs ovGUILLEMONT
12-55pm **MIA**(2Lt B McPherson **POW**) left 11-25am,
POW:MacPherson ["SE5" claim combat
MARTINPUICH 1-05pm Hpt W Reinhard Ja6]

A7401   DH4   57Sqn
B combat with EA BAPAUME **MIA(2Lt E Whitfield
KIA/Lt WCF Nicol-Hart **KIA**) left 7-30am, shot down
nrACHIET-LE-PETIT ["Bristol" claim combat
ACHIET-LE-PETIT 8am Vzfw F Hemer Ja6]

A7872   DH4   57Sqn
B seen nrBAPAUME **MIA(2Lt DP Trollip **KIA**/Lt JD
Moses **KIA**) left 8-20am [?"DH4" claim combat
GREVILLERS 9am Ltn HJ Wolff Ja11]

          DH4   57Sqn
** (/2Lt A Leach **WIA**)

A6398   FE2b   58Sqn
**NB left 8-05pm DOUAI engine hit EoL but returned
WoL ftl cr o't(Lt GL Castle OK/Lt FC Dixon **inj**)head,
a'c shelled but salvable

D1811   Sopwith Camel   65Sqn
OP left 6-30am seen ovMOREUIL **MIA(2Lt PR Cann
DoW 2.4.18) ["Camel" claim combat seFOUILLOY
8am Ltn E Siempelkamp Ja4]

D1817   Sopwith Camel   65Sqn
+* combat with AlbatrosDIII[+ooc] FROISSY sBRAY
4-25pm? OK(Lt TM Williams SA.) many of his 9 claims
in this a'c

D6474   Sopwith Camel   65Sqn
OP left 10-50am seen ovDEMUIN **MIA(2Lt JR
Greasley **KIA**)

C1681   Sopwith Camel   80Sqn
P left 3-15pm seen ovMOREUIL **MIA(2Lt JJ
Meredith US. **WIA POW**)

          A.W.FK8   82Sqn
** (/2Lt RT Langdon **WIA**)

B174   SE5a   84Sqn
**OP left 4-30pm combat with EA cr wood
nrMEZIÈRES **MIA**(2Lt SH Winkley **KIA**) to AMIENS-
ST QUENTIN ["SE5" claim combat MOREUIL
WOOD 5pm Ltn HJ Wolff Ja11]

A5624, A5643, A5786 FE2bs 101Sqn
** all a'c damaged by enemy bombing of a'dr

These three machines were damaged by enemy
bombing on 101 Squadron's aerodrome shortly
before dawn. It is possible the enemy machines
followed the last FE back as it returned from the
lines. The Official History notes that three personnel were killed and another two wounded, but their
names have not yet been established.

B3798   Sopwith Camel   203Sqn
** cr nLOOS then a'c shelled(FSLt OP Adam **KIA**)

B7198   Sopwith Camel   203Sqn
+* combat with Fokker DrI[+cr destr] 3m eOPPY 2pm
OK(FCdr RA Little)

2nd April
GENERAL FOCH'S DICTUM ON THE USE OF AIR POWER

On the 2nd of April RAF headquarters received
General Foch's instructions for the employment of
British and French air services in the battle area.
They were a landmark in strategic air thinking, but
through their very insight they highlighted the
central weakness of the Allied air effort. This was
the lack of co-ordination between the two air
services which, had it existed, could have greatly
enhanced their capability. As the Official History
deftly describes, this would have enabled the
building up of a strategic reserve capable of being
deployed to sections of the front where it was most
needed. Such co-operation as ensued could be
better described as improved demarcation.
Germany succeeded as much as it did with its
numerically smaller air force because it had this
unity of direction.

The inherent wisdom of Foch's dictums on
bombing and air fighting would nevertheless guide
Allied thinking for the remainder of the war. The
order for air fighting stated that "At the present
time the first duty of fighting aeroplanes is to assist
troops on the ground by incessant attacks . . . Air
fighting is not to be sought except so far as neces-

sary for the fulfiment of this duty." Interestingly, there was no mention of protecting corps machines. His bombing directive stated that "The essential condition of success is the concentration of every resource of the British and French bombing formations on such few of the most important of the enemy's railway junctions as it may be possible to put out of action with certainty, and keep out of action. Effort should not be dispersed against a large number of targets . . ."

D3429   SE5a   2Sqn AFC
+* combat with 2Str[+des] AMIENS-CORBIE 5-30pm OK(Capt AG Clark) shared

C3522   A.W.FK8   10Sqn
CAP shot up ground mg 1-20pm fire wr ShD.27.d.7.0.(Lt ED Jones **KIA/2Lt W Smith **KIA**)

C4862   Bristol F2b   11Sqn
COP seen dive on EA **MIA(2Lt AR Knowles **KIA**/Lt EA Matthews **KIA**) left 5pm to seALBERT? [?"BF" claim combat neBRAY 6-05pm Ltn P Wenzel Ja6]

A7286   Bristol F2b   22Sqn
OP VAUVILLERS combat with Fokker DrI then seen in flames after **MIA(2Lt F Williams **KIA**/2Lt R Critchley **KIA**) left 3-15pm [?"F2b" claim combat MORCOURT-FRAMVILLE 4-50pm Ltn HJ Wolff Ja11][?"F2b" claim combat MORCOURT-HARBONNIÈRES 5pm Ltn H Weiss Ja11]

B1162   Bristol F2b   22Sqn
+*OP combat with Fokker DrIs[++ooc] wVAUVILLERS 4-45pm OK(2Lt JE Gurdon/2Lt AJH Thornton) this was the first of 28 victories by Gurdon on two-seaters

               SE5a   29Sqn
** (Lt HR Uttley **WIA**)

C8293   Sopwith Camel   43Sqn
SpM left 12-20pm **MIA(2Lt AK Lomax **POW**)

B1269   Bristol F2b   48Sqn
OP left 5-05pm VILLERS BRETONNEAUX combat with EA shot up ftl(2Lt KWD Pope **WIA/2Lt WJ Buttle **WIA**)

C4707   Bristol F2b   48Sqn
OP combat with HA ftl cr nrLines(2Lt GBB Stiles **WIA/2Lt FF Walker **WIA**) left 5-05pm VILLERS BRETONNEAUX, unsalvable

A3868   RE8   52Sqn
BP left 12pm **MIA(2Lt ED Jones **KIA**/2Lt RF Newton **KIA**) ["RE" claim combat neMOREUIL 12-35pm Rittm M Fr vRichthofen JG1]

D6505   Sopwith Camel   54Sqn
**OP left 6-05pm sMOREUIL seen go down in control MIA but OK(2Lt RN Maclean OK?)

B8236   SE5a   60Sqn
OP VRELY-ROSIÈRES combat with EA 6-16pm **MIA(2Lt EW Christie **KIA**) left 5-30pm ["SE5" claim

combat wHARBONNIÈRES 6-20pm Ltn H Kirschstein Ja6][?"SE" claim combat VILLERS BRETONNEAUX 6-15pm Vzfw J Putz Ja34]

C5388   SE5a   60Sqn
**OP combat with HA BERTANGLES dam ftl 6-45pm OK(2Lt KP Campbell)

C8227   Sopwith Camel   65Sqn
OP left 8-40am Flak? ftl seen ldg Sh62D c.8.0.4 nrLines(2Lt JC Burney-Cummings **WIA)a'c unsalvable

C8524   A.W.FK8   82Sqn
Rec (Capt GI Paterson **KIA/Lt TI Findley **WIA**) was MIA[?"Bristol" claim combat BOIS DE VAIRE 9-40am Ltn F Piechulek Ja56]

3rd April

Rain and cloud restricted flying.

C3682   A.W.FK8   35Sqn
P combat with EA ftl(Lt RMC MacFarlane **WIA/2Lt AE Lancashire **WIA**) left 9am VILLERS BRETONNEAUX, burnt a'c ["AW" claim combat BLANGY-TRONVILLE 10-05am Ltn V vPressentin Ja4]

C8457   A.W.FK8   35Sqn
**CP AMIENS combat with EA shot through ftl OK(2Lt Phillips/2Lt M Balston) left 2pm, returned 5-20pm

D1797   Sopwith Camel   54Sqn
**OP left 3-45pm combat with AlbatrosD[+ftl nrMEZIÈRES] 4-50pm then combat with AlbatrosD[+cr nrROSIÈRES] 5-10pm shot up ftl ST POL OK(2Lt RT Cuffe) [?"Sopwith 1Str" claim combat Ltn W Böning Ja76]

C8230   Sopwith Camel   65Sqn
OP left 11am seen eDEMUIN-MOREUIL Flak? **MIA(2Lt H? Dean **POW**) initials JE? [2 "Camel" claims combat MEZIÈRES 12-18pm Ltn K Schwartz Ja22][?"Sopwith 1Str" claim combat VILLERS BRETONNEAUX Ltn K Schattauer Ja16]

C8294   Sopwith Camel   65Sqn
OP left 11am seen eDEMUIN-MOREUIL flak? **MIA(Lt LNF Towne **POW**) [2 "Camel" claims combat LA NEUVILLE 12-30pm Ltn K Schwartz Ja22]["Camel" claim combat CACHY 12-36pm Ltn A Lenz Ja22]

There was a single big fight on the 3rd, between twenty-seven machines of 65 and 84 Squadron and maybe thirty enemy fighters. The encounter began at only 1,500 feet and was continued for about an hour, in which time five enemy were claimed shot down. Two claimed by Capt RA Grosvenor are given below. The British lost Dean and Towne from 65 Squadron. Other German patrols were seen higher up but the one which descended to make this attack was notably large. This experience caused headquarters to order more offensive

patrols for the following day with the objective of engaging enemy aircraft. With Foch's directives ringing in their ears they were to ". . . seek out and destroy enemy formations". What is more, the patrols were to gather together machines of several squadrons, and from this time larger British formations of fighters became common.

B8408   SE5a   84Sqn
+* combat with PfalzDIIIs[+flames+des] btwn ROSIÈRES A'dr-eVILLERS BRETONNEAUX 11-50am OK(Capt RA Grosvenor)

A5559   FE2b   101Sqn
**NB mg fire auxiliary fuel tank hit ftl nrBERTANGLES cr dam OK(Capt ED Hall/Lt WS Aulton)

4th April

Low clouds and rain promised to hinder flying for another day, but as German forces launched their final assault on the British lines south of the Somme, some contact patrols were attempted over the fighting and low bombing and strafing was possible in the afternoon when the weather cleared.

D214   SE5a   2Sqn AFC
**P combat with AlbatrosDV[+des] VILLERS BRETONNEAUX oil tank shot up ftl dam OK(Lt LJ Primrose)

C1653   Sopwith Camel   3Sqn
**LowB left 2-05pm shot up mg dam returned a'dr 3-15pm OK(Capt CM Leman)

B8411   SE5a   24Sqn
+* combat RumplerC[+capt] ST NICHOLAS 5-30pm OK(Lt RT Mark) shared, made 14 victory claims

**   A.W.FK8   35Sqn**
** (/2Lt ED Stevens WIA)

**   Sopwith Camel   54Sqn**
** (2Lt WN Plenderleith WIA)

D6552   Sopwith Camel   65Sqn
**B left 3pm combat C-type[+flames] VAIRE WOOD 3-30pm then shot down cr Sh62D P.16.d.(2Lt JG Kennedy KIA) [?"Sopwith 1Str" claim combat WARFUSÉE Ltn G Geigl Ja16]

**   Sopwith Camel   73Sqn**
** (2Lt JC Collier WIA)

5th April

The German Army extended the scope of its attack on the Somme on the 5th in a last desperate attempt to destabilise the British Line. Mist and rain made RAF involvement in this battle impossible. Some ground was gained, but at tremendous cost, and from this point the fighting was destined to die away in a series of intermittent and localised attacks. The thrust towards Amiens had

been finally blocked at Villers Bretonneaux. The British suffered casualties of 178,000 men, 70,000 of whom had fallen prisoner. The French had lost 77,000. Germany's losses were estimated at 250,000, many of whom were highly trained assault troops on whom so much had depended. These losses were so significant that there would be no real recovery for Germany from this position. It would ride the momentum of its efforts for some months, for its army was huge and amazingly resilient. The German Commander Ludendorff and his staff would also display great agility as they marshalled and drove their forces. Driven by the dictum best described when he later wrote "We must not get drawn into a battle of exhaustion", the Allies would have to resist another four major offensives in the west before the end of July. The failure to take Amiens and to divide the two Allied armies in March 1918, however, was the first and greatest stumble because so much had been risked. In retrospect, it made a gradual decline into surrender inevitable.

A7553   DH4   55Sqn
**B LUXEMBURG MIA(2Lt PH O'Lieff POW/2Lt SR Wells POW)

6th April

It has been noted that the German attacks near Arras from the 28th of March had been associated with a new offensive planned to take place in the north. Ludendorff hoped to capture the high ground between Arras and Lens which overlooked the chosen setting for this fighting — the plain of the River Lys in Flanders. With the consummate failure of these attacks his plan was modified and reduced, so that they now prepared to strike directly westwards across the plain between Armentières and La Bassée. The target was the important rail centre of Hazebrouck, away to the north-west.

Air reports from the 31st of March had detected this change of emphasis as a wholesale redeployment northwards of men, guns, and supplies took place around the rear of Lens, as well as southwards from Lille. One observer at dawn on the 1st of April counted fifty-four separate trains converging on the Armentières-La Bassée front. Ludendorff knew that the British line here, comprising the First Army, was severely weakened. The Official History notes that forty-six of the fifty-eight divisions in France had been withdrawn to fight in the Somme battles, and the Flanders sector had been drained more than any other. Positioned thinly along six crucial miles of this front was a

single Portuguese Division, which it was planned to relieve on the 9th or 10th.

At first, the British General Headquarters believed they were watching a diversionary tactic in all this activity — they could hardly believe the German Army could be abandoning the Amiens offensive so close to such a crucial objective. This caused some vital hesitation in commencing to bomb the German concentrations. Instead, most of the day and night bombing work concentrated on the rail network behind Vimy, where for a while the next attack seemed most likely.

Reports came in on the 6th, however, to suggest a major offensive was coming, and that it was the Portuguese weak point further north which the Germans were preparing to attack. Enemy fighter activity began to increase in the north as well, endeavouring to prevent RAF reconnaissance of the build-up as much as possible. There was precious little RAF fighter strength to counter this, only promises of transfers northwards once the attack began. Already, however, some low-bombing and machine-gun attacks had begun around Lens and the La Bassée Canal. 4 AFC Camel pilots who were now experts in this work were particularly involved. The only corps units in the sector were those of 1 (Corps) Wing, namely Nos. 2 (FK8s) and 4 and 42 (RE8s). All three did a great deal of work registering enemy batteries and making reconnaissance and photographic flights.

A.W.FK8   2Sqn
** (/2Lt CFG Doran **WIA**)

C1577   Sopwith Camel   3Sqn
LowB left 2-45pm seen nrLA MOTTE **MIA(2Lt DG Gold **POW**) [?"Camel" claim neWARTISSE? 3-25pm Ltn H Kirschstein Ja6]

C1609   Sopwith Camel   3Sqn
**LowB left 2-45pm Third Army area mg dam returned 4-35pm OK(2Lt GR Riley)

C4570   RE8   13Sqn
A4570? **Phot left 10am **MIA**(Lt ST Payne **DoW**/2Lt R Hilton **DoW** 29.4.18) XVII Corps front

Bristol F2b   22Sqn
** (/2Lt BCM Ward **WIA**)

B6878   SPAD 13   23Sqn
OP AA wDOMART ftl sAMIENS 2pm a'c shelled(2Lt ER Varley MC **WIA) combat?

B157   SE5a   40Sqn
+* combat with 2Str[+des] BREBIÈRES 10-35am OK(Capt I Napier) Napier made 12 victory claims, many in this a'c

B2431   Sopwith Camel   43Sqn
SpM left 3-10pm **MIA(Lt FD Hudson **POW DoW**) Ja11 ["Camel" claim combat eLAMOTTE 4pm Ltn H

Weiss Ja11][?"Sopwith" claim combat CERISY 4-05pm Vzfw E Scholtz Ja11]

C8247   Sopwith Camel   43Sqn
SpM left 2pm down in controlled glide nABANCOURT smoke 800′ **MIA(Lt HS Lewis **KIA**) Ja11 ["Camel" claim combat HAMEL 2-15pm Ltn E Udet Ja11]

C8248   Sopwith Camel   43Sqn
SpM left 3-15pm shot down **MIA(Lt TRV Hill **WIA POW**) severely WIA, Ja11 [?"Camel" claim combat neSAILLY 5-50pm Ltn H Weiss Ja11]

C8281   Sopwith Camel   43Sqn
SpM left 3-15pm **MIA(Lt E Mather **KIA**) Ja11

D6452   Sopwith Camel   43Sqn
SpM left 3-10pm **MIA(Lt MF Peiler **POW**) Ja11["Camel" claim combat MERICOURT 4-10pm Ltn E Just Ja11]

D6491   Sopwith Camel   46Sqn
LowP seen ovLAMOTTE shot down in flames 3-30pm **MIA(Capt SP Smith **KIA**) combat with Fokker DrI? ["Camel" claim combat BOIS DE HAMEL 3-45pm Rittm M Fr vRichthofen JG1, other options exist, eg Ja11 claims of 43Sq a'c]

B1299   Bristol F2b   48Sqn
+* combat with Fokker DrI[+flames] sLAMOTTE 3-40pm shot up(Lt JE Drummond **WIA**/2Lt HF Lumb OK)ankle, Drummond claimed 6 victories

C4864   Bristol F2b   48Sqn
OP combat with 3 Fokker DrIs LAMOTTE 3-50pm(2Lt BGA Bell **KIA/2Lt GG Bartlett **KIA**) left 2-35pm, seen eVILLERS BRETONNEAUX, Wolff Ja11 [?"F2b" claim combat neVAUVILLERS 3-55pm Ltn HJ Wolff Ja11]

Sopwith Camel   65Sqn
** (2Lt JL Jewkes **WIA**)

Sopwith Camel   65Sqn
** (2Lt GM Knocker **WIA**)

C8252   Sopwith Camel   70Sqn
EscLowP left 3-05pm CERISY-LAMOTTE **MIA(2Lt DV Gillespie **KIA**) buried Sh62D J.35.A.2.1. [?"Camel" claim combat eLAMOTTE 3-55pm Ltn HJ Wolff Ja11]

C3939   Sopwith Dolphin 79Sqn
OP left 4-10pm **MIA(2Lt HG Dugan US. **POW**) [?"SE5" claim combat DEMUIN 5-15pm Vzfw Hemer Ja6]

Sopwith Camel   80Sqn
** (Capt WA Forsyth **WIA**)

B2479   Sopwith Camel   80Sqn
P left 4-15pm LAMOTTE **MIA(2Lt EL Smithers **POW**)

C1772   SE5a   84Sqn
+* combat with LVGC[+cr capt] nHANGARD 11-20am OK(Lt JF Larsen US.) shared, EA from FAb(A)205, last of 9 claims

B6419   Sopwith Camel   201Sqn
** combat with Fokker DrIs MERICOURT 6-05pm dam
OK(FSLt MH Findlay) [?"Camel" claim combat
seMORCOURT 6pm Ltn A Delling Ja34]

B7231   Sopwith Camel   203Sqn
+* combat with DFWCV[+shot down in flames] 3m
neLENS 12-30pm OK(FCdr RA Little)

A7620   DH4   205Sqn
B left 3-14pm LAMOTTE **MIA(Lt GM Cartmell
KIA/AGL A Lane **KIA**)

B7187   Sopwith Camel   208Sqn
**OP combat with 6 Fokker DrIs[+ooc] LENS 11-30am
but shot down in flames **MIA**(FSLt WH Sneath **KIA**)
dead nrLOISON? [?"Camel" claim LENS Ltn Hertz
Ja59], pilot had 5 victory claims

7th April
PREPARATIONS FOR THE GERMAN OFFENSIVE IN FLANDERS: THE BATTLES OF THE LYS

The Royal Air Force support for the First Army
was supplied by I Brigade, made up of the 10th
(Army) Wing and the 1st (Corps) Wing. The corps
units have been noted above. The fighter
squadrons of the army wing had been depleted to
fight on the Somme: 2 AFC and 43 Squadron had
departed (see below), but 22 Squadron, which had
been transferred to III Brigade, would now be
ordered back. In early April 208 and 210 Squadrons (Sopwith Camels) from Dunkirk, and 19
Squadron (Sopwith Dolphins) and 41 Squadron
(SE5as) came as replacements. 10th (Army) Wing
had also retained 40 Squadron (SE5as) and 18
Squadron (DH4s). Two further fighter units, Nos.
46 (Sopwith Camels) and 64 (SE5as) were to be
available once fighting started.

Machines from 9th (Headquarters) Wing, which
was now renamed IX Brigade, were also available
for the fighting. IX Brigade was divided into 9th
(Day) Wing (Nos. 32, 73, 79; 62; and 25 and 27
Squadrons), and 54th (Night) Wing (Nos. 58 and
83 Squadrons, with I Flight, a Special Duties Flight
for intelligence and espionage work). Finally, the
units of the new 51st Wing behind Arras would be
available. These were Nos. 43 and 80 Squadrons
(Sopwith Camels), and AFC 2 (SE5as).

From the 7th of April German guns were
ominously silent whenever attempts were made to
draw their fire — they were concealing their final
positions for the attack. The enemy were also
known to be hurrying their preparations so as to
have the best chance of meeting the Portuguese

before they could be relieved. The attack became
ever more imminent as an intense bombardment of
mustard gas shells occurred through the night of
the 7th/8th.

C1083   SE5a   1Sqn
**OP combat with EA burst into flames 2000'
HOLLEBEKE 2pm **MIA**(Capt GB Moore Can. **KIA**)
left 12-52pm

B5635   Sopwith Camel   4Sqn AFC
LowB left 11am AA down nrILLIES in flames **MIA(Lt
JC Courtney **KIA**) LILLE-LA BASSÉE Rd,
nrBETHUNE, hit by "flaming onion"

C3678   A.W.FK8   8Sqn
**CP mg shot up nBUIRE 10-30am fuel tank hit ftl
Sh62D D.23.d. wr OK(2Lt LC Hooton/2Lt EI Wells) left
6-20am

B5824   A.W.FK8   10Sqn
**CAP AA mg fire fuel tank hit ftl J.1.d.4.8. cr wr
OK(2Lt S Jukes/2Lt WH Stanley)shaken

B63   SE5a   24Sqn
OP left 3pm seen ovMOREUIL WOOD **MIA(2Lt PJ
Nolan **KIA**) ["SE5" claim combat MOREUIL 3-45pm
Ltn F Putter Ja68]

B79.Y   SE5a   24Sqn
+* combat with AlbatrosDV[+ooc] MOREUIL WOOD
3pm OK(2Lt WC Lambert US.) first of 18 claims

B3601   Nieuport 27   29Sqn
*SpP left 6-57pm ovHOLLEBEKE 7-15pm **MIA**(Lt AG
Wingate-Grey **POW**)

                    RE8   42Sqn
** (Lt EC Musson **WIA**)

B3423   RE8   52Sqn
**Rec combat shot down nrLines(2Lt T Killeen OK/2Lt
J Napier **KIA**)a'c abandoned, left 8-15am

A7876   DH4   57Sqn
**Phot 5EA shot up BEAUVOIR ftl 73Sq dam OK(2Lt
FAW Mann/2Lt JT White) left 10-25am

D6550   Sopwith Camel   73Sqn
**OP combat with EA ftl 1500yd wVILLERS
BRETONNEAUX wr OK(2Lt AV Gallie) left 10-10am
[?"SE5" claim, but usual Lt Nolan 24Sq's time does not
fit, "ATL":possible 73Sq Camel? combat VILLERS
BRETONNEAUX 11-30am Rittm M Fr vRichthofen
JG1: claim still a mystery]

D6554   Sopwith Camel   73Sqn
**OP left 10am seen about to attk EA LAMOTTE
MIA(Lt RGH Adams **POW**) ["Sopwith" claim combat
sPROYART 11-45am Ltn H Kirschstein Ja6]

B5687   Sopwith Camel   203Sqn
**P ground mg fuel tank & engine shot up dam ftl(FSLt
RC Berlyn **WIA**)slight

D3336   Sopwith Camel   203Sqn
** shot up ftl BEAUVAIS dam OK(FSLt AN Webster)

B6417   Sopwith Camel   208Sqn
**OP combat with HA engine hit? ftl in control neLOOS
Sh36C H.26 12-10pm **MIA**(FSLt DC Hopewell **POW**)
left 9-45am ["Camel" claim combat eHULLUCH
11-10am? Ltn P Billik Ja52]

N6349   Sopwith Camel   213Sqn
** left formation nwZEEBRUGGE **MIA**(Lt KR Cole
POW)

8th April

There was rain through most of the day, all but
eliminating flying. The shared attack on the kite
balloon noted below was a rare report of air
activity.

C6730   Sopwith Camel   3Sqn
+* attacked KB[+flames] eMORY 6-55am OK(Capt DJ
Bell MC) shared with B7248

B7248   Sopwith Camel   201Sqn
+* attacked KB[+des] eBOYELLES 6-45am OK(Capt
CB Ridley) shared with C6730

9th April
THE BATTLE OF THE LYS

After a dawn bombardment, which included
extensive gas-shelling into the rear areas, the
enemy launched its offensive at 8-45am, striking
between Armentières and Givenchy on the the La
Bassée Canal. In mist and rain, which precluded
any air co-operation, the Germans swept through
the Portuguese-held line and opened up a critical
breach. The thinnest of British reinforcements
managed only to delay progress near Armentières
through the morning, so that the Lys at Bac St
Maur had been reached and crossed by 2-20pm.
The line was more firmly held at Givenchy, but
nevertheless was driven back onto the La Lawe
River.

The advance caught the RAF awkwardly — nine
squadrons being forced to relocate. Despite this,
contact patrolling began about 2pm and some low
patrols were organised through the afternoon and
evening. The greatest loss for the RAF on the 9th
were the machines of 208 Squadron. This unit had
been at La Gorgue, where the La Lawe and Lys
rivers met, and fog had prevented evacuation. The
Squadron commander was eventually forced to
assemble their entire strength of Camels in the
centre of the airfield and have them burnt. The
fighters of the German Air Force were also
seriously handicapped by the conditions and their
deployment was plagued by poor communications.
Their most effective work was done in protection of
their co-operation machines.

A8933   SE5a   1Sqn
**SpM left 5-30pm seen swARMENTIÈRES ovLYS
~6-30pm **MIA**(Lt GA Mercer **POW**)

SE5a   1Sqn
** ground mg fire(2Lt HW McKeague **WIA**)

RE8   4Sqn
Visiting Battery: gased(2Lt JL Parren **WIA/Lt HG
Burgess **WIA**) crew?

B7395   Sopwith Camel   4Sqn AFC
**B left 4-40pm shot up dam returned a'dr 5-35pm
OK(Lt JW Weingarth)

B1221   Bristol F2b   20Sqn
** combat with EA shot up cr sandhills
nrWIMEREUX(2Lt RH Harmer **WIA**/Lt N Peters **inj**)

D3554   SE5a   40Sqn
B left 5pm **MIA(Lt RE Bion **KIA**) Casualty Card gives
D3534, but in error?

A3658   RE8   42Sqn
**AP mg fire dam ldg ok CHOCQUES a'dr
5pmOK(Capt RA Archer/2Lt DG Smith) left 2-45pm

A4212   RE8   42Sqn
AP mg fire LA FOSSE ftl(Lt W Beart **WIA/Lt GW
Gotch OK)

**B3773, B3785, B3794, B3853, B3936,
B6260, B7189, B7193, B7196, B7201,
B7253, D3330, D3335, D3339, D3352,**

N6342   Sopwith Camels   208Sqn
All Camels of 208 Squadron caught fog-bound on LA
GORGUE A'dr and ordered burnt before evacuation

10th April

On the 10th of April the German Fourth Army
attacked sections of the British Second Army
further north, through Ploegsteert and Messines.
The defences in this sector were stronger than had
been available to the Fifth Army on the Somme,
but reserves were now very low. From 1pm
Armentières had to be abandoned and there was
also enemy progress in the area beyond Bac St
Maur, where they had crossed the Lys the day
before. Despite this, on the edges of the salient the
Allies held their ground. The weather was very bad
again — low mist and clouds limiting the effectiveness of air co-operation — but there was some
contact patrolling carried out.

Fighter Squadrons of II Brigade came into the
action on the 10th. These were Nos. 1 (SE5as), 29
(Nieuports), 54 (Sopwith Camels), and 20
Squadrons (Bristol Fighters). All the fighter units
concentrated on ground attacks which were known
to be making the life of the German infantry worse
than appalling. Machines were driven very low by
the conditions and naturally became targets for

unusually heavy ground fire. The more accomplished of the pilots used the low cloud as cover from which to launch sudden and precise attacks, keeping their exposure to hostile fire to a minimum. The enemy was also active on similar patrols, however, and there were many opportunities for air fighting throughout the day. All these factors combined to produce a high number of air casualties on both sides. The German Air Force chose to concentrate on the protection of its ground forces and this work drew in ever greater numbers of fighters to confront the low flying British aircraft. As a consequence, the number left to provide direct protection of the army co-operation units was reduced.

B8371   SE5a   1Sqn
LowP left 9-40am combat with EA ARMENTIÈRES **MIA(Capt WD Patrick **POW**) seen nrMESSINES, Patrick had claimed 7 victories with 1Sqn

**   SE5a   1Sqn**
** ground mg fire(Lt DM Bissett **WIA**)

**   SE5a   1Sqn**
P ground mg fire(2Lt FP Magoun **WIA)

**   RE8   4Sqn**
** ground mg fire(/2Lt CS White **WIA**)

**   RE8   4Sqn**
** (/Lt WAS McKerrell **DoW**)

B5649   Sopwith Camel   4Sqn AFC
BOP left 8-35am attacking transport AA? ground fire? seen zoom then nd & ooc cr **MIA(Lt FS Woolhouse **KIA**)

B9302   Sopwith Camel   4Sqn AFC
BOP attacking transport AA? engine cut ftl ldg ok but hit fence o't eLAVENTIEcr **MIA(Lt HK Love **POW**) left 8-35am

A7989   DH4   18Sqn
**B ground mg dam ftl cr 12-45pm OK(2Lt L Balderson/ Lt G Bullen) left 12pm First Army area

**   DH4   18Sqn**
** ground mg fire(Capt AF Brooke **WIA**/Capt EC Powell **WIA**)

B6860   SPAD 13   23Sqn
BOP AA Fokker DrI? 3-02pm seen eVILLERS BRETONNEAUX 12000' **MIA(2Lt GG MacPhee **POW**)

B6864   SPAD 13   23Sqn
B left 5-20pm AA **MIA(2Lt FJ Hopgood **POW**)

C8520   A.W.FK8   35Sqn
**P AMIENS fuel tank shot up 3pm dam OK(2Lt MC Sonnenberg/2Lt D Wills) left 1-55pm

C8528   A.W.FK8   35Sqn
**P combat with EA ovVILLERS BRETONNEAUX engine shot up ~10-55am ftl OK(2Lt JE Phillips/2Lt HW White) left 8-30am [?possible "RE" claim combat

ROUVREL 9-30am? Ltn J Veltjens Ja15]

D5011   A.W.FK8   35Sqn
P combat with EA 10-55am shot down MERVILLE BOIS(2Lt A MacGregor OK/2Lt JH Shooter **KIA)

**   SE5a   40Sqn**
ground mg fire(Lt H Carnegie **WIA)

C5437   SE5a   40Sqn
B engine failed EoL GORRE ftl(Lt CO Rusden **POW) a'c abandoned, Rusden had destroyed a 2Str in this a'c the previous day

A4306   RE8   42Sqn
CP rifle ground mg returned a'dr(2Lt NMcC Anderson **WIA/Lt MJ Pottie **WIA**) left 6-05am

B5099   RE8   42Sqn
AP left 11-50am **MIA(2Lt AR Holthouse **KIA**/2Lt DG Smith **KIA**)

**   RE8   42Sqn**
** ground mg fire(Lt LP Rendell **WIA**/Cpl G Alston **WIA**)

C1661   Sopwith Camel   46Sqn
**LowP left 9-20am controls shot up dam returned a'dr 10-05am? OK(2Lt GA Lamburn) returned 10-47am?

B6641   RE8   52Sqn
Rec combat with 9 Fokker DrIs ftl(2Lt HL Taylor **WIA/2Lt WIE Lane **WIA**) ["RE8" claim combat AMIENS Ltn W Göttsch Ja19]

**   RE8   59Sqn**
** (/2Lt WL Kingswill **WIA**)

**   Untraced RAF Sqn**
** **MIA**(Lt G Thomas **POW**) repat 14.12.18 Christian name Geraint

11th April

The week of poor weather continued, so that yet again it was not until late afternoon that conditions cleared. Then followed a few hours of very intense air fighting. Operations were similar to those of the previous day but many more enemy formations were met, including some at high level. Bombing and ground strafing was concentrating on two areas: the Lys Valley, including bombing of bridges; and on attacking enemy troop concentrations around La Bassée in the south, where it was critical the Allies held fast.

B243   A.W.FK8   2Sqn
*prac hit by own AA ovANNEQUIN ftl wr OK(2Lt JWD Farrell/Lt F Ambler)

**   RE8   3Sqn AFC**
** combat with 6 Albatros ovHENENCOURT shot up(2Lt AW Rees **WIA**/Lt GA Paul **WIA**)

**   RE8   4Sqn**
P ground mg(2Lt CA Mason **WIA/Lt CR Pilcher-Hemingway **WIA**)

RE8   **4Sqn**
P ground mg(2Lt AC Nye **WIA)

RE8   **4Sqn**
** AA(/2Lt S Ramsden **WIA**)

B5123   **RE8**   **5Sqn**
Phot combat with EA shot up returned a'dr(2Lt JF Good **WIA/Lt AW Mackay **WIA**)

B4033   **RE8**   **7Sqn**
FlRec left 4-50pm **MIA(2Lt LM Gerson **POW**/2Lt H Inman **POW**)

B6489   **RE8**   **7Sqn**
*OP mg fire? NIEPPE ftl abandoned OK(Capt AWF Glenny MC/2Lt JP Bosman) burnt by Infantry

RE8   **7Sqn**
** ground fire(/2Lt GN Lloyd-Rees **WIA**)

A.W.FK8   **10Sqn**
** ground mg(/2Lt IS Black **WIA**)

B5087   **RE8**   **13Sqn**
**AOb left 5-20pm shot up eARRAS ftl OK(Capt Douglas/Lt Daria)

B844   **RE8**   **15Sqn**
ShootP combat with EA CONTAY 6-35pm controls shot away ftl(2Lt RG Hart **WIA?/2Lt HF Handford **WIA**)

B6522   **RE8**   **16Sqn**
AOb combat with 3EA 5-15pm shot down br down wr(Capt TB Jones **KIA/Lt V King **KIA**) [?"RE" claim wOSTENDE 5-05pm combat Ltn J Jacobs Ja7]

B1275   **Bristol F2b**   **20Sqn**
OP ground mg shot up NEUVE EGLISE ftl wr(Maj JA Dennistoun **WIA/Lt JJ Scaramanga **WIA**?) a'c shelled on ground

C5042   **RE8**   **21Sqn**
**CAP YPRES AA rifle fire dam returned a'dr 8-35am OK(Capt LH Jones/Lt PH Clarke) left 7-40am

C3629   **A.W.FK8**   **35Sqn**
**P AA mg CACHY 6-30pm shot through ftl OK(2Lt EC Grimes/2Lt N Bowden)

B4021   **RE8**   **53Sqn**
CAP ground fire 10-25am ftl wr(Lt RD Best **WIA/Capt CG White MC OK)

B8890   **RE8**   **53Sqn**
CAP combat with EA shot down in flames ARMENTIÈRES 5-05pm cr destroyed nrBETHUNE(2Lt J Craig **KIA/Lt K Hall **WIA**)

RE8   **53Sqn**
** mg fire(/2Lt WR McCoo **WIA**)

E18   **RE8**   **53Sqn**
**CAP ground mg hit prop 3-05pm ftl cr shell hole OK(Lt RS Barlow/2Lt F Pashley) to HOLLEBEKE-WYTSCHAETE

C8287   **Sopwith Camel** **54Sqn**

OP ground mg fire ftl cr nose ldg(Lt TR Hostetter US. **WIA)to hospital

D6453   **Sopwith Camel** **54Sqn**
**SpP:HAP left 5-50pm combat with EA shot up mg dam OK(Maj RS Maxwell MC)

C5445   **SE5a**   **60Sqn**
OP left 3-35pm combat with 2EAs? seen BUCQUOY **MIA(Capt K Crawford **KIA**) ["SE5" claim combat BAPAUME 5-15pm Vzfw O Koennecke Ja5][?"SE5" claim combat nwALBERT 5-45pm Ltn W Böning Ja76]

D1827   **Sopwith Camel** **73Sqn**
OP left 5-25pm not seen leaving formation **MIA(2Lt RG Lawson **POW**) [?"Sopwith 1Str" claim combat VILLERS-AUX-ERUBLES 7-25pm Ltn F Pütter Ja68]

B8233   **SE5a**   **84Sqn**
+* combat with Fokker DrIs[+ooc] eALBERT 5-05pm OK(Capt JV Sorsoleil Can.) Ja76?, half of his 14 claims were in this a'c

B6409   **Sopwith Camel** **201Sqn**
**OP AA shot up ftl 20Sq dam OK(FSLt F Newton)

B7277   **Sopwith Camel** **203Sqn**
SpM combat with 6 AlbatrosDV ovNEUVE EGLISE 2pm in flames **MIA(FSLt S Smith **KIA**) left 1-45pm

B5750   **Sopwith Camel** **210Sqn**
LowB seen eARMENTIÈRES 2-30pm shot down **MIA(FSLt MT McKelvey **WIA POW**) left 1-30pm ["Sopwith 1Str" claim combat neSTEENWERCK 2-55pm Ltn A Dietlen Ja58]

3119   **H.P. 0/100**   **214Sqn**
*NB ZEEBRUGGE cr o't a'c burnt **MIA**(Capt ER Barker **INT**/Lt FH Hudson **INT**/Lt DC Kinmond **INT**) left 11-50pm

1462   **H.P. 0/100**   **215Sqn**
NB ZEEBRUGGE AA?, fire started, engine failed ftl sea 7 miles off OSTENDE 12am sank(FCom JR Allen **KIA/Capt P Bewsher **inj**/2Lt MC Purvis OK) left 10-40pm, a'c on loan from 207Sq

The night of the 11th of April had been chosen for the naval attack on Zeebrugge whereby ships would be rammed into the mole in order to block the harbour. Preparations had been made in great secrecy and involved RAF aircraft in a number of ways. During the attack, fleet protection patrols, anti-submarine patrols, and low bombing raids of German seaplane bases were to be carried out. Additionally, heavy bombers were to attack the area of the mole itself in the hope that this would drive the defenders into cover and generally cause chaos. Handley Page 1462 duly began its bombing but the weather was worsening and it is likely that the machine was hit by anti-aircraft fire. An engine failed and a forced landing on the sea was made, from which the crew was rescued. Other Handley Pages from 214 and 215 Squadrons took off shortly

before midnight, as the weather really began to close in. One of these was No.3119 above, which was forced down and crashed in Holland, where the crew was interned. Ironically, the weather caused the Navy to postpone its attack and none of the other air operations were commenced. The raid would be delayed another eleven days and this would affect the size of the force the RAF was subsequently able to offer. By that time the containment of the enemy offensive towards Hazebrouck and the coast had passed through a critical stage, one aspect of which was that the personnel of two of the previously available bomber squadrons had been evacuated to England as a precautionary measure (the units were 207 and 215 Squadrons, and their machines were allotted to 214 and 216 Squadrons).

12th April

The 12th of April was the most critical day of the new offensive. Reinforcements were on their way, but a supreme effort would be needed to contain the advance for another day. Merville had fallen, and it was expected the big push on Hazebrouck would now be made by what was an optimistic German Army. Haig issued a special Order of the Day which included the words "There is no other course open to us but to fight it out. Every position must be held to the last man: there must be no retirement. With our backs to the wall and believing in the justice of our cause each one of us must fight on to the end."

Virtually the entire air fighting effort was thrown into attacks around Merville, Estaires and Neuf Berguin. The weather was fine at last, so that squadrons carried out their relentless attacks from dawn until dusk. The way in which the RAF grasped its duties is illustrated by the fact that in this twenty-four hours the air arm flew a record number of hours for the war, took more photographs than ever before, and dropped a record number of bombs. Fighters carried out strong offensive patrols high above the battle but the most intense air fighting was low down. Forty-nine enemy machines were claimed brought down with another twenty-five down out of control. Capt HW Woollett of 43 Squadron claimed six of the enemy shot down in two separate engagements. The fine weather also enabled widespread artillery co-operation and gave the contact patrols an excellent appreciation of the state of the battle.

C9610   SE5a   1Sqn
**OP left 11-55am BAILLEUL shot up returned a'dr 1-18pm OK(Lt RB Donald)

SE5a   1Sqn
** (2Lt WL Harrison **WIA**)

C3552   A.W.FK8   2Sqn
**AP LOCON combat with 7EA mg dam 4-50pm OK(Lt LJ Money/2Lt RL Davies) left 3-05pm

B5580   Sopwith Camel   3Sqn
COP left 5-40pm seen ovAVELUY WOOD **MIA(Lt AAMcD Arnott **KIA**) DoW?

RE8   4Sqn
** ground mg(/2Lt D Henderson **WIA**)

D4692   RE8   4Sqn
P left 12-50pm **MIA(2Lt PC Westhofen **KIA**/2Lt AW Miller **POW**)

B271   A.W.FK8   10Sqn
CAP left 3-30pm **MIA(Capt AM Maclean **KIA**/2Lt FB Wright **KIA**) [+"Armstrong" claim combat nBAILLEUL 5pm Ltn Lotz Ja7, but see C3552?]

C3548   A.W.FK8   10Sqn
CAP mg engine hit ftl 6-50am(Lt EC Harrison **WIA/2Lt JC Anderson OK)unsalvable

A.W.FK8   10Sqn
** ground mg(/2Lt ELH McLeod **WIA**)

RE8   15Sqn
** (/2Lt AW Bolitho **WIA**)

A7800   DH4   18Sqn
B combat with EA mg dam ldg ok(2Lt EN? Wilton **WIA/Lt W Miller OK) nrESTAIRES? in am?, initials GN?

B1257   Bristol F2b   20Sqn
LowB nrNEUF BERGUIN **MIA(Lt AL Pemberton **POW**/Cpl F Archer **POW**) left 3-10pm ["Camel" claim combat CALONNE 4-50pm Ltn O Creutzmann Ja43]

C4605   Bristol F2b   20Sqn
**SpM enemy fire shot up dam returned a'dr OK(Lt DG Cooke/Lt HG Crowe) left 3-14pm, Cooke claimed over a dozen victories

A4578   RE8   21Sqn
**CAP mg fire YPRES ftl dam OK(Lt HA Marshall Can./Lt C Whiting) left 5-45am

C1081   SE5a   24Sqn
+* combat with PfalzDIII[+des] nMOREUIL A'dr 11am OK(Lt GB Foster Can.) made several other victory claims

SE5a   24Sqn
** (2Lt ET Hendrie **WIA**)

B178   SE5a   40Sqn
+* combat with AlbatrosDV[+des] eESTAIRES 7-25pm OK(Maj RS Dallas)

40 Squadron made seven claims through the day, including four Pfalz DIIIs in a big fight over Bethune at about 5-30pm.

D6402.S   Sopwith Camel   43Sqn
+* combat with AlbatrosDVs[+des+flames] & 2Str[+ des] neLA GORGUE ~10-35am then in afternoon: combat with AlbatrosDVs[+++des] neLA GORGUE 5pm OK(Capt HW Woollett) six EAs claimed in one day, 23 of his 35 claims in this a'c

D6428   Sopwith Camel   43Sqn
**OP left 9-35am MIA(Lt AC Dean POW)

D6558   Sopwith Camel   43Sqn
**OP left 9-35am MIA(1Lt GH Kissell USAS. KIA)

RE8   53Sqn
** ground mg(/2Lt FE Pashby WIA) name Pashley?, and see previous day's entry for this observer?

B5424   Sopwith Camel   54Sqn
**OP seen ok about to dive on EA eARMENTIÈRES 8-20am shot down nrWAMBRECHIES MIA(1Lt JR Sanford USAS. KIA) name Sandford?, left 7-50am ["Sopwith" claim combat WAMBRECHIES 8-30am Ltn H-G Marwitz Ja30]

C1559   Sopwith Camel   54Sqn
**OP troop straffe seen in control wESTAIRES MIA(Lt I MacNair KIA) left 10-15am [?"Sopwith 1Str" claim combat FRELINGHIEN 10-20am Vzfw F Ehmann Ja47]

C1603   Sopwith Camel   54Sqn
**OP left 7-50am mg shot up dam OK(Lt NF Spurr)

D6509   Sopwith Camel   54Sqn
**GndP left 10-15am mg shot up wESTAIRES ftl OK(Lt JR Moore)

C5430.V   SE5a   56Sqn
**OP mg engine failed cr ldg QUERRIEU 11-20am dam OK(Capt LW Jarvis) left 9-35am Third Army area

FE2b   58Sqn
** ground mg(/2Lt JO Holliday WIA)

C2254   RE8   59Sqn
**Phot left 10-30am combat with EA shot down(Lt C Curtis WIA/2Lt EG Thomas OK)to hospital

C8282   Sopwith Camel   65Sqn
**CP shell hit nrHANGARD ftl CACHY OK(Capt TEW Withington)shelled, left 6-45pm, unsalvable, off strength

D1850   Sopwith Camel   73Sqn
**OP seen wVIELLE CHAPELLE 12000' MIA(2Lt MF Korslund US. KIA) left 11-05am, first time EoL ["Sopwith 1Str" claim combat AUBERS 11-25am Ltn H-G Marwitz Ja30]

B173   SE5a   74Sqn
+* combat with AlbatrosDV[+des] eMERVILLE 8-25am OK(Lt HE Dolan)

C5396   SE5a   74Sqn
+* combat with AlbatrosDV[+des] seDEULEMONT 11-40am OK(Maj KL Caldwell NZ.)

This was Caldwell's first claim with 74 Squadron, made on the day that the unit itself began scoring.

His final overall total by the end of the war was most likely twenty-four victories.

D278   SE5a   74Sqn
+* combat with AlbatrosDV[+destr] eMERVILLE 9am OK(Capt EC Mannock) Mannock scored 17 victories in this a'c

B5154   Sopwith Camel   80Sqn
**P left 3-30pm MERVILLE-RADINGHEM MIA(2Lt GL Murray KIA)

C1683   Sopwith Camel   80Sqn
**P left 3-30pm MERVILLE MIA but OK(2Lt AL Code)

C1699   Sopwith Camel   80Sqn
**P seen in combat ovPARADIS MIA(2Lt WA Pell KIA) left 3-30pm MERVILLE-RADINGHEM

C3680   A.W.FK8   82Sqn
**OP mg shot down CERTELLES wr OK(2Lt S Haigh/ 2Lt W Spencer) unsalvable

C1094   SE5a   84Sqn
**OP left 4-45pm seen ldg ok nwPLESSIER MIA(Lt CM McCann POW) Roll of Honour: KIA? ["SE5" claims combat VILLERS-AUX-ERUBLES 6-10pm Ltn F Pütter & Vzfw W Stör Ja68]

C9519   SE5a   84Sqn
+* combat with DFWC[+ooc] BAPAUME 11-50am OK(Lt CL Stubbs) possible earlier 2Str nHANGARD 11-20am, Stubbs made 6 claims

DH9   98Sqn
**B NEUF BERQUIN ground mg(/Lt V Brent WIA)to hospital

This was the first casualty suffered in action by 98 Squadron and the first on the de Havilland DH9 bomber. The Squadron had made its first raid the day previously.

A5728   FE2b   101Sqn
**NB French AA spiralled down cr wr(2Lt JP Owen-Holdsworth KIA/2Lt HJ Collins inj)

B7202   Sopwith Camel   210Sqn
** attacked KBs[++des] shot up dam OK(Capt AW Carter DSC)

A special patrol to attack German kite balloons in the forward area was sent out at 1-05pm. Seven Camels from 210 Squadron made the raid, escorted by five SE5as from 40 Squadron.

3129   H.P. 0/100   214Sqn
**NB shot up & bad weather ftl FORT MARDYCKE nrDUNKIRK wr OK(Lt EF McIlraith/Lt WH Matthews/Lt AR Clark) left 12-33am

13th April

After the exertions of the 12th, the efforts of the German Army slackened and there was also no

enemy air activity to speak of. The weather closed in again, limiting Allied flying.

A.W.FK8   2Sqn
** (2Lt HS Woodman **WIA**)

A.W.FK8   10Sqn
** (/2Lt JP Mackenzie **WIA**)

Bristol F2b   22Sqn
** mg fire(2Lt HF Davison **WIA**)

D6461   **Sopwith Camel**   54Sqn
OP seen ok ovNEUF BERGUIN 3-55pm shot down **MIA(Capt EZ Agar **KIA**)

A5632   **FE2b**   101Sqn
*NB French AA on way out ftl cr ldg LONGRE(Lt GEP Elder **inj**/2Lt SM Sproat **shaken**) left 2-45am ERCHIES

D3347   **Sopwith Camel**   203Sqn
SpM mg shot up ESTAIRES-MERVILLE cr ldg WoL Sh36A H.5.A(FSLt J Denison **KIA) found with bullet in head

D1840   **Sopwith Camel**   208Sqn
**SpLP left 12-45pm mg shot up ST VERANT fuel tank hit ftl 1400yd WoL cr wr OK(FSLt WEG Mann) unsalvable

14th April

Mist and rain and low clouds persisted to make flying difficult, but most squadrons of I Brigade continued to make reconnaissance and low attacks. In the next few days the enemy progressed no further beyond Merville and it looked as though Hazebrouck had been saved. Their biggest gains were in the Second Army area where on the 15th they took Bailleul. The offensive was being held, however, and survival in Flanders was to be finally assured after the arrival of the British 5th and 33rd Divisions and the 1st Australian Division.

C3530   **A.W.FK8**   2Sqn
AP mg fire LOCON ftl(2Lt T Rawsthorne OK/Lt AH McLachan **WIA)

A.W.FK8   2Sqn
AOb ground mg(2Lt HS Montgomerie **WIA/)

B4879   **SE5a**   40Sqn
Rec BAILLEUL STN dive on lorry ground mg shot up but returned a'dr ok(Maj RS Dallas **WIA)back

15th April

B218   **A.W.FK8**   2Sqn
**AP heavy AA shot up ovLOCON 9am dam OK(2Lt FH Baguley/Lt RL Rice) left 5-40am

B248   **A.W.FK8**   2Sqn
**LP heavy AA fuel tank & radiator hit 7-10am ftl CHOCQUES a'dr OK(2Lt GH Allison/Lt FW Gundiff) left 5-40am LOCON

C3651   **A.W.FK8**   2Sqn
AP heavy AA mg? shot up dam(2Lt JH Jennings OK/2Lt H Stanners **WIA)

A.W.FK8   2Sqn
B ground mg(/Lt J Thomson **WIA)

A.W.FK8   2Sqn
B rifle fire(/2Lt JA Weatherley **WIA)

A.W.FK8   2Sqn
** ground mg(2Lt R Allan **WIA**)

C4557   **RE8**   4Sqn
P left 3-40pm XV Corps front **MIA(2Lt W Naylor **KIA**/Lt D Elliot **KIA**)

B3903   **Sopwith Camel**   4Sqn AFC
**B shot up FESTUBERT-NEUVE CHAPELLE dam ftl OK(Lt R Sly)

C4808   **Bristol F2b**   22Sqn
OP hit by British infantry fire wr 2-30pm Sh36A J.28.c.(2Lt GN Traunweiser **KIA/Sgt S Belding **KIA**)

C4817   **Bristol F2b**   22Sqn
**OP First Army area shot through OK(2Lt WS Hill-Tout/2Lt PS Williams)

C4606   **Bristol F2b**   48Sqn
**LowRec CHAULNES mg dam returned 12-45pm OK(2Lt ACG Brown/2Lt W Hart) left 11-30am

RE8   53Sqn
** (2Lt CE Lovick **WIA**)

C1573   **Sopwith Camel**   54Sqn
**OP mg fire dh to prop NIEPPE FOREST ftl trees OK(Lt JR Moore) left 8-05am

C1601   **Sopwith Camel**   54Sqn
**OP left 8-05am mg fire shot down NIEPPE FOREST OK(Lt NF Spurr) WIA on 17.4.18?

D1845   **Sopwith Camel**   208Sqn
this a'c? ** ground mg(2Lt GJ Glazier **WIA**)

N6376   **Sopwith Camel**   210Sqn
B combat with EA or ground fire(FLt HT Mellings **WIA)

16th April

From the 16th of April German time reverted to being one hour ahead of British time (all times given are British time).

B532   **SE5a**   1Sqn
LowB HA & mg? seen ovFLETRE 1-40pm shot up ftl **MIA(Lt FR Knapp **POW**) left 1-10pm FLETRE-MESSINES

SE5a   1Sqn
LowP (Capt JS Windsor MC **WIA)

D5026   **A.W.FK8**   2Sqn
B heavy mg combat? ftl cr(2Lt JL Walton **WIA/Lt AE Cripps shaken)

A.W.FK8   **10Sqn**
** ground mg(/2Lt EK Harker **WIA**)

B6737   **SPAD 7**   **23Sqn**
**prac:View Lines, left 4-40pm AA ftl nrLines P.31.b.4.5. OK(Lt RA Way)

D1799   **Sopwith Camel**   **65Sqn**
OP seen AA hit 4000′ DOMART 5-20pm cr(Lt B Balfour **KIA)

17th April

Ludendorff had made significant inroads into Flanders, including the recovery in ten days of fighting of virtually all the territory the British had won so dearly the previous autumn — even the Passchendaele Ridge was returning into German hands. He had also forced the Allies to divert large and vital resources from other sectors of the defence. On the other hand, the salient he had created was a distinct strategic liability and in order to straighten the line somewhat he was forced to undertake a number of costly attacks around Mount Kemmel which crucially prolonged and wearied his efforts on this front. These began on the 17th and were temporarily frustrated by the defenders. Most air fighting on the 17th in connection with this occurred in the few hours of clear weather in the morning. Following this there was a week of relative quiet before the next big attack on Kemmel was launched. In the meantime the attention returned to the fighting in front of Amiens where an increasingly desperate Ludendorff was about to set a third major offensive in motion.

B5776   **A.W.FK8**   **2Sqn**
*AOb ground mg ovBELLERIVE engine hit fire ftl CHOCQUES 10-15am dam OK(Lt DS Thompson/Lt AJ Melanson) left 9-30am

A.W.FK8   **2Sqn**
** ground mg(Lt GA Barry **WIA**)

B830   **RE8**   **4Sqn**
P combat with 7EA ovSh36A D.17.d.93 shot up ftl(2Lt ML James **WIA/2Lt OA? Broomhall **WIA**) initials DA?, left 11-30am [?possible "Camel" claim combat neNÍEPPE 2pm Ltn P Strähle Ja57]

C2274   **RE8**   **5Sqn**
AP combat with 5EA shot down FARBUS WOOD(2Lt AGE Edwards **WIA/Lt N Sworder **DoW**) left 7-50am ["RE" claim combat wFARBUS 10-25am Ltn E Koch Ja32]

B5048   **RE8**   **7Sqn**
OP shot down sMERRIS(Lt ASN Coombe **KIA/Lt SS Wright DCM **KIA**) left 11-45am HAZEBROUCK, shot down ovHAZEBROUCK? ["RE8" claim combat HAZEBROUCK 1-10pm Ltn G Schlenker Ja3]

B5065   **RE8**   **7Sqn**

OP ground mg fire shot up dam(Capt FJ Watts OK/ Lt D Gardner MC **WIA)

C4699   **Bristol F2b**   **20Sqn**
+* combat with AlbatrosDVs[++des] seHAZEBROUCK 2pm OK(Capt TP Middleton/Capt F Godfrey) pilot claimed 27 victories including 7 with 48Sqn

B6365   **Sopwith Camel**   **54Sqn**
**OP left 10-35am mg fire shot up dam OK(Lt CS Bowen)

D1837   **Sopwith Camel**   **54Sqn**
OP left 6am combat with HA seen in control wBAILLEUL **MIA(Lt CC Lloyd **KIA**) ["Camel" claim combat neVIEUX-BERQUIN Ltn P Strähle Ja57]

D1848   **Sopwith Camel**   **54Sqn**
OP left 5-15pm seen leaving **MIA(Lt WHG Liddell **KIA**)

D6512   **Sopwith Camel**   **54Sqn**
**OP left 8-05am mg shot up dam OK(Lt RFW Moore)

D6523   **Sopwith Camel**   **54Sqn**
*OP left 8am mg shot up dam OK(Lt TS Howe MC)

D6583   **Sopwith Camel**   **54Sqn**
OP combat with HA neOUTERSTEENE **MIA(Lt TSC Howe MC **KIA**) left 12-15pm

C6087   **DH9**   **98Sqn**
*B BAILLEUL controls shot away LYNDE ftl wr OK(Lt SB Welsh/Lt C deCruise) left 12pm, 18.4?

N6000.B1 **DH4**   **205Sqn**
**B LA MOTTE A'dr combat with EA shot up rudder controls shot away ftl CORBIE hit wires dam OK(Capt CR Lupton/AG AG Wood) left 12-37pm

DH9   **206Sqn**
** ground mg(/Sgt JJ Ryan **WIA**)

DH9   **206Sqn**
B (2Lt VFA Rolandi **WIA)

Surprisingly, these were the first casualties in action for 6 (Naval)/206 Squadron since it had been re-formed as a day-bomber unit in January. It had been on active duty for six weeks.

18th April

There was a German attack on Bethune on the 18th, a last attempt to widen the southern extremity of their salient. It was beaten off with very heavy casualties to the attackers. Snow and sleet fell through the fighting, but machines of I Brigade still managed significant bombing and ground strafing.

A8929   **SE5**   **1Sqn**
**LowB left 11-58am shot up dam ftl 42Sq OK(Lt RB Donald)

19th April

B5214   Sopwith Camel   54Sqn
**OP left 5-45pm mg shot up dam OK(Lt RFW Moore)

20th April

148 Squadron arrived in France with their FE2b light night bombing machines on the 20th of April. They were the sixth of eight such units to operate in France. The others to use the FE2b in a night role were Nos. 58, 83, 100, 101, and 102 Squadrons, as well as 38 and 149 Squadrons who would arrive shortly.

B7393   Sopwith Camel   3Sqn
"RHODESIA" **COP combat with EA fuel tank hit shot down in flames 1m neVILLERS BRETONNEAUX cr **MIA**(2Lt DG Lewis **WIA**? **POW**) left 5-30pm VILLERS BRETONNEAUX ["Camel" claim combat VILLERS BRETONNEAUX 5-43pm? Rittm M Fr vRichthofen JG1]

2Lt Lewis was the eightieth and last victory of the Red Baron, Manfred von Richthofen.

D6439   Sopwith Camel   3Sqn
COP combat with EA ~6pm ovVILLERS BRETONNEAUX in flames(Maj R Raymond-Barker MC **KIA) left 5-30pm, MvR79 ["Camel" claim combat swBOIS DE HAMEL 5-40pm? Rittm M Fr vRichthofen JG1]

D6475   Sopwith Camel   3Sqn
COP combat with EA shot up ~6pm returned a'dr(2Lt GR Riley **WIA) [?"Camel" claim combat swBOIS DE HAMEL 5-40pm? Ltn H Weiss Ja11] made 13 victory claims

RE8   4Sqn
** (/Lt JEG Mosby **WIA**)

RE8   4Sqn
** (2Lt L Gowsell **KIA**)

C5086   RE8   13Sqn
**Phot left 9-25am combat with EA shot up returned a'dr OK(Capt F Hyde/2Lt WTC Blake)

C8503   A.W.FK8   35Sqn
CP left 6-05pm combat with EA VILLERS BRETONNEAUX ftl(2Lt JE Phillips OK/2Lt HW White **WIA)

A.W.FK8   35Sqn
** mg fire(2Lt CT Bremickar **WIA**)

D3510   SE5a   40Sqn
**OP combat with 2 Albatros C-types shot up ovBOIS DE PACAUT dam OK(Lt RG Landis US.) left 12-35pm, returned 1-35pm

D5578   DH9   49Sqn
B combat with EA shot down cr LEKE-GHISTELLES EoL **MIA(Lt BW Robinson **WIA POW**/Sgt T? Wills **KIA**) initials TJ?, left 4-30pm THOROUT, badly WIA

A5605   FE2b   83Sqn
NB ARMENTIÈRES mg engine hit ftl cr Sh36B E.19.b wr(2Lt GW Higgs **inj/2Lt PA Bankes MC **inj**)to hospital

D270   SE5a   84Sqn
OP AA hit GLISY 7-15am shot down(Capt EH Tatton **KIA)

21st April

C8512   A.W.FK8   2Sqn
*Phot combat with 7EA mg ovLACOUTURE 11-30am dam OK(2Lt JWD Farrell/Lt F Ambler) left 10-20am

C5069   RE8   5Sqn
**AOb mg THELUS 6-55pm engine failed cr OK(2Lt RS Durno MC/Capt L Oerbling)

B4051   RE8   12Sqn
**AOb combat with 8EA ovBOYELLES 7500' 10-30am controls shot up dam ftl SIMERCOURT OK(2Lt HR Caffyn/2Lt WA Armit)

RE8   12Sqn
Phot (2Lt CA Brook **WIA)

C3799   Sopwith Dolphin   19Sqn
+* combat with PfalzDIII[+flames] STEENWERCK 7pm OK(2Lt GB Irving) scored many of his 12 victories in this a'c

C3833   Sopwith Dolphin   19Sqn
+* combat with PfalzDIII[+ooc] STEENWERCK 7-15pm OK(Lt JA Aldridge)

C1084   SE5a   24Sqn
"BABE CINCINATTI USA" +* attacked KB[+des] LE QUESNEL 11am OK(Capt GO Johnson Can.) claimed 11 victories including several in this a'c

SE5a   24Sqn
P (2Lt HB Redler **WIA)

A7563   DH4   25Sqn
*Rec VALENCIENNES-BUSIGNY **MIA**(2Lt CJ Fitzgibbon **POW**/2Lt W Rudman MC **POW**)

A8078   DH4   25Sqn
B combat with 10HAs SERNY 3-15pm shot up then cr ldg by observer(2Lt JD Dingwall **KIA/Lt CM Sinclair **WIA**)

DH4   25Sqn
B shot up(2Lt WF Gonzalez **WIA)

C5037   RE8   53Sqn
CAP KEMMEL was heard to call Sqn **MIA(Lt EHN Stroud **KIA**/Capt CG White MC **KIA**) left 6-45am

B9315   Sopwith Camel   54Sqn
OP combat with 8 Fokker DrIs seen 3000' in control ovESTAIRES **MIA(Lt RJ Marion **KIA**) left 11-40am

D6569   Sopwith Camel   54Sqn
OP combat with 8 Fokker DrIs swBAILLEUL 12-30pm seen ok **MIA(Lt CJ Mason **KIA**) left 11-40am [?"Sopwith" claim combat wBAILLEUL 12-50pm Ltn K

Gallwitz Ja2][?"Sopwith 1Str" claim combat eARMENTIÈRES, but 10-10am? Ltn C Degelow Ja40]

B1234   Bristol F2b   62Sqn
OP AA nrARMENTIÈRES ftl cr wr(Lt DA Savage **inj/2Lt LM Thompson **inj**)

D269   SE5a   74Sqn
**OP combat with HA MARIE CAPPELLE shot up ftl OK(Lt CEL Skeddon) [?"SE5" claim combat seHAZEBROUCK 3-30pm Vzfw F Ehmann Ja47]

D281   SE5a   74Sqn
OP seen in combat with HA 13000' down in flames ARMENTIÈRES **MIA(Lt SCH Begbie **POW DoW** 22.4.18) left 5-20pm ARMENTIÈRES-LAVENTIE

Lt Begbie was the first 74 Squadron pilot lost in action.

B4617   Sopwith Camel   80Sqn
OP MERCATEL-ARMENTIÈRES mg fire ftl nrLines(2Lt AL Code **WIA) left 8-50am, combat?

C6108   DH9   98Sqn
+* combat with Fokker DrI[+ooc] BAILLEUL-ARMENTIÈRES 7am OK(Lt AM Phillips/Lt CP Harrison)

C6199   DH9   98Sqn
B combat with EA[+ooc] BAILLEUL-ARMENTIÈRES 7am shot up dam(Lt CJ Stanfield OK/Lt FH Wrigley **WIA)leg

These two victories were the first in air fighting by 98 Squadron.

B6319   Sopwith Camel   203Sqn
** combat with PfalzDIII[+ooc] wBAILLEUL 3pm contols shot up ftl nLILLERS Sh36A D.156 wr OK(FCdr RA Little)

B7245   Sopwith Camel   209Sqn
HOP combat with EAs shot up dam but ldg ok?(Lt WJ Mackenzie **WIA) [?possible "Camel" claim combat sHAMELET 10-50am Ltn HJ Wolff Ja11]

B7270   Sopwith Camel   209Sqn
** dive on Red Fokker DrI WARFUSÉE-ABANCOURT[+? claimed capt] OK(Capt AR Brown Can. DFC) EA cr VAUX-SUR-SOMME 10-45am, claimed victory over Rt Manfred Fr von Richthofen, but most likely claim is from Australian machine gun fire from ground

D3328   Sopwith Camel   209Sqn
+* being chased by EA piloted by Richthofen at the time of his death OK(2Lt WR May)

THE DEATH OF MANFRED VON RICHTHOFEN

It was at some time during this engagement that Germany's great air fighter, leader of Jagdgeschwader I and the most famous ace of the First World War, met his death from a single bullet.

There have been conflicting claims ever since concerning exactly who it was that brought him down. At the time of being hit he was in Fokker Triplane 425/17 pursuing a fleeing Camel of 209 Squadron west of the lines. This was Camel D3328 piloted by 2Lt WR May. Capt AR Brown had dived to attack the triplane which shortly afterwards crashed at Vaux-sur-Somme. There was known to have been intense ground fire directed at the machine from Australian trenches, and it may have been an Australian machine-gunner who delivered the fatal shot. The machine was shelled for some hours before it was eventually retrieved and then stripped by souvenir hunters. JG1 had been fighting in the Amiens offensive but on the 13th had been ordered up to Kemmel. They had been kept south ostensibly by the poor weather, but as they were about to depart on the 15th they received orders to remain in the area for the renewed attack around Villers Bretonneaux.

The news of Richthofen's death spread quickly to all corners of the Western Front. The men of his Jagdgeschwader were stunned to learn of it and could scarcely believe he had been killed. Germany lost not only a very great air fighter but also a tactician and leader of exceeding skill.

22nd April

**   SE5a   1Sqn**
** (Lt RB Donald **WIA**) inj?

D5005   A.W.FK8   2Sqn
AOb AA LE BREBIS 6-30pm ftl wr(2Lt R Allan **KIA/2Lt C Sheil **DoW**)

C2276   RE8   4Sqn
**P combat with 5EA 8-10am shot up dam OK(TLt FWMC Chesney/2Lt JC Stack) left 5-20am XV Corps area

C8445   A.W.FK8   8Sqn
**AP AA shot up ftl wr OK(Lt FMS West/2Lt JAG Haslam)

B6853   SPAD 13   23Sqn
+* combat with AlbatrosDV[+ooc] ROSIÈRES 7-20pm OK(Lt RA Way)

This was the last SPAD victory for 23 Squadron before the unit fully re-equipped with Sopwith Dolphins.

B6857   SPAD 13   23Sqn
BOP last seen 5000' nwCORBIE 7-40pm **MIA(2Lt LW Prescott US. **KIA**) left 6-43pm

B2073   DH4   27Sqn
B combat with EA shot up bad dam(2Lt EJ Smith OK/2Lt ECW Deacon **KIA)

B2110   DH4   27Sqn
****B left 7am ROULERS AA dam OK(2Lt CH
Gannaway/2Lt WI Crawford) turned back before
objective**

C1584   Sopwith Camel   54Sqn
*OP combat with EA mg shot up(Lt CS Bowen **WIA**)to
hospital

C4045   Sopwith Dolphin   79Sqn
**OP left 10-45am ARMENTIÈRES AA dam ftl(Capt C
Faber **WIA**)

**   Sopwith Dolphin   79Sqn**
** (2Lt B Holding **WIA**)

B6428   Sopwith Camel   201Sqn
**OP left 10-20am combat with HA nrHANGARD
MIA(Capt GA Magor **KIA**) [?"Camel" claim combat
MOREUIL WOOD 10-58am Ltn H Weiss Ja11]

N6377   Sopwith Camel   201Sqn
**OP left 10-20am combat with HA HANGARD
MIA(2Lt WH Easty **KIA**)

B7228   Sopwith Camel   203Sqn
**OP mg ovMERVILLE ftl FLORINGHEM
9-30am(2Lt NC Dixie **WIA**)slight

A8063   DH4   217Sqn
this a'c? **B enemy trawler snd cr sea nZEEBRUGGE
MOLE **MIA**(Lt CStC Parsons **POW**/GL GS Gladwin
POW) crew picked up and taken prisoner by enemy
trawler

The main naval attacks on Zeebrugge mole and
Ostende harbour were carried out in the evening of
the 22nd. 217 Squadron were undoubtedly
involved in keeping the Channel clear of any enemy
presence and this crew were lost attacking an
enemy trawler. The attack failed to close Ostende
but Zeebrugge was partly blocked. Efforts would
continue through early summer to complete this
work, including some aerial bombing of the submarines thus trapped in Bruges Docks by 5 Group.
The latter were to be hampered by lack of aircraft,
however, for despite powerful representations no
reinforcements were forthcoming. The Admiralty
were desperate to strike at this enemy stronghold,
but by the end of May all that had been offered was
38 night-bomber Squadron with their FE2bs, and
a brief loan of 98 Squadron. It was an opportunity
missed. Nevertheless, in May, thirty-six tons of
bombs were dropped on Bruges, thirty-two on
Zeebrugge, and nine on Ostende. 214 Squadron
Handley Pages were regularly deployed to Bruges,
for instance, but also suffered several casualties
from enemy fire over these highly defended bases.

23rd April

87 Squadron arrived in France on the 23rd of April
equipped with the Sopwith Dolphin fighter.

D6511   Sopwith Camel   46Sqn
**COP left 10-05am First Army area shot up dam
returned a'dr 11-35am OK(2Lt RK McConnell)

C1086   SE5a   56Sqn
**OP combat with Albatros & Fokker DrIs ovBRAY
MIA(Capt KW Junor **KIA**) left 4-30pm ["SE5" claim
combat SAILLY-LAURETTE 5-55pm Ltn E Koepsch
Ja4]

D8406   DH4   57Sqn
**B BAPAUME AA shot down cr fire(2Lt WH
Townsend US. **DoI**/2Lt C Souchette **KIA**)

**   Sopwith Camel   70Sqn**
P (2Lt HL Whiteside **WIA)

D1829   Sopwith Camel   70Sqn
**LP AVELUY WOOD mg fire ftl dam returned a'dr
2-45pm OK(2Lt WE Woods)

**   SE5a   84Sqn**
** (Lt LdeS Duke **WIA**)

A6408   FE2b   101Sqn
**NB crashed in action DOMMARTIN 11-50pm
wr(Capt JA Middleton **inj**/Lt RE Smith **KIA**) left
11-50pm, reason for crash unknown, a'c shelled &
unsalvable

A7933   DH4   205Sqn
**B CHAULNES STATION combat with HA
BELLEVUE ftl(2Lt LF Cocks **WIA**/AG HF Taylor OK)
left 5-30pm

N6004   DH4   205Sqn
+*B combat with Fokker DrI[+flames] & PfalzDIII[+
broke up] CHAULNES 7-50pm OK(Capt J Gamon/Lt
R Scott)

B7586   DH9   206Sqn
**B cr nrBUSNES on return, fire destroyed(Lt LM
Whittington **inj**/AG S Jones **WIA**)

**   DH4   217Sqn**
+* combat with AlbatrosDV[+des] OSTENDE OK(Lt
RG Shaw/GL Tallboys)

This was the first enemy fighter claimed shot down
by 217 Squadron.

24th April

The German attack towards Amiens briefly
renewed itself on the 24th. After a bombardment
there was a direct attack just south of Villers
Bretonneaux, and this village was soon taken. The
enemy used tanks to create a breakthrough in this
assault, which also had the benefit of fog. The town
was promptly recovered, however, after a night
counter-attack spearheaded by Australian troops.
On both days air activity was made difficult by the
conditions. Airmen were driven low and casualties
were reasonably high from ground fire. There was
little enemy air presence. After this fighting,

activity on the front died away. Ludendorff's efforts to make sense of his gains in Flanders, principally his attacks on the Kemmel range, had probably robbed him of his chance to resume the attack at Amiens successfully.

218 Squadron arrived at Petite Synthe on the 24th of April equipped with DH9 day-bombers.

A.W.FK8   **35Sqn**
** ground mg(/2Lt FG Brown **WIA**)

A7114   Bristol F2b   48Sqn
**COP mg shot up on return 2-10pm OK(2Lt TG Jackson/Lt AE Ansell) left 1-10pm VILLERS BRETONNEAUX

C4886   Bristol F2b   48Sqn
**COP mg shot up dam on return 12pm OK(2Lt FC Ransley/2Lt CW Davies) left 11-25am VILLERS BRETONNEAUX, Ransley claimed 9 victories, 3 with Davies

Bristol F2b   48Sqn
** rifle fire(2Lt WL Thomas **WIA**)

D6436   Sopwith Camel   65Sqn
OP left 11-20am seen ovVILLERS BRETONNEAUX **MIA(Lt HBD Harrington **POW**)

A.W.FK8   82Sqn
** ground mg(/Lt KC Herron **KIA**)

C1794   SE5a   84Sqn
**OP AMIENS-ST QUENTIN ground mg 12-30pm dam OK(Capt AW Beauchamp-Proctor) left 12-05pm

C9623   SE5a   84Sqn
**OP left 3-30pm ground mg dam return 4-35pm OK(Capt KA Lister-Kaye) to VILLERS BRETONNEAUX

SE5a   84Sqn
** ground mg(Lt WL Sumsion **WIA**)

B6311   Sopwith Camel   209Sqn
SpM left 4-45pm Fourth Army front combat? with Pfalz **MIA(Lt FC Stovin **KIA**)

D3331   Sopwith Camel   209Sqn
**SpM combat with PfalzDIII[+cr] WARFUSÉE-ABANCOURT 6-50pm but shot up dam ftl cr OK(Lt CG Edwards)

25th April
FIGHTING FOR
THE KEMMEL RIDGE

The battle for the Kemmel Ridge recommenced on the 25th with an intense bombardment and an attack by thirteen German divisions. Mount Kemmel was the key position and was captured in the afternoon from its defenders who were mostly French. Elsewhere, the British were driven back to a line running in front of Dickebusch Lake, La

Clytte, the Sherpenberg, and Locre. German aircraft were very active in the evening, attacking Corps machines and ground strafing troop concentrations. II Brigade machines (from 1, 54, and 74 Squadrons) were busiest in trying to counter this, but in general, the German Air Force retained its control of the air on the first day.

Two new RAF squadrons arrived in France on the 25th: No. 88 with Bristol Fighters and No. 99 with DH9 bombers. The latter joined 41st Wing and moved to its base at Tantonville on the 3rd of May from where it flew its first raid on the 21st. It subsequently became a part of the Independent Force.

B8254.O   SE5a   1Sqn
+* combat with PfalzDIII[+ooc] HOUTHEM 6-55pm OK(Lt JC Bateman) made several claims

B8410   SE5a   1Sqn
+* combat with PfalzDIII[+ooc] HOUTHEM 6-50pm OK(Capt CC Clark)

C1104   SE5a   1Sqn
+* combat with PfalzDIII[+ooc] HOUTHEM 6-55pm OK(Lt F Nesbitt)

C5374   SE5a   1Sqn
+* combat with Fokker DrI[+des] BECELAERE-DADIZEELE 6-45pm OK(Lt KC Mills)

B5102   RE8   4Sqn
CP combat with HA Sh17 W.28.1.08 at 7-45am shot down wr(2Lt CB Hunt **KIA/2Lt PH Whitwell **KIA**)

C8553   A.W.FK8   10Sqn
CAP mg fire 10-45am ftl cr shell hole Sh28.N.5.a(Lt HW Holmes **WIA/Lt HG Hooker OK)

C9518   SE5a   24Sqn
**LowGndP Fourth Army area shot up dam returned a'dr 5-25pm OK(Lt W Selwyn) left 4-15pm

C8552   A.W.FK8   35Sqn
AP AA shell hit CACHY **MIA(2Lt AEG Williams **KIA**/2Lt N Bowden **KIA**)

B1126   Bristol F2b   48Sqn
OP dive on EA 8000' ovWIENCOURT 5pm **MIA(Capt T Colvill-Jones **POW DoW** 24.5/1AM F Finney **POW**) left 4-05pm, Colvill-Jones made 11 claims

B6615   RE8   53Sqn
CAP combat HA? KEMMEL(Capt HM Gibbs **WIA/Lt A Lomax **WIA**)to hospital, left 9-15am ["RE" claim combat eRENINGHELST 9-50am Ltn K Schattauer Ja16]

B7827   RE8   53Sqn
**CAP combat with 2EA shot up 8-45am OK(2Lt GWT Glasson/2Lt WW Porter) to ST JANS CAPPELL-DRANOUTRE

RE8   53Sqn
** (2Lt GJ Hutcheson **WIA**)

D6517   Sopwith Camel   54Sqn
+* combat with LVGC[+ooc] seBAILLEUL 7-30am
OK(Capt GH Hackwill)

D1801   Sopwith Camel   65Sqn
*OP left 5pm combat with 5 Albatros engine shot up ftl
Sh62D T.24 OK(2Lt MA Newnham) ["Sopwith 1Str"
claim combat DOMART 5-25pm Ltn J Mai Ja5]

D1776   Sopwith Camel   73Sqn
**OP seen ok starting combat with Fokker DrIs
eMESSINES **MIA**(Lt AN Baker **KIA**) left 12pm
[?"Camel" claim combat NEUVE EGLISE 1-25pm Ltn
K Bolle Ja2]

D276   SE5a   84Sqn
**OP combat with HA VILLERS BRETONNEAUX
5-15pm engine shot up ftl then hit pole ldg cr wr(Capt KA
Lister-Kaye **WIA**)

C6079   DH9   98Sqn
**B GHELUVELT engine failed far EoL: seen glide
down going west ovGHELUWE **MIA**(Lt CJ Gillan
POW/Lt W Duce **POW**) left 11-30am

26th April

For three days following the 26th the weather was
very bad, seriously limiting flying.

27th April

C1104   SE5a   1Sqn
**OP left 6pm combat with EA REXPOEDE shot up
dam ftl(Lt FW Nesbitt **WIA**)

D5015   A.W.FK8   8Sqn
**LP mg shot up dam ftl Sh62D U.18.v.13. OK(2Lt J
Stuart/Lt HL Cox) left 5-15pm, returned a'dr 6-45pm

B79.Y   **SE5a   24Sqn**
**OP left 10-15am shot down nrLONGUEAU 11-15am
cr OK(Lt JAER Daley) Daley had several victories in this
a'c

29th April
THE GERMAN OFFENSIVE IN FLANDERS HELD

Attacks in Flanders reached their peak of intensity
on the 29th with what proved to be a final great
push against the front from Locre almost to Ypres.
The weather had improved and air activity was the
heaviest for several days. This attack was completely shattered however, and Ludendorff's second
offensive, and his last against the British front,
came to an end. On the 30th Locre was recaptured
by the Allies and after this time the front quietened.
   In just under six weeks Germany had flung one
hundred and forty divisions at the combined
British and French forces. Fifty-five British infantry
divisions and three cavalry divisions had resisted

and survived the attacks of one hundred and nine
German divisions. The third great German
campaign in the west had been defeated.
   The Allies had withstood the very hardest blows
the enemy could deliver, but at terrible cost. British
casualties amounted to nearly 250,000 killed,
wounded, and missing; they had lost 80,000
prisoners. The losses were equally as devastating
for the German Army numerically, but infinitely
more damaging to the contracting options left to
Ludendorff. From this time onwards the German
war programme increasingly gambled on finding
quick success through a succession of other offensives, for time was indeed running out. In April
nearly 120,000 American troops landed in France,
over 220,000 in May, and 275,000 in June. By the
beginning of June over a million American troops
would have sailed, bringing with them the certainty
of Allied victory.
   The aircraft losses suffered by the RFC and RAF
since the March offensive had begun are quoted in
the Official History as being 1,032 from all causes.
This should be compared with the number of
machines the RFC had on strength in France on
the 21st of March, which was 1,232.
   The contribution the RAF made during the
Battle of the Lys was obviously restricted by the
weather, a factor which limited operations on
nearly every day of the offensive. On the one day
on which flying was possible throughout, the RAF
set records in nearly every aspect of its work. As in
the fighting on the Somme, the taking of air
superiority and then using it to gradually wither
the German attack had won both time and material
advantage for the Allies. There had been more air
fighting in the Lys, but again the German Air Force
had lost its effectiveness after a few days — lack of
liaison with infantry and artillery and difficulty in
bringing air units up closer to the battle zone as the
advance progressed being at the heart of the
problem. Again, by the time this organisation
began to filter through, the RAF had also reinforced its own fighter strength.

C4555   RE8   4Sqn
**P combat with 6EA Sh27 Q23.x.7.5. at 1-30pm dam(Lt
TD Henderson OK/Lt A Fleming **DoW**)

B3327   A.W.FK8   10Sqn
**FlRec dh shell 8-20am ftl dam OK(Lt FW Burdick/
ProbAG C Liston)

B5789   A.W.FK8   35Sqn
**CP combat with EA Sh62A 619 at 11-10am ftl(2Lt RW
Truebridge **DoW** 6.5.18/2Lt H Gittons OK)

C1617   Sopwith Camel   46Sqn
**COP left 11-20am ground mg fire Sh51B B.4 seen spin

down in flames cr just WoL(2Lt FJ? Smith **KIA**) initials FE?

D5571   DH9   98Sqn
****B MENIN seen going E ok GHELUWE-WERVICQ
MIA(Lt CG Tysoe **POW**/2Lt CV Carr **WIA POW**) left
7-50am

B3809   Sopwith Camel   210Sqn
BOP left 1pm Flak seen cr Sh36A F.11 **MIA(TLt HL
Nelson **KIA**)

B7195   Sopwith Camel   210Sqn
*BOP AA dam OK(TLt HA Patey)

30th April

A.W.FK8   2Sqn
** AA(2Lt JH Mitchell **WIA**)

RE8   53Sqn
Rec (/2Lt RA Carter **WIA)

May 1918

Germany's greatest fighter of the war, the Fokker
DVII, began to appear in numbers on the Western
Front in May. It had an excellent rate of climb,
and although at first slower than most Allied
fighters it was highly manoeuvrable at all altitudes
and speeds. When upgrades utilising the 185hp
BMW engine began to appear later in the summer,
an extremely good fighter became a brilliant one.
Its high altitude perfomance was particularly
impressive. The Fokker's operational use was to be
widespread and timely, if slow to start — eight
hundred Fokker DVIIs were serving with forty-
eight Jagdstaffeln by September, and its introduction greatly boosted the morale of the German
Air Force as it faced an increasingly difficult task.
At this time, its best pilots and its most effective
aircraft were still heavily concentrated on the
Amiens front. Although they were often deployed
very successfully here in large formations, the
numerical superiority of the Allies ensured the
latter would never be overwhelmed in the air on
the critical fronts, whilst elsewhere, the Allies could
operate very effectively against a depleted enemy.
It was an equation the German Air Force would
find insoluble as air activity gradually climbed
along the entire Western Front.

2nd May

RE8   15Sqn
P (Lt A Young **WIA/Lt JA Fitzherbert **WIA**) crew?

C3829   Sopwith Dolphin   19Sqn
+* combat with PfalzDIII[+ooc] sARMENTIÈRES
5-45pm OK(Capt J Leacroft) last of 22 claims

B2482   Sopwith Camel   43Sqn
prac left 6-05pm **MIA(Lt G Hamilton **POW**)

B178   SE5a   40Sqn
+* combat with AlbatrosDV[+des] BREBIÈRES
2-50pm OK(Maj RS Dallas Aust.)

Prior to this combat Dallas had challenged enemy
fighter pilots at La Brayelle aerodrome to a
combat. He had done this by first strafing the
hangars and then dropping a pair of boots with a
message attached which read "If you won't come
up here and fight, herewith one pair of boots for
work on the ground. Pilots — for the use of." He
then returned to further shoot up and bomb the
airfield.

C1685   Sopwith Camel   46Sqn
**COP left 4-25pm seen attack 6HAs ESTAIRES
5pm(2Lt LC Hickey **KIA**) [?"Camel" claim combat
LOCON 5-15pm Vzfw H Juhnke Ja52]

C1096   SE5a   56Sqn
+* combat with PfalzDIII[+des] seMARTINPUICH
11-25am OK(Lt HJ Burden) first of his 13 claims in this
a'c

C1796   SE5a   56Sqn
**SpM seen in combat with HA MARTINPUICH
11-30am **MIA**(Maj R Balcombe-Brown **KIA**) left
10-40am["SE5" claim combat nMONTAUBAN
11-30am Ltn E Loewenhardt Ja10]

C1100.A SE5a   64Sqn
**OP left 10-15am seen ovBIACHE going east 11-30am
but returned MIA but OK(Lt JFT Barrett)

C8296   Sopwith Camel   65Sqn
**OP combat with EA shot down 11-35am
HAMEL:CGE 68.B OK(2Lt P Whiteley)unsalvable

D6546   Sopwith Camel   65Sqn
**OP combat with 12EA HAMEL-CERISY 1-25pm
MIA(2Lt WH Duncan-Knight **KIA**) left 11-40am
["Camel" claim combat MORCOURT 1-15pm Ltn J
Mai Ja5][?"Camel" claim combat VILLERS
BRETONNEAUX Ltn F Rumey Ja5]

C4126   Sopwith Dolphin   79Sqn
OP on fire BERNICOURT nd cr(2Lt ACR Tate **KIA)

B6421   Sopwith Camel   201Sqn
+* combat with 2Str[+ooc] nALBERT 10-10am OK(Lt
RCB Brading) shared, first of 13 claims by Brading with
201Sqn

B7276   Sopwith Camel   213Sqn
** seen cr nrZEEBRUGGE **MIA**(FLt EF Bensly **POW**)

3rd May

B188   SE5a   2Sqn AFC
**OP combat with Fokker DrI[+des] 11-30am then more
4EA controls shot away shot down ooc n.m.l.

nrMETEREN but ldg ok OK(Lt ED Cummings)
unsalvable, left 10-05am

RE8   5Sqn
** (Lt WRW Henderson **WIA**/Lt AM Morgan **WIA**)

RE8   7Sqn
P (/Lt FE Gauntlett **WIA)

C8583   A.W.FK8   8Sqn
*AP combat with 6EA shot up nrMERICOURT dam
OK(Capt JT Quick/2Lt CP Henzell) left 6-05am,
returned 8-45am

C3641   A.W.FK8   10Sqn
**FlRec ground mg shot up dam returned a'dr OK(Lt
FW Burdick/Prob AC Clinton) left 6-45pm
VIERSTRAAT & N.10.d.

C2361   RE8   15Sqn
**Phot combat with 3 Fokker DrIs BUIRE shot down in
flames **MIA**(Lt HJ Browne **KIA**/Lt LJ Derrick **KIA**) left
8-40am

C3828   Sopwith Dolphin 19Sqn
**OP combat with EA then seen wNEUVE CHAPELLE
MIA(Capt G Chadwick **WIA POW**) left 5-04pm
["Sopwith 1Str" claim combat nLA BASSÉE 5-30pm Ltn
P Billik Ja52]

This was the first Sopwith Dolphin casualty for 19
Squadron.

C4818   Bristol F2b   20Sqn
**OP combat with HA fuel tank shot through ftl
WORMHOUDT cr OK(Lt FE Boulton/AM WH
Foster) left 4-05pm

B5585   Sopwith Camel   46Sqn
**OP left 11-25am badly shot up CHOCQUES dam ftl
OK(Lt JR Cote)

B7357   Sopwith Camel   46Sqn
**OP left 11-25am combat with HA nwDON 1pm
MIA(2Lt RLG Skinner **POW DoW**) ["Camel" claim
combat ESTAIRES 1pm Ltn P Billik Ja52]

C1637   Sopwith Camel   46Sqn
+* combat with HalbC[+des] nwDON 1pm OK(2Lt
VM Yeates) shared with Capt DR MacLaren, first claim
for Yeates, best known for his book *Winged Victory*

C814.12   Bristol F2b   48Sqn
Rec **MIA(2Lt ACG Brown **POW DoW** 7.5.18/Cpl AW
Sainsbury **WIA POW**) left 9-40am VILLERS
BRETONNEAUX [?"BF" claim claim PROYART
11-15am OffSt P Aue Ja10]

C2311   RE8   53Sqn
**Phot ABEELE combat with HA 11-05am shot down
dam(Lt HT Rushton **WIA**/Prob JB Sanders **WIA**)

C4709.8   Bristol F2b   62Sqn
.8? **OP combat with EA controls shot up dam ftl wr
OK(Capt H Rees-Jones/2Lt Bruce-Norton) left 9-55am
FONTAINE-LES-BOUBINS

C4744   Bristol F2b   62Sqn
**OP ARMENTIÈRES combat with EA seen spin EoL
MIA(Lt Hampton **WIA POW**/Lt LC Lane **WIA POW**)
left 9-55am, JG1

Bristol F2b   62Sqn
P (Lt CH Arnison OK/2Lt S Parry **KIA) crew?

Bristol F2b   62Sqn
** ground mg(Lt HK Spoonley **WIA**/Lt EG Grant
WIA?) crew?

B2.2   **SE5a**   **64Sqn**
**OP combat with EA engine shot through DAINVILLE
ftl trenches wr OK(Lt WC Daniel)

D6480   Sopwith Camel   73Sqn
**OP combat with HA MESSINES 12-50pm seen
ARMENTIÈRES-YPRES going west in control **MIA**(Lt
AF Dawes **POW**) left 11-30am [?"Camel" claim combat
NIEPPE 12-45pm Ltn K Bolle Ja2]

D6536   Sopwith Camel   73Sqn
**OP seen before combat PLOEGSTEERT WOOD
12-40pm **MIA**(Lt RR Rowe **KIA**) left 11-30am

C6085   DH9   98Sqn
**B combat with HA shot down WESTULETEREN
dam(Lt FA Loughlin OK/2Lt TRG Cooke **WIA**)

C6101   DH9   98Sqn
**B MENIN combat with 18EA EoL ooc broke up seen
going down vertically in flames ovGHELUWE **MIA**(Lt
RA Holiday **KIA**/Lt CB Whyte **KIA**) left 12pm, observer
fell [?possible unconfirmed "DH9" claim combat
FREZENBERG 1-10pm Ltn K Bolle Ja2]

FE2b   148Sqn
NB (/2Lt FH Stock **WIA)

Stock was the first casualty in action for 148
Squadron.

B3855   Sopwith Camel   203Sqn
+* combat with Fokker DrI[+ooc] ARMENTIÈRES-
NEUVE EGLISE 11-35am OK(Capt HF Beamish NZ.)
claimed 11 victories, many in this a'c

D3360   Sopwith Camel   203Sqn
**OP combat with Fokker DrI fuel tank hit
ovARMENTIÈRES shot down ftl Sh36B F.7.A cr
11-45am OK(FSLt JD Breakey) Breakey made several
victory claims

D9237   DH4   205Sqn
+* combat with PfalzDIIIs[+ooc+des] CHAULNES-
ROSIÈRES 3-45pm OK(Capt E Dickson NZ./AGL CV
Robinson) Dickson claimed 18 victories

D9243   DH4   205Sqn
flat spin ovCHAULNES Stn(Lt RJ Scott **KIA/2Lt TA
Humphreys **KIA**) left 4-10pm

C2157   DH9   206Sqn
**B left 5-41pm ARMENTIÈRES going down in flames
BAILLEUL-KEMEL **MIA**(Lt AE Steel **KIA**/2Lt AE
Slinger **KIA**)

D1663   DH9   206Sqn
**B AA shot up dam OK(Lt T Roberts/Sgt J Chapman DFM)

4th May

A.W.FK8   2Sqn
P ground mg(/2Lt GA Hunter **WIA)

B5629   Sopwith Camel   4Sqn AFC
BOP combat with EA shot down in flames cr nrVIEUX BERQUIN 6-05pm(Lt BW Wright **KIA) left 5-35pm ["Camel" claim combat NIEPPE WOOD 5-50pm Ltn H Müller Ja18]

Bristol F2b   11Sqn
** (2Lt R Fiton **WIA**)

C1793   SE5a   24Sqn
OP left 5-30pm **MIA(2Lt RA Slipper **WIA POW**)severe [?"SE5" claim combat MAMETZ 6-30pm Ltn A Heldmann Ja10]

A4452   RE8   53Sqn
**CAP KEMMEL mg rifle fire dam OK(Lt SF Pickup/ Lt CE . . .?) left 10-30am, returned a'dr, Surname cannot be made out on RAF Casualty Report

N5985   DH4   202Sqn
** combat with 2 Albatros ftl BRAY DUNES cr sea 6-20pm o't badly dam(Lt JP Everitt **WIA**/Lt WR Stennett **KIA**)

N5989   DH4   202Sqn
Esc combat with EA shot up nrZEEBRUGGE(Capt GW Biles OK/Lt EE Gowing **WIA)

5th May

B2092   DH4   27Sqn
**B combat with EA engine dam ftl nKEMMEL cr wr OK(2Lt GE Ffrench/Sgt V Cummins) left 6-30am, fell out of formation, unsalvable

6th May

C1074   SE5a   1Sqn
**OP fuel tank shot up storm ftl cr trees CLAIRMARAIS A'dr dam OK(Lt BD Clark) left 2-55pm

C5374   SE5a   1Sqn
**OP left 1-40pm AA shot up ftl dam OK(Lt KC Mills)

A4404   RE8   3Sqn AFC
P 4 Fokker DrIs came from clouds SAILLY LE SEC shot down ooc in flames(Capt HDE Ralfe **KIA/Lt WAJ Buckland **KIA**) left 6-35am, not A4494 as AIR1/969/204/ 5/1101?, left 6-35am ["RE" claim combat MERICOURT 7-15am Ltn V vPressentin Ja4]

RE8   5Sqn
AOb shot up(/2Lt RD Stewart **WIA)

D5956   SE5a   29Sqn
LP left 2-15pm combat ovNIEPPE FOREST 2-45pm **MIA(Sgt AS Carno)

C4156   Sopwith Dolphin 87Sqn
+* combat Rumpler[+ooc] GHELUVELT 5-40pm OK(Lt L Murray-Stewart) shared

C4157   Sopwith Dolphin 87Sqn
+* combat Rumpler[+ooc] GHELUVELT 5-40pm OK(Capt AAND Pentland Aust.)

C4163   Sopwith Dolphin 87Sqn
+* combat Rumpler[+ooc] GHELUVELT 5-40pm OK(Lt CK Oliver) shared

The three shared claims above were the first made by 87 Squadron.

C6276, D1700 DH9   98Sqn
** damaged in enemy bombing raid overnight

C9787   FE2b   101Sqn
SpNRec left 9-10pm ESTRÉES BRIE **MIA(Lt SA Hustwitt **POW**/Lt NA Smith **POW**)

D3374   Sopwith Camel 210Sqn
**OP AA aileron controls shot away ftl Sh20.s.28. 6-20pm OK(Lt J Hollick) left 5-25pm

7th May

C1849   SE5a   1Sqn
+* combat with 2Str[+des] 1m eKEMMEL shot up(2Lt KC Mills **WIA**) last of 5 claims

C8521   A.W.FK8   10Sqn
FlRec combat with EA PESELHOEK controls shot up 2-45pm ftl(Lt W Hughes OK/Lt HG Hooker **WIA)

B1164   Bristol F2b   22Sqn
+* combat with several D-types[+++destr++shot down in flames] 10m neARRAS 6-45pm to 6-50pm OK(2Lt AC Clayburn Can./2Lt CG Gass) the first victories for this crew for 22 Sqn, sharing in a total of 29 in under a month

B1253   Bristol F2b   22Sqn
+* combat with D-types[++destr+shot down in flames]eARRAS 6-45pm OK(2Lt JE Gurdon/2Lt AJH Thornton) the famous "two versus twenty fight", this a'c seems to have taken part in at least 28 victories

RE8   53Sqn
P ground mg(Lt GWT Glasson **WIA)

8th May

B8410   SE5a   1Sqn
OP left 6-15am combat with EA neKEMMEL 7-45am **MIA(Capt CC Clark **WIA POW**)slight [?"SE5" claim combat KEMMEL 7-35am Ltn H vBülow Ja36] Clark made a few of his 10 claims in this a'c

C1095   SE5a   1Sqn
**OP left 6-15am combat with HA shot up dam OK(Lt PJ Clayson) Ja26?

C6408   SE5a   1Sqn
OP combat with HA 7-45am neKEMMEL EoL **MIA(Lt JC Wood **WIA POW**)slight, Ja26? [?"SE5" claim combat ST ELOI 7-20am Ltn K Bolle Ja2]

RE8   **4Sqn**
Rec (2Lt S Moxey **WIA)

B138   SE5a   41Sqn
**OP combat with EA shot up dam returned a'dr 3-15pm
OK(Lt WG Shields) left 1-15pm

C8298   Sopwith Camel   43Sqn
**OP left 12-20pm ooc eBAILLEUL seen going down
MIA(Lt TM O'Neill **KIA**) ["Camel" claims combat
wSTEENWERCK 1-20pm Ltn K Bolle & Ltn F Kempf
both Ja2]

B8097   RE8   53Sqn
**CAP mg KEMMEL fuel tank hit ftl 4-45pm OK(Lt
GL Dobell/Lt CE Willows)

B8373   SE5a   74Sqn
**OP left 7-35am combat with 10EA eZILLEBEKE
8-35am **MIA**(Lt RE Bright **KIA**) [?"SE5" claim
BECELAERE 8-37am Vzfw E Buder Ja26]["SE5" claim
combat sZILLEBEKE LAKE 8-45am Ltn H Lange &
Ltn F Loerzer Ja26]

B8502   SE5a   74Sqn
**OP mg shot through ftl 16.B.94 destr on ground OK(Lt
JR Piggott) left 4-35am

C1078   SE5a   74Sqn
OP combat with 10EA eZILLEBEKE 8-35am **MIA(Lt
PJ Stuart-Smith **KIA**) left 7-35am [?"SE5" claim
GHELUVELT 8-40am Vzfw F Classen Ja26]

C6406   SE5a   74Sqn
+* combat with 2Str[+flames] BAILLEUL-NIEPPE
6-25pm OK(Lt JIT Jones) Jones' first of 37 claims in 3
months

C6108   DH9   98Sqn
**B ROULERS-MENIN combat with 20EAs
AlbatrosDV[+flames] MENIN-WERVICQ 7-20pm shot
up(2Lt NC Macdonald **WIA**/Lt CP Harrison OK)

B7595   DH9   206Sqn
**LP AA nrMERVILLE dam OK(Lt EA Burn/2Lt AH
Mitchener)

D1845   Sopwith Camel   208Sqn
+* combat with AlbatrosDV[+ooc] PROVIN 11-15am
OK(Lt WEG Mann) first of 13 victories

D1852   Sopwith Camel   208Sqn
**SpLRec combat with 2EA low ovPROVIN 11-15am
MIA(Capt R McDonald Can. **KIA**) left 10-30am
[?"Sopwith" claim combat nrPROVIN OffSt J Trotzky
Ja43] had made several claims on Triplanes & Camels
with 8(N) & 208Sqn

B6276   Sopwith Camel   210Sqn
*OP combat with EA nrARMENTIÈRES shot up dam
OK(Capt ES Arnold)

9th May

B5792   A.W.FK8   2Sqn
**AOb seen RUE DE MARAIS 11-50am, combat with
4EA nILLIES shot down in flames 12pm(Lt RL Johnson

KIA/Lt AJ Melanson **KIA**) left 11-15am ["AW" combat
NEUVE CHAPELLE 11-55am Ltn P Billik Ja52]

RE8   3Sqn AFC
**Phot combat with 4 Fokker DrI ftl CACHY(Capt JR
Duigan MC **WIA**/Lt AS? Paterson **WIA**) initials AF?
["RE" claim combat eCACHY 11-30am Ltn F Hemer
Ja6]

Duigan built the first Australian aircraft to fly. His
"Duigan Biplane" flew for the first time on the 16th
of July 1910.

A.W.FK8   10Sqn
P mg fire(2Lt HG Jackson **WIA)

B1164   Bristol F2b   22Sqn
**OP combat with PfalzDIII[+ooc] nDOUAI 6-45pm
but shot up dam(Lt SFH Thompson OK/Sgt L Kendrick
WIA)arm, to First Army area, Thompson eventually
claimed 30 victories, 2 with Kendrick

B1253   Bristol F2b   22Sqn
+*OP combat with D-types[++ooc+destr in flames]
LILLE 9-40am OK(2Lt AC Atkey Can./2Lt CG Gass)
shot down 2 more D-types nDOUAI 6-40pm, making
second 5-EA haul in 3 days. These were first of 18
victories for this crew in this a'c with 22Sqn, the last on
2.6.18

D301   SE5a   29Sqn
**OP ARMENTIÈRES mg fire shot up dam OK(Lt CJ
Venter)

D3566   SE5a   29Sqn
**OP left 8-40am combat ARMENTIÈRES 9-50am
MIA(Lt T Ratcliffe **POW**)

D5966   SE5a   29Sqn
**LP combat with EA controls shot up OSTREVILLE
ftl 6-45am cr OK(Lt LE Bickel) Ja29 ["SE5" claim
swLAVENTIE 9-05am Ltn G Schuster Ja29]

D1790   Sopwith Camel   43Sqn
OP left 2-25pm combat shot down **MIA(Lt S Birch
POW) Ja29 ["Camel" claim combat seLESTREM
3-15pm Untoff K Pech Ja29]

D1821   Sopwith Camel   43Sqn
OP combat with HA in flames seALBERT **MIA(Lt A
Whitford-Hawkey **KIA**) left 5-40pm [?"Camel" claim
combat HAMEL 6-50pm Ltn E Loewenhardt
Ja10][?"Camel" claim combat wMORLANCOURT
7pm Oblt W Reinhard JGI]

D6588   Sopwith Camel   43Sqn
**pracform hit by AA ftl Sh36A 36C.4.2.(2Lt EP Pycroft
inj)shaken, left 11-25am, fainted on ldg?

C4750   Bristol F2b   48Sqn
**OP combat with Fokker DrIs[+++ooc]
WIENCOURT-MERICOURT 3-40pm shot up dam
returned 5pm OK(Capt CGD Napier/Sgt W Beales) left
3-10pm WIENCOURT-MERICOURT [?"BF" claim
combat CORBIE Vzfw R Heibert Ja46]

C6094   DH9   49Sqn
**B combat with EA 12-10pm seen glide down eBRAY

MIA(Lt GA Leckie **KIA**/Lt GR Cuttle MC **KIA**) left 9-40am [?"DH9" claim combat WIENCOURT 12-15pm Ltn V vPressentin Ja4]

A8068   DH4   57Sqn
**Phot combat with 15EA shot up cr ldg 12-15pm wr OK(Lt CM Powell/Sgt EEAG Bridger) left 9-30am

D8411   DH4   57Sqn
Phot controls shot away ftl spun on ldg at a'dr 12-20pm cr wr OK(2Lt LdeV Wiener **inj/Lt RW Rumsby **DoI**) left 10-05am

C1860.D SE5a   64Sqn
+* combat with PfalzDIII[+des] & RumplerC[+ooc] BOIRY ~10-40am OK(Lt T Rose) made 11 claims

C9517.B SE5a   64Sqn
+* combat with HalbC[+ooc] & PfalzDIII[+ooc] BOIRY 10-43am OK(Lt CA Bissonette US.) made 6 claims

C5446   SE5a   84Sqn
**OP combat with Albatros shot up dam returned a'dr 3-30pm OK(Lt SB Echert) left 1-30pm VILLERS BRETONNEAUX

B7280   Sopwith Camel   201Sqn
**OP combat with PfalzDIII[+ooc] ovBAPAUME but then AA 1-05pm ftl BERTRANCOURT cr Sh57D 528 OK(Lt JH Forman Can.) made 9 claims

D3375   Sopwith Camel   201Sqn
OP left 10-30am combat with 8 Pfalz BAPAUME shot down **MIA(2Lt F Newton **KIA**)

B7637   DH9   211Sqn
B combat with EA shot up dam(Lt FJ Islip OK/2Lt E Cooke **inj) to OSTENDE-NIEUPORT, observer injured in combat

          DH9   211Sqn
+* combat with Fokker DrI[+flames] ZEEBRUGGE MOLE OK(Lt W Gillan/2Lt R Lardner)

This was the first combat victory for 211 Squadron.

10th May

C4851   Bristol F2b   20Sqn
OP combat shot up ftl HAZEBROUCK dam(Lt DE Smith OK/Pbr FJ Ralph **WIA) left 3-55pm [?combat HOUTHULST WOOD 5-40pm Ja56]

A7514   DH4   27Sqn
B combat with 20-30EAs swPERONNE then seen going down **MIA(Capt GBS McBain DSC MC **KIA**/2Lt W Spencer **KIA**) left 5-05pm ["DH9" claim combat ROSIÈRES 7-30pm Ltn V vPressentin Ja4]

B2078   DH4   27Sqn
B running combat ftl by EA(2Lt SW Taylor OK/2Lt WH Gibson **WIA) left 5-05pm BERTANGLES

B2081   DH4   27Sqn
B combat with 20-30EAs swPERONNE seen going down **MIA(Lt LE Dunnett **KIA**/Lt DH? Prosser **KIA**)

initials HD?, left 5-05pm ["DH9" claim combat CHAULNES 7-30pm Ltn E Loewenhardt Ja10]

B2087   DH4   27Sqn
B combat with 20-30EA swPERONNE seen going down after combat **MIA(Lt AH Hill **KIA**/1AM GS Richmond **KIA**) left 5-05pm [?"DH9" claim combat CHAULNES 7pm Ltn P Wenzel Ja6]

B1299   Bristol F2b   48Sqn
BOP combat with EA MARICOURT down spin(Lt NG Stransom **KIA/Pte CV Taylor **KIA**) left 2-30pm, Ja4 ["DH9" claim combat CHUIGNES 3-40pm Ltn V vPressentin Ja4]

D5993   SE5a   56Sqn
OP combat with 2EA BRAY 8pm then broke up(Lt BW Harmon Can. **KIA) left 6-25pm ["SE5" claim combat eHAMEL Ltn F Rumey Ja5]

B2463   Sopwith Camel   80Sqn
OP left 5pm SOMME **MIA(Lt AW Rowdon **KIA**) [?"Camel" claim combat CERISY pm Oblt E vWedel Ja11][?"Camel" claim combat CHERISY?(CERISY?) 6-50pm Vzfw F Hemer Ja6]

B7322   Sopwith Camel   80Sqn
**OP dusk combat with HA BEAUVAL ftl cr o't OK(Lt CSL Coulson)

B9243   Sopwith Camel   80Sqn
**OP left 5pm SOMME gunfire dam returned a'dr OK(Lt TS Nash)

D6419   Sopwith Camel   80Sqn
OP left 5pm SOMME **MIA(2Lt GA Whateley **KIA**) ["Camel" claim combat CHIPILLY 6-50pm Ltn H Kirschstein Ja6]

D6457   Sopwith Camel   80Sqn
OP left 5pm SOMME **MIA(2Lt AV Jones **WIA POW**) ["Camel" claim combat nCERISY pm Ltn W Steinhauser Ja11]

D6481   Sopwith Camel   80Sqn
+* combat with Fokker DrIs[+flames+ooc] MORCOURT ~6-40pm OK(Capt OC Bridgeman) claimed 5 victories

D6591   Sopwith Camel   80Sqn
OP left 5pm combat with HA EoL BOUZENCOURT shot down cr(Lt HV Barker **WIA?) inj?

D6619   Sopwith Camel   80Sqn
OP left 5pm SOMME burnt to death EoL **MIA(Lt CGS Shields **KIA**) [?"Camel" claim combat sSAILLY-LAURETTE Ltn HJ Wolff Ja11, NB: Ja11 claims given here non-specifically]

B7650   DH9   98Sqn
**B MENIN AA shrapnel hit EoL dam returned 6-30pm OK(Lt FA Laughlin/1AM Weston) left 5-30pm

11th May

C1113   SE5a   1Sqn
+* combat with AlbatrosDV[+ooc] BAILLEUL 5-15pm

OK(Capt HA Rigby Aust.) last of 6 claims, most in this a'c

C6444   SE5a   1Sqn
**OP combat ovBAILLEUL shot down in flames 5-15pm
MIA(Lt CA Pelletier KIA) left 4pm, Ja20? [?"SE5" claim
combat BAILLEUL 5-25pm Ltn K Mendel
Ja18][?"SE5" claim combat MESSINES 5-35pm Vzfw F
Ehmann Ja47, but see D3442?]

B7480   Sopwith Camel   4Sqn AFC
**BOP seen ovARMENTIÈRES combat? shot down in
flames 7-45pm MIA(Lt OC Barry KIA) left 6-40pm,
Ja29?

D3442   SE5a   41Sqn
**OP combat with EA shot up ECQUEDECQUES
5-20pm(Lt RH Stacey WIA)to hospital,
ESQUELBECQ? ["SE5" claim combat BAILLEUL
5-25pm Ltn K Monnington Ja18]

RE8   42Sqn
** (/Lt L Patterson MC WIA)

C1112   SE5a   74Sqn
+* combat with PfalzDIII[+flames]
neARMENTIÈRES 5-40pm OK(Capt EC Mannock)
Ltn O Aeckerle Ja47, first of 5 victories in this a'c

C4131.T Sopwith Dolphin 79Sqn
+* combat with Fokker DrI[+des] BRAY OK(Capt
WM Fry) Fry's last victory, only one with 79Sqn

B7587   DH9   206Sqn
**B combat with 2EA ARMENTIÈRES shot up dam
ftl(Lt GA Pitt OK/2Lt CE Anketell KIA) left 5-07pm

B7252   Sopwith Camel   210Sqn
**OP combat with EA[+ooc] mist ftl cr Sh27c.4 wr
OK(Lt LP Coombes)

B7192   Sopwith Camel   213Sqn
Dunkirk ** combat with EA neNIEUPORT 2-45pm shot
down MIA(Lt J Reid KIA) [?combat off BREEDENE
4-02pm Oblt T Osterkamp MFJaII]

12th May

103 Squadron arrived in France on the 12th of May
equipped with DH9 day-bombers.

A.W.FK8   2Sqn
**Phot (/Lt F Ambler WIA)

DH4   18Sqn
** (/Capt MSE Archibald DoW)

B1162   Bristol F2b   22Sqn
**OP ARMENTIÈRES AA? seen ARMENTIÈRES-
MERVILLE 7pm MIA(2Lt CE Tylor WIA POW/2Lt
AP Bollins POW) left 6-20pm

B497   FE2b   58Sqn
**NB left 9-20pm MIA(Lt J Handley WIA POW/2Lt JB
Birkhead WIA POW) Handley in Karlsruhe

B7733   SE5a   74Sqn
**OP left 5-35pm combat with HA cr

nrWULVERGHEM MIA(Lt HE Dolan MC KIA) seen
4m eDICKEBUSCH LAKE 6-30pm ["SE5" claim
combat sDICKEBUSCH 6pm Ltn R Fr vBarnekow
Ja20]

14th May

A.W.FK8   2Sqn
**Phot (Lt D McGregor WIA)

B5213   Sopwith Camel   4Sqn AFC
**SpM shot up nrYPRES dam returned a'dr 6-50pm
OK(2Lt RG Smallwood) left 5-50pm

D1818   Sopwith Camel   4Sqn AFC
**SpM seen eZILLEBEKE shot down 6-10pm MIA(Lt
LR Sinclair US. WIA POW) left 5-30pm [?combat
swERQUINGHEM 6-20pm Ja28]

RE8   16Sqn
**P (/2Lt FL Norden WIA)

A7998   DH4   18Sqn
**Phot combat HA? NIEPPE FOREST 6-7pm(Lt FJ
Morgan DoW 16.5.18/2Lt STJ Helmore KIA)

C4178   Sopwith Dolphin 87Sqn
**P left 4-40pm NIEUPORT-OSTENDE shot up dam
returned a'dr 6-30pm OK(Lt RA Hewat)

B7223   Sopwith Camel   209Sqn
**IOP left 6-25pm AA wing hit broke up 8000' spun
down cr ~Sh62D E.15 wMEAULTE MIA(Lt EV Bell
KIA) to north & south SOMME

15th May

C845   Bristol F2b   11Sqn
**DOP combat with EA ovBOUCHOU MIA(Lt HW
Sellars KIA/Lt CC Robson MC POW) left 3-40pm
seALBERT ["F2b" claim combat CONTALMAISON
5-15pm OffSt J Mai Ja5] this crew had shared several
victory claims in F2b C4673

C867   Bristol F2b   11Sqn
+* combat with PfalzDIII[+ooc] seALBERT 5-22pm
OK(Lt JP Seabrook/Lt C Wrigglesworth) Seabrook
claimed 5 victories

C4882   Bristol F2b   11Sqn
**DOP combat with Fokker DrI[+?ooc
~5-20pm]ovBOUCHOU? MIA(Capt JV Aspinall KIA/
Lt PV de la Cour KIA) left 3-40pm seALBERT [?"BF"
claim combat OVILLERS 5-20pm Ltn H Kirschstein
Ja6]

D5963   SE5a   29Sqn
+* combat with 2Str[+flames] seMERRIS 3-05pm
OK(Capt RH Rusby)

This was the first SE5a victory for 29 Squadron.

D3956   SE5a   40Sqn
**P seen dive on EA nLORGIES 5-30am MIA(2Lt WL
Andrew POW) left 4-45am

B2522   Sopwith Camel   46Sqn
+* combat with PfalzDIII[++ooc] ARMENTIÈRES

12-45pm OK(Lt AG Vlasto) Vlasto made 8 claims

Bristol F2b   48Sqn
** (Lt WA MacMichael **WIA**)

Bristol F2b   48Sqn
** (/2Lt HF Lumb **WIA**)

B1337   Bristol F2b   48Sqn
OP in flames ovLAMOTTE **MIA(Capt CGD Napier MC **KIA**/Sgt P Murphy **KIA**) left 1pm, Ja6? [?"BF" claim combat seCAIX 2-15pm Ltn H Kirschstein Ja6] Napier claimed 9 victories on F2bs with 48Sqn

C855   Bristol F2b   48Sqn
OP spin with 2EA on tail down nrLAMOTTE **MIA(2Lt CL Glover **KIA**/2Lt JC Fitton **KIA**) left 1pm, Ja6?(too late?) [?"BF" claim combat seGUILLAUCOURT 2-15pm Oblt E vWedel Ja11][?"BF" claim combat wGUILLAUCOURT 2-10pm Ltn HJ Wolff Ja11]

C6177   DH9   49Sqn
Phot left 7-50am(Capt WG Chambers **KIA/Lt RJ Burky USAS. **KIA**) [?possible "DH4" claim combat AVELUY 9-30am Ltn P Wenzel Ja6]

A7645   DH4   57Sqn
Phot combat with EA shot down WoL **MIA(Lt FL Mond **KIA**/Lt EM Martyn **KIA**) unsalvable, left 9-50am BOYERCOURT-CORBIE [?"BF" claim combat nHAMEL 11-50am Ltn J Janzen Ja6]

A7725   DH4   57Sqn
Phot left 9-50am **MIA(Lt EH Piper **KIA**/2Lt HLB Crabbe **KIA**) [?possible "DH9" claim combat MAMETZ 12-25pm Ltn E Loewenhardt Ja10]

C8217   Sopwith Camel   70Sqn
+* combat with PfalzDIII[+smoking] Sh57D.R.4 7am OK(2Lt HNC Robinson) Robinson made most of his 10 claims with 46Sqn

D6438   Sopwith Camel   70Sqn
COP combat HA? seen cr Sh57D L.22(2Lt JW Williamson **KIA) left 6-35am [?"Camel" claim combat nwALBERT 7-15am Ltn F Friedrichs Ja10]

C780   Bristol F2b   88Sqn
+* combat with AlbatrosDIII[+des] GHISTELLES 6-30am OK(Lt RJ Cullen/2Lt EH Ward)

This was the first victory claim for 88 Squadron.

B498   FE2b   100Sqn
travel to OCHEY **MIA(2Lt DS Anderson **POW**/AM2 H O'Connor **POW**) left 5-50pm from VILLESNEUX

DH4   205Sqn
** (/2Lt HP Bennett **WIA**)

B5666   Sopwith Camel   209Sqn
HOP seen enter combat with Fokker DrIs ovIGNAUCOURT(2Lt OG Brittorous **KIA) left 9-30am north & south SOMME [?"Camel" claim combat AUBERCOURT? 11-15am Ltn V vPressentin Ja4]

B6257   Sopwith Camel   209Sqn
**HOP seen enter combat with Fokker DrIs

ovIGNAUCOURT spin down?(Lt G Wilson **KIA**) left 9-30am to north & south SOMME [?"Camel" claim combat eDEMUIN 11-05am Ltn H Kirschstein Ja6]

D3373   Sopwith Camel   209Sqn
+* combat with EA[+] nrFLAUCOURT 10-15am shot up(Capt OW Redgate **WIA**)

B7160   Sopwith Camel   210Sqn
*OP AA? air collision with Camel D3385 lost wings cr(Lt MA Kelly **KIFA**) left 6-45pm

D3385   Sopwith Camel   210Sqn
*OP air collision with B7160(this a'c hit by AA?) cr R.34.b.5.5.(Lt FV Hall **KIFA**) Hall had made several victory claims, the last in this a'c the previous day

D3342   Sopwith Camel   213Sqn
**OP combat with 2 AlbatrosDVs MIDDELKERKE 7-50pm ailerons shot up ftl cr hangar OK(Lt AR Talbot)

16th May

A.W.FK8   2Sqn
** (/Lt HA Deakin **WIA**)

RE8   7Sqn
** (/2Lt RC Mais **WIA**)

B1232   Bristol F2b   20Sqn
OP left 12pm seen cross Lines ~12-30pm **MIA(2Lt FE Boulton **POW**/Pbr HG Holman **WIA POW**)

C8557   A.W.FK8   35Sqn
**P ALBERT combat with EA shot up dam returned 11am OK(2Lt JM Walker/2Lt TH McNay) left 7-50am

B123   SE5a   41Sqn
**OP combat with EA FLORINGHEM 8-50am controls shot away ftl cr OK(Lt WE Shields)

A7477   DH4   55Sqn
B in flames ovSAARBRÜCKEN **MIA(2Lt RC Sansom **KIA**/2AM GC Smith **KIA**) left 6-35am

DH4   55Sqn
** (/2Lt J Bradley **WIA**)

DH4   55Sqn
B SAARBRÜCKEN shot up(/2Lt WI Parke **WIA)

DH4   55Sqn
B SAARBRÜCKEN shot up(/2Lt FW Roaks **WIA)

B183.A   SE5a   56Sqn
COP left 6-50pm seen attack Fokker DrIs neALBERT **MIA(Capt T Durrant **KIA**) ["SE5" claim combat CONTALMAISON 8-10pm Ltn H Kirschstein Ja6] Durrant claimed most of his 11 victories in this a'c

B4880   SE5a   56Sqn
**prac combat with EA prop shot away ftl cr tree BOIS DE LA NAOURS 6-55pm OK(1Lt RH Ritter USAS.)

D3912   SE5a   60Sqn
OP BEUGNY-BAPAUME combat ovBAPAUME **MIA(Lt HNJ Proctor **KIA**) left 3pm [?"SE5" claim combat swCOURCELETTE Ltn F Rumey Ja5]

C886   Bristol F2b   62Sqn
**LP shot up ftl PICQUIGNY dam OK(Lt JA Chubb/
2Lt E Dumville) left 12-25pm

C4859   Bristol F2b   62Sqn
**OP combat with EA shot up ftl CORBIE(Lt CH
Arnison **WIA**/Lt CD Wells MC **KIA**) left 12-15pm, a'c
abandoned on ground & shelled ["BF" claim combat
SAILLY-LE-SEC 1-40pm Ltn H Kirschstein Ja6]
Arnison claimed several victories in this a'c in barely two
months

C1859.X **SE5a   64Sqn**
**OP plane spar broke in dive on EA ftl 59Sqn 10-05am
dam OK(Lt SB Reece) left 8-05am ["SE5" claim combat
HAMBLAIN 9-50am Ltn M Gossner Ja23] [?"SE5"
claim combat TILLOY 9-55am Ltn O Kissenberth Ja23]

The time of Ltn Kissenberth's claim would seem to
make this SE5a the most likely to be involved.
Kissenberth was known to be flying a captured
Sopwith Camel in action at this time and his SE5a
claim on this day is believed to have been made in
this machine. It had been a 3 (Naval) Squadron
aircraft, possibly B7230 lost on the 10th of March.
He would, incidentally, have a serious crash in this
Camel on the 29th of May.

D1886   Sopwith Camel   70Sqn
**LowP left 4-45am WIA cr ldg 1000yd sBAISIEUX
wr(Lt WS Dann **DoW**)

C1847   SE5a   84Sqn
**OP combat with HA engine shot up cr n.m.l. fire
destr(Capt HP Smith **WIA**) VILLERS
BRETONNEAUX [?"SE5" claim combat sBOIS DE
VAIRE 6-30pm Ltn R Wenzl Ja11]

C6103   DH9   98Sqn
**B combat with HA shot down in flames 4m
wCOURTRAI **MIA**(2Lt W Lamont **POW**/Lt HBB
Wilson **POW**) seen below formation nrCOURTRAI
7-30am, "plane leaving centre section"

D3353   Sopwith Camel   203Sqn
**OP combat with 6 Pfalz nLA BASSÉE 11-20am
MIA(Capt PR White **POW**) left 10-30am

D3341   Sopwith Camel   204Sqn
**SpM NIEUPORT-MIDDELKERKE combat with
EA badly shot up ftl OK(Lt WF Robinson)

DH4   205Sqn
B (/2Lt LH Jones **WIA)

D9540   Sopwith Camel   208Sqn
**OP left 6-30am combat with 2HA on tail nLA BASSÉE
seen 500' diving west in control **MIA**(Lt WE Cowan
POW) ["Sopwith 1Str" claim combat LORGIES 7-40am
Ltn H-G Marwitz Ja30]

3132   H.P. 0/100   214Sqn
**NB BRUGES AA & searchlights shot down
ovBRUGES DOCKS **MIA**(Capt CG Rushton **KIA**/Maj
JI Harrison **KIA**/Lt WJ King **KIA**) left 12-45am

RAF
** **MIA**(Lt WA Leslie **POW**) repat 30.12.18

17th May

Bristol F2b   11Sqn
** (Maj RFS Morton **WIA**)

RE8   13Sqn
AOb (/Lt PW Booth **WIA)

C1105   SE5a   24Sqn
**OP combat with Fokker DrIs glide down in flames
FOUCAUCOURT(Lt E Harrison **KIA**) left 3pm
[?"SE5" claim combat eFOUCAUCOURT 4-15pm Ltn
V vPressentin Ja4]

B8393   SE5a   32Sqn
OP left 4-45am VITRY-MAMETZ **MIA(2Lt DJ
Russell **POW**)

D268   SE5a   32Sqn
OP left 4-45am VITRY-MAMETZ **MIA(Lt AS Cross
POW)

D3535   SE5a   40Sqn
**OP left 7am seen attacking EA formation nrBOIS DE
BIEZ nLENS 8-45am **MIA**(Lt L Seymour **POW**) had
fired Red Verys

RE8   52Sqn
Phot (Capt AFW Gregory **WIA)

B37.U **SE5a   56Sqn**
+* combat with AlbatrosDV[+ooc] FRESNOY 2-45pm
OK(Capt WS Fielding-Johnson) claimed his 6 victories
in this a'c

D1791   Sopwith Camel   65Sqn
**OP combat with HA seen 1000' going down in control
ovBECORDEL 5-20pm **MIA**(Lt HJ Leavitt US. **POW**)
left 5pm

B7471   Sopwith Camel   70Sqn
**LowP BEAUMONT-MIRAUMONT RD ground mg
shot up dam OK(2Lt VC Chapman) left 4-30am,
returned 5-30am

C8242   Sopwith Camel   70Sqn
**COP combat seen 1m eAVELUY WOOD 2-20pm
going west **MIA**(Lt VWH Hillyard **POW**) left 12-35pm

C1854   SE5a   74Sqn
**OP AA hit 2-30pm diving in flames cr Sh36A Q.26.c(Lt
LF Barton **KIA**)

C6404   SE5a   74Sqn
**OP seen ovESTAIRES 9-40am combat with HA ovLA
GORGUE? in flames 9-45am **MIA**(Lt LM Nixon **KIA**)
left 8-30am [?"SE5" claim combat LE PARC? 9-45am
UntOff M Schumm Ja52]

C821   Bristol F2b   88Sqn
+* combat with AlbatrosDV[+ooc] eMIDDELKERKE
7-45am OK(Capt A Hepburn Aust./2Lt GW Lambert)
Hepburn's first of 16 claims on F2bs, all in this a'c (last
on 4.11.18)

C6142   DH9   98Sqn
**B ARMENTIÈRES AA shot up on returned dam
OK(Lt RE Dubber/Sgt ER MacDonald) left 4-35am

**   DH9   98Sqn**
B ARMENTIÈRES(/Lt HP Roberts **WIA)

D1667   DH9   98Sqn
**B left 4-30am ARMENTIÈRES AA shot up EoL on
return dam OK(Lt FH Reilly/Lt RMcK Hall)

D5630   DH9   98Sqn
HighRec shot down sTHIEPVAL **MIA(Capt N Bell
KIA/Lt AA Malcolm **KIA**) left 4-30am HAZEBROUCK

B492   FE2b   100Sqn
NB THIONVILLE railways & town **MIA(2Lt JC
Williamson **POW**/Lt NF Penruddocke **POW**) left
10-35pm

100 Squadron made this raid with the Handley
Pages of 216 Squadron. Between them they caused
some heavy damage as well as casualties.

B7782   FE2b   102Sqn
**NB AA engine failed n.m.l. ftl nrDOUCHY-LES-
AYETTE Sh11.I.A at 2-50am OK(Lt AS Kelly/Lt WJ
Harvey) left 1-20am

B6408   Sopwith Camel   203Sqn
**OP combat with 15 Fokker DrI shot down
nrMERVILLE in control? ~11-20am **MIA**(2Lt ER
Prideaux **KIA**) left 10-30am, Ja29 ["Sopwith" claim
combat MERVILLE 11-25am Oblt H Auffahrt
Ja29][?"SE5" claim combat MORBECQUE 11-30am
Vzfw K Pech Ja29]

C61   Sopwith Camel   203Sqn
**OP combat with EA shot up dam OK(2Lt CF Brown)

D3362   Sopwith Camel   203Sqn
**OP left 10-30am combat with 15 Fokker DrI shot down
nrST VENANT OK(2Lt R Stone) [?possible "SE5"
claim combat MORBECQUE 11-30am Vzfw K Pech
Ja29]

**   DH4   205Sqn**
** (/2Lt JA Whalley **WIA**)

18th May

**   1Sqn**
? (1Lt GA Roper USAS. **KIA?) given in US sources
only

C2329   RE8   4Sqn
** damaged in enemy bombing raid on a'dr

**   RE8   4Sqn**
** (Maj RE Saul **WIA**)

C8261   Sopwith Camel   4Sqn AFC
** AA fire shot up(Capt GF Malley **WIA**)

B1279   Bristol F2b   20Sqn
**OP shot up VLAMERTINGHE ftl(Lt TW Williamson
OK/Cpl WH Foster **WIA**) left 6-15am

B2129   DH4   27Sqn
**B engine cut ovVALENCIENNES seen ftl EoL nr
ARRAS(2Lt FJ Bull **POW**/2Lt CB Law **POW**)

C9615   SE5a   32Sqn
OP combat ETAING bits off in spin **MIA(Capt
Viscount EWCGdeVP Glentworth **KIA**)

D331   SE5a   32Sqn
**OP engine shot up 10-30am ftl cr Sh51C L2.c. OK(Lt
GEB Lawson)

D6413   Sopwith Camel   46Sqn
**OP left 5-25am First Army area AA dam returned
7-15am OK(Lt G Hudson)

A7593   DH4   55Sqn
B KÖLN shot up cr nr a'dr(Lt CE Reynolds **inj/2Lt
JE Reynolds **KIA**) pilot inj in cr, observer shot

55 Squadron's raid to Köln was a fine feat of
endurance — the outward journey to the target
taking two and a half hours. The formation was
attacked three times on their flight but were not
prevented from launching a substantial attack on
the heart of the city. It was the first daylight raid
on Köln since 1914 and caused considerable
distress and damage. Forty people were killed and
over one hundred injured, and the impact of the
raid reverberated along the Rhineland which
suddenly felt itself exposed and vulnerable. One of
the advantages of this deep bombing offensive of
the Allies was that reports became exaggerated and
a natural state of anxiety arose in the common
people. After this particular raid the German
government came under great pressure to reduce
its own strategic bombing in the hope of a
reciprocal gesture.

C6470.4 **SE5a   64Sqn**
**OP left 6pm shot up dam returned a'dr 8-15pm OK(Lt
WP Southall)

D336.5   **SE5a   64Sqn**
**OP steep dive on EA:leading edges shred ftl u'c broke
ldg a'dr 8-15pm(Lt WC Daniel **shaken**) left 6pm First
Army front

B7178   Sopwith Camel   65Sqn
**OP left 9am combat with 12EA ALBERT-BRAY
10-15am **MIA**(Lt KP Hunt **POW**) ["Sopwith 1Str" claim
combat sMORLANCOURT Vzfw R Heibert
Ja46]["Sopwith" claim combat seALBERT Vzfw O
Hennrich Ja46]

C8256   Sopwith Camel   65Sqn
**OP seen in combat with 12EA ALBERT-BRAY
10-15am **MIA**(Lt WF Scott-Kerr **POW**) left 9am

C8278   Sopwith Camel   65Sqn
+* combat with AlbatrosDV[+des] eBRAY 10-20am &
2Str[+des] eLAMOTTE 10-30am) OK(Capt JI
Gilmour) last of 13 claims in this a'c

B8408   SE5a   84Sqn
+* combat with AlbatrosDV[+ooc] CHAULNES
11-30am then combat with 2Str[+des] seMOREUIL
12pm OK(Capt RA Grosvenor) last of 16 claims with
84Sqn

C780   Bristol F2b   88Sqn
**OP YPRES combat EoL engine cut 7000' then glided
west ftl BUSSEBOOM cr OK(Lt RJ Cullen/2Lt EH
Ward) left 6-30am

C783   Bristol F2b   88Sqn
**P combat with HA YPRES snd seen going down ooc
nrLANGEMARCK **MIA**(2Lt LGS Gadpaille **KIA**/2Lt S
Griffin **KIA**)

This was the first loss in combat for 88 Squadron.

D8401 . DH4   205Sqn
B seen nrAUBERCOURT **MIA(2Lt HCR Conron
KIA/2Lt J Finnigan **KIA**) left 9-55am CHAULNES Stn

D3390   Sopwith Camel   210Sqn
SpM left 9-30am combat shot down **MIA(Lt J Hollick
KIA) Ja29 ["Sopwith" claim combat LESTREM
10-45am Vzfw K Pech Ja29]

D3391   Sopwith Camel   210Sqn
SpM left 9-30am combat shot down **MIA(Lt MF
Sutton **WIA POW**) Ja29 ["Camel" claim combat
MERVILLE 10-50am Vzfw K Pech Ja29]

D3410   Sopwith Camel   210Sqn
+* combat with PfalzDIII[+ooc] BAC ST MAUR
15000' 8-05pm OK(Lt HB Maund) 203Sqn confirmed,
Maund claimed 4 of his 8 EAs in this a'c

19th May

104 Squadron arrived from England to bolster the
41st Wing strategic bombing group. Its first
operation was to the Metz-Sablon triangle on the
8th of June.

C1655   Sopwith Camel   3Sqn
+* combat with 2Str[+ftl] 6-50am OK(Capt JW Aldred)
shared, EA captured Sh57D.R.13

D6433   Sopwith Camel   3Sqn
**WTInt combat with several HAs MESNIL then seen
going down in flames ooc(Lt FJ Brotheridge **KIA**) left
6-30am [?"Sopwith" claim combat CHUIGNOLLES Fw
R Heibert Ja46]

A.W.FK8   10Sqn
AOb (/2Lt FW Rushton **WIA)

RE8   16Sqn
B (/Lt LE Evans **WIA)

C3796   Sopwith Dolphin 19Sqn
+* combat with PfalzDIII[+ooc] eLA BASSÉE 10-15am
OK(Lt AW Blake SA.) made 5 claims

C4017   Sopwith Dolphin 19Sqn
**OP left 9-11am last seen eLA BASSÉE going down in
slow spirals **MIA**(Maj AD Carter Can. DSO **POW**)

["Dolphin" claim combat WINGLES 10-10am Ltn P
Billik Ja62] Carter had achieved many of his 29 claims in
this a'c

C843   Bristol F2b   20Sqn
+* combat with PfalzDIII[+des] ESTAIRES 10-45am
OK(Lt WM Thomson Can./2Lt GH Kemp) pilot made
half of his 26 claims in this a'c

D3942   SE5a   29Sqn
**OP combat with PfalzDIII[+air coll, broke up]
BAILLEUL 11-40am then ftl cr Sh27.Q.22 dam
OK(Capt HG White) [Vzfw Kech Ja29], White claimed
several victories

D5965   SE5a   29Sqn
**OP ESTAIRES mg shot up dam OK(Lt HM Hutton)

A.W.FK8   35Sqn
** ground mg(Capt RCStJ Dix **WIA**)

Bristol F2b   48Sqn
** (2Lt ER Stock **WIA**)

D1002   DH9   49Sqn
B BRAY seen HARBONNIÈRES **MIA(Lt FD Nevin
KIA/Sgt H Barfoot **KIA**) left 5-05pm ["DH9" claim
neMARCELCAVE 7-10pm Vzfw W Gabriel
Ja11]["DH9" claim combat VILLERS
BRETONNEAUX 7-10pm Ltn W Steinhauser Ja11]

B7649   DH9   49Sqn
**B combat shot up 11-25am ftl BERTANGLES cr(Lt N
Braithwaite **WIA**/2Lt FP Bellingham **inj**)to hospital

C6181   DH9   49Sqn
*B combat with HA RAINEVILLE 7-10pm engine ftl(Lt
CG Capel **WIA**/1AM J Knight **WIA**) [?"DH9" claim
combat 7-10pm Vzfw W Gabriel Ja11]

B1336   Bristol F2b   62Sqn
**OP combat with AlbatrosDV[+ooc] BRAY then dive
on 2EAs ftl CORBIE 10-15am OK(Lt DA Savage MC/
Lt EW Collis) attacked while diving on 2EAs [?"F2b"
claim combat VILLERS BRETONNEAUX Vzfw O
Koennecke Ja5], Savage claimed several victories

C796   Bristol F2b   62Sqn
**OP seen ok CORBIE combat with HAs 10-15am ftl
MIA(Lt HC Hunter **WIA POW**/Sgt J Lake **KIA**) left
8-15am ["BF" claim combat HAMEL 10-30am Ltn W
Steinhauser Ja11][?"BF" claim combat
GUILLAUCOURT 9-10am Oblt Ritt vGreim JGr10]

C4630.J Bristol F2b   62Sqn
**OP combat with HA 10-15am seen nrCORBIE ok, ftl
EoL(Lt HA Clarke **POW**/Capt H Claye **POW**) left
8-15am, a'c captured [?F2b claim: AA or combat
swHENGEST 10-45am Ltn A Delling Ja34]

C4751.T Bristol F2b   62Sqn
**OP seen nrCORBIE ok 10-15am? combat with HAs
ftl(2Lt F Atkinson **POW DoW**/Sgt CC Brammer
POW)Ja34, left 8-15am, a'c captured ["BF" claim
combat PROYART 9-15am? Vzfw M Kahlow Ja34]

B2429   Sopwith Camel   80Sqn
prac left 6-50pm seen nrDOULLENS **MIA(2Lt AJ Patenaude **POW**)

C6449   SE5a   84Sqn
P left 8-10am seen dive on EA eWIENCOURT EoL **MIA(1Lt EM Hammer USAS. **KIA**) to VILLERS BRETONNEAUX ["SE5" claim combat BOIS DE HANGARD 9-40am Ltn F Pütter Ja68]

B7594   DH9   206Sqn
B combat with HA shot up **MIA(Lt FG Reddie **KIA**/Lt AC Howell-Jones **KIA**) left 6-15pm, seen nrLines-MENIN ~7-40pm

C6136   DH9   206Sqn
B AA combat with HA? TETEGHEM ftl(Lt PW Birkbeck **OK/2Lt W Susman **WIA**) left 6-15pm

C6159   DH9   206Sqn
B seen nwROULERS in combat going west 7-10am **MIA(Lt BF Dunford **KIA**/2Lt FF Collins **KIA**) left 5-42am ["BF" claim combat swZONNEBEKE 7-20am Ltn K Bolle Ja2]

C6161   DH9   206Sqn
B combat with HA nrMENIN **MIA(Lt H Mitchell **POW**/AG CF Costen **POW**) left 6-15pm, seen leave formation WoL and turn back ["DH" claim combat HOUTHEM-KEMMEL 7-30pm Ltn P Strähle Ja57]

D2784   DH9   211Sqn
B seen in formation OSTENDE-NIEUPORT 12pm **MIA(Lt NA Taylerson **KIA**/2Lt CL Bray **KIA**) left 11am, later to 1ASD?,[?combat UYTKERKE 12-30pm FlM K Engelfried SFS]

C65   Sopwith Camel   213Sqn
+* combat with AlbatrosDV[+flames] 1m sWOUMEN 5-35pm **OK**(Capt JW Pinder) shared, EA from Ja16, Pinder's 1st with 213Sqn

C3487   H.P. 0/400   214Sqn
NB shot down nrZEEBRUGGE **MIA(Capt VE Sieveking **KIA**/Lt HA Havilland-Roe **KIA**/AM F Spencer **WIA POW**) left 12-28am to SOLWEY WORKS at ZEEBRUGGE, a'c captured

20th May

B8876   RE8   3Sqn AFC
AOb combat with Fokker DrI shot up cr a'dr(Capt EJ Jones **WIA/Lt ALD? Taylor **KIA**) initials KLD?

D6506   Sopwith Camel   4Sqn AFC
+* combat with PfalzDIII[+ooc] KEMMEL-NEUVE EGLISE 7-55am **OK**(Lt ER King) King's first of 26? victories

A7975   DH4   18Sqn
B combat shot up dam ldg ok 8-45pm **OK(2Lt G Leitch/Capt D Gale) left 7-05pm First Army area

C4747   Bristol F2b   22Sqn
OP left 6-15pm combat? AA ftl cr **OK(2Lt CH Dunster/2Lt JH Umney) to First Army area

C3807   Sopwith Dolphin   23Sqn
IOP combat with 7DrIs[+des] LE HAMEL but shot down in flames Sh62D 028 btwn 10am & 10-15am (Lt CA Crysler **KIA)a'c unsalvable

This was the first Sopwith Dolphin victory for 23 Squadron.

C5367   SE5a   24Sqn
OP left 7-30am Fourth Army area combat with EA canvas off wing ftl in control 84Sq cr 9-15am **OK(Lt RT Mark MC)

D275   SE5a   24Sqn
OP left 7-30am Fourth Army area combat with EA shot up **OK(Capt CN Lowe) returned 9-05am, Lowe claimed several victories

D9239   DH4   25Sqn
B hit by AA 15000' down in flames cr AULNOYE EoL(Lt AH Herring **KIA/2Lt RS Lasker **KIA**) left 8am

D3438   SE5a   40Sqn
OP combat with 3EA ovHINGES shot down ooc 9-40am cr(Lt G Watson **KIA) left 8-05am ["SE5" claim combat VIELLE CHAPELLE 10am Ltn H Oberländer Ja30

D6418   Sopwith Camel   46Sqn
+* combat with DFWC[+des] nLA BASSÉE 5pm then attacked KBs[++des] sSTEENWERCK 5-05pm **OK**(Capt DR MacLaren Can.) 17 of his claims made in this a'c

D1876   Sopwith Camel   65Sqn
OP seen in combat with 5 Fokker DrIs seALBERT 6-20pm **MIA(Capt LE Whitehead **KIA**) left 5-15pm, Whitehead had claimed 5 victories, 4 in this a'c in May

C3901   Sopwith Dolphin   79Sqn
OP combat with 3EA fuel tank shot up ftl cr o't field WIPPENBACH **OK(Capt HP Rushforth)

**   DH9   103Sqn**
B (/2Lt JK Clarke **WIA)

C6179   DH9   103Sqn
+* attacked KB[+des] SECLIN 11am **OK**(Capt JS Stubbs/2Lt CC Dance)

C6186   DH9   103Sqn
B AA dam(Lt Sparkes **OK/2Lt Wrighton **WIA**)

During a raid on the 20th, 103 Squadron achieved its first victory but also suffered its first casualties.

21st May

C9621   SE5a   1Sqn
SpM combat with EA shot up 9-09am dam **OK(Lt KJP Laing)

D9251   DH4   25Sqn
Rec lost AA hit EA ftl Sh17 R.19.D. wr 10-45am **OK(Lt LLK Straw/2Lt HH Watson)

D5968   SE5a   40Sqn
**OP eLENS combat with EA shot up btwn ~8-15am &

8-30am dam OK(Lt DF Murman) left 7am

C883   Bristol F2b   48Sqn
+* combat with Fokker DrI[+des] 1m nMERICOURT
6-53pm OK(Lt HA Oaks Can./Lt CS Bissett) first claim
of 10 for Oaks, possibly had earlier claim of Fokker DrI
at 6-15pm ovCARNOY

A7791   DH4   55Sqn
**B CHARLEROI seen in control nVERDUN MIA(2Lt
HE Townsend POW/AM J Greenway POW)

B8419   SE5a   60Sqn
**OP left 7-30am combat shot up dam returned 9-30am
OK(2Lt RG Lewis)

B7737   SE5a   64Sqn
**OP seen ovSCARPE RIVER 3m EoL 12000' MIA(2Lt
SB Reece POW) left 6-30pm

D6604   Sopwith Camel   73Sqn
**OP seen eARMENTIÈRES going west in control
7-35pm MIA(Lt JL Brewster KIA) left 5-30pm
[?"Camel" claim combat STEENWERCK 7-30pm Ltn H
Viebig Ja57][?Camel claim combat sBAILLEUL 7-25pm
Ltn J Gildemeister Ja20]

D9539   Sopwith Camel   73Sqn
**OP seen LA BASSÉE in control going north 6-30pm
MIA(Lt TG Drew-Brook WIA POW) left 5-30pm

B1341   Bristol F2b   88Sqn
**P intense combat with 12EA OSTENDE not seen after
MIA(Lt CG Scobie KIA/2Lt FJD Hudson KIA) left
6-15pm [?unconfirmed "Bristol" claim at sea Ltn
Tinschert MFJaI]

C839   Bristol F2b   88Sqn
**P intense combat with 12EA OSTENDE MIA(Lt KO
Millar KIA/2Lt S Davidson KIA) left 6-15pm [?possible
"DH4" claim combat at sea Ltn Saschenberg MFJaI]

C6166   DH9   98Sqn
**B ROULERS Rlwy Stn AA? lost cowl glided down cr
wr ldg F.24.c.9.7. OK(Lt AM Phillips/Lt NC McDonald)

C62   Sopwith Camel   210Sqn
+* attacked KB[+des] eLESTREM 5-10pm OK(Lt CW
Payton) shared, made 11 claims

B7604   DH9   211Sqn
** combat with 5EA BOETSCHOUCK AA ftl back
WoL OK(Lt RFC Metcalfe/2Lt DR Bradley) left
10-20am

B7661   DH9   211Sqn
**B seen ovVARSSANAERE MIA(2Lt HE Tansley
POW/2Lt NB Harris POW) left 10-15am, got behind,
seen over target [?combat MARIAKERKE Oblt zS G
Sachsenberg MFJa1]

3134.B3   H.P. 0/100   216Sqn
**NB AA nrKROPPEN 4am ftl MIA(Lt HL LeRoy
POW/Lt RW Peat POW/AG WJL Twite POW) left
9-20pm THIONVILLE

A direct hit was made on the Oppau Works on this

raid which caused major damage after a gas main
ruptured.

22nd May

85 Squadron came to France with their SE5a
fighters on the 22nd of May.

B7382   Sopwith Camel   4Sqn AFC
**OP mg fire 8-30am engine cut ftl nrLines burnt a'c
OK(Lt EV Culverwell)

D1909   Sopwith Camel   4Sqn AFC
**BOP air collision with Camel D1924 ovNEUF
BERGUIN 11-30am MIA(Lt G Nowland KIA) left
10-35am

D1924   Sopwith Camel   4Sqn AFC
**BOP air collision with Camel D1909 ovNEUF
BERGUIN 11-30am MIA(Lt A Finnie KIA) left
10-35am

C8628   A.W.FK8   35Sqn
**P shell hit ALBERT ftl OK(Capt LS Kigwell/2Lt JA
Weller)

C874   Bristol F2b   62Sqn
+* combat with LVGC[+des] nLAVENTIE 8am
OK(Lt WE Staton/Lt JR Gordon) Staton claimed several
of his 26 victories in this a'c, many with Gordon

B132.V   SE5a   64Sqn
**OP left 9-30am seen 8m EoL MIA(2Lt GA Rainier
POW) [?"SE5" claim combat ARMENTIÈRES 11-20am
Ltn H Boy Ja14][?"SE5" claim combat seLA GORGUE
11-30am Vzfw P Rothe Ja14]

B495   FE2b   83Sqn
**NB fuel pipe shot away ftl cr ~11-30am OK(Lt NS
Jones/2Lt TH Singleton) fuel ran out

A5587   FE2b   102Sqn
**NB shot up dam OK(Capt AL Chick/Lt WO Patey)

D5605   DH9   103Sqn
+* combat with AlbatrosDV[+ooc] DOUAI 11am
OK(Lt EA Windridge/2Lt VW Allen)

C6163   DH9   206Sqn
** AA shrapnel ACQUIN ftl dam OK(Capt GLE
Stevens/Lt LA Christian) left 12-05pm

23rd May

C8526   A.W.FK8   2Sqn
**AOb combat with 5EA mg ovLE TOURET 10am dam
ftl(Lt TH Crossman OK?/Lt LC Spence MC DoW
25.5.18) left 8-55am ["Bristol" claim combat nwLA
BASSÉE 10-10am Ltn H Seywald Ja23]

A7840   DH4   27Sqn
**B combat with EA in dive wMARIA AELTRE
MIA(Capt AE Palfreyman KIA/2Lt WI Crawford WIA
POW) left 6-10am THOUROUT-
ALBERT?(sic)(AELTRE?), observer severely wounded

D5616   DH9   27Sqn
*B engine fell off cr wr SAINS-LES-PERNES(2Lt GE
Ffrench **KIFA**/Cpl FY McLauchlan **KIFA**) left 6-10am
MARIA AELTRE [?"Bristol" claim MARIA AELTRE
8-30am Ltn D Collin Ja56]

C8446   A.W.FK8   35Sqn
**Shoot FLEISELLES a'dr combat dam OK(Lt A
MacGregor/2Lt GF Sharp) left 10am, returned 11-40am

D1902   Sopwith Camel   70Sqn
**COP left 9am AA? COURCELETTE seen dive past
other a'c, broke up cr(Lt AL Stockenstrom **KIA**)

A5779   FE2b   100Sqn
**NB left 9-05pm MIA but OK(Lt LD Kirk/Lt W
Richards)? Squadron History gives 23.5?; Casualty
Report gives 27.5?

A5649   FE2b   102Sqn
**NB shrapnel hit prop engine failed ftl FICHEUX 11pm
OK(Lt AB Whiteside MC/Lt EF Howard MC) left
10-30pm

B7250   Sopwith Camel   209Sqn
**SpM dive on 2Str EA HAMEL ROAD shot down ooc
in flames cr sLE HAMEAU Sh62D.p.18 nLAMOTTE
9am(2Lt AW Aird **KIA**) left 8-25am to intercept EA

24th May

**   DH9   99Sqn**
**B HAGENDINGEN Blast Furnaces combat with EAs
over objective(2Lt O Jones **WIA**/Lt MR Skinner **WIA**)

These were the first casualties in action for 99
Squadron.

25th May

**   RE8   5Sqn**
ground mg (/2Lt ARA Millar **WIA)

**   RE8   6Sqn**
** (2Lt HW Chattaway **WIA**)

A8000   DH4   18Sqn
**B HOUDAIN combat with EA 12pm shot up ftl cr
dam u'c OK(2Lt J Waugh/2Lt F Walker)

D3927   SE5a   41Sqn
+* combat with 2Str[+ooc] ESTAIRES 2-15pm OK(Lt
FRG McCall Can.) his first victory with 41Sqn, including
20 in this a'c in 6 weeks

D1903   Sopwith Camel   65Sqn
+* combat with AlbatrosDV[+ftl captured] SENLIS
7-50pm OK(Lt AA Leitch Can.) EA from Ja76 (Vzfw K
Koller) Leich made most of his 7 claims in this a'c

C4128   Sopwith Dolphin 79Sqn
**OP combat with EA YPRES ground fire? ftl hit
ditch(Lt PDP Hamilton **WIA**) left 10-30am

C6266   DH9   104Sqn
*travel from UK engine failure then lost, ftl PONT À
MAISON EoL **MIA**(Lt W Bruce **KIA**/SgtMaj DG
Smith **KIA**) left SEZANNE 10am

This was the first aircraft lost on active duty by 104
Squadron.

9060   Short 184   Dunkirk Seaplane Stn
engine failed ftl nr U-boat 20m nDUNKIRK **MIA(FLt
C Laurence **POW**/SLt LJ Bennett **POW**) crew taken by
U-boat

26th May

**   Bristol F2b   20Sqn**
AA fire(/2Lt W Jacklin **WIA)

**   RE8   21Sqn**
** (/2Lt JFA Hall **WIA**)

D6861.Y SE5a   64Sqn
+* combat with AlbatrosDV[+?ooc] ERQUINGHEM
7-30pm OK(Lt ED Atkinson) pilot claimed 10 victories

C6450   SE5a   74Sqn
** combat with EA shot up seMETEREN dam returned
a'dr OK(Lt AC Kiddie SA.) left 6-17pm

D1693   DH9   211Sqn
**test with extra driftwires, shot down? broke up 20' cr
wr on Lines PERVYSE(Capt TF LeMesurier **DoI**/2Lt R
Lardner **KIFA**) KIA? left 10-10am, a'c salvable?

27th May

THE GERMAN OFFENSIVE
ON THE AISNE

The German offensive on the French front on the
Aisne commenced with a surprise assault on the
27th of May. In broad terms it hoped to widen the
front against Paris; whether Paris was its goal at
this time is open to question, for Ludendorff knew
he must defeat the British in Flanders if he was to
have any chance of victory, and this offensive
would, in the meantime, surely draw the French
out of that sector, leaving the British more
vulnerable.

In May, Britain had begun rebuilding and
resting its shattered armies. With cruel irony, three
of the five British divisions which had been
removed from the Somme in order to recuperate
had been transferred to the front line in this sector,
namely to serve with the French Sixth Army. With
them had come a solitary RAF Squadron of RE8s,
No.52, who were now based at Fismes. Opposite
the army the terrain was heavily wooded and
unfamiliar, and their reconnaissances had reported
little that was unusual — some clouds of dust had
been noticed, but nothing more. The peace and
calm of this part of the line was suddenly shattered
by a stupendous bombardment from 1am, lasting
one hundred and sixty minutes. Once more the
same battle-weary troops found themselves beneath
withering artillery fire, awaiting a huge attack.

The assault came at 3-40am, and within a few hours the German Army had torn a gaping hole in the Franco-British front. It crossed the Aisne with relative ease and by nightfall had swallowed up a phenomenal twelve miles of enemy territory. Twelve German fighter units had been secretly moved to the front, and on the first day of the battle gave their army nearly complete aerial supremacy. The Schlachtstaffeln below were able to drive the infantry forward with their low attacks. 52 Squadron, in contrast, had only been able to carry out the most desultory co-operation and in the afternoon were bombed out of their aerodrome.

C6730   Sopwith Camel   3Sqn
WTInt combat C-type shot down broke up seTHIEPVAL cr Sh57A R32 **MIA(Capt DJ Bell MC **POW DoW**) left 12-10pm

B4100   RE8   4Sqn
**AOb combat with 5EA ovVIEUX BERQUIN shot up 9-40am OK(TLt AH Maltby/2Lt JBP Simms) left 8-10am XV Corps Area (serial as per Casualty Report) [?"RE" claim combat METEREN, but 7-30pm? Ltn F Ray Ja49]

**   A.W.FK8   8Sqn**
B (2Lt LC Hooton **WIA)

B2277   RE8   15Sqn
**AP mg fuel pipe dam ftl ENGELBELMER 2-30pm cr shell hole, a'c shelled OK(Lt GA Griffin/2Lt JH Wilkinson)

**   Sopwith Dolphin 19Sqn**
P (2Lt WH Barlow **WIA)

B1193   Bristol F2b   20Sqn
OP left 6pm EA shot up ftl(Sgt A Starsfield OK/Pbr J Tulloch **WIA) CLAIRMARAIS SOUTH

C8588   A.W.FK8   35Sqn
Shoot ground mg BUIRE 11-25am controls shot up ftl wr(Lt AB Hughes **WIA/2Lt GF Sharp **WIA**)to hospital, a'c shelled on ldg, WIA?

B38   SE5a   41Sqn
+* combat with Fokker DrI[+ooc] eESTAIRES 7-15pm OK(Lt WG Claxton Can.) first of 37 victories all with 41Sqn

**   SE5a   41Sqn**
P (Capt CN Russell **WIA)

**   Bristol F2b   48Sqn**
** (/Lt CJR Gibson **WIA**)

**   RE8   52Sqn**
** **MIA**(/1AM GR Anthony **POW**)

D4970   RE8   52Sqn
* a'c left on FISMES a'dr then destroyed by shell fire

B5147   RE8   52Sqn
BP left 5-05am **MIA(2Lt CCA Beaumont **KIA**/2Lt F Whitehouse **KIA**)

D1825   Sopwith Camel   70Sqn
**COP combat with 2Str[+des] ovHAMELINCOURT 12-45pm shot up dam OK(Lt WW McConnachie)

C6490   SE5a   85Sqn
+* combat with 2Str[+des] ePASSCHENDAELE 4-32pm OK(Maj WA Bishop Can.) Bishop achieved 12 victories in this a'c

Bishop's was the first 85 Squadron air combat victory.

C6137   DH9   99Sqn
B combat with EAs nDIEUZE chased down in spin from 2000' **MIA(Lt DA MacDonald Can. **POW**/2Lt FH Blaxill **POW**) left 9-55am, ldg ok?

D3416   Sopwith Camel   203Sqn
** left 10-30pm cr found NOEUX 5am next day wr(Capt RA Little DSO CdG **DoW**) NB to attack EA bomber FILESCAMP FARM A'dr, WIA by mg fire

C74   Sopwith Camel   204Sqn
+* combat with AlbatrosDIII[+ooc] OSTENDE 7-20pm OK(Capt CRR Hickey Can. DFC) first of several victories in this a'c in a total over 20

28th May

C8582   A.W.FK8   2Sqn
**Phot AA ovAUCHY 4pm bad dam OK(Lt CE Preece/ Lt HS Woodman) left 3-30pm

C8586   A.W.FK8   8Sqn
**B combat with EA ovFRICOURT 10-15am ftl OK(Lt R Grice/2Lt SH Smith) left 8-50am

C4763   Bristol F2b   20Sqn
OP left 9-17am seen nrNEUF BERQUIN ~10-30am **MIA(Lt RG Bennett **KIA**/Lt GCT Salter MC **KIA**) Bennett claimed 9 victories

D3444   SE5a   24Sqn
+* combat with Fokker DVII[+ooc] MARICOURT ~6am OK(Capt IDR McDonald) first of 7 claims in this a'c, in total of 20

B8394   SE5a   41Sqn
OP combat with 2EAs 11-45am FRESNES LES MONTAUBAN **MIA(Lt RS Milani **WIA POW**) left 10-45am, serious WIA, repat 17.12.18 ["SE5" claim combat ETERPIGNY 11-45am Ltn E Koch Ja32]

C6455   SE5a   64Sqn
OP left 7am combat with EA LOCON shot down in flames(Lt WP Southall **KIA) ["SE5" claim combat LOCON 7-50am Ltn P Billik Ja52]

C8280   Sopwith Camel   65Sqn
OP left 8-30am steep dive on EA wLAMOTTE 9-30am(Lt WB Craib **KIA)

C1772   SE5a   84Sqn
**OP AA ALLONVILLE dam prop ftl ldg ok OK(Capt AFW Beauchamp-Proctor SA.) had achieved 10 victories in this a'c

SE5a	84Sqn

** (Lt B Stefanson **WIA**)

D259   SE5a   84Sqn
+* combat with AlbatrosDVs[++collided]
seWARFUSÉE 9-20am OK(Lt R Manzer Can.) made 11
victory claims

B7674   DH9   98Sqn
**B BRUGES combat with 2EA[+?] shot down in flames
ovZEEBRUGGE **MIA**(Lt FFH Reilly **KIA**/Lt RMcK
Hall **KIA**) left 4am

B448   FE2b   100Sqn
NB left 11-15pm METZ **MIA(2Lt VR Brown **POW**/
Pte AJ Johnson **POW**)

A8065   DH4   217Sqn
**LowB left 2-35am ZEEBRUGGE MOLE, shot down
MIA(LtCol PFM Fellowes **WIA POW**/Sgt FN Pritchard
POW)

The crew noted above shared a daring raid on
Zeebrugge mole on the 28th. A 214 Squadron
Handley Page, piloted by a Canadian Capt CH
Darley (in 0/100 3135?), glided in at the lock gates
from the sea at about two hundred feet and
dropped three bombs. One exploded near the
gates. Ten minutes later, this DH4 crew came in
on another low attack and dropped two more
bombs. One may have hit the target. Fellowes, who
was the Commanding Officer of 61st Wing, and
Pritchard were shot down and taken prisoner.

29th May

B3382   A.W.FK8   8Sqn
**B left 6-15 am AA dam returned 7-55pm OK(Lt HN
Young/2Lt LW Norman)

C856   Bristol F2b   20Sqn
**OP left 6-12pm HA shot up dam ftl nr a'dr OK(Lt TC
Traill/2Lt PG Jones)

B876   RE8   42Sqn
**Phot combat with EA shot up MERVILLE 3-15pm ftl
cr ldg TREIZENNES(Lt FV Sheard **WIA**/Lt MC Sexton
WIA)

DH4	55Sqn

** (Lt W Wild **WIA**)

Sopwith Camel	70Sqn

** (Capt JGSC Smith-Grant **WIA**)

D5064   A.W.FK8   HQ Communications Flt
**travel, hit by nearby shelling on ground(Lt SS
Turnbull **WIA**) pilot was waiting for Maj Miles

30th May

D6483   Sopwith Camel   3Sqn
**Esc combat with 6HA seen shot down in flames
eACHIET-LE-PETIT Sh57C G15.L3(Lt CP Macklin
KIA) left 10-15am [?second "Camel" claim combat
BRAY Ltn W Böning Ja76]

D1929   Sopwith Camel   4Sqn AFC
+* attacked KB[+flames] sESTAIRES 4-50pm then
combat with AlbatrosDV[+flames cr] ESTAIRES
4-57pm OK(Capt AH Cobby) first of 14 victories in 6
weeks for Cobby in this a'c

C8522   A.W.FK8   10Sqn
**AOb hit by shell 4-15pm G1.c.68.? ftl dam(Lt LH
Short MC **WIA**/Pbr2Lt AC Clinton **WIA**)

DH4	18Sqn

** (A/Sgt GL Braithwaite **WIA**)

C961   Bristol F2b   22Sqn
+* combat with PfalzDIII[+ooc] ARMENTIÈRES
7-40pm OK(2Lt EC Bromley/2Lt JH Umney) both this
crew claimed over 10EA

SE5a	29Sqn

P (2Lt EAW Kent **WIA)

C8262   Sopwith Camel   43Sqn
+* combat with AlbatrosDV[+des] nCOMBLES
2-50pm OK(Lt GG Bailey) Bailey achieved most of his 8
claims in this a'c

D1793   Sopwith Camel   43Sqn
**OP left 1-40pm seen start combat with EA ovFLEURS
MIA(2Lt PT Bruce **KIA**) ["Camel" claim combat
CONTALMAISON Ltn W Böning Ja76]

Sopwith Camel	46Sqn

** (2Lt GR Priestley **WIA**)

C871   Bristol F2b   48Sqn
**OP combat ST MOREUIL 10-30am shot down in
flames nrBOIS DE SENECAT **MIA**(2Lt WB Yuille
KIA/2Lt WD Davidson **KIA**) left 9-25am, Ja68?

D462   DH9   49Sqn
B shell? 12000' broke up(Lt RHB Stevens **KIA/1AM
LC Norman **KIA**) air collision?

A3447   RE8   52Sqn
**SituationP AA? hit ovCHAMBERY ftl for hospital for
observer(Lt HP Illsley OK/2Lt JW Benton **WIA**) left
7-10am, a'c shelled

52 Squadron had been unable to operate since the
28th because of incessant moves imposed by the
retreat. When work commenced again on the 30th
they carried out low machine-gun and bombing
strafes as well as reconnaissance.

DH4	55Sqn

** (/Lt LF Short **WIA**)

C1670   Sopwith Camel   70Sqn
+* combat with AlbatrosDVs[+flames+des] ALBERT-
BRUAY 11-10am OK(Capt J Todd MC) Todd made 18
claims with 70Sqn, most in this a'c

D6640   Sopwith Camel   70Sqn
**DOP left 11-10am combat seen ok eALBERT 11am
MIA(Lt WA Scott **POW**)

C8554   A.W.FK8   82Sqn
** combat with 8EA incl Fokker DrI CORBIE ftl as

blood obscured pilot's vision(Lt HF Flowers **WIA**/2Lt SG Dyson **WIA**)

C1862   SE5a   85Sqn
HAP:lone? left 6-55pm **MIA(Capt EL Benbow MC **KIA**) [?"SE5" claim combat NIEPPE WOOD 7-35pm Oblt H-E Gandert Ja51]

This was the first loss in action for 85 Squadron.

A8071   DH4   205Sqn
**B AA shot up dam OK(Lt GE Siedle/Sgt CV Middleton)

31st May

By the 29th the advance in the battle of the Aisne had reached Soissons and was making for the Marne. The diversionary nature of this offensive had been forgotten under a spell of success, however, and the German High Command had resolved to exploit the stunning advance and move on Paris. Notably, it was to be American reinforcements, rushed into the fighting at Château Thierry, who finally halted the onrush. This was the 2nd Division who had been in reserve north-west of Paris. On the 31st they were rushed to Meux and on the following morning were inserted into the line across the road from Château Thierry to the capital. They were followed into the area by the 3rd US Division and increasing numbers of French as well. From the 4th of June the two armies shared a series of vigorous counter-attacks around Belleau Wood which finally closed down the German advance. 52 Squadron was rested through the latter part of June before joining III Brigade at Auxi-le-Château on the 30th.

38 Squadron arrived in France on the 31st of May. It had been continuously engaged in home defence work until only a few days before, when it was suddenly called to the Western Front. It quickly assembled three Flights of FE2b night-bombers, mostly acquired from 192 (Night Training) Squadron, and flew to Dunkirk where it operated in the north alongside naval units.

B7717   RE8   7Sqn
**AOb combat with EA tanks shot up ftl OK(Lt RV Facey/2Lt WE Barnes) left 12-35pm, ftl Sh28 B22.c

A7256   Bristol F2b   22Sqn
**OP EA fire shot up dam returned a'dr 10-50am OK(2Lt OStC Harris/Sgt Shannan) left 8-30am First Army area

            SE5a   . 29Sqn
** (2Lt HA Whittaker **WIA**)

A7825   DH4   55Sqn
B combat with EA shot down in flames ovKARLSRUHE **MIA(Lt JLK? Anderson **POW DoW**/Sgt H Nelle **KIA**) initials JLH?

The original target for this strategic raid had been chemical works at Mannheim. The patrol encountered thick cloud north of Pirmasens and so the leader changed the target to Karlsruhe. Here, one of the bombs made a direct hit on the munitions factory and it was blown to pieces. The patrol met about fourteen enemy fighters and the crew noted above was shot down in the fighting.

C8217   Sopwith Camel   70Sqn
COP left 9am EA? shot down? sALBERT **MIA(2Lt WE Taylor US. **KIA**) [?"Camel" claim combat sALBERT am Ltn H Steinbrecher Ja46]

D1925   Sopwith Camel   70Sqn
**COP left 9am ALBERT combat with EA dam returned 10-45am OK(2Lt CL Frank)

            Sopwith Dolphin 79Sqn
** (Capt WAC Morgan MC **WIA**)

C4158   Sopwith Dolphin 87Sqn
+* combat with LVGC[+des] GENTELLES 11am OK(Capt CJW Darwin)

B7657   DH9   98Sqn
B BRUGES AA down in spin **MIA(Capt GD Horton **KIA**/2Lt HJ McConnell **KIA**) left 12-15pm

D1013   DH9   98Sqn
**B BRUGES DOCKS left 12-15pm AA shot up dam returned 3pm OK(Lt LIA Peers US./1AM Wentworth DFM) DFM for act of gallantry on this operation

                        52Sqn?
** **MIA**(Lt HCE Bockett-Pugh **POW**) May.18? repat 29.11.18

June 1918

1st June

B525   SE5a   2Sqn AFC
OP left 6pm seen 15m eVILLERS BRETONNEAUX shot down **MIA(Lt AR Rackett **POW**)

C8231   Sopwith Camel   4Sqn AFC
OP seen ok BAC ST MAUR 14000' 3-30pm down in control **MIA(2Lt A Rintoul **POW**) left 2-10pm [?"Camel" claim combat LAVENTIE 3-10pm ObFlM K Schoenfelder Ja7]

D6600   Sopwith Camel   4Sqn AFC
+* combat with PfalzDIII[+des] BAC ST MAUR 3-30pm OK(Capt GF Malley MC) EA broke up, last of 6 victories

C4846.6 **Bristol F2b   11Sqn**
Rec **MIA but OK: ftl?(Lt RF Mullins/2Lt FCB Phillips) left 7-05pm [?"Bristol" claim sALBERT pm Ltn A Hets Ja37]

            Bristol F2b   20Sqn
** (/2Lt GH Kemp **KIA**)

C4749   Bristol F2b   20Sqn
**OP combat shot up ovPOPERINGHE dam ftl OK(Lt

TC Traill/2Lt PG Jones) left 5-24am ["BF" claim combat nwDICKEBUSCH 6-40am Ltn J Jacobs Ja7]

D3530   SE5a   40Sqn
OP combat with 3 Fokker DrIs LIEVIN 12pm nd cr(Maj RS Dallas **KIA)head ["SE5" claim combat seLENS 11-35pm Ltn J Werner Ja14]

B7738   RE8   52Sqn
AP EA shot down ROMMERY fire(2Lt A Nugent **KIA/2Lt GAB Ross **KIA**)left 1pm, a/c destroyed [?unconfirmed "RE8" claim combat LA FERTE MILON OffSt G Doerr Ja45]

B8888   RE8   52Sqn
**AP left 2-40pm 3EA eDOMERY shot down OK(Lt TE Sharp/2Lt WH Bentley) ROMMERY?

A7482   DH4   55Sqn
B dive broke up nrMETZ **MIA(2Lt LdeG Godet **KIA**/2Lt A Haley **KIA**) [?possible "DH4" claim combat ANTULLEN? 5-50am Ltn G Weiner Kest3]

C6443   SE5a   74Sqn
OP combat with EA neESTAIRES 4-25pm broke up(Capt WJ Cairnes Irl. **KIA) ["SE5" claim combat eMERVILLE 4-40pm Ltn P Billik Ja52]

B7346   Sopwith Camel   80Sqn
+* combat with PfalzDIII[+des] CURLU-ECLUSIER 8-15am OK(Lt HA Whistler) Whistler made 23 claims

C6472   SE5a   85Sqn
+* combat with PfalzDIIIs[++des] LA GORGUE 8-10pm OK(Capt MC McGregor NZ.) first victories with 85Sqn

C6271   DH9   98Sqn
B left 11-45am BRUGES **MIA(2Lt LIA Peers US. **POW**/Pte Wentworth **POW**)

**   DH9   99Sqn**
** METZ-SABLON AA fire(/Lt HT Melville **WIA**)

B7234   Sopwith Camel   213Sqn
+* combat with PfalzDIIIs[++?ooc] BRUGES 2-20pm OK(Capt JdeC Paynter) both shared, last of 10 claims

2nd June

149 Squadron arrived in France on the 2nd of June equipped with FE2b night-bombers.

C1113   SE5a   1Sqn
OP seen ok BAILLEUL 3-55pm **MIA(Capt KS Henderson **KIA**) Ja51["SE5" claim combat swBAILLEUL 3-30pm Oblt H-E Gandert Ja51]

C6479   SE5a   1Sqn
**OP combat dive with 3EA on tail wSTEENWERCKE fuel tank hit shot down OK(1Lt D Knight USAS.) left 8am, many of his 10 victories with 1Sqn in this a'c

D3962   SE5a   2Sqn AFC
+* combat with PfalzDIII[+des] CLERY 7-05pm then Fokker DrI[+des] ESTRÈES 7-30pm OK(Capt AT Cole) first of several claims

**   RE8   3Sqn AFC**
P AA fire(Capt TL Simpson **WIA)

D5074   A.W.FK8   8Sqn
**B AA hit rudder controls dam ftl nrBRESLE cr OK(2Lt HN Young/2Lt HB Davies) left 4-45pm, unsalvable

A7882   DH4   25Sqn
B CAMBRAI engine failed nrCAMBRAI ftl EoL ~5-40am ldg ok & burnt a'c(Lt JR Zieman **POW/2Lt H Tannenbaum **POW**) left 4am [?possible "BF" claim combat wGRAND-SEC-BOIS 6-10am Ltn A Fr vBrandenstein Ja49]

**   A.W.FK8   35Sqn**
AObs ground mg(/2Lt RV Hepburn **WIA)

**   A.W.FK8   35Sqn**
** (/Lt P Pickering **WIA**)

D6562   Sopwith Camel 65Sqn
OP combat with HA shot down in flames ovMEZIÈRES 7pm **MIA(2Lt A Devitt **KIA**) left 5-30pm ["Camel" claim combat sHANGARD 6-45pm? Ltn J Mai Ja5][?"Camel" claim combat HANGARD 6-45pm? Vzfw F Rumey Ja5]

C4029   Sopwith Dolphin 79Sqn
**OP combat with 7EA ovBAILLEUL shot up dam returned a'dr 6-20am OK(TLt CA Howse) left 5-40am

C785   Bristol F2b   88Sqn
P EA & mg OSTENDE shot up cr(Lt JP Findlay OK/2Lt GW Lambert **WIA) returned to a'dr

D1854   Sopwith Camel   208Sqn
P left 11am combat with Albatros MERVILLE-ESTAIRES seen after combat ovESTAIRES **MIA(Lt PM Dennett **KIA**)

3rd June

The Allies were still in a very precarious position, although the moment of crisis had passed, and indeed lessened, as each division of American troops entered the fighting. The enemy was nevertheless within forty miles of Paris, and still threatened Hazebrouck and Amiens. The Allied Command also knew with certainty that Germany would launch further big attacks before it bowed to the inevitable. There was still fighting on all the fronts that had been ignited since March, especially in the air, for there was an onus on the air forces of both sides to be ever vigilant of developments. The continuing volume of British air casualties listed here is testament to the fact that there were to be no quiet fronts in this war. More than the forces on the ground, the air arms were now to be largely marshalled and disposed to wherever the fighting was most needful of them. Liaison and organisation made this increasingly possible, and for the British there would now be an unending

flow of machines and trained personnel to carry out the work.

The next opportunity for this process to occur was in expectation of the next German offensive. The salient Ludendorff's army had created in the south was a deep and awkward one for him to supply and maintain. It was criss-crossed with damaged roads and railways and was poorly linked to the salient south-east of Amiens. Already, the German Air Force was experiencing some supply restrictions of its own which would soon tell on its effectiveness.

The Germans were expected to attempt to expand their gains by a drive towards Compiègne. This time, however, the Allies would be ready for them. Foch called for direct RAF operations with the French, and planned to launch attacks and bombing raids on the enemy around Nesle and Roye. In return, he guaranteed French air support if the British lines received the greatest blow. As a consequence, several squadrons of the Headquarters IX Brigade were made available, namely Nos. 27 (DH4s); 49 and 103 (DH9s); 43, 73, and 80 (Sopwith Camels); and 2 AFC and 32 (SE5as). All units moved into place in the south on the 3rd.

D6621   Sopwith Camel   54Sqn
LP left 7pm shot down THIEUSHOUK ftl(Lt WA Hunter US. **WIA)to hospital

C4159   Sopwith Dolphin 87Sqn
+* combat with Fokker DrI[+des] BRAY & AlbatrosDV[+?ooc] BRAY-HERBECOURT 6-35pm OK(Lt AW Vigers) made over a dozen claims in this a'c

C6274   DH9   98Sqn
B seen in spin ovBRUGES **MIA(Lt BA Bird **WIA** **POW**/Lt AR Cowan **POW**) left 1-45pm [?claim combat ZUIDSCHOOTE? FlM C Kairies SFS]

B6369   Sopwith Camel   209Sqn
+* combat with Pfalz[+destr] FIGNIÈRES 8pm OK(Lt JH Siddall) pilot scored several victories

4th June

E38   RE8   4Sqn
AOb HA? shot down in flames Sh36A K9.d.3.3. at 4pm(Lt AH Maltby **KIA/2Lt JPB Simms **KIA**) left 3-15pm

A7930   DH4   202Sqn
**EscP combat with EA rudder shot away ftl nrFORT MARDYCKE cr beach 8pm dam OK(Lt LH Pearson/ GL SE Allanson)

D8402   DH4   202Sqn
** shot up dam ftl(Lt TA Warne-Browne OK/Cpl W Bowman **WIA**)slight

N5997.M DH4   202Sqn
** combat with EA off ZEEBRUGGE(Lt JP Everitt OK/ Lt IH McClure **WIA**)

5th June

107 Squadron arrived in France on the 5th of June equipped with DH9 day-bombers.

C6416   SE5a   1Sqn
LP left 11-05am combat with HA ftl nHAZEBROUCK(2Lt AF Scroggs **WIA)

D337   SE5a   1Sqn
LP seen above clouds in combat with EAs HAZEBROUCK **MIA(Lt HS Hennessey **KIA**) left 11-05am, Ja18? [?"SE5" claim combat BAILLEUL 12pm Vzfw H Juhnke Ja52]

B1114   Bristol F2b   20Sqn
 OP left 4-25pm shot down seen nrARMENTIÈRES **MIA(Lt JEW Sugden **POW**/Sgt W O'Neill **POW**) ["BF" claim combat LESTREM 5-40pm Vzfw H Juhnke Ja52]

C817   Bristol F2b   20Sqn
OP seen ARMENTIÈRES **MIA(Lt EA Magee **POW**/ Pbr.2Lt RJ Gregory **POW**) left 4-30pm

B5897   RE8   21Sqn
**AP engine shot up dam cr ldg 4-50pm OK(2Lt P? Brown/2Lt A Summerfelt) left 1-50pm

A7243   Bristol F2b   22Sqn
OP combat with EA shot up ftl(Lt JE Gurdon OK/Sgt Hall **WIA) [?"BF" claim combat nVIOLAINES 11-05am Ltn K Monnington Ja18]

B1253   Bristol F2b   22Sqn
OP going down in control towards LESTREMok 7-15pm **MIA(Lt CH Dunster **WIA POW**/Sgt LAF Young **KIA**) left 6pm BETHUNE-LESTREM

D5992.E SE5a   60Sqn
+* attacked KB[+des] IRLES 9-25am OK(Capt WJA Duncan Can.) last of 11 claims

C8204   Sopwith Camel   70Sqn
**COP ALBERT combat with EA shot up dam returned a'dr 9am OK(2Lt GC Morris) left 7-50am

C2158, C6134, C6198, C6212,
C6248   DH9s   98Sqn
** All damaged by enemy bombing overnight on COUDEKERQUE A'dr 5/6Jun.18

As has been noted, 98 Squadron had been temporarily loaned to the Dunkirk command to assist in the bombing offensive on Zeebrugge, Bruges, and Ostende. The spate of attacks on the U-boat bases brought their own retaliation, and a number of airfields in the Dunkirk area were bombed on the 4th, 5th and 6th of May. 98 Squadron itself had five aircraft damaged or destroyed, but the total of slightly damaged machines was officially put at thirty-seven. The unit returned south the following day.

C6203   DH9   103Sqn
**B combat glide with 4EA on tail down over wood

WARSY-LIGLIÈRES ok? **MIA**(Capt H Turner **KIA**/
2Lt G Webb **KIA**) left 6-55pm

B7220   Sopwith Camel   203Sqn
**OP combat with HA from clouds nrRICHEBOURG-
ST VAAST, shot down seen spin ooc wLA BASSÉE
11-10am **MIA**(FSLt AN Webster **KIA**) left 10am

D9256   DH4   205Sqn
**B combat with Fokker DrI OMNICOURT shot up ftl
1km sCAGNY OK(Lt WV Theron/Sgt HF Monday)
[?"DH9" claim combat nST JUST Hpt R Berthold JGII]

              Sopwith Camel   210Sqn
SpM (2Lt A Bird **WIA)

6th June
THE FORMATION OF
THE INDEPENDENT FORCE

The Independent Force of the Royal Air Force
came into being on the 6th of June. This recognised
and promoted the valuable strategic bombing
programme of targets in Germany which until now
had been carried out by the 41st Wing. It came
under the command of Major General Sir HM
Trenchard and comprised two wings of the new
VIII Brigade, namely 41st Wing, which was now
to contain day squadrons Nos. 55 (DH4s), 99, and
104 (both DH9s); and 83rd Wing, which contained
the night bombing units Nos. 100 (FE2bs) and 216
(HP 0/400s). From this time onwards, all entries
relating to the Independent Force will have
"(I.F.)" after the squadron number.

Trenchard summarised and explained the role
he designed for his new force in a memorandum.
Its chief objective was "the breakdown of the
German Army in Germany, its Government, and
the crippling of its sources of supply". It then
described why so many different industrial centres
had been chosen for attack, as opposed to a steady
wiping out of one centre after another. Reasons
included the undoubted moral effect which widely
dispersed attacks would have on the populace, and
that the same uncertainty would force the allocation of defensive measures wastefully throughout
the country. Trenchard was also aware of the
limitations of his machines and other technology at
his disposal — deep flights into foreign territory
were amongst the most demanding operations
imaginable, as well as being heavily reliant on the
weather for success. In view of these factors,
Trenchard knew the greatest effectiveness of his
bombing programme would not come from a few
spectacular raids which could not be followed up,
but rather by a steady wearing away at crucial
targets. As to these, he sought "attacks which
would have the greatest effect in hastening the end

of hostilities. . . . railways were first in order of
importance, and next in importance the blast
furnaces." Good targets of both kinds were to be
found reasonably close to the front as well as being
relatively easy to find at night.

Some of their later raids were also delivered to
enemy aerodromes and this more tactical use of
their strength has been debated over the years. In
fact, forty per cent of their bombs were dropped on
these rather vulnerable targets and they undoubtedly made some highly damaging raids. The
question is, would these bombs have inflicted more
destruction of the German war machine if they had
been dropped on factories and railways instead? Of
course, many such raids were made by 100
Squadron FE2bs, which in any case did not have
the capability to raid more distant targets in
Germany.

The promise of a truly independent bombing
force was never to be fulfilled; at its maximum
strength it would consist of nine squadrons, a mere
shadow of the forty or so which had first been
proposed in 1917. As the Official History also
points out, it was always composed of makeshift
aircraft; early promises of high specification,
purpose-built long distance bombers were lost in
compromise and confused debate about the priority
between day and night work. Many of its day
bombing elements, like most of those in the RAF,
were also severely and fundamentally let down by
the de Havilland DH9 — the machine they had to
take into battle.

C4129   Sopwith Dolphin 19Sqn
+* combat with DFWC[+ooc] VIEUX BERQUIN
5-15pm OK(Lt CV Gardner) first of 10 victories claimed
with 19Sqn

B2071.R **DH4**   **27Sqn**
**B HA shot up ovBEAUVOIS ftl(Maj GD Hill OK/2Lt
CHF Nesbit **WIA**)

B2080   DH4   **27Sqn**
**B left formation EoL seen in control CHAULNES
MIA(Lt MF Cunningham **KIA**/Lt WJ Stockins **KIA**)
left 8-20am [?"DH" claim combat ASSAINVILLERS
Ltn O vB-Marconnay Ja15][?"DH4" claim combat
FERRIÈRES 10-40am Ltn G vHantelmann Ja15]

              DH4   **27Sqn**
** (2Lt DB Robertson **WIA**)

D5970   SE5a   **29Sqn**
+* combat with PfalzDIII[+des] nwESTAIRES 6pm
OK(Lt AE Reed SA.) Reed made 19 claims with 29Sqn

B8374.B **SE5a**   **32Sqn**
+* combat with Fokker DVIIs[+flames+ooc]
MONTDIDIER ~6-45pm OK(Capt WA Tyrell) also
shared PfalzDIII[+flames] ROMOQNIES 5-50am that
morning, last of 17 claims, 12 in this a'c

C1791   SE5a   32Sqn
**OP MONTDIDIER-LASSIGNY combat with EA
shot up dam OK(Lt REL MacBean) left 6pm, returned
6-50pm [?"SE5" claims: combat swMONTDIDIER
6-50pm Vzfw J Klein & Ltn J Veltjens Ja15]

D4812   RE8   59Sqn
**P hit by AA in dive on mg dam: extensions lost ftl cr
wr Sh57D F.20.D.Cent OK(Lt HM Golding/2Lt AJ
Bridge) left 3-55pm

D6504   Sopwith Camel   73Sqn
**OP left 9-45am eMONTDIDIER combat with EA[+]
badly shot up OK(Lt AV Gallie)

A8012   DH4   217Sqn
**dam on a'dr in air raid (see 98 Squadron entries for
5th June)

7th June

C4576   RE8   5Sqn
**P AA shot up dam OK(Lt KMA Ramsey/2Lt AT
Sprangle)

B611   SE5a   24Sqn
**OP left 10-45am seen EoL nrROSIÈRES 7000'
MIA(2Lt JJ Dawe KIA) ["SE5" claim combat
ROSIÈRES Ltn F Rumey Ja5] had claimed several
victories, including some in this a'c

D9266   DH4   25Sqn
**B AA swVALENCIENNES seen going down in control
MIA(Lt LA Hacklett POW/Sgt WC Elliott POW) left
8-30am

D3941   SE5a   40Sqn
**OP ESTAIRES combat with 2Str shot up dam OK(Lt
DS Poler) left 6-35am

C6114.M   DH9   49Sqn
**B FRESNOY-LE-ROYE AA ftl 11-45am OK(Lt AH
Curtis/Sgt A Davis) left 9-30am

C6184   DH9   49Sqn
**BPhot combat with EA seen down ooc MIA(Lt GC
McEwan KIA/Lt TF Harvey KIA) combat 10-45am
ovAPPILY ["English EA" claim combat sNOYON
10-50am Ltn J Veltjens Ja15][?possible "DH" claim
combat MERY Ltn A Lenz Ja22]

B144   SE5a   56Sqn
**COP left 8-20am combat with EA dam returned a'dr
10-10am OK(Lt C Parry) to Third Army area

A7771   DH4   57Sqn
**B left 2-10pm BAPAUME AA ftl OK(Capt H Liver/
Sgt PS Tidy)

D9763   FE2b   58Sqn
**NB AA ftl cr dam OK(Lt WA Leslie/Lt F Wilkinson)

D1817   Sopwith Camel   65Sqn
**OP left 5-30am combat with 2EA shot up dam
OK(TLt CL Morley)

9970   BE2c   214Sqn
* bombed by EA on a'dr overnight 7/8

8th June

B130   SE5a   1Sqn
**LP left 7-50am combat with EA EoL shot up dam
OK(Lt BH Moody)

DH4   25Sqn
**Rec (/2Lt WH Dixon WIA)

C882   Bristol F2b   88Sqn
**Esc OSTENDE AA shot down cr OK(Lt RJ Cullen/
2Lt FA Lewis) returned a'dr dam ldg

DH9   104Sqn (I.F.)
**B METZ-SABLON Triangle AA? shot up(/2Lt RK
Pollard WIA)

This was the first raid carried out by 104 Squadron.
The formation was hit by accurate AA over the
target and then followed back by three German
fighters whose pilots occasionally launched attacks.

9th June
THE FOURTH GERMAN
OFFENSIVE:
BATTLE OF THE MATZ

The anticipated German offensive, the fourth of
1918, was launched at 3-20am towards the Matz.
Early progress was again remarkable, penetrating
six miles on the first day. This time, however, the
French were ready for the attack and launched
counter-strokes on the 10th with tanks and low
flying air support that stopped the advance. In the
three days in which IX Brigade contributed to the
battle it dropped sixteen tons of bombs and fired
120,000 rounds of ammunition. Some of the
heaviest air fighting was undertaken by 73
Squadron on the 11th. There was some notable
confusion in the joint operations conducted by the
British and the French. It was realised that on
occasions fire had been exchanged between the
two, both in the air and from the ground.

The German Army had suffered heavy casualties
for their meagre gains, but despite this, Ludendorff
had one more battle to launch — the fifth and final
German offensive in the west would come five
weeks later. The British were also certain there was
to be a final supreme effort to overwhelm their
front. Events would ultimately prove otherwise, but
for now, matters were moving at such pace and on
such an enormous scale that to relax might still
prove fatal. In order to anticipate from where the
attack might be launched, the RAF was ordered to
be extremely vigilant in its day and night reconnaissance work and photographic patrols were
redoubled. A bombing programme of carefully
selected railway targets was also instigated which

called for raids to be continued around the clock.

C4134 **Sopwith Dolphin 19Sqn**
LP AA shot down(2Lt WA Hunter **WIA)to hospital

DH4 **25Sqn**
** (2Lt JFV Alkinson **WIA**) spelt Ahlkinson?

B8391.B **SE5a** **32Sqn**
GndStr mg fire ovMAGNELAY 7am then dived from 1000′ cr burnt(Capt WA Tyrell **KIA) WIA: fainted?

D6867 **SE5a** **32Sqn**
GndStr ground mg fire shot up ftl 43Sq(2Lt SW Graham **WIA)leg, to hospital, left 4-30am MONTDIDIER-LASSIGNY

D5959.W **SE5a** **41Sqn**
**OP combat with EA BERRY 7-30am engine shot up ftl OK(Lt FRG McCall MC Can.)

D1844 **Sopwith Camel** **43Sqn**
*SpM left 7-55am down EoL **MIA**(Lt JH Johnson **POW DoW**)

DH9 **49Sqn**
B AA fire(ACapt HL Rough **WIA)

B5244 **Sopwith Camel** **73Sqn**
LowStr left 7-30pm seen in control wTRICOT going s-w towards Lines nrRESSONS **MIA(2Lt RA Baring **KIA**) [?"Camel" claim combat 8pm Ltn A Delling Ja34]

D6592 **Sopwith Camel** **73Sqn**
**LowStr dhAA EoL glide towards GODENVILLERS cr destroyed OK(Lt H Jenkinson) left 7-30am, a'c shelled, burnt

C6155 **DH9** **103Sqn**
**B left 6-25pm shot up dam returned 7-45pm OK(Lt Chrispin/Lt Wadsworth) [?"DH" claim Ltn R Francke Ja8]

D1007 **DH9** **103Sqn**
B seen EoL going east ok **MIA(Lt EA Windridge **KIA**/Lt VW Allen MC **KIA**) left 7-45pm

B7163 **Sopwith Camel** **210Sqn**
OP combat with EA ovPLOEGSTEERT WOOD down ooc swESTAIRES 8-30am **MIA(2Lt C Marsden **POW**) [?"Sopwith" claim combat VIEUX BERQUIN 8-11am Ltn H-G Marwitz Ja30]

D3348 **Sopwith Camel** **210Sqn**
P combat ovPLOEGSTEERT WOOD 8-30am ooc **MIA(2Lt W Breckenridge USAS. **WIA POW**) left 7am, not seen going down [?"English EA" claim combat LA GORGUE 8-20am Ltn Katzenstein Ja30]

D3410 **Sopwith Camel** **210Sqn**
+* combat with PfalzDIIIs[+ooc+des] nePLOEGSTEERT WOOD btwn 8-20am & 8-30am OK(Capt JG Manuel Can.) last of 13 victories before KIFA 10.6.18

10th June

RE8 **15Sqn**
Phot (/2Lt JHT Davies **WIA)

A7676.G **DH4** **27Sqn**
B broke up nrGOURNEY cr wr(2Lt T Noad **KIA/Sgt T Sterling **KIA**) left 6-50pm

C6169 **DH9** **27Sqn**
**LowStr BOULOGNE shot up dam returned 7pm OK(Lt FG Powell/Sgt J Little) left 4-20pm

C1884.C **SE5a** **32Sqn**
**left 6am combat with EA shot up seCOMPIÈGNE ftl OK(Lt AA Callender US.)

C9626 **SE5a** **32Sqn**
GndStr combat with HA ovSOREL CHÂTEAU 5-15am shot down **MIA(1Lt P Hooper USAS. **KIA**) seen spiral down & cr

D1785 **Sopwith Camel** **43Sqn**
+* combat with AlbatrosDV[+ooc] CUVILLY wRESSONS 7-25pm OK(Lt GA Lingham Aust.) last of 6 claims

D1809 **Sopwith Camel** **43Sqn**
*SpM combat with EA fuel tank shot up ftl OK(Lt CC Banks MC)a'c burnt destr

D5585 **DH9** **49Sqn**
** EA AA(Lt LR Charron OK/Lt FE Dennison US. **WIA**)

D1963 **Sopwith Camel** **73Sqn**
LowStr attached to SE5a Sqn ooc **MIA(1Lt BWdeB Leyson USAS. **POW**) left 6am [?"Camel" claim combat sPOPERINGHE 7-45am Ltn J Jacobs Ja7]

D8117 **Sopwith Camel** **73Sqn**
**LowStr left 6-40am combat with AlbatrosDVs[++ooc] swROLLOT 7-05am but shot up ftl cr OK(Lt J Balfour)

B7249 **Sopwith Camel** **210Sqn**
P air collision with Camel D9590 diving on EA LAVENTIE-NEUVE CHAPELLE **MIA(Capt JG Manuel **KIA**) left 5-10pm

D9590 **Sopwith Camel** **210Sqn**
OP air collision with B7249 diving on EA broke up LAVENTIE-NEUVE CHAPELLE **MIA(2Lt FC Dodd **KIA**) left 5-10pm

11th June

C2303 **RE8** **7Sqn**
AOb left 12-50pm combat with EA dam(2Lt WW Saunders **WIA/Pbr EL Goulder OK)

D7222 **DH9** **27Sqn**
**LowStr MONTDIDIER shot through dam OK(Lt F Carr/Lt JH Holland) left 1-50pm, returned 4-15pm

C2185 **DH9** **49Sqn**
B combat with EA shot up FOUQUEROLLES 1-30pm ftl(Lt RC Stokes **inj/Lt CE Pullen **inj**)

D7201 **DH9** **49Sqn**
LowB EA controls shot up ovMONTIERZ 3-30pm engine ftl(Lt C Bowman OK/Lt LV Gordon **WIA)

B2351   Sopwith Camel   73Sqn
**LowStr left 1-30pm combat with HA nROLLOT seen
in control EoL nrCUVILLY **MIA**(Lt JI Carpenter
USAS. **KIA**) [?"Sopwith 1Str" claim combat
FAVEROLLES pm Oblt C Menckhoff Ja72]

D1832   Sopwith Camel   73Sqn
**LowStr left 1-45pm ROLLOT combat with 2Str[+des]
eMERY 2-15pm shot up dam OK(Lt OM Baldwin)

D1841   Sopwith Camel   73Sqn
**OP left 3pm combat with Fokker DVII[+des] 3m
neROLLOT 4pm shot up dam OK(Capt WH Hubbard)

D1922   Sopwith Camel   73Sqn
+* combat with Fokker DVII[+des] eBUS-ROLLOT
4pm OK(Lt RN Chandler) made 7 claims

D1962   Sopwith Camel   73Sqn
LowStr diving on 2Str nrMERY 2-15pm **MIA(Lt
CWH Douglas USAS. **KIA**) ["Sopwith" claim combat
MERY 2-10pm Ltn O Fr vB-Marconnay Ja15]

D6636   Sopwith Camel   73Sqn
**OP left 9-40am AA dam ooc cr ldg OK(Lt H Jenkinson
USAS)

D9382   Sopwith Camel   73Sqn
**LowStr LE MESNIL combat with Fokker DVII[+
ooc] ROLLOT, se MONTDIDIER shot up dam ftl(1Lt
JH Ackerman USAS. **WIA**) left 1-15pm

D3417   Sopwith Camel   203Sqn
+* combat with PfalzDIIIs[+destr+ooc]
OUTTERSTEENE 6-35pm OK(Maj R Collishaw Can.)
second EA shared, first of Collishaw's victories with
203Sqn & first of possibly 19 in this machine

12th June

D3960   SE5a   2Sqn AFC
**OP left 9-10am combat with 8 Pflaz & 4 Fokker DrIs,
seen ovNOYON after combat **MIA**(Lt TJ Hammond
KIA)

D6860   SE5a   2Sqn AFC
+* combat with Fokker DrIs[++des] GURY 10-40am
OK(Capt RC Phillips) claimed many of 15 victories in
this a'c

B5646   Sopwith Camel   4Sqn AFC
**BOP seen nrBAILLEUL 12-05pm combat with Pfalz
shot down nrMETEREN **MIA**(Lt WS Martin **KIA**)
["Camel" claim combat wMETEREN 12pm Ltn R Fr
vBarnekow Ja20]

D1961   Sopwith Camel   4Sqn AFC
+* attacked KB[+flames] 11-50am then combat with
PfalzDIII[+des] BAILLEUL-ESTAIRES 12pm OK(Lt
EJ Kingston-McCloughry) first of 21 claims, most in this
a'c

D6023.A SE5a   41Sqn
+* combat with AlbatrosDV[+?ooc] GUERBIGNY
1pm OK(Lt WE Shields Can.) possible first claim for this
24 victory ace

D1885   Sopwith Camel   43Sqn
**OP RIBECOURT combat with HA 11-15am dam
returned a'dr 12-40pm OK(Lt JG Beck) left 10-25am

D1917   Sopwith Camel   43Sqn
**OP combat shot up eCOMPIÈGNE 12-30pm dam ftl
o't corn OK(Lt PWR Arundel) [3 "Sopwith 1Str"
claims?combat neCOMPIÈGNE 12-15pm Ltn O Fr vB-
Marconnay, Ltn G vHantelmann, & Ltn J Veltjens all
Ja15]

A7650   DH4   55Sqn (I.F.)
**Height test combat with EA WoL shot up dive cr
MIA(Lt MG Jones MC **KIA**/2Lt TE Brewer **KIA**)
caught in height test ovCHENEURIÈRES

C2240   RE8   59Sqn
**Phot left 10-45am combat with 5 Fokker DrIs dam
OK(Lt GF Thomas/2Lt JC Walker)

C6497   SE5a   74Sqn
**OP combat shot down nwARMENTIÈRES spin
15000' **MIA**(2Lt GF Thompson US. **POW**) left 7-05pm

D9762   FE2b   83Sqn
NRec left 10-34pm **MIA(A.Capt J Weaver **POW**/2Lt
JL Brown **POW**) WT message 10-50pm jammed by
BRUGES

C1208   DH9   98Sqn
**B combat with HA? going down EoL sBOIS DE BIEZ
MIA but OK(Lt FC Wilton/Sgt Reed) left 10am

C6172   DH9   103Sqn
B found nrMONTDIDIER **MIA(2Lt WR McGee
KIA/2Lt H Thomson **KIA**) left 2-30pm

A7632   DH4   202Sqn
** AA hit ovOSTENDE(Capt CF Brewerton OK/Lt MG
English **WIA**)

**   DH9   206Sqn**
** (1Lt JW Leach **WIA**/) inj?

B7272   Sopwith Camel   213Sqn
**HOP combat with 16EA 18000' shot down
PERVYSE(Lt JN Nelson **DoW** 14.6.18) left 6-05pm

B7660   DH9   218Sqn
**B AA OSTENDE dam OK(Capt JF Chisholm Can./
GL LH Lecke)

C6321   DH9   218Sqn
**B shrapnel hit, combat?, dam OK(Lt CLW Brading/
Sgt RS Joysey) [?"DH4" claim combat off OSTENDE
Oblt zS G Sachsenberg MFJa1]

13th June

B8508   SE5a   1Sqn
**OP combat with EA seen ldg sLAVENTIE 8-50am
MIA(Lt ETS Kelly **KIA**) left 7-48am ["Sopwith 1Str"
claim combat swAUBERS 8-50am Ltn O Creutzmann
Ja43]

C889   Bristol F2b   20Sqn
+* combat with AlbatrosDV[+ooc]
nwARMENTIÈRES 8am OK(Capt W Beaver Can./Sgt

EA Deighton) this was the last claim of 19 for Beaver, Deighton went on to make 16

D1723   DH9   49Sqn
B RICQUESBOURG seen going down in control nrORVILLIERS **MIA(1Lt HH Gile USAS. **POW**/2Lt EM Nicholas **POW**) left 10-55am

A7466   DH4   55Sqn (I.F.)
B TREVES seen in control over target then combat with EAs down in flames **MIA(2Lt W Legge **KIA**/2Lt A McKenzie **KIA**)

C9566   SE5a   56Sqn
**OP EA shot up ftl 57D.67 11-40am OK(Lt CB Stenning)

C9498   SE5a   60Sqn
OP ABLAINCOURT engine? ftl down nrCHAULNES or HARBONNIÈRES EoL cr 5am **MIA(Lt RG Lewis **POW**) left 4-15am

D5988.N SE5a   60Sqn
OP left 4-15am combat with two 2strs[+des] 4m eALBERT 4-45am but shot down **MIA(Capt JD Belgrave MC **KIA**) seen on tail of 2Str, shared, Belgrave had made 18 claims

B7830   SE5a   85Sqn
OP left 5-20pm seen ok YPRES-BAILLEUL 6-55pm **MIA(Lt CR Hall **POW**)

DH9   103Sqn
** (2Lt CJ Bayly **WIA**)

C6267   DH9   104Sqn (I.F.)
B HAGENDINGEN combat with HA shot up ftl(2Lt WJ Rivett-Carnac **WIA/2AM WE Flexman **DoW**)

14th June

C8545   A.W.FK8   35Sqn
DuskP combat ftl cr(Lt MC Sonnenberg OK/2Lt JT Thursfield **WIA)to hospital

D6420   Sopwith Camel   80Sqn
OP left 6-20pm seen ovDRESLINCOURT **MIA(2Lt AR Melbourne? **KIA**) name Melbourn? ["Sopwith 1Str" claim combat DRESLINCOURT 7-10pm Ltn U Neckel Ja12]

D6597   Sopwith Camel   80Sqn
OP left 6-20pm combat with EA ftl cr ldg, to hospital(Lt PR Beare **WIA) ["Sopwith 1Str" claim combat DRESLINCOURT 7-15pm Ltn U Neckel Ja12]

15th June

C1835   SE5a   1Sqn
+* attacked KB[+des] sESTAIRES 1-15pm OK(Lt HA Kullberg US.), shared, scored several of his 19 claims in this a'c

C920   Bristol F2b   4Sqn
Rec combat with 3EA shot up nr MERVILLE-NEUF BERQUIN(Lt HN Loch OK/2Lt CH White **WIA) left 3-35pm XV Corps area

A.W.FK8   10Sqn
** (2Lt HL Storrs **DoW**) DoW this date?

DH4   18Sqn
** (/Lt WH Lyell **WIA**)

C2310   RE8   53Sqn
**B KEMMEL combat with 3EA 2-35pm shot through ftl dam OK(TLt B Pepper/Pbr JW Perks)

D4811   RE8   53Sqn
**B combat with 3EA KEMMEL 2-40pm shot through ftl dam OK(Lt HH Blackwell/Pbr DC Burke)

DH4   57Sqn
** AA fire(/Sgt PS Tidy **WIA**)

C1904.Z SE5a   85Sqn
+* combat with PfalzDIII[+des] eESTAIRES 6-55pm OK(Maj WA Bishop) Bishop achieved his last 13 victories in this a'c

FE2b   101Sqn
LRec (/Lt M McConville **WIA)

16th June

The first Flight of 151 Squadron Sopwith Camel night fighters arrived in France on the 16th of June. From its hasty formation at Hainault Farm on the 12th of June, from elements drawn from Nos. 44, 78, and 112 Home Defence Squadrons, it was operating as a complete unit against enemy night-bombers just nine days later (see below).

B823   RE8   4Sqn
Rec British shell hit broke up ovMERRIS(Lt P Bertrand? **KIA/Pbr C Levick **KIA**) hit 4-45am, Casualty Cards: Birtrand

B6656   RE8   4Sqn
Phot AA 3-10pm cr n.m.l. Sh27 X.25.b.98 **MIA(Capt FW Burdick MC **KIA**/Lt SC Shillingford **KIA**) left 2-45pm, body found

DH4   25Sqn
Phot (/Sgt CAF Johnson **WIA)

B2113   DH4   25Sqn
B ROYE combat with EA shot up(Capt J Anderson **WIA/Lt JH Holland **WIA**) ["DH4" claim combat ERCHES 11am Ltn J Veltjens Ja15]

A7597   DH4   27Sqn
B combat with EA 2m wROYE seen shot down in flames(Lt CH Gannaway **KIA/Sgt WEA Brooks **KIA**) left 8-55am ["DH4" claim combat ROYE 11am Ltn O Fr vB-Marconnay Ja15][?"DH4" combat BRACHES 10-50am Ltn H Schaefer Ja15][?"DH4" claim combat GRIVESNES 11am Vzfw J Klein Ja15]

C6109   DH9   27Sqn
B EA on tail 2m wROYE spin **MIA(2Lt H Wild **KIA**/Sgt E? Scott **KIA**) initials F?, left 8-55am [?"DH9" claim combat BUS Ltn K Bolle Ja2]

C6346   DH9   27Sqn
B seen in combat with EA wROYE in flames **MIA(Lt

H Vick **WIA POW**/Lt FRG Spurgin **KIA**) left 8-55am

DH4   27Sqn
B (2Lt EA Coghlan **WIA/2Lt HM Stewart **KIA**)

D6088   SE5a   56Sqn
COP dive on 2Str EA broke up nBOYELLES **MIA(Lt FC Tarbutt US. **KIA**) left 4-45am

C788   Bristol F2b   62Sqn
OP seen with formation during combat with EAs MONTDIDIER **MIA(Lt JM Goller **KIA**/2Lt M Ross-Jenkins **KIA**) left 6-15am ["BF" claim combat POPINCOURT 8am Ltn H Viebig Ja57]

B7347   Sopwith Camel   65Sqn
B seen ok going east towards FOUCAUCOURT 7-30pm **MIA(Lt JA Sykes **KIA**) left 6-55pm, 17.6?

B2524   Sopwith Camel   80Sqn
OP left 7-30am NOYON in spin ovSUZOY **MIA(2Lt GH Glasspoole **POW**)

A5780   FE2b   83Sqn
NB CAMBRAI **MIA(Sgt SC Bracey **DoW**/2Lt P Kemp **WIA POW**) left 10-27pm, Bracey buried ST QUENTIN

D6859   SE5a   85Sqn
+* attacked KB[+des] KRUISECKE 12-30pm OK(Lt AS Cunningham-Reid) first of 7 claims

D6876   SE5a   85Sqn
OP with patrol going towards MENIN ROAD intense mg ftl uncertainly o't KRUISECKE, on YPRES-MENIN ROAD **MIA(Lt HE Thomson **POW**) left 11-50am

A6424   FE2d?   101Sqn
NRec left 10-30pm PERONNE **MIA(Capt RO Purry **POW**/2Lt WHA Rickett **POW**)

C2200   DH9   103Sqn
B ROYE seen btwn ROYE & Lines **MIA(2Lt V Mercer-Smith **WIA POW**/Sgt J Hamilton **WIA POW**) left 10am

C6192   DH9   103Sqn
B left 10am dh?AA seen ovCRAPE-AU-MESUIL **MIA(2Lt S Hirst **KIA**/2Lt JM Hughes **KIA**)

B7808   FE2b   148Sqn
NB left 10pm seen approaching Lines **MIA(Lt CE Wharton **POW**/Lt JW Pryor **POW**)

D5401   H.P.0/400   214Sqn
**NB left 10-56pm BRUGES DOCKS AA hit port engine ftl on return on beach OOSTDUNKERQUE BAINS OK(Lt WSB Freer/Cpl WE Wardrop/Lt R Binckes) a/c shelled, destroyed

17th June

A.W.FK8   2Sqn
P ground mg(2Lt JH Jennings **WIA)

B2300   RE8   13Sqn
**Phot left 9-20am AA hit ftl 10-45am OK(Lt Johnson/Lt Viveash)

Sopwith Dolphin 19Sqn
** (2Lt FW Leach **WIA**)

C4062   Sopwith Dolphin 19Sqn
**OP shot down RICQOUNGHEN ftl dam OK(Lt DP Laird)

C4228   Sopwith Dolphin 19Sqn
OP shot down LOOS dam(2Lt WF Lead **WIA)to hospital [?"Dophin" claim combat LOOS 9-15am Ltn J Werner Ja14]

C4185   Sopwith Dolphin 23Sqn
**IP combat with EA ftl Sh62D N.28 12-15pm dam OK(Lt CF Walton)

D3955.W SE5a   41Sqn
OP left 9-15am seen diving on KB CHUIGNES(Lt JS Turnbull **KIA) [?"SE5" claim on 17.6? combat VILLERS BRETONNEAUX 10am Ltn A Delling Ja34]

C914   Bristol F2b   48Sqn
**OP AA engine shot up ftl QUERIEU OK(Lt RH Davies/2Lt G Rider)

D461   DH9   49Sqn
**B left 1-45pm AA returned a'dr 4-05pm OK(Lt HAP Estlin/Lt RHV Scherk)

D6410   Sopwith Camel   54Sqn
**OP left 8-50am combat with EA shot up dam OK(TLt PC Mitchell)

E5845?   SE5a   74Sqn
this a'c? +* combat with HannoverC[+destr] ARMENTIÈRES 9-45am OK(Capt EC Mannock) Mannock's last victory with 74Sqn

SE5a   84Sqn
** AA fire(2Lt CFS Wilson **WIA**)

B9332   DH9   98Sqn
B CAMBRAI Rlwy Station combat with 20 EAs shot down ftl in control EoL **MIA(2Lt WJT Atkins **POW**/Sgt JH Read? **WIA POW**) left 7-15am, name Reed?

D1694   DH9   98Sqn
B CAMBRAI Rlwy Stn combat with 20HA shot down in flames **MIA(Lt DA MacCartney? **KIA**/2Lt JR Jackman **POW DoW**) name Macartney?, left 7-15am, both in Cemetery

A6409   FE2d?   148Sqn
NB ESTAIRES left 10-20pm seen WoL making for Lines **MIA(Lt HB Evans **POW**/Lt HS Collett **POW**)

N5997.M DH4   202Sqn
+* combat with EA[+] then engine ftl eLA PANNE OK(Lt HS Round/2Lt W Taylor)

D9277   DH4   205Sqn
B hit by AA shot up dam(Capt J Gamon **WIA)

D3381   Sopwith Camel   210Sqn
OP left 7am combat with HA shot down Sh36H 30.c.9.6.(2Lt KT Campbell **KIA) [?"Camel" claim combat DICKEBUSCHSEE 8-10am Ltn Hillmann Ja7]

D3424   Sopwith Camel   210Sqn
**OP left 7am combat with HA mg ftl cr Sh36b
S.9.c.2.9.(2Lt CH Strickland **WIA**) [?"Camel" claim
combat DICKEBUSCHSEE 8-20am UntOff Eigenbrodt
Ja7]

                DH9   **211Sqn**
** (/2Lt JS Muir **WIA**)

A7935.2   **DH4**   **217Sqn**
B ZEEBRUGGE chased by 4 Pfalz ftl cr **MIA(Lt GB?
Coward **INT**/Lt JF Reid **INT**) initials GD?, chased then
shot down by Dutch troops, interned Holland [?combat
3-30pm Ltn P Achilles SFS]

18th June

C1631   Sopwith Camel   3Sqn
**COP ground fire shot up last seen ovNEUVILLE ST
VAAST cr Sh51B a.14. 4pm **MIA**(Lt OH Nicholson
KIA) left 3pm

D6665   Sopwith Camel   3Sqn
**COP seen ovNEUVILLE ST VAAST 51B a.9.a. 4pm
MIA(Lt RL Leigh **KIA**) left 3pm

B5768   A.W.FK8   8Sqn
**B combat with EA ovMERICOURT shot up dam
OK(2Lt FA Whittall/2Lt AJ Ord) left 8-30am, returned
10-20am

B2288   RE8   13Sqn
**P left 3-10am XIII Corps mg fire OK(Lt KW Murray/
Pbr HL Wilson) returned 5-55am

C776   Bristol F2b   22Sqn
**OP combat with EA fuel tank & radiator shot up cr wr
OK(Capt WFJ Harvey DFC/Lt AP Stoyle) left 7am First
Army area [?"BF" claim combat SUZANNE 10am? Oblt
Ritt vGreim JGr 10]

C8870   SE5a   29Sqn
**OP combat engine dam AA ftl nrLines Sh31A E.28.a
unsalvable OK(Lt RG Pierce) left 7-30am [?"SE" claim
combat VIEUX BERQUIN 8-30am Ltn C Degelow
Ja40]

B7171   Sopwith Camel   54Sqn
**OP shot up 8am dam OK(TLt MG Burger)

D6487   Sopwith Camel   54Sqn
**OP seen dive in control nARMENTIÈRES fr 17000'
8-45am **MIA**(2Lt JM Connolly **WIA POW**) left 8am
[?possible "Camel" claim combat nKEMMELBERG
9am Ltn Nebgen Ja7]

D6098   SE5a   56Sqn
**COP SUZANNE a'dr combat with EA cr AVELUY
WOOD seen hit 9-10am **MIA**(Lt HJ Mulroy **KIA**) left
7-45am

C1117.T   **SE5a**   **74Sqn**
+* combat with DFWC[+des] nBAILLEUL 12-30pm
OK(Lt JIT Jones) last of 15 claims in this a'c

                A.W.FK8   **82Sqn**
B (/Lt LCJ Barlow **KIA)

C1923   SE5a   84Sqn
**OP left 9-45am combat with 2EA neABANCOURT
MIA(Lt P Nielsen **KIA**) [?"SE5" claim combat this
a'c or D259 VILLERS BRETONNEAUX 10-55am
Ltn O Fr vB-Marconnay Ja15][?SE5a claim VILLERS
BRETONNEAUX 10-50am combat Hpt R Berthold
JGII]

D259   SE5a   84Sqn
**OP combat with EA seABANCOURT EoL 12000'
MIA(2Lt RJ Fyfe **KIA**) left 9-45am [?"SE5" claim
combat VILLERS BRETONNEAUX 10-55am Hpt R
Berthold JGII][?"SE" claim combat HAMEL 11am
Vzfw J Putz Ja34]

C1883   SE5a   85Sqn
**OP left 9-15am seen in combat with EA MENIN
1-50pm? **MIA**(Capt JM Grider USAS. **KIA**)

C3827.G   **Sopwith Dolphin** **87Sqn**
**SpP left 7am combat with RumplerCs[++ooc]
DONVILLE-swARRAS 8-40am shot through dam
OK(Capt AAND Pentland) Pentland achieved 13
victories with 87Sqn

D7226   DH9   103Sqn
**B left 1-15pm EA shot up returned 4pm OK(Capt KT
Dowding/Lt CE Eddy)

D9587   Sopwith Camel   201Sqn
**B AA ftl cr wr Sh57D o.12 at 7pm OK(Lt R
McLaughlin)

                DH9   **211Sqn**
B BRUGES DOCKS shot up(2Lt JS Forgie **WIA)

19th June

C1101   SE5a   1Sqn
**OP AA fuel tank hit ftl Sh27L 1.a.3.9. OK(Lt EM
Newman)

                RE8   **3Sqn AFC**
AObs ground fire(Lt WW Duff **WIA/)

20th June

D1843   Sopwith Camel   65Sqn
**OP left 5pm lost formation combat with 6EA shot up
dam OK(TLt ML Green)

C8636   A.W.FK8   82Sqn
**B eMORLANCOURT AA dam OK(Capt RT Fagan/
Lt MH Ely) left 4-30pm

D3405   Sopwith Camel   209Sqn
HOP left 5-25pm seen nrPROYART **MIA(2Lt H
Mason **POW**) [?"Camel" claim combat wCERISY
5-50pm Ltn E Thuy Ja28]["Sopwith 1Str" claim
combat ABLAINCOURT 6pm Ltn K Christ Ja28]

21st June

The balance of 151 (Night Fighter) Squadron
arrived in France on the 21st of June. Its role was
now to protect the Abbeville area from night bomb-

ing activity. This had been creating increasing anxiety for some months, in a region whose railways were essential to the sustenance of the British defence of Flanders. The Squadron had been dispatched to France within eight days of its formation. At first it was found that the searchlights and air defence batteries around Abbeville were too numerous for effective fighter cover, so a new system of highly co-ordinated defence between air and ground was originated, based around offensive patrols at night which intercepted enemy bombers as they returned from their raids. The Camels began to inflict heavy casualties — so serious that they eventually halted the night bombing operations.

B6326   Sopwith Camel   54Sqn
OP seen ok going east nrYPRES ok 7000′ **MIA(Lt WK Wilson **POW**) left 4-20pm [?"Camel" claim combat 5-15pm Oblt H-E Gandert Ja51]

**   Sopwith Camel   151Sqn**
travel from UK (Lt HS Bannister **KIA) inj?

B7227.C Sopwith Camel   210Sqn
HP left 12-40pm then not seen **MIA(2Lt RG Carr **POW**) escaped 1.7.18 [?"Camel" claim combat MENIN 1-45pm ObFlM K Schoenfelder Ja7]

D3410   Sopwith Camel   210Sqn
**SpM AA shot up dam OK(Capt HA Patey)

B7245   Sopwith Camel   213Sqn
** seen 7m neNIEUPORT 19000′ 2-45pm **MIA**(Lt KWJ Hall **POW**)

22nd June

C2293   RE8   53Sqn
**NP STEENWERCK ground mg shot up dam OK(TLt GL Dobell/Pbr AW Baker) left 12-15pm

23rd June

The bombing of the enemy rail network was reviewed at this time and it was decided that a programme aimed at hindering enemy concentrations behind the line between La Bassée and Ypres should be begun. It was to last about two weeks and was of special note for the fact that detailed records were to be kept of the effectiveness of these raids so as to provide a test-bed for exploring operational planning and bombing techniques. The units involved were from IX Brigade, namely the day-bombers of Nos. 49, 98, 103, and 107 Squadrons (all DH9s), and night-bombers of Nos. 58 and 83 Squadrons (FE2bs) and 207 Squadron (HP 0/400s).

B1122   Bristol F2b   20Sqn
*OP fuel tank shot up? ftl TILQUES cr OK(Lt HC

McCreary/Sgt JDC Summers) or fuel simply ran out?

C929   Bristol F2b   22Sqn
**OP left 7pm combat with PfalzDIII[+ooc] LA BASSÉE 8-45pm shot up OK(Lt SFH Thompson/Sgt RM Fletcher) to First Army area, Thompson & Fletcher claimed 8 EAs in this a'c

**   DH4   57Sqn**
** AA fire(Lt E Erskine **WIA**)

A7742   DH4   57Sqn
B combat with Fokker DrI driven down wMONTAUBAN seen BAPAUME going south **MIA(Lt CW Peckham **POW**/2Lt AJ Cobbin **POW DoW** 14.7) left 3-40am

D9276   DH4   57Sqn
B BAPAUME seen going south **MIA(2Lt ADR Jones **POW**/Sgt JT Ward **POW**?) left 3-40am

D6182   SE5a   60Sqn
** AA ftl BERTANGLES 7-45am OK(Lt KP Campbell)

D5573   DH9   99Sqn (I.F.)
**B METZ 6-15pm AA shot up OK(Lt HD West Can./2Lt J Levy)

D9777   FE2b   149Sqn
NB ARMENTIÈRES **MIA(Lt JW Thompson **POW**/2Lt LJW Ingram **POW**) left 11-36pm

This crew were the first casualties in action for 149 Squadron.

24th June

A3665   RE8   3Sqn AFC
**AP left 3pm mg top longeron ov nCERISY ftl OK(Lt FM Lock/2Lt AG Barrett)

**   Sopwith Dolphin   23Sqn**
** (2Lt CJ Rae **WIA**)

C8558   A.W.FK8   35Sqn
AP radiator hit RAINNEVILLE ftl(2Lt CF Brown OK/2Lt HH Creighton **inj) hit tree re-take off cr wr

A5689   FE2b   38Sqn
NB OSTENDE-THOUROUT **MIA(2Lt WC Tempest **POW**/2Lt W Turner **POW**) left 12-26am

C8874.Y SE5a   41Sqn
**OP left 7-25am SUZANNE shot up dam OK(Lt EJ Stephens)

D8388   DH4   55Sqn (I.F.)
**B METZ AA hit dam returned a'dr ok OK(2Lt JR Bell/Sgt E Clare)

D8028   Bristol F2b   62Sqn
OP combat with 4-5EA LILLE **MIA(Lt F Williams **KIA**/2Lt E Dumville **KIA**) left 6-15am [?"BF" claim combat MERIGNIES? 7-20am Ltn P Billik Ja52]

D7229   DH9   104Sqn (I.F.)
**B SAARBRÜCKEN RAILWAYS & FACTORIES

combat with EA shot up but returned to land ok nr a'dr
AZELOT(Lt OJ Lange **WIA**/Sgt GT Smith **WIA**) pilot
slight WIA

Thick mist meant a compass course had to be
steered to the target at Saarbrücken. Nine of the
twelve original DH9s made the objective but
were attacked by four enemy fighters over the
town. At least one was claimed shot down in
flames.

D1012   DH9   206Sqn
**LRec left 3-30am down EoL **MIA(Lt WC Cutmore
KIA/2Lt WG Duncan **KIA**) ["English EA" claim
eMONTDIDIER 6-30am combat Ltn P Strähle Ja57]

D3367   Sopwith Camel   210Sqn
**SpM combat with 3EA wings folded cr
neZILLEBEKE LAKE(Lt GA Learn **KIA**) left 9am

25th June

C1102   SE5a   1Sqn
**OP left 4-35pm seen ok BAC ST MAUR 5-25pm
MIA(1Lt HB Bradley USAS. **KIA**) ["SE5" claim
combat DOULIEU?(DEULEMONT?) 5-26pm Ltn P
Billik Ja52]

C1800   SE5a   24Sqn
**OP combat WoL BOUZINCOURT fuel tank on fire
ftl(Lt EB Wilson **WIA**)burnt, left 9-45am, a'c destr
["SE5" claim combat wALBERT Ltn F Rumey Ja5]

C6452   SE5a   24Sqn
**OP AA prop off ftl cr Sh57D N.10.c 11-20am OK(Capt
CN Lowe MC)

Bristol F2b   48Sqn
** (/2Lt JW Whitmarsh **WIA**)

C789   Bristol F2b   48Sqn
**OP FOUCAUCOURT seen start combat with EA
then down ooc **MIA**(2Lt F Cabburn **KIA**/Sgt WE
Lawder **KIA**) left 10-40am, JGII ["BF" claim combat
eALBERT 11-40am Ltn U Neckel Ja12]

C983   Bristol F2b   48Sqn
+* combat with Fokker DVII[+des] FOUCAUCOURT
11-45am OK(2Lt N Roberts/2Lt CC Walmsley) EA pilot
UntOff W Hertsch of Ja12 became POW, Roberts made
5 claims

C4719   Bristol F2b   48Sqn
BOP seen start combat with EA then ooc **MIA(2Lt
NH Muirden **WIA POW**/2Lt E Roberts **POW**) left
10-40am, FOUCAUCOURT, JGII ["BF" claim
combat sALBERT Ltn K Hetze Ja13]

B7164   Sopwith Camel   54Sqn
OP seen ok 10000' wBAILLEUL 7pm **MIA(Lt WH
Stubbs **POW DoW**) left 6-15pm

C8238   Sopwith Camel   54Sqn
OP seen ok NIEPPE FOREST 7pm **MIA(Lt OJF
Jones-Lloyd **POW**) left 6-15pm [?"Camel" claim
combat ZANDVOORDE 7-25pm Ltn C Degelow Ja40]

B7866   DH4   55Sqn (I.F.)
**B KARLSRUHE combat ovSAARBRÜCKEN driven
down **MIA**(2Lt GA Sweet **KIA**/2Lt CRF Goodyear
KIA)

C6170   DH9   98Sqn
**B COURTRAI Rlwy Station left 4-10pm combat with
EA shot up dam OK(Lt G Richmond/Sgt F Sefton)

DH9   99Sqn (I.F.)
B OFFENBURG shot up(/2Lt WWL Jenkins **DoW)

D5570   DH9   99Sqn (I.F.)
**B OFFENBURG several EAs shot down
sSTRASBURG steam emiting chased down in control
MIA(Lt NS Harper Can. **KIA**/2Lt DG Benson Can.
KIA) left 4-45am

99 Squadron was attacked over Offenburg but
the objective was still heavily bombed. Two
enemy fighters were claimed.

C2170   DH9   104Sqn (I.F.)
**B KARLSRUHE 5EA met on return engine hit? down
eVOSGES EoL **MIA**(Lt SCM Pontin **POW**/2Lt J
Arnold **POW**) left 9-35am

C6260   DH9   104Sqn (I.F.)
**B KARLSRUHE combat with 5EA
MARONCOURT? shot up ftl cr(Lt EW Mundy **WIA**/
2Lt HAB Jackson **DoW**)

D1675   DH9   104Sqn (I.F.)
B KARLSRUHE shot up(2Lt AW Robertson **WIA/Lt
MH? Cole OK) these casualties on the 24.6?

B7278   Sopwith Camel   201Sqn
**SpM combat with 7EA eVILLERS BRETONNEAUX
7pm seen going down in flames **MIA**(Lt E Nightingale
KIA) ["Sopwith 1Str" claim combat eVILLERS
BRETONNEAUX 7pm Ltn U Neckel Ja12]

C2176   DH9   211Sqn
**B seen hit by heavy AA 2m eOSTENDE 5000'
11-30am **MIA**(2Lt F Daltrey **WIA POW**/AG R
Shepherd **KIA**) left 9-35am

26th June

C1116   SE5a   29Sqn
+* combat with HannoverC[+des] seMT KEMMEL
5-45pm OK(Lt CJ Venter SA.) Venter claimed 16EAs

C8869   SE5a   40Sqn
+* combat with DFWC[+destr] 500yds seANNAY
6-55am OK(Capt GEH McElroy) first of many victories
in this a'c

C818   Bristol F2b   48Sqn
**Rec left 3-45am AA ovVILLERS BRETTONEAUX
target ~5am **MIA**(Lt JE Doe **POW**/2Lt AJ Elvin **POW**)

A8073   DH4   55Sqn (I.F.)
**B KARLSRUHE seen in control sSTRASBURG ldg
field nSAVERNE **MIA**(2Lt FFH Bryan **POW**/Sgt A
Boocock **POW**) [?"DH4" claim combat HAGUENAU
Ltn W Rosenstein Kest.1b]

B1273   Bristol F2b   62Sqn
**OP combat shot up LILLE ftl nrSENLECQUES
Dummy a'dr cr(Lt TH Broadley OK/Sgt FR Bower
WIA) left 6-15am

D6630   Sopwith Camel   65Sqn
OP combat with Pfalzes neALBERT 8-30pm **MIA(Lt
EC Eaton **KIA**) left 7-30am pm? [?"Camel" claim
combat eBOUZINCOURT 8-25pm? Ltn F Rumey
Ja5]

D1777   Sopwith Camel   80Sqn
**OP left 6-30am ANNEQUIN AA shot down wr
destr(2Lt B Critchley **DoW**) combat with EA?

A5745   FE2b   101Sqn
**LowNRec mg engine hit dam ftl cr OK(Capt R Affleck/
Maj AB Mason) to VILLERS BRETONNEAUX, 26/27
Jun

C6256   DH9   104Sqn (I.F.)
B KARLSRUHE down EoL **MIA(2Lt CG Jenyns
WIA POW/2Lt HC Davis **KIA**)

All three Independent Force day bombing
squadrons attacked Karlsruhe on the 26th, but
only twenty of the thirty-six crews who set out
finally reached the objective. The DH9s were
either plagued with engine trouble or failed to
rendezvous properly.

D2783   DH9   206Sqn
** combat with EA shot up ftl ESTRÉE BLANCHE
OK(Lt C Eaton/2Lt EW Tatnall) left 6-08pm

B7153.X Sopwith Camel   210Sqn
+* combat with Fokker DVIIs[+des+ooc] then combat
with PfalzDIII[++ooc] 1m wARMENTIÈRES 7-20pm
OK(Lt IC Sanderson) all shared, final total of 11 EAs
claimed

D3387   Sopwith Camel   210Sqn
+* combat with Fokker DVIIs[+des+ooc] 1n
wARMENTIÈRES 7-20pm & PfalzDIIIs[+ooc]
YPRES-DICKEBUSCH 7-45pm OK(Capt LP
Coombes) shared, claimed 15EAs, 7 in this a'c

D9608   Sopwith Camel   210Sqn
+* combat with Fokker DVII[+des] 1m
wARMENTIÈRES 7-20pm then combat with Fokker
DVII[+ooc] & PfalzDIIIs[++] YPRES-
DICKEBUSCH 7-45pm OK(Lt KR Unger US.) shared,
the first of 14 claims

D9614   Sopwith Camel   210Sqn
**OP ARMENTIÈRES-LILLE seen
ovARMENTIÈRES 7-10pm shot down EoL **MIA**(2Lt
CD Boothman **POW DoW**) left 6-15pm [?"Camel"
claim combat MENIN 7-15pm Ltn J Jacobs Ja7]

27th June

A3661   RE8   3Sqn AFC
**AOb combat with 2 Pfalz ovCORBIE shot up(Lt PH
Kerr **WIA**/Lt AO'C Brook **KIA**) combat 7pm(9pm?)

wr ldg PONT NOYELLES H24.d.4.5. ["English EA"
claim combat VILLERS BRETONNEAUX 6pm?
Vzfw A Haussmann Ja13]

D9510   Sopwith Camel   4Sqn AFC
LP left 8-40am **MIA(Lt JSMcD Browne Can. **KIA**)

RE8   5Sqn
*trav cr(Capt RS Durno **inj**/2Lt FWP Clark **inj**)

DH4   18Sqn
** (/Lt PW Anderson **WIA**)

D3691   Sopwith Dolphin   23Sqn
**OP seen engaging in low combat with 2Str
nrPERONNE going east 300'-400' 11-15am **MIA**(Lt
SCK Welinkar? **POW DoW** 30.6.18) name Welinker?,
left 9-45am [?"Dolphin" claim combat nrSOMME
Ltn F Rumey Ja5]

A7670   DH4   25Sqn
Phot LANDRECIES **MIA(Lt J Webster **POW**/2Lt
GM Gray **POW**) left 5-15pm

C8859   SE5a   29Sqn
+* combat with HalbC[+flames] eESTAIRES 9-25am
OK(Lt TS Harrison SA.) first of 22 victory claims

C9573   SE5a   29Sqn
**OP combat with EA seen in slow spin ooc
seBAILLEUL 7000' 8-45am(Lt FR Brand **KIA**) left
8am [?"SE5" claim combat 8-40am Ltn C Degelow
Ja40]

C877   Bristol F2b   48Sqn
OP combat with HA shot down in flames **MIA(1Lt JM
Goad USAS. **KIA**/Sgt C Norton **KIA**) left 4-30pm
VILLERS BRETONNEAUX ["BF" claim combat
VILLERS BRETONNEAUX 6-05pm Ltn U Neckel
Ja12]

C935   Bristol F2b   48Sqn
OP combat with EA shot down in flames **MIA(Lt EA
Foord **KIA**/Sgt L James **KIA**) left 4-30pm VILLERS
BRETONNEAUX

B9334   DH9   49Sqn
**B AA hit 10-50am down ooc ovSECLIN but ok later?
MIA(Lt JC Robinson **POW**/2Lt LG Cocking **POW**)

C8268   Sopwith Camel   70Sqn
+* combat with AlbatrosDV[+ooc] & Pfalz[+ooc]
eALBERT btwn 8-30pm & 8-40pm OK(Lt ST
Liversedge) claimed over a dozen victories

D1905   Sopwith Camel   70Sqn
**Esc12Sq combat with EA COURCELLES shot down
in flames Sh57C A.15.b. at 5-35pm **MIA**(Lt CMcW
McMillan **KIA**) left 4pm

D6532   Sopwith Camel   70Sqn
**DOP left 7-05pm seen eALBERT combat with EA EoL
MIA(Lt CS Sheldon **KIA**) ["Camel" claim combat
THIEPVAL 8-30pm Ltn J Mai Ja5]["Camel" claim
combat BRAY-SUR-SOMME Ltn F Rumey Ja5]

D9396   Sopwith Camel   70Sqn
**DOP left 7-05pm seen eALBERT combat with EA

MIA(2Lt J Fulton **WIA POW**)

C8249   Sopwith Camel   73Sqn
**OP ok swLILLE combat with EA down in flames
MIA(Lt FS Ganter **KIA**) Ja29?, left 8-45am

C3806   Sopwith Dolphin   79Sqn
**OP left 7-45am ovARMENTIÈRES 8-30am
MIA(Capt WA Forsyth **POW DoW**)

C3816   Sopwith Dolphin   79Sqn
**OP left 7-45am combat with EA shot through returned
9am OK(TLt LR Lang) ["Dolphin" claim
ARMENTIÈRES 8-45am Ltn H Gilly Ja40]

D1789   Sopwith Camel   80Sqn
OP BETHUNE seen ok LENS-LA BASSÉE **MIA(2Lt
WR Archibald **KIA**) left 9-30am

B8408   SE5a   84Sqn
**OP combat with EA dam then heavy ldg 10am OK(Lt
CRJ Thompson SA.) left 8-15am VILLERS
BRETONNEAUX [?"SE5" claim Ltn U Neckel Ja12]

C6453   SE5a   84Sqn
**OP AA PETIT BLANGY shot up 9-45am & combat?
ftl(Lt DB Jones DCM **DoW** 3.7.18?)

D333   SE5a   84Sqn
**OP VILLERS BRETONNEAUX combat with
Pfalz[+ooc] neVILLERS BRETONNEAUX 9-30am
then shot down ftl fire destroyed? OK(Capt JS Ralston)
left 8-15am

D6902   SE5a   84Sqn
**OP VILLERS BRETONNEAUX combat with EA
dam returned 10am OK(Lt R Manzer Can.) left 8-15am

DH9   99Sqn (I.F.)
**B THIONVILLE Station & workshops mg fire(Lt H
Sanders **WIA**)

D1669   DH9   99Sqn (I.F.)
**OP combat with EA eTHIONVILLE shot down in
flames broke up **MIA**(Lt EA Chapin US. **KIA**/2Lt TH
Wiggins **KIA**) name Wiggin? ["DH4" claim combat
DIEDENHOFEN 4-25pm Ltn H Müller Ja18]

A7868   DH4   202Sqn
**Esc combat with 5EAs nrMIDDELKERKE 5pm(Lt
LA Ashfield OK/Lt NH Jenkins DSM **WIA**)

A8025.Z   DH4   **202Sqn**
**Esc combat with 5HA nrMIDDELKERKE dam ftl
OK(Lt LH Pearson/2Lt E Darby)

A8079   DH4   202Sqn
*PhotRec combat shot up ovZEEBRUGGE OK(Capt J
Robinson DFC OK/Lt FS Russell **WIA**)

N5996.E   DH4   **202Sqn**
** combat with 5 Pfalz WESTENDE(Lt JF Moffett
USNR OK/Lt WD Jeans **WIA**)

D3345   Sopwith Camel   209Sqn
+* combat with PfalzDIII[+flames] WARFUSÉE
8-05pm OK(Capt EB Drake)

Ltn Steinbrecher of Jagdstaffel 46 made the first

operational parachute escape to survive this
combat.

B7620.A   DH9   **211Sqn**
**B BRUGES seen bomb target then AA hit engine ftl
nrBRESKENSAND **MIA**(Capt JA Gray **INT**/2Lt JJ
Comerford **INT**) left 2pm, seen waving "washout",
interned Holland

B7186   Sopwith Camel   213Sqn
** combat with Pfalz 4m nBLANKENBERGHE
10-20am ooc in spin **MIA**(Lt WG Evans **KIA**) [Camel
claim combat off WENDUYNE Oblt T Osterkamp &
VzfM A Zenses MFJaII]

C65   Sopwith Camel   213Sqn
+* combat with Fokker DVIIs[+shot down into sea]
BLANKENBERGHE-OSTENDE 10-20am OK(Capt
JW Pinder) Fokker DVII had just shot down DH9 D5687
of 218Sqn (see below)

D3411   Sopwith Camel   213Sqn
**HOP left 6-50pm combat with 4EA YPRES ftl
WORMHOUT dam OK(Lt BA Hewett)

D5683   DH9   218Sqn
+* combat with Fokker DVII[+ooc] ZEEBRUGGE
10-20am OK(Capt MG Baskerville/2Lt Cunningham)

D5687   DH9   218Sqn
**B dive on Fokker DVII folded ovBLANKENBERGHE
broke up **MIA**(Lt C Briggs **KIA**/2Lt WH Warner **KIA**)
then Fokker DVII shot down by Camel C65 [?combat
BLANKENBERGHE VzfM A Zenses MFJaII]

The crews above were involved in fighting
which brought the first victory, as well as the
first casualties, to 218 Squadron.

28th June

D5061   A.W.FK8   2Sqn
**AP AA ovRICHEBOURG ST VAAST shot up ftl ok
8-25am OK(Lt MW Richardson/2Lt JC Gleave) left
6-05am

C4593   RE8   4Sqn
**AP combat with EA shot down in flames JOBBERY
CROSSING Sh36A E.4.d.54 wr(Lt RS Burch **KIA**/Pbr
T Garlick **KIA**) left 6-45am

C2465   RE8   7Sqn
** left 2-45am CAP ST JULIAN ground fire shot down
OK(Lt WG Allanson/2Lt SE Grand) returned a'dr
5-20am

RE8   42Sqn
** mg fire(/2Lt HH Stephens **KIA**)

B4612   Sopwith Camel   54Sqn
OP seen ok 1m NIEPPE FOREST 2000' 2pm **MIA(Lt
PC Mitchell **POW**)

SE5a   56Sqn
** (2Lt OC Holleran **WIA**)

B8421   SE5a   56Sqn
**OP seen nrMIRAUMONT AA 14000' 4-45am
MIA(Lt AL Garrett **WIA POW**) seen prior to heavy
shelling

D283   SE5a   56Sqn
**DOP combat with EA engine shot up 8-30pm ftl
OK(Lt TD Hazen)

D6086   SE5a   56Sqn
**DOP seen in combat with EA BRAY-FRICOURT
8-35pm **MIA**(Lt H Austin **WIA POW**) [?"Camel" claim
8pm Ltn F Büchner Ja13]

C4880   Bristol F2b   88Sqn
**OP seen HOUTHULST WOOD combat with EA
CLERKEN shot down in flames 2000' 7-55pm **MIA**(2Lt
JP West US. **KIA**/AGnr AJ Loton **KIA**) left 6-30pm
[?F2b claim combat sePERVYSE on 28.6.18?:nil on 29.9
Oblt T Osterkamp MFJaII][?combat sBLANKARTSEE
VzfM A Zenses MFJaII]

D3327   Sopwith Camel   209Sqn
*SpM combat with EA shot up dam OK(Lt LC Story)

D3420   Sopwith Camel   209Sqn
**SpM combat with EA 2Str LAMOTTE shot up dam
OK(Lt JP Naish)

A8023   DH4   217Sqn
** combat with EA shot down in sea 5m off coast
OSTENDE 6pm(Lt AE Bingham **POW**/2Lt LJ Smith
POW)

29th June

A7913   DH4   25Sqn
Phot BRUGES 4-40pm **MIA(Lt BL Lindley MC
KIA/2Lt D Boe **POW**)

B425   FE2b   38Sqn
NB ZEEBRUGGE **MIA(2Lt G Ballance **POW**/2Lt
EG Turner **POW**) left 12-50am

D4834   RE8   53Sqn
**Shoot, seen going down in flames 7pm cr Sh36A
D.5.c.0.6. destr(2Lt JN Gatecliff **KIA**/2Lt J Harrison
KIA) to XV Corps front

B7829   Sopwith Camel   65Sqn
**OP left 7-30pm seen ovGUILLAUCOURT 8-45pm
MIA(Lt RP Whyte **POW**) ["Camel" claim combat
wCAIX Vzfw M Kahlow Ja34]

C983   Bristol F2b   88Sqn
**OP combat with EA ovBEVEREN 2000' ftl cr
OK(Capt KR Simpson/Sgt C Hill) [?combat
seDIXMUDE VzfM A Zenses MFJaII]

D8022   Bristol F2b   88Sqn
**P Coast-YPRES combat with Fokker DVIIs[+++des]
nrGHISTELLES 2000' 8-10pm brought down ST
JACQUES CAPPELLE Sh20.H.22 6-30pm (left
6-30pm?) ftl 300yd WoL(2Lt RJ Cullen **WIA**/2Lt EH
Ward OK) 1 shared, this crew made 5 claims with
88Sqn

C1177   DH9   206Sqn
LRec left 2-15pm mg fire **MIA(Lt C Eaton **POW**/2Lt
EW Tatnall **POW**)

**B7175, B7200, B7203, B7215, B7274, D1866, D3356,
D3364, D3369, D3398, D3407,
D3412   Sopwith Camels   213Sqn**
** burnt and destroyed in an enemy bombing raid on
DUNKIRK

C1211.VI   DH9   218Sqn
**B ZEEBRUGGE AA ovBELGIUM engine ftl cr u'c
dam **MIA**(Lt WF Purvis **INT**/2AM LH Locke **INT**)

30th June

B1307.K   Bristol F2b   20Sqn
+* combat with PfalzDIIIs[+des++ooc] WERVICQ-
COMINES 7-30am OK(Lt DJ Weston/Lt W Noble)
Weston claimed 13 victories

C938   Bristol F2b   20Sqn
**OP fuel tank shot up ST MONELIN-METZ ftl OK(Lt
TC Traill/2Lt PG Jones)

D5961.X   SE5a   41Sqn
**OP combat shot up dam returned a'dr 9-40am OK(Lt
EJ Stephens) left 7-40am

C8212   Sopwith Camel   70Sqn
**DOP combat with HA ftl 8-55pm nrBRAY Sh57D
P.17.c(2Lt JW Gibson **WIA**)

D6564   Sopwith Camel   70Sqn
**DOP left 7pm eALBERT combat with EA diving
eBRAY **MIA**(Lt JE Sydie **POW**) diving with Lt
Liversedge ["Camel" claim combat eALBERT pm Vzfw
H Steinbrecher Ja46]

D1008   DH9   104Sqn (I.F.)
**B LANDAU Station combat with EA shot up dam
returned a'dr ok OK(2Lt FH Beaufort US./Lt CGV
Pickard) left 5am, formation attacked both on way out
and on return

D5720   DH9   104Sqn (I.F.)
**B LANDAU Station combat with 20EAs on return shot
down in flames? EoL **MIA**(1Lt WL Deetjen USAS. **KIA**/
Lt MH? Cole **KIA**) initials EH? left 5am, target 78m EoL

D3359   Sopwith Camel   204Sqn
** combat with EA nrZEEBRUGGE air collision with
ooc Fokker DVII **MIA**(Lt JM Wilson **KIA**) left 1-15pm
[?possible claim combat BLANKENBERGHE pm LtnzS
W Thone MFJaI]

D3361   Sopwith Camel   204Sqn
** combat with EA seen spin dive ooc sGHISTELLES
MIA(Lt S Harston **KIA**) left 1-30pm [?possible second
claim combat NIEUPORT pm LtnzS W Thone MFJaI]

D5609   DH9   206Sqn
**LRec left 2-14pm combat with EA ftl cr n.m.l.(Lt EA
Burn **inj**/2Lt CO Shelswell OK) unsalvable

C9648   H.P. 0/400   214Sqn
**NB MARIAKERKE A'dr ftl beach nrVALKENISSE

MIA(Lt JD Vance INT/2Lt SB Potter INT/Sgt RG Kimberley INT) left 9-45pm

A8013　　DH4　　　　217Sqn
** combat with HA shot down ooc broke up shot down in sea 5m off OSTENDE MIA(Lt CJ Moir KIA/Pte EE Hunnisett KIA) left 5pm ?combat MARIAKERKE 7-40pm FlgM H Goerth MFJaIII][?combat MIDDELKERKE 7-40pm VzfM A Zenses MFJaII]

Untraced Casualties in France in June 1918

** MIA(2Lt A Johnson POW) Jun.18? repat 13.12.18

** MIA(Lt F Clarke POW) Jun.18? repat?

July 1918

1st July

C5090　　RE8　　　　13Sqn
**P AA ooc cr EoL wMONCHY MIA(Lt KW Murray KIA/2Lt HL Wilson KIA) left 7-45am [?"RE8" claim combat nwARRAS 9-07am Ltn R Stark Ja35]

**　　　　RE8　　　　13Sqn**
** AA fire(Lt DH Howitt WIA)

C3824.U　Sopwith Dolphin　23Sqn
+* combat with AlbatrosDVs[+des+ooc] HANGEST btwn 11-35am to 11-40am OK(Lt JW Pearson US.) his first few victories of 12 were made in this a'c before it was wiped out that evening (see below)

C3824.U　Sopwith Dolphin　23Sqn
**OP dive on mg then fog lost ftl dark cr PAILLART 9-35pm dam OK(Lt CF Walton) left 7-26pm, initials CE?

C3871　　Sopwith Dolphin　23Sqn
**OP combat with 7EA nrHANGEST seen ldg EoL ~11-30am MIA(Capt HV Puckridge POW)

C4181　　Sopwith Dolphin　23Sqn
**OP combat with 7EA HANGEST ~11-30am broke up MIA(Lt CLA Sherwood US. KIA) left 10-55am ?combat 11-50am OffSt E Nathanael Ja5]

A8054　　DH4　　　　25Sqn
**Phot BRUGES MIA(Lt GE Dobeson KIA/2Lt JE Pilling KIA) left 6-35am [?"BF or DH" claim combat RUDDEVORDE 8-20am Vzfw F Piechulek Ja56]

C4849　　Bristol F2b　　35Sqn
*?combat COISY shot up 7-30pm ftl(Lt A MacGregor inj/Lt RJ Fitzgerald MC KIA) pilot inj in cr, observer killed in air

A6483　　FE2b　　　　58Sqn
**NRec LILLE MIA(Lt GL Castle POW/Lt AH Harrison POW) left 11-10pm 30.6.18, last WT message 12-40am: "engine konked out — impossible to make lines . . ."

C8264　　Sopwith Camel　65Sqn
**OP left 6-30pm ok ovMORLANCOURT 7-15pm MIA(Lt HH Borden KIA) [?"Camel" claim combat Ltn F Rumey Ja5]

D1687　　DH9　　　　98Sqn
**B AA dam ftl OK(Lt CH Roberts/Sgt GW Slater) left 4-30pm

C6262　　DH9　　　　104Sqn (I.F.)
**B seen going down btwn METZ and Line MIA(Lt GC Body POW/2Lt WG Norden POW)

C6307　　DH9　　　　104Sqn (I.F.)
**B combat? ovMETZ seen glide down EoL MIA(Lt TL McConchie POW/2Lt KCB Woodman POW)

104 Squadron was allotted rail targets at Karthaus on the 1st, but the formation was attacked at Conflans and then again over Metz. Besides the two machines lost in this fighting, two DH9s had returned with engine trouble: one was wrecked taking off, and a fourth was forced to land west of the lines. The leader found his attacking force reduced to four aircraft so they dropped their bombs on rail targets around Metz-Sablon and made for home.

D3343　　Sopwith Camel　　203Sqn
** combat with EA AUCHY nrLA BASSÉE 7-40am ftl OK(Lt NC Dixie)

B6369　　Sopwith Camel　　209Sqn
**Esc left 6-05am combat with 3EA sALBERT shot down in flames(2Lt LC Story KIA) seen breaking up ["1Str" claim combat sALBERT pm Ltn W Niethammer Ja13]

2nd July

92 Squadron arrived in France on the 2nd of July equipped with SE5a fighters. It carried out its first operations in the Dunkirk area but then moved to Serny in early August where it contributed to the air support for the Amiens offensive.

C850　　Bristol F2b　　20Sqn
** left 7-49am HALLUIN seen GHELUWE 9am MIA(Lt BT Davidson KIA/Sgt J Helsby KIA) ["Bristol" claim combat YPRES 8-55am Ltn D Collin Ja56][?"Bristol" claim combat neWERVICQ 8-40am Ltn F Piechulek Ja56]

**　　　　Bristol F2b　　　20Sqn**
** (/2Lt PG Jones KIA)

D8090　　Bristol F2b　　20Sqn
** left 7-48am HALLUIN seen GHELUWE 9am MIA(Lt HC McCreary KIA/Sgt WJH Barter KIA) Ja56?

B8524　　SE5a　　　　29Sqn
**HighOP combat with EA 7am shot down WoL Sh28 H.23.c.8.G.(Lt WE Durant KIA) unsalvable [?"SE5" claim combat KRUISSTRAAT 7-40am Ltn C Degelow Ja40]

D8444　　SE5a　　　　29Sqn
**OP left 7-10pm combat with HA shot down Sh27 Q.31.D.5.5.(Lt RG Pierce KIA)

C808　　Bristol F2b　　48Sqn
**OP combat with EA fuel tank shot up dam OK(Lt ED

Shaw USAS./Sgt TW Smith) left 6-25pm VILLERS BRETONNEAUX, returned 8-25pm

RE8   **53Sqn**
** AA fire(/Lt IB Macbean **WIA**)

B151 **SE5a**   **60Sqn**
** combat with Pfalz VILLERS BRETONNEAUX 10-50am shot up ftl 2AFC a'dr(Lt FK Read USAS. **WIA**)

D9404 **Sopwith Camel** **65Sqn**
OP left 7-30pm seen ok ovPROYART 8-25pm **MIA(2Lt AMcB Sutherland **KIA**)

D3671 **Sopwith Dolphin** **87Sqn**
SpP left 10-15am down in flames nrALBERT **MIA(Maj JC Callaghan Irl. MC **KIA**) [?"English EA" claim combat Ltn F Büchner Ja13]

This was the first casualty suffered in action by 87 Squadron — remarkable for the fact that the unit had been fighting in France for well over two months.

3rd July

A.W.FK8   **2Sqn**
** (Lt L Daly **WIA**)

C3903 **Sopwith Dolphin** **23Sqn**
** combat with EA VILLERS BRETONNEAUX 8-15pm down EoL **MIA**(Lt JT McKay **KIA**) left 7-30pm, seen 300' ovVILLERS BRETONNEAUX a'dr after combat going west [?"Dolphin" claim combat CHERISY?(CERISY) Ltn A Fr vBrandenstein Ja49, but time and on 4.7 in Abschusse?]

DH9   **103Sqn**
BRec spin observer fell out at 10000'(/2Lt TH? Souter **KIFA?) initials TA?, name Souther?

4th July
THE BATTLE FOR HAMEL

A small but very influential British attack was carried out to near perfection on the 4th. This was an assault on the small village of Hamel, just south of the Somme. Its aim was to correct a small bulge in the line of the Fourth Army, for the purposes of assisting future artillery work, and its architect was the Australian, Lieutenant General John Monash. At his disposal on the ground were just eight divisions of Australian and American troops, but at the heart of his strategy was a belief that relatively small numbers of well trained men, blended with an array of "mechanical resources" to support them, could achieve success. To assist his troops in the attack he assembled sixty new Mark V tanks, artillery, and air support, which would be carrying out not only the usual ground attacks and bombing, but ammunition drops as well, which on this scale was completely novel. To cover the noise of

the tanks being brought up into position, 101 Squadron FE2bs flew forward of the battle area through much of the night.

The artillery bombardment began at 3am and, in well drilled cohesion, the infantry and tanks advanced as one on the enemy positions behind a creeping barrage. No.9 Squadron had the special duty of making the ammunition drops, which they did with parachutes onto prearranged sites, ninety-three boxes being dropped through the day. Its crews suffered heavily for this work for their targets were deep amongst the fighting and their presence became well known to enemy guns. 3 AFC provided the tactical co-operation with the advancing troops, whilst 8 Squadron did the same for the tanks. Fighter units strafed and bombed troops. The operation met every expectation, all objectives being taken in ninety minutes with relatively light casualties to the attacking infantry. This precise, co-ordinated, many-faceted assault, based on teamwork and economy of means, was a blueprint for the future.

D6894 **SE5a**   **1Sqn**
*OP left 7-09pm AA shot up ftl dam OK(Capt Sison)

RE8   **9Sqn**
SpM(Ammunition Drop) shot up(Lt HE Pryce **WIA)

RE8   **9Sqn**
SpM(Ammunition Drop) ground mg shot up(/2Lt RE Hagley **WIA)

RE8   **9Sqn**
SpM(Ammunition Drop) shot up (/2Lt ER Moore **WIA)

B5073 **RE8**   **9Sqn**
SpM(Ammunition Drop) ground fire? shot down Sh62d P9/10(Lt HH Riekie **KIA/Lt W Knowles **KIA**) left 3 AFC A'dr 9-30am

C4580 **RE8**   **9Sqn**
SpM(Ammunition Drop) combat with EAs shot down(Lt SE Harris **KIA/2Lt DE Bell USAS. **KIA**) left 9-30am [?"BE" claim combat sHAMEL 9-30am Ltn M Dehmisch Ja58]

C5086 **RE8**   **9Sqn**
**B ground mg shot up dam OK(Capt R Hilton/2Lt A Easterbrook) left 8-10am SAILLY-LAURETTE & CERISY-GAILLY on SOMME River

C842 **Bristol F2b** **22Sqn**
**OP combat with EA radiator shot up ftl nrBURBURE 7-10pm dam OK(Lt IO Stead/2Lt WA Cowie) left 6pm First Army area

C1893 **SE5a**   **24Sqn**
**OP/GndStr left 8am ground mg shot up dam returned 10-10am OK(Capt W Selwyn)

D3444 **SE5a**   **24Sqn**
+* combat with Fokker DVII[+ooc] sCERISY 8-50am

OK(Capt TF Hazell Irl.) first victory for this ace since joining 24Sqn

B2086   DH4   27Sqn
**B LILLE AA combat with EA shot up dam OK(2Lt R Turner/Sgt V Cummins) left 3pm, returned 5-45pm

D6000.F   SE5a   41Sqn
+* attacked KB[+des] MERICOURT 6-55am OK(Lt SA Puffer Can.) last of 7 claims

D6023.A   SE5a   41Sqn
+* combat with Fokker DVII[++ooc] PROYART 1-30pm OK(Lt EFH Davis Can.) shared

C6135   DH9   49Sqn
**B FIVES Rlwy Jctn combat with shot through cr ldg 5-30pm OK(Lt CAB Beattie/Sgt FL Roberts) left 3pm

D1948   Sopwith Camel   54Sqn
+* combat with HannoverC[+ooc] HERLEVILLE 2-30pm OK(Lt EJ Salter Can.) claimed several victories

D6479   Sopwith Camel   54Sqn
+* combat with HannoverC[+?ooc] HARBONNIÈRES 2-30pm OK(Capt GH Hackwill) claimed several victories

D6494   Sopwith Camel   54Sqn
**OP ESTRÉES-DOMPIERRE combat with Fokker DVII 16000′ 7pm seen spin down ooc ovESTRÉES MIA(2Lt CH Atkinson KIA) [?"Dolphin" claim combat ESTRÉES 7pm Oblt C Menckhoff Ja72]

C1848   SE5a   56Sqn
**OP ALBERT-SUZANNE combat with EA dam ftl 9-20pm OK(Capt CM Crowe MC) left 7-30pm

D8160   Sopwith Camel   65Sqn
**OP seen eHAMEL 12-45pm combat? down EoL Sh62d p.12 MIA(Lt HAH Tuckwell KIA) left 12-05pm

B3852   Sopwith Camel   151Sqn
**P ETAPLES British AA ftl LE TOUQUET fire burnt(Lt WGDH Nicol inj)to hospital

B7248   Sopwith Camel   201Sqn
+* combat with Fokker DVII[+ooc] FOUCAUCOURT 7-15pm OK(Capt CB Ridley Can. DSC) last of 11 claims

D3370   Sopwith Camel   203Sqn
**OP seen in combat with Fokker DVII 2m eYPRES seen diving with Fokker shot down 8-55pm MIA(Lt AJ Fricker POW) left 7-45pm

**   Sopwith Camel   209Sqn**
** (Lt JP Naish WIA)

B3858   Sopwith Camel   209Sqn
**LP combat with Fokker DVII seen 1000′ sMORCOURT 1-15pm shot down MIA(2Lt HR Frank KIA) left 12-45pm [?"Sopwith" claim combat swCERISY 1-15pm Ltn E Thuy Ja28]

D3345   Sopwith Camel   209Sqn
**LP left 7am ground mg shot up ftl bad ground ORESMAUX, nrCERISY cr o't OK(Lt JA Fenton)

D3373   Sopwith Camel   209Sqn
**LP shot up combat? dam OK(Capt JK Summers)

**   DH9   211Sqn**
** AA fire (2Lt HH Palmer WIA) (14.7? in D2782?)

5th July

C8847   SE5a   1Sqn
**LP left 7-45am combat with EA shot up dam OK(Lt NT Trembath)

**   RE8   3Sqn AFC**
** combat with EA shot up(/Lt GR Blundell WIA)

C2285   RE8   7Sqn
**CAP ground mg shot up EoL nrLines dam OK(2Lt CS Bolsby/2Lt CG Strange) left 8-05pm, returned 10-20pm

B6675   RE8   15Sqn
**Phot AA hit wing 9-30am dive planes folded cr Sh57D w.13.d(Capt CC Snow inj/2Lt G Crowther inj) left 8-10am

**   Sopwith Dolphin   23Sqn**
** (Lt RD McPherson WIA) [?"Bristol" claim combat sMEMEL Vzfw F Huffzky/Vzfw G Ehmann Sh15]

C791   Bristol F2b   48Sqn
**Rec VILLERS BRETONNEAUX shot down EoL MIA(2Lt BS Hillis KIA/Sgt SJ Pratt KIA) left 7-15pm, Ja5 ["BF" claim combat GUILLEMONT 8-20pm OffSt J Mai Ja5]

C4574   RE8   53Sqn
**CAP ground mg fuel tank shot up dam OK(TLt DC Dunlop/Hon.Lt BE Scott MC) left 4am MESSINES

D1947   Sopwith Camel   54Sqn
**OP EA shot up ftl 84Sq(2Lt SHF Jones WIA)to hospital

D6126   SE5a   56Sqn
+* combat with Fokker DVIII[+destr] DOMPIERRE 8-30pm OK(Capt GJC Maxwell) last of 26 victories, all with 56Sqn

C2174   DH9   98Sqn
** bombed by EA on a'dr overnight dam

D5690   DH9   103Sqn
**B fuel tank & rudder shot up ftl 6-15pm dam OK(Lt CT Houston/Lt JF? Clarke) left 4-15pm, initials JT?

D9238   DH4   205Sqn
+* combat with PfalzDIII[+flames] sBRAY 7-58pm shot up(Lt CJ Heywood OK/2Lt EA Dew WIA)

B7677   DH9   218Sqn
**B OSTENDE shot up dam OK(Lt BH Stata/2Lt CVR Browne)

6th July

C4136.J   Sopwith Dolphin   87Sqn
+* combat with Fokker DVII[+ooc] BAPAUME 11-35am OK(Lt LN Hollinghurst) first of several victories in this a'c

D9631   Sopwith Camel   210Sqn
**OP combat with 5 Pfalz 11-55am chased down in steep

down dive with EA on tail ovLESTREM **MIA**(2Lt WJ Saunders **WIA POW**) left 10-30am, Ja29 ["Camel" claim combat ESTAIRES 11-50am Ltn E Siempelkamp Ja29]

7th July

D3511   SE5a   40Sqn
+* combat with LVGC[+capt] LENS 9-25am OK(Capt GH Lewis) shared, last of 12 claims

C1895.V SE5a   41Sqn
+* combat with AlbatrosC[+ooc] LA BOISSIÈRE 12-15pm OK(Lt WJ Gillespie Can.) shared

B1135   Bristol F2b   48Sqn
**AS EA AMIENS radiator shot up ftl 4k sAMIENS 12pm OK(2Lt BE Sharwood-Smith/Sgt E Collinson) left 10am

A5636   FE2b   58Sqn
NRec engine failure ftl BETHUNE cr house wr(Lt HG Jeffery Can. **KIA/2Lt H Booth **inj**) left 12am LILLE, message 12-30am: "Beyond Lines" but returned WoL before crashing

B137   SE5a   60Sqn
OP seen ok after combat 6-50pm seen VILLERS BRETONNEAUX **MIA(Lt HA Gordon **KIA**) left 6pm LA MOTTE-ALBERT

D1812   Sopwith Camel   73Sqn
+* combat with Fokker DrI[+ooc] LA MOTTE 12pm OK(Capt GAH Pidcock) claimed 6 victories

C1900   SE5a   85Sqn
**OP left 7-30pm combat with EA shot up ST MARIE CAPELLE ftl OK(Capt AC Randell)

E1295   SE5a   85Sqn
+* combat with Fokker DVIIs[+des+ooc] DOULIEU 8-20pm OK(Maj EC Mannock) first of Mannock's victories with 85 Sqn, of which all were in this a'c

D2868   DH9   104Sqn (I.F.)
B KAISERSLAUTERN combat with EA down ovHOMBURG-DIEUZE **MIA(Lt A Moore **POW**/Lt FP Cobden **KIA**) patrol attacked on both outwards and return journey, one DH9 shot down nrPIRMASENS

D2878   DH9   104Sqn (I.F.)
B KAISERSLAUTERN combat with EAs ovHOMBURG-DIEUZE down in control **MIA(Lt MJ Ducray **POW**/2Lt NH Wildig **KIA**)

Following several day raids by the Independent Force early in the month, attempts to reach some of the more distant targets such as Köln and Stuttgart were thwarted for the rest of the month. Heavy cloud over the Rhine Valley was the reason for this. After Nos. 99 and 104 Squadrons made the above raid to Kaiserslautern there were virtually no more until the middle of the month. They were then handicapped by storms, strong winds, and cloud, and forced landings, and other problems were common. Towards the end of the month

conditions made most deep flying impractical and very few allotted targets were actually bombed. Enemy air activity also increased markedly through July, the most serious losses occurring on the last day of the month (see below).

D1730   DH9   206Sqn
LRec left 4-40pm **MIA(Lt JR Harrington **KIA**/2Lt CL Bray **KIA**) ?combat NIEUPORT Flgm H Goerth MFJaIII]

C8279   Sopwith Camel   209Sqn
Int combat with EAs 11-15am seen driven down neWARFUSÉE **MIA(Lt DY Hunter **KIA**) left 10am to intercept WEA nrCERISY ["Camel" claim combat neWARFUSÉE am Ltn U Neckel Ja12]

D3329   Sopwith Camel   209Sqn
SpM combat with EA seen come down in spiral fr 1500', cr HAMEL Sh62D P.10. at 11-15am(Lt MS Taylor Can. **KIA) left 10am, a'c shelled, unsalvable ["Sopwith" claim combat HAMEL Ltn F Büchner Ja13] Taylor had claimed the last 2 of 7 victories in this a'c

8th July

C8550   A.W.FK8   2Sqn
**Phot AA hit ovLA BASSÉE 1-30pm shot up dam OK(Lt J Stuart/2Lt AWG Luke)

          SE5a   2Sqn AFC
** (Lt FR Smith **WIA**)

          RE8   4Sqn
** ground mg(2Lt JE Hammond **WIA**)

          SE5a   29Sqn
OP (2Lt FT Arnold **WIA)

B8346   SE5a   32Sqn
OP left 6-30am seen return ovARRAS 8-40am **MIA(Lt HW Burry **POW**)

C1089   SE5a   32Sqn
OP seen CARVIN-SECLIN 4-5000' 8-15am **MIA(Capt A Claydon Can. **KIA**) ["SE5" claim combat ENNEVELIN? 7-50am? Ltn P Billik Ja52] Claydon made several claims in this a'c

D6185   SE5a   40Sqn
**OP MAROEUIL-NEUVILLE ST VAAST dhAA 5m EoL ftl cr nrMAROEUIL 11-45am dam OK(Lt NS Cameron) left 11am

E98   RE8   42Sqn
AOb mg fire shot up ftl 8-20am dam(Lt A de Niverville **WIA/Lt J Blair OK) left 5-05am

C1002   Bristol F2b   62Sqn
OP combat with EAs CARVIN seen diving with 3EAs on tail nrSECLIN cr **MIA(Lt JA Chubb **POW**/Sgt J Borwein **POW**) left 6-10am ["BF" claim combat LORGIES? 7-30am Ltn P Billik Ja52]

B2473   Sopwith Camel   73Sqn
OP combat with HA 10000' ooc nPONT À VENDIN 7-50am **MIA(2Lt EG Reynolds **KIA**) left 6-10am

C4020   Sopwith Dolphin   79Sqn
**OP left 9am mg fire low ovBAILLEUL dam returned
11am OK(Lt Robinson)

DH9   103Sqn
B (/2Lt WS Marshall **WIA)

D5577   DH9   103Sqn
+* combat with PfalzDII[+des] HAUBOURDIN -BAC
ST MAUR 9-50am OK(2Lt JGH Crispin/2Lt EA
Wadsworth)

D1813   Sopwith Camel   208Sqn
**OP combat with EA shot up dam OK(Lt WA
Crundall)

D1955   Sopwith Camel   208Sqn
OP left 7am combat? engine? 7-50am ftl EoL **MIA(2Lt
HK Scrivener **POW**) MEURCHIN-EPINOY, cause not
seen: "unlikely shot down as EA below"

D9607   Sopwith Camel   209Sqn
**LOP left 4-55am ground mg CORBIE engine hit ftl
cr(Capt JK Summers MC **WIA**) Summers claimed
several victories

9th July

C3581   A.W.FK8   2Sqn
**Phot HA shot up eBETHUNE 10am ftl(Lt J Stuart
WIA/2Lt AWG Luke OK)

E1416?   Sopwith Camel   4Sqn AFC
this a'c? +* attacked 2 2Strs[+des] neLA BASSÉE
7-40pm then shot up whilst attacking KB dam OK(Capt
AH Cobby) EA cr nGRAVELIN

German artillery observation aircraft were
especially important targets in the air war over the
expansive and flattened northern battlefields
because so many features, as well as any movement
through it, could be so easily discerned. 4 AFC
often went hunting both balloons and enemy two-
seaters in early morning patrols over the Lys.

B1113   Bristol F2b   48Sqn
Rec combat with 3 Pfalz ALBERT shot down **MIA(1Lt
ED Shaw USAS. **KIA**/Sgt TW Smith **KIA**) left 6pm
[?possible "Dolphin" claim combat neALBERT Ltn O
Koennecke Ja5]

C1126   SE5a   60Sqn
*deliv engine failed on take off, bank then snd cr
5-30pm(Maj JTB McCudden VC DSO MC MM **DoI**)

The accidental death of James McCudden was the
first of two deaths for the RAF in the space of
eighteen days which took perhaps its finest fighters
from their comrades. The second was to be Mick
Mannock. McCudden had spent the entire war in
service of the air arm. In April 1913 he had been
accepted into the fledgling RFC as an engine fitter,
had come to France on the 13th of August 1914 and
was flying operational sorties as an observer with 3

Squadron by the summer of 1915. He qualified as
a pilot in early 1916 and by the time of the First
Battle of the Somme was flying DH2s with 29
Squadron. His first of fifty-seven victories came on
the 6th of September, and from that time his skills
quickly grew to full maturity. His was a fully
rounded talent, combining an innate understanding of his machine and its armament with a
deadly eye and great flying skills. Overlaying all
was a bravery driven by an unflawed devotion to
duty. As with Mannock, one of the most valuable
aspects of his legacy was the knowledge and understanding he imparted to those put in his care. He
was awarded the Victoria Cross on the 29th of
March not simply for his outstanding achievements
in air fighting but for his leadership as well.

Ironically, McCudden died in a flying accident
which occurred as he was making his way to 60
Squadron at Boffles. He had landed briefly at Auxi-
le-Château to ask directions and as he took off
again he made a low turn and side-slipped to the
ground. He was taken from the wreckage unconscious but never recovered, dying the same day.

C1950   SE5a   74Sqn
**OP left 9am combat with HA NEUVE EGLISE
9-30am **MIA**(Lt AJ Battel **KIA**) ["SE5" claim combat
swDICKEBUSCH 9-25am Ltn J vBusse Ja3]

DH9   98Sqn
**B FIVES combat with 9EA ovLILLE dam brought a'c
back(Lt AE Simpson **WIA**/Lt HA Lamb **KIA**) crew?

D1023   DH9   103Sqn
Rec seen WoL going north **MIA(2Lt RH Dunn **POW**/
2Lt HE Hinchliffe **POW**) left 3-40am

D1734   DH9   107Sqn
+* combat with Fokker DVII[+flames] LILLE 10-50am
OK(2Lt JR Brown/AM JP Hazell)

This was the first air combat victory for 107
Squadron.

D6544   Sopwith Camel   208Sqn
**WT AA hit CHOCQUES ftl cr blown over ldg OK(Lt
WR Allison) left 9-50am

B7598   DH9   211Sqn
**B AA hit dam OK(Lt H Axford/Cpl F Wilkinson) to
BRUGES-OSTENDE

10th July

D6512   Sopwith Camel   4Sqn AFC
**BOP shell hit wing 11-30am ftl cr nrROBECQ dam
OK(Lt R Moore) Moore attached from RAF

No. 4 Squadron AFC were making daily attacks on
enemy infantry around Merville and Estaires,
bombing and machine-gunning transport, forward
trenches, gun positions and billeting villages in the
area.

C795   **Bristol F2b**   **22Sqn**
OP seen going south MERVILLE **MIA(Lt HM Dickinson **KIA**/Lt MHK Kane MC **POW**) left 7-50am

C1003   **Bristol F2b**   **22Sqn**
OP left 8am combat with EA shot up(Lt JE Gurdon **WIA/Lt JJ Scaramanga **DoW**)

D9279   **DH4**   **25Sqn**
Phot left 7-55am **MIA(Lt J Loupinsky **WIA POW**/Sgt JR Wright **POW**)

D9500   **Sopwith Camel**   **43Sqn**
OP engine failed EoL seen glide eLENS going west **MIA(Lt CB Ridley **POW**) left 8-50am

D6463   **Sopwith Camel**   **80Sqn**
OP left 8-20am nrLA BASSÉE ftl then **MIA(Lt LL McFaul **KIA**)

D1725   **DH9**   **107Sqn**
B LILLE combat with Fokker DVIIs controls shot up cr 79Sqn a'dr(Lt SR Coward OK/2Lt PA Hand **KIA) AIR1/969/204/5/1101 gives 9.7?

2Lt Hand was the first casualty in action for 107 Squadron.

11th July

D468   **DH9**   **98Sqn**
**B DON shot up ST VENANT EoL engine failed glide WoL cr OK(2Lt F Carpenter/Lt Donkin) left 5-25am

D1724   **DH9**   **98Sqn**
B DON AA combat with EAs[++] shot up ESSARS ftl(2Lt FC Wilton OK/2Lt EV Austin **KIA) left 5-25am, a'c shelled [?"DH9" claim combat wLA BASSÉE 7-35am? Oblt A Gutkneckt Ja43]

D1731   **DH9**   **98Sqn**
+*B DON combat with EA[+ooc] 7-30am OK(Capt OCW Johnson/Capt GHP Whitfield)

C2182   **DH9**   **107Sqn**
B TOURNAI combat with HA? seen ovTOURNAI **MIA(2Lt JD Cook **KIA**/2Lt HH Ankrett **KIA**) Ja29, left 6-25am

C2183   **DH9**   **107Sqn**
B HA? TOURNAI **MIA(Lt RA Arnott **WIA POW**/ 2Lt HR Whitehead **WIA POW**) left 6-25am, badly WIA, Arnott repat 9.18, Ja29

D5647   **DH9**   **107Sqn**
B seen ovTOURNAI **MIA(2Lt AT Simons **WIA POW**/Lt TF Blight **WIA POW**)to hospital, left 6-20am, combat with HA?, Ja29 [?possible "DH9" claim combat MOLEMBAIX 8-15am Ltn E Siempelkamp Ja29]

D5651   **DH9**   **107Sqn**
+* combat with Fokker DVII[+ooc] BLENDAIN swTOURNAI 8-45am OK(Lt Holden/2Lt H Bradbury)

D5666   **DH9**   **107Sqn**
+* combat with AlbatrosDV[+ooc] TOURNAI 8-20am OK(Capt WH Dore/Lt JE Wallace)

B7398   **Sopwith Camel**   **US 17th Pursuit Sqn**
** AA hit dam OK(2Lt WH Shearman)

12th July

A.W.FK8   **35Sqn**
** (/2Lt JA Wilson **WIA**)

D6908   **SE5a**   **74Sqn**
OP left 8am seen ovWARNETON 8-30am **MIA(Lt FJ Church **KIA**) [?"SE5" claim combat nBAILLEUL 8-55am Ltn J vBusse Ja20, combat date 13.7?]

13th July

C3829   **Sopwith Dolphin**   **19Sqn**
+* combat with Fokker DVII[+ooc] BOIS DE BIEZ 8-05pm OK(Capt JD dePencier Can.) last of 8 claims

C4835   **Bristol F2b**   **22Sqn**
**OP AA hit LILLERS 7-25pm ftl OK(Lt CF Hurst/Lt SG Birch)

B191   **SE5a**   **40Sqn**
+* combat with PfalzDIII[+des] eBREBIÈRES 8-05pm OK(Lt GJ Strange) also shared HannoverC[+des] wESTAIRES 6-45am that day, brother of Col. LA Strange, scored several victories

D6865   **SE5a**   **64Sqn**
**OP BETHUNE combat with HA controls shot up 6am ftl cr OK(Lt GW Wood)

C1818   **SE5a**   **85Sqn**
OP left 7-15pm combat seARMENTIÈRES down EoL(Lt WS Robertson **KIA)

D3386   **Sopwith Camel**   **204Sqn**
** air collision with B6389 ovZEEBRUGGE broke up diving towards Holland **MIA**(2Lt JH Mesham **KIA**) at 4-40pm

B6389   **Sopwith Camel**   **204Sqn**
SpM air collision with D3386 ovZEEBRUGGE 4-40pm broke up cr sea in flames **MIA(Lt GW Graham **KIA**)

B9346   **DH9**   **211Sqn**
B AA 5-15pm seen glide down 4m nNIEUPORT & ditch in sea **MIA(2Lt WJ Gilman **KIA**/Pte WJ Atkinson **KIA**)drowned, left 3-20pm OSTENDE [DH9 claim WENDYNE 5-05pm FlM E Blaas MFJaIII]

DH9   **211Sqn**
** (/2Lt CWT Colman **WIA**)

14th July

C1114.N   **SE5a**   **1Sqn**
+* combat with Fokker DVII[+?ooc] NEUF BERQUIN- ESTAIRES 5-35pm OK(Capt PJ Clayson) last of possibly 15 victories in this a'c

C2444   **RE8**   **4Sqn**
AOb combat shot down Sh36a E.19 7-45am(Lt S Moxey **KIA/Lt JE Weston **KIA**)

D1927   Sopwith Camel   4Sqn AFC
+* combat AgoC[+des] LAVENTIE 7-15am OK(Lt
NC Trescowthick) first of several claims

E1410   Sopwith Camel   4Sqn AFC
**BOP seen ok swESTAIRES 11am ground fire shot
down **MIA**(Lt RC Nelson **POW**) left 9-45am, shooting
up transport

A7900   DH4   18Sqn
**B combat LIGNY 10-20am engine shot through then
hit railway ldg o't dam OK(2Lt A Duncan/2Lt JH
Dunbar)

A7939   DH4   18Sqn
**B seen nrARRAS going east, AA? brought down Sh57
6.B.6 9-40am ldg ok? **MIA**(2Lt D Mallett **POW**/2Lt JS
Burn **POW**)

C9575   SE5a   29Sqn
**OP mg fire 10-10am magneto shot up ftl cr corn Sh27
V.24.c.8.4. 10-10am o't OK(Lt CM Wilson Can.) left
9-15am

**   SE5a   29Sqn**
** (Lt HA Whittaker **WIA**)

D6064   SE5a   56Sqn
**COP combat with EA HENDECOURT 6am shot
down in flames **MIA**(Lt LN Franklin **KIA**) left 4-10am,
buried sCROISILLES

C6447.1 SE5a   64Sqn
OP left 8am First Army area **MIA(2Lt BN Garrett
POW) [?combat wMERVILLE 8-40am Ltn C Degelow
Ja40]

F5920   Sopwith Camel   73Sqn
**trav left PLANQUES fuel ftl 1m NOGHENT then
MIA(Lt RA Yates **POW**) no news after ldg for oil &
petrol

C6490   SE5a   85Sqn
OP seen in combat nESTAIRES 8-35am **MIA(2Lt
NH? Marshall **POW**) initials WN?, left 8-05am [?"SE5"
claim combat seVIEUX BERQUIN 8-35am Ltn C
Degelow Ja40][?"SE5" claim combat seVIEUX
BERQUIN 8-30am Ltn W Rosenstein Ja40] [combat
V.BERQUIN 8-40am Ltn H Gilly Ja40]

D2782   DH9   211Sqn
** flak shot up dam(2Lt HH Palmer **WIA**/2Lt WC
Snowden OK)

B7673   DH9   218Sqn
** Flak ZEEBRUGGE 7-30am(Lt AM Anderson OK/
2Lt CJ Swatridge **WIA**)

15th July .
THE FINAL GERMAN
OFFENSIVE ON THE MARNE

When the final German offensive in the west was
launched it came not on the British but on the

French Army around Rheims. The British had
again agreed to provide air co-operation for the
French and to extend offensive patrolling southwards as it became clear their front was to be the
focus of the attack. General Haig was ill at ease
with the scope of the commitment requested but
nevertheless complied with it. IX Brigade again
supplied the aircraft, and on the 14th, through
heavy rain, its squadrons had struggled south to
the impending battle zone. The units involved were
Nos. 32 (SE5as); 43, 54, 73, and 80 (all Sopwith
Camels; and 27, 49, 98, and 107 Squadrons (all
DH9s). Reinforcements of British infantry were
also requested and dispatched, and 82 Squadron
(FK8s) was sent in support.

After a bombardment which lasted four hours
German attacks were launched to either side of the
cathedral city. That to the east was completely
shattered by General Gouraud whose army exer-
cised well learnt lessons of elastic defence to near
perfection. The advance between Rheims and
Château Thierry, however, made good early
progress, to which the German Air Force contributed significantly. The Allied presence in the air,
mostly French, was numerically larger, but in the
initial advance its formations were repeatedly
pushed back. Only as Allied air reinforcements
grew did they begin to impose their will once more.
By the 17th ground attacks and bombing of the
Marne bridges were beginning to stifle the German
advance, but in the air the German Air Force was
having some of its greatest battles with the French.
Of the British squadrons involved, both bombers
and fighters suffered reasonably light casualties in
early fighting.

**   RE8   4Sqn**
** (/2Lt FH Foster **WIA**)

D469   DH9   27Sqn
B seen seDORMANS **MIA(Lt HGS Phipson **KIA**/2Lt
NCK Auster **KIA**) left 4-15pm

D1778   Sopwith Camel   43Sqn
**SpM left 12-35pm combat with 5 Pfalz nrSOILLY
MIA(2Lt TE Babbitt **KIA**) ["Camel" claim combat
DORMANS 1-30pm Rtm K Bolle Ja2]

D2872   DH9   49Sqn
**Learn Lines AA hit & gunshot MONTMORT 7-20pm
ftl cr(Lt CC Conover OK/Sgt RS? Dobbie **WIA**) initials
RO?

D1945   Sopwith Camel   54Sqn
**OP seen ok PAROY 1200' 12-30pm combat with EA
MIA(2Lt MB Lewis US. **KIA**)

D9401   Sopwith Camel   54Sqn
**OP seen ok 2000' ovCOURTHIEZY 12-30pm
MIA(Sgt PH Williams **KIA**) [?"Camel" claim combat

nDORMANS 12-07pm Ltn E Löwenhardt Ja10]

D6910   SE5a   74Sqn
OP left 8am seen ovROULERS 8-50pm combat with EA **MIA(2Lt RH Gray **POW**)

A6487   FE2d   101Sqn
**B radiator shot through on return ftl dam OK(Lt EH Lyon-Hall/Lt E Clark) left 10-25pm

16th July

D1835.2   **Sopwith Camel   3Sqn**
+* combat with 2Str[+des] Sh57c.A.15.? 12-10pm OK(Lt CG Brock) shared, last of 6 claims

              RE8   15Sqn
** AA fire(Lt F Fowler **WIA**)

D8380   DH4   25Sqn
Phot TOURNAI **MIA(Capt E Waterlow **KIA**/Lt JM Mackie **KIA**) left 1-20pm [?possible "DH4" claim combat PILCKEM 2-40pm Vzfw F Piechulek Ja56]

              DH4   27Sqn
** (/Sgt V Cumming **WIA**)

              DH9   49Sqn
LowB shot up(/2Lt JT Peacock **KIA)

              DH9   49Sqn
** (/Lt EH Tredcroft **WIA**)

B9335   DH9   49Sqn
B MARNE BRIDGES **MIA(2Lt J Aitken **KIA**/Sgt SW Melbourne **KIA**) left 3-50pm

D1727   DH9   49Sqn
**B HA shot up PETIT BECURRE ftl cr(Lt CAB Beattie/Sgt F? Roberts) initials TL?, left 7-10pm

C1609   Sopwith Camel   54Sqn
OP seen in control ROZOY 4000' 4-45pm **MIA(Capt RA James **KIA**) left 3-40pm

D6511   Sopwith Camel   54Sqn
OP left 6-30pm going down in flames 4m wCOURTHIEZY **MIA(Lt JH Spence **KIA**)

D9437   Sopwith Camel   54Sqn
OP seen ok 4000' nrROZAY then cr 5pm(Lt RB Thompson **WIA)legs, to hospital, left 3-40pm, a'c found nrCOURBOIN on 22.7

C4225   Sopwith Dolphin 87Sqn
SpP left 10-25am **MIA(Lt EB Crickmore **POW**)

D1717   DH9   98Sqn
B combat with 12EAs sSOILLY down spiral ooc **MIA(Capt EBG Morton **KIA**/Lt FA Shaw **KIA**) left 4-40pm

D3056   DH9   98Sqn
+*B DORMANS-VINCELLES attacked KB[+des] 2k nwTIELOUP 5-45pm OK(Lt WV Thomas/2Lt HTG Robey)

              DH9   107Sqn
** (/2AM J Hazell **WIA**)

D1734   DH9   107Sqn
B combat with EA LE BREUIL 6-30pm shot up ftl(Lt BE Gammell/2Lt W Middleton **DoW) explosive bullets used, pilot's name Gamnell?

              DH9   107Sqn?
104Sqn? **B (1Lt DF Taber USAS. **WIA**)

A7868   DH4   202Sqn
Phot combat with EA OSTENDE(Lt LA Ashfield DFC **KIA/Lt MG English **KIA**) MFJaIII [?combat ZEVECOTE 5-25pm Flgm H Goerth MFJaIII][?combat MIDDELKERKE LtnzS H Wessels MFJaI]

B7673   DH9   218Sqn
** ZEEBRUGGE left formation lost **MIA**(Lt JA Pugh **POW**/Lt J Ankers **KIA**) [?DH9 claim combat ZEEBRUGGE 11-30am Ltn R Poss MFJaIV]

17th July

D6919   SE5a   2Sqn AFC
+* combat with Fokker DrI[+flames] ARMENTIÈRES 5-30pm OK(Lt CO Stone) [Ltn O Francke Ja30 KIA], first of several claims in this a'c

C3792   Sopwith Dolphin 19Sqn
OP left 5-02pm **MIA(2Lt RE White **POW**)

              DH4   27Sqn
** (Lt R Turner **WIA**/Sgt WB Harold **WIA**) crew?

              RE8   42Sqn
** AA fire(/2Lt AN Thomson **WIA**)

C8254   Sopwith Camel   80Sqn
OP left 7am FÈRE EN TARDENOIS **MIA but OK(Lt EG Hayes **WIA**)

D6917   SE5a   84Sqn
+* attacked KB[+des] PROYART 10-35am OK(Lt NWR Mawle) first of a dozen victories mostly in this a'c in 3 weeks, including 4 kite balloons

              DH9   211Sqn
B ZEEBRUGGE mg fire(/2Lt JG Breeze **WIA)

18th July

The evident progress of the German forces to the west of Rheims was driven to a complete standstill by a combined Allied counter-attack launched on the 18th. This was a decisive and well-prepared blow, delivered eastwards from the forest of Villers-Cotterets, between the Marne and the Aisne. French and American troops spearheaded the attack but British and Italian forces were also involved. Following a brief bombardment a devastating assault, which included two hundred and twenty-five tanks, took the German Army by complete surprise. 82 Squadron for their part made contact patrols and attacked enemy troops with bombs and machine-gun fire wherever possible. IX Brigade machines concentrated on low attacks in

the initial stages of the counter-attack, but as the rout developed they turned their attention to bombing lines of communications, enemy aerodromes, and dumps. British casualties climbed on the 18th, and were particularly high on this work.

In two days over six miles of territory had been recovered from the Germans and Soissons was being abandoned. This was the rail centre on which all the enemy's operations in the Marne depended, and without it their campaign was in tatters. By the beginning of August the German Army had been forced back across the Marne in retreat and soon afterwards were driven further north, over the Vesle. Their salient in the south had soon dissolved into memory, taking with it the last expectations of success. Paris was no longer threatened, and for the first time in a year the initiative was firmly back with the Allies.

C1830 SE5a 32Sqn
OP left 11-30am seen in control nrNEUILLY **MIA(Lt FJ Connelly USAS. **POW**)

F6060 SE5a 32Sqn
OP left 4-15pm NEUILLY seen nrGRISOLLES **MIA(2Lt WA Anderson **KIA**) [?"SE5" claim Ltn W Blume Ja9]

B431 FE2b 38Sqn
NB OSTENDE **MIA(Lt LWDT Tratman **POW**/2Lt H Bosher **POW**) left 11-01pm

B186 SE5a 60Sqn
**OP left 4am combat with EA shot up dam returned 6am OK(Lt RK Whitney)

D3503 SE5a 60Sqn
OP AA 5-45am fuel tank hit ftl FORTEL cr corn dam(Lt JS Griffith US. **inj) had made several victory claims

C2221 DH9 98Sqn
+* combat with PfalzDIII[+des] FORÊT DE FÈRE 8am OK(Lt FC Wilton/Lt CP Harrison)

C6252 DH9 107Sqn
B left 6-33am COURMONT-FÈRE EN TARDENOIS **MIA(Lt FN Mollett **KIA**/2Lt B Rawlings **KIA**)

D5684 DH9 107Sqn
B left 6-33am **MIA(Capt RE Dubber **KIA**/Lt CB Dickie **KIA**)

F5849 DH9 107Sqn
**B left 6-33am MIA but OK?(Lt SS George/AM PG Mackie)

D3779 FE2b 149Sqn
NB left 10-30pm not seen **MIA(Lt RA Vosper **POW**/Lt A Smith **POW**)

E1404 Sopwith Camel 208Sqn
WT AA hit MERVILLE 6-30am fell ooc EoL **MIA(Lt WSK Scudamore **KIA**)

D6653 Sopwith Camel US 17th Pursuit Sqn
**P HA instruments shot up seNIEUPORT 9-30am engine failed ftl cr OK(1Lt FM Showalter)

C9665 H.P. 0/400 207Sqn
NB left 10-51pm VALENCIENNES-MONS Rlwy **MIA(Lt F Kemp **POW**/Lt WMF Bayliss **POW**/Lt G Rose **POW**)

3139 H.P. 0/100 216Sqn (I.F.)
*NB SAARBRÜCKEN ftl nrLUNEVILLE after raid wr MIA but OK(Lt JA Stronech/Sgt EC Carpenter/Lt B Norcross)

19th July

F6150 Sopwith Camel 43Sqn
SpM left 9-30am a Camel? seen going down in flames **MIA(Lt VRvT Irvine US. **KIA**) [?possible "Sopwith" claim combat NANTEUIL 10-50am Vzfw J Schwendemann Ja41: 43Sqn ops in south]

D6681 Sopwith Camel 46Sqn
BOP AA? seen dive on BAC dump 8000′ 5-45pm **MIA(2Lt HL Cross **POW**) left 5pm

E3921 SE5a 64Sqn
OP left 7am **MIA(2Lt JA vanTilburg **POW**)

D6896 SE5a 74Sqn
OP combat with HA shot up nABEELE 9-15am ftl(2Lt LA Richardson US. **WIA)to hospital

D6922 SE5a 74Sqn
+* attacked KB[+des] sARMENTIÈRES 5-40am OK(Lt S Carlin) 5 of his 10 claims were balloons

E5948 SE5a 74Sqn
OP left 8am seen ovMENIN 8-25am **MIA(Lt AM Roberts USAS. **POW**) [?"SE5" claim combat MOORSLEDE 8-30am Ltn J Jacobs Ja7]

E5940 SE5a 85Sqn
OP left 5pm seen ok MERVILLE 5-30pm **MIA(Lt DJ Trapp **KIA**)

D9586 Sopwith Camel 201Sqn
**KBP left 11-50am [+KB] AA fuel tank hit ftl AVELUY WOOD OK(Lt RSS Orr)

A7811 DH4 205Sqn
Phot AA then combat with 3 Fokker DVII[+ooc] RANCOURT 8-45am cr ldg OK(Lt JC Wilson **WIA/2Lt JB Leach OK) controls hit, spun 300′ ldg

C193 Sopwith Camel 209Sqn
SpM seen ovCAPPY a'dr 4-45am shot down **MIA(2Lt DB Griffith **KIA**) left 4-15am [Flak]

D9629 Sopwith Camel 209Sqn
SpM left 4-15am shot down ovCAPPY a'dr 4-45am **MIA(Lt E Scadding **POW**) hit by Flak?

3136 H.P. 0/100 216Sqn (I.F.)
NB SAARBRÜCKEN engine? forced to return ftl EoL **MIA(Lt AR Jones **POW**/Sgt G Harvey **POW**/Sgt JS Ayre **POW**)

20th July

B9273   Sopwith Camel   46Sqn
**B seen ok ovARMENTIÈRES going west 9000' 10am
MIA(Lt AJ Cyr **POW**) left 8am, DROs give date 19.7?
["Camel" claim combat ERQUINGHEM 10am UntOff
M Schumm Ja52]

D7234   DH9   49Sqn
**B combat with EA ovGRAND ROZOY 2000' seen
going down in control **MIA**(Sgt SJ Oliver **POW**/Sgt A
Davis **POW**) left 5-20pm SAPENEY

A7427   DH4   55Sqn (I.F.)
**B OBERNDORF mg shot down wr(Lt AD Keep MC
WIA/2Lt JF Pollock **KIA**)

A7876   DH4   55Sqn (I.F.)
B OBERNDORF seen neCOLMAR **MIA(Sgt FE
Nash **POW**/Sgt WE Baker **KIA**)

D9275   DH4   55Sqn (I.F.)
B shot down in flames ovOBERNDORF **MIA(Lt C
Young **KIA**/Lt RA Butler **KIA**)

55 Squadron was bombing the Oberndorf munition
works and was attacked over the target.

B7865   DH4   57Sqn
**BPhot RIENCOURT seen on return ovBAPAUME
11-10am **MIA**(Lt JT Kirkland **KIA**/2Lt EJ? Riley **POW**)
initials EI? left 9-25am ["DH4" claim combat ACHIET
LE PETIT 11-05am OffSt J Mai Ja5]

B5572   Sopwith Camel   70Sqn
**OP left 7-50am dived on by 3EA sPOELCAPPELLE
seen dive & land EoL after combat **MIA**(2Lt KR Angus
POW) [?"Camel" claim of driven down EA neYPRES
UntOff Huttenrauch Ja7?, but D6502 below more likely?]

C1670   Sopwith Camel   70Sqn
**BOP left 7-50am NE Army front combat with EA shot
up dam OK(2Lt RW Whalley) returned 9-30am

D6502   Sopwith Camel   70Sqn
**OP left 7-50am combat with EA eYPRES ~9-15am
MIA(2Lt T Conlan **POW**) [?"Camel" claim combat
PASSCHENDAELE 9-15am Ltn J vBusse
Ja20][?"Camel" claim combat nYPRES 9-15am UntOff
P Huttenrauch Ja7, but see B5572 above]

C3662   A.W.FK8   82Sqn
*CP left 7am rifle fire POUREY ftl wr OK(Lt EC
Grimes/2Lt GT Carr)

C1166   DH9   98Sqn
**B left 6-15am BAZOCHES Rlwy Jctn & A'dr AA hit
combat with EA dam OK(Lt F Carpenter/Lt Donkin)

F5843   DH9   98Sqn
**B left 6-15am BAZOCHES A'dr AA then EA cr dam
OK(Lt Roberts-Taylor/Lt Bates)

D1679   DH9   99Sqn (I.F.)
**B OFFENBURG Railways seen ovMOLCHEN
MIA(Lt FG Thompson **POW**/2Lt SC Thornley **POW**)
EAs attacked formation near objective, released POW?

[?"DH9" claim combat MORFAIN? 7-30am Ltn H
Drekmann Ja4]

C6200   DH9   103Sqn
**B combat ooc slow spin down ovARMENTIÈRES
wing crumpled **MIA**(2Lt SE Carson **KIA**/2Lt T Hawkins
KIA) left 8am [?"BF" claim combat WARNETON 10am
Ltn P Billik Ja52]

B7624   DH9   211Sqn
** combat with EA engine dam ftl LA PANNE
Beach(Capt HM Freland OK/Maj R Loraine **WIA**)

D9618   Sopwith Camel   203Sqn
+* combat with DFWCV[+des] seLESTREM 6pm
OK(Capt LH Rochford DSC DFC) shared

D1938   Sopwith Camel   US 17th Pursuit Sqn
**Esc(211Sqn) combat with 5 Fokker DVIIs
seOSTENDE 9am then seen nd 20000' EoL **MIA**(1Lt GP
Glenn **KIA**) left 8am ?combat eNIEUPORT 9-25am
Oblt T Osterkamp MFJaII]

D6595.N Sopwith Camel   US 17th Pursuit Sqn
**Esc(211Sqn) combat with 5 Fokker DVIIs[+flames?,+
ooc] 3m eOSTENDE 16000' 9-45am OK(1Lt RD
Williams)

17th Pursuit Squadron lost its first airman in this
fighting but also achieved its first combat victory.

21st July

E136   RE8   21Sqn
** **MIA**(Lt A Lewis **POW**/2Lt A Summerfelt **POW**)

C974   Bristol F2b   48Sqn
OP left 7-25pm LA MOTTE **MIA(2Lt BM Battey?
USAS. **POW**/2Lt J Gondre **POW**) name Batty?, seen in
formation going east ovLines with no EA about

B2490   Sopwith Camel   54Sqn
OP left 6pm seen in control ovFÈRE **MIA(2Lt B
Fisher **KIA**) ["Camel" claim combat nrFÈRE 7-15pm
Ltn W vRichthofen Ja11]

F2103   Sopwith Camel   54Sqn
**OP left 6-15pm combat with EA shot up cr nr a'dr
wr(Lt RT Cuffe **KIA**) killed in cr ldg

F2160   Sopwith Camel   54Sqn
OP left 6pm seen in control ovFÈRE 13000' **MIA(Lt
FW Dougall MC **KIA**?)

D1918   Sopwith Camel   73Sqn
**OP left 6-45pm combat with EA then seen ok going
north ok wBELLEAU but **MIA**(Maj RH Freeman **KIA**)
["Sopwith" claim combat FÈRE-EN-TARDENOIS Ltn
H vBülow Ja36]

C8647   A.W.FK8   82Sqn
**CP rifle fire POUREY cr n.m.l. OK(Capt JE Hibbert
MC/Lt LW Edmonds) left 7am, a'c shelled destroyed,
unsalvable

B500   FE2b   102Sqn
**NB left 10-35pm MIA but OK?(Lt JA Hoogterp/Lt EC
Harris)

** **MIA**(Lt Jackson **INT**/Lt Williams **INT**) interned
Holland, crew?

** **MIA**(2Lt E Dawson **INT**) interned Holland, repat
26.12.18, but see 5.11.1918?

22nd July

A day of fine weather in the Lys Valley saw some
heavy air fighting at all levels taking place. Australian SE5as and Camels typically met enemy during
their frequent low strafing and bombing attacks as
well as high up on offensive patrols. They made
several claims through the day.

108 Squadron arrived in France on the 22nd of
July equipped with DH9 day-bombers. Its first
operation would be a raid on Ostende Docks on the
12th of August.

| A.W.FK8 | | 2Sqn |
** (2Lt JC Gleave **WIA**)

| A7862 | DH4 | 18Sqn |
**B EA neLA BASSÉE & AA? seen spin down with EA
behind 4-20pm **MIA**(2Lt HC Tussaud **POW**/Sgt LG
Vredenburg **POW**) left 2-40pm ["DH4" claim combat
SANTE 4-30pm Ltn P Billik Ja52]

| F5832 | DH4 | 25Sqn |
**Phot engine shot through ftl 7-10pm OK(Lt S Jones/
Lt MF StClair-Fowles) left 5-10pm LANDRECIES

| D490 | DH9 | 27Sqn |
**B combat with EA MORT NOTRE DAME seen going
down in flames **MIA**(2Lt SM Feurer **KIA**/2Lt HB
Steckley **KIA**) left 3-55pm [?possible "DH" claim combat
CELLES 4pm Ltn K Seit Ja80]

| B180 | SE5a | 40Sqn |
**OP combat with Fokker DVII CARVIN 8-50am shot
down in flames **MIA**(Lt IL Roy **KIA**) left 8am, Ja29?
[?"SE5" claim combat LOOS 8-40am Oblt H Auffarth
Ja29][?"SE5" claim combat COURRIÈRES 8-40am
Vzfx Gregor Ja29] Roy had claimed his 10 victories in
this a'c in 2 weeks in July

| E1318 | SE5a | 40Sqn |
+* combat with Fokker DVII[+des] CARVIN 8-50am
OK(Lt RG Landis US.) EA from Ja30, achieved maybe
a dozen victories, mostly in this a'c

| D8087 | Bristol F2b | 52Sqn |
**AOb AA hit MONCHY 6-30pm ftl(Lt LR Brereton
WIA/2Lt GR LaCecilia **WIA**) made good ldg

| RE8 | | 53Sqn |
** (/2Lt JA Lewis **WIA**)

| D6183 | SE5a | 60Sqn |
**OP combat with Fokker DVII AVEDY WOOD
57c.N.18 at 5-25am **MIA**(Lt JEC MacVicker **KIA**) left
4-15am, combat with Pfalz? [?"SE5" claim combat ST
MARTIN 5-45am Ltn E Koch Ja32]

| F5810 | Bristol F2b | 62Sqn |
**OP seen dive on 3HA ovLAVENTIE 16000' 8-30am

MIA(2Lt WE Coulson **POW**/2Lt WHE Labatt **POW**)
left 7am ["BF" claim combat LESTREM 8-30am Ltn C
Degelow Ja40][?"BF" claim combat BUCQUOY? Ltn G
Meyer Ja37]

| D9478 | Sopwith Camel | 73Sqn |
**OP left 5pm seen sBAZOCHES combat with EA shot
down(Lt WSG Kidder **WIA POW**) [?"Sopwith 1Str"
claim combat QUESNOY 6-10pm Rtm K Bolle Ja2]

| D9492 | Sopwith Camel | 73Sqn |
+* combat with Fokker DVIIs[+ooc+des] BAZOCHES
6-10pm OK(Lt GL Graham) made 13 claims

| A.W.FK8 | | 82Sqn |
** (/2Lt P Evans **WIA**)

| DH9 | | 98Sqn |
**B FOREST DE NESLE AA fire shot up(/2Lt H Ridley
WIA)

| | | 99Sqn (I.F.) |
** hit on ground(2Lt FA Wood **WIA**)

| DH9 | | 103Sqn |
B AA fire(/2Lt JY Round **WIA)

| C1213 | DH9 | 103Sqn |
**B combat with HA going down EoL seen cr
HOUPLINES **MIA**(Lt CT Houston **KIA**/Lt JF? Clarke
KIA) initials JT? left 6am [?possible "DH" claim
combat YPRES 9am UntOff Reuss Ja7]

| C6179 | DH9 | 103Sqn |
**B shot up dam returned a'dr 8-30am OK(Lt Hallawell/
Sgt Watkinson) left 6am

| D3415 | Sopwith Camel | 203Sqn |
+* combat with DFWC[+des] BAUVIN 6-45am
OK(Capt LD Bawlf Can.)

| D9624 | Sopwith Camel | 203Sqn |
**OP left 9am combat with Fokker DVIIs ovCARVIN
10-35am **MIA**(Lt AE Rudge **KIA**) [?"Sopwith" claim
combat sLA BASSÉE 10-45am Vzfw E Wiehle Ja43]

| DH9 | | 206Sqn |
** (/Lt WH Binnie **KIA**)

| D9626 | Sopwith Camel | 210Sqn |
**OP combat with 2 Fokker DVIIs ROULERS 7000'
5-30pm **MIA**(2Lt EH Bullen USAS **POW**) to
OSTENDE [?"Camel" claim combat 5-20pm Ltn L
Beckmann Ja56]

| F5914.S | Sopwith Camel | 210Sqn |
**OP combat with 12 Fokker DVII 200' 5m sOSTENDE
7-30pm **MIA**(Capt HT Mellings DSC **KIA**) left 6-20pm
[?"Camel" claim combat COOLSCAMP but 5-20pm?
Ltn L Beckmann Ja56], Mellings had made his last few
of 15 victories in this a'c, including 2 that morning

23rd July

| D5108 | A.W.FK8 | 8Sqn |
TankCP left 6-10am **MIA(Lt HW Walker **KIA**/2Lt
GG Ashton **KIA**)

24th July

| | RE8 | 12Sqn |
** AA fire(Lt CR Pithey DFC **WIA**)

C4604   Bristol F2b   20Sqn
OP seen nARMENTIÈRES 8-20pm **MIA(Sgt HD Aldridge **POW**/Sgt MS Samson **POW**) left 7pm ["BF" claim combat ARMENTIÈRES 8pm Oblt H-E Gandert Ja51]

D7902   Bristol F2b   48Sqn
OP combat with EA ovFOUCAUCOURT seen fall in flames **MIA(2Lt SN Waddy **KIA**/Sgt WJ Shuker **KIA**) left 6am [?"BF" claim combat BRAY 7-30am Ltn G Meyer Ja37]

| | RE8 | 59Sqn |
** AA fire(Capt EH Leake MC **WIA**)

D6900   SE5a   64Sqn
OP seen 6-05pm combat shot down wSECLIN EoL **MIA(Capt PS Burge MC **KIA**) left 5pm [?possible "SE5" claim combat sHULLUCH UntOff M Schumm Ja52]

C3679   A.W.FK8   82Sqn
CP HA? gunshots ftl n.m.l.(2Lt ST Rekofski **WIA/2Lt MStJ Ross OK)

25th July

C976   Bristol F2b   20Sqn
OP shot down ovMENIN ~8-55am(Lt FJ Shearer **KIA/Sgt D Malpas **KIA**) left 7-51am ["Bristol" claim combat GHELUVELT 8-50am Ltn F Ritt vRöth Ja16]

| | DH4 | 27Sqn |
** (Lt RC Rogers **WIA**)

E5966   SE5a   32Sqn
OP combat with 7EAs FISMES 4000' 7-25pm **MIA(Lt HM Struben **POW**) left 5-45pm ["SE5" claim combat LOUPEIGNE 7-20pm Ltn R Klimke Ja27]

D1870   Sopwith Camel   43Sqn
OP left 5-45pm SOISSONS **MIA(Lt RE Meredith **KIA**?) [?"Sopwith" claim combat Ltn C Bolle Ja2]

D1894   Sopwith Camel   43Sqn
OP left 5-45pm SOISSONS **MIA(Lt FS Coghill **POW**) [?"Camel" claim combat Ltn H Frommherz Ja2]

D8197   Sopwith Camel   43Sqn
OP left 5-45pm SOISSONS **MIA(2Lt N Wilson **POW DoW** 18.10.18) ["Sopwith 1Str" claim combat FÈRE-EN-TARDENOIS pm Ltn G Bassenge Ja2]

C1929   SE5a   64Sqn
OP left 7am **MIA(Lt WR Henderson **WIA**? **POW**)

C6475   SE5a   64Sqn
OP combat with EA HESDIGNEUL 8-30am ftl cr ldg(Lt ML Howard **DoW)

C8734   SE5a   64Sqn
**OP left 7am combat with EA shot up dam returned a'dr 9am OK(Lt AS Barrett) [?possible combat nLORGIES 8-15am UntOff M Schumm Ja52]

B7874   Sopwith Camel   73Sqn
OP left 6pm combat with HA FISMES **MIA(2Lt KS Laurie **POW**) [?"Sopwith 1Str" claim combat FÈRE-EN-TARDENOIS pm Ltn K Bolle Ja2]["Camel" claim combat FISMES 6-50pm Ltn L Fr vRichthofen Ja11]

D1794   Sopwith Camel   73Sqn
OP left 6pm combat with HA FISMES **MIA(2Lt WA Armstrong **KIA**)

D9398   Sopwith Camel   73Sqn
OP left 6pm combat with HA FISMES **MIA(Lt RF Lewis **KIA**)

D9438.B   Sopwith Camel   73Sqn
+* combat with Fokker DVIIs[+des+ooc] sVILLERS 7pm OK(Lt EJ Lussier Can.) first of 11 claims

F6148   Sopwith Camel   80Sqn
OP combat with EA dam(2Lt WA Hallgren US. **WIA)slight

D5114   A.W.FK8   82Sqn
**Phot AA CHAUMAZY ftl dam OK(Capt WE Joseph/ 2Lt M StJ Ross)

D6914   SE5a   84Sqn
OP VILLERS BRETONNEAUX attacked KB[+des] sWARVILLERS 6-30am then combat with EA ftl wr(Capt JS Ralston MC **WIA) left 5-30am, last of 12 claims in SE5as

| | SE5a | 85Sqn |
** mg fire(Capt CBR Macdonald **WIA**)

B7583   DH9   98Sqn
B combat with 30EA CHÂTEAU THIERRY shot up dam(Lt Nichlos? OK/2Lt GK Carruthers **KIA) left 4-50am, name 2Lt JH Nicholass?

C6349   DH9   98Sqn
**B FÈRE? left 4-50am combat with 30EA EoL shot up dam OK(Capt OCW Johnson/Capt GHP Whitfield)

D7224.H   DH9   98Sqn
B left 4-30pm FÈRE? combat with 30EA shot up(Lt CH Roberts OK/Sgt GW Slater **DoW) DoW a few days later

D9585   Sopwith Camel   203Sqn
OP combat with EAs then going down in control EoL ftl 3000yd nwLA BASSÉE? 7-40am **MIA(Lt CF Brown **POW DoW** 3.8.18) left 6-30am ["Camel" claim combat GIVENCHY 7-40am Ltn P Billik Ja52][?"SE5" claim combat nLA BASSÈE UntOff M Hutterer Ja23]

| | DH4 | 205Sqn |
** AA fire(/2Lt PS Hartley **WIA**)

C6121   DH9   206Sqn
B combat with HA? 2m nGHELUWE 8-15am **MIA(2Lt FT Heron **KIA**/2Lt CJ Burne **KIA**) left 6-29am

D1889   Sopwith Camel   208Sqn
WT left 7-25am ESTAIRES ground mg? shot down ovWYTSCHAETE **MIA(Lt WA Carveth **POW**)

[?"Camel" claim combat WYTSCHAETE 8-35am Ltn C Degelow Ja40]

D9621   Sopwith Camel   209Sqn
OP seen in combat with HA eYPRES 8-40am shot down **MIA(2Lt AGS Blake **POW**) ["Camel" claim combat GHELUWE 8-55am Ltn L Beckmann Ja56]

D9636   Sopwith Camel   209Sqn
OP combat with HA swHOUTHEM 8-40am **MIA(Lt JH Siddall **KIA**) [?"SE" claim combat wYPRES 8-40am Ltn D Collin Ja56]

D2781.M DH9   211Sqn
B AA nrRAMSCAPELLE ftl **MIA(Sgt RS Gude **INT**/ Sgt HM Partridge **INT DoW**) left 11-35am, hit in rear cockpit, interned Holland

D9685?   H.P.0/400   215Sqn
** ground mg shot up(/2Lt FE King **WIA**/)

26th July

E1294   SE5a   85Sqn
**OP left 5-10am low combat with 2Str[+destr] LESTREM shot up ftl nr Lines ST FLORES OK(Lt DC Inglis NZ.)

E1295   SE5a   85Sqn
OP COLONNE-LESTREM combat with 2Str[+ destr] LESTREM then ground mg shot down in flames EoL cr **MIA(Maj EC Mannock MC DSO VC **KIA**) left 5-10am, all 8 victories by Mannock with 85Sqn claimed in this a'c

The second great English ace to be killed in July was Major Edward "Mick" Mannock. At the time of his death he had claimed around sixty enemy machines shot down but his final total may have been higher. Any assessment of this great pilot, however, extends far beyond a tally of his victories, for he inspired admiration in all who flew with him. He was a wonderful teacher and a selfless leader, and brought the very best out of his men. Undoubtedly, he had a dark side — he hated and loathed his enemy, and this instinct drove his skills.

Mannock had been given command of 85 Squadron on the 3rd of July, and in a very short time had moulded his men into a formidable fighting outfit. In the early light of the 26th, Mannock took off with a young New Zealander, Donald Inglis, to search the lines for enemy aircraft. Over the lines, Mannock spotted a two-seater and signalled the attack. Inglis and Mannock shot it down in flames, very low, and came out through heavy ground fire. Mannock was hit at this time, Inglis reporting that the last he saw of his commander was his machine catching fire and crashing. The final resting place of this great pilot has yet to be established. In 1919 he was posthumously awarded the Victoria Cross.

D1891   Sopwith Camel   209Sqn
OP combat shot down nCOMINES 7-30~7-40am **MIA(2Lt G Travers **POW**) [?"Camel" claim combat Serg Körner/Ltn Schulz FAbA258]

D6495   Sopwith Camel   209Sqn
P combat with Fokker DVII[+ooc] nCOMINES 7-20am shot up(2Lt AL Porter US. **WIA) shared with B7471 & C198

27th July

D8022   Bristol F2b   88Sqn
**OP combat with EA ftl BEVEREN 8pm cr nrLines OK(Lt RJ Cullen/Lt EH Ward)unsalvable

28th July

Sopwith Camel   3Sqn
Prac ldg (2Lt JG Galbraith **WIA)

D1901   Sopwith Camel   4Sqn AFC
B ARMENTIÈRES RLY combat with LVGC[+cr] 4-20am & ground fire cr ST POL(Lt GS Jones-Evans Can. **WIA) crawled 1m to safety

D6632   Sopwith Camel   4Sqn AFC
B seen ok CANDEN ABBÉ 4-35am AA engine hit: lagging ftl EoL by EAs ovESTAIRES **MIA(2Lt AFG McCulloch UK. **POW**)

A7911   DH4   18Sqn
B combat shot up 5-30am ftl cr(2Lt A Pickin **inj/Sgt W Dyke DCM **WIA**) ESTRÉE-COUCHY

B2065   DH4   18Sqn
B seen ok VITRY-QUIERY LA MOTTE ~7-45am then ftl EoL **MIA(Lt RV Irwin **POW**/Sgt GH Tench MM **POW DoW**) left 6am ["DH4" claim combat CROISILLES 7-45am Ltn E Koch Ja32]

E5964   SE5a   29Sqn
+* combat with 2Str[+ooc] swMERVILLE 8-15am OK(Lt HC Rath Can.) shared, first of 12 claims, many in this a'c

C8296   Sopwith Camel   73Sqn
P seen in combat with 7 Fokker DVIIs[+flames] ovFÈRE-EN-TARDENOIS 2pm but shot down **MIA(Lt WS Stephenson Can. MC **POW**) left 6-20pm ["Camel" claim combat eSAPONAY 6-50pm Ltn J Grassmann Ja10], claimed 12 EA, 9 in this a'c in July

Bristol F2b   88Sqn
** AA fire(/Lt CB Marshall **WIA**)

E1408   Sopwith Camel   208Sqn
** left 8am seen ok going east ovLILLERS **MIA**(Sgt D Tottman **POW**)

29th July

D5021   A.W.FK8   2Sqn
**AReg AA ftl MAZINGARBE dam ldg ALG 12-45pm OK(Lt HJC Spencer/2Lt TB Lamble) left 10-50am

D9442   Sopwith Camel   70Sqn
+* combat with Fokker DVII[+des] eARMENTIÈRES

7-15pm OK(Capt WM Carlaw) made 12 claims

D9498   Sopwith Camel   73Sqn
OP left? 4pm combat with EA FISMES **MIA(2Lt E
Cotton **KIA**) [?"Camel" claim combat Ltn F Büchner
Ja13]

C6496   SE5a   84Sqn
+* combat with LVGC[+des] nBOIS DE TAILLES
nrBRAY 8am OK(Capt HWL Saunders SA.) last of 15
claims by this pilot

D8402   DH4   202Sqn
**EscRec combat with 8EA[++ooc] TERVAETE
9-30am shot up ftl ROUSBRUGGE(Lt W Chalaire
USNR. **WIA**/Pte AE Humphrey **WIA**) ?combat
sGUDEKAPELLE? Oblt T Osterkamp MFJaII]

**   DH9   206Sqn**
B (/Cpl H Williams **WIA /Sgt LH Rowe **WIA**), crew?

B7668   DH9   206Sqn
**B seen ovCOURTRAI wMENIN nrROULERS
ROAD 7-20pm **MIA**(1Lt G Cheston USAS. **KIA**/Cpl
JW Pacey **WIA**? **POW**?) left 5-35pm [?"BF" claim
combat GHELUVELT 7-35pm Ltn F Ritt vRöth Ja16]

F5848   DH9   206Sqn
**B shot up ROUSBRUGGE-HARINGHE ftl(Lt RH
Stainbank **inj**/2Lt EW Richardson **inj**) left 5-35pm

A7863   DH4   217Sqn
+*SubP combat Brandenburg W29 seaplane[+des]
7-40pm OK(Lt AMcM Phillips Can./Lt NS Dougall)
shared, this was a new monoplane fighter seaplane

A7941   DH4   217Sqn
+*SubP combat Brandenburg W29 seaplane[+des]
7-40pm OK(Lt RG Shaw/Lt VGA Tonge) shared

30th July

C904   Bristol F2b   20Sqn
P seen in flames **MIA(1Lt GH Zellers USAS. **KIA**/Sgt
JD Cormack **KIA**) left 6-25pm

E2471   Bristol F2b   20Sqn
** broke up in flames 10000' **MIA**(Sgt JJ Cowell MM
KIA/Cpl C Hill **KIA**) left 6-25pm ["BF" claim combat
sYPRES 8pm Ltn F Ritt vRöth Ja16] Cowell made 16
claims, the last the day before

F6087   Sopwith Camel   43Sqn
OP left 5-25pm combat?(Lt LH Parsons **inj?) was MIA
[?"Camel" claim combat SAPONAY 7-10pm Ltn E
Loewenhardt Ja10]

E2   RE8   52Sqn
B MARTINPUICH **MIA(Capt RT Barlow **KIA**/2Lt
HG Scott **KIA**) left 9-25am

C2237   RE8   52Sqn
**B combat with HA shot down destroyed by fire(2Lt
STC Roberts **KIA**/2Lt DP Ogilvy **KIA**) left 9-25am
MARTINPUICH ["RE" claim combat nwROMAN
ROAD Vzfw O Hennrich Ja46]

C5056   RE8   52Sqn
**B combat with HA shot down destroyed by fire(Lt KV
King **KIA**/2Lt J Kelly **KIA**) left 9-25am MAILLY-
MAILLET [?"BF" claim combat swALBERT Vzfw M
Hutterer Ja23]

E53   RE8   52Sqn
**B combat with EA shot up dam(Lt RW Frean OK/2Lt
HH Fitzsimmons **WIA**)to hospital

B7867   Sopwith Camel   73Sqn
**OP left 6pm fuel tank shot up dam OK(Lt GW
Gorman)

D9480   Sopwith Camel   73Sqn
OP left 1-30pm seen ovFÈRE EoL going west **MIA(Lt
KWA Symons **KIA**) FÈRE-EN-TARDENOIS [?"Camel"
claim combat ARCY 2-10pm Ltn E Loewenhardt Ja10]

D6895   SE5a   74Sqn
**SpM gunfire dam combat RumplerC[+flames]
CASSELL-YPRES 12-10pm then LVGC[+des]
MERVILLE 12-30pm then ftl cr 12-50pm OK(Capt JIT
Jones) left 11-30am [?"SE5" claim combat nwLE
QUESNEL Offst R Heibert Ja46] last of 13 victories in
this a'c

E1400   SE5a   74Sqn
+* combat with PfalzDIII[+des] MERVILLE 11-45am
OK(Capt AC Kiddie SA.) scored over a dozen victories

C6210   DH9   99Sqn (I.F.)
**B mg radiator hit on return cr ldg JAENINENIE
wr(2Lt G Martin **WIA**/2Lt SG Burton **KIA**)

D7223   DH9   99Sqn (I.F.)
**B combat with 5EAs broke up nwSCHLETTSTADT,
eLILLE **MIA**(1Lt P Dietz USAS. **KIA**/2Lt HW Batty
KIA)

99 Squadron had set out to bomb Stuttgart but
found low cloud as they neared the target. The
town of Lahr was therefore bombed instead, but
their activities attracted a large formation of enemy
fighters. Three enemy were claimed destroyed and
another two shot down out of control, but the above
crew was also lost east of the lines.

31st July

**   Sopwith Camel   4Sqn AFC**
** combat with LVGC[+des] WAVRIN then Fokker
DVII[+des] eESTAIRES shot up(Capt EJ Kingston-
McCloughry **WIA**)

E1482   Sopwith Camel   4Sqn AFC
+* combat with Fokker DVII[+ooc] swESTAIRES
11-35am OK(Lt TCR Baker) first of 6 victories in this a'c

These and several other claims were made in
fighting for possession of the sky over Aubers
Ridge. Eight LVGs being escorted by nine Fokkers
were met and fought in the morning by 4 Squadron
AFC. 2 AFC were also active in the same area.

C2420, D4735 RE8s   5Sqn
** destroyed by enemy bombing on a'dr burnt

13Sqn
** (/2Lt WN Van Someren **WIA**) wounded in enemy
bombing raid

DH4   18Sqn
** (/Capt D Gale **WIA**)

C859   Bristol F2b   20Sqn
OP seen ok? seMERVILLE 7-30pm **MIA(Lt WH Shell
POW/Sgt JDC Summers **POW**) left 5-45pm
[?Ja18][?"BF" claim combat VIEUX BERQUIN
7-30pm Oblt H Auffahrt Ja29]

E1310   SE5a   40Sqn
**OP:lone left 8-15am combat with HannoverC[+destr]
LAVENTIE then shot down EoL **MIA**(Capt GEH
McElroy Irl. MC DFC **KIA**) buried sLAVENTIE-
ARMENTIÈRES RLWY, his last of probably 47
victories [?"SE5" claim combat ARMENTIÈRES
9-05am Vzfw Gullmann Ja56]

C2308   RE8   53Sqn
**NF:experimental British AA? accident? cr 10-30pm
MIA(Lt KA Ranney **KIA**/2Lt HS Smith **KIA**)

C8274   Sopwith Camel   70Sqn
OP left 6-35pm seen ok eZILLEBEKE **MIA(2Lt WJ
Hutchinson **POW**) [?"Camel" claim combat
swROULERS 7-30pm, but see 204Sq a'c, Ltn K Plauth
Ja20]

D6602   Sopwith Camel   70Sqn
**BOP left 4-35pm combat with EA shot up dam
returned 6-30pm OK(Lt RW Whalley)

C6145   DH9   99Sqn (I.F.)
**B SAARBRÜCKEN shot down 6000' ovSTAVOLD
MIA(Lt EL Doidge Can. **KIA**/Lt HT Melville **KIA**)

C6149   DH9   99Sqn (I.F.)
B combat with EA nDIEUZE **MIA(2Lt TM Ritchie
POW/2Lt LWG Stagg **DoW**)

C6196   DH9   99Sqn (I.F.)
B shot up ovSTAVOLD radiator hit ftl **MIA(Lt WJ
Garrity Can. **POW**/2Lt GH Stephenson **POW**)

C6278   DH9   99Sqn (I.F.)
B combat with EA nDIEUZE **MIA(Lt SMcB Black
Can. **POW**/2Lt E Singleton **POW**)

D1029   DH9   99Sqn (I.F.)
B engine hit ovSTAVOLD ftl **MIA(2Lt F Smith
POW/2Lt KH Ashton **POW**)

D1032   DH9   99Sqn (I.F.)
B combat ~40EAs nDIEUZE **MIA(2Lt LR Dennis
KIA/2Lt FW Woolley **KIA**) [?DH9 claim combat
GROSSBLITTERSDORF? Ltn K Monnington Ja18]

D3039   DH9   99Sqn (I.F.)
**B combat shot down in control ovPUTTELANG
MIA(Lt MTS Papenfus DFC **WIA POW**/Lt AL
Benjamin **POW**) pilot hit in back & temporarily
collapsed over controls, but managed to make forced ldg

The heaviest air fighting involving a squadron of
the Independent Force in July took place on a raid
by 99 Squadron. Twelve machines had set out at
5-30am for Mainz but three had dropped away
with engine trouble before the lines were reached.
The first enemy attacks came over Saaralbe where
the first DH9 was lost. The eight remaining
machines pressed on, only to be met by a huge
formation waiting for them near Saarbrücken. The
enemy machines numbered about forty, and three
more DH9s were shot down before the patrol could
move on. The leader decided that the bombs
should be dropped on Saarbrücken itself and the
railway station was hit. After the raid the group
was attacked once more, and this time another
three machines were eventually shot down, leaving
two from the original twelve to recross the
lines

The loss of fourteen officers in a single raid was
a terrible disaster for the Squadron. It is understood that many were newly arrived with the unit
and their inexperience of formation flying in war
conditions may have cost them dearly. The casualties for the Independent Force in the coming weeks
were to be generally heavy. In particular, it was
shaken by the continuing losses suffered in DH9s.
Another unit equipped with the type, 104
Squadron, was forced to stop active duties on three
separate occasions in order to regroup after losses.
The DH9's faults in combination made it a terrible
aircraft for the role it had been given, and most of
these were caused in some way by its weak and
unreliable engine. This unreliability meant that
many machines were forced to drop out of operations long before the target was even approached.
Its poor performance also meant that crews could
not keep up in formation, which was the key to
defensive survival in day bombing. Its low operational ceiling also drew it down into comfortable
attacking levels for the enemy fighters. Matters
finally came to a head in August when Trenchard
insisted the DH9 be withdrawn as a service type.
This could not be achieved overnight, or even in
several weeks, and crews battled on with them until
the end of the war. The DH9A was the notional
replacement, but it was introduced very slowly
and, it will be seen, had its own baptism of fire with
the Independent Force (see 110 Squadron entries
in September).

DH9   103Sqn
** (/2Lt K Nixon **WIA**)

203Sqn
** (2Lt W Towell **WIA**)
** (Lt CH Lick **WIA**)
** (Lt YES Kirkpatrick **WIA**)

All the above were wounded in an enemy bombing raid.

B7234   Sopwith Camel   204Sqn
"LAURA" ** combat with 10 Fokker DVIIs ovROULERS
& mg **MIA**(Lt RL Hollingsworth **POW**) left 6pm
[?"Camel" claim combat swROULERS 7-30pm, but see 70Sq a'c, Ltn K Plauth Ja20]

D3394   Sopwith Camel   204Sqn
** combat with 10 Fokker DVIIS ovROULERS then shot down mg **MIA**(Lt JE Gow **POW DoW** 10.8.18) left 6pm

D8182   Sopwith Camel   204Sqn
** combat with 10 Fokker DVIIs ovROULERS then shot down by mg **MIA**(Lt J Farquhar **POW DoW** 1.8.18) left 6pm [?"Camel" claim combat HOOGLEDE 7-40pm UntOff P Huttenrauch Ja7]

F1314   Sopwith Camel   208Sqn
OP combat LA BASSÉE seen spin ooc ovBETHUNE **MIA(Lt LC Gilmour **POW**) left 10-45am

D3326   Sopwith Camel   213Sqn
** combat with EA ftl(Lt ML Cooper Irl. **WIA**) had made 6 claims

D5717   DH9   218Sqn
B ZEEBRUGGE AA hit engine ftl **MIA(Lt LWC Pearce **INT**/2Lt FH Bugge **INT**) interned Holland

2ASD
** (Sgt FJ Wallis **WIA**)

D1046   DH9   2ASD
ferrying to IX Brigade area when south **MIA(Lt DC Townley **POW**) a'c captured

August 1918

THE TIDE TURNS:
THE AMIENS OFFENSIVE

After the victories on the Marne the tide of war turned decisively in favour of the Allies. The German Army was poised on the edge of disarray, although its reserves still left it a formidable threat. The dilemma facing the German Air Force was a microcosm of this. Most of its best fighter forces were now concentrated into the huge Marne-Amiens salient, but they could never again be employed in massed large scale attacks as had once been possible. All their efforts were to be directed towards fighting an ever growing and more numerous enemy in order to protect their army from destruction.

Before a decisive blow could be delivered, however, the Allies would have to tear at the German Army's real inner strength, which at this time rested in the advance it had made on the Somme. To this end, Foch handed the initiative to Haig, who had been secretly planning an attack on the Amiens front. Late July had already seen some encouraging recovery of territory by the Allies. Meteren, near Bailleul in the Lys, had been recaptured on the 19th, and south of Amiens, the French had pushed the German forces back to the Avre River. A more damaging attack was needed, however, before Germany properly reorganised for its survival. In fact, Haig now believed Germany could be beaten in months, and an offensive which drove them from around Amiens would give proper security to the supply networks in order to achieve this.

The date set for the attack was the 8th of August and it was to be carried out by Rawlinson's Fourth Army and the French First Army. The Fourth Army's original objective had been to occupy and make secure the old Amiens defence line, between Mericourt and Hengest. Whilst this remained the initial focus for attack, Allied optimism soon extended the plan and objectives then moved successively deeper. Chaulnes and Roye were encompassed and then, days before the battle, Haig made distant Ham on the Somme river the final objective. The confusion during preparations which derived from these revisions introduced a crucial flaw into the battle plans: some commanders becoming uncertain about the extent and purpose of the attack. Rawlinson, for instance, continued to prepare his Fourth Army for success in the early battle whilst at the highest command levels it was the extended phase following the exploitation of the breakthrough which increasingly held their interest. This diversity of understanding naturally filtered down to the commands of the different RAF brigades who were to support the Army.

The lessons of economy and co-ordination in Monash's attack on Villers Bretonneaux had been well absorbed and would provide the techniques for the battle. A massed tank and aircraft assault would again replace the preliminary bombardment, artillery coming to its fullest use from the time of the advance. The RAF would play a pivotal role, supporting the highly organised infantry and attacking in unison with the tank advance. Three additional British divisions would be available in reserve to exploit the early progress which was expected.

1st August

Sopwith Dolphin 23Sqn
** combat(Capt JM McAlery **WIA**)

C1116 SE5a 29Sqn
**OP left 7-55pm AA hit controls ftl cr dam OK(Lt WW Lauer)

SE5a 64Sqn
B (2Lt GT Oldmstead **DoW)

D2960 DH9 104Sqn (I.F.)
B formation met 24EAs fuel tank hit ovMETZ seen dive for Line **MIA(Lt WH Goodale **KIA**/2Lt LC Prentice USAS. **KIA**) [possible "DH4" claim combat WIEGINGEN UntOff H Marwede Ja67]

104 Squadron's target of Karthaus was found covered in mist when reached, so Trèves railway workshops were bombed instead. The formation was attacked over Trèves and again near Boulay aerodrome.

B3884 Sopwith Camel 201Sqn
OP left 7-45am combat with HA ftl nrBOESCHAPE Sh27.R.16.b.(Lt BL McCarthy **WIA)to hospital

DH9 206Sqn
** combat(/2Lt FJ Paget **WIA**)

D2855 DH9 206Sqn
B seen MENIN 8-40am **MIA(Capt JW Mathews **KIA**/2Lt WA John **KIA**) left 6-40am [?unconfirmed "DH4" claim combat YPRES 8-45am Ltn L Beckmann Ja56][?possible unconfirmed DH9 claim combat LOVENINGEN? 8-40am Ltn K Seit Ja80]

2nd August

RAF
exNaval Unit? ** **MIA**(Capt EP Hardman **POW**) repat 20.11.18

B1168 Bristol F2b 20Sqn
OP shot up? ftl sAIRE 36A 03.1(Lt JJ Quinn **WIA/Pbr K Penrose **WIA**)

3rd August

A.W.FK8 2Sqn
** AA(2Lt DM Pinkerton **WIA**)

RE8 7Sqn
** mg fire(/2Lt AB Mellor **WIA**)

D4882 RE8 9Sqn
LRec left 4-15pm **MIA(Lt AF Forsyth **WIA POW**/2Lt ES Coombes **POW**)

C2518 RE8 16Sqn
AOb driven down by 3HA eVIMY T.22 cr 6-55pm(Lt PC West **KIA/Lt CV Todman **KIA**) ["RE" claim combat VIMY 6-40pm Ltn P Billik Ja52]

RE8 21Sqn
** mg fire(Lt RE Norman **WIA**)

D9411 Sopwith Camel 46Sqn
**OP left 6-05pm Fifth Army area combat with Fokker DVII[+des] eLENS 6-35pm shot up dam returned 7-50pm OK(Lt CH Sawyer) first of 6 claims

RE8 53Sqn
** mg ground fire(/2Lt C Whitehead **WIA**)

DH4 57Sqn
** combat(/Sgt CG Sowden **WIA**)

C3887 Sopwith Dolphin 79Sqn
+* attacked KB[+des] nESTAIRES 7-35am OK(Lt FW Gillet US.) first victory for this high scoring Dolphin ace

E5159 Sopwith Camel US 17th Pursuit Sqn
OP combat shot down in flames 1.5m sROULERS 9-15am **MIA(Lt MK Spidle **KIA**) seen in formation [?"Camel" claim combat STADENBERG 8-40am Ltn L Beckmann Ja56]

4th August

RE8 12Sqn
** AA fire(/2Lt GG Traviss **WIA**) name Travins?

D6154.C SE5a 41Sqn
**OP MOREUIL AA shot up dam ftl 1-25pm OK(Lt A Goby) left 11-30am

D6958 SE5a 74Sqn
+* combat with HannoverC[+des] wESTAIRES 5-10pm OK(Capt JIT Jones) last few of 37 victories in this a'c

C3879.Q Sopwith Dolphin 79Sqn
+* combat with Fokker DVII[+des] NEUVE EGLISE 8-40am OK(Lt RB Bannerman) first of 17 claims, most in this a'c

D4567 H.P.0/400 215Sqn
NB FIVES Rlwy Stn **MIA(Lt HL Hammond **KIA**/2Lt WH Brinkworth **KIA**/Sgt HT Pheby **KIA**) left 11-50pm 3.8.18

RAF
ex Naval Unit? ** **MIA**(Capt H Rampling **INT**) interned Holland, repat?

5th August

RE8 7Sqn
** mg ground fire(2Lt KVC Lewis **WIA**)

RE8 42Sqn
** mg ground fire(Capt D Puckle **WIA**)

6th August

AIR SUPPORT FOR THE BATTLE OF AMIENS

Tactical surprise was an essential ingredient of the planned attack for the enemy was known to have significant reserves in the north, some of which could be quickly brought down. For the British and French to achieve such a large build-up of men, weapons, and equipment as they did in these circumstances showed a new tactical sophistication. The RAF contributed to maintaining

security in a number of ways. On the the 27th of July secret orders had been issued which intended to draw attention away from the Somme. These provided for the RAF presence and general activity in Flanders, especially that with the Second Army, to be artificially increased until the 6th of August. From the 6th until the 8th, activity over the First and Fifth Armies was also built up. It was essential to prevent any enemy air reconnaissance of what was happening. Poor weather in the first week of August greatly assisted in this, and only on the 7th did German aircraft threaten to detect the growing army. These were soon seen off by British fighters. Some RAF patrols east of the lines were made specifically to check that the build-up was remaining invisible from the enemy's air space.

The plans for the use of the RAF on the first day of the battle show that a lucid understanding of the value of air power had now been achieved. That its main role was crucially redirected after only several hours of fighting does not essentially detract from this. The tasks allotted were so precise and appropriate to an unfolding air offensive that it is worth referring to the Official History:

(i) At daybreak the bomber squadrons were to attack aerodromes on the Fourth Army front, with the fighter squadrons giving their support. These were at St Christ, Ennemain, Bray Station, and Moislains.

(ii) The fighter squadrons afterwards were to stand by ready to operate on the Fourth Army front if enemy activity became important (namely, offensive patrolling in protection of low flying aircraft), and

(iii) The day-bomber squadrons were to attack in the evening, with the help of the fighter squadrons, the railway stations at Peronne and Chaulnes, Marchelepot, Villers Carbonnel, and Etricourt.

In order to allay suspicion of an attack, build-ups of aircraft into the Fourth Army front were delayed as long as possible, their markings altered, and their use restricted to the operations related to those mentioned above. This was why the enemy airfields in the sector were to be attacked at the outset — it would be the first real chance to strike at the enemy. Attacks on the rail system were also to be delayed until the evening because it was reasoned that substantial reinforcements would only begin arriving at that time. To ensure maximum effectiveness for the fighters they also were to be brought up closer to the fighting and would operate from advanced landing grounds.

The British air concentration assembled for the battle was considerable, indicating the very important role it was to play in support of the Fourth

Army. It was made up of the following units: V Brigade consisted of 15 (Corps) Wing, being Nos. 3 AFC, 5, 6, and 9 Squadrons (RE8s), and 8 and 35 Squadrons (FK8s). Of these, special duties were to be performed by 8 and 9 Squadrons. 8 Squadron would co-operate with the tank advance. Three hundred and twenty-four heavy tanks and ninety-six small Whippet Tanks would take part, and this work was still in its pioneering stages. 9 Squadron would repeat its ammunition dropping to the infantry. V Brigade also included 22 (Army) Wing, with the following fighter squadrons: Nos. 23 (Sopwith Dolphins), 24, 41, and 84 (SE5as), and 65, 80, 201, and 209 (Sopwith Camels), as well as 48 Squadron (Bristol Fighters on fighter-reconnaissance), 205 Squadron (DH4 day-bombers), and No. 101 Squadron (FE2bs) carrying out night bombing.

IX Brigade was also available, consisting of fighter squadrons Nos. 1 and 32 (SE5as), 43, 54, and 73 Squadrons (Sopwith Camels), as well as 151 Squadron (Night Fighter Sopwith Camels). In the same brigade fighter reconnaissance was supplied by Nos. 25 (DH4) and 62 Squadrons (Bristol Fighters), day bombing by Nos. 27, 49, 98, and 107 (all DH9), and night bombing by Nos. 58 and 83 Squadrons (FE2bs) and 207 and 215 Squadrons (HP 0/400s). The night before the attack 207 Squadron's Handley Page twin-engined bombers were to fly about the front to muffle the sound of massing tanks. It transpired that it was a filthy night for this work, and the two pilots who managed to get their bombers aloft and complete almost three hours of flying in dense fog both received the DFC. These were Canadians Lt GA Flavelle and Lt WJ Peace (see entries below).

Yet another nine squadrons were to be made available as required from adjacent fronts. From III Brigade there were the fighter squadrons Nos. 3 (Sopwith Camels), 56 and 60 (SE5as), and 87 (Sopwith Dolphins), 11 Squadron (Bristol Fighters) in fighter reconnaissance, 57 (DH4) day bombing, and 102 Squadron (FE2bs) as night-bombers. Finally, day bombing units Nos. 18 (DH4) and 103 (DH9) came from I and X Brigade respectively. The total strength of British aircraft available for the offensive was eight hundred.

By the time the Allies began their offensive in front of Amiens the German Air Force was in serious decline. The Official History gives the figure of German aircraft in the area of the fighting on the 8th of August as only three hundred and sixty-five, of which only one hundred and forty-five were fighters. This lack of enemy air presence certainly assisted in keeping the build-up secret.

However, these figures are misleading for there were many more machines on nearby fronts, particularly in Champagne. Indeed, by the afternoon of the 8th substantial numbers of units began to arrive, so that by the evening a little under three hundred new aircraft were available. The speed with which Germany assembled its reinforcements was one factor underestimated by the Allies. Many of these were actually operational by 4-30pm and the formidable Fokker DVII, now powered by the 185hp BMW engine, was common amongst them. It was an aircraft capable of inflicting tremendous damage, the new engine lifting its top speed to 125 miles per hour and giving it an unsurpassed rate of climb. Nevertheless, the fact remained that they were now opposing forces with overwhelming reserves — the RAF had almost eighteen hundred machines, the Americans over seven hundred, and the French three thousand. Whatever combat success a combination of great aircraft and individual bravery might now give the German Air Force, the numerical superiority of the Allies would now always prevail.

D8248   Sopwith Camel   65Sqn
**OP air collision with Camel F6069
ovCARDONNETTE wr(Lt ML Green **KIA**)

F6069   Sopwith Camel   65Sqn
**OP air collision with Camel D8248
ovCARDONNETTE wr 7-30pm(2Lt SA Smith **KIA**)

7th August

C2307   RE8   4Sqn
Rec left 4-45am spin cr 5-15am(2Lt WA Isaac **KIA/
2Lt CG Weir **KIA**) KIFA?

C6279   DH9   27Sqn
**B AA shot through IZEL LE HAMEAU 11am ftl
OK(2Lt HM Brown/Sgt HW Cornell)

C1944   SE5a   84Sqn
**OP seen dive East ovLE QUESNEL 9-50am(Sgt HJN
Guy **WIA POW**) ["SE5" claim combat HANGARD 9am
Oblt Ritt vGreim JGr 9]

B7813   FE2b   101Sqn
NB left 9-30pm **MIA(2Lt JD Anderson **POW**/2Lt
CEA Lovell **POW**)

C6289   DH9   206Sqn
B seen NEUVE EGLISE **MIA(Lt FA Brock MM
KIA/Pte CH Cullimore **KIA**) left 5-30am

D5816   DH9   206Sqn
**B combat with EA forced down cr nrGRASSE
PAYELLE wr(Lt JFS Percival **inj**/2Lt J Lowthian **inj**)
left 5-30am

8th August
THE BATTLE OF AMIENS

The Amiens offensive opened with a deafening artillery barrage from over two thousand guns at 4-20am. Moments later, the combined assault of infantry and tanks commenced along a twenty-mile front between Morlancourt and La Neuville on the Avre. Australian and Canadian Corps were the main strike force and would fight magnificently. There was a heavy ground mist which hid the attackers until they were well advanced onto their initial targets — the German Army was in any case taken by complete surprise and offered slight opposition. By the end of a catastrophic day for them they had been pushed back between seven and eight miles in places.

For the RAF it was to be one of the most important and complex days of fighting the RAF had ever undertaken. The manner in which they threw themselves into the desperate events of the 8th is nowhere better illustrated than by the thick file of RAF Casualty Reports from the fighting which resides in the Public Record Office in London. There is no other day on which casualties remotely approach those sustained this day.

Their main role was to carry out an unprecedented level of liaison with troops and tanks in support of the general ground assault through contact patrolling and low attack work. As well as this close co-operation its more conventional tasks were everywhere to be carried out. These included artillery work, bombing, and offensive patrolling to interfere with enemy reconnaissance gathering as well as to intercept enemy fighters and attack aircraft before they could inflict damage. Aircraft had already been in the air as the guns began, but their early effectiveness was hindered by the gloomy conditions. These cleared around 9am, and after that time, contact patrolling and registering of enemy guns as they came into action began in earnest. The fluid and fast evolving state of the fighting was to make Corps work increasingly difficult. Bombing of enemy aerodromes took place early as planned, but the mist left the results confused and uncertain. The crippling of the enemy air force was certainly not achieved, and the machines which escaped were to form the basis of some tellingly stiff opposition.

To aid control, the front was divided up into Northern, Central, and Southern sectors. To help understand where air attacks were being carried out, the V Brigade fighter squadrons were allocated these areas as follows: 48 and 80 Squadrons in the northern; 41, 84, and 201 Squadrons the Central;

and 23, 24, and 209 Squadrons the Southern. 65 Squadron was operating with the Cavalry and one flight of 48 Squadron was allocated for low reconnaissance work. After the fog cleared these fighter squadrons, all from 22 Wing, concentrated on low ground attacks, for which they had a special responsibility. Their pilots soon found they were flying over a chaotic rout which offered an abundance of targets. Fighters operated in pairs and a constant stream of patrols was carried out. There were many hundreds of bombing and machine-gun attacks on troops, trains, gun positions, and along roads crowded with the escaping army. The first British objective had been reached with crushing speed in a few hours. This was the line Demuin-Marcelcave-Cerisy-Morlancourt. Those who had made the successful assault stood aside to permit the reserves to come through and continue the attack.

About midday, reconnaissance reports were coming in of enormous activity on the bridges across the Somme — there were eleven of these. The initial assault had been launched with extraordinary success, and now a chance was offered to richly exploit the situation by destroying these life lines for the enemy.

The RAF had dominated the air through the morning. In the early afternoon, however, a most important event occurred, for Major-General Salmond ordered the cancellation of all IX Brigade day-bombing planned for the afternoon and the commencement of a new offensive against these bridges on the Somme which were to be bombed to destruction. It was anticipated that by this action, absolute chaos at these centres of activity would be caused and the German retreat dealt a devastating blow.

The problems which then ensued for the Air Force mirrored something of the confusion about objectives which was surfacing on the ground. By ordering the air assaults on the bridges the crucial bombing programme against reinforcements was to be delayed, whilst the fighter squadrons of IX Brigade were also ordered to join the bombing raids — not as escorts but as bombers themselves — so their planned work was similarly abandoned. The early morning bombing of aerodromes would also never be repeated.

The support of the advance, although in theory a separate task for the RAF, suffered from these changes. If the attacks on the bridges had been successful then the battle may well have ended in disaster for the enemy, but in general it has to be said success was limited. Two hundred and five individual bombing flights were made on the

bridges on the 8th, and twelve tons of bombs were dropped. All bridges still stood by the evening however, and others were being constructed, and throughout the battle the RAF was to be met by a blistering defence in the air. By the time the attacks were being hastily dispatched, the German Air Force was increasingly active in the battle. Fighter reinforcements including Jagdgeschwader 1 were now present, and their orders were to come down low and assist their artillery and contact patrols. It would have been soon apparent to these pilots, however, that the threat posed to the crossings was of the direst kind, and almost immediately their entire effort was turned over to the defence of the bridges.

The task for the German fighters was also helped by the fact that a number of their aerodromes were relatively near the river. Furthermore, the RAF was bombing at low levels and so could be engaged moments after a warning of an attack had been received. The German fighters flew ceaselessly through the day — they needed to. Some of their pilots recorded ten hours in the air, and in consequence of the commitment by both sides there were some titanic struggles in the afternoon and evening. A number of these are touched on in the entries and the heavy losses involved to both sides are all too evident. About two-thirds of the forty-five RAF machines lost on the 8th were shot down in fighting for the crossings, whilst the German units suffered terribly as well. One reason for this, which shows a transformation in the air war as profound as any which had been experienced, was that the German Air Force was finally forced to abandon its policy of selective offence in this fighting: the situation suddenly demanded a bare-fisted fight for survival. As the Official History says, ". . . the German pilots, for the first time in the war, stayed to fight without calculation". The way it had survived until this time against a numerically superior enemy had been to select the moment and the place and the extent of the fight. It had mostly thrived on this tactic, but now it became almost reckless and, although it put up a magnificent fight, its true decline began with the damage inflicted in this battle. Within a few days, for example, JG1 had been reduced from fifty to eleven serviceable machines and was withdrawn from the fighting.

C1894   SE5a   1Sqn
**SpM:B left 3-40pm PERONNE **MIA(Lt GR
Touchstone USAS. **WIA POW**) [?"SE5" claim combat
FONTAINE-LES-CAPPY 4-30pm Ltn E Udet
Ja4][?"SE5" claim combat PROYART 4-25pm Vzfw H
Juhnke Ja52]

D6962   SE5a   1Sqn
SpM left 4-45pm CAPPY-PERONNE **MIA(Capt KC
Mills **KIA**) [?"SE5" claim combat 4-45pm Ltn L Fr
vRichthofen Ja11]

C8225   Sopwith Camel   3Sqn
**COP seen ok wVILLERS BRETONNEAUX 1500'
going east **MIA**(Lt AT? Sampson **KIA**) initials AP?, left
6-25pm

D6655.1   Sopwith Camel   3Sqn
**COP seen just before combat with 7HA PROYART
6pm **MIA**(Lt A Hamilton **KIA**) left 5-35pm

C2309   RE8   3Sqn AFC
 **CP combat with 9 Fokker DVIIs shot down
nrMERICOURT ~12pm **MIA**(Lt EJ Bice **KIA**/2Lt JE
Chapman **KIA**) left 11-05am ["RE" claim combat
sMORCOURT 12-50pm Oblt Ritt R vGreim JGr 9]

D1920   Sopwith Camel   4Sqn AFC
**SpM AA controls shot up SWARTENBRAUCH
10-50am ftl OK(2Lt S Howard)

D6747   RE8   5Sqn
CP left 7-10am combat with EA EoL **MIA(Lt FC
Russell **POW**/Lt LJF Oertling **DoW**)

F5908   RE8   5Sqn
CP left 10-30am **MIA(Lt AD Robinson **KIA**/Lt ACS
Estcourt **KIA**)

B7716   RE8   6Sqn
**CRec elevators shot through heavy ldg cr OK(Lt Holt/
Lt WT Saville) left 6-15pm ROUVROY-ROSIÈRES

C8648   A.W.FK8   8Sqn
**Phot ground mg shot up dam returned 1-48pm OK(Lt
A Swales/2Lt JC Ferguson) left 11-25am

D5110   A.W.FK8   8Sqn
**Rec mg fire FOUILLOY ftl(Lt JRMG MacCallum
OK/2Lt H Faulks **DoW**) left 10-50am

8 Squadron was detailed to carry out co-operation
duties with tanks. As radio communication with
tanks was still impractical one can imagine the
difficulties they faced. A particularly useful task
they performed was the laying of smoke screens in
front of the enemy anti-tank batteries from the air.
Nos. 3 AFC, 5, and 9 Squadrons also did valuable
smoke-laying work for the infantry.

B6494   RE8   9Sqn
**B BRAY combat with EA shot through(Capt R Hilton
OK/2Lt F Ibbotson **WIA**)

C2709   RE8   12Sqn
**P LOG EAST WOOD shot through dam OK(Lt EO
Haskail/2Lt TT Eales) left 1-15pm, returned 4pm

DH4   18Sqn
** combat(/Sgt E Homer **WIA**)

RE8   21Sqn
** mg fire(/Lt JFA Hall **WIA**)

C4148   Sopwith Dolphin 23Sqn
**LOP/B left 10-26am mg? engine shot through ftl Sh62D
V17 OK(Lt GS Roden)a'c salvable

C8070   Sopwith Dolphin 23Sqn
LOP/B left 11-55am AA ftl(Lt O Pearson **WIA)to
hospital

C8073   Sopwith Dolphin 23Sqn
**LOP/B seen ok GUILLAUCOURT-CAYEUX shot
down? **MIA**(Lt EW Helmer **KIA**) left 1-35am, buried
Sh62.0. W.26.A.39

C8074   Sopwith Dolphin 23Sqn
**LOP/B left 9-07am mg fire engine ftl Sh62D W8.c. dam
salvable OK(Capt AJ Brown MC)

C8111   Sopwith Dolphin 23Sqn
**LOP/B shot down in flames Sh66E D24. wr(Capt AC
St Clair-Morford MC **WIA**) left 11-55am, pilot burnt

D3715   Sopwith Dolphin 23Sqn
**LOP left 11-25am engine shot up ftl V.3.c.62D dam
OK(Lt HA White US.)ac' salvable

D3738   Sopwith Dolphin 23Sqn
**LOP/B mg? engine shot through Sh62D W7.d ftl
dam(Capt B Ankers DCM **WIA**)

C1084   SE5a   24Sqn
**GndStr AA fuel tank shot up 11-40am cr Sh66E D.10.b
OK(Lt WC Lambert US.) left 10-50am Fourth Army
area

C6481   SE5a   24Sqn
**GndStr AA? 1-30pm cr BEAUCOURT OK(Lt HD
Barton)

D6937   SE5a   24Sqn
**GndStr combat with 9 Fokker DVIIs nrLIHONS shot
down WARFUSÉE cr 3-05pm OK(Lt CMG Farrell
Can.) salvable, left 1pm Fourth Army area, this was his
4th raid for the day, awarded DFC for his work

D6943   SE5a   24Sqn
**GndTarg left 12-05pm ground fire shot up dam OK(Lt
JH Southey) returned 1-15pm

E1388   SE5a   24Sqn
**GndTarg combat shot up cr OK(Capt TF Hazell MC)
left 6-30pm Fourth Army area, returned 7-55pm

E5971   SE5a   24Sqn
**GndStr AA? 1-10pm eBEAUCOURT(2Lt JR Watkins
WIA) [?"SE5" claim combat FOUCAUCOURT 1pm
Oblt A Gutknecht Ja43]

E5975   SE5a   24Sqn
GndStr left 6-30pm Fourth Army area shot up **MIA(Lt
FE Beauchamp Can. **POW**) [?"SE5" claim combat
ESTRÉES 7-03pm Ltn O Fruhner Ja26]

B2133   DH4   27Sqn
LowB left 5-20pm **MIA but OK(Lt BM Bowyer-
Smith/Lt LJ Edwards) Ja29?, at one point thought to be
POWs

D1719   DH9   27Sqn
**LowB VOYENNES MIA(Lt LH Forest POW/Lt SWP Foster-Sutton POW) left 5-30pm [?possible "DH" claim combat GENERMONT? 6-40pm Ltn R Wenzl Ja6]

D7317   DH9   27Sqn
**LowB combat with 2EAs ovVOYENNES MIA(2Lt HM Brown POW/2Lt DE Chase POW) left 5-20pm, ovSOMME, Ja28? [?"BF" claim combat PROYART 7-15pm Vzfw C Mesch Ja26]

Nos. 27 and 73 Squadrons attacked bridges at Voyennes, Pithon, and Offoy. Two raids were made and the formation was broken up by enemy fighters on both occasions.

E1255   SE5a   29Sqn
**OP left 8-20am attkg 2EA WARNETON 9-10am MIA(2Lt M Tison POW)

D5120   A.W.FK8   35Sqn
**P MORLANCOURT MIA(2Lt H Elliott? POW/Lt FI Rogers POW) name Elliot? left 12-05pm

E1289.F SE5a   41Sqn
**OP shot up engine dam ftl BERTANGLES 11-15am OK(Capt FRG McCall DSO MC DFC) left 10-05am

E1300   SE5a   41Sqn
+* combat with yellow Fokker DVII[+flames] wPROYART 11-45am then combat with Fokker DVII[+capt] MORCOURT 12-30pm OK(Capt FO Soden Can.) second victory shared with Lt A Goby of 41Sqn

E1309.D SE5a   41Sqn
**OP seen ok ovPROYART 10-50am MIA(2Lt GL Carter POW) left 10-05am

E1326.1 SE5a   41Sqn
**OP left 2pm seen climb into clouds AMIENS 2-10pm combat with EA? shot down wMORLANCOURT(Lt WA Foot WIA)

41 Squadron was in continuous heavy fighting over the Australian sector throughout the day. It claimed three enemy aircraft, including the two above, and a kite balloon.

D1855   Sopwith Camel 43Sqn
**SpM ENNENAIN combat 2pm shot up ftl 2-45pm dam OK(Lt PWR Arundel) left 1-10pm

D9456   Sopwith Camel 43Sqn
**SpM left 4pm MIA(Lt PWR Arundel KIA)

F5919   Sopwith Camel 43Sqn
**SpM left 4pm MIA(Lt CHB? Lefroy WIA POW) initials CBH? ["Camel" claim combat wPERONNE 4-30pm Ltn L Fr vRichthofen Ja11]

All the above occurred in afternoon bombing raids on the bridges at Peronne, made with 1 and 98 Squadrons.

C786   Bristol F2b   48Sqn
**LOP LA MOTTE MIA(Lt JC Nuttall POW/2Lt BC

Pearson WIA POW) left 4-35pm [?"BF" claim combat CHAULNES 5-30pm Ltn J Grassmann Ja10]

C876   Bristol F2b   48Sqn
**LowOP mg ftl BONNOY fire OK(2Lt GE? Sharwood-Smith/2Lt JN Kier) left 8-15am, initials BE?

C947   Bristol F2b   48Sqn
**LOP combat with Fokker DVII[+capt] neLA MOTTE 12-05pm AA ftl cr shell hole wr OK(Lt CG Imeretinsky/Lt A Urinowsky) ["BF" claim MERICOURT 11-50am Ltn A Scheicher Ja34, also had local F2b earlier claim, 8am]

D8061   Bristol F2b   48Sqn
**LowP seen dive FOUCAUCOURT EoL MIA(2Lt BJ McCutcheon KIA/2Lt VS Gray KIA) left 9-05am

C2152   DH9   49Sqn
**B going down DRESLINCOURT in control & ldg MIA(Lt JA Yates POW/2Lt GR Schooling POW) left 2pm

C2196   DH9   49Sqn
**B AA AMIENS 4-45pm shot through ftl(Lt MD Allen OK/2Lt J Ross KIA)

C6110   DH9   49Sqn
**B left 2-05pm BETHENCOURT BRIDGE MIA(Lt HP Mallett WIA POW/2Lt R Kelly WIA POW) both slight WIA

D457   DH9   49Sqn
**LowB shot up dam ftl returned a'dr 4-15pm OK(Lt GS Ramsay/2Lt BT Gillman) left 2pm BETHENCOURT BRIDGE

D7231   DH9   49Sqn
**B seen going down in flames cr nrBETHENCOURT BRIDGE MIA(Lt GS Ramsey KIA/2Lt WM Hartley KIA) left 5-55pm

49 Squadron twice attempted to bomb Bethencourt bridge with SE5as of 32 Squadron. On each occasion German fighters ensured only a few aircraft reached their target, and when they did they were very heavily shot up.

D6575   Sopwith Camel 54Sqn
**SpB seen in control BRIE 1-45pm 2000' MIA(Capt ME Gonne POW DoW)

Nos. 54, 107, and 205 Squadrons to bomb the bridge at Brie. Although some of the raids were made in terrible rain storms a number of pilots made three trips.

D9481   Sopwith Camel 54Sqn
**SpB seen ok WARFUSÉE entering clouds going east 5000' 7-30pm MIA(Lt RE Taylor POW) ["Camel" claim combat seFOUCAUCOURT 7-40pm Ltn E Udet Ja4]

B8423   SE5a   56Sqn
**COP combat with HA neCHAULNES 7-30pm cr wr(1Lt TJ Herbert USAS. WIA) [?possible "SE5" claim combat NESLE 6-55pm Ltn R Klimke Ja27]

D6096   SE5a   56Sqn
+* combat with Fokker DVII[+ooc] neCHAULNES
7-05pm OK(Capt WO Boger Can.) last of 5 claims

D8382   DH4   57Sqn
+*LowB combat with Fokker DVII[+ooc]
MOISLAINS A'dr 8-05am OK(Sgt DE Edgley/2Lt FG
Craig)

D8398   DH4   57Sqn
+*LowB combat with Fokker DVII[+ooc]
MOISLAINS A'dr 8-10am OK(Lt A MacGregor/Lt JFB
Tanqueray Can.)

D8419   DH4   57Sqn
+*LowB combat with Fokker DVII[+des]
MOISLAINS A'dr 8-15am OK(Capt FMcDC Turner/
2Lt HS Musgrove Can.) EA collided?

F6059   DH4   57Sqn
**Phot seen in combat ovMOISLAINS A'dr 1000'
MIA(Lt LL Brown Can. DFC **POW**/2Lt AE Doncaster
POW) left 7-10am MOISLAINS

57 Squadron was one of the few squadrons on early
morning bombing raids to be attacked. Only one
crew was lost whilst three enemy fighters were
claimed.

B151   SE5a   60Sqn
**OP seen ok sFOUCAUCOURT 1500' 4-40pm
MIA(2Lt JG Hall US. **KIA**) combat?
FOUCAUCOURT-WANCOURT [?"SE5" claim
combat seBARLEUX 5-30pm Ltn E Udet
Ja4][?"Camel" claim combat ESTRÉES 5-50pm Ltn L
Fr vRichthofen Ja11]

D6945.U SE5a   60Sqn
+* combat with Fokker DVII[+des] FOLIER-
ROSIÈRES 12-55pm OK(Capt A Beck) made 11 claims

E3916.L SE5a   60Sqn
+* combat with 2Str[+des] CHAULNES 1-15pm
OK(Capt AW Saunders)

**   Sopwith Camel   65Sqn**
** ground rifle fire(Lt EGK Weakley **WIA**)

B7875   Sopwith Camel   65Sqn
**OP left 3-10pm rifle fire shot up dam(Lt FB Miseroy
WIA)

C8250   Sopwith Camel   65Sqn
OP seen nrHARBONNIÈRES 10-30am **MIA(2Lt VS
Stevens **WIA POW**)

D1875   Sopwith Camel   65Sqn
**OP controls shot up ftl cr FOUCHAMP dam OK(2Lt
AS Sinclair) left 1-30pm

D8107   Sopwith Camel   65Sqn
**OP ground fire shot up dam ftl Q.24.Cent-Q.30.d.Cent
OK(Maj HV Champion de Crespigny) left 9-40am

D8119   Sopwith Camel   65Sqn
OP seen nHARBONNIÈRES 2-30pm **MIA(Capt EG
Brookes **KIA**)

D8204   Sopwith Camel   65Sqn
**OP left 9am engine shot up dam ftl cr P.32.D.48 dam
OK(Lt DM John)

F6068   Sopwith Camel   65Sqn
**OP left 9-40am shot up on return dam OK(2Lt CFW
Illingworth)

65 Squadron came in for some of the heaviest
casualties of the day, caused by a variety of enemy
activity. Their low attacks were, admittedly, very
dangerous work. A formation of six of their Camels
also shot down a Fokker DVII over Proyart at 12-
25pm, but there was only one other possible air
victory for the unit that day, by the South African
Capt TM Williams.

B5568   Sopwith Camel   73Sqn
BOP left 1-50pm seen ovMARQUION? **MIA(Lt A
McConnell-Wood **POW**) "MARCAIN"?

B7868   Sopwith Camel   73Sqn
BOP left 1-50pm seen eSOMME BRIDGE **MIA(Lt
GW Gorman Can. **POW**) [?"Camel" claim
wMERICOURT Ltn A Scheicher Ja34, but slim
evidence]

Ten 73 Squadron Camels were attacked by eight
German fighters on the first bombing raid of the
afternoon and suffered these two losses. The only
Squadron claim was a two-seater on the second
raid.

B2396   Sopwith Camel   80Sqn
OP left BRAY 9-45am **MIA(2Lt HE Hudson **KIA**)

D6453   Sopwith Camel   80Sqn
**OP seen sMORLANCOURT going West 1500'
MIA(2Lt G Wignall **POW**) left 9-15am

B5587   Sopwith Camel   80Sqn
**OP left 10-15am combat with Fokker DVII[+des]
sMORCOURT then attacked by 4 more Fokker DVIIs
mg fire? cr **MIA**(Lt TS Nash **DoW**)

C8732   SE5a   84Sqn
**OP AMIENS-ST QUENTIN RD ldg ok EoL?
MIA(Capt R Manzer DFC Can. **POW**) left 11am,
bombing and straffing troops nrPROYART when
possibly hit by ground fire [?consider "SE5" claim
combat CHIPILLY 1-15pm Ltn O Creutzmann Ja46]

D6856   SE5a   84Sqn
+* attacked KB[+destr] ROSIÈRES 2-40pm OK(Capt
AW Beauchamp-Proctor) first of 16 victories in this a'c

**   SE5a   84Sqn**
OP ground mg fire(Lt NWR Mawle **WIA) initials
NRW?

C870   Bristol F2b   88Sqn
OP left 5pm AA dam 6pm(Lt HR Little **WIA/Pte WJ
Spalding **WIA**)

C2203   DH9   98Sqn
**B PERONNE Rlwy seen rising above clouds

nrAMIENS **MIA**(Lt W Goffe **POW**/Sgt JL May **WIA POW**) left 5am [?possibly one of the three "Bristol" claims combat MERICOURT-VILLERS BRETONNEAUX btwn 8-30am & 9-15am Ltn G Meyer Ja37, other Jasta claims around St Christ a'dr, to which 98 Sqn went in morning]

This was 98 Squadron's only loss from their early morning raids to bomb airfields with 43 Squadron. Some were found to have had the aircraft on them dispersed and bombing had little effect. It is possible this crew was not lost to enemy action.

D622   DH9   98Sqn
+*B PERONNE Rlwy Bridge combat with HalbC[+des] ovFOY 3-05pm OK(Lt F Carpenter/Lt NC MacDonald)

D3060   DH9   98Sqn
+*B PERONNE Rlwy Bridge combat with PfalzDIII[+des] swPERONNE 3-20pm OK(Sgt HW Bush/Sgt ER MacDonald)

D3078   DH9   98Sqn
B PERONNE Rlwy Bridge **MIA(Capt FG Powell **WIA POW**/Capt GHP Whitfield **WIA POW**) left 12-50pm [?"DH4" claim combat BIACHES 1-45pm Ltn P Billik Ja52]

Nos. 1, 43, and 98 Squadrons bombed the road and railway bridges at Peronne. It is important to note that the fighter squadrons were not escorting the bombers but dropping bombs themselves. The DH9 squadrons suffered the worst casualties of any in these raids.

D5668   DH9   107Sqn
B left 12-40pm BRIE BRIDGE nrPERONNE in terrible rain combat with Fokker DVIIs **MIA(Lt JK Gaukroger **KIA**/Lt EL Doncaster **KIA**) [?possible "DH4" claim combat swESTRÉES 1-05pm Oblt A Gutknecht Ja43]

B5425   Sopwith Camel   201Sqn
LowP left 11-35am combat with 8 Fokker DVIIs ftl EoL **MIA(Lt JM McKay **POW**?)

B7157   Sopwith Camel   201Sqn
LowP left 11-20am **MIA(Lt W Cox **POW**) [?possible "Sopwith" claim combat neBAYONVILLERS 11-40am Oblt Ritt R vGreim JGr 9, but see B2396]

D1804   Sopwith Camel   201Sqn
LP MERINCOURT Rly then spin ooc ePROYART 11-05am **MIA(2Lt NOM Foggo Can. **POW**) left 10-50am

D3419   Sopwith Camel   201Sqn
LowP seen ok ovHARBONNIÈRES 10-30am **MIA(Lt RH Hemmens **POW**)

D9645   Sopwith Camel   201Sqn
LowOP seen in flames eVILLERS BRETONNEAUX **MIA(Lt RSS Orr **KIA**) left 6am

D9652   Sopwith Camel   201Sqn
**LP AA & mg? seen cr eBAYONVILLERS 9-05am

MIA(Lt LH Riddell **POW**) left 8-30am

D9656   Sopwith Camel   201Sqn
**AerialSentry shot down in flames HARBONNIÈRES MIA but OK(Lt R McLaughlin) left 11-20am

201 Squadron operated in the Australian sector. They suffered the highest casualties of all the squadrons engaged in close support patrolling.

F6070   DH4   205Sqn
+*B combat with PfalzDIII[+flames] ROSIÈRES-CHAULNES 7-15pm OK(Lt AR McPhee/Sgt L Murphy)

C9657?   HP 0/400   207Sqn
this a'c? +*Tank Camouflage AMIENS OK(Lt GA Flavelle Can./Lt Garrett?/?) left before dawn, Flavelle was flying this a'c a few days later

D5409   HP 0/400   207Sqn
+*Tank Camouflage AMIENS left 1-09am in atrocious condtions, fog to very low levels OK(Lt WJ Peace Can./Lt Fawcett/?)

These two crews performed the operation noted above whereby the sound of their engines camouflaged the positioning of the tanks before the offensive.

**   Sopwith Camel   209Sqn**
SpM (Lt WR May Can. **WIA)

C194   Sopwith Camel   209Sqn
**LowP left 11-15am mg ftl n.m.l. nrBEAUCOURT OK(Lt WA Rollason) a'c noted unsalvable but later collected. Rollason may be 209Sqn pilot who force-landed in No Man's Land and subsequently joined cavalry for attack

C198   Sopwith Camel   209Sqn
**LowP ground fire shot up dam OK(Capt JK Summers MC)

D3421   Sopwith Camel   209Sqn
LowP ground fire shot up by explosive bullets dam(2Lt WM Wormald **WIA)

D9619   Sopwith Camel   209Sqn
LP seen ok nWARFUSÉE-MARCELCAVE RLWY **MIA(2Lt L Thompson **KIA**) left 9-30am

D9644   Sopwith Camel   209Sqn
LP sSOMME seen ok ovGUILLAUCOURT 200' about to bomb infantry **MIA(Lt WL Brookes **KIA**) left 9-55am

D9670   Sopwith Camel   209Sqn
**LowP ground mg fire CAIX-ROSIÈRES nrCONTY ftl dam OK(Lt MA Toomey) salvable, left 2pm

B7624   DH9   211Sqn
B AA BRUGES engine seized ftl SAS VAN GHENT burnt a'c **MIA(2Lt LK Davidson **INT**/2Lt WL Bing **INT**) interned Holland

9th August

The bombing offensive on the bridges was continued through the night and then maintained from first light. There had been no further RAF losses for the night bombing squadrons, and there were additional measures on the second day to give more protection to the bombers. One of the key lessons from the previous day's work seemed to have been learnt and the fighters were no longer to carry bombs but to provide escort protection from German air attacks. By this time, however, the German Air Force had mustered an additional two hundred and ninety-four machines for use in the battle. Thirty-four of these were night-bombers.

The day's raids were to be again flawed, however, this time through a lack of co-ordination. Fighter escorts failed to appear or were drawn off on at least three crucial occasions. There had been no opportunity to practice this close co-operation and the aircraft involved found it very difficult to remain in contact. 73 Squadron Camels were ordered to successively protect 27 and then 49 Squadrons on their early morning raids but failed to meet either formation (see below). 54 Squadron failed to give adequate protection to 107 Squadron DH9s, both units losing seven machines between them, including five DH9s. Finally, 57 Squadron was to bomb the bridge at Peronne, escorted by Bristol Fighters of 11 Squadron, but called the attack off when eight Fokkers drew the escort off. With a better record, 205 Squadron DH4s, which frequently bombed without escort, had their second day with no casualties. In the morning they bombed the bridge at Brie, and in the afternoon and evening also attacked that at St Christ. On the 9th, this unit recorded ninety-five hours of active flying.

The serious problems of the morning caused a change of tactics in the afternoon. It was decided to mount a carefully timed mass attack at 5pm with bombing machines from 27, 49, 98, and 107 Squadrons. The measures to assist these crews this time were elaborately planned and had substantially swelled numbers of IX Brigade fighters available for close protection. This was made possible by bringing down I Brigade fighters (from 19, 22, 40, and 64 Squadrons) to carry out the higher offensive Line Patrols for the afternoon. One can see from the entries below, however, that these units were involved in minimal fighting — they made no claims — for the action was all beneath them.

27 Squadron was once more allotted 73 Squadron for escort. Again, 73 Squadron lost them, but despite being attacked by eight Fokkers their casualties were light. Their bombing of their target of Bethencourt Bridge was inconclusive because of the enemy disruption. 49 Squadron were escorted to the bridge at Falvy by 32 Squadron, but they also lost touch with each other. No. 49 then met and fought its second big enemy formation for the day. Raids to the other bridges seemed to avoid serious fighting, but again, results were inconclusive and there were losses.

As the battle had raged on the ground the progress eastwards was variable. By the evening of the 9th the French had made substantial progress towards Roye and the British Fourth Army had regained the outskirts of Proyart, from where the line now ran down to Bouchoir. The British advance had slowed, however. The attacks were less co-ordinated and they were also beginning to meet the old Somme battlefields of 1916 which were full of difficulties. Another reason for the slowing of the advance was that the fighter squadrons working with the Fourth Army were having to contend with sizeable German air reinforcements which were now reaching the sector, and increasingly turned to higher offensive patrolling to keep the battle area secure. As a result, their close attacking work with the army was reduced, and as this was a key ingredient of the co-ordinated battle plan, the advance faltered. The German forces on the ground had been swelled as well, ensuring enough troops were reaching the battle area to provide some resistance. At least sixteen new German divisions reached the area by the evening of the 11th.

Bombing of the bridges continued again through the night, and included raids by the heavy bombers of 207 Squadron. It began to be conceded, however, that the bombing offensive had failed in its objective and, what is more, the shift in emphasis had caused the British to postpone their attacks on the rail centres until it was too late — the serious bombing of these targets would only begin the following day. The feeling grew that had these been attacked as planned it might have had an ultimately greater influence on the battle. On the other hand, major elements of the German Air Force had been sacrificed in the fighting, driven to suffer losses from which it was never likely to recover. Had the fighting remained more conventional it is very likely the German Air Force would have remained a more potent force for longer.

97 Squadron arrived in France on the 9th equipped as a Handley Page heavy bombing squadron. It joined the Independent Force.

C8843	SE5a	1Sqn

**OP combat with HA ftl 4-20pm dam OK(Lt Boyd)

RE8		5Sqn

** mg fire(Lt R Cook **WIA**)

B6502   RE8   6Sqn
CRec ROSIÈRES **MIA(Lt JET Sutcliffe **POW**/2Lt
LA Clack **POW**) left 2-15pm [?"RE" claim combat
ROSIÈRES Oblt K Bolle Ja2]

E4   RE8   6Sqn
CRec ROSIÈRES combat with EA shot down **MIA(Lt
RC Wickett **KIA**/Lt GB Barre **KIA**) left 12-10pm

            RE8   7Sqn
** combat(/2Lt A Bendlestein **WIA**)

            A.W.FK8   8Sqn
** gunshot(/2Lt JC Ferguson **WIA**) but see previous
day?

B4175   A.W.FK8   8Sqn
TankP ftl BAYONVILLERS(2Lt GAH Nudds **WIA/
2Lt P Lawrence **KIA**) left 3-30pm, salvable

C8566   A.W.FK8   8Sqn
**LRec AA fuel tank shot through ftl OK(Lt FA
Whittell/Lt WT Mitchell) left 9-45am WIENCOURT

D5138   A.W.FK8   8Sqn
**TankP mg engine shot up ftl nrCAIX dam OK(Capt
FMF West/Lt JAG Haslam) left 10-30am

D5140   A.W.FK8   8Sqn
LRec mg fire CAIX ftl(Capt FB Wilson **WIA/Lt WL
Norman OK) left 7-35am, a'c salvable

C931   Bristol F2b   11Sqn
**EscB(57Sqn) EA fuel tank shot up ST JUST 9am ftl
cr in corn OK(Sgt RS Hutt/Sgt RA Watson) fumes
overcame pilot

D3669   Sopwith Dolphin 23Sqn
**BOP left 6-10pm combat with EA shot up dam
returned 6-50pm OK(Lt AW Blake)

C1316   DH9   27Sqn
 **B AUXI-LE-CHÂTEAU mg fire shot up ftl(Lt CB
Sanderson OK/Sgt A Dobell **WIA**) left 4-15pm

B8374.B   SE5a   32Sqn
OP ok ovLICOURT 11am HA? **MIA(2Lt PTA
Reveley **WIA POW**) [?"SE5" claim combat
ROSIÈRES 11-30am Vzfw C Mesch Ja26]

E1327   SE5a   32Sqn
** OP seen ok MISERY 4-40pm 5000' HA? **MIA**(1Lt
RL Paskill USAS. **KIA**) [?"SE5" claim combat
sBRAY 5-12pm Ltn R Klimke Ja27]

Paskill was probably lost whilst escorting 49
Squadron to bomb the bridge at Brie.

C8454   A.W.FK8   35Sqn
**P mg shot through MORLANCOURT controls hit ftl
nd cr 50yds WoL wr(2Lt JT Duckworth/2Lt HH Davies)
left 4-30am, shaken

C8593   A.W.FK8   35Sqn
**Phot sMEAULTE combat shot up on return 8-50pm
OK(2Lt JM Brown US./2Lt A Gilchrist) left 6-50pm
[?"AW" claim combat MERICOURT Ltn O Löffler Ja2]

F3472   A.W.FK8   35Sqn
P left 6pm **MIA(Lt LH Button **POW**/2Lt B Hall
POW)

D6179   SE5a   41Sqn
+* combat with Fokker DVII[+ooc] CAPPY 5-30pm
OK(Maj GH Bowman)

D8446   SE5a   41Sqn
+* combat with DFWC[+des] sCONTALMAISON
5-55am OK(Capt AS Hemming)

E1362.3   SE5a   41Sqn
OP combat with EAs eESTRÉES 4-30pm **MIA(Lt
FWH Martin Can. **KIA**)

E3966.4   SE5a   41Sqn
**OP combat with Fokker DVIIs[+ooc] nBRAY 6-15pm
then another[+flames] CARNOY-SUZANNE 6-30pm
then ground fire shot up dam returned a'dr 6-55pm
OK(Capt FRG McCall Can. DSO MC DFC) left 5-30pm

F5910   SE5a   41Sqn
+* attacked KB[+des] neBRAY 7-45am OK(Lt WG
Claxton Can.) later in the day attacked and shot down a
Fokker DVII in flames eESTRÉES 4-25pm

41 Squadron recorded the highest number of
victories in fighting over the battle on the 9th —
some very experienced pilots achieving these
victories. Significant groups of German fighters
often managed to penetrate the offensive shield and
operate low down over the forward area, most
commonly flying in groups of eight to ten.

            DH9   49Sqn
+*B FALVY & BETHENCOURT BRIDGES combat
with 25-30EAs[+flames ovMARCHELEPOT then [+
flames nrABLAINCOURT] further fighting[++ooc cr
nrSOYECOURT] badly shot up engine hit ftl nrLA
MOTTE-EN-SANTERRE OK(Lt JA Keating US./2Lt
EA Simpson) left at dawn: 5-15am?, attacked by
10-15EAs on approach to objective who were then joined
by a further 10-15 EAs after drop, running fight
developed

            DH9   49Sqn
** combat(/Lt CE Pullen **WIA**)

            DH9   49Sqn
** combat(Lt RC Stokes **WIA**)

These two observers may have been hit during
the big afternoon raid in which 49 Squadron
had been allotted the bridge at Falvy. They
were attacked by twenty enemy fighters and
forced to drop their bombs near Fresnes.

F2167   Sopwith Camel 54Sqn
OP seen ok ESTRÉES 6000' 6-40am **MIA(Lt ACR
Hawley **KIA**) [?"Camel" claim combat ESTRÉES
6-40am Ltn E Loewenhardt Ja10]

F6152   Sopwith Camel 54Sqn
**OP seen ok ESTRÉES 6000' 6-40am down EoL

MIA(2Lt RRC Winter **KIA**)

Both of the above were lost on the third raid to the bridge at Brie whilst escorting 107 Squadron (see below).

D8416 DH4 57Sqn
Phot left 8-15am down EoL **MIA(Lt WJ Pitt-Pitts **KIA**/2Lt HS Musgrove **POW DoW**) 57 Squadron was bombing PERONNE BRIDGE [?"DH4" claim combat BAUCOURT? 10-05am Ltn P Billik Ja52]

D1810 Sopwith Camel 65Sqn
OP diving through clouds VAUVILLERS 3000′ **MIA but OK(Lt GOD Tod US. **WIA**) seen 11-25am HARBONNIÈRES, thought ldg WoL, Tod made 5 claims with 65Sqn

D8161 Sopwith Camel 65Sqn
OP left 7-50pm **MIA(2Lt AS Sinclair **POW**) [?"Camel" claim combat seHERLEVILLE 8-20pm Ltn E Udet Ja4]

E1548 Sopwith Camel 65Sqn
OP seen ok HARBONNIÈRES 7-15am but shot down **MIA(Lt CFW Illingworth **POW**) ["Sopwith 1Str" claim combat eFRAMERVILLE 8-10am Ltn W Neuenhofen Ja27]

F5952 Sopwith Camel 65Sqn
OP seen nrVAUXVILLERS with EA on tail 5-30pm shot down ooc **MIA(Lt HE Dempsey Can. **POW**) left 5pm

The four losses on the 9th were 65 Squadron's last before being withdrawn for a rest on the 12th.

Sopwith Camel 80Sqn
** ground rifle fire(Lt CSL Coulson **WIA**)

D9429 Sopwith Camel 80Sqn
OP left 6-30pm SOMME RIVER ground mg seen going down in fast spin cr swETINEHEM **MIA(Lt JR Orr **KIA**)

D9099 FE2b 83Sqn
**NB EA shot up engine ftl cr trenches nrMOREUIL wr(Capt AO Lewis-Roberts DFC/2Lt EN Lohmeyer DFC) left 10pm, shaken

B682 SE5a 84Sqn
**OP ground fire combat with EA dam returned 4-20pm OK(1Lt AF Matthews USAS.) left 3-30pm AMIENS-ST QUENTIN RD

C4060 Sopwith Dolphin 87Sqn
**COP ESTRÉES DENIERCOURT combat shot through dam OK(Lt CA Bryant) left 4-40pm, returned 6-40pm

D1054 DH9 98Sqn
B FEUILLÈRES Bridge glide going west EoL with steam coming from radiator **MIA(Lt F Carpenter **POW**/ Sgt ER MacDonald **POW**?) left 5-30am

Six DH9s were escorted by five Camels of 43 Squadron on this raid.

C6320 DH9 107Sqn
B left 5-40am BRIE BRIDGE down EoL **MIA(2Lt SJ Hill **POW**/2AM FA Ellery **DoW**) observer was reported **WIA POW** but died [?"DH9" claim HERLEVILLE 7-10am combat Ltn H Frommherz Ja27]

C6343 DH9 107Sqn
B BRIE BRIDGE nrPERONNE combat ~25 Fokker DVIIs[++flames+ooc] FRESNES btwn 6-55am & 7-15am on return shot up cr(Lt G Beveridge **WIA/Lt SL Dunlop DFC Can. OK) left 5-40am, VILLERS BRETONNEAUX, pilot fainted, requiring ldg by observer [?"DH9" claim combat MORCOURT Vzfw A Lux Ja27]

D1049 DH9 107Sqn
+* combat ~6 Fokker DVIIs[+des] swVILLERS CARBONNEL 6-05am OK(2Lt FT Stott/AM WJ Palmer)

D1722 DH9 107Sqn
B left 5-40am BRIE BRIDGE **MIA(Lt H Butterworth **KIA**/Lt RO Baird **KIA**) ["DH9" claim combat PROYART 7-10am Ltn R Klimke Ja27]

D2856 DH9 107Sqn
+* combat ~6 Fokker DVIIs[+flames] 2m wHAPLINCOURT 5-50am OK(Capt FM Carter/Lt AWH Arundell) EA shot down with front gun

D5666 DH9 107Sqn
B seen going down in flames EoL **MIA(Capt WH Dore **KIA**/Lt JE Wallace **KIA**) left 5-40am ["DH" claim VILLERS-CARBONNEL 6-30am combat Ltn L Fr vRichthofen Ja11]

E621 DH9 107Sqn
B left 5-40am BRIE BRIDGE **MIA(Lt JE Emtage **KIA**/Lt P Willis MM Can. **KIA**)

E633 DH9 107Sqn
B left 5-40am BRIE BRIDGE believed ftl VILLERS BRETONNEAUX & laid out wounded **MIA(Lt SR Coward **WIA POW**/Lt LG Cooper **POW DoW**)

The most severe losses inflicted during the early morning raids on the Somme bridges were to 107 Squadron crews. It was believed that the German Air Force concentrated their attacks on DH9 formations rather than on DH4s because they knew they could expect higher success. 54 Squadron Camels were escorting 107 Squadron raids to the bridge at Brie which were leaving at thirty-minute intervals. The first left at 5am and was met by twelve Fokkers and totally disrupted, the second had to fight its way home, and the third, no doubt by now expected, was brutally dealt with: three of the five DH9s which were lost, as well as the two

Camels shot down, were on this last raid. The crew of C6343 which crash-landed after combat also belonged to this last raid.

F6066   DH9   107Sqn
B left 4-15pm **MIA(Capt AJ Mayo **KIA**/Lt JW Jones **KIA**) ["DH" claim combat FOUCAUCOURT 5-40pm Ltn L Fr vRichthofen Ja11]

This crew was shot down in the big evening raid on the bridges. In the hectic fighting of the morning they had achieved two victories over Fokker DVIIs south west of Peronne at 7-30am

D6520   Sopwith Camel   201Sqn
LowP left 2-45pm combat with Fokker DVIIs spin down in flames nROSIÈRES cr **MIA(Lt R Stone **KIA**) attacking troops nROSIÈRES

D9589   Sopwith Camel   201Sqn
LP left 5pm combat with formation of Fokker DVIIs eFOUCAUCOURT **MIA(2Lt MS Misener Can. **KIA**) [?"Camel" claim combat sCERISY 5-55pm Ltn E Loewenhardt Ja10] "Sopwith" claims: [?combat nBEAUCOURT 5-15pm Ltn O Fr vB-Marconnay Ja15][?combat BEAUCOURT Hpt R Berthold JGII]

D1834   Sopwith Camel   208Sqn
**OP combat with EA 12pm shot up dam OK(Lt WEG Mann)

The first additional bombing squadrons for the Independent Force began to arrive in France in August. A preference for increased capability for heavy night bombing was very apparent from the units which were dispatched — three of the four to arrive in August were equipped with twin-engined Handley Page 0/400s, and 100 Squadron was also in the process of exchanging its FE2bs for the same type. The first new squadron was No. 97, and it arrived on the 9th. Others to follow were Nos. 215, 115, and 110 Squadrons, and their dates of joining the Expeditionary Force are given where appropriate.

10th August

On the 10th, the bombing of the bridges was abandoned by all but the DH4s of 205 Squadron. From this time the day-bombers turned their attention to the stations at Peronne and Equancourt, and the rail network between Bapaume and Epehy. Peronne was a key rail centre and received repeated attacks. In the morning it was bombed by a formation of twelve bombers from 27 and 49 Squadrons escorted by forty fighters from 32 and 62 Squadrons. They met about fifteen Fokkers over the target and although seven SE5as of 56 Squadron came to their assistance there were five casualties

from this raid, suffered mostly by the fighters. In the evening, 18 and 103 Squadrons bombed it again, and then overnight both 83 and 207 Squadrons made it their target. There were no casualties on these later raids.

The first British reinforcements of aircraft, consisting of ninety extra fighters, arrived in the sector on the 10th.

B7399.Z   Sopwith Camel   3Sqn
COP seen attkg 20EA nrSOYECOURT 10-40am **MIA(Lt VB McIntosh **KIA**) left 9-50am [?"Camel" claim combat sMORCOURT 10-30am Ltn E Udet Ja4]

C2275   RE8   3Sqn AFC
CP mg fire shot down VAUVILLERS ldg ok(Lt JL Smith **WIA/Lt OG White? OK) left 5-20am, combat?

C2339   RE8   5Sqn
**CAP combat with EA shot through returned a'dr OK(Lt LR Evershed/Lt EP Everleigh) left 1pm

C5069   RE8   5Sqn
CAP left 3-50pm **MIA(2Lt CF Grant **KIA**/2Lt WH Webber **KIA**)

B5893   RE8   6Sqn
LRec snd fr 500′(Lt AR Thompson **KIA/2Lt WT Saville **WIA**)

C8602   A.W.FK8   8Sqn
TankP combat with several EAs ovCAIX shot up ftl cr(Capt FMF West MC VC **WIA/Lt JAG Haslam MC **WIA**) left 8am

West was awarded the Victoria Cross for his efforts on the 10th. He and his observer were on contact patrol with tanks moving on Roye. They were both highly experienced men, and that morning had been bombing and shooting up enemy troops and assessing the strength of the force in front of the advance. As they were returning with their information they were attacked by several fighters. West was hit in his leg by five explosive bullets and severely wounded. The attacks continued and Haslam did what he could with his gun to fend them off — he was subsequently wounded as well. West was now in a terrible state, unable to control the aircraft because of his leg. He managed to lift it out of the way and, almost unconscious with pain, made a forced landing in a field near Canadian troops. He was hurried to a casualty station where he insisted on giving his report. As a result of his injuries his leg needed to be amputated. He was to have a distinguished career in the diplomatic side of the RAF.

E8821   A.W.FK8   8Sqn
TankCP left 12-55pm shot up ftl dam(Lt HN Young **WIA/Lt HB Davis OK)

D4844   RE8   9Sqn
**OP combat with EA shot dn Sh62D x.20.a(2Lt STH
Roberts OK/2Lt SJ West **inj**) left 12pm

D4862   RE8   9Sqn
**B mg shot up dam OK(Lt G Milner/2Lt LF Rowsell)
name Rowswell?, EA involved?

A7226   Bristol F2b   11Sqn
**COP AA ovMONCHY-AU-BOIS shot up dam ftl cr
8am OK(Lt BSB Thomas MC/2Lt CE Spinks) left
7-30am

C8838   SE5a   32Sqn
OP seen ok PERONNE 11-30am 14000′ **MIA(Lt P
MacFarlane **KIA**)

D6921   SE5a   32Sqn
OP seen ok PERONNE 11-30am 14000′ **MIA(Lt WE
Jackson Can. **POW**)

E5950   SE5a   32Sqn
**OP PERONNE combat with EA shot up dam OK(2Lt
JB Bowen)

These three pilots were involved in action whilst
escorting 27 and 49 Squadrons to bomb Peronne.
The unit claimed four enemy shot down in this
dogfight.

B8399   SE5a   41Sqn
**OP combat with EA shot up dam returned a'dr 8-40pm
OK(Capt AS Hemming DFC) left 6-45pm

D6120.6 SE5a   41Sqn
**OP combat 6-40pm engine cut ftl TREUX OK(Lt B
Slightholm) a'c shelled

B9344   DH9   49Sqn
B seen ovPERONNE **MIA(2Lt H Hartley **POW**/Sgt
OD Beetham **POW**?) left 9-15am [?"DH" claim
combat ABLAINCOURT 11-30am Hpt R Berthold
JGII]

B8429   SE5a   56Sqn
**COP seen attkg HA 11-30am MARCHELEPOT
MIA(Capt WO Boger **KIA**) [?"SE5" combat
CHAULNES 11-15am Ltn E Loewenhardt Ja10 but
then air collision with Ja11 a'c & **KIA**]

C1096   SE5a   56Sqn
+* combat with Fokker DVIIs[++des] nrCHALUS
10am then 20 Fokker DVIIs[+des] PUZEAUX 12000′
10-30am OK(Capt HJ Burden Can.) shot down another
two Fokker DVIIs eROYE at 8-10pm to make five
victories in the day

D6094   SE5a   56Sqn
**COP seen going into combat with HA
ovMARCHELEPOT 11-30am **MIA**(Lt HT Flintoft
POW) left 11am Third Army area [?"SE5" claim
combat ARVILLERS 11-45am Ltn J Veltjens Ja15]

E1286   SE5a   56Sqn
**COP left 9am seen in combat with HA CHAULNES

10-30am **MIA**(Lt H Allen **KIA**)

D9278   DH4   57Sqn
**B combat with HA AA? dam ftl FROHEN LE
GRAND 8pm(2Lt DU Thomas OK/2Lt JK Mitchell
KIA) left 5pm

C8862   SE5a   60Sqn
**OP combat shot up ESQUINNOY ftl 7-10am(2Lt H
Buckley **WIA**) left 5-55am Fourth Army area

D1783   Sopwith Camel   73Sqn
**OP combat with HA going down ok?
wCHUIGNOTTES 12-10pm **MIA**(Lt SA Dawson **KIA**)
down ooc? ["Camel" claim combat PROYART
12-10pm Oblt H Auffahrt Ja29]

**   Sopwith Camel   80Sqn**
** ground mg fire(2Lt LK Baker **WIA**)

D6184   SE5a   84Sqn
**OP mg engine shot up VILLERS BRETONNEAUX
14000′ ftl OK(Lt SW Highwood) left 9-35am

D6904   SE5a   84Sqn
**OP combat ftl LA FLACQUE 10am(Lt R? Chesters
WIA) initial J?

C4176   Sopwith Dolphin   87Sqn
**COP left 8-45am seen ok FOUCAUCOURT 9-40am
MIA(Lt TT Shipman **POW**) ["Dolphin" claim
combat PUZEAUX 9-40am Vzfw A Lux
Ja27][?"Sopwith" claim combat 9-40am Ltn W
Neuenhofen Ja27]

D3774   Sopwith Dolphin   87Sqn
*P seen in steep dive with prop stopped ovBELLOY
1000′ 9-15am **MIA**(1Lt GS Harvey USAS. **POW**)
["Dolphin" claim combat PUZEAUX (PUISIEUX?)
9-40am Ltn F Noltenius Ja27]

D6573   Sopwith Camel   151Sqn
+* attacked Staaken RXIV 43/17[+flames] cr 1m west
of No.22 Lighthouse TALMAS OK(Capt AB Yuille)
Staaken R-type giant plane belonging to Rfa 501, EA
crew killed

This was the first of two German giant planes
brought down in the war by the RAF. In many
ways a staggering technological achievement for
the time, the RXIVs and RXIVas were one of the
more successful series of giant bomber types. The
machine shot down was powered by five engines,
its wing span was almost one hundred and forty
feet, and there were six machine-gun positions. Its
range with 1000 kg of bombs was over eight
hundred miles.

F5934   Sopwith Camel   201Sqn
**OP seen in combat with 10 Fokker DVIIs
ovASSEVILLERS 6-45pm **MIA**(Lt CL Wood US. **DoW**
17.8.18) left 5-45pm, died at TOURNAI [?"Camel"
claim combat eFAY? 6-45pm Ltn E Udet Ja4]

D8412   DH4   205Sqn
**B combat with Pfalz shot down ooc 3-40pm(Lt JG Kerr

OK/2Lt HW Hopton **DoW** 12.8.18)

C199   Sopwith Camel   209Sqn
**LowP shot up dam OK(Lt MA Toomey)

E4389   Sopwith Camel   209Sqn
**LowP left 2-15pm ground mg fire ftl cr BOUCHOIR
OK(Lt JW Sole)

11th August
THE USE OF AIR POWER
AT AMIENS

Raids on the rail centres, with particular emphasis
on Bapaume, continued on the 11th. Cambrai and
Equancourt were also attacked. 98 Squadron
suffered two casualties, but the air fighting was
notable for its lowering intensity. It mirrored the
increasing stalemate on the ground, in which the
Allies now considered they had pushed as far as
they were likely to manage without substantial
reinforcements of men and tanks and the reorganisation of their artillery and supply. The German
Army was also offering its stiffest opposition, finally
closing down the Allied advance. The RAF bombing of the railways was yielding diminishing returns
and the close support work of the fighters was
almost in abeyance. On the 11th, Haig called for
the postponement of operations indefinitely and the
battle ended.

The British and French Armies had advanced
twelve miles into the heart of the German defences
in the west and dealt it a near mortal blow. Amiens
had been saved and the new line ran just west of
Albert-Chaulnes-Roye. The German Air Force had
fought bravely but the will of the Allies had finally
prevailed: it had been drawn into a fight it could
not win. The RAF, on the other hand, had certainly
been denied its full effectiveness: after playing a
highly useful and important part in the initial
assault, its casualties had then dramatically risen
whilst its influence had correspondingly declined.
There is no doubt it was a great and promising
victory, but its flaws left it an unfulfilled one as
well.

As had happened before on the Western Front,
to lose focus after success was a stumbling block
few had been able to avoid. Ludendorff had
changed his battle plans tempted by the prospect
of swift victory in his spring battles, only to find he
had unbalanced his offensive and opened the way
for the Allies' reserves to regroup. The British in
their turn also failed to profit from stunning success
at Cambrai because they lacked both the means
and the understanding to exploit it. At Amiens they
began a battle in which the objectives were con-

fused; the air arm was more crucial to the fighting
than ever before and therefore suffered as much as
any one from this. Orders to shift the air effort to
the bridges brought many problems to the surface,
and a dislocation of effort was certain. A superbly
structured and co-ordinated offensive was
effectively halted by the removal of one of its key
elements — the aeroplane — in order to seek a
speedier solution. The target of the bridges was in
itself an extremely difficult and demanding one
technically. Its choice assumed bombing skills
beyond the means of the RAF at the time, and an
underestimation of the fight the Germans would be
capable of mounting in their defence. The British
lost a decisive opportunity on the 8th and it was
also very costly for the RAF. For instance, of the
ninety-seven aircraft deleted from strength on the
first day, seventy were from squadrons involved in
attacks on the bridges. Nevertheless, the RAF
endured the demands of the four days of fighting
with great courage and determination, and as a
whole, the battle was far from being a disaster. It
was, after all, a crushing and demoralising defeat
for Germany, and the first battle of the Allied
campaign to victory.

D4853   RE8   3Sqn AFC
**CAP shot up shrapnel dam returned 8-55pm OK(Lt
LP Chase/2Lt JP Jeffers) left 7pm

C8300   Sopwith Camel   4Sqn AFC
**BOP combat with EAs, escaped into clouds but then
AA ftl HAZEBROUCK 10-40am(Lt L Wharton MC
WIA) first 1EA then 6EAs, AA fragment hit head

C8530   A.W.FK8   8Sqn
TankP mg fire? VRELY ftl wr(Lt EL Munslow **WIA/
2Lt WA Mercer **WIA**) left 4-50pm, 10.8?

**   RE8   9Sqn**
LowP ground mg fire(/2Lt R Brandon **KIA)

D5076   A.W.FK8   10Sqn
**Phot combat with EA 5-45pm shot up ldg 27J.6.c.67.K
cr(2Lt HW Sheard **KIA**/2Lt H Goodwin OK)

B7876   Sopwith Dolphin 19Sqn
**OP left 4-14pm combat with EA eALBERT 5-50pm
MIA(Lt MS Gregory **KIA**) ["Dolphin" claim combat
ECLUSIER 5-55pm Ltn J Grassmann Ja10]

C4026   Sopwith Dolphin 19Sqn
**OP left 4-15pm shot up cr ldg 6-25pm OK(Lt DP
Laird)

C4043   Sopwith Dolphin 19Sqn
OP left 4-12pm seen in combat eALBERT **MIA(Lt RK
Douglas **KIA**) DoW as POW? ["Dolphin" claim
combat eFRISE 6pm Ltn A Heldman Ja10]

E4432   Sopwith Dolphin 19Sqn
**OP combat with EA eALBERT shot down in flames

EoL(Capt GB Irving **KIA**) left 4-15pm

E2467   Bristol F2b   20Sqn
+* attacked KB[+des] wCOURTRAI 5-40pm OK(Capt HP Lale/2Lt J Hills) this was the only balloon Lale shot down out of 23 victories

C8844   SE5a   24Sqn
**OP left 7-15pm Fourth Army area ground fire dam OK(2Lt TM Harries) returned a'dr 8-35pm

E1386   SE5a   29Sqn
**SpM radiator shot up ovCAMBRAI engine seized ftl ABEELE OK(Lt BR Rolfe)

         Bristol F2b   48Sqn
P combat(/2Lt H Knowles **DoW)

C2265   RE8   53Sqn
AReg EA AA? down in flames ooc 8pm cr nrFOETRE 27.s.E.2c(Lt GL Dobell **KIA/2Lt AW Baker **KIA**)

B9267   Sopwith Camel   54Sqn
delivery from 2ASD became lost **MIA(2Lt JB Risk **POW**)

C8886   SE5a   60Sqn
OP combat with EA neCHAULNES ftl 48Sqn A'dr BERTANGLES 10-05am(2Lt RK Whitney **WIA)to hospital, left 8-25am [?"SE5a" claim Ltn G Meyer Ja37]

D375   SE5a   92Sqn
OP seen going down in control nrNESTLE **MIA(Lt GF Metson **POW**) left 5-45 ALLONVILLE

This was the first loss in action for 92 Squadron.

D6925   SE5a   92Sqn
+* combat with Fokker DVII[+des] NESTLE 11-30am OK(Lt HB Good)

         DH9   98Sqn
B CLERY? combat(/Sgt EA Swayne **WIA)

C2206   DH9   98Sqn
**B CLERY combat with EA shot up sFALOISE ftl cr ground OK(Lt HJ Fox/Lt WR Sellar) left 6-30am

D1721   DH9   98Sqn
B left 6-30am CLERY **MIA(2Lt JD Connolly **POW**/2Lt EH Clayton **POW DoW**) [?"DH" claim combat CHAULNES 9am Ltn E Udet Ja4]

D3097   DH9   98Sqn
B left 6-30am CLERY **MIA(2Lt BC Geary **KIA**/2Lt EH Edgell **KIA**) ["DH" claim combat 8-30am Ltn L Fr vRichthofen Ja11]

C2199   DH9   206Sqn
LRec left 5-05am **MIA(Lt EHP Bailey **KIA**/2Lt R Milne **KIA**) [?"DH9" claim combat nLILLE 7-50am Ltn K Plauth Ja20]

D3423   Sopwith Camel   209Sqn
HOP combat with 5HA ftl Lines BAYONVILLERS(Lt JA Watt **WIA)slight

C1207   DH9   218Sqn
** AA hit ZEEBRUGGE in flames **MIA**(Lt H Fawdry **KIA**/Lt JS Cryan **KIA**)

D1028   DH9   218Sqn
**B AA engine failed ftl beach 1.5m wNIEUPORT OK(Lt WS Mars/2Lt HE Power) a'c shelled & destroyed, tide submerged it

** **MIA**(Lt WW Bradford **POW**) repat 26.11.18

** **MIA**(2Lt JE Parke **POW**) repat 26.11.18

12th August

E234   RE8   3Sqn AFC
**CP mg? shot down MORCOURT Sh62D Q18.A5.5 OK(Lt FM Lock/Lt AG Barrett) left 5am

         DH4   25Sqn
** combat(/Sgt T Lumley **WIA**)

         DH4   25Sqn
** combat(/Sgt WB Gray **WIA**)

         DH4   27Sqn
** combat(/Lt NF Frome **WIA**)

D6944   SE5a   29Sqn
OP shot up 27.R.5.a.45.10 at 9-30am ftl fainted 100' cr(Capt FJ Davies **WIA)to hospital, Davies had made 12 claims

A5743   FE2b   38Sqn
**NB ftl in sea off CALAIS BEACH then shot up by HA when in water OK(Lt HC McDonald/2Lt ER Bull) a'c sank

C9803   FE2b   38Sqn
**NB ftl in sea off CALAIS BEACH by HA OK(Lt H McAndrew/Sgt Harris) a'c sank

D6193   SE5a   40Sqn
OP seen nrBRIE 9am **MIA(Lt HH Wood **POW**) [?"SE5" claim combat nwROYE 5-10pm Ltn Brandes Ja24]

E3984   SE5a   40Sqn
OP seen nrBRIE 9am down EoL **MIA(Capt IF Hind **KIA**) [?"SE5" claim combat PERONNE 10-30am Ltn E Udet Ja4]

E3949.6   SE5a   41Sqn
OP several EAs on tail MORCOURT 7-20pm being chased west **MIA(Lt JA Gordon **KIA**) left 6pm

C8331   Sopwith Camel   46Sqn
WTInt seen dive on 2Str 12-30pm then down ooc **MIA(2Lt R Moore US. **KIA**) left 12-10pm

E2468   Bristol F2b   62Sqn
EscB combat nPERONNE shot down in flames **MIA(Lt AB Cort **KIA**/2Lt JN Mitchell **KIA**)

D6952.6   SE5a   64Sqn
+* combat with Fokker DVII[+des] CHAULNES 7-15am OK(Capt CW Cudemore) made half of his 15 claims in this a'c

D6969   SE5a   84Sqn
**OP mg VILLERS BRETONNEAUX 8-40pm engine ftl cr trench OK(Lt IP Corse)

D6875   SE5a   85Sqn
LP combat with 5 Fokker DVII 7-35am PASSCHENDAELE **MIA(Lt TC Martin **KIA**) left 7am ["SE5" claim combat LANGEMARCK 7-40am Ltn F Ritt vRöth Ja16]

D6862   SE5a   92Sqn
**OP ALLONVILLE shot up wr OK(Lt WS Philcox)salvable

D6883   SE5a   92Sqn
**OP ALLONVILLE shot up wr OK(Maj A Coningham DSO MC)

D2931.S DH9   104Sqn (I.F.)
B combat with 23EAs fuel tank hit? shot down **MIA(2Lt OF Meyer **POW**/Sgt AC Wallace **POW**) a'c captured, Ja18 ["DH9" claim combat BUHL a'dr Ltn K Monnington Ja18]

D3084   DH9   104Sqn (I.F.)
B combat with 23EAs 5m EoL fuel tank hit **MIA(Lt GH Patman **POW**/2Lt JMS Macpherson **POW**) one report: fell out, 40 minute combat caused re-direction of target to HAGENAU A'dr

B3894   Sopwith Camel   204Sqn
** combat with Fokker DVIIs[++flames+ooc] BLANKENBERGHE 10-55am shot up(Capt JEL Hunter DSC **WIA**)

D3355   Sopwith Camel   204Sqn
** left 9-10am combat with EA OSTENDE **MIA**(Lt SCJ Askin **POW**)

D6624   Sopwith Camel   204Sqn
** left 9-10am combat with EA shot down off OSTENDE PIER **MIA**(Lt RAG Hill **KIA**)

D9648   Sopwith Camel   204Sqn
** combat with EA[+ooc] bad shot up ftl MARDYKE BEACH dam OK(Lt WA Pomeroy) [?Camel claim combat off WESTENDE Flm G Hubrich SFS, but see US17 Camels]

D7315   DH9   206Sqn
B left 8-55am seen just WoL but cr EoL **MIA(Lt JC Ivens **POW**/2Lt CA Atkins **POW**) later salvaged by 103Sq in n.m.l. 7.9.18

B7471   Sopwith Camel   209Sqn
HOP seen in combat with 4 Fokker DVIIs ePERONNE 8-30am **MIA(Lt DK Leed **KIA**) [?"Dolphin" claim combat nwPERONNE 8-30am Ltn L Fr vRichthofen Ja11][?"English EA" claim combat ePERONNE 8-35am Ltn E Just Ja11]

D9657   Sopwith Camel   209Sqn
HOP combat with 4 Fokker DVIIs ePERONNE 8-30am **MIA(Lt KM Walker **KIA**) [?"Dolphin" claim combat nwMISERY 8-50am Ltn L Fr vRichthofen Ja11]

D9668   Sopwith Camel   209Sqn
HOP combat with Fokker DVIIs ePERONNE 8-30am **MIA(Capt JK Summers MC **POW**) LvR[?"Camel" claim combat nwPERONNE 8-30am Ltn L Fr vRichthofen Ja11]

D9608   Sopwith Camel   210Sqn
** flak dam ftl(2Lt HR Hughes **WIA**)slight

D1691   DH9   218Sqn
**B OSTENDE combat with EA bad shot up fire dam OK(Ens Moseley/Lt MM Lowry) [?DH9 claim combat off OSTENDE 11-55am Oblt zS G Sachsenberg MFJa1]

**   Sopwith Camel   US 17th Pursuit Sqn**
EscB(DH9s) combat with 2 Fokker DVIIs shot up ftl hit DH9 ldg PETITE SYNTHE A'dr dam(1Lt WJ Armstrong USAS **WIA)back & arm

D9495.C Sopwith Camel   US 17th Pursuit Sqn
EscB(DH9s) combat with EAs o'shot ldg PETITE SYNTHE cr dam(1Lt RW Snoke **inj)to hospital

D9507   Sopwith Camel   US 17th Pursuit Sqn
EscB seen in combat with 2 Fokker DVII nrOSTENDE 11-45am **MIA(1Lt RD Gracie **KIA**) escorting 211Sqn to BRUGES [?combat off OSTENDE 11-53am Oblt zS G Sachsenberg MFJa1]

**   Sopwith Camel   US 17th Pursuit Sqn**
** combat with EAs shot up ftl nrNIEUPORT(1Lt HB Alderman **WIA**)buttocks, to hospital: visited by King George who asked where he had been wounded: Alderman replied "Over Ostende, Your Majesty"

13th August

D6948   SE5a   2Sqn AFC
OP combat? then engine failed ftl field cr dam(Lt F Alberry DCM **inj)

B8885   RE8   9Sqn
**B shell engine hit & failed dam ftl OK(2Lt RN Essell/2Lt R Rawlinson)

A7907   DH4   18Sqn
B seen going s-w in combat with 15EA nrALBERT **MIA(Lt CF Drabble **KIA**/2Lt RW Rawley **KIA**) left 9am

This DH4 was lost during a dogfight in which machines of 18 and 22 Squadrons were attacked by many enemy fighters. 22 Squadron were escorting No. 18 on a bombing raid to Somain when they spotted and chased a two-seater near the lines. The enemy machine appeared to fire a light at which German fighters came up from near Douai and made an attack. The enemy two-seater is likely to have been performing a form of sentry duty. 22 Squadron claimed five enemy shot down on the 13th, shared between ten crews. The most intense fighting took place over Auberchicourt around 11-20am.

Sopwith Dolphin 19Sqn
air collision nrALLONVILLE(2Lt PJE Pierce **KIA)
KIA?

Sopwith Dolphin 19Sqn
air collision nrALLONVILLE(/2Lt WG Lance **KIA)
KIA?

D3927.B SE5a 41Sqn
**OP combat with HA? shot up ftl ST VAAST 8-15am
OK(Lt EH Barksdale) [?"SE5" claim combat
sZUYDSCHOOTE 7-50am UntOff P Huttenrauch Ja7]

C940 Bristol F2b 48Sqn
+* combat with Fokker DVIIs[+des++ooc] eROYE
5pm OK(Capt CR Steele/Lt JB Jameson) last of several
claims by pilot

Bristol F2b 48Sqn
** combat(/Capt MS Anthony **WIA**)

SE5a 56Sqn
** combat(2Lt VH Hervey **WIA**)

D6979.H SE5a 60Sqn
**OP combat with Fokker DVIIs CHAULNES 4-20pm
shot down in flames ROUVROY-EN-SANTERRE
MIA(Lt JR Anderson **KIA**) ["SE5" claim combat
FOUCHÈRES? 4-15pm Vzfw O Fruhner Ja26]

E1308 SE5a 60Sqn
**OP seen in combat with 15EAs nCHAULNES 4-20pm
MIA(Lt EJC McCracken **POW**) left 3-30pm

D9919 FE2b 101Sqn
**NRec engine shot through ftl nrAUBERCOURT
OK(2Lt LH Phillips/2Lt RG Miller), left 11pm
12.8, a'c salvable

D2881 DH9 104Sqn (I.F.)
B dh AA broke up then fell on D7229 **MIA(2Lt FH
Beaufort US. **KIA**/2Lt SO Bryant **KIA**) after bombing
EHRANGE(sic) Rlwy Junction [2 "DH4" claims combat
ARRICH?-ARNAVILLE 4-05pm Ltn K Monnington
Ja18]

D3088 DH9 104Sqn (I.F.)
B METZ-SABLON **MIA(2Lt EO Clarke **KIA**/Lt JLC
Sutherland **POW**) [?"DH9" claim combat ROYE
5-20pm Ltn R Klimke Ja27]

D7229 DH9 104Sqn (I.F.)
B hit by D2881 **MIA(2Lt HPG Leyden **KIA**/Sgt AL
Windridge **KIA**) D2881 had been hit by AA, after
bombing EHRANGE(sic) Rlwy Junction [2 "DH4"
claims combat ARRICH?-ARNAVILLE 4-05pm Ltn K
Monnington Ja18]

F5844 DH9 104Sqn (I.F.)
B THIONVILLE mg ftl wr(2Lt JC Uhlman **WIA/2Lt
P Sutherland USAS. **WIA**)

The target for 104 Squadron had been the Benz
works at Mannheim, but Thionville was bombed
instead. The enemy formation attacked the patrol
on the return journey, but of the three DH9s lost,
one was hit by AA and collided with another,

taking it down as well. Three enemy machines were
claimed destroyed or out of control.

D9642 Sopwith Camel 201Sqn
**SpM(showing Lines) combat with many Fokker
DVIIs[+++] wROSIÈRES 11am **MIA**(Maj CD Booker
DoW) ["Camel" claim combat LE QUESNEL 12pm Ltn
U Neckel Ja12]

A7573 DH4 205Sqn
PhotRec shot down cr Sh66E.L 29.a.8.4. **MIA(Lt T
Fattorini **KIA**/2Lt SJ Parkes **KIA**) left 5-12pm, buried
beside cr a'c

D8429 DH4 205Sqn
**B PERONNE Stn combat with Fokker DVIIs 11am
shot up(Lt FO McDonald **WIA**/Sgt FG Manning **KIA**)

DH9 206Sqn
** combat(2Lt E Calvert **DoW** 14.8.18)

D5590 DH9 206Sqn
B left 5-11pm **MIA(Lt CS Johnson **KIA**/2Lt AB
Sangster **KIA**)

In order to deal a blow at enemy air reinforcements
in the Dunkirk area, a very large raid was carried
out on Varssenaere aerodrome — west of Bruges,
on the 13th. The raid involved bombers from 211
and 218 Squadron and fifty Sopwith Camels from
Nos. 210, 213, and US 17th Pursuit Squadron who
would bomb from low levels. Additionally, 204
Squadron Camels patrolled at 5000 feet to protect
from attack above. The Camels left at dawn and
once rendezvoused they made for the aerodrome
where they arrived with complete surprise. Fokker
DVIIs were lined up on the ground in front of their
hangars. The raid caused great chaos and destruction yet not a single Allied machine was lost.

14th August

RE8 6Sqn
** combat(2Lt D Bradbury **WIA**)

B4160 A.W.FK8 8Sqn
LP left 2-35pm **MIA(2Lt EG Renton **KIA**/2Lt GE
Cave **KIA**)

D7912 Bristol F2b 11Sqn
** combat with HA ftl cr VERT GALAND(Lt ES Coler
US. OK/2Lt CW Gladman **WIA**) at 9-10am, injured in
crash?, pilot claimed a few of his 16 victories in this a'c

C2507 RE8 12Sqn
**CP AA dam ftl cr GOUYER ARTOIS(Maj HS Lees-
Smith **inj**/2Lt AJ Baxter **inj**)to hospital, left 5-45pm

A7856 DH4 18Sqn
B EA? AA hit going down ovLA BASSÉE cr **MIA(1Lt
T Kearney USAS. **KIA**/Sgt H Hammond **KIA**) left
5-35am

A7903 DH4 18Sqn
Phot left 9-05am down EoL **MIA(Capt HR Gould MC

KIA/2Lt EWF Jinman **KIA**)

C987   Bristol F2b   20Sqn
OP left 5pm **MIA(Lt DE Smith **KIA**/2Lt J Hills
POW) [?possible "BF" claim combat WERVICQ
6-15pm Ltn Schramm Ja56]

B3539   SPAD 7   23Sqn
+* combat with AlbatrosDV[+ooc]
PASSCHENDAELE 7pm then combat with 2Str[+des]
eST JULIEN 7-15pm OK(2Lt GID Marks Can.) 2Str
shared, last of several victories

C1085   SE5a   24Sqn
**OP combat shot up ftl ALLONVILLE 8pm dam
OK(Lt TTB Hellett)

D6631   Sopwith Camel   46Sqn
**OP combat with EA going down in flames seBRAY
8000' 5-45pm **MIA**(2Lt JE Crouch **KIA**) ["Sopwith"
claim combat CHAULNES 5-40pm Vzfw A Haussmann
Ja13]

F2086   Sopwith Camel   46Sqn
**OP seen dive west in control seBRAY 8000' 5-45pm
MIA(2Lt GAR Hill **POW**)

F2112   Sopwith Camel   46Sqn
**OP seen ooc diving west seBRAY 8000' 5-45pm
MIA(2Lt CE Thorpe **POW**) ["Sopwith" claimed
CHAULNES 5-40pm Ltn R Büchner Ja13]

D2861   DH9   49Sqn
**B combat shot down in flames broke up
ovHAVRINCOURT WOOD **MIA**(2Lt JG Andrews
KIA/2Lt J Churchill **KIA**) left 8-30am ["DH9" claim
combat BERTINCOURT 10-20am Ltn W Sommer
Ja39]

E4434   Sopwith Dolphin 87Sqn
SpP left 9-25am ARRAS-ALBERT **MIA(Lt RA Hewat
KIA)

C852   Bristol F2b   88Sqn
**OP combat with 11EA 5-45pm seen going down
vertically ovAMIENS-ST QUENTIN RD **MIA**(Lt AR
Stedman **POW**/2Lt GR Howard **POW**) ["BF" claim
combat VERMANDOVILLERS 6pm Ltn E Udet Ja4]

C1888   SE5a   92Sqn
**OP elevator shot away swPERONNE going down EoL
FIENVILLERS? **MIA**(Lt HA O'Shea **POW**) [?"SE5"
claim combat CHAULNES 11-05am Ltn U Neckel Ja12]

D6173   SE5a   92Sqn
**OP combat with Fokker DVII[+flames] sPERONNE
11-30am shot up ftl dam OK(Lt OJ Rose US.) Rose
claimed 16 EAs

D1701   DH9   211Sqn
**Rec combat with 6HA shot up ftl cr FORTHEM-
LOO: seFURNES OK(Lt AF Bonnalie USAS/2Lt TB
Dodwell) left 2-35pm

B7614   DH9   211Sqn
**PhotRec combat with 6HA shot up ftl cr
OUDECAPPELLE wr(Lt CH Miller **WIA**/Cpl SJ Bence

KIA) left 2-35pm

D9455   Sopwith Camel   US 17th Pursuit Sqn
**EscB combat with 6 Fokker DVIIs air collision with
DVII seen ooc 14000' cr swBRUGES 11-30am **MIA**(1Lt
LE Case **KIA**) left 10-25am, Fokker DVII had just been
hit by Lt GD Wicks in Camel B9166

F2134   Sopwith Camel   US 17th Pursuit Sqn
**OP seen dive on EA[+?des] sBRUGES 11-30am
MIA(2Lt WH Shearman **POW DoW**)

15th August
FIGHTING AT AMIENS DRAWN TO A CLOSE

The lessons for the Royal Air Force from the
Amiens offensive were quickly assimilated as it
learned from its inconclusive assault on the Somme
bridges and derived confidence from the impact it
had undoubtedly had in the early stages. They key
elements which had made these low level attacks
so effective had been a relatively good understanding of the battlefield and the expected course
of the battle, and the advantage of surprise. As soon
as enemy resistance stiffened their use was less
influential and more costly.

The work of the corps squadrons was also considered. Contact patrolling associated with the
infantry had been effective within the limitations
imposed by the weather and the fluid state of the
battle. It was realised, however, that improved co-
operation with tanks was essential. In August 1918
this was as much as anything a technological
question limited by wireless telegraphy. Improved
air protection for tanks was also essential, particularly through the laying of smoke screens. There
should also be attacks on anti-tank guns, and 73
Squadron was henceforth allocated to the Tank
Corps to carry out this offensive work. A final
important development of this assessment of the
corps squadrons' work was the setting up of the
Wireless Central Information Bureau to co-
ordinate the information about enemy activities
that was coming in throughout the battle. It was
felt that valuable time had been wasted whilst news
about a useful target found its way to fighter
squadrons who could attack it. These might be an
enemy formation in the sky as much as a target on
the ground.

C2490   RE8   3Sqn AFC
**CAP shot up dam returned a'dr 10-45am OK(Lt DF
Dimsey/Lt RFC Machin)

Sopwith Camel   4Sqn AFC
** shot up(2Lt F Howard **WIA**)

D1927   Sopwith Camel   4Sqn AFC
**KB[+des] SAILLY then AA shot up ftl fainted cr
SERNY(Lt RG Smallwood **WIA**) [?possible "Camel"
claim combat HERLEVILLE 4-15pm Ltn E Udet Ja4]

Bristol F2b   20Sqn
** AA(Lt WH Markham **WIA**)

A7891   DH4   25Sqn
Rec left 5am DOUAI **MIA(Lt TJ Arthur **POW**/2Lt
AG Lawe **POW**)

D6122   SE5a   40Sqn
*trav low stall snd cr fire(Maj AW Keen MC **DoI**
12.9.18) Keen claimed his last 2 of 14 EAs in this a'c

C1825   SE5a   74Sqn
*OP AA prop shot off ftl cr Sh27Q 18.B.55. at 6-10am(Lt
WE Bargett **WIA**)slight

D3048   DH9   99Sqn (I.F.)
B cr on return wr(2Lt EL McCowen **WIA/2Lt W Shaw
WIA) inj?

A6570   FE2b   101Sqn
**NRec AA ftl cr fire nrAILLY SUR NOYE 3-15am
destroyed OK(2Lt PJ Williams/2Lt RL Williams) left
2am

B7176   Sopwith Camel   204Sqn
** combat with Fokker DVII[+ooc] 6m eYPRES
8-25am(Lt JR Robinson **WIA**)

D9628   Sopwith Camel   204Sqn
**HOP combat NIEUPORT-YPRES shot up ftl dam ldg
ok ●K(Lt HWM Cumming)

D9630   Sopwith Camel   204Sqn
** left 6-50am shot down eYPRES **MIA**(Lt CD
Darlington **KIA**)

E4405   Sopwith Camel   204Sqn
** combat with EA eYPRES shot down **MIA**(Lt DE
Culver **POW**) [?"Camel" claim combat
ePASSCHENDAELE 6-35pm Ltn K Plauth Ja20]

D1871   Sopwith Camel   213Sqn
** last seen ok as combat with 15EA DIXMUDE-YPRES
started 6-50pm shot down **MIA**(Lt CH Denny **POW**) left
5-15pm [?possible "Camel" claim ST JULIEN Ltn
Schramm Ja56]

E1409   Sopwith Camel   US 148th Pursuit Sqn
**P AA fuel tank shot up ftl Sh66E.F.10A (1Lt LT Wyly
WIA)

16th August

** **MIA**(Lt H Burton **POW**) repat?

A.W.FK8   2Sqn
** combat(2Lt EC Gordon **WIA**)

D6579   Sopwith Camel   3Sqn
**COP left 5-15am mg fire ftl returned a'dr 7-15am(1Lt
MC Kinney USAS. **WIA**)

D9443.F Sopwith Camel   3Sqn

**COP seen ok sARRAS-CAMBRAI RD going s-e in
control 1000' 3-30pm **MIA**(Lt AT Partridge **POW**)

RE8   5Sqn
** (/Lt RW Jackson **WIA**)

B6575   RE8   6Sqn
**LRec combat with EA LA MOTTE shot up ftl dam(Lt
Bradley **WIA**/Lt Lucy OK) left 6-30pm

C8620   A.W.FK8   8Sqn
**LP AA hit u'c ftl cr ldg wr OK(Lt VA Grundy/Lt WL
Norman) left 4pm

RE8   9Sqn
** ground mg fire(/2Lt LF Rowsell **WIA**)

C2407   RE8   21Sqn
Shoot AA? Q29.B.68 **MIA(Lt WH Pollard **POW**/Lt K
Macdonald **KIA**) left 3pm, grave at Sh36A Q.24.d.2.6.

A7781   DH4   55Sqn (I.F.)
**B DARMSTADT combat with EAs shot down
sMANNHEIM **MIA**(2Lt JB McIntyre **KIA**/2Lt HH
Bracher **KIA**)

A7813   DH4   55Sqn (I.F.)
**B DARMSTADT combat with EAs shot down in
control sMANNHEIM **MIA**(2Lt J Campbell **POW**/2Lt
JR Fox **DoW** as **POW**)

D9273   DH4   55Sqn (I.F.)
**B DARMSTADT combat with EAs MANNHEIM
MIA(2Lt EA Browhill **KIA**/2Lt WT Madge **KIA**)

DH4   55Sqn (I.F.)
B shot up (1Lt GC Sherman USAS. **WIA/) 16.6?

F5703   DH4   55Sqn (I.F.)
**B DARMSTADT mg shot up wr on ldg?(2Lt AC
Roberts **WIA**/2Lt N Wallace **WIA**?)

These very heavy casualties for 55 Squadron
occurred on a morning raid which bombed the
railway at Darmstadt. The original target had been
Köln, but low cloud made the leader choose the
alternative target of Mannheim instead and, as
conditions improved, they pressed on a little
further and hit Darmstadt. Throughout August,
enemy opposition on these raids was increasing
daily, and on the way home, near Mannheim, they
were attacked by twenty fighters who shot four
DH4s down and wounded other crew.

E4626   DH4   57Sqn
**RecB combat on return dam hit hangar ldg cr(2Lt JP
Ferreira/Sgt NM Belcher **WIA**) left 8-45am
SANCOURT DUMP

DH4   57Sqn
** combat(/Sgt EEAG Bridger **KIA**)

D9267   DH4   57Sqn
**RecB seen ok QUESNOY 14000' 11-10am then down
in control going n-e **MIA**(Lt WH Kilbourne **POW**/2Lt
DE Stephens **POW DoW**)

C6496   SE5a   84Sqn
**OP combat with 2Str spin broke up
FOUCAUCOURT(Lt JL Payton **KIA**) right planes shot
away

D5973?   SE5a   92Sqn
this a'c? **SpM (Capt JM Robb **WIA**) had made several
victory claims

D9595   Sopwith Camel   203Sqn
**Esc combat with Fokker DVIIIs seen shot down
nrPERONNE in control 11-35am **MIA**(Sgt PM Fletcher
POW) escorting 205Sqn [+?"Camel" claim combat
MESNIL 11-30am Ltn Rolff Ja6]

B7623.L DH9   211Sqn
**B neBRUGES AA seen glide down ok ftl
ZOUDEKERQUE **MIA**(1Lt DR Harris USAS. **INT**/
2Lt J Munro **INT**) left 10-30am, interned Holland
[?"DH9" claim CADZAND Oblt zS G Sachsenberg
MFJa1]

B7679   DH9   211Sqn
** (Lt GH Baker **WIA**?)inj?

C6348.C DH9   211Sqn
**B flak BRUGES engine ftl sea WIELINGEN
MIA(Capt RM Wynne-Eaton **INT**/2Lt TB Dodwell
WIA INT) left 10-30am, rescued

D1708   DH9   218Sqn
** engine failed ftl cr wr **MIA**((Lt AC Lloyd **INT**/2Lt
MG Wilson **INT**) interned Holland ?combat off
BLANKENBERGHE Oblt T Osterkamp MFJaII]

17th August
PREPARATIONS FOR THE BATTLE OF BAPAUME

Skirmishes naturally continued on the old Amiens
front as the armies settled down into their
positions. Foch had wanted the British to make
their next attacks in the Roye-Chaulnes area but
Haig believed they should come further north in
order to straighten the line and exert greater
pressure on Peronne. If an assault was launched
between Albert and Arras a number of other
advantageous aspects could be exploited. Firstly,
this region lent itself to a tank advance; secondly,
it would put pressure on the major strategic prizes
of Cambrai and St Quentin; and thirdly, wholesale
readjustments of armies, air force, and equipment
need not be necessary, for surprise would again
play a key role. Foch was convinced by these
arguments and ordered preparations to begin in
order for a main attack to commence on the 23rd.
The French would attack in co-operation in the
south.

Some RAF units which had been in the thick of
fighting at Amiens were retired to recuperate on
other fronts, others coming in by way of exchange.

In general, however, all that was required to
provide support for the Third and Fourth Armies,
who were to make the attack, was some strengthening of III Brigade. Most of those already active
north of the Somme would keep fighting. Two US
Aero Squadrons who had been flying Sopwith
Camels with the British, Nos. 17 and 148 Pursuit
Squadrons, were moved to the Third Army area,
and four additional RAF fighter squadrons joined
III Brigade as well, so that besides the Americans
there were Nos. 1, 3, 54, 73, and 201 (Sopwith
Camels), Nos. 1, 56, 60 (SE5as), and No. 87
(Sopwith Dolphins) on its strength. Other units
strengthening III Brigade were 11 Squadron
(Bristol Fighters), 57 Squadron (DH4s), and 102
Squadron (FE2b night-bombers). III Brigade's
Corps Units were Nos. 12, 13, 15, and 59 (all
RE8s). The four fighter units of I Brigade were to
provide high offensive patrolling from their bases
in the adjacent sector. All the units which would
be involved in the fighting needed to ensure that
none of their activity would create suspicion.
Operations were therefore continued in front of all
three of the Fourth, Third, and First Armies.

D1961   Sopwith Camel   4Sqn AFC
BOP ground fire ovLOMME A'dr 8-25am **MIA(Lt
EPE McCleery **KIA**)

                RE8   15Sqn
** (/2Lt H Atkinson **WIA**)

E4014   SE5a   41Sqn
**LP Fokker DVII on tail? going east ovZONNEBEKE
9-45am **MIA**(Lt TM Alexander **KIA**) to
LANGEMARCK-NIEPPE WOOD, combat possible
9-45am

E4018.F   SE5a   41Sqn
+* combat with LVGC[+ooc] DEULEMONT-
OUTTERSTEENE 9-20am OK(Capt FRG McCall
Can.) McCall's last of 35 victories

F5910.A   SE5a   41Sqn
OP seen ok sYPRES 9am 10000' **MIA(Lt WG Claxton
Can. **POW**) pilot had scored his 37th victory 4 days
previously [?"SE5" claim combat wWERVICQ 9am Ltn
K Plauth Ja20][?"SE5" claim combat eWERVICQ 9am
Ltn J Gildemeister Ja20]

D6976   SE5a   74Sqn
+* combat with Fokker DVII[+ooc] nHOUTHULST
WOOD 9-05am OK(Capt B Roxburgh-Smith) claimed
22 EAs with 74Sqn

E2183   Bristol F2b   88Sqn
** (/Pte E Hoare **WIA**?) inj?

D9094?   FE2b   100Sqn (I.F.)
B aerodromes **MIA(1Lt JJ vanSchaack USAS. **POW**/
Capt JA King USAS. **POW**), possible D9094 as a'c went
off strength the next day?

This was the last FE2b lost to 100 Squadron before re-equipping with the Handley Page 0/400.

18th August

D6965   SE5a   29Sqn
OP seen ok KEMMEL-BAILLEUL 4000' 12-15pm going west for lines **MIA(Capt CJ Venter **POW**)

D7302   DH9   108Sqn
B EA AA OSTENDE dam seen going down fast nr OSTENDE 3-53pm **MIA(Capt RSS Ingram **POW**/2Lt AW Wyncoll **POW**)

This was the first crew lost to enemy action by 108 Squadron.

19th August

215 Squadron joined the Independent Force at Xaffevillers on the 19th. In March and April it had operated from Dunkirk but was sent to England on the 23rd of April to be brought up to strength. It returned to France on the 4th of July and had been operating from Alquines. On its redeployment it remained a heavy night-bomber squadron and its Handley Pages flew their first raid to Mannheim only a few nights later, on the 25th/26th.

On the eve of the operations at Bapaume there was encouraging news of progress in the Lys Valley where the German Army was being decisively pushed out of its salient. A key victory occurred here on the 19th with the fall of Merville. The French Army under Mangin was also forcing its way forward between Soissons and Noyon.

E120   RE8   3Sqn AFC
Phot left 3-15pm **MIA(Lt JC Peel **KIA**/2Lt JP Jeffers **KIA**)

**   RE8   13Sqn**
** (Lt CH Tyreman **WIA**)

E6006   SE5a   24Sqn
+* combat with Fokker DVII[+ooc] FRESNOY 11-30am OK(2Lt TM Harries) claimed several EAs

E3947   SE5a   40Sqn
+* attacked KBs[++des] eMERVILLE then in afternoon KBs[++des] ~1-40pm OK(Lt L Bennett US.) Bennett made 12 claims in 10 days, including 9 balloons

C926   Bristol F2b   48Sqn
OP air collision with D8027: locked together wPERONNE 10000' **MIA(2Lt ES Glasse **KIA**/2Lt CW Woodend **KIA**) left 5-10am [?double "BF" claim combat LIHONS? 7-05am OffSt J Mai Ja5]

D8027   Bristol F2b   48Sqn
OP air collision with C926: locked together wPERONNE 10000' **MIA(Lt RH Davis **KIA**/2Lt EG Locke **KIA**) left 5-10am [?2 "BF" claims combat LIHONS? 7-05am OffSt J Mai Ja5]

D1715   DH9   49Sqn
**B AA ERINCOURT? 8-10am engine cut ftl OK(Lt ER Wallington/2Lt JD Hall) a'c abandoned

F2169   Sopwith Camel   54Sqn
OP seen ok eROISELLE 9-35am **MIA(2Lt AC Porter **POW**)

E1348   SE5a   56Sqn
COP seen in combat with many Fokker DVIIs eBAPAUME 12000' 7-45am down ooc flat spin **MIA(Lt TD Hazen **KIA**) ["SE5" claim combat LE TRANSLOY 7-35am OffSt J Mai Ja5][?possible "SE5" claim combat AVELUY 8am Ltn A Heldman Ja10]

E2216   Bristol F2b   88Sqn
+* combat with Fokker DVII[+ooc] then Fokker DrI[+ooc] nrOIGNIES 10-25am OK(Lt KB Conn Can./2Lt BH Smyth) Conn claimed maybe 20 EAs, over half in this F2b

D3045   DH9   98Sqn
**B left 6-30am ROISEL Stn combat with EA shot up dam OK(Lt JM Brown/2Lt H Lawrence)

D504   DH9   104Sqn (I.F.)
B combat with Fokker DVII WoL down in flames ovROISELLE **MIA(Lt CH Roberts **KIA**/Lt JH Davies **KIA**) left 6-40am

E602   DH9   108Sqn
B combat? AA hit nrBRUGES dam going down into sea off JABBEKE nrOSTENDE **MIA(2Lt JM Dunlop **POW**/Lt FF Schorn **WIA? POW**) left 5-05pm, failed to reach Holland

3127   H.P. 0/100   216Sqn (I.F.)
**NB probably ftl MIA but OK(Lt HG Sawyer/2Lt RSV McKenna/Sgt SF Mills)

There was extremely bad weather on the night of the 19th and the targets for 216 Squadron of Koln and Frankfurt were abandoned in preference of Boulay aerodrome.

20th August

C2596   RE8   5Sqn
P shell AA WARVILLERS(Lt WT Fothergill **KIA/Lt GWH Parlee **KIA**)

A7867   DH4   217Sqn
** spun into sea 3m neDUNKIRK 6-45am(Ens TN McKinnon USNRF **KIA**/Yeo ME O'Connor **KIA**) drowned, EA?

21st August
PRELIMINARY FIGHTING
FOR THE BATTLE

The first fighting in the battle of Bapaume was a preliminary operation to capture the Arras-Albert railway, launched on the 21st. In an effort to preserve secrecy, none of the air units involved had

been advised that fighting was imminent until the previous evening. At that time, night flying to cover the noise of tanks being brought up was again provided, but may have been less successful than before.

Rain and low mist hung over the battlefield on the morning of the assault, hindering the early low attacks of the aircraft but helping the tanks. Much work had been done to identify more accurately where enemy reinforcements might best be attacked from the air as they swarmed up to the line, but these operations were delayed until around 10am, almost six hours after the advance had begun. Pairs of aircraft from Nos. 3, 56, and 60 Squadrons made the attacks and incidentally met the most enemy air activity. The German Air Force was also concentrating on low protection and attack work. The SE5as were not as suited to this work as the Sopwith Camel because their manoeuvrability at low level was inferior. As a consequence they took heavy punishment. On the other hand, a telling quote is given in Wise's *Canadian Airmen*, extracted from the contemporary diary of Karl Bodenschatz, which pleaded that "The German Luftwaffe is choking to death under the weight of enemy strength in the air. There is little left that can be done." In addition to these low raids, there were also high offensive patrols mounted by US 17 and 148 Squadrons, and 11 and 87 Squadrons, and day and night bombing typically targeted Aubigny-au-Bac and Marquion rail centres.

D1835? **Sopwith Camel** **3Sqn**
this a'c? **LowB attacking transport, ground fire shot up, managed to return to a'dr(Lt CG Brock Can. **WIA**)knee

Sopwith Camel **3Sqn**
** (Lt WH Hubbard Can. **WIA**)

F1960 **Sopwith Camel** **3Sqn**
KBP last seen ok diving steeply on KB BAPAUME 12-20pm **MIA(Lt LH McIntyre Can. **KIA**)

D4738 **RE8** **6Sqn**
CP mg hit shot up 500yd wACHIET WOOD 1-15pm ftl(Lt HF Longbottom **WIA/Lt Anderson OK)unsalvable

C8540 **A.W.FK8** **8Sqn**
CAP AA ftl Sh51C X.19.c dam(Lt WP Packenham OK/2Lt AE Shirley **WIA) left 11-25am

RE8 **12Sqn**
** mg fire(/Lt LG Hummerstone **KIA**)

E232 **RE8** **12Sqn**
P air collision with KB cable cr BIENVILLERS-MONCHY RD(Lt FV Bird **KIA/2Lt LM Stubley **KIA**) left 4-25pm

E2158 **Bristol F2b** **20Sqn**

+* combat with Fokker DVII[+des] nMENIN 7-20pm OK(Lt JH Colbert/2Lt HL Edwards) last of 6 claims by Colbert, notably Edwards went on to make 21

C1942 **SE5a** **29Sqn**
**OP AA hit u'c dam ftl cr ldg 2-45pm OK(Lt AE Reed) left 12-35pm

B442 **FE2b** **38Sqn**
**NB AA ftl LA PANNE dam OK(Lt E Everatt/2Lt W Marginson) 21/22Aug

SE5a **56Sqn**
** combat(2Lt NF Bishop **WIA**)

C8884 **SE5a** **56Sqn**
LowP shot up ovSAILLY 4-10pm seen cr(1Lt RH Ellis USAS. **POW) killed?

D6128 **SE5a** **56Sqn**
**LowGndStr shot up bad dam returned 32Sq a'dr 4-15pm OK(Lt CB Stenning) left 3-45pm Third Army area

C1131 **SE5a** **60Sqn**
LowP combat with HA AA? shot down 500' ERVILLERS 1-30pm(Lt SW Keen MC **DoW 28.8.18?)

D6992 **SE5a** **60Sqn**
**LowP AA shot up dam returned a'dr 3-20pm OK(Lt FE Smith) left 2-05pm Sixth Army area

E3916.L **SE5a** **60Sqn**
**LowP EA? shot up COURCELLES 2-50pm ftl OK(Capt FW Clarke) unsalvable

E5941.U **SE5a** **64Sqn**
+* combat with Fokker DVII[+des] neDOUAI 4-30pm OK(Capt WH Farrow) Farrow made several claims

D5414 **H.P.0/400** **97Sqn (I.F.)**
NB BUHL A'dr **MIA(Lt ME Burnham **POW**/2Lt CK David **POW**/Lt JS Andrews **POW**) 21/22Aug.18

This was the first crew lost to enemy action by 97 Squadron.

F6112 **DH9** **107Sqn**
B left 2-25pm ROISEL-CLERY-VITRY **MIA(Lt HC Curtis **KIA**/Lt FG Davies **KIA**) Station targets, patrol met 8 Fokker DrIs [?"DH9" claim combat PERONNE 4pm Oblt Ritt vGreim JGr 9][?"DH4" claim combat MOISLAINS 3-45pm Vzfw G Staudacher Ja1]

D8420 **DH4** **202Sqn**
** combat with Fokker DVII BLANKENBERGHE-ZEEBRUGGE 1-10pmshot up dam(Lt GR Hurst OK/Sgt LA Allen **WIA**) [?combat Ltn T Osterkamp MJaII]

D8387 **DH4** **205Sqn**
** heavy AA ftl dam(Lt AN Hyde/2Lt WW Harrison)

D3380 **Sopwith Camel** **213Sqn**
** seen in combat with 11EA on coast 7-15pm **MIA**(Lt J Wooding **POW**) [Camel claim combat off WESTENDE Flm G Hubrich SFS]

D9659 **Sopwith Camel** **213Sqn**
**HOP combat with 11HA shot up dam ftl cr nr a'dr

BE12 6547 belonged to the 9th Wing Special Duty Flight and was lost in the early hours of 9 August 1917. The pilot 2AS Bean was taken prisoner.

A German Drachen kite balloon. Such balloons were usually heavily defended and were difficult and frequent targets for Allied fighter pilots.

This Sopwith Triplane with German markings is believed to be N5429 of 1(Naval) Sqn which was shot down and captured on 13 September 1917. The pilot was FSLt JR Wilford.

4. Twelve inmates of Schweidnitz, with dates of capture in brackets: 2Lt AJ Savory (11.7.17), 2Lt EAL? Lloyd, Lt Hardy?, ?, FLt HC Vereker (1.1.17), Lt Smith, 2Lt HG Tinney (13.8.17), 2Lt CR Dougall (19.3.17), Lt CH Beldam (31.7.17), Lt OD Maxted (12.4.17), Lt L Dodson (3.4.17), Lt JG Young (14.8.17).

1. Lt Hammond's SE5 in German hands. (See caption below).

2. Canadian 2Lt JL Haight was shot down and captured in this crashed DH5, A9276 of 41 Sqn, on 28 September 1917.

3. Lt HT Bunny Hammond of 60 Sqn, taken in 1916. He was shot down in combat whilst flying SE5 A8918 on 14 September 1917 and taken prisoner.

4. The forty-victory ace Capt PF Fullard of 1 Sqn at Bailleul in October 1917.

Line up of officers of 1 (Naval) Squadron in front of ⌐pwith Triplanes at Bailleul on 28 October 1917. Left to ⌐ht: FSLts SM Kinkead, Canadian JH Forman (POW in ⌐ Sqn Camel C8239 on 4.9.18), H Wallace, AJA Spence, ⌐Everett, FCdr HV Rowley, FSLts P Luard, Magrath?, ⌐F Crundall, WH Sneath? (KIA in 208 Sqn Camel B7187 ⌐ 6.4.18), E Burton, HR Adee, Canadian SW Rosevear, ⌐dr RP Minifie (POW in Camel B6420 on 17.3.18), ⌐dr RS Dallas (KIA 1.6.18), FCdr CB Ridley, FSLts ⌐deWilde, Canadian JB White, Lt WH Holden?

Two German troops examine the battered remains of a ⌐5 of 64 Squadron down in enemy lines - possibly one of the ⌐eral machines which that unit lost on 20 November 1917.

3. Two captured British machines at an enemy aerodrome: in the foreground is DH5 A9474 of 41 Sqn in which 2Lt FS Clark was wounded and taken prisoner on 29 October 1917; behind is SE5a B4876 of 84 Sqn, lost on 20 October, when 2Lt WE Watts was POW. There appears to be a third British aircraft, a Sopwith Pup, behind the SE5a.

4. Capt AC Youdale of 21 Sqn points to shell damage on the nose of his RE8, probably incurred in October 1917. Youdale was killed in action on 23 December 1917 in B5088 with his regular observer Lt JE Mott.

1. Lt HG Reeves, an ace of 1 Sqn, in October 1917. He was killed in an accident on 24 January 1918.

2. Lt WG Meggitt MC of 22 Sqn, taken after the war. He was wounded and taken prisoner in F2b B1123 on 8 November 1917 after heavy combat. His observer, Capt FA Durrad, was killed in the air and thrown out on landing.

3. DH4 A2170 of 25 Sqn came down in enemy lines on 2 November 1917. The crew of 2Lt R Main and 1AM GP Leach were taken prisoner. *(K Molson, via JMB/GSL)*

4. Sopwith Triplane N533, possibly at Petite Synthe in la[te] 1917. This was 'Black Maria' of 10 (Naval) Sqn, flown b[y] the Canadian ace FLt R Collishaw.

1

2

3

4

German Albatros DVa brought down by Lt JLM Sandy
~~d~~ Sgt HF Hughes of 69 (Australian) Sqn on 17 December
~~17~~ in RE8 D3816. Both Australian airmen were killed
~~on~~ after but the RE8 landed itself fifty miles away (see
~~xt~~). The Albatros is now in the Australian War Museum.

2Lt LG Nixon of 3 Sqn was captured after being forced

down in this Camel B6234 on 5 December 1917.

3. A DFW CIV rides high above a patchwork of fields and
roads. The abundance of visible tracks probably means it
is flying over support positions close to the lines.

4. B Flight of 7 Sqn in front of an RE8 in 1918.

1. 2Lt FM Ohrt of 54 Sqn was shot down and captured in Sopwith Camel B5423 on 19 January 1918. It is seen here in German hands.

2. Six officers of C Flight 56 Sqn in February or March 1918, left to right: Lt ME Mealing (KIA in SE5a B182 on 24.3.18), Capt WS Fielding-Johnson, Lt HJ Walkerdine, Lt LW Jarvis, Lt LN Franklin (KIA in SE5a D6064 on 14.7.18), Lt AL Garrett (WIA POW in SE5a B8421 on 28.6.18).

3. The German ace Hpt von Tutschek stands at the nose of SPAD B6732 of 23 Sqn which he had just forced to land east of the lines on 26 February 1918. The pilot, 2Lt DC Doyle, was taken prisoner. *(A Imrie, via JMB/GSL)*

4. Officers of A(Naval) Sqn, later 16 (Naval) Sqn, at Ochey in early 1918. Standing left to right: SLt Pilkington, FSLt GA Flavelle (Can.), FSLt LR Shoebottom (Can.), FSLt HH Costain (Can.), SLt JW Adams (Can.), SLt Todd, WO O'Donnel, WO Fry, Lt Harper RFC, Lt Best RFC; seated: FSLt Babee, FLt Rawlings, FLt Gilligan, FLt Digby, SCdr HA Buss, LCdr EW Steadman, FLt McLelland, Lt Gibbons, Lt Samson RFC, FSLt Halley. *(GA Flavelle, via R Bernard)*

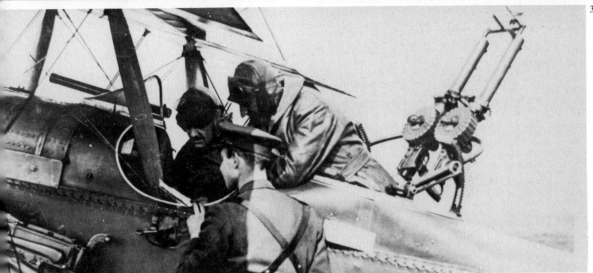

A line-up of 9 Fokker DrIs of Jasta 11 at Awoingt in ~~arch~~ 1918. In the distance are Albatros DVas and Pfalz IIIs of Jasta 4.

This SE5a crashed in enemy territory is believed to be a ~~Sqn~~ machine lost in March 1918. The most likely ~~entity~~ is one of the two SE5as lost on 24 March, one of ~~hich~~ was claimed by Manfred von Richthofen and ~~escribed~~ as losing its wings and falling out of control. It ~~uld~~ be C6399, in which 2Lt DC Tucker was killed, and it

may be von Richthofen standing fourth from left, half facing the camera.

3. Lts Hobbs and Chippendale in their RE8 reporting to Maj. Solomon, the CO of 15 Sqn, on 25 March 1918 during the battle of Bapaume.

4. A study of a Sopwith Camel from 65 Sqn. Pilot and aircraft serial are unknown.

1. Group of 213 Sqn officers at Bergues in May 1918.
From left to right: Lt Taylor, Lt WE Gray, Capt Horstman, Capt JW Pinder, Lt Talbot, Lt MN Hancocks.

2. No. 40 Sqn officers at Bruay in April 1918. Left to right: Capt WL Harrison, Lt GAB Wheldon, ?, Lt HS Cameron, Lt CW Usher, Lt JW Walwork, Lt JH Tudhope, Capt GH Lewis, Major RS Dallas (KIA 1.6.1918); Padre BW Keymer; Lt LH Sutton.

3. The captured 3 (Naval) Sqn Sopwith Camel flown in action by Ltn O Kissenberth of Jasta 23. It may be B7230. In the background is an Albatros D-type with that unit's markings.

4. The wreckage of Handley Page 0/100 3132 shot down over Bruges in the early hours of 16 May 1918. The crew from 214 Sqn, who were all killed, were Capt CG Rushton, Major JI Harrison, and Lt WJ King.

he crew of this Bristol Fighter, C4630 of 62 Sqn, made
rced landing east of the lines after combat on 19 May
3. The crew of Lt HA Clarke and Capt H Claye were
n prisoner.

x Canadians of 41 Sqn at Conteville, June 1918. From
to right they are Lt SA Puffer; Lt ME Gadd; Lt WE
lds; Lt WG Claxton DFC (POW 17.8.1918); Capt FRG
all MC DFC; Lt EFH Davies. These pilots claimed
100 victories between them.

3. The topsy-turvy world of a night bombing unit: a group
of 58 Sqn airmen having arisen about noon relax in their
pyjamas in the summer of 1918. From left to right: Capt
GN McBlain, Lt KY Gliddon, Capt WE Leslie, Sgt EE
Jones, Capt CC Cole, 2Lt RK Fletcher, ?, Lt AH Padley,
Lt SGE Inman-Knox.

4. An FE2b of 58 Sqn being bombed up with eight 25-lb
bombs for a night raid in 1918.

1. A signalling lighthouse of the type used to guide night bombing crews. Known to be dash dot dot dot.

2. A Sopwith Ship's Pup is prepared for launching on the forward flying-off deck of HMS *Pegasus*.

3. Lt F Currie of 2 Sqn, AFC stands beside his SE5a No. B8392 of C Flight.

4. A Sopwith Strutter takes off from the gun platform of HMS *Queen Elizabeth* in the summer of 1918.

pwith Camels of C Flight 210 Sqn at Teteghem in mid
. F5914 was lost on 22 July 1918 when Lt HT Mellings
killed during air combat, whilst in B7153 behind it, Lt
anderson accounted for four enemy machines on 26
1918.

e Irish ace Capt GEH McElroy MC DFC on the right,
ng to an unidentified officer in front of a SE5a at 3
ing School, Sedgeford. McElroy was killed in combat
July 1918 in SE5a E1310 of 40 Sqn.

3. Believed to be one of the two 9 Sqn RE8s shot down at
Hamel on 4 July 1918 whilst carrying out ammunition
drops. The photo was taken by Australian forward
positions.

4. Capt RGD Francis of 3 Sqn AFC with his usual RE8
A4397. This machine flew over 440 hours on active
service on the Western Front, a record for any aircraft,
mostly with Francis at the controls and involving 147 trips
across the lines.

1. The Australian ace Capt AAND Pentland of Nos. 16, 19, and 87 Sqns. He was wounded twice: on 26 September 1917 and again on 25 August 1918.

2. Four officers from 84 Sqn: Lt Simpson, 2Lt SW Highwood, South African Capt AW Beauchamp-Proctor VC DSO DFC MC, 54 victories (WIA in SE5a C1911 on 8 October 1918), and Lt JE Boudwin USAS.

3. Five pilots of 19 Sqn in front of Sopwith Dolphin C8087

in autumn 1918. From left to right: Lt JA Aldridge, C RA de L'Haye, Lt C Montgomery-Moore, Capt JW C (KIA 30.10.18 in Dolphin B7855), Lt WF Gordon.

4. A group of officers at Turnberry, left to right: Capt Chappell of 41 Sqn (WIA 13 January 1918); Capt HW Saunders, of 84 Sqn; Capt JV Sorsoleil, Canadian of 8 Sqn; Capt AB Yuille, who shot down a Staaken Giant plane in France in night-fighter Sopwith Camel D6573 151 Sqn on 10 August 1918; and Capt PJ Clayson of 1

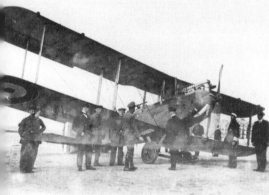

1. Believed to be two Handley Page 0/400s of the night bombing unit 214 Squadron in 1918. *(via R Bernard)*

2. This captured DH9, with Flight markings N on the nose, is likely to be D7320 of 108 Sqn, known to have been forced down onto Ostende beach on 30 August 1918. The crew of 2Lt KAW Leighton and 2Lt WR Jackson were taken prisoner.

3. Believed to be 46 Sqn Sopwith Camel B9271, probably in early 1918. Lt PH Goodhugh of that unit was later shot down in combat in this machine and died of his wounds on 30 August 1918.

4. Lt LF Pendred testing a DH4 of A Flight of 202 Sqn at Varssenaeres airfield in late 1918.

1

2

3

4

1. Freshly dug graves somewhere in France: in the foreground is one of about six aviators' graves identifiable in the scene by the use of cut down propellers for crosses.

2. Bristol Fighter E2260 of 48 Sqn, with the crew of Lt MFJR Mahony and 2Lt JN Keir, came down in enemy lines on 20 September 1918. Ltn Carl Degelow of Jasta 40, who was responsible, stands fourth from left.

3. An aerodrome destroyed prior to evacuation – systematically ploughed and bombed to prevent use by enemy. The location is unknown.

4. This captured Sopwith Camel sits semi-derelict on a German airfield in late 1918, possibly that of Jasta 35b. The original shows that the cockade has been cut out. flight marking is either a B or a P.

...ajor GH Bowman, the British ace of 56 and 41 Sqns,
...n the wheel of a Fokker DVII brought down by Lt
...oden.

...member of a heavy bomber unit stands in front of two
...dley Page 0/400s.

...DH4 day bomber with a Puma engine flanked by
...nd crew.

4. A group of officers from 3 Sqn AFC in November 1918.
From left to right: Lts Cole, CE Frazer, W Palstra, SJ?
Moir, Wilson, Capt HN Wrigley, Lts AR MacDonald,
Charles, CEA Fossett, Lonergan, ?.

5. Commanding Officer of 65 Sqn, Major HV Champion
de Crespigny, on the left, with Capt AG Jones-Williams,
also of that unit, in front of Sopwith Camel F3991 at the
end of 1918.

1. An example of an Albatros-built Fokker DVII, the great German fighter of the last stages of the war, being tested and flown at Cologne airfield in early 1919. Note overpainted cockade on fuselage and wings.

2. Sopwith Dolphin E4587 of 87 Squadron, photographed after the war at 204 Training Depot Squadron, Eastchurch.

3. A Bristol Fighter pursuing a Bristol Fighter. Both machines are from 48 Sqn.

4. For the Allies too, with the war over, it was time to reduce to produce. Literally dozens of wings are set blazing in a bonfire.

5. The remarkable sight of a Zeppelin hangar-full of impounded German aircraft at the end of 1918.

7-15pm OK(Lt WA Rankin) [?claim combat off BLANKENBERGHE Flm C Kairies SFS]

C3492   H.P. 0/400   214Sqn
B AA short of fuel ftl sea(Lt J Betherington OK/2Lt BC Fletcher **Kld/Lt CH Kennedy OK) left 9-10pm, floated 2.5hr: observer drowned

C9797   FE2b   I Flt
**SpM shot up engine cut cr nrFAUQUEMBERQUES OK(Lt J Wingate/Capt CC Cole)

I Flight was a little known intelligence gathering Flight whose work also included spy dropping. Throughout the second half of 1918 it operated with Headquarters FE2b night bombing and reconnaissance squadrons and as well as having specialist personnel it would utilise crew from these units as required. Its FE2bs were also specially adapted so as to carry pigeon holders, extra pistols, elaborate transmitting equipment and an assortment of other peculiar gadgets. Occasionally, a night bombing crew would need to use one of these machines on a normal raid, and there was great trepidation concerning their fate if they were ever forced to land in enemy territory. Flying such a machine they would doubtless be taken for spies, for which death was the likely penalty. This crew was on a special reconnaissance when it was shot up but managed to nurse their machine home again. Lt Wingate seems to have been in command of this Flight.

E1478   Sopwith Camel   US 148th Pursuit Sqn
P left 6-45pm patrol had combat with 7 Fokker DVIIs nrVELU shot up: passed out until 300′ ftl trenches cr Sh51b.M.27(2Lt TW Imes **WIA)arm & head, "EA camped on Imes' tail," a'c abandoned [?possible "Dolphin" claim combat COURCELLES 6-15pm? Ltn E Udet Ja4]

22nd August

Albert was recaptured in very heavy fighting on the 22nd. Progress continued through the day and the foundations for the main battle were achieved.

C1698   Sopwith Camel   3Sqn
+* attacked KB[+des] TILLOY 9-55am OK(Capt HleR Wallace) shared, last of over a dozen claims

D4912   RE8   12Sqn
P combat with HA COURCELLES shot down in flames **MIA(Capt CE Pither **KIA**/2Lt LJ Lavington **KIA**) left 12pm

RE8   15Sqn
CP (/2Lt WRS Fox **DoW)

D7993   Bristol F2b   20Sqn
OP left 7-30am seen nrMENIN **MIA(Capt D Latimer MC DFC **POW**/Lt TC Noel MC **KIA**) [?"BF" claim combat WESTROOSEBEKE Ltn Nebgen Ja7] high

scoring two-seater crew with 28 & 27 claims respectively

C8644   A.W.FK8   35Sqn
**P mg through radiator ALBERT ftl OK(Lt GJ Gunyon/2Lt EJ Richardson) left 4-10pm

E3979   SE5a   40Sqn
+* attacked KB[+des] HANTAY 6-05am OK(Capt GC Dixon Can.) made several victory claims

Sopwith Camel   43Sqn
** combat(Lt JG Beck **WIA**)

C2516   RE8   59Sqn
mg engine shot up ADINFER WOOD ftl (2Lt NM McDougall **inj/2Lt EG Thomas)OK left 12-25pm

F5890   RE8   59Sqn
P mg shot up ST ARMAND engine cut ftl(2Lt TG Hobbs **inj/Lt CRA Wallis **inj**) left 4-45am

E3943   SE5a   60Sqn
**LowP fuel tank shot up AA? ftl field GOUY-EN-ARTOIS 8pm cr OK(Lt FW McCarthy) left 7-15pm

B1216   Bristol F2b   62Sqn
**EscOP combat with 4EA PRONVILLE controls shot up ftl dam OK(Lt C Allday/2Lt L Millar) EAs followed back a'c WoL

C895   Bristol F2b   62Sqn
EscB(27Sqn) combat with Fokker DVIIs[+ooc+ flames] PRONVILLE 7-45am shot up ftl burnt a'c(Capt ET Morrow Can. **WIA/2Lt LM Thompson Can. OK) left 6-05am, Morrow wounded in leg, a'c spun down but recovered. Thompson fought flames on descent. Morrow claimed 7 EA, 4 with Thompson

C953   Bristol F2b   62Sqn
Esc/OP combat with EA wCAMBRAI DAINVILLE shot up dam ftl(Lt SAR Solomon **WIA/2Lt L Egan OK) left 6-05am CAMBRAI

62 Squadron was escorting 27 Squadron DH9s on the rail network around Cambrai when the formation was heavily attacked.

SE5a   64Sqn
** combat(Lt KJ Isaac **WIA**) [?"SE5" claim combat CAPPY SUR SOMME 4-45pm Ltn Kohlbach Ja10]

E5177   Sopwith Camel   80Sqn
OP ground fire dam returned a'dr(Lt HW Phear **WIA)

F1969   Sopwith Camel   80Sqn
pracP left 6-45am **MIA(2Lt AL Tupman **KIA**) ["Camel" claim combat nBRAY 7-30am Ltn E Udet Ja4]

C6454   SE5a   85Sqn
+* combat with Fokker DVII[+ooc] MARICOURT 4-50pm OK(Capt AC Randall) made 10 claims, many in this a'c

B8803   H.P. 0/400   97Sqn (I.F.)
NB AA **MIA(Lt DF Burton **POW**/2Lt LG Taylor **POW**/2Lt RF Glazebrook **POW**) possibly shot down in flames, this a'c also given as a'c MIA 30.8.18, but almost certainly wrongly?

D8304   H.P.0/400   97Sqn (I.F.)
NB ftl EoL PECHELBRONN, ALSACE **MIA(Capt
SG Gilmour **POW**/2Lt GE Rochester **POW**/Sgt JW
Chalmers **POW**) 22/23Aug

This raid was only the third attempted by 97
Squadron and brought to three the number of
crews lost. The Squadron bombed Volpersweiler
aerodrome and the railway at Herzing.

C2179   DH9   104Sqn (I.F.)
**B MANNHEIM combat ~15EAs from approach to
target **MIA**(Lt GHB Smith **POW**/Sgt W Harrop MM
POW)

C6202   DH9   104Sqn (I.F.)
B MANNHEIM combat with EAs on return **MIA(2Lt
J Valentine **POW**/2Lt CG Hitchcock **POW**)

D1048   DH9   104Sqn (I.F.)
B MANNHEIM combat with EAs **MIA(2Lt RT?
Searle **POW**/2Lt CGV? Pickard **KIA**) RJ? Searle, GG?
Pickard

D1729   DH9   104Sqn (I.F.)
**B MANNHEIM combat with EAs on return radiator
hit spin down but ldg ok **MIA**(Capt JB Home-Hay MC
DFC **POW**/Sgt WT Smith DCM MM **POW**?) patrol
followed him down to 6000' & became separated: 10 min
combat

D2812   DH9   104Sqn (I.F.)
**B combat with 8EAs 5m EoL on way out radiator hit
going down VOSGES in control **MIA**(Capt EA McKay
MC DFC **POW**/Lt RAC Brie **POW**) ftl 40m EoL, taken
prisoner by peasants with pitchforks & Sythes

D2917   DH9   104Sqn (I.F.)
B MANNHEIM combat with EAs **MIA(1Lt HP Wells
USAS. **POW**/2Lt JJ Redfield USAS. **WIA POW**)

D5729   DH9   104Sqn (I.F.)
B MANNHEIM combat with EAs **MIA(Lt E
Cartwright **KIA**/Lt AGL Mullen **KIA**)

These extremely heavy losses to 104 Squadron were
their worst of the war. They were attacked on their
way to the objective and again whilst they were
bombing, at one point there were perhaps forty
enemy fighters engaging them. Two DH9s were
lost before Mannheim and another five over it.

**   DH9   206Sqn**
B AA fire(2Lt LR Curtis **WIA/)

**   Sopwith Camel   US 17th Pursuit Sqn**
** combat(2Lt HC Knotts USAS **WIA**)

D9399   Sopwith Camel   US 17th Pursuit Sqn
**OP shot up dam returned a'dr 11am OK(Lt JF
Campbell) left 9-10am, co-operating with 6Sqn RE8's
~Sh57c.H.22

23rd August
THE BATTLE OF BAPAUME
The battle of Bapaume began in earnest on the

23rd, involving thirty-three miles of British front
from its boundary with the French at Lihons up to
Mercatel, just below Arras. In the south, the
French line of advance stretched as far as Soissons.
A new confidence, built of the knowledge that the
German war machine was beginning to unravel,
was clearly evident in the Allied battle plan. This
is nowhere better summed up than in Haig's
telegram to his commanders on the eve of the
battle, which in part read, ". . . The methods which
we have followed hitherto in our battles with
limited objectives when the enemy was strong are
no longer suited to his present condition. The
enemy has not the means to deliver counter-attacks
on an extended scale nor has he the numbers to
hold a continuous position against the very extended advance which is now being directed upon
him. To turn the present situation to account the
most resolute offensive action is everywhere
desirable . . . each division should be given a
distant objective which must be reached independently of its neighbour and even if one's flank is
thereby exposed for the time being. Reinforcements
must be directed on the points where our troops are
gaining ground, not where they are checked. A
vigorous offensive against the sectors where the
enemy is weak will cause hostile strong points to
fall and in due course our whole army will be able
to continue its advance."

The Allies began their assault at 4-45am. With
this new offensive spirit abroad, General Byng's
Third Army drove in at Bapaume and captured the
town by the 29th. South on the Somme the Australian Divisions pressed along the margins of the
river and had entered Peronne by the 1st of
September.

The progress on the first day had not matched
that enjoyed on the 8th, but that which followed
was more sustained and suffered fewer interrup-
tions. It was a steady and often remorseless
advance, made behind what one German historian
described as "a mighty curtain of fire" and composed of infantry, tanks, cavalry, and aircraft
rolling forward as one. By the first evening the
advance had reached a line through Boiry,
Ervillers, Bihucourt, and Irles, and the Australians
had recovered Bray. The German strong point of
Thiepval was therefore outflanked and, in the
manner predicted by Haig's dispatch, fell on the
24th. General Horne's First Army then struck east
from Arras on the 26th. In this manner the Allied
armies moved forward so that by the end of the
month they had driven thirty-five German
divisions back across the entire width of the old
Somme battlefield in just ten days.

D5177   A.W.FK8   2Sqn
**AReg dhAA VERMELLES 2-40pm snd flames cr wr
MIA(2Lt EH Pepper **KIA**/2Lt WS Melvin **KIA**)

F4264   A.W.FK8   2Sqn
**Phot AA circled dive cr swLA BASSÉE Sh44A
A.17.d.2.7. at 12-56pm **MIA**(Lt EO Drinkwater **KIA**/2Lt
DO Duthie **KIA**) left 11-45am

A.W.FK8   8Sqn
** combat(/2Lt SHJ Garne **WIA**)

D5175   A.W.FK8   8Sqn
**CAP left 5am(Lt JR? McCallum KIA/2Lt HS Scott
OK?) pilot's initials JRRG?, crew was **MIA**? [?"BF"
claim on 22.8? combat sMOREUIL 7-35am Vzfw J Putz
Ja34]

C2269   RE8   12Sqn
**CP combat with EA EoL shot up dam(2Lt AV Stupart
WIA/Lt AA Neilson **DoW**) left 9-55am, returned
12-40pm

C2519   RE8   12Sqn
**CP mg shot up ftl cr shell hole X29.U.55 dam OK(Lt
Allen/Lt Stubbings) left 6-20pm, name Stubbins?

E115   RE8   12Sqn
**COP left 6-05pm mg shot up ftl cr RANSART-
ADINFER RD dam(Lt Smith OK/Lt Shaw **inj**)

B1330   Bristol F2b   22Sqn
 **OP AA hit Sh51B G11.d.71 at 7-30am ftl(Lt JS
Tarbolton **WIA**/Sgt T Hooton sick)to hospital

C2194   DH9   27Sqn
**B combat with EA DUISANS shot up engine ftl OK(Lt
PV Holder/2Lt H Pitkin) left 5-30am

C6315   DH9   49Sqn
**B combat OSTERVILLE shot up dam ftl OK(2Lt ST
Franks/2Lt SP Scott) 7-30pm

Nos. 27, 49, and 107 Squadrons bombed the
important railway centres of Valenciennes,
Somain, and Cambrai through the day. The attack
was typically taken up in the evening by the night-
bombers of IX Brigade.

C2738   RE8   59Sqn
**CP mg BUCQUOY shot up ftl dam(2Lt TG Hobbs
DoW 24.8.18/Lt CRA Wallis OK) left 3pm

RE8   59Sqn
** combat(/2Lt JB Hyslop **WIA**)

D4740   RE8   59Sqn
**P mg MIRAUMONT-IRLES and dam OK(2Lt JCG
Drummond/2Lt HS Hudson)

D4856   RE8   59Sqn
**P mg MIRAUMONT dam OK(Capt GJ Scott/Lt JBV
Clements)

F6158   Bristol F2b   62Sqn
**EscOP combat with EA DENAIN-DOUAI shot up
dam OK(Lt JK Stewart/2Lt EM Buckley) left 6am

D3055   DH9   108Sqn
**Phot left 7-30am ARDOYE Dump AA hit dam lost
control cr ldg OK(2Lt R Russell/2Lt GB Pike)

D6660   Sopwith Camel   151Sqn
+* combat Friedrichshafen[+flames] nDOULLENS-
ARRAS 1-15am OK(Lt CRW Knight) EA crew from
Bogohl VI/8 all killed

D9445   Sopwith Camel   151Sqn
+* combat GothaGVb[+des] BEAUQUESNE 12-35am
OK(Lt W Aitken) crew from Bogohl III/17: 1 killed, 2
POW, burnt a'c

D9671   Sopwith Camel   203Sqn
**SpM(Low Attacks on Fourth Army front) AA hit shot
up nBRAY 1-05pm spun in cr(Capt JP Hales Can. **KIA**)

A7518   DH4   205Sqn
**B BARLEUX dhAA ftl cr dam OK(Lt EO Danger/
2Lt AD Hollingsworth)

D9674   Sopwith Camel   210Sqn
**LP AA prop shot off POPERINGHE ftl cr dam OK(Lt
L Yerex)

C9659   H.P. 0/400   215Sqn (I.F.)
**NB FOLPESWEILER A'dr forced to return because
of weather ftl **MIA**(2Lt FE Rees **KIA**/2Lt J Stott **KIA**/
Sgt G Hare **POW**) 22/23Aug

D6595   Sopwith Camel   US 17th Pursuit Sqn
**LowB ground mg fire fuel tank hit cr ldg 3Sqn a'dr(1Lt
RD Williams USAS **WIA**)back, flew back with finger in
hole in tank, to hospital

D1941   Sopwith Camel   US 17th Pursuit Sqn
**LowB mg hit nd ovWARLENCOURT 12-15pm(1Lt
ML Campbell **KIA**) left 11-35am co-operating with 6Sqn
RE8's

These two casualties were, remarkably, the only
two incurred this day from ground attack work on
the Third Army front, the other squadrons
involved being Nos. 1, 3, 54, and 73. No.73
Squadron was operating in co-ordination with the
tank assault. The low flying attacks made by corps
machines during their co-operation work suffered
more, with those inflicted on 59 Squadron RE8
crews being typical (see above).

24th August

The Third and Fourth Armies continued their
advance by launching night attacks at 1am. There
was rain overnight and the IX Brigade night-
bombers could not operate. These conditions
continued until the middle of the day, restricting
air work. Some day-bomber squadrons were given
a day's rest.

D6878   SE5a   1Sqn
**SpM left 4pm fuel tank shot up ftl nrCANDAS dam
OK(Lt BH Moody)

D6970　SE5a　　　1Sqn
**SpM left 5-30pm seen ovBAPAUME shot down EoL
MIA(1Lt RH Ritter USAS. **KIA**) POW?, Ja28? [?"SE5"
claim combat neBAPAUME 6-20pm Ltn O Koennecke
Ja5, but see D6121?]

C2299　RE8　　　6Sqn
**LRec left 5-30am combat with EA shot up dam OK(Lt
Howard/Lt MA Waterer)

**　　　RE8　　　9Sqn**
** mg fire(/2Lt F Marshall **WIA**)

D4736　RE8　　　15Sqn
**CP AA shot up dam returned a'dr 4-30pm OK(Lt AR
Cross/Lt HF Griffith) left 2-20pm

D5154　A.W.FK8　　　35Sqn
**AmmDrop mg ftl cr trench dam OK(Lt MGW
Stewart/2Lt HS Howard) left 3-15pm

E3947　SE5a　　　40Sqn
**BOP attkg KB[++des] PROVIN-HANTAY btwn
12-25pm & 12-30pm then AA whilst making for a third:
shot down in flames nrGRAND MOISNET **MIA**(Lt L
Bennett US. **DoW**) left 12-15pm, ovHAISNIES?

**　　　　　48Sqn**
**Died of Wounds
(2Lt A Urinowsky, Lt JB Jameson)

** Wounded by enemy bombing
(Lt H Hood, Lt E Vickers, Lt T Beck, Lt FD Kilby, 2Lt
JN Kier, Capt CR Steele, Capt HA Oakes, Lt CG
Imeretinsky, 2Lt EG Weller, 2Lt SH Whipple US., 2Lt
DT Turnbull, Lt MFJR Mahony, 2Lt HY Lewis)

All of the above were casualties of an enemy
bombing raid.

**C886, C940, C4629, D7909, E2472, E2480,
F5811**.3, **F6094, F6118,
F6404?　Bristol F2bs　　48Sqn**
**all a'c destroyed by enemy bombing on aerodrome

Night bombing on the 24th/25th was carried out in
force, Nos. 58, 83, 102, 148, and 207 Squadrons all
raiding stations and main roads. Night fighter
Camels of 151 Squadron were also very active, for
enemy night bombing formations were numerous
in the bright moonlight. Very great damage was
done, however, by one enemy raid from Schlacht-
staffel 16 who bombed Bertangles, starting a fire
which destroyed five hangars containing Bristol
Fighters of 48 Squadron. There was also a direct
hit on stores, offices and hutments in which further
aircraft of 48 Squadron, and an SE5a of 84
Squadron (see below), were burnt. The worst blow
for 48 Squadron was however the loss of so many
of its flying personnel, for fifteen were wounded.
Two of these men subsequently died. 84 Squadron
also lost a pilot and had another wounded. Such
losses in these circumstances were unparalleled in
the British air services throughout the entire war,

and 48 Squadron was temporarily withdrawn to
Boisdinghem to be re-equipped. The remarkable
fact is that the unit was flying at the front again
two days later.

D3056　DH9　　　49Sqn
**B shot up dam ftl 1ASD 7-50pm OK(Lt AR Spurling/
Sgt FW Bell) left 4-35pm

E5174　Sopwith Camel　54Sqn
**SpB left 4-55pm AA hit dam cr OK(Lt AH Belliveau)

B8414　SE5a　　　56Sqn
LowB seen ovLE SARS 2300′ 2-15pm **MIA(Lt HJW
Roberts **POW**)

D6121　SE5a　　　56Sqn
LowB seen ooc ovBARASTRE 5000′ 5-20pm **MIA(2Lt
DC Collier **KIA**)

**　　　RE8　　　59Sqn**
** mg fire(2Lt R Calrow **WIA**/)

B6674　RE8　　　59Sqn
**CP ground fire shot up dam OK(Capt LM Woodhouse
MC/Lt GM Thompson DFC) left 9-45am IRLES-
MIRAUMONT RLWY

D5176　A.W.FK8　　　82Sqn
B AA hit WARNETON 7pm in flames? **MIA(2Lt T
McCarthy **KIA**/2Lt CW Somerville **KIA**) left 5-25pm
["AW" claim combat neWARNETON 7-30pm Ltn K
Plauth Ja20]

**　　　　　84Sqn**
** in hostile bomb raid(1Lt AF Matthews USAS. **KIA**)

in hostile bomb raid(Lt CB Bateman **WIA)

E4012　SE5a　　　84Sqn
** damaged in hostile bomb raid on a'dr

For details of this raid see 48 Squadron entries
above.

**　　　FE2b　　　101Sqn**
** (/2Lt PK Chapman **WIA**)

F6102　Sopwith Camel　151Sqn
+*NF attacked Gotha GVb[+shot down] nrHAUTE
AVESNES, ARRAS 10-20pm OK(Lt FC Broome)
assisted by Capt DV Armstrong in Camel C6713,
German crew from Bogohl III/15: 1 killed, 2 taken POW

Also see second claim later that night listed under
25th August.

D7204.J　DH9　　　211Sqn
B AA ovBRUGES ftl ZUIDZANDE 4-30pm **MIA(Lt
JA Dear **INT**/2Lt JFJ Peters **INT**) left 1-30pm, seen
going down towards Holland & interned

D1940　Sopwith Camel　US 17th Pursuit Sqn
**KBP attacked KB[+des] eBAPAUME 2-10pm
followed KB down, seen hit by AA? mg? ~2-30pm then
ooc 4m nBAPAUME **MIA**(1Lt LA Hamilton DFC DSC
KIA) KB at Sh57c.I.34, made 10 claims, many in this a'c

F5985 Sopwith Camel US 17th Pursuit Sqn
P(LowB) EoL seen nrCOURCELLES 4pm **MIA(2Lt
GT Wise **POW**) left 3pm ["Sopwith" claim combat
nwBAPAUME 5-15pm Oblt Ritt vGreim JG]

B7869 Sopwith Camel US 148th Pursuit Sqn
**B left 5-20pm seen crossing lines nrBAPAUME 5-35pm
MIA(1Lt MK Curtis **POW**)

25th August

In retaliation for the night bombing of Bertangles
aerodrome, raids were launched by escorted IX
Brigade day-bombers at German counterparts.
Nos. 27 and 49 Squadrons attacked Bombengeschwader 1 at Etreux and Nos. 98 and 107
Squadron attacked Bombengeschwader 4 at Mont
d'Origny. SE5as from 32 and 40 Squadrons would
make offensive patrols of the St Quentin-Marcoing
area and then escort the bombers home. 62
Squadron F2bs were to give support over the
aerodromes during the raid. The attacks were of
mixed success, and seriously hampered by very bad
conditions (see below). Of twenty-four DH9s which
left to bomb Mont d'Origny, only eight reached the
destination, all from 98 Squadron. Many had
suffered engine problems and had to return. The
43 Squadron Camels due to escort these formations
also flew into clouds and never found them.

D9432 Sopwith Camel 4Sqn AFC
**OP AA shell splinter hit 6pm cr canal LOCON ftl(Lt
TR Edols **WIA**)hand

C2611 RE8 12Sqn
**NP combat with EA mg shot up dam(2Lt WJ McLean
WIA/Lt Godson OK) [?possible "RE" claim combat
ETERPIGNY Ltn E Thuy Ja28]

D4914 RE8 12Sqn
**CP left 3-30pm AA wST LEGER dam OK(Lt Haskall/
2Lt Marsland)

DH4 18Sqn
** combat(/2Lt GA Duthie **WIA**)

E4026 SE5a 32Sqn
+* combat with Fokker DVII[+des] HANCOURT 7pm
OK(Lt FL Hale)

E5939 SE5a 32Sqn
+* combat with Fokker DVII[+des] HANCOURT
6-50pm? OK(2Lt JC Donaldson US.) EA pilot jumped
with parachute

32 Squadron missed its rendezvous with 49
Squadron because it met a formation of Fokkers
south of this point. These claims were made from
this fighting.

F7374 A.W.FK8 35Sqn
**P combat shot down MONCHY WOOD(Lt CR
Strudwick **WIA**/2Lt JA Weller **WIA**) left 7-25am

C9260 SE5a 41Sqn
**OP seen ok? ovBAILLEUL going East 10-20am
MIA(Lt AV Trimble **KIA**) COMINES-BAILLEUL

DH9 49Sqn
** combat(/Lt F Maudesley **WIA**)

DH9 49Sqn
** combat(/Sgt RW Buchan **WIA**)

C6209 DH9 49Sqn
**B combat with EA tail planes shot away then slow spin
ovMOIVRES **MIA**(Lt SB Welch **KIA**/2Lt DC Roy
KIA) left 4-05pm BOURLON WOOD

D1075 DH9 49Sqn
**B EA AA? CAMBRAI seen going down control?
ovMAZINGHEM **MIA**(Lt CH Stephens **POW**/2Lt AB
Henderson **POW**) left 4-05pm

D3164 DH9 49Sqn
**B AA cr IZEL LE HAMEAU 7-35pm dam OK(Lt CC
Conover/2Lt SP Scott) left 4-05pm ETREUX

49 Squadron had some heavy fighting to contend
with on its homeward journey from Etreux. As
mentioned above, its fighter escort was prevented
from reaching it and the flight was also made in a
thunderstorm. 49 Squadron claimed one enemy
shot down in flames.

A2131 DH4 55Sqn (I.F.)
B LUXEMBOURG mg fire ftl wr(/2Lt JA Lee **KIA)

B3967 DH4 55Sqn (I.F.)
**B LUXEMBOURG mg fire shot up(/Sgt AS Allan
WIA)

D8392 DH4 55Sqn (I.F.)
B LUXEMBOURG cr after raid(2Lt E Wood **WIA?/
2Lt GS Barber OK) injured in crash?

The original target for this raid was Köln, but over
Trèves the leader decided the wind was too strong
to reach the allotted objectives and the six DH4s
bombed Luxembourg instead. All the Independent
Force squadrons were finding it difficult to reach
their targets because of the weather, engine
problems, or simply the range limitations of the
aircraft. The latter was a particular dilemma for 55
Squadron with their DH4s. Some of the objectives
they had been given in August — for instance
Düren and Frankfurt — were at the very limits of
what could be reached with the five and a half
hours' worth of fuel which could be carried. Such
destinations left little room for error once the
decision was taken to try and reach them, which is
why many allotted targets were abandoned.

C3314 Sopwith Camel 73Sqn
OP left 6pm seen attkg EA neBAPAUME **MIA(Lt
HLM Dodson **KIA**) [?"Camel" claim combat
COURCELLES pm Ltn E Thuy Ja28]

D6484   Sopwith Camel   73Sqn
+* combat with LVGC[+des] COHAN 7-45pm OK(2Lt N Cooper US.) shared, made several claims, real name was ES Tooker

D8150   Sopwith Camel   73Sqn
**OP left 6-05pm ne BAPAUME shot up dam OK(2Lt FM Stieber)

D3727.J   Sopwith Dolphin   79Sqn
**OP AA mg fire 5-25pm seen ldg ok? EoL MIA(Lt E Taylor US. KIA) left 4-30pm, Taylor had claimed a few KBs in this a'c in August

F6184   Sopwith Camel   80Sqn
** mg fire(Lt AW Chadwick WIA)

C8109   Sopwith Dolphin   87Sqn
**SpP left 8-30am combat with EA mg ftl o't n.m.l. nrALBERT OK(Lt DC Mangan) escaped to safety

D3718   Sopwith Dolphin   87Sqn
** combat with DFWC[+des] LE SARS 9am then combat with Fokker DVII[+des] sGUEDECOURT 9-25am shot up(Capt AAND Pentland Aust. WIA) last of 23 victories, may have been WIA later in day?

D6660   Sopwith Camel   151Sqn
+* combat FriedrichshafenG[+flames] cr eARRAS 12-33am OK(Lt CRW Knight) EA exploded on crashing

See also Sopwith Camel F6102 on the previous day.

B6358   Sopwith Camel   213Sqn
**HOP seen in combat with 5EA 10m sOSTENDE MIA(Lt EC Toy KIA) ?combat ICHTEGHEM Flm C Kairies SFS]

26th August
THE BATTLE OF THE SCARPE

The Allied advance continued steadily, but low clouds for most of this week restricted RAF activity. Low flying patrols by fighters continued, as well as close corps support, but day and night bombing was mostly washed out.

Further north, the British First Army launched an attack eastwards from Arras. This was known as the battle of the Scarpe and formed an extension of the general offensive. Nevertheless it was given significant and experienced air support. Nos. 8 and 73 Squadrons, with appropriate specialist skills, were moved up to support the tanks and attack the anti-tank defences. Henceforth they came under the command of I Brigade. Nos. 5 and 52 Squadron provided tactical support to the Canadian Corps who were to spearhead the assault, and 6 Squadron came north with the British cavalry corps who were also involved. The fighter component of I Brigade was also enlarged, so that for the battle it included Nos. 40, 54, 64, 208, and 209 Squadrons, and 22 fighter reconnaissance Squadron. 40 and 22

Squadrons were to carry out offensive patrols whilst the remainder were to rotate co-ordinated low attacks, notably under the control of a single officer for the first time. It also had use of the day-bombers of 18 Squadron, which would attack rail targets, and those of IX Brigade who planned to concentrate on German aerodromes north of Cambrai in the morning and then switch to the railways as well. I Brigade's night bombing was provided by 148 Squadron.

The attack was launched at 3am and made very good progress. For the RAF, however, the weather was terrible, there being a strong south-west wind, low clouds and rain. The bombing of aerodromes was abandoned but all those involved in corps and low fighter work struggled into battle valiantly, often working from a few hundred feet. The first of the low bombing attacks was made by 209 Squadron from 6-50am, then followed Nos. 64, 54, and 208 Squadrons respectively through the morning. There was very little enemy opposition and few casualties in this work.

E104   RE8   9Sqn
**NF mg shot through ftl Sh66E F.17.c.54 dam OK(Lt SA Desmore/2Lt WO Goldthorpe) left 3-05pm

E158   RE8   13Sqn
**OP shot through(Lt TS Symons OK/2Lt WTC Blake WIA) name Symonds?

D9475   Sopwith Camel   54Sqn
**SpB left 1-45pm combat with EA shot up dam(2Lt CS? Leslie WIA)back, to hospital, initials SC?

D8388   DH4   55Sqn (I.F.)
**B combat with EA shot up(2Lt N Wallace WIA)

D6978.V   SE5a   64Sqn
**OP BEHAGNIES-SAPIGNIES AA shell fire shot down cr 3-30pm OK(Lt JB Edwards) left 2-30pm First Army area, unsalvable

DH9   104Sqn (I.F.)
**B (/2Lt P Sutherland WIA)severe

E1468   Sopwith Camel   208Sqn
**LowB left 7pm heavy mg fire & AA nrST LEGER dam ftl OK(Lt JW Marshall) a'c being shelled Sh57C B.2.c.0.8.

D9637   Sopwith Camel   209Sqn
**LowP ground mg cr shell hole nwMONCHY fire(Capt TC Luke MC inj) left 7-15am, unsalvable

D9676   Sopwith Camel   209Sqn
**LowP left 6-55pm HA? broke up cr nrMONCHY(Lt RW Whalley WIA) unsalvable

E4392   Sopwith Camel   209Sqn
**LowP shot up 8pm dam OK(Lt RL Scharff)

F6028   Sopwith Camel   209Sqn
**LowP AA hit 7-30am cr trees nrREMY MIA(Lt L Belloc KIA)

B5428   Sopwith Camel   US 17th Pursuit Sqn
**P seen in combat with 5 Fokker DVIIs eBAPAUME
Sh57C.E. 5-25pm **MIA**(1Lt LC Roberts USAS **KIA**)
other EAs joined fighting [?"Camel" claim combat
BEUGNY Oblt K Bolle Ja2][?"Camel" claim combat
BEUGNY Oblt B Loerzer JGIII]

C141   Sopwith Camel   US 17th Pursuit Sqn
**P seen in combat with 5 Fokker DVIIs eBAPAUME
ov Sh57C.E. 5-30pm **MIA**(1Lt HB Frost **WIA POW**)
other EAs joined fighting, severe WIA

D6595.N   Sopwith Camel   US 17th Pursuit Sqn
**P seen in combat with 5 Fokker DVIIs[+des]
BAPAUME-QUEANT ov Sh57C.E at 5-25pm cr
nCAMBRAI-BAPAUME RD wr **MIA**(2Lt RM Todd
US. **POW**) high winds, guns salvable ["Camel" claim
combat nBEUGNY 4-55pm Ltn R Klimke Ja27][also Ja2
in fight]

F1958   Sopwith Camel   US 17th Pursuit Sqn
**P seen in combat with 5 Fokker DVIIs eBAPAUME
ovSh57CE at 5-25pm **MIA**(2Lt HH Jackson **KIA**)

F1964   Sopwith Camel   US 17th Pursuit Sqn
**P combat with 5 Fokker DVIIs eBAPAUME 5-25pm
shot down(2Lt HP Bittinger **POW DoW**) message that
he was dead went to A.A.S. HQ

F5951   Sopwith Camel   US 17th Pursuit Sqn
**P seen in combat with 5 Fokker DVIIs & others[++
des] eBAPAUME-QUEANT 5pm ovSh57.CE 5-25pm
fuel tank shot up ftl **MIA**(1Lt WD Tipton **WIA
POW**)legs, Combat Reports give time 5pm
ovSh57c.D.15, Tipton sent card from imprisonment
detailing losses

17th Pursuit Squadron had one of their worst days
on the 26th, meeting a formation of Fokker DVIIs
whilst on offensive patrol between Peronne and
Cambrai. Six pilots were lost.

D9516   Sopwith Camel   US 148th Pursuit Sqn
B left 4-15pm forced to return? **MIA(1Lt GV Seibold
KIA) this was probably the Camel which 17th Aero Sqn
saw being attacked & came to assist

27th August

In fighting on the Scarpe the Germans chose the
27th to mount a desperate defence of their
positions. For the next two days the Canadians
pressed with equal determination, assisted by
extremely heavy bombardments of enemy positions
and a redoubled British effort in the air. Low
attacks were ordered to be made at squadron
strength throughout the day. Despite the continuing bad weather, the five fighter units
(including 73 Squadron) dropped six hundred and
forty-six 25-lb bombs and fired 47,570 rounds of
ammunition.

E5965.X   SE5a   2Sqn AFC
+* combat with Fokker DVIIs[+flames+ooc] SAINS

LES MARQUION ~10-50am & with PfalzDIII[+ooc]
LECLUSE 10-55am OK(Lt G Cox) initials GJ?

D6627.R   Sopwith Camel   3Sqn
**LowP combat with 2Str shot up ftl Sh57C G.36 OK(Lt
WH Hubbard) unsalvable, left 12-15pm

                    A.W.FK8   8Sqn
** (/2Lt G Storey **WIA**)

C2313   RE8   13Sqn
**CP left 12-25pm XVII Corps area mg dam OK(Lt JJ
Elder/Lt MJ Sheehan) returned 3-25pm

F5876   RE8   16Sqn
P left 2-30pm dh British shell(2Lt DS Reid **KIA/2Lt
WD Houston **KIA**)

E2454   Bristol F2b   22Sqn
+* combat with Fokker DVII[+ooc] DOUAI 1-45pm
OK(Lt FG Gibbons/Lt J McDonald) Gibbons made 14
claims with 22Sqn

E2514   Bristol F2b   22Sqn
OP going down ok seARRAS **MIA(Lt FM Sellars
POW/2Lt TB Collis **KIA**?) left 5-40am, a'c captured,
Fromherz kept tail canvas as trophy ["BF" claim combat
GRAINCOURT 7-05am Ltn H Frommherz Ja27]

C8882   SE5a   40Sqn
**OP combat with Fokker DVII 7-20am going down
Sh51B P.32.d **MIA**(2Lt RA Anderson USAS. **WIA
POW**) [?"SE5" claim combat CROISILLES 7-40am
Vzfw F Classen Ja26]

F5940   Sopwith Camel   54Sqn
**SpB seen ok wETAING 2000' down in control 9-30am
MIA(Lt AH Belliveau **POW**) left 8-50am [?"Sopwith"
claim combat MERCATEL Ltn C Reimer Ja26]

F6149   Sopwith Camel   54Sqn
**SpB left 8-50am combat with Fokker DVII shot down
ftl 51A.N4 OK(Lt EC Crosse)

D8106   Sopwith Camel   73Sqn
**GndStr seen going east ok ~7-30am combat seARRAS
MIA(2Lt AR Heaver **POW**) Ja36?

                    SE5a   84Sqn
** combat(Lt MH Goudie **WIA**)

                    DH9   108Sqn
B OSTENDE AA fire(/2Lt G Ritchie **WIA)neck

D1928   Sopwith Camel   208Sqn
**B left 7am combat with Fokker DVIIs 7-50am seen ooc
4000' with 4EA chasing down cr eVIS-EN-ARTOIS
MIA(Lt J Mollison **KIA**) "Camel" claims: [?combat
TILLOY 6-40am?Ltn H-G Marwitz Ja30] [?combat
CROISILLES 7-40am Ltn H Lange Ja26] [?combat
wCHERISY 7-50am Ltn J Jensen Ja57, & others?]

D6606   Sopwith Camel   208Sqn
**SpLowB left 7am VITRY combat with EA shot up
dam OK(Lt AH Hiscox)

B6371   Sopwith Camel   209Sqn
**LowP dh by shell 200' broke up sRIVER SCARPE

12-15pm(Lt CG Edwards DFC **KIA**) broke up sJIGSAW WOOD

F5925   Sopwith Camel   209Sqn
**LowP mg? fuel tank shot through ftl AGNY dam OK(Lt JE Walker)

D8180   Sopwith Camel   US 148th Pursuit Sqn
+* combat with 2Str[+des] REMY 1-05pm OK(1Lt HR Clay) shared, made several victory claims

28th August

The weather continued very poor along all main battle fronts.

C2505   RE8   13Sqn
AP left 2-55pm **MIA(Lt TA Johnson **KIA**/2Lt AJ Viveash **KIA**)

F5878   RE8   13Sqn
AP left 10-45am cr **MIA(Lt JB Cuthbert **KIA**/Lt T Pim **KIA**) bodies found [?possible RE8 claim Oblt H-E Gandert Ja51]

C8840.V   SE5a   24Sqn
+* combat with PfalzDIII[+des] nrBARLEUX Sh62c.N. 7-15pm OK(Capt HD Barton SA.) made most of his last 19 claims in this a'c

**   A.W.FK8   35Sqn**
** mg fire(/2Lt F Powell **WIA**)

N5962   DH4   202Sqn
** left 6-10am storm seen nrENGEL DUMP **MIA**(Lt R Ringrose **KIA**/2Lt H Hollings **KIA**)

F3948   Sopwith Camel   213Sqn
** left 7-15am shot down **MIA**(Lt WA Rankin **POW**)

29th August

Clearer conditions enabled a fuller day's air activities in the battle of the Scarpe, including escorted day-bomber raids to Cambrai, Valenciennes, and Somain. Substantial enemy formations were met on most of these, but the heaviest casualties by far were inflicted on the raid to Somain, made by 98 Squadron escorted by 43 Squadron (see below). Further south, the Germans began to abandon Peronne.

**   A.W.FK8   8Sqn**
** combat(Lt LGB Spence **WIA**/)

F5804   A.W.FK8   8Sqn
Phot AA combat? ftl cr dam(Lt A Swales **WIA/2Lt SE Gillmar OK)

**   RE8   9Sqn**
** mg fire(/2Lt JW Johnson **WIA**)

**   Bristol F2b   11Sqn**
** combat(2Lt EWC Sharpe **WIA**/)

A7957   DH4   18Sqn

B HA HERDAN nrLILLE 11-15am engine shot through dam ldg(Lt W Hogg OK/2Lt WE Baldwin DoW) Baldwin **DoW 25.8?

E2453   Bristol F2b   22Sqn
OP ARRAS-CAMBRAI RD seen in control? **MIA(Lt JJ Borrowman **KIA**/2Lt J Amos **KIA**) left 8-50am

C8215   Sopwith Camel   43Sqn
EscB left 7-10am(Capt LG Loudoun **POW) ["Sopwith" claim combat wMONCHY 10-25am Ltn C Reimer Ja26]

D1785.Z   Sopwith Camel   43Sqn
EscB left 7-10am(Sgt ACT? Harbour **POW) initials AGT? [?2 "Camel" claims combat BREBIÈRES Ltn P Strähle Ja57]

D1956   Sopwith Camel   43Sqn
+*EscB left 7-10am combat with Fokker DVII[+des] SOMAIN 8-25am OK(Lt EG Weaver)

D6542   Sopwith Camel   43Sqn
EscB left 7-10am **MIA(Lt WK MacFarlane **POW**)

D9470   Sopwith Camel   43Sqn
EscB left 7-10am(Lt SE Crookell **POW)

D9474   Sopwith Camel   43Sqn
**EscB nrDOULLENS combat with EA shot up ftl cr a'dr 9-10am wr OK(Lt AC Macaulay), left 7-10am, cr on return because of damage

D9514   Sopwith Camel   43Sqn
**EscB combat with Fokker DVII[+des] nrSOMAIN 8-30am shot up dam returned 9-35am OK(Lt CC Banks MC) left 7-10am, EA pilot was Vzfw Knobel WIA Ja57

E1485   Sopwith Camel   43Sqn
EscB left 7-10am shot down FIENVILLERS(2Lt W Omerod **KIA) [?"Camel" claim combat ANICHE 8-40am Ltn E Koch Ja32]

The five pilots lost in defence of 98 Squadron were the last casualties on Sopwith Camels for 43 Squadron before they converted to the new Sopwith Snipe fighter.

**   Sopwith Camel   46Sqn**
** (Lt AL Aldridge **WIA**)

D8425   DH4   57Sqn
B combat with Fokker DVII[+flames] YTRES 8am(Lt FO Thornton OK/2Lt WH Thornton **WIA)

D9262   DH4   57Sqn
+*B combat with Fokker DVII[+ooc] YTRES 8am OK(Capt WE Green/Lt AM Barron MC) this was Green's 8th claim

F5825   DH4   57Sqn
B chased down in control? by 2EAs DENAIN-DOVEY nrDOUAI 8000' 7-45am **MIA(Lt J Caldwell **KIA**/Sgt AT Wareing **KIA**) ["DH4" claim combat SOMAIN 7-45am Vzfw G Staudacher Ja1]

F6167   DH4   57Sqn
**B combat with EAs DENAIN-DOVEY nrDOUAI in

formation 7-45am **MIA**(Sgt THC Davies **POW**/2Lt WTS Lewis **POW**) [?"DH4" claim combat WAVRECHAIN Obt H-H vBoddien Ja59]

It is possible 57 Squadron was attacked by enemy fighters who subsequently mauled 43 and 98 Squadrons.

C9061.4 **SE5a**   **64Sqn**
****OP combat with HA 7-06am flames cr Sh51C c.7
MIA(Lt EA Parnell **KIA**) left 6-40am [?possible claim combat HAPLINCOURT 7-10am Ltn H-G Marwitz Ja30]

D374   **SE5a**   **85Sqn**
**OP left 7-35pm AA mg shot up dam OK(Lt GM Baldwin)

D2858   **DH9**   **98Sqn**
B SOMAIN combat with 30-40 Fokker DVII dam ftl DAINVILLE(2Lt TW Sleigh OK/Lt AA Douglas **WIA) left 6-10am

D3096   **DH9**   **98Sqn**
B combat with EA ALBERT driven down EoL? **MIA(2Lt HJ Fox **WIA**/2Lt WR Sellar **KIA**) left 6-15am, but made Lines?

D5829   **DH9**   **98Sqn**
B SOMAIN Rlwy Stn combat with 30EA[+bu+ flames] DOUAI btwn 8-45am & 8-54am elevators shot up dam ftl Lines nrMORY unsalvable(Lt JM Brown OK/2Lt H Lawrence **WIA) left 6-10am MORY-VAULX VRAUCOURT

All 98 Squadron crews recovered the lines after the heated combat of the morning, but the damage and injuries took their toll and there were some forced landings.

B7680   **DH9**   **206Sqn**
+* combat with Fokker DVII[+ooc] ROULERS 4-05pm shot up(2Lt AJ Garside **WIA** /Sgt WS Blythe **WIA**)

D7322   **DH9**   **206Sqn**
*LRec AA EA fire shot up 5-15pm OK(Lt CL Cumming OK/2Lt B Knee **WIA**)

F5965   **Sopwith Camel   209Sqn**
SpM AA mg fire? shot up cr nFEUCHY CHAPEL(2Lt MA Toomey **WIA)

30th August

No. 58 night-bomber Squadron began to receive Handley Pages 0/400s in exchange for its old FE2b pushers on the 30th. Some night bombing units would continue to use the FE2b until the end of the war — for example, 83, 101, 102, 148, and 149 Squadrons. In its own way the FE was an excellent machine for night operations: it gave both pilot and observer an unsurpassed view, it was easy to fly and extremely sturdy in landing — all essential characteristics for this work. Both 58 and 100

Squadrons, however, were given the new type and, remarkably, worked up on the Handley Pages without a break in their war flying. How this was possible, given the great disparity between the types, gives an insight into the world of night bombing. 58 Squadron, for instance, took two or three 0/400s at a time, gradually shedding its Flights of FEs. With the help of experienced Handley Page air crew borrowed, and in some cases transferred, from 207 Squadron, they worked up under their guidance for about three weeks. At the same time, a great influx of technical staff joined the unit and, whilst bombing continued at night, training took place throughout the day. It is remarkable that so many FE2b pilots from 58 Squadron were able to learn to fly the larger type despite the sustained pressures of their duties. The first Handley Page raid by the unit was flown on the 20th of September and for the old FE2b pilots the increased capability was a revelation.

C2413   **RE8**   **3Sqn AFC**
**AOb shrapnel shot up ftl returned a'dr OK(Lt KA Roberts/Lt GS Bell UK.) left 12-15pm

C4586   **RE8**   **3Sqn AFC**
**AP mg shot up ftl SUZANNE OK(Lt J Gould-Taylor/Lt BG Thomson)

C2650   **RE8**   **6Sqn**
**LRec left 5-30pm AA eARRAS shot up dam OK(Lt HH Scott/Lt Chard)

E8   **RE8**   **6Sqn**
CP GAVRELLE-FONTAINES LES CROISILLES combat **MIA(2Lt BJ Macdonald **POW KIA**?/2Lt FC Cook **POW**?) left 4-35pm, observer's fate untraced

F3490   **A.W.FK8**   **8Sqn**
**CP ground mg shot up dam returned 8-50am OK(Capt SE Toomer/Lt WJT Shirlaw) left 8am

E21   **RE8**   **9Sqn**
**NF mg shot up ABLANCOURT ftl dam OK(Lt C Dotzert/2Lt KS Hill) left 5-50am

D7981   **Bristol F2b**   **11Sqn**
**EscB AA shot up dam returned a'dr 7-15pm OK(Lt CR Smythe/2Lt WT Barnes) left 5-20pm BOURLON WOOD

B9271   **Sopwith Camel   46Sqn**
SpM combat seen under 8EA sPERONNE 2000' **MIA(Lt PH Goodhugh **POW DoW**) left 7-15am Fourth Army front

D3170   **DH9**   **49Sqn**
**B BUSIGNY EA gun fire dam OK(2Lt ST Franks/2Lt A Dewhirst) left 3-55pm, returned 7-30pm

D3227   **DH9**   **49Sqn**
**B EA gun fire dam returned a'dr 7-10pm OK(Lt CC Conover/2Lt SP Scott) left 3-55pm

A7589   DH4   55Sqn (I.F.)
**B THIONVILLE Sidings combat with EAs shot down MIA(2Lt WW Tanney USAS. POW/2Lt AJC Gormley POW)

A7708.K   DH4   55Sqn (I.F.)
**B THIONVILLE Sidings combat with EAs MIA(2Lt HH Doehler USAS POW/2Lt AS Papworth POW) [Ja18?]

A7783   DH4   55Sqn (I.F.)
**B THIONVILLE Sidings shot down wr(2Lt PJ Cunningham KIA/2Lt JG Quinton DoW)

A7972   DH4   55Sqn (I.F.)
**B THIONVILLE Sidings combat with EAs MIA(2Lt TH Laing KIA/2Lt TFL Myring KIA)

A8069   DH4   55Sqn (I.F.)
**B THIONVILLE Sidings shot up dam(/2Lt HTC Gompertz WIA)

D8396   DH4   55Sqn (I.F.)
**B THIONVILLE-CONFLANS MIA(2Lt RIA Hickes KIA/2Lt TA Jones KIA)

F5711   DH4   55Sqn (I.F.)
**B THIONVILLE-CONFLANS combat with EAs(/ 2Lt CE Thorp DoW)

High winds and generally adverse weather meant the original target of Köln or Coblenz was dropped in favour of the rail sidings at Thionville. The eleven aircraft which reached the town were attacked before and after bombing and four of these were shot down and other crew wounded. Three of the enemy were also claimed.

D8385   DH4   57Sqn
**Phot combat with Fokker DVII[+ooc] BANCOURT controls shot up nrGOMMECOURT ~5-30pm ftl hit trees cr wr(Lt LK Devitt WIA/Sgt AC Loveday? inj) name Lovesey? [?"BF" claim combat sETAING 4-50pm Ltn F Noltenius Ja27]

C6456.C   SE5a   64Sqn
**OP left 4pm(Lt RB Luard POW) [?"SE5" claim combat INCHY 4-50pm Ltn O Fruhner Ja26]

D9482   Sopwith Camel   65Sqn
**OP HA? seen ok in dive ovGHISTELLES 1-05pm MIA(2Lt HG Pike KIA) [Camel claim wHANDZAEME 1-40pm Flgm H Goerth MFJaIII]

F6151   Sopwith Camel   80Sqn
**OP left 8am mg fire WARLOY engine ftl cr wr(2Lt VG Brindley DoW)

D3764   Sopwith Dolphin   87Sqn
**OP left 5-05pm combat with EA shot through dam returned a'dr OK(Lt FW Ferguson)

D4583   H.P.0/400   97Sqn (I.F.)
**NB ftl French A'dr ORGELET in JURA MIA but OK(Lt H Cooper WIA?/2Lt AE Alderslade OK/Pte1 Taylor OK) 30/31Aug

The relevant Casualty Report and a Casualty Card at Hendon RAF Museum gives this crew MIA in B8803, but it was not operating this night, having gone missing on 22.8.18.

D3215   DH9   99Sqn (I.F.)
**B CONFLANS & DONCOURT A'drs combat with EAs near targets(/2Lt CG Russell KIA)

Cloud was encountered near the targets so each flight attacked an enemy aerodrome. That which bombed Conflans was attacked by enemy fighters.

D7320   DH9   108Sqn
**B ZEEBRUGGE AA OSTENDE engine hit seen diving nrOSTENDE beach 11-30am & ldg 100yds wOSTENDE PIER MIA(2Lt KAW Leighton POW/2Lt WR Jackson POW)

31st August

The German salient in the Lys Valley continued to crumble as August ended. Bailleul had fallen on the 30th, Mount Kemmel on the 31st, and Ploegsteert Wood would be taken on the 4th of September.

A magnificent battle which took the German stronghold of Mont St Quentin the following day was launched by the 5th Australian Infantry Brigade on the 30th. This victory opened the way to Peronne. Involved in support of this force was 3 AFC Squadron and wet weather and low clouds drove its crews to dangerously low levels. An additional problem now being encountered was a diminishing intelligence picture of the country being moved through. This made contact work all the more difficult. Counter-battery work on the 30th, which was carried out in very trying conditions, played a major part in wearing down the defenders during the following day.

RE8   3Sqn   AFC
**CP combat with 13 Fokker DVIIs shot up engine hit ftl(Lt GE Kilburn OK/Lt WP Moore WIA)

F5886   RE8   5Sqn
**Phot combat with EA ftl cr Sh51B P19a(Lt T Killeen OK/Lt RJ Evans WIA) left 6pm, unsalvable

C2727   RE8   6Sqn
**CP GAVRELLE-FONTAINE MIA(2Lt GE Herring POW/Capt WG Shedel POW) left 1-25pm [?possible "RE" claim HAYNECOURT Ltn A Lindenberger Ja2] [?"RE8" claim combat FREMICOURT 1-50pm Ltn H Steinbrecher Ja46]

F5891   RE8   13Sqn
**NF mg fire EA? ftl Sh51B.u.14D wr destr OK(Lt JJ Elder/2Lt MJ Sheehan) left 2-50pm

               Sopwith Dolphin   23Sqn
**? (Lt AO Bentley WIA) inj?

               Sopwith Dolphin   23Sqn
**? (Lt FC Troup WIA) inj?

D3687   Sopwith Dolphin 23Sqn
**OP combat with EA ePERONNE shot down in flames
EoL 6-45pm MIA(2Lt CHA Bridge POW DoW)
["Dolphin" claim combat swPERONNE 6-45pm Oblt E
vWedel Ja11]

D3752   Sopwith Dolphin 23Sqn
**OP combat with EA shot up engine lost ftl 01a.2.3.67C?
dam OK(Lt WNL Cope) left 6-08pm

D5232   Sopwith Dolphin 23Sqn
**OP combat with EA shot up bad ftl A.L.G. dam
OK(Capt AJ Brown)

D6975   SE5a   24Sqn
**OP mg PROYART 3-50pm fuel tank shot up ftl cr
trench OK(Lt JPalmer)

C8869   SE5a   40Sqn
**OP combat with EA lost ftl DOMELIERS to ask:
c'wind o't OK(Lt JV Price) left 10-45am

E2469   Bristol F2b   48Sqn
**OP AA ftl 8pm cr ELVERDINGHE bad ground dam
OK(2Lt JB Cowan/Sgt RLG White) left 6-10pm MENIN

E4001   SE5a   60Sqn
**OP BAPAUME combat dam returned a'dr 7-30pm
OK(Lt JE Smith) left 6-10pm

E5977.5   SE5a   64Sqn
**OP left 2pm combat with EA down in flames
nSCARPE? MIA(Capt TStP Bunbury KIA) buried
JIGSAW WOOD Sh51B.134 ["SE5" claim combat
ROEUX 2-05pm? Ltn F Noltenius Ja27]

F1413   Sopwith Camel   70Sqn
**BOP mg fire NIEPPE 1pm ftl cr o't OK(2Lt CA
Crichton)

D6977   SE5a   84Sqn
**OP mg PERONNE fuel tank shot up ftl cr shell hole
OK(Lt JE Robbins) left 3-15pm

D6927   SE5a   85Sqn
** left 2-45pm MIA but OK?(Capt GD Brewster MC)

E1271   SE5a   85Sqn
**OP left 2-45pm ground mg shot up dam returned a'dr
4pm OK(Lt DC Inglis)

E4374   Sopwith Camel   203Sqn
**SpM ground mg shot down ovPERONNE cr
Sh62c.014.d wr(2Lt DH Woodhouse inj) left 7-15pm, a'c
shelled

D8196   Sopwith Camel   US 148th Pursuit Sqn
**GndStr shot up dam returned a'dr 2-20pm OK(Lt GC
Dorsey) left 1-15pm

Untraced casualties in France in August 1918

** MIA(Capt R Marshall POW) Aug.18?
** MIA(2Lt Z Miller POW) Aug.18? (may be American
from 27th US Aero on 27.7.18?)

Two additional bombing squadrons arrived in

France at the end of August to serve with the
Independent Force. The first was 115 Squadron,
which departed England on the 29th. Its Handley
Pages were safely at Roville-aux-Chene four days
later. 110 Squadron then arrived at Bettencourt on
the 31st of August. It was the first unit to be fully
equipped with the DH9A day-bomber, and all its
machines were, incidentally, made as a gift by the
Nizam of Hyderabad.

September 1918

1st September

RE8   5Sqn
** shot up in action(Lt EA Locke-Waters WIA/)

A.W.FK8   8Sqn
** combat(2Lt T Brandon WIA/)

D4895   RE8   13Sqn
**PhotAOb left 3-55pm combat with EA dam OK(Lt GN
Dennis/2Lt JM Brown) to XVII Corps area, returned
5-15pm

E67   RE8   15Sqn
**CAP ground mg ftl Sh57C N.34 at 6-45pm dam
OK(Capt CC Snow/2Lt RC Capel-Cure) salvaged

B7890   SE5a   32Sqn
**OP seen ok CAMBRAI 15000' 2-40pm MIA(Lt EC
Klingman USAS. POW) Ja36

SE5a   32Sqn
** combat(Lt AE Sandys-Winsch WIA)

E5939.B SE5a   32Sqn
**OP seen ok CAMBRAI 2-40pm(2Lt JOW Donaldson
USAS. POW) a'c captured, pilot later escaped ?combat
sPRONVILLE 2-55pm Ltn T Quandt Ja36], made
several victory claims

D5134   A.W.FK8   35Sqn
**P AA MORVAL shot up dam engine ftl OK(2Lt H
Phillips/2Lt H Griffiths)

Bristol F2b   48Sqn
** AA fire(/2Lt JN Kier WIA)

C2244   RE8   53Sqn
**LP AA shot up 3-45pm dam returned a'dr(TLt SW
Cowper-Coles WIA/TLt GL Pargeter OK) to X Army
area

RE8   53Sqn
** AA fire(/2Lt DC Burke WIA)

DH4   57Sqn
** shot up in action(/Lt J Howard-Brown WIA)

D8382   DH4   57Sqn
**B CAMBRAI ANNEX STN combat with EA 2-55pm
dam(Sgt DE Edgley OK/Sgt N Sandison WIA) left
12-10pm

F6096   DH4   57Sqn
**B combat chased down in control by 6EA
seCAMBRAI **MIA**(2Lt JG Dugdale **POW**/2Lt FB
Robinson **POW**) left 12-10pm

E2479   Bristol F2b   62Sqn
**EscOP combat with EA seen going down in control
1-40pm **MIA**(2Lt LB Raymond **POW**/2Lt DS Hamilton
KIA) left 12-15pm CAMBRAI [?"BF" claim combat
sLECLUSE Ltn E Bormann Ja2]

E2494   Bristol F2b   62Sqn
**EscOP combat with EA MONCHY AU BOIS 1-40pm
shot through cr ldg dam(Lt LW Hudson OK/2Lt J Hall
WIA) left 12-15pm

        Bristol F2b   62Sqn
** combat(2Lt JK Stewart **WIA**/)

D1922   Sopwith Camel   73Sqn
GndStr seen ok CAGNICOURT shot down **MIA(Lt
HV Fellowes **POW**) left 6-20am

        SE5a   74Sqn
** combat(Lt J Adamson **WIA**)

E4433   Sopwith Dolphin   79Sqn
prac left 4-45pm **MIA(Lt DA Martin US. **POW**)

C9790   FE2b   101Sqn
NB left 11-05pm **MIA(Lt ME Challis **POW**/2Lt RD
Hughes **POW**)

        DH9   108Sqn
** combat(/Lt FD McClinton **WIA**)

E1538   Sopwith Camel   208Sqn
+* combat with Fokker DVII[+ooc] ECOURT ST
QUENTIN 3-50pm OK(Capt GK Cooper) made 7
claims

E4388   Sopwith Camel   209Sqn
HOP left 3pm seen ok nrHAMBLIN 16000' **MIA(2Lt
HV Peeling **POW**)

E4393   Sopwith Camel   209Sqn
**HOP seen dive on 7 Fokker DVII BOIRY-NOTRE
DAME **MIA**(2Lt RL Scharff **POW**) left 3pm, repat
30.12.18, Ja36? [?combat Ltn Quandt Ja36]

E2521   Bristol F2b   L Flt
**Phot combat with several EAs ovSENSÉE CANAL
down ooc **MIA**(Lt GL Barritt **POW**/2Lt RHG Boys
POW) left 11am

        Bristol F2b   L Flt
** combat(/2Lt M Wallace **WIA**)

2nd September
FIGHTING ON THE DROCOURT-QUEANT LINE

The pressure for a withdrawal to a defensive line
behind Bapaume had become so unendurable that
Ludendorff had been forced to make the order at
the end of the previous month. The pull-back
encompassed country as far south as Noyon. On
the 2nd, however, the Canadian Corps attacked
and broke through the long-established Drocourt-
Queant line abreast the Arras-Cambrai road.
Between this attack and open country stood only
the barriers of the waterways, and Ludendorff was
left no option but to pull his armies back still
further to positions established eighteen months
previously. On this day, in demonstration of the
weight of arms descending on the German forces,
the British Army fired 943,857 shells.

The RAF was highly active in this fighting, its
corps units suffering some of their heaviest losses of
the war. Some were from ground fire, but the
majority appear to have been from attacks by
enemy fighters who had penetrated the net of offensive patrolling. These were infrequent, but intense
when they came. Some significant dogfights took
place in the morning between the attackers looking
for access to the battle and fighters from I and III
Brigades who were patrolling higher up (namely,
from Nos. 22 and 40, and Nos. 3, 56, 60, 87, 201,
US17, and US148 Squadrons). These are noted
where possible below.

Where casualties were highest, they had been
mostly inflicted by the large and well organised
formations of Jagdgeschwader III. Their groups
that morning were often as strong as thirty aircraft,
containing a high proportion of experienced and
competent war flyers. Wherever possible, the
German Air Force was still operating its fundamental strategy whereby its strength was drawn
together for selective actions of greatest worth, and
on this occasion they were very successful. However, the RAF also remained absolutely committed
to its own abiding doctrine of highly planned
offensive flying, which in time would wear down all
the efforts of the enemy. Co-ordinated low patrols
were made once again by fighters from I Brigade,
each pilot attacking particular prearranged targets
in the enemy positions with an abiding tactical
sophistication simply unapproached by the enemy.
These included the fortified villages, trains, kite
balloons, and low level enemy air formations which
were found counter-attacking the advance. The
Official History records that at one point there
were ninety-two Allied fighters involved in attacks
on enemy troops and positions in front of the
Canadians. Through the day these single-seaters
dropped eight tons of bombs.

It was to become obvious in the next day or two
that a great victory had been achieved, for reports
flooded in of the enemy in widespread retreat. For
the RAF there had been a high price to pay,
especially on the 2nd of September, when there

were forty-two airmen dead, missing, or wounded in the sector.

C8344   Sopwith Camel   3Sqn
LowP seen ok then combat with EA Sh51B V.11 at 9-20am then seen going s-w 800' after **MIA(Lt VH McElroy **KIA**) [?Camel claim combat ETAING but 10am? Ltn F Noltenius Ja27]

F6190   Sopwith Camel   3Sqn
LowP seen dive steeply on ground target AA? dive broke up cr Sh51B V.17c 5pm **MIA(Lt GF Young **KIA**)

C2536   RE8   5Sqn
CP combat with EA ftl 09d 90.40 wr(Lt CC Fraser OK/2Lt AJ Bishop **WIA) left 11-50am

C2729   RE8   5Sqn
AP left 10-50am **MIA(Lt L Coleman **KIA**/2Lt CE Garden **KIA**) to Corps front, buried Sh51B P.32.B.9.8. [?possible RE8 claim combat FAMPOUX 11-20am Ltn W Sommer Ja39]

C4590   RE8   5Sqn
**CP EA & ground mg fire ftl 09d.40.40 wr OK(Lt J Town/Lt AC Pollard) left 1-15pm

RE8   5Sqn
** in action(/2Lt GJ Carr **WIA**)

Nos. 5 and 52 Squadrons operated with the attacking Canadian Corps.

C5072   RE8   6Sqn
** combat fuel tank shot up eARRAS ftl Sh51B P21c OK(Lt Pettit/Lt Clarke) left 8am, unsalvable [?claim combat BAILLEUL 10-25am Vzfw R Jorke Ja39]

RE8   6Sqn
** mg fire(/Lt CE Clegg **WIA**)

E91   RE8   6Sqn
**CP AA ftl ShD36 4.b.59 dam unsalvable OK(Lt Martin/Lt Churchward) left 3-30pm, unsalvable due to mg fire

F5880   RE8   6Sqn
**P combat with EA fuel tank shot through dam returned a'dr OK(Lt Fenwick/2Lt JA Holmes) left 10-55am, 6 Sqn co-operating with cavalry

RE8   7Sqn
** AA fire(/2Lt J McAslan **WIA**)

D6735   RE8   7Sqn
**CAP ground mg dam OK(2Lt CS Bolsby/Lt JMG Bell MC)

A.W.FK8   8Sqn
** AA fire(/Lt HA Mould **WIA**)

B4161   A.W.FK8   8Sqn
**CP mg BOYELLES ftl cr shell hole OK(2Lt WL Chapman/2Lt FEL Elliot) salvable, left 8-35am

D5121   A.W.FK8   8Sqn
CP mg shot up dam returned a'dr 6-45am(Lt Spriggs OK/2Lt JA Cogan **WIA) left 5-30am

D5185   A.W.FK8   8Sqn
CP EA AA? shot down eVAULX VRAUCOURT wr(Capt GH Dykes **WIA/Lt Birkett OK) left 7-05am

F4268   A.W.FK8   8Sqn
**CP mg wBULLECOURT water pipe shot through cooling system damaged ftl OK(Lt Spriggs/Lt Glover) left 10-50am

F7394   A.W.FK8   8Sqn
CAP left 9-15am **MIA(2Lt CFW Appley US. **KIA**/2Lt RF Talbot **KIA**)

8 Squadron was, as usual, co-operating tactically with tanks during the assault on the Drocourt-Queant line, and they were therefore drawn into some of the heaviest fighting. They took their heaviest ever casualties on this day.

F4263   A.W.FK8   10Sqn
CAP mg & shells 2pm down WIENHANT CROSSROADS Sh28 N.11 a'c shelled(2Lt RA Coulthurst **WIA/2Lt AR Macpherson OK)

RE8   13Sqn
** (/Lt FPJ Travis **WIA**)

F5978   RE8   13Sqn
CP left 5pm **MIA(2Lt JS Stringer **POW**/Lt RAB Pope MC **POW**) with the XVII Corps, offering artillery support to Canadian advance

DH4   18Sqn
** combat(/Lt RL Aslin **WIA**)

Bristol F2b   20Sqn
** (/Sgt L Bradshaw **WIA**)

D7908   Bristol F2b   22Sqn
+*OP combat with Fokker DVII[+des] ARRAS-CAMBRAI Road 9-15am OK(Lt HH Beddow/2Lt TJ Birmingham)

D7990   Bristol F2b   22Sqn
OP seen ok eCAMBRAI going into clouds **MIA(Capt BL Dowling **KIA**/Lt VStB Collins **KIA**) left 8-25am

E2516   Bristol F2b   22Sqn
OP combat with Fokker DVII[+ooc] ARRAS-CAMBRAI Road 9-15am shot up ftl 9-30am(2Lt IO Stead OK/2Lt WA Cowie **WIA)

All the above action occurred during a big combat near Marquion around 9-30am. Somewhat over two hours later, 22 Squadron was involved in more fighting in the same area (see entries for US 148th Pursuit Sqn below). In this fighting, another three claims were made by its crews but none was lost.

B4174   A.W.FK8   35Sqn
P combat with EA driven down FREIGECOURT cr ldg(2Lt H Nattrass **WIA/Lt FA Lawson **WIA**) left 7-30am, were MIA

D8445   SE5a   40Sqn
**OP combat with 12EA steam ooc nwCAMBRAI

9-30am **MIA**(Lt HW Clarke **DoW**)

SE5a   **41Sqn**
** combat(1Lt EH Barksdale USAS. **WIA**)

C943   **Bristol F2b**   **48Sqn**
**OP combat with EA[+ooc] eMENIN 7-45pm shot up
dam OK(2Lt JB Cowan/2Lt TL Jones) left 6-10pm
MENIN

E2214   **Bristol F2b**   **48Sqn**
**OP MENIN seen in combat with EA eLILLE 7-15pm
MIA(2Lt O O'Connor **POW**/2Lt JJ Ambler **POW**) left
6-10pm

E2455   **Bristol F2b**   **48Sqn**
**OP MENIN combat with HA 7-15pm seen eLILLE
MIA(2Lt IMB McCulloch **POW**/2Lt LP Perry **KIA**) left
6-10pm

C2467   **RE8**   **52Sqn**
**B combat with EA shot down BREBIÈRES Sh51B
b.31d(2Lt RG Walton **WIA**/2Lt G Bradbury **WIA**) left
11am

D4899   **RE8**   **52Sqn**
**B combat shot down BREBIÈRES Sh51B H17
OK(2Lt JB Elton/2Lt WE China) left 11am, salvaged?

F6015   **RE8**   **52Sqn**
**B BREBIÈRES combat with EA shot down
Sh51B.b.31d wr(2Lt JC Garlake OK/2Lt L Sharp **WIA**)
left 11am [RE8 claim combat VIS-EN-ARTOIS 12-30pm
Ltn M Dehmisch Ja58]

D4903   **RE8**   **53Sqn**
**NF AA dam ftl Sq.28 at 4pm OK(2Lt AJ Macqueen/
2Lt DA Lawson)

F2145   **Sopwith Camel**   **54Sqn**
**SpB mg fire shot up 8-15am ftl OK(2Lt WJ Densham)

F5968   **Sopwith Camel**   **54Sqn**
**SpB left 9-15am mg fire shot up ftl(Capt EJ Salter
WIA)

C8706   **SE5a**   **56Sqn**
COP seen ok nDOUAI 8000' 9-45am **MIA(Lt WM
Strathearne **POW**) [?SE5 claim combat VILLERS
9-25am Ltn O Fruhner Ja26] [?SE5 claim combat
VILLERS 9-15am Ltn H Lange Ja26]

C2502   **RE8**   **59Sqn**
**CAP ground mg ovLE TRANSLOY-VILLERS AU
FLOS shot through dam OK(Lt A Ibbotson/2Lt WJ
Carruthers) left 5-15am

D6956.Z **SE5a**   **60Sqn**
**OP combat with EA shot up dam returned a'dr
10-45am OK(Capt B McEntegart) left 9am Third Army
area

D8114   **Sopwith Camel**   **73Sqn**
**GndStr left 9-55am seen ok ovSANTEMONT
MIA(2Lt DB Sinclair **POW**)

C6468   **SE5a**   **74Sqn**
**OP left 5-30pm mg fire combat ftl Sh27 F.8 cr? 5-50pm

dam OK(Capt S Carlin)

B1879   **FE2b**   **148Sqn**
**NB mg prop dam ftl SOUCHEZ cr wr 2-15am OK(Lt
E Alder OK/Lt AV Collins **inj**) left 12-15am, Collins
WIA?

148 Squadron were also performing tank camou-
flage operations for the attack on the Drocourt-
Queant line using the sound of their engines as they
went to and from their night bombing targets.
These were the defended villages of Saudemont,
Ecourt St Quentin, and Palleul.

E4399   **Sopwith Camel**   **201Sqn**
**OP mg? seen low going east ovBOURIES 7am
MIA(2Lt WA Hall **POW**) left 5-45am Third Army front

D3226   **DH9**   **206Sqn**
EscRec seen nrDUNKIRK **MIA(2Lt HA Scrivener
WIA POW/Sgt CH Davidson **POW DoW**) left 7-20am

D1873.U **Sopwith Camel**   **208Sqn**
**LowB left 9-30am heavy combat SAUDEMONT
MIA(2Lt JW Marshall **WIA**)

E1545   **Sopwith Camel**   **208Sqn**
**LowB left 6am combat with EA SAUDEMONT shot
up ftl nrLAGNICOURT **MIA**(2Lt CH Living **POW**)

E4381   **Sopwith Camel**   **209Sqn**
**LP seen in combat with EA ovECOURT ST
QUENTIN 7-30am down in flames **MIA**(Lt WM
Wormald **KIA**)?combat ECOURT ST QUENTIN
7-20am Ltn T Quandt Ja36]

F5970   **Sopwith Camel**   **209Sqn**
**LP seen in combat with EA ovECOURT ST
QUENTIN 7-30am down in flames **MIA**(Capt RC Grant
KIA)

D6700   **Sopwith Camel**   **US 148th Pursuit Sqn**
**OP seen in combat with EA btwn RUMAUCOURT
& ARRAS-CAMBRAI ROAD 12-10pm **MIA**(2Lt JD
Kenyon **POW**) [?Camel claim combat neBARALLE
11-45am Ltn H Lange Ja26][?"Camel" claim combat
wHAVRINCOURT pm Ltn E Borman Ja2]

D8245   **Sopwith Camel**   **US 148th Pursuit Sqn**
**OP left 11am combat with EA[+cr smoking] 11-50am
shot up dam returned a'dr 1pm OK(1Lt FE Kindley)

E1412   **Sopwith Camel**   **US 148th Pursuit Sqn**
**OP RUMAUCOURT seen in combat btwn
RUMAUCOURT-ARRAS-CAMBRAI Road 12-10pm
MIA(1Lt LH Forster **KIA**) left 11am [?"Camel" claim
combat HANCOURT 11-40am Oblt T Dahlmann
JGIII][?also 3 Camel claims incl combat SAUCHY-
LESTRÉE pm Ltn E Bormann Ja2]

E1414   **Sopwith Camel**   **US 148th Pursuit Sqn**
**OP left 11am RUMAUCOURT seen in combat with
EA btwn RUMAUCOURT & CAMBRAI-ARRAS
Road 12-10pm **MIA**(2Lt O Mandel **POW**) [?"Camel"
claim combat swDURY Ltn E Bormann Ja2]

E1471   Sopwith Camel   US 148th Pursuit Sqn
**OP RUMAUCOURT seen in combat with EA
MIA(2Lt JE Frobisher **POW DoW** 10.9.18) left 11am
["Camel" claim combat BEUGNATRE 12pm Ltn O
Löffler Ja2]

Of the squadrons involved in combats on the 2nd,
US 148th Pursuit suffered the highest casualties.
The unit joined fight in support of a group from 64
Squadron and 22 Squadron who had met around
fifteen enemy fighters a little before midday. 5
Squadron RE8s also became involved. Five
German machines are believed to have been shot
down. American casualties were similar.

3rd September

The German Army evacuated Lens on the 3rd of
September. Fighting in the air continued with
steady intensity. The RAF not only fought off
German machines attempting to cover the retreat
of their armies, but were also an important part of
the Allied strike force of the advance. In consequence, fighters on offensive patrols and day-
bombers attacking the withdrawal continued to
take some casualties but corps machines had a less
critical day. Progress was inevitable as the German
armies pulled back and, by that evening, the
British line ran northwards from Peronne roughly
along the Canal du Nord and crossed the Sensée
river near Ecourt St Quentin. This point having
been reached, operations were halted on the First
Army front. On the Somme south of Peronne, the
German Army withdrew eastwards back over the
river as both the British and French continued to
harass them, and in a matter of days had crossed
it as well.

F5899   RE8   3Sqn AFC
**CP ground mg dam returned a'dr OK(Lt DF Dimsey/
Lt RFC Machin) left 5-45pm

E1407   Sopwith Camel   4Sqn AFC
+* attacked KB[+des] LE PLOUICH 7-05am OK(Lt
LTE Taplin) another KB shot down at HERLIES at
7pm, made most of his 12 claims in this a'c

RE8   4Sqn
** AA fire(2Lt PFf Gyles **WIA**/)

F5885   RE8   5Sqn
**AP mg NEUVILLE VITASSE shot up then became
lost, low fuel ftl cr dam OK(Lt J Scholes/Lt R Boyle) left
5-35am

A.W.FK8   10Sqn
** mg fire(/2Lt WJ Mills **DoW** 4.9.18)

B7888   RE8   12Sqn
CAP left 7-20am **MIA(Lt AW Macnamara **KIA**/Lt H
Jonsson MC **KIA**) [?RE8 claim combat BEUGNY Ltn
H Frommherz Ja27]

C2699   RE8   12Sqn
**CAP combat with 4EA Sh57C NW mg shot up ftl
dam(Lt TS Bulman **WIA**/Lt Smith **WIA**?) left 3-05pm
to Sh57cNW J.5.d [?RE8 claim combat BEUGNATRE
Ltn H Frommherz Ja27]

F5839   DH4   18Sqn
Phot AA? shot down wBOURLON WOOD **MIA(Lt
FM Macfarland **KIA**/2Lt A Peterson **KIA**) left 1-55pm

B1344   Bristol F2b   20Sqn
**OP left 4-26pm seen ok? ovHAVRINCOURT WOOD
combat with EA **MIA**(Lt WF Washington **KIA**/2Lt K
Penrose **KIA**) Ja3? [?BF claim combat
wHAVRINCOURT 5-40pm Ltn Vollbracht Ja5][?BF
claim combat ETERPIGNY Ltn T Quandt Ja36]

Bristol F2b   20Sqn
** combat(/2Lt FJ Ralph DFC **KIA**)

D9235   DH4   25Sqn
**prac combat with 5EA DIXMUDE 5-15pm ftl dam(Lt
S Crosfield OK/2Lt EF Boyce **KIA**)

C1124   SE5a   32Sqn
OP seen CAMBRAI 13000' 4-45pm **MIA(Capt JHLW
Flynn Can. **KIA**)

D6935   SE5a   32Sqn
OP seen CAMBRAI 13000' 4-45pm **MIA(2Lt FC
Pacey Can. **KIA**)

C9259.5   **SE5a   41Sqn**
**OP seen with 2EA on tail spinning eARRAS 7pm(2Lt
CE Turner **WIA**) left 6-30am, was **MIA** but seen spin
out of combat [?combat GUEMAPPE 7pm Oblt H
Auffahrt Ja29][?SE5a claim swNOREUIL 7-35pm Vzfw
O Hennrich Ja46]

D3269   DH9   49Sqn
**B DOUAI STN AA cr a'dr 5-10pm OK(2Lt BG Pool/
Sgt RA Campbell) left 2-25pm

C2377   RE8   53Sqn
**FlRec mg dam(Lt DC Dunlop OK/2Lt BE Scott MC
DFC **WIA**)

C8867   SE5a   56Sqn
**EscB left 1-45pm Third Army area combat with EA
shot up dam OK(1Lt LG Bowen USAS.) returned
3-50pm

D338   SE5a   56Sqn
+* combat with Fokker DVIIs[++des] ETAING-
HAYNECOURT 7-10am OK(Capt WR Irwin Can.)
Irwin's last of 11 victories

E4064   SE5a   56Sqn
**COP combat with EA spiral 10000' seen chased down
ooc by EA wHAYNECOURT 7-20am **MIA**(Lt A Vickers
KIA) left 6-15am

F5874   RE8   59Sqn
P ground mg shot up dam(Capt GJ Scott **WIA/2Lt JN
Schofield **WIA**) left 8-10am

RE8   59Sqn
B in action(/2Lt A Dewhirst **WIA)

B8503   SE5a   60Sqn
**OP combat controls shot up ftl nrBUISY cr o't Sh51B
V17.0.2.3. at 5-20pm OK(Lt CS Hall) left 4-10pm Third
Army area

E6000   SE5a   60Sqn
**OP combat with HA nrCAGNICOURT engine dam
ftl 11am OK(Lt JFM Kerr) left 9am Third Army area
[SE5a claim combat NOREUIL 10-25am Ltn T Quandt
Ja36]

D5174   A.W.FK8   82Sqn
**B seen ARMENTIÈRES 10-45am MIA(2Lt D Rose
POW/2Lt JB Cockin POW) left 9-30am [?"AW" claim
combat LOMME 11-30am Ltn Nebgen Ja7]

C1834   SE5a   84Sqn
+* combat RumplerC[+des] sMANANCOURT-
NURLU Road 6-15am then KB[+des] FINS 6-45am
OK(Capt WA Southey SA.) 2Str shared, shot down
another KB nFINS 3-30pm, Southey's final claims
numbered 20

C4163   Sopwith Dolphin   87Sqn
**COP seen ovEPINOY 7000' going down control?
MIA(Lt FW Ferguson KIA) left 5pm [?Dolphin claim
combat MARCOING 7-05pm Vzfw M Hutterer Ja23]

D2863   DH9   98Sqn
**B CAMBRAI-VILLE Rlwy Jctn combat with EA[+?]
shot up ftl CAPPY dam(Lt CG Gowing OK/2Lt JGW
Halliday KIA) left 3-30pm, operating again 4 days later
[?DH claim combat EPHEY 3-25pm Ltn O Löffler Ja2]

D7202   DH9   98Sqn
**B CAMBRAI-VILLE Rlwy Jctn 5-55pm combat with
6EA but shot down by AA in spin ooc wCAMBRAI
MIA(2Lt RT Ingram KIA/2Lt KJW Dennitts KIA) left
3-30pm [DH9 claim nBERTINCOURT 5-47pm combat
Ltn F Rumey Ja5]

D511   DH9   108Sqn
**B OSTENDE DOCKS AA? seen going down at 9000'
towards seOSTENDE MIA(2Lt A Preston POW/Sgt H
Stewart POW) left 10-16am

4th September

C8333.8 Sopwith Camel   3Sqn
**OP left 8-50am combat with EA ftl cr shell hole Sh51B
u.19d wr(2Lt RN Tedbury DoW) [?possible combat
sRAILLENCOURT 10am Ltn R Wenzl Ja6][?possible
Camel claim combat SAILLY-CAMBRAI 10-10am Vzfw
G Staudacher Ja1]

F1972   Sopwith Camel   3Sqn
**OP combat fuel tank shot up ftl Sh51B V.23 OK(Lt
DJ Hughes) left 8-50am, a'c shelled & abandoned?: a'c
still with 3Sqn 10.18

E111   RE8   4Sqn
**AOb combat with EAs forced down Sh28.T.22c
8-15am dam(Lt EL Barrington MC WIA/2Lt WG
Greenaway WIA)

E1416   Sopwith Camel   4Sqn AFC

+* combat with Fokker DVII[+ooc] nrWATTIGNIES
7-15am OK(Capt AH Cobby) last of 29 victories for this
Australian ace

**   A.W.FK8   10Sqn**
** (/Lt AHE King WIA?) inj?

**   RE8   13Sqn**
** (/2Lt H Dobing WIA)

A7853   DH4   18Sqn
**B shot down in flames cr Sh51b Q.9.c.7.4. MIA(Lt WB
Hogg KIA/2Lt AE Stock KIA) left 8-30am, bodies
unrecognisable

**   DH4   18Sqn**
** combat(/Sgt GA Cribbes WIA)

F5838   DH4   18Sqn
**Phot EA shot up dam ftl SERNY a'dr 2pm OK(2Lt C
Mason/Lt EA Collis MM) left 10-15am First Army area

E4026   SE5a   32Sqn
+* combat with Fokker DVIIs[+flames+ooc]
nCAMBRAI-seARRAS btwn 9-45am & 9-50am OK(Lt
FL Hale)

B5434   Sopwith Camel   46Sqn
**LowP seen ovPRONVILLE following 7EA MIA(Lt
CHP Killick POW) left 8-30am [?Camel claim combat
RECOURT Ltn H Frommherz Ja27]

E2611   Bristol F2b   48Sqn
** combat with EA[+des] wARMENTIÈRES 9-40am
shot up(Lt GF Manning OK/2Lt PA Clayson WIA)

C2364   RE8   53Sqn
**CAP combat with EA shot up & mg dam ftl
CLAIRMARAIS Sh28 T.14.B.8.4. OK(TLt JB Pierce/
TLt MW Wakeman)

E5991   SE5a   60Sqn
**OP combat QUEANT 7am prop shot off ftl Sh51B
D1.B2.8. OK(Lt OP Johnson) [?combat QUEANT Ltn
T Quandt Ja36]

D7899   Bristol F2b   62Sqn
+*EscB attacked by ~25 Fokker DVIIs[+ooc]
ovMARQUETTE 9-30am OK(Capt WE Staton MC
DFC/Lt LE Mitchell) attacked just after crossing lines

D7945   Bristol F2b   62Sqn
**EscB combat with Fokker DVIIs nCAMBRAI engine
hit ftl seen going down in control nCAMBRAI MIA(Lt
WK Swayze POW/2Lt WE Hall POW) left 8-15am
CAMBRAI-DOUAI [?combat EMERCHICOURT a'dr
10am Ltn M Dehmisch Ja58]

E2128   Bristol F2b   62Sqn
+*EscB attacked Fokker DVII[+ooc cr 3m
nCAMBRAI] 9-10am OK(Lt RO Schallaire Can./2Lt R
Lowe)

E2457   Bristol F2b   62Sqn
+*EscB combat with Fokker DVIIs[+des+ooc]
ABANCOURT-nCAMBRAI 9-30am OK(Capt GE
Gibbons/2Lt T Elliott) first victory was over Fokker

DVII attacking D7945, whose prop had stopped, pilot claimed 17 victories

Nos. 32 and 62 Squadrons were escorting 107 Squadron on a IX Brigade day bombing raid to Valenciennes station. There was heavy fighting, involving losses to both sides.

E1273.V **SE5a** **64Sqn**
OP left 5-40am air collision with D6988 EoL 6-45am MIA(Lt AM Stahl **KIA)

E4002Z **SE5a** **64Sqn**
OP left 5-40am MIA(Lt HT McKinnie **POW?) pilot's fate untraced

E5979.5 **SE5a** **64Sqn**
OP left 8-05am MIA(2Lt V Harley **POW) in F5978? [?combat PELVES 10am Ltn E Bormann Ja2]

B9269 **Sopwith Camel** **70Sqn**
OP seen ECAILLON 5m eDOUAI MIA(Lt J Leveson-Gower Can. **POW) left 7-20am [?combat MONCHECOURT 8-20am Oblt B Loerzer JGIII][2 Camels claim CANTIN ~8-15am Vzfw E Buder Ja26]

C8239 **Sopwith Camel** **70Sqn**
P left 7-20am seen nrECAILLON 5m eDOUAI MIA(Capt JH Forman Can. **POW) [?combat CANTIN 8-18am Vzfw F Classen Ja26][?2 Camel claims Oblt TH Dahlmann JG111]

D1930 **Sopwith Camel** **70Sqn**
OP left 7-20am seen ECAILLON 5m eDOUAI MIA(Lt R McPhee Can. **POW) [3 Camel claims combat CANTIN 8-15am, sDOUAI 8-20am, wCORBEHEM 8-30am Ltn O Fruhner Ja26]

D3406 **Sopwith Camel** **70Sqn**
OP left 7-20am seen ECAILLON 5m eDOUAI MIA(2Lt WM Herriot **DoW)

D9416 **Sopwith Camel** **70Sqn**
OP left 7-20am seen ECAILLON 5m eDOUAI MIA(Lt JA Spilhaus **KIA)

D9418 **Sopwith Camel** **70Sqn**
OP left 7-20am seen ECAILLON 5m eDOUAI MIA(Lt SW Rochford **POW)

D9458 **Sopwith Camel** **70Sqn**
OP left 7-20am seen ECAILLON 5m eDOUAI MIA(2Lt KH Wallace **KIA)

E1472 **Sopwith Camel** **70Sqn**
OP left 7-20am last seen in combat with Fokker DVII[+des] ECAILLON 5m eDOUAI 8-15am MIA(Lt DHS Gilbertson **KIA) shared with D8175

E7173 **Sopwith Camel** **70Sqn**
+*OP combat with Fokker DVII[+flames] ECAILLON 8-15am OK(Lt KB Watson)

These extremely heavy losses were suffered by 70 Squadron in a single combat whilst on an offensive patrol. They were on temporary attachment from

II Brigade and met perhaps thirty Fokkers over the First Army front.

Sopwith Dolphin **79Sqn**
** combat(Lt VG Snyder **WIA**)

D9501 **Sopwith Camel** **80Sqn**
**OP combat with EA PARGNY? dam ftl fire ldg destr OK(2Lt EO Champagne) left 12pm

B9355 **DH9** **104Sqn (I.F.)**
** shot up? cr wr(/Sgt FHI Denny **WIA**)

C6169 **DH9** **107Sqn**
B left 7-35am MIA(Lt BE Gammell **KIA/2Lt F Player **KIA**) [?DH9 claim combat NEUF BERQUIN 8-30am Oblt F Ritt vRöth Ja16]

D3106 **DH9** **107Sqn**
B left 7-35am MIA(2Lt JC Boyle **POW/2Lt FCB Eaton **KIA**) [?DH9 claim combat ST AUBERT 9-15am Gfr H Nülle Ja39]

F6172 **DH9** **107Sqn**
B left 7-35am VALENCIENNES-MARGUETTE MIA(Lt ERL Sproule **POW/2Lt GT Coles **POW**)

107 Squadron was being escorted by Nos. 32 and 62 Squadrons when it suffered these losses (see above).

D9641 **Sopwith Camel** **203Sqn**
+* combat with Fokker DVII[+des] TRESCAULT eHAVRINCOURT WOOD 4-15pm OK(Capt AT Whealy Can.) last of 27 claims

5th September

A pause in the main Allied advance was called on the 5th of September. The progress had been enormous and profound, and it was time to rest and recover where possible, assess the enemy's dispositions, and to prepare for perhaps a decisive blow. The RAF fighter squadrons were ordered to stop low bombing and attack work, but a watchful air offensive would continue. It would concentrate less on the seeking out and destroying of the enemy air force and more on excluding the enemy two-seaters and on the protection of the RAF corps machines from attack. The latter would be needed to assist the armies through their artillery and reconnaissance work as they prepared for the next phase. This was no easy matter, for once again the Allies in the British sector had come face to face with the formidable defences of the main Hindenburg Line, along which Germany now assembled its best and most determined troops. Theses forces would make the British armies pay dearly for the victories to come.

F6032.R **Sopwith Camel** **3Sqn**
+* combat with AlbatrosC[+flames] PERONNE 12-05pm OK(Lt WH Hubbard) made 10 claims on Camels

B778　　Sopwith Camel　4Sqn AFC
**OP combat with 8 Fokker DVIIs BREBIÈRES 6-05pm
shot down in flames? **MIA**(2Lt MH Eddie **KIA**) ?combat
seHENIN-LIETARD 6-05pm Vzfw F Classen Ja26]

D8136　　Sopwith Camel　4Sqn AFC
**OP combat with 8 Fokker DVIIs[?+] BREBIÈRES
6-05pm shot down ooc **MIA**(2Lt AH Lockley **KIA**)
[?Camel claim combat MARQUION 6pm Ltn H
Frommherz Ja27]

E1407　　Sopwith Camel　4Sqn AFC
**OP big combat with 8 Fokker DVII BREBIÈRES
6-05pm then shot down by ground fire **MIA**(Lt LTE
Taplin DFC **WIA POW**)hand, ?combat CUINCY 6pm
Vzfw C Mesch Ja26]

E7174　　Sopwith Camel　4Sqn AFC
**OP combat with 8 Fokker DVII BREBIÈRES 6-05pm
shot down in flames? **MIA**(Lt DC Carter **KIA**)

C2427　　RE8　　　　　6Sqn
**CP eARRAS shot up dam returned a'dr OK(Lt Owen/
Lt Sterling) left 5-45pm

D7998　　Bristol F2b　　22Sqn
+* combat with Fokker DVII[+ooc] DOUAI 5pm
OK(Lt HH Beddow/Lt WV Tyrrell) last of 10 claims by
pilot, many in this a'c

**　　　　　DH4　　　　　57Sqn**
** combat(/Sgt JH Bowler **WIA**)

**　　　　　DH4　　　　　57Sqn**
** combat(/Lt GAF Riley **WIA**)

D8419　　DH4　　　　　57Sqn
+* combat with Fokker DVII[+flames] wAVESNES-
LES-SEC 4-05pm OK(Capt A MacGregor/Sgt J Grant)
EA pilot from Ja4 failed attempt to bale out

C1876　　SE5a　　　　　60Sqn
**OP seen ok wHAYENCOURT going west 10-30am
combat? **MIA**(2Lt SA Thomson **KIA**) [?claim combat
BUGNICOURT 10-10am OffSt J Mai Ja5]

**　　　　　SE5a　　　　　60Sqn**
** combat(Lt RC Blessley **WIA**)

D6953.A SE5a　　　　　60Sqn
+* combat with Fokker DVII[+flames+ooc]
AVESNES-LES-SEC OK(Capt JW Rayner)

D6960.P SE5a　　　　　60Sqn
+* combat with Fokker DVIIs[+des+ooc] AVESNES
~6-20pm OK(Capt GM Duncan) made 8 claims

C1909.D SE5a　　　　　64Sqn
OP left 8am combat with 2EA neCAMBRAI **MIA(Lt
WAF Cowgill **POW**) [?SE5a claim combat
nBOUCHAIN 9-05am Ltn F Rumey Ja5]

**　　　　　SE5a　　　　　64Sqn**
** combat(Lt TG Sifton **WIA**)

F5945　　Sopwith Camel　73Sqn
**OP left 10am combat? seen down ooc MARQUION
MIA(2Lt TKG Oliver **KIA**)

F2133　　Sopwith Camel　80Sqn
OP left 4-25pm ST QUENTIN **MIA(2Lt AR Thatcher
POW)

F2143　　Sopwith Camel　80Sqn
**OP left 8-55am FLESQUIÈRES combat with EA shot
up dam OK(Lt GB Wootten) name Wooten?

B8428　　SE5a　　　　　92Sqn
OP seen dive on EA CAMBRAI 11am **MIA(Capt GA
Wells **POW**) [?SE claim combat INCHY 11-10am Oblt
B Loerzer JGIII][?combat eHAVRINCOURT 11am Ltn
G Meyer Ja37]

D372　　　SE5a　　　　　92Sqn
**OP seen diving on Fokker DVII formation
nrCAMBRAI 11-10am **MIA**(Lt HB Good **KIA**) to LE
HAMEAU

D6889　　SE5a　　　　　92Sqn
OP seen dive on EA nrCAMBRAI 11-10am **MIA(Lt
EV Holland **POW**)

E4024　　SE5a　　　　　92Sqn
**OP combat with EA shot up fuel line 5m eVERT
GALAND ftl OK(Lt Shapard) left 10am

B7280　　Sopwith Camel　210Sqn
** seen nrABEELE a'dr combat with EA shot down
MIA(Capt HA Patey DSC **POW**) a'c captured ["Camel"
claim combat VOORMEZELE 5-27pm Ltn L Beckmann
Ja56][?"Camel" claim combat LENVELERE? 5-25pm
UntOff Jeckert Ja56], Patey claimed several of his 11
victories in this a'c

E4390　　Sopwith Camel　210Sqn
** combat with EAs[+ooc] neROULERS then seen dive
ABEELE 2000′ 5pm on EA? **MIA**(Lt L Yerex **POW**)

D1824　　Sopwith Camel　213Sqn
** combat with 3HAs shot down 10m seOSTENDE
2-40pm ooc **MIA**(2Lt CE Fancis **POW**) [?combat
STALHILLE FlgM Mayer MJaIII]

C1294　　DH9　　　　　218Sqn
**B BRUGES heavy combat with EAs dam ftl
VROUWENPOLDER **MIA**(Lt JG Munro INT/2Lt TW
Brodie INT) interned Holland [?combat wKNOCKE
FlM K Engelfried MFJaV]

6th September

**　　　　　SE5a　　　　　2Sqn AFC**
** combat with EA(Lt JSL Ross **WIA**)

D6968　　SE5a　　　　　2Sqn AFC
+* combat with Fokker DVII[+ooc] 2m nwDOUAI
7pm OK(Lt JJ Wellwood) made 6 victory claims

C4745　　Bristol F2b　　11Sqn
**Rec ch by several EAs ovCAMBRAI going west
MIA(Lt CB Seymour **KIA**/2Lt EG Bugg **KIA**) left
8-40am LE CATEAU [?"BF" claim combat
nwBOURLON WOOD Ltn O Löffler Ja2]

D7906　　Bristol F2b　　11Sqn
**Rec chased west ovCAMBRAI by several EA 10-30am

MIA(Lt EN Underwood **KIA**/2Lt CM Coleman **KIA**) left 8-40am LE CATEAU [?combat wCANTIN Ltn P Bäumer Ja2]

A7815　　DH4　　　　　　　18Sqn
B combat with EA MONCHY controls shot up ftl cr shell hole dam(Capt GWF Darvill DFC OK/Lt WN Miller **WIA)

E2213　　Bristol F2b　　　20Sqn
+* combat with Fokker DVIIs[+?ooc+des] nCAMBRAI-ST QUENTIN btwn 8-30am & 8-35am OK(Capt AT Iaccaci US./Sgt A Newland) first of 7 victories for this crew in this a'c

E2470　　Bristol F2b　　　20Sqn
+* combat with Fokker DVIIs[+des+ooc] CAMBRAI-ST QUENTIN btwn 8-30am & 8-50am OK(Lt PT Iaccaci US./Lt A Mills) both Iaccaci brothers in crews which shot down 2 EAs each this day, both achieved 16 or 17 victories

F5820　　Bristol F2b　　　22Sqn
**OP AA ftl Sh57C o.13 dam(Lt LC Rowney OK/Sgt J Goodman inj)to hospital

C8166　　Sopwith Dolphin　　23Sqn
OP combat steep dive ovST QUENTIN 13000′ **MIA(Capt N Howarth **KIA**) [?combat eST QUENTIN 8-45am Ltn W vRichthofen Ja11]

D6991.A　SE5a　　　　　32Sqn
+* combat RumplerC[+ooc] eROISEL 11am OK(Lt B Rogers US.) also claimed Fokker DVII[+flames] HOLNON nwST QUENTIN 5pm on this day

E2492　　Bristol F2b　　　48Sqn
**OP AA 7-15pm shot up ovPOPERINGHE dam ftl cr(2Lt WS Rycroft inj/2Lt HC Wood OK) left 6pm COMINES

C2479　　RE8　　　　　　52Sqn
AOb combat with HA mg shot down Sh51B o.23.A 12-25pm(Lt J Talbot **WIA/Sgt HJ Sampson **WIA**) to hospital [?combat MONCHY 12-40pm Ltn M Dehmisch Ja58]

**　　　　　DH4　　　　　　57Sqn**
** AA fire(Lt G Anderson **WIA**/)

D9483　　Sopwith Camel　　80Sqn
OP left 8-50am combat ovLE CATELET shot down **MIA(Lt JA McGill **KIA**)

**　　　　　Sopwith Camel　　201Sqn**
** combat(2Lt LG Tearle **WIA**)

**　　　　　H.P.0/400　　　　207Sqn**
** combat(/Sgt.Mech CJEJ Jones **WIA**)

**　　　　　H.P.0/400　　　　207Sqn**
** combat(Lt C Roberts **WIA**/)

D9484　　Sopwith Camel　　208Sqn
OP left 5pm combat with many Fokker DVIIs CANAL DU NORD **MIA(Lt AH Hiscox **KIA**) a'c recovered? [Camel claim combat LAGNICOURT pm Ltn A

Lindenberger Ja2][?combat nwBOURLON WOOD Ltn E Bormann Ja2]

D3379　　Sopwith Camel　　210Sqn
**OP left 12-35pm ZEVECOTE AA hit ftl returned a'dr dam OK(Capt SC Joseph DFC)

7th September

D9271　　DH4　　　　　　25Sqn
Rec combat with 30EA shot up dam(2Lt CH Saffery OK/2Lt J Harrington **WIA)

C1123　　SE5a　　　　　　32Sqn
SpLP left 11am **MIA(2Lt JB Bowen USAS. **POW DoW**)

D1887　　Sopwith Camel　　65Sqn
**OP left 8-05am AA ftl field dam OK(Capt A Jones-Williams) for ZOETENAEY?-LAMPERNISSE?

**　　　　　Sopwith Dolphin　　79Sqn**
** AA fire(FComm.Capt HP Rushforth **WIA**)

C8895　　SE5a　　　　　　84Sqn
OP left 6pm combat ST QUENTIN ooc **MIA(2Lt WB Aldred **DoW** 20.9.18) [?claim combat LE CATELET 6-45pm Oblt E vWedel Ja11]

D6917　　SE5a　　　　　　84Sqn
OP left 6pm combat? in flames ST QUENTIN **MIA(Lt EC Bateman **KIA**)

D2916　　DH9　　　　　　99Sqn (I.F.)
B MANNHEIM 6EAs from behind, seen going down in control nrSAVERNE **MIA(Lt G Broadbent **WIA POW**/2Lt MA Dunn **POW**) [?possible DH claim Ltn G Weiner Ja3]

B7653　　DH9　　　　　　104Sqn (I.F.)
B MANNHEIM **MIA(2Lt JE Kemp **POW**/2Lt EB Smailes **POW DoW** 13.9.18) [?possible DH claim Ltn K Seit Ja80]

D3268　　DH9　　　　　　104Sqn (I.F.)
B MANNHEIM combat with EAs **MIA(Sgt E Mellor **KIA**?/Sgt J Bryden **POW**)

D7210　　DH9　　　　　　104Sqn (I.F.)
B MANNHEIM combat with EAs **MIA(2Lt WEL Courtney **POW**/2Lt AR Sabey **POW**) [?second possible DH9 claim Ltn G Weiner Ja3]

D7318　　DH9　　　　　　104Sqn (I.F.)
B MANNHEIM shot up(Lt JW? Richards OK/Sgt WE Reast **DoW 9.9.18)

Most of September was unsuitable for deep bombing because of the weather. The Official History notes that raids were prevented on nineteen days and eighteen nights because of low clouds, rain, and high winds. The operations on the 7th were again very damaging to 104 Squadron, who continued to have a terrible record with the DH9. On this joint raid with 99 Squadron, to the Badische Aniline and Soda Factory at Mannheim,

both units were attacked relentlessly throughout their journey. Fifteen enemy were met over the target and three were claimed shot down.

A7587   DH4   205Sqn
Rec left 8-30am **MIA(Lt DJT Mellor **KIA**/2Lt JC Walker **POW**)

D2918   DH9   211Sqn
B shot down sea neGRAVELINES(Lt ES Morgan DFC **KIA/2Lt R Simpson **KIA**) left 9-50am, possible air collision, found 7-9m neGRAVELINES by French

8th September

** **MIA**(Lt RA Henry **POW**) repat 8.12.18

D4814   RE8   3Sqn AFC
**CP mg ftl Sh62C P.30.d dam ldg OK(Lt JJ Pengilley/ Lt OG Witcomb) left 5-30am

D4923   RE8   13Sqn
**P XVII Corps area mg shot up returned a'dr OK(Lt GJ Millar/Lt HW Wynn) left 6-35am

D4847.15 RE8   15Sqn
**CAP mg 9-20am ftl Sh57c W1B.55 dam OK(Capt AR Cross/Lt HA Coysh) unsalvable

D6693   Sopwith Camel 46Sqn
+* combat RumplerC[+flames] sPERONNE 7am OK(Lt RK McConnell Can.) last of 7 claims

**   DH9   206Sqn**
** combat(2Lt JD Russell **WIA**/)

9th September

B4179   A.W.FK8   35Sqn
P AA 4pm ftl cr EPEHY 62C E.3.d(Lt PE Mercer **WIA/2Lt AE Harris inj)

10th September

D4852   RE8   4Sqn
**Rec AA shelled 11-20am ftl 28.I.30c OK(2Lt J Sharp/ Lt S Leslie)

D5149   A.W.FK8   8Sqn
**LP AA ftl 4.4A.22a shelled OK(Lt Stacey/Lt Mann) unsalvable, left 12-50pm

**   RE8   59Sqn**
** mg fire(/2Lt SE Rowley **WIA**)

F1399   Sopwith Camel 208Sqn
WT left 2-50pm seen nrLENS **MIA(Lt JP Lloyde **POW**)

11th September

**   RE8   3Sqn AFC**
CP mg fire shot up ftl nrBOUVINCOURT(Lt TL Baillieu **WIA/2Lt FA Sewell **WIA**)

12th September
THE ST MIHIEL OFFENSIVE IN THE SOUTH

Foch had been anxious to expand the scope of the Allied offensive. In the north and in front of Cambrai and St Quentin the German Army's increasing preoccupation with survival was a continual drain on its reserves. From the very beginning the Allied offensive's first objectives had been the recovery of Ludendorff's salients and the removal of the German stranglehold on the rail link eastwards to Nancy. The threat to Amiens had been eradicated, but the St Mihiel salient in the south still enabled control of the railway. Germany had held this territory since 1914, and the Allies resolved it was time it was recovered. It would be an unexpected blow to the extremities of the German line and a first necessary phase of any major southern offensive. Finally, it was an ideal battle for the American Army, now rivalling the French and British armies for size and able to assume responsibility for the right wing of the Allied front.

On the 12th of September the First American Army, with the assistance of the French, launched what was to prove an unstoppable assault on the salient, which had collapsed within a day or two. This now permitted the secure redeployment of the American forces along the southern flank of the Western Front in preparation for a much bigger attack. As this was taking place the first German overtures for peace crossed the Atlantic — the huge reserves of her Army had been reduced and dismantled by blow upon blow so that it now faced exhaustion and ruin.

At this turning point in the war, however, Foch and his commanders could think of nothing but their plans for a great culminating effort in which a series of co-ordinated attacks would be launched from the Meuse all the way into Flanders. These would strike not only into armies which would be shattered under the weight of arms, but also target the transportation network which the German Army had used for four years to transfer and co-ordinate its war effort. A French and American attack in the Argonne would aim at Mezières and Sedan, where the southern end of the main railway ran. The British Army would attempt to break clean through the Hindenburg Line around Cambrai, with the northern section of the same rail network at Maubeuge as the target. As these battles were absorbing the strength of the German Army, a general offensive in Flanders would begin. If all went to plan, the German forces here would

be not only critically depleted, but also isolated. The primary objective in the north was the recovery of the Belgian coast. All three attacks were to be launched between the 26th and 28th of September.

Most work in advance of major fighting needed to be undertaken by the British Third and Fourth Armies. To enable a proper and direct assault on the Hindenburg defences, Havrincourt and Epehy needed to be taken, and fighting for these began on the 12th of September. Rain and stormy weather prevented much air activity in connection with this until the 15th.

E2527   Bristol F2b   48Sqn
OP thunderstorm seen in clouds 6-30pm lost EoL ftl **MIA(Lt HA Cole **POW**/2Lt CR Gage **POW**) left 5-15pm MENIN

13th September

Bristol F2b   48Sqn
** in action(/2Lt GC Schofield **WIA**)

RE8   52Sqn
? ftl(/2Lt B Hurdus **WIA?)

B9347.T   DH9   99Sqn (I.F.)
B combat with EA(2Lt JL Hunter Can. **WIA/) rail targets

D1668.6   DH9   99Sqn (I.F.)
** AA (/Lt HS Notley **WIA**)

D1670   DH9   99Sqn (I.F.)
B broke up crashed in American Lines **MIA(2Lt EE Crosby **KIA**/2Lt CP Wogan-Brown **KIA**) [?DH claim combat THIAUCOURT Ltn H Müller Ja18]

D3218   DH9   99Sqn (I.F.)
B METZ-SABLON Rlwy shot down after bombing **MIA(2Lt FA Wood USAS. **KIA**/2Lt C Bridgett **KIA**)

D1050   DH9   104Sqn (I.F.)
B METZ-SABLON(/2Lt TJ Bond **WIA)to hospital

In support of the French and American attack on the St Mihiel Salient, the Independent Force was requested to shift its bombing programme temporarily to the Lorraine front. This work was due to begin on the evening before the offensive but the night was very stormy. On the 12th, daylight raids were attempted but machines were driven back by rain and low cloud. On the night of the 12/13th, with the weather little better, heavy raids were nevertheless launched on the Metz-Sablon rail networks. Some IX Brigade heavy bombers also took part, including a Handley Page from 207 Squadron which dropped a 1,650-lb bomb on Le Cateau Station. On the 13th, 99 Squadron's allotted target was Courcelles, but repeated attempts to reach it were thwarted by the weather

and other targets, such as at Ars and Arnaville had to suffice. Enemy fighters were met over both these towns and inflicted casualties.

14th September

RE8   4Sqn
** combat(Lt TO Henderson **WIA**/2Lt F Butterworth **KIA**) crew? [?"RE" claim combat seYPRES Ltn Kresse Ja7]

B7434   Sopwith Camel   80Sqn
OP left 1-30pm AA cr nr a'dr wr(Maj FI Tanner **inj)

D6131   SE5a   84Sqn
OP left 9am seen ok BANTOUZELLE going west **MIA(Lt JE Reid **POW**) [?SE5a claim sLE CATELET 10-10am combat Ltn F Rumey Ja5]

SE5a   92Sqn
** combat(2Lt LS Davis **WIA**)

D3064?   DH9   99Sqn (I.F.)
D3264? **B seen going down in control ovMETZ-SABLON **MIA**(Lt WF Ogilvy **POW**/2Lt GA Shipton **POW**)

99 Squadron launched two raids to Metz-Sablon and this machine was lost on the first. They were attacked by an enemy formation but this aircraft may have lost its way in mist and bombed Ars Junction where it met heavy ground fire.

D3215   DH9   99Sqn (I.F.)
B METZ-SABLON shot up(2Lt JG Dennis **WIA/2Lt HG Ramsey **WIA**)to hospital

D5581   DH9   99Sqn (I.F.)
B METZ-SABLON AA hit(2Lt GH Knight **WIA/)

E4391   Sopwith Camel   201Sqn
** fired Verys then seen going down cr Sh57C K.17.10.8.7. o't 11-55am **MIA**(2Lt WA Johnston **POW**)

3131   H.P. 0/100   216Sqn (I.F.)
NB shot down ovMETZ **MIA(Lt RW Heine **POW**/1Lt FF Jewett USAS. **POW**/Lt EA Marchant **POW**)

15th September

The weather cleared on the 15th and brought aircraft into the Somme skies. Balloon attacks were common from both sides on the First and Third Army fronts, and the RAF additionally attacked German aerodromes. There were other balloon claims further north, including the two noted below by 41 and 70 Squadrons. 73 Squadron was very busy in the fighting, its Camel pilots making a total of nine claims.

C1875   SE5a   1Sqn
**OP left 3-25pm combat with HA DURY controls shot away ftl OK(Lt W Newby) [?SE5a claim combat ST LEGER 5-10pm Vzfw M Hutterer Ja23]

C2789   RE8   5Sqn
Phot combat with EA ftl(Capt CF Galbraith **DoW/
2Lt EGW Coward OK) left 5-25pm, a'c shelled destroyed

F5894   RE8   5Sqn
Phot combat with EA ftl cr wr(Lt JM Bright **WIA/2Lt
EP Eveleigh **WIA**) left 5-35pm, ftl P25.d.18 [RE claim
combat PALLEUL 6-05pm Ltn O Fruhner Ja26]

D5314   Sopwith Dolphin 19Sqn
OP ch down by EA nrFERMEGHEM **MIA(2Lt GF
Anderson **POW**) left 2-30pm

D7939.P Bristol F2b   20Sqn
**OP AA? engine ftl neEPEHY(SLt ABD Campbell
POW/Sgt TA Stac **POW**) left 4-30pm

E2512   Bristol F2b   20Sqn
OP seen ok nrST QUENTIN **MIA(Lt FE Finch **WIA
POW**/2Lt CG Russell **POW**) left 10-20am [F2b claim
combat 11-35am Ltn U Neckel Ja12]

F5816   Bristol F2b   20Sqn
**OP left 10-20am combat with EA ftl(Lt ARD Campbell
OK/Sgt AJ Winch **WIA**)

B8505   SE5a   24Sqn
+* combat with Hannover[+des] HANNESCOURT
WOOD 6-55pm OK(2Lt HL Bair US.) shared, last of 5
claims in this a'c

E4079   SE5a   29Sqn
**OP combat with Fokker DVII eYPRES 17000' 6-45pm
then seen after **MIA**(Lt EF Wright **POW**)

C1912   SE5a   41Sqn
+* combat with Fokker DVIII[+ooc] HOUTHEM
4-45pm OK(Capt WE Shields Can.) first of 11 victories in
this a'c

C1913   SE5a   41Sqn
+* attacked KB[+des] BEAUCAMPS 5pm OK(Capt
FO Soden Can.)

C2649   RE8   42Sqn
**AP combat with EA shot down dam (2Lt RM Marshall
WIA/2Lt A Mulholland OK) left 10-55am, shot down
Sh36.C7 [claim combat wARMENTIÈRES 11-30am Ltn
H Leptien Ja63]

F2137   Sopwith Camel 46Sqn
+* combat with Fokker DVII[+ooc]
nGOUZEAUCOURT 2-15pm OK(Capt DR MacLaren
Can.) pilot scored several of 54 victories in this Camel

C2341   RE8   52Sqn
**LP combat with EA shot up dam(2Lt JB Smith OK/
2Lt B Shaw **WIA**)to hospital

E5173   Sopwith Camel 54Sqn
**OP left 10-05am combat with HA shot up ARRAS
dam(2Lt B Dixon **WIA**)to hospital

F2144   Sopwith Camel 54Sqn
**OP left 5-25pm combat with EA shot up dam OK(Capt
GH Hackwill MC)

C8866   SE5a   56Sqn

**LowB seen ok attkg ESTOURMEL a'dr 3-30pm
MIA(1Lt LG Bowen USAS. **KIA**)

SE5a   56Sqn
P combat(Capt WR Irwin **WIA)

E1291   SE5a   56Sqn
**LowB seen ldg ESTOURMEL a'dr ~3-45pm
MIA(Capt OC Holleran US.? **POW**)

56 Squadron attacked aerodromes opposite the
First and Third Armies in the afternoon. Hangars
at Estourmel were left burning.

D6981   SE5a   60Sqn
**OP combat?, wing off broke up in steep dive
BOURLON WOOD ovFONTAINE NOTRE DAME
6-35pm **MIA**(2Lt H Stuart-Smith **KIA**) [?SE5a claim
REMY Vzfw C Mesch Ja26][?combat BOURLON
6-45pm Ltn G Meyer Ja37][SE5a claim BOURLON
WOOD 6-40pm Ltn W Neuenhofen Ja27][SE5a claim
PALLEUL 6-20pm Ltn C Reimer Ja26]

E2525   Bristol F2b   62Sqn
**OP combat with 20 Fokker DVIIs neCAMBRAI
4-30pm seen going down in control **MIA**(Lt TH Broadley
KIA/2Lt RH Dilloway **KIA**)

E7182   Sopwith Camel 70Sqn
+* attacked KB[+des] eARMENTIÈRES 6-30pm
OK(2Lt MJ Ward) black balloon

D1898   Sopwith Camel 73Sqn
+* combat with Fokker DVIIs[+des+ooc] CAMBRAI
then 2Str[+des] nrLA FOLIE btwn 11-05am & 11-20am
OK(Lt OM Baldwin) also claimed Fokker DVII[+des]
6-15pm sGOUY-SOUS-BELLONE, most of his 15
claims in this a'c

F6107   Sopwith Camel 73Sqn
OP left 10am seen ok nrCAMBRAI **MIA(2Lt JA
Matthews **POW**) [?possible Camel claim combat
MARQUETTE 11-05am Ltn H Seyward Ja23]

D5234   Sopwith Dolphin 79Sqn
**OP combat & mg KEMMEL RIDGE 6-45pm ftl cr o't
2000' WoL OK(Lt FW Gillett)

D9485   Sopwith Camel 80Sqn
+* attacked KB[+des] ETRICOURT 1-20pm OK(Capt
HA Whistler)

C8571   A.W.FK8   82Sqn
B seen ovPASSCHENDAELE 6-05pm **MIA(2Lt HT
Hempsall **POW**/Lt JHM Yeomans MC **POW**) ["AW"
claim combat PASSCHENDAELE 6-10pm Ltn J Jacobs
Ja7]

C6420   SE5a   84Sqn
**OP attacked KB[+des] eST QUENTIN 9-55am then
combat with Fokker DVII shot up ftl cr ldg a'dr(2Lt CRJ
Thompson SA. **WIA**) 9-50am?, had claimed several
victories

C1911   SE5a   85Sqn
+* attacked KB[+des] BELLICOURT 8-50am

OK(Capt AW Beauchamp-Proctor) shared with Capt D Carruthers

D3783   FE2b   101Sqn
NB **MIA(Lt EJ Stockman **POW**/2Lt P Payne **POW**)

            FE2b   102Sqn
** combat(Capt RT Jones **WIA**/)

D532   DH9   104Sqn (I.F.)
B METZ-SABLON combat many EAs cr wr(2Lt AA Baker **WIA/Sgt HE Longe **WIA**) to hospital

D3211   DH9   104Sqn (I.F.)
B METZ-SABLON(/2Lt WE Jackson **DoW)

D3245   DH9   104Sqn (I.F.)
B METZ-SABLON combat many EAs **MIA(2Lt LG Hall USAS. **POW died**?/2Lt WD Evans **POW**) Hall wounded severely, Casualty Card says he died? [?DH claim combat swMETZ 11-10am Ltn H Schaefer Ja15][DH claim combat sMETZ 11-15am Ltn G vHantelmann Ja15]

D3263   DH9   104Sqn (I.F.)
B METZ-SABLON combat many EAs **MIA(2Lt AD MacKenzie **KIA**/2Lt CE Bellord **KIA**)

D7205   DH9   104Sqn (I.F.)
B METZ-SABLON combat many EAs **MIA(2Lt RH Rose **POW**/2Lt EL Baddeley **POW**)

Over the target a very large formation of enemy fighters was met. They shot down three DH9s in fighting and subsequently three more needed to make forced landings once they reached the safety of the lines whilst another crashed on landing.

D1733   DH9   108Sqn
B AA ovBRUGES ftl **MIA(Capt WRE Harrison **INT**/2Lt C Thomas **INT**) left 2-15pm interned Holland [?DH9 claim combat WALCHEREN 4-10pm FlM K Engelfried MFJaV]

D3107.P DH9   108Sqn
B BRUGES ftl SOUBURG cr canal **MIA(2Lt FB Cox **WIA INT**/Lt JJ Lister **INT**) left 2-15pm, interned Holland

D7336   DH9   108Sqn
B BRUGES AA ftl cr ZIERVIKSEE **MIA(Lt JJ McDonald **INT**/Lt GE McManus **INT**) left 2-15pm, interned Holland

E4404   Sopwith Camel   203Sqn
KBP combat with 4 Fokker DVIIs neBOURLON WOOD ovCAMBRAI 11-45am flames **MIA(Sgt RR Lightbody **KIA**) ["Camel" claim combat CANTAING 11-50am Ltn W Kohlbach Ja10]

C74   Sopwith Camel   204Sqn
**HOP left 5pm AA heavy dam ftl OK(Capt CRR Hickey DFC)

D8221   Sopwith Camel   204Sqn
LP left 10-05am mg fire shot down nrNIEUPORT(Lt RE Hodgson **KIA) salvable

D9496   Sopwith Camel   204Sqn
HOP AA RAMSCAPELLE badly shot up ftl cr wr(2Lt LP Worthington **inj) left 5pm

E4418   Sopwith Camel   204Sqn
HOP combat shot down in sea nrBLANKENBERGHE flames(Lt RC Pattulo **KIA) [?Camel claim combat ZEEBRUGGE 3-10pm Ltn R Poss MFJaIV]

F1009   DH9A   205Sqn
+* combat with 2Str[+flames] wROISEL 5pm OK(2Lt FO McDonald/2Lt JB Leach)

This was the first combat victory for the new DH9A day-bomber.

D3210   DH9   211Sqn
B BRUGES shot up ftl cr hedge nr a'dr(2Lt JM Payne OK/Lt CT Linford **WIA)

C9673   H.P. 0/400   215Sqn (I.F.)
NB KAISERSLAUTERN? **MIA(2Lt AG Harrison **KIA**/2Lt H Davies **POW**/2Lt C Guild **POW**) "Harrison **KIA** nr KOKELARE"

C9683   H.P. 0/400   215Sqn (I.F.)
NB COURCELLES **MIA(2Lt A Tapping **POW**/2Lt WJN Chalkin **POW**/2Lt JB Richardson **POW**) failed to return

C2158   DH9   218Sqn
B combat with 2EA ZEEBRUGGE fuel tank hit ftl mouth of SHELDE RIVER off WALCHEREN **MIA(Lt WS Mars **inj INT**/2Lt HE Power **inj INT**)

16th September

From the 16th of September until the 5th of October German and British times were the same (all times given are British time). Air fighting was much heavier on the 16th as German reconnaissance machines attempted to penetrate the air space over the Third Army. Eight enemy machines were claimed shot down, including another two by a DH9A crew from 205 Squadron.

            A.W.FK8   2Sqn
** combat(2Lt RP Nowell **WIA**/)

D6995.Y SE5a   2Sqn AFC
+* combat with Fokker DVII[+sh down in flames] nwLILLE 7-30pm OK(Lt F Alberry Aust.) first of 7 victories on this a'c for this Australian who was wounded and lost a leg in July 1916 and became a pilot

F5958   Sopwith Camel   3Sqn
COP seen ok 2m nwCAMBRAI 10000' going west 12-30pm **MIA(Lt JR Montgomery **KIA**) ?combat MARQUION 12-35pm Ltn F Rumey Ja5]

F4270   A.W.FK8   8Sqn
**LP AA engine hit ftl Sh62C K.26.s dam OK(Lt JR Desy/Lt North) left 4-40am

C878   Bristol F2b   11Sqn
Rec CAMBRAI-LE CATEAU down EoL **MIA(2Lt L
Arnott **KIA**/2Lt GL Bryars **KIA**) left 7am [?F2b claim
combat FONTAINE 8-45am Ltn O Fruhner Ja26]

C946   Bristol F2b   11Sqn
Rec CAMBRAI-LE CATEAU **MIA(Lt JC Stanley
USAS. **WIA POW**/2Lt EJ Norris **POW**) left 7am [F2b
claim combat neQUIEVY 8-50am Ltn H Lange Ja26]

E2215   Bristol F2b   11Sqn
**Rec combat radiator hit ftl BEUGNY cr o't(Capt ES
Coler US. **inj**/2Lt EJ Corbett **inj**)

F5977   RE8   13Sqn
P left 5-15am **MIA(Lt JJ Elder **KIA**/Lt A Ostler MC
KIA)

C4718   Bristol F2b   20Sqn
**OP combat with EA dam ftl VIGNACOURT a'dr dam
OK(Lt HE Johnston/2Lt ES Harvey) left 7-27am

C978   Bristol F2b   22Sqn
**OP combat with EA shot up dam returned 10-15am
OK(Lt LN Caple/Lt GS Routhier) left 8-05am First
Army area

          Bristol F2b   22Sqn
** combat(/Sgt.Mech M Jones **WIA**)

E2519   Bristol F2b   22Sqn
OP combat with EA eCAMBRAI seen ooc **MIA(2Lt
W Kellow **KIA**/2Lt HA Felton **KIA**) left 2-30pm

F5824   Bristol F2b   22Sqn
**OP combat with EA shot up dam ftl 16Sqn OK(Lt TD
Smith/2Lt SC Barrow) left 8-05am First Army area

C8157   Sopwith Dolphin   23Sqn
+* combat with Fokker DVIIs[+ooc+flames] ST
QUENTIN 8-30am OK(Lt HA White US.) shared first
claim with Lt AP Pehrson in Dolphin F5965, claimed
several victories with 23 Sqn

Two other Fokker DVIIs were claimed shot down
by 23 Squadron in this combat.

A7788   DH4   25Sqn
Phot left 8-30am **MIA(Capt RL Whalley **KIA**/2Lt EB
Andrews **KIA**)

D8378   DH4   25Sqn
**Rec combat MONT ST ELOI 8-30am ftl(Lt C Brown
OK/Lt EW Griffin **KIA**)

E6002   SE5a   29Sqn
**OP seen in combat with 2 Fokker DVIIs LINSELLES
8-40am **MIA**(2Lt PJA Fleming **POW**) [?"SE" claim
combat wMENIN 8-40am Ltn J Jacobs Ja7, also Vzfw
Lieber & UntOff Peisker of Ja7 involved?]

E4026   SE5a   32Sqn
+* combat with Fokker DVII[+des] BRUNEMONT
6-10pm OK(Lt FL Hale)

D5146   A.W.FK8   35Sqn
P AA hit fell burnt(Capt JE Phillips **KIA/2Lt RV
Hepburn **KIA**) left 10am, cr Sh57c F.25.A5

D1946   Sopwith Camel   54Sqn
**LP:KB AA fuel tank shot up BOUVELLES ftl OK(2Lt
BH Matthews) left 10-40am

F1962   Sopwith Camel   54Sqn
**OP AA shot up dam 9-30am OK(Lt JC McLennan)

E8434   DH9A   55Sqn (I.F.)
B MANNHEIM (/2Lt HM Kettener **WIA)

This is the first record of a casualty to 55 Squadron
crew flying DH9As.

F5712   DH4   55Sqn (I.F.)
**B MANNHEIM shot up nrHAGUENAU seen going
down in control cr **MIA**(2Lt WE Johns **WIA POW**/2Lt
AE Amey **KIA**) [DH claim combat ALTEKENDORF
1-30pm Ltn G Weiner Ja3]

B8499   SE5a   56Sqn
**COP combat with EA 16000' left wing buckled ooc
broke up eHAVRINCOURT WOOD 6pm **MIA**(2Lt NF
Bishop **KIA**)

F2634   DH4   57Sqn
Phot EA? cr Sh57C o.12 wr(Lt G Anderson **KIA/Sgt
JS Macdonald **inj**)

A7987   DH4   57Sqn
**B combat with Fokker DVIIs shot down in flames 1m
eMARCOING(2Lt JP Ferreira **KIA**/2Lt LB Simmonds
KIA) left 10-30pm

F7597   DH4   57Sqn
**B combat with Fokker DVIIs[+flames]
HAVRINCOURT WOOD 12-15pm (Lt PWJ Timson
WIA/2Lt IS Woodhouse OK)

Three other claims were made by 57 Squadron in
this fighting.

          Bristol F2b   62Sqn
** combat with Fokker DVII[+des] shot up (2Lt CH
Moss **WIA**/2Lt R Lowe)

E2244   Bristol F2b   62Sqn
**EscOP combat with EA down in control 10m
neDOUAI **MIA**(2Lt RN Stone **POW**/2Lt NF Adams
POW) left 7-45am

E1597   Sopwith Camel   70Sqn
**KBP nARMENTIÈRES seen eYPRES 2-30pm
MIA(Lt J Glen **KIA**) left 1-45pm

B8420   SE5a   84Sqn
+* combat RumplerC[+des] SELENOY 6-30am OK(Lt
CFC Wilson) shared with C6490

C6490   SE5a   84Sqn
+* combat RumplerC[+des] SELENOY 6-30am
OK(2Lt SW Highwood) shared with B8420

E6024   SE5a   84Sqn
+* combat with Fokker DVII[+ooc] MONTIGNY 2pm
OK(Capt CF Falkenburg Can.) made several of 17 claims
in this a'c

C8163.A   Sopwith Dolphin   87Sqn
+* combat with Fokker DVII[+des] wABANCOURT

5-30pm OK(Capt HJ Larkin Aust.) last of 11 victories

C9728   H.P. 0/400   97Sqn (I.F.)
**NB FRANKFURT? ftl cr MIA but OK(2Lt A Hinder
DoI/Lt H Cooper **inj**/2Lt OF Bendall **inj**) DoI hospital
DIJON, but NOTE: Roll of Honour & official POW lists
state "Lt Hinder" died as POW 16.9.18?

C2221   DH9   98Sqn
**B left 8am VALENCIENNES Rlwy Stn combat with
20EA shot up dam OK(2Lt WV Thomas/Sgt CHO
Allwork)

D3262   DH9   98Sqn
+*B combat with PfalzDIII[+des] 4m
wVALENCIENNES 10-35am OK(2Lt JH Nicholass/2Lt
APC Bruce)

D3267   DH9   98Sqn
**B VALENCIENNES Rlwy Stn seen ok sDOUAI
combat ~20EAs **MIA**(2Lt FJ Keble **POW**/2Lt CH
Senecal **POW**) left 8am [?possible claim combat
neARRAS Ltn O Löffler Ja2][?possible claim combat
wCANTIN 11-55am Ltn H Seyward Ja23]

D5825   DH9   98Sqn
+*B VALENCIENNES combat ~20EA[+ooc] 10-35am
OK(2Lt TW Sleigh/2Lt AH Fuller)

D8302   H.P.0/400   100Sqn (I.F.)
**NB FRESCATY ZEPPELIN SHEDS engine failed ftl
field & burnt a'c **MIA**(Lt FR Johnson **POW**/Lt RC
Pitman **POW**/2Lt FH Chainey **POW**)

This was the only 100 Squadron Handley Page
crew to be shot down. The unit had exchanged
their FE2bs for 0/400s towards the end of August.
The crew was on the run for four nights before
turning themselves in to the authorities in a state
of exhaustion.

A5610   FE2b   102Sqn
NRec left 1-15am **MIA(Lt CB Naylor **POW**/Lt H
Mercer **POW**)

D489   DH9   103Sqn
**B seen ooc spin down LILLE but flattened out 2000'
MIA(2Lt WH Cole **KIA**/Sgt S Hookway **KIA**?) left 8am
[?DH claim combat ARMENTIÈRES Ltn K Plauth
Ja20]

D3254   DH9   103Sqn
B ooc spin down & flatten 1000' LOMME **MIA(Capt
FA Ayrton **POW**/2Lt BP Jenkins **POW DoW**) left 8am,
died ACHEN

E8410   DH9A   110Sqn (I.F.)
B down with tail off nrMANNHEIM **MIA(Sgt A
Haigh **KIA**/Sgt J West **KIA**)

F997   DH9A   110Sqn (I.F.)
B shot down nrMANNHEIM smoke cr **MIA(Lt HV
Brisbin **POW**/2Lt RS Lipsett **POW**)

D9689   H.P.0/400   115Sqn (I.F.)
**NB METZ-SABLON Rlwy flak nrTHIONVILLE ftl
MIA(Lt RL Cobham **INT**/Lt EE Taylor **INT**/Lt EG

Gallagher **INT**) crew were hidden but captured, interned
Luxembourg, Casualty Report and Casualty Card both
give serial D9698 but this is incorrect

B7764   DH4   205Sqn
**B BUSIGNY combat with EA shot up ftl
nrGERMAINE(Lt GC Matthews **WIA**/Lt AG
Robertson **KIA**)

A7964?   DH4   205Sqn
this a'c? ** in action(/2Lt HS Mullen **WIA**)

D8429   DH4   205Sqn
**B BUSIGNY combat with EA shot up dam(Lt EO
Danger **WIA**/Lt AD Hollingsworth OK)

D9250   DH4   205Sqn
B BUSIGNY with 2EA on tail **MIA(2Lt FF Anslow
POW/Sgt L Murphy **KIA**) left 7-30am [?DH9 claim
combat nwBELLENGLISE 8-40am Ltn H Böhning
Ja79]

D9255   DH4   205Sqn
+* combat with Fokker DVII[+ooc] 10m wBRAY
OK(2Lt KG Nairn/2Lt NR McKinley)

F1016   DH9A   205Sqn
+*B combat with HannoverC[+flames] 2m nST
QUENTIN then Fokker DVII[+broke up] sST
QUENTIN 8-45am OK(Lt WE Macpherson/2Lt CF
Ambler)

D9634   Sopwith Camel   209Sqn
**HOP AA hit? engine shot up ftl cr nrARRAS dam
OK(Lt G Knight)

B7271   Sopwith Camel   210Sqn
** seen 14000' ovBRUGES 9-25am combat with EA
MIA(2Lt EB Markquick **KIA**) [?2 Camel claim combat
COXYDE(to West) Oblt T Osterkamp MFJaII]
[?combat ZERKEGHEM 9-15am Vzfw H Goerth MFJaIII]

D3357   Sopwith Camel   210Sqn
** seen in combat with 15EA ovZEEBRUGGE 18000'
11-05am **MIA**(2Lt JA Lewis **KIA**) [?2 Camel claim
combat COXYDE(to West) Oblt T Osterkamp MFJaII]

DH9   211Sqn
** in action(/2Lt HM Moodie **KIA**)

C9658   H.P. 0/400   215Sqn (I.F.)
NB FRESCATY A'dr shot down **MIA(Lt HR Dodd
KIA/2Lt EC Jeffkins **POW**/2Lt A Fairhurst **POW**) left
7-35pm

C9727   H.P. 0/400   215Sqn (I.F.)
**NB KÖLN AA hit nrBONN engine hit ftl
OOSTERHOOT nrBREDA destr **MIA**(2Lt CC Fisher
INT/2Lt RS Oakley **INT**/2Lt CJ Locke **INT**) left
7-48pm, interned Holland

D4566   H.P.0/400   215Sqn (I.F.)
**NB KÖLN then hit by AA after bombing? shot down
burnt a'c **MIA**(Lt HB Monaghan **POW**/2Lt GW
Mitchell **POW**/Lt HE Hyde **POW**) left 7-46pm

D9684   H.P.0/400   215Sqn (I.F.)
NB MANNHEIM **MIA(2Lt JB Lacy **POW**/2Lt CN

Yelverton **POW**/2Lt RT Down **POW**) left 7-35pm

C9662   H.P. 0/400   216Sqn (I.F.)
****B METZ railways shot down ovMETZ cr nose
MIA(Lt B Norcross **POW**/2Lt RH Cole **DoW** 30.9.18/
Sgt? G Hall **POW**) 16/17Sep.18 rank Pte Hall?,
"Visibility good but becoming misty. Wind strong and
gusty", allocated target of Köln abandoned, a'c captured

The heaviest losses for Handley Pages in the war
were experienced on the night of the 16th/17th
September. Seven were lost, all from the Independent Force, including the five listed above from
Nos. 215 and 216 Squadrons (see also Nos. 100 and
115 Squadrons' entries above). These raids ended
the British bombing carried out in co-ordination
with the St Mihiel Offensive.

B7671   DH9   218Sqn
****B AA dam OK(Lt HD McLaren/Sgt G Barlow)

E1479   Sopwith Camel   US 148th Pursuit Sqn
****B combat with EA shot up ftl front lines MIA but
OK(1Lt GC Dorsey **WIA**)arm

17th September

D8088   Bristol F2b   11Sqn
****Rec AA shot up dam returned a'dr 11-50am OK(Capt
A Morrison/Sgt R Allan) left 9-10am CAMBRAI-LE
CATEAU

B8412   SE5a   24Sqn
****OP seen ovVERMAND combat with HA FRESNOY
LE VETRE(2Lt WJ Miller **KIA**) left 11am

A7820   DH4   25Sqn
****Phot combat with EA HAUTE AVESNES 10-30am
shot up ftl(Lt R Dobeson OK/Lt AG Grant **WIA**)

A8031   DH4   25Sqn
****Phot left 9-35am MIA but OK(Lt JH Latchford/2Lt J
Pullar)

E4053   SE5a   40Sqn
****OP seen in combat with EA seCAMBRAI 9-55am
MIA(2Lt FW King **WIA POW**) [?SE5a claim
RUMILLY 9-05am combat Ltn F Rumey Ja5]

F2130   Sopwith Camel   46Sqn
****OP seen in combat wBOURLON WOOD 2000'
7-05pm **MIA**(Lt H Toulmin MC **KIA**) [?combat
swCAMBRAI 7-10pm Ltn F Rumey Ja5]

F6226   Sopwith Camel   46Sqn
****OP seen in combat wBOURLON WOOD 2000'
7-05pm **MIA**(2Lt CE Usher-Somers **POW**)

F6133   DH4   57Sqn
**B seen ok nrARRAS going s-w **MIA(2Lt WA Wilson
POW/2Lt HH Senior **POW**) left 11-30am

F5971   RE8   59Sqn
****P combat with Fokker DVII ovRIBECOURT shot up
dam ftl ALG OK(Lt A Ibbotson/2Lt WJ Carruthers) left
9-25am

C9297.G **SE5a**   **60Sqn**
****OP combat with Fokker DVII ovMARQUION
12-50pm **MIA**(Lt JE Smith **KIA**)

E2218   Bristol F2b   62Sqn
****OP combat ftl cr shell hole REMY OK(2Lt RA
Boxhall/2Lt L Millar) left 4-35pm

D6030.Y **SE5a**   **64Sqn**
****SpM(LowB) left 6am EMERCHICOURT A'dr
MIA(Lt WW Chrieman **POW**)

Fighters from 64 and 209 Squadrons, escorted by
Bristol Fighters of 22 Squadron, bombed and
strafed Emerchicourt aerodrome. This was part of
a continued offensive against the German Air Force
on the ground prior to the main attack on Epehy
and Havrincourt.

C6480   SE5a   84Sqn
AS left 8-15am PERONNE **MIA(Sgt A Jex **POW)

C9069   SE5a   84Sqn
**AS left 8-15am PERONNE **MIA(Sgt FS Thomson
POW)

D8062   Bristol F2b   88Sqn
****Phot combat with 6EA TREIZENNES dam cr OK(Lt
F Jeffreys/Lt FW Addison) left 8-10am

F5863   FE2b   101Sqn
****NB left 10-40pm AA ftl trenches cr OK(Lt AW Allen/
Lt EH Clarke) salvaged

C6713   Sopwith Camel   151Sqn
+*NP attacked FriedrG[+ftl captured] FLETRE
10-40pm OK(Capt D'UV Armstrong DFC SA.) EA from
8/BG VI, scored a few night-fighter victories in this a'c,
but also KIFA in it on 13.11.18

151 Squadron night fighters shot down three of the
German bombers who had launched raids against
Allied lines of communications behind the Third
and Fourth Armies. The Squadron had operated
until this time in defence of the area around
Abbeville but had been brought down to operate
over a new searchlight barrier system along the
central British front.

D8421   DH4   205Sqn
****B BUSIGNY combat with HA shot up ftl(Lt HF
Taylor OK/2Lt HS Millen **WIA**) then dam by storm
after ldg

E4382   Sopwith Camel   209Sqn
****LowB seen in control ovEMERCHICOURT A'dr
6-30am **MIA**(Lt JE Walker **KIA**) (see 64Sqn entry
above)

E1405   Sopwith Camel   210Sqn
** shot up(Lt IC Sanderson **WIA)

E4406   Sopwith Camel   210Sqn
****OP AA OSTENDE shot up ftl TETEGHEM 6-35pm
dam OK(Capt E Swale)

E4407   Sopwith Camel   210Sqn
+* combat with Fokker DVIIs[++flames] sOSTENDE
6-30pm OK(Lt WS Jenkins Can.) Jenkins claimed 12EA

F3931   Sopwith Camel   210Sqn
** combat with 2EA ovGHISTELLES 6-30pm MIA(2Lt
JE Harrison KIA) MFJa4? [?claim combat 6-33pm Flm
G Hubrich MFJaIV]

D9513   Sopwith Camel   US 17th Pursuit Sqn
**P combat MONT ST ELOI 3-40pm controls shot up
ftl OK(2Lt JA Ellison)

18th September
THE BATTLE OF HAVRINCOURT AND EPEHY

The attack on the outlying fortifications of the
Hindenburg Line began on the 18th. It was a
preparatory battle to the main assault but was
given plentiful means to succeed, including tanks
and full air cover. The British attack was made
along a seven-mile front between Holnon and
Gouzeaucourt, with the French advancing to the
south. It was launched at 7am in heavy rain and
although it made generally good progress it met
very stiff resistance in front of Epehy. This was
gradually worn away through an intense day's
fighting in which all objectives were kept within
reach. The conditions limited the RAF's best work
to some vital artillery co-operation.

C2490   RE8   3Sqn AFC
**CP left 10am mg fire ~10am ftl dam(Lt DF Dimsey
OK/Lt RFC Machin KIA) to HINDENBURG
OUTPOST LINE, observer hit in back

C951   Bristol F2b   20Sqn
**OP combat with EA dam 5-30pm returned a'dr OK(Lt
AR Strachan/Lt BW Wilson)

F7395   A.W.FK8   35Sqn
**Phot combat shot down in flames cr Sh62c F.25.b(Lt
MC Sonnenberg DoW 19.9.18/2Lt J Clarke KIA) left
10am, observer fell out [?"AW" claim combat UntOff P
Hüttenrauch Ja7]

C5357   SE5a   40Sqn
**OP combat with EA shot up(2Lt LC Band WIA)arm

D9405   Sopwith Camel   46Sqn
**OP combat with EA eHESBECOURT 11-50am seen
shot down in flames at 5000' MIA(Lt HC Saunders KIA)

D6971   SE5a   92Sqn
**OP AA shot down spun into ground nPONT À
VENDIN EoL MIA(Lt CM Holbrook POW) left 9am

C9834   FE2b   101Sqn
**NB mg AA ftl EoL escaped back to lines(Capt HW
Stockdale/2Lt Shergold)

D5572?   DH9   103Sqn
**B seen AA hit 11-40am spin nwLILLE 15000' MIA(Lt

TM Phillips KIA/2Lt RE Owen KIA) left 9-50am

D3341   Sopwith Camel   213Sqn
+* attacked KB[+des] nrLA BARRIÈRE 10-50am
OK(Lt GS Hodson) shared, burning KB set fire to 3
hangars, claimed 10 victories

19th September

F6045   RE8   5Sqn
**AP combat with EA shot down cr Sh51B Q.196
destr(Lt HW Driver KIA/2Lt R Greenyer WIA) left
10-30am

C2718   RE8   6Sqn
**AP eARRAS combat with EA shot up cr dam OK(Lt
Owen/Lt Sterling) left 5-30am

**   FE2b   101Sqn**
** shot up? MIA but OK(2Lt FA Browning DoW
22.9.18/2Lt BML Bunting)

20th September

Poor weather restricted flying during this week
except for the 20th, when clearer weather brought
some large German formations westwards. This
was to be a growing trend as September closed.
The biggest dogfight involved about twenty
Fokkers against an equal number from Nos. 20 and
84 Squadrons. Many 20 Squadron Bristol fighter
crews made claims, accounting for perhaps six
enemy fighters. One crew's claims are given below,
along with the single machine from that unit which
was lost.

F6007   RE8   9Sqn
**CAP shot up cr dam(Lt C Dotzert OK/2Lt KS Hill
WIA)

B4172   A.W.FK8   10Sqn
**FlRec combat with 7 Fokker DVIIs shot up dam ftl
Sh28 O.21.b.7.6. at 7-40pm OK(2Lt L Reader/2Lt ER
Airey) left 6-15pm

E2158   Bristol F2b   20Sqn
**OP combat shot down in flames(Lt AR Strachan KIA/
2Lt DM Calderwood KIA) left 9-30am [?"BF" claim
combat FRESNOY LE GRAND 9-37am Oblt O Schmidt
Ja5][also "BF" claim CROIX FONSOMME 9-40am
UntOff Leicht Ja5]

E2258   Bristol F2b   20Sqn
+*OP combat with Fokker DVIIs[+des] MESNIL 10am
then further combat with Fokker DVIIs [+flames]
MESNIL-ST QUENTIN 10-15am OK(Lt FG Harlock/
Lt AS Draisey)

**   RE8   21Sqn**
** mg fire(2Lt FLW Dowling WIA/)

E4072   SE5a   24Sqn
**OP seen under EAs sCAMBRAI going down EoL
MIA(Lt EP Larrabee US. POW) left 6am

E4000   SE5a   29Sqn
**OP AA hit 9-40am ftl 28.T.17 OK(Lt CG Ross
DFC)unsalvable

E5974   SE5a   29Sqn
**OP AA fuel tank hit RUBROUCK 2-45pm ftl dam
OK(Lt EO Amm)

E2260   Bristol F2b   48Sqn
**OP combat ovROUBAIX 11am seen diving on EA ftl
MIA(Lt MFJR Mahony **POW**/2Lt JN Keir **POW**) left
9-20am COMINES [?combat nANNAPPES 10-55am
Ltn C Degelow Ja40]

**   RE8   59Sqn**
** mg fire(/2Lt WG Brown **WIA**)

D6945.U SE5a   60Sqn
**OP left 6-25am combat with EA 8am shot up ftl(2Lt
HFV Battle **WIA**) ftl 59Sq at FREMICOURT [?combat
nHERMIES 8am Ltn G Meyer Ja37]

F5472   SE5a   60Sqn
**OP left 6-15am combat with EA then seen ldg but cr
nMARCOING-HAVRINCOURT RD o't **MIA**(Lt GFC
Caswell **WIA POW**)

C6429   SE5a   84Sqn
+* combat with Fokker DVIIs[+des] eMONT
D'ORIGNY ~10am OK(Lt WJB Mel)

E6024   SE5a   84Sqn
+* combat with Fokker DVIIs[+ooc+des] MONT
D'ORIGNY btwn 10-15am & 10-30am OK(Capt CF
Falkenburg)

E2183   Bristol F2b   88Sqn
**OP combat with EA engine hit ftl STRAZEELE cr
dam OK(Lt A Williamson/2Lt KC Craig) left 6-05am

**   FE2b   148Sqn**
** mg fire(Lt HR Hern **WIA**/)

C125.H Sopwith Camel   201Sqn
**OP comb10 Fokker DVII sBOURLON WOOD cr
nrSERANVILLERS 7-30am **MIA**(Lt J Mill **KIA**) left
6-15am [?combat MARCOING 7-45am Ltn H
Frommherz Ja27][Camel claim combat PROVILLE
7-45am Ltn W Neuenhofen Ja27][ditto MARCOING
7-45am Ltn F Noltenius Ja27]

E4377   Sopwith Camel   203Sqn
**OP seen in combat with Fokker DVIIs
ovHAYNECOURT 3-30pm **MIA**(2Lt CG Milne **POW**)
[?combat ECOURT 3-40pm Ltn F Brandt Ja26][?Camel
claim eRUMAUCOURT 3-50pm Ltn P Bäumer Ja2]

E4409   Sopwith Camel   203Sqn
**P combat with Fokker DVIIs ovHAYNECOURT
3-30pm **MIA**(Lt MG Cruise **KIA**) [Camel claim combat
eCAGNICOURT 3-45pm Ltn O Fruhner Ja26]

B6319   Sopwith Camel   204Sqn
** shot up WoL WINCKEM ftl cr(Lt DF Tysoe **WIA**)

D3387   Sopwith Camel   204Sqn
** seen in combat with EA 5m neDIXMUDE 8-30am
MIA(2Lt EG Rolph **POW**)

D8205   Sopwith Camel   204Sqn
** combat with EA 5m neDIXMUDE 8-30am **MIA**(2Lt
CL Kelly **KIA**) [Camel claim combat PRAET BOSCH?
Ltn T Osterkamp MFJaII]

F3243   Sopwith Camel   204Sqn
** combat with Fokker DVII[+] 5m eDIXMUDE
10-25am OK(2Lt HG Clappison) DVII shot down had
yellow stripes [?Camel claim in this combat PERVYSE
10-05am, but none lost, Vzf K Scharon MFJaII]

F5986   Sopwith Camel   209Sqn
**OP combat with Fokker DVIIs ECOURT ST
QUENTIN shot down in flames **MIA**(Lt DC Ware **KIA**)
left 4-45pm

F6192   Sopwith Camel   US 148th Pursuit Sqn
**KBP combat with 4 Fokker DVIIs AUBIGNY brought
down in flames **MIA**(1Lt H Jenkinson **KIA**) left 1-50pm
[Camel claim combat AUBIGNY AU BAC 2-45pm Ltn
F Noltenius Ja27]

21st September

E5965.X SE5a   2Sqn AFC
**OP left 10-05am engine seen low ARMENTIÈRES
going west ftl EoL **MIA**(Lt G Cox **POW**)

F5976   RE8   7Sqn
**Phot combat with 5 Fokker DVIIs 10am down in
flames(Lt WG Allanson **KIA**/2Lt WL Anderson MC
KIA) ST JULIEN-ZONNEBEKE [?combat nYPRES
10-45am Ltn C Degelow Ja40][?combat STADEN 12pm
Ltn K Plauth Ja20]

F7405   A.W.FK8   8Sqn
**CP left 6am ground mg dam returned a'dr OK(Lt JR
Desy/Lt North)

**   A.W.FK8   8Sqn**
CP mg fire(/2Lt AB McDonald **WIA)

**   A.W.FK8   35Sqn**
** mg fire(/2Lt AE Harris **WIA**) but see 9.9.18?

F5827   DH4   57Sqn
**B down in flames eBOURLON WOOD-CAMBRAI
6-45pm **MIA**(2Lt OMcI Turnbull **KIA**/Lt DFV Page
KIA) [?combat eBOURLON WOOD Ltn P Bäumer
Ja2]

D6958   SE5a   74Sqn
**OP left 5-55pm combat with EA wLILLE shot down
6-50pm **MIA**(Capt S Carlin **POW**) left 5-55pm [?SE5
claim combat HANTAY? 6-45pm Untoff S Westphal
Ja29]

F5853   FE2b   83Sqn
**NB AA shot up nrCAMBRAI EoL on return wr(Lt
DDA Greig/2Lt WA Armstrong) left 8-45pm, shaken

F6557   FE2b   83Sqn
**NB radiator hit ftl shell hole cr GREVILLERS
shaken(Lt LGW Howles/2Lt JR Crowe) left 8pm

Word had been received that Germany intended to
bomb Paris at night with large numbers of incen-

diary bombs, and in response it was decided to bomb aerodromes from which these attacks might be launched. Nos. 58, 83, and 207 Squadrons of IX Brigade carried out this work for several nights at this time.

D3092   DH9   108Sqn
B combat with 15EA ovZARREN shot down **MIA(2Lt DA Shanks **KIA**/Sgt RJ Sear **KIA**) left 10-30am LICHTERVELDE, spiral chased down by 2EA 10000' [DH9 claim combat DIXMUDE 11-10am, & another unconfirmed 10 mins later Ltn J Jacobs Ja7]

D5759   DH9   108Sqn
B dhAA broke up seen fall ooc 11000' wLICHTERVELDE **MIA(2Lt HL McLellan **KIA**/2Lt FX Jackson **KIA**) left 10-27am

D6423   Sopwith Camel   151Sqn
+* combats with FriedrichshafenG[+capt] & AEGG[+capt] GOUZEAUCOURT ~9-30pm OK(Maj CJQ Brand SA.) made a dozen claims, including several night-fighter victories in this a'c

A8089   DH4   205Sqn
B combat with 12 Fokker DVII seen dive with 2EA on tail ovLE CATELET 6-45pm broke up **MIA(Lt AN Hyde **KIA**/2Lt WW Harrison **KIA**) left 5-35pm VILLERS OUTREAUX [?combat LE CATELET 6-40pm OffSt J Mai Ja5][?combat eBOURLON WOOD Ltn P Bäumer Ja2]

DH4   205Sqn
** combat(/2Lt W Tunstall **WIA**)

D9599   Sopwith Camel   209Sqn
**OP combat with Fokker DVII[+ooc] sSCARPE River ovECOURT ST QUENTIN 6-35pm shot up dam OK(Capt WR May Can.)

C9732   H.P. 0/400   215Sqn (I.F.)
NB FRESCATY A'dr shot down in flames ovMETZ **MIA(2Lt ACG Fowler **KIA**/2Lt CC Eaves **KIA**/2Lt JS Ferguson **KIA**) 20/21Sep, crew buried METZ, NB: not H.P. C9723

22nd September

45 Squadron returned from Italy and was attached to the Independent Force from the 22nd of September. It was to be used in escort duties, but it was decided to wait until its Camels could be exchanged for specially adapted Sopwith Snipes which would have an endurance of four and a half hours. This re-equipment did not occur before the end of the war and its activities were confined to the front line areas.

E7191   Sopwith Camel   4Sqn AFC
**OP combat with 4 Fokker DVII[++ooc] ARMENTIÈRES 8-20am engine shot up driven down ftl NEUVE EGLISE 8-35am OK(2Lt TH Barkell) EA was firing to within 100ft of ldg [?claim combat sNEUVE EGLISE 8-15am Ltn H-G Marwitz Ja30]

E6012   SE5a   24Sqn
**OP fuel tank shot up 11-20am ftl n.m.l. Sh57C 11c.16c abandoned OK(Lt WC Sterling)

C9133   SE5a   41Sqn
OP left 12-45pm COMINES **MIA(Lt DA Neville **POW**)

C2604   RE8   52Sqn
**CP left 6am ground mg shot up dam OK(Lt WH Buckeridge/2Lt TH Barry) returned 8-10am

C2506   RE8   53Sqn
NF mg engine hit 8-30am ftl cr PROVEN(2Lt JP Sharp **inj/TLt SA Bird OK) to X Army area

C8864   SE5a   56Sqn
COP combat with EA then seen ovHAMEL going west ok 12pm **MIA(2Lt JC Gunn **POW**)

F5453   SE5a   74Sqn
**OP oil tank shot through ABEELE 7-35pm ftl OK(Lt FJ Hunt)

E4493   Sopwith Dolphin   87Sqn
+* combat with Fokker DVIIs[++des] BOURLON WOOD 8-40am OK(Capt HAR Biziou) made 8 claims, many in this a'c

F2157   Sopwith Camel   US 17th Pursuit Sqn
P seen in combat seFONTAINE-NOTRE DAME 9am **MIA(1Lt TE Tillinghurst **POW**) escaped to UK by 4.11.18 [2 Camel claims combat nEPEHY but ~7-55am Vzfw K Bohnenkamp Ja22]

F5969   Sopwith Camel   US 17th Pursuit Sqn
P seen ok seFONTAINE-NOTRE DAME 8-45am then dive on EA formation 9am **MIA(2Lt GP Thomas **KIA**) [Camel claim combat wSAUCHY-LESTRÉE 8-50am Ltn C Reimer Ja26]

F6034.N   Sopwith Camel   US 17th Pursuit Sqn
**OP combat ~18 Fokker DVIIs ovRUMILLY[+cr Sh57c.F.22,+flames swCAMBRAI] 8-45am to 8-55am OK(Lt GA Vaughn) Vaughn made 13 claims

23rd September

F6029   Sopwith Camel   3Sqn
COP seen 6000' 6-35am then cr in flames nrBOURSIES Sh57C K.2.a. **MIA(2Lt SH Richardson **KIA**)

E2562   Bristol F2b   20Sqn
OP combat with EA seen going down nrVILLERS OUTREUX in flames **MIA(Lt J Nicolson **KIA**/2Lt BW Wilson **KIA**)Ja29?, left 4-45pm ["BF" claim combat LEVERGIES 5-25pm Vzfw Ungewitter Ja24]

Bristol F2b   20Sqn
** combat(/Sgt NC Dodds **WIA**)

C2300   RE8   42Sqn
Phot combat with EA Sh36a N2C at 5-15pm shot down in flames **MIA(2Lt DA Newson **KIA**/2Lt GEM Browne **KIA**) [RE claim combat sFLEURBAIX 5-10pm Ltn H Leptien Ja63]

D5432   H.P.0/400   58Sqn
**NB BAC ST MAUR A'dr chased back to Lines by 2EA
in running fight shot up OK(2Lt MP Fraser/2Lt A
Spotswood/Sgt TH Barron) bomb bay later found
damaged

F2174   Sopwith Camel   80Sqn
**OP ST QUENTIN dive on 2EA ovVENDEUIL
MIA(2Lt FA Fairburn **KIA**) left 5-30

D3741   Sopwith Dolphin   87Sqn
**COP left 4-55pm combat with EA dam shot down ftl
QUEANT(Lt FW Goodman **WIA**) [?combat
swBARALLE-QUEANT 6-15pm Ltn F Rumey Ja5]

H7275   Sopwith Camel   US 17th Pursuit Sqn
**P left 8-15am ground mg shot up dam ftl 12Sq 8-45am
OK(Lt MC Giesecke)

24th September
ALLIED PREPARATIONS FOR
ATTACKING THE
HINDENBURG LINE

The German Air Force was very active again in
front of the Hindenburg Line on the 24th. RAF
offensive patrols accounted for eighteen enemy
machines in a number of intense combats. As larger
and more aggressive enemy formations were
becoming more commonplace, and dogfights with
these would dominate air fighting until the war's
end, it is interesting to note some of the tactics
which were being used to counter them. Brigadier-
General Longcroft issued instructions to his III
Brigade on the 22nd which read in part: "The
present policy of the enemy air patrols on this front
seems to be to put very strong patrols (20 to 40
machines) into the air at varying times of the day
with a view to making offensive demonstrations
and occasionally attacking small patrols of our
machines when obviously at a disadvantage. This
system makes the work of our small patrols difficult
as they are not in sufficient strength to attack the
enemy or no enemy are found in the air to attack."
To counter this, large offensive patrols consisting
of at least two fighter squadrons would operate east
of the lines in the proximity of enemy airfields.
Their main objective, however, would be to find
and attack enemy machines. They would patrol at
two levels: in the upper air the SE5a or Dolphin
squadrons would act as protecting sentries of those
below. The latter would always be formations of
Camels, who were responsible for initiating all
attacks. If no enemy were about, then their airfields
were bombed and strafed. It was not only offensive-
minded, it was a system full of provocation,
designed to draw the German Air Force into
fighting.

The moment of truth was fast approaching for
the Allies as they moved into their final positions
for their great attack down the whole length of the
Western Front. The Americans and the French
were preparing for their offensive on the Lorraine
from the south, whilst the British would first attack
east of Cambrai and St Quentin, and then in
Flanders. To summarise, these three phased offensives had the double purpose of driving back and
exhausting the enemy whilst at the same time
aiming to destroy his communication and supply
network.

The most difficult and challenging element of the
German defences, the Hindenburg Line, was to be
tackled by three British armies. The most formidable sections lay straddled along the Canal de St
Quentin, between St Quentin and Bantouzelle.
The natural barrier of the canal had been
developed and integrated into a complex defence
zone often five miles deep. The way the waterway
and its tunnels and other features had been made
use of showed particular ingenuity. The line was
organised north and south so as to offer the best
protection to the most vital zone in the centre.

On the more northern section facing the British
First and Third Armies, the trenches faced south-
west, and utilised part of the Hindenburg Line
itself, as well as other extremely strong defensive
positions to protect the town of Cambrai. This area
would form the objective for the first assault for it
not only protected the more southerly Hindenburg
Line but was slightly less impregnable. Its capture
would enable artillery to be brought up for an
assault on the main section of the line, in front of
the Fourth Army to the right. This part was truly
formidable and left no option but for a lengthy
bombardment as a precursor to attack. Another
obstacle facing the British was the relative unsuit-
ability of the area for tank warfare and successful
use of artillery throughout the battle would be vital.
To confuse the enemy, however, the bombardment
would commence all along the front.

Reflecting the demands of the fighting to be
undertaken, the majority of Royal Air Force units
were concentrated onto the Cambrai-St Quentin
front. I Brigade with the First Army had twelve
squadrons, with a total of two hundred and thirty-
six aircraft. Beside it with the Third Army, III
Brigade had fifteen squadrons, with two hundred
and sixty-one aircraft. The V Brigade with the
Fourth Army had been bolstered to seventeen
squadrons for the battle, with three hundred and
thirty-seven aircraft. IX Brigade was also fully
devoted to this front, adding a further thirteen
squadrons with two hundred and twenty-four

aircraft, so that the RAF strength therefore amounted to one thousand and fifty-eight machines when sundry additional flights were added.

C1948   SE5a   2Sqn AFC
+* combat with AlbatrosC[+ooc] LA BASSÉE-BETHUNE 10-30am OK(Capt RL Manuel) last of 12 claims, many in this a'c

Sopwith Camel   4Sqn AFC
B combat with EA shot up ftl ST VENANT(Capt EJ Kingston-McCloughry **WIA) after bombing train at LILLE ["Camel" claim combat SAILLY-SUR-LYS Ltn P Bäumer Ja2]

E8837   A.W.FK8   8Sqn
CP left 6-20am **MIA(Lt WFR Robinson **KIA**/Lt JH Roberts **KIA**)

E2363   Bristol F2b   11Sqn
Phot AA BEELEVUE 6-30pm ftl(2Lt C Johnson OK/ Sgt GH Hampson **WIA) shot up by EA?, inj in cr?

F6165   DH4   18Sqn
**Phot combat with EA shot up dam returned a'dr 1-35pm OK(Lt RC Bennett/Lt A Lilley) left 10-45am

E2181   Bristol F2b   20Sqn
**OP combat with EA 3-10pm dam returned a'dr OK(Lt HE Johnston/2Lt ES Harvey) ground fire?

Bristol F2b   22Sqn
** combat(/Capt G McCormack **WIA**)

D6983   SE5a   32Sqn
**OP combat with EA fuel tank shot up ftl cr Sh57C D.11.B.9.9. 9-30am OK(Lt DS Atkinson)abandoned, left 7-30am

E6010   SE5a   32Sqn
+* combat with Fokker DVII[++ooc] nBOURLON WOOD btwn 5-05pm & 5-10pm OK(Capt AA Callender US.) last of 8 claims

E4054   SE5a   40Sqn
BOP combat with Fokker DVIIs[+] CAMBRAI-DOUAI 7am shot down in flames **MIA(Capt GJ Strange **KIA**) left 6-15am, 'Ben' Strange [?combat ABANCOURT 7-30am Lt M Dehmisch Ja58, who was then shot down]

E4074.O   SE5a   41Sqn
OP combat with EA nwLILLE 6pm **MIA(Capt C Crawford **POW**) left 5-20pm [?combat nrZILLEBEKE LAKE 6pm Ltn C Degelow Ja40][?SE5a claim ANNEUX? Obt H-H vBoddien Ja59]

DH9   49Sqn
B combat(/2Lt L Eteson **WIA)

DH9   49Sqn
B combat(/2Lt LC Belcher **WIA)

DH9   49Sqn
B combat(1Lt EC Moore USAS. **WIA/)

E658   DH9   49Sqn
B AULNOYE Junction **MIA(Lt HJ Bennett **POW** DoW**/2Lt RH Armstrong **POW**) left 6-50am [?combat

swCLARY Ltn P Bäumer Ja2]

E8869   DH9   49Sqn
B AULNOYE Junction combat with EAs wFORÊT DE MORMAL on return **MIA(Capt ED Asbury **KIA**/ 2Lt BT Gillman **KIA**) left 2-50pm

F6098   DH9   49Sqn
B AULNOYE Junction seen in combat with EAs wFORÊT DE MORMAL on return **MIA(Lt CC Conover **POW**/2Lt HJ Pretty **WIA POW**) left 2-50pm

F5488   SE5a   56Sqn
COP left 9am combat with EA shot up dam ftl(Lt FA Sedore **WIA)

A8088   DH4   57Sqn
**PhotB left 6-45am BEAUVOIS a'dr combat with EA shot up dam OK(Lt FG Pym) returned 8-30am [?possible DH9 combat sBEAUVOIS, but "4-30pm"? OffSt J Mai Ja5]

Bristol F2b   62Sqn
EscB combat with 30EA[+ooc] eCAMBRAI on return shot up(Capt WE Staton **WIA/2Lt LE Mitchell OK)

E2457   Bristol F2b   62Sqn
**OP combat many EAs 8am radiator shot up ftl 107Sq OK(Lt LW Hudson/2Lt AW Palmer) left 6-55am

E2515   Bristol F2b   62Sqn
EscOP seen ok CAMBRAI 8am **MIA(Lt NN Coope **WIA POW**/2Lt HS Mantle **WIA POW**) both slight WIA

E4071   SE5a   84Sqn
+* attacked KBs[++des] CAMBRAI 1-50pm OK(2Lt SW Highwood) also shot down another KB at 9-15am that day nrGOUY, over half his 16 victories were balloons

D9921   FE2b   101Sqn
NB left 9-25pm **MIA(Lt BH Kewley **POW**/2Lt JW Brown **POW**)

D2877   DH9   103Sqn
B seen in combat **MIA(Lt CH Heebner **KIA**/2Lt D Davenport **KIA**) left 9-30am [DH claim LORGIES Ltn J vBusse Ja20][DH claim combat LORGIES 10-50am Ltn J Gildemeister Ja20]

F5842   DH9   103Sqn
B had damaged tail 4000' then seen attkd by 4EA **MIA(Lt HC Noel **KIA**/Sgt LC Ovens? **POW**?) name Owers?, left 9-20am [?DH9 claim combat VERMAND 10-40am Vzfw K Bohnenkamp Ja22][?combat LA BASSÉE-SAINGHIN 10-40am Ltn K Plauth Ja20]

D7208   DH9   108Sqn
B combat chased down by 2EA in controlled dive nrROULERS seen at 6000' ovTHOUROUT **MIA(2Lt JM Dandy **POW**/Sgt CP Crites **POW**) left 2-47pm ?combat 4-20pm Ltn P Achilles MFJaV]

H.P.0/400   207Sqn
B (/2Lt JM Mackinnon **WIA?) inj?

D8147   Sopwith Camel   210Sqn
+* combat with EA shot up ftl dam(TCapt SC Joseph
DSC **WIA**) [?combat Ltn Wilhelm MJaIV]

D3251   DH9   211Sqn
**B BRUGES AA engine dam, seen going north gliding
down nBRUGES, ftl BRESKENS **MIA**(2Lt J
Olorenshaw **INT**/2Lt RL Kingham **INT**) left 1-30pm

25th September

Bristol F2b   20Sqn
** combat(/Lt R Gordon-Bennett **WIA**)

E2536   Bristol F2b   20Sqn
+* combat with Fokker DVIIs[+++des] neST
QUENTIN-MAGNY btwn 6-15pm & 6-30pm OK(Capt
GH Hooper Aust./2Lt HL Edwards) Hooper & Edwards
claimed another 3 EAs on the 29th in this a'c

A8051   DH4   25Sqn
**Phot combat ftl cr after ldg(Capt S Jones OK/2Lt J
Pullar **WIA**) ldg ok but ran on & crashed as pilot helped
observer away

D3163   DH9   27Sqn
B BOHAIN seen in control LE CATELET **MIA(2Lt
CB Sanderson **POW DoW** 17.10.18/Sgt J Wilding **WIA**
POW) left 3-50pm [DH9 claim sESCAUFOURT
6-15pm combat Oblt Ritt vGreim JGr 9]

E8857   DH9   27Sqn
B combat wBOHAIN flames **MIA(2Lt AV Cosgrove
KIA/2Lt SC Read **KIA**) left 4pm [DH9 claim combat
FRESNOY 6pm Ltn S Garsztka Ja31]

D8356   DH4   55Sqn (I.F.)
B KAISERSLAUTERN **MIA(2Lt JB Dunn **KIA**/2Lt
HS Orange **KIA**)

D8386   DH4   55Sqn (I.F.)
B KAISERSLAUTERN wr(/2Lt GS Barber **KIA)

D8388   DH4   55Sqn (I.F.)
B KAISERSLAUTERN AA? **MIA(2Lt RC Pretty
POW/2Lt GR Bartlett **POW**)

D8392   DH4   55Sqn (I.F.)
**B KAISERSLAUTERN shot up(/2Lt JTL Attwood
KIA)

D8413   DH4   55Sqn (I.F.)
B KAISERSLAUTERN AA? **MIA(2Lt AJ Robinson
KIA/2Lt HR Burnett **KIA**)

F5714   DH4   55Sqn (I.F.)
B KAISERSLAUTERN Works AA? **MIA(2Lt GB
Dunlop **POW**/2Lt AC Heyes **POW**)

Twelve DH4s of 55 Squadron had been bombing
ammunition factories at Kaiserslautern when they
were attacked on the way home by enemy fighters.
Four crews were lost but the formation was also
subjected to heavy anti-aircraft fire which may
have done most damage.

F5892   RE8   59Sqn
**Phot mg ftl nr Lines Sh57c Q.27 OK(Lt J Stanley/2Lt
JW Elias) left 4-20pm, unsalvable

D3270   DH9   99Sqn (I.F.)
B (/2Lt JLMcI Oliphant **WIA)

D9922   FE2b   102Sqn
**NB engine shot up ftl SAILLEAUMONT on return
OK(2Lt W Lloyd-Williams/Lt O Reilly-Patey DFC) left
11-30pm

E8420   DH9A   110Sqn (I.F.)
**B FRANKFURT shot up wr(/Sgt WH Neighbour
KIA)

E8422   DH9A   110Sqn (I.F.)
B FRANKFURT **MIA(Sgt HW Tozer **KIA**/Sgt W
Platt **KIA**)

E9660   DH9A   110Sqn (I.F.)
B FRANKFURT shot down **MIA(Lt CBE Lloyd
POW/2Lt HJC Elwig **POW**)

F992   DH9A   110Sqn (I.F.)
B FRANKFURT shot down **MIA(Lt LS Brooke
POW/2Lt A Provan **POW**)

F993   DH9A   110Sqn (I.F.)
**B FRANKFURT combat with EAs[++] shot down(/
Lt RF Casey **WIA**) to hospital

F1000.B   DH9A   110Sqn (I.F.)
B FRANKFURT shot down(Lt HJ Cockman **WIA/)
repairable

F1030   DH9A   110Sqn (I.F.)
B FRANKFURT **MIA(Capt A Lindley **POW**/Lt CR
Gross **POW**)

110 Squadron suffered these very heavy losses on a
raid to factories and rail targets at Frankfurt. The
formation was attacked more or less continuously
throughout the journey.

B7232   Sopwith Camel   204Sqn
** AA hit ftl ss cr LAMPERNISSE wr OK(Lt OJ Orr)

C66   Sopwith Camel   204Sqn
** seen 5m seDIXMUDE 6-50pm **MIA**(2Lt T
Warburton **POW**) [?"Camel" claim combat
CORTEMARCK 6-50pm Ltn F Piechulek Ja56]

B7252   Sopwith Camel   213Sqn
** combat with 7 Fokker DVIIs 3m wTHOUROUT
5-45pm **MIA**(Lt CP Sparkes **POW**) [?combat
WYNENDAELE 6pm VzfM A Zenses MFJaII]

D3360   Sopwith Camel   213Sqn
** seen attacking HA 10000' 3m seOSTENDE 6-35pm
MIA(2Lt JC Sorley **KIA**) [?combat nwROULERS
6-05pm Ltn P Achilles MFJaV]

D8189   Sopwith Camel   213Sqn
+* combat with Fokker DVII[+ooc] 4m
wTHOUROUT 5-45pm OK(Lt WE Gray)

D8216   Sopwith Camel   213Sqn
** seen in combat with 7 Fokker DVIIs 3m seOSTENDE

6-35pm **MIA**(Lt LC Scroggie **KIA**) [?combat
HOOGLEDE 5-50pm Ltn P Achilles MFJaV]

D9649   Sopwith Camel   213Sqn
**test combat with 2Str[+flames] ovNIEUPORT 6pm ftl
dam OK(Lt DS Ingalls USNRF)

E4385   Sopwith Camel   213Sqn
** seen 3m wTHOUROUT 5-45pm 7 Fokker DVIIs
attacked patrol **MIA**(2Lt G Illiff **KIA**)

26th September

' **C2800   RE8   3Sqn AFC**
**CAP combat with 3 Fokker DVIIs ovBELLENGLISE
~7pm? ftl dam(Lt GM Deans OK/Lt TH Prince **WIA**)
Pfalzes?

RE8   5Sqn
** mg fire(Capt GN Moore **WIA**/)

E2155   Bristol F2b   20Sqn
**OP combat nwST QUENTIN flames?(2Lt LG Smith
POW/2Lt ES Harvey **KIA**) left 12-33pm

H7243   Sopwith Dolphin   23Sqn
**OP seen ok BELLICOURT going n-w 13000' 11-45am
MIA(Lt E Fulford **POW**)

DH4   25Sqn
Rec (/2Lt CW Blasdale **WIA?) inj?

D6939   SE5a   29Sqn
**OP HA? radiator shot up VLAMERTINGHE 7pm ftl
trenches OK(Capt EC Hoy Can. DFC) several victories
for 29Sqn in this a'c, including his first on 12.8.18

E2282   Bristol F2b   48Sqn
**OP combat with 8EA[+] eMENIN engine shot up ftl
12pm cr OK(2Lt JB Cowan/Lt LN Jones) left 9-55am
HAZEBROUCK

RE8   52Sqn
** mg fire(Lt WEC Coombs **WIA**/)

DH4   57Sqn
** combat(/2Lt EG Perret **WIA**)

D8419   DH4   57Sqn
**B combat with EA ovCAMBRAI 6-20pm shot down in
control from 1000' **MIA**(Lt PWJ Timson **KIA**/Lt AN
Eyre **KIA**)

F6187   DH4   57Sqn
**PhotB AWOIGNT combat with EA down in control
from 10000' ovCAMBRAI 6-20pm **MIA**(Lt FG Pym
WIA POW/Sgt WCE Mason **POW DoW**)

A5647   FE2b   58Sqn
*NB engine ftl on return cr 3am wr(Lt AH Thompson
KIA/2Lt LH Bell **KIA**)

C9788   FE2b   58Sqn
*NB fuel pump failed EoL but returned ftl ammunition
dump cr 2-15am OK(2Lt EE Jones/2Lt J Warren)

E1552   Sopwith Camel   65Sqn
OP seen ok CLEMSKERKE 11am **MIA(2Lt WR
Thornton **POW**)

F1975   Sopwith Camel   80Sqn
**OP left 4-30pm combat with EA nST QUENTIN
flames **MIA**(2Lt H Walker **KIA**) [?combat FRESNOY
5-40pm Ltn S Garsztka Ja31]

B9347.T **DH9   99Sqn (I.F.)**
**B METZ-SABLON combat with 20-30 EAs
MIA(Capt PE Welchman MC DFC **WIA POW**/2Lt TH
Swann **WIA POW**)leg, Welchman DoW to lungs soon
after Armistice, Swann still noted as being severely
wounded

B9366.Y **DH9   99Sqn (I.F.)**
**B METZ-SABLON combat with 30-40EAs heavily
shot up ftl cr PONT À MOUSSON wr(2Lt S McKeever
WIA/Lt Boniface OK)foot, a'c was almost destroyed by
mg

C6272   DH9   99Sqn (I.F.)
B METZ-SABLON combat with 30-40EAs **MIA(2Lt
CRG Abrahams **KIA**/2Lt CH Sharp **KIA**) [?possible
DH9 claim combat KUBERN 5-27pm OffSt A Ulmer
Ja77]

D544   DH9   99Sqn (I.F.)
**B METZ-SABLON combat with 30-40EAs(Lt HD
West Can. OK/2Lt JW Howard **KIA**) this was the only
a'c of 7 which crossed lines to return to base at AZELOT

D3213   DH9   99Sqn (I.F.)
B METZ-SABLON combat with 30-40EAs **MIA(2Lt
WHC Gillett **WIA POW**/2Lt H Crossley **WIA POW**)
[?2DH claims combat sMETZ ~5-10pm Ltn E Udet Ja4]

D5573   DH9   99Sqn (I.F.)
**B combat many EAs METZ-SABLON shot down
MIA(2Lt LG Stern **KIA**/Lt FO Cook **KIA**) buried
nrPULLINGEN, raid re-routed from THIONVILLE

E632   DH9   99Sqn (I.F.)
B METZ-SABLON Rlwy combat many EAs **MIA(Lt
SC Gilbert **KIA**/2Lt R Buckby **KIA**) [DH claim combat
MANNINGEN? 5-25pm Ltn M Gossner Ja77]

D7232.3 **DH9   104Sqn (I.F.)**
**B METZ-SABLON Rlwys attacked by EAs, seen ooc
ovVERNY **MIA**(Lt OL Malcolm **KIA**/2Lt GV Harper
KIA)

The Independent Force was involved in further
operations with the French and the Americans on
the 26th, in connection with their offensive around
Verdun. They were given objectives of the rail
junctions around Mezières and at Thionville, Ars,
Audun-le-Roman, and Metz-Sablon, as well as the
enemy aerodrome at Frescaty. Their bombing
began at dawn and continued through the day and
evening. The day-bombers met fierce opposition,
99 Squadron, for instance, being attacked by thirty
to forty fighters on their outward journey. Railways
and bridges at Thionville were their allotted target,
but three machines had turned back and another
was shot down in this first attack, so the remaining
six machines bombed Metz instead. They were

attacked again on the return journey and lost another five DH9s.

The evening bombing was somewhat thwarted by poor conditions but no aircraft were lost. The remaining days of the month were too poor for long distance work, although another series of night raids was unsuccessfully attempted on the 30th. September had seen terrible losses for the Independent Force. Sixteen DH9s and five DH4s had been lost, along with eleven 0/400s and six DH9As.

D1016   DH9   107Sqn
**B ST QUENTIN combat with EA dam ftl cr OK(2Lt H Gill/2Lt J Thompson)

A7632   DH4   202Sqn
** seen in combat with 5EA OSTENDE 16500' 11am **MIA**(Lt FAB Gasson **KIA**/2Lt S King **KIA**)

D9611   Sopwith Camel   203Sqn
**SpM LIEU ST AMAND A'dr AA 2pm ftl Sh57C D.25 OK(Lt FJS Britnell) ldg trenches nBAPAUME-CAMBRAI RD, had earlier claimed Fokker DVII[+ flames] HAYNECOURT 1-15pm, made 9 claims

D9632   Sopwith Camel   203Sqn
**SpM LIEU ST AMAND a'dr AA 1-30pm ftl cr trenches on return Sh57C.NE D.17.c.2.5. OK(Lt NC Dixie)

D9640   Sopwith Camel   203Sqn
SpM combat with Fokker DVII[+] ~1-30pm seen ldg in control? neCAMBRAI **MIA(2Lt WH Coghill **POW**) or in flames? [?combat nCAMBRAI Ltn E Bormann Ja2]

C75   Sopwith Camel   204Sqn
** left 8-25am combat with HA BLANKENBERGHE **MIA**(2Lt GEC Howard **KIA**) ?combat WENDUYNE-NEUMUNSTER 10-30am FlM K Engelfried & FlM C Kairies MFJaV, but possible D3374]

D3374   Sopwith Camel   204Sqn
** combat with EA shot down ovBLANKENBERGHE(Lt WB Craig **KIA**) left 8-25am [?combat FlgM Engelfried MJaV] Craig claimed several victories in this a'c

D8168   Sopwith Camel   208Sqn
OP combat with EA ftl VILLECHOTTES cr wr(Capt A Storey **WIA) left 2pm ST QUENTIN [?combat wST QUENTIN 2-33pm Vzfw C Mesch Ja26]

D3271   DH9   218Sqn
B BRUGES AA on return engine hit ftl VLISSINGEN **MIA(Capt JF Chisholm DFC **INT**/Sgt HJ Williams **INT**)

D5742   DH9   218Sqn
B **MIA(2Lt JT Aitken **KIA**/2Lt OP Hibbert **POW**)

E2163   Bristol F2b   L Flt
pracPhot combat nBOURLON WOOD shot up **MIA(2Lt CA Harrison **POW**/Lt JA Parkinson **POW**) left 11-55am

27th September
THE BATTLE OF THE CANAL DU NORD

The British attack on the Hindenburg Line began with the advance of the First and Third Armies towards Cambrai on the 27th. The assault was made on a thirteen-mile front between Ecourt St Quentin down to Gouzeaucourt. The Canal du Nord formed a defended barrier immediately in front of the army and was too substantial to be stormed, and the attack was therefore concentrated into a desperate attempt to force a single crossing at Moeuvres. Once again, the brilliant fighting skills of the Canadian Corps meant they were chosen to lead this work. Assisting them and the four other British Corps involved were Nos. 5, 12, 13, 52, and 59 Squadrons. The battle went very much as planned. The infantry had moved off at 5-30am after a tremendous artillery barrage. Although it had rained during the night, it had cleared by dawn, and air support was therefore plentiful and well co-ordinated, as one had come to anticipate after four years of war. Contact patrols relayed back a clear picture of the advance, enabling quick reinforcement where it was needed or else bringing in barrages to protect or assist the infantry. Artillery and counter-battery patrols were laying accurate fire within twenty minutes of the assault beginning.

The work of the fighter squadrons in the battle offered an interesting comparison in approach between the two Brigades. On the First Army front, the squadrons deployed on low-flying attacks had been once again concentrated on a single airfield, in the same way as had been found effective on the Scarpe. Most of the same units were involved (Nos. 40, 54, 64, 203, and 209 Squadrons), and were again under the overall operational command of a single commander, Major BE Smythies of 64 Squadron. Work was rotated through the different squadrons, and every patrol, at flight strength, had a series of specific tactical objectives to attack. On the first day of the battle, these particularly included the crossings on the Sensée and Schelde Canals, traffic around Bantigny and Ramillies, and kite balloons. I Brigade's offensive patrols were laid on by Nos. 19 and 22 Squadrons. They were also to attack balloons, but their primary role was to protect the low-flying aircraft and day-bombers by offensive action against enemy machines. They were ordered to fly as one large formation at particular times through the day, which no doubt dissipated their overall effect.

III Brigade operated a more co-ordinated and

unified approach, whereby only a single squadron, No. 201, was specifically allocated low patrol work, and instead had fighters incorporate this work into the start and finish of their offensive patrols. In this way, flights from pairs of squadrons would take off through the day, first proceeding to attack kite balloons or ground targets and then ascend to search out opponents in the upper sky and other more usual work. Squadrons operating together in this way were typically Nos. 3 and 56, 60 and 148 US, and 87 and 17 US Squadrons. 11 Squadron also made offensive patrols at near squadron strength.

The final RAF air group of substance operating on the 27th was IX Brigade. Its work had started the previous night with bombing raids to stations at Denain, Busigny, and Le Cateau and reconnaissances of the main enemy communications lines. Its day-bomber squadrons then continued this work, with fighter escort, but widened its scope to include enemy aerodromes in the morning. These relatively deep intrusions to targets such as Emerchicourt, Bevillers, and Bertry, attracted some of the heaviest air fighting of the day. Fighter escorts drawn from 32 and 40 Squadrons claimed high numbers of victories but were also mauled.

By the evening, the attack centred on Moeuvres had been highly successful and the Allied armies were across the Canal du Nord and fanning eastwards to enclose Cambrai.

F5503   SE5a   1Sqn
**OP combat with EA ftl BEUGNATRE A'dr 8-50am dam OK(Lt W Newby) left 8-05am

F2153.7 Sopwith Camel   3Sqn
+* attacked KBs[+++des] at Sh57B.M.14 btwn 8-05am & 8-20am OK(Lt GR Riley) made 13 claims

F2158   Sopwith Camel   3Sqn
**SpM left 7am combat with EA 4000' Sh57C L.27 then seen ok 8-05am low after combat MIA(Lt TR Hostetter US. KIA) [Camel claim combat sMASNIÈRES 8-15am Oblt Ritt vGreim JGr 9]

F6117   Sopwith Camel   3Sqn
**SpM left 7am combat with Fokker DVII 4000' seen ok low at 8-05am after combat, controls shot away ftl Sh57C L.27 MIA(2Lt JO Wood POW)

C2672   RE8   4Sqn
**CP mg fuel tank shot up 8-30am ftl Sh28 T28 a.2.3. OK(2Lt FE Winter/2Lt WTJ Hall)

A.W.FK8   8Sqn
** mg fire(/2Lt SF Blackwell WIA)

RE8   12Sqn
** combat(Lt CR Pithey WIA/Lt H Rhodes WIA)

D4939   RE8   13Sqn
**CAP combat shot up? fainted cr(Lt RE Britton WIA/

2Lt B Hickman WIA)

D4942   RE8   13Sqn
**P combat with EA shot up dam returned a'dr 5-55pm OK(Lt EG Plum/Lt WG Campbell) left 4-20pm XVII Corps area

F6005   RE8   13Sqn
**NF left 6-15am shot up dam(Lt Daniel OK/2Lt HF Lea WIA)

A7887   DH4   18Sqn
**Phot combat with EA badly shot up returned a'dr 1-25pm OK(2Lt JKS Smith/2Lt A Lilley) left 10-25am First Army area

A7899   DH4   18Sqn
**B combat with several EAs SANCOURT seen going n-w after combat MIA(Lt RC Bennett DFC POW/Lt NW Helwig DFC POW?) left 6-10am

Nos. 18 and 103 Squadrons made high level bombing raids on Wasnes-au-Bac.

E4501   Sopwith Dolphin   19Sqn
**OP combat with EA shot up BAPAUME dam(Capt CV Gardiner DoW 30.9.18)

E4713   Sopwith Dolphin   19Sqn
+* combat with Fokker DrIs[+des++ooc] & KB[+des] neCAMBRAI 7-15am OK(Lt LH Ray Can.) claimed 7 victories

E2566   Bristol F2b   20Sqn
**OP seen neST QUENTIN combat with EA MIA(Lt FE Turner KIA/2Lt CE Clarke KIA) left 9-30am, but a'c with 22Sq late 10.18

D8089   Bristol F2b   22Sqn
**OP seen ovCAMBRAI going east MIA(2Lt GJ? Smith POW/Lt GB Shum POW) initials GF? left 2-30pm [?combat CATTENIÈRES 3-50pm Oblt O Schmidt Ja5]

E2243   Bristol F2b   22Sqn
**OP seen ovCAMBRAI going east MIA(Lt JR Drummond KIA/2Lt CH Wilcox POW) left 2-30pm [F2b claim combat NEUVILLY 4pm Vzfw O Hennrich Ja46]

E2477   Bristol F2b   22Sqn
**OP seen going east ovCAMBRAI MIA(Capt SFH Thompson KIA/2Lt CJ Tolman KIA) left 2-30pm, pilot made several of his 30 claims in this a'c

A8031   DH4   25Sqn
**Rec left 7-45am MONS MIA(Lt DH Hazell KIA/2Lt DB Robertson KIA)

25 Squadron carried out strategic reconnaissance and photography for the attack.

B8355   SE5a   32Sqn
**OP seen in combat with 6EA ovCAMBRAI 6000' 5-45pm MIA(2Lt CF Cawley POW) Cawley had claimed his first Fokker DVII in the morning combats over EMERCHICOURT at 9-40am?[combat wCAMBRAI 5-50pm UntOff K Treiber Ja5][?combat sSAILLY 5-35pm Vzfw F Classen Ja26]

E1399.A **SE5a**   **32Sqn**
+* combat with Fokker DVIIs[++flames]
EMERCHICOURT A'dr 9-30am OK(Capt GEB
Lawson SA.) claimed 6 victories

E4026.A **SE5a**   **32Sqn**
+* combat with Fokker DVIIs[+des++ooc] CAMBRAI
5-20pm OK(Lt FL Hale US.) made 7 victories in this a'c

B8442 **SE5a**   **40Sqn**
BOP seen ok CAMBRAI-DOUAI 8-20am **MIA(Lt
ND Willis **POW**)

C9135 **SE5a**   **40Sqn**
BOP seen ok CAMBRAI-DOUAI 8-20am **MIA(2Lt
PB Myers **KIA**) [?this or B8442 combat 8-30am Ltn R
vBarnekow Ja1]

D8440 **SE5a**   **40Sqn**
+*BOP combat with Fokker DVII[+des]
AUBERCHEUL-AU-BAC 8-45am OK(Capt JL
Middleton)

E1345 **SE5a**   **40Sqn**
BOP seen ok 8-20am CAMBRAI-DOUAI **MIA(1Lt R
Mooney USAS **WIA POW**)

E1350 **SE5a**   **40Sqn**
B seen ok 8-30am CAMBRAI-DOUAI **MIA(2Lt GMJ
Morton **KIA**)

E3946 **SE5a**   **40Sqn**
+*B combat with Fokker DVII[+ooc] OISY-LE-
VERGER 9-30am OK(2Lt GS Smith)

E8028 **Sopwith Snipe**   **43Sqn**
** combat with Fokker DVIIs[+ooc] CAMBRAI 9-25am
OK(Capt CC Banks MC) shared, claimed a dozen
victories

E8031 **Sopwith Snipe**   **43Sqn**
+* combat with Fokker DVIIs[+ooc] CAMBRAI
9-25am OK(Capt CF King MC) pilot shared, made over
20 victory claims

This shared victory was the first on Sopwith Snipes
for 43 Squadron.

                RE8   **52Sqn**
** mg fire(Lt JWH Scales **WIA**/)

B6421 **Sopwith Camel**   **54Sqn**
**SpB combat with EA 12-10pm shot down ooc spin
2000' nwCAMBRAI **MIA**(Lt P McCaig **KIA**) [?Camel
claim combat MARQUION Ltn H Vallendor
Ja2][?combat eMARQUION 12-08pm Ltn F Rumey
Ja5][?combat seOISY-LE-V Ltn E Bormann Ja2]

F2135 **Sopwith Camel**   **54Sqn**
**SpB left 11-35am EA fire shot up dam returned a'dr
OK(2Lt JM Stevenson)

F5482 **SE5a**   **56Sqn**
**COP combat with EA shot up dam returned a'dr
8-45am OK(Lt JA Pouchot DCM) left 6-50am Third
Army area

F5495 **SE5a**   **56Sqn**
**COP in combat with 3EA on tail ovBOURLON

WOOD 6000' 8-20am in control **MIA**(Lt GO Mackenzie
KIA) [?"SE5" claim combat NOYELLES Ltn G
Bassenge Ja2]

A8085 **DH4**   **57Sqn**
B combat 6-30pm shot up ftl wr(2Lt GJ Dickens **inj/
2Lt AH Aitken OK)

A8086 **DH4**   **57Sqn**
**B left 4-30pm shot up dam(2Lt FdeM Hyde OK/2Lt
LH Eyres **WIA**)

F6114 **DH4**   **57Sqn**
**BPhot combat with EA dam ftl 62Sq 6-30pm(Lt EM
Coles OK/2Lt C Wilkinson **WIA**) to Sh57b B.26.a.3.0.

57 Squadron, attached to the Third Army, was
allotted Rumilly and German headquarter targets.

F6011 **RE8**   **59Sqn**
CP flames wr(Capt LM Woodhouse MC DFC **KIA/Lt
WS Peel MC **KIA**) left 8-40am

C944   **Bristol F2b**   **62Sqn**
OP attkg EA eDOUAI **MIA(2Lt PS Manley **POW**/
Sgt GF Hines **POW**) left 8-15am [?"BF" claim combat
MARCY-POMTAINE 9-20am OffSt F Altemeier Ja24]

          Bristol F2b   **62Sqn**
** (/2Lt RF Hunter **WIA**?) inj?

E1549 **Sopwith Camel** **65Sqn**
**OP 2 Fokker DVIIs diving on him GHISTELLES
11-50am **MIA**(2Lt RO Campbell US. **KIA**) [Camel
claim combat nwTHOUROUT 12-50pm Ltn F
Piechulek Ja56]

D9460 **Sopwith Camel** **70Sqn**
**LP seen ZILLEBEKE LAKE-PLOEGSTEERT
WOOD 6-45am **MIA**(2Lt PM Wallace **POW**) left 6am

C6723 **Sopwith Camel** **73Sqn**
*GndStr combat with EA 1-30pm shot up dam OK(2Lt
TC McNeale)

D9472 **Sopwith Camel** **73Sqn**
**GndStr AA? seen in flames BOIS DE BOURLON
MIA(2Lt WA Brett **KIA**) left 8-25am [?Camel claim
combat nBOURLON WOOD am Ltn H Vallendor Ja2]

F1917 **Sopwith Camel** **73Sqn**
**GndStr British shell hit u'c & combat ftl cr a'dr
OK(Capt WH Hubbard DFC) left 6am

H7249 **SE5a**   **85Sqn**
**OP left 4-55pm combat with 2EA eST QUENTIN
MIA(Lt EG Robertson **KIA**)

E2153 **Bristol F2b**   **88Sqn**
**SpM combat with EA nrABANCOURT seen in
control **MIA**(Lt C Foster **KIA**/Sgt T Proctor **KIA**) left
12-55pm [?combat VALENCIENNES Ltn C Degelow
Ja40]

D1106 **DH9**   **98Sqn**
**B left 7-30am BERTRY A'dr combat with 8EA dam
OK(Lt G Richmond/2Lt P Fish)

D7334   DH9   98Sqn
**B combat GREVILLERS ftl cr shell hole(2Lt EAR Lee
inj/2Lt EG Banham **inj**) left 7-15am

          DH9   103Sqn
** combat(/2Lt HS Crees **WIA**)

E669   DH9   108Sqn
**B AA ooc ovCORTEMARCK-THOUROUT but in
partial control? **MIA**(2Lt AS Jones **KIA**/Sgt R
Richardson **KIA**?) left 10-30am

E4375   Sopwith Camel   201Sqn
**LowOP mg fire fuel tank hit cr o't EoL amongst British
tank barrage Sh57C K.15.b.95.50. & escaped OK(Lt
WAW Carter)

F5941.E Sopwith Camel   201Sqn
**KBP KB[+flames] shot up 11-30am(Capt GB Gates
DFC **WIA**) KB at Sh57C.L.12c, scored over a dozen
victories, many in this a'c

E4407   Sopwith Camel   210Sqn
**OP AA prop fail ftl snd 1m sWULPEN wr OK(2Lt HE
Light)to hospital

28th September
THE BATTLES IN FLANDERS

The final Allied campaign in Flanders began on the
28th. It was the last of the series of battles designed
to break the German Army's fighting capability
and spirit. Ludendorff had perilously weakened his
armies in Flanders in order to defend Cambrai and
the Meuse. The moment when the pressure was
greatest on Cambrai was therefore chosen for the
start of fighting in Flanders. The attack was
planned for the front between Dixmude and St
Eloi, and was made by Belgian and French armies
and the British Second Army. The RAF provided
air support principally from II Brigade, but it has
to be said that supply difficulties were by now
affecting both sides on this front, and additional
aircraft for use by the Belgian Army were drawn
from Naval 5 Group operating on the coast. Its
units were the bombers of 82nd Wing: Nos. 38
(FE2bs), 214 (HP 0/400s), and 218 Squadrons
(DH9s), and the 61st Wing, being Nos. 204, 210,
and 213 Squadrons (Sopwith Camels), and Nos.
202 and 217 Squadrons (DH4s).

The RAF units of II Brigade involved in the
Flanders battles were: the 11th (Army) Wing,
containing Squadrons 29, 41, and 74 (SE5as), 70
(Sopwith Camels), 79 (Sopwith Dolphins), 48
(Bristol Fighters), 206 (DH9s), and 149 (FE2bs);
the 65th (Army) Wing, with 65 Squadron (Sopwith
Camels), 108, and 211 Squadrons (DH9s); and the
2nd (Corps) Wing, with Squadrons 4, 7, and 53
(RE8s), and 10, and 82 (A.W. FK8s).

Secrecy had been maintained to the utmost, so
that when the third major Allied offensive in three
days began at dawn it took the enemy by almost
complete surprise. Progress was extremely good:
the enemy was capable of little resistance and was
driven back with such speed that by evening the
limits of the old battlefields of 1917 had been
reached and exceeded. The British had reached
Kruiseik and Becelaere, whilst the Belgians had
taken Houthulst Wood.

The conditions for flying had been very poor, but
airmen spent the entire day fighting. Great risks
were taken by the corps squadrons who were driven
low to do their work, and the low fighter patrols
everywhere attacked and harried the enemy in
retreat. The day's losses for this work, however,
were amongst the heaviest for 1918 — many were
the victim of anti-aircraft and ground fire, but
explanation also lay in a violent storm which
patrols met in the morning. The rail network was
also bombed throughout the day. A notable feature
of the RAF units assembled for the fighting was the
high proportion of bombers, which could be used
to disrupt the inward flow of reinforcements. It was
clear that the German Army in Flanders was weak
and extremely vulnerable, and that progress was
ensured for as long as it could not be effectively
relieved. Day and night-bombers attacked
Thourout, Cortemarck, Menin, Roulers, Thielt,
and Ingelmunster, and just as many more important rail junctions. The raids were mostly
continuous and unmolested.

On the Cambrai-St Quentin front, rain and low
cloud had persisted through the night, making the
job of the night-bomber crews exceedingly difficult.
They had managed to bomb their main objective
of Busigny station to some effect, and brought back
reports of other stations on fire and the roads
clogged to bursting point with the movement of
men and supplies. Further progress was made in
early fighting and a major shift in fortune in the
battle was reported by a crew from 13 Squadron
on contact patrol (see below). Soon before midday,
they detected that the German Army was with-
drawing to positions east of the Schelde Canal. The
division they were shadowing, the 57th, therefore
made a rapid advance into new ground, and were
only prevented from immediately going further by
a lack of materials to bridge the canal.

Low-flying attacks continued on the 28th, but
were only made by Nos. 54, 203, and 209
Squadrons for the First Army whose targets were
the crossings on the Schelde Canal. The other
squadrons were ordered to turn their attention to
offensive patrols against kite balloons for the next
few days but there was little enemy presence in the

air. As the army secured its gains through the afternoon and evening, the pressure mounted on Cambrai. It was far too strong a fortress to fall immediately, but it was now flanked so menacingly that it could no longer be used as a rail head. With these objectives gained, the artillery necessary for the main central assault on the Hindenburg Line began to be brought forward and registered. Fighting continued on the First and Third Army fronts; by the end of the month the Germans had withdrawn their centre at Gonnelieu and Villers Guislain, but it was the task of the British Fourth Army to the south which now took centre stage.

Sopwith Camel　3Sqn
** (2Lt RL McLeod **WIA**?) inj?

C5036　RE8　　　　4Sqn
CAP left 5-10pm combat with EA dam(Lt RH Shroder OK/2Lt BR Jones **KIA)

C2530　RE8　　　　7Sqn
CAP shot up(2Lt HM Matthews **WIA/2Lt C Fletcher **DoW**) left 7-15am, was MIA

RE8　　　　7Sqn
** mg fire ground(/2Lt S Kennan **WIA**)

D6741　RE8　　　　7Sqn
CAP combat with EA mg dam(2Lt WK Rose **WIA/ 2Lt AE Jenkins **DoW**)

E273　RE8　　　　7Sqn
CAP combat ftl cr shell hole in Belgian Lines(2Lt JAG Henry **KIA/Lt A Westall **WIA**) left 2-15pm

D5152　A.W.FK8　　　　10Sqn
CAP mg shot up ftl cr dam(Lt CFJ Lisle **WIA/2Lt M deVerteuil OK) hit 1-45pm Sh28 P8.09

C2715　RE8　　　　12Sqn
**CAP left 9am Sixth Army ground mg shot up OK(Lt SD Evans/Lt Stubbings)

C2712　RE8　　　　13Sqn
**P engine shot up dam returned 11-15am OK(Lt GJ Farmer/Lt WG Campbell) left 7-50am XVII Corps area

RE8　　　　13Sqn
**CP SCHELDE CANAL OK(Capt GB Bailey/Lt JWG Clark) working with advance of 57th Division, reconnaissance of enemy lines showed retreat eastwards of canal had occurred(see text above)

RE8　　　　13Sqn
** gunshot wound(2Lt J Nicole **WIA**)

D7894　Bristol F2b　22Sqn
**OP combat with EA shot up dam cr OK(2Lt TD Smith/Lt B Caillard) left 5pm First Army area, returned 6-35pm

DH9　　　　27Sqn
** (2Lt CM Allan **WIA**?/) inj? 27.9?

C1914　SE5a　　　　29Sqn
**OP seen in combat with Fokker DVII seMENIN

12000′ 4-30pm **MIA**(Capt EC Hoy DFC **POW**)[?combat eYPRES 5-50pm Ltn J Raesch Ja43]

D6947　SE5a　　　　29Sqn
OP left 6-50am ovLINSELLES going east in rain **MIA(2Lt WL Dougan **POW**)

D6949　SE5a　　　　29Sqn
**OP AA hit 8-05am ftl cr OK(Lt DM Layton) ftl Sh44A 6 17.A.6.9.

D6984　SE5a　　　　29Sqn
+* combat with Fokker DVII[+flames] sMENIN then Fokker DVII[+des] MENIN-GHELUVELT Rd 5-30pm OK(Lt CG Ross SA.) Ross claimed 20 victories

F5456　SE5a　　　　29Sqn
OP seen LINSELLES going east in rain **MIA(Lt BR Rolfe **POW**) left 6-50am

F5480　SE5a　　　　29Sqn
OP seen LINSELLES going east in rain **MIA(Lt DA O'Leary US. **POW**) left 6-50am

C8887.D　SE5a　　　　41Sqn
OP left 8-30am **MIA(2Lt HB Hewat **POW**) [?2 SE5 claims combat MOORSLEDE Ltn J Jacobs Ja7, but other possibilities]

E4048.Z　SE5a　　　　41Sqn
OP left 8-30am **MIA(Lt AF Smith **POW**)

E4061.B　SE5a　　　　41Sqn
OP left 8-30am **MIA(Lt PB Cooke **POW**)

E4076　SE5a　　　　41Sqn
**OP combat with EA shot up then lost ftl QUAEDYPRE 9-30am cr dam OK(Lt WA Morris) left 8-30am

F5484　SE5a　　　　41Sqn
OP left 8-30am **MIA(Lt HC Telfer **POW**)

F5506　SE5a　　　　41Sqn
OP left 8-30am **MIA(2Lt W Mitchell **POW DoW**)

C9294　SE5a　　　　56Sqn
**LowB dam by own bombs exploding on target ftl Sh57C.E 15a OK(Lt DW Grinnell-Milne)

SE5a　　　　56Sqn
** mg fire(Lt JC Speaks US. **WIA**)

B7900.B　SE5a　　　　64Sqn
OP left 8-05am **MIA(2Lt AT Sheldrake **KIA**)

B7864　Sopwith Camel　65Sqn
OP left 6-55am **MIA(2Lt F Edsted? US. **POW**) name Edstead?

D8145　Sopwith Camel　65Sqn
OP left 6-55am seen seOSTENDE **MIA(2Lt JC Malcolmson **POW**)

D8158　Sopwith Camel　65Sqn
OP left 6-55am seen seOSTENDE **MIA(2Lt RC Mitten **POW**)

E1487　Sopwith Camel　65Sqn
** left 6-55am seen seOSTENDE 8000′ **MIA**(Lt JMcM

Maclennan DFC **POW**)

F1324 Sopwith Camel 65Sqn
**OP left 6-55am OOSTKERKE-LAMPERNISSE AA
ftl dam OK(Lt CR Tolley)

F1542 Sopwith Camel 65Sqn
**OP left 6-55am cr WATERLANDKERJE WR
MIA(Lt DM John **inj INT**) interned Holland

H7288 Sopwith Camel 65Sqn
OP left 6-55am seen seOSTENDE 8000′ **MIA(2Lt WJ
Brookes **KIA**)

Sopwith Camel 70Sqn
** (Lt CL Frank **WIA**?) **inj**?

D8175 Sopwith Camel 70Sqn
**LowP left 2-55pm seen ok nGHELUWE circled
MIA(2Lt JS Wilson **DoW**)

E1593 Sopwith Camel 70Sqn
**LowP combat with EA shot up dam ftl cr ldg nose a'dr
9-30am OK(2Lt EDA Mackay) left 8-05am
HANDZEAME

E7173 Sopwith Camel 70Sqn
**LowP EA fire shot up dam returned a'dr 8-35am
OK(2Lt RM Atwater) left 8-05am PASSCHENDAELE
area

E7199 Sopwith Camel 70Sqn
LowP left 8am PERENCHIES seen eYPRES **MIA(Sgt
AC Hall **POW**)

C4127 Sopwith Dolphin 79Sqn
+* combat with PfalzDIII[+des] WERCKEN 1-15pm
OK(Capt FI Lord US.) last of 12 claims

F6020 Sopwith Dolphin 79Sqn
LowB left 12-30am seen straff 3m wSTADEN **MIA(Lt
RJ Morgan US. **POW**) rank of Captain? [?combat
ROULERS 5-45pm ObflM A Buhl MFJaIV]

C8643 A.W.FK8 82Sqn
**NFP combat with EA YPRES 6-30pm shot down(Lt J
Sangster **WIA**/2Lt LJ Skinner **WIA**)

C8115 Sopwith Dolphin 87Sqn
OP left 4-25pm seen nwCAMBRAI **MIA(2Lt DA
Thompson **POW**)

D6959 SE5a 92Sqn
**OP sPROYART followed EA ST QUENTIN 6-20pm
then fuel ftl cr R.29.c.50. OK(Lt OJ Rose) left 4-45pm

D5622 DH9 108Sqn
**B HA? seen going down in control 28m nROULERS
4pm wr MIA but OK(2Lt PL Phillips/2Lt PCS McCrea)

A7849 DH4 202Sqn
** combat with 5EA ooc cr ENGEL DUMP **MIA**(Lt AM
Stevens **KIA**/2Lt WHL Halford **KIA**) left 1-35pm
[?"DH4" claim combat WERVICQ Ltn F Piechulek
Ja56]

A8025.Z DH4 202Sqn
** storm lost EoL seen nrENGEL DUMP **MIA**(Capt AV
Bowater **POW**/Lt DL Melvin **POW**) left 6-35am

A8066 DH4 202Sqn
** storm seen ovNIEUPORT 7-25am **MIA**(Lt CR
Moore **POW**/2Lt E Darby **POW**)

F3220 Sopwith Camel 203Sqn
**SpM combat with 16 Fokker DVII ovHAM
LANGELET 8-30am **MIA**(Sgt WN Mayger MM **KIA**)
[?combat HAM-LENGELET 8-35am Ltn G Bassenge
Ja2]

D8186 Sopwith Camel 204Sqn
** shot up dam(Lt RMcI Gordon **WIA**)

D9600 Sopwith Camel 204Sqn
+* combat with Fokker DVIIs[+des+ooc] WERCKEN
12-30pm OK(Capt AJB Tonks) last of 11 claims

F5937 Sopwith Camel 209Sqn
**LowP seen 7-45am ovEPINOY going east after
bombing sSCARPE RIVER AA? **MIA**(Lt JA Fenton
KIA)

E8936 DH9 211Sqn
B seen ok? wSTADEN in control afterwards **MIA(2Lt
WJ Johnson **POW DoW**/Sgt WE Jones MM **POW**) left
11-30am

D3326 Sopwith Camel 213Sqn
** left 7-15am lost EoL **MIA**(2Lt A Fletcher **POW**)

D3372 Sopwith Camel 213Sqn
** left 7-15am shot down **MIA**(Lt PC Jenner **POW**)
[?combat Ltn M Lampel]

D8217 Sopwith Camel 213Sqn
**OOAB left 7-15am combat fuel tank shot up ftl
MOERES OK(Lt MN Hancocks)

A7924 DH4 217Sqn
** combat with 16EAs shot down in flames 4m
eTHOUROUT **MIA**(1Lt JE Gregory USAS. **KIA**/2Lt E
Martin-Bell **KIA**)

C1206 DH9 218Sqn
** combat with EAs shot up dam(2Lt F Nelms USMCR
WIA/2Lt CC Barr USMC **DoW** 6.10.18)

2Lt Barr was the first US Marine aviator to be
killed by enemy action.

D5654 DH9 218Sqn
*B THOUROUT down ~12pm **MIA**(2Lt TM Steele
POW/2Lt G Gedge **POW**)

D5712 DH9 218Sqn
** combat with EAs ovCORTEMARCK shot up
dam(1Lt ER Brewer USMC **WIA**/Sgt HB Wersheimer
USMC **WIA**)

F1934 Sopwith Camel US 148th Pursuit Sqn
**LowStr left 6-30am shot up dam returned 8-50am
OK(1Lt PE Cunnius)

29th September
THE BATTLE FOR
THE HINDENBURG LINE

On the 29th, the Fourth Army extended the

fighting between Cambrai and St Quentin with its direct assault onto the Hindenburg Line. It was one of the most crucial battles of the war — for the Allies, it had to succeed if they were to end the fighting before winter; for the German Army, the Hindenburg Line was their last great defensive asset, and for their people it was the centrepiece of public morale.

As well as British troops, the Fourth Army would again use three Australian Corps to drive the assault, with the help of an additional American Corps as well. 1,634 pieces of artillery had been assembled and were expected to play a vital role. There were also over two hundred tanks, to be used mainly in the initial assault with the Australians. The air support available to the Fourth Army, as noted earlier, consisted of the three hundred and thirty-seven aircraft of V Brigade. Its fighter squadrons included Nos. 23, 24, 84, 80, 201, 209, as well as 20 Squadron (fighter-reconnaissance), and 205 Squadron (day-bombers). The Corps Squadrons with this army were Nos. 3 AFC, 9 and 35 Squadrons, with 6 Squadron supporting the Cavalry, and 8 and 73 (Fighter) Squadron supporting the tanks. 15 Squadron were operating with the right flank of the Third Army who would also be involved. As well as their usual roles, corps squadrons were ordered to be especially vigilant for any signs of counter-attacks forming. The day and night bombing squadrons of IX Brigade, for whom there was no rest, were ordered to attack aerodromes and rail targets from midnight onwards, and once fighting began, the German kite balloons were to be especially singled out for attack by fighters. This was because many enemy batteries were known to be entirely dependent on these. Gun positions were in fact designated as overriding targets for all low patrols.

The attack was launched at 5-50am on the 29th. One of the greatest advantages the attacking force carried with it against these most formidable defences was a comprehensive understanding of them. The small but vital advances recently made just to the north of St Quentin meant the front line ran along, or just west of, the St Quentin Canal. This made a turn at Bellenglise, and it was here that the enemy had one of their key defensive positions. It was taken by a British division swarming en masse across the canal, towing rafts behind them, and carrying their equipment over. Fog helped the attack, and through the break they had formed, reserves pushed eastwards to take a section of the rear defences in the most successful move of the day. Some way to the north lay the Le Tronquoy tunnel, three and a half miles long and

in some ways the heart of this section of the Hindenburg Line. It quartered thousands of troops and from it spread a network of passages and other works from which the defence was managed. Tanks managed to cross on the ground above this and joined in the attack which eventually won the northern entrance after intense fighting.

The area over and around the tunnel, between Bellicourt and Vendhuille, was where the Australian and American troops launched their critical attack. Decisive progress was made here, but the American Corps drove on with perhaps too much enthusiasm and became separated and isolated from the body of the attack. Uncertain lest they become targets of the British guns, the artillery barrage was forced to contract by these events. From this time onwards progress was much more difficult as the complexity of the defences compounded these other problems. Nevertheless, a breach had been made in the Hindenburg Line sufficient for the British Army to exploit, and incidentally so damaging that it significantly aided the French attack on nearby St Quentin.

If the conditions had been better this may well have been an occasion when the RAF corps machines could have offered vital assistance. As it was, the desperate and confused fighting was made almost indecipherable by smoke, mist and rain, and only minimal air support could be given. The best work was done in a few hours in the afternoon when the sky briefly cleared. This was enough for reconnaissance to establish the line of the advance, but it also failed to locate the American troops. Offensive air activity was more effective. SE5as of 84 Squadron attacked kite balloons in the morning — a speciality of the unit by this time — and met and fought ten Fokkers who attempted to come to their defence. This fighting was done by two flights from 84 Squadron operating above in protection and a Fokker was shot down. The Official History notes that five balloons were destroyed as well. There was also a second, bigger dogfight involving twenty-nine British fighters against twenty German machines, as well as other more minor engagements throughout the afternoon.

C8841	SE5a	1Sqn

OP seen nrBOHAIN 9-40am HA? **MIA(Lt LN Elworthy **POW**)[?combat BOHAIN 9-40am Ltn K Odebrett Ja42]

E4023	SE5a	1Sqn

+* combat with Fokker DVIIs[+ooc] BOHAIN 9-45am OK(Lt DM Bissett)

H7257	SE5a	1Sqn

+* combat with Fokker DVIIs[+ooc] BOHAIN 9-45am OK(2Lt DE Cameron)

1 Squadron was escorting 98 Squadron on a bombing raid to Montigny aerodrome. The group was attacked over the target; all the bombing machines returned but 1 Squadron lost a machine.

RE8 3Sqn AFC
** ground mg fire nBELLICOURT shot up(2Lt SH Deamer **WIA**/Lt Fullerton OK) Deamer born UK

F6175 Sopwith Camel 3Sqn
**LowP combat with Fokker DVII shot up bad ftl cr bad ground Sh51B W.29.b.9.2. at 9-45am OK(2Lt AW Tinham)shelled, left 8-15am Third Army area

C2693 RE8 5Sqn
**AP combat at 2pm fuel tank shot up ftl W2c 00 dam OK(2Lt EA Harrison/2Lt EM Patterson)

RE8 6Sqn
** combat(/2Lt WM Sanderson **WIA**)

D4734 RE8 6Sqn
LRec nST QUENTIN **MIA(2Lt HH Scott **KIA**/2Lt ACJ Payne **POW**) left 7-15am

A.W.FK8 8Sqn
** mg fire(/2Lt JB Ballantyne **WIA**)

D5147 A.W.FK8 8Sqn
**OP left 12-05am ground mg dam returned 2pm OK(Lt Peffers/2Lt R Lister)

D5151 A.W.FK8 10Sqn
**CP mg 5-25pm ftl Sh28.H.18c dam OK(Lt T Shields/2Lt RA Thomas)left exposed

F5814 Bristol F2b 11Sqn
COP CAMBRAI down EoL **MIA(2Lt TT Smith **KIA**/Lt JL Bromley **KIA**) left 7-20am [?combat eCAUDRY 8-50am OffSt J Mai Ja5]

C2559 RE8 12Sqn
**CP mg shot up over front dam OK(Lt Metcalfe/Lt Hopkins) left 11-25am Sixth Army area

E2561 Bristol F2b 20Sqn
OP seen ok Sh62B N2.c.97 ovLines going west **MIA(2Lt NS Boulton **KIA**/2Lt CH Case **KIA**) left 9-05am, pilot made 6 claims, including 3 on 23.9

E2266 Bristol F2b 22Sqn
OP combat with Fokker DVIIs eCAMBRAI shot down EoL **MIA(1Lt E Adams USAS. **KIA**/Sgt GH Bissell **KIA**) left 10am [possible "BF" claims eIRONY UntOff P Keusen & CAGNOEULLES? UntOff Fevers Ja2]

E2517 Bristol F2b 22Sqn
OP seen in combat with Fokker DVII eCAMBRAI **MIA(Lt CWM Thompson **POW**/Lt LR James **POW**) left 10am [?"BF" claim combat MARCOING Ltn P Bäumer Ja2] Thompson made 12 claims with 22Sqn

DH4 27Sqn
** (/2Lt CE Robinson **WIA**?) inj?

D3172 DH9 27Sqn
B seen shot down ovBUSIGNY **MIA(2Lt HS Thomas **KIA**/2Lt T Brown **KIA**?) left 6-30am [DH9 claim combat nCAUDRY 8-45am UOff K Treiber Ja5]

D3237 DH9 27Sqn
B BUSIGNY shot up had to bank to miss a'c ldg 9-30am cr dam(2Lt J Cocksedge OK/2Lt EC Robinson **WIA) left 6-30am

27 Squadron was escorted to Busigny by 62 Squadron.

C1133 SE5a 29Sqn
+* attacked KB[+des] eCOMINES 2-10pm OK(Lt CW Wareing) last of 9 claims, had shot down another KB that morning seARMENTIÈRES in SE5a D6940

D6942 SE5a 29Sqn
**OP mg eHOUTHULST FOREST 5-50pm ftl cr shell hole OK(Capt RCL Holme MC)

E5690 SE5a 29Sqn
**OP AA ftl 10-15am cr shell hole Sh28H 16.A.5.5 dam OK(Lt RG Robertson)

The air activity in Flanders was heavily restricted by rain in the coming days. As Wise notes in *Canadian Airmen*, however, air support was hardly needed in this fighting as the defeated enemy was pushed back so comprehensively. In many areas the speed of the advance was limited more by poor ground than by enemy resistance.

C2372 RE8 42Sqn
**TrStr mg shot up dam returned a'dr 1-30pm OK(Lt R Hall/2Lt FL Strangward) left 12-05pm

D6572 Sopwith Camel 46Sqn
OP seen ok going west with no EAs about 800′ 4-45pm but ftl EoL **MIA(2Lt NF Moxon **POW**)

F5960 Sopwith Camel 46Sqn
OP seen ok EoL going west 4000′ 4-45pm **MIA(2Lt AM Allan **POW**) repat 12.12.18, but report in AIR1/969/204/5/1102: buried CAPPY?

D6820 RE8 59Sqn
**CAP bullet in fuel tank dam ftl OK(2Lt HSR Burt/2Lt WC Kidd) left 2-15pm

F5872 RE8 59Sqn
CP combat with EA Sh53 M2a shot down(Capt TS Symons DFC **KIA/2Lt FW Chadwick **KIA**?) left 5-30pm

E2509 Bristol F2b 62Sqn
LP hit by shell? dive broke up ovDURY(Lt RH O'Reilly **KIA/2Lt LE Mitchell **KIA**) left 7-05am

D9485 Sopwith Camel 80Sqn
+* combat with Fokker DVII[+des] nFONTAINE 10-15am then another Fokker DVII[+des] JONCOURT 10-35am OK(Capt HA Whistler)

F6188 Sopwith Camel 80Sqn
SpM left 12-10pm ESTRÉES **MIA(Capt HJ Welch **KIA**)

H7274 Sopwith Camel 80Sqn
OP left 9am seen in combat ovJONCOURT **MIA(2Lt R Bramwell **KIA**)

C9293   SE5a   84Sqn
**OP left 9-45am seen dive on KB[+des]
nrBEAUREVOIR 10-10am **MIA**(2Lt DC Rees **KIA**) to
BELLICOURT-ST QUENTIN, shared with E4071
[?"SE5" claim combat 10-20am Oblt H vWedel
Ja24][?SE5 claim combat BELLENGLISE Ltn A Lenz
Ja22, time?]

D6982   SE5a   84Sqn
OP left 4-30pm seen ok? MONTBREHAIN **MIA(2Lt
FR Christiani US. **KIA**) [SE5a claim VILLERS
OUTREAUX 10-20am Vzfw O Hennrich Ja46]

E4071   SE5a   84Sqn
+* attacked KB[+des] BEAUREVOIR 10-10am
OK(2Lt SW Highwood)

F5489   SE5a   84Sqn
+* attacked KB[+des] nVILLERS OUTREAUX
9-50am OK(Lt JG Coots)

84 Squadron made claims for destroying five kite
balloons on this raid, some of which are noted
above. These brought to thirteen the number it had
claimed in the previous six days.

C4155   Sopwith Dolphin   87Sqn
OP left 6-30am seen ok swCAMBRAI **MIA(Lt RM
MacDonald **POW**)

**   DH9   103Sqn**
** combat(Capt J Austin-Sparkes **WIA**/2Lt B Russell
WIA)

D8187   Sopwith Camel   204Sqn
*LowB left 6-30am storm seen slow ovYPRES **MIA**(Lt
RM Bennett **KIFA**) cr KIA? [?combat WOUMEN
6-15pm FlgM Pfeiffer MJaIII]

E8419   DH9A   205Sqn
Rec (Lt HG Kirkland **WIA/2Lt CO'N Daunt **KIA**)

205 Squadron was bombing the villages of
Brancourt and Beaurevoir on this day.

**   DH9   206Sqn**
** AA fire(/2Lt AG Squire **WIA**)

E4376   Sopwith Camel   209Sqn
**LowP left 12-30pm seen ovCAMBRAI 1-15pm
MIA(Capt EB Drake **KIA**) [?combat sSAILLY Ltn P
Bäumer Ja2]

D3422   Sopwith Camel   210Sqn
+* combat with 15 Fokker DVIIs[+des+ooc]
WIJNENDAELE WOOD ~8am OK(Lt A Buchanan)
last of 7 claims

D9664   Sopwith Camel   210Sqn
** diving on 15EA ZARREN-WIJNENDAELE WOOD
8am **MIA**(2Lt JF Stafford US. **KIA**)

D482   DH9   211Sqn
**B dhAA YPRES-ROULERS ftl WoL cr
Sh28NW.B.21.D.55. (2Lt JL McAdam OK/2Lt TW
Kelly **KIA**) left 7am

D565   DH9   211Sqn
**B COURTRAI running combat with EA shot down in
flames YPRES-COURTRAI **MIA**(Lt W Henley-Mooney
USAS. **WIA POW**/2Lt VAM Fair MC **KIA**) left
11-30am

D3093   DH9   211Sqn
**B COURTRAI combat with 40-50EA YPRES-
CAMBRAI 12pm? seen with smoking fuselage but down
in control **MIA**(Lt AG White **KIA**/2Lt JB Blundell **KIA**)
left 11-30am

D5714   DH9   211Sqn
*B YPRES-COURTRAI AA? shot up after bombing ftl
cr OK(2Lt VGH Phillips/2Lt AF Taylor)

D7338   DH9   211Sqn
**B ROULERS combat ST POL-SUR-MER shot up
controls dam ftl nr a'dr 7am cr o't OK(2Lt JM Payne/
2Lt WG Gadd)

B7677   DH9   218Sqn
** combat with Fokker DVII[+sh down in flames]
ovCORTEMARCK 9-40am OK(1Lt FP Mulcahy
USMCR/Cpl TL McCullough USMCR)

This was the first US Marine air crew to shoot
down an enemy aircraft.

D3272   DH9   218Sqn
*?combat with EAs LICHTERVELDE seen dive with
5EAs on tail **MIA**(2Lt JC Pritchard **KIA**/2Lt AE Smith
KIA)

E8883   DH9   218Sqn
*B THOUROUT ftl Eol~12pm **MIA**(Lt HP Brummell
POW/Sgt RS Joysey **POW**)

30th September

Fighting through the night the IX Corps captured
the whole of the tunnel defence system as well as
Le Tronquoy. This key achievement was exploited
in the morning and the various elements of the
Allied assault began to link up. Some groups were
two miles east of the canal by nightfall, and further
north, stiff resistance had been overcome at
Vendhuile, near Le Catelet, so that it was abandoned. The poor weather continued for another
day, limiting the air co-operation possible. The
American troops who had exceeded the advance on
the first day were still not found.

E121   RE8   9Sqn
**CAP ground fire shot through 4-15pm dam OK(Capt
JE Croden/2Lt L Eastwood)

C2442   RE8   12Sqn
CAP flames EoL **MIA(2Lt TH Jacques **KIA**/Lt FN
Billington **KIA**) left 4-40pm [RE8 claim combat
CREVECOEUR 5pm Ltn H Henkel Ja37]

**   Bristol F2b   48Sqn**
** mg fire(2Lt WS Rycroft **WIA**/2Lt HC Wood **WIA**)
name Ryecroft?

October 1918

1st October
PROGRESS ON ALL FRONTS

The weather improved on the 1st and the assault between Cambrai and St Quentin was intensified and widened. Air co-operation with the ground forces and the artillery was comprehensive and undoubtedly helped progress. There were also several large dogfights. St Quentin was finally abandoned to the French and ANZAC and British troops took Rumilly south of Cambrai, and the Canadians Blicourt to the north. The heart of the German line was crumbling and in retreat, and with the loss of the Hindenburg Line, Germany's defeat could be only weeks away. In contrast, it became increasingly apparent that their front along the Meuse from Verdun to Mezières was to be their last key battleground, for this now provided their flank for a retreat back into Germany. To be defeated here would make for unacceptable disaster. This was why fighting was so intense in the south and the defence of Flanders, drained of fighting capability, so weak. The Allied armies were overwhelming what was left of the German war machine, but their strategy of strangling its supply had also worked.

By the evening of the 1st of October, the line in Flanders ran from Dixmude to Staden and to the left bank of the Lys at Comines. The advance had never been easy due to the lack of good roads and other problems they had encountered, but it had been enormous for all that. It was recognised, however, that it was time to call a temporary halt whilst communications were put in order and preparations for a final push were finalised. The battle would be resumed again on the 14th of October.

The final progress preceding the decision to halt had been substantial and the air activity had been higher than of late because the weather had improved. Word came that some Belgian and French divisions had exhausted their supplies of food, so ration drops were organised. Nos. 82 and 218 Squadrons helped in this work and a staggering total of thirteen tons of food had been dropped by shortly before the following midday. It was clear that there were increased numbers of enemy fighters operating in Flanders, but they made only limited impression on the low bombing and strafing attacks of the RAF. More of their energies were directed at defending the railway centres, and 108 Squadron suffered a particularly devastating attack over Thielt. As the Allied bombing offensive gained ever more importance and momentum in the final weeks of fighting, losses were to be exceedingly high. The day-bomber squadrons of both the RAF and the Independent Force were admired and pitied for the casualties they were sustaining, and the deficiencies of the DH9 remained one of the root causes of their problems.

The German Air Force concentrated increasingly on containing the bombing offensive and was mounting some of its most spirited and bravely fought battles as a result. Nevertheless, its effectiveness was being restricted as much by its own dwindling supplies and lack of operational intelligence as by anything else. It was being forced to be increasingly selective against opposition with ultimately overwhelming strength and reserves. Its own army, although apparently broken, had surprising fight in it still, as the Allies would come to know in the next month. Its forces had suffered a catastrophe, however, from which they had no chance of recovery — the Official History records that in the fighting since the middle of July the German Army had lost nearly 4,000 guns, 25,000 machine-guns, and a quarter of a million of its troops had been taken prisoner. From Lille to Cambrai, and down to the Argonne in the south, it was being driven back into its homeland.

B8427 SE5a 1Sqn
**OP combat with HA? seen ovAULNOYE 4-55pm MIA(Lt W Joffe DSO KIA) [?SE5a claim combat FERME DE PAVILLON? 5-55pm Oblt O Schmidt Ja5]

C2564 RE8 4Sqn
**CAP AA ovSh28 T.29.b. mg engine seized ftl dam OK(TLt HT Townsend/T2Lt RW Lane) left 12-20pm XV Corps area

C2698 RE8 5Sqn
**CP dh by 18-lb shell! neSAILLY 6-55am ftl wr OK(2Lt J Town DFC/Lt AC Pollard)

F6046 RE8 5Sqn
**AP combat with EA shot down in flames cr Sh51C E.29 destr(2Lt EA Harrison KIA/2Lt A Johnson WIA) left 5-05pm

H7267 RE8 7Sqn
**CAP combat with EA DADIZEELE engine hit ftl ldg ok OK(2Lt CS Bolsby/2Lt AM McIntyre) left 5-55pm

E2250 Bristol F2b 10Sqn
**Phot combat with 16 Fokker DVIIs dam(Lt AW Bennett WIA/2Lt GHE Kime MM WIA)

E2366 Bristol F2b 11Sqn
**Rec LE CATEAU-CAMBRAI AA shot up dam OK(Sgt A Cridlan/2Lt W Connor) left 7am, returned 9-25am

B3406   RE8   13Sqn
PhotP left 10-20am **MIA(2Lt JS King **KIA**/2Lt HW
Wynn **KIA**)

D4898   RE8   13Sqn
P left 5pm **MIA(2Lt WG McCaig **KIA**/2Lt MJ
Sheehan **KIA**)

D5236   Sopwith Dolphin   19Sqn
+* combat with PfalzDIII[+ooc] eCAMBRAI 8-50am
OK(Capt RA De L'Haye) last of 9 claims

E4659   Sopwith Dolphin   19Sqn
OP left 8-05am ftl dam ldg(2Lt DP Laird **WIA)

E5657   SE5a   32Sqn
**OP CAMBRAI shot up dam OK(Lt C Wilderspin)

F1966   Sopwith Camel   46Sqn
**OP combat shot up ftl Sh62C R.28.D 5-45pm OK(Lt
BS Smallman) to Fourth Army area

E2265   Bristol F2b   48Sqn
OP MENIN combat with HA ovTHIELT **MIA(Capt
W Buckingham **POW**/Lt T Beck **POW DoW**) left
4-15pm

E2531   Bristol F2b   48Sqn
**OP MENIN combat with EA shot up dam OK(Lt EC
Shurley Can./Sgt RLG White) left 11am, returned
12-45pm

C2325   RE8   52Sqn
 **Phot combat with EA shot down in flames 10-30am(Lt
GS Day **KIA**/2Lt FS Occomore DFC **KIA**) shot down
Sh51b Q.20.C7

C2549   RE8   53Sqn
**CAP mg shot up 8-20am ftl Sh28M 34.d.5.5. dam
OK(Lt GC Brown/2Lt LF Raby)

F6123   Sopwith Camel   54Sqn
**SpB left 6-30am AA fuel tank hit dam OK(2Lt HR
Abey)

D9269   DH4   57Sqn
B combat with HA neBEAUVOIS **MIA(2Lt AH
Mills-Adams **KIA**/Lt P Sherek **KIA**) left 7am, combat
after bombing going west ?combat nwST QUENTIN
10-15am Vzfw K Bohnenkamp Ja22]

F5451.2 SE5a   64Sqn
**OP AA? ftl shell holes 5pm Sh51B U.56 dam OK(2Lt
WG Graham)

E1272   SE5a   74Sqn
OP left 9-30am **MIA(2Lt RJ Hagenbush USAS.
POW)

F5464   SE5a   74Sqn
OP left 1-30pm **MIA(Lt AM Sanderson **KIA**)
[?combat MENIN 2-20pm SE5a claim Ltn C Degelow
Ja40]

E4590   Sopwith Dolphin   79Sqn
**OP left 12pm AA ftl eYPRES 200yd WoL OK(Lt W
Gilbert)

F6026   Sopwith Camel   80Sqn
OP left 2pm BELLICOURT **MIA(2Lt RE Thompson
KIA)

          A.W.FK8   82Sqn
** mg fire(2Lt CR McInnes **WIA**/Capt WE Joseph
WIA?)

D6961   SE5a   85Sqn
**OP left 3-45pm BELLINGHAM-WIENCOURT AA
ftl OK(Capt EF Nichol)

F5479   SE5a   84Sqn
OP left 3-15pm seen BELLICOURT **MIA but
OK(2Lt CW Kerr **WIA**)

D7324   DH9   103Sqn
Rec combat HAZEBROUCK ftl(Capt JA Sparks **inj/
Lt JB Russell DFC **inj**) left 6am

D1055   DH9   107Sqn
**P combat HAM 5-55pm fuel tank shot up engine seized
ftl OK(2Lt LE Gosden/2Lt WA Smith)

The four day-bomber squadrons of IX Brigade,
Nos. 27, 49, 98, and 107, mounted two attacks on
rail centres which were most notable for the very
poor light they threw on the DH9 aircraft which
were mostly used. The two morning raids were to
Aulnoye junction, and of the twenty DH9s which
left, seven turned back with engine problems. The
second raid there saw fifteen out of twenty-nine
turn back, and another crew return due to illness.
The remaining machines pressed on with their
SE5a escorts only to be heavily attacked and forced
to drop their bombs short of the target and retreat.
A third raid in the afternoon was more successful,
targets in Aulnoye junction, including an ammunition train, being blown up. 207 Squadron Handley
Pages returned there again in the evening, and
amongst bombs dropped was a single 1,650-lber.

D5835   DH9   108Sqn
**B THIELT combat with 33 Fokker DVIIs
INGELMUNSTER **MIA**(Lt F Hopkins **KIA**/Lt JW
Firth **KIA**) left 3-24pm [?DH9 claim combat
HOUTHULST 5-20pm Flm E Blaas MFJaIII][DH9
claims combat seROULERS 5-25pm Ltn R Poss & Flm
G Hubrich MFJaIV]

D5847   DH9   108Sqn
**B seen in combat with 33 Fokker DVIIs
ovINGELMUNSTER **MIA**(Lt AM Matheson **POW**/
2Lt FR Everleigh **POW**) left 3-24pm THIELT [?DH9
claim combat Ltn K Plauth Ja51]

D7342   DH9   108Sqn
**B THIELT combat with 33 Fokker DVIIs
ovINGELMUNSTER seen in control nrROULERS
MIA(Lt GA Featherstone **KIA**/2Lt F Owen **KIA**) left
3-24pm [DH9 claim combat sHOUTHULST 5-25pm
Vzfw H Goerth MFJaIII]

F5847   DH9   108Sqn
** combat with EA "SPAD" MIA but returned(2Lt CS

Whellock **WIA**/2Lt JW White **WIA**) DROs give this a'c MIA, this crew in this a'c?

D1883   Sopwith Camel   210Sqn
** combat with 12EAs ovHOUTHULST FOREST 5-50pm cr **MIA**(Maj RDG Sibley **KIA**) [?combat HOUTHULST 5-30pm FlgM E Blaas MFJaIII][Camel claim combat sHANDZAEME 5-50pm Vzfw H Goerth MFJaIII]

E4421   Sopwith Camel   210Sqn
** combat with 12-15 Fokker DVIIs[+des] ovHOUTHULST FOREST 9-55am shot up dam OK(2Lt CW Payton)

F3235   Sopwith Camel   210Sqn
** combat with 11EAs ovROULERS 5-10pm **MIA**(2Lt RW Johnson **KIA**)

D3331   Sopwith Camel   213Sqn
**OOAB shot up ftl dam OK(2Lt RA Pearce)

D8189   Sopwith Camel   213Sqn
**LowB combat with Fokker DVII[+ooc] mg? shot up ftl cr HOUTHULST WOOD OK(Lt WE Gray) left 1pm, unsalvable

D8219   Sopwith Camel   213Sqn
**OOAB combat with EA shot up ftl dam OK(Capt JR Swanston)

F3110   Sopwith Camel   213Sqn
**OOAB shot up ftl PETITE SYNTHE OK(2Lt WH Herd)

D-1   DH-4   218Sqn
**B LICHTERVELDE Rlwy Yards OK(Capt RS Lytle USMC/Sgt A Wiman USMC)

This was the first Marine Aviation operation with its own aircraft. Its machine serial D-1 was operating with 218 Sqaudron.

C2414   RE8   HQ Communication Flt
SpP engine failed shot down in flames cr 1000yd EoL nCAMBRAI **MIA(Lt B Pepper **KIA**/Maj B Kirkpatrick **KIA**) SpP with GHQ, left 7-30am

F6185   Sopwith Camel   US 148th Pursuit Sqn
B left 8-25am last seen ovSERANVILLERS shot down by ground fire? EoL **MIA(1Lt WR Avery **POW**) taken prisoner seCAMBRAI, made several attempts to escape, eventually reaching WoL 11.11.18

2nd October

D8159   Sopwith Camel   4Sqn AFC
+* attacked KB[+des] CAPINGHEM-WEZ MACQ 6-15am OK(Capt HG Watson DFC NZ.) last of 14 claims

F7410   A.W.FK8   10Sqn
**CAP mg 11am ftl 28 I.12.c OK(Capt LH Short MC/ Lt FC Peacock MC) shaken

E5779   SE5a   41Sqn
OP combat WoL 10-45pm shot down cr Sh78N 14.a.5.0.(Lt WA Morris **DoW)

C2822   RE8   42Sqn
** **MIA**(Lt R Hall **POW**/2Lt FL Strang-Ward **POW**)

F1977   Sopwith Camel   46Sqn
OP combat with EA going down ok sST QUENTIN 15000' **MIA(2Lt JK Shook **POW**) left 9am Fourth Army area, going down ooc? sCAMBRAI [?combat CROIX-FONSOMME(nrBUSIGNY) 12pm UOff B Bartels Ja44]

DH9   49Sqn
** combat(2Lt BG Pool **WIA**/)

C2475   RE8   52Sqn
Shoot hit by British shell 11-20am down in flames cr Sh51B J.34(Lt WH Buckeridge **KIA/2Lt AG Malcolm **KIA**)

C2742   RE8   53Sqn
CAP left 7-50am **MIA(Lt JB Pierce **KIA**/2Lt MW Wakeman **KIA**) [?RE8 claim GHELUVELT combat Ltn K Plauth Ja51]

F5926   Sopwith Camel   54Sqn
SpB ch by 2 Fokker DVIIs swTHUN 11-30am cr **MIA(2Lt WJ Densham **KIA**) [?combat CAMBRAI 11-30am Ltn R Fr vBarnekow Ja1][?Camel claim combat CAMBRAI 11-25am Ritt K vDöring Ja1]

A8090   DH4   57Sqn
B combat with EA 8-25am shot down in flames nr objective SANTZOI, seCAMBRAI **MIA(2Lt FHA Weale **KIA**/2Lt E Preece **KIA**)

DH4   57Sqn
** combat(/Lt MG Robson MC **WIA**)

F7597   DH4   57Sqn
B seen ok seCAMBRAI 8-30am **MIA(Lt JWMcN Ramsay US. **KIA**/Sgt JF Turner **KIA**)

C1874.W   SE5a   64Sqn
**OP mg fire fuel tank shot up ftl Sh57B A2 OK(Lt JB Forrester)shelled

E1531   Sopwith Camel   65Sqn
** combat(Capt NE Chandler **WIA**)

F5478   SE5a   74Sqn
OP dhAA VLAMERTINGHE 1-40pm cr ldg dam(Lt GR Hicks **WIA)

F5921   Sopwith Camel   80Sqn
OP left 12pm mg fire ftl **MIA(2Lt JE Jennings **POW**)

D1080   DH9   108Sqn
B seen wMENIN 3000' last seen flying West above clouds, lost? **MIA(2Lt ATW Boswell **KIA**/2Lt RP Gundill **KIA**) left 12-07pm MENIN [?possible DH9 claim combat STADEN Ltn J Jacobs Ja7]

D9638.II Sopwith Camel   203Sqn
OP combat many Fokker DVIIs[+shot down] neCAMBRAI then cr ldg MORENCHIES nr CAMBRAI 8-50am, a'c shelled(2Lt HW Skinner **WIA) to hospital

D9658   Sopwith Camel   210Sqn
** shot down mg fire COURTRAI flames 10am **MIA**(Lt

CW Payton **KIA**) after silencing AA position

D568   DH9   211Sqn
**B AA ovMENIN dam cr OK(2Lt PM Keary/2Lt RM Alston)

F3121   Sopwith Camel   213Sqn
**Rec left 5-30am shot up ftl 6-50am OK(Capt ML Cooper) [?combat ROULERS Camel claim Ltn C Degelow Ja40]

F3951   Sopwith Camel   213Sqn
B spun on train being bombed 200′ ground fire? cr 8-10am 1m neGITSBERG **MIA(Capt ML Cooper DFC **KIA**)

D2922   DH9   218Sqn
** shot up(Lt FG Burden **WIA**)

E8465   DH9A   218Sqn
First US Marine Aviation Force (their Serial: E-1)
*FoodDrop OK(Capt RS Lytle USMC/Sgt A Wiman USMC) 2-3Oct

This food drop to French and Belgian troops involved around eighty aircraft and was done under heavy fire.

E8958   DH9   218Sqn
FoodDrop STADENBERG down EoL **MIA(Capt WF Cleghorn DFC **KIA**/Lt FH Stringer DFC **POW**) left am

3rd October

By the 3rd of October the Fourth Army had developed their initial penetrations of a few days earlier into a six-mile-wide opening in the Beaurevoir Line, namely the third and last major support system of Hindenburg Line. Desperate and ceaseless fighting had brought the army to the verge of a very great victory. Within two days, Beaurevoir itself would fall, along with the German stronghold of Montbrehain.

           A.W.FK8   2Sqn
** combat(/2Lt AP Quaife **WIA**)

F7458   A.W.FK8   2Sqn
LP combat with 5EA seBERCLAU 12-45pm spin down in flames wr(Capt AB Clark MC **KIA/2Lt WMR Hey **WIA**)

E224   RE8   3Sqn AFC
AP shell hit **MIA(Lt J Gould-Taylor **KIA**/Lt BG Thomson **KIA**) left 6-05am to bomb BEAUREVOIR MILL, buried nrESTRÉES

           RE8   4Sqn
** combat(/2Lt AE Garrison MC **WIA**)

D4905   RE8   5Sqn
AP left 6-15am **MIA(Lt WM Difford **KIA**/2Lt EM Patterson **WIA POW**?) to Corps front

F5888   RE8   6Sqn
**AP BEAUREVOIR AA dam returned a'dr OK(2Lt JM McChlery/2Lt JV Gardenner) left 7-15am

           RE8   7Sqn
** combat(/Lt JMG Bell MC **WIA**)

F6204   RE8   12Sqn
**NF AA over Fourth Army area shot through dam OK(Lt Townsend/Lt Stannard) left 10-05am Sixth Army area

D3769   Sopwith Dolphin   19Sqn
OP left 8-30am **MIA(2Lt ES Farrand **POW**)

E1268   SE5a   24Sqn
** left 7-40am **MIA**(Lt E Carpenter **KIA**) [?combat SEBONCOURT 9am Vzfw K Ungewitter Ja24]

F5517   SE5a   24Sqn
GndTarg dhAA 4000′ seen cr Sh62B B.2.a.(Lt WC Sterling **KIA) left 9-25am

A8052   DH4   25Sqn
Rec MAUBEUGE **MIA(Sgt FP Clarke **KIA**/Lt EWAG Middlecote **KIA**) left 3-15pm

F3475   A.W.FK8   35Sqn
P AA wing off cr LE CATELET at Sh62B A.23wr 1pm **MIA(Lt JM Brown US. DFC **KIA**/2Lt A Gilchrist **KIA**)

F7383   A.W.FK8   35Sqn
P mg GILLEMONT FARM shot down cr(Lt CS Booker **DoW/2Lt R Whitfield OK) left 1pm

E2523   Bristol F2b   48Sqn
OP combat with EAs INGELMUNSTER 6-30pm **MIA(2Lt JB Cowan **KIA**?/Lt LN Jones **KIA**) seen nrINGELMUNSTER 5-30pm

E636   DH9   49Sqn
**B left 11-45am VALENCIENNES AA dam OK(2Lt LWD Peacock/Sgt R Read) returned a'dr 2-50pm

C2534   RE8   53Sqn
**NF combat with EA 6-40am shot up dam ftl Sh28.K.7.d.3. OK(2Lt BR Ronald/2Lt H Walpole)

           Sopwith Camel   73Sqn
** combat(2Lt G Roberts **WIA**)

           Sopwith Dolphin   79Sqn
** combat(2Lt HMS Parsons US. **WIA**)

E2533   Bristol F2b   88Sqn
+* combat with Fokker DVII[+des] MEURCHIN 5-30pm OK(Capt EC Johnston Aust./Lt IWF Agabeq) last of 20 victories for Johnston

E5758   SE5a   92Sqn
OP left 7-30am combat with EA sPROYART ftl dam(Lt A Scott **WIA)

           KB 10KB   Coy
** gased(Lt WS Eastaugh **WIA**)

E4403   Sopwith Camel   201Sqn
OP combat with EA 11-20am fuel tank shot up ftl shell hole Sh57C H.22.d.(2Lt AH Griffiths **WIA)

D6626   Sopwith Camel   204Sqn
** dive through cloud led to air collision with Camel D8188 ovNIEUPORT 12000′ cr swRAMSCAPELLE

MIA(Capt CRR Hickey DFC **KIA**)

D8188   Sopwith Camel   204Sqn
** air collision with Camel D6626 ovNIEUPORT 12000'
cr swRAMSCAPELLE **MIA**(2Lt SE Matthey **KIA**)

D8223   Sopwith Camel   204Sqn
** shot up ftl(Lt WJP Jenner **WIA**)

**   DH9   211Sqn**
** combat(/2Lt DJ Avery **WIA**)

F1024   DH9A   205Sqn
** combat with EA shot up(/Sgt WJH Middleton **DoW**
4.10.18)

F1159   DH9   206Sqn
**B seen ok EoL, seen WoL nrDEULEMONT 4-15pm
MIA(Sgt R Walker **WIA POW**/Cpl AF Bailey **KIA**?) left
3-42pm [?DH9 claim Ltn A Burkard Ja29][?combat
nROULERS VzfM A Zenses MFJaII]

F6249   Sopwith Camel   US 17th Pursuit Sqn
**B CAUDRY seen near A.L.G. 9-30am lost formation
after dropping bombs & ftl BOREST, nrSENLIS MIA
but OK(2Lt AG White) returned to Sqn 4.10.18

**   Bristol F2b   N Flt**
** combat(2Lt TC Sutcliffe **WIA**/2Lt NJ Dalgleish
WIA)

4th October

E240   RE8   7Sqn
**NF mg 5-30pm dam ftl 28J 35.c OK(Lt GV Howard/
2Lt LF Williamson)

A8057   DH4   25Sqn
Rec left 6-35am MAUBEUGE **MIA(Lt L Young
KIA?/Sgt HE Whitehead **POW**?)

D7347   DH9   27Sqn
**B AA MOEUVRES engine seized ftl wr OK(Lt E
Bryant/2Lt WJ Diment) left 6-45am

C8406   A.W.FK8   35Sqn
**P mg bad dam ftl 3-25pm OK(Capt MGW Stewart
DFC/2Lt AE Sherwood) left 1pm CAMBRAI

**   A.W.FK8   35Sqn**
** mg fire(/2Lt LA Higgs **DoW**)

F5494   SE5a   41Sqn
**OP combat with HA 6pm mg sump hit ftl Sh28B
22.c(Capt E Gribbin **WIA**)slight?

D6519   Sopwith Camel 46Sqn
**OP air collision with Camel H771 ST QUENTIN
MIA(Maj AH O'Hara-Wood **KIA**) left 10-50am,
Squadron Commander

H771   Sopwith Camel 46Sqn
**OP ST QUENTIN air collision with Camel D6519
MIA(2Lt LL Saunders **KIA**) left 10-50am

E2498   Bristol F2b   48Sqn
**OP combat with EAs INGELMUNSTER 6-30pm
MIA(Lt JA Sykes **KIA**/Sgt S Kitchen **KIA**?)

F1988   Sopwith Camel 54Sqn
**OP left 9-45am combat with EA eTILLOY ftl a'c
abandoned OK(2Lt HJ Fuller)

E4100.E   SE5a   64Sqn
**OP AA 9-25pm ftl cr shell holes o't Sh51B H.28.
OK(Capt D Lloyd-Evans) several victories in this a'c

E1596   Sopwith Camel 65Sqn
**OP seen in flames neMENIN nrLENDELSEDGE
11000' 5-50pm **MIA**(2Lt SJ Hill **KIA**)

F1990   Sopwith Camel 80Sqn
**OP BEAUREVOIR-REMANCOURT cr ESNES EoL
MIA(Lt JW Andrews **KIA**) left 9am [?this or F5954
combat CAMBRAI 11-30am Lt R Fr vBarnekow Ja1]

F5954   Sopwith Camel 80Sqn
**OP BEAUREVOIR-REMANCOURT folded cr EoL
MIA(2Lt TW Whitman US. **KIA**) left 9am, down with
crumpled wing ovLIVERGES

D6985   SE5a   85Sqn
** seen with patrol ovBUSIGNY 12pm **MIA**(2Lt FL
LeLievre **KIA**)

E3922   SE5a   85Sqn
P seen with formation ovBUSIGNY 12pm **MIA(Lt JW
Warner **KIA**) [?combat MONTBREHAIN Ltn P Bäumer
Ja2][?combat JONCOURT Ltn G Bassenge Ja2]

F5520   SE5a   85Sqn
P seen with formation ovBUSIGNY 12pm **MIA(Lt
CW Davison **KIA**) [?combat LE CATELET Vzfw A
Hübner Ja36][?this a'c or E3992 in combat JONCOURT
Ltn G Bassenge Ja2]

E2474   Bristol F2b   88Sqn
+* combat with Fokker DVII[+des] & HalbC[+des] 1m
seLILLE 5-45pm OK(Lt JP Findlay SA./2Lt RE Hasell)
Findlay claimed 5EAs

D3358   Sopwith Camel 204Sqn
**LowB AA hit LICHTERVELDE bad dam ftl OK(Lt
HJ Gemmel)

D9648   Sopwith Camel 204Sqn
**LowB heavy mg fire LICHTERVELDE dam ftl
OK(Lt JR Robinson)

D3341   Sopwith Camel 213Sqn
** left 8-20am combat with 20HAs nwROULERS flames
MIA(Lt WG Upton **KIA**) [?combat nwROULERS Ltn
C Degelow Ja40]

D8177   Sopwith Camel 213Sqn
+* combat with Fokker DVIIs[+flames++des]
RUMBEKE 9-30am OK(Capt CP Brown) last of 14
claims

D9601   Sopwith Camel 213Sqn
** seen ROULERS 4pm **MIA**(2Lt KG Ibison **KIA**)

F3965   Sopwith Camel 213Sqn
*HOP left 2-35pm dhAA 4-24pm but OK(Lt AF Chick)

E8465   DH9A   218Sqn
from First Marine Aviation Force (US), their Serial: E-1

**B THOUROUT combat with EAs[+] OK(1Lt R Talbot USMC/Cpl RG Robinson)

This was the first victory in combat for the FMAF.

E8881   DH9   218Sqn
*B LICHTERVELDE combat with 7EAs ovCORTEMARCK dam(Lt HD McLaren DFC OK/Sgt G Barlow **WIA**)

5th October

F6012   RE8   4Sqn
**FlRec combat 1-20pm ftl Sh28 S.11.68 dam OK(2Lt S Lee/Lt S Leslie)

              RE8   7Sqn
** combat(Lt LH Brown **WIA**/2Lt JG Clayton **WIA**)

              A.W.FK8   10Sqn
** combat(/2Lt P Hinde **WIA**)

C3829   Sopwith Dolphin   19Sqn
+* combat with Fokker DVII[+flames] eCAMBRAI 8-05am OK(Capt FM McQuistan) last of 10 victories, most in this a'c

F859   SE5a   41Sqn
LP combat with 2Str? wMENIN Sh28Q 18.c at 7-35am then seen ldg **MIA(2Lt CVA Bucknall **POW**)

E5708   SE5a   56Sqn
EscB seen seCAMBRAI 9000' 1-30pm **MIA(Lt JA Pouchot DCM **KIA**)

H7253   SE5a   56Sqn
SpM seen diving on KB eBOHAIN 1-05pm **MIA(Lt IW Awde **WIA POW**) left 12-30pm

D6922   SE5a   74Sqn
LP left 8-35am seen 3m seROULERS 9-30am **MIA(Lt FE Bond **POW**)

C3702   A.W.FK8   82Sqn
FlRec combat with HA shot down GHELUVELT(2Lt LT Wilson **WIA/2Lt A Hogg **WIA**) shot down Sh28J 23.c

F5485   SE5a   85Sqn
** combat(Capt EF Nichol **WIA**?)

E8439   DH9A   110Sqn (I.F.)
B KAISERSLAUTERN-PIRMASENS heavy combats with EAs & poor weather **MIA(2Lt DP Davies **POW**/ 2Lt HMD Speagell **POW**)

F980   DH9A   110Sqn (I.F.)
B KAISERSLAUTERN-PIRMASENS heavy combats with EAs & poor weather **MIA(2Lt A Brandrick **POW**/ 2Lt HC Eyre **KIA**)

F1010   DH9A   110Sqn (I.F.)
B KAISERSLAUTERN-PIRMASENS heavy combat shot down(Capt AG Inglis **POW/2Lt WGL Bodley **POW**) [?DH9A claim combat HEIMBACH Ltn G Weiner Ja3]

The October bombing programme for the Independent Force was to be even more disrupted by bad weather than in the previous month. Fog and mist was very prevalent, particularly affecting night work. 110 Squadron suffered the loss of another three machines on the above raid. Their objective had been factories at Koln but concern grew about the weather and they were so heavily attacked that they were forced to bomb Pirmasens and Kaiserslautern instead. Four of the enemy were claimed shot down as well. On the 5th of October the 85th Wing of the Independent Force was formed, taking over Nos. 45 and 110 Squadrons.

B7678   DH9   206Sqn
B left 7-40am **MIA(2Lt HL Prime **POW DoW**/2Lt C Hancock **POW**) Ja29 [?"DH9a" MARKE 8-30am Ltn A Burkard Ja29][?"DH9" claim combat AELBEKE 8-30am UntOff S Westphal Ja29]

C2193   DH9   206Sqn
B AA 9-35am radiator hit ftl cr Sh28I 11.d (Sgt G Packman **inj/2Lt JW Kennedy OK)

D560   DH9   206Sqn
B combat with EA shot down nrAELBEKE **MIA(1Lt CT Knight USAS. **POW**/2Lt JH Perring **POW**) left 7-45am [?combat AELBEKE 8-30am Oblt H Auffahrt Ja29]

D1718   DH9   206Sqn
**B AA controls shot away ftl cr shell holes nrYPRES 9am OK(Capt RNG Atkinson MC DFC/2Lt JS Blanford)

C1168   DH9   211Sqn
** combat(Lt JL McAdam **WIA**/Sgt.Mech H Lindsay **WIA**)

E8872   DH9   211Sqn
B combat with EA EoL shot up 10am on return ftl just WoL nrROULERS(2Lt VGH Phillips **WIA/2Lt AF Taylor **WIA**) [?DH9 claim combat GHENT Ltn C Degelow Ja40]

F5967.M Sopwith Camel   US 17th Pursuit Sqn
OP air collision with Camel F6194 ovLIGNY ooc cr **MIA(Lt GD Wicks **KIA**) date as per RAF Casualty Report & American Battle Monuments Com. Other date of 6.10.18 often given is probably error

F6194   Sopwith Camel   US 17th Pursuit Sqn
P air collision F5967 ovLIGNY 4-50pm ooc cr Sh57B I.31.d. **MIA(1Lt HG Shoemaker **KIA**) date via RAF Casualty Report: see Camel F5967

6th October

From the 6th of October until the 11th of November German time reverted to being one hour ahead of British time (all times given are British time).

              A.W.FK8   2Sqn
** combat(2Lt AG Johnston **WIA**/2Lt JL Irving **WIA**)

RE8   **7Sqn**
** combat(/2Lt CR Palmer **WIA**)

F5979   RE8   12Sqn
**NF mg controls shot up dam returned a'dr OK(Lt Nelson/Lt Kelly) left 10-30am Sixth Army area

Bristol F2b   20Sqn
** combat(/Capt H Dinwoodie MC **WIA**)

D4687   RE8   59Sqn
NF left 8-30pm **MIA(Lt R Calrow **POW**/2Lt WTS Cairns **POW**)

F2177   Sopwith Camel   80Sqn
OP left 3-45pm **MIA(2Lt OV Judkins **POW**)

E8934   DH9   108Sqn
Rec:solo left 3-30pm **MIA(2Lt W Freer **KIA**/2Lt JW Neil **KIA**)

D9581   Sopwith Camel   203Sqn
**OP mg AA? MONCHY 9am ftl trenches nrFOSSE FARM dam OK(2Lt PB Calder)

7th October

B8392.1 **SE5a**   **2Sqn AFC**
OP own bomb fragments damaged fuel tank NOYELLES 6-40am ftl(Lt AL Long **inj)

A.W.FK8   10Sqn
** combat(2Lt CN Glidewell **WIA**/)

E2591   Bristol F2b   11Sqn
Rec left 9-50am CAMBRAI **MIA(Sgt AL Cridlan **KIA**/Sgt GE Fuller **KIA**)[?combat AVESNES 11-10am Ltn R Fr vBarnekow Ja1]

E1537   Sopwith Camel   65Sqn
OP seen 5-15pm COURTRAI-ROULERS dam ldg **MIA(2Lt B Lockey **INT**)

H7001   Sopwith Camel   65Sqn
OP seen eYPRES going west 11-30am **MIA(2Lt LSR Jones **KIA**)

E7176   Sopwith Camel   70Sqn
BOP left 8am seen nrLICHTERVELDE **MIA(2Lt HD Lackey **KIA**) [?Camel claim combat GHENT 10-30am Ltn C Degelow Ja40][?Camel claim combat GHENT Ltn W Rosenstein Ja40]

DH9   211Sqn
** combat(/2Lt HB Shaw **WIA**)

8th October
THE SECOND BATTLE
OF LE CATEAU

The British Third and Fourth Armies, with the French First Army on their right, launched their next major attack on the 8th of October. This was on a seventeen-mile front south of Cambrai, and through a hard day's fighting, progress of a further four miles was made. Air co-operation was exten-

sive and played a vital part. Contact patrolling was particularly effective, and offensive patrols were flown at two or three squadron strength. Enemy air activity was relatively light, but fighting did claim some casualties. The weather was poor enough to wash out the intended raids of the IX Brigade day-bombers. With this advance, the German Army was decisively detached from the Hindenburg Line and their retreat for the next few days was extremely strained.

C2749   RE8   6Sqn
**CP SERAIN-PREMONT AA dam returned a'dr OK(Capt Munden/Lt Clark) left 8-20am

C2792   RE8   6Sqn
**CP left 3-50pm mg TUMULUS engine failed ftl OK(Lt Mulvey/Lt King)

F5904   RE8   6Sqn
CP mg wings off cr Sh62B M.I.d dam(2Lt JM McChlery **KIA/Lt Gardenner **DoW** 1.9.18) left 7am

F6013   RE8   6Sqn
CP SERAIN-BOHAIN **MIA(Capt W Walker DFC **KIA**/Lt MA Waterer **DoW** 10.10.18) left 11-10am, DoW 11.10?

C2894   RE8   7Sqn
Phot combat with Pfalz[+] then shot down ftl cr Sh28 L.8 at 3-20pm wr(2Lt J Graham **WIA/Lt MA O'Callaghan **WIA**)

A.W.FK8   10Sqn
** combat(/2Lt FJ Walsh **WIA**)

E233   RE8   13Sqn
CAP left 10-40am dam(Capt RF Browne **WIA/2Lt EH Sansom OK)

F5896   RE8   13Sqn
CP mg ftl cr ldg ShF19 d.1.1(2Lt RE Britton **WIA/Lt JP Thomas OK) left 8-45am

D4944   RE8   15Sqn
**CAP AA ftl cr hit tree Sh57C N26.B.4 OK(Capt AR Cross/2Lt HV Alder)shaken

E2420   Bristol F2b   20Sqn
OP left 3-40pm combat with EA **MIA(Lt FW Ely **KIA**/2Lt JG McBride **KIA**) [?combat BRANCOURT 4-30pm OffSt F Altemeier Ja24]

F5508   SE5a   24Sqn
+* attacked KB[+des] sBUSIGNY 7-30am OK(Capt WH Longton) pilot scored several victories

C1133.2 **SE5a**   **29Sqn**
OP seen going north ovYPRES 2-40pm **MIA(Lt JP Murphy **POW**) [?possible claim combat PLOEGSTEERT WOOD 2-15pm? Ltn H-G Marwitz Ja30]

D3992   SE5a   40Sqn
BOP combat with HA? 2-50pm ftl n.m.l. wr(Lt WV Trubshawe **WIA) [?possible SE5a claim combat

sCAMBRAI, but 2pm Oblt A Gutkneckt Ja43]

F5545   SE5a   41Sqn
+* combat with DFWC[+des] LEDEGHEM 12-33pm
OK(Capt FO Soden) shared, claimed 27 victories

F5481   SE5a   56Sqn
**GndStrCOP ground mg shot up ftl bad ground 8-30am
dam OK(Lt DW Grinnell-Milne) left 6-30am Third
Army area

C9710   HP 0/400   58Sqn
**NB VALENCIENNES AA over target OK(2Lt FG
Prince/2Lt JS Rough/Sgt JL Isaacs) left 9-20pm, dropped
1,650-lb bomb onto trackway & sidings: first such by 58
Sqn

NIGHT BOMBING IN THE CLOSING WEEKS

2Lt FG Prince was to make a speciality of carrying
and dropping this single huge bomb. To illustrate
a typical night's bombing at this time, the details
of 58 Squadron raids were as follows: its Handley
Pages made two operations to Valenciennes, the
first involving six crews who had been delayed by
cloud until 9-20pm, but the last had got away by
9-50pm. The crew above was the last to leave. All
machines returned by 12-20am and then all but
Prince's crew made a second raid on Valenciennes,
leaving between 1-25am and 2-10am. The last
aircraft home landed at 4am. Both raids encountered troublesome searchlights over Douai, and
attracted heavy anti-aircraft fire over the target and
over Denain. Bombs were dropped from between
3,500 feet and 7,000 feet, all seen to fall on and
around the target, fifteen direct hits being claimed.
The weight of bombs dropped on this night was
over ten tons, and apart from the 1,650-lber,
amounted to one hundred and fifty-nine 112-lbers
and one hundred and fourteen 25-lb bombs.
Additionally, the crews fired off the phenomenal
quantity of 10,700 rounds of ammunition at searchlights, anti-aircraft batteries and, of course, the
target.

The programme of night bombing in support of
the Allied advances had been constantly curtailed
by the poor weather. In early October, as the
British Army prepared for the battles which would
finally break their enemy's resolve, bombing was
essential to maintain the crippling disruption of
Germany's war effort. Valenciennes and other
main junctions were typically hit whenever
conditions permitted, but after the 8th of October,
night flying was severely restricted for the remainder of the month. 58 Squadron, for instance, could
operate on only another four nights before
November. These long periods of washed-out

operations were doubtless intensely frustrating to
the crews, who were more keen than ever to be out
bombing. They sensed they were part of a coming
victory, which was at last promising an end to the
war. From their unique position, flying above the
conflict, they could see solid evidence that the
Allies were overwhelming the enemy. Its dis-
heartened and depleted armies were now in their
last defensive positions, and whatever the airmen
could contribute now might be decisive. The
general appearance of the front line, seen from their
aircraft, was no longer the continuous line of noise
and flashing artillery fire it had been all year,
indicating that at last a remarkable change was
occurring.

**   RE8   59Sqn**
** combat with EA mg(Lt GO Wood **WIA**/2Lt WJ
Carruthers **KIA**)

E229   RE8   59Sqn
SmokeScreen shot up WAMBAIX **MIA(2Lt JCG
Drummond **KIA**/2Lt P Chavasse **KIA**) WAMBEKE?
left 6am [?RE8 claim combat LOOS 6-50am Oblt O
Schmidt Ja5][?RE8 claim combat GHELUVELT Oblt F
Ritt vRöth Ja16]

F5887   RE8   59Sqn
**CP shell splinter ovBRISEUX WOOD when low dam
OK(Lt FE Robinson/Lt AL Wilmshurst) left 6am

H7264   RE8   59Sqn
**CAP mg dam ftl Sh57B M.18 OK(Lt WL Christian/
Lt WF Wilson) left 2-30pm

E6029   SE5a   60Sqn
** AA? BEAUVOIR ftl 15Sq a'dr OK(Capt A Beck)

**   Sopwith Camel   70Sqn**
** combat(Lt GWK Smith **WIA**)

D1856   Sopwith Camel   73Sqn
GndStr left 7-45am shot down **MIA(2Lt GDN Snyman
KIA) Ja51? [?combat Ltn K Plauth Ja51]

F6251   Sopwith Camel   80Sqn
**OP FRESNOY shot up controls dam ftl a'dr OK(2Lt
HR Messinger) left 7am

C1911   SE5a   84Sqn
** combat RumplerC[+destr] neMAMETZ 11-30am
then ground fire(Capt AW Beauchamp-Proctor SA. VC
DSO DFC MC **WIA**) his last of 54 victories, including
16 kite balloons.

Beauchamp-Proctor was subsequently awarded the
Victoria Cross for his repeatedly brave and
brilliant work in the air.

C1143   SE5a   85Sqn
+* attacked KB[+des] eMARETZ 1pm OK(Capt MC
McGregor NZ.) shared, pilot claimed 11 victories

C9291   SE5a   92Sqn
**OP combat with EA shot up sPROYART dam ftl

8Sq(Lt JO MacAndrew **WIA**) left 1-30pm

E8955   DH9   103Sqn
B left 11-42am AA ftl cr wr(Sgt J McKie **KIA/2Lt M Pitot **DoW**) inj in ldg?

E4378   Sopwith Camel   209Sqn
LP seen dive West ovABANCOURT with Fokker DVII on tail 2-30pm **MIA(2Lt F Cornwell **POW**) to CAMBRAI [?combat nREMAUCOURT? 3-40pm Ltn W Blume Ja9]

E4423   Sopwith Camel   209Sqn
LowP air collision with Camel H7278 cr wBOURLON E11. c.00 at 3pm(Capt DGA Allen **KIA) left 1pm

H7278   Sopwith Camel   209Sqn
LP left 1pm air collision with Camel E4423 wBOURLON 3pm(2Lt RGA Bingham **KIA)

D1868   Sopwith Camel   210Sqn
** combat with Fokker DVIIs[+shot down] seen going west 4m neROULERS 9-25am then shot down **MIA**(2Lt CF Pineau US. **POW**) shot down by Fokker DrI?

D3332   Sopwith Camel   210Sqn
+* combat with Fokker DVII[+flames] 4m neROULERS OK(Capt E Swale) last of 17 victory claims with 210Sqn

D3382   Sopwith Camel   210Sqn
** combat with EA ROULERS 9-20am **MIA**(2Lt RW Hopper **POW**) [?Camel claim combat YPRES Ltn C Degelow Ja40]

N6376   Sopwith Camel   213Sqn
**HOP combat with 8 Fokker DVII 9-30am spun down ftl ldg ok OK(2Lt EB Holden) [?Camel claim combat Ltn K Plauth Ja51]

F2141.L   Sopwith Camel   US 17th Pursuit Sqn
**P left 11-35am Third Army mg shot up dam returned 12-55pm OK(1Lt H Burdick) claimed 8 victories, many in this a'c

F6249   Sopwith Camel   US 17th Pursuit Sqn
B CAGNONCLES-NAVES Road shot up(2Lt EG White **WIA)to hospital

9th October

Canadian troops entered Cambrai overnight and from dawn the advance continued along the whole front. Most of the air activity was in low attacks on vast columns of retreating German troops, swarming towards Le Cateau. Near here however, on the River Selle, the Germans were preparing a defensive resistance. The weather was very poor in the next few days and prevented all but a few low attacks on the enemy here in support of the advance. Localised fighting gradually won sections of the river and by the 13th there were some Allied bridgeheads established.

There was more air fighting further north, where the Allies prepared to resume their offensive in Flanders in a few days time.

E7190   Sopwith Camel   4Sqn AFC
SpP combat with 2str ovNIEPPE[+] 5-50am hit wires ldg cr(2Lt HN Kerr **inj)

RE8   6Sqn
** mg fire(2Lt EE Welby **WIA**/)

D5144   A.W.FK8   8Sqn
LP combat with EA shot up dam(2Lt GA Ballantyne **WIA/2Lt WC Treen **WIA**)

RE8   12Sqn
** combat(2Lt NH Bain **WIA**/)

RE8   15Sqn
** combat(/2Lt CHA Collyns **WIA**)

SE5a   40Sqn
** (Lt WD Archer **WIA**)

B8445   SE5a   40Sqn
**BOP left 3pm mg fire ftl neCAMBRAI abandoned OK(Lt WH Jordan)

E4037   SE5a   40Sqn
BOP left 3pm AA HA? neCAMBRAI ftl abandoned(2Lt WL Field **WIA)inj?

E4089   SE5a   40Sqn
**BOP mg 4-45pm PETIT FONTAINE engine hit ftl o't shell hole OK(Lt WD Archer US.) inj?

D8240   Sopwith Camel   45Sqn (I.F.)
+* combat RumplerC[+ooc] XAFFEVILLERS 3pm OK(Capt JW Pinder)

This was the first combat victory for 45 Squadron after joining the Independent Force.

E2510   Bristol F2b   48Sqn
**OP COURTRAI combat with EA[+des] 4-50pm shot up dam OK(2Lt H Thomas/2Lt FHV Coomer) left 3-45pm, returned 5pm

DH9   49Sqn
** combat(/2Lt J Warren **WIA**)

D1108   DH9   49Sqn
**B left 5-55am AULNOYE JCTN shot up dam returned a'dr 8-55am OK(2Lt WA Crich/SgtMech HL Dodson)

D6804   RE8   53Sqn
NF combat with HA Sh28I 36.B 6-30am(Lt GC Brown **DoW 10.10.18/2Lt LF Raby **KIA**)

F1976   Sopwith Camel   54Sqn
**SpB left 4-20pm mg fire MARQUION ftl OK(Lt HTB Lockwood)

Bristol F2b   62Sqn
** combat(/2Lt RA Clarke **WIA**)

E2256   Bristol F2b   62Sqn
OP combat with EA ovFORÊT DE MORMAL going down ok **MIA(Capt L Campbell **KIA**/2Lt W Hodgkinson **KIA**) left 6-45am [?Ja29][?combat PRESEAU Ltn P Bäumer Ja2]

E2528   Bristol F2b   62Sqn
**EscOP combat with EAs seCAMBRAI seen going
down ooc seCAMBRAI 8am **MIA**(Lt JE Sitch **POW**/2Lt
DS Fox **POW**) Fox escaped by 14.11

E7219   Sopwith Camel   70Sqn
**BOP combat with EA neCOURTRAI 9-30am shot
down? seen o't **MIA**(2Lt JM Poe **KIA**)

E7277.8   Sopwith Camel   70Sqn
+* combat with Fokker DVIIs[++des+capt]
nrROULERS btwn 9-40am & 9-45am OK(Lt OP
Heron) made 13 claims

F6397   Sopwith Camel   73Sqn
GndStr left 5-30am **MIA(2Lt TC McNeale **KIA**)

D6976   SE5a   74Sqn
OP left 8-20am **MIA(Lt WE Bardgett **POW**) repat
25.11.18

E5695   SE5a   85Sqn
**OP mg fire fuel tank shot through ftl Sh62B B.7.a. dam
OK(Lt PD d'Albenas)

F5541   SE5a   92Sqn
**OP left 4-05pm combat shot up dam returned
ESTRÉES a'dr OK(Lt Shapard)

D1107   DH9   107Sqn
B left 10-58am MONS STN **MIA(2Lt DE Webb **KIA**/
2Lt JH Thomson **KIA**) [?possible "DH9" claim combat
THULIN 1-40pm Ltn O Löffler Ja2]

F5846   DH9   107Sqn
B left 10-58am MONS STN **MIA(2Lt C Houlgrave
POW/2Lt WM Thompson **KIA**) [?possible "DH9" claim
combat SEBOURG 1-40pm Ltn H Vallendor Ja2]

B9417   DH9   108Sqn
**B left 8-05am MOUSCRON AA eZILLEBEKE ftl cr
shell hole nrYPRES OK(Lt JG Kershaw/2Lt WL
Walker) salvaged?

F1014   DH9A   205Sqn
+* combat with Fokker DVII[+des] BUSIGNY 8-30am
OK(Lt RLM Barbour/Capt MFM Wright) Barbour
claimed 6 victories, 3 in DH9As

F3223   Sopwith Camel   209Sqn
**LowP VILLERS-LES-CAGNICOURT hit KB cable
cr wr(2Lt JE Gibbons **KIA**) left 2pm

10th October

C8621   A.W.FK8   2Sqn
**PhotCP shell fire ftl Sh34c 6. dam OK(Lt Bates/Lt
Mercer) left 2pm

D6918   SE5a   24Sqn
**GndTarg left 2-45pm controls shot away cr 3-20pm
OK(2Lt AL Bloom) to Fourth Army area

E6006   SE5a   24Sqn
**GndTarg ground mg & combat with Fokker DVII dam
ftl 3-05pm OK(2Lt WB Thomson) left 1-30pm Fourth
Army area

D3161   DH9   27Sqn
**B combat with EA ovAULNOYE dam OK(Lt BM
Bowyer-Smythe/Lt WG Lacey) left 6-05am

E1267   SE5a   85Sqn
OP left 2-40pm shot up? **MIA(2Lt RAH Lloyd **DoW**)

11th October

**   RE8   4Sqn**
** gas(/2Lt AH Winham **WIA**)

C2740   RE8   6Sqn
**Cavalry Contact mg engine shot up BERTRY ftl
OK(Lt Martin/Lt H Mottershaw) left 2-15pm

E5156   Sopwith Camel   54Sqn
**SpB ground mg shot up 5-55pm dam OK(Lt JC Green)

C2263   RE8   59Sqn
*CAP ground mg ftl n.m.l. cr(Lt NM McDougall **inj**/2Lt
SF Kidd **inj**)unsalvable, left 5-45am

C2721   RE8   59Sqn
**CAP left 11-30am ground mg EoL dam OK(2Lt HSR
Burt/2Lt WC Kidd)

F872   SE5a   85Sqn
OP left 7am combat with EA cr Sh57B Q.26. **MIA(Lt
PD d'Albenas **KIA**)

12th October

C2603   RE8   13Sqn
**P AA ftl V.7d? OK(Lt CA Brown/Capt GAR
Slimming) left 6-40am, a'c shelled destroyed

D4890   RE8   59Sqn
**CP left 3-35pm ground mg shot up dam OK(Lt GT
Williams/2Lt GW Elias)

E5761   SE5a   74Sqn
**OP AA? HA? MOORSLEDE 9-25am ftl dam
OK(Capt CB Glynn)

D9449   Sopwith Camel   80Sqn
**OP AA controls shot up ftl LE CATEAU cr OK(2Lt
HP Sharkey) left 5-30am

13th October

C2499   RE8   52Sqn
**AP mg fire ftl IWVY observer landed a'c Sh51a 08d
11am wr(2Lt T Phillips **KIA**/2Lt KWI Howie **inj**)
Howie escaped to WoL

D4694   RE8   52Sqn
**CP mg AVESNES LE SEC 7-30am shot down OK(Lt
JA MacGregor/Lt JL Sutherland) unsalvable

**   208Sqn**
** shell fire(Maj C Draper DSC **WIA**) on ground?

D2921   DH9   218Sqn
**B MELLE AA fire shot up ftl ST POL(Lt W Bentley
WIA/)

14th October
THE FINAL FIGHTING IN FLANDERS

The Allied offensive in Flanders recommenced on the 14th with a big attack launched along the whole front from Dixmude to the Lys. The weather was good during the day and the RAF was out in force, its work being almost entirely offensive. The enemy fell back in disarray, its retreating army presenting a gruesome target for bombing, strafing and artillery fire, which the corps squadrons directed onto it largely unopposed. Most of the air fighting took place between single-seaters, in which the Allies held a vast air superiority. Bombing of the rail network behind the battle also increasingly trapped the German retirement, so that in all it looked as though a few days' more punishment at this intensity might bring wholesale disaster on its army in the north. The most important rail target was Melle, south-east of Ghent, which received attention around the clock. Other stations attacked included Thielt, Deynze, Lichtervelde, Courtrai, and Mouscron.

C6473   SE5a   2Sqn AFC
+* combat with Fokker DVIIs[+des++ooc] CYSOING-HERTAIN btwn 10-10am & 10-20am OK(Capt ED Cummings) made 9 claims, mostly in this a'c

D6968   SE5a   2Sqn AFC
**OP combat with 12 Fokker DVIIs ovTOURNAI shot down nrHAVRON? MIA(Lt JAH McKeown KIA) left 3-15pm, combat ovSCHELDT RIVER, cr bank wr [?SE5a claim nrROULERS 4pm combat Oblt A Gutkneckt Ja43]

E5989   SE5a   2Sqn AFC
**OP seen wTOURNAI combat with EA shot down inexperienced wr MIA(Capt EW Cornish POW) left 3-15pm, 'reckless fighting'

D4924   RE8   7Sqn
**AmmDp AA? ovMOORSEELE down in flames cr(2Lt HA Townsley KIA/2Lt FJ Jackson KIA) left 2-25pm

E33   RE8   7Sqn
**NF combat with EA shot down LEDEGHEM(Capt SW Cowper-Coles KIA/2Lt RW Davidson KIA) left 9-55am [?claim Oblt H Auffahrt Ja29]

B8941   Bristol F2b   11Sqn
**Rec LE CATEAU MIA(Sgt R McCondach KIA/2Lt CE Wainwright DoW) left 2-40pm

**   RE8   21Sqn**
** AA fire(2Lt AW Kilpatrick WIA/2Lt JR Wilkinson WIA)

A7637   DH4   25Sqn
**Phot AA LE HAMEAU 3pm shot up ftl dam OK(Lt LLK Straw/2Lt J Skidmore)

**   DH4   27Sqn**
** (/2Lt HG Biltcliffe WIA?) inj?

E4084   SE5a   29Sqn
+* combat with Fokker DVIIs[+des+ftl] nrROULERS btwn 8-35am & 8-50am OK(Capt CHR Lagesse) second EA captured, Lagesse made at least 20 claims, of which these were the last

F5497   SE5a   29Sqn
**OP left 7-45am AA hit dam ftl(2Lt HC Parks WIA)to hospital

F5516   SE5a   29Sqn
**OP seen in combat with EA eROULERS 8-30am MIA(Lt CM Wilson DFC KIA) [?possible combat YPRES Ltn M Johns Ja65]

**   SE5a   29Sqn**
** combat(2Lt T Stead WIA)

E2507   Bristol F2b   48Sqn
+* combat with Fokker DVIIs[+ooc] wTHIELT 8-55am OK(Capt FJ Cunninghame/Lt TL Jones) last of 5 claims by pilot

F1940   Sopwith Camel   70Sqn
**BOP left 1pm seen nrHOUTHULST MIA(2Lt DDA Mackay KIA) [?2 Camel claims combat HOUTHULST WOOD Ltn R Poss MFJaIV]

F6144   Sopwith Dolphin   79Sqn
**OP AA ELVERDINGHE 2-15pm radiator hit ftl cr a'dr OK(Lt SB Croyden) hit mast ldg

C8557   A.W.FK8   82Sqn
**FlRec combat ovLEDEGHEM 11am shot down(Capt HF Flowers KIA/2Lt AR Bennett KIA)

D5161   A.W.FK8   82Sqn
**B combat with EA COURTRAI 3-50pm shot down MIA(2Lt W Debussey KIA/2Lt GT Carr KIA)

D5194   A.W.FK8   82Sqn
**B combat with EA COURTRAI shot down ftl 3-50pm dam(Capt EGE Donaldson WIA/2Lt WV Hunt DoW 17.10.18)

E4493   Sopwith Dolphin   87Sqn
**Esc(57Sqn) shot up BAPAUME 9-05am engine failed ftl dam OK(Lt CA Bryant)

E4636   Sopwith Dolphin   87Sqn
**Esc(57Sq) combat with EA LE QUESNOY 8-40am flames MIA(Lt RJ Farquharson POW) [claims combat ROULERS Obfl A Buhl & Flm G Hubrich MFJaIV]

E605   DH9   108Sqn
**B AUDINARDE combat with EA seen going down in flames eCOURTRAI MIA(2Lt HW Bingham KIA/2Lt FW Woolley KIA) left 6-22am [DH9 claim combat LEDEGHEM Oblt F Ritt vRöth Ja16]

E8871   DH9   108Sqn
**B AUDINARDE combat with EA ovCOURTRAI seen spiral down ooc with EA on tail MIA(2Lt PL

Phillips **POW**/2Lt PCS McCrea **POW**) left 6-22am, one report saw them in control

H7286   **Sopwith Camel**   **203Sqn**
OP left 9-30am AA ftl WARCOURT cr shell holes wr(Lt RB Wiggins **inj)

D3400   **Sopwith Camel**   **204Sqn**
+* combat with EA[+] GITS 6-30am shot up(Lt HC Smith **WIA**)

F3116   **Sopwith Camel**   **210Sqn**
LowStrB seen straffe ovPITTHEM 7-30am **MIA(2Lt CC Fountain **KIA**) [?Camel claim combat EEGHEM, but see 213Sqn, Ltn K Plauth Ja51]

F3117   **Sopwith Camel**   **210Sqn**
LowP shot up **MIA(2Lt HH Whitlock **POW**)

B7272   **Sopwith Camel**   **213Sqn**
+* combat with Fokker DVIIs[++des+ooc] LEKE 2-30pm OK(Lt CJ Sims)

D3378   **Sopwith Camel**   **213Sqn**
** seen in combat with 17 Fokker DVIIs nrLA BARRIÈRE 10-15am **MIA**(2Lt WT Owen Can. **KIA**) [?Camel claim combat ISEGHEM FlM G Hubrich MFJaIV]

D3409   **Sopwith Camel**   **213Sqn**
** seen in combat with 17 Fokker DVIIs shot up flames? **MIA**(Capt JE Greene DFC **KIA**)

D8177   **Sopwith Camel**   **213Sqn**
?** seen in combat with 17 Fokker DVIIs PERVYSE 2-30pm **MIA**(2Lt FRL Allen **KIA**)

D9673   **Sopwith Camel**   **213Sqn**
NOP seen in solo combat with 7 Fokker DVIIs 2m nDIXMUDE 2-30pm shot down **MIA(Lt K MacLeish USNRF **KIA**) left 1-30pm, combat after his patrol had fought 14EA, body found nrGHISTELLES

D9677   **Sopwith Camel**   **213Sqn**
**LowB left 6am mg fire shot up dam OK(Maj R Graham)

F3120.5   **Sopwith Camel**   **213Sqn**
** seen in combat with 17EA PERVYSE-THOUROUT 10-15am **MIA**(2Lt JCJ McDonald **KIA**) [?Camel claim ZARREN Ltn R Poss MFJaIV]

F5987   **Sopwith Camel**   **213Sqn**
** combat with 17EA 10-15am ARDOYE-THOUROUT **MIA**(2Lt EB McMurty **KIA**)

D3328   **Sopwith Camel**   **US 17th Pursuit Sqn**
BOP left 12-55pm engine ftl EoL Sh51a.P.28 **MIA(2Lt HC Knotts **POW**) seen get out of a'c

The date of the 14th is via the RAF Casualty Report — the frequently given date of the 15th is incorrect. Knotts destroyed seven Fokker DVIIs by setting fire to a train on his way to prison and was almost executed as a result.

15th October

Mist and rain set in for most of the following three days and thereby saved a disaster for the German Army. Flying was heavily restricted until the 17th, when widespread bombing again took place, but after this, the weather in Flanders closed in for about ten days. These circumstances enabled countless thousands of German soldiers, who otherwise might well have been decimated by artillery and air attacks, to be evacuated eastwards to safety.

F7373   **A.W.FK8**   **2Sqn**
**CAP shot up engine ftl HULLUCH dam OK(Lt Robinson/Lt Mercer) left 11-20am

F7392   **A.W.FK8**   **82Sqn**
FlRec ground mg LEDEGHEM shot down 1-45pm cr(2Lt GW Kitchen **inj/2Lt MStJ Ross OK)

16th October

D4929   **RE8**   **16Sqn**
**CP left 12-15pm ground mg shot up OK(2Lt H Pattinson/2Lt WN Hicks)

E271   **RE8**   **16Sqn**
**CP ground mg rifle dam returned 5pm OK(2Lt SH Hughes/2Lt TPT Jones) left 3-05pm

17th October

B4170   **A.W.FK8**   **8Sqn**
LP shell hit cr Sh57B K.32.c(Capt RI Dines **inj/2Lt TM Baker **KIA**) left 2pm, observer thrown out by shell hit

D6799   **RE8**   **53Sqn**
NF left 7-50am **MIA(Lt GWE Whitehead **KIA**/2Lt RH Griffiths **KIA**)

F1941.P   **Sopwith Camel**   **73Sqn**
**GndStr left 6am shell fire dam ftl OK(Capt RN Chandler)

F7413   **A.W.FK8**   **82Sqn**
AmmDp HA? ground mg? ftl WINKEL 1pm(Capt R Johnstone **WIA/2Lt R Alcock **WIA**) also food drop

F3108   **Sopwith Camel**   **204Sqn**
** AA shot up(Lt JR? Robertson **WIA**) initials AE?

18th October

D6860   **SE5a**   **2Sqn AFC**
**OP oil tank shot up engine ftl BOIS GRENIER 1-20pm dam OK(Lt EE Davies) left 11-40am TOURNAI

F5457.1   **SE5a**   **2Sqn AFC**
+* combat with Fokker DVII[+des] sTOURNAI 12-30pm OK(Capt GH Blaxland) made 8 claims

C2866   **RE8**   **4Sqn**
Rec left 12-15pm **MIA(2Lt S Hall **KIA**/2Lt GP Blake **KIA**?)

RE8   **16Sqn**
** mg fire(/Lt RNK Jones **WIA**)

D4909   RE8   59Sqn
NF mg fire EA? ftl(Lt TH Upfill **KIA/2Lt JC Walker **KIA**)unsalvable, left 2-30pm, shot down at D12.c.5.0. [RE8 claim combat wSOLESMES 4-45pm Ltn H Henkel Ja37]

E5807   SE5a   85Sqn
** AA hit(Lt EC Brown **KIA**)

Bristol F2b   88Sqn
** combat(Capt JP Findlay **WIA**/)

E2579   Bristol F2b   88Sqn
**SpM TOURNAI ground mg dam OK(Capt A Hepburn/2Lt D Varasour) left 11-35am

D530   DH9   104Sqn (I.F.)
B (Lt JW Richards OK/2Lt AM Mitchell **WIA) 19.10?

N5997.M DH4   202Sqn
B mg ZEEBRUGGE MOLE 300' 7-05am shot down **MIA(Lt R Coulthard **POW**/2Lt L Timmins **POW**) ZEEBRUGGE MOLE

19th October

F6126   Sopwith Camel   213Sqn
** left 10am ftl off ZEEBRUGGE MOLE swam in **MIA**(Lt AR Talbot **POW**) seen hanging on tail of Camel

F8502   Sopwith Camel   213Sqn
** seen ZEEBRUGGE 11-45am cr but ok **MIA** but OK(Lt AH Pownall)

21st October

E60   RE8   16Sqn
**CP left 1-05pm ground mg shot up dam OK(2Lt H Pattinson/2Lt WN Hicks)

Bristol F2b   22Sqn
** (/2Lt JA Oliver **WIA**?) inj?

F863   SE5a   56Sqn
+* combat with Fokker DVII[+des] nBOURSIES 3pm OK(Lt DW Grinnell-Milne) this notable pilot scored 5 victories with 56Sqn in late 1918

F5463   SE5a   56Sqn
LowB seen ooc? 12m eLE CATEAU 3pm **MIA(Lt MH Winkler US. **POW**)

E8484   DH9A   110Sqn (I.F.)
B FRANKFURT **MIA(2Lt AWR Evans **POW**/Lt RWL Thomson **POW**)

F984   DH9A   110Sqn (I.F.)
B FRANKFURT **MIA(Lt SL Mucklow **POW**/2Lt R Riffkin **POW**)

F985   DH9A   110Sqn (I.F.)
B FRANKFURT shot down **MIA(Maj LGS Reynolds **POW**/2Lt MW Dunn **POW**)

F986   DH9A   110Sqn (I.F.)

B FRANKFURT shot down **MIA(2Lt JORS Saunders **KIA**/2Lt WJ Brain **KIA**)

F1005   DH9A   110Sqn (I.F.)
B FRANKFURT fuel tank hit ftl **MIA(Capt WE Windover **POW**/2Lt JA Simpson **POW**)

F1021   DH9A   110Sqn (I.F.)
B FRANKFURT combat with EA shot up **MIA(2Lt P King **POW**/2Lt RG Vernon **POW DoW**)to hospital

F1029   DH9A   110Sqn (I.F.)
B FRANKFURT **MIA(Lt J McLaren-Pearson **POW**/Sgt TW Harman **POW**?)

110 Squadron suffered its worst losses on this raid — in fact there were none worse in the entire bombing programme of the Independent Force. Heavy clouds led to the formation becoming broken up on its way to Koln and eventually Frankfurt was bombed by only five of the thirteen DH9As which had set out. The patrol was hit severely by enemy formations, and German records noted at least five aircraft brought down north of Frankfurt. These included one in flames at Dillenburg, one at Berenbach, one near Lauterbach, and two near Weiler.

22nd October

RE8   5Sqn
** AA fire(2Lt H Proudlove **WIA**/)

RE8   42Sqn
** (/2Lt FL McHenry **WIA**?) inj?

C8387   Sopwith Camel   80Sqn
 prac accident? cr wr found 4m swMONTDIDIER **MIA but OK(2Lt TM MacIntyre)

D1110   DH9   108Sqn
Rec:solo left 6-23am GHENT **MIA(Lt CF Cave **KIA**/2Lt H McNish **KIA**?) [?combat nBELLEM? Ltn P Achilles MFJaV]

DH4   205Sqn
** combat(/2Lt A Hesketh **WIA**)

23rd October

Allied operations had resumed on the Le Cateau front on the 17th. The Fourth Army, with the French First Army to its right, attacked along the Selle River to the south, and three days later, the First and Third Armies came gradually into action north of Le Cateau. Here they took Solesmes in fierce fighting, whilst the enemy was driven across the Sambre-et-Oise Canal along most of its length south of Catillon. Poor weather continued to restrict the support the RAF could give to these advances, and this was especially telling when the next main push was begun on the 23rd. It had been planned to make a major attack all along the line, from the boundary with the French Army near

Catillon, up along the western face of Mormal Wood, to Valenciennes. Counter-battery work in preparation for this had been virtually negligible, and when the assault began the British infantry were heavily shelled with gas and high explosive. On the day itself, conditions were fine, if not very clear, and there was some very heavy air fighting.

C2445　RE8　　　　　6Sqn
 Phot combat with EA shot up dam(Lt Fenwick OK/ 2Lt JA Holmes **WIA)

C2923　RE8　　　　　6Sqn
**Phot combat with HA? seen eROBERSART 3pm MIA but OK?(2Lt GE Dunn/2Lt E Souter)

D4930　RE8　　　　　6Sqn
Phot seen 1500yd eROBERSART 3pm combat with HA? **MIA(Lt JT Sorley **POW**/2Lt FH Reid **POW**) left 2pm

F6279　RE8　　　　　6Sqn
Phot seen in combat with HA eROBERSART 3pm **MIA(Lt RN Cresswell **KIA**/Lt RW Silk **POW**)

E8830　A.W.FK8　　　　8Sqn
CAP combat with EA shot up 2-55pm dam(Lt Glen OK/Lt GH Carr **WIA) left 2-50pm

E2470　Bristol F2b　　　20Sqn
OP combat seen low AULNOYE **MIA(Lt HL Pennal **KIA**/Sgt G Aitken **KIA**) left 2-33pm

20 Squadron met a large formation of Fokkers over Aulnoye Station which they had been attacking with 112-lb bombs. Five enemy fighters were claimed shot down in the dogfight.

D3581　Sopwith Dolphin　23Sqn
OP left 9am air collision at 5000′ 10-20am spin **MIA(2Lt EL Howells **KIA**)

C1911　SE5a　　　　　84Sqn
OP left 3-45pm seen going west ovABATTOIR **MIA(2Lt JC Collins **POW**) to ENGLEFONTAINE-PRISCHES

H7251　SE5a　　　　　85Sqn
**OP left 1-45pm combat shot up dam returned 3-25pm OK(Capt CBR Macdonald)

**　　　　DH9　　　　　98Sqn**
B HIRSON Rlwy Stn (/2Lt AH Fuller **WIA?)inj?

**　　　　DH9　　　　　98Sqn**
+*B HIRSON Rlwy Stn combat with Fokker DVIIs[+ ooc] eTOURNAI 4-50pm OK(Sgt WJ MacNeil/2Lt J Davison)

C2204　DH9　　　　　98Sqn
+*B HIRSON Rlwy Stn combat with Fokker DVIIs[+ flames] eTOURNAI 4-50pm OK(2Lt LW Marchant/2Lt EA Slater)

D3262　DH9　　　　　98Sqn
**B HIRSON Rlwy Stn combat? seen glide down in

control? nrGUISE **MIA**(2Lt HH Rofe **POW**/2Lt APC Bruce **POW**) left 2-05pm

D7346　DH9　　　　　98Sqn
B HIRSON Rlwy Stn combat with EA formation shot up dam(2Lt FC Wilton OK/Capt GH Gillis **WIA?) left 2-05pm, inj?

D7377　DH9　　　　　98Sqn
+*B HIRSON Rlwy Stn combat with Fokker DVII[+ flames+ooc] LEUZE 4-50pm OK(Sgt TW Haines/2Lt DC McDonald)

98 Squadron bombed Hirson railway junction with 107 Squadron.

D539　DH9　　　　　103Sqn
B left 3-10pm dam(Capt DM Darroch **WIA/Lt FM Loly **WIA**)

D2932　DH9　　　　　104Sqn (I.F.)
B met EAs over objective, seen going down ooc ovMETZ **MIA(2Lt BS Case **POW DoW** 31.10.18/2Lt H Bridger **WIA POW**) but Roll of Honour gives Case DoW 10.11.18? [?DH claim combat FOURASSE? WOOD 12-15pm Ltn K Monnington Ja18]

C6314　DH9　　　　　108Sqn
Rec:solo left 10-35am **MIA(Capt GC Haynes **KIA**/2Lt G Brown **KIA**) [?DH9 claim combat VOSSELAERE Ltn K Plauth Ja51][?DH9 claim Oblt zS G Sachsenberg MFJa1]

E9034　DH9　　　　　108Sqn
**B MELLE AA? GHENT seen going down ok MIA but OK?(Capt R Russell/2Lt GB Pike) left 9-36am, "seen steering n-w with water streaming from radiator", MIA cancelled in AIR1/969/204/5/1102

C197　Sopwith Camel　　203Sqn
+* combat with Fokker DVIIs[++ooc] VERTAIN 4-35pm OK(Lt W Sidebottom) many of his 14 claims were in this a'c

D8223　Sopwith Camel　　204Sqn
HOP left 8-30am combat with 12EA nrTERMONDE in mist after bombing **MIA(Sgt CMA Mahon **KIA**) [?Camel claim combat ROUSELE? Vzfw K Scharon MFJaII][?3 Camel claims combats ~MERENDSEE? VzfM A Zenses MFJaII]

D9608　Sopwith Camel　　204Sqn
HOP left 8-30am combat with 12EA TERMONDE in mist after bombing **MIA(Capt TW Nash DFC **KIA**)

D9613　Sopwith Camel　　204Sqn
HOP left 8-30am combat with 12HA shot down nrTERMONDE in mist after bombing **MIA(Lt OJ Orr **KIA**)

E4420　Sopwith Camel　　204Sqn
HOP left 8-30am combat with 12HA TERMONDE after bombing **MIA(Lt FG Bayley **KIA**) [2 Camel claims combat Oblt zS G Sachsenberg MFJa1]

F3101　Sopwith Camel　　204Sqn
**HOP combat with 12HA air collision? TERMONDE

in mist after bombing **MIA**(2Lt G Sutcliffe US. **KIA**) left 8-30am, possibly 2 a'c collided [?2 Camel claims combat Oblt zS G Sachsenberg MFJa1]

24th October

Enemy air activity was light on the Le Cateau front for the next two days. This permitted some valuable RAF artillery and photo-reconnaissance work to take place.

RE8   6Sqn
** AA fire(2Lt HE Peer **WIA**/)

RE8   13Sqn
** (/Lt HD Hewett **WIA**?)inj?

RE8   21Sqn
** mg fire(/2Lt B Heaton **WIA**)

C2935   RE8   53Sqn
**CAP shot up dam ftl COUCOU a'dr OK(Lt AH Alban/TLt RA Neilson) left 10-10am X Army area

RE8   59Sqn
** (/2Lt WH Adderley **DoW**)

H7254.ASE5a   64Sqn
**OP mg fuel tank shot up 4-15pm LASCELLES ftl OK(Lt RH Channing)

Sopwith Camel   204Sqn
** (Lt D Price **WIA**?)inj?

H.P.0/400   207Sqn
** (/2Lt W Whichelow **WIA**)

25th October

D6737   RE8   10Sqn
**FlRec mg shot up dam ftl Sh29 O.30.b.3.3. at 12-25pm OK(2Lt RJ Davey/Lt DA Mackenzie)

E2534   Bristol F2b 48Sqn
**LP AA DEERLYCK 2-45pm ftlOK(2Lt G Thornton-Norris/Sgt RLG White)

RE8   59Sqn
** mg fire(/2Lt AJ Bridge **WIA**)

E1102   RE8   59Sqn
**CP mg LE QUESNOY fuel tank shot up dam ftl OK(Lt FE Robinson/Lt AL Wilmshurst) left 3-55pm

E1276   SE5a   60Sqn
OP left 8-20am seen ok BERLAIMONT going sw **MIA(Lt LH Smith **POW**) [?SE5 claim combat nMORMAL WOOD 9-45am UOff K Treiber Ja5]

F6241   Sopwith Camel 80Sqn
**OP left 12pm combat with HA ST SOUPLET shot up ftl OK(2Lt HP Sharkey)

A.W.FK8   82Sqn
** mg fire(/2Lt WM Brewer **WIA**)

D2652   Bristol F2b P Flt
** dhAA ftl dam OK(2Lt JT Brown/2Lt Gutheridge)

H830   Sopwith Camel (NF)   US 17th Pursuit Sqn
+* combat with Fokker DVII[+flames] MORMAL WOOD 10-55am OK(1Lt H Burdick) last of 8 claims

26th October

B7909   SE5a   1Sqn
trav seen ok ePERONNE 10-50am **MIA(Lt HH Hunt **KIA**)

D406   SE5a   2Sqn AFC
**OP left 2-05pm CONDE ground mg dam ftl 4pm OK(Capt EL Simonson)

E8032   Sopwith Snipe 4Sqn AFC
** combat with Fokker DVIIs[+flames+ooc] eTOURNAI 3-45pm shot up ftl PERONNE(2Lt TH Barkell **WIA**)

F7480   A.W.FK8   8Sqn
Phot left 9-55am **MIA(2Lt JR Desy **KIA**/2Lt R Lister **KIA**)

C1915   SE5a   29Sqn
OP air collision? with F900 ovTOURNAI 12000' **MIA(Lt HC Rath **KIA**) left 11-15am

F900   SE5a   29Sqn
OP air collision? with SE5a C1915 TOURNAI 12000' **MIA(2Lt RSG MacLean US. **KIA**) left 11-15am [?SE5a claim combat VELENNES Ltn J Raesch Ja43]

F5536   SE5a   40Sqn
BOP left 1-30pm seen ok wVALENCIENNES **MIA(Lt TH Turnbull **KIA**)

C2557   RE8   42Sqn
**LowRec combat with 7 Fokker DVIIs mg dam OK(Lt AD MacDonald/2Lt G Riley) left 2-20pm, shot up returned a'dr 4-30pm

D4917   RE8   42Sqn
AOb combat with 7 Fokker DVIIs shot down 4-20pm(2Lt HE Chaffey **KIA/2Lt HP Turnbull **KIA**) left 3pm, combat shot down N.6.d.2.2.

E2532   Bristol F2b 48Sqn
OP seen 1-30pm **MIA(2Lt H Thomas US? **POW**/2Lt FHV Coomer **POW**) left 12-15pm

H7005   Sopwith Camel 65Sqn
OP combat 1-40pm ESSEGHEM seen going down in flames **MIA(2Lt AE Moir **KIA**) ?combat ESSENGHEM Ltn F Rumey Ja5]

C1910   SE5a   74Sqn
+* combat with Fokker DVIIs[+++des] CORDESneTOURNAI btwn 2-55pm & 3-10pm OK(Lt JE Ferrand)

E3942   SE5a   74Sqn
OP seen in combat ovCORDES 1500' 1-45pm ftl **MIA(2Lt M Maclean **POW**)

Sopwith Dolphin   79Sqn
** mg fire(2Lt WLN Cope **WIA**)

DH9   108Sqn
B MELLE? AA fire(2Lt CR Knott **WIA/)

27th October

D6950.V   **SE5a**   **2Sqn AFC**
**OP left 7am seen ok TOURNAI going west shot down
MIA(Lt F Howard **KIA**)

  A.W.FK8   **10Sqn**
** gunshot(Lt CT Aulph **WIA**/)

C2322   **RE8**   **16Sqn**
**CP left 8-45am AA shot up(Lt H Pattinson OK/2Lt
WN Hicks **DoW**)

E8415   **DH9A**   **18Sqn**
**PhotB combat with EA ovMONS 11am dam ftl
207Sqn(Lt R Johnson OK/2Lt A Toes **KIA**)

D5236   **Sopwith Dolphin**   **19Sqn**
OP seen in steep dive wQUROUBLE smoke **MIA(2Lt
WJ Nesbitt **KIA**) left 10-50am [?Dolphin claim combat
11-20am Vzfw K Bohnenkamp Ja22]

F5901   **RE8**   **21Sqn**
**Phot shot up returned a'dr cr dam(Lt SC Rainbow
OK/Lt EE Davis **DoW**)

B7894   **Sopwith Dolphin**   **23Sqn**
**OP seen ok with patrol LE CATEAU on return 2000'
10-35am **MIA**(2Lt AR Pratt **POW**)

H676   **SE5a**   **29Sqn**
**OP combat with Fokker DVII eTOURNAI 1500'
9-20am **MIA**(Capt GW Wareing DFC **KIA**) [?combat
eTOURNAI 9-30am Ltn J Raesch Ja43]

  A.W.FK8   **35Sqn**
** (2Lt HG Harper **WIA**/2Lt EJ Richardson **KIA**)

E8838   **A.W.FK8**   **35Sqn**
**P combat with 2EA shot up ftl Sh57B P.2.D(2Lt CF
Brown OK/2Lt EMS Kearney **KIA**) left 5-50am

F7401   **A.W.FK8**   **35Sqn**
**P to Sh57B A.15 ground shot up dam OK(Lt J Officer/
2Lt GI Thompson) left 6am

F5547.Y   **SE5a**   **41Sqn**
OP left 9-10am TOURNAI **MIA(Lt EWO Hall **POW**)

E2609   **Bristol F2b**   **48Sqn**
LP seen ovRIVER SCHELDT 7-45am **MIA(2Lt W
Saunders **POW**/2Lt HG Lewis **POW**) left 6am

  RE8   **52Sqn**
** combat(/2Lt DV Clawson **WIA**)

C6464   **SE5a**   **56Sqn**
**COP left 8-15am combat with Fokker DVII then broke
up ooc **MIA**(2Lt TH Rogers **KIA**)

  DH4   **57Sqn**
** combat(/2Lt E Till **WIA**)

  DH4   **57Sqn**
** combat(Lt AE? Bourns **WIA**/), initials AW?

  DH4   **57Sqn**
** combat(2Lt SCH Biddle **WIA**/)

F2633   **DH4**   **57Sqn**

**B left formation going west ok seen ovST VAAST LA
VALLÉE **MIA**(2Lt DU Thomas **KIA**/2Lt AH Aitken
KIA) left 8-45am

E1587   **Sopwith Camel**   **70Sqn**
**KBP left 7am AMIENS combat with EA shot up
MIA(2Lt CA Crichton **WIA POW**)

  A.W.FK8   **82Sqn**
** mg fire(/Lt B Charlton **KIA**)

  SE5a   **92Sqn**
** AA fire(Lt A Scott **WIA**)

  SE5a   **92Sqn**
** AA fire(Lt B Mignault **WIA**)

E8102   **Sopwith Snipe**   **201Sqn**
+* combat with 2Str[+broke up] then wounded by
Fokker DVII and fell down into two successive
formations of ~15 Fokker DVIIs[+++shot down in
flames] ovMORMAL WOODS 8-25am to 8-30am shot
up, made escape, ftl cr WoL(Maj WG Barker Can. DSO
MC VC **WIA**)

This famous fight earned Barker the Victoria
Cross. It was also the Sopwith Snipe's finest hour,
for four enemy machines were shot down in lone
combat, and another two driven down indecisively.
What became a series of most desperate dogfights
began with the attack and destruction of a two-
seater at 21,000 feet. One of the enemy was seen to
make his escape by parachute. Barker was then
wounded the first time by fire from a Fokker below,
and spun down only to recover in the midst of an
enemy formation which he then began to fight. He
was wounded again, but not before he had shot one
fighter down in flames. He lost consciousness for a
few moments and spun down again only to find
himself facing a further twelve to fifteen of the
enemy. He shot down another Fokker and was
seriously wounded in the elbow and fell out of
control a third time. Yet another patrol of enemy
machines awaited him at 12000 feet, where he came
to and fought them whilst smoke began to come
from his machine. He tried to ram one of his
attackers, but managed instead to shoot it down in
flames from very close range. In order to escape
westwards he had to fight off a last enemy patrol
of about eight machines, and with this accomplished, he returned to British lines almost at
ground level where he finally crashed near a kite
balloon.

C144   **Sopwith Camel**   **204Sqn**
**HOP combat with 30-40EA ovST DENIS WESTREM
9-10am **MIA**(2Lt N Smith **POW**) left 8-10am [?combat
sDEYNZE? VzfM A Zenses MFJaII]

D9600   **Sopwith Camel**   **204Sqn**
+* combat with Fokker DVIIs[+des+ooc] sGHENT
9-10am OK(Capt CP Allen) made 7 claims

E4387   Sopwith Camel   204Sqn
**HOP combat with 30-40 Fokker DVIIs ST DENIS
WESTREM sGHENT 9-10am **MIA**(2Lt PF Cormack
KIA) [?Camel claim combat WYNGHENE Ltn C
Degelow Ja40][?Camel claim combat WYNYHENE
9-15am Ltn W Rosenstein Ja40]

F3112   Sopwith Camel   204Sqn
**HOP combat with 30-40 Fokker DVIIs ovST DENIS
WESTREM sGHENT 9-10am **MIA**(2Lt AJF Ross **KIA**)
[?Camel claim combat ST DENYZE? Vzf K Scharon
MFJaII]

F3929   Sopwith Camel   204Sqn
"FUMS UP"! +* combat with Fokker DVII[+flames]
sGHENT 9-10am OK(Lt RMcI Gordon **WIA**) last of
several claims

F3940   Sopwith Camel   204Sqn
**HOP combat with 30-40 Fokker DVIIs ST DENIS
WESTREM GHENT 9-15am **MIA**(2Lt HG Murray
KIA) left 8-10am

H7082   Sopwith Camel   204Sqn
**HOP ch by 3 Fokker DVIIs[+] RUYSSLED 20-100'
9am ftl cr wr OK(Lt AA Argles) 1 Fokker hit tree

F8647   Sopwith Camel   213Sqn
**HOP AA 5m nGHENT 10-30am glided back & spun
in wr OK(Lt JFT Fenn) tail shot off

28th October
THE HEAVIEST DAYS
OF AIR FIGHTING

The closing days of October saw some of the
heaviest air fighting of the entire war. There was a
lull in the advance on the ground as these events
occurred — the British artillery had been progres-
sively brought up and was now able to devastate
the enemy back areas and lines of communications
almost at will. The corps squadrons facilitated this
work with a precision borne of long experience.
Meanwhile, the day and night bombing squadrons
also launched big attacks on these targets, and it
was in these overwhelming circumstances that the
German Air Force fought in a last desperate series
of battles to protect its beleaguered and dying
army.

The fighting grew from the 28th onwards, until
on the 30th the heaviest single day of air fighting
of the Great War took place. Some of the enemy
fighter formations operating above the most critical
rail centres, namely Namur and Liége, contained
over fifty aircraft. It was a strategy which would
bleed the last life out of the German Air Force but,
after all, a brave final effort to protect the remnants
of its army was a more meaningful sacrifice than
anything else it could now achieve.

The main bottlenecks of the German Army with-

drawal spread back westwards from Namur and
Liége, to Charleroi, Mariembourg, up to Louvain,
Termonde and Mons. Over all these centres very
great air battles took place. These towns were now
being bombed from the air around the clock, but
enemy fighters reserved most of their attention for
the DH9 day-bombers. This was perhaps the
RAF's most vulnerable and most disappointing
machine of 1918, and all their raids required fighter
escorts. The German Air Force chose wisely, for
although several other raids did penetrate this
enemy fighter screen and bomb to plan, notably
those by 205 Squadron DH9As, only one DH9 raid
in three days was allowed to reach the target. This
was a formation of 107 Squadron on the 30th,
escorted by Nos.1 and 43 Squadrons to Mariembourg. All the other raids, as noted below, were
abandoned after depletion through engine
problems or forced to drop their bombs early and
make their escape.

B8501   SE5a   1Sqn
+* combat with Fokker DVIIs[+ooc] TRELOU
1-35pm OK(Lt BH Moody SA.)

D6951   SE5a   1Sqn
**OP HIRSON combat with Fokker DVIIs[++des]
HIRSON 1-30pm then shot down ovTRELOU 1-45pm
MIA(Lt NT Trembath **POW**)

F5578   SE5a   1Sqn
+* combat with Fokker DVIIs[+ooc] ANOR 1-40pm
OK(Lt FP McGoun)

H7257   SE5a   1Sqn
+* combat with Fokker DVII[+des] TRELOU 1-35pm
OK(Lt DE Cameron)

1 Squadron was escorting 107 Squadron back from
an attempted raid on Mariembourg. No. 107 had
left with 43 Squadron for its outward journey but
were so reduced by machines suffering engine
failures that Hirson was bombed instead. 107 and
1 Squadrons were then attacked all the way home.

D5104   A.W.FK8   2Sqn
**P left 8-15am mg fire dam OK(Lt MW? Richardson/
Lt HA Deakin) returned 11-40am

E8050.A   Sopwith Snipe   4Sqn AFC
+* combat with Fokker DVIIs[+des+flames]
eBUISSENAL btwn 1-15pm & 1-20pm OK(Capt ER
King) several of his 26? victories made in this Snipe

E8092   Sopwith Snipe   4Sqn AFC
+* combat with Fokker DVIIs[+ooc+des] ATH btwn
2-55pm & 3pm OK(Capt TCR Baker) also earlier victory
Fokker DVII[+des] seTOURNAI 12pm

RE8   7Sqn
** mg fire(Capt JW Foreman **WIA**/)

F7412   A.W.FK8   10Sqn
**Phot combat with EA ftl 11-30am dam(Lt CC
Summers OK/2Lt DA Mackenzie **KIA**) ftl Sh29 C.24

E252   RE8   16Sqn
**AA LA BROISETTE 8-30am ftl dam OK(2Lt H
Laycock/2Lt BW Thwaites) ftl Sh17 b.5.6.

D535   DH9   27Sqn
B combat with EA radiator hit ovMONS **MIA(2Lt
CM Allan **POW**/2Lt JP Coleman **POW**) left 9-40am
MONS, seen going down in control loosing radiator water

D1092   DH9   27Sqn
**B left 9-35am MONS AA dam OK(Capt JR Webb/2Lt
LJ Edwardes) returned a'dr 12-30pm

27 and 49 Squadron DH9s were escorted by 32
Squadron SE5as. The formation was met by
around thirty Fokkers over Mons.

D7000   SE5a   29Sqn
**OP AA hit 4pm ftl Sh37Q 26.a. a'c abandoned(2Lt T
Stead **WIA**)

E5999   SE5a   29Sqn
+* combat with Fokker DVII[+des] swAVELGHEM
4pm OK(Lt SM Brown US.)

E6033   SE5a   29Sqn
**OP seen cross Lines nrMOEN 8000' going west 11am
MIA but OK?(2Lt C Keene) left 9-10am, MIA cancelled
in AIR1/969/204/5/1102

F862   SE5a   29Sqn
OP AA 4pm engine cut ftl Sh37Q 26.a **MIA(Lt RB
Lovemore **POW**?)

           A.W.FK8   35Sqn
** mg fire(Lt J Officer **WIA**/)

D3223   DH9   49Sqn
**B ST GHISLAM shot up dam OK(2Lt WE
McDermott/2Lt RH StAmory) left 9-35am, returned a'dr
12-15pm

           RE8   59Sqn
** mg fire(/Lt CRA Wallis **WIA**)

E1105   RE8   59Sqn
PhotNF shot up? cr fire(Lt F Whitburn **WIA/2Lt CA
Firmin **WIA**)to hospital, left 12pm, pilot burnt in cr

H690   SE5a   60Sqn
**Esc57Sq seen ok ovMAUBEUGE 14000' going west
12-50pm **MIA**(2Lt LG Stockwell **POW**)

F869.6   SE5a   64Sqn
**OP left 3-30pm AA shot up dam returned a'dr 4-35pm
OK(Capt CW Cudemore) to First Army area

D8167   Sopwith Camel   70Sqn
**BOP seen ok QUARTES combat with EA shot down
MIA(2Lt N Greaves **KIA**) left 10-40am, buried Sh37J
31.b.61

E7222   Sopwith Camel   70Sqn
BOP left 10-40am seen ok nrQUARTES **MIA(2Lt RF
Russell **KIA**)

D7919   Bristol F2b   N Flt
AOb left 10-40am **MIA(Lt J Thompson **KIA**/2Lt AF
Perry **KIA**)

E1539.B Sopwith Camel   US 148th Pursuit Sqn
+* combat with Fokker DVII[+des cr] VILLERS POL
12-05pm OK(1Lt FE Kindley) shared, his last of a dozen
victories

F6176   Sopwith Camel   US 148th Pursuit Sqn
+*combat with Fokker DVII[+des] nwJENLAIN
12-05pm OK(1Lt JO Creech) shared, scored several
victories

29th October

D6973   SE5a   1Sqn
+* combat with Fokker DVII[+flames] LANDRECIES
2-20pm OK(Lt WA Smart) last of 5 claims, and during
1Sqn's last successful air combat

E5799   SE5a   1Sqn
+* combat with Fokker DVII[+des] POMMEREUIL
2-30pm OK(Capt RTC Hoidge Can.) last of 27 victories

F5476   SE5a   1Sqn
**OP seen in combat with EA nrLANDRECIES 2-30pm
MIA(Lt W Newby **KIA**) [?combat CATILLON 2-40pm
Ltn H vFreden Ja50]

1 Squadron was again escorting 107 Squadron
when it was attacked over Anor. The raid was a
failure.

           A.W.FK8   2Sqn
** mg fire(/2Lt GG Shaw **WIA**)

C8375   Sopwith Camel   3Sqn
**OP combat with EA 1500' 10-30am seen shot down in
flames Sh51A F.19 **MIA**(2Lt JH Hampton **KIA**) left
9-30am

H7270   Sopwith Camel   3Sqn
**OP combat with Fokker DVII 1500' 10-30am flames
cr Sh51A K.9 **MIA**(2Lt HC Maisey **KIA**) left 9-30am

H7021   RE8   4Sqn
**CAP left 3-20pm MIA but OK(2Lt AV Heslop/2Lt
RW Lane) MIA cancelled in AIR1/969/204/5/1102: see
9.11.18?

E8070   Sopwith Snipe   4Sqn AFC
**OP combat with EA neTOURNAI[+] 4-10pm shot
down **MIA**(Lt PJ Sims **KIA**)

F6218   RE8   13Sqn
CP combat ftl Sh57B R.8.c(Lt VL Watts **WIA/Lt J
Evans **DoW**)unsalvable, left 8-15am

C2695   RE8   42Sqn
**Phot combat with 8EA 4-30pm but returned a'dr(Capt
GWT Glasson **WIA**/Lt WJ Hagen **WIA**) name Hagan?
[?possible RE8 claim Ltn H Frommherz Ja27]

E2367   Bristol F2b   48Sqn
**LP AA 3pm DEERLYDE ftl OK(Lt IO Gaze/2Lt CW
Newstead)

E254   **RE8**   **52Sqn**
**P ground mg dam returned a'dr 7-50am OK(Capt R
Harrison/2Lt JA Guymer) left 5-55am, found dam after
ldg

D8398   **DH4**   **57Sqn**
**PhotB AA seen hit 2-30pm down in control
MAUBEUGE Sh51 U.2. **MIA**(Capt CH Stokes **KIA**/2Lt
LH Eyres **POW**)

               Sopwith Camel   **70Sqn**
** combat(2Lt JJ Luckley **WIA**)

C1142   **SE5a**   **92Sqn**
+* combat with Fokker DVII[+ooc] MORMAL
WOOD 9-30am then combat with Fokker DVIIs[+des+
ooc] eLE QUESNOY 10-30am OK(Capt WE Reed) last
of several victories

E5792   **SE5a**   **92Sqn**
+* combat with Fokker DVII[+ooc] eLE QUESNOY
10-30am OK(Lt EF Crabb Can.)

E7056   **FE2b**   **101Sqn**
NB **MIA(Lt J Malley-Martin **KIA**/2Lt TLW Leonard
KIA) left 10-25pm

E8978   **DH9**   **104Sqn (I.F.)**
B **MIA(2Lt HD Arnott **KIA**/2Lt B Johnson **KIA**)
[?DH claim Ltn G Meyer Ja37]

               DH9   **107Sqn**
**B MARIEMBOURG combat with Fokker DVIIs
ovANOR shot up(/2Lt RB Williamson **KIA**)

C9720   **H.P. 0/400**   **215Sqn (I.F.)**
NB THIONVILLE Rlwy Jctn **MIA(2Lt JB Vickers
POW/2Lt SJ Goodfellow **POW**/Sgt RE Culshaw **POW**)
Formation met very heavy AA, weather was also poor

E7329   **Sopwith Camel**   **US 148th Pursuit Sqn**
**OP to Third Army area combat with EA shot up dam
returned 1-45pm OK(1Lt CL Bissell) left 10-30am,
Bissell claimed 6 victories

F6191   **Sopwith Camel**   **US 148th Pursuit Sqn**
**OP combat fuel tank shot up chased down cr Sh51A
Q.5.B dam OK(2Lt LT Wyly) left 10-30am Third Army
area

30th October

This was the heaviest day of air fighting of the war.
The Official History notes that sixty-seven enemy
machines were claimed destroyed on the British
front whilst forty-one RAF machines were struck
off by the end of the day as a result of enemy action.
The raids carried out by the IX Brigade bombing
squadrons and their escorts have been noted, but
others were as intently engaged. Taking virtually
all their attention were the stations and junctions
along the great arterial rail system linking Ghent
in the north to Avesnes, south of Le Cateau. II
Brigade in the north attacked Melle, Audenarde,
and Sotteghem; X Brigade attacked between Ath

and Tournai; I Brigade hit Mons; III Brigade,
Maubeuge; and V Brigade, Avesnes. Escorted
bombing raids to all these destinations met attacks
at some stage in the day. One of the heaviest was
given to a formation of 98 Squadron DH9s escorted
by 19 Squadron Dolphins as they returned from a
raid on Mons. Despite ten Fokkers being claimed,
nine RAF machines were lost and others were so
badly shot up that they crashed on landing.

The biggest single operation of the day was
mounted by the squadrons of X Brigade, operating
with the Fifth Army, north of the First Army. A
great deal of enemy air activity was detected in the
morning on Rebaix aerodrome, north of Ath, and
it was decided that the entire 80th Wing would
attack it. The raid took place at 2-30pm and
involved sixty-two aircraft, led by the indomitable
Wing Commander, Lt. Co. LA Strange in his
personal Sopwith Camel, No. D1943. Bombing was
made by Nos. 2 AFC, 54, and 103 Squadrons, who
were escorted by 4 AFC and 88 Squadrons. Three
hangars were left burning and numerous enemy
machines were doubtless destroyed. Enemy fighters
were active in the air throughout the attack and
many combats on several layers above the aerodrome were known to have taken place — nine
German fighters were claimed. The formation then
returned at low level, shooting up enemy transport
and troop columns as they went.

C8846.M SE5a   **1Sqn**
**OP left 8-15am combat with EA shot up dam OK(Lt
Phinney)

E8071   **Sopwith Snipe**   **4Sqn AFC**
**OP combat with Fokker DVII ovLEUZE 2-55pm ftl
EoL **MIA**(2Lt MJ Kilsby **POW**) left 1-55pm

E4511   **Sopwith Dolphin**   **19Sqn**
OP left 10-15am seen in combat nrMONS **MIA(2Lt F
Lynn **POW**) [Dolphin claim combat MONS Ltn W
Neuenhofen Ja27]

E4552   **Sopwith Dolphin**   **19Sqn**
**OP left 10-15am seen in combat with EA nrMONS
MIA(2Lt CN Boyd **POW**)

E4637   **Sopwith Dolphin**   **19Sqn**
OP left 10-20am seen in combat nrMONS **MIA(2Lt
RB Murray **POW**)

B7855   **Sopwith Dolphin**   **19Sqn**
**OP left 10-15am seen in combat with EA MONS
MIA(Capt JW Crane **KIA**) [Dolphin claim combat
nrMONS 11-20am? Ltn H Frommherz Ja27][claim
MONS 11-20am Fw W Kahle Ja27]

               Sopwith Dolphin   **19Sqn**
** (2Lt H Walmsley **WIA**?)inj?

D3768   **Sopwith Dolphin**   **19Sqn**
OP left 10-15am combat with EA MONS **MIA(2Lt
RW Duff **POW**)

D5237   Sopwith Dolphin   19Sqn
this a'c? +*EscB(98Sqn) combat with Fokker DVIIs[+
+flames] btwn MONS & front lines ~11-30am OK(Capt
JDI Hardman)

E4495   Sopwith Dolphin   19Sqn
+*EscB combat with Fokker DVIIs[+des+ooc] MONS
btwn 11-20am & 11-25am OK(Lt WF Hendershot)

E4514   Sopwith Dolphin   19Sqn
+*EscB combat with Fokker DVIIs[+flames] MONS
11-20am OK(Lt C Montgomery-Moore)

E4713   Sopwith Dolphin   19Sqn
+*EscB combat with Fokker DVII[+des] MONS
11-20am OK(Lt RC Davies)

19 Squadron was escorting 98 Squadron to Mons
when these casualties and combats occurred — all
claims have been given as well for comparison.
They met Jagdgeschwader III and had a bitter
twenty-minute fight. They were the last losses and
aerial combat victories for 19 Squadron.

E2407   Bristol F2b   20Sqn
+* combat with Fokker DVIIs[++des] sAVESNES
12-05pm OK(Capt HP Lale/2Lt CG Boothroyd) this air
crew scored several victories

F6040   Bristol F2b   22Sqn
**OP combat with EA shot up dam OK(Lt OH
Williamson/Capt GB Crawford) left 6am First Army
area, returned 8-10am

F5739   DH4   25Sqn
**Rec MAUBEUGE combat with EA shot up dam
OK(Lt DS Crumb/Lt TA Chilcott) left 7-20am, returned
10-05am

E6010   SE5a   32Sqn
**OP combat with EA 1000' ovGHISLAIN 9-20am
MIA(Capt AA Callender US. DoW) [?"SE5" claim
combat FRESNES Oblt vGriesheim Ja2]

D3440   SE5a   32Sqn
**OP left 8-25am ok ovGHISLAIN 12000' 9-20am
MIA(2Lt W Amory POW) [?SE5a claim combat
COURTRAI Ltn C Degelow Ja40]

D6132   SE5a   32Sqn
**OP combat with EA 1000' ovGHISLAIN 9-20am
MIA(Lt RW Farquhar KIA) left 8-25am [?"SE5" claim
combat nNEUVILLE Ltn E Bormann Ja2]

E6010   SE5a   32Sqn
** shot up(Capt AA Callender US. DoW)

E5804   SE5a   41Sqn
**OP combat with EA & AA 10-45am shot down
Sh37.C.16 MIA(Lt AL Pink KIA)

E8028   Sopwith Snipe   43Sqn
**OP AULNOYE combat shot up dam returned a'dr
2-40pm OK(Capt CC Banks MC) left 12-40pm

C2970   RE8   42Sqn
**AP mg fire 2-05pm engine cut ftl(Lt EA Goodwill

WIA/2Lt HJ Andrews WIA?) cr H20.d.3.9., inj in
accident?

D502   DH9   49Sqn
**B combat with EA swMONS seen in flames MIA(2Lt
BW Cotterell KIA/Sgt WH Gumbley KIA) left 7-25am
[?combat nQUIEVRAIN Ltn O Löffler Ja2]

D3260   DH9   49Sqn
**B ST DENIS combat with EA shot up dam OK(Capt
H Ford/2Lt J Whitehead) left 7-25am, returned 9-45am

D3265   DH9   49Sqn
**B ST DENIS combat with EA shot through dam
OK(2Lt JF Higgins/2Lt EN Andrews) left 7-25am,
returned 9-45am

C2558   RE8   53Sqn
**Phot AA shot up ftl COUCOU A'dr dam(Lt HH
Blackwell OK/TLt PG Hutson WIA) left 9-25am X
Army area

D361.L   SE5a   60Sqn
**OP combat? prop shot up ftl 92Sq dam OK(2Lt EWC
Densham) left 7-30am Third Army area, prop destroyed
by own fire?

C1135.Z   SE5a   64Sqn
**OP left 2-30pm MIA but OK(2Lt TA Priestley WIA)

E7279   Sopwith Camel   65Sqn
+* combat with Fokker DVIIs[+ooc+des] wMULLEM
1-20pm OK(Capt MA Newnham) pilot made 18 claims

H831   Sopwith Camel (NF)   80Sqn
**OP mg fire? ftl POMMEREUIL cr shell hole dam(Lt
GB Wootten WIA) left 9am CATILLON-
PERENCHIES

B7902   SE5a   84Sqn
**OP left 9am seen ok going east ETREUX MIA(2Lt
HJC Thorn KIA)

H7256   SE5a   84Sqn
**OP combat with EA shot up dam(Sgt JM Tarver
WIA)

E2451   Bristol F2b   88Sqn
**OP combat with Fokker DVIIs[+?shot down]
neFROIDMONT? fuel tanks shot up ftl 400yd from
enemy outpost, a'c shelled unsalvable(Lt GF Anderson
DFC SA. WIA/2Lt CMW Elliot WIA) left 7-55am,
Casualty Report:"neFRIEDMONT"?, pilot had made
several combat victories, Ja36 [?"BF" claim combat
TOURNAI 9-10am Vzfw A Hübner Ja36]

E2533   Bristol F2b   88Sqn
+* combat with Fokker DVIIs[+flames] HAVINNES
8-55am OK(Capt C Findlay/Lt IWF Aqaberq) the last of
over a dozen victories for Findlay

88 Squadron, of X Brigade, met nine enemy scouts
over Tournai. The fight intensified when another
eight Fokkers arrived. The outcome was confused
because of the tight nature of the dogfight, but 88
Squadron made nine claims — five down in flames
and four crashed.

DH9   **98Sqn**
B AA fire(2Lt WG Davies **WIA/)

DH9   **98Sqn**
+*B MONS Rlwy Stn combat with 30EAs[+flames]
wMONS 11-30am OK(Lt HW Whitlock/Sgt F Sefton)

D557   DH9   **98Sqn**
+*B MONS Rlwy Stn combat with 30EAs[+des] MONS
11-30am OK(2Lt JM Brown/Sgt T Tedder)

D692   DH9   **98Sqn**
+*B MONS Rlwy Stn combat with Fokker DVIIs[++
des] wMONS 11-30am OK(2Lt FC Wilton/Capt GH
Gillis)

D3239   DH9   **98Sqn**
**B MONS Rlwy Stn combat with 30EAs[+des flames]
wMONS 11-30am AA fire shot up controls hit but
returned a'dr dam(2Lt WV Thomas OK/2Lt WS
Woodall **WIA**)wrist, left 9-15am

D7323   DH9   **98Sqn**
**B MONS Rlwy Stn combat with EAs wMONS on
return **MIA**(Lt EAR Lee **KIA**/Lt AA Douglas **KIA**) left
9-30am

D7325   DH9   **98Sqn**
**B MONS Rlwy Stn combat with 30EAs wMONS on
return **MIA**(Lt DW Holmes **KIA**/Lt JE Prosser **KIA**) left
9-30am [?possible combat CRESPIN 11-30am Ltn H
Lange Ja26]

D7335   DH9   **98Sqn**
**B MONS Rlwy Stn heavy combat with 30EAs ftl
ODAMEZ OK(Lt EW Langford/Lt J Andrews)shelled,
unsalvable

E8863   DH9   **98Sqn**
**B MONS Rlwy Stn combat with EAs on return
ovMONS **MIA**(Lt HF Mulhall **POW**/Lt JC Pritchard
KIA) left 9-30am

F6055   DH9   **98Sqn**
**B MONS Rlwy Stn combat with EAs on return MONS
MIA(Lt TW Sleight **POW**/Lt EPW Dyke **KIA**) left
9-30am

See also the casualties and victories for 19 Squadron who were escorting 98 Squadron. Most of the
attacking formation were Fokker DVIIs.

D550   DH9   **103Sqn**
+* combat with Fokker DVII[+des] MONTREUIL AU
BOIS, nLEUZE 2-30pm OK(Capt JS Stubbs/Lt CG
Bannermann) last of 8 claims by Stubbs

D5569   DH9   **103Sqn**
**B TOURNAI seen in combat ovBARCY going west
14000' MIA but OK(Sgt WJ McNiell/Sgt EG Stevens)
left 7-50am

D5749   DH9   **103Sqn**
B seen sTOURNAI going west 2000' **MIA(Sgt CS
Silvester **POW**?/2Lt H Lansdale **POW**) left 7-50am

D7249   DH9   **103Sqn**

**B combat with Fokker DVIIs[++des] nwLEUZE
2-40pm shot up(Lt GB Hett OK/2Lt JJ Nichols **KIA**)
DoW 31.10.18? Roll of Honour: Nicholls?

DH9   **107Sqn**
** combat(2Lt RC Creamer **WIA**/)

C6240   DH9   **206Sqn**
**B AA hit nr target, radiator dam, dropped behind then
running combat with 3 Fokker DVIIs[+broke up]
nrGHENT ftl crAELTRE-PUCQUES OK(Sgt G
Packman/2Lt JW Kennedy)

DH9   **206Sqn**
** combat(/2Lt WJ Jackson **KIA**)

D3336   Sopwith Camel   210Sqn
+* combat with Fokker DVII[+des] ROMBIES-
ESTREAUX 11-15am OK(Capt SC Joseph) last of over
a dozen victories

F3242   Sopwith Camel   210Sqn
**LP combat with 7 Fokker DVIIs eVALENCIENNES
11-15am **MIA**(Lt A Buchanan DFC **POW**) [?combat
SEBOURG 11-20am Vzfw M Hutterer Ja23]

31st October

Worsening conditions in the following days
reduced the scope for air fighting, but essential
bombing of the rail network continued.

94 Squadron RAF arrived at Senlis from
England on the 31st of October but was to carry
out no operational flying before hostilities ended. It
was equipped with SE5a fighters.

F622   A.W.FK8   **10Sqn**
**FlRec mg 11-50am shot up ftl ShV13 b.7.8. dam
OK(2Lt CD Neill/2Lt MG Ryan)

F625   A.W.FK8   **10Sqn**
**FlRec mg fire shot up ftl cr ldg Sh29 03.b.3.2.(Lt L
Reader **inj**/2Lt F Fletcher **WIA**) hit 9-05am, combat?

RE8   **21Sqn**
** mg fire(Lt EM Mullen **WIA**/)

E1303   SE5a   **32Sqn**
**OP left 8-25am combat with EA shot down
SOLESMES cr(Lt C Wilderspin **WIA**) 30.10?

C1139.2, **E1400, E5976,**
H681   SE5a   **74Sqn**
** all damaged by enemy bombing on a'dr

F3928   Sopwith Camel   204Sqn
**LowB mg engine dam? seen going down low ok
eDEYNZE going West towards Lines **MIA**(2Lt HJ
Gemmell **POW**) left 6-15am, combat? 4m eDEYNZE

November 1918

1st November

E5765.A **SE5a**   **2Sqn AFC**
+* combat with LVGC[+ooc] ANTOING 2-15pm
OK(Capt EE Davies) Davies made several victory claims

RE8   **15Sqn**
** (2Lt LES Burns **WIA**?/) inj?

F6116   Bristol F2b   20Sqn
OP left 11-30am combat with EA seen in steep dive ovFORÊT DE MORMAL **MIA(Lt P Segrave **KIA**/2Lt JF Kidd **KIA**)

F1068   DH9A   25Sqn
PhotRec AVESNES **MIA(2Lt RG Dobeson **POW**/2Lt FG Mills **POW**) left 12-35pm [?possible DH claim Ltn O Könnecke Ja5]

H7164   SE5a   29Sqn
OP combat? cr ldg TOURNAI(Lt DM Layton **WIA)to hospital

E4004   SE5a   32Sqn
OP combat with EA 6m eVALENCIENNES 15000' 1-25pm **MIA(2Lt SE Burden **KIA**) [?possible "SE5" claim combat wHARCHIES Ltn C Bolle Ja2]

E5662   SE5a   32Sqn
**OP left 12-05pm VALENCIENNES combat shot up dam OK(Capt CL Veitch)

E5811   SE5a   32Sqn
OP combat with EA 6m eVALENCIENNES 1-25pm **MIA(Lt H Wilson Can. **KIA**?) [?possible "SE5" claim combat swHARCHIES Ltn A Lindenberger Ja2]

C1150.3 **SE5a   64Sqn**
OP left 11am **MIA(Lt GW Graham **KIA**) [?combat swVALENCIENNES 11-40am Vzfw M Hutterer Ja23]

DH9   **98Sqn**
B MONS Rlwy combat with 20EAs shot up(/Capt AWB Becher **WIA)

D1109   DH9   98Sqn
**B combat with EA BOUVIGNIES radiator shot up engine seized ftl dam OK(2Lt HW Whitlock/Maj Crewdson) left 11-30am

D484   DH9   103Sqn
Rec combat with EA **MIA(2Lt PS Tennant **WIA POW**/2Lt GLP Drummond **WIA POW**) left 6-10am

D5798   DH9   108Sqn
**B AA DENTERGHEM shot up 10-26am oil tank hit ftl WoL dam OK(Lt JG Kershaw/Lt WL Walker) left 9-41am SOLTEGHEM

D9596   Sopwith Camel   204Sqn
+* combat with Fokker DVII[+ooc] SOFFEGHEM 1-50pm OK(2Lt HG Clappison Can.)

D517   DH9   211Sqn
Phot combat with 4EA ovMAUBEUGE 14000' dam(2Lt PM Keary OK/2Lt AK Robinson **WIA) left 11am

D3241   DH9   211Sqn
Phot combat sMAUBEUGE going down in control with 10 EA attacking **MIA(2Lt JM Payne **POW**/2Lt WG Gadd **POW**) left 11am

2nd November

On the 2nd and the 3rd the weather was too poor to permit high bombing, but all fighter squadrons bombed rail stations in addition to their normal low attack work.

Sopwith Dolphin   19Sqn
** combat with EA shot down(2Lt L Reader **WIA**)

D378   SE5a   24Sqn
** dam by shell fire on a'dr

H7079   Sopwith Camel   54Sqn
OP seen ok sTOURNAI going down in control 6000' 3-30pm **MIA(2Lt HR Abey **POW**)

E5941.U **SE5a   64Sqn**
**OP left 3-10pm AA shot up dam returned a'dr 3-50pm OK(Lt JW Bell)

3rd November

E1107   RE8   5Sqn
AP seen cr Sh44 W18.b.9.2. **MIA(Lt E Milner **KIA**/2Lt DE Coe **KIA**) left 1-25pm

RE8   **12Sqn**
** rifle fire(/2Lt CA Stubings **WIA**)

E5739   SE5a   40Sqn
OP had EA on tail 3-45pm nwVALENCIENNES **MIA(Lt PG Greenwood **POW**) left 3-05pm, seen in combat ovST AMAND

RE8   **53Sqn**
** in action(Lt AH Alban **WIA**/)

RE8   **59Sqn**
** mg fire(2Lt FW Dey **WIA**/)

F864.5 **SE5a   64Sqn**
OP left 2-20pm **MIA(Lt J Bullough **KIA**) buried VALENCIENNES

SE5a   **92Sqn**
** AA fire(Capt WE Reed **WIA**)

4th November
THE FINAL ALLIED ASSAULTS

The 4th of November was the day on which the last great air fights of the First World War took place. The mist cleared, and it was reasonably fine, and the German Air Force came out for a final intense confrontation. The last acts of the war were about to be played out, and its fighter pilots could only gather the last of their reserves and their courage and skill to lessen the disaster which was unfolding. Ultimately, there was little they could do to restrict the constant and deadly attacks of the RAF. The casualties inflicted on the 4th were very heavy, but the important fighting on the ground was little hindered by it. The German Air Force had made only minimal attacks on British troops for some

time — all their work was now desperately defensive and could no longer influence the course of the war.

It was in these circumstances that the British Fourth, Third, and First Armies commenced what was to be their decisive and ultimately crushing blow on the German centre on the same day. Valenciennes had fallen two days previously, and the attack was continued along a thirty-mile front stretching south to Oisy on the River Sambre from where the French launched their own attacks. Under this enormous pressure the German resistance was finally broken. By the first evening Landrecies and Le Quesnoy fell, Mormal Wood had been entered, and as position after position crumbled and was overrun, the battle turned into a pursuit. After the 4th the sky was comprehensively in the hands of Allied fighters and bombers, whose scope to wreak increasing damage would be limited only by the weather.

C1129   SE5a   2Sqn AFC
+* combat with Fokker DVII[+des] TOMBELLE 8-10am OK(Capt EL Simonson)

E8038   Sopwith Snipe   4Sqn AFC
**OP seen eBUISSERAL 1-15pm combat with 12 Fokker DVIIs MIA(Lt PW Symons KIA) [?"Snipe" claim combat wRENAIX Ltn E Bormann Ja2]

E8062   Sopwith Snipe   4Sqn AFC
**OP combat with 12 Fokker DVII seen cr Sh37C H.d. 1-15pm MIA(Capt TCR Baker MM KIA) Baker made half of his 12 claims on Snipes

E8064   Sopwith Snipe   4Sqn AFC
**OP seen eBUISSERAL 1-15pm combat with 12 Fokker DVIIs MIA(Lt AJ Palliser KIA) left 11-40am

E8072   Sopwith Snipe   4Sqn AFC
**OP seen neTOURNAI 10-15am combat but AA hit shot down cr Canal TOURNAI MIA(Lt EJ Goodson POW) born UK [?2 Snipe claims combats nTOURNAI Oblt K Bolle Ja2]

E8073   Sopwith Snipe   4Sqn AFC
**OP seen neTOURNAI 10-15am combat with 7 Fokker DVII shot down MIA(Lt CW Rhodes POW)

E9705   DH9A   25Sqn
**PhotRec left 8-15am MAUBEUGE MIA(Lt LLK Straw KIA/2Lt P Cartwright KIA)

F957   DH9A   25Sqn
+*Phot combat with AlbatrosC[+des?] wMAUBEUGE 9-55am ftl? dam OK(Lt JH Latchford/Lt HL Tate)

D572   DH9   27Sqn
**B combat VALENCIENNES shot up ftl OK(2Lt HD Williams/2Lt HB Smith) left 12-25pm

D7355   DH9   27Sqn
**B seen ovST SYMPHOMEN A'dr shot down

MIA(2Lt JG Symonds KIA/Lt WG Lacey MC KIA) left 12-25pm, JG1?

D7356   DH9   27Sqn
**B seen ovST SYMPHOMEN A'dr MIA(2Lt WJ Potts POW/Sgt CW Metcalfe POW?) left 12-25pm, JG1?

E5756   SE5a 29Sqn
*GndTarg left 3-55pm ground mg fuel tank shot up dam returned a'dr OK(2Lt A Wren) to Fourth Army area

A.W.FK8   35Sqn
** mg fire(Capt FH Hodgson WIA/)

H683   SE5a   41Sqn
+* attacked KBs[++destr] PIPAIX & BAUGNIES ~11-25am OK(Lt MP MacLeod Can.) first KB shared, made several victories, most in this a'c

E8004   Sopwith Snipe   43Sqn
**OP ok gliding westwards MAUBEUGE 9000' 1-50pm MIA(2Lt AC MacAulay POW) left 12pm

B5446   Sopwith Camel   46Sqn
**LowB left 12-05pm AA? sudden dive cr(2Lt TG Brooke WIA) was MIA

D6455   Sopwith Camel   46Sqn
**LowB combat with EA seen with EA behind 11-35am MIA(2Lt J O'Donoghue KIA) left 11am

E2583   Bristol F2b   48Sqn
**OP TOURNAI-ATH combat ovLESSINES 3-15pm MIA(Lt IO Gaze POW/2Lt CW Newstead POW) left 1-45pm

E2592   Bristol F2b   48Sqn
**OP TOURNAI-ATH combat ovLESSINES 3-15pm MIA(Lt JF McNamara POW/2Lt J Pugh POW) left 1-45pm

E2625   Bristol F2b   48Sqn
**OP TOURNAI-ATH combat ovLESSINES 3-15pm MIA(Capt AA Harcourt-Vernon POW/2Lt DM Dee POW) left 1-45pm

C61   Sopwith Camel   54Sqn
+* combat with PfalzDXII[+ooc] ATHIES 7-30am OK(Capt RM Foster DFC) shared, last of 7 victories in this a'c

F1987   Sopwith Camel   54Sqn
** mg fire shot up(Capt ADC Browne WIA)

F5631   SE5a   56Sqn
**COP combat LE QUESNOY shot up 10-15am MIA but OK(Lt RF Shutes WIA) [?one of 2 SE5a claims combat ENGLEFONTAINE? Oblt K Bolle Ja2]

F6276   SE5a   56Sqn
**COP left 8-30am AA hit down in slow spin cr Sh51 G.3.A MIA(2Lt O Price KIA)

A7652   DH4   57Sqn
**PhotRec MIA(Lt AE Bourns KIA/Capt R Colville-Jones KIA) left 9-20am [?possible DH claim combat MORMAL WOOD 10-45am Ltn O Könnecke Ja5]

F5719   DH4   57Sqn
** left 9-20am **MIA**(2Lt W Kinghorn **KIA**/2Lt W
Rushton **KIA**)

F5727   DH4   57Sqn
** left 9-20am **MIA**(Lt LdeV Wiener **KIA**/2Lt HG
Dixon **KIA**)

F5833   DH4   57Sqn
**prac left 1-25pm MIA but OK(2Lt LS Harvey/2Lt F
Heath MM)

C4560   RE8   59Sqn
**CP ground mg ovLE QUESNOY dam OK(Lt WL
Christian/Lt WF Wilson) returned a'dr

D7948   Bristol F2b   62Sqn
**EscOP combat with 2EA[+] on tail swMONS 8-50am
MIA(Lt FCD Scott **KIA**/2Lt C Rigby **KIA**) had just got
EA then seen go down control

E2513   Bristol F2b   62Sqn
**EscOP combat with EA swMONS 8-50am then seen
going down with wing broken **MIA**(Lt F Sumsion **KIA**/
Capt WG Walford **KIA**) [?possible F2b claim combat
VIEUX RENGTS? 9-15am Ltn H Lange Ja26]

E7160   Sopwith Camel   65Sqn
+* combat with Fokker DVIIs[+ooc+flames]
seGHENT 8-55am OK(2Lt WH Bland) last of several
claims

E7193   Sopwith Camel   65Sqn
** seen ok ovSOTTEGEM 8-45am **MIA**(Lt J Reid US.
KIA)

F1936   Sopwith Camel   65Sqn
**OP seen ftl nrSOTTEGEM 8-45am abandoned(2Lt
HG Luther **WIA POW**) right hand amputated

F6355   Sopwith Camel   65Sqn
**P combat with Fokker DVIIs[+ooc] seGHENT
~8-50am shot up(2Lt FR Pemberton US. **WIA**)

H7007   Sopwith Camel   65Sqn
this a'c? +* combat with Fokker DVIIs[+des++
flames+ooc] seGHENT ~8-50am OK(Capt JLM White)

**   Sopwith Camel   73Sqn**
** combat(2Lt J Cockburn **WIA**)

C8382   Sopwith Camel   80Sqn
**OP combat? FORÊT DE MORMAL shot up dam
returned a'dr OK(Capt HA Whistler) left 10-15am

D9635   Sopwith Camel   80Sqn
**OP left 10-15am combat with EA shot down FORÊT
DE MORMAL **MIA**(2Lt HCR Grant **KIA**)

F2139   Sopwith Camel   80Sqn
**OP left 6-05am FORÊT DE MORMAL combat shot
up dam OK(2Lt GA Hodgetts)

F6110   Sopwith Camel   80Sqn
**OP left 10-15am combat? FORÊT DE MORMAL
MIA but OK?(Lt RC Fyson)

F6292   Sopwith Camel   80Sqn
**OP LANDRECIES mg shot up dam returned

BERTRY a'dr OK(2Lt GA Muschamp) left 2-45pm

E5766   SE5a   84Sqn
**OP BAVAI-LA CAPELLE ground mg shot up 3-15pm
dam OK(Capt SW Highwood DFC) left 2-30pm, initials
SH?

E5963   SE5a   84Sqn
**OP left 10-45am seen FORÊT DE MORMAL
MIA(Sgt AJ Wing **KIA**)

C8165   Sopwith Dolphin 87Sqn
**OP left 9am shot down in flames ovLE QUESNOY
MIA(2Lt HJ Curtis **KIA**) [?combat
SCHELDEWINDEKE ObFlg A Buhl MFJaIV]

F889   SE5a   92Sqn
B mist seen dive nr ground BERTRY **MIA but
OK(Capt WS Philcox **WIA**) left 6am

**   DH9   98Sqn**
PhotRec combat with EAs(2Lt EW Langford **WIA/2Lt
J Andrews **WIA**)

C2224   DH9   103Sqn
B left 12pm down LOUVAIN **MIA(Lt JG Carey
POW/2Lt DC McDonald **POW**) [?DH claim combat
DUTCH border Ltn C Degelow Ja40]

C2205   DH9   108Sqn
**B British AA 3-40pm engine seized ftl cr BAERLE
OK(Lt Thomson/Lt Donald)

F1118   DH9   108Sqn
**B combat with 6EA ovHUNDELGEM 10am radiator
hit down in control **MIA**(2Lt W Shackleton **POW**/Lt JE
Radley **POW**)

E4384   Sopwith Camel   204Sqn
**OP MELLE combat with 24 Fokker DVIIs 12000'
8-45am then AA ftl MOULIN DE VOORDE OK(Lt JR
Chisman) a'c shelled

F6257   Sopwith Camel   204Sqn
**OP combat with 20-30 Fokker DVIIs ovMELLE
12000' 8-45am then seen after **MIA**(2Lt JD Lightbody
KIA) left 8am, claimed several victories

F1025   DH9A   205Sqn
+* combat with Fokker DVII[+des] MAUBEUGE
3-35pm OK(Maj EG Joy/2Lt LA Drain) Joy had made 7
previous claims with 57Sqn

F1157   DH9   211Sqn
TacRec left 11-30am **MIA(2Lt CC Brouncker **KIA**/
2Lt CD Macdonald **KIA**)

5th November

C2823   RE8   6Sqn
AP left 7am AULNOYE-DOMPIERRE **MIA(2Lt HJ
Berry **POW**/2Lt HA Hamlet **POW**)

**   Bristol F2b   20Sqn**
** mg fire(/Sgt.Mech W Gibson **WIA**)

E7244   Sopwith Camel   45Sqn (I.F.)
+* combat RumplerC[+des] nPARROY 3-50pm

OK(Capt JW Pinder) last of 17 claims, on the last successful day of fighting for 45Sqn

E7198   Sopwith Camel   70Sqn
LP mg fire hit fuel tank ftl spun in cr Sh29 P.32.c at 11-50am(2Lt RR Thomson **KIA)

        SE5a   85Sqn
** mg fire(2Lt RV Lane **WIA**)

E3945   SE5a   85Sqn
OP left 11-45am **MIA(2Lt E Dawson **POW**?) Casualty Cards give POW, but other sources give MIA but OK?

E8421   DH9A   110Sqn (I.F.)
B KAISERSLAUTERN-PIRMASENS heavy combats & poor weather **MIA(Lt RCP Ripley **KIA**?/2Lt FS Towler **KIA**)

D7884   Bristol F2b   P Flt
**P dhAA ftl Sh36 T.3.Cent dam OK(2Lt JT Brown/2Lt HV Irving)

6th November

C2529   RE8   59Sqn
**CAP mg eSOMBRE RIVER 6-45am controls shot up ftl dam OK(Lt RA Spencer/Lt WF Wilson)

F858   SE5a   92Sqn
**OP BERTRY badly shot up dam OK(Lt TS Horry DFC) Horry had claimed at least 6EAs in this a'c in October

D3040   DH9   99Sqn (I.F.)
B **MIA(2Lt CEW Thresher **POW**/2Lt W Glew **DoW** 7.11.18) [?2 DH9 claims combat IBINGEN? 2pm Vzfw H Nülle Ja39]

D1050   DH9   104Sqn (I.F.)
B shot down **MIA(2Lt HL Wren **POW**/2Lt WH Tresham **POW**)

D3101   DH9   104Sqn (I.F.)
B **MIA(2Lt A Hemingway **KIA**/Sgt GA Smith **KIA**)

F3930   Sopwith Camel   210Sqn
**SpM AA fuel tanks shot up ftl dam OK(TLt KR Unger)

C1013   Bristol F2b   P Flt
**P mg ftl Sh37 U.1F 10-30am fire OK(Capt LH Jones/2Lt V Lockey)

        81st Wing RAF
** (LtCol RA Cooper **WIA**?) inj?

7th November

F7385   A.W.FK8   10Sqn
CAP mg fire ftl cr Sh29 Q.7.d.5.5. at 1-20pm(2Lt H Parsons **WIA/2Lt LA Harris OK) a'c shelled

8th November

The British Army had advanced twelve miles further eastwards from Landrecies by the 8th. Avesnes was occupied, and the outskirts of Maubeuge and other points along the Belgian border were being reached. Further north, Conde was captured and Tournai would fall the next day. Towards the coast the armies were deep into Belgium.

E7161   Sopwith Camel   70Sqn
LP combat with EA? 12-10pm **MIA(2Lt J Burt **KIA**)

F6261   Sopwith Camel   80Sqn
OP AVESNES seen attkg transport 500' **MIA(Lt HW Russell DFC **POW**) left 12-30pm

E5775   SE5a   84Sqn
**OP GIVRY-FOURMIES ground mg shot up 3-30pm dam OK(Sgt PJ Palmer) left 2-15pm

9th November

80th Wing made another massed attack on the 9th, this time directed at the retreating army around Enghien as well as airfields in the area. It was led by Major RS Maxwell of 54 Squadron and his unit, in unison with Nos. 103 and 2 AFC Squadrons, spearheaded the attack. They were escorted by 4 AFC Snipes and 88 Squadron Bristol Fighters. The latter were so unoccupied that they eventually came down and joined the attack.

C6403   SE5a   2Sqn AFC
OP left 2pm seen ENGHIEN ground mg shot down **MIA(Capt FR Smith **POW**) but returned through Lines 14.11.18, Smith claimed over a dozen victories in this a'c incl 4 on 14.10.18, in a total of 16

C2774   RE8   4Sqn
CAP AA? cr Sh37 D.6(2Lt JG Leckerby **KIA/2Lt GC Watson MC **WIA**?)inj?

C2690   RE8   4Sqn
 CAP combat with HA? down in flames Sh36 F3.c.4.2. cr destr(2Lt AV Heslop **KIA/2Lt RW Lane **KIA**) at 12-15pm

        RE8   5Sqn
** combat(/2Lt A Berry **WIA**)

        A.W.FK8   8Sqn
** mg fire(2Lt EF Newman **WIA**)

C2796   RE8   15Sqn
**NF AA? shot down ftl 57 S.8.8.5. wr OK(Lt JC Deremo/2Lt WJ Wreford) left 8-15am, unsalvable

C2967   RE8   15Sqn
CAP combat with EA shot down cr Sh51A 20.A.8.8., seen totally wr **MIA(Lt JCH Holmes **KIA**/2Lt EE Richardson **KIA**) left 11am

        RE8   21Sqn
** combat(/2Lt WV Wood **WIA**)

E5999   SE5a   29Sqn
OP combat with EA eMUNTE 10-30am **MIA(2Lt WA Howden **KIA**) btwn MUNTE & Lines?

F853   SE5a   29Sqn
OP combat with EA eMUNTE? 10-30am **MIA(Lt EO Amm SA. **POW**) escaped at Armistice, Amm scored 10 victories

H700   SE5a   29Sqn
+* combat RumplerC[+flames] then Fokker DVII[+des] LAETHEN-ST MARIE btwn 10am & 10-05am OK(Lt EG Davies) made 10 claims

29 Squadron made seventeen claims this day.

E1109   RE8   53Sqn
**NF mg 8-10am ftl 37B 9.c.6.3. dam OK(Lt V Foster/2Lt GW Pearce)

F5982   Sopwith Camel 54Sqn
? (2Lt GA Milbank **WIA)inj?

C8336   Sopwith Camel 54Sqn
+* combat with AlbatrosC[+des] CROISETTE 2-35pm OK(Mjr RS Maxwell) pilot made several claims, including a few on two-seaters in 1916

E5795   SE5a   56Sqn
COP seen ok 2m eMAUBEUGE 3-05pm **MIA(2Lt JC Crawford **KIA**) WIA?

E5805   SE5a   56Sqn
**COP combat shot up 3-30pm ftl Sh57A D.11.d.8.0 cr o't OK(2Lt DN King)

C2537   RE8   59Sqn
CAP combat shot up dam(Lt JS Robson **WIA/2Lt HN Mitchell **WIA**)

**   SE5a   60Sqn**
** combat(Lt FW McCarthy **WIA**) initials WF?

D6953.A   SE5a   60Sqn
**LowP ground fire shot up dam OK(2Lt SJ Mason) left 11-45am Third Army area, returned 1-50pm

F5454.F   SE5a   60Sqn
**LowP left 11-45am ground fire shot up dam OK(Lt BS Johnston) to Third Army front, returned 1-55pm

B9421   DH9   98Sqn
**Rec left 10-15am combat with EA dam OK(Lt HW Whitlock/Lt Bocock) [?possible DH9 claim combat BEAUMONT Ltn H vFreden Ja50]

D9929   FE2b   101Sqn
NB left 5-30pm **MIA(2Lt HT Eyres **KIA**/2Lt GE Williams)

E7078   FE2b   101Sqn
**NB ftl cr wr MIA but OK(2Lt J Cave/2Lt BML Bunting) left 6-15pm

D3036   DH9   107Sqn
prac cr French Lines MIA but OK(2Lt WA Oates USAS. **inj/2Lt WJB Penman **inj**) left 11-10am

**   DH9   108Sqn**
B DENDERLEEUWE combat with 13 Fokker DVIIs just before target shot up(/Lt HS Gargett **WIA)wrist, two explosive bullets through wrist, first raid left 9-30am

**   DH9   108Sqn**
B DENDERLEEUWE combat with 13 Fokker DVIIs just before target shot up(/2Lt FLP Smith **KIA)head, first raid left 9-30am, also heavy AA

E8980   DH9   108Sqn
B DENDERLEEUWE combat with 12 Fokker DVIIs then hit by AA AUDENARDE shot up ftl(2Lt JD Sloss **DoW ~16.11.18/2Lt JD Todd **WIA**)arm, left 1-05pm, second raid left 2-20pm?

**   DH9   108Sqn**
B DENDERLEEUWE AA fire(Lt W Marsden **WIA/)

F1022   DH9A   205Sqn
B combat with EA seen ok going east nrFLORENNES **MIA(Lt EH Johnson **KIA**/Sgt GE Grundy **KIA**) left 8-35am

D3400   Sopwith Camel 213Sqn
+* combFokker DVII[+des] 10m neGHENT 10-30am OK(Lt HC Smith) last of 5 claims

F5913   Sopwith Camel 213Sqn
**HOP shot up engine hit dam ftl neCOURTRAI OK(2Lt GC Garner)

10th November

C2691   RE8   12Sqn
CAP left 11-30am **MIA(Lt AB Agnew US. **POW**/2Lt S Coates **POW**)

C2873   RE8   12Sqn
** mg fire 7-25am ftl Sh51 K.30 dam OK(Lt Townsend/Lt Steele)

E2429   Bristol F2b   20Sqn
+* combat with Fokker DVIIs[+des+flames] wLOUERVAL swCHARLEROI btwn 11am & 11-35am OK(Lt GE Randall/Lt GV Learmond) last victories of 11 for Randall

F4421   Bristol F2b   20Sqn
** left 10-15am seen in combat with EA ovCHARLEROI **MIA**(Lt EAC Britton **POW**/Sgt RS Dodds **KIA**) pilot escaped

F6195   Bristol F2b   20Sqn
OP combat with EA ovCHARLEROI **MIA(2Lt AW McHardy **KIA**/2Lt WA Rodger Can. **KIA**) left 10-20am

C1212   DH9   27Sqn
**B AA shot up ST REMY-M-B ftl dam OK(2Lt IL Dutton/2Lt GH Wilson) left 6-45am

C2409   RE8   42Sqn
**Rec mg shot up 9am ftl EoL wr(2Lt GC Upson/2Lt HJ Clements) escaped back over Lines

**   Sopwith Camel 46Sqn**
** mg fire(Capt CA Brown **WIA**)

C8391   Sopwith Camel 46Sqn
OP left 9am air collision with Camel F6285 ovSh57 D8.B.7.8. **MIA(2Lt GE Dowler **KIA**)

F6285   Sopwith Camel   46Sqn
**LowB left 9-05am air collision with Camel C8391 cr
Sh57D 8.B.7.8. **MIA**(2Lt WG Coulthurst **KIA**)

F2083   Sopwith Camel   54Sqn
**SpB left 1-35pm mg fire? ldg ok wBASSILY MIA but
OK?(Lt JC MacLennan)

F5725   DH4   55Sqn (I.F.)
B THIONVILLE-METZ going down ok **MIA(Capt
DRG Mackay DFC **POW DoW** 11.11.18/2Lt HTC
Gompertz **POW**) observer "returned"

Low clouds, mist, and heavy AA prevented the
formation of twelve DH4s from reaching their
objective of Koln. Instead, railways around Ehrang
were bombed.

F855   SE5a   84Sqn
+* combat with Fokker DVII[+des] seFAYNOLLE
10am OK(Lt FH Taylor Can.) last of 10 claims, & last
for 84Sqn

F5515   SE5a   84Sqn
**OP left 2-25pm shot down wMARIENBURG seen ldg
in control **MIA**(Lt AM Rosenbleet US. **POW**)

E5771   SE5a   92Sqn
**OP mg radiator shot up ftl SOLRE LE CATEAU cr
OK(Capt OJ Rose)unsalvable

F5623   SE5a   92Sqn
**OP mg shot up LANDRECIES engine seized ftl dam
OK(Lt TS Horry)

F8509   Sopwith Camel   210Sqn
**OP seen going s-e nrBOIS DE WAUHU ovMONS
Sh46.s.23. at 9-10am **MIA**(Lt JE Pugh **KIA**) to MONS-
MAUBEUGE

D7362   DH9   211Sqn
Phot AA ftl swCHARLEROI EoL **MIA(2Lt CH
Thomas **POW**/2Lt JHR Smith **KIA**) left 9-45am, repat
28.2.19

D9648   Sopwith Camel   213Sqn
+* combat with LVGC[+des] 7m seGHENT 10-40am
OK(Capt GC Mackay Can.) shared, last of 18 claims

11th November

The British Army ended the war on the Western
Front much where it had first begun it. As dawn
rose, the Canadians captured Mons, and at 11am
the Armistice brought fighting on the ground and
in the air to a close. The news that the war was
ended caused ecstatic celebrations to erupt in
Britain. In France, Allied squadrons up and down
the line, as well as those in the Mediterranean and
the Middle East, no doubt celebrated their victory
well that day. Although not unexpected, the news
could hardly be believed, however, and it was met
with a mixture of exhaustion and relief, as much as
with jubilation.

A great victory had been achieved in which
airmen had been rarely far from the heart of the
action. True, their work had been above the ground
fighting where the worst excesses and demands of
this terrible war had been played out, but their
unremitting devotion to duty and their skills and
talents had never been offered with a less than full
commitment. In somewhat over four years their
roles had changed out of all recognition and the
weight of responsibility on them increased enormously. The eight thousand-odd separate
casualties listed in this book are testimony to the
victorious sacrifice of those who made the sky their
battlefield.

A.W.FK8   2Sqn
** mg fire(/2Lt S Soothill **WIA**)

Untraced Casualties in France in 1918

(Lt J Martin **POW**) .18?, to Holland, repat 12.18
(Capt WE Foster **POW**) .18? repat 27.11.18
(Lt JB Hulme **POW**) .18? repat 27.11.18
(Capt CB Wilson **POW**) .18? repat 19.11.18
(Lt A Copley **POW**) .18? repat 9.2.19
(Lt G Wallace-Simpson **POW**) .18? repat 9.2.19

Part II

AMERICANS IN THE GREAT WAR 1916–1918

Section A
L'ESCADRILLE LAFAYETTE 1916–1917

The Escadrille Americaine was officially authorised on the 21st of March 1916 to bring together a unit of American volunteers within the French Air Service. It formally came into being on the 17th of April, and it rose on a tide of opinion in the United States, which sought in a public and overt way to lend support to the Allied cause. Most of the funding for its formation and subsequent training organisation came from voluntary contributions, helped considerably by the active promotion of several prominent and influential citizens. After complaints about its name from many in America, including the German Ambassador, it was to be re-titled the Lafayette Escadrille by the end of the year. The French numbered it Escadrille N.124.

It was to become a focus not only for Americans with aspirations to fly in France, but also for the many who were already serving with the French. It offered sponsorship for training of air crew in France, as well as entry to a fighting unit for those who made the grade. At first, the scale of recruitment meant that these were placed in the Escadrille Lafayette, but within months the numbers involved became so great that the American airmen could be farmed out to other French units. Americans eventually served in nearly one hundred escadrilles. One source of confusion for some is that whilst all Americans who passed through the system were members of the "Lafayette Flying Corps", many of these never flew with the "Lafayette Escadrille" itself.

1916
May

13th May

The first patrol of the Lafayette was flown to the Mulhouse area on the 13th of May, led by Cpl K Rockwell. It met some AA fire but was otherwise uneventful.

18th May

        Nieuport 11   N.124
** combat with LVG 2Str[+shot down smoking cr nrTHANN] between MULHOUSE-HARTMANNSWEILERKOPF shot up OK(Cpl KY Rockwell) only 4 rounds fired before jam, but enough

This was the first victory for the unit.

24th May

        Nieuport Scout N.124
P attacked EA 2Strs shot up(Cpl KY Rockwell **WIA)face

        Nieuport Scout N.124
P combat with EA 2Strs shot up(Cpl VE Chapman **WIA)arm

        Nieuport Scout N.124
P combat with EA 2Strs shot up engine & fuel tank hit shot down(Sgt W Thaw **WIA)arm, to hospital

A patrol of five machines, led by the Commanding Officer Capt G Thenault, spotted several German two-seaters near Etain and some Nieuports apparently broke formation in order to attack them. The whole patrol was therefore drawn into the fight; most of the casualties, the first for the unit, occurred as the chasing aircraft passed down through the enemy group.

June

19th June

Nieuport   N.124

P combat with many EAs nVERDUN shot up ftl nrFORT CHOISEUL(Sgt C Balsley **WIA)thigh, hit by explosive bullet, recovered out of spin in descent

23rd June

Nieuport   N.124

P patrol met 5EAs nrTHIAUMONT then when other Nieuports retired he attacked EA & then seen fall ooc cr wr(Sgt V Chapman **KIA) left 12-15pm

This was the first death in combat for the Lafayette. There were three other Nieuports flying that day, and as the enemy was engaged the patrol became separated. The other three were uncertain of Chapman's fate when the fighting ended and headed for home. Later, however, another French unit reported that one of the four Nieuports had been seen making a final attack and then going down out of control until it crashed.

July

30th July

Nieuport   N.124

** combat with 2Str[+] FORÊT D'ETAIN OK(Sgt GR Lufbery)

This was Lufbery's first victory.

September

23rd September

Nieuport   N.124

P combat with EAs then 2nd combat with 2Str EA ~9am shot up broke up cr nrRODERN(SLt K Rockwell **KIA) hit in chest

Rockwell had begun the patrol with Lufbery. They had met and engaged some enemy, but Lufbery was forced to withdraw with a gun jam and landed at Esc.49. Rockwell followed him down, but then turned eastwards again and sought out an enemy two-seater. In his dive on it he almost collided with its tail. There was an exchange of fire and Rockwell was hit in the chest with an explosive bullet. His Nieuport shed a wing on the way down.

Nieuport 17 Scouts began to come on strength late September 1916.

October

12th October

Nieuport 17   N.124

EscB OBERNDORF Small Arms Works, forced to land in darkness on return at CORCIEUX A.L.G. cr wr(SLt N Prince LdH **DoI 15.10.16) thrown from a'c, died in hospital

There were sixty machines involved in this raid.

November

The first SPAD 7 machines came on strength in November 1916. Patrols were continued until the middle of the month when fog and rain began to restrict operations. Action was minimal until January, when the unit was moved to Just-en-Chaussée on the Oise-Aisne sector.

1917
March

19th March

Nieuport   N.124

OP shot up(Sgt EEC Genet **WIA)slight, initials ECC?

Nieuport 17   N.124

OP combat with EA ovDOUCHY shot down nrFLAVY-LE-MARTEL **MIA(Sgt JR McConnell **KIA**)

McConnell was the last of the original pilots still to be on strength and the last to be lost before the United States of America entered the war on the 6th of April 1917.

April

On April the 7th the unit moved to Ham to be nearer the new Hindenburg Line, on the Somme front. They remained in this sector for two months before returning to the Aisne.

16th April

Nieuport   N.124

** AA ovST QUENTIN(Sgt EEC Genet **KIA**) 17.4?

23rd April

Morane Parasol   N.124

** combat with EA shot down(Sgt R Hoskier **KIA**/Sgt J Dressy **KIA**)

This Morane was normally only used for training and gunnery practice. Dressy was de Laage de Meux's orderly, who was the Assistant Commanding Officer (Laage de Meux's death is noted below).

May

23rd May

> SPAD 7   N.124
> *test engine failed at 250' after take off at HAM A'dr ss cr(Lt A de Laage de Meux **KIFA**)

June

Some Nieuport 28C.1s were assigned in June.

25th June

> Nieuport 17   N.124
> **P joined EA formation in error, shot down(Sgt JN Hall **WIA**)severe

July

17th July

> Nieuport 17   N.124
> **travelling, became separated then attacked 2EAs who were attacking Allied KB, but shot down WoL(Cpl JR Doolittle)

Doolittle was shot down on his first flight, during the unit's move to St Pol to co-operate in the Flanders Offensive. In this month its official designation altered to Spa.124 in recognition of the fact that they were mostly equipped with SPADs.

August

18th August

Yet another move for the Escadrille came on August the 11th, back to Senard to take part in the French offensive at Verdun, on the edge of the Argonne forest.

> Nieuport   N.124
> **EscB combat with EAs shot down nrDUN-SUR-MEUSE(Sgt HB Willis **POW**) running fight

> Nieuport   N.124
> **EscB combat with EAs shot up ovDUN-SUR-MEUSE(Sgt S Bigelow **WIA**)severe

September

24th September

> 2119   SPAD 7   Spa.124
> ** combat nrTHIAUCOURT shot down **MIA**(Sgt D MacMonagle **KIA**)

The unit was reassigned to Chandon on the Aisne to prepare for the Malmaison offensive.

October

1st October

> Ni3578?   Nieuport 17   N.124
> ** combat with 2Str nSOISSONS cr marshes nrFORT MALMAISON shot down (Sgt AC Campbell **KIA**) [shot down by Sch.Staffel 8]

December

With America preparing to bring its own aero squadrons into action in France it was clear that the Escadrille Lafayette had served its purpose and that a redeployment of its personnel was in order. In early December its American pilots were released from the French military in order to transfer to the American Air Service. Only one, 2Lt EC Pearson, remained with the French, to fly with Escadrille Spa.3. Due to bureaucratic lethargy the pilots' commissions were held up for two months, so that they flew effectively as civilians.

On February 18th 1918 the Escadrille Lafayette passed out of being, the pilots becoming the nucleus of the 103rd US Aero Squadron. Escadrille Spa.124 returned to a wholly French affair, renamed the Escadrille Jeanne d'Arc.

Section B
UNITED STATES
AIR SERVICE AERO SQUADRONS 1918

These entries exclude information relating to the US 17th and 148th Pursuit Squadrons who were operating with the Royal Air Force. Details of airmen with these units are given in Part I: THE WESTERN FRONT.

March 1918

9th March

3144   SPAD 7   95th Pursuit Sqn
HAP attacked by 2Strs nrCRAONNE shot down in spin ovBERRIEUX WOODS cr EoL **MIA(Capt JE Miller **KIA**) left 10am, gun jam

Miller was the first US Air Service flying officer killed in action in France.

12th March

**   SPAD   103rd Pursuit Sqn**
AntiGothaP ovPARIS seen cr sCHÂTEAU THIERRY ~1-30pm(Capt P Collins **KIA)

April 1918

14th April

Ni6164.10   **Ni28C.1**   **94th Pursuit Sqn**
**P combat with Pfalz[+] & AlbatrosDV ovGENGOULT A'dr OK(1Lt D Campbell) Vzfw A Wroniecki of Ja64 shot down

This was the first combat victory for 94th US.

29th April

Ni6153.17   **Ni28C.1**   **94th Pursuit Sqn**
**P combat with AlbatrosD?[+shot down in flames] ST BAUSSANT 6-10pm OK(Capt JN Hall) shared victory with 1Lt EV Rickenbacker, Pfalz DIII?

Ni6159.12   **Ni28C.1**   **94th Pursuit Sqn**
** combat with AlbatrosD?[+shot down in flames] ST BAUSSANT 6-10pm OK(1Lt EV Rickenbacker CMH) shared victory with Capt JN Hall, Pfalz DIII?

This Albatros was Rickenbacker's first of twenty-two aircraft and four balloon victories, making him the highest scoring ace of the US Air Service.

May 1918

2nd May

Ni6144.14   **Ni28C.1**   **94th Pursuit Sqn**
**Esc combat with 2Hannovers[+shot down in flames] ovFORÊT DE VENCHÈRES lost fabric upper wing ftl OK(1Lt JA Meissner) [EA of FAb(A)298b]

3rd May

Ni6138.0   **Ni28C.1**   **94th Pursuit Sqn**
P combat with 4Albatros shot down in flames AMENONCOURT ~10-25am(2Lt CW Chapman DSC **KIA) Ja80b [?"SPAD" claim Oblt E Wenig Ja80b]

7th May

Ni6153.17   **Ni28C.1**   **94th Pursuit Sqn**
P combat ovVIEVILLE-EN-HAYE driven down then AA hit engine ftl cr(Capt JN Hall **inj POW) wing damaged, down btwn QUELLENLAGER-VIEVILLE [Flak 54]["Nieu" claim combat VIEVILLE 8-05am Ltn F Hengst Ja64]

11th May

**   SPAD   103rd Pursuit Sqn**
P combat with 3EAs engine failed ftl seYPRES EoL 3-40pm **MIA(1Lt PW Eaton **WIA POW**) had joined Camel flight in error, then met EAs on way home, confirmed POW by later letter

12th May

**   Ni28C.1   95th Pursuit Sqn**
* cr(1Lt RA Blodgett **KIA**) 17.5?, possibly killed in accidental crash

14th May

**   Dorand AR-1 12th Observation Sqn**
** **MIA**(2Lt CM Angel **KIA**/2Lt WKB Emerson **KIA**) crew?

15th May

**   SPAD 13   103rd Pursuit Sqn**
P combat with 2Str then 2nd 2Str shot up ftl nrYPRES 11-30am(Capt CJ Biddle **WIA)leg, to hospital, was with Lafayette FC [combat w FAb(A)221?]

19th May

Ni6178.16 **Ni28C.1** **94th Pursuit Sqn**
**HAP left 9am chased EA 2Str fuel tank hit shot down
in flames nrMARON ~9-20am(Maj GR Lufbery **KIA**)
jumped from a'c, borrowed a'c to chase EA from
ReihenbildzeugC, EA later brought down by French Spa68

22nd May

SPAD 13 **103rd Pursuit Sqn**
** combat with ~8Albatros shot down nrLAVENTIE
9-35am **MIA**(1Lt EA Giroux **KIA**) [?"SPAD" claim
combat eBRETAGNE? 9-53am Ltn H Muller Ja18]

SPAD 13 **103rd Pursuit Sqn**
** patrol met Albatros[+] nrLAVENTIE then controls
hit shot down cr EoL 9-45am **MIA**(1Lt PF Baer DFC **inj
POW**) Baer's 9th & last victory, he had served with
Lafayette FC [?"Camel" claim combat FLEURBAIX
10-05am Gefr Deberitz Ja18]

27th May

Ni6142.23 **Ni28C.1** **94th Pursuit Sqn**
**HAP combat with 4Albatros ovMONTSEC-
HEUDICOURT ~10am shot up ftl
RAMBUCOURT?(1Lt WD Hill **WIA**)leg, Ja65
explosive bullet? [?"SPAD" claim Ltn O Fitzner Ja65]

28th May

Ni6144.8 **Ni28C.1** **94th Pursuit Sqn**
**HAP combat with EA[+gng down] ~8-55am
eTHIAUCOURT shot up lost fabric ftl OK(1Lt JA
Meissner) Ja65, name Meisner?

Ni28C.1 **95th Pursuit Sqn**
? (Capt JA Hambleton **WIA) only in Gorrell

30th May

Ni28C.1 **95th Pursuit Sqn**
**P dive on 2EAs[+] when top plane fabric tore: spin ftl
EoL **MIA**(1Lt WV Casgrain **POW**) shared victory with
4 others

June 1918

2nd June

Ni6193.2 **Ni28C.1** **94th Pursuit Sqn**
**HAP combat with EA shot down in flames(2Lt PW
Davis **KIA**) Ja64 ["Nieu" claim combat nMONTSEC
3-15pm Ltn F Hengst Ja64] had been Lufbery's regular a'c

SPAD 13 **103rd Pursuit Sqn**
**P combat with 7EAs shot up nrMONT KEMMEL
5-25pm(1Lt FO'D Hunter **WIA**) bullet splinter to forehead

5th June

Ni28C.1 **147th Pursuit Sqn**
OP AA fire? dam prop, became lost ftl **MIA(2Lt JF
Ashenden **INT**) 24.6? A Flt, left to meet French
Photographic a'c from METZ, interned Switzerland

6th June

Ni6158.0 **Ni28C.1** **94th Pursuit Sqn**
**P combat with 2EA ovEPLEY? 18000' shot up ftl(1Lt
D Campbell **WIA**)back, hit by explosive bullet, returned
to USA [FAb12]

12th June

Salmson 2A2 **91st Observation Sqn**
**EscPhot testing guns on return & destroyed prop ftl
EoL **MIA**(1Lt BB Battle **POW**/1Lt JF Williamson
POW) German message came 3 weeks later

13th June

Ni28C.1 **27th Pursuit Sqn**
**P became separated combat with EA shot up dam ftl
EoL **MIA**(2Lt WH Plyler **POW**) fabric shredded on wing

24th June

Caproni **US Italy**
IV Caproni Group(or XIV Grp) based nrPADUA **B
troops nrFALSE DE PIAVE engine failed mist ftl in
Austrian lines on River PIAVE ~5-30pm **MIA**(1Lt CM
Young **POW**/) with Italian observer & bombadier,
controls fouled?, first American POW on Italian front

25th June

SPAD 13 **103rd Pursuit Sqn**
**P AA? shot up cr seYPRES 7-35pm(1Lt WT Hobbs
KIA)

July 1918

1st July

Ni6271.7 **Ni28C.1** **94th Pursuit Sqn**
**P combat with Pfalzes[+?] nrCHARLY ~4-30pm shot
down WoL ftl cr wires o't wr(1Lt HH Tittmann
WIA)severe, WIA lung, arm & foot, thrown 30' in seat
in cr, Ja66 [?"Nieu" claims by Ltn A Laumann & Ltn W
Preuss Ja66]

2nd July

Ni28C.1 **27th Pursuit Sqn**
**P left 6-15am combat with 9 Fokker DVIIs
neCHÂTEAU THIERRY 7-15am **MIA**(1Lt EB Elliott
KIA) combat lasted 30mins, Ja4

Ni6347 **Ni28C.1** **27th Pursuit Sqn**
**P left 6-15am combat with 9 Fokker DVIIs
neCHÂTEAU THIERRY 7-15am **MIA**(1Lt WB
Wanamaker **WIA POW**) combat lasted 30mins, Ja4
["Nieu" claim combat BEZU-ST-GERMAINE 7-15am
Ltn E Udet Ja4]

Salmson 2A2 **91st Observation Sqn**
LRec combat with 9EAs shot up ftl EoL **MIA(2Lt HG
Mayes **WIA POW**/1Lt FF Shilling **KIA**) Mayes WIA
head & legs, to hospital, became separated from other a'c

5th July

Salmson 2A2   **12th Observation Sqn**
** (/1Lt BP Harwood **WIA**)

Ni28C.1   **95th Pursuit Sqn**
** (1Lt C Rhodes **POW**)

Ni28C.1   **95th Pursuit Sqn**
** **MIA**(1Lt SP Thompson **KIA**) was thought POW

7th July

Ni6181.15   Ni28C.1   **94th Pursuit Sqn**
P brought down EoL(1Lt WW Chalmers **POW) a'c captured in tact

Ni28C.1   **95th Pursuit Sqn**
** combat with EAs[++] 10-10am shot up **MIA**(1Lt SE McKeown **WIA POW**) to hospital

8th July

Ni28C.1   **147th Pursuit Sqn**
** shot down EoL **MIA**(2Lt MO Parry **KIA**)

10th July

Breguet 14B2   **96th Bombardment Sqn**
B CONFLANS Rlwy Yards lost ftl nrCOBLENZ **MIA(1Lt RL Browning **POW**/1Lt JE Duke **POW**) crew?

Breguet 14B2   **96th Bombardment Sqn**
B CONFLANS wind lost dark ftl 9pm **MIA(Maj HM Brown **POW**/2Lt HA McChesney **POW**) both captured at bridge into Luxemburg trying to escape

Breguet 14B2   **96th Bombardment Sqn**
B CONFLANS wind lost ftl **MIA(1Lt DL MacDonald **POW**/2Lt RH Tucker **POW**) crew?

Breguet 14B2   **96th Bombardment Sqn**
B CONFLANS wind lost ftl **MIA(1Lt HC Lewis **POW**/1Lt CH Tichenor **POW**) crew?

Breguet 14B2   **96th Bombardment Sqn**
B CONFLANS wind lost ftl **MIA(1Lt HD Smith **POW**/Lt GI Ratterman **POW**) crew?

Breguet 14B2   **96th Bombardment Sqn**
B CONFLANS wind lost ftl **MIA(1Lt JM Mellen **POW**/2Lt AR Strong **POW**) crew?

At this time the 96th Squadron *was* the American bombing effort, so these six losses were a disaster. The aircraft known to be involved in this raid were Breguets 4003, 4005, 4012, 4015, 4019, and 4020. Each crew was forced down at different times after the patrol had met strong westerly winds in growing darkness and lost formation.

14th July

.14   **Ni28C.1**   **95th Pursuit Sqn**
** became separated from patrol combat with 7EAs shot down **MIA**(1Lt Q Roosevelt **KIA**)head ["Nieu 1Str" claim Untoff Graper] only Nieuport claim of day: some

say Sgt K Thom Ja21 but his nearest claim was 2Str SPAD on 15.7

15th July

Ni6206   Ni28C.1   **147th Pursuit Sqn**
** combat with Fokker DVIIs[+?ooc] btwn 6pm to 7-30pm OK(2Lt TJ Abernethy) [Ja36]

16th July

Ni28C.1   **27th Pursuit Sqn**
GndStrafe **MIA(1Lt MB Gunn **KIA**)

Ni28C.1   **27th Pursuit Sqn**
P combat with 12EAs ovEPERNAY 18000'-1500' shot down EoL **MIA(1Lt RF Raymond DSC **POW**) in pm [?poss "Nieu" claim 12-20pm? Ltn W Blume & Untoff Schneck Ja9]

Salmson 2A2   **91st Observation Sqn**
Rec combat with 4 Fokker DVIIs 16000' shot up(1Lt JW van Huevel **WIA/2Lt FK Hirth **KIA**)heart, Van Hueval hit in head & came to in dive, but pulled out and landed, crew?

Ni28C.1   **147th Pursuit Sqn**
OP combat with EAs shot up cr(1Lt DW Cassard **KIA)

17th July

SPAD   **139th Pursuit Sqn**
DeepRec ftl EoL **MIA(1Lt HG McClure **POW**)

18th July

Sopwith Strutter 88th Observation Sqn
CP ground fire shot up(1Lt FE Evans **WIA/1Lt HW Merrill OK)pilot WIA leg:severe, guided back by observer

19th July

Ni28C.1   **27th Pursuit Sqn**
** combat with Fokker DVIIs? ~2pm?(1Lt RS Schmitt **WIA**) severe

SPAD 13   **95th Pursuit Sqn**
** **MIA**(1Lt HL Richards **POW**)

20th July

Salmson 2A2   **1st Observation Sqn**
CP ground fire(/1Lt HJ Boldt **KIA) 21.7?

Ni28C.1   **27th Pursuit Sqn**
ftgprac left 6-55pm combat with 7Albatros nrSOISSONS shot down **MIA(1Lt J MacArthur DSC **KIA**) following RAF formation but lost them, 30mph wind from sw, led eastwards then lost

Ni28C.1   **27th Pursuit Sqn**
ftgprac left 6-55pm combat with 7Albatros[++] nrSOISSONS 7-30pm to 7-45pm then brought down **MIA(1Lt ZR Miller **POW**)

Ni28C.1　　**27th Pursuit Sqn**
**ftgprac left 6-55pm combat with EAs shot down EoL
MIA(1Lt FW Norton DSC **DoW** 22.7.18) possibly DoW
23.7.18 [?"Nieu" claim FÈRE-EN-TARDENOIS
7-50pm Ltn R Klimke Ja27]

22nd July

Ni28C.1　　**94th Pursuit Sqn**
? (1Lt WW Palmer **WIA) only in Gorrell

25th July

Salmson 2A2　　**12th Observation Sqn**
** shot down(1Lt AN Joerg **KIA**/2Lt AJ Bradford **KIA**)

SPAD 13　　**95th Pursuit Sqn**
** **MIA**(1Lt GC Vann **KIA**) Gorrell: 14.10?

26th July

.24　　**SPAD 13**　　**95th Pursuit Sqn**
**P patrol met EAs combat with Rumpler[+ftl] 7am shot
up ftl **MIA**(1Lt GW Puryear **POW**) shared victory with
4 others, landed for confirmation thinking he was WoL,
escaped to Switzerland 11.18, first American airman to
do so

27th July

Salmson 2A2　　**91st Observation Sqn**
? (/1Lt WH Lawson **WIA) only in Gorrell

28th July

Salmson 2A2　　**12th Observation Sqn**
**AP combat with Fokker DVIIs 7pm shot up ftl EoL
MIA(2Lt AP Baker **WIA POW**/2Lt JC Lumsden **KIA**)
crew?

Salmson 2A2　　**12th Observation Sqn**
**AP combat with Fokker DVIIs[++] low ovFÈRE EN
TARDENOIS 7pm shot up ftl OURCQ River(1Lt JC
Miller **DoW**/1Lt SW Thompson **WIA**)leg, Miller hit in
stomach, shared victories, observer hit but brought a'c
down

31st July

SPAD?　　**94th Pursuit Sqn**
** combat with several EAs EoL late pm **MIA**(2Lt AF
Winslow **WIA POW**)arm, arm was amputated

SPAD 13　　**95th Pursuit Sqn**
** **MIA**(1Lt PH Montague **POW**)

Ni28C.1　　**147th Pursuit Sqn**
OP shot up **MIA(2Lt JH Stevens **KIA**)

August 1918

1st August

Salmson 2A2　　**1st Observation Sqn**
**Phot FÈRE-EN-TARDENOIS heavy combat with

Fokker DVIIs shot up ftl(1Lt WP Erwin OK/1Lt EB
Spencer **WIA**)severe:side, escort by US 27Sqn, 42 bullet
holes in a'c

Salmson 2A2　　**1st Observation Sqn**
**Phot combat with several Fokker DVIIs nrSOISSONS
MIA(1Lt EG Wold **DoW** 2.8.18/1Lt JC Wooten **KIA**)

Salmson 2A2　　**1st Observation Sqn**
**Phot combat with several Fokker DVIIs nrSOISSONS
MIA(21Lt WP Miller **DoW** 3.8.18/2Lt JJ Sykes **KIA**)
crew?

Ni28C.1　　**27th Pursuit Sqn**
**EscPhot left ~7am FISMES combat with 8 Fokker
DVIIs[+] chased it down then headed West but met 2
Fokker DVIIs fuel tank hit ftl cr **MIA**(1Lt AL Whiton
POW) escorting Salmsons, deliberate cr

Ni28C.1　　**27th Pursuit Sqn**
**EscPhot nrFISMES combat with 5 Fokker DVIIs
nrSOISSONS engine hit ftl cr **MIA**(1Lt CA McElvain
POW) escorting Salmsons ["Nieu" claim nrARCY
8-40am Ltn R Fleischer Ja17]

This combat, and its remarkable aftermath of
friendship, is described in Vol 3, No 3 of the
American Cross and Cockade journal.

Ni28C.1　　**27th Pursuit Sqn**
**EscPhot nrFISMES combat with 8 Fokker DVIIs
eFÈRE 8-10am shot up fainting ftl **MIA**(1Lt RC Martin
WIA POW)hand & shoulder, escorting Salmsons [Ja17]

Ni28C.1　　**27th Pursuit Sqn**
**EscPhot nrFISMES combat with 8 Fokker DVIIs shot
up ret a'dr cr ldg(1Lt OT Beauchamp **Kld**) escorting
Salmsons, seen w 2EAs on tail then keel over but returned
only to crash

Ni28C.1　　**27th Pursuit Sqn**
**EscPhot nrFISMES combat with 8 Fokker DVIIs[+
?spin down] FÈRE-EN-TARDENOIS shot up then
Rumpler[+wing off] then ground fire then Rumpler[+
shot down cr] OK(1Lt D Hudson) combat 8-10am to
8-30am

Ni28C.1　　**27th Pursuit Sqn**
**EscPhot nrFISMES combat with EAs fuel? ftl?
MIA(1Lt JS Hunt **KIA**)

Ni6275.2 Ni28C.1　　**27th Pursuit Sqn**
**EscPhot nrFISMES combat with EAs shot down in
flames EoL nrBRANGES(1Lt CB Sands **KIA**)

4th August

4609　　**SPAD 13**　　**213th Pursuit Sqn**
? (1Lt Albertson **POW) Aug.18

9th August

Salmson 2A2　　**88th Observation Sqn**
**Rec combat with 6Pfalz[+ooc] ovBAZOCHES(1Lt
RCM Page DFC OK/1Lt JI Rancourt DFC **WIA**)severe,
WIA on 10.8?, WIA 3 times in leg

10th August

95th Pursuit Sqn
** cr(1Lt IR Curry **KIA**) KIFA?

SPAD 13   **95th Pursuit Sqn**
** shot up(1Lt CS Gill **WIA**)

11th August

Salmson 2A2   **88th Observation Sqn**
**PhotRec FISMES combat with 11 Fokker DVIIs
control surfaces shot up but returned FERME-DE-
GRÈVES A'dr(1Lt RW Hitchcock OK/2Lt JSD Burns
KIA)

Salmson 2A2   **88th Observation Sqn**
**PhotRec FISMES combat with 11Fokker DVIIs shot
up cr VILLE SAVOYE(1Lt JH McClendon **KIA**/2Lt
CW Plummer **KIA**) Ja2? Bolle30? [?"SPAD" claim
combat VILLESAVAGE Oblt Rt K Bolle Ja2]

Salmson 2A2   **88th Observation Sqn**
**PhotRec FISMES combat with 11Fokker DVIIs shot
up(1Lt JW Jordan **WIA**/)severe

SPAD 13   **95th Pursuit Sqn**
** **MIA**(1Lt WM Russell **KIA**)

4524?   **SPAD 13**   **103rd Pursuit Sqn**
3435? ** combat with 2AlbatrosC[+ooc cr] & Fokker
DVII ovFLIREY 10-05am then shot down ftl
nrEUVEZIN 10-10am **MIA**(1Lt vW Todd **POW**) shared
victory with 1Lt EG Tobin & 1Lt GW Furlow

12th August

Salmson 2A2   **91st Observation Sqn**
**Rec combat with 4Pfalzes shot up(1Lt JH Lambert
OK/1Lt HT Baker **DoW** 14.8.18?) 14.8?, Baker hit in
stomach

16th August

DH-4   **135th Observation Sqn**
**Phot combat with AlbatrosD engine hit shot up dam
glide down ftl WoL(2Lt DB Cole **WIA**/2Lt PG Hart DSC
OK) WIA leg & thigh

17th August

Caproni   **US Italy**
6th Sqn, XI Caproni Group **B shrapnel hit(1Lt AD
Farquhar **WIA**/)head, back on strength in one week, a'c
called PURPLE HEART afterwards

25th August

Breguet 14B2   **96th Bombardment Sqn**
B LONQUYON AA shot up(1Lt DH Young **WIA/)
shrapnel through seat

DH-4   **135th Observation Sqn**
**Phot LAHAYVILLE-BOUILLONVILLE combat
with 4EAs rudder shot up spin ftl cr trenches(2Lt WC
Suiter OK/1Lt LA Smith **WIA**)thigh

30th August

Breguet 14B2   **96th Bombardment Sqn**
**B CHAMBLEY AA shot up ftl got back WoL(1Lt CR
Codman OK/)

September 1918

2nd September

SPAD 13   **22nd Pursuit Sqn**
**P combat with EA[+shot down smoking]
nrARNACOURT-BEY OK(2Lt AR Brooks)

This was the first Squadron victory for 22nd US.

Salmson 2A2   **88th Observation Sqn**
**Rec AA then combat with 9Hannover 12k EoL shot up
then last seen in vert nd(1Lt RW Hitchcock **KIA**/2Lt FM
Moore **KIA**) [FAb2, or Ja45?]

Salmson 2A2   **88th Observation Sqn**
**Rec AA then combat with 9Hannover[+] 12k EoL
OK(1Lt GM Comey/1Lt RB Bagby) shared victory, EAs
from FAb2

Salmson 2A2   **88th Observation Sqn**
**Rec AA then combat with 9Hannover[+] 12k EoL shot
up dam ftl French a'dr nrRHEIMS OK(1Lt RCM Page/
1Lt PF Carl) EAs from FAb2, or Ja45?

4th September

Salmson 2A2   **91st Observation Sqn**
**Rec combat with 3EAs nPONT-À-MOUSSON shot
up ftl EoL **MIA**(1Lt FV Foster **POW**/2Lt RR Sebring
KIA) 5.9?, crew?

Breguet 14B2   **96th Bombardment Sqn**
**B CONFLANS combat with 4Pfalzes shot up(/2Lt AN
Hexter **WIA DoW**?)severe:head, then other EAs

Breguet 14B2   **96th Bombardment Sqn**
**B CONFLANS combat with 4Pfalzes shot up(1Lt AH
Alexander **WIA**/2Lt JC McClennan **WIA**)legs, then
other EAs, Pilot WIA back, both WIA severe

Breguet 14B2   **96th Bombardment Sqn**
**B CONFLANS combat with 4Pflazes shot up(/2Lt DD
Warner **WIA**)severe:hips, then other EA

7th September

SPAD 13   **49th Pursuit Sqn**
** **MIA**(2Lt WT Kent **KIA**)

8th September

aaa   **SPAD 13**   **22nd Pursuit Sqn**
**P METZ AA broke patrol & lost attacked EA on
a'dr[+] shot up then combat with 10 Fokker DVIIs shot
up & hit WIA passed out cr WoL(1Lt JM Swabb **WIA**)
back with Sqn in 2 weeks

Salmson 2A2   **88th Observation Sqn**
Phot (1Lt EW Wagner **WIA)

Salmson 2A2   91st Observation Sqn
Rec **MIA(1Lt AW Lawson **POW**/1Lt HW Verwohlt **WIA POW**) crew?

SPAD 13   95th Pursuit Sqn
P AA ftl **MIA(1Lt NS Archibald **POW**) Gorrell: 24.9?

9th September

Salmson 2A2   12th Observation Sqn
** (1Lt WS Lockhart **WIA**/)

12th September

3203   Salmson 2A2   1st Observation Sqn
Rec shot up fuel tank hit shot down in flames cr(1Lt HS Aldrich **WIA/1Lt D Ker **KIA**) pilot thrown clear

DH-4   8th Observation Sqn
** combat with EAs in pm? **MIA**(1Lt HW Mitchell **POW**/2Lt JW Artz **WIA POW**)

DH-4   20th Bombardment Sqn
CP ST MIHIEL rain clouds 300' ftl EoL **MIA(1Lt GM Crawford **POW**/2Lt JG O'Toole **WIA POW**) O'Toole temporarily with 20US from 96US when lost, one record has him KIA, but error?

SPAD 13   22nd Pursuit Sqn
**P combat with Hannover[+shot down] ~6-55am then ground fire engine hit ftl OK(Capt RC Bridgman)

This was the first combat victory of the offensive for the AEF.

SPAD 13   22nd Pursuit Sqn
P lost control landing after op cr 5-30am(2Lt VR McCormick **WIA? **KIFA**) possibly WIA in morning combats

SPAD 13   27th Pursuit Sqn
+*KB attacked KB[+shot down after 3 passes] ovMARIEVILLE 8-09am OK(2Lt F Luke) his first balloon victory, immediately landed WoL for confirmation

DH-4   50th Observation Sqn
CP hit by ground fire? shot down crTHIONVILLE **MIA(1Lt HleN Stevens **KIA**/2Lt EH Gardiner **KIA**) left 10-30am? supporting 82nd Div.

Breguet 14B2   96th Bombardment Sqn
B troops BUXIÈRES combat with 8 Fokker DVIIs in mist ovCOMMERCY on return shot down in flames ~12pm(1Lt AH Gundelach DSC **DoW/2Lt PH Way DSC **KIA**) volunteered for operation. despite high winds & low cloud, Gundelach jumped & was killed, Way was burnt to death

Breguet 14B2   96th Bombardment Sqn
*B ftl dark cr ldg nrGONDECOURT(1Lt EM Cronin **KIFA**/1Lt LC Bleeker **OK**)

Salmson 2A2   104th Observation Sqn
** rain mist lost shot up ovLAMARVILLE ftl EoL **MIA**(1Lt D Johnston **KIA**/Cpl Johnson **inj**) left am, Cpl Johnson found injured in German dug-out by advancing US troops next day

DH-4   135th Observation Sqn
ARec lost ftl Switzerland **MIA(1Lt TJD Fuller **INT**/1Lt V Brookhart **INT**) low clouds & wind, interned Switzerland, Fuller on first operation EoL

DH-4   135th Observation Sqn
CP hit low by US shell & blew up cr fire(2Lt JE Bowyer **KIA/1Lt AT Johnson **KIA**) left 5-30am, forced low by clouds, event described in History of the 89th Division

DH-4   135th Observation Sqn
**CP? combat with 6 Fokker DVIIs[+] shot up but returned ok OK(1Lt GM Chritzman/1Lt MJ Reed)

DH-4   135th Observation Sqn
LRec combat with 6 Fokker DVIIs shot down in flames nrVILCEY-SUR-TREY(1Lt WC Suiter DSC **KIA/2Lt GE Morse DSC **KIA**) filthy weather, had completed operation but "went back for another look"?, believed attacked over own a'dr, pilot hit in head, observer thrown out

SPAD 13   139th Pursuit Sqn
LowP shooting up troops combat with Fokker DVIIs[+] 6-30pm shot up **MIA(1Lt DE Putnam **KIA**)

13th September

The opening ground assault of the St Mihiel Offensive began at 1am on the 13th of September. This battle is described in more detail in Part I: The Western Front. Of great relevance to this section is the fact that almost fifteen hundred French and American aircraft took part in enormous raids in the opening fighting of this very successful campaign. The American Air Service was to be plagued with bad weather in the remaining months of the war: of the sixty-one days between the 12th of September and the 11th of November, eleven were fair, twenty cloudy, fifteen foggy, and fifteen rainy.

DH-4   8th Observation Sqn
** (1Lt EG West **WIA**) to hospital

DH-4   8th Observation Sqn
** running combat with Fokker DVIIs **MIA**(1Lt HB Rex **KIA**/2Lt WF Gallagher **KIA**)

SPAD 13   13th Pursuit Sqn
P combat with Fokker DVIIs[++ooc,+dr down] 6-35pm to 6-55pm shot up ftl **MIA(1Lt RRS Converse **POW**) shared victory with 4 others

DH-4   50th Observation Sqn
CP rifle fire shot up ftl(1Lt DC Beebe **OK/2Lt FK Bellows **KIA**) ftl near lines to help observer but found dead

Salmson 2A2   88th Observation Sqn
** (1Lt PH McNulty **KIA**) 13.9.18?

7577   SPAD 13   93rd Pursuit Sqn
** **MIA**(2Lt CP Nash **POW**)

Breguet 14B2   96th Bombardment Sqn
B left 3-15pm CHAMBLEY combat with 14 Fokker DVIIs[+] 4000' 4pm then shot down in flames cr **MIA(2Lt ST Hopkins **KIA**/1Lt BR Williams **KIA**) shared victory

.13   **Breguet 14B2   96th Bombardment Sqn**
B left 3-15pm CHAMBLEY combat with 15 Fokker DVIIs shot down 4000'(1Lt TH Farnsworth **KIA/2Lt RE Thompson **KIA**) seen going down in control, Pilot thrown out on ldg & died shortly after, Thompson killed on Friday 13th, in a'c No13, on 13th raid

SPAD 13   103rd Pursuit Sqn
**P combat with Pfalzes & Albatros[+ooc] ovST JULIEN 5-10pm shot up ftl ORCHIES dam OK(1Lt HN Kenyon)

SPAD 13   103rd Pursuit Sqn
Rec shot down nrCHAREY last seen 5-10pm **MIA(1Lt EB Jones **KIA**) ["SPAD" claim combat swTHIAUCOURT Ltn G vHantelmann Ja15]

SPAD 13   139th Pursuit Sqn
? (1Lt RC Lindsay **WIA) only in Gorrell

14th September

DH-4   11th Bombardment Sqn
B CONFLANS combat with Fokker DVIIs shot down spiral fr 8000' **MIA(1Lt FT Shoemaker **WIA POW**/2Lt RH Groner **inj POW**) EAs came fr behind formation, patrol saved further damage by arrival of US SPADs, one of this crew unconscious for 5 days from crash

DH-4   11th Bombardment Sqn
B CONFLANS combat with Fokker DVIIs[+] shot down(2Lt H Shidler **POW/2Lt HH Sayre **KIA**) shared victory

SPAD 13   13th Pursuit Sqn
** combat with Fokker DVIIs? ~8-05am **MIA**(1Lt AA Brody **POW**)

SPAD 13   13th Pursuit Sqn
** combat with Fokker DVIIs? ~8-05am **MIA**(1Lt CW Drew **WIA POW**)

SPAD 13   13th Pursuit Sqn
** combat with Fokker DVIIs? ~8-05am **MIA**(1Lt HB Freeman **POW**)

4562   **SPAD 13   13th Pursuit Sqn**
"HELEN AIR" ** combat with Fokker DVIIs? ~8-05am **MIA**(1Lt GP Kull **KIA**)

SPAD 13   22nd Pursuit Sqn
**P combat with 12 Fokker DVIIs shot up OK(1Lt AC Kimber)

SPAD 13   22nd Pursuit Sqn
**P combat with 12 Fokker DVIIs[+ooc] 3-20pm shot up controls dam ftl OK(2Lt AR Brooks) shared victory

7580   **SPAD 13   22nd Pursuit Sqn**
**P combat with several Fokker DVIIs[++cr] MARS-LA-TOUR EoL 3-20pm fuel tank hit? by explosive bullet

MIA(1Lt PE Hassinger **KIA**) both shared

Salmson 2A2   24th Observation Sqn
** combat with EA scout shot down **MIA**(1Lt JJ Goodfellow **KIA**/1Lt EM Durand **KIA**)

15206   **SPAD 13   28th Pursuit Sqn**
** (1Lt WB Stephenson **KIA**)

15241   **SPAD 13   28th Pursuit Sqn**
LowB troops ARNEVILLE-WARVILLE & trenches nrCARNY ground fire shot up ftl **MIA(1Lt GB Woods **POW**) 13.9?, left 12-50pm, last seen nrCARNY

Salmson 2A2   88th Observation Sqn
EscPhot combat with 5EAs ovCONFLANS rad shot up dam ftl(Capt K Littauer DFC OK/2Lt TE Boyd DFC **WIA)severe:legs & arms

Salmson 2A2   91st Observation Sqn
Rec **MIA(1Lt PJ Hughey **KIA**/2Lt? K Roper **KIA**) Capt Roper?, crew?

99th Observation Sqn
Phot combat with EA shot up(1Lt CC Kahle OK/1Lt RC Hill **KIA) 13.9?

SPAD 13   213th Pursuit Sqn
P combat with several EAs shot up dam seen drop away & dive, cr woods eST MIHIEL EoL **MIA(1Lt FW Sidler **KIA**) 14.8?

15th September

Salmson 2A2   1st Observation Sqn
** (/1Lt JW Corley **WIA**)

Salmson 2A2   24th Observation Sqn
** combat with Pfalz?[+] 7-50am OK(2Lt REW Wells/2Lt AW Swinebroad)

This was the first Squadron victory for 24th US.

Salmson 2A2   91st Observation Sqn
? (/1Lt GB Merrill **WIA)severe, inj?

Salmson 2A2   91st Observation Sqn
? (/Capt A Tabachnik **WIA) only in Gorrell

Salmson 2A2   91st Observation Sqn
Rec (2Lt PD Coles **WIA/)

Salmson 2A2   99th Observation Sqn
** (1Lt HM Sanford **WIA**/)

15221?   **SPAD 13   147th Pursuit Sqn**
** **MIA**(1Lt EA Love **KIA**)

16th September

SPAD 13   13th Pursuit Sqn
** (1Lt RH Stiles **KIA**)

DH-4   20th Bombardment Sqn
**B CONFLANS AA nrETAIN down ooc but recovered then engine failed ftl cr just WoL OK(1Lt AF Seaver DSC/1Lt JY Stokes DSC) through drop-outs had reached target alone, were also chased back by EAs

Breguet 14B2   96th Bombardment Sqn
B CONFLANS combat with EAs 4200' fuel tank hit shot down in flames **MIA(1Lt CP Anderson **KIA**/1Lt HS Thompson **KIA**) after dropping bombs

Breguet 14B2   96th Bombardment Sqn
B combat with EAs 4200m shot down smoking(1Lt NC Rogers **KIA/1Lt KP Strawn **KIA**)

Breguet 14B2   96th Bombardment Sqn
B combat with EAs ovCONFLANS 4200m controls hit shot down cr field **MIA(1Lt CR Codman **WIA POW**/2Lt SA McDowell **WIA POW**)thighs

Breguet 14B2   96th Bombardment Sqn
B combat attacked by 3EAs nrCONFLANS 4200m shot down smoking(1Lt RC Taylor **KIA/1Lt WA Stewart **KIA**) chased down by 2EA after pilot hit

SPAD 13   213th Pursuit Sqn
Troop strafe, left 12-15pm combat with EAs[+++] shot up **MIA(1Lt DM McClure **POW**) 13.9?, low mist hid until late, word came McClure was KIA, but turned up after war, also with confirmation of his 3 victories!

17th September

1150   Salmson 2A2   1st Observation Sqn
** **MIA**(1Lt WB Cowart **KIA**/2Lt HW Dahringer **KIA**) crew?

Salmson 2A2   24th Observation Sqn
** combat? shot down EoL **MIA**(1Lt WL Bradfield **POW**/1Lt AL Clark? **POW**) name Clarks?

SPAD 13   95th Pursuit Sqn
** combat with Fokker DVIIs guns failed shot up ftl cr field **MIA**(1Lt WH Heinrichs **WIA POW**) to hospital, severe WIA to cheek, arm & leg

18th September

DH-4   11th Bombardment Sqn
B LA CHAUSSÉE combat with ~10 Fokker DVIIs controls shot up flames ftl nrOLLEY cr EoL(1Lt TD Hooper **WIA POW/1Lt RR Root **WIA POW**)face,leg, Hooper CO of 11US Aero, Pilot WIA foot, 17 a'c left, 1 forced to return, 10 failed to reach target, 5 out of 6 shot down, 3 shot down in flames

DH-4   11th Bombardment Sqn
B LA CHAUSSÉE combat with ~10 Fokker DVIIs shot down in flames **MIA(1Lt JC Tyler **KIA**/1Lt HH Strauch **KIA**)

DH-4   11th Bombardment Sqn
B LA CHAUSSÉE combat with ~10 Fokker DVIIs shot down in flames **MIA(1Lt LS Harter **KIA**/1Lt McR Stephenson **KIA**) inexperienced, all found cloud conditions difficult

DH-4   11th Bombardment Sqn
B LA CHAUSSÉE combat with ~10 Fokker DVIIs shot down fuel tank hit then AA ftl **MIA(1Lt RF Chapin **POW**/2Lt CB Laird **POW**) this a'c led patrol, clouds made keeping formation difficult

.12   DH-4   11th Bombardment Sqn
**B LA CHAUSSÉE combat with ~10 Fokker DVIIs fought back to lines nrDAMLOUE then ftl OK(1Lt VP Oatis/2Lt RJ Guthrie) only crew to survive this combat, possibly shot down 1EA

.14   DH-4   11th Bombardment Sqn
B LA CHAUSSÉE combat with ~10 Fokker DVIIs shot down in flames **MIA(1Lt ET Comegys **KIA**/2Lt AR Carter **KIA**) [Ltn H Besser Ja12]

SPAD 13   27th Pursuit Sqn
+*KBP left 4pm attacked 2KBs[++] nrLABEUVILLE then combat with several EAs[++ nd cr, then saw 2nd dive also] nrST HILAIRE then combat with 2Str[+cr seVERDUN] OK(2Lt F Luke Jnr) 14 victories in 10 days

7555   SPAD 13   27th Pursuit Sqn
+*KBP left 4pm attacked 2KBs[++] nrLABEUVILLE then attacked by EAs combat nrST HILAIRE ~4-40pm? shot down in flames(1Lt JF Wehner DSC **KIA**) patrolling w Frank Luke

SPAD 13   95th Pursuit Sqn
** **MIA**(1Lt WH Taylor **KIA**)

19th September

SPAD 13   28th Pursuit Sqn
SpB troops nrCHAMBLEY & MARS-LE-TOUR met EAs over target shot down in flames? or ooc **MIA(1Lt F Philbrick **KIA**) 18.9?, left 4-30pm, operation w 213Sqn RAF

25th September

SPAD 13   93rd Pursuit Sqn
** (1Lt HB Merz **WIA**) to hospital

26th September

Salmson 2A2   1st Observation Sqn
CP shot down ovVARENNES **MIA(1Lt JF Richards **KIA**/2Lt AF Hanscom **KIA**) Hanscom KIA 17.8?

SPAD 13   13th Pursuit Sqn
** (1Lt TP Evans **POW**)

SPAD 13   13th Pursuit Sqn
** (2Lt vH Burgin **POW**)

32286   DH-4   20th Bombardment Sqn
B DUN-SUR-MEUSE combat with 12 Fokker DVIIs[+] 10-55am shot up **MIA(2Lt GB Wiser **POW**/1Lt GR Richardson **POW**) combat lasted 35mins, shared victory

32492   DH-4   20th Bombardment Sqn
B DUN-SUR-MEUSE combat with 12 Fokker DVIIs[+] 10-55am after drop engine hit in flames ooc but recov(Capt MC Cooper **WIA:burnt **POW**/1Lt EC Leonard **WIA POW**) patrol had taken sharp turn after drop and caused break up of formation, Cooper about to jump but saw observer alive

32584   DH-4   20th Bombardment Sqn
**B combat with 12 Fokker DVIIs[+] 10-55am shot up

ftl(1Lt SC Howard OK/1Lt EA Parrott **KIA**)mouth, shared victory, Parrot killed early & fell onto dual controls forcing a'c to fly east for 35 mins before pilot able to move him & turn

32792   DH-4   20th Bombardment Sqn
B combat with 12 Fokker DVIIs[+] 10-55am shot up **MIA(2Lt DB Harris **KIA**/2Lt E Forbes **KIA**) shared victory

32819   DH-4   20th Bombardment Sqn
B combat with 12 Fokker DVIIs[+] nrCLERY-LA-GRAND 10-55am shot up **MIA(1Lt RP Matthews **KIA**/2Lt EA Taylor **KIA**) shared victory, all losses were from 2nd attacking Flight, following Breguets

32915   DH-4   20th Bombardment Sqn
B combat with 12 Fokker DVIIs[+] 10-55am shot up **MIA(1Lt PN Rhinelander **KIA**/1Lt HC Preston **KIA**)

**   SPAD 13   22nd Pursuit Sqn**
P hit by American barrage? **MIA(1Lt AC Kimber **KIA**) no enemy AA, formation was flying through American barrage

**   Salmson 2A2   24th Observation Sqn**
Rec rail system ETAIN-STENAY combat shot up(/1Lt CW Higgins **WIA) to hospital

7519   SPAD 13   27th Pursuit Sqn
+*KBP combat with several EAs CONSENVOYE-SIVRY shot down **MIA**(2Lt IA Roberts **KIA**) patrolling w Frank Luke in pm, never found

**   SPAD 13   49th Pursuit Sqn**
** (1Lt IJ Roth **KIA**)

**   Salmson 2A2   91st Observation Sqn**
Rec rail system ETAIN-STENAY-DUN-SUR-MEUSE AA shot up(1Lt AE Kelty **KIA/2Lt FB Lowry **KIA**)

**   SPAD 13   94th Pursuit Sqn**
** **MIA**(1Lt A Nutt **KIA**)

.7   Breguet 14B2   96th Bombardment Sqn
B bridge on MEUSE? combat with 10 Pfalz[+ooc] nrDUN-SUR-MEUSE 10-15am shot up dam(2Lt HJ Forshay OK/2Lt PJ O'Donnell **KIA) shared victory

**   SPAD 13   139th Pursuit Sqn**
** combat with EAs **MIA**(1Lt HE Petree **KIA**) Gorrell: 22.9?

**   SPAD 13   139th Pursuit Sqn**
** combat with EAs **MIA**(1Lt HR Sumner **KIA**?) POW?

**   SPAD 13   139th Pursuit Sqn**
** combat with EAs incl DFW[+] 11-40am shot up **MIA**(1Lt HA Garvie **KIA**?) POW?, shared victory

27th September

**   Salmson 2A2   91st Observation Sqn**
Rec combat with Fokker DVIIs[+shot down in flames] 4pm shot up(1Lt WF Baker OK/2Lt RS Jannopulo **WIA) shared victory

**   Salmson 2A2   99th Observation Sqn**
** (/1Lt ER Case **WIA**)severe

28th September

**   Salmson 2A2   12th Observation Sqn**
** **MIA**(1Lt W Morris **POW DoW**/1Lt CH Styles **POW**) crew?

**   SPAD 13   27th Pursuit Sqn**
** (1Lt PV Stout **WIA**)severe

**   SPAD 13   27th Pursuit Sqn**
+*KBP attacked KB[+] nrBANTHEVILLE(2Lt F Luke Jnr) last combat report of 2Lt Frank Luke

**   SPAD 13   28th Pursuit Sqn**
** (2Lt LP Moriarty **WIA**)

**   Salmson 2A2   88th Observation Sqn**
CP shot down in flames nrMANTILLOIS **MIA(2Lt HE Loud **DoW** 28.9.18?/Capt CT Trickey **WIA**) DoW of burns, possibly DoW 29.9.18?, Trickey saved himself by climbing onto wing

29th September

**   Salmson 2A2   1st Observation Sqn**
** (/1Lt AW Duckstein **WIA**)severe, 14.10?

**   SPAD 13   13th Pursuit Sqn**
** (1Lt EF Richards **WIA**)severe, only in Gorrell?

**   SPAD 13   27th Pursuit Sqn**
+*KBP attacked KB[+] DUN-SUR-MEUSE,2nd KB[+] BRIÈRE Farm,3rd KB[+] MILLY ground fire ftl(2Lt F Luke Jnr DSC CMH **KIA**) had taken off, despite grounding, having obtained permission for attack from Maj. Hartney; Luke resisted surrender but shot dead, had final total of 14KBs & 4EAs shot down

**   SPAD 13   49th Pursuit Sqn**
** **MIA**(1Lt TA Gabel **KIA**)

**   Salmson 2A2   88th Observation Sqn**
Rec ground mg shot up(/2Lt CC Gifford **WIA)leg:severe

7613.3   SPAD 13   93rd Pursuit Sqn
P combat with Albatros 2Str[+] 4-25pm shot up **MIA(1Lt RH Fuller **KIA**) shared victory

**   SPAD 13   95th Pursuit Sqn**
KBP attacked balloon[+] 6pm shot down? **MIA(2Lt GO Woodard **POW**)

15304.23 SPAD 13   213th Pursuit Sqn
** (2Lt JW Ogden **POW**)

30th September

**   Breguet(Ren)   9th Observation Sqn**
Rec combat with 5 Fokker DVIIs neMONTFALCON engine hit shot down cr(2Lt LD Warrender **WIA/2Lt HC Crumb **DoW** 1.10.18?) 28.9?, pilot WIA severe, Crumb hit in abdomen (crew based on C&C US vol.12 No.2 but date re-appraised?)

Breguet(Ren)   9th Observation Sqn
**Rec combat with 5 Fokker DVIIs neMONTFALCON shot down cr o't wr OK(2Lt HA Dolan/2Lt DB Woon) 28.9?

Breguet(Ren)   9th Observation Sqn
Rec shot up(1Lt RW Wright **WIA/)severe

Breguet(Ren)   9th Observation Sqn
Rec shot up(2Lt MF Saunders **POW?/) only in Gorrell

Salmson 2A2   104th Observation Sqn
Rec combat with 4 Fokker DVIIs nrJAMEZ engine shot up in flames ftl **MIA(Capt ER Haslett **WIA POW**/ 1Lt RE Davis **POW**) left in high wind

Salmson 2A2   104th Observation Sqn
**Rec wing hit by shell dam ftl OK(1Lt CH Reynolds/ 1Lt HA Nichols)

SPAD 13   213th Pursuit Sqn
** (1Lt IW Fish **WIA**) 13.9?

October 1918

1st October

Salmson 2A2   1st Observation Sqn
** (1Lt RF Fox **KIA**/1Lt WA Phillips **KIA**)

SPAD 13   13th Pursuit Sqn
** (1Lt CA Brodie **KIA**)

7890   SPAD 13   13th Pursuit Sqn
** (1Lt GD Stivers **KIA**)

2nd October

Breguet(Ren)   9th Observation Sqn
** (1Lt HW Thayer **WIA**/1Lt GB Atkinson **WIA**) crew?

Breguet 14B2   96th Bombardment Sqn
** (/2Lt JB Walden **WIA**) only in Gorrell

Salmson 2A2   99th Observation Sqn
** (1Lt CC Kahle **KIA**/1Lt CE Spencer **WIA**)severe crew?

3rd October

SPAD 13   94th Pursuit Sqn
** **MIA**(1Lt ER Scroggie **WIA POW**)

SPAD 13   95th Pursuit Sqn
KBP attacked balloon[+prob] 5-48pm shot down? **MIA(1Lt WL Avery **POW**)

4th October

Salmson 2A2   1st Observation Sqn
** (1Lt JH Michener **WIA**/)

Salmson 2A2   12th Observation Sqn
** (/2Lt SA Bowman **WIA**) 3.10?

SPAD 13   13th Pursuit Sqn
P combat with Fokker DVIIs[+ooc] 9-55am shot down **MIA(1Lt HG Armstrong **KIA**) shared victory

SPAD 13   22nd Pursuit Sqn
P combat with Fokker DVIIs[+] 4-10pm shot down **MIA(1Lt JA Sperry **POW**) other victory earlier in day at 9-15am

7625.17 **SPAD 13   28th Pursuit Sqn**
LowP became separated, ftl or shot down? **MIA(1Lt JF Merrill **KIA**) left 6-15am

SPAD 13   49th Pursuit Sqn
P combat with Fokker DVIIs[+] 9-15am to 10am shot up **MIA(1Lt CA Kinney **KIA**) shared victory, possibly lost on 5.10?

Salmson 2A2   91st Observation Sqn
Rec combat with 9 Fokker DVIIs shot down **MIA(2Lt SG Frierson **WIA POW**/1Lt RG Scott **KIA**)

5th October

Salmson 2A2   1st Observation Sqn
? (1Lt CA Henry **WIA/1Lt EJ Groteclose **WIA**)

SPAD 13   22nd Pursuit Sqn
P combat with EAs **MIA(1Lt HB Hudson **KIA**) never found

SPAD 13   27th Pursuit Sqn
** ?combat with Fokker DVIIs(1Lt WS McKimmon **WIA**)

DH-4   50th Observation Sqn
**CP shot down cr BINARVILLE OK(1Lt GR Phillips/ 2Lt MH Brown) search for "Lost Battalion" of 308th Regt trapped in ravine by enemy fire

DH-4   50th Observation Sqn
**CP shot down cr VIENNE-LE-CHÂTEAU OK(1Lt SC Bird/1Lt WA Bolt) search for "Lost Battalion"

6th October

Salmson 2A2   1st Observation Sqn
** (2Lt JM Richardson **WIA**/2Lt JW Corley? OK)severe, Corley was usual gunner

DH-4   50th Observation Sqn
CP ground fire shot up(1Lt M Graham OK/2Lt JE McCurdy **WIA)neck, WIA severe, searching for "Lost Battalion"

DH-4   50th Observation Sqn
CP ground fire shot down nrBINARVILLE **MIA(2Lt HE Goettler CMH **KIA**/2Lt ER Bleckley CMH **DoW**) searching for "Lost Battalion" of the 308th Regt: lost going out a second time in search

7th October

Salmson 2A2   12th Observation Sqn
** (/2Lt RC Keely **WIA**) 6.10?

DH-4   50th Observation Sqn
**CP shot up OK(1Lt RM Anderson/1Lt WJ Rogers) located the "Lost Battalion" of 308th Regt

4540   SPAD 13   103rd Pursuit Sqn
**P last seen 2000m ovARGONNE FOREST shot down

12-30pm **MIA**(2Lt W MacFadden? **KIA**) name McFadden?

8th October

1203   **Salmson 2A2**   **24th Observation Sqn**
** combat with 4 Fokker DVIIs[+shot down] eVERDUN ~3-45pm shot up dam ftl cr ETAIN-VERDUN **MIA**(1Lt HW Riley **WIA POW**/2Lt SR Keesler **WIA DoW** 10.10.18?) Keesler hit in chest & abdomen, then again on the ground when Germans continued attack

    DH-4   **50th Observation Sqn**
CP/FoodDrop shot up(1Lt FC Slater **WIA)foot

9th October

    Salmson 2A2   **24th Observation Sqn**
CP combat? **MIA(1Lt SvW Peters **WIA POW**/)

    SPAD 13   **213th Pursuit Sqn**
**P combat with Fokker DVII fuel tank hit in flames but exting in long dive then ftl wMARRE MIA but OK(1Lt R Phelan)

10th October

    DH-4   **8th Observation Sqn**
** patrol attacked by 12 Fokker DVIIs shot down in flames **MIA**(1Lt CS Garrett **KIA**/1Lt RJ Cochran **KIA**) Infantry reported seeing pilot on wing holding strut and attempting to control a'c, until he fell off at 50'

    DH-4   **20th Bombardment Sqn**
B rail yards MILLY-DEVANT-DUN combat with 12 Fokker DVIIs shot down **MIA(1Lt WC Potter DSC **KIA**/1Lt HW Wilmer **KIA**)

32503   **DH-4**   **20th Bombardment Sqn**
B rail yards MILLY-DEVANT-DUN combat with 12 Fokker DVIIs[+] 12-26pm shot up dam(1Lt LB Edwards OK/2Lt EB Christian **WIA) US SPADS came to assistance, shared victory

32748   **DH-4**   **20th Bombardment Sqn**
B rail yards MILLY-DEVANT-DUN combat with 12 Fokker DVIIs[+] 12-25pm shot up(1Lt SC Howard OK/2Lt SC Hicks **WIA) US SPADS came to assistance, shared victory

    SPAD 13   **49th Pursuit Sqn**
** combat with EAs ~4-10pm? **MIA**(1Lt GO West **KIA**)

    Breguet 14B2   **96th Bombardment Sqn**
** (/2Lt AE Newell **DoW**?) only in Gorrell

    Salmson 2A2   **104th Observation Sqn**
Rec combat with EAs shot up(1Lt JL Johnson OK/2Lt CE Rust **DoW 11.10.18)arm

7588?   **SPAD 13**   **147th Pursuit Sqn**
OP combat with EAs collided w Fokker DVII in attack 3-50pm cr(2Lt WW White DSC **KIA) leading patrol ovDUN-SUR-MEUSE, both a'c fell locked together, 8 victory ace

8502   **SPAD 13**   **147th Pursuit Sqn**
** combat with Rumpler[+shot down] 11-30am shot up dam(2Lt WE Brotherton **KIA**)

12th October

    Salmson 2A2   **99th Observation Sqn**
** (/1Lt WB Gaither **DoW**)

14th October

D-1   **DH-4**   **US-FMAF**
B THIELT combat with 12EAs[+shot down] on return shot up ftl HONDSCHOOTE(2Lt R Talbot CMH OK/Cpl R Robinson CMH **WIA) WIA in arm, then stomach & thigh, another EA unconfirmed

D-3?   **DH-4**   **US-FMAF**
**B THIELT combat with 12EAs on return shot up engine failed ftl then ground fire & AA ldg ok nrPERVYSE OK(Capt RS Lytle USMC/Cpl A Wiman USMC) a'c salvaged with some difficulty

15th October

4541   **SPAD 13**   **103rd Pursuit Sqn**
** ground fire shot down nrREMBERCOURT ~1-40pm **MIA**(2Lt CW Ford **POW**)

15255.2   **SPAD 13**   **103rd Pursuit Sqn**
** ground fire shot down nrREMBERCOURT **MIA**(1Lt KM Palmer **KIA**)

18th October

    Salmson 2A2   **12th Observation Sqn**
** (/1Lt AL Hopkins **WIA**) Gorrell: WIA 24.6?

    Salmson 2A2   **12th Observation Sqn**
** (/2Lt HS Bean **WIA**) 19.10?

    Salmson 2A2   **91st Observation Sqn**
Rec (1Lt HJ Watson **KIA?/) Gorrell gives KIFA?

21st October

    Salmson 2A2   **90th Observation Sqn**
** **MIA**(1Lt HDG Broomfield **KIA**/1Lt EB Cutter **KIA**)

    Salmson 2A2   **91st Observation Sqn**
Rec **MIA(2Lt JD Adams **POW**/1Lt HE Bash **POW**) crew?

22nd October

    SPAD 13   **49th Pursuit Sqn**
** **MIA**(1Lt HR Kendall **POW**)

    Salmson 2A2   **91st Observation Sqn**
Rec **MIA(1Lt JW Wallis **WIA**/) pilot?

7662.1   **SPAD 13**   **93rd Pursuit Sqn**
P eMEUSE River combat with EAs in heavy rain ftl EoL **MIA(1Lt OJ Gude **POW**) last seen flying east [Ja65]

7708   **SPAD 13**   **94th Pursuit Sqn**
** **MIA**(1Lt RJ Saunders **KIA**)

SPAD 13	213th Pursuit Sqn

P seen ~9am in snow storm **MIA(1Lt LC Dudley **POW**) seen by 1Lt JC Lee

D-4	DH-4	US-FMAF

B MELLE in dense fog AA & combat ovGHENT attacked by 3EAs after bombing shot up cr nrBRUGES-GHENT Canal **MIA(1Lt HC Norman **KIA**/1Lt CW Taylor **KIA**) left 8-40am

23rd October

Salmson 2A2	1st Observation Sqn

B? **MIA(1Lt CG Johnson **KIA**/2Lt CH Kennedy **KIA**)

DH-4	20th Bombardment Sqn

B combat with Fokker DVIIs nrBUZANCY radiator shot up(Capt CG Sellers DSC OK/1Lt PH Buckley **WIA)

31062	DH-4	20th Bombardment Sqn

B combat with Fokker DVIIs nrBUZANCY shot down in flames ooc nrBAYONVILLE(2Lt JH Weimer **KIA/1Lt HE Turner **KIA**) 7 Breguets & 30 DH-4s left to bomb troops BUZANCY-BOIS DE BARRICOURT in pm

32962	DH-4	20th Bombardment Sqn

B combat with Fokker DVIIs[+] nrBUZANCY 3-25pm shot up(1Lt KG West OK/1Lt WF Frank **WIA)slight

Salmson 2A2	91st Observation Sqn

? (1Lt WF Baker **WIA/) only in Gorrell?

DH-4	166th Bombardment Sqn

** (/2Lt RW Steele **WIA**?) inj?

DH-4	166th Bombardment Sqn

B shot up(/1Lt G Todd **WIA)

24th October

SPAD 13	49th Pursuit Sqn

** (1Lt HL Fontaine **WIA**)

Salmson 2A2	91st Observation Sqn

Rec (1Lt E Houghton **WIA/)

25th October

Salmson 2A2	12th Observation Sqn

** (/2Lt WB Harwell **WIA**?)

Salmson 2A2	99th Observation Sqn

** (/1Lt BL Atwater **WIA**)

26th October

SPAD 13	147th Pursuit Sqn

** **MIA**(2Lt ML Dowd **KIA**)

27th October

DH-4	11th Bombardment Sqn

B BRIQUENAY combat with Fokker DVIIs shot up ftl cr(1Lt DC Malcolm OK/1Lt LW Springer **WIA)shoulder, attacked after bombing

SPAD 13	28th Pursuit Sqn

*P combat with EA shot up ftl CLERMONT strong winds mis-judged ldg hit hangar cr wr(1Lt HC Allein **DoW**) left 12-45pm, had been hit in combat

7708	SPAD 13	94th Pursuit Sqn

** hit by AA shell, a'c exploded in flames **MIA**(Capt HR Coolidge **KIA**) 8 victory ace

Breguet 14B2	96th Bombardment Sqn

** (/1Lt HR Pancoast **WIA**)severe

Caproni	US Italy

B combat with 5 Austrian 1Strs[++2 shot down] fuel tanks hit shot down in flames ovREVINE nrVITTORIO(1Lt DeW Coleman **KIA/1Lt JL Bahl **KIA**/Italian **KIA**) Caproni was unescorted

D-11	DH-4	US-FMAF

B LOKEREN Rlwy Yards AA shot up ftl Holland **MIA(2Lt F Nelms **INT**/2Lt JF Gibbs **INT**)

28th October

Salmson 2A2	90th Observation Sqn

** (1Lt H Connover **WIA**/)severe

13271?	SPAD 13	147th Pursuit Sqn

** **MIA**(1Lt CW McDermott **KIA**)

29th October

Salmson 2A2	12th Observation Sqn

** **MIA**(1Lt SW Beauclerk **KIA**/1Lt RA Patterson **POW**) crew?

4608.12	SPAD 13	93rd Pursuit Sqn

P combat with Fokker DVIIs[+] 3-45pm shot down **MIA(1Lt AB Patterson **KIA**)

7708	SPAD 13	94th Pursuit Sqn

** **MIA**(1Lt EG Garnsey **KIA**)

Breguet 14B2	96th Bombardment Sqn

** (/1Lt WB Ten Eyck **WIA**) only in Gorrell

Salmson 2A2	99th Observation Sqn

** (1Lt JW McElroy **KIA**/2Lt HI Kinne **KIA**) crew?

DH-4	135th Observation Sqn

PhotRec MARS LA TOUR combat with 7 Fokker DVIIs shot up ftl(1Lt EC Landon OK/1Lt PH Aldrich DSC **KIA) Landon was Aldrich's usual pilot

SPAD 13	139th Pursuit Sqn

** **MIA**(1Lt KJ Schoen **DoW**) 7 victory ace

30th October

Salmson 2A2	12th Observation Sqn

** (1Lt RL Davidson **WIA**?)

Salmson 2A2	12th Observation Sqn

AOb ovBUZANCY combat with 18 Fokker DVIIs engine failed ftl cr **MIA(1Lt HD Muller **POW**/1Lt JM Foy **POW**) Foy was radio officer of 1st Corps Observation Group & had volunteered for observer work: first time EoL

SPAD 13   22nd Pursuit Sqn
Esc BUZANCY combat with 8 Fokker DVIIs shot down cr nrOUTHE on road BRIEULLES-ST PIERREMONT in ARDENNES **MIA(1Lt JD Beane **KIA**) met Circus?

SPAD 13   22nd Pursuit Sqn
**Esc combat with 8 Fokker DVIIs shot up OK(2Lt AR Brooks) 27 bullet holes

SPAD 13   22nd Pursuit Sqn
P BUZANCY combat with 8 Fokker DVIIs[+] 3-40pm shot down cr **MIA(1Lt RdeB Vernam DSC **POW DoW** 1.12.18) met Circus?, WIA in groin, taken to hospital at LONGWY & then abandoned in evacuation

Salmson 2A2   104th Observation Sqn
Rec ground fire & first combat[+?ftl] nrLANDRES ET ST GEORGE then returned for 2nd look & attacked by more EAs shot up(2Lt EM Morris OK/1Lt FLA? Andrew **WIA)chin, initials FCA?, WIA on 2nd sortie, flying btwn 9-10am to 11-30am

F1430   Sopwith Camel   185th Pursuit Sqn
KBP nrBEAUMONT met Fokker DVIIs ovVILLERS-DEVANT-DUN shot down cr **MIA(1Lt EH Kelton **inj POW**) left at dusk

31st October

SPAD 13   13th Pursuit Sqn
** (1Lt WS Cousins **POW**)

SPAD 13   27th Pursuit Sqn
** cr a'dr after sortie, fire(1Lt SW White **DoW** 1.11.18) exploding ammunition prevented rescue until severely burned

Salmson 2A2   88th Observation Sqn
Phot ANDEVANNE heavy AA shot up(1Lt JM Murphy **WIA/)foot & knee

.10   Breguet 14B2   96th Bombardment Sqn
B? (1Lt G Stanley **WIA/2Lt HT Folger **WIA**) bombing to TAILLY-BARRICOURT?, possibly 29.10?

Salmson 2A2   99th Observation Sqn
** (2Lt FE Kuntz **WIA**/1Lt LGE Reilly **KIA**) crew?, Gorrell: Kuntz possibly WIA on 1.11?

DH-4   166th Bombardment Sqn
B TAILLY-BARRICOURT combat with 13 Fokker DVIIs shot up(1Lt S Pickard **WIA/2Lt SL Cockrane **KIA**) EAs seen using BARRICOURT-BAYONVILLE Road as air-strip

SPAD 13   213th Pursuit Sqn
B shot down in flames **MIA(1Lt R Phelan **KIA**)

SPAD 13   213th Pursuit Sqn
P shot down **MIA(1Lt AM Weirick **WIA? POW**)

Unspecified date in October 1918?

Salmson 2A2   104th Observation Sqn
** (2Lt RE Spell **WIA**)slight Oct.18?

November 1918

1st November

DH-4   168th Observation Sqn
** (1Lt RM Armstrong **WIA**/) 5.11?

2nd November

SPAD 13   213th Pursuit Sqn
B ftl JULVECOURT then re-took off 10-30am & not seen again **MIA(1Lt RT Aldworth **POW**)

3rd November

Salmson 2A2   1st Observation Sqn
** **MIA**(2Lt WD Walsh **POW**/1Lt JH East **POW**) crew?

Salmson 2A2   1st Observation Sqn
CP? shot up(1Lt JF McCormick **KIA/1Lt RW Booze **WIA**) crew?

.24   Salmson 2A2   1st Observation Sqn
"*GERTRUDE R*" **CP VAUX-BUZANCY combat with 4 Fokker DVIIs[+shot down] sVAUX 12-10pm ank shot up dam chased back WoL ftl CHEVIÈRES(1Lt AJ Coyle **WIA?**/1Lt AE Easterbrook **WIA**)slight, left 11am, observer suffered graze on cheek, Easterbrook was an observer ace

DH-4   8th Observation Sqn
** **MIA**(2Lt WW Royce **POW**/2Lt JJ McIlvaine **POW**)

SPAD 13   22nd Pursuit Sqn
B BEAUMONT combat with many Fokker DVIIS shot up cr 15m swBEAUMONT **MIA(2Lt EB Gibson **DoW**) target 25m EoL, either WIA ov target & passed out on return, or attacked again on return

SPAD 13   22nd Pursuit Sqn
B BEAUMONT combat with many Fokker DVIIs[+ ?] 3-20pm shot down **MIA(2Lt G Tiffany **POW**)

16508   SPAD 13   22nd Pursuit Sqn
B BEAUMONT combat with many Fokker DVIIS shot down **MIA(1Lt HR Clapp **KIA**) target 25m EoL

Salmson 2A2   99th Observation Sqn
? (/1Lt FG Voeks **WIA) only in Gorrell, there is a 1Lt FG Voeks noted in US27?

15297   SPAD 13   103rd Pursuit Sqn
LowB LOUPPY-REMOIVILLE met 4 Fokker DVIIs shot up nrFONTAINES ~3-55pm ftl nrCHAUMONT-SUR-AIRE(1Lt JN Koontz **WIA)leg

DH-4   168th Observation Sqn
** (/1Lt EA Hassett **WIA**)

DH-4   168th Observation Sqn
**LowRec attacked KB[+shot down in flames] 9-30am OK(1Lt ER Clark/1Lt BF Giles) shared victory

DH-4   168th Observation Sqn
**LowRec attacked KB[+shot down in flames] 9-30am OK(2Lt RG Conant/Lt.Col JF Curry) shared victory

SPAD 13   213th Pursuit Sqn
**B combat with Fokker DVIIs shot up dam ftl field
CLERMONT(1Lt HC Smith **WIA**)shoulder, possibly
balloon attack?

4th November

DH-4   11th Bombardment Sqn
**B CHEVENEY LE CHÂTEAU AA shot down
MIA(1Lt CJ Gatton **KIA**/1Lt GE Bures **KIA**) left late
[Ja11?]

DH-4   11th Bombardment Sqn
**B CHEVENEY LE CHÂTEAU combat with 18 Fokker
DVIIs shot up(1Lt Newby **WIA**/1Lt JR Pearson
WIA)severe, both hit in leg

DH-4   11th Bombardment Sqn
**B CHEVENEY LE CHÂTEAU combat with 18 Fokker
DVIIs[+?] heavily shot up fuel tank on fire shot down in
flames cr nrSTENAY **MIA**(1Lt DE Coates **KIA**/2Lt LR
Thrall **KIA**) combined operation of 30 a'c with US11 &
US166

DH-4   50th Observation Sqn
** **MIA**(2Lt DC Beebe **POW**/2Lt MK Lockwood **POW**)

Salmson 2A2   90th Observation Sqn
** (1Lt LM Carver **WIA**)

Breguet 14B2   96th Bombardment Sqn
** (/1Lt HJ Spalding **WIA**)

DH-4   168th Observation Sqn
** (/1Lt E Pendell **WIA**) 5.11?

5th November

DH-4   20th Bombardment Sqn
**B MOUZON combat with Fokker DVIIs 12000' after
drop engine hit shot down partly ooc then ss & cr
MARTINCOURT (1Lt SP Mandell **DoW**/2Lt RW?
Fulton **POW**) initials RB?, attacked by third of 3 patrols,
Mandell killed by German infantrymen?

This was the final operation of the 1st Day Bombardment Group.

DH-4   20th Bombardment Sqn
**B MOUZON combat with Fokker DVIIs 13000' after
drop: shot up by 2nd patrol shot down in flames(1Lt KG
West **KIA**/1Lt WF Frank **KIA**) chased down by EA

DH-4   20th Bombardment Sqn
**B combat with Fokker DVIIs MOUZON-STENAY

fuel tank & engine shot up ftl EoL(1Lt LB Edwards **POW**/
1Lt KC Payne **POW**) hit by 3rd patrol

.14?   DH-4   20th Bombardment Sqn
**B MOUZON combat with Fokker DVIIs[+] DUN-
SUR-MEUSE 9-25am to 9-45am(2Lt LP Koepfgen OK/
Cpl RC Alexander **WIA**)slight, shared victory

7655.9   SPAD 13   93rd Pursuit Sqn
** combat with Fokker DVIIs[+] 9-20am to 9-40am shot
down? **MIA**(1Lt LL Carruthers **POW**?) ?Gorrell: POW

6th November

7528.4   SPAD 13   28th Pursuit Sqn
**P combat with EAs[+2Str cr] 10-55am then chased by 4
Fokker DVIIs very low shot up dam ooc cr **MIA**(1Lt BE
Brown **POW**) left 9-30am, weather reduced patrol to 3 a'c,
had followed EA down ["SPAD" claim combat
BETHELAINVILLE 10-30am Ltn U Neckel Ja6]

4611.7   SPAD 13   95th Pursuit Sqn
** combat with Hannovers[+] 3-30pm shot down(1Lt
WH Vail **WIA**) shared victory

SPAD 13   213th Pursuit Sqn
**B? combat with 3 Fokker DVIIs 3000m down to ground
mist, seen chased into mist by Fokker **MIA**(1Lt AM
Treadwell **KIA**)

7th November

Salmson 2A2   91st Observation Sqn
? (/1Lt AC Kincaid **WIA)severe, only in Gorrell?

8th November

DH-4   8th Observation Sqn
** **MIA**(2Lt CB Robinson **POW**/2Lt DD Watson **POW**)
crew?

SPAD 13   93rd Pursuit Sqn
** shot down? **MIA**(2Lt WE Case **POW**?) Gorrell: POW

7739.20 SPAD 13   93rd Pursuit Sqn
B GIBENY ftl n.m.l. **MIA(1Lt CB Maxwell **POW**)
walked back to squadron after Armistice

10th November

Salmson 2A2   91st Observation Sqn
Rec **MIA(2Lt LM Bruck **KIA**/2Lt WA White **KIA**)
crew?

Section C
AMERICANS KNOWN TO HAVE BEEN
CASUALTIES WHILST SERVING WITH THE
FRENCH AIR FORCE IN 1918

Entry via the Lafayette Flying Corps

January

French Unit
** (Soldat FE Starrett US. **KIA**?) 3Jan.18

French N.150
** (Cpl D Spencer US. **KIA**) 22Jan.18 22.6?

French Spa.67
** (Cpl PP Benney US. **DoW**) 26Jan.18

February

French Spa.67
** (Sgt WH Tailer US. **KIA**) 5Feb.18

French N.314
** **MIA**(Sgt? HJ McKee US. **POW**) 8Feb.18

French Spa.84
** (Sgt EJ Loughran US. **KIA**) 18Feb.18

March

French Spa.87
** (Sgt? T Hitchcock US. **WIA POW**) 6Mar.18

French Spa.156
** (Cpl WC Winter US. **KIA**) 8Mar.18

French Br.117
** **MIA**(Sgt? CW Kerwood US. **POW**) 31Mar.18

April

French Spa.94
** (Cpl HH Woodward US. **KIA**) 1Apr.18

French Spa.96
** (Sgt S Lee US. **KIA**) 12Apr.18

French Spa.12
** (Sgt DE Stone US. **KIA**) 21Apr.18

May

French Spa.77
** (Sgt? TG Buffum US. **POW**) 4May.18

French Spa.85

** (1Lt JA Bayne US. **KIA**) 18May.18

French Spa.31
** (Cpl SR Drew US. **KIA**) 19May.18

French N.99
** (Sgt? CB Shoninger US. **POW**) 29May.18

French N.97
** (Sgt AD Pelton Can. **KIA**) 31May.18

June

French Spa.85
** (Sgt AH Nichols US. **KIA**) 2Jun.18

French Br.227
** (Sgt A Bluthenthal US. **KIA**) 5Jun.18

French Spa.3
** (Sgt FL Baylies US. **KIA**) 17Jun.18

French Spa.85
** (Sgt CF Chamberlain US. **KIA**) 13Jun.18

French Spa.17
** (Sgt DG Tucker US. **KIA**) 8Jul.18

July

French Spa.98
** (Sgt JH Baugham US. **DoW**) 2Jul.18

French Spa.96
** (Sgt V Booth US. **DoW**) 10Jul.18

French Spa.38
** **MIA**(Sgt? LL Byers US. **POW**) 18Jul.18

French Spa.85
** (Sgt SM Tyson US. **KIA**) 19Jul.18

August

French C.46
** (Cpl WJ McKerness US. **KIA**) 15Aug.18

French N.158
** (1Lt SE Edgar US. **KIA**) 17Aug.18

Section D
AMERICANS KNOWN TO HAVE BEEN CASUALTIES WHILST SERVING WITH THE FRENCH AIR FORCE IN 1917–1918

Direct entry

1917

December

SPAD   **French Spa.84**
** combat with 2Strs[+] ovSAINT SOUPLET shot

down EoL **MIA**(Cpl S Walcott US. **KIA**) 12Dec.17

1918

March

French Unit
** (2Lt RH Whitner US. **KIA**/) 13Mar.18

April

SPAD   **French Spa.77**
** combat with EAs shot down ovMONTDIDIER
MIA(Cpl H Whitmore US. **POW**) 6Apr.18 ["SPAD"
claim combat MONTDIDIER Offst Sporbert Ja62]

May

Salmson 2A2   **French SAL.51**
** (/1Lt LA Gunderson US. **WIA**) 3May.18

Salmson 2A2?   **French GB9**
** (/2Lt RB Parker US. **KIA**?) 4May.18 POW?

SPAD   **French Spa.77**
** combat with EAs shot down eMONTDIDIER
MIA(Cpl Buffum US. **POW**) 4May.18 [?"SPAD" claim
combat seMONTDIDIER 8pm Ltn H Pippart Ja19]

French Unit
? (1Lt JA Bayne US. **Kld) 8May.18

Breguet 14B2   **French Br.111**
** **MIA**(/1Lt RM Noble US. **KIA**) 14May.18

French Unit
** (/1Lt HF Johnson US. **KIA**) 21May.18

French Unit
** **MIA**(1Lt CL Ovington US. **KIA**/) 29May.18

June

Salmson 2A2   **French SAL.4**
** (/2Lt CH Eyman US. **KIA**) 5Jun.18

Salmson 2A2?   **French Sop.251?**
** combat with 6EAs[+] EoL shot up (/2Lt CL Miller US.
Ld'H **WIA**)arm 6Jun.18 a'c had 103 bullet holes in it,
airman possibly linked to US99?

Salmson 2A2?   **French GB9**
** (1Lt RL Moore US. **WIA**/) 21Jun.18

SPAD   **French Spa.69**
** combat with EAs shot up (1Lt JD Beane US.
WIA)fingers 30Jun.18

July

SPAD   **French Spa.90**
P combat with 4EAs 4000m shot down **MIA(1Lt GN
Jerome US. **KIA**) 11Jul.18

Breguet 14B2   **French Br.117**
** (1Lt M Lehr US. **KIA**) 15Jul.18

Breguet 14B2   **French Br.129**
B hit by mg fire(/2Lt RW Moody US. **DoW 16.7.18)
15Jul.18

11043   SPAD 7   **French Spa.33**
P combat with EAs shot down EoL **MIA(1Lt LD
Layton US. **KIA**) 18Jul.18 airman linked with US138?

SPAD   **French Spa.38**
P shot down nrMARQUISES EoL **MIA(Cpl LL Byers
US. **POW**) 18Jul.18

French   **6th Armee**
** (/1Lt FM Dixon US. **WIA**)severe 22Jul.18, airman
later with US99

SPAD   **French Spa.38**
? **MIA(Adj G Sitterly US. **POW**) 28Jul.18

SPAD   **French Spa.100**
** combat with 3EAs shot down ovCHOUY?(1Lt GC
Davidson US. **KIA**) 31Jul.18 buried in garden of priest's
house CHOUY

SPAD   **French Spa.3**
** (Capt HC Ferguson US. **WIA**) Jul.18

August

Salmson 2A2?   **French GB6**
** combat with EAs[+?] shot up (/1Lt AH Keith US.
Ld'H **WIA**)severe:stomach 6Aug.18 shot down EA while
wounded

Breguet 14B2   **French Br.29**
**LowB combat with EAs[+] shot up (/2Lt EW Porter
US. **WIA**)jaw:severe 9Aug.18 continued firing after being
hit & brought down EA

French AR108
LowB AA shot down flames(2Lt NC Barber US. **KIA/)
11Aug.18 on "low altitude long distance bombardment"

French C.46
** (2Lt P Penfield US. **KIA**) 15Aug.18

SPAD   **French Spa.12**
B shot through head EoL(/1Lt HW Craig US. **DoW)
20Aug.18

Breguet 14B2   **French Br.108**
B combat with 4EAs shot up (1Lt SR Halley US. **WIA/)
arm:slight 24Aug.18

September

Breguet 14B2   **French Br.66**
B shot up (/2Lt LD Schaeffer US. **WIA)severe 3Sep.18
29.8?

SPAD   **French Spa.164**
**P combat with DVIIs ovSOMME-AY 4000m shot up
(1Lt RC McCormick US. **WIA**)leg 5Sep.18

Breguet 14B2   **French Br.131**
** (/2Lt GM Newell US. **WIA**) 14Sep.18 19.9?

Breguet 14B2   **French Br.123**
** (/1Lt EM Powell US. **WIA**) 22Sep.18

SPAD   **French Spa.38**
P ftl EoL **MIA(Cpl JJ Bach US. **POW**) 23Sep.18

October

Breguet 14B2   **French Br.117**
** combat with EAs shot down EoL **MIA**(1Lt EM Manier
US. **KIA**) 2Oct.18 making last flight at own request before
returning to US

SPAD   **French Spa.38**
**KBP attacked KB then combat with 10DVIIs swLAON
shot down **MIA**(Sgt WJ Schafer US. **KIA**?) 3Oct.18 *name*
Schaffer?, in via the Lafayette?

Breguet 14B2   **French Br.129**
** (1Lt CT Buckley US. **KIA**) 10Oct.18

Untraced date

Salmson 2A2?   **French GB9**
** (2Lt HH Eymann US. **WIA**) .18

Part III

UNITED KINGDOM and HOME WATERS
1914–1918

1914
August

12th August

260   Bleriot Tandem XI-2   3Sqn
* ss dive cr after take off from NETHERAVON for
mobilisation at DOVER(2Lt. RR Skene **KIFA**/AM RK
Barlow **KIFA**) Barlow thrown out

These were the first casualties on active service for
the RFC after the declaration of war.

September

5th September

Farman   RNAS
*Night Patrol ovLONDON OK(FSLt. C Graham-
White/FSLt. RT Gates)

This was the first ever night patrol. Gates was
Graham-White's manager in his aviation business.

December

25th December

664·   Vickers FB4   7Sqn
**Home Defence, intercepted & shot up EA FF29
seaplane ovERITH on the THAMES ESTUARY, caused
damage & drove it off until gun jam, then shot up by
either British AA or EA bullet? OK(2Lt. MR Chidson/
Cpl Martin) left Joyce Green 12-35pm 25.12.14, German
crew of OblzS S Prondynski & FzS vonFrankenberg in
FF29 #203, were on their second raid over England. Von
Frankenberg was WIA in elbow.

This was the prototype Vickers FB4 pusher, fitted
with a Maxim machine-gun. As such it was the

only operational British aircraft of the time so
armed.

1915
January

19th January

1617   FB5   7Sqn (HomeDefence)
**ZepP to pursue Zeppelins, became lost, engine failed &
fell into snd but recovered at 600′ then heavy ldg cr(Capt
WHC Mansfield **inj**/QMSgt HE Chaney **inj**) left
JOYCE GREEN 9-17pm, also shot up by London's AA

This was the first Zeppelin raid made on the
United Kingdom, Zeppelins L3 and L4 bombing
East Anglia. Another 7 Squadron FB5 went aloft
but this, too, was forced down with engine trouble.

1916
March

19th March

3964   Nieuport   10 RNAS
+*HAP chased Friedrichshafen Seaplane [+ftl captured]
OK(FCdr RJ Bone) German crew of FlM Ponater/Ltn
Herrenkrecht

6364   FE2b   Lympne
+*Delivery to France, left 1-30pm, combat with
Brandenberg Seaplane[+chased down "into" Channel,
engine smoking] 4000′ 2-30pm engine failing so pulled
out OK(2Lt R Collis/FSgt AC Emery) crew knew they
had been unseen by EA because it fired no mg in
defence[German Report: radiator hit, ftl, then repair was
effected and made OSTENDE] RFC Combat Report in
1Sqn Combats

April

15th April

39 Squadron RFC was formed at Hounslow to defend London.

25th April

3108	Short 827	Yarmouth

** a'c shelled by German Fleet off SCARBOROUGH cr(FSLt HG Hall **inj**/OSLt DC Evans OK)

May

6th May

8038	Short 184	Dover RNAS

** ftl and then captured by U-boat(FSLt ATM Cowley **POW**/Lt RM Inge **POW**) both to Holland 30.4.18

August

2nd August

8953	Bristol Scout D	HMS *Vindex*

**HD attacked Zeppelin L.17 engine failed ftl ditched nrNORTH HINDER OK(FSLt CT Freeman) picked up & taken to Holland, but released 6.8.16

This was the first carrier-borne Home Defence operation.

September

2nd September

2092 or 2693	BE2c	39 HD Sqn

Suttons Farm **ZepP attacked Army Airship SL11[+ shot down in flames] ovCUFFLEY, Herts ~1-30am OK(Lt W Leefe-Robinson VC) 2/3Sep, left ~11pm patrolling across the THAMES to JOYCE GREEN, made three attacks before airship was brought down

This was the first German airship to be shot down over Great Britain by an aircraft. Leefe-Robinson was awarded the Victoria Cross for his accomplishment. For full details of all encounters with Zeppelins in the course of home defence in the Great War reference should be made to the excellent book *The Air Defence of Britain 1914-1918* by C Cole and EF Cheesman.

23th September

4112	BE2c	39 HD Sqn

Suttons Farm **ZepP attacked Zeppelin L.32[+shot down in flames] nrBILLERICAY 13000' ~1am shot up

OK(2Lt F Sowrey) 23/24Sep, left 11-30pm, made two attacks, Zeppelin cr 1-20am, seen falling from eighty miles

This aircraft is now preserved in the Canadian War Museum. On the same night, Zeppelin L33 was also forced to land and crash after receiving a direct hit from an AA battery in east London and being attacked by home defence aircraft on its journey. It came down at Little Wigborough, north of the Blackwater estuary.

October

1st October

4577	BE2c	39 HD Sqn

North Weald **ZepP attacked Navy Airship L.31[+shot down cr 11-54pm] ovPOTTERS BAR 12700' then spin to avoid airship ftl cr 12-10am dam OK(2Lt WJ Tempest) 1/2Oct, left 10pm, fire delivered from very close range and beneath, hull went up "like an enormous Chinese lantern" which very nearly fell on him

November

27th November

2738	BE2c	36 HD Sqn

Seaton Carew **ZepP attacked Navy Zeppelin L.34[+ shot down in flames in sea off HARTLEPOOL] ~9800' 11-30pm OK(2Lt IV Pyott SA.) 27/28Nov, left 10-22pm, BE2c was close enough for Pyott's face to be scorched

28th November

8626	BE2c	Bacton

**ZepP chased Navy Zeppelin L.21 to 8m off LOWESTOFT[+shot down in flames cr sea 6-42am] OK(FSLt E Pulling DSO) left 4-45am, shared victory with Cadbury

8420	BE2c	Burgh Castle

**ZepP chased Navy Zeppelin L.21 to 8m off LOWESTOFT but guns jammed OK(FSLt GWR Fane DSC) left 4-35am, scorched by flames

8625	BE2c	Burgh Castle

**ZepP chased Navy Zeppelin L.21 to 8m off LOWESTOFT[+shot down in flames cr sea 6-42am] 8500' OK(FSLt E Cadbury DSC) left 6-18am, shared victory with Pulling but most likely caused the crucial damage

3324	Short 827	Felixstowe

P ftl dam **MIA(FSLt G Llewellyn-Davies **POW**/Lt AC Stevens **POW**)

1917
March

17th March

7181   BE2c   78HD Sqn
Telscombe Cliffs **HD left 12-01am cr 9 mins after take
off fire wr(2Lt DD Fowler **KIA**)

This was the first operation for 78 Squadron.

June

14th June

8677   Curtiss H12   Felixstowe
+* attacked Zeppelin L.43[+shot down in flames] off
VLIELAND OK(FSLt BD Hobbs DSC/FSLt RFL
Dickey/2AM HM Davis/1AM AW Goody) left 5-15am,
attacked from above

July

7th July

A8271   Sopwith Strutter   37HD Sqn
Rochford ** combat with 22 Gothas? or British AA?, shot
down in sea nrMALPIN LIGHT SHIP(2Lt JER Young
KIA/2AM CC Taylor **DoI**) left 9-31am [?possible
"English 1Str" nrLONDON Vzfw Gaede/Ltn Radke
KG13]

A6230   Sopwith Pup   63 Trg Sqn
Joyce Green **HD combat with Gothas shot up ftl cr
Joyce Green(2Lt WG Salmon **DoW**) hit in head, almost
landed [?"Sopwith 1Str" claim in Gotha am OffSt R
Klimke/Oblt Leon KG13]

August

12th August

B3798   Sopwith Camel   Eastchurch
**HD left 5-30pm shot up by Gotha off Kent dam ftl
7-45pm OK(FCdr AF Bettington)

N6333   Sopwith Camel   Manston
**attacked Gothas but guns jammed, engine shot up dam
ftl OK(FLt AA Wallis)

21st August

N6430   Sopwith Pup   HMS *Yarmouth*
** attacked Airship L.23[+shot down in flames in sea]
off LODBJERG, DENMARK OK(FSLt BA Smart)
attacked from above and infront & narrowly avoided
collision, picked up by TDB Prince

September

25th September

A6461   FE2d   36 HD Sqn
Seaton Carew **HD chased Zeppelin?, ran out of fuel?
MIA(2Lt HJ Thornton **KIA**/2Lt CA Moore **KIA**) 24/
25Sep, left 1-50am, never found

October

1st October

9810   Porte FB2   Felixstowe
** combat with 3EAs shot up engines hit ftl sea(/WTOp
HM Davies **WIA**) towed to shore [combat 5-10pm Oblt
F Christiansen SFL1]

14th October

N1661   Short 184   Dundee
*Anti-SubP bombed submarine then ftl OK(FSLt A
Holland/OSL L Ritson)

24th October

8693   Curtiss H12   Felixstowe
SubP engine ftl then saved by Dutch **MIA(FLt W
Perham **INT**/FSLt HC Gooch **INT**/LM CW Sivyer **INT**/
AM BM Millichamp **INT**) crew destroyed a'c, interned
Holland

November

6th November

A5719   FE2b   36 HD Sqn
Seaton Carew *NFP blown out to sea? **MIA**(2Lt HD
Crisp **KIA**) left 5pm

December

18th December

B5192   Sopwith Camel   44 HD Sqn
Hainault A Flt +* combat with GothaGIII[+ftl] off
FOLKESTONE ~9pm OK(Capt GW Murlis Green)
EA ditched & captured, Murlis Green's last of 8 victories,
the others in Macedonia

1918
January

3rd January

A5698   FE2b   38 HD Sqn
Stamford **Rec hit by British Home Defence AA ftl cr
OK(Lt EF Wilson) 3/4Jan, on cross-country trg flight

28th January

C4638   Bristol F2b   39HD Sqn
North Weald **HD combat with HA btwn NORTH
WEALD-PASSINGFORD BRIDGE 11-50pm shot up
mg fuel tank hit ftl(2Lt JG Goodyear OK/1AM WT
Merchant **WIA**)arm, WIA slight but to hospital ["EA"
claim combat btwn LONDON-GRAVESEND Vzfw
Eschenderlein/Ltn Radke/Ltn Genth BSt13]

The enemy aircraft encountered was the German
Staaken Giant R.IV 12/15, on its inward journey
to bomb London. The crew sighted the machine
between Sawbridgeworth and Sutton's Farm but
came under fire from its many machine-guns and
was forced to land. The Staaken continued on to
London where one of its bombs exploded in
Odham's Printing Works in Lond Acre and caused
thirty-eight deaths and injured another ninety.

B2402   Sopwith Camel   44 HD Sqn
Hainault +*HD attacked GothaG[+cr,capt] FRUND'S
FARM, WICKFORD 10-10pm OK(Capt GH Hackwill)
28/29Jan, shared victory, 10 minute combat, Gotha
shot down was GV 938/16, both pilots awarded MCs for
victory

B3827   Sopwith Camel   44 HD Sqn
Hainault +*HD attacked GothaG[+cr,capt] FRUND'S
FARM WICKFORD 10-10pm OK(Lt CC Banks) 28/
29Jan, shared victory

February

18th February

6610   BE12   37 HD Sqn
Goldhanger **HAP engine? ftl crTOLLESHUNT
MANOR 1-10am (2Lt S Armstrong **KIFA**) pilot burnt,
was initially believed Armstrong had been in combat
ovTIPTREE

March

8th March

C3208   BE12   37 HD Sqn
Stow Maries **HD collided w B679 ovRAYLEIGH,
Essex cr wr(Capt AB Kynoch **KIA**) left 11-29pm 7.3.18
Kynoch may have been chasing Staaken R.VI 27/16:
KIFA?

B679   SE5a   61 HD Sqn
Rochford **HD:NFP combat with EA collided with BE12
C3208 ovRAYLEIGH, Essex 12-30am(Capt HC Stroud
KIA) left 11-30pm 7.3.18, KIFA?

10th March

C3116   BE12   50 HD Sqn
HD:NFP fog flew out to sea **MIA(Lt JAC Kempe-

Roberts **KIA**) left SHEFFIELD for BEKESBOURNE
12-25am

April

12th April

A5707   FE2b   38 HD Sqn
Buckminster **HD:ZepP chased Zeppelin shot up? AA
ftl cr nrCOVENTRY ~1-30am(Lt CH Noble-Campbell
WIA) left 11-25pm, pilot believed he had been hit by fire
from Zeppelin but may have been victim of British AA

24th April

8677   Curtiss H12   Felixstowe
** combat with 7EAs ovNORTH HINDER shot
down(Capt NA Magor **KIA**/Ens S Potter USN. **KIA**/
LM R Lucas **KIA**/1AM JG Strathearn **KIA**) [claim
combat 9-10am Oblt F Christiansen SFL1]

May

10th May

N4291   Felixstowe F2A   Killingholme
+*ZepP took off to track & chase Zeppelin
ovHELIGOLAND Mine Fields OK(Capt TC Pattinson/
Capt AH Munday/Sgt HR Stubbington/AM.WT
Johnson) left 1-20pm, Zeppelin L62 seen go down in
flames nrBORKUM DEEP

This crew was credited with chasing and shooting
down Zeppelin L62. Wise in *Canadian Airmen* notes
that the airship this crew actually chased was L56.
L62 was destroyed on this day, but it is likely to
have blown up after being hit by lightning.

19th May

D6423   Sopwith Camel   112 HD Sqn
Throwley +*HD attacked GothaGIV[+flames]
nrFAVERSHAM 11-26pm OK(Maj CJQ Brand SA.) left
11-15pm, pilot's face and moustache scorched by flames

C4636.A6 Bristol F2b   39 HD Sqn
North Weald +*HD attacked GothaGIV[+shot dn]
nrROMAN ROAD, EAST HAM heavily shot up OK(Lt
AJ Arkell/1AM ATC Stagg) left 10-56pm, Gotha engine
hit, cr 12-20am 20.5.18

C851   Bristol F2b   141 HD Sqn
Biggin Hill +*HD attacked GothaGIV[+shot down]
then landed DETLING OK(Lt EE Turner/Lt HB
Barwise) left 11-02pm, Gotha shot up ~12-30am 20.5.18
& cr btwn FRINSTED-HARRIETSHAM ~12-40am

Three Gothas were shot down and a fourth crashed
through bad flying on the night of the 19th/20th
May.

30th May

8660   Curtiss H12   Yarmouth
**Rec BORKUM engine trouble, ftl on sea then shot up
by 3EA Seaplanes(Capt CT Young **KIA**/Ens JT Roe
USN **POW**/Pte JE Money **POW**/Pte WF Chase **KIA**/
Cpl F Grant **POW**) Chase was drowned, other fatalities
by fire from enemy seaplanes whilst flying boat was on
water, Roe and Money also **KIA**? details related in *The
Story of a North Sea Air Station* by CF Snowden Gamble

June

4th June

8689   Curtiss H12   Felixstowe
**ZepP HAAKS LIGHT VESSEL shot down ftl
NORTH SEA off VLIELAND **MIA**(Lt RJR Duff-Fyfe
INT/FSLt JF Pattison **INT**/Ens JA Eaton USN. **INT**/
Sgt AJ Brown **INT**/1AM EJ Strewthers **INT**) (see below)

N4533   Felixstowe F2A   Felixstowe
**ZepP HAAKS LIGHT VESSEL engine failure ftl on
sea then shot up by EA while taxying fire **MIA**(Capt RFL
Dickey **INT**/Capt RJ Paul **INT**/Lt AG Hodgson **INT**/
2AM EPC Burton **INT**/FW ACH Russell **INT**) [shot up
off TERSCHELLING by Obt F Christiansen SFL1]

A group of five flying boats from Felixstowe and
Yarmouth had set off in the afternoon to investigate
wireless activity, possibly coming from airships.
N4533 above was forced to land with a broken feed
pipe, and about this time the patrol was attacked
by a small group of enemy seaplanes. These were
driven off, or rather, went for reinforcements, with
the Curtiss H12 8689 in pursuit. The latter was
eventually forced down in Dutch waters and the
crew interned. N4533 meanwhile had received a
message from the patrol leader to taxi to shore in
Holland but to destroy his flying boat on nearing
land. As the remainder of the patrol were shepherd-
ing it towards Holland they were engaged by at
least ten enemy seaplanes about 4-30pm. There
followed the biggest seaplane air battle of the war,
in which one large enemy type was forced down to
land heavily in the sea and another seaplane was
shot down. It is likely that N4533 was shot up by
a German seaplane near Holland, and the machine
was certainly set on fire and the crew interned. The
remainder of the patrol eventually limped back to
the mainland, but not before one had been forced
down temporarily to make repairs.

6th June

N4345   Curtiss H12B   Felixstowe
this a'c? ** combat with 4 enemy Seaplanes shot down
nrINNER GABBARD ftl cr OK(LtCol EDM Robertson/
Maj CJ Galpin) rescued next day after clinging to
wreckage for eight hours, Robertson was Felixstowe

Station Commanding Officer [?claim OblMt Metzing/
FlMt Walker]

7th June

8417   BE2c   273Sqn
Burgh Castle +*SubP attacked by 5 enemy Seaplanes
seCROSS SANDS 5-35am OK(Lt GF Hodson) unarmed
bombing patrol, escaped & returned to Yarmouth (see
below)

N1693   Short 320   Yarmouth
** combat with 5 enemy Seaplanes ~5-35am shot down
ftl sea nrLOWESTOFT(2Lt RWA Ivermere **WIA**/2AM
SE Bourne **WIA**) EA Seaplanes from Zeebrugge, crew
was strafed after ldg for ten minutes but saved by motor
launch

This crew came to the assistance of the unarmed
BE2c 8417 on anti-submarine patrol being attacked
by five enemy seaplanes.

17th June

The Official History cites the pilot of a Sopwith
Camel which flew off HMS *Galatea* becoming
interned in Denmark on the 17th. The light cruiser
had been attacked by German seaplanes and it sent
the Camel aloft to pursue them. The pilot found
one of these alighting in Ringkjobblink Fjord but
was prevented from attack by gun jams. He met a
heavy rain storm as he set out seawards again to
find his ship and eventually force-landed on the
shore at Fjaltring where he was interned. His
identity and that of his aircraft are yet to be
established.

19th June

N6810   Sopwith Camel 2F1   HMS *Furious*
** chased 2 enemy Seaplanes, combat then ftl sea OK(Lt
MW Basedon) a'c salvaged by HMS *Wolfhound*

July

4th July

N4297   Felixstowe F2A   Felixstowe
** combat with 4 enemy seaplanes ftl sea seNORTH
HINDER OK, crew not yet established [combat 5-10pm
Obt F Christiansen SFL1]

N4513   Felixstowe F2A   Felixstowe
** combat with 4 enemy seaplanes ftl sank in tow 20m
seNORTH HINDER (Lt S Anderson **WIA**/Lt KL
Williams **WIA**/BoyMech AEV Hilton **WIA**/2AM AC
Cokeley **KIA**) [combat with SFL1]

N4540   Felixstowe F2A   Felixstowe
** combat with 4EA seaplanes seNORTH HINDER but
returned YARMOUTH OK, crew not yet established
[combat 5-20pm Obt F Christiansen SFL1]

18th July

B5601   Sopwith Camel   Manston
+*EscP combat with 7 enemy Seaplanes[+cr vertically]
seKENTISH KNOCK OK(Lt FC Vincent)

B7269   Sopwith Camel   Manston
+*EscP combat with 7 enemy Seaplanes seKENTISH
KNOCK OK(Lt CFA Wagstaff)

N2927   Short 184   Westgate
**P combat with 7 enemy Seaplanes shot down ftl sea
seKENTISH KNOCK fire(Lt JAH Pegram **KIA**/2Lt LA
Thrower **KIA**) broke ldg gear, fire started [combat
9-30am Obt F Christiansen SFL1]

N2937   Short 184   Westgate
**P combat with 7 enemy Seaplanes shot down sea
seKENTISH KNOCK OK(Lt JAE Vowles/2Lt JGM
Farrall) [combat 9-30am Obt F Christiansen SFL1]

This patrol of two Shorts, escorted by two Camels,
was met by six Brandenburg seaplane fighters of
Flanders I. There was confusion during and after
the fight, in which the escorts mistook the Short
which had been shot down for an enemy machine
and a retreating Brandenburg for a Short, so they
too left the scene. Of interest is the fact that these
German claims were later substantiated by photographs taken by one Christiansen's men who
recorded some of the action with his camera.

19th July

Sopwith Camel 2F1   HMS *Furious*
**B TONDERN Airship Base ftl in sea? on return
MIA(Lt WA Yeulett **KIA**) left 3-22am, one report stated
he came down near TONDERN, another that his a'c was
salvaged from the sea nrHOYER, but neither he nor his
a'c were actually found

Sopwith Camel 2F1   HMS *Furious*
**B TONDERN Airship Base returned safely OK(Capt
BA Smart DSO) left 3-22am

Sopwith Camel 2F1   HMS *Furious*
**B TONDERN Airship Base returned safely OK(Capt
WF Dickson) left 3-14am

Sopwith Camel 2F1   HMS *Furious*
**B TONDERN Airship Base returned early with engine
trouble OK(Capt TK Thyne) left 3-22am

N6605   Sopwith Camel 2F1   HMS *Furious*
**B TONDERN Airship Base low fuel ftl
nrSCALLINGER, DENMARK **MIA**(Lt NE Williams
INT) left 3-14am, interned Denmark

N6771   Sopwith Camel 2F1   HMS *Furious*
**B TONDERN Airship Base low fuel ftl nrEBSJERG,
DENMARK **MIA**(Capt WD Jackson **INT**) left 3-14am,
burnt a'c on ldg, interned Denmark

N6823   Sopwith Camel 2F1   HMS *Furious*
**B TONDERN Airship Base ftl nrRINKJOBING,

DENMARK **MIA**(Lt S Dawson **INT**) left 3-22am,
interned Denmark

A daring raid on the two Zeppelin sheds at
Tondern was made on the 19th by seven Ships'
Camels flying off HMS *Furious*. The raid had been
delayed for some weeks by terrible weather on two
previous attempts. Machines in two formations
began leavng the aircraft carrier at 3-14am to begin
their eighty-mile flight across open sea to the
enemy base. All Camels and pilots involved are
given above. One machine turned back with engine
trouble, but six duly arrived over the sheds and
dropped their bombs. There were no protecting
enemy fighters at Tondern, although ground fire
was plentiful. Each aircraft carried two specially
made 60-lb Cooper bombs, and two Zeppelins, L54
and L60, were destroyed in huge explosions in one
of the sheds. Of the first flight of three Camels, only
Dickson's returned safely, the others being forced
to land in Denmark. Of the second group of three,
another was also interned, one came down in the
sea on the return journey and was drowned, and
only Capt Smart made it back to a British ship.
Clouds and poor visibility may have contributed to
the losses.

31st July

N4305   Felixstowe F2A   Yarmouth
** combat with 5EA off LOWESTOFT shot down,
caught fire sank(Capt EA Mossop OK/Lt G Hodson
OK/Pte Greenwood OK/Pte RRN Cooper **died**/Pte
WHD Dingley **died**) crew drowned [combat 4-45pm Obt
F Christiansen SFL1]

August

2nd August

N4299   Felixstowe F2A   Felixstowe
ZepP ftl **MIA(Lt DW Wilson **INT**/Lt LC Bower
INT/3AM RA Wootton **INT**/3AM HB May **INT**)

5th August

N6620   Sopwith Camel   273Sqn
Burgh Castle **HD:ZepP **MIA**(Lt GF Hodgson **KIFA**)
left 9-05pm

A8032   DH4   Yarmouth
+*HD:ZepP attacked Zeppelin L.70[+shot down in
flames] 8m off WELLS-NEXT-THE-SEA, NORTH
NORFOLK 18,000' OK(Maj E Cadbury/Capt R Leckie)
left 9-05pm, Cadbury came down through cloud with
difficulty and landed SEDGEFORD

Leckie had already been involved in the shooting
down of a Zeppelin, L22, which was brought down
over the North Sea in May 1917.

A8039   DH4   Yarmouth
+*HD:ZepP attacked Zeppelin L.70[+?des] OK(Lt RE
Keys/AM AT Harman) left 8-55pm

D5802   DH9   Yarmouth
HD:ZepP ftl **MIA(Capt DGB Jardine **KIA**/Lt ER
Munday **KIA**) left 8-55pm

The 5th of August saw the last night of Zeppelin
raids on England of the war. Five Zeppelins made
attacks and one of them, the L70, was shot down.
The crew of A8039 made a counter-claim for the
destruction of L70 and it is accepted that they also
attacked it shortly before it was destroyed. Thick
cloud and poor conditions have, nevertheless,
obscured the detail of what happened through this
night.

11th August

N6812   Sopwith Ship's Camel   HM TBD*Redoubt*
**ZepP attacked Zeppelin L.53[+shot down in flames]
off HELIGOLAND BIGHT 19000′ 9-41am OK(Lt SD
Culley) left 8-41am, took off from towed lighter for attack
only eleven days after this feat had been achieved for the
first time

28th August

B9983   Blackburn Kangaroo   246Sqn

Seaton Carew **Anti-SubP dropped 520lb bomb onto
submerged submarine 54-31 N. 0.40 W. OK(Lt EF
Waring/2Lt HJ Smith/Sig Reed) air bubbles and oil
rising, HMS *Ouse* then dropped depth charge to destroy,
submarine was the U.C.70

October

2nd October

N4302   Felixstowe F2A Felixstowe
HAP ftl off VLIELAND **MIA(Capt AT Barker **KIFA**/
t VFA Galvayne **KIFA**/Pte Hopkins **INT**?)

N4551   Felixstowe F2A 232Sqn
Felixstowe ** eng failed ftl 10m nnwNORDWIJK
MIA(2Lt TN Enright **INT**/2Lt W Pendleton **INT**/Lt
JC Stockman **INT**/1AM HL Curtis **INT**/3AM WA
Mitchell **INT**) interned Holland

November

9th November

N4543   Felixstowe F2A 230Sqn
** low fuel ftl sea & sank seSMITH'S KNOLL **MIA**(2Lt
FB Candy **INT**/2Lt OL Coleman **INT**/2Lt J Freeman
INT/Sgt RH Thomas **INT**/2AM LA Christmas **INT**)
interned Holland

Part IV

ITALY AND THE ADRIATIC 1917–1918

1917
November 1917
THE BEGINNINGS OF BRITISH INVOLVEMENT IN ITALY

Five squadrons of the Royal Flying Corps arrived
in northern Italy in November 1917. They had
been rushed from the Western Front when it
appeared the Italian war effort might be disinte-
grating. The Italian front stretched three hundred
and seventy-five miles from Switzerland to the
Adriatic, and a state of war with the Austro-

Hungarian Empire had existed for two and a half
years. Activity was mostly concentrated into
fighting around the enemy salient at Trentino and
in battles for control of Trieste. No less than twelve
separate battles were fought in the key regions
around Isonzo before the arrival of the British, and
it was due to the autumn fighting here that both
Germany and Britain felt it necessary to become
involved. First, in the 11th battle of Isonzo in
September, the Austrian forces had themselves
nearly collapsed, and as a consequence seven
German divisions under the command of General
von Below arrived in the Alps. They brought significant amounts of artillery and aeroplanes with

them and their presence completely altered the balance of power in the region.

The most important development to flow from this was a devastating defeat inflicted on the Italians in the 12th battle of Isonzo, which began on the 24th of October. The German forces extracted 275,000 prisoners in the fighting, and hundreds of thousands of Italian soldiers were wounded and killed, or deserted. It was a disaster for the Allies, and demanded immediate action to prevent a complete loss of the front. Britain offered two divisions, to be known as the XIV Corps, with artillery and air support provided by the newly formed VII Brigade.

The first squadrons to arrive were a fighter unit, No. 28 (Sopwith Camels), and a reconnaissance unit, No. 34 (RE8s), forming 51st Wing. It was very quickly realised as events unfolded, however, that these were not enough, and another three were ordered to Italy along with a further Corps, the XIth. These squadrons were Nos. 42 (RE8s), 45, and 66 (both with Sopwith Camels). These moves were completed by the end of November 1917, which time also saw the first active flying begun. The first operation, a photographic reconnaissance by 34 Squadron over the Montello front, escorted by 28 Squadron, took place on the 29th of that month. By this time the Italians had stabilised their front along the River Piave, and on a more general note, had begun to rebuild their native instinct for resistance and survival.

The magnificent wild and mountainous terrain which made up much of the battle area called for a completely different approach from that which had been learnt on the Western Front. Even more than in the rolling river valleys and fields of northern France, the work of artillery observation and reconnaissance was totally crucial to effective warfare in these conditions. Of great benefit to the RFC, in their efforts to master the new circumstances, was that all units sent to Italy had experienced war flying in France. They also arrived in Italy with high quality, battle proven aircraft. Both these factors were naturally invaluable, and they quickly asserted themselves against an Austrian and German foe who was used to having control of the air. There was no doubting that the determined enemy would have to be fought out of the sky, but in time that is what the RFC managed to do.

29th November

B6313.N **Sopwith Camel   28Sqn**
+*EscRec combat with AlbatrosDV[+des] PIAVE DI SOLIGO, neSERNAGLIA 12-15pm OK(Capt WG

Barker Can.) 29Nov.17 patrol attacked by ~12 EAs, EA broke up

This was Barker's first combat victory in Italy, on the first day of operations. Barker was to become by far the highest scoring ace on this front, accounting for forty-two enemy machines before being withdrawn and rested in late 1918.

December 1917

8th December

B2363   Sopwith Camel   66Sqn
+* combat with AlbatrosDV[+ooc] VALSTAGNA-ASIAGO OK(2Lt HK Boysen)

This was the first victory claim for 66 Squadron in Italy.

B4604   Sopwith Camel   66Sqn
** (2Lt JAM Robertson **POW**) ["Sopwith" claim combat PEZZAR Vzfw W Hippert Ja39]["Sopwith" claim combat VILLAMATTA 1-30pm Oblt H Kummetz Ja1]

Robertson was the first British airman lost in combat in the Italian campaign whilst Boysen's claim was the first for 66 Squadron.

16th December

B5223   Sopwith Camel   66Sqn
+* combat with AlbatrosDV[+ooc] neCASA DE FELICE 2pm OK(2Lt HB Bell Can.) Bell's first of 10 claims in Italy

19th December

B6425   Sopwith Camel   66Sqn
** AA hit 3000' ooc **MIA**(Lt LB May **POW**)

31st December

A3614   RE8   34Sqn
** destroyed in enemy bomb raid

B6238.C **Sopwith Camel   45Sqn**
Clubs symbol on tail +* combat with AlbatrosDV[+ooc] PIAVE DE SOLIGO 9-45am then combat with AlbatrosDV[+capt] PARDERNO 10-30am OK(2Lt HM Moody) second Albatros was Ltn A Thurm KIA Ja31, Moody made most of his 8 victory claims in Italy

These were the first victories for 45 Squadron in Italy.

1918

January 1918

1st January

B6414   Sopwith Camel   66Sqn
** seen behind EA ovVITTORIO 6000' **MIA**(Capt R

& 2. The wrecked Nieuport 28 of 1Lt Quentin Roosevelt with the dead pilot laid out beside it after being shot down a 14 July 1918; also his grave. He was a member of the 5th Pursuit Sqn and the son of the former President of the nited States.

DH-4 32286 of the 20th US Bombardment Sqn, forced own in German territory in an extremely heavy gagement on 26 September 1918 in which the unit lost veral machines and crews. The crew of this DH-4 were

2Lt GB Wiser and 1Lt GR Richardson, both POWs.

4. Some men of 258th Aero Sqn possibly at Toul aerodrome flanked by a visiting Caproni Ca46 heavy bomber and a Liberty-engined DH-4.

5. Officers of the American Expeditionary Force stand in front of a row of Salmson 2A2s in late 1918. The nearest aircraft has 'MC "MACK"' painted beneath the cockpit.

PART III · GREAT BRITAIN

1. Lt Myers of the AEF poses in front of a SPAD 13 in late 1918.

2. This photo was taken in June 1919 but shows a Salmson 2A2 No. 8 of 1 US Aero Sqn. It is believed that Lt WP Erwin and Lt AL Easterbrook were the crew.

3. A group from 258th Aero Sqn displaying their selection of souvenirs of the Great War in December 1918.

4. 2Lt CC White in a BE12 adapted for home defence duties in the United Kingdom. White flew anti-Zeppelin night sorties in this machine in early 1917 for 50 Sqn HQ Flight at Dover. Note the Lewis gun and the three launching tubes for Le Prieur rockets. The use of these was practised but never used in home defence work - the burden on performance being too great.

1. An airman honing his skills on the range at the School of Aerial Gunnery at Marske. Note the rocking fuselage.

2. A German Gotha GIV bomber is pushed into position by mechanics. It was this type of machine which carried out the infamous Gotha raids on London in 1917. It is not an R-type as noted on the original Sanke card.

3. A group of officers of 44 Home Defence Sqn relax in front of two of their Sopwith Camels in the summer of 1917 at Hainault Farm. There were some notable fliers in this unit, including a few in this photograph. They included Lt LF Lomas, Lt CCC Banks, Lt RGH Adams, Lt CA Lewis, and Capt CJQ Brand. In Camel B3827 seen behind, Lt CCC Banks shared a Gotha over Wickford on 28 January 1918.

4. Major GW Murlis Green when CO of 44 HD Sqn. Beside home defence, this distinguished airman served in France and was also one of the most successful combat pilots on the Macedonian front.

5. Capt GAH Pidcock of Nos. 60, 1, and 73 Squadrons. He claimed six victories in France but is probably seen here immediately after the war.

PART IV · ITALY

1. A further group of 44 HD Sqn personnel: Lt? Buck, Lt d'UV Armstrong, Lt LF Lomas, Lt Thomas, Lt RS Bozman, and Capt CJQ Brand.

2. A Blackburn Kangaroo, most likely at Catterick in late 1918, in its role as a torpedo-carrying bomber.

3. The North Sea airship NS11, designed for long sea patrolling, returning to England in 1919. She had set the world flight endurance record with a voyage of over 100 hours in February 1919. She was destroyed in a storm on 15 July 1919 with ten dead.

4. Bristol Fighter D7966 of 139 Sqn was forced down by Austrian fire on 23 August 1918 on the Italian front. The crew of Lt CEG Gill and 2Lt T Newey were taken prisoner.

PART V · DARDANELLES

PART VI · MACEDONIA

1. This Bristol Scout D 8996 of 2 Wing RNAS was lost in combat over the Dardanelles on 17 February 1917. The pilot FSLt GT Bysshe was taken prisoner. *(E Ferko, via MB/GSL)*

2. Two-seater Sopwith Strutter N5108 may be that belonging to F Sqn which was lost near Smyrna on 1 August 1917. It is sometimes referred to as being shot down by Eschwege. The crew is yet to be substantiated.

3. The wreckage of the German airship LZ85 brought down in the marshes near Vardar in Salonica on 5 May 1916. Fire from the British Navy accounted for the Zeppelin and the troops seen in the photograph are French and Serbian.

4. The RFC airfield at Mikra Bay in Macedonia in 1917, the home of 17 Sqn.

1. A pilot of 17 Sqn stands beside a BE12 at Salonica. It is likely to be one of the RFC machines drawn into E Sqn. Note the Lewis guns mounted on their sides.

2. Capt GW Murlis Green of 17 Sqn in Macedonia in spring 1917.

3. A Naval Sopwith Strutter of E Sqn in Macedonia in August 1917. These two-seaters were sent to form part of the Composite Fighting Unit with the RFC in Macedonia April 1917.

4. Thought to be Major FA Bates at work in his office, the Commanding Officer of 17 Sqn in late 1918.

Bristol Scout C 4684 of 67 (Australian) Sqn at eliopolis in late 1916.

BE2e 6825 of 14 Sqn in Egypt in the late spring of 1917.

Lt EA Floyer? and 2Lt CB? Palmer of 14 Sqn taken isoner in Palestine. Here they are seen as the guests of

Hpt Felmy and others of FAb. 300 Pascha on 15 February 1917. Felmy is fourth from left.

4. Starting up a Vickers FB19 of 111 Sqn, possibly A5231, in Palestine in October 1917.

1. The captured Albatros DIII 636/17 being brought in by the Australian Light Horse in Egypt on 8 October 1917. This machine was forced down by Canadian Lt RC Steele and Lt JJ Lloyd-Williams of 111 Sqn on 8 October 1917 in Bristol Fighter A7194.

2. RE8 B5854 of 67 (Australian) Sqn shot down in enemy territory in Palestine on 4 January 1918. The pilot Lt JDS Potts was killed and lies in front of his machine. The observer 2Lt VJ Parkinson of New Zealand was taken prisoner.

3. Lt FW Haig and Lt RT Challinor in Bristol Fighter A7196 of 1 Sqn AFC at El Mejdel in Palestine in Februa[ry] 1918. It was in this aircraft that this crew attempted to rescue Rutherford and McElligott on 1 May 1918 but all four were captured.

4. A Felixstowe F3 flying boat in late 1918 at Alexandria Seaplane Base. The aircraft is possibly N4360.

5. The undercarriage of a Short Seaplane at Alexandria Seaplane Base. The bomb load is three 112-lbers.

Erskine **DoW**) [2 "Sopwith" claims combats
sVITTORIO 10-05am Ltn Fr vStenglin & unconfirmed
claim by Oblt Kummetz both Ja1]

On the 1st of January, ten RE8s from 42 Squadron made a bombing raid on the German 14th Army Headquarters at Vittorio. They were escorted by Sopwith Camels of 28 and 66 Squadron. Erskine was lost in fighting on this raid but there were also three claims for enemy machines.

10th January

B6282　Sopwith Camel　45Sqn
+* combat with AlbatrosDIII[+ooc] PORTO
BUFFOLE ~4pm OK(2Lt TF Williams) first victory
claim of 10 in Italy, including several with 28Sqn

11th January

B2436　Sopwith Camel　45Sqn
EscPhot seen dive nrVITTORIO **MIA(2Lt DW Ross
Can. **KIA**) nrFIOR DI SOPRA [?"Camel" claim combat
CIMADOLMO 11-45am Vzfw W Hippert Ja39]

B2494.S　Sopwith Camel　45Sqn
** combat with Albatros[+des] VITTORIO 11-45am,
then seen go down in steep dive but ok(Lt HT Thompson
WIA) to hospital [see B6414: Ja1]

45 Squadron was escorting RE8s on a photo-reconnaissance of aerodromes when the formation was attacked and heavy fighting broke out. There were four other claims made by Camel pilots.

B6372.H　Sopwith Camel　45Sqn
+* combat with AlbatrosDIII[+des] MOTTA 3-30pm
OK(Capt MB Frew) early victory in Italy for Frew, who
had scored several on Camels with 45Sqn in France

12th January

A4445　RE8　42Sqn
** **MIA**(Lt GN Goldie **POW**/Lt JD Barnes **POW**)

Work of the corps units was substantial in the early months of 1918 as the enemy positions and communications in the new terrain were learnt. Strategic reconnaissances and photographic patrols were carried out. Fighting on the British front was essentially trench-based so that in addition there was artillery co-operation to be done. Both sides were engaging in bombing of aerodromes and command centres but the Allied units continued to retain general control of the air. The key to this, of course, was the Sopwith Camel, which could bomb and strafe from low levels as well as carry out a range of offensive patrols. About this time VII Brigade instituted a programme of these to ensure the enemy was constrained, and at the same time, provoked, for it incorporated some attacking of enemy airfields to draw his machines into fighting.

The present intensity of warfare on the front, combined with offensive patrolling, meant a minimum of effort was required to protect corps machines.

14th January

B4609.F　Sopwith Camel　45Sqn
+* combat with AlbatrosDIII[+flames cr] CIMETTA-
CADOGNE 3pm OK(2Lt CE Howell Aust.) first victory
of 19 in Italy

B2475　Sopwith Camel　66Sqn
* shot down by Italian pilot(Maj R Gregory **Kld**)

28th January

B2472　Sopwith Camel　66Sqn
** (Lt HK Boysen US. **WIA**) [?possible "Sopwith" claim
combat nVOLPAGO Ltn Meyer/Vzfw Glode FAbA219]

29th January

B6487　RE8　34Sqn
** shot down in flames ovPIAVE cr eNERVESA **MIA**(Lt
RS Gaisford **KIA**/Lt LWB Moore **KIA**)

February 1918

The weather was poor in February, but the RFC Camel pilots continued to hound and overwhelm their Austrian opponents. In January the RFC claimed to have destroyed twenty-nine enemy machines and two kite balloons for the loss of four machines. During February this figure markedly increased. Prominent in the scoring through the following months were the Canadians William Barker and Harold Hudson who flew and worked together very often. It has to be said there were many other Camel pilots building up large tallies of claims at this time and, where possible, some of their victories are noted in this record.

2nd February

B6207　Sopwith Camel　66Sqn
** seen in spin 7000' ftl wST VETO **MIA**(Lt FDC Gore
POW)

4th February

B2494.S　Sopwith Camel　45Sqn
**EscRE8s combat with AlbatrosDVs[+ooc]
SUSEGANA 11-10am then hit by shell cr burnt nrSAN
CROCE(Lt DG McLean **KIA**) patrol in 30 min combat

12th February

B6313　Sopwith Camel　28Sqn
+*gun test, attacked KBs[+++++des]
FOSSAMERLO 2-45pm OK(Capt WG Barker Can.)

attack made in ground mist, shared victories

B6356   Sopwith Camel   28Sqn
+*gun test, attacked KBs[+++++des]
FOSSAMERLO 2-45pm OK(2Lt HB Hudson Can.)
shared victories, kite balloon victories included 3 small
round balloons, nearly all of his 13 victories were in this
a'c

19th February

One notable aerodrome raid carried out by
Sopwith Camels occurred on the 19th when eleven
machines from 28 and 66 Squadrons bombed the
enemy airfield at Casarsa. This caused great
damage and prompted plans for a series of further
such attacks.

20th February

B5193   Sopwith Camel   28Sqn
** shot down ovCONEGLIANO MIA(Lt DC Wright
POW DoW 22.2.18) DoW in Vienna

21st February

B2514   Sopwith Camel   66Sqn
** hit tree sPORTO GRUARO wr(2Lt AB Reade KIFA)
was reported MIA

22nd February

B6362.C2   Sopwith Camel   28Sqn
** down nMONTE BELLUNA MIA(2Lt H Butler KIA)

B4628   Sopwith Camel   66Sqn
** MIA(Capt KB Montgomery POW)

25th February

B5099   RE8   42Sqn
** (Capt EC Stonehouse WIA)

27th February

B6354.N   Sopwith Camel   45Sqn
+* combat with AlbatrosDIII[+des+ooc] ODERZO-
PONTE DI PIAVE 12-50pm OK(Maj AM Vaucour)
made 7 victory claims

March 1918

10th March

B2377   Sopwith Camel   66Sqn
** seen nrMASERADO 10000' "WoL" MIA(2Lt WG
Francis KIA)

11th March

B5190   Sopwith Camel   66Sqn
+* combat with BergD[+ooc] nVALSTAGNA 11-40am
OK(2Lt GF Apps) first of 10 victories in Italy

14th March

Events on the Western Front at this time naturally
dominated the war efforts of all the protagonists.
Although Italy had recovered much of its sense of
purpose and strength, the Italian front fell
relatively quiet for some time and both sides
evidently used the opportunity to resettle and
organise themselves. The near total air ascendency
which the RFC had achieved could not be turned
to any great effect for neither side was contem-
plating an offensive. British Army divisions had
been moved wholesale back to France, and on the
14th, 42 (Corps) Squadron returned as well. 51st
Wing Headquarters and a balloon company had
already left and before the end of the month the
headquarters staff of VII Brigade had returned. To
compensate for these losses, a Flight of Bristol
Fighters was sent to Italy and arrived in the last
days of March. It was initially attached as a fourth
Flight to 28 Squadron on the 28th, but was soon
transferred to 34 Squadron and became known
as "Z" Flight, its principal duties being long
reconnaissances.

About this time Italian forces were made available to relieve the British on the Piave, and through
March the troops were redeployed onto the
mountain plateau between Canove and Asiago.
Here the line pressed hard against the magnificent
southern foothills of the Dolomites, defending the
approaches to the Lombardy plain.

The 14th Wing naturally moved there with the
army, and continuous offensive patrols were flown
to prevent any enemy air reconnaissance from
detecting these events. Once the move had been
made the RFC set about building air supremacy
above its new sector. The Allied Command had in
mind an offensive on Trentino, in order to facilitate
a more major attack across the Piave at some future
date. At the same time however, there were some
confusing signs emanating from the Austrian
forces, which in time suggested that they too might
be preparing for an offensive. In the coming month
an effort was made to elucidate these, but reconnaissance was to be seriously hindered by fog and
storms in April and the position was left unclear.

30th March

B5648.E   Sopwith Camel   66Sqn
**OP MANSUE A'dr combat with many
AlbatrosDIIIs[?+++des] btwn 11-40am & 11-50am
shot down 4m wMANSUE A'dr cr MIA(Lt A Jerrard
WIA POW) a'c captured [combat Ltn BF vonFernbrugg
Flik51J]

Alan Jerrard claimed six victories in this machine

before he was shot down on the 30th. For his effort in this air fight low down over the enemy airfield at Mansue he was awarded the Victoria Cross. There are some differences between the Austrian and British records of the fighting which took place and the details remain uncertain. The aircraft was certainly heavily shot up, and Jerrard's survival was miraculous. Examined by the Germans after it had been brought down, it was found to have one hundred and sixty-three bullet holes, including twenty-seven in the tank.

> **B7353**.L   **Sopwith Camel**   **66Sqn**
> +* combat with AlbatrosDIII[+des] MT MALETTO 1-15pm OK(Lt F Symondson) half of his 13 victories in Italy in this a'c

April 1918

The Royal Air Force came into being on the 1st of April. In Italy, April was another month of very high claims by its fighter pilots, whilst the corps squadrons operated with substantial impunity.

3rd April

> **B1185**   **Bristol F2b**   **34Sqn**
> Z Flt **Rec left 8-45am MIA but OK(2Lt WL Vorster/ Lt CleG Amy)

4th April

> **B1214**   **Bristol F2b**   **34Sqn**
> Z Flt ** combat with AlbatrosDV[+ooc] STRIGUS(Lt TC Lowe OK/Lt HVN? Bankes **WIA**) initials HM? HVA?

This was the first combat victory for Z Flight.

17th April

> **B6342**   **Sopwith Camel**   **28Sqn**
> ** combat with EA shot down cr **MIA**(Lt WG Hargrave **KIA**)

> **B6313**.N   **Sopwith Camel**   **66Sqn**
> +* combat with AlbatrosDIII[+des] eVITTORIO 11am OK(Capt WG Barker)

Capt Barker moved to 66 Squadron as a Flight Commander on the 10th of April and continued to score heavily. This was his first victory for the unit.

23rd April

> **B5401**.E   **Sopwith Camel**   **28Sqn**
> ** seen 6000' going nw ovFONZASS AA hit **MIA**(Capt CJ Thomsen **POW**)

24th April

> **B1212**   **Bristol F2b**   **34Sqn**

> Z Flt ** left 10-10am **MIA**(2Lt PG Ratliff **POW**/Lt HVN Bankes **POW**)

May 1918

During May the RAF was to claim sixty-four enemy machines shot down, but the vast air superiority it enjoyed was ultimately of no great benefit. Reconnaissance continued to tell a shifting and uncertain story, and the mountains generally made work difficult — in particular it affected artillery co-operation. Enemy positions were well camouflaged and hard to locate precisely with map co-ordinates. It was also often impossible to see where shells were landing when directing fire. The momentum for a British offensive nevertheless continued to grow through May until the enemy's intentions became suddenly clearer towards the end of the month. In a matter of days his activity on the Piave grew notably, and it was obvious that Austria was intending to launch its own large offensive in that area. It also became clear that the British should expect a simultaneous attack in the mountains. With this news plans for the Allied offensive on the Asiago plateau were effectively abandoned.

3rd May

> **C4756**   **Bristol F2b**   **34Sqn**
> *Rec left 6-05am NOVE AA dam OK(Lt TC Lowe/2Lt T Newey)

8th May

> **B7358**   **Sopwith Camel**   **66Sqn**
> ** trench rifle fire nrZENSEN(Lt VS Parker **WIA**)

10th May

> **B6363**.K   **Sopwith Camel**   **28Sqn**
> +* attacked KB[+des] MARENO 2-25pm OK(Lt P Wilson) claimed several victories, most in this a'c

11th May

> **C4755**   **Bristol F2b**   **34Sqn**
> **Rec combat with 4EA LEVICO 16000' 8-15am **MIA**(Lt JB Guthrie **KIA**/Lt HV Thornton **KIA**) left 6-40am

> **B5187**   **Sopwith Camel**   **28Sqn**
> **EscRec combat with AlbatrosD[+cr in flames] FOLLINA 10am then low fuel ftl cr(Lt OW Frayne **inj**)

> **B2455**.X   **Sopwith Camel**   **28Sqn**
> ** last seen 10-05am **MIA**(Lt EG Forder **POW**) a'c captured [combat Oblt F Linke-Crawford Flik51J]

> **DH4**   **224Sqn?**   **Adriatic**
> **B shipping at KUMBOR in CATTARO BAY **MIA** crew not yet estasblished

OPERATIONS IN THE ADRIATIC

The first of twelve raids on the enemy naval base at Cattaro was made on the 11th of May. It was an ambitious target, involving a four hundred-mile round trip over sea by the land aircraft which carried them out. The strategic purpose of this and other raids like it was to reduce attacks on Allied shipping in the Adriatic, and by June they had been halved. On this occasion six DH4s bombed ships and submarines but one crew was lost and taken prisoner. Their identity has not yet been established, but some of the names given in the list of untraced prisoners in the Balkans at the end of Part VI: Macedonia and the Aegean may be candidates.

13th May

B8875   RE8   34Sqn
** AA **MIA**(Lt WRB Amesby/Lt E Hamilton)

16th May

C5070   RE8   34Sqn
** EA shot up(Lt HC Kelly OK/2Lt LH Moreton **KIA**)

17th May

B3872   Sopwith Camel   45Sqn
+* combat with AlbatrosDIII[+ooc] ODERZO 9-15am OK(Capt JR Brownell Aust.) claimed 12 victories

19th May

D1911   Sopwith Camel   28Sqn
+* combat with AlbatrosDVs[+flames+des] ARSIE 7-15am OK(Lt AG Cooper) claimed 7 victories

23rd May

B6413   Sopwith Camel   28Sqn
+* combat with AlbatrosDV[+des] 2km wGRIGNO 7-25am OK(Capt S Stanger Can.) made 12 claims in Italy

26th May

B6344.1   Sopwith Camel   28Sqn
+* combat with AlbatrosDIII[+flames] 2m nARCADE 8-45am OK(Capt J Mitchell) EA from Flik42J, pilot made 8 claims in Italy

30th May

B7360   Sopwith Camel   45Sqn
** ground mg shot up(Lt J Cottle **WIA**)

On the morning of the 30th, thirty-five Camels carried off a low bombing raid to enemy positions in Val d'Assa. A ton of bombs was dropped and 9,000 rounds of ammunition fired. The units involved were Nos. 28, 45, and 66.

B5180   Sopwith Camel   66Sqn
+* combat with AlbatrosDIII[+des] MORENO 3-55pm OK(Lt HK Boysen US.) last of 5 claims

June 1918

As an important part of the build-up for the Austrian offensive the enemy air presence greatly increased. A concerted effort was being made to gather reconnaissance and it was decided this must be stopped. In June therefore, a new programme of offensive patrolling began, whereby close and long offensive patrols were mounted. The close patrols were effectively barrage patrols operating tightly along the British line between Forni and Gallio with instructions to stray only in order to directly attack enemy machines. The long offensive patrols took place some five miles deeper into enemy territory, in a looser zone between Casotto and Cismon. These operations were effective in restricting enemy access to the front but also led to an escalation in air fighting.

1st June

B6423.T   Sopwith Camel   45Sqn
** down in flames **MIA**(Lt EMcN Hand **POW**) ldg burning

2nd June

C4700   Bristol F2b   34Sqn
Z Flt +* combat with AlbatrosDIII[+?shot down] OK(2Lt EM Brown/2Lt H Milburn) not confirmed

6th June

B7353.L   Sopwith Camel   66Sqn
** seen combat with EA sPORDENONE 11500' **MIA**(Lt AF Bartlett **POW**)

8th June

D9394   Sopwith Camel   45Sqn
+* combat with PhonixDI[+des] & BergDI[+des] nrMT TOMBA 8am OK(Lt CE Howell Aust.) first of 10 victories in this a'c

B2316.H   Sopwith Camel   28Sqn
** seen dive on EA 12000' **MIA**(Lt GD McLeod **POW**)

9th June

C4700   Bristol F2b   34Sqn
Esc last seen combat with EA shot down ovTRENTO 2000' 9am **MIA(Lt EM Brown **POW**/2Lt CA Gordon **POW**)

C4757 Bristol F2b 34Sqn
Z Flt +* combat with AlbatrosDIII[+ooc] OK(Lt G
Robertson/2Lt H Milburn)

C4758 Bristol F2b 34Sqn
Z Flt +* combat with AlbatrosDIII[+des] TRENTO
OK(2Lt AE Ryan/2Lt T Newey)

This was the last victory claim for Z Flight before
the formation of 139 Squadron (see below).

B7387 Sopwith Camel 66Sqn
+* combat with AlbatrosDV[+flames] sSEBASTIANO
7-10am OK(Capt P Carpenter) almost half of
Carpenter's 19 claims in Italy were in this machine

10th June

C916 Bristol F2b 34Sqn
Z Flt ** AA hit(Lt WL Vorster OK/Lt R Murdoch **WIA**)

15th June
THE AUSTRIAN OFFENSIVES: AIR FIGHTING ON THE PIAVE

On the morning of the 15th an Austrian bombardment commenced along the entire front from the
Adriatic to the Asiago Plateau, which was followed
shortly afterwards by an infantry attack. In the
British sector in the mountains fog and low clouds
at first helped the attackers. The RAF co-operation
was restricted by the conditions but 34 Squadron
laid down some very effective artillery fire in places
and Camels bombed and strafed troop lines. Most
of the small gains made by the Austrian Army on
the 15th were to be wrested back the following day.

More serious events were happening down on
the Piave, from where news came that the
Austrians had crossed the river opposite the
Montello mountain and were establishing numerous bridgeheads. With conditions worsening for air
work in the British sector it was decided to send all
available assistance to the Italians on the Piave.
Soon after midday, Camels of 45 Squadron were
bombing and attacking targets along the river. The
diversion of aircraft grew through the afternoon
until at 4pm, for instance, thirty-three Camels and
several RE8s were working with the Italian air
service. Bridges, rafts, boats, and enemy troop
concentrations and working parties were strafed
and disrupted in repeated raids. The result of this
effort was that by evening, although a number of
bridges were still standing and substantial bodies
of enemy troops had fought their way across, a
much greater assault had been prevented. Most
important for the events as they unfolded was the
fact that the enemy had been delayed.

B6356 Sopwith Camel 28Sqn
** ground mg fire(2Lt CS Style **WIA**)

D8111 Sopwith Camel 28Sqn
+* combat with AlbatrosDV[+flames] 5k wFELTRE
8-05am OK(Lt J Mackereth) made 7 claims in Italy

C5077 RE8 34Sqn
** ground mg shot up(Capt HA Pearson MC OK/2Lt
RB Carey **WIA**)

B5181 Sopwith Camel 45Sqn
+* combat with 2Str[+ooc] PONTE DI PIAVE 1-30pm
OK(Lt FS Bowles) made 5 claims in Italy

B6412.D Sopwith Camel 45Sqn
+* combat with AviatikC[+des] MT CAMPO-
POSELARO 7-45am OK(2Lt RG Dawes Can.) last of 9
claims

D9392 Sopwith Camel 45Sqn
+* combat with AviatikC[+ooc] MT CAMPO-
POSELARO 7-45am OK(Lt CG Catto US.) made 6
claims in Italy

16th June

Fighting along the Piave continued in desperate
fashion through the 16th. The job of the Camel
pilots was made more dangerous by anti-aircraft
guns which had now been brought up, but their
bombing operations continued — some two tons of
bombs were dropped from the air this day.

B5204 Sopwith Camel 28Sqn
** shot up wr(Lt SW Ellison **DoW**)

C4757 Bristol F2b 34Sqn
Z Flt **B shot up ovPIAVE dam OK(Lt CEG Gill/Lt T
Newey)repairable

C4758 Bristol F2b 34Sqn
Z Flt **B left 9-10am shot down ovPIAVE cr, a'c shelled
wr OK(Lt Wood/Lt CleG Amy)

17th June

The delays imposed on the enemy by the RAF
offensive on the crossings finally brought reward on
the 17th, albeit through an Act of God. Rain
poured throughout the day and by evening the
river had become a raging torrent in full spate.
Through the night and the following morning
nearly all the bridges were destroyed, leaving the
Austrian Army effectively stranded. With its
supply lines in tatters, the offensive was stopped in
its tracks. An Italian counter-attack was launched
to exploit the blow which fate had dealt and the
enemy was pressed back relentlessly onto the river.
During this time the RAF made continuous and
very heavy attacks on the retreating troops, suffering very light casualties in the process. By the 23rd
the Austrian Command ordered a general withdrawal across the river and this was managed on
the night of the 22nd/23rd. This victory was seen
as a great achievement for the Italian Army for it

demonstrated the recovery it had made since the calamities of Caporetto. It also gave heart to the Allies who at that time in France had virtually all their victories of 1918 still ahead of them. Undeniably, it was also one of the great battles of the Royal Air Force, and it may well have influenced RAF Headquarters to feel confident in attacking the Somme bridges in the August offensive.

19th June

B9310.D **Sopwith Camel** **28Sqn**
** seen ovVIGONOVO 9000′ ground fire? **MIA**(Lt SM Robins **POW**)

D8112   **Sopwith Camel** **28Sqn**
+* combat with BergDIs[+flames+ooc] CALDONAZZO 8-45am OK(Lt CM McEwan Can.) first of several claims in this a'c in a total of 27

21st June

D8101.P **Sopwith Camel** **66Sqn**
+* combat with AlbatrosDV[+des] ODERZO MOTTA 9-30am OK(Lt GA Birks Can.) last of 12 claims in Italy, Barker & Apps also claimed victories in this fight but the enemy recorded a single loss: Oblt F Dechant KIA of Flik51J

22nd June

B7283   **Sopwith Camel** **66Sqn**
+* combat with BrandenburgC[+flames] BASSANO 3-55pm OK(Lt HR Eycott-Martin) last of 8 claims in Italy

28th June

C993   **Bristol F2b**   **34Sqn**
EscRec AA shot down in flames nr S POLO, wODERZO on the PIAVE 6pm **MIA(Lt FS Williams **KIA**/2Lt D Thomas **KIA**)

July 1918

3rd July

139 Squadron was formed on the 3rd of July from reinforcements sent from England and France, and elements of "Z" Flight. The latter had grown to two Flights of Bristol Fighters in June and the potential of the new unit was enhanced greatly when Major WG Barker DSO MC assumed command on the 14th of July, bringing Sopwith Camel B6313 with him. 139 Squadron was typically involved in Fighter reconnaissance duties, but towards the end of the confict it also participated in bombing and photography. July was a relatively quiet month on the Italian front in terms of ground fighting. As had

been the case elsewhere, however, the RAF continued an active offensive air policy of patrols and reconnaissance. There was always work to do. 34 Squadron was loaned for a few weeks to work with the Italian forces on the southern Piave and, owing to the scarcity of aircraft in the sector, they remained there into September. Camel patrols bombed aerodromes and engaged the enemy in the air at every opportunity, and the number of claims made by pilots continued to reach remarkable levels. The indicative combat claims given in this list are a mere fraction of the total made and are there to draw attention to a few of the notable airmen who were involved. The high numbers of claims not only reflected the advantage which the superb Camel fighter gave its pilots over less potent opposition. Another factor was the game and courageous tactics of the Austrian fighter pilots who usually stayed to fight, although the odds were increasingly stacked against them.

4th July

C916   **Bristol F2b**   **139Sqn**
+* combat with AlbatrosDIII[+des] nrASOLO OK(Lt HCW Walters/Lt C Beagle) pilot made 6 victory claims in Italy

C999   **Bristol F2b**   **139Sqn**
+* combat with Albatros[+ooc] LEVICO OK(Lt WC Simon US./Lt W Smith)

These were the first combat claims for 139 Squadron.

5th July

Adriatic
Naval ** **MIA**(Lt BT Anderson **WIA POW**/Lt CS Sivil **WIA POW**)

This crew may have been lost in connection with the Italian campaign in Albania. All crew and aircraft not directly required for anti-submarine work in the Otranto region were made available to the Italian forces in this theatre. The Italian attack began on the 6th, however. These two airmen are noted on Casualty Cards held in the RAF Museum.

12th July

D8240   **Sopwith Camel** **45Sqn**
+*combat with Berg[+des] then PhonixD[+des] FELTRE 8-05am OK(Lt A Rice-Oxley) first of 6 claims in Italy

13th July

D8209   **Sopwith Camel** **28Sqn**
** **MIA**(Lt AR Strang **POW**)

14th July

D1974   Sopwith Camel   45Sqn
+* combat with D-type[+des] MT CISMON 9-45am
OK(Lt E Masters) made 7 of his 8 claims in Italy

16th July

D8102   Sopwith Camel   45Sqn
* killed by Italian pilot(Maj AM Vaucour MC DFC **Kld**)

B7358   Sopwith Camel   66Sqn
** combat[+] shot up(2Lt GF Apps **WIA**)

18th July

B6313.N Sopwith Camel   139Sqn
+* attacked 2Strs[++des] nrGALLIO 8-05am to
8-10am OK(Maj WG Barker)

These were the first victories for Barker in B6313
after joining 139 Squadron.

20th July

D8211   Sopwith Camel   45Sqn
+* combat with AlbatrosDV[++des] eFELTRE 7-20am
OK(Lt MR James Can.) most of his 11 claims in Italy in
this a'c

23rd July

C4759   Bristol F2b   139Sqn
Rec shot down ovTRENTO **MIA(Lt WL Vorster
KIA/Sgt HG Frow **KIA**) left 7-45am

C4762   Bristol F2b   139Sqn
**SpRec left 7-30am seen wBELLUNO going East shot
down **MIA**(Lt vD Fernald **KIA**/Lt WC Watkins **KIA**)

29th July

C990   Bristol F2b   139Sqn
**Phot combat with EA NOVE shot up ftl cr(Lt AE Ryan
WIA/Lt CleG Amy OK)

30th July

C916   Bristol F2b   139Sqn
**Rec combat with EA SACCA ~6pm? wr(Lt HCW
Walters **WIA**/2Lt WF Davies OK) left 5-30am, combat
swPORTO GURNARO

C999   Bristol F2b   139Sqn
**OP combat with AlbatrosDs[+des+ooc] & 2Str[+ooc]
MOTTA 6-30am shot up(Lt WC Simon US. OK/Lt WW
Smith **WIA**) Smith hit by 2Str, this crew had several
victories

August 1918

1st August

B2433   Sopwith Camel   66Sqn
+* combat with AlbatrosDVs[++des]

FONTANELETTO btwn 11-55am to 12-10pm OK(Lt C
McEvoy) last of 9 claims

D8081   Bristol F2b   139Sqn
**Esc66 combat with EA ftl cr Italian GROSSA A'dr
~3pm dam (Lt MO Ramsay **inj**/2Lt FF Crump **inj**) left
2-40pm, down SO. PIETRO IN GU with only 2hr 25min
on clock

2nd August

                    Italy
*B Austrian Base **MIA**(/Pte JF Hartley **POW**)

5th August

B6354   Sopwith Camel   66Sqn
** seen 13000' eVAZZOLA **MIA**(Lt GC Easton **KIA**)

8th August

D8084.S Bristol F2b   139Sqn
+*combat with AlbatrosDV[+flames] LEVICO &
AlbatrosDV[+flames] CALDONAZZO OK(Capt S
Dalrymple/2Lt H Baldwin) also probably shot down
another EA in 2nd fight, crew made other victory claims

These combats took place whilst reconnoitring
Pergine aerodrome. Four Bristol Fighters were
attacked by three Albatros single-seaters. The
Official History mentions that the Albatroses were
flying a protective patrol over the aerodrome whilst
Emperor Karl was there on an inspection tour.

10th August

D9412   Sopwith Camel   45Sqn
** AA hit shot down cr "WoL"(Lt AJ Haines **KIA**) made
6 claims in Italy

14th August

D9406   Sopwith Camel   66Sqn
** ground mg shot up(Lt AJ Gates **WIA**)

16th August

D8069   Bristol F2b   139Sqn
**B combat with 4EA TRENTO shot down in flames(Lt
CRH Jackson **KIA**/Lt WF Keepin **KIA**) left 7-05am

21st August

D8234   Sopwith Camel   45Sqn
+* combat with AlbatrosDVs[+des+ooc] GHIARONA
8-15am OK(Capt NC Jones) last of 9 claims in Italy

22nd August

D8236   Sopwith Camel   66Sqn
** mg fire shot up dam(Lt CS Cot **WIA**)

D8075   Bristol F2b   139Sqn
Rec seen 4000' on return **MIA(Lt NE Gwyer **POW**/
2Lt TR Hilton **POW**) left 7am for PIAVE

23rd August

D7966   Bristol F2b   139Sqn
Rec left 6-55am gear shot away ftl **MIA(Lt CEG Gill **POW**/2Lt T Newey **POW**)

30th August

D2793   DH9   226Sqn Adriatic
Taranto **B CATTARO forced to return **MIA**(2Lt GVV Cooper/Pte WA Easman **KIA**)

D2802   DH9   226Sqn Adriatic
B CATTARO ftl **MIA(Lt J McDonald DFC **POW**/Pte GLE Sutcliffe **KIA**)

31st August

D8211   Sopwith Camel 45Sqn
+* combat with AlbatrosDVs[++des] MT SEGUGIO-ARSIERO 9-45am OK(Lt MR James)

D8237.D Sopwith Camel 45Sqn
+* combat with AlbatrosDIIIs[+des] PERALTO 9-35am then AlbatrosDIII[++capt] ARSIERO-POSINO 9-45am then combat with 2Str[+ooc] VALSUGANA 10-25am OK(Capt J Cottle) claimed 13 victories in Italy

D9386   Sopwith Camel 45Sqn
+* combat with AlbatrosDVs[+ooc] ARSIERO 9-45am OK(Lt RG Davis)

These seven victories, made in a short sharp engagement in which all opposing aircraft were shot down, brought 45 Squadron's account in Italy to a close before being returned to France. During its service on the Italian front it had claimed one hundred and fourteen victories for the loss of only three of its own aircraft to enemy action. It left as part of the British force withdrawn for service on the Western Front in September. The unit departed on the 20th and joined the Independent Force where it was earmarked for an escort role — one it was actually never to fulfil. Refer Part I: The Western Front, September 1918.

E1496   Sopwith Camel 66Sqn
** (Capt J Mackereth **WIA**? **POW**)

September 1918

September was a relatively quiet month on the Italian front.

1st September

B6313.N Sopwith Camel 139Sqn
+* combat with D-types[+++shot down in flames]nrFELTRE 10am to 10-05am OK(Maj WG Barker)

These were the last of Major Barker's forty-six

victories in B6313. The machine was finally taken off strength of the unit on the 8th of October with 404hrs 10mins on log. Barker left Italy for England, with the prospect of a desk job for the remainder of the war, on the 30th of September. Understandably restless, he cajoled officialdom to permit him another short period of active service, joining 201 Squadron on the Western Front. On the day he was due to return to England after this, on the 27th of October, he had a titanic series of engagements with enemy formations whilst on lone patrol and for his efforts was awarded the Victoria Cross. See Part I: Western Front.

C992   Bristol F2b   139Sqn
**Rec left 7-30am shot up bad ftl dam OK(Lt Martyn/ Lt Kayl)

6th September

D2795   DH9   224Sqn Adriatic
Taranto **B CATTARO shot up(/2Lt RJ Gray **WIA**)

N6418   DH4   Malta
B CATTARO shot down in flames **MIA(Lt RB Picken **KIA**/Lt AF Hodgskin **KIA**)

14th September

D7975   Bristol F2b   139Sqn
**Rec combat with EAs[++] shot up dam strained OK(Lt HV Jellicoe/Sgt FH Shanks)

15th September

C134   Sopwith Camel 28Sqn
** combat with Albatros[+] SUSEGANA then ground mg shot up 6-55pm(2Lt EL Roberts **WIA inj**) 16.9?

D8078.X Bristol F2b   139Sqn
** AA hit(Lt GRB Playford **WIA**/AM JC Ings OK)

18th September

D9406   Sopwith Camel 66Sqn
** (2Lt N Howarth **WIA**) inj?

21st September

D1772   DH4   224Sqn Adriatic
Taranto ** ftl nwFIERI "EoL" **MIA**(2Lt AL Mawer **POW**/2Lt GE Hughes **POW**)

22nd September

D8170.7 Sopwith Camel 28Sqn
.7? ** combat with EA(Lt AR Bell **KIA**) KIFA?

30th September

E7211   Sopwith Camel 66Sqn
+* combat with LVGC[+des] neCONEGLIANO 6-15pm OK(Lt HK Goode) first of 8 victories in this a'c in one month, including 6 balloons

October 1918

VICTORY IN ITALY:
THE BATTLE OF THE PIAVE

The Italian Supreme Command waited until the end of October to deliver its final blow on the Austrian Army. By this time the extent of Allied successes in France portended a great victory and every day brought increasing disintegration of the German and Hapsburg Empires. The Italian battle plan was simple enough: whilst the enemy was contained on the Trentino front the main advance would be across the Piave River, driving a wedge between the Austrian forces on the plain and in the mountains. One British division remained on the Asiago plateau, but the other two joined French and American units in support of the Italians on the Piave. To allay suspicion, the British troops wore Italian uniforms and the air support for the battle was kept in the Asiago area from where it could be quickly deployed. The four RAF squadrons involved were Nos. 28 and 66 (Sopwith Camels), 34 (RE8s) and 139 (Bristol Fighters), as well as two Balloon Sections.

4th October

A preliminary blow was delivered to the opposing air forces by two raids carried out by RAF on the 4th and 5th. These attacked two advanced training schools of the Austrian Air Force. On the 4th, twenty-three Camels of 28 and 66 Squadron attacked that at Campoformido with phosphorus and high explosive bombs and great destruction was caused. Some aircraft which had come up to attack the formation were also shot down. On the 5th, the school at Egna in the Adige Valley was bombed and shot up by twenty-two Camels. Two of the casualties noted below were caused on these raids.

> B5638   Sopwith Camel   28Sqn
> **LowB CAMPOFORMIDO Training School AA shot
> down cr MIA(Lt JH Bryant KIA) left 12-20pm, bombs
> exploded on ldg

> D8244   Sopwith Camel   28Sqn
> ** combat with EA? AA? last seen ooc nROTZO 7-50am
> MIA(Lt A Latimer KIA)

5th October

> E1581   Sopwith Camel   28Sqn
> **LowB EGNA Training School ground fire mg shot up
> cr nrRIVOLI(Lt CS Style WIA)

7th October

> C46   Sopwith Camel   66Sqn
> +* combat with AlbatrosDV[+ooc] ODERZO
> ~10-30am OK(Capt CM Maud) last of 11 victories in
> Italy

> D8215   Sopwith Camel   66Sqn
> ** combat with 4DVs seen on fire ovLISON MIA(Lt WJ
> Courtenay KIA) as POW? [combat sDONA DI PIAVE
> Oblt L Hautzmeyer Flik61J]

> E1498   Sopwith Camel   66Sqn
> ** TRENTO MIA(2Lt GR Leighton KIA)

8th October

> D7957   Bristol F2b   139Sqn
> **RecB combat with EA[+] BORGO shot up
> 8-25am(Capt SH Holland OK/2Lt RG Fullagar WIA)

22nd October

> E1576   Sopwith Camel   66Sqn
> **KBP attacked KB[+des] swVAZZOLA 4-45pm then
> ground fire shot up ftl on island in PIAVE RIVER cr o't
> wr(Capt HH James WIA) shared KB victory

> E7167.S   Sopwith Camel   66Sqn
> ** forced to return, last seen in combat with AlbatrosDV
> cr CONEGLIANO MIA(2Lt JM Kelly POW)

> E7211   Sopwith Camel   66Sqn
> +*KBP attacked KB[+des] swVAZZOLA 4-45pm
> OK(Lt HK Goode)

> C994   Bristol Fighter   139Sqn
> **Rec eng cut ftl PIAVE cr MIA but OK(Lt HV Jellicoe/
> Sgt FH Shanks)

23rd October

The Allied offensive on the Piave was originally planned to take place on the 25th, but first some preparatory operations were set in motion. The first was a feinted attack by Italian and French troops in the area around Mount Grappa in order to draw the enemy. More importantly, an assault was launched on the night of the 23rd/24th on the island of Grave di Papadopoli — a key possession if the crossing of the Piave was to be attempted. By late on the 25th it was finally occupied but bad weather set in and the major stages of the assault were postponed for two days. The weather had been generally poor throughout October, limiting the support the RAF could provide. Crucially, a thorough photographic reconnaissance of the Piave, planned to be undertaken by 139 Squadron, had been delayed until only a few days before these events. Once it was possible to fly, however, the unit worked unceasingly, photographing the entire corps area on the Piave throughout the 22nd.

25th October

B5182   Sopwith Camel   66Sqn
** (Lt HE Hastie **POW**)

27th October

On the 27th the decisive assault of the Allied armies across the Piave began at 6-45am. It was to be known as the battle of the Vittorio Veneto. The barrier of the river still presented a considerable logistical problem to the attackers, and in the same way in which the RFC had attacked the bridges in June, the Austrian Air Service now strafed and bombed the troops as they attempted to cross. All the bridges remained intact, however, and despite some early anxiety about co-ordination between the Italian and British forces, by the middle of the day substantial numbers of infantry and cavalry were in possession of the north bank. 34 Squadron carried out extremely accurate contact patrols with the advancing troops on the first day of fighting, although these also suffered attacks from enemy fighters. In addition, they co-operated with the artillery and made occasional ammunition drops. The fighter squadrons were naturally active as well, having begun the day with their first strikes at the enemy kite balloon line and then concentrating their low attacks into the area behind the immediate battlefield. Their role was as much to monitor enemy troop movements as to bomb and strafe them, although the latter task grew in intensity throughout the day as targets increasingly presented themselves. It was apparent as the breach grew by the hour that the Austrian front on the Piave was collapsing. The enemy forces had very quickly become disordered and were soon in retreat. In this state they were left highly vulnerable to attack from the air. Most of the claims for air fighting on this day are given below along with the casualties, which again were very light.

D4906   RE8   34Sqn
AP ground fire shot up(Capt RC Cain DFC OK/2Lt M Nicol Can. **WIA)

D4906   RE8   34Sqn
AP combat with 2 AlbatrosDVs 9-55am shot up(Capt RC Cain DFC **WIA/2Lt LJ Shepard Can. OK)

Cain had returned from his earlier patrol in which Nicol had been wounded and returned to the battle with Shephard only to be wounded himself in combat with enemy fighters.

E7216   Sopwith Camel   28Sqn
+* combat with 5AlbatrosDV[+ooc] eng hit ftl PAPADOPOLI OK(Lt NH Hamley) possibly slightly **WIA** in finger?

E235   RE8   34Sqn
** ftl EoL **MIA**(Capt LMC King Can. **POW**/Lt KO Bracken Can. **POW**) left 6-20am, both evaded capture and escaped back to lines

E1579   Sopwith Camel   66Sqn
+*KBP attacked KB[+des] 1pm OK(2Lt AG Kettles)

E1582   Sopwith Camel   66Sqn
+* combat with LVGC[+ooc] sPOLO DI PIAVE 10-10am OK(Lt JS Lennox)

E7211   Sopwith Camel   66Sqn
+*KBP attacked KBs[+des] 8-15am OK(Lt HK Goode)

E7213   Sopwith Camel   66Sqn
+* combat with LVGC[+ooc smoking] SUSEGANA OK(Lt NS Taylor)

E7214   Sopwith Camel   66Sqn
+*KBP attacked KBs[++des] btwn 1pm & 1-30pm OK(Lt A Paget)

D7969   Bristol Fighter   139Sqn
+* combat with EA Scout[+ooc] CIMALDOLMO OK(Lt AA Bartram/2Lt CA Sander)

28th October

D8212   Sopwith Camel   28Sqn
+* combat with 2Str[+ooc] DANELA sVISNA OK(Lt AF White) 28th Oct.18

E7216   Sopwith Camel   28Sqn
+* combat with Albatros DV[+ooc] ovRAI 11am OK(Lt NH Hamley)

E1579   Sopwith Camel   66Sqn
OP forced to return shot down in flames? eGODEGA A'dr 8-50am **MIA(Lt GA Goodman **KIA**)

29th October

The battle on the Piave turned on the 29th as the Austrian forces attempted a final resistance on the Monticano but were finally broken. Although enemy reinforcements had been brought up to hold the line, a breach was made which fundamentally split the two Austrian armies, and a rout quickly developed. Low attacking Camels, which had played a vital role in the morning attack on the Monticano, then began a deadly programme against the retreating army in which they too suffered a number of casualties. This was carried out in combination with bombing aircraft of the Italian Air Service and continued with little abatement until an Armistice brought the war in northern Italy to a close on the 4th of November. Enemy airfields were overrun and, following this, the air was left almost entirely to the Allies to wreak absolute havoc on the retreating columns. Many of the infantry who streamed back towards Austria, down roads piled and choked with their own dead

and dying, were no longer armed, and what they had hoped to drag back with them into their country was soon abandoned by the roadside. In such conditions of intense panic and disaster, experienced on a vast scale, there was no escape from the attacks of the airmen, and in truth those who saw it knew it to be a terrible and shocking moment for humanity as many hundreds were killed. The war in Italy was brought to a close with great carnage.

B6344.G **Sopwith Camel   28Sqn**
GndStr flying so low that a'c hit truck **MIA(Capt J Hallonquist **WIA POW**) injured as well, left behind in enemy hospital in retreat and escaped

30th October

C3290   Sopwith Camel   66Sqn
LowB:transport combat with EA shot up **MIA(2Lt A Paget **KIA**)

C4760   Bristol F2b   139Sqn
B shot down then burnt a'c(2Lt JB Isaacs **POW/Capt MGMcL Cahill-Byrne **POW**) left 12-20pm

D7969   Bristol F2b   139Sqn
B shot up TREVISO ftl cr dam(Capt LF Hursthouse **WIA/Lt WW Smith OK) left 11-25am

D8048   Bristol F2b   139Sqn
OP shot up eng seized ftl cr ldg CONEGLIANO wr(Maj HH Kitchener OK/Lt HH Dowse **WIA)

November 1918

1st November

E1503   Sopwith Camel   28Sqn
** AA(Lt NH Hamley **WIA**)

E7170   Sopwith Camel   28Sqn
** AA fire CASARSA(Lt W McBain **KIA**)

E7245   Sopwith Camel   66Sqn
LowB attacking transport cr trees beside road CORVA **MIA(2Lt AE Sissing **KIA**)

E7246   Sopwith Camel   66Sqn
** combat with EA shot up(2Lt SJ Osborne **DoW**)

E2187   Bristol F2b   139Sqn
** (2Lt H Baldwin **WIA**)

4th November

The Armistice requested by Austro-Hungary came into effect on the 4th of November 1918 and fighting halted on the Italian front.

Part V

THE DARDANELLES and THE TURKISH COAST 1915–1918

1915

February 1915

British naval efforts to force an entrance into the Dardanelles only really gained momentum by the end of February 1915. It was the first essential step in order to establish a new front — one which would help Russia contend with the Turks. By February, a naval strike force had been assembled in the region, including a new ship, the *Ark Royal*, which was the world's first aircraft carrier. In the

absence of landing grounds, the *Ark Royal*'s complement of eight machines were to supply air reconnaissance for the venture. She had reached the Dardanelles on the 17th February, and air operations began immediately, reconnoitring the Turkish defences and exploring the Straits. She brought six two-seater seaplanes and two land aircraft, but from virtually the first day of their arrival, all but one proved woefully inadequate for the rigours of war flying.

17th February

172   **Wight A1 Seaplane   HMS *Ark Royal***

**Rec Turkish forts, dropped 20lb bomb OK(FLt GR Bromet/FCdr HA Williamson) only one of four a'c launched that took to the air.

This was the first air operation in the Dardanelles. Others followed fitfully when the weather permitted launching.

March 1915

5th March

808	Sopwith 807	RNAS

AOb lost propeller at 3000' ftl cr sea(FLt WHS Garnett **inj/FCdr HA Williamson **inj**)

922	Sopwith 807	RNAS

AOb rifle fire shot up dam ftl(FLt N Sholto-Douglas **WIA/FLt EH Dunning OK)

Both these incidents occurred whilst observing fire for HMS *Queen Elizabeth*. They were attempting the first such operation in the Straits. 922 took to the air after the crash of 808, but also failed to convey any real messages and the day's work was lost.

The lack of success suffered by the *Ark Royal*'s machines paled into insignificance against the apparent failure of the overall battle plan. It became obvious that the Navy alone could not prise open the Straits: army reinforcements would be needed. A series of organisational blunders led to the late dispatch of these troops from Egypt, by which time the enemy had been given a priceless month to dig itself in. This hiatus was to prove of great importance.

As part of the reinforcements, the first elements of 3 Squadron RNAS arrived at Tenedos on the 24th of March under the command of Cdr CR Samson. Their aircraft were a mixture of Henri Farmans, Maurice Farmans, BE2 types, Sopwith Tabloids, and an experimental Breguet bomber. They were given the task of providing the air reconnaissance of the Straits, although their location placed them at the extremities of operational distance from the battle scene. They were flying by the end of March. The unit was re-named No.3 Wing RNAS on the 21st of June.

April 1915

April 25th saw the landing at Gaba Tepe, later known as Anzac, by troops of the Australian and New Zealand Army Corps. The commencement of their assault on Turkish territory became a famous day in the history of Australian nationhood. The ANZACs found themselves fighting against tremendous odds and soon began to take the first of very many casualties. Their attempts to gain a foothold evolved into an increasingly desperate battle, for the Turkish positions were formidable.

16th April

176	Whight A1	RNAS

**Spotting for HMS *Lord Nelson* at GALLIPOLI, shot up wings & floats ftl dam OK(FLt R Whitehead/SLt W Parke)

27th April

136	Short 135	RNAS

**Spotting for HMS *Triumph*, rifle fire shot up ftl heavy sea OK(Lt EH Dunning/SLt W Parke) a'c never flew convincingly again.

May 1915

2nd May

	3Sqn RNAS

** intercepted & drove down enemy seaplane nrKEPHEZ POINT but then shot up by ground fire nrCHANAK OK(FLt RLG Marix) seaplane was approaching TENEDOS, enemy observer shot and killed once seaplane was on water

17th May

Breguet	3Sqn RNAS

**B AK BASHI LIMAN Port OK(FCdr RLG Marix/ Cdr CR Samson)

A makeshift landing strip had been laid out near Helles by early May so that aircraft could operate more effectively with the ground forces. This was one raid which was highly disruptive and successful. After dropping their bombs they flew on to find large enemy reinforcements massing to attack the ANZAC forces. This intelligence was vital to their subsequent resistance.

June 1915

4th June

	3Sqn RNAS

**B submarine OK(Cdr CR Samson)

21st June

No.3 Squadron RNAS was renamed No.3 Wing RNAS on the 21st of June.

22nd June

Voisin	3 Wing RNAS

**P attacked EA with rifle fire[+EA hit in engine and

brought down nrACHI BABA] OK(Cdr CH Collet/Maj RET Hogg) EA later destroyed by French shelling

In support of the British attack on Helles in late June, thirty-one hours of flying were carried out. Work included bombing of troops and batteries as well as artillery spotting. Already, however, some air fighting was taking place, and the victory above was the first achieved in the Dardanelles.

late June?

11 (Fin No.)   Henri Farman   3 Wing RNAS
** shot up by Turkish gunfire GALLIPOLI dam ftl OK(Cdr RLG Marix DSO/Lt.Hon M Knatchbull-Hugessen MC) landed safely (via photograph at IWM)

July 1915

3 Wing RNAS
Phot shot up hit by shrapnel(FLt CH Butler **WIA) July.15?, via *Fights and Flights*, by CR Samson

August 1915

4th August

3 Wing RNAS moved to Imbros on the 4th of August, leaving only a Repair Section at Tenedos. The onerous nature of 3 Wing's duties at this time is well illustrated in a passage from Commander Samson's memoirs, *Fights and Flights*.

"In August [1915] two new pilots arrived to reinforce, and badly they were needed, when it is remembered that the maximum number I ever had was eleven, counting myself, with the average of seven and we now had to work
1)   For the ships firing at shore targets.
2)   In co-operation with Helles, Anzac, and Suvla.
3)   On frequent anti-aircraft patrols, to keep enemy aircraft from observing our position.
4)   On reconnaissance.
"Really, at least three Squadrons were required. The situation would have been improved if I had had more aeroplanes, also of a more suitable type for the work in hand. Another difficulty I always had was a complete lack of spare parts".

12th August

842   Short 184   HMS *Ben-my-Chree*
**TorpP attacked shipping in Straits launching from 15' at 300yds OK(FCdr CHK Edmonds) flew from GULF OF XEROS

Edmonds was the first man to torpedo shipping from the air. He and another pilot made another raid five days later.

17th August

184   Short 184   HMS *Ben-my-Chree*
**Torpedo Attack: engine problems ftl, then attacked Turkish tug while taxying[+destroyed] then was shot up heavily but managed take off after 2mile run OK(FCdr GB Dacre)

842   Short 184   HMS *Ben-my-Chree*
**Torpedo Attack: attacked one of three steamers heading for AK BASHI LIMAN[+set on fire & destroyed] OK(FCdr CHK Edmonds)

2 Wing RNAS arrived on Imbros in the Dardanelles in late August, bringing vital additional machines to the region. Both they and 3 Wing could use the newly constructed aerodrome on Imbros for their operations. 2 Wing were equipped with Morane Parasols, BE2cs, Caudrons, and Bristol Scouts. Some of the latter were armed with Lewis guns. It was in the Dardanelles campaign, rather than on the Western Front, that the first armed RNAS machines took part in regular air combat. By the last months of the year armed French-built Nieuport 11s would also be flying with the RNAS in the East.

November 1915

8th November

Maurice Farman   RNAS
**B bridge at MARITZA River on BERLIN-CONSTANTINOPLE Rlwy OK(Cdr CR Samson/Capt IAE Edwards)

Short 184   RNAS
**B bridge at MARITZA River on BERLIN-CONSTANTINOPLE Rlwy OK(FLt GB Dacre)

Short 184   RNAS
**B bridge at MARITZA River on BERLIN-CONSTANTINOPLE Rlwy OK(FCdr CHK Edmonds)

13th November

BE2c   2Wing RNAS
**NB bridge at MARITZA River on BERLIN-CONSTANTINOPLE Rlwy OK(FCdr JRW Smyth-Pigott)

All the above raids, including the last, which was carried out by moonlight, attacked a vital bridge on the Berlin to Constantinople railway. For the seaplanes it involved a flight of one hundred and twenty miles, all but the first ten over land. For the land aeroplanes, a round trip of some one hundred and eighty miles was necessary, the machines being fitted with auxiliary fuel tanks. On no occasion was a proper hit on the bridge achieved, although several subsequent raids were undertaken. Turkish

AA was brought up to defend it and little could be achieved once this was in place.

19th November

HF H5   Horace Farman   3 Wing RNAS
**B FEREJIK Rail Junction BUGARIA engine shot up ftl, destroyed a'c then rescued by FCdr Bell-Davies OK(FSLt GF Smylie DSC)

3172   Nieuport 12   3 Wing RNAS
Tenedos **B FEREJIK Rail Junction: carried out rescue of FSLt GF Smylie DSC OK(FCdr R Bell-Davies VC)

Bell-Davies was awarded the Victoria Cross for his rescue of FSLt Smylie. Having had his machine seriously shot up, Smylie had been forced to land, although he still carried one of his two bombs. Once on the ground he saw Turkish soldiers approaching, so set fire to his Farman. Bell-Davies calmly landed and took off again with Smylie crouching under the petrol tank.

By the beginning of November it was clear that the campaign in the Dardanelles was grinding to failure, profligate of resources and dreadfully wasteful of men. It was decided that an evacuation must be attempted, so preparations for that dangerous operation were put in hand.

December 1915

8th December

979   BE2c   2 Wing RNAS
possibly this a'c?: **B CHANAK lost Narrows-HELLES MIA(FCdr CE Robinson KIA) a'c salvable

20th December

3168   Nieuport 10   2 Wing RNAS
Imbros **ANZAC-SUVLA-IMBROS MIA(FSLt F Beeson KIA/PO W Auger? WIA)

The evacuation of the Expeditionary Force from around Anzac and Suvla Bay was carried out on the 19th of December. That from Cape Helles was made three weeks later, on the 9th of January 1916. Every RNAS machine that could be flown patrolled as continuously as possible to prevent news of these operations reaching the enemy. In general the work was very successful. Six Bristol Scouts armed with machine-guns had recently arrived and these were invaluable in seeing off enemy machines. All the troops were eventually removed without loss, but there were casualties in the air, particularly in connection with the Cape Helles evacuation.

1916

January 1916

The pressures on the airmen protecting the withdrawal are well demonstrated by the losses they suffered in the last days on the Peninsula. German Fokker E-types had also found their way into the area and these contributed to the sudden toll of casualties. The Official History draws attention to the peculiar fact that all seven of the RNAS airmen shot down in this month had surnames beginning with the letter "B".

6th January

RNAS
**B of Turkish troops came down sea? MIA(FCdr HA Busk KIA)

8th January

8502   Voisin LAS   2 Wing RNAS
**Spotting combat nrCAPE HELLES ftl a'c destroyed by crew OK(FSLt FDH Bremner/MS HE Burnaby) [combat Oblt T Croneiss FAb6]

11th January

Farman   RNAS
** combat with 2EA shot down SEDD-EL-BAHR off HELLES (FSLt CH Brinsmead KIA) [FAb6]

Farman   RNAS
** combat with 2EA shot down SEDD-EL-BAHR off HELLES (FLt NH Boles KIA) [FAb6]

12th January

RNAS
** shot down off HELLES MIA(FSLt JS Bolas KIA/MS DM Branson WIA POW) [FAb6]

18th January

No.2 Wing RNAS absorbed the equipment and resources of No.3 Wing RNAS on the 18th of January when the latter returned to England and was disbanded. No.2 Wing RNAS was operating from Mudros in May, where it remained in a long and continuous period of service. It became No.62 Wing on the formation of the RAF on the 1st of April 1918.

March 1916

17th March

3921   Nieuport 10   2 Wing RNAS
Imbros **Rec GALLIPOLI combat with Fokker shot up

dam (FSLt HK Thorold OK/SLt RH Portal **WIA**)

As the army at Gallipoli had dispersed, the Navy and its air arm remained in the Eastern Mediterranean to continue operations.

1917

February 1917

11th February

N3175   Nieuport 12   2 Wing RNAS
Stavros +* combat with Albatros[+smoking] nrANGISTA(FLt CE Wood/2Lt EP Hyde RFC)

12th February

N3021   Henri Farman F27   2 Wing RNAS
Imbros ** combat with Fokker shot down nrCHANAK **MIA**(FLt CA Maitland-Heriot **POW**/FLt WC Jameson **POW**) in the Dardanelles [?combat nrCHANAK Ltn E Meinecke FAb6]

17th February

8996   Bristol Scout D   2 Wing RNAS
Imbros, 2 Lewis **Esc combat with EA shot down nrCHANAK(FSLt GT Bysshe **POW**) in the Dardanelles, a'c captured [combat nrHAMIDGE? Ltn E Meinecke FAb6]

March 1917

30th March

9203   Nieuport 12   2 Wing RNAS
** combat with Fokker SMYRNA shot down(FLt JE Morgan **KIA**/FSLt A Sandell **KIA**) ["English Nieu" claim combat nrSMYRNA Hpt H-J Buddecke FAb5]

N3024   Henri Farman F27   2 Wing RNAS
Mudros ** combat with EA shot down nrSMYRNA **MIA**(FSLt BA Trechmann **POW**/LM WA Jones **POW**) ["English Farman" claim combat in Fokker SMYRNA Hpt H-J Buddecke FAb5]

August 1917

1st August

N5108?   Sopwith Strutter F Sqn RNAS
EscB HALKA BOUNAN Rlwy blgs ground fire shot down **MIA(crew **KIA**) crew not yet established

In July 1917 F Squadron RNAS arrived at Thermi from Mudros for bombing operations near Smyrna, on the west coast of Turkey. On the 1st of August bombing Sopwith Strutters, with fighter Strutters

for escort, bombed railway workshops at Halka Bounan. Effective fires were started, but one escort was lost.

September 1917

2nd September

Henri Farman   Mudros
B CHANAK **MIA(FSLt E Foster? **POW**) this pilot?

In response to several enemy bombing attacks on the Mudros base on this day, four Henri Farmans took off to bomb Chanak. One did not return. Foster was known to have been made a prisoner in the Middle East, probably in September 1917, and he may have been the pilot lost.

30th September

3124   HP 0/100   2 Wing RNAS
B engine failure AA? ftl sea swam shore **MIA(FLt JW Alcock **POW**/FSLt HR Aird **POW**/WO SJ Wise **POW**) bombed CONSTANTINOPLE, down in GULF OF XEROS

This Handley Page had been flown out from England in the summer to take part in a bombing offensive in the area around Constantinople. It was based at Mudros on the island of Lemnos, with other elements of F Squadron and a Greek naval squadron from Thasos. The first raid it carried out was on the night of the 3rd of July on the Gallipoli area when engine problems forced it down for an emergency landing. Its first effective raid was made on the 9th of July and then many others followed. On the 30th of September the crew had set out to bomb the two main stations at Constantinople but an engine failed and the pilot turned back. He was forced to make an emergency landing in the sea, however, and when no rescue arrived the crew eventually set off on an hour-long swim to the shore where they were captured.

October 1917

11th October

8021   Short 184   HMS *Empress*
Turkey, this a'c? **OP AA shot down ovALEXANDRETTA cr "EoL" **MIA**(Cdr AW Clemson **POW**/2Lt EA Newton **POW**) to ADANA-KARATASH BURNU

December 1917

10th December

N5618   Sopwith Strutter 2Wing RNAS
Imbros ** combat EA cr ldg(FCdr PC Douglass **KIA**/
OSLt W Hinsley **inj**)

1918

January 1918

10th January

RNAS
Dardanelles? ** (Lt P Parkinson **POW**)

20th January

N1445   Sopwith Baby   Mudros
**B attkg Cruiser *Goeben* combat with 6 enemy
seaplanes shot down in flames(TFSLt W Johnston **KIA**)
[?combat off NAGARA POINT Ltn E Meinecke FAb6]

Sopwith Baby   Mudros
**B attkg Cruiser *Goeben* combat with 6 enemy
seaplanes engine failure ftl taxied back to IMBROS
OK(FSLt RW Peel)

Sopwith Camel   Z(Greek) Sqn Mudros
**Esc attacked 6 enemy seaplanes defending *Goeben* fuel
tank shot up dam returned IMBROS OK(Cdr A
Moraintinis Grk.) Commander of Greek personnel, may
have shot down some of the enemy seaplanes

The RNAS aircraft at Mudros were most commonly occupied with routine anti-submarine
patrols and reconnaissance, but in January the
news was received that two German cruisers, the
Goeben and the *Dreslau*, had left the Dardanelles to
shell British shipping and positions at Imbros. All
available aircraft of 2 (Naval) Wing were hurriedly
drawn to the island, including several Greek pilots
and their aircraft from Thasos, and attacks were
commenced on the two ships. Two Sopwith Baby
seaplanes allotted to this work were attacked by
enemy seaplanes and one RNAS crew was shot
down in flames. Their escorting Camel, piloted by
Cdr Moraintinis, managed to protect the other so
that it could return to base. The *Dreslau* was
eventually harried into minefields and ostensibly
destroyed, and the *Goeben* had grounded in shallow

water. Many bombing attacks on the ship were
made in the next five days but she eventually got
off on the 26th and sailed to safety. The bombs
available to the aircraft had been too light to
seriously harm the German cruiser, but on the
other hand, she never left the Dardanelles in anger
again. A Greek pilot, FSLt Hamblas, had been lost
on these raids when hit by Turkish anti-aircraft
fire. Subsequent patrols were made to keep an eye
on the ship and another crew was very likely lost
on one of these on the 22nd of March (see below).

23rd January

Sopwith Camel   Z(Greek) Sqn
Aegean **B *Goeben* shot down by Turkish AA(FSLt
Hambas)

28th January

N1582   Short 184   HMS *Empress*
Dardanelles, this a'c? ** mg shot down **MIA**(Lt CG
Bronson **POW**/Lt LH Pakenham-Walsh) searching for
"Goeben"

This aircraft was possibly lost whilst diverting
attention from British submarine *E14* which was
entering the Dardanelles to search for the *Goeben*.

March 1918

22nd March

N6410   DH4   2 Wing RNAS
Mudros, this a'c? **Rec shot down **MIA**(Cdr TR
Hackman **POW**/Lt TH Piper **POW**) searching for *Goeben*

July 1918

29th July

Aegean
** **MIA**(Lt CG Clark **POW**)

September 1918

5th September

D2804   DH9   RAF
Stavros ** **MIA**(Lt HT Williams **KIA**)

Part VI

MACEDONIA and THE AEGEAN
1916–1918

THE ORIGINS OF
BRITISH INVOLVEMENT IN THE BALKANS

The Allies became involved in Macedonia as an inevitable result of the volatility of the region. The Balkans had harboured the primary unrest which had led to the original outbreak of war, and tensions there were deep seated and virtually intractable. Germany had enticed Bulgaria into the war with the promise of being given the Serbian nation in return. But Serbia had already repulsed Austrian efforts to overwhelm it and were not about to submit to the Bulgars. At the time of these events, in late 1915, British troops were becoming increasingly available from the Dardanelles, and on the 5th of October of that year they began arriving in Salonika. Alongside a sizeable French army they began digging in before the Bulgarian forces. Numbers grew dramatically in the early months of 1916, until Allied forces reached almost 300,000. The Bulgarian positions were formidable, dooming their enemies in this theatre to years of unrewarded effort against a chain of fortified strongholds in often mountainous terrain. The British section of the front was roughly ninety miles long, running up the Sturma Valley from the sea, across the southern shore of Lake Dojran to the Vardar River.

1916

July 1916

Air support for the Allied armies was important in this difficult terrain, and until the summer of 1916 it was mostly supplied by French machines with some additional seaplanes operating from HMS *Ark Royal*. The French had around one hundred and sixty machines. Any RFC aircraft would have to come from Egypt, and it was not until the 2nd and 17th of July respectively that an advanced detachment of two Flights of 17 Squadron finally left Cairo for Macedonia. They took up quarters at Mikra Bay, near Salonika, and although their duties were nominally those of a corps squadron, namely reconnaissance and artillery observation, all the units in this theatre were expected to carry out the full range of air activities. Therefore, although they were equipped with already obsolete machines like the BE2c and BE12, these had also to be used for bombing, and even the occasional air combat. Pitted against them were around fifty German aircraft, located at Monastir, Hudova, and Xanthi aerodromes. This number was increasing, and included the superior Halberstadt fighter, so that air fighting was to be very uneven when it occurred. The Macedonian front was to remain a low priority for British equipment for at least another eighteen months, putting tremendous demands on the units there. Air fighting was rare at first, its threat minor when compared with the effort required to keep the old machines operational.

August 1916

The political situation affecting the Macedonian front underwent an important change in August, with Romania drawn directly into the conflict. It

joined the Allies on certain conditions, one of which was a guarantee of protection from Bulgaria by the opening of an Allied offensive from Salonika. In this way, the British, and thus the RFC and RNAS, found themselves on a new front line. Reinforcements into the area continued as Romania began its own campaign against Germany's allies on the 28th of August. This soon proved disastrous however, and the hopes built up around Romania's entry into the war faded. On the other hand, the Macedonian offensive, centred around Monastir, proceeded very well. By the 18th of November the town had been taken.

October 1916

A second RFC squadron, No. 47, had arrived in Macedonia on the 20th of September. It was to carry out corps duties of reconnaissance, photography and artillery co-operation, but the demands of the theatre meant its tasks were typically broader than this. The 17th Balloon Section also arrived. With this increase in strength the whole RFC presence in Salonika was reorganised and redistributed along the British front in October.

5th October

BE2c	17Sqn	

** AA shot up(2Lt DD Fowler **WIA**/2Lt J Hutchins OK)

23rd October

8913   Nieuport 12   2 Wing RNAS
Rec BUK shot down nrDRAMA **MIA(FSLt GK Bands **WIA POW**/Lt RG Blakesley **POW**)

November 1916

19th November

3979   Nieuport 11   2 Wing RNAS
B DRAMA A'dr combat with EA ftl **MIA(FSLt Whetnall **KIA**) 18.11? [combat DRAMA Ltn R vEschwege FAb66]

21st November

3783   Sopwith Schneider   HMS *Empress*
Stavros +*SubP combat with EA Seaplane[+ FF Seaplane ftl destroyed] eTENEDOS OK(FSLt AF Brandon) EA destroyed by shelling from ship

This Friedrichshafen seaplane was pursued back out to sea after it had bombed the airship shed on Mudros. It was accompanied by an aeroplane which escaped.

29th November

3905   Henri Farman   2 Wing RNAS
Thasos **B GERAVIZ Seaplane Base ftl **MIA**(FLt EJ Cooper **POW**/Lt Lord Torrington **POW**) 1.12?

3916   Henri Farman   2 Wing RNAS
Thasos **B GERAVIZ Seaplane Base ftl **MIA**(FSLt CW Greig **POW Died** 12.9.18/2Lt RW Frazier RNVR **POW**) 1.12?

The German seaplane base at Geraviz was about thirty-five miles from Thasos and the forces there posed a constant threat to RNAS operations in the area. The Official History notes that on the 29th of November two Henri Farmans bombed the base from below one thousand feet and the ensuing fire caught hold and destroyed most of the buildings there. One must assume these crews were responsible, although one source has their loss as being on the 1st of December.

December 1916

10th December

BE2c	17Sqn	

**Rec nrDRAMA combat with EA[+shot down ooc cr] on return OK(Lt WS Scott/Greek Officer) looking for location to drop spy, EA had come up from DRAMA A'dr

13th December

BE12	17Sqn	

**P combat with EA[+shot down cr gully nrFORT RUPEL] OK(Capt GW Murlis Green) on the STRUMA front

23rd December

	47Sqn	

**P combat with 2Str[+shot down] OK(Capt WDM Bell)

These few victories noted above were probably the first for both squadrons in Macedonia.

1917
January 1917

5th January

FK3	47Sqn	

B dumps at HADOVA STATION AA ftl "EoL" **MIA(2Lt AND Pocock **POW**) destroyed a'c [?"AW 1939" engine failed ftl nrGJEVGJELI]

15th January

FK3	47Sqn	

EscRec combat with EA shot down "EoL" **MIA(2Lt

SJM White **KIA**/2Lt H Matthews **KIA**) later German
note dropped with bombs on SNEVCHE a'dr notified
RFC of their deaths ["EA" claim combat SMOLARI,
nrLAKE DOJRAN Oblt F-K Burckhardt Ja25]

27th January

4533   **BE2d**   **17Sqn**
** **MIA**(2Lt S Smith **POW**) [?BE claim combat
nrYENISHIR Ltn E Meinecke FAb6]

February 1917

11th February

6196   **FK3**   **47Sqn**
**B combat with EA shot down eHUDSOO(Maj MA
Black **KIA**) ["AW 6166"(but 6196 correct) claim combat
sHUDOVA nrBALINCE(Bardar) Ltn O Brauneck
Ja25]

12th February

6219?   **FK3**   **47Sqn**
** seen going North DEMIR HISODA ftl "EoL"
MIA(2Lt AC Stopher **POW**) ["AW 6219" forced to land
sDEMIRHISAR 12.2.17]

18th February

A589   **BE12a**   **17Sqn**
**P DRAMA A'dr combat with EA AA shot down ftl
"EoL" nrDRAMA A'dr **MIA**(Lt JCF Owen Can. **POW**)
set fire to a'c, POW with Bulgarians ["BE 1Str 5289"(viz:
error, 5289 is a FB9) claim combat DRAMA Ltn R
vEschwege FAb30]

This was the first victory over an RFC pilot by this
notable German airman. Owen had set out in
company with Capt Murlis Green to challenge von
Eschwege over his aerodrome but in the fighting
Murlis Green's machine-gun jammed and Owen
was shot down.

26th February

        47Sqn
** bombing raid on JANESH A'dr(2Lt EMcH Howes
WIA) Equipment Officer

Howes was wounded during a big enemy bombing
raid on the RFC airfield at Janesh. Seven
mechanics were killed and another nine wounded.
It was carried out by twenty machines of the newly
arrived bombing group Kampfgeschwader I. This
unit operated its own bombers and fighter escort
and its headquarters and stores were housed on a
train. Earlier in the day the same group had
attacked a French aerodrome, and on the 27th it
made a devastating raid on the British military
camp at Salonika causing three hundred and

seventy-six casualties. The raids continued through
March and April.

March 1917

12th March

        FK3   **47Sqn**
B shot down "EoL" **MIA(2Lt DE Glasson
DoW)stomach [?"AW 250" claim combat over German
a'dr Ltn Hinsen KG1]

Kampfgeschwader I was bombing Vertekop on the
Salonika-Monastir railway on the 12th, and their
targets included a British field hospital. Glasson
was shot down in retaliatory bombing raids to
Hudova airfield after this attack.

18th March

A4007   **BE12a**   **17Sqn**
+* combat with FriedG[+des] WHITE SCAR HILL
5-15pm then another FriedG[+ooc] VOLUVAR?
5-45pm OK(Capt GW Murlis Green) shot down
AlbatrosC in this a'c the next day

22nd March

N3182   **Nieuport 12**   **2 Wing RNAS**
Thasos ** combat with Halberstadt shot down **MIA**(SLt
SG Beare **POW**/2Lt EP Hyde **POW**) combat
ovDRAMA-MAVALA Rd, observer attached from
17Sqn ["Nieu 3182" claim combat DOKSAT Ltn R
vEschwege FAb30]

30th March

N5223   **Sopwith Strutter**   **2 Wing RNAS**
**Rec combat with EA XANTHI shot down(FSLt JM
Ingham **KIA**/SLt JE Maxwell **KIA**) ["Sopwith" claim
combat XANTHI-PHILIPPOPEL Ltn R vEschwege
FAb30]

April 1917

5th April

        47Sqn
** combat with EA shot up(2Lt WH Farrow **WIA**)

N5111   **Sopwith Strutter**   **2 Wing RNAS**
Aegean ** combat with EA shot up dam ftl OK(FLt CE
Wood/Capt Hicks RFC)

8th April

        BE12   **17Sqn**
** combat with EA(Capt FG Saunders **WIA**) to hospital

KGI attacked Janesh railhead on the 8th. Saunders
was wounded, but other airmen of the composite
flight managed to force down a Friedrichshafen.

22nd April

N5087   Sopwith Strutter 2 Wing RNAS
** combat with EA shot up(FSLt WV Simonds OK/1AM
A Carder **WIA**) Carder wounded during KGI raid on
advanced troop bivouacs in the XII Corps area

24th April

The battle of Dojran commenced on the 24th of
April. It began with a night attack, for which the
RFC could offer little assistance other than to make
preparatory reconnaissances during the bombardment. This work was done by 47 Squadron.

25th April

6810   BE2e   17Sqn
**B combat with Fokker 8000' shot down "EoL" diving
in flames **MIA**(Lt GA Radcliffe **KIA**) in pm, 17Sqn had
set out to bomb dumps at BOGDANCI but met KGI on
the way to the raid: Radcliffe lost in this fighting [?"BE"
claim PALSORKA, LAKE DOJRAN Ltn Weltz]

At the end of April a concerted effort was made to
end the German raids of Kampfgeschwader I. The
RFC had already appealed for assistance to the
Eastern Mediterranean Squadron. This naval
group sent four RNAS Sopwith Strutters and a
Sopwith Triplane at the end of March to
strengthen the fighting element of the Salonika
force, and the listings show that the Strutters were
already active. It was given the name "E
Squadron". A composite fighting unit was formed
combining the RNAS machines with three 17
Squadron BE12s and two DH2s from 47 Squadron.
This group had some success but the enemy
bombing continued, its Halberstadt fighter escorts
being particularly effective. A genuine RNAS
bombing group, known as "F Squadron", was
therefore established out of 2 Wing. From the 29th
of April until the 5th of May enemy bases, dumps,
and their aerodrome at Hudova were heavily and
consistently raided. Their efforts were rewarded
with the news on the 10th of May that Kampfgeschwader I had abandoned Hudova and been
withdrawn from the region.

May 1917

2nd May

9748   Sopwith Strutter RNAS Otranto, att 47Sqn
** AA shot down nrHIRSOVA broke up(TFSLt HL
Gaskell **KIA**/2Lt J Watt **KIA**)

9th May

FK3   47Sqn

** combat with EA shot up dam(2Lt HJ Scales OK/2Lt
EES Wheatley **WIA**)

10th May

BE2c   17Sqn
** combat with HA shot up(Lt WS Scott OK/Capt
KWM Pickthorn **WIA**) [?"BE" claim combat
nrVORNA, wTAHINOS LAKE Ltn R vEschwege
FAb30]

18th May

N5532   Sopwith Strutter 2 Wing RNAS
Aegean **B DRAMA A'dr AA hit fainted but ftl
dam(FSLt GA Magor **WIA**) came to and landed

After the departure of the German bombing group
the British flyers made efforts to assert themselves,
but the poor equipment always restricted them.
Anything approaching control of the air would
have to await better aircraft being sent to the
Macedonian front, which occurred only in early
1918 with the operational introduction of the SE5a
fighter. Disaster occurred on the 27th when five
bomb-laden Strutters and three other fighters were
destroyed in a hangar fire on Marian aerodrome.
Four men were killed and several seriously injured.
This accident brought not only loss of life but a
decimation of the British air fighting force in
Macedonia.

For the remainder of 1917 the RFC battled on
with their odd assortment of old fighter aircraft.
These, coupled with the Armstrong Whitworth
FK3s and BE2e two-seaters, often left them at a
disadvantage in the air. In May, however, the
Allied offensives in Macedonia came rather hastily
to a halt and for the remainder of the year the front
saw only sporadic action. There was some commensurate reorganisation of the air services in the
region as operations settled into a regular pattern
of reconnaissance and bombing. Fighter escorts
were often provided for this work. In fact, most of
the British action in Macedonia in the second half
of 1917 took place in the air.

20th May

Henri Farman   HMS *Raglan*
Thasos **Spotting for HMS *Raglan* in shelling of
KAVALLA attacked by EA shot down & thrown
out(crew both **KIA**) crew yet to be established [claim
combat KAVALLA Ltn R vEschwege FAb30] (source:
Official History & War Flying in Macedonia)

Naval bombing operations on selected targets
continued through the year. This raid on Kavalla
was mounted in response to the intelligence that
submarines were being erected in the Customs
House buildings in the town. All RNAS units in the

area were involved, including the Raglan, whose duties in the raid were to attack the enemy gun positions.

30th May

A4771   **DH2**   **47Sqn**
+* combat with HalberstadtDII[+ooc] BOGDARCI 10-45am OK(Capt EE Clarke)

June 1917

11th June

6677   **BE12**   **17Sqn**
** attacked by Halberstadt ovLAKE TAHINOS 10-30am shot up ftl 500yd wAHINOS OK(Capt EV Longinette)

18th June

       BE2e   **17Sqn**
** left formation **MIA**(Lt A Leslie-Moore **POW**)

24th June

       FK3   **17Sqn**
** AA fire shelled(2Lt SC Fowler? OK/Lt AC Dent **WIA**)severe, name Forler?

29th June

A4772   **DH2**   **47Sqn**
+* combat with HalberstadtDII[+ooc] BOGDARCI 11am OK(2Lt HJ Gibson)

July 1917

8th July

       BE2e   **17Sqn**
** combat with HA "EoL" ftl control? **MIA**(Capt JEA O'Dwyer **WIA**? **POW**) [2 "unconfirmed English EAs" behind Turkish Lines]

                 47Sqn
** a'c broke up after combat with EA **MIA**(Lt HC Brufton **KIA**) [2 "unconfirmed English EAs" behind Turkish Lines]

August 1917

9th August

The 17 Squadron aerodrome at Orlyak was shelled on the 9th and the gun positions attacked in the afternoon.

       BE12   **17Sqn**
** combat with EA shot up(Lt PML Edmunds **WIA**) [?"BE 1Str" claim combat nrIVERON? Ltn R vEschwege FAb30]

18th August

A huge fire enveloped the town of Salonika for three days leaving 80,000 inhabitants homeless.

20th August

N3743   **Nieuport 27**   **17Sqn**
French Nieuport 120hp on loan **EscB combat with EA ftl ooc "EoL" nrPRILEP **MIA**(2Lt JL Bamford **KIA**?) ["Nieuport" claim combat sPRILEP Ltn G Fieseler Ja25]

A1466   **FK8**   **47Sqn**
EscB MONASTIR combat with AlbatrosDIII[+ooc] PRILEP? then shot up ftl(Lt FWH Thomas MC **DoW 5.1.18/2Lt HA Jones **WIA**) FK8 was covering rear of formation and was heavily shot up. Thomas passed out but recovered to fly back "WoL" and land safely 50mins after being wounded.

From mid-August the RFC operated in the Monastir area with the French. Work consisted mostly of escorted bombing raids on German aerodromes and billets. On the 20th, the German headquarters in Prilep were attacked, but additional French escorts failed to appear and the British aircraft were heavily attacked by German fighters.

October 1917

3rd October

       BE2e   **17Sqn**
** combat with EA nrSERES shot down "EoL" **MIA**(Lt IL Stockhausen **KIA**/2Lt CVM Watson **KIA**) seen EoL [?"BE" claim combat wSARMUSAKLI Ltn R vEschwege FAb30]

5th October

       FK8   **47Sqn**
B CESTOVO Dump combat with 3 Halberstadts shot up engine hit nrLAKE DOJRAN ftl cr(2Lt GC Gardiner **WIA/2Lt AS Clark Can. OK) 3 other Allied a'c came to assist, WIA in leg, to hospital, 3.10?

6th October

       FK3   **47Sqn**
** AA hit shot up(Lt ER Wilkinson MC **DoW** 7.10.17/ 2Lt GS Bennett OK)

29th October

A4040   **BE12a**   **47Sqn**
B CESTOVO Dump combat with EA ftl Bulgarian lines **MIA(2Lt PD Montague **KIA**) [?unconfirmed claim CERNISTE]

       FK8   **47Sqn**
B CESTOVO Dump shot down "EoL" **MIA(2Lt JRF Gubbin **POW DoW** 20.11.17/2AM TH Bury **POW**) [?unconfirmed "BE" claim combat HODZ OBASI]

Five aircraft of 47 Squadron attacked Cestovo dump again but were met by eight Halberstadt and Albatros fighters from Hudova aerodrome.

November 1917

Greece finally entered the fighting in the Balkans in November; taking over the Struma front from the British greatly lessened the RFC burden. SE5a fighters and RE8 two-seaters were also beginning to arrive, opening the way for the British to take control of the air in 1918.

11th November

17KBS, Salonika
** killed in parachute descent in EA attack(Capt CH Gimingham **KIA**)

14th November

BE12　　　　　　**47Sqn**
** AA shrapnel hit(2Lt E Brewer? **WIA**) name Bewer?

19th November

Sopwith Strutter?　　**17Sqn**
** combat with EA(2Lt HJ Gates **KIA**) [?"Sopwith 1Str" claim combat KALENDRA wSERES Ltn R vEschwege FAb30]

21st November

After incessant German fighter attacks on kite balloons one was left booby-trapped with explosives and when approached they were detonated. This destroyed the German machine and killed its pilot, Ltn von Eschwege, the highest scoring enemy ace on the Macedonian front.

30th November

47Sqn
** combat with EA shot up(Capt RM Wynne-Eyton **WIA**/2Lt WD Robertson **WIA**)

December 1917

19th December

A4046　　**BE12a**　　　　**17Sqn**
+* combat with AlbatrosDIII[+ooc] wLAKE DOJRAN 12-30pm OK(2Lt FD Travers)

This was the last BE12 victory in Macedonia but 47 Squadron continued to fly the type into January 1918.

1918
January 1918
THE ALLIED
BOMBING OFFENSIVE

In the absence of military operations in Macedonia for the first months of 1918 the British used air power to maintain pressure on the enemy, achieved primarily through a programme of bombing. Until the summer, however, this was limited by the available resources. For much of this time Nos. 17 and 47 Squadrons remained the only units in the region, and corps and fighter duties were divided thinly amongst their various Flights. Urgent requests for fighters and bombers to enable a more expansive air offensive had brought only a few SE5a single-seaters by early January, insufficient to impose air superiority. Only by spring were there enough British fighters in the region for the RAF finally to take the initiative, following the formation of 150 fighter Squadron on the 1st of April (see below). More effective bombing aircraft were even longer in arriving — a few DH9s came on strength in Macedonia only in August. Until this time, the Armstrong Whitworths had struggled on with these duties, but as they could only operate as bombers if no observer was carried, they needed fighter escort. Once 150 Squadron gained control of the air in the summer the situation eased somewhat, and the corps machines were able to go about their work in greater safety.

22nd January

B28　　**SE5a**　　　　　　**17Sqn**
+* combat with DFWC[+des] PORNA 1-40pm
OK(Capt FG Saunders) first of 4 victories in this a'c

This was the first SE5a victory in Macedonia.

28th January

B613　　**SE5a**　　　　　　**17Sqn**
+* combat with DFWC[+ftl des] sANGISTA 11-30am
OK(Lt BE Gibbs) first of 10? victories for 17Sqn

March 1918

24th March

B690　　**SE5a**　　　　　　**17Sqn**
+* combat with AlbatrosDIII[+ooc] TOLOS 7am
OK(Lt AG Goulding Can.) made 9 victory claims with 17Sqn & 150Sqn

April 1918

1st April

150 Squadron was formed on the 1st of April. It operated somewhat notionally for several weeks, for it consisted initially of a fighter Flight from each of Nos. 17 and 47 Squadrons, which effectively continued to operate from within those units. On the 7th of May a Flight of Sopwith Camels was added and from this time it became independent. As will be seen from the entries which follow, it also maintained a few other disparate fighter types it had inherited from its parent units. These included the Bristol M1C monoplane and the DH12, both long obsolete for use on the Western Front, but still fighting in theatres of the Middle East Brigade late into 1918. Losses on the Macedonian front were very light until the autumn offensives, which is why a selection of RAF combat victories have been given here in order to record some of the individuals involved in the air fighting.

13th April

B30   **SE5a**   **150Sqn**
+* combat with AlbatrosDIII[+des] 1500yd
sBRAJKOVIC 7-30am OK(Lt CB Green Can. DFC)
first of 11 victories, the balance being with 150 Sqn

B692   **SE5a**   **150Sqn**
+* combat with AlbatrosDIII[+des] sBRAJKOVIC
7-30am OK(Lt GG Bell Can.) shared victory, first in
fighters for this 16 victory ace(others as observer with
22Sqn in 1917)

This shared victory was the first for 150 Squadron, although these two machines were still effectively operating as 47 Squadron aircraft. Bell was the unit's highest scoring ace.

14th April

                        Balkans
** (2Lt G Hannan **POW**)

25th April

B690   **SE5a**   **150Sqn**
+* combat with DFWC[+ooc] ANGISTA 10am OK(Lt
AG Goulding) shared victory

C4913   **Bristol M1C**   **17Sqn**
+* combat with DFWC[+ooc] ANGISTA 10am OK(Lt
AEdeM Jarvis) shared victory, repeated victory the next
day

May 1918

6th May

C1587   **Sopwith Camel**   **150Sqn**

+* combat with DFWC[+ooc] nCERNISTE 9-50am
OK(Lt CB Green) shared victory

This was the first Sopwith Camel claim in Macedonia.

C4963   **Bristol M1C**   **150Sqn**
+* combat with AlbatrosDV[+ooc] nCERNISTE
9-50am OK(Lt W Ridley)

13th May

B695   **SE5a**   **150Sqn**
+* combat with AlbatrosDIII[+des] LIVANOVO 8am
OK(Lt GG Bell Can.)

Naval air detachments from Stavros and Thasos sometimes operated in co-operation with the RAF in Macedonia, and one example of this was the series of bombing raids made by ten naval machines on the 13th and 14th. They attacked dumps and stations in association with all three RAF units. The combat above may have been part of these raids.

June 1918

1st June

Air activity increased briefly in June as signs grew that Bulgaria was preparing for an offensive in the Dojran region. There was much more air fighting as well, but by this time the RAF was in the ascendant and suffered not a single casualty. The threat of the offensive faded away as the month closed, intelligence being received that enemy troops had mutinied.

B692   **SE5a**   **150Sqn**
+*EscB combat with 12EAs[+flames] CASANDULE
3-05pm OK(Capt GG Bell Can.)

B695   **SE5a**   **150Sqn**
+*EscB combat with 12EAs[++ooc] CASANDULE
~3-08pm OK(Lt CB Green Can.) first of 6 victories by
Green in this a'c

6th June

C1598   **Sopwith Camel**   **150Sqn**
+* combat with AlbatrosDIII[+ooc] MRAVINCA
11-30am OK(Lt GC Gardiner) Gardiner claimed 6
victories

12th June

C1599   **Sopwith Camel**   **150Sqn**
+* combat with AlbatrosDV[+flames] MILETKOVO-
MRZENCI 6-55am then AlbatrosDV[+des]
nGUEVGUELI 8am OK(Lt DA Davies) Davies claimed
most of his 10 victories in this a'c

July 1918

17th July

B3357   A.W.FK8   17Sqn
** AA hit **MIA**(Capt SR Penrose-Welsted **KIA**/Lt HG
Hall **KIA**)

26th July

C3671   A.W.FK8   47Sqn
** (Capt GH Taylor **WIA**) inj?

August 1918

July and August had continued quietly on the
ground, but typically, air operations were maintained. There were some reasonably large bombing
raids at this time, involving as many as twenty
aircraft, whose targets were dumps, railways and
aerodromes. In August, preparations for an Allied
offensive were finally developing, and therefore
artillery work and photographic reconnaissance
gained in importance. The first DH9s were
arriving, enabling the first deep reconnaissances to
be carried out as well.

17th August

                                    150Sqn
** combat(Lt JP Cavers **WIA**)

18th August

D6643   Sopwith Camel   150Sqn
+* combat with SSDIII[++] nLAKE DOJRAN then
combat with AlbatrosDVs[+++ooc] LAKE DOJRAN-
PIRAVO 7-45am OK(Lt JC Preston) shared victory,
pilot made 7 claims

September 1918

PREPARATIONS FOR
THE ALLIED OFFENSIVE

The Allied offensive in Macedonia began unfolding
in September. The most crucial fighting was to take
place along the eighty miles of front between
Monastir and to the east of Lake Dojran. The
objective of the fighting was the town of Gradsko
on the Vardar River. It was an ambitious target,
being thirty-five miles away across a rugged
mountain terrain and with formidable defensive
positions protecting the valley approaches. If
taken, though, it would threaten key enemy lines of
communications and divide the Bulgarian Army.
Rather than attack along the river valleys it was

decided to launch an assault over the mountains,
and the Serbian Army, alongside the French, was
chosen to spearhead this most difficult operation.
Other attacks would be launched simultaneously
— the British for instance would attack along their
front from Lake Dojran back to the Vardar — but
these were to confine the enemy to his positions
away from the main assault and to draw in his
reserves. Facing the British were some very well
constructed defences and progress against them
was expected to be slight. In the air, the Allies had
a substantial numerical superiority — about two
hundred aircraft as against about eighty.

1st September

The first preliminary skirmishes were undertaken
on the 1st of September, almost three weeks before
the main assault. In these, the British successfully
attacked a small salient on the Vardar Valley in
order to suggest to the enemy that the main attack
might occur in this region. Contact patrolling,
bombing, and some low patrolling accompanied
the ground attack which began in the late afternoon. Several enemy fighters came out to confront
this activity but the air fighting was generally
inconclusive.

2nd September

C4907   Bristol M1C   150Sqn
+* combat with LVGC[+flames] NIHOR 8-15am
OK(Lt JP Cavers) shared victory

C4976   Bristol M1C   150Sqn
+* combat with LVGC[+flames] NIHOR 8-15am
OK(Lt FD Travers) shared victory

3rd September

C4907   Bristol M1C?   150Sqn
**EscPhot attacked by 6 EAs shot down into LAKE
DOJRAN(Lt JP Cavers **KIA**)

The Official History notes that Cavers survived the
crash into the lake but was killed by subsequent
fire from the enemy fighters as he tried to swim
away from his machine. These events were witnessed by a fighter patrol on escort duty from 150
Squadron who then attacked the enemy formation
and shot four of them down. The known details of
these claims are given below.

             SE5a?   150Sqn
+*EscB combat with 6AlbatrosDVs[+des] nwLAKE
DOJRAN 8-15am then another[+des] 8-20am
eCERNISTE OK(Lt FD Travers)

B163   SE5a   150Sqn
+*EscB combat with 6AlbatrosDVs[+des] 1m nLAKE
DOJRAN 8am OK(Lt W Ridley)

D6549 Sopwith Camel 150Sqn
+*EscB combat with 6AlbatrosDVs[+des] 8-20am
wCERNISTE Hosp. OK(Capt GC Gardiner)

15th September

After a day of heavy bombardment of the Bulgarian positions in the mountains, the main assault on the Franco-Serbian front began at dawn. The Serbian First and Second Armies were fired with anticipation at ridding their country of the invader and stormed up through most difficult terrain to take the whole Bulgarian front line by nightfall. French gains followed on the 16th, so that by that evening the advance had pressed several miles into the mountains in places. A day later the French and Serbian Armies had forced a wedge twenty-five miles deep.

16th September

C4976 Bristol M1C 150Sqn
+* combat with DVII[+ooc] LAKE DOJRAN 12-05pm
OK(Lt FD Travers) [Ltn A Ebert KIA DRAMA], last of
9 claims, at least 3 in this Bristol M1C

This was the last combat victory claim in a Bristol M1C on this front. The type had first appeared in late 1916 but following staunch opposition to it from Trenchard it had never been flown in anger on the Western Front.

18th September

The main attack on the British front, on the strong and well defended positions around Lake Dojran and the Vardar Valley, began on the 18th. The various corps duties in support of the army were shared between the flights of 17 and 47 Squadrons thus: A & B Flights of 17 Squadron were on hand to carry out low bombing and machine-gunning as required, whilst C Flight contact patrolled in support of the XVI Corps. A Flight of 47 Squadron made strategic reconnaissances, B Flight contact patrolled with the XII Corps, and C Flight was responsible for all artillery work. Preliminary air operations had been proceeding for the previous four days; in particular these had involved the bombing of Hudova aerodrome as well as stations and dumps, whilst on the day before the attack a programme of artillery registration was carried out.

Air support was commendably laid on throughout the fighting, but against such formidable positions the British attack could bring only minimal gains at first. The attack had the desired effect, however, of pinning down the local Bulgarian forces. The fighting was heavy, and much air work was done from very low levels, with crews subjected to intense fire. The Armstrong Whitworth noted below was nevertheless the only crew lost. There was a notable lack of enemy fighters over the battle — the main engagement occurred in the morning when four RAF fighters who were protecting the contact patrol machines met five enemy single-seaters. Two of the attackers were shot down in what was to be the last dogfight on the Macedonian front. From this time the enemy fighters withdrew from the region.

C3590 A.W.FK8 47Sqn
** AA MIA(Lt JA Brandt KIA/2Lt H Gerhardt KIA)
[?FK8 claim Ltn F Thiede Ja38]

B692 SE5a 150Sqn
+* combat with DVII[+ooc] KARALI 7am OK(Lt L
Hamilton)

D3495 SE5a 150Sqn
+* combat with DVII[+flames] KARALI 6-30am
OK(Capt GG Bell Can.)

D5954? SE5a 150Sqn
+* combat with DVII[+flames] KARALI 6-15am
OK(Capt GM Brawley)

These were the last combat victories in Macedonia.

19th September

17Sqn
**SpyDrop ldg nrPETRIC dropped passenger but forced to take off again by enemy troops shot up eng hit ftl cr RUPEL PASS MIA(Lt WJ Buchanan POW/unnamed Sgt POW?) left 5pm

20th September

D2889 DH9 Mudros
** MIA(Lt SPO? Haughton POW/Gnr A Weller POW)
21.9? initials EPO?

Naval bombing machines operated on this front from Mudros during the final week of fighting.

21st September

On the ground a lull followed the heavy fighting on the opening day of the British offensive. In the air, however, bombing of aerodromes, particulary Hudova, and reconnaissance work continued. On the 21st these flights began to bring in reports indicating that the enemy was about to begin a general retreat. Troops were on the move everywhere, and key positions were being torched and blown up throughout the countryside. Upon this news the British corps were immediately ordered to rest in preparation for a general advance, whilst the normal corps work in the air was also mostly abandoned and all available machines began bombing troops and transport. Routes of retreat for

the Bulgarian forces offered little cover and great damage was soon inflicted, particularly where troops were massing to cross key bridges.

22nd September

Bombing recommenced on the 22nd in spite of high winds. By noon the enemy was in full retreat along the entire line from Monastir to Lake Dojran, with no apparent intention of making a stand. Now that the Bulgarian troops were without defensive air cover they became highly exposed to attack, and through the following days were driven rather bloodily from the region. Bombing and low machine-gunning of the enemy continued for a week whilst the Bulgarian government, now desperate for an end to hostilities, strove for an agreement. This was finalised on the 29th, and came into being on the 30th, at which time fighting in the Balkans came to an end.

27th September

N1746? **Short 184** **Mudros**
this a'c? ** **MIA**(Maj JPB Ferrand **POW**) 27/28Sep.18

October 1918

17th October

D7213 **DH9** **Mudros**
** ftl "EoL" **MIA**(Lt W Bamber **POW**/Lt KG Withers **POW**)

Untraced Naval Prisoners in the Balkans in 1918?

** (FLt BJ Brady **POW**) .18?
** (SFLt LL Marsh **POW**) .18?
** (Capt GB Baker **POW**) .18?
** (SLt G Blandy **POW**) .18? repat 10.18

Part VII

EGYPT AND PALESTINE 1914–1918

1914

The first reconnaissance flight in Egypt was made on the 27th of November when an aircraft from Ismailia flew along the Canal Defence Zone. A single Flight of aeroplanes had been dispatched from England at the beginning of the month to help discern the enemy's early intentions in the region. The general impression was that Turkey would attempt to capture part of the Suez Canal and destroy its usefulness by sinking ships within it. With this patrol began years of air operations in the East, virtually all of which would exert an influence on affairs and stretch into every corner of the theatre. Air reconnaissance was to prove particularly effective in this harsh and terrible environment where conditions made any equivalent scope of reconnoitre on the ground completely impossible. The machines available, often very obsolete, would be driven to their limits. At this time, they included Maurice and Henri Farmans, with a few seaplanes being flown from ships.

1915 THE BUILD-UP OF AIR FORCES IN EGYPT

Concentrations of Turkish troops were first seen on reconnaissances from around the middle of the month, principally massing at Beersheba, 100 miles or so east of the Canal, and within days it was clear they were on the move towards it. As they followed their progress, machines also dropped bombs on the troops on several occasions. By early February, one seaplane observer reported seeing some 35,000 troops at

Beersheba. It was at this time, however, that matters on the Gallipoli Peninsula began to dominate the concerns of the region, and the Canal Zone quietened as the Turks rushed to defend the Dardanelles. When substantial sections of the British Army also departed the region, the RFC detachment at Ismailia remained. On the 24th of March this detachment became known as 30 Squadron RFC. Although it was now unlikely Suez would be threatened in the immediate future, this unit commenced a programme of routine desert reconnaissances east of the Canal. There were skirmishes on the ground in April in which it assisted, but the Sinai front was generally quiet for the remainder of the year.

The early involvement of British air units in the various campaigns of the Middle East is not always easy to follow, so a brief overview might be useful. Although the forces involved were initially very meagre the usefulness of aircraft was recognised from the earliest days. As will be often apparent, the aeroplane was able to perform reconnaissance in conditions and over territory where any other normal option would have been extremely hazardous. They lent themselves to desert work.

For the first three years of the war in the East, aircraft were precious commodities. It was not the policy of the Allies to commit sophisticated machines to these theatres, preferring to concentrate them on the Western Front. In contrast, the Germans ensured that some high quality armed two-seaters, and even some Fokker monoplane fighters reached Egypt months before Britain sent any machines which could match them. In the East, the British squadrons also remained multi-functional in character long after specialisation of types into discrete squadrons and groups had occurred in France. Each squadron had machines capable of carrying out a full variety of tasks such as reconnaissance, bombing, and escorting, and later, some scouts were merged into these units to add some token offensive capability. No genuine fighting component was really added until late 1916.

In the early days the scarcity of machines meant that resources were thus spread very thinly, with not simply squadrons, but individual flights being sent off in opposite directions, often several hundreds of miles apart. The regions within the Middle East where trouble variously arose were spread over an enormous area.

The first air patrols in the Middle East had been seen over the highly sensitive Canal Zone in late 1914, but when the campaign in the Dardanelles began the following February the first concerted and important reconnaissance flying took place there. Flying was mostly carried out by machines operating from Royal Navy ships, and then land-based RNAS units. The first air losses in the region due to enemy action occurred in the Dardanelles.

By late 1916 a second significant area of conflict had also opened up — in Mesopotamia. The Australian "Mesopotamian Half Flight" was operating here, along with one Flight of 30 Squadron RFC. By the end of 1915 these two had amalgamated and 30 Squadron was destined to remain in Mesopotamia for the rest of the war. Reinforcements in the form of Fifth Wing RFC also arrived in the Middle East at this time. It consisted of 14 Squadron, which arrived on the 19th of November, and 17 Squadron, which followed on the 11th of December. The third and last Flight of 30 Squadron had left Ismailia for Mesopotamia in October, and its duties were taken over by one of the new Flights of 14 Squadron. Within days, however, two of this Flight's BE2cs were ordered along the coast to join the Western Frontier Force at Matruh. The first reconnaissance was carried out from here on December the 5th — so beginning several months of fighting against hostile Arab groups, in particular the Senussi.

As the Dardanelles quietened after the evacuation of the British in early 1916, and then as Kut fell a few months later, Egypt again took centre stage. Accordingly, the RFC forces there were gradually built up. With the Canal apparently secure, and recalcitrant Arabs being contained in the Western Desert, the attack could be taken to the Turks in Sinai in an offensive on Palestine. No.1 Australian Squadron would arrive in Egypt in April 1916, and a single Flight of 17 Squadron found itself in the Sudan for a while before the whole unit was posted to Macedonia in October. All these movements are dealt with in more detail when they occurred.

1916

In January, the main camp of the Senussi was located by aerial reconnaissance and an attacking force immediately assembled. Fighting commenced on the 23rd, and over the next months the enemy was pursued into submission. It was then decided to move on the regional town of Sollum. The route was over very demanding country, and aeroplanes were used not only to spy out Arab positions, but also to provide information about the difficult terrain which could be expected in the advance. The town was taken on the 14th of March.

January 1916

26th January

Egypt
(** 2AM WC Pass **POW Died**) in Turkey

April 1916

British activity in Egypt had increased greatly by April. As regards the Royal Flying Corps, the Fifth Wing was installed in Ismailia and several new aerodromes had been constructed in the Canal Zone, housing a Flight each of 14 and 17 Squadron. Pressuring these events was the fact that substantial Turkish forces had also been freed for fighting, and their objectives once again appeared to include the Suez Canal. Germany had also begun to invest resources into the region, including a number of air units which were to cause many problems for the Allies. Their machines not only included superior two-seater Rumpler reconnaissance types but, more importantly, Fokker Eindekkers, some of which had reached the Middle East by mid-April. The first of five German units to be sent to the region in 1916 was Flieger Abteilung 300 Pascha, based at Beersheba. Almost immediately, as the entries will show, air fighting increased, forcing LtGen Sir GF Gorringe to concede within weeks that the German machines had given the Turkish air superiority. The enemy held this for over a year, until a few Bristol Fighters arrived in Egypt.

Air reconnaissances showed the Turkish forces moving westwards, and on the 20th one patrolling BE2c was heavily shot up from the ground. For a few days following, fighting burst out around Qatiya, in which time the two RFC flights, with their eight aircraft, flew sixty-eight hours of operations. Little came of these events, however, and the blistering heat of summer set in to add a new burden to the flyers.

14th April

The personnel of No.1 Squadron Australian Flying Corps had arrived by ship at Suez on the 14th of April. Immediately upon arrival its technical staff were dispersed amongst local British squadrons for training and the majority of air crew sent on to England for training as well. It was still uncertain where this squadron would eventually be sent, nor was it to be allocated any aircraft for several weeks. However, when 17 Squadron was ordered to Salonika on the 12th of June, 1 Squadron AFC took over its machines and its Canal stations, as well as

its headquarters at Heliopolis. For some months following this, the unit was split up and its flights dispersed across Egypt, as was typical in this theatre. Elements were sent as far as Sherika in Upper Egypt, where they continued the operations against the Senussi in the Western Desert. More routine flying was carried out along the Canal Zone where, for lack of aircraft and other resources, 1 Squadron AFC mostly shared the machines of 14 Squadron. It was not until December 1916 that it came together again to begin operations as a single entity.

May 1916

A Half-Flight of 14 Squadron was established at Port Said late in the month in response to German bombing of the town.

3rd May

	BE2c	14Sqn

** combat with EA shot down (Lt CR Rowden **WIA**)

4419	BE2c	14Sqn

PhotRec EL ARISH rifle fire, sump hit shot down ftl "EoL" nr coast **MIA(Lt CW Hill Aust. **POW**) from Kantara, had extra fuel tank, destroyed a'c on ldg

THE SUDAN IN MAY 1916

The remaining area of the Middle East to flare up into hostilities in the first half of 1916 was the Sudan. The Sultan of neighbouring Darfur had given all the appearances of a man about to invade the borders of this country. His was not a huge force, but it needed to be contained and controlled. It was decided a move should be made on his stronghold at El Fasher, and as usual air power was an essential tool in this operation. The British Army not only wanted information gathered about the enemy but was hoping that the mere presence of "iron horses", as the Sultan called aeroplanes, would have a salutary effect on the rebels. The logistics of moving machines and supplies into this area was a daunting prospect. For most of the final stages it would involve transportation by camels. Operations would also occur at the very hottest time of the year, and then run on into the rainy season. C Flight of 17 Squadron were chosen to undertake the work, and it took a journey of almost three weeks to reach the region from Suez. The first reconnaissance to El Fasher was flown on the 12th May by Lt F Bellamy in a BE2c.

17th May

BE2c   **17Sqn**
Sudan **Rec ground fire ovMELIT prop hit but bombed
& shot up troops on ground OK(Capt EJ Bannatyne)
spent total of nine hours in air through the day

23rd May

5413   **BE2c**   **17Sqn**
Sudan **Rec attacked & shot up enemy cavalry then shot
up & bombed troops at EL FASHER, shot up by rifle fire
ftl(2Lt JC Slessor **WIA**) thigh

Slessor's attack proved to be a very important one.
The main forces of the Sultan had been broken the
day before, but this bombing caused such panic in
the enemy ranks that the British were subsequently
able to enter El Fasher virtually unopposed. All
danger to the Sudan from the Sultan of Darfur ended
with this incident.

June 1916

15th June

BE2c   **17Sqn**
*trav to A.L.G. at KHARGA lost ftl(2Lt SG Ridley **Died**/
1AM J Garside **Died**) died of exposure by 19th or 20th

This crew was lost during operations against the
Senussi in the Western Desert. Two machines had
left for the advanced landing ground at Kharga but
had come down for the night after becoming lost. In
the morning the engine of this BE2c could not be
started and the other crew went on with the
intention of returning with help. In the morning the
crew had been able to take off but were forced down
again, and could not be located before they were
found dead.

Short 184   **HMS *Ben-My-Chree***
**PhotB Turkish trenches before JEDDAH then ground
fire shot up dam engine hit ftl sea OK(Cdr CR Samson
DSO/Capt J Wedgwood-Benn) also shot up from trenches,
Samson removed bullet from boot heel

HMS *Ben-my-Chree* and other ships were in the area
to assist an Arab siege of Turks in Jeddah. The
seaplanes played a crucial part in its fall. The Arab
revolt had begun on the 5th of June.

18th June

2691   **BE2c**   **17Sqn**
**B EL ARISH A'dr heavy ground fire, rifle bullet in sump
ftl beach rescued by crew of BE2c 2700 OK(Capt HA
vanRyneveld SA.)

2700   **BE2c**   **14Sqn**
**B EL ARISH OK(Capt S Grant-Dalton DSO/Lt DK

Paris MC) landed beside in BE2c 2691 and eventually
managed take off with rescued pilot and returned 90miles
to QANTARA.

2116   **BE2c**   **14Sqn**
**B EL ARISH A'dr heavy ground fire shot up ftl nr a'dr
MIA(Capt RJ Tipton **POW**) burnt a'c before capture

4506   **BE2c**   **17Sqn**
**B EL ARISH A'dr shot up ftl sea OK(2Lt M Minter)
rescued by motor launch.

These events occurred during a bombing raid to El
Arish aerodrome in response to a bombing raid on
two British garrisons. A total of eleven BE2cs were
involved, three of which were hit by ground fire.
Relatively little damage was caused on the ground,
so these losses were hard to justify.

July 1916

The RFC Middle East Brigade was formed on the
1st July, to control the continued expansion of the
air arm in the region. At formation in Egypt it
included Fifth Wing (14 and 17 Squadron, and No.1
Australian Squadron), 20th Reserve Wing (training), "X" Aircraft Park and "X" Aircraft Depot.
Elsewhere it included 30 Squadron in Mesopotamia
and 26 Squadron in East Africa. Individual Flights
of the various squadrons were typically spread
throughout the various regions.

At this time a definite build-up of Turkish forces
was perceived in the Eastern Desert, east of the
Canal Zone. The reconnaissance below was the one
which brought conclusive proof of this when it
spotted some 8,000 troops at Bir Bayud and elsewhere. It now looked as though the long expected
Turkish offensive was about to take place. By the
end of the month enemy troops numbered around
13,000, and within days the crucial battle of Romani
would be fought. From this time the RFC began
bombing and attacking troops. Until now they had
been ordered to hold their fire, however, so as to lure
the Turks into a prepared battle plan.

19th July

BE2c   **14Sqn**
**Rec BIR BAYUD-BIR GAMEIL ground rifle fire shot
up (/BrigGen EWC Chaytor NZ **WIA**) shoulder, bullet
grazed shoulder, Chaytor was Commander of New
Zealand Mounted Rifles Brigade

24th July

BE2c   **14Sqn**
** combat with EA(2Lt RP Wilcock **WIA**/2Lt TJ West
WIA) crew?

August 1916

2nd August

4609   DH1A   14Sqn
**P attacked Fokker[+?fuel tank hit shot down but
recovered] nrROMANI 4pmOK(Lt MacLaren/Lt TJ
West) EA ftl nrSALMANA [German crew was Ltn H
Henkel (Merkel?)/Oblt Stalter FAb300]

This was the first Allied claim in air fighting over
the Egyptian front.

3rd August

BE2c   14Sqn
**B KATIA AA shot up OK(Lt Edwards) AFC1
personnel attached to 14 Sqn also involved in this raid

THE BATTLE OF ROMANI

The Turks began their attack in the battle of
Romani on the night of 3rd August, but after a day
of very hard fighting their initial efforts failed. On
the 5th, the British counter-attack commenced. This
advanced successfully for over a week, until the
Turkish forces had been decisively pushed back, the
battle won, and over four thousand taken prisoner.
During the fighting, as many as seventeen Allied
machines were active, including some from 1
Australian Squadron, for whom this was the first
concerted fighting. RFC casualties sustained during
sporadic air fighting included six RFC pilots
wounded, one of whom later died. One British
machine was shot down by AA twelve miles east of
the lines, but the crew managed to walk out to safety
after destroying their aircraft. Finally, one enemy
machine was shot down in combat. What is known
of these events is given below.

10th August

BE2c   14Sqn
**Rec combat with EA SINAI shot up(2Lt LF Hursthouse
WIA/2Lt G McDiarmid **WIA**)

11th August

BE2c   14Sqn
**Rec attacked by EA ovBIR EL ABD shot up dam ftl(2Lt
EW Edwards **WIA**/Lt J Brown **DoW**) 2EA?

Edwards had been hit possibly seven times but had
still gone off to search for help for his more critically
wounded observer. Brown then refused treatment
when it arrived, until he had given his report. He
was concerned that if his chest wound was touched
he would faint. This brave man died two hours later.

September 1916

The Sinai front remained relatively quiet on the
ground for the remainder of 1916, but was generally
characterised by steady Allied progress into
Turkish-held territory. Air operations were maintained by both sides as a way of keeping pressure on
the enemy. Much bombing of a strategic nature was
carried out, and the German pilots in the region also
continued to fly aggressively and with purpose. On
one raid to bomb Turkish water works at Maghara,
one BE2c was forced to land in the desert, and
another, attempting to rescue the pilot, was also
damaged. Two other BE2cs then had to land and
pick them up, all four officers flying safely back to
Ismailia.

A big surprise raid on the Turkish garrison at Bir
El Mazar was planned for the middle of the month,
and in support, 14 Squadron was required to ensure
that no German aeroplanes left El Arish which could
give away British intentions. The region around the
town was reconnoitred constantly through
September and the aerodrome was bombed on the
night of the 15th/16th September. On the 16th,
interception patrols were begun. These were a
failure, as two BE2cs had to land, one being hit by
fire from a German aircraft. The screen was penetrated and the element of surprise lost.

17th September

8135   Sopwith Schneider   HMS *Ben-my-Chree*
Mediterranean, Sopwith Baby? **EscSpot combat with
EA shot down in flames eEL ARISH(FLt JT Bankes-Price
KIA) escorting Short spotting for monitors at EL-ARISH,
attacked soon after start of spotting, Bankes-Price killed by
jumping from a'c [combat eEL ARISH Ltn W vBulow/
FAb300, 2nd a'c ftl (see below)]

Sopwith Schneider   HMS *Ben-my-Chree*
**EscSpot combat with EA chased down ftl sea OK(FSLt
AJ Nightingale) picked up by monitor, a'c salvaged

Short184   HMS *Ben-my-Chree*
**Spot combat with EA OK(FLt Maskell/SLt Kerry)
escorted by above Sopwiths, saw EA off after they had been
accounted for

German aircraft became increasingly active in this
month, and in response Samson began training his
naval pilots in techniques of formation and combat
flying. The Fokkers involved in the casualties above
caused considerable problems for the Royal Navy in
their bombardment of El Arish. *Ben-my-Chree*'s
seaplanes were spotting for two separate targets ten
miles apart. The first Fokker not only accounted for
two aircraft but when joined by another three

German machines, all dropped bombs on four of the warships. The attempted shelling from the sea had failed but ground forces, including Australian light horse, eventually forced the Turkish garrison to leave Bir El Mazar by the 21st. No.1 AFC and 14 Squadrons had assisted by reconnoitring and bombing the town during attacks.

November 1916

By November the British had advanced nearly half the distance from the Nile to the Palestine frontier. The problems posed by the local Arabs in the Western Desert had eased to the point where it was decided that control could be maintained by simple regular air patrolling. This freed considerable resources for redeployment eastwards, to assist in the drive for Palestine. The first step was to take El Arish and use it as a base for further attacks into Syria. The various Flights of No.1 Australian Squadron now began coming together on the 8th of November and the unit was renamed 67 (Australian) Squadron. It and two Flights of 14 Squadron then made wholesale movements eastwards, which saw them begin operating on an extensive new frontier.

2nd November

14Sqn

** combat with EAs shot up fuel tank hit dam, eventually ftl nrRAFA "EoL" then burnt a'c OK(Capt FF Minchin) Capt Freeman drove off EAs and escorted Minchin back until forced to land, then rescued him and flew him back "WoL" sitting on cowl of Martinsyde

Martinsyde G100 14Sqn

** combat with EAs shot up OK(Capt RH Freeman) landed & rescued Capt Minchin who had been forced down

25th November

Egypt

** (Sgt TN Palmer **POW Died**)Turkey

A detachment of six aircraft from 14 Squadron was sent to support the Arab defence of Rabigh on the Red Sea on the 13th of November. It was feared the Turks were planning an attack to retake Mecca which they had evacuated in September. Their advance would need to take Rabigh, and indeed there was fighting in the region which kept this flight on the Red Sea until March. They mostly carried out reconnaissance and photographic work.

December 1916

Concentrations to attack El-Arish continued to build through November and December. The activity brought out the German Air Force and there were many fights of an inconclusive nature. On the 20th of December, however, namely on the eve of the attack, air reconnaissance revealed that the town appeared deserted, and so it proved. A few days before Christmas 1916 the British entered El-Arish unopposed, and in the following days the light horse moved out to take Magdhaba and other enemy positions which air patrols showed were also being abandoned. It became apparent that a general withdrawal was being made to a line between Gaza and Beersheba, and the latter town became the objective for the new year.

2nd December

8372	Short 184	HMS *Empress*

Rec dhAA ovRAMLEH shot down ooc(FSLt AJ Nightingale **POW/Lt PM Woodland **POW**)

8080	Short 184	HMS *Ben-my-Chree*

** search for Short 8372 AA shot up OK(FCdr TH England DFC/Capt J Wedgwood-Benn)

A few pilots of both 14 and 67 (Australian) Squadron had been using Mustabig aerodrome to carry out some daringly deep raids into enemy territory. For instance, the Hejaz railway on the far side of the Dead Sea had been bombed by two Martinsydes on the 24th of November (by Maj RH Freeman and Capt SK Muir of 14 and 67 Squadron respectively). With the exception of the detachment which had been sent to the Red Sea in November, 14 Squadron was moved to Mustabig by the end of November. On the 17th of December, the Australian unit was also moved there in its entirety, in preparation for the advance across the Sinai peninsula into Palestine. The move finally brought this Squadron together as a fighting unit and it also coincided with the re-equipment of the Squadron with BE2es and some BE12s. Increased numbers of Martinsydes arrived and some Bristol Scouts came on strength, so that optimism about the coming year's fighting naturally grew. These types, of course, were already approaching obsolescence on the Western Front.

1917

THE ALLIED MOVE ON GAZA AND PALESTINE

Attacks on Gaza and the general advance into Palestine consumed the Allied efforts in eastern Egypt through 1917. These occurred intermittently

over many months and lacked cohesion and drive, and only as the year closed did they meet with any real success as Jerusalem was captured. The lack of good British aircraft, coupled with sparse facilities and few air personnel in the region, directly contributed to these failures. The units in place worked hard and tenaciously, but were denied real effectiveness because of the quality enemy machines they faced and by the unfolding nature of the battles. The eventual successes which were achieved, however, owed immeasurably to their efforts.

Reconnaissance and air photography of the country ahead of the advance enabled very rapid progress on occasions. On the other hand, any advance eastwards around the Mediterranean had to be a measured one. Progress was only worth making if the logistical means to support it followed smoothly behind. These included the building of the railway through Sinai and water pipelines — waiting for various stages of these to be completed was to hinder the timing of the British campaign throughout 1917.

At this time the War Office was planning to defer the advance into Palestine until the autumn, but to keep the enemy distracted by regular action in the region. The main fighting was to involve an attack on Gaza, but waiting for progress to be made on the railway gave the Turks time to reinforce and build their defences by the time the attack came in late March. In the meantime, the Royal Flying Corps was kept at the head of the advance, feeling the way forward by reconnaissance, and bombing and harassing the enemy along its front.

January 1917

The year began encouragingly enough with a successful assault on the important Turkish garrison town of Rafah on the 9th of January. This was an extremely well managed attack which owed much to the air support provided. Not only was very effective fire directed onto the Turkish defences but enemy reinforcements were spotted approaching the town and the attack was redoubled and driven through before these troops could effect the outcome. Capt Kingsley, noted below, was probably wounded in this operation. After this victory the way eastwards was cleared, but fighting on the ground again subsided and air activity became the chief offensive weapon. Aerodromes were bombed, in particular that at Beersheba, to the point where the German Air Force evacuated it in the middle of the month and moved to Er Ramle. The British meanwhile concentrated on the construction of their

railway across Sinai.

10th January

		Martinsyde	14Sqn

** combat shot up(Capt SG Kingsley **WIA**)

23rd January

8004	Short 184	HMS *Anne*

** Turkish rifle fire shot up(FSLt E King OK/Lt NW Stewart **DoW**)

24th January

	BE2c	67 (Australian) Sqn

LRec gunshot(Lt EG Roberts OK/Lt GN Mills **WIA)

February 1917

11th February

	Martinsyde	14Sqn

** a'c on fire ftl **MIA**(2Lt AJ Lazarus-Barlow **POW**) escaped to Alexandria 9.1.19

15th February

	14Sqn

** cr burnt a'c **MIA**(Lt EA Floyer? **POW**/2Lt CB? Palmer **POW**) 15.2.17?, 5.3?, name Hoyer?, initials CV?

March 1917

There was evidence the Turks were continuing a slow fall back towards Gaza where strong defences were known to be in the course of construction. RFC machines were sufficiently close now to be able to carry out a daily tactical reconnaissance of both this town and Beersheba, and all the enemy positions were carefully photographed and mapped. It was also noticed that the enemy was constructing a branch line of its own to supply the Gaza region and Junction Station, between Jerusalem and the sea, and this became the target for heavy bombing in March. The British had been about to attack Turkish positions at Shellal on the 5th of March when air reconnaissance showed that a wholesale evacuation was in progress.

9th March

6295?	BE2e	67 (Australian) Sqn

this a'c? **B JUNCTION STATION engine failed ftl nGAZA **MIA**(2Lt LW Heathcote **POW**)

Bombing was carried out day and night on Junction Station, as many as thirty aircraft being involved through the week.

20th March

4479	BE2c		67 (Australian) Sqn

*B engine failed ftl, eventually flown back to a'dr with McNamara's help OK (Capt DW Rutherford) pilot saved by Lt FH McNamara VC

7486	Martinsyde G100	67 (Australian) Sqn

B rail network nrTELL EL HESI ground fire shot up, descended to rescue Capt DW Rutherford but a'c crashed on take off (Lt FH McNamara VC **WIA) a'c abandoned

Lt FH McNamara was awarded the Victoria Cross for his rescue of Rutherford. Machines from the Australian unit were bombing the enemy rail network near Tell el Hesi when Rutherford was forced down with engine trouble. McNamara came down to his assistance through ground fire and landed despite being wounded in the thigh. His wound prevented him from leaving his aircraft to help start Rutherford's, so the latter climbed onto the Martinsyde and they attempted to take off. McNamara was unable to control the machine because of his leg and it crashed and turned over. The two men struggled back to the BE2c, receiving some covering fire from the other aircraft above, and with McNamara flying the machine they finally managed to take off. He was losing a great deal of blood but somehow held himself together long enough to fly back to his aerodrome seventy miles away. He was rushed to hospital from where he gradually recovered his health.

24th March

	Martinsyde G100	14Sqn

**EscRec AA fuel tank hit engine failed ftl 4m nASHKELON in sea OK (Lt WEL Seward) escaped capture by swimming out to sea for 4 hours, returned to shore and eventually walked down the coast past GAZA to safety

26th March
THE FIRST BATTLE OF GAZA

The first battle of Gaza began on the 26th of March. In preparation, two flights of 67 (Australian) Squadron had moved to the aerodrome at Rafah on the 25th so as to be closer, and there were other elements of 5th Wing available. However, only twelve Allied aircraft were allocated for direct co-operation with the ground forces, being ordered to carry out contact, reconnaissance and patrol work. Their machines were typically obsolete and in marked contrast to the Halberstadt fighters and various two-seaters which the German Air Force had in the area.

When the ground advance began in the morning both sides struggled for air intelligence through thick fog, but in general, the German airmen had the best of it. In the previous two weeks they had been able to patrol more or less unmolested and had brought in clear indications of the intended British attack. As a result, the lightly defended Turkish garrison at Gaza had been substantially reinforced and this soon told on the attack. By the 27th it was clear Gaza was not to be taken as further Turkish reinforcements flooded into the area. The lack of an effective British air counter to the enemy reconnaissance work had cost them dearly. The German air effort could have been much worse for the Allies, but they were clearly conserving their resources for the fighting ahead. Many more attacks might have been made on the old British machines, but on the other hand, it had not been necessary.

28th March

BE2c	67 (Australian) Sqn

AOb attacked by Aviatik from below shot up (Capt DW Rutherford **WIA/Lt WR Hyam **DoW** 30.3.17)

This was the first serious air combat involving the Australian Squadron.

April 1917
THE SECOND BATTLE OF GAZA

After the first battle of Gaza a major change in British policy for the region occurred. It was decided there would now be a general offensive with the aim of taking Jerusalem by the end of the year. The importance of the region had also escalated for the Turkish, however, and the area around Gaza had become an entrenched front line for them, with defences now stretching the twelve miles to the sea. This situation greatly changed the character of the fighting as a more methodical and extensive campaign evolved. Its first stage was an effective siege of Gaza, with much greater use of artillery. This naturally needed increased air co-operation as well as a comprehensive programme of air photography, but German air superiority continued unchallenged and this gave them a clear advantage. On the ground, the Turks themselves brought up significant reinforcements of their own. These developments may have impelled the British to attack before time for the preliminary advance for the second battle of Gaza was completed by the 17th of April and the direct assault began on the 19th. Their insufficient resources told, however, and the attack failed.

20th April

A1583　　　Martinsyde G102　　　67 (Australian) Sqn
this a'c? **Bombing cavalry, AA shot down "EoL"
MIA(2Lt NL Steele POW DoW)

The Allied airmen were able to contribute more widely in this battle, its more traditional structure lending itself to air co-operation. Their work included some very vital reconnaissance work which for instance on the 20th prevented a dangerous Turkish counter-attack. Large enemy troop concentrations were spotted and then bombed, and the casualty above was caused in the course of this action. In general, however, the RFC could do little to prevent the lack of progress on the ground.

May 1917

After the failure of the assault on Gaza the fighting in Palestine settled into six months of protracted trench warfare. In this time the decision was finally taken to increase and reorganise the air strength in the region. From this a complete air supremacy for the Allies would eventually flow, but in the meantime, the units in place continued operations typical of a quiet theatre. The Australian Squadron made long distance reconnaissances and bombing raids whilst 14 Squadron carried out tactical work and artillery co-operation as required.

11th May

Martinsyde G100　　　67 (Australian) Sqn
** combat with Fokker shot up then Very Light exploded ftl(Lt JV Tunbridge MC WIA)burnt, invalided to Australia ["Mart" claim combat nr TEL EL SHERIA, BEERSHEBA Ltn F Schleiff/Oblt Daum FAb300]

16th May

Martinsyde G100　　　67 (Australian) Sqn
** combat with EA shot up ftl(Capt AM Jones MC WIA)leg [?"English EA" combat nrGALJUN Oblt Felmy FAb300]

30th May

6781?　　　BE2e　　　　　67 (Australian) Sqn
this a'c? **AObAA shot down "WoL" ovGAZA(Lt GC Stones KIA/2Lt JA? Morgan KIA) initials AJ?

June 1917

25th June

BE12a　　　　　　　67 (Australian) Sqn
**EscRec combat with 3 Fokkers nrTEL EL SHERIA shot down "EoL"(Lt JS Brasell KIA) shot through head [?combat seKAFIE Ltn F Schleiff FAb300]

July 1917

25th June

A6321　　　BE12a　　　　　　67 (Australian) Sqn
this a'c? ** combat with EAs driven down "EoL"
MIA(2Lt CH Vautin POW) ["BE" claim combat nrBET HANUN Oblt Felmy FAb300]

Martinsyde　　　67 (Australian) Sqn
** combat with EA tail collapsed cr(Capt CA Brookes UK. KIA) Brookes attached from RFC [?possible "English 1Str" nr TEL EL SHERIA Oblt K Jancke/Offst Kern FAb300]

23rd July

BE2e　　　　　　14Sqn
** dhAA swGAZA MIA(Capt RN Thomas KIA/2Lt JW Howells KIA)

August 1917

1st August

No. 111 Squadron was formed at Deir-el-Belah on the 1st of August from a nucleus Flight provided by personnel of No.14 Squadron. It was to be a new fighter unit to operate under 5th Wing. It had no aircraft at its foundation but within a week began to acquire a mixture of types including Vickers FB19 Bullets, Bristol M1Cs, DH2s, and a Bristol Scout for testing purposes. These were sufficient to form two Flights. As an active fighter squadron it needed significantly better machines than these if it was to exert an influence, and on the 25th of September its first three Bristol Fighters came on strength. With these aircraft the slower machines could be given safe escort. More Bristols followed, and as its personnel became more familiar with the country and settled into their routines on their F2bs increasing numbers of German machines began to be attacked and shot down. On the 29th of September the German Commander of the Sinai front would inform his superiors that "The mastery of the air has unfortunately for some weeks completely passed over to the British . . . Our airmen estimate the number of British aircraft at from thirty to forty." There would still be only a single Flight at this time.

8th August

DH2　　　　　111Sqn
+*Esc combat with 2EAs[+?driven off ooc] OK(2Lt RC Steele)

This was the first recorded air fight for 111 Squadron and, incidentally, very likely to be the last

combat claim made on the most venerable DH2 pusher type. The aircraft may have been A2628 which had been acquired from 14 Squadron the day before and which was sent to X Aircraft Park on the 11th, after it had been perhaps shot up.

12th August

BE2e   14Sqn
** combat with EA ALEXANDRIA(2Lt WI Jamieson WIA/2Lt JH Maingot OK) combat over tank redoubt

25th August

111 Squadron took delivery of its first three Bristol Fighters (A7190, A7194, and A7196).

September 1917

The ongoing reorganisation of the Allied arm in the area saw the creation of the Palestine Brigade. This included all RFC forces east of the Suez Canal. A new corps Squadron, No. 113, was additionally formed in September.

1st September

A6311   BE12a   67(Australian) Sqn
+* combat with AlbatrosDIII[+des] BEERSHEBA 9-20am OK(Lt RM Smith)

This was the first air combat victory for 67 (Australian) Squadron.

October 1917

4th October

A5233   Vickers FB19   111Sqn
+* combat with AlbatrosDIII[+ooc] HUJ-BEIT HANUN 11-40am OK(Lt CR Davidson)

8th October

A7194   Bristol F2b   111Sqn
+* combat with AlbatrosDIII[+capt] OK(2Lt RC Steele Can./Lt JJ Lloyd-Williams)

Following 2Lt Steele's driving down of an enemy aircraft on the 8th of August there had been a further two possible enemy driven down by Lt CR Davidson in one of the unit's Vickers FB19s, but these had been inconclusive. On the 8th, Steele and Lloyd Williams drove down an Albatros DIII and this time it was captured. The German serial was 636/17 and the pilot was Oblt Ditmar. This was the first enemy machine captured in Egypt and Steele was awarded the DSO.

30th October

N1262   Short 184   HMS *Raglan*
Port Said **ArtSpot GAZA combat with Halberstadt after spotting shot up ftl sea & salvaged(FLt EJ Burling OK/ Capt WR Kempson **WIA**) a'c wrecked once back on board

THE THIRD BATTLE OF GAZA

The third battle of Gaza began on the 31st of October with an infantry attack on Beersheba. Naval forces were heavily involved in bombardments of Gaza's defences and rail facilities, and this seaplane was spotting for the *Raglan* on the eve of fighting.

The keys to the British battle plan were the effective deception of the enemy in the weeks preceding the attack and the speed of the assault to prevent Turkish reinforcements coming into play. Both these relied on careful planning, in which the air arm played a vital part. The Turkish defences were now formidable and detailed air photography was used to locate their weakest parts. These were around Beersheba and formed the target of the attack. To allay enemy suspicions various ruses were played out to indicate interest in other sections of the line. From the 27th the RFC was expected to prevent all German aircraft from obtaining intelligence about the Beersheba front. One enemy machine got through on the 30th and made a reconnaissance, but was then shot down by Peck and Lloyd-Williams as it was recrossing the lines. Worrying news also came at this time that the German air units in the area were about to be substantially enhanced, but there were no machines forthcoming to counter this.

The attack on Beersheba began on the 31st, for which both the RFC and offshore RNAS machines offered artillery co-operation, as well as strategic and tactical reconnaissance which proved vital. There was also offensive patrolling and contact work. The taking of Beersheba was achieved and attention turned immediately towards Gaza on the coast. An initial night attack on the town was launched on the 1st/2nd of November, with the moon so bright and brilliant that air support could be used.

November 1917

The first week of November saw a continued advance through the lines of Turkish defences and the steady disintegration of their resistance. By the 8th the Turkish Army was in full retreat. As in France at this time, the RFC found itself increasingly involved in ground attacks and strafing

of enemy positions and personnel. On all fronts, the aircraft was becoming a powerful battlefield weapon. For a few days the rout which had been induced behind Gaza gave ample scope for this work, as well as an opportunity for low level bombing of enemy air fields and communications. The chance was taken to damage the retreating enemy air force as much as possible, and they were largely bombed out of the fighting. Ground strafing was also used to draw enemy fire with the aim of exposing the enemy positions. On a more general level the appearance of harassing, attacking aircraft low over the retreating Turkish infantry had the same psychological effect as elsewhere. It caused heightened and material panic, and contributed to the grim news of disaster that was now spreading all the way back to Jerusalem.

10th November

BE2e   14Sqn
B shot up dam(2Lt HJ Hammer **WIA)rib slight, bullet hit cigarette case

BE2e   14Sqn
B mg fire **MIA(2Lt HLC McConnell **DoW** 24.11.17) DoW in Damascus

These casualties came about during an attack on the railway bridge near Junction Station, over the Wadi es Sarar. This important station was being bombed to hinder the Turkish withdrawal and the destruction of the bridge would have additionally isolated an important railway centre. The raid was not a success, none of the bombs exploding.

In the coming days Junction Station became the focus for the advance, for taking it would have the effect of dividing the two Turkish armies. A successful attack was carried out by the 14th. General Allenby then decided to contain the Turkish 8th Army on the coast and make an all out drive against the 7th Army, with the goal of reaching Jerusalem itself. To lend assistance, all RFC Squadrons began to move forward with ground forces.

24th November

111Sqn
** combat with EA(Lt Horan **WIA**)

The German Air Force became more active from the 24th. They were operating from a new aerodrome at Tul Karm, and this was bombed on the 28th and 29th.

28th November

BE2e   14Sqn
** rifle fire(Lt JW Mitchell **WIA**/Lt Bates OK)

29th November

111Sqn
** combat with EA(2Lt Gilham **WIA**)

A7184   Bristol F2b   111Sqn
this a'c? ** (Cpl W Richards **WIA**/2AM PL Smith **WIA**)

113Sqn
** (Sgt AJ Sampson **DoW**)

In late November SE5as came on strength of the Palestine Brigade.

December 1917

THE CAPTURE OF JERUSALEM

The main attack to capture Jerusalem began on the 8th of December. It was accompanied by a few days of heavy rain which left the exposed RFC machines mostly sodden and useless. Some brave attempts were made to get one or two machines into the air, but the Command was conscious of how precious they were and little flying was done until the rain stopped. Operations included reconnaissance and low strafing and bombing of troops. By the evening of the 8th the Turkish forces began abandoning Jerusalem to the attackers and on the 11th General Allenby walked through the Jaffa gate to take possession of the city for the Allies.

4th December

B26   SE5a   111Sqn
+* combat with AlbatrosDIII[+ooc] JUNCTION STN 12pm OK(Capt AH Peck)

12th December

A7202   Bristol F2b   111Sqn
+* combat with AlbatrosDVs[+ooc++des] TUL KERAM-WADI AUJA btwn 10-30am & 10-45am OK(Capt RM Drummond Aust./2AM FJ Knowles)

17th December

A7192   Bristol F2b   111Sqn
+* combat with 2Str[+ftl des] 5m nBIREH 11-15am OK(Lt CR Davidson/2Lt A Simmons) made 3 claims in this a'c in late December

1918
January 1918
PLANS FOR AN ATTACK ON JERICHO

Allenby was not content with the great victory his army had won in Jerusalem — he knew he must

push further northwards in order to remove the threat of Turkish artillery. Despite very heavy rains which hindered and delayed this consolidation, the army had driven the enemy a further ten miles north of the city by the new year, at which distance the exhausted Turks seemed prepared to remain. Another benefit this final push had yielded for the British was that the lateral supply line from Jaffa on the coast to Jerusalem was now secure.

The weather encountered during these operations had meant the air support had been restricted. Corps work included artillery co-operation and reconnaissance, and all units had at some time carried out strafing and bombing of retreating troops. Some of the latter operations had involved as many as thirty-six aircraft in a day, but there had not been a single loss in action.

At the start of 1918 the Palestine Brigade consisted of 14 Squadron at Junction Station, and 113 Squadron at Deiran, making up the 5th (Corps) Wing. The 40th (Army) Wing was at Julis, comprising 67 (Australian) Squadron, and 111 Squadron. One of the main priorities for the RFC at this time was the photographing and proper mapping of the surrounding enemy positions, and 67 (Australian) Squadron carried out this work in the last two weeks of January. The area most concentrated upon was the Jordan Valley and Jericho to the east, for this was where Allenby was planning to launch his next attack. The regions to the north were the main objective of the Palestine campaign, but they were presently flooded, and in any case Allenby would need more resources for that campaign than were presently available. By taking Jericho and crossing the Jordan he would secure his flank in depth, and disrupt important lines of enemy communications. It also meant that British forces could finally link up with friendly Arab forces who were fighting the Turks near the Dead Sea. So although there was little fighting on the ground in this period of preparation, the work of the airmen was very intense as much needed to be done. Typically, the aerial bombing offensive aimed at wearing down the enemy also continued despite the general hiatus on the ground. His anti-aircraft batteries and aircraft attempted to hinder this work and very many combats took place in the first three months of the year. Some of these are noted below in order to record a few of the notable airmen on the front.

3rd January

B1128   Bristol F2b   67(Australian) Sqn
+*EscB EL AFULE A'dr combat with 2AlbatrosDVs[+ shot down cr] 9-20am OK(Lt RA Austin/Lt LW

Sutherland) EA cr near railway btwn EL AFULE & JENIN

This was the first enemy aircraft conclusively destroyed in combat by the Australian Squadron.

4th January

B5854   RE8   67(Australian) Sqn
this a'c? **B JENIN a'dr MIA(Lt JDS Potts KIA/2Lt VJ Parkinson NZ. inj POW) left 7-05am, air collision with EA which had attacked 113Sqn RE8, observer died?

9th January

14Sqn
**Phot mg(Lt T Owen WIA)

Bristol F2b   111Sqn
** combat shot up(Lt CR Davidson WIA/Capt JJ Lloyd-Williams OK) pilot had made several victory claims in late 1917

10th January

A3796   RE8   67(Australian) Sqn
**Rec left 8am KERAM AA shot up(Lt AV Tonkin OK/ Lt G Finlay WIA) KERAM & KALKILIEH: both "renowned hot-pots", Finlay WIA twice

17th January

A7192   Bristol F2b   111Sqn
+* combat with 2Str[+des] KALKILIEH 9-20am OK(Capt AL Fleming/Cpl FJ Knowles) this crew claimed again the following day in F2b A7148

A575   BE12a   67(Australian) Sqn
+*Phot combat with AlbatrosDIII[+?down in vertical dive] ovNABLUS HILLS 12000' shot up OK(Lt LTE Taplin) in morning, went on with photography after combat

This was one of the last combats for 67 Squadron in a BE12a before being fully equipped with Bristol Fighters.

A7194   Bristol F2b   67(Australian) Sqn
+*RecNABLUS combat with 5AlbatrosDIIIs[+?ooc] EL LUBBAR 11000' 9-15am OK(Lt LMS Potts/Lt FW Hancock) attacked by other EA so could not follow down

20th January

A7202   Bristol F2b   67(Australian) Sqn
**Rec nrCOAST AA eng hit ftl "EoL" the destroyed a'c(2Lt AA Poole POW/Lt FW Hancock POW) left 8-30am, AA from TUL KERAM or KALKILIEH

Lt AR Brown & Lt G Finlay in another Bristol Fighter attempted to rescue this crew by proposing to land, but enemy troops were too near.

23rd January

B538   SE5a   111Sqn
+* combat with AlbatrosDIII[+des] TUL KERAM
11-45am OK(Capt AL Fleming)

This was the first SE5a victory for 111 Squadron. Its use of the Bristol Fighter was being phased out after three months' service, and instead it was to be fully equipped with single-seat fighters. Its Vickers Bullets and Bristol M1Cs were also replaced, so that by the end of February its equipment consisted of a single Flight of Nieuport 17s and two Flights of SE5as. With these aircraft it became a potent fighting force.

Henri Farman   Aden
** brought down "EoL" flames(2Lt JB? Thomas **KIA**/Sgt Hartley **KIA**)

Henri Farman   Aden
** shot up ftl wr(Lt Mann OK/Lt Owden **WIA**)

February 1918

2nd February

142 Squadron was formed at Ismailia on the 2nd of February. It was taken on strength of 40th (Army) Wing on the 13th and provisionally allotted the remaining BE12as of 67 (Australian) Squadron. It was destined to become a corps squadron in June, carrying out army co-operation work in the Jordan Valley.

6th February

67 (Australian) Squadron was redesignated 1 Squadron, Australian Flying Corps on the 6th of February.

19th February
THE TAKING OF JERICHO

The march towards Jericho began on the 19th, with 14 Squadron providing air support to the advance. This was immediately handicapped by four days of gales, but there had been early signs that the Turkish forces were in any case abandoning the city, and so it proved. On the 21st the cavalry entered Jericho and secured the British right flank.

March 1918

The further objective of creating a sizeably clear front north of the Dead Sea in order to attack east of the Jordan had not yet been achieved, however, and this occupied the following month. Allenby moved northwards against stiffening Turkish opposition on the 8th, towards the Wadi El Auja tributary. Aiding him in this attack were the machines of 1 AFC, 111 and 142 Squadrons, who repeatedly patrolled and bombed the enemy from the air, and 113 Squadron who had carefully registered the enemy positions in advance and directed highly accurate artillery fire. There was some enemy activity in the air opposing these operations but most fighting was inconclusive. All squadrons nevertheless made claims in March. In only a few days' fighting the general line had been advanced a further seven miles along a twenty-six mile front, and the British Army was in a strong position, for the first time able to strike both north and eastwards.

19th March

B1128   Bristol F2b   1Sqn AFC
this a'c? **EscB(142Sqn) EL KUTRANI **MIA**(Capt RA Austin MC **POW**/Lt OM Lee **POW**) landed to help Evans but broke wheel, burnt a'c

A3960   Martinsyde G102 142Sqn
this a'c? **B EL KUTRANI eng fai ftl "EoL" nrKERAK(Capt AJ Evans **POW**) burnt a'c

The story of the mishaps which befell these airmen is told in *The Escaping Club* by AJ Evans.

21st March

By March the Arab revolt the Allies had promoted was gaining momentum. Allenby therefore desired to drive it forward by continuing his campaign east of the Jordan. For his own purposes he also hoped fighting in this region would force the enemy to deploy greater numbers of troops there, thus depriving the coastal region where his ultimate objectives lay. The first attack across the river was launched on the 21st with the aim of destroying the Hejaz railway at Amman. The second was planned for April and would capture key Turkish garrisons in the Es-Salt region. The attack on Amman was plagued from the start by bad weather. The river was swollen and extremely difficult to cross, so that three vital days were wasted in this effort whilst Turkish reinforcements flowed into the area. Wind and rain also made air support tenuous, but they bombed bridges and reconnoitred where possible. Es-Salt was temporarily taken enroute on the 26th. One New Zealand raiding party reached the railway and blew up a section, but all other subsequent attempts failed, as did an attempt to take Amman itself. A withdrawal was ordered on the 30th and by the 2nd of April all troops were back west of the

Jordan. This was the first setback in Palestine for a year.

23rd March

B52   SE5a   111Sqn
+* combat with AlbatrosDIIIs[++ooc] & 2Str[+ooc]
nJERICHO ~9-30am OK(Capt AH Peck) 23.4?, last of 8
victories with 111Sqn

27th March

B3597   Nieuport 17   111Sqn
+*HAP combat with Rumpler & 6AlbatrosDVs[+des+
ooc] TEIYIBEH btwn 8-30am & 8-45am OK(Capt RM
Drummond Aust. DSO MC) last of 8 claims

This Rumpler had been seen patrolling over Jaffa and Drummond and another pilot went up to drive it off. They chased it back to its aerodrome at Tul Keram, and Drummond believed he wounded its observer. During this attack, six Albatros fighters arrived from the north and began a dogfight with Drummond in which he shot two of them down. The combat was too hot, however, his single machine-gun and failing engine leaving him vulnerable. He was forced down and eventually spun and landed on the German aerodrome. He was about to give himself up when his engine recovered a little and he decided to make a break for it. Flying only a few feet above the ground he gained half a mile on the enemy fighters before they realised what he had done. He eventually regained the lines, having landed a further four times in enemy territory owing to his engine and the effects of intense ground fire which he suffered for most of his trip home.

April 1918

In the early summer the RAF fighter squadrons in Palestine carried out some of their heaviest sustained fighting of the campaign. The main British offensive was now intended for September and there was little to be gained in fighting on the ground before that time. Thousands of troops were being shipped back to fight on the Western Front, and most efforts by the army were geared towards securing their positions and preparing for the great attack. In the air, in contrast, the British and Australian airmen were required to apply constant pressure to the enemy by bombing, reconnoitring, and harassing along his entire front, one aim of which was to draw German fighters into combat. Aerial superiority was wholly in Allied hands, and whilst this could be used to thoroughly expose the enemy's intentions, it had also to be used to destroy

his own ability to observe. In the three months of April to June, 111 Squadron, for instance, claimed to have engaged the enemy forty-five times, in which seventeen enemy machines were destroyed for the loss of three of their own.

10th April

B3594   Nieuport 17   111Sqn
** MIA(2Lt TL Steele DSO **KIA**)

12th April

B8242   SE5a   111Sqn
+* combat with AlbatrosDVs[++ooc] TUL KERAM
btwn 7-15am & 7-20am OK(Capt AL Fleming Can.) last
of 8 claims

15th April

B3595   Nieuport 17   111Sqn
+* combat with 2Str[+des] seTUL KERAM 5pm
OK(Capt AJ Bott Can.)

B3595?   Nieuport 17   111Sqn
this a'c?: this was his usual machine ** combat shot down
MIA(Capt AJ Bott **POW**)

25th April

B6601   RE8   142Sqn
test MIA(Maj ER? McGregor-Turnbull **POW/Lt CT
Repton **KIA**) initials MR?

28th April

C4626   Bristol F2b   1Sqn AFC
+* combat with 3AlbatrosDIIIs[+ooc] sNABLUS
5-45pm OK(Lt EP Kenny?/Lt FC Hawley) name Kenny?,
first of several claims for pilot in this a'c

30th April

Allenby launched a second, stronger attack across the Jordan at Es-Salt on the 30th. This also failed because of the weight of enemy reinforcements which eventually opposed it. Air reconnaissance also failed to detect some of the early key movements of Turkish forces but then gave invaluable assistance in the retreat. There were also two Australian crews lost on the 1st (see below). A withdrawal was ordered on the 3rd of May and completed the next day.

May 1918

1st May

A7196   Bristol F2b   1Sqn AFC
this a'c? **Rec ldg to aid B1146? then cr on re-take off
burnt a'c MIA(Lt FW Haig **POW**/Lt RT Challinor
POW)

B1146   Bristol F2b   1Sqn AFC
this a'c? **Rec ground mg nrAMMAN ftl burnt a'c
MIA(Capt DW Rutherford **POW**/2Lt J McElligott
POW) Haig tried rescue the crew above

The two crews above were dropping leaflets on the
Beni Sakr Arabs when Rutherford's machine was hit
by ground fire and forced to land. Haig came down
to rescue them but a wheel broke on take-off and the
machine turned on its nose. Both aircraft were burnt
before the four airmen were taken prisoner.

3rd May

B1149   Bristol F2b   1Sqn AFC
+*EscB AMMAN combat with 2Str[+des]
swSUWEILAH 7am then shot up AMMAN A'dr &
troops OK(Capt AR Brown/Lt G Finlay)

4th May

**   1Sqn AFC**
** Enemy bomb raid(1AM WH Fell **KIA**)

**   142Sqn**
** (2Lt RC van der Ben **WIA**)

7th May

B1129   Bristol F2b   1Sqn AFC
+* combat with 2Str[+flames] 1m seJENIN A'dr 3-15pm
OK(Capt RM Smith/Lt EA Mustard) shared victory,
pilot's first of 10 victories in this a'c

23rd May

C4627   Bristol F2b   1Sqn AFC
+* combat with AlbatrosDVs[+ooc+ftl des] NABLUS
btwn 7am & 7-15am OK(Lt CS Paul NZ./Lt WJA Weir)
the 2nd EA was probably from Ja1F (Vzfw Schneidewind)
this crew made several claims

June 1918

4th June

B1276   Bristol F2b   1Sqn AFC
**Rec combat with RumplerC gun jam shot up engine
hit(Lt AV Tonkin OK/Lt RA Camm **WIA**) left 5-30am

9th June

B614   SE5a   111Sqn
this a'c? ** HAP **MIA**(Lt EW Greswell **KIA**)

11th June

B1681?   Nieuport 17   111Sqn
this a'c? ** dhAA cowling knocked off and caught in the
empennage, spin ooc but shaken lose and ftl cr wr OK(Lt
AD Gledhill) pilot made a claim in this a'c on 8.6.18

26th June

C4623   Bristol F2b   1Sqn AFC
**P combat with AlbatrosC ovRAMLEH 18000' shot
up(Lt AW Murphy OK/Lt AWK Farquhar **KIA**) left
11-45am, EA observer was also hit?

27th June

A7236   Bristol F2b   1Sqn AFC
**EscRec combat with 2AEG 2Strs[+?ftl] 4000' then hit
by ground fire cr **MIA**(Lt GV Oxenham **KIA**/Lt LH
Smith **WIA POW**) seen in distant combat with other AEG
by B1149

B1149   Bristol F2b   1Sqn AFC
**EscRec combat with 2AEG 2Strs[+smoking] 4000'
OK(Capt AR Brown/Lt G Finlay)

July 1918

17th July

B696   SE5a   111Sqn
+* combat with AlbatrosDV[+des] BEIT DEGAR
7-35am OK(Lt HL Swinburne) [Ltn Kruger Ja1F **KIA**]

This was the last combat victory for 111 Squadron.
The unit was becoming less involved in offensive
and line patrolling, and concentrating more on low
bombing work. The unit was to be heavily engaged
in the fighting of the final offensive, but although
there were some other unconfirmed claims made,
they were less likely to meet the enemy in their
changing role. The mantle of responsibility to take
the fight to the enemy in the air passed to the
Australian unit.

**   111Sqn**
** (Lt AD Gledhill **WIA**)

29th July

**   RE8   14Sqn**
B attacking AA Section136 shot down **MIA(Capt SL
Pettit **POW**/Lt GJ Williams **POW**) Turkey, repat
16.12.18

August 1918

14th August

144 Squadron was formed as a DH9 bombing unit
at Junction Station on the 14th of August. It became
part of 40th (Army) Wing for Allenby's offensive in
September and was to play a vital role in the wholesale destruction of the enemy communications
systems. Prior to the attack, however, in common
with all other units, it was not openly used on the
active front in order to keep Allied intentions secret.
One Flight of a new SE5a fighter squadron, No. 145,

was also incorporated into the 40th Wing on the same day. In the coming battle it was to work mostly with 111 Squadron.

22nd August

B1222   Bristol F2b   1Sqn AFC
this a'c? **P combat with 2Str fuel tank shot up seen going down in flames to sw from SAMEIL(Lt JM Walker **KIA**/ Lt HA Letch MC **KIA**)

B1284   Bristol F2b   1Sqn AFC
+* combat with RumplerC[+capt] RAMLEH 1-15pm OK(Capt AR Brown/Lt G Finlay) Brown claimed 5 EA with this squadron

24th August

C4623   Bristol F2b   1Sqn AFC
+* combat with PfalzDIIIs[+flames+ftl,des] KALKILIEH 8-30am OK(Lt PJ McGinness/Lt HB Fletcher) McGinness claimed several victories on F2bs

ALLIED AIR SUPREMACY BEFORE THE MAIN BATTLE

The few entries based on combat reports which are given occasionally in this record bear no real relation to the tremendous amount of air fighting which the RAF carried out through the summer. With it, they had gradually built up their influence to a point of complete air superiority. 111 Squadron fighters had slowly stemmed enemy air activity in the first months, after which the Australian Flying Corps had positively withered it in the autumn. Every machine shot down in Palestine in the two months before Allenby's offensive was at the hands of an Australian crew.

In the previous five months the German air forces in the region had been dealt a terrible blow. They operated with high quality machines and fought with notable bravery — they had made desperate and costly efforts to cross the lines in August — but any hopes they had of securing superiority of the skies had long since faded. In the spring they had shown every intention of carrying out a full programme of reconnaissance, repeatedly challenging the Allies for air space. 1 AFC records quoted in Cutlack noted that in one week in June ". . . hostile aeroplanes had crossed our lines one hundred times — mainly on the tip-and-run principle. They came over at altitudes (16,000 to 18,000 feet) from which accurate observation was impossible." By August the number of visits recorded in a week had dropped to eighteen.

The Allied campaign in Palestine which would lead to victory was about to commence. What was achieved in its two weeks of remorseless and bloody

advance owed a great deal to the fact that the enemy air force had been resoundingly driven from from the sky. It not only meant that vast British preparations had been able to proceed almost completely unobserved, it also enabled a crushing killer blow to be delivered from the air once the Turkish armies were pushed into headlong retreat.

September 1918

16th September

RE8?   Egypt
MIA(/2Lt J Topping **KIA)

Topping is possibly one of a crew from 144 Squadron lost at this time and described in Cutlack (p167).

19th September
VICTORY IN PALESTINE

General Allenby's decisive offensive was launched on the 19th of September. It was a classic of co-operation between ground and air forces, which is why this part of the book closes with a short study of what happened. It combined surprise with superb preparation, so that a devastating attack which swept through the enemy lines could be brilliantly exploited — the result was that three Turkish armies were annihilated. In the circumstances it was as much the Royal Air Force as any other body which was responsible for the destruction. From their position of complete dominance of the air they carefully helped and influenced its planning, oversaw its execution, and then destroyed the armies as they fled along the valleys.

Allenby's intention was to position the greater part of his strike force on eight miles of line running in from the sea on the extreme left of the front. From here he would create a breach by launching an overwhelming infantry attack which his cavalry would then exploit by driving north-eastwards towards Nazareth, destroying enemy communications and cutting off the lines of retreat of the Turkish Seventh and Eight Armies. Away to the north the most important centre of rail communications was Der'a, where the Palestine and Hejaz railways met, and this would be entrusted to the Arabs under Feisal and led by Colonel TE Lawrence — "Lawrence of Arabia."

The success of this plan was predicated on factors of surprise and preparation, which have been mentioned. Great care was taken to give the impression that the next great attack, when it came,

would be on the Jordan, and the Turks had moved thousands of men there in anticipation. Instead, however, the British and Arab forces would rush in with tremendous force from opposite corners of Palestine, giving the enemy no option but to be driven into a trap. To force the disintegration of the enemy control structure, his transport system was to be crippled early in the battle and his command posts and telephone systems bombed to destruction. Once the expected rout began, the final objective of this campaign was to be the effective annihilation of the Turkish armies in Palestine.

It becomes immediately apparent why control of the air was so vital in this battle — air support was a key factor in each of these stages. Because no enemy airman had been permitted to reconnoitre Allenby's preparations they were totally unexpected. When the attack came, the assault was to be carefully driven through the Turkish positions by close contact patrolling and low bombing and strafing. When the cavalry was set in motion it would move into enemy territory at lightning speed. Months of patient air reconnaissance and mapping which had now been carried out, as well as careful contact work, were crucial to the success of this stage.

It was essential that the Turkish Command be kept ignorant of the extent of this advance until it was well underway, and the air force again played a part in restricting all enemy access to eastern Palestine. The aerial bombing offensive, which began before dawn on the day of the battle, was also vitally important to progress because it was the main means of destroying the enemy's communications. Their efforts were to be brilliantly successful. With no way left of organising its defence, the Turkish Army would be forced to retreat in chaos, and at this time the RAF would become a deadly tactical battlefield weapon, raining death onto the shell of an army. With little variation, this was how the battle unfolded and the air arm, extremely well deployed and managed, played its full part.

There had been little Allied air activity in the preceding days beyond that required to hold the enemy, as all units made their machines as ready as possible. The squadrons which Allenby had at his disposal were as follows. The strengthened 40th Wing consisted of four units: these were Nos.111 and 145 Squadrons (both SE5as), who patrolled over and around the enemy aerodrome at Jenin all day, thereby preventing any enemy air support from developing. They also attacked a plentiful selection of ground targets. 1 AFC (Bristol Fighters) carried out all strategic reconnaissance and bombing, and in effect drove the air offensive forward. 144

Squadron (DH9s) bombed the railway station and main telephone exchange at El Affule, as well as destroying the Turkish headquarters at Nablus. To help in the bombing offensive the RAF also had the use of a Handley Page heavy bomber which had been flown out from England at the end of July. This was on strength of the Australian Flying Corps and in fact it launched the offensive by bombing El Affule in the early hours of the morning. Details of this raid are given below.

The Fifth Wing corps units in the battle were 113 Squadron with the XXI Corps on the coast, 14 Squadron with XX Corps further inland; two Flights of 142 Squadron with the Desert Mounted Corps who exploited the initial assault, and the remaining flight of No. 142 was with the army on the Jordan. All these corps units participated in bombing as well — for instance 142 Squadron bombed headquarters at Tul Karem. In consequence of all this action the Turkish Army Command had lost all communications with Nazareth by 7am, and by the time it was sketchily restored at noon the British army was through their lines and heading north. The German Air Force was also stunned into inaction by the raids of the fighter squadrons — not a single aircraft left the ground.

By early afternoon sections of the Turkish Army were seen abandoning their positions en masse and attempting to retreat. This had been fully anticipated, with the result that every available aircraft was ordered into the sky to launch attacks on these troops. In the months before the battle, all possible routes which now lay open to the Turk had been minutely photographed from the air and studied to reveal where maximum damage from these attacks might be inflicted. Aircraft were sent in great numbers to these points. Selected attacking aircraft carried wireless sets so that headquarters knew almost from moment to moment where bombing could best be directed. The attacks were often flown in pairs, relieved every half hour, and strengthened regularly with larger attacking formations of around six aircraft. There were minimal air casualties on these raids because the Turkish divisions had been driven into disarray.

The regular work of the corps squadrons on this day should also not be forgotten — for instance 113 Squadron flew a record one hundred and five hours on active duty through the day, its machines making fifty-one separate flights. By nightfall the British cavalry had penetrated deeply and begun its arc to the north-east. The following day it would meet this retreating army in the rear and bar its escape.

C9681   H.P. 0/400   1Sqn AFC
**B central telephone exchange of the enemy army group

EL AFFULE OK (Capt RM Smith/Lt EA Mulford/Lt MD Lees/Lt AV McCann) left 1-15am, dropped 16 112-lb bombs

Bristol F2b	1Sqn AFC

LowB TUL KERAM? ground fire ftl **MIA(Lt DR Dowling **WIA**/Lt EA Mulford **WIA**)

According to Cutlack, this crew was wounded and forced to land in enemy territory. They were taken prisoner but recaptured and freed a few hours later by the Australian light horse.

20th September

The Turkish withdrawal widened on the 20th and attacks upon it intensified. On this day, the RAF dropped ten tons of bombs on retreating troops and transport and fired 40,000 rounds of ammunition. The first elements of the cavalry began to intercept the Turks from behind. El Affule was taken and the old German airfield there became an advanced landing ground for reconnaissance machines. After barely a day's fighting the RAF was using an aerodrome which had been forty miles behind enemy lines. This was a true measure of the speed of the advance, and of the part the air service had played in it, and yet the next day's fighting was to be greater still for it saw the crushing of two Turkish armies. This was made possible by an all-out bombing campaign spearheaded by the Australian squadron which in essence finally blocked the main roads of retreat. In consequence, the remnants of the armies were driven onto the Jordan by the 24th and reduced to abject defeat.

C6305	DH9	144Sqn

** **MIA**(Lt KMH Marriott **KIA**) 28.9?

SE5a	145Sqn

**LowB JENIN-EL AFFULE Road eng fail ftl burnt a'c then chased and taken by Turkish soldiers but released again when retreat met elements of cavalry blocking it MIA but OK(2Lt ER Stafford) left 11-30am

22nd September

B1278	Bristol F2b	1Sqn AFC

+* combat with DFWC[+des] 8m nDERAA 5pm OK(Lt GC Peters/Lt JH Traill) then killed German crew on ground with mg fire, last of several claims by Peters

B1286	Bristol F2b	1Sqn AFC

+* combat with 2Str[+flames] MAFRAK-NABIB 10am OK(Lt ES Headlam/Lt WH Lilly) 2Str shared

B1229	Bristol F2b	1Sqn AFC

+* combat with 2Str[+des] MAFRAK 10am then later combat with PfalzDIII[+des+ftl] MAFRAK 10-45am OK(Capt RM Smith/Lt EA Mustard) 2Str shared

This day saw some of the last fighting efforts of the enemy forces in the air. These were to no avail, however, as several machines were shot down, particularly in morning engagements. At dawn a Flight of Bristol Fighters had flown to Lawrence's main Arab encampment at Um es Surab. It was their intention to fly on from there and bomb the German Air Force group at Der'a, which consisted of three Pfalz fighters and a few DFWs. A patrol from Der'a was reported approaching the camp and Smith and Headlam took off with their observers and chased and shot down a two-seater. After this they returned and completed their breakfast which the combat had interrupted. Another flight of Pfalzes was sighted and Smith and Mustard set off again and drove two of them down. Der'a was visited and shot up and then in the afternoon another DFW, which had bombed the Arab camp, was chased by Peters in B1278 and sent down smoking. In this way the German Air Force was reduced to the absolute minimum of effectiveness. RAF bombing raids on enemy aerodromes increased greatly after this time, completing the misery inflicted on these forces. It was later revealed that by now the enemy had begun the withdrawal of much of his air force deep back into Palestine and Syria. Here too, however, they were threatened this time by Arab forces, and eventually retired to the Lebanon.

29th September

C6231	DH9	142Sqn?

** (2Lt JS Wesson **POW**/Lt W Steele **POW**) crew?

30th September

Most RAF units accompanied Allenby's army on its inexorable march northwards. Its speed was only limited by the logistics of servicing its great strides and by the capacity of its horses and men. These constraints naturally affected the work of the RAF as well. On this day Nos. 14 and 113 Squadrons ferried 928 gallons of petrol and 156 gallons of oil to units in the field. The SE5as of 111 Squadron at Ramleh were simply put out of range by the advance and, because of the rationing of resources which was necessary, it was detained there until the end of the fighting. When possibilities for bombing also diminished, 144 Squadron proceeded to Mudros.

News reached the Allies on the 30th that the Turkish forces were retreating from Damascus.

October 1918

19th October

B1229	Bristol F2b	1Sqn AFC

+*combat with DFWC[+des] 25m swALEPPO 18000′
10-30am OK (Capt RM Smith/Lt AV McCann) shared
victory

B1295 Bristol F2b 1Sqn AFC
+*combat with DFWC[+des] 25m swALEPPO 18000′
10-30am OK (Lt ES Headlam/Lt WH Lilly) shared
victory, last of Headlam's 5 claims

This air fighting occurred in advance of the attack
on Aleppo which was begun on the 20th. They
forced the two-seater to land and then, coming down
beside it to accept the surrender of its crew, McCann
set light to it with Very lights and they departed,
leaving the German crew to make the best of it.

23rd October

C4626 Bristol F2b 1Sqn AFC

+*combat with DFWCs[?++forced down to land]
BABANNIT A'dr nALEPPO 6am OK (Lt SH Harper/Lt
WH Lilly) then shot up and bombed these & others on a'dr

These were the last combat claims for 1 Squadron
Australian Flying Corps in the Great War. The unit
had hardly seen an enemy aeroplane in the air for a
month before this last flurry of activity.

25th October

Aleppo was entered on the 25th.

31st October

Turkey surrendered on the 31st of October, bringing
fighting in Palestine to an end.

Part VIII

MESOPOTAMIA 1915–1918

May 1915

OPERATIONS BEGIN IN
MESOPOTAMIA

The first appearance of the Australian Flying Corps
in the Great War was not in France, but in Mesopotamia. Australia had barely conceived of an air
arm as the war began. Only a few rudimentary steps
had been taken towards a flying force which in a few
years would be one of the most admired and
respected of the war. By early 1915 there were still
only a handful of officers, so it came as some surprise
when the Indian Government requested assistance
from Australia in the form of an air unit. It was to
help fight the Turks in Mesopotamia.

Hasty preparations enabled a tiny force of four
flying officers and forty-one other personnel to arrive
at Basra on May 26th. The pilots were Capt TW
White, Lt GP Merz, Lt HA Petre, and Lt WH
Treloar. It would be known as the Mesopotamian
Half Flight, and in the absence of being able to bring
aircraft of their own, the unit began with three
decrepit machines of the Indian Army: two Maurice
Farman Shorthorns and a Longhorn. Two
Caudrons were added on the 4th July. At Basra they
were joined by more flying officers: Capt PWL
Broke-Smith and Capt HL Reilly both of the Indian

Army, and from New Zealand, Lt WWA Burn.

By this time the ground campaign on the Tigris
river was in full spate — that is, as full a spate as
the terrible and debilitating conditions could
permit. Tremendous and unrelenting heat and dust,
a difficult enemy, and a logistical vacuum at the
centre of operations, made progress extremely
difficult. For the flyers, the conditions were to take
a huge toll on machines as well as on their own
stamina as they began active patrolling within a
week of arrival.

July – September 1915

30th July

IFC 3 Caudron G3 AFC Half Flt
*Rec NASIRIYEH engine problems ftl 25m from re-filling
station and helped by friendly Arabs OK (Capt HL Reilly/
Sgt.Mech)

IFC 4 Caudron G3 AFC Half Flt
Rec NASIRIYEH ftl on return **MIA (Lt GP Merz **DoW**/
Lt WWA Burn **DoW**)

The crew of IFC4 were the first casualties suffered
by the Australian Flying Corps on flying operations.
The two Caudrons had been reconnoitring near
Nasiriyeh following its fall on the 24th of July. They
were returning to Basra when they became
separated and then both suffered engine problems.

Reilly and his observer were saved, but little is known about Merz and Burn. One eyewitness said they came down and were immediately attacked by Arabs. After a running battle of several miles, with only service revolvers to defend themselves, they had been captured and murdered. Their bodies were never found, but their wrecked Caudron was eventually located and salvaged.

The Australian Half Flight was absorbed into 30 Squadron RFC in August. Towards the end of the month it received four Martinsyde single-seater scouts as reinforcement, but their performance was very poor. In the coming months they were plagued by equipment problems and losses.

16th September

IFC 3   Caudron G3   AFC Half Flt (att 30Sqn)
Rec ES-SINN rifle fire? engine dam ftl **MIA(Capt WH Treloar **POW**/Capt BS Atkins **POW**) left am?, mishandled by Arabs before being taken prisoner, a'c destroyed, Atkins repatriated 7.12.18

KUT-EL-AMARA TAKEN BY THE BRITISH FORCES

This crew was taken whilst reconnoitring Turkish trenches and emplacements on the Tigris River, on the stretches below Kut. It had been decided in July that the capture of Kut was an absolute necessity, and by the 12th of September concentrations of troops were in place to make the assault. The few aircraft that could be assembled were a vital component in the plans, for they would expose the Turkish strength. Treloar and Atkins' reconnaissance was one of the last Major-General Townsend was seeking in order to finalise his battle plan. When they failed to return, Major Reilly, in the last surviving Caudron, made another recce in the evening, and brought back plans of elaborate Turkish preparations for a defence. The advance commenced on the 26th and the Turks were met two days later. On the 29th, the Turkish defenders abandoned their positions and Kut was entered. Throughout these operations, as well as in subsequent weeks, the few aeroplanes available to the British gave them a vital advantage.

October 1915

10th October

Seaplane Sqn
** (/2Lt.Sir RJ Paul **POW**)

Preparations for the next phase of the campaign in Mesopotamia progressed through October. An attempt would be made to take Baghdad, but first the Turkish forces at Ctesiphon would have to be defeated. The remaining flights of 30 Squadron all reached Mesopotamia at this time, with long awaited reinforcements of aircraft, albeit consisting of four BE2cs and four pilots. Every available machine would be needed to assess the opposing Turkish forces.

November 1915

13th November

IFC 2   MFLH   AFC Half Flt (Att30Sqn)
**SpM:sabotage of telegraph lines nrBAGHDAD
MIA(Capt TW White DFC **POW**/Capt FCC Yeats-Brown DFC **POW**) left at dawn, succeeded in cutting wires, tried ground run escape but failed, destroyed a'c

As well as reconnaissance work there were also some special operations carried out prior to the offensive. One of these was an attempt to isolate Baghdad by blowing up the main telegraph lines north and west of the city, carried out by White and Yeats-Brown. After a long and dangerous flight to the target they unexpectedly found the lines running along a well used road, rather than through the desert. At great risk they carried on and made a landing, but their aircraft ran into a telegraph pole. Although under fire, they managed to blow up the line and then attempted an escape by ground-running the damaged Farman across the desert. The same crew had made a similar amazing escape weeks previously, travelling some fifteen miles through enemy territory to reach safety. This time, however, the attempt failed, and they were taken prisoners. TW White's book, *Guests of the Unspeakable*, is a remarkable account of his service in the East and his subsequent imprisonment after these events.

21st November

IFC 6   Martinsyde S1   AFC Half Flt (Att 30Sqn)
Rec ground fire AA splinter? shot down ftl(Maj HL Reilly NZ. **POW) attempted escape on foot but was captured

23rd November

IFC 8   Martinsyde S1   AFC Half Flt (Att 30Sqn)
Rec CTESIPHON gunfire shot down engine hit ftl (Capt EJ Fulton **POW) including AA?, 20.11?

A very bad month for the Australian Flying Corps continued with the loss of another two pilots and their machines one week later, at the start of the assault on Ctesiphon. Major Reilly's loss was

particularly serious as he had proved himself an able and reliable flyer. The capture of such an experienced man no doubt contributed to the reversals of the following days. With Fulton lost as well, A Flight of 30 Squadron consisted of a single operational Maurice Farman, IFC7, and one pilot, Capt Petre. He flew as much as possible as the 6th Division attempted to advance, but could only watch as Turkish reinforcements slowly ground their efforts to a halt. Eventually a full retreat back to Kut was inevitable.

Kut became the British base in the region, and as such was the focus for a terrible Turkish siege which would last for six months. In the battle to take Ctesiphon the 6th Division had lost a third of their number dead or wounded. The remnants of the Australian Half Flight, along with the elements of 30 Squadron, also quartered themselves in the town. As the siege tightened, however, it was ordered that any machines which could be flown out should immediately depart, and this occurred on the 7th of December.

December 1915

THE TURKISH SIEGE OF KUT-EL-AMARA BEGINS

Some of the Half Flight aircraft in Kut at the time of the evacuation are given below. Along with the few machines left and abandoned were several British pilots, observers, and most of the non-commissioned officers and mechanics, all of whom would have to face a terrible fate. The Turkish forces intended to starve the British garrison to death.

7th December

IFC 7	MFSH	AFC Half Flt (Att 30Sqn)
* flown out of KUT (Capt HA Petre)

| IFC 9 | Martinsyde S1 | AFC Half Flt (Att 30Sqn) |
* damaged so abandoned in KUT

| IFC12 | BE2c | AFC Half Flt (Att 30Sqn) |
possibly one of two BE2cs damaged so abandoned in KUT

| IFC12A | BE2c | AFC Half Flt (Att 30Sqn) |
was 4361, possibly one of two BE2cs damaged so abandoned in KUT

| IFC14 | BE2c | AFC Half Flt (Att 30Sqn) |
was 4363, possibly one of two BE2cs damaged so abandoned in KUT

January – March 1916

An attempt to relieve the Kut garrison was begun in January, and a new corps was formed for the purpose, the "Tigris Corps". The sad fact was that

the RFC could muster only two aircraft to work with this unit, a Maurice Farman and a BE2c, as many of their vital personnel as well as three of their machines were trapped in Kut itself. Two more RNAS aircraft reinforced the two Shorts already at Basra, and the air services combined into a Composite Flight. Misfortune plagued this unit from the start, with nearly every aircraft assembled for the operation crashing or malfunctioning in the opening weeks. Only with the arrival of two all-steel Henri Farmans in February did consistent patrolling begin.

The first enemy bombs were dropped on the Kut garrison on the 13th February. The German unit, Flieger Abteilung 2, was now operating in the region, with machines including monoplane scouts such as the Pfalz Parasol and subsequently the Fokker Eindekker.

5th March

Vs 1541	Voisin	30Sqn
** shot down cr Turkish lines (2Lt RH Peck **KIA**/Capt WG Palmer **KIA**) ["British Voisin" claim on Turkish front FAb2, also Turkish machine-gunners claimed a RFC Voisin at ES-SINN on same day] full correspondence in AIR1/505/16/3/34

April 1916

KUT-EL-AMARA FALLS

The siege of Kut-el-Amara came to an end on the 29th of April, after one hundred and forty-six days of increasing misery for the British garrison. Floods on the Tigris had limited the effectiveness of the relief forces in the final weeks, and their attempts ultimately failed. Notably, aircraft had been used in the last two weeks to deliver food, but these operations had attracted fierce opposition from German machines after the 24th. One hundred and forty food drops were achieved in all, but the feverish desperation which accompanied these efforts to supply the garrison took a great physical toll on those involved.

At the time of the fall, 13,309 persons surrendered, including 3,776 casualties, most of whom were near death. For the injured and wounded troops the end of the siege brought a little care and attention, but it also saw most of the native inhabitants butchered by the Turks. Those who could walk began an enforced march across the Middle East into captivity in Turkey, a journey from which almost five thousand would not return.

26th April

8044	Short 184	D Force
Food Drop into KUT shot down (2Lt CB Gasson **WIA

POW/2Lt AC Thouless **KIA**) [?combat KUT Hpt H
Schüz FAb2]

    BE2c   **30Sqn**
**FoodDrop into KUT controls shot up but ldg ok at
ORA(Lt DAL Davidson **WIA**) BE2c probably unarmed
[?BE claim combat KUT Hpt H Schüz FAb2]

28th April
    BE2c   **30Sqn**
** captured at KUT(Capt B Winfield-Smith **POW**/Capt
SCP Munday **POW**)

    Voisin   **30Sqn**
** captured at KUT(Capt TR Wells MC **POW**/2Lt
CHC? Munro **POW**) initials MH?

                Mesopotamia
** Cpl A Reid **POW**, Died 5.5.16 of enteritis at
SHUMARN nr KUT

29th April
                30Sqn
** (Cpl HL Morris **POW**) captured at KUT, interned
Turkey

                Mesopotamia
** (2AM W Haynes **POW**) interned Turkey

May 1916
7th May
    4558   **BE2c**   **30Sqn**
** in combat with EA ovEUPHRATES RIVER shot up
ftl OK [?2 BE claims combat Hpt H Schüz FAb2] Allied
crew not yet established

RFC Prisoners of War in the Middle East noted in early 1916
                Mesopotamia
** 2AM W Keefe **POW** captured at KUT, died of enteritis
7.5.16

                Middle East
** 1AM FG Draper **POW** interned Turkey ~ 30.5.16

                Middle East
** 2AM RG Nicholls **POW** interned Turkey ~30.5.16

                Middle East
** Sgt FE Read **POW** at BAGTCHE? **DoW** 31.5.17?

August 1916
13th August
    BE2c   **30Sqn**
** combat with "Fokker" ovSHUMRAN A'dr shot up
dam OK(Lt.Hon JHB Rodowney **WIA**/) EA probably a
Pfalz monoplane

    BE2c   **30Sqn**
** combat with "Fokker"[+shot down] ovSHUMRAN
A'dr OK(Lt TE? Lander/Lt EAD Barr) EA had been
attacking Rodowney

This was the first enemy aircraft shot down on the
Mesopotamian front. Shumran airfield was bombed
the next night, the three pilots involved, Capt H de
Havilland, Maj JE Tennant and Capt JH Herring
being heavily shot up by ground fire.

    8054   **Short 184**   **HMS** *Ben-my-Chree*
B BUREIR CAMP engine failed ftl cr **MIA(Cdr GB
Dacre **POW**)

Commander Dacre was lost during the second of
two big bombing operations on this day planned by
Samson. The first hit El Afuleh rail junction. Ten
seaplanes took off and, splitting into two groups,
pressed on through heavy ground fire to cause
considerable damage over the target. A second
raiding patrol of seven seaplanes attacked Bureir
Camp and a railway viaduct at Wadi El Hesi.
Dacre's engine failed on the return journey.

September 1916
Early September
                30Sqn
** 2AM W Fairhead Dead ~9.9.16 previously presumed
POW

23rd September
    Voisin   **30Sqn**
**AP attacked by EA monoplane shot up rudder dam ooc
but recovered for ldg ok OK(Capt JH Herring/Capt L
King-Harman)

December 1916

A continual build-up of forces in Mesopotamia had
proceeded so well that by December all was ready
to renew the Allied offensive towards Baghdad. The
immediate task was to pursue the Turks up the Hai
River. Lines of communication back to Basra had
been strengthened, troops and equipment had been
forthcoming, and a plan of battle settled, so that the
British felt ready to resume the attack. An air
offensive against the German Air Force had won and
maintained air superiority, so that the full range of
reconnaissances, co-operation with artillery, and
bombing had been possible, especially since August,
once 30 Squadron had begun to be supplied with
adequate numbers of machines. The Turkish forces
had also been reinforcing their positions, and would
no doubt defend in strength. Bombardment of their
positions began on the 13th December, and the next
day the ground offensive began.

30 Squadron carried out continuous close reconnaissances and bombing as the infantry advanced,
including a night reconnaissance on the14/15th by

Capt JH Herring. Through December a foothold was gradually established on the Hai.

15th December

BE2c   30Sqn

** rifle fire in the HAI(/Lt JA Ainscow **WIA**) to hospital

January – March 1917

27th January

BE2c   30Sqn

**AP EL SINN attacked by Albatros & Fokker shot up ftl cr "WoL" OK (Lt Baldwin)

1st February

BE2c   30Sqn

+*AReg ovHAI Salient attacked by FokkerE[+shot down] OK (Lt JR Burns/Lt L Beevor-Potts) crew?, took 5 shots to bring down EA

This machine was attacked whilst registering artillery at the moment of an assault on the Turkish third line of the Hai salient. The combat took place over the fighting and greatly boosted the morale of the British troops.

24th February

30Sqn

LowB attacked retreating troops ovEUPHRATES shot up(/Lt AR Rattray **WIA) NB not 24.2.1918 as some sources

THE ATTACK ON BAGHDAD

Consolidation of the right bank of the Tigris was also complete by the middle of February and the decision was taken to attack the formidable enemy forces on the other side. This required an initial assault in order to permit the construction of a bridge, essential to the success of the operation. Work on it was able to begin on the 23rd. The RFC played a vital part in preventing German aircraft from finding out about its existence until it was mostly complete. Through February and March a series of battles then proceeded to roll up the enemy forces along the left bank, until on the 11th of March Baghdad was finally entered. 30 Squadron had continued to be the sole unit available for these operations, with each Flight specialising in a particular duty. From the time of the crossing of the Tigris, with air superiority gained, they had exerted their full influence on events. The featureless terrain across which these operations took place offered no concealment for the enemy, and their movements well back behind the fighting could be easily reconnoitred. By the time the advance reached these areas the airmen could direct artillery co-operation onto

well understood positions. 30 Squadron now moved their base to Baghdad and over the next six weeks consolidated the surrounding country.

April 1917

The balance of air superiority in Mesopotamia altered in April with the arrival of new German fighters. With these the enemy air activity greatly increased for they were better than any machines with which the RFC could oppose them. As a consequence some Bristol Scouts were hastily transferred from Egypt and some SPADs were promised.

3rd April

4585   BE2c   30Sqn

**Rec combat with Fokker ovBELED shot up and collided with enemy ftl OK (Lt LSM Page/Lt AR Rattray) returned KHASIRIN [claimed he rammed BE in combat BALAD, TIGRIS RIVER 6-30am Hpt H Schüz FAb2] German recovered from being out of control and reportedly returned with a piece of BE2c wing attached.

15th April

4500   BE2c   30Sqn

Rec BASRA combat nrSAMARA (Capt CL Pickering **KIA/Lt HW Craig **KIA**) ["BE" claim combat SAMARA, TIGRIS front Hpt H Schuez FAb2, and buried by him]

This aircraft had been operating in Mesopotamia since before the battle of Ctesiphon in 1915

22nd April

Bristol Scout   30Sqn

** combat HalberstadtD[+broke up,des] OK (2Lt ML Maguire MC) EA crashed nrISTABULAT

This combat took place during the final fighting for Samarra, and was again in full view of the troops.

28th April

Bristol Scout   30Sqn

** BELED combat **MIA** (2Lt ML Maguire MC **POW DoW** 5.17) [?unconfirmed "EA" claim combat TIGRIS Hpt H Schüz FAb2]

30Sqn

** shot down in combat OK? (2Lt JB Lloyd)

May – September 1917

6th May

7466?   Martinsyde   30Sqn

** BELED combat with EA **MIA** (Lt TE Lander MC **WIA POW**) probably this a'c as it was in combats on 4.2.17 & in May 1917, and was known to be lost only to be re-captured from the Turks on 6.11.17

The Royal Flying Corps in Mesopotamia became the 31st Wing RFC on the 15th of June.

The summer of 1917 in the Tigris-Euphrates basin proved to be extremely hot and arduous for all those unlucky enough to be stationed there. After the successes of the battles for Baghdad most of the troops were moved to cooler parts to be rested, but 30 Squadron remained in the desert in order to carry out an extensive programme of photography. This they did by flying in the early morning and evening, and by late summer most of the enemy territory relevant for the autumn campaigns had been recorded and mapped. Some of the machines used in this work began to disintegrate in the heat.

63 Squadron had arrived in Mesopotamia on the 13th of August. Amongst the aircraft they brought were RE8s which held out the hope of greatly improved performance. The fate that befell its personnel, however, was indicative of the problems the weather caused that summer for within weeks the unit was reduced by sickness and exhaustion to a bare handful of men. The Squadron had worked up and trained in Northumberland, only to be delivered into almost unendurable conditions, in which some of their number actually died. Those few still able to work struggled on with the erection of their machines, which like many others already there were soon also deteriorating. These factors delayed the start of operations for the unit and are bound to have contributed to some of its early losses. The first completed RE8s reached Samarra airfield in Baghdad on the 14th of September. It had two reconnaissance Flights of these machines, as well as a fighting Flight of SPADs, Bristol Scouts and Martinsyde G100s. The first reconnaissance the unit carried out was on the 25th, and both machines involved were lost.

25th September

RE8   **63Sqn**
Rec combat with Halberstadt ovTEKRIT **MIA(Capt JR Philpott **POW DoW** 15.1.18/Lt LN Baillon **POW**) wings of one of the RE8s involved folded in a diving attack

RE8   **63Sqn**
Rec combat with Halberstadt ovTEKRIT shot down **MIA(Lt MG Begg MC **POW**/ACpl OW Grant **POW**) engine possibly failed then ftl

October 1917

As the weather cooled a number of campaigns recommenced, making use of the hard won intelligence gathered by the RFC through the summer. The first of these had been on Ramadi, but by October most of the action was on the Tigris front. 63 Squadron provided most of the air support for these activities, including reconnaissance, bombing, and contact patrolling during engagements. 30 Squadron were concentrated on the Euphrates and Diyala fronts.

5th October

RE8   **63Sqn**
** ftl nrCHAI KHANA on the ADHAIM **MIA**(2Lt JW Blake **POW**/Lt JDG MacRae **POW**)

16th October

Martinsyde G100   **63Sqn**
**B KIFRI A'dr shot up fuel tank hit ftl then burnt a'c OK(Lt AEL Skinner) rescued by Welman

Martinsyde G100   **63Sqn**
**B KIFRI A'dr ground fire shot up OK(Lt JB Welman) landed to rescue other pilot who had been shot down

German aircraft had become more numerous and active again on the Diyala and Tigris fronts. In response to this the enemy airfield at Kifri was bombed by three Martinsydes on the 16th, when these casualties resulted. The raid caused little damage.

19th October

                 RNAS
** (2Lt P Price **POW**)

31st October

Martinsyde G100   **63Sqn**
**B KIFRI A'dr OK(Lt F Nuttall) landed to rescue Adams and returned ok

BE2e   **30Sqn**
**B KIFRI A'dr combat with EA shot up ftl then destroyed a'c OK(2Lt AP Adams) rescued by Nuttall

Martinsyde G100   **63Sqn**
**B KIFRI A'dr hit by AA ftl EoL OK(Lt C Cox) landed still 18 miles into enemy territory but walked out in six and three-quarter hours

Martinsyde G100   **63Sqn**
B KIFRI A'dr combat with EA ftl on a'dr(2Lt JB Welman **WIA POW)

2Lt Welman was lost as I Corps was about to attack on the Tigris front. To draw attention from these plans another raid was made on Kifri aerodrome, the home of FAb13. This involved six aircraft, most of which were involved in incidents after a German scout ascended to confront them.

The BE2es of 30 Squadron also began to be replaced by RE8s as the year closed.

December 1917

17th December

RE8?   **63Sqn**
B HUMR A'dr met by 3 Halberstadts shot up(Lt JH Caldwell OK/Lt Griffiths **WIA) on TIGRIS front,

combined operation with 30 & 63 Sqns

Bombing raids took place on the 17th, 27th, and 28th of December.

Untraced RNAS prisoners in Mesopotamia in 1917

** (SLt H Burns **POW**) .17?
** (Lt BA Treachman **POW**) .17?

January 1918

By the start of 1918 the overall situation in Mesopotamia had been complicated by the revolution in Russia in the previous October. From December, armistices between Russia and Turkey came into effect and at a stroke the Allies lost their means of defending Persia and her rich oilfields. The withdrawal of the Russian presence on this front also gave access for Turkish and German forces to threaten the British right flank. Political efforts were begun to galvanise local forces in Georgia and Armenia into providing a measure of protection. Meanwhile, a British force had reached Kermanshah, on the Persian Plateau, from where RE8s could at least reconnoitre enemy movements in this region.

The year opened with a flurry of retaliatory bombing raids shared between the protagonists. Nos. 30 and 63 Squadrons for their part bombed the enemy aerodromes at either Humr or Kifri on the 3rd, 21st, and 25th of the month, whilst German machines bombed British aerodromes and other targets in Baghdad. Some combats developed during the course of these raids but were mostly inconclusive. The Official History notes that four aircraft were forced to land in enemy territory in January owing to engine trouble. Besides Capt Caldwell, and the crew of Taylor and Mills, it may be that some of the airmen involved in these landings are included in the list of untraced prisoners for 1918 given at the end of this section.

12th January

A8811   SPAD 7   63Sqn
*B HUMR A'dr ftl in desert nrFATHA, TIGRIS(Capt JH Caldwell **Died**)

Captain Caldwell's mutilated and naked body was found, after being left by Arabs to die of exposure.

17th January

RE8   30Sqn
B shot down ovEUPHRATES ftl(2Lt W Taylor **POW/Lt AS Mills **POW**) engine failure?, burnt & destroyed a'c, almost escaped

RE8   30Sqn
**B ROMADIE shot up ovEUPHRATES(Capt G

Merton MC **WIA**/Lt D Craik **WIA**)

21st January

DH4   30Sqn
B KIFRI A'dr dhAA 7000'(2Lt WS Bean **KIA/2AM RG Castor **KIA**)

This crew was killed when twelve machines from 30 Squadron bombed Kifri aerodrome.

25th January

DH4   30Sqn
**NB KIFRI A'dr engine caught fire 1000' ftl desert nrQUARA TEPE OK(Capt F Nuttall/Lt RBB Sievier) 25/26Jan.18 walked 24 miles to safety

This crew came down in the desert during one of the raids to enemy aerodromes. They burnt their machine and then set course by the stars carrying their two Lewis guns and ammunition they had salvaged from the DH4. Over the next two days they walked to within a mile or two of the British lines and after signalling to patrols they were brought in. At this time there had been only two DH4s in the region, and both had now been lost in a week.

February 1918

19th February
THE ADVANCE ON THE EUPHRATES

The British advance intended to take the western Euphrates began on the 19th with a move on the enemy garrison at Hit. A composite unit of two Flights of 30 Squadron and one from 63 Squadron co-operated in the fighting by intensively bombing and machine-gunning enemy strongholds. This programme continued until the 27th when the machines from 63 Squadron returned to the Tigris, and from this time onwards, 30 Squadron concentrated on bombing and reconnaissance.

March 1918

72 Squadron arrived in Mesopotamia on the 2nd of March. It brought, in part, a welcome additional fighter component to the RFC in the region, although its machines were a typically mixed bunch of mostly semi-obsolete types. Its best aircraft were the DH4s and SE5as of A Flight which went to operate at Samarra on the Tigris. B Flight, made up of Martinsydes, operated from Baghdad, and C Flight, with Bristol M1C monoplanes, went to Mirjana on the Diyala river close to the Persian border.

The British were making good progress towards their objectives around Hit when on the 8th of

March a reconnaissance brought in the news that the enemy was retreating from its positions around the town and an advance was ordered to take it. In support of these actions 30 Squadron bombed and harassed troops repeatedly. For instance, on the 9th, the unit dropped one hundred and forty-seven 20-lb or 25-lb bombs and fired 7,000 rounds of ammunition. In the following days the enemy was driven back in a continuing rout. Air attacks were made easier when 30 Squadron moved to Hit and were joined again by a Flight from 63 Squadron. The Turkish forces attempted to make a stand at Khan Baghdadi on the 26th but these fortifications were also stormed by the 11th Cavalry Brigade in a very demanding but completely successful rear attack. Detailed contact patrols and reconnaissance work by 30 Squadron were instrumental in the success of this assault, in which many thousands of prisoners were taken. This victory opened the way forward along the Euphrates Valley and in the following days mobile units, with air support, pressed as far as Ana, driving the Turkish forces from the region.

4th March

RE8   30Sqn
** ftl **MIA**(Capt WL Haight **POW**/Lt HJW Hancock **POW**) Haight rescued from Turks 28.3.18?(also see below?)

25th March

DH4   30Sqn
Rec BAGHDADI engine hit ftl **MIA(LtCol JE Tennant **POW**/Maj PCS Hobart **POW**) burnt a'c, rescued on the 28.3.18

These two senior officers had set out on a reconnaissance of the Baghdadi positions the day before the intended assault when they were brought down by heavy ground fire and taken prisoners. After interrogation they had been taken to Ana and then conveyed westwards towards Aleppo and imprisonment. When Ana was reached and taken by the armoured cars of the British advance on the 27th the priority then became the recovery of the two officers. Eight armoured cars then rushed in pursuit and eventually managed to recapture the men on the 28th after encountering the group thirty-two miles west of Ana.

April 1918

A sudden, large gale swept the Euphrates on the night of the 31st of March/1st of April, destroying several hangars containing 30 Squadron aircraft. Three were lost and several damaged. Fortunately, most of the British objectives for the present had been achieved by the time of this mishap. Elsewhere

in Mesopotamia, operations planned for April were to be handicapped more than once by such weather. Pressure was growing for Allied activity which would stifle Turkish intentions in Persia. It was decided there should be an attack on the Kifri-Qara Tepe region at the end of the month and Flights from all three squadrons were drafted in to assist. Bombing from the air began in the middle of the month, some of the targets being chosen so as to mislead the enemy about the planned attacks. The advance on the ground began on the 26th and was supported with reconnaissance and low bombing from the air. In these raids 72 Squadron Bristol M1Cs carried out their first active operations. By the evening of the 29th the Turks had been driven from their positions as far north as Tuz Khurmatli and a halt was called to the British advance so as to assess the situation.

27th April

Martinsyde?   30Sqn
LowB TUZ KHURMATLI shot up(Capt F Nuttall MC DFC **WIA)

May 1918

The enemy had fallen back to Kirkuk, and although to pursue them as far as this town — barely one hundred miles south of Mosul — would stretch British lines of communications to their limit, it was decided an attack must be made. Only with the Turks driven back into Kurdistan would pressure on Persia be relieved. The RAF moved forward in support of this plan, so that by the 2nd parts of both 30 and 72 Squadron were at Tuz. The fighter element provided by the Bristol monoplanes of 72 Squadron was in order to protect 30 Squadron RE8s on their reconnaissance work. A number of German Albatros fighters were known to have reached the area and, as will be seen, air fighting intensified in the coming month. At the same time, an advance was made on the Tigris towards Tikrit in order to tie up the Turkish forces there.

2nd May

RE8   30Sqn
Rec KIRKUK ground mg shot down(Capt AS Edwards **POW DoW/Maj GA Beazeley **POW DoW**) 14.5.18, Beazeley Royal Engineers

4th May

The advance on Kirkuk was begun on the 4th and the town occupied on the 7th after some very heavy fighting. Its inhabitants were found in a dreadful state and efforts were made to feed them with what little was available. The move on Kirkuk was indeed

to prove too demanding on British resources and, being unable to supply and hold the town safely, a withdrawal was made towards the end of the month. Before this was carried out, however, a number of aircraft from 30 Squadron were moved forward to the abandoned aerodrome in the town and made some extremely valuable photographic reconnaissances as far as Mosul. There was an increasing enemy presence in the air during these operations as they regained their organisation, and a number of air crew were lost or wounded in attacks. Tikrit was also occupied in May but similarly abandoned once the enemy had been severely struck and driven from the area.

15th May

B5872   RE8   30Sqn
B combat with EA shot down(Lt JO Allison MC **KIA/ Lt MC Atherton MC **KIA**) from KIRKUK [?"RE8" claim combat Hpt H Schüz FAb13][?"RE8" claim combat PALESTINE Ltn H Kunz Ja1F]

RE8   30Sqn
** combat with EA shot up (/1AM F Sutherst **KIA**) date?

21st May

30Sqn
** (/Lt RRB Siever MC **WIA**) 21.5?

July – October 1918
THE "DUNSTERFORCE"

Summer in Mesopotamia inevitably drew operations on the ground mostly to a standstill. The season was not as punishing as it had been in 1917, however, and a few minor schemes were pursued by the British in the coming months. In the air, a major photgraphic reconnaissance of the region was completed and air support was also lent to operations on the Caspian and in northern Persia known as the "Dunsterforce". This body amounted to little more than a brigade, under the command of Major General LC Dunsterville, sent to Hamadan in order to exert influence, and if necessary, force, upon the local Persian tribes. The region was especially volatile at this time as Russia was only now completing its withdrawal from Persia. It was deemed essential to have a presence against the Turks in the oilfields and to continue the protection of the British right flank. In effect, it extended a weak British front all the way to the Caspian Sea. The force took with it Martinsydes from "B" Flight of 72 Squadron, to which three RE8s from "A" Flight 30 Squadron were subsequently added in September. Through a hot and difficult summer it operated at the very limits of a six hundred-mile-long logistical

lifeline. Hamadan also stood at an altitude of 6,500 feet so that machines sometimes required a take-off of half a mile before reaching flying speed.

15th July

RE8   Middle East
Palestine/Mesopotamia ** **MIA**(Lt JN Garnett **POW**/2Lt HG Penwarden **POW**) Casualty Cards at the RAF Museum give 17.7?

31st August

72Sqn
** shot down BAKU **MIA**(Lt AA Cullen **POW**) repat 7.4.19, via Casualty Card at RAF Museum

Dunsterville's force was having ever greater demands placed on it, for in late July the oil centre at Baku on the Caspian came under dire threat from Turkish forces and help was requested from the British. A small force landed at Baku on the 4th of August and proceeded to hold the town in combination with Russian troops. To help them, Dunsterville later sent two Martinsydes from 72 Squadron which were ready for operations by the 20th. These could reconnoitre the country, be used to keep the command in touch, and perhaps encourage the support of the locals.

Although British troop reinforcements also reached Baku at this time, there was a series of increasingly damaging Turkish attacks and, on the 31st, ground was lost in a very heavy battle. It was probably during fighting on this day that Lt Cullen was shot down and taken prisoner, although the Official History gives the two 72 Squadron pilots operating at Baku as Lt MC Mackay and Lt RPP Pope. Baku was finally abandoned by the Allies in an evacuation on the night of the 14th/15th of September, but vital time had been gained by this resistance, for the Turkish empire was showing the first signs of collapse from within. The 72 Squadron Martinsydes were involved in fighting in Baku up until the last day. Their pilots were out reconnoitring and machine-gunning Turkish positions but by early afternoon neither machine was in an airworthy state, having been shot up so much. They were destroyed and the pilots, taking the machine-guns and cameras with them, joined the ground forces in the fighting. Subsequently, they and the other RAF personnel were evacuated.

15th September

C9564   SE5a   72Sqn
Persia A Flt *Rec OK(Lt Thomas)

Thomas is mentioned in these records beause he was one of the most active fighter pilots on the Mesopotamian front.

6th October

Martinsyde G100   72Sqn

Persia **EscRec TABRIZ Road shot up troops but engine
failed ftl 40m "EoL" MIA but OK (Lt TL Williams)
walked out in 4 days

72 Squadron had been reinforced in Persia by three
30 Squadron RE8s on the 17th of September.
Williams was escorting one of these on the 6th when
he lost sight of it. Whilst searching for the RE8 he
came across a body of enemy troops which he began
to shoot up. His engine then failed and he was forced
to come down in enemy territory. He attempted to
walk out but eventually had to ask for help from the
local people. He was directed on his way, in disguise,
after leaving most of his possessions with them. He
took four days to walk out to safety, reaching the
British lines in a state of exhaustion.

11th October

RE8   30Sqn

Persia +*LowB landed to help 72 Sqn pilot but crashed
on re-take off MIA but OK (Lt AE Morgan/Lt JC
Chacksfield) left in patrol of 3 a'c, 3 airmen walked out

Martinsyde G100   72Sqn

Persia +*EscLowB shot up troops but engine failed ftl
MIA but OK (Lt KM Pennington) RE8 crew of 30 Sqn
above landed to rescue but this crashed on take off, 3
airmen walked out

Another three airmen walked to safety in Persia after
coming down on a patrol on the 11th. The
Martinsyde escort was forced down and Morgan
came down to rescue the pilot. When the RE8 took
off again it crashed, and these three airmen walked
an unbelievable one hundred and twenty miles to
safety in seven days.

18th October
VICTORY IN MESOPOTAMIA

The final Allied campaign of victory in Mesopotamia began in late October. This centred on a
general assault up the Tigris River against Turkish
fortifications at the Fat-ha Gorge, some thirty-five
miles further north of the British railhead which had
been established at Tikrit. Across the Middle East
and Asia Minor the situation was grave for the
enemy. Allenby had made devastating advances in
Palestine; Bulgaria had sued for an Armistice and
stopped fighting; and Turkey was everywhere
driven back in defence of itself. In such circumstances, with a rested British Army and the weather
cooling, an offensive would be perfectly timed. All
three squadrons, Nos. 30, 63, and 72, contributed
machines to the battle, which began with a move
forward on the 18th. 63 and part of 72 operated from

the aerodrome at Tikrit, well placed to support the
main attack. No. 30, and the remainder of 72
Squadron flew from Kifri, aiding an advance
protecting the eastern flank of the river. Fat-ha
Gorge was stormed on the night of the 23rd/24th
and enemy troops were pouring from its defences by
morning. Through the 24th they were bombed and
raked with fire from the air — routes out of the gorge
having been destroyed in order to handicap the
retreat.

25th October

Attacks continued on the 25th, but not without
casualties. The Official History notes that two
SE5as and a Sopwith Camel from 72 Squadron were
so heavily shot up by ground fire during an attack
on Humr Bridge that one SE5a had to be force-
landed and the pilot of the Camel was slightly
wounded in the leg. The identity of these pilots and
their aircraft have yet to be established, but the
Camel pilot might be the Canadian Lt HW Price
who is mentioned elsewhere as being wounded in
action on the 24th in this theatre. Another pilot, Lt
McDonald from 30 Squadron, was also forced down
by ground fire behind enemy lines but was rescued
by the RE8 crew of Capt AP Adams and Capt AH
Mellows who flew him to safety whilst he crouched
on their machine's lower plane.

In the following days, the Turkish troops were
gradually surrounded in their attempts to retreat to
Mosul. Resources for the RAF units were low in the
region by this time, but they were used carefully and
effectively, for instance bombing and shooting up
enemy positions from the air shortly before the
launching of infantry attacks. They also bombed
Turkish camps and provided general contact patrolling and reconnaissance. Despite fighting with great
tenacity and desperation in order to break through
the British line the enemy was finally driven to
surrender on the 30th. An Armistice came into effect
on the 31st — the Turks had been defeated in
Mesopotamia.

Untraced Prisoners in Mesopotamia 1918

** (Lt E Robinson **POW**) .18

** (Capt AJ Everard **POW**) .18?

** (Lt A Ward **POW**) .18? repat 7.12.18, but see Lt AA
Ward in Part I, 14.10.17?

** (Lt EP Osmond **POW**) .18? repat 11.18

** (Capt LJ Bayly **DoW**) .18, Mesopotamia?

30Sqn

** (/2Lt EC Kinghorn **WIA**) 4.11? inj?. 1917?

Part IX

EAST AFRICA 1914–1917

November 1914

Curtiss F Flying Boat   RNAS
*Rec search for *Königsberg* OK (FSLt. HD Cutler)
~24Nov.14

Cutler had been a pre-war aviator in South Africa. At the outbreak of the war the flying boat he had been using had been requisitioned and he himself given a commission in the RNAS. The German light cruiser *Königsberg* had been operating with deadly effect in the Gulf of Aden, and in September had sunk HMS *Pegasus* off Zanzibar. She was believed to have retired into the Rufiji delta, and Cutler and his machine were a way of spying her out. He had set out on the 22nd on his first reconnaissance, but he was flying without a compass and eventually force-landed near a remote island. By considerable chance he was rescued, and then within days attempted another sortie. It was on this flight that he discovered the *Königsberg*. Much of the next six months of effort expended by the RNAS in East Africa was in assisting in the destruction of this vessel.

April – December 1915

122   Short S85 Seaplane   RNAS
this a'c? **PhotRec for *Königsberg* up RUFIJI DELTA rifle fire from bank engine dam ftl towed to safety OK (FCdr JT Cull/AM EHA Boggis)

5th May

119   Short Folder   East Africa
** shot up from beach at RAS T WARA rudder hit ftl sea broke up and sank (FLt HEM Watkins/Air Mech)

The crew were rescued after three hours by FCdr JT Cull in Short Folder Seaplane 122, who taxied out to sea with them until he could leave them with a patrolling whaler.

11th July

SA/9/HF Henri Farman   RNAS
non-RFC number **Spotting for attack on *Königsberg*, enemy shell exploded nr a'c engine hit shot down ftl on river in RUFIJI DELTA o't sank OK (FLt JT Cull/FSLt HJ Arnold) left 11-50am, spotting corrections continued to be sent in descent

10th December

Curtiss F Flying Boat   RNAS
** engine trouble ftl in mouth of KIKUNJA River (FSLt HD Cutler **POW**) a'c salvaged. Cutler had been a pre-war aviator in South Africa. He had made the first discovery of the *Königsberg* in his flying boat on the 22nd November 1914.

January – August 1917

27th January

3882   Caudron GIII   East Africa
**B engine failed ovSALAITA ground fire shot up ftl wr OK (FSLt LO Brown)

31st January

26 Squadron RFC arrived in East Africa, flying BE2cs.

6th January

8254   Short 827   HMS *Himalaya*
at ZANZIBAR ** engine failed ftl creek nrKIOMBINI (FLt ER Moon **POW**/Cdr.Hon OBR Bridgeman DSO **Kld**) drowned, Moon swam to bank, a'c destroyed by fire

8th August

N1078   FBA Flying Boat   Malta
SubP ftl sea nrTRIPOLI (FLt WE Robinson **POW/SLt JCA Jenks **POW**) ftl nrMISURATA, on African coast

Casualty of Unknown date in 1917 in East Africa

** (2Lt CF Strangham **POW**) .17
** (Lt GS Frame **POW**) .17

Part X

THE NAME INDEX

This section indexes the 10,800 individuals who are mentioned in this book. The chronological entries and the accompanying text can be read as the unfolding story of the air war. For those additionally interested in personnel, however, the name index is the key method of finding one's way around the book. It links a name with a date in a particular theatre of war which can then be looked up in the body of the work. It is more than a simple index, however, because in addition, it gives all relevant casualty-related information for every name, notes the flyer's nationality if it was known to be other than British, and gives a range of other details where relevant (these are described below).

The index entries are ordered by surname and then by initial, with the relevant rank inserted between the two. Then follows any casualty data, followed by a Roman numeral "in italics" referring to the part of the book. For ease of access, the parts are given at the top of every page of the index. Considering the very first name in the index, for example.

Abbot, FSLt.ED, **WIA POW** 13Sep.17-*I*

This entry tells one that FSLt. ED Abbott was wounded in action and taken prisoner on the 13th of September 1917 whilst serving on the Western Front. One simply looks up this date in Part I and locates Abbot's entry to find out more details. Here one is told the following:

B3933   **Sopwith Camel**   **10 (Naval) Sqn**
**OP combat with EAs wROULERS 3000' 7-10am **MIA(FSLt ED
Abbot **WIA POW**) seen at rear of formation about to be attacked,
in control after? ["Sopwith 1Str" claim combat TERHAND,
nrBECELAERE 7-10am Ltn W vBülow Ja36]

If no initials have been substantiated for a particular surname then these examples are listed first for that name. In these cases a squadron number in italics is given as a cross reference. Squadron numbers are similarly provided in instances where two different airman have the same name and initials.

It is not uncommon for an airman to have multiple date references. A great deal of effort has been taken to tie up diverse entries relating to what is in fact a single individual. Even in cases of two men with identical names and initials, however, an occasional apparently obvious link has proved erroneous. If there is any doubt in this respect the two have been kept as separate entries and provided with the relevant squadron numbers and dates for cross-referencing. With so may names there are bound to be some details which will be open to further research and revelation.

When *Died of Wounds* (**DoW**) is noted after a name, if there is a second date given in a different format from usual, typically using all numbers and the full year, as in 12.6.1917, then this is the date on which the individual actually died. In the example.

Addams,2Lt.VH, **POW DoW** 5.5.1917 4May.17-*I*

Adams was wounded and captured on the 4th of May 1917 but he died of his wounds on the 5th of May. If this special format date does not appear then the individual died on the same day as the relevant incident.

Spelling and case names are as per those most usually found in the primary sources. Thus, for example, both *MacLennan* and *Maclennan* will be found. In addition to the date, casualty, nationality, and theatre information, any queries relating to name spelling, initials, ranks, or dates are noted. This supplementary information is always given in italics. Entries also include mentions of individuals in the text.

A

Abbott,FSLt.ED, **WIA POW** 13Sep.17-*I*
Abbot,FSLt.RFP, **WIA** 17Aug.17-*I*
Abbott,2Lt.TW, **KIA** 18Aug.17-*I*
Abell,Lt.CE, 9Nov.17-*I*
Abercromby,Capt., *5Sqn.* 27Jul.15-*I*
Abernethy,2Lt.TJ, *US.* 15Jul.18-*IIB*
Abey,2Lt.HR, 1Oct.18-*I*, **POW** 2Nov.18-*I*
Abrahams,Sgt.CJ, **KIA** 19May.17-*I*
Abrahams,2Lt.CRG, **KIA** 26Sep.18-*I*
Abram,Lt.RK, **WIA** 4May.17-*I*
Achton,2Lt., *12Sqn.* 22Mar.18-*I*
Ackerman,1Lt.JH, *USAS.* **WIA** 11Jun.18-*I*
Ackers,Lt.CHS, **WIA**? **POW** 26Feb.18-*I*
Ackland,2Lt.,Lt.WHD, 9May.15-*I*, 1Jun.15-*I*, 2Jun.15-*I*, **WIA**? 20Jun.15-*I*
Ackroyd,Lt., **POW**? *16Sqn.* 19Jun.15-*I*
Acland,Lt.WHW, 10May.15-*I*, 29May.15-*I*
Adam,Lt.AR, **POW DoW** 3Jul.17-*I*
Adam,FSLt.OP, **KIA** 1Apr.18-*I*
Adams,FSgt., *23Sqn.* 1Jul.16-*I*
Adams,Lt.AB, 25Apr.16-*I*
Adams,2Lt.,Capt.AP, 25Oct.18-*VIII*, 31Oct.17-*VIII*
Adams,2Lt.AW, **WIA** 27Mar.18-*I*
Adams,Lt.B, 25Jan.16-*I*
Adams,2Lt.D, **WIA** 22Mar.18-*I*
Adams,1Lt.E, *USAS.* **KIA** 29Sep.18-*I*
Adams,2Lt.F, *1Sqn.* **POW** 10Jan.16-*I*
Adams,2Lt.F, *11Sqn.* **WIA** 9Aug.17-*I*
Adams,2Lt.F, *53Sqn.* **KIA** 12May.17-*I*
Adams,Lt.FM, 6Jun.15-*I*
Adams,Lt.FP, **INT** 3Jul.15-*I*
Adams,2Lt.HC, 21Mar.18-*I*
Adams,2Lt.HT, **KIA** 28Mar.18-*I*
Adams,Lt.HT, **POW** 5Apr.17-*I*
Adams,2Lt.JD, *US.* **POW** 21Oct.18-*IIB*
Adams,2Lt.JPF, **KIA** 14Oct.17-*I*
Adams,2Lt.NF, **POW** 16Sep.18-*I*
Adams,2Lt.RGH, 12Jan.16-*I*, 19Jan.16-*I*, **POW** 7Apr.18-*I*
Adams,Capt.RN, 20May.16-*I*, **KIA** 10Oct.16-*I*
Adams,Capt.TD, **KIA** 7Nov.15-*I*
Adams,2Lt.VH, **POW DoW** 5.5.1917 4May.17-*I*
Adamson,2Lt.CL, **WIA** 15Jun.17-*I*
Adamson,2Lt.CP, **WIA POW** 20Aug.17-*I*
Adamson,Lt.J, **WIA** 1Sep.18-*I*
Adamson,Lt.WC, *6Sqn.* 20Apr.15-*I*, 3May.15-*I*, **KIA** 5Sep.15-*I*
Adderley,2Lt.WH, **DoW** 24Oct.18-*I*
Addison,Lt.FW, 17Sep.18-*I*
Addison,2AM.W, **KIA** 15Aug.17-*I*
Adeney,2Lt.RE, **DoW** 11Apr.17-*I*
Adkin,2Lt.CW, **WIA** 25Aug.17-*I*
Adlam,FSLt.LE, **KIA** 9Sep.17-*I*
Adler,Lt.E, **WIA** 12May.17-*I*
Affleck,Lt.,Capt.R, 7Dec.16-*I*, 26Jun.18-*I*
Agabeq,Lt.IWF, 3Oct.18-*I*
Agar,Capt.EZ, **KIA** 13Apr.18-*I*
Agnew,2Lt.ICF, *Aust.* **POW** 2Oct.17-*I*
Agnew,Lt.AB, *US.* **POW** 10Nov.18-*I*
Aikins,2Lt.JR, **KIA** 26Mar.18-*I*
Ainger,Lt.HC, **KIA** 4Oct.17-*I*
Ainscow,Lt.JA, **WIA** 15Dec.16-*VIII*
Aird,2Lt.AW, **KIA** 23May.18-*I*
Aird,FSLt.HR, **POW** 30Sep.17-*V*
Airey,2Lt.ER, 20Sep.18-*I*
Airth,Lt.RA, **DoW** 29Jul.17-*I*
Aitken,2Lt.AH, 27Sep.18-*I*, **KIA** 27Oct.18-*I*
Aitken,Sgt.G, **KIA** 23Oct.18-*I*
Aitken,2Lt.J, **KIA** 16Jul.18-*I*
Aitken,2Lt.JT, **KIA** 26Sep.18-*I*
Aitken,Lt.W, 23Aug.18-*I*
Aizlewood,Capt.LP, **WIA** 10Feb.17-*I*
Aked,Lt.HLC, **POW** 21May.16-*I*
Akers,FSLt.FW, **KIA** 20Jul.17-*I*
Akester,FSLt.JC, **WIA POW** 26Sep.17-*I*
Alban,Lt.AH, 24Oct.18-*I*, **WIA** 3Nov.18-*I*
Alberry,Lt.F, DCM *Aust.* **inj** 13Aug.18-*I*, 16Sep.18-*I*
Albertson,1Lt., *USAS. 213thUS.* **POW** 4Aug.18-*IIB*
Alcock,FLt.JW, *Aust.* **POW** 30Sep.17-*V*
Alcock,2Lt.R, **WIA** 17Oct.18-*I*
Alcock,2Lt.W, 24Jan.16-*I*
Alder,2Lt., *16Sqn.* 6May.17-*I*
Alder,Lt.E, 2Sep.18-*I*
Alder,2Lt.HV, **inj** 8Oct.18-*I*
Alder,2Lt.S, **WIA POW** 25Jan.17-*I*
Alderman,1Lt.HB, *USAS.* **WIA** 12Aug.18-*I*
Alderslade,2Lt.AE, 30Aug.18-*I*
Alderson,2Lt.AGD, **POW** 6Feb.18-*I*
Aldred,Sgt.B, 12May.17-*I*, **KIA** 23May.17-*I*
Aldred,Lt.JA, 16Feb.17-*I*
Aldred,Capt.JW, 19May.18-*I*
Aldred,2Lt.WB, **DoW** 20.9.1918 7Sep.18-*I*
Aldrich,1Lt.HS, *US.* **WIA** 12Sep.18-*IIB*
Aldrich,1Lt.PH,DSC *US.* **KIA** 29Oct.18-*IIB*
Aldridge,2Lt.AER, **WIA** 30Nov.17-*I*
Aldridge,Lt.AL, **WIA** 29Aug.18-*I*
Aldridge,Sgt.HD, **POW** 24Jul.18-*I*
Aldridge,Lt.JA, 21Apr.18-*I*
Aldworth,1Lt.RT, *US.* **POW** 2Nov.18-*IIB*
Alexander,1Lt.AH, *US.* **WIA** 4Sep.18-*IIB*
Alexander,Lt.D, **WIA** 9Oct.17-*I*
Alexander,2Lt.EHEJ, **WIA POW** 5Feb.16-*I*
Alexander,1AM.H, **WIA** 10Nov.16-*I*
Alexander,Cpl.RC, *US.* **WIA** 5Nov.18-*IIB*
Alexander,Lt.TM, **KIA** 17Aug.18-*I*
Alexander,FCdr.WM, *Can.* 6Mar.18-*I*
Alkinson,2Lt.JFV, **WIA** 9Jun.18-*I*
Allabarton,2Lt.SF, **POW** 19May.17-*I*
Allan,2Lt.AM, **POW** 29Sep.18-*I*
Allan,Sgt.AS, **WIA** 25Aug.18-*I*
Allan,2Lt.CM, **WIA**? 28Sep.18-*I*, **POW** 28Oct.18-*I*
Allan,FSLt.JAM, **WIA** 12Jul.17-*I*
Allan,2Lt.LE, **KIA** 26Apr.17-*I*
Allan,2Lt.R, **WIA** 15Apr.18-*I*, **KIA** 22Apr.18-*I*
Allan,Sgt.R, 17Sep.18-*I*
Allanson,GL.SE, 4Jun.18-*I*
Allanson,Lt.WG, 28Jun.18-*I*, **KIA** 21Sep.18-*I*
Allcock,2Lt.W, 11Nov.15-*I*, 2Dec.15-*I*, 12Jan.16-*I*
Allcock,Capt.WT, 12Mar.16-*I*
Allcock,Capt.WTL, **KIA** 5Jun.17-*I*
Allday,Lt.C, 22Aug.18-*I*
Allein,1Lt.HC, *US.* **DoW** 27Oct.18-*IIB*
Allen,1AM., 22Mar.17-*I*
Allen,Lt., *12Sqn.* 23Aug.18-*I*
Allen,2Lt.AA, **KIA** 11Oct.17-*I*
Allen,Capt.AS,MC *Can.* **KIA** 30Apr.17-*I*
Allen,Lt.AW, 17Sep.18-*I*
Allen,2Lt.C, **KIA** 13Mar.18-*I*
Allen,Capt.CP, 27Oct.18-*I*
Allen,Lt.DG, 4May.17-*I*
Allen,Capt.DGA, **KIA** 8Oct.18-*I*
Allen,Lt.DL, 27Jul.15-*I*
Allen,2Lt.EF, 31May.16-*I*
Allen,2Lt.FRL, **KIA** 14Oct.18-*I*
Allen,2Lt.GM, **WIA** 3Aug.15-*I*, **KIA** 2Sep.16-*I*
Allen,Capt.GWD, 24Aug.16-*I*, 17Mar.17-*I*
Allen,Lt.H, **KIA** 10Aug.18-*I*
Allen,Lt.JB, 24Mar.18-*I*
Allen,2Lt.JM, **POW** 26Feb.18-*I*
Allen,FCdr.JR, **KIA** 11Apr.18-*I*
Allen,Sgt.LA, **WIA** 21Aug.18-*I*
Allen,Lt.LG, 5Apr.17-*I*
Allen,Lt.LW, **WIA** 24May.17-*I*
Allen,Lt.MD, 8Aug.18-*I*
Allen,2Lt.RGR, **KIA** 16Nov.16-*I*
Allen,Lt.SH, **KIA** 12Oct.17-*I*
Allen,2Lt.,Lt.VW, MC, 22May.18-*I*, **KIA** 9Jun.18-*I*
Allison,2Lt.GH, 15Apr.18-*I*
Allison,FSLt.JL, **KIA** 18Mar.18-*I*
Allison,Lt.JO,MC **KIA** 15May.18-*VIII*
Allison,Lt.WR, 9Jul.18-*I*
Allport,2Lt.M, **KIA** 10Nov.16-*I*
Allsop,2Lt.G, **WIA** 12Jun.17-*I*
Allum,2AM.TE, **WIA** 29Apr.17-*I*
Allwork,Sgt.CHO, 16Sep.18-*I*
Alston,Cpl.G, **WIA** 10Apr.18-*I*
Alston,2Lt.RM, 2Oct.18-*I*
Alton,Cpl., *15Sqn.* 7Feb.16-*I*
Ambler,2Lt.CF, 16Sep.18-*I*
Ambler,Lt.E, 7Sep.16-*I*
Ambler,Lt.F, 11Apr.18-*I*, 21Apr.18-*I*, **WIA** 12May.18-*I*
Ambler,2Lt.JJ, **POW** 2Sep.18-*I*
Amesby,Lt.WRB, 13May.18-*IV*
Amey,2Lt.AE, **KIA** 16Sep.18-*I*
Amm,Lt.EO, *SA.* 20Sep.18-*I*, **POW** 9Nov.18-*I*
Amory,2Lt.W, **POW** 30Oct.18-*I*
Amos,2Lt.J, **KIA** 29Aug.18-*I*
Amy,Lt.CleG, 3Apr.18-*IV*, 16Jun.18-*IV*, 29Jul.18-*IV*
Anderson,Lt., *6Sqn.* 21Aug.18-*I*
Anderson,Lt.A, **inj POW** 3Nov.16-*I*
Anderson,Lt.AM, 14Jul.18-*I*
Anderson,Lt.BT, **WIA POW** 5Jul.18-*IV*
Anderson,1Lt.CP, *US.* **KIA** 16Sep.18-*IIB*
Anderson,2Lt.DS, **POW** 15May.18-*I*
Anderson,Lt.FStK, 17Oct.17-*I*, **WIA** 31Oct.17-*I*
Anderson,Lt.G, **WIA** 6Sep.18-*I*, **KIA** 16Sep.18-*I*
Anderson,2Lt.GF, **POW** 15Sep.18-*I*
Anderson,Lt.GF, DFC SA. **WIA** 30Oct.18-*I*
Anderson,2Lt.GN, **WIA** 2Sep.16-*I*
Anderson,Capt.J, **WIA** 16Jun.18-*I*
Anderson,2Lt.JC, 12Apr.18-*I*
Anderson,2Lt.JD, **POW** 7Aug.18-*I*
Anderson,Lt.JLK?, **POW DoW**, *initials* JLH? 31May.18-*I*
Anderson,Lt.JR, **KIA** 13Aug.18-*I*
Anderson,2Lt.NMcC, **WIA** 10Apr.18-*I*
Anderson,Lt.PW, **WIA** 27Jun.18-*I*
Anderson,2Lt.RA, *USAS.* **WIA POW** 27Aug.18-*I*
Anderson,Lt.RH, 18Mar.16-*I*
Anderson,1Lt.RM, *US.* 7Oct.18-*IIB*
Anderson,2Lt.RWL, **KIA** 11Jun.17-*I*
Anderson,Lt.S, **WIA** 4Jul.18-*III*
Anderson,Lt.W,MC **POW** 17Mar.17-*I*
Anderson,2Lt.WA, **KIA** 18Jul.18-*I*
Anderson,Lt.WF, 7Jun.17-*I*
Anderson,2Lt.WL,MC **KIA** 21Sep.18-*I*
Andrew,1Lt.FLA?, *US.* **WIA** 30Oct.18-*IIB*
Andrew,Lt.WB, **KIA** 12Feb.18-*I*
Andrew,2Lt.WL, **POW** 15May.18-*I*
Andrews,2Lt.,Lt. *5Sqn.* 26Apr.15-*I*, 5May.15-*I*, 9May.15-*I*, 10May.15-*I*, 16Jun.15-*I*
Andrews,2Lt.CB, **WIA** 27Sep.17-*I*
Andrews,2Lt.EB, **KIA** 16Sep.18-*I*
Andrews,2Lt.EN, 30Oct.18-*I*
Andrews,2Lt.FC, **POW** 26Sep.17-*I*
Andrews,Lt.FS, **DoW** 29.4.1917 16Apr.17-*I*
Andrews,FSLt.G, **POW** 26Oct.17-*I*
Andrews,2Lt.HJ, **WIA**? 30Oct.18-*I*
Andrews,2Lt.,Lt.J, 30Oct.18-*I*, **WIA** 4Nov.18-*I*
Andrews,2Lt.JG, **KIA** 14Aug.18-*I*
Andrews,Capt.JO, 31Jul.16-*I*, 31Aug.16-*I*
Andrews,Lt.JW, **KIA** 4Oct.18-*I*
Angel,2Lt.CM, *US.* **KIA** 14May.18-*IIB*
Angier,2Lt.GM, **inj** 20Jul.16-*I*
Angstrom,2Lt.LC, **WIA** 22Jun.16-*I*
Angus,2Lt.KR, **POW** 20Jul.18-*I*
Angus,Lt.RE, **KIA** 20Nov.17-*I*
Ankers,Capt.B,DCM **WIA** 8Aug.18-*I*
Ankers,Lt.J, **KIA** 16Jul.18-*I*
Anketell,2Lt.CE, **KIA** 11May.18-*I*
Ankrett,2Lt.HH, **KIA** 11Jul.18-*I*
Annesley,SLt.Earl of, **KIA** 5Nov.14-*I*
Ansell,Lt.AE, 24Apr.18-*I*
Ansell,Lt.L, **WIA** 17Jun.17-*I*
Anslow,2Lt.FF, **POW** 16Sep.18-*I*
Anstey,Lt.CW, **WIA** 30Apr.15-*I*
Anthony,FSLt.E, **WIA** 20Sep.17-*I*
Anthony,1AM.GR, **POW** 27May.18-*I*
Anthony,Lt.JR, **POW DoW** 25May.17-*I*
Anthony,Capt.MS, **WIA** 13Aug.18-*I*
Appleton,2Lt.A, **KIA** 17Mar.17-*I*
Appley,2Lt.CFW, *US.* **KIA** 2Sep.18-*I*
Applin,2Lt.R, **KIA** 29Apr.17-*I*
Apps,2Lt.GF, 11Mar.18-*IV*, **WIA** 16Jul.18-*IV*
Aqaberq,Lt.IWF, 30Oct.18-*I*
Archer,Cpl.F, **POW** 12Apr.18-*I*
Archer,Lt.,Capt.RA, 10Sep.15-*I*, 9Apr.18-*I*
Archer,Lt.WD, *US.* 9Oct.18-*I*
Archer,Lt.WD, **WIA** 9Oct.18-*I*
Archibald,2Lt.LM, **POW** 24Oct.17-*I*
Archibald,Capt.MSE, **DoW** 12May.18-*I*
Archibald,1Lt.NS, *US.* **POW** 8Sep.18-*IIB*
Archibald,2Lt.WR, **KIA** 27Jun.18-*I*
Ardley,2Lt.EL, **WIA** 7Jul.17-*I*
Argles,Lt.AA, 27Oct.18-*I*
Arkell,Lt.AJ, 19May.18-*III*
Arkwright,Lt., *5Sqn.* 27Nov.14-*I*
Arkwright,Capt., *8Sqn.* 4Jun.15-*I*
Armit,2Lt.WA, 21Apr.18-*I*
Armitage,2Lt.E, **DoW** 4.10.1917 30Sep.17-*I*
Armstrong,Capt.D'UV, DFC *SA.* 17Sep.18-*I*
Armstrong,FCdr.FC, 23Mar.18-*I*, **KIA** 25Mar.18-*I*
Armstrong,2Lt.GW, 20Nov.17-*I*
Armstrong,2Lt.GW, **POW** 12Oct.17-*I*
Armstrong,1Lt.HG, *US.* **KIA** 4Oct.18-*IIB*
Armstrong,2Lt.JA, 20May.17-*I*
Armstrong,2Lt.JLP, **POW DoW** 22Jun.16-*I*
Armstrong,2Lt.MH, 28Apr.17-*I*
Armstrong,2Lt.RH, **POW** 24Sep.18-*I*
Armstrong,1Lt.RM, *US.* **WIA** 1Nov.18-*IIB*
Armstrong,2Lt.S, **KIFA** 18Feb.18-*III*
Armstrong,2Lt.WA, 21Sep.18-*I*
Armstrong,2Lt.WA, **KIA** 25Jul.18-*I*
Armstrong,1Lt.WJ, *USAS.* **WIA** 12Aug.18-*I*
Arnison,Lt.CH, 3May.18-*I*, **WIA** 16May.18-*I*
Arnold,Capt.ES, 8May.18-*I*
Arnold,2Lt.FT, **WIA** 8Jul.18-*I*
Arnold,2Lt.HE, **Kld** 26Dec.16-*I*
Arnold,FSLt.HJ, 11Jul.15-*IX*
Arnold,2Lt.J, **POW** 25Jun.18-*I*
Arnott,Lt.AAMcD, **KIA** 12Apr.18-*I*
Arnott,2Lt.HD, **KIA** 29Oct.18-*I*
Arnott,2Lt.L, **KIA** 16Sep.18-*I*
Arnott,Lt.RA, **WIA POW** 11Jul.18-*I*
Arthur,2Lt.HN, 27Mar.18-*I*, **WIA** 28Mar.18-*I*
Arthur,2Lt.NA, **WIA** 6Nov.17-*I*
Arthur,Lt.TJ, **POW** 15Aug.18-*I*
Artz,2Lt.JW, *US.* **WIA POW** 12Sep.18-*IIB*
Arundell,Lt.AWH, 9Aug.18-*I*
Arundel,Lt.PWR, 12Jun.18-*I*, **KIA** 8Aug.18-*I*
Asbury,Capt.ED, **KIA** 24Sep.18-*I*
Ash,FSLt.CFD, **WIA** 19Sep.17-*I*
Ashby,Lt.GSM, **WIA** 14Nov.15-*I*
Ashby,2Lt.RSCD, **WIA inj** 15Sep.17-*I*
Ashenden,2Lt.JF, *US.* **INT** 5Jun.18-*IIB*
Asher,2Lt.RS, **KIA** 21Sep.17-*I*
Ashfield,Lt.LA, DFC 27Jun.18-*I*, **KIA** 16Jul.18-*I*
Ashton,Lt.EE, 20Nov.17-*I*
Ashton,2Lt.GG, **KIA** 23Jul.18-*I*
Ashton,2Lt.KH, **POW** 31Jul.18-*I*
Askin,Lt.SCJ, **POW** 12Aug.18-*I*
Aslin,Lt.RL, **WIA** 2Sep.18-*I*
Aspinall,Capt.JV, **KIA** 15May.18-*I*
Atherton,Lt.MC,MC **KIA** 15May.18-*VIII*
Atkey,2Lt.AC, *Can.* 19Sep.17-*I*, 4Feb.18-*I*, 9May.18-*I*
Atkins,Capt.BS, UK. **POW** 16Sep.15-*VIII*
Atkins,2Lt.CA, **POW** 12Aug.18-*I*
Atkins,2Lt.GC, **POW** 19Jun.17-*I*
Atkins,2Lt.WJT, **POW** 17Jun.18-*I*
Atkinson,2Lt.CH, **KIA** 4Jul.18-*I*
Atkinson,Lt.DS, 24Sep.18-*I*
Atkinson,Capt.ED, **WIA** 1May.17-*I*
Atkinson,Lt.ED, 26May.18-*I*
Atkinson,2Lt.F, **POW DoW** 19May.18-*I*
Atkinson,1Lt.GB, *US.* **WIA** 2Oct.18-*IIB*
Atkinson,2Lt.H, **WIA** 17Aug.18-*I*
Atkinson,2Lt.JD, 23Apr.17-*I*
Atkinson,Lt.JM, **POW** 12Oct.17-*I*
Atkinson,Lt.KP, 7Sep.14-*I*
Atkinson,Capt.RNG,MC DFC 5Oct.18-*I*
Atkinson,Lt.TL, **POW** 22Nov.17-*I*
Atkinson,Pte.WJ, **KIA** 13Jul.18-*I*
Attwater,Sgt.S, **POW** 29Apr.17-*I*
Attwood,2Lt.JTL, **KIA** 25Sep.18-*I*
Atwater,1Lt.BL, *US.* **WIA** 25Oct.18-*IIB*
Atwater,2Lt.RM, 28Sep.18-*I*
Atwell,2AM.GF, **KIA** 23Apr.16-*I*
Auger?,PO.W, **WIA** 20Dec.15-*V*
Aulph,Lt.CT, **WIA** 27Oct.18-*I*
Aulton,Lt.WS, 3Apr.18-*I*
Austen,FSLt.VG, **WIA POW** 29Jul.17-*I*
Auster,2Lt.NCK, **KIA** 15Jul.18-*I*
Austin,2Lt.EV, **KIA** 11Jul.18-*I*
Austin,2Lt.FH, **WIA** 24May.17-*I*
Austin,2Lt.FM, 9Feb.17-*I*

Austin,Lt.H, **WIA POW** 28Jun.18-*I*
Austin,Lt.,Capt.RA, MC *Aust.*, 3Jan.18-*VII*, **POW** 19Mar.18-*VII*
Austin-Sparkes,Capt.J, **WIA** 29Sep.18-*I*
Austin-Sparks,Capt.RH, **WIA** 10Jul.15-*I*
Avery,2Lt.DJ, **WIA** 3Oct.18-*I*
Avery,1Lt.WL, *US.* **POW** 3Oct.18-*IIB*
Avery,1Lt.WR, *USAS.* **POW** 1Oct.18-*I*
Awcock,Lt.CH, 3May.15-*I*, 8May.15-*I*, 6Jul.15-*I*
Awde,Lt.IW, **WIA POW** 5Oct.18-*I*
Axford,Lt.H, 9Jul.18-*I*
Ayre,Sgt.JS, **POW** 19Jul.18-*I*
Ayres,Lt.SW, *Aust.* **DoW** 24.11.17 23Nov.17-*I*
Ayrton,Capt.FA, **POW** 16Sep.18-*I*

B

Babbage,2Lt.FF, 12May.17-*I*
Babbitt,2Lt.TE, **KIA** 15Jul.18-*I*
Babington,Capt., *2Sqn.* 10Oct.15-*I*, 11Nov.15-*I*, 13Feb.16-*I*, 24Feb.16-*I*, 29Feb.16-*I*
Babington,FCdr.,SCdr.JT, 21Nov.14-*I*, 16Mar.17-*I*
Bach,Cpl.JJ, *US.* **POW** 23Sep.18-*IID*
Backhouse,Sgt.WDA, **KIA** 7Jul.17-*I*
Bacon,Lt.DH, **KIA** 16Nov.16-*I*
Bacon,2Lt.ES, **KIA** 31Aug.17-*I*
Bacon,2Lt.LG, **WIA POW** 5May.17-*I*
Baddeley,2Lt.EL, **POW** 15Sep.18-*I*
Baer,1Lt.PF, *US.* DFC **inj POW** 22May.18-*IIB*
Baerlein,2Lt.AA, **WIA** 24Mar.17-*I*, **POW** 28Apr.17-*I*
Bagby,1Lt.RB, *US.* 2Sep.18-*IIB*
Bagot,Lt.HE, **WIA** 26Feb.17-*I*
Baguley,2Lt.FH, 15Apr.18-*I*
Bahl,1Lt.JL, *US.* **KIA** 27Oct.18-*IIB*
Bailey,Cpl.AF, **KIA**? 3Oct.18-*I*
Bailey,Lt.CF, **KIA** 6Apr.17-*I*
Bailey,Lt.EHP, **KIA** 11Aug.18-*I*
Bailey,Capt.GB, 28Sep.18-*I*
Bailey,Capt.GC, **WIA** 14Feb.17-*I*
Bailey,Lt.GG, 30May.18-*I*
Bailey,2Lt.JB, **KIA** 20Sep.17-*I*
Bailey,FLt.JF, **POW** 24Jul.16-*I*
Bailey,Capt.WI, **WIA** 8Jun.17-*I*
Baillie,Lt.W, 9Nov.16-*I*
Baillieu,Lt.TL, *Aust.* **WIA** 11Sep.18-*I*
Baillon,Lt.LN, **POW** 25Sep.17-*VIII*
Baily,2Lt.LJ, **WIA** 10Nov.15-*I*
Bain,1AM.LJW, **POW**? 5Feb.18-*I*
Bain,2Lt.NH, **WIA** 9Oct.18-*I*
Bainbridge,2Lt.EF, **KIA** 5Sep.16-*I*
Baines,2Lt.C, **WIA** 21Sep.16-*I*
Baines,2Lt.G, 20May.17-*I*, **DoW** 3.6.1917 27May.17-*I*
Baines,Lt.MT, **WIA** 24Aug.16-*I*
Bair,2Lt.HL, *US.* 15Sep.18-*I*
Baird,2Lt.J, 6Mar.18-*I*
Baird,Lt.RO, **KIA** 9Aug.18-*I*
Baker,2Lt.AA, **WIA** 15Sep.18-*I*
Baker,Capt.AF, **KIA** 11Apr.17-*I*
Baker,Lt.AN, **KIA** 25Apr.18-*I*
Baker,2Lt.AP, *US.* **WIA POW** 28Jul.18-*IIB*
Baker,2Lt.AR, **KIA** 16Aug.17-*I*
Baker,2Lt.AW, **KIA** 11Aug.18-*I*
Baker,Pbr.AW, 22Jun.18-*I*
Baker,Capt.BE, 27Jul.17-*I*
Baker,2Lt.ET, **KIA** 19Jan.18-*I*
Baker,Capt.FC, 5Aug.16-*I*, 16Sep.16-*I*
Baker,2Lt.FG, **POW** 6Nov.17-*I*
Baker,Capt.GB, **POW** .18-*VI*
Baker,Lt.GBA, 6Sep.16-*I*
Baker,2Lt.GC, 14Sep.16-*I*
Baker,Lt.GH, **WIA**? **inj**? 16Aug.18-*I*
Baker,1Lt.HT, *US.* **DoW** 14.8.1918? 12Aug.18-*IIB*
Baker,2Lt.LK, **WIA** 10Aug.18-*I*
Baker,Lt.RP, **WIA POW** 24Mar.17-*I*
Baker,Lt.,Capt.TCR, MM. *Aust.*, 31Jul.18-*I*, 28Oct.18-*I*, **KIA** 4Nov.18-*I*
Baker,2Lt.TM, **KIA** 17Oct.18-*I*
Baker,2Lt.VC, **WIA** 3Jan.18-*I*
Baker,Sgt.WE, **KIA** 20Jul.18-*I*
Baker,1Lt.WF, *US.* 27Sep.18-*IIB*, **WIA** 23Oct.18-*IIB*
Bakewell,Lt.GJ, **DoI** 16.11.1917 15Nov.17-*I*
Balaam,Lt.AO, **KIA** 24Oct.17-*I*
Balcombe-Brown,2Lt.,Maj.,R, 7Sep.15-*I*, 23Nov.17-*I*, **KIA** 2May.18-*I*
Balden,2Lt.WR, **WIA** 16Apr.17-*I*
Balderson,2Lt.L, 10Apr.18-*I*
Balderstone,2Lt.J, 6Mar.18-*I*
Baldwin,Lt., *30Sqn.* 27Jan.17-*VIII*
Baldwin,Sgt.CG, **KIA** 3Nov.16-*I*
Baldwin,Lt.GM, 29Aug.18-*I*
Baldwin,2Lt.H, 8Aug.18-*IV*
Baldwin,2Lt.H, **WIA** 1Nov.18-*IV*
Baldwin,Lt.OM, 11Jun.18-*I*, 15Sep.18-*I*
Baldwin,2Lt.WE, **DoW** 29Aug.18-*I*
Balfour,Lt.AS, **KIA** 13Jan.18-*I*
Balfour,Lt.B, 24Mar.17-*I*, 12Nov.17-*I*, **KIA** 16Apr.18-*I*
Balfour,Capt.HH, 16Feb.18-*I*
Balfour,Lt.J, 10Jun.18-*I*
Ball,2Lt.,Lt.,Capt.A, VC DSO MC, 16May.16-*I*, 22May.16-*I*, 29May.16-*I*, 1Jun.16-*I*, 8Jun.16-*I*, 2Jul.16-*I*, 3Jul.16-*I*, 16Aug.16-*I*, 17Aug.16-*I*, 21Aug.16-*I*, 22Aug.16-*I*, 25Aug.16-*I*, 15Sep.16-*I*, 23Apr.17-*I*, 6May.17-*I*, **KIA** 7May.17-*I*
Ball,2Lt.AC, **POW** 5Feb.18-*I*
Ball,2AM.AJ, **DoI** 21Mar.17-*I*
Ball,2Lt.OFG, **KIA** 5Apr.17-*I*
Ballance,2Lt.G, **POW** 29Jun.18-*I*
Ballantyne,2Lt.GA, **WIA** 9Oct.18-*I*
Ballantyne,2Lt.JB, **WIA** 29Sep.18-*I*
Balmain,2Lt.WF, 23Sep.15-*I*, 25Nov.15-*I*
Balsley,Sgt.C, *US.* **WIA** 19Jun.16-*IIA*
Balston,2Lt.M, 1Apr.18-*I*, 3Apr.18-*I*
Bamber,Lt.W, **POW** 17Oct.18-*VI*
Bamford,2Lt.JL, **KIA**? 20Aug.17-*VI*
Bampfylde-Daniel,FSLt.J, **WIA POW** 11May.17-*I*
Banbury,FCdr.FE, *Can.* 23Nov.17-*I*
Bancroft,Sgt.JW, **POW** 20Sep.17-*I*
Band,2Lt.LC, **WIA** 18Sep.18-*I*
Bands,FSLt.GK, **WIA POW** 23Oct.16-*VI*
Banfield,2Lt.CB, **POW DoW** 21Mar.18-*I*
Banham,2Lt.EG, **inj** 27Sep.18-*I*
Bankes,2Lt.PA, MC **inj** 20Apr.18-*I*
Bankes,Lt.HVN?, *34Sqn.*, *initials* HVA? HM? **WIA** 4Apr.18-*IV*, **POW** 24Apr.18-*IV*
Bankes-Price,FLt.JT, **KIA** 17Sep.16-*VII*
Banks,Capt.CC, MC 28Jan.18-*III*, 10Jun.18-*I*, 29Aug.18-*I*, 27Sep.18-*I*, 30Oct.18-*I*
Bannatyne,Capt.EJ, 17May.16-*VII*
Bannerman,Lt.RB, 4Aug.18-*I*
Bannermann,Lt.CG, 30Oct.18-*I*
Bannister,Lt.HS, **KIA** 21Jun.18-*I*
Banagar,Lt.FB, **WIA** 3Sep.17-*I*
Barber,Lt.BKB, **KIA** 4Sep.17-*I*
Barber,2Lt.GS, 25Aug.18-*I*, **KIA** 25Sep.18-*I*
Barber,2Lt.NC, *US.* **KIA** 11Aug.18-*IID*
Barbour,2Lt.HD, **KIA** 21Oct.17-*I*
Barbour,Lt.RLM, 9Oct.18-*I*
Bardgett,Lt.WE, **POW** 9Oct.18-*I*
Barfield,2Lt.CH, 6Jun.15-*I*
Barfoot,Sgt.H, **KIA** 19May.18-*I*
Barford,2Lt.KP, **KIA** 27Mar.18-*I*
Bargett,Lt.WE, **WIA** 15Aug.18-*I*
Baring,2Lt.RA, **KIA** 9Jun.18-*I*
Baring-Gould,2Lt.JH, **WIA** 25May.17-*I*
Barkell,2Lt.TH, *Aust.* 22Sep.18-*I*,. **WIA** 26Oct.18-*I*
Barker,Capt., *2Sqn.* 19Aug.15-*I*
Barker,2Lt.AF, *41Sqn.* 2May.17-*I*
Barker,2Lt.AF, **WIA** 28Jan.17-*I*
Barker,Capt.AT, **KIFA** 2Oct.18-*III*
Barker,Capt.ER, **INT** 11Apr.18-*I*
Barker,2Lt.FE, 27Jul.17-*I*, **WIA** 26Aug.17-*I*
Barker,Lt.FL, **WIA** 2Jul.17-*I*
Barker,Lt.GBA, 15Sep.16-*I*
Barker,Lt.HV, **WIA**? 10May.18-*I*
Barker,Lt.J, **WIA** 31Oct.17-*I*
Barker,2Lt.P, **WIA** 4Feb.18-*I*
Barker,Capt.,Maj.WG, *Can.* 20Oct.17-*I*, 29Nov.17-*IV*, 12Feb.18-*IV*, 17Apr.18-*IV*, 18Jul.18-*IV*, 1Sep.18-*IV*, 27Oct.18-*I*
Barksdale,1Lt.EH, *USAS.* 13Aug.18-*I*, **WIA** 2Sep.18-*I*
Barlow,2Lt.AN, **POW** 10Aug.17-*I*
Barlow,2Lt.CA, **DoW** 17Aug.17-*I*
Barlow,Sgt.G, 16Sep.18-*I*, **WIA** 4Oct.18-*I*
Barlow,Lt.HC, **KIA** 18Jun.17-*I*
Barlow,2Lt.,Lt.JL, 9Jun.17-*I*, **KIA** 23Sep.17-*I*
Barlow,Lt.LCJ, **KIA** 18Jun.18-*I*
Barlow,2Lt.LM, 24Apr.17-*I*, 26Jul.17-*I*
Barlow,AM.RK, **KIFA** 12Aug.14-*III*
Barlow,Lt.RS, 11Apr.18-*I*
Barlow,2Lt.,Capt.RT, 6Aug.17-*I*, **KIA** 30Jul.18-*I*
Barlow,1AM.T, **KIA** 2Oct.17-*I*
Barlow,2Lt.TW, **WIA** 26Mar.18-*I*
Barlow,2Lt.WH, **WIA** 27May.18-*I*
Barltrop,Lt.EA, **KIFA** 23Apr.17-*I*
Barnard,Sgt.BF, **KIA** Aug.15-*I*
Barnard,2Lt.EA, **KIA** 29Sep.17-*I*
Barnard,2Lt.FL, **inj** 22Oct.16-*I*
Barnes,Capt.EE, **KIA** 7Nov.17-*I*
Barnes,2AM.EW, **POW** 6Apr.17-*I*
Barnes,Lt.JD, **POW** 12Jan.18-*IV*
Barnes,Lt.,Capt.JS, 14Sep.16-*I*, **WIA** 16Aug.17-*I*
Barnes,Sgt.WA, **KIA** 13Apr.17-*I*
Barnes,2Lt.WE, 31May.18-*I*
Barnes,2Lt.WT, 30Aug.18-*I*
Barnet,Lt.DG, **DoW**? 28Dec.17-*I*
Barnett,Capt.JCL, 20Nov.17-*I*
Barnett,Lt.PJ, 10Jun.17-*I*
Barnett,2Lt.WA, **DoW** 15Nov.17-*I*
Barney,2Lt.LW, 3Apr.17-*I*
Baron,FSLt.MN, **KIA** 14Aug.17-*I*
Barr,2Lt.CC, *USMC.* **DoW** 6.10.1918 28Sep.18-*I*
Barr,Lt.EAD, 13Aug.16-*VIII*
Barr,2Lt.HC, **KIA** 11Dec.16-*I*
Barraclough,Lt., *6Sqn.* 31Jul.17-*I*
Barrager,2Lt.F, 2Jun.17-*I*
Barratt,Capt.M, 1Aug.15-*I*, 11Oct.15-*I*
Barre,Lt.GB, **KIA** 9Aug.18-*I*
Barrell,AG.Sgt.TH, *Aust.* **WIA** 24Nov.17-*I*
Barrett,2Lt.AG, *Aust.* 24Jun.18-*I*, 12Aug.18-*I*
Barrett,Lt.AS, 25Jul.18-*I*
Barrett,Capt.EW, **KIA** 29May.16-*I*
Barrett,2Lt.,Lt.JFT, 17Mar.18-*I*, 2May.18-*I*
Barrie,2Lt.F, **POW** 2Jun.17-*I*
Barrie,2AM.VN, **KIA** 6Apr.17-*I*
Barrington,Lt., *3Sqn.* 3May.17-*I*
Barrington,Lt.EL, MC **WIA** 4Sep.18-*I*
Barrington-Kennett,Lt.,Maj.VA, 12Mar.15, 3May.15-*I*, 4May.15-*I*, **KIA** 13Mar.16-*I*
Barritt,2Lt.GL, 13Apr.17-*I*, **POW** 1Sep.18-*I*
Barron,Lt.AM, MC 29Aug.18-*I*
Barron,Sgt.TH, 23Sep.18-*I*
Barrow,2Lt.SC, 16Sep.18-*I*
Barry,Lt.C, **KIA** 21Aug.17-*I*
Barry,Lt.GA, 25Mar.18-*I*, **WIA** 17Apr.18-*I*
Barry,Lt.OC, *Aust.* **KIA** 11May.18-*I*
Barry,Lt.JV, **WIA** 16Nov.16-*I*
Barry,2Lt.TH, 22Sep.18-*I*
Barter,Sgt.WJH, **KIA** 2Jul.18-*I*
Bartlett,Lt.AF, **POW** 6Jun.18-*IV*
Bartlett,2Lt.CH, **POW** 18Oct.17-*I*
Bartlett,FCdr.CPO, 28Mar.18-*I*
Bartlett,2Lt.EBW, **WIA** 20May.17-*I*
Bartlett,2Lt.GC, 22Mar.18-*I*
Bartlett,2Lt.GG, **KIA** 6Apr.18-*I*
Bartlett,2Lt.GR, **POW** 25Sep.18-*I*
Barton,Lt.,Capt., *4Sqn.* 15Oct.14-*I*, 1Nov.14-*I*, 11Mar.15-*I*
Barton,Lt.AES, **POW** 16Aug.17-*I*
Barton,2Lt.BCL, **WIA** 22Aug.17-*I*
Barton,Lt.CH, **KIA** 26Oct.17-*I*
Barton,Sgt.F, **KIA** 16Oct.16-*I*
Barton,Capt.HD, *SA.* 28Aug.18-*I*
Barton,Lt.HD, 8Aug.18-*I*
Barton,Lt.LF, **KIA** 17May.18-*I*
Barton,2Lt.R, **KIA** 12Jan.16-*I*
Bartram,Lt.AA, 27Oct.18-*IV*
Barwell,Capt.FL, **KIA** 29Apr.17-*I*
Barwell,Capt.HWE, MC **KIA** 25Mar.18-*I*
Barwise,Lt.HB, 19May.18-*III*
Basden,2Lt.MD, **KIA** 20May.16-*I*
Basedon,Lt.MW, 19Jun.18-*III*
Bash,1Lt.HE, *US.* **POW** 21Oct.18-*IIB*
Baskerville,Capt.MG, 27Jun.18-*I*
Bassett,Lt.WE, *Aust.* **WIA** 1Jun.17-*I*
Bassinger,Cpl.HG, **POW** 18Aug.17-*I*
Bastick,Sgt?, *59Sqn.* **POW** 30Nov.17-*I*
Batchelor,Lt.HC?, **WIA** 21Mar.18-*I*
Bate,2Lt.GB, 23Apr.17-*I*, **KIA** 29Apr.17-*I*
Bateman,Lt.CB, **WIA** 24Aug.18-*I*
Bateman,Lt.EC, **KIA** 7Sep.18-*I*
Bateman,Lt.JC 25Apr.18-*I*
Bates,Lt., *2Sqn.* 10Oct.18-*I*
Bates,Lt., *14Sqn.* 28Nov.17-*VII*
Bates,Lt., *98Sqn.* 20Jul.18-*I*
Bates,2Lt.AH, **KIA** 13Apr.17-*I*
Bath,Capt.EL, **WIA** 3Nov.17-*I*
Batson,2Lt.HT, **KIA** 11Sep.17-*I*
Battel,Lt.AJ, **KIA** 9Jul.18-*I*
Batten,2AM.WJ, **WIA** 13Apr.17-*I*
Battersby,Lt.PW, **KIA** 7Jul.17-*I*
Battey?,2Lt.BM, *USAS.* **POW** 21Jul.18-*I*
Battle,1Lt.BB, *US.* **POW** 12Jun.18-*IIB*
Battle,2Lt.HFV, **WIA** 20Sep.18-*I*
Batty,2Lt.HW, **KIA** 30Jul.18-*I*
Baudry,FLt.RGA, **KIA** 2Aug.16-*I*
Baugham,Sgt.JH, *US.* **DoW** 2Jul.18-*IIC*
Baumann,2Lt.MO, **KIA** 13Jul.17-*I*
Bawlf,Capt.LD, *Can.* 22Jul.18-*I*
Baxter,2Lt.AJ, **inj** 14Aug.18-*I*
Bayes,1AM., 3Sep.16-*I*
Bayetto,Sgt.,2Lt.TH, 5Jan.16-*I*, 2Mar.16-*I*, 2Jul.16-*I*
Bayley,Lt.FG, **KIA** 23Oct.18-*I*
Bayley,2Lt.LJ, **WIA** 22Mar.18-*I*
Bayley,2Lt.V, 23Jun.16-*I*
Baylies,Sgt.FL, *US.* **KIA** 17Jun.18-*IIC*
Baylis,2Lt.CJ, **KIA** 6Jun.17-*I*
Bayliss,Lt.WMF, **POW** 18Jul.18-*I*
Bayly,Lt.CGG, **KIA** 22Aug.14-*I*
Bayly,2Lt.CJ, **WIA** 13Jun.18-*I*
Bayly,Capt.LJ, **DoW** .18-*VIII*
Bayne,1Lt.JA, *US.* **KIA** 18May.18-*IIC*
Bayne,1Lt.JA, *US.* **Kld** 8May.18-*IID*
Baynton,2Lt.GR, **POW** 23Sep.17-*I*
Beagle,Lt.C, 4Jul.18-*IV*
Beal,2Lt.,Lt.LW, 4Mar.17-*I*, 11Mar.17-*I*, **WIA** 26Apr.17-*I*
Beales,Cpl.,Sgt.W, 23Mar.18-*I*, **WIA** 28Mar.18-*I*, 9May.18-*I*
Beamish,FSLt.,Capt.HF, *NZ.* 4Mar.17-*I*, 3May.18-*I*
Bean,2Lt.BH, **KIA** 18Jun.17-*I*
Bean,Lt.CAS, **POW** 9Aug.17-*I*
Bean,2Lt.CO, **WIA** 30Sep.17-*I*
Bean,Capt.HHW, **WIA** 13Feb.18-*I*
Bean,2Lt.HS, *US.* **WIA** 18Oct.18-*IIB*
Bean,Lt.HWW, **WIA** 26Aug.17-*I*
Bean,2Lt.WS, **KIA** 21Jan.18-*VIII*
Beane,1Lt.JD, *US.* **WIA** 30Jun.18-*IID*, **KIA** 30Oct.18-*IIB*
Beanlands,Capt.BPG, 30Nov.17-*I*, 21Mar.18-*I*, **WIA** 22Mar.18-*I*
Beare,Lt.PR, **WIA** 14Jun.18-*I*
Beare,SLt.SG, **INT** 25Apr.16-*I*
Beare,FSLt.SG, **POW** 22Mar.17-*VI*
Beart,Lt.W, **WIA** 9Apr.18-*I*
Beattie,FSLt.AG, **POW** 3Jan.18-*I*
Beattie,Lt.CAB, 4Jul.18-*I*, 16Jul.18-*I*
Beattie,Lt.JO, **KIA** 24Jan.18-*I*
Beatty,2Lt.BG, **KIA** 28Jul.17-*I*
Beatty,2Lt.CJ, **KIA** 15Sep.16-*I*
Beauchamp,Cpl.C, **WIA** 17May.17-*I*, **WIA** 24May.17-*I*
Beauchamp,Lt.FE, *Can.* **POW** 8Aug.18-*I*
Beauchamp,1Lt.OT, *US.* **Kld** 1Aug18-*IIB*
Beauchamp-Proctor,2Lt.,Capt.AFW, *SA.* VC DSO DFC MC 22Nov.17-*I*, 3Jan.18-*I*, 24Apr.18-*I*, 28May.18-*I*, 8Aug.18-*I*, 15Sep.18-*I*, **WIA** 8Oct.18-*I*
Beauclerk,1Lt.SW, *US.* **KIA** 29Oct.18-*IIB*
Beaufort,2Lt.FH, *US.* 30Jun.18-*I*, **KIA** 13Aug.18-*I*
Beaufort,Capt.JM, **inj** 25Aug.17-*I*
Beaulah,Capt.EA, **WIA** 23Jan.17-*I*
Beaumont,2Lt.CCA, **KIA** 27May.18-*I*
Beaumont,Lt.F, **POW** 1Apr.18-*I*
Beaver,2Lt.,Capt.W, *Can.* 29Nov.17-*I*, 13Jun.18-*I*

Beazeley,Maj.GA, POW 2May.18-VIII
Becher,Capt.AWB, WIA 1Nov.18-I
Beck,2Lt.,Capt.A, 9Aug.17-I, 8Aug.18-I, 8Oct.18-I
Beck,Lt.JG, 12Jun.18-I, WIA 22Aug.18-I
Beck,Lt.T, WIA 24Aug.18-I, POW DoW 1Oct.18-I
Beddow,Lt.HH, 2Sep.18-I, 5Sep.18-I
Bedson,Capt.EH, 31Jul.17-I, KIA 7Aug.17-I
Beebe,1Lt.DC, US. 13Sep.18-IIB, POW 4Nov.18-IIB
Beebee,Cpl.A, KIA 29Apr.17-I
Beeson,FSLt.F, KIA 20Dec.15-V
Beetham,Sgt.OD, POW? 10Aug.18-I
Beeton,2Lt.V, WIA 23Mar.18-I
Beevor,FLt.CF, 27Sep.14-I, KIA 5Nov.14-I
Beevor-Potts,Lt.L, 1Feb.17-VIII
Begbie,Lt.SCH, POW DoW 22.4.1918 21Apr.18-I
Begg,2Lt.HB, KIA 23Nov.16-I
Begg,Lt.MG, MC 3Sep.16-I, POW 25Sep.17-VIII
Belchamber,1AM.WJ, POW? 24Jan.18-I
Belcher,2Lt.LC, WIA 24Sep.18-I
Belcher,Sgt.NM, WIA 16Aug.18-I
Beldam,Lt.CH, POW 31Jul.17-I
Belding,Sgt.S, KIA 15Apr.18-I
Belgrave,Capt.JD,MC KIA 13Jun.18-I
Bell,CPO., 25Dec.14-I
Bell,Lt.AR, KIA 22Sep.18-IV
Bell,2Lt.BGA, KIA 6Apr.18-I
Bell,2Lt.DE, USAS. KIA 4Jul.18-I
Bell,Capt.DJ,MC SA. 24Mar.18-I, 8Apr.18-I, POW DoW 27May.18-I
Bell,2Lt.EA, KIA 22Sep.17-I
Bell,2Lt.EAV, POW 8Apr.17-I
Bell,Lt.EV, KIA 14May.18-I
Bell,Sgt.FW, 24Aug.18-I
Bell,Lt.,Capt.GG, Can. 29Jul.17-I, 13Apr.18-VI, 13May.18-VI, 1Jun.18-VI, 18Sep.18-VI
Bell,Lt.GS, UK. 30Aug.18-I
Bell,2Lt.HB, Can. 16Dec.17-IV
Bell,Capt.J, Aust. DoW 27.12.1917 20Nov.17-I
Bell,Lt.JMG,MC 2Sep.18-I, WIA 3Oct.18-I
Bell,2Lt.JR, 24Jun.18-I
Bell,Sgt.JV?, WIA 11Apr.17-I
Bell,2Lt.,Lt.JW, WIA 11Mar.18-I, 2Nov.18-I
Bell,2Lt.LH, KIA 26Sep.18-I
Bell,2Lt.N, KIA 18Aug.17-I
Bell,Capt.N, KIA 17May.18-I
Bell,2Lt.SH, 30Apr.17-I
Bell,2Lt.VD, 17Jan.16-I
Bell,Capt.WDM, 23Dec.16-VI
Bell-Davies,SCdr.R, VC DSO WIA 23Jan.15-I, 19Nov.15-V
Bell-Irving,2Lt.AD, MC Can. 20Sep.15-I, 22Sep.15-I, 26Sep.15-I, WIA 14Dec.15-I, WIA 9Nov.16-I
Bell-Irving,Lt.M, 17Jun.15-I
Bell-Irving,2Lt.,Lt.,Capt.MMcB, Can. 28Apr.15-I, 7May.15-I, 19Jul.15-I, 26Jul.15-I, 1Aug.15-I, 26Aug.15-I, WIA 19Dec.15-I, WIA 17Jun.16-I
Bellamy,Lt.F, 12May.16-VII
Bellerby,Sgt.H, 22Sep.16-I, KIA 23Sep.16-I
Bellingham,2Lt.FP, inj 19May.18-I
Belliveau,Lt.AH, 24Aug.18-I, POW 27Aug.18-I
Belloc,Lt.L, KIA 26Aug.18-I
Bellord,2Lt.CE, KIA 15Sep.18-I
Bellows,2Lt.FK, US. KIA 13Sep.18-IIB
Belton,2AM.CS, WIA 15Mar.17-I
Bembridge,FSLt.FEA, inj 22Mar.18-I
Beminster,2AM.C, 13May.17-I, POW 20May.17-I
Bemridge,Lt.G, 9Mar.18-I
Benbow,Lt.EL,MC WIA 21Mar.17-I, KIA 30May.18-I
Bence,Cpl.SJ, KIA 14Aug.18-I
Bendall,2Lt.OF, inj 16Sep.18-I
Bendlestein,2Lt.A, WIA 9Aug.18-I
Benett,2Lt., 4Sqn. 12May.15-I
Benge,2Lt.AN, 20Dec.16-I
Benger,Rfn.,Sgt,WJ, inj 25Jun.17-I, POW DoW 17Oct.17-I
Bengough,2Lt.NJ, 20Sep.15-I, 30Sep.15-I
Benjamin,Lt.AL, POW 31Jul.18-I
Benjamin,Lt.L, Aust. 1Dec.17-I
Bennet,Lt.TM, KIA 10Nov.16-I
Bennett,Cpl.T?, 16Sqn. 28Sep.15-I
Bennett,2Lt.AR, KIA 14Oct.18-I
Bennett,Lt.AW, WIA 1Oct.18-I
Bennett,2Lt.CD, WIA POW 14Feb.17-I
Bennett,Lt.CN, WIA 2Jun.17-I
Bennett,Lt.HJ, POW DoW 24Sep.18-I
Bennett,2Lt.HP, WIA 15May.18-I
Bennett,Lt.L, US. 19Aug.18-I, DoW 24Aug.18-I
Bennett,SLt.LJ, POW 25May.18-I
Bennett,Lt.RC, DFC 24Sep.18-I, POW 27Sep.18-I
Bennett,Lt.RG, KIA 28May.18-I
Bennett,2Lt.RJ, Aust.? WIA 29Jul.16-I
Bennett,Lt.RM, KIFA 29Sep.18-I
Bennett,FSLt.S, 11Apr.17-I
Bennett,FSLt.SL, KIA 29Apr.17-I
Bennett,Cpl.T, 16Jun.15-I, WIA? 21Oct.15-I
Bennett,Sgt.WG, WIA 4May.17-I
Bennetto,2AM.HV, WIA 27Jul.17-I
Bennetts,FSLt.EA, KIA 17Aug.17-I
Benney,Cpl.PP, US. DoW 26Jan.18-IIC
Bennie,Lt.RS, KIA 5Jun.17-I
Bensly,FLt.EF, POW 2May.18-I
Benson,2Lt.DG, Can. KIA 25Jun.18-I
Bent,2Lt.HKR, WIA 12Aug.17-I
Bentham,2Lt.GA, KIA 3Nov.16-I
Bentley,Lt.AO, WIA 31Aug.18-I
Bentley,2Lt.GW, KIFA 13Jan.17-I
Bentley,Lt.W, WIA 13Oct.18-I
Bentley,2Lt.WH, 1Jun.18-I
Benton,2Lt.JW, 29Mar.18-I, WIA 30May.18-I
Berlyn,FSLt.RC, WIA 7Apr.18-I
Berrington,Lt.NT, 23Mar.18-I
Berry,2Lt.A, WIA 9Nov.18-I
Berry,2Lt.FH, POW 9Oct.17-I
Berry,2Lt.HJ, POW 5Nov.18-I
Berry,2Lt.OW, KIA 8Apr.17-I
Bertie,Capt.CP, KIA 19Mar.17-I
Bertrand?,Lt.P, KIA 16Jun.18-I
Best,Lt.FB, 28Jul.17-I, KIA 29Jul.17-I
Best,Lt.RD, 11Apr.18-I
Best,Lt.RD, WIA 11Apr.18-I
Bestford,AG.2AM.R, KIA 12Aug.17-I
Betherington,Lt.J, 21Aug.18-I
Betley,2Lt.E, KIA 28Mar.18-I
Bettington,FCdr.AF, 12Aug.17-III
Bevan,2Lt.BJ, WIA 23Mar.18-I
Bevan,2Lt.W, KIA 3Dec.17-I
Beveridge,Lt.G, WIA 9Aug.18-I
Beveridge,FSLt.JE, WIA 22Jan.18-I
Bevington,Lt.RJ, POW 7Apr.17-I
Bewes,Lt.RCH, DoW 23May.15-I
Bewsher,Capt.P, inj 11Apr.18-I
Beynon,Lt.LF, WIA 13Apr.17-I
Bibby,2Lt.GMG, KIA 6Mar.17-I
Bice,Lt.EJ, Aust. KIA 8Aug.18-I
Bickel,Lt.LE, 9May.18-I
Bickerton,2Lt.FH, WIA 20Sep.17-I
Bickerton,2Lt.JH, WIA 31Jul.16-I
Biddington,2Lt.HV, POW 13Jan.18-I
Biddle,Capt.CJ, US. WIA 15May.18-IIB
Biddle,2Lt.SCH, WIA 27Oct.18-I
Bidmead,2Lt.B, WIA 11Mar.18-I
Bidmead,2Lt.CH, KIA 10Nov.16-I
Biedermann,2Lt.HE, KIA 10Aug.17-I
Biette,2Lt.FC, 15Sep.16-I, WIA 1Oct.16-I
Bigelow,Sgt.S, US. WIA 18Aug.17-IIA
Bigsworth,SCdr.AW, 26Aug.15-I
Bigwood,Lt.PH, KIA 21Jun.17-I
Biheller?,Capt., Sqn? POW 19Jan.18-I
Biles,Capt.GW, 4May.18-I
Bill,Lt.AG, inj 12Jul.17-I
Billinge,Lt.HF, 7Feb.16-I, 13Feb.16-I, WIA 14Mar.16-I
Billings,2Lt.HB, POW DoW 9Aug.17-I
Billington,Lt.FN, KIA 30Sep.18-I
Biltcliffe,2Lt.HG, WIA? 14Oct.18-I
Binckes,Lt.R, 16Jun.18-I
Bing,2Lt.WL, INT 8Aug.18-I
Bingham,Lt.AE, POW 28Jun.18-I
Bingham,2Lt.HW, KIA 14Oct.18-I
Bingham,2Lt.RGA, KIA 8Oct.18-I
Binkley,Lt.BW, KIA 12Jul.17-I
Binney,Capt.FB, WIA POW 26Sep.15-I
Binnie,Capt.A, WIA POW 14Apr.17-I
Binnie,Lt.A, WIA 10Aug.17-I
Binnie,Lt.J, 11Sep.17-I
Binnie,Lt.WH, KIA 22Jul.18-I
Binns,2Lt.JH, KIA 4Sep.17-I
Bion,Lt.RE, KIA 9Apr.18-I
Birch,Lt., 12Sqn. 10Sep.15-I
Birch,2Lt.DC, POW 6Apr.17-I
Birch,Lt.S, POW 9May.18-I
Birch,Sgt.S, WIA 15Nov.16-I
Birch,Lt.SG, 13Jul.18-I
Birch,2Lt.W, WIA 23May.17-I, WIA 14Jul.17-I
Birch,Lt.,Capt.WCK, 10Mar.15-I, 30Nov.15-I
Bird,2Lt.A, WIA 5Jun.18-I
Bird,Lt.AF, POW 3Sep.17-I
Bird,Lt.BA, WIA POW 3Jun.18-I
Bird,Lt.CB, MC 14Sep.16-I, POW DoW 28Jan.17-I
Bird,Lt.EH, DoW 27.6.1916 26Jun.16-I
Bird,Sgt.F, KIA 23May.17-I
Bird,Lt.FV, KIA 21Aug.18-I
Bird,Lt.JDJ, KIA 27Jun.17-I
Bird,TLt.SA, 22Sep.18-I
Bird,1Lt.SC, US. 5Oct.18-IIB
Birdwood,Lt.HF, KIA 2Mar.16-I
Birkbeck,Lt.PW, 19May.18-I
Birkbeck,Capt.RA, 1Oct.17-I
Birkett,Lt., 8Sqn. 2Sep.18-I
Birkett,Lt.W, inj 17Jun.17-I
Birkhead,2Lt.JB, WIA POW 12May.18-I
Birks,Lt.GA, Can. 21Jun.18-IV
Birks,Lt.NA, WIA POW 5Apr.17-I
Birley,2Lt.TEH, POW 22Mar.18-I
Birmingham,2Lt.TJ, 2Sep.18-I
Bishop,2Lt., 16Sqn. 21Apr.17-I, 30Apr.17-I
Bishop,2Lt.AJ, WIA 2Sep.18-I
Bishop,2Lt.BB, KIA 9Sep.17-I
Bishop,2Lt.NF, WIA 21Aug.18-I, KIA 16Sep.18-I
Bishop,Lt.,Capt.,Maj.WA, Can. 25Mar.17-I, 31Mar.17-I, 20Apr.17-I, 12Jul.17-I, 28Jul.17-I, 27May.18-I, 15Jun.18-I
Bishop,2Lt.WR, KIA 2Oct.17-I
Bissell,1Lt.CL, USAS. 29Oct.18-I
Bissell,Sgt.GH, KIA 29Sep.18-I
Bisset,2Lt.EGW, DoW 7Jan.17-I
Bissett,Lt.CS, 21May.18-I
Bissett,Lt.DM, 26Mar.18-I, WIA 10Apr.18-I, 29Sep.18-I
Bissonette,Lt.CA, US. 9May.18-I
Bittinger,2Lt.HP, USAS. POW DoW 26Aug.18-I
Biziou,Capt.HAR, 22Sep.18-I
Black,2Lt.IS, WIA 11Apr.18-I
Black,Maj.MA, KIA 11Feb.17-VI
Black,FSLt.N, DoW 12.10.1917 11Oct.17-I
Black,Lt.SMcB, Can. POW 31Jul.18-I
Black,2Lt.W, WIA POW 20Oct.16-I
Blackall,2Lt.JH, WIA POW 21May.17-I
Blackburn,2Lt.HD, KIA 5Apr.17-I
Blackledge,2Lt.EJ, KIA 23Nov.17-I
Blackwell,Lt.HH, 15Jun.18-I, 30Oct.18-I
Blackwell,2Lt.SF, WIA 27Sep.18-I
Blagrove,FSLt.CR, 23Apr.16-I, KIA 7Feb.17-I
Blain,2Lt.CW, POW 7Aug.16-I
Blair,Lt.J, 8Jul.18-I
Blake,2Lt.AGS, POW 25Jul.18-I
Blake,Lt.AW, SA. 19May.18-I, 9Aug.18-I
Blake,2Lt.CL, 31May.16-I, 1Jul.16-I
Blake,2Lt.GP, KIA? 18Oct.18-I
Blake,2Lt.HP, POW 24Mar.18-I
Blake,2Lt.JE, KIA 6Apr.17-I
Blake,2Lt.JW, POW 5Oct.17-VIII
Blake,Pte.WC, POW 7May.17-I
Blake,2Lt.WTC, 20Apr.18-I, WIA 26Aug.18-I
Blakesley,Lt.RG, POW 23Oct.16-VI
Bland,2Lt.WH, 4Nov.18-I
Blandy,SLt.G, POW .18-VI
Blanford,2Lt.JS, 5Oct.18-I
Blasdale,2Lt.CW, WIA? 26Sep.18-I
Blatherwick,2AM.CA, KIA 19Sep.17-I
Blatherwick,Pte.C, 17Aug.17-I
Blaxill,2Lt.FH, POW 27May.18-I
Blaxland,Capt.GH, Aust. 18Oct.18-I
Blaxland,2Lt.LB, 15Feb.17-I
Blayney,2Lt.BW, POW 24Nov.16-I
Bleckley,2Lt.ER, US. CMH DoW 6Oct.18-IIB
Bleeker,1Lt.LC, US. 12Sep.18-IIB
Blencowe,2Lt.FP, inj 28Jul.17-I
Blenkiron,2Lt.AV, WIA 29Jan.17-I
Blessley,Lt.RC, WIA 5Sep.18-I
Blight,Lt.TF, WIA POW 11Jul.18-I
Bliss,2Lt.G, 4Sep.17-I
Blitch,Lt.WJ, WIA 21Feb.18-I
Blodgett,1Lt.RA, US. KIA 12May.18-IIB
Blofeld,2Lt.H, WIA 27May.17-I
Bloom,2Lt.AL, 10Oct.18-I
Bloomfield,2Lt.,Capt.WSR, NZ. WIA 29Feb.16-I, POW 6Mar.17-I
Blount,Capt.CHB, 22Jul.16-I, 15Sep.16-I
Blundell,Lt.GR, Aust.? WIA 5Jul.18-I
Blundell,2Lt.JB, KIA 29Sep.18-I
Blunden,2AM.FA, WIA 23Apr.17-I
Bluthenthal,Sgt.A, US. KIA 5Jun.18-IIC
Blyth,2Lt.EJ, KIA 26Mar.18-I
Blyth,FSLt.RA, KIA 23Jan.18-I
Blythe,2Lt.H, POW DoW 10.2.1917 2Feb.17-I
Blythe,Sgt.WS, WIA 29Aug.18-I
Bockett-Pugh,Lt.HCE, POW May.18-I
Bocock,Lt., 98Sqn. 9Nov.18-I
Boddam-Whitham,Capt., 16Sqn. 14Dec.15-I
Boddy,2Lt.,Lt.JAV, 22Nov.16-I, WIA 23Nov.17-I
Bodley,2Lt.WGL, POW 5Oct.18-I
Body,Lt.GC, WIA 18Jun.17-I, POW 1Jul.18-I
Boe,2Lt.D, POW 29Jun.18-I
Boger,Capt.RA, 8Sep.14-I, POW 5Oct.14-I
Boger,Lt.,Capt.WO, Can., WIA 20Dec.16-I, 8Aug.18-I, KIA 10Aug.18-I
Boggis,AM.EHA, 25Apr.15-IX
Bolam,2Lt.WH, WIA 6Jun.17-I
Bolas,FSLt.JS, KIA 12Jan.16-V
Boldison,2Lt.A, WIA POW 5Apr.17-I
Boldt,1Lt.HJ, US. KIA 20Jul.18-IIB
Boles,2Lt.HF, DoW 24.5.15 23May.15-I
Boles,FLt.NH, KIA 11Jan.16-V
Bolitho,2Lt.AW, WIA 12Apr.18-I
Bolitho,2Lt.GR, 30Jul.16-I, WIA 25Aug.16-I, KIA 25Oct.16-I
Bollins,2Lt.AP, POW 12May.18-I
Bolsby,2Lt.CS 5Jul.18-I, 2Sep.18-I, 1Oct.18-I
Bolt,1Lt.WA, US. 5Oct.18-IIB
Bolton,Capt.AC, WIA POW 9Nov.16-I
Bolton,2AM.JH, 2Apr.17-I, KIA 5Apr.17-I
Bolton,2Lt.Lt.,Capt.NA, 20Nov.15-I, 17Jan.16-I, 9Feb.16-I, 29May.16-I, 22Jun.16-I, WIA 23Jun.17-I
Bond,Lt.FE, POW 5Oct.18-I
Bond,2Lt.TJ, WIA 13Sep.18-I
Bond,1AM.W, 23Apr.17-I, KIA 10May.17-I
Bond,Lt.WA, MC 9Jun.17-I, KIA 22Jul.17-I
Bond,2AM.WJ, KIA 24Apr.17-I
Bone,FSLt.JT, Kld 18Oct.15-I
Bone,FCdr.RJ, 19Mar.16-III
Bonham-Carter,Lt.IM, WIA 6Nov.14-I
Boniface,Lt., 99Sqn. 26Sep.18-I
Bonnalie,Lt.AF, USAS 14Aug.18-I
Bonner,2Lt.A, KIA 30Apr.17-I
Bonner,1AM.P, KIA 2Apr.17-I
Boocock,Sgt.A, POW 26Jun.18-I
Booker,FCdr.,Maj.CD, 11Aug.17-I, 27Sep.17-I, DoW 13Aug.18-I
Booker,Lt.CS, DoW 3Oct.18-I
Boote,2Lt.RSL, POW 8Jun.17-I
Booth,2Lt.EB, Can. 12Oct.17-I
Booth,FSLt.F, KIA 3Jan.18-I
Booth,Lt.GB, inj 20Oct.17-I
Booth,2Lt.H, inj 5Jul.18-I
Booth,FSLt.HH, POW 25Aug.17-I
Booth,Sgt.L, KIA 24Jan.17-I
Booth,Lt.PW, WIA 17May.18-I
Booth,Pte.TA, KIA 15Feb.17-I
Booth,Sgt.V, US. DoW 10Jul.18-IIC
Booth,2Lt.WA, KIA 23Nov.17-I
Boothman,2Lt.CD, POW DoW 26Jun.18-I
Boothroyd,2Lt.CG, 30Oct.18-I
Booze,1Lt.RW, US. WIA 3Nov.18-IIB
Borden,Lt.HH, KIA 1Jul.18-I
Borrowman,Lt.JJ, KIA 29Aug.18-I

Borthistle,Lt.WJ, **KIA** 29Jan.18-*I*
Borton,Lt.,Capt.AE, 5Feb.15-*I*, **WIA** 7Jun.15-*I*
Borton, 2Lt. CVJ, **WIA** 19Jul.16-*I*
Borwein,Cpl.J, 25Mar.18-*I*, 28Mar.18-*I*
Borwein,Sgt.J, **POW** 8Jul.18-*I*
Bosher,2Lt.H, **POW** 18Jul.18-*I*
Bosman,2Lt.JP, 11Apr.18-*I*
Boston,2Lt.WH, **WIA** 5Mar.18-*I*
Boswell,2Lt.ATW, **KIA** 2Oct.18-*I*
Bott,Lt.,Capt.AJ, *Can.* 24Aug.16-*I*, 2Sep.16-*I*, 15Apr.18-*VII*, **POW** 22Apr.18-*VII*
Bottomley,2Lt.ER, **KIA** 2Jun.17-*I*
Bottrell,2Lt., *4Sqn.* 26Nov.15-*I*, *4Sqn.* 29Dec.15-*I*
Boucher,Lt.N, **WIA** 17Jun.17-*I*
Boult,Cpl., *52Sqn.* 29Jan.17-*I*
Boultbee,Lt.AE, **KIA** 17Mar.17-*I*
Boulton,2Lt.FE, **POW** 16May.18-*I*
Boulton,2Lt.NS, **KIA** 29Sep.18-*I*
Boulton,Lt.FE, 3May.18-*I*
Boumphrey,Capt.GM, 5Feb.17-*I*
Boumphrey,Lt.JW, **POW** 30Sep.17-*I*
Bourinot,Lt.AS, *Can.* **POW** 3Jun.17-*I*
Bourne, 2Lt. GHT, **KIA** 18Mar.17-*I*
Bourne, 2AM. SE, **WIA** 7Jun.18-*III*
Bourns,Lt.AE, **WIA** 27Oct.18-*I*, **KIA** 4Nov.18-*I*
Bousfield,2Lt.C, 25Apr.17-*I*
Bousfield,Lt.JK, MC **POW** 6Apr.17-*I*
Bousher,Sgt.EV, 21Jul.17-*I*, **WIA** 21Aug.17-*I*
Boustead,Lt.HAR, **DoW** 5.4.1917 5Apr.17-*I*
Bovill,Capt., *6Sqn.* 20Apr.15-*I*, 2May.15-*I*, 3May.15-*I*, 9May.15-*I*
Bowater,Capt.AV, **POW** 28Sep.18-*I*
Bowden,2Lt.HGG?, **KIA** 11Mar.17-*I*
Bowden,2Lt.N, 11Apr.18-*I*, **KIA** 25Apr.18-*I*
Bowen,Lt.CS, 17Apr.18-*I*, **WIA** 22Apr.18-*I*
Bowen,Lt.EG, **WIA**? 7Dec.15-*I*
Bowen,Lt.EGA, **KIA** 8Sep.16-*I*
Bowen,2Lt.JB, *USAS.* 10Aug.18-*I*, **POW DoW** 7Sep.18-*I*
Bowen,1Lt.LG, *USAS.* 3Sep.18-*I*, **KIA** 15Sep.18-*I*
Bower,Cpl.AO, **WIA** 4Dec.16-*I*
Bower,2Lt.F, **DoW** 31.3.1917 30Mar.17-*I*
Bower,Sgt.FR, **WIA** 26Jun.18-*I*
Bower,Lt.LC, **INT** 2Aug.18-*III*
Bowerman,Lt.AJ, **KIA** 9Sep.16-*I*
Bowers,Lt.PT, **POW** 30Apr.17-*I*
Bowes,1AM., *2Sqn.* 11Nov.15-*I*
Bowler,Cpl.JH, **WIA** 21Mar.18-*I*
Bowler,Sgt.JH, **WIA** 5Sep.18-*I*
Bowles,Lt.FS, 15Jun.18-*IV*
Bowles,FSLt.G, **INT** Feb.17-*I*
Bowles,Cpl.J, 11Mar.18-*I*
Bowman,2Lt.,Lt.C, 25Mar.18-*I*, 11Jun.18-*I*
Bowman,FSLt.GG, **KIA** 19May.17-*I*
Bowman,Capt.,Maj.GH, 15Aug.17-*I*, 17Aug.17-*I*, 27Jul.17-*I*, 9Aug.18-*I*
Bowman,Lt.LS, **KIA** 25Jun.17-*I*
Bowman,2Lt.SA, *US.* **WIA** 4Oct.18-*IIB*
Bowman,Cpl.W, **WIA** 4Jun.18-*I*
Bowman,Lt.WP, 19Sep.16-*I*, **KIA** 17Oct.16-*I*
Bowring,2Lt.JV, **WIA POW** 14Sep.16-*I*
Bowyer,2Lt.F, **KIA** 25Jul.16-*I*
Bowyer,2Lt.FH, **WIA POW** 15Sep.16-*I*
Bowyer,2Lt.JE, *US.* **KIA** 12Sep.18-*IIB*
Bowyer-Bowyer,Capt.EW, **KIA** 19Mar.17-*I*
Bowyer-Smith,Lt.BM, 8Aug.18-*I*, *but name?:*
Bowyer-Smythe,Lt.BM, 10Oct.18-*I*
Boxall,1AM.A, **WIA** 28Mar.18-*I*
Boxall,AG.2AM.SC, **WIA** 22Aug.17-*I*
Boxhall,2Lt.RA, 17Sep.18-*I*
Boyce,2Lt.EF, **KIA** 3Sep.18-*I*
Boyce,Lt.HBP, **POW** 12Mar.18-*I*
Boyd,Lt., *1Sqn.* 9Aug.18-*I*
Boyd,2Lt.CN, **POW** 30Oct.18-*I*
Boyd,CPO.EA, **POW** 24Sep.17-*I*
Boyd,Lt.J, **POW** 12Jan.18-*I*
Boyd,Lt.JW, **DoW** 5.2.1917 4Feb.17-*I*
Boyd,Capt.OT, 2Jul.16-*I*, 29Jul.16-*I*
Boyd,Lt.PB, **KIA** 13Apr.17-*I*
Boyd,2Lt.TE, *US.* DFC **WIA** 14Sep.18-*IIB*
Boyd,2Lt.WW, 25May.17-*I*
Boyd-Moss,Maj.LB, 26Aug.14-*I*
Boyle,2Lt., *16Sqn.* 30Apr.17-*I*
Boyle,2Lt.JC, **POW** 4Sep.18-*I*
Boyle,Lt.R, 3Sep.18-*I*
Boys,2Lt.RHG, **POW** 1Sep.18-*I*
Boysen,2Lt.,Lt.HK, *US.* 8Dec.17-*IV*, **WIA** 28Jan.18-*IV*, 30May.18-*IV*
Boyton,2Lt.Lt., *7Sqn.* 20Nov.15-*I*, 5Jan.16-*I*
Brabrook,2Lt., *8Sqn.* 28Mar.18-*I*
Brabrook,Lt.EJ, 31Mar.18-*I*
Bracey,Sgt.SC, **DoW** 16Jun.18-*I*
Bracher,2Lt.HH, **KIA** 16Aug.18-*I*
Bracken,Lt.KO, *Can.* **POW** 27Oct.18-*IV*
Brackley,FSLt.HG, 7Sep.16-*I*
Bradbury,2Lt.D, **WIA** 14Aug.18-*I*
Bradbury,2Lt.G, **WIA** 2Sep.18-*I*
Bradbury,2Lt.H, 11Jul.18-*I*
Braddyll,Lt.EC, 28Jul.15-*I*, 31Jul.15-*I*, **POW DoW** 5Sep.15-*I*
Bradfield,1Lt.WL, *US.* **POW** 17Sep.18-*IIB*
Bradford,2Lt.AJ, *US.* **KIA** 25Jul.18-*IIB*
Bradford,2Lt.GWB, **KIA** 4Feb.17-*I*
Bradford,Lt.WW, **POW** 11Aug.18-*I*
Brading,Lt.CLW, 12Jun.18-*I*
Brading,Lt.RCB,2May.18-*I*
Bradley,Lt., *6Sqn.* **WIA** 16Aug.18-*I*
Bradley,Capt., *16Sqn.* 29May.15-*I*
Bradley,2Lt.DR, 21May.18-*I*
Bradley,2Lt.GP, **KIA** 27Oct.17-*I*
Bradley,1Lt.HB, *USAS.* **KIA** 25Jun.18-*I*
Bradley,2Lt.J, **WIA** 16May.18-*I*
Bradley,LCpl.R, **KIA** 20May.17-*I*
Bradshaw,Sgt.L, **WIA** 2Sep.18-*I*
Brady,FLt.BJ, **POW** .18-*VI*
Braebrook,Lt.EJ, **WIA** 1Apr.18-*I*
Brain,1AM.NL, **DoW** 22Oct.16-*I*
Brain,2Lt.WJ, **KIA** 21Oct.18-*I*
Braithwaite,2Lt.BF, **WIA POW** 14Oct.17-*I*
Braithwaite,ASgt.GL, **WIA** 30May.18-*I*
Braithwaite,Lt.N, **WIA** 19May.18-*I*
Bramley,2Lt.SLJ, **KIA** 23Sep.17-*I*
Brammer,Sgt.CC, **POW** 19May.18-*I*
Bramwell,2Lt., *7Sqn.* **WIA** 1Apr.16-*I*
Bramwell,2Lt.R, **KIA** 29Sep.18-*I*
Brand,Capt.CJQ, *SA.* **WIA** 1May.17-*I*, 19May.18-*III*, 21Sep.18-*I*
Brand,Lt.FR, **KIA** 27Jun.18-*I*
Brander,Lt.ES, **WIA** 6Nov.17-*I*
Brandon,FSLt.AF, 21Nov.16-*VI*
Brandon,Lt.ETC, *SA.* **KIA** 3Apr.17-*I*
Brandon,2Lt.R, **KIA** 11Aug.18-*I*
Brandon,2Lt.T, **WIA** 1Sep.18-*I*
Brandrick,2Lt.A, **POW** 5Oct.18-*I*
Brandt,Lt.JA, **KIA** 18Sep.18-*VI*
Branford,FSLt.FV, **INT** 1Mar.17-*I*
Bransby-Williams,Capt.WD,MC **KIA** 12May.17-*I*
Branson,MS,DS, **WIA POW** 12Jan.16-*V*
Brasell,Lt.JS, *Aust.* **KIA** 25Jun.17-*VII*
Brasington,2Lt.FT, **KIA** 9Oct.17-*I*
Brawley,Capt.GM, 18Sep.18-*VI*
Bray,2Lt.CL, *206Sqn.* **KIA** 7Jul.18-*I*
Bray,2Lt.CL, *211Sqn.* **KIA** 19May.18-*I*
Bray,FSLt.F, **KIA** 15Jul.17-*I*
Brayshay,Capt.WS, **KIA** 6Apr.17-*I*
Brazier,2Lt.LG, 2Sep.17-*I*
Breakey,FSLt.JD, 3May.18-*I*
Breakfield,2AM.GD, **KIA** 9May.17-*I*
Brearley,2Lt.N, **WIA** 9Nov.16-*I*
Breckenridge,2Lt.W, *USAS.* **WIA POW** 9Jun.18-*I*
Bredner,2Lt.NJ, **WIA** 11Mar.17-*I*
Breen-Turner,2Lt.WG, 7Jun.17-*I*
Breese,SqCdr.CD, **WIA** 1Jun.17-*I*
Breeze,2Lt.JG, **WIA** 17Jul.18-*I*
Bremickar,2Lt.CT, **WIA** 20Apr.18-*I*
Bremner,FSLt.FDH, 8Jan.16-*V*
Brent,Lt.J, **INT** Dec.17-*I*
Brent,Lt.V, **WIA** 12Apr.18-*I*
Brereton,Lt.LR, **WIA** 22Jul.18-*I*
Brett,AG.Cpl.S, **KIA** 13Jul.17-*I*
Brett,2Lt.WA, **KIA** 27Sep.18-*I*
Brettell,2Lt.W, **WIA** 15Apr.17-*I*
Brettingham-Moore,Lt.G, *Aust.* 27Mar.18-*I*
Brewer,Capt.CH,MC **inj WIA** 10Mar.18-*I*
Brewer?,2Lt.E, **WIA** 14Nov.17-*VI*
Brewer,1Lt.ER, *USMC* **WIA** 28Sep.18-*I*
Brewer,2Lt.TE, **KIA** 12Jun.18-*I*
Brewer,2Lt.WM, **WIA** 25Oct.18-*I*
Brewerton,Capt.CF, 12Jun.18-*I*
Brewis,Lt.JAG, **KIA** 29Apr.17-*I*
Brewster,Capt.GD,MC 31Aug.18-*I*
Brewster,Lt.JL, **KIA** 21May.18-*I*
Brewster-Joske,Lt.,Capt.CA, *Aust.* 2Jun.17-*I*, 22Sep.17-*I*
Brichta,Lt.GJO, *Can.* **KIA** 6Mar.17-*I*
Bridge,2Lt.AJ, 6Jun.18-*I*, **WIA** 25Oct.18-*I*
Bridge,2Lt.CHA, **POW DoW** 31Aug.18-*I*
Bridge,Capt.MF, **WIA** 27Mar.18-*I*
Bridgeman,2Lt.,Capt.OC, **WIA** 25Aug.17-*I*, 10May.18-*I*
Bridgeman,Cdr.Hon.OBR, DSO **Kld** 6Jan.17-*IX*
Bridger,Sgt.EEAG, 9May.18-*I*, **KIA** 16Aug.18-*I*
Bridger,2Lt.H, **WIA POW** 23Oct.18-*I*
Bridgett,2Lt.C, **KIA** 13Sep.18-*I*
Bridgman,Capt.RC, *US.* 12Sep.18-*IIB*
Brie,Lt.RAC, **POW** 22Aug.18-*I*
Briggs,Lt.C, **KIA** 27Jun.18-*I*
Briggs,1AM.H, **WIA** 19Feb.16-*I*
Briggs,Lt.LR, **WIA POW** 11Sep.16-*I*
Briggs,2Lt.,Lt.RW, 21Mar.18-*I*, 28Mar.18-*I*, 1Apr.18-*I*
Briggs,2Lt.SP, **POW** 26Aug.16-*I*
Brigham,Lt.KB, **WIA** 1Feb.17-*I*
Bright,2AM.HH, **KIA** 23Sep.17-*I*
Bright,2Lt.H, 4Nov.15-*I*, 5Feb.16-*I*
Bright,Lt.JM, **WIA** 15Sep.18-*I*
Bright,Lt.RE, **KIA** 8May.18-*I*
Brimmell,Pte.AW, **KIA** 4Sep.17-*I*
Brindle,2AM.P, **WIA** 1Nov.16-*I*
Brindley,2Lt.VG, **DoW** 30Aug.18-*I*
Brink,Lt.JHE, **DoW** 11.4.1917 9Apr.17-*I*
Brinkworth,2Lt.WH, **KIA** 4Aug.18-*I*
Brinsmead,FSLt.CH, **KIA** 11Jan.16-*V*
Brisbin,Lt.HV, **POW** 16Sep.18-*I*
Briscoe,Lt.MW, **KIA** 23Jul.17-*I*
Britnell,Lt.FJS, 26Sep.18-*I*
Britton,Lt.AF, **WIA** 27Jul.17-*I*, 18Aug.17-*I*, **WIA** 20Aug.17-*I*
Britton,Lt.EAC, **POW** 10Nov.18-*I*
Britton,Lt.RE, **WIA** 27Sep.18-*I*, **WIA** 8Oct.18-*I*
Britton,2Lt.WKM, **WIA** 19Dec.16-*I*
Brittorous,2Lt.OG, **KIA** 15May.18-*I*
Broad,FSLt.HS, **WIA** 11May.17-*I*
Broad,Sgt.AG, 21Jul.17-*I*
Broadbent,Lt.G, **WIA POW** 7Sep.18-*I*
Broadbent,Capt.S, **KIA** 18Feb.18-*I*
Broadberry,Capt.EW, **WIA** 12Jul.17-*I*
Broadhurst,2Lt.DS, **WIA** 10Mar.18-*I*
Broadley,Lt.TH, 26Jun.18-*I*, **KIA** 15Sep.18-*I*
Brock,Lt.CG, *Can.*, 16Jul.18-*I*, **WIA** 21Aug.18-*I*
Brock,Lt.FA, MM **KIA** 7Aug.18-*I*
Brockbank?,Sgt.A, *name* Brocklebank? **KIA**, 13Mar.18-*I*
Brockhurst,2Lt.GN, **WIA POW** 11Apr.17-*I*
Brocklebank,Sgt.A, *see* Brockbank
Broder,Lt.PA, **POW** 29Jul.15-*I*
Brodie, 1Lt.CA, *US.* **KIA** 1Oct.18-*IIB*
Brodie,2Lt.TW, **INT** 5Sep.18-*I*
Brody,1Lt.AA, *US.* **POW** 14Sep.18-*IIB*
Broke-Smith,Capt.PWL, UK. May.15-*VIII*
Brokensha,Capt.H, **WIA** 5Dec.17-*I*
Bromet,FLt.GR, 17Feb.15-*V*
Bromley,Sgt., *7Sqn.* **DoW** 2Nov.16-*I*
Bromley,2Lt.EC, 8Nov.17-*I*, 30May.18-*I*
Bromley,Lt.JL, **KIA** 29Sep.18-*I*
Bronskill,2Lt.FH, **POW** 1Feb.17-*I*
Bronson,Lt.CG, **POW** 28Jan.18-*V*
Brook,2Lt.AO'C, *Aust.* **WIA** 21Feb.18-*I*,. **KIA** 27Jun.18-*I*
Brook,2Lt.CA, **WIA** 21Apr.18-*I*
Brooke,Capt.AF, **WIA** 10Apr.18-*I*
Brooke,Lt.GA, 28Jul.17-*I*, 23Aug.17-*I*
Brooke,Lt.LS, **POW** 25Sep.18-*I*
Brooke,2Lt.TG, **WIA** 4Nov.18-*I*
Brooke-Murray,Capt.A, **DoW** 23.9.1916 16Sep.16-*I*
Brooker,Lt.J, 9Apr.17-*I*
Brookes,Capt.CA, UK. **KIA** 8Jul.17-*VII*
Brookes,Capt.EG, **KIA** 8Aug.18-*I*
Brookes,2Lt.GE, **WIA** 5Apr.17-*I*
Brookes,2Lt.LW, **KIA** 6Jul.17-*I*
Brookes,2Lt.RB, **KIA** 13Mar.18-*I*
Brookes,2Lt.WJ, **KIA** 28Sep.18-*I*
Brookes,Lt.WL, **KIA** 8Aug.18-*I*
Brookes,2Lt.WR, **WIA** 16Aug.17-*I*
Brookhart,1Lt.V, *US.* **INT** 12Sep.18-*IIB*
Brooking,2Lt.WA, **KIA** 19Jan.16-*I*
Brooks,2Lt.AR, *US.* 2Sep.18-*IIB*, 14Sep.18-*IIB*, 30Oct.18-*IIB*
Brooks,AM.H, **POW** 30Oct.17-*I*
Brooks,Sgt.WEA, **KIA** 16Jun.18-*I*
Broome,Lt.FC, 24Aug.18-*I*
Broomfield,1Lt.HDG, *US.* **KIA** 21Oct.18-*IIB*
Broomhall,2Lt.OA?, **WIA** 17Apr.18-*I*
Brotheridge,Lt.FJ, **KIA** 19May.18-*I*
Brothers,2AM.H, 3Sep.16-*I*
Brotherton,2Lt.WE, *US.* **KIA** 10Oct.18-*IIB*
Broughall,FSLt.HS, 6Sep.17-*I*, **POW** 20Sep.17-*I*
Broughton,2Lt.CB, **WIA POW** 11Apr.17-*I*
Brouncker,2Lt.CC, **KIA** 4Nov.18-*I*
Browhill,2Lt.EA, **KIA** 16Aug.18-*I*
Brown,2Lt.ACG, **WIA** 22Mar.18-*I*, 15Apr.18-*I*, **POW DoW** 7.5.1918 3May.18-*I*
Brown,Capt.AJ, MC 6Mar.18-*I*, 8Aug.18-*I*, 31Aug.18-*I*
Brown,Sgt.AJ, **INT** 4Jun.18-*III*
Brown,2Lt.AR, **KIA** 6Apr.17-*I*
Brown,Lt.,Capt.AR, *Aust.* 20Jan.18-*VII*, 3May.18-*VII*, 27Jun.18-*VII*, 22Aug.18-*VII*
Brown,Capt.AR, *Can.* DFC 21Apr.18-*I*
Brown,2Lt.,Lt.AW, 22Sep.15-*I*, 26Oct.15-*I*, 27Oct.15-*I*
Brown,Lt.AW, **WIA POW** 10Nov.15-*I*
Brown,1Lt.BE, *US.* **POW** 6Nov.18-*IIB*
Brown,2Lt.C, *25Sqn. observer* 6Apr.17-*I*
Brown,Lt.C, *25Sqn. pilot* 16Sep.18-*I*
Brown,Lt.CA, 12Oct.18-*I*, **WIA** 10Nov.18-*I*
Brown,Lt.CAF, **KIA** 26Dec.16-*I*
Brown,2Lt.CF, *203Sqn.* 17May.18-*I*, **POW DoW** 3.8.1918 25Jul.18-*I*
Brown,2Lt.CF, *35Sqn.* 24Jun.18-*I*, 27Oct.18-*I*
Brown,Lt.CH, *5Sqn.* **WIA** 1Apr.18-*I*
Brown,2Lt.CH, *70Sqn.* **WIA INT** 28Nov.17-*I*
Brown,Lt.CH, *70Sqn.* 23Mar.18-*I*
Brown,Capt.CP, 4Oct.18-*I*
Brown,2Lt.DG, **WIA** 30Mar.18-*I*
Brown,Lt.EC, **KIA** 18Oct.18-*I*
Brown,2Lt.EJ, 10Aug.17-*I*
Brown,2Lt.EM, 2Jun.18-*IV*, **POW** 9Jun.18-*IV*
Brown,Capt.FE,MC *Can. 84Sqn.* 22Mar.18-*I*
Brown,Lt.FE, *12Sqn.* 2Apr.17-*I*
Brown,2Lt.FG, **WIA** 24Apr.18-*I*
Brown,2Lt.FP, **WIA** 7Jun.17-*I*
Brown,2AM.G, *23Sqn.* **WIA** 6Mar.17-*I*
Brown,2Lt.G, **KIA** 23Oct.18-*I*
Brown,AG.1AM.G, *22Sqn.* **WIA** 21Aug.17-*I*
Brown,Lt.GC, 1Oct.18-*I*, **DoW** 10.10.1918 9Oct.18-*I*
Brown,2Lt.HM, 7Aug.18-*I*, **POW** 8Aug.18-*I*
Brown,Maj.HM, *US.* **POW** 10Jul.18-*IIB*
Brown,2Lt.HO, **WIA** 22Aug.17-*I*
Brown,Lt.J, **DoW** 11Aug.16-*VII*
Brown,2Lt.JA, **KIA** 25Jul.16-*I*
Brown,2Lt.JL, **POW** 12Jun.18-*I*
Brown,2Lt.JM, *13Sqn.* 1Sep.18-*I*
Brown,2Lt.,Lt.JM, DFC *US. 35Sqn.* 9Aug.18-*I*, **KIA** 3Oct.18-*I*
Brown,Lt.JM, *98Sqn.* 19Aug.18-*I*, 29Aug.18-*I*, 30Oct.18-*I*
Brown,2Lt.JR, 9Jul.18-*I*
Brown,2Lt.JT, 25Oct.18-*I*, 5Nov.18-*I*
Brown,Lt.JVR, **WIA** 27Mar.18-*I*
Brown,2Lt.,Lt.JW, *8Sqn.* 9May.17-*I*, **KIA** 14May.17-*I*
Brown,2Lt.JW, *101Sqn.* **POW** 24Sep.18-*I*
Brown,2Lt.LGH, **KIA** 6Dec.17-*I*
Brown,Lt.LH, **WIA** 5Oct.18-*I*
Brown,2Lt.LL, *15Sqn.* **WIA** 11Feb.17-*I*
Brown,Lt.LL, *Can. 57Sqn.* DFC **POW** 8Aug.18-*I*
Brown,FSLt.LO, 27Jan.16-*IX*

Brown,2Lt.MH, *US.* 5Oct.18-*IIB*
Brown,2Lt.P?, 5Jun.18-*I*
Brown,Lt.RSS, 22Nov.17-*I*, **WIA** 3Jan.18-*I*
Brown,2Lt.SF, 21Jul.17-*I*
Brown,Lt.SM, *US.* 28Oct.18-*I*
Brown,2Lt.T, **KIA**? 29Sep.18-*I*
Brown,Lt.V, **WIA** 14Sep.18-*I*
Brown,2Lt.VR, **POW** 28May.18-*I*
Brown,2Lt.WG, **WIA** 20Sep.18-*I*
Brown,2Lt.WH, *Can.* 10Mar.18-*I*
Browne,Lt.AA, *name* Brown?, 20Nov.17-*I*, **WIA** 30Nov.17-*I*
Browne,Capt.ADC, **WIA** 4Nov.18-*I*
Browne,2Lt.AR, **WIA** 30Sep.17-*I*
Browne,2Lt.ARH, *Aust.* **DoW** 5Dec.15-*I*
Browne,2Lt.CVR, 5Jul.18-*I*
Browne,2Lt.GEM, **KIA** 23Sep.18-*I*
Browne,Lt.HJ, **KIA** 3May.18-*I*
Browne,2Lt.HW, **POW** 30Mar.18-*I*
Browne,Lt.JSMcD, *Can.* **KIA** 27Jun.18-*I*
Browne,Capt.RF, **WIA** 8Oct.18-*I*
Browne,Lt.WA, **KIA** 21Sep.17-*I*
Brownell,Capt.JR, *Aust.* 17May.18-*IV*
Browning,2Lt.FA, **DoW** 22.9.1918 19Sep.18-*I*
Browning,1Lt.RL, *US.* **POW** 10Jul.18-*IIB*
Browning,Capt.SF, **KIA** 3May.17-*I*
Browning-Paterson,Capt.NA, **KIA** 21Jul.16-*I*
Bruce,Capt., *10Sqn.* 14Oct.15-*I*, 28Nov.15-*I*
Bruce,2Lt.APC, 16Sep.18-*I*, **POW** 23Oct.18-*I*
Bruce,Lt.CT, **DoW** 5May.17-*I*
Bruce,2Lt.PT, **KIA** 30May.18-*I*
Bruce,2Lt.TB, **POW** 6Nov.17-*I*
Bruce,Lt.W, **KIA** 25May.18-*I*
Bruce-Norton,2Lt.J, 27Mar.18-*I*
Bruck,2Lt.LM, *US.* **KIA** 10Nov.18-*IIB*
Brufton,Lt.HC, **KIA** 8Jul.17-*VI*
Brummell,Lt.HP, **POW** 29Sep.18-*I*
Brunwin-Hales,Capt.GO, **KIA** 24Mar.17-*I*
Bryan,2Lt.FFH, **POW** 26Jun.18-*I*
Bryant,Lt.CA, 9Aug.18-*I*, 14Oct.18-*I*
Bryant,Capt.CE, DSO 6Mar.17-*I*
Bryant,Lt.E, 4Oct.18-*I*
Bryant,Lt.JH, **KIA** 4Oct.18-*IV*
Bryant,2Lt.SO, **KIA** 13Aug.18-*I*
Bryant,2Lt.WEG, **WIA** 30Jul.16-*I*
Bryars,2Lt.GL, **KIA** 16Sep.18-*I*
Bryden,Sgt.J, **POW** 7Sep.18-*I*
Brydone,2Lt.J, **POW** 28Dec.17-*I*
Bryers,2Lt.G, 15Feb.17-*I*
Brymer,Lt., *6Sqn.* 22Jun.16-*I*
Bryom,Lt.JF, 19Aug.17-*I*
Bryson,Lt.OC, 16Aug.17-*I*
Bryson,Capt.RE, **WIA** 21Mar.18-*I*
Buchan,Sgt.RW, **WIA** 25Aug.18-*I*
Buchanan,Lt.A, DFC 29Sep.18-*I*, **POW** 30Oct.18-*I*
Buchanan,2Lt.L, **KIA** 22Nov.17-*I*, **POW** 10Jan.18-*I*
Buchanan,Lt.WJ, **POW** 19Sep.18-*VI*
Buchannan,Sgt.C, **WIA** 16Mar.17-*I*
Buck,Lt.CM, **KIA** 24Jan.17-*I*
Buck,Lt.GS, 13Apr.17-*I*
Buck,2Lt.R, 1Jun.16-*I*
Buckby,2Lt.R, **KIA** 26Sep.18-*I*
Buckerfield,1AM., *5Sqn.* 22Aug.15-*I*
Buckeridge,2Lt.,Lt.WH, 31Jul.16-*I*, 22Sep.18-*I*, **KIA** 2Oct.18-*I*
Buckingham,Capt.W, **POW** 1Oct.18-*I*
Buckland,Lt.WAJ, *Aust.* **KIA** 6May.18-*I*
Buckley,1Lt.CT, *US.* **KIA** 10Oct.18-*IID*
Buckley,FSLt.EJK, 27Jul.17-*I*
Buckley,2Lt.EM, 23Aug.18-*I*
Buckley,2Lt.H, **WIA** 10Aug.18-*I*
Buckley,1Lt.PH, *US.* **WIA** 23Oct.18-*IIB*
Buckley,Lt.SE, 15Nov.15-*I*, **POW** 30Nov.15-*I*
Bucknall,2Lt.CVA, **POW** 5Oct.18-*I*
Buckton,2Lt.NC, 13Apr.17-*I*, 28Apr.17-*I*
Budd,Sgt.BC, **WIA** 20May.17-*I*
Budd,2Lt.EFC, **DoW** 11Sep.17-*I*
Budden,Lt.G, 11Jun.17-*I*, **WIA** 5Aug.17-*I*
Budds,CPO., 25Dec.14-*I*
Buddwin,2Lt.LA, 23Mar.18-*I*
Budgen,2Lt.HK, **WIA** 31Jul.17-*I*
Budgett,Lt., **inj** 23Apr.17-*I*

Buffum,Cpl., *US., Spa.77* **POW** 4May.18-*IID*
Buffum,Sgt?,TG, *US.* **POW** 4May.18-*IIC*
Bugg,2Lt.EG, **KIA** 6Sep.18-*I*
Bugge,2Lt.FH, **INT** 31Jul.18-*I*
Bull,2Lt.ER, 12Aug.18-*I*
Bull,2Lt.FJ, **POW** 18May.18-*I*
Bullen,2Lt.EH, *USAS* **POW** 22Jul.18-*I*
Bullen,Lt.G, 10Apr.18-*I*
Buller,Lt.JAR, **WIA** 23Sep.16-*I*
Bullock,2Lt.RN, **WIA** 20Aug.17-*I*
Bullock-Webster?,Lt.F, **DoW** 20Sep.17-*I*
Bullough,Lt.J, **KIA** 3Nov.18-*I*
Bulman,2Lt.PWS, **WIA** 29Jan.18-*I*
Bulman,Lt.TS, **WIA** 3Sep.18-*I*
Bulmer,2Lt.GW, *US.* 6Mar.18-*I*
Bunbury,Capt.TStP, **KIA** 31Aug.18-*I*
Bundy,Lt.JI, 12Nov.17-*I*
Buntine,2Lt.WHC, **WIA** 9Sep.16-*I*
Bunting,2Lt.BML, 19Sep.18-*I*, 9Nov.18-*I*
Bunting,2Lt.SW, **WIA** 5Mar.18-*I*
Burbury,Lt.AV,MC **POW** 26Apr.17-*I*
Burch,Lt.RS, **KIA** 28Jun.18-*I*
Burcher,2Lt.LC, 7Sep.16-*I*
Burden,Lt.FG, **WIA** 2Oct.18-*I*
Burden,Lt.,Capt.HJ, *Can.* 2May.18-*I*, 10Aug.18-*I*
Burden,2Lt.SE, **KIA** 1Nov.18-*I*
Burdett,1AM.WR, **WIA** 20Jul.17-*I*
Burdick,Lt.,Capt.FW, MC 8Dec.17-*I*, 29Apr.18-*I*, 3May.18-*I*, **KIA** 16Jun.18-*I*
Burdick,1Lt.H, *USAS.* 8Oct.18-*I*, 25Oct.18-*I*
Bures,1Lt.GE, *US.* **KIA** 4Nov.18-*IIB*
Burge,2Lt.,Capt.PS, MC 17Mar.18-*I*, **KIA** 24Jul.18-*I*
Burger,TLt.MG, 18Jun.18-*I*
Burgess,Lt.DL, 7Jul.17-*I*
Burgess,Lt.HG, **WIA** 9Apr.18-*I*
Burgess,Sgt.HP, **KIA** 11Mar.17-*I*
Burgess,Lt.R, **DoW** 1Jul.16-*I*
Burgess,2Lt.VW, 16Aug.17-*I*, **inj** 31Aug.17-*I*
Burgin,2Lt.vH, *US.* **POW** 26Sep.18-*IIB*
Burke,Pbr.,2Lt.DC, 15Jun.18-*I*, **WIA** 1Sep.18-*I*
Burke,2Lt.EW, **KIA** 14Sep.16-*I*
Burkett,2Lt.GTW, 27Jul.17-*I*
Burky,Lt.RJ, *USAS.* **KIA** 15May.18-*I*
Burleigh,Lt.R, **KIA** 28Aug.16-*I*
Burling,FLt.EJ, 30Oct.17-*VII*
Burlton,Lt.AV, 10Nov.16-*I*
Burn,Lt.EA, 8May.18-*I*, **inj** 30Jun.18-*I*
Burn,2Lt.JS, **POW** 14Jul.18-*I*
Burn,Lt.WWA,*NZ.* 8May.15-*VIII*, **DoW** 30Jul.15-*VIII*
Burnaby,MS,HE, 8Jan.16-*V*
Burnand,2Lt., *16Sqn.* 15Aug.17-*I*
Burnand,Lt.GA, 7Apr.17-*I*
Burnard,2Lt.RA, 24Mar.18-*I*, 27Mar.18-*I*, **WIA POW** 31Mar.18-*I*
Burne,2Lt.CJ, **KIA** 25Jul.18-*I*
Burnett,2Lt.HR, **KIA** 25Sep.18-*I*
Burnett,FSLt.WG?, **KIA** 26Sep.17-*I*
Burney,Capt.GA, 7Jul.16-*I*
Burney,Lt.GA, 25Jan.16-*I*
Burney-Cummings,2Lt.JC, **WIA** 4Apr.18-*I*
Burnham,Lt.ME, **POW** 21Aug.18-*I*
Burnie,2Lt.AJ, **POW** 11Oct.15-*I*
Burns,Lt.JR, 1Feb.17-*VIII*
Burns,2Lt.JSD, *US.* **KIA** 11Aug.18-*IIB*
Burns,2Lt.LES, **WIA**? 1Nov.18-*I*
Burns,2Lt.VLA, **POW** 29Apr.17-*I*
Burns,FSgt.W, **DoW** 28Sep.15-*I*
Burr,FSLt.RE, **DoW** 20.2.1918 18Feb.18-*I*
Burrell,Lt.EL, **WIA** 29Sep.17-*I*
Burrell,AG.ACpl.H, **KIA** 18Oct.17-*I*
Burrill,Lt.TF, **POW** 6Apr.17-*I*
Burrow?,2Lt.AN, **WIA** 20Sep.17-*I*
Burry,Lt.HW, **POW** 8Jul.18-*I*
Burt,FSLt.AC, 22Sep.17-*I*
Burt,2Lt.HSR, 29Sep.18-*I*, 11Oct.18-*I*
Burt,2Lt.J, **KIA** 8Nov.18-*I*
Burt,Lt.OL, **KIA** 23Jul.17-*I*
Burton,Sgt.A, 16Mar.18-*I*
Burton,2Lt.AE, 27Mar.18-*I*
Burton,Lt.DF, **POW** 22Aug.18-*I*

Burton,2Lt.E, **POW** 2Sep.16-*I*
Burton,2AM.EPC, **INT** 4Jun.18-*III*
Burton,Lt.H, **POW** 16Aug.18-*I*
Burton,FSLt.HM, **POW** .16-*I*
Burton,2Lt.SG, **KIA** 30Jul.18-*I*
Bury,2Lt.N, **WIA** 25Mar.18-*I*
Bury,2AM.TH, **POW** 29Oct.17-*VI*
Busby,FSLt.EW, **KIA** 10Jul.17-*I*
Buschmann,2Lt.AKAM, **WIA** 12Jul.17-*I*
Bush,2Lt., *10Sqn.* 19Jan.16-*I*
Bush,2Lt.JC,MC **KIA** 7Oct.17-*I*
Bush,Capt.JSdeL, **POW DoW** 25.8.1917 25Aug.17-*I*
Bush,2Lt.RFL, **WIA** 3Sep.17-*I*
Bush,Sgt.HW, 8Aug.18-*I*
Bushe,2Lt.JF, **POW** 30Sep.17-*I*
Busk,FCdr.HA, **KIA** 6Jan.16-*V*
Busk,Lt., *70Sqn.* 6Sep.16-*I*
Buswell,2Lt.TH, **KIA** 26Mar.18-*I*
Butler,Sgt.C, 23Nov.16-*I*
Butler,FLt.CH **WIA** Jul.15?-*V*
Butler,Sgt.CJ, **POW** 21Oct.17-*I*
Butler,2Lt.H, **KIA** 22Feb.18-*IV*
Butler,Lt.H, 24Mar.17-*I*, **KIA** 25Mar.17-*I*
Butler,Lt.JO, **POW DoW** 11.4.1918 24Mar.18-*I*
Butler,Lt.L, **POW** 8Apr.17-*I*
Butler,Lt.RA, **KIA** 20Jul.17-*I*
Butler,2Lt.WM, 28Mar.18-*I*
Butt,2Lt.LAK, 23Sep.15-*I*, 19Dec.15-*I*
Butterworth,FSLt.CH, **WIA POW** 12Oct.16-*I*
Butterworth,2Lt.F, **KIA** 14Sep.18-*I*
Butterworth,Lt.H, **KIA** 9Aug.18-*I*
Butterworth,2Lt.HA, **WIA** 16Jul.16-*I*
Butterworth,2Lt.N, **KIA** 10May.17-*I*
Buttle,2Lt.WJ, **WIA** 2Apr.18-*I*
Button,Lt.LH, **POW** 9Aug.18-*I*
Buxton,2Lt.GB, **KIA** 28Jul.17-*I*
Byers,Cpl.LL, *US.* **POW** 18Jul.18-*IID*
Byrne,2Lt.E, **KIA** 11Mar.17-*I*
Byrne,Lt.PAL, 23Sep.16-*I*, **KIA** 16Oct.16-*I*
Byron,2Lt.JF, 16Sep.17-*I*
Bysshe,FSLt.GT, **POW** 17Feb.17-*V*

C

Cabburn,2Lt.F, **KIA** 25Jun.18-*I*
Cadbury,FSLt.,Maj.E, DSC 28Nov.16-*III*, 5Aug.18-*III*
Caffyn,2Lt.HR, 21Apr.18-*I*
Cahill-Byrne,Capt.MGMcL, **POW** 30Oct.18-*IV*
Cahusac,Capt.EB, **POW** 27Mar.18-*I*
Caillard,Lt.B, 28Sep.18-*I*
Cain,Capt.RC, DFC 27Oct.18-*IV*, **WIA** 27Oct.18-*IV*
Cairne-Duff,2Lt.A, **WIA POW** 31May.16-*I*
Cairnes,Capt., *16Sqn.* 26May.15-*I*
Cairnes,Capt.WJ, *Irl.* 19Mar.17-*I*, **KIA** 1Jun.18-*I*
Cairns,Lt.DS, **POW** 29Aug.16-*I*
Cairns,2Lt.JA, **POW** 27Apr.17-*I*
Cairns,2Lt.WTS, **POW** 6Oct.18-*I*
Caldecott,2Lt.R, **POW** 10Mar.18-*I*
Calder,Lt.A, **KIA** 10Aug.17-*I*
Calder,2Lt.PB, 6Oct.17-*I*
Calderwood,2Lt.DM, **KIA** 20Sep.18-*I*
Caldwell,Lt.J, **KIA** 29Aug.18-*I*
Caldwell,Lt.Capt.JH, 17Dec.17-*VIII*, **Died** 12Jan.18-*VIII*
Caldwell,2Lt.,Lt.,Maj.KL, *NZ.* 27Jan.17-*I*, 14Jun.17-*I*, 12Apr.18-*I*
Callaghan,2Lt.EC, 24Aug.16-*I*, **KIA** 26Aug.16-*I*
Callaghan,2Lt.,Maj.JC, *Irl.* MC 26Apr.16-*I*, MC **KIA** 2Jul.18-*I*
Callender,Lt.,Capt.AA, *US.* 10Jun.18-*I*, 24Sep.18-*I*, **DoW** 30Oct.18-*I*
Callender,Lt.GG, *NZ.* **WIA** 20Oct.16-*I*
Calrow,2Lt.R, **WIA** 24Aug.18-*I*, **POW** 6Oct.18-*I*
Calvert,FSLt.CWL, **WIA** 26Sep.17-*I*
Calvert,2Lt.E, **DoW** 14.8.1918 13Aug.18-*I*
Calvert,2Lt.TW, **WIA POW** 7Dec.17-*I*
Calvey,Lt.H, 25Mar.17-*I*
Cambray,2Lt.WC, 26Sep.17-*I*
Cameron,FSLt.AW, 5Nov.17-*I*
Cameron,2Lt.CH, 15Aug.17-*I*

Cameron,2Lt.CW, **KIA** 18Dec.17-*I*
Cameron,2Lt.D, **KIA** 25Mar.18-*I*
Cameron,2Lt.DE, 29Sep.18-*I*, 28Oct.18-*I*
Cameron,Lt.DR, **POW** 3Jun.17-*I*
Cameron,2Lt.ID, **POW** 18Dec.17-*I*
Cameron,2Lt.IG, **POW DoI** 9Nov.16-*I*
Cameron,Lt.NS, 8Jul.18-*I*
Cameron,Lt.PG, **KIA** 14Aug.17-*I*
Camm,Lt.RA, *Aust.* **WIA** 4Jun.18-*VII*
Campbell,2Lt.A, 10Aug.17-*I*
Campbell,SLt.ABD, **POW** 15Sep.18-*I*
Campbell,Sgt.AC, *US.* **KIA** 1Oct.17-*IIA*
Campbell,Lt.ARD, 15Sep.18-*I*
Campbell,2Lt.CB, *Aust.* **KIA** 29Nov.17-*I*
Campbell,2Lt.CStG, **KIA** 6Apr.17-*I*
Campbell,1Lt.D, *US.* 14Apr.18-*IIB*, **WIA** 6Jun.18-*IIB*
Campbell,Lt.DG, 5Feb.18-*I*, **KIA** 19Feb.18-*I*
Campbell,2Lt.EJ, **WIA** 10Sep.16-*I*
Campbell,Lt.HJQ, **WIA** 11Apr.17-*I*
Campbell,2Lt.ID, **KIA** 30Nov.17-*I*
Campbell,2Lt.J, **POW** 16Aug.18-*I*
Campbell,Lt.JF, *USAS.* 22Aug.18-*I*
Campbell,Cpl.JK, 3Sep.16-*I*
Campbell,2Lt.JK, **KIA** 28Jul.17-*I*
Campbell,Capt.JS, **KIA** 28Sep.17-*I*
Campbell,FSLt.KD, **POW** 10Mar.18-*I*
Campbell,Lt.,Lt.KP,2Apr.18-*I*, 23Jun.18-*I*
Campbell,2Lt.KT, **KIA** 14Apr.17-*I*
Campbell,2Lt.Capt.L, 24Mar.18-*I*, **KIA** 9Oct.18-*I*
Campbell,1Lt.ML, *USAS.* **KIA** 23Aug.18-*I*
Campbell,Sgt.RA, 3Sep.18-*I*
Campbell,2Lt.RO, *US.* **KIA** 27Sep.18-*I*
Campbell,Lt.W, **KIA** 6Jul.17-*I*
Campbell,2Lt.WA, **KIA** 26Apr.17-*I*
Campbell,2Lt.WA, **DoW** 21Sep.17-*I*
Campbell,2Lt.WC, DSO MC 16Jun.17-*I*, **WIA** 31Jul.17-*I*
Campbell,Lt.WG, 27Sep.18-*I*, 28Sep.18-*I*
Campbell-Dick,Lt.JW, 27Mar.18-*I*
Campbell-Martin,Lt.PC, **POW** 3Feb.18-*I*
Campbell-Orde,FSLt.AC, **WIA** 26Jul.17-*I*, 14Sep.17-*I*
Candy,2Lt.FB, **INT** 9Nov.18-*III*
Candy,2Lt.JGS, 21Jul.17-*I*, 24Oct.17-*I*
Cann,2Lt.L, **KIA** 13Mar.18-*I*
Cann,2Lt.PR, **DoW** 2.4.1918 1Apr.18-*I*
Canning,2Lt.S, 18Sep.17-*I*
Canning,AM.SA, **KIA** 25Aug.17-*I*
Canon,FSLt.RP, 21Nov.14-*I*
Cantle,Lt.LH, **KIA** 8Apr.17-*I*
Cantlon,Lt.FH,MC *Can.* **KIA** 18Mar.18-*I*
Capel,2Lt., *4Sqn.* 23May.15-*I*, 26Jul.15-*I*
Capel,Lt.CG, **WIA** 19May.18-*I*
Capel,Lt.K, 9Apr.17-*I*
Capel-Cure,2Lt.RC, 1Sep.18-*I*
Caple,Lt.LN, 16Sep.18-*I*
Capon,2Lt.RS, **WIA** 31Aug.16-*I*, **WIA POW** 24Apr.17-*I*
Capp,1AM.PJ, **Kld** 11Mar.18-*I*
Capper,Cpl., **inj** 21Jul.16-*I*
Capper,2Lt.EW, 22Oct.16-*I*, **KIA** 14Apr.17-*I*
Carbert,Capt.CM, MC **inj** 27Dec.16-*I*, **KIA** 1Feb.17-*I*
Carbery,2Lt.DHM, 25Jan.17-*I*
Carbines,2Lt.H, **KIA** 27Mar.18-*I*
Carden,2Lt., *12Sqn.* 20May.16-*I*
Carder,1AM.A, **WIA** 22Apr.17-*VI*
Carey,2Lt.AS, **KIA** 27May.17-*I*
Carey,Lt.JG, **POW** 4Nov.18-*I*
Carey,2Lt.RB, **WIA** 15Jun.18-*IV*
Carl,1Lt.PF, *US.* 2Sep.18-*IIB*
Carlaw,Capt.WM, 29Jul.18-*I*
Carley,2Lt.TE, **inj** 27Mar.18-*I*
Carlin,Lt.,Capt.S, 19Jul.18-*I*, 2Sep.18-*I*, **POW** 21Sep.18-*I*
Carline,2Lt.RS, **WIA** 31Aug.16-*I*
Carlisle,FSgt.TFB, 19Mar.16-*I*, 30Mar.16-*I*, 12Mar.16-*I*, 30Apr.16-*I*, 18May.16-*I*
Carlton,2Lt.WM, *Can.* **KIA** 26Oct.16-*I*
Carlyle,2Lt.WM, *Can.* **KIA** 26Oct.16-*I*
Carmichael,Capt.GI, 10Mar.15-*I*

Carmichael,Lt.GR, 3Sep.17-*I*
Carmichael,2Lt.WRC, **WIA POW** 2Oct.16-*I*
Carmichael-MacGregor,2Lt.J, **inj** 9Aug.17-*I*
Carnegie,Lt.H, **WIA** 10Apr.18-*I*
Carno,Sgt.AS, 6May.18-*I*
Carpenter,Lt.E, **KIA** 3Oct.18-*I*
Carpenter,Sgt.EC, 18Jul.18-*I*
Carpenter,Cpl.A,Lt.F, 11Jul.18-*I*, 20Jul.18-*I*, 8Aug.18-*I*, **POW** 9Aug.18-*I*
Carpenter,Lt.JI, *USAS.* **KIA** 11Jun.18-*I*
Carpenter,Lt.P, 15Nov.17-*I*
Carpenter,Capt.P, 9Jun.18-*IV*
Carr,2Lt.CV, **WIA POW** 29Apr.18-*I*
Carr,2Lt.F, 1Apr.18-*I*, 11Jun.18-*I*
Carr,Lt.GH, **WIA** 23Oct.18-*I*
Carr,2Lt.GJ, **WIA** 2Sep.18-*I*
Carr,2Lt.GT, 20Jul.18-*I*, **KIA** 14Oct.18-*I*
Carr,2AM.,Sgt.JF, 6Apr.17-*I*, **WIA** 22Apr.17-*I*, **KIA** 12Jul.17-*I*
Carr,FSLt.JHT, **POW** 25Jan.18-*I*
Carr,2Lt.RG, **POW** 21Jun.18-*I*
Carre,Lt.EM, **KIA** 16Oct.16-*I*
Carroll,2Lt.CE, **POW** 6Oct.17-*I*
Carroll,FSLt.JG, **KIA** 28Mar.18-*I*
Carroll,Lt.JM, **WIA** 19Feb.18-*I*, **WIA** 10Mar.18-*I*
Carruthers,2Lt.DA, 20Mar.16-*I*, 18May.16-*I*
Carruthers,2Lt.GK, **KIA** 25Jul.18-*I*
Carruthers,1Lt.LL, *US.* **POW**? 5Nov.18-*IIB*
Carruthers,2Lt.WJ, 2Sep.18-*I*, 17Sep.18-*I*, **KIA** 8Oct.18-*I*
Carse,2Lt.WK, **KIA** 13Feb.17-*I*
Carson,2Lt.SE, **KIA** 20Jul.18-*I*
Carson,2Lt.TL, **KIA** 31Jul.17-*I*
Carter,2Lt., *16Sqn.* 6May.17-*I*
Carter,Capt.,Maj.AD, *Can.* DSO 29Dec.17-*I*, **POW** 19May.18-*I*
Carter,2Lt.AR, *US.* **KIA** 18Sep.18-*IIB*
Carter,Capt.AW, DSC 12Apr.18-*I*, 27Jul.17-*I*
Carter,Lt.DC, *Aust.* **KIA** 28Oct.16-*I*
Carter,2Lt.FL, **KIA** 22Apr.17-*I*
Carter,Capt.FM, 9Aug.18-*I*
Carter,2Lt.G, 26Mar.18-*I*
Carter,2Lt.GA, **DoW** 5Dec.17-*I*
Carter,2Lt.GL, **POW** 8Aug.18-*I*
Carter,SR, **KIA** 14Apr.17-*I*
Carter,2Lt.LL, **WIA** 26Feb.17-*I*
Carter,2Lt.RA, **WIA** 30Apr.18-*I*
Carter,Lt.RB, *Can.* **KIA** 19Aug.17-*I*
Carter,2Lt.RN, **POW** 20Sep.16-*I*
Carter,Lt.WAW, 27Sep.18-*I*
Carthew,Capt.T?, *4Sqn.* 18Apr.15-*I*
Carthew,Capt.T, DSO 23Oct.15-*I*, 26Jul.15-*I*, 7Oct.15-*I*, 2Dec.15-*I*
Cartledge,Lt.RA, **POW** 27Oct.18-*I*
Cartmell,FSLt.,Lt.GM, **WIA** 16Mar.18-*I*, **KIA** 6Apr.18-*I*
Cartwright,AM., *12Sqn.* 16Aug.17-*I*
Cartwright,Lt.E, **KIA** 22Aug.18-*I*
Cartwright,2Lt.P, **KIA** 4Nov.18-*I*
Cartwright,2Lt.RWStG, **KIA** 26Feb.18-*I*
Carver,1Lt.LM, *US.* **WIA** 4Nov.18-*IIB*
Carveth,Lt.WA, **POW** 25Jul.18-*I*
Case,2Lt.BS, **POW DoW** 31.10.1918? 23Oct.18-*I*
Case,2Lt.CH, **KIA** 29Sep.18-*I*
Case,1Lt.ER, *US.* **WIA** 27Sep.18-*IIB*
Case,1Lt.LE, *USAS.* **KIA** 14Aug.18-*I*
Case,2Lt.WE, *US.* **POW**? 8Nov.18-*IIB*
Casey,FSLt.FD, 17Mar.17-*I*
Casey,2Lt.PJ, **POW** 24Sep.17-*I*
Casey,Lt.RF, **WIA** 25Sep.18-*I*
Casgrain,FSLt.HR, **POW** 8Mar.18-*I*
Casgrain,1Lt.WV, *US.* **POW** 30May.18-*IIB*
Cassard,1Lt.DW, *US.* **KIA** 16Jul.18-*IIB*
Cassels,2Lt.HK, **POW** 22Mar.18-*I*
Cassidy,Lt.DM, MC 22Mar.18-*I*
Casswell,Lt.EDS, **KIA** 7Nov.17-*I*
Caster,Lt.WS, 19Mar.17-*I*
Castle,2Lt.AF, **POW** 24Dec.17-*I*
Castle,2Lt.GL, **WIA** 28May.17-*I*
Castle,2Lt.GL, 1Apr.18-*I*, **POW** 1Jul.18-*I*
Castle,2Lt.JS, **WIA POW** 30Mar.18-*I*
Castle,2Lt.VWB, 13Mar.17-*I*

Castle,2Lt.WFL, **POW** 3Jul.16-*I*
Castor,2AM.RG, **KIA** 21Jan.18-*VIII*
Casty,1AM.N, 26Apr.16-*I*
Caswell,2Lt.BH, **WIA** 1Oct.17-*I*
Caswell,Lt.GFC, **WIA POW** 20Sep.18-*I*
Catherall,2Lt., *16Sqn.* 26Oct.15-*I*, 14Dec.15-*I*
Cathie,2Lt.AJ, **WIA** 19Sep.16-*I*
Cathie,Cpl.AJ, 1Jul.16-*I*
Cato,Lt.GMWG, **KIA** 6Nov.17-*I*
Caton,2Lt., *16Sqn.* 5Jan.16-*I*
Catterall,2Lt.F, 21Mar.18-*I*
Catto,Lt.CG, *US.* 15Jun.18-*IV*
Catton,1AM.S, 21Apr.16-*I*, **KIA** 29Apr.16-*I*
Caudwell,Capt.NG?, **WIA** 27May.17-*I*
Caulfield,2Lt.TSC, **KIA** 16Jun.17-*I*
Caulfield-Kelly,2Lt.ET, 9May.17-*I*
Caunt,2Lt.HV, **POW** 15Dec.17-*I*
Caunter,Capt.JCA, **KIA** 28Oct.18-*I*
Cavaghan,2Lt.C, 10Mar.18-*I*
Cave,Lt.CF, **KIA** 22Oct.18-*I*
Cave,2Lt.,Lt.EHP, 20Nov.15-*I*, 30Nov.15-*I*, 5Dec.15-*I*, 19Dec.15-*I*, 28Dec.15-*I*, **WIA** 17Jan.16-*I*
Cave,2Lt.GE, **KIA** 14Aug.18-*I*
Cave,2Lt.J, 9Nov.18-*I*
Cave,2Lt.TW, **WIA** 5Mar.18-*I*
Cavers,Lt.JP, **WIA** 17Aug.18-*VI*, 2Sep.18-*VI*, **KIA** 3Sep.18-*VI*
Cawdwell,Lt.P, 28Oct.16-*I*
Cawley,2Lt.CF, **POW** 27Sep.18-*I*
Cawley,2Lt.J, **WIA** 13Aug.17-*I*
Caws,2Lt.SW, **KIA** 21Sep.15-*I*
Cawson,2Lt.GA, **KIA** 30Nov.17-*I*
Cayley,2Lt.PJ, **WIA** 20Nov.17-*I*
Cemlyn-Jones,2Lt.,Lt.JS, 21Aug.15-*I*, 22Aug.15-*I*, 25Aug.15-*I*, **WIA** 28Sep.15-*I*
Chacksfield,Lt.JC, 11Oct.18-*VIII*
Chadwick,Lt., *2Sqn.* 10Oct.15-*I*, 11Nov.15-*I*
Chadwick,Lt., *25Sqn.* 16Jul.16-*I*
Chadwick,FSLt.,FCdr.AJ 2Oct.16-*I*, **Drowned** 27Jul.17-*I*
Chadwick,Lt.AW, **WIA** 25Aug.18-*I*
Chadwick,2Lt.FW, **KIA**? 29Sep.18-*I*
Chadwick,Capt.G, **WIA** 4Jun.17-*I*, **WIA POW** 3May.18-*I*
Chadwick,2AM.H, **KIA** 26Jun.18-*I*
Chadwick,2Lt.S, 22Sep.17-*I*
Chaffey,2Lt.HE, **KIA** 26Oct.18-*I*
Chainey,2Lt.FH, **POW** 16Sep.18-*I*
Chalaire,Lt.W, *USNR.* **WIA** 29Jul.18-*I*
Chalk,Lt.WJ, **KIA** 13Apr.17-*I*
Chalkin,2Lt.WJN, **POW** 15Sep.18-*I*
Challinor,Lt.RT, *Aust.* **POW** 1May.18-*VII*
Challis,Lt.ME, **POW** 1Sep.18-*I*
Chalmers,2Lt.BG, **POW** 5Jun.17-*I*
Chalmers,Sgt.JW, **POW** 22Aug.18-*I*
Chalmers,1Lt.WW, *US.* **POW** 7Jul.18-*IIB*
Chaloner,Capt.TWPL, **POW** 1Jul.16-*I*
Chamberlain,Sgt.CF, *US.* **KIA** 13Jun.18-*IIC*
Chambers,2Lt.FW, **WIA** 18Feb.18-*I*
Chambers,Capt.PW, **POW DoW** 11Aug.18-*I*
Chambers,Lt.WD, **POW** 9Oct.17-*I*
Chambers,Capt.WG, **KIA** 15May.18-*I*
Champagne,2Lt.EO, 4Sep.18-*I*
Champion,2Lt.HF, **POW** 29Feb.16-*I*
Chance,Lt.WHS, 14Sep.16-*I*, **POW** 17Sep.18-*I*
Chancellor,2Lt.G, 14Mar.18-*I*
Chandler,Capt.NE, **WIA** 2Oct.18-*I*
Chandler,Capt.RN, 17Oct.18-*I*
Chandler,Lt.RN, 11Jun.18-*I*
Chaney,QMSgt.HE, **inj** 19Jan.15-*III*
Channing,Lt.RH, 24Oct.18-*I*
Chant,Lt.EM, **POW** 25Mar.18-*I*
Chapin,Lt.EA, *US.* **KIA** 27Jun.18-*I*
Chapin,1Lt.RF, *US.* **POW** 18Sep.18-*IIB*
Chaplin,2Lt., *100Sqn.* 4Jun.17-*I*
Chapman,2Lt.AJ, **KIA** 18Sep.17-*I*
Chapman,2Lt.CW, *US.* **DSC KIA** 3May.18-*IIB*
Chapman,1AM.DAR, 20May.16-*I*, 31May.16-*I*
Chapman,2Lt.J, **POW** 27Jul.17-*I*
Chapman,Sgt.J, DFM 3May.18-*I*
Chapman,2Lt.JE, *Aust.* **KIA** 8Aug.18-*I*

Chapman,2Lt.LC?, 23Oct.15-*I*
Chapman,2Lt.LC, 8Jul.16-*I*, **POW DoW** 16.4.1917 14Apr.17-*I*
Chapman,2Lt.PK, **WIA** 24Aug.18-*I*
Chapman,Sgt.V, *US.* **KIA** 23Jun.16-*IIA*
Chapman,2Lt.VC, 17May.18-*I*
Chapman,Cpl.VE, *US.* **WIA** 24May.16-*IIA*
Chapman,2Lt.WL, 2Sep.18-*I*
Chapman,Lt.WW, **KIA** 7Oct.17-*I*
Chappell,2Lt.RW, 27Sep.16-*I*
Chappell,Capt.RW, *SA.* **WIA** 13Jan.18-*I*, 25Mar.18-*I*
Chard,Lt., *6Sqn.* 30Aug.18-*I*
Chard,Lt., *21Sqn.* 9Nov.17-*I*
Chard,2Lt.WT, **WIA** 28Mar.18-*I*
Charles,Capt.LS, **POW DoW** 30Jul.16-*I*
Charlton,Lt.B, **KIA** 27Oct.18-*I*
Charron,Lt.LR, 10Jun.18-*I*
Chase,2Lt.DE, **POW** 8Aug.18-*I*
Chase,Lt.LP, *Aust.* 11Aug.18-*I*
Chase,Pte.WF, **KIA** 30May.18-*III*
Chattaway,2Lt.HW, **WIA** 25May.18-*I*
Chavasse,2Lt.P, **KIA** 8Oct.18-*I*
Chaworth-Musters,2Lt.,Lt.RM, 8Jul.16-*I*, 28Jul.16-*I*, **KIA** 7May.17-*I*
Chaytor,BrigGen.EWC,NZ **WIA** 19Jul.16-*VII*
Cheatle,2Lt.CC, **KIA** 5May.17-*I*
Chegwidden,1AM., *34Sqn.* 11Aug.17-*I*
Chesney,TLt.FWMC, 22Apr.18-*I*
Chester,Lt.WH, 25May.17-*I*
Chester-Walsh,2Lt.JH, 3Sep.16-*I*
Chesters,Lt.R?, **WIA** 10Aug.18-*I*
Cheston,1Lt.G, *USAS.* **KIA** 29Jul.18-*I*
Chick,Lt.AF, 4Oct.18-*I*
Chick,Capt.AL, 22May.18-*I*
Chick,2Lt.JS, 12Mar.18-*I*
Chidlaw-Roberts,Capt.Lt.RL, 21Sep.17-*I*
Chidson,2Lt.MR, 25Dec.14-*III*, **POW** 28Feb.15-*I*
Chilcott,Lt.TA, 30Oct.18-*I*
Child,Lt., *8Sqn.* 29Dec.15-*I*
Child,2Lt.Capt.HR, 5Dec.17-*I*, **KIA** 27Mar.18-*I*
Child,Capt.J, 30Nov.17-*I*
China,2Lt.WE, 2Sep.18-*I*
Chinnery,Capt.EF, 4Oct.14-*I*, **KIA** 18Jan.15-*I*
Chisam,FLt.WH, **WIA** 26Mar.18-*I*
Chisholm,Capt.JF, *Can.* DFC 12Jun.18-*I*, **INT** 26Sep.18-*I*
Chisman,Lt.JR, 4Nov.18-*I*
Chisnall,Lt.CA, **WIA** 25Mar.18-*I*
Chivers,2Lt.W, **KIA** 17Aug.17-*I*
Chown,2Lt.FG, 16Sep.17-*I*
Chown,2Lt.FJ, **KIA** 20Sep.17-*I*
Chrieman,Lt.WW, **POW** 17Sep.18-*I*
Chrispin,Lt., *103Sqn.* 9Jun.18-*I*
Christian,2Lt.EB, *US.* **WIA** 10Oct.18-*IIB*
Christian,Lt.LA, 22May.18-*I*
Christian,2Lt.Lt.WL, 27Mar.18-*I*, 8Oct.18-*I*, 4Nov.18-*I*
Christiani,2Lt.FR, *US.* **KIA** 29Sep.18-*I*
Christie,2Lt.DM, **WIA** 29Dec.17-*I*
Christie,2Lt.EW, **KIA** 2Apr.18-*I*
Christie,2Lt.HL, 23Mar.18-*I*
Christmas,2AM.LA, **INT** 9Nov.18-*III*
Chritzman,1Lt.GM, *US.* 12Sep.18-*IIB*
Chrysler,Lt.CA, 20May.18-*I*
Chubb,Lt.JA, 16May.18-*I*, **POW** 8Jul.18-*I*
Church,2Lt.EH, **WIA** 6Jan.18-*I*
Church,Lt.FJ, **KIA** 12Jul.18-*I*
Churchill,2Lt.J, **KIA** 14Aug.18-*I*
Churchward,2Lt.HA, 12Aug.17-*I*, **KIA** 16Aug.17-*I*
Churchward,Lt., *6Sqn.* 7Aug.18-*I*
Chuter,2Lt.,Lt.HA, 31Oct.16-*I*, **KIA** 25Mar.17-*I*
Clack,2Lt.LA, **POW** 9Aug.18-*I*
Clapham,2Lt.G, 11Sep.17-*I*
Clapp,1Lt.HR, *US.* **KIA** 3Nov.18-*IIB*
Clapperton,Lt.CR, **WIA** 16Oct.16-*I*
Clapperton,FSLt.WM, **WIA** 27Oct.17-*I*
Clappison,2Lt.HG, *Can.* 20Sep.18-*I*, 1Nov.18-*I*
Clare,Sgt.E, 24Jun.18-*I*
Clark,AM, 1Apr.16-*I*
Clark,Lt., *6Sqn.* 8Oct.18-*I*
Clark,Capt.AB, MC **KIA** 3Oct.18-*I*
Clark,2Lt.AE, **WIA** 28Apr.17-*I*

Clark,Capt.AG, *Aust.* 2Apr.18-*I*
Clark,Lt.AL, **POW** 13Dec.17-*I*
Clark,?1Lt.AL, *US.* **POW** 17Sep.18-*IIB*
Clark,Lt.AR, 12Apr.18-*I*
Clark,Lt.AS, *Can.* 5Oct.17-*VI*
Clark,Lt.BD, 6May.18-*I*
Clark,Capt.CC, 25Apr.18-*I*, **WIA POW** 8May.18-*I*
Clark,Lt.CG, **POW** 29Jul.18-*V*
Clark,2Lt.DG, *Aust.* **KIA** 22Nov.17-*I*
Clark,Lt.E, 15Jul.18-*I*
Clark,1Lt.ER, *US.* 3Nov.18-*IIB*
Clark,2Lt.EV, **KIA** 29Nov.17-*I*
Clark,2Lt.FS, **WIA POW** 29Oct.17-*I*
Clark,2Lt.FS, 15Mar.18-*I*
Clark,2Lt.FWP, **inj** 27Jun.18-*I*
Clark,FSLt.JG, **POW** 12Dec.17-*I*
Clark,Lt.JWG, 28Sep.18-*I*
Clark,2Lt.LL, **KIA** 2Aug.16-*I*
Clark,2Lt.LVW, 21Sep.17-*I*
Clark,Lt.N, *Aust.*? 2Sep.17-*I*
Clark,2Lt.N, **KIA** 18Mar.18-*I*
Clark,2Lt.RB, **DoW** 1.5.1917 24Apr.17-*I*
Clark,2Lt.WB, **POW** 26Nov.16-*I*
Clark,2Lt.WH, **KIA** 6Jul.17-*I*
Clarke,Lt., *6Sqn.* 2Sep.18-*I*
Clarke,Capt.AC, **WIA** 8Jun.18-*I*
Clarke,2Lt.AFG, **POW** 23Mar.18-*I*
Clarke,Lt.CE, 11Oct.15-*I*
Clarke,2Lt.CE, **KIA** 27Sep.18-*I*
Clarke,2Lt.CH, **POW** 23Mar.18-*I*
Clarke,2Lt.D?, **KIA** 26Apr.16-*I*
Clarke,2Lt.,Lt.ED, 23Aug.17-*I*, **WIA** 26Oct.17-*I*
Clarke,Capt.EE, 30May.17-*VI*
Clarke,2Lt.EH, 17Sep.18-*I*
Clarke,2Lt.EO, **KIA** 13Aug.18-*I*
Clarke,Lt.F, **POW** Jun.18-*I*
Clarke,Lt.FCE, **DoW** 11.10.1917 11Oct.18-*I*
Clarke,Sgt.FP, **KIA** 3Oct.18-*I*
Clarke,Capt.FW, 21Aug.18-*I*
Clarke,Sgt.H, **KIA** 27Sep.17-*I*
Clarke,Lt.HA, **POW** 19May.18-*I*
Clarke,2Lt.HC, **KIA** 6Jul.17-*I*
Clarke,Lt.HW, **DoW** 2Sep.18-*I*
Clarke,2Lt.J, **KIA** 18Sep.18-*I*
Clarke,Lt.JF?, *initials* JT? 5Jul.18-*I*, **KIA** 22Jul.18-*I*
Clarke,2Lt.JK, **WIA** 20May.18-*I*
Clarke,1AM.JS, **KIA** 10Oct.17-*I*
Clarke,Lt.PH, 11Apr.18-*I*
Clarke,2Lt.RA, **WIA** 9Oct.18-*I*
Clarke,Lt.SH, 25Aug.16-*I*
Clarke,Lt.TH, **POW** 20Nov.16-*I*
Clarke,Sgt.WR, **WIA** 28Jul.17-*I*
Clarkson,Sgt.A, **KIA** 30Sep.16-*I*
Clarkson,FSgt.LC, **KIA** 1Aug.16-*I*
Claudet,Lt.J, 27Dec.16-*I*
Clawson,2Lt.DV, **WIA** 27Oct.18-*I*
Claxton,Lt.WG, *Can.* 27May.18-*I*, 9Aug.18-*I*, **POW** 17Aug.18-*I*
Clay,1Lt.HR, *USAS.* 27Aug.18-*I*
Clayburn,2Lt.AC, *Can.* 7May.18-*I*
Claydon,Lt.A, *Can.* 20Sep.17-*I*, 11Nov.17-*I*, **KIA** 8Jul.18-*I*
Claye,Lt.CG, **WIA** 9May.17-*I*
Claye,Capt.H, 21Feb.18-*I*, **POW** 19May.18-*I*
Clayson,2Lt.PA, **WIA** 4Sep.18-*I*
Clayson,2Lt.,Lt.,Capt.PJ, 16Feb.18-*I*, 8May.18-*I*, 14Jul.18-*I*
Clayton,Sgt.A, **KIA** 26Apr.17-*I*
Clayton,2Lt.EH, **POW DoW** 11Aug.18-*I*
Clayton,2Lt.G, **POW** 17Oct.16-*I*
Clayton,2Lt.JG, **WIA** 5Oct.18-*I*
Clear,Sgt.AL, **POW** 12Oct.17-*I*
Clear,Lt.EA, 15Mar.18-*I*
Cleary,2Lt.MH, **KIA** 28Mar.18-*I*
Cleaver,2Lt.,Lt.CT, MC 1Aug.15-*I*, 28Aug.15-*I*, 5Sep.15-*I*, 11Oct.15-*I*, 19Dec.15-*I*, 20Aug.16-*I*, **WIA** 9Oct.16-*I*, **WIA** 3May.17-*I*
Cleaver,2Lt.CT?, *3Sqn.* 16Sep.16-*I*
Clegg,Lt.CE, **WIA** 2Sep.18-*I*
Cleghorn,FSLt.Capt.WF, DFC 20Jul.17-*I*, **KIA** 2Oct.18-*I*
Cleland,2Lt.EMcL, **WIA** 11Mar.18-*I*

Clement,2Lt.,Capt.CM, Can. 8Aug.16-I, 3Sep.16-I, 5Jun.17-I, 29Jul.17-I, KIA 19Aug.17-I
Clement,Pte.DW, 17Sep.17-I
Clements,2Lt.HJ, 10Nov.18-I
Clements,Lt.JBV, 23Aug.18-I
Clements-Finnerty,Lt.H, POW 19Jul.16-I
Clementz,2Lt.DM, KIA 6Mar.18-I
Clemons,2Lt.HS, WIA POW 25Jan.18-I
Clemson,Cdr.AW, POW 11Oct.17-V
Cleobury,2Lt.S, WIA 3Sep.17-I
Clifford,2Lt.AEI, WIA 25Mar.18-I
Clifford,2Lt.WJ, KIA 25Apr.17-I
Clifton,Lt.N, 11Aug.15-I
Clifton,2Lt.WGT, DoW 31Mar.17-I
Clinton,Pbr2Lt.AC, 3May.18-I, WIA 30May.18-I
Cloete,2Lt.DC, 20May.16-I, 31May.16-I
Cluncy,Pte.G, KIA 4Jun.17-I
Clutterbuck,2Lt.LCF, WIA POW 12Mar.18-I
Coates,1Lt.DE, US. KIA 4Nov.18-IIB
Coates,2Lt.JA, WIA 26Jun.16-I
Coates,Capt.LC, WIA 14Apr.17-I
Coates,2Lt.S, POW 10Nov.18-I
Coates,Lt.WH, NZ. KIA 22Jul.17-I
Coath,Lt.RD, 21Jul.17-I, WIA 23Nov.17-I
Cobbin,2Lt.AJ, POW DoW 14.7.1918 23Jun.18-I
Cobbold,Lt.EFW, KIA 12Jan.16-I
Cobbold,Lt.FRC, 16Nov.16-I, WIA POW 8Nov.17-I
Cobby,Lt.,Capt.AH, Aust. 21Mar.18-I, 30May.18-I, 9Jul.18-I, 4Sep.18-I
Cobden,Lt.FP, KIA 7Jul.18-I
Cobham,Lt.RL, INT 16Sep.18-I
Cochran,1Lt.RJ, US. KIA 10Oct.18-IIB
Cochrane,2Lt.AB, 3Jan.18-I
Cock,Capt.GH, MC WIA? POW 22Jul.17-I
Cock,2Lt.JH, NZ. KIA 14Apr.17-I
Cockburn,Lt.GA, KIA 8Nov.17-I
Cockburn,2Lt.J, WIA 4Nov.18-I
Cockerell,Sgt.S, WIA 10Oct.16-I
Cockerell,Lt.S, 25May.17-I
Cockey,FSLt.LH, WIA 4Jun.17-I
Cockin,2Lt.JB, POW 2Sep.18-I
Cocking,2Lt.LG, POW 27Jun.18-I
Cockman,Lt.HJ, WIA 25Sep.18-I
Cockrane,2Lt.SL, US. KIA 31Oct.18-IIB
Cocks,2Lt.LF, WIA 23Apr.18-I
Cocksedge,2Lt.J, 29Sep.18-I
Code,2Lt.AL, 28Mar.18-I, 12Apr.18-I, WIA 21Apr.18-I
Codman,1Lt.CR, US. 30Aug.18-IIB, WIA POW 16Sep.18-IIB
Cody,2Lt.SF, KIA 23Jan.17-I
Coe,2Lt.DE, KIA 3Nov.18-I
Cogan,2Lt.JA, WIA 2Sep.18-I
Coghill,Lt.FS, POW 25Jul.18-I
Coghill,2Lt.WH, POW 26Sep.18-I
Coghlan,2Lt.EA, WIA 16Jun.18-I
Coghlan,GL.JL, POW KIA? 14Apr.17-I
Cogswell,2Lt.ES, inj 24May.17-I
Cokeley,2AM.AC, KIA 4Jul.18-III
Colbert,Lt.JH, 21Aug.18-I
Colbert,2Lt.LA, POW 30Sep.17-I
Cole,Capt.AT, Aust. 2Jun.18-I
Cole,Lt.BS, WIA 27Mar.18-I
Cole,Capt.CC, 21Aug.18-I
Cole,2Lt.DB, US. WIA 16Aug.18-IIB
Cole,Lt.HA, POW 12Sep.18-I
Cole,Lt.JE, WIA 8Dec.17-I
Cole,Lt.KR, POW 7Apr.18-I
Cole,2Lt.MB, WIA 26May.17-I
Cole,2Lt.MG, KIA 18May.17-I
Cole,Lt.MH?, initials EH? 25Jun.18-I, KIA 30Jun.18-I
Cole,2Lt.RH, DoW 30.9.1918 16Sep.18-I
Cole,2Lt.WH, KIA 16Sep.18-I
Coleman,2Lt.CB, WIA POW 31Mar.18-I
Coleman,2Lt.CM, KIA 6Sep.18-I
Coleman,1Lt.DeW, US. KIA 27Oct.18-IIB
Coleman,2AM.ERA, POW 30Mar.16-I
Coleman,2Lt.JP, POW 28Oct.18-I
Coleman,Lt.L, KIA 2Sep.18-I
Coleman,2Lt.OL, INT 9Nov.18-III
Coler,Lt.,Capt.ES, US. 14Aug.18-I, inj 16Sep.18-I
Coles,Lt.EM, 27Sep.18-I
Coles,2Lt.GT, POW 4Sep.18-I
Coles,2Lt.PD, US. WIA 15Sep.18-IIB
Coles,Lt.RH, KIA 9May.17-I
Colin,Lt.JP, 29Jul.17-I
Colledge,2Lt.G 12Jul.17-I, POW 11Aug.17-I
Collen,2Lt.J, KIA 25Oct.16-I
Coller,Lt.BT, 8Jul.16-I, 16Jul.16-I, 20Jul.16-I, 23Jul.16-I, 9Sep.16-I, KIA 26Sep.16-I
Collet,Lt.,Cdr.CH, DSO 22Sep.14-I, 10Jan.15-I, 22Jun.15-V
Collett,Capt.CF, NZ. MC 27Jul.17-I, 31Aug.17-I, WIA 9Sep.17-I
Collett,Lt.HS, POW 17Jun.18-I
Collier,2Lt.AC, 28Aug.15-I, POW 22Oct.15-I
Collier,2Lt.DC, KIA 24Aug.18-I
Collier,2Lt.JC, WIA 4Apr.18-I
Collier,Lt.JT, WIA 4May.17-I
Collier,2Lt.L, WIA 31Jul.17-I
Collier,Lt.S, MC KIA 28Mar.18-I
Collins,2Lt.AD, WIA 25Mar.17-I
Collins,Lt.AV, inj 2Sep.18-I
Collins,2Lt.FF, KIA 19May.18-I
Collins,Lt.HG, KIA 9Apr.17-I
Collins,2Lt.HJ, inj 12Apr.18-I
Collins,2Lt.HJW, WIA? 29Jul.16-I
Collins,Capt.J, 21Jul.15-I
Collins,2Lt.JC, POW 23Oct.18-I
Collins,Cpl.JW, WIA 12Jun.17-I
Collins,Capt.P, US. KIA 12Mar.18-IIB
Collins,2Lt.VH, 15 Feb.17-I
Collins,Lt.VStB, KIA 2Sep.18-I
Collinson,Sgt.E, 7Jul.18-I
Collinson,2AM.F, WIA 28Jul.16-I
Collis,Lt., 6Sqn. 27Aug.15-I, 6Sqn. 28Aug.15-I
Collis,2Lt.DP, inj 24Jun.17-I, POW 10Aug.17-I
Collis,Lt.EA, MM 4Sep.18-I
Collis,Lt.EW, 19May.18-I
Collis,2Lt.R, 19Mar.16-III
Collis,2Lt.TB, KIA? 27Aug.18-I
Collishaw,SLt.,FCdr.,Maj.R, DSC DSO Can. 6Jun.17-I, 27Jul.17-I, 11Jun.18-I
Collison,Pte.J, WIA 4Mar.17-I
Collison,Lt.WE, 23Apr.16-I
Collon-Minchin,Lt.W, 28Aug.15-I
Collyns,2Lt.CHA, WIA 9Oct.18-I
Colman,2Lt.CWT, WIA 13Jul.18-I
Colson,2Lt.NH, WIA 17Mar.17-I
Colvill-Jones,Capt.T, POW DoW 24.5.1918 25Apr.18-I
Colville-Jones,Capt.R, KIA 4Nov.18-I
Comegys,1Lt.ET, US. KIA 18Sep.18-IIB
Comerford,Sgt.CJ, KIA 18Aug.17-I
Comerford,2Lt.JJ, INT 27Jun.18-I
Comey,1Lt.GM, US. 2Sep.18-IIB
Compston,FCdr.RJO, 1Jan.18-I
Conant,2Lt.RG, US. 3Nov.18-IIB
Conder,2Lt.RE, WIA 6Jun.17-I
Coningham,Capt.,Maj.,A, DSO MC WIA 30Jul.17-I, 12Aug.18-I
Conlan,2Lt.T, POW 20Jul.18-I
Conlin,2AM.J, WIA POW 8Nov.17-I
Conn,Lt.KB, Can. 19Aug.18-I
Connelly,Lt.FJ, USAS. POW 18Jul.18-I
Connolly,2Lt.JD, POW 11Aug.18-I
Connolly,2Lt.JM, WIA POW 18Jun.18-I
Connor,2Lt.W, 1Oct.18-I
Connover,1Lt.H, US. WIA 28Oct.18-IIB
Conover,Lt.CC, 15Jul.18-I, 25Aug.18-I, 30Aug.18-I, POW 24Sep.18-I
Conran,Capt.EL, 10Mar.15-I, WIA 26Mar.15-I
Conron,2Lt.HCR, KIA 18May.18-I
Constable,2Lt.RA, KIA 17Mar.17-I
Converse,1Lt.RRS, US. POW 13Sep.18-IIB
Convery,Lt.JA, KIA 11Mar.18-I
Cooch,Lt.TA, 6May.17-I, WIA 17Mar.17-I
Cook,2Lt.AB, 55Sqn. 20Aug.17-I
Cook,Capt.AB, 57Sqn. WIA 27Oct.17-I
Cook,2Lt.CR, WIA 7Sep.16-I
Cook,2Lt.CW, POW 24Mar.18-I
Cook,Lt.FAV, 9Apr.17-I
Cook,2Lt.FC, POW? 30Aug.18-I
Cook,Lt.FO, KIA 26Sep.18-I
Cook,2Lt.JD, KIA 11Jul.18-I
Cook,2Lt.LCL, WIA POW 3Nov.16-I
Cook,Lt.R, WIA 9Aug.18-I
Cook,Sgt.EA, KIA 5Jun.17-I
Cooke,Lt.BA, WIA 10Mar.18-I
Cooke,Lt.DG, 12Apr.18-I
Cooke,2Lt.E, inj 9May.18-I
Cooke,2Lt.EA, POW 21Sep.17-I
Cooke,2Lt.HC, 25Mar.18-I
Cooke,2Lt.J, DoW 20Jun.16-I
Cooke,Lt.PB, POW 28Sep.18-I
Cooke,2Lt.TRG, WIA 3May.18-I
Cooke,Lt.WR, 27Jul.17-I, inj 13Aug.17-I
Cooksey,Lt.KB, KIA 8Apr.17-I
Coolidge,Capt.HR, US. KIA 27Oct.18-IIB
Coombe,Lt.ASN, KIA 17Apr.18-I
Coombe,Lt.JG, 28Jan.18-I
Coomber,Capt.HB, KIA 12Oct.17-I
Coombes,2Lt.ES, POW 3Aug.18-I
Coombes,Lt.LP, 11May.18-I, 26Jun.18-I
Coombs,2Lt.HM, WIA 30Apr.17-I
Coombs,Lt.VC, WIA POW 15Jul.17-I
Coombs,Lt.WEC, WIA 26Sep.18-I
Coomer,2Lt.FHV, 9Oct.18-I
Coomer,2Lt.FHV, POW 26Oct.18-I
Coomer-Weare,Sgt.M, WIA 7Oct.17-I
Coop,2Lt.R, 20Nov.17-I
Coop,2Lt.R, WIA 30Nov.17-I
Coope,Lt.NN, WIA POW 24Sep.18-I
Cooper,2Lt., 5Sqn. 19Dec.15-I
Cooper,Capt., 13Sqn. 1Apr.16-I
Cooper,Cpl.A, KIA 17Mar.17-I
Cooper,2Lt.,Lt.AG, 27Oct.17-I, 19May.18-IV
Cooper,2Lt.AK, 9Mar.18-I
Cooper,FLt.EJ, POW 29Nov.16-VI
Cooper,FSLt.,Capt.GK, 1Jan.18-I, 1Sep.18-I
Cooper,2Lt.GVV, 30Aug.18-IV
Cooper,Lt.H, inj 16Sep.18-I, WIA? 30Aug.18-I
Cooper,2Lt.HA, 23Aug.15-I, 31Aug.15-I, 4Sep.15-I, 5Sep.15-I, 8Sep.15-I, 26Nov.15-I
Cooper,2Lt.,Capt.HA, 11Sqn. 17Jan.16-I, 10Apr.16-I, 19May.16-I
Cooper, Lt.HA, 48Sqn. pilot, WIA POW 5Apr.17-I
Cooper, 2Lt.HA, 48Sqn. observer 8Mar.18-I
Cooper, 2Lt.JH, WIA 10Apr.17-I
Cooper, Capt.JO, KIA 21Jul.16-I
Cooper, 2Lt.,Lt.JS, 31Oct.16-I, KIA 25Mar.17-I
Cooper, Lt.LG, POW DoW 9Aug.18-I
Cooper, Capt. MC, US. WIA POW 26Sep.18-IIB
Cooper, Lt. ML, DFC Irl. WIA 31Jul.18-I, KIA 2Oct.18-I
Cooper, 2Lt. N, US. 25Jul.18-I
Cooper, LtCol. RA, WIA? 6Nov.18-I
Cooper,Pte.RRN, Died 31Jul.18-III
Cooper, 2Lt. S, WIA 9Apr.17-I
Cooper-King,2Lt.,Capt.MK, 25Jul.15-I, 1Aug.15-I, 2Aug.15-I, 27Aug.15-I, 12Sep.15-I, WIA 17Nov.15-I
Cooper-Wilson,2Lt.J, KIA 17Oct.16-I
Coops,2Lt.FC, POW 11Mar.17-I
Coote,Lt.MH, 27Sqn. WIA 23Apr.17-I
Coote,Lt.MH, 56Sqn. 8Nov.17-I
Coots,Lt.JG, 29Sep.18-I
Cope,2Lt.WLN, WIA 26Oct.18-I
Cope,Lt.WNL, 31Aug.18-I
Copeland,Lt.AHM, Can. WIA POW 10Oct.16-I
Copeland,Lt.WHK, WIA 8Feb.17-I
Copley,Lt.A, POW .18-I
Corbet,2Lt.JH, KIA 13Jan.18-I
Corbett,Flt.Hon,AC, KIA 4Dec.16-I
Corbett,2Lt.EJ, inj 16Sep.18-I
Corbett,2Lt.R, WIA 14Nov.15-I
Corbett,Lt.R, WIA POW 22Nov.16-I
Corbett-Wilson,Lt.D, KIA 10May.15-I
Corbishley,2Lt.RH, KIA 28Jul.17-I
Corbold,2Lt.HM, Can. POW DoW 26Aug.16-I
Corley,2Lt.,1Lt.JW, US. WIA 15Sep.18-IIB, 6Oct.18-IIB
Cormack,Cpl., 15Sqn. 8Feb.16-I, 21Feb.16-I
Cormack,Sgt.JD, KIA 30Jul.18-I
Cormack,2Lt.PF, KIA 27Oct.18-I
Cornell,2Lt.HC, Aust. 30Nov.17-I
Cornell,Sgt.HW, 7Aug.18-I
Corner,2Lt.WG, WIA 5Jun.17-I
Cornford,Lt.R, KIA 17Aug.17-I
Cornforth,2Lt.NL, KIA 18Jan.18-I
Cornish,Capt.EW, Aust. POW 14Oct.18-I
Cornish,2Lt.WO, DoW 20Sep.17-I
Cornwell,2Lt.F, POW 8Oct.18-I
Corry,2Lt.FC, WIA 10Oct.16-I
Corse,Lt.IP, 12Aug.18-I
Corson,Sgt.AL, 14Aug.17-I
Cort,Lt.AB, KIA 12Aug.18-I
Cosgrove,2Lt.AV, KIA 25Sep.18-I
Costello,Capt.WH, POW 24Mar.17-I
Costen,AG.CF, POW 19May.18-I
Cot,Lt.CS, WIA 22Aug.18-IV
Cote,Lt.JR, 3May.18-I
Cotterell,2Lt.BW, KIA 30Oct.18-I
Cotterill,Lt.HGK, KIA DoW? 6Jun.17-I
Cottier,Capt.ER, WIA 23Nov.17-I
Cottingham,Cpl.GO, WIA 11Feb.17-I
Cottle,Capt.J, 31Aug.18-IV
Cottle,Lt.J, WIA 30May.18-IV
Cotton,2Lt.E, KIA 29Jul.18-I
Cotton,Lt.H, WIA POW 28May.17-I
Cotton,Lt.JC, WIA 14Apr.17-I
Cotton,2Lt.WMV, Can. KIA 21Dec.16-I
Coulson,2Lt.,Lt.CSL, 21Mar.18-I, 10May.18-I, WIA 9Aug.18-I
Coulson,2Lt.WE, POW 22Jul.18-I
Coulthard,Lt.R, POW 18Oct.18-I
Coulthurst,2Lt.RA, WIA 2Sep.18-I
Coulthurst,2Lt.WG, KIA 10Nov.18-I
Coupal,2Lt.AB, inj 4Feb.17-I
Coupal,Sgt., 11Sqn. 19Sep.16-I
Coupland,2Lt.JCG, KIA 6May.17-I
Court,1AM.,Sgt.LS, 20Jul.16-I, 5Aug.16-I, 27Sep.16-I
Court-Freath,Lt.C, 23Apr.15-I, WIA 23May.15-I
Courtenay,Lt.WJ, KIA 7Oct.18-IV
Courtis,2Lt.,Lt.WJH, 15Oct.17-I, 18Nov.17-I
Courtneidge,Capt.C, 20Nov.17-I, WIA 23Nov.17-I
Courtney,Sgt.F, DoW 21Oct.15-I
Courtney,Lt.JC, NZ. KIA 7Apr.18-I
Courtney,2Lt.WEL, POW 7Sep.18-I
Cousans,2Lt.GN, KIA 9Sep.16-I
Cousins,1Lt.WS, US. POW 31Oct.18-IIB
Couston,2Lt.A, Aust. POW 21Feb.18-I
Coutts,Lt.RW, POW 22Mar.18-I
Cowan,Lt.AR, POW 3Jun.18-I
Cowan,2Lt.JB, 31Aug.18-I, 2Sep.18-I, 26Sep.18-I, KIA? 3Oct.18-I
Cowan,Capt.PC, KIA 8Nov.17-I
Cowan,2Lt.RH, POW 18Dec.17-I
Cowan,2Lt.,Capt.SE, 4May.16-I, WIA 9Aug.16-I, KIA 17Nov.16-I
Cowan,Lt.WE, POW 16May.18-I
Coward,2Lt.EGW, 15Sep.18-I
Coward,Lt.GB?, INT initials GD? 17Jun.18-I
Coward,2Lt.JB, KIA 26Mar.18-I
Coward,Lt.SR, 10Jul.18-I, WIA POW 9Aug.18-I
Cowart,1Lt.WB, US. KIA 17Sep.18-IIB
Cowell,Sgt.J, 6Jun.17-I
Cowell,Sgt.JJ, MM KIA 30Jul.18-I
Cowgill,Lt.WAF, POW 5Sep.18-I
Cowie,2Lt.G, KIA 22Oct.17-I
Cowie,2Lt.JD, WIA 9Nov.16-I
Cowie,2Lt.WA, 4Jul.18-I, WIA 2Sep.18-I
Cowley,FSLt.ATM, POW 6May.16-III
Cowper,2Lt.,Capt.AK, MC Aust. 27Sep.17-I, 17Mar.18-I, 24Mar.18-I
Cowper-Coles,TLt.SW, WIA 1Sep.18-I, KIA 14Oct.18-I
Cox,2Lt.BH, 10Feb.16-I
Cox,Lt.C, 31Oct.17-VIII
Cox,Lt.CHL, 28Mar.18-I
Cox,Sgt.CJ, inj 26Jan.17-I
Cox,2Lt.DP, KIA 21Aug.17-I
Cox,2Lt.FB, WIA INT 15Sep.18-I
Cox,Pte.FD, WIA 17Nov.16-I
Cox,Lt.G, Aust., initials GJ? 27Aug.18-I, POW 21Sep.18-I

Cox,Lt.GM, 15Nov.17-I
Cox,Lt.HL, 27Apr.18-I
Cox,2Lt.RC, WIA 17Mar.17-I
Cox,Lt.W, POW 8Aug.18-I
Cox,1AM.WH, POW 5Dec.15-I
Coxe,2Lt.CH, DoW 1Jul.16-I
Coyle,1Lt.AJ, US. WIA? 3Nov.18-IIB
Coysh,Lt.HA, 8Sep.18-I
Crabb,Lt.EF, Can. 29Oct.18-I
Crabbe,2Lt.HLB, KIA 15May.18-I
Crabbie,2Lt.WM, WIA POW 14Jul.15-I
Crafter,Lt.J, MC POW DoW 7Jul.17-I
Craib,Lt.WB, KIA 28May.18-I
Craig,2Lt.ADK, inj 5Sep.17-I
Craig,2Lt.FC, POW 22Apr.17-I
Craig,2Lt.FG, 8Aug.18-I
Craig,2Lt.GB, US. POW DoW 22.2.1918 21Feb.18-I
Craig,Lt.GE, 1Mar.17-I
Craig,Lt.HW, KIA 15Apr.17-VIII
Craig,1Lt.HW, US. DoW 20Aug.18-IID
Craig,2Lt.J, KIA 11Apr.18-I
Craig,2Lt.KC, 20Sep.18-I
Craig,Lt.WB, KIA 26Sep.18-I
Craik,Lt.D, WIA 17Jan.18-VIII
Cramb,2Lt.WB, 22Mar.17-I, KIA 14Jul.17-I
Crammond,Lt.GR, POW 13Mar.18-I
Crane,2Lt.CG, POW 2Oct.17-I
Crane,Capt.JW, KIA 30Oct.18-I
Crang,2Lt.JG, 16Aug.17-I
Cranswick,2Lt.GA, KIA 18Nov.17-I
Craven,Sgt., 2Sqn. 11Oct.15-I
Crawford,Capt.C, POW 24Sep.18-I
Crawford,Capt.GB, 30Oct.18-I
Crawford,1Lt.GM, US. POW 12Sep.18-IIB
Crawford,2Lt.JC, KIA WIA? 9Nov.18-I
Crawford,2Lt.K, WIA 26Oct.16-I
Crawford,Capt.K, KIA 11Apr.18-I
Crawford,2Lt.,Lt.OGS, WIA 6Mar.17-I, POW 14Feb.18-I
Crawford,2Lt.WC, KIA 17Nov.16-I
Crawford,2Lt.WI, 22Apr.18-I, WIA POW 23May.18-I
Creaghan,Lt.TC, WIA 20Nov.17-I
Creamer,2Lt.RC, WIA 30Oct.18-I
Crean,Capt.T, 15Oct.14-I, KIA 26Oct.14-I
Creech,1Lt.JO, USAS. 28Oct.18-I
Creery,2Lt.CJ, Can. KIA 20Oct.16-I
Creery,2Lt.,Lt.KA, 15Sep.15-I, 27Dec.16-I
Crees,2Lt.HS, WIA 27Sep.18-I
Creighton,2Lt.CP, 25Jul.16-I, 5Nov.16-I
Creighton,2Lt.HH, inj 24Jun.18-I
Cresswell,Lt.RN, KIA 23Oct.18-I
Crewdson,Maj., 98Sqn? 1Nov.18-I
Cribb,2Lt.AG, POW 6Nov.17-I
Cribbes,Sgt.GA, WIA 4Sep.18-I
Crich,2Lt.WA, 9Oct.18-I
Crichton,2Lt.CA, 31Aug.18-I, WIA POW 27Oct.18-I
Crichton,Lt.CJW, 3Sep.16-I
Crickmore,Lt.EB, POW 16Jul.18-I
Cridlan,Sgt.A, 1Oct.18-I
Cridlan,Sgt.AL, KIA 7Oct.18-I
Cripps,Lt.AE, inj 16Apr.18-I
Crisp,2Lt.AE, WIA POW 20Apr.17-I
Crisp,2Lt.AR, POW 15Oct.16-I
Crisp,2Lt.F, 22Nov.16-I
Crisp,2Lt.HD, KIA 6Nov.17-III
Crispin,2Lt.JGH, 8Jul.18-I
Critchley,2Lt.B, DoW 26Jun.18-I
Critchley,Sgt.EP, 6Mar.17-I, WIA 24Mar.17-I
Critchley,2Lt.R, 29Mar.18-I, KIA 2Apr.18-I
Crites,Sgt.CP, POW 24Sep.18-I
Croden,Capt.JE, 30Sep.18-I
Croft,Lt., 12Sqn. 9Apr.17-I
Croft,2Lt.GW, KIA 16Feb.18-I
Croft,2Lt.HA, KIA 14Feb.17-I
Croft,FSLt.JC, 13Jul.15-I, POW 4Jan.17-I
Crofts,2Lt.HJ, 19Feb.18-I
Croker,2Lt.FR, KIA 27Apr.17-I
Crole,Capt.GB, MC WIA POW 22Nov.17-I
Crole,Lt.GB, 25Jun.17-I
Croll,1AM.EP, ? 14Sep.17-I
Crompton,2Lt.HD, KIA 4Dec.16-I

Cronin,1Lt.EM, US. KIFA 12Sep.18-IIB
Cronyn,Lt.VP, 10Aug.17-I, 23Sep.17-I
Crookell,Lt.SE, POW 29Aug.18-I
Cropper,2Lt.A, DoW 22Oct.16-I
Crosbee,Lt.JB, 4Mar.17-I
Crosbie?,2Lt.CH, see Crossbee
Crosbie,Lt.,Capt.DSK, 9Sep.14-I, 28Sep.14-I, WIA POW 30Apr.15-I
Crosby,2Lt.EE, KIA 13Sep.18-I
Crosfield,Lt.S, 3Sep.18-I
Cross,Lt.AR, 24Aug.18-I, 8Sep.18-I, 8Oct.18-I
Cross,Lt.AS, POW 17May.18-I
Cross,2Lt.HL, POW 19Jul.18-I
Cross,2Lt.JH, inj 11Mar.17-I
Cross,2Lt.RW, POW 17Mar.17-I
Crossbee?,2Lt.CH, name Crosbie? POW 26Feb.18-I
Crosse,Lt.EC, 27Aug.18-I
Crossley,AM., 5Sqn. 7Feb.16-I
Crossley,2Lt.H, WIA POW 26Sep.18-I
Crossley-Meates,FLt.B, INT 24Mar.15-I
Crossman,Lt.TH, 23May.18-I
Crouch,2Lt.JE, KIA 14Aug.18-I
Crow,2Lt.CM, 16Sqn. KIA 23Apr.17-I
Crow,2Lt.NH, KIA 14Sep.17-I
Crowe,Capt.CM, 8Sqn. 28Dec.15-I, 5Jan.16-I
Crowe,Capt.CM, MC 56Sqn. 24May.17-I, 4Jul.18-I
Crowe,2Lt.,Lt.HG, 1Apr.18-I, 12Apr.18-I
Crowe,2Lt.JR, 21Sep.18-I
Crowther,2Lt.G, inj 5Jul.18-I
Crowther,TFLt.OH, KIA 20Aug.16-I
Crowther,2Lt.SL, KIA 20Sep.17-I
Crowther,Lt.W, Can. KIA 31Oct.17-I
Croyden,Lt.SB, 14Oct.18-I
Cruikshank,Capt.GL, DSO MC 8Jul.16-I, KIA 15Sep.16-I
Cruickshank,2Lt.AJT, WIA DoW 8Jul.16-I
Cruickshank,Cpl.J, KIA 12Mar.18-I
Cruickshank,2Lt.KG, POW DoW 12.7.1917 11Jul.17-I
Cruise,Lt.MG, KIA 20Sep.18-I
Crumb,Lt.DS, 30Oct.18-I
Crumb,2Lt.HC, US. DoW 1.10.1918? 30Sep.18-IIB
Crump,2Lt.FF, inj 1Aug.18-IV
Crundall,FSLt.ED, 28Jul.17-I, WIA 10Aug.17-I
Crundall,Lt.WA, 8Jul.18-I
Cryan,Lt.JS, KIA 11Aug.18-I
Crysler,Lt.CA, KIA 20May.18-I
Cubbon,Capt.FR, MC KIA 9Jun.17-I
Cudemore,Capt.CW, 12Aug.18-I, 28Oct.18-I
Cudmore,2Lt.EO, POW 5Feb.18-I
Cuffe,2Lt.,Lt.RT, 3Apr.18-I, KIA 21Jul.18-I
Cull,Capt.AT, KIA 11May.17-I
Cull,FCdr.JT, 25Apr.15-IX, 11Jul.15-IX
Cullen,Lt.AA, POW 31Aug.18-VIII
Cullen,Lt.RJ, 15May.18-I, 18May.18-I, 8Jun.18-I, WIA 29Jun.18-I, 27Jul.18-I
Cullen,2Lt.WD, POW 12Aug.17-I
Culley,Lt.SD, 11Aug.18-III
Cullimore,Pte.CH, KIA 7Aug.18-I
Culling,FLt.TG, DSC KIA 8Jun.17-I
Culshaw,Sgt.RE, POW 29Oct.18-I
Culver,Lt.DE, POW 15Aug.18-I
Culverwell,Lt.EV, 22May.18-I
Cumberland,Sgt.JR, 27May.17-I
Cumming,Lt.CL, 29Aug.18-I
Cumming,Lt.HWM, 15Aug.18-I
Cumming,Sgt.V, WIA 16Jul.18-I
Cummings,Capt.ED, Aust. 14Oct.18-I
Cummings,Lt.ED, 3May.18-I
Cummings,Lt.PH, 26Nov.17-I
Cummins,Sgt.V, 5May.18-I, 4Jul.18-I
Cunnell,2Lt.,Capt.DC, 27Dec.16-I, 6Jul.17-I, KIA 12Jul.17-I
Cunniffe,Sgt.JA, 3Apr.17-I, WIA 13Apr.17-I
Cunningham,Lt., 6Sqn. 5May.15-I
Cunningham,2Lt., 218Sqn. 27Jun.18-I
Cunningham,2Lt.EA, KIA 28Jan.18-I
Cunningham,Capt.,Maj.JA, 28Nov.15-I, 28Dec.15-I, 29Dec.15-I, 23Jan.16-I, 25Jan.16-I, 5Feb.16-I, 2Mar.16-I, 17Mar.18-I
Cunningham,2Lt.JC, KIA 14Mar.16-I
Cunningham,2Lt.JN, DoW 19.10.1917 11Oct.17-I

Cunningham,Lt.MF, KIA 6Jun.18-I
Cunningham,2Lt.PJ, KIA 30Aug.18-I
Cunningham-Reid,Lt.AS, 16Jun.18-I
Cunningham-Reid,Lt.DF, KIA 19Dec.15-I
Cunninghame,Capt.FJ, 14Oct.18-I
Cunnius,1Lt.PE, USAS. 28Sep.18-I
Curlewis,2Lt.I, WIA POW 9Nov.16-I
Curling,Lt.ET, WIA 13Apr.17-I
Curphey,Capt.WGS, MC WIA 4Feb.17-I, POW DoW 15.5.1917 14May.17-I
Currie,Lt.JD, POW 24Mar.18-I
Currington,2Lt.JR, WIA 16Jun.17-I
Curruthers,2Lt.A, inj 12Jun.17-I
Curry,1Lt.IR, US. KIA 10Aug.18-IIB
Curry,LtCol.JF, US. 3Nov.18-IIB
Curry,2Lt.RA, WIA 23Mar.18-I
Curtis,Lt.AH, 7Jun.18-I
Curtis,Lt.C, 13Sqn. WIA 11Apr.17-I
Curtis,Lt.C, 59Sqn. WIA 12Apr.18-I
Curtis,2Lt.FW, KIA 14Aug.17-I
Curtis,Lt.HC, KIA 21Aug.18-I
Curtis,2Lt.HJ, KIA 4Nov.18-I
Curtis,1AM.HL, INT 2Oct.18-III
Curtis,2Lt.HN, KIA 25Jul.17-I
Curtis,2Lt.LR, WIA 22Aug.18-I
Curtis,1Lt.MK, USAS. POW 24Aug.18-I
Curtis,2Lt.RL, POW DoW 21Sep.17-I
Curtis,FSLt.WA, Can. 15Oct.17-I
Cushing,2Lt.D, Can. POW 16Sep.16-I
Cushny,2Lt.,Lt.J, 18Oct.17-I, WIA 22Nov.17-I
Cutbill,2Lt.EH, POW 6Nov.17-I
Cuthbert,Lt.CR, 21Mar.18-I
Cuthbert,Lt.JB, KIA 28Aug.18-I
Cuthbertson,Lt.,Capt.GC, MC 1Mar.18-I, WIA 1Apr.18-I
Cutler,Lt.HC, KIA 10May.17-I
Cutler,FSLt.HD, ~24Nov.14-IX, POW 10Dec.15-IX
Cutler,Capt.SleG, 31Jul.17-I
Cutmore,Lt.WC, KIA 24Jun.18-I
Cutter,1Lt.EB, US. KIA 21Oct.18-IIB
Cuttle,Lt.GR, MC KIA 9May.18-I
Cuzner,FSLt.AE, KIA 29Apr.17-I
Cyr,Lt.AJ, POW 20Jul.18-I

D

d'Albenas,Lt.PD, name d'Alberas? 9Oct.18-I, KIA 11Oct.18-I
D'Arcy,2Lt.LG, KIA 20Dec.16-I
D'Arcy,2Lt.Hon,SH, WIA 7Jun.17-I
D'Arcy-Levy,FSLt.JM, POW 12Aug.15-I
Da Costa,2Lt.WRC, 31Jul.16-I
Dabbs,2Lt.DH, WIA 8Sep.16-I
Dacre,FCdr.,FLt.GB, 17Aug.15-V, 8Nov.15-V, POW 25Aug.16-VIII
Daffey,Gnr.GE, KIA 28Mar.18-I
Daggett,2Lt.HCE, WIA 26Mar.18-I
Dagleish,2Lt., 59Sqn. 8Nov.17-I
Dahringer,2Lt.HW, US. KIA 17Sep.18-IIB
Daley,Lt.JEAR, 26Mar.18-I, 27Apr.18-I
Dalgleish,2Lt.NJ, WIA 3Oct.18-I
Dalkeith-Scott,Lt.C, KIA 30Sep.17-I
Dallas,FSLt.,SCdr.,Maj.RS, Aust. 20Feb.16-I, 23Apr.16-I, 20May.16-I, 1Jul.16-I, 30Sep.16-I, 9Jul.16-I, 21Oct.16-I, 15Nov.17-I, 12Apr.18-I, 2May.18-I, WIA 14Apr.18-I, KIA 1Jun.18-I
Dalley,2Lt.,Lt.JP, 27Sep.17-I, KIA 15Oct.17-I
Dalrymple,Capt.S, 8Aug.18-IV
Dalton,2Lt.MJ, 5Jun.17-I
Daltrey,2Lt.F, WIA POW 25Jun.18-I
Daly,2Lt.APV, 8Sqn. POW 3Sep.16?-I
Daly,Capt.APV, 29Sqn. WIA POW 1Feb.17-I
Daly,FSLt.IdeB, inj 1Jun.16-I
Daly,Lt.JAER, 9Apr.17-I
Daly,Lt.L, WIA 3Jul.18-I
Daly,FSLt.RH, DSC WIA 26Sep.17-I
Dalzell,Lt.W, POW 6Aug.15-I
Dalziel,2Lt.RG, WIA 3May.17-I, WIA 25May.17-I
Dame,2AM.FW, 2May.17-I
Dampier,2Lt.GW, KIA 11Dec.16-I

Danby,Lt., 6Sqn. 4Nov.15-I, 17Jan.16-I, 20Jan.16-I
Danby,2Lt.C, 15Sqn. 8Feb.16-I
Dance,2Lt.CC, 20May.18-I
Dancy,2Lt.W, WIA 31Mar.18-I
Dandy,2Lt.H, WIA 19Sep.17-I
Dandy,2Lt.JM, POW 24Sep.18-I
Danger,Lt.EO, 23Aug.18-I, WIA 16Sep.18-I
Dangerfield,Sgt.J, POW 20Apr.17-I
Daniel,Lt., 13Sqn. 27Sep.18-I
Daniel,2Lt.HC, SA. 24Mar.18-I
Daniel,Lt.WC, 3May.18-I, inj 18May.18-I
Dann,Lt.WS, DoW 16May.18-I
Danzey,AC2.,WC, POW DoW 6.12.1917 25Apr.17-I
Darby,2Lt.E, 27Jun.18-I, POW 28Sep.18-I
Daria,Lt., 13Sqn. 11Apr.18-I
Dario,Lt.G, 21Mar.18-I
Darley,Capt.CC, 7Sep.15-I, 12Sep.15-I, 19Sep.15-I, WIA POW 26Oct.15-I
Darley,Capt.CH, Can. 28May.18-I
Darley,FSLt.R, 15Nov.16-I
Darlington,Lt.CD, KIA 15Aug.18-I
Darnell,2Lt.CV, KIA 25Apr.17-I
Darroch,Capt.DM, WIA 23Oct.18-I
Darvill,Capt.GWF, DFC 6Sep.18-I
Darwin,Capt.CJW, 31May.18-I
Daunt,2Lt.CO'N, KIA 29Sep.18-I
Davenport,2Lt.D, KIA 24Sep.18-I
Davenport,2Lt.ES, KIA 3Jan.18-I
Davey,Lt., 2Sqn. 18Nov.15-I, 5Jan.16-I, 12Jan.16-I, 19Jan.16-I
Davey,Lt.HB, 23Jun.16-I
Davey,2Lt.RJ, 25Oct.18-I
Davey,2Lt.WC, DoW 21.11.1917 20Nov.17-I
Davidson,2Lt.,Lt.AGB, 14Jul.17-I, WIA 19Jul.17-I, KIA 9Sep.17-I
Davidson,Lt.BT, KIA 2Jul.18-I
Davidson,Sgt.CH, POW DoW 2Sep.18-I
Davidson,Lt.CR, Can.? 18Mar.16-I
Davidson,Lt.CR, 4Oct.17-VII, 17Dec.17-VII, WIA 9Jan.18-VII
Davidson,Lt.,Capt.DAL, MC WIA 26Apr.16-VIII, KIA 30Apr.17-I
Davidson,Lt.DG, 17Jun.17-I
Davidson,1Lt.GC, US. KIA 31Jul.18-IID
Davidson,Capt.JF, WIA 25May.17-I
Davidson,2Lt.LK, INT 8Aug.18-I
Davidson,1Lt.RL, US. WIA? 30Oct.18-IIB
Davidson,2Lt.RW, KIA 14Oct.18-I
Davidson,2Lt.S, KIA 21May.18-I
Davidson,Capt.T, POW 19Jun.17-I
Davidson,Lt.W, KIA 31Oct.17-I
Davidson,2Lt.WD, 28Mar.18-I, KIA 30May.18-I
Davies,Lt.AW, 29Jul.15-I, 11Aug.15-I, 22Aug.15-I
Davies,2Lt.CW, 24Apr.18-I
Davies,Lt.DA, 12Jun.18-VI
Davies,Lt.DB, KIA 11Aug.17-I
Davies,2Lt.DE, KIA 29Apr.17-I
Davies,2Lt.DP, POW 5Oct.18-I
Davies,Lt.,Capt.EE, Aust. 18Oct.18-I, 1Nov.18-I
Davies,Lt.EG, 9Nov.18-I
Davies,Lt.FG, KIA 21Aug.18-I
Davies,Capt.FJ, WIA 12Aug.18-I
Davies,Capt.FWK, 16Jun.15-I
Davies,Capt.G, 15Jul.17-I
Davies,2Lt.GAH, KIA 7Jun.17-I
Davies,2Lt.H, POW 15Sep.18-I
Davies,2Lt.HB, 2Jun.18-I
Davies,2Lt.HD, POW 13Apr.17-I
Davies,2Lt.HE, POW 13Jan.18-I
Davies,2Lt.HH, 9Aug.18-I
Davies,Lt.HR 11Mar.17-I, 19Mar.17-I, POW 14Apr.17-I
Davies,2Lt.JE, POW 29Apr.17-I
Davies,Lt.JH, KIA 19Aug.18-I
Davies,2Lt.JHT, WIA 10Jun.18-I
Davies,2Lt.LC, MC WIA 11Mar.17-I
Davies,2Lt.LG, 5Jun.17-I, 29Jul.17-I
Davies,2Lt.RB, WIA 11Dec.16-I, KIA 1May.17-I
Davies,2Lt.RC, WIA 2Oct.17-I, 30Oct.18-I
Davies,Lt.RH, 17Jun.18-I
Davies,2Lt.RL, 12Apr.18-I
Davies,2Lt.RS, inj 13Jun.17-I

Davies,2Lt.RWM, KIA 6Apr.17-I
Davies,2Lt.TEH, 9Mar.15-I, POW 20Mar.15-I
Davies,Sgt.THC, POW 29Aug.18-I
Davies,2Lt.WE, KIA 14Apr.17-I
Davies,2Lt.WE, 7Sqn. WIA 17Jun.17-I
Davies,Lt.WE, 25Sqn. KIA 11May.17-I
Davies,2Lt.WF, 30Jul.18-IV
Davies,2Lt.WG, WIA 30Oct.18-I
Davies,Lt.WH, WIA 14Aug.17-I
Davies,WTOp.HM, WIA 1Oct.17-III
Davin,2AM.AG, initials FG? 4Mar.17-I, WIA 11Mar.17-I
Davis,Lt., 102Sqn. 27Oct.17-I
Davis,Sgt.A, 7Jun.18-I, POW 20Jul.18-I
Davis,Lt.BR, KIA 20Sep.17-I
Davis,Lt.DW, Can. WIA POW 21Dec.16-I
Davis,Lt.EE, DoW 27Oct.18-I
Davis,Lt.EFH, Can. 4Jul.18-I
Davis,2Lt.,Lt.ER, 4May.16-I, 17May.16-I
Davis,Lt.G, POW 14Jul.17-I
Davis,Lt.HB, 10Aug.18-I
Davis,2Lt.HC, KIA 26Jun.18-I
Davis,2Lt.HJ, KIA 6Feb.17-I
Davis,2AM.HM, 14Jun.17-III
Davis,Rfn.H, KIA 21Jul.17-I
Davis,2Lt.LS, WIA 14Sep.18-I
Davis,2Lt.PW, US. KIA 2Jun.18-IIB
Davis,2Lt.R, KIA 20Oct.16-I
Davis,1Lt.RE, US. POW 30Sep.18-IIB
Davis,Lt.RG, 31Aug.18-IV
Davis,Lt.RH, KIA 19Aug.18-I
Davison,Lt.CW, KIA 4Oct.18-I
Davison,2Lt.HF, WIA 13Apr.18-I
Davison,2Lt.J, 23Oct.18-I
Davyes,2Lt.,Lt.CW, Aust. 13Aug.17-I, WIA POW 21Aug.17-I
Dawe,2Lt.JJ, KIA 7Jun.18-I
Dawes,Lt.AF, POW 3May.18-I
Dawes,Lt.L, 22Aug.14-I, 28Sep.14-I, 9Sep.14-I, 12Sep.14-I
Dawes,2Lt.RG, Can. 15Jun.18-IV
Dawson,2Lt.E, INT 21Jul.18-I
Dawson,2Lt.E, POW? 5Nov.18-I
Dawson,Lt.S, INT 19Jul.18-III
Dawson,Lt.SA, KIA 10Aug.18-I
Day,Lt.GS, KIA 1Oct.18-I
Day,FSLt.H, DSC KIA 5Feb.18-I
Day,2Lt.HJ, inj 10Jul.17-I, DoW 8.8.1917 7Aug.17-I
Day,2Lt.JC, KIA 9May.17-I
Day,2Lt.JFA, WIA 11Mar.17-I
Day,FCdr.MJG, DSC 25Jan.18-I, KIA 27Feb.18-I
Day,Lt.WL, DoW 6Apr.17-I
de Boutiny,Lt., French. WIA 1Jul.15-I
de Brasseur,Lt.RH, 5Jan.16-I
de Carteret,Lt.HGS, 5Aug.17-I
de Conway,2Lt.JH, 2Apr.17-I, WIA 15May.17-I, KIA 15Jun.17-I
de Crespigny,2Lt.,Capt.,Maj.HVC, 13Dec.15-I, 14Jan.16-I, 20Jan.16-I, 31Mar.16-I, 5May.16-I, 8Aug.18-I
de Cruise,Lt.C, 17Apr.18-I
de Escofet,2Lt.PA, WIA 22Apr.17-I
de Halpert,2Lt.RV, 26May.15-I, inj 20Jun.15-I
de Halpert,Lt.RV, 2Jun.15-I
de Havilland,Capt.H, 19Jan.16-I, 25Jan.16-I, 13Aug.16-VIII
De L'Haye,Capt.RA, 1Oct.18-I
de la Cour,Lt.PV, KIA 15May.18-I
de Laage de Meux,Lt.A, French. KIFA 23May.17-IIA
de Lacey,2Lt.JM, KIA 23Sep.17-I
de Lavison,Lt.AMN, WIA 24Apr.17-I
de Lisle,Lt.ACNMP, KIA 20Nov.17-I
de Niverville,Lt.A, WIA 8Jul.18-I
de Pencier,2Lt.,Lt.,Capt.JD, Can. 7Jun.17-I, WIA 23Nov.17-I, 26Feb.18-I, 13Jul.18-I
de Pomeroy,2Lt.NR, KIA 20Oct.16-I
de Puechredon,Lt., French. 10Jan.15-I
de Rochie,Lt.CM, KIA 14Jul.17-I
de Roeper,FSLt.BPH, WIA 25May.17-I
de Ross,Lt.AD, 16Dec.16-I
de Ross,Lt.AGS, KIA 14Feb.17-I
de Selincourt,Capt.A, WIA POW 28May.17-I
de Watteville,2Lt.JE, WIA 8Apr.17-I
de Wilde,FSLt.JS, KIA 27Sep.17-I
Deacon,2Lt.ECW, KIA 22Apr.18-I
Deakin,Lt.HA, WIA 16May.18-I, 28Oct.18-I
Deakin,Lt.RH, KIA 22Jul.17-I
Deal,2AM.ER, WIA 26Jul.16-I
Deamer,2Lt.SH, UK. WIA 29Sep.18-I
Dean,Lt.AC, POW 12Apr.18-I
Dean,2Lt.H?, POW 3Apr.18-I
Deane,2Lt.GS, POW 26Nov.16-I
Deane,Capt.W, 26Feb.18-I, WIA 23Mar.18-I
Deans,Lt.GM, Aust. 26Sep.18-I
Deans,Lt.JH, Can. KIA 8Nov.17-I
Dear,Lt.JA, INT 24Aug.18-I
Dearing,1AM.F, 8Sep.16-I, WIA 26Sep.16-I
Dearlove,2Lt.CJS, 21Mar.18-I
Deason,Lt.TG, POW 15Sep.17-I
Debussey,2Lt.W, KIA 14Oct.18-I
Dee,2Lt.DM, POW 4Nov.18-I
Deeks,2Lt.HC, 25Mar.18-I
Deetjen,1Lt.WL, USAS. KIA 30Jun.18-I
Deighton,Sgt.EA, 13Jun.18-I
Deighton-Simpson,2Lt.HR, initials HD? 25Sep.15-I, 5Feb.16-I
Delamere,2Lt.WP, 24Oct.17-I
Dell,AM.LA, 25Feb.17-I
Dempsey,Lt.HE, Can. POW 9Aug.18-I
Dempsey,Sgt.J, POW 13Apr.17-I
Dempster,2Lt.IM, KIA 24Feb.18-I
Denavon,2Lt.AMcN, WIA 15Jun.17-I
Dendrino,2Lt.S, POW DoW 27Sep.16-I
Denison,2Lt.A, WIA 24Jan.17-I
Denison,2Lt.EB, POW 11Sep.17-I
Denison,FSLt.J, KIA 13Apr.18-I
Denison,Lt.NC, WIA POW 2Apr.17-I
Denne,2Lt.RA, WIA 14Jan.16-I
Dennett,FSLt.PM, 3Jan.18-I
Dennett,Lt.PM, KIA 2Jun.18-I
Dennett,2Lt.TFP, DoW 5.8.1917 4Aug.17-I
Dennett,2Lt.WC, WIA 23Mar.18-I, KIA 27Mar.18-I
Dennis,StfSgt., 34Sqn. 11Mar.17-I
Dennis,2Lt.CC, KIA 25Sep.17-I
Dennis,2Lt.E, KIA 22Mar.18-I
Dennis,Lt.GN, 1Sep.18-I
Dennis,2Lt.JG, WIA 14Sep.18-I
Dennis,2Lt.LR, KIA 31Jul.18-I
Dennison,Lt.FE, US. WIA 10Jun.18-I
Dennistoun,Maj.JA, 1Apr.18-I
Dennistoun,2Lt.JR, 7Sqn. KIA 4May.16-I
Dennistoun,Lt.JR, 23Sqn. POW DoW 9.8.1916 26Jun.16-I
Dennistoun,Maj.JA, WIA 11Apr.18-I
Dennitts,2Lt.KJW, KIA 3Sep.18-I
Denny,Lt.CH, POW 15Aug.18-I
Denny,Sgt.FHI, WIA 4Sep.18-I
Denovan,2Lt.AMcN, Can. KIA 26Mar.18-I
Densham,2Lt.EWC, 30Oct.18-I
Densham,2Lt.WJ, 2Sep.18-I, KIA 2Oct.18-I
Dent,Lt.AC, WIA 24Jun.17-VI
Deremo,Lt.JC, 9Nov.18-I
Derrick,Lt.LJ, KIA 3May.18-I
Derwin,Lt.ECE, WIA 11Apr.17-I
Desbarats,FSLt.EW, POW 20Sep.17-I
Desborough,Lt.LV, KIA 30Nov.17-I
des Brisay,Sap.EM, KIA 3Aug.16-I
Desmore,Lt.SA, 26Aug.18-I
Desy,2Lt.,Lt.JR, 16Sep.18-I, 21Sep.18-I, KIA 26Oct.18-I
Detmold,2Lt.EJ, 16Sep.17-I
Devenish,Lt.GW, KIA 6Jun.17-I
deVerteuil,2Lt.M, 28Sep.18-I
Devitt,2Lt.A, KIA 2Jun.18-I
Devitt,Lt.LK, WIA 30Aug.18-I
Devlin,Lt.HL, KIA 19Sep.17-I
Dew,2Lt.EA, WIA 5Jul.18-I
Dewhirst,2Lt.A, 30Aug.18-I, WIA 3Sep.18-I
Dexter,Lt.WE, WIA 3Dec.17-I
Dey,2Lt.FW, WIA 3Nov.18-I
di Balme,2Lt.Count.LTB, POW 7Jun.17-I
Diamond,2Lt.WEdeB, WIA POW 9Sep.17-I
Diamond,Lt.J, MC KIA 8Oct.17-I
Dick,Lt.GM, KIA 29May.17-I
Dickens,2Lt.GJ, inj 27Sep.18-I
Dickens,Lt.MW, KIA 27Feb.18-I
Dickey,FSLt.,Capt.RFL, 14Jun.17-III, INT 4Jun.18-III
Dickie,Lt.CB, KIA 18Jul.18-I
Dickinson,Lt.HM, KIA 10Jul.18-I
Dickinson,Lt.TM, WIA POW 4Jun.17-I
Dicksee,2Lt.HJH, WIA 27Dec.16-I
Dickson,Capt.E, NZ. 3May.18-I
Dickson,Capt.WF, 19Jul.18-III
Dietz,1Lt.P, USAS. KIA 30Jul.18-I
Difford,Lt.WM, KIA 3Oct.18-I
Digby,1AM.BC, 10Oct.15-I, POW 9Oct.16-I
Digby-Johnson,Capt.E, 17Sep.16-I
Dillnutt,Lt.EJ, POW 25Apr.17-I
Dilloway,2Lt.RH, KIA 15Sep.18-I
Diment,2Lt.WJ, 4Oct.18-I
Dimsey,Lt.DF, Aust. 15Aug.18-I, 3Sep.18-I, 18Sep.18-I
Dines,Capt.RI, inj 17Oct.18-I
Dingley,2Lt.RL, POW 19Oct.16-I
Dingley,Pte.WHD, died 31Jul.18-III
Dingwall,2Lt.JD, KIA 21Apr.18-I
Dinsmore,2Lt.GH, 29Apr.17-I
Dinwoodie,Capt.H, MC WIA 6Oct.18-I
Dissette,FSLt.IS, KIA 2Jun.17-I
Dix,Lt.,Capt.RCStJ., 26Mar.18-I, WIA 19May.18-I
Dixie,2Lt.,Lt.NC, WIA 22Apr.18-I, 1Jul.18-I, 26Sep.18-I
Dixon,FSLt.AJ, KIA 4Jan.18-I
Dixon,2Lt.B, WIA 15Sep.18-I
Dixon,Capt.CH, 25Sqn. 1Aug.16-I
Dixon,Lt.CH, 9Sqn. 16Aug.17-I, KIA 28Nov.17-I
Dixon,Lt.FC, 27Mar.18-I, inj 1Apr.18-I
Dixon,1Lt.FM, US. WIA 22Jul.18-IID
Dixon,2Lt.G, inj 14Mar.18-I
Dixon,Capt.GC, Can. 22Aug.18-I
Dixon,2Lt.H, 4May.16-I
Dixon,2Lt.HG, KIA 4Nov.18-I
Dixon,AM.JM, 7Nov.17-I
Dixon,2Lt.RM, WIA 10Jun.17-I
Dixon,2Lt.WH, WIA 8Jun.18-I
Dobbie,Sgt.RS?, WIA 15Jul.18-I
Dobell,Sgt.A, WIA 9Aug.18-I
Dobell,TLt.,Lt.GL, 8May.18-I, 22Jun.18-I, KIA 11Aug.18-I
Dobell,LCdr.H, POW 12May.15-I
Dobeson,Lt.GE, KIA 1Jul.18-I
Dobeson,Lt.R, 17Sep.18-I
Dobeson,2Lt.RG, POW 1Nov.18-I
Dobing,2Lt.H, WIA 4Sep.18-I
Doble,2Lt.AJS, WIA 6Mar.18-I
Dobson,2Lt.AEJ, 4Jun.17-I, KIA 7Jun.17-I
Dobson,Sgt.EH, KIA 12Aug.16-I
Docker,Pte., 6Sqn. 17Oct.17-I
Docking,Lt.RJ, DoW 10Feb.17-I
Dockree,Pte.HG, WIA 31Oct.17-I
Dodd,2Lt.FC, KIA 10Jun.18-I
Dodd,Lt.HR, KIA 16Sep.18-I
Dodd,GL.HL, POW 30Oct.17-I
Dodd,2Lt.WdeC, POW DoW 31Oct.17-I
Dodds,Lt.A, POW 29Nov.17-I
Dodds,Sgt.NC, WIA 23Sep.18-I
Dodds,Lt.R, Can. 3Sep.17-I
Dodds,Sgt.RS, KIA 10Nov.18-I
Dodson,SgtMech.HL, 9Oct.18-I
Dodson,Lt.HLM, KIA 25Aug.18-I
Dodson,Lt.L, WIA POW 3Apr.17-I
Dodwell,2Lt.TB, 14Aug.18-I, WIA INT 16Aug.18-I
Doe,Lt.JE, POW 26Jun.18-I
Doehler,2Lt.HH, USAS POW 30Aug.18-I
Dogherty,2Lt.FW, POW 22Jan.18-I
Doidge,Lt.EL, Can. KIA 31Jul.18-I
Dolan,Pte.AM, WIA 12Jun.17-I
Dolan,2Lt.HA, 30Sep.18-IIB
Dolan,Lt.HE, MC 12Apr.18-I, KIA 12May.18-I
Dollingsworth,2Lt.C, POW 6Aug.15-I
Don,Capt.FP, WIA POW 5Jun.17-I
Donald,Lt., 108Sqn. 4Nov.18-I
Donald,Lt.RB, 12Apr.18-I, 18Apr.18-I, WIA 22Apr.18-I
Donald,AM.,Cpl.TH, DCM 7Nov.15-I, 13Dec.15-I, WIA POW 14Dec.15-I
Donaldson,2Lt.CTL, KIA 14Apr.17-I
Donaldson,Lt.,Capt.EGE, WIA 16Apr.16-I, WIA 14Oct.18-I
Donaldson,2Lt.JC, US. 25Aug.18-I
Donaldson,2Lt.JOW, USAS. POW 1Sep.18-I
Doncaster,2Lt.AE, POW 8Aug.18-I
Doncaster,Lt.EL, KIA 8Aug.18-I
Donkin,Lt., 98Sqn. 11Jul.18-I, 20Jul.18-I
Donnet,2Lt.AN, WIA 20Aug.17-I
Donovan,2Lt.HR, inj 26Dec.17-I
Doolittle,Cpl.JR, US. 17Jul.17-IIA
Doran,2Lt.CFG, WIA 6Apr.18-I
Doran,Lt.FB, KIA 14Aug.17-I
Dore,Maj.ASW, 25Apr.16-I
Dore,2Lt.GL, WIA 12Oct.17-I
Dore,Capt.WH, 11Jul.18-I, KIA 9Aug.18-I
Dormer,2Lt.FA, WIA 5Nov.17-I
Dormor,Lt., 3Sqn. 23Nov.16-I
Dorsey,Lt.GC, USAS. 31Aug.18-I, WIA 16Sep.18-I
Dotzert,Lt.C, 30Aug.18-I, 20Sep.18-I
Douch,2Lt.EJH, 10Sep.16-I
Dougall,2Lt.CR, POW 19Mar.17-I
Dougall,Lt.FW, MC KIA? 21Jul.18-I
Dougall,2Lt.HF, POW 26Feb.18-I
Dougall,Lt.NS, 29Jul.18-I
Dougan,2Lt.WL, POW 28Sep.18-I
Doughty,2Lt.G, KIA 20Nov.16-I
Doughty,2Lt.RC, 4Mar.17-I, WIA 29Apr.17-I
Douglas,Capt., 13Sqn. 11Apr.18-I
Douglas,Lt., 16Sqn. 18Aug.17-I
Douglas,2Lt.A, KIA 16Oct.16-I
Douglas,Lt.AA, WIA 29Aug.18-I, KIA 30Oct.18-I
Douglas,Capt.BC, 4Nov.17-I
Douglas,Lt.CKM, WIA 16Oct.16-I, 22Nov.17-I, 30Nov.17-I
Douglas,Lt.CWH, USAS. KIA 11Jun.18-1
Douglas,2Lt.J, WIA 15Aug.17-I
Douglas,2Lt.Lord,CC, 24Mar.18-I
Douglas,2Lt.P, 12Mar.18-I
Douglas,Lt.RK, KIA 11Aug.18-I
Douglas,Lt.WS, 28Nov.15-I
Douglas,Lt.WT?, 14Dec.15-I
Douglass,FCdr.PC, KIA 10Dec.17-V
Doune,2Lt.,Lt.Lord., 29Apr.16-I, 4Jun.16-I
Dowd,2Lt.ML, US. KIA 26Oct.18-IIB
Dowding,Capt.KT, 18Jun.18-I
Dowler,2Lt.GE, KIA 10Nov.18-I
Dowling,Capt.BL, 29Jan.17-I, KIA 2Sep.18-I
Dowling,Lt.DR, Aust. WIA 19Sep.18-VII
Dowling,2Lt.FLW, WIA 20Sep.18-I
Down,2Lt.RT, POW 16Sep.18-I
Down,Lt., 5Sqn. 11Jul.17-I
Downing,Lt.GGB, 13Aug.16-I, WIA 2Sep.16-I
Downing,2Lt.HG, MC KIA 6Nov.17-I
Dowse,Lt.HH, WIA 30Oct.18-IV
Doyle,2Lt.DC, POW 26Feb.18-I
Drabble,Lt.CF, KIA 13Aug.18-I
Dracup,Lt.GF, DoW 28Jul.17-I
Drain,2Lt.LA, 4Nov.18-I
Draisey,Lt.AS, 20Sep.18-I
Drake,Capt.EB, 27Jun.18-I, KIA 29Sep.18-I
Draper,1AM.FG, POW 30May.16-VIII
Draper,Maj.C, DSC WIA 13Oct.18-I
Drenon,2Lt.,Lt.LC, 22Sep.15-I, 28Dec.15-I
Dreschfield,2Lt.SE, 13Oct.17-I
Dressy,Sgt.J, KIA 23Apr.17-IIA
Drew,1Lt.CW, US. WIA POW 14Sep.18-IIB
Drew,Sgt.J, 3Nov.16-I
Drew,Cpl.SR, US. KIA 19May.18-IIC
Drew-Brook,Lt.TG, WIA POW 21May.18-I
Drewitt,Capt.HFS, NZ. 17Mar.18-I, 24Mar.18-I
Drinkwater,Lt.AT, Aust. 21Sep.17-I
Drinkwater,Lt.EO, KIA 23Aug.18-I
Driver,Lt.HW, KIA 19Sep.18-I
Driver,2Lt.,Lt.PS, 7Nov.17-I, 3Jan.18-I, KIA 26Mar.18-I
Dronsfield,2Lt.SW, POW 12Sep.17-I
Drummond,2Lt.GLP, WIA POW 1Nov.18-I
Drummond,2Lt.JCG, 23Aug.18-I, KIA 8Oct.18-I
Drummond,Lt.JE, WIA 6Apr.18-I
Drummond,Lt.JR, KIA 27Sep.18-I

Drummond,Lt.L, 7May.17-*I*, **KIA** 18May.17-*I*
Drummond,Capt.RM, DSO MC *Aust.* 12Dec.17-*VII*, 27Mar.18-*VII*
Drury,2Lt.DD, **POW** 16Aug.15-*I*
Drury-Lowe,2Lt.DRC, 21Jun.17-*I*
Drysdale,Lt., *60Sqn.* **WIA** 25Aug.16-*I*
Drysdale,2Lt.JM, 3Aug.16-*I*
Drysdale,2Lt.NM, **WIA** 22Mar.18-*I*
Dubber,Lt.RE, 17May.18-*I*, **KIA** 18Jul.18-*I*
Duce,Lt.W, **POW** 25Apr.18-*I*
Duckstein,1Lt.AW, *US.* **WIA** 29Sep.18-*IIB*
Duckworth,2Lt.JT, 9Aug.18-*I*
Ducray,Lt.MJ, **POW** 7Jul.18-*I*
Dudley,1Lt.LC, *US.* **POW** 22Oct.18-*IIB*
Duff,Dvr.RA, **DoI** 30Jan.18-*I*
Duff,Capt.1AJ, **WIA** 9Apr.16-*I*, **WIA** 27Oct.17-*I*
Duff,2Lt.RW, **POW** 30Oct.18-*I*
Duff,Capt.TR, **WIA** 14Oct.16-*I*
Duff,1Lt.WW, *Aust.?* **WIA** 19Jun.18-*I*
Duff-Fyfe,Lt.RJR, **INT** 4Jun.18-*III*
Duffus,Lt.AA, 23Nov.17-*I*
Duffus,2Lt.CS, 30Sep.16-*I*
Dugan,2Lt.HG, *US.* **POW** 6Apr.18-*I*
Dugdale,2Lt.JG, **POW** 1Sep.18-*I*
Duggan,2Lt.ES, **WIA** 19Sep.16-*I*
Duggan,2Lt.JHW, **WIA** 6Nov.17-*I*
Duguid,2Lt.A, 19Dec.15-*I*, 5Feb.16-*I*
Duigan,Capt.JR, MC *Aust.* **WIA** 9May.18-*I*
Duke,1Lt.JE, *US.* **POW** 10Jul.18-*IIB*
Duke,Lt.LdeS, **WIA** 23Apr.18-*I*
Duke,Lt.RE, **POW** 6Mar.18-*I*
Dumbell,2Lt.HC, **WIA** 26Aug.17-*I*
Dumville,2Lt.E, 16May.18-*I*, **KIA** 24Jun.18-*I*
Dunbar,2Lt.JH, 14Jul.18-*I*
Duncan,2Lt.A, 14Jul.18-*I*
Duncan,Capt.GM, 5Sep.18-*I*
Duncan,2Lt.HD, 20Jun.17-*I*
Duncan,Lt.HF, **DoW** 29.3.1917 24Mar.17-*I*
Duncan,Lt.HJ?, MC *ISqn.* **WIA** 18May.17-*I*
Duncan,Lt.HJ, *5Sqn.* 26Sep.16-*I*
Duncan,2Lt.J, 10Nov.16-*I*
Duncan,Lt.J, **WIA** 14Oct.17-*I*
Duncan,Lt.W, 6Nov.17-*I*
Duncan,2Lt.WG, **KIA** 24Jun.18-*I*
Duncan,Capt.WIA, *Can.* 5Jun.18-*I*
Duncan-Knight,2Lt.WH, **KIA** 2May.18-*I*
Dunford,1AM.EJ, 24Oct.17-*I*
Dunford,2Lt.ET, **POW DoW** 23.4.1917 11Apr.17-*I*
Dunford,Lt.BF, **KIA** 19May.18-*I*
Dunkerley,Lt.JS, **WIA** 27Mar.18-*I*
Dunlop,TLt.LDC, 5Jul.18-*I*, 3Sep.18-*I*
Dunlop,2Lt.GB, **POW** 25Sep.18-*I*
Dunlop,2Lt.JM, **POW** 19Aug.18-*I*
Dunlop,Lt.SL, DFC *Can.* 9Aug.18-*I*
Dunn,2Lt.GE, 23Oct.18-*I*
Dunn,2Lt.JB, **KIA** 25Sep.18-*I*
Dunn,2Lt.MA, **POW** 7Sep.18-*I*
Dunn,2Lt.MW, **POW** 21Oct.18-*I*
Dunn,Sgt.R, 31Oct.16-*I*, 4Mar.17-*I*, **KIA** 2Apr.17-*I*
Dunn,2Lt.RH, **POW** 9Jul.18-*I*
Dunn,Sgt.WH, **POW** 13May.17-*I*
Dunnett,Lt.LE, **KIA** 10May.18-*I*
Dunning,FLt.EH, 5Mar.15-*V*, 27Apr.15-*V*
Dunsford,2Lt.CW, **WIA** 27Nov.17-*I*
Dunstan,2Lt.H, **WIA** 12Aug.17-*I*, **KIA** 18Aug.17-*I*
Dunster,2Lt.,Lt.CH, 20May.18-*I*, **WIA POW** 5Jun.18-*I*
du Peuty,Capt., *French.* **WIA** 1Jul.15-*I*
Durand,1Lt.EM, *US.* **KIA** 14Sep.18-*IIB*
Durand,2Lt.W, 6Jul.17-*I*
Durant,Lt.WE, **KIA** 2Jul.18-*I*
Durham,2Lt.JO, 22Oct.17-*I*
Durkin,Lt.FV, **POW** 7Jun.17-*I*
Durno,2Lt.Capt.RS, MC 25Mar.18-*I*, 21Apr.18-*I*, **inj** 27Jun.18-*I*
Durrad,Capt.FA, 11Oct.17-*I*, **KIA** 8Nov.17-*I*
Durrand,2Lt.W, 8Jun.17-*I*, 21Sep.17-*I*
Durrant,Capt.T, **KIA** 16May.18-*I*
Dusgate,Lt.RE, 23Nov.17-*I*, **POW DoW** 19.12.17 30Nov.17-*I*
Duthie,2Lt.DO, **WIA** 23Nov.17-*I*, **KIA** 23Aug.18-*I*

Duthie,2Lt.GA, **WIA** 25Aug.18-*I*
Duthie,2Lt.WG, **WIA** 26Feb.18-*I*
Dutton,2Lt.IL, 10Nov.18-*I*
Dutton,2Lt.R, **KIA** 19Aug.17-*I*
Duxbury,2Lt.HC, **KIA** 11May.17-*I*
Dyer,2Lt.HA, **KIA** 6Dec.17-*I*
Dyke,Lt.EPW, **KIA** 30Oct.18-*I*
Dyke,Sgt.W, **DCM WIA** 28Jul.18-*I*
Dykes,Capt.GH, **WIA** 2Sep.18-*I*
Dyson,2Lt.SG, **WIA** 30May.18-*I*

E

Eales,Capt.C, 20Nov.17-*I*
Eales,2Lt.TT, 8Aug.18-*I*
Eardley-Wilmot,Lt.L, 17Jan.16-*I*
Earle,2Lt.WS, **KIA** 16Apr.16-*I*
Easman,Pte.WA, **KIA** 30Aug.18-*IV*
Eason?,Lt.AT, **POW** 28Sep.16-*I*
East,1Lt.JH, *US.* **POW** 3Nov.18-*IIB*
Eastaugh,Lt.WS, **WIA** 3Oct.18-*I*
Easterbrook,1Lt.AE, *US.* **WIA** 3Nov.18-*IIB*
Easterbrook,1Lt.A, 4Jul.18-*I*
Easton,Lt.GC, **WIA** 5Aug.18-*IV*
Eastwood,Lt.,Capt.GH, 10Oct.15-*I*, 28Nov.15-*I*, 14Dec.15-*I*, 19Dec.15-*I*
Eastwood,2Lt.GH?, **INT** 8Mar.15-*I*
Eastwood,2Lt.L, 30Sep.18-*I*
Eastwood,2Lt.WP, 1May.17-*I*
Easty,2Lt.WH, **KIA** 22Apr.18-*I*
Eaton,Lt.C, 26Jan.18-*I*, **POW** 29Jun.18-*I*
Eaton,Lt.EC, **KIA** 26Jun.18-*I*
Eaton,2Lt.FCB, **KIA** 4Sep.18-*I*
Eaton,Ens.JA, *USN.* **INT** 4Jun.18-*III*
Eaton,1Lt.PW, *US.* **WIA POW** 11May.18-*IIB*
Eaves,2Lt.CC, **KIA** 21Sep.18-*I*
Eberli,Lt.FH, **POW** 9May.15-*I*
Eccles,Lt.CG, **KIA** 25May.17-*I*
Eccles,2Lt.HEK, **WIA** 8May.17-*I*
Echert,Lt.SB, 9May.18-*I*
Echlin,2Lt.FStJFN, **KIA** 26Sep.16-*I*
Eddie,2Lt.MH, *Aust.* **KIA** 5Sep.18-*I*
Eddington,Sgt., *6Sqn.* **WIA?** 5Nov.17-*I*
Eddy,Lt.CE, 18Jun.18-*I*
Edelsten,2Lt.J, **WIA** 25Mar.18-*I*
Edelston,2Lt.ERH, **POW** 23Mar.18-*I*
Edelston,Lt.TS, **WIA** 10Feb.17-*I*
Edens,Lt.LA, 18Mar.18-*I*
Edgar,1Lt.SE, *US.* **KIA** 17Aug.18-*IIC*
Edgell,2Lt.EH, **KIA** 11Aug.18-*I*
Edgington,Sgt.SF, **WIA** 11Sep.17-*I*
Edgley,Sgt.DE, 8Aug.18-*I*, 1Sep.18-*I*
Edmonds,FCdr.CHK, 12Aug.15-*V*, 17Aug.15-*V*, 8Nov.15-*V*
Edmonds,2Lt.EPP, **WIA POW** 10Mar.18-*I*
Edmonds,Lt.LW, 21Jul.18-*I*
Edmunds,Lt.PML, **WIA** 9Aug.17-*VI*
Edols,Lt.TR, *Aust.* **WIA** 25Aug.18-*I*
Edson,2Lt.CR, *Aust.* **DoW** 17Aug.17-*I*
Edsted?,2Lt.F, *US.* **POW** 28Sep.18-*I*
Edwardes,1Lt.LJ, 28Oct.18-*I*
Edwards,2AM., 26Apr.16-*I*
Edwards,Lt., *14Sqn.* 3Aug.16-*VII*
Edwards,Cpl., *15Sqn.* 19Jan.16-*I*
Edwards,2Lt.AGE, 17Apr.18-*I*
Edwards,Capt.AS, **POW DoW** 14.5.18 2May.18-*VIII*
Edwards,2Lt.AW, **KIA** 10Oct.17-*I*
Edwards,2Lt.CG, DFC 24Apr.18-*I*, **KIA** 27Aug.18-*I*
Edwards,Capt.DW, MC **KIA** 6Apr.17-*I*
Edwards,2Lt.EL, **POW** 1May.17-*I*
Edwards,2Lt.EW, **WIA** 11Aug.16-*VII*
Edwards,2Lt.G, **KIA** 24Sep.16-*I*
Edwards,2Lt.GR, **WIA POW** 21Oct.17-*I*
Edwards,FSLt.H, **POW** 14Apr.17-*I*
Edwards,2Lt.HJ, 13Jul.17-*I*
Edwards,2Lt.HL, 21Aug.18-*I*, 25Sep.18-*I*
Edwards,Capt.IAE, 8Nov.15-*V*
Edwards,Lt.JB, 26Aug.18-*I*
Edwards,Rfn.Q, **KIA?** 16Jun.17-*I*
Edwards,1Lt.LB, *US.* 10Oct.18-*IIB*, **POW** 5Nov.18-*IIB*

Edwards,Lt.LJ, 8Aug.18-*I*
Edwards,2Lt.RH, 3Sep.16-*I*, **KIA** 22Sep.16-*I*
Edwards,FCdr.ST, *Can.* 21Sep.17-*I*
Edwards,LM.WJ, **WIA** 7Jul.17-*I*
Egan,2Lt.L, 22Aug.18-*I*
Egan,1AM.SW, **WIA** 17Feb.18-*I*
Egerton,Lt.R, 5Feb.16-*I*, 10Feb.16-*I*
Eglington,2Lt.,Lt.DC, MC 20May.17-*I*, 16Jun.17-*I*
Ekins,2AM.AW, **KIA** 6May.17-*I*
Ekins,2Lt.CCF, **WIA** 25Mar.18-*I*
Elder,Lt.GEP, **inj** 13Apr.18-*I*
Elder,Lt.JJ, 27Aug.18-*I*, 31Aug.18-*I*, **KIA** 16Sep.18-*I*
Elder-Hearn,2Lt.T, **WIA** 15Nov.17-*I*
Elgey,Lt.E, **KIA** 19Mar.17-*I*
Elias,2Lt.GW, 12Oct.18-*I*
Elias,Capt.IG, **inj** 15Jun.17-*I*
Elias,2Lt.JW, 25Sep.18-*I*
Ellam,2Lt.HJ, **WIA POW** 5Aug.17-*I*
Ellen,CPO., *RNAS* 18Jun.16-*I*
Ellerbeck,2Lt.EAV, **POW** 29Sep.17-*I*
Ellery,2AM.FA, **DoW** 9Aug.18-*I*
Elliot,2Lt.CMW, **WIA** 30Oct.18-*I*
Elliot,2Lt.CW, **KIA** 12Aug.17-*I*
Elliot,Lt.D, **KIA** 15Apr.18-*I*
Elliot,Lt.FE, **WIA** 3May.17-*I*
Elliot,2Lt.FEL, 2Sep.18-*I*
Elliot,FSLt.GL, **POW** 1Feb.17-*I*
Elliot,2Lt.HS, 6Mar.17-*I*
Elliot,2Lt.JMcC, **KIA** 16Apr.17-*I*
Elliot,2Lt.RD, 21Oct.16-*I*
Elliot,Cpl.WA, **WIA** 12Nov.17-*I*
Elliott,1Lt.EB, *US.* **KIA** 2Jul.18-*IIB*
Elliott,2Lt.EEF?, **WIA** *initials* GEF? 21Mar.18-*I*
Elliott?,2Lt.H, **POW** 8Aug.18-*I*
Elliott,2Lt.HS, 24Mar.17-*I*
Elliott,2Lt.T, 4Sep.18-*I*
Elliott,Sgt.WC, **POW** 7Jun.18-*I*
Ellis,AM.FG, 9May.17-*I*
Ellis,Lt.HEO, 13Apr.17-*I*
Ellis,FSLt.OB, **KIA** 19May.17-*I*
Ellis,Lt.PC, 17Oct.16-*I*
Ellis,1Lt.RH, *USAS.* **POW** 21Aug.18-*I*
Ellis,Lt.RW, **KIA** 18Jun.17-*I*
Ellis,2Lt.S, 2Nov.17-*I*
Ellis,2Lt.SH, *NZ.* **WIA POW** 3Jul.16-*I*
Ellis,Lt.WB, **POW** 3Jul.16-*I*
Ellison,2Lt., *2Sqn.* 11Oct.15-*I*
Ellison,2Lt.JA, *USAS.* 17Sep.18-*I*
Ellison,Lt.SW, **DoW** 16Jun.18-*IV*
Ellwood,FSLt.AB, 22Mar.18-*I*
Elphinston,2Lt.C, **WIA POW** 15Sep.16-*I*
Elphinstone,Maj.M, **KId** 22Mar.17-*I*
Elsley,Lt.L, **KIA** 5Apr.17-*I*
Elton,2Lt.JB, 2Sep.18-*I*
Elton,Sgt.EJ, 29Mar.18-*I*
Elvin,2Lt.AJ, **POW** 26Jun.18-*I*
Elwig,2Lt.HJC, **POW** 25Sep.18-*I*
Elworthy,Lt.LN, **POW** 29Sep.18-*I*
Ely,Lt.FW, **KIA** 8Oct.18-*I*
Ely,Lt.MH, 20Jun.18-*I*
Emerson,2Lt.WKB, *US.* **KIA** 14May.18-*IIB*
Emery,FSgt.AC, 19Mar.16-*III*
Emmerson,1Lt.AE, **DoW** 4Apr.17-*I*
Emsden,Sgt.L, **WIA** 1May.17-*I*
Emtage,Lt.JE, **KIA** 9Aug.18-*I*
England,2Lt.NH, **WIA** 25May.17-*I*
England,FCdr.TH, DFC 2Dec.16-*VII*
English,Capt.AA, **WIA** 25Sep.17-*I*
English,Lt.MG, **WIA** 12Jun.18-*I*, **KIA** 16Jul.18-*I*
English,2Lt.W, **WIA POW** 24Sep.17-*I*
Enright,2Lt.TN, **INT** 2Oct.18-*III*
Epps,2Lt.AM, *Aust.* **WIA** 19Aug.17-*I*
Eppstein,FSLt.MWW, **KIA** 12May.17-*I*
Erlebach,2Lt.EE, **KIA** 7Feb.17-*I*
Errol Boyd,FSLt.JED, **INT** 3Oct.15-*I*
Erskine,Lt.E, **WIA** 23Jun.18-*I*
Erskine,Capt.R, **WIA** 14Jan.16-*I*, **DoW** 1Jan.18-*IV*
Erskine-Childers,Lt.R, 25Dec.14-*I*
Erwin,1Lt.WP, *US.* 1Aug.18-*IIB*
Essell,2Lt.RN, 13Aug.18-*I*
Estcourt,Lt.ACS, **KIA** 8Aug.18-*I*

Estlin,Lt.HAP, 17Jun.18-*I*
Etches,2Lt.AJE, **KIA** 11Apr.17-*I*
Eteson,2Lt.L, **WIA** 24Sep.18-*I*
Etheridge,2Lt.CJG, 16Aug.17-*I*
Evans,1AM., *8Sqn.* 30Mar.16-*I*
Evans,Lt.AJ, *3Sqn.* **INT** 22Jan.15-*I*
Evans,Capt.AJ, *3Sqn.* 14Jul.16-*I*, **POW** 16Jul.16-*I*
Evans,Capt.AJ, *142Sqn.* **POW** 19Mar.18-*VII*
Evans,AM.AM *100Sqn.* **KId** 22Jul.17-*I*
Evans,2Lt.AWR, **POW** 21Oct.18-*I*
Evans,Lt.B, **KIA** 8Apr.17-*I*
Evans,Sgt.C, **WIA** 31May.17-*I*
Evans,Sgt.CE, 11May.17-*I*
Evans,OSL.DC, 25Apr.16-*III*
Evans,2Lt.ELP, 19Sep.17-*I*
Evans,1Lt.FE, *US.* **WIA** 18Jul.18-*IIB*
Evans,Sgt.FH, **POW** 6Apr.17-*I*
Evans,2Lt.FW, **DoW** 23May.17-*I*
Evans,Lt.HB, **POW** 17Jun.18-*I*
Evans,2Lt.HC, DSO *Can.* 8Aug.16-*I*, **KIA** 3Sep.16-*I*
Evans,2Lt.HF, **POW** 9Nov.16-*I*
Evans,Lt.J, **DoW** 29Oct.18-*I*
Evans,2Lt.JE, 2Jul.16-*I*
Evans,Lt.LE, **WIA** 19May.18-*I*
Evans,2Lt.P, **WIA** 22Jul.18-*I*
Evans,Lt.RJ, **WIA** 31Aug.18-*I*
Evans,Sgt.RS, **KIA** 16Nov.16-*I*
Evans,Lt.SD, 28Sep.18-*I*
Evans,1Lt.TP, *US.* **POW** 26Sep.18-*IIB*
Evans,Lt.WD, **POW** 15Sep.18-*I*
Evans,Lt.WG, **KIA** 27Jun.18-*I*
Eveleigh,2Lt.EP, **WIA** 15Sep.18-*I*
Everard,Capt.AJ, **POW** .18-*VIII*
Everatt,Lt.E, 21Aug.18-*I*
Everingham,2Lt.G, **KIA** 8Apr.17-*I*
Everitt,Lt.JP, **WIA** 4May.18-*I*, 4Jun.18-*I*
Everix,Sgt.MH, **POW** 5Dec.17-*I*
Everleigh,Lt.EP, 10Aug.18-*I*
Everleigh,2Lt.FR, **POW** 1Oct.18-*I*
Evershed,Lt.LR, 10Aug.18-*I*
Ewart,2Lt.KP, **KIA** 4Jan.18-*I*
Exley,2Lt.GA, 21Apr.16-*I*
Eycott-Martin,Lt.HR, 22Jun.18-*IV*
Eyman,2Lt.CH, *US.* **KIA** 5Jun.18-*IID*
Eymann,2Lt.HH, *US.* **WIA** .18-*IID*
Eyre,Lt.AN, **KIA** 26Sep.18-*I*
Eyre,FCdr.CA, **KIA** 7Jul.17-*I*
Eyre,FSLt.EG, **KIA** 21Oct.17-*I*
Eyre,2Lt.HC, **KIA** 5Oct.18-*I*
Eyre,2Lt.HT, **WIA** 9Nov.18-*I*
Eyres,2Lt.LH, **WIA** 27Sep.18-*I*, **POW** 29Oct.18-*I*

F

Faber,2Lt.C, *9Sqn.* 5Feb.16-*I*, **WIA** 10Feb.16-*I*
Faber,Capt.C, *79Sqn.* **WIA** 22Apr.18-*I*
Facey,Lt.RV, 31May.18-*I*
Fagan,Capt.RT, 20Jun.18-*I*
Fair,2Lt.VAM, MC **KIA** 29Sep.18-*I*
Fairbairn,2Lt.,Lt.CO, *Aust.* 31Aug.15-*I*, **WIA** 19Dec.15-*I*
Fairbairn,2Lt.JV, **WIA POW** 14Feb.17-*I*
Fairburn,2Lt., *10Sqn.* 31Aug.15-*I*
Fairburn,2Lt.FA, 23Sep.18-*I*
Fairclough,Lt.AB, *Can.* 23Sep.18-*I*
Fairhurst,2Lt.A, **POW** 16Sep.18-*I*
Falkenberg,2Lt.GD, **POW** 12Mar.18-*I*
Falkenburg,Capt.CF, *Can.* 16Sep.18-*I*, 20Sep.18-*I*
Falkiner,2Lt.FB, MC **KIA** 21Aug.17-*I*
Fall,FSLt.,FCdr.JST, 11Apr.17-*I*, 3Sep.17-*I*
Fancis,2Lt.CE, **POW** 5Sep.18-*I*
Fane,FSLt.GWR,DSC 28Nov.16-*III*
Faraday,2Lt.MS, **WIA POW** 27Sep.16-*I*
Farmer,2Lt.B, **WIA** 19Mar.17-*I*, 14Jul.17-*I*
Farmer,Lt.ER, **POW** 30Jul.16-*I*
Farmer,2AM.F, **DoW** 17.9.1917 16Sep.17-*I*
Farmer,Lt.GJ, 30Mar.17-*I*, 23Apr.17-*I*, 28Sep.18-*I*
Farnes,Lt.HC, **KIA** 6Jul.17-*I*
Farnsworth,1Lt.TH, *US.* **KIA** 13Sep.18-*IIB*
Farquhar,1Lt.AD, *US.* **WIA** 17Aug.18-*IIB*

Farquhar,Lt.AWK, *Aust.* **KIA** 26Jun.18-*VII*
Farquhar,Lt.J, **POW DoW** 1.8.1918 31Jul.18-*I*
Farquhar,Lt.RW, **KIA** 30Oct.18-*I*
Farquharson,2Lt.FB, **POW** 20Oct.17-*I*
Farquharson,Lt.RJ, **POW** 14Oct.18-*I*
Farrall,2Lt.JGM, 18Jul.18-*III*
Farrand,2Lt.ES, **POW** 3Oct.18-*I*
Farrell,Lt.CMG, *Can.* 8Aug.18-*I*
Farrell,2Lt.JWD, 11Apr.18-*I*, 21Apr.18-*I*
Farrier,2Lt.AV, **WIA** 6Nov.17-*I*
Farrow,Lt., *12Sqn.* 20May.16-*I*
Farrow,2Lt.WH, **WIA** 5Apr.17-*VI*
Farrow,Capt.WH, 21Aug.18-*I*
Fasson,Capt., *35Sqn.* 23Mar.18-*I*
Fattorini,Lt.T, **KIA** 13Aug.18-*I*
Faulks,2Lt.H, **DoW** 8Aug.18-*I*
Faure,Lt., *2Sqn.* 5Feb.16-*I*
Faure,Capt.DM, 1Apr.18-*I*
Fauvel,2Lt.,Lt.LG, **inj** 26Jan.17-*I*, **WIA** 3May.17-*I*, 13May.17-*I*, **inj** 25May.17-*I*
Fawcett,Lt., *207Sqn.* 8Aug.18-*I*
Fawdry,Lt.H, **KIA** 11Aug.18-*I*
Fawkner,2Lt.LC, **KIA** 26Oct.16-*I*
Fear,2Lt.RS, **DoW** 5Mar.18-*I*
Featherstone,Lt.GA, **KIA** 1Oct.18-*I*
Featherstone-Briggs,SCdr.E, DSO **POW** 21Nov.14-*I*
Feez,Lt.CM, *Aust.* **POW** 28Mar.18-*I*
Fell,1AM.WH, *Aust.* **KIA** 4May.18-*VII*
Fellowes,Lt.HV, **POW** 1Sep.18-*I*
Fellowes,LtCol.PFM, **WIA POW** 28May.18-*I*
Fellows,Dvr.WA, MC **DoW** 29.7.1917 28Jul.17-*I*
Felton,2Lt.CT, **WIA POW** 17Jul.17-*I*
Felton,2Lt.HA, **KIA** 16Sep.18-*I*
Feltum?,2Lt.L, 19Jan.16-*I*
Fendall,2Lt.DJ, **DoW** 7Aug.17-*I*
Fenelon,2Lt.LM, 8Dec.17-*I*
Fenlow,2Lt.L, 26Mar.18-*I*
Fenn,Capt.RP, **KIA** 25Mar.18-*I*
Fenn,Lt.JFT, 27Oct.18-*I*
Fenn-Smith,2Lt.WK, **KIA** 18Jan.18-*I*
Fenton,2Lt.AH, **KIA** 4Mar.17-*I*
Fenton,2Lt.CB, **POW** 12Mar.18-*I*
Fenton,Lt.H, 27Mar.18-*I*
Fenton,Lt.JA, 4Jul.18-*I*, **KIA** 28Sep.18-*I*
Fenton,Lt.JB, **WIA** 26Oct.17-*I*
Fenwick,Lt., *6Sqn.* 2Sep.18-*I*
Fenwick,2Lt.TB, **POW** 26Sep.17-*I*
Fenwick,2Lt.WC, **KIA** 7Oct.16-*I*
Fenwick,Lt., *6Sqn.* 23Oct.18-*I*
Fereman,2Lt.AE, **POW** 30Apr.17-*I*
Ferguson,2Lt.CE, **KIA** 18Oct.17-*I*
Ferguson,Lt.FW, 30Aug.18-*I*, **KIA** 3Sep.18-*I*
Ferguson,2Lt.GW, **WIA** 6Jan.18-*I*
Ferguson,Capt.HC, *US.* **WIA** Jul.18-*IID*
Ferguson,Lt.JAA, **WIA POW** 12Mar.18-*I*
Ferguson,2Lt.JC, 8Aug.18-*I*, **WIA** 9Aug.18-*I*?
Ferguson,Lt.JF, **WIA DoW**? 26Feb.17-*I*
Ferguson,2Lt.JS, **KIA** 21Sep.18-*I*
Fernald,Lt.vD, **KIA** 23Jul.18-*IV*
Fernauld,2Lt.VD, 24Mar.17-*I*
Fernihough,2Lt., 14Dec.15-*I*
Ferrand,FSLt.JBP, 28Dec.15-*I*
Ferrand,Lt.JE, 26Oct.18-*I*
Ferrand,Maj.JPB, **POW** 27Sep.18-*VI*
Ferreira,2Lt.JP, 16Aug.18-*I*, **KIA** 16Sep.18-*I*
Ferrie,2Lt.,Lt.RLM, MC 23Nov.17-*I*, **KIA** 3Jan.18-*I*
Ferriman,2Lt.FS, **KIA** 7Jun.17-*I*
Fetch,2Lt.EHM, **WIA** 19Jan.18-*I*
Feurer,2Lt.SM, **KIA** 22Jul.18-*I*
Ffolliott,Lt.CRH, 4Feb.18-*I*, **KIA** 10Mar.18-*I*
Ffrench,2Lt.GE, 5May.18-*I*, **KIFA** 23May.18-*I*
Field,Capt.ACW, 3Jul.16-*I*, **WIA** 25Sep.16-*I*
Field,Capt.AW, **KIA** 9Jan.18-*I*
Field,Lt.CVG, **KIA** 12Jan.16-*I*
Field,2Lt.N, **KIA** 14Aug.17-*I*
Field,2Lt.WL, **WIA inj**? 9Oct.18-*I*
Fielding,Lt.WW, **WIA** 27Nov.17-*I*
Fielding-Clarke,2Lt.A, **POW** 9Feb.18-*I*
Fielding-Johnston,Lt.,Capt.WS, 26Oct.15-*I*, 17Feb.18-*I*
Fiennes,Capt.Hon.LJE, 24Jul.15-*I*, late Sep.15-*I*
Filley,2Lt.OD, 6Jul.15-*I*, 31Jul.15-*I*, **WIA** 15Nov.15-*I*
Finch,Lt.FE, **WIA POW** 15Sep.18-*I*
Finch,2Lt.JB, **WIA** 25Aug.17-*I*
Fincham,2Lt.GEH, 19Dec.15-*I*, 2Mar.16-*I*, **WIA** **KIA** 9Mar.16-*I*
Findlay,2Lt.AL, 10Sep.15-*I*, 23Sep.15-*I*, 21Oct.15-*I*, 26Oct.15-*I*
Findlay,Capt.C, 30Oct.18-*I*
Findlay,Capt.F, 5Feb.17-*I*
Findlay,Lt.,Capt.JP, *SA.* 2Jun.18-*I*, 4Oct.18-*I*, **WIA** 18Oct.18-*I*
Findlay,FSLt.MH, 6Apr.18-*I*
Findlay,Lt.WF, **WIA** 3Oct.17-*I*
Findley,Lt.TI, 21Mar.18-*I*
Findley,Lt.TI, **WIA** 2Apr.18-*I*
Finer,2Lt.HJ, **inj** 22Sep.16-*I*
Fineran,Cpl., *5Sqn.* 6Jun.15-*I*, 11Oct.15-*I*
Finlay,Lt.G, *Aust.* **WIA** 10Jan.18-*VII*, 20Jan.18-*VII*, 3May.18-*VII*, 27Jun.18-*VII*, 22Aug.18-*VII*
Finnemore,2Lt.HJ, **DoW** 27Mar.18-*I*
Finney,1AM.F, **POW** 25Apr.18-*I*
Finnie,Lt.A, *Aust.* **KIA** 22May.18-*I*
Finnigan,2Lt.J, **KIA** 18May.18-*I*
Firbank,2Lt.GJ, 1Jul.16-*I*, **KIA** 11Sep.16-*I*
Firmin,2Lt.CA, **WIA** 28Oct.18-*I*
Firstbrook,Lt.JH, *Can.* **WIA POW** 1Jul.16-*I*
Firth,Lt.JCB, 5Jun.17-*I*, 22Jul.17-*I*, 15Nov.17-*I*
Firth,Lt.JW, **KIA** 1Oct.18-*I*
Fish,1Lt.IW, *US.* **WIA** 30Sep.18-*IIB*
Fish,2Lt.P, 27Sep.18-*I*
Fish,2Lt.,Capt.WR, 10Aug.17-*I*, 16Oct.17-*I*, **WIA** 19Nov.17-*I*, **KIA** 27Mar.18-*I*
Fisher,2Lt.AJ, **KIA** 25Oct.16-*I*
Fisher,2Lt.B, **KIA** 21Jul.18-*I*
Fisher,2Lt.CC, **INT** 16Sep.18-*I*
Fiske,2Lt.H, **KIA** 20Dec.16-*I*
Fiton,2Lt.R, **WIA** 4May.18-*I*
Fitton,2Lt.JC, **KIA** 15May.18-*I*
Fitz-Morris,Capt.J, MC 7Jul.17-*I*, 24Mar.18-*I*
Fitzgerald,Cpl., *1Sqn.* 18Apr.15-*I*
Fitzgerald,2Lt.JJ, **POW** 5Oct.17-*I*
Fitzgerald,Lt.RJ, MC **KIA** 1Jul.18-*I*
Fitzgerald,2Lt.WW, **WIA** 16Nov.16-*I*, **KIA** 27Jul.17-*I*
Fitzgerald-Uniacke,2Lt.DP, **WIA POW** 21Sep.17-*I*
Fitzgibbon,2Lt.CJ, **WIA** 26Mar.18-*I*, **POW** 21Apr.18-*I*
Fitzherbert,Lt.JA, **WIA** 2May.18-*I*
Fitzherbert,Capt.WW, **KIA** 7Jul.17-*I*
Fitzmaurice,Lt.AH, **KIA** 12Mar.18-*I*
Fitzsimmons,2Lt.HH, **WIA** 30Jul.18-*I*
Flavelle,Lt.GA, *Can.* 8Aug.18-*I*
Fleming,Lt.A, **DoW** 29Apr.18-*I*
Fleming,Capt.AL, *Can.* 17Jan.18-*VII*, 23Jan.18-*VII*, 12Apr.18-*VIII*
Fleming,Capt.GRS, **POW DoW** 17.4.1917 14Apr.17-*I*
Fleming,2Lt.JAM, **POW** 25Oct.17-*I*
Fleming,2Lt.JW, **KIA** 12Jul.17-*I*
Fleming,2Lt.PJA, **POW** 16Sep.18-*I*
Fleming,Cpl.RD, **KIA** 26Jan.17-*I*
Fleming,Capt.WA, MC **KIA** 10Aug.17-*I*
Flere,2Lt.CH, **POW** 10Mar.18-*I*
Fletcher,2Lt.A, **POW** 28Sep.18-*I*
Fletcher,FSLt.AHV, **WIA POW** 29Apr.17-*I*
Fletcher,2Lt.BC, **Kld** 21Aug.18-*I*
Fletcher,2Lt.C, **DoW** 28Sep.18-*I*
Fletcher,Capt.E, **WIA** 26Feb.17-*I*
Fletcher, 2Lt. F, **WIA** 31Oct.18-*I*
Fletcher, 2Lt. GH, **KIA**? 2Jun.17-*I*
Fletcher, Lt. HB, *Aust.* 24Aug.18-*VII*
Fletcher, Bdr.E, **KIA** 13Jul.17-*I*,
Fletcher, Sgt. PM, **POW** 16Aug.18-*I*
Fletcher, 2Lt. RK, 3Feb.18-*I*
Fletcher, Sgt. RM, 23Jun.18-*I*
Fletcher, Lt. WF, 24Mar.17-*I*, **WIA** 22Apr.17-*I*
Flexman,2AM.WE, **DoW** 13Jun.18-*I*
Flight,2Lt.OT, *Aust.* **POW** 28Mar.18-*I*
Flintoft,Lt.HT, **POW** 10Aug.18-*I*
Flower,2Lt.FG, **KIA** 18Dec.17-*I*
Flowers,Lt.,Capt.HF, **WIA** 30May.18-*I*, **KIA** 14Oct.18-*I*
Floyd,2Lt.J, **DoW** 11.7.1916 9Jul.16-*I*
Floyer?,Lt.EA, **POW** 15Feb.17-*VII*
Fluke,Lt.WG, DSO **POW** 24Mar.18-*I*
Flynn,Capt.JHLW, *Can.* **KIA** 3Sep.18-*I*
Foden,2Lt.JC, *Aust.* **WIA** 27Jul.17-*I*
Fogarty,2Lt.GJ, 16Aug.17-*I*, **KIA** 25Aug.17-*I*
Foggin,2Lt.CE, **WIA** 27Apr.16-*I*
Foggo,2Lt.NOM, *Can.* **POW** 8Aug.18-*I*
Foley?, 1AM., **POW** 12Sep.14-*I*
Foley, Lt. RG, MC **KIA** 8Mar.18-*I*
Folger,2Lt.HT, *US.* **WIA** 31Oct.18-*IIB*
Follit,Lt.RW, **DoW** 28Apr.17-*I*
Fontaine,1Lt.HL, *US.* **WIA** 24Oct.18-*IIB*
Foord,Lt.EA, 17Mar.17-*I*, 19Aug.17-*I*, **KIA** 27Jun.18-*I*
Foot,Lt.,Capt.EL, MC 21Jul.15-*I*, 24Jul.15-*I*, 23Sep.15-*I*, 28Sep.16-*I*, 26Oct.16-*I*
Foot,Lt.WA, **WIA** 8Aug.18-*I*
Forbes, 2Lt.E, *US.* **KIA** 26Sep.18-*IIB*
Forbes, Capt.EW, 18Mar.16-*I*, **WIA** 16May.16-*I*
Forbes, 2Lt.GW, **POW** 18Oct.17-*I*
Ford,2Lt.CW, *US.* **POW** 15Oct.18-*IIB*
Ford,Capt.H, 30Oct.18-*I*
Forder,Lt.EG, **POW** 11May.18-*IV*
Foreman,2Lt.GW, 19May.17-*I*
Foreman,Capt.JW, **WIA** 28Oct.18-*I*
Forest,Lt.LH, **POW** 8Aug.18-*I*
Forgie,2Lt.JS, **WIA** 18Jun.18-*I*
Forman,FSLt.,Lt.,Capt.JH, *Can.* **WIA** 28Jul.17-*I*, 12Nov.17-*I*, 9May.18-*I*, **POW** 4Sep.18-*I*
Formilli,Lt.GC, **WIA POW** 5Jan.16-*I*
Forrest,Lt.H, 7May.17-*I*
Forrest,Lt.HG, *Aust.* 22Mar.18-*I*
Forrester,Lt.JB, 2Oct.18-*I*
Forsaith,Lt.HJ, **KIA** 18Aug.17-*I*
Forshaw,Lt., *3Sqn.* 23Nov.16-*I*
Forshay,2Lt.HJ, *US.* 26Sep.18-*IIB*
Forster,2Lt.F, **WIA** 5Sep.17-*I*
Forster,1Lt.LH, *USAS.* **KIA** 2Sep.18-*I*
Forsyth,Lt.AF, **WIA POW** 3Aug.18-*I*
Forsyth,2Lt.RA, **KIA** 28Nov.17-*I*
Forsyth,Capt.WA, **WIA** 6Apr.18-*I*, **POW DoW** 27Jun.18-*I*
Fosse,2Lt.EL, **POW** 17Oct.17-*I*
Foster,FSLt.B, **POW** 24Sep.17-*I*
Foster,Lt.C, **KIA** 27Sep.18-*I*
Foster,2Lt.F, 31Aug.17-*I*
Foster,2Lt.FH, *4Sqn.* **WIA** 15Jul.18-*I*
Foster,2Lt.FH, *45Sqn.* **KIA** 3Jun.17-*I*
Foster,2Lt.FJ, 17Jun.17-*I*, **inj** 10Jul.17-*I*
Foster,1Lt.FV, *US.* **POW** 4Sep.18-*IIB*
Foster,Lt.GB, *Can.* 12Apr.18-*I*
Foster,Lt.PLaT, **POW** 9Mar.18-*I*
Foster,2Lt.,Capt.RM, DFC 6Apr.17-*I*, 4Nov.18-*I*
Foster,Lt.V, 9Nov.18-*I*
Foster,Capt.WE, **POW** .18-*I*
Foster,AM.,Cpl.WH, 3May.18-*I*, **WIA** 18May.18-*I*
Foster-Sutton,Lt.SWP, **POW** 8Aug.18-*I*
Foster?,FSLt.E, **POW** 2Sep.17-*V*
Fothergill,Lt.WT, **KIA** 20Aug.18-*I*
Fotheringham,Lt.JB, **KIA** 7Jul.17-*I*
Foulsham,Sgt.HS, **WIA**? **POW** 3Sep.17-*I*
Fountain,2Lt.CC, **KIA** 14Oct.18-*I*
Fowler,2Lt.ACG, **KIA** 21Sep.18-*I*
Fowler,2Lt.CJ, 16Oct.17-*I*
Fowler,2Lt.DD, **WIA** 5Oct.16-*VI*, **KIA** 17Mar.17-*III*
Fowler,Lt.F, **WIA** 16Jul.18-*I*
Fowler,Capt.H, 2Apr.17-*I*
Fowler,FSLt.HHS, *Can.* 5Feb.18-*I*
Fowler,2Lt.JO, **KIA** 19Aug.17-*I*
Fowler?,2Lt.SC, 24Jun.17-*VI*
Fox,Capt.AG, **KIA** 9May.15-*I*
Fox,2Lt.CF, 2Apr.17-*I*
Fox,2Lt.DS, **POW** 9Oct.18-*I*
Fox,Lt.,2Lt.HJ, 11Aug.18-*I*, **WIA** 29Aug.18-*I*
Fox,2Lt.JR, **DoW** as **POW** 16Aug.18-*I*
Fox,1Lt.RF, *US.* **KIA** 1Oct.18-*IIB*
Fox,FSLt.WN, **WIA** 20Oct.17-*I*
Fox,2Lt.WRS, **DoW** 22Aug.18-*I*
Fox-Russell,Capt.HT, 23Nov.17-*I*
Foy,Lt.AW, 22Mar.18-*I*
Foy,1Lt.JM, *US.* **POW** 30Oct.18-*IIB*
Foy,2Lt.TAW, 26Feb.18-*I*
Frame,Lt.GS, **POW** .17-*IX*
Francis,Lt.AH, **WIA** 21May.16-*I*
Francis,2Lt.D, **WIA** 28Nov.17-*I*
Francis,2Lt.JW, 16Nov.16-*I*
Francis,2Lt.WG, **KIA** 10Mar.18-*IV*
Frank,2Lt.,Lt.CL, 31May.18-*I*, **WIA**? 28Sep.18-*I*
Frank,2Lt.HR, **KIA** 4Jul.18-*I*
Frank,1Lt.WF, *US.* **WIA** 23Oct.18-*IIB*, **KIA** 5Nov.18-*IIB*
Franklin,Lt.BL, **KIA** 4May.17-*I*
Franklin,Lt.LN, **KIA** 14Jul.18-*I*
Franklin,2Lt.RV, **WIA** 10Oct.16-*I*, **WIA** 1Nov.16-*I*, 4Dec.16-*I*
Franklin,Lt.W, **WIA** 22Apr.17-*I*
Franks,AG.1AM.H, **WIA** 9Nov.17-*I*
Franks,2Lt.ST, 23Aug.18-*I*, 30Aug.18-*I*
Frantz,Sgt., *French.* 5Oct.14-*I*
Fraser,2Lt.A, **WIA POW** 3May.17-*I*
Fraser,2Lt.AW, **WIA** 16Mar.18-*I*
Fraser,Lt.CC, 2Sep.18-*I*
Fraser,2Lt.MP, 23Sep.18-*I*
Fraser,Lt.SMcK, **WIA** 6Mar.17-*I*
Fraser,2Lt.W, **KIA** 25Oct.16-*I*
Fraser,2AM.WA, **WIA** 27Sep.17-*I*
Frayne,Lt.OW, **inj** 11May.18-*IV*
Frazer,Sgt.A, 11Sep.17-*I*
Frazier,2Lt.RW, *RNVR* **POW** 29Nov.16-*VI*
Frean,Lt.RW, 30Jul.18-*I*
Freehill,2Lt.MM, 13Mar.18-*I*, 23Mar.18-*I*
Freeman,Capt., *5Sqn.* 10Oct.15-*I*
Freeman,FSLt.CT, 2Aug.16-*VIII*
Freeman,1Lt.HB, *US.* **POW** 14Sep.18-*IIB*
Freeman,2Lt.J, **INT** 9Nov.18-*VIII*
Freeman,Capt.,Maj.RH, 2Nov.16-*VII*, 17Dec.16-*VII*, **KIA** 21Jul.18-*I*
Freeman,Lt.WR, 12Sep.14-*I*, 3Nov.14-*I*
Freemantle,2Lt.RPC, **KIA** 30Apr.17-*I*
Frecr,2Lt.AP, 6Mar.18-*I*, 24Mar.18-*I*
Freer,2Lt.W, **KIA** 6Oct.18-*I*
Freer,Lt.WSB, 16Jun.18-*I*
Freland,Capt.HM, 20Jul.18-*I*
French,Lt.CE, **POW** 20May.17-*I*
French,Lt.GS, **WIA POW** 1May.17-*I*
French,Lt.H, 10Oct.15-*I*
Frew,2Lt.JGE?, **WIA POW** 16Apr.17-*I*
Frew,2Lt.,Capt.MB, 5Jun.17-*I*, 28Jul.17-*I*, 11Jan.18-*IV*
Fricker,Lt.AJ, **POW** 4Jul.18-*I*
Friend,1AM.H, 3Apr.17-*I*, **KIA** 21Sep.17-*I*
Frierson,2Lt.SG, *US.* **WIA POW** 4Oct.18-*IIB*
Frith,2Lt.RG, **WIA POW** 5Nov.17-*I*
Frobisher,2Lt.JE, *USAS.* **POW DoW** 10.9.1918 2Sep.18-*I*
Frome,Lt.NF, **WIA** 12Aug.18-*I*
Frost,Capt.GW, **inj** 12Aug.17-*I*
Frost,Lt.HA, **WIA POW** 1Apr.16-*I*
Frost,1Lt.HB, *USAS.* **WIA POW** 26Aug.18-*I*
Frost,2Lt.JW, **INT** 29Sep.17-*I*
Frow,Sgt.HG, **KIA** 23Jul.18-*IV*
Fry,Lt., *35Sqn.* 6Mar.18-*I*
Fry,2Lt.JLS, 27Mar.18-*I*
Fry,Capt.WM, 11May.18-*I*
Fryer,Capt.FE, **INT** 8Mar.15-*I*
Fudge,Lt.A, **DoW** 22.2.1918 21Feb.18-*I*
Fulford,Lt.E, **POW** 26Sep.18-*I*
Fullagar,2Lt.RG, **WIA** 8Oct.18-*IV*
Fullard,Lt.,Capt.PF, 26May.17-*I*, 13Jul.17-*I*, 22Aug.17-*I*, 15Nov.17-*I*
Fuller,2Lt.AH, 16Sep.18-*I*, **WIA**? **inj**? 23Oct.18-*I*
Fuller,Sgt.GE, **KIA** 7Oct.18-*I*
Fuller,2Lt.HJ, 4Oct.18-*I*
Fuller,2Lt.LA, **KIA** 17May.17-*I*
Fuller,1Lt.RH, *US.* **KIA** 29Sep.18-*IIB*
Fuller,1Lt.TJD, *US.* **INT** 12Sep.18-*IIB*
Fullerton,Lt., *Aust.* *3AFC.* 29Sep.18-*I*
Fullerton,2Lt.WFH, *Can.* **KIA** 22Oct.16-*I*
Fulton,Capt.EJ, *Irl.* **POW** 23Nov.15-*VIII*
Fulton,2Lt.EP, *Aust.* **POW** 10Aug.17-*I*
Fulton,2Lt.J, **WIA POW** 27Jun.18-*I*
Fulton,2Lt.RW?, *US.*, *initials* RB? **POW** 5Nov.18-*IIB*
Furby,GL.RA, **KIA** 19Dec.17-*I*
Furlonger,2Lt.CAM, **POW** 9May.17-*I*

Furniss,2Lt.KR, POW DoW 22Apr.17-I
Furse,Maj.EW, WIA 30Sep.15-I
Fyfe,2Lt.RJ, KIA 18Jun.18-I
Fyffe,AM.A, KIA 11Apr.17-I
Fyson,Lt.RC, 4Nov.18-I

G

Gabel,1Lt.TA, US. KIA 29Sep.18-IIB
Gabell,2Lt.DRC, inj 1Mar.17-I
Gadd,2Lt.WG, 29Sep.18-I, POW 1Nov.18-I
Gadpaille,2Lt.LGS, KIA 18May.18-I
Gage,2Lt.CR, POW 12Sep.18-I
Gagne,2Lt.J, KIA 24May.17-I
Gagnier,FSLt.OJ, inj 11May.17-I
Gaisford,Lt.RS, KIA 29Jan.18-IV
Gaither,1Lt.WB, US. DoW 12Oct.18-IIB
Galbraith,Capt.CF, DoW 15Sep.18-I
Galbraith,FSLt.DHMB, Can. 15Jul.16-I, 28Sep.16-I, 22Oct.16-I
Galbraith,2Lt.JG, WIA 28Jul.18-I
Gale,Capt.AWG, DSO KIA 9Apr.16-I
Gale,Capt.D, 20May.18-I, WIA 31Jul.18-I
Gale,2Lt.JH, KIA 14Sep.16-I
Galer,2Lt.HE, POW 29Dec.17-I
Gallagher,Lt.EG, INT 16Sep.18-I
Gallagher,2Lt.WF, US. KIA 13Sep.18-IIB
Galley,2Lt.E, 6Feb.17-I
Galley,2Lt.,Lt.EDG, WIA 24Mar.17-I, 23Mar.18-I, 24Mar.18-I
Gallie,2Lt.AV, 7Apr.18-I, 6Jun.18-I
Gallie,2Lt.GC?, initials JC? KIA 22Aug.15-I
Galpin,Maj.CJ, 6Jun.18-VIII
Galvayne,Lt.VFA, KIFA 2Oct.18-VIII
Gammell,Lt.BE, 16Jul.18-I, KIA 4Sep.18-I
Gamnell?, see Gammell
Gamon,Capt.J, 23Apr.18-I, WIA 17Jun.18-I
Gannaway,2Lt.,Lt.CH, 22Apr.18-I, KIA 16Jun.18-I
Ganter,Lt.FS, KIA 27Jun.18-I
Garden,2Lt.CE, KIA 2Sep.18-I
Gardenner,2Lt.JV, 3Oct.18-I, DoW 8Oct.18-I
Gardiner,Capt.CV, DoW 30.9.1918 27Sep.18-I
Gardiner,2Lt.D, 10Mar.18-I
Gardiner,2Lt.EH, US. KIA 12Sep.18-IIB
Gardiner,2Lt.GC, WIA 5Oct.17-VI, 6Jun.18-VI, 3Sep.18-VI
Gardiner,2Lt.PJ, WIA 16Jun.17-I
Gardiner,2Lt.SJ, 21Oct.17-I
Gardner,2Lt.AW, 20May.17-I
Gardner,Capt.CH, WIA 14Aug.17-I, WIA 20Sep.17-I
Gardner,Lt.CV, 6Jun.18-I
Gardner,Lt.D, MC WIA 17Apr.18-I
Gardowner,Sgt.HJ, 25Jan.16-I
Gargett,Lt.HS, WIA 9Nov.18-I
Garlake,2Lt.JC, 2Sep.18-I
Garland,2Lt.EH, POW 22Aug.17-I
Garland,2Lt.EJ, 31Jul.16-I
Garlick,2Lt.FAA, KIA 20Feb.16-I
Garlick,Pbr.T, KIA 28Jun.18-I
Garne,2Lt.SHJ, WIA 23Aug.18-I
Garner,PO.EJ, 26Sep.17-I
Garner,2Lt.GC, 9Nov.18-I
Garnett,Lt.JN, POW 15Jul.18-VIII
Garnett,FLt.WHS, inj 5Mar.15-V
Garnett,Lt.WP, KIA 30Mar.17-I
Garnsey,1Lt.EG, US. KIA 29Oct.18-IIB
Garratt,2Lt.RH, KIA 20Sep.17-I
Garrett?,Lt., 207Sqn. 8Aug.18-I
Garrett,Lt.AL, WIA POW 28Jun.18-I
Garrett,2Lt.BN, POW 14Jul.18-I
Garrett,1Lt.CS, US. KIA 10Oct.18-IIB
Garrett,2Lt.HT, KIA 20May.17-I
Garrett,2Lt.JC, WIA POW 14Oct.17-I
Garrison,2Lt.AE, MC WIA 3Oct.18-I
Garrity,Lt.WJ, Can. POW 31Jul.18-I
Garros,Lt.R, French. 1Apr.15-I, POW 18Apr.15-I
Garside,1AM.J, Died 15Jun.16-VII
Garside,2Lt.AJ, WIA 29Aug.18-I
Gartside-Tippinge,2Lt.F, KIA 6Nov.17-I
Garvie,1Lt.HA, US. KIA? 26Sep.18-IIB

Gaskain,2Lt.CS, KIA 7May.17-I
Gaskell,TFSLt.HL, KIA 2May.17-VI
Gaskell,2Lt.LN, DoW 1.3.1918 27Feb.18-I
Gaskell-Blackburn,FSLt.V, 25Dec.14-I
Gass,2Lt.CG, 7May.18-I, 9May.18-I
Gasson,2Lt.CB, WIA POW 26Apr.16-VIII
Gasson,Lt.FAB, KIA 26Sep.18-I
Gatecliff,2Lt.JN, KIA 29Jun.18-I
Gates,Lt.AJ, WIA 14Aug.18-IV
Gates,Capt.GB, DFC WIA 27Sep.18-I
Gates,2Lt.HJ, KIA 19Nov.17-VI
Gates,2Lt.HR, 19Dec.17-I
Gates,FSLt.RT, 5Sep.14-VIII
Gatton,1Lt.CJ, US. KIA 4Nov.18-IIB
Gaukroger,Lt.JK, KIA 8Aug.18-I
Gaulter,Lt.CV, KIA 7May.17-I
Gaunt,Lt.W, WIA 2Jul.17-I
Gauntlett,Lt.FE, WIA 3May.18-I
Gavaghan,2Lt.A, KIA 13Mar.18-I
Gay,Lt.BC, WIA 19Sep.17-I
Gay,2Lt.FH, 4Dec.16-I, DoW 24Mar.17-I
Gay,2Lt.J, 7Sep.15-I, 11Sep.15-I, 27Sep.15-I, DoW 10Oct.15-I
Gaye,Capt.AD, WIA 15May.15-I, INT 2Jun.15-I
Gayford,2Lt.DB, POW 9Mar.16-I
Gayner,2Lt.WJ, KIA 9May.17-I
Gaynor,2Lt.JJ, WIA 7Jun.17-I
Gaze,Lt.IO, 29Oct.18-I, POW 4Nov.18-I
Geary,2Lt.BC, KIA 11Aug.18-I
Geddes,Lt.JR, WIA 4May.17-I
Gedge,2Lt.G, POW 28Sep.18-I
Gedge,2Lt.LSV, 17Aug.17-I
Gee,2Lt.GRD, KIA 4Jun.17-I
Geen,2Lt.C, POW 13Aug.16-I
Gemmel,2Lt.Lt.HJ, 4Oct.18-I, POW 31Oct.18-I
Genet,Sgt.EEC, initials ECC WIA 19Mar.17-IIA, KIA 16Apr.17-IIA
George,Lt.FA, WIA 27Nov.16-I
George,Lt.HDK, POW DoW 6.4.1917 5Apr.17-I
George,2Lt.OC, WIA 27Oct.17-I
George,Lt.SS, 18Jul.18-I
Gerhardt,2Lt.H, KIA 18Sep.18-VI
Gerrard,FCdr.TFN, 4Jun.17-I
Gerson,2Lt.LM, POW 11Apr.18-I
Gethin,2Lt.,Capt.PEL, 2Dec.15-I, 7Dec.15-I, 1Apr.16-I, 24Apr.16-I
Gibbes,2Lt.FW, 19Aug.17-I, KIA 13Oct.17-I
Gibbon,2Lt.JT, KIA 6Feb.17-I
Gibbons,Lt.FG, 27Aug.18-I
Gibbons,Lt.,Capt.GE, 11Apr.17-I, 4Sep.18-I
Gibbons,2Lt.JE, KIA 9Oct.18-I
Gibbons,2Lt.SA, WIA 1Sep.16-I, WIA 7Oct.16-I
Gibbs,Lt.BE, 28Jan.18-VI
Gibbs,2Lt.FJ, 2Jun.17-I
Gibbs,Capt.HM, WIA 25Apr.18-I
Gibbs,2Lt.JF, US. INT 27Oct.18-IIB
Gibson,Lt.CJR, WIA 27May.18-I
Gibson,Lt.CM, 22Jun.16-I
Gibson,2Lt.EB, US. DoW 3Nov.18-IIB
Gibson,2Lt.EV, WIA 9Aug.17-I
Gibson,2Lt.HJ, 29Jun.17-VI
Gibson,Lt.JG, DoW 11.8.1917 10Aug.17-I
Gibson,2Lt.JW, WIA 30Jun.18-I
Gibson,Sgt.Mech.W, WIA 5Nov.18-I
Gibson,2Lt.WH, WIA 10May.18-I
Giesecke,Lt.MC, USAS. 23Sep.18-I
Gifford,2Lt.CC, US. WIA 29Sep.18-IIB
Gilbert,Sgt., French. 10Jan.15-I
Gilbert,2Lt.AH, KIA 21Sep.17-I
Gilbert,2Lt.CG, POW 25Mar.17-I
Gilbert,2Lt.,Lt.EM, 19Sep.15-I, 2Oct.15-I, 7Oct.15-I, 11Nov.15-I
Gilbert,2Lt.FC, POW 16Feb.18-I
Gilbert,Lt.JD, KIA 18Oct.17-I
Gilbert,2Lt.RS, POW 11Oct.17-I
Gilbert,Lt.SC, KIA 26Sep.18-I
Gilbert,Lt.W, 1Oct.18-I
Gilbertson,Lt.DHS, KIA 4Sep.18-I
Gilchrist,2Lt.A, 9Aug.18-I, KIA 3Oct.18-I
Gilchrist,2AM.E, KIA 6Jul.17-I
Gilchrist,2Lt.W, WIA POW 25May.17-I
Gile,1Lt.HH, USAS. POW 13Jun.18-I

Giles,Cpl.A, Can. KIA 3Jun.17-I
Giles,1Lt.BF, US. 3Nov.18-IIB
Giles,2Lt.WB, 1Jun.17-I
Gilham,2Lt., 111Sqn. WIA 29Nov.17-VII
Gilham,2Lt.G, WIA 10Mar.18-I
Gill,Lt.CEG, 16Jun.18-IV, POW 23Aug.18-IV
Gill,1Lt.CS, US. WIA 10Aug.18-IIB
Gill,2Lt.H, 26Sep.18-I
Gill,Lt.HG, KIA 12Mar.18-I
Gillan,Lt.CJ, POW 25Apr.18-I
Gillan,Lt.W, 9May.18-I
Gillespie,2Lt.DV, KIA 6Apr.18-I
Gillespie,2Lt.GW, KIA 13Apr.17-I
Gillespie,2Lt.JW, POW 19Aug.17-I
Gillespie,Lt.WJ, Can. 7Jul.18-I
Gillet,Lt.FW, US. name Gillett? 3Aug.18-I, 15Sep.18-I
Gillett,2Lt.WHC, WIA POW 26Sep.18-I
Gillie,Lt.GD, 5Aug.17-I
Gillings,2Lt.GA, WIA 30Sep.17-I
Gillis,Capt.GH, WIA? 23Oct.18-I, 30Oct.18-I
Gillman,2Lt.BT, 8Aug.18-I, KIA 24Sep.18-I
Gillmar,2Lt.SE, 29Aug.18-I
Gilman,2Lt.WJ, KIA 13Jul.18-I
Gilmour,Lt.AC, KIA 6Mar.18-I
Gilmour,Lt.J, 6Mar.17-I
Gilmour,2Lt.,Capt.JI, 18Dec.17-I, 4Jan.18-I
Gilmour,Lt.LC, POW 31Jul.18-I
Gilmour,Capt.SG, WIA 1Jul.16-I, WIA 12Aug.16-I, POW 22Aug.18-I
Gilray,T2Lt.SA, 2Oct.17-I
Gilroy,Capt.WH, 8Aug.17-I
Gilson,2Lt.AJ, KIA 17Mar.17-I
Gimingham,Capt.CH, KIA 11Nov.17-VI
Giroux,1Lt.EA, US. KIA 22May.18-IIB
Girvan,2Lt.CCG, WIA 7Jun.17-I
Gittons,2Lt.H, 29Apr.18-I
Gladman,2Lt.CW, WIA 14Aug.18-I
Gladstone,2Lt.CA, POW 30Apr.15-I
Gladwin,GL.GS, POW 22Apr.18-I
Glanville?,Lt.HF, 27Nov.14-I, WIA 9May.15-I
Glasse,2Lt.ES, KIA 19Aug.18-I
Glasson,2Lt.DE, DoW 12Mar.17-VI
Glasson,2Lt.,Lt,Capt.GWT, 25Apr.18-I, WIA 7May.18-I, WIA 29Oct.18-I
Glasspoole,2Lt.GH, POW 16Jun.18-I
Glazebrook,2Lt.RF, POW 22Aug.18-I
Glazier,2Lt.GJ, WIA 15Apr.18-I
Gleave,2Lt.JC, 28Jun.18-I, WIA 22Jul.18-I
Gledhill,Lt.AD, 11Jun.18-VII, WIA 17Jul.18-VII
Gleed,Lt.JVA, KIA 7Jul.17-I
Glen,Lt., 8Sqn. 23Oct.18-I
Glen,2Lt.DA, 22Sep.15-I, 25Sep.15-I, 22Oct.15-I, KIA 29Dec.15-I
Glen,Lt.J, KIA 16Sep.18-I
Glenday,Capt.FG, 28Aug.16-I, KIA 15Sep.16-I
Glendinning,2Lt.JG, POW DoW 16.12.1917 2Dec.17-I
Glenn,1Lt.GP, USAS. KIA 20Jul.18-I
Glenn,2Lt.WW, WIA 8Apr.17-I
Glenny,2Lt., 5Sqn. 19Dec.15-I
Glenny,Capt.AWF, MC 11Apr.18-I
Glentworth,Capt.EWCGdeVP, KIA 18May.18-I
Glew,2Lt.W, DoW 7.11.1918 6Nov.18-I
Glidewell,2Lt.CN, WIA 7Oct.18-I
Gloster,2Lt.FB, KIA 3Dec.17-I
Glover,Lt., 8Sqn. 2Sep.18-I
Glover,Lt.AMT, KIA 17Aug.17-I
Glover,2Lt.BE, KIA 13Mar.16-I
Glover,2Lt.CL, KIA 15May.18-I
Glover,Sgt.JE, KIA 17Sep.16-I
Glynn,Capt.CB, 12Oct.18-I
Goad,1Lt.JM, USAS. KIA 27Jun.18-I
Goble,SCdr.SJ, Aust. DSO DSC 16Mar.18-I
Goby,Lt.A, 4Aug.18-I
Godard,Lt.JS, 4Jul.17-I, POW 24Oct.17-I
Godet,2Lt.LdeG, KIA 1Jun.18-I
Godfrey,Lt.AE, Can. 28May.17-I
Godfrey,Capt.F, 17Apr.18-I
Godfrey,2Lt.OC, KIA 23Sep.16-I
Godlee,2Lt.J, Aust. DoW 19Jul.16-I
Godson,Lt., 12Sqn. 25Aug.18-I
Godwin,2Lt.CC, 27Nov.15-I, 17Jan.16-I, KIA 17Oct.16-I
Godwin,Lt.TE, KIA? 21Aug.17-I
Goettler,2Lt.HE, US. CMH KIA 6Oct.18-IIB
Goffe,2AM.C, WIA 8Apr.17-I
Goffe,AG.Cpl.CR, WIA 16Aug.17-I
Goffe,Lt.W, POW 8Aug.18-I
Gogarty,2Lt.HJ, WIA 28Apr.17-I
Gold,2Lt.DG, POW 6Apr.18-I
Goldie,2Lt.AH, 10Sep.15-I
Goldie,2Lt.GN, WIA 28Jul.17-I
Goldie,Lt.GN, POW 12Jan.18-IV
Golding,Lt.E, KIA 19Sep.17-I
Golding,Lt.HM, WIA 29Jan.17-I, 6Jun.18-I
Golding,2Lt.KL, POW 24Oct.17-I
Golding,2Lt.WA, WIA 4Mar.17-I
Goldthorpe,2Lt.WO, 26Aug.18-I
Goller,Lt.JM, KIA 16Jun.18-I
Gompertz,2Lt.AVH, 28Mar.17-I
Gompertz,2Lt.HTC, WIA 30Aug.18-I, POW 10Nov.18-I
Gondre,2Lt.J, POW 21Jul.18-I
Gonne,Capt.ME, POW DoW 8Aug.18-I
Gonzalez,2Lt.WF, WIA 21Apr.18-I
Gooch,FSLt.HC, INT 24Oct.17-VIII
Good,Lt.HB, 11Aug.18-I, KIA 5Sep.18-I
Good,2Lt.JF, WIA 11Apr.18-I
Goodale,Lt.WH, KIA 1Aug.18-I
Goodall,Lt.JHH, POW 24May.17-I
Goodban,2Lt.MS, KIA 19May.17-I
Goodbehere,2Lt.P, POW 22Oct.17-I
Goodchap,2Lt.AF, POW 3Dec.17-I
Goodchild,FSgt.D, POW 12Sep.14-I
Goode,Lt.GM, KIA 24May.17-I
Goode,Lt.HK, 30Sep.18-IV, 22Oct.18-IV, 27Oct.18-IV
Goode,2Lt.,Lt.HM, 17Jun.15-I, WIA POW 14Jul.15-I
Goode,Lt.RJEP, POW 27Oct.17-I
Goodeve,Lt.SM, Can. KIA 20Nov.17-I
Goodfellow,2Lt.A, 30Mar.16-I
Goodfellow,1Lt.JJ, US. KIA 14Sep.18-IIB
Goodfellow,2Lt.SJ, POW 29Oct.18-I
Goodhugh,Lt.PH, POW DoW 30Aug.18-I
Goodison,2Lt.FB, POW DoW 26.5.1917 8Apr.17-I
Goodison,2Lt.HAF, 30Mar.18-I
Goodman,Lt.FW, WIA 23Sep.18-I
Goodman,Sgt.G, WIA 16Mar.17-I
Goodman,Lt.GA, KIA 28Oct.18-IV
Goodman,Sgt.J, inj 6Sep.18-I
Goodman,2Lt.JE, KIA 14Aug.17-I
Goodrich,2Lt.FE, 19Jan.16-I, 21Feb.16-I
Goodson,2Lt.AR, 14Dec.15-I
Goodson,2Lt.C, POW 3Jun.16-I
Goodson,Lt.EJ, Aust. POW 4Nov.18-I
Goodwill,Lt.EA, WIA 30Oct.18-I
Goodwin,2Lt.AS, 24Jun.17-I
Goodwin,2Lt.H, 11Aug.18-I
Goodwin,2Lt.LF, 21Mar.18-I
Goodwin,Lt.NW, KIA 16Sep.17-I
Goody,1AM.AW, 14Jun.17-VIII
Goodyear,2Lt.CRF, KIA 25Jun.18-I
Goodyear,Lt.DM, KIA 29Jun.17-I
Goodyear,2Lt.JG, 28Jan.18-VIII
Goolden,Lt.GE, WIA 9Nov.16-I
Gopsill,2Lt.KL, 1Jul.16-I, inj 25Jun.16-I, 24Sep.16-I
Gordon,2Lt.AW, inj DoW 12.8.1917 30Jul.17-I
Gordon,2Lt.CA, POW 9Jun.18-IV
Gordon,Lt.D, KIA 14Aug.17-I
Gordon,2Lt.DS, KIA 21Feb.18-I
Gordon,2Lt.EC, WIA 16Aug.18-I
Gordon,Lt.EGS, POW 6Nov.17-I
Gordon,2Lt.GS, KIA 19Aug.17-I
Gordon,Lt.HA, KIA 7Jul.18-I
Gordon,Lt.JA, KIA 12Aug.18-I
Gordon,Lt.JR, 22May.18-I
Gordon,Lt.LV, WIA 11Jun.18-I
Gordon,Lt.RMcI, WIA 28Sep.18-I, WIA 27Oct.18-I
Gordon-Bell,Capt.C, 19Sep.15-I, 13Oct.15-I, 7Nov.15-I, 15Nov.15-I, 28Nov.15-I, 30Nov.15-I, 28Dec.15-I, 17Jan.16-I, 19Jan.16-I, 25Jan.16-I
Gordon-Bennett,Lt.R, WIA 25Sep.18-I
Gordon-Burge,Lt.C, 12Oct.15-I

Gordon-Kidd,Capt.AL, DSO DoW 27.8.1917 23Aug.17-I
Gordon-Scaife,2Lt.TE, 5Feb.16-I, 10Feb.16-I, 1Jul.16-I, 7Jul.16-I, 16Jul.16-I, 20Jul.16-I, 23Jul.16-I, 9Sep.16-I, KIA 26Sep.16-I
Gordon-Smith,Lt.N, KIA 19Dec.15-I
Gore,Lt.FDC, POW 2Feb.18-IV
Gorman,Lt.GW, Can. 30Jul.18-I, POW 8Aug.18-I
Gormley,2Lt.AJC, POW 30Aug.18-I
Gornall,2Lt.G, KIA 27Mar.18-I
Gorringe,2Lt.FC, 15Nov.17-I, 18Dec.17-I
Gosden,2Lt.LE, 1Oct.18-I
Gosney,2AM.HV, KIA 24Mar.17-I
Goss,Cpl.LS, POW DoW 19Sep.17-I
Gossett,Lt.WE, 12Jun.17-I
Gostling,Sgt.H, KIA 13Mar.18-I
Gotch,Lt.GW, 9Apr.18-I
Gotch,2Lt.JH, 5Jun.17-I
Goudie,Lt.MH, WIA 27Aug.18-I
Goudie,2Lt.PL, WIA 11Apr.17-I
Gough,2Lt.HS, WIA 17Aug.17-I
Gould,Lt., 3Sqn. 28Dec.15-I
Gould,Capt.HR, MC KIA 14Aug.18-I
Gould,Capt.JR, WIA 26Dec.16-I
Gould,Lt.LN, 28Nov.15-I, 8Mar.16-I, KIA 15Oct.17-I
Gould,Lt.LTN, WIA 28Jul.16-I
Gould,Capt.,Lt?RG, 10Sqn. 13Oct.15-I, 28Nov.15-I, 30Nov.15-I, 2Dec.15-I, 13Dec.15-I, 26Apr.16-I, 1Jun.16-I
Gould,Lt.RG, 2Sqn. WIA 8Jul.16-I
Gould,Lt.WHR, KIA 26Sep.17-I
Gould-Taylor,Lt.J, Aust. 30Aug.18-I, KIA 3Oct.18-I
Goulder,Pbr.EL, 11Jun.18-I
Goulding,Lt.AG, Can. 24Mar.18-VI, 25Apr.18-VI
Gove,2Lt.FDC, 12Oct.17-I
Gow,Lt.JE, POW DoW 10.8.1918 31Jul.18-I
Gower,Lt.WE, MC inj 7Jan.17-I
Gowing,Lt.CG, 3Sep.18-I
Gowing,Lt.EE, WIA 4May.18-I
Gowsell,2Lt.L, KIA 20Apr.18-I
Grace,FSLt.EJV, KIA? 19Sep.17-I
Gracie,1Lt.RD, USAS. KIA 12Aug.18-I
Graham,FSLt.CW, 14Dec.15-I
Graham,Lt.G, WIA 15May.15-I
Graham,Lt.GL, 21Mar.18-I, 22Jul.18-I
Graham,Lt.GW, 64Sqn. KIA 1Nov.18-I
Graham,Lt.GW, 204Sqn. KIA 13Jul.18-I
Graham,2Lt.J, WIA 8Oct.18-I
Graham,2Lt.JB, 22Oct.16-I
Graham,2Lt.LN, WIA POW 30Jul.16-I
Graham,1Lt.M, US. 6Oct.18-IIB
Graham,FCdr.,Maj.R, 25Sep.17-I, 14Oct.18-I
Graham,Lt.RL, KIA 16Sep.17-I
Graham,2Lt.SW, WIA 9Jun.18-I
Graham,2Lt.WG, 1Oct.18-I
Graham-Gilmour,Lt.S, 26Apr.15-I, 8May.15-I, 9May.15-I, 8Jun.15-I, 9Jun.15-I, 22Aug.15-I
Graham-White,FSLt.C, 5Sep.14-VIII
Grand,2Lt.SE, 28Jun.18-I
Grandin,2Lt.RJ, KIA 18May.17-I
Grant,Lt.AG, WIA 17Sep.18-I
Grant,2Lt.CF, KIA 10Aug.18-I
Grant,Capt.DL, POW 1Jun.16-I
Grant,Lt.EG, WIA? 3May.18-I
Grant,2Lt.EH, 14Nov.15-I
Grant,Cpl.F, POW 30May.18-VIII
Grant,2Lt.,Capt.FD, WIA 17Oct.17-I, WIA 19Jan.18-I
Grant,2Lt.HCR, KIA 4Nov.18-I
Grant,Sgt.J, 5Sep.18-I
Grant,ACpl.OW, POW 25Sep.17-VIII
Grant,Capt.RC, KIA 2Sep.18-I
Grant,Lt.RM, WIA 8Apr.17-I
Grant,Capt.T?, WIA initial J? 30Nov.17-I
Grant-Dalton,Capt.S, DSO 18Jun.16-VII
Grantham,2Lt.VM, POW 11Nov.15-I
Graves,Lt.CL, KIA 24Apr.17-I
Graves,Maj.EP, KIA 6Mar.17-I
Gray,2Lt.A, 5Nov.16-I
Gray,FSLt.AT, POW DoW 16Aug.17-I
Gray,2Lt.CGD, WIA POW 20Sep.17-I
Gray,Capt.DB, POW 17Sep.16-I
Gray,Lt.DH, Aust. KIA 3Jul.16-I
Gray,2Lt.GM, POW 27Jun.18-I
Gray,2Lt.GR, POW DoW 31Oct.17-I
Gray,2Lt.GT, KIA 24Mar.17-I
Gray,Capt.JA, INT 27Jun.18-I
Gray,Lt.KW, WIA POW 12Jan.16-I
Gray,Sgt.L, KIA 7Jun.17-I
Gray,Lt.LS, WIA 23Mar.18-I
Gray,Lt.LV, KIA 16Aug.17-I
Gray,2Lt.RH, POW 15Jul.18-I
Gray,2Lt.RJ, WIA 6Sep.18-IV
Gray,2Lt.VS, KIA 8Aug.18-I
Gray,Sgt.WB, WIA 12Aug.18-I
Gray,Lt.WE, 25Sep.18-I, 1Oct.18-I
Gray,2Lt.WJ, Can. POW 20Sep.16-I
Gray,2Lt.WMR, SA. POW 26Mar.18-I
Greasley,2Lt.JR, KIA 1Apr.18-I
Greaves,2Lt.N, KIA 28Oct.18-I
Green,Lt.CB, Can. DFC 13Apr.18-VI, 6May.18-VI, 1Jun.18-VI
Green,Lt.EG, MC POW 3Feb.18-I
Green,2Lt.HJ, KIA 4Mar.17-I
Green,Lt.JC, 11Oct.18-I
Green,TLt.,Lt.ML, 20Jun.18-I, KIA 6Aug.18-I
Green,2Lt.W, WIA 16Apr.17-I
Green,Capt.WE, 29Aug.18-I
Green,2Lt.WH, WIA POW 13Apr.17-I
Greenall,Capt.JE, WIA? 31Mar.18-I
Greenaway,2Lt.WG, WIA 4Sep.18-I
Greene,2Lt.AW, KIA 17Feb.18-I
Greene,FSLt.,Capt.JE, DFC Can. 4Dec.17-I, 29Jan.18-I, KIA 14Oct.18-I
Greenheus,2Lt.EB, KIA 25Aug.17-I
Greenhow,2Lt.DE, DoW 6Mar.17-I
Greenhow,2Lt.MW, POW 25Sep.15-I
Greenner,AG.Pte.H, WIA 21Aug.17-I
Greenslade,Lt., 8Sqn. 24May.15-I, 6Jul.15-I
Greenslade,Capt.AA, WIA 22Jul.17-I
Greenslade,Lt.RS, POW 24Oct.17-I
Greensmith,FSLt.RE, INT 4May.16-I
Greenway,AM.J, POW 21May.18-I
Greenwood,Pte.,RNAS. 31Jul.18-VIII
Greenwood,Lt.JP, 21Oct.15-I, 4Dec.16-I, WIA 16Dec.16-I
Greenwood,Lt.PB, 26Aug.15-I
Greenwood,Lt.PG, POW 3Nov.18-I
Greenyer,2Lt.R, WIA 19Sep.18-I
Greg,Capt.AT, KIA 23Apr.17-I
Gregor,2Lt.AJ, 21Oct.16-I
Gregory,Pbr.2Lt.RJ, POW 5Jun.18-I
Gregory,2Lt.,Capt.AFW, 8Mar.18-I, WIA 17May.18-I
Gregory,1Lt.JE, USAS. KIA 28Sep.18-I
Gregory,Capt.JS, 16Feb.18-I, KIA 19Feb.18-I
Gregory,Lt.MS, KIA 11Aug.18-I
Gregory,2Lt.,Capt.,Maj.R, 25Sep.16-I, 30Mar.17-I, Kld 23Jan.18-IV
Gregson,Lt.WCS, WIA 21Feb.18-I
Greig,Lt., 5Sqn. 18Aug.15-I
Greig,FSLt.CW, POW Died 12.9.18 29Nov.16-VI
Greig,Lt.DDA, 21Sep.18-I
Greig,Capt.O, POW 24Jan.17-I
Grenfell,Lt.,Capt.EO, MC 12Mar.15-I, 10Jul.15-I, 19Oct.15-I, 11Nov.15-I, 7Dec.15-I, 17Jan.16-I, 13Sep.15-I, 30Sep.16-I, WIA 11Dec.16-I
Greswell,Lt.EW, KIA 9Jun.18-VII
Grevelink,Lt.EJY, KIA 6Jun.17-I
Grey,Capt.R, POW 5Oct.14-I
Grey,Lt.AAD, POW Nov.17-I
Grey-Edwards,2Lt.HBR, 21Sep.15-I, 18Oct.15-I
Gribbin,Capt.E, WIA 4Oct.18-I
Grice,2Lt.,Lt.R, 22Mar.18-I, 28May.18-I
Grider,Capt.JM, USAS. KIA 18Jun.18-I
Grierson,2Lt.CD, POW 5Jun.17-I
Griffin,Lt.EW, KIA 16Sep.18-I
Griffin,Lt.GA, 27May.18-I
Griffin,2Lt.RT, Can. WIA POW 20Aug.16-I
Griffin,2Lt.S, KIA 18May.18-I
Griffith,2Lt.DB, KIA 19Jul.18-I
Griffith,Lt.HF, 24Aug.18-I
Griffith,2Lt.HH, 22Oct.16-I
Griffith,2Lt.JC, POW 12Jul.17-I
Griffith,Lt.JS, US. inj 18Jul.18-I
Griffiths,Lt., 63Sqn. WIA 17Dec.17-VIII
Griffiths,2Lt.AH, WIA 3Oct.18-I
Griffiths,2Lt.CD, POW 7Aug.16-I
Griffiths,2Lt.FW, POW 2Sep.16-I
Griffiths,2Lt.GA, KIA 2Jun.17-I
Griffiths,2Lt.H, 1Sep.18-I
Griffiths,2Lt.JC, 31May.16-I, 24Sep.16-I, WIA 7Dec.16-I
Griffiths,2Lt.RH, KIA 17Oct.18-I
Griggs,Lt.A, US. DoW 23.11.1917 23Nov.17-I
Grimes,2Lt.,Lt.EC, 11Apr.18-I, 20Jul.18-I
Grimwade,Lt.FN, WIA POW 1Apr.16-I
Grimwood,Lt.,2Lt.BCR, MC WIA 16Aug.17-I, KIA 7Nov.17-I
Grinell-Milne,Capt.D, POW 16May.16-I
Grinnell-Milne,Lt.DW, 15Nov.15-I, 20Nov.15-I, 25Nov.15-I, 28Nov.15-I, POW 1Dec.15-I, 28Sep.18-I, 8Oct.18-I, 21Oct.18-I
Groner,2Lt.RH, US. inj POW 14Sep.18-IIB
Grose,2Lt.AG, POW DoW 9.11.1917 7Nov.17-I
Gross,Lt.CR, POW 25Sep.18-I
Grossberg,2Lt.S, WIA 5Jan.18-I
Grossett,Lt.WE, POW 17Jul.17-I
Grosvenor,2Lt.T, KIA 17Sep.17-I
Grosvenor,Capt.RA, 3Apr.18-I, 18May.18-I
Groteclose,1Lt.EJ, US. WIA 5Oct.18-IIB
Grout,SLt.EJ, POW 15May.17-I
Groves,FLt.JO, POW 12May.15-I
Groves,2AM.SA, 15Jun.17-I, 7Jul.17-I
Grundy,1AM.A, KIA 26Sep.16-I
Grundy,Lt.VA, 16Aug.18-I
Grundy,Sgt.GE, KIA 9Nov.18-I
Grune,Lt.GDJ, KIA 13Mar.16-I
Gubbin,2Lt.JRF, POW DoW 20.11.1917 29Oct.17-VI
Gude,1Lt.OJ, US. POW 22Oct.18-IIB
Gude,Sgt.RS, INT 25Jul.18-I
Guest,Capt.OM, WIA 14Dec.15-I
Guild,2Lt.C, POW 15Sep.18-I
Guillon,Lt.GM, WIA 3Sep.17-I
Guillon,Lt.S, WIA 19Mar.17-I
Gumbley,Sgt.WH, KIA 30Oct.18-I
Gundelach,1Lt.AH, US. DSC DoW 12Sep.18-IIB
Gunderson,1Lt.LA, US. WIA 3May.18-IID
Gundiff,Lt.FW, 15Apr.18-I
Gundill,2Lt.RP, KIA 2Oct.18-I
Gunn,2Lt.JC, POW 22Sep.18-I
Gunn,1Lt.MB, US. KIA 16Jul.18-IIB
Gunn,2Lt.MG, KIA 7Dec.17-I
Gunner,Lt.ER, WIA 11Apr.17-I
Gunner,2Lt.WH, MC WIA 3Jun.17-I, KIA 29Jul.17-I
Gunton,2Lt.JW, 22Jul.16-I, KIA 9Aug.16-I
Gunyon,Lt.GJ, 22Aug.18-I
Gurdon,2Lt.,Lt.JE, 2Apr.18-I, 7May.18-I, 5Jun.18-I, WIA 10Jul.18-I
Gutheridge,2Lt., PFlt. 25Oct.18-I
Guthrie,Lt.JB, KIA 11May.18-IV
Guthrie,2Lt.RJ, US. 18Sep.18-IIB
Guy,Lt.CG, POW DoW 12.8.1917 11Aug.17-I
Guy,Sgt.HJN, WIA POW 7Aug.18-I
Guyat,2AM.JC, POW 18Feb.18-I
Guymer,2Lt.JA, 29Oct.18-I
Gwilt,2Lt.ELC, 6Apr.17-I
Gwyer,2Lt.NE, WIA 6Jan.18-I, POW 22Aug.18-IV
Gyles,2Lt.PFF, WIA 3Sep.18-I
Gyles,Lt.RR, WIA 2Jun.17-I

H

Hacklett,Lt.LA, POW 7Jun.18-I
Hackman,Cdr.TR, POW 22Mar.18-V
Hackman,2Lt.WGC, 15Sep.17-I, WIA 9Oct.17-I
Hackwill,Capt.GH, MC 28Jan.18-III, 25Apr.18-I, 4Jul.18-I, 15Sep.18-I
Haddow,2Lt.W, 9Mar.18-I
Hadlow,2AM.F, 25Mar.17-I, POW 1Apr.17-I
Hadrill,2Lt.GCT, POW 9May.17-I
Hadwick,2Lt.HC, 22Jun.16-I
Hagan,Sgt.C, WIA 26Feb.18-I
Hagen,Lt.WJ, name Hagan? WIA 29Oct.18-I
Hagenbush,2Lt.RJ, USAS. POW 1Oct.18-I
Hagley,2Lt.RE, WIA 4Jul.18-I
Hagon,2Lt., 7Sqn. 5Jan.16-I
Haig,Lt.FW, Aust. POW 1May.18-VII
Haigh,Sgt.A, KIA 16Sep.18-I
Haigh,2Lt.S, 12Apr.18-I
Haight,2Lt.JL, WIA POW 28Sep.17-I
Haight,Capt.WL, POW 4Mar.18-VIII
Haines,Lt.AJ, KIA 10Aug.18-IV
Haines,Lt.CL, KIA 26May.17-I
Haines,Sgt.TW, 23Oct.18-I
Hainsby,2Lt.FW, Can. KIA 26Mar.18-I
Hair,2Lt.NB, POW 7Jun.17-I
Halahan,Capt.JC, 28Nov.15-I
Halcrow,Lt.JW, KIA 7Jul.16-I
Hale,Lt.FL, US. 25Aug.18-I, 4Sep.18-I, 16Sep.18-I, 27Sep.18-I
Hales,Capt.JP, Can. KIA 23Aug.18-I
Haley,Lt., 6Sqn. 5Sep.17-I
Haley,2Lt.A, KIA 1Jun.18-I
Halford,2Lt.EA, POW 29Mar.16-I
Halford,2Lt.WHL, KIA 28Sep.18-I
Hall,FSgt., 3Sqn. WIA 6Jul.16-I
Hall,Sgt., 22Sqn. WIA 5Jun.18-I
Hall,Sgt.AC, POW 28Sep.18-I
Hall,2Lt.B, POW 9Aug.18-I
Hall,Lt.CR, POW 13Jun.18-I
Hall,2Lt.CS, KIA 7Apr.17-I
Hall,Lt.CS, 3Sep.18-I
Hall,Capt.DDG, MC DoW 27.3.1918 26Mar.18-I
Hall,2Lt.,Lt.,Capt.DS, 19Dec.15-I, 18Aug.17-I, KIFA 20Nov.17-I
Hall,Capt.ED, 3Apr.18-I
Hall,Lt.EWO, POW 27Oct.18-I
Hall,2Lt.F, 16Sep.16-I, DoW 22Sep.16-I
Hall,Lt.FH, WIA 13Jan.18-I
Hall,FSLt.,Lt.FV, WIA 23May.17-I, KIFA 15May.18-I
Hall,2Lt.G, 28Apr.17-I, 27Mar.18-I
Hall,Sgt?,G, rank Pte? POW 16Sep.18-I
Hall,Lt.GH, 30Dec.15-I, 23Jan.16-I
Hall,2Lt.GS, POW DoW 30.11.1916 20Nov.16-I
Hall,2Lt.GW, KIA 20Nov.17-I
Hall,FSLt.,Lt.HG, inj 25Apr.16-III, KIA 17Jul.18-VI
Hall,2Lt.J, WIA 1Sep.18-I
Hall,2Lt.JD, 19Aug.18-I
Hall,2Lt.,Lt.JFA, WIA 26May.18-I, WIA 8Aug.18-I
Hall,2Lt.JG, US. KIA 8Aug.18-I
Hall,Sgt.,Capt.JN, US. WIA 26Jun.17-IIA, 29Apr.18-IIB, inj POW 7May.18-IIB
Hall,Lt.K, WIA 11Apr.18-I
Hall,Lt.KWJ, POW 21Jun.18-I
Hall,2Lt.LG, USAS. POW died? 15Sep.18-I
Hall,FSLt.ND, POW 3Sep.17-I
Hall,Lt.R, 29Sep.18-I, POW 2Oct.18-I
Hall,Lt.RMcK, 17May.18-I, KIA 28May.18-I
Hall,Lt.,Capt.RWP, 22Mar.17-I, WIA 15Jul.17-I
Hall,2Lt.S, KIA 18Oct.18-I
Hall,2Lt.WA, POW 2Sep.18-I
Hall,2Lt.WE, 15Sqn. POW 24Sep.17-I
Hall,2Lt.WE, 62Sqn. POW 4Sep.18-I
Hall,2Lt.WTJ, 27Sep.18-I
Hallam,2AM.C, KIA 21Aug.17-I
Hallam,2Lt.EW, WIA 25May.17-I
Hallam,2Lt.HA, POW 9Nov.16-I
Hallam,2Lt.W, WIA 26Oct.15-I
Hallawell,Lt., 103Sqn. 22Jul.18-I
Haller,2Lt.ED, KIA 3Jun.17-I
Halley,2Lt.CRB, WIA 11Sep.17-I, KIA 2Oct.17-I
Halley,1Lt.SR, US. WIA 24Aug.18-IID
Hallgren,2Lt.WA, US. WIA 25Jul.18-I
Halliday,2Lt.JGW, KIA 3Sep.18-I
Halliday,Lt.MFJ, KIA 7Jun.17-I
Halliwell,2Lt.EJ, KIA 11Sep.17-I
Hallonquist,Capt.J, WIA POW 29Oct.18-IV
Halse,2Lt.CH, KIA 24Apr.17-I
Halstead,FSgt., 6Sqn. 8Jun.17-I, 13Oct.17-I
Halstead,FSgt.GW, 4Sqn. WIA 4Dec.16-I
Hamar,Lt.AJ, DoW 8Apr.17-I
Hambas,FSLt., ZSqn. Grk. 23Jan.18-V
Hambleton,Capt.JA, US. WIA 28May.18-IIB

Hamel,2Lt.EB, inj 7Jun.17-I
Hamel,2Lt.HPJG, KIA 10Jan.18-I
Hamer,2Lt.HW, WIA 12Aug.17-I
Hamer,Sgt.JH, KIA 9Sep.17-I
Hamersley,Capt.HA, Aust. 18Mar.18-I
Hamilton,Lt.A, KIA 8Aug.18-I
Hamilton,2Lt.CW, WIA 10Oct.17-I
Hamilton,2Lt.DS, KIA 1Sep.18-I
Hamilton,Lt.E, 13May.18-IV
Hamilton,2Lt.EH, KIA 15Feb.17-I
Hamilton,Lt.G, POW 2May.18-I
Hamilton,2Lt.HD, WIA POW 6Apr.17-I
Hamilton,Capt.HJ, 26Mar.18-I
Hamilton,Sgt.J, WIA POW 16Jun.18-I
Hamilton,Lt.L, 18Sep.18-VI
Hamilton,1Lt.LA, USAS. DFC DSC KIA 24Aug.18-I
Hamilton,Lt.PDP, WIA 25May.18-I
Hamilton?,1AM.W, WIA 21Aug.17-I
Hamilton,Lt.WN, POW 29Apr.17-I
Hamlet,2Lt.HA, POW 5Nov.18-I
Hamley,Lt.NH, 27Oct.18-IV, 28Oct.18-IV, WIA 1Nov.18-IV
Hammer,1Lt.EM, USAS. KIA 19May.18-I
Hammer,2Lt.HJ, WIA 10Nov.17-VII
Hammersley,Lt.FJB, WIA POW 8Nov.17-I
Hammersley,Capt.HA, 23Sep.17-I
Hammersley,Lt.RG, 23Mar.18-I
Hammond,Lt.AW, MC WIA 27Mar.18-I
Hammond,Rfn.P, DoW 15Jun.17-I
Hammond,Sgt.H, KIA 14Aug.18-I
Hammond,Lt.HB, MC WIA 5Jun.17-I
Hammond,Lt.HL, KIA 4Aug.18-I
Hammond,Lt.HT, POW 14Sep.17-I
Hammond,2Lt.JE, WIA 8Jul.18-I
Hammond,Lt.TJ, Aust. KIA 12Jun.18-I
Hampson,Sgt.GH, WIA 24Sep.18-I
Hampson,2Lt.HN, DoW 7Apr.17-I
Hampton,Lt., 62Sqn. WIA POW 3May.18-I
Hampton,2Lt.GWB, 14Feb.17-I, KIA 11Mar.17-I
Hampton,2Lt.JH, KIA 29Oct.18-I
Hanafy,2Lt.SR, 20Nov.17-I
Hanafy,Lt.SR, DoW 23Nov.17-I
Hancock,2Lt.C, POW 5Oct.18-I
Hancock,Lt.FW, Aust. 17Jan.18-VII, POW 20Jan.18-VII
Hancock,Lt.HJW, POW 4Mar.18-VIII
Hancocks,Lt.MN, 28Sep.18-I
Hand,Lt.EMcN, Can. 15Nov.17-I, POW 1Jun.18-IV
Hand,2Lt.PA, KIA 10Jul.18-I
Handford,2Lt.HF, WIA 11Apr.18-I
Handley,2Lt.FAW, POW 29Apr.17-I
Handley,Lt.J, WIA POW 12May.18-I
Hanis,Lt.SHB, 16Mar.16-I
Hankin,Lt.HM?, 4Sqn., initials HF? 18Apr.15-I, 11May.15-I, POW 26Jul.15-I
Hanley,1AM., KIA May.15-I
Hanlon,Lt.DR, 10Mar.15-I
Hanman,2Lt.JLS, 21Mar.18-I
Hann,2Lt.CC, DoW 22Oct.16-I
Hanna,2Lt.AG, 24Mar.18-I, 27Mar.18-I, POW 31Mar.18-I
Hannan,2Lt.G, POW 14Apr.18-VI
Hanning,Lt.JE, 27Mar.18-I
Hanning,2Lt.JT, Can. KIA 27Nov.16-I
Hanscom,2Lt.AF, US. KIA 26Sep.18-IIB
Hanson,2Lt.H, 23Mar.18-I, WIA 24Mar.18-I
Harbour,Sgt.ACT?, POW 29Aug.18-I
Harcourt-Vernon,Capt.AA, POW 4Nov.18-I
Hardeman,Sgt.ET, KIA 16Feb.18-I
Hardie,2Lt., 16Sqn. 10Oct.15-I
Hardie,2Lt.DW, KIA 18Nov.17-I
Hardie,Capt.FR, DSO WIA 11Mar.17-I
Hardie,Lt.RC, 23Nov.17-I
Hardie,Lt.RG, 20Nov.17-I
Harding,2Lt.FL, 24Mar.17-I
Harding,2Lt.GH, US. KIA 27Mar.18-I
Harding,Lt.GP, MC POW 1May.17-I
Hardinge,1AM.L, 10Oct.16-I, POW 15Oct.16-I
Hardioe,2Lt.FR, 28Nov.15-I
Hardman,Capt.EP, POW 2Aug.18-I
Hardman,Capt.JDI, 30Oct.18-I
Hardwick,2Lt.GN, 23Mar.18-I
Hardy,2Lt.P, WIA 29Mar.18-I
Hare,2Lt.EF?, KIA 24Mar.17-I
Hare,Cpl.EJ, inj 29Jan.17-I
Hare,Sgt.G, POW 23Aug.18-I
Harel,2Lt.LO, KIA 18Aug.17-I
Hargrave,Lt., 6Sqn. 23Apr.15-I 2May.15-I, 9May.15-I
Hargrave,Lt.WG, KIA 17Apr.18-IV
Hargreaves,2Lt.CA, DoW 15Aug.17-I
Hargreaves,FSgt.JM, 28Jul.15-I, 31Aug.15-I, 19Sep.15-I, 21Sep.15-I, 22Sep.15-I, 30Sep.15-I
Harker,Lt.B, POW 21Oct.17-I
Harker,2Lt.EK, WIA 16Apr.18-I
Harker,2Lt.GT, POW 23Jun.17-I
Harker,2Lt.HR, 24Mar.17-I
Harkness,FLt.DE, NZ. WIA INT 17Sep.16-I
Harle,2Lt., 16Sqn. 15Aug.17-I
Harle,Lt.W, WIA POW 14Jul.17-I
Harley,Lt.FW, KIA 3Jun.17-I
Harley,2Lt.,Lt.V, POW 4Sep.18-I
Harlock,Lt.FG, 20Sep.18-I
Harlock?,Lt.AG, see Horlock
Harman,Lt., 12Sqn. 12Jan.18-I, 9Feb.18-I, 7Mar.18-I
Harman,AM.AT, 5Aug.18-III
Harman,Sgt.TW, POW? 21Oct.18-I
Harmer,Lt.H, KIA 6Jun.17-I
Harmer,2Lt.RH, WIA 9Apr.18-I
Harmer,2Lt.WTV, inj 10Dec.17-I
Harmon,Lt.BW, Can. KIA 10May.18-I
Harms,2Lt.W, KIA 4Mar.17-I
Harold,Lt.JPB, WIA 28Jan.18-I
Harold,Sgt.WB, WIA 17Jul.18-I
Harper,2Lt.GV, KIA 26Sep.18-I
Harper,2Lt.HG, WIA 27Oct.18-I
Harper,Lt.NS, Can. KIA 25Jun.18-I
Harper,Lt.SA, MC WIA POW 4Sep.17-I
Harper,Lt.SH, Aust. 23Oct.18-VII
Harper,Lt.WE, WIA 24Aug.16-I
Harries,2Lt.TM, 11Aug.18-I, 19Aug.18-I
Harriman,2Lt.CH, KIA 29Oct.17-I
Harrington,Lt.HBD, POW 24Apr.18-I
Harrington,2Lt.J, WIA 7Sep.18-I
Harrington,Lt.JR, KIA 7Jul.18-I
Harris,Sgt., 38Sqn. 12Aug.18-I
Harris,2Lt.AE, inj 9Sep.18-I, WIA 21Sep.18-I?
Harris,Capt.AT, 13Aug.17-I
Harris,2Lt.DB, US. KIA 26Sep.18-IIB
Harris,1Lt.DR, USAS. INT 16Aug.18-I
Harris,Lt.EC, 21Jul.18-I
Harris,2Lt.H, WIA POW 5Jun.17-I
Harris,2Lt.IM, WIA 13Aug.16-I
Harris,2AM.J, 8Jun.17-I
Harris,2Lt.LA, 7Nov.18-I
Harris,2Lt.NB, POW 21May.18-I
Harris,2Lt.OStC, 31May.18-I
Harris,2Lt.PG, KIA 11Aug.17-I
Harris,Lt.SE, KIA 4Jul.18-I
Harris,Lt.SHB, initials SNB? 29Mar.16-I, WIA 30Apr.16-I
Harris,2AM.W, POW 12Jul.17-I
Harrison,Cpl., 5Sqn. 21Sep.15-I
Harrison,2Lt.AG, KIA 15Sep.18-I
Harrison,Lt.AH, POW 1Jul.18-I
Harrison,2Lt.AR, WIA 30Mar.18-I
Harrison,2Lt.CA, POW 26Sep.18-I
Harrison,2Lt.CJL, WIA 28Jul.17-I
Harrison,Lt.CP, 21Apr.18-I, 8May.18-I, 18Jul.18-I
Harrison,Lt.E, KIA 17May.18-I
Harrison,2Lt.EA, 29Sep.18-I
Harrison,2Lt.EA, KIA 1Oct.18-I
Harrison,Lt.EC, WIA 12Apr.18-I
Harrison,2Lt.GH, WIA 6Mar.17-I
Harrison,2Lt.J, KIA 29Jun.18-I
Harrison,2Lt.JE, KIA 17Sep.18-I
Harrison,Maj.JI, KIA 16May.18-I
Harrison,Bdr.A, KIA 23Jan.17-I
Harrison,2Lt.LG, WIA 2May.17-I
Harrison,Lt.NV, 14Oct.17-I
Harrison,Capt.R, 29Oct.18-I
Harrison,Lt.TS, SA. 27Jun.18-I
Harrison,2Lt.VW, 27Sep.16-I
Harrison,FSgt.WH, 26Nov.15-I, 28Nov.15-I
Harrison,2Lt.WL, 1Sqn. WIA 12Apr.18-I
Harrison,2Lt.WL, 40Sqn. Can. 1Apr.18-I
Harrison,Lt.WL, 65Sqn. POW 6Nov.17-I
Harrison,2Lt.WRE, WIA 22Aug.16-I
Harrison,Capt.WRE, INT 15Sep.18-I
Harrison,2Lt.WW, 21Aug.18-I, KIA 21Sep.18-I
Harrison-Mitchell,2Lt.E, 28Aug.15-I
Harrop,AG.2AM.W, 20Sqn. WIA 5Sep.17-I
Harrop,Sgt.W, MM 104Sqn. POW 22Aug.18-I
Harrover,FSLt.GS, WIA 23Sep.17-I
Harrow-Bunn,Lt.AL, WIA 23Nov.16-I
Harry,2Lt.RC, KIA 28Aug.16-I
Harryman,2Lt.S, POW DoW 24.3.1917 19Mar.17-I
Harston,Lt.S, KIA 30Jun.18-I
Hart,Lt.CJ, 16Apr.16-I, KIA 9Aug.16-I
Hart,2Lt.PG, US. DSC 16Aug.18-IIB
Hart,2Lt.RG, WIA? 11Apr.18-I
Hart,2Lt.W, 15Apr.18-I
Hart Collins,Lt.C, WIA 19Feb.16-I
Hart-Davies,2Lt.HR, WIA POW 19Aug.17-I
Harter,1Lt.LS, US. KIA 18Sep.18-IIB
Hartigan,Lt.EP, KIFA 20Nov.17-I
Hartley,Sgt., Aden. KIA 23Jan.18-VII
Hartley,2Lt.H, POW 10Aug.18-I
Hartley,2Lt.HH, KIA 14Mar.18-I
Hartley,LM.RL, INT 17Dec.14-I
Hartley,2Lt.J, 5Jun.17-I
Hartley,Pte.JF, POW 2Aug.18-IV
Hartley,2Lt.JH, KIA 22Jul.17-I
Hartley,2Lt.PS, WIA 25Jul.18-I
Hartley,2Lt.RStJ, WIA 7Oct.16-I
Hartley,2Lt.WM, KIA 8Aug.18-I
Hartnett,Lt.MC, KIA 19Sep.17-I
Hartney,Lt.,Capt.HE, Can. 20Oct.16-I, inj 14Feb.17-I
Hartridge,Lt., 41Sqn. inj 19Jun.17-I
Harvey,Cpl., 5Sqn. 18May.16-I
Harvey,AG.2AM.CN, KIA 30Jan.18-I
Harvey,2Lt.EB, 16Mar.16-I, POW 2Jul.16-I
Harvey,2AM.ED, 6Mar.17-I, POW 20Apr.17-I
Harvey,2Lt.ES, 16Sep.18-I, 24Sep.18-I, KIA 26Sep.18-I
Harvey,Sgt.G, POW 19Jul.18-I
Harvey,1Lt.GS, USAS. POW 10Aug.18-I
Harvey,Lt.JBBdeM, POW 9May.17-I
Harvey,Lt.JS, 1Jun.17-I
Harvey,2Lt.LS, 4Nov.18-I
Harvey,2Lt.PGA, 20Mar.16-I
Harvey,Lt.RP, WIA 20Oct.16-I
Harvey,Lt.TF, KIA 7Jun.18-I
Harvey,Lt.WA, WIA POW 11Nov.15-I
Harvey,2Lt.,Capt.WFJ, DFC 16Mar.18-I, 18Jun.18-I
Harvey,Lt.WJ, 17May.18-I
Harvey-Bathurst,Sgt.AR, WIA 9Aug.17-I
Harvey-Kelly,Lt.,Maj.HD, DSO 25Aug.14-I, 9Sep.14-I, DoW 29Apr.17-I
Harwell,2Lt.WB, US. WIA? 25Oct.18-IIB
Harwood,1Lt.BP, US. WIA 5Jul.18-IIB
Harwood,AM.EM?, 8Sqn. 1Feb.17-I
Harwood,2Lt.EM, 10Apr.17-I
Haseler,2Lt.GF, POW 9Mar.17-I
Hasell,2Lt.RE, 4Oct.18-I
Haskail,Lt.EO, 8Aug.18-I
Haskall,Lt., 12Sqn. 25Aug.18-I
Haslam,Lt.H, KIA 16Sep.17-I
Haslam,2Lt.,Lt.JAG, MC 22Apr.18-I, 9Aug.18-I, WIA 10Aug.18-I
Hassett,1Lt.EA, US. WIA 3Nov.18-IIB
Haslett,Capt.ER, US. WIA POW 30Sep.18-IIB
Hassinger,1Lt.PE, US. KIA 14Sep.18-IIB
Hastie,Lt.HE, POW 25Oct.18-IV
Hatch,2Lt.ML, 16Aug.17-I
Hatch,Lt.GJ, KIA 6Apr.17-I
Hatcher,2Lt.WO, WIA 18May.17-I
Hatfield,Capt.AC, POW 21Sep.17-I
Hathaway,2Lt.S, KIA 12Jan.16-I
Haughan,2Lt.JH, WIA 13Jan.18-I
Haughton,Lt.SPO?, POW 20Sep.18-VI
Havens,Cpl.P, 20May.16-I
Havilland-Roe,Lt.HA, KIA 19May.18-I
Haward?,2Lt.RS, name Howard? 25Sep.16-I
Hawgood,2Lt.WP, WIA 5Aug.17-I
Hawker,Lt.,Capt.,Maj.LG, VC 18Apr.15-I, WIA 25Apr.15-I, 26Apr.15-I, 7Jun.15-I, 12Jun.15-I, 20Jun.15-I, 22Jun.15-I, 25Jul.15-I, 31Jul.15-I, 2Aug.15-I, 9Aug.15-I, 11Aug.15-I, 7Sep.15-I, KIA 23Nov.16-I
Hawkins,Lt., 6Sqn. 23Apr.15-I, 28Apr.15-I
Hawkins,2AM.AC, KIA Mar.15-I
Hawkins,2AM.AW, POW 10Aug.17-I
Hawkins,Lt.GHA, WIA 8Aug.16-I
Hawkins,Capt.HR, POW 26Apr.17-I
Hawkins,2Lt.T, KIA 20Jul.18-I
Hawksley,2Lt.GE, WIA 10May.17-I
Hawley,2Lt.,Lt.ACR, 27Mar.18-I, WIA 29Mar.18-I, KIA 9Aug.18-I
Hawley,Lt.FC, Aust. 28Apr.18-VII
Hawtrey,2Lt.JJA, POW DoW 17.9.1917 16Sep.17-I
Haxton,Sgt.E, KIA 10Oct.16-I
Hay,Capt.BM, 26May.16-I
Hay,Lt.DY, inj 30Apr.17-I
Hay,2Lt.J, Aust. KIA 23Jan.17-I
Hay,FSLt.JF, POW 25Mar.16-I
Hay,Lt.JM, KIA 24Mar.18-I
Hay,Lt.OD, WIA 15Aug.17-I
Hay,Lt.RB, MC DoW 17Jul.17-I
Haydon,Sgt.GL, 31May.17-I
Hayes,Lt.EG, WIA 17Jul.18-I
Hayes,Lt.R, KIA 22Jul.17-I
Hayne,FSLt.ET, SA. 22Aug.17-I
Hayne,2Lt.M, KIA 10Oct.16-I
Haynes,Lt., 7Sqn. 19Dec.15-I
Haynes,Lt.CC, 19Oct.15-I
Haynes, Capt. GC, KIA 23Oct.18-I
Haynes, Lt. JLP, KIA 11Mar.18-I
Haynes, 2Lt. T, WIA 9Nov.16-I
Haynes, 2AM. W, POW 29Apr.16-VIII
Hayward, 2Lt. CC, 1Sqn. KIA 17Jan.16-I
Hayward, 2Lt. CC, 18Sqn. Aust. DoI 16Sep.16-I
Hayward, Lt. GS, 18Mar.18-I
Hayward, 2Lt. JH, WIA 29Apr.17-I
Hazell, Lt. DH, KIA 27Sep.18-I
Hazell, 2AM. J, WIA 16Jul.18-I
Hazell, AM. JP, 9Jul.18-I
Hazell, 2Lt.,Capt. TF, MC Irl. 24Apr.17-I, 16Aug.17-I, 4Jul.18-I, 8Aug.18-I
Hazen,Lt.TD, 28Jun.18-I, KIA 19Aug.18-I
Head,Lt.B, WIA 11Nov.17-I
Head,Lt.BT, 21Mar.18-I
Head,2Lt.M, KIA 28Dec.15-I
Headlam,Lt.ES, Aust. 22Sep.18-VII, 19Oct.18-VII
Headley,2Lt.HM, KIA 11Mar.17-I
Heagerty,2Lt.JS, POW 8Apr.17-I
Heakes,Lt.FV, WIA 28Mar.18-I
Heald,Lt.I, KIA 4Dec.16-I
Heald,Lt.TP, KIA 13Oct.17-I
Heard,2Lt.SF, 19Sep.16-I
Hearn,2Lt.ETH, KIA 11Sep.17-I
Hearson,Capt.JG, 21Jul.15-I, 29Jul.15-I, 11Aug.15-I, 19Aug.15-I
Heaston,Lt.CG, WIA? 7Dec.15-I
Heath, Lt. EE, WIA POW 13Mar.18-I
Heath, 2Lt. F, MM 4Nov.18-I
Heath, Lt. RC, WIA 9Apr.17-I
Heathcote,2Lt.LW, Aust. POW 9Mar.17-VII
Heather?,Lt.RT, 22Aug.15-I
Heaton,2Lt.B, WIA 24Oct.18-I
Heaven,2Lt.AC, name Heavan? 18Mar.17-I, 24Apr.17-I
Heaver,2Lt.AR, POW 27Aug.18-I
Hedderwick,2Lt.G, KIA 22Sep.16-I
Hedges,2Lt.RBT, WIA 1Apr.18-I
Hedley,Capt.JH, 17Feb.18-I, POW 27Mar.18-I
Heebner,Lt.CH, KIA 24Sep.18-I
Heedy,2AM.J, KIA 4Sep.17-I
Hegan,2Lt.R, 21Mar.18-I
Heigham-Plumptre,2Lt.FL, WIA 22Mar.18-I
Heine,Lt.RW, POW 14Sep.18-I
Heinrichs,1Lt.WH, US. WIA POW 17Sep.18-IIB
Helder,Lt.LB, POW 17Sep.16-I
Hele-Shaw,Lt.HR, KIA 19Jul.16-I
Helingoe,FSgt.J, WIA 21Oct.16-I
Hellett,Lt.TTB, 14Aug.18-I
Helliwell,2Lt.MR, WIA 17Nov.16-I
Hellyer,Lt.FE, 26Jul.15-I, WIA 26Sep.15-I

Helmer,Lt.EW, KIA 8Aug.18-I
Helmore,2Lt.STJ, KIA 14May.18-I
Helsby,Sgt.J, KIA 2Jul.18-I
Helwig,Lt.NW, DFC POW? 27Sep.18-I
Hemingway,2Lt.A, KIA 6Nov.18-I
Hemmens,Lt.RH, POW 8Aug.18-I
Hemming,2Lt., 2Sqn. 12Jan.16-I
Hemming,2Lt.,Capt.AS, DFC 6Jan.18-I, 9Aug.18-I, 10Aug.18-I
Hempel,2Lt.AE, POW 21Oct.17-I
Hempsall,2Lt.HT, POW 15Sep.18-I
Hendershot,Lt.WF, 30Oct.18-I
Henderson,2Lt., 2Sqn. 5Feb.16-I
Henderson,2Lt.AB, POW 25Aug.18-I
Henderson,2Lt.D, WIA 12Apr.18-I
Henderson,2Lt.EG, 27Oct.17-I
Henderson,2Lt.,Capt.EJ, 9Sep.16-I, 21Oct.16-I, KIA 25Mar.17-I
Henderson,Capt.G, 19Jan.16-I
Henderson,Lt.GLP, 28Nov.15-I, WIA 2Dec.15-I
Henderson,Lt.H, 19Dec.15-I
Henderson,Capt.IHD, 24Aug.16-I, 26Aug.16-I, 3Sep.16-I
Henderson,2Lt.,Capt.KS, Aust. 1Jul.16-I, 9Sep.16-I, 3Mar.17-I, KIA 2Jun.18-I
Henderson,2Lt.LJF, POW 10Aug.17-I
Henderson,Lt.M, WIA POW 20Feb.16-I
Henderson,2Lt.NP, inj 26Apr.17-I
Henderson,2Lt.T, 10Oct.15-I, 8Dec.15-I
Henderson,Lt.TD, 29Apr.18-I
Henderson,Lt.TO, WIA 14Sep.18-I
Henderson,Lt.WR, WIA? POW 25Jul.18-I
Henderson,Lt.WRW, WIA 3May.18-I
Hendrie,2Lt.ET, WIA 12Apr.18-I
Hendrie,2Lt.KGP, 29Mar.18-I
Henley-Mooney,Lt.W, USAS. WIA POW 29Sep.18-I
Hennessey,Lt.HS, KIA 5Jun.18-I
Henney,2Lt.WJ, 7Nov.17-I, 3Jan.18-I
Henry,1Lt.CA, US. WIA 5Oct.18-IIB
Henry,Lt.FR, WIA POW 8Apr.17-I
Henry,2Lt.JAG, KIA 28Sep.18-I
Henry,Lt.RA, POW 8Sep.18-I
Henry,2Lt.SS, POW 15Nov.17-I
Henzell,2Lt.CP, 3May.18-I
Hepburn,Capt.A, Aust. 17May.18-I, 18Oct.18-I
Hepburn,2Lt.RV, WIA 2Jun.18-I, KIA 16Sep.18-I
Heppel,2Lt.PF, WIA POW 26Oct.16-I
Hepple,Lt.TR, inj 2Dec.17-I
Hepworth,2Lt.AH, WIA 18Oct.17-I
Herbert,Lt.EG, WIA 28Jan.17-I
Herbert,2Lt.LA, 18Feb.18-I, WIA 24Feb.18-I
Herbert,1Lt.TJ, USAS. WIA 8Aug.18-I
Herd,2Lt.WH, 1Oct.18-I
Herman,2Lt.RD, 6Sep.16-I, 14Sep.16-I, DoW as POW 22Sep.16-I
Hern,Lt.HR, WIA 20Sep.18-I
Heron,2Lt.FT, KIA 25Jul.18-I
Heron,Lt.OP, 9Oct.18-I
Herring,Lt.AH, KIA 20May.18-I
Herring,2Lt.ES, WIA 22Mar.18-I
Herring,2Lt.GE, POW 31Aug.18-I
Herring,2Lt.JH, 8Sqn. WIA 14Jan.16-I
Herring,Capt.JH, 30Sqn. 13Aug.16-VIII, 23Sep.16-VIII, 14Dec.16-VIII
Herring,2Lt.RS, WIA 26Mar.18-I
Herriot,2Lt.WM, DoW 4Sep.18-I
Herron,Lt.KC, KIA 24Apr.18-I
Hervey,2Lt.HE, 60Sqn. 7Apr.17-I, POW 8Apr.17-I
Hervey,2Lt.VH, WIA 13Aug.18-I
Heseltine,2Lt.GC, 29Apr.17-I, 5May.17-I, WIA 13May.17-I
Hesketh,2Lt.A, WIA 22Oct.18-I
Hesketh,2Lt.JEB, DoW 22Apr.17-I
Heslop,2Lt.AV, 29Oct.18-I, KIA 9Nov.18-I
Hett,Lt.GB, 30Oct.18-I
Hewat,2Lt.HB, POW 28Sep.18-I
Hewat,2Lt.,Lt.RA, Can. 7Jun.17-I, WIA 26Oct.17-I, 14May.18-I, KIA 14Aug.18-I
Hewett,Lt.BA, 27Jun.18-I
Hewett,Lt.HD, WIA? inj? 24Oct.18-I
Hewett,2Lt.JD, 11Mar.17-I
Hewitt,2Lt.HA, POW 19Feb.18-I
Hewitt,FSLt.NDM, POW 6Apr.17-I
Hewitt,2AM.W, WIA POW 11Oct.17-I
Hewson,2Lt.CV, KIA 9Jul.16-I
Hewson,2Lt.FAA, WIA POW 22Sep.16-I
Hewson,Lt.T, Aust. KIA 7Jul.17-I
Hexter,2Lt.AN, US. WIA DoW? 4Sep.18-IIB
Hey,2Lt.WMR, WIA 3Oct.18-I
Heyes,2Lt.AC, POW 25Sep.18-I
Heys,Lt.GDA, WIA 30Oct.17-I
Heyward,FSLt.CJ, 30Mar.18-I
Heywood,Lt.AJ, 16Aug.17-I
Heywood,FSLt.AP, WIA 29Apr.17-I
Heywood,Lt.AT, KIA 3Sep.17-I
Heywood,Lt.CJ, 5Jul.18-I
Heywood,Lt.LR, POW 9Mar.16-I
Heyworth,Lt.EL, WIA POW 3Apr.17-I
Hiatt,Capt.CAA, 3Jul.16-I
Hibbard,Lt.SR, POW 1Jan.17-I
Hibbert,Capt.JE, MC 21Jul.18-I
Hibbert,2Lt.OP, POW 26Sep.18-I
Hickes,2Lt.RIA, KIA 30Aug.18-I
Hickey,Capt.CRR, Can. DFC 27May.18-I, 15Sep.18-I, KIA 3Oct.18-I
Hickey,2Lt.LC, KIA 2May.18-I
Hickling,2AM.R, DoW 7May.17-I
Hickman,2Lt.B, WIA 27Sep.18-I
Hicks,Capt., RFC 5Apr.17-VI
Hicks,Lt.ED, WIA 8Sep.16-I
Hicks,Lt.GE, POW 24Apr.17-I
Hicks,Lt.GR, WIA 2Oct.18-I
Hicks,2Lt.HR, KIA 12Oct.17-I
Hicks,2Lt.SC, US. WIA 10Oct.18-IIB
Hicks,2Lt.WN, 16Oct.18-I, 21Oct.18-I, DoW 27Oct.18-I
Higginbottom,2Lt.F, DoW 6.4.1917 5Apr.17-I
Higgins,2Lt.CD, KIA 22Sep.16-I
Higgins,1Lt.CW, US. WIA 26Sep.18-IIB
Higgins,2Lt.JF, 30Oct.18-I
Higgins,Maj.JFA, WIA 30Oct.14-I
Higginson,2Lt.WCV, KIA 20Nov.17-I
Higgs,2Lt.GW, inj 20Apr.18-I
Higgs,2Lt.LA, DoW 4Oct.18-I
Higham,2Lt.JA, 7Nov.17-I, WIA 12Nov.17-I
Highton,2Lt.HV, KIA 25Mar.18-I
Highwood,2Lt.,Lt.,Capt.SW, DFC 10Aug.18-I, 16Sep.18-I, 24Sep.18-I, 29Sep.18-I, 4Nov.18-I
Hilborn,2Lt.CL, 27Mar.18-I
Hill,2Lt.AB, 17Jul.17-I, POW 24Jul.17-I
Hill,Lt.AH, KIA 10May.18-I
Hill,Lt.BW, KIA 4Mar.17-I
Hill,Cpl.C, 20Sqn. KIA 30Jul.18-I
Hill,Sgt.C, 88Sqn. 29Jun.18-I
Hill,Lt.CW, Aust. POW 3May.16-VII
Hill,2Lt.GAR, POW 14Aug.18-I
Hill,Maj.GD, 6Jun.18-I
Hill,2Lt.HAV, WIA 14Jul.16-I
Hill,2Lt.HO, KIA 23Apr.17-I
Hill,Lt.,Capt.HOW, MC 10Aug.17-I, KIA 21Oct.17-I
Hill,2Lt.KS, 30Aug.18-I, WIA 20Sep.18-I
Hill,Lt.RAG, KIA 12Aug.18-I
Hill,1Lt.RC, US. KIA 14Sep.18-IIB
Hill,Lt.RF, POW 9Oct.17-I
Hill,Lt.RIV, POW 11Oct.17-I
Hill,2Lt.SJ, 65Sqn. KIA 4Oct.18-I
Hill,2Lt.SJ, 107Sqn. POW 9Aug.18-I
Hill,Lt.TRV, WIA POW 6Apr.18-I
Hill,1Lt.WD, US. WIA 27May.18-IIB
Hill-Tout,2Lt.WS, 15Apr.18-I
Hillaby,FSLt.EC, KIA 6Jul.17-I
Hillier,2Lt.JF, 21Jun.17-I
Hillis,2Lt.BS, KIA 5Jul.18-I
Hills,2Lt.FE, POW 6Mar.17-I
Hills,2Lt.J, 11Aug.18-I, POW 14Aug.18-I
Hills,2Lt.OM, MC POW 21Oct.17-I
Hills,2Lt.WB, POW 9Mar.17-I
Hills,Lt.WFW, KIA 6Mar.17-I
Hillyard,Lt.VWH, POW 17May.18-I
Hilton,Lt.R, WIA 27Jun.16-I
Hilton,2Lt.R, DoW 29.4.1918 6Apr.18-I
Hilton,Capt.R, 4Jul.18-I, 8Aug.18-I
Hilton,2Lt.TR, POW 22Aug.18-IV
Hilton,2Lt.VK, 25Mar.18-I, WIA 27Mar.18-I
Hilton,BoyMech.AEV, WIA 4Jul.18-III
Hinchcliff,2Lt.JB, WIA 1Aug.16-I
Hinchliffe,2Lt.HE, POW 9Jul.18-I
Hinchliffe,FLt.WGR, 3Feb.18-I
Hind,Capt.IF, KIA 12Aug.18-I
Hinde,2Lt.P, WIA 5Oct.18-I
Hinder,2Lt.A, DoI? 16Sep.18-I
Hine,2Lt.JB, POW 28Jul.17-I
Hines,Sgt.GF, POW 27Sep.18-I
Hinkley,2Lt.DR, KIFA 13Jan.17-I
Hinshelwood,FLt.T, 22Jun.16-I
Hinsley,OSLt.W, inj 10Dec.17-V
Hird,Lt.FL, 16Mar.18-I
Hirst,2Lt.H, WIA 20Oct.17-I
Hirst,2Lt.S, KIA 16Jun.18-I
Hirth,2Lt.FK, US. KIA 16Jul.18-IIB
Hiscock,Lt.FH, WIA 12Oct.17-I
Hiscox,Lt.AH, 27Aug.18-I, KIA 6Sep.18-I
Hitchcock,2Lt.CG, POW 22Aug.18-I
Hitchcock,Capt.GEW, WIA 20Nov.17-I
Hitchcock,1Lt.RW, 11Aug.18-IIB, US. KIA 2Sep.18-IIB
Hitchcock,Sgt?,T, US. WIA POW 6Mar.18-IIC
Hoare,Pte.E, WIA? inj? 17Aug.18-I
Hobart,Maj.PCS, POW 25Mar.18-VIII
Hobart-Hampden,Lt.GMA, 1Mar.17-I
Hobbs,2Lt.AV, 10Sep.15-I, 23Sep.15-I, 10Nov.15-I, KIA 15Dec.15-I
Hobbs,FSLt.BD, DSC 14Jun.17-III
Hobbs,2Lt.RW, MC 26Mar.18-I
Hobbs,2Lt.TG, inj 22Aug.18-I, DoW 24.8.1918 23Aug.18-I
Hobbs,1Lt.WT, US. KIA 25Jun.18-IIB
Hoblyn,Mid.SE, POW 25Mar.16-I
Hobson,Capt.FH, 25Mar.18-I
Hodge,FLt.GGG, POW 10Nov.16-I
Hodge,Sgt.H, POW 24Mar.18-I
Hodges,FSLt.CRW, KIA 18Aug.17-I
Hodgetts,2Lt.GA, 4Nov.18-I
Hodgkinson,Lt.JR, WIA 7Dec.17-I
Hodgkinson,2Lt.W, KIA 9Oct.18-I
Hodgskin,Lt.AF, KIA 6Sep.18-IV
Hodgson,Sgt., 2Sqn. 11Nov.15-I
Hodgson,2Lt., 13Sqn. 26Apr.16-I
Hodgson,Lt.AG, INT 4Jun.18-III
Hodgson,Lt.EE, INT 5Jun.15-I
Hodgson,2Lt.,Capt.FH, WIA 6Sep.16-I, WIA 4Nov.18-I
Hodgson,Capt.GB, KIA 13Apr.17-I
Hodgson,Lt.GF, KIFA 5Aug.18-III
Hodgson,Lt.RE, KIA 15Sep.18-I
Hodgson,Cpl.W, KIA 14Apr.17-I
Hodkinson,2Lt.L, KIA 14Sep.17-I
Hodson,Lt.G, 31Jul.18-III
Hodson,Lt.GF, 7Jun.18-III
Hodson,Lt.GS, 10Mar.18-I, 18Sep.18-I
Hogan,Lt.PL, WIA 8Apr.17-I
Hogarth,2Lt.FG, WIA 23Jul.16-I
Hogg,2Lt.A, WIA 5Oct.18-I
Hogg,Lt.AW, WIA 9Jun.17-I
Hogg,Maj.RET, 22Jun.15-V
Hogg,Lt.W, 29Aug.18-I
Hogg,Lt.WB, KIA 4Sep.18-I
Hoidge,Capt.RTC, Can. 28Jul.17-I, 29Oct.18-I
Hoidge,Lt.RTC, 27Jul.17-I
Holbrook,Lt.CM, POW 18Sep.18-I
Holbrow,Lt., 2Sqn. 1Sep.14-I
Holcroft,FSLt.AB, WIA POW 24Jun.17-I
Holden,Lt., 107Sqn. 11Jul.18-I
Holden,2Lt.A, POW 11Mar.17-I
Holden,2Lt.EB, 8Oct.18-I
Holden,Lt.LH, Aust. MC 20Nov.17-I, 23Nov.17-I, 28Mar.18-I
Holden,1AM.W, POW 28Dec.15-I
Holder,2Lt.FD, 31Jul.16-I, 7Sep.16-I
Holder,Lt.PV, 23Aug.18-I
Holding,2Lt.B, WIA 22Apr.18-I
Holdsworth,2Lt.E, KIA 23Sep.17-I
Holiday,Lt.RA, KIA 3May.18-I
Holland,FSLt.A, 14Oct.17-III
Holland,2Lt.,Capt.C, 17Sep.16-I, WIA 18Mar.17-I
Holland,2Lt.CB, WIA POW 11Apr.17-I
Holland,Lt.EV, POW 5Sep.18-I
Holland,2Lt.,Lt.JH, 25Jan.18-I, 1Apr.18-I, 11Jun.18-I, WIA 16Jun.18-I
Holland,Cpl.PH, KIA 10May.17-I
Holland,Capt.SH, 8Oct.18-IV
Holland,2Lt.VJ, MC WIA 9Jun.17-I
Holland,Capt.WTF, WIA 27Jun.17-I
Holleran,2Lt.,Capt.OC, US.? WIA 28Jun.18-I, POW 15Sep.18-I
Holley,Lt.TG, WIA POW 2Feb.17-I
Hollick,Lt.J, 6May.18-I, KIA 18May.18-I
Holliday,Lt.FP, 9May.17-I
Holliday,2Lt.JO, WIA 12Apr.18-I
Hollinghurst,2Lt.CS, WIA 13Sep.16-I
Hollinghurst,Lt.LN, 6Jul.18-I
Hollings,2Lt.H, KIA 28Aug.18-I
Hollingworth,Lt.A, 9May.17-I
Hollingsworth,2Lt.,Lt.AD, 23Aug.18-I, 16Sep.18-I
Hollingsworth,2Lt.FE, KIA 15Sep.16-I
Hollingsworth,2Lt.PC, WIA 26Jan.17-I
Hollingsworth,Lt.RL, POW 31Jul.18-I
Hollis,2Lt.A, POW 26Mar.18-I
Hollis,Lt.JA, POW 20Dec.16-I
Hollis,Sgt.JK, WIA POW 22Apr.17-I
Holman,Lt.GC, KIA 17Sep.17-I
Holman,Pbr.HG, WIA POW 16May.18-I
Holman,2Lt.L, WIA POW 24May.17-I
Holme,2Lt.McL, 17Jun.15-I
Holme,Capt.RCL, MC 29Sep.18-I
Holmes,2Lt.A, KIA 4Feb.18-I
Holmes,2Lt.CWD, POW 14Apr.17-I
Holmes,Lt.DW, KIA 30Oct.18-I
Holmes,Lt.HW, WIA 25Apr.18-I
Holmes,2Lt.JA, 2Sep.18-I, WIA 23Oct.18-I
Holmes,Lt.JCH, KIA 9Nov.18-I
Holmes,2Lt.JDV, POW 18May.17-I
Holmes,Lt.KW, Aust. KIA 11Aug.17-I
Holmes,Lt.TG, KIA 6May.17-I
Holmes,Sgt.WN, 17Mar.18-I
Holoway,2Lt.CE, KIA 11Aug.17-I
Holroyde,2Lt.JS, KIA 10May.17-I
Holt,Lt., 6Sqn. 8Aug.18-I
Holt,Capt., 7Sqn. 19Sep.15-I, 11Oct.15-I
Holt,Capt.FV, 22Jan.15-I
Holt,Lt.HG, MC KIA 6Oct.17-I
Holt,2Lt.JL, KIA 17Mar.18-I
Holt,Capt.WP, KIA 24Jun.17-I
Holthom,2Lt.JN, KIA 22Oct.16-I
Holthouse,2Lt.AR, KIA 10Apr.18-I
Home-Hay,Capt.JB, MC DFC POW 22Aug.18-I
Homer,Sgt.E, WIA 8Aug.18-I
Homersham,Lt.AJ, KIA 18Feb.18-I
Hone,Lt.JA, 17Aug.17-I
Honer,2Lt.DJ, KIA 4Jun.17-I
Honeyman,2Lt.HTA, KIA 10Dec.17-I
Hood,Lt.H, WIA 24Aug.18-I
Hood,Lt.J, KIA 18Aug.17-I
Hood,2Lt.RP, 5Aug.17-I, KIA 28Sep.17-I
Hood,FSLt.TSS, KIA 25Apr.17-I
Hoogterp,Lt.JA, 21Jul.18-I
Hooker,1AM., 10Sqn. 25Feb.16-I, 9Apr.16-I
Hooker,Lt.HG, 25Apr.18-I, WIA 7May.18-I
Hookway,2AM.,1AM.S, 12Aug.17-I, WIA 12Nov.17-I
Hookway,Sgt.S, KIA? 16Sep.18-I
Hooper,Capt.GH, Aust. 25Sep.18-I
Hooper,1Lt.P, USAS. KIA 10Jun.18-I
Hooper,1Lt.TD, US. WIA POW 18Sep.18-IIB
Hooten,2Lt., 8Sqn. 23Mar.18-I
Hooton,2Lt.LC, 27Mar.18-I, 7Apr.18-I, WIA 27May.18-I
Hooton,Sgt.T, 23Aug.18-I
Hopcroft,SLt.,FLt.EG, 20Mar.16-I, 23Mar.16-I, 26Sep.17-I
Hope,Lt.AT, 19Mar.17-I
Hope,Lt.HBT, KIA 26Apr.17-I
Hope,FLt.WH, POW DoW 23Nov.16-I
Hopewell,FSLt.DC, POW 7Apr.18-I
Hopgood,2Lt.FJ, POW 10Apr.18-I
Hopkins,Lt., 12Sqn. 29Sep.18-I
Hopkins,Pte., RNAS. INT? 2Oct.18-III

Hopkins,1Lt.AL, *US.* **WIA** 18Oct.18-*IIB*
Hopkins,Lt.F, **KIA** 1Oct.18-*I*
Hopkins,2Lt.GM, 3Apr.18-*I*, **POW** 26Apr.17-*I*
Hopkins,2Lt.JR, 12Oct.16-*I*
Hopkins,2Lt.ST, *US.* **KIA** 13Sep.18-*IIB*
Hopper,Sgt.F, 21Sep.17-*I*, **WIA** 6Dec.17-*I*
Hopper,2Lt.RW, **POW** 8Oct.18-*I*
Hopton,2Lt.HW, **DoW** 12.8.1918 10Aug.18-*I*
Hopwood,Capt.RG, **KIA** 24Aug.16-*I*
Horan,Lt., *111Sqn.* **WIA** 24Nov.17-*VII*
Hore,Lt.CA, MC **WIA** 22Mar.18-*I*
Hore,2Lt.CH, 12Mar.18-*I*
Horlock,Lt.AG, **WIA**, *name* Harlock? 1Apr.18-*I*
Horn,2Lt., *7Sqn.* 19Dec.15-*I*
Horn,2Lt.EE, **KIA** 4Mar.17-*I*
Horn,Lt.SB, 2May.17-*I*
Horncastle,2Lt.LH, MC **KIA** 20May.17-*I*
Horne,Lt.HGH, **KIA** 13Apr.17-*I*
Horne,2Lt.JL, 1Mar.18-*I*
Horner,2Lt.KC, **DoW** 4Apr.17-*I*
Horry,Lt.TS, DFC 6Nov.18-*I*, 10Nov.18-*I*
Horsbrough?,2Lt., *7Sqn.* 19Dec.15-*I*
Horsfall,Capt.ED, 29Dec.15-*I*, 19Feb.16-*I*
Horsfall,2Lt.GR, **WIA** 3Oct.17-*I*, **KIA** 20Nov.17-*I*
Horsfield,Lt.HT, 16Oct.16-*I*
Horsley,Capt.WP, MC **KIA** 2Jul.17-*I*
Horton,Capt.GD, **KIA** 31May.18-*I*
Hoskier,Sgt.R, **KIA** 23Apr.17-*IIA*
Hosking,Lt.CG, **KIA** 26Oct.14-*I*
Hosking,2Lt.T, *Aust.* **KIA** 28Mar.18-*I*
Hoskins,2Lt.GC, **KIA** 11Mar.17-*I*
Hostetter,Lt.TR, *US.* **WIA** 11Apr.18-*I*, **KIA** 27Sep.18-*I*
Hough,FSLt.JEC, **KIA** 24Oct.17-*I*
Houghton,2Lt.DL, **POW** 29Apr.17-*I*
Houghton,1Lt.E, *US.* **WIA** 24Oct.18-*IIB*
Houghton,2Lt.J, **WIA** 25Jan.17-*I*
Houlgrave,2Lt.C, **POW** 9Oct.18-*I*
Houston,Lt.CT, 5Jul.18-*I*, **WIA** 22Jul.18-*I*
Houston,2Lt.WD, **KIA** 27Aug.18-*I*
Houston-Stewart,FSLt.W, **KIA** 26May.17-*I*
Howard,Lt., *6Sqn.* 24Aug.18-*I*
Howard,Lt.EF, MC 23May.18-*I*
Howard,2Lt.,Lt.F, *Aust.* **WIA** 15Aug.18-*I*, **KIA** 27Oct.18-*I*
Howard,2Lt.S, *Aust.* 8Aug.18-*I*
Howard,2Lt.GEC, **KIA** 26Sep.18-*I*
Howard,Capt.GR, 22Sep.18.3Sep.16-*I*
Howard,2Lt.GR, *88Sqn.* **POW** 14Aug.18-*I*
Howard,Lt.GV, 4Oct.18-*I*
Howard,2Lt.HS, 24Aug.18-*I*
Howard,2Lt.JK, **KIA** 11Feb.17-*I*
Howard,2Lt.JW, **KIA** 26Sep.18-*I*
Howard,Lt.ML, **DoW** 25Jul.18-*I*
Howard,2Lt.RS, *see* Haward 25Sep.18-*I*
Howard,Lt.,Capt.RW, *Aust.* MC 16Oct.17-*I*, 22Nov.17-*I*, 29Nov.17-*I*, **DoW** 22Mar.18-*I*
Howard,2Lt.S, *Aust.* 8Aug.18-*I*
Howard,1Lt.SC, *US.* 26Sep.18-*IIB*, 10Oct.18-*IIB*
Howard-Brown,Lt.J, **WIA** 1Sep.18-*I*
Howarth,2Lt.N, 7Feb.16-*I*, 8Feb.16-*I*
Howarth,Capt.N, **KIA** 6Sep.18-*I*
Howarth,2Lt.N, **WIA inj**? 18Sep.18-*IV*
Howarth,2Lt.W, **WIA** 23May.17-*I*
Howden,2Lt.WA, **KIA** 9Nov.18-*I*
Howe,2Lt.G, **WIA** 11Mar.17-*I*
Howe,2Lt.HB, **inj** 20May.17-*I*
Howe,2Lt.,Lt.TS, MC 29Feb.16-*I*, 17Apr.18-*I*
Howe,Lt.TSC, MC **KIA** 17Apr.18-*I*
Howell,2Lt.,Lt.CE, *Aust.* 14Jan.18-*IV*, 8Jun.18-*IV*
Howell,2Lt.HA, **WIA** 9Sep.16-*I*
Howell,2Lt.JG, 11May.18-*I*
Howell-Evans,Lt.H, **KIA** 5Apr.17-*I*
Howell-Jones,Lt.AC, **WIA** 19May.18-*I*
Howells,2Lt.EL, **KIA** 23Oct.18-*I*
Howells,2Lt.GJ, **KIA** 23Nov.17-*I*
Howells,2Lt.JW, **WIA** 23Jul.17-*VII*
Howes,2Lt.EMcH, **WIA** 26Feb.17-*VI*
Howes,Lt.WH, **POW** 9Aug.17-*I*
Howett,Capt.JR, 5Feb.16-*I*, **inj** 9Mar.16-*I*, 14Mar.16-*I*
Howey,Lt.JEP, 26Oct.15-*I*, 4Nov.15-*I*, 5Nov.15-*I*, **WIA POW** 11Nov.15-*I*

Howie,2Lt.KWI, **inj** 13Oct.18-*I*
Howitt,Lt.DH, **WIA** 1Jul.18-*I*
Howitt,Lt.FD, **WIA** 19Jan.18-*I*
Howitt,Lt.FW, 6Jan.18-*I*
Howles,Lt.LGW, 21Sep.18-*I*
Howlett,Sgt.FA, 17Mar.17-*I*
Howsam,2Lt.GR, *Can.* 28Dec.17-*I*, **WIA** 24Mar.18-*I*
Howse,TLt.CA,2Jun.18-*I*
Howson,2Lt.CJ, 29Jan.18-*I*
Hoy,Lt.CA, **inj** 25May.17-*I*, 27Jul.17-*I*, 8Aug.17-*I*
Hoy,Capt.EC, *Can.* DFC 26Sep.18-*I*, **POW** 28Sep.18-*I*
Hoyles,2Lt.AHC, **KIA** 2Dec.17-*I*
Hubbard,Maj.TO'B, 2Apr.16-*I*
Hubbard,Lt.WH, *3Sqn. Can.* **WIA** 21Aug.18-*I*, 27Aug.18-*I*, 5Sep.18-*I*
Hubbard,2Lt.,Lt.WH, *5Sqn.* 9Sep.16-*I*, **WIA** 26Dec.16-*I*
Hubbard,Capt.WH, DFC *73Sqn.* 11Jun.18-*I*, 27Sep.18-*I*
Hucklebridge,2Lt.EC, 21Mar.18-*I*
Hudd,Lt.RS, 7Jun.17-*I*
Hudson,Lt., *18Sqn.* 16Feb.18-*I*
Hudson,Capt.AR, **POW** 16Aug.17-*I*
Hudson,1Lt.D, *US.* 1Aug.18-*IIB*
Hudson,Lt.FD, **PoW DoW** 6Apr.18-*I*
Hudson,Lt.FH, **INT** 11Apr.18-*I*
Hudson,2Lt.FJD, **KIA** 21May.18-*I*
Hudson,2Lt.,Capt.FN, MC 19Jan.16-*I*, 25Jan.16-*I*, 7Feb.16-*I*, **WIA** 21Feb.16-*I*, **POW** 13Jul.17-*I*
Hudson,2Lt.FR, **WIA** 17Mar.17-*I*
Hudson,Lt.G, 18May.18-*I*
Hudson,2Lt.HB, *Can.* 12Feb.18-*IV*
Hudson,1Lt.HB, *US.* **KIA** 5Oct.18-*IIB*
Hudson,Lt.HK, **KIA** 8Aug.18-*I*
Hudson,2Lt.HS, 23Aug.18-*I*
Hudson,2Lt.LW, 1Sep.18-*I*, 24Sep.18-*I*
Hudson,2Lt.RJ, 23Aug.16-*I*, 27Aug.16-*I*
Hudson,2Lt.TJ, **KIA** 20May.17-*I*
Huggard,2Lt.JC, **POW** 5Sep.17-*I*
Hughes,2Lt.A, 21Jul.16-*I*, **WIA** 30Jul.16-*I*
Hughes,Lt.AB, **WIA** 27May.18-*I*
Hughes,FSLt.AM, 20Mar.16-*I*
Hughes,Lt.DJ, 4Sep.18-*I*
Hughes,Lt.EY, 1Dec.17-*I*
Hughes,2Lt.GE, **POW** 21Sep.18-*IV*
Hughes,2Lt.GJ, **WIA** 25Apr.18-*I*
Hughes,Capt.GF, *Aust.* 21Feb.18-*I*
Hughes,Sgt.HF, *Aust.* **KIA** 17Dec.17-*I*
Hughes,Lt.HR, **WIA** 12Aug.18-*I*
Hughes,2Lt.JL, **KIA** 1Oct.17-*I*
Hughes,2Lt.JM, **KIA** 16Jun.18-*I*
Hughes,Lt.RD, **POW** 1Sep.18-*I*
Hughes,2Lt.SH, 16Oct.18-*I*
Hughes,2AM.T, **WIA POW** 10Aug.17-*I*
Hughes,Lt.TMcK, 7Sep.15-*I*, **KIA** 5Feb.18-*I*
Hughes,2Lt.V, 31May.17-*I*
Hughes,Lt.VH, 16Aug.17-*I*
Hughes,Lt.W, 7May.18-*I*
Hughes-Chamberlain,2Lt.,Lt.JLMdeC, 14Jan.16-*I*, 20Jan.16-*I*, 31Mar.16-*I*, 2Apr.16-*I*, **WIA** 27Jul.17-*I*
Hughes-Chamberlain,2Lt.R, *initials* REAW? 23Sep.15-*I*
Hughes-Chamberlain,Capt.REAW, **WIA** 16Aug.16-*I*
Hughes-Hallett,Capt.HH, 8Nov.14-*I*, **WIA** 19Nov.14-*I*
Hughesden,Sgt.A, **KIA** 17Feb.18-*I*
Hughey,1Lt.PJ, *US.* **WIA** 14Sep.18-*IIB*
Hugill,2Lt.V, **KIA** 16Oct.16-*I*
Hulme,2Lt.B, **POW** .18-*I*
Humble,Sgt.G, **POW** 29Apr.17-*I*
Humble,2Lt.T, **POW** 19Sep.17-*I*
Hume,Lt.R, **KIA** 6Apr.17-*I*
Hume,2Lt.RC, **POW** 28Jul.17-*I*
Hume,2Lt.SS, **POW** 27May.17-*I*
Hummerstone,Lt.LG, **KIA** 21Aug.18-*I*
Humphrey,Pte.AE, **WIA** 29Jul.18-*I*
Humphrey,2Lt.EG, **WIA** 22Jul.17-*I*, **WIA** 13Mar.18-*I*, **WIA** 28Mar.18-*I*
Humphreys,2Lt.Dd'H, **WIA** 22Oct.17-*I*
Humphreys,Lt.GN, 30Oct.14-*I*, 9Mar.15-*I*, **POW** 20Mar.15-*I*

Humphreys,Lt.GN, **WIA**, *name* JN Humphries? 18Nov.14-*I*
Humphreys,2Lt.TA, **KIA** 3May.18-*I*
Humphries,2Lt.LG, **KIA** 16Sep.17-*I*
Humphries?,Lt.JN, *see* Humphreys?
Hunnisett,Pte.EE, **KIA** 30Jun.18-*I*
Hunt,Lt.BPG, **WIA POW** 11Dec.16-*I*
Hunt,2Lt.CB, **KIA** 25Apr.18-*I*
Hunt,2Lt.EWA, **KIA** 1May.17-*I*
Hunt,Lt.FJ, 22Sep.18-*I*
Hunt,Lt.HH, **KIA** 26Oct.18-*I*
Hunt,1Lt.JS, *US.* **KIA** 1Aug.18-*IIB*
Hunt,2Lt.KF, **POW** 22Sep.16-*I*
Hunt,Lt.KP, **POW** 18May.18-*I*
Hunt,Capt.REB, 13Jul.15-*I*, **INT** 21Jul.15-*I*
Hunt,2Lt.WV, **DoW** 17.10.1918 14Oct.18-*I*
Hunter,Lt.DY, **KIA** 7Jul.18-*I*
Hunter,1Lt.FO'D, *US.* **WIA** 21Jun.18-*IIB*
Hunter,Lt.GA, **WIA** 4May.18-*I*
Hunter,2Lt.GD, **WIA POW** 6May.17-*I*
Hunter,Lt.HC, **WIA POW** 19May.18-*I*
Hunter,FLt.,Capt.JEL, DFC 3Sep.17-*I*, 22Sep.17-*I*, **WIA** 12Aug.18-*I*
Hunter,2Lt.JL, *Can.* **WIA** 13Sep.18-*I*
Hunter,2Lt.RF, **WIA**? 27Sep.18-*I*
Hunter,2Lt.SJ, 6Mar.18-*I*
Hunter,Lt.TV, 12Jul.17-*I*
Hunter,2Lt.WA, *19Sqn.* **WIA** 9Jun.18-*I*
Hunter,2Lt.WA, *42Sqn.* **WIA** 27May.17-*I*
Hunter,Lt.WA, *US. 54Sqn.* **WIA** 3Jun.18-*I*
Hupper,AG.Sgt., *25Sqn.* **WIA** 5Feb.18-*I*
Hurdus,2Lt.R, **WIA** 13Sep.18-*I*
Hurley,2Lt.A, **WIA** 20Jun.17-*I*
Hurley,1AM.JV, **KIA** 23Aug.17-*I*
Hurr,2Lt.DF, **WIA** 17Feb.18-*I*
Hurrell,2Lt.WG, 26Mar.18-*I*
Hurst,2Lt.CF, 13Jul.18-*I*
Hurst,Lt.GR, 21Aug.18-*I*
Hurst,2Lt.HB, 20Dec.16-*I*
Hursthouse,2Lt.,Capt.LF, **WIA** 10Aug.16-*VII*, **WIA** 30Oct.18-*IV*
Huskinson,Capt.P, MC 15Nov.17-*I*, 6Jan.18-*I*
Huston,Lt.VH, 17Mar.17-*I*
Hustwitt,Lt.SA, **POW** 6May.18-*I*
Hutcheson,Capt., *18Sqn.* 19Jan.16-*I*
Hutcheson,2Lt.GJ, **WIA** 25Apr.18-*I*
Hutcheson,Lt.WB, 17Jun.17-*I*, **POW** 21Aug.17-*I*
Hutchins,2Lt.J, 5Oct.16-*VI*
Hutchinson,Lt.A, **KIA** 19Jan.18-*I*
Hutchinson,2Lt.CD, **PoW DoW** 12.8.1917 10Aug.17-*I*
Hutchinson,2Lt.WJ, **POW** 31Jul.18-*I*
Hutchison,Lt.FF, 16Mar.18-*I*
Hutson,TLt.PG, **WIA** 30Oct.18-*I*
Hutt,Sgt.RS, 9Aug.18-*I*
Hutton,Lt.HM, 19May.18-*I*
Huxley,Lt.FG, *Aust.* 22Nov.17-*I*
Hyam,Lt.WR, *Aust.* **DoW** 30.3.17 28Mar.17-*VII*
Hyatt,2Lt.V, **KIA** 24Mar.18-*I*
Hyde,Lt.AN, 21Aug.18-*I*, **KIA** 21Sep.18-*I*
Hyde,2Lt.C, *US.* **KIA** 1Dec.17-*I*
Hyde,Lt.CW, 16Nov.16-*I*
Hyde,2Lt.,Lt.EL, **WIA** 25Sep.15-*I*, **WIA** 8Apr.17-*I*
Hyde,2Lt.EP, 11Feb.17-*V*, **POW** 22Mar.17-*VI*
Hyde,Capt.F, 20Apr.18-*I*
Hyde,2Lt.FdeM, 27Sep.18-*I*
Hyde,Lt.HE, **POW** 16Sep.18-*I*
Hyland,2Lt.FH, **DoW** 23May.15-*I*
Hynes,2Lt.ESP, **KIA** 10Nov.16-*I*
Hyslop,2Lt.JB, **WIA** 23Aug.18-*I*

I

Iaccaci,Capt.AT, *US.* 6Sep.18-*I*
Iaccaci,Lt.PT, *US.* 6Sep.18-*I*
Ibbotson,2Lt.F, **WIA** 8Aug.18-*I*
Ibbotson,2Lt.H, **POW** 15Sep.17-*I*
Ibbotson,Lt.A, 2Sep.18-*I*, 17Sep.18-*I*
Ibison,2Lt.KG, **KIA** 4Oct.18-*I*
Iliff,2Lt.G, **KIA** 25Sep.18-*I*
Illingworth,2Lt.,Lt.CFW, 8Aug.18-*I*, **POW** 9Aug.18-*I*

Illingworth,2Lt.FW, **WIA POW** 7Jun.17-*I*
Illsley,Lt.HP, *34Sqn.* **KIA** 23Apr.17-*I*
Illsley,Lt.HP, *52Sqn.* 30May.18-*I*
Imeretinsky,Lt.CG, 8Aug.18-*I*, **WIA** 24Aug.18-*I*
Imes,2Lt.TW, *USAS.* **WIA** 21Aug.18-*I*
Impey,2Lt., *6Sqn.* 19Oct.15-*I*
Ince,FSLt.AS, 14Dec.15-*I*
Ingalls,1Lt.DS, *USNRF* 25Sep.18-*I*
Inge,Lt.RM, **POW** 6May.16-*III*
Ingham,FSLt.JM, **KIA** 30Mar.17-*VI*
Inglefield,Lt.JP, **WIA** 18Nov.15-*I*
Ingleson,FSLt.W, **POW** 26Sep.17-*I*
Inglis,Capt.AG, **POW** 5Oct.18-*I*
Inglis,Lt.DC, *NZ.* 26Jul.18-*I*, 31Aug.18-*I*
Inglis,2Lt.RA, **KIA** 21Sep.17-*I*
Inglis,2Lt.WL, **KIA** 2Oct.17-*I*
Ingram,2Lt.LJW, **POW** 23Jun.18-*I*
Ingram,Capt.RSS, **POW** 18Aug.18-*I*
Ingram,2Lt.RT, **KIA** 3Sep.18-*I*
Ings,AM.JC, 15Sep.18-*IV*
Inman,2Lt.H, **POW** 11Apr.18-*I*
Insall,2Lt.AJ, 23Aug.15-*I*, 31Aug.15-*I*, 4Sep.15-*I*, 5Sep.15-*I*, 8Sep.15-*I*, 9Sep.15-*I*, 26Nov.15-*I*, 13Dec.15-*I*, 2Apr.16-*I*
Insall,2Lt.,Lt.GSM, VC 6Sep.15-*I*, 2Oct.15-*I*, 7Nov.15-*I*, **WIA POW** 14Dec.15-*I*
Insoll,FSLt.FN, **POW** 26Dec.16-*I*
Ireland,2AM.R, **KIA**? 5Feb.18-*I*
Ireland,AG.2AM.R **WIA** 28Dec.17-*I*
Irons,2Lt.TR, 2Jul.16-*I*
Irvine,Lt.VRvT, *US.* **KIA** 19Jul.18-*I*
Irvine,2Lt.WM, 21Mar.18-*I*, **KIA** 22Mar.18-*I*
Irving,2Lt.,Capt.GB, 21Apr.18-*I*, **KIA** 11Aug.18-*I*
Irving,2Lt.GG, 9Mar.18-*I*
Irving,2Lt.HV, 5Nov.18-*I*
Irving,2Lt.JL, **WIA** 6Oct.18-*I*
Irving,FSLt.LH, 9Jul.16-*I*
Irwin,2Lt.ACS, **WIA** 27Jul.17-*I*
Irwin,Sgt.B, **KIA**? 17Sep.16-*I*
Irwin,Lt.RV, **POW** 28Jul.18-*I*
Irwin,Capt.WR, *Can.* 3Sep.18-*I*, **WIA** 15Sep.18-*I*
Isaac,Lt.KJ, **WIA** 22Aug.18-*I*
Isaac,2Lt.WA, **WIA** 7Aug.18-*I*
Isaacs,2Lt.JB, **POW** 30Oct.18-*IV*
Isaacs,Sgt.JL, 8Oct.18-*I*
Isbell,Lt.AT, **WIA POW** 31Mar.18-*I*
Islip,Lt.FJ, 9May.18-*I*
Ivamy,2Lt.WG, **WIA** 18Jan.18-*I*, **POW** 18Mar.18-*I*
Ivens,2Lt.JC, **POW** 12Aug.18-*I*
Ivermere,2Lt.RWA, **WIA** 7Jun.18-*III*

J

Jack,2Lt.RLM, **DoW** 27.2.1917 26Feb.17-*I*
Jacklin,2Lt.W, **WIA** 26May.18-*I*
Jackman,2Lt.JR, **POW DoW** 17Jun.18-*I*
Jacks,2Lt.M, 31Jul.15-*I*, 7Oct.15-*I*, 27Nov.15-*I*
Jackson,Lt., *Sqn?* **INT** 21Jul.18-*I*
Jackson,Lt.CRH, **KIA** 16Aug.18-*IV*
Jackson,Lt.FH, **WIA INT** 21Jul.15-*I*
Jackson,2Lt.FJ, **KIA** 14Oct.18-*I*
Jackson,2Lt.FT, **WIA** 25Mar.18-*I*
Jackson,2Lt.FX, **KIA** 21Sep.18-*I*
Jackson,Lt.GG, **POW** 18Feb.18-*I*
Jackson,2Lt.GW, **KIA** 7May.17-*I*
Jackson,Capt.H, **DoW** 7Jun.17-*I*
Jackson,2Lt.HAB, **DoW** 25Jun.18-*I*
Jackson,2Lt.HG, **WIA** 9May.18-*I*
Jackson,2Lt.HH, *USAS.* **KIA** 26Aug.18-*I*
Jackson,2Lt.,Lt.HM, 31May.17-*I*, **KIA** 18Jun.17-*I*
Jackson,2Lt.JB, **KIA** 7Jun.17-*I*
Jackson,2Lt.JL, **WIA** 10May.15-*I*
Jackson,Lt.RW, **WIA** 16Aug.18-*I*
Jackson,2Lt.TG, 24Apr.18-*I*
Jackson,Capt.WD, **INT** 19Jul.18-*III*
Jackson,2Lt.WE, *32Sqn. Can.* **POW** 10Aug.18-*I*
Jackson,2Lt.WE, *104Sqn.* **DoW** 15Sep.18-*I*
Jackson,2Lt.WJ, **KIA** 30Oct.18-*I*
Jackson,2Lt.WR, **POW** 30Aug.18-*I*
Jacob,2Lt.GH, **WIA** 11Apr.17-*I*
Jacot,2Lt.E, **KIA** 6Jun.17-*I*

Jacques,2Lt.TH, KIA 30Sep.18-*I*
James,Cpl., *3Sqn.* 19Jan.16-*I*
James,Lt.AR, POW? 24Mar.18-*I*
James,Lt.AWH, 14Dec.15-*I*, 19Dec.15-*I*, 17Jan.16-*I*, 19Jan.16-*I*
James,2Lt.BG, 26Jul.15-*I*, WIA 31Aug.15-*I*, KIA 26Sep.15-*I*
James,Capt.BT, 6Jul.15-*I*, KIA 13Jul.15-*I*
James,Capt.BT?, *6Sqn.* 9May.15-*I*
James,Capt.CEH, 21Apr.16-*I*, POW 21May.16-*I*
James,2Lt.,Lt.,Capt.HH, 31Aug.15-*I*, WIA 31Jul.17-*I*, WIA 22Oct.18-*IV*
James,Sgt.L, KIA 27Jun.18-*I*
James,Lt.LR, POW 29Sep.18-*I*
James,2Lt.ML, WIA 17Apr.18-*I*
James,Lt.MR, *Can.* 20Jul.18-*IV*, 31Aug.18-*IV*
James,AGL.L, 18Mar.18-*I*
James,Capt.RA, KIA 16Jul.18-*I*
James,Lt.WFT, WIA 5Jan.17-*I*
Jameson,2Lt.H, MC KIA 5Jan.17-*I*
Jameson,2Lt.J, 11May.17-*I*
Jameson,Lt.JB, 13Aug.18-*I*, DoW 24Aug.18-*I*
Jameson,FLt.WC, POW 12Feb.17-*V*
Jamieson,FSLt.CW, INT 25Aug.16-*I*
Jamieson,2Lt.WI, WIA 12Aug.17-*VII*
Jannopulo,2Lt.RS, *US.* WIA 27Sep.18-*IIB*
Jardine,Capt.DGB, KIA 5Aug.18-*III*
Jardine,Lt.DGE, 4Sep.17-*I*
Jardine,2Lt.RG, 16Jul.17-*I*
Jardine,Lt.RG, KIA 20Jul.17-*I*
Jarvis,Capt.AB, KIA 10Aug.17-*I*
Jarvis,Capt.LW, 12Apr.18-*I*
Jarvis,Lt.AEdeM, 25Apr.18-*VI*
Jarvis,Lt.RH, 7Sep.16-*I*, 14Sep.16-*I*
Jay,2Lt.TW, WIA POW 19Mar.17-*I*
Jeans,Lt.WD, WIA 27Jun.18-*I*
Jeff,2Lt.RNW, 20May.17-*I*, POW 11Aug.17-*I*
Jefferd,Capt.WW, POW 10Jul.16-*I*
Jeffers,2Lt.,Lt.JP, *Aust.* 11Aug.18-*I*, KIA 19Aug.18-*I*
Jeffery,Lt.HG, *Can.* KIA 5Jul.18-*I*
Jeffery,Lt.RE, KIA 25May.17-*I*
Jeffkins,2Lt.EC, POW 16Sep.18-*I*
Jeffreys,Lt.F, 17Sep.18-*I*
Jeffs,Cpl.BGF, KIA 10Oct.16-*I*
Jeffs,2Lt.CH, POW 5Oct.17-*I*
Jellicoe,Lt.HV, 14Sep.18-*IV*, 22Oct.18-*IV*
Jenkin,Lt.,Capt.LF, MC 23May.17-*I*, 28Jul.17-*I*, KIA 11Sep.17-*I*
Jenkins,2Lt.AE, DoW 28Sep.18-*I*
Jenkins,2Lt.BP, POW DoW 16Sep.18-*I*
Jenkins,Capt.CH, DoW 23.5.1917 20May.17-*I*
Jenkins,Lt.GD, WIA 27Mar.18-*I*
Jenkins,2Lt.HF, WIA 24Oct.17-*I*
Jenkins,Capt.L, 7Feb.16-*I*
Jenkins,Lt.LF, 3Jun.17-*I*
Jenkins,Lt.NH, DSM WIA 27Jun.18-*I*
Jenkins,2Lt.RB, DoW 18.1.1916 17Jan.16-*I*
Jenkins,Lt.WE, 29Jul.17-*I*
Jenkins,Lt.WS, *Can.* 17Sep.18-*I*
Jenkins,2Lt.WWL, DoW 25Jun.18-*I*
Jenkinson,1Lt.H, *USAS.* 9Jun.18-*I*, 11Jun.18-*I*, KIA 20Sep.18-*I*
Jenks,Lt.AN, 8Jun.17-*I*, 21Sep.17-*I*
Jenks,SLt.JCA, POW 8Aug.17-*IX*
Jenner,Lt.PC, POW 28Sep.18-*I*
Jenner,Lt.WJP, WIA 3Oct.18-*I*
Jenning,Lt.MRM, 15Oct.17-*I*
Jennings,Capt.A, KIA 7Apr.17-*I*
Jennings,2Lt.ED, POW 30Apr.17-*I*
Jennings,2Lt.JE, POW 2Oct.18-*I*
Jennings,2Lt.JH, 15Apr.18-*I*, WIA 17Jun.18-*I*
Jenyns,2Lt.CG, WIA POW 26Jun.18-*I*
Jerome,1Lt.GN, *US.* KIA 11Jul.18-*IID*
Jerrard,Lt.A, WIA POW 30Mar.18-*IV*
Jervis,Lt.JC, KIA 26Oct.16-*I*
Jessop,Lt.AJ, KIA 12May.17-*I*
Jewett,1Lt.FF, *USAS.* POW 14Sep.18-*I*
Jewkes,2Lt.JL, WIA 6Apr.18-*I*
Jex,Sgt.A, POW 17Sep.18-*I*
Jillings,SgtMaj.DS, WIA 22Aug.14-*I*
Jinman,2Lt.EWF, KIA 14Aug.18-*I*
Joel,2Lt., *13Sqn.* 21Apr.16-*I*
Joerg,1Lt.AN, *US.* KIA 25Jul.18-*IIB*
Joffe,Lt.W, DSO KIA 1Oct.18-*I*
John,Lt.DM, 8Aug.18-*I*, inj INT 28Sep.18-*I*
John,2Lt.WA, KIA 1Aug.18-*I*
Johns,Pte.FJ, POW 5Oct.17-*I*
Johns,Lt.RAP, WIA POW 23May.17-*I*
Johns,Lt.TM, POW 31Oct.16-*I*
Johns,2Lt.WE, WIA POW 16Sep.18-*I*
Johnson,2Lt.,Lt., *13Sqn.* 15Dec.15-*I*, 17Jun.18-*I*
Johnson,Lt., *68Sqn. Aust.* 6Dec.17-*I*
Johnson,Cpl., *US. 104thUS* inj 12Sep.18-*IIB*
Johnson,2Lt.A, *Sqn.?* POW Jun.18-*I*
Johnson,2Lt.A, WIA 1Oct.18-*I*
Johnson,Pte.AJ, POW 28May.18-*I*
Johnson,1Lt.AT, *US.* KIA 12Sep.18-*IIB*
Johnson,2Lt.B, KIA 29Oct.18-*I*
Johnson,2Lt.C, 24Sep.18-*I*
Johnson,Sgt.CAF, WIA 16Jun.18-*I*
Johnson,1Lt.CG, *US.* KIA 23Oct.18-*IIB*
Johnson,2Lt.CL, *Aust.* WIA 21Oct.17-*I*
Johnson,Lt.CS, KIA 13Aug.18-*I*
Johnson,2Lt.DS, KIA 4Dec.16-*I*
Johnson,Lt.EH, KIA 9Nov.18-*I*
Johnson,Cpl.F, *22Sqn.* 30Sep.16-*I*
Johnson,Sgt.F, *20Sqn.* 17Feb.18-*I*
Johnson,Lt.FR, POW 16Sep.18-*I*
Johnson,Capt.GO, *Can.* 21Apr.18-*I*
Johnson,2Lt.HA, KIA 27Feb.17-*I*
Johnson,1Lt.HF, *US.* KIA 21May.18-*IID*
Johnson,Sgt.HN, WIA 25Jun.16-*I*
Johnson,2Lt.HR?, 10Oct.15-*I*
Johnson,Lt.JH, POW DoW 9Jun.18-*I*
Johnson,1Lt.JL, 10Oct.18-*IIB*
Johnson,2Lt.JT, WIA 20May.17-*I*, WIA 21Oct.17-*I*
Johnson,2Lt.JW, WIA 29Aug.18-*I*
Johnson,Capt.OCW, 11Jul.18-*I*, 25Jul.18-*I*
Johnson,Lt.OP, 4Sep.18-*I*
Johnson,2Lt.PCE, KIA 28Jan.17-*I*
Johnson,Lt.R, 27Oct.18-*I*
Johnson,2Lt.RH, 25Aug.16-*I*, WIA 2Sep.16-*I*
Johnson,Lt.RL, KIA 9May.18-*I*
Johnson,AM/WT., *RNAS.* 10th May.18-*III*
Johnson,2Lt.RW, KIA 1Oct.18-*I*
Johnson,Lt.TA, KIA 28Aug.18-*I*
Johnson,2Lt.WJ, POW DoW 28Sep.18-*I*
Johnson-Gilbert,Lt.IA, 22Oct.17-*I*
Johnston,2Lt.AG, WIA 6Oct.18-*I*
Johnston,2Lt.AR, KIA 24Apr.17-*I*
Johnston,Lt.BS, 9Nov.18-*I*
Johnston,2Lt.CH, 17Jan.16-*I*
Johnston,1Lt.D, *US.* KIA 12Sep.18-*IIB*
Johnston,Capt.EC, *Aust.* 3Oct.18-*I*
Johnston,Lt.HE, 16Sep.18-*I*, 24Sep.18-*I*
Johnston,Pte.J, KIA 19May.17-*I*
Johnston,Capt.JE, *20Sqn.* inj POW 2Dec.17-*I*
Johnston,2Lt.JE, *32Sqn.* WIA 5Oct.17-*I*
Johnston,FLt.,FCdr.PA, 12Jul.17-*I*, KIA 17Aug.17-*I*
Johnston,Lt.RE, inj 25May.17-*I*
Johnston,2Lt.TP, KIA 20May.17-*I*
Johnston,TFSLt.W, KIA 20Jan.18-*V*
Johnston,2Lt.WA, POW 14Sep.18-*I*
Johnstone,2Lt.BI, 24Mar.18-*I*
Johnstone,2Lt.DK, 21Feb.16-*I*
Johnstone,FSLt.EG, 3Feb.18-*I*
Johnstone,2Lt.GG, KIA 30Jan.18-*I*
Johnstone,2Lt.J, WIA POW 25May.17-*I*
Johnstone,2Lt.JA, KIA 20May.15-*I*
Johnstone,2Lt.M, KIA 5Apr.17-*I*
Johnstone,Cpl.R, *4Sqn.* KIA 8Jul.16-*I*
Johnstone,Capt.R, *82Sqn.* WIA 17Oct.18-*I*
Jones,Lt., *3Sqn.* 3May.17-*I*
Jones,Pte., *70Sqn.* 25Sep.16-*I*
Jones,2Lt.ADR, POW 23Jun.18-*I*
Jones,2AM.AH?, KIA? 8Apr.17-*I*
Jones,Capt.AM, MC *Aust.* WIA 16May.17-*VII*
Jones,Lt.AR, POW 19Jul.18-*I*
Jones,2Lt.AS, KIA 27Sep.18-*I*
Jones,2Lt.AV, WIA POW 10May.18-*I*
Jones,2Lt.BC, WIA 13Jul.17-*I*
Jones,2Lt.BHM, WIA 24Nov.16-*I*
Jones,2Lt.BR, KIA 28Sep.18-*I*
Jones,2Lt.C, 8Aug.15-*I*, 11Aug.15-*I*
Jones,Lt.,Capt.CN, WIA 1Nov.16-*I*, WIA 27Oct.17-*I*
Jones,Lt.DB, DCM DoW 3.7.1918? 27Jun.18-*I*
Jones,Cpl.,Sgt.E, 22Oct.15-*I*, POW 29Dec.15-*I*
Jones,1Lt.EB, *US.* KIA 13Sep.18-*IIB*
Jones,Lt.ED, *10Sqn.* KIA 2Apr.18-*I*
Jones,2Lt.ED, *52Sqn.* 26Mar.18-*I*, KIA 2Apr.18-*I*
Jones,2Lt.EE, 26Sep.18-*I*
Jones,2Lt.EH, WIA 24May.17-*I*
Jones,Capt.EJ, *Aust.* WIA 20May.18-*I*
Jones,2Lt.ETL, WIA 10Aug.17-*I*
Jones,2Lt.HA, WIA 20Aug.17-*VI*
Jones,2Lt.HE, DOW? 11Sep.17-*I*
Jones,2Lt.HV, 14Jul.17-*I*
Jones,Capt.HWG, MC 1Oct.16-*I*, WIA 15Feb.17-*I*, WIA 21Mar.17-*I*
Jones,2Lt.JH, 28Apr.17-*I*
Jones,2Lt.JHO, 30Mar.17-*I*
Jones,Lt.,Capt.JIT, 8May.18-*I*, 18Jun.18-*I*, 30Jul.18-*I*, 4Aug.18-*I*
Jones,Lt.JW, KIA 9Aug.18-*I*
Jones,2Lt.LE, WIA 24Mar.18-*I*
Jones,Capt.LH, *21Sqn.* 11Apr.18-*I*
Jones,2Lt.LH, *205Sqn.* WIA 16May.18-*I*
Jones,Capt.LH, *PFlt.* 6Nov.18-*I*
Jones,Lt.LN, WIA 6Mar.18-*I*, 26Sep.18-*I*, KIA 3Oct.18-*I*
Jones,2Lt.LSR, KIA 7Oct.18-*I*
Jones,Sgt.Mech.M, WIA 16Sep.18-*I*
Jones,Lt.MG, MC KIA 12Jun.18-*I*
Jones,Capt.NC, 21Aug.18-*IV*
Jones,Lt.NS, 22May.18-*I*
Jones,2Lt.O, WIA 24May.18-*I*
Jones,2Lt.PG, 29May.18-*I*, 1Jun.18-*I*, 30Jun.18-*I*, KIA 2Jul.18-*I*
Jones,LM.WA, POW 30Mar.17-*V*
Jones,Lt.RNK, WIA 18Oct.18-*I*
Jones,Capt.RT, WIA 15Sep.18-*I*
Jones,2Lt.S, *9Sqn.* WIA 6Mar.18-*I*
Jones,Lt.S, 22Jul.18-*I*
Jones,Capt.S, 25Sep.18-*I*
Jones,AG.S, *206Sqn.* WIA 23Apr.18-*I*
Jones,2Lt.SHF, WIA 5Jul.18-*I*
Jones,Sgt.T, 16Sep.16-*I*, inj DoW 29.9.1916 22Sep.16-*I*
Jones,2Lt.TA, KIA 30Aug.18-*I*
Jones,2Lt.,Capt.TB, WIA 24Dec.16-*I*, KIA 11Apr.18-*I*
Jones,2Lt.TL, 2Sep.18-*I*
Jones,2Lt.TPT, 16Oct.18-*I*
Jones,Lt.W, 19Sep.17-*I*, WIA 26Sep.17-*I*
Jones,2Lt.WE, *23Sqn.* 4Mar.17-*I*
Jones,Sgt.WE, *211Sqn.* MM POW 28Sep.18-*I*
Jones,2Lt.WH, 22Sep.17-*I*, POW 24Oct.17-*I*
Jones,SgtMech.CJEJ, WIA 6Sep.18-*I*
Jones,AG.S, WIA 23Apr.18-*I*
Jones,AGL.TW, WIA 30Mar.18-*I*
Jones,2Lt.WR, 16Nov.17-*I*
Jones,2Lt.WW, 24Mar.18-*I*
Jones-Evans,Lt.GS, *Can.* WIA 28Jul.18-*I*
Jones-Lloyd,Lt.OJF, POW 25Jun.18-*I*
Jones-Williams,Capt.A, 7Sep.18-*I*
Jonsson,Lt.H, MC KIA 3Sep.18-*I*
Jordan,1Lt.JW, *US.* WIA 11Aug.18-*IIB*
Jordan,Lt.WH, 9Oct.18-*I*
Jordan,FSLt.WL, 28Jun.17-*I*, WIA 24Sep.17-*I*, 28Dec.17-*I*, 19Jan.18-*I*, 18Feb.18-*I*
Jordan,2Lt.WT, *name* Jourdan? 20Oct.16-*I*, inj 14Feb.17-*I*
Joseph,TCapt.,Capt.SC, DFC DSC 6Sep.18-*I*, WIA 24Sep.18-*I*, 30Oct.18-*I*
Joseph,Capt.WE, 25Jul.18-*I*, WIA? 1Oct.18-*I*
Joske,2Lt.CB, 29Feb.16-*I*, 12Mar.16-*I*
Joslyn,Lt.HW, *Can.* 17Jun.17-*I*, 27Jul.17-*I*, KIA 17Aug.17-*I*
Joubert de la Ferte,2Lt.JC, INT 21Mar.15-*I*
Joubert de la Ferte,Capt.PB, 19Aug.14-*I*
Jourdan,2Lt.WT, *see* Jordan
Jowett,Lt.EC, KIA 8Jul.16-*I*
Joy,Maj.EG, 28Jul.17-*I*, 17Aug.17-*I*, 4Nov.18-*I*
Joyce,2Lt.NR, KIA 1Apr.18-*I*
Joyce,2Lt.,Lt.PS, 2Nov.16-*I*, KIA 6Mar.17-*I*
Joyce,Lt.WJ, WIA POW 30Mar.16-*I*
Joysey,Sgt.RS, 12Jun.18-*I*, POW 29Sep.18-*I*
Judge,Cpl.V, 6Jul.15-*I*, DoW 21Jul.15-*I*
Judkins,2Lt.OV, POW 6Oct.18-*I*
Judson,2Lt.DS, WIA 18Feb.18-*I*
Jukes,2Lt.S, 7Apr.18-*I*
Junor,Lt.,Capt.KW, 22Mar.18-*I*, 24Mar.18-*I*, KIA 23Apr.18-*I*

K

Kahle,1Lt.CC, *US.* 14Sep.18-*IIB*, KIA 2Oct.18-*IIB*
Kaizer,2Lt.MM, POW 7May.17-*I*
Kane,Lt.MHK, MC POW 10Jul.18-*I*
Kann,Lt.EH, KIA 21Oct.17-*I*
Kann,Lt.RV, WIA 25Apr.17-*I*
Kantel,Lt.FW, POW 30May.17-*I*
Kay,2Lt.GP, 4Mar.17-*I*
Kay,Lt.MA, KIA 30Apr.17-*I*
Kay,Sgt.R, WIA 12Jul.17-*I*
Kayl,Lt., *139Sqn.* 1Sep.18-*IV*
Kearley,2Lt.H, KIA 3Feb.18-*I*
Kearney,2Lt.EMS, KIA 27Oct.18-*I*
Kearney,1Lt.T, *USAS.* KIA 14Aug.18-*I*
Kearton,2Lt.R, 20Nov.17-*I*
Keary,2Lt.PM, 2Oct.18-*I*, 1Nov.18-*I*
Keast,2Lt.WR, DoW 21.8.1917 8Jul.17-*I*
Keast,2Lt.WR, KIA 21Aug.17-*I*
Keating,Lt.JA, 9Aug.18-*I*
Kebblewhite,2Lt.FE, KIA 14Aug.17-*I*
Keble,2Lt.FJ, POW 16Sep.18-*I*
Keefe,2AM.W, POW died 7.5.16 April.16-*VIII*
Keely,2Lt.RC, *US.* WIA 7Oct.18-*IIB*
Keen,Lt.,Maj.AW, MC 28Aug.16-*I*, DoI 12.9.1918 15Aug.18-*I*
Keen,2Lt.FF, 27Mar.18-*I*
Keen,Lt.LC, 22Mar.18-*I*, 25Mar.18-*I*
Keen,Lt.SW, MC DoW 28.8.1918? 21Aug.18-*I*
Keene,2Lt.C, 28Oct.18-*I*
Keens,FSLt.JH, WIA 7Jun.17-*I*
Keep,Lt.AD, MC WIA 20Jul.18-*I*
Keep,2Lt.EW, WIA? 22Mar.18-*I*
Keepin,Lt.WF, KIA 16Aug.18-*IV*
Keesler,2Lt.SR, *US.* WIA DoW 10.10.1918? 8Oct.18-*IIB*
Keeton,2Lt.H, WIA 16Dec.17-*I*
Keir,Lt.EH, KIA 28Oct.17-*I*
Keir,2Lt.JN, POW 20Sep.18-*I*
Keith,1Lt.AH, *US.* Ld'H WIA 6Aug.18-*IID*
Keith,2Lt.F, WIA 24Mar.18-*I*
Keller,Lt.CF, POW 23Nov.17-*I*
Kellog,2Lt.WB, WIA, *name* Kellogg? 24Dec.16-*I*, WIA POW 31Jul.17-*I*
Kellow,2Lt.W, KIA 16Sep.18-*I*
Kelly,Lt., *12Sqn.* 6Oct.18-*I*
Kelly,2Lt.,Lt.AP, 29Jul.16-*I*, WIA 21Mar.18-*I*
Kelly,Lt.AS, 17May.18-*I*
Kelly,2AM.C, KIA 13Aug.17-*I*
Kelly,2Lt.CL, KIA 20Sep.18-*I*
Kelly,Lt.EC, WIA 28May.17-*I*
Kelly,Lt.ETS, KIA 13Jun.18-*I*
Kelly,Lt.HC, 16May.18-*IV*
Kelly,2Lt.J, KIA 30Jul.18-*I*
Kelly,2Lt.JM, POW 22Oct.18-*IV*
Kelly,Capt.JU, WIA 14Jul.16-*I*
Kelly,Lt.MA, KIFA 15May.18-*I*
Kelly,2Lt.OR, KIA 12May.17-*I*
Kelly,2Lt.R, WIA POW 8Aug.18-*I*
Kelly,2Lt.TW, KIA 29Sep.18-*I*
Kelsall,Sgt., *49Sqn.* 25Mar.18-*I*
Kelton,1Lt.EH, *US.* inj POW 30Oct.18-*IIB*
Kelty,1Lt.AE, *US.* KIA 26Sep.18-*IIB*
Kelway-Bamber,2Lt.CH, 4Nov.15-*I*, KIA 11Nov.15-*I*
Kember,Lt.W, KIA 1Sep.17-*I*
Kemp,2Lt.EC, KIA 6Sep.16-*I*
Kemp,Lt.F, POW 18Jul.18-*I*
Kemp,2Lt.GH, 19May.18-*I*, KIA 1Jun.18-*I*
Kemp,2Lt.HT, 2Oct.15-*I*, 4Nov.15-*I*, WIA POW 12Jan.16-*I*
Kemp,2Lt.JE, POW 7Sep.18-*I*
Kemp,2Lt.NH, POW 31Oct.17-*I*

Kemp,2Lt.P, **WIA POW** 16Jun.18-*I*
Kempe-Roberts,Lt.JAC, **KIA** 10Mar.18-*III*
Kempson,Capt.WR, **WIA** 30Oct.17-*VII*
Kemsley,2Lt.N, 15Sep.16-*I*
Kendall,FSLt.EK, **KIA** 12Jul.17-*I*
Kendall,1Lt.HR, *US.* **POW** 22Oct.18-*IIB*
Kendall,2Lt.S, **WIA POW** 5Dec.17-*I*
Kendrick,Sgt.L, **WIA** 9May.18-*I*
Kennan,2Lt.S, **WIA** 28Sep.18-*I*
Kennard,2Lt.C, **WIA POW** 9Oct.16-*I*
Kennard,2Lt.WD, 11Jul.17-*I*
Kennedy,Lt,Capt., *4Sqn.* 31May.15-*I*, 12Jun.15-*I*, 29Jul.15-*I*
Kennedy,Cpl., *15Sqn.* 8Feb.16-*I*
Kennedy,2Lt.CE, **WIA** 20Nov.17-*I*
Kennedy,2Lt.CH, *US. 1stAero.* **KIA** 23Oct.18-*IIB*
Kennedy,Lt.CH, *214Sqn.* 21Aug.18-*I*
Kennedy,2Lt.CJ, **POW** 15Sep.16-*I*
Kennedy,AM.D, **POW** 1Jan.17-*I*
Kennedy,2Lt.,Capt.DS, 6Apr.17-*I*, **KIA** 12Mar.18-*I*
Kennedy,Lt.HA, **KIA** 22Aug.17-*I*
Kennedy,2Lt.JG, **KIA** 4Apr.18-*I*
Kennedy,2Lt.JW, 5Oct.18-*I*, 30Oct.18-*I*
Kennedy,2Lt.RD, **KIA** 27Mar.18-*I*
Kennedy,Lt.SNS, **WIA** 24May.17-*I*
Kennedy-Cochran-Patrick,Capt.WJC, MC 13Jul.17-*I*
Kenney?,Lt.EP, *Aust.*, *name* Kenny? 28Apr.18-*VII*
Kenny,Lt.MJ, **POW DoW** 23Sep.16-*I*
Kent,2Lt.EAW, **WIA** 30May.18-*I*
Kent,2Lt.PF, **KIA** 6Feb.18-*I*
Kent,GL.GA, **POW** 26Oct.17-*I*
Kent,FSLt.RL, **POW** 11Jul.17-*I*
Kent,2Lt.TJ, **POW** 20Nov.17-*I*
Kent,2Lt.WM, **KIA** 21Feb.18-*I*
Kent,2Lt.WT, *US.* **KIA** 7Sep.18-*IIB*
Kent,2Lt.WW, **KIA** 26Oct.17-*I*
Kent-Jones,2Lt.DW, **POW** 23Mar.18-*I*
Kenyon,1Lt.HN, *US.* 13Sep.18-*IIB*
Kenyon,2Lt.JD, *USAS.* **POW** 2Sep.18-*I*
Ker,1Lt.D, *US.* **KIA** 12Sep.18-*IIB*
Kernahan,2Lt.JEA, **WIA** 22Mar.18-*I*
Kerr,2Lt.C, **POW** 11Jul.16-*I*
Kerr,2Lt.CW, **WIA** 1Oct.18-*I*
Kerr,2Lt.HN, *Aust.* **inj** 9Oct.18-*I*
Kerr,Lt.JFM, 3Sep.18-*I*
Kerr,Lt.JG, 10Aug.18-*I*
Kerr,Lt.PH, *Aust.* **WIA** 27Jun.18-*I*
Kerr,Lt.SH, **WIA** 15Mar.18-*I*
Kerry,SLt., RNAS. 17Sep.16-*VII*
Kershaw,2Lt.CD, **WIA** 24Aug.16-*I*
Kershaw,Lt.JG, 9Oct.18-*I*, 1Nov.18-*I*
Kert,Lt.L, **POW** 27Nov.17-*I*
Kerwood,Sgt?,CW, *US.* **POW** 31Mar.18-*IIC*
Kettener,2Lt.HM, **WIA** 16Sep.18-*I*
Kettles,2Lt.AG, 27Oct.18-*IV*
Kewley,Lt.BH, **POW** 24Sep.18-*I*
Key,2Lt.R, 25Mar.18-*I*, 28Mar.18-*I*
Keys,Lt.RE, 5Aug.18-*III*
Kiburz,Lt.LA, 5Jun.17-*I*
Kidd, 2Lt. AL, **POW** 1Jan.18-*I*
Kidd, 2Lt. JF, **KIA** 1Nov.18-*I*
Kidd, Lt. LC, **KIA** 12Oct.16-*I*
Kidd, 2Lt. SF, **inj** 11Oct.18-*I*
Kidd, 2Lt. WC, 29Sep.18-*I*, 11Oct.18-*I*
Kidder,Lt.WSG, **WIA POW** 22Jul.18-*I*
Kiddie,Lt.,Capt.AC, SA. 26May.18-*I*, 30Jul.18-*I*
Kier,2Lt.JN, 8Aug.18-*I*, **WIA** 24Aug.18-*I*, **WIA** 1Sep.18-*I*
Kiggell,2Lt.,Capt.LS, 21Mar.18-*I*, 22May.18-*I*
Kilbourne,Lt.WH, **POW** 16Aug.18-*I*
Kilburn,Lt.GE, *Aust.* 31Aug.18-*I*
Kilby,Lt.FD, **WIA** 24Aug.18-*I*
Kilkelly,Capt.JGJ, **KIA** 26Mar.18-*I*
Killeen,2Lt.,Lt.T, 7Apr.18-*I*, 31Aug.18-*I*
Killick,Lt.CHP, **POW** 4Sep.18-*I*
Kilner,FCdr.CF, 25Dec.14-*I*
Kilpatrick,2Lt.AW, **WIA** 14Oct.18-*I*
Kilsby,2Lt.MJ, *Aust.* **POW** 30Oct.18-*I*
Kimbell,2Lt.RE, **KIA** 16Apr.17-*I*
Kimber,1Lt.AC, *US.* 14Sep.18-*IIB*, **KIA** 26Sep.18-*IIB*
Kimberley,Sgt.RG, **INT** 30Jun.18-*I*
Kime,2Lt.GHE, MM **WIA** 1Oct.18-*I*
Kincaid,1Lt.AC, *US.* **WIA** 7Nov.18-*IIB*
Kindley,1Lt.FE, *USAS.* 2Sep.18-*I*, 28Oct.18-*I*
King,Lt., *6Sqn.* 8Oct.18-*I*
King,2Lt., *16Sqn.* 14Mar.16-*I*
King,Lt.AHE, **WIA**? 4Sep.18-*I*
King,2Lt.B, 1May.17-*I*
King,2Lt.,Capt.CF, MC **WIA** 28Mar.18-*I*, 27Sep.18-*I*
King,Lt.D, **WIA** 9Aug.17-*I*
King,Capt.DB, 20Nov.17-*I*, **POW** 30Nov.17-*I*
King,2Lt.DN, 9Nov.18-*I*
King,FSLt.E, 23Jan.17-*VII*
King,Lt.,Capt.ER, *Aust.* 20May.18-*I*, 28Oct.18-*I*
King,2AM.F, 16Mar.17-*I*, **KIA**? 17Mar.17-*I*
King,2Lt.FE, **WIA** 25Jul.18-*I*
King,2Lt.FW, **WIA POW** 17Sep.18-*I*
King,2Lt.G, 1Oct.16-*I*
King,Capt.JA, *USAS.* **POW** 17Aug.18-*I*
King,2Lt. JS, **KIA** 1Oct.18-*I*
King,Lt.KV, **KIA** 30Jul.18-*I*
King,Capt.LMC, *Can.* **POW** 27Oct.18-*IV*
King,2Lt.P, **POW** 21Oct.18-*I*
King,2Lt.S, **KIA** 26Sep.18-*I*
King,Lt.V, **KIA** 11Apr.18-*I*
King,Lt.WJ, **KIA** 16May.18-*I*
King-Harman,Capt.L, 23Sep.16-*VIII*
Kingdon,2Lt., *12Sqn.* **KIA** 12Jan.16-*I*
Kingham,2Lt.RL, **INT** 24Sep.18-*I*
Kinghorn,2Lt.EC, **WIA** 4Nov.18-*VIII*
Kinghorn,2Lt.W, **KIA** 4Nov.18-*I*
Kingsland,2Lt.WR, **WIA POW** 8Nov.17-*I*
Kingsley,Capt.SG, **WIA** 10Jan.17-*VII*
Kingston-McCloughry,Lt.,Capt.EJ, *Aust.* 12Jun.18-*I*, **WIA** 31Jul.18-*I*, **WIA** 24Sep.18-*I*
Kingwell,2Lt.WL, MC 27Mar.18-*I*, **WIA** 10Apr.18-*I*
Kinkead,FSLt.SM, DSC 15Nov.17-*I*
Kinmond,Lt.DC, **INT** 11Apr.18-*I*
Kinne,2Lt.HI, *US.* **KIA** 29Sep.18-*IIB*
Kinnear,Lt.,Capt., *6Sqn.* 28Apr.15-*I*, 20Jun.15-*I*, 21Sep.15-*I*, 19Oct.15-*I*, 26Oct.15-*I*, 5Nov.15-*I*, 14Dec.15-*I*
Kinnear,2Lt.,Lt.AM, 30Nov.17-*I*, **WIA** 1Dec.17-*I*, 22Dec.17-*I*, 14Mar.18-*I*, 27Mar.18-*I*
Kinney,1Lt.CA, *US.* **KIA** 4Oct.18-*IIB*
Kinney,1Lt.MC, *USAS.* **WIA** 16Aug.18-*I*
Kirby,AM., *4Wg RNAS.* 15Nov.16-*I*
Kirby,AM.FC, **WIA** 25Apr.17-*I*
Kirby,2Lt.FW, **KIA** 21Sep.17-*I*
Kirby,2Lt.H, **POW** 12May.17-*I*
Kirk,Lt.JH, 11Jul.17-*I*
Kirk,Lt.LD, 23May.18-*I*
Kirk,Capt.PG, **KIA** 13Aug.17-*I*
Kirkaldy,2Lt.RH, **KIA** 25Mar.18-*I*
Kirkbride,1AM.H, **KIA** 5Dec.15-*I*
Kirkham,Lt.FJ, **WIA POW** 28Apr.17-*I*
Kirkland,Lt.HG, **WIA** 29Sep.18-*I*
Kirkland,Lt.JT, **KIA** 20Jul.18-*I*
Kirkman,Capt.RK, **POW** 27Mar.18-*I*
Kirkness,2Lt.TR, **KIA** 18Aug.17-*I*
Kirkpatrick,Maj.B, **KIA** 1Oct.18-*I*
Kirkpatrick,Lt.JC, 25Sep.17-*I*, 9Oct.17-*I*, **KIA** 10Dec.17-*I*
Kirkpatrick,Lt.YES, **WIA** 31Jul.18-*I*
Kirton,AG.2AM.G, **WIA** 27Oct.17-*I*
Kirton,2Lt.JT, 13Feb.16-*I*
Kirwan,AG.2AM., *42Sqn.* 7Jun.17-*I*
Kissell,1Lt.GH, *USAS.* **KIA** 12Apr.18-*I*
Kitchen,2Lt.GW, **inj** 15Oct.18-*I*
Kitchen,Sgt.S, **KIA**? 4Oct.18-*I*
Kitchener,2Lt.,Maj.HH, 19Oct.15-*I*, 30Oct.18-*IV*
Kitchin,Lt.FL, **KIA** 11Apr.17-*I*
Kitsun,2AM., *53Sqn.* **WIA**? 31Oct.17-*I*
Kitto,Lt.FM, 17Aug.17-*I*
Klingenstein,Lt.G, **WIA POW** 15Sep.16-*I*
Klingman,Lt.EC, *USAS.* **POW** 1Sep.18-*I*
Knaggs,2Lt.KJ, **WIA** 16Jun.17-*I*, **KIA** 16Mar.18-*I*
Knapp,Lt.FR, **POW** 16Apr.18-*I*
Knatchbull-Hugessen,Lt.Hon.M, MC Jun.15-*V*
Knee,2Lt.B, **WIA** 29Aug.18-*I*
Kneller,2Lt.FK, **POW DoW** 21Mar.18-*I*
Knight,Capt.AG, *29Sqn.* **KIA** 20Dec.16-*I*
Knight,2Lt.AG, *53Sqn.* **WIA** 2Jul.17-*I*
Knight,Lt.,2Lt.CC, 7Jun.17-*I*, **POW** 22Jul.17-*I*
Knight,FSLt.CG, **POW** 25Mar.16-*I*
Knight,Lt.CRW, 23Aug.18-*I*, 25Aug.18-*I*
Knight,1Lt.CT, *USAS.* **POW** 5Oct.18-*I*
Knight,1Lt.D, *USAS.* 2Jun.18-*I*
Knight,Lt.G, 16Sep.18-*I*
Knight,Lt.GF, **POW** 9Nov.16-*I*
Knight,2Lt.GH, **WIA** 14Sep.18-*I*
Knight,1AM.J, **WIA** 19May.18-*I*
Knight,2Lt.NL, **WIA POW** 28Mar.17-*I*
Knight,2Lt.,Lt.OR, MC **WIA** 6Mar.17-*I*, **WIA** 28Mar.17-*I*, **KIA** 6Apr.17-*I*
Knivecon,Lt., *35Sqn.* 6Mar.18-*I*
Knocker,2Lt.GM, 3Feb.18-*I*, **WIA** 6Apr.18-*I*
Knott,2Lt.CR, **WIA** 26Oct.18-*I*
Knotts,2Lt.HC, *USAS.* **WIA** 22Aug.18-*I*, **POW** 14Oct.18-*I*
Knowlden,2Lt.WE, **WIA POW** 3Nov.16-*I*
Knowles,2Lt.AR, **KIA** 2Apr.18-*I*
Knowles,2AM.,Cpl.FJ, 12Dec.17-*VII*, 17Jan.18-*VII*
Knowles,2Lt.H, **DoW** 11Aug.18-*I*
Knowles,Capt.MB, **POW** 7Apr.17-*I*
Knowles,Capt.RM, MC **WIA** 24Apr.17-*I*
Knowles,Lt.W, **KIA** 4Jul.18-*I*
Knox,2Lt.CD, **KIA** 17Mar.17-*I*
Knox,Capt.W, *13Sqn.* **KIA** 20Feb.16-*I*
Knox,2Lt.W, *54Sqn.* **KIA** 24Mar.18-*I*
Koch,2Lt.A, *6Sqn.* **WIA** 22Oct.16-*I*
Koch,2Lt.,Lt.A, *Can.* 23Mar.18-*I*, **WIA** 27Mar.18-*I*
Koepfgen,2Lt.LP, 5Nov.18-*IIB*
Koontz,1Lt.JN, *US.* **WIA** 3Nov.18-*IIB*
Korslund,2Lt.MF, *US.* **KIA** 12Apr.18-*I*
Krohn,2Lt.EO, 15Oct.17-*I*, **KIA** 28Feb.18-*I*
Kull,1Lt.GP, *US.* **KIA** 14Sep.18-*IIB*
Kullberg,Lt.HA, *US.* 15Jun.18-*I*
Kuntz,2Lt.FE, *US.* **WIA** 31Oct.18-*IIB*
Kydd,2Lt.FJ, 29Apr.17-*I*, 5May.17-*I*
Kynoch,Capt.AB, **KIA** 8Mar.18-*III*

L

La Cecilia,2Lt.GR, **WIA** 22Jul.18-*I*
Labatt,2Lt.WHE, **POW** 22Jul.18-*I*
Lacey,Lt.WG, MC 10Oct.18-*I*, **KIA** 4Nov.18-*I*
Lackey,2Lt.HD, **KIA** 7Oct.18-*I*
Lacy,2Lt.JB, **POW** 16Sep.18-*I*
Lagesse,Capt.CHR, 14Oct.18-*I*
Laing,2Lt.JD, **POW DoW** 28.1.1918 24Oct.17-*I*
Laing,Lt.KJP, 21May.18-*I*
Laing,2Lt.TH, **KIA** 30Aug.18-*I*
Laird,2Lt.CB, *US.* **POW** 18Sep.18-*IIB*
Laird,2Lt.,Lt.DP, 17Jun.18-*I*, 11Aug.18-*I*, **WIA** 1Oct.18-*I*
Lake,Sgt.J, **WIA** 14Mar.18-*I*, **KIA** 19May.18-*I*
Lale,Capt.HP, 11Aug.18-*I*, 30Oct.18-*I*
Lally,Capt.CT, MC **WIA** 8Dec.17-*I*
Lamb,Lt.HA, **KIA** 9Jul.18-*I*
Lamb,2Lt.HHG, **WIA** 21Aug.17-*I*
Lambe,2Lt.L, **WIA** 3Jan.18-*I*
Lambert,Gnr.1AM.FARC, 7May.17-*I*
Lambert,2Lt.GW, 17May.18-*I*, **WIA** 2Jun.18-*I*
Lambert,1Lt.JH, *US.* 12Aug.18-*IIB*
Lambert,2Lt.,Lt.WC, *US.* 7Apr.18-*I*, 8Aug.18-*I*
Lambeth,Sgt.GE, **KIA** 9Sep.17-*I*
Lamble,2Lt.TB, 29Jul.18-*I*
Lambourne,Lt.H, **WIA** 4Mar.17-*I*
Lamburn,2Lt.GA, 10Apr.18-*I*
Lamont,2Lt.W, **POW** 16May.18-*I*
Lancashire,2Lt.AE, 24Mar.18-*I*, **WIA** 3Apr.18-*I*
Lance,2Lt.WG, **KIA** 13Aug.18-*I*
Lander,Lt.TE, MC *30Sqn.* 13Aug.16-*VIII*, **WIA POW** 6May.17-*VIII*
Landis,Lt.RG, *US.* 20Apr.18-*I*, 22Jul.18-*I*
Landon,1Lt.EC, *US.* 29Oct.18-*IIB*
Lane,2Lt.CW, *22Sqn.* **POW** 9May.17-*I*
Lane,Lt.,Capt.CW, *11Sqn.* 1Aug.15-*I*, 28Aug.15-*I*, 8Sep.15-*I*, 23Sep.15-*I*, 2Oct.15-*I*
Lane,2Lt.DW, **WIA** 20Nov.17-*I*
Lane,AGL.A, **KIA** 6Apr.18-*I*
Lane,Lt.LC, **WIA POW** 3May.18-*I*
Lane,2Lt.RV, **WIA** 5Nov.18-*I*
Lane,T2Lt.,2Lt.RW, 1Oct.18-*I*, 29Oct.18-*I*, **KIA** 9Nov.18-*I*
Lane,2Lt.WIE, **WIA** 10Apr.18-*I*
Lang,TLt.LR, 27Jun.18-*I*
Lang,2Lt.R, MM *UK.* **WIA** 21Feb.18-*I*
Langdon,2Lt.RT, **WIA** 1Apr.18-*I*
Lange,Lt.OJ, **WIA** 24Jun.18-*I*
Langford,2Lt.EW, **WIA** 4Nov.18-*I*
Langford,Lt.EW, 30Oct.18-*I*
Langford,Lt.GC, **WIA** 25Sep.17-*I*
Langlands,2Lt.D, 22Jul.17-*I*, **WIA** 25Jul.17-*I*
Langridge,Cpl.E, **KIA** 6Apr.17-*I*
Langton,2Lt.ESW, **WIA** 25Apr.17-*I*
Langwill,Lt.T, **POW DoW** 17.4.1917 16Apr.17-*I*
Lankshear,AG.Pte.F, **DoW** 21Aug.17-*I*
Lansdale,Lt.EC, **POW DoW** 1.12.1916 30Sep.16-*I*
Lansdale,2Lt.H, **POW** 30Oct.18-*I*
Lardner,2Lt.R, 9May.18-*I*, **KIFA** 26May.18-*I*
Larkin,Capt.HJ, *Aust.* 16Sep.18-*I*
Larkin,2Lt.RS, 2Nov.17-*I*
Larrabee,Lt.EP, *US.* **POW** 20Sep.18-*I*
Larsen,Lt.JF, *US.* 6Apr.18-*I*
Lascelles,Lt., *12Sqn.* 5Apr.17-*I*
Lascelles,2Lt.EH, **WIA** 2Aug.16-*I*
Lascelles,Capt.GA, **WIA** 31Jul.17-*I*
Lascelles,2Lt.,Lt.JF, 17Apr.15-*I*, 15Jun.15-*I*, 20Jun.15-*I*, 6Jul.15-*I*
Lasker,2Lt.RS, **KIA** 20May.18-*I*
Latchford,Lt.JH, 17Sep.18-*I*, 4Nov.18-*I*
Lathean,2AM., *15Sqn.* 17Jan.16-*I*, 25Jan.16-*I*
Latimer,Lt.A, **KIA** 4Oct.18-*IV*
Latimer,Capt.D, MC DFC **POW** 22Aug.18-*I*
Latta,2Lt.J, *5Sqn.* 20Mar.16-*I*
Latta,2Lt.,Capt.JD, MC 1Jun.16-*I*, 8Jun.16-*I*, 9Nov.16-*I*, **WIA** 8Jun.17-*I*
Lauer,Lt.WW, 1Aug.18-*I*
Laughlin,Lt.FA, 10May.18-*I*
Laughton,SLt.DB, **DoW** 1Oct.17-*I*
Laughton,Lt.PS, 2May.17-*I*
Laurence,FLt.C, **POW** 25May.18-*I*
Laurence,Capt.FH, 3Sep.17-*I*
Laurie,2Lt.KS, **POW** 25Jul.18-*I*
Lavarack,Lt., 23Apr.17-*I*
Lavers,Lt.CSI, 14Jul.17-*I*, 15Jul.17-*I*
Lavington,2Lt.LJ, **KIA** 22Aug.18-*I*
Law,2Lt.CB, **POW** 18May.18-*I*
Law,Lt.ER, **WIA POW** 13Apr.17-*I*
Law,Capt.JK, 20Sep.17-*I*, **KIA** 21Sep.17-*I*
Law,Lt.JR, **POW** 26Feb.18-*I*
Law,Cpl.LO, **POW** 22Sep.16-*I*
Lawder,Sgt.WE, **KIA** 25Jun.18-*I*
Lawe,2Lt.AG, **POW** 15Aug.18-*I*
Lawes,2Lt., *4Sqn.* 29Jul.15-*I*
Lawledge,2Lt.FM, **DoW** 10Oct.16-*I*
Lawrence,Lt., *2Sqn.* 1Sep.14-*I*
Lawrence,AG.2AM.G, **WIA** 7Dec.17-*I*
Lawrence,Capt.GAK, 10Sep.15-*I*, 26Sep.15-*I*, 12Oct.15-*I*, 17Jan.16-*I*
Lawrence,2Lt.H, 19Aug.18-*I*, **WIA** 29Aug.18-*I*
Lawrence,2Lt.NA, **KIA** 30Apr.17-*I*
Lawrence,2Lt.P, **KIA** 9Aug.18-*I*
Lawrence,2Lt.WG, **KIA** 23Oct.15-*I*
Lawson,FSLt.AHS, **WIA** 7Jan.17-*I*
Lawson,1Lt.AW, *US.* **POW** 8Sep.18-*IIB*
Lawson,2Lt.DA, 2Sep.18-*I*
Lawson,2Lt.DF, **WIA** 28Jan.18-*I*
Lawson,Lt.FA, **WIA** 2Sep.18-*I*
Lawson,Lt.,Capt.GEB, *SA.* 18May.18-*I*, 27Sep.18-*I*
Lawson,2Lt.J, 7Apr.17-*I*
Lawson,2Lt.RG, **POW** 11Apr.18-*I*
Lawson,1Lt.WH, *US.* **WIA** 27Jul.18-*IIB*
Lawton,Lt.JB, 25Sep.16-*I*, **POW** 10Oct.16-*I*
Laycock,2Lt.H, 28Oct.18-*I*
Layfield,2Lt.HD, **WIA** 21Sep.17-*I*
Layton,2Lt., *7Sqn.* 18Sep.15-*I*, 26Sep.15-*I*
Layton,Lt.DM, 28Sep.18-*I*, **WIA** 1Nov.18-*I*
Layton,1Lt.LD, *US.* **KIA** 18Jul.18-*IID*
Lazarus-Barlow,2Lt.AJ, **POW** 11Feb.17-*VII*
Le Bas,Lt.OV, **KIA** 7Nov.15-*I*

Le Blanc-Smith,2Lt.,Capt.M, 19Dec.15-I, 10Mar.18-I
Le Fevre,Lt.FE, MC POW 24Jan.18-I
Le Lievre,2Lt.FL, KIA 4Oct.18-I
Le Mesurier,Capt.TF, DoI 26May.18-I
Le Roy,Lt.HL, POW 21May.18-I
Lea,2Lt.HF, WIA 27Sep.18-I
Lea,2AM.TH, 18Sep.17-I
Leach,2Lt.A, 27Mar.18-I, WIA 1Apr.18-I
Leach,2Lt.FW, WIA 17Jun.18-I
Leach,1AM.GP, POW? 23Nov.17-I
Leach,2Lt.JB, 19Jul.18-I, 15Sep.18-I
Leach,Lt.JM, WIA POW 15Nov.17-I
Leach,Lt.JO, MC WIA 7May.17-I
Leach,1Lt.JW, WIA 12Jun.18-I
Leacroft,Capt.J, 2May.18-I, 3Sep.17-I
Lead,2Lt.WF, WIA 17Jun.18-I
Leake,Lt.EG, 25Mar.18-I, 28Mar.18-I, 8Apr.17-I, WIA 4May.17-I, WIA 7Jun.17-I
Leake,Capt.EH, MC WIA 24Jul.18-I
Leal,2Lt.G, 31Jul.17-I, KIA 7Aug.17-I
Learmond,Lt.GV, 10Nov.18-I
Learmount,2Lt.,Maj.LW, DSO MC 31Jul.15-I, 26Sep.15-I, 30Dec.15-I, WIA 9Mar.18-I, WIA 10May.17-I
Learn,Lt.GA, KIA 24Jun.18-I
Leask,Capt.KMGStCG, 23Mar.18-I
Leather,FLt.GV, 20Oct.16-I
Leathey,Lt.F, 30Apr.17-I, 28Jul.17-I, 17Aug.17-I
Leavitt,Lt.HJ, US. POW 17May.18-I
Lecke,GL.LH, 12Jun.18-I
Leckerby,2Lt.JG, KIA 9Nov.18-I
Leckie,Lt.G, 21Sqn. 31May.17-I, KIA 7Jul.17-I
Leckie,Lt.GA, 49Sqn. KIA 9May.18-I
Leckie,Capt.R, 5Aug.18-III
Leckler,2Lt.AN, WIA POW 5Apr.17-I
Ledger,2Lt.HP, KIA 20Nov.17-I
Lee,Lt.AC, 13May.17-I, POW 20May.17-I
Lee,Lt.AG, 4Sep.17-I
Lee,2Lt.,Capt.AS, WIA 26May.17-I, 26Nov.17-I
Lee,Capt.ASG, 22Nov.17-I
Lee,2Lt.,Lt.EAR, inj 27Sep.18-I, KIA 30Oct.18-I
Lee,2Lt.EB, POW 18Mar.18-I
Lee,2Lt.JA, KIA 25Aug.18-I
Lee,Lt.OM, Aust. POW 19Mar.18-VII
Lee,2AM.RT, KIA? 10Dec.17-I
Lee,2Lt.S, 4Sqn. 5Oct.18-I
Lee,Sgt.S, US. KIA 12Apr.18-IIC
Leech,Capt.JC, POW 4Jul.15-I
Leech,2Lt.WF, DoW 18.8.1917 16Aug.17-I
Leed,Lt.DK, KIA 12Aug.18-I
Leefe-Robinson,Lt.,Capt.W, VC 2Sep.16-III, POW 5Apr.17-I
Lees,Lt., 6Sqn. 8Jun.17-I
Lees,Capt.A, 25Jan.17-I, WIA POW 4Mar.17-I
Lees,2Lt.DW, 27Mar.18-I, WIA 30Mar.18-I
Lees,2Lt.JC, WIA POW 20Nov.16-I
Lees,Lt.MD, Aust. 19Sep.18-VII
Lees-Smith,Maj.HS, inj 14Aug.18-I
Leeson,Lt.D, Can. 27Aug.15-I, 7Sep.15-I, 11Sep.15-I, 27Sep.15-I, WIA POW 10Oct.15-I
Leete,2Lt.SJ, KIA 28Jul.17-I
Leete,Capt.WW, WIA 7May.17-I
Lefroy,Lt.CHB?, WIA POW 8Aug.18-I
Leggat,2Lt.M, 21Mar.18-I, KIA 26Mar.18-I
Leggatt,2Lt.CW, POW 10Jan.18-I
Leggatt,2Lt.,Capt.EW, 25Jul.15-I, 1Aug.15-I, 2Aug.15-I, 29Feb.16-I, 9Apr.16-I, POW 9Aug.16-I
Legge,Lt.AR, KIA 24Mar.17-I
Legge,Sgt.FV,? 10Oct.17-I
Legge,2Lt.W, KIA 13Jun.18-I
Leggett,Lt.E, 15Apr.17-I
Lehr,1Lt.M, US. KIA 15Jul.18-IID
Leigh,Sgt.J, WIA 20Nov.17-I
Leigh,Lt.RL, KIA 18Jun.18-I
Leigh-Pemberton,Lt.RD, WIA 26Mar.18-I
Leighton,2Lt.GR, KIA 7Oct.18-IV
Leighton,2Lt.KAW, POW 30Aug.18-I
Leighton,Lt.RT, WIA POW 17Aug.17-I
Leighton,2Lt.WH, 21Mar.18-I
Leishman,Lt.GE, WIA 5Jun.17-I
Leitch,Lt.AA, Can. 25May.18-I
Leitch,GL.CA, KIA 30Jan.18-I
Leitch,2Lt.G, 20May.18-I
Leith,2Lt.JL, 1Mar.17-I
Leman,Capt.CM, 21Mar.18-I, 4Apr.18-I
Lennox,2Lt.AD, KIA 18Oct.17-I
Lennox,Lt.JS, 27Oct.18-IV
Leonard,1Lt.EC, US. WIA POW 26Sep.18-IIB
Leonard,2Lt.TLW, KIA 29Oct.18-I
Lerwill,2Lt.O, POW 25Mar.16-I
Leslie,2Lt.CS?, WIA 26Aug.18-I
Leslie,Lt.S, 10Sep.18-I, 5Oct.18-I
Leslie,Lt.WA, 58Sqn. 7Jun.18-I
Leslie,Lt.WA, Sqn.?(not 58Sqn.) POW 16May.18-I
Leslie-Moore,Lt.A, POW 18Jun.17-VI
Letch,Lt.HA, MC Aust. KIA 22Aug.18-VII
Letts,Lt.EM, WIA 22Aug.17-I
Letts,Lt.,Capt.JHT, 9Apr.17-I, WIA? 11May.17-I, 24May.17-I, inj 22Aug.17-I
Leveson-Gower,Lt.J, Can. POW 4Sep.18-I
Levick,Pbr.C, KIA 16Jun.18-I
Levy,2Lt.J, 23Jun.18-I
Lewis,Lt.A, POW 21Jul.18-I
Lewis,FSLt.ADM, POW 25Aug.17-I
Lewis,Lt.CA, 5May.17-I, WIA 7Jul.17-I
Lewis,Lt.DF, POW Sep.17?-I
Lewis,2Lt.DG, WIA? POW 20Apr.18-I
Lewis,Lt.,Lt.Col.DS, DSO 13Sep.14-I, KIA 9Apr.16-I
Lewis,2Lt.E, WIA 29Jul.16-I
Lewis,2Lt.EL, KIA 26Dec.16-I
Lewis,2Lt.EP, KIA 6Oct.17-I
Lewis,2Lt.FA, US. 53Sqn. KIA 5Feb.18-I
Lewis,2Lt.FA, 88Sqn. 8Jun.18-I
Lewis,FSLt.FC, KIA 21Aug.17-I
Lewis,Capt.GH, 7Jul.18-I
Lewis,1Lt.HC, US. POW 10Jul.18-IIB
Lewis,2Lt.HG, POW 27Oct.18-I
Lewis,2Lt.HM, POW 12Jul.17-I
Lewis,Lt.HS, KIA 6Apr.18-I
Lewis,2Lt.HV, WIA 29Mar.18-I
Lewis,2Lt.HY, WIA 24Aug.18-I
Lewis,Sgt.J, POW 24May.17-I
Lewis,2Lt.JA, 53Sqn. WIA 22Jul.18-I
Lewis,2Lt.JA, 210Sqn. KIA 16Sep.18-I
Lewis,2Lt.JE, inj 11Mar.17-I
Lewis,2Lt.KVC, WIA 5Aug.18-I
Lewis,2Lt.M, POW 6Apr.17-I
Lewis,2Lt.MB, US. KIA 15Jul.18-I
Lewis,2Lt.OG, Aust. WIA 9Aug.17-I, WIA 14Aug.17-I
Lewis,Lt.RF, KIA 25Jul.18-I
Lewis,2Lt.RG, 21May.18-I, POW 13Jun.18-I
Lewis,2Lt.TAMS, 5Jun.17-I, 27Jul.17-I
Lewis,2Lt.WTS, POW 29Aug.18-I
Lewis-Roberts,Capt.AO, DFC 9Aug.18-I
Ley,2Lt.CFH, WIA 3Jun.17-I
Leycester,2Lt.PW, 28Nov.17-I
Leyden,2Lt.HPG, KIA 13Aug.18-I
Leyson,1Lt.BWdeB, USAS. POW 10Jun.18-I
Lick,Lt.CH, WIA 31Jul.18-I
Liddell,Lt.,Capt.JA, 29Jul.15-I, DoW 31.8.15 31Jul.15-I
Liddell,Lt.WHG, KIA 17Apr.18-I
Lidsey,2Lt.WJ, DoW 22.3.1917 21Mar.17-I
Light,2Lt.HE, 27Sep.18-I
Lightbody,2Lt.JD, KIA 4Nov.18-I
Lightbody,Sgt.RR, KIA 15Sep.18-I
Lilley,2Lt.,Lt.A, 24Sep.18-I, 27Sep.18-I
Lillis,Lt.MMA, 26Sep.16-I, KIA 11Apr.17-I
Lilly,Lt.WH, Aust. 22Sep.18-VII, 19Oct.18-VII, 23Oct.18-VII
Lillywhite,2Lt.RJ, 26Oct.15-I, 19Dec.15-I, 15Jan.16-I
Lindfield,Sgt.ASC, 12Jul.17-I
Lindley,2Lt.A, 55Sqn. WIA 10Apr.17-I
Lindley,Capt.A, 110Sqn. POW 25Sep.18-I
Lindley,2Lt.BL, MC 27Mar.18-I, KIA 29Jun.18-I
Lindley,2Lt.EW, POW DoW 18.2.1917 16Feb.17-I
Lindop,Lt.VSE, POW 7Sep.14-I
Lindsay,2Lt.ATW, POW 26Mar.18-I
Lindsay,Lt.EE, 24Mar.18-I
Lindsay,FSLt.LL, 7Jul.17-I
Lindsay,Sgt.Mech.H, WIA 5Oct.18-I
Lindsay,1Lt.RC, US. WIA 13Sep.18-IIB
Lindsay,2Lt.RE, WIA 27Mar.18-I
Lindsey,2Lt.WJ, 4Dec.16-I
Lines,2Lt.TH, POW 18May.17-I
Linford,Lt.CT, WIA 15Sep.18-I
Lingard,2Lt.JR, POW 30Apr.17-I
Lingard,2Lt.M, WIA 4Jul.17-I
Lingham,2Lt.,Lt.GA, Aust. 22Mar.18-I, 10Jun.18-I
Linlay,Cpl.AJ, KIA 16Sep.17-I
Linnell,FSLt.HGB, POW 24Oct.17-I
Lipsett,2Lt.GA, WIA 3Feb.18-I
Lipsett,2Lt.RS, POW 16Sep.18-I
Lisle,Lt.CFJ, WIA 28Sep.18-I
Lister,2Lt.BS, WIA POW 1Jun.17-I
Lister,Lt.E, KIA? 15-I
Lister,Lt.JJ, INT 15Sep.18-I
Lister,2Lt.R, 29Sep.18-I, KIA 26Oct.18-I
Lister-Kaye,Capt.KA, 24Apr.18-I, WIA 25Apr.18-I
Liston,ProbAG.C, 29Apr.18-I
Littauer,Capt.K, US. DFC 14Sep.18-IIB
Little,2Lt.AW, WIA 5Aug.17-I
Little,Lt.HR, WIA 8Aug.18-I
Little,Sgt.J, 10Jun.18-I
Little,FSLt.,FCdr.,Capt.RA, DSO CdG Aust. 9Jul.16-I, 23Nov.16-I, 27Jul.17-I, 1Apr.18-I, 6Apr.18-I, 21Apr.18-I, DoW 27May.18-I
Little,Lt.RH, 6Mar.18-I
Littlejohn,2Lt.R, WIA 25Mar.17-I
Littler,2Lt.T, KIFA 3Jul.17-I
Littlewood,Lt.SCT, POW 1Jun.16-I
Liver,Capt.H, 7Jun.18-I
Liversedge,Lt.ST, 27Jun.18-I
Living,2Lt.CH, POW 2Sep.18-I
Livingstone,2Lt.AF, WIA 26Sep.16-I
Livock,Lt.ES, KIA 8Nov.17-I
Llewellyn-Davies,FSLt.G, POW 28Nov.16-III
Lloyd,Lt.AC, INT 16Aug.18-I
Lloyd,Capt.AT, KIA 28Sep.17-I
Lloyd,Pte.C, 13May.17-I, 3Jun.17-I, 5Jun.17-I, POW 7Jun.17-I
Lloyd,Lt.CBE, POW 25Sep.18-I
Lloyd,Lt.CC, KIA 17Apr.18-I
Lloyd,Lt.DRC, KIA 16Jun.17-I
Lloyd,2Lt.EAL, WIA POW 27May.17-I
Lloyd,Capt.GL, 7Oct.17-I
Lloyd,2Lt.JB, 28Apr.17-VIII
Lloyd,2Lt.RAH, DoW 10Oct.18-I
Lloyd,2Lt.RH, WIA 28Mar.17-I
Lloyd,2Lt.RS, KIA 18Jun.17-I
Lloyd,FSLt.SH, KIA 14Aug.17-I
Lloyd-Evans,Capt.D, 4Oct.18-I
Lloyd-Rees,2Lt.GN, WIA 11Apr.18-I
Lloyd-Williams,2Lt., 10Sqn. 10Oct.15-I, WIA 26Oct.15-I
Lloyd-Williams,Lt.,Capt.JJ, 8Oct.17-VII, 9Jan.18-VII
Lloyd-Williams,2Lt.W, 24Sep.18-I
Lloyde,Lt.JP, POW 10Sep.18-I
Loch,Lt.HN, 15Jun.18-I
Lock,Lt.FM, Aust. 24Jun.18-I, 12Aug.18-I
Locke,2Lt.CJ, INT 16Sep.18-I
Locke,2Lt.EG, KIA 19Aug.18-I
Locke,2AM.LH, INT 29Jun.18-I
Locke-Waters,Lt.EA, WIA 1Sep.18-I
Lockey,2Lt.B, INT 7Oct.18-I
Lockey,2Lt.V, 6Nov.18-I
Lockhart,Capt.GB, KIA 14Apr.17-I
Lockhart,Lt.JW, WIA 6Mar.17-I
Lockhart,1Lt.WS, US. WIA 9Sep.18-IIB
Lockley,2Lt.AH, Aust. KIA 5Sep.18-I
Lockwood,Lt.HTB, 9Oct.18-I
Lockwood,2Lt.MK, US. POW 4Nov.18-IIB
Lockyer,AM.AG, POW 14Apr.17-I
Lodge,Lt.CF, 29Jan.17-I, POW 17Mar.17-I
Logan,2Lt.D, WIA 14Jul.17-I
Logan,2Lt.GC, Can. POW 21Feb.18-I
Logan,2Lt.,Lt.RA, 13Mar.16-I, POW 8Apr.17-I
Logan,Lt.TE, WIA 22Mar.18-I
Lohmeyer,2Lt.EN, DFC 9Aug.18-I
Loly,Lt.FM, WIA 23Oct.18-I
Lomax,Lt.A, WIA 25Apr.18-I
Lomax,2Lt.AK, 22Mar.18-I, POW 2Apr.18-I
Lomax,2Lt.CNL, 13Jul.17-I, POW 26Sep.17-I
Lombridge,Capt.TE, 26Aug.15-I
Lomer,Capt.HC, KIA 5May.17-I
Long,Lt.AL, Aust. inj 7Oct.18-I
Long,2Lt.CP, KIA 13Apr.17-I
Long,2Lt.GR, WIA POW 6Oct.17-I
Long,Lt.HO, 30Nov.15-I, 19Dec.15-I, WIA 14Jul.16-I, POW 16Jul.16-I
Long,2Lt.JT, WIA 10Aug.17-I
Long,Sgt.LSD, WIA POW 12Mar.18-I
Long,2Lt.PJ, WIA 4Dec.16-I
Long,Capt.SH, 27Jan.17-I
Long,1AM.WT, POW 21Oct.17-I
Longbottom,Lt.HF, WIA 21Aug.18-I
Longcroft,Maj., 2Sqn. 22Aug.14-I, 1Sep.14-I
Longe,Sgt.HE, WIA 15Sep.18-I
Longinette,Capt.EV, 11Jun.17-VI
Longman,2Lt.R, WIA 21Feb.18-I
Longmore,SCdr.AM, 30Sep.14-I
Longton,Lt.AJ, 6Jul.17-I, KIA 31Jul.17-I
Longton,Capt.WH, 8Oct.18-I
Lonsdale,2Lt.VO, POW 6Mar.17-I
Loraine,Capt.,Maj.R, 11Oct.15-I, 26Oct.15-I, 8Feb.16-I, WIA 20Jul.18-I
Lord,Capt.FI, US. 28Sep.18-I
Loton,AGnr.AJ, KIA 28Jun.18-I
Loud,2Lt.HE, US. DoW 28.9.1918? 28Sep.18-IIB
Loudoun,Capt.LG, POW 29Aug.18-I
Loughlin,Lt.FA, 3May.18-I
Loughlin,2AM.JW, WIA POW 9May.17-I
Loughran,Sgt.EJ, US. KIA 18Feb.18-IIC
Loupinsky,Lt.J, WIA POW 10Jul.18-I
Loutit,2Lt.JA, WIA 9Jun.17-I
Love,1Lt.EA, US. KIA 15Sep.18-IIB
Love,Lt.HK, Aust. POW 10Apr.18-I
Loveday?,Sgt.AC, inj 30Aug.18-I
Loveland,2AM.C, KIA 21Sep.17-I
Loveland,Lt.H, 4Mar.17-I, KIA 2Apr.17-I
Lovell,2Lt.CEA, POW 7Aug.18-I
Lovell,2Lt.LG, KIA 11Apr.17-I
Lovell,2Lt.WL, KIA 27Jul.17-I
Lovelock,AM1.HG, KIA 22Mar.18-I
Lovemore,Lt.RB, POW? 28Oct.18-I
Lovick,2Lt.CE, WIA 15Apr.18-I
Lowcock,Capt.RJ, MC WIA 26Apr.17-I, WIA 20Jul.17-I
Lowe,Capt.CN, 22Oct.16-I, inj 24Mar.17-I, 20May.18-I, 25Jun.18-I
Lowe,Sgt.J, WIA 6Mar.18-I
Lowe,Lt.M, KIA 27Jun.17-I
Lowe,2Lt.R, 4Sep.18-I, 16Sep.18-I
Lowe,Lt.TC, 4Apr.18-IV, 3May.18-IV
Lowery,Capt.AM, DoW 24Mar.17-I
Lownds,2Lt.RH, KIA 17Mar.17-I
Lowry,2Lt.FB, US. KIA 26Sep.18-IIB
Lowry,Lt.MM, 12Aug.18-I
Lowson,2Lt.CPF, 8Aug.16-I
Lowson,2Lt.JH, WIA POW 27Sep.16-I
Lowther,FSLt.C, KIA 21Aug.17-I
Lowthian,2Lt.J, inj 7Aug.18-I
Loyd,Lt.EEF, POW 15Sep.17-I
Luard,Lt.RB, POW 30Aug.18-I
Lubbock,Lt.,Capt.Hon.EFP, MC 26Oct.15-I, 4Nov.15-I, 28Nov.15-I, 19Dec.15-I, 20Oct.16-I, 9Feb.17-I, 6Mar.17-I, KIA 11Mar.17-I
Lucas,2Lt.AJ, WIA 3May.17-I
Lucas,Capt.Lord.AT, KIA 3Nov.16-I
Lucas,Capt.GB, DoW 16May.16-I
Lucas,LM.R, KIA 24Apr.18-III
Lucas,Lt.TCH, KIA 6Feb.17-I
Luchford,Lt.,Capt.HGET, MC 5Jun.17-I, 27Jul.17-I, 16Aug.17-I, KIA 2Dec.17-I
Luckley,2Lt.JJ, WIA 29Oct.18-I
Lucy,Lt., 6Sqn. 16Aug.18-I
Lucy,Lt.,Capt.RS, 1Apr.16-I, 10May.17-I
Ludlow-Hewitt,Capt.ER, 12Mar.15-I, 23Apr.15-I, 18Apr.15-I
Lufbery,Sgt.,Maj.GR, US. 30Jul.16-IIA, KIA 19May.18-IIB
Luke,2Lt.AWG, 8Jul.18-I, 9Jul.18-I
Luke,2Lt.F, Jnr. DSC CMH US. 12Sep.18-IIB, 18Sep.18-IIB, 28Sep.18-IIB, KIA 29Sep.18-IIB

Luke,2Lt.T, MC 66Sqn. WIA 28Jul.17-I
Luke,Capt.TC, MC 209Sqn. inj 26Aug.18-I
Lumb,2Lt.HF, 6Apr.18-I, WIA 15May.18-I
Lumley,Sgt.T, WIA 12Aug.18-I
Lumsden,2Lt.JC, US. KIA 28Jul.18-IIB
Lund,Lt.RJS, WIA 25Feb.17-I
Lupton,Capt.CR, 17Apr.18-I
Lussier,Lt.EJ, Can. 25Jul.18-I
Lusted,Sgt.GJ, 25Nov.15-I
Luther,2Lt.HG, WIA POW 4Nov.18-I
Lutyens,2Lt.AC, MC WIA 13Apr.17-I
Lutyens,Lt.FD, 22Oct.16-I
Luxmoore,Capt.FL, POW 18Mar.18-I
Luxton,Lt.WH, inj 16Aug.17-I
Luyt,2Lt.HVC, WIA 5Feb.18-I
Lyell,Lt.WH, WIA 15Jun.18-I
Lygon,Lt.Hon.H, 8Mar.15-I, 10May.15-I, 12May.15-I, 15May.15-I
Lyle,2Lt.JN, KIA 23Jan.17-I
Lynn,2Lt.F, POW 30Oct.18-I
Lyon-Hall,Lt.EH, 15Jul.18-I
Lytle,Capt.RS, USMC. 1Oct.18-I, 2Oct.18-I, 14Oct.18-IIB
Lytton,2Lt.,Lt. 16Sqn. 30Apr.17-I, 6May.17-I
Lytton,2Lt.PAB, KIA 4Feb.18-I
Lywood,Lt.GWG, 12May.15-I, 21Jul.15-I

M

M'Alery,Capt.JM, WIA 30Oct.17-I
Maasdorp,2Lt.CR, POW DoW 28Mar.18-I
MacAulay,2Lt.AC, POW 4Nov.18-I
MacAloney,Lt.CW, WIA 9Oct.17-I
MacAndrew,2Lt.CGO, KIA 2Oct.17-I
MacAndrew,Lt.JO, WIA 8Oct.18-I
MacArthur,1Lt.J,DSC US. KIA 20Jul.18-IIB
Macartney?,Lt.DA, see MacCartney
Macaskie,2Lt.DSC, WIA POW 20Jul.16-I
Macaulay,Lt.AC, 29Aug.18-I
Macbean,Lt.IB, WIA 2Jul.18-I
MacBean,Lt.REL, 6Jun.18-I
MacBrayne,2Lt.DCH, KIA 21Jun.17-I
MacCallum,Capt., 7Sqn. 2Aug.16-I
MacCallum,Lt.JRMG, 8Aug.18-I
MacCartney?,Lt.DA, KIA name Macartney? 17Jun.18-I, 29Jun.18-I
MacClintock,Lt., 2Sqn. 13Feb.16-I, 24Feb.16-I, 29Feb.16-I
MacDaniel,2Lt.JR, KIA 18Aug.17-I
MacDonald,Lt.AD, 26Oct.18-I
MacDonald,FSLt.AF, WIA 25Sep.17-I
Macdonald,2Lt.,Capt.AL, MC 18Jul.16-I, KIA 26Aug.17-I
Macdonald,2Lt.BJ, POW KIA? 30Aug.18-I
Macdonald,Capt.CBR, WIA 25Jul.18-I, 23Oct.18-I
Macdonald,2Lt.CD, KIA 4Nov.18-I
MacDonald,FSLt.CG, Kld 11Mar.18-I
MacDonald,Lt.DA, Can. POW 27May.18-I
MacDonald,1Lt.DL, US. POW 10Jul.18-IIB
MacDonald,2Lt.DP, POW 3Apr.17-I
MacDonald,Sgt.ER, 17May.18-I, 8Aug.18-I, POW? 9Aug.18-I
Macdonald,2Lt.GK, WIA 1Sep.16-I
Macdonald,2Lt.HB, 14Aug.17-I, 5Sep.17-I
MacDonald,2Lt.HO, 16Mar.18-I
MacDonald,Lt.IDR, 10Dec.17-I
Macdonald,Sgt.JS, inj 16Sep.18-I
Macdonald,Lt.K, KIA 16Aug.18-I
MacDonald,Capt.KG, inj KIA? 12Jun.17-I
MacDonald,Lt.KW, POW DoW 3Sep.17-I
Macdonald,2Lt.NC, 98Sqn. WIA 8May.18-I
MacDonald,Lt.NC, 98Sqn. 8Aug.18-I
MacDonald,2Lt.R, POW 16Feb.18-I
MacDonald,Lt.RM, POW 29Sep.18-I
Macdonald,2Lt.WF, KIA 23May.17-I
Macdonell,Capt., 4Sqn. 20Jun.15-I
Macdonnell,Capt., 6Sqn. 9May.15-I
MacDonnell,Capt.HC, DoW 23.5.15 20May.15-I
MacDonnell,Lt.IC, KIA 2Jul.16-I
MacDougall,2Lt.PA, WIA 24Oct.17-I, 12Mar.18-I
MacFadden?,2Lt.W, US. KIA 7Oct.18-IIB
Macfarland,Lt.FM, KIA 3Sep.18-I
Macfarlane,2Lt.,Capt.AL, 54Sqn. 10Aug.17-I, WIA 18Aug.17-I
Macfarlane,Lt.JL, 22Sqn. POW DoW 26.9.1917 17Aug.17-I
MacFarlane,Lt.P, KIA 10Aug.18-I
MacFarlane,Lt.RMC, name McFarlane? 24Mar.18-I, WIA 3Apr.18-I
MacFarlane,Lt.WK, POW 29Aug.18-I
Macfie,2Lt.JDA, WIA POW 31Aug.16-I
MacGeorge,2Lt., 34Sqn. 19Mar.17-I
MacGown,Lt.JC, inj POW 7Jul.17-I
MacGregor,2Lt.,Lt.A, 35Sqn. 10Apr.18-I, 23May.18-I, inj 1Jul.18-I
MacGregor,Lt.,Capt.A, 57Sqn. 8Aug.18-I, 5Sep.18-I
Macgregor,Lt.DADI, KIA 30Nov.17-I
MacGregor,Lt.IC, WIA 22Sep.17-I
MacGregor,Lt.JA, 13Oct.18-I
MacGregor,FSLt.NM, 22Mar.17-I, 15Sep.17-I
Macgregor,2Lt.RR, POW 21Sep.17-I
MacGregor,2Lt.TCS, KIA 8Jun.17-I
Machin,Lt.RFC, Aust. 15Aug.18-I, 3Sep.18-I, KIA 18Sep.18-I
MacIlwaine,Capt.JM, KIA 22Mar.18-I
Macintosh,Lt.PD, WIA 17Jul.17-I
MacIntosh,2Lt.RR, POW 26May.17-I
Macintyre,2Lt.DH, WIA POW 9Jul.16-I
MacIntyre,2Lt.TM, 22Oct.18-I
Mack,AFCdr.RG, inj POW 12Apr.17-I
Mackain,2Lt.HF, KIA 27Feb.17-I
Mackay,Lt.AG, KIA 18May.17-I
Mackay,2Lt.,Lt.AW, WIA 25Aug.17-I, WIA 11Apr.18-I
MacKay,Capt.CJ, 2Sqn. WIA 27May.16-I
MacKay,Capt.CJ, 4Sqn. 21Jul.16-I, 29Jul.16-I, 30Jul.16-I, 31Jul.16-I
Mackay,2Lt.DDA, KIA 14Oct.18-I
Mackay,Capt.DRG, DFC POW DoW 11.11.1918 10Nov.18-I
Mackay,2Lt.EDA, 28Sep.18-I
Mackay,Capt.GC, Can. 10Nov.18-I
Mackay,2Lt.GF, WIA 18Aug.17-I
Mackay,2Lt.HAD, 25Jan.16-I, 7Feb.16-I, 25Jan.17-I
Mackay,Lt.HS, see Strathy Mackay
Mackay,Lt.HWM, DoW Mar.18-I
Mackay,2Lt.JA, KIA 11Sep.17-I
MacKay,Capt.JE, 6Mar.17-I
Mackay,Lt.MC, Aug.18-VIII
Mackay,2Lt.WA, 1Oct.16-I
Mackay,Lt.WB, POW 27Jul.17-I
MacKenzie,2Lt., 16Sqn. 21Apr.17-I
MacKenzie,2Lt.AD, KIA 15Sep.18-I
Mackenzie,Lt.AS, KIA 1Apr.17-I
Mackenzie,FLt.,FCdr.CR, 4Dec.16-I, KIA 24Jan.17-I
Mackenzie,2Lt.,Lt.DA, 25Oct.18-I, KIA 28Oct.18-I
Mackenzie,Lt.GO, KIA 27Sep.18-I
MacKenzie,Lt.J, KIA 1Dec.17-I
Mackenzie,2Lt.JP, WIA 13Apr.18-I
MacKenzie,2Lt.KI, KIA 8Apr.17-I
MacKenzie,Lt.RW, Aust. 1Dec.17-I
MacKenzie,2Lt.WG, 20Feb.18-I, 30Mar.18-I
Mackenzie,Lt.WJ, WIA 21Apr.18-I
Mackereth,Lt.,Capt.J, 15Jun.18-IV, WIA? POW 31Aug.18-IV
Mackie,1AM.G, 30Dec.15-I, 23Jan.16-I, 25Jan.16-I
Mackie,2AM.J, WIA 3Apr.17-I
Mackie,AM.PG, 18Jul.18-I
Mackie,Lt.JM, KIA 16Jul.18-I
Mackinnon,2Lt.JF, KIA 28Nov.17-I
Mackinnon,2Lt.JM, WIA? inj? 24Sep.18-I
Mackintosh,2Lt.C, KIA 5Apr.17-I
Macklin,Lt.CP, KIA 30May.18-I
Mackrow,Lt.NH, WIA 29Apr.17-I
MacLanachan,2Lt.,Lt.W, 12Jul.17-I, 12Nov.17-I
MacLaren,Lt., 14Sqn. 2Aug.16-VII
MacLaren,2Lt.,Capt.DR, Can. 6Mar.18-I, 20May.18-I, 15Sep.18-I
Maclaren,2Lt.WFEdeB, WIA 16Jun.17-I
MacLaughlin,2Lt.AW, KIA 29Oct.17-I
Maclean,Capt.AM, KIA 12Apr.18-I
Maclean,Capt.AP, POW DoW 18Mar.18-I
Maclean,Lt.D, 20Nov.17-I, 31Mar.18-I, WIA 1Apr.18-I
Maclean,2Lt.EV, WIA 5Aug.16-I
MacLean,Capt.LJ, 3Feb.18-I
MacLean,Lt.LJ, 19Jun.17-I
Maclean,2Lt.M, POW 26Oct.18-I
Maclean,Lt.MS, WIA 29Mar.18-I
Maclean,2Lt.RN, 2Apr.18-I
MacLean,2Lt.RSG, US. WIA 26Aug.17-I, KIA 26Oct.18-I
Maclean,2Lt.WA, WIA POW 16Aug.15-I
Macleay,Lt.HW, 23Nov.17-I
MacLeish,Lt.K, USNRF KIA 14Oct.18-I
Maclennan,AFCdr.GC, KIA 20Jul.17-I
MacLennan,Lt.JC, 10Nov.18-I
MacLennan,Lt.JE, POW 24Jan.17-I
Maclennan,Lt.JMcM, DFC POW 28Sep.18-I
MacLeod,2Lt.EG, 8Nov.17-I
MacLeod,Pte.J, 16Jun.17-I
MacLeod,Lt.MP, Can. 4Nov.18-I
Macloud,Pte.J, KIA 23Jun.17-I
MacMichael,Lt.WA, WIA 15May.18-I
Macmillan,2Lt.N, 5Jun.17-I, 21Aug.17-I, 25Aug.17-I
MacMillan,FSLt.RE, POW 19Sep.17-I
MacMonagle,Sgt.D, US. KIA 24Sep.17-IIA
MacMurchy,2Lt.IU, KIA 9Oct.17-I
MacNair,Lt.I, KIA 12Apr.18-I
Macnamara,Lt.AW, KIA 3Sep.18-I
MacNeil,Sgt.WJ, 23Oct.18-I
Macniell,2Lt.DA, KIA 16Nov.16-I
MacNiven,2Lt.AO, KIA 5Sep.17-I
MacPhee,2Lt.GG, POW 10Apr.18-I
Macpherson,2Lt.AR, 2Sep.18-I
MacPherson,2Lt.HD, KIA 14Oct.17-I
Macpherson,2Lt.JMS, POW 12Aug.18-I
Macpherson,2Lt.RC, 21Jul.15-I, POW 29Jul.15-I
Macpherson,Lt.WE, 16Sep.18-I
Macqueen,2Lt.AJ, 2Sep.18-I
MacQueen,Lt.NA, KIA 25Mar.17-I
Macrae,2Lt.CE, KIA 10Nov.16-I
MacRae,Lt.JDG, POW 5Oct.17-VIII
MacVicker,Lt.JEC, KIA 22Jul.18-I
Maddocks,Capt.HH, 3Jan.18-I
Madeley,2Lt.CN, KIA 19Jan.18-I
Maden,2Lt.,Lt.F, 26Aug.17-I, 20Sep.17-I
Madge,Lt.JBC, WIA POW 1Sep.17-I
Madge,2Lt.WT, KIA 16Aug.18-I
Madill,Lt.RMcK, 5Jun.17-I, KIA 23Jul.17-I
Magee,Lt.EA, POW 5Jun.18-I
Magenais,2Lt.FM, WIA 11May.17-I
Magor,Capt.GA, KIA 22Apr.18-I
Magor,Capt.NA, KIA 24Apr.18-III
Magor,FSLt.GA, WIA 18May.17-VI
Magoun,2Lt.FP, WIA 10Apr.18-I
Magrath,FSLt.WS, POW 9Nov.17-I
Maguire,2Lt.ML, MC 22Apr.17-VIII, POW DoW 5.17 28Apr.17-VIII
Mahon,Sgt.CMA, KIA 23Oct.18-I
Mahony,Lt.MFJR, WIA 24Aug.18-I, POW 20Sep.18-I
Mahony-Jones,Capt.GJ, KIA 7Apr.17-I
Main,2Lt.R, POW 23Nov.17-I
Maingot,2Lt.JH, 12Aug.17-VII
Mainwaring,2Lt.HTW, 21Mar.18-I
Mais,2Lt.RC, WIA 16May.18-I
Maisey,2Lt.HC, KIA 29Oct.18-I
Maitland-Heriot,FLt.CA, POW 12Feb.17-V
Makepeace,2Lt.RM, 11Jul.17-I, 27Jul.17-I, 3Sep.17-I
Malcolm,Lt.AA, KIA 17May.18-I
Malcolm,2Lt.AG, KIA 2Oct.18-I
Malcolm,1Lt.DC, US. 27Oct.18-IIB
Malcolm,Lt.OL, KIA 26Sep.18-I
Malcolmson,2Lt.JC, POW 28Sep.18-I
Malcomson,Capt.TS, 30Nov.17-I, 10Dec.17-I
Mallett,2Lt.D, POW 14Jul.18-I
Mallett,Lt.HP, WIA POW 8Aug.18-I
Malley,Capt.GF, MC Aust. WIA 18May.18-I, 1Jun.18-I
Malley-Martin,Lt.J, KIA 29Oct.18-I
Malloch,Lt.AC, WIA POW 28Jul.17-I
Mallous,2Lt.CG, POW 10Aug.17-I
Malone,FSLt.JJ, DSO KIA 30Apr.17-I
Malpas,Sgt.D, KIA 25Jul.18-I
Maltby,TLt.,Lt.AH, KIA 27May.18-I, 4Jun.18-I
Maltby,Capt.PC, 19Jan.16-I, 25Jan.16-I
Malthouse,Lt.PW, WIA 15Oct.17-I
Manby,Lt.RA, WIA 8Apr.17-I
Mandel,2Lt.O, USAS. POW 2Sep.18-I
Mandell,1Lt.SP, US. DoW 5Nov.18-IIB
Manfield,Lt.NP, KIA 9Sep.16-I
Mangan,Lt.DC, 25Aug.18-I
Manier,1Lt.EM, US. KIA 2Oct.18-IID
Manley,Lt., 52Sqn. 20Jul.17-I
Manley,2Lt.G, 6Sep.15-I
Manley,2Lt.GAC, POW 9Feb.18-I
Manley,2Lt.J, WIA 20Jul.16-I
Manley,2Lt.PS, POW 27Sep.18-I
Mann,Lt., 8Sqn. 10Sep.18-I
Mann,Lt., 12Sqn. 7May.17-I
Mann,Lt., Aden 23Jan.18-VII
Mann,2AM.A, POW DoW? 22Jan.18-I
Mann,2Lt.FA, POW 7Jan.17-I
Mann,2Lt.FAW, 7Apr.18-I
Mann,2Lt.HB, 17Mar.17-I
Mann,Lt.IA, KIA 9Aug.16-I
Mann,Sgt.R, WIA 8Jun.17-I
Mann,2Lt.SW, 3Sep.16-I, KIA 1Nov.16-I
Mann,FSLt.,Lt.WEG, 13Apr.18-I, 8May.18-I, 9Aug.18-I
Mann,2Lt.WG, KIA 28Nov.17-I
Manners-Smith,Lt.JA, WIA POW 21Aug.17-I
Manning,Capt.ER, Aust. 22Apr.17-I, 20May.17-I
Manning,Lt.ER, WIA 19Jul.16-I
Manning,Sgt.FG, KIA 13Aug.18-I
Manning,Lt.GF, 4Sep.18-I
Mannock,Lt.,Capt.,Maj.EC, MC DSO VC 7May.17-I, 7Jun.17-I, 12Jul.17-I, 23Sep.17-I, 25Sep.17-I, 1Jan.18-I, 12Apr.18-I, 11May.18-I, 17Jun.18-I, 7Jul.18-I, KIA 26Jul.18-I
Mansbridge,2Lt.LM, WIA 3Jun.17-I
Mansell,2Lt.WS, WIA 6Aug.16-I, 21Aug.17-I, KIA 11Sep.17-I
Mansell-Moullin,2Lt.O, POW 12Mar.15-I
Mansfield,Lt., 6Sqn. 31Jul.15-I
Mansfield,Capt., 7Sqn. 19Sep.15-I, 11Oct.15-I, 15Nov.15-I
Mansfield,Capt.JA, WIA 23Nov.17-I
Mansfield,Capt.WHC, inj 19Jan.15-III
Mantle,2Lt.HS, WIA POW 24Sep.18-I
Manuel,Capt.JG, Can. 9Jun.18-I
Manuel,Capt.JG, KIA 10Jun.18-I
Manuel,Capt.RL, 24Sep.18-I
Manzer,Lt.,Capt.R, DFC Can. 28May.18-I, 27Jun.18-I, POW 8Aug.18-I
Maplestowe,2Lt.AN, WIA 15Aug.17-I
Mapplebeck,Lt.,Capt.GW, 19Aug.14-I, 20Sep.14-I, WIA 22Sep.14-I, POW 11Mar.15-I
Mapplebeck,Capt.T, WIA POW 9Nov.16-I
Marburg,Lt., 3Sqn. WIA inj? 7Dec.15-I
March,2Lt.CH, WIA POW 15Feb.17-I
March,2Lt.JGW, WIA 25Mar.18-I
March,2Lt.WFG, POW DoW 24Oct.17-I
Marchand,2Lt.EF, POW 22Nov.17-I
Marchant,Lt.EA, POW 14Sep.18-I
Marchant,2Lt.FWG, DoW 25.10.1916 22Oct.16-I
Marchant,2Lt.LW, 23Oct.18-I
Mardock,FLt.FW, POW 24Jul.16-I
Mare-Montembault,2Lt.MJJG, 10Oct.16-I, POW 6Mar.17-I
Margerison,2Lt.T, KIA 13Apr.17-I
Marginson,2Lt.W, 21Aug.18-I
Margolouth,2Lt.AH, KIA 2Apr.17-I
Marion,Lt.RJ, KIA 21Apr.18-I
Marix,FLt.,FCdr.RLG, DSO 8Oct.14-I, 8Oct.15-I, 2May.15-V, 17May.15-V, Jun.15-V
Mark,Lt.RT, MC 26Mar.18-I, 4Apr.18-I, 20May.18-I
Markham,Lt.WH, WIA 15Aug.18-I
Markquick,2Lt.EB, KIA 16Sep.18-I
Marks,Capt.CH, KIA 23Oct.15-I
Marks,2Lt.GID, Can. 14Aug.18-I
Marm,Lt., 12Sqn. 16Aug.17-I
Marnham,2Lt.HC, 3Jun.16-I, KIA 23Aug.16-I
Marriott,Lt.KMH, KIA 20Sep.18-VII
Mars,Lt.WS, 11Aug.18-I, inj INT 15Sep.18-I

Marsden,2Lt.C, *46Sqn.* **inj** 28Mar.18-*I*
Marsden,2Lt.C, *210Sqn.* **POW** 9Jun.18-*I*
Marsden,2Lt.CC, *7Sqn.* **WIA** 27Jul.17-*I*
Marsden,Lt.W, **WIA** 9Nov.18-*I*
Marsh,2Lt.GRT, **POW** 24Feb.18-*I*
Marsh,SFLt.LL, **POW** .18-*VI*
Marsh,Lt.RM, **POW** 7Jun.17-*I*
Marshall,Capt., *8Sqn.* 7Jun.15-*I*
Marshall,2Lt.BS, MC **KIA** 7Jun.17-*I*
Marshall,Lt.CB, **WIA** 28Jul.18-*I*
Marshall,Capt.E, **POW** 21Sep.17-*I*
Marshall,2Lt.F, **WIA** 24Aug.18-*I*
Marshall,Lt.HA, *Can.* 12Apr.18-*I*
Marshall,2Lt.JA, **KIA** 6Apr.17-*I*
Marshall,2Lt.,Lt.JW, 26Aug.18-*I*, **WIA** 2Sep.18-*I*
Marshall,2Lt.L, **KIA** 23Nov.17-*I*
Marshall,2Lt.NH?, **POW** 14Jul.18-*I*
Marshall,Capt.R, **POW** Aug.18-*I*
Marshall,Lt.R, 21Jul.15-*I*, 29Jul.15-*I*
Marshall,2Lt.RM, **WIA** 15Sep.18-*I*
Marshall,2Lt.WS, **WIA** 8Jul.18-*I*
Marshall-Lewis,2Lt.F, **inj** 13Aug.17-*I*, **KIA** 13Sep.17-*I*
Marsland,2Lt., *12Sqn.* 25Aug.18-*I*
Martin,Lt., *6Sqn.* 2Sep.18-*I*, 11Oct.18-*I*
Martin,Cpl., *7Sqn.* 25Dec.14-*III*
Martin,2Lt.AD, 12Aug.17-*I*
Martin,Lt.AW, **POW** 7May.17-*I*
Martin,2Lt.CH, *Aust.* **KIA** 17Feb.18-*I*
Martin,Lt.DA, *US.* **POW** 1Sep.18-*I*
Martin,2Lt.FA, **WIA** 2Oct.17-*I*
Martin,Lt.FJ, **WIA** 3Jun.17-*I*
Martin,2Lt.FR, **KIA** 29Jun.17-*I*
Martin,Lt.FWH, *Can.* **KIA** 9Aug.18-*I*
Martin,2Lt.G, **WIA** 30Jul.18-*I*
Martin,Lt.J, **POW** .18-*I*
Martin,Lt.JB, **WIA** 28Mar.18-*I*
Martin,1Lt.RC, *US.* **WIA POW** 1Aug.18-*IIB*
Martin,Capt.RH, **KIA** 24Mar.18-*I*
Martin,Lt.TC, **KIA** 12Aug.18-*I*
Martin,2Lt.WH, **WIA** 17Feb.18-*I*
Martin,Lt.WS, *Aust.* **KIA** 12Jun.18-*I*
Martin-Bell,2Lt.E, **KIA** 28Sep.18-*I*
Martin-Massey,2Lt.H, **inj** 22Oct.16-*I*, **inj** 4Feb.17-*I*
Martyn,Lt., *139Sqn.* 1Sep.18-*IV*
Martyn,Lt.EM, **KIA** 15May.18-*I*
Martyn,2Lt.TJC, 27Sep.17-*I*
Marvin,Lt.HL, **KIA** 26Oct.17-*I*
Mase,Lt.HF, **POW** 28Aug.16-*I*
Maskell,FLt., *RNAS.* 17Sep.16-*VII*
Mason,Lt., *16Sqn.* **KIA** 28Apr.17-*I*
Mason,Maj.AB, 26/27Jun.18-*I*
Mason,2Lt.AW, **KIA** 11May.17-*I*
Mason,Lt.B, **inj** 16Aug.17-*I*
Mason,2Lt.C, 4Sep.18-*I*
Mason,2Lt.CA, **WIA** 11Apr.18-*I*
Mason,Lt.CJ, **KIA** 21Apr.18-*I*
Mason,2Lt.EB, 14Oct.16-*I*
Mason,2Lt.H, **POW** 20Jun.18-*I*
Mason,Cpl.J, 20Nov.17-*I*
Mason,2Lt.SJ, 9Nov.18-*I*
Mason,Sgt.WCE, **POW DoW** 26Sep.18-*I*
Massey,2Lt., *16Sqn.* 2Aug.16-*I*
Masson,2Lt.RG, **KIA** 23May.17-*I*
Master,Lt.CFO, **WIA** leg 3May.15-*I*
Masters,Lt.E, 14Jul.18-*IV*
Masters,2Lt.G, *NZ.* 24Mar.17-*I*, **KIA** 3Apr.17-*I*
Masters,2Lt.GA, **WIA** 26Dec.16-*I*
Mather,FSLt.AS, **POW** 1May.17-*I*
Mather,Lt.E, **KIA** 6Apr.18-*I*
Mather,Lt.TG, 20Jan.18-*I*
Matheson,Lt.AM, **POW** 1Oct.18-*I*
Matheson,Lt.AP, **KIA** 13Jul.17-*I*
Matheson,2Lt.WD, **WIA** 16Mar.17-*I*
Mathew,Lt.CG, **POW** 13Jul.17-*I*
Mathews,2Lt.EVD, **WIA** 24Aug.16-*I*
Mathews,2Lt.G, *55Sqn.* **KIA** 2Oct.17-*I*
Mathews,Capt.JW, **KIA** 1Aug.18-*I*
Matson,2Lt.AW, **POW** 18Mar.18-*I*
Matt,2Lt.AO, **inj** 21Mar.18-*I*
Matthews,2Lt.A, **WIA** 29Jan.17-*I*
Matthews,1Lt.AF, *USAS.* 9Aug.18-*I*, **KIA** 24Aug.18-*I*

Matthews,2Lt.BH, 16Sep.18-*I*
Matthews,Lt.CB, **WIA** 22Mar.18-*I*
Matthews,Lt.EA, **KIA** 2Apr.18-*I*
Matthews,2Lt.F, **WIA POW** 11Apr.17-*I*
Matthews,2Lt.FA, **KIA** 24Apr.17-*I*
Matthews,Lt.GC, **WIA** 16Sep.18-*I*
Matthews,2Lt.H, **KIA** 15Jan.17-*VI*
Matthews,2AM.HF, **KIA** 6Sep.17-*I*
Matthews,2Lt.HM, **WIA** 28Sep.18-*I*
Matthews,2Lt.JA, **POW** 15Sep.18-*I*
Matthews,1Lt.RP, *US.* **KIA** 26Sep.18-*IIB*
Matthews,Lt.WH, 12Apr.18-*I*
Matthews,2Lt.WJ, **WIA** 13Nov.17-*I*
Matthewson,2Lt.K, **KIA** 3Aug.16-*I*
Matthewson,2Lt.RWB, **POW** 12Oct.17-*I*
Matthey,2Lt.SE, **KIA** 3Oct.18-*I*
Maud,Capt.CM, 7Oct.18-*IV*
Maudesley,Lt.F, **WIA** 25Aug.18-*I*
Maudsley,2Lt.JB, 12Jul.17-*I*, **WIA** 22Jul.17-*I*
Maule,Lt.EB, **KIA** 6Feb.17-*I*
Maund,Lt.HB, 18May.18-*I*
Mawdsley, *see* Maudsley
Mawer,2Lt.AL, **POW** 21Sep.18-*IV*
Mawle,Lt.NWR, *initials* NRW? 17Jul.18-*I*, **WIA** 8Aug.18-*I*
Maxted,Lt.OD, **POW** 12Apr.17-*I*
Maxwell,Mjr.RS, 9Nov.18-*I*
Maxwell,1Lt.CB, *US.* **POW** 8Nov.18-*IIB*
Maxwell,Cpl.G, **WIA POW** 31May.16-*I*
Maxwell,Capt.GJC, 5Jul.18-*I*
Maxwell,SLt.JE, **KIA** 30Mar.17-*VI*
Maxwell,Maj.RS, MC 11Apr.18-*I*
Maxwell,2Lt.WS, **KIA** 27Mar.18-*I*
Maxwell-Pike,2Lt.R, 5May.15-*I*, 10May.15-*I*, 26May.15-*I*, 29Jul.15-*I*, **DoW** 9Aug.15-*I*
May,Cpl., *20Sqn.* 14Mar.16-*I*
May,3AM.HB, **INT** 2Aug.18-*III*
May,Sgt.JL, **WIA POW** 8Aug.18-*I*
May,Lt.LB, **POW** 19Dec.17-*IV*
May,Sgt.T, **WIA** 9Mar.16-*I*
May,FSLt.TC, **KIA** 24Jul.17-*I*
May,2Lt.WR, 21Apr.18-*I*
May,Lt.,Capt.WR, *Can.* **WIA** 8Aug.18-*I*, 21Sep.18-*I*
Mayberry,Lt.R, **inj** 26Dec.16-*I*, **WIA** 11Mar.17-*I*, **KIA** 15Nov.17-*I*
Maybery,Lt.,Capt.RA, MC 7Jul.17-*I*, 27Jul.17-*I*, 23Sep.17-*I*, **KIA** 19Dec.17-*I*
Mayes,2Lt.HG, *US.* **WIA POW** 2Jul.18-*IIB*
Mayger,Sgt.WN, MM **KIA** 28Sep.18-*I*
Mayne,Lt.HGL, **POW** 27Oct.14-*I*
Mayne,2Lt.RA, **WIA POW** 16Mar.18-*I*
Mayo,Capt.AJ, **KIA** 9Aug.18-*I*
Mayoss,2Lt.WF, **WIA** 20Nov.17-*I*, **WIA** 9Mar.18-*I*
McAdam,2Lt.,Lt.JL, 29Sep.18-*I*, **WIA** 5Oct.18-*I*
McAlery,Lt.,Capt.JM, 26Sep.16-*I*, **WIA** 1Aug.18-*I*
McAndrew,Lt.H, 12Aug.18-*I*
McArdle,Lt.HF, **KIA** 18Sep.17-*I*
McArthur,2Lt., *12Sqn.* 26Sep.15-*I*
McArthur,Capt.JH, **KIA** 27Feb.17-*I*
McArthur,Capt.LW, MC **KIA** 27May.17-*I*
McAslan,2Lt.J, **WIA** 2Sep.18-*I*
McBain,Capt.GBS,DSC MC **KIA** 10May.18-*I*
McBain,Lt.W, **KIA** 1Nov.18-*IV*
McBlain,Lt.GN, 27Mar.18-*I*
McBride,2Lt.JG, **KIA** 8Oct.18-*I*
McCaig,Lt.P, **KIA** 27Sep.18-*I*
McCaig,2Lt.WG, **KIA** 1Oct.18-*I*
McCall,Lt.,Capt.FRG, MC DSO DFC *Can.*, 21Mar.18-*I*, *Can.* 25May.18-*I*, 9Jun.18-*I*, 8Aug.18-*I*, 9Aug.18-*I*, 17Aug.18-*I*
McCall,Lt.JD, 8Nov.17-*I*
McCall,2Lt.M, **inj** 25Jun.17-*I*, **WIA** 23Jul.17-*I*
McCallum,2Lt.AHK, **POW** 8Apr.17-*I*
McCallum,Lt.JR?, **KIA** *initials* JRRG? 23Aug.18-*I*
McCallum,Capt.KC, 6Apr.17-*I*, **WIA** 22Apr.17-*I*
McCann,Lt.AV, *Aust.* 19Sep.18-*VII*, 19Oct.18-*VII*
McCann,Lt.CM, **POW** 12Apr.18-*I*
McCarthy,Lt.BL, **WIA** 1Aug.18-*I*
McCarthy,Lt.FW, *initials* WF? 22Aug.18-*I*, **WIA** 9Nov.18-*I*
McCarthy,2Lt.T, **KIA** 24Aug.18-*I*
McCash,Lt.JW, **KIA** 23Nov.17-*I*

McChesney,2Lt.HA, *US.* **POW** 10Jul.18-*IIB*
McChlery,2Lt.JM, 3Oct.18-*I*, **KIA** 8Oct.18-*I*
McCleery,Lt.EPE, *Aust.* **KIA** 17Aug.18-*I*
McClendon,1Lt.JH, *US.* **KIA** 11Aug.18-*IIB*
McClennan,2Lt.JC, *US.* **WIA** 4Sep.18-*IIB*
McClintock,Capt.RStC, 10Mar.18-*I*
McClinton,Lt.FD, **WIA** 1Sep.18-*I*
McClure,1Lt.DM, *US.* **POW** 16Sep.18-*IIB*
McClure,1Lt.HG, *US.* **POW** 17Jul.18-*IIB*
McClure,Lt.IH, **WIA** 4Jun.18-*I*
McConchie,Lt.TL, **POW** 1Jul.18-*I*
McCondach,Sgt.R, **KIA** 14Oct.18-*I*
McCone,2Lt.JP, *US.* **KIA** 24Mar.18-*I*
McConkey,Lt.TW, **WIA** 11May.17-*I*
McConnachie,Lt.WW, 27May.18-*I*
McConnell,2Lt.HJ, **KIA** 31May.18-*I*
McConnell,2Lt.HLC, **DoW** 24.11.17 10Nov.17-*VII*
McConnell,Sgt.JR, *US.* **KIA** 19Mar.17-*IIA*
McConnell,2Lt.,Lt.RK, *Can.* 21Mar.18-*I*, 23Apr.18-*I*, 8Sep.18-*I*
McConnell-Wood,Lt.A, **POW** 8Aug.18-*I*
McConnochie,Lt., *5Sqn.* 4Nov.15-*I*
McConville,Lt.M, **WIA** 15Jun.18-*I*
McCoo,2Lt.WR, **WIA** 11Apr.18-*I*
McCormack,Capt.G, **WIA** 24Sep.18-*I*
McCormick,Lt.EJ, **KIA** 14May.17-*I*
McCormick,1Lt.JF, *US.* **KIA** 3Nov.18-*IIB*
McCormick,1Lt.RC, *US.* **WIA** 5Sep.18-*IID*
McCormick,2Lt.VR, *US.* **WIA? KIFA** 12Sep.18-*IIB*
McCowen,2Lt.EL, **WIA** 15Aug.18-*I*
McCracken,Lt.EJC, **POW** 13Aug.18-*I*
McCrea,2Lt.PCS, 28Sep.18-*I*, **POW** 14Oct.18-*I*
McCreary,Lt.FL, 15Aug.17-*I*, **WIA** 25Sep.17-*I*
McCreary,Lt.HC, 23Jun.18-*I*, **KIA** 2Jul.18-*I*
McCubbin,2Lt.GR, 18Jun.16-*I*, **WIA** 26Jun.16-*I*
McCudden,2Lt.JA, MC 19Feb.18-*I*, **KIA** 18Mar.18-*I*
McCudden,Sgt.,Capt.,Maj.JTB,VC DSO MC MM 19Jul.15-*I*, 19Dec.15-*I*, 5Jan.16-*I*, 6Sep.16-*I*, 26Jul.17-*I*, 18Aug.17-*I*, 5Sep.17-*I*, 23Sep.17-*I*, 21Oct.17-*I*, 18Nov.17-*I*, 5Dec.17-*I*, 26Feb.18-*I*, **DoI** 9Jul.18-*I*
McCulloch,2Lt.AFG, *Aust.* **POW** 28Jul.18-*I*
McCulloch,2Lt.IMB, **POW** 2Sep.18-*I*
McCullough,2Lt.FJ, **KIA** 8Nov.17-*I*
McCullough,Cpl.TL, *USMCR* 29Sep.18-*I*
McCurdy,2Lt.JE, *US.* **WIA** 6Oct.18-*IIB*
McCutcheon,2Lt.BJ, **KIA** 8Aug.18-*I*
McCutcheon,2Lt.HE, **KIFA** 3Sep.16-*I*
McDermott,1Lt.CW, *US.* **KIA** 28Oct.18-*IIB*
McDermott,2Lt.WE, 28Oct.18-*I*
McDiarmid,2Lt.G, **WIA** 10Aug.16-*VII*
McDonald,Lt., *30Sqn.* 25Oct.18-*VIII*
McDonald,FSLt.A, **POW** 24Oct.17-*I*
McDonald,2Lt.AB, **WIA** 21Sep.18-*I*
McDonald,2Lt.DC, 23Oct.18-*I*, **POW** 4Nov.18-*I*
McDonald,Lt.FO, **WIA** 13Aug.18-*I*, 15Sep.18-*I*
McDonald,Lt.HC, 12Aug.18-*I*
McDonald,Lt.HO, **POW** 29Jul.17-*I*
McDonald,Capt.IDR, 28May.18-*I*
McDonald,Lt.J, *22Sqn.* 27Aug.18-*I*
McDonald,Lt.J, DFC *226Sqn.* **POW** 30Aug.18-*IV*
McDonald,2Lt.JCJ, **KIA** 14Oct.18-*I*
McDonald,Lt.JJ, **INT** 15Sep.18-*I*
McDonald,Lt.NC, 21May.18-*I*
McDonald,Capt.R, *Can.* **KIA** 8May.18-*I*
McDonald,Lt.WN, **WIA** 6Feb.17-*I*
McDougall,2Lt.,Lt.NM, **inj** 22Aug.18-*I*, **inj** 11Oct.18-*I*
McDowell,2Lt.SA, *US.* **WIA POW** 16Sep.18-*IIB*
McElligott,2Lt.J, *Aust.* **POW** 1May.18-*VII*
McElroy,2Lt.,Capt.GEH, MC DFC *Irl.* 28Dec.17-*I*, 21Feb.18-*I*, 26Jun.18-*I*, **KIA** 31Jul.18-*I*
McElroy,1Lt.JW, *US.* **KIA** 29Sep.18-*IIB*
McElroy,Lt.VH, **KIA** 2Sep.18-*I*
McElvain,1Lt.CA, *US.* **POW** 1Aug.18-*IIB*
McEntee,2Lt.GO, **POW** 26Apr.17-*I*
McEntegart,Capt.B, 2Sep.18-*I*
McEvoy,Lt.C, 1Aug.18-*IV*
McEwan,Lt.CM, *Can.* 19Jun.18-*IV*
McEwan,Lt.GC, **KIA** 7Jun.18-*I*
McEwan,2Lt.JG, 7Oct.15-*I*, **WIA POW** 10Jan.16-*I*
McEwan,Capt.JHF, **POW** 16Jul.16-*I*

McEwen,2Lt.BC, 26Oct.15-*I*
McFarlane, *see* MacFarlane?
McFaul,Lt.LL, **KIA** 10Jul.18-*I*
McFerran,2Lt.TM, **KIA** 21Jun.17-*I*
McGavin,2Lt.PL, **KIA** 14Aug.17-*I*
McGee,2Lt.WR, **KIA** 12Jun.18-*I*
McGill,Lt.JA, **KIA** 6Sep.18-*I*
McGinness,Lt.PJ, *Aust.* 24Aug.18-*VII*
McGoun,Lt.FP, 28Oct.18-*I*
McGovern,2Lt.T, **WIA** 9Mar.18-*I*
McGrath,1AM.T, 19Sep.17-*I*
McGregor,2Lt.A, 1Apr.18-*I*
McGregor,Lt.D, **WIA** 14May.18-*I*
McGregor,Capt.DU, *Can.* 26Aug.17-*I*
McGregor,Capt.MC, *NZ.* 1Jun.18-*I*, 8Oct.18-*I*
McGregor-Turnbull,Maj.ER?, **POW** 25Apr.18-*VII*
McHardy,2Lt.AW, **KIA** 10Nov.18-*I*
McHenry,2Lt.FL, **WIA?** 22Oct.18-*I*
McIlraith,Lt.EF, 12Apr.18-*I*
McIlvaine,2Lt.JJ, *US.* **POW** 3Nov.18-*IIB*
McInnes,2Lt.CR, **WIA** 1Oct.18-*I*
McIntosh,Lt.DD, 20May.17-*I*
McIntosh,2Lt.FG, **WIA POW** 31Aug.16-*I*
McIntosh,Lt.VB, **KIA** 10Aug.18-*I*
McIntyre,2Lt.AM, 1Oct.18-*I*
McIntyre,2Lt.JB, **KIA** 16Aug.18-*I*
McIntyre,Lt.LH, *Can.* **KIA** 21Aug.18-*I*
McKay,Capt.AE, 19Nov.17-*I*, **KIA** 28Dec.17-*I*
McKay,Capt.EA, MC DFC **POW** 22Aug.18-*I*
McKay,Lt.JM, **POW?** 8Aug.18-*I*
McKay,Lt.JT, **KIA** 3Jul.18-*I*
McKeague,2Lt.HW, **WIA** 9Apr.18-*I*
McKechnie,Lt.WGB, **WIA** 11Sep.17-*I*
McKee,Sgt?,HJ, *US.* **POW** 8Feb.18-*IIC*
McKeever,Lt.,Capt.AE, *Can.* 20Jun.17-*I*, 26Jun.17-*I*, 16Oct.17-*I*, 30Nov.17-*I*
McKeever,2Lt.S, **WIA** 26Sep.18-*I*
McKelvey,FSLt.MT, **WIA POW** 11Apr.18-*I*
McKelvie,Lt.JA, 19Mar.16-*I*, 30Mar.16-*I*
McKenna,2Lt.JM, **KIA** 2Oct.17-*I*
McKenna,2Lt.RSV, 19Aug.18-*I*
McKenna,Lt.T, 28Nov.15-*I*
McKenzie,2Lt.A, **KIA** 13Jun.18-*I*
McKenzie,2Lt.GW, **KIA** 20Sep.17-*I*
McKenzie,Lt.RW, *Aust.* 6Dec.17-*I*
McKeown,2Lt.CJW, **POW** 18Feb.18-*I*
McKeown,Lt.JAH, *Aust.* **KIA** 14Oct.18-*I*
McKeown,1Lt.SE, *US.* **WIA POW** 7Jul.18-*IIB*
McKerness,Cpl.WJ, *US.* **KIA** 15Aug.18-*IIC*
McKerrell,Lt.WAS, **DoW** 10Apr.18-*I*
McKie,Sgt.J, **KIA** 8Oct.18-*I*
McKim,2Lt.JNB, **KIA** 10Mar.18-*I*
McKimmon,1Lt.WS, *US.* **WIA** 5Oct.18-*IIB*
McKinley,2Lt.NR, 16Sep.18-*I*
McKinnie,Lt.HT, **POW?** 4Sep.18-*I*
McKinnon,Ens.TN, *USNRF* **KIA** 20Aug.18-*I*
McKissock,2Lt.CW, **POW** 6May.17-*I*
McKissock,Lt.WE, **KIA** 1Jun.17-*I*
McLachan,Lt.AH, **WIA** 14Apr.18-*I*
McLaren,2Lt.FM, **KIA** 12Aug.17-*I*
McLaren,Lt.HD, DFC 16Sep.18-*I*, 4Oct.18-*I*
McLaren,2Lt.WS, **DoW** 19.11.1917 18Nov.17-*I*
McLaren-Pearson,Lt.J, **POW** 21Oct.18-*I*
McLauchlan,Cpl.FY, **KIFA** 23May.18-*I*
McLaughlin,Pte.A, **KIA?** 22Jul.17-*I*
McLaughlin,Lt.R, 18Jun.18-*I*, 8Aug.18-*I*
McLaurin,2Lt.D, **POW** 21Oct.17-*I*
McLean,Lt.DG, **KIA** 4Feb.18-*IV*
McLean,2Lt.JM, **WIA** 15Aug.17-*I*
McLean,2Lt.TW, **KIA** 21Sep.17-*I*
McLean,2Lt.WJ, **WIA** 25Aug.18-*I*
McLeay,2Lt.DM, **KIA** 23Mar.17-*I*
McLellan,2Lt.HL, **KIA** 21Sep.18-*I*
McLennan,Lt.JC, 16Sep.18-*I*
McLeod,Capt., *4Sqn.* 28Nov.15-*I*
McLeod,2Lt.AA, *Can.* **DoW** 6.11.1918 AW
McLeod,Lt.DW, 30Apr.17-*I*, **WIA** 23May.17-*I*
McLeod,2Lt.ELH, **WIA** 12Apr.18-*I*
McLeod,Lt.GD, **POW** 8Jun.18-*IV*
McLeod,2Lt.RL, **WIA?** 28Sep.18-*I*
McLintock,2Lt.JL, **KIA** 26Feb.18-*I*
McMaking,Lt.OL, 22Jul.17-*I*, **KIA** 11Sep.17-*I*

McManus,Lt.GE, **INT** 15Sep.18-*I*
McMaster,Cpl.D, **POW** 16May.16-*I*
McMechan,AM.J, 9Oct.17-*I*
McMichael,Lt.GB, **POW** 15Sep.17-*I*
McMillan,2AM.AG, **inj** 24Mar.17-*I*
McMillan,Lt.CMcW, **KIA** 27Jun.18-*I*
McMillan,Capt.JC, **DoW** 6.2.1917 3Feb.17-*I*
McMurty,Maj., *16Sqn.* **KIA** 28Apr.17-*I*
McMurty,2Lt.EB, **KIA** 14Oct.18-*I*
McNally,Lt.PB, **KIA** 13Aug.17-*I*
McNamara,Lt.FH, *Aust.* VC 20Mar.17-*VII*
McNamara,2Lt.JC, **KIA** 2Jun.17-*I*
McNamara,Lt.JF, **POW** 4Nov.18-*I*
McNamara,2Lt.KP, **KIA** 29Jun.16-*I*
McNaughton,2Lt.,Capt.NG, MC 14Mar.16-*I*, 18Mar.16-*I*, **WIA** 21Apr.16-*I*, **KIA** 24Jun.17-*I*
McNay,2Lt.TH, 16May.18-*I*
McNeale,2Lt.TC, 27Sep.18-*I*, **KIA** 9Oct.18-*I*
McNeil,2Lt.FG, **KIA** 8Mar.18-*I*
McNeil,FSLt.PG, **KIA** 3Jun.17-*I*
McNiell,Sgt.WJ, 30Oct.18-*I*
McNish,2Lt.H, **KIA**? 22Oct.18-*I*
McNulty,1Lt.PH, *US.* **KIA** 13Sep.18-*IIB*
McPhee,Lt.AR, 8Aug.18-*I*
McPhee,Lt.R, *Can.* **POW** 4Sep.18-*I*
McPherson, 2Lt.B, **POW** 1Apr.18-*I*
McPherson, 2Lt.LA, **KIA** 28Jul.17-*I*
McPherson,Lt.RD, **WIA** 5Jul.18-*I*
McQuistan,2Lt.F, **WIA** 9May.17-*I*
McQuistan,Capt.FM, 5Oct.18-*I*
McRae,Lt.DJ, *Can.* **DoW** 2.2.1917 1Feb.17-*I*
McRae,Lt.JP, **WIA POW** 20Nov.17-*I*
McRae, 2Lt.WG, 21Sep.17-*I*
McTavish,2Lt.AM, 30Mar.18-*I*
McTavish,2Lt.D, **WIA POW** 30Apr.17-*I*
McVittie,2Lt.AE, 5Aug.17-*I*
Meakin,2Lt.GER, 6Jun.15-*I*, **INT** 3Jul.15-*I*
Mealing,2Lt.,Lt.ME, 2Apr.17-*I*, 16Mar.18-*I*, **KIA** 24Mar.18-*I*
Mearns,Lt.AH, **KIA** 24Jun.17-*I*
Mearns,2Lt.EA, 4Mar.17-*I*, 15Mar.17-*I*
Medhurst,2Lt.CEH, 8Dec.15-*I*
Medlen,2Lt.LL, **KIA** 22Dec.17-*I*
Medlicott,2Lt.HW, 19Sep.15-*I*, 22Sep.15-*I*, 2Oct.15-*I*, 10Oct.15-*I*, 11Oct.15-*I*, **POW** 10Nov.15-*I*
Mee,AG.Cpl.S, **WIA** 20Jul.17-*I*
Meek,2Lt.ES, *Can.* 12Oct.17-*I*
Meggitt,Lt.WG, MC 11Oct.17-*I*, **WIA POW** 8Nov.17-*I*
Meintjes,Capt.H, **WIA** 7May.17-*I*
Meissner,1Lt.JA, *US.* 2May.18-*IIB*, 28May.18-*IIB*
Mel,Lt.WJB, 20Sep.18-*I*
Melanson,Lt.AJ, 17Apr.18-*I*, **KIA** 9May.18-*I*
Melbourne?,2Lt.AR, *name* Melbourn? **KIA** 14Jun.18-*I*
Melbourne,Sgt.SW, **KIA** 16Jul.18-*I*
Mellen,1Lt.JM, *US.* **POW** 10Jul.18-*IIB*
Mellings,FLt,Capt.HT,DSC **WIA** 15Apr.18-*I*, **KIA** 22Jul.18-*I*
Mellor,2Lt.AB, **WIA** 3Aug.18-*I*
Mellor,Lt.DJT, **KIA** 7Sep.18-*I*
Mellor,Sgt.E, **KIA**? 7Sep.18-*I*
Mellows,Capt.AH, 25Oct.18-*VIII*
Melville,Lt.HT, **WIA** 1Jun.18-*I*, **KIA** 31Jul.18-*I*
Melvin,Lt.DL, **POW** 28Sep.18-*I*
Melvin,2Lt.WS, **KIA** 23Aug.18-*I*
Menendez,Lt.FTS, 21Sep.17-*I*
Mercer,Lt., *2Sqn.* 10Oct.18-*I*, 2Sqn. 15Oct.18-*I*
Mercer,Lt.GA, **POW** 9Apr.18-*I*
Mercer,Lt.H, **POW** 16Sep.18-*I*
Mercer,2Lt.LWK, **WIA** 26Apr.17-*I*
Mercer,Lt.PE, **WIA** 9Sep.18-*I*
Mercer,2Lt.WA, **WIA** 11Aug.18-*I*
Mercer-Smith,2Lt.V, **WIA POW** 16Jun.18-*I*
Merchant,2Lt.AW, 24Jul.17-*I*
Merchant,1AM.WT, **WIA** 28Jan.18-*III*
Meredith,2Lt.JJ, *US.* **WIA POW** 1Apr.18-*I*
Meredith,2Lt.OW, **KIA** 20Nov.17-*I*
Meredith,Lt.PR, **WIA** 3Jul.16-*I*
Meredith,Lt.RE, **KIA**? 25Jul.18-*I*
Merrill,1Lt.GB, *US.* **WIA** 15Sep.18-*IIB*
Merrill,1Lt.HW, *US.* 18Jul.18-*IIB*
Merrill,1Lt.JF, *US.* **KIA** 4Oct.18-*IIB*
Merritt,Lt.HE, 28Mar.18-*I*
Merton,2Lt.G, 26Oct.15-*I*, 11Nov.15-*I*, 14Nov.15-*I*, 20Nov.15-*I*, 25Jan.16-*I*
Merton,Capt.G, MC **WIA** 17Jan.18-*VIII*
Merz,Lt.GP, *Aust.* May.15-*VIII*, **DoW** 30Jul.15-*VIII*
Merz,1Lt.HB, *US.* **WIA** 25Sep.18-*IIB*
Mesham,2Lt.JH, **KIA** 13Jul.18-*I*
Messervy,Capt.ED, 12Jul.17-*I*, **KIA** 20Jul.17-*I*
Messinger,2Lt.HR, 8Oct.18-*I*
Messiter,FSLt.LC, 24Mar.18-*I*
Metcalf,Capt.JN, 23Jan.18-*I*
Metcalfe,Lt., *12Sqn.* 29Sep.18-*I*
Metcalfe,Sgt.CW, **POW**? 4Nov.18-*I*
Metcalfe,Lt.RFC, 21May.18-*I*
Metford,Lt.CKS, **WIA** 19Mar.18-*I*
Metheral,Lt.TA, **KIA** 5Jun.17-*I*
Metson,Lt.GF, **POW** 11Aug.18-*I*
Meyer,2Lt.OF, **POW** 12Aug.18-*I*
Miall-Smith,Lt.GE, **KIA** 25Sep.17-*I*
Michener,1Lt.JH, *US.* **WIA** 4Oct.18-*IIB*
Middis,Sgt.FH, 25Jan.16-*I*
Middlebrook,2Lt.N, **POW** 10Oct.16-*I*
Middlecote,Lt.EWAG, **KIA** 3Oct.18-*I*
Middleton,2Lt.AH, 8Nov.17-*I*, **POW** 3Dec.17-*I*
Middleton,Sgt.CV, 30May.18-*I*
Middleton,Capt.JA, **inj** 23Apr.18-*I*
Middleton,Capt.JL, 27Sep.18-*I*
Middleton,Lt.JR, **POW DoW** 21.6.1917 24Mar.17-*I*
Middleton,2Lt.LW, **KIA** 8Nov.17-*I*
Middleton,Capt.TP, 17Apr.18-*I*
Middleton,2Lt.W, **DoW** 16Jul.18-*I*
Middleton,Sgt.WJH, **DoW** 4.10.1918 3Oct.18-*I*
Mighell,Lt.P, **DoW** 12.10.1917 11Oct.17-*I*
Mignault,Lt.B, **WIA** 27Oct.18-*I*
Milani,2Lt.,Lt.RS, **WIA POW** 28May.18-*I*
Milbank,2Lt.GA, **WIA inj**? 9Nov.18-*I*
Milburn,2Lt.H, 2Jun.18-*IV*, 9Jun.18-*IV*
Miles,2Lt.AA, **POW** 24Mar.18-*I*
Miles,2Lt.,Capt.CC, 2Oct.15-*I*, **WIA** 10Nov.15-*I*, 20Aug.16-*I*, **WIA** 25Aug.16-*I*
Miles,Lt.GH, **KIA** 12Sep.17-*I*
Miles,Lt.HL, 19Feb.18-*I*
Miley,FLt.AJ, 25Dec.14-*I*
Mill,Lt.J, **KIA** 20Sep.18-*I*
Millar,Capt., *3Sqn.* **WIA** 15Sep.16-*I*
Millar,2Lt.ARA, **WIA** 25May.18-*I*
Millar,2Lt.E, 25Jan.16-*I*
Millar,Lt.GJ, 8Sep.18-*I*
Millar,Lt.KO, **KIA** 21May.18-*I*
Millar,2Lt.L, 17Sep.18-*I*, 22Aug.18-*I*
Millar,2Lt.TS, **POW** 25May.17-*I*
Millen,2Lt.HS, **WIA** 17Sep.18-*I*
Miller,Capt.AM, *3Sqn.* 14Jul.16-*I*, 15Sep.16-*I*
Miller,2Lt.AT, 31Jul.17-*I*
Miller,2Lt.AW, **POW** 12Apr.18-*I*
Miller,Lt.AWB, **KIA** 13Jul.17-*I*
Miller,Lt.CH, **WIA** 14Aug.18-*I*
Miller,2Lt.CL, *US.* Ld'H **WIA** 6Jun.18-*IID*
Miller,2Lt.D, **WIA POW** 2Dec.17-*I*
Miller,2Lt.FD, **KIA** 4Feb.18-*I*
Miller,2Lt.G, **POW DoW** 31.3.1918 25Mar.18-*I*
Miller,2Lt.GB, **KIA** 1May.17-*I*
Miller,1Lt.JC, *US.* **DoW** 28Jul.18-*IIB*
Miller,Capt.JE, *US.* **KIA** 9Mar.18-*IIB*
Miller,2Lt.JMR, **WIA** 2Feb.17-*I*
Miller,2Lt.RG, 13Aug.18-*I*
Miller,Lt.W, 12Apr.18-*I*
Miller,Lt.WD, **KIA** 2Oct.16-*I*
Miller,2Lt.WJ, **KIA** 17Sep.18-*I*
Miller,Lt.WN, **WIA** 6Sep.18-*I*
Miller, 21Lt.WP, *US.* **DoW** 3.8.1918 1Aug.18-*IIB*
Miller,2Lt.Z, **POW** Aug.18-*I*
Miller,1Lt.ZR, *US.* **POW** 20Jul.18-*IIB*
Millett,2Lt.JNL, **KIA** 13Mar.18-*I*
Millichamp,AM.BM, **INT** 24Oct.17-*III*
Milligan,2Lt.CN, **WIA** 21Apr.17-*I*
Milligan,2Lt.FJ, **DoW** 13Mar.18-*I*
Milling,2Lt.,Lt.HB, **WIA** 14Jan.16-*I*, 31Mar.16-*I*, **POW** 29Apr.17-*I*
Millington,2Lt.CCR, 25Mar.18-*I*
Millington,Sgt.PWE, **inj** 9May.17-*I*
Milliship,2Lt.WG, **KIA** 7Jun.17-*I*
Millman,Capt.NC, *Can.* 8Mar.18-*I*
Mills,Lt.A, 24Mar.18-*I*, 6Sep.18-*I*
Mills,Lt.AS, **POW** 17Jan.18-*VIII*
Mills,2Lt.FG, **POW** 1Nov.18-*I*
Mills,Capt.GD, 28Apr.15-*I*, 21Jul.15-*I*, 18Sep.15-*I*, 26Sep.15-*I*
Mills,Lt.GN, *Aust.* **WIA** 24Jan.17-*VII*
Mills,2Lt.,Lt.,Capt.KC 25Apr.18-*I*, 6May.18-*I*, **WIA** 7May.18-*I*, **KIA** 8Aug.18-*I*
Mills,Capt.RNF, **KIA** 21Sep.17-*I*
Mills,Lt.RP, 22Jan.15-*I*
Mills,Sgt.SF, 19Aug.18-*I*
Mills,2Lt.WJ, **DoW** 4.9.1918 3Sep.18-*I*
Mills,Lt.WL, **KIA** 9May.17-*I*
Mills-Adams,2Lt.AH, **KIA** 1Oct.18-*I*
Millward,FSLt.KH, **KIA** 7Jul.17-*I*
Milne,Lt.,Capt., *2Sqn.* 26Jul.15-*I*, 11Aug.15-*I*, 2Dec.15-*I*
Milne,2AM.1AM, *16Sqn.* 26Oct.15-*I*, 14Nov.15-*I*, 20Mar.16-*I*
Milne,2Lt.CG, **POW** 20Sep.18-*I*
Milne,2AM.J, **KIA** 7Feb.17-*I*
Milne,Capt.JT, MC 20Aug.17-*I*, **KIA** 24Oct.17-*I*
Milne,2Lt.R, **KIA** 11Aug.18-*I*
Milne,Capt.W, **WIA** 17May.16-*I*
Milne-Henderson,2Lt.JM, **KIA** 28Jan.18-*I*
Milner,Lt.E, **KIA** 3Nov.18-*I*
Milner,Lt.G, 10Aug.18-*I*
Milner,2Lt.J, **KIA** 26Apr.16-*I*
Milnes,Sgt.HA, **WIA** 28May.17-*I*
Milot,Maj.JAA, **KIA** 8Apr.17-*I*
Milton,Capt.AV, 27Mar.18-*I*
Milton,Pte.W, **WIA** 29Jul.17-*I*
Milton,Lt.WA, 27Mar.18-*I*
Minchin,Capt.FF, 2Nov.16-*VII*
Minchin,Lt.,Capt.JHC, 22Oct.16-*I*, **WIA** 12Oct.17-*I*
Minifie,AFCdr.RP, DSC **POW** 17Mar.18-*I*
Minot,2Lt.,Capt.L, 9Aug.16-*I*, 28Oct.16-*I*, 27Jul.17-*I*, **KIA** 28Jul.17-*I*
Minter,2Lt.M, 18Jun.16-*VII*
Misener,2Lt.MS, *Can.* **KIA** 9Aug.18-*I*
Miseroy,Lt.FB, **WIA** 8Aug.18-*I*
Mitchell,2Lt., *4Sqn.* 23May.15-*I*
Mitchell,Capt., *10Sqn.* 11Oct.15-*I*, 14Oct.15-*I*, 28Nov.15-*I*, 13Dec.15-*I*, 19Dec.15-*I*
Mitchell,2Lt.AM, **WIA** 18Oct.18-*I*
Mitchell,Lt.AP, **WIA POW** 7Jun.17-*I*
Mitchell,2Lt.EH, **WIA** 26Sep.15-*I*
Mitchell,2Lt.GW, **POW** 16Sep.18-*I*
Mitchell,Lt.H, **POW** 19May.18-*I*
Mitchell,2Lt.HBO, **WIA POW** 26Oct.16-*I*
Mitchell,2Lt.HN, **WIA** 9Nov.18-*I*
Mitchell,1Lt.HW, *US.* **POW** 12Sep.18-*IIB*
Mitchell,2Lt.J, *18Sqn.* **WIA** 26Apr.16-*I*
Mitchell,2Lt.J, *27Sqn.?* **WIA** 26Mar.18-*I*
Mitchell,Lt.,Capt.J, *28Sqn.* 20Oct.17-*I*, 26May.18-*IV*
Mitchell,2Lt.JH, **WIA** 30Apr.18-*I*
Mitchell,2Lt.JK, **KIA** 10Aug.18-*I*
Mitchell,2Lt.JN, **KIA** 12Aug.18-*I*
Mitchell,2Lt.JPC, **KIA** 21Apr.17-*I*
Mitchell,Lt.JW, **WIA** 28Nov.17-*VII*
Mitchell,2Lt.,Lt.LE, 4Sep.18-*I*, 24Sep.18-*I*, **KIA** 29Sep.18-*I*
Mitchell,TLt.,Lt.PC, 17Jun.18-*I*, **POW** 28Jun.18-*I*
Mitchell,2Lt.RG, **WIA** 26Mar.18-*I*
Mitchell,2Lt.W, **POW DoW** 28Sep.18-*I*
Mitchell,3AM.WA, **INT** 2Oct.18-*III*
Mitchell,Lt.WGS, 30Sep.14-*I*, 8Nov.14-*I*, 19Nov.14-*I*, 15Jun.15-*I*
Mitchell,Lt.WT, 9Aug.18-*I*
Mitchener,2Lt.AH, 8May.18-*I*
Mitten,2Lt.RC, **POW** 28Sep.18-*I*
Moffatt,Lt., *7Sqn.* 15Nov.15-*I*, 14Dec.15-*I*, 19Dec.15-*I*, 30Dec.15-*I*
Moffett,Lt.JF, *USNR* 27Jun.18-*I*
Moir,Sgt.AAL, 16Aug.17-*I*, **WIA** 5Sep.17-*I*
Moir,2Lt.AE, **KIA** 26Oct.18-*I*
Moir,FLt.CJ, *4Naval.* **KIA** 10May.17-*I*
Moir,Lt.CJ, *217Sqn.* **KIA** 30Jun.18-*I*
Moir,2Lt.JA, **WIA** 1Mar.18-*I*
Moir-Paton,Lt.D, **KIA** 24Sep.17-*I*
Molesworth,Capt.WE, *Irl.* 29Jun.17-*I*, 23Jul.17-*I*, 8Nov.17-*I*
Moller,2Lt.FS, *name* Miller? 13Feb.16-*I*, **WIA** 23Nov.16-*I*
Mollett,Lt.FN, **KIA** 18Jul.18-*I*
Mollison,Lt.J, **KIA** 27Aug.18-*I*
Mollison,Sgt.W, **POW** 21Jun.17-*I*
Molloy,2Lt.TPL, **POW** 17Sep.16-*I*
Moloney,2Lt.PJ, **WIA** 22Nov.17-*I*
Molyneux,2Lt.ET, **WIA** 16Aug.17-*I*
Monaghan,Lt.HB, **POW** 16Sep.18-*I*
Monckton,2Lt.C, **KIA** 1Jul.16-*I*
Monckton,Lt.MH, **KIA** 9Jul.15-*I*
Moncrieff,Lt., *6Sqn.* 19Dec.15-*I*
Mond,Lt.FL, **KIA** 15May.18-*I*
Monday,Sgt.HF, 5Jun.18-*I*
Money,2Lt.DG, **WIA** 6Jul.17-*I*, **KIA** 16Feb.18-*I*
Money,Pte.JE, **POW** 30May.18-*III*
Money,Lt.LJ, 12Apr.18-*I*
Money,Lt.RRN, **POW** 17Sep.16-*I*
Money-Kyrle,2Lt.RE, **WIA** 12Jul.17-*I*
Monk,Capt.EW, **KIA** 29Mar.18-*I*
Monkhouse,2Lt.B, 21Oct.17-*I*
Monks,Cpl.H, 4Nov.15-*I*, 17Jan.16-*I*
Monkton,2Lt., *8Sqn.* 4Jun.15-*I*
Montague,1Lt.PH, *US.* **POW** 31Jul.18-*IIB*
Montague,2Lt.PD, **KIA** 29Oct.17-*VI*
Montgomerie,2Lt.HS, **WIA** 14Apr.18-*I*
Montgomery,Lt.JR, **KIA** 16Sep.18-*I*
Montgomery,2Lt.,Lt.,Capt.KB, 23Aug.17-*I*, 20Sep.17-*I*, 22Sep.17-*I*, 26Sep.17-*I*, 15Nov.17-*I*, **POW** 22Feb.18-*IV*
Montgomery,Lt.RM, **WIA** 26Mar.18-*I*
Montgomery-Moore,Lt.C, 30Oct.18-*I*
Moodie,2Lt.HM, **KIA** 16Sep.18-*I*
Moody,2Lt.BC, **WIA POW** 21May.17-*I*
Moody,Lt.BH, *SA.* 8Jun.18-*I*, 24Aug.18-*I*, 28Oct.18-*I*
Moody,2Lt.CA, **KIA** 21Aug.17-*I*
Moody,2Lt.HM, 31Dec.17-*IV*
Moody,Sgt.RJ, **KIA** 4Mar.17-*I*
Moody,2Lt.RW, *US.* **DoW** 16.7.1918 15Jul.18-*IID*
Moon,FLt.ER, **POW** 6Jan.17-*IX*
Mooney,1Lt.R, *USAS* **WIA POW** 27Sep.18-*I*
Moore,Capt., *6Sqn.*, *name* Moor, 19Dec.15-*I*, 17Jan.16-*I*
Moore,Lt., *21Sqn.* 13Oct.17-*I*
Moore,Lt.A, **POW** 7Jul.18-*I*
Moore,2Lt.BJ, 22Jun.16-*I*, 25Jun.16-*I*, 3Jul.16-*I*
Moore,2Lt.CA, **KIA** 25Sep.17-*III*
Moore,2Lt.CG, **KIA** 15Aug.17-*I*
Moore,Lt.CR, **POW** 28Sep.18-*I*
Moore,1Lt.EC, *USAS.* **WIA** 24Sep.18-*I*
Moore,2Lt.ER, **WIA** 4Jul.18-*I*
Moore,2Lt.ES, 2May.17-*I*, **POW** 11May.17-*I*
Moore,AG.Dvr,FJ, **WIA** 22Aug.17-*I*
Moore,2Lt.FM, *US.* **KIA** 2Sep.18-*IIB*
Moore,2Lt.GB, *Can.* 2Oct.17-*I*, **KIA** 7Apr.18-*I*
Moore,Capt.GM, **WIA** 1Feb.17-*I*
Moore,2Lt.,Capt.GN, **WIA** 4Sep.17-*I*, **WIA** 26Sep.18-*I*
Moore,2Lt.JMJ, 21Mar.18-*I*
Moore,2Lt.,Lt.JR, **inj** 13Mar.18-*I*, 12Apr.18-*I*, 15Apr.18-*I*
Moore,Lt.LWB, **KIA** 29Jan.18-*IV*
Moore,Lt.M, **POW** 22Jul.17-*I*
Moore,Lt.R, *UK. 4AFC.* 10Jul.18-*I*
Moore,2Lt.R, *US. 46Sqn.* **KIA** 12Aug.18-*I*
Moore,Lt.RFW, 17Apr.18-*I*, 19Apr.18-*I*
Moore,1Lt.RL, *US.* **WIA** 21Jun.18-*IID*
Moore,Lt.WP, *Aust.* **WIA** 31Aug.18-*I*
Moore-Kelly,2Lt.C, **WIA POW** 16Oct.16-*I*
Moorhead,Lt.WB, 21Feb.16-*I*
Moraintinis,Cdr.A, *Grk.* 20Jan.18-*V*
Morang,FSLt.GH, **KIA** 27Oct.17-*I*
Moreton,2Lt.LH, **KIA** 16May.18-*IV*
Morey,Lt.AW, **KIA** 24Jan.18-*I*
Morgan,Cpl.A, **KIA** 22Apr.17-*I*
Morgan,2Lt.AB, **KIA** 21Apr.17-*I*
Morgan,Lt.AE, 11Oct.18-*VIII*
Morgan,2Lt.,Lt.AM, **WIA** 26Feb.17-*I*, **WIA** 3May.18-*I*
Morgan,Lt.ES, DFC **KIA** 7Sep.18-*I*
Morgan,Lt.FJ, **DoW** 16.5.1918 14May.18-*I*

Morgan,Lt.HR, KIA 8Nov.17-I
Morgan,2Lt.JA, Aust. initials AJ? KIA 30May.17-VII
Morgan,FLt.JE, KIA 30Mar.17-V
Morgan,2Lt.LL, WIA 24May.17-I
Morgan,Lt.RC?, 21Sep.15-I
Morgan,Lt.RJ, US. POW 28Sep.18-I
Morgan,2Lt.RWC, DoW 27Jul.17-I
Morgan,2Lt.TP, POW 15Nov.17-I
Morgan,Capt.WAC, MC WIA 31May.18-I
Morgan,2Lt.WG, POW DoW 23.10.1917 12Oct.17-I
Moriarty,2Lt.LP, US. WIA 28Sep.18-IIB
Morice,Lt.CS, 30Apr.17-I
Morley,2Lt., 66Sqn. 24Apr.17-I
Morley,2AM.A, 28Apr.17-I, KIA 30Sep.17-I
Morley,TLt.CL, 7Jun.18-I
Morrell,2Lt.CM, INT 5Jun.15-I
Morrice,Lt.W, 9Mar.17-I
Morris,Lt., 3Sqn. 15Mar.17-I
Morris,Lt.AC, KIA 17Feb.18-I
Morris,Lt.CH, KIA 13Apr.17-I
Morris,2Lt.EHS, 20Feb.18-I, 30Mar.18-I
Morris,2Lt.EM, US. 30Oct.18-IIB
Morris,2Lt.EP, KIA 1May.17-I
Morris,2Lt.EW, KIA 9Nov.17-I
Morris,2Lt.GC, 5Jun.18-I
Morris,Lt.GT, KIA 11Apr.17-I
Morris,Cpl.HL, POW 29Apr.16-VIII
Morris,2Lt.JE, 25Jan.16-I
Morris,2Lt.,Capt.JF, 29Dec.15-I, 30Mar.18-I
Morris,2Lt.LBF, POW DoW 17Sep.16-I
Morris,Lt.NG, WIA 6Mar.18-I
Morris,2Lt.RSV, 21Aug.17-I, 14Sep.17-I, 21Sep.17-I
Morris,2Lt.VC, POW 3Apr.17-I
Morris,1Lt.W, US. POW DoW 28Sep.18-IIB
Morris,Lt.WA, 28Sep.18-I, DoW 2Oct.18-I
Morrison,2Lt., 11Sqn. 25Mar.17-I
Morrison,Lt., 13Sqn. 15Dec.15-I
Morrison,Capt.A, 17Sep.18-I
Morrison,Lt.AH, 14Nov.15-I
Morrison,Lt.DG, WIA 13Oct.17-I
Morrison,Lt.KS, WIA POW 12Nov.17-I
Morrison,Lt.NW, KIA 14Apr.17-I
Morrow,2Lt.ET, Can. 28Mar.18-I
Morrow,Capt.ET, Can. WIA 22Aug.18-I
Morse,Lt.FJ, 11May.17-I, 21Aug.17-I
Morse,2Lt.GE, US. DSC KIA 12Sep.18-IIB
Morse,Lt.TW, WIA POW 20Nov.17-I
Mortimer,2Lt.GJ, WIA 25Mar.18-I
Mortimer-Phelan,2Lt.WC, 1Apr.16-I, POW 23Apr.16-I
Morton,Lt., 6Sqn. 23Apr.15-I
Morton,Capt., 8Sqn. 13Mar.16-I
Morton,Capt.EBG, KIA 16Jul.18-I
Morton,Cpl.,Sgt.GJ, 29Dec.15-I, 1Apr.16-I, 9Sep.16-I, WIA POW 17Sep.16-I
Morton,2Lt.GMJ, KIA 27Sep.18-I
Morton,Maj.RFS, WIA 17May.18-I
Morton,2Lt.RJ, 14Mar.16-I
Mosby,Lt.JEG, 5Mar.18-I, WIA 20Apr.18-I
Moseley,Ens., 218Sqn. 12Aug.18-I
Moseley,2Lt.GF, WIA 22Mar.18-I
Moser,2Lt.,Lt.GR, 2Feb.16-I, 3May.16-I
Moses,Lt.JD, KIA 1Apr.18-I
Moss,2Lt.CH, WIA 16Sep.18-I
Moss,2Lt.L, WIA 8Dec.15-I
Mossop,Capt.EA, 31Jul.18-III
Mott,2Lt.,Lt.JE, 1Oct.17-I, 4Oct.17-I, 12Oct.17-I, 13Oct.17-I, 28Oct.17-I, KIA 23Dec.17-I
Mott,Lt.LW, KIA 23Apr.17-I
Mottershaw,Lt.H, 11Oct.18-I
Mottershead,Sgt.TT, VC DoI 12.1.1917 7Jan.17-I
Mould,Lt.HA, WIA 2Sep.18-I
Moult,2AM.A, WIA? POW 28Apr.17-I
Moult,Lt.OM, POW? 12Mar.16-I
Mounsey,2Lt.RJ, 3May.16-I
Mowatt,2Lt.MM, POW DoW 16May.16-I
Mowle,Lt.AWM, WIA 22Jul.17-I
Moxey,2Lt.,Lt.S, WIA 8May.18-I, KIA 14Jul.18-I
Moxon,2Lt.NF, POW 29Sep.18-I
Moyes,2Lt.WB, KIA 7Apr.17-I
Moyle,FSLt.WA, KIA 22Mar.18-I
Mucklow,Lt.SL, POW 21Oct.18-I
Muff,2AM., 101Sqn. 22Sep.17-I
Muff,Sgt.AH, 8Mar.18-I
Muff,Sgt.AM, WIA 28Mar.18-I
Muir,2Lt.A, POW 24Nov.17-I
Muir,2Lt.JH, KIA 7Apr.17-I
Muir,2Lt.JS, WIA 17Jun.18-I
Muir,2Lt.JW, KIA 12Mar.18-I
Muir,Capt.SK, 17Dec.16-VII
Muirden,2Lt.NH, 22Mar.18-I, WIA POW 25Jun.18-I
Muirhead,2Lt.J, KIA 18Mar.17-I
Mulcahy,1Lt.FP, USMCR 29Sep.18-I
Mulcahy-Morgan,Lt.,Capt.TW, 19Jan.15-I, 10Sep.15-I, WIA POW 13Sep.15-I
Mulford,Lt.EA, Aust. WIA 19Sep.18-VII
Mulhall,Lt.HF, POW 30Oct.18-I
Mulholland,2Lt.A, 15Sep.18-I
Mulholland,Capt.DO, 22Sep.16-I
Mullen,Lt.AGL, KIA 22Aug.18-I
Mullen,Lt.EM, WIA 31Oct.18-I
Mullen,2Lt.HS, WIA 16Sep.18-I
Mullen,2Lt.JW, WIA 10Aug.17-I
Mullens,SLt.CJA, KIA 5May.16-I
Muller,1Lt.HD, US. POW 30Oct.18-IIB
Mulligan,2Lt.CA, WIA 26Nov.17-I
Mullins,CPO., POW 25Mar.16-I
Mullins,Lt.RF, 1Jun.18-I
Mulock,Lt.HC, 29Jan.17-I, KIA 15Feb.17-I
Mulock,FSLt.RH, 6Sep.15-I, 30Dec.15-I, 24Jan.16-I, 26Jan.16-I, 21May.16-I
Mulroy,Lt.HJ, KIA 18Jun.18-I
Mulvey,Lt., 6Sqn. 8Oct.18-I
Mumford,Lt.GW, WIA POW 19Sep.17-I
Mumford,Cpl.,Sgt.R, 24Feb.16-I, 3Jul.16-I
Munday,Capt.AH, 10May.18-III
Munday,Lt.ER, KIA 5Aug.18-III
Munday,FLt.RB, Aust. 2Sep.17-I
Munday,Capt.SCP, POW 28Apr.16-VIII
Munden,Capt., 6Sqn. 8Oct.18-I
Mundie,2Lt.J, WIA 20May.17-I
Mundy,Lt.EW, WIA 25Jun.18-I
Munk,Cpl.G, WIA 19Sep.16-I
Munn,2Lt.LV, KIA 16Feb.17-I
Munro,2Lt.CHC?, POW, initials MH? 28Apr.16-VIII
Munro,2Lt.J, INT 16Aug.18-I
Munro,Lt.JG, INT 5Sep.18-I
Munro,FSLt.KR, KIA 9Aug.17-I
Munro,2Lt.RNL, WIA 16Mar.17-I
Munroe,Lt.FF, 4Sep.17-I
Munslow,Lt.EL, WIA 11Aug.18-I
Murchie,2Lt.CP, 9Nov.16-I
Murdoch,Lt.R, WIA 10Jun.18-IV
Murlis Green,2Lt.,Lt.,Capt.GW 19Dec.15-I, 12Jan.16-I, 17Jan.16-I, 19Jan.16-I, 13Dec.16-VI, 18Dec.17-III, 18Feb.17-VI, 18Mar.17-VI
Murman,Lt.DF, 21May.18-I
Murphy,Capt., 4Sqn. 12May.15-I
Murphy,Lt.AW, Aust. 26Jun.18-VII
Murphy,1Lt.JM, US. WIA 31Oct.18-IIB
Murphy,Lt.JP, POW 8Oct.18-I
Murphy,Sgt.L, 8Aug.18-I, KIA 16Sep.18-I
Murphy,Sgt.P, KIA 15May.18-I
Murray,Lt., 7Sqn. 28Apr.15-I
Murray,2Lt.A, 1Sep.15-I, 7Sep.15-I
Murray,Lt.AA, DoW 19Mar.17-I
Murray,Sgt.BF, DoW 25Aug.16-I
Murray,Lt.DCG, WIA POW 27Jun.17-I
Murray,FLt.DG, INT 17Feb.15-I
Murray,Lt.GIL, Aust. WIA 10Aug.17-I
Murray,2Lt.GL, KIA 12Apr.18-I
Murray,Lt.HG, 12Sqn. KIA 16Dec.16-I
Murray,2Lt.HG, 204Sqn. KIA 27Oct.18-I
Murray,2Lt.JL, KIA 29May.17-I
Murray,2Lt.KDP, 22Sep.15-I, 11Nov.15-I, 29Dec.15-I
Murray,Lt.KW, 18Jun.18-I, KIA 1Jul.18-I
Murray,Lt.PW, POW DoW 2.2.1917 1Feb.17-I
Murray,2Lt.RB, POW 30Oct.18-I
Murray-Stewart,Lt.L, 6May.18-I
Murton,FSLt.HS, POW 4May.17-I
Muschamp,2Lt.GA, 4Nov.18-I
Musgrove,2Lt.HS, Can. 8Aug.18-I, POW DoW 9Aug.18-I
Muspratt,Lt.KK, 31Oct.17-I
Mussared,2Lt.WJ, POW 9Jun.17-I
Musson,Lt.EC, WIA 7Apr.18-I
Musson,Lt.JM, 9Apr.17-I, WIA 29Apr.17-I
Mustard,Lt.EA, Aust. 7May.18-VII, 22Sep.18-VII
Mutch,Lt.G, DSO KIA 6Jul.17-I
Myburgh,2Lt.JA, DoW 10.4.1917 8Apr.17-I
Myers,2Lt.FM, KIA 14Feb.17-I
Myers,2Lt.PB, KIA 27Sep.18-I
Myring,2Lt.TFL, KIA 30Aug.18-I

N

Nairn,2Lt.KG, 16Sep.18-I
Naish,Lt.JP, 28Jun.18-I, WIA 4Jul.18-I
Nalder,FSLt.JF, WIA 7Jun.17-I
Napier,2Lt.,Capt.CGD, MC 21Mar.18-I, 9May.18-I, KIA 15May.18-I
Napier,Capt.I, 26Mar.18-I, 6Apr.18-I
Napier,2Lt.J, KIA 7Apr.18-I
Nash,2Lt.CP, US. POW 13Sep.18-IIB
Nash,Bdr.EA, DoW 27Sep.17-I
Nash,Sgt.FE, POW 20Jul.18-I
Nash,2Lt.FM, POW 3Oct.17-I
Nash,FSLt.GE, WIA POW 25Jun.17-I
Nash,Lt.TS, 10May.18-I, DoW 8Aug.18-I
Nash,Capt.TW, DFC KIA 23Oct.18-I
Nash,2Lt.WH, 5Feb.18-I
Nasmyth,Lt.AW, 2Apr.17-I, KIA 12Oct.17-I
Nason,Capt.JWN, KIA 26Dec.16-I
Nattrass,2Lt.H, WIA 2Sep.18-I
Naylor,AGL.W, 28Mar.18-I
Naylor,Lt.CB, POW 16Sep.18-I
Naylor,2Lt.F, KIA 23Mar.18-I
Naylor,2Lt.W, KIA 15Apr.18-I
Neale,2Lt.AL?, 11Sqn. 28Aug.15-I, 8Sep.15-I, 23Oct.15-I, 14Dec.15-I
Neale,2Lt.RE, KIA 18Mar.18-I
Neighbour,Sgt.WH, KIA 25Sep.18-I
Neil,2Lt.JW, KIA 6Oct.18-I
Neill,2Lt.CD, 31Oct.18-I
Neill,Lt.JWF, WIA POW 5Sep.17-I
Neill,2Lt.RM, KIA 3Jun.17-I
Neilson,Lt.AA, DoW 23Aug.18-I
Neilson,TLt.RA, 24Oct.18-I
Neily,2Lt.FE, KIA 22Dec.17-I
Nelle,Sgt.H, KIA 31May.18-I
Nelles,FSLt.DAH,DSC INT 22Apr.17-I
Nelms,2Lt.F, USMCR WIA 28Sep.18-I, INT 27Oct.18-IIB
Nelson,Lt., 12Sqn. 6Oct.18-I
Nelson,TLt.HL, KIA 29Apr.18-I
Nelson,Lt.JN, DoW 14.6.1918 12Jun.18-I
Nelson,Lt.RC, Aust. POW 14Jul.18-I
Nesbit,2Lt.CHF, WIA 6Jun.18-I
Nesbitt,Lt.A, 13Mar.16-I, 16Sep.16-I
Nesbitt,Lt.AN, WIA 9Feb.17-I
Nesbitt,Lt.F, 25Apr.18-I
Nesbitt,Lt.FW, WIA 27Apr.18-I
Nesbitt,2Lt.WJ, KIA 27Oct.18-I
Nethersole,2Lt., 5Sqn. 12Jan.16-I
Neve,2Lt.RE, WIA 9Mar.17-I
Nevile-Smith,2Lt.L, 17Mar.17-I
Neville,Lt.DA, POW 22Sep.18-I
Neville,2Lt.HG, DoW 10.5.1917 9May.17-I
Neville,2Lt.LR, WIA 6Jun.17-I
Neville,Capt.RG, 6Jul.17-I
Nevin,Lt.FD, KIA 19May.18-I
New,Lt.HB, KIA 31Oct.17-I
Newbold,2Lt.LA, POW 29Feb.16-I
Newbury,2Lt.GG, POW 25Mar.18-I
Newby,1Lt., US. 11th US. WIA 4Nov.18-IIB
Newby,Lt.W, 15Sep.18-I, 27Sep.18-I, KIA 29Oct.18-I
Newcomb,2Lt.M, POW 12Oct.17-I
Newell,2Lt.AE, US. DoW? 10Oct.18-IIB
Newell,2Lt.GM, US. WIA 14Sep.18-IID
Newenham,2Lt.GA, WIA POW 20Apr.17-I
Newey,2Lt.T, 3May.18-IV, 9Jun.18-IV, 16Jun.18-IV, POW 23Aug.18-IV
Newland,Sgt.A, 6Sep.18-I
Newling,Lt.PT, WIA 5Jun.17-I
Newman,FLt.CD, POW 12Oct.16-I
Newman,2Lt.EF, WIA 9Nov.18-I
Newman,Lt.EM, 19Jun.18-I
Newnham,2Lt.,Capt.MA, 25Apr.18-I, 30Oct.18-I
Newson,2Lt.DA, KIA 23Sep.18-I
Newstead,2Lt.CW, 29Oct.18-I, POW 4Nov.18-I
Newton,2Lt.EA, POW 11Oct.17-V
Newton,FSLt.,2Lt.F, 11Apr.18-I, KIA 9May.18-I
Newton,2Lt.HI, 16Nov.16-I
Newton,2Lt.HJ, KIA 2Aug.16-I
Newton,1AM.JW, KIA 14Mar.16-I
Newton,Lt.ME, KIA 18Jun.17-I
Newton,2Lt.RF, KIA 2Apr.18-I
Newton,2Lt.TMB, 18May.16-I
Nichlos?,Lt., 98Sqn., name 2Lt.JH Nicholass? 25Jul.18-I
Nichol,Capt.EF, 1Oct.18-I, WIA? 5Oct.18-I
Nichol,2Lt.RW, POW 9Jul.16-I
Nicholas,2Lt.EM, POW 13Jun.18-I
Nicholass?,2Lt.JH, see Nichlos? 25Jul.18-I, 16Sep.18-I
Nicholl,2Lt., 8Sqn. 6Jul.15-I
Nicholl,2Lt.HR, 24May.15-I, 14Sep.15-I
Nicholls,1AM., 5Sqn. 18Aug.15-I, 28Dec.15-I
Nicholls,2Lt.ECHR, WIA 1May.17-I
Nicholls,Lt.LB, WIA 30Nov.17-I
Nicholls,2AM.RG, POW ~30May.16-VIII
Nicholls,2Lt.WG, WIA 24Jun.17-I
Nicholls,2Lt.WH, Aust. POW 16Mar.18-I
Nichols,Sgt.AH, US. KIA 2Jun.18-IIC
Nichols,1Lt.HA, US. 30Sep.18-IIB
Nichols,2Lt.JJ, KIA 30Oct.18-I
Nichols,2Lt.SL, KIA 12Aug.17-I
Nicholson,Lt., 16Sqn. 26May.15-I
Nicholson,2Lt.,Lt.GAS, 15Aug.17-I, DoW 22.8.1917 21Aug.17-I
Nicholson,Lt.GH, POW 31Oct.16-I
Nicholson,Lt.HR, KIA 24Apr.17-I
Nicholson,2Lt.M, KIA 18Aug.17-I
Nicholson,Lt.OH, KIA 18Jun.18-I
Nicholson,Lt.T, WIA 16Feb.18-I
Nickalls,Lt.HQ, 27Jan.17-I, WIA 26Feb.17-I, KIA 29Jul.17-I
Nicol,2Lt.M, Can. WIA 27Oct.18-IV
Nicol,2AM.W, POW 15Oct.17-I
Nicol,Lt.WGDH, inj 4Jul.18-I
Nicol-Hart,Lt.WCF, KIA 1Apr.18-I
Nicole,2Lt.J, WIA 28Sep.18-I
Nicolson,Lt.J, KIA 23Sep.18-I
Nielsen,Lt.P, KIA 18Jun.18-I
Nightingale,FSLt.AJ, 17Sep.16-VII, POW 2Dec.16-VII
Nightingale,Lt.E, KIA 25Jun.18-I
Nixon,2Lt.AWL, KIA 1Jun.17-I
Nixon,2Lt.JHC, WIA 16Aug.17-I
Nixon,2Lt.K, WIA 31Jul.18-I
Nixon,2Lt.LG, POW 5Dec.17-I
Nixon,Lt.LM, KIA 17May.18-I
Nixon,Lt.O, 6Sqn. 5Dec.15-I
Nixon,2Lt.O, 15Sqn. 17Jan.16-I
Nixon,2Lt.O, 70Sqn. KIA 17Sep.16-I
Nixon,2Lt.WE, 24Sqn. WIA 18Jun.16-I, 23Sep.16-I
Nixon,Lt.WE, 32Sqn. WIA 15Oct.16-I
Nixon,Capt.WE, 40Sqn. KIA 7May.17-I
Nixon,2Lt.WH, KIA 19Sep.15-I
Noad,2Lt.T, KIA 10Jun.18-I
Noakes,Sgt., 5Sqn. 7Feb.16-I
Nobbs,2Lt.CHF, POW 20Sep.17-I
Noble,2Lt.HT, KIA 28Sep.17-I
Noble,1Lt.RM, US. KIA 14May.18-IID
Noble,2Lt.,Lt.W, 17Feb.18-I, 30Jun.18-I
Noble-Campbell,Lt.CH, WIA 12Apr.18-III
Noel,Lt.HC, KIA 24Sep.18-I
Noel,2Lt.MW, 22Aug.14-I
Noel,Lt.TC, MC KIA 22Aug.18-I
Nolan,2Lt.PJ, 12Mar.18-I, WIA 14Mar.18-I, 22Mar.18-I, KIA 7Apr.18-I
Noon,2Lt.G, KIA 29Nov.17-I
Norcross,Lt.B, 18Jul.18-I, POW 16Sep.18-I
Norden,2Lt.FL, WIA 14May.18-I
Norden,2Lt.WG, POW 1Jul.18-I

Norman,Lt.,Capt.GH, 13Dec.15-*I*, 29Dec.15-*I*, **WIA** 9Nov.16-*I*
Norman,2Lt.GR, 24Mar.18-*I*, **POW** 26Mar.18-*I*
Norman,1Lt.HC, *US.* **KIA** 22Oct.18-*IIB*
Norman,1AM.LC, **KIA** 30May.18-*I*
Norman,2Lt.LW, 29May.18-*I*
Norman,Lt.RE, **WIA** 3Aug.18-*I*
Norman,Lt.WL, 9Aug.18-*I*, 16Aug.18-*I*
Norris,Lt., *25Sqn.* 31Mar.16-*I*
Norris,2Lt.EJ, **POW** 16Sep.18-*I*
Norris,2Lt.LA, **KIA** 25Mar.17-*I*
North,Lt., *8Sqn.* 16Sep.18-*I*, 21Sep.18-*I*
Northam,2Lt.NF, 22Sep.17-*I*
Northcote,2Lt.TF, **WIA** 23Jan.17-*I*
Norton,2Lt.BL, 21Mar.18-*I*, 28Mar.18-*I*, 1Apr.18-*I*
Norton,Sgt.C, **KIA** 27Jun.18-*I*
Norton,FSLt.EW, 23Jan.16-*I*, 20Oct.16-*I*
Norton,1Lt.FW, *US.* DSC **DoW** 22.7.1918 20Jul.18-*IIB*
Norton,Lt.H, **KIA** 24Mar.17-*I*
Norton,Lt.JH, 9Apr.17-*I*
Norton,2Lt.OI, **inj** 6Dec.17-*I*
Norton,2Lt.PC, 5Sep.17-*I*
Norton,2Lt.PC, **POW** 13Oct.17-*I*
Norvill,Lt.VA, *Aust.* **WIA POW** 29Jun.17-*I*
Norwood,2Lt.,Lt.OD, 17Mar.17-*I*, **WIA** 9Apr.17-*I*
Nosworthy,Lt.CWM, **DoW** 6Dec.17-*I*
Notley,Lt.HS, **WIA** 13Sep.18-*I*
Nott,Cpl.CN, DCM **WIA** 19Jan.16-*I*
Nowell,2Lt.RE, **KIA** 22Sep.17-*I*
Nowell,2Lt.RP, **WIA** 16Sep.18-*I*
Nowland,Lt.G, *Aust.* **KIA** 22May.18-*I*
Nudds,2Lt.GAH, **WIA** 9Aug.18-*I*
Nuding,2Lt.EG, 8Jun.17-*I*
Nugent,2Lt.A, **KIA** 1Jun.18-*I*
Nunn,Sgt.CH, 16Mar.17-*I*
Nunn,Lt.FAW, **Kld** 29Mar.18-*I*
Nunnerley,2Lt.WK, **KIA** 5Dec.17-*I*
Nutkins,Lt.VWG, **WIA** 14Jul.17-*I*
Nutt,1Lt.A, *US.* **KIA** 26Sep.18-*IIB*
Nuttall,Capt.F, MC DFC 25Jan.18-*VIII*, **WIA** 27Apr.18-*VIII*
Nuttall,Lt.F, 31Oct.17-*VIII*
Nuttall,Lt.JC, **POW** 8Aug.18-*I*
Nuttall,Lt.W, **WIA** 12Aug.17-*I*
Nye,2Lt.AC, **WIA** 11Apr.18-*I*

O

O'Beirne,Lt.AJL, **DoW** 28.7.1917 27Jul.17-*I*
O'Beirne,2Lt.JIM, **KIA** 3Apr.17-*I*
O'Brien,2Lt.ASH, **WIA** 15Mar.17-*I*
O'Brien,Lt.CR, **POW** 1May.17-*I*
O'Brien?,FLt.Hon.D, **KIA** 16Feb.15-*I*
O'Brien,2Lt.PA, **POW** 17Aug.17-*I*
O'Brien,2Lt.TD, 21Sep.15-*I*
O'Byrne,2Lt.AJ, **WIA POW** 31Aug.16-*I*
O'Callaghan,2Lt.,Lt.MA, 31Jul.17-*I*, 1Dec.17-*I*, **WIA** 8Oct.18-*I*
O'Connor,Yeo.ME, **KIA** 20Aug.18-*I*
O'Connor,2Lt.O, **POW** 2Sep.18-*I*
O'Connor,AM2.H, **POW** 15May.18-*I*
O'Donnell,2Lt.PJ, *US.* **KIA** 26Sep.18-*IIB*
O'Donoghue,2Lt.J, **KIA** 4Nov.18-*I*
O'Dwyer,Capt.JEA, **WIA**? **POW** 8Jul.17-*VI*
O'Giollagain,Cpl., *Sqn?* **WIA** ~10Dec.15-*I*
O'Grady,2Lt.SC, *Irl.* 26Aug.17-*I*
O'Hara-Wood,2Lt., *10Sqn.* 3Jun.16-*I*
O'Hara-Wood,Capt.,Maj.AH, *Aust.* 24Jan.18-*I*, **KIA** 4Oct.18-*I*
O'Leary,Lt.DA, *US.* **POW** 28Sep.18-*I*
O'Lieff,2Lt.PH, **POW** 5Apr.18-*I*
O'Longan,2Lt.PCS, **KIA** 1Jun.17-*I*
O'Malley,2Lt.HMD, 26Nov.15-*I*, 28Nov.15-*I*
O'Neill,Lt.TM, **KIA** 8May.18-*I*
O'Neill,Sgt.W, **POW** 5Jun.18-*I*
O'Reilly,Lt.RH, **KIA** 29Sep.18-*I*
O'Shea,Lt.HA, **POW** 14Aug.18-*I*
O'Sullivan,2Lt., 28Apr.17-*I*
O'Toole,2Lt.JG, *US.* **WIA POW** 12Sep.18-*IIB*
O'Toole,2Lt.W, 3Jul.17-*I*, 20Aug.17-*I*
Oades,2Lt.SA, **WIA** 5Mar.18-*I*
Oake,2Lt.E, 26Jun.17-*I*
Oakes,Capt.HA, **WIA** 24Aug.18-*I*
Oakes,2Lt.RC, **KIA** 19Jul.16-*I*
Oakley,2Lt.RS, **INT** 16Sep.18-*I*
Oakley,FSLt.WEB, **POW** 15Oct.17-*I*
Oaks,Lt.HA, *Can.* 21May.18-*I*
Oates,2Lt.WA, *USAS.* **inj** 9Nov.18-*I*
Oatis,1Lt.VP, *US.* 18Sep.18-*IIB*
Occomore,2Lt.FS, DFC **KIA** 1Oct.18-*I*
Ocling,2Lt., *70Sqn.* 11Jul.16-*I*
Odell,2Lt.CW, 5Sep.17-*I*, 23Nov.17-*I*
Odling,Lt.VG, **POW** 28Aug.16-*I*
Oerbling,Capt.L, 21Apr.18-*I*
Oertling,Lt.LJF, **DoW** 8Aug.18-*I*
Officer,Lt.J, 27Oct.18-*I*, **WIA** 28Oct.18-*I*
Ogden,2Lt.CE, 15Nov.17-*I*, **POW** 5Dec.17-*I*
Ogden,2Lt.JW, *US.* **POW** 29Sep.18-*IIB*
Ogg,2Lt.GJ, 10Oct.16-*I*
Ogilvy,2Lt.DP, **KIA** 30Jul.18-*I*
Ogilvy,Lt.WF, **POW** 14Sep.18-*I*
Ohrt,2Lt.FM?, **POW**, *initials* AM? 19Jan.18-*I*
Okenden,Lt.HGP, *Aust.* **WIA** 25May.17-*I*
Oldfield,1AM., *1WgRNAS.* 28Dec.15-*I*
Oldham,Sgt.J, 17Sep.17-*I*
Oldmstead,2Lt.GT, **DoW** 1Aug.18-*I*
Oliphant,2Lt.JLMcI, **WIA** 25Sep.18-*I*
Oliver,2Lt.BCD, 24Mar.18-*I*
Oliver,Lt.CK, 6May.18-*I*
Oliver,FCdr.DA, 25Dec.14-*I*
Oliver,Capt.DH, 21Mar.18-*I*
Oliver,2Lt.E, 26Oct.17-*I*
Oliver,2Lt.FL, **WIA** 23Apr.17-*I*, 10May.17-*I*, **KIA** 13Jul.17-*I*
Oliver,2Lt.JA, **WIA**? 21Oct.18-*I*
Oliver,2AM.K, **KIA** 24Apr.17-*I*
Oliver,2Lt.RCD, **POW** 26Mar.18-*I*
Oliver,Sgt.SJ, *49Sqn.* **POW** 20Jul.18-*I*
Oliver,2Lt.SJ, *66Sqn.* **KIA** 10Aug.17-*I*
Oliver,2Lt.,Lt.,Capt.TA, 20Mar.16-*I*, 3Jul.16-*I*, 11Aug.17-*I*, **KIA** 14Aug.17-*I*
Oliver,2Lt.TKG, **KIA** 5Sep.18-*I*
Oliver-Jones,Lt.AV, **KIA** 21Jul.16-*I*
Olley,Sgt.GP, 26Jun.17-*I*
Olorenshaw,2Lt.J, **INT** 24Sep.18-*I*
Omerod,2Lt.W, **KIA** 29Aug.18-*I*
Orange,2Lt.HS, **KIA** 25Sep.18-*I*
Orchard,FSLt.WE, **DoW** 2Jun.17-*I*
Ord,2Lt.AFT, **WIA** 11Apr.17-*I*
Ord,2Lt.AJ, 21Mar.18-*I*, 30Mar.18-*I*, 18Jun.18-*I*
Ord,2Lt.B, **WIA** 27May.17-*I*
Orde,2Lt.LAJ, 23Sep.15-*I*
Orde,2Lt.MAJ?, *6Sqn.* 19Oct.15-*I*
Orde,2Lt.MAJ, *8Sqn.* **WIA POW** 13Mar.16-*I*
Ordish,2Lt.BWA, **POW** 3Nov.16-*I*
Organ,2Lt.AF, 2Mar.16-*I*, **POW** Sep.16-*I*
Organ,FSgt.W, **POW** 23Aug.17-*I*
Orlebar,Lt.,Capt.AH, 24Mar.17-*I*, 13Mar.18-*I*, **WIA** 22Mar.18-*I*
Ormerod,Lt.A, **KIA** 13Apr.17-*I*
Ormerod,FCdr.LW, DSC **KIA** 16Mar.18-*I*
Ormsby,Lt.JAN, *Can.* **POW DoW** 5.8.1916 2Aug.16-*I*
Orr,Lt.DW, **WIA** 25Mar.18-*I*
Orr,Lt.JR, **KIA** 9Aug.18-*I*
Orr,Lt.OJ, 25Sep.18-*I*, **KIA** 23Oct.18-*I*
Orr,Lt.RSS, 19Jul.18-*I*, **KIA** 8Aug.18-*I*
Orr-Ewing,2Lt.AI, **POW** 21Sep.17-*I*
Orrel,Lt.JR, 6Aug.17-*I*
Orrell,2Lt.JT, **KIA** 2Dec.17-*I*
Ortweiler,Lt.FJ, **POW** 16Oct.17-*I*
Osborn,2Lt.CCF, **POW** 24May.17-*I*
Osborne,2Lt.SJ, **DoW** 1Nov.18-*IV*
Osborne,Gnr.WG, **WIA** 7Oct.17-*I*
Osbourne,Capt.HP, **KIA** 7Jul.17-*I*
Osman,2Lt.LW, **WIA** 14Jul.17-*I*
Osmaston,2Lt.RS, **KIA** 24Sep.16-*I*
Osmond,FLt.E, 30Sep.14-*I*
Osmond,Lt.EP, **POW** .18-*VIII*
Ostler,Lt.A, MC **KIA** 16Sep.18-*I*
Ottey,2Lt.RG, **KIA** 28Jul.17-*I*
Ottey,1AM.SWT, **WIA** 9Sep.17-*I*
Ovens?,Sgt.LC, **POW**? 24Sep.18-*I*
Ovington,1Lt.CL, *US.* **KIA** 29May.18-*IID*
Owden,Lt., Aden. **WIA** 23Jan.18-*VII*
Owen,Lt., *6Sqn.* 5Sep.18-*I*, 19Sep.18-*I*
Owen,Capt., *55Sqn.* 27Sep.17-*I*
Owen,Gnr.A, **DoW** 15Aug.17-*I*
Owen,Capt.D, **POW** 21Oct.17-*I*
Owen,2Lt.F, **KIA** 1Oct.18-*I*
Owen,2Lt.H, 31Aug.17-*I*
Owen,Capt.HLH, 26Dec.16-*I*, **WIA** 22Apr.17-*I*
Owen,SLt.HW, **POW** 28Mar.17-*I*
Owen,2Lt.IR, **DoW** 7May.17-*I*
Owen,Lt.JCF, *Can.* **POW** 18Feb.17-*VI*
Owen,2Lt.RE, **KIA** 18Sep.18-*I*
Owen,2Lt.RJ, **POW** 28Mar.18-*I*
Owen,Lt.T, *4Sqn.* 21Sep.17-*I*
Owen,Lt.T, *14Sqn.* **WIA** 9Jan.18-*VII*
Owen,2Lt.TJ, **KIA** 8Apr.17-*I*
Owen,2Lt.WT, *Can.* **KIA** 14Oct.18-*I*
Owen-Holdsworth,2Lt.JP, **KIA** 12Apr.18-*I*
Owles,Capt.ET, MC **WIA** 21Mar.18-*I*
Oxenham,Lt.GV, *Aust.* **KIA** 27Jun.18-*VII*
Oxley,2Lt.MGM, **KIA** 19Sep.17-*I*
Oxspring,Capt.R, 24Apr.17-*I*

P

Pacey,2Lt.FC, *Can.* **KIA** 3Sep.18-*I*
Pacey,Cpl.JW, **WIA**? **POW**? 29Jul.18-*I*
Packenham,Lt.WP, 21Aug.18-*I*
Packman,Sgt.G, **inj** 5Oct.18-*I*, 30Oct.18-*I*
Page,2Lt.,Lt.DA, 5Aug.17-*I*, **POW DoW** 14Aug.17-*I*
Page,Lt.DFV, **KIA** 21Sep.18-*I*
Page,FSLt.JA, **KIA** 22Jul.17-*I*
Page,Lt.LSM, 3Apr.17-*VIII*
Page,1Lt.RCM, DFC *US.* 9Aug.18-*IIB*, 2Sep.18-*IIB*
Paget,2Lt.,Lt.A, 27Oct.18-*IV*, **KIA** 30Oct.18-*IV*
Paget,2Lt.FJ, **WIA** 1Aug.18-*I*
Pailthorpe,FSLt.HA, **KIA** 23May.17-*I*
Paine,2Lt.JJ, **inj** 22Apr.17-*I*
Paine,FSLt.LP, DSC **POW** 19Jun.17-*I*
Pakenham,Capt.MM, **WIA** 25Mar.18-*I*
Pakenham-Walsh,Lt.LH, 28Jan.18-*V*
Palfreyman,Capt.AE, **KIA** 23May.18-*I*
Palfreyman,2Lt.GA, **KIA** 26Oct.16-*I*
Paling,Lt.,Capt.LG, 23Nov.17-*I*, 23Mar.18-*I*
Palliser,Lt.AJ, *Aust.* **KIA** 4Nov.18-*I*
Palmer,2Lt.AW, *13Sqn.* **POW** 7Dec.17-*I*
Palmer,2Lt.AW, *62Sqn.* 24Sep.18-*I*
Palmer,2Lt.CB?, **POW** 15Feb.17-*VII*
Palmer,2Lt.CF, **inj** 28Mar.18-*I*
Palmer,2Lt.CR, **WIA** 6Oct.18-*I*
Palmer,Lt.CW, **POW DoW** ~29.3.1916 2Mar.16-*I*
Palmer,2Lt.DH?, **POW** 14Jul.17-*I*
Palmer,2Lt.HH, **WIA** 4Jul.18-*I*, **WIA** 14Jul.18-*I*
Palmer,Lt.J 31Aug.18-*I*
Palmer,1Lt.KM, *US.* **KIA** 15Oct.18-*IIB*
Palmer,2Lt.,Lt.PE, 16Jul.17-*I*, **KIA** 17Jul.17-*I*
Palmer,Sgt.PJ, 8Nov.18-*I*
Palmer,Lt.PR, **KIA** 25May.17-*I*
Palmer,Sgt.TN, **POW** 25Nov.16-*VII*
Palmer,Capt.WG, **KIA** 5Mar.16-*VIII*
Palmer,AM.WJ, 9Aug.18-*I*
Palmer,1Lt.WW, *US.* **WIA** 22Jul.18-*IIB*
Pancoast,1Lt.HR, *US.* **WIA** 27Oct.18-*IIB*
Panter,Lt.GW, **WIA** 2Jul.16-*I*
Papenfus,Lt.MTS, DFC **WIA POW** 31Jul.18-*I*
Papworth,2Lt.AS, **POW** 30Aug.18-*I*
Parfitt,2AM.HE, **KIFA** 16Aug.14-*I*
Pargeter,TLt.GL, 1Sep.18-*I*
Paris,Lt.DJ, MC **POW** 30Apr.17-*I*
Paris,Lt.DK, MC 18Jun.16-*VII*
Park,Cpl.JT, **KIA** 6Jul.17-*I*
Park,Lt.KR, *NZ.* 24Jul.17-*I*
Park,2Lt.SM, **POW** 18Oct.17-*I*
Parke,Sgt., *11Sqn.* 19Sep.16-*I*
Parke,2Lt.EA, 7Feb.16-*I*
Parke,2Lt.JE, **POW** 11Aug.18-*I*
Parke,Lt.W, 16Apr.15-*V*, 27Apr.15-*V*
Parke,2Lt.WI, **WIA** 16May.18-*I*
Parker,Capt., *5Sqn.* 10Oct.15-*I*
Parker,Lt.CA, 22Apr.17-*I*
Parker,2Lt.D, **inj** 6Dec.17-*I*
Parker,2Lt.,Lt.,Capt.GA, 24May.15-*I*, 10Sep.15-*I*, 21Apr.16-*I*, 26Apr.16-*I*, 27Aug.15-*I*, 28Aug.15-*I*, 29Mar.16-*I*, 3Jun.15-*I*, 6Jun.15-*I*, 16Jun.15-*I*, 20Jun.15-*I*, **KIA** 27Nov.16-*I*
Parker,2Lt.GH, **KIA** 24Mar.18-*I*
Parker,2Lt.JK, **WIA POW** 17Oct.16-*I*
Parker,2Lt.JR, **POW DoW** 21Jul.15-*I*
Parker,Lt.JR?, *4Sqn.* 23May.15-*I*
Parker,2Lt.L, *1Sqn.* **WIA** 28Apr.15-*I*
Parker,2Lt.L, *4Sqn.* **WIA** 29Apr.15-*I*
Parker,Maj.L, **KIA** 7Jan.17-*I*
Parker,FSLt.LH, **KIA** 14Jun.17-*I*
Parker,2Lt.RB, *US.* **KIA**? 4May.18-*IID*
Parker,Lt.SR, **WIA** 22Mar.18-*I*
Parker,2Lt.VS, 8Dec.17-*I*
Parker,Lt.VS, **WIA** 8May.18-*IV*
Parker,Lt.WLO, **KIA** 31Oct.17-*I*
Parkes,Lt.F, 23Jul.17-*I*
Parkes,Lt.GAH, **WIA POW** 15Jul.17-*I*
Parkes,2Lt.SJ, **KIA** 13Aug.18-*I*
Parkes,1AM.T, **KIA** 14Mar.16-*I*
Parkhouse,2Lt.R, 28Mar.18-*I*
Parkinson,2Lt.,Lt.C, 30Sep.16-*I*, 17Mar.17-*I*
Parkinson,Lt.JA, **POW** 26Sep.18-*I*
Parkinson,Lt.P, **POW** 10Jan.18-*V*
Parkinson,2Lt.VJ, *NZ.* **inj POW** 4Jan.18-*VII*
Parks,2Lt.HC, **WIA** 14Oct.18-*I*
Parlee,Lt.GWH, **KIA** 20Aug.18-*I*
Parnell,Lt.EA, **KIA** 29Aug.18-*I*
Parnell,2Lt.IW, **WIA** 17Mar.17-*I*
Parren,2Lt.JL, **WIA** 9Apr.18-*I*
Parrott,1Lt.EA, *US.* **KIA** 26Sep.18-*IIB*
Parry,Sgt.AE, **POW DoW** 29Jul.17-*I*
Parry,Lt.C, 7Jun.18-*I*
Parry,Lt.HA, 26Nov.17-*I*
Parry,2Lt.HR, 7May.17-*I*
Parry,2Lt.MO, *US.* **KIA** 8Jul.18-*IIB*
Parry,2Lt.S, **KIA** 3May.18-*I*
Parsons,Lt.CStC, **POW** 22Apr.18-*I*
Parsons,2Lt.FG, **KIA** 26Oct.16-*I*
Parsons,2Lt.H, **WIA** 7Nov.18-*I*
Parsons,2Lt.HM, 24Apr.16-*I*
Parsons,2Lt.HMS, *US.* **WIA** 3Oct.18-*I*
Parsons,Lt.LH, **inj**? 30Jul.18-*I*
Parsons,2Lt.LWB, **WIA** 8Aug.16-*I*
Partington,Lt.OJ, **WIA POW** 17Jul.17-*I*
Partridge,Lt.AT, **POW** 16Aug.18-*I*
Partridge,Sgt.HM, **INT DoW** 25Jul.18-*I*
Pascoe,2Lt.A, 17Mar.17-*I*, **WIA** 16Apr.17-*I*
Pascoe,2Lt.EJ, 5Apr.17-*I*, **KIA** 14Apr.17-*I*
Pascoe,2Lt.FGB, **KIA** 2Jul.17-*I*
Pashley,2Lt.FE, *name* Pashby? **WIA** 12Apr.18-*I*
Pashley,2Lt.F, 11Apr.18-*I*
Paskill,1Lt.RL, *USAS.* **KIA** 9Aug.18-*I*
Pass,2AM.WC, **POW Died** 26Jan.16-*VII*
Patch,Capt.H, 19Aug.17-*I*, **POW DoW** 19.10.1917 18Oct.17-*I*
Pateman,2Lt.HL, **KIA** 6Feb.17-*I*
Patenaude,2Lt.AJ, **POW** 19May.18-*I*
Paterson,2AM.A, **KIA** 28Jan.18-*I*
Paterson,Lt.AS, *Aust. initials* AF? **WIA** 9May.18-*I*
Paterson,2Lt.DWS, **KIA** 20Jun.16-*I*
Paterson,Capt.GI, 21Mar.18-*I*, **KIA** 2Apr.18-*I*
Patey,TLt.,Capt.HA, DSC 29Apr.18-*I*, 21Jun.18-*I*, **POW** 5Sep.18-*I*
Patey,Lt.WO, 22May.18-*I*
Patman,Lt.GH, **POW** 12Aug.18-*I*
Paton,2Lt.HF, **KIA** 4Jun.17-*I*
Paton,2Lt.MDR, **DoW** 12.6.1917 1Jun.17-*I*
Patrick,Capt.WD, 9Jan.18-*I*, **POW** 10Apr.18-*I*
Patrick,Capt.WJCKC, 14Sep.16-*I*, 15Sep.16-*I*, 16Nov.16-*I*
Pattern,2Lt.JA, 28Nov.17-*I*
Patterson,2Lt.AA, **DoW** 9Nov.16-*I*
Patterson,1Lt.AB, *US.* **KIA** 29Oct.18-*IIB*
Patterson,2Lt.AFA, **POW DoW** 25.9.1916 17Sep.16-*I*
Patterson,2Lt.EM, 29Sep.18-*I*, **WIA POW**? 3Oct.18-*I*
Patterson,Lt.L, MC **WIA** 11May.18-*I*
Patterson,1Lt.RA, *US.* **POW** 29Oct.18-*IIB*
Patterson,Lt.RJ, **WIA** 19Sep.17-*I*

Pattinson,2Lt.,Lt.H, 16Oct.18-I, 21Oct.18-I, 27Oct.18-I
Pattinson,2Lt.,Lt.,Capt.LA, 22Aug.15-I, 10Sep.15-I, 22Sep.15-I, 26Oct.15-I, 19Dec.15-I, 29Dec.15-I, 25Jan.16-I, 21Feb.16-I, 30Apr.16-I, 19May.16-I
Pattinson,Capt.TC, 10May.18-III
Pattison,FSLt.CE, WIA 20May.17-I
Pattison,FSLt.JF, INT 4Jun.18-III
Pattisson,2Lt.PB, 6Mar.17-I, WIA 10Apr.17-I
Pattisson,FSLt.WLH, DFC KIA 16Mar.18-I
Pattulo,Lt.RC, KIA 15Sep.18-I
Paul,2Lt.AR, POW DoW 22Jan.18-I
Paul,Lt.CS, NZ. 23May.18-VII
Paul,Lt.GA, Aust. WIA 11Apr.18-I
Paul,Capt.RJ, INT 4Jun.18-III
Paul,2Lt.Sir RJ, POW 10Oct.15-VIII
Pawley,2AM.G, KIA 25Apr.17-I
Payn,Lt.HJ, 2Aug.15-I, 4Nov.15-I
Payne,2Lt.ACJ, POW 29Sep.18-I
Payne,2Lt.CB, KIA 20Aug.17-I
Payne,2Lt.HA, KIA 18Mar.18-I
Payne,2Lt.JD, inj 10Aug.17-I, 18Oct.17-I
Payne,2Lt.JM, 15Sep.18-I, 29Sep.18-I, POW 1Nov.18-I
Payne,1Lt.KC, US. POW 5Nov.18-IIB
Payne,2Lt.LA, 8Mar.18-I
Payne,Capt.LGS, 28Sep.17-I
Payne,2Lt.P, POW 15Sep.18-I
Payne,Lt.ST, DoW 6Apr.18-I
Payne,2Lt.WSL, MC KIA 4Sep.17-I
Paynter,2Lt.HS, 5Jan.16-I
Paynter,FSLt.,Capt.JdeC, WIA 9Apr.17-I, 1Jun.18-I
Paynton,2Lt.HS, 25Jan.16-I
Payton,2Lt.,Lt.CW, 21May.18-I, 1Oct.18-I, KIA 2Oct.18-I
Payton,Lt.JL, KIA 16Aug.18-I
Payze,2Lt.A, 22Jun.15-I, WIA 3Jul.15-I
Pea,Pte., 16Sqn. 26Apr.17-I
Peace,Lt.AG, 5Aug.17-I
Peace,Lt.WJ, Can. 8Aug.18-I
Peacock,Lt.FC, MC 2Oct.18-I
Peacock,2Lt.JT, KIA 16Jul.18-I
Peacock,2Lt.LWD, 3Oct.18-I
Peacock,2Lt.MA, POW 9Oct.17-I
Pearce,Gnr.CR, Can. KIA 24Aug.16-I
Pearce,2Lt.ESC, KIA 31Mar.18-I
Pearce,2Lt.GW, 9Nov.18-I
Pearce,Lt.LWC, INT 31Jul.18-I
Pearce,2Lt.RA, 1Oct.18-I
Pearce,AG.Sgt.SD, WIA 21Sep.17-I
Pearson,2Lt.AJ, MC 3Mar.17-I, KIA 9Mar.17-I
Pearson,2Lt.BC, WIA POW 8Aug.18-I
Pearson,Lt.CW, KIA 3Jan.18-I
Pearson,2Lt.EC, US. .18-IIA
Pearson,Lt.FG, 1Jun.16-I
Pearson,2Lt.,Capt.HA, MC 22Oct.16-I, 15Jun.18-IV
Pearson,1Lt.JR, US. WIA 4Nov.18-IIB
Pearson,Lt.JW, US. 1Jul.18-I
Pearson,Lt.LH, 4Jun.18-I, 27Jun.18-I
Pearson,2Lt.LJ, POW 5Feb.16-I
Pearson,Lt.O, WIA 8Aug.18-I
Pearson,2Lt.OC, KIA 10Sep.17-I
Pearson,2Lt.TS, 22Jul.16-I
Pearson,2Lt.WJ, WIA 14Feb.17-I
Pearson,Lt.,Capt.WRG, 27Jul.17-I, 5Dec.17-I
Peat,Lt.RW, POW 21May.18-I
Peck,Capt.AH, 4Dec.17-VII, 23Mar.18-VII
Peck,2Lt.RH, 7Sqn. WIA 6Jul.15-I, 27Jul.15-I, 31Jul.15-I
Peck,2Lt.RH, 30Sqn. KIA 5Mar.16-VIII
Peckham,Lt.CW, POW 23Jun.18-I
Peden,2Lt.,Lt.JKvonI, 13Mar.18-I, WIA 21Mar.18-I, KIA 28Mar.18-I
Peel,2Lt.AE, Aust. WIA 10Aug.17-I
Peel,2Lt.EO, 9Sep.17-I
Peel,Lt.JC, KIA 19Aug.18-I
Peel,FSLt.RW, 20Jan.18-V
Peel,Lt.WS, MC KIA 27Sep.18-I
Peeling,2Lt.HV, POW 1Sep.18-I
Peer,2Lt.HE, WIA 24Oct.18-I
Peers,2Lt.,Lt.LIA, US. 31May.18-I, US. POW 1Jun.18-I
Peffers,Lt., 8Sqn. 29Sep.18-I
Pegram,Lt.JAH, KIA 18Jul.18-III
Peile,2Lt.AH, POW 21Jan.18-I
Peiler,Lt.MF, POW 6Apr.18-I
Pelger,FSLt.CR, KIA 12Jul.17-I
Pell,2Lt.HS, KIA 6Apr.17-I
Pell,2Lt.WA, 24Mar.18-I, KIA 12Apr.18-I
Pelletier,Lt.CA, KIA 11May.18-I
Pelton,Sgt.AD, Can. KIA 31May.18-IIC
Pember,Lt.EH, KIA 30Sep.17-I
Pember?,Lt.WG, see Pender
Pemberton,2Lt., 5Sqn. 19Dec.15-I, 28Dec.15-I
Pemberton,Capt.AJM, Can. KIA 3Nov.16-I
Pemberton,Lt.AL, POW 12Apr.18-I
Pemberton,Capt.FD, WIA 11May.17-I, KIA 21Aug.17-I
Pemberton,2Lt.FR, US. WIA 4Nov.18-I
Pendell,1Lt.E, US. WIA 4Nov.18-IIB
Pender,2Lt.GW, 26Sep.16-I
Pender,Capt.JMcAM, WIA 11Aug.17-I
Pender,2Lt.,Capt.WG, MC WIA 10Jul.16-I, 11Jul.17-I, MC KIA 15Aug.17-I
Pendleton,2Lt.W, INT 2Oct.18-III
Penfield,2Lt.P, US. KIA 15Aug.18-IID
Pengilley,Lt.JJ, Aust. 8Sep.18-I
Penman,2Lt.WJB, inj 9Nov.18-I
Pennal,Lt.HL, KIA 23Oct.18-I
Pennell,Capt.ER, 22Nov.17-I
Pennington,Lt.KM, 11Oct.18-VIII
Penny,2Lt.AR, 23Jul.17-I, WIA 5Aug.17-I
Penrose,Pbr.,2Lt.K, WIA 2Aug.18-I, KIA 3Sep.18-I
Penrose-Welsted,Capt.SR, KIA 17Jul.18-VI
Penruddocke,Lt.NF, POW 17May.18-I
Pentecost,2Lt.CG, KIA 27Mar.18-I
Pentland,2Lt.,Capt.AAND, Aust. 10Jun.16-I, 12Aug.17-I, 16Aug.17-I, 24Sep.17-I, WIA 26Sep.17-I, 6May.18-I, 18Jun.18-I, WIA 25Aug.18-I
Penwarden,2Lt.HG, POW 15Jul.18-VIII
Pepler,Lt.SJ, KIA 6Mar.17-I
Pepper,2Lt.AC, POW 6Apr.17-I
Pepper,TLt.,Lt.B, 15Jun.18-I, KIA 1Oct.18-I
Pepper,2Lt.EH, KIA 23Aug.18-I
Percival,2Lt., 7Sqn. 1Nov.16-I
Percival,2Lt.E, POW 29Apr.17-I
Percival,Lt.JFS, inj 7Aug.18-I
Perham,FLt.W, INT 24Oct.17-III
Perkins,2Lt.ACT, MC WIA 23Nov.17-I
Perkins,Sgt.AJ, WIA 17Mar.18-I
Perkins,2Lt.JFRI, KIA 8Mar.18-I
Perkins,2Lt.T, 20May.17-I
Perks,Pbr.JW, 15Jun.18-I
Perney,2Lt.ED, KIA 23Nov.17-I
Perret,2Lt.EG, WIA 26Sep.18-I
Perrin,Capt.EC, 19Dec.15-I
Perring,2Lt.JH, POW 5Oct.18-I
Perrott,2AM.BG, KIA 30Apr.17-I
Perrott,AG.2AM.E, WIA 18Aug.17-I
Perry,2Lt.AF, KIA 28Oct.18-I
Perry,2Lt.BB, POW 18Oct.17-I
Perry,1AM.EG, POW 27Apr.17-I
Perry,2Lt.EO, 24Apr.17-I, WIA 29Apr.17-I
Perry,2Lt.EWC, KIFA 16Aug.14-I
Perry,2Lt.LP, KIA 2Sep.18-I
Perryman,2Lt.AC, inj 28Apr.17-I
Peter,Lt., inj 24Mar.17-I
Peterkin,2Lt.SMacG, WIA 19Sep.17-I
Peters,Lt.GC, Aust. 22Sep.18-VII
Peters,2Lt.JFJ, INT 24Aug.18-I
Peters,Lt.N, inj 9Apr.18-I
Peters,1Lt.SvW, US. WIA POW 9Oct.18-IIB
Petersen,2Lt.GGW, POW 2Dec.17-I
Peterson,2Lt.A, KIA 3Sep.18-I
Petit,2Lt., 16Sqn. 14Mar.16-I
Petre,Lt.,Capt.HA, Aust. May.15-VIII, 23Nov.15-VII
Petree,1Lt.HE, US. KIA 26Sep.18-IIB
Pettit,Capt.SL, POW 29Jul.18-VII
Pettit,Lt., 6Sqn. 2Sep.18-I
Pettitt,2Lt.MS, WIA 27Mar.18-I
Peverell,Lt.EH, 23Mar.18-I
Pfrimmer,Lt.VR, KIA 1May.17-I
Phalen,2Lt.RU, KIA 28May.17-I
Phear,Lt.HW, WIA 22Aug.18-I
Pheby,Sgt.HT, KIA 4Aug.18-I
Phelan,1Lt.R, US. 9Oct.18-IIB, KIA 31Oct.18-IIB
Phelan,2Lt.RS, WIA POW 17Aug.17-I
Phelps,Lt.LH, WIA 18Nov.17-I
Philbrick,1Lt.F, US. KIA 19Sep.18-IIB
Philcox,Lt.CL, 30Nov.17-I
Philcox,Lt.,Capt.WS, 12Aug.18-I, WIA 4Nov.18-I
Philip,2Lt.ET, KIA 18Jun.17-I
Phillipi,2Lt.G, WIA 26Sep.16-I
Phillippo,Lt.AJCE, 7Jan.17-I, KIA 7Jun.17-I
Phillips,Lt.AM, 21Apr.18-I, 21May.18-I
Phillips,Lt.AMcM, Can. 29Jul.18-I
Phillips,2Lt.AW, 23Sqn. 23Nov.16-I
Phillips,FSLt.AW, Dunkirk POW 24Sep.17-I
Phillips,2Lt.CI, KIA 27Oct.17-I
Phillips,2Lt.FCB, 1Jun.18-I
Phillips,Lt.FES, KIA 12Oct.16-I
Phillips,1Lt.GR, US. 5Oct.18-IIB
Phillips,2Lt.H, 1Sep.18-I
Phillips,2Lt.,Capt.JE?, 3Apr.18-I, 10Apr.18-I, 20Apr.18-I, KIA 16Sep.18-I
Phillips,Pte.JVW, WIA 3Sep.16-I
Phillips,2Lt.LH, 13Aug.18-I
Phillips,2Lt.NA, 15Feb.17-I, KIA 25Mar.17-I
Phillips,2Lt.PL, 28Sep.18-I, POW 14Oct.18-I
Phillips,Capt.RC, Aust. 7Aug.17-I, 12Jun.18-I
Phillips,2Lt.RO, WIA 18Dec.17-I
Phillips,2Lt.T, KIA 13Oct.18-I
Phillips,Lt.TM, KIA 18Sep.18-I
Phillips,2Lt.VGH, 29Sep.18-I, WIA 5Oct.18-I
Phillips,1Lt.WA, US. KIA 1Oct.18-IIB
Phillips,2Lt.WO, 23Jun.16-I
Philpott,Lt., 12Sqn. 21Jul.16-I, 12Sqn. 30Jul.16-I
Philpott,Capt.JR, POW DoW 15.1.18 25Sep.17-VIII
Phinney,Lt., 1Sqn. 30Oct.18-I
Phipson,Lt.HGS, KIA 15Jul.18-I
Pickard,2Lt.,Lt.CGV, 30Jun.18-I, KIA 22Aug.18-I
Pickard,1Lt.S, US. WIA 31Oct.18-IIB
Picken,Lt.RB, KIA 6Sep.18-IV
Pickering,Lt.AE, 7Jun.17-I
Pickering,Capt.CL, KIA 15Apr.17-VIII
Pickering,Lt.P, WIA 2Jun.18-I
Pickett,Lt.AC, 10Aug.17-I, POW 3Sep.17-I
Pickford,2Lt.A, WIA 8Nov.17-I
Pickford,2Lt.EW, POW 28Mar.18-I
Pickin,2Lt.A, inj 28Jul.18-I
Pickles,2Lt.H, WIA 28Mar.18-I
Pickstone,2Lt.C, KIA 3Sep.17-I
Pickthorn,Lt.CEM, WIA 6Mar.17-I, 11Mar.17-I
Pickthorn,2Lt.GM, 29Jun.16-I
Pickthorn,Capt.KWM, WIA 10May.17-VI
Pickup,Lt.SF, 4May.18-I
Picot,2Lt.,Lt.MR?, 22Dec.17-I, 22Mar.18-I
Pidcock,Capt.GAH, 7Apr.18-I
Pierce,TLt.,Lt.JB, 4Sep.18-I, KIA 2Oct.18-I
Pierce,2Lt.PJE, KIA 13Aug.18-I
Pierce,Lt.RG, 18Jun.18-I, KIA 2Jul.18-I
Pierce,Lt.W, WIA 9Aug.17-I
Pierson,Gnr.H, WIA 11Apr.17-I
Piggott,Lt.JCC, WIA 26May.17-I
Piggott,Lt.JR, 8May.18-I
Pike,Lt.CA, 4Sep.17-I
Pike,2Lt.GB, 23Aug.18-I, 23Oct.18-I
Pike,2Lt.HG, KIA 30Aug.18-I
Pilbrow,Pte.SE, 27Jul.17-I, KIA 15Aug.17-I
Pilcher,2Lt.TF, WIA 24Nov.17-I
Pilcher,Lt.CR, WIA 8Mar.18-I
Pilcher-Hemingway,Lt.CR, WIA 11Apr.18-I
Pilditch,2Lt.G, 26Mar.18-I
Pile,Lt.CJ?, DoW 1.5.1917 29Apr.17-I
Pilkington,LCpl.G, WIA 12Oct.16-I
Pilkington,Lt.JO, KIA 6Sep.17-I
Pilling,2Lt.JE, KIA 1Jul.18-I
Pim,Lt.T, KIA 28Aug.18-I
Pinder,2Lt.FG, WIA POW 29Mar.16-I
Pinder,Capt.JW, 19May.18-I, 27Jun.18-I, 9Oct.18-I, 5Nov.18-I
Pinder,2Lt.SR, KIA 19Feb.18-I
Pineau,2Lt.CF, US. POW 8Oct.18-I
Pink,Lt.AL, KIA 30Oct.18-I
Pinkerton,2Lt.AL, POW 16Sep.16-I
Pinkerton,2Lt.DM, WIA 3Aug.18-I
Pinsent,2Lt.PR, DoW 23Sep.16-I
Pinson,2Lt.IL, DoW 4May.17-I
Piper,Cpl., 4Sqn. 4Oct.14-I
Piper,Sgt., 15Sqn. KIA 17Jan.16-I
Piper,Lt.EH, KIA 15May.18-I
Piper,Lt.TH, POW 22Mar.18-V
Pirie,Capt.GC, 13Aug.17-I
Pirie,2Lt.JB, 17Sep.16-I
Pitcher,Capt.DLeG, 30Sep.14-I
Pither,2Lt.,Capt.CE, 31May.16-I, KIA 22Aug.18-I
Pither,2Lt.SE, 28Dec.15-I
Pithey,Lt.CR, DFC WIA 24Jul.18-I, WIA 27Sep.18-I
Pitkin,2Lt.H, 23Aug.18-I
Pitman,Capt.AFE, KIA 3Jan.18-I
Pitman,Lt.RC, 25Sep.17-I, POW 16Sep.18-I
Pitot,2Lt.M, DoW 8Oct.18-I
Pitt,2Lt.BW, KIA 10May.17-I
Pitt,Lt.GA, 11May.18-I
Pitt,Lt.GH, WIA 12Nov.17-I
Pitt,2Lt.GL, KIA 28Dec.15-I
Pitt-Pitts,Lt.WJ, KIA 9Aug.18-I
Pivette,Serg.L, French. 16Mar.17-I
Pixley,Capt.RGH, MC inj 10May.17-I, KIA 4Jun.17-I
Pizey,2Lt.NM, KIA 27Jul.17-I
Platel,1AM.SH, WIA 31Oct.17-I
Platt,Capt.LS, KIA 13Apr.17-I
Platt,Sgt.W, KIA 25Sep.18-I
Player,2Lt.F, KIA 4Sep.18-I
Playfair,Lt.L, 23Apr.15-I, KIA 6Jul.15-I
Playfair,Lt.,Capt.PHL, 8Nov.14-I, 21Aug.15-I, 25Aug.15-I, 1Sep.15-I, 7Sep.15-I, 9Sep.15-I, 21Oct.15-I
Playford,Lt.ERB, 22Oct.17-I
Playford,Lt.GRB, WIA 15Sep.18-IV
Playne,2Lt.L, KIA 27Mar.18-I
Plenderleith,2Lt.WN, WIA 4Apr.18-I
Plenty,2Lt.,Lt.EP, 29Feb.16-I, 27Apr.16-I
Plum,Lt.EG, 27Sep.18-I
Plummer,2Lt.CW, US. KIA 11Aug.18-IIB
Plyler,2Lt.WH, US. POW 13Jun.18-IIB
Pocock,2Lt.AND, POW 5Jan.17-VI
Poe,2Lt.JM, KIA 9Oct.18-I
Pohlmann,Lt.HE, 6Mar.18-I
Pohlmann,2Lt.RP, KIA 5Feb.18-I
Poland,Lt.TG, WIA 5May.17-I
Poler,Lt.DS, 7Jun.18-I
Pollack,2Lt.,Capt.ERH, name Pollak? 25Jul.16-I, 1Mar.18-I
Pollard,Lt.AC, 2Sep.18-I, 1Oct.18-I
Pollard,2Lt.GH, POW DoW 7Jun.17-I
Pollard,2Lt.RK, WIA 8Jun.18-I
Pollard,Lt.WH, POW 16Aug.18-I
Pollitt,1AM.F, WIA POW 21Oct.17-I
Pollock,2Lt.JF, KIA 20Jul.18-I
Pomeroy,Lt.WA, 12Aug.18-I
Pontin,Lt.SCM, POW 25Jun.18-I
Pool,2Lt.BG, 3Sep.18-I, WIA 2Oct.18-I
Poole,2Lt.AA, Aust. POW 20Jan.18-VII
Poole,2Lt.BG, KIA 22Mar.18-I
Poole,2Lt.CJ, 11Mar.17-I
Poole,Lt.HWL, inj 21Mar.17-I
Poole,2AM.WH, WIA 16Jun.17-I
Pope,2Lt.AD, 25Mar.18-I, 27Mar.18-I, POW 28Mar.18-I
Pope,2Lt.EA, KIA 27Feb.17-I
Pope,2Lt.,Capt.EEE, 2Apr.17-I, POW 4Jan.18-I
Pope,2Lt.KWD, WIA 2Apr.18-I
Pope,Lt.RAB, MC POW 2Sep.18-I
Pope,Lt.RPP, Aug.18-VIII
Pope,2Lt.SLG, Irl. WIA 18Nov.17-I
Porkess,Lt.WA, KIA 10Feb.17-I
Porri,Lt.C, 4Nov.15-I, 14Dec.15-I, 19Dec.15-I
Portal,SLt.RH, WIA 17Mar.16-V
Porter,Capt., 16Sqn. 29May.15-I
Porter,2Lt.AC, POW 19Aug.18-I
Porter,2Lt.AL, US. WIA 26Jul.18-I
Porter,2Lt.EW, US. WIA 9Aug.18-IID
Porter,Lt.GA, KIA 5Dec.15-I
Porter,Capt.GT, 26Oct.15-I, 18Nov.15-I, 2Dec.15-I, 19Dec.15-I, POW 27Dec.15-I

Porter,Lt.HS, **KIA** 18Jul.17-*I*
Porter,Capt.L, **POW DoW** 24.10.1916 22Oct.16-*I*
Porter,Lt.LE, **WIA** 23Apr.17-*I*
Porter,2Lt.W, **KIA** 24Mar.18-*I*
Porter,2Lt.WW, 25Apr.18-*I*
Portsmouth,AM1.RS, **KIA** 25Feb.17-*I*
Postons,1AM.HL, **KIA** 31Oct.17-*I*
Potter,2Lt., *82Sqn.* 27Mar.18-*I*
Potter,FLt.E, 25Feb.17-*I*
Potter,2AM.FA, 27Jul.17-*I*
Potter,Lt.J, 11Mar.17-*I*, 1Jun.17-*I*
Potter,Lt.R, **POW** 10Oct.15-*I*
Potter,Ens.S, *USN*. **KIA** 24Apr.18-*III*
Potter,2Lt.SB, **INT** 30Jun.18-*I*
Potter,Lt.SLH, **WIA** 19Feb.18-*I*
Potter,1Lt.WC, DSC *US*. **KIA** 10Oct.18-*IIB*
Pottie,Lt.MJ, **WIA** 10Apr.18-*I*
Potts,Lt.JDS, *UK*. **KIA** 4Jan.18-*VII*
Potts,Lt.LMS, *UK*. 17Jan.18-*VII*
Potts,2Lt.WJ, *27Sqn.* **POW** 4Nov.18-*I*
Potts,Lt.WJ, *56Sqn.* **KIA** 21Sep.17-*I*
Potvin,FSLt.JE, **KIA** 19Jun.17-*I*
Pouchot,Lt.JA,DCM 27Sep.18-*I*, **KIA** 5Oct.18-*I*
Poulter,2Lt.WF, **POW DoW** 6.3.1918 5Mar.18-*I*
Poundall,Capt.WAL, MC **KIA** 31Oct.17-*I*
Powell,Lt., *57Sqn.* 27Mar.18-*I*
Powell,2Lt.CH?, **KIA** 15Jun.17-*I*
Powell,Lt.CM, 9May.18-*I*
Powell,Lt.DG, **POW** 9Oct.17-*I*
Powell,Capt.EC, **WIA** 10Apr.18-*I*
Powell,1Lt.EM, *US*. **WIA** 22Sep.18-*IID*
Powell,2Lt.EW, **KIA** 31Oct.17-*I*
Powell,2Lt.F, **WIA** 28Aug.18-*I*
Powell,Lt.FG, 10Jun.18-*I*, **WIA POW** 8Aug.18-*I*
Powell,Lt.,Capt.,Maj.FJ, MC 19Sep.15-*I* 3Oct.15-*I*, 11Oct.15-*I*, 4Nov.15-*I*, 28Nov.15-*I*, 19Dec.15-*I*, 12Jan.16-*I*, 17Jan.16-*I*, 20Jan.16-*I*, 5Feb.16-*I*, 7Feb.16-*I*, 29Feb.16-*I*, 12Mar.16-*I*, **WIA POW** 2Feb.18-*I*
Powell,2Lt.LA, *11Sqn.* 16Oct.17-*I*, 30Nov.17-*I*
Powell,FSLt.LA, *3Naval* **DoW** 7.3.1917 4Mar.17-*I*
Powell,2Lt.,Lt.LC, 29Mar.16-*I*, **KIA** 31May.16-*I*
Powell,Lt.PJG, **KIA** 2Apr.17-*I*
Powell,2Lt.RA, **WIA** 7Jun.17-*I*
Power,2Lt.HE, 11Aug.18-*I*, **inj INT** 15Sep.18-*I*
Power,2Lt.HR, **KIA** 22Aug.17-*I*
Power-Clutterbuck,2Lt.JE, **KIA** 25Jun.17-*I*
Powers,Lt.BA, **KIA** 25Sep.17-*I*
Powles,FSLt.GP, 17Nov.16-*I*, **INT** 26Feb.17-*I*
Pownall,Lt.AH, 19Oct.18-*I*
Powney,2Lt.AJ, **DoW** 15Sep.17-*I*
Prance,Sgt.JE, **WIA** 4Mar.17-*I*
Pratt,Lt.AJ, *Aust*. **inj** 22Nov.17-*I*
Pratt,2Lt.AR, **POW** 27Oct.18-*I*
Pratt,2Lt.HJ, 31Aug.17-*I*
Pratt,2Lt.SH, 15Feb.17-*I*
Pratt,Sgt.SJ, **KIA** 5Jul.18-*I*
Preece,Lt.CE, 28May.18-*I*
Preece,2Lt.E, **KIA** 2Oct.18-*I*
Prentice,2Lt.LC, *USAS*. **KIA** 1Aug.18-*I*
Prescott,Lt.CE, 12Oct.17-*I*
Prescott,2Lt.FA, 6Mar.17-*I*
Prescott,2Lt.LW, *US*. **KIA** 22Apr.18-*I*
Preston,2Lt.A, **POW** 3Sep.18-*I*
Preston,1Lt.HC, *US*. **KIA** 26Sep.18-*IIB*
Preston,Lt.JC, 18Aug.18-*VI*
Preston,Lt.RA, 14Nov.15-*I*, **KIA** 15Sep.16-*I*
Preston,Lt.TF, **KIA** 24Jan.17-*I*
Preston-Cobb,2Lt.RJ, 5Oct.17-*I*, **KIA** 11Oct.17-*I*
Prestwich,Lt.J, **DoW** 7Feb.16-*I*
Pretty,2Lt.HJ, **WIA POW** 24Sep.18-*I*
Pretty,2Lt.RC, **POW** 25Sep.18-*I*
Pretyman,Lt.,Capt.,Maj.GF, 26Aug.14-*I*, 9Sep.14-*I*, 15Sep.14-*I*, 10Mar.15-*I*, 5May.15-*I*, 16Jun.15-*I*, 24Feb.16-*I*
Price,Lt.D, **WIA? inj?** 24Oct.18-*I*
Price,2Lt.,Lt.G, 20Nov.15-*I*, 19Dec.15-*I*, 17Jan.16-*I*, 20Jan.16-*I*, 25Jan.16-*I*, 7Feb.16-*I*, 8Feb.16-*I*, 2Mar.16-*I*, **WIA** 9Mar.16-*I*
Price,FCdr.GW, DSC 18Jun.16-*I*, 16Feb.18-*I*, **KIA** 18Feb.18-*I*
Price,2Lt.HJ, **POW** 26Apr.17-*I*
Price,Lt.HW, *Can*. 25Oct.18-*VIII*
Price,2Lt.JCE, 19Feb.18-*I*
Price,2Lt.JHR, **WIA** 22Aug.17-*I*
Price,Lt.JV, 31Aug.18-*I*
Price,2Lt.O, **KIA** 4Nov.18-*I*
Price,2Lt.P, **POW** 19Oct.17-*VIII*
Price,2Lt.WT, **WIA** 9May.17-*I*
Prickett,Capt.L, 2Oct.15-*I*
Prideaux,2Lt.ER, **KIA** 17May.18-*I*
Prier,2Lt.WJ, **POW** 28Mar.18-*I*
Priestley,2Lt.GR, **WIA** 30May.18-*I*
Priestley,2Lt.TA, **WIA** 30Oct.18-*I*
Prime,2Lt.HL, **POW DoW** 5Oct.18-*I*
Primeau,2Lt.CW, 24Sep.17-*I*, **KIA** 27Oct.17-*I*
Primrose,Lt.LJ, 4Apr.18-*I*
Prince,2Lt.FG, 8Oct.18-*I*
Prince,SLt.N,LdH **DoI** 15.10.1916 12Oct.16-*IIA*
Prince,Lt.TH, *Aust*. **WIA** 26Sep.18-*I*
Prince-Smith,Lt.DSP, **KIA** 24Oct.17-*I*
Prior,Capt.LP, **DoW** 7Jun.17-*I*
Pritchard,2Lt.CF, **KIA** 17Sep.17-*I*
Pritchard,2Lt.EW, **WIA** 15Aug.17-*I*
Pritchard,Capt.FH, **INT** 2Jun.15-*I*
Pritchard,Sgt.FN, **POW** 28May.18-*I*
Pritchard,2Lt.JC, **KIA** 29Sep.18-*I*
Pritchard,Lt.JC, **KIA** 30Oct.18-*I*
Pritt,2Lt.WA, 21Aug.17-*I*
Probyn,2Lt.HM, **WIA** 23Aug.16-*I*
Proctor,2Lt.HF, 29Mar.18-*I*, **WIA** 1Apr.18-*I*
Proctor,Lt.HNJ, **KIA** 16May.18-*I*
Proctor,Sgt.T, **KIA** 27Sep.18-*I*
Prosser,Lt.DH?, **KIA**, *initials* HD? 10May.18-*I*
Prosser,Lt.JE, **KIA** 30Oct.18-*I*
Prothero,Lt.,Capt.PB, 6Jul.16-*I*, 23May.17-*I*, **KIA** 26Jul.17-*I*
Protheroe,Lt.WB, **KIA** 12Jun.17-*I*
Proud,2Lt.JRS, **DoW** *as* **POW** 6Apr.17-*I*
Proudlove,2Lt.H, **WIA** 22Oct.18-*I*
Provan,2Lt.A, **POW** 25Sep.18-*I*
Pruden,2Lt.WC, **POW** 8Nov.17-*I*
Pryce,Lt.HE, **WIA** 4Jul.18-*I*
Pryor,Lt.AD, **WIA** 8Apr.17-*I*
Pryor,Lt.JW, **POW** 16Jun.18-*I*
Puckle,Capt.D, **WIA** 5Aug.18-*I*
Puckridge,2Lt.,Capt.HV, **WIA** 9Feb.17-*I*, **POW** 1Jul.18-*I*
Puffer,Lt.SA, *Can*. 4Jul.18-*I*
Pugh,2Lt.J, **POW** 4Nov.18-*I*
Pugh,Lt.JA, **POW** 16Jul.18-*I*
Pugh,Lt.JE, **KIA** 10Nov.18-*I*
Pughe-Evans,2Lt.H, **POW** 12Oct.17-*I*
Pugsley,2Lt.CG, **DoW** 26.3.1918 26Mar.18-*I*
Pullan,Lt.JA, **KIA** 28Nov.17-*I*
Pullar,2Lt.J, 17Sep.18-*I*, **WIA** 25Sep.18-*I*
Pullen,Lt.CE, **inj** 11Jun.18-*I*, **WIA** 9Aug.18-*I*
Pullen,2Lt.CJ, **KIA** 4Sep.17-*I*
Pullen,Lt.FJ, **WIA** 24Mar.18-*I*
Pulleyn,2Lt.JL, **KIA** 17Oct.16-*I*
Pulling,FSLt.E, DSO 28Nov.16-*III*
Purry,Capt.RO, **POW** 16Jun.18-*I*
Purves,2Lt.SSB, **POW** 19Mar.17-*I*
Purvis,2Lt.MC, 11Apr.18-*I*
Purvis,2Lt.RC, 23Aug.17-*I*
Purvis,Lt.WF, **INT** 29Jun.18-*I*
Puryear,1Lt.GW, *US*. **POW** 26Jul.18-*IIB*
Putnam,1Lt.DE, *US*. **KIA** 12Sep.18-*IIB*
Pybus,2Lt.E, 24Mar.18-*I*
Pycroft,2Lt.EP, **inj** 9May.18-*I*
Pym,Lt.ACM, **WIA** 13Jul.17-*I*
Pym,Lt.FG, 24Sep.18-*I*, **WIA POW** 26Sep.18-*I*
Pyott,2Lt.,Lt.IV, DSO *SA*. 27Nov.16-*III*, 23Apr.17-*I*

Q

Quaife,2Lt.AP, **WIA** 3Oct.18-*I*
Quelch,2Lt.LM, 19Aug.17-*I*
Quenault,Cpl., *French*. 5Oct.14-*I*
Quested,2Lt.,Capt.JB, 14Dec.15-*I*, 27Dec.16-*I*
Quick,Lt.,Capt.JT, 21Mar.18-*I*, 25Mar.18-*I*, 28Mar.18-*I*, 30Mar.18-*I*, 3May.18-*I*
Quicke,Sgt.SH, **KIA** 21Mar.17-*I*
Quigley,2Lt.,Capt.FG, *Can*. 10Oct.17-*I*, 9Mar.18-*I*, **WIA** 27Mar.18-*I*
Quilter,2Lt.EGC, *initials* EDC 25Aug.17-*I*, **WIA POW** 6Sep.17-*I*
Quinlan,2Lt.JF, **KIA** 3Jul.16-*I*
Quinlan,2Lt.JS, 25Jan.16-*I*
Quinn,Lt.JJ, **WIA** 2Aug.18-*I*
Quinnell,2Lt.,Capt.JC, 13Sep.15, 16Mar.16-*I*, **WIA** 10Jul.16-*I*
Quinton,2Lt.JG, **DoW** 30Aug.18-*I*

R

Rabagliati,Lt.CEC, 1Nov.14-*I*
Raby,2Lt.LF, 1Oct.18-*I*, **KIA** 9Oct.18-*I*
Rackett,Lt.AR, *Aust*. **POW** 1Jun.18-*I*
Radcliff,2Lt.RSFD, **KIA** 25Mar.18-*I*
Radcliffe,Lt.GA, **KIA** 25Apr.17-*VI*
Radley,Lt.JE, **POW** 4Nov.18-*I*
Rae,2Lt.CJ, **WIA** 24Jun.18-*I*
Rainbow,Lt.SC, 27Oct.18-*I*
Rainey,Lt.,FLt.TA, 1Oct.14-*I*, **INT** 17Dec.14-*I*
Rainier,2Lt.GA, **POW** 22May.18-*I*
Raleigh,Maj.GH, 25Aug.14-*I*, 19Jan.15-*I*
Ralfe,Capt.HDE, *Aust*. **KIA** 6May.18-*I*
Ralph,Pbr,2Lt.FJ, DFC **WIA** 10May.18-*I*, **KIA** 3Sep.18-*I*
Ralphs,Lt.A, **KIA** 23Apr.17-*I*
Ralston,Capt.JS, MC **WIA** 16Feb.18-*I*, 27Jun.18-*I*, **WIA** 25Jul.18-*I*
Ramage,2Lt.LW, 13Aug.17-*I*
Rampling,Capt.H, **INT** 4Aug.18-*I*
Ramsay,FSLt.DW, **KIA** 7Jul.17-*I*
Ramsay,Lt.GS, 8Aug.18-*I*
Ramsay,Lt.JWMcN, *US*. **KIA** 2Oct.18-*I*
Ramsay,Lt.MO, **inj** 1Aug.18-*IV*
Ramsden,2Lt.S, **WIA** 11Apr.18-*I*
Ramsden,Cpl.T, 17Mar.18-*I*, 27Mar.18-*I*
Ramsey,Lt.GS, **KIA** 8Aug.18-*I*
Ramsey,2Lt.HG, **WIA** 14Sep.18-*I*
Ramsey,Lt.KMA, 7Jun.18-*I*
Rancourt,1Lt.JI, DFC *US*. **WIA** 9Aug.18-*IIB*
Randall,2Lt.,Capt.AC, **WIA** 11Mar.17-*I*, 22Aug.18-*I*
Randall,Lt.BFtH, 22Sep.16-*I*
Randall,Lt.GE, 10Nov.18-*I*
Randall,2Lt.GV, **KIA** 20Jul.16-*I*
Randall,2Lt.SW, **KIA** 31Oct.17-*I*
Randell,Capt.AC, 7Jul.18-*I*
Randell,Sgt.CL, **KIA** 23Aug.17-*I*
Randell,2Lt.WB, *Aust*. **POW** 24Feb.18-*I*
Raney,Lt.PH, **KIA** 21Aug.17-*I*
Rankin,Lt.FS, 1Sep.16-*I*, 30Sep.16-*I*, **KIA** 22Oct.16-*I*
Rankin,Lt.WA, 21Aug.18-*I*, **POW** 28Aug.18-*I*
Ranney,Lt.KA, **KIA** 31Jul.18-*I*
Ransford,FSLt.RB, **KIA** 18Mar.18-*I*
Ransley,2Lt.FC, 24Apr.18-*I*
Ransom,2Lt.HW, **KIA** 27Mar.18-*I*
Raper,2Lt.SE, **KIA** 17Aug.17-*I*
Ratcliffe,Lt.T, **POW** 9May.18-*I*
Rath,Lt.HC, *Can*. 28Jul.18-*I*, **KIA** 26Oct.18-*I*
Rathborne,FLt.C, **POW** 14Apr.17-*I*
Rathbone,LtCol.CEH, **POW** Apr.17-*I*
Rathbone,Lt.GH, **KIA** 29Apr.17-*I*
Ratliff,2Lt.PG, **POW** 24Apr.18-*IV*
Ratterman,Lt.GI, *US*. **POW** 10Jul.18-*IIB*
Rattray,Lt.AR, **WIA** 24Feb.17-*VIII*, 3Apr.17-*VIII*
Rawley,2Lt.RW, **KIA** 13Aug.18-*I*
Rawlings,2Lt.B, **KIA** 18Jul.18-*I*
Rawlins,Lt.ACC, 13May.17-*I*
Rawlinson,2Lt.R, 13Aug.18-*I*
Rawson-Shaw,Lt.K, **POW** 27Oct.14-*I*
Rawsthorne,2Lt.T, 14Apr.18-*I*
Ray,Lt LH, *Can*. 27Sep.18-*I*
Ray,Lt.PO, **KIA** 13Apr.17-*I*
Raymond,FSgt., *16Sqn.* 31Oct.15-*I*
Raymond,Lt.AB, **POW** 13May.17-*I*
Raymond,2Lt.LB, **POW** 1Sep.18-*I*
Raymond,1Lt.RF, *US*. DSC **POW** 16Jul.18-*IIB*
Raymond-Barker,2Lt., *6Sqn.* 17Jan.16-*I*
Raymond-Barker,2Lt.AB, **WIA POW** 21Oct.16-*I*
Raymond-Barker,Capt.,Maj.R, MC 20May.17-*I*, **KIA** 20Apr.18-*I*
Rayner,2Lt.CO, **KIA** 1Oct.17-*I*
Rayner,2Lt.NR, **KIA** 27Jul.17-*I*
Rayner,Capt.JW, 5Sep.18-*I*
Read,Capt., *5Sqn.* 22Aug.15-*I*, 10Oct.15-*I*, 14Dec.15-*I*
Read,Capt.AM, *Sqn?* **KIA** 25Sep.15-*I*
Read,2Lt.CS, **KIA** 6Dec.17-*I*
Read,Lt.EH, **KIA** 26Dec.17-*I*
Read,Sgt.FE, **POW DoW** 31.5.17? 30May.16-*VIII*
Read,Lt.FK, *USAS*. **WIA** 2Jul.18-*I*
Read,Capt.HE, **KIA** 10Aug.17-*I*
Read?,Sgt.JH, **WIA POW** *name* Reed? 17Jun.18-*I*
Read,2Lt.L, **POW** 12Aug.17-*I*
Read,Lt.NH, 17Mar.17-*I*
Read,Sgt.R, 3Oct.18-*I*
Read,2Lt.SC, **KIA** 25Sep.18-*I*
Read,Lt.WR, **WIA?** 3Nov.14-*I*
Reade,2Lt.AB, **KIFA** 21Feb.18-*IV*
Reader,2Lt.,Lt.L, 20Sep.18-*I*, **inj** 31Oct.18-*I*, **WIA** 2Nov.18-*I*
Reading,2Lt.VJ, 21Mar.18-*I*, **KIA** 26Mar.18-*I*
Reast,Sgt.WE, **DoW** 9.9.1918 7Sep.18-*I*
Reay,2Lt.S, **KIA** 28Jan.18-*I*
Reddie,Lt.FG, **KIA** 19May.18-*I*
Redfield,2Lt.JJ, *USAS*. **WIA POW** 22Aug.18-*I*
Redgate,FSLt.,Capt.OW, 21Sep.17-*I*, **WIA** 15May.18-*I*
Redler,2Lt.HB,SA. 15Mar.18-*I*, 26Mar.18-*I*, **WIA** 21Apr.18-*I*
Redpath,Lt.HS, 25Mar.18-*I*, 27Mar.18-*I*, **POW** 28Mar.18-*I*
Reece,2Lt.CM, **POW** 28Apr.17-*I*
Reece,2Lt.,Lt.SB, 16May.18-*I*, **POW** 21May.18-*I*
Reed,Sgt., *98Sqn.* 12Jun.18-*I*
Reed,Sig., *264Sqn.* 28Aug.18-*III*
Reed,Lt.AE, SA. 6Jun.18-*I*, 21Aug.18-*I*
Reed,2Lt.DL, **WIA** 11Sep.16-*I*
Reed?,Sgt.JH, *see* Read 29Jun.18-*I*
Reed,1Lt.MJ, *US*. 12Sep.18-*IIB*
Reed,Lt.,Capt.WE, **WIA** 23Apr.17-*I*, 29Oct.18-*I*, **WIA** 3Nov.18-*I*
Rees,Capt., *5Sqn.* 2Jun.15-*I*
Rees,2Lt.AW, *Aust*. **WIA** 11Apr.18-*I*
Rees,2Lt.DC, **KIA** 29Sep.18-*I*
Rees,2Lt.FE, **KIA** 23Aug.18-*I*
Rees,Capt.,Maj.LWB, 28Jul.15-*I*, 1Aug.15-*I*, 31Aug.15-*I*, 19Sep.15-*I*, 21Sep.15-*I*, 22Sep.15-*I*, 30Sep.15-*I*, 22Oct.15-*I*, 23Oct.15-*I*, 31Oct.15-*I*, **WIA** 1Jul.16-*I*
Rees,Lt.T, **KIA** 17Sep.16-*I*
Rees-Jones,Capt.H, 3May.18-*I*
Reese,Capt., *4Sqn.* 29Jul.15-*I*
Reeve,Lt.A, 5Dec.17-*I*, **KIA** 27Mar.18-*I*
Reeve,2Lt.FHE, **WIA** 4Mar.17-*I*
Reeves,FLt.FP, **KIA** 6Jun.17-*I*
Reeves,Capt.HG, **KIFA** 24Jan.18-*I*
Reeves,2Lt.JH, **WIA?** 21Mar.18-*I*, **WIA** 22Mar.18-*I*
Reeves,2Lt.WA, **WIA POW** 1Feb.17-*I*
Reid,Cpl.A, **POW**, **Died** 5.5.16 28Apr.16-*VIII*
Reid,2Lt.AW, **KIA** 4Mar.17-*I*
Reid,Lt.CW, **POW** 21Jan.18-*I*
Reid,2Lt.DS, **KIA** 27Aug.18-*I*
Reid,FSLt.EV, DSC *Can*. DSC 27Jul.17-*I*, **KIA** 28Jul.17-*I*
Reid,2Lt.FH, **POW** 23Oct.18-*I*
Reid,FLt.GH, **POW** 25Mar.16-*I*
Reid,2Lt.GPS, 7Feb.16-*I*
Reid,Lt.J, *65Sqn*. *US*. **KIA** 4Nov.18-*I*
Reid,Lt.J, *213Sqn.* **KIA** 11May.18-*I*
Reid,Lt.JE, **POW** 14Sep.18-*I*
Reid,Lt.JF, **INT** 17Jun.18-*I*
Reid,2Lt.JL, **DoW** 15Jul.16-*I*
Reid,2Lt.RW, 29Apr.17-*I*
Reid,2Lt.W, **WIA POW** 1Aug.15-*I*
Reid-Walker,2Lt.A, 18Nov.17-*I*
Reilly,Lt.FFH, **KIA** 28May.18-*I*
Reilly,Lt.FH, 17May.18-*I*
Reilly,Capt.,Maj.HL, *NZ*. May.15-*VIII*, 30Jul.15-*VIII*, **POW** 21Nov.15-*VIII*
Reilly,1Lt.LGE, *US*. **KIA** 31Oct.18-*IIB*
Reilly-Patey,Lt.O, DFC 24Sep.18-*I*
Reincke,Capt.LF, **KIA** 17Aug.17-*I*

Rekofski,2Lt.ST, WIA 24Jul.18-*I*
Remington,Sgt.A, 27Mar.18-*I*
Rendell,Lt.LP, WIA 10Apr.18-*I*
Rendle,AGL.AM, KIA 27Mar.18-*I*
Rennie,2Lt., *4Sqn.* inj 3Sep.16-*I*
Renton,2Lt.EG, KIA 14Aug.18-*I*
Rentoul,Lt.A, KIA 27Mar.18-*I*
Repton,Lt.CT, KIA 25Apr.18-*VII*
Reveley,2Lt.PTA, WIA POW 9Aug.18-*I*
Revill,Capt.JA, WIA 9Aug.17-*I*
Rex,1Lt.HB, *US.* KIA 13Sep.18-*IIB*
Reynell,2Lt.AW, POW 26Aug.16-*I*
Reynish,2Lt.HJC, KIA 23Mar.18-*I*
Reynolds,Lt.CE, inj 18May.18-*I*
Reynolds,1Lt.CH, *US.* 30Sep.18-*IIB*
Reynolds,2Lt.EG, KIA 8Jul.18-*I*
Reynolds,2Lt.JE, KIA 18May.18-*I*
Reynolds,2Lt.L, 25Sep.16-*I*
Reynolds,Maj.LGS, POW 21Oct.18-*I*
Rhinelander,1Lt.PN, *US.* KIA 26Sep.18-*IIB*
Rhodes Moorhouse,2Lt.WB, DoW 27.4.15 26Apr.15-*I*
Rhodes,1Lt.C, *US.* POW 5Jul.18-*IIB*
Rhodes,Lt.CW, *Aust.* POW 4Nov.18-*I*
Rhodes,Lt.H, WIA 27Sep.18-*I*
Rhys Davids,Lt.APF, MC DSO 27May.17-*I*, 12Jul.17-*I*, 23Sep.17-*I*, 11Oct.17-*I*, KIA 27Oct.17-*I*
Riach,2AM.CC, WIA 24Mar.17-*I*
Rice,2Lt., *2Sqn.* 25Jan.16-*I*
Rice,2Lt.AH, KIA 29Nov.17-*I*
Rice,2Lt,Capt..BC, 10Oct.15-*I*, 11Nov.15-*I*, 29Dec.15-*I*, 12Jan.16-*I*, 24Jan.16-*I*, 24Apr.17-*I*
Rice,2Lt.EA, 8Jun.16-*I*
Rice,Lt.LR, 25Mar.18-*I*
Rice,Lt.RL, 15Apr.18-*I*
Rice-Oxley,2Lt.,Lt.A, WIA 7Oct.16-*I*, 12Jul.18-*IV*
Richard,Lt., *1Sqn.* 3May.15-*I*
Richards,2Lt.ARM, WIA POW 6Apr.17-*I*
Richards,Lt.CR, MC *Aust.* 6Jul.17-*I*, 17Jul.17-*I*, WIA POW 19Aug.17-*I*
Richards,1Lt.EF, *US.* WIA 29Sep.18-*IIB*
Richards,1Lt.HL, *US.* POW 19Jul.18-*IIB*
Richards,2Lt.HLE, WIA 2May.17-*I*
Richards,2Lt.HS, DoW 3Apr.17-*I*
Richards,1Lt.JF, *US.* KIA 26Sep.18-*IIB*
Richards,Lt.JW, 7Sep.18-*I*, 18Oct.18-*I*
Richards,2Lt.RC, WIA 26Mar.18-*I*
Richards,Lt.W, *100Sqn.* 23May.18-*I*
Richards,Cpl.W, *111Sqn.* WIA 29Nov.17-*VII*
Richardson,Lt.DD, 29Nov.17-*I*, POW 28Mar.18-*I*
Richardson,2Lt.EA, 6Mar.18-*I*, WIA 22Mar.18-*I*
Richardson,2Lt.EE, KIA 9Nov.18-*I*
Richardson,Lt.EG, inj 28Jul.17-*I*
Richardson,2Lt.EJ, 22Aug.18-*I*, KIA 27Oct.18-*I*
Richardson,2Lt.EW, inj 29Jul.18-*I*
Richardson,2Lt.G, WIA 23Mar.18-*I*
Richardson,1Lt.GR, *US.* POW 26Sep.18-*IIB*
Richardson,2Lt.GT, 19Sep.16-*I*
Richardson,2Lt.,Lt.HB, 21Mar.18-*I*, 26Mar.18-*I*
Richardson,2Lt.HJ, *US.* WIA 25Mar.18-*I*
Richardson,GL.GA, INT 12May.17-*I*
Richardson,2Lt.JB, POW 15Sep.18-*I*
Richardson,2Lt.JL, KIA 21Aug.17-*I*
Richardson,2Lt.JM, *US.* WIA 6Oct.18-*IIB*
Richardson,2Lt.LA, *US.* WIA 19Jul.18-*I*
Richardson,2Lt.,Capt.LL, *Aust.* WIA 20Jul.16-*I*, KIA 13Apr.17-*I*
Richardson,Lt.MW, 28Jun.18-*I*, 28Oct.18-*I*
Richardson,Sgt.R, KIA? 27Sep.18-*I*
Richardson,Lt.RH, *6Sqn.* KIA 6Nov.17-*I*
Richardson,2Lt.RH, *102Sqn.* POW 6Oct.17-*I*
Richardson,2Lt.SH, KIA 23Sep.18-*I*
Richardson,FSLt.SS, KIA 19Dec.17-*I*
Richman,2AM.W, WIA 17Mar.17-*I*, WIA POW 11Aug.17-*I*
Richmond,Lt.G, 25Jun.18-*I*, 27Sep.18-*I*
Richmond,1AM.GS, KIA 10May.18-*I*
Rickards,2Lt., *3Sqn.* 19Jul.16-*I*
Rickards,Capt.AT, KIA 13Sep.17-*I*
Rickards,2Lt.,Lt.HB, *initials* HG? 9Sep.16-*I*, 23Sep.16-*I*, WIA 16Nov.16-*I*
Rickards,2Lt.HWB, KIA 28Jul.17-*I*
Rickenbacker,1Lt.EV, *US.* CMH 29Apr.18-*IIB*
Rickett,2Lt.WHA, POW 16Jun.18-*I*
Riddell,Lt.LH, POW 8Aug.18-*I*
Rider,2Lt.G, 17Jun.18-*I*
Ridewood,Capt.OE, WIA 16Mar.18-*I*
Ridgeway,Gnr.F, KIA 7Feb.17-*I*
Ridgway,Sgt.JF, WIA 24Mar.17-*I*
Ridley,2Lt.,Lt.CA, 27Aug.15-*I*, 28Aug.15-*I*, WIA 5Sep.15-*I*, POW 3Aug.16-*I*
Ridley,FLt.,Capt.CB, DSC *201Sqn. Can.* 8Apr.18-*I*, 29Apr.17-*I*, 4Jul.18-*I*
Ridley,Lt.CB, *43Sqn.* POW 10Jul.18-*I*
Ridley,2Lt.H, WIA 22Jul.18-*I*
Ridley,2Lt.SG, Died 15Jun.16-*VII*
Ridley,Lt.W, 6May.18-*VI*, 3Sep.18-*VI*
Riekie,2Lt.,Lt.HH, 16Apr.17-*I*, KIA 4Jul.18-*I*
Riffkin,2Lt.R, POW 21Oct.18-*I*
Rigby,2Lt.C, KIA 4Nov.18-*I*
Rigby,Capt.HA, *Aust.* 11May.18-*I*
Rigby,2Lt.TF, KIA 27Mar.18-*I*
Riggall,FLt.EG, KIA 16Feb.15-*I*
Rilett,2Lt.WH, 5Aug.16-*I*
Riley,2Lt.A, 3Jul.17-*I*
Riley,2Lt.CG, WIA 31Jul.16-*I*
Riley,2Lt.EJ?, POW 20Jul.18-*I*
Riley,2Lt.G, 26Oct.18-*I*
Riley,Lt.GAF, WIA 5Sep.18-*I*
Riley,2Lt.,Lt.GR, 6Apr.18-*I*, WIA 20Apr.18-*I*, 27Sep.18-*I*
Riley,1Lt.HW, *US.* WIA POW 8Oct.18-*IIB*
Riley,Lt.RCB, WIA 26Jun.16-*I*
Rimer,2Lt.JC, KIA 17Mar.17-*I*
Ringer,2Lt.ECS, POW 25Oct.17-*I*
Ringrose,Lt.R, KIA 28Aug.18-*I*
Rintoul,2Lt.A, *Aust.* POW 1Jun.18-*I*
Ripley,2Lt.ER, KIA 31Oct.17-*I*
Ripley,Lt.RCP, KIA? 5Nov.18-*I*
Risk,2Lt.JB, POW 11Aug.18-*I*
Risteen,2Lt.CF, KIA 26Sep.17-*I*
Ritch,Lt., *18Sqn.* 28Jan.18-*I*
Ritchie,2Lt.G, WIA 27Aug.18-*I*
Ritchie,Lt.LMcC, WIA 27Feb.18-*I*
Ritchie,2Lt.TM, POW 31Jul.18-*I*
Ritson,OSL.L, 14Oct.17-*III*
Ritter,1Lt.RH, *USAS.* 16May.18-*I*, KIA 24Aug.18-*I*
Rivers,2Lt.LA, 2Dec.17-*I*
Rivett-Carnac,2Lt.WJ, WIA 13Jun.18-*I*
Roach,FSLt.ED, KIA 1May.17-*I*
Roach,FSLt.G, KIA 27Jul.17-*I*
Roadley,Lt.TS, KIA 17Aug.17-*I*
Roaks,2Lt.FW, WIA 16May.18-*I*
Robarts,Capt.GW, MC WIA 8Jul.17-*I*
Robb,Capt.JM, WIA 11Mar.17-*I*, WIA 16Aug.18-*I*
Robb,2AM.R, POW 8Apr.17-*I*
Robb,2Lt.RE, KIA 4Jan.18-*I*
Robbins,2Lt.CR, 19Jan.16-*I*, 25Apr.16-*I*
Robbins,Lt.JE, 31Aug.18-*I*
Roberton,2Lt.JL, KIA 6Sep.16-*I*
Roberts,Cpl., *3Sqn.* 26Aug.15-*I*, 27Aug.15-*I*, WIA 10Oct.15-*I*
Roberts,Capt., *18Sqn.* 28Jan.18-*I*
Roberts,2Lt.AC, WIA 16Aug.18-*I*
Roberts,Lt.AM, *USAS.* POW 19Jul.18-*I*
Roberts,Lt.C, WIA 6Sep.18-*I*
Roberts,Lt.CH, 1Jul.18-*I*, 25Jul.18-*I*, KIA 19Aug.18-*I*
Roberts,2Lt.CL, POW 17Oct.16-*I*
Roberts,2Lt.E, *10Sqn.* KIA 10Feb.17-*I*
Roberts,2Lt.E, *48Sqn.* POW 25Jun.18-*I*
Roberts,Lt.EG, *Aust.* 24Jan.17-*VII*
Roberts,2Lt.EJ, KIA 23Sep.16-*I*
Roberts,2Lt.EL, WIA inj 15Sep.18-*IV*
Roberts,Lt.EP, WIA 22Nov.16-*I*
Roberts,Sgt.F?, *initials* TL? 16Jul.18-*I*
Roberts,Sgt.FL, 4Jul.18-*I*
Roberts,2Lt.G, WIA 3Oct.18-*I*
Roberts,2Lt.GB, KIA 26Sep.17-*I*
Roberts,Lt.HJW, POW 24Aug.18-*I*
Roberts,Lt.HP, WIA 17May.18-*I*
Roberts,2Lt.IA, *US.* KIA 26Sep.18-*IIB*
Roberts,Lt.JH, KIA 24Sep.18-*I*
Roberts,Lt.KA, *Aust.* 30Aug.18-*I*
Roberts,1Lt.LC, *USAS* KIA 26Aug.18-*I*
Roberts,2Lt.N, 17Mar.18-*I*, 25Jun.18-*I*
Roberts,2Lt.P, 17Feb.18-*I*
Roberts,Lt.RM, POW 28May.17-*I*
Roberts,2Lt.STC, KIA 30Jul.18-*I*
Roberts,2Lt.STH, 10Aug.18-*I*
Roberts,Lt.T, 3May.18-*I*
Roberts,Lt.VC, WIA 31Jul.17-*I*
Roberts-Taylor,Lt., *98Sqn.* 20Jul.18-*I*
Robertson,2Lt.A, DoW 17.8.1917 16Aug.17-*I*
Robertson,2Lt.AG, KIA 8Jun.17-*I*
Robertson,Lt.AR, *66Sqn.* WIA 31Oct.17-*I*
Robertson,Lt.AG, *205Sqn.* KIA 16Sep.18-*I*
Robertson,2Lt.AW, WIA 25Jun.18-*I*
Robertson,Capt.CE, KIA 12Jul.17-*I*
Robertson,2Lt.DB, *25Sqn.* KIA 27Sep.18-*I*
Robertson,2Lt.DB, *27Sqn.* WIA 6Jun.18-*I*
Robertson,2Lt.DH, 1Feb.17-*I*
Robertson,2Lt.DN, POW DoW 16Apr.17-*I*
Robertson,Lt.Col.EDM, 6Jun.18-*III*
Robertson,Lt.EG, KIA 27Sep.18-*I*
Robertson,Lt.G, 9Jun.18-*IV*
Robertson,2Lt.GM, WIA POW 26May.17-*I*
Robertson,2Lt.GP, POW 10Sep.17-*I*
Robertson,2Lt.,Capt.HS, 23Apr.17-*I*, WIA 20Nov.17-*I*
Robertson,2Lt.JAM, POW 8Dec.17-*IV*
Robertson,2Lt.JG, WIA POW 25Jul.16-*I*
Robertson,2Lt.JH, DoW 11Mar.18-*I*
Robertson,Lt.JR, *66Sqn.* KIA 12May.17-*I*
Robertson,Lt.JR?, *initials* AE? *204Sqn.* WIA 17Oct.18-*I*
Robertson,Lt.NL, WIA 24Apr.17-*I*
Robertson,Lt.RG, 29Sep.18-*I*
Robertson,2AM.TC, KIA? 21Oct.17-*I*
Robertson,Lt.WA, *Aust.* 20Nov.17-*I*, 1Dec.17-*I*
Robertson,2Lt.WD, WIA 30Nov.17-*VI*
Robertson,Lt.WS, KIA 13Jul.18-*I*
Robeson,2Lt.VAH, 10Feb.16-*I*
Robey,2Lt.HTG, 16Jul.18-*I*
Robin,2Lt.GD, WIA 26Mar.18-*I*
Robins,2Lt.ER, *initials* EK? WIA 3Jun.17-*I* WIA? 9Jun.17-*I*
Robins,Lt.SM, POW 19Jun.18-*IV*
Robinson,Lt., *2Sqn.* 15Oct.18-*I*
Robinson,2Lt., *4Sqn.* 26Nov.15-*I*
Robinson,Lt., *8Sqn.* 13Mar.16-*I*
Robinson,Lt., *79Sqn.* 8Jul.18-*I*
Robinson,Lt.AD, KIA 8Aug.18-*I*
Robinson,2Lt.AJ, KIA 25Sep.18-*I*
Robinson,2Lt.AK, WIA 1Nov.18-*I*
Robinson,Lt.BW, WIA POW 20Apr.18-*I*
Robinson,2Lt.CB, *US.* POW 8Nov.18-*IIB*
Robinson,2Lt.CE, WIA? 29Sep.18-*I*
Robinson,FCdr.CE, KIA 8Dec.15-*V*
Robinson,AGL.CV, 3May.18-*I*
Robinson,2Lt.DO, WIA 28Mar.18-*I*
Robinson,2Lt.,Lt.E, *11Sqn.* 7Sep.15-*I*, 12Sep.15-*I*, 19Sep.15-*I*, 2Oct.15-*I*, 19Dec.15-*I*
Robinson,Lt.E, *Sqn?* POW .18-*VIII*
Robinson,2Lt.EC, WIA 29Sep.18-*I*
Robinson,2Lt.EDS, KIA 4Sep.17-*I*
Robinson,2Lt.FB, POW 1Sep.18-*I*
Robinson,Lt.FE, 8Oct.18-*I*, 25Oct.18-*I*
Robinson,2Lt.HG, POW 8Nov.17-*I*
Robinson,2Lt.HNC, 23Nov.17-*I*, 15May.18-*I*
Robinson,Capt.J, DFC 27Jun.18-*I*
Robinson,2Lt.JB, POW 2Nov.15-*I*
Robinson,Lt.JC, POW 27Jun.18-*I*
Robinson,Lt.JR, WIA 15Aug.18-*I*, 4Oct.18-*I*
Robinson,2AM.N?, WIA POW 18Jun.16-*I*
Robinson,2Lt.P, WIA? 27Apr.17-*I*
Robinson,Capt.PD, MC KIA 31Mar.18-*I*
Robinson,Cpl.R, *US?* CMH WIA 14Oct.18-*IIB*
Robinson,Cpl.RG, 4Oct.18-*I*
Robinson,2Lt.TN, 31Jul.17-*I*, WIA 16Aug.17-*I*
Robinson,FLt.WE, POW 8Aug.17-*IX*
Robinson,Lt.WF, *204Sqn.* 16May.18-*I*
Robinson,Lt.WFR, *8Sqn.* KIA 24Sep.18-*I*
Robinson,2Lt.WL, WIA 8May.15-*I*
Robison,2Lt.ND, 19May.17-*I*
Robson,Lt.CC, MC POW 15May.18-*I*
Robson,Lt.JS, WIA 9Nov.18-*I*
Robson,Lt.MG, MC WIA 2Oct.18-*I*
Robson,1AM.RW, WIA 23Apr.17-*I*
Roche,2Lt.CPV, WIA 30Sep.16-*I*
Roche,Lt.,Capt.HJA, 7Sep.14-*I*, KIA 19Jan.15-*I*
Roche,2Lt.S, POW 11Apr.17-*I*
Rochelle,2Lt.W, 6Mar.18-*I*
Rochester,2Lt.GE, POW 22Aug.18-*I*
Rochford,FLt.,FCdr.,Capt.LH, DSC DFC 5Sep.17-*I*, 30Jan.18-*I*, 20Jul.18-*I*
Rochford,Lt.SW, POW 4Sep.18-*I*
Rock,Lt.JMJCJI, WIA 10Feb.17-*I*
Rockey,FSLt.J, POW 12Oct.16-*I*
Rockwell,Cpl.,SLt.KY, *US.* 13May.16-*IIA*, 18May.16-*IIA*, WIA 24May.16-*IIA*, KIA 23Sep.16-*IIA*
Roden,Lt.GS, 8Aug.18-*I*
Rodger,Lt.KM, WIA POW 29Jan.18-*I*
Rodger,2Lt.WA, *Can.* KIA 10Nov.18-*I*
Rodmell,Lt.GE, inj 6Jan.18-*I*
Rodney,2Lt.Hon.FW, KIA 9May.15-*I*
Rodocanachi,2Lt.PJ, KIA 27Jul.17-*I*
Rodowney,Lt.Hon.JHB, WIA 13Aug.16-*VIII*
Roe,Ens.JT, *USN.* POW 30May.18-*III*
Roebuck,Sgt.WH, KIA 11Sep.17-*I*
Rofe,2Lt.HH, POW 23Oct.18-*I*
Rogers,1AM., *5Sqn.* 8May.15-*I*, 10May.15-*I*
Rogers,Lt.B, *US.* 6Sep.18-*I*
Rogers,Lt.CE, KIA 18Jun.16-*I*
Rogers,2Lt.CVdeB, 5Apr.17-*I*, KIA 21Apr.17-*I*
Rogers,Lt.FI, POW 8Aug.18-*I*
Rogers,2Lt.G, WIA 2Jun.17-*I*
Rogers,Capt.GC, *16Sqn.* KIA 21Apr.17-*I*
Rogers,Capt.GC, *52Sqn.* WIA 27Oct.17-*I*
Rogers,1Lt.NC, *US.* KIA 16Sep.18-*IIB*
Rogers,Lt.RC, MC *2Sqn.* WIA 26May.17-*I*
Rogers,Lt.RC, *27Sqn.* WIA 25Jul.18-*I*
Rogers,Lt.T, KIA 19Jun.17-*I*
Rogers,2Lt.TH, KIA 27Oct.18-*I*
Rogers,1Lt.WJ, *US.* 7Oct.18-*IIB*
Rogers,2Lt.WW, *Can.* 12Jul.17-*I*
Rogerson,Lt.H, POW 14Jun.17-*I*
Rolandi,2Lt.VFA, WIA 17Apr.18-*I*
Rolfe,Lt.BR, 11Aug.18-*I*, POW 28Sep.18-*I*
Rolfe,2AM.HHR, DoI 25Sep.16-*I*
Rollason,Lt.WA, 8Aug.18-*I*
Rollo,2Lt.DJ, WIA 23Nov.17-*I*
Rolph,2Lt.EG, POW 20Sep.18-*I*
Ronald,2Lt.BR, 3Oct.18-*I*
Rook,2Lt.FW, KIA 21Jul.17-*I*
Rooper,Capt.WVT, DoW 25.10.1917 9Oct.17-*I*
Roosevelt,1Lt.Q, *US.* KIA 14Jul.18-*IIB*
Root,1Lt.RR, *US.* WIA POW 18Sep.18-*IIB*
Roper,1Lt.GA, *USAS.* KIA? 18May.18-*I*
Roper,2Lt.?K, *US.* KIA 14Sep.18-*IIB*
Rose,Sgt.AT, 17Jun.17-*I*
Rose,2Lt.D, POW 2Sep.18-*I*
Rose,Lt.G, POW 18Jul.18-*I*
Rose,2Lt.GA, POW 18Aug.17-*I*
Rose,Lt.,Capt.OJ, *US.* 14Aug.18-*I*, 28Sep.18-*I*, 10Nov.18-*I*
Rose,2Lt.RH, POW 15Sep.18-*I*
Rose,Lt.T, 9May.18-*I*
Rose,2Lt.WK, WIA 28Sep.18-*I*
Rosenbleet,Lt.AM, *US.* POW 10Nov.18-*I*
Rosenthal,2Lt.A, KIA 23Nov.17-*I*
Rosevear,FSLt.SW, *Can.* 5Dec.17-*I*
Roskelly,Lt.WM, KIA 29Jul.17-*I*
Ross,2Lt.AC, DoW 6Dec.17-*I*
Ross,2Lt.AJF, KIA 27Oct.18-*I*
Ross,2Lt.C, 6Mar.18-*I*
Ross,Lt.CG, DFC *SA.* 20Sep.18-*I*, 28Sep.18-*I*
Ross,Lt.CM, KIA 19Aug.17-*I*
Ross,2Lt.DN, DCM MM KIA 17Feb.18-*I*
Ross,2Lt.DW, *Can.* KIA 11Jan.18-*IV*
Ross,2Lt.GAB, KIA 1Jun.18-*I*
Ross,2Lt.J, KIA 8Aug.18-*I*
Ross,2Lt.JH, WIA 7Jul.16-*I*
Ross,2Lt.JK, DoW 9.4.1917 5Apr.17-*I*
Ross,Lt.JSL, *Aust.* WIA 6Sep.18-*I*
Ross,2Lt.MStJ, 24Jul.18-*I*, 25Jul.18-*I*, 15Oct.18-*I*

Ross,2Lt.PC, DoW 26Jun.17-I
Ross,Lt.W, POW 19Feb.18-I
Ross-Jenkins,2Lt.M, KIA 16Jun.18-I
Rossi,2Lt.JA, WIA 23Apr.17-I
Roth,1Lt.IJ, US. KIA 26Sep.18-IIB
Rothery,2Lt.H, POW DoW? 23Sep.17-I
Rothwell,1AM.F, KIA 2Dec.17-I
Rothwell,2Lt.J, 13Apr.17-I, inj 22Apr.17-I
Rough,2Lt.JS, 8Oct.18-I
Rough,Capt., 11Sqn. 3Jul.16-I
Rough,ACapt.HL, WIA 9Jun.18-I
Roulstone,Capt.A, MC WIA 17Mar.18-I
Round,Lt.HS, 17Jun.18-I
Round,2Lt.JY, WIA 22Jul.18-I
Rouquette,2Lt.DG, KIA 26Sep.17-I
Routh,Capt.EJD, WIA 21Apr.17-I
Routhier,Lt.GS, 16Sep.18-I
Roux,Lt.F, DoW as POW? 26Apr.17-I
Rowan,Lt.OA, 27Sep.17-I
Rowden,Lt.CR, WIA 3May.16-VII
Rowden,Lt.RCG, KIA 30Nov.17-I
Rowdon,Lt.AW, KIA 10May.18-I
Rowe,2Lt.BF, KIA 1Jun.17-I
Rowe,Sgt.LH, WIA 29Jul.18-I
Rowe,Lt.RR, KIA 3May.18-I
Rowe,Lt.WC, inj 9May.17-I
Rowell,Capt., 12Sqn. 16May.16-I
Rowles,Lt.SW, DoW 13.12.1917 3Dec.17-I
Rowley,FSLt.,FLt.HV, 29Apr.17-I, 12Mar.18-I
Rowley,2Lt.SE, WIA 10Sep.18-I
Rowney,Lt.LC, 6Sep.18-I
Rowsell,2Lt.LF, name Rowswell? 10Aug.18-I, WIA 16Aug.18-I
Roxburgh-Smith,Capt.B, 17Aug.18-I
Roy,2Lt.DC, KIA 25Aug.18-I
Roy,Lt.IL, KIA 22Jul.18-I
Royce,2Lt.WW, US. POW 3Nov.18-IIB
Royffe,2Lt.HS, 16Sep.16-I
Rudge,Lt.AE, KIA 22Jul.18-I
Rudman,2Lt.W, MC POW 21Apr.18-I
Rumsby,Lt.RW, DoI 9May.18-I
Rundle-Woolcock,2Lt.DTC, 25Jan.18-I
Runnels-Moss,2Lt.CVG, KIA 5Dec.17-I
Rusby,Capt.RH, WIA 24Jan.17-I, WIA 6Jan.18-I, 23Mar.18-I, 15May.18-I
Rusden,Lt.CO, 26Mar.18-I, POW 10Apr.18-I
Rush,2Lt.AW, POW 28Oct.17-I
Rushbrooke,2Lt.LA, WIA 7Jul.17-I
Rushby,Capt.RH, 22Oct.16-I
Rushforth,Capt.HP, 20May.18-I, WIA 7Sep.18-I
Rushton,Capt.CG, KIA 16May.18-I
Rushton,2Lt.FW, WIA 19May.18-I
Rushton,Lt.HT, WIA 3May.18-I
Rushton,2Lt.W, KIA 4Nov.18-I
Rushworth,Capt.HN, WIA POW 18Aug.17-I
Russell,2AM., 3Nov.16-I
Russell,2Lt.,Lt.AL, 8Mar.15-I, 26Oct.15-I, 27Oct.15-I, 11Nov.15-I, 5Jan.16-I
Russell,2Lt.B, WIA 29Sep.18-I
Russell,2Lt.CG, 20Sqn. POW 15Sep.18-I
Russell,2Lt.CG, 99Sqn. KIA 30Aug.18-I
Russell,Capt.CN, WIA 27May.18-I
Russell,2Lt.DJ, POW 17May.18-I
Russell,1AM.F, 18Sqn. KIA 24Mar.17-I
Russell,1AM.F, 45Sqn. KIA 16Apr.17-I
Russell,AG.LCpl.F, DoW 2Jul.17-I
Russell,Sgt.F, POW 7May.17-I
Russell,Lt.FC, POW 8Aug.18-I
Russell,2Lt.FG, KIA 28Jan.17-I
Russell,Lt.FS, WIA 27Jun.18-I
Russell,2Lt.G, inj 2Feb.18-I, KIA 18Mar.18-I
Russell,Lt.HB, 22Sep.15-I, 11Oct.15-I, WIA POW 26Jun.16-I
Russell,Lt.HW, DFC POW 8Nov.18-I
Russell,FW.ACH, INT 4Jun.18-III
Russell,Lt.JB, DFC inj 1Oct.18-I
Russell,2Lt.JD, WIA 8Sep.18-I
Russell,2Lt.LD, NZ.? DoW 2.9.1916 26Aug.16-I
Russell,2Lt.PA, KIA 2Apr.17-I
Russell,2Lt.,Capt.R, 23Aug.18-I, 23Oct.18-I
Russell,2Lt.RF, KIA 28Oct.18-I
Russell,Lt.W, WIA 8Jun.16-I
Russell,1Lt.WM, US. KIA 11Aug.18-IIB
Russell,Lt.WO, POW 14Apr.17-I
Rust,2Lt.CE, US. DoW 11.10.1918 10Oct.18-IIB
Rutherford,Capt.DW, Aust. 20Mar.17-VII, WIA 28Mar.17-VII, POW 1May.18-VII
Rutherford,Lt.WJ, Can. 22Sep.17-I
Rutter,2Lt.,Capt.DC, MC 25Sep.15-I, KIA 7Jun.17-I
Ryall,2Lt.AG, POW 6Mar.17-I
Ryan,2Lt.,Lt.AE, 9Jun.18-IV, WIA 29Jul.18-IV
Ryan,Lt.BW, KIA 20Sep.17-I
Ryan,Lt.,Capt.CE, 19Sep.15-I?, WIA 4Nov.15-I
Ryan,Sgt.J, 18Mar.18-I, KIA 24Mar.18-I
Ryan,Lt.JH, DoW 2.5.1917 30Apr.17-I
Ryan,Sgt.JJ, WIA 17Apr.18-I
Ryan,2Lt.MG, 31Oct.18-I
Ryckman,2Lt.EG, KIA 4May.16-I
Rycroft,Lt., 12Sqn. 5Apr.17-I
Rycroft,2Lt.WS, name Ryecroft? inj 6Sep.18-I, WIA 30Sep.18-I

S

Sabey,2Lt.AR, POW 7Sep.18-I
Sadler,2Lt.F, KIA 21Apr.17-I
Saffery,2Lt.CH, 7Sep.18-I
Sage,2Lt.DM, KIA 18Dec.17-I
Saidler,Lt.WT, KIA 26Mar.18-I
Sainsbury,Cpl.AW, WIA POW 3May.18-I
Saint,2Lt.WB, 20Jul.16-I, DoW 15Sep.16-I
Saint,FLt.HJT, WIA 16Aug.17-I
Salmon,2Lt.WG, DoW 7Jul.17-III
Salmond,Capt.HA, 28Aug.16-I
Salmond,Capt.HG, WIA POW 2Sep.16-I
Salmond,Maj.JM, 10Mar.15-I
Salt,2Lt.TE, 22Jul.17-I, 28Jul.17-I
Salter,Lt.,Capt.EJ, Can. 4Jul.18-I, WIA 2Sep.18-I
Salter,Lt.GCT, MC KIA 28May.18-I
Salter,FSLt.HP, POW 6Nov.17-I
Salter,2Lt.JHR, KIA 13Oct.17-I
Salter,Capt.WE, 24Mar.17-I
Sampson,Lt., 5Sqn. 1Jun.15-I, 5Sqn. 2Jun.15-I
Sampson,Sgt.AJ, DoW 29Nov.17-VII
Sampson,Lt.AT?, KIA 8Aug.18-I
Sampson,Lt.HA, 19Feb.18-I
Sampson,Sgt.HJ, WIA 6Sep.18-I
Sampson,2Lt.RD, WIA 29Apr.16-I
Sams,2Lt.FDH, POW 3Sep.16-I
Samson,Cdr.CR, DSO 21Dec.14-I, 17May.15-V, 4Jun.15-V, 8Nov.15-V, 15Jun.16-VII
Samson,Sgt.MS, POW 24Jul.18-I
Samuel,Lt.JR, POW 14Apr.17-I
Samuels,2Lt.GB, 20Oct.16-I, KIA 22Oct.16-I
Samways,AM.WAE, KIA 29Nov.17-I
Sanday,2Lt.,Lt.WDS, 2Sqn. 11Oct.15-I, 11Nov.15-I
Sanday,Capt.WJS, 70Sqn. 6Sep.16-I
Sandell,FSLt.A, KIA 30Mar.17-V
Sander,2Lt.CA, 27Oct.18-IV
Sanders,2Lt.APM, WIA 20May.17-I
Sanders,2Lt.DCW, POW 28Feb.15-I
Sanders,Lt.H, WIA 27Jun.18-I
Sanders,Capt.JDG?, 23Apr.15-I
Sanders,Lt.JW, POW 16Sep.16-I
Sanders,Lt.NM, WIA 22Dec.17-I
Sanders,Prob.JB, WIA 3May.18-I
Sanderson,2Lt.AC, WIA 6May.17-I
Sanderson,Lt.AM, KIA 1Oct.18-I
Sanderson,2Lt,Lt.CB, 9Aug.18-I, POW DoW 17.10.1918 25Sep.18-I
Sanderson,Lt.IC, 26Jun.18-I, WIA 17Sep.18-I
Sanderson,2Lt.WM, WIA 29Sep.18-I
Sandford?,1Lt.JR, see Sanford 12Apr.18-1
Sandison,Sgt.N, WIA 1Sep.18-I
Sands,1Lt.CB, US. KIA 1Aug.18-IIB
Sands,FSLt.LA, KIA 22Mar.18-I
Sandy,2Lt.BF, WIA 14Aug.17-I
Sandy,Lt.JLM, Aust. KIA 17Dec.17-I
Sandys,Lt.WE, KIA 5Sep.17-I
Sandys-Thomas,2Lt.CI, WIA POW 20Jul.16-I
Sandys-Winsch,Lt.AE, WIA 1Sep.18-I
Sanford,1Lt.HM, US. WIA 15Sep.18-IIB
Sanford,1Lt.JR, USAS. KIA name Sandford? 12Apr.18-I
Sanford,Lt.SA, POW 9May.15-I
Sangster,2Lt.AB, KIA 13Aug.18-I
Sangster,Lt.J, WIA 28Sep.18-I
Sansom,2Lt.EH, 8Oct.18-I
Sansom,2Lt.RC, 18Mar.18-I, KIA 16May.18-I
Sant,2Lt.EM, KIA 1Sep.17-I
Sargant,2Lt.FHStC, WIA 11Jul.17-I
Satchell,Lt.HL, 5Jun.17-I, 8Jun.17-I
Sattin,Lt.A, WIA 5Dec.17-I
Saul,Maj.RE, WIA 18May.18-I
Saunby,Lt.RHMS, WIA 31Jul.16-I
Saundby,2Lt.WSF, KIA 17Nov.16-I
Saunders,Lt., 3Sqn. 19Jul.15-I, 26Aug.15-I, 19Dec.15-I
Saunders,Capt.AW, 8Aug.18-I
Saunders,Capt.FG, 22Jan.18-VI, WIA 8Apr.17-VI
Saunders,Lt.HC, KIA 18Sep.18-I
Saunders,Capt.HWL, SA. 29Jul.18-I
Saunders,Capt.JD, 27Nov.15-I
Saunders,2Lt.JORS, KIA 21Oct.18-I
Saunders,2Lt.LL, KIA 4Oct.18-I
Saunders,2Lt.MF, US. POW? 30Sep.18-IIB
Saunders,Capt.RA, 20Feb.16-I, 26Feb.16-I, 29Feb.16-I, 2Mar.16-I, 12Mar.16-I, WIA DoW 14Mar.16-I
Saunders,FSLt.RG, KIA 24Jun.17-I
Saunders,1Lt.RJ, US. KIA 22Oct.18-IIB
Saunders,2Lt.W, POW 27Oct.18-I
Saunders,2Lt.WJ, WIA POW 6Jul.18-I
Saunders,2Lt.WW, WIA 11Jun.18-I
Savage,Lt.DA, MC inj 21Apr.18-I, 19May.18-I
Savage,2Lt.JRB, DoW 18Jun.16-I
Savile,Lt.WAB, 8Mar.18-I, WIA 26Mar.18-I
Saville,2Lt.,Lt.WT, 8Aug.18-I, WIA 10Aug.18-I
Savory,2Lt.AJ, POW 11Jul.17-I
Saward,Lt.NC, WIA? POW 9Sep.17-I
Sawden,Lt.WW, DoW 5Jun.17-I
Sawlor?,Lt.RH, KIA? 11Aug.17-I
Sawyer,Lt.CH, 3Aug.18-I
Sawyer,Lt.HG, 19Aug.18-I
Saxby,Capt.AG, name Saxty? 10Nov.16-I, 24Mar.17-I
Sayer,2Lt.HL, KIA 17Aug.17-I
Sayer,2Lt.JH, KIA 3Apr.17-I
Sayers,2AM.,Sgt.EH, 24Apr.17-I, inj 30Apr.17-I, 8Jun.17-I
Sayers,2Lt.KR, KIA 9Sep.17-I
Sayre,2Lt.HH, US. KIA 14Sep.18-IIB
Scadding,Lt.E, POW 19Jul.18-I
Scaife,2Lt.TEG, (see Gordon-Scaife)
Scales,2Lt.HJ, 9May.17-VI
Scales,Lt.JWH, WIA 27Sep.18-I
Scandrett,2Lt.H, WIA 1Oct.17-I
Scaramanga,Lt.JJ, WIA? 11Apr.18-I, DoW 10Jul.18-I
Scarborough,2Lt.F, POW 3Sep.17-I
Schaeffer,2Lt.LD, US. WIA 3Sep.18-IID
Schafer,Sgt.WJ, US. name Schaffer? KIA? 3Oct.18-IID
Schallaire,Lt.RO, Can. 4Sep.18-I
Scharff,2Lt.RL 26Aug.18-I, POW 1Sep.18-I
Schell,Lt.FS, 2Sep.16-I
Scherk,Lt.RHV, 17Jun.18-I
Schmitt,1Lt.RS, US. WIA 19Jul.18-IIB
Schoen,1Lt.KJ, US. DoW 29Oct.18-IIB
Schofield,2Lt.GC, WIA 13Sep.18-I
Schofield,2Lt.JN, WIA 3Sep.18-I
Scholefield,2Lt.ERC, 23Aug.15-I, 30Aug.15-I, POW 1Sep.15-I
Scholes,Lt.J, 3Sep.18-I
Scholte,2Lt.OJF, 19Dec.15-I, POW 20Feb.16-I, 2May.17-I
Scholtz,2Lt.E, POW 17Oct.17-I
Schooley,2Lt.SJ, 26Aug.17-I, 4Nov.17-I
Schooling,2Lt.GR, POW 8Aug.18-I
Schorn,Lt.FF, WIA? POW 19Aug.18-I
Schreiber,Lt.RTB, POW 6Apr.17-I
Schweitzer,Capt.VE, 4Jul.17-I
Scobie,Lt.CG, KIA 21May.18-I
Scott,Capt., 10Sqn. 1Apr.16-I
Scott,Lt.A, WIA 3Oct.18-I, WIA 27Oct.18-I
Scott,Maj.AJL, MC 28May.17-I, WIA 10Jul.17-I
Scott,2Lt.BE, MC DFC WIA 3Sep.18-I
Scott,Hon.Lt.BE, MC 5Jul.18-I
Scott,Capt.CLM, KIA 15Feb.17-I
Scott,Lt.DH, 28Aug.16-I, KIA 12Nov.17-I
Scott,Sgt.E?, KIA 16Jun.18-I
Scott,2Lt.ED, KIA 30Oct.17-I
Scott,AG.2AM.F, WIA 6Sep.17-I
Scott,Lt.FCD, KIA 4Nov.18-I
Scott,FSLt.GBG, KIA 3Sep.17-I
Scott,Capt.GJ, 23Aug.18-I, WIA 3Sep.18-I
Scott,2Lt.HG, KIA 30Jul.18-I
Scott,Lt.HH, 30Aug.18-I, KIA 29Sep.18-I
Scott,2Lt.HS, 23Aug.18-I
Scott,Lt.JS, Can. 3Jul.16-I
Scott,Pte.JW, 2Dec.17-I
Scott,Capt.MDG, 11Sep.17-I
Scott,2Lt.PG, 13Feb.16-I
Scott,Lt.R, 23Apr.18-I
Scott,1Lt.RG, US. KIA 4Oct.18-IIB
Scott,Lt.RJ, KIA 3May.18-I
Scott,2Lt.SP, 23Aug.18-I, 25Aug.18-I, 30Aug.18-I
Scott,Capt.TM, 12Oct.16-I
Scott,2Lt.TR, WIA 13Dec.17-I
Scott,Lt.VW, MC KIA 16Mar.18-I
Scott,Lt.WA, POW 30May.18-I
Scott,2Lt.WP, inj 24May.17-I
Scott,Lt.WS, 10Dec.16-VI, 10May.17-VI
Scott-Brown,2Lt.NAG?, POW 23Apr.16-I
Scott-Foxwell,2Lt.B, WIA 13Apr.17-I
Scott-Kerr,Lt.WF, POW 18May.18-I
Scrivener,2Lt.HA, WIA POW 2Sep.18-I
Scrivener,2Lt.HK, POW 8Jul.18-I
Scrivener,2Lt.JA, 21Mar.18-I
Scroggie,1Lt.ER, US. WIA POW 3Oct.18-IIB
Scroggie,Lt.LC, KIA 25Sep.18-I
Scroggs,2Lt.AF, WIA 5Jun.18-I
Scudamore,2Lt.HD, inj, initials HG? 16Aug.17-I
Scudamore,Lt.WSK, KIA 18Jul.18-I
Scutt,Lt.GHH, 8Mar.18-I
Seabrook,Lt.JP, 15May.18-I
Seagrave,Capt.H, WIA 31Mar.16-I
Sear,Sgt.RJ, KIA 21Sep.18-I
Searle,2Lt.RT?, POW 22Aug.18-I
Seaver,1Lt.AF, US. DSC 16Sep.18-IIB
Sebring,2Lt.RR, US. KIA 4Sep.18-IIB
Seddon,SCdr.JW, INT 17Dec.14-I
Sedore,Lt.FA, WIA 24Sep.18-I
Seedhouse,2Lt.CW, WIA 5Mar.16-I
Seeman-Green,Lt.T, KIA 13Feb.17-I
Sefton,Sgt.F, 25Jun.18-I, 30Oct.18-I
Segrave,Lt.P, KIA 1Nov.18-I
Seguin,2Lt.UH, KIA 6Apr.17-I
Seibold,1Lt.GV, USAS. KIA 26Aug.18-I
Selby,2Lt., 70Sqn. 11Jul.16-I
Selby,2Lt.CWP, 5Feb.16-I, WIA POW 16Apr.16-I
Sellar,2Lt.,Lt.WR, 11Aug.18-I, KIA 29Aug.18-I
Sellars,Lt.FM, POW 27Aug.18-I
Sellars,Lt.HW, KIA 15May.18-I
Sellers,Capt.CG, US. DSC 23Oct.18-IIB
Sellers,2Lt.H, 16Nov.16-I
Selous,2Lt.,Capt.FHB, MC 25Sep.16-I, KIA 4Jan.18-I
Selwyn,2Lt.,Lt.,Capt.W, 16Mar.18-I, 25Apr.18-I, 4Jul.18-I
Sen,2Lt.ESC, Ind. POW 14Sep.17-I
Senecal,2Lt.CH, POW 16Sep.18-I
Senior,2Lt.HH, POW 17Sep.18-I
Senior,2Lt.,Lt.J, 23Jan.17-I, DoW 9May.17-I
Senior,Capt.N, WIA 10May.17-I
Sercombe-Smith,FSLt.JS, POW Oct.17-I
Seth-Smith,Lt.KA, WIA 23Mar.18-I
Seth-Ward,2Lt.E, KIA 10Aug.17-I
Settle,2Lt.RW, KIA 23Jul.16-I
Severs,2Lt.AG, KIA 28Mar.17-I
Seward,Lt.WEL, 24Mar.17-VII
Sewell,2Lt.FA, Aust. WIA 11Sep.18-I
Sewell,Lt.WA, KIA 12Nov.17-I
Sexton,Lt.MC, WIA 29May.18-I
Seymour,Lt.CB, KIA 6Sep.18-I
Seymour,Lt.L, POW 17May.18-I
Shackill,Lt.FC, KIA 23May.17-I
Shackleton,2Lt.W, POW 4Nov.18-I
Shadwell,2Lt.LM, POW 16Sep.17-I

Shakesby,2Lt.CV, **POW** 16Mar.18-*I*
Shand,2Lt., *101Sqn.* 30Nov.17-*I*
Shanks,2Lt.,Lt.D, **inj** 21Oct.17-*I*, **WIA** 31Jan.18-*I*
Shanks,2Lt.DA, **KIA** 21Sep.18-*I*
Shanks,Sgt.FH, 14Sep.18-*IV*, 22Oct.18-*IV*
Shannan,Sgt., *22Sqn.* 31May.18-*I*
Shapard,Lt., *92Sqn.* 5Sep.18-*I*, 9Oct.18-*I*
Sharkey,2Lt.HP, 12Oct.18-*I*, 25Oct.18-*I*
Sharland,2Lt.FJ, **KIA** 24Oct.17-*I*
Sharman,FCdr.JE, DSO **KIA** 22Jul.17-*I*
Sharp,Capt.CC, **WIA POW** 4Sep.17-*I*
Sharp,2Lt.CH, **KIA** 26Sep.18-*I*
Sharp,AG.Rfn.E, **DoW** 27Jun.17-*I*
Sharp,2Lt.GF, 23May.18-*I*, **WIA** 27May.18-*I*
Sharp,2Lt.J, 10Sep.18-*I*
Sharp,2Lt.JP, **inj** 22Sep.18-*I*
Sharp,2Lt.L, **WIA** 2Sep.18-*I*
Sharp,Lt.TE, 1Jun.18-*I*
Sharpe,2Lt.EWC, **WIA** 29Aug.18-*I*
Sharpe,Lt.F, **WIA POW** 9Jun.17-*I*
Sharpe,2Lt.JG, 5Aug.17-*I*
Sharpe,2Lt.M, **KIA** 28Oct.16-*I*
Sharpe,2Lt.SA, **POW** 3Apr.17-*I*
Sharpe,Capt.TS, DFC 22Mar.18-*I*, **WIA POW** 27Mar.18-*I*
Sharples,Lt.N, 14Aug.17-*I*, **KIA** 20Sep.17-*I*
Sharwood-Smith,2Lt.BE, *initials* GE? 7Jul.18-*I*, 8Aug.18-*I*
Shaumer,2Lt.CG, 10Oct.16-*I*, 4Mar.17-*I*
Shaw,Lt., *12Sqn.* **inj** 23Aug.18-*I*
Shaw,2Lt.B, **WIA** 15Sep.18-*I*
Shaw,2Lt.CL, **WIA** 29Oct.17-*I*
Shaw,Lt.ED, *USAS.* 2Jul.18-*I*, **KIA** 9Jul.18-*I*
Shaw,2Lt.EL, **WIA** 1Dec.17-*I*
Shaw,Lt.FA, **KIA** 16Jul.18-*I*
Shaw,2Lt.GG, **WIA** 29Oct.18-*I*
Shaw,Lt.GM, **WIA POW** 26Feb.18-*I*
Shaw,2Lt.HB, **WIA** 7Oct.18-*I*
Shaw,2AM.HV, **KIA** 5Jun.17-*I*
Shaw,1AM.J, 19Sep.15-*I*, 3Oct.15-*I*, **WIA** 11Oct.15-*I*
Shaw,Sgt.JF, **KIA** 4Feb.17-*I*
Shaw,Lt.JW, **POW** 7Jun.17-*I*
Shaw,1AM.P, **POW** 13Mar.16-*I*
Shaw,Lt.RG, 23Apr.18-*I*, 29Jul.18-*I*
Shaw,2Lt.TG, **KIA** 17Mar.18-*I*
Shaw,2Lt.W, **WIA** 15Aug.18-*I*
Sheard,Lt.FV, **WIA** 29May.18-*I*
Sheard,2Lt.HW, **KIA** 11Aug.18-*I*
Shearer,Lt.FJ, **KIA** 25Jul.18-*I*
Shearman,2Lt.WH, *USAS.* 11Jul.18-*I*, **POW DoW** 14Aug.18-*I*
Shedel,Capt.WG, **POW** 31Aug.18-*I*
Sheehan,2Lt.DJ, **KIA** 10May.17-*I*
Sheehan,2Lt.,Lt.MJ, 27Aug.18-*I*, 31Aug.18-*I*, **KIA** 1Oct.18-*I*
Sheil,2Lt.C, **DoW** 22Apr.18-*I*
Sheldon,Lt.CS, **KIA** 27Jun.18-*I*
Sheldrake,2Lt.AT, **KIA** 28Sep.18-*I*
Shell,Lt.WH, **POW** 31Jul.18-*I*
Shelswell,2Lt.CO, 30Jun.18-*I*
Shelton,Lt.K, 4Sep.17-*I*, 17Oct.17-*I*
Shepard,2Lt.LJ, *Can.* 27Oct.18-*IV*
Shepard,2Lt.T, **POW** 9Mar.17-*I*
Shephard,Capt.GS, 24Aug.14-*I*, 4Nov.14-*I*
Shepherd,Lt., *10Sqn.* 11Oct.15-*I*, 2Dec.15-*I*, 7Dec.15-*I*
Shepherd,2Lt.ALM, **POW DoW** 3.11.1916 22Oct.16-*I*
Shepherd,2Lt.,Lt.AS, DSO MC *Aust.* 11May.17-*I*, **POW DoW** 20Jul.17-*I*
Shepherd,2Lt.FH, *Aust.* 20Nov.17-*I*
Shepherd,Capt.JME, **KIA** 15Feb.17-*I*
Shepherd,AG.R, **KIA** 25Jun.18-*I*
Shepherd,2Lt.RMS, 22Jul.16-*I*, **KIA** 9Aug.16-*I*
Sherek,Lt.P, **KIA** 1Oct.18-*I*
Shergold,2Lt., *101Sqn.* 18Sep.18-*I*
Sheridan,Lt.JW, **WIA** 14Sep.17-*I*
Sherman,1Lt.GC, *USAS.* **WIA** 16Aug.18-*I*
Sherman,2Lt.P, **KIA** 30Apr.17-*I*
Sherren,Lt.PC, 19Aug.16-*I*
Sherwell,2Lt.R, 26Jun.16-*I*, **KIA** 3Jul.16-*I*
Sherwin,2Lt.CE, **WIA** 15Jan.16-*I*
Sherwood,2Lt.AE, 4Oct.18-*I*
Sherwood,Lt.CLA, *US.* **KIA** 1Jul.18-*I*
Sherwood,Lt.WB, **KIA** 27Oct.17-*I*
Shewell,2Lt.,Lt.AV, 16Sep.16-*I*, **WIA** 17Nov.16-*I*
Shidler,2Lt.H, *US.* **POW** 14Sep.18-*IIB*
Shield,2Lt.HS, 16Jun.15-*I*, 27Aug.15-*I*, 28Sep.15-*I*, Oct.15-*I*
Shields,Lt.CGS, **KIA** 10May.18-*I*
Shields,FSLt.DM, **WIA** 1May.17-*I*
Shields?,2AM.HG, **KIA** Oct.15-*I*
Shields,Lt.T, 29Sep.18-*I*
Shields,Lt.W, **KIA** 5Sep.17-*I*
Shields,Lt.,Capt.WE, *Can.* 16May.18-*I*, 12Jun.18-*I*, 15Sep.18-*I*
Shields,Lt.WG, 8May.18-*I*
Shilling,1Lt.FF, *US.* **KIA** 2Jul.18-*IIB*
Shillingford,Lt.SC, **KIA** 16Jun.18-*I*
Shillington,Lt.TC, **POW** 19Nov.15-*I*
Shipman,Lt.TT, **POW** 10Aug.18-*I*
Shipton,2Lt.GA, **POW** 14Sep.18-*I*
Shipwright,Lt.AT, **POW** 16Aug.17-*I*
Shirlaw,2Lt.,Lt.WJT, 25Mar.18-*I*, 30Aug.18-*I*
Shirley,2Lt.AE, **WIA** 21Aug.18-*I*
Shirley,2Lt.AV, 7Jun.17-*I*, **KIA** 8Jun.17-*I*
Shirley,Capt.FLJ, **WIA** 12Apr.17-*I*
Shirtcliffe,2Lt.AW, 29Jan.17-*I*
Shives,2Lt.RK, **WIA** 30Apr.16-*I*
Shoemaker,1Lt.FT, *US.* **WIA POW** 14Sep.18-*IIB*
Shoemaker,1Lt.HG, *USAS.* **KIA** 5Oct.18-*I*
Sholto-Douglas,FLt.N, **WIA** 5Mar.15-*V*
Sholto-Douglas,Lt.WS, 29Dec.15-*I*
Shone,Lt.GB, 11Oct.17-*I*, **DoW** 19.10.1917 18Oct.17-*I*
Shoninger,Sgt?,CB, *US.* **POW** 29May.18-*IIC*
Shook,FCdr.AM, 4Jun.17-*I*, 5Jun.17-*I*, **WIA** 21Oct.17-*I*
Shook,2Lt.JK, **POW** 2Oct.18-*I*
Shooter,2Lt.JH, **KIA** 10Apr.18-*I*
Short,2Lt.,Lt.CW, MC 21Feb.16-*I*, **DoW** 6Mar.17-*I*
Short,Lt.LF, **WIA** 30May.18-*I*
Short,Capt.LH, MC 2Oct.18-*I*
Short,Lt.LH, MC **WIA** 30May.18-*I*
Short,2Lt.SH, *Can.* **WIA** 10Aug.17-*I*
Shorter,Lt.WJ, 21Mar.18-*I*
Showalter,1Lt.FM, *USAS.* 18Jul.18-*I*
Shreeve,2Lt.FD, **POW** 28Mar.18-*I*
Shroder,Lt.RH, 28Sep.18-*I*
Shuker,Sgt.WJ, **KIA** 24Jul.18-*I*
Shum,2Lt.CAR, **POW** 11Mar.17-*I*
Shum,Lt.GB, **POW** 27Sep.18-*I*
Shurley,Lt.EC, *Can.* 1Oct.18-*I*
Shutes,Lt.RF, **WIA** 4Nov.18-*I*
Sibley,Pte.R, 6Apr.17-*I*
Sibley,Maj.RDG, **KIA** 1Oct.18-*I*
Sibley,Pte.RE, **KIA** 13Apr.17-*I*
Sibley,2Lt.SJ, 2Apr.16-*I*
Sibley,Capt.SJ, **POW** 14Feb.18-*I*
Siddall,Lt.JH, 3Jun.18-*I*, **KIA** 25Jul.18-*I*
Sidebottom,Lt.W, 23Oct.18-*I*
Sidler,1Lt.FW, *US.* **KIA** 13Sep.18-*IIB*
Sidney,2Lt.LP, **KIA** 2Oct.17-*I*
Siedle,LtGE, 30May.18-*I*
Sieveking,FLt.LG **POW** 30Oct.17-*I*
Sieveking,Capt.VE, **KIA** 19May.18-*I*
Siever,Lt.RRB, MC **WIA** 25Jan.18-*VIII*, 21May.18-*VIII*
Sievwright,2Lt.RH, 15Jul.16-*I*
Sifton,Lt.TG, **WIA** 5Sep.18-*I*
Silk,Lt.RW, **POW** 23Oct.18-*I*
Sillem,2Lt.SC, **KIA** 12Aug.17-*I*
Silly,Lt.BJ, MC DFC 4May.17-*I*
Silvester,Sgt.CS, **POW**? 30Oct.18-*I*
Sim,2Lt.JM, **KIA** 25Mar.17-*I*
Simmonds,2Lt.LB, **KIA** 16Sep.18-*I*
Simmons,2Lt.A, 17Dec.17-*VII*
Simms,FSLt.HR, 23Jan.16-*I*, 29Feb.16-*I*, **KIA** 5May.16-*I*
Simms,2Lt.JBP, 27May.18-*I*, **KIA** 4Jun.18-*I*
Simon,2Lt.GP, **POW** 27Jun.17-*I*
Simon,2Lt.NES, **WIA** 25Sep.16-*I*
Simon,Lt.WC, *US.* 4Jul.18-*IV*, 30Jul.18-*IV*
Simonds,FSLt.WV, 22Apr.17-*VI*
Simons,2Lt.AT, **WIA POW** 11Jul.18-*I*
Simons,Lt.H, 14Sep.16-*I*
Simonson,Capt.EL, *Aust.* 26Oct.18-*I*, 4Nov.18-*I*
Simpson,Capt., *5Sqn.* 26Oct.15-*I*
Simpson,Lt.AE, **WIA** 9Jul.18-*I*
Simpson,2Lt.CB, **KIA** 6Nov.17-*I*
Simpson,Capt.FWH, 25Jan.17-*I*
Simpson,FSLt.GG, 4Dec.16-*I*
Simpson,Lt.GK, **DoW** 7.3.1917 1Mar.17-*I*
Simpson,2Lt.JA, *10Sqn.* 3Sep.16-*I*, **DoW** 22.10.1916 21Oct.16-*I*
Simpson,2Lt.JA, *110Sqn.* **POW** 21Oct.18-*I*
Simpson,Lt.JRM, **WIA** 15Sep.17-*I*
Simpson,Capt.KR, 29Jun.18-*I*
Simpson,2Lt.R, **KIA** 7Sep.18-*I*
Simpson,Capt.TL, *Aust.* **WIA** 2Jun.18-*I*
Sims,Lt.BW, **WIA** 30Mar.18-*I*
Sims,Lt.CJ, 14Oct.18-*I*
Sims,2AM.GL, 28Dec.17-*I*
Sims,Lt.PJ, *Aust.* **KIA** 29Oct.18-*I*
Sincay,Lt.Compte de 28Nov.15-*I*
Sinclair,2Lt.AS, 8Aug.18-*I*, **POW** 9Aug.18-*I*
Sinclair,Lt.CM, **WIA** 21Apr.18-*I*
Sinclair,2Lt.DB, **POW** 2Sep.18-*I*
Sinclair,Lt.DMF, **KIA** 30Mar.17-*I*
Sinclair,1AM.H, **POW**? 27Mar.18-*I*
Sinclair,Lt.LR, *US.* **WIA POW** 14May.18-*I*
Singh-Malik,2Lt.HE, *Ind.* 20Oct.17-*I*, **WIA** 26Oct.17-*I*
Singleton,2Lt.E, **POW** 31Jul.18-*I*
Singleton,2Lt.TH, 22May.18-*I*
Sippe,FLt.SV, 21Nov.14-*I*
Sisley,2Lt.AJS, **KIA** 10Sep.17-*I*
Sisley,2Lt.DL, **KIA** 6Mar.18-*I*
Sison,Capt., *1Sqn.* 4Jul.18-*I*
Sison,Lt.HM, 14Dec.15-*I*
Sissing,2Lt.AE, **KIA** 1Nov.18-*IV*
Sitch,Lt.JE, **POW** 9Oct.18-*I*
Sitterly,Adj.G, *US.* **POW** 28Jul.18-*IID*
Sivil,Lt.CS, **WIA POW** 5Jul.18-*IV*
Sivyer,LM.CW, **INT** 24Oct.17-*III*
Skeate,Lt., *5Sqn.* 23Sep.16-*I*
Skeate,Lt.WA, 22Sep.15-*I*, 22Oct.15-*I*, 23Oct.15-*I*
Skeddon,Lt.CEL, 21Apr.18-*I*
Skeffington,Lt.HNS, **KIA** 28Jul.17-*I*
Skelton,Lt.EK, **KIA** 9Jan.18-*I*
Skelton,2Lt.JEL, **WIA** 15Sep.17-*I*
Skene,2Lt.RR, **KIFA** 12Aug.14-*III*
Skidmore,2Lt.J, 14Oct.18-*I*
Skinner,Capt.A, **KIA** 31Aug.16-*I*
Skinner,Lt.AEL, 16Oct.17-*VIII*
Skinner,2Lt.AH, **WIA POW** 16Sep.17-*I*
Skinner,2Lt.CD, **WIA** 3Jan.18-*I*
Skinner,2Lt.HW, **WIA** 2Oct.18-*I*
Skinner,2Lt.LJ, **WIA** 28Sep.18-*I*
Skinner,Lt.MR, **WIA** 24May.18-*I*
Skinner,2Lt.RLG, **POW DoW** 3May.18-*I*
Skinner,Lt.WMB, 12Oct.17-*I*
Skinner,2Lt.WRK, **POW** 9Aug.17-*I*
Slade,2Lt.RB, **WIA inj** 20Oct.17-*I*
Slade,2Lt.RJ, 23Oct.15-*I*, **POW** 26Oct.15-*I*
Slater,2Lt.EA, 23Oct.18-*I*
Slater,1Lt.FC, *US.* **WIA** 8Oct.18-*IIB*
Slater,Sgt.GW, 1Jul.18-*I*, **DoW** 25Jul.18-*I*
Slater,2Lt.,Capt.JA, 17Jan.16-*I*, 30Nov.17-*I*, 21Mar.18-*I*
Slater,FSLt.RK, **WIA POW** 5Apr.17-*I*
Slee,2Lt.FD, **POW** 8Jun.17-*I*
Sleigh,2Lt.,Lt.TW, 29Aug.18-*I*, 16Sep.18-*I*, **POW** 30Oct.18-*I*
Slessor,2Lt.JC, **WIA** 23May.16-*VII*
Slightholm,Lt.B, 10Aug.18-*I*
Slimming,Capt.GAR, 12Oct.18-*I*
Slinger,2Lt.AE, **KIA** 3May.18-*I*
Slingsby,FSgt.F, 23Jan.17-*I*, 24Jan.17-*I*
Slipper,2Lt.RA, **WIA POW** 4May.18-*I*
Sliter,Lt.ED, **WIA POW** 13Jul.17-*I*
Sloan,2Lt.CR, **KIA** 12May.17-*I*
Sloley,2Lt.RH, 14Aug.17-*I*, **KIA** 1Oct.17-*I*
Sloss,2Lt.JD, **DoW** 16.11.1918 9Nov.18-*I*
Sly,Lt.R, *Aust.* 15Apr.18-*I*
Smailes,2Lt.EB, **POW DoW** 13.9.1918 7Sep.18-*I*
Small,Capt., *4Sqn.* 25Aug.14-*I*
Small,2Lt., *11Sqn.* 23Sep.15-*I*
Small,Lt.FG, **WIA** 22Nov.14-*I*
Smallman,Lt.BS, 1Oct.18-*I*
Smallwood,2Lt.RG, *Aust.* 14May.18-*I*, **WIA** 15Aug.18-*I*
Smart,FSLt.,Capt.BA, DSO 21Aug.17-*III*, 19Jul.18-*III*
Smart,2Lt.EJ, 9May.17-*I*
Smart,2Lt.ET, **KIA** 27Mar.18-*I*
Smart,2Lt.GO, **KIA** 7Apr.17-*I*
Smart,Lt.WA, 29Oct.18-*I*
Smith,Lt., *4Sqn.* 1Nov.14-*I*
Smith,2Lt., *5Sqn.* **WIA** 26Oct.16-*I*
Smith,Lt., *12Sqn.* 23Aug.18-*I*, **WIA**? 3Sep.18-*I*
Smith,1AM., *18Sqn.* 28Nov.15-*I*
Smith,Lt.A, **POW** 18Jul.18-*I*
Smith,2Lt.AE, **KIA** 29Sep.18-*I*
Smith,2Lt.AEP, **WIA** 10Feb.17-*I*
Smith,Lt.AF, **POW** 28Sep.18-*I*
Smith,Capt.AH, MC **KIA** 21Aug.17-*I*
Smith,2Lt.AW, **WIA** 17Jun.16-*I*
Smith,Lt.B, **WIA POW** 5Jun.17-*I*
Smith,Lt.BH, **KIA** 22Jul.17-*I*
Smith,2Lt.B*US*, **WIA** 27Sep.16-*I*
Smith,2Lt.C, **POW** 25Aug.16-*I*
Smith,2Lt.CF, **POW** 26May.17-*I*
Smith,2Lt.CK, **WIA** 14Aug.17-*I*
Smith,Lt.DE, **KIA** 14Aug.18-*I*
Smith,Lt.DE, 10May.18-*I*
Smith,2Lt.DG, *42Sqn.* 9Apr.18-*I*, **KIA** 10Apr.18-*I*
Smith,SgtMaj.DG, *104Sqn.* **KIA** 25May.18-*I*
Smith,2Lt.EALF, *Can.* **POW** 26Oct.17-*I*
Smith,GL.EE, **POW** 24Oct.17-*I*
Smith,2Lt.EJ, 22Apr.18-*I*
Smith,Pte.F, *57Sqn.* **WIA POW** 6Apr.17-*I*
Smith,2Lt.F, *99Sqn.* **POW** 31Jul.18-*I*
Smith,Sgt.FC, **POW** 25Apr.17-*I*
Smith,Lt.FE, 21Aug.18-*I*
Smith,2AM.FJ, *55Sqn.* **DoW** 20Aug.17-*I*
Smith,2Lt.FJ?, *initials* FE? *46Sqn.* **KIA** 29Apr.18-*I*
Smith,2Lt.FL, **INT** 29Sep.17-*I*
Smith,2Lt.FLP, **KIA** 9Nov.18-*I*
Smith,Lt.,Capt.FR, *Aust.* **WIA** 8Jul.18-*I*, **POW** 9Nov.18-*I*
Smith,Sgt.GA, **KIA** 6Nov.18-*I*
Smith,Lt.GC, MC *6Sqn.* **DoW** 31Jul.17-*I*
Smith,2AM.GC, *55Sqn.* **KIA** 16May.18-*I*
Smith,Lt.GHB, **POW** 22Aug.18-*I*
Smith,2Lt.GJ?, **POW** 27Sep.18-*I*
Smith,Capt.GK, MC **KIA** 21Aug.17-*I*
Smith,2Lt.GM, **POW** 16Aug.17-*I*
Smith,2Lt.GS, *40Sqn.* 27Sep.18-*I*
Smith,FSLt.GS, *ASqn.RNAS.* **KIA** 24Oct.17-*I*
Smith,Sgt.GT, **WIA** 24Jun.18-*I*
Smith,Lt.GWK, **WIA** 8Oct.18-*I*
Smith,2Lt.HB, 4Nov.18-*I*
Smith,2Lt.HC, *52Sqn.* **KIA** 11Sep.17-*I*
Smith,Lt.HC, *204Sqn.* **WIA** 14Oct.18-*I*
Smith,Lt.HC, *213Sqn.* 9Nov.18-*I*
Smith,1Lt.HC, *US. 213thUS.* **WIA** 3Nov.18-*IIB*
Smith,1Lt.HD, *US.* **POW** 10Jul.18-*IIB*
Smith,Sgt.HG, **WIA** 16Feb.17-*I*
Smith,2Lt.HJ, 28Aug.18-*III*
Smith,FSLt.HL, **KIA** 24May.17-*I*
Smith,Sgt.HO, **WIA POW** 25Jan.18-*I*
Smith,Capt.HP, **WIA** 16May.18-*I*
Smith,2Lt.HS, **KIA** 31Jul.18-*I*
Smith,Lt.HW, **WIA** 2Oct.17-*I*
Smith,2Lt.JB, *43Sqn.* **KIA** 15Aug.17-*I*
Smith,2Lt.JB, *52Sqn.* 15Sep.18-*I*
Smith,2Lt.JC, 26Jul.17-*I*, **KIA** 28Jul.17-*I*
Smith,Lt.JE, 31Aug.18-*I*, **KIA** 17Sep.18-*I*
Smith,Lt.JH, *46Sqn.* 21Mar.18-*I*
Smith,2Lt.JHR, *211Sqn.* **KIA** 10Nov.18-*I*
Smith,2Lt.JK, *46Sqn.* **WIA** 20Nov.17-*I*
Smith,2Lt.JKS, *18Sqn.* 27Sep.18-*I*
Smith,Lt.JL, *Aust.* 1Apr.18-*I*, **WIA** 10Aug.18-*I*
Smith,FSLt.JM, **POW** 24Oct.17-*I*
Smith,2Lt.JR, **WIA** 11Apr.17-*I*
Smith,AGL.G, **KIA** 18Mar.18-*I*
Smith,1Lt.LA, *US. 135thUS.* **WIA** 25Aug.18-*IIB*
Smith,Capt.LA, *66Sqn.* **POW** 24May.17-*I*

Smith,FSLt.LE, POW DoI 25Feb.17-I
Smith,FSLt.LFW, DSC KIA 13Jun.17-I
Smith,2Lt.LG, POW 26Sep.18-I
Smith,Lt.LH, UK. 1AFC. WIA POW 27Jun.18-VII
Smith,Lt.LH, 60Sqn. POW 25Oct.18-I
Smith,2Lt.LJ, POW 28Jun.18-I
Smith,Lt.LT, 12Apr.17-I
Smith,2Lt.LTS, WIA 23Aug.16-I
Smith,2Lt.N, 204Sqn. POW 27Oct.18-I
Smith,Lt.NA, 101Sqn. POW 6May.18-I
Smith,2Lt.PJ, DoI 16Sep.16-I
Smith,2AM.PL, WIA 29Nov.17-VII
Smith,2Lt.R, 18Sqn. KIA 20Dec.16-I
Smith,2Lt.R, 20Sqn. KIA 6Apr.17-I
Smith,2Lt.RB, US? POW 27Mar.18-I
Smith,Lt.RE, KIA 23Apr.18-I
Smith,2Lt.RJ, 17Mar.18-I
Smith,2Lt.RM, 23Sqn. POW 31Oct.17-I
Smith,Lt.,Capt.RM, 1AFC. 1Sep.17-VII, 7May.18-VII, 19Sep.18-VII, Aust. 22Sep.18-VII, 19Oct.18-VII
Smith,Lt.RNS, WIA 14Apr.17-I
Smith,2Lt.S, 17Sqn. POW 27Jan.17-VI
Smith,FSLt.S, 203Sqn. KIA 11Apr.18-I
Smith,2Lt.SA, KIA 6Aug.18-I
Smith,2Lt.SH, 28May.18-I
Smith,2Lt.SM, WIA 12Oct.16-I
Smith,Capt.SP, 6Sqn. 26Jan.17-I, WIA 1May.17-I
Smith,Capt.SP, 46Sqn. KIA 6Apr.18-I
Smith,Lt.TD, 16Sep.18-I, 28Sep.18-I
Smith,2Lt.TE, KIA 14Jul.17-I
Smith,2Lt.TT, KIA 29Sep.18-I
Smith,Capt.TW, 2Sqn. 29Jul.15-I, 11Aug.15-I
Smith,Sgt.TW, 48Sqn. 2Jul.18-I, KIA 9Jul.18-I
Smith,Lt.V, WIA POW 28May.17-I
Smith,2Lt.W, 10Sqn. KIA 2Apr.18-I
Smith,Lt.W, 139Sqn. 4Jul.18-IV
Smith,Lt.WA, 9Sqn. 24Jun.17-I
Smith,2Lt.WA, 107Sqn. 1Oct.18-I
Smith,2Lt.WC, WIA POW 13Jul.17-I
Smith,2Lt.WRS, KIA 22Oct.17-I
Smith,2Lt.WS, KIA 9Jan.18-I
Smith,Pbr.WT, 45Sqn. 11Aug.17-I
Smith,Sgt.WT,DCM MM 104Sqn. POW? 22Aug.18-I
Smith,Lt.WW, WIA 30Jul.18-IV, 30Oct.18-IV
Smith-Grant,Capt.JGSC, WIA 29May.18-I
Smither,2Lt.H, KIA 6Jul.17-I
Smithers,2Lt.EL, POW 6Apr.18-I
Smithett,2Lt.GCE, KIA 12Oct.17-I
Smylie,FSLt.GF, DSC 19Nov.15-V
Smyth,2Lt., 19Sqn. 9Sep.16-I
Smyth,2Lt.BH, 19Aug.18-I
Smyth,2Lt.J, KIA 11Mar.17-I
Smyth,2Lt.PJ, 15Sep.16-I
Smyth-Pigott,FCdr.JRW, 13Nov.15-V
Smythe,Lt.C, MC POW 14Oct.17-I
Smythe,Lt.CR, 30Aug.18-I
Smythe,2Lt.EB, WIA 9Apr.17-I
Sneath,FSLt.WH, KIA 6Apr.18-I
Snelgrove,2Lt.HDB, KIA 15Aug.17-I
Snelling,Pte.E, POW 6Apr.17-I
Snoke,1Lt.RW, USAS. inj 12Aug.18-I
Snook,Capt.CW, POW 2Aug.16-I
Snoulton,AG.Pte.CM, WIA 30Oct.17-I
Snow,Capt.CC, inj 5Jul.18-I, 1Sep.18-I
Snow,Capt.WR, MC WIA 22Jul.17-I
Snowden,Lt.HJ, WIA 31Jul.17-I
Snowden,2Lt.WC, 14Jul.18-I
Snowdon,Sgt.P, KIA 22Oct.16-I
Snyder,Lt.FCH, KIA 7Jul.17-I
Snyder,Lt.VG, WIA 4Sep.18-I
Snyman,2Lt.GDN, KIA 8Oct.18-I
Soar,FSLt.RR, 26Jan.17-I
Soden,Lt.,Capt.FO, Can. 1Jan.18-I, 8Aug.18-I, 15Sep.18-I, 8Oct.18-I
Sogno,2Lt.GF, DoW 9Oct.17-I
Sole,Lt.JW, 10Aug.18-I
Solly,Lt.AN, 30Apr.16-I, 13May.17-I, 31May.16-I, WIA 1Jul.16-I
Solomon,Lt.SAR, WIA 22Aug.18-I
Somervell,2Lt.WE, WIA POW 5Jan.16-I
Somerville,2Lt.CW, KIA 24Aug.18-I
Somerville,2Lt.HA, MC KIA 30Mar.18-I
Sommervail,Lt.A, 19Sep.15-I, WIA 30Sep.15-I
Sonnenberg,2Lt.,Lt.MC, 10Apr.18-I, 14Jun.18-I, DoW 19.9.1918 18Sep.18-I
Soothill,2Lt.S, WIA 11Nov.18-I
Sorley,2Lt.JC, KIA 25Sep.18-I
Sorley,Lt.JT, POW 23Oct.18-I
Sorsoleil,Capt.JV, Can. 11Apr.18-I
Souchette,2Lt.C, KIA 23Apr.18-I
Soulby,2Lt.HW, 20Oct.16-I
Souray,FSLt.R, 16Apr.16-I
Souter,2Lt.E, 23Oct.18-I
Souter,Lt.JM, KIA 11Apr.17-I
Souter,2Lt.TH?, KIFA? 3Jul.18-I
Southall,Lt.WP, 18May.18-I, KIA 28May.18-I
Southam,Lt.RC, KIA 9Jan.18-I
Southey,Lt.JH, 8Aug.18-I
Southey,Capt.WA, SA. 3Sep.18-I
Southon,Capt.HG, WIA POW 6Mar.17-I
Southorn,Lt.TN, POW 28May.17-I
Soutten,2Lt.B, WIA 30Apr.17-I
Sowden,Sgt.CG, WIA 3Aug.18-I
Sowerby,AM.J, Kld 22Jul.17-I
Sowrey,2Lt.,Capt.F, 23Sep.16-III, 21Jul.17-I
Spalding,1Lt.HJ, US. WIA 4Nov.18-IIB
Spalding,Pte.WJ, WIA 8Aug.18-I
Spanner,Lt.,Capt.H, Can. 6Aug.16-I, 27Sep.16-I, KIA 28Dec.16-I
Sparkes,Lt., 103Sqn. 20May.18-I
Sparkes,Lt.CP, POW 25Sep.18-I
Sparks,2Lt.HJ, MC POW 12Mar.18-I
Sparks,Capt.JA, inj 1Oct.18-I
Speagell,2Lt.HMD, POW 5Oct.18-I
Speaks,Lt.JC, US. WIA 28Sep.18-I
Spearpoint,Lt.HD, POW 17Jun.17-I
Speer,Lt.HTL, KIA 9Jul.16-I
Spell,2Lt.RE, US. WIA Oct.18-IIB
Speller,2Lt.L, WIA 10May.17-I
Spence,Lt.CB, KIA 9May.15-I
Spence,Lt.JH, KIA 16Jul.18-I
Spence,Lt.LC, MC DoW 25.5.1918 23May.18-I
Spence,Lt.LGB, WIA 29Aug.18-I
Spence,2Lt.WS, KIA 26Apr.17-I
Spencer,1Lt.CE, US. WIA 2Oct.18-IIB
Spencer,Cpl.D, US. KIA 22Jan.18-IIC
Spencer,1Lt.EB, US. WIA 1Aug.18-IIB
Spencer,AM.F, WIA POW 19May.18-I
Spencer,Lt.GR, WIA 24Jul.17-I, 27Jul.17-I
Spencer,Lt.HJC, 29Jul.18-I
Spencer,Lt.MJ, KIA 3Nov.16-I
Spencer,Lt.RA, 6Nov.18-I
Spencer?,FSLt.T, KIA 16Feb.15-I
Spencer,2Lt.W, 12Apr.18-I, KIA 10May.18-I
Spencer,2Lt.WAL, WIA POW 2Sep.17-I
Spencer Grey,SCdr.DA, 8Oct.14-I
Spensley,Pte.R, POW? 18Oct.17-I
Sperry,1Lt.JA, US. POW 4Oct.18-IIB
Spicer,2Lt.ED, KIA 1Feb.17-I
Spidle,Lt.MK, USAS. KIA 3Aug.18-I
Spiers,Lt.R, WIA 17Sep.16-I
Spilhaus,Lt.JA, KIA 4Sep.18-I
Spinks,2Lt.CE, 10Aug.18-I
Spiro,2Lt.SG, POW 2Dec.17-I
Spooner,2Lt.RW, KIA 8Jun.17-I
Spoonley,Lt.HK, WIA 3May.18-I
Spotswood,2Lt.A, 23Sep.18-I
Sprangle,2Lt.AT, 7Jun.18-I
Spratt,Lt.,Capt.NC, WIA 30Apr.15-I, 22Sep.15-I, 26Sep.15-I, WIA POW 28Sep.15-I
Spriggs,Lt., 8Sqn. 2Sep.18-I
Springer,1Lt.LW, US. WIA 27Oct.18-IIB
Sproat,2Lt.SM, inj 13Apr.18-I
Sproule,Lt.ERL, POW 4Sep.18-I
Spurgin,Lt.FRG, KIA 16Jun.18-I
Spurling,Lt.AR, 24Aug.18-I
Spurr,2Lt.,Lt.NF, WIA? 1Apr.18-I, 12Apr.18-I, 15Apr.18-I
Spurway,2Lt.SM, KIA 21Sep.17-I
Squire,2Lt.AG, WIA 29Sep.18-I
St Amory,2Lt.RH, 28Oct.18-I
St Clair,2Lt.LCF, DoW 4Aug.17-I
St Clair-Morford,Capt.AC, MC WIA 8Aug.18-I
Stac,Sgt.TA, POW 15Sep.18-I
Stacey,Lt., 8Sqn. 10Sep.18-I
Stacey,Lt.RH, WIA 11May.18-I
Stack,2Lt.JC, 22Apr.18-I
Stackard,FSLt.HF, 6Jun.17-I, WIA 8Jun.17-I, 24Sep.17-I
Stafford,2Lt.EJE, WIA 11Apr.17-I
Stafford,2Lt.ER, 20Sep.18-VII
Stafford,2Lt.JF, US. KIA 29Sep.18-I
Stagg,1AM.ATC, 19May.18-III
Stagg,2Lt.LWG, DoW 31Jul.18-I
Stahl,Lt.AM, KIA 4Sep.18-I
Stainbank,Lt.RH, inj 29Jul.18-I
Stalker,Lt.RM, KIA 8Sep.16-I
Stammers,Lt.HV, 3Oct.15-I, 11Oct.15-I
Stammers,Capt.SR, 29Feb.16-I
Stanes,2Lt.EH, 24Mar.18-I
Stanfield,Lt.CJ, 21Apr.18-I
Stanger,Capt.S, Can. 23May.18-IV
Stanley,Sgt.AO, KIA 30Sep.17-I
Stanley,1Lt.G, US. WIA 31Oct.18-IIB
Stanley,Lt.J, 25Sep.18-I
Stanley,Lt.JC, USAS. WIA POW 16Sep.18-I
Stanley,2Lt.SE, POW DoW 19.10.1917 17Oct.17-I
Stanley,2Lt.WH, 7Apr.18-I
Stanley-Clarke,Lt.A, 30Mar.16-I
Stannard,Lt., 12Sqn. 3Oct.18-I
Stanners,2Lt.H, WIA 15Apr.18-I
Stanton,2Lt.VG, POW DoW 29.3.1918 28Mar.18-I
Stapylton,2Lt.GC, 26Jun.16-I
Starey,Capt.SH, 16Jul.17-I
Starfield,2Lt.B, KIA 19Jan.18-I
Starley,2Lt.DR, 16Aug.17-I
Starrett,Soldat.FE, US. KIA? 3Jan.18-IIC
Starsfield,Sgt.A, 27May.18-I
Stata,Lt.BH, 5Jul.18-I
Statham,2Lt.WH, inj 10Nov.17-I
Staton,Lt.,Capt.WE, MC DFC 22May.18-I, 4Sep.18-I, WIA 24Sep.18-I
Stead,Sgt.G, KIA 29Apr.17-I
Stead,2Lt.GC, POW 7Jun.17-I
Stead,2Lt.,Lt.IO, 4Jul.18-I, 2Sep.18-I
Stead,Lt.JK, KIA 1Feb.17-I
Stead,2Lt.MWB, POW 20Nov.17-I
Stead,2Lt.T, WIA 14Oct.18-I, WIA 28Oct.18-I
Steben,2Lt.FL, WIA 16Sep.17-I
Steckley,2Lt.HB, KIA 22Jul.18-I
Stedman,Lt.AR, POW 14Aug.18-I
Stedman,2Lt.F, Aust.? POW 27Apr.17-I
Stedman,2Lt.RA, 27Jul.17-I
Stedman,2Lt.RdeL, WIA 11Sep.17-I
Steel,Lt.AE, KIA 3May.18-I
Steel,2Lt.RA, KIA 27Mar.18-I
Steele,Lt., 12Sqn. 12Jan.18-I, 10Nov.18-I
Steele,2Lt.AH, 10Nov.16-I, DoW 5.2.1917 4Feb.17-I
Steele,Capt.CR, 24Mar.18-I, 13Aug.18-I, WIA 24Aug.18-I
Steele,2Lt.HW, 27Sep.17-I
Steele,2Lt.NL, Aust. POW DoW 20Apr.17-VII
Steele,2Lt.RB, POW DoW 22.10.1917 21Oct.17-I
Steele,2Lt.RC, Can. 8Aug.17-VII, 8Oct.17-VII
Steele,2Lt.RW, US. WIA? 23Oct.18-IIB
Steele,2Lt.TL, DSO KIA 10Apr.18-VII
Steele,2Lt.TM, POW 28Sep.18-I
Steele,Lt.W, POW 29Sep.18-VII
Steele,2Lt.WH, 22Nov.17-I
Steeves,2Lt.DT, POW 4Jun.17-I
Steeves,FSLt.GT, POW 18Mar.18-I
Stefanson,Lt.B, WIA 28May.18-I
Steinbach-Mealing,Capt., 3Sqn. 19Dec.15-I
Stennett,Lt.WR, KIA 4May.18-I
Stenning,Lt.CB, 13Jun.18-I, 21Aug.18-I
Stephen,2Lt.JP, KIA 23May.17-I
Stephens,Lt.CH, POW 25Aug.18-I
Stephens,2Lt.DE, POW DoW 16Aug.18-I
Stephens,Lt.EJ, 24Jun.18-I, 30Jun.18-I
Stephens,2Lt.,Lt.FH, Can. 20Nov.17-I, KIA 23Nov.17-I
Stephens,Lt.HC, 20May.17-I
Stephens,Lt.HH, KIA 28Jun.18-I
Stephenson,2Lt.GH, POW 31Jul.18-I
Stephenson,1Lt.McR, US. KIA 18Sep.18-IIB
Stephenson,Sgt.TF, 31Oct.17-I, KIA 20Nov.17-I
Stephenson,1Lt.WB, US. KIA 14Sep.18-IIB
Stephenson,2Lt.,Lt.WS, MC Can. 24Mar.18-I, POW 28Jul.18-I
Sterling,Lt., 6Sqn. 5Sep.18-I, 19Sep.18-I
Sterling,Sgt.T, KIA 10Jun.18-I
Sterling,Lt.WC, 22Sep.18-I, KIA 3Oct.18-I
Stern,2Lt.LG, KIA 26Sep.18-I
Steuart,2Lt.WW, DoW 5.3.1917 4Mar.17-I
Stevens,Lt., 8Sqn. 30Mar.16-I
Stevens,Lt.AC, POW 28Nov.16-III
Stevens,Lt.AM, KIA 28Sep.18-I
Stevens,2Lt.,Lt.CA?, 10May.17-I, 14Aug.17-I
Stevens,2Lt.DE, KIA 13Mar.18-I
Stevens,2Lt.ED, WIA 4Apr.18-I
Stevens,Sgt.EG, 30Oct.18-I
Stevens,2Lt.EH, 8Jul.16-I, 21Aug.16-I, 7Sep.16-I, POW DoW 16.6.1917 28May.17-I
Stevens,Capt.FD, 20Sep.17-I
Stevens,Capt.GLE, 22May.18-I
Stevens,1Lt.HleN, US. KIA 12Sep.18-IIB
Stevens,2Lt.JH, US. KIA 31Jul.18-IIB
Stevens,2Lt.JMSG, DoW 14.7.1917 7Jul.17-I
Stevens,Lt.RHB, KIA 30May.18-I
Stevens,2Lt.VS, WIA POW 8Aug.18-I
Stevenson,Capt., 12Sqn. 15Sep.17-I
Stevenson,2Lt.DB, KIA 11Mar.17-I
Stevenson,2Lt.JG, POW 5Oct.17-I
Stevenson,2Lt.JM, 27Sep.18-I
Stevenson,2Lt.WH, KIA 5Jun.17-I
Stewardson,Lt.EA, POW 1Jun.17-I
Stewart,2Lt., 16Sqn. 30Apr.17-I
Stewart,2Lt.CE, WIA 8Nov.17-I
Stewart,2Lt.CG, WIA 24May.17-I
Stewart,Lt.D, POW 2Sep.16-I
Stewart,2Lt.DA, 18Sqn. 23Nov.17-I, 6Mar.18-I
Stewart,Lt.DA, 70Sqn. 28Aug.16-I
Stewart,Lt.DJ, WIA POW 5Apr.17-I
Stewart,Capt.G, KIA 11Apr.17-I
Stewart,2Lt.GS, 29Nov.17-I, KIA 28Mar.18-I
Stewart,Sgt.H, POW 3Sep.18-I
Stewart,2Lt.HE, 21Mar.18-I, WIA 27Mar.18-I
Stewart,2Lt.HGH, 3Sep.16-I, 9Sep.16-I
Stewart,2Lt.HM, KIA 16Jun.18-I
Stewart,Lt.JA, WIA 7Oct.16-I
Stewart,2Lt.JCM, 23Sqn. KIA 3Jul.16-I
Stewart,2Lt.JCM, 25Sqn. 26May.16-I
Stewart,2Lt.JDM, POW 26Apr.17-I
Stewart,2Lt.JK, WIA 1Sep.18-I
Stewart,Lt.JK, 23Aug.18-I
Stewart,2Lt.,Lt.,Capt.MGW, DFC 22Mar.18-I, 25Mar.18-I, 24Aug.18-I, 4Oct.18-I
Stewart,2Lt.MS, 5Jul.15-I
Stewart,Lt.NW, DoW 23Jan.17-VII
Stewart,Capt.O, 25Sep.17-I
Stewart,2Lt.,Lt.RD, 25Mar.18-I, WIA 6May.18-I
Stewart,2Lt.RJG, WIA POW 3Jan.18-I
Stewart,2Lt.SJ, WIA 1May.17-I
Stewart,2Lt.VF, 30Apr.17-I, KIA 13May.17-I
Stewart,1Lt.WA, US. KIA 16Sep.18-IIB
Steytler,2Lt.ED, KIA 25Jul.16-I
Stieber,2Lt.FM, 25Aug.18-I
Stiles,2Lt.CDB, 21Feb.18-I, WIA 1Apr.18-I
Stiles,2Lt.GBB, WIA 2Apr.18-I
Stiles,1Lt.RH, US. KIA 16Sep.18-IIB
Stivers,1Lt.GD, US. KIA 1Oct.18-IIB
Stock,2Lt.AE, KIA 4Sep.18-I
Stock,Lt.E, 21Mar.18-I
Stock,2Lt.EE, WIA 1Apr.18-I
Stock,2Lt.ER, 28Mar.18-I, WIA 19May.18-I
Stock,2Lt.FH, WIA 3May.18-I
Stockdale,Capt.HW, 18Sep.18-I
Stockenstrom,Lt.AL, KIA 23May.18-I
Stocker,FSLt.EC, KIA 27Mar.18-I
Stockhausen,Lt.IL, KIA 3Oct.17-VI
Stockins,Lt.WJ, KIA 6Jun.18-I
Stockman,Lt.EJ, POW 15Sep.18-I
Stockman,Lt.JC, INT 2Oct.18-III
Stocks,2Lt.SJ, WIA 22Mar.17-I
Stockwell,2Lt.LG, POW 28Oct.18-I
Stoddard,2Lt.RC, KIA 3Jul.16-I
Stoddart,Capt.DE, 5Jul.15-I

Stokes,Capt.CH, KIA 29Oct.18-I
Stokes,1Lt.JY, US. DSC 16Sep.18-IIB
Stokes,Lt.RC, inj 11Jun.18-I, WIA 9Aug.18-I
Stolt,Capt., 8Sqn. 14Sep.15-I
Stone,Lt.CO, Aust. 17Jul.18-I
Stone,Sgt.DE, US. KIA 21Apr.18-IIC
Stone,2Lt.HJ, DoI 15Nov.17-I
Stone,Lt.R, 201Sqn. KIA 9Aug.18-I
Stone,2Lt.R, 203Sqn. 17May.18-I
Stone,2Lt.RN, POW 16Sep.18-I
Stone,Lt.RS, WIA 24Apr.17-I
Stonehouse,Capt.EC, WIA 25Feb.18-IV
Stones,Lt.GC, Aust. KIA 30May.17-VII
Stonier,2Lt.WJ, 2Apr.17-I, KIA 27Apr.17-I
Stopher,2Lt.AC, POW 12Feb.17-VI
Storey,Capt.A, WIA 26Sep.18-I
Storey,2Lt.G, WIA 27Aug.18-I
Storrs,2Lt.HL, DoW 15Jun.18-I
Story,2Lt.AES, 27Jun.16-I
Story,2Lt.,Lt.LC, 28Jun.18-I, KIA 1Jul.18-I
Stott,2Lt.FT, 9Aug.18-I
Stott,2Lt.J, KIA 23Aug.18-I
Stott,Capt.JNS, WIA 1Jun.15-I, WIA 21Jun.15-I, WIA POW 19Sep.15-I
Stout,2Lt.GRY, KIA 30Apr.17-I
Stout,1Lt.PV, US. WIA 28Sep.18-IIB
Stovin,Lt.FC, KIA 24Apr.18-I
Stoyle,Lt.AP, 18Jun.18-I
Strachan,Lt.AR, 18Sep.18-I, KIA 20Sep.18-I
Strachan,Lt.B, KIA 18May.17-I
Strang,Lt.AR, POW 13Jul.18-IV
Strang-Ward,2Lt.FL, POW 2Oct.18-I
Strange,2Lt.CG, 5Jul.18-I
Strange,Lt.GJ, 13Jul.18-I, KIA 24Sep.18-I
Strange,2Lt.HM, POW 31Aug.16-I
Strange,Lt.,Capt.,LtCol.LA, 22Aug.14-I, 22Nov.14-I, 10Mar.15-I, 16Apr.15-I, 23Apr.15-I, 28Apr.15-I, 30Apr.15-I, 3May.15-I, 8May.15-I, 10May.15-I, 24May.15-I, 3Jun.15-I, 6Jun.15-I, 16Jun.15-I, 28Jul.15-I, 30Oct.18-I
Strange,Lt.LAT, POW 31Mar.17-I
Strangham,2Lt.CF, POW .17-IX
Strangward,2Lt.FL, 29Sep.18-I
Stransom,Lt.NG, KIA 10May.18-I
Strathearn,1AM.JG, KIA 24Apr.18-III
Strathearne,Lt.WM, POW 2Sep.18-I
Strathy,FSLt.FS, KIA 17Aug.17-I
Strathy,Spr.JM, KIA 14Sep.16-I
Strathy Mackay,Lt.H, KIA 9Sep.16-I
Strauch,1Lt.HH, US. KIA 18Sep.18-IIB
Strauss,2Lt.,Lt.VA, 8Jul.16-I, KIA 27Nov.16-I
Straw,Lt.LLK, 21May.18-I, 14Oct.18-I, KIA 4Nov.18-I
Strawn,1Lt.KP, US. KIA 16Sep.18-IIB
Stream,Lt.JH, KIA 19Feb.18-I
Streatfield,Capt.GHB, WIA 30Mar.18-I
Streather,2Lt.EHP, KIA 11Sep.17-I
Street,Lt.CC, KIA 26Jun.17-I
Streeter,Lt.H, Aust. KIA 17Feb.18-I
Strewthers,1AM.EJ, INT 4Jun.18-III
Strickland,2Lt.CH, WIA 17Jun.18-I
Strickland,2Lt.HCW, 2Apr.17-I
Strickland,2Lt.WA, WIA POW 12Jul.17-I
Stringer,Lt.CH, WIA 28Mar.15-I
Stringer,Lt.FH, DFC POW 2Oct.18-I
Stringer,2Lt.JS, POW 2Sep.18-I
Stronech,Lt.JA, 18Jul.18-I
Strong,2Lt.AR, US. POW 10Jul.18-IIB
Strong,Capt.CC, 20Nov.15-I, 25Nov.15-I, 28Nov.15-I, POW 1Dec.15-I
Stroud,Lt.EHN, KIA 21Apr.18-I
Stroud,2Lt.H, WIA 17Jun.17-I
Stroud,Capt.HC, KIA 8Mar.18-III
Strover,Lt.EJ, POW 28Dec.15-I
Strover?,Lt.G, 28Nov.15-I
Struben,2Lt.LF, 14Oct.16-I, KIA 16Nov.16-I
Struben,Lt.HM, POW 25Jul.18-I
Strudwick,Lt.CR, WIA 25Aug.18-I
Strugnell,2Lt.VS, 15Sep.15-I, 5Feb.16-I, 20Feb.16-I
Strugnell,Capt.WV, 11May.17-I
Stuart,2Lt.CE, POW 26Sep.17-I
Stuart,Lt.J, 2Sqn. 8Jul.18-I, WIA 9Jul.18-I
Stuart,2Lt.J, 8Sqn. 27Apr.18-I
Stuart,2Lt.J, 15Sqn. 25Jan.16-I, 8Feb.16-I
Stuart,Capt.JD, KIA 6Mar.17-I
Stuart,Capt.JM, KIA 13Apr.17-I
Stuart-Smith,2Lt.H, KIA 15Sep.18-I
Stuart-Smith,Lt.PJ, KIA 8May.18-I
Stubbings,Lt., name Stubbins?, 12Sqn. 23Aug.18-I, 28Sep.18-I
Stubbington,Sgt.HR, 10May.18-III
Stubbins, see Stubbings
Stubbs,Lt.CL, 12Apr.18-I
Stubbs,Lt.EW, 30Nov.15-I
Stubbs,2Lt.HB, POW 28Sep.15-I
Stubbs,Capt.JS, 20May.18-I, 30Oct.18-I
Stubbs,2Lt.RA, DoW 8Jun.16-I
Stubbs,Lt.WH, POW DoW 25Jun.18-I
Stubings,2Lt.CA, WIA 3Nov.18-I
Stubley,2Lt.LM, KIA 21Aug.18-I
Studholme,Sgt.W, WIA 17Jun.17-I, 6Jul.17-I, DoW 5.9.1917 3Sep.17-I
Stupart,2Lt.AV, WIA 23Aug.18-I
Sturdee,GL., 3WgRNAS. 12Oct.16-I
Sturgess,2Lt.TM, POW 24Jun.17-I
Sturrock,2Lt.J, WIA 7Dec.17-I
Sturrock,2Lt.TGG, KIA 16Oct.16-I
Sturruck,LCpl.C, WIA POW 28May.17-I
Sturt,Lt.CG, WIA 29Apr.17-I
Style,2Lt.,Lt.CS, WIA 15Jun.18-IV, WIA 5Oct.18-IV
Styles,1Lt.CH, US. POW 28Sep.18-IIB
Styles,2Lt.WB, WIA POW 18Aug.17-I
Sugden,Lt.JEW, POW 5Jun.18-I
Sugden-Wilson,Lt.WH, 13Sep.15-I, WIA POW 21Sep.15-I
Suiter,2Lt.WC, US. DSC 25Aug.18-IIB, KIA 12Sep.18-IIB
Sullivan,2Lt.FO, KIFA 23Apr.17-I
Sully,Lt.JA, 12Jun.17-I
Summerfelt,2Lt.A, 5Jun.18-I, POW 21Jul.18-I
Summers,Capt.ASM, KIA 15Sep.16-I
Summers,Lt.CC, 28Oct.18-I
Summers,Sgt.JDC, 23Jun.18-I, POW 31Jul.18-I
Summers,2Lt.,Lt.,Capt..JK, MC 22Jun.15-I, 3Jul.15-I, 28Aug.15-I, 16Sep.16-I, 25Sep.16-I, 4Jul.18-I, WIA 8Jul.18-I, 8Aug.18-I, POW 12Aug.18-I
Summers,Cpl.W, WIA POW 3Sep.16-I
Summers,Capt.WA, MC 8Jul.16-I, 28Jul.16-I, KIA 1Aug.16-I
Sumner,1Lt.HR, US. KIA? 26Sep.18-IIB
Sumsion,Lt.F, KIA 4Nov.18-I
Sumsion,Lt.WL, WIA 24Apr.18-I
Surgey,Lt.F, WIA 22Oct.16-I
Surne?,Capt.GW, 21Nov.17-I
Susman,2Lt.W, WIA 19May.18-I
Sutcliffe,1AM., 5Sqn. 9May.15-I, 29May.15-I, 8Jun.15-I, 9Jun.15-I
Sutcliffe,2Lt.AL, WIA POW 26Sep.17-I
Sutcliffe,2Lt.CA, POW 19Sep.17-I
Sutcliffe,Maj.CE, KIA 6Jun.17-I
Sutcliffe,Capt.FR, POW 26Feb.18-I
Sutcliffe,2Lt.G, US. KIA 23Oct.18-I
Sutcliffe,Pte.GLE, KIA 30Aug.18-IV
Sutcliffe,Lt.JET, POW 9Aug.18-I
Sutcliffe,2Lt.S, KIA 2Oct.17-I
Sutcliffe,2Lt.TC, WIA 3Oct.18-I
Sutherland,2Lt.AM, 29Sqn. POW 13May.17-I
Sutherland,2Lt.AMcB, 65Sqn. KIA 2Jul.18-I
Sutherland,FSLt.IF, WIA 15Oct.17-I
Sutherland,Lt.JL, 52Sqn. 13Oct.18-I
Sutherland,Lt.JLC, 104Sqn. POW 13Aug.18-I
Sutherland,Lt.LW, Aust. 3Jan.18-VII
Sutherland,2Lt.P, USAS. WIA 13Aug.18-I, WIA 26Aug.18-I
Sutherst,1AM.F, KIA 15May.18-VIII
Sutton,Capt.BE, DSO MC WIA 5Sep.17-I
Sutton,Capt.C, WIA? 24Feb.18-I
Sutton,Lt.GEF, 3Jul.16-I, 7Jul.16-I
Sutton,Lt.MF, WIA POW 18May.18-I
Sutton,Lt.OM, 24May.17-I
Sutton,Capt.SJ?, 16Aug.17-I
Sutton-Gardner,2Lt.W, KIA 6Mar.17-I
Swabb,1Lt.JM, US. WIA 8Sep.18-IIB
Swain,Sgt.FJ, KIA 27Feb.18-I
Swaine,2Lt.SW, 22Mar.18-I
Swale,Capt.E, 17Sep.18-I, 8Oct.18-I
Swales,Lt.A, 8Aug.18-I, WIA 29Aug.18-I
Swann,2Lt.GH, KIA 18Oct.17-I
Swann,Lt.GWW, DoW 24Mar.17-I
Swann,2Lt.TH, WIA POW leg 26Sep.18-I
Swanston,Capt.JR, 1Oct.18-I
Swart,2Lt.OB, POW 9Feb.18-I
Swart,Lt., 5Sqn. 16Jun.15-I, 26Oct.15-I
Swart,Capt.JG, 6Aug.16-I
Swatridge,2Lt.CJ, WIA 14Jul.18-I
Swayne,Sgt.EA, WIA 11Aug.18-I
Swayze,Lt.WK, POW 4Sep.18-I
Sweet,2Lt.GA, KIA 25Jun.18-I
Sweet,Capt.LH, KIA 22Jun.16-I
Sweeting,2Lt.AE, WIA 30Mar.18-I
Swift,2AM.WH, KIA 20Nov.17-I
Swinebroad,2Lt.AW, US. 15Sep.18-IIB
Swinburne,Lt.HL, 17Jul.18-VII
Swinburne,FSLt.TR, KIA 8Jun.17-I
Sworder,Lt.HP, KIA 2Apr.17-I
Sworder,Lt.N, DoW 17Apr.18-I
Sydie,Lt.JE, POW 30Jun.18-I
Sykes,Lt.JA, 48Sqn. KIA 4Oct.18-I
Sykes,Lt.JA, 65Sqn. KIA 16Jun.18-I
Sykes,2Lt.JJ, US. KIA 1Aug.18-IIB
Sykes,FSLt.R, WIA 20Sep.17-I
Symington,2Lt.DAC, 19Oct.15-I, 10Nov.15-I, 20Nov.15-I, 19Dec.15-I
Symonds,2Lt.JG, KIA 4Nov.18-I
Symonds,2Lt.SLH, KIA 12Nov.17-I
Symonds,Lt.TS, 59Sqn., see Symons
Symondson,Lt.F, 30Mar.18-IV
Symons,Lt.,Capt.HL, Can. 15Nov.17-I, 21Feb.18-I
Symons,2Lt.JW, 17Mar.18-I
Symons,Lt.KWA, KIA 30Jul.18-I
Symons,Lt.PW, Aust. KIA 4Nov.18-I
Symons,2Lt.SW, WIA 28Mar.18-I
Symons,Lt.,Capt.TS, DFC 26Aug.18-I, KIA 29Sep.18-I

T

Tabachnik,Capt.A, US. WIA 15Sep.18-IIB
Taber,1Lt.DF, USAS. WIA 16Jul.18-I
Tagent,2Lt.HW, 2Aug.16-I, KIA 24Mar.17-I
Tailer,Sgt.WH, US. KIA 5Feb.18-IIC
Talbot,1AM., 20Sqn. 18Mar.16-I
Talbot,Lt.AR, 15May.18-I, POW 19Oct.18-I
Talbot,2Lt.FW, POW 12Oct.17-I
Talbot,Lt.J, WIA 6Sep.18-I
Talbot,1Lt.R, CMH USMC. 4Oct.18-I, US. 14Oct.18-IIB
Talbot,2Lt.RF, 8Sqn. KIA 2Sep.18-I
Talbot,2Lt.,Lt.RF, 19Sqn. 22Aug.16-I, KIA 26Aug.16-I
Tallboys,GL., 217Sqn. 23Apr.18-I
Tambling,2Lt.HG, POW 23Aug.17-I
Tanfield,Lt.AH, KIA 13Apr.17-I
Tanglin,Lt.J, WIA 28May.17-I
Tannenbaum,2Lt.H, POW 2Jun.18-I
Tanner,Maj.FI, inj 14Sep.18-I
Tanner,FSLt.JC, DoI 7Jul.17-I
Tanner,2Lt.KE, 21Jul.17-I
Tanner,Capt.PV, KIA 27Mar.18-I
Tanney,2Lt.WW, USAS. POW 30Aug.18-I
Tanqueray,Lt.JFB, Can. 8Aug.18-I
Tansley,2Lt.HE, POW 21May.18-I
Taplin,Lt.LTE, DFC Aust. 17Jan.18-VII, 3Sep.18-I, WIA POW 5Sep.18-I
Tapp,Lt.HD, KIA 24Jul.17-I
Tappin,Pte., 45Sqn. 10Aug.17-I
Tapping,2Lt.A, POW 15Sep.18-I
Tapscott,FSLt.HV, INT 12May.17-I
Tarbolton,Lt.JS, WIA 23Aug.18-I
Tarbutt,Lt.FC, US. KIA 16Jun.18-I
Tarrant,Lt.FJ, KIA 17Feb.18-I
Tarver,Sgt.JM, WIA 30Oct.18-I
Tasker,2Lt.WTB, POW 5Apr.17-I
Tate,2Lt.ACR, KIA 2May.18-I
Tate,Lt.HL, 4Nov.18-I
Tate,2Lt.RM, WIA 8Mar.18-I
Tatham,2Lt.LCS, KIA 10Jan.18-I
Tatnall,2Lt.EW, 26Jun.18-I, POW 29Jun.18-I
Tatton,Capt.EH, KIA 20Apr.18-I
Tatton?,Lt.H, WIA 15Sep.16-I
Tayler,2Lt.CC, 14May.17-I, WIA 31Jul.17-I
Tayler,Lt.HM, WIA POW 15Jul.17-I
Tayler,Lt.,Capt.StCC, 11Jul.17-I, KIA 17Mar.18-I
Taylerson,Lt.NA, KIA 19May.18-I
Taylor,Pte1., 97Sqn. 30Aug.18-I
Taylor,2Lt.A, POW 26Sep.17-I
Taylor,2Lt.AD, WIA 23Apr.17-I
Taylor,2Lt.AF, 29Sep.18-I, WIA 5Oct.18-I
Taylor,2Lt.AGV, POW DoW 17Oct.17-I
Taylor,Lt.ALD, Aust., initials KLD? KIA 20May.18-I
Taylor,2Lt.ALT, POW 16Mar.18-I
Taylor,2Lt.AVG, 19Sep.17-I
Taylor,2AM.CC, DoI 7Jul.17-III
Taylor,Pte.CV, KIA 10May.18-I
Taylor,1Lt.CW, US. KIA 22Oct.18-IIB
Taylor,Lt.D, 22Nov.17-I
Taylor,Lt.DPB, KIA 14Mar.16-I
Taylor,2Lt.E, 23Sqn. DoW 26.9.1917 26Sep.17-I
Taylor,Lt.E, US. 79Sqn. KIA 25Aug.18-I
Taylor,2Lt.EA, US. KIA 26Sep.18-IIB
Taylor,Lt.EE, INT 16Sep.18-I
Taylor,2Lt.EF, WIA 9Mar.18-I
Taylor,2Lt.ER, 20Sep.17-I
Taylor,2Lt.ET, 18Nov.17-I
Taylor,2Lt.FG, 11Mar.17-I
Taylor,2Lt.FG, WIA 23Mar.17-I
Taylor,Lt.FH, Can. 23Mar.18-I, 10Nov.18-I
Taylor,2Lt.FJ, inj 14Feb.17-I
Taylor,2Lt.FT, 6Mar.18-I
Taylor,Capt.GH, WIA 26Jul.18-VI
Taylor?,Lt.H, 3Sqn. 15Sep.16-I
Taylor,Sgt.H, 25Sqn. WIA POW 18Jun.16-I
Taylor,Lt.H, 68(A)Sqn. Aust. 20Nov.17-I
Taylor,2Lt.HA, KIA 27Sep.16-I
Taylor,Lt.HF, 17Sep.18-I
Taylor,Sgt.HG, WIA 1May.17-I
Taylor,2Lt.HL, WIA 10Apr.18-I
Taylor,FSLt.HW, 21Jun.17-I, WIA 20Jul.17-I
Taylor,2Lt.JB, KIA 28Mar.18-I
Taylor,2Lt.JC, WIA 26Aug.16-I, WIA POW 6Sep.16-I
Taylor,2Lt.JY, KIA 6Jul.17-I
Taylor,2Lt.LG, 97Sqn. POW 22Aug.18-I
Taylor,Lt.LG, 100Sqn. POW 24Jan.18-I
Taylor,Lt.MS, Can. KIA 7Jul.18-I
Taylor,2Lt.NJ, WIA POW 19Sep.17-I
Taylor,Lt.NS, 27Oct.18-IV
Taylor,Capt.NW, 26Mar.18-I
Taylor,AG.HF, 23Apr.18-I
Taylor,2Lt.PS, inj 26Dec.16-I, inj 17Mar.17-I
Taylor,1Lt.RC, US. KIA 16Sep.18-IIB
Taylor,2Lt.RC, POW 6Nov.17-I
Taylor,2Lt.RE, 41Sqn. KIA 17Sep.17-I
Taylor,Lt.RE, 54Sqn. POW 8Aug.18-I
Taylor,Sgt.RW, KIA 20Nov.17-I
Taylor,2Lt.SH, POW 14Sep.17-I
Taylor,Capt.StCC, 10Mar.18-I
Taylor,2Lt.SW, 10May.18-I
Taylor,2Lt.T, KIA 28Mar.18-I
Taylor,2AM.TH, POW 3Sep.17-I
Taylor,2Lt.W, 202Sqn. 17Jun.18-I
Taylor,2Lt.W, 30Sqn. POW 17Jan.18-VIII
Taylor,2Lt.WDB, WIA 28Mar.17-I
Taylor,2Lt.WE, US. KIA 31May.18-I
Taylor,1Lt.WH, US. 95thUS. KIA 18Sep.18-IIB
Taylor,2Lt.WH, 83Sqn. POW 16Mar.18-I
Teale,2Lt.G, 30Dec.15-I, 5Jan.16-I, 12Jan.16-I, 25Jan.16-I
Tearle,2Lt.LG, WIA 6Sep.18-I
Tebbit,2Lt.TL, 21Aug.17-I
Tedbury,2Lt.RN, DoW 4Sep.18-I
Tedder,Sgt.T, 30Oct.18-I
Telfer,Lt.HC, POW 28Sep.18-I
Temperley,Capt.CJ, WIA 28Oct.17-I
Tempest,2Lt.ED?, initials ER? 17Jan.16-I
Tempest,Lt.,Capt.ER, 25Jan.16-I, 30Nov.17-I
Tempest,2Lt.WC, POW 24Jun.18-I

Tempest,2Lt.WJ, 1Oct.16-*III*
Ten Eyck,1Lt.WB, *US.* **WIA** 29Oct.18-*IIB*
Tench,Sgt.GH, MM **POW DoW** 28Jul.18-*I*
Tennant,2Lt.J, 16Aug.17-*I*
Tennant,Capt.,Maj.,Lt.Col.JE, 19Feb.16-*I*, 13Aug.16-*VIII*, **POW** 25Mar.18-*VIII*
Tennant,2Lt.PS, **WIA POW** 1Nov.18-*I*
Tester,Dvr.G, **KIA** 28Sep.17-*I*
Tetlow,Lt.CL, **KIA** 23Aug.16-*I*
Thackrah,2Lt.NH, **POW** 24Mar.18-*I*
Thamer,2Lt.O, **INT** 6Jan.18-*I*
Thatcher,2Lt.AR, **POW** 5Sep.18-*I*
Thaw,Sgt.W, *US.* **WIA** 24May.16-*IIA*
Thayer,1Lt.HW, *US.* **WIA** 2Oct.18-*IIB*
Thayre,Lt.FH, *16Sqn.* 18Mar.16-*I*
Thayre,Capt.FJH, MC *20Sqn.* **KIA** 9Jun.17-*I*
Thenault,Capt.G, *French.* 24May.16-*IIA*
Theron,Lt.WV, 5Jun.18-*I*
Thierry,Lt.LH, **KIA** 10Dec.17-*I*
Thiery,2Lt.FG, **KIA** 17Sep.16-*I*
Thom,2Lt.,Lt.WD, 28Apr.17-*I*, 11Aug.17-*I*
Thomas,Lt., *72Sqn.* 15Sep.18-*VIII*
Thomas,Lt.BSB, MC 10Aug.18-*I*
Thomas,2Lt.C, **INT** 15Sep.18-*I*
Thomas,2Lt.CH, **POW** 10Nov.18-*I*
Thomas,2Lt.CLS, **KIA** 6Sep.16-*I*
Thomas,2Lt.CR, **POW DoW** 17Aug.17-*I*
Thomas,2Lt.D, **KIA** 28Jun.18-*IV*
Thomas,2Lt.DU, 10Aug.18-*I*, **KIA** 27Oct.18-*I*
Thomas,Lt.EA, **WIA** 13Apr.17-*I*
Thomas,2Lt.EG, 12Apr.18-*I*, 22Aug.18-*I*
Thomas,Capt.FS, **KIA** 16Feb.18-*I*
Thomas,Lt.FWH, MC **DoW** 5.1.18 20Aug.17-*VI*
Thomas,Lt.G, *Sqn?* **POW**, *first name* Geraint 10Apr.18-*I*
Thomas,Lt.GF, 12Jun.18-*I*
Thomas,2Lt.GP, *USAS. 17thUS.* **KIA** 22Sep.18-*I*
Thomas,2Lt.GPF, *55Sqn.* **POW** 10Mar.18-*I*
Thomas,2Lt.H, *US?* 9Oct.18-*I*, **POW** 26Oct.18-*I*
Thomas,2Lt.HS, **KIA** 29Sep.18-*I*
Thomas,2Lt.JB?, **KIA** 23Jan.18-*VII*
Thomas,1AM.JM?, 29Nov.17-*I*
Thomas,Lt.JP, 8Oct.18-*I*
Thomas,Lt.M, 19Aug.17-*I*
Thomas,Lt.MN, **KIA** 5Aug.16-*I*
Thomas,2Lt.,Lt.MW 12Sep.15-*I*, 20Nov.15-*I*, 8Jul.16-*I*
Thomas,2Lt.OV, 22Jun.16-*I*
Thomas,2Lt.RA, 29Sep.18-*I*
Thomas,Sgt.RH, **INT** 9Nov.18-*III*
Thomas,Capt.RN, **KIA** 23Jul.17-*VII*
Thomas,2Lt.WL, 11Mar.18-*I*, **WIA** 24Apr.18-*I*
Thomas,2Lt.,Lt.WV, 16Jul.18-*I*, 16Sep.18-*I*, 30Oct.18-*I*
Thompson,2Lt.A, 27Oct.17-*I*, **POW** 9Nov.17-*I*
Thompson,Capt.AAB, 5Jan.16-*I*, 18Sep.15-*I*, 21Sep.15-*I*, 23Sep.15-*I*
Thompson,Lt.AH, **KIA** 26Sep.18-*I*
Thompson,Lt.AR, **KIA** 10Aug.18-*I*
Thompson,Lt.CAW, **inj** 26Dec.16-*I*
Thompson,Lt.CD, **POW** 16Aug.17-*I*
Thompson,Lt.CRJ, *Aust. 19Sqn* 15Jun.17-*I*
Thompson,2Lt.,Lt.CRJ, SA. *84Sqn* 27Jun.18-*I*, **WIA** 15Sep.18-*I*
Thompson,Lt.CWM, **POW** 29Sep.18-*I*
Thompson,2Lt.DA, **POW** 28Sep.18-*I*
Thompson,Lt.DS, 17Apr.18-*I*
Thompson,2Lt.F, 13May.17-*I*
Thompson,Lt.FG, **POW** 20Jul.18-*I*
Thompson,Capt.GE, MC 21Mar.18-*I*
Thompson,2Lt.GF, *US.* **POW** 12Jun.18-*I*
Thompson,2Lt.GI, 27Oct.18-*I*
Thompson,Lt.GM, DFC 24Aug.18-*I*
Thompson,2Lt.H, *Can.* **POW DoW** 18.9.1916 17Sep.16-*I*
Thompson,Lt.HK, 8Aug.17-*I*
Thompson,1Lt.HS, *US.* **KIA** 16Sep.18-*IIB*
Thompson,Lt.HT, **WIA** 11Jan.18-*IV*
Thompson,2Lt.HV, **KIA** 26Sep.17-*I*
Thompson,2Lt.J, *19Sqn.* **KIA** 16Oct.16-*I*
Thompson,Lt.J, *45Sqn.* 6Mar.17-*I*, **KIA** 11Mar.17-*I*
Thompson,2Lt.J, *107Sqn.* 26Sep.18-*I*
Thompson,Lt.J, *NFlt.* **KIA** 28Oct.18-*I*
Thompson,Lt.JC, **WIA POW** 27Mar.18-*I*
Thompson,2Lt.JRW, **DoW** 22Mar.18-*I*
Thompson,Lt.JW, **POW** 23Jun.18-*I*
Thompson,2Lt.L, **KIA** 8Aug.18-*I*
Thompson,2Lt.LM, **inj** *Can.* 21Apr.18-*I*, 22Aug.18-*I*
Thompson,Capt.P, **KIA** 23Mar.18-*I*
Thompson,Lt.RB, **WIA** 16Jul.18-*I*
Thompson,2Lt.RE, *80Sqn.* **KIA** 1Oct.18-*I*
Thompson,2Lt.RE, *US. 96thUS.* **KIA** 13Sep.18-*IIB*
Thompson,2Lt.S, *27Sqn.* **POW** 21Aug.17-*I*
Thompson,2Lt.S, *43Sqn.* 12Jul.17-*I*, **WIA inj** 14Sep.17-*I*
Thompson,2AM.S, *45Sqn.* **WIA POW** 5Jun.17-*I*
Thompson,2Lt.SF, *20Sqn.* **WIA POW** 19Aug.17-*I*
Thompson,Lt.,Capt.SFH, *22Sqn.* 9May.18-*I*, 23Jun.18-*I*, **KIA** 27Sep.18-*I*
Thompson,1Lt.SP, *US.* **KIA** 5Jul.18-*IIB*
Thompson,1Lt.SW, *US.* **WIA** 28Jul.18-*IIB*
Thompson,2Lt.VW, 23Nov.17-*I*
Thompson,2Lt.WC, 13Aug.17-*I*
Thompson,Lt.WG, **KIA** 14Jul.17-*I*
Thompson,2Lt.WM, **KIA** 9Oct.18-*I*
Thomsen,Capt.CJ, **POW** 23Apr.18-*IV*
Thomson,Lt., *12Sqn.* 17Mar.17-*I*
Thomson,Lt., *108Sqn.* 4Nov.18-*I*
Thomson,2Lt.AN, **WIA** 17Jul.18-*I*
Thomson,Lt.BG, *Aust.* 30Aug.18-*I*, **KIA** 3Oct.18-*I*
Thomson,2Lt.EG, 20Nov.17-*I*
Thomson,Sgt.FS, **POW** 17Sep.18-*I*
Thomson,2Lt.H, **KIA** 12Jun.18-*I*
Thomson,Lt.HE, **POW** 16Jun.18-*I*
Thomson,Lt.J, **WIA** 15Apr.18-*I*
Thomson,2Lt.JH, **KIA** 9Oct.18-*I*
Thomson,2Lt.RR, **KIA** 5Nov.18-*I*
Thomson,Lt.RWL, **POW** 21Oct.18-*I*
Thomson,2Lt.SA, **KIA** 5Sep.18-*I*
Thomson,2Lt.,Lt.T, **inj** 16Dec.16-*I*, **KIA** 25Apr.17-*I*
Thomson,Lt.TC, 14Jul.17-*I*
Thomson,2Lt.WB, *Aust.* 10Oct.18-*I*
Thomson,Lt.WD, **KIA** 5Jan.17-*I*
Thomson,Lt.WM, *Can.* 19May.18-*I*
Thomson-Glover,Capt.JW, **WIA** 6Sep.17-*I*
Thorburn,Capt.J, **KIA** 11Feb.17-*I*
Thorn,2Lt.HJC, **KIA** 30Oct.18-*I*
Thorne,Lt.AB, 8Jun.17-*I*
Thorne,FSLt.AL, 3Sep.16-*I*, **KIFA** 9Apr.17-*I*
Thorne,Capt.GS, **DoW** 18Mar.17-*I*
Thornely,FLt.RR, 11Sep.17-*I*
Thornley,2Lt.SC, **POW** 20Jul.18-*I*
Thornton,2Lt.AJH, 2Apr.18-*I*, 7May.18-*I*
Thornton,2Lt.CP, 4Mar.17-*I*, **POW** 5Apr.17-*I*
Thornton,Lt.FO, 29Aug.18-*I*
Thornton,Sgt.G, **DoW** 21Oct.15-*I*
Thornton,2Lt.HJ, **KIA** 25Sep.17-*III*
Thornton,Lt.HV, **KIA** 11May.18-*IV*
Thornton,2Lt.WH, **WIA** 29Aug.18-*I*
Thornton,2Lt.WR, **POW** 26Sep.18-*I*
Thornton-Norris,2Lt.G, 25Oct.18-*I*
Thorold,FSLt.HK, 17Mar.16-*V*
Thorowgood,2Lt.LV, **WIA** 21Sep.17-*I*
Thorp,2Lt.CE, **DoW** 30Aug.18-*I*
Thorp,2Lt.FH, **DoW** 31.3.1918 30Mar.18-*I*
Thorpe,2Lt.CE, **POW** 14Aug.18-*I*
Thouless,2Lt.AC, **KIA** 26Apr.16-*VIII*
Thrall,2Lt.LR, *US.* **KIA** 4Nov.18-*IIB*
Thresher,2Lt.CEW, **POW** 6Nov.18-*I*
Thrower,2Lt.LA, **KIA** 18Jul.18-*III*
Thuell,2Lt.WJ, **KIA** 22Oct.16-*I*
Thursfield,2Lt.JT, **WIA** 14Jun.18-*I*
Thwaites,2Lt.BW, 28Oct.18-*I*
Thwaytes,2Lt.J, **KIA** 18Mar.17-*I*
Thyne,Capt.TK, 19Jul.18-*III*
Tibbetts,2Lt.JL, **WIA POW** 23Sep.16-*I*
Tibbles,AG.2AM.A, **WIA** 20Jul.17-*I*
Tibbs,Capt.TL, 9Apr.17-*I*
Tichenor,1Lt.CH, *US.* **POW** 10Jul.18-*IIB*
Tidmarsh,2Lt.,Capt.DM, MC 2Apr.16-*I*, 21Apr.16-*I*, 30Apr.16-*I*, **POW** 11Apr.17-*I*
Tidswell,Capt.CR, 12Aug.16-*I*, 6Sep.16-*I*, **KIA** 16Oct.16-*I*
Tidy,Sgt.PS, 7Jun.18-*I*, **WIA** 15Jun.18-*I*
Tiffany,2Lt.G, *US.* **POW** 3Nov.18-*IIB*
Till,2Lt.E, **WIA** 27Oct.18-*I*
Tillard,2Lt.TA, **WIA** 6Jul.16-*I*
Tillet,2Lt.RAW, **KIA** 24Mar.17-*I*
Tilley,2AM.H, **inj** 27Apr.17-*I*
Tillie,2Lt.,Capt.AR, 28Nov.15-*I*, 29Feb.16-*I*, **KIA** 11May.16-*I*
Tillinghurst,1Lt.TE, *USAS.* **POW** 22Sep.18-*I*
Tilney,2Lt.,Maj.LA, 8Aug.15-*I*, 11Aug.15-*I*, **KIA** 9Mar.18-*I*
Timmins,2Lt.L, **POW** 18Oct.18-*I*
Timmis,2Lt.LW, **POW** 30Nov.17-*I*
Tims,2Lt.LC, 9Nov.17-*I*
Timson,Lt.PWJ, **WIA** 16Sep.18-*I*, **KIA** 26Sep.18-*I*
Tinham,2Lt.AW, 29Sep.18-*I*
Tinney,2Lt.HG, **POW** 13Aug.17-*I*
Tipping,Lt.FB, **KIA** 19Aug.17-*I*
Tiptaft,2Lt.CP, MC **WIA** 23Nov.17-*I*
Tipton,Capt.RJ, *14Sqn.* **POW** 18Jun.16-*VII*
Tipton,Capt.RJ, *40Sqn.* **WIA** 9Mar.18-*I*
Tipton,1Lt.WD, *USAS.* **WIA POW** legs 26Aug.18-*I*
Tison,2Lt.M, **POW** 8Aug.18-*I*
Tittmann,1Lt.HH, *US.* **WIA** 1Jul.18-*IIB*
Tivy,2Lt.RV, **WIA** 17Nov.16-*I*
Tobin-Willis,2Lt.JG, **DoW** 17Aug.17-*I*
Tod,Lt.GOD, *US.* **WIA** 9Aug.18-*I*
Todd,Lt.A, MC **POW DoW** 16.4.1917 12Apr.17-*I*
Todd,FLt.AS, **KIA** 4Jan.17-*I*
Todd,2Lt.FG, **KIA** 12Feb.18-*I*
Todd,1Lt.G, *US.* **WIA** 23Oct.18-*IIB*
Todd,2Lt.HC, 9Mar.17-*I*, 6Apr.17-*I*, 7Apr.17-*I*
Todd,2Lt.,Capt.J, MC 24Feb.18-*I*, 30May.18-*I*
Todd,2Lt.JD, **WIA** 9Nov.18-*I*
Todd,2Lt.RM, *USAS.* **POW** 26Aug.18-*I*
Todd,1Lt.vW, *US.* **POW** 11Aug.18-*IIB*
Todman,Lt.CV, **KIA** 3Aug.18-*I*
Toes,2Lt.A, **KIA** 27Oct.18-*I*
Tolhurst,Lt.BJ, **KIA** 22Apr.17-*I*
Tollemache,2Lt.AHW, **KIA** 19Jul.16-*I*
Tollerbey,Sgt.AG, **KIA** 23Apr.17-*I*
Tollerfield,Cpl.R, **WIA** 22Apr.17-*I*
Tollerfield,2AM.RE, 22Oct.16-*I*
Tolley,Lt.CR, 28Sep.18-*I*
Tolman,2Lt.CJ, **KIA** 27Sep.18-*I*
Tomer,2Lt.SE, 20Apr.17-*I*
Tomkies,2Lt.HL, **KIA** 25Apr.17-*I*
Tomlin,2Lt.HF, 14Sep.17-*I*, **KIA** 28Sep.17-*I*
Tomlinson,Capt.H, MC **POW DoW** 2Apr.17-*I*
Tomson,Lt.WJM, **inj POW** 10Jul.16-*I*
Tonge,Lt.VGA, 29Jul.18-*I*
Tonkin,Lt.AV, *Aust.* 10Jan.18-*VII*, 4Jun.18-*VII*
Tonks,Capt.AJB, 28Sep.18-*I*
Tonks,2Lt.HAC, *Aust.* 21Jun.17-*I*
Toogood,2Lt.Y?, **WIA POW** 26May.17-*I*
Tooke,FLt.BC, **POW** 20Aug.16-*I*
Tooley,AM., *11Sqn.* 25Mar.17-*I*
Toomer,Capt.SE, 30Aug.18-*I*
Toomey,2Lt.,Lt.MA, 8Aug.18-*I*, 10Aug.18-*I*, **WIA** 29Aug.18-*I*
Tooms,Sgt.CS, **KIA** 24Jan.17-*I*
Toone,2Lt.JW, 31Mar.16-*I*, **POW** 2Jul.16-*I*
Topham,2Lt.M, **KIA** 13Apr.17-*I*
Topliffe,Sgt.G, **POW** 22Jun.16-*I*
Topliss,2Lt.RH, **WIA POW** 8Mar.18-*I*
Topping,2Lt.J, **KIA** 16Sep.18-*VII*
Torrington,Lt.Lord, **POW** 29Nov.16-*VI*
Torry,2Lt.AJD, MC **KIA** 9Oct.17-*I*
Tottman,Sgt.D, **POW** 28Jul.18-*I*
Touchstone,Lt.GR, *USAS.* **WIA POW** 8Aug.18-*I*
Toulmin,Lt.H, MC **KIA** 17Sep.18-*I*
Towell,2Lt.W, **WIA** 31Jul.18-*I*
Tower,Capt.HC, **KIA** 19Sep.16-*I*
Towler,2Lt.FS, **KIA** 5Nov.18-*I*
Towler,FLt.HF, 20Mar.16-*I*, 23Mar.16-*I*
Town,2Lt.,Lt.J, DFC 2Sep.18-*I*, 1Oct.18-*I*
Towne,Lt.LNF, **POW** 3Apr.18-*I*
Townesend,Lt.EJD, **WIA POW** 5Apr.17-*I*
Townley,Lt.DC, **POW** 31Jul.18-*I*
Townsend,Lt., *12Sqn.* 3Oct.18-*I*, 10Nov.18-*I*
Townsend,2AM.A, **WIA** 6Nov.17-*I*
Townsend,2Lt.D, **KIA** 16Aug.17-*I*
Townsend,2Lt.HE, **POW** 21May.18-*I*
Townsend,TLt.HT, 1Oct.18-*I*
Townsend,2Lt.RGR, **inj** 20Sep.17-*I*
Townsend,Capt.RTR, 20Nov.17-*I*, **KIA** 30Nov.17-*I*
Townsend,2Lt.WH, *US.* **DoI** 23Apr.18-*I*
Townsley,2Lt.HA, **KIA** 14Oct.18-*I*
Toy,Lt.EC, **KIA** 25Aug.18-*I*
Tozer,Sgt.HW, **KIA** 25Sep.18-*I*
Trafford-Jones,Lt.E, **KIA** 16May.16-*I*
Traill,Lt.TC, 29May.18-*I*, 1Jun.18-*I*, 30Jun.18-*I*
Trapp,Lt.DJ, **KIA** 19Jul.18-*I*
Trapp,FSLt.GL, **KIA** 12Nov.17-*I*
Tratman,Lt.LWDT, **POW** 18Jul.18-*I*
Trattles,2Lt.A, **POW** 11Jul.17-*I*
Trattles,2Lt.R, **inj** 21Jun.17-*I*
Traunweiser,2Lt.GN, **KIA** 15Apr.18-*I*
Travers,2Lt.CT, **inj** 30Mar.18-*I*
Travers,2Lt.,Lt.FD, 19Dec.17-*VI*, 2Sep.18-*VI*, 3Sep.18-*VI*, 16Sep.18-*VI*
Travers,2Lt.G, **POW** 26Jul.18-*I*
Travis,Lt.FPJ, **WIA** 2Sep.18-*I*
Traviss,2Lt.GG, **WIA** 4Aug.18-*I*
Traynor,FSLt.WE, **KIA** 2Feb.17-*I*
Treachman,Lt.BA, **POW** .17?-*VIII*
Treadwell,1Lt.AM, *US.* **KIA** 6Nov.18-*IIB*
Treadwell,Lt.RN, **DoW** 9.9.1917 11Aug.17-*I*
Trechmann,FSLt.BA, **POW** 30Mar.17-*V*
Tredcroft,Lt.EH, **WIA** 16Jul.18-*I*
Treen,2Lt.WC, **WIA** 9Oct.18-*I*
Treloar,Lt.,Capt.WH, *Aust.* May.15-*VIII*, **POW** 16Sep.15-*VIII*
Trembath,Lt.NT, 5Jul.18-*I*, **POW** 28Oct.18-*I*
Trescowthick,Lt.NC, *Aust.* 14Jul.18-*I*
Tresham,2Lt.WH, **POW** 6Nov.18-*I*
Trevethan,2Lt.,Lt.RM, 27Jul.17-*I*, 8Aug.17-*I*
Trickey,Capt.CT, *US.* **WIA** 28Sep.18-*IIB*
Trimble,Lt.AV, **KIA** 25Aug.18-*I*
Trollip,2Lt.DP, **KIA** 1Apr.18-*I*
Trollope,Capt.JL, 24Mar.18-*I*, **WIA POW** 28Mar.18-*I*
Trollope,2Lt.WK, **DoW** 3.5.1917 30Apr.17-*I*
Trotter,Lt.MT, **WIA** 1Jun.17-*I*
Trotter,Lt.SF, 17Jun.17-*I*, **DoW** 6Jul.17-*I*
Troup,Lt.FC, 11Apr.17-*I*, **WIA** 31Aug.18-*I*
Troup,2Lt.JG, **KIA** 13May.17-*I*
Trubshawe,Lt.WV, **WIA** 8Oct.18-*I*
Truebridge,2Lt.RW, **DoW** 6.5.1918 29Apr.18-*I*
Truesdale,Pte.WH, **WIA** 16Jul.16-*I*
Trulock,2Lt.JC, 7Jun.17-*I*, **POW** 22Jul.17-*I*
Truscott,2Lt.FG, MC **DoW** 6Apr.17-*I*
Trusson,1AM.A, **KIA** 11May.17-*I*
Tubbs,Lt.HVL, 26Feb.18-*I*, **WIA** 21Mar.18-*I*
Tucker,2Lt.DC, **KIA** 24Mar.18-*I*
Tucker,Sgt.DG, *US.* **KIA** 8Jul.18-*IIC*
Tucker,Cpl.L, **WIA** 6Jun.17-*I*
Tucker,2Lt.NP, **WIA** 1Jul.16-*I*
Tucker,2Lt.RH, *US.* **POW** 10Jul.18-*IIB*
Tuckwell,Lt.HAH, **KIA** 4Jul.18-*I*
Tudhope,Lt.JH, *SA.* 22Sep.17-*I*
Tudor-Hart,Lt.WO, **WIA POW** 1Jul.16-*I*
Tudor-Jones,2Lt.CEG, 10Nov.15-*I*, **KIA** 15Dec.15-*I*
Tuffield,Lt.TCS, 3Sep.17-*I*, 11Sep.17-*I*
Tullis,2Lt.JK, **POW** 6Sep.16-*I*
Tulloch,Pbr.J, **WIA** 27May.18-*I*
Tulloch,2Lt.KE, **POW** 29Aug.16-*I*
Tunbridge,Lt.JV, MC *Aust.* **WIA** 11May.17-*VII*
Tunstall,2Lt.W, **WIA** 21Sep.18-*I*
Tupman,2Lt.AL, **KIA** 22Aug.18-*I*
Turk,2Lt.HH, 28Aug.16-*I*
Turnbull,2Lt.AM, **KIA** 25Apr.17-*I*
Turnbull,2Lt.DT, **WIA** 24Aug.18-*I*
Turnbull,2Lt.HP, **KIA** 26Oct.18-*I*
Turnbull,2Lt.JOM, **WIA** 3Feb.18-*I*
Turnbull,2Lt.,Lt.JS, **inj** 7Jun.17-*I*, **WIA** 12Jul.17-*I*, **KIA** 17Jun.18-*I*
Turnbull,2Lt.OMcI, **KIA** 21Sep.18-*I*
Turnbull,2Lt.RBE, **WIA** 21Mar.18-*I*
Turnbull,Lt.SS, **WIA** 29May.18-*I*
Turnbull,Lt.TH, **KIA** 26Oct.18-*I*
Turnbull,2Lt.W, **KIA** 12Jun.17-*I*
Turner,Lt., *12Sqn.* 16May.16-*I*
Turner,2Lt.AE, MC **WIA**? 11Mar.17-*I*, **WIA** 27Jul.17-*I*

Turner,2Lt.C,*32Sqn.* 25Aug.17-*I*
Turner,2Lt.CE, *41Sqn.* **WIA** 3Sep.18-*I*
Turner,Lt.EE, 19May.18-*III*
Turner,2Lt.EG, **POW** 29Jun.18-*I*
Turner,2Lt.ET, **WIA** 23Apr.17-*I*
Turner,Lt.FE, **KIA** 27Sep.18-*I*
Turner,Capt.FMcDC, 8Aug.18-*I*
Turner,2Lt.GD, **WIA** 20Sep.17-*I*
Turner,2Lt.GF, **POW** 24Dec.17-*I*
Turner,Lt.H, *9Sqn.* 14Aug.17-*I*
Turner,Capt.H, *103Sqn.* **KIA** 5Jun.18-*I*
Turner,2Lt.HD, **KIA** 20Aug.17-*I*
Turner,1Lt.HE, *US.* **KIA** 23Oct.18-*IIB*
Turner,Lt.JC, 29Jul.16-*I*, **POW DoW** 3Aug.16-*I*
Turner,Lt.JE, 2May.17-*I*
Turner,Sgt.JF, **KIA** 2Oct.18-*I*
Turner,GL.V, **KIA** 14Apr.17-*I*
Turner,Lt.KK, **POW** 25Aug.16-*I*
Turner,Capt.MH, **WIA** 26Mar.18-*I*
Turner,Lt.MW, 17Aug.17-*I*
Turner,2Lt.R, 4Jul.18-*I*, **WIA** 17Jul.18-*I*
Turner,2Lt.RP, 8Mar.16-*I*, **KIA** 9Mar.16-*I*
Turner,2Lt.W, **POW** 24Jun.18-*I*
Turner,2Lt.WGD, **KIA** 24May.17-*I*
Turner-Coles,Lt.W, **POW** 17Jun.17-*I*
Turney,FSLt.KV, 22Sep.17-*I*
Turton,Lt.GH, 3Oct.15-*I*
Turvey,2Lt.AE, **POW** 11Oct.17-*I*
Tussaud,2Lt.HC, **POW** 22Jul.18-*I*
Twite,AG.WJL, **POW** 21May.18-*I*
Tylee,2Lt.AK, 19May.16-*I*
Tyler,Lt., *6Sqn.* 9Oct.17-*I*
Tyler,1Lt.JC, *US.* **KIA** 18Sep.18-*IIB*
Tylor,2Lt.CE, **WIA POW** 12May.18-*I*
Tyrell,2Lt.,Capt.WA, 29Mar.17-*I*, 6Jun.18-*I*, **KIA** 9Jul.18-*I*
Tyrell,Lt.WA, 5Dec.17-*I*
Tyreman,Lt.CH, **WIA** 19Aug.18-*I*
Tyrrell,2AM.A, **POW** 15May.17-*I*
Tyrrell,Lt.WV, 5Sep.18-*I*
Tysoe,Lt.CG, **POW** 29Apr.18-*I*
Tysoe,Lt.DF, **WIA** 20Sep.18-*I*
Tyson,Capt.EG, **WIA** 15Sep.16-*I*
Tyson,Maj.EJ, DSO MC **DoW** 11.3.1918 11Mar.18-*I*
Tyson,Sgt.SM, *US.* **KIA** 19Jul.18-*IIC*
Tyssen,Capt.JHS, 5May.15-*I*, **WIA** 29May.15-*I*, 25Aug.16-*I*
Tyzack,2Lt.ED, **KIA** 15Sep.17-*I*

U

Uhlman,2Lt.JC, **WIA** 13Aug.18-*I*
Umney,2Lt.JH, 20May.18-*I*, 30May.18-*I*
Underwood,Lt.EN, **KIA** 6Sep.18-*I*
Underwood,2Lt.GM, **KIA** 6Mar.17-*I*
Unger,Lt.KR, *US.* 26Jun.18-*I*
Unger,TLt.KR, 6Nov.18-*I*
Unwin,Capt.EF, 8May.15-*I*, 9May.15-*I*, 10May.15-*I*, **inj** 15May.15-*I*, **WIA** 24Jun.15-*I*
Upfull,2Lt.,Lt.TH, 25Mar.18-*I*, 28Mar.18-*I*, **KIA** 18Oct.18-*I*
Upson,2Lt.GC, 10Nov.18-*I*
Upson,2Lt.RH, **POW** 30Apr.17-*I*
Upton,Lt.WG, **KIA** 4Oct.18-*I*
Urinowsky,2Lt.,Lt.A, 8Aug.18-*I*, **DoW** 24Aug.18-*I*
Urquhart,2Lt.A, *Aust.* **KIA** 17Aug.17-*I*
Urwin,2Lt.TA, **POW DoW** 15.1.1918 12Jan.18-*I*
Usborne,Lt.CO, 4Mar.17-*I*
Usher,Lt.RHC, **WIA** 31Jul.16-*I*
Usher-Somers,2Lt.CE, **POW** 17Sep.18-*I*
Uttley,Lt.HR, **WIA** 2Apr.18-*I*

V

Vail,1Lt.WH, *US.* **WIA** 6Nov.18-*IIB*
Vaisey,2Lt.AH, **WIA** 29Jun.16-*I*
Valentine,2Lt.J, **POW** 22Aug.18-*I*
van Allen,FSLt.KM, **POW DoW** 11.5.1916 4May.16-*I*
van Baerle,2Lt.PEH, **POW** 18Mar.17-*I*

Vance,Lt.JD, **INT** 30Jun.18-*I*
van der Ben,2Lt.RC, **WIA** 4May.18-*VII*
van der Byl,2Lt.RI, **WIA** 9Oct.17-*I*
van der Hoff,2Lt.CL, **KIA** 29Jan.18-*I*
Vandyke,1Lt.CS, **WIA** 12Oct.17-*I*
van Goethem,2Lt.HE, 25Feb.16-*I*
van Huevel,1Lt.JW, *US.* **WIA** 16Jul.18-*IIB*
van Nostrand,Lt.CJ?, *Can.* 14Mar.16-*I*, **POW** 1Jul.16-*I*
van Tilburg,2Lt.JA, **POW** 19Jul.18-*I*
Vane-Tempest,Lt.CS, **DoW** 27.3.17 25Mar.17-*I*
Vann,1Lt.GC, *US.* **KIA** 25Jul.18-*IIB*
van Ryneveld,Capt.,Maj.HA, SA. 18Jun.16-*VII*, **WIA** 18Aug.17-*I*
van Schaack,1Lt.JJ, *USAS.* **POW** 17Aug.18-*I*
van Someren,2Lt.WN, **WIA** 31Jul.18-*I*
Varasour,2Lt.D, 18Oct.18-*I*
Varley,2Lt.ER, MC 29Mar.18-*I*, **WIA** 24Mar.18-*I*, **WIA** 6Apr.18-*I*
Vaucour,Lt., *108Sqn.* 13Oct.15-*I*, 28Nov.15-*I*, 30Nov.15-*I*, 2Dec.15-*I*, 13Dec.15-*I*
Vaucour,2Lt.,Maj.AM, MC DFC 2Sep.16-*I*, 24Aug.16-*I*, 25Aug.16-*I*, 27Feb.18-*IV*, **Kld** 16Jul.18-*IV*
Vaughan,2Lt.JD, **POW** 27Mar.18-*I*
Vaughan,Lt.,Capt.RM, 30Oct.14-*I*, **WIA** 1Nov.14-*I*, 17Apr.15-*I*, 11May.15-*I*, 12Jun.15-*I*, 29Jul.15-*I*
Vaughan-Jones,2Lt.G, **KIA** 26Feb.17-*I*
Vaughn,Lt.GA, *USAS.* 22Sep.18-*I*
Vautin,2Lt.CH, *Aust.* **POW** 8Jul.17-*VII*
Veacock,Lt.S, **POW** 17Oct.17-*I*
Veitch,Lt., *16Sqn.* 27Nov.15-*I*, 14Dec.15-*I*
Veitch,Lt.,Capt.CL, **inj** 13Aug.17-*I*, 1Nov.18-*I*
Veitch,Lt.DMV, **INT** 21Mar.15-*I*, **KIA** 8Jul.16-*I*
Venmore,2Lt.WC, **WIA** 17Mar.18-*I*
Venter,Lt.CJ, *SA.* 9May.18-*I*, 26Jun.18-*I*, **POW** 18Aug.18-*I*
Vereker,FLt.HC, **POW** 1Jan.17-*I*
Vernam,1Lt.RdeB, *US.* DSC **POW DoW** 1.12.1918 30Oct.18-*IIB*
Vernham,2Lt.NMH, **KIA** 4Feb.17-*I*
Vernon,2Lt.LGH, **POW** 11Sep.16-*I*
Vernon,2Lt.RG, **POW DoW** 21Oct.17-*I*
Vernon-Lord,2Lt.T, **POW** 15Oct.17-*I*
Verwohlt,1Lt.HW, *US.* **WIA POW** 8Sep.18-*IIB*
Vick,Lt.H, **WIA POW** 16Jun.18-*I*
Vick,2Lt.WW, **POW** 13Oct.17-*I*
Vickers,Lt.A, **KIA** 3Sep.18-*I*
Vickers,Lt.E, **WIA** 24Aug.16-*I*
Vickers,2Lt.GR, **KIA** 6Jan.18-*I*
Vickers,2Lt.JB, **POW** 29Oct.18-*I*
Vickers,2Lt.OHD, 17Aug.17-*I*
Vickery,2Lt.FWA, 24Sep.16-*I*, **WIA** 6Feb.17-*I*,
Vickery,2Lt.HC, 10Apr.16-*I*, **WIA** 16Apr.16-*I*
Vigers,Lt.AW, 3Jun.18-*I*
Villiers,Lt.HL, **KIA** 4Feb.17-*I*
Villiers,2Lt.SA, 29Mar.16-*I*, 21Apr.16-*I*, 26Apr.16-*I*
Vincent,Lt.FC, 18Jul.18-*III*
Viney,FSLt.TE, 28Nov.15-*I*
Vinson,2Lt., *15Sqn.* 16Sep.16-*I*
Vinson,2Lt.AH, 6Apr.17-*I*
Vinter,Lt.NO, 20Sep.17-*I*
Vipond,2Lt.FE, **POW** 27Jun.17-*I*
Virgo,2Lt.CP, **WIA** 6Mar.18-*I*
Vitty,GL., *3WgRNAS* **POW?** 12Oct.16-*I*
Viveash,2Lt.AJ, **KIA** 28Aug.18-*I*
Viveash,Lt., *13Sqn.* 17Jun.18-*I*
Vlasto,Lt.AG, 15May.18-*I*
Voeks,1Lt.FG, *US.* **WIA** 3Nov.18-*IIB*
Vorster,2Lt.,Lt.WL, 3Apr.18-*IV*, 10Jun.18-*IV*, **KIA** 23Jul.18-*IV*
Vosper,Lt.RA, **POW** 18Jul.18-*I*
Vowles,Lt.JAE, 18Jul.18-*III*
Vredenburg,Sgt.LG, **POW** 22Jul.18-*I*

W

Waddell,2Lt.LN, **WIA** 9Sep.17-*I*, 11Sep.17-*I*
Wadden,Lt.G, **POW** 11Oct.16-*I*
Waddington,2Lt.MW, 2Jul.17-*I*, 3Sep.17-*I*
Waddy,2Lt.SN, **KIA** 24Jul.18-*I*

Wade,2Lt.OJ, **KIA** 22Oct.16-*I*
Wade,2Lt.RC, **KIA** 26Feb.18-*I*
Wadham,Lt.NW, **WIA** 9Oct.17-*I*
Wadham,2Lt.,Capt.VHN, 5Feb.15-*I*, **KIA** 17Jan.16-*I*
Wadsworth,Lt., *103Sqn.* 9Jun.18-*I*
Wadsworth,2Lt.EA, 8Jul.18-*I*
Wagner,2Lt.EGS, **KIA** 7Jan.17-*I*
Wagner,1Lt.EW, *US.* **WIA** 8Sep.18-*IIB*
Wagstaff,Lt.CFA, 18Jul.18-*III*
Wainwright,2Lt.BM, **POW** 28Aug.16-*I*
Wainwright,2Lt.CE, **DoW** 14Oct.18-*I*
Wainwright,2Lt.,Lt.RBW, 15Nov.16-*I*, **WIA** 15Feb.17-*I*
Wait,Lt.GE, 26Mar.18-*I*
Wait,Sgt.TE, **POW** 12May.17-*I*
Waite,Lt.HL, **WIA** 16Aug.17-*I*
Wakeman,2Lt.,Lt.FT, **WIA** 2Jul.17-*I*, **KIA** 30Oct.17-*I*
Wakeman,2Lt.,TLt.MW, 4Sep.18-*I*, **KIA** 2Oct.18-*I*
Walcott,Cpl.S, *US.* **KIA** 12Dec.17-*IIC*
Walden,2Lt.JB, *US.* **WIA** 2Oct.18-*I*
Waldron,Capt.,Maj.FF, 9Sep.14-*I*, **POW DoW** 3Jul.16-*I*
Walford,Capt.WG, **KIA** 4Nov.18-*I*
Walker,1AM.A, **KIA** 30Mar.16-*I*
Walker,Sgt.A, **KIA** 2Aug.16-*I*
Walker,2AM.AG, **POW** 11Mar.17-*I*
Walker,Sgt.DB, **POW** 15Sep.16-*I*
Walker,Lt.EGS, 3May.15-*I*, 16Jun.15-*I*, 19Jun.15-*I*, **POW** 4Jul.15-*I*
Walker,2Lt.F, *185Sqn.* 25May.18-*I*
Walker,2Lt.FF, *48Sqn.* **WIA** 2Apr.18-*I*
Walker,Lt.FR, 22Oct.17-*I*
Walker,Lt.GH, **KIA** 28Jul.17-*I*
Walker,2Lt.GK, 6Mar.17-*I*
Walker,2Lt.H, **KIA** 26Sep.18-*I*
Walker,Lt.HW, **KIA** 23Jul.18-*I*
Walker,2AM.J, *185Sqn.* **KIA** 12Apr.17-*I*
Walker,2Lt.JC, *593Sqn.* 12Jun.18-*I*, **KIA** 18Oct.18-*I*
Walker,2Lt.JC, *205Sqn.* **POW** 7Sep.18-*I*
Walker,1Lt.JE, 27Aug.18-*I*, **KIA** 17Sep.18-*I*
Walker,2Lt.JM, *35Sqn.* 16May.18-*I*
Walker,Lt.JM, *IAFC. Aust.* **KIA** 22Aug.18-*VII*
Walker,2Lt.JQF, **KIA** 31Mar.18-*I*
Walker,Lt.KM, **KIA** 12Aug.18-*I*
Walker,Sgt.R, **WIA POW** 3Oct.18-*I*
Walker,Lt.RD, **inj** 21Jul.16-*I*, **POW** 25Aug.16-*I*
Walker,2Lt.RU, 29Apr.16-*I*, **WIA** 4Jun.16-*I*
Walker,Sgt.T, **POW** 12Jul.17-*I*
Walker,AG.2AM.W, **inj** 17Sep.17-*I*
Walker,Capt.W, DFC **KIA** 8Oct.18-*I*
Walker,Capt.WH, *Can.* 10Jun.16-*I*, **POW?** 18Aug.17-*I*
Walker,2Lt.WL, 9Oct.18-*I*, 1Nov.18-*I*
Walker,FSLt.WR, **POW** 14May.17-*I*
Walkerdine,Lt.HJ, 27Mar.18-*I*
Wall,Capt.AHW, 9May.17-*I*
Wallace,Sgt.AC, **POW** 1Jan.18-*I*
Wallace,2Lt.EE, **WIA** 18Aug.17-*I*
Wallace,Capt.HIeR, 22Aug.18-*I*
Wallace,Lt.JE, 11Jul.18-*I*, **KIA** 9Aug.18-*I*
Wallace,SLt.K, 11Jun.17-*I*, 13Jul.17-*I*
Wallace,2Lt.KH, **KIA** 4Sep.18-*I*
Wallace,2Lt.M, **WIA** 1Sep.18-*I*
Wallace,2Lt.N, **WIA**? 16Aug.18-*I*, **WIA** 8Aug.18-*I*
Wallace,2Lt.PM, **POW** 27Sep.18-*I*
Wallace,2Lt.R, 24Mar.18-*I*
Wallace,2Lt.RH, **WIA** 2Nov.16-*I*
Wallace,2Lt.W, 3Aug.17-*I*, **WIA** 18May.17-*I*
Wallace,2Lt.WM, **KIA** 22Aug.15-*I*
Wallace-Simpson,Lt.G, **POW** .18-*I*
Waller,Capt., *16Sqn.* 22Oct.16-*I*
Waller,Cpl.JH, 16Apr.16-*I*, 18Jun.16-*I*, 26Jun.16-*I*
Wallington,Lt.ER, 19Aug.18-*I*
Wallis,FLt.AA, 12Aug.17-*III*
Wallis,Lt.CRA, **inj** 22Aug.18-*I*, 23Aug.18-*I*, **WIA** 28Oct.18-*I*
Wallis,2Lt.FB, **WIA** 18Nov.17-*I*
Wallis,Sgt.FJ, **WIA** 31Jul.18-*I*
Wallis,1Lt.JW, *US.* **WIA** 22Oct.18-*IIB*
Wallwork,2Lt.JW, 6Mar.18-*I*

Walmsley,2Lt.CC, 25Jun.18-*I*
Walmsley,2Lt.H, **WIA? inj?** 30Oct.18-*I*
Walpole,2Lt.H, 3Oct.17-*I*
Walrond-Skinner,Capt.DD, **POW** 5Oct.17-*I*
Walsh,2Lt.A, **DoW** 8.8.1917 7Aug.17-*I*
Walsh,2Lt.FJ, **WIA** 8Oct.18-*I*
Walsh,2Lt.WD, *US.* **POW** 3Nov.18-*IIB*
Walter,2Lt.DP, **WIA** 6Apr.17-*I*
Walter,FSLt.EBJ, **KIA** 24Apr.17-*I*
Walter,2Lt.HL, **WIA** 21Oct.17-*I*
Walter,Lt.SRP, **WIA** 23Jun.16-*I*, 14Jul.17-*I*
Walters,2Lt.AM, 20Jul.16-*I*
Walters,Lt.HCW, 4Jul.18-*IV*, **WIA** 30Jul.18-*IV*
Walthew,2Lt.JS, **KIA** 19Sep.17-*I*
Walton,Lt.CF, *initials* CE? 17Jun.18-*I*, 1Jul.18-*I*
Walton,2Lt.JL, **WIA** 16Apr.18-*I*
Walton,2Lt.OT, **KIA** 12Apr.17-*I*
Walton,2Lt.RG, **WIA** 2Sep.18-*I*
Walton,Capt.RN, **WIA** 21Nov.17-*I*
Walworth,FSLt.CR, **KIA** 18Feb.18-*I*
Wambolt,FLt.HR, **KIA** 4Mar.17-*I*
Wanamaker,1Lt.WB, *US.* **WIA POW** 2Jul.18-*IIB*
Waner,2Lt.GRF, **DoW** 2.3.1917 1Mar.17-*I*
Wanklyn,Lt.HG, 31May.15-*I*
Warberton,Lt.P, 31Jul.17-*I*
Warburton,2Lt.ED, **POW** 5Apr.17-*I*
Warburton,2Lt.T, **POW** 25Sep.18-*I*
Ward,2Lt., *2Sqn.* 2Feb.16-*I*
Ward,2Lt.AA, *6Sqn.* **POW** 14Oct.17-*I*
Ward,Lt.A, *Mesop?* **POW**.18-*VIII*
Ward,2Lt.BCM, **WIA** 6Apr.18-*I*
Ward,2Lt.CE, 10Oct.16-*I*, **WIA** 31Oct.16-*I*
Ward,Cpl.CGS, **KIA** 9Nov.16-*I*
Ward,Lt.CT, 4Jun.17-*I*
Ward,2Lt.EAH, *22Sqn.* 29Jul.17-*I*, **KIA** 11Aug.17-*I*
Ward,2Lt.EH, *9Sqn.* **KIA** 5Jun.17-*I*
Ward,2Lt.,Lt.EH, *88Sqn.* 15May.18-*I*, 18May.18-*I*, 29Jun.18-*I*, 27Jul.18-*I*
Ward,Maj.GB, MC **KIA** 21Sep.17-*I*
Ward,Lt.GF, **inj** 3Sep.17-*I*
Ward,2Lt.HE, **WIA** 17Mar.17-*I*
Ward,2Lt.HS, 10Oct.15-*I*, 27Nov.15-*I*, **WIA POW** 30Nov.15-*I*
Ward,Sgt.JT, **POW?** 23Jun.18-*I*
Ward,2Lt.LN, *Aust.* **inj** 20Nov.17-*I*
Ward,2Lt.MJ, 15Sep.18-*I*
Ward,2Lt.PHB, **KIA** 19May.17-*I*
Ward-Price,Lt.LS, **KIA** 25Mar.17-*I*
Warden,Capt.RH, **inj** 6Dec.17-*I*
Wardlaw,1AM.AH, **KIA** 30Sep.17-*I*
Wardrop,Cpl.WE, 16Jun.18-*I*
Wardrope,2Lt.WHM, **WIA** 27Mar.18-*I*
Ware,2Lt.,Capt.DC, *21Sqn.* 8Sep.14-*I*, **WIA** 31Mar.18-*I*
Ware,Lt.DC, *203Sqn.* **KIA** 20Sep.18-*I*
Wareing,Sgt.AT, **KIA** 29Aug.18-*I*
Wareing,Lt.CW, 29Sep.18-*I*
Wareing,Capt.GW, DFC **KIA** 27Oct.18-*I*
Waring,Lt.EF, 28Aug.18-*III*
Waring,2Lt.HEA, **WIA? POW** 19Aug.17-*I*
Warman,2Lt.CW, *US.* **WIA** 20Aug.17-*I*
Warminger,1AM.HP, **DoW** 25Aug.16-*I*
Warn,Lt.WG, **KIA** 23Sep.16-*I*
Warne-Browne,Lt.TA, 4Jun.18-*I*
Warneford,FSLt.RAJ, 7Jun.15-*I*
Warner,2Lt.DD, *US.* **WIA** 4Sep.18-*IIB*
Warner,Lt.JW, **KIA** 4Oct.18-*I*
Warner,2Lt.WF, 23Mar.18-*I*
Warner,2Lt.WH, **KIA** 27Jun.18-*I*
Warrand,Lt.AStJM, **POW DoW** 19.3.15 11Mar.15-*I*
Warren,2Lt.AP, **POW** 23Apr.17-*I*
Warren,2Lt.CF, **WIA** 27Mar.18-*I*
Warren,2Lt.J, 26Sep.18-*I*, **WIA** 9Oct.18-*I*
Warren,Lt.JW, 7Apr.17-*I*
Warren,2Lt.LG, 21Mar.18-*I*
Warrender,2Lt.LD, *US.* **WIA** 30Sep.18-*IIB*
Warter,2Lt.JG, **KIA** 30Sep.17-*I*
Wasey,Capt.CWC, **KIA** 28Oct.17-*I*
Washington,2Lt.JN, **POW DoW** 2.10.15 25Sep.15-*I*
Washington,1Lt.WF, **KIA** 3Sep.18-*I*
Waterer,Lt.MA, 24Aug.18-*I*, **DoW** 10.10.1918? 8Oct.18-*I*

Waterfall,2Lt.VE, KIA 22Aug.14-I
Waterlow,Capt.E, KIA 16Jul.18-I
Waters,Lt.CB, POW 16Aug.17-I
Waters,2Lt.EG, KIA 24Jan.17-I
Waters,2Lt.HE, POW 2Jun.17-I
Watkins,FLt.HEM, 5May.15-IX
Watkins,2Lt.,Lt.HH, 29Jul.15-I, 31Jul.15-I, WIA 28Jul.16-I
Watkins,2Lt.JR, WIA 8Aug.18-I
Watkins,FLt.SR, 16Mar.18-I
Watkins,Lt.WC, KIA 23Jul.18-IV
Watkinson,Sgt., 103Sqn. 22Jul.18-I
Watlington,2Lt.HJ, KIA 6Jul.17-I
Watson,Lt.A, WIA POW 13Apr.17-I
Watson,2Lt.AT, 31May.16-I, 1Jul.16-I
Watson,2Lt.AW, 23Apr.17-I
Watson,Lt.C, MC WIA 1Oct.17-I
Watson,2Lt.CVM, KIA 3Oct.17-VI
Watson,2Lt.DD, US. POW 8Nov.18-IIB
Watson,Lt.G, KIA 20May.18-I
Watson,2Lt.GC, MC WIA? inj? 9Nov.18-I
Watson,Capt.GL, WIA 22Nov.16-I
Watson,AG.2AM.H, WIA 15Jul.17-I
Watson,2Lt.,Capt.HG, DFC, NZ. 25Mar.18-I, 2Oct.18-I
Watson,2Lt.HH, 21May.18-I
Watson,1Lt.HJ, US. KIA? 18Oct.18-IIB
Watson,2Lt.JK, 29Mar.18-I
Watson,Lt.KB, 4Sep.18-I
Watson,FSLt.MJ, POW 5Oct.17-I
Watson,Lt.NT, WIA POW 13Mar.18-I
Watson,Sgt.RA, 9Aug.18-I
Watson,GL.RH, POW DoW 25Apr.17-I
Watson,2Lt.T, KIA 28Mar.18-I
Watt,2Lt.CM?, KIA, initials GM? 17Mar.17-I
Watt,2Lt.J, 47Sqn. KIA 2May.17-VI
Watt,Lt.JA, 209Sqn. WIA 11Aug.18-I
Watt,2Lt.NL, DoW 27Jul.17-I
Watt,2Lt.WH, WIA POW 31Jul.17-I
Watts,2Lt.AE, KIA 6Mar.17-I
Watts,Capt.FJ, 17Apr.18-I
Watts,2Lt.FP, WIA 20Sep.17-I
Watts,1AM.O, KIA 27Nov.16-I
Watts,2Lt.R, POW 22Oct.16-I
Watts,Lt.VL, WIA 29Oct.18-I
Watts,2Lt.W, KIA 17Jan.16-I
Watts,2Lt.WE, POW 20Oct.17-I
Watts,Lt.WPT, WIA 23Apr.17-I
Wattson,2Lt.CB, KIA 8Oct.17-I
Waugh,2Lt.J, 25May.18-I
Way,2Lt.PH, US. DSC KIA 12Sep.18-IIB
Way,2Lt.,Lt.RA, WIA 10Feb.16-I, 16Apr.18-I, 22Apr.18-I
Weakley,Lt.EGK, WIA 8Aug.18-I
Weale,2Lt.FHA, KIA 2Oct.18-I
Wear,2Lt.AE, 6Jul.17-I, 17Jul.17-I
Weare,Capt.FGC, 18Mar.18-I
Wearne,2Lt.A, Aust. POW 26Jul.17-I
Weatherley,2Lt.JA, WIA 15Apr.18-I
Weaver,A.Capt.J, POW 12Jun.18-I
Weaver,Lt.EG, 29Aug.18-I
Webb,2Lt.DE, KIA 9Oct.18-I
Webb,2AM.F, KIA 28Jul.17-I
Webb,2Lt.G, KIA 5Jun.18-I
Webb,Capt.GW, KIA 1Jul.16-I
Webb,Capt.JR, 28Oct.18-I
Webb,Capt.NW, MC 12Jul.17-I, 26Jul.17-I, KIA 16Aug.17-I
Webb,2Lt.PFH, 5Jun.17-I, WIA 13Aug.17-I
Webb,2Lt.T, 23Apr.17-I, KIA 10May.17-I
Webb,FSgt.WG, KIA 26Jan.17-I
Webber,2Lt.WH, KIA 10Aug.18-I
Webster,Lt., 12Sqn. 7May.17-I, 15Sep.17-I
Webster,FSLt.AN, 7Apr.18-I, KIA 5Jun.18-I
Webster,Lt.J, POW 27Jun.18-I
Webster,2Lt.TM, WIA POW 5Sep.17-I
Wedderspoon,Lt.JHB, KIA 6Apr.17-I
Wedgwood,2Lt.FCB, WIA POW 27Mar.18-I
Wedgwood,Lt.J, WIA 28Mar.18-I
Wedgwood,2Lt.WA, KIA 9Jul.16-I
Wedgwood-Benn,Capt.J, 15Jun.16-VII, 2Dec.16-VII
Wehner,1Lt.JF, US. DSC KIA 18Sep.18-IIB
Weightman,2Lt.H, WIA 9Sep.17-I
Weil,Capt.B, 16Aug.17-I
Weil,FSLt.LMB, KIA 6Apr.17-I
Weimer,2Lt.JH, US. KIA 23Oct.18-IIB
Weingarth,Lt.JW, Aust. 9Apr.18-I
Weir,Lt.AG, POW 26Jul.15-I
Weir,2Lt.CG, KIA 7Aug.18-I
Weir,FSLt.CH, POW DoI 21.8.1917 20Aug.17-I
Weir,Lt.WJA, Aust. 23May.18-VII
Weirick,1Lt.AM, US. WIA? POW 31Oct.18-IIB
Welby,2Lt.EE, WIA 9Oct.18-I
Welch,Cpl., 2Sqn. 26Oct.15-I
Welch,2Lt.EA, KIA 23Apr.17-I
Welch,2Lt.H, 1Sqn. KIA 28Mar.17-I
Welch,2Lt.H, 18Sqn. 30Dec.15-I
Welch,Capt.HJ, KIA 29Sep.18-I
Welch,Lt.SB, KIA 25Aug.18-I
Welch,2Lt.ST, 19Oct.15-I
Welchman,Capt.PE, MC DFC WIA POW 26Sep.18-I
Weld,Lt.DS, POW 12Jul.17-I
Welford,Pte., 22Sqn. inj 31Jul.16-I
Welinkar?,Lt.SCK, POW DoW 30.6.1918 name Welinker? 27Jun.18-I
Welinker?,Lt.SCK, see Welinkar
Wellby,Lt.HS, POW 15Oct.17-I
Weller,Gnr.A, POW 20Sep.18-VI
Weller,2Lt.EG, WIA 24Aug.18-I
Weller,2Lt.JA, 22May.18-I, WIA 25Aug.18-I
Weller,2Lt.WH, WIA 16Sep.17-I
Wells,Lt.CD, MC KIA 16May.18-I
Wells,2Lt.EI, 14Mar.18-I, 7Apr.18-I
Wells,Lt.FW, 25Sep.17-I
Wells,2Lt.,Capt.GA, WIA 11Aug.17-I, POW 5Sep.18-I
Wells,2Lt.HE, WIA 7Jun.17-I
Wells,2Lt.HMW, KIA 15Sep.16-I
Wells,1Lt.HP, USAS. POW 22Aug.18-I
Wells,2Lt.NB, POW 13Mar.18-I
Wells,2Lt.REW, US. 15Sep.18-IIB
Wells,2Lt.SR, POW 5Apr.18-I
Wells,Capt.TR, MC POW 28Apr.16-VIII
Wells,Capt.WL, 23Mar.18-I, WIA 28Mar.18-I
Wells-Bladen,2Lt., 1Sqn. 4May.15-I
Wellwood,Lt.JJ, Aust. 6Sep.18-I
Welman,2Lt.,Lt.JB, 16Oct.17-VIII, WIA POW 31Oct.17-VIII
Welsford,2Lt.GJL, KIA 30Mar.16-I
Welsford,2Lt.GK, KIA 20Oct.16-I
Welsh,Lt.SB, 17Apr.18-I
Welsh,FCdr.WL, 26Apr.17-I
Welshman,Capt.PE, WIA 26Sep.16-I
Wenden,Lt., 6Sqn. 5May.15-I
Wenger,Lt.NJ, inj 7Jun.17-I
Wensley,Lt.JH, POW 18Mar.18-I
Wentworth,Pte., POW 1Jun.18-I
Wentworth,1AM.D, DFM 31May.18-I
Wersheimer,Sgt.HB, USMC WIA 28Sep.18-I
Wessell,Lt.FF, WIA 20Apr.17-I
Wesson,2Lt.JS, POW 29Sep.18-VII
West,2Lt.AM, 20May.17-I
West,1Lt.EG, US. WIA 13Sep.18-IIB
West,Capt.FMF, MC VC 9Aug.18-I, WIA 10Aug.18-I
West,Lt.FMS, 22Apr.18-I
West,1Lt.GO, US. KIA 10Oct.18-IIB
West,Lt.HD, Can. 23Jun.18-I, 26Sep.18-I
West,Sgt.J, KIA 16Sep.18-I
West,2Lt.JP, US. KIA 28Jun.18-I
West,1Lt.KG, US. 23Oct.18-IIB, KIA 5Nov.18-IIB
West,2Lt.MS, 9Aug.17-I
West,Lt.PC, KIA 3Aug.18-I
West,2Lt.PH, WIA 23Apr.17-I
West,2Lt.RWG, WIA 20May.17-I
West,2Lt.SJ, inj 10Aug.18-I
West,2Lt.T, 11Sep.16-I, 14Sep.16-I, KIA 24Sep.16-I
West,2Lt.,Lt.TJ, WIA 24Jul.16-VII, 2Aug.16-VII
West-White,2Lt.E, 27May.17-I
Westall,Lt.A, WIA 28Sep.18-I
Westaway,2Lt.HW, WIA 14Sep.17-I
Westcott,2Lt.G, 2Aug.16-I
Westcott,2Lt.,Lt.GF, 1Jun.16-I, POW 29Sep.17-I
Westfield,Lt.FJ, WIA POW 27Mar.18-I
Westhofen,2Lt.PC, KIA 12Apr.18-I
Westing,2Lt.CF, POW 24Mar.18-I
Westlake,Lt.AN, MC KIA 4Jan.18-I
Westlake,Lt.JH, DoW 7.5.1917 29Apr.17-I
Westmoreland,2Lt.E, KIA 19Feb.18-I
Weston,1AM., 98Sqn. 10May.18-I
Weston,Lt.DJ, 30Jun.18-I
Weston,Lt.JE, KIA 14Jul.18-I
Whalley,2Lt.JA, WIA 17May.18-I
Whalley,Capt.RL, KIA 16Sep.18-I
Whalley,2Lt.,Lt.RW, 20Jul.18-I, 31Jul.18-I, WIA 26Aug.18-I
Wharram,2Lt.,Lt.CE, WIA 10Aug.17-I, KIA 26Mar.18-I
Wharton,Lt.CE, POW 16Jun.18-I
Wharton,Lt.L, MC Aust. WIA 11Aug.18-I
Whateley,2Lt.GA, KIA 10May.18-I
Whatley,Sgt.HA, KIA 2Jul.17-I
Whealy,FLt.,Capt.AT, Can. 24Mar.18-I, 4Sep.18-I
Wheatley,2Lt.EES, WIA 9May.17-VI
Wheeler,2Lt.LF, WIA POW 16Sep.17-I
Wheldon,2Lt.EG, 3Sep.16-I, WIA 23Nov.16-I
Whellock,2Lt.CS, WIA 1Oct.18-I
Whetnall,FSLt., 2Wg RNAS, KIA 19Nov.16-VI
Whichelow,2Lt.W, WIA 24Oct.18-I
Whidborne,2Lt.CSL, WIA? 27Jul.15-I
Whipple,2Lt.SH, US. WIA 24Aug.18-I
Whistler,Lt.AH, WIA 29Jan.17-I
Whistler,Capt.HA, 16Dec.16-I, 1Jun.18-I, 15Sep.18-I, 29Sep.18-I, 4Nov.18-I
Whitaker,Capt.VJ, KIA 6Apr.17-I
Whitaker,2Lt.W, KIA 6Dec.17-I
Whitburn,Lt.F, WIA 28Oct.18-I
White,Lt.AF, 28th Oct.18-IV
White,Lt.AG, 211Sqn. KIA 29Sep.18-I
White,2Lt.AG, 17thUS Sqn. USAS. 3Oct.18-I
White,2Lt.AT, 25Nov.15-I
White,2Lt.BW, KIA 8Apr.17-I
White,FSlt.JB, Can. 24Jan.18-I
White,Capt.CG, MC 11Apr.18-I, KIA 21Apr.18-I
White,2Lt.CH, WIA 15Jun.18-I
White,2Lt.CM, WIA 23Mar.17-I
White,2Lt.CS, WIA 10Apr.18-I
White,2Lt.EG, USAS. WIA 8Oct.18-I
White,Lt.HA, US. 8Aug.18-I, 16Sep.18-I
White,Capt.HG, 19May.18-I
White,2Lt.HW, 10Apr.18-I, WIA 20Apr.18-I
White,Lt.JF, 27Mar.18-I
White,2Lt.JG, KIA 26Aug.17-I
White,Capt.JLM, 4Nov.18-I
White,FSLt.JP, KIA 4Mar.17-I
White,2Lt.JT, 7Apr.18-I
White,2Lt.JW, WIA 1Oct.18-I
White,Spr.AG, KIA 27Sep.17-I
White,2Lt.MA, KIFA 23Apr.17-I
White?,Lt.OG, Aust.? 10Aug.18-I
White,GL.HW, POW 6Nov.17-I
White,Capt.PR, POW 16May.18-I
White,2Lt.RE, POW 17Jul.18-I
White,Sgt.RLG, 31Aug.18-I, 1Oct.18-I, 25Oct.18-I
White,Lt.RW, WIA POW 25Jan.17-I
White,2Lt.SJM, KIA 15Jan.17-VI
White,1Lt.SW, US. DoW 1.11.1918 31Oct.18-IIB
White,2Lt.TW, 56Sqn. POW 27Jul.17-I
White,Capt.TW, Aust. May.15-VIII, POW 13Nov.15-VIII
White,2Lt.WA, US. KIA 10Nov.18-IIB
White,2Lt.WW, US. DSC KIA 10Oct.18-IIB
Whiteford,Pte.J, KIA 27Feb.17-I
Whitehead,Cpl., 15Sqn. 27Aug.16-I
Whitehead,Lt., 55Sqn. 14Aug.17-I, 5Sep.17-I
Whitehead,Lt.AD, WIA POW 11Mar.17-I
Whitehead,Capt.AG, KIA 29Jan.18-I
Whitehead,2Lt.C, WIA 3Aug.18-I
Whitehead,2Lt.EA, KIA 13Mar.18-I
Whitehead,2Lt.F, WIA 4Nov.17-I
Whitehead,Lt.GWE, KIA 17Oct.18-I
Whitehead,Sgt.HE, POW? 4Oct.18-I
Whitehead,Lt.HH, Can. POW DoW 21.8.1916 20Aug.16-I
Whitehead,2Lt.HR, WIA POW 11Jul.18-I
Whitehead,2Lt.J, 30Oct.18-I
Whitehead,Lt.,Capt.LE, 26Jul.16-I, WIA 30Jul.16-I, KIA 20May.18-I
Whitehead,FLt.R, 16Apr.15-V
Whitehead,2Lt.RM, 18Oct.17-I
Whitehead,Lt.WHN, Can. POW 19Oct.16-I
Whitehouse,2AM.AG, MM WIA 10May.17-I
Whitehouse,2Lt.F, KIA 27May.18-I
Whitehouse,2Lt.SL, WIA POW 27Oct.17-I
Whiteley,2Lt.P, 2May.18-I
Whitelock,2Lt.AT, 23Sep.15-I, 14Dec.15-I
Whiteman,Sgt.T, WIA 30Apr.17-I
Whiteside,Lt.AB, MC 23May.18-I
Whiteside,2Lt.HL, WIA 23Apr.18-I
Whiteside,Lt.HS, POW 24Mar.17-I
Whiteside,2Lt.RC, KIA 20Dec.16-I
Whitfield,2Lt.E, KIA 1Apr.18-I
Whitfield,Capt.GHP, 11Jul.18-I, 25Jul.18-I, WIA POW 8Aug.18-I
Whitfield,2Lt.R, 3Oct.18-I
Whitford-Hawkey,Lt.A, KIA 9May.18-I
Whiting,Lt.C, 12Apr.18-I
Whiting,Lt.JO, KIA 22Sep.17-I
Whitlock,2Lt.HH, POW 14Oct.18-I
Whitlock,2Lt.,Lt.HW, 30Oct.18-I, 1Nov.18-I, 9Nov.18-I
Whitman,2Lt.TW, US. KIA 4Oct.18-I
Whitmarsh,2Lt.JW, WIA 25Jun.18-I
Whitmore,Cpl.H, US. POW 6Apr.18-IID
Whitner,2Lt.RH, US. KIA 13Mar.18-IID
Whitney,2Lt.,Lt.RK, 18Jul.18-I, WIA 11Aug.18-I
Whitney,2Lt.RT, POW 2Feb.17-I
Whiton,1Lt.AL, US. POW 1Aug.18-IIB
Whittaker,2Lt.,Lt.HA, WIA 31May.18-I, WIA 14Jul.18-I
Whittaker,Lt.J, 16Mar.17-I
Whittaker,Capt.JTP, 1Jul.16-I, 7Jul.16-I, 21Aug.16-I, WIA 25Aug.16-I
Whittall,2Lt.,Lt.FA, 18Jun.18-I, 9Aug.18-I
Whittall,2Lt.NC, KIA 12Sep.17-I
Whittington,Lt.LM, inj 23Apr.18-I
Whittington,AG.Pte.W, WIA 16Aug.17-I
Whittle,Capt.OL, POW 31Aug.16-I
Whittle,2Lt.WK, 30Nov.17-I
Whittome,2Lt.HL, 24Mar.18-I
Whitty,Lt.JL, DoW 8Jul.16-I
Whitwell,2Lt.PH, KIA 25Apr.18-I
Whitworth,Lt.H, POW 5Dec.17-I
Whitworth-Jones,2Lt.J, 18Aug.17-I
Whyte,Lt.CB, KIA 3May.18-I
Whyte,Lt.RP, POW 29Jun.18-I
Whytehead,2Lt.HH, KIA 12Jul.17-I
Wickenden,2Lt.CRF, 27Oct.17-I
Wickett,Lt.RC, KIA 9Aug.18-I
Wickett,Lt.TH, WIA POW 10May.17-I
Wickham,Sgt.WS, 22Jul.17-I, KIA 25Jul.17-I
Wicks,Lt.GD, USAS. KIA 5Oct.18-I
Wiener,2Lt.,Lt.LdeV, inj 9May.18-I, KIA 4Nov.18-I
Wigan,2Lt.APC, POW 6Mar.18-I
Wiggin?,2Lt.TH, see Wiggins
Wiggins,Lt.RB, inj 14Oct.18-I
Wiggins,2Lt.TH, KIA name Wiggin? 27Jun.18-I
Wightman,2Lt.JF, KIA 4Sep.17-I
Wigle,2Lt.GB, WIA 10Oct.17-I
Wigley,2Lt.L, POW 23Aug.17-I
Wignall,2Lt.G, POW 8Aug.18-I
Wilcock,2Lt.RP, WIA 24Jul.16-VII
Wilcox,2Lt.CH, POW 27Sep.18-I
Wilcox,AGL.RB, WIA 16Mar.18-I
Wild,2Lt.H, KIA 16Jun.18-I
Wild,Lt.W, WIA 29May.18-I
Wilderspin,Lt.C, 1Oct.18-I, WIA 31Oct.18-I
Wildig,2Lt.NH, KIA 7Jul.18-I
Wilding,Sgt.J, WIA POW 25Sep.18-I
Wilford,FSLt.JR, WIA POW 13Sep.17-I
Wilkin,2Lt.BO, POW 11Oct.15-I
Wilkins,2Lt.FS, 10Nov.16-I
Wilkins,Capt.HOD, 13Jul.17-I, POW 28Jul.17-I
Wilkinson,Capt.A, 5Apr.17-I
Wilkinson,2Lt.C, WIA 27Sep.18-I
Wilkinson,Lt.CB, KIA 29Mar.18-I
Wilkinson,Lt.DS, POW DoW 26.8.1917 17Aug.17-I

Wilkinson,Lt.ER, MC **DoW** 7.10.17-*VI*
Wilkinson,Lt.ES, **KIA** 12Jan.16-*I*
Wilkinson,Lt.F, *58Sqn.* 7Jun.18-*I*
Wilkinson,Cpl.F, *21TSqn.* 9Jul.18-*I*
Wilkinson,2Lt.,Lt.GM, **WIA** 28May.17-*I*, **KIA** 10Oct.17-*I*
Wilkinson,2Lt.GN, 31Aug.17-*I*
Wilkinson,2Lt.HR, **WIA** 9May.17-*I*
Wilkinson,2Lt.JH, 27May.18-*I*
Wilkinson,2Lt.JR, **WIA** 14Oct.18-*I*
Willans,Lt.A, **WIA** 20Sep.17-*I*
Willard,2Lt.KH, **KIA** 12Oct.17-*I*
Willcox,Lt.PW, 5Jun.17-*I*
Willcox,2Lt.WT, **POW** 22Oct.16-*I*
Williams,Lt., *Sqn?* **INT** 21Jul.18-*I*
Williams,Lt., *55Sqn.* 21Sep.15-*I*
Williams,Lt., *16Sqn.* 18Aug.17-*I*
Williams,2Lt.AEG, **KIA** 25Apr.18-*I*
Williams,2Lt.AT, *19Sqn.* 31Aug.16-*I*, 2Sep.16-*I*
Williams,2Lt.AT, *25Sqn.* **DoW** 4Sep.18-*I*
Williams,1Lt.BR, *US.* 13Sep.18-*IIB*
Williams,Lt.C, **KIA** 30Jul.16-*I*
Williams,2Lt.CP, **KIA** 26Aug.17-*I*
Williams,2Lt.F, *22Sqn.* **KIA** 2Apr.18-*I*
Williams,Lt.F, *62Sqn.* **KIA** 24Jun.18-*I*
Williams,2Lt.FGS, 18May.16-*I*
Williams,Lt.FJ, 18Mar.18-*I*
Williams,Lt.FS, **KIA** 28Jun.18-*IV*
Williams,FSLt.FTP, **KIA** 30Jan.18-*I*
Williams,2Lt.GE, 9Nov.18-*I*
Williams,Capt.GGA, 24Aug.16-*I*, **WIA** 6Sep.16-*I*
Williams,2Lt.GJ, **POW** 29Jul.18-*VII*
Williams,Lt.GT, 12Oct.18-*I*
Williams,Cpl.H, **WIA** 29Jul.18-*I*
Williams,2Lt.HD, 4Nov.18-*I*
Williams,Sgt.HJ, **INT** 26Sep.18-*I*
Williams,Lt.HT, **WIA** 5Sep.18-*V*
Williams,Lt.KL, **WIA** 4Jul.18-*III*
Williams,2Lt.LB, **WIA** 20Nov.17-*I*
Williams,Lt.LJ, **POW** 28Jan.18-*I*
Williams,2Lt.NE, *5Sqn.* **KIA** 9Nov.17-*I*
Williams,Lt.NE, *RNAS.* **INT** 19Jul.18-*III*
Williams,Sgt.PH, **KIA** 15Jul.18-*I*
Williams,2Lt.PJ, 15Aug.18-*I*
Williams,2Lt.PS, 15Apr.18-*I*
Williams,1Lt.RD, *USAS.* 20Jul.18-*I*, **WIA** 23Aug.18-*I*
Williams,2Lt.RH, **WIA** 17Feb.18-*I*
Williams,2Lt.RL, 15Aug.18-*I*
Williams,Capt.RM, **KIA** 12Aug.17-*I*
Williams,2Lt.SG, MC **POW** 21Feb.18-*I*
Williams,2Lt.SN, **KIA** 25Oct.16-*I*
Williams,Lt.SW, **POW** 3Sep.17-*I*
Williams,2Lt.TF, 10Jan.18-*IV*
Williams,Lt.TL, 6Oct.18-*VIII*
Williams,Lt.,Capt.TM, *SA.* 1Apr.18-*I*, 8Aug.18-*I*
Williams,2Lt.VF, **KIA** 2Apr.17-*I*
Williams,Capt.WGB, 23Jan.17-*I*
Williams,2Lt.WHT, **POW DoW** 22.8.1917 16Aug.17-*I*
Williamson,Lt.A, *3Sqn.* 26Sep.16-*I*
Williamson,Lt.A, 20Sep.18-*I*
Williamson,2Lt.GA, **DoW** 1Jan.18-*I*
Williamson,2Lt.HA, *9Sqn.* **KIA** 2Jul.16-*I*
Williamson,FCdr.HA, *RNAS.* 17Feb.15-*V*, **inj** 5Mar.15-*V*
Williamson,2Lt.JC, **POW** 17May.18-*I*
Williamson,2Lt.JF, *US.* **POW** 12Jun.18-*IIB*
Williamson,2Lt.JW, **KIA** 15May.18-*I*
Williamson,2Lt.LF, 4Oct.18-*I*
Williamson,Lt.OH, 30Oct.18-*I*
Williamson,2Lt.RB, **KIA** 29Oct.18-*I*
Williamson,Lt.RH?, 31Jul.17-*I*
Williamson,Lt.TW, 18May.18-*I*
Williamson-Jones,1Lt.CE, **WIA** 7Jun.17-*I*
Willis,2Lt.GR, **WIA** 28Jul.17-*I*
Willis,Sgt.HB, *US.* **POW** 18Aug.17-*IIA*
Willis,Lt.ND, **POW** 27Sep.18-*I*
Willis,Lt.P, MM *Can.* **KIA** 9Aug.18-*I*
Willis,Cpl.TW, **inj** 17Mar.17-*I*
Willmott,2Lt.FB, **POW** 13Jan.18-*I*
Willows,Lt.CE, 8May.18-*I*
Wills,2Lt.D, 10Apr.18-*I*

Wills,Capt.RP, 19Jan.15-*I*
Wills,2Lt.ST, **POW** 30Apr.17-*I*
Wills,Sgt.T?, **KIA**, *initials* TJ? 20Apr.18-*I*
Wilmer,1Lt.HW, *US.* 10Oct.18-*IIB*
Wilmot,2Lt.,Lt.EP, MC 15Mar.17-*I*, **POW** 6Nov.17-*I*
Wilmot,FSLt.WH, **KIA** 3Feb.18-*I*
Wilmott,Lt.S, **WIA** 2Sep.17-*I*
Wilmshurst,Lt.AL, 8Oct.18-*I*, 25Oct.18-*I*
Wilsdon,2Lt.CJ, **WIA** 27Mar.18-*I*
Wilson,Cpl.A, **POW** 1Apr.17-*I*
Wilson,Lt.AP, **KIA** 14Apr.17-*I*
Wilson,Lt.BA, **WIA** 7May.17-*I*
Wilson,2Lt.,Lt.BW, 18Sep.18-*I*, **KIA** 23Sep.18-*I*
Wilson,Lt.,Capt.CB, 17Jan.16-*I*, **POW** .18-*I*
Wilson,2Lt.CE, **KIA** 16Apr.17-*I*
Wilson,Lt.CFC, 16Sep.18-*I*
Wilson,2Lt.CFS, **WIA** 17Jun.18-*I*
Wilson,Lt.CM, DFC *Can.* 14Jul.18-*I*, **KIA** 14Oct.18-*I*
Wilson,Lt.CW, **WIA POW** 19Jan.16-*I*
Wilson,Lt.DW, **INT** 2Aug.18-*III*
Wilson,2Lt.E, **inj** 20Sep.17-*I*
Wilson,2Lt.EB, **WIA** 25Jun.18-*I*
Wilson,Lt.EF, 3Jan.18-*III*
Wilson,2Lt.,Capt.FB, 27Mar.18-*I*, **WIA** 9Aug.18-*I*
Wilson,Lt.FH, **POW** 19Mar.17-*I*
Wilson,Capt.FJC, 30Aug.15-*I*, **POW** 1Sep.15-*I*
Wilson,Lt.FWW, 9Nov.17-*I*
Wilson,Lt.G, **KIA** 15May.18-*I*
Wilson,2Lt.GH, 10Nov.18-*I*
Wilson,Lt.GR, 26Jun.17-*I*
Wilson,Lt.H, *Can.* **KIA?** 1Nov.18-*I*
Wilson,Lt.HBB, **POW** 16May.18-*I*
Wilson,2Lt.HDW, 29Feb.16-*I*
Wilson,2Lt.,Lt.HH, 16Feb.18-*I*, **KIA** 19Feb.18-*I*
Wilson,Pbr.,2Lt.HL, 18Jun.18-*I*, **KIA** 1Jul.18-*I*
Wilson,2Lt.JA, **WIA** 12Jul.18-*I*
Wilson,Lt.JG, **WIA** 19Jul.18-*I*
Wilson,Lt.JM, **KIA** 30Jun.18-*I*
Wilson,2Lt.JR, *6Sqn.* **WIA** 7Jun.17-*I*
Wilson,Capt.JR, *70Sqn.* **KIA** 20Oct.17-*I*
Wilson,2Lt.JS, **DoW** 28Sep.18-*I*
Wilson,Lt.LT, **WIA** 5Oct.18-*I*
Wilson,2Lt.MG, **INT** 16Aug.18-*I*
Wilson,2Lt.MW, 23Apr.17-*I*
Wilson,2Lt.N, **POW DoW** 18.10.1918 25Jul.18-*I*
Wilson,Lt.P, 10May.18-*IV*
Wilson,Capt.RE, **POW** 24Sep.18-*I*
Wilson,Lt.TC, **WIA POW** 30Mar.16-*I*
Wilson,Lt.TS, **WIA POW** 13Mar.18-*I*
Wilson,2Lt.WA, **POW** 17Sep.18-*I*
Wilson,Lt.WF, 8Oct.18-*I*, 4Nov.18-*I*, 6Nov.18-*I*
Wilson,FLt.WH, 21Dec.14-*I*, 10Jan.15-*I*
Wilson,Lt.WK, **POW** 21Jun.18-*I*
Wilson-Browne,2Lt.RM, **POW DoW** 21.7.1916 21Jul.16-*I*
Wilton,Lt.EN?, **WIA** 12Apr.18-*I*
Wilton,2Lt.,Lt.FC, 12Jun.18-*I*, 11Jul.18-*I*, 18Jul.18-*I*, 23Oct.18-*I*, 30Oct.18-*I*
Wiman,Cpl.A, *USMC.* 14Oct.18-*IIB*
Wiman,Sgt.A, *USMC.* 1Oct.18-*I*, 2Oct.18-*I*
Wimbush,FSLt.LEB, **WIA** 9May.17-*I*
Winch,Sgt.AJ, **WIA** 15Sep.18-*I*
Windle,2Lt.BCW, **POW** 21Feb.18-*I*
Windover,Capt.WE, **POW** 21Oct.18-*I*
Windridge,Sgt.AL, **KIA** 13Aug.18-*I*
Windridge,Lt.EA, 22May.18-*I*, **KIA** 9Jun.18-*I*
Windrum,Lt.CH, 17Nov.16-*I*, **POW** 20Dec.16-*I*
Windsor,Capt.HTO, 4Jan.18-*I*
Windsor,Capt.JS, MC **WIA** 16Apr.18-*I*
Winfield-Smith,Capt.B, **POW** 28Apr.16-*VIII*
Wing,Sgt.AJ, **KIA** 4Nov.18-*I*
Wing,FSLt.WR, **POW** May.17-*I*
Wingate,Lt.J, 21Aug.18-*I*
Wingate-Grey,Lt.AG, **POW** 7Apr.18-*I*
Wingfield,2Lt.EN, **POW** 24Sep.16-*I*
Wingfield,Lt.LA, **POW** 1Jul.16-*I*
Winham,2Lt.AH, **WIA** 11Oct.18-*I*
Winkler,Lt.MH, *US.* **POW** 21Oct.18-*I*
Winkler,2Lt.,Lt.WOB, 2May.17-*I*, **POW KIA** 11May.17-*I*
Winkley,2Lt.SH, **KIA** 1Apr.18-*I*

Winn,FSLt.JH, **KIA** 19Sep.17-*I*
Winnicott,Lt.R, 6Sep.17-*I*, 18Oct.17-*I*, 22Nov.17-*I*
Winser,2Lt.FE, **KIA** 20Aug.17-*I*
Winslow,2Lt.AF, *US.* **WIA POW** 31Jul.18-*IIB*
Winter,2Lt.CG, **inj** 28Jul.17-*I*
Winter,2Lt.FE, 27Sep.18-*I*
Winter,AFCdr.RR, **KIA** 3Feb.18-*I*
Winter,2Lt.RRC, **KIA** 9Aug.18-*I*
Winter,2Lt.WA, 10Apr.17-*I*
Winter,Cpl.WC, *US.* **KIA** 8Mar.18-*IIC*
Winter,2Lt.WH, **POW** 11Oct.17-*I*
Winterbotham,Lt.FW, **POW** 13Jul.17-*I*
Winterbottom,Cpl.A, **KIA** 22Sep.16-*I*
Wischer,2Lt.JV, *Aust.* **WIA POW** 28Apr.17-*I*
Wise,2Lt.GT, *USAS.* **POW** 24Aug.18-*I*
Wise,WO.SJ, **POW** 30Sep.17-*V*
Wiser,2Lt.GB, *US.* **POW** 26Sep.18-*IIB*
Wisnekowitz,2Lt.H, 23Mar.18-*I*, 27Mar.18-*I*
Witcomb,Lt.OG, *Aust.* 8Sep.18-*I*
Withers,Lt.JL, 1Apr.18-*I*
Withers,Lt.KG, **POW** 17Oct.18-*VI*
Withington,Capt.TEW, 12Apr.18-*I*
Wodehouse,FSLt.CE, **WIA** 18Mar.18-*I*
Wodehouse,2Lt.FJA, **KIA** 26May.17-*I*
Wogan-Brown,2Lt.CP, **KIA** 13Aug.18-*I*
Wold,1Lt.EG, *US.* **DoW** 2.8.1918 1Aug.18-*IIB*
Wollen,2Lt.DC, **KIA** 13Apr.17-*I*
Wolstenholm,Lt.J, **KIA** 23Sep.17-*I*
Wood,Lt., *12Sqn.* 9Feb.18-*I*
Wood,Lt., *34Sqn.* 16Jun.18-*IV*
Wood,AG.AG, 17Apr.18-*I*
Wood,FSLt.AR, 11Sep.17-*I*
Wood,Lt.AW, **WIA POW** 22Apr.17-*I*
Wood,FLt.CE, 11Feb.17-*V*, 5Apr.17-*VI*
Wood,2Lt.CG, **WIA** 24Oct.17-*I*
Wood,Lt.CL, *US.* **DoW** 17.8.1918 10Aug.18-*IIB*
Wood,2AM.E, *11Sqn.* **KIA** 6Apr.17-*I*
Wood,2Lt.E, *55Sqn.* **WIA?** 25Aug.18-*I*
Wood,2Lt.FA, *USAS.* **WIA** 22Jul.18-*I*, **KIA** 13Sep.18-*I*
Wood,2Lt.G, **KIA** 6May.17-*I*
Wood,2Lt.GH, 9Aug.16-*I*, **DoW** 2Nov.16-*I*
Wood,Lt.GO, **WIA** 8Oct.18-*I*
Wood,2Lt.GSW, **WIA** 23Aug.16-*I*
Wood,Lt.GW, 13Jul.18-*I*
Wood,2Lt.HC, 6Sep.18-*I*, **WIA** 30Sep.18-*I*
Wood,Lt.HH, **POW** 12Aug.18-*I*
Wood,Lt.JC, **WIA POW** 8May.18-*I*
Wood,2Lt.JO, **POW** 24Sep.18-*I*
Wood,Lt.LG, 26Sep.16-*I*
Wood,Capt.MH, **KIA** 13Apr.17-*I*
Wood,2Lt.PL, **KIA** 4Mar.17-*I*
Wood,2Lt.RW, **POW** 17Sep.16-*I*
Wood,Lt.WB, 9Aug.17-*I*
Wood,2Lt.WV, **WIA** 9Nov.18-*I*
Woodall,2Lt.WS, **WIA** 30Oct.18-*I*
Woodard,2Lt.GO, *US.* **POW** 29Sep.18-*IIB*
Woodend,2Lt.CW, **KIA** 19Aug.18-*I*
Woodhouse,Lt., *52Sqn.* 27Jan.17-*I*
Woodhouse,2Lt.DH, **inj** 31Aug.18-*I*
Woodhouse,2Lt.IS, 16Sep.18-*I*
Woodhouse,2Lt.JW, 23Sep.15-*I*, 3Oct.15-*I*, 28Dec.15-*I*
Woodhouse,Capt.LM, MC DFC 24Aug.18-*I*, **KIA** 27Sep.18-*I*
Woodhouse,FSLt.MG, **KIA** 9Aug.17-*I*
Woodhouse,2Lt.PW, 23Mar.18-*I*, **KIA** 28Mar.18-*I*
Wooding,Lt.J, **POW** 21Aug.18-*I*
Woodiwiss,2Lt.IN, **KIA** 10May.15-*I*
Woodland,Lt.PM, **POW** 2Dec.16-*VII*
Woodman,Lt.AC, 17Mar.17-*I*
Woodman,2Lt.D, **KIA** 11Apr.17-*I*
Woodman,2Lt.HS, **WIA** 13Apr.18-*I*, 28May.18-*I*
Woodman,2Lt.KCB, **POW** 1Jul.18-*I*
Woods,Lt.CHC, **KIA?** 21Sep.17-*I*
Woods,1Lt.GB, *US.* **POW** 14Sep.18-*IIB*
Woods,2Lt.ME, **inj POW** 6Feb.17-*I*
Woods,2Lt.WE, 23Apr.18-*I*
Woodward,Cpl.HH, *US.* **KIA** 1Apr.18-*IIC*
Woodward,2AM.W, 26Jun.17-*I*
Wookey,2Lt.HC, **POW** 17Oct.17-*I*

Woolhouse,Lt.FS, *Aust.* **KIA** 10Apr.18-*I*
Woollett,Capt.HW, 12Apr.18-*I*
Woolley,Lt.DB, **POW** 17Mar.17-*I*
Woolley,2Lt.FW, *99Sqn.* **KIA** 31Jul.18-*I*
Woolley,2Lt.FW, *108Sqn.* **KIA** 14Oct.18-*I*
Woolley,FSLt.SJ, 20Mar.16-*I*
Woolliams,2Lt.FD, **POW** 9May.17-*I*
Woolner,2Lt.FM, **WIA** 28Jan.18-*I*
Woon,2Lt.DB, 30Sep.18-*IIB*
Wooten,1Lt.JC, *US.* **KIA** 1Aug.18-*IIB*
Wooten,Lt.GB, *name* Wooten? 5Sep.18-*I*, **WIA** 30Oct.18-*I*
Wootton,3AM.RA, **INT** 2Aug.18-*III*
Wordsworth,2Lt.JCD, **KIA** 6Apr.17-*I*
Workman,1Lt.CS, MC 15Jun.17-*I*, 7Jul.17-*I*, **DoW** 17Jul.17-*I*
Wormald,2Lt.WM, **WIA** 8Aug.18-*I*, **KIA** 2Sep.18-*I*
Worrall,1Lt.EA, **WIA** 29May.17-*I*
Worsley,2Lt., *12Sqn.* 7Mar.18-*I*
Worsley,2Lt.RSL, *48Sqn.* **POW** 13Apr.17-*I*
Worthing,2AM.G, **KIA** 5May.17-*I*
Worthington,2Lt.BR, 27Aug.17-*I*, 13Oct.17-*I*
Worthington,Lt.FP, 25Sep.17-*I*
Worthington,2Lt.LP, **inj** 15Sep.18-*I*
Wray,2Lt.AM, **WIA** 28May.17-*I*
Wray,Lt.TE, **KIA** 4Sep.17-*I*
Wreford,2Lt.WJ, 9Nov.18-*I*
Wren,2Lt.A, 4Nov.18-*I*
Wren,2Lt.HL, **POW** 6Nov.18-*I*
Wren,2Lt.LR, 26Sep.16-*I*
Wrigglesworth,Lt.C, 15May.18-*I*
Wright,Lt., *6Sqn.* 5Sep.17-*I*
Wright,Capt.AB, **WIA** 17Jun.17-*I*
Wright,Capt.AC, **WIA** 6Apr.17-*I*
Wright,Lt.BW, *Aust.* **KIA** 4May.18-*I*
Wright,2Lt.DC, **POW DoW** 22.2.18-*IV*
Wright,2Lt.EF, **POW** 15Sep.18-*I*
Wright,2Lt.FA, **KIA** 19Sep.17-*I*
Wright,2Lt.FB, **KIA** 12Apr.18-*I*
Wright,2Lt.FCA, 25Apr.16-*I*, 26Apr.16-*I*, **WIA** 16May.16-*I*
Wright,Sgt.JR, **POW** 10Jul.18-*I*
Wright,Lt.JW, DFC *Aust.* **WIA** 26Mar.18-*I*
Wright,Capt.MFM, 9Oct.18-*I*
Wright,2Lt.MT, **POW** 16Aug.17-*I*
Wright,Lt.PA, **WIA** 3Sep.16-*I*
Wright,1Lt.RW, *US.* **WIA** 30Sep.18-*IIB*
Wright,Lt.S, MC *48Sqn.* **KIA** 24Oct.17-*I*
Wright,Lt.SS, DCM *75Sqn.* **KIA** 24Oct.17-*I*
Wright,2Lt.WA, 30Apr.17-*I*, 9May.17-*I*, 16Jun.17-*I*
Wrighton,2Lt., *103Sqn.* 20May.18-*I*
Wrigley,Lt.FH, **WIA** 21Apr.18-*I*
Wyatt,Capt.F, **KIA** 2Jul.17-*I*
Wyatt,AG.2AM.G, **WIA** 12Nov.17-*I*
Wyatt,2Lt.WJ, 25May.17-*I*
Wylde,Lt.TE, **DoW** 27Jun.17-*I*
Wylie,2Lt.AE, **KIA** 18Jan.18-*I*
Wylie,2Lt.AL, MC **KIA** 20Nov.17-*I*
Wyllie,Capt., *6Sqn.* 26Apr.15-*I*, 28Apr.15-*I*
Wyllie,Capt.H, 31May.16-*I*, 1Jul.16-*I*
Wyly,2Lt.,1Lt.LT, *USAS.* **WIA** 15Aug.18-*I*, 29Oct.18-*I*
Wyman,2Lt.JBH, **WIA POW** 15Sep.17-*I*
Wyncoll,2Lt.AW, **POW** 18Aug.18-*I*
Wynn,2Lt.AE, 5Feb.16-*I*
Wynn,2Lt.EA, **KIA** 1Nov.16-*I*
Wynn,2Lt.,Lt.HW, 8Sep.18-*I*, **KIA** 1Oct.18-*I*
Wynn,2AM.JH, **DoW** 30Apr.17-*I*
Wynn,Capt.TS, MC **WIA** 3Jul.17-*I*, 28Sep.17-*I*
Wynne,Lt.AF, **POW** 4Jan.18-*I*
Wynne,Capt.AM, **WIA** 1Apr.17-*I*
Wynne-Eyton,Lt., *2Sqn.* 5Jan.16-*I*, 12Jan.16-*I*, 19Jan.16-*I*, 25Jan.16-*I*, 1Feb.16-*I*, 29Feb.16-*I*
Wynne-Eyton,Capt.RM, **WIA** 30Nov.17-*VI*, **INT** 16Aug.18-*I*

Y

Yates,Lt.JA, **POW** 8Aug.17-*I*
Yates,Lt.RA, **POW** 14Jul.18-*I*
Yates,2Lt.VM, 25Mar.18-*I*, 3May.18-*I*